PHILIP'S

WORLD ATLAS

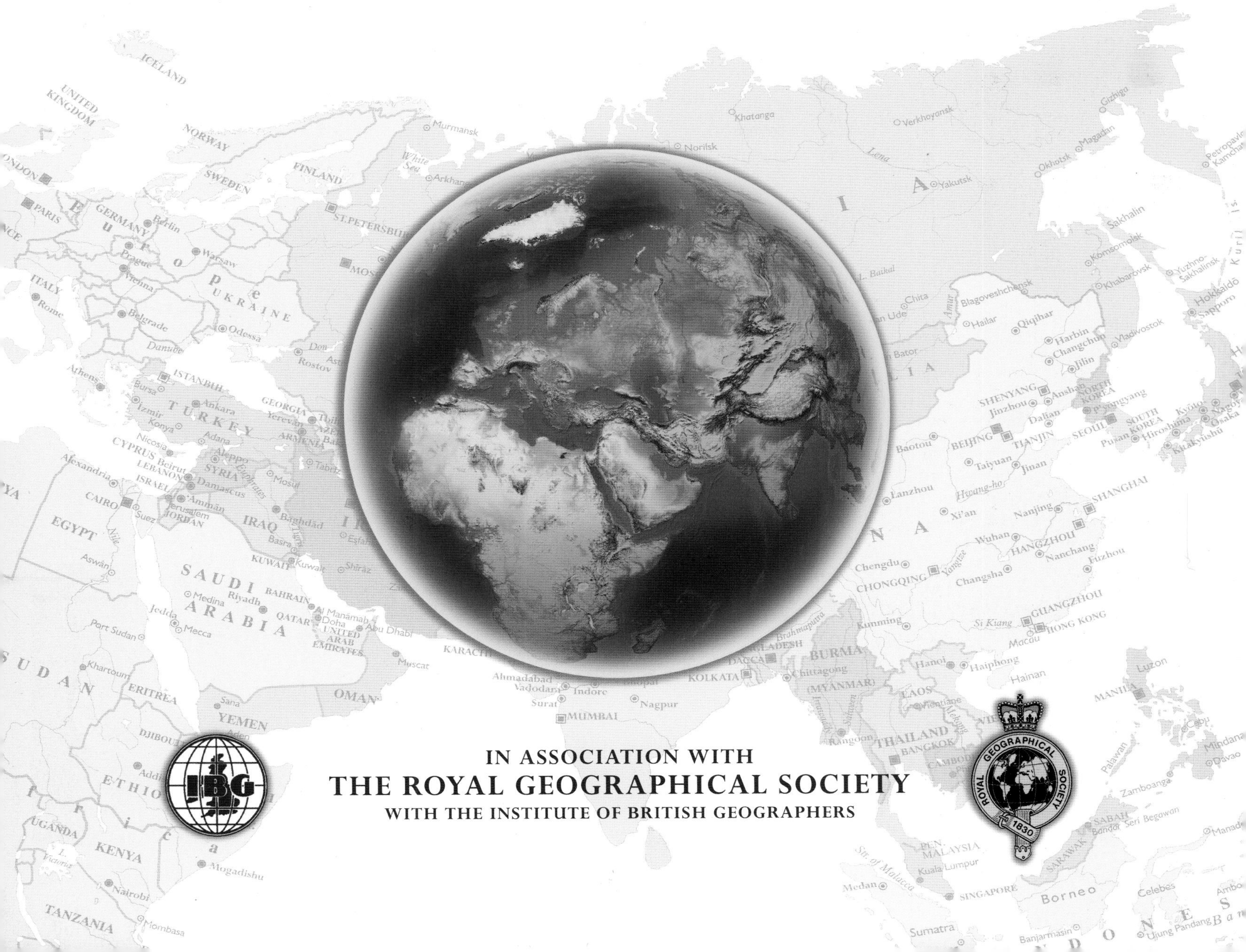

IN ASSOCIATION WITH
THE ROYAL GEOGRAPHICAL SOCIETY
WITH THE INSTITUTE OF BRITISH GEOGRAPHERS

Contents

World Statistics

Countries   vi
Physical Dimensions   vii
User Guide   viii

The World in Focus

Planet Earth   2–3
Restless Earth   4–5
Landforms   6–7
Oceans   8–9
Climate   10–11
Water and Vegetation   12–13
Environment   14–15
Population   16–17
The Human Family   18–19
Wealth   20–21
Quality of Life   22–23
Energy   24–25
Production   26–27
Trade   28–29
Travel and Tourism   30–31

World Cities

Amsterdam   2
Athens   2
Atlanta   3
Baghdad   3
Bangkok   3
Barcelona   4
Beijing   4
Berlin   5
Boston   6
Brussels   6
Budapest   7
Buenos Aires   7
Cairo   7
Cape Town   8
Copenhagen   8
Chicago   9
Delhi   10
Dublin   10
Edinburgh   11
Guangzhou   11
Helsinki   11
Hong Kong   12
Istanbul   12
Jakarta   12
Jerusalem   13
Johannesburg   13
Karachi   13
Kolkata   14
Lagos   14
Las Vegas   14
Lima   14
London   15
Lisbon   16
Los Angeles   16
Madrid   17
Manila   17
Melbourne   18
Mexico City   18
Miami   18
Milan   19
Moscow   19
Montréal   20
Mumbai   20
Munich   21
New Orleans   21
New York   22
Orlando   23
Osaka   23
Oslo   23
Paris   24
Prague   25
Rio de Janeiro   25
Rome   26
San Francisco   26
St Petersburg   27
Santiago   27
São Paulo   27
Seoul   27
Shanghai   28
Singapore   28
Stockholm   29
Sydney   29
Tokyo   30
Tehran   31
Toronto   31
Vienna   32
Warsaw   32
Washington   33
Wellington   33
Index to City Maps   34–39
World Cities Satellite Images   40–48

World Maps

Map Symbols   1

The World: Political
1:95 000 000   2–3

Arctic Ocean
1:35 000 000   4

Antarctica
1:35 000 000   5

Europe

Europe: Physical
1:20 000 000   6

Europe: Political
1:20 000 000   7

Scandinavia 1:6 000 000
Iceland 1:6 000 000
Færoe Islands 1:6 000 000

8–9

Ireland 1:2 000 000

10

Scotland 1:2 000 000
11

England and Wales
1:2 000 000
12–13

British Isles 1:5 000 000

14

Netherlands, Belgium and
Luxembourg 1:2 500 000
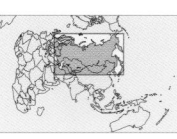
15

Central Europe 1:5 000 000

16–17

Eastern Europe and Turkey
1:10 000 000

18–19

France 1:5 000 000

20

Spain and Portugal
1:5 000 000
21

Italy and the Balkan States
1:5 000 000
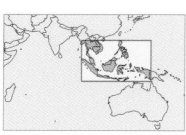
22–23

The Balearics, the Canaries and
Madeira 1:1 000 000 / 1:2 000 000

24

Malta, Crete, Corfu, Rhodes
and Cyprus
1:1 000 000 / 1:1 300 000
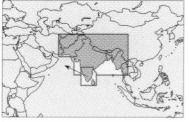
25

Asia

Asia: Physical 1:47 000 000   26

Asia: Political 1:47 000 000   27

Russia and Central Asia
1:20 000 000
28–29

Japan 1:5 000 000
30–31

China and the Far East
1:15 000 000
Hong Kong and Macau 1:1 000 000
32–33

Northern China and Korea
1:6 000 000
34–35

Indonesia and the Philippines
1:12 500 000
Java and Madura 1:7 500 000
Bali 1:2 000 000
36–37

Mainland South-east Asia
1:6 000 000
Ko Phuket 1:1 000 000
Ko Samui 1:1 000 000
Pinang 1:1 000 000
Singapore 1:1 000 000
38–39

South Asia 1:10 000 000
40–41

MAP PAGES

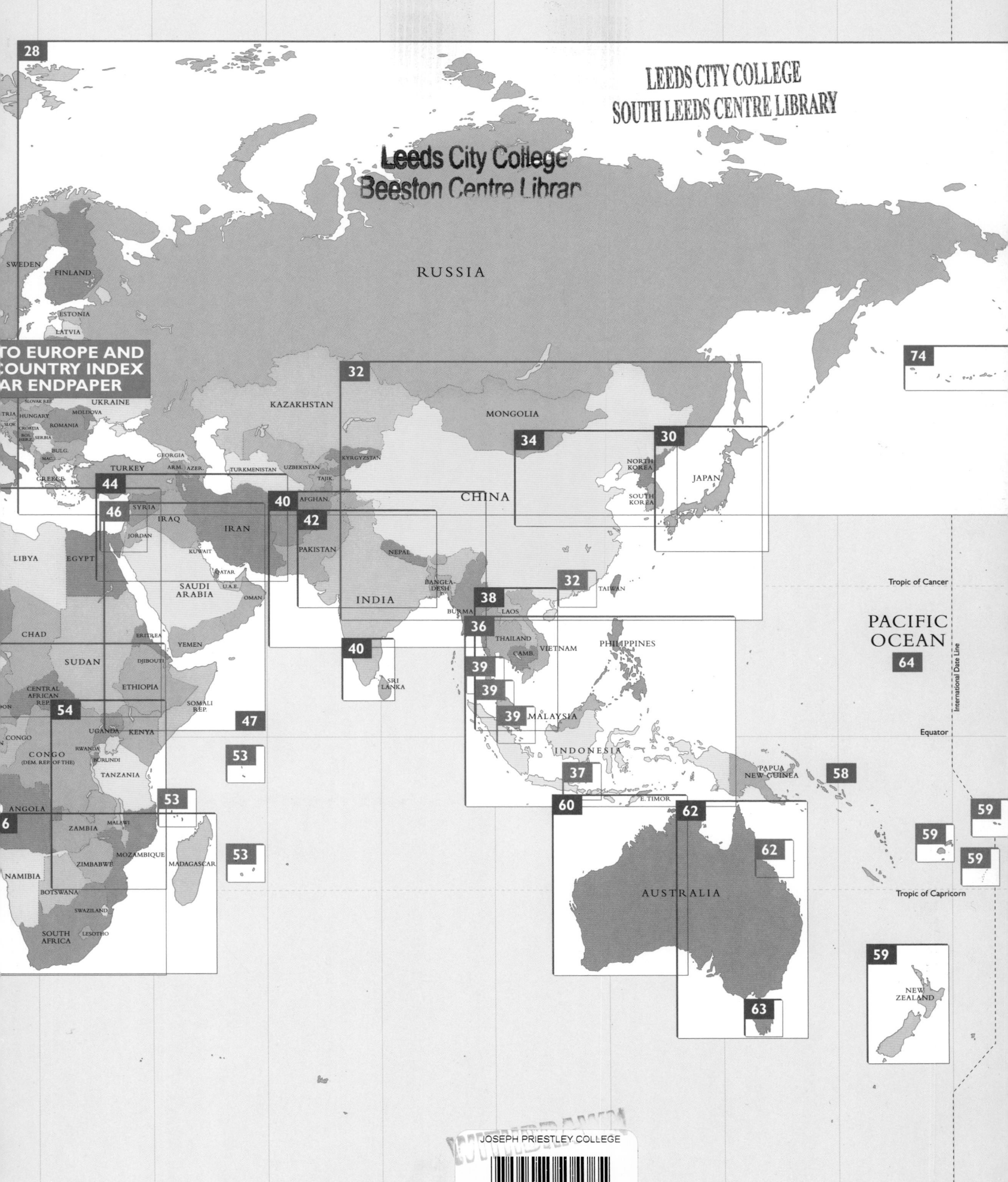

28

74

TO EUROPE AND
COUNTRY INDEX
AR ENDPAPER

SWEDEN
FINLAND
ESTONIA
LATVIA

RUSSIA

32
KAZAKHSTAN
MONGOLIA

34
30

NORTH
KOREA
JAPAN

SOUTH
KOREA

SLOVAK REP.
TRIA HUNGARY MOLDOVA
SLOK CROATIA ROMANIA
BOS. SERBIA
HERZ.
BULG.
MAC.
GREECE
UKRAINE

GEORGIA
TURKEY ARM. AZER.
TURKMENISTAN UZBEKISTAN
KYRGYZSTAN
TAJIK.

CHINA

44
46 SYRIA
IRAQ
JORDAN

40 AFGHAN.
42
IRAN

KUWAIT
QATAR
U.A.E.
OMAN
SAUDI
ARABIA

LIBYA
EGYPT

PAKISTAN

NEPAL
BANGLA-
DESH
BURMA

32
TAIWAN

Tropic of Cancer

PACIFIC
OCEAN

CHAD

SUDAN
ERITREA
YEMEN
DJIBOUTI

INDIA

38 LAOS
36
THAILAND
CAMB.
VIETNAM

40
SRI
LANKA

64

CENTRAL
AFRICAN
REP.
ETHIOPIA
SOMALI
REP.

54
UGANDA KENYA

CONGO
RWANDA
(DEM. REP. OF THE) BURUNDI
TANZANIA

47

53

PHILIPPINES

39
39
39 MALAYSIA

INDONESIA

Equator

ANGOLA
6
ZAMBIA
MALAWI

53
MOZAMBIQUE
ZIMBABWE MADAGASCAR
NAMIBIA
BOTSWANA
SWAZILAND

53

37

60
62
62

AUSTRALIA

PAPUA
NEW GUINEA
58

59

59

59

Tropic of Capricorn

International Date Line

SOUTH
AFRICA LESOTHO

E. TIMOR

63

59
NEW
ZEALAND

WORLD ATLAS

Philip's are grateful to the following for acting as specialist geography consultants on '*The World in Focus*' front section:

Professor D. Brunsden, Kings College, University of London, UK
Dr C. Clarke, Oxford University, UK
Dr I. S. Evans, Durham University, UK
Professor P. Haggett, University of Bristol, UK
Professor K. McLachlan, University of London, UK
Professor M. Monmonier, Syracuse University, New York, USA
Professor M-L. Hsu, University of Minnesota, Minnesota, USA
Professor M. J. Tooley, University of St Andrews, UK
Dr T. Unwin, Royal Holloway, University of London, UK

THE WORLD IN FOCUS
Cartography by Philip's

Picture Acknowledgements
NASA/GSFC page 14

Illustrations: Stefan Chabluk

WORLD CITIES
Cartography by Philip's

Page 10, Dublin: The town plan of Dublin is based on Ordnance Survey Ireland by permission of the Government Permit Number 8186. © Ordnance Survey Ireland and Government of Ireland.

Page 11, Edinburgh, and page 15, London:
This product includes mapping data licensed from Ordnance Survey® with the permission of the Controller of Her Majesty's Stationery Office. © Crown copyright 2007. All rights reserved. Licence number 100011710.

Vector data courtesy of Gräfe and Unser Verlag GmbH, München, Germany
(city-centre maps of Bangkok, Beijing, Cape Town, Jerusalem, Mexico City, Moscow, Singapore, Sydney, Tokyo and Washington D.C.)
The following city maps utilize base data supplied courtesy of MapQuest.com, Inc. (© MapQuest)
(Las Vegas, New Orleans, Orlando)

All satellite images in this section courtesy of NPA Group, Edenbridge, Kent (www.satmaps.com)

Published in Great Britain in 2007
by Philip's,
a division of Octopus Publishing Group Limited,
2–4 Heron Quays, London E14 4JP
An Hachette Livre UK Company

Copyright © 2007 Philip's

Cartography by Philip's

ISBN-13 978–0–540–09010–5
ISBN-10 0–540–09010–7

A CIP catalogue record for this book is available from the British Library.

Printed in Hong Kong

Details of other Philip's titles and services can be found on our website at: www.philips-maps.co.uk

Philip's World Atlases are published in association with The Royal Geographical Society (with The Institute of British Geographers).

The Society was founded in 1830 and given a Royal Charter in 1859 for 'the advancement of geographical science'. It holds historical collections of national and international importance, many of which relate to the Society's association with and support for scientific exploration and research from the 19th century onwards. It was pivotal in establishing geography as a teaching and research discipline in British universities close to the turn of the century, and has played a key role in geographical and environmental education ever since.

Today the Society is a leading world centre for geographical learning – supporting education, teaching, research and expeditions, and promoting public understanding of the subject.

The Society welcomes those interested in geography as members. For further information, please visit the website at: www.rgs.org

Northern India, Pakistan and Nepal
1:6 000 000
Jammu and Kashmir 1:6 000 000

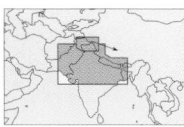

42–43

The Middle East
1:7 000 000

44–45

The Near East 1:2 500 000

46

Arabia and the Horn of Africa 1:15 000 000

47

Africa

Africa: Physical
1:42 000 000   48

Africa: Political
1:42 000 000   49

Northern Africa
1:15 000 000
Azores 1:15 000 000
Cape Verde Islands 1:10 000 000

50–51

Central and Southern Africa
1:15 000 000
Seychelles 1:2 500 000
Réunion 1:2 500 000
Mauritius 1:2 500 000
Comoros 1:8 000 000

52–53

East Africa 1:8 000 000

54–55

Southern Africa
1:8 000 000
Madagascar 1:8 000 000

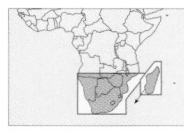

56–57

Australia and Oceania

Australia and Oceania: Physical and Political
1:50 000 000   58

New Zealand 1:6 000 000
Samoan Islands 1:6 000 000
Fiji 1:6 000 000
Tonga 1:6 000 000
Tahiti and Moorea 1:1 000 000

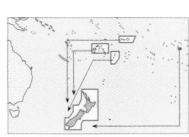

59

Western Australia
1:8 000 000

60–61

Eastern Australia
1:8 000 000
Whitsunday Islands 1:2 500 000
Tasmania 1:8 000 000

62–63

Pacific Ocean
1:54 000 000   64–65

North America

North America: Physical
1:35 000 000   66

North America: Political
1:35 000 000   67

Canada 1:15 000 000

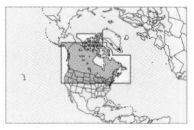

68–69

Western Canada 1:7 000 000

70–71

Eastern Canada 1:7 000 000

72–73

United States 1:12 000 000
Hawai'i 1:10 000 000
Alaska 1:30 000 000

74–75

United States – West
1:6 700 000

76–77

Central and Southern California and Western Washington
1:2 500 000

78–79

United States – Midwest and North-east
1:6 700 000

80–81

North-eastern United States
1:2 500 000

82–83

United States – South
1:6 700 000

84–85

Mexico 1:8 000 000

86–87

Central America and the West Indies 1:8 000 000
Jamaica 1:3 000 000
Guadeloupe 1:2 000 000
Martinique 1:2 000 000
Puerto Rico 1:3 000 000
Virgin Islands 1:2 000 000
St Lucia 1:2 000 000
Barbados 1:2 000 000

88–89

South America

South America: Physical
1:35 000 000   90

South America: Political
1:35 000 000   91

South America – North
1:16 000 000
Trinidad and Tobago 1:2 500 000

92–93

Central South America
1:8 000 000

94–95

South America – South
1:16 000 000

96

Index to World Maps

97–176

World: Regions in the News   177

World Statistics: Countries

This alphabetical list includes the principal countries and territories of the world. If a territory is not completely independent, the country it is associated with is named. The area figures give the total area of land, inland water and ice. The population figures are 2006 estimates where available. The annual income is the Gross Domestic Product per capita in US dollars. The figures are the latest available, usually 2006 estimates.

Country/Territory	Area km² Thousands	Area miles² Thousands	Population Thousands	Capital	Annual Income US $
Afghanistan	652	252	31,057	Kabul	800
Albania	28.7	11.1	3,582	Tirana	5,600
Algeria	2,382	920	32,930	Algiers	7,700
American Samoa (US)	0.20	0.08	58	Pago Pago	5,800
Andorra	0.47	0.18	71	Andorra La Vella	38,800
Angola	1,247	481	12,127	Luanda	4,300
Anguilla (UK)	0.10	0.04	13	The Valley	8,800
Antigua & Barbuda	0.44	0.17	69	St John's	10,900
Argentina	2,780	1,074	39,922	Buenos Aires	15,000
Armenia	29.8	11.5	2,976	Yerevan	5,400
Aruba (Netherlands)	0.19	0.07	72	Oranjestad	21,800
Australia	7,741	2,989	20,264	Canberra	32,900
Austria	83.9	32.4	8,193	Vienna	35,500
Azerbaijan	86.6	33.4	7,962	Baku	7,300
Azores (Portugal)	2.2	0.86	236	Ponta Delgada	15,000
Bahamas	13.9	5.4	304	Nassau	21,300
Bahrain	0.69	0.27	699	Manama	25,300
Bangladesh	144	55.6	147,365	Dhaka	2,200
Barbados	0.43	0.17	280	Bridgetown	18,200
Belarus	208	80.2	10,293	Minsk	7,800
Belgium	30.5	11.8	10,379	Brussels	31,800
Belize	23.0	8.9	288	Belmopan	8,400
Benin	113	43.5	7,863	Porto-Novo	1,100
Bermuda (UK)	0.05	0.02	66	Hamilton	69,900
Bhutan	47.0	18.1	2,280	Thimphu	1,400
Bolivia	1,099	424	8,989	La Paz/Sucre	3,000
Bosnia-Herzegovina	51.2	19.8	4,499	Sarajevo	5,500
Botswana	582	225	1,640	Gaborone	11,400
Brazil	8,514	3,287	188,078	Brasília	8,600
Brunei	5.8	2.2	379	Bandar Seri Begawan	25,600
Bulgaria	111	42.8	7,385	Sofia	10,400
Burkina Faso	274	106	13,903	Ouagadougou	1,300
Burma (Myanmar)	677	261	47,383	Rangoon/Naypyidaw	1,800
Burundi	27.8	10.7	8,090	Bujumbura	700
Cambodia	181	69.9	13,881	Phnom Penh	2,600
Cameroon	475	184	17,341	Yaoundé	2,400
Canada	9,971	3,850	33,099	Ottawa	35,200
Canary Is. (Spain)	7.2	2.8	1,682	Las Palmas/Santa Cruz	19,900
Cape Verde Is.	4.0	1.6	421	Praia	6,000
Cayman Is. (UK)	0.26	0.10	45	George Town	43,800
Central African Republic	623	241	4,303	Bangui	1,100
Chad	1,284	496	9,944	Ndjaména	1,500
Chile	757	292	16,134	Santiago	12,700
China	9,597	3,705	1,313,974	Beijing	7,600
Colombia	1,139	440	43,593	Bogotá	8,400
Comoros	2.2	0.86	691	Moroni	600
Congo	342	132	3,702	Brazzaville	1,300
Congo (Dem. Rep. of the)	2,345	905	62,661	Kinshasa	700
Cook Is. (NZ)	0.24	0.09	21	Avarua	9,100
Costa Rica	51.1	19.7	4,075	San José	12,000
Croatia	56.5	21.8	4,495	Zagreb	13,200
Cuba	111	42.8	11,383	Havana	3,900
Cyprus	9.3	3.6	784	Nicosia	22,700
Czech Republic	78.9	30.5	10,235	Prague	21,600
Denmark	43.1	16.6	5,451	Copenhagen	37,000
Djibouti	23.2	9.0	487	Djibouti	1,000
Dominica	0.75	0.29	69	Roseau	3,800
Dominican Republic	48.5	18.7	9,184	Santo Domingo	8,000
East Timor	14.9	5.7	1,063	Dili	800
Ecuador	284	109	13,548	Quito	4,500
Egypt	1,001	387	78,887	Cairo	4,200
El Salvador	21.0	8.1	6,822	San Salvador	4,900
Equatorial Guinea	28.1	10.8	540	Malabo	5,200
Eritrea	118	45.4	4,787	Asmara	1,000
Estonia	45.1	17.4	1,324	Tallinn	19,600
Ethiopia	1,104	426	74,778	Addis Ababa	1,000
Faroe Is. (Denmark)	1.4	0.54	47	Tórshavn	31,000
Fiji	18.3	7.1	906	Suva	6,100
Finland	338	131	5,231	Helsinki	32,800
France	552	213	60,876	Paris	30,100
French Guiana (France)	90.0	34.7	200	Cayenne	8,300
French Polynesia (France)	4.0	1.5	275	Papeete	17,500
Gabon	268	103	1,425	Libreville	7,200
Gambia, The	11.3	4.4	1,642	Banjul	2,000
Gaza Strip (OPT)*	0.36	0.14	1,429	–	1,500
Georgia	69.7	26.9	4,661	Tbilisi	3,800
Germany	357	138	82,422	Berlin	31,400
Ghana	239	92.1	22,410	Accra	2,600
Gibraltar (UK)	0.006	0.002	28	Gibraltar Town	27,900
Greece	132	50.9	10,668	Athens	23,500
Greenland (Denmark)	2,176	840	56	Nuuk	20,000
Grenada	0.34	0.13	90	St George's	3,900
Guadeloupe (France)	1.7	0.66	453	Basse-Terre	7,900
Guam (US)	0.55	0.21	171	Agana	15,000
Guatemala	109	42.0	12,294	Guatemala City	4,900
Guinea	246	94.9	9,690	Conakry	2,000
Guinea-Bissau	36.1	13.9	1,442	Bissau	900
Guyana	215	83.0	767	Georgetown	4,700
Haiti	27.8	10.7	8,309	Port-au-Prince	1,800
Honduras	112	43.3	7,326	Tegucigalpa	3,000
Hungary	93.0	35.9	9,981	Budapest	17,300
Iceland	103	39.8	299	Reykjavik	38,100
India	3,287	1,269	1,095,352	New Delhi	3,700
Indonesia	1,905	735	245,453	Jakarta	3,800
Iran	1,648	636	68,688	Tehran	8,900
Iraq	438	169	26,783	Baghdad	2,900
Ireland	70.3	27.1	4,062	Dublin	43,600
Israel	20.6	8.0	6,352	Jerusalem	26,200
Italy	301	116	58,134	Rome	29,700
Ivory Coast (Côte d'Ivoire)	322	125	17,655	Yamoussoukro	1,600
Jamaica	11.0	4.2	2,758	Kingston	4,600
Japan	378	146	127,464	Tokyo	33,100
Jordan	89.3	34.5	5,907	Amman	4,900
Kazakhstan	2,725	1,052	15,233	Astana	9,100
Kenya	580	224	34,708	Nairobi	1,200
Kiribati	0.73	0.28	105	Tarawa	2,700
Korea, North	121	46.5	23,113	Pyŏngyang	1,800
Korea, South	99.3	38.3	48,847	Seoul	24,200
Kuwait	17.8	6.9	2,418	Kuwait City	21,600
Kyrgyzstan	200	77.2	5,214	Bishkek	2,000
Laos	237	91.4	6,368	Vientiane	2,100
Latvia	64.6	24.9	2,275	Riga	15,400
Lebanon	10.4	4.0	3,874	Beirut	5,500
Lesotho	30.4	11.7	2,022	Maseru	2,600
Liberia	111	43.0	3,042	Monrovia	1,000
Libya	1,760	679	5,901	Tripoli	12,700
Liechtenstein	0.16	0.06	34	Vaduz	25,000
Lithuania	65.2	25.2	3,586	Vilnius	15,100
Luxembourg	2.6	1.0	474	Luxembourg	68,800
Macedonia (FYROM)	25.7	9.9	2,051	Skopje	8,200
Madagascar	587	227	18,595	Antananarivo	900
Madeira (Portugal)	0.78	0.30	241	Funchal	22,700
Malawi	118	45.7	13,014	Lilongwe	600
Malaysia	330	127	24,386	Kuala Lumpur/Putrajaya	12,700
Maldives	0.30	0.12	359	Malé	3,900
Mali	1,240	479	11,717	Bamako	1,200
Malta	0.32	0.12	400	Valletta	20,300
Marshall Is.	0.18	0.07	60	Majuro	2,900
Martinique (France)	1.1	0.43	436	Fort-de-France	14,400
Mauritania	1,026	396	3,177	Nouakchott	2,600
Mauritius	2.0	0.79	1,241	Port Louis	13,500
Mayotte (France)	0.37	0.14	201	Mamoundzou	4,900
Mexico	1,958	756	107,450	Mexico City	10,600
Micronesia, Fed. States of	0.70	0.27	108	Palikir	2,300
Moldova	33.9	13.1	4,467	Chişinău	2,000
Monaco	0.001	0.0004	33	Monaco	30,000
Mongolia	1,567	605	2,832	Ulan Bator	2,000
Montenegro	14.0	5.4	631	Podgorica	3,800
Montserrat (UK)	0.10	0.04	9	Plymouth	3,400
Morocco	447	172	33,241	Rabat	4,400
Mozambique	802	309	19,687	Maputo	1,500
Namibia	824	318	2,044	Windhoek	7,400
Nauru	0.02	0.008	13	Yaren District	5,000
Nepal	147	56.8	28,287	Katmandu	1,500
Netherlands	41.5	16.0	16,491	Amsterdam/The Hague	31,700
Netherlands Antilles (Neths)	0.80	0.31	222	Willemstad	16,000
New Caledonia (France)	18.6	7.2	219	Nouméa	15,000
New Zealand	271	104	4,076	Wellington	26,000
Nicaragua	130	50.2	5,570	Managua	3,000
Niger	1,267	489	12,525	Niamey	1,000
Nigeria	924	357	131,860	Abuja	1,400
Northern Mariana Is. (US)	0.46	0.18	82	Saipan	12,500
Norway	324	125	4,611	Oslo	47,800
Oman	310	119	3,102	Muscat	14,100
Pakistan	796	307	165,804	Islamabad	2,600
Palau	0.46	0.18	21	Koror	7,600
Panama	75.5	29.2	3,191	Panamá	7,900
Papua New Guinea	463	179	5,671	Port Moresby	2,700
Paraguay	407	157	6,506	Asunción	4,700
Peru	1,285	496	28,303	Lima	6,400
Philippines	300	116	89,469	Manila	5,000
Poland	323	125	38,537	Warsaw	14,100
Portugal	88.8	34.3	10,606	Lisbon	19,100
Puerto Rico (US)	8.9	3.4	3,927	San Juan	19,100
Qatar	11.0	4.2	885	Doha	29,400
Réunion (France)	2.5	0.97	788	St-Denis	6,200
Romania	238	92.0	22,304	Bucharest	8,800
Russia	17,075	6,593	142,894	Moscow	12,100
Rwanda	26.3	10.2	8,648	Kigali	1,600
St Kitts & Nevis	0.26	0.10	39	Basseterre	8,200
St Lucia	0.54	0.21	168	Castries	4,800
St Vincent & Grenadines	0.39	0.15	118	Kingstown	3,600
Samoa	2.8	1.1	177	Apia	2,100
San Marino	0.06	0.02	29	San Marino	34,100
São Tomé & Príncipe	0.96	0.37	193	São Tomé	1,200
Saudi Arabia	2,150	830	27,020	Riyadh	13,800
Senegal	197	76.0	11,987	Dakar	1,800
Serbia	88.4	34.1	9,396	Belgrade	4,400
Seychelles	0.46	0.18	82	Victoria	7,800
Sierra Leone	71.7	27.7	6,005	Freetown	900
Singapore	0.68	0.26	4,492	Singapore City	30,900
Slovak Republic	49.0	18.9	5,439	Bratislava	17,700
Slovenia	20.3	7.8	2,010	Ljubljana	23,400
Solomon Is.	28.9	11.2	552	Honiara	600
Somalia	638	246	8,863	Mogadishu	600
South Africa	1,221	471	44,188	Cape Town/Pretoria	13,000
Spain	498	192	40,398	Madrid	27,000
Sri Lanka	65.6	25.3	20,222	Colombo	4,600
Sudan	2,506	967	41,236	Khartoum	2,300
Suriname	163	63.0	439	Paramaribo	7,100
Swaziland	17.4	6.7	1,136	Mbabane	5,500
Sweden	450	174	9,017	Stockholm	31,600
Switzerland	41.3	15.9	7,524	Bern	33,600
Syria	185	71.5	18,881	Damascus	4,000
Taiwan	36.0	13.9	23,036	Taipei	29,000
Tajikistan	143	55.3	7,321	Dushanbe	1,300
Tanzania	945	365	37,445	Dodoma	800
Thailand	513	198	64,632	Bangkok	9,100
Togo	56.8	21.9	5,549	Lomé	1,700
Tonga	0.65	0.25	115	Nuku'alofa	2,200
Trinidad & Tobago	5.1	2.0	1,066	Port of Spain	19,700
Tunisia	164	63.2	10,175	Tunis	8,600
Turkey	775	299	70,414	Ankara	8,900
Turkmenistan	488	188	5,043	Ashkhabad	8,900
Turks & Caicos Is. (UK)	0.43	0.17	21	Cockburn Town	11,500
Tuvalu	0.03	0.01	12	Fongafale	1,600
Uganda	241	93.1	28,196	Kampala	1,800
Ukraine	604	233	46,711	Kiev	7,600
United Arab Emirates	83.6	32.3	2,603	Abu Dhabi	49,700
United Kingdom	242	93.4	60,609	London	31,400
United States of America	9,629	3,718	301,139	Washington, DC	43,500
Uruguay	175	67.6	3,432	Montevideo	10,700
Uzbekistan	447	173	27,307	Tashkent	2,000
Vanuatu	12.2	4.7	209	Port-Vila	2,900
Venezuela	912	352	25,730	Caracas	6,900
Vietnam	332	128	84,403	Hanoi	3,100
Virgin Is. (UK)	0.15	0.06	23	Road Town	38,500
Virgin Is. (US)	0.35	0.13	109	Charlotte Amalie	14,500
Wallis & Futuna Is. (France)	0.20	0.08	16	Mata-Utu	3,800
West Bank (OPT)*	5.9	2.3	2,460	–	1,500
Western Sahara	266	103	273	El Aaiún	N/A
Yemen	528	204	21,456	Sana'	900
Zambia	753	291	11,502	Lusaka	1,000
Zimbabwe	391	151	12,237	Harare	2,000

*OPT = Occupied Palestinian Territory   N/A = Not available

World Statistics: Physical Dimensions

Each topic list is divided into continents and within a continent the items are listed in order of size. The bottom part of many of the lists is selective in order to give examples from as many different countries as possible. The order of the continents is the same as in the atlas, beginning with Europe and ending with South America. The figures are rounded as appropriate.

World, Continents, Oceans

	km²	miles²	%
The World	509,450,000	196,672,000	–
Land	149,450,000	57,688,000	29.3
Water	360,000,000	138,984,000	70.7
Asia	44,500,000	17,177,000	29.8
Africa	30,302,000	11,697,000	20.3
North America	24,241,000	9,357,000	16.2
South America	17,793,000	6,868,000	11.9
Antarctica	14,100,000	5,443,000	9.4
Europe	9,957,000	3,843,000	6.7
Australia & Oceania	8,557,000	3,303,000	5.7
Pacific Ocean	155,557,000	60,061,000	46.4
Atlantic Ocean	76,762,000	29,638,000	22.9
Indian Ocean	68,556,000	26,470,000	20.4
Southern Ocean	20,327,000	7,848,000	6.1
Arctic Ocean	14,056,000	5,427,000	4.2

Ocean Depths

Atlantic Ocean	m	ft
Puerto Rico (Milwaukee) Deep	9,220	30,249
Cayman Trench	7,680	25,197
Gulf of Mexico	5,203	17,070
Mediterranean Sea	5,121	16,801
Black Sea	2,211	7,254
North Sea	660	2,165

Indian Ocean	m	ft
Java Trench	7,450	24,442
Red Sea	2,635	8,454

Pacific Ocean	m	ft
Mariana Trench	11,022	36,161
Tonga Trench	10,882	35,702
Japan Trench	10,554	34,626
Kuril Trench	10,542	34,587

Arctic Ocean	m	ft
Molloy Deep	5,608	18,399

Southern Ocean	m	ft
South Sandwich Trench	7,235	23,737

Mountains

Europe		m	ft
Elbrus	Russia	5,642	18,510
Mont Blanc	France/Italy	4,808	15,774
Monte Rosa	Italy/Switzerland	4,634	15,203
Dom	Switzerland	4,545	14,911
Liskamm	Switzerland	4,527	14,852
Weisshorn	Switzerland	4,505	14,780
Taschorn	Switzerland	4,490	14,730
Matterhorn/Cervino	Italy/Switzerland	4,478	14,691
Mont Maudit	France/Italy	4,465	14,649
Dent Blanche	Switzerland	4,356	14,291
Nadelhorn	Switzerland	4,327	14,196
Grandes Jorasses	France/Italy	4,208	13,806
Jungfrau	Switzerland	4,158	13,642
Grossglockner	Austria	3,797	12,457
Mulhacén	Spain	3,478	11,411
Zugspitze	Germany	2,962	9,718
Olympus	Greece	2,917	9,570
Triglav	Slovenia	2,863	9,393
Gerlachovka	Slovak Republic	2,655	8,711
Galdhøpiggen	Norway	2,469	8,100
Ben Nevis	UK	1,342	4,403

Asia		m	ft
Everest	China/Nepal	8,850	29,035
K2 (Godwin Austen)	China/Kashmir	8,611	28,251
Kanchenjunga	India/Nepal	8,598	28,208
Lhotse	China/Nepal	8,516	27,939
Makalu	China/Nepal	8,481	27,824
Cho Oyu	China/Nepal	8,201	26,906
Dhaulagiri	Nepal	8,167	26,795
Manaslu	Nepal	8,156	26,758
Nanga Parbat	Kashmir	8,126	26,660
Annapurna	Nepal	8,078	26,502
Gasherbrum	China/Kashmir	8,068	26,469
Broad Peak	China/Kashmir	8,051	26,414
Xixabangma	China	8,012	26,286
Kangbachen	Nepal	7,858	25,781
Trivor	Pakistan	7,720	25,328
Pik Imeni Ismail Samani	Tajikistan	7,495	24,590
Demavend	Iran	5,604	18,386
Ararat	Turkey	5,165	16,945
Gunong Kinabalu	Malaysia (Borneo)	4,101	13,455
Fuji-San	Japan	3,776	12,388

Africa		m	ft
Kilimanjaro	Tanzania	5,895	19,340
Mt Kenya	Kenya	5,199	17,057
Ruwenzori (Margherita)	Ug./Congo (D.R.)	5,109	16,762
Meru	Tanzania	4,565	14,977
Ras Dashen	Ethiopia	4,533	14,872
Karisimbi	Rwanda/Congo (D.R.)	4,507	14,787
Mt Elgon	Kenya/Uganda	4,321	14,176
Batu	Ethiopia	4,307	14,130
Toubkal	Morocco	4,165	13,665
Mt Cameroun	Cameroon	4,070	13,353

Oceania		m	ft
Puncak Jaya	Indonesia	5,029	16,499
Puncak Trikora	Indonesia	4,730	15,518
Puncak Mandala	Indonesia	4,702	15,427
Mt Wilhelm	Papua New Guinea	4,508	14,790
Mauna Kea	USA (Hawai'i)	4,205	13,796
Mauna Loa	USA (Hawai'i)	4,169	13,681
Aoraki Mt Cook	New Zealand	3,753	12,313
Mt Kosciuszko	Australia	2,230	7,316

North America		m	ft
Mt McKinley (Denali)	USA (Alaska)	6,194	20,321
Mt Logan	Canada	5,959	19,551
Pico de Orizaba	Mexico	5,610	18,405
Mt St Elias	USA/Canada	5,489	18,008
Popocatépetl	Mexico	5,452	17,887
Mt Foraker	USA (Alaska)	5,304	17,401
Iztaccihuatl	Mexico	5,286	17,343
Mt Lucania	Canada	5,226	17,146
Mt Steele	Canada	5,073	16,644
Mt Bona	USA (Alaska)	5,005	16,420
Mt Whitney	USA	4,418	14,495
Tajumulco	Guatemala	4,220	13,845
Chirripó Grande	Costa Rica	3,837	12,589
Pico Duarte	Dominican Rep.	3,175	10,417

South America		m	ft
Aconcagua	Argentina	6,962	22,841
Bonete	Argentina	6,872	22,546
Ojos del Salado	Argentina/Chile	6,863	22,516
Pissis	Argentina	6,779	22,241
Mercedario	Argentina/Chile	6,770	22,211
Huascarán	Peru	6,768	22,204
Llullaillaco	Argentina/Chile	6,723	22,057
Nudo de Cachi	Argentina	6,720	22,047
Yerupaja	Peru	6,632	21,758
Sajama	Bolivia	6,520	21,391
Chimborazo	Ecuador	6,267	20,561
Pico Cristóbal Colón	Colombia	5,800	19,029
Pico Bolivar	Venezuela	5,007	16,427

Antarctica		m	ft
Vinson Massif		4,897	16,066
Mt Kirkpatrick		4,528	14,855

Rivers

Europe		km	miles
Volga	Caspian Sea	3,700	2,300
Danube	Black Sea	2,850	1,770
Ural	Caspian Sea	2,535	1,575
Dnepr (Dnipro)	Black Sea	2,285	1,420
Kama	Volga	2,030	1,260
Don	Black Sea	1,990	1,240
Petchora	Arctic Ocean	1,790	1,110
Oka	Volga	1,480	920
Dnister (Dniester)	Black Sea	1,400	870
Vyatka	Kama	1,370	850
Rhine	North Sea	1,320	820
N. Dvina	Arctic Ocean	1,290	800
Elbe	North Sea	1,145	710

Asia		km	miles
Yangtze	Pacific Ocean	6,380	3,960
Yenisey–Angara	Arctic Ocean	5,550	3,445
Huang He	Pacific Ocean	5,464	3,395
Ob–Irtysh	Arctic Ocean	5,410	3,360
Mekong	Pacific Ocean	4,500	2,795
Amur	Pacific Ocean	4,442	2,760
Lena	Arctic Ocean	4,402	2,735
Irtysh	Ob	4,250	2,640
Yenisey	Arctic Ocean	4,090	2,540
Ob	Arctic Ocean	3,680	2,285
Indus	Indian Ocean	3,100	1,925
Brahmaputra	Indian Ocean	2,900	1,800
Syrdarya	Aral Sea	2,860	1,775
Salween	Indian Ocean	2,800	1,740
Euphrates	Indian Ocean	2,700	1,675
Amudarya	Aral Sea	2,540	1,575

Africa		km	miles
Nile	Mediterranean	6,695	4,180
Congo	Atlantic Ocean	4,670	2,900
Niger	Atlantic Ocean	4,180	2,595
Zambezi	Indian Ocean	3,540	2,200
Oubangi/Uele	Congo (D.R.)	2,250	1,400
Kasai	Congo (D.R.)	1,950	1,210
Shaballe	Indian Ocean	1,930	1,200
Orange	Atlantic Ocean	1,860	1,155
Cubango	Okavango Delta	1,800	1,120
Limpopo	Indian Ocean	1,770	1,100
Senegal	Atlantic Ocean	1,640	1,020

Australia		km	miles
Murray–Darling	Southern Ocean	3,750	2,330
Darling	Murray	3,070	1,905
Murray	Southern Ocean	2,575	1,600
Murrumbidgee	Murray	1,690	1,050

North America		km	miles
Mississippi–Missouri	Gulf of Mexico	5,971	3,710
Mackenzie	Arctic Ocean	4,240	2,630
Missouri	Mississippi	4,088	2,540
Mississippi	Gulf of Mexico	3,782	2,350
Yukon	Pacific Ocean	3,185	1,980
Rio Grande	Gulf of Mexico	3,030	1,880
Arkansas	Mississippi	2,340	1,450

		km	miles
Colorado	Pacific Ocean	2,330	1,445
Red	Mississippi	2,040	1,270
Columbia	Pacific Ocean	1,950	1,210
Saskatchewan	Lake Winnipeg	1,940	1,205

South America		km	miles
Amazon	Atlantic Ocean	6,450	4,010
Paraná–Plate	Atlantic Ocean	4,500	2,800
Purus	Amazon	3,350	2,080
Madeira	Amazon	3,200	1,990
São Francisco	Atlantic Ocean	2,900	1,800
Paraná	Plate	2,800	1,740
Tocantins	Atlantic Ocean	2,750	1,710
Orinoco	Atlantic Ocean	2,740	1,700
Paraguay	Paraná	2,550	1,580
Pilcomayo	Paraná	2,500	1,550
Araguaia	Tocantins	2,250	1,400

Lakes

Europe		km²	miles²
Lake Ladoga	Russia	17,700	6,800
Lake Onega	Russia	9,700	3,700
Saimaa system	Finland	8,000	3,100
Vänern	Sweden	5,500	2,100

Asia		km²	miles²
Caspian Sea	Asia	371,000	143,000
Lake Baikal	Russia	30,500	11,780
Tonlé Sap	Cambodia	20,000	7,700
Lake Balqash	Kazakhstan	18,500	7,100
Aral Sea	Kazakhstan/Uzbekistan	17,160	6,625

Africa		km²	miles²
Lake Victoria	East Africa	68,000	26,300
Lake Tanganyika	Central Africa	33,000	13,000
Lake Malawi/Nyasa	East Africa	29,600	11,430
Lake Chad	Central Africa	25,000	9,700
Lake Bangweulu	Zambia	9,840	3,800
Lake Turkana	Ethiopia/Kenya	8,500	3,290

Australia		km²	miles²
Lake Eyre	Australia	8,900	3,400
Lake Torrens	Australia	5,800	2,200
Lake Gairdner	Australia	4,800	1,900

North America		km²	miles²
Lake Superior	Canada/USA	82,350	31,800
Lake Huron	Canada/USA	59,600	23,010
Lake Michigan	USA	58,000	22,400
Great Bear Lake	Canada	31,800	12,280
Great Slave Lake	Canada	28,500	11,000
Lake Erie	Canada/USA	25,700	9,900
Lake Winnipeg	Canada	24,400	9,400
Lake Ontario	Canada/USA	19,500	7,500
Lake Nicaragua	Nicaragua	8,200	3,200

South America		km²	miles²
Lake Titicaca	Bolivia/Peru	8,300	3,200
Lake Poopo	Bolivia	2,800	1,100

Islands

Europe		km²	miles²
Great Britain	UK	229,880	88,700
Iceland	Atlantic Ocean	103,000	39,800
Ireland	Ireland/UK	84,400	32,600
Novaya Zemlya (N.)	Russia	48,200	18,600
Sicily	Italy	25,500	9,800
Corsica	France	8,700	3,400

Asia		km²	miles²
Borneo	South-east Asia	744,360	287,400
Sumatra	Indonesia	473,600	182,860
Honshu	Japan	230,500	88,980
Sulawesi (Celebes)	Indonesia	189,000	73,000
Java	Indonesia	126,700	48,900
Luzon	Philippines	104,700	40,400
Hokkaido	Japan	78,400	30,300

Africa		km²	miles²
Madagascar	Indian Ocean	587,040	226,660
Socotra	Indian Ocean	3,600	1,400
Réunion	Indian Ocean	2,500	965

Oceania		km²	miles²
New Guinea	Indonesia/Papua NG	821,030	317,000
New Zealand (S.)	Pacific Ocean	150,500	58,100
New Zealand (N.)	Pacific Ocean	114,700	44,300
Tasmania	Australia	67,800	26,200
Hawai'i	Pacific Ocean	10,450	4,000

North America		km²	miles²
Greenland	Atlantic Ocean	2,175,600	839,800
Baffin Is.	Canada	508,000	196,100
Victoria Is.	Canada	212,200	81,900
Ellesmere Is.	Canada	212,000	81,800
Cuba	Caribbean Sea	110,860	42,800
Hispaniola	Dominican Rep./Haiti	76,200	29,400
Jamaica	Caribbean Sea	11,400	4,400
Puerto Rico	Atlantic Ocean	8,900	3,400

South America		km²	miles²
Tierra del Fuego	Argentina/Chile	47,000	18,100
Falkland Is. (E.)	Atlantic Ocean	6,800	2,600

User Guide

The reference maps which form the main body of this atlas have been prepared in accordance with the highest standards of international cartography to provide an accurate and detailed representation of the Earth. The scales and projections used have been carefully chosen to give balanced coverage of the world, while emphasizing the most densely populated and economically significant regions. A hallmark of Philip's mapping is the use of hill shading and relief colouring to create a graphic impression of landforms: this makes the maps exceptionally easy to read. However, knowledge of the key features employed in the construction and presentation of the maps will enable the reader to derive the fullest benefit from the atlas.

Map sequence

The atlas covers the Earth continent by continent: first Europe; then its land neighbour Asia (mapped north before south, in a clockwise sequence), then Africa, Australia and Oceania, North America and South America. This is the classic arrangement adopted by most cartographers since the 16th century. For each continent, there are maps at a variety of scales. First, physical relief and political maps of the whole continent; then a series of larger-scale maps of the regions within the continent, each followed, where required, by still larger-scale maps of the most important or densely populated areas. The governing principle is that by turning the pages of the atlas, the reader moves steadily from north to south through each continent, with each map overlapping its neighbours.

Map presentation

With very few exceptions (for example, for the Arctic and Antarctica), the maps are drawn with north at the top, regardless of whether they are presented upright or sideways on the page. In the borders will be found the map title; a locator diagram showing the area covered; continuation arrows showing the page numbers for maps of adjacent areas; the scale; the projection used; the degrees of latitude and longitude; and the letters and figures used in the index for locating place names and geographical features. Physical relief maps also have a height reference panel identifying the colours used for each layer of contouring.

Map symbols

Each map contains a vast amount of detail which can only be conveyed clearly and accurately by the use of symbols. Points and circles of varying sizes locate and identify the relative importance of towns and cities; different styles of type are employed for administrative, geographical and regional place names. A variety of pictorial symbols denote features such as glaciers and marshes, as well as man-made structures including roads, railways, airports and canals.

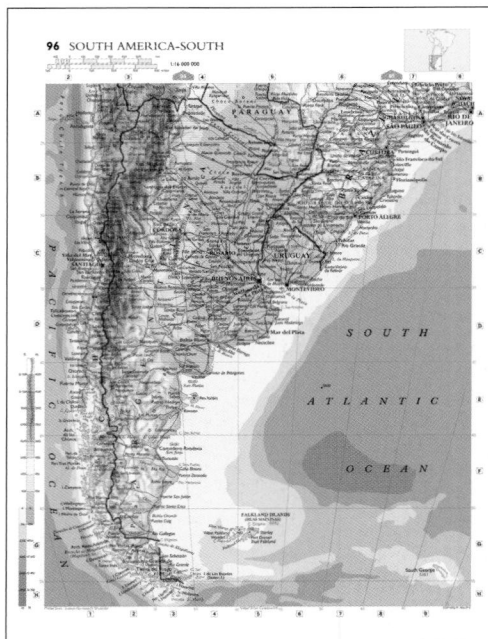

International borders are shown by red lines. Where neighbouring countries are in dispute, for example in the Middle East, the maps show the *de facto* boundary between nations, regardless of the legal or historical situation. The symbols are explained on the first page of the World Maps section of the atlas.

Map scales

The scale of each map is given in the numerical form known as the 'representative fraction'. The first figure is always one, signifying one unit of distance on the map; the second figure, usually in millions, is the number by which the map unit must be multiplied to give the equivalent distance on the Earth's surface. Calculations can easily be made in centimetres and kilometres, by dividing the Earth units figure by 100 000 (i.e. deleting the last five 0s). Thus 1:1 000 000 means 1 cm = 10 km. The calculation for inches and miles is more laborious, but 1 000 000 divided by 63 360 (the number of inches in a mile) shows that the ratio 1:1 000 000 means approximately 1 inch = 16 miles. The table below provides distance equivalents for scales down to 1:50 000 000.

LARGE SCALE		
1:1 000 000	1 cm = 10 km	1 inch = 16 miles
1:2 500 000	1 cm = 25 km	1 inch = 39.5 miles
1:5 000 000	1 cm = 50 km	1 inch = 79 miles
1:6 000 000	1 cm = 60 km	1 inch = 95 miles
1:8 000 000	1 cm = 80 km	1 inch = 126 miles
1:10 000 000	1 cm = 100 km	1 inch = 158 miles
1:15 000 000	1 cm = 150 km	1 inch = 237 miles
1:20 000 000	1 cm = 200 km	1 inch = 316 miles
1:50 000 000	1 cm = 500 km	1 inch = 790 miles
SMALL SCALE		

Measuring distances

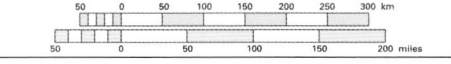

Although each map is accompanied by a scale bar, distances cannot always be measured with confidence because of the distortions involved in portraying the curved surface of the Earth on a flat page. As a general rule, the larger the map scale (i.e. the lower the number of Earth units in the representative fraction), the more accurate and reliable will be the distance measured. On small-scale maps such as those of the world and of entire continents, measurement may only be accurate along the 'standard parallels', or central axes, and should not be attempted without considering the map projection.

Latitude and longitude

Accurate positioning of individual points on the Earth's surface is made possible by reference to the geometrical system of latitude and longitude. Latitude *parallels* are drawn west-east around the Earth and numbered by degrees north and south of the Equator, which is designated 0° of latitude. Longitude *meridians* are drawn north–south and numbered by degrees east and west of the *prime meridian*, 0° of longitude, which passes through Greenwich in England. By referring to these co-ordinates and their subdivisions of minutes ($\frac{1}{60}$th of a degree) and seconds ($\frac{1}{60}$th of a minute), any place on Earth can be located to within a few hundred metres. Latitude and longitude are indicated by blue lines on the maps; they are straight or curved according to the projection employed. Reference to these lines is the easiest way of determining the relative positions of places on different maps, and for plotting compass directions.

Name forms

For ease of reference, both English and local name forms appear in the atlas. Oceans, seas and countries are shown in English throughout the atlas; country names may be abbreviated to their commonly accepted form (for example, Germany, not The Federal Republic of Germany). Conventional English forms are also used for place names on the smaller-scale maps of the continents. However, local name forms are used on all large-scale and regional maps, with the English form given in brackets only for important cities – the large-scale map of Russia and Central Asia thus shows Moskva (Moscow). For countries which do not use a Roman script, place names have been transcribed according to the systems adopted by the British and US Geographic Names Authorities. For China, the Pin Yin system has been used, with some more widely known forms appearing in brackets, as with Beijing (Peking). Both English and local names appear in the index, the English form being cross-referenced to the local form.

THE WORLD IN FOCUS

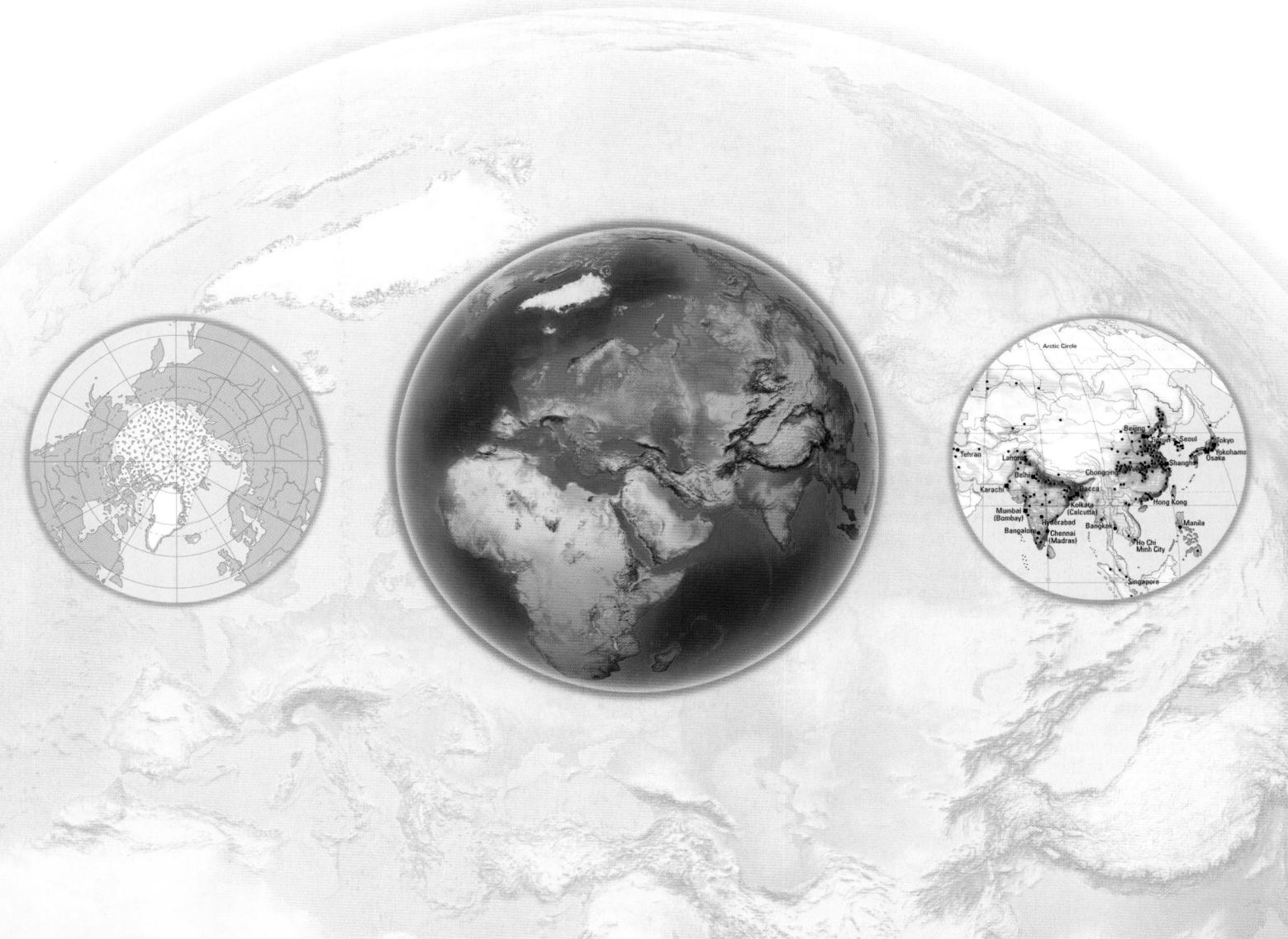

PLANET EARTH	2	WATER & VEGETATION	12	QUALITY OF LIFE	22
RESTLESS EARTH	4	ENVIRONMENT	14	ENERGY	24
LANDFORMS	6	POPULATION	16	PRODUCTION	26
OCEANS	8	THE HUMAN FAMILY	18	TRADE	28
CLIMATE	10	WEALTH	20	TRAVEL & TOURISM	30

Planet Earth

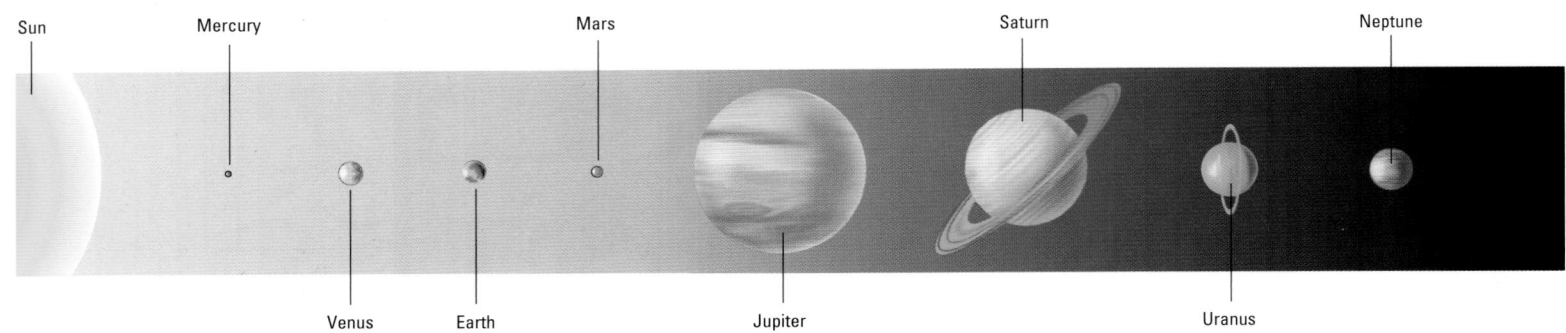

Sun   Mercury   Mars   Saturn   Neptune

Venus   Earth   Jupiter   Uranus

The Solar System

A minute part of one of the billions of galaxies (collections of stars) that populate the Universe, the Solar System lies about 26,000 light-years from the centre of our own galaxy, the 'Milky Way'. Thought to be about 5 billion years old, it consists of a central Sun with eight planets and their moons revolving around it, attracted by its gravitational pull. The planets orbit the Sun in the same direction – anti-clockwise when viewed from above the Sun's north pole – and almost in the same plane. Their orbital distances, however, vary enormously.

The Sun's diameter is 109 times that of the Earth, and the temperature at its core – caused by continuous thermonuclear fusions of hydrogen into helium – is estimated to be 15 million degrees Celsius. It is the Solar System's only source of light and heat.

Profile of the Planets

	Mean distance from Sun (million km)	Mass (Earth = 1)	Period of orbit (Earth days/years)	Period of rotation (Earth days)	Equatorial diameter (km)	Number of known satellites*
Mercury	57.9	0.06	87.97 days	58.65	4,879	0
Venus	108.2	0.82	224.7 days	243.02	12,104	0
Earth	149.6	1.00	365.3 days	1.00	12,756	1
Mars	227.9	0.11	687.0 days	1.029	6,792	2
Jupiter	778	317.8	11.86 years	0.411	142,984	63
Saturn	1,427	95.2	29.45 years	0.428	120,536	59
Uranus	2,871	14.5	84.02 years	0.720	51,118	27
Neptune	4,498	17.2	164.8 years	0.673	49,528	13

* Number of known satellites at mid-2007

All planetary orbits are elliptical in form, but only Mercury follows a path that deviates noticeably from a circular one. In 2006, Pluto was demoted from its former status as a planet and is now regarded as a member of the Kuiper Belt of icy bodies at the fringes of the Solar System.

The Seasons

Seasons occur because the Earth's axis is tilted at an angle of approximately 23½°. When the northern hemisphere is tilted to a maximum extent towards the Sun, on 21 June, the Sun is overhead at the Tropic of Cancer (latitude 23½° North). This is midsummer, or the summer solstice, in the northern hemisphere.

On 22 or 23 September, the Sun is overhead at the equator, and day and night are of equal length throughout the world. This is the autumnal equinox in the northern hemisphere. On 21 or 22 December, the Sun is overhead at the Tropic of Capricorn (23½° South), the winter solstice in the northern hemisphere. The overhead Sun then tracks north until, on 21 March, it is overhead at the equator. This is the spring (vernal) equinox in the northern hemisphere.

In the southern hemisphere, the seasons are the reverse of those in the north.

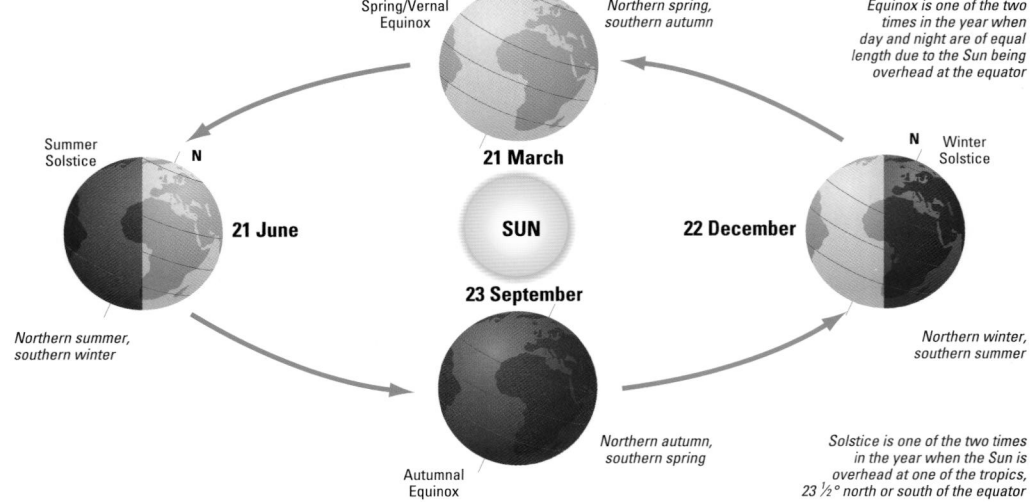

Equinox is one of the two times in the year when day and night are of equal length due to the Sun being overhead at the equator

Spring/Vernal Equinox — Northern spring, southern autumn

21 March

Summer Solstice — N

21 June

SUN

23 September

Winter Solstice — N

22 December

Northern summer, southern winter

Autumnal Equinox — Northern autumn, southern spring

Northern winter, southern summer

Solstice is one of the two times in the year when the Sun is overhead at one of the tropics, 23 ½° north or south of the equator

Day and Night

The Sun appears to rise in the east, reach its highest point at noon, and then set in the west, to be followed by night. In reality, it is not the Sun that is moving but the Earth rotating from west to east. The moment when the Sun's upper limb first appears above the horizon is termed sunrise; the moment when the Sun's upper limb disappears below the horizon is sunset.

At the summer solstice in the northern hemisphere (21 June), the Arctic has total daylight and the Antarctic total darkness. The opposite occurs at the winter solstice (21 or 22 December). At the equator, the length of day and night are almost equal all year.

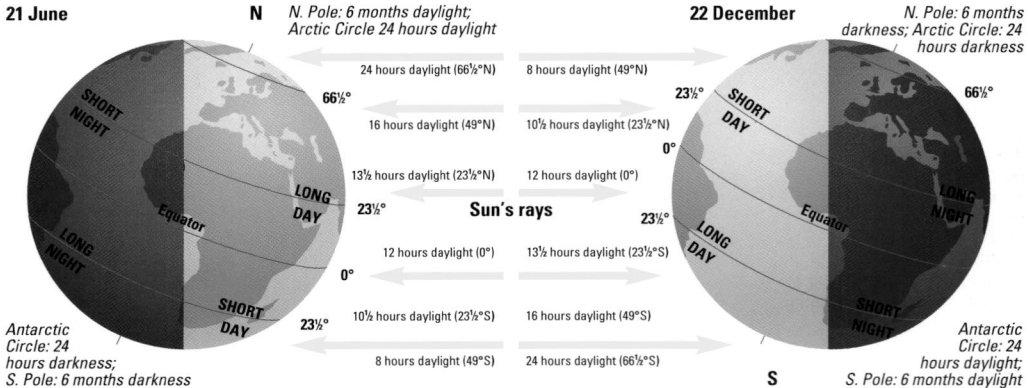

21 June   N   N. Pole: 6 months daylight; Arctic Circle 24 hours daylight

SHORT NIGHT   66½°

24 hours daylight (66½°N)   8 hours daylight (49°N)

16 hours daylight (49°N)   10½ hours daylight (23½°N)

LONG DAY   23½°   13½ hours daylight (23½°N)   12 hours daylight (0°)

Equator   Sun's rays

LONG NIGHT   0°   12 hours daylight (0°)   13½ hours daylight (23½°S)

SHORT DAY   23½°   10½ hours daylight (23½°S)   16 hours daylight (49°S)

Antarctic Circle: 24 hours darkness; S. Pole: 6 months darkness   8 hours daylight (49°S)   24 hours daylight (66½°S)

22 December   N. Pole: 6 months darkness; Arctic Circle: 24 hours darkness

23½°   SHORT DAY   66½°

0°

Equator   LONG NIGHT

23½°   LONG DAY

SHORT NIGHT   Antarctic Circle: 24 hours daylight; S. Pole: 6 months daylight   S

Time

Year: The time taken by the Earth to revolve around the Sun, or 365.24 days.

Leap Year: A calendar year of 366 days, 29 February being the additional day. It offsets the difference between the calendar and the solar year.

Month: The 12 calendar months of the year are approximately equal in length to a lunar month.

Week: An artificial period of 7 days, not based on astronomical time.

Day: The time taken by the Earth to complete one rotation on its axis.

Hour: 24 hours make one day. The day is divided into hours a.m. (ante meridiem or before noon) and p.m. (post meridiem or after noon), although most timetables now use the 24-hour system, from midnight to midnight.

Sunrise

Sunset

The Moon

The Moon rotates more slowly than the Earth, taking just over 27 days to make one complete rotation on its axis. Since this corresponds to the Moon's orbital period around the Earth, the Moon always presents the same hemisphere towards us, and we never see the far side. The interval between one New Moon and the next is 29½ days – this is called a lunation, or lunar month. The Moon shines only by reflected sunlight, and emits no light of its own. During each lunation the Moon displays a complete cycle of phases, caused by the changing angle of illumination from the Sun.

Phases of the Moon

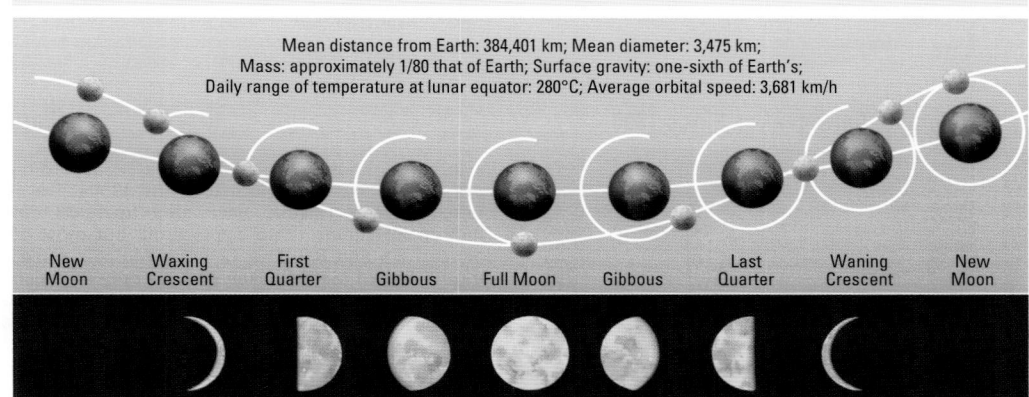

Mean distance from Earth: 384,401 km; Mean diameter: 3,475 km; Mass: approximately 1/80 that of Earth; Surface gravity: one-sixth of Earth's; Daily range of temperature at lunar equator: 280°C; Average orbital speed: 3,681 km/h

New Moon — Waxing Crescent — First Quarter — Gibbous — Full Moon — Gibbous — Last Quarter — Waning Crescent — New Moon

Eclipses

When the Moon passes between the Sun and the Earth, the Sun becomes partially eclipsed (1). A partial eclipse can become a total eclipse if the Moon covers the Sun completely (2) and the dark central part of the lunar shadow touches the Earth. The broad geographical zone covered by the Moon's outer shadow (P) has only a very small central area (often less than 100 km wide) that experiences totality. Totality can never last for more than 7½ minutes, and it is usually briefer than this. Lunar eclipses take place when the Moon moves through the shadow of the Earth, and can also be partial or total. Any single location on Earth can experience a maximum of four solar and three lunar eclipses in any single year, while a total solar eclipse occurs an average of once every 360 years for any given location.

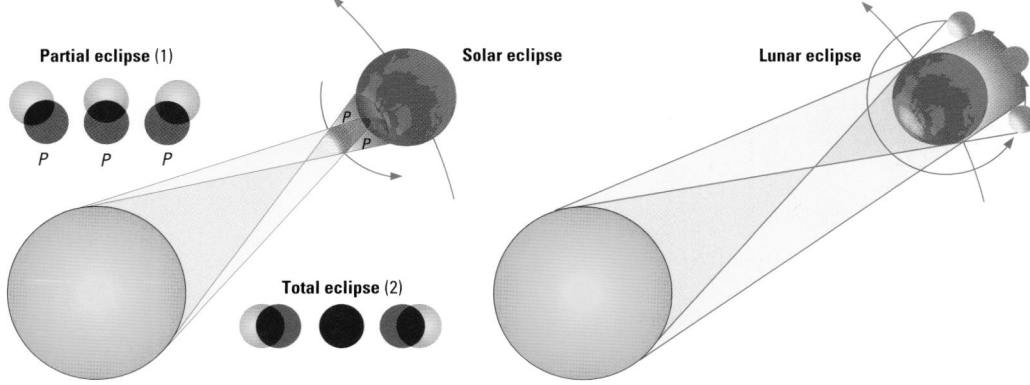

Tides

The daily rise and fall of the ocean's tides are the result of the gravitational pull of the Moon and that of the Sun, though the effect of the latter is not as strong as that of the Moon. This effect is greatest on the hemisphere facing the Moon and causes a tidal 'bulge'.

When the Sun, Earth and Moon are in line, spring tides occur: high tide reaches the highest values, and low tide falls to low levels. When lunar and solar forces are least coincidental with the Sun and Moon at an angle (near the Moon's first and third quarters), neap tides occur, which have a small tidal range.

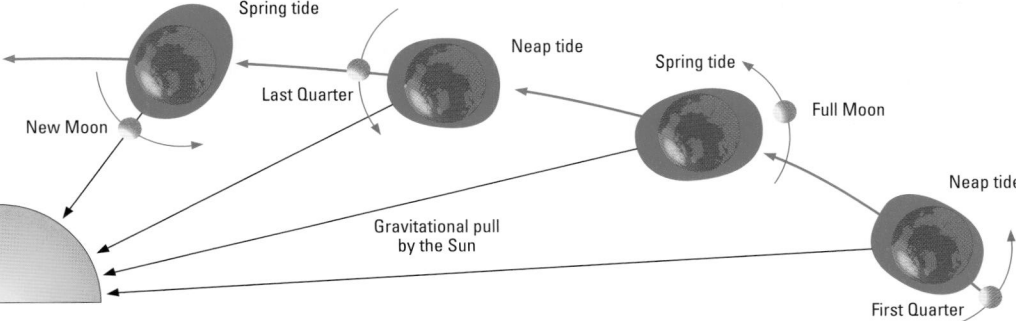

Restless Earth

The Earth's Structure

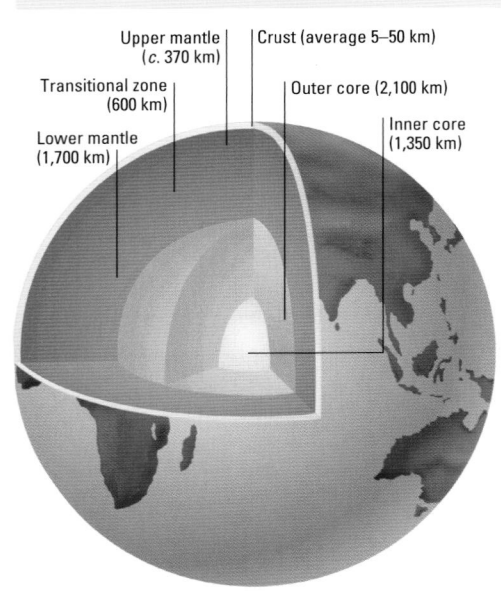

Upper mantle (c. 370 km)
Crust (average 5–50 km)
Transitional zone (600 km)
Outer core (2,100 km)
Lower mantle (1,700 km)
Inner core (1,350 km)

Continental Drift

About 200 million years ago the original Pangaea landmass began to split into two continental groups, which further separated over time to produce the present-day configuration.

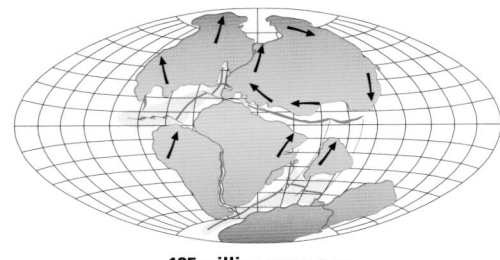

135 million years ago

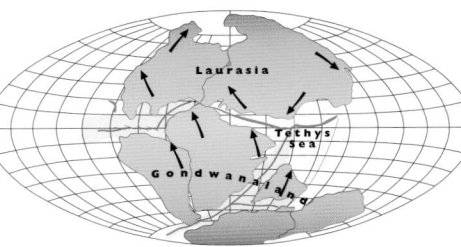

180 million years ago

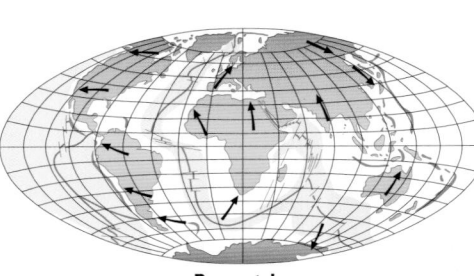

Present day

Trench
Rift
New ocean floor
Zones of slippage

Notable Earthquakes Since 1900

Year	Location	Richter Scale	Deaths
1906	San Francisco, USA	8.3	3,000
1906	Valparaiso, Chile	8.6	22,000
1908	Messina, Italy	7.5	83,000
1915	Avezzano, Italy	7.5	30,000
1920	Gansu (Kansu), China	8.6	180,000
1923	Yokohama, Japan	8.3	143,000
1927	Nan Shan, China	8.3	200,000
1932	Gansu (Kansu), China	7.6	70,000
1933	Sanriku, Japan	8.9	2,990
1934	Bihar, India/Nepal	8.4	10,700
1935	Quetta, India (now Pakistan)	7.5	60,000
1939	Chillan, Chile	8.3	28,000
1939	Erzincan, Turkey	7.9	30,000
1960	S. W. Chile	9.5	2,200
1960	Agadir, Morocco	5.8	12,000
1962	Khorasan, Iran	7.1	12,230
1964	Anchorage, USA	9.2	125
1968	N. E. Iran	7.4	12,000
1970	N. Peru	7.8	70,000
1972	Managua, Nicaragua	6.2	5,000
1974	N. Pakistan	6.3	5,200
1976	Guatemala	7.5	22,500
1976	Tangshan, China	8.2	255,000
1978	Tabas, Iran	7.7	25,000
1980	El Asnam, Algeria	7.3	20,000
1980	S. Italy	7.2	4,800
1985	Mexico City, Mexico	8.1	4,200
1988	N.W. Armenia	6.8	55,000
1990	N. Iran	7.7	36,000
1992	Flores, Indonesia	6.8	1,895
1993	Maharashtra, India	6.4	30,000
1994	Los Angeles, USA	6.6	51
1995	Kobe, Japan	7.2	5,000
1995	Sakhalin Is., Russia	7.5	2,000
1996	Yunnan, China	7.0	240
1997	N. E. Iran	7.1	2,400
1998	Takhar, Afghanistan	6.1	4,200
1998	Rostaq, Afghanistan	7.0	5,000
1999	Izmit, Turkey	7.4	15,000
1999	Taipei, Taiwan	7.6	1,700
2001	Gujarat, India	7.7	14,000
2002	Baghlan, Afghanistan	6.1	1,000
2003	Boumerdes, Algeria	6.8	2,200
2003	Bam, Iran	6.6	30,000
2004	Sumatra, Indonesia	9.0	250,000
2005	N. Pakistan	7.6	74,000
2006	Java, Indonesia	6.4	6,200

Earthquakes

Earthquake magnitude is usually rated according to either the Richter or the Modified Mercalli scale, both devised by seismologists in the 1930s. The Richter scale measures absolute earthquake power with mathematical precision: each step upwards represents a tenfold increase in shockwave amplitude. Theoretically, there is no upper limit, but most of the largest earthquakes measured have been rated at between 8.8 and 8.9. The 12–point Mercalli scale, based on observed effects, is often more meaningful, ranging from I (earthquakes noticed only by seismographs) to XII (total destruction); intermediate points include V (people awakened at night; unstable objects overturned), VII (collapse of ordinary buildings; chimneys and monuments fall), and IX (conspicuous cracks in ground; serious damage to reservoirs).

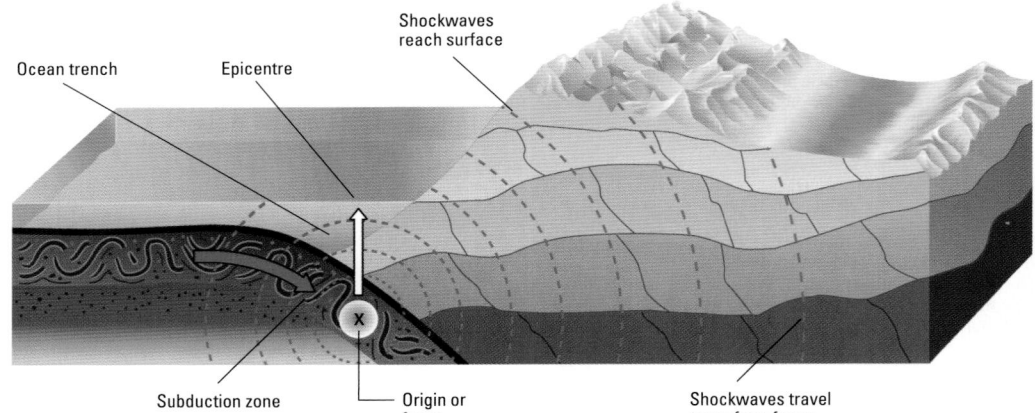

Shockwaves reach surface
Ocean trench
Epicentre
Subduction zone
Origin or focus
Shockwaves travel away from focus

Structure and Earthquakes

Mobile land areas
Submarine zones of mobile land areas
Stable land platforms
Submarine extensions of stable land platforms
Mid-oceanic volcanic ridges
Oceanic platforms

1976° Principal earthquakes and dates (since 1900)

Earthquakes are a series of rapid vibrations originating from the slipping or faulting of parts of the Earth's crust when stresses within build up to breaking point. They usually happen at depths varying from 8 km to 30 km. Severe earthquakes cause extensive damage when they take place in populated areas, destroying structures and severing communications. Most initial loss of life occurs due to secondary causes such as falling masonry, fires and flooding.

Projection: Interrupted Mollweide

Plate Tectonics

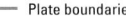

Plate boundaries   PACIFIC   Major plates

Direction of plate movements and rate of movement (cm/year)

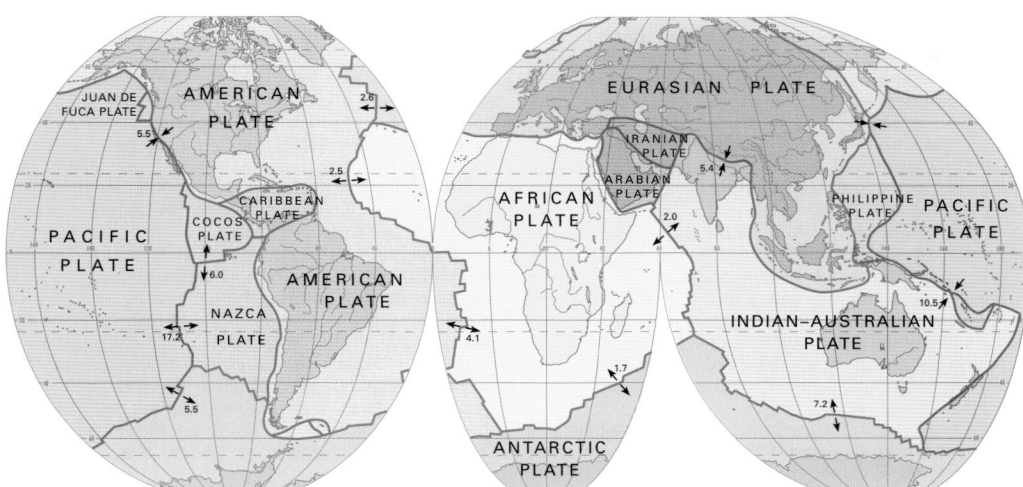

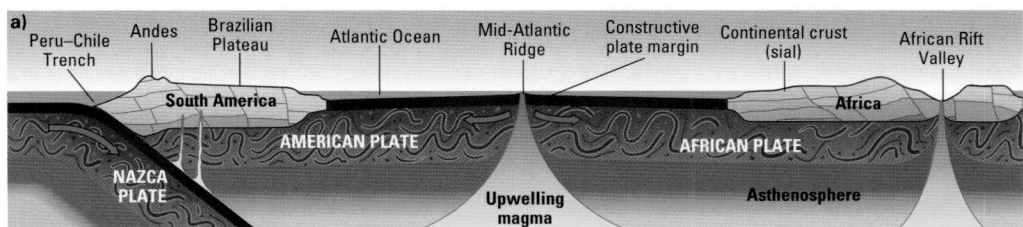

a) Peru–Chile Trench | Andes | Brazilian Plateau | Atlantic Ocean | Mid-Atlantic Ridge | Constructive plate margin | Continental crust (sial) | African Rift Valley
South America — AMERICAN PLATE — AFRICAN PLATE — Africa
NAZCA PLATE — Upwelling magma — Asthenosphere

The drifting of the continents is a feature that is unique to Planet Earth. The complementary, almost jigsaw-puzzle fit of the coastlines on each side of the Atlantic Ocean inspired Alfred Wegener's theory of continental drift in 1915. The theory suggested that the ancient super-continent, which Wegener named Pangaea, incorporated all of the Earth's landmasses and gradually split up to form today's continents.

The original debate about continental drift was a prelude to a more radical idea: plate tectonics. The basic theory is that the Earth's crust is made up of a series of rigid plates which float on a soft layer of the mantle and are moved about by continental convection currents within the Earth's interior. These plates diverge and converge along margins marked by seismic activity. Plates diverge from mid-ocean ridges where molten lava pushes upwards and forces the plates apart at rates of up to 40 mm [1.6 in] a year.

The three diagrams, left, give some examples of plate boundaries from around the world. Diagram (a) shows sea-floor spreading at the Mid-Atlantic Ridge as the American and African plates slowly diverge. The same thing is happening in (b) where sea-floor spreading at the Mid-Indian Ocean Ridge is forcing the Indian–Australian plate to collide into the Eurasian plate. In (c) oceanic crust (sima) is being subducted beneath lighter continental crust (sial).

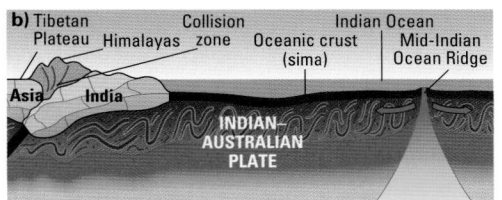

b) Tibetan Plateau | Himalayas | Collision zone | Oceanic crust (sima) | Indian Ocean | Mid-Indian Ocean Ridge
Asia | India
INDIAN–AUSTRALIAN PLATE

Volcanoes

Volcanoes occur when hot liquefied rock beneath the Earth's crust is pushed up by pressure to the surface as molten lava. Some volcanoes erupt in an explosive way, throwing out rocks and ash, whilst others are effusive and lava flows out of the vent. There are volcanoes which are both, such as Mount Fuji. An accumulation of lava and cinders creates cones of variable size and shape. As a result of many eruptions over centuries, Mount Etna in Sicily has a circumference of more than 120 km [75 miles].

Climatologists believe that volcanic ash, if ejected high into the atmosphere, can influence temperature and weather for several years afterwards. The 1991 eruption of Mount Pinatubo in the Philippines ejected more than 20 million tonnes of dust and ash 32 km [20 miles] into the atmosphere and is believed to have accelerated ozone depletion over a large part of the globe.

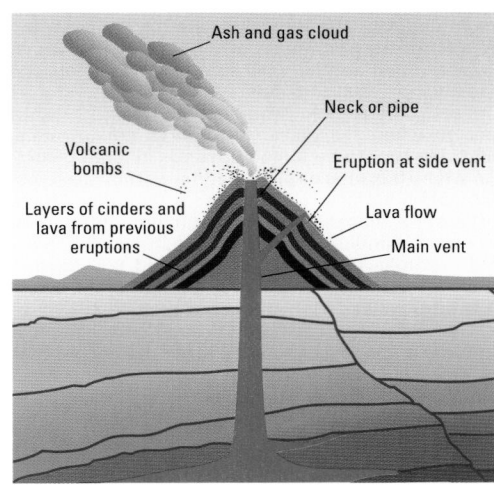

Ash and gas cloud
Neck or pipe
Volcanic bombs
Eruption at side vent
Layers of cinders and lava from previous eruptions
Lava flow
Main vent

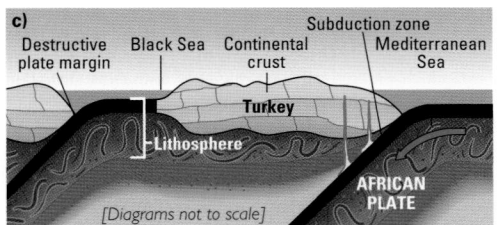

c) Destructive plate margin | Black Sea | Continental crust | Subduction zone | Mediterranean Sea
Turkey
Lithosphere
AFRICAN PLATE
[Diagrams not to scale]

Distribution of Volcanoes

Volcanoes today may be the subject of considerable scientific study but they remain both dramatic and unpredictable: in 1991 Mount Pinatubo, 100 km [62 miles] north of the Philippines capital Manila, suddenly burst into life after lying dormant for more than six centuries. Most of the world's active volcanoes occur in a belt around the Pacific Ocean, on the edge of the Pacific plate, called the 'ring of fire'. Indonesia has the greatest concentration with 90 volcanoes, 12 of which are active. The most famous, Krakatoa, erupted in 1883 with such force that the resulting tidal wave killed 36,000 people and tremors were felt as far away as Australia.

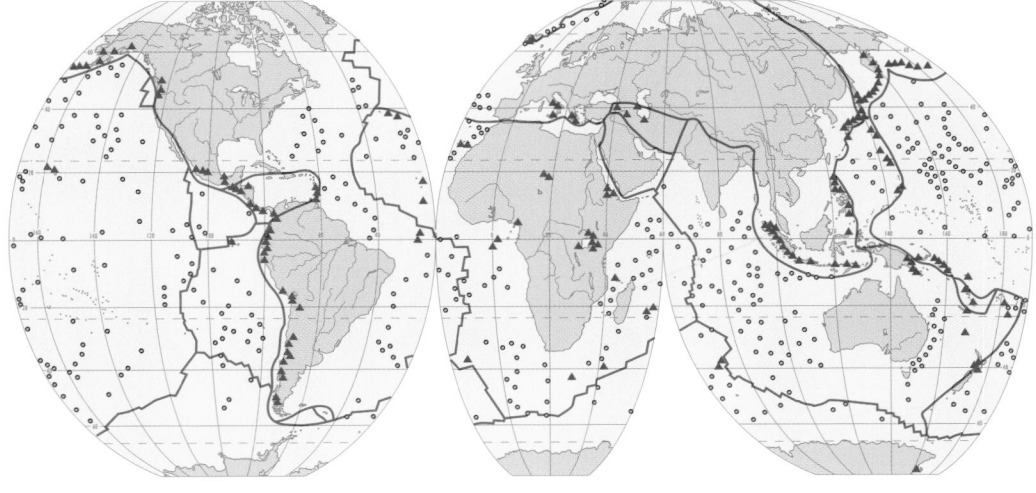

○ Submarine volcanoes

▲ Land volcanoes active since 1700

— Boundaries of tectonic plates

Landforms

The Rock Cycle

James Hutton first proposed the rock cycle in the late 1700s after he observed the slow but steady effects of erosion.

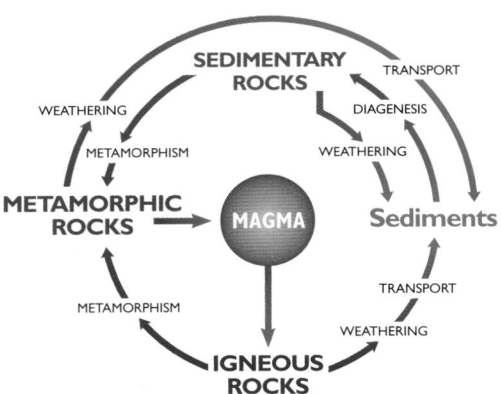

Above and below the surface of the oceans, the features of the Earth's crust are constantly changing. The phenomenal forces generated by convection currents in the molten core of our planet carry the vast segments or 'plates' of the crust across the globe in an endless cycle of creation and destruction. A continent may travel little more than 25 mm [1 in] per year, yet in the vast span of geological time this process throws up giant mountain ranges and creates new land.

Destruction of the landscape, however, begins as soon as it is formed. Wind, water, ice and sea, the main agents of erosion, mount a constant assault that even the most resistant rocks cannot withstand. Mountain peaks may dwindle by as little as a few millimetres each year, but if they are not uplifted by further movements of the crust they will eventually be reduced to rubble and transported away.

Water is the most powerful agent of erosion – it has been estimated that 100 billion tonnes of sediment are washed into the oceans every year. Three

Asian rivers account for 20% of this total; the Huang He, in China, and the Brahmaputra and Ganges in Bangladesh.

Rivers and glaciers, like the sea itself, generate much of their effect through abrasion – pounding the land with the debris they carry with them. But as well as destroying they also create new landforms, many of them spectacular: vast deltas like those of the Mississippi and the Nile, or the deep fjords cut by glaciers in British Columbia, Norway and New Zealand.

Geologists once considered that landscapes evolved from 'young', newly uplifted mountainous areas, through a 'mature' hilly stage, to an 'old age' stage when the land was reduced to an almost flat plain, or peneplain. This theory, called the 'cycle of erosion', fell into disuse when it became evident that so many factors, including the effects of plate tectonics and climatic change, constantly interrupt the cycle, which takes no account of the highly complex interactions that shape the surface of our planet.

Mountain Building

Mountains are formed when pressures on the Earth's crust caused by continental drift become so intense that the surface buckles or cracks. This happens where oceanic crust is subducted by continental crust or, more dramatically, where two tectonic plates collide: the Rockies, Andes, Alps, Urals and Himalayas resulted from such impacts. These are all known as fold mountains because they were formed by the compression of the rocks, forcing the surface to bend and fold like a crumpled rug. The Himalayas are formed from the folded former sediments of the Tethys Sea which was trapped in the collision zone between the Indian and Eurasian plates.

The other main mountain-building process occurs when the crust fractures to create faults, allowing rock to be forced upwards in large blocks; or when the pressure of magma within the crust forces the surface to bulge into a dome, or erupts to form a volcano. Large mountain ranges may reveal a combination of these features; the Alps, for example, have been compressed so violently that the folds are fragmented by numerous faults and intrusions of molten igneous rock.

Over millions of years, even the greatest mountain ranges can be reduced by the agents of erosion (most notably rivers) to a low rugged landscape known as a peneplain.

Types of faults: Faults occur where the crust is being stretched or compressed so violently that the rock strata break in a horizontal or vertical movement. They are classified by the direction in which the blocks of rock have moved. A normal fault results when a vertical movement causes the surface to break apart; compression causes a reverse fault. Horizontal movement causes shearing, known as a strike-slip fault. When the rock breaks in two places, the central block may be pushed up in a horst fault, or sink (creating a rift valley) in a graben fault.

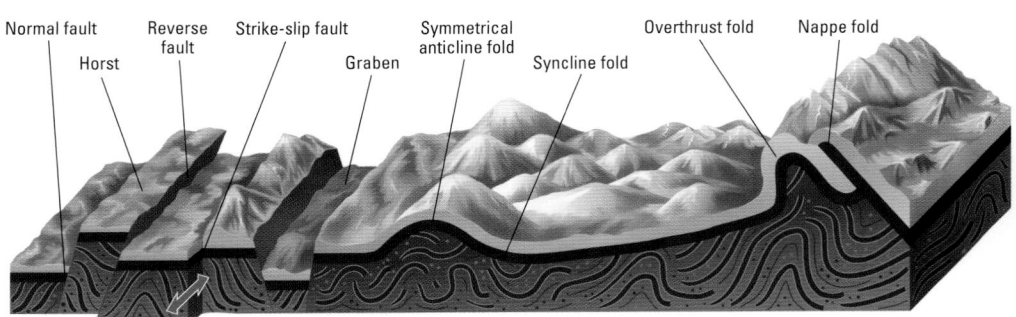

Types of fold: Folds occur when rock strata are squeezed and compressed. They are common, therefore, at destructive plate margins and where plates have collided, forcing the rocks to buckle into mountain ranges. Geographers give different names to the degrees of fold that result from continuing pressure on the rock. A simple fold may be symmetric, with even slopes on either side, but as the pressure builds up, one slope becomes steeper and the fold becomes asymmetric. Later, the ridge or 'anticline' at the top of the fold may slide over the lower ground or 'syncline' to form a recumbent fold. Eventually, the rock strata may break under the pressure to form an overthrust and finally a nappe fold.

Continental Glaciation

Ice sheets were at their greatest extent about 200,000 years ago. The maximum advance of the last Ice Age was about 18,000 years ago, when ice covered virtually all of Canada and reached as far south as the Bristol Channel in Britain.

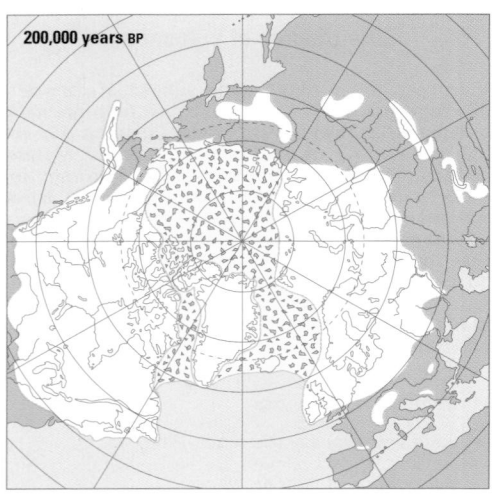

200,000 years BP

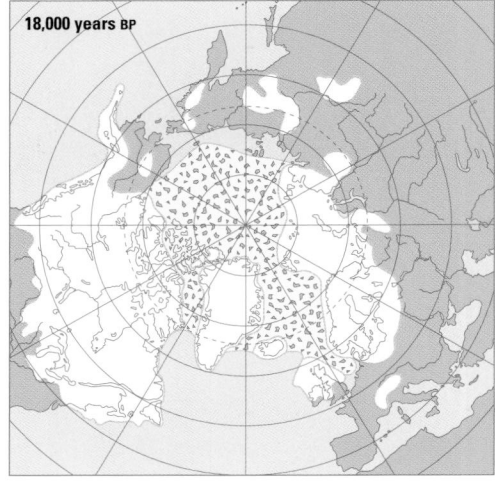

18,000 years BP

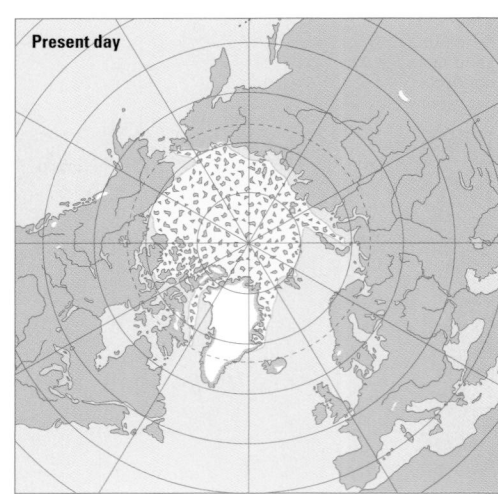

Present day

Natural Landforms

A stylized diagram to show a selection of landforms found in the mid-latitudes.

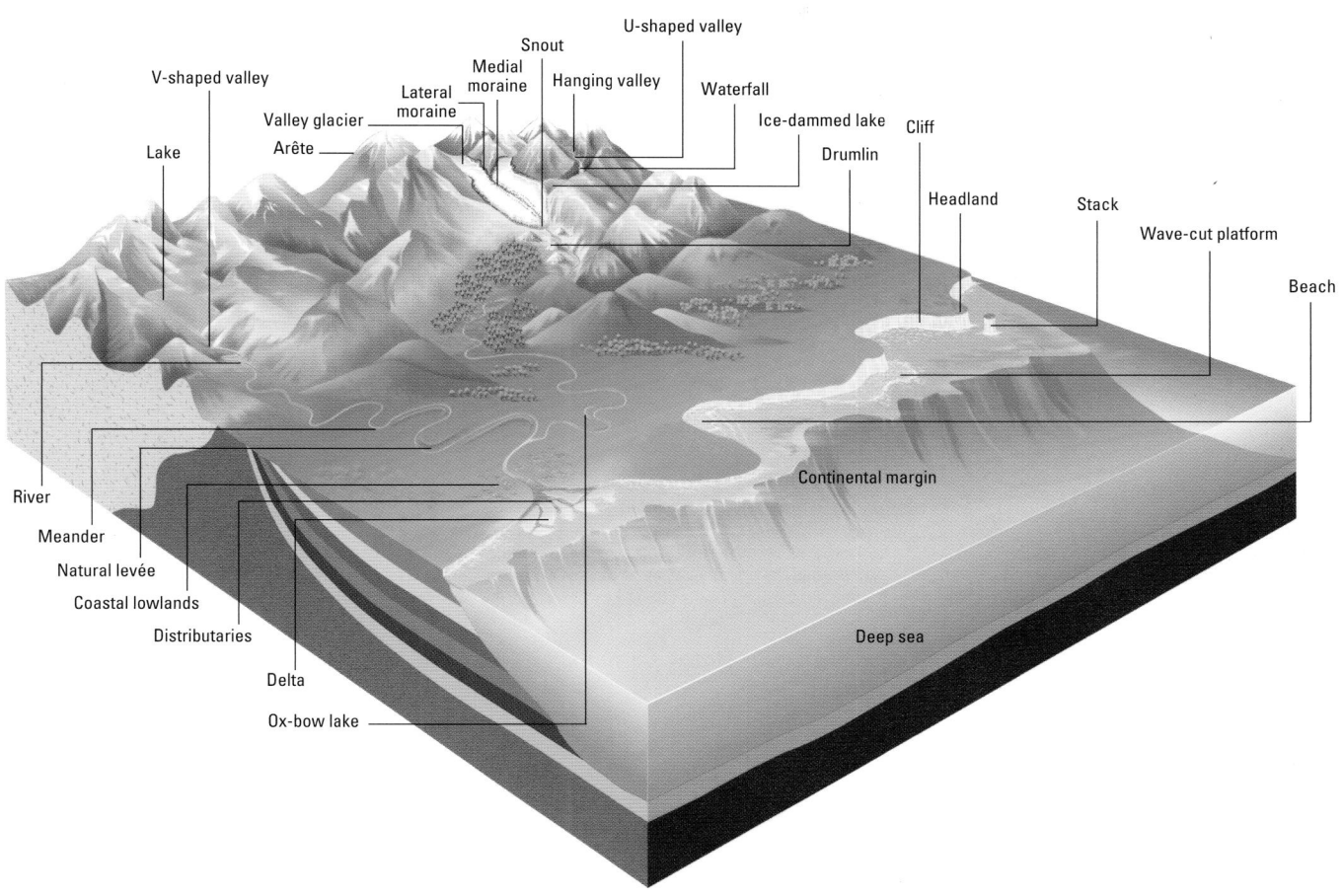

Desert Landscapes

The popular image that deserts are all huge expanses of sand is wrong. Despite harsh conditions, deserts contain some of the most varied and interesting landscapes in the world. They are also one of the most extensive environments – the hot and cold deserts together cover almost 40% of the Earth's surface.

The three types of hot desert are known by their Arabic names: sand desert, called *erg*, covers only about one-fifth of the world's desert; the rest is divided between *hammada* (areas of bare rock) and *reg* (broad plains covered by loose gravel or pebbles).

In areas of *erg*, such as the Namib Desert, the shape of the dunes reflects the character of local winds. Where winds are constant in direction, crescent-shaped *barchan* dunes form. In areas of bare rock, wind-blown sand is a major agent of erosion. The erosion is mainly confined to within 2 m [6.5 ft] of the surface, producing characteristic mushroom-shaped rocks.

Erg

Hammada

Reg

Surface Processes

Catastrophic changes to natural landforms are periodically caused by such phenomena as avalanches, landslides and volcanic eruptions, but most of the processes that shape the Earth's surface operate extremely slowly in human terms. One estimate, based on a study in the United States, suggested that 1 m [3 ft] of land was removed from the entire surface of the country, on average, every 29,500 years. However, the time-scale varies from 1,300 years to 154,200 years depending on the terrain and climate.

In hot, dry climates, mechanical weathering, a result of rapid temperature changes, causes the outer layers of rock to peel away, while in cold mountainous regions, boulders are prised apart when water freezes in cracks in rocks. Chemical weathering, at its greatest in warm, humid regions, is responsible for hollowing out limestone caves and decomposing granites.

The erosion of soil and rock is greatest on sloping land and the steeper the slope, the greater the tendency for mass wasting – the movement of soil and rock downhill under the influence of gravity. The mechanisms of mass wasting (ranging from very slow to very rapid) vary with the type of material, but the presence of water as a lubricant is usually an important factor.

Running water is the world's leading agent of erosion and transportation. The energy of a river depends on several factors, including its velocity and volume, and its erosive power is at its peak when it is in full flood. Sea waves also exert tremendous erosive power during storms when they hurl pebbles against the shore, undercutting cliffs and hollowing out caves.

Glacier ice forms in mountain hollows and spills out to form valley glaciers, which transport rocks shattered by frost action. As glaciers move, rocks embedded into the ice erode steep-sided, U-shaped valleys. Evidence of glaciation in mountain regions includes cirques, knife-edged ridges, or arêtes, and pyramidal peaks.

Oceans

The Great Oceans

Relative sizes of the world's oceans

- Pacific
- Atlantic
- Indian
- Southern
- Arctic

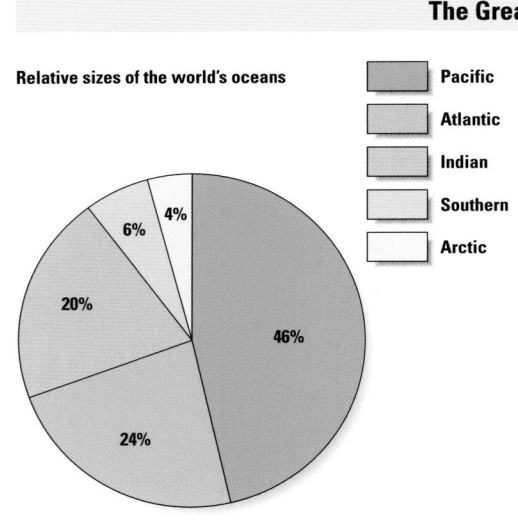

From ancient times to about the 15th century, the legendary 'Seven Seas' comprised the Red Sea, Mediterranean Sea, Persian Gulf, Black Sea, Adriatic Sea, Caspian Sea and Indian Sea.

The Earth is a watery planet: more than 70% of its surface – over 360,000,000 sq km [140,000,000 sq miles] – is covered by the oceans and seas. The mighty Pacific alone accounts for nearly 36% of the total, and more than 46% of the sea area. Gravity holds in around 1,400 million cu. km [320 million cu. miles] of water, of which over 97% is saline.

The vast underwater world starts in the shallows of the seaside and plunges to depths of more than 11,000 m [36,000 ft]. The continental shelf, part of the landmass, drops gently to around 200 m [650 ft]; here the seabed falls away suddenly at an angle of 3° to 6° – the continental slope. The third stage, called the continental rise, is more gradual with gradients varying from 1 in 100 to 1 in 700. At an average depth of 5,000 m [16,500 ft] there begins the aptly-named abyssal plain – massive submarine depths where sunlight fails to penetrate and few creatures can survive.

From these plains rise volcanoes which, taken from base to top, rival and even surpass the tallest continental mountains in height. Mauna Kea, on Hawai'i, reaches a total of 10,203 m [33,400 ft], some 1,355 m [4,500 ft] more than Mount Everest, though scarcely 40% is visible above sea level.

In addition, there are underwater mountain chains up to 1,000 km [600 miles] across, whose peaks sometimes appear above sea level as islands, such as Iceland and Tristan da Cunha.

The Ocean Depths

Average and maximum depths of the world's great oceans, in metres

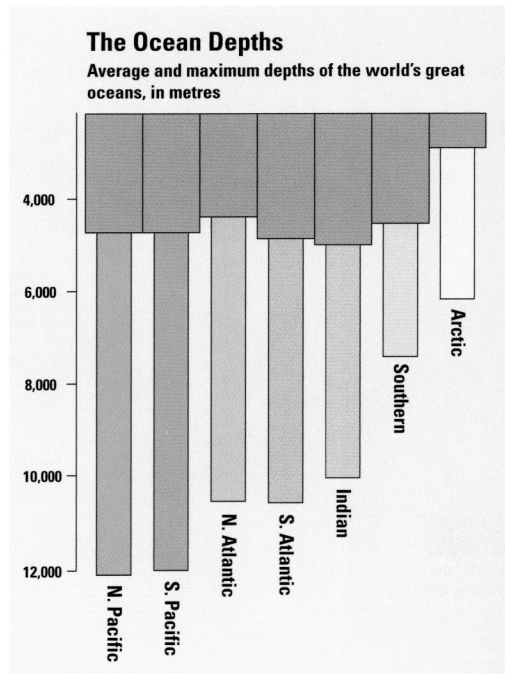

Ocean Currents

January ocean currents

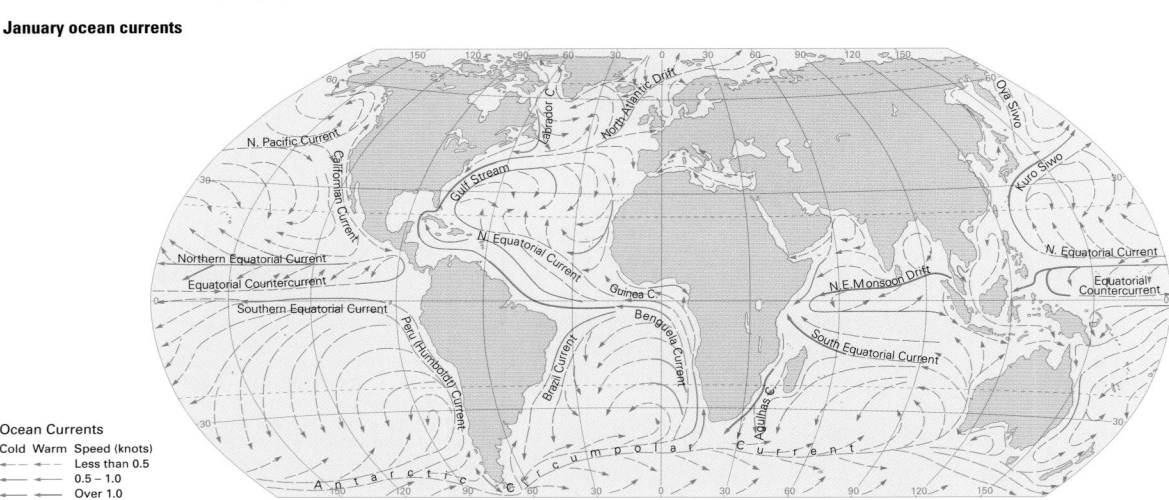

Ocean Currents
Cold Warm Speed (knots)
- Less than 0.5
- 0.5 – 1.0
- Over 1.0

July ocean currents

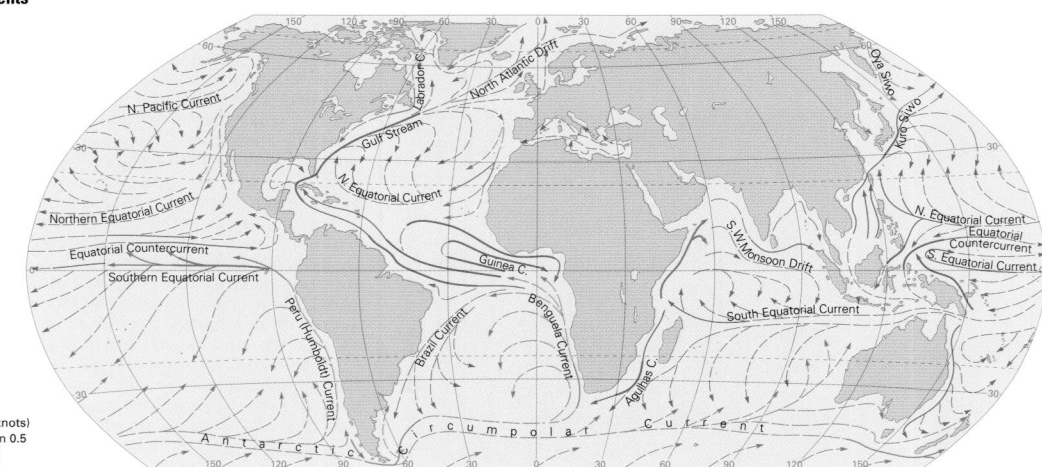

Ocean Currents
Cold Warm Speed (knots)
- Less than 0.5
- 0.5 – 1.0
- Over 1.0

Moving immense quantities of energy as well as billions of tonnes of water every hour, the ocean currents are a vital part of the great heat engine that drives the Earth's climate. They themselves are produced by a twofold mechanism. At the surface, winds push huge masses of water before them; in the deep ocean, below an abrupt temperature gradient that separates the churning surface waters from the still depths, density variations cause slow vertical movements.

The pattern of circulation of the great surface currents is determined by the displacement known as the Coriolis effect. As the Earth turns beneath a moving object – whether it is a tennis ball or a vast mass of water – it appears to be deflected to one side. The deflection is most obvious near the Equator, where the Earth's surface is spinning eastwards at 1,700 km/h [1,050 mph]; currents moving polewards are curved clockwise in the northern hemisphere and anti-clockwise in the southern.

The result is a system of spinning circles known as gyres. The Coriolis effect piles up water on the left of each gyre, creating a narrow, fast-moving stream that is matched by a slower, broader returning current on the right. North and south of the Equator, the fastest currents are located in the west and in the east respectively. In each case, warm water moves from the Equator and cold water returns to it. Cold currents often bring an upwelling of nutrients with them, supporting the world's most economically important fisheries.

Depending on the prevailing winds, some currents on or near the Equator may reverse their direction in the course of the year – a seasonal variation on which Asian monsoon rains depend, and whose occasional failure can bring disaster to millions.

World Fishing Areas

Main commercial fishing areas (numbered FAO regions)

Catch by top marine fishing areas, million tonnes (2004)

1.	Pacific, NW	[61]	21.6	22.7%
2.	Pacific, SE	[87]	15.5	16.3%
3.	Pacific, WC	[71]	11.0	11.6%
4.	Atlantic, NE	[27]	10.0	10.5%
5.	Indian, E	[57]	5.6	5.9%
6.	Indian, W	[51]	4.1	4.3%
7.	Atlantic, EC	[34]	3.4	3.6%
8.	Pacific, NE	[67]	3.1	3.3%
9.	Atlantic, NW	[21]	2.4	2.5%
10.	Atlantic, WC	[31]	2.1	2.2%

Principal fishing areas

Leading fishing nations

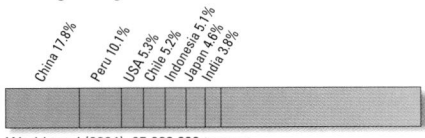

China 17.8% Peru 10.1% USA 5.3% Chile 5.2% Indonesia 5.1% Japan 4.6% India 3.6%

World total (2004): 95,000,000 tonnes
(Marine catch 90.3% Inland catch 9.7%)

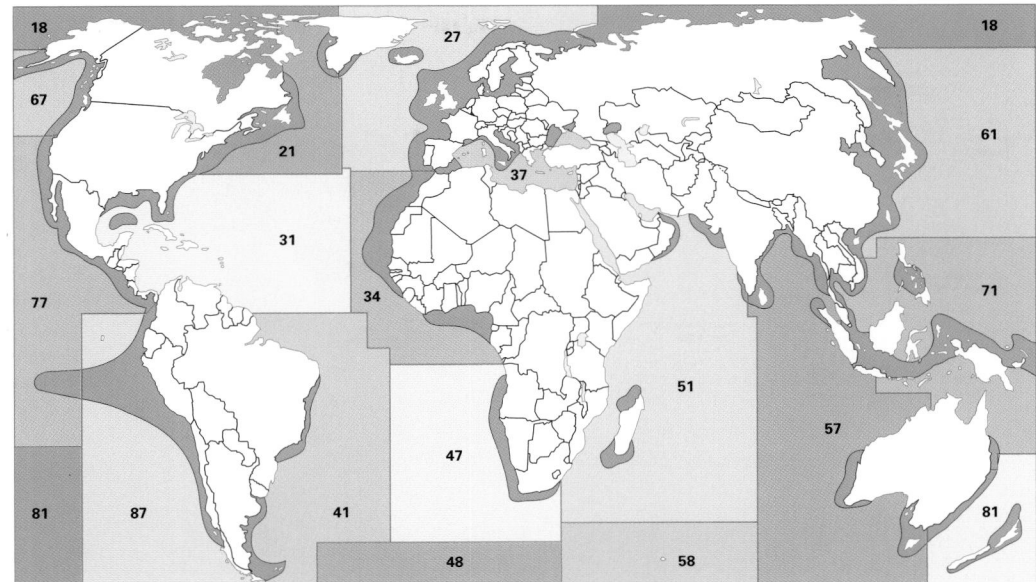

Marine Pollution

Sources of marine oil pollution

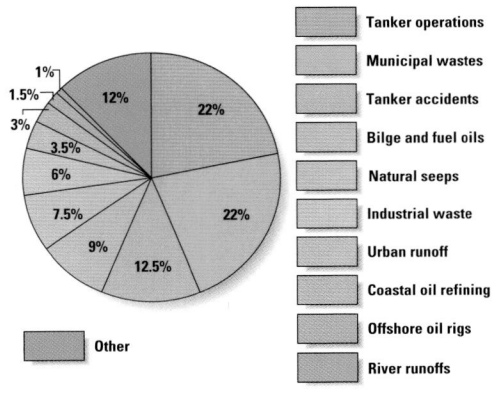

- Tanker operations
- Municipal wastes
- Tanker accidents
- Bilge and fuel oils
- Natural seeps
- Industrial waste
- Urban runoff
- Coastal oil refining
- Offshore oil rigs
- River runoffs
- Other

Oil Spills

Major oil spills from tankers and combined carriers

Year	Vessel	Location	Spill (barrels) *	Cause
1979	Atlantic Empress	West Indies	1,890,000	collision
1983	Castillo De Bellver	South Africa	1,760,000	fire
1978	Amoco Cadiz	France	1,628,000	grounding
1991	Haven	Italy	1,029,000	explosion
1988	Odyssey	Canada	1,000,000	fire
1967	Torrey Canyon	UK	909,000	grounding
1972	Sea Star	Gulf of Oman	902,250	collision
1977	Hawaiian Patriot	Hawaiian Is.	742,500	fire
1979	Independenta	Turkey	696,350	collision
1993	Braer	UK	625,000	grounding
1996	Sea Empress	UK	515,000	grounding
2002	Prestige	Spain	463,250	storm

Other sources of major oil spills

1983	Nowruz oilfield	Persian Gulf	4,250,000[†]	war
1979	Ixtoc 1 oilwell	Gulf of Mexico	4,200,000	blow-out
1991	Kuwait	Persian Gulf	2,500,000[†]	war

* 1 barrel = 0.136 tonnes/159 lit./35 Imperial gal./42 US gal. [†] estimated

River Pollution

Sources of river pollution, USA

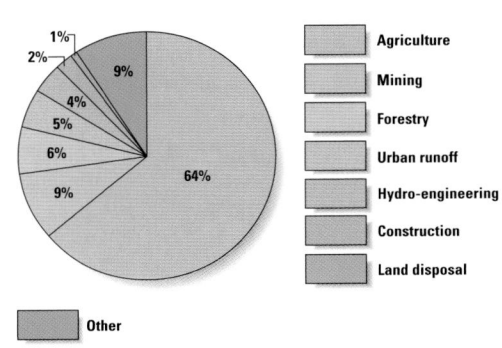

- Agriculture
- Mining
- Forestry
- Urban runoff
- Hydro-engineering
- Construction
- Land disposal
- Other

Water Pollution

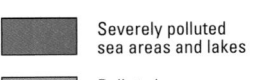
Severely polluted
sea areas and lakes

Polluted sea
areas and lakes

Areas of frequent oil pollution
by shipping

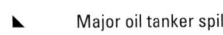
Major oil tanker spills

▲ Major oil rig blow-outs

▼ Offshore dumpsites for industrial
and municipal waste

Severely polluted
rivers and estuaries

The most notorious tanker spillage of the
1980s occurred when the *Exxon Valdez* ran
aground in Prince William Sound, Alaska,
in 1989, spilling 267,000 barrels of crude oil
close to shore in a sensitive ecological area.
This rates as the world's 28th worst spill in
terms of volume.

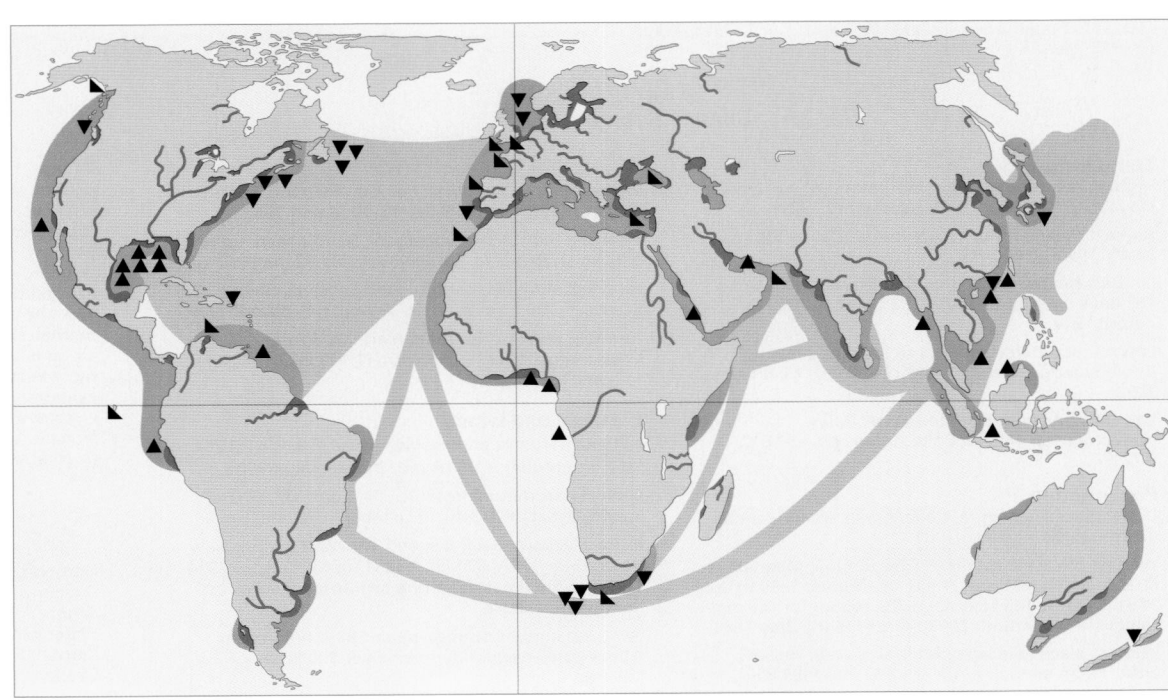

Climate

Climatic Regions

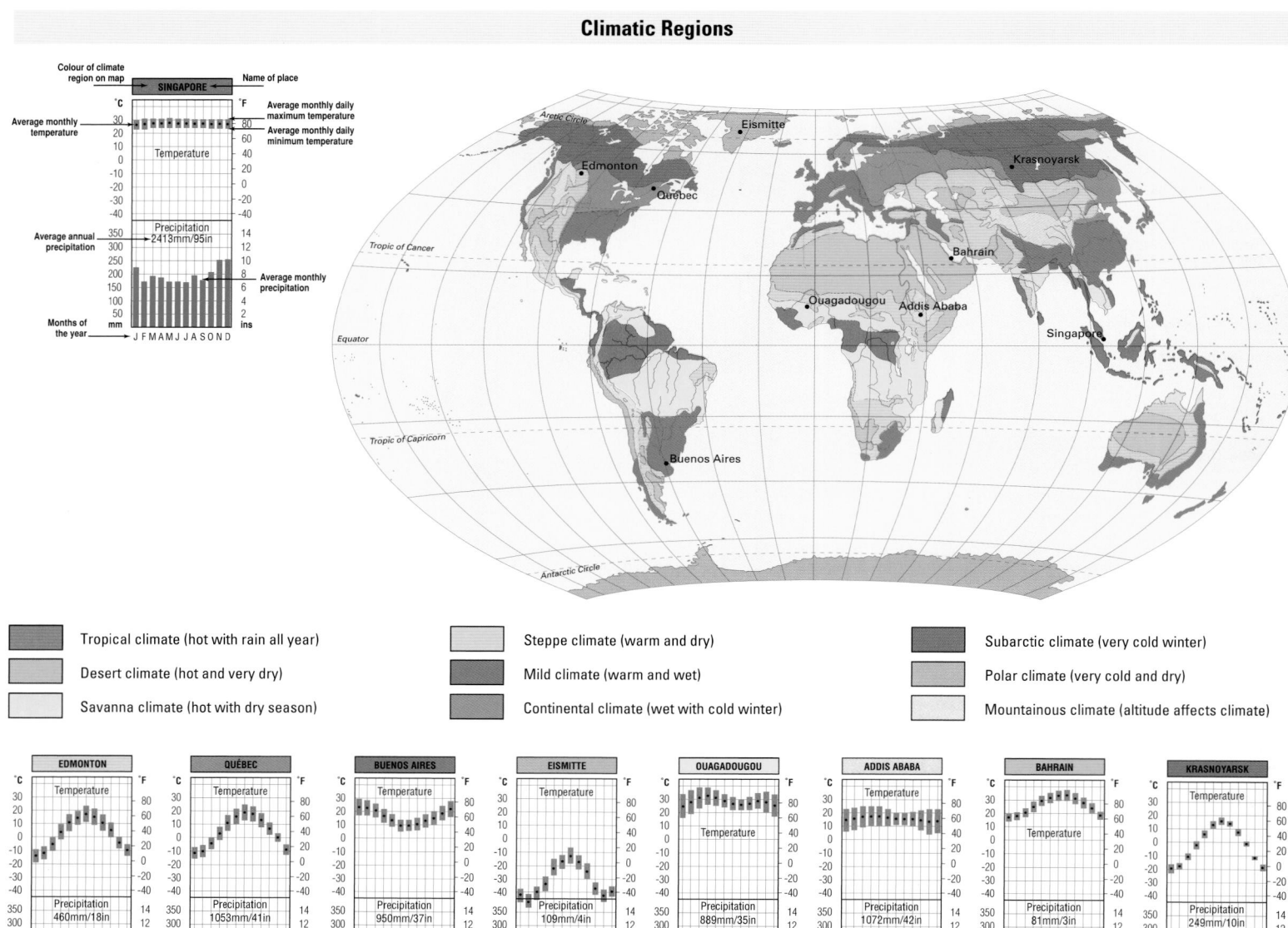

Tropical climate (hot with rain all year)

Desert climate (hot and very dry)

Savanna climate (hot with dry season)

Steppe climate (warm and dry)

Mild climate (warm and wet)

Continental climate (wet with cold winter)

Subarctic climate (very cold winter)

Polar climate (very cold and dry)

Mountainous climate (altitude affects climate)

Climate Records

Temperature
Highest recorded shade temperature: Al Aziziyah, Libya, 57.7°C [135.9°F], 13 September 1922.

Highest mean annual temperature: Dallol, Ethiopia, 34.4°C [94°F], 1960–66.

Longest heatwave: Marble Bar, W. Australia, 162 days over 38°C [100°F], 23 October 1923 to 7 April 1924.

Lowest recorded temperature (outside poles): Verkhoyansk, Siberia, –69.8°C [–93.6°F], 7 February 1892.

Lowest mean annual temperature: Polus Nedostupnosti, Pole of Cold, Antarctica, –57.8°C [–72°F].

Precipitation
Driest place: Quillagua, Chile, mean annual rainfall 0.5 mm [0.02 in], 1964–2001.

Wettest place (12 months): Cherrapunji, Meghalaya, N. E. India, 26,461 mm [1,042 in], August 1860 to July 1861. Cherrapunji also holds the record for the most rainfall in one month: 2,930 mm [115 in], July 1861.

Wettest place (average): Mt Wai-ale-ale, Hawai'i, USA, mean annual rainfall 11,680 mm [459.8 in].

Wettest place (24 hours): Fac Fac, Réunion, Indian Ocean, 1,825 mm [71.9 in], 15–16 March 1952.

Heaviest hailstones: Gopalganj, Bangladesh, up to 1.02 kg [2.25 lb], 14 April 1986 (killed 92 people).

Heaviest snowfall (continuous): Bessans, Savoie, France, 1,730 mm [68 in] in 19 hours, 5–6 April 1969.

Heaviest snowfall (season/year): Mt Baker, Washington, USA, 28,956 mm [1,140 in], June 1998 to June 1999.

Pressure and winds
Highest barometric pressure: Agata, Siberia (at 262 m [862 ft] altitude), 1,083.8 mb, 31 December 1968.

Lowest barometric pressure: Typhoon Tip, Guam, Pacific Ocean, 870 mb, 12 October 1979.

Highest recorded wind speed: Mt Washington, New Hampshire, USA, 371 km/h [231 mph], 12 April 1934. This is three times as strong as hurricane force on the Beaufort Scale.

Windiest place: Commonwealth Bay, Antarctica, where gales frequently reach over 320 km/h [200 mph].

Climate

Climate is weather in the long term: the seasonal pattern of hot and cold, wet and dry, averaged over time (usually 30 years). At the simplest level, it is caused by the uneven heating of the Earth. Surplus heat at the Equator passes towards the poles, levelling out the energy differential. Its passage is marked by a ceaseless churning of the atmosphere and the oceans, further agitated by the Earth's diurnal spin and the motion it imparts to moving air and water. The heat's means of transport – by winds and ocean currents, by the continual evaporation and recondensation of water molecules – is the weather itself. There are four basic types of climate, each of which can be further subdivided: tropical, desert (dry), temperate and polar.

Composition of Dry Air

Nitrogen	78.09%	Sulphur dioxide	trace
Oxygen	20.95%	Nitrogen oxide	trace
Argon	0.93%	Methane	trace
Water vapour	0.2–4.0%	Dust	trace
Carbon dioxide	0.03%	Helium	trace
Ozone	0.00006%	Neon	trace

El Niño

In a normal year, south-easterly trade winds drive surface waters
westwards off the coast of South America, drawing cold, nutrient-
rich water up from below. In an El Niño year (which occurs every
2–7 years), warm water from the west Pacific suppresses upwelling in the east, depriving the region of nutrients. The water is
warmed by as much as 7°C [12°F], disturbing the tropical atmos-
pheric circulation. During an intense El Niño, the south-east trade
winds change direction and become equatorial westerlies, resulting in climatic extremes in many regions of the world, such as
drought in parts of Australia and India, and heavy rainfall in south-
eastern USA. An intense El Niño occurred in 1997–8, with resultant
freak weather conditions across the entire Pacific region.

Normal year

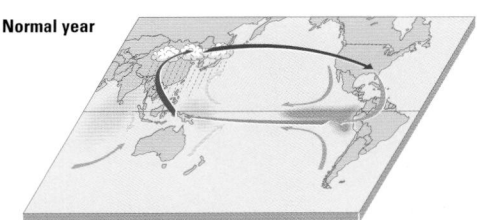

El Niño event

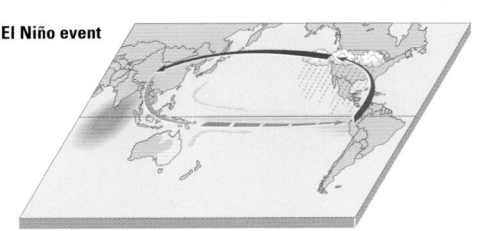

Beaufort Wind Scale

Named after the 19th-century British naval officer who
devised it, the Beaufort Scale assesses wind speed
according to its effects. It was originally designed as an aid
for sailors, but has since been adapted for use on the land.

Scale	Wind speed km/h	mph	Effect
0	0–1	0–1	**Calm** Smoke rises vertically
1	1–5	1–3	**Light air** Wind direction shown only by smoke drift
2	6–11	4–7	**Light breeze** Wind felt on face; leaves rustle; vanes moved by wind
3	12–19	8–12	**Gentle breeze** Leaves and small twigs in constant motion; wind extends small flag
4	20–28	13–18	**Moderate** Raises dust and loose paper; small branches move
5	29–38	19–24	**Fresh** Small trees in leaf sway; wavelets on inland waters
6	39–49	25–31	**Strong** Large branches move; difficult to use umbrellas
7	50–61	32–38	**Near gale** Whole trees in motion; difficult to walk against wind
8	62–74	39–46	**Gale** Twigs break from trees; walking very difficult
9	75–88	47–54	**Strong gale** Slight structural damage
10	89–102	55–63	**Storm** Trees uprooted; serious structural damage
11	103–117	64–72	**Violent storm** Widespread damage
12	118+	73+	**Hurricane**

Conversions
°C = (°F − 32) × 5/9; °F = (°C × 9/5) + 32; 0°C = 32°F
1 in = 25.4 mm; 1 mm = 0.0394 in; 100 mm = 3.94 in

Temperature

Average temperature in January

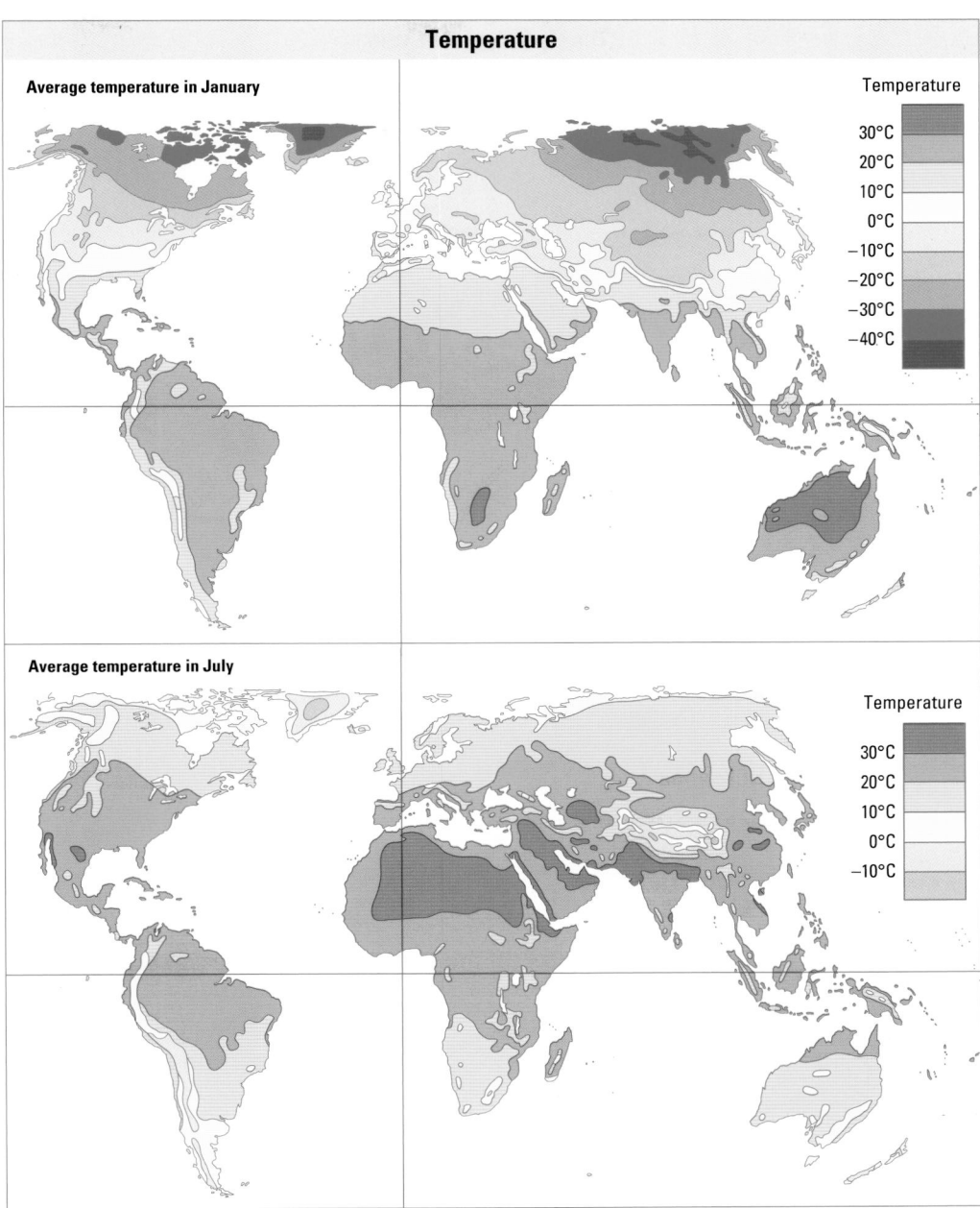

Temperature

	30°C
	20°C
	10°C
	0°C
	−10°C
	−20°C
	−30°C
	−40°C

Average temperature in July

Temperature

	30°C
	20°C
	10°C
	0°C
	−10°C

Precipitation

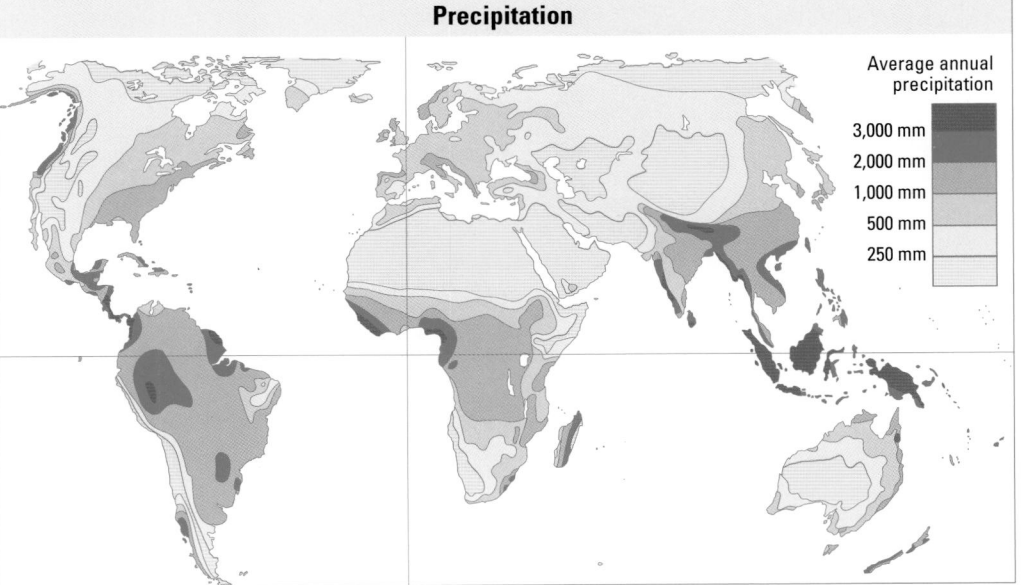

Average annual
precipitation

	3,000 mm
	2,000 mm
	1,000 mm
	500 mm
	250 mm

Water and Vegetation

The Hydrological Cycle

The world's water balance is regulated by the constant recycling of water between the oceans, atmosphere and land. The movement of water between these three reservoirs is known as the hydrological cycle. The oceans play a vital role in the hydrological cycle: 74% of the total precipitation falls over the oceans and 84% of the total evaporation comes from the oceans.

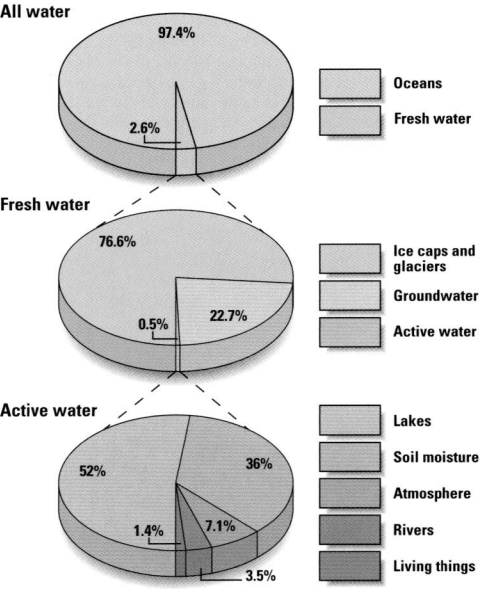

Water Distribution

The distribution of planetary water, by percentage. Oceans and ice caps together account for more than 99% of the total; the breakdown of the remainder is estimated.

All water
- 97.4% Oceans
- 2.6% Fresh water

Fresh water
- 76.6% Ice caps and glaciers
- 22.7% Groundwater
- 0.5% Active water

Active water
- 36% Lakes
- 52% Soil moisture
- 1.4% Atmosphere
- 7.1% Rivers
- 3.5% Living things

Water Utilization

Domestic Industrial Agriculture

The percentage breakdown of water usage by sector, selected countries (2002)

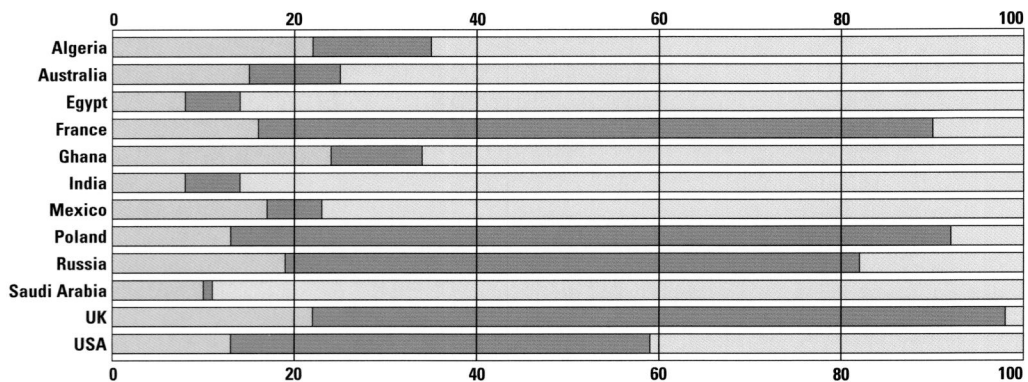

Algeria, Australia, Egypt, France, Ghana, India, Mexico, Poland, Russia, Saudi Arabia, UK, USA

Water Usage

Almost all the world's water is 3,000 million years old, and all of it cycles endlessly through the hydrosphere, though at different rates. Water vapour circulates over days, even hours, deep ocean water circulates over millennia, and ice-cap water remains solid for millions of years.

Fresh water is essential to all terrestrial life. Humans cannot survive more than a few days without it, and even the hardiest desert plants and animals could not exist without some water. Agriculture requires huge quantities of fresh water: without large-scale irrigation most of the world's people would starve. In the USA, agriculture uses 41% and industry 46% of all water withdrawals.

According to the latest figures, the average North American uses 1.3 million litres per year. This is more than six times the average African, who uses just 186,000 litres of water each year. Europeans and Australians use 694,000 litres per year.

Water Supply

Percentage of total population with access to safe drinking water (2004)

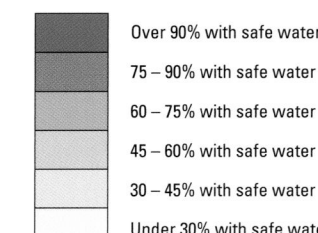

- Over 90% with safe water
- 75 – 90% with safe water
- 60 – 75% with safe water
- 45 – 60% with safe water
- 30 – 45% with safe water
- Under 30% with safe water

- ◊ Under 80 litres per person per day domestic water consumption
- ▲ Over 320 litres per person per day domestic water consumption

NB: 80 litres of water a day is considered necessary for a reasonable quality of life.

Least well-provided countries

Afghanistan	13%	Papua New Guinea	39%
Ethiopia	22%	Cambodia	41%
Western Sahara	26%	Somalia	42%

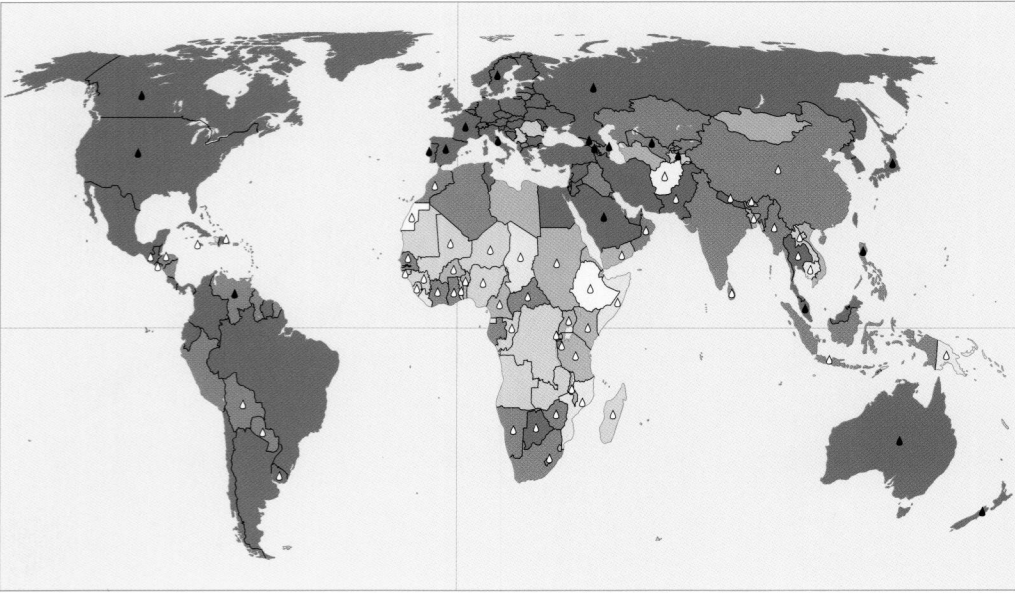

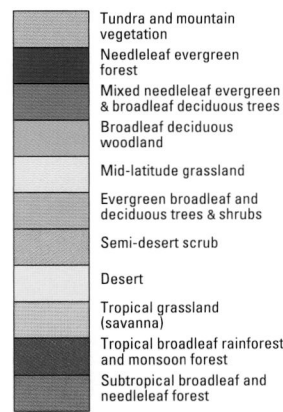

Regional variation in vegetation

- Tundra and mountain vegetation
- Needleleaf evergreen forest
- Mixed needleleaf evergreen & broadleaf deciduous trees
- Broadleaf deciduous woodland
- Mid-latitude grassland
- Evergreen broadleaf and deciduous trees & shrubs
- Semi-desert scrub
- Desert
- Tropical grassland (savanna)
- Tropical broadleaf rainforest and monsoon forest
- Subtropical broadleaf and needleleaf forest

The map shows the natural 'climax vegetation' of regions, as dictated by climate and topography. In most cases, however, agricultural activity has drastically altered the vegetation pattern. Western Europe, for example, lost most of its broadleaf forest many centuries ago, while irrigation has turned some natural semi-desert into productive land.

Land Use by Continent (2004)

- Forest
- Permanent pasture
- Permanent crops
- Arable
- Other

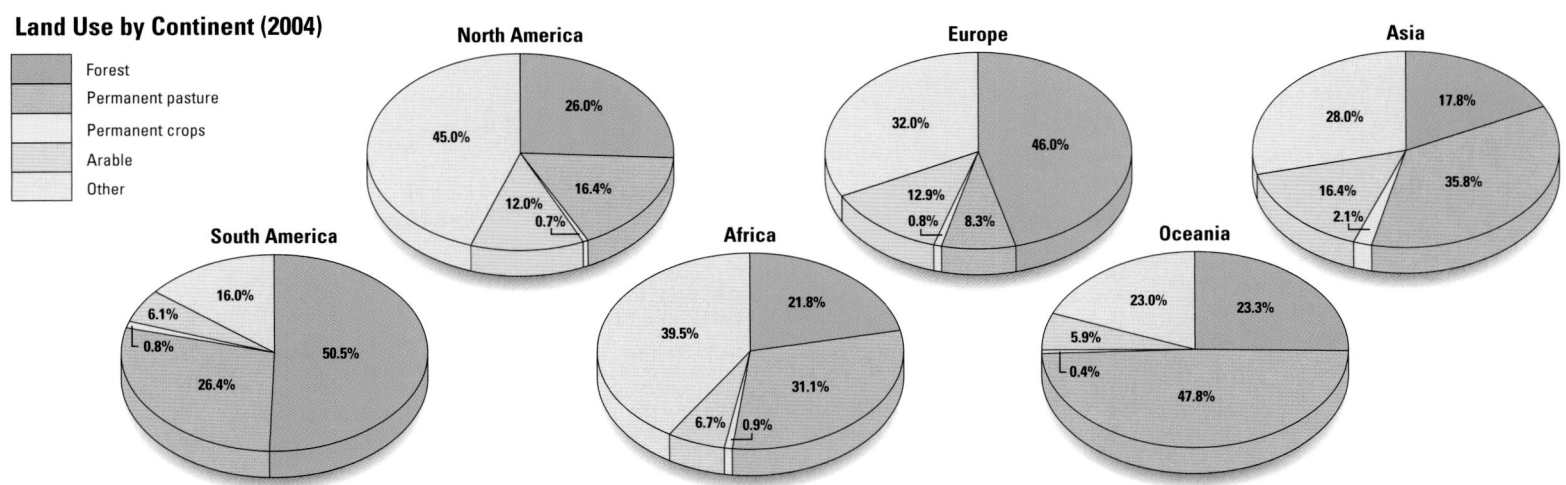

North America: 26.0%, 16.4%, 0.7%, 12.0%, 45.0%

Europe: 46.0%, 8.3%, 0.8%, 12.9%, 32.0%

Asia: 17.8%, 35.8%, 2.1%, 16.4%, 28.0%

South America: 16.0%, 6.1%, 0.8%, 26.4%, 50.5%

Africa: 21.8%, 31.1%, 0.9%, 6.7%, 39.5%

Oceania: 23.3%, 47.8%, 0.4%, 5.9%, 23.0%

Forestry: Production

Forest and woodland (million hectares)	Annual production (2005, million cubic metres)	
	Fuelwood	Industrial roundwood*
World **3,869.5**	*1,792.1*	*1710.6*
Europe 1,039.3	117.3	544.0
S. America 885.6	192.8	186.7
Africa 649.9	563.3	69.4
N. & C. America 549.3	130.2	623.6
Asia 547.8	779.5	237.5
Oceania 197.6	9.0	49.4

Paper and Board

Top producers (2005)**		Top exporters (2005)**	
USA	81,437	Canada	15,731
China	53,463	Germany	12,205
Japan	29,295	Finland	11,155
Germany	21,679	Sweden	10,593
Canada	19,673	USA	9,610

* roundwood is timber as it is felled
** in thousand tonnes

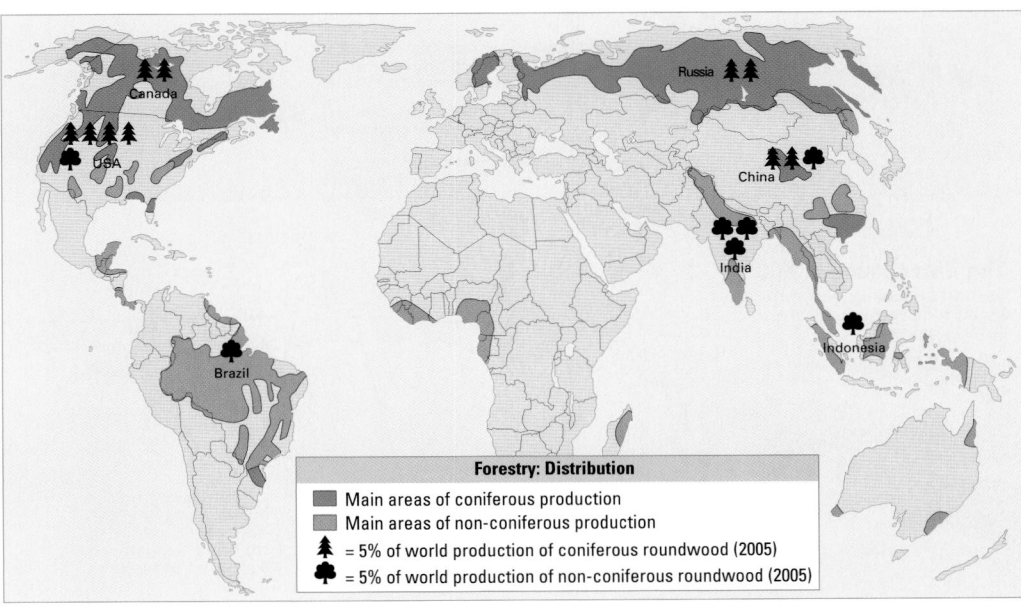

Forestry: Distribution

- Main areas of coniferous production
- Main areas of non-coniferous production
- ♣ = 5% of world production of coniferous roundwood (2005)
- ♠ = 5% of world production of non-coniferous roundwood (2005)

Environment

Humans have always had a dramatic effect on their environment, at least since the development of agriculture almost 10,000 years ago. Generally, the Earth has accepted human interference without obvious ill effects: the complex systems that regulate the global environment have been able to absorb substantial damage while maintaining a stable and comfortable home for the planet's trillions of lifeforms. But advancing human technology and the rapidly-expanding populations it supports are now threatening to overwhelm the Earth's ability to compensate.

Industrial wastes, acid rainfall, desertification and large-scale deforestation all combine to create environmental change at a rate far faster than the great slow cycles of planetary evolution can accommodate. As a result of overcultivation, overgrazing and overcutting of groundcover for firewood, desertification is affecting as much as 60% of the world's croplands. In addition, with fire and chain-saws, humans are destroying more forest in a day than their ancestors could have done in a century, upsetting the balance between plant and animal, carbon dioxide and oxygen, on which all life ultimately depends.

The fossil fuels that power industrial civilization have pumped enough carbon dioxide and other so-called greenhouse gases into the atmosphere to make climatic change a near-certainty. As a result of the combination of these factors, the Earth's average temperature has risen by approximately 0.5°C [1°F] since the beginning of the 20th century, and it is still rising.

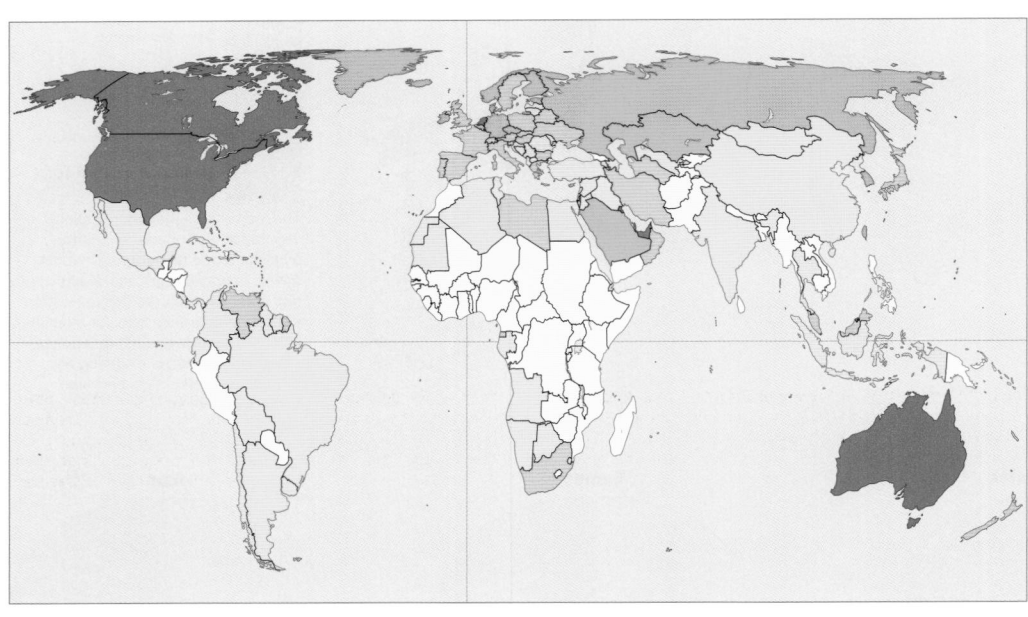

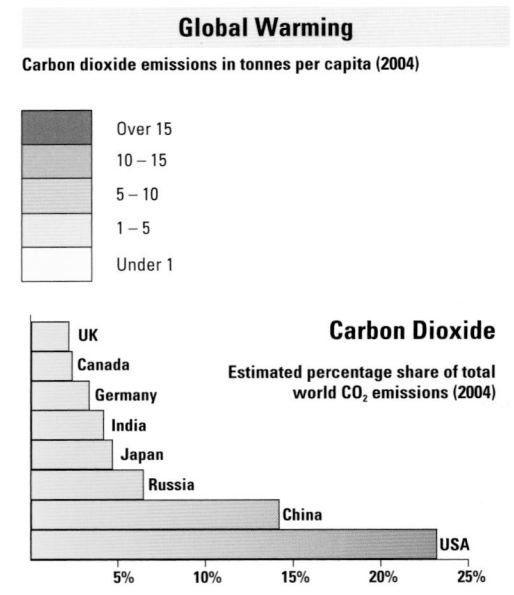

Global Warming

Carbon dioxide emissions in tonnes per capita (2004)

- Over 15
- 10 – 15
- 5 – 10
- 1 – 5
- Under 1

Carbon Dioxide

Estimated percentage share of total world CO₂ emissions (2004)

UK
Canada
Germany
India
Japan
Russia
China
USA

5%   10%   15%   20%   25%

Temperature Rise

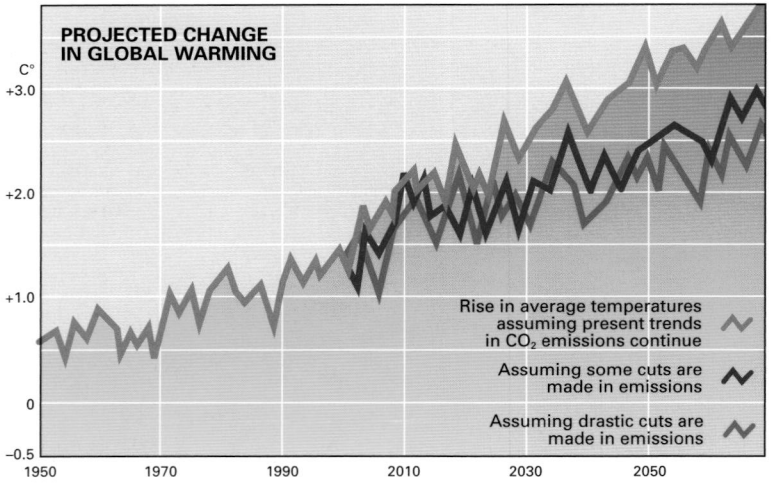

PROJECTED CHANGE IN GLOBAL WARMING

C°
+3.0
+2.0
+1.0
0
-0.5
1950   1970   1990   2010   2030   2050

Rise in average temperatures assuming present trends in CO₂ emissions continue

Assuming some cuts are made in emissions

Assuming drastic cuts are made in emissions

Sea Level Rise

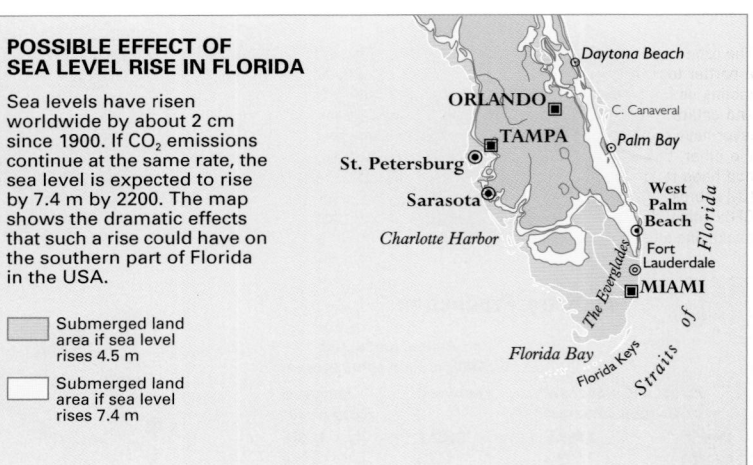

POSSIBLE EFFECT OF SEA LEVEL RISE IN FLORIDA

Sea levels have risen worldwide by about 2 cm since 1900. If CO₂ emissions continue at the same rate, the sea level is expected to rise by 7.4 m by 2200. The map shows the dramatic effects that such a rise could have on the southern part of Florida in the USA.

Submerged land area if sea level rises 4.5 m

Submerged land area if sea level rises 7.4 m

Daytona Beach
ORLANDO
C. Canaveral
TAMPA
Palm Bay
St. Petersburg
Sarasota
West Palm Beach
Charlotte Harbor
Fort Lauderdale
MIAMI
Florida Bay
The Everglades
Florida Keys
Straits of Florida

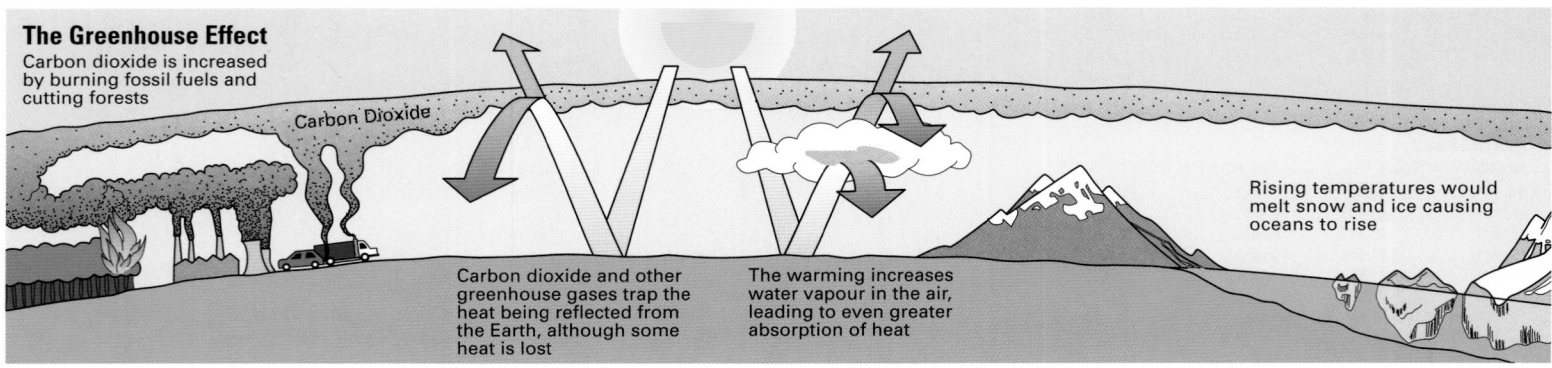

The Greenhouse Effect

Carbon dioxide is increased by burning fossil fuels and cutting forests

Carbon Dioxide

Rising temperatures would melt snow and ice causing oceans to rise

Carbon dioxide and other greenhouse gases trap the heat being reflected from the Earth, although some heat is lost

The warming increases water vapour in the air, leading to even greater absorption of heat

Desertification

- Existing deserts
- Areas with a high risk of desertification
- Areas with a moderate risk of desertification
- Former areas of rainforest
- Existing rainforest

Forest Clearance

Thousands of hectares of forest cleared annually, tropical countries surveyed 1980–85, 1990–95 and 2000–05. Loss as a percentage of remaining stocks is shown in figures on each column. Gain is indicated as a minus figure.

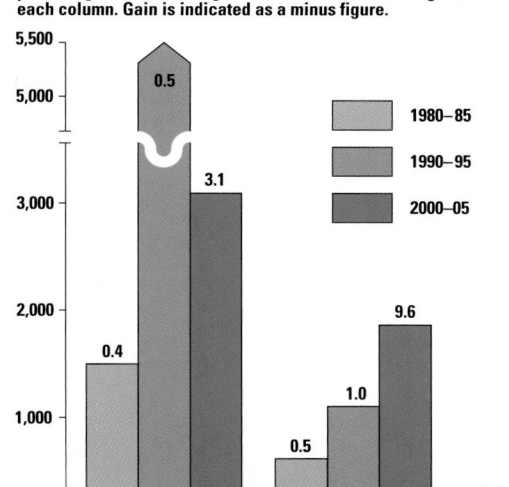

Legend:
- 1980–85
- 1990–95
- 2000–05

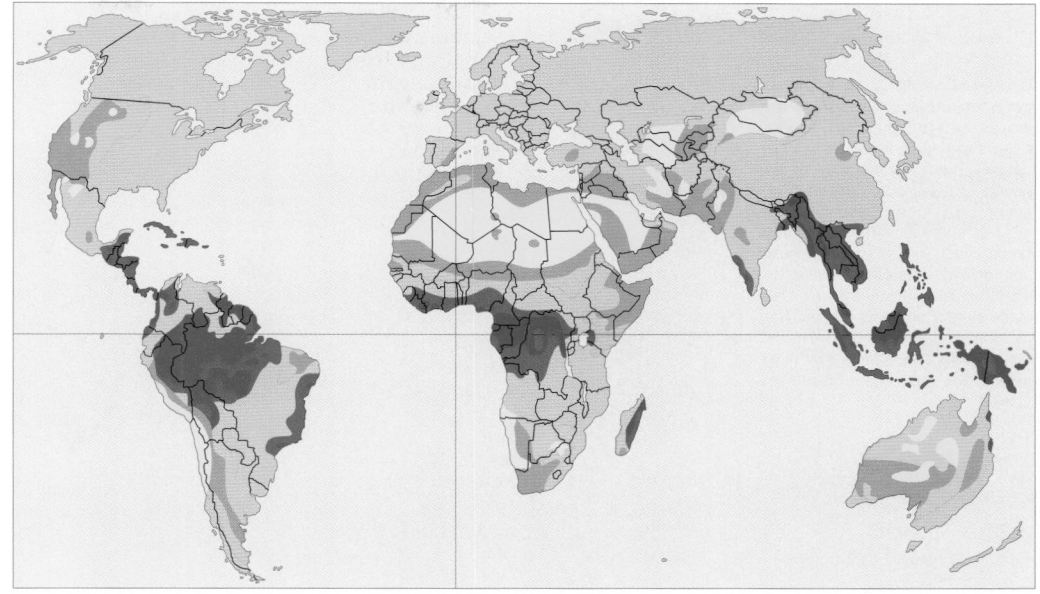

Deforestation

The Earth's remaining forests are under attack from three directions: expanding agriculture, logging, and growing consumption of fuelwood, often in combination. Sometimes deforestation is the direct result of government policy, as in the efforts made to resettle the urban poor in some parts of Brazil; just as often, it comes about despite state attempts at conservation. Loggers, licensed or unlicensed, blaze a trail into virgin forest, often destroying twice as many trees as they harvest. Landless farmers follow, burning away most of what remains to plant their crops, completing the destruction. Some countries such as Vietnam and Costa Rica have successfully implemented reafforestation programmes.

Ozone Depletion

The ozone layer, 25–30 km [15–18 miles] above sea level, acts as a barrier to most of the Sun's harmful ultra-violet radiation, protecting us from the ionizing radiation that can cause skin cancer and cataracts. In recent years, however, two holes in the ozone layer have been observed during winter: one over the Arctic and the other, the size of the USA, over Antarctica. By 1996, ozone had been reduced to around a half of its 1970 amount. The ozone (O_3) is broken down by chlorine released into the atmosphere as CFCs (chlorofluorocarbons) – chemicals used in refrigerators, packaging and aerosols.

Air Pollution

Sulphur dioxide is the main pollutant associated with industrial cities. According to the World Health Organization, at least 600 million people live in urban areas where sulphur dioxide concentrations regularly reach damaging levels. One of the world's most dangerously polluted urban areas is Mexico City, due to a combination of its enclosed valley location, 3 million cars and 60,000 factories. In May 1998, this lethal cocktail was added to by nearby forest fires and the resultant air pollution led to over 20% of the population (3 million people) complaining of respiratory problems.

Acid Rain

Killing trees, poisoning lakes and rivers, and eating away buildings, acid rain is mostly produced by sulphur dioxide emissions from industry and volcanic eruptions. By the mid 1990s, acid rain had sterilized 4,000 or more of Sweden's lakes and left 45% of Switzerland's alpine conifers dead or dying, while the monuments of Greece were dissolving in Athens' smog. Prevailing wind patterns mean that the acids often fall many hundred kilometres from where the original pollutants were discharged. In parts of Europe acid deposition has slightly decreased, following reductions in emissions, but not by enough.

World Pollution

Acid rain and sources of acidic emissions (latest available year)

Acid rain is caused by high levels of sulphur and nitrogen in the atmosphere. They combine with water vapour and oxygen to form acids (H_2SO_4 and HNO_3) which fall as precipitation.

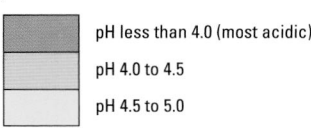

- Regions where sulphur and nitrogen oxides are released in high concentrations, mainly from fossil fuel combustion
- Major cities with high levels of air pollution (including nitrogen and sulphur emissions)

Areas of heavy acid deposition

pH numbers indicate acidity, decreasing from a neutral 7. Normal rain, slightly acid from dissolved carbon dioxide, never exceeds a pH of 5.6.

- pH less than 4.0 (most acidic)
- pH 4.0 to 4.5
- pH 4.5 to 5.0
- Areas where acid rain is a potential problem

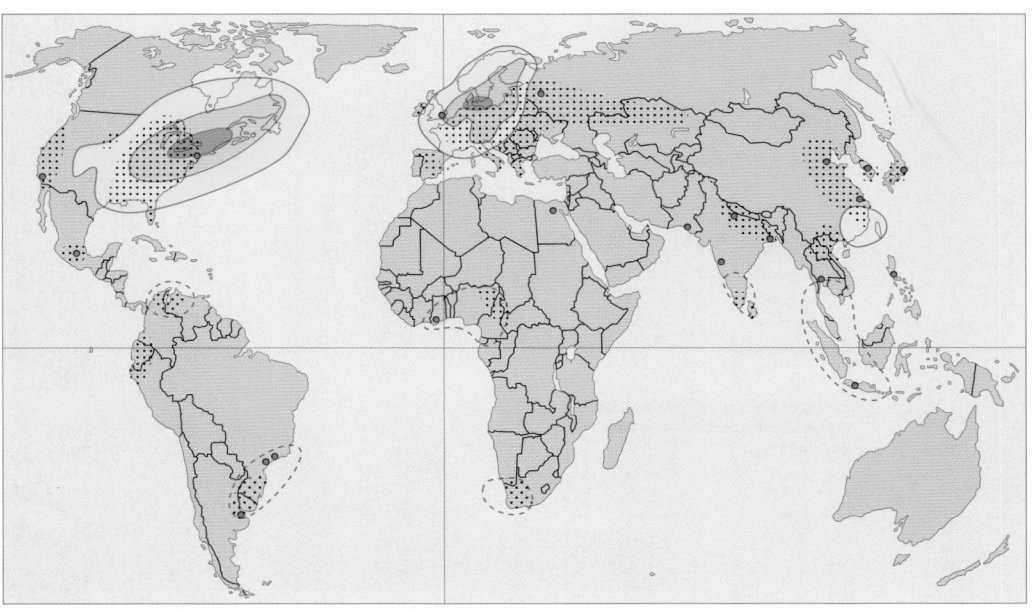

Population

Demographic Profiles

Developed nations such as the UK have populations evenly spread across the age groups and, usually, a growing proportion of elderly people. The great majority of the people in developing nations, however, are in the younger age groups, about to enter their most fertile years. In time, these population profiles should resemble the world profile (even Nigeria has made recent progress by reducing its birth rate), but the transition will come about only after a few more generations of rapid population growth.

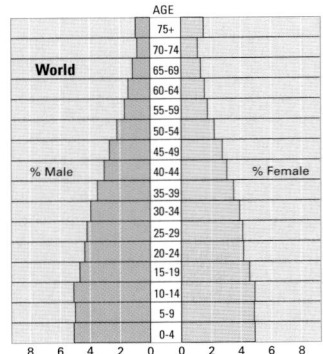

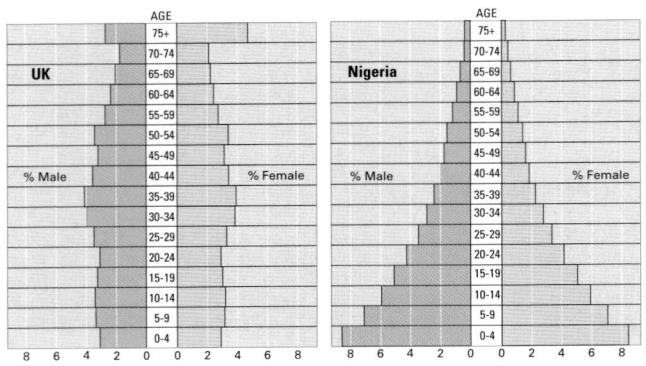

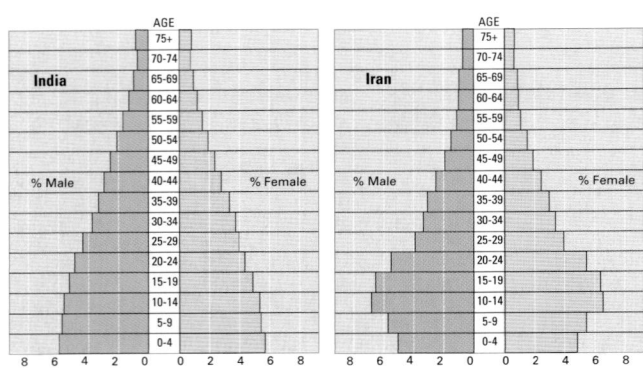

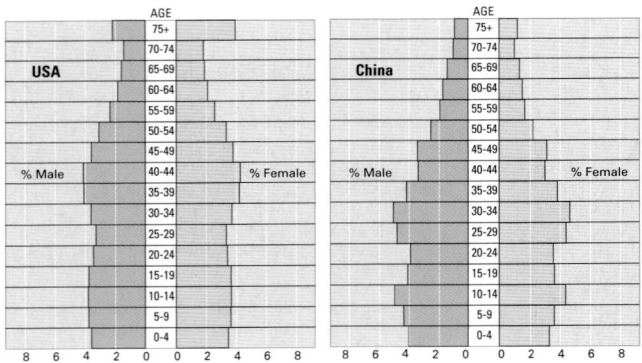

Most Populous Nations, in millions (2006 estimates)

1.	China	1,314	9. Nigeria	132	17. Turkey	70
2.	India	1,095	10. Japan	127	18. Iran	69
3.	USA	301	11. Mexico	107	19. Thailand	65
4.	Indonesia	245	12. Philippines	89	20. Congo (Dem. Rep.)	63
5.	Brazil	188	13. Vietnam	84	21. France	61
6.	Pakistan	166	14. Germany	82	22. UK	61
7.	Bangladesh	147	15. Egypt	79	23. Italy	58
8.	Russia	143	16. Ethiopia	75	24. South Korea	49

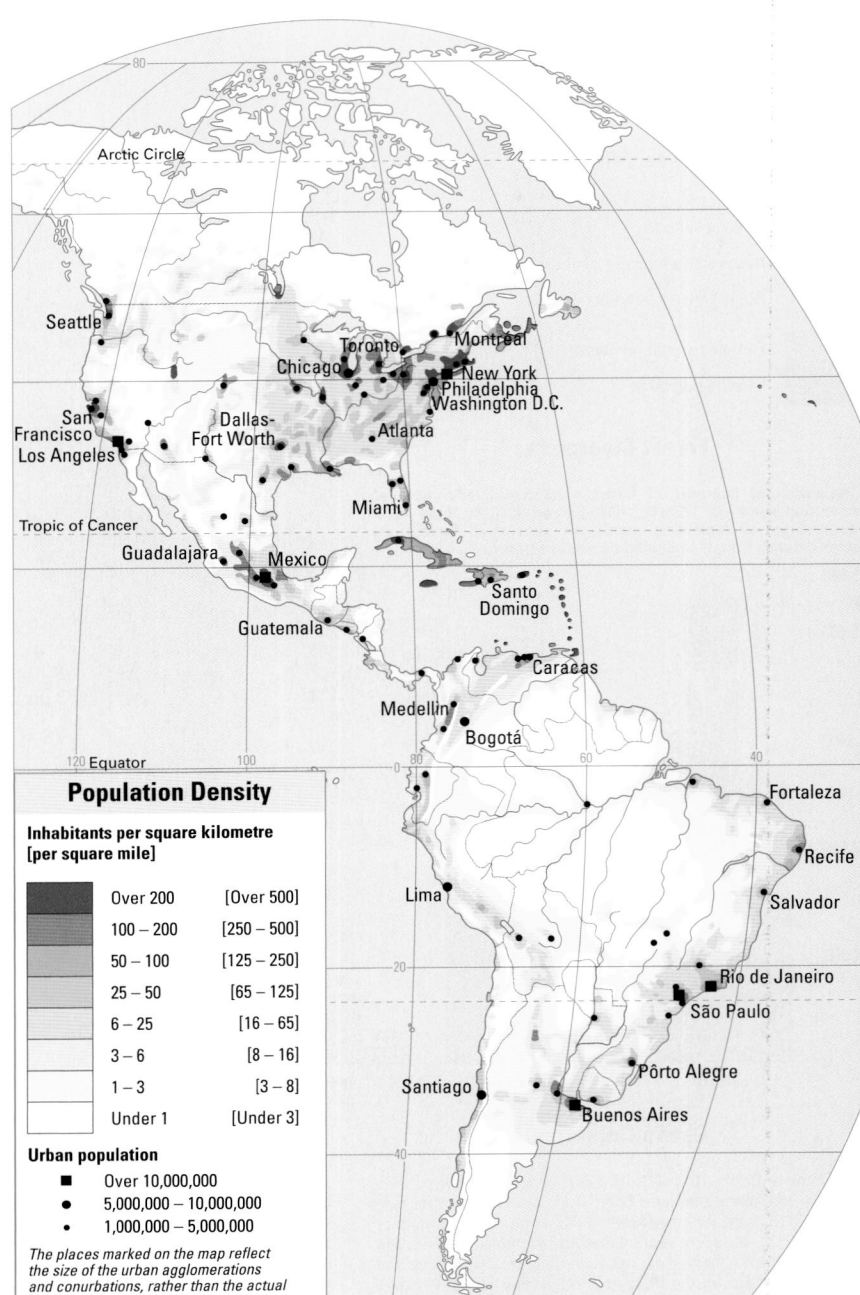

Population Density

Inhabitants per square kilometre [per square mile]

Over 200	[Over 500]
100 – 200	[250 – 500]
50 – 100	[125 – 250]
25 – 50	[65 – 125]
6 – 25	[16 – 65]
3 – 6	[8 – 16]
1 – 3	[3 – 8]
Under 1	[Under 3]

Urban population

- ■ Over 10,000,000
- ● 5,000,000 – 10,000,000
- • 1,000,000 – 5,000,000

The places marked on the map reflect the size of the urban agglomerations and conurbations, rather than the actual city limits.

Continental Comparisons

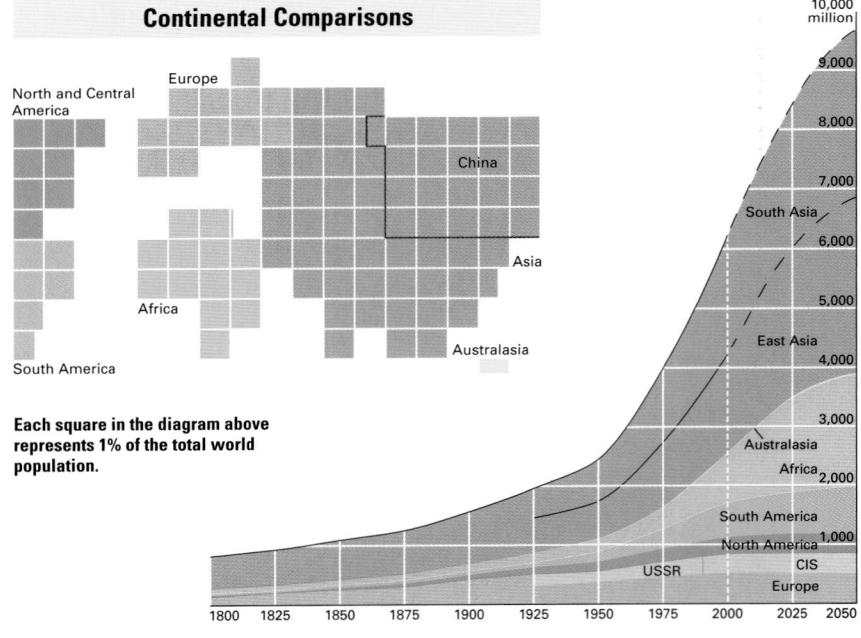

Each square in the diagram above represents 1% of the total world population.

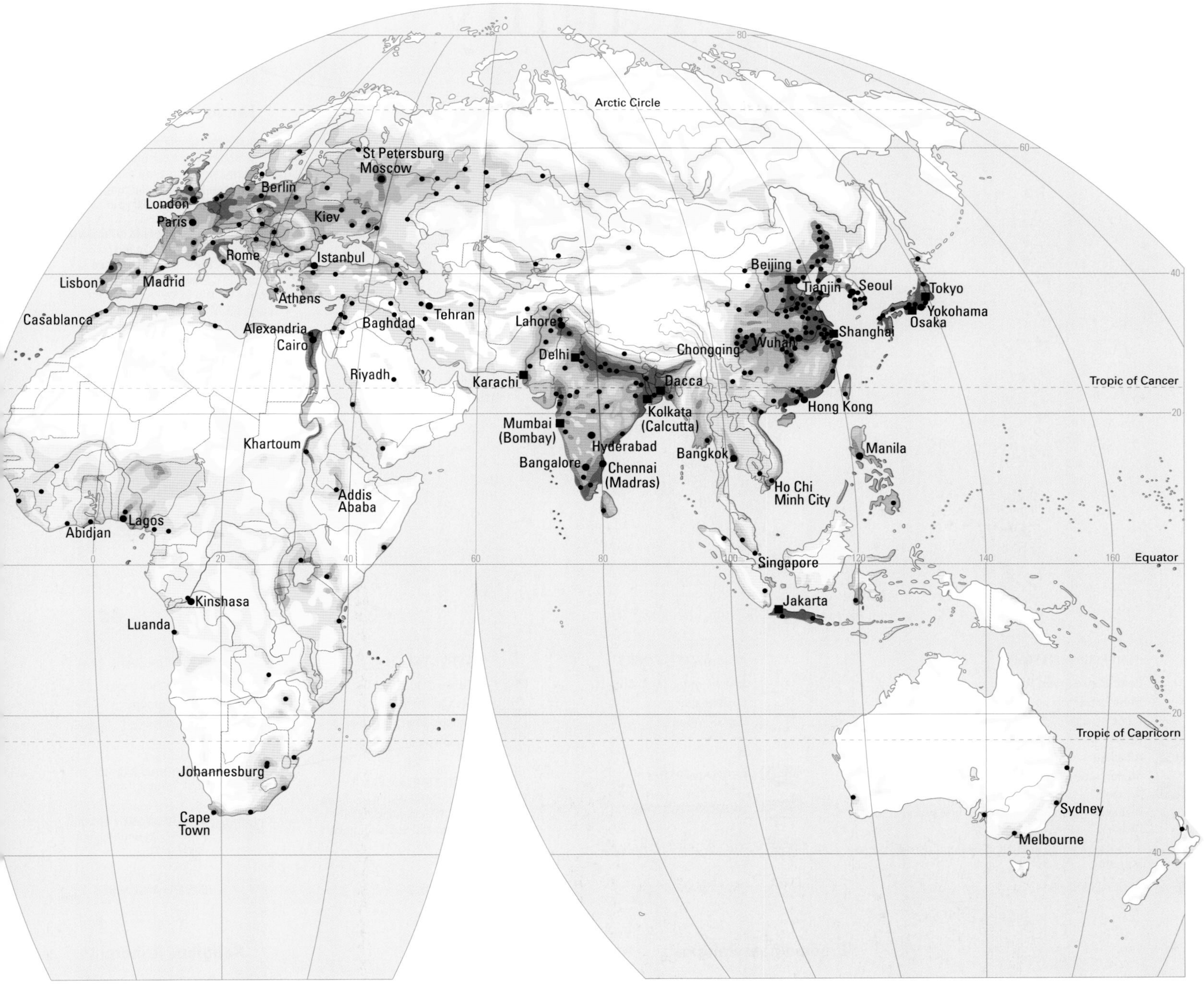

Arctic Circle

London
Paris
Berlin
St Petersburg
Moscow
Kiev
Rome
Istanbul
Lisbon
Madrid
Athens
Casablanca
Alexandria
Cairo
Baghdad
Tehran
Lahore
Beijing
Tianjin
Seoul
Tokyo
Yokohama
Osaka
Chongqing
Wuhan
Shanghai
Delhi
Riyadh
Karachi
Dacca
Tropic of Cancer
Khartoum
Mumbai
(Bombay)
Kolkata
(Calcutta)
Hong Kong
Hyderabad
Bangalore
Chennai
(Madras)
Bangkok
Manila
Addis
Ababa
Ho Chi
Minh City
Lagos
Abidjan
Singapore
Equator
Kinshasa
Jakarta
Luanda
Johannesburg
Sydney
Cape
Town
Tropic of Capricorn
Melbourne

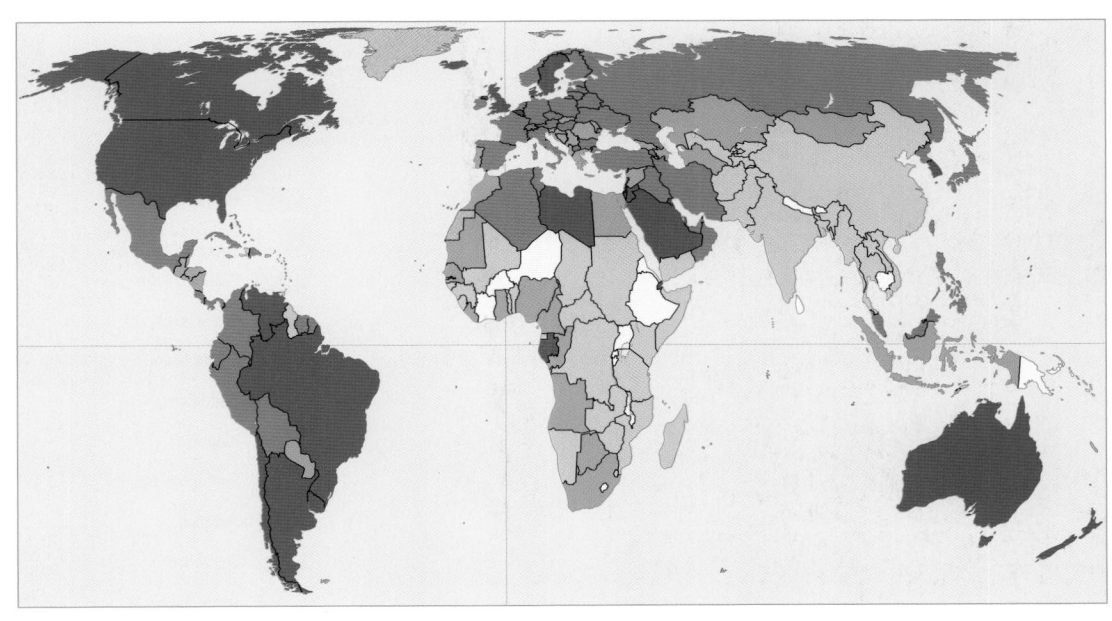

Urban Population

Percentage of total population living in towns and cities (2004)

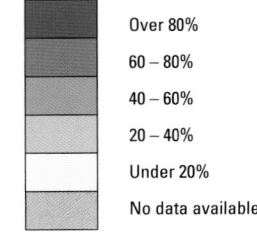

Over 80%

60 – 80%

40 – 60%

20 – 40%

Under 20%

No data available

Most urbanized		Least urbanized	
Singapore	100%	Burundi	10%
Kuwait	97%	Bhutan	11%
Belgium	97%	Trinidad & Tobago	12%
Bahrain	96%	Uganda	13%
Qatar	95%	Papua New Guinea	13%

The Human Family

Predominant Languages

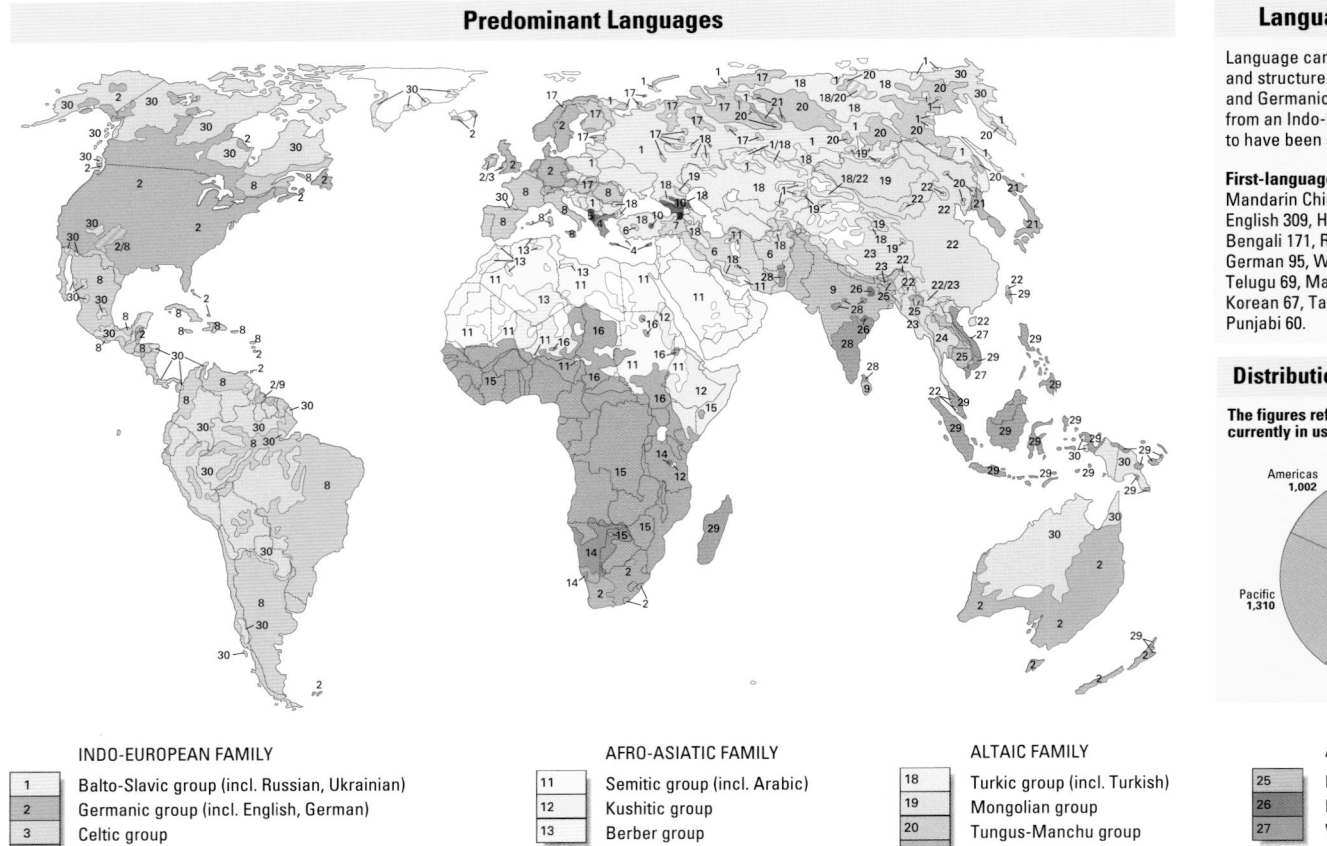

Languages of the World

Language can be classified by ancestry and structure. For example, the Romance and Germanic groups are both derived from an Indo-European language believed to have been spoken 5,000 years ago.

First-language speakers in millions (2004)
Mandarin Chinese 873, Spanish 322, English 309, Hindi 180, Portuguese 177, Bengali 171, Russian 145, Japanese 122, German 95, Wu Chinese 77, Javanese 75, Telugu 69, Marathi 68, Vietnamese 67, Korean 67, Tamil 66, French 64, Italian 61, Punjabi 60.

Distribution of Living Languages

The figures refer to the number of languages currently in use in the regions shown

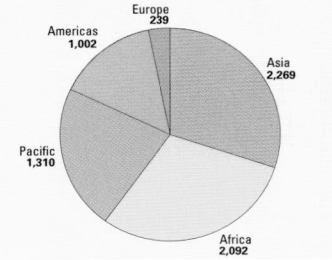

Europe 239
Americas 1,002
Asia 2,269
Pacific 1,310
Africa 2,092

INDO-EUROPEAN FAMILY

1	Balto-Slavic group (incl. Russian, Ukrainian)
2	Germanic group (incl. English, German)
3	Celtic group
4	Greek
5	Albanian
6	Iranian group
7	Armenian
8	Romance group (incl. Spanish, Portuguese, French, Italian)
9	Indo-Aryan group (incl. Hindi, Bengali, Urdu, Punjabi, Marathi)
10	CAUCASIAN FAMILY

AFRO-ASIATIC FAMILY

11	Semitic group (incl. Arabic)
12	Kushitic group
13	Berber group
14	KHOISAN FAMILY
15	NIGER-CONGO FAMILY
16	NILO-SAHARAN FAMILY
17	URALIC FAMILY

ALTAIC FAMILY

18	Turkic group (incl. Turkish)
19	Mongolian group
20	Tungus-Manchu group
21	Japanese and Korean

SINO-TIBETAN FAMILY

22	Sinitic (Chinese) languages (incl. Mandarin, Wu, Yue)
23	Tibetic-Burmic languages
24	TAI FAMILY

AUSTRO-ASIATIC FAMILY

25	Mon-Khmer group
26	Munda group
27	Vietnamese
28	DRAVIDIAN FAMILY (incl. Telugu, Tamil)
29	AUSTRONESIAN FAMILY (incl. Malay-Indonesian, Javanese)
30	OTHER LANGUAGES

Predominant Religions

Religious Adherents

Religious adherents in millions (2005)

Christianity	2,100	Hindu	832
Roman Catholic	*1,050*	Chinese folk	394
Protestant	*396*	Buddhism	329
Orthodox	*240*	Ethnic religions	300
Anglican	*73*	New religions	103
Others	*341*	Sikhism	23
Islam	1,070	Judaism	15
Sunni	*940*	Spiritism	12
Shi'ite	*120*	Baha'i	6
Others	*10*	Confucianism	6
Non-religious/		Jainism	5
Agnostic/Atheist	1,100	Shintoism	3

▲	Roman Catholicism
	Orthodox and other Eastern Churches
•	Protestantism
	Sunni Islam
	Shi'ite Islam
	Buddhism
	Hinduism
	Confucianism
✶	Judaism
	Shintoism
	Tribal Religions

United Nations

Created in 1945 to promote peace and co-operation and based in New York, the United Nations is the world's largest international organization, with 192 members and an annual budget of US $1.9 billion (2006). Each member of the General Assembly has one vote, while the five permanent members of the 15-nation Security Council – China, France, Russia, UK and USA – hold a veto. The Secretariat is the UN's principal administrative arm. The 54 members of the Economic and Social Council are responsible for economic, social, cultural, educational, health and related matters. The UN has 16 specialized agencies – based in Canada, France, Switzerland and Italy, as well as the USA – which help members in fields such as education (UNESCO), agriculture (FAO), medicine (WHO) and finance (IFC). By the end of 1994, all the original 11 trust territories of the Trusteeship Council had become independent.

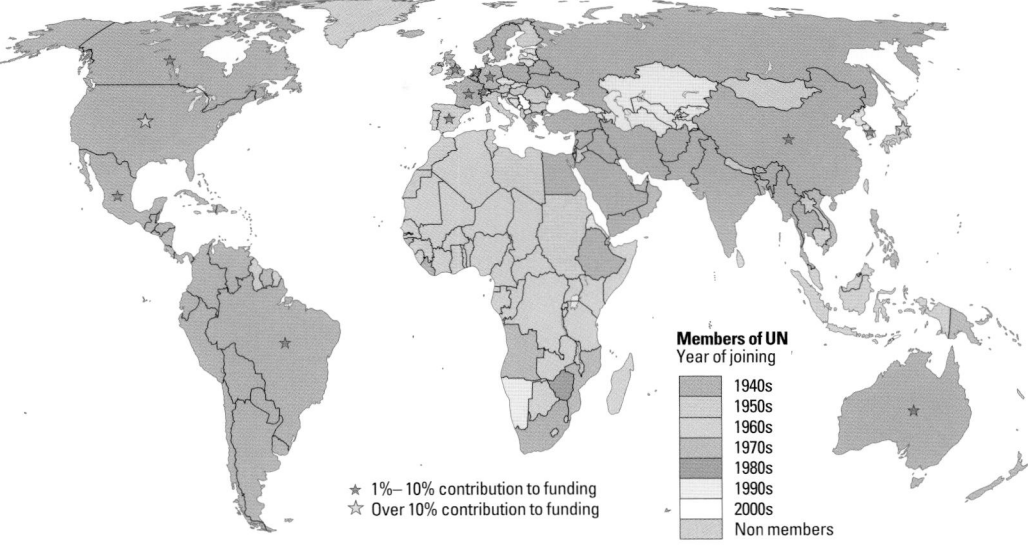

Members of UN
Year of joining
- 1940s
- 1950s
- 1960s
- 1970s
- 1980s
- 1990s
- 2000s
- Non members

★ 1%– 10% contribution to funding
☆ Over 10% contribution to funding

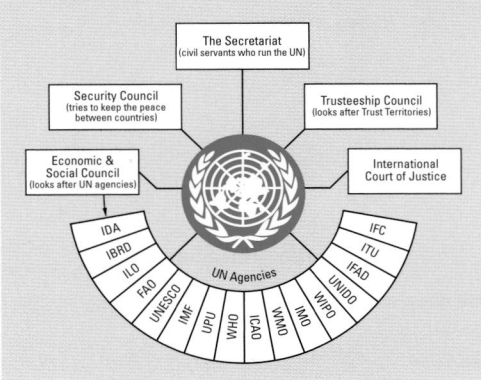

MEMBERSHIP OF THE UN In 1945 there were 51 members; by the end of 2006 membership had increased to 192 following the admission of East Timor, Switzerland and Montenegro. There are 2 independent states which are not members of the UN – Taiwan and the Vatican City. All the successor states of the former USSR had joined by the end of 1992. The official languages of the UN are Chinese, English, French, Russian, Spanish and Arabic.

FUNDING The UN regular budget for 2006 was US$1.9 billion. Contributions are assessed by the members' ability to pay, with the maximum 22% of the total (USA's share), the minimum 0.01%. The European Union pays over 37% of the budget.

PEACEKEEPING The UN has been involved in 61 peacekeeping operations worldwide since 1948.

International Organizations

ACP African-Caribbean-Pacific (formed in 1963). Members have economic ties with the EU.

APEC Asia-Pacific Economic Co-operation (formed in 1989). It aims to enhance economic growth and prosperity for the region and to strengthen the Asia-Pacific community. APEC is the only intergovernmental grouping in the world operating on the basis of non-binding commitments, open dialogue, and equal respect for the views of all participants. There are 21 member economies.

ARAB LEAGUE (formed in 1945). The League's aim is to promote economic, social, political and military co-operation. There are 22 member nations.

ASEAN Association of South-east Asian Nations (formed in 1967). Cambodia joined in 1999.

AU The African Union replaced the Organization of African Unity (formed in 1963) in 2002. Its 53 members represent over 94% of Africa's population. Arabic, French, Portuguese and English are recognized as working languages.

COLOMBO PLAN (formed in 1951). Its 25 members aim to promote economic and social development in Asia and the Pacific.

COMMONWEALTH The Commonwealth of Nations evolved from the British Empire. Pakistan was suspended in 1999, and Zimbabwe in 2002. In response to its continued suspension, Zimbabwe left the Commonwealth in December 2003. Pakistan was reinstated in 2004, but Fiji Islands was suspended in December 2006 following a military coup. It now comprises 16 Queen's realms, 31 republics and 6 indigenous monarchies, giving a total of 53 member states.

EU European Union (evolved from the European Community in 1993). Cyprus, the Czech Republic, Estonia, Hungary, Latvia, Lithuania, Malta, Poland, the Slovak Republic and Slovenia joined the EU in May 2004; Bulgaria and Romania joined in January 2007. The other members are Austria, Belgium, Denmark, Finland, France, Germany, Greece, Ireland, Italy, Luxembourg, Netherlands, Portugal, Spain, Sweden and the UK – together these 27 countries aim to integrate economies, co-ordinate social developments and bring about political union.

LAIA Latin American Integration Association (1980). Its aim is to promote freer regional trade.

NATO North Atlantic Treaty Organization (formed in 1949). It continues after 1991 despite the winding up of the Warsaw Pact. Bulgaria, Estonia, Latvia, Lithuania, Romania, the Slovak Republic and Slovenia became members in 2004.

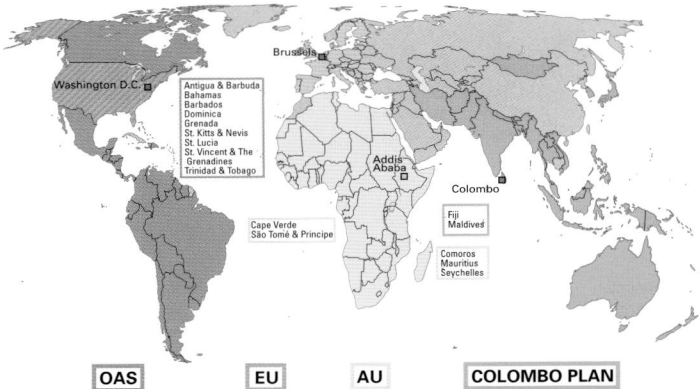

| OAS | EU | AU | COLOMBO PLAN |

OAS Organization of American States (formed in 1948). It aims to promote social and economic co-operation between developed countries of North America and developing nations of Latin America.

OECD Organization for Economic Co-operation and Development (formed in 1961). It comprises 30 major free-market economies. Poland, Hungary and South Korea joined in 1996, and the Slovak Republic in 2000. 'G8' is its 'inner group' of leading industrial nations, comprising Canada, France, Germany, Italy, Japan, Russia, UK and USA.

OPEC Organization of Petroleum Exporting Countries (formed in 1960). It controls about three-quarters of the world's oil supply. Gabon left the organization in 1996.

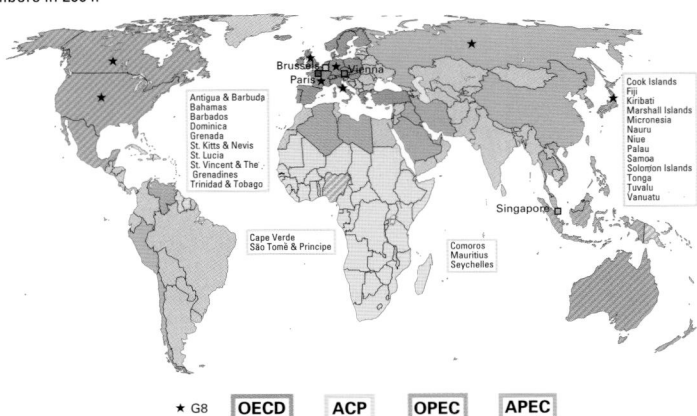

| ★ G8 | OECD | ACP | OPEC | APEC |

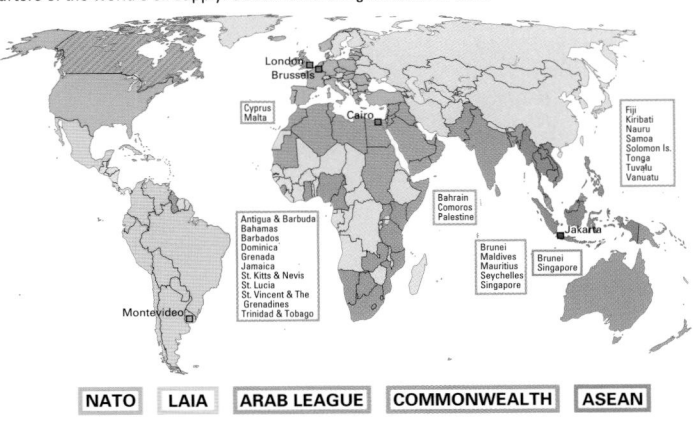

| NATO | LAIA | ARAB LEAGUE | COMMONWEALTH | ASEAN |

Wealth

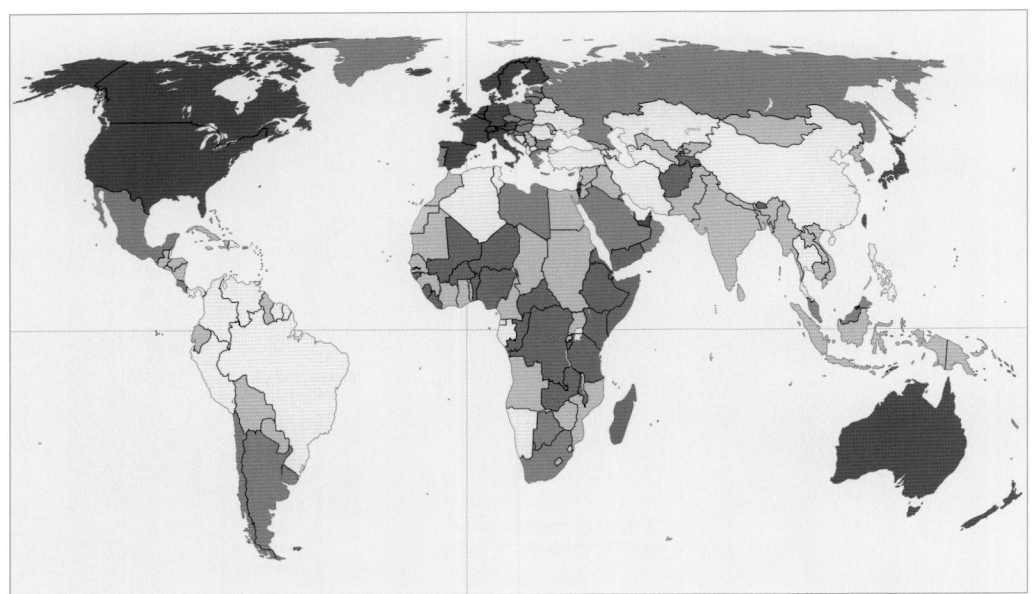

Levels of Income

Gross Domestic Product per capita: the annual value of goods and services divided by the population, using purchasing power parity (PPP) (2006)

 Over 250% of world average

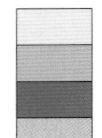 100% – 250% of world average

[World average per person US$10,000]

50% – 100% of world average

15% – 50% of world average

Under 15% of world average

No data available

Wealth Creation

The Gross Domestic Product (GDP) of the world's largest economies, US$ million (2006)

1.	USA	12,980,000	23.	Poland	543,000
2.	China	10,000,000	24.	Netherlands	512,000
3.	Japan	4,220,000	25.	Philippines	443,000
4.	India	4,042,000	26.	Pakistan	427,000
5.	Germany	2,585,000	27.	Saudi Arabia	374,000
6.	UK	1,903,000	28.	Colombia	367,000
7.	France	1,871,000	29.	Ukraine	356,000
8.	Italy	1,727,000	30.	Bangladesh	331,000
9.	Russia	1,723,000	31.	Belgium	330,000
10.	Brazil	1,616,000	32.	Egypt	328,000
11.	South Korea	1,180,000	33.	Malaysia	309,000
12.	Canada	1,165,000	34.	Sweden	285,000
13.	Mexico	1,134,000	35.	Austria	280,000
14.	Spain	1,070,000	36.	Vietnam	259,000
15.	Indonesia	935,000	37.	Algeria	253,000
16.	Taiwan	686,000	38.	Hong Kong	253,000
17.	Australia	666,000	39.	Switzerland	253,000
18.	Turkey	627,000	40.	Greece	252,000
19.	Iran	610,000	41.	Czech Republic	221,000
20.	Argentina	599,000	42.	Norway	207,000
21.	Thailand	586,000	43.	Portugal	203,000
22.	South Africa	576,000	44.	Chile	203,000

The Wealth Gap

The world's richest and poorest countries, by Gross Domestic Product per capita in US $ (2006)

Richest countries		Poorest countries	
1. Luxembourg	68,800	1. Somalia	600
2. UAE	49,700	2. Malawi	600
3. Norway	47,800	3. Comoros	600
4. Ireland	43,600	4. Congo (Dem. Rep.)	700
5. USA	43,500	5. Burundi	700
6. Andorra	38,800	6. Tanzania	800
7. Iceland	38,100	7. East Timor	800
8. Denmark	37,000	8. Afghanistan	800
9. Hong Kong (China)	36,500	9. Yemen	900
10. Austria	35,500	10. Sierra Leone	900
11. Canada	35,200	11. Madagascar	900
12. San Marino	34,100	12. Guinea-Bissau	900
13. Switzerland	33,600	13. Zambia	1,000
14. Japan	33,100	14. Niger	1,000
15. Australia	32,900	15. Liberia	1,000
16. Finland	32,800	16. Ethiopia	1,000
17. Belgium	31,800	17. Eritrea	1,000
18. Netherlands	31,700	18. Djibouti	1,000
19. Sweden	31,600	19. Central African Rep.	1,100
20. Germany	31,400	20. Benin	1,100
21. UK	31,400	21. Mali	1,200

Continental Shares

Shares of population and of wealth (GNI) by continent

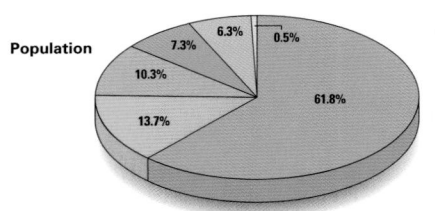

Population

7.3% 6.3% 0.5%
10.3%
13.7%
61.8%

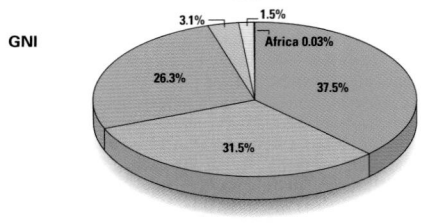

GNI

3.1% 1.5% Africa 0.03%
26.3% 37.5%
31.5%

Europe   Asia   South America

Australia   Africa   North America

Inflation

Average annual rate of inflation (2006)

Over 20%

10% – 20%

5% – 10%

2.5% – 5%

Under 2.5%

No data available

Highest inflation		Lowest inflation	
Zimbabwe	976%	Nauru	–3.6%
Iraq	65%	Vanuatu	–1.6%
Guinea	29%	San Marino	–1.5%
Burma (Myanmar)	21%	Barbados	–0.5%
Congo (Dem. Rep.)	18%	Dominica	–0.1%

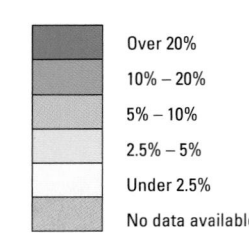

International Aid

Official Development Assistance (ODA) provided and received, per capita (2004)

Over $100 per person
$50 – $100 per person
$20 – $50 per person
→ Providers

Under $10 per person
$10 – $25 per person
$25 – $50 per person
Over $50 per person
↓ Receivers

No data available

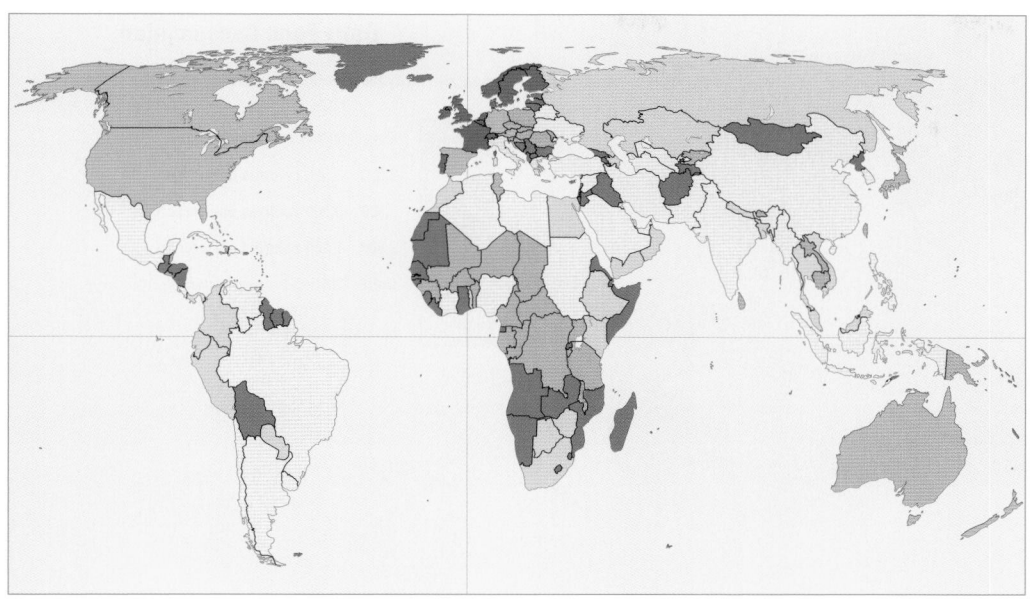

Debt and Aid

International debtors and the aid they receive

Although aid grants make a vital contribution to many of the world's poorer countries, they are usually dwarfed by the burden of debt that the developing economies are expected to repay. It is estimated that the total debt burden of developing countries is US$523 billion.

Debt, US $ per capita (2004)

Aid, US $ per capita (2004)

$12,906
$8,028
$3,538

$3,500
$3,000
$2,500
$2,000
$1,500
$1,000
$500
0

Algeria, Cameroon, Papua New Guinea, Zambia, Bolivia, Syria, Nicaragua $229, Ivory Coast, Sudan, Honduras, Mauritania, Colombia, Angola, Peru, Jordan, El Salvador, Ecuador, Guyana $193, Kazakhstan, Lebanon, Israel

$40
$80
$120
$160

Distribution of Spending

Percentage share of household spending, selected countries

Food
Clothing
Energy & Housing
Medicine & Education
Transport
Other

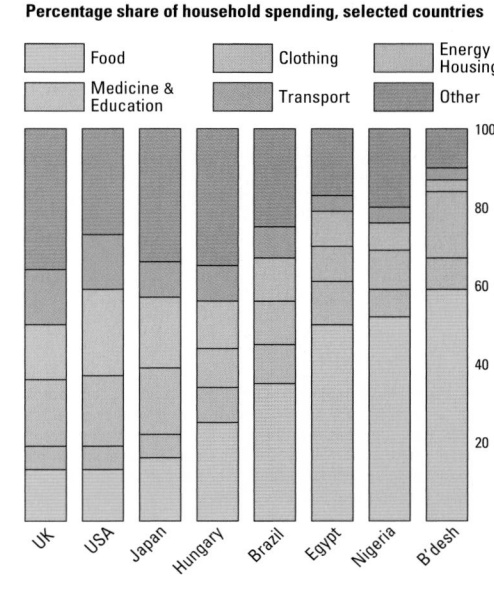

UK, USA, Japan, Hungary, Brazil, Egypt, Nigeria, B'desh

100
80
60
40
20

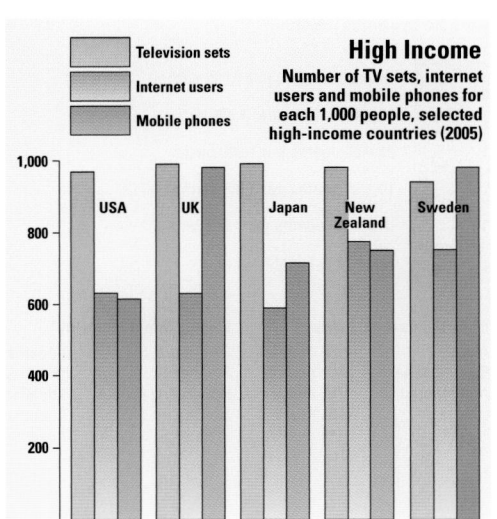

Television sets
Internet users
Mobile phones

High Income

Number of TV sets, internet users and mobile phones for each 1,000 people, selected high-income countries (2005)

1,000
800
600
400
200

USA, UK, Japan, New Zealand, Sweden

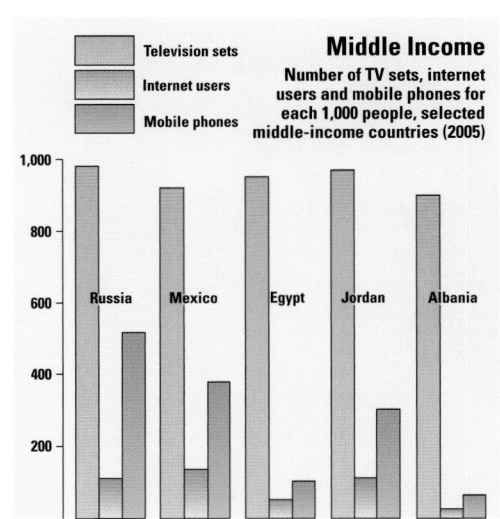

Television sets
Internet users
Mobile phones

Middle Income

Number of TV sets, internet users and mobile phones for each 1,000 people, selected middle-income countries (2005)

1,000
800
600
400
200

Russia, Mexico, Egypt, Jordan, Albania

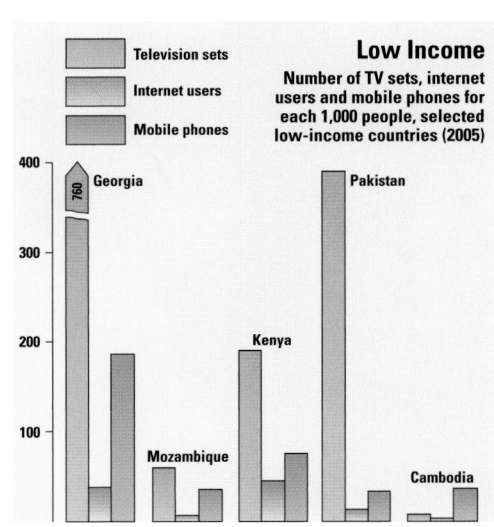

Television sets
Internet users
Mobile phones

Low Income

Number of TV sets, internet users and mobile phones for each 1,000 people, selected low-income countries (2005)

400
760
300
200
100

Georgia, Pakistan, Kenya, Mozambique, Cambodia

Quality of Life

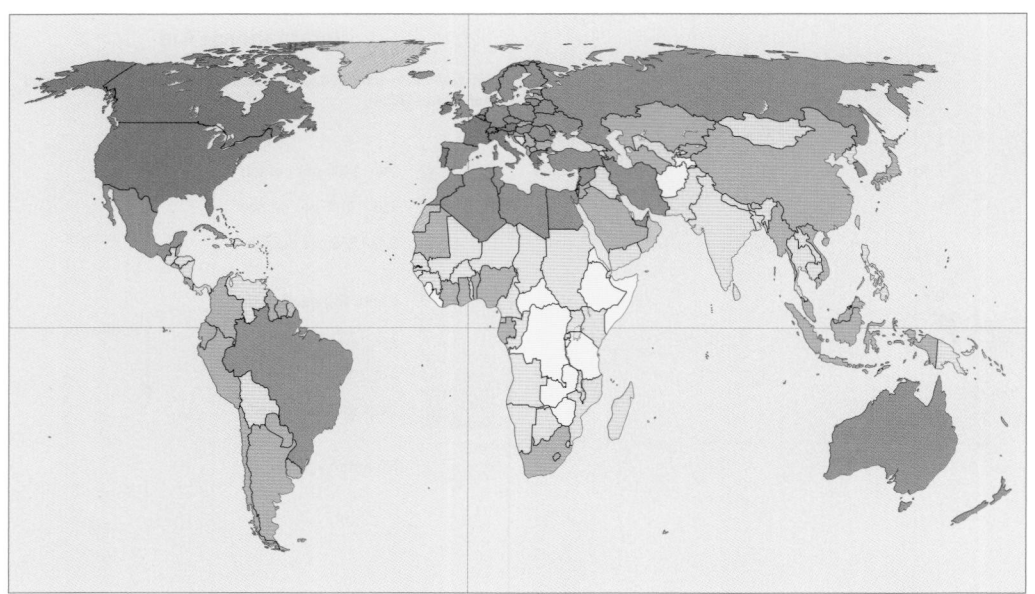

Daily Food Consumption

Average daily food intake in calories per person (2003)

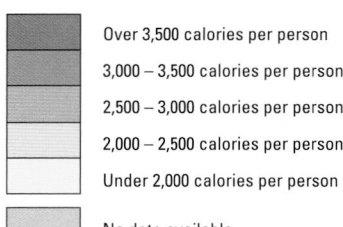

Over 3,500 calories per person

3,000 – 3,500 calories per person

2,500 – 3,000 calories per person

2,000 – 2,500 calories per person

Under 2,000 calories per person

No data available

Hospital Capacity

Hospital beds available for each 1,000 people (2003)

Highest capacity		Lowest capacity	
Monaco	19.6	Nepal	0.2
Japan	14.7	Bangladesh	0.3
North Korea	13.6	Somalia	0.4
Niue	13.0	Afghanistan	0.4
Belarus	11.3	Guatemala	0.5
Russia	10.5	Cambodia	0.5
Germany	8.9	Yemen	0.6
Ukraine	8.8	Burma (Myanmar)	0.6
Lithuania	8.7	Sudan	0.7
Czech Republic	8.6	Pakistan	0.7

Although the ratio of people to hospital beds gives a good approximation of a country's health provision, it is not an absolute indicator. Raw numbers may mask inefficiency and other weaknesses: the high availability of beds in Belarus, for example, has not prevented infant mortality rates over three times as high as in the United Kingdom and the United States.

Life Expectancy

Years of life expectancy at birth, selected countries (2005)

The chart shows combined data for both sexes. On average, women live longer than men worldwide, even in developing countries with high maternal mortality rates. Overall, life expectancy is steadily rising, though the difference between rich and poor nations remains dramatic.

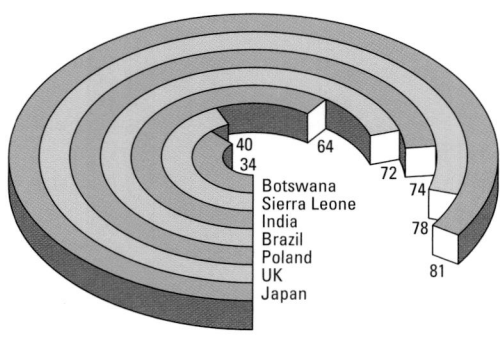

40
34
64
72
74
78
81

Botswana
Sierra Leone
India
Brazil
Poland
UK
Japan

Causes of Death

Causes of death for selected countries by percentage

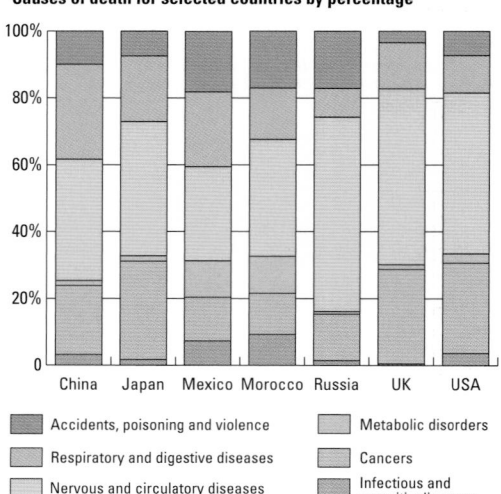

China Japan Mexico Morocco Russia UK USA

- Accidents, poisoning and violence
- Metabolic disorders
- Respiratory and digestive diseases
- Cancers
- Nervous and circulatory diseases
- Infectious and parasitic diseases

Infant Mortality

Number of babies who died under the age of one, per 1,000 live births (2006)

Over 100 deaths per 1,000 births

50 – 100 deaths per 1,000 births

25 – 50 deaths per 1,000 births

10 – 25 deaths per 1,000 births

Under 10 deaths per 1,000 births

No data available

Highest infant mortality		Lowest infant mortality	
Angola	185 deaths	Singapore	2 deaths
Sierra Leone	160 deaths	Sweden	3 deaths
Afghanistan	160 deaths	Hong Kong (China)	3 deaths
Liberia	156 deaths	Japan	3 deaths
Niger	118 deaths	Iceland	3 deaths

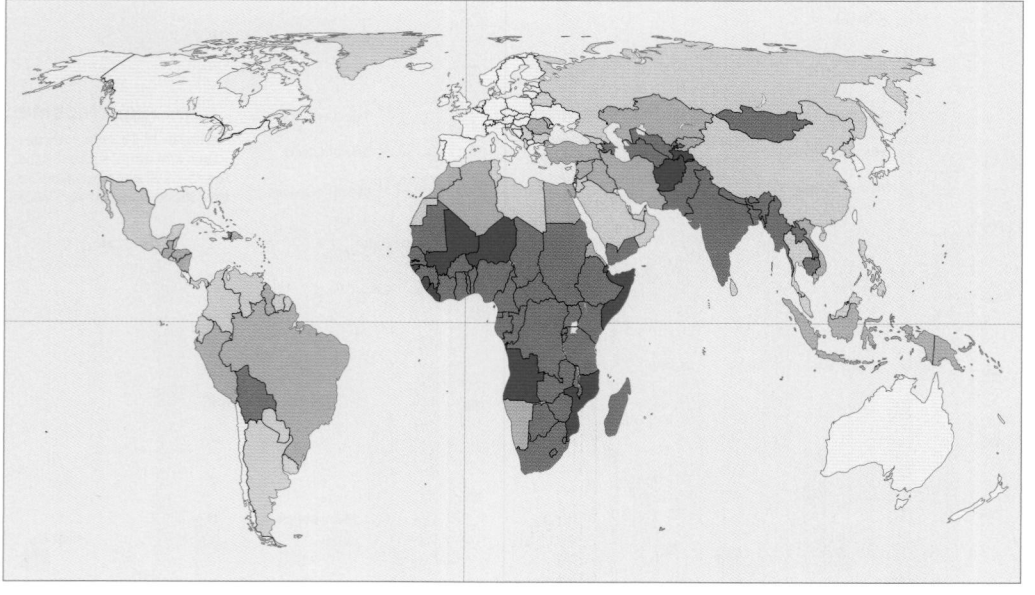

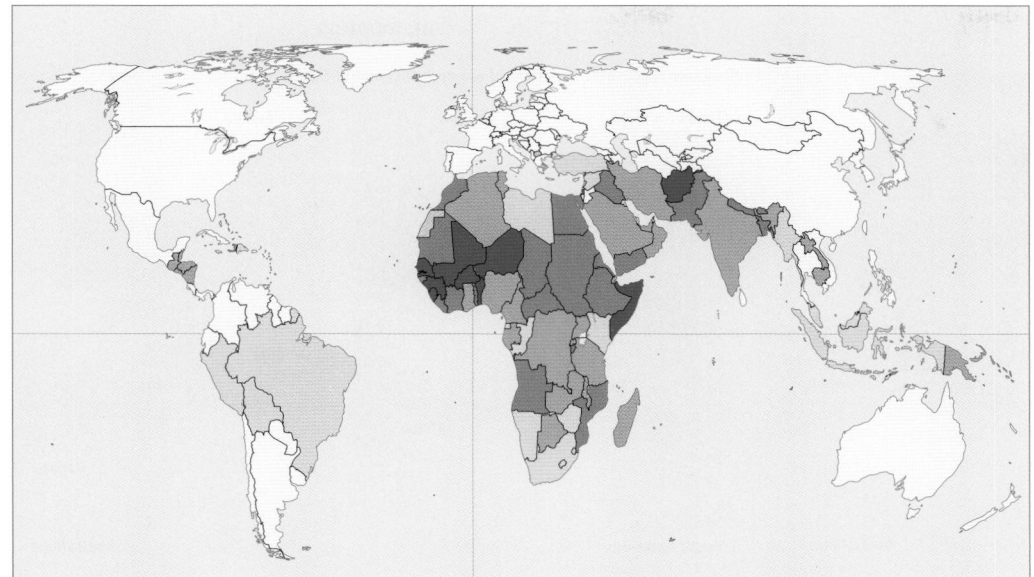

Illiteracy

Percentage of the total adult population unable to read or write (2004)

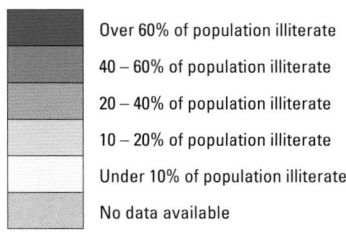

- Over 60% of population illiterate
- 40 – 60% of population illiterate
- 20 – 40% of population illiterate
- 10 – 20% of population illiterate
- Under 10% of population illiterate
- No data available

Countries with the highest and lowest illiteracy rates

Highest		Lowest	
Burkina Faso	87	Australia	0
Niger	83	Denmark	0
Mali	81	Finland	0
Sierra Leone	69	Liechtenstein	0
Guinea	64	Luxembourg	0

Fertility and Education

Fertility rates compared with female education, selected countries (2000–05)

- Percentage of females aged 12–17 in secondary education
- Fertility rate: average number of children borne per woman

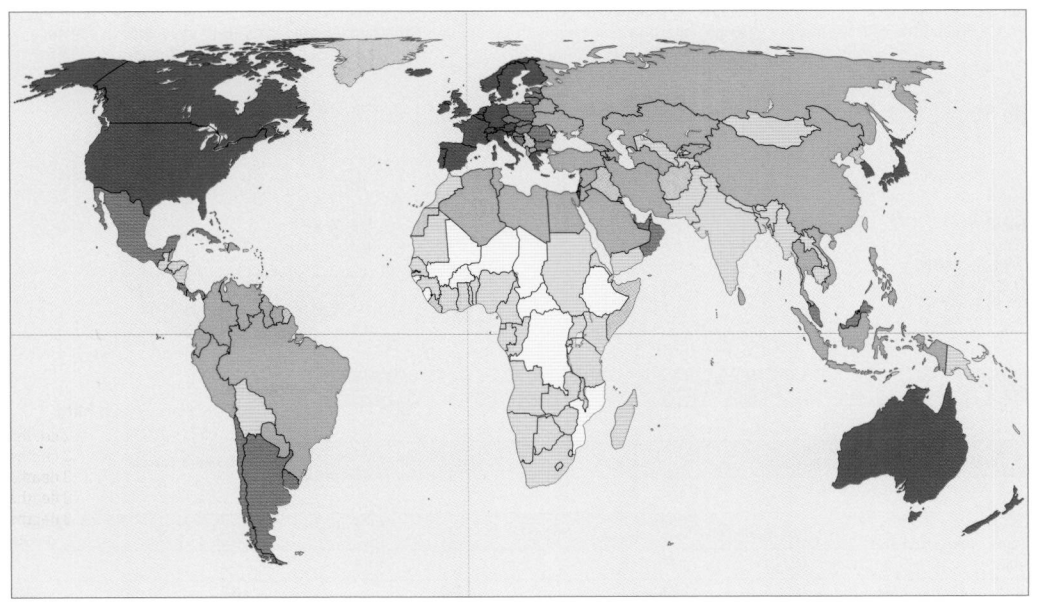

Living Standards

At first sight, most international contrasts in living standards are swamped by differences in wealth. The rich not only have more money, they have more of everything, including years of life. Those with only a little money are obliged to spend most of it on food and clothing, the basic maintenance costs of their existence; air travel and tourism are unlikely to feature on their expenditure lists. However, poverty and wealth are both relative: slum dwellers living on social security payments in an affluent industrial country have far more resources at their disposal than an average African peasant, but feel their own poverty nonetheless. A middle-class Indian lawyer cannot command a fraction of the earnings of a counterpart living in New York, London or Rome; nevertheless, he rightly sees himself as prosperous.

The rich not only live longer, on average, than the poor, they also die from different causes. Infectious and parasitic diseases, all but eliminated in the developed world, remain a scourge in the developing nations. On the other hand, more than two-thirds of the populations of OECD nations eventually succumb to cancer or circulatory disease.

Human Development Index

The Human Development Index (HDI), calculated by the UN Development Programme, gives a value to countries using indicators of life expectancy, education and standards of living (2004). Higher values show more developed countries.

- Over 0.9
- 0.8 – 0.9
- 0.7 – 0.8
- 0.4 – 0.7
- Under 0.4
- No data available

Highest values		Lowest values	
Norway	0.965	Niger	0.311
Iceland	0.960	Sierra Leone	0.335
Australia	0.957	Mali	0.338
Ireland	0.956	Burkina Faso	0.342
Sweden	0.951	Guinea-Bissau	0.349

Energy

Production

Each square represents 1% of world energy production (2005)

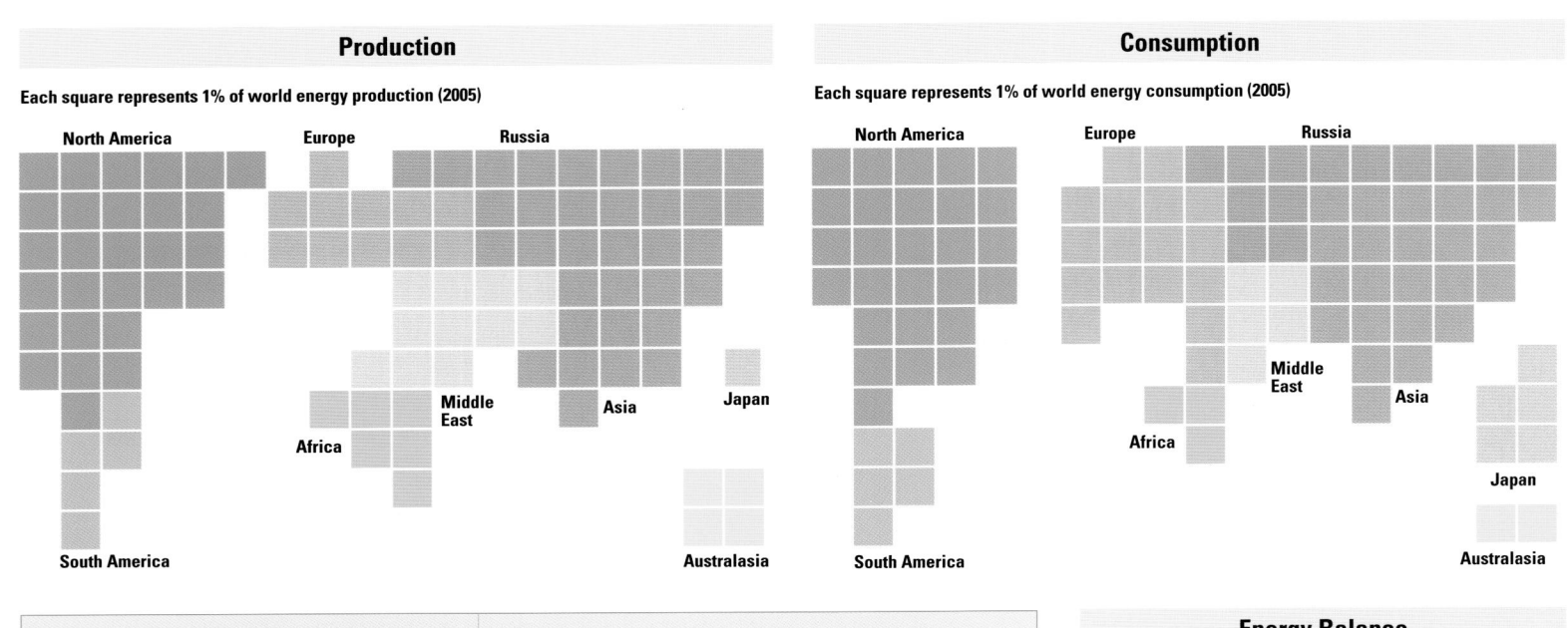

North America   Europe   Russia   Middle East   Asia   Japan   Africa   South America   Australasia

Consumption

Each square represents 1% of world energy consumption (2005)

North America   Europe   Russia   Middle East   Asia   Africa   South America   Japan   Australasia

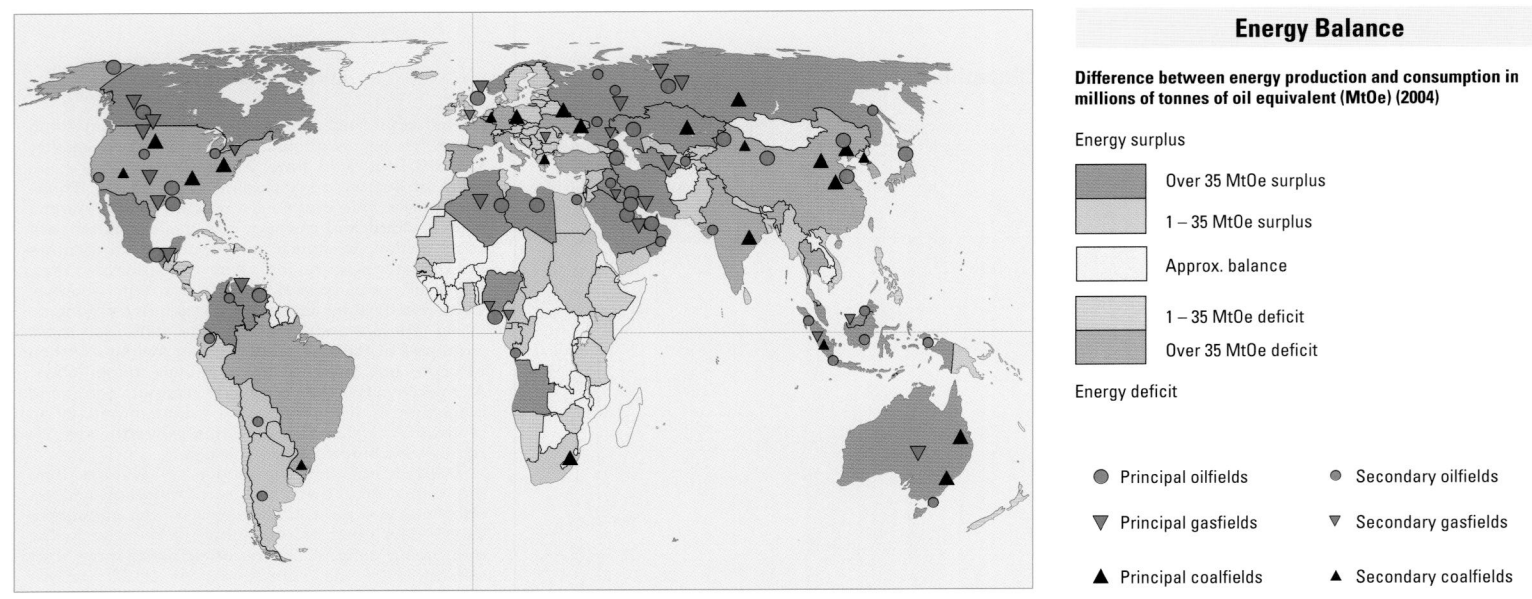

Energy Balance

Difference between energy production and consumption in millions of tonnes of oil equivalent (MtOe) (2004)

Energy surplus

- Over 35 MtOe surplus
- 1 – 35 MtOe surplus
- Approx. balance
- 1 – 35 MtOe deficit
- Over 35 MtOe deficit

Energy deficit

- ● Principal oilfields
- ● Secondary oilfields
- ▽ Principal gasfields
- ▽ Secondary gasfields
- ▲ Principal coalfields
- ▲ Secondary coalfields

World Energy Consumption

Energy consumed by world regions, measured in million tonnes of oil equivalent in 2005. Total world consumption was 10,537 MtOe. Only energy from oil, gas, coal, nuclear and hydroelectric sources are included. Excluded are fuels such as wood, peat, animal waste, wind, solar and geothermal which, though important in some countries, are unreliably documented in terms of consumption statistics.

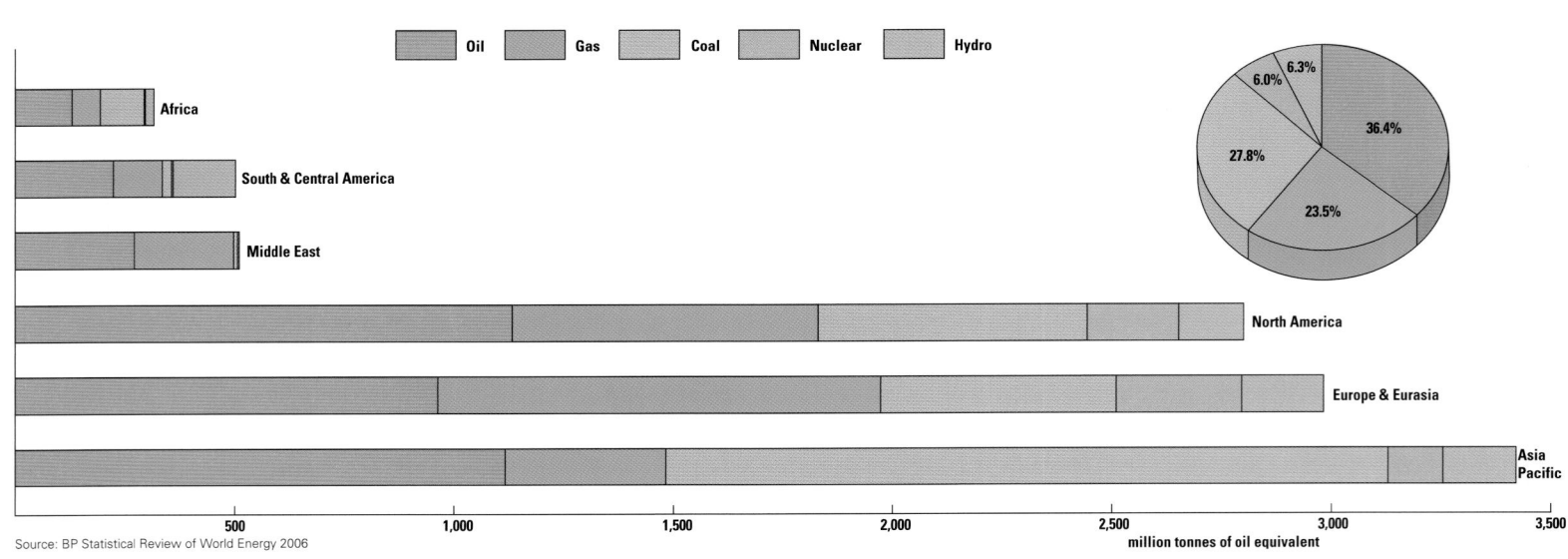

Oil   Gas   Coal   Nuclear   Hydro

Africa   South & Central America   Middle East   North America   Europe & Eurasia   Asia Pacific

6.3%   6.0%   27.8%   36.4%   23.5%

500   1,000   1,500   2,000   2,500   3,000   3,500

million tonnes of oil equivalent

Source: BP Statistical Review of World Energy 2006

Energy

Energy is used to keep us warm or cool, fuel our industries and our transport systems, and even feed us; high-intensity agriculture, with its use of fertilizers, pesticides and machinery, is heavily energy-dependent. Although we live in a high-energy society, there are vast discrepancies between rich and poor; for example, a North American consumes 13 times as much energy as a Chinese person. But even developing nations have more power at their disposal than was imaginable a century ago.

The distribution of energy supplies, most importantly fossil fuels (coal, oil and natural gas), is very uneven. In addition, the diagrams and map opposite show that the largest producers of energy are not necessarily the largest consumers. The movement of energy supplies around the world is therefore an important component of international trade. In 2005, total world movements in oil amounted to 2,462 million tonnes.

As the finite reserves of fossil fuels are depleted, renewable energy sources, such as solar, hydro-thermal, wind, tidal and biomass, will become increasingly important around the world.

Nuclear Power

Major producers by percentage of world total and by percentage of domestic electricity generation (2004)

Country	% of world total production	Country	% of nuclear as proportion of domestic electricity
1. USA	30.1%	1. Lithuania	80.6%
2. France	16.3%	2. France	78.8%
3. Japan	10.4%	3. Belgium	57.1%
4. Germany	6.1%	4. Slovak Rep.	56.2%
5. Russia	5.2%	5. Sweden	58.8%
6. South Korea	4.7%	6. Ukraine	45.9%
7. Canada	3.3%	7. Switzerland	41.3%
8. Ukraine	3.2%	8. Armenia	38.6%
9. UK	2.8%	9. Bulgaria	37.2%
= Sweden	2.8%	10. South Korea	36.0%

Although the 1980s were a bad time for the nuclear power industry (major projects ran over budget and fears of long-term environmental damage were heavily reinforced by the 1986 disaster at Chernobyl), the industry picked up in the early 1990s. Whilst the number of reactors is still increasing, however, orders for new plants have shrunk. Sixteen countries currently rely on nuclear power to supply over 25% of their electricity requirements.

Hydroelectricity

Major producers by percentage of world total and by percentage of domestic electricity generation (2004)

Country	% of world total production	Country	% of hydroelectric as proportion of domestic electricity
1. Canada	12.2%	1. Bhutan	100%
2. China	11.9%	= Paraguay	100%
3. Brazil	11.6%	= Lesotho	100%
4. USA	9.8%	4. Mozambique	99.8%
5. Russia	6.0%	5. Congo	99.7%
6. Norway	3.9%	= Congo (Dem. Rep.)	99.7%
7. Japan	3.4%	= Uganda	99.7%
8. India	3.0%	8. Nepal	99.6%
9. Sweden	2.3%	9. Zambia	99.5%
10. France	2.2%	10. Norway	98.8%

Countries heavily reliant on hydroelectricity are usually small and non-industrial: a high proportion of hydroelectric power more often reflects a modest energy budget than vast hydroelectric resources. The USA, for instance, produces only 6.7% of its power requirements from hydroelectricity; yet that 6.7% amounts to more than seven times the hydropower generated by most of Africa.

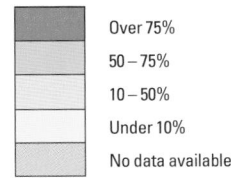

Fuel Exports

Fuels as a percentage of total value of exports (2004)

- Over 75%
- 50 – 75%
- 10 – 50%
- Under 10%
- No data available

In the 1970s, oil exports became a political issue when OPEC sought to increase the influence of developing countries in world affairs by raising oil prices and restricting production. But its power was short-lived, following a fall in demand for oil in the 1980s, due to an increase in energy efficiency and development of alternative resources. However, with the heavy energy demands of the Asian economies early in the 21st century, both oil and gas prices have risen sharply.

Conversion Rates

1 barrel = 0.136 tonnes or 159 litres or 35 Imperial gallons or 42 US gallons

1 tonne = 7.33 barrels or 1,185 litres or 256 Imperial gallons or 261 US gallons

1 tonne oil = 1.5 tonnes hard coal or 3.0 tonnes lignite or 12,000 kWh

1 Imperial gallon = 1.201 US gallons or 4.546 litres or 277.4 cubic inches

Measurements

For historical reasons, oil is traded in 'barrels'. The weight and volume equivalents (shown right) are all based on average-density 'Arabian light' crude oil.

The energy equivalents given for a tonne of oil are also somewhat imprecise: oil and coal of different qualities will have varying energy contents, a fact usually reflected in their price on world markets.

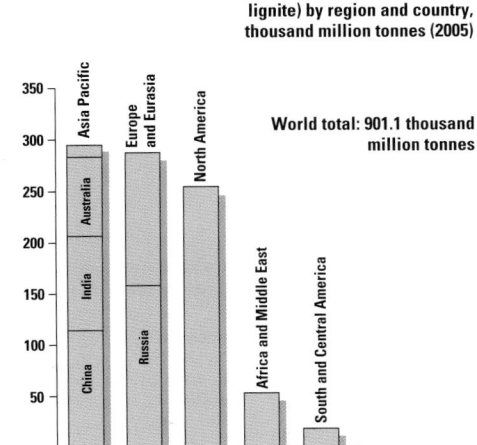

World Coal Reserves

World coal reserves (including lignite) by region and country, thousand million tonnes (2005)

World total: 901.1 thousand million tonnes

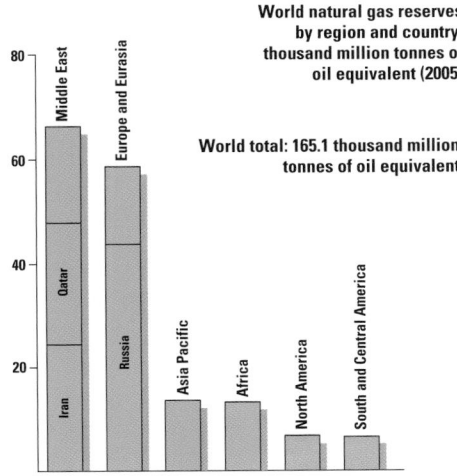

World Gas Reserves

World natural gas reserves by region and country, thousand million tonnes of oil equivalent (2005)

World total: 165.1 thousand million tonnes of oil equivalent

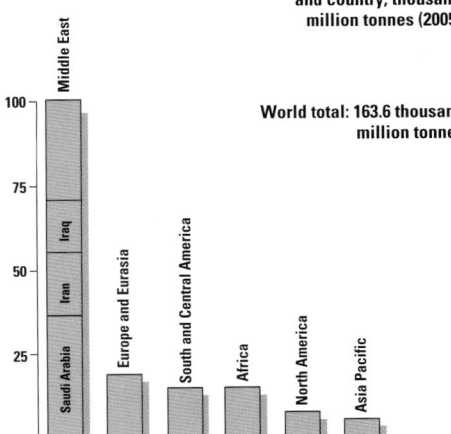

World Oil Reserves

World oil reserves by region and country, thousand million tonnes (2005)

World total: 163.6 thousand million tonnes

Production

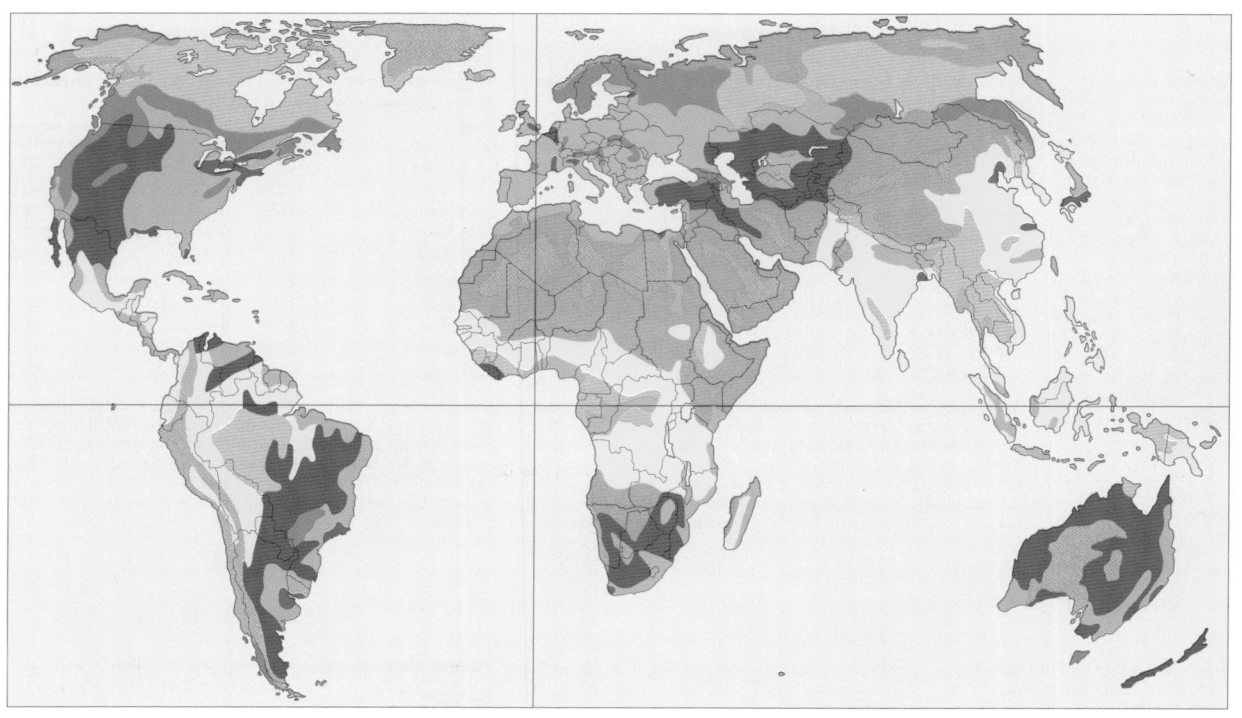

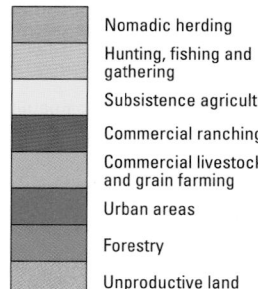

CARTOGRAPHY BY PHILIP'S. COPYRIGHT PHILIP'S

Agriculture

Predominant type of farming or land use

- Nomadic herding
- Hunting, fishing and gathering
- Subsistence agriculture
- Commercial ranching
- Commercial livestock and grain farming
- Urban areas
- Forestry
- Unproductive land

The development of agriculture has transformed human existence more than any other. The whole business of farming is constantly developing: due mainly to the new varieties of rice and wheat, world grain production has more than doubled since 1965. New machinery and modern agricultural techniques enable relatively few farmers to produce enough food for the world's 6 billion or so people.

Staple Crops

Wheat
China 15.7% India 11.6% USA 9.2% Russia 7.7% France 5.9% Canada 4.3% Australia 4.0%

World total (2005): 622,561,430 tonnes

Maize
USA 39.8% China 19.7% Brazil 5.0%

World total (2005): 709,366,400 tonnes

Oats
Russia 19.1% Canada 14.4% USA 7.0% Poland 5.5% Australia 5.9% Finland 4.5% Germany 4.0%

World total (2005): 23,882,000 tonnes

Millet
India 34.1% Nigeria 23.7% Niger 8.8% China 5.9%

World total (2005): 30,233,000 tonnes

Rice
China 15.7% India 11.6% USA 9.2% Russia 7.7% France 5.9% Canada 4.3% Australia 4.0%

World total (2005): 622,561,430 tonnes

Potatoes
USA 39.8% China 19.7% Brazil 5.0%

World total (2005): 709,366,400 tonnes

Soya
Russia 19.1% Canada 14.4% USA 7.0% Poland 5.5% Australia 5.9% Finland 4.5% Germany 4.0%

World total (2005): 23,882,000 tonnes

Cassava
India 34.1% Nigeria 23.7% Niger 8.8% China 5.9%

World total (2005): 30,233,000 tonnes

Sugars

Sugar cane
Brazil 33.4% India 18.3% China 6.9% Pakistan 3.7% Mexico 3.6% Thailand 3.4%

World total (2005): 1,267,211,000 tonnes

Sugar beet
Brazil 33.4% India 18.3% China 6.9% Pakistan 3.7% Mexico 3.6% Thailand 3.4%

World total (2005): 1,267,211,000 tonnes

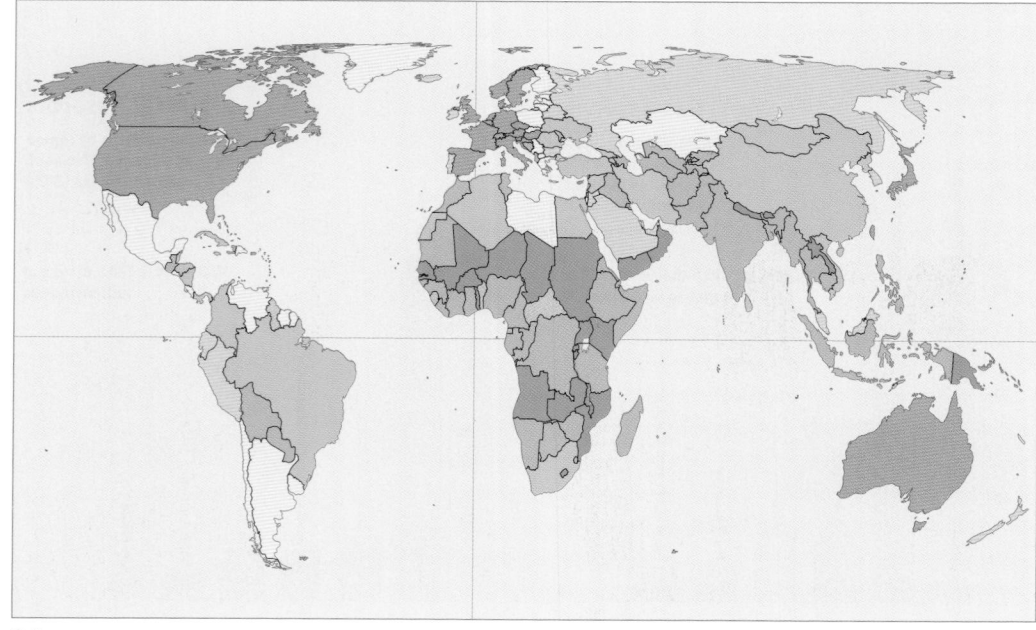

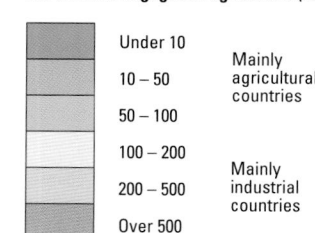

Employment

The number of workers employed in manufacturing for every 100 workers engaged in agriculture (2005)

- Under 10
- 10 – 50 — Mainly agricultural countries
- 50 – 100
- 100 – 200
- 200 – 500 — Mainly industrial countries
- Over 500

Countries with the highest and lowest number of workers employed in manufacturing per 100 workers engaged in agriculture (2005)

Highest		Lowest	
Bahrain	7,900	Burundi	2.5
San Marino	4,200	Yemen	5.0
Micronesia	3,822	Oman	5.0
USA	3,271	Rwanda	5.6
Liechtenstein	2,350	Malawi	5.6

Mineral Production

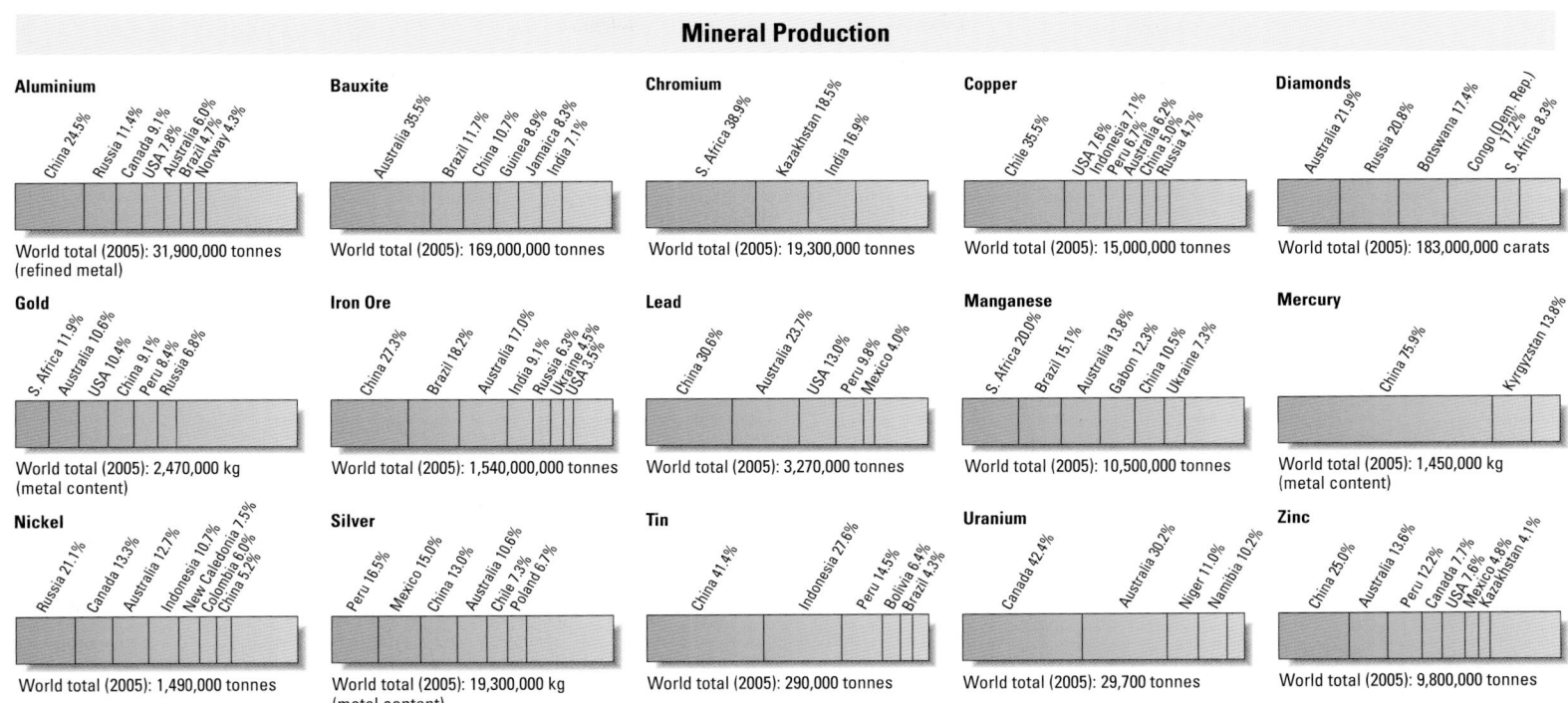

Aluminium
China 24.5% Russia 11.4% Canada 9.1% USA 7.8% Australia 6.0% Brazil 4.7% Norway 4.3%
World total (2005): 31,900,000 tonnes (refined metal)

Bauxite
Australia 35.5% Brazil 11.7% China 10.7% Guinea 8.9% Jamaica 8.3% India 7.1%
World total (2005): 169,000,000 tonnes

Chromium
S. Africa 38.9% Kazakhstan 18.5% India 16.9%
World total (2005): 19,300,000 tonnes

Copper
Chile 35.5% USA 7.6% Indonesia 7.1% Peru 6.7% Australia 6.2% China 5.0% Russia 4.7%
World total (2005): 15,000,000 tonnes

Diamonds
Australia 21.9% Russia 20.8% Botswana 17.4% Congo (Dem. Rep.) 17.2% S. Africa 8.3%
World total (2005): 183,000,000 carats

Gold
S. Africa 11.9% Australia 10.6% USA 10.4% China 9.1% Peru 8.4% Russia 6.8%
World total (2005): 2,470,000 kg (metal content)

Iron Ore
China 27.3% Brazil 18.2% Australia 17.0% India 9.1% Russia 6.3% Ukraine 4.5% USA 3.5%
World total (2005): 1,540,000,000 tonnes

Lead
China 30.6% Australia 23.7% USA 13.0% Peru 9.8% Mexico 4.0%
World total (2005): 3,270,000 tonnes

Manganese
S. Africa 20.0% Brazil 15.1% Australia 13.8% Gabon 12.3% China 10.5% Ukraine 7.3%
World total (2005): 10,500,000 tonnes

Mercury
China 75.9% Kyrgyzstan 13.8%
World total (2005): 1,450,000 kg (metal content)

Nickel
Russia 21.1% Canada 13.3% Australia 12.7% Indonesia 10.7% New Caledonia 7.5% Colombia 6.0% China 5.2%
World total (2005): 1,490,000 tonnes

Silver
Peru 16.5% Mexico 15.0% China 13.0% Australia 10.6% Chile 7.3% Poland 6.7%
World total (2005): 19,300,000 kg (metal content)

Tin
China 41.4% Indonesia 27.6% Peru 14.5% Bolivia 6.4% Brazil 4.3%
World total (2005): 290,000 tonnes

Uranium
Canada 42.4% Australia 30.2% Niger 11.0% Namibia 10.2%
World total (2005): 29,700 tonnes

Zinc
China 25.0% Australia 13.6% Peru 12.2% Canada 7.7% USA 7.6% Mexico 4.6% Kazakhstan 4.1%
World total (2005): 9,800,000 tonnes

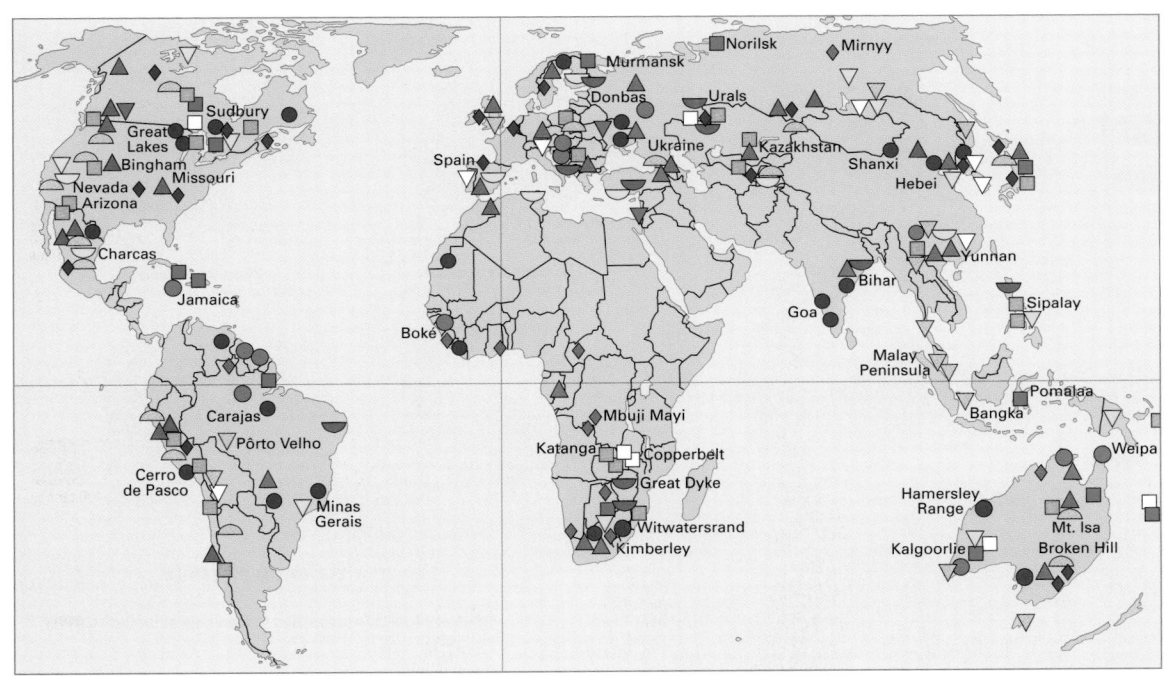

Mineral Distribution

The map shows the richest sources of the most important minerals (major mineral locations are named)

- ● Bauxite
- ◗ Chromium
- ☐ Cobalt
- ▣ Copper
- ◆ Diamonds
- ▽ Gold
- ● Iron ore
- ▲ Lead
- ▲ Manganese
- ◡ Mercury
- ▲ Molybdenum
- ▪ Nickel
- ▼ Potash
- ◠ Silver
- ▽ Tin
- ▽ Tungsten
- ◆ Zinc

The map does not show undersea deposits, most of which are considered inaccessible.

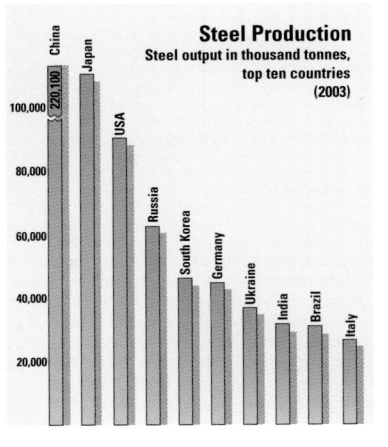

Steel Production
Steel output in thousand tonnes, top ten countries (2003)
China 220,100

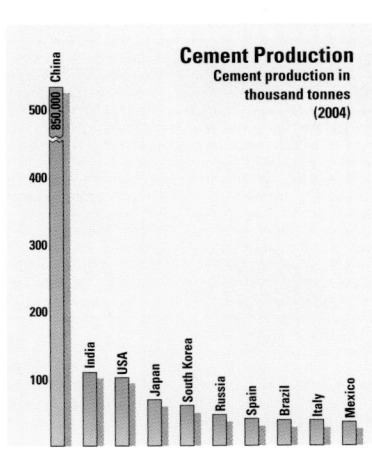

Cement Production
Cement production in thousand tonnes (2004)
China 850,000

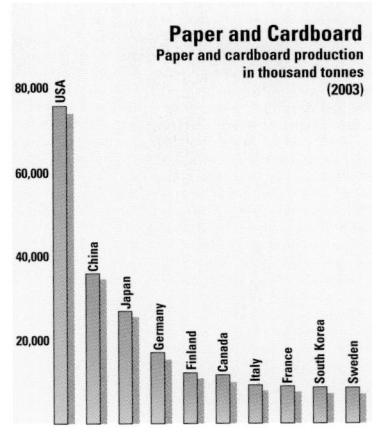

Paper and Cardboard
Paper and cardboard production in thousand tonnes (2003)

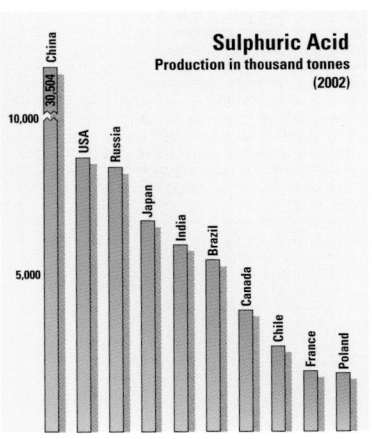

Sulphuric Acid
Production in thousand tonnes (2002)
China 30,504

Trade

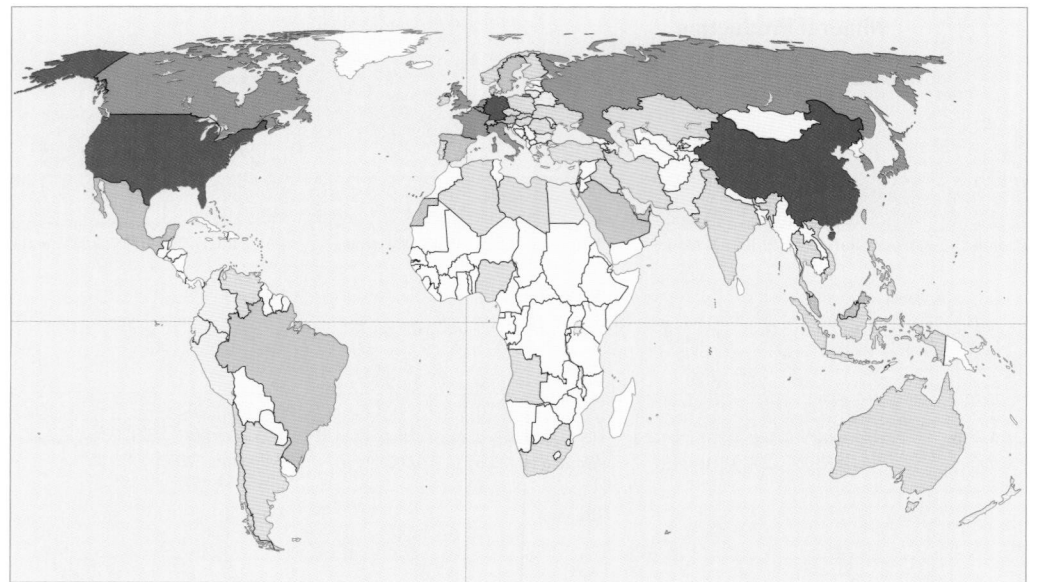

Share of World Trade

Percentage share of total world exports by value (2006)

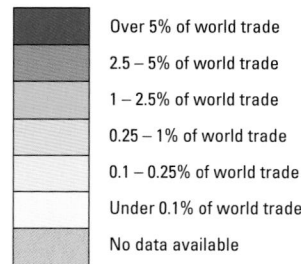

- Over 5% of world trade
- 2.5 – 5% of world trade
- 1 – 2.5% of world trade
- 0.25 – 1% of world trade
- 0.1 – 0.25% of world trade
- Under 0.1% of world trade
- No data available

Largest share of world trade		Smallest share of world trade	
Germany	9.1%	East Timor	0.0%
USA	8.2%	Eritrea	0.0%
China	7.8%	Burundi	0.0%
Hong Kong (China)	4.9%	Rwanda	0.0%
Japan	4.8%	Guinea-Bissau	0.0%

The Main Trading Nations

The imports and exports of the top ten trading nations as a percentage of world trade (2006). Each country's trade in manufactured goods is shown in dark blue

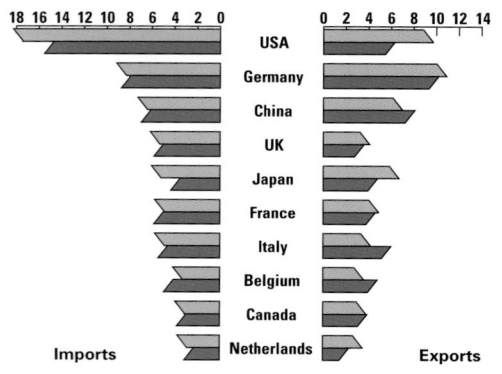

Imports / Exports

USA, Germany, China, UK, Japan, France, Italy, Belgium, Canada, Netherlands

Major exports

Leading manufactured items and their exporters (2004)

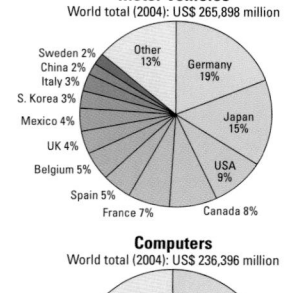

Motor Vehicles
World total (2004): US$ 265,898 million

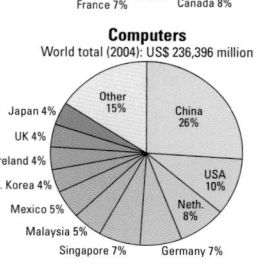

Computers
World total (2004): US$ 236,396 million

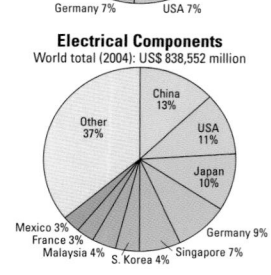

Telecommunications Gear
World total (2004): US$ 405,989 million

Electrical Components
World total (2004): US$ 838,552 million

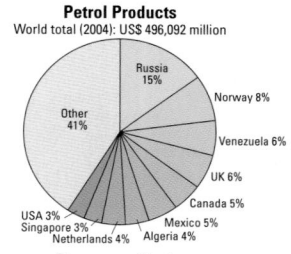

Petrol Products
World total (2004): US$ 496,092 million

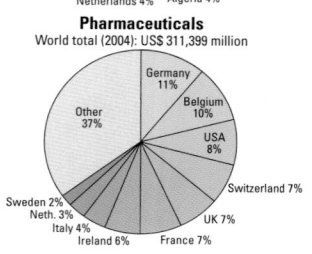

Pharmaceuticals
World total (2004): US$ 311,399 million

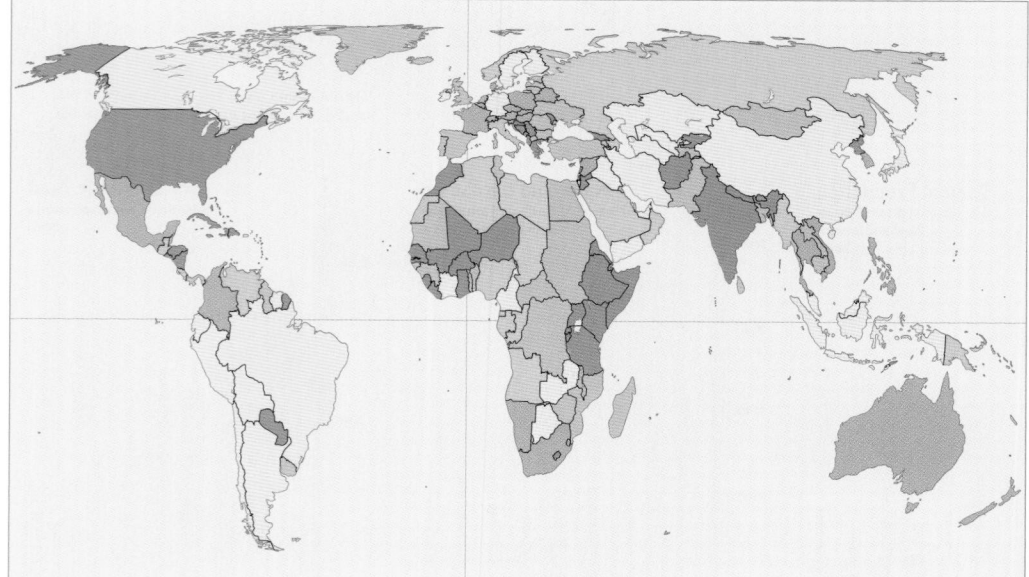

Balance of Trade

Value of exports in proportion to the value of imports (2006)

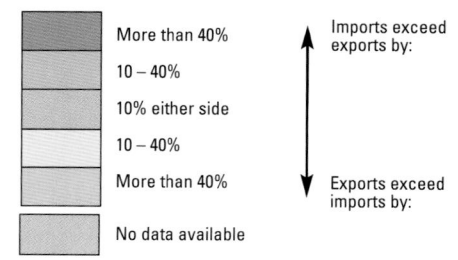

- More than 40% — Imports exceed exports by:
- 10 – 40%
- 10% either side
- 10 – 40%
- More than 40% — Exports exceed imports by:
- No data available

The total world trade balance should amount to zero, since exports must equal imports on a global scale. In practice, at least $100 billion in exports go unrecorded, leaving the world with an apparent deficit and many countries in a better position than public accounting reveals. However, a favourable trade balance is not necessarily a sign of prosperity: many poorer countries must maintain a high surplus in order to service debts, and do so by restricting imports below the levels needed to sustain successful economies.

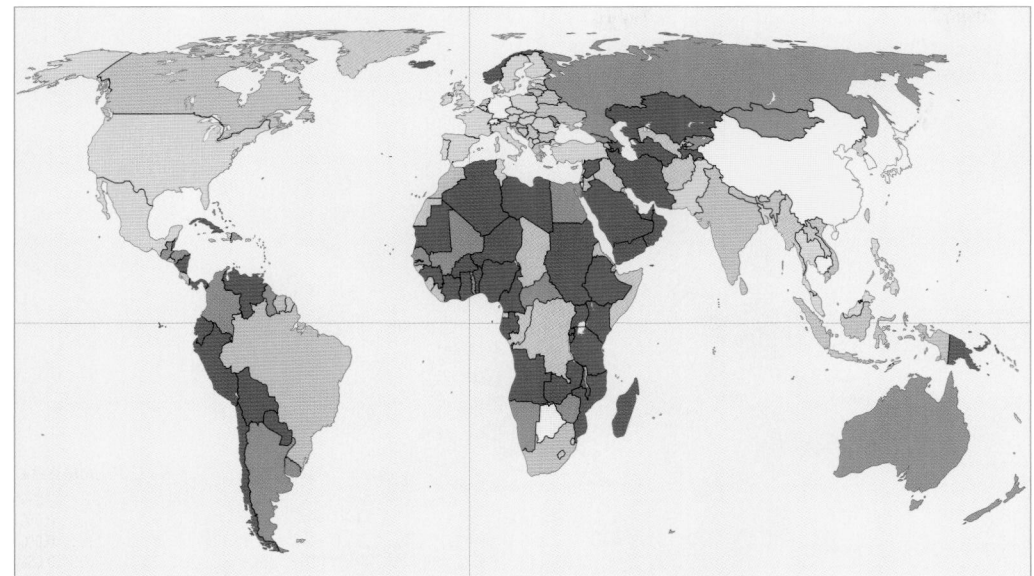

Primary exports as a percentage of total export value (2004)

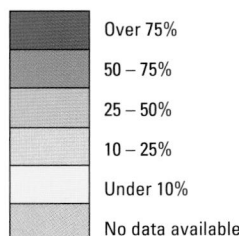

Over 75%

50 – 75%

25 – 50%

10 – 25%

Under 10%

No data available

Primary exports are raw materials or partly processed products that form the basis for manufacturing. They are the necessary requirements of industries and include agricultural products, minerals, fuels and timber, as well as many semi-manufactured goods such as cotton, which has been spun but not woven, wood pulp or flour. Many developed countries have few natural resources and rely on imports for the majority of their primary products. The countries of South-east Asia export hardwoods to the rest of the world, while many South American countries are heavily dependent on coffee exports.

Merchant Fleets

Merchant fleets in thousand gross registered tonnage (2006). Although a large number of vessels are registered in Liberia and Panama, they are not part of the national fleet

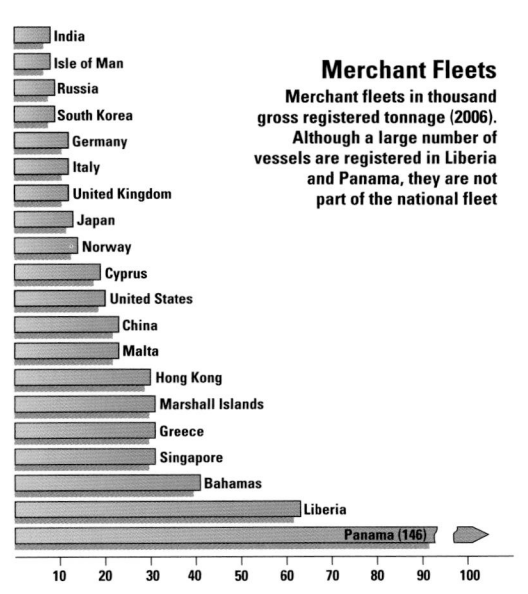

India
Isle of Man
Russia
South Korea
Germany
Italy
United Kingdom
Japan
Norway
Cyprus
United States
China
Malta
Hong Kong
Marshall Islands
Greece
Singapore
Bahamas
Liberia
Panama (146)

10 20 30 40 50 60 70 80 90 100

Top Ten Ports

Total container traffic, in million TEU (2004) ('TEU' stands for Twenty-foot Equivalent Unit, the equivalent of a standard container)

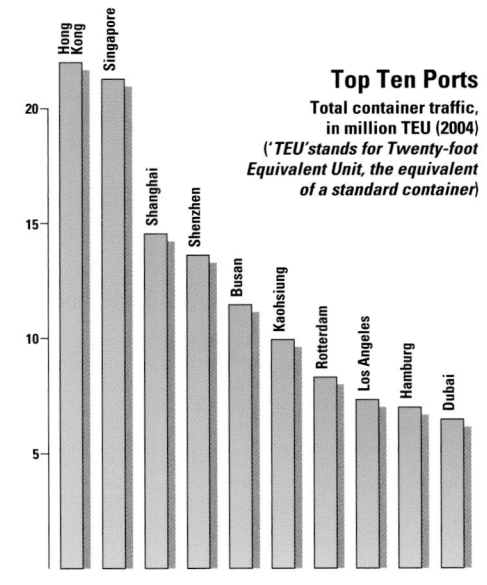

Hong Kong
Singapore
Shanghai
Shenzhen
Busan
Kaohsiung
Rotterdam
Los Angeles
Hamburg
Dubai

Types of Vessels

World fleet by type of vessel (2006)

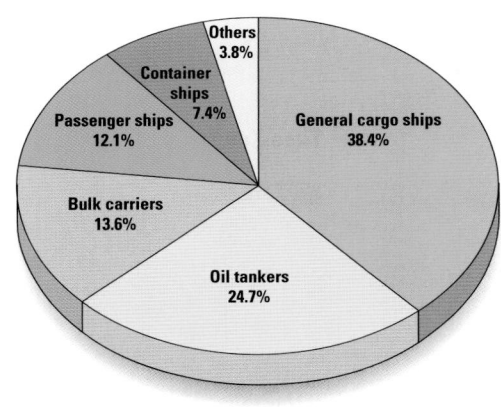

Others 3.8%
Container ships 7.4%
Passenger ships 12.1%
Bulk carriers 13.6%
Oil tankers 24.7%
General cargo ships 38.4%

Exports Per Capita

Value of exports in US $, divided by total population (2006)

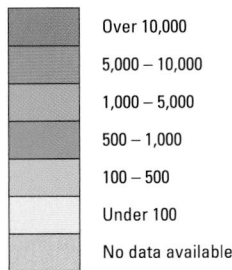

Over 10,000

5,000 – 10,000

1,000 – 5,000

500 – 1,000

100 – 500

Under 100

No data available

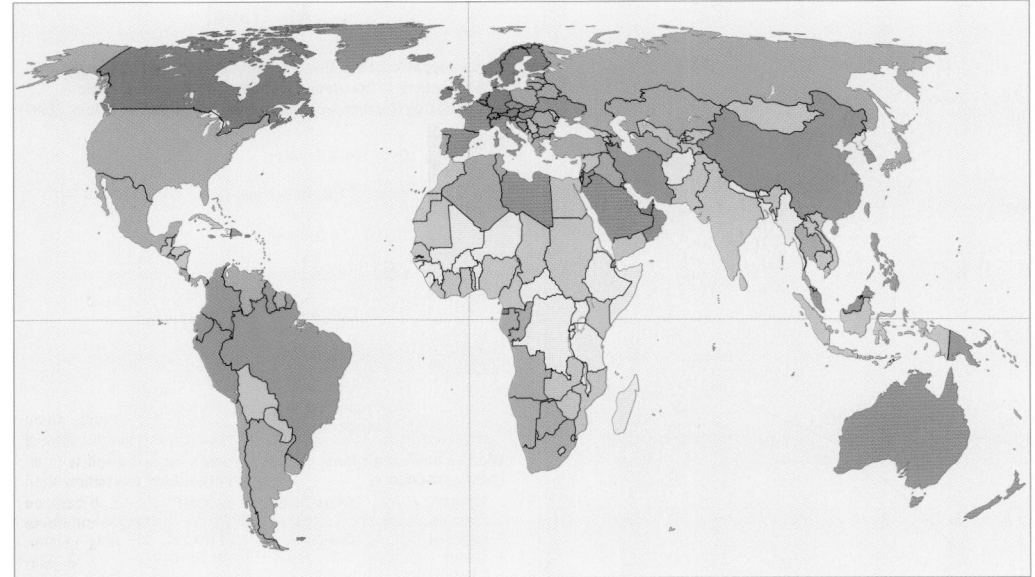

Highest per capita

Hong Kong	$88,121
Liechtenstein	$72,675
Singapore	$63,132
United Arab Emirates	$52,676
Luxembourg	$41,209

Travel and Tourism

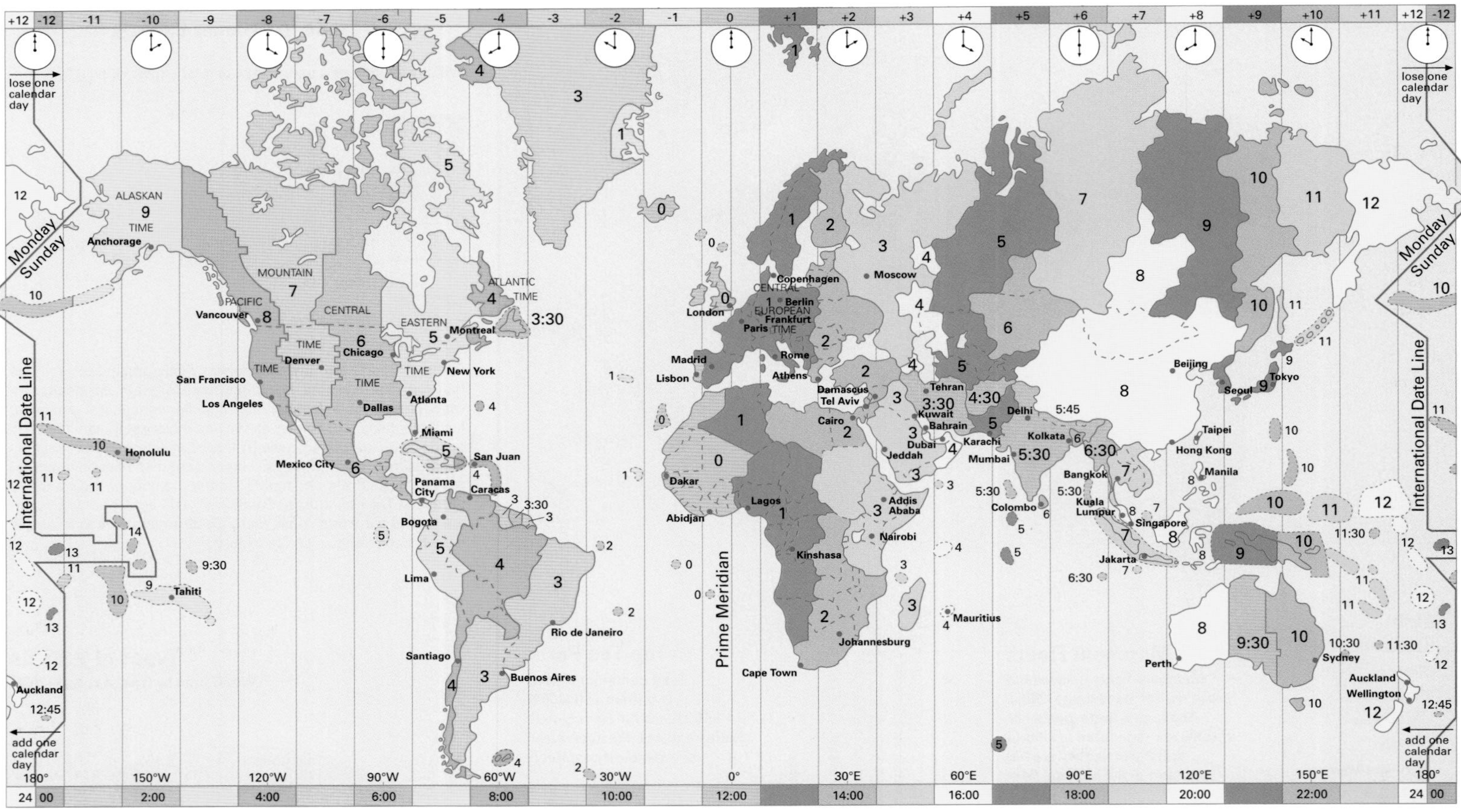

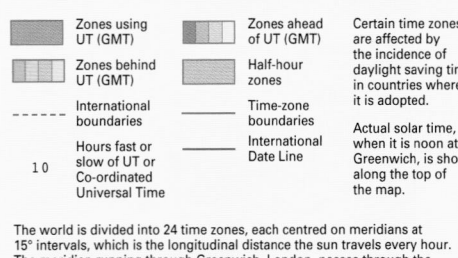

Projection: Mercator

Time Zones

▨ Zones using UT (GMT)	▨ Zones ahead of UT (GMT)	Certain time zones are affected by the incidence of daylight saving time in countries where it is adopted.
▨ Zones behind UT (GMT)	▨ Half-hour zones	
- - - International boundaries	Time-zone boundaries	
Hours fast or slow of UT or Co-ordinated Universal Time	International Date Line	Actual solar time, when it is noon at Greenwich, is shown along the top of the map.
1 0		

The world is divided into 24 time zones, each centred on meridians at 15° intervals, which is the longitudinal distance the sun travels every hour. The meridian running through Greenwich, London, passes through the middle of the first zone.

Rail and Road: The Leading Nations

Total rail network ('000 km)	Passenger km per head per year	Total road network ('000 km)	Vehicle km per head per year	Number of vehicles per km of roads
1. USA 233.8	Japan 1,891	USA 6,378.3	USA..............12,505	Hong Kong.........287
2. Russia 85.5	Switzerland 1,751	India 3,319.6	Luxembourg 7,989	Qatar.................284
3. Canada 73.2	Belarus 1,334	China 1,765.2	Kuwait 7,251	UAE....................232
4. India 63.1	France 1,203	Brazil 1,724.9	France 7,142	Germany 195
5. China 60.5	Ukraine............1,100	Canada..........1,408.8	Sweden 6,991	Lebanon 191
6. Germany 36.1	Russia 1,080	Japan 1,171.4	Germany 6,806	Macau................172
7. Argentina 34.2	Austria 1,008	France 893.1	Denmark 6,764	Singapore 167
8. France............29.3	Denmark 999	Australia 811.6	Austria 6,518	South Korea 160
9. Mexico 26.5	Netherlands 855	Spain 664.9	Netherlands 5,984	Kuwait 156
10. South Africa.........22.7	Germany 842	Russia 537.3	UK 5,738	Taiwan 150
11. Brazil 22.1	Italy 811	Italy 479.7	Canada 5,493	Israel 111
12. Ukraine 22.1	Belgium..............795	UK 371.9	Italy.................4,852	Malta 110

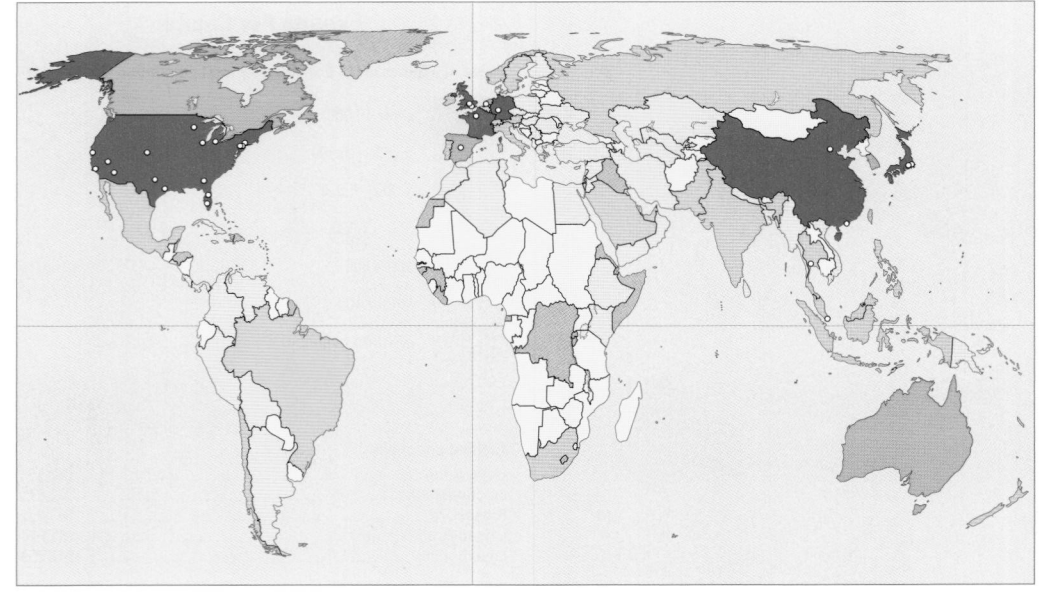

Air Travel

Passenger kilometres flown on scheduled flights (the number of passengers in thousands – international and domestic – multiplied by the distance flown from the airport of origin) (2002)

▨	Over 100,000 million
▨	50,000 – 100,000 million
▨	10,000 – 50,000 million
▨	1,000 – 10,000 million
▨	Under 1,000 million
▨	No data available
○	Major airports (handling over 30 million passengers)

World's busiest airports (total passengers)		World's busiest airports (international passengers)	
1. Atlanta	(Hartsfield)	1. London	(Heathrow)
2. Chicago	(O'Hare)	2. Paris	(Charles de Gaulle)
3. London	(Heathrow)	3. Frankfurt	(International)
4. Tokyo	(Haneda)	4. Amsterdam	(Schipol)
5. Los Angeles	(International)	5. Hong Kong	(International)

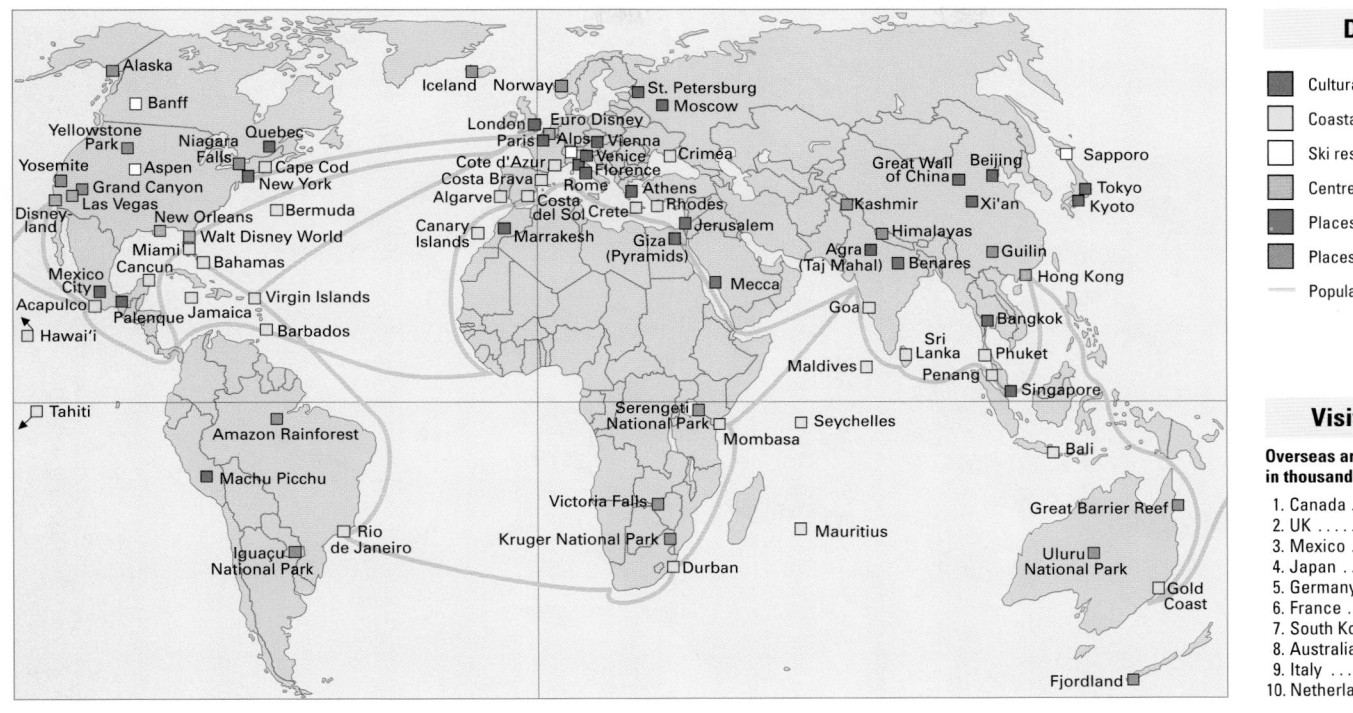

Destinations

- Cultural and historical centres
- Coastal resorts
- Ski resorts
- Centres of entertainment
- Places of pilgrimage
- Places of great natural beauty
- Popular holiday cruise routes

Visitors to the USA

Overseas arrivals to the USA, in thousands (2004)

1.	Canada	13,849
2.	UK	4,302
3.	Mexico	3,993
4.	Japan	3,748
5.	Germany	1,319
6.	France	775
7.	South Korea	627
8.	Australia	520
9.	Italy	470
10.	Netherlands	424

Tourist Spending

Countries spending the most on overseas tourism, US$ million (2004)

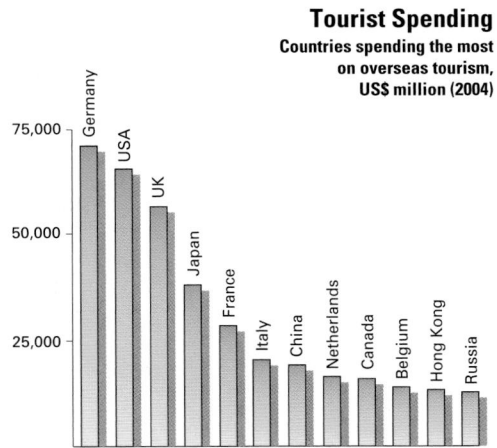

Importance of Tourism

		Arrivals from abroad (2004)	% of world total (2004)
1.	France	75,121,000	9.9%
2.	Spain	53,599,000	7.1%
3.	USA	46,077,000	6.1%
4.	China	41,761,000	5.5%
5.	Italy	37,071,000	4.9%
6.	UK	27,755,000	3.7%
7.	Hong Kong	21,811,000	2.9%
8.	Mexico	20,618,000	2.7%
9.	Germany	20,137,000	2.7%
10.	Austria	19,373,000	2.6%
11.	Canada	19,150,000	2.5%
12.	Turkey	16,826,000	2.2%

After 3 years of stagnant growth, international tourist arrivals reached an all-time record of 763 million in 2004, almost 11% more than in 2003. Growth was common to all regions, but particularly strong in Asia and the Pacific, and in the Middle East.

Tourist Earnings

Countries receiving the most from overseas tourism, US$ million (2004)

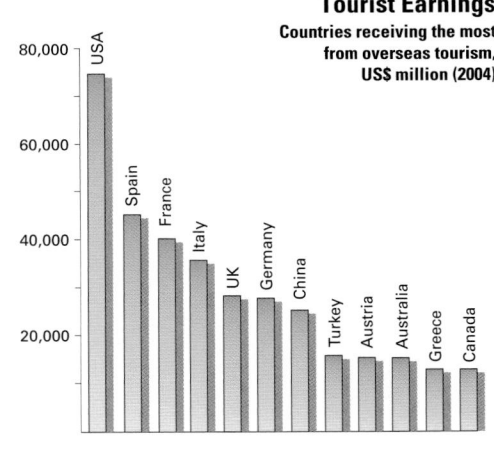

Tourism

Tourism receipts as a percentage of Gross National Income (2005)

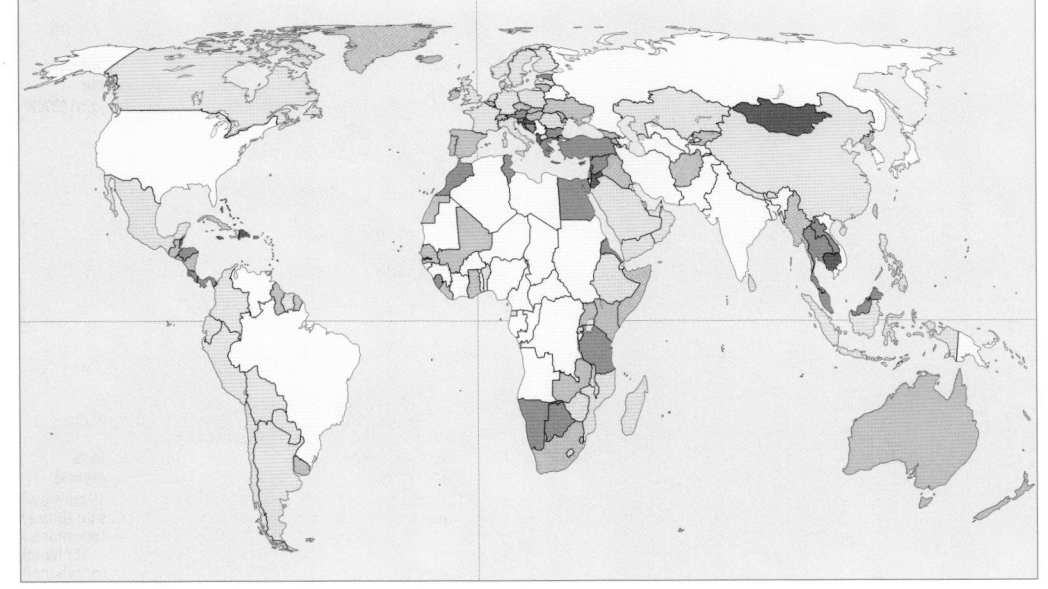

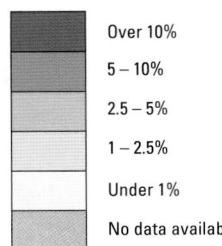

- Over 10%
- 5 – 10%
- 2.5 – 5%
- 1 – 2.5%
- Under 1%
- No data available

Percentage change in tourist arrivals from 2004 to 2005 (top six countries in total number of arrivals)

France	+1.2%
Spain	+3.7%
USA	+0.02%
China	+8.5%
Italy	–1.5%
UK	+8.0%

WORLD CITIES

AMSTERDAM	2	HONG KONG	12	MUMBAI	20	TEHRAN	31
ATHENS	2	ISTANBUL	12	MUNICH	21	TORONTO	31
ATLANTA	3	JAKARTA	12	NEW ORLEANS	21	VIENNA	32
BAGHDAD	3	JERUSALEM	13	NEW YORK	22	WARSAW	32
BANGKOK	3	JOHANNESBURG	13	ORLANDO	23	WASHINGTON	33
BARCELONA	4	KARACHI	13	OSAKA	23	WELLINGTON	33
BEIJING	4	KOLKATA	14	OSLO	23		
BERLIN	5	LAGOS	14	PARIS	24	INDEX	34–39
BOSTON	6	LAS VEGAS	14	PRAGUE	25		
BRUSSELS	6	LIMA	14	RIO DE JANEIRO	25		
BUDAPEST	7	LONDON	15	ROME	26	WORLD CITIES	
BUENOS AIRES	7	LOS ANGELES	16	SAN FRANCISCO	26	SATELLITE IMAGES	
CAIRO	7	LISBON	16	ST PETERSBURG	27	CAPE TOWN	40
CAPE TOWN	8	MADRID	17	SANTIAGO	27	CHICAGO	41
COPENHAGEN	8	MANILA	17	SÃO PAULO	27	KARACHI	42
CHICAGO	9	MELBOURNE	18	SEOUL	27	LONDON	43
DELHI	10	MEXICO CITY	18	SHANGHAI	28	NEW YORK	44
DUBLIN	10	MIAMI	18	SINGAPORE	28	SAN FRANCISCO	45
EDINBURGH	11	MILAN	19	STOCKHOLM	29	SANTIAGO	46
GUANGZHOU	11	MOSCOW	19	SYDNEY	29	SYDNEY	47
HELSINKI	11	MONTRÉAL	20	TOKYO	30	TOKYO	48

CITY MAPS

Motorway, freeway, expressway with toll – with road number	A10
Motorway, freeway, expressway – with European road number	E51
Road junction	
Under construction	
Tunnel	
Primary road – with road number dual carriageway single carriageway	14 / 14
Secondary road – with road number dual carriageway single carriageway	96 / 96
Other road	
Ferry	
Railroad	
Principal station	Estación del Norte
Height above sea level (m)	705
Airport	
Airfield	
Central area coverage	
Urban area	
Woodlands and parks	

CENTRAL AREA MAPS

Motorway, freeway, expressway	
Through route	
Secondary road	
Dual carriageway	
Other road	
Tunnel	
Limited access/pedestrian road	
Parking (Europe only)	P
Railroad	
Rail/bus station	
Underground, metro station	M S T
Funicular	
Cable car	
Abbey, cathedral	
Church of interest	
Synagogue	
Shrine, temple	
Mosque	
Public building	
Tourist information	
Place of interest	Palace

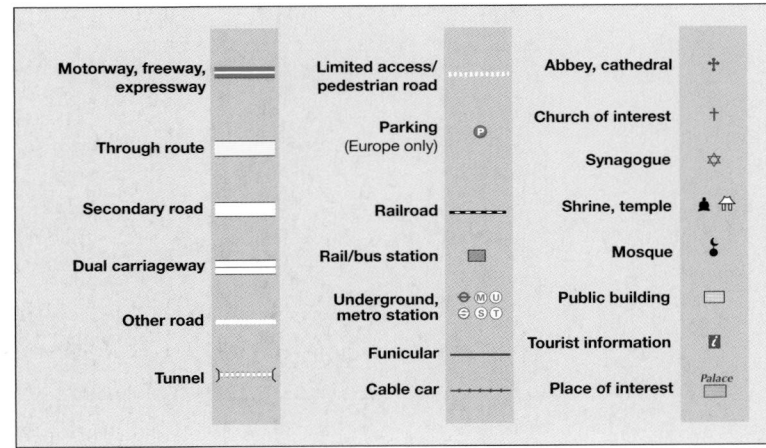

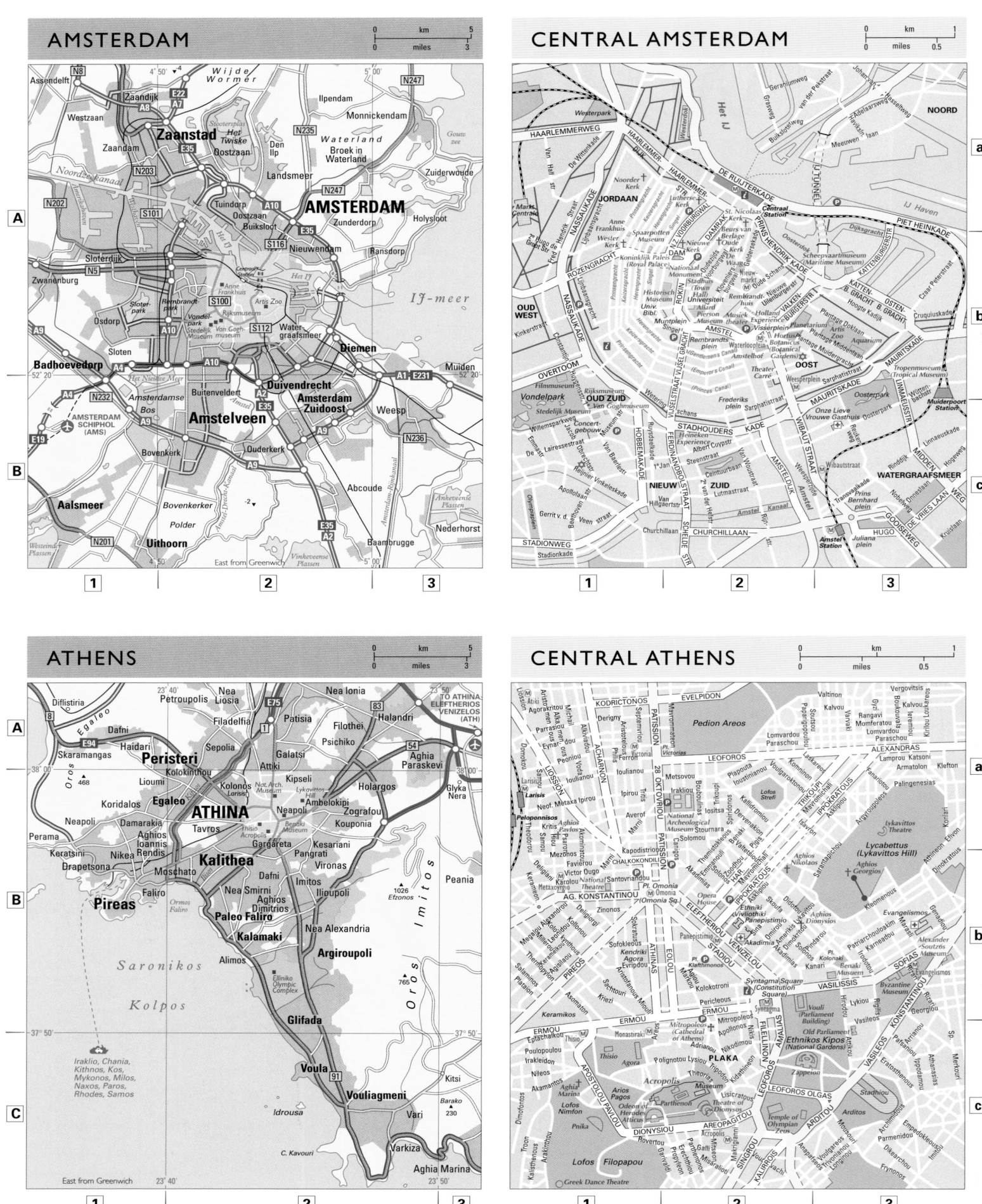

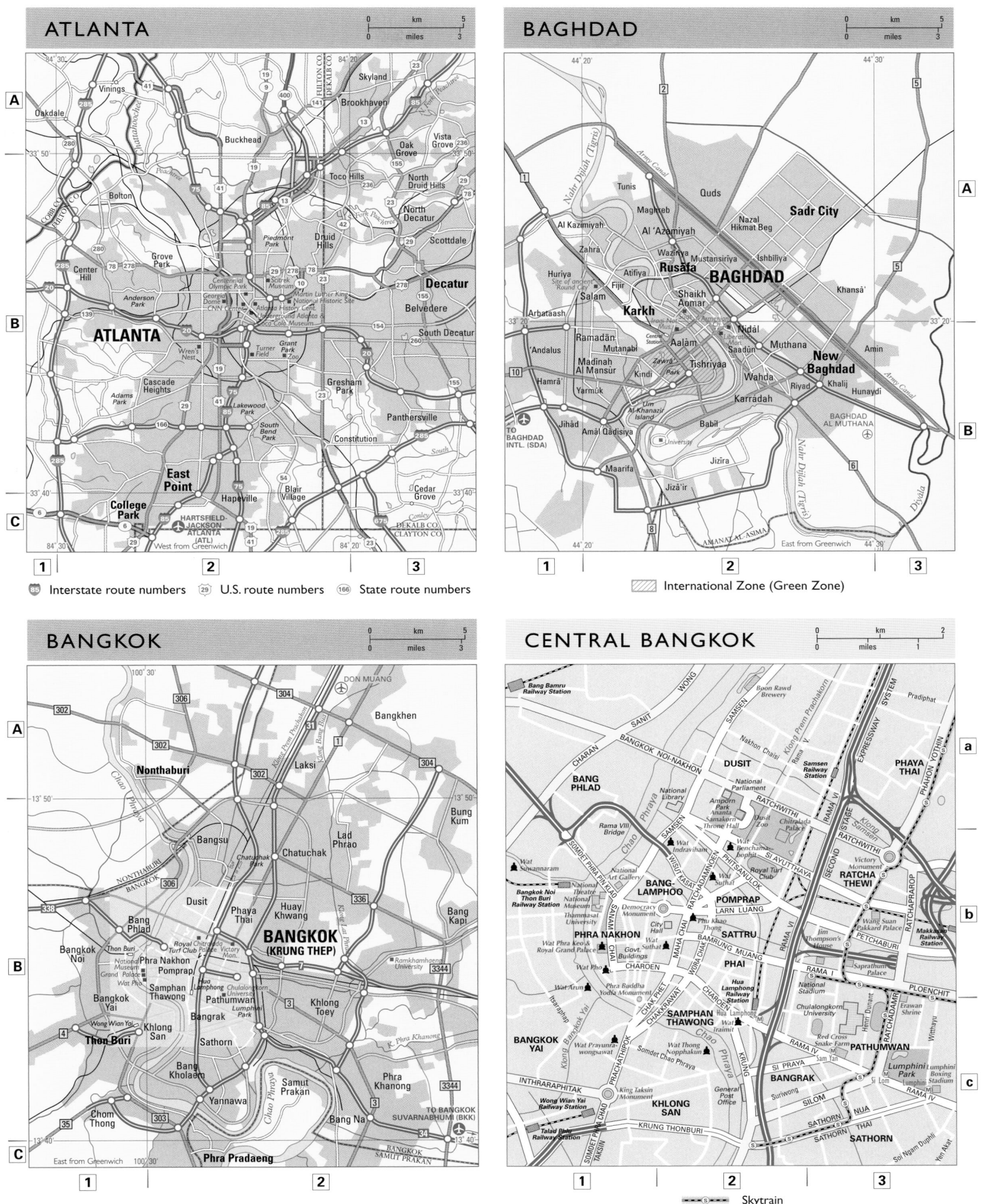

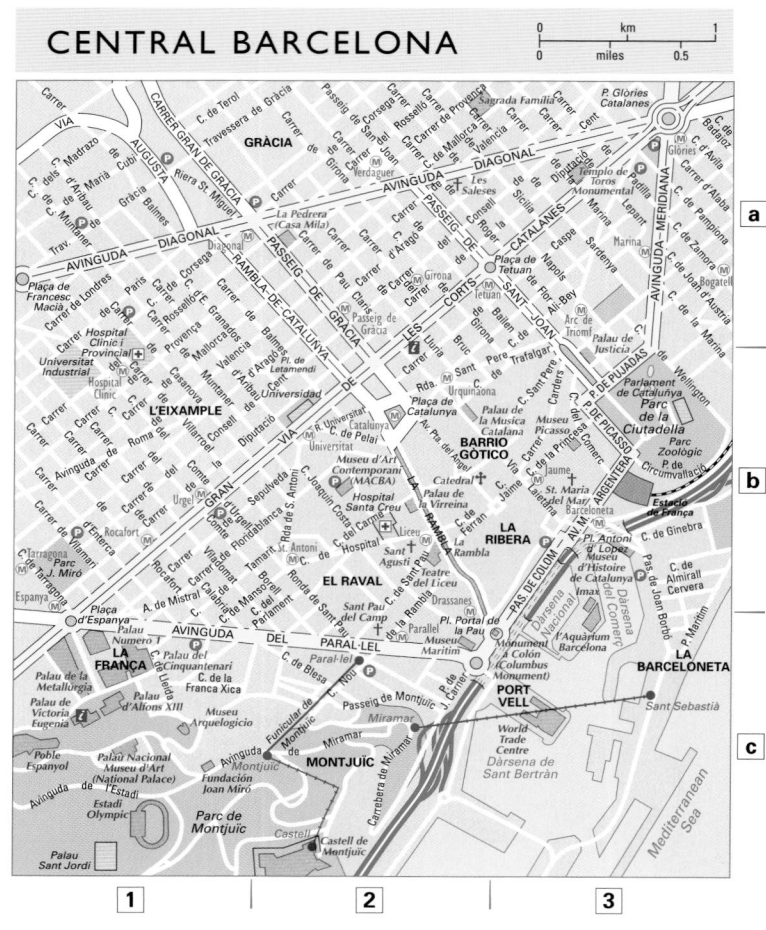

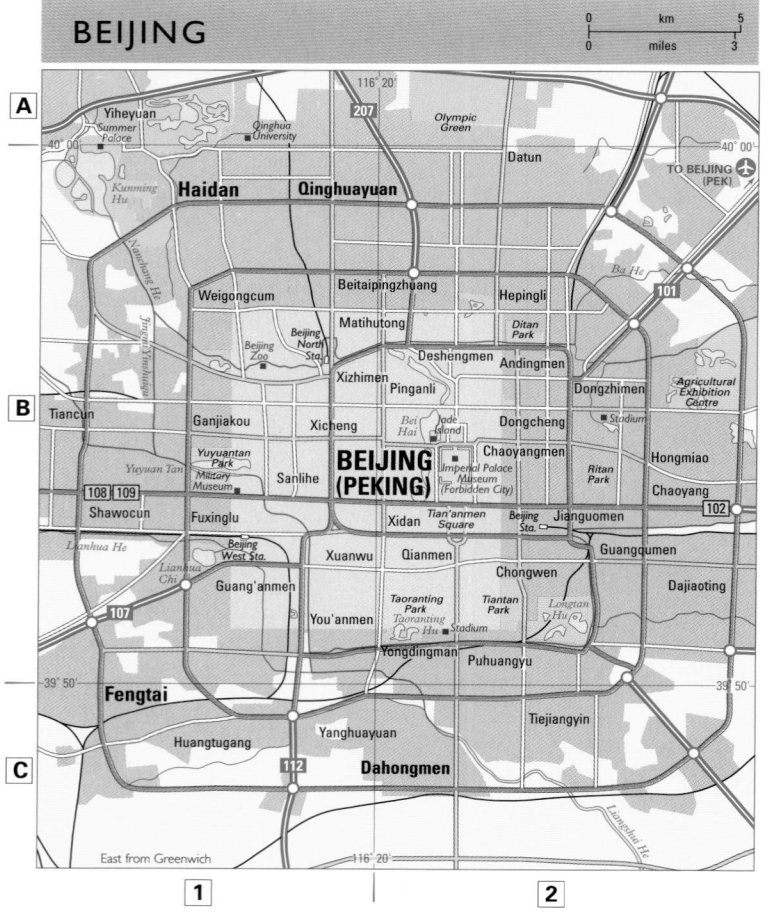

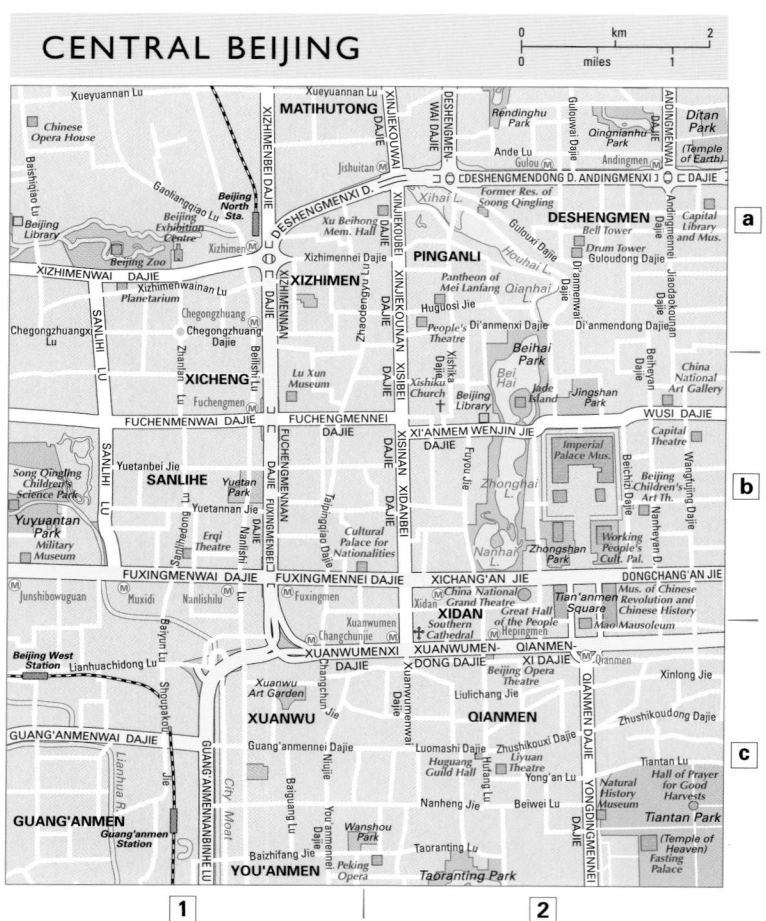

BERLIN

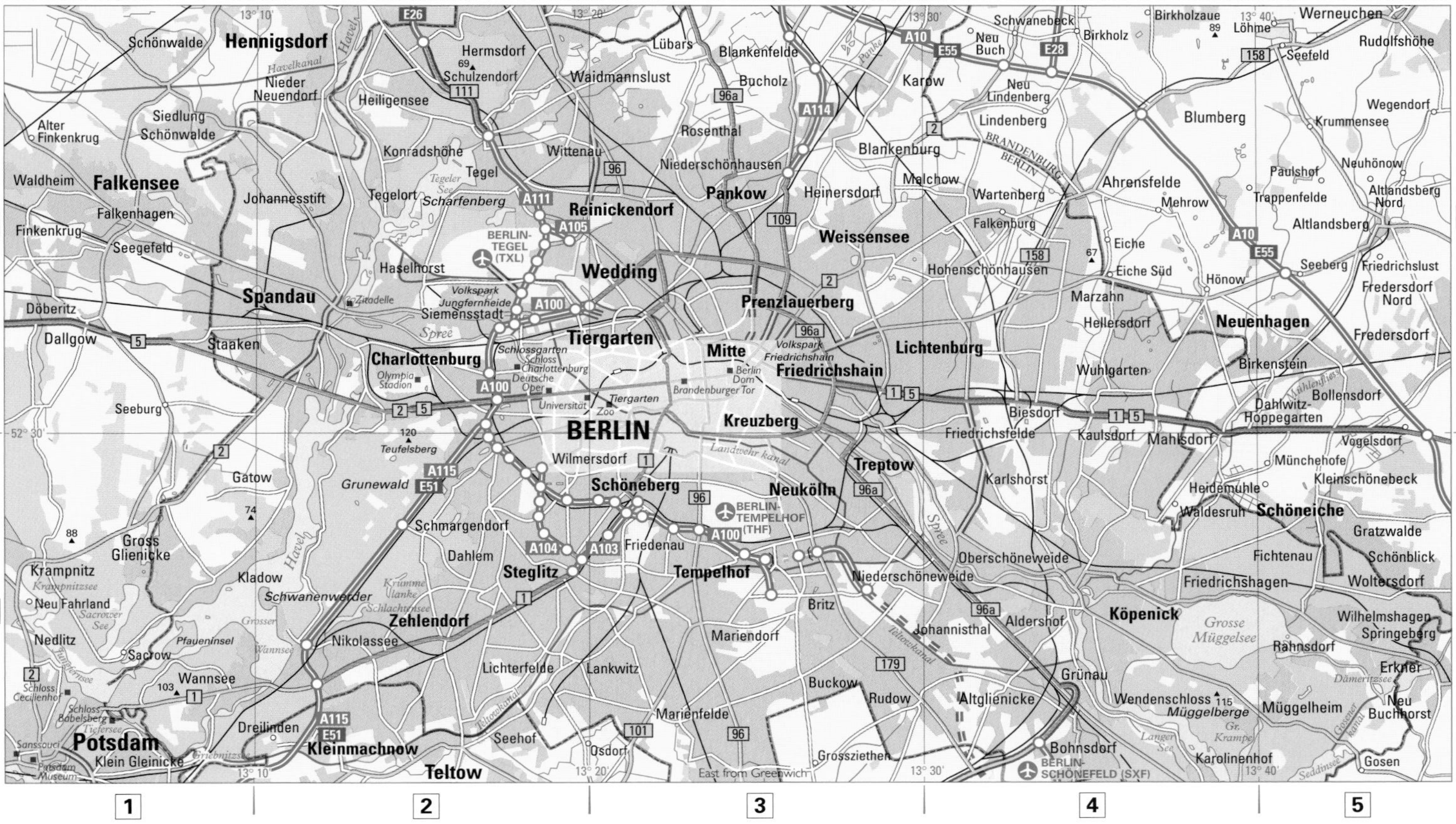

km 5
miles 3

Schönwalde · Hennigsdorf · Hermsdorf · Lübars · Blankenfelde · Schwanebeck · Birkholzaue · Werneuchen
E26 · Schulzendorf · Waidmannslust · Bucholz · Birkholz · Löhme
Nieder Neuendorf · 111 · Heiligensee · Rosenthal · Niederschönhausen · Karow · Neu Lindenberg · E55 · E28 · 158 · Seefeld · Rudolfshöhe
Alter Finkenkrug · Siedlung Schönwalde · 96a · A114 · Lindenberg · Blumberg · Krummensee
Waldheim · **Falkensee** · Johannesstift · Tegelort · Tegel · Wittenau · 96 · Blankenburg · Heinersdorf · Malchow · Wartenberg · Ahrensfelde · Paulshof · Neuhönow
Finkenkrug · Falkenhagen · BERLIN-TEGEL (TXL) · **Pankow** · Falkenberg · 158 · Eiche · Mehrow · Trappenfelde · Altlandsberg Nord
Seegefeld · Haselhorst · A105 · 109 · **Weissensee** · Hohenschönhausen · 67 · Eiche Süd · Hönow · A10 · E55 · Seeberg · Friedrichslust
Spandau · Siemensstadt · Volkspark Jungfernheide · **Wedding** · **Prenzlauerberg** · Marzahn · Neuenhagen · Fredersdorf Nord
Döberitz · Zitadelle · A100 · Volkspark Friedrichshain · Hellersdorf · **Neuenhagen** · Birkenstein · Bollersdorf
Dallgow · Stäaken · Schlossgarten · **Tiergarten** · **Mitte** · **Lichtenburg** · Wuhlgarten · Dahlwitz-Hoppegarten
5 · **Charlottenburg** · Schloss Charlottenburg · Deutsche Oper · Berlin Dom · **Friedrichshain** · Biesdorf · 1 5 · Vogelsdorf
Olympia Stadion · A100 · Universität · Tiergarten Zoo · Brandenburger Tor · Friedrichsfelde · Kaulsdorf · Mahlsdorf · Münchehofe
Seeburg · 2 5 · Teufelsberg · 120 · **BERLIN** · **Kreuzberg** · Karlshorst · Kleinschönebeck
Gatow · 2 · Grunewald · Wilmersdorf · 1 · **Treptow** · Heidemühle · **Schöneiche**
74 · A115 · E51 · **Schöneberg** · **Neukölln** · 96a · Waldesruh · Gratzwalde
Gross Glienicke · Schmargendorf · 96 · BERLIN-TEMPELHOF (THF) · Oberschöneweide · Fichtenau · Schönblick
Krampnitz · Neu Fahrland · Dahlem · A104 · A103 · A100 · Friedenau · **Tempelhof** · Niederschöneweide · Friedrichshagen · Woltersdorf
Nedlitz · Sacrow · 103 · **Steglitz** · Britz · 96a · **Köpenick** · Grosse Müggelsee · Rahnsdorf · Wilhelmshagen · Springeberg
Schwanenwerder · **Zehlendorf** · Lichterfelde · Mariendorf · Aldershof · Erkner · Neu Buchhorst
Wannsee · Nikolassee · Lankwitz · Johannisthal · 179 · Grünau · Wendenschloss · 115 · Müggelheim
Schloss Cecilienhof · Sacrow · Buckow · Rudow · Altglienicke · Müggelberge · Müggelheim
Potsdam · Klein Gleinicke · **Kleinmachnow** · Dreilinden · A115 · E51 · Seehof · Osdorf · Marienfelde · 96 · Bohnsdorf · BERLIN-SCHÖNEFELD (SXF) · Gosen
Sanssouci · Babelsberg · **Teltow** · 101 · Grossziethen · Karolinenhof

East from Greenwich
13° 10 · 13° 20 · 13° 30' · 13° 40

A B
1 2 3 4 5

CENTRAL BERLIN

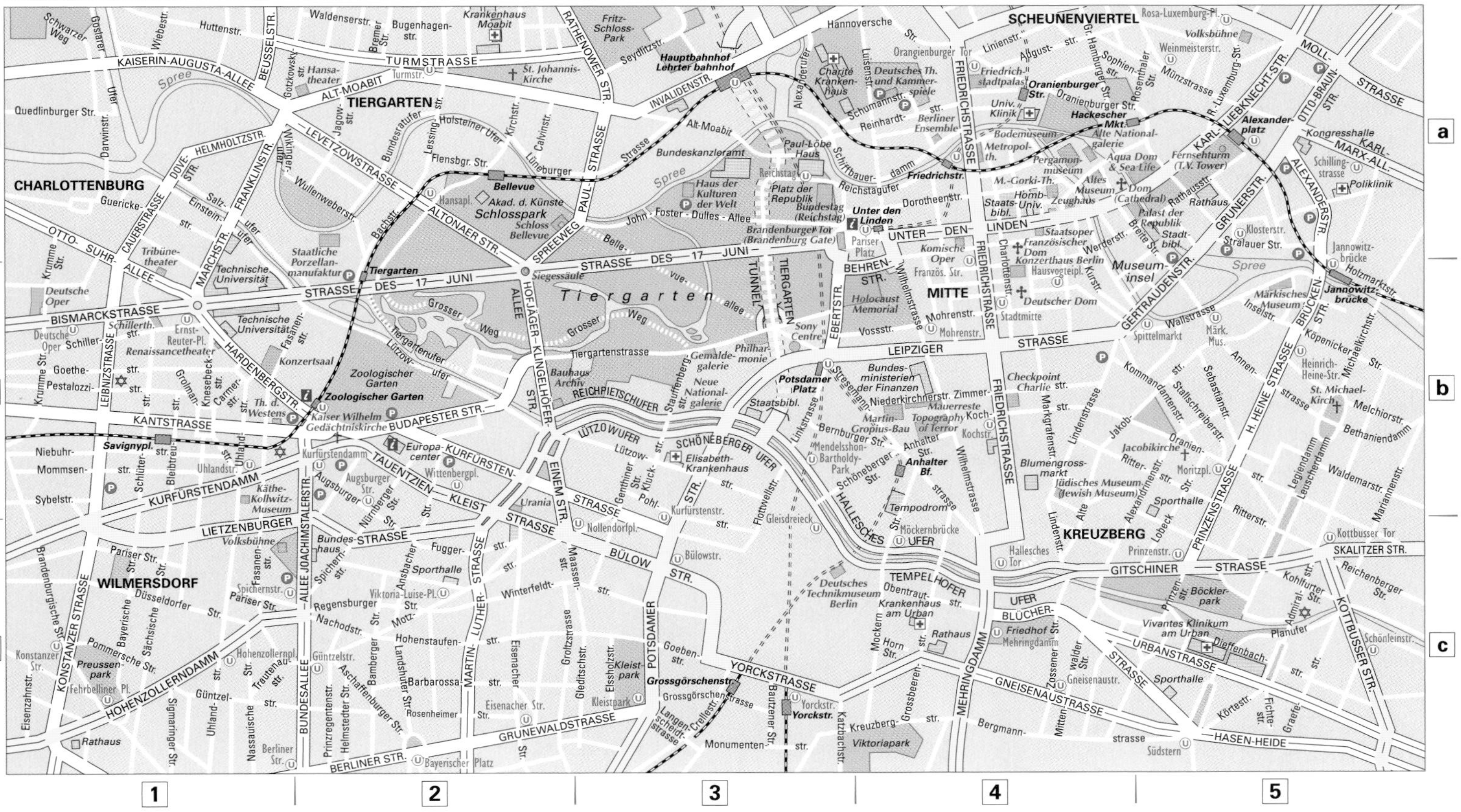

km 1
miles 0.5

SCHEUNENVIERTEL · Rosa-Luxemburg-Pl. · Volksbühne
CHARLOTTENBURG · **TIERGARTEN** · Hauptbahnhof Lehrter bahnhof · Oranienburger Tor · Charité Krankenhaus · Deutsches Th. & Kammerspiele · Oranienburger Str. · Hackescher Mkt. · **Alexanderplatz** · Kongresshalle
KAISERIN-AUGUSTA-ALLEE · Spree · St. Johannis-Kirche · INVALIDENSTR. · Univ. Klinik · Berliner Ensemble · Metropol-th. · Pergamon museum · Aqua Dom & Sea Life · Fernsehturm (T.V. Tower) · Poliklinik
ALT-MOABIT · Alt Moabit · Bundeskanzleramt · Paul-Löbe Haus · Alte Nationalgalerie · M-Gorki-Th. · Altes Museum · Dom (Cathedral) · Rathaus
Schlosspark Bellevue · Akad. d. Künste · Haus der Kulturen der Welt · Reichstag · Platz der Republik (Reichstag) · Staats-Univ. · Palast der Republik · Stadt-bibl.
Tiergarten · Grosser Weg · Tiergarten allee · Brandenburger Tor (Brandenburg Gate) · UNTER-DEN-LINDEN · Staatsoper · Konzerthaus Berlin · **Museum-insel** · Spree
STRASSE DES 17 JUNI · TUNNEL · Komische Oper · BEHRENSTR. · **MITTE** · Deutscher Dom
Technische Universität · Zoologischer Garten · Holocaust Memorial · Sony Centre · MOHRENSTR. · LEIPZIGER STRASSE
Kaiser Wilhelm Gedächtniskirche · Gemäldegalerie · Philharmonie · Potsdamer Platz · Bundesministerium der Finanzen · Checkpoint Charlie · St. Michael-Kirche
KURFÜRSTENDAMM · Europa center · Bauhaus Archiv · Neue Nationalgalerie · Topography Koch- · **KREUZBERG**
Savignypl. · TAUENTZIEN · Urania · Anhalter Bf. · Jüdisches Museum (Jewish Museum) · Sporthalle
KANTSTRASSE · Nollendorfpl. · HALLESCHES UFER · Tempodrom · Halleschen Tor
WILMERSDORF · BÜLOW STR. · Deutsches Technikmuseum Berlin · Krankenhaus am Urban · Vivantes Klinikum am Urban · Böckler park
KURFÜRSTENDAMM · Viktoria-Luise-Pl. · Winterfeldt str. · Kleist park · YORCKSTRASSE · GNEISENAUSTRASSE · Sporthalle
GRUNEWALDSTRASSE · Bayerischer Platz · **Grossgörschenstr.** · **Yorckstr.** · Viktoriapark · HASEN-HEIDE

a b c
1 2 3 4 5

COPYRIGHT PHILIP'S

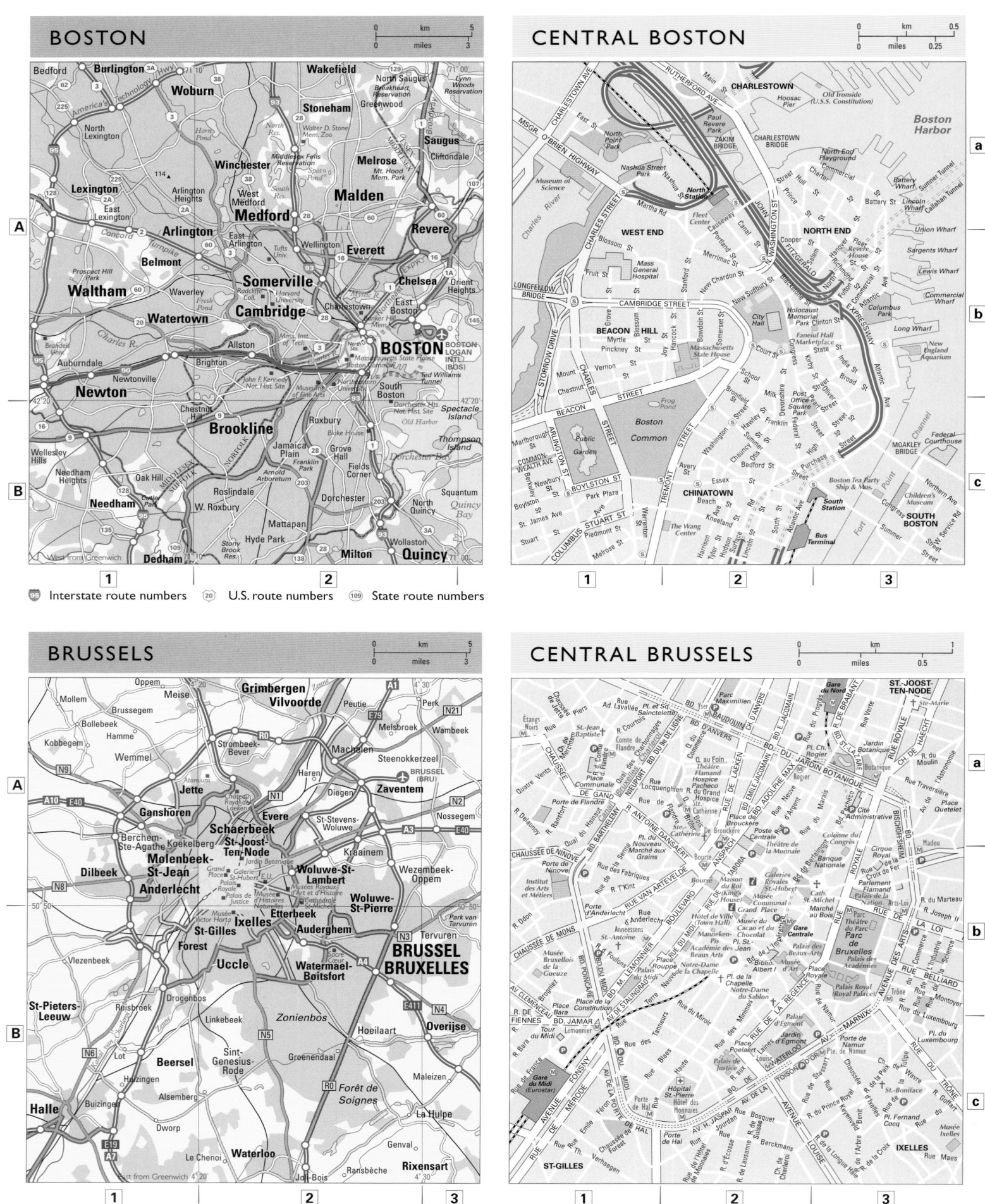

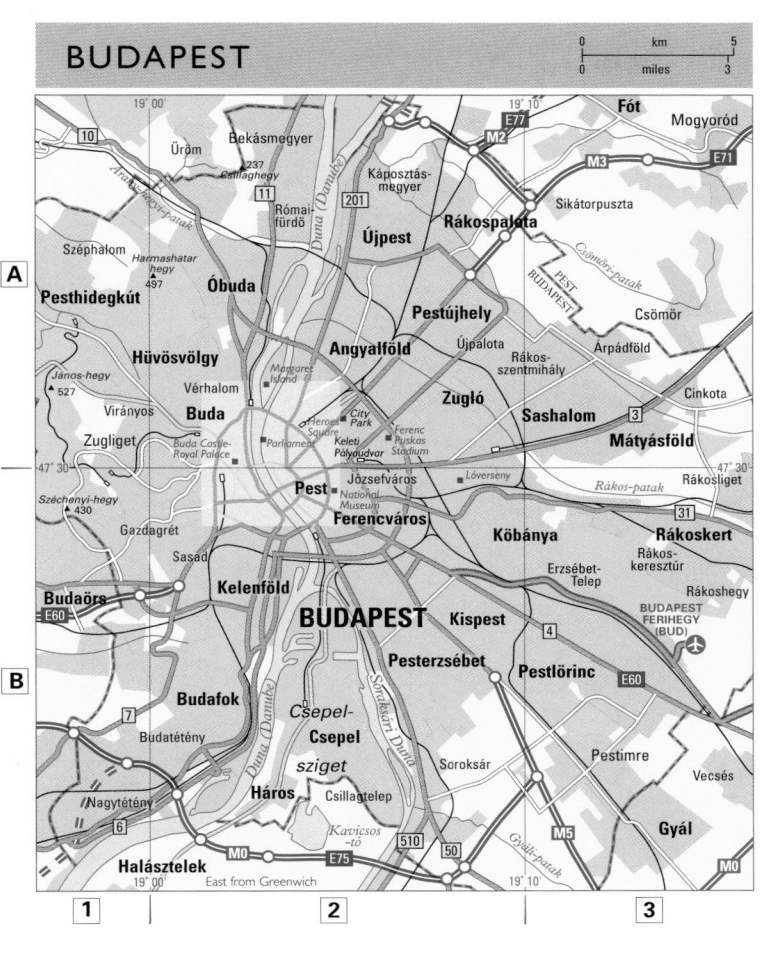

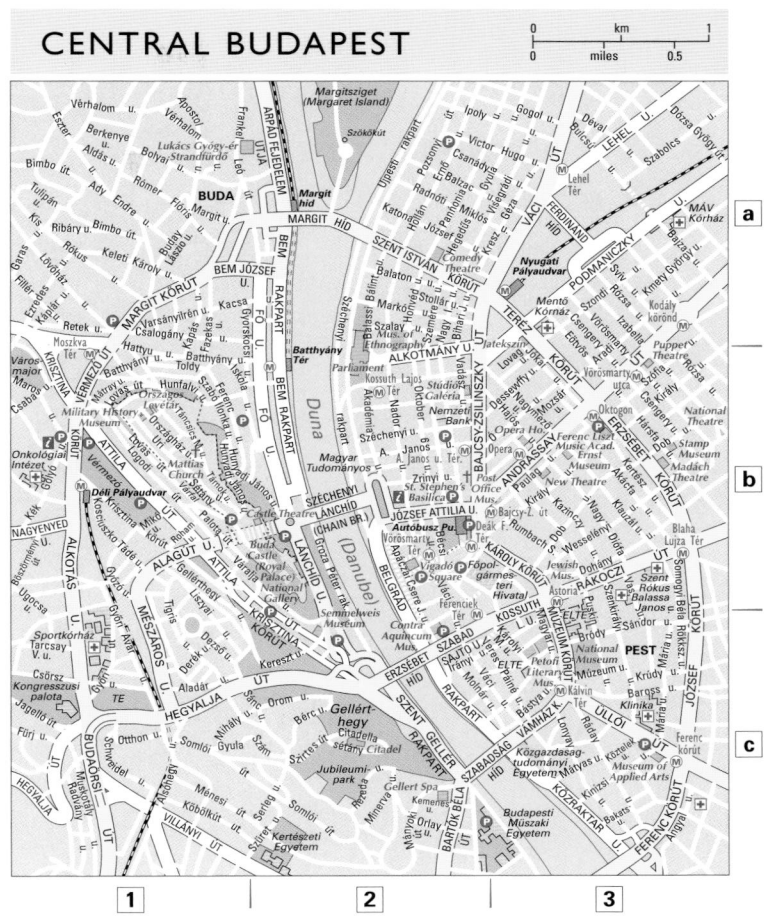

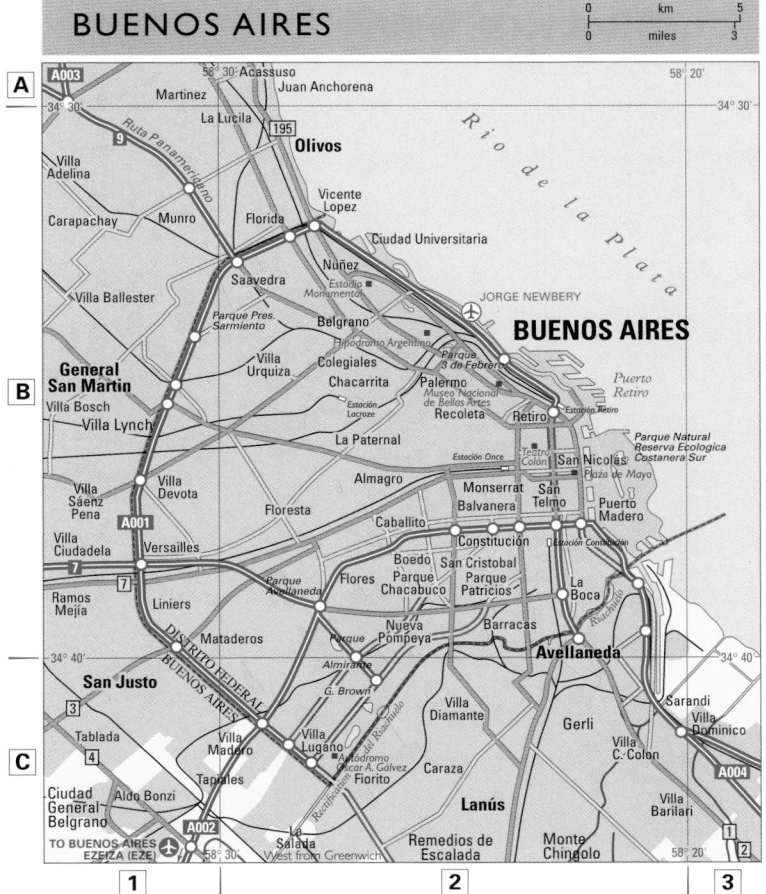

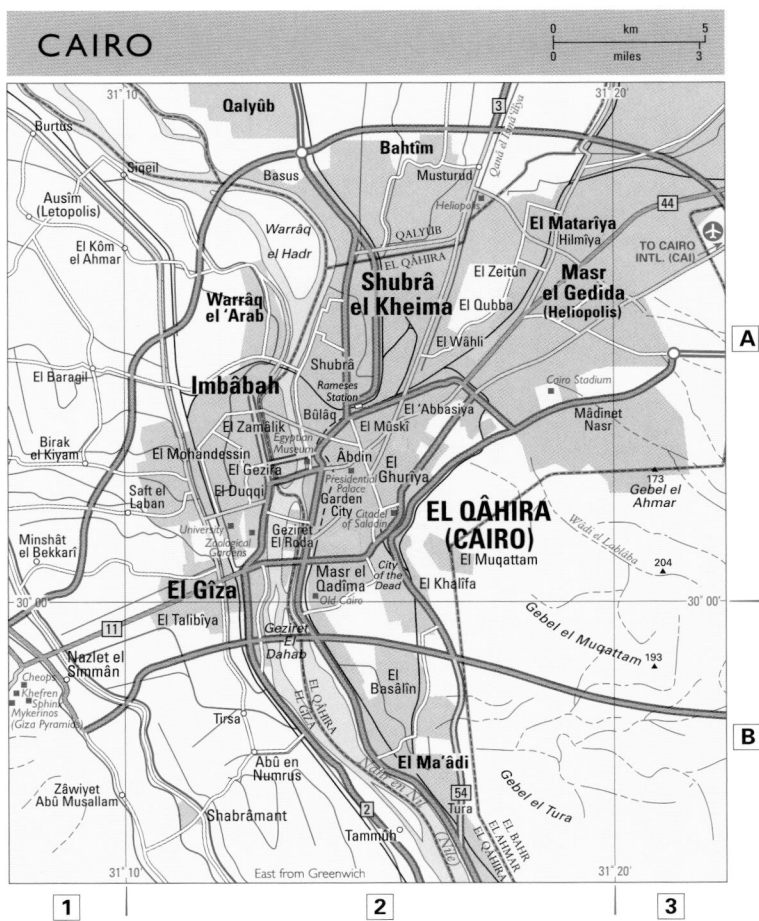

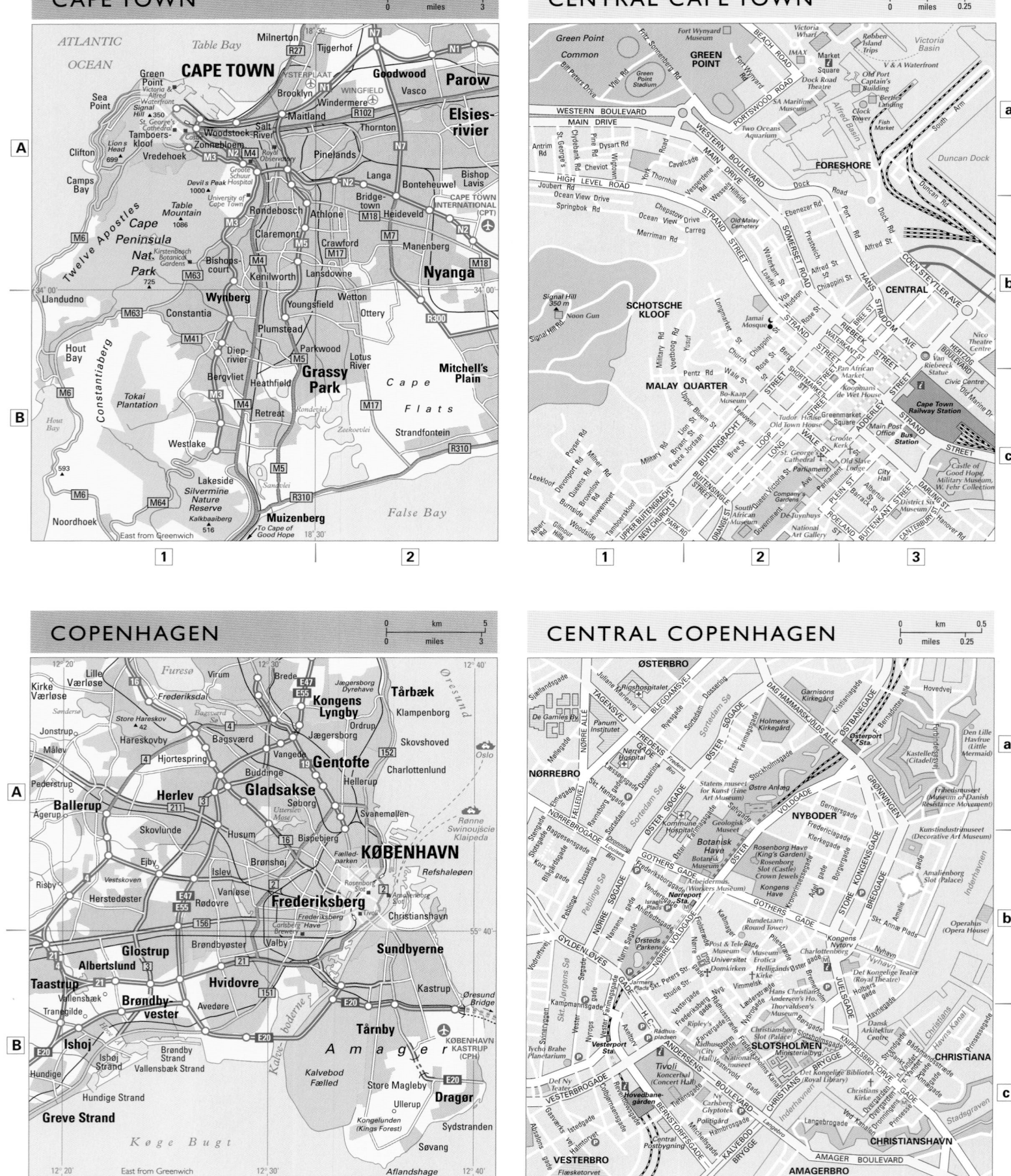

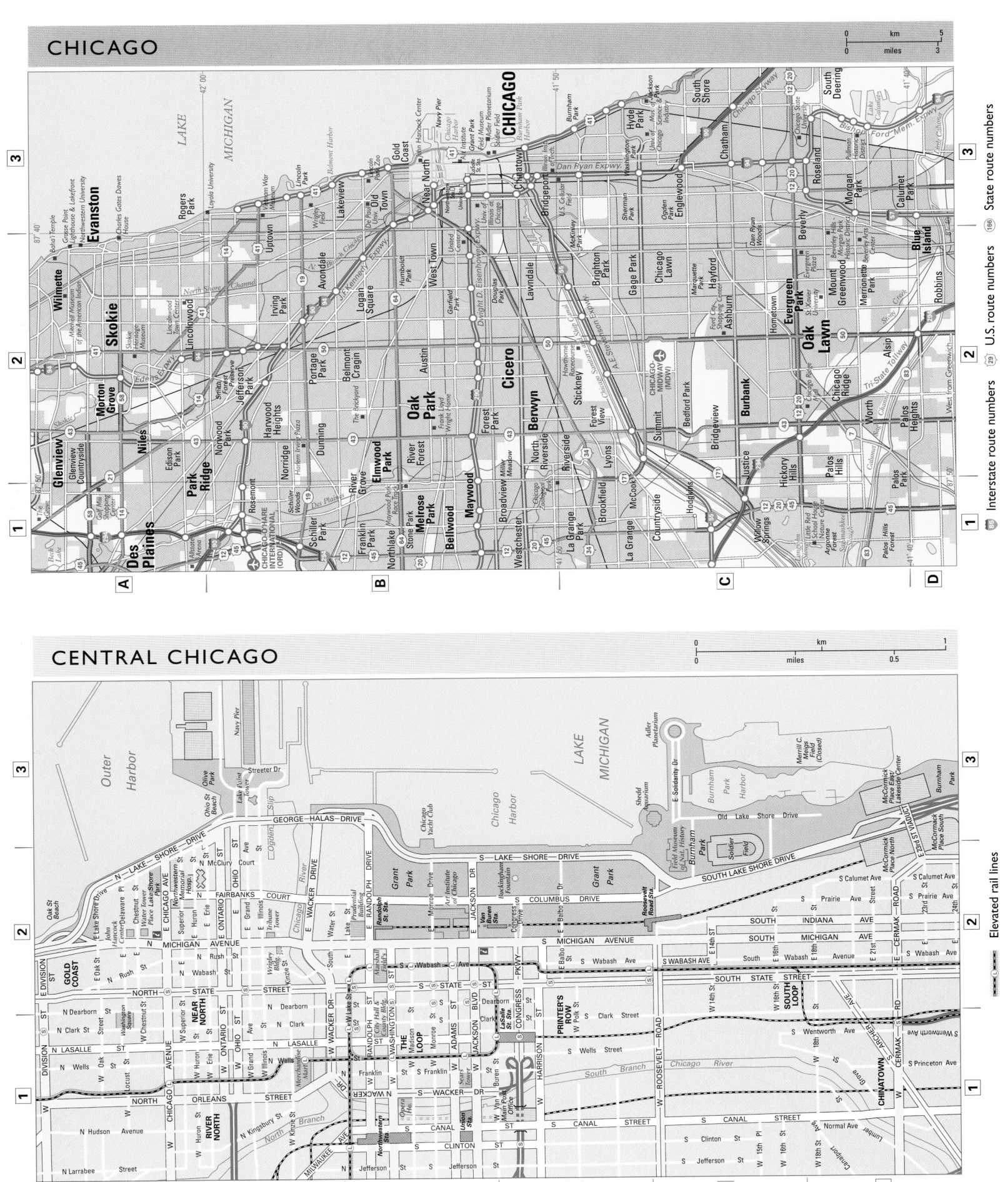

CHICAGO

0 km 5
0 miles 3

Map key (right margin)

- Interstate route numbers
- U.S. route numbers
- State route numbers

CENTRAL CHICAGO

0 km 1
0 miles 0.5

Elevated rail lines

DELHI

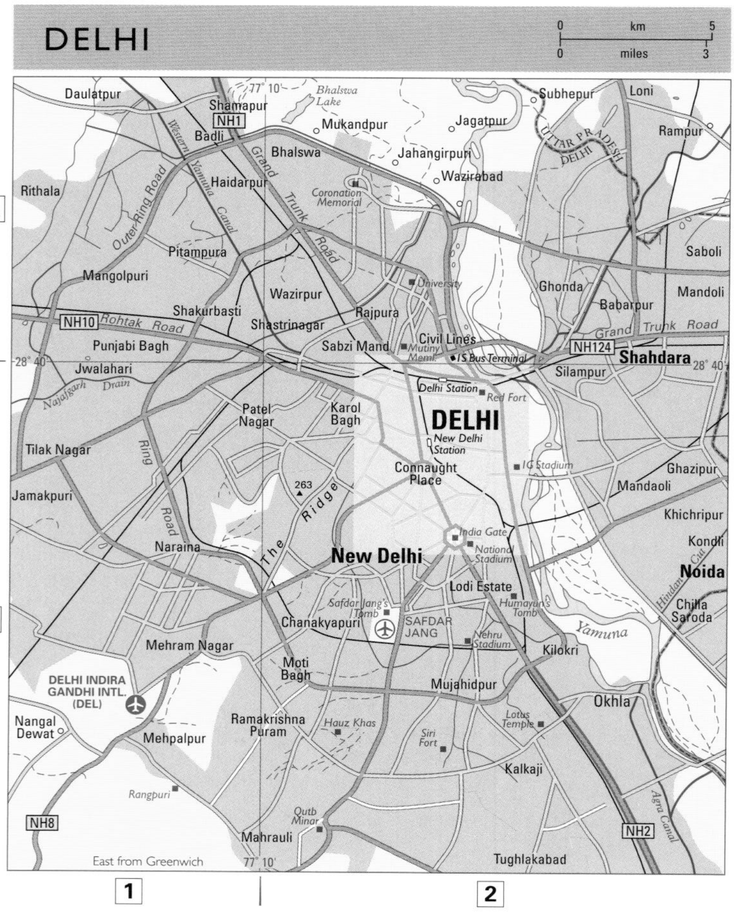

km 5 / miles 3

CENTRAL DELHI

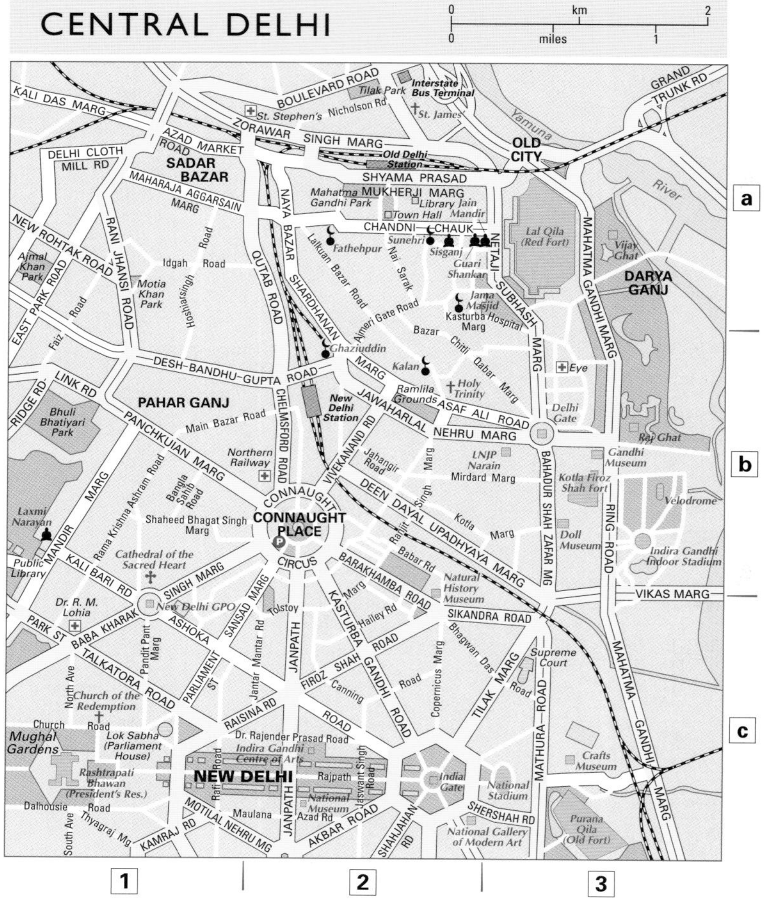

km 2 / miles 1

DUBLIN

km 5 / miles 3

CENTRAL DUBLIN

km 0.5 / miles 0.25

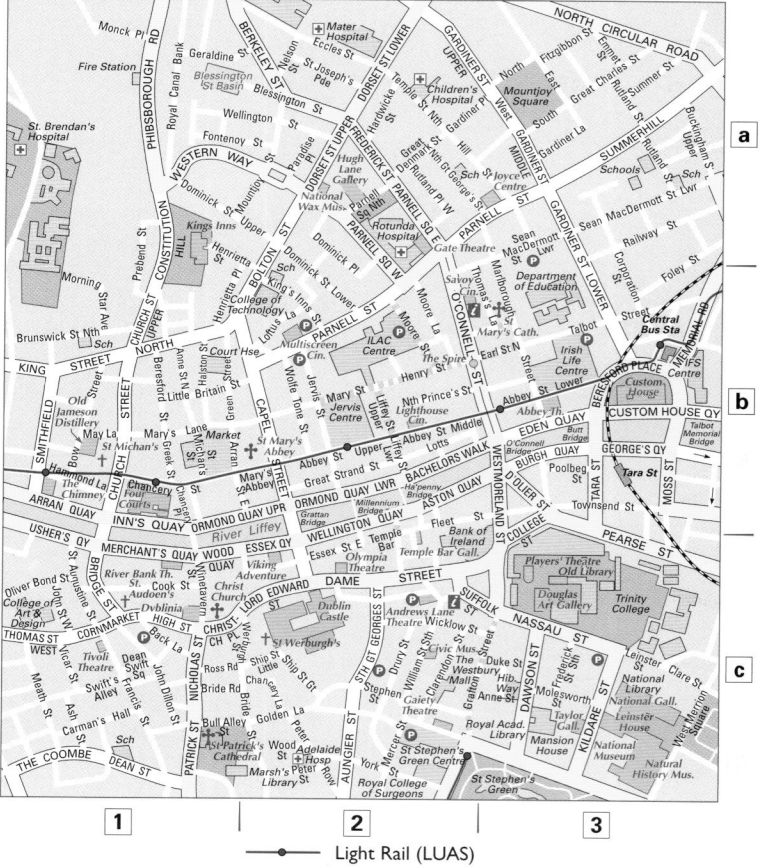

Light Rail (LUAS)

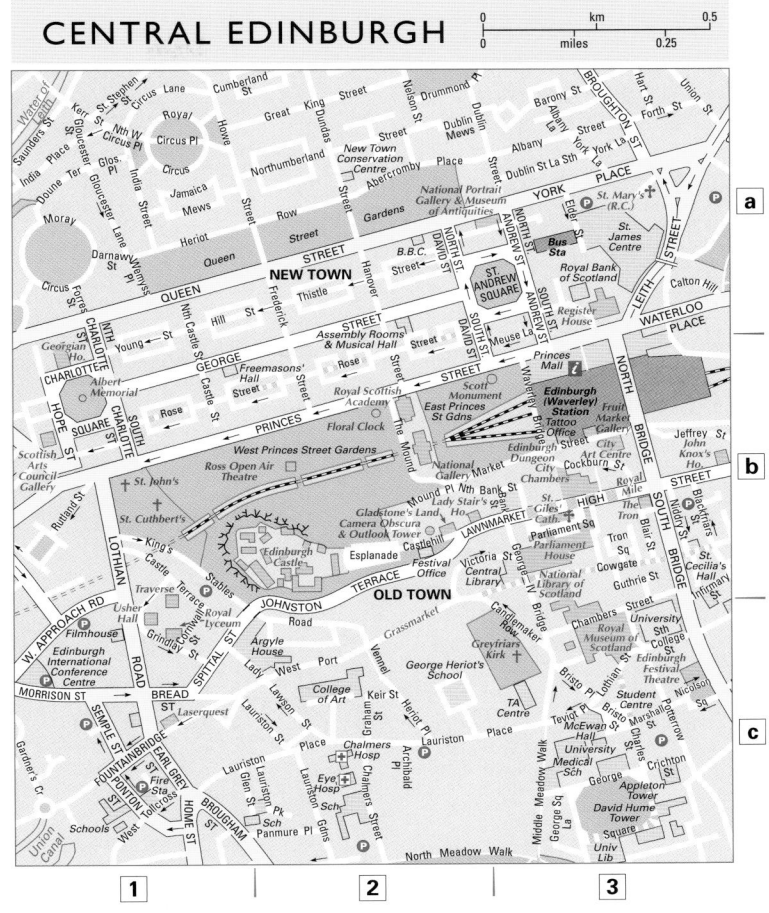

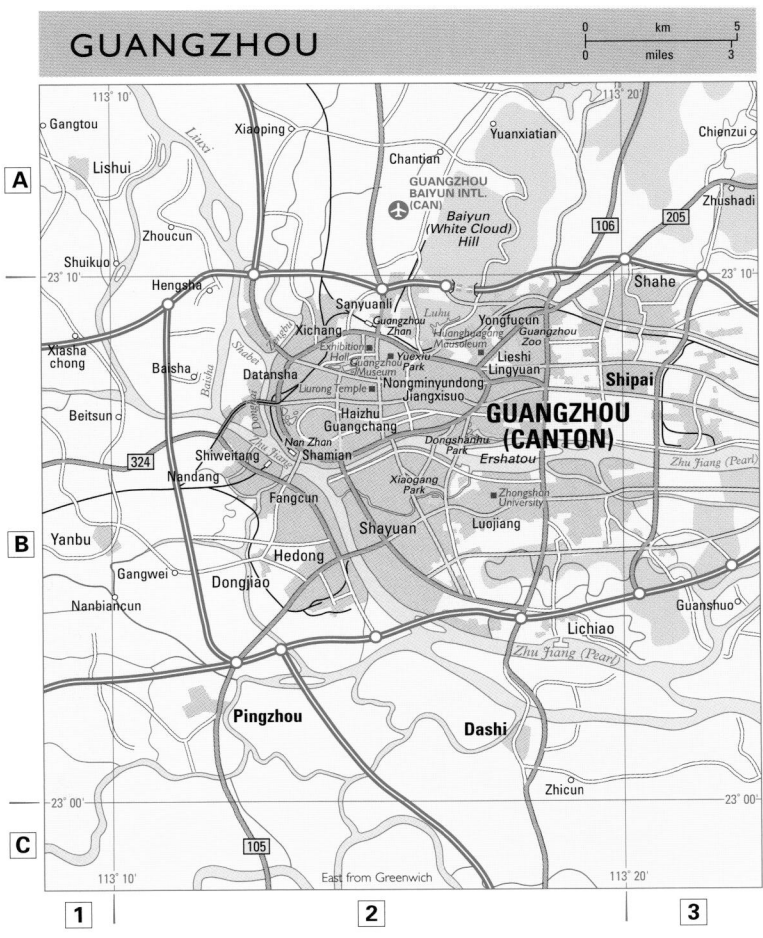

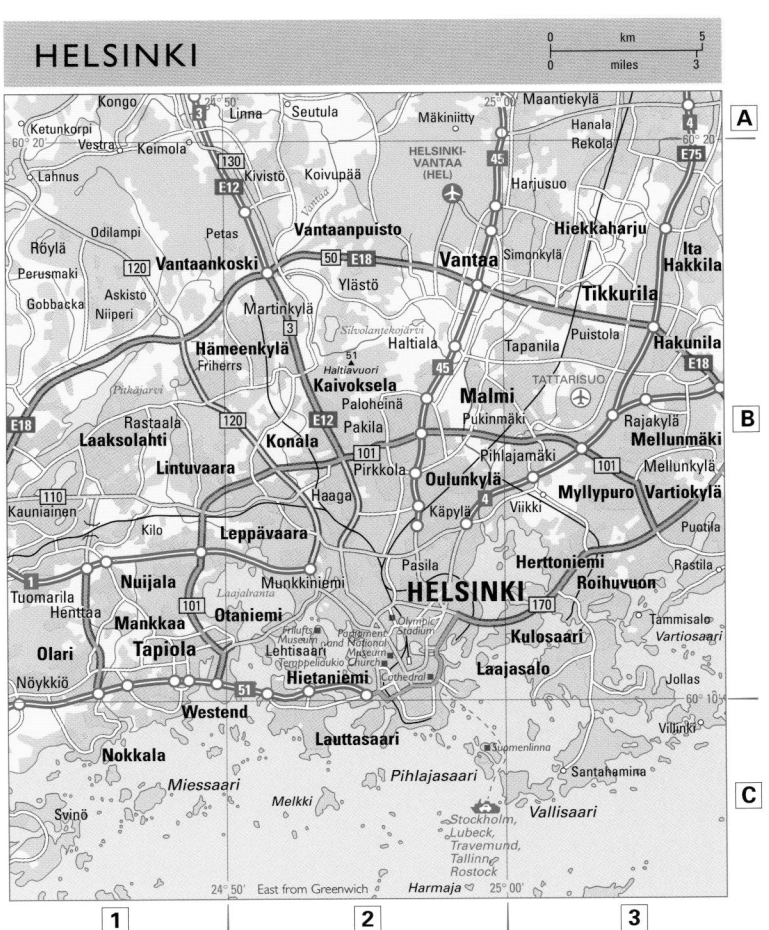

COPYRIGHT PHILIP'S

HONG KONG

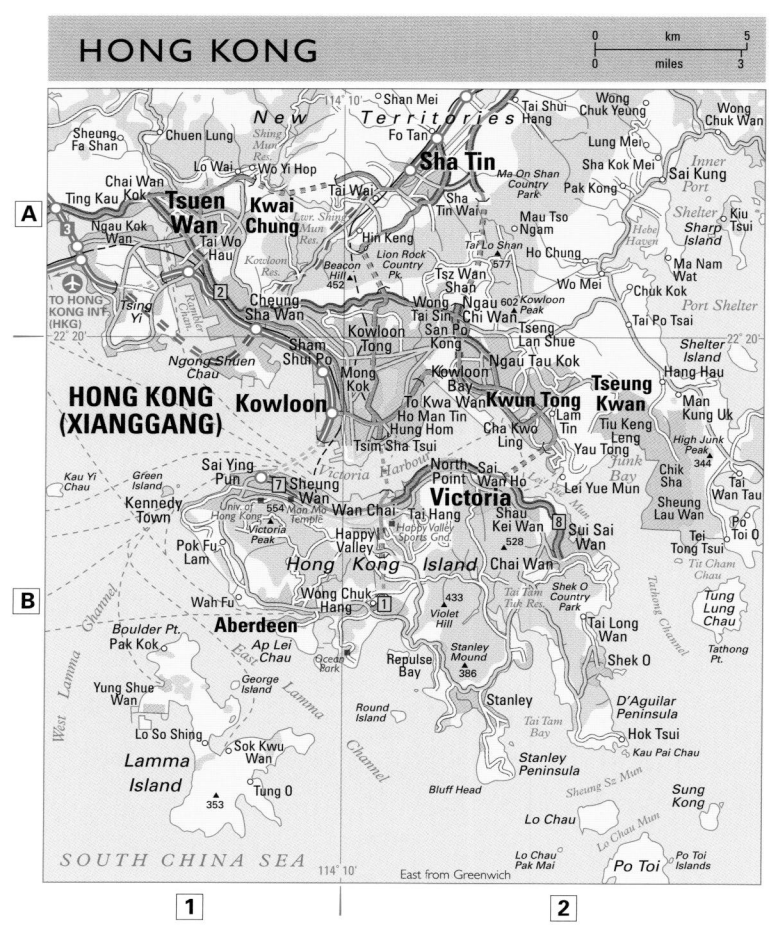

CENTRAL HONG KONG

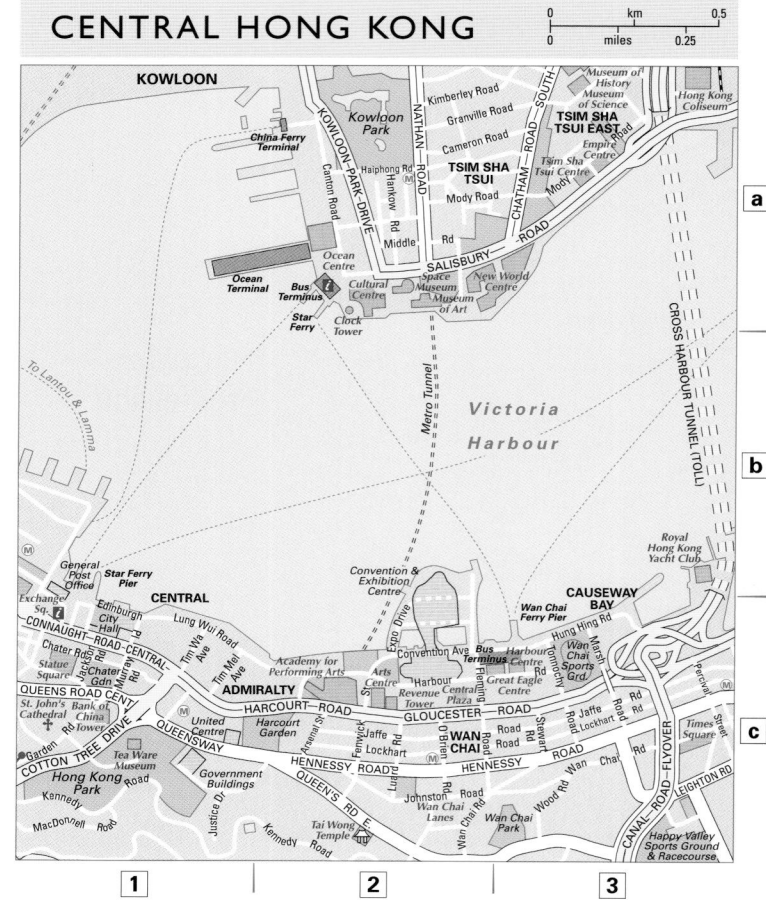

ISTANBUL

JAKARTA

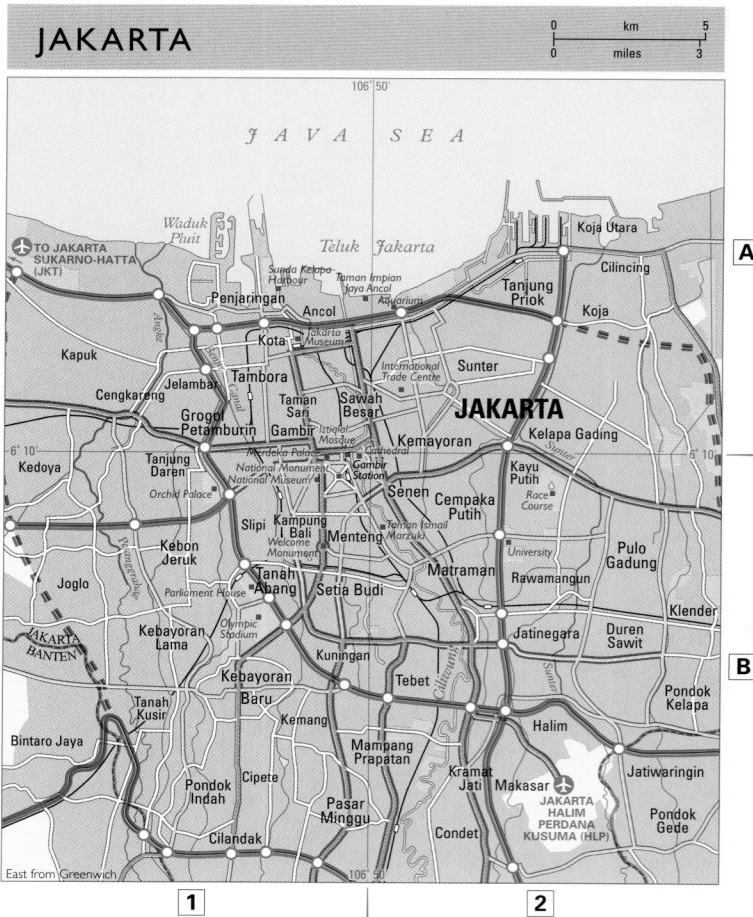

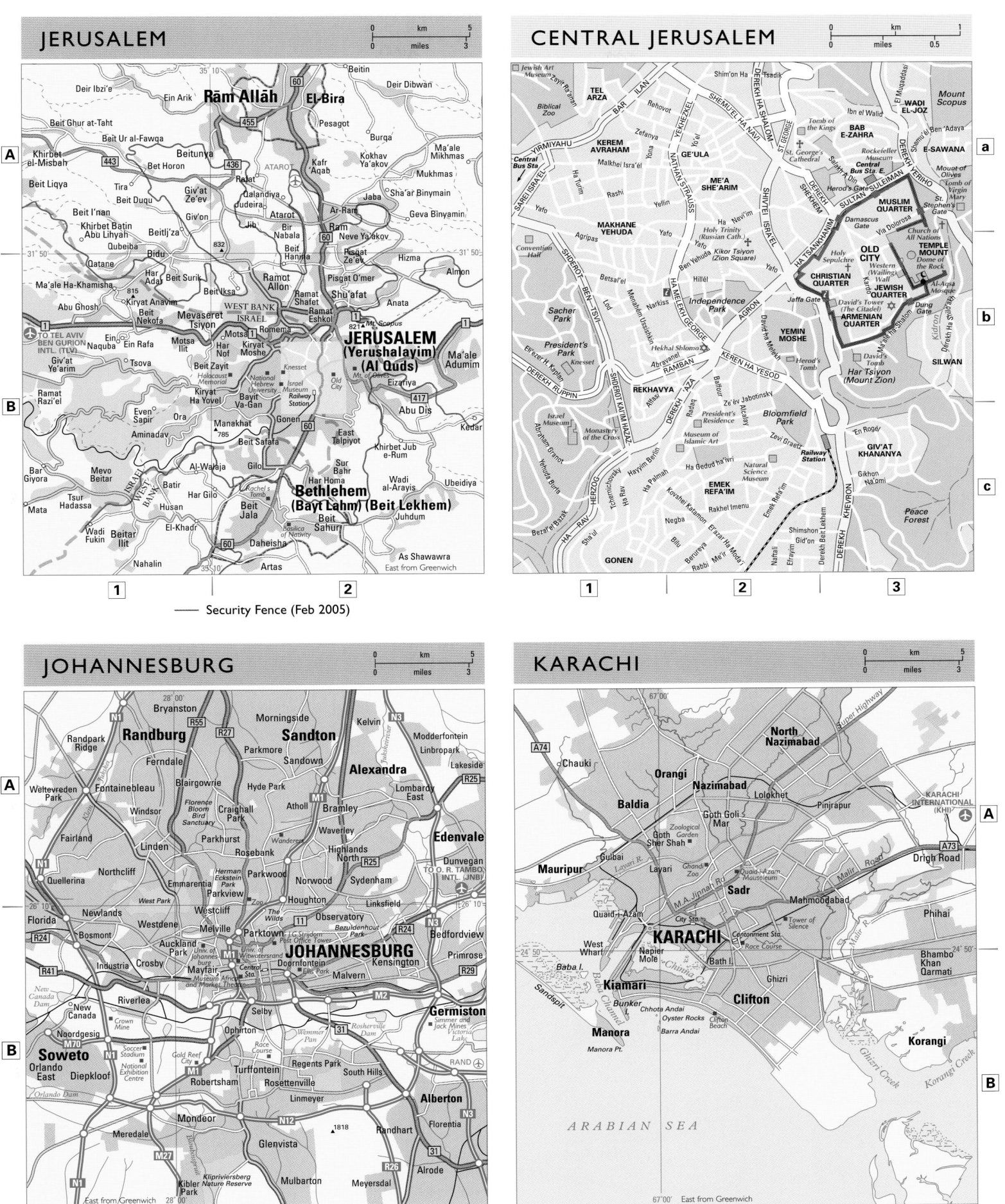

KOLKATA

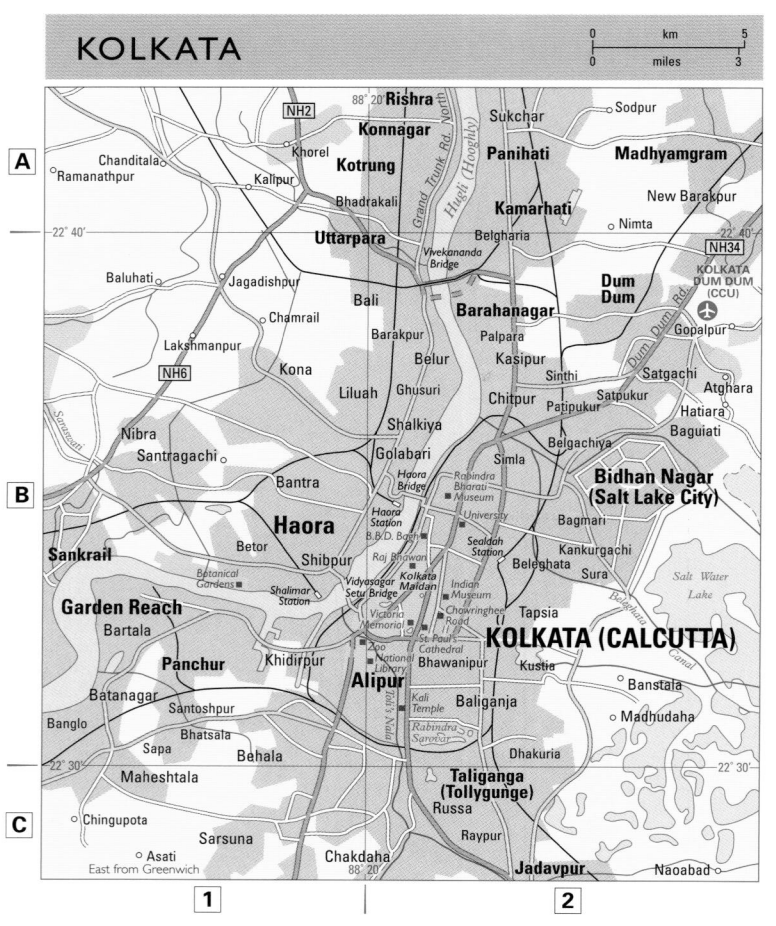

LAGOS

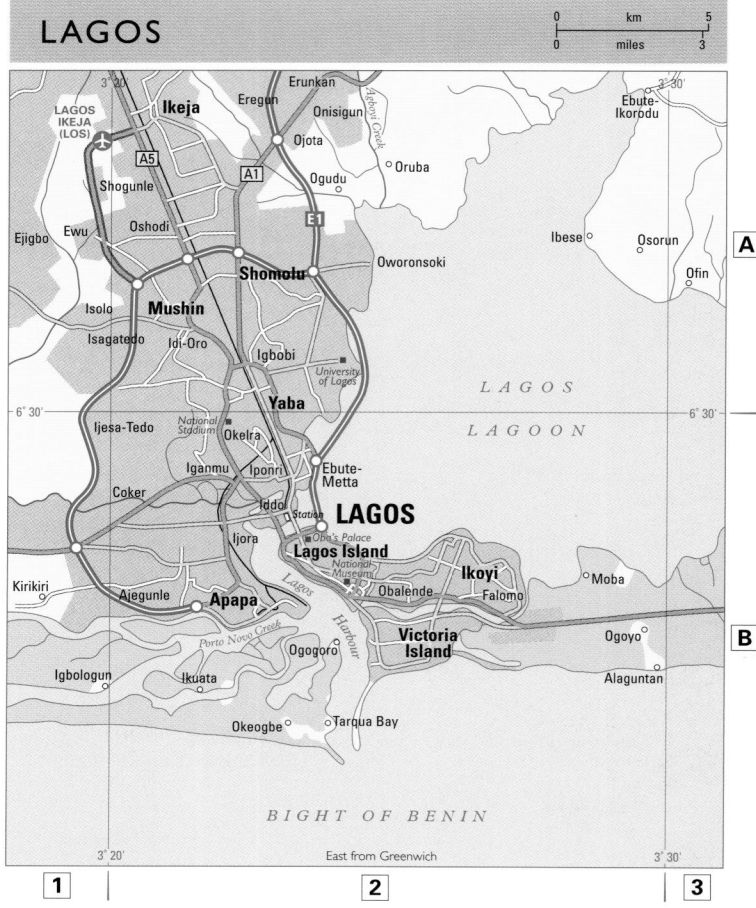

LAS VEGAS

LIMA

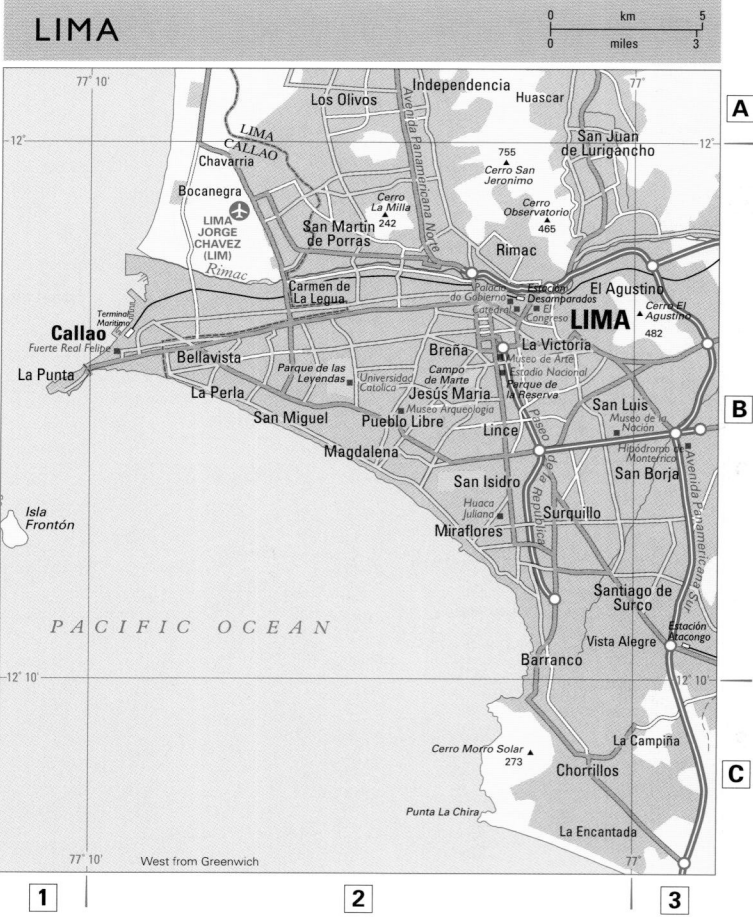

 Interstate route numbers   U.S. route numbers   State route numbers

LONDON

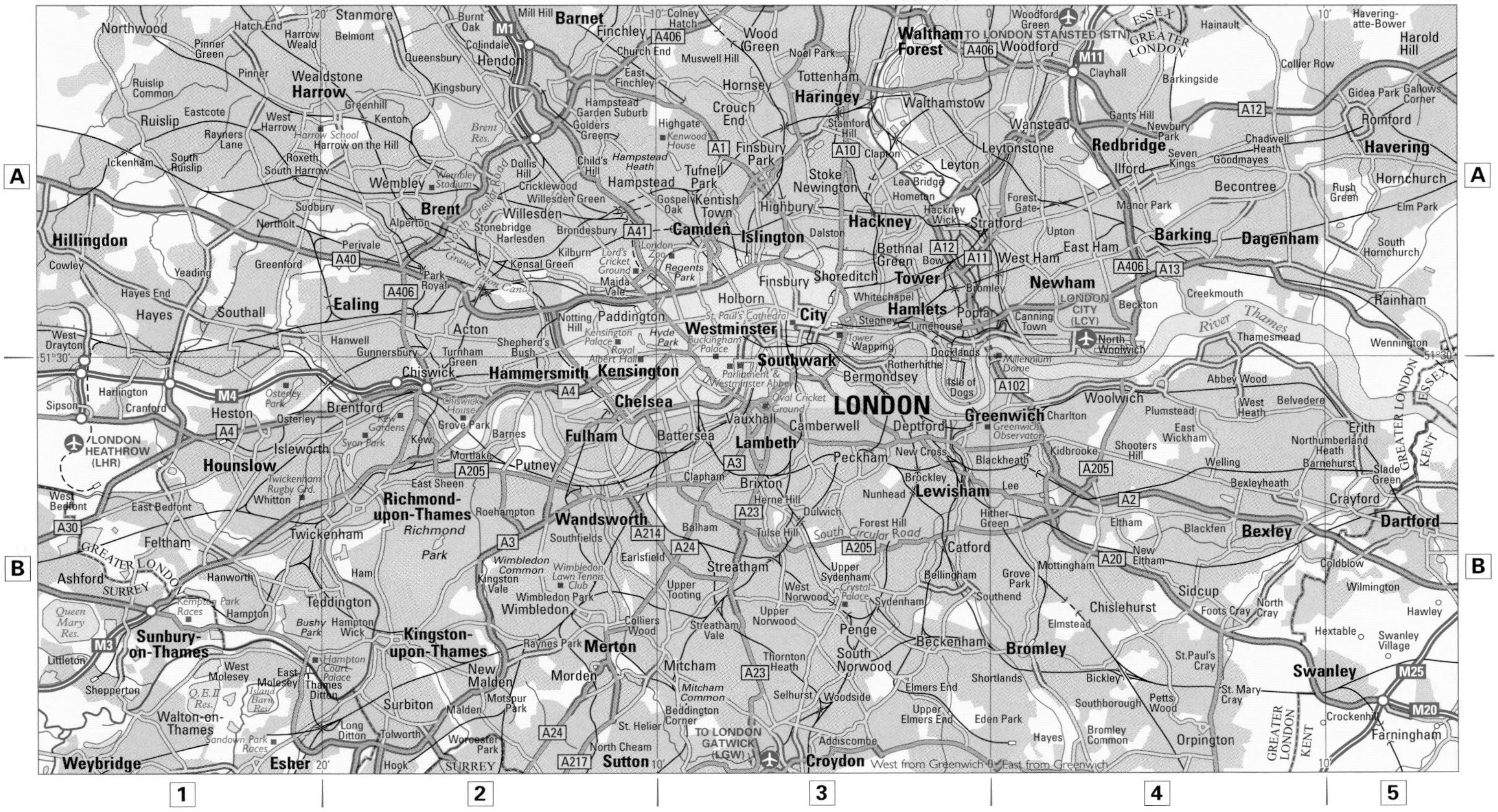

km 0 — 5
miles 0 — 3

A

Northwood Stanmore Mill Hill Barnet Finchley Church End Colney Hatch Wood Green Noel Park Waltham Forest TO LONDON STANSTED (STN) Woodford Green Hainault Havering-atte-Bower Harold Hill
Pinner Green Hatch End Harrow Weald Belmont Burnt Oak Colindale Hendon A406 Muswell Hill Hornsey Tottenham Woodford M11 Clayhall Barkingside Gidea Park Collier Row Romford Gallows Corner
Ruislip Common Wealdstone Harrow Greenhill Kenton Brent Res. Crouch End Haringey Walthamstow Wanstead Gants Hill Newbury Park Chadwell Heath Goodmayes Seven Kings A12 Havering Hornchurch
Eastcote Rayners Lane Wembley Cricklewood Hampstead Garden Suburb Golders Green Highgate Kenwood House Stoke Newington Leyton Leytonstone Redbridge Ilford A12 Becontree Rush Green Elm Park
Hillingdon Cowley Yeading Greenford Perivale Willesden Harlesden Kensal Green Maida Vale Finsbury Park Highbury Hackney Stratford East Ham Barking Dagenham South Hornchurch Rainham

Ealing Acton Shepherd's Bush Notting Hill Paddington Holborn City Tower Hamlets Poplar Newham Canning Town LONDON CITY (LCY) North Woolwich Thamesmead

Hounslow Chiswick Hammersmith Kensington Chelsea Westminster Southwark Bermondsey Isle of Dogs Greenwich Charlton Woolwich Plumstead Abbey Wood West Heath Belvedere Erith
LONDON HEATHROW (LHR) Brentford Fulham Battersea Lambeth LONDON Camberwell Deptford Greenwich Observatory Blackheath Kidbrooke Shooters Hill East Wickham Welling Bexleyheath Northumberland Heath Crayford

B

Feltham Twickenham Richmond-upon-Thames Putney Wandsworth Clapham Brixton Herne Hill Dulwich Forest Hill Catford Eltham Blackfen Bexley Dartford
Ashford Hanworth Ham Wimbledon Common Streatham Upper Norwood Crystal Palace Sydenham Grove Park Mottingham Sidcup Wilmington
Queen Mary Res. Sunbury-on-Thames Teddington Kingston-upon-Thames Wimbledon Upper Tooting Colliers Wood Streatham Vale Penge Beckenham Bromley Chislehurst Hextable Swanley Village
Shepperton Walton-on-Thames East Molesey Surbiton New Malden Morden Mitcham Thornton Heath South Norwood Shortlands Bickley St. Paul's Cray Swanley M25
Weybridge Esher Hook Worcester Park North Cheam TO LONDON GATWICK (LGW) Addiscombe Elmers End Hayes Orpington GREATER LONDON KENT Farningham M20
SURREY Sutton Croydon West from Greenwich 0 East from Greenwich

1 2 3 4 5

CENTRAL LONDON

km 0 — 2
miles 0 — 1

a

QUEEN'S PARK ST. JOHN'S WOOD Regent's Park London Zoo King's Cross St. Pancras PENTONVILLE RD HOXTON SHOREDITCH
WEST KILBURN MAIDA VALE London Mosque Euston British Library CITY ROAD CLERKENWELL
WESTBOURNE GREEN Madame Tussaud's BLOOMSBURY FARRINGDON Barbican Moorgate
PADDINGTON Marylebone Wallace Collection British Museum HOLBORN Barbican LIVERPOOL ST. Whitechapel Art Gall.

b

BAYSWATER Marble Arch SOHO Covent Garden STRAND Temple Fenchurch St. CITY
NOTTING HILL Kensington Gardens Hyde Park MAYFAIR PICCADILLY CIRCUS Charing Cross Blackfriars Tate Modern The Monument Tower of London
KENSINGTON Kensington Palace Serpentine Gallery Green Park ST. JAMES Trafalgar Sq. Waterloo East SOUTHWARK London Bridge Tower Bridge
Holland Park Albert Memorial KNIGHTSBRIDGE Buckingham Palace Westminster Abbey Waterloo International BOROUGH The Design Museum

c

WEST KENSINGTON BROMPTON BELGRAVIA PIMLICO Victoria Tate Britain LAMBETH Elephant & Castle NEWINGTON BERMONDSEY
SOUTH KENSINGTON CHELSEA Victoria Coach Sta. VAUXHALL KENNINGTON The Oval WALWORTH
Chelsea Bridge River Thames Vauxhall Bridge OLD KENT ROAD Burgess Park

1 2 3 4 5

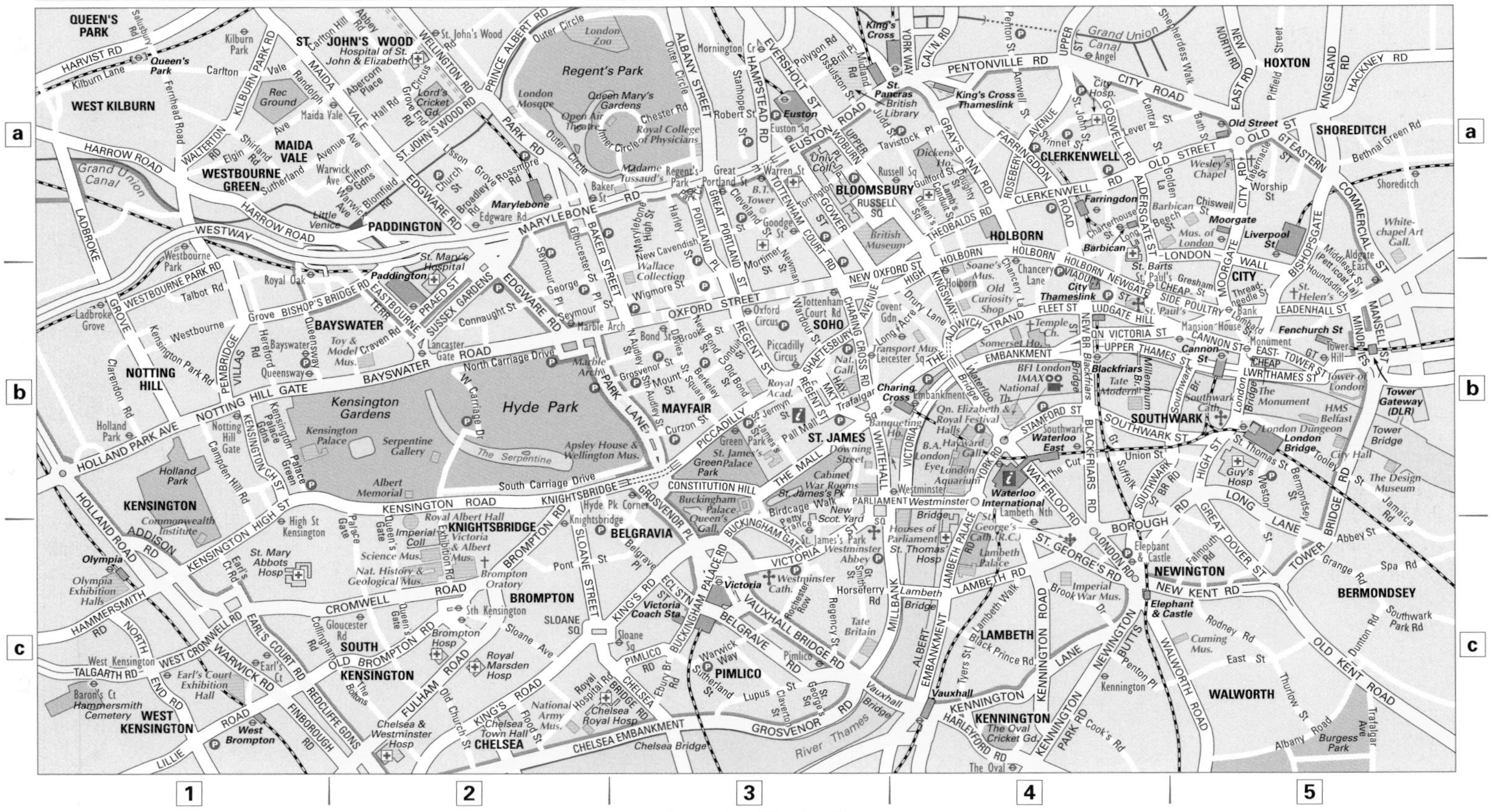

— Congestion Charging Zone

COPYRIGHT PHILIP'S

LISBON

km 5
miles 3

São Julião do Tojal
Botica Sete
Almargem do Bispo
Santo Antão do Tojal
Sta. Iria da Azóia
Sabugo
Tapada Piedade
320
Montemor 357
Camarões
Loures
Unhos
Apelação
Caneças
Póvoa de Santo Adrião
Amoreira
Camarate
Ada Beja
Odivelas
Charneca
Rio de Mouro
Venda Seca
Belas
Massamá
Lumiar
Pontinha
Carnide
Moscavide
Parque das Nações (Park of Nations)
Ponte Vasco da Gama
Amadora
Carnide
Campo Grande
Olivais
Queluz
Benfica
Damaia
University
Campo Pequeno
Matinha
Monsanto
Parque Florestal de Monsanto
Alto do Pina
Beato
Carnaxide
Campolide
Rato
Xabregas
Bairro Lopes
LISBOA
Talaide
Leião
Barcarena
Castelo de S. Jorge
Estação Santa Apolónia
Ajuda
Alcântara
Santo Amaro
Estação do Rossio
Praça do Comércio
Linda-a-Pastora
Algés
Mosteiro dos Jerónimos
Estação Cais do Sodré
Caxias
Terrugem
Belém
Cacilhas
Oeiras
Porto Brandão
Almada
Paço de Arcos
Trafaria
Cova de Piedade
Lavradio
Torre de Belém (Tower of Belém)
Padrão dos Descobrimentos (Discoveries Monument)
Banática
Raposo 125
Caparica
38°40
Bugio
Barreiro
Coina
Quinta de Santo António
Sobreda
Laranjeiro
Costa da Caparica
Capuchos
Corroios
Seixal
Santo André
ATLANTIC OCEAN
West from Greenwich
Amora
Cruz de Pau
Palhais
Arrentela
Charneca
9°10

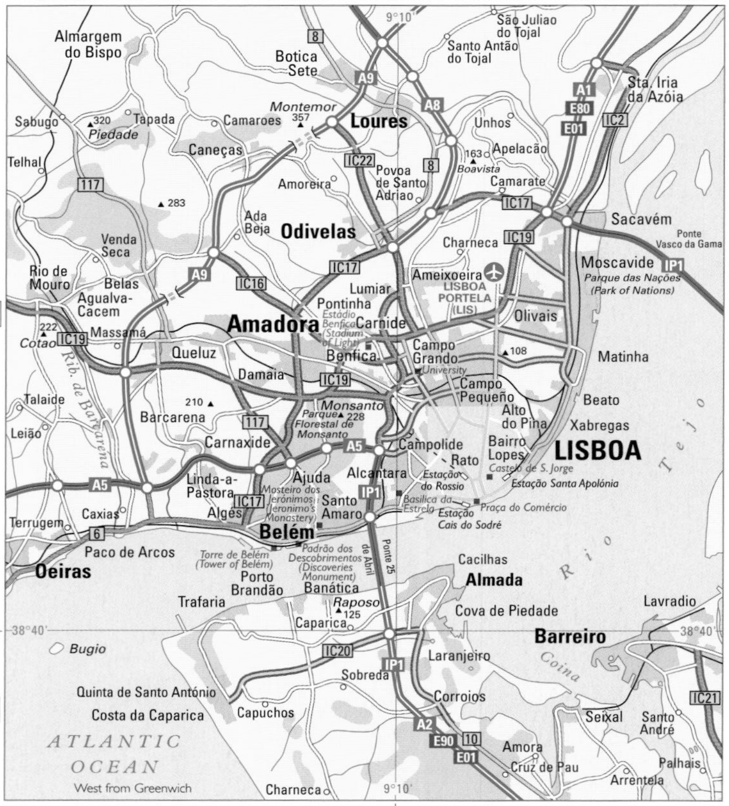

CENTRAL LISBON

km 1
miles 0.5

Palácio de Penitenciária
Palácio de Justiça
R. Pinheiro Chagas
Praça Duque Saldanha
Instituto Superior Técnico
Hosp. Infantil
Maternidade
ESTEFÂNIA
PENHA FRANÇA
Parque Eduardo VII
Pavilhão dos Desportos
AMOREIROS
Praça Marquês de Pombal
ANJOS
Hospital de Santa Marta
Hospital M. Bombarda
RATO
Academia das Ciências
Jardim Botânico
Hosp. dos Capuchos
GRAÇA
BAIRRO LOPES
Palácio de Assembleia Nacional
Instituto de Medicina Legal
Igreja de Graça
BAIRRO ALTO
Museu du Arqueológico
Theatro Nac. de Dona Maria II
Castelo de São Jorge (St. George's Castle)
Igreja Sta. Engrácia
Estação Santa Apolónia
Elevador de Santa Justa
Hospital de S. José
Teatro Nac. de São Carlos
ALFAMA
Museu de Arte Decorativas
Museu Antoniano (St. Anthony Mus.)
Military Trigo Museum
Biblioteca Nacional
Museu do Chiado
Sé Catedral
AV. VINTE E QUATRO DE JULHO
BAIXA
RUA DO ARSENAL
Estação Cais do Sodré
AV. RIBEIRA DAS NAUS
Dom José I
Estação Fluvial
Rio Tejo (Tagus)

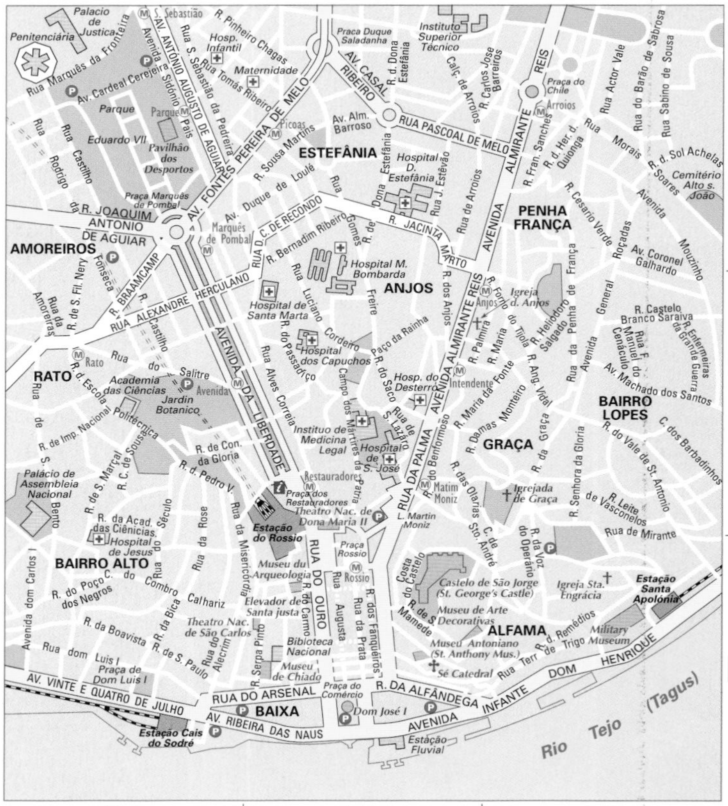

a
b
c
1 2 3

LOS ANGELES

km 5
miles 3

Tarzana
Sepulveda Dam Rec. Area
Van Nuys
Burbank
Verdugo Mts.
Altadena
Eaton Canyon Park
San Gabriel Mts.
34°10
Encino
San Fernando Valley
North Hollywood
N.A.C. Studios
Disney Studios
San Rafael Hills
Flint Peak 575
Rose Bowl
Pasadena
Sierra Madre
216
Studio City
C.B.S.
Fox Studios
Zoo
Warner Brothers Studios
Glendale
134
California Institute of Technology
Monrovia
Encino Reservoir
Sherman Oaks
Universal Studios
Cahuenga Peak 555
Glendale Galleria
Eagle Rock
Santa Anita Park
Arcadia
Stone Canyon Reservoir
Griffith Park
Lake Hollywood
Griffith Observatory
Highland Park
Garvanza
South Pasadena
San Marino
19
Temple City
Topanga State Park
Santa Monica Mts.
Nat. Rec. Area 459
Franklin Reservoir
Hollywood Bowl
Hollywood
Mann's Chinese Theatre
Hollywood Blvd.
Sunset Blvd.
Silver Lake Reservoir
Southwest Museum
El Sereno
San Gabriel
Rosemead
The Getty Center
Bel Air
Beverly Glen
Beverly Hills
West Hollywood
Santa Monica Blvd.
Paramount Studios
Hollywood Fwy.
Elysian Park
Dodger Stadium
Pasadena Fwy.
Arroyo Secco Park
Alhambra
University of California Los Angeles
Westwood Village
Los Angeles County Art Museum
Wilshire Blvd.
MacArthur Park
Lincoln Heights
California State University
San Bernardino Fwy.
Monterey Park
El Monte
405
LOS ANGELES
Civic Center
110
South San Gabriel
South El Monte
Pacific Palisades
Brentwood Park
Convention Center
710
Whittier Narrows
Flood Control Basin
60
Montebello Town Center
Bicentennial Park
Santa Monica
Museum of Art
Santa Monica Fwy.
University of Southern California
California Space & Science Center
Exposition Park
Boyle Heights
East Los Angeles
Montebello
605
Puente Hills
Santa Monica Pier
California Heritage Museum
SANTA MONICA
Sony Picture Studio
Baldwin Hills Reservoir
View Park
Vernon
Commerce
72
Pico Rivera
Pio Pico State Historic Park
Venice
Baldwin Hills
Windsor Hills
Maywood
19
Whittier
Venice Boardwalk
Ladera Heights
Huntington Park
Florence
Bell Gardens
Los Nietos
PACIFIC OCEAN
Marina del Rey
Westchester
42
Walnut Park
Bell
Cudahy
LOS ANGELES INTERNATIONAL (LAX)
University of West Los Angeles
Great Western Forum
Inglewood
107
South Gate
110
Downey
Santa Fe Springs
Lennox
West from Greenwich
118°20

Interstate route numbers   State route numbers

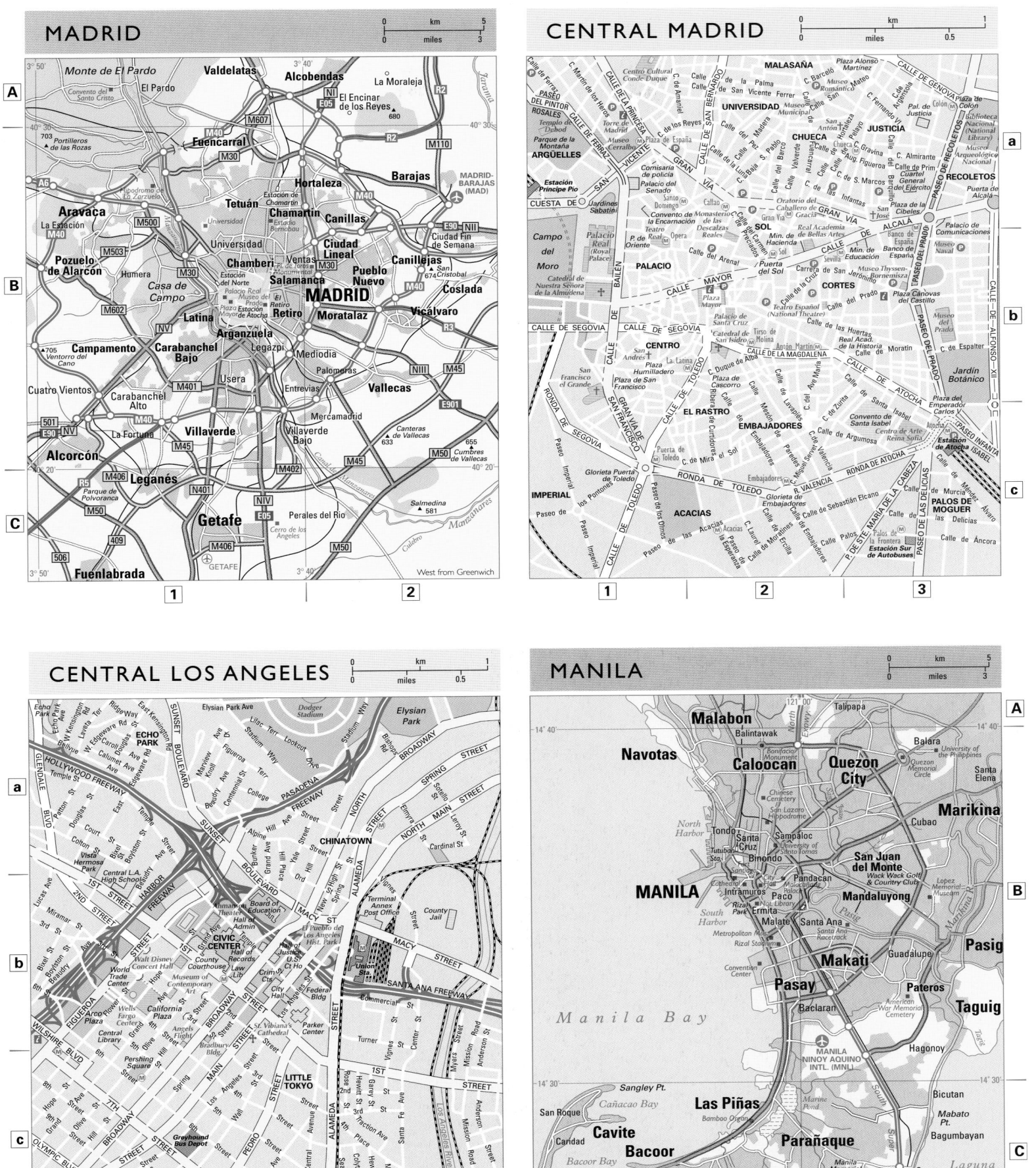

COPYRIGHT PHILIP'S

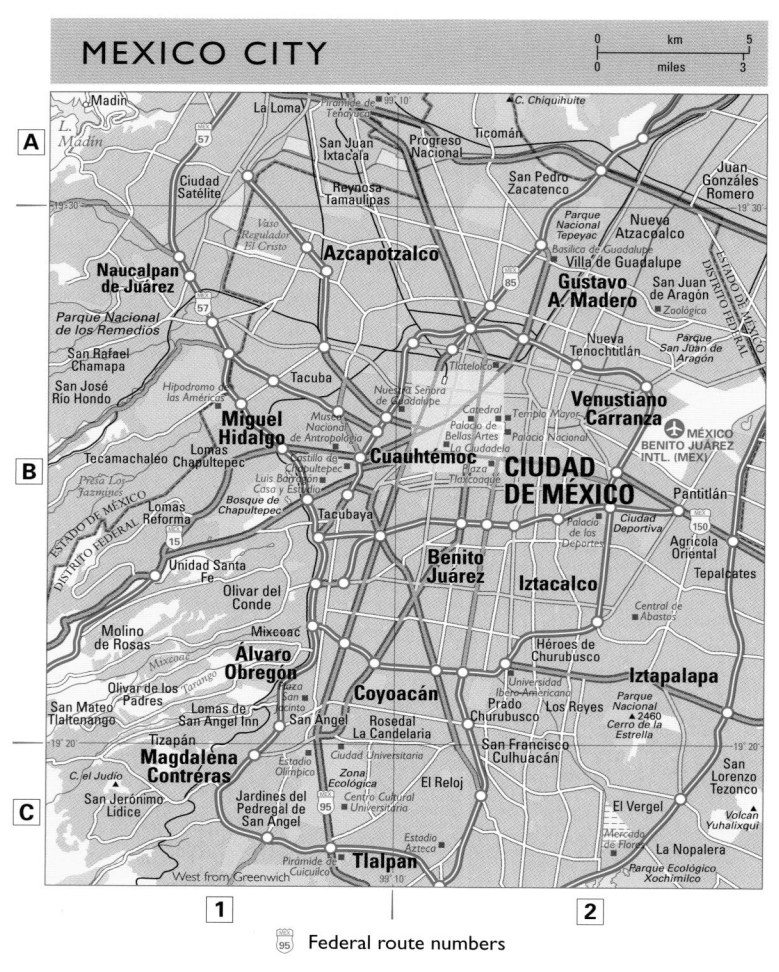

MEXICO CITY

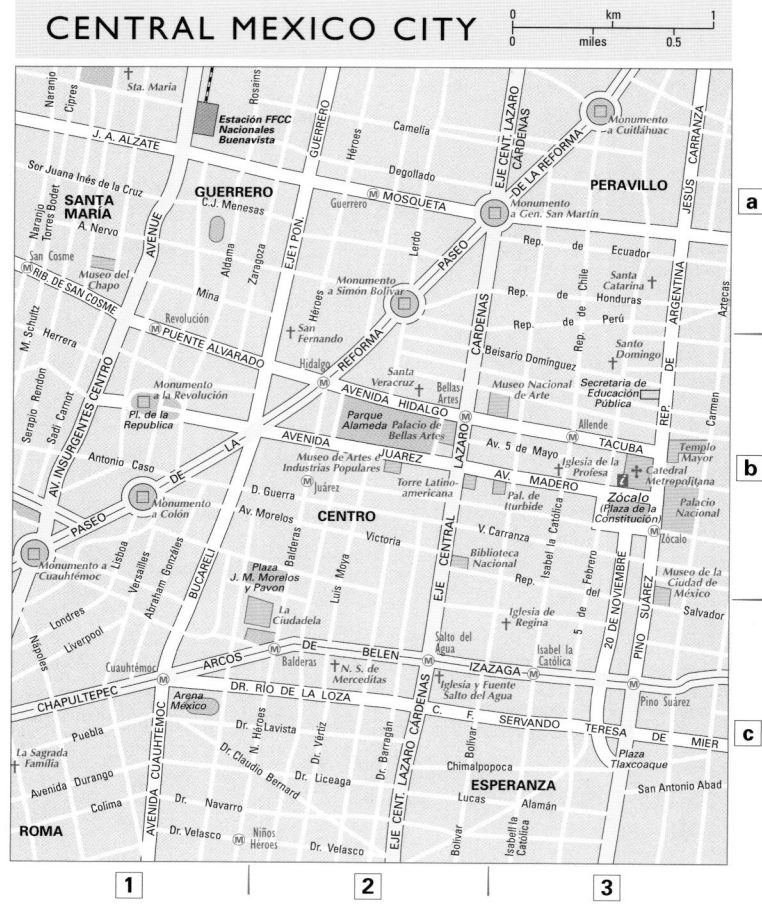

CENTRAL MEXICO CITY

95 Federal route numbers

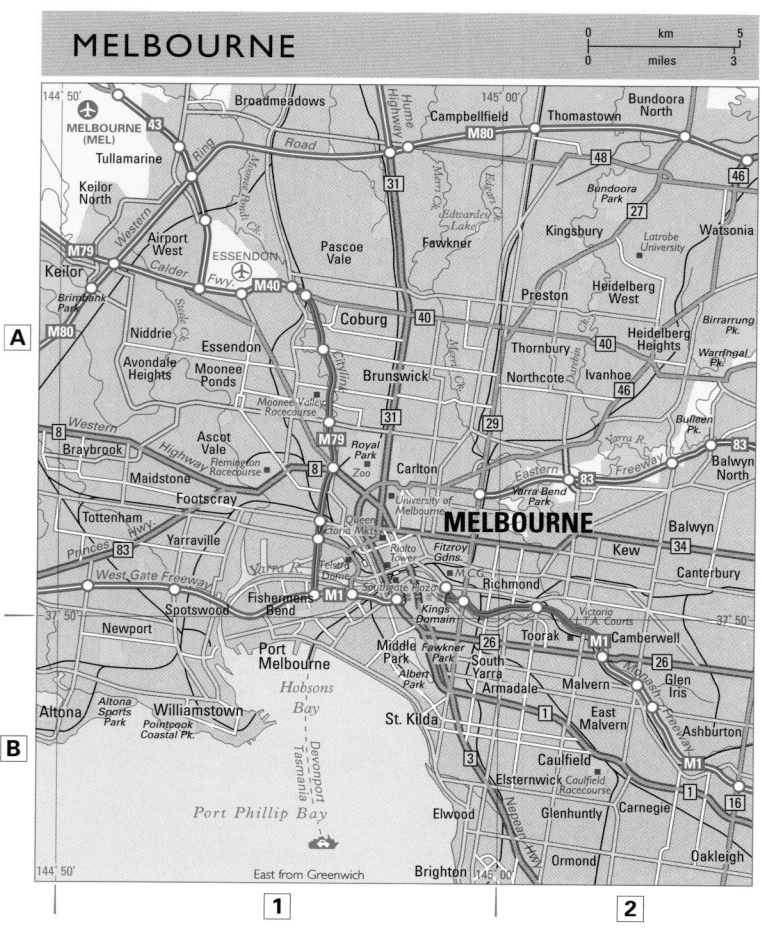

MELBOURNE

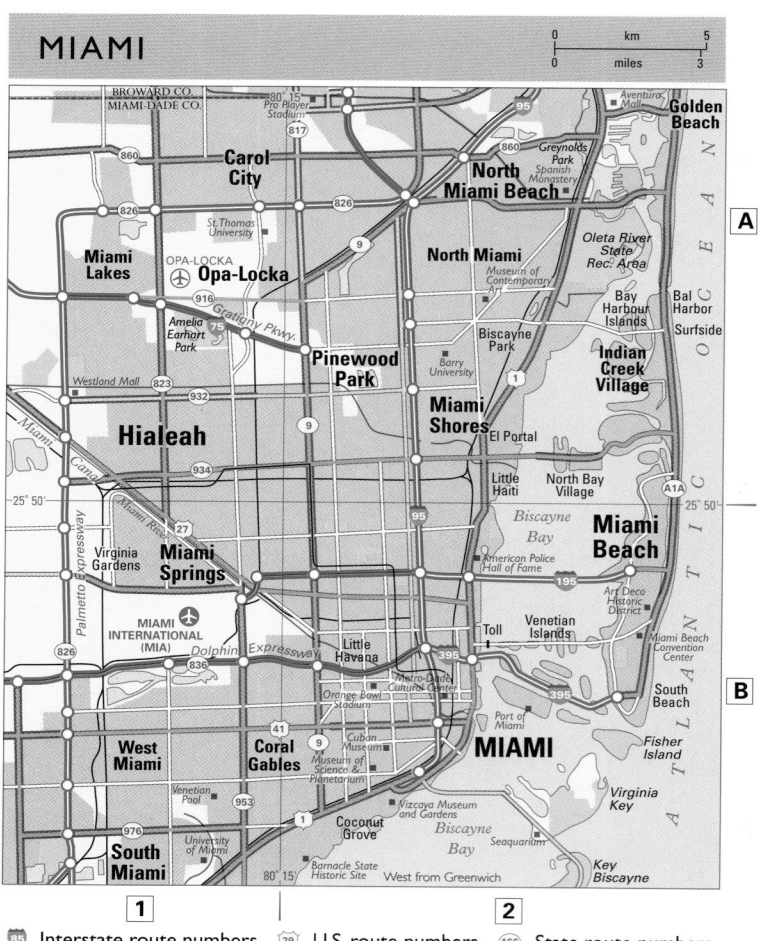

MIAMI

85 Interstate route numbers   29 U.S. route numbers   166 State route numbers

MILAN

km 0 — 5
miles 0 — 3

Coronno · Cesate · Pertusella · **Limbiate** · Varedo · 527 · **Muggiò** · **Monza** · Concorezzo · Autodromo
Garbagnate Milanese · Senago · Palazzolo · Incirano · **Nova Milanese** · 36 · 527
Lainate · 233 · Amata · Cassina Nuova · **Dugnano** · A52 · San Fruttuoso · E66 · A4
Bollate · **Paderno** · **Cusano Milanino** · **Cinisello Balsamo** · **Brughério** · A51
Passirana · Arese · Cormano · **Bresso** · San Maurizio al Lambro
Rho · Terrazzano · Ospiate · A8 · Bruzzano · Parco Regionale · **Cologno Monzese**
Cornaredo · Pero · **Novate Milanese** · Áffori · **Sesto San Giovanni** · Precotto · Vimodrone · **Pioltello**
Vighignolo · Figino · Trenno · Musocco · **Boldinasco** · Bovisa · Greco · Crescenzago · Milano Due
Séttimo Milanese · E35 · 11 · A50 · **MILANO** · Loreto · Parco Lambro · Segrate
Seguro · Quinto Romano · San Siro · Fiera Camp. · Sta. Ferrovie Nord · Città degli Studi · **Segrate**
Monzoro · **Cesano Boscone** · Bággio · Assiano · San Cristóforo · Morivione · Calvairate · Lambrate · Ortica · Milano San Felice · San Bóvio
Cúsago · Quartiere Zingone · **Córsico** · A7 · Vigentino · Gamboláita · MILANO LINATE (LIN) · San Donato Milanese
494 · Romano Banco · Chiaravalle Milanese · Triulzo · Metanopoli · **San Donato Milanese**
Trezzano sul Naviglio · Buccinasco · Assago · 412 · Gratosóglio · Poasco · 415 · Peschiera Borromeo
Gaggiano · San Novo · Quinto de Stampi · **San Giuliano Milanese**
Barate · San Pietro Cúsico · Gudo Gamb. · E35 · Mirasole · 9 · Mediglia · Zivido
Tainate · Pontesesto · Opera · A50 · Sesto Ulteriano · San Brera
Zibido San Giacomo · **Rozzano** · Fizzonasco · A1 · E35 · Mezzano
Noviglio · Mairano · Tolcinasco · 9° 10' East from Greenwich · Locate di Triulzi · Zúnico

1 · **2**

CENTRAL MOSCOW

km 0 — 1
miles 0 — 0.5

SAD-SAMOTECHNAYA · SAD-SUHAREVSKAYA · SAD-SPASSKAYA
Svetnoy Boulevard · Old Moscow Circus · Suharevskaya · SVETNOY BOULEVARD
SAD-TRIUMFALNAYA ULITSA · CHEKHOVA U. · PETROVSKIY BOULEVARD · Sergievskiy Per. · U. SRETENKA · Kostyanskiy Per.
Mayakovskiy Ploshchad · Tchaikovsky Concert Hall · Russian Cinema · Trubnaya Pl. · 'BOULEVARD RING' ROZHDESTVENSKIY BOULEVARD · Turgenevskaya · Turgenev-skaya Pl. · Chisty Prudy
BOULEVARD RING · Mayakovskaya · Pushkinskaya · STRASTNOY BULVAR · Varsonofevsky Per.
Youth Theatre · TVERSKAYA · Pushkin Ploshchad · PUSHKINSKAYA ULITSA · NEGLINNAYA ULITSA · PETROVKA · ROZHDESTVENKA · Convent of the Nativity of the Virgin · U. ZHDANOVA
Sadovnikov · Museum of the Revolution · Pushkin Ploshchad · Chekovskaya · Kuznetsky Most · Detskiy Theatre · LUBYANKA · Lubyanka · U. MYASNITSKAYA · Komsomolskaya Blvd.
MAL. BRONNAYA ULITSA · Gorky Theatre · Chekho Theatre · Okhotny Ryad · Petrovskiy Passage · Bolshoy Theatre · Teatralnaya · ULITSA ILINKA · NOVAYA PL. · Polytechnic Museum · Nogina
TVERSKOY BOULEVARD · Ulitsa Stanislavskovo · Central Post Office · Ulitsa Ogaryova · Ermolovey Theatre · Theatre · TEATRALNIY PROJ. · Ploshchad Lubyanskaya · LUBYANSKY PROSPEKT · Kitai Gorod
Gorky House Museum · Balinstogo Ul · Manezhnaya Ploshchad · Revolution Square · Pl. Revolyutsiy · Slavansky Bazar · Gum Shopping Arcade · SLAVYANSKAYA PL.
GERSENA · Historical Museum · Lenin Museum · Ul. Nikolskaya · Bolshoy Per. Devyatinsky · Vishnevyra Pereulok
Moscow Conservatoire · GERSENA ULITSA · University · Central Exhibition Hall · Red Square · Ulitsa Ilinka
NIKITSKIY BLD. · Semashko Ulitsa · OKHOTNIY RYAD · Arsenal · Council of Ministers · Lenin Mausoleum · ULITSA VARVARKA
Arbatskaya Ploshchad · VOZDVIZHENKA U. · Aleksandrovsky Sad · Ivan Square · Presidium of the Supreme Soviet · St. Basil's Cathedral · Central Concert Hall
U. ZNAMENA · Arbatskaya · Alexander Garden · Palace of Congress · Terem Palace · Kremlin · Archangel Cathedral · KITAISK. PEREULOK
ULITSA ARBAT · Lenin State Library · MANEZHNAYA · Armoury Palace · Cathedral Square · Kremlin Palace · MOSKVORETS. NAB.
GOGOLEVSKY BOULEVARD · BOLSHOY KAMENNY MOST · Marx Engels Ulitsa · Borovitskaya Ploshchad · Moskva (Moscow) · RAUSHSKAYA NAB.
BOULEVARD RING · Pushkin Fine Arts Museum · KREMLEVSKAYA NABEREZHNAYA · SADOVNICHESKAYA
Ryleyev Ulitsa · VOLKHONKA ULITSA · Lenka Ulitsa · SOFIYSKAYA NABEREZHNAYA · OVCHINNIKOVSKAYA
Kropotkinskaya · Moscow Swimming Pool · BOLOTNAYA NAB. · Vodootvodny · BOLOTNAYA UL. · KADASHEVSKAYA NAB.

1 · **2** · **3**

a · b · c

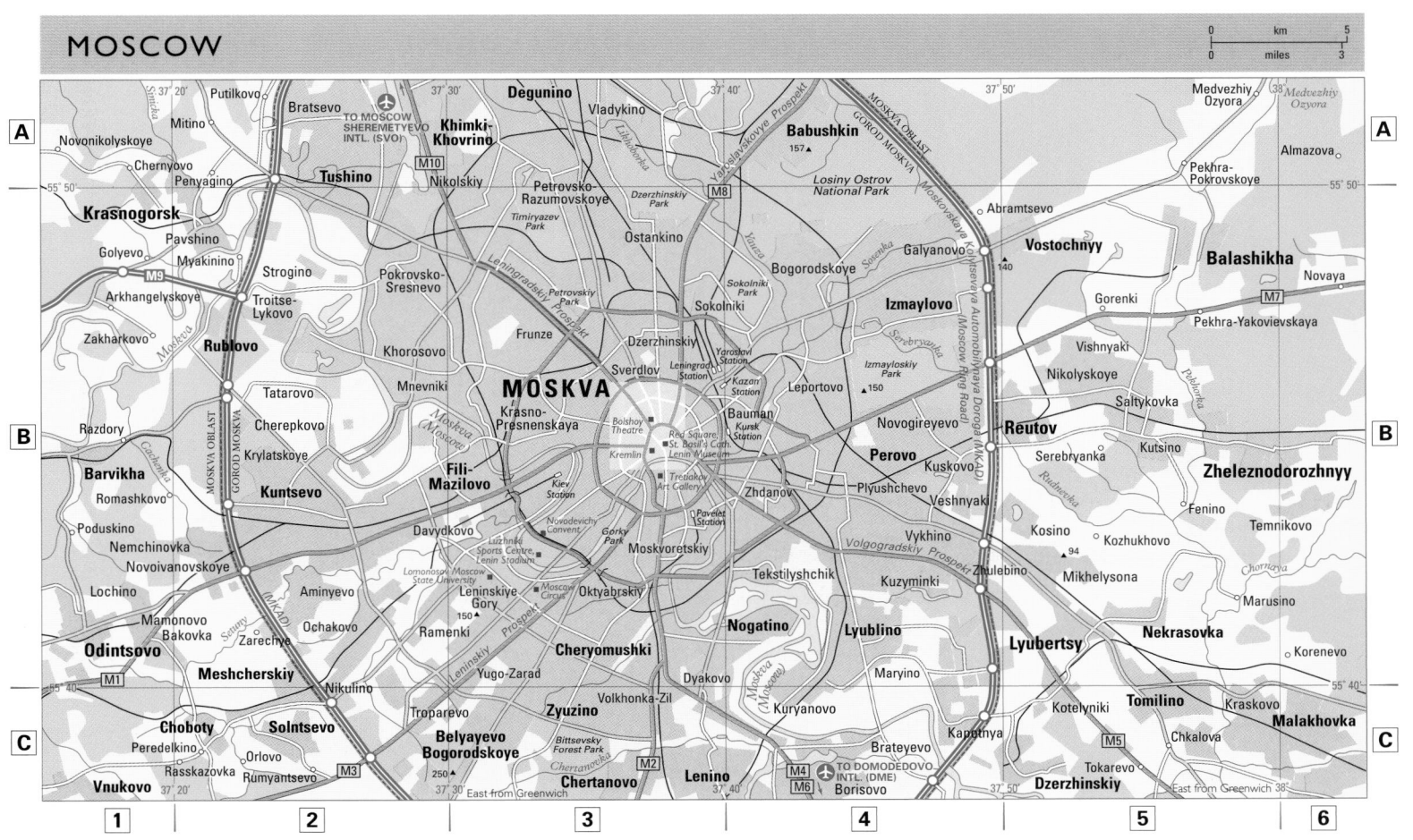

MOSCOW

km 0 — 5
miles 0 — 3

Putilkovo · 37° 20' · 37° 30' · **Degunino** · Vladykino · 37° 40' · Moskva Prospekt · 37° 50' · 38° · **Medvezhiy Ozyora** · Medvezhiy Ozyora
Novonikolyskoye · Mitino · Bratsevo · TO MOSCOW SHEREMETYEVO INTL. (SVO) · **Khimki-Khovrino** · **Babushkin** · 157 · GOROD MOSKVA · MOSKVA OBLAST · Almazova
Chernyovo · Penyaging · M10 · **Tushino** · Nikolsky · Petrovsko-Razumovskoye · M8 · Losiny Ostrov National Park · Pekhra-Pokrovskoye · 55° 50'
Krasnogorsk · Pavshino · Strogino · Timiryazev Park · Dzerzhinskiy Park · Ostankino · Abramtsevo
Golyevo · Myakinino · M9 · Pokrovsko-Sresnevo · Leningradskiy Prospekt · Petrovskiy Park · **Vostochnyy** · 140 · Gorenki · **Balashikha**
Arkhangelskoye · Troitse-Lykovo · Frunze · Sokolniki Park · Bogorodskoye · Galyanovo · **Izmaylovo** · M7 · Novaya
Zakharovo · **Rublovo** · Khorosovo · Sokolniki · **Moskva** · Izmaylovskiy Park · Pekhra-Yakovievskaya
Barvikha · Tatarovo · Cherepkovo · Mnevniki · **Krasno-Presnenskaya** · Dzerzhinskiy · Yaroslavl Station · Leningrad Station · Kazan Station · Leportovo · 150 · Vishnyaki
Romashkovo · Krylatskoye · Sverdlov · Bolshoy Theatre · Red Square, St. Basil's Cath., Lenin Museum · Bauman · Kursk Station · **Reutov** · Nikolskoye · Saltykovka
Kuntsevo · **Fili-Mazilovo** · Kremlin · Kiev Station · Zhdanov · Novogireyevo · **Perovo** · Kuskovo · Kutsino
Poduskino · Davydkovo · Tretyakov Art Gallery · **Zheleznodorozhnyy** · Serebryanka
Nemchinovka · Novoivanovskoye · Novodevichy Convent · Pavelet Station · Plyushchevo · Veshnyak · Fenino
Lochino · **Kuntsevo** · Gorky Park · Moskvoretskiy · Vykhino · Temnikovo · 55° 50'
Mamonovo · Bakovo · Aminyevo · Lomonosov Moscow State University · Leninskiye Gory · Moscow Circus · Oktyabrskiy · Kuzyminki · Zhulebino · 94 · Mikhelysona
Odintsovo · Zarechie · Ochakovo · 150 · Ramenki · Yugo-Zarad · **Nogatino** · **Lyublino** · **Lyubertsy** · **Nekrasovka** · Korenevo
Meshcherskiy · M1 · Nikulino · **Cheryomushki** · Dyakovo · Maryino · Kotelniki · **Tomilino** · Kraskovo
Choboty · **Solntsevo** · Troparevo · **Zyuzino** · Volkhonka-Zil · Kuryanovo · Kapptnya · **Malakhovka** · 55° 40'
Peredelkino · Orlovo · **Belyayevo Bogorodskoye** · Bittsevsky Forest Park · M2 · **Lenino** · Brateyevo · Chkalova
Vnukovo · Rasskazovka · Rumyantsevo · M3 · 250 · **Chertanovo** · TO DOMODEDOVO INTL. (DME) · M5 · Tokarevo
37° 20' · 37° 30' East from Greenwich · M4 · M6 · Borisovo · 37° 40' · **Dzerzhinskiy** · 37° 50' · East from Greenwich 38°

A · B · C

1 · **2** · **3** · **4** · **5** · **6**

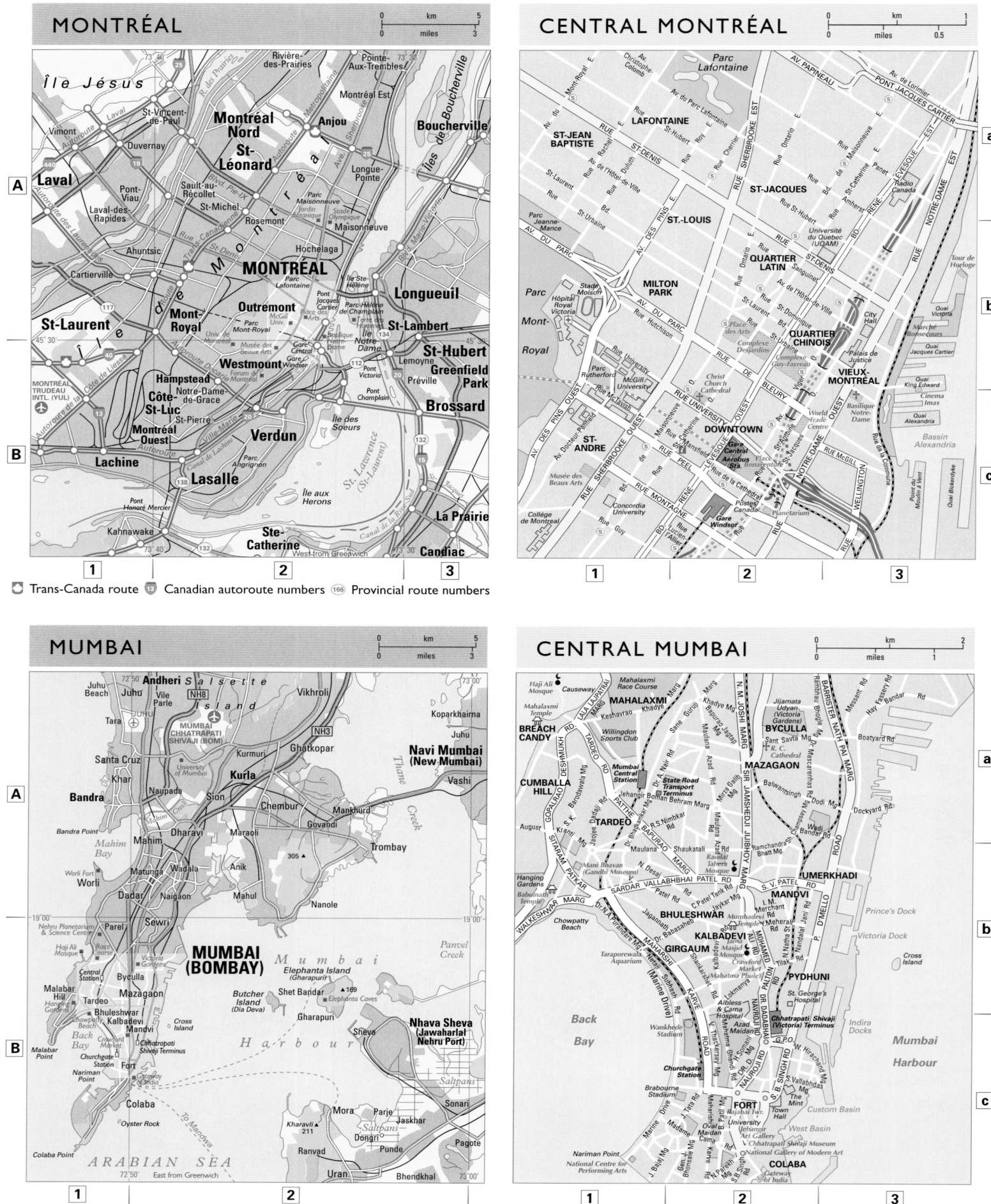

MUNICH

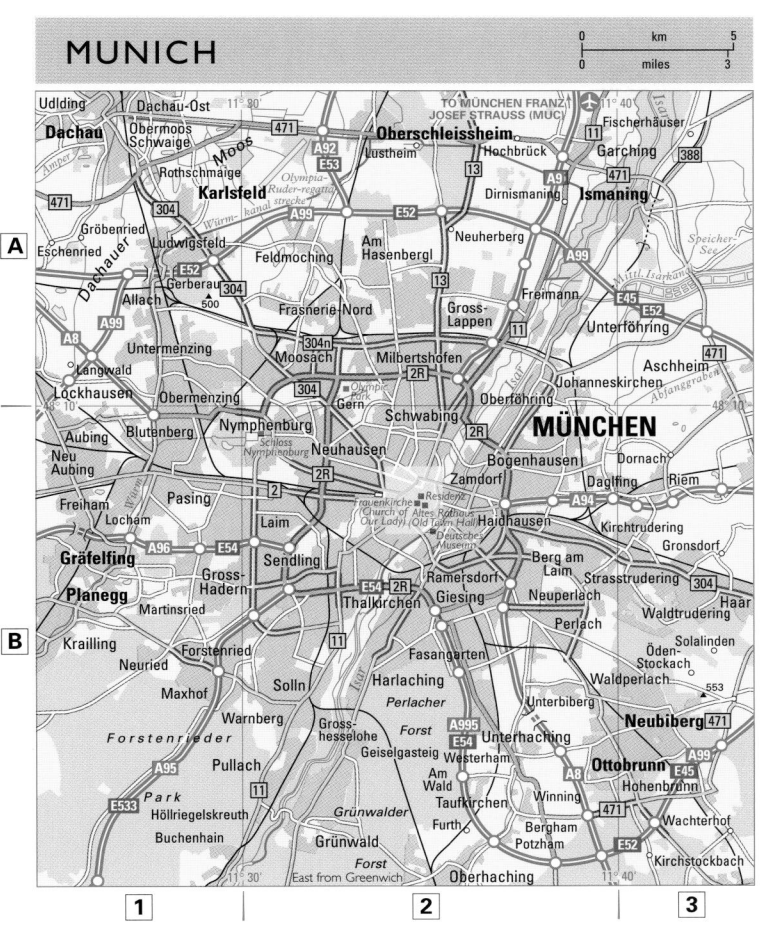

CENTRAL MUNICH

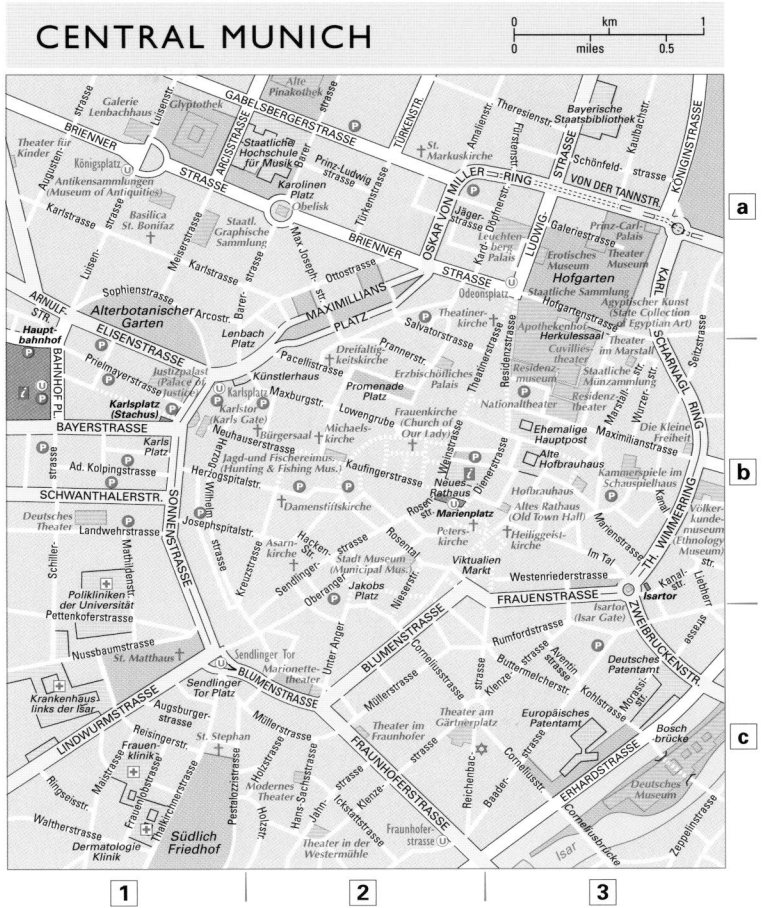

NEW ORLEANS

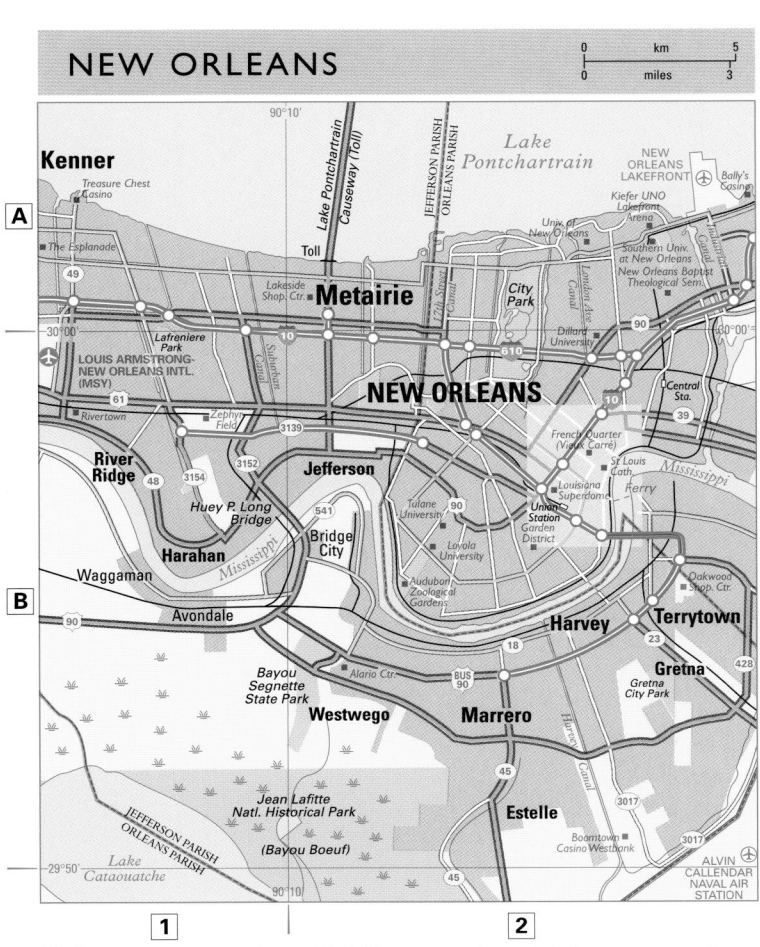

CENTRAL NEW ORLEANS

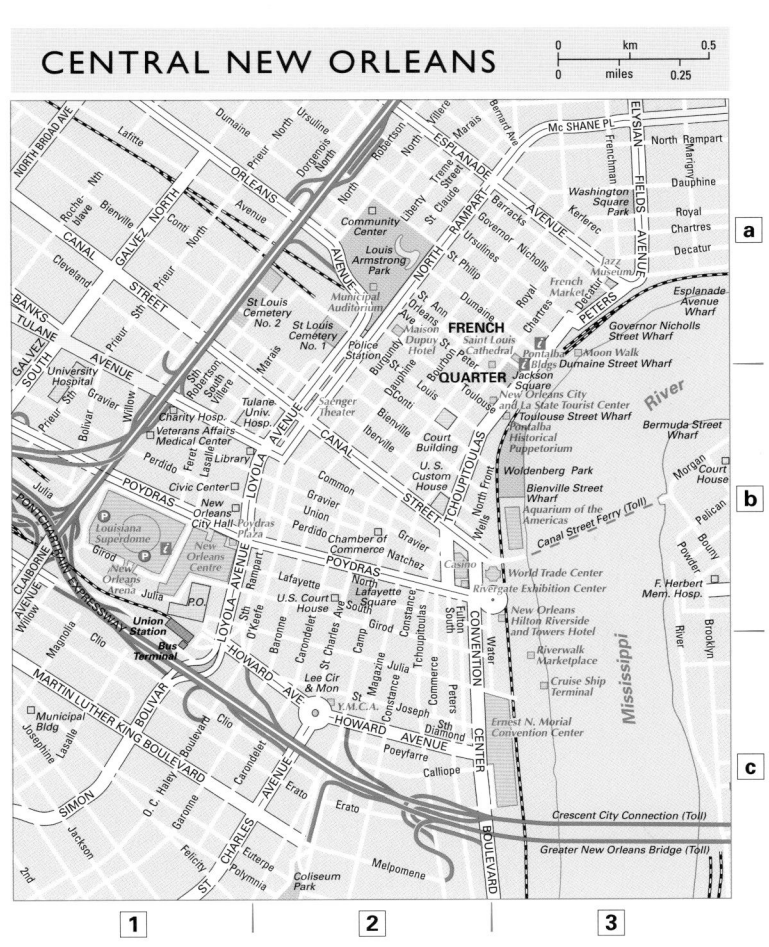

Interstate route numbers   U.S. route numbers   State route numbers

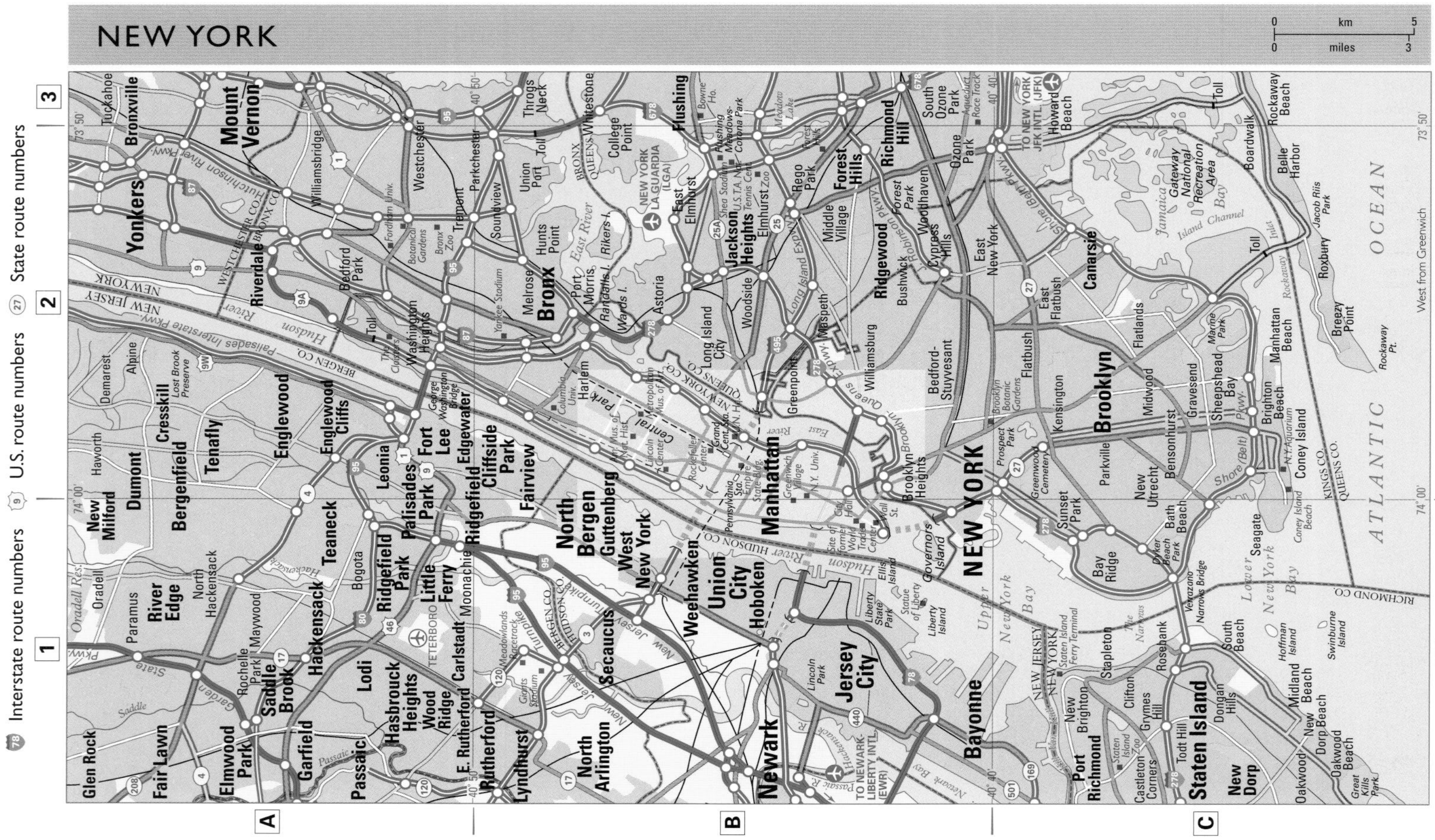

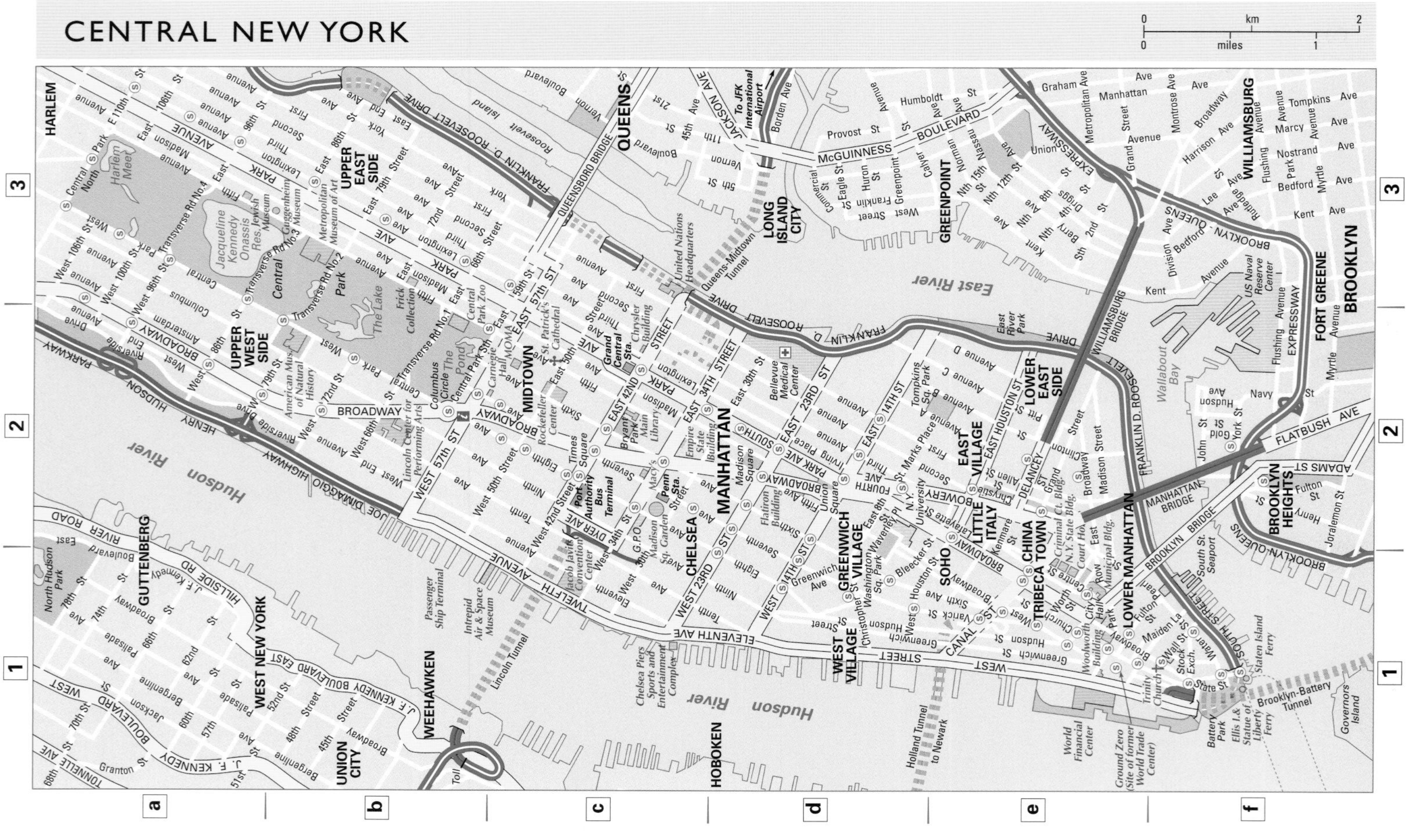

NEW YORK

km 5
miles 3

State route numbers
U.S. route numbers
Interstate route numbers

Yonkers, Bronxville, Mount Vernon, Westchester, Throgs Neck, Whitestone, Flushing, College Point, Richmond Hill, Ozone Park, South Ozone Park, JFK INTL (JFK), Howard Beach, Rockaway Beach, Boardwalk, Belle Harbor

Riverdale, Williamsbridge, Trappent, Southview, New York LA GUARDIA (LGA), East Elmhurst, Rego Park, Forest Hills, Forest Park, Woodhaven, East New York, Canarsie, Roxbury, Breezy Point, Rockaway Pt.

Demarest, Alpine, Cresskill, Bergenfield, Englewood, Englewood Cliffs, Fort Lee, Leonia, Washington Heights, Harlem, Central Park, Manhattan, Long Island City, Astoria, Woodside, Jackson Heights, Elmhurst, Middle Village, Ridgewood, Bushwick, Bedford-Stuyvesant, Brooklyn, Midwood, Gravesend, Sheepshead Bay, Brighton Beach, Coney Island, Manhattan Beach

New Milford, Dumont, Teaneck, Palisades Park, Ridgefield Park, Cliffside Park, Fairview, Edgewater, North Bergen, Guttenberg, West New York, Weehawken, Union City, Hoboken, New York, Sunset Park, New Utrecht, Bath Beach, Bay Ridge, Dyker Park, Manhattan

Glen Rock, Fair Lawn, Elmwood Park, Garfield, Passaic, Lyndhurst, North Arlington, Rutherford, Carlstadt, E. Rutherford, Wood Ridge, Hasbrouck Heights, Lodi, Saddle Brook, Rochelle Park, Maywood, Hackensack, Bogota, River Edge, New Hackensack, Oradell, Paramus, Teterboro, Little Ferry, Moonachie, Secaucus, North Bergen, Jersey City, Newark, Bayonne, New Brighton, Port Richmond, Castleton Corners, Staten Island, Todt Hill, New Dorp, Oakwood, Great Kills Park

Newark NEWARK LIBERTY INTL (EWR), Bayonne, Upper New York Bay, Lower New York Bay, Governor's Island, Ellis Island, Liberty State Park, Statue of Liberty, Verrazano Narrows Bridge, ATLANTIC OCEAN

A   B   C

CENTRAL NEW YORK

km 2
miles 1

HARLEM, Harlem Meer, Central Park, Jacqueline Kennedy Onassis Res., The Lake, The Pond, UPPER WEST SIDE, UPPER EAST SIDE, Metropolitan Museum of Art, Guggenheim Museum, Frick Collection, Central Park Zoo, American Museum of Natural History, Lincoln Center for the Performing Arts, Columbus Circle, QUEENS, LONG ISLAND CITY, GREENPOINT, WILLIAMSBURG, BROOKLYN, FORT GREENE

MIDTOWN, St Patrick's Cathedral, Rockefeller Center, Grand Central Station, Chrysler Building, Empire State Building, United Nations Headquarters, Bellevue Medical Center, Times Square, Port Authority Bus Terminal, Penn Station, G.P.O., Madison Square Garden, Jacob Javits Convention Center, MANHATTAN, CHELSEA, GREENWICH VILLAGE, WEST VILLAGE, EAST VILLAGE, LOWER EAST SIDE, SOHO, LITTLE ITALY, CHINA TOWN, TRIBECA, NOBBLE, BOWERY, LOWER MANHATTAN, Flatiron Building, Union Square, Washington Square, Criminal Courts, Municipal Building, City Hall, Brooklyn Bridge, Manhattan Bridge, Williamsburg Bridge, BROOKLYN HEIGHTS

Hudson River, East River, FRANKLIN D. ROOSEVELT DRIVE, HENRY HUDSON PARKWAY, JOE DiMAGGIO HIGHWAY, TWELFTH AVENUE, ELEVENTH AVE, WEST STREET, BROADWAY, Lincoln Tunnel, Holland Tunnel, Brooklyn-Battery Tunnel, Battery Park, Statue of Liberty Ferry, Ellis Island Ferry, Staten Island Ferry, World Financial Center, World Trade Center, Ground Zero, Trinity Church, N.Y. Stock Exchange, South Street Seaport, Governors Island

WEST NEW YORK, WEEHAWKEN, UNION CITY, GUTTENBERG, HOBOKEN, North Hudson Park, Boulevard East, J. F. KENNEDY BOULEVARD EAST, Intrepid Air & Space Museum, Chelsea Piers Sports and Entertainment Complex, Passenger Ship Terminal

a   b   c   d   e   f

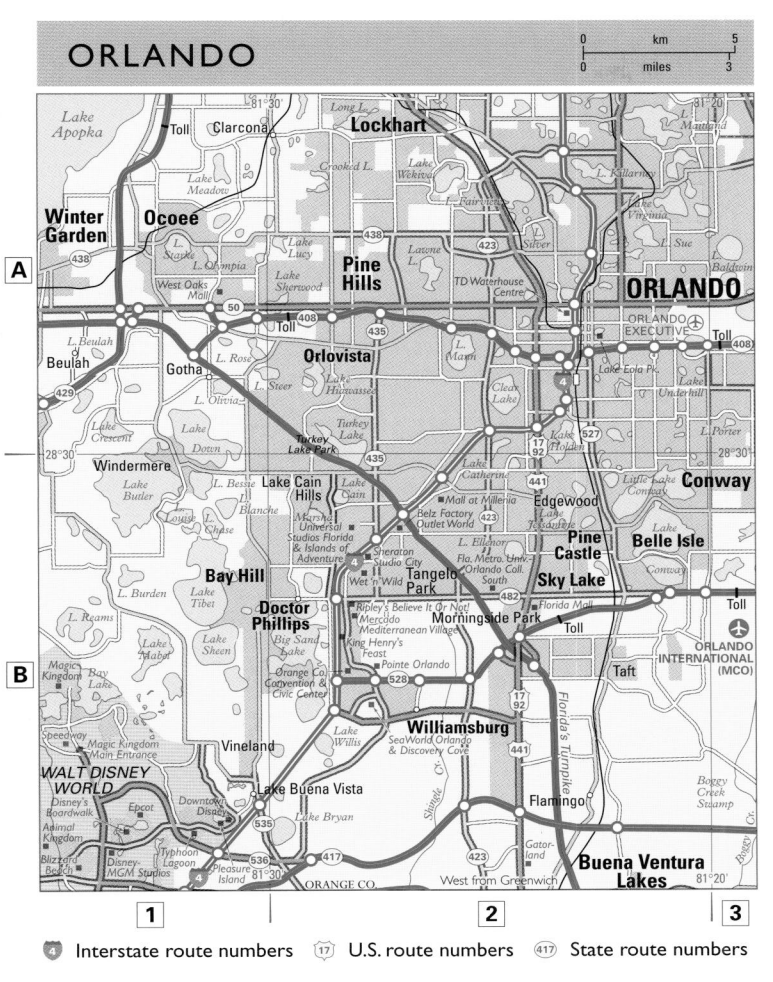

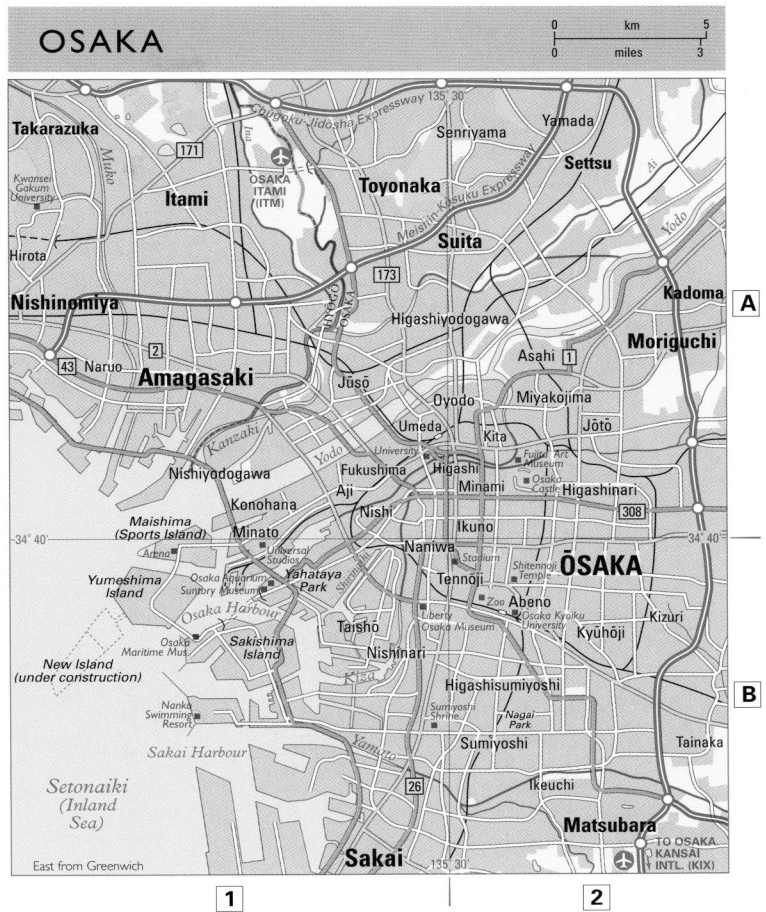

🛡4 Interstate route numbers   ⬭17 U.S. route numbers   ⬭417 State route numbers

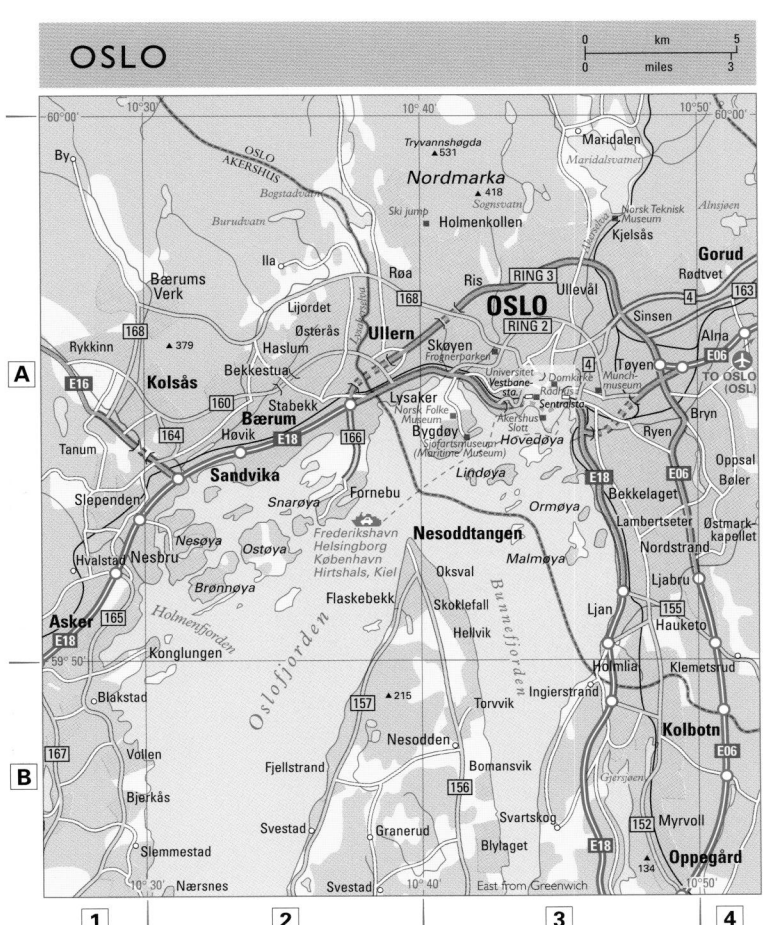

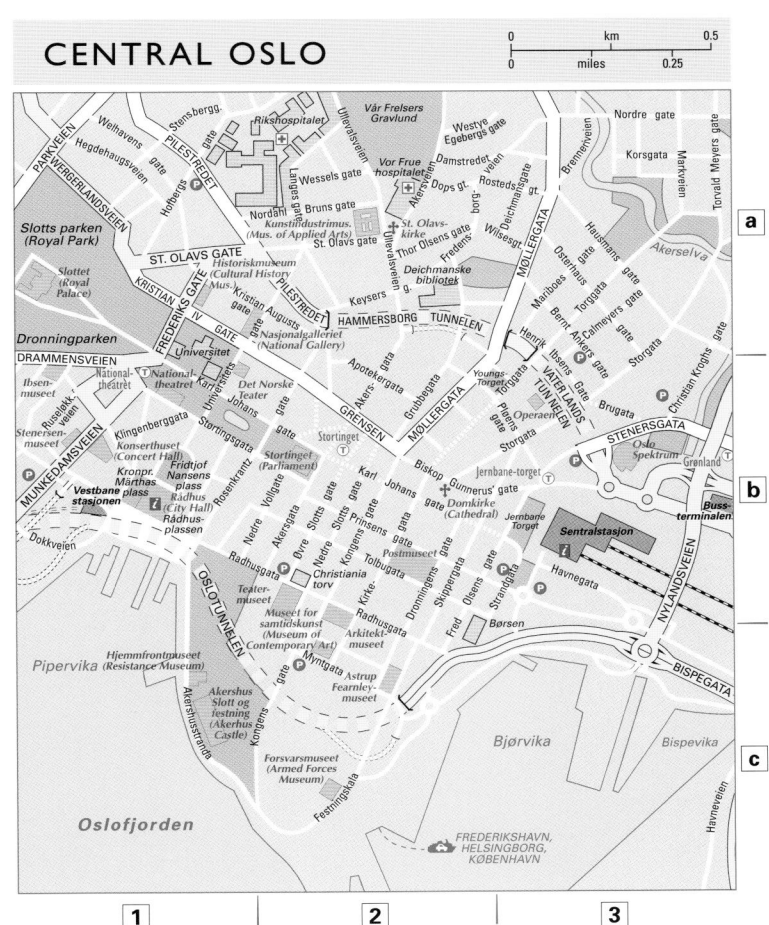

COPYRIGHT PHILIP'S

PARIS

km 5
miles 3

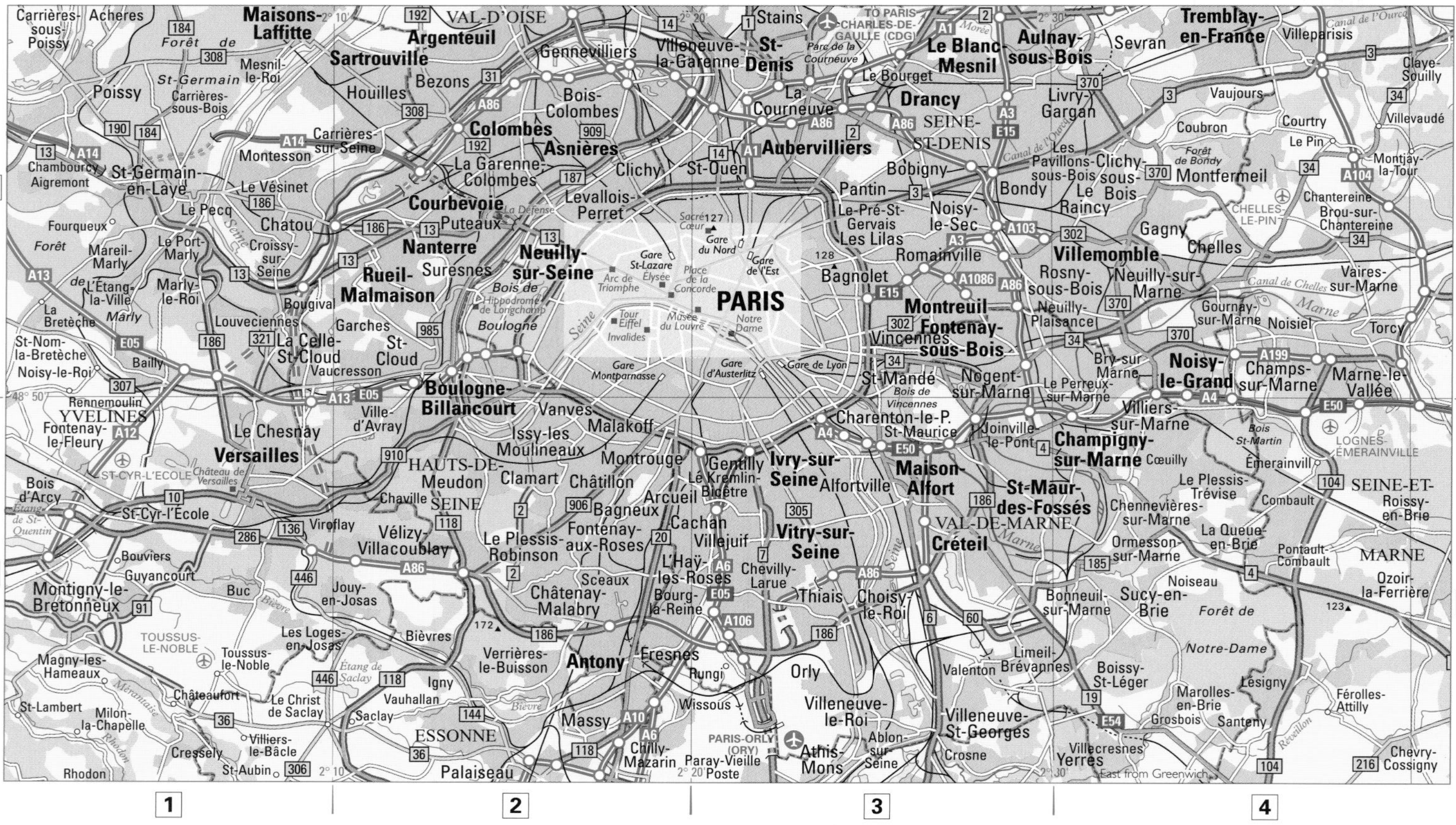

Carrières-sous-Poissy · Achères · Maisons-Laffitte · VAL-D'OISE · Gennevilliers · Villeneuve-la-Garenne · Stains · TO PARIS CHARLES-DE-GAULLE (CDG) · Tremblay-en-France · Villeparisis
Forêt de · Argenteuil · Bezons · St-Denis · Parc de la Courneuve · Le Blanc Mesnil · Aulnay-sous-Bois · Sevran · Claye-Souilly
Poissy · St-Germain · Sartrouville · Houilles · Bois-Colombes · Le Bourget · Le Blanc · Livry-Gargan · Vaujours · Courtry · Villevaudé
Carrières-sous-Bois · Colombes · Asnières · La Courneuve · Drancy · SEINE-ST-DENIS · Le Pin · Montjay-la-Tour
Montesson · La Garenne-Colombes · Clichy · Aubervilliers · Bobigny · Les Pavillons-sous-Bois · Clichy-sous-Bois · Montfermeil
St-Germain-en-Laye · Le Vésinet · Courbevoie · Levallois-Perret · St-Ouen · Pantin · Le Pré-St-Gervais Les Lilas · Noisy-le-Sec · Le Bois Raincy · Gagny · Chelles · Chanterine Brou-sur-Chantereine
Chambourcy Aigremont · Le Pecq · Chatou · Nanterre · Puteaux · Sacré Cœur · Gare du Nord · Gare de l'Est · Romainville · Villemomble · Neuilly-sur-Marne
Fourqueux · Croissy-sur-Seine · Rueil-Malmaison · Neuilly-sur-Seine · Arc de Triomphe · Gare St-Lazare · Place de la Concorde · Bagnolet · Rosny-sous-Bois · Neuilly-Plaisance · Vaires-sur-Marne
Mareil-Marly · Le Port-Marly · Suresnes · Bois de Boulogne · Tour Eiffel Invalides · PARIS · Notre Dame · Montreuil · Le Perreux-sur-Marne · Gournay-sur-Marne · Noisiel · Torcy
L'Étang-la-Ville · Marly-le-Roi · Garches · St-Cloud · Boulogne · Montparnasse · Gare de Lyon · Fontenay-sous-Bois · Vincennes · Bry-sur-Marne · Champs-sur-Marne · Marne-le-Vallée
La Bretèche · Louveciennes · La Celle-St-Cloud · Vaucresson · Gare d'Austerlitz · St-Mandé · Nogent-sur-Marne · Noisy-le-Grand · LOGNES EMERAINVILLE
St-Nom-la-Bretèche Noisy-le-Roi · Bailly · Boulogne-Billancourt · Ville-d'Avray · Vanves · Malakoff · Charenton-le-P. St-Maurice · Joinville-le-Pont · Villiers-sur-Marne · Émerainville · SEINE-ET-Roissy-en-Brie
Rennemoulin · YVELINES · Fontenay-le-Fleury · Le Chesnay · Meudon · HAUTS-DE-SEINE · Issy-les-Moulineaux · Montrouge · Gentilly Kremlin-Bicêtre · Ivry-sur-Seine · Alfortville · Maison-Alfort · Le Plessis-Trévise · Cœuilly · La Queue-en-Brie · Combault
Bois d'Arcy · Versailles · Château de Versailles · Chaville · Clamart · Châtillon · Arcueil · Cachan · Vitry-sur-Seine · Créteil · St-Maur-des-Fossés · Chennevières-sur-Marne · Ormesson-sur-Marne · MARNE
Étang de St-Quentin · St-Cyr-l'École · Viroflay · Vélizy-Villacoublay · Bagneux · Fontenay-aux-Roses · Villejuif · VAL-DE-MARNE · Bonneuil-sur-Marne · Noiseau · Sucy-en-Brie · Ozoir-la-Ferrière
Montigny-le-Bretonneux · Bouviers · Guyancourt · Buc · Jouy-en-Josas · Le Plessis-Robinson · Sceaux · L'Haÿ-les-Roses · Bourg-la-Reine · Chevilly-Larue · Thiais · Choisy-le-Roi · Forêt de Notre-Dame
Magny-les-Hameaux · Toussus-le-Noble · Les Loges-en-Josas · Bièvres · Châtenay-Malabry · Antony · Fresnes · Rungis · Orly · Valenton · Brévannes · Boissy-St-Léger · Marolles-en-Brie · Grosbois · Santeny · Férolles-Attilly
St-Lambert · Milon-la-Chapelle · Châteaufort · Le Christ de Saclay · Igny · Vauhallan · ESSONNE · Massy · Wissous · Villeneuve-le-Roi · Villeneuve-St-Georges · Lésigny
Rhodon · St-Aubin · Saclay · Palaiseau · Chilly-Mazarin · Paray-Vieille Poste · PARIS-ORLY (ORY) Aéro · Athis-Mons · Ablon-sur-Seine · Crosne · Yerres · Villecresnes · Chevry-Cognigny
East from Greenwich

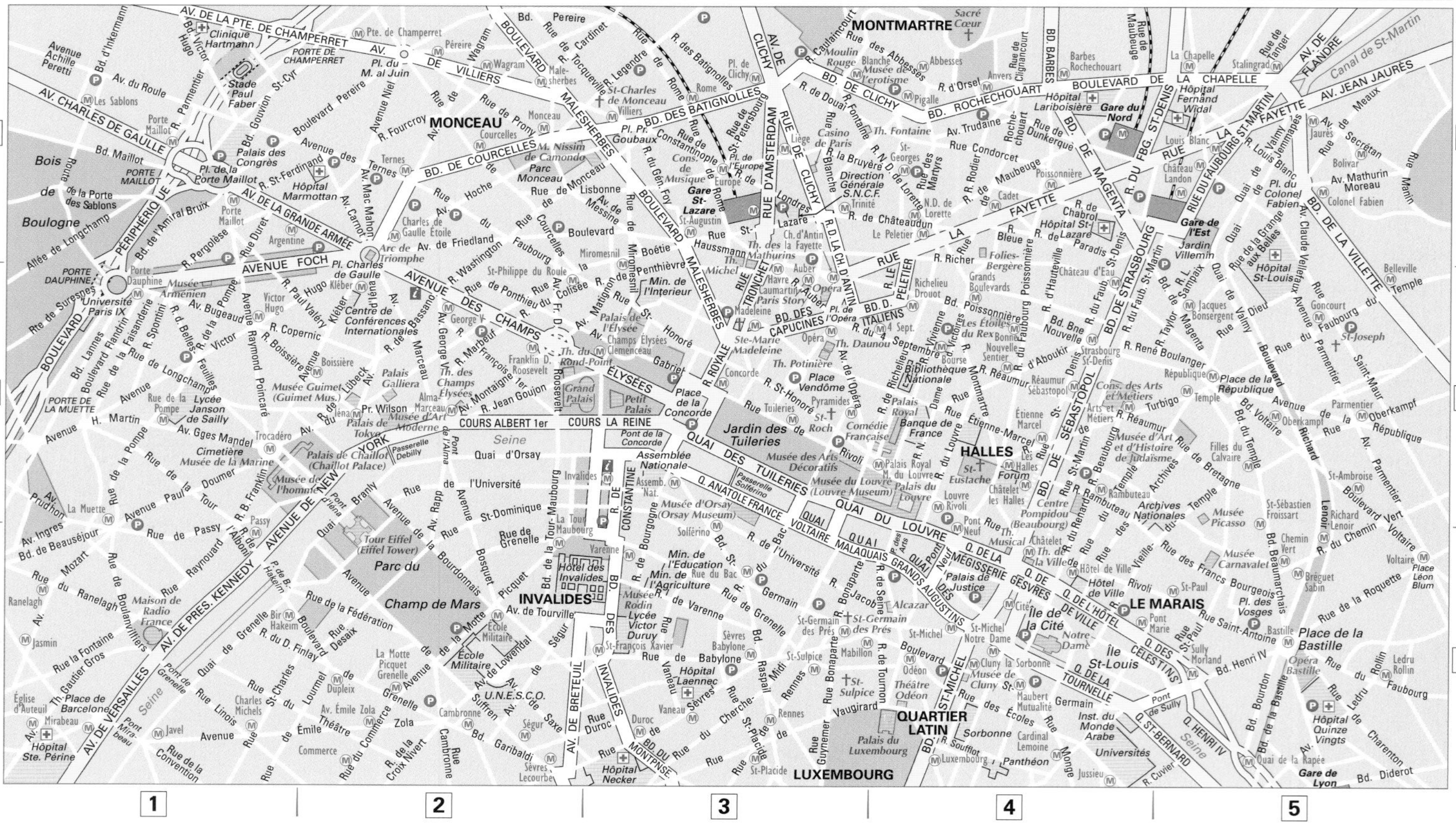

CENTRAL PARIS

km 1
miles 0.5

PTE. DE CHAMPERRET · Clinique Hartmann · MONTMARTRE · Sacré Cœur · Gare du Nord · AV. DE FLANDRE · Canal de St-Martin
MONCEAU · Parc Monceau · Gare St-Lazare · Gare de l'Est · AV. JEAN JAURÈS
Bois de Boulogne · PORTE MAILLOT · Arc de Triomphe · Pl. Charles de Gaulle Étoile · L'Opéra · HALLES · Belleville Temple
PORTE DAUPHINE · AVENUE FOCH · AVENUE DES CHAMPS ÉLYSÉES · Palais de l'Élysée · Bibliothèque Nationale · Centre Pompidou (Beaubourg) · Musée Picasso · Place de la République
PORTE DE LA MUETTE · Palais de Chaillot (Chaillot Palace) · ÉLYSÉES · Place de la Concorde · Jardin des Tuileries · Musée du Louvre (Louvre Museum) · Hôtel de Ville · LE MARAIS · Place de la Bastille
Tour Eiffel (Eiffel Tower) · Parc du Champ de Mars · INVALIDES · Musée d'Orsay (Orsay Museum) · Assemblée Nationale · Notre Dame · Île de la Cité · Île St-Louis · Opéra Bastille
Maison de Radio France · École Militaire · U.N.E.S.C.O. · QUARTIER LATIN · LUXEMBOURG · Panthéon · Sorbonne · Gare de Lyon

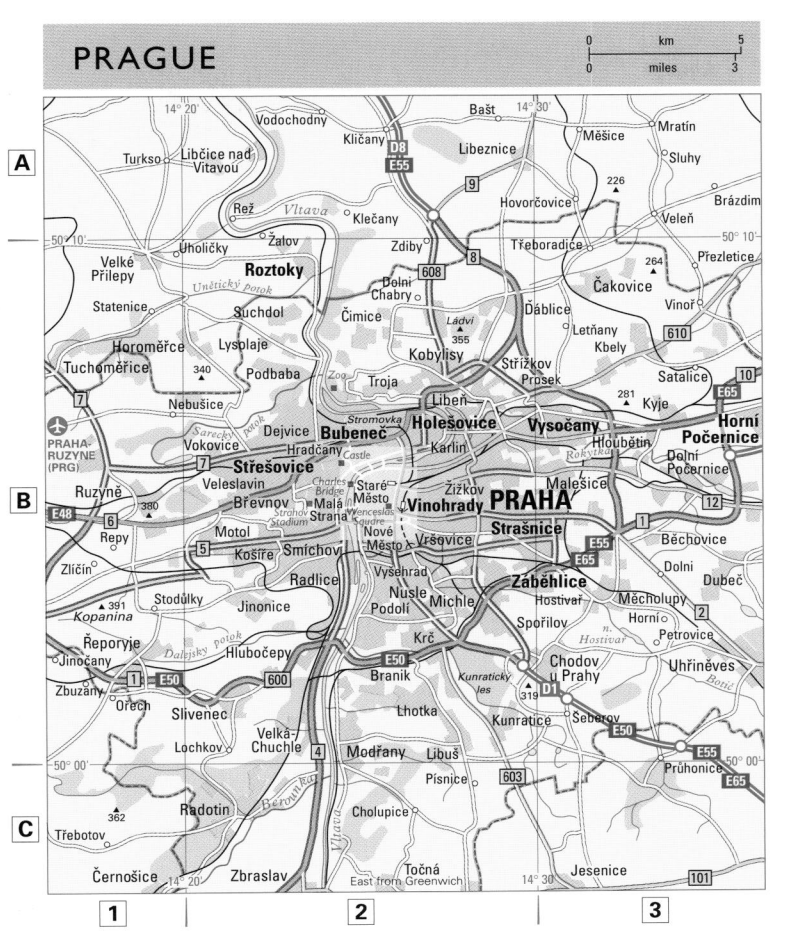

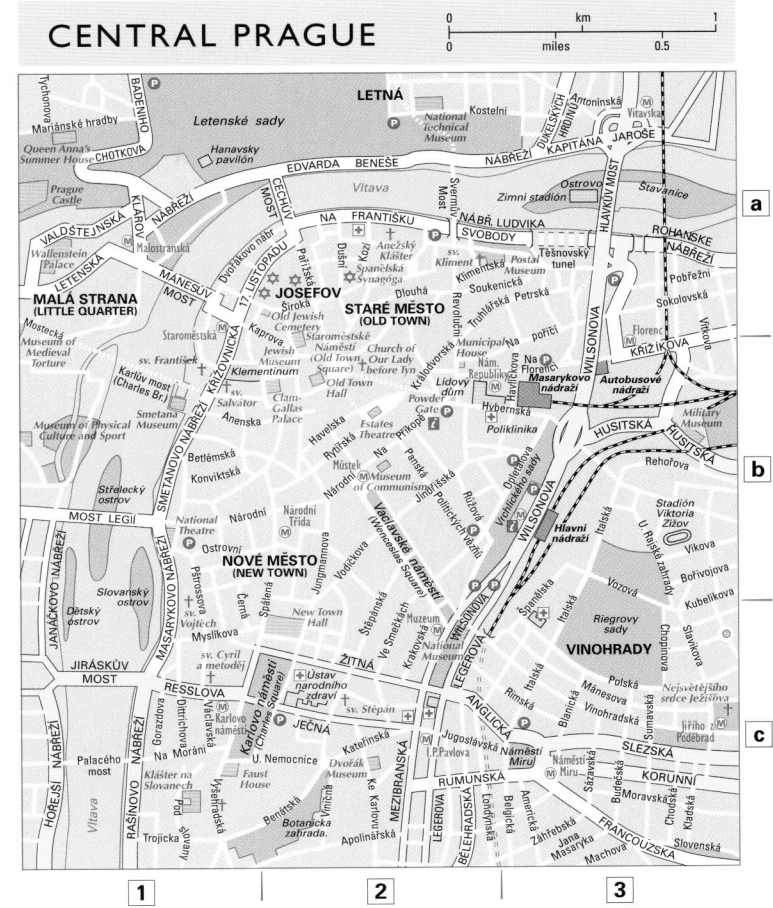

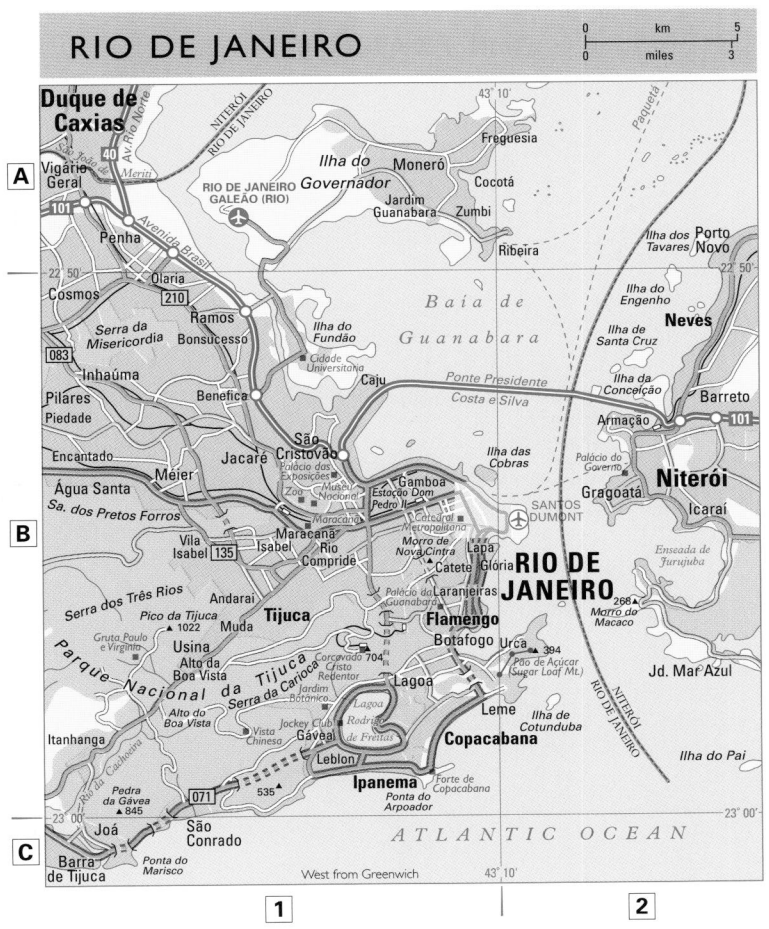

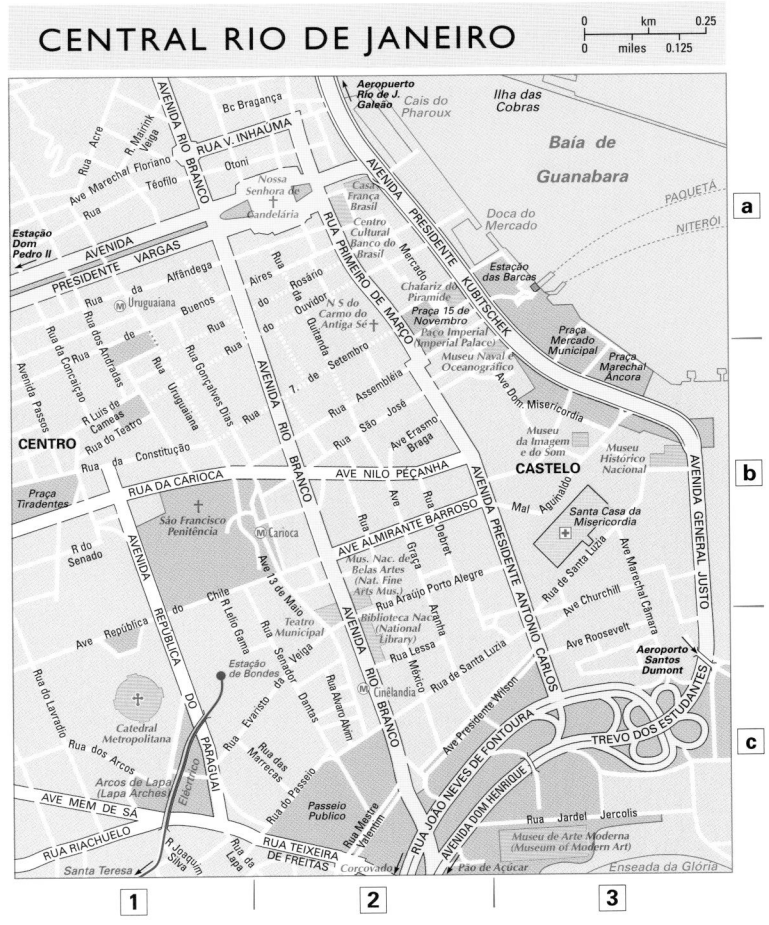

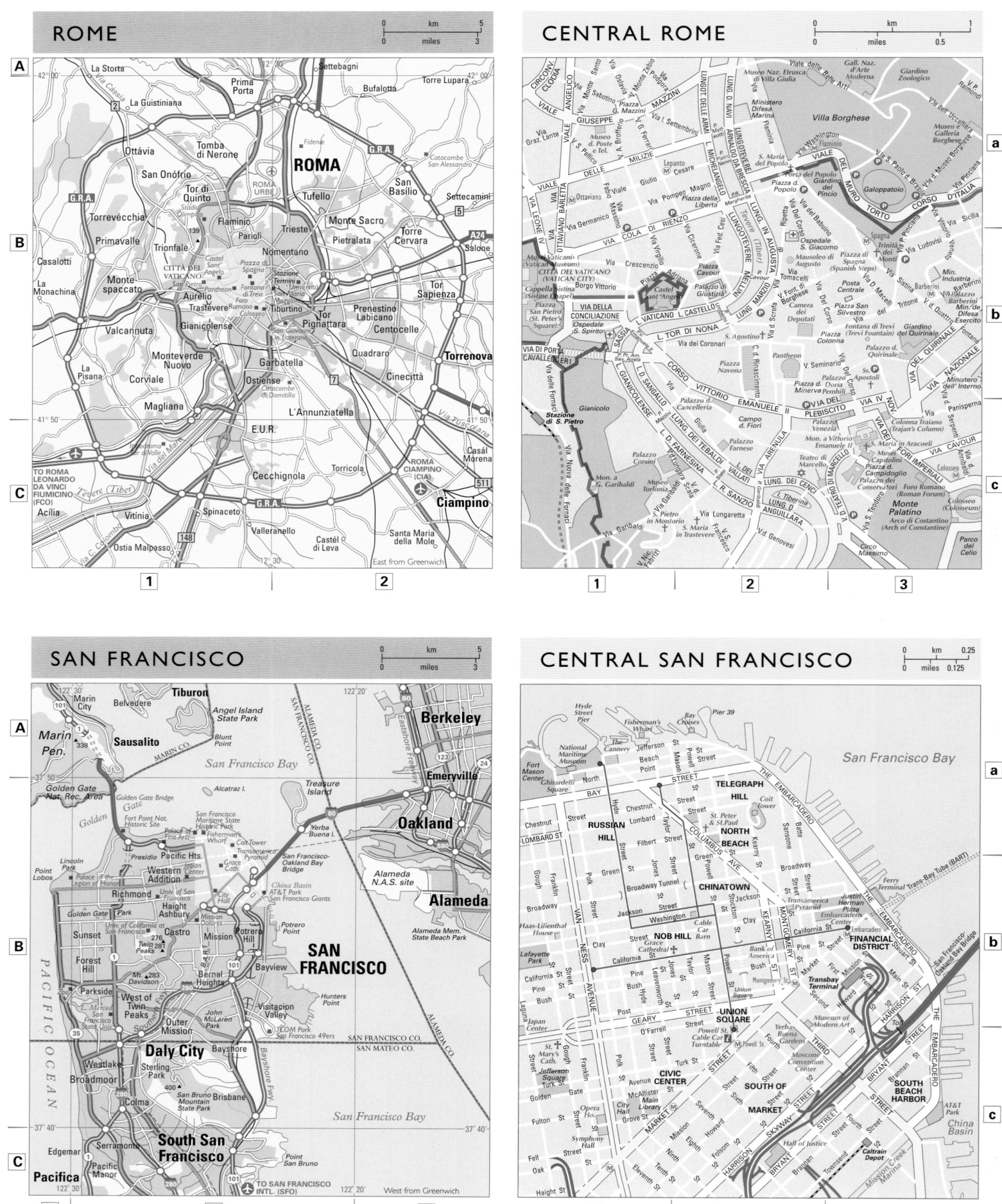

ROME

CENTRAL ROME

SAN FRANCISCO

CENTRAL SAN FRANCISCO

Interstate route numbers   U.S. route numbers   State route numbers

Cable Car route

COPYRIGHT PHILIP'S

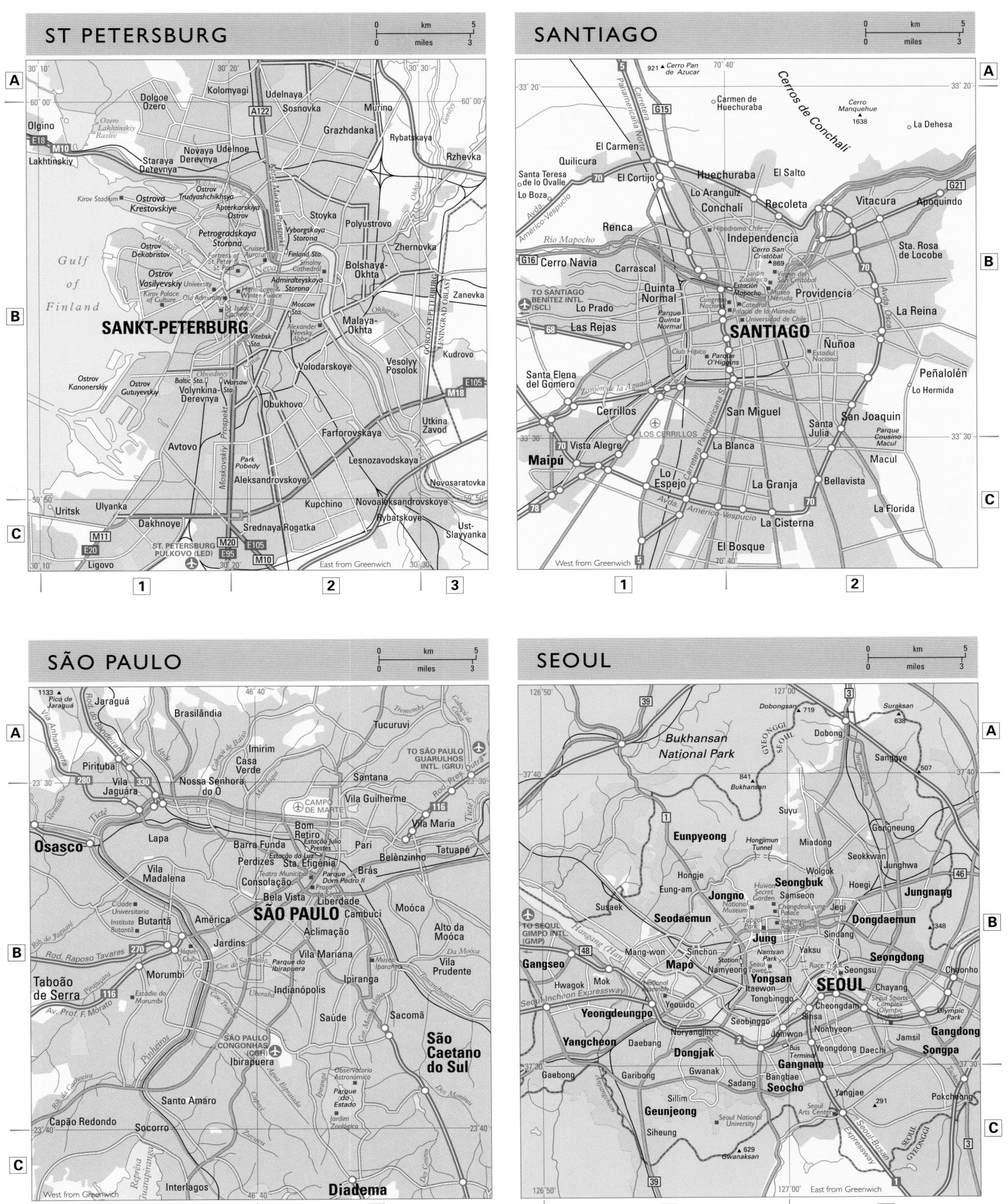

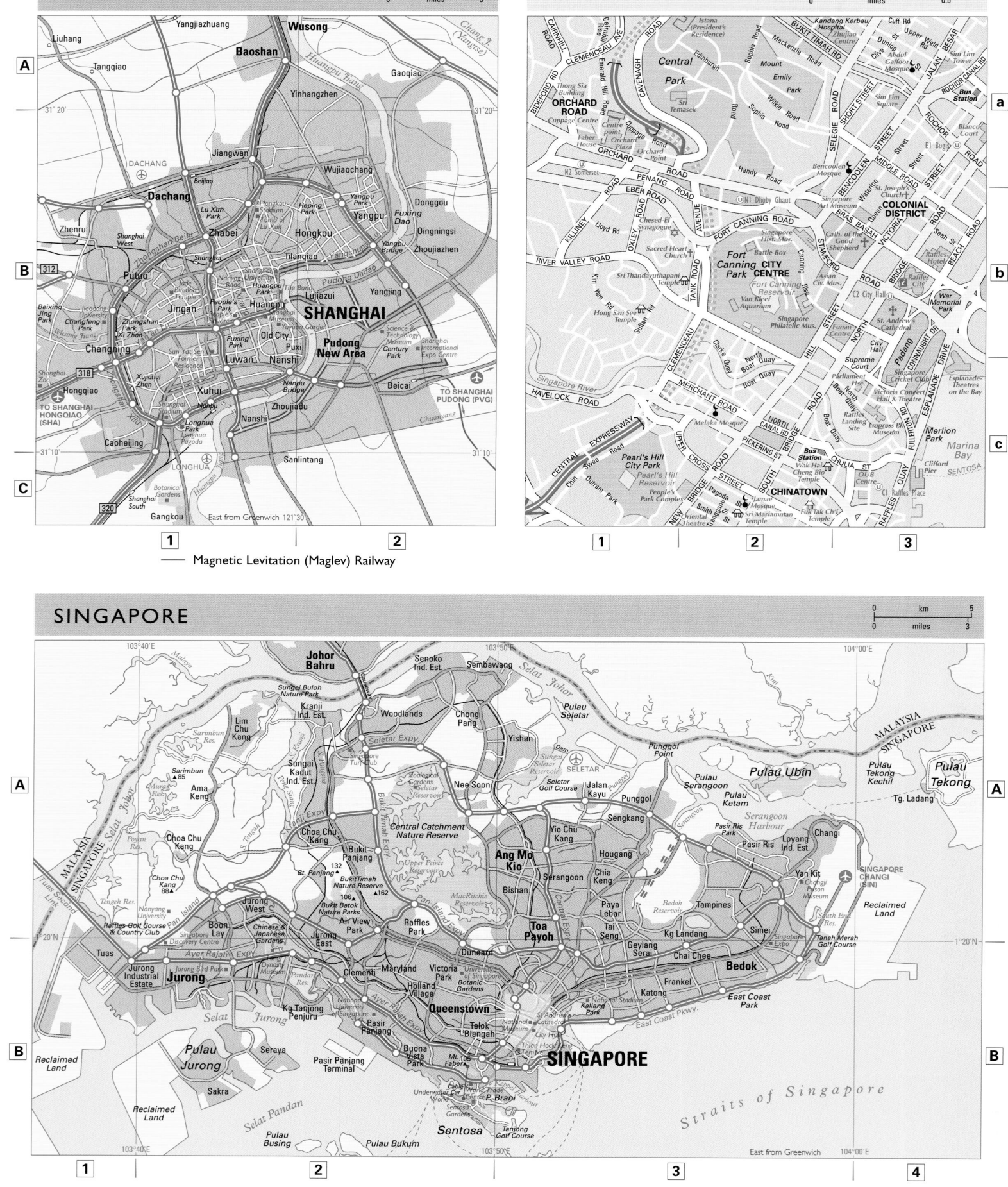

SHANGHAI

km 5 / miles 3

Liuhang
Yangjiazhuang
Wusong
Baoshan
Tangqiao
Gaoqiao
Yinhangzhen
A
31°20'
31°20'
Huangpu Jiang
Chang J. (Yangtse)
Jiangwan
DACHANG
Beijiao
Wujiaochang
Dachang
Hongkou Stadium
Heping Park
Yangpu Park
Yangpu
Donggou
Fuxing Dao
Zhenru
Lu Xun Park
Tomb of Lu Xun
Zhabei
Hongkou
Dingningsi
Shanghai West
Yangpu Bridge
Zhoujiazhen
Putuo
Nanjing University Rd
Huangpu The Bund
Tilangiao
Yangjing
B
312
Shanghai Museum
Pudong Dadao
Beixing Jing Park
Jade Buddha
People's Park
Huangpu
Lujiazui
Changfeng Park
Jingan
Yuyuan Garden
Zhongshan Park
People's Square
SHANGHAI
Xi Zhan
Zhongshan Park
Former Residence
Old City
Puxi
Science Technology Museum
Changning
318
Sun Yat-Sen's Former Residence
Fuxing Park
Luwan
Nanshi
Pudong New Area
Shanghai Century Park
Shanghai International Expo Centre
Shanghai Zhan
Xujiahui Zhan
Xuhui
Nanpu Bridge
Beicai
Hongqiao
TO SHANGHAI HONGQIAO (SHA)
Shanghai Stadium
Nanpu
Zhoujiadu
C
Longhua Park
Longhua Pagoda
Nanshi
TO SHANGHAI PUDONG (PVG)
Chuanyang
31°10'
31°10'
Caoheijing
Sanlintang
320
Shanghai South
Gangkou
Botanical Gardens
LONGHUA
East from Greenwich 121°30'

1 **2**

—— Magnetic Levitation (Maglev) Railway

CENTRAL SINGAPORE

km 1 / miles 0.5

CAIRNHILL ROAD
CLEMENCEAU AVE
Kandang Kerbau Hospital
Istana (President's Residence)
BUKIT TIMAH RD
Cuff Rd
Upper Weld Rd
Sim Lim Tower
A / a
BIDEFORD RD
Thong Sia Building
Emerald Hill
Edinburgh
Sophia Road
Mackenzie Road
Dunlop
Clive
Jalan Besar
Abdul Gaffoor Mosque
ORCHARD ROAD
Cuppage Centre
Centre point
Orchard Plaza
Orchard Point
Mount Emily Park
Wilkie Road
SELEGIE ROAD
SHORT STREET
Sim Lim Square
ROCHOR CANAL RD
Faber House
ORCHARD ROAD
Handy Road
Sophia Road
Bencoolen Mosque
BENCOOLEN
Waterloo
MIDDLE ROAD
Bus Station
Blanco Court
N2 Somerset
PENANG ROAD
EBER ROAD
U1 Dhoby Ghaut
Singapore Art Museum
St. Joseph's Church
BRAS BASAH
COLONIAL DISTRICT
b
KILLINEY ROAD
Chesed-El synagogue
FORT CANNING ROAD
Singapore Hist. Mus.
Cath. of the Good Shepherd
VICTORIA
Seah Rd
Raffles Hotel
BEACH ROAD
RIVER VALLEY ROAD
OXLEY ROAD
Lloyd Rd
Sacred Heart Church
Sri Thandayuthapani Temple
TANK ROAD
Fort Canning Park
Battle Box
Fort Canning Reservoir
Van Kleef Aquarium
Asian Civ. Mus.
CITY CENTRE
STAMFORD ROAD
Funan Centre
NORTH BRIDGE ROAD
C2 City Hall
St. Andrew's Cathedral
Raffles City
War Memorial Park
Kim
Yen
Hong San See Temple
Sultan Rd
Singapore Philatelic Mus.
CANNING
City Hall
Supreme Court
Padang
Singapore Cricket Club
CONNAUGHT DRIVE
Esplanade-Theatres on the Bay
CLEMENCEAU
Clarke Quay
Parliament Hse.
North Boat Quay
South Boat Quay
Victoria Concert Hall & Theatre
Express Mus.
Singapore River
MERCHANT ROAD
HILL STREET
Raffles Landing Site
Boat Quay
Merlion Park
HAVELOCK ROAD
Melaka Mosque
NORTH CANAL RD
SOUTH CANAL RD
PICKERING ST
Boat Quay
Fullerton Rd
Marina Bay
c
CENTRAL EXPRESSWAY
Pearl's Hill City Park
UPPER CROSS ROAD
NEW BRIDGE ROAD
SOUTH BRIDGE ROAD
Bus Station
Wak Hai Cheng Bio Temple
CHULIA ST
Fullerton Rd
OUB Centre
RAFFLES QUAY
Clifford Pier
SENTOSA
Swee Road
Chin
Outram Park
Pearl's Hill Reservoir
People's Park Complex
Pagoda St
PAGODA
Jamae Mosque
Sri Mariamman Temple
CHINATOWN
Fuk Tak Ch'i Temple
C1 Raffles Place
Oriental Theatre

1 **2** **3**

SINGAPORE

km 5 / miles 3

103°40'E
Malaysia
103°50'E
Selat Johor
104°00'E
Johor Bahru
Senoko Ind. Est.
Sembawang
Pulau Seletar
MALAYSIA
SINGAPORE
Sungai Buloh Nature Park
Kranji Ind. Est.
Woodlands
Chong Pang
Yishun
Punggol Point
Pulau Tekong Kechil
Pulau Tekong
Sarimbun Res.
Lim Chu Kang
Sungai Kadut Ind. Est.
Seletar Expy.
Singapore Turf Club
Upper Seletar Reservoir
Dam
SELETAR
Punggol
A
Sarimbun 85
Ama Keng
Sungai Seletar
Jurong Canal
Gardens Seletar Reservoir
Seletar Golf Course
Jalan Kayu
Pulau Serangoon
Pulau Ubin
Pulau Ketam
Pulau Tekong
Poyan Res.
Choa Chu Kang
Sungei Tengeh
Nee Soon
Serangoon
Tg. Ladang
Tengeh Res.
Black Timah Expy.
Central Catchment Nature Reserve
Sengkang
Pasir Ris Park
Serangoon Harbour
Changi
Nanyang University
Choa Chu Kang
Bukit Panjang
Upper Peirce Reservoir
Yio Chu Kang
Hougang
Chia Keng
Pasir Ris
Loyang Ind. Est.
Choa Chu Kang 88
Bt. Panjang 132
BukitPanjang Nature Reserve
Bukit Timah 162 Nature Reserve
MacRitchie Reservoir
Ang Mo Kio
Bishan
Serangoon
Paya Lebar
Tai Seng
Kg Landang
Bedok Reservoir
Tampines
SINGAPORE CHANGI (SIN)
Changi Prison Museum
Reclaimed Land
Jurong West
Boon Lay
Raffles Golf Course & Country Club
Singapore Discovery Centre
Chinese & Japanese Gardens
Jurong Bird Park
Air View Park
Raffles Park
Pan-Island Expy.
Dunearn
Toa Payoh
Geylang Serai
Chai Chee
Simei
Tanah Merah Golf Course
1°20'N
Tuas
Jurong Industrial Estate
Jurong
Ayer Rajah Expy.
Jurong East
Dynoo Museum
Pandan Res.
Clementi
Maryland
Holland Village
Victoria Park
University of Singapore
Singapore Botanic Gardens
Bedok
Frankel
Katong
National Stadium
East Coast Park
South East Res.
Singapore Expo
1°20'N
Pulau Damar Laut
Kg Tanjong Penjuru
National University of Singapore
Pasir Panjang
Pasir Panjang Terminal
Buona Vista Park
Queenstown
Telok Blangah
Mt. 105 Faber
Kallang Park
East Coast Pkwy.
B
Reclaimed Land
Pulau Jurong
Seraya
Sakra
Pasir Panjang
Mt. 105 Faber
Global Sentosa World Trade Centre
Underwater World Car
SINGAPORE
St. Andrew's
Thian Hock Keng Temple
City Hall
National Mus.
B
Selat Jurong
Reclaimed Land
Selat Pandan
Pulau Busing
Pulau Bukum
P. Brani
Sentosa
Sentosa Gardens
Tanjong Golf Course
103°50'E
Straits of Singapore
East from Greenwich
104°00'E

1 **2** **3** **4**

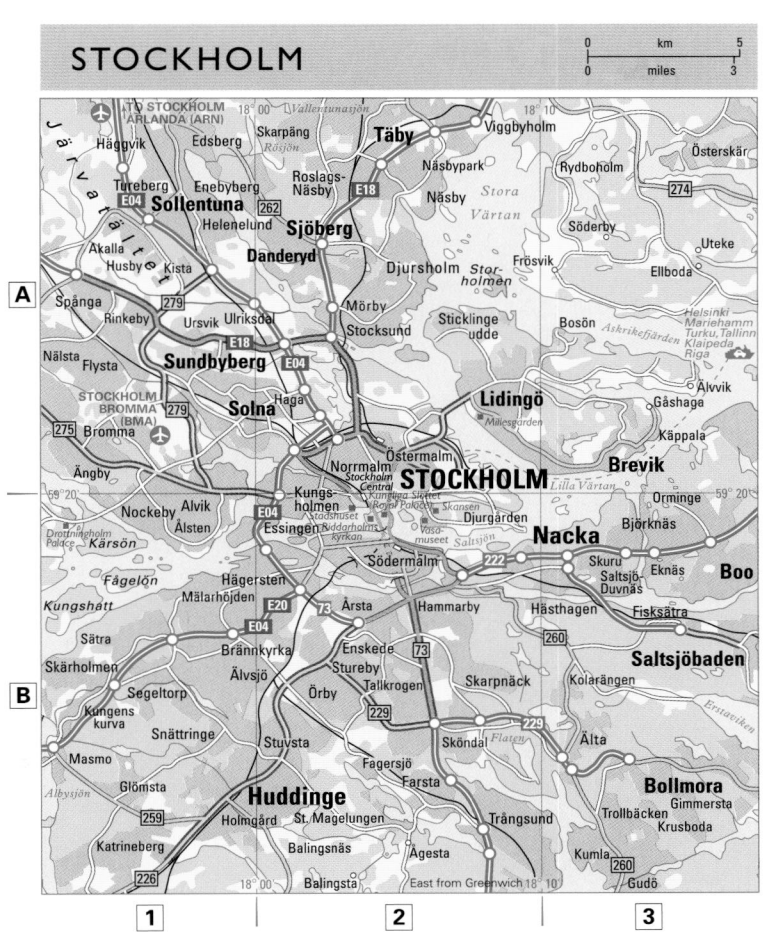

STOCKHOLM

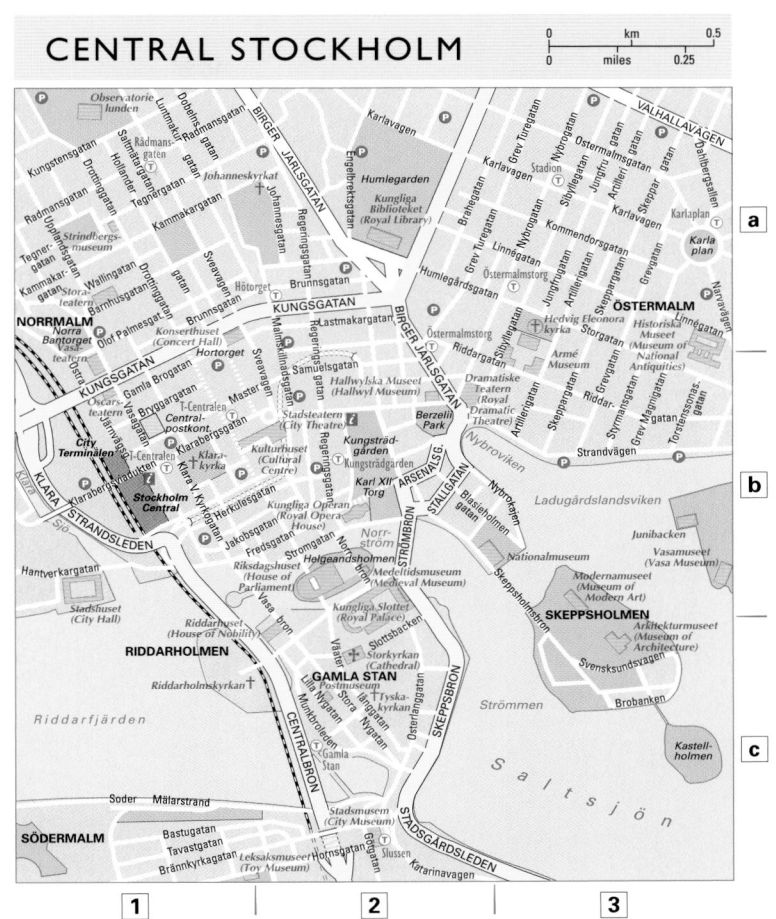

CENTRAL STOCKHOLM

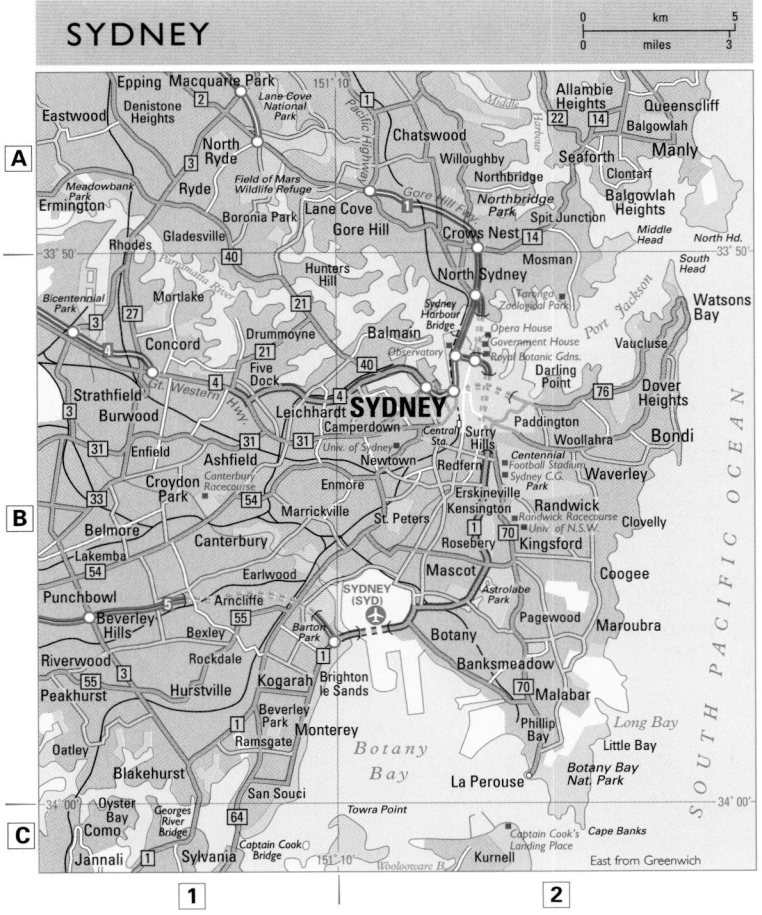

SYDNEY

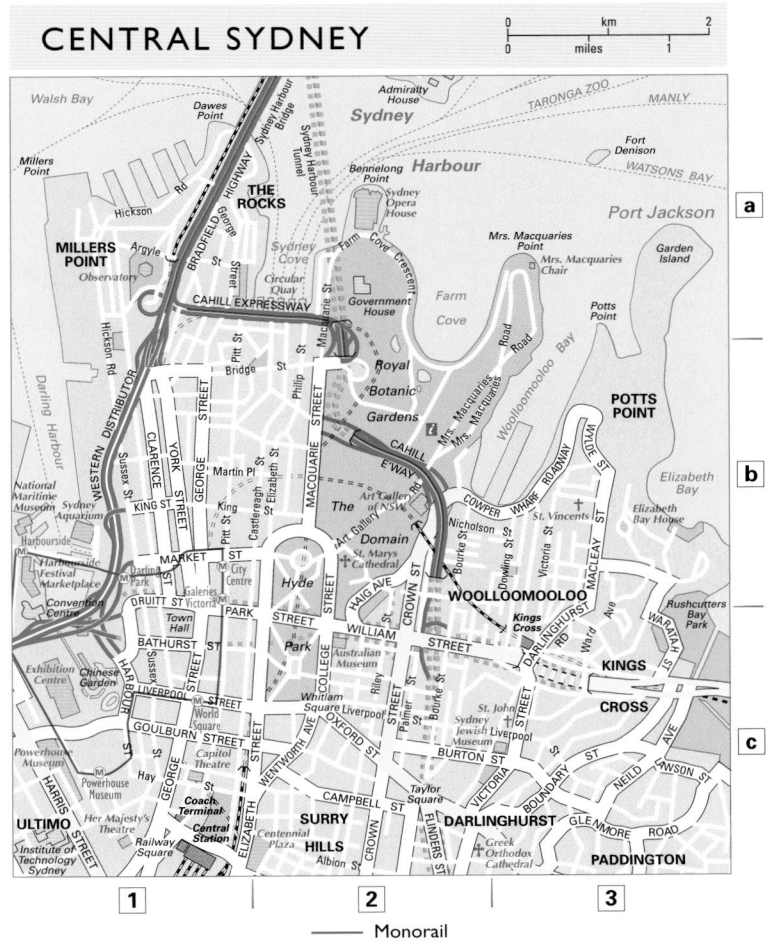

CENTRAL SYDNEY

— Monorail

COPYRIGHT PHILIP'S

TOKYO

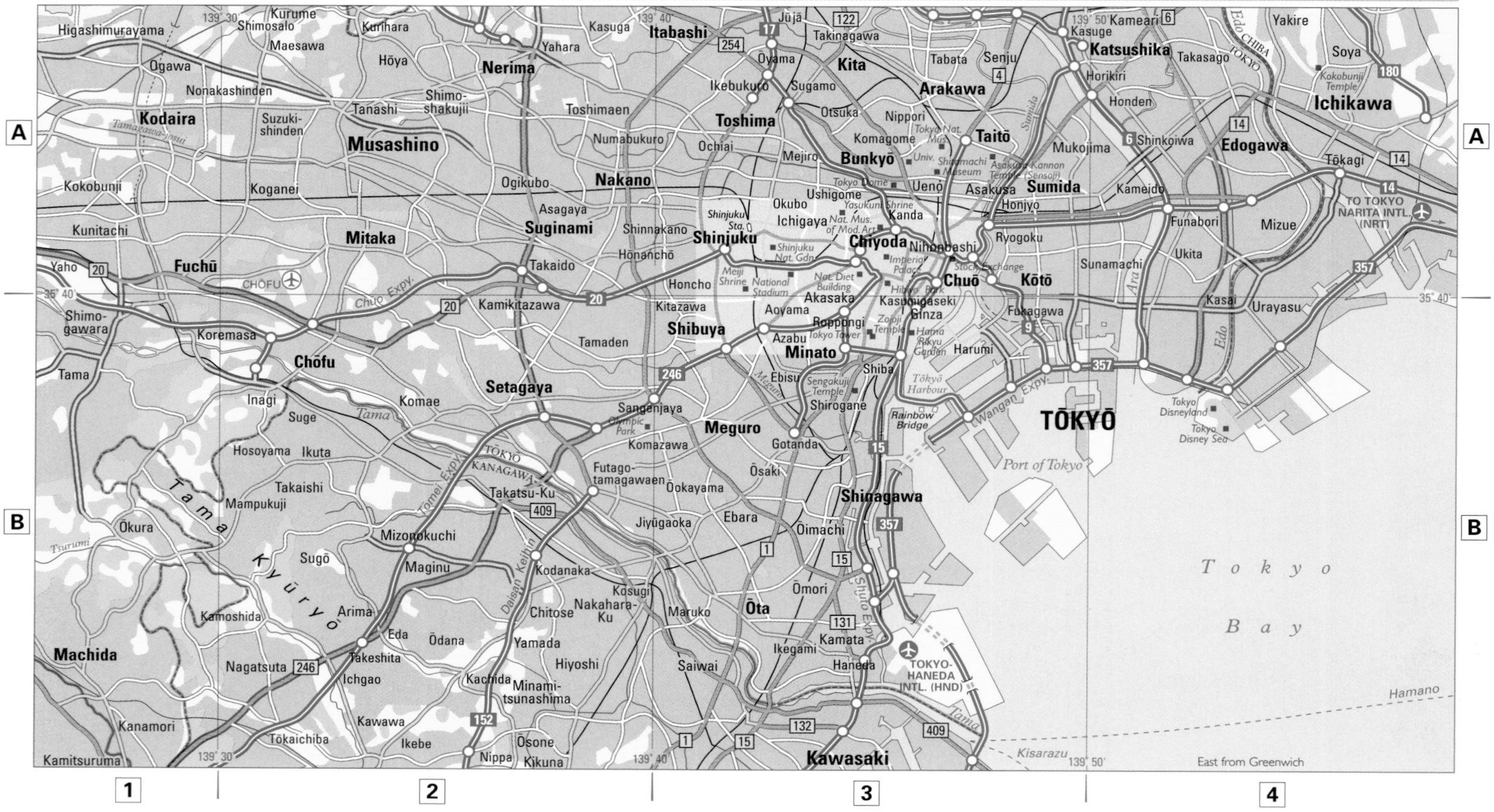

km 5
miles 3

Higashimurayama · Kurume · Shimosalo · Kasuga · Itabashi · Jūjō · 122 · 139 50 Kameari · 6 · Yakire
Kuribara · Takinogawa · Kasuge · Katsushika · Takasago · Soya
Ogawa · Maesawa · Yahara · Kita · Tabata · Senju · Horikiri · Honden · Kokubunji Temple · 180
Nonakashinden · Hōya · Shimo-shakujii · Ōyama · 254 · Ikebukuro · Sugamo · Otsuka · Arakawa · Nippori · Mukojima · Shinkoiwa · 14 · Ichikawa
Kodaira · Suzuki-shinden · Nerima · Toshimaen · Numabukuro · Toshima · Mejiro · Ochiai · Komagome · Taitō · 14 · Edogawa · Tōkagi · 14
Musashino · Nakano · Asagaya · Shinnakano · Ōkubo · Ushigome · Ueno · Asakusa · Sumida · Kameido · Mizue
Mitaka · Suginami · Takaido · Honchō · Shinjuku · Ichigaya · Chiyoda · Nihonbashi · Ryogoku · Honjo · Funabori · NRT TO TOKYO NARITA INTL
Fuchū · 20 · CHOFU · Kamikitazawa · 20 · Kitazawa · Akasaka · Kasumigaseki · Chūō · Kōtō · 357
Shimo-gawara · Koremasa · Shibuya · Aoyama · Roppongi · Ginza · Fukagawa · Kasai · Urayasu
Tama · Chōfu · Komae · Tamaden · Minato · Ebisu · Shiba · Harumi · TŌKYŌ · Tokyo Disneyland · Tokyo Disney Sea
Inagi · Setagaya · Sangenjaya · Meguro · Shirogane · Rainbow Bridge · Tōkyō Harbour · Port of Tokyo
Hosoyama · Ikuta · Komazawa · Gotanda · 15
Takaishi · Mizonokuchi · Futago-tamagawaen · Ōokayama · Ōsaki
Mampukuji · Maginu · Jiyūgaoka · Ebara · Shinagawa
Okura · Sugō · Kodanaka · Ōimachi · 357 · Tokyo Bay
Kamoshida · Arima · Eda · Chitose · Nakahara-Ku · Maruko · Ōmori · 15
Machida · Takeshita · Ōdana · Yamada · Hiyoshi · Ikegami · Kamata · Ōta
Nagatsuta · 246 · Ichgao · Kachida · Minami-tsunashima · Saiwai · Haneda · TOKYO-HANEDA INTL (HND)
Kanamori · 152 · Ikebe · Kawawa · 131
Kamitsuruma · Tōkaichiba · Nippa · Kikuna · Kusazu · Kawasaki · Hamano · Kisarazu · East from Greenwich

CENTRAL TOKYO

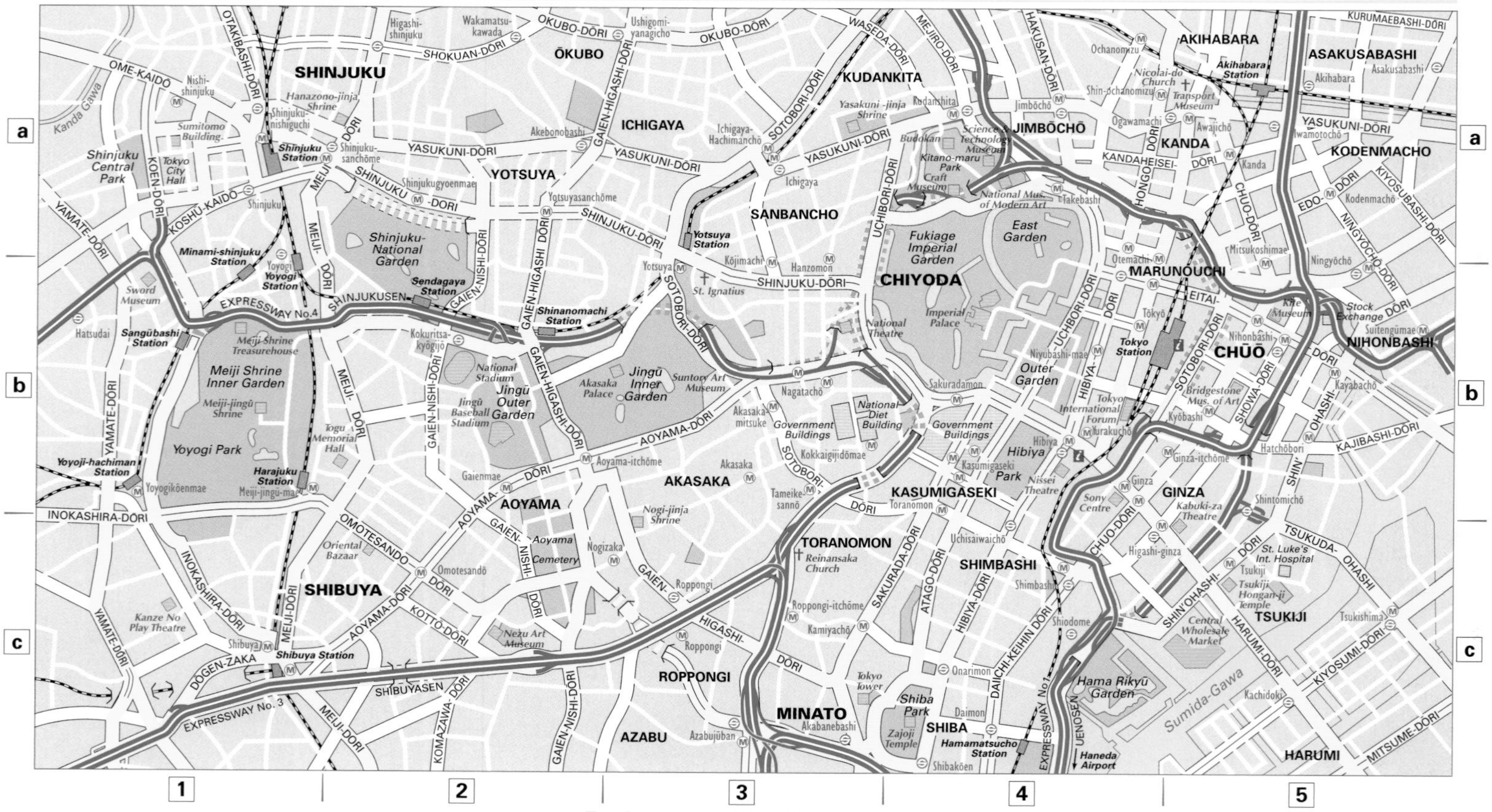

km 0.5
miles 0.25

Toei Subway
Tokyo Metro

COPYRIGHT PHILIP'S

TEHRAN

km 5
miles 3

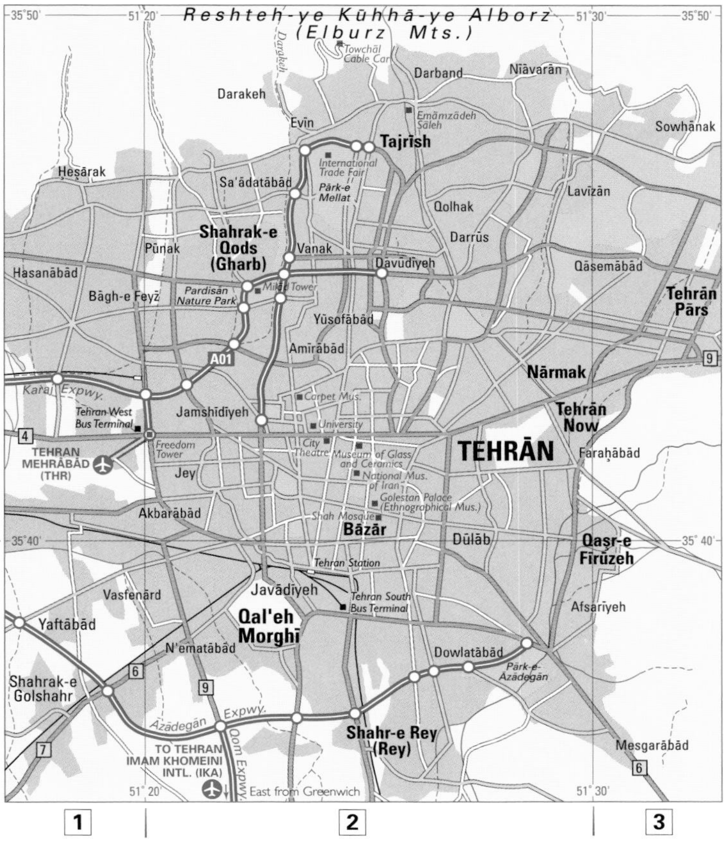

Reshteh-ye Kūhhā-ye Alborz
(Elburz Mts.)

35°50' 51°20' 51°30' 35°50'

Towchāl Cable Car
Darband
Darakeh
Niāvarān
Sowhānak
Evīn
Emāmzādeh Sāleh
Tajrīsh
International Trade Fair
Pārk-e Mellat
Sa'ādatābād
Qolhak
Lavīzān
Heşārak
Shahrak-e Qods (Gharb)
Vanak
Darrūs
Qāsemābād
Pūnak
Davūdīyeh
Tehrān Pārs
Hasanābād
Pardīsan Nature Park
Yūsofābād
A
Bāgh-e Feyż
Mīlād Tower
Amīrābād
A01
Nārmak
Karaj Expwy.
Jamshīdīyeh
Carpet Mus.
University
Tehrān Now
9
Tehrān West Bus Terminal
Freedom Tower
City Theatre
Museum of Glass and Ceramics
National Mus. of Iran
TEHRĀN
Farahābād
4
TEHRAN MEHRĀBĀD (THR)
Jey
Golestan Palace (Ethnographical Mus.)
Akbarābād
Shah Mosque
Bāzār
Dūlāb
Qaşr-e Fīrūzeh
35°40' 35°40'
Tehran Station
Vasfenārd
Javādīyeh
Tehran South Bus Terminal
Afsarīyeh
Yaftābād
Qal'eh Morghi
N'ematābād
Dowlatābād
Pārk-e Āzādegān
B
6
9
Shahrak-e Golshahr
Āzādegān Expwy.
Dowlatābād
7
Shahr-e Rey (Rey)
Mesgarābād
TO TEHRAN IMAM KHOMEINI INTL. (IKA)
Qom Expwy.
6
51°20' East from Greenwich 51°30'

1   **2**   **3**

CENTRAL TORONTO

km 0.5
miles 0.25

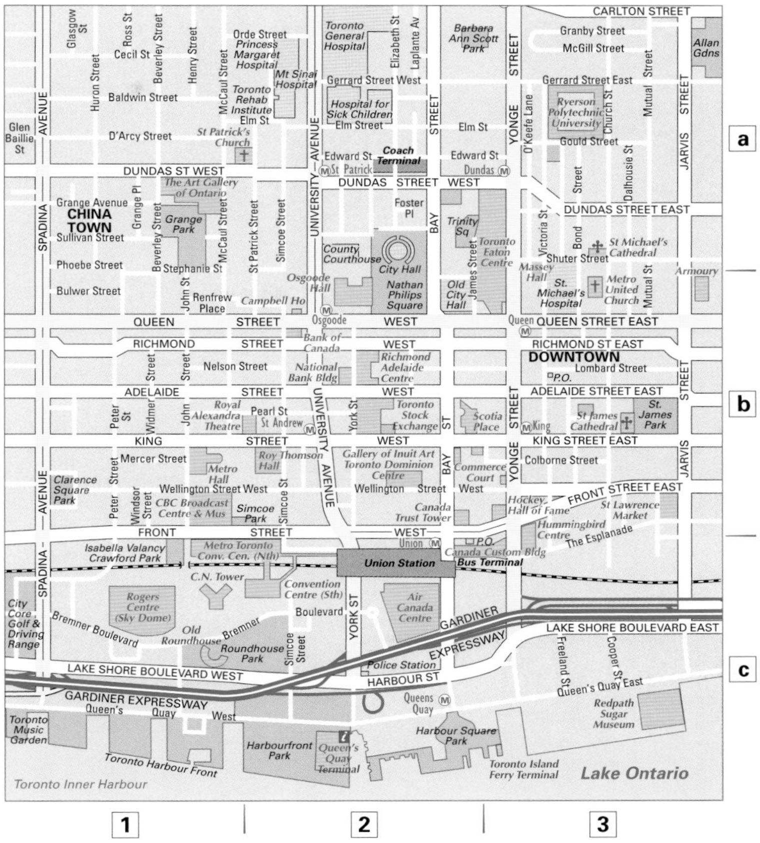

CARLTON STREET
Glasgow St
Ross St
Cecil St
Orde Street
Toronto General Hospital
Granby Street
McGill Street
Allan Gdns
Beverley Street
Princess Margaret Hospital
Elizabeth St
Laplante Av
Barbara Ann Scott Park
Huron Street
Henry Street
McCaul Street
Gerrard Street West
Mt Sinai Hospital
Gerrard Street East
Baldwin Street
Toronto Rehab Institute
Hospital for Sick Children
STREET
Ryerson Polytechnic University
Glen Baillie St
D'Arcy Street
St Patrick's Church
Elm St
Elm St
YONGE
O'Keefe Lane
Gould Street
Edward St
Coach Terminal
Edward St
a
Grange Avenue
CHINA TOWN
DUNDAS ST WEST
DUNDAS
STREET
WEST
DUNDAS STREET EAST
The Art Gallery of Ontario
Grange Pl
Foster Pl
Trinity Sq
Victoria
Bond
St Michael's Cathedral
SPADINA
Sullivan Street
Grange Park
Beverley Street
McCaul Street
St Patrick Street
Simcoe Street
County Courthouse
City Hall
Toronto Eaton Centre
Mutual
Phoebe Street
Stephanie St
Osgoode Hall
Nathan Phillips Square
Old City Hall
St. Michael's Hospital
Metro United Church
Massey Hall
Armoury
Bulwer Street
John St
Renfrew Place
Campbell Ho
AVENUE
QUEEN
STREET
WEST
Osgoode
QUEEN STREET EAST
Bank of Canada
RICHMOND
STREET
WEST
National Bank Bldg
Richmond Adelaide Centre
RICHMOND ST EAST
Lombard Street
DOWNTOWN
P.O.
Nelson Street
ADELAIDE
STREET
WEST
UNIVERSITY
Peter St
Widmer St
Royal Alexandra Theatre
Pearl St
St Andrew
Toronto Stock Exchange
YORK ST
Scotia Place
ADELAIDE STREET EAST
JARVIS
St King
St James Cathedral
St James Park
KING
STREET
Mercer Street
John Street
Metro Hall
Roy Thomson Hall
BAY
Commerce Court West
YONGE
KING STREET EAST
Clarence Square Park
Peter Street
Windsor Street
Wellington Street West
Simcoe Street
Gallery of Inuit Art Toronto Dominion Centre
Wellington St
Colborne Street
AVENUE
CBC Broadcast Centre & Mus
Hockey Hall of Fame
Canada Trust Tower
FRONT STREET EAST
FRONT
STREET
WEST
Hummingbird Centre
St Lawrence Market
Isabella Valancy Crawford Park
Metro Toronto Conv. Cen. (Nth)
Union Station
P.O.
Canada Custom Bldg
The Esplanade
SPADINA
City Core Golf & Driving Range
Rogers Centre (Sky Dome)
Bremner Boulevard
C.N. Tower
Old Roundhouse
Convention Centre (Sth)
Boulevard
Air Canada Centre
Bus Terminal
LAKE SHORE BOULEVARD EAST
c
Bremner
Simcoe Street
YORK ST
Police Station
GARDINER
Freeland St
Cooper St
Roundhouse Park
EXPRESSWAY
Queen's Quay East
Redpath Sugar Museum
LAKE SHORE BOULEVARD WEST
HARBOUR ST
Toronto Music Garden
GARDINER EXPRESSWAY
Queen's Quay
Queens Quay
West
Harbourfront Park
Queen's Quay Terminal
Harbour Square Park
Toronto Harbour Front
Toronto Island Ferry Terminal
Lake Ontario
Toronto Inner Harbour

1   **2**   **3**

TORONTO

km 5
miles 3

79°40' 79°30' 79°20' 79°10'
Boyd Conservation Area
7
407
Metro Toronto Zoo
401
Fairport
Thornhill
The Promenade
East Don
Brown
Glen Rouge Park
West Rouge
Rouge Hill
Vaughan
Concord
Markham
27
Pine Grove
7
Edgeley
Newtonbrook
48
Port Union
Woodbridge
407
Fisherville
11
Willowdale
Agincourt
Malvern
401
Highland Creek
2A
Humber Summit
York University
G. Ross Lord Park
East Don Parkland
404
Fairview Mall
Morningside Park
Black Creek Pioneer Village
Northmount
Scarborough Town Centre
Woburn
West Hill
Beaumonde Heights
Northwood Park
North York
Lansing
401
Bendale
Thistletown
400
DOWNSVIEW C.A.F.B.
Armour Heights
York Mills
Wexford
Scarborough
2
Eastpoint Park
A
Humberwood Park
427
Woodbine Centre
Kipling Heights
Downsview
Lawrence Heights
Don Mills
Cliffside
Malton
Rexdale
Humberlea
401
Yorkdale Shopping Centre
York Univ. Glendon
Wilket Creek Park
Sunnybrook Health Science Centre
Ontario Science Centre
Danforth
Bluffers Park
Woodbine Race Track
27
Weston
11A
Forest Hill
Leaside
Thorncliffe
409
Cedarvale Park
Dentonia Park
Scarborough Bluffs
401
11
York
East York
Birch Cliff
TORONTO LESTER B. PEARSON INTL. (YYZ)
Humber Valley Village
Mount Dennis
Casa Loma
Kew Gardens
2
43°40' 43°40'
410
Hanlon
Lambton Mills
Swansea
Royal Ontario Museum
Riverdale Park
Ashbridge's Bay Park
401
Etobicoke
Kingsway
High Park
University of Toronto
Parliament Buildings
B
Islington
Old City Hall
C.N. Tower & Rogers Centre
Old Fort York
Union Stn
Tommy Thompson Park
TORONTO
Markland Wood
427
Humber Bay
Parkdale
Exhibition Place
TORONTO CITY CENTRE (ISLAND)
Toronto Harbour
403
Burnhamthorpe
Summerville
5
Humber Bay Park
Ontario Place
Toronto Islands
LAKE ONTARIO
10
Mimico
Gibraltar Point
Square One
Dixie
New Toronto
Humber College
Samuel Smith Park
Mississauga
Cooksville
Long Branch
79°40' 79°30' 79°20' West from Greenwich 79°10'

1   **2**   **3**   **4**

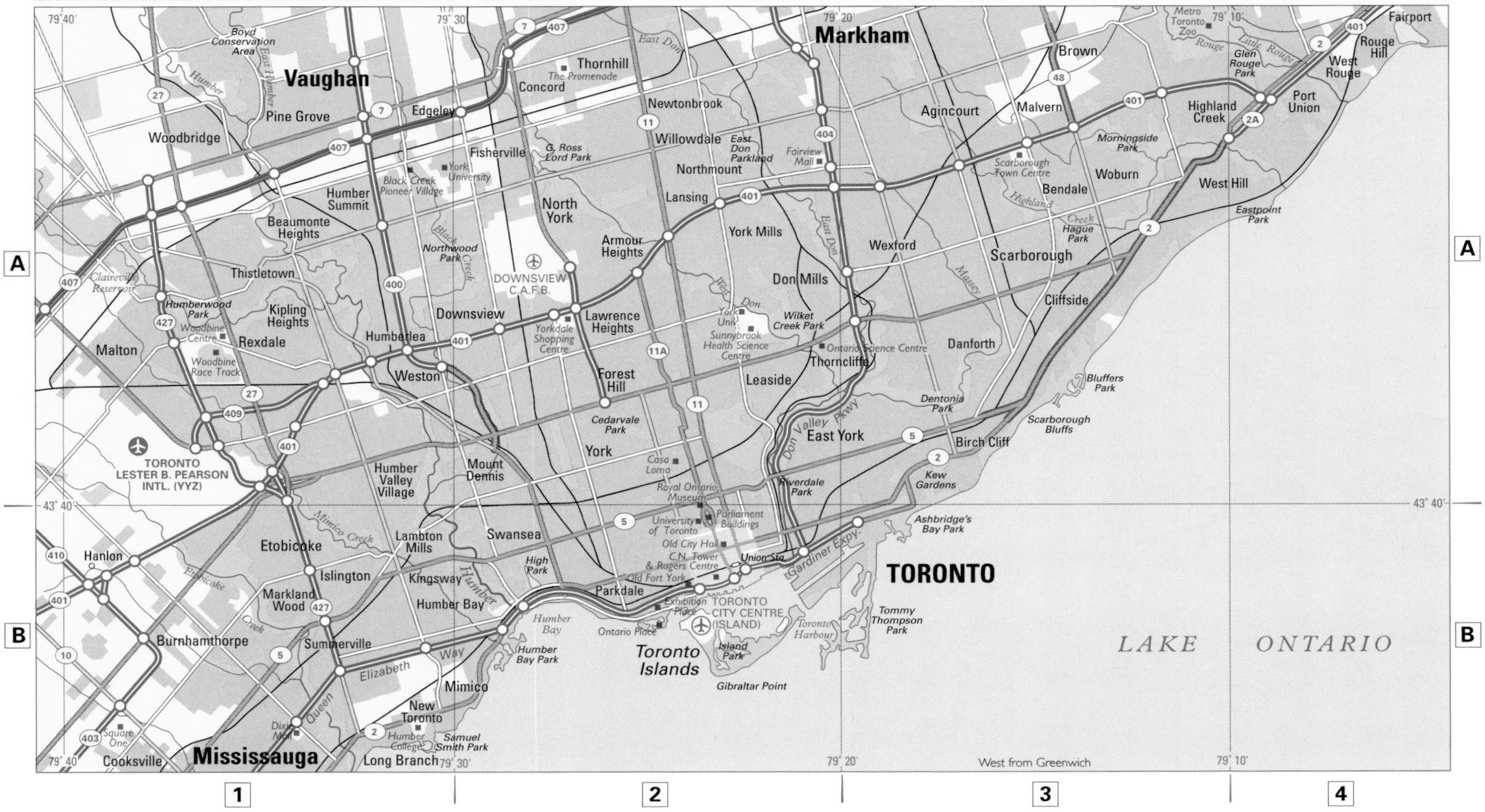

(427) Provincial route numbers

32 VIENNA, WARSAW

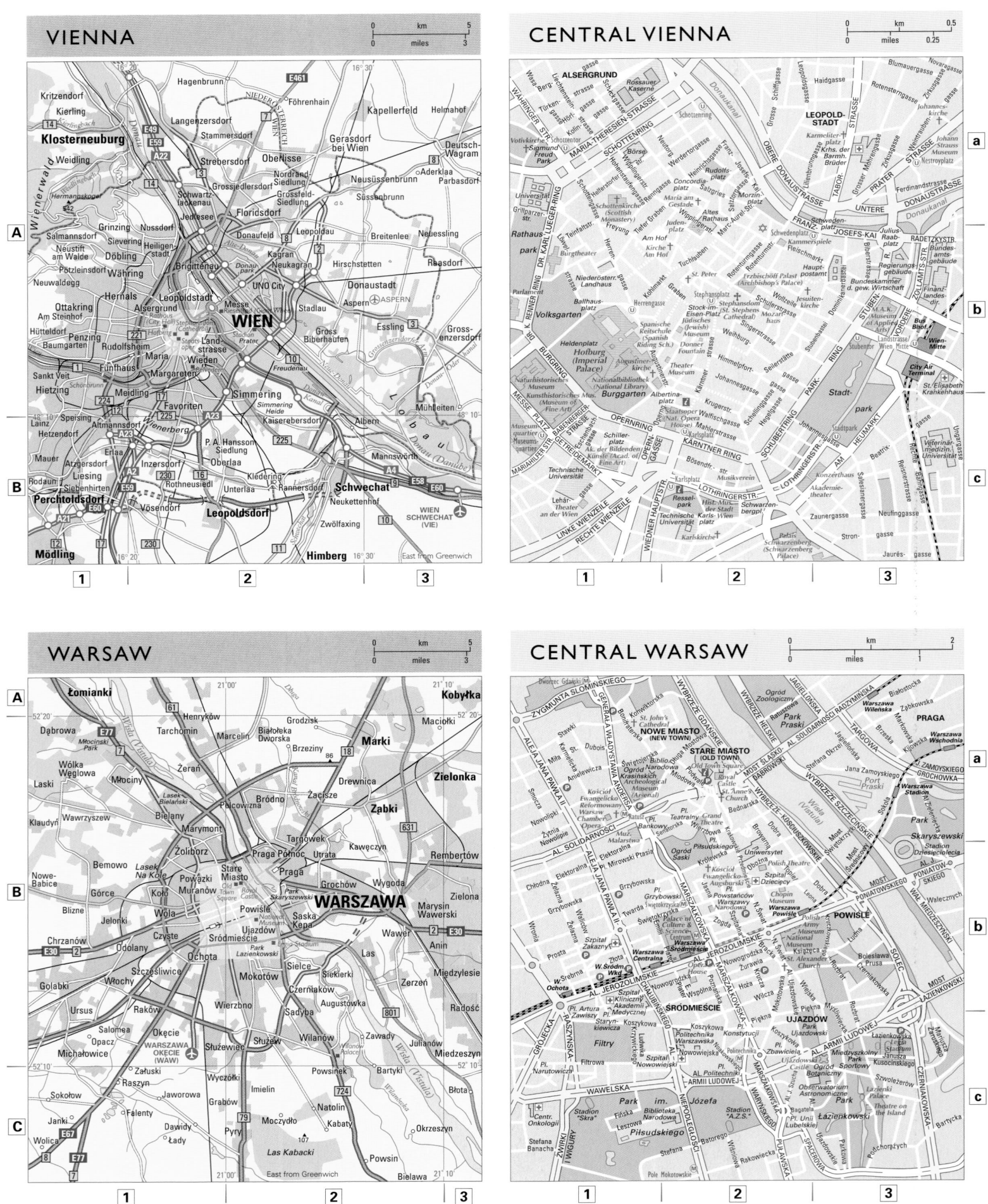

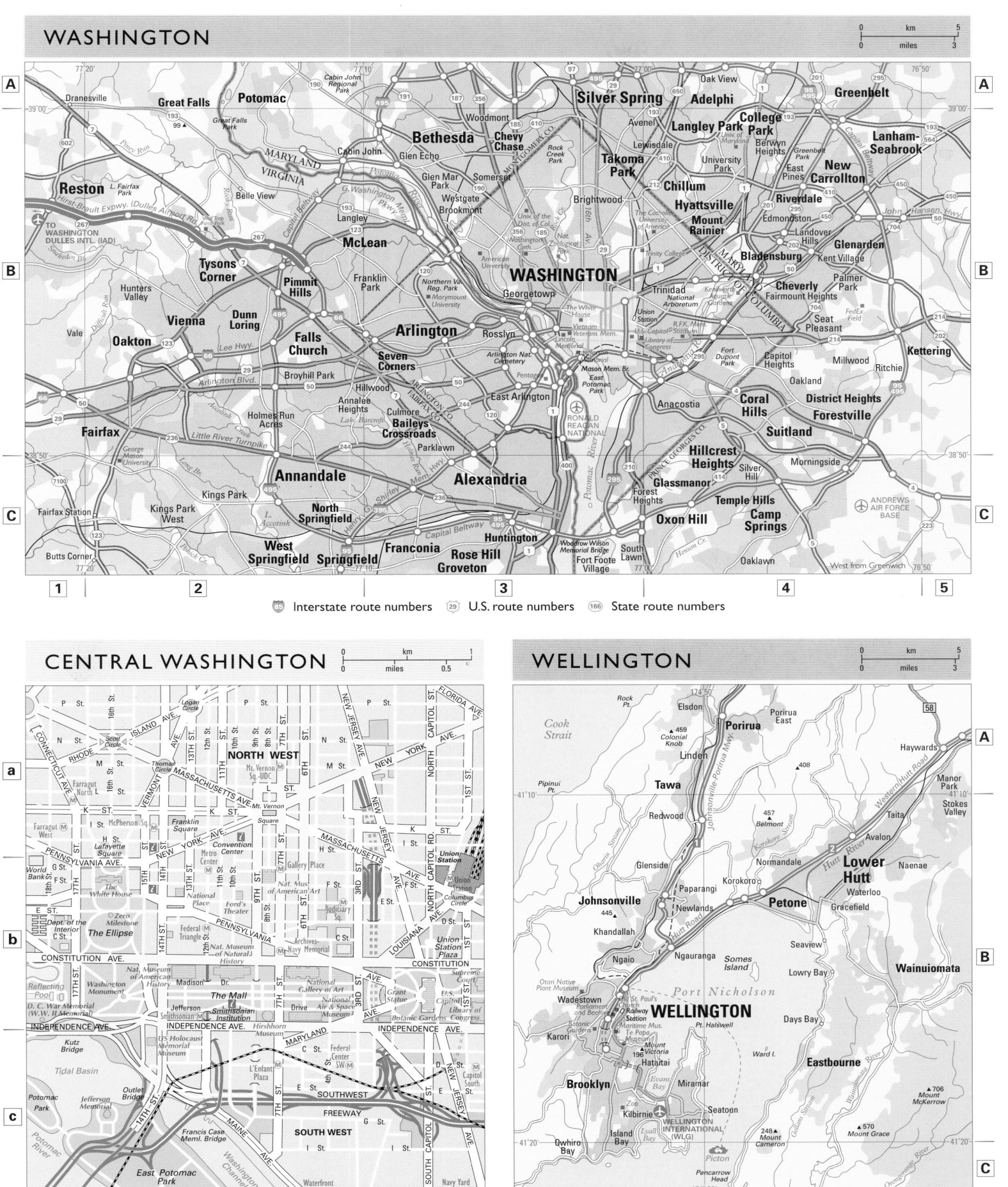

INDEX TO CITY MAPS

The index contains the names of all the principal places and features shown on the City Maps. Each name is followed by an additional entry in italics giving the name of the City Map within which it is located.

The number in bold type which follows each name refers to the number of the City Map page where that feature or place will be found.

The letter and figure which are immediately after the page number give the grid square on the map within which the feature or place is situated.

The letter represents the latitude and the figure the longitude. The full geographic reference is provided in the border of the City Maps.

The location given is the centre of the city, suburb or feature and is not necessarily the name. Rivers, canals and roads are indexed to their name. Rivers carry the symbol → after their name.

An explanation of the alphabetical order rules and a list of the abbreviations used are to be found at the beginning of the World Map Index.

A

Aalām *Baghdad* **3** B2
Abbey Wood *London* **15** B4
Abcoude *Amsterdam* **2** B2
Ābdīn *Cairo* **7** A2
Abeno *Osaka* **23** B2
Aberdeen *Hong Kong* **12** B1
Aberdour *Edinburgh* **11** A2
Aberdour Castle *Edinburgh* **11** A2
Abfanggraben → *Munich* **21** A3
Ablon-sur-Seine *Paris* **24** B3
Abramtsevo *Moscow* **19** B3
Abu Dis *Jerusalem* **13** B2
Abû en Numrus *Cairo* **7** B2
Abu Ghosh *Jerusalem* **13** B1
Acassuso *Buenos Aires* **7** A1
Accotink, L. *Washington* **33** C2
Accotink Cr. → *Washington* **33** B2
Achères *Paris* **24** A1
Acilia *Rome* **26** C1
Aclimação *São Paulo* **27** B2
Acropolis *Athens* **2** B2
Acton *London* **15** A2
Açúcar, Pão de *Rio de Janeiro* **25** B2
Ada Beja *Lisbon* **16** A1
Adams Park *Atlanta* **3** B2
Addiscombe *London* **15** B3
Adelphi *Washington* **33** A4
Aderklaa *Vienna* **32** A3
Adler Planetarium *Chicago* **9** B3
Admiralteyskaya Storona *St. Petersburg* **27** B2
Affori *Milan* **19** A2
Aflandshage *Copenhagen* **8** B3
Afsarīyeh *Tehran* **31** B2
Agboyi Cr. → *Lagos* **14** A2
Ågerup *Copenhagen* **8** A1
Ågesta *Stockholm* **29** B2
Aghia Marina *Athens* **2** C3
Aghia Paraskevi *Athens* **2** A2
Aghios Dimitrios *Athens* **2** B2
Aghios Ioannis Rendis *Athens* **2** B1
Agincourt *Toronto* **31** A3
Agra Canal *Delhi* **10** B2
Agricola Oriental *Mexico City* **18** B2
Agua Espraiada → *São Paulo* **27** B2
Agualva-Cacem *Lisbon* **16** A1
Agustino, Cerro El *Lima* **14** B3
Ahrensfelde *Berlin* **5** A4
Ahuntsic *Montreal* **20** A1
Ai → *Osaka* **23** A2
Aigremont *Paris* **24** A1
Air View Park *Singapore* **28** A2
Airport West *Melbourne* **18** A1
Ajegunle *Lagos* **14** B2
Aji *Osaka* **23** A1
Ajuda *Lisbon* **16** A1
Akalla *Stockholm* **29** A1
Akasaka *Tokyo* **30** A3
Akbarābād *Tehran* **31** A2
Akershus Castle = Akershus Slott *Oslo* **23** A3
Akershus Slott *Oslo* **23** A3
Al 'Azamīyah *Baghdad* **3** A2
Al Quds = Jerusalem *Jerusalem* **13** B2
Al-Walaja *Jerusalem* **13** B1
Alaguntan *Lagos* **14** B2
Alameda *San Francisco* **26** B3
Alameda Memorial State Beach Park *San Francisco* **26** B3
Albern *Vienna* **32** B2
Albert Park *Melbourne* **18** B1
Alberton *Johannesburg* **13** B2
Albertslund *Copenhagen* **8** B2
Albysjön *Stockholm* **29** B1
Alcantara *Lisbon* **16** A1
Alcatraz I. *San Francisco* **26** B2
Alcobendas *Madrid* **17** A2
Alcorcón *Madrid* **17** B1
Aldershof *Berlin* **5** B4
Aldo Bonzi *Buenos Aires* **7** C1
Aleksandrovskoye *St. Petersburg* **27** B2
Alexander Nevsky Abbey *St. Petersburg* **27** B2
Alexandra *Johannesburg* **13** A2
Alexandra *Singapore* **28** B2
Alexandria *Washington* **33** C3
Alfortville *Paris* **24** B3
Algés *Lisbon* **16** A1
Alhambra *Los Angeles* **16** B4
Alibey → *Istanbul* **12** B1
Alibey Barajı *Istanbul* **12** B1
Alibeyköy *Istanbul* **12** B1
Alimos *Athens* **2** B2
Alipur *Kolkata* **14** B1
Allach *Munich* **21** A1
Allambie Heights *Sydney* **29** A2
Allermuir Hill *Edinburgh* **11** B2
Allstate Arena *Chicago* **9** A1
Allston *Boston* **6** A2
Almada *Lisbon* **16** A2
Almagro *Buenos Aires* **7** B2
Almargem do Bispo *Lisbon* **16** A1
Almirante G. Brown, Parque *Buenos Aires* **7** C2
Almon *Jerusalem* **13** B2
Almond → *Edinburgh* **11** B2
Alna *Oslo* **23** A4
Alnsjøen *Oslo* **23** A4
Alperton *London* **15** A2
Alpine *New York* **22** A2
Alrode *Johannesburg* **13** B2
Alsemberg *Brussels* **6** B1
Alsergrund *Vienna* **32** A2
Alsip *Chicago* **9** C2
Älsten *Stockholm* **29** B1
Älta *Stockholm* **29** B3
Altadena *Los Angeles* **16** A4
Alte-Donau → *Vienna* **32** A2
Alter Finkenkrug *Berlin* **5** A1
Altes Rathaus *Munich* **21** B2
Altglienicke *Berlin* **5** B4
Altlandsberg *Berlin* **5** A5
Altlandsberg Nord *Berlin* **5** A5
Altmannsdorf *Vienna* **32** B1
Alto da Boa Vista *Rio de Janeiro* **25** B1
Alto da Moóca *São Paulo* **27** B2
Alto do Pina *Lisbon* **16** A2
Altona *Melbourne* **18** B1
Alvik *Stockholm* **29** B1
Älvsjö *Stockholm* **29** B2
Älvvik *Stockholm* **29** A3
Am Hasenbergl *Munich* **21** A2
Am Steinhof *Vienna* **32** A1
Am Wald *Munich* **21** B2
Ama Keng *Singapore* **28** A2
Amadora *Lisbon* **16** A1
Amagasaki *Osaka* **23** A1
Amager *Copenhagen* **8** B3
Amāl Qādisiya *Baghdad* **3** B2
Amalienborg Slot *Copenhagen* **8** A3
Amata *Milan* **19** A1
Ambelokipi *Athens* **2** B2
Ameixoeira *Lisbon* **16** A2
América *São Paulo* **27** B1
American Police Hall of Fame *Miami* **18** B2
American University *Washington* **33** B3
Amin *Baghdad* **3** B2
Aminadav *Jerusalem* **13** B1
Amīrābād *Tehran* **31** A2
Amora *Lisbon* **16** B2
Amoreira *Lisbon* **16** A1
Amper → *Munich* **21** A1
Amstel-Drecht-Kanaal *Amsterdam* **2** B2
Amstelveen *Amsterdam* **2** B2
Amsterdam *Amsterdam* **2** A2
Amsterdam ✕ (AMS) *Amsterdam* **2** B1
Amsterdam-Rijnkanaal *Amsterdam* **2** B3
Amsterdam Zuidoost *Amsterdam* **2** B2
Amsterdamse Bos *Amsterdam* **2** B1
Anacosta → *Washington* **33** B4
Anacostia *Washington* **33** B4
Anadoluhisarı *Istanbul* **12** B2
Anadolukavağı *Istanbul* **12** A2
Anata *Jerusalem* **13** B2
Ancol *Jakarta* **12** A1
'Andalus *Baghdad* **3** B1
Andaraí *Rio de Janeiro* **25** B1
Anderlecht *Brussels* **6** A1
Anderson Park *Atlanta* **3** B2
Andingmen *Beijing* **4** B2
Ang Mo Kio *Singapore* **28** A3
Ängby *Stockholm* **29** A1
Angel I. *San Francisco* **26** A2
Angel Island State Park ⌂ *San Francisco* **26** A2
Angke, Kali → *Jakarta* **12** A1
Angyalföld *Budapest* **7** A2
Anik *Mumbai* **20** A2
Anin *Warsaw* **32** B2
Anjou *Montreal* **20** A2
Annalee Heights *Washington* **33** B2
Annandale *Washington* **33** C2
Anne Frankhuis *Amsterdam* **2** A2
Antony *Paris* **24** B2
Aoyama *Tokyo* **30** B3
Ap Lei Chau *Hong Kong* **12** B1
Apapa *Lagos* **14** B2
Apelação *Lisbon* **16** A2
Apopka, L. *Orlando* **23** A1
Apoquindo *Santiago* **27** B2
Apterkarskiy Ostrov *St. Petersburg* **27** B2
Ar Kazimiyah *Baghdad* **3** B1
Ar Ram *Jerusalem* **13** A2
Ara → *Tokyo* **30** A4
Arakawa *Tokyo* **30** A3
Arany-hegyi-patak → *Budapest* **7** A2
Aravaca *Madrid* **17** B1
Arbataash *Baghdad* **3** A1
Arc de Triomphe *Paris* **24** A2
Arcadia *Los Angeles* **16** B4
Arcueil *Paris* **24** B2
Arese *Milan* **19** A1
Arganzuela *Madrid* **17** B1
Argenteuil *Paris* **24** A2
Argiroupoli *Athens* **2** B2
Argonne Forest *Chicago* **9** C1
Arima *Tokyo* **30** B2
Arlanda ✕ (ARN) *Stockholm* **29** A1
Arlington *Boston* **6** A1
Arlington *Washington* **33** B3
Arlington Heights *Boston* **6** A1
Arlington Nat. Cemetery *Washington* **33** B3
Armação *Rio de Janeiro* **25** B2
Armadale *Melbourne* **18** B2
Armour Heights *Toronto* **31** A2
Arncliffe *Sydney* **29** B1
Arnold Arboretum *Boston* **6** B2
Árpádföld *Budapest* **7** A3
Arrentela *Lisbon* **16** B2
Arroyo Seco Park *Los Angeles* **16** B3
Årsta *Stockholm* **29** B2
Art Institute *Chicago* **9** B3
Artane *Dublin* **10** A2
Artas *Jerusalem* **13** B2
Arthur's Seat *Edinburgh* **11** B3
Arts, Place des *Montreal* **20** A2
As Shawawra *Jerusalem* **13** B2
Asagaya *Tokyo* **30** A2
Asahi *Osaka* **23** A2
Asakusa *Tokyo* **30** A3
Asati *Kolkata* **14** C1
Aschheim *Munich* **21** A3
Ascot Vale *Melbourne* **18** A1
Ashbridge's Bay Park *Toronto* **31** B3
Ashburn *Chicago* **9** C2
Ashburton *Melbourne* **18** B2
Ashfield *Sydney* **29** B1
Ashford *London* **15** B1
Ashtown *Dublin* **10** A2
Askisto *Helsinki* **11** B1
Askrikefjärden *Stockholm* **29** A3
Asnières *Paris* **24** A2
Aspern *Vienna* **32** A2
Aspern ✕ *Vienna* **32** A3
Assago *Milan* **19** B1
Assendelft *Amsterdam* **2** A1
Assiano *Milan* **19** B1
Astoria *New York* **22** B2
Astrolabe Park *Sydney* **29** B2
Atarot *Jerusalem* **13** A2
Atarot ✕ *Jerusalem* **13** A2
Atghara *Kolkata* **14** B2
Athens = Athina *Athens* **2** B2
Athina *Athens* **2** B2
Athina ✕ (ATH) *Athens* **2** A3
Athínai = Athina *Athens* **2** B2
Athis-Mons *Paris* **24** B3
Athlone *Cape Town* **8** A2
Atholl *Johannesburg* **13** A2
Atifiya *Baghdad* **3** A2
Atişalen *Istanbul* **12** B1
Atlanta *Atlanta* **3** B2
Atlanta Hartsfield Int. ✕ (ATL) *Atlanta* **3** C2
Atlanta Zoo *Atlanta* **3** B2
Atomium *Brussels* **6** A2
Attiki *Athens* **2** A2
Atzgersdorf *Vienna* **32** B1
Aubervilliers *Paris* **24** A3
Aubing *Munich* **21** B1
Auburndale *Boston* **6** A1
Auchendinny *Edinburgh* **11** B2
Auckland Park *Johannesburg* **13** B2
Auderghem *Brussels* **6** B2
Augustówka *Warsaw* **32** B2
Aulnay-sous-Bois *Paris* **24** A3
Aurelio *Rome* **26** B1
Ausim *Cairo* **7** A1
Austerlitz, Gare d' *Paris* **24** A3
Austin *Chicago* **9** B2
Avalon *Wellington* **33** B2
Avedøre *Copenhagen* **8** B2
Avellaneda *Buenos Aires* **7** C2
Avenel *Washington* **33** B4
Avondale *Chicago* **9** B2
Avondale Heights *Melbourne* **18** A1
Avtovo *St. Petersburg* **27** B1
Ayazağa *Istanbul* **12** B1
Ayer Chawan, Pulau *Singapore* **28** B2
Ayer Merbau, Pulau *Singapore* **28** B2
Azabu *Tokyo* **30** B3
Azcapotzalco *Mexico City* **18** B1
Azteca, Estadia *Mexico City* **18** C2
Azucar, Cerro Pan de *Santiago* **27** A1

B

Baambrugge *Amsterdam* **2** B2
Baba Ch. *Karachi* **13** B1
Baba I. *Karachi* **13** B1
Babarpur *Delhi* **10** A2
Babushkin *Moscow* **19** A3
Back B. *Mumbai* **20** B1
Baclaran *Manila* **17** B2
Bacoor *Manila* **17** C1
Bacoor B. *Manila* **17** C1
Badalona *Barcelona* **4** A2
Badhoevedorp *Amsterdam* **2** A1
Badli *Delhi* **10** A1
Bærum *Oslo* **23** A2
Bağcılar *Istanbul* **12** B1
Bàggio *Milan* **19** B1
Bāgh-e-Feyz *Tehran* **31** A1
Baghdād *Baghdad* **3** A2
Baghdad al Muthana ✕ *Baghdad* **3** B2
Baghdad Int. ✕ (SDA) *Baghdad* **3** B1
Bagmari *Kolkata* **14** B2
Bagneux *Paris* **24** B2
Bagnolet *Paris* **24** A3
Bagsværd *Copenhagen* **8** A2
Bagsværd Sø *Copenhagen* **8** A2
Baguiati *Kolkata* **14** B2
Bagumbayan *Manila* **17** C2
Baha'i Temple *Chicago* **9** A2
Bahçeköy *Istanbul* **12** A1
Bahçelievler *Istanbul* **12** B1
Bahtim *Cairo* **7** A2
Baile Atha Cliath = Dublin *Dublin* **10** A2
Baileys Crossroads *Washington* **33** B3
Bailly *Paris* **24** A1
Bairro Lopes *Lisbon* **16** A2
Baisha *Guangzhou* **11** B2
Baiyun Hill *Guangzhou* **11** B2
Baiyun Int. ✕ (CAN) *Guangzhou* **11** A2
Bakırköy *Istanbul* **12** C1
Bal Harbor *Miami* **18** A2
Balara *Manila* **17** B2
Baldia *Karachi* **13** A1
Baldoyle *Dublin* **10** A3
Baldwin, L. *Orlando* **23** A3
Baldwin Hills *Los Angeles* **16** B2
Baldwin Hills Res. *Los Angeles* **16** B2
Balgowlah *Sydney* **29** A2
Balgowlah Heights *Sydney* **29** A2
Balham *London* **15** B3
Bali *Kolkata* **14** B1
Baliganja *Kolkata* **14** B2
Balingsnäs *Stockholm* **29** B2
Balingsta *Stockholm* **29** B2
Balintawak *Manila* **17** B1
Ballerup *Copenhagen* **8** A2
Ballinteer *Dublin* **10** B2
Ballyboden *Dublin* **10** B2
Ballybrack *Dublin* **10** B3
Ballyfermot *Dublin* **10** A1
Ballymorefinn Hill *Dublin* **10** B1
Ballymun *Dublin* **10** A2
Balmain *Sydney* **29** B2
Baluhati *Kolkata* **14** B1
Balvanera *Buenos Aires* **7** B2
Balwyn *Melbourne* **18** A2
Balwyn North *Melbourne* **18** A2
Banática *Lisbon* **16** A1
Bandra *Mumbai* **20** A1
Bandra Pt. *Mumbai* **20** A1
Bang Kapi *Bangkok* **3** B2
Bang Na *Bangkok* **3** B2
Bangbae *Seoul* **27** C1
Bangkhen *Bangkok* **3** A2
Bangkok *Bangkok* **3** B2
Bangkok Noi *Bangkok* **3** B1
Bangkok Yai *Bangkok* **3** B1
Banglo *Kolkata* **14** B1
Bangrak *Bangkok* **3** B2
Bangsu *Bangkok* **3** B2
Banks, C. *Sydney* **29** C2
Banksmeadow *Sydney* **29** B2
Banstala *Kolkata* **14** B2
Bantra *Kolkata* **14** B1
Baoshan *Shanghai* **28** A1
Bar Giyora *Jerusalem* **13** B1
Barahanagar *Kolkata* **14** B2
Barajas *Madrid* **17** B2
Barajas, Madrid ✕ (MAD) *Madrid* **17** B2
Barakpur *Kolkata* **14** A2
Barcarena *Lisbon* **16** A1
Barcarena, Rib. de → *Lisbon* **16** A1
Barcelona *Barcelona* **4** A2
Barcelona-Prat ✕ (BCN) *Barcelona* **4** B1
Barceloneta *Barcelona* **4** A2
Barcroft, L. *Washington* **33** B3
Barking *London* **15** A4
Barkingside *London* **15** A4
Barnes *London* **15** B2
Barnet *London* **15** A2
Barra Andai *Karachi* **13** B2
Barra Funda *São Paulo* **27** B2
Barracas *Buenos Aires* **7** B2
Barrackpur = Barakpur *Kolkata* **14** A2
Barranco *Lima* **14** B2
Barreiro *Lisbon* **16** B2
Barreto *Rio de Janeiro* **25** B2
Bartala *Kolkata* **14** B1
Barton Park *Sydney* **29** B1
Bartyki *Warsaw* **32** C2
Basus *Cairo* **7** A2
Batanagar *Kolkata* **14** B1
Bath Beach *New York* **22** C1
Bath I. *Karachi* **13** B2
Batir *Jerusalem* **13** B1
Batok, Bukit *Singapore* **28** A2
Battersea *London* **15** B3
Bauman *Moscow* **19** B3
Baumgarten *Vienna* **32** A1
Bay, L. *Orlando* **23** A2
Bay Harbour Islands *Miami* **18** A2
Bay Hill *Orlando* **23** B1
Bay Ridge *New York* **22** C1
Bayit Va-Gan *Jerusalem* **13** B2
Bayonne *New York* **22** B1
Bayrampaşa *Istanbul* **12** B1
Bayshore *San Francisco* **26** B2
Bayt Lahm *Jerusalem* **13** B2
Bayview *San Francisco* **26** B2
Bāzār *Tehran* **31** A2
Beacon Hill *Hong Kong* **12** A2
Beato *Lisbon* **16** A2
Beaumont *Dublin* **10** A2
Beaumonte Heights *Toronto* **31** A1
Bebek *Istanbul* **12** B2
Běchovice *Prague* **25** B3
Beck L. *Chicago* **9** A1
Beckenham *London* **15** B3
Beckton *London* **15** A4
Becontree *London* **15** A4
Beddington Corner *London* **15** B3
Bedford *Boston* **6** A1
Bedford Park *Chicago* **9** C2
Bedford Park *New York* **22** A2
Bedford Stuyvesant *New York* **22** B2
Bedford View *Johannesburg* **13** B2
Bedok *Singapore* **28** B3
Bedok, Res. *Singapore* **28** A3
Beersel *Brussels* **6** B1
Behala *Kolkata* **14** B1
Bei Hai *Beijing* **4** B2
Beicai *Shanghai* **28** B2
Beijing *Beijing* **4** B1
Beit Duqu *Jerusalem* **13** A1
Beit Ghur at-Taht *Jerusalem* **13** A1
Beit Ghur el-Fawqa *Jerusalem* **13** A1
Beit Hanina *Jerusalem* **13** B2
Beit Ij'za *Jerusalem* **13** A1
Beit Iksa *Jerusalem* **13** B2
Beit I'nan *Jerusalem* **13** A1
Beit Jala *Jerusalem* **13** B2
Beit Lekhem = Bayt Lahm *Jerusalem* **13** B2
Beit Liqya *Jerusalem* **13** A1
Beit Nekofa *Jerusalem* **13** B1
Beit Sahur *Jerusalem* **13** B2
Beit Sofafa *Jerusalem* **13** B2
Beit Surik *Jerusalem* **13** B1
Beit Ur al-Fawqa *Jerusalem* **13** A1
Beit Zayit *Jerusalem* **13** B1
Beitaipingzhuan *Beijing* **4** B1
Beitar Illit *Jerusalem* **13** B1
Beitin *Jerusalem* **13** A2
Beitsun *Guangzhou* **11** B2
Beitunya *Jerusalem* **13** A2
Beixing Jing Park *Shanghai* **28** B1
Békásmegyer *Budapest* **7** A2
Bekkelaget *Oslo* **23** A3
Bekkestua *Oslo* **23** A2
Bel Air *Los Angeles* **16** B2
Bela Vista *São Paulo* **27** B2
Bélanger *Montreal* **20** A1
Belas *Lisbon* **16** A1
Beleghata *Kolkata* **14** B2
Belém *Lisbon* **16** A1
Belém, Torre de *Lisbon* **16** A1
Belènzinho *São Paulo* **27** B2
Belgachiya *Kolkata* **14** B2
Belgharia *Kolkata* **14** B2
Belgrano *Buenos Aires* **7** B2
Bell *Los Angeles* **16** C3
Bell Gardens *Los Angeles* **16** C4
Bellavista *Lima* **14** B2
Bellavista *Santiago* **27** C2
Belle Harbor *New York* **22** C2
Belle Isle *Orlando* **23** B2
Belle View *Washington* **33** B2
Bellingham *London* **15** B3
Bellwood *Chicago* **9** B1
Belmont *Boston* **6** A1
Belmont *London* **15** A2
Belmont, Mt. *Wellington* **33** B2
Belmont Cragin *Chicago* **9** B2
Belmont Harbor *Chicago* **9** B3
Belmore *Sydney* **29** B1
Belur *Kolkata* **14** B2
Belvedere *Atlanta* **3** B3
Belvedere *London* **15** B4
Belvedere *San Francisco* **26** A2
Belyayevo Bogorodskoye *Moscow* **19** C2
Bemowo *Warsaw* **32** B1
Benaki Museum *Athens* **2** B2
Bendale *Toronto* **31** A3
Benefica *Rio de Janeiro* **25** B1
Benfica *Lisbon* **16** A1
Benito Juárez *Mexico City* **18** B2
Benito Juárez, Int. ✕ (MEX) *Mexico City* **18** B2
Bensonhurst *New York* **22** C2
Berchem-Ste-Agathe *Brussels* **6** A1
Berg am Laim *Munich* **21** B2
Bergenfield *New York* **22** A2
Bergham *Munich* **21** B2
Bergvliet *Cape Town* **8** B1
Beri *Barcelona* **4** A1
Berkeley *San Francisco* **26** A3
Berlin *Berlin* **5** A3
Berlin Dom *Berlin* **5** A3
Berlin Tegel ✕ (TXL) *Berlin* **5** A2
Berlin Tempelhof ✕ (THF) *Berlin* **5** B3
Bermondsey *London* **15** B3
Bernabeu, Estadio *Madrid* **17** B1
Bernal Heights *San Francisco* **26** B2
Berwyn *Chicago* **9** B2
Berwyn Heights *Washington* **33** B4
Besiktas *Istanbul* **12** B2
Besós → *Barcelona* **4** A2
Bessie, L. *Orlando* **23** B1
Bet Horon *Jerusalem* **13** A1
Bethesda *Washington* **33** B3
Bethlehem = Bayt Lahm *Jerusalem* **13** B2
Bethnal Green *London* **15** A3
Betor *Kolkata* **14** B1
Beulah *Orlando* **23** A1
Beulah, L. *Orlando* **23** A1
Beverley Hills *Sydney* **29** B1
Beverley Park *Sydney* **29** B1
Beverly *Chicago* **9** C3
Beverly Arts Center *Chicago* **9** C2
Beverly Glen *Los Angeles* **16** B2
Beverly Hills *Los Angeles* **16** B2
Beverly Hills -Morgan Park Historic District *Chicago* **9** C2
Bexley *Sydney* **29** B1
Bexley □ *London* **15** B4
Bexleyheath *London* **15** B4
Beykoz *Istanbul* **12** B2
Beylerbeyi *Istanbul* **12** B2
Beyoğlu *Istanbul* **12** B1
Bezons *Paris* **24** A2
Bezuidenhout Park *Johannesburg* **13** B2
Bhadrakali *Kolkata* **14** A2
Bhalswa *Delhi* **10** A2
Bhambo Khan Qarmati *Karachi* **13** B2
Bhatsala *Kolkata* **14** B1
Bhawanipur *Kolkata* **14** B2
Bhendkhal *Mumbai* **20** B2
Bhuleshwar *Mumbai* **20** B1
Białołeka Dworska *Warsaw* **32** B2
Bicentennial Park *Los Angeles* **16** B4
Bicentennial Park *Sydney* **29** B1
Bickley *London* **15** B4
Bicutan *Manila* **17** C2
Bidhan Nagar *Kolkata* **14** B2
Bidu *Jerusalem* **13** A1
Bielany *Warsaw* **32** B1
Bielawa *Warsaw* **32** C2
Biesdorf *Berlin* **5** A4
Bièvre → *Paris* **24** B1
Bièvres *Paris* **24** B2
Big Sand Lake *Orlando* **23** B2
Bilston *Edinburgh* **11** B2
Binacayan *Manila* **17** C1
Binondo *Manila* **17** B1
Bintaro Jaya *Jakarta* **12** B1
Bir Nabala *Jerusalem* **13** A2
Birak el Kiyam *Cairo* **7** A1
Birch Cliff *Toronto* **31** A3
Birkenstein *Berlin* **5** A5
Birkholz *Berlin* **5** A4
Birkholzaue *Berlin* **5** A4
Birrarung Park *Melbourne* **18** A2
Biscayne Park *Miami* **18** A2
Bishop Lavis *Cape Town* **8** A2
Bishopscourt *Cape Town* **8** A1
Bispebjerg *Copenhagen* **8** A3
Bittsevsky Forest Park *Moscow* **19** C2
Björknas *Stockholm* **29** B3
Black Cr. → *Toronto* **31** A2
Black Creek Pioneer Village *Toronto* **31** A1
Blackfen *London* **15** B4
Blackheath *London* **15** B4
Blackrock *Dublin* **10** B2
Bladensburg *Washington* **33** B4
Blair Village *Atlanta* **3** C2
Blairgowrie *Johannesburg* **13** A2
Blake House *Boston* **6** B2
Blakehurst *Sydney* **29** B1
Blakstad *Oslo* **23** B1
Blanche, L. *Orlando* **23** B1
Blankenburg *Berlin* **5** A3
Blankenfelde *Berlin* **5** A3
Blizne *Warsaw* **32** B1
Błota *Warsaw* **32** C3
Blue Island *Chicago* **9** D2
Blue Mosque = Sultanahme Camil *Istanbul* **12** B1
Bluebell *Dublin* **10** B1
Bluff Hd. *Hong Kong* **12** B2
Bluffers Park *Toronto* **31** A3
Blumberg *Berlin* **5** A4
Blunt Pt. *San Francisco* **26** A2
Blutenberg *Munich* **21** B1
Blylaget *Oslo* **23** B3
Boa Vista, Alto do *Rio de Janeiro* **25** B1
Boardwalk *New York* **22** C3
Boavista *Lisbon* **16** A2
Bobigny *Paris* **24** A3
Bocanegra *Lima* **14** B2
Boedo *Buenos Aires* **7** B2
Bogenhausen *Munich* **21** B2
Boggy Creek Swamp *Orlando* **23** B2
Bogorodskoye *Moscow* **19** B3
Bogota *New York* **22** A1
Bogstadvatnet *Oslo* **23** A2
Bohnsdorf *Berlin* **5** B4
Bois-Colombes *Paris* **24** A2
Bois-d'Arcy *Paris* **24** B1
Boissy-St-Léger *Paris* **24** B4
Boldinasco *Milan* **19** B1
Bøler *Oslo* **23** A4
Bollate *Milan* **19** A1
Bollebeek *Brussels* **6** A1
Bollensdorf *Berlin* **5** A5
Bollmora *Stockholm* **29** B3
Bolshaya Okhta *St. Petersburg* **27** B2
Bolton *Atlanta* **3** B2
Bom Retiro *São Paulo* **27** B2
Bombay = Mumbai *Mumbai* **20** B2
Bondi *Sydney* **29** B2
Bondy *Paris* **24** A3
Bondy, Forêt de *Paris* **24** A4
Bonifacio Monument *Manila* **17** B1
Bonneuil-sur-Marne *Paris* **24** B4
Bonnington *Edinburgh* **11** B1
Bonnyrigg and Lasswade *Edinburgh* **11** B3
Bonsucesso *Rio de Janeiro* **25** B1
Bonteheuwel *Cape Town* **8** A2
Boo *Stockholm* **29** A3
Booterstown *Dublin* **10** B2
Borisovo *Moscow* **19** C3
Borle *Mumbai* **20** A2
Boronia Park *Sydney* **29** A1
Bosmont *Johannesburg* **13** B1
Bosön *Stockholm* **29** A3
Bosporus = İstanbul Boğazı *Istanbul* **12** B2
Bostancı *Istanbul* **12** C2
Boston *Boston* **6** A2
Boston Common *Boston* **6** A2
Boston Logan Int. ✕ (BOS) *Boston* **6** A2
Botafogo *Rio de Janeiro* **25** B1
Botany *Sydney* **29** B2
Botany B. *Sydney* **29** B2
Botany Bay Nat. Park △ *Sydney* **29** B2
Botič → *Prague* **25** B3
Botica Sete *Lisbon* **16** A1
Boucherville *Montreal* **20** A3
Boucherville, Îs. de *Montreal* **20** A3
Bougival *Paris* **24** A1
Boulder Pt. *Hong Kong* **12** B1
Boulogne, Bois de *Paris* **24** A2
Boulogne-Billancourt *Paris* **24** A2
Bourg-la-Reine *Paris* **24** B2
Bouviers *Paris* **24** B1
Bovenkerk *Amsterdam* **2** B2
Bovenkerker Polder *Amsterdam* **2** B2
Bovisa *Milan* **19** A2
Bow *London* **15** A3
Boyacıköy *Istanbul* **12** B2
Boyd Conservation Area *Toronto* **31** A1
Boyle Heights *Los Angeles* **16** B3
Braepark *Edinburgh* **11** B2
Braid *Edinburgh* **11** B2
Bramley *Johannesburg* **13** A2
Brandeis University *Boston* **6** A1
Brandenburger Tor *Berlin* **5** A3
Brani, Pulau *Singapore* **28** B3
Branik *Prague* **25** B2
Brännkyrka *Stockholm* **29** B2
Brás *São Paulo* **27** B2
Brasilândia *São Paulo* **27** A1
Brateyevo *Moscow* **19** C3
Braybrook *Melbourne* **18** A1
Brázdim *Prague* **25** A3
Breakheart Reservation *Boston* **6** A2
Brede *Copenhagen* **8** A3
Breezy Point *New York* **22** C2
Breitenlee *Vienna* **32** A3
Breña *Lima* **14** B2
Brent □ *London* **15** A2
Brent Res. *London* **15** A2
Brentford *London* **15** B2
Brentwood Park *Los Angeles* **16** B2
Brera *Milan* **19** B2
Bresso *Milan* **19** A2
Brevik *Stockholm* **29** A3
Břevnov *Prague* **25** B2
Brickyard, The *Chicago* **9** B2
Bridgeport *Chicago* **9** B3
Bridgetown *Cape Town* **8** A2
Bridgeview *Chicago* **9** C2
Brighton *Boston* **6** A2
Brighton *Melbourne* **18** B1
Brighton Beach *New York* **22** C2
Brighton le Sands *Sydney* **29** B1
Brighton Park *Chicago* **9** C2
Brightwood *Washington* **33** B3
Brigittenau *Vienna* **32** A2
Brimbank Park *Melbourne* **18** A1
Brisbane *San Francisco* **26** B2
Britz *Berlin* **5** B3
Brixton *London* **15** B3
Broadmeadows *Melbourne* **18** A1
Broadmoor *San Francisco* **26** B2
Broadview *Chicago* **9** B1
Brockley *London* **15** B3
Bródno *Warsaw* **32** B2
Bródnowski, Kanal *Warsaw* **32** B2
Broek *Amsterdam* **2** A2
Bromley □ *London* **15** B4
Bromley Common *London* **15** B4
Bromma *Stockholm* **29** A1
Bromma ✕ *Stockholm* **29** A1
Brøndby Strand *Copenhagen* **8** B2
Brøndbyøster *Copenhagen* **8** B2
Brøndbyvester *Copenhagen* **8** B2
Brondesbury *London* **15** A2
Brønnøya *Oslo* **23** A2
Brønshøj *Copenhagen* **8** A2
Bronxville *New York* **22** A3
Brookfield *Chicago* **9** C1
Brookhaven *Atlanta* **3** A2
Brookline *Boston* **6** B2
Brooklyn *Cape Town* **8** A1
Brooklyn *New York* **22** C2
Brooklyn *Wellington* **33** B1
Brooklyn Heights *New York* **22** B2
Brookmont *Washington* **33** B3
Brossard *Montreal* **20** B3
Brou-sur-Chantereine *Paris* **24** A4
Brown *Toronto* **31** A3
Broyhill Park *Washington* **33** B2
Brughério *Milan* **19** A2
Brunswick *Melbourne* **18** A1
Brussegem *Brussels* **6** A1
Brussel *Brussels* **6** A2
Brussel ✕ (BRU) *Brussels* **6** A2
Brussels = Brussel *Brussels* **6** A2
Bruxelles = Brussel *Brussels* **6** A2
Bruzzano *Milan* **19** A2
Bry-sur-Marne *Paris* **24** A4
Bryan, L. *Orlando* **23** B2
Bryanston *Johannesburg* **13** A1
Bryn *Oslo* **23** A1
Brzeziny *Warsaw* **32** B2
Bubeneč *Prague* **25** B2
Buc *Paris* **24** B1
Buchenhain *Munich* **21** B1
Buchholz *Berlin* **5** A3
Buckhead *Atlanta* **3** A2
Buckingham Palace *London* **15** A3
Buckow *Berlin* **5** B3
Buda *Budapest* **7** A2
Buda Castle = Budaváripalota *Budapest* **7** A2
Budafok *Budapest* **7** B2
Budaörs *Budapest* **7** B1
Budapest *Budapest* **7** B2
Budapest ✕ (BUD) *Budapest* **7** B3
Budatétény *Budapest* **7** B2
Budaváripalota *Budapest* **7** A2
Buddinge *Copenhagen* **8** A3
Buena Ventura Lakes *Orlando* **23** B2
Buena Vista *San Francisco* **26** B2
Buenos Aires *Buenos Aires* **7** B2
Bufalotta *Rome* **26** B2
Bugio *Lisbon* **16** B1
Buiksloot *Amsterdam* **2** A2
Buitenveldert *Amsterdam* **2** B2
Buizingen *Brussels* **6** B1
Bukhansan *Seoul* **27** B1
Bukit Panjang Nature Reserve *Singapore* **28** A2
Bukit Timah Nature Reserve *Singapore* **28** A2
Bukum, Pulau *Singapore* **28** B2
Būlāq *Cairo* **7** A2
Bule *Manila* **17** C2
Bulim *Singapore* **28** A2
Bullen Park *Melbourne* **18** A2
Bund, The *Shanghai* **28** B1
Bundoora North *Melbourne* **18** A2
Bundoora Park *Melbourne* **18** A2
Bunker Hill Memorial *Boston* **6** A2
Bunker I. *Karachi* **13** B1
Bunkyō *Tokyo* **30** A3
Bunnefjorden *Oslo* **23** A3
Buona Vista Park *Singapore* **28** B2
Burbank *Chicago* **9** C2
Burbank *Los Angeles* **16** A3
Burden, L. *Orlando* **23** B1
Burlington *Boston* **6** A1
Burnham Park *Chicago* **9** C3
Burnham Park Harbor *Chicago* **9** B3
Burnhamthorpe *Toronto* **31** B1
Burnt Oak *London* **15** A2
Burntisland *Edinburgh* **11** A2
Burnwynd *Edinburgh* **11** B1
Burqa *Jerusalem* **13** B2
Burtus *Cairo* **7** A1
Burudvatn *Oslo* **23** A2
Burwood *Sydney* **29** B1
Bushwick *New York* **22** B2
Bushy Park *London* **15** B1
Butantã *São Paulo* **27** B2
Butcher I. *Mumbai* **20** B2
Butler, L. *Orlando* **23** B1
Butts Corner *Washington* **33** C2
Büyükdere *Istanbul* **12** B2
Bycula *Mumbai* **20** B2
Bygdøy *Oslo* **23** A3

C

C.B.S. Fox Studios *Los Angeles* **16** B2
C.N.N. Center *Atlanta* **3** B2
C.N. Tower *Toronto* **31** B2
Caballito *Buenos Aires* **7** B2
Cabin John *Washington* **33** B2
Cabin John Regional Park ⌂ *Washington* **33** A2
Cabinteely *Dublin* **10** B3
Cabra *Dublin* **10** A2
Cabuçú de Baixo → *São Paulo* **27** A1
Cabuçú de Cima → *São Paulo* **27** A2
Cachan *Paris* **24** B2
Cachoeira, Rib. da → *São Paulo* **27** B1
Cacilhas *Lisbon* **16** A2
Cahuenga Park *Los Angeles* **16** B3
Cain, L. *Orlando* **23** B2
Cairo = El Qâhira *Cairo* **7** A2
Cairo Int. ✕ (CAI) *Cairo* **7** A3
Caju *Rio de Janeiro* **25** B1
Čakovice *Prague* **25** B3
Calcutta = Kolkata *Kolkata* **14** B2
California Inst. of Tech. *Los Angeles* **16** B4
California Los Angeles, University of *Los Angeles* **16** B2
California State University *Los Angeles* **16** B3
Callao *Lima* **14** B2
Caloocan *Manila* **17** B1
Calumet L. *Chicago* **9** C3
Calumet Park *Chicago* **9** C3

Calumet Sag Channel → *Chicago* 9 C2
Calvairate *Milan* 19 B2
Camarate *Lisbon* 16 A2
Camaroes *Lisbon* 16 A1
Camberwell *London* 15 B3
Camberwell *Melbourne* 18 B2
Cambridge *Boston* 6 A2
Cambuci *São Paulo* 27 B2
Camden □ *London* 15 A3
Cameron, Mt. *Wellington* 33 B2
Çamlıca *Istanbul* 12 B2
Camp Springs *Washington* 33 C4
Campamento *Madrid* 17 B1
Campbellfield *Melbourne* 18 A1
Camperdown *Sydney* 29 B2
Campo, Casa de *Madrid* 17 B1
Campo F.C. Barcelona *Barcelona* 4 A1
Campo Grando *Lisbon* 16 A2
Campo Pequeño *Lisbon* 16 A2
Campolide *Lisbon* 16 A2
Camps Bay *Cape Town* 8 A1
C'an San Joan *Barcelona* 4 A2
Cañacao B. *Manila* 17 C1
Canarsie *New York* 22 C2
Candiac *Montreal* 20 B3
Caneças *Lisbon* 16 A1
Canillas *Madrid* 17 B2
Canillejas *Madrid* 17 B2
Canning Town *London* 15 A4
Canteras de Vallecas *Madrid* 17 B2
Canterbury *Melbourne* 18 A2
Canterbury *Sydney* 29 B1
Canton = Guangzhou *Guangzhou* 11 B2
Caoheijing *Shanghai* 28 B1
Capão Redondo *São Paulo* 27 B1
Caparica *Lisbon* 16 A2
Caparica, Costa da *Lisbon* 16 B1
Cape Flats *Cape Town* 8 B2
Cape Peninsula △ *Cape Town* 8 A1
Cape Town *Cape Town* 8 A1
Cape Town Int. ✕ (CPT) *Cape Town* 8 A2
Capitol Heights *Washington* 33 B4
Captain Cook Bridge *Sydney* 29 C1
Captain Cook Landing Place Park *Sydney* 29 C2
Capuchos *Lisbon* 16 B1
Carabanchel Alto *Madrid* 17 B1
Carabanchel Bajo *Madrid* 17 B1
Carapachay *Buenos Aires* 7 B1
Caraza *Buenos Aires* 7 C2
Caridad *Manila* 17 C1
Carioca, Sa. da *Rio de Janeiro* 25 B1
Carlstadt *New York* 22 A1
Carlton *Melbourne* 18 A1
Carmen de Huechuraba *Santiago* 27 B1
Carmen de la Legua *Lima* 14 B2
Carnaxide *Lisbon* 16 A1
Carnegie *Melbourne* 18 B2
Carnide *Lisbon* 16 A1
Carol City *Miami* 18 A1
Carrascal *Santiago* 27 B1
Carrickmines *Dublin* 10 B3
Carrières-sous-Bois *Paris* 24 A1
Carrières-sous-Poissy *Paris* 24 A1
Carrières-sur-Seine *Paris* 24 A2
Carrigeen B. *Dublin* 10 A3
Cartierville *Montreal* 20 A1
Casa Loma *Toronto* 31 A2
Casa Verde *São Paulo* 27 A1
Casál Morena *Rome* 26 C2
Casalotti *Rome* 26 B1
Cascade Heights *Atlanta* 3 B2
Castèl di Leva *Rome* 26 C2
Castèl Sant'Angelo *Rome* 26 B1
Castleknock *Dublin* 10 A1
Castleton Corners *New York* 22 C1
Catete *Rio de Janeiro* 25 B1
Catford *London* 15 B3
Catherine, L. *Orlando* 23 B2
Caulfield *Melbourne* 18 B2
Cavite *Manila* 17 C1
Caxias *Lisbon* 16 A1
Cebecci *Istanbul* 12 B1
Cecchignola *Rome* 26 C2
Cecilienhof, Schloss *Berlin* 5 B1
Cedar Grove *Atlanta* 3 C3
Cedarvale Park *Toronto* 31 A2
Cempaka Putih *Jakarta* 12 B2
Çengelköy *Istanbul* 12 B2
Cengkareng *Jakarta* 12 A1
Centennial Olympic Park *Atlanta* 3 B2
Centennial Park *Sydney* 29 B2
Center Hill *Atlanta* 3 B2
Centocelle *Rome* 26 B2
Central, Gare *Montreal* 20 B2
Central Park *New York* 22 B2
Cerdanyola del Vallès *Barcelona* 4 A1
Cerillos *Santiago* 27 B1
Cerro de la Estrella, Parque Nacional △ *Mexico City* 18 B2
Cerro de los Angeles *Madrid* 17 C1
Cerro Navia *Santiago* 27 B1
Cesano Boscone *Milan* 19 B1
Cesate *Milan* 19 A1
Cha Kwo Ling *Hong Kong* 12 B2
Chacarrita *Buenos Aires* 7 B2
Chadwell Heath *London* 15 A4
Chai Chee *Singapore* 28 B3
Chai Wan *Hong Kong* 12 B2
Chai Wan Kok *Hong Kong* 12 A1
Chakdaha *Kolkata* 14 C1
Chamartín *Madrid* 17 B1
Chamberí *Madrid* 17 B1
Chambourcy *Paris* 24 A1
Champigny-sur-Marne *Paris* 24 B4
Champlain, Pont *Montreal* 20 B2
Champs-sur-Marne *Paris* 24 A4
Chamrail *Kolkata* 14 B1
Chanakyapuri *Delhi* 10 B2
Chanditala *Kolkata* 14 A1
Changfeng Park *Shanghai* 28 B1
Changhai = Shanghai *Shanghai* 28 B2
Changi *Singapore* 28 A3
Changi, Singapore ✕ (SIN) *Singapore* 28 A3
Changning *Shanghai* 28 B1
Chantereine *Paris* 24 A4
Chantian *Guangzhou* 11 A2
Chaoyang *Beijing* 4 B2
Chaoyangmen *Beijing* 4 B2
Chapelizod *Dublin* 10 A1
Chapultepec, Bosque de *Mexico City* 18 B1
Chapultepec, Castillo de *Mexico City* 18 B1
Charenton-le-Pont *Paris* 24 B3
Charleroi, Kanal de → *Brussels* 6 B1
Charles Bridge = Karlův most *Prague* 25 B2
Charles Gates Dawes House *Chicago* 9 A2
Charlestown *Boston* 6 A2
Charlottenburg *Berlin* 5 A2
Charlottenburg, Schloss *Berlin* 5 A2
Charlottenlund *Copenhagen* 8 A3
Charlton *London* 15 B4
Charneca *Lisbon* 16 A2
Chase, L. *Orlando* 23 B1
Châteaufort *Paris* 24 B1
Châtenay-Malabry *Paris* 24 B2
Chatham *Chicago* 9 C3
Chatillon *Paris* 24 B2
Chatou *Paris* 24 A1
Chatpur *Kolkata* 14 B2
Chatswood *Sydney* 29 A2
Chatuchak *Bangkok* 3 B2
Chatuchak Park *Bangkok* 3 B2
Chauki *Karachi* 13 A1
Chavarria *Lima* 14 B2
Chaville *Paris* 24 B2
Chayang *Seoul* 27 B2
Chelles *Paris* 24 A4
Chelles, Canal de *Paris* 24 A4
Chells-le-Pin ✕ *Paris* 24 A4
Chelsea *Boston* 6 A2
Chelsea *London* 15 B2
Chembur *Mumbai* 20 A2
Chennevières-sur-Marne *Paris* 24 B4
Cheongdam *Seoul* 27 B2
Cheonho *Seoul* 27 B2
Cheops *Cairo* 7 B1
Chertanovka → *Moscow* 19 C2
Chertanovo *Moscow* 19 C2
Cheryomushki *Moscow* 19 B2
Chestnut Hill *Boston* 6 B1
Cheung Sha Wan *Hong Kong* 12 A1
Cheverly *Washington* 33 B4
Chevilly-Larue *Paris* 24 B3
Chevry-Cossigny *Paris* 24 B4
Chevy Chase *Washington* 33 B3
Chhatrapati Shivaji, Mumbai ✕ (BOM) *Mumbai* 20 A2
Chia Keng *Singapore* 28 A3
Chiaravalle Milanese *Milan* 19 B2
Chicago *Chicago* 9 B3
Chicago, University of *Chicago* 9 C3
Chicago Harbor *Chicago* 9 B3
Chicago Lawn *Chicago* 9 C2
Chicago-Midway ✕ (MDW) *Chicago* 9 C2
Chicago O'Hare Int. ✕ (ORD) *Chicago* 9 B1
Chicago Ridge *Chicago* 9 C2
Chicago River, North Branch → *Chicago* 9 B2
Chicago Sanitary and Ship Canal *Chicago* 9 C2
Chicago State University *Chicago* 9 C3
Chicago Zoo *Chicago* 9 B1
Chienzui *Guangzhou* 11 A3
Chik Sha *Hong Kong* 12 B2
Child's Hill *London* 15 A2
Chilla Saroda *Delhi* 10 B2
Chillum *Washington* 33 B4
Chilly-Mazarin *Paris* 24 B2
China Basin *San Francisco* 26 B2
Chingupota *Kolkata* 14 C1
Chinna Cr. → *Karachi* 13 B2
Chiquihuite, Cerro *Mexico City* 18 A2
Chislehurst *London* 15 B4
Chiswick *London* 15 B2
Chiswick House *London* 15 B2
Chitose *Tokyo* 30 B2
Chitralada Palace *Bangkok* 3 B2
Chiyoda *Tokyo* 30 A3
Choa Chu Kang *Singapore* 28 A2
Chodov u Prahy *Prague* 25 B3
Chōfu *Tokyo* 30 B2
Choisy-le-Roi *Paris* 24 B3
Cholupice *Prague* 25 C2
Chom Thong *Bangkok* 3 B1
Chong Pang *Singapore* 28 A2
Chongwen *Beijing* 4 B2
Chorrillos *Lima* 14 C2
Chowpatty Beach *Mumbai* 20 B1
Christianshavn *Copenhagen* 8 A3
Chrzanów *Warsaw* 32 B1
Chuen Lung *Hong Kong* 12 A1
Chuk Kok *Hong Kong* 12 A2
Chulalongkorn Univ. *Bangkok* 3 B2
Chuō *Tokyo* 30 A3
Church End *London* 15 A2
Churchtown *Dublin* 10 B2
Ciampino *Rome* 26 C2
Ciampino ✕ *Rome* 26 C2
Cicero *Chicago* 9 B2
Cilandak *Jakarta* 12 B1
Cilincing *Jakarta* 12 A2
Ciliwung → *Jakarta* 12 B2
Čimice *Prague* 25 B2
Cinecittà *Rome* 26 B2
Cinisello Bálsamo *Milan* 19 A2
Cinkota *Budapest* 7 A3
Cipete *Jakarta* 12 B1
Citta degli Studi *Milan* 19 B2
Città del Vaticano = Vatican City ■ *Rome* 26 B1
City, The *London* 15 A3
City of the Dead *Cairo* 7 A2
Ciudad de México *Mexico City* 18 B2
Ciudad Deportiva *Mexico City* 18 B2
Ciudad Fin de Semana *Madrid* 17 B2
Ciudad General Belgrano *Buenos Aires* 7 C1
Ciudad Lineál *Madrid* 17 B2
Ciudad Satélite *Mexico City* 18 A1
Ciudad Universitaria *Buenos Aires* 7 B2
Ciudad Universitaria *Mexico City* 18 C1
Claireville Res. *Toronto* 31 A1
Clamart *Paris* 24 B2
Clapham *London* 15 B3
Clapton *London* 15 A3
Claremont *Cape Town* 8 A1
Clayhall *London* 15 A4
Clear, L. *Orlando* 23 A2
Clermiston *Edinburgh* 11 B2
Clichy *Paris* 24 A2
Clichy-sous-Bois *Paris* 24 A4
Cliffside *Toronto* 31 A3
Cliffside Park *New York* 22 B2
Clifton *Cape Town* 8 A1
Clifton *Karachi* 13 B2
Clifton *New York* 22 C1
Clifton Beach *Karachi* 13 B2
Cliftondale *Boston* 6 A2
Clonskeagh *Dublin* 10 B2
Clontarf *Dublin* 10 A2
Clontarf *Sydney* 29 A2
Clovelly *Sydney* 29 B2
Cobras, I. das *Rio de Janeiro* 25 B2
Coburg *Melbourne* 18 A1
Cocotá *Rio de Janeiro* 25 A1
Cœuilly *Paris* 24 B4
Coina *Lisbon* 16 B2
Coker *Lagos* 14 B2
Colaba *Mumbai* 20 B1
Colaba Pt. *Mumbai* 20 B1
Colegiales *Buenos Aires* 7 B2
Colindale *London* 15 A2
Colinton *Edinburgh* 11 B2
College Park *Atlanta* 3 C2
College Park *Washington* 33 B4
College Point *New York* 22 B2
Collégien *Paris* 24 A4
Collier Row *London* 15 A4
Colliers Wood *London* 15 B2
Colma *San Francisco* 26 B2
Colney Hatch *London* 15 A3
Cologno Monzese *Milan* 19 A2
Colombes *Paris* 24 A2
Colonia Güell *Barcelona* 4 A1
Colonial Knob *Wellington* 33 A1
Colosseo *Rome* 26 B1
Colosseum = Colosseo *Rome* 26 B1
Combault *Paris* 24 B4
Comércio, Praça do *Lisbon* 16 A2
Commerce *Los Angeles* 16 B4
Como *Sydney* 29 C1
Conceição, I. da *Rio de Janeiro* 25 B2
Conchalí *Santiago* 27 B2
Concord *Sydney* 29 B1
Concord *Toronto* 31 A2
Concorde, Place de la *Paris* 24 A2
Concorezzo *Milan* 19 A2
Condet *Jakarta* 12 A2
Coney Island *New York* 22 C2
Congonhas São Paulo ✕ (CGH) *São Paulo* 27 B2
Conley → *Atlanta* 3 C3
Connaught Place *Delhi* 10 B2
Consolação *São Paulo* 27 B2
Constantia *Cape Town* 8 B1
Constitución *Buenos Aires* 7 B2
Constitution *Atlanta* 3 B2
Convention Center *Los Angeles* 16 B3
Conway *Orlando* 23 B2
Conway, L. *Orlando* 23 B2
Coogee *Sydney* 29 B2
Cooksville *Toronto* 31 B1
Coolock *Dublin* 10 A2
Copacabana *Rio de Janeiro* 25 B1
Copenhagen = København *Copenhagen* 8 A2
Coral Gables *Miami* 18 B2
Coral Hills *Washington* 33 B4
Corcovado, Cristo Redentor *Rio de Janeiro* 25 B1
Corduff *Dublin* 10 A1
Cormano *Milan* 19 A2
Cornaredo *Milan* 19 A1
Córsico *Milan* 19 B1
Corstorphine *Edinburgh* 11 B2
Corviale *Rome* 26 B1
Coslada *Madrid* 17 B2
Cossigny *Paris* 24 B4
Cotao *Lisbon* 16 A1
Côte-St-Luc *Montreal* 20 B2
Cotunduba, I. de *Rio de Janeiro* 25 B2
Coubron *Paris* 24 A4
Countryside *Chicago* 9 C1
County Art Museum *Los Angeles* 16 B2
Courbevoie *Paris* 24 A2
Courtry *Paris* 24 A4
Cowley *London* 15 A1
Coyoacán *Mexico City* 18 B2
Craighall Park *Johannesburg* 13 A2
Craiglockhart *Edinburgh* 11 B2
Craigmillar *Edinburgh* 11 B3
Cramond *Edinburgh* 11 B2
Cramond Bridge *Edinburgh* 11 B1
Cramond I. *Edinburgh* 11 B2
Cranford *London* 15 B1
Crawford *Cape Town* 8 A2
Crayford *London* 15 B5
Creekmouth *London* 15 A4
Crescent, L. *Orlando* 23 A1
Crescenzago *Milan* 19 A2
Cressely *Paris* 24 B1
Cresskill *New York* 22 A2
Créteil *Paris* 24 B3
Cricklewood *London* 15 A2
Cristo Redentor, Estatua do *Rio de Janeiro* 25 B1
Crockenhill *London* 15 B4
Croissy-Beaubourg *Paris* 24 B4
Croissy-sur-Seine *Paris* 24 A1
Crosby *Johannesburg* 13 B1
Crosne *Paris* 24 B3
Cross I. *Mumbai* 20 B2
Crouch End *London* 15 A3
Crown Mine *Johannesburg* 13 B1
Crows Nest *Sydney* 29 A2
Croydon *London* 15 B3
Croydon Park *Sydney* 29 B1
Cruagh Mt. *Dublin* 10 B2
Crumlin *Dublin* 10 B2
Cruz de Pau *Lisbon* 16 B2
Crystal Palace *London* 15 B3
Csepel *Budapest* 7 B2
Csepelsziget *Budapest* 7 B2
Csillaghegy *Budapest* 7 A2
Csillagtelep *Budapest* 7 B2
Csömör *Budapest* 7 A3
Csömöri-patak → *Budapest* 7 A3
Cuatro Vientos *Madrid* 17 B1
Cuauhtémoc *Mexico City* 18 B2
Cuban Museum *Miami* 18 B2
Cubao *Manila* 17 B2
Çubuklu *Istanbul* 12 B2
Cudahy *Los Angeles* 16 C3
Cuicuilco, Pirámido de *Mexico City* 18 C1
Culmore *Washington* 33 B3
Culver City *Los Angeles* 16 B2
Cumbres de Vallecas *Madrid* 17 B2
Cupecé *São Paulo* 27 B1
Currie *Edinburgh* 11 B2
Cusago *Milan* 19 B1
Cusano Milanino *Milan* 19 A2
Cutler Park *Boston* 6 B1
Çuvuşabaşi → *Istanbul* 12 B1
Cypress Hills *New York* 22 B2
Czerniaków *Warsaw* 32 B2
Czyste *Warsaw* 32 B1

D

Da Moóca → *São Paulo* 27 B2
Ďáblice *Prague* 25 B2
Dąbrowa *Warsaw* 32 B1
Dachang *Shanghai* 28 B1
Dachang ✕ *Shanghai* 28 B1
Dachau *Munich* 21 A1
Dachau-Ost *Munich* 21 A1
Dachauer Moos *Munich* 21 A1
Dadar *Mumbai* 20 A1
Daebang *Seoul* 27 B1
Daechi *Seoul* 27 B2
Dafní *Athens* 2 B2
Dagenham *London* 15 A4
Daglfing *Munich* 21 B2
Dahab, Gezîret el *Cairo* 7 B2
Daheisha *Jerusalem* 13 B2
Dahlem *Berlin* 5 B2
Dahlwitz-Hoppegarten *Berlin* 5 A5
Dahongmen *Beijing* 4 C2
Dajiaoting *Beijing* 4 B2
Dakhnoye *St. Petersburg* 27 C1
Dalejsky potok → *Prague* 25 B2
Dalgety Bay *Edinburgh* 11 A1
Dalkeith *Edinburgh* 11 B3
Dalkey *Dublin* 10 B3
Dalkey I. *Dublin* 10 B3
Dallgow *Berlin* 5 A1
Dalmeny *Edinburgh* 11 B1
Dalston *London* 15 A3
Daly City *San Francisco* 26 B2
Damaia *Lisbon* 16 A1
Damarakia *Athens* 2 B1
Dämeritzsee *Berlin* 5 B5
Dan Ryan Woods *Chicago* 9 C2
Danderhall *Edinburgh* 11 B3
Danderyd *Stockholm* 29 A2
Danforth *Toronto* 31 A3
Darakeh *Tehran* 31 A2
Darband *Tehran* 31 A2
Darling Point *Sydney* 29 B2
Darndale *Dublin* 10 A2
Darrūs *Tehran* 31 A2
Dartford *London* 15 B5
Dashi *Guangzhou* 11 B2
Datansha *Guangzhou* 11 B2
Datun *Beijing* 4 B2
Daulatpur *Delhi* 10 A1
Davidson, Mt. *San Francisco* 26 B2
Davidson's Mains *Edinburgh* 11 B2
Dāvūdiyeh *Tehran* 31 A2
Davydkovo *Moscow* 19 B1
Dawidy *Warsaw* 32 C1
Days Bay *Wellington* 33 B2
Decatur *Atlanta* 3 B3
Dedham *Boston* 6 B1
Degunino *Moscow* 19 A2
Deir Dibwan *Jerusalem* 13 A2
Deir Ibzi'e *Jerusalem* 13 A1
Dejvice *Prague* 25 B2
Dekabristov, Ostrov *St. Petersburg* 27 B1
Delhi *Delhi* 10 B2
Demarest *New York* 22 A2
Den Ilp *Amsterdam* 2 A2
Denistone Heights *Sydney* 29 A1
Dentonia Park *Toronto* 31 A3
DePaul University *Chicago* 9 B3
Deptford *London* 15 B3
Des Plaines *Chicago* 9 A1
Deshengmen *Beijing* 4 B2
Deutsch-Wagram *Vienna* 32 A3
Deutsche Oper *Berlin* 5 A2
Deutscher Museum *Munich* 21 B2
Devil's Peak *Cape Town* 8 A1
Dhakuria *Kolkata* 14 B2
Dharavi *Mumbai* 20 A2
Diadema *São Paulo* 27 C2
Diegem *Brussels* 6 A2
Diemen *Amsterdam* 2 A2
Diepkloof *Johannesburg* 13 B1
Dieprivier *Cape Town* 8 B1
Difficult Run → *Washington* 33 B2
Dilbeek *Brussels* 6 A1
Dilli = Delhi *Delhi* 10 B2
Dirnismaning *Munich* 21 A2
Disney-M.G.M. Studios *Orlando* 23 B1
Disney Studios *Los Angeles* 16 B3
District Heights *Washington* 33 B4
Djakarta = Jakarta *Jakarta* 12 A2
Djursholm *Stockholm* 29 A2
Döberitz *Berlin* 5 A1
Döbling *Vienna* 32 A2
Dobong *Seoul* 27 B2
Dobongsan *Seoul* 27 A2
Docklands *London* 15 A3
Doctor Phillips *Orlando* 23 B2
Dodder → *Dublin* 10 B1
Dodger Stadium *Los Angeles* 16 B3
Dogs, Isle of *London* 15 B3
Dolgoe Ozero *St. Petersburg* 27 A1
Dollis Hill *London* 15 A2
Dollymount *Dublin* 10 A2
Dolni *Prague* 25 B3
Dolni Chabry *Prague* 25 B2
Dolni Počernice *Prague* 25 B3
Dolphins Barn *Dublin* 10 B2
Dom Pedro II, Parque *São Paulo* 27 B2
Don Mills *Toronto* 31 A2
Don Muang Int. ✕ (BKK) *Bangkok* 3 A2
Donaghmede *Dublin* 10 A3
Donau-Oder Kanal *Vienna* 32 A3
Donaufeld *Vienna* 32 A2
Donaupark *Vienna* 32 A2
Donaustadt *Vienna* 32 A2
Dongan Hills *New York* 22 C1
Dongcheng *Beijing* 4 B2
Dongdaemung *Seoul* 27 B2
Donggou *Shanghai* 28 B2
Dongjak *Seoul* 27 B1
Dongjiao *Guangzhou* 11 B2
Dongri *Mumbai* 20 B2
Dongshanhu Park *Guangzhou* 11 B2
Dongzhimen *Beijing* 4 B2
Donnybrook *Dublin* 10 B2
Doornfontein *Johannesburg* 13 B2
Dorchester *Boston* 6 B2
Dorchester B. *Boston* 6 B2
Dorchester Heights Nat. Historical Site △ *Boston* 6 B2
Dornach *Munich* 21 B3
Dorval Int., Montréal ✕ (YUL) *Montreal* 20 B1
Dos Couros → *São Paulo* 27 C2
Dos Moninos → *São Paulo* 27 C2
Douglas Park *Chicago* 9 B2
Dover Heights *Sydney* 29 B2
Dowlatābād *Tehran* 31 B2
Down, L. *Orlando* 23 A1
Downey *Los Angeles* 16 C4
Downsview *Toronto* 31 A1
Downsview C.A.F.B. ✕ *Toronto* 31 A2
Dragør *Copenhagen* 8 B3
Drancy *Paris* 24 A3
Dranesville *Washington* 33 A1
Drapetsona *Athens* 2 B1
Dreilinden *Berlin* 5 B2
Drewnica *Warsaw* 32 B2
Drigh Road *Karachi* 13 A2
Drimnagh *Dublin* 10 B2
Drogenbos *Brussels* 6 B1
Druid Hills *Atlanta* 3 B2
Drumcondra *Dublin* 10 A2
Drummoyne *Sydney* 29 B1
Drylaw *Edinburgh* 11 B2
Dubeč *Prague* 25 B3
Dublin *Dublin* 10 A2
Dublin ✕ (DUB) *Dublin* 10 A2
Dublin B. *Dublin* 10 B3
Dublin Harbour *Dublin* 10 A2
Duddingston *Edinburgh* 11 B3
Dugnano *Milan* 19 A2
Duivendrecht *Amsterdam* 2 B2
Dūlāb *Tehran* 31 B2
Dulwich *London* 15 B3
Dum Dum *Kolkata* 14 B2
Dum Dum Int. ✕ (CCU) *Kolkata* 14 B2
Dumont *New York* 22 A2
Dún Laoghaire *Dublin* 10 B3
Dundrum *Dublin* 10 B2
Dunearn *Singapore* 28 B2
Dúnleary = Dún Laoghaire *Dublin* 10 B3
Dunn Loring *Washington* 33 B2
Dunning *Chicago* 9 B2
Dunvegan *Johannesburg* 13 A2
Duomo *Milan* 19 B2
Duque de Caxias *Rio de Janeiro* 25 A1
Duren Sawit *Jakarta* 12 A2
Dusit *Bangkok* 3 B2
Dworp *Brussels* 6 B1
Dyakovo *Moscow* 19 B2
Dyker Beach Park *New York* 22 C1
Dzerzhinskiy *Moscow* 19 B2
Dzerzhinskiy Park *Moscow* 19 B2

E

E.U.R. = Esposizione Universale di Roma *Rome* 26 C1
Eagle Rock *Los Angeles* 16 B3
Ealing □ *London* 15 A2
Earlsfield *London* 15 B2
Earlwood *Sydney* 29 B1
East Arlington *Boston* 6 A2
East Arlington *Washington* 33 B3
East Bedfont *London* 15 B1
East Boston *Boston* 6 A2
East Don → *Toronto* 31 A2
East Don Parkland *Toronto* 31 A2
East Elmhurst *New York* 22 B2
East Finchley *London* 15 A2
East Flatbush *New York* 22 C2
East Ham *London* 15 A4
East Humber → *Toronto* 31 A1
East Lamma Channel *Hong Kong* 12 B1
East Lexington *Boston* 6 A1
East Los Angeles *Los Angeles* 16 B3
East Molesey *London* 15 B1
East New York *New York* 22 B2
East Pines *Washington* 33 B4
East Point *Atlanta* 3 B2
East Potomac Park *Washington* 33 B3
East River → *New York* 22 B2
East Rutherford *New York* 22 A1
East Sheen *London* 15 B2
East Talpiyot *Jerusalem* 13 B2
East Wickham *London* 15 B4
East York *Toronto* 31 A2
Eastbourne *Wellington* 33 B2
Eastcote *London* 15 A1
Easter Howgate *Edinburgh* 11 B2
Eastpoint Park *Toronto* 31 A4
Eastwood *Sydney* 29 A1
Eaton Canyon Park *Los Angeles* 16 A4
Ebara *Tokyo* 30 B3
Ebisu *Tokyo* 30 B3
Ebute-Ikorodu *Lagos* 14 A2
Ebute-Metta *Lagos* 14 B2
Eda *Tokyo* 30 B2
Edendale *Johannesburg* 13 A2
Edenmore *Dublin* 10 A2
Edgars Cr. → *Melbourne* 18 A1
Edgeley *Toronto* 31 A1
Edgemar *San Francisco* 26 C2
Edgewater *New York* 22 B2
Edgewood *Orlando* 23 B2
Edinburgh *Edinburgh* 11 B2
Edinburgh ✕ (EDI) *Edinburgh* 11 B1
Edinburgh Castle *Edinburgh* 11 B2
Edison Park *Chicago* 9 A2
Edmondston *Washington* 33 B4
Edmondstown *Dublin* 10 B2
Edo → *Tokyo* 30 B4
Edogawa *Tokyo* 30 A4
Edsberg *Stockholm* 29 A1
Edwards L. *Melbourne* 18 A1
Efzonos *Athens* 2 B2
Egaleo *Athens* 2 B2
Egaleo, Oros *Athens* 2 B1
Eiche *Berlin* 5 A4
Eiche Süd *Berlin* 5 A4
Eiffel, Tour *Paris* 24 A2
Ein Arik *Jerusalem* 13 A1
Ein Naquba *Jerusalem* 13 B1
Ein Rafa *Jerusalem* 13 B1
Eizariya *Jerusalem* 13 B2
Ejby *Copenhagen* 8 A2
Ejigbo *Lagos* 14 A1
Ekeberg *Oslo* 23 A3
Eknäs *Stockholm* 29 B3
El 'Abbasiya *Cairo* 7 A2
El Agustino *Lima* 14 B2
El Baragil *Cairo* 7 A1
El Basâtîn *Cairo* 7 B2
El Bira *Jerusalem* 13 A2
El Bosque *Santiago* 27 C2
El Carmen *Santiago* 27 B1
El Cortijo *Santiago* 27 B1
El Cristo, Vaso Regulador *Mexico City* 18 B1
El Duqqi *Cairo* 7 A2
El Encinar de los Reyes *Madrid* 17 A2
El Gezira *Cairo* 7 A2
El Ghurîya *Cairo* 7 A2
El Gîza *Cairo* 7 A2
El Khadr *Jerusalem* 13 B1
El Khalîfa *Cairo* 7 A2
El Kôm el Ahmar *Cairo* 7 A2
El Ma'âdi *Cairo* 7 B2
El Matarîya *Cairo* 7 A2
El Mohandessin *Cairo* 7 A2
El Monte *Los Angeles* 16 B4
El Muqattam *Cairo* 7 A2
El Mûski *Cairo* 7 A2
El Pardo *Madrid* 17 A1
El Portal *Miami* 18 A2
El Prat de Llobregat *Barcelona* 4 B1
El Qâhira *Cairo* 7 A2
El Qubba *Cairo* 7 A2
El Reloj *Mexico City* 18 C2
El Retiro *Madrid* 17 B1
El Salto *Santiago* 27 B2
El Sereno *Los Angeles* 16 B3
El Talibîya *Cairo* 7 B2
El Vergel *Mexico City* 18 C2
El Wâhli *Cairo* 7 A2
El Zamâlik *Cairo* 7 A2
El Zeitûn *Cairo* 7 A2
Elephanta Caves *Mumbai* 20 B2
Elephanta I. *Mumbai* 20 B2
Ellboda *Stockholm* 29 A3
Ellenor, L. *Orlando* 23 B2
Elliniko Olympic Complex *Athens* 2 B2
Ellis I. *New York* 22 B1
Elm Park *London* 15 A5
Elmers End *London* 15 B3
Elmhurst *New York* 22 B2
Elmstead *London* 15 B4
Elmwood Park *Chicago* 9 B2
Elmwood Park *New York* 22 A1
Elsdon *Wellington* 33 A1
Elsiesrivier *Cape Town* 8 A2
Elsternwick *Melbourne* 18 B2
Eltham *London* 15 B4
Elwood *Melbourne* 18 B1
Élysée *Paris* 24 A2
Elysian Park *Los Angeles* 16 B3
Emāmzādeh Sāleh *Tehran* 31 A2
Émerainville *Paris* 24 B4
Emeryville *San Francisco* 26 A3
Eminönü *Istanbul* 12 B1
Emirgan *Istanbul* 12 B2
Emmarentia *Johannesburg* 13 A2
Empire State Building *New York* 22 B2
Encantado *Rio de Janeiro* 25 B1
Encino *Los Angeles* 16 B2
Encino Res. *Los Angeles* 16 B1
Enebyberg *Stockholm* 29 A1
Enfield *Sydney* 29 B1
Engenho, I. do *Rio de Janeiro* 25 B2
Englewood *Chicago* 9 C3
Englewood *New York* 22 A2
Englewood Cliffs *New York* 22 A2
Enmore *Sydney* 29 B2
Enskede *Stockholm* 29 B2
Entrevias *Madrid* 17 B1
Epcot *Orlando* 23 B1
Epping *Sydney* 29 A1
Eregun *Lagos* 14 A2
Erenköy *Istanbul* 12 C2
Erith *London* 15 B5
Erlaa *Vienna* 32 B1
Ermington *Sydney* 29 A1
Ermita *Manila* 17 B1
Ershatou *Guangzhou* 11 B2
Erskineville *Sydney* 29 B2
Erunkan *Lagos* 14 A2
Erzsébet-Telep *Budapest* 7 B3
Eschenried *Munich* 21 A1
Esenler *Istanbul* 12 B1
Esher *London* 15 B1
Eskbank *Edinburgh* 11 B3
Esplugas *Barcelona* 4 A1
Esposizione Universale di Roma *Rome* 26 C1
Essendon *Melbourne* 18 A1
Essendon ✕ (MEB) *Melbourne* 18 A1
Essingen *Stockholm* 29 B1
Essling *Vienna* 32 A3
Est, Gare de l' *Paris* 24 A3
Estado, Parque do *São Paulo* 27 B2
Estrela, Basilica da *Lisbon* 16 A2
Etobicoke *Toronto* 31 B1
Etobicoke Cr. → *Toronto* 31 B1
Etterbeek *Brussels* 6 B2
Eung-am *Seoul* 27 B1
Eunpyeong *Seoul* 27 B1
Evanston *Chicago* 9 A2
Even Sapir *Jerusalem* 13 B1
Evere *Brussels* 6 A2
Everett *Boston* 6 A2
Evergreen Park *Chicago* 9 C2
Evīn *Tehran* 31 A2
Ewu *Lagos* 14 A1
Exhibition Place *Toronto* 31 B2
Exposições, Palácio das *Rio de Janeiro* 25 B1
Eyüp *Istanbul* 12 B1
Ezeiza ✕ (EZE) *Buenos Aires* 7 B2

F

Fabour, Mt. *Singapore* 28 B2
Fælledparken *Copenhagen* 8 A3
Fågelön *Stockholm* 29 B1
Fagersjö *Stockholm* 29 B2
Fair Lawn *New York* 22 A1
Fairfax *Washington* 33 B2
Fairfax Station *Washington* 33 C2
Fairland *Johannesburg* 13 A1
Fairmilehead *Edinburgh* 11 B2
Fairmount Heights *Washington* 33 B4
Fairport *Toronto* 31 A4
Fairview *New York* 22 B2
Fairview, L. *Orlando* 23 A2
Falenty *Warsaw* 32 C1
Faliro *Athens* 2 B1
Faliro, Ormos *Athens* 2 B2
Falkenburg *Berlin* 5 A4
Falkenhagen *Berlin* 5 A1
Falkensee *Berlin* 5 A1
Falls Church *Washington* 33 B2
Falomo *Lagos* 14 B2
False Bay *Cape Town* 8 B2
Fangcun *Guangzhou* 11 B2
Farahābād *Tehran* 31 A2
Farforovskaya *St. Petersburg* 27 B2
Farningham *London* 15 B5
Farsta *Stockholm* 29 B2
Fasanerie-Nord *Munich* 21 A2
Fasangarten *Munich* 21 B2
Fatih *Istanbul* 12 B1
Favoriten *Vienna* 32 B2
Fawkner *Melbourne* 18 A1
Fawkner Park *Melbourne* 18 B1
FedEx Stadium *Washington* 33 B4
Feijó *Lisbon* 16 B2
Feldkirchen *Munich* 21 B3
Feldmoching *Munich* 21 A2
Feltham *London* 15 B1
Fener *Istanbul* 12 B1
Fenerbahçe *Istanbul* 12 C2
Fengtai *Beijing* 4 C1
Ferencváros *Budapest* 7 B2
Ferihegy, Budapest ✕ (BUD) *Budapest* 7 B3
Ferndale *Johannesburg* 13 A2
Férolles-Attilly *Paris* 24 B4
Fichtenau *Berlin* 5 B5
Field Museum of Natural History *Chicago* 9 B3
Fields Corner *Boston* 6 B2
Fiera Camp *Milan* 19 B1
Figino *Milan* 19 B1
Fijir *Baghdad* 3 A2
Filadelfia *Athens* 2 A2
Fili-Mazilovo *Moscow* 19 B1
Filothei *Athens* 2 A2
Finchley *London* 15 A2
Fine Arts, Museum of *Boston* 6 A2
Finglas *Dublin* 10 A2
Finsbury *London* 15 A3
Finsbury Park *London* 15 A3
Fiorito *Buenos Aires* 7 C2
Firhouse *Dublin* 10 B2
Fischerhäuser *Munich* 21 A3
Fisher Island *Miami* 18 B2
Fishermans Bend *Melbourne* 18 A1
Fisherville *Toronto* 31 A2
Fisksätra *Stockholm* 29 B3
Fitzroy Gardens *Melbourne* 18 A1
Five Dock *Sydney* 29 B1
Fjellstrand *Oslo* 23 B2
Flamengo *Rio de Janeiro* 25 B1
Flamingo *Orlando* 23 B2
Flaminio *Rome* 26 B1
Flaskebekk *Oslo* 23 A2
Flatbush *New York* 22 C2
Flaten *Stockholm* 29 B2
Flatlands *New York* 22 C2
Flemington Racecourse *Melbourne* 18 A1
Flint Pk. *Los Angeles* 16 B3
Florence *Los Angeles* 16 C3
Florence Bloom Bird Sanctuary △ *Johannesburg* 13 A2
Florentia *Johannesburg* 13 B2
Flores *Buenos Aires* 7 B2
Flores, Mercado de *Mexico City* 18 C2
Floresta *Buenos Aires* 7 B2
Florida *Buenos Aires* 7 B2
Florida *Johannesburg* 13 B1
Floridsdorf *Vienna* 32 A2
Flushing *New York* 22 B3
Flushing Meadows Corona Park *New York* 22 B2
Flysta *Stockholm* 29 A1
Fo Tan *Hong Kong* 12 A2
Föhrenhain *Vienna* 32 A2
Fontainebleau *Johannesburg* 13 A1
Fontenay-aux-Roses *Paris* 24 B2
Fontenay-le-Fleury *Paris* 24 B1
Fontenay-sous-Bois *Paris* 24 A3
Foots Cray *London* 15 B4
Footscray *Melbourne* 18 A1
Forbidden City = Imperial Palace Museum *Beijing* 4 B2
Forest *Brussels* 6 B1
Forest Gate *London* 15 A4
Forest Heights *Washington* 33 C3
Forest Hill *London* 15 B3
Forest Hill *Toronto* 31 A2
Forest Hills *New York* 22 B2
Forest Park *Chicago* 9 B2
Forest Park *New York* 22 B2
Forest View *Chicago* 9 C2
Forestville *Washington* 33 B4
Fornebu *Oslo* 23 A2
Foro Romano *Rome* 26 B1
Forstenried *Munich* 21 B1
Forstenrieder Park *Munich* 21 B1
Fort *Mumbai* 20 B1
Fort Dupont Park *Washington* 33 B4
Fort Foote Village *Washington* 33 C3
Fort Lee *New York* 22 A2
Forth, Firth of *Edinburgh* 11 A2
Forth Rail Bridge *Edinburgh* 11 A1
Forth Road Bridge *Edinburgh* 11 A1
Fót *Budapest* 7 A3
Fourqueux *Paris* 24 A1
Foxrock *Dublin* 10 B2
Franconia *Washington* 33 C3
Frank Lloyd Wright Home *Chicago* 9 B2
Frankel *Singapore* 28 B3
Franklin Park *Boston* 6 B2
Franklin Park *Chicago* 9 B1
Franklin Park *Washington* 33 B3
Franklin Res. *Los Angeles* 16 B2
Frauenkirche *Munich* 21 B2
Frederiksberg *Copenhagen* 8 A3
Frederiksdal *Copenhagen* 8 A2
Fredersdorf *Berlin* 5 A5
Freguesia *Rio de Janeiro* 25 A1
Freidrichshain, Volkspark *Berlin* 5 A3
Freiham *Munich* 21 B1
Freimann *Munich* 21 A2
French Quarter *New Orleans* 21 B2
Fresh Pond *Boston* 6 A2
Fresnes *Paris* 24 B2
Freudenau *Vienna* 32 A2
Friarstown *Dublin* 10 B1
Friedenau *Berlin* 5 B3
Friedrichsfelde *Berlin* 5 B4
Friedrichshagen *Berlin* 5 B4
Friedrichshain *Berlin* 5 A3
Friedrichslust *Berlin* 5 A5
Friherrs *Helsinki* 11 B1
Frilufts Museum *Helsinki* 11 B2
Frontón, I. *Lima* 14 B1
Frunze *Moscow* 19 B2
Fūchū *Tokyo* 30 A1
Fuencarral *Madrid* 17 B1
Fuenlabrada *Madrid* 17 C1
Fukagawa *Tokyo* 30 B3
Fukushima *Osaka* 23 A1
Fulham *London* 15 B2
Funabori *Tokyo* 30 A4
Fundão, I. do *Rio de Janeiro* 25 B1
Fünfhaus *Vienna* 32 A2
Fureso *Copenhagen* 8 A2
Fürth *Munich* 21 B2
Futago-tamagawaen *Tokyo* 30 B2
Fuxing Dao *Shanghai* 28 B2
Fuxing Park *Shanghai* 28 B1
Fuxinglu *Beijing* 4 B1

G

G. Ross Lord Park *Toronto* 31 A2
Gaebong *Seoul* 27 C1
Gage Park *Chicago* 9 C2
Gagny *Paris* 24 A4
Galata *Istanbul* 12 B1
Galata Tower *Istanbul* 12 B1
Galatsi *Athens* 2 A2
Galeão, Int. de ✕ (GIG) *Rio de Janeiro* 25 A1
Galyanovo *Moscow* 19 B3
Gambir *Jakarta* 12 A1
Gamboa *Rio de Janeiro* 25 B1
Gambolóita *Milan* 19 B2
Gamlebyen *Oslo* 23 A3
Gangdong *Seoul* 27 B2
Gangnam *Seoul* 27 B1
Gangseo *Seoul* 27 B1
Gangtou *Guangzhou* 11 A1
Gangwei *Guangzhou* 11 B2
Ganjiakou *Beijing* 4 B1
Ganshoren *Brussels* 6 A1
Gants Hill *London* 15 A4
Gaoqiao *Shanghai* 28 A2
Garbagnate Milanese *Milan* 19 A1
Garbatella *Rome* 26 B2
Garches *Paris* 24 A2
Garching *Munich* 21 A3
Garden City *Cairo* 7 A2
Garden Reach *Kolkata* 14 B1
Garder *Oslo* 23 B2
Garfield *New York* 22 A1
Garfield Park *Chicago* 9 B2
Gargareta *Athens* 2 B2
Garibong *Seoul* 27 C1
Garvanza *Los Angeles* 16 B3
Gåshaga *Stockholm* 29 A3
Gateway △ *New York* 22 C2
Gateway of India *Mumbai* 20 B2
Gatow *Berlin* 5 B1
Gavà *Barcelona* 4 B1
Gávea *Rio de Janeiro* 25 B1
Gávea, Pedra da *Rio de Janeiro* 25 B1
Gazdagrét *Budapest* 7 B1
Gaziosmanpaşa *Istanbul* 12 B1
Gebel el Ahmar *Cairo* 7 A3
Gebel el Muqattam *Cairo* 7 A2
Gebel el Tura *Cairo* 7 B2
Geiselgasteig *Munich* 21 B2
General San Martín *Buenos Aires* 7 B1
Gennevilliers *Paris* 24 A2
Gentilly *Paris* 24 B3
Gentofte *Copenhagen* 8 A3
Genval *Brussels* 6 B2
George I. *Hong Kong* 12 B1
Georges River Bridge *Sydney* 29 C1
Georgetown *Washington* 33 B3
Georgia Dome *Atlanta* 3 B2
Gerasdorf bei Wien *Vienna* 32 A2
Gerberau *Munich* 21 A1
Gerli *Buenos Aires* 7 C2
Germiston *Johannesburg* 13 B2
Gern *Munich* 21 B2
Getafe *Madrid* 17 C1
Getty Center, The *Los Angeles* 16 B2
Geunjeong *Seoul* 27 C1
Geva Binyamin *Jerusalem* 13 A2
Geylang Serai *Singapore* 28 B3
Gharapuri *Mumbai* 20 B2
Gharb = Shahrak-e Qods *Tehran* 31 A2
Ghatkopar *Mumbai* 20 A2
Ghazipur *Delhi* 10 B2
Ghizri *Karachi* 13 B2
Ghizri Cr. → *Karachi* 13 B2
Ghonda *Delhi* 10 A2
Ghusuri *Kolkata* 14 B2
Gianicolense *Rome* 26 B1
Giant Wheel = Riesenrad *Vienna* 32 A2
Gibraltar Pt. *Toronto* 31 B2
Gidea Park *London* 15 A5
Giesing *Munich* 21 B2
Gilmerton *Edinburgh* 11 B3
Gilo *Jerusalem* 13 B2
Gimmersta *Stockholm* 29 B3
Ginza *Tokyo* 30 B3
Giv'at Ram *Jerusalem* 13 B2
Giv'at Ye'arim *Jerusalem* 13 B1
Giv'at Ze'ev *Jerusalem* 13 A2
Giv'on *Jerusalem* 13 A1
Giza = El Gîza *Cairo* 7 A2
Giza Pyramids *Cairo* 7 B1
Gjersjøen *Oslo* 23 B3
Gladesville *Sydney* 29 B1
Gladsakse *Copenhagen* 8 A2
Glasnevin *Dublin* 10 A2
Glassmanor *Washington* 33 C4
Glasthule *Dublin* 10 B3
Glen Iris *Melbourne* 18 B2
Glen Mar Park *Washington* 33 B3
Glen Rock *New York* 22 A1
Glen Rouge Park *Toronto* 31 A4
Glenarden *Washington* 33 B4
Glenasmole Reservoirs *Dublin* 10 B1
Glencorse Res. *Edinburgh* 11 B2
Glencullen *Dublin* 10 B2
Glendale *Los Angeles* 16 B3
Glendoo Mt. *Dublin* 10 B2
Glenhuntly *Melbourne* 18 B2
Glenside *Wellington* 33 B1
Glenview *Chicago* 9 A2
Glenview Countryside *Chicago* 9 A2
Glenvista *Johannesburg* 13 B2
Glifada *Athens* 2 B2
Glömsta *Stockholm* 29 B1
Glostrup *Copenhagen* 8 B2
Gogar *Edinburgh* 11 B2
Göktürk *Istanbul* 12 A1
Golabari *Kolkata* 14 B2
Golabki *Warsaw* 32 B1
Gold Coast *Chicago* 9 B3
Golden Gate *San Francisco* 26 B2
Golden Gate △ *San Francisco* 26 A2
Golden Gate Bridge *San Francisco* 26 B2
Golden Gate Park *San Francisco* 26 B2
Golden Horn = Haliç *Istanbul* 12 B1
Golders Green *London* 15 A2
Golestan Palace *Tehran* 31 A2
Gollans Stream → *Wellington* 33 B2
Gonen *Jerusalem* 13 B2
Gongneung *Seoul* 27 B2
Goodmayes *London* 15 A4
Goodwood *Cape Town* 8 A2
Gopalpur *Kolkata* 14 B2
Górce *Warsaw* 32 B1
Gore Hill *Sydney* 29 A2

Gorelyy → St. Petersburg 27 A3
Gorgie Edinburgh 11 B2
Gorky Park Moscow 19 B2
Gosen Berlin 5 B5
Gosener kanal Berlin 5 B5
Gospel Oak London 15 A3
Gotanda Tokyo 30 B3
Goth Goli Mar Karachi 13 A2
Goth Sher Shah Karachi 13 A1
Gotha Orlando 23 A1
Gournay-sur-Marne Paris 24 A4
Governador, I. do Rio de Janeiro 25 A1
Governors I. New York 22 B1
Grabów Warsaw 32 C1
Grace, Mt. Wellington 33 B2
Gracefield Wellington 33 B2
Gracia Barcelona 4 A2
Gräfelfing Munich 21 B1
Gragoatá Rio de Janeiro 25 B2
Grand Bazaar = Kapali Carsi Istanbul 12 B1
Grand Central Station New York 22 B2
Grand Palace Bangkok 3 B1
Grande Place Brussels 6 A2
Grankulla = Kauniainen Helsinki 11 B1
Grant Park Chicago 9 B3
Granton Edinburgh 11 B2
Grassy Park Cape Town 8 B2
Gratosóglio Milan 19 B2
Gratzwalde Berlin 5 B5
Gravesend New York 22 C2
Grazhdanka St. Petersburg 27 B2
Great Falls Washington 33 B2
Great Falls Park Washington 33 B2
Great Western Forum Los Angeles 16 C2
Greco Milan 19 A2
Green I. Hong Kong 12 B1
Green Point Cape Town 8 A1
Greenbelt Washington 33 A4
Greenbelt Park Washington 33 B4
Greenfield Park Montreal 20 B3
Greenford London 15 A1
Greenhill London 15 A2
Greenhills Dublin 10 B1
Greenpoint New York 22 B2
Greenwich □ London 15 B3
Greenwich Observatory London 15 B3
Greenwich Village New York 22 B2
Greenwood Boston 6 A2
Grefsen Oslo 23 A3
Gresham Park Atlanta 3 B2
Greve Strand Copenhagen 8 B1
Griebnitzsee Berlin 5 B1
Griffith Park Los Angeles 16 B3
Grimbergen Brussels 6 A2
Grinzing Vienna 32 A2
Gröbenried Munich 21 A1
Grochów Warsaw 32 B2
Grodzisk Warsaw 32 B2
Groenendaal Brussels 6 B2
Grogol Petamburin Jakarta 12 A1
Gronsdorf Munich 21 B3
Grorud Oslo 23 A4
Gross-Glienicke Berlin 5 B1
Gross-Hadern Munich 21 B1
Gross-Lappen Munich 21 A2
Grosse Krampe Berlin 5 B5
Grosse Müggelsee Berlin 5 B4
Grosse Point Lighthouse Chicago 9 A2
Grossenzersdorf Vienna 32 A3
Grossenzersdorfer Arm → Vienna 32 A3
Grosser Biberhaufen Vienna 32 A2
Grosser Wannsee Berlin 5 B2
Grossfeld-Siedlung Vienna 32 A2
Grosshesselohe Munich 21 B2
Grossjedlersdorf Vienna 32 A2
Grossziethen Berlin 5 B3
Ground Zero New York 22 B1
Grove, The Chicago 9 A1
Grove Hall Boston 6 B2
Grove Park Atlanta 3 B2
Grove Park Hounslow, London 15 B2
Grove Park Lewisham, London 15 B4
Groveton Washington 33 C3
Grünau Berlin 5 B4
Grunewald Berlin 5 B2
Grünwald Munich 21 B2
Grünwalder Forst Munich 21 B2
Grymes Hill New York 22 C1
Guadalupe Manila 17 B2
Guadalupe, Basilica de Mexico City 18 B2
Guanabara, B. de Rio de Janeiro 25 B1
Guanabara, Jardim Rio de Janeiro 25 A1
Guanabara, Palácio da Rio de Janeiro 25 B1
Guang'anmen Beijing 4 B1
Guangqumen Beijing 4 B2
Guangzhou Guangzhou 11 B2
Guanshuo Guangzhou 11 B3
Gudö Stockholm 29 B3
Güell, Parque de Barcelona 4 A2
Guinardó Barcelona 4 A2
Gulbai Karachi 13 A1
Güngören Istanbul 12 B1
Gunnersbury London 15 B2
Gustavo A. Madero Mexico City 18 B2
Guttenberg New York 22 B1
Gutuyevskiy, Ostrov St. Petersburg 27 B1
Guyancourt Paris 24 B1
Gwanak Seoul 27 C1
Gwanaksan Seoul 27 C1
Gyál Budapest 7 B3
Gyáli-patak → Budapest 7 B2

H

Haaga Helsinki 11 B2
Haar Munich 21 B3
Habay Manila 17 C1
Hackbridge London 15 B3
Hackensack New York 22 A1
Hackensack → New York 22 B1
Hackney □ London 15 A3
Hackney Wick London 15 A3
Hadr, Warrâq el Cairo 7 A2
Haga Stockholm 29 A2
Hagenbrunn Vienna 32 A2
Hägersten Stockholm 29 B1
Häggvik Stockholm 29 A1
Hagonoy Manila 17 B2
Hague Park Toronto 31 A3
Haidian Beijing 4 B1
Haidari Athens 2 A1
Haidarpur Delhi 10 A1
Haidhausen Munich 21 B2
Haight-Ashbury San Francisco 26 B2
Hainault London 15 A4
Haizhu Guangchang Guangzhou 11 B2
Hakunila Helsinki 11 B3
Halandri Athens 2 A2
Halásztelek Budapest 7 B1
Haliç Istanbul 12 B1
Halim Perdana Kusuma Int. ✈ (HLP) Jakarta 12 B2
Halle Brussels 6 B1
Haltiala Helsinki 11 B2
Haltiavuori Helsinki 11 B2
Ham London 15 B2
Hämeenkylä Helsinki 11 B1
Hammarby Stockholm 29 B2
Hamme Brussels 6 A1
Hammersmith London 15 B2
Hampstead London 15 A2
Hampstead Montreal 20 B2
Hampstead Garden Suburb London 15 A2
Hampstead Heath London 15 A2
Hampton London 15 B1
Hampton Court Palace London 15 B1
Hampton Wick London 15 B2
Hamrā' Baghdad 3 B1
Hanala Helsinki 11 A3
Haneda Tokyo 30 B3
Haneda, Tōkyō ✈ (HND) Tokyo 30 B3
Hang Hau Hong Kong 12 B2
Hanging Gardens Mumbai 20 B1
Hanlon Toronto 31 B1
Hanwell London 15 A1
Hanworth London 15 B1
Haora Kolkata 14 B1
Hapeville Atlanta 3 C2
Happy Valley Hong Kong 12 B2
Har Adar Jerusalem 13 B1
Har Gilo Jerusalem 13 B2
Har Homa Jerusalem 13 B2
Har Nof Jerusalem 13 B2
Haren Brussels 6 A2
Hareskovby Copenhagen 8 A2
Haringey □ London 15 A3
Harjusuo Helsinki 11 B3
Harlaching Munich 21 B2
Harlaw Res. Edinburgh 11 B2
Harlem New York 22 B2
Harlesden London 15 A2
Harlington London 15 B1
Harmaja Helsinki 11 C2
Harmashatar hegy Budapest 7 A2
Harolds Cross Dublin 10 B2
Háros Budapest 7 B2
Harperrig Res. Edinburgh 11 B1
Harrow □ London 15 A1
Harrow on the Hill London 15 A1
Harrow School London 15 A1
Harrow Weald London 15 A1
Hartsfield-Atlanta Int. ✈ (ATL) Atlanta 3 C2
Harumi Tokyo 30 B3
Harvard University Boston 6 A2
Harwood Heights Chicago 9 B2
Hasanābād Tehran 31 A1
Hasbrouck Heights New York 22 A1
Haselhorst Berlin 5 A2
Hasköy Istanbul 12 B1
Hasle Oslo 23 B2
Haslum Oslo 23 A2
Hästhagen Stockholm 29 B2
Hataitai Wellington 33 B1
Hatch End London 15 A1
Hatiara Kolkata 14 B2
Hauketo Oslo 23 A3
Hauz Khas Delhi 10 B2
Havel → Berlin 5 A2
Havelkanal Berlin 5 A2
Havering □ London 15 A5
Havering-atte-Bower London 15 A5
Haworth New York 22 A2
Hawthorne Racecourse Chicago 9 C2
Hayes Bromley, London 15 B4
Hayes Hillingdon, London 15 A1
Hayes End London 15 A1
Hayford Chicago 9 C2
Haywards Wellington 33 A2
Heathfield Cape Town 8 B1
Heathrow, London ✈ (LHR) London 15 B1
Hebe Haven Hong Kong 12 A2
Hedong Guangzhou 11 B2
Heidelberg Heights Melbourne 18 A2
Heidelberg West Melbourne 18 A2
Heidemühle Berlin 5 B5
Heideveld Cape Town 8 A2
Heiligensee Berlin 5 A2
Heiligenstadt Vienna 32 A2
Heinersdorf Berlin 5 A3
Hélène de Champlain, Parc △ Montreal 20 A2
Helenelund Stockholm 29 A1
Heliopolis = Masr el Gedida Cairo 7 A2
Hellersdorf Berlin 5 A4
Hellerup Copenhagen 8 A3
Helmahof Vienna 32 A3
Helsingfors = Helsinki Helsinki 11 B2
Helsinki Helsinki 11 B2
Helsinki-Vantaa ✈ (HEL) Helsinki 11 B2
Hendon London 15 A2
Hengsha Guangzhou 11 B2
Hennigsdorf Berlin 5 A2
Henryków Warsaw 32 B1
Henson Cr. → Washington 33 C4
Herttua Helsinki 11 B1
Heping Park Shanghai 28 B2
Hepingli Beijing 4 B2
Herlev Copenhagen 8 A2
Herman Eckstein Park Johannesburg 13 A2
Hermannskogel Vienna 32 A1
Hermiston Edinburgh 11 B2
Hermitage and Winter Palace St. Petersburg 27 B1
Hermsdorf Berlin 5 A2
Hernals Vienna 32 A2
Herne Hill London 15 B3
Héroes de Churubusco Mexico City 18 B2
Herons, Î. aux Montreal 20 B2
Herstedøster Copenhagen 8 A2
Herttoniemi Helsinki 11 B3
Heşārak Tehran 31 A1
Heston London 15 B1
Hetzendorf Vienna 32 B1
Hextable London 15 B5
Hialeah Miami 18 A1
Hiawassa, L. Orlando 23 A2
Hickory Hills Chicago 9 C2
Hiekkaharju Helsinki 11 B3
Hietaniemi Helsinki 11 B2
Hietzing Vienna 32 A1
Higashi Osaka 23 A2
Higashimurayama Tokyo 30 A1
Higashinari Osaka 23 A2
Higashisumiyoshi Osaka 23 B2
Higashiyodogawa Osaka 23 A1
High Park Toronto 31 B2
Highbury London 15 A3
Highgate London 15 A3
Highland Cr. → Toronto 31 A3
Highland Creek Toronto 31 A3
Highland Park Los Angeles 16 B3
Highlands North Johannesburg 13 A2
Hillcrest Heights Washington 33 C4
Hillend Edinburgh 11 A1
Hillingdon □ London 15 A1
Hillwood Washington 33 B3
Hilmīya Cairo 7 A2
Hin Keng Hong Kong 12 A2
Hirota Osaka 23 A1
Hirschstetten Vienna 32 A2
History Center Atlanta 3 B2
Hither Green London 15 B3
Hiyoshi Tokyo 30 B2
Hizma Jerusalem 13 B2
Hjortekær Copenhagen 8 A3
Hjortespring Copenhagen 8 A2
Hlubočepy Prague 25 B2
Ho Chung Hong Kong 12 A2
Ho Man Tin Hong Kong 12 B2
Hoboken New York 22 B1
Hobsons B. Melbourne 18 B1
Hochbrück Munich 21 A2
Hochelaga Montreal 20 A2
Hodgkins Chicago 9 C1
Hoegi Seoul 27 B2
Hoeilaart Brussels 6 B2
Hofburg Vienna 32 A2
Hoffman I. New York 22 C1
Hohenbrunn Munich 21 B3
Hohenschönhausen Berlin 5 A4
Holargos Athens 2 B2
Holborn London 15 A3
Holden, L. Orlando 23 B2
Holešovice Prague 25 B2
Holland Village Singapore 28 B2
Höllriegelskreuth Munich 21 B1
Hollywood Los Angeles 16 B3
Hollywood Bowl Los Angeles 16 B2
Holmenkollen Oslo 23 A3
Holmes Run Acres Washington 33 B2
Holmgård Stockholm 29 B1
Holmlia Oslo 23 B3
Holocaust Memorial Jerusalem 13 B2
Holyrood House, Palace of Edinburgh 11 B3
Holysloot Amsterdam 2 A3
Homerton London 15 A3
Hometown Chicago 9 C2
Hōnanchō Tokyo 30 A2
Honcho Tokyo 30 A3
Honden Tokyo 30 A4
Hondo, Rio → Los Angeles 16 B4
Hong Kong Hong Kong 12 B1
Hong Kong, Univ. of Hong Kong 12 B1
Hong Kong I. Hong Kong 12 B2
Hongje Seoul 27 B1
Hongjimun Tunnel Seoul 27 B1
Hongkou Shanghai 28 B1
Hongmiao Beijing 4 B2
Hongqiao Shanghai 28 B1
Honjyo Tokyo 30 A3
Honoré Mercier, Pont Montreal 20 B1
Hönow Berlin 5 A4
Hook London 15 B2
Horikiri Tokyo 30 A4
Horn Pond Boston 6 A1
Hornchurch London 15 A5
Horni Prague 25 B3
Horni Počernice Prague 25 B3
Hornsey London 15 A3
Horoměřice Prague 25 B1
Hortaleza Madrid 17 B2
Hosoyama Tokyo 30 B2
Hostafrancs Barcelona 4 A1
Hostivař Prague 25 B3
Houbětin Prague 25 B3
Houghton Johannesburg 13 B2
Houilles Paris 24 A2
Hounslow □ London 15 B1
Hout Bay Cape Town 8 B1
Hove Å → Copenhagen 8 A1
Hovedøya Oslo 23 A3
Høvik Oslo 23 A2
Hovorčovice Prague 25 A3
Howard Beach New York 22 C2
Howrah = Haora Kolkata 14 B1
Howth Dublin 10 A3
Howth Hd. Dublin 10 A3
Hōya Tokyo 30 A2
Hradčany Prague 25 B2
Huanghuagang Mausoleum Guangzhou 11 B2
Huangpu Shanghai 28 B2
Huangpu Jiang → Shanghai 28 B1
Huangpu Park Shanghai 28 B1
Huangtugang Beijing 4 C1
Huascar Lima 14 A2
Huay Khwang Bangkok 3 B2
Huddinge Stockholm 29 B2
Huechuraba Santiago 27 B1
Huertas de San Beltran Barcelona 4 A1
Huizingen Brussels 6 B1
Humayun's Tomb Delhi 10 B2
Humber → Toronto 31 A1
Humber B. Toronto 31 B2
Humber Bay Toronto 31 B2
Humber Bay Park Toronto 31 B2
Humber College Toronto 31 B1
Humber Summit Toronto 31 A1
Humber Valley Village Toronto 31 A1
Humberlea Toronto 31 A1
Humberwood Park Toronto 31 A1
Humboldt Park Chicago 9 B2
Humera Madrid 17 B1
Hunaydī Baghdad 3 B2
Hundige Copenhagen 8 B1
Hundige Strand Copenhagen 8 B2
Hung Hom Hong Kong 12 B2
Hunters Hill Sydney 29 B1
Hunters Pt. San Francisco 26 B2
Hunters Valley Washington 33 B2
Huntington Washington 33 C3
Huntington Park Los Angeles 16 C3
Hurīya Baghdad 3 A1
Hurstville Sydney 29 B1
Husan Jerusalem 13 B1
Husby Stockholm 29 A1
Husum Copenhagen 8 A2
Hutt → Wellington 33 B2
Hütteldorf Vienna 32 A1
Hűvösvölgy Budapest 7 A2
Huwon Secret Garden Seoul 27 B1
Hvalstad Oslo 23 A1
Hvalstrand Oslo 23 A2
Hvidovre Copenhagen 8 B2
Hwagok Seoul 27 B1
Hyattsville Washington 33 B4
Hyde Park Boston 6 B2
Hyde Park Chicago 9 C3
Hyde Park Johannesburg 13 A2
Hyde Park London 15 A2
Hyde Park Sydney 29 B2

I

Ibese Lagos 14 A2
Ibirapuera São Paulo 27 B1
Ibirapuera, Parque do São Paulo 27 B2
Icarai Rio de Janeiro 25 B2
İçerenköy Istanbul 12 C2
Ichgao Tokyo 30 B2
Ichigaya Tokyo 30 A3
Ichikawa Tokyo 30 A4
Ickenham London 15 A1
Iddo Lagos 14 B2
Idi-Oro Lagos 14 A2
Iganmu Lagos 14 B2
Igbobi Lagos 14 A2
Igbologun Lagos 14 B1
Igny Paris 24 B2
IJ, Het → Amsterdam 2 A2
IJ-meer Amsterdam 2 A3
Ijesa-Tedo Lagos 14 B1
Ijora Lagos 14 B2
Ikebe Tokyo 30 B2
Ikebukuro Tokyo 30 A3
Ikegami Tokyo 30 B3
Ikeja Lagos 14 A2
Ikeuchi Osaka 23 B2
Ikoyi Lagos 14 B2
Ikuata Lagos 14 B2
Ikuno Osaka 23 A2
Ikuta Tokyo 30 B2
Ila Oslo 23 A2
Ilford London 15 A4
Ilioupoli Athens 2 B2
Illinois at Chicago, University of Chicago 9 B3
Illinois Institute of Technology Chicago 9 B3
Ilpendam Amsterdam 2 A2
Ilsos → Athens 2 B2
Imbābah Cairo 7 A2
Imielin Warsaw 32 C2
Imirim São Paulo 27 A2
Imitos Athens 2 B2
Imitos, Oros Athens 2 B2
Imperial Palace Museum Beijing 4 B2
Inagi Tokyo 30 B2
Inchcolm Edinburgh 11 A2
Inchicore Dublin 10 A1
Inchkeith Edinburgh 11 A3
Inchmickery Edinburgh 11 A2
Incirano Milan 19 A1
Independencia Lima 14 A2
Independencia Santiago 27 B2
India Gate Delhi 10 B2
Indian Creek Village Miami 18 A2
Indianópolis São Paulo 27 B2
Indira Gandhi Int. ✈ (DEL) Delhi 10 B1
Industria Johannesburg 13 B1
Ingierstrand Oslo 23 B3
Inglewood Los Angeles 16 C3
Ingliston Edinburgh 11 B1
Inhaúma Rio de Janeiro 25 B1
Inner Port Shelter Hong Kong 12 A2
Interlagos São Paulo 27 C1
Intramuros Manila 17 B1
Invalides Paris 24 A2
Inverkeithing Edinburgh 11 A1
Inzersdorf Vienna 32 B2
Ipanema Rio de Janeiro 25 B1
Ipiranga São Paulo 27 B2
Ipiranga → São Paulo 27 B2
Iponri Lagos 14 B2
Ireland's Eye Dublin 10 A3
Irving Park Chicago 9 B2
Isabel Rio de Janeiro 25 B1
Isagatedo Lagos 14 A1
Isar → Munich 21 A3
Ishbīliya Baghdad 3 A2
Ishøj Strand Copenhagen 8 B2
Island Bay Wellington 33 B1
Island Park Toronto 31 B2
Islev Copenhagen 8 A2
Isleworth London 15 B2
Islington Toronto 31 B1
Islington □ London 15 A3
Ismaning Munich 21 A3
Ismayloskiy Park Moscow 19 B3
Isolo Lagos 14 A1
Issy-les-Moulineaux Paris 24 B2
İstanbul Istanbul 12 C1
İstanbul Boğazı Istanbul 12 B2
Istinye Istanbul 12 B2
Itä Hakkila Helsinki 11 B3
Itaewon Seoul 27 B1
Itami Osaka 23 A1
Itanhanga Rio de Janeiro 25 B1
Ivanhoe Melbourne 18 A2
Ivry-sur-Seine Paris 24 B3
Ixelles Brussels 6 B2
Izmaylovo Moscow 19 B3
Iztacalco Mexico City 18 B2
Iztapalapa Mexico City 18 B2

J

Jaba Jerusalem 13 A2
Jacaré Rio de Janeiro 25 B1
Jackson Heights New York 22 B2
Jackson Park Chicago 9 C3
Jacques-Cartier Montreal 20 A3
Jacques-Cartier, Pont Montreal 20 A2
Jadavpur Kolkata 14 C2
Jade Buddha Temple Shanghai 28 B1
Jægersborg Copenhagen 8 A3
Jægersborg Dyrehave Copenhagen 8 A3
Jagadishpur Kolkata 14 B1
Jagatpur Delhi 10 A2
Jaguaré, Rib. do → São Paulo 27 B1
Jahangirpur Delhi 10 A2
Jakarta Jakarta 12 A2
Jakarta, Teluk Jakarta 12 A1
Jalan Kayu Singapore 28 A3
Jamaica B. New York 22 C3
Jamaica Plain Boston 6 B2
Jamakpuri Delhi 10 B1
Jamshīdīyeh Tehran 31 A2
Jamsil Seoul 27 B2
Jamwon Seoul 27 B2
Janki Warsaw 32 C1
Jannali Sydney 29 C1
Jaraguá São Paulo 27 A1
Jaraguá, Pico de São Paulo 27 A1
Jardim Paulista São Paulo 27 B1
Järvatältet Stockholm 29 A1
Jaskhar Mumbai 20 B2
Jatinegara Jakarta 12 B2
Javādīyeh Tehran 31 B2
Jaworowa Warsaw 32 C1
Jedlesee Vienna 32 A2
Jefferson Memorial Washington 33 B3
Jefferson Park Chicago 9 B2
Jegi Seoul 27 B2
Jelambar Jakarta 12 A1
Jelonki Warsaw 32 B1
Jerónimos, Mosteiro dos Lisbon 16 A1
Jersey City New York 22 B1
Jerusalem Jerusalem 13 B2
Jessamine, L. Orlando 23 B2
Jésus, Î. Montreal 20 A1
Jesús María Lima 14 B2
Jette Brussels 6 A1
Jey Tehran 31 B2
Jianguomen Beijing 4 B2
Jiangwan Shanghai 28 B1
Jib Jerusalem 13 A2
Jihād Baghdad 3 B1
Jingan Shanghai 28 B1
Jinočany Prague 25 B1
Jinonice Prague 25 B2
Jiulong = Kowloon Hong Kong 12 B1
Jiyūgaoka Tokyo 30 B3
Jīzā'ir Baghdad 3 B2
Jīzīra Baghdad 3 B2
Joglo Jakarta 12 B1
Johannesburg Johannesburg 13 B2
Johannesburg, Univ. of Johannesburg 13 B2
Johanneskirchen Munich 21 A2
Johannestift Berlin 5 A2
Johannisthal Berlin 5 B4
John F. Kennedy Nat. Historic Site △ Boston 6 A2
John McLaren Park San Francisco 26 B2
Johnsonville Wellington 33 B1
Joinville-le-Pont Paris 24 B3
Joli-Bois Brussels 6 B2
Jollas Helsinki 11 B3
Jongmyo Royal Shrine Seoul 27 B1
Jongno Seoul 27 B1
Jonstrup Copenhagen 8 A2
Joppa Edinburgh 11 B3
Jorge Chavez, Int. ✈ (LIM) Lima 14 B2
Jorge Newbery ✈ Buenos Aires 7 B2
Józefa Piłsudskiego Park Warsaw 32 B1
Jōtō Osaka 23 A2
Jouy-en-Josas Paris 24 B2
Juan Anchorena Buenos Aires 7 A2
Juan González Romero Mexico City 18 A2
Juárez Int. ✈ (MEX) Mexico City 18 B2
Judeira Jerusalem 13 A2
Juhdum Jerusalem 13 B2
Juhu Mumbai 20 A2
Jūjā Tokyo 30 A3
Jukskeirivier → Johannesburg 13 A2
Julianów Warsaw 32 B2
Jung Seoul 27 B1
Jungfernheide, Volkspark Berlin 5 A2
Jungfernsee Berlin 5 B1
Junghwa Seoul 27 B2
Jungnang Seoul 27 B2
Jungnangcheon → Seoul 27 B1
Juniper Green Edinburgh 11 B2
Junk B. Hong Kong 12 B2
Jurong Singapore 28 B2
Jurong, Selat Singapore 28 B2
Jurong Industrial Estate Singapore 28 B1
Jurujuba, Enseada de Rio de Janeiro 25 B2
Jūsō Osaka 23 A1
Justice Chicago 9 C2
Jwalahari Delhi 10 B1

K

Kaapstad = Cape Town Cape Town 8 A1
Kabaty Warsaw 32 C2
Kadıköy Istanbul 12 C2
Kadoma Osaka 23 A2
Kafr 'Aqab Jerusalem 13 A2
Kâğıthane Istanbul 12 B1
Kâğıthane → Istanbul 12 B1
Kagran Vienna 32 A2
Kahnawake Montreal 20 B1
Kaimes Edinburgh 11 B2
Kaiserebersdorf Vienna 32 B2
Kaivoksela Helsinki 11 B2
Kalamaki Athens 2 B2
Kalbadevi Mumbai 20 B1
Kalipur Kolkata 14 A1
Kalithea Athens 2 B2
Kalkaji Delhi 10 B2
Kalvebod Fælled Copenhagen 8 B3
Kalveboderne Copenhagen 8 B3
Kamarhati Kolkata 14 A2
Kamata Tokyo 30 B3
Kameari Tokyo 30 A4
Kameido Tokyo 30 A4
Kami-Itabashi Tokyo 30 A3
Kamikitazawa Tokyo 30 B2
Kamitsuruma Tokyo 30 B1
Kamoshida Tokyo 30 B2
Kampong Landang Singapore 28 A3
Kampong Tanjong Penjuru Singapore 28 B2
Kampung Bali Jakarta 12 B1
Kanamori Tokyo 30 B1
Kanda Tokyo 30 A3
Kandilli Istanbul 12 B2
Kankurgachi Kolkata 14 B2
Kanlıca Istanbul 12 B2
Kanonerskiy, Ostrov St. Petersburg 27 B1
Kanzaki → Osaka 23 A1
Kapali Carsi Istanbul 12 B1
Kapellerfeld Vienna 32 A2
Káposztásmegyer Budapest 7 A2
Kapotnya Moscow 19 C3
Käppala Stockholm 29 A3
Kapuk Jakarta 12 A1
Käpylä Helsinki 11 B2
Karachi Karachi 13 A2
Karachi Int. ✈ (KHI) Karachi 13 A2
Karkh Baghdad 3 A2
Karlin Prague 25 B2
Karlsfeld Munich 21 A1
Karlshorst Berlin 5 B4
Karlův most Prague 25 B2
Karol Bagh Delhi 10 B2
Karolinenhof Berlin 5 B4
Karori Wellington 33 B1
Karow Berlin 5 A3
Karrādah Baghdad 3 B2
Kärsön Stockholm 29 B1
Kasai Tokyo 30 B4
Kasipur Kolkata 14 B2
Kastrup Copenhagen 8 B3
Kastrup, København ✈ (CPH) Copenhagen 8 B3
Kasuga Tokyo 30 A2
Kasuge Tokyo 30 A3
Kasumigaseki Tokyo 30 B3
Katong Singapore 28 B3
Katrineberg Stockholm 29 B1
Katsushika Tokyo 30 A4
Kau Pai Chau Hong Kong 12 B2
Kau Yi Chau Hong Kong 12 B1
Kaulsdorf Berlin 5 B4
Kauniainen Helsinki 11 B1
Kawasaki Tokyo 30 B3
Kawawa Tokyo 30 B2
Kawęczyn Warsaw 32 B2
Kayu Putih Jakarta 12 B2
Kbely Prague 25 B3
Kebayoran Baru Jakarta 12 B1
Kebayoran Lama Jakarta 12 B1
Kebon Jeruk Jakarta 12 B1
Kedar Jerusalem 13 B2
Kedoya Jakarta 12 B1
Keilor Melbourne 18 A1
Keilor North Melbourne 18 A1
Keimola Helsinki 11 A1
Kelapa Gading Jakarta 12 A2
Kelenföld Budapest 7 B2
Kelvin Johannesburg 13 A2
Kemang Jakarta 12 B1
Kemayoran Jakarta 12 B2
Kemerburgaz Istanbul 12 B1
Kempton Park Races London 15 B1
Kenilworth Cape Town 8 A1
Kennedy Town Hong Kong 12 B1
Kensal Green London 15 A2
Kensington Johannesburg 13 B2
Kensington London 15 B2
Kensington New York 22 C2
Kensington Sydney 29 B2
Kensington Palace London 15 A2
Kent Village Washington 33 B4
Kentish Town London 15 A3
Kenton London 15 A2
Kenwood House London 15 A3
Kepa Warsaw 32 B2
Keppel Harbour Singapore 28 B2
Kesariani Athens 2 B2
Kettering Washington 33 B5
Kew London 15 B2
Kew Melbourne 18 A2
Kew Gardens London 15 B2
Kew Gardens Toronto 31 A3
Key Biscayne Miami 18 B2
Khalīj Baghdad 3 B2
Khandallah Wellington 33 B1
Khansā' Baghdad 3 A2
Kharavli Mumbai 20 B2
Khefren Cairo 7 B1
Khichripur Delhi 10 B2
Khidirpur Kolkata 14 B1
Khimki-Khovrino Moscow 19 A2
Khirbet Batin Abu Lihyah Jerusalem 13 A1
Khirbet el-Misbah Jerusalem 13 A1
Khirbet Jub e-Rum Jerusalem 13 B2
Khlong San Bangkok 3 B2
Khlong Toey Bangkok 3 B2
Khorel Kolkata 14 A1
Khorosovo Moscow 19 B1
Kiamari Karachi 13 B1
Kierling Vienna 32 A1
Kierlingbach → Vienna 32 A1
Kifisos → Athens 2 B2
Kikuna Tokyo 30 B2
Kilbarrack Dublin 10 A3
Kilbirnie Wellington 33 B1
Kilburn London 15 A2
Killakee Dublin 10 B2
Killester Dublin 10 A2
Killiney Dublin 10 B3
Killiney B. Dublin 10 B3
Kilmacud Dublin 10 B2
Kilmainham Dublin 10 A2
Kilmainham Gaol Dublin 10 A2
Kilmashogue Mt. Dublin 10 B2
Kilmore Dublin 10 A2
Kilnamanagh Dublin 10 B1
Kilo Helsinki 11 B1
Kilokri Delhi 10 B2
Kiltiernan Dublin 10 B2
Kimmage Dublin 10 B2
Kindi Baghdad 3 B2
Kinghorn Edinburgh 11 A2
Kings Domain Melbourne 18 A1
Kings Forest = Kongelunden Copenhagen 8 B3
Kings Park Washington 33 C2
Kings Park West Washington 33 C2
Kingsbury London 15 A2
Kingsbury Melbourne 18 A2
Kingsford Sydney 29 B2
Kingsford Smith, Sydney ✈ (SYD) Sydney 29 B2
Kingston-upon-Thames □ London 15 B2
Kingston Vale London 15 B2
Kingsway Toronto 31 B1
Kinsaley Dublin 10 A2
Kipling Heights Toronto 31 A1
Kipseli Athens 2 B2
Kirchstockbach Munich 21 B3
Kirchtrudering Munich 21 B3
Kirikiri Lagos 14 B1
Kirke Værløse Copenhagen 8 A1
Kirkhill Edinburgh 11 B2
Kirkliston Edinburgh 11 B1
Kirknewton Edinburgh 11 B1
Kirov Palace of Culture St. Petersburg 27 B1
Kiryat Anavim Jerusalem 13 B1
Kiryat Ha Yovel Jerusalem 13 B1
Kısıklı Istanbul 12 B2
Kispest Budapest 7 B2
Kista Stockholm 29 A1
Kita Osaka 23 A2
Kita Tokyo 30 A3
Kitazawa Tokyo 30 B3
Kiu Tsiu Hong Kong 12 A2
Kivistö Helsinki 11 B2
Kızıltoprak Istanbul 12 C2
Kizuri Osaka 23 B2
Kjelsås Oslo 23 A3
Kladow Berlin 5 B1
Klampenborg Copenhagen 8 A3
Klaudyń Warsaw 32 B1
Klecany Prague 25 A2
Kledering Vienna 32 B2
Klein Jukskei → Johannesburg 13 A1
Kleinmachnow Berlin 5 B2
Kleinschönebeck Berlin 5 B5
Klemetsrud Oslo 23 A4
Klender Jakarta 12 A2
Kličany Prague 25 A2
Klipriviersberg Nature Reserve Johannesburg 13 B2
Klosterneuburg Vienna 32 A1
Kőbánya Budapest 7 B2
Kobbegem Brussels 6 A1
København Copenhagen 8 A2
København ✈ (CPH) Copenhagen 8 B3
Kobylisy Prague 25 B2
Kobyłka Warsaw 32 A3
Kodaira Tokyo 30 A1
Kodanaka Tokyo 30 B2
Koekelberg Brussels 6 A1
Koganei Tokyo 30 A2
Kogarah Sydney 29 B1
Koivupää Helsinki 11 B2
Koja Jakarta 12 A2
Koja Utara Jakarta 12 A2
Kokhav Ya'akov Jerusalem 13 A2
Kokobunji Tokyo 30 A1
Kokobunji-Temple Tokyo 30 A4
Kolarängen Stockholm 29 B3
Kolbotn Oslo 23 B3
Kolkata Kolkata 14 B2
Kolkata Dum Dum Int. ✈ (CCU) Kolkata 14 B2
Kolkata Maidan Kolkata 14 B1
Koło Warsaw 32 B1
Kolokinthou Athens 2 B2
Kolomyagi St. Petersburg 27 A1
Kolonos Athens 2 B2
Kolsås Oslo 23 A1
Komae Tokyo 30 B2
Komagome Tokyo 30 A3
Komazawa Tokyo 30 B3
Kona Kolkata 14 B1
Konala Helsinki 11 B2
Kondli Delhi 10 B2
Kongelunden Copenhagen 8 B3
Kongens Lyngby Copenhagen 8 A3
Kongo Helsinki 11 A1
Konnagar Kolkata 14 A2
Konohana Osaka 23 A1
Konradshöhe Berlin 5 A2
Kopanina Prague 25 B1
Koparkhairna Mumbai 20 A2
Köpenick Berlin 5 B4
Korangi Karachi 13 B2
Koremasa Tokyo 30 B1
Koridalos Athens 2 B1
Korokoro Wellington 33 B2
Korokoro Stream → Wellington 33 B2
Kosino Moscow 19 B4
Kosugi Tokyo 30 B2
Kota Jakarta 12 A1
Kōtō Tokyo 30 A3
Kotrung Kolkata 14 A2
Kouponia Athens 2 B2
Kowloon Hong Kong 12 B1
Kowloon Park Hong Kong 12 A2
Kowloon Res. Hong Kong 12 A1
Kowloon Tong Hong Kong 12 A2
Kraainem Brussels 6 A2
Krailling Munich 21 B1
Krampnitz Berlin 5 B1
Krampnitzsee Berlin 5 B1
Kranji, Sungei → Singapore 28 A2
Kranji Industrial Estate Singapore 28 A2
Krasno-Presnenskaya Moscow 19 B2
Krč Prague 25 B2
Kremlin Moscow 19 B2
Krestovskiy, Ostrov St. Petersburg 27 B1
Kreuzberg Berlin 5 A3
Kritzendorf Vienna 32 A1
Krumme Lanke Berlin 5 B2
Krummensee Berlin 5 A5
Krung Thep = Bangkok Bangkok 3 B2
Krusboda Stockholm 29 B3
Kuangchou = Guangzhou Guangzhou 11 B2
Küçükköy Istanbul 12 B1
Küçüksu Istanbul 12 B2
Kudrovo St. Petersburg 27 B3
Kulosaari Helsinki 11 B3
Kumla Stockholm 29 B3
Kungens kurva Stockholm 29 B1
Kungliga Slottet Stockholm 29 B2
Kungshatt Stockholm 29 B1
Kungsholmen Stockholm 29 A2
Kuningan Jakarta 12 B1
Kunitachi Tokyo 30 A1
Kunming Hu Beijing 4 B1
Kunratice Prague 25 B2
Kupchino St. Petersburg 27 B2
Kurbağalı → Istanbul 12 C2
Kurihara Tokyo 30 A2
Kurla Mumbai 20 A2
Kurmuri Mumbai 20 A2
Kurume Tokyo 30 A2
Kuryanovo Moscow 19 C3
Kuskovo Moscow 19 B3
Kusta Kolkata 14 B2
Kuzguncuk Istanbul 12 B2
Kuzyminki Moscow 19 B3
Kwai Chung Hong Kong 12 A1
Kwangchow = Guangzhou Guangzhou 11 B2
Kwun Tong Hong Kong 12 B2
Kyje Prague 25 B3
Kyūhōji Osaka 23 B2

L

La Blanca Santiago 27 C2
La Boca Buenos Aires 7 B2
La Bretèche Paris 24 A1
La Campiña Lima 14 C2
La Celle-St-Cloud Paris 24 A1
La Cisterna Santiago 27 C2
La Courneuve Paris 24 A3
La Dehesa Santiago 27 B2
La Encantada Lima 14 C2
La Estación Madrid 17 B1
La Floresta Barcelona 4 A1
La Florida Santiago 27 C2
La Fortuna Madrid 17 B1
La Fransa Barcelona 4 A1
La Garenne-Colombes Paris 24 A2
La Giustiniana Rome 26 B1
La Grange Chicago 9 C1
La Grange Park Chicago 9 C1
La Granja Santiago 27 C2
La Guardia, New York ✈ (LGA) New York 22 B2
La Hulpe Brussels 6 B2
La Llacuna Barcelona 4 A2
La Loma Mexico City 18 A1
La Lucila Buenos Aires 7 B2
La Maladrerie Paris 24 A1
La Milla, Cerro Lima 14 B2
La Monachina Rome 26 B1
La Moraleja Madrid 17 A2
La Nopalera Mexico City 18 C2
La Paternal Buenos Aires 7 B2
La Perla Lima 14 B2
La Perouse Sydney 29 B2
La Pineda Barcelona 4 B1
La Pisana Rome 26 B1
La Prairie Montreal 20 B3
La Punta Lima 14 B1
La Puntigala Barcelona 4 A2
La Queue-en-Brie Paris 24 B4
La Reina Santiago 27 B2
La Ribera Barcelona 4 A1
La Sagrera Barcelona 4 A2
La Salada Buenos Aires 7 C2
La Scala Milan 19 B2
La Storta Rome 26 A1
La Taxonera Barcelona 4 A2
La Victoria Lima 14 B2
Laajalahti Helsinki 11 B1
Laajasalo Helsinki 11 B3
Laaksolahti Helsinki 11 B1
Lablâba, W. el → Cairo 7 A2
Lachine Montreal 20 B1
Lachine, Canal de Montreal 20 B2
Lad Phrao Bangkok 3 B2
Ladera Heights Los Angeles 16 C2
Ládví Prague 25 B2
Łady Warsaw 32 C1
Lafontaine, Parc Montreal 20 A2
Lagoa Rio de Janeiro 25 B1
Lagos Lagos 14 B2
Lagos Harbour Lagos 14 B2
Lagos-Ikeja ✈ (LOS) Lagos 14 A1
Lagos Island Lagos 14 B2
Lagos Lagoon Lagos 14 B2
Laguna de B. Manila 17 C2
Laim Munich 21 B2
Lainate Milan 19 A1
Lainz Vienna 32 B1
Lake Buena Vista Orlando 23 B1
Lake Cain Hills Orlando 23 B2
Lake Fairfax Park Washington 33 B2
Lakemba Sydney 29 B1
Lakeside Cape Town 8 B1
Lakeside Johannesburg 13 A2
Lakeview Chicago 9 B3
Lakewood Park Atlanta 3 B2
Lakhtinskiy St. Petersburg 27 B1
Lakhtinskiy Razliv, Oz. St. Petersburg 27 B1
Lakshmanpur Kolkata 14 B1
Laksi Bangkok 3 A2
Lal Qila Delhi 10 B2
Lam Tin Hong Kong 12 B2
Lambert Oslo 23 A3
Lambeth □ London 15 B3
Lambrate Milan 19 B2
Lambro, Parco Milan 19 B2
Lambton Mills Toronto 31 B1
Lamma I. Hong Kong 12 B1
Landover Hills Washington 33 B4
Landsmeer Amsterdam 2 A2
Landstrasse Vienna 32 A2
Landwehr kanal Berlin 5 B3
Lane Cove Sydney 29 A1
Lane Cove National Park △ Sydney 29 A1
Langa Cape Town 8 A2
Langenzersdorf Vienna 32 A2
Langer See Berlin 5 B4
Langley Washington 33 B2
Langley Park Washington 33 B4
Langwald Munich 21 A1
Lanham Washington 33 B4
Lankwitz Berlin 5 B3
L'Annunziatella Rome 26 C2
Lansdowne Cape Town 8 A2
Lansing Toronto 31 A2
Lanús Buenos Aires 7 C2
Lapa Rio de Janeiro 25 B1
Laranjeiras Rio de Janeiro 25 B1
Las Warsaw 32 B2
Las Corts Barcelona 4 A1
Las Kabacki Warsaw 32 C2
Las Piñas Manila 17 C1
Las Rejas Santiago 27 B1
Lasalle Montreal 20 B2
LaSalle Street Station Chicago 9 B3
Lasek Bielański Warsaw 32 B1
Lasek Na Kole Warsaw 32 B1
Laski Warsaw 32 B1
Latina Madrid 17 B1
Lauttasaari Helsinki 11 C2
Laval-des-Rapides Montreal 20 A1
Lavizān Tehran 31 A2
Lavradio Lisbon 16 A2
Lawndale Chicago 9 B2
Lawne L. Orlando 23 A2
Lawrence Heights Toronto 31 A2
Layari Karachi 13 B1
Layari → Karachi 13 A1
Łazienkowski Park Warsaw 32 B2
Le Blanc-Mesnil Paris 24 A3
Le Bourget Paris 24 A3
Le Chenoi Brussels 6 B2
Le Chesnay Paris 24 B1
Le Christ de Saclay Paris 24 B2
Le Kremlin-Bicêtre Paris 24 B3
Le Mesnil-le-Roi Paris 24 A1
Le Pecq Paris 24 A1
Le Perreux Paris 24 A3
Le Pin Paris 24 A4
Le Plessis-Robinson Paris 24 B2
Le Plessis-Trévise Paris 24 B4
Le Port-Marly Paris 24 A1
Le Pré-St-Gervais Paris 24 A3
Le Raincy Paris 24 A4
Le Vésinet Paris 24 A1
Lea Bridge London 15 A3
Leaside Toronto 31 A2
Leblon Rio de Janeiro 25 B1
Lee London 15 B4
Leganés Madrid 17 C1
Legazpi Madrid 17 B1
Lehtisaari Helsinki 11 B2
Lei Yue Mun Hong Kong 12 B2
Leião Lisbon 16 A1

Leichhardt *Sydney* 29 B1
Leith *Edinburgh* 11 B3
Leme *Rio de Janeiro* 25 B1
Lemoyne *Montreal* 20 B3
Lenin *Moscow* 19 B2
Lenino *Moscow* 19 C2
Leninskiye Gory *Moscow* 19 B2
Lennox *Los Angeles* 16 C2
Leonia *New York* 22 A2
Leopardstown *Dublin* 10 B2
Leopoldau *Vienna* 32 A2
Leopoldsdorf *Vienna* 32 B2
Leopoldstadt *Vienna* 32 A2
Leportovo *Moscow* 19 B3
Leppävaara *Helsinki* 11 B1
Les Lilas *Paris* 24 A3
Les Loges-en-Josas *Paris* 24 B1
Les Pavillons-sous-Bois *Paris* 24 A4
Lésigny *Paris* 24 B4
Lesnozavodskaya *St. Petersburg* 27 B2
Lester B. Pearson Int., Toronto ✈ (YYZ) *Toronto* 31 A1
L'Étang-la-Ville *Paris* 24 A1
Letňany *Prague* 25 B3
Letopolis = Ausîm *Cairo* 7 A1
Levallois-Perret *Paris* 24 A2
Levent *Istanbul* 12 B2
Lewisdale *Washington* 33 B4
Lewisham □ *London* 15 B3
Lexington *Boston* 6 A1
Leyton *London* 15 A3
Leytonstone *London* 15 A4
L'Haÿ-les-Roses *Paris* 24 B3
L'Hospitalet de Llobregat *Barcelona* 4 A1
Lhotka *Prague* 25 B2
Liangshui He → *Beijing* 4 C2
Lianhua Chi *Beijing* 4 B1
Lianhua He → *Beijing* 4 B1
Libčice nad Vltavou *Prague* 25 A2
Libeň *Prague* 25 B2
Liberdade *São Paulo* 27 B2
Liberton *Edinburgh* 11 B3
Liberty I. *New York* 22 B1
Liberty Osaka Museum *Osaka* 23 B1
Liberty State Park ⌂ *New York* 22 B1
Libeznice *Prague* 25 A2
Libuš *Prague* 25 B2
Lichiao *Guangzhou* 11 B2
Lichtenburg *Berlin* 5 A4
Lichterfelde *Berlin* 5 B2
Lidingö *Stockholm* 29 A2
Lieshi Lingyuan *Guangzhou* 11 B2
Liesing *Vienna* 32 B1
Liesing → *Vienna* 32 B2
Ligovo *St. Petersburg* 27 C1
Lijordet *Oslo* 23 A2
Likhoborka → *Moscow* 19 A2
Liljeholmen *Stockholm* 29 B2
Lilla Värtan *Stockholm* 29 A3
Lille Værløse *Copenhagen* 8 A2
Liluah *Kolkata* 14 B1
Lim Chu Kang *Singapore* 28 A2
Lima *Lima* 14 B2
Limbiate *Milan* 19 A1
Limehouse *London* 15 A3
Limeil-Brévannes *Paris* 24 B3
Linate, Milano ✈ (LIN) *Milan* 19 B2
Linbropark *Johannesburg* 13 A2
Lincoln Center for Performing Arts *New York* 22 B2
Lincoln Heights *Los Angeles* 16 B3
Lincoln Memorial *Washington* 33 B3
Lincoln Park *Chicago* 9 B3
Lincoln Park *New York* 22 B1
Lincoln Park *San Francisco* 26 B1
Lincoln Park Zoo *Chicago* 9 B3
Lincolnwood *Chicago* 9 A2
Linda-a-Pastora *Lisbon* 16 A1
Linden *Johannesburg* 13 A2
Linden *Wellington* 33 A1
Lindenberg *Berlin* 5 A4
Lindøya *Oslo* 23 A3
Liniers *Buenos Aires* 7 B1
Linkebeek *Brussels* 6 B2
Linksfield *Johannesburg* 13 A2
Linmeyer *Johannesburg* 13 B2
Linna *Helsinki* 11 A2
Lintuvaara *Helsinki* 11 B1
Lion Rock Country Park ⌂ *Hong Kong* 12 A2
Lion's Head *Cape Town* 8 A1
Lioumi *Athens* 2 B2
Lisboa *Lisbon* 16 A2
Lisboa ✈ (LIS) *Lisbon* 16 A2
Lisbon = Lisboa *Lisbon* 16 A2
Lishui *Guangzhou* 11 A1
Little B. *Sydney* 29 B2
Little Calumet → *Chicago* 9 D3
Little Ferry *New York* 22 A1
Little Lake Conway *Orlando* 23 B2
Little Red School House Nature Center *Chicago* 9 C1
Little Rouge → *Toronto* 31 A4
Liuhang *Shanghai* 28 A1
Liurong Temple *Guangzhou* 11 B2
Livry-Gargan *Paris* 24 A4
Ljan *Oslo* 23 A3
Llano de Can Gineu *Barcelona* 4 A2
Lo Aranguiz *Santiago* 27 B2
Lo Boza *Santiago* 27 B1
Lo Chau *Hong Kong* 12 B2
Lo Chau Pak Mai *Hong Kong* 12 B2
Lo Espejo *Santiago* 27 C1
Lo Hermida *Santiago* 27 B2
Lo Prado *Santiago* 27 B1
Lo So Shing *Hong Kong* 12 B1
Lo Wai *Hong Kong* 12 A1
Loanhead *Edinburgh* 11 B3
Lobau *Vienna* 32 A3
Lobos, Pt. *San Francisco* 26 B1
Locham *Munich* 21 B1
Lochkov *Prague* 25 B2
Lockhausen *Munich* 21 A1
Lodi *New York* 22 A1
Lodi Estate *Delhi* 10 B2
Logan Int., Boston ✈ (BOS) *Boston* 6 A2
Logan Square *Chicago* 9 B2
Lognes-Émerainville ✈ *Paris* 24 B4
Löhme *Berlin* 5 A5
Lolokhet *Karachi* 13 A2
Lomas Chapultepec *Mexico City* 18 B1
Lomas de San Angel Inn *Mexico City* 18 B1
Lombardy East *Johannesburg* 13 A2
Lomianki *Warsaw* 32 A1
Lomus Reforma *Mexico City* 18 B1
London *London* 15 B3
London City ✈ (LCY) *London* 15 A4
London Heathrow ✈ (LHR) *London* 15 B1
London Zoo *London* 15 A3
Long B. *Sydney* 29 B2
Long Branch *Toronto* 31 B1
Long Brook → *Washington* 33 C2
Long Ditton *London* 15 B2
Long Island City *New York* 22 B2
Longchamp, Hippodrome de *Paris* 24 A2
Longhua Pagoda *Shanghai* 28 B1
Longhua Park *Shanghai* 28 B1
Longjohn Slough *Chicago* 9 C1
Longtan Hu → *Beijing* 4 B2
Longue-Pointe *Montreal* 20 A2
Longueuil *Montreal* 20 A3
Longueuil-St-Hubert = St-Hubert *Montreal* 20 B3
Loni *Delhi* 10 A2
Loop, The *Chicago* 9 B3
Lord's Cricket Ground *London* 15 A2
Loreto *Milan* 19 B2
Los Angeles *Los Angeles* 16 B3
Los Angeles Int. ✈ (LAX) *Los Angeles* 16 C2
Los Cerrillos ✈ (ULC) *Santiago* 27 B1
Los Nietos *Los Angeles* 16 C4
Los Olivos *Lima* 14 A2
Los Reyes *Mexico City* 18 B2
Losiny Ostrov △ *Moscow* 19 A3
Lot *Brussels* 6 B1
Lotus River *Cape Town* 8 B2
Lotus Temple *Delhi* 10 B2
Loughlinstown *Dublin* 10 B3
Louise, L. *Orlando* 23 B1
Louisiana Superdome *New Orleans* 21 B2
Loures *Lisbon* 16 A1
Louveciennes *Paris* 24 A1
Louvre, Musée du *Paris* 24 A3
Lower B. *New York* 22 C1
Lower Hutt *Wellington* 33 B2
Lower New York B. = Lower B. *New York* 22 C1
Lower Shing Mun Res. *Hong Kong* 12 A1
Lowry Bay *Wellington* 33 B2
Loyola University *Chicago* 9 B3
Lu Xun, Tomb of *Shanghai* 28 B1
Lu Xun Park *Shanghai* 28 B1
Lübars *Berlin* 5 A3
Lucy, L. *Orlando* 23 A2
Ludwigsfeld *Munich* 21 A1
Luhu *Guangzhou* 11 B2
Lumiar *Lisbon* 16 A2
Lundtofte *Copenhagen* 8 A3
Lung Mei *Hong Kong* 12 A2
Luojiang *Guangzhou* 11 B2
Lustheim *Munich* 21 A2
Luwan *Shanghai* 28 B1
Luzhniki Sports Centre *Moscow* 19 B2
Lyndhurst *New York* 22 B1
Lynn Woods Res. *Boston* 6 A2
Lyon, Gare de *Paris* 24 A3
Lyons *Chicago* 9 C2
Lysaker *Oslo* 23 A2
Lysakerselva → *Oslo* 23 A2
Lysolaje *Prague* 25 B2
Lyublino *Moscow* 19 B3

M

Ma Nam Wat *Hong Kong* 12 A2
Ma On Shan Country Park ⌂ *Hong Kong* 12 A2
Ma'ale Adumim *Jerusalem* 13 B2
Ma'ale Ha Khamisha *Jerusalem* 13 B1
Ma'ale Mikhmas *Jerusalem* 13 A2
Maantiekylä *Helsinki* 11 A3
Maarifa *Baghdad* 3 B2
Mabato Pt. *Manila* 17 C2
Mabel, L. *Orlando* 23 B1
Macaco, Morro do *Rio de Janeiro* 25 B2
McCook *Chicago* 9 C2
McGill University *Montreal* 20 A2
Machelen *Brussels* 6 A2
Machida *Tokyo* 30 B1
Maciołki *Warsaw* 32 B2
McKerrow, Mt. *Wellington* 33 B2
McKinley Park *Chicago* 9 C2
McLean *Washington* 33 B2
Macopocho → *Santiago* 27 B1
MacRitchie Res. *Singapore* 28 A2
Macul *Santiago* 27 C2
Madhudaha *Kolkata* 14 B2
Madhyamgram *Kolkata* 14 A2
Madīn *Mexico City* 18 A1
Madīn, L. *Mexico City* 18 A1
Madīnah Al Mansūr *Baghdad* 3 B2
Mâdinet Nasr *Cairo* 7 A2
Madrid *Madrid* 17 B1
Madrid Barajas ✈ (MAD) *Madrid* 17 B2
Madrona *Barcelona* 4 A1
Maesawa *Tokyo* 30 A2
Magdalena *Lima* 14 B2
Magdalena Contreras *Mexico City* 18 C1
Maghreb *Baghdad* 3 A2
Maginu *Tokyo* 30 B2
Magliana *Rome* 26 B1
Magny-les-Hameaux *Paris* 24 B1
Maheshtala *Kolkata* 14 C1
Mahim *Mumbai* 20 A2
Mahim B. *Mumbai* 20 A1
Mahlsdorf *Berlin* 5 A4
Mahmoodabad *Karachi* 13 A2
Mahrauli *Delhi* 10 B2
Mahul *Mumbai* 20 A2
Maida Vale *London* 15 A2
Maidstone *Melbourne* 18 A1
Maipú *Santiago* 27 C1
Maisonneuve, Parc *Montreal* 20 A2
Maisons-Alfort *Paris* 24 B3
Maisons-Laffitte *Paris* 24 A1
Maissoneuve *Montreal* 20 A2
Maitland *Cape Town* 8 A1
Makasar *Jakarta* 12 A2
Makati *Manila* 17 B2
Mäkiniitty *Helsinki* 11 A2
Malá Strana *Prague* 25 B2
Malabar *Sydney* 29 B2
Malabar Hill *Mumbai* 20 B1
Malabar Pt. *Mumbai* 20 B1
Malabon *Manila* 17 B1
Malacañang Palace *Manila* 17 B1
Malahide *Dublin* 10 A3
Malakoff *Paris* 24 B2
Mälarhöjaen *Stockholm* 29 B1
Malate *Manila* 17 B1
Malaya Neva *St. Petersburg* 27 B1
Malaya Okhta *St. Petersburg* 27 B2
Malchow *Berlin* 5 A3
Malden *Boston* 6 A2
Malden *London* 15 B2
Maleizen *Brussels* 6 B3
Malešice *Prague* 25 B3
Malir → *Karachi* 13 B2
Malleny Mills *Edinburgh* 11 B2
Malmi *Helsinki* 11 B2
Malmøya *Oslo* 23 A3
Måløv *Copenhagen* 8 A2
Malton *Toronto* 31 A1
Malvern *Johannesburg* 13 B2
Malvern *Melbourne* 18 B2
Malvern *Toronto* 31 A3
Mampang Prapatan *Jakarta* 12 B1
Mampukuji *Tokyo* 30 B2
Man Budrukh *Mumbai* 20 A2
Man Khurd *Mumbai* 20 A2
Manakhat *Jerusalem* 13 B2
Mandaluyong *Manila* 17 B2
Mandaoli *Delhi* 10 B2
Mandaqui → *São Paulo* 27 A2
Mandoli *Delhi* 10 A2
Mandvi *Mumbai* 20 B2
Manenberg *Cape Town* 8 A2
Mang Kung Uk *Hong Kong* 12 B2
Mang-won *Seoul* 27 B1
Mangpuri *Delhi* 10 A1
Manguinhos ✈ *Rio de Janeiro* 25 B1
Manhattan *New York* 22 B2
Manhattan Beach *New York* 22 C2
Manila *Manila* 17 B1
Manila Ninoy Aquino Int. ✈ (MNL) *Manila* 17 B2
Mankkaa *Helsinki* 11 B1
Manly *Sydney* 29 A2
Mann, L. *Orlando* 23 A2
Mann's Chinese Theatre *Los Angeles* 16 B2
Mannswörth *Vienna* 32 B3
Manor Park *London* 15 A4
Manor Park *Wellington* 33 A2
Manora *Karachi* 13 B1
Manora Pt. *Karachi* 13 B1
Manquehue, Cerro *Santiago* 27 B2
Manzanares, Canal de *Madrid* 17 C2
Mapo *Seoul* 27 B1
Maracanã *Rio de Janeiro* 25 B1
Maraoli *Mumbai* 20 A2
Marcelin *Warsaw* 32 B1
Mareil-Marly *Paris* 24 A1
Margareten *Vienna* 32 A2
Maria *Vienna* 32 A2
Maridalen *Oslo* 23 A3
Maridalsvatnet *Oslo* 23 A3
Mariendorf *Berlin* 5 B3
Marienfelde *Berlin* 5 B3
Marikina *Manila* 17 B2
Marikina → *Manila* 17 B2
Marin City *San Francisco* 26 A1
Marin Pen. *San Francisco* 26 A1
Marina del Rey *Los Angeles* 16 C2
Marino *Dublin* 10 A2
Marisco, Ponta do *Rio de Janeiro* 25 C1
Markham *Toronto* 31 A2
Marki *Warsaw* 32 B2
Markland Wood *Toronto* 31 B1
Marly, Forêt de *Paris* 24 A1
Marly-le-Roi *Paris* 24 A1
Marne-la-Vallée *Paris* 24 A4
Marolles-en-Brie *Paris* 24 B4
Maroubra *Sydney* 29 B2
Marquette Park *Chicago* 9 C2
Marrickville *Sydney* 29 B1
Marsfield *Sydney* 29 A1
Marsha, L. *Orlando* 23 B2
Marte, Campo de *São Paulo* 27 B2
Martesana, Navíglio della *Milan* 19 A2
Martin Luther King Nat. Historic Site ⌂ *Atlanta* 3 B2
Martinez *Buenos Aires* 7 A1
Martinkylä *Helsinki* 11 B2
Martinsried *Munich* 21 B1
Maruko *Tokyo* 30 B3
Maryino *Moscow* 19 B3
Maryland *Singapore* 28 B2
Marymont *Warsaw* 32 B1
Marysin Wawerski *Warsaw* 32 B2
Marzahn *Berlin* 5 A4
Mascot *Sydney* 29 B2
Masmo *Stockholm* 29 B1
Maspeth *New York* 22 B2
Masr el Gedida *Cairo* 7 A2
Masr el Qadima *Cairo* 7 A2
Massachusetts Inst. of Tech. *Boston* 6 A2
Massamá *Lisbon* 16 A1
Massey → *Toronto* 31 A3
Massy *Paris* 24 B2
Mata *Jerusalem* 13 B1
Matihutong *Beijing* 4 B1
Matinha *Lisbon* 16 A2
Matramam *Jakarta* 12 B2
Matsubara *Osaka* 23 B2
Mattapan *Boston* 6 B2
Mátyásföld *Budapest* 7 A3
Mau Tso Ngam *Hong Kong* 12 B2
Mauer *Vienna* 32 B1
Mauripur *Karachi* 13 A1
Maxhof *Munich* 21 B1
Mayfair *Johannesburg* 13 B2
Mayor, Plaza *Madrid* 17 B1
Maywood *Chicago* 9 B1
Maywood *Los Angeles* 16 C3
Maywood *New York* 22 A1
Maywood Park Race Track *Chicago* 9 B1
Mazagaon *Mumbai* 20 B2
Meadowbank Park *Sydney* 29 A1
Měcholupy *Prague* 25 B3
Měčice *Prague* 25 A3
Mecidiyeköy *Istanbul* 12 B2
Medford *Boston* 6 A2
Mediodia *Madrid* 17 B2
Meguro *Tokyo* 30 B3
Meguro → *Tokyo* 30 B3
Mehpalpur *Delhi* 10 B1
Mehrābād ✈ (THR) *Tehran* 31 A1
Mehram Nagar *Delhi* 10 B1
Mehrow *Berlin* 5 A4
Meidling *Vienna* 32 A2
Méier *Rio de Janeiro* 25 B1
Meiji Shrine *Tokyo* 30 A3
Meise *Brussels* 6 A1
Mejiro *Tokyo* 30 A3
Melbourne *Melbourne* 18 A1
Melbourne ✈ (MEL) *Melbourne* 18 A1
Melkki *Helsinki* 11 C2
Mellunkylä *Helsinki* 11 B3
Mellunmäki *Helsinki* 11 B3
Melrose *Boston* 6 A2
Melrose *New York* 22 B2
Melrose Park *Chicago* 9 B1
Melsbroek *Brussels* 6 A2
Melville *Johannesburg* 13 B2
Menteng *Jakarta* 12 B1
Mérantaise → *Paris* 24 B1
Mercamadrid *Madrid* 17 B2
Merced, L. *San Francisco* 26 B2
Meredale *Johannesburg* 13 B1
Merlimau, Pulau *Singapore* 28 B2
Merri Cr. → *Melbourne* 18 A1
Merrion *Dublin* 10 B2
Merrionette Park *Chicago* 9 C2
Merton □ *London* 15 B2
Mesgarābād *Tehran* 31 B3
Messe *Vienna* 32 A2
Metanópoli *Milan* 19 B2
Metro-Dade Cultural Centre *Miami* 18 B2
Metro Toronto Zoo *Toronto* 31 A3
Metropolitan Museum of Art *New York* 22 B2
Meudon *Paris* 24 B2
Mevaseret Tsiyon *Jerusalem* 13 B1
Mevo Beitar *Jerusalem* 13 B1
México *Mexico City* 18 B2
México, Ciudad de *Mexico City* 18 B2
Mexico City Int. ✈ (MEX) *Mexico City* 18 B2
Meyersdal *Johannesburg* 13 B2
Mezzate *Milan* 19 B2
Miadong *Seoul* 27 B2
Miami *Miami* 18 B2
Miami Beach *Miami* 18 B2
Miami Canal *Miami* 18 A1
Miami Int. ✈ (MIA) *Miami* 18 B1
Miami Shores *Miami* 18 A2
Miami Springs *Miami* 18 B1
Miasto *Warsaw* 32 B2
Michałowice *Warsaw* 32 B1
Michle *Prague* 25 B2
Middle Harbour *Sydney* 29 A2
Middle Hd. *Sydney* 29 A2
Middle Park *Melbourne* 18 B1
Middle Village *New York* 22 B2
Middlesex Fells Reservation *Boston* 6 A2
Midland Beach *New York* 22 C1
Midwood *New York* 22 C2
Miedzeszyn *Warsaw* 32 B3
Międzylesie *Warsaw* 32 B3
Miessaari *Helsinki* 11 C1
Miguel Hidalgo *Mexico City* 18 B1
Milan = Milano *Milan* 19 B1
Milanese, Parco Regionale ⌂ *Milan* 19 B1
Milano *Milan* 19 B1
Milano Due *Milan* 19 B2
Milano Linate ✈ (LIN) *Milan* 19 B2
Milano San Felice *Milan* 19 B2
Milbertshofen *Munich* 21 A2
Mill Hill *London* 15 A2
Millennium Dome *London* 15 A4
Miller Meadow *Chicago* 9 B2
Millerhill *Edinburgh* 11 B3
Milltown *Dublin* 10 B2
Millwood *Washington* 33 B4
Milnerton *Cape Town* 8 A1
Milon-la-Chapelle *Paris* 24 B1
Milton *Boston* 6 B2
Milton Bridge *Edinburgh* 11 B2
Mimico *Toronto* 31 B2
Mimico Creek → *Toronto* 31 B1
Minami *Osaka* 23 A2
Minamitsunashima *Tokyo* 30 B2
Minato *Osaka* 23 B1
Minato *Tokyo* 30 B3
Minshât el Bekkarî *Cairo* 7 A1
Miraflores *Lima* 14 B2
Miramar *Wellington* 33 B1
Misericordia, Sa. da *Rio de Janeiro* 25 B1
Mission *San Francisco* 26 B2
Mississauga *Toronto* 31 B1
Mitaka *Tokyo* 30 A2
Mitcham *London* 15 B2
Mitcham Common *London* 15 B3
Mitchell Museum of the American Indian *Chicago* 9 A2
Mitchell's Plain *Cape Town* 8 B2
Mitte *Berlin* 5 A3
Mittel Isarkanal → *Munich* 21 A3
Mixcoac *Mexico City* 18 B1
Miyakojima *Osaka* 23 A2
Mizonokuchi *Tokyo* 30 B2
Mlocinski Park *Warsaw* 32 B1
Młociny *Warsaw* 32 B1
Mnevniki *Moscow* 19 B1
Moba *Lagos* 14 B2
Moczydło *Warsaw* 32 C2
Modderfontein *Johannesburg* 13 A2
Modřany *Prague* 25 B2
Mogyoród *Budapest* 7 A3
Moinho Velho, Cor. → *São Paulo* 27 B2
Mok *Seoul* 27 B1
Mokotów *Warsaw* 32 B2
Molenbeek-St-Jean *Brussels* 6 A1
Molino de Rosas *Mexico City* 18 B1
Mollem *Brussels* 6 A1
Mollins de Rey *Barcelona* 4 A1
Mondeor *Johannesburg* 13 B2
Moneda, Palacio de la *Santiago* 27 B2
Monerò *Rio de Janeiro* 25 A1
Mong Kok *Hong Kong* 12 B2
Monkstown *Dublin* 10 B3
Monnickendam *Amsterdam* 2 A3
Monrovia *Los Angeles* 16 B4
Monsanto *Lisbon* 16 A1
Monsanto, Parque Florestal de *Lisbon* 16 A1
Mont-Royal *Montreal* 20 A2
Mont-Royal, Parc *Montreal* 20 A2
Montana de Montjuich *Barcelona* 4 A1
Montcada i Reixac *Barcelona* 4 A2
Monte Chingolo *Buenos Aires* 7 C2
Montebello *Los Angeles* 16 B4
Montemor *Lisbon* 16 A1
Monterey Park *Los Angeles* 16 B4
Montespaccato *Rome* 26 B1
Montesson *Paris* 24 A1
Monteverde Nuovo *Rome* 26 B1
Montfermeil *Paris* 24 A4
Montigny-le-Bretonneux *Paris* 24 B1
Montjay-la-Tour *Paris* 24 A4
Montparnasse, Gare *Paris* 24 A2
Montréal *Montreal* 20 A2
Montréal, Î. de *Montreal* 20 A2
Montréal, Université de *Montreal* 20 B2
Montréal Est *Montreal* 20 A2
Montréal-Nord *Montreal* 20 A2
Montréal-Ouest *Montreal* 20 B1
Montréal Trudeau Int. ✈ (YUL) *Montreal* 20 B1
Montreuil *Paris* 24 A3
Montrouge *Paris* 24 B2
Montserrat *Buenos Aires* 7 B2
Monza *Milan* 19 A2
Monzoro *Milan* 19 B1
Moóca *São Paulo* 27 B2
Moonachie *New York* 22 B1
Moonee Ponds *Melbourne* 18 A1
Moonee Valley Racecourse *Melbourne* 18 A1
Moosach *Munich* 21 A2
Mora *Mumbai* 20 B2
Moratalaz *Madrid* 17 B2
Mörby *Stockholm* 29 A2
Morden *London* 15 B2
Morée → *Paris* 24 A3
Morgan Park *Chicago* 9 C3
Moriguchi *Osaka* 23 A2
Morivione *Milan* 19 B2
Morningside *Edinburgh* 11 B2
Morningside *Johannesburg* 13 A2
Morningside *Washington* 33 C4
Morningside Park *Orlando* 23 B2
Morningside Park *Toronto* 31 A3
Morro Solar, Cerro *Lima* 14 C2
Mortlake *London* 15 B2
Mortlake *Sydney* 29 B1
Morton Grove *Chicago* 9 A2
Morumbi *São Paulo* 27 B1
Moscavide *Lisbon* 16 A2
Moschato *Athens* 2 B2
Moscow = Moskva *Moscow* 19 B2
Moskva *Moscow* 19 B2
Moskvoretskiy *Moscow* 19 B2
Mosman *Sydney* 29 A2
Móstoles *Madrid* 17 C1
Moti Bagh *Delhi* 10 B2
Motol *Prague* 25 B1
Motsa *Jerusalem* 13 B2
Motsa Ilit *Jerusalem* 13 B1
Motspur Park *London* 15 B2
Mottingham *London* 15 B4
Mount Dennis *Toronto* 31 A2
Mount Greenwood *Chicago* 9 C2
Mount Hood Memorial Park ⌂ *Boston* 6 A2
Mount Merrion *Dublin* 10 B2
Mount Rainier *Washington* 33 B4
Mount Vernon *New York* 22 A3
Müggelberge *Berlin* 5 B4
Müggelheim *Berlin* 5 B5
Muggiò *Milan* 19 A2
Mühleiten *Vienna* 32 A3
Mühlenfliess → *Berlin* 5 A5
Muiden *Amsterdam* 2 A3
Muizenberg *Cape Town* 8 B1
Mujahidpur *Delhi* 10 B2
Mukandpur *Delhi* 10 A2
Mukhmas *Jerusalem* 13 A2
Muko → *Osaka* 23 A1
Mukojima *Tokyo* 30 A3
Mulbarton *Johannesburg* 13 B2
Mumbai *Mumbai* 20 B2
Mumbai Chhatrapati Shivaji Int. ✈ (BOM) *Mumbai* 20 A2
Mumbai Harbour *Mumbai* 20 B2
Munch Museum *Oslo* 23 A3
Münchehofe *Berlin* 5 B5
München *Munich* 21 B2
München Franz Josef Straus ✈ (MUC) *Munich* 21 A2
Munich = München *Munich* 21 B2
Munkkiniemi *Helsinki* 11 B2
Munro *Buenos Aires* 7 B1
Muntinlupa *Manila* 17 C2
Murai Res. *Singapore* 28 A2
Muranów *Warsaw* 32 B1
Murino *St. Petersburg* 27 B2
Murrayfield *Edinburgh* 11 B2
Musashino *Tokyo* 30 A2
Museu Nacional *Rio de Janeiro* 25 B1
Mushin *Lagos* 14 A2
Musocco *Milan* 19 B1
Mustansirīya *Baghdad* 3 A2
Musturud *Cairo* 7 A2
Muswell Hill *London* 15 A3
Mutanabi *Baghdad* 3 B2
Muthana *Baghdad* 3 B2
Mykerinos *Cairo* 7 B1
Myllypuro *Helsinki* 11 B3
Mystic → *Boston* 6 A2

N

Nacka *Stockholm* 29 B3
Naenae *Wellington* 33 B2
Nærsnes *Oslo* 23 B1
Nagatsuta *Tokyo* 30 B2
Nagytétény *Budapest* 7 B1
Nahalin *Jerusalem* 13 B1
Najafgarh Drain → *Delhi* 10 B1
Nakahara *Tokyo* 30 B2
Nakano *Tokyo* 30 A2
Namsan Park *Seoul* 27 B1
Namyeong *Seoul* 27 B1
Nanbiancun *Guangzhou* 11 B1
Nanchang He → *Beijing* 4 B1
Nandang *Guangzhou* 11 B2
Nangal Dewat *Delhi* 10 B1
Naniwa *Osaka* 23 B1
Nanole *Mumbai* 20 A2
Nanpu Bridge *Shanghai* 28 B2
Nanshi *Shanghai* 28 B1
Nanterre *Paris* 24 A2
Naoabad *Kolkata* 14 C2
Napier Mole *Karachi* 13 B1
Naraina *Delhi* 10 B1
Nariman Point *Mumbai* 20 B1
Nariman Pt. *Mumbai* 20 B1
Nārmak *Tehran* 31 A2
Naruo *Osaka* 23 A1
Näsby *Stockholm* 29 A2
Näsbypark *Stockholm* 29 A2
National Arboretum *Washington* 33 B3
National Zoological Park *Washington* 33 B3
Nativity, Basilica of *Jerusalem* 13 B2
Natolin *Warsaw* 32 C2
Naucalpan de Juárez *Mexico City* 18 B1
Naupada *Mumbai* 20 A2
Navi Mumbai *Mumbai* 20 A2
Navíglio di Pavia *Milan* 19 B1
Navíglio Grande *Milan* 19 B1
Navotas *Manila* 17 B1
Navy Pier *Chicago* 9 B3
Nazal Hikmat Beg *Baghdad* 3 A2
Nazimabad *Karachi* 13 A2
Nazlet el Simmân *Cairo* 7 B1
Nea Alexandria *Athens* 2 B2
Nea Ionia *Athens* 2 A2
Nea Liosia *Athens* 2 A2
Nea Smirni *Athens* 2 B2
Neapoli *Athens* 2 B2
Near North *Chicago* 9 B3
Nebušice *Prague* 25 B1
Nederhorst *Amsterdam* 2 B3
Nedlitz *Berlin* 5 B1
Nee Soon *Singapore* 28 A2
Needham *Boston* 6 B1
Needham Heights *Boston* 6 B1
N'ematābād *Tehran* 31 B2
Nerima *Tokyo* 30 A3
Nesodden *Oslo* 23 B3
Nesoddtangen *Oslo* 23 A3
Nesøya *Oslo* 23 A2
Neu Aubing *Munich* 21 B1
Neu Buch *Berlin* 5 A4
Neu Buchhorst *Berlin* 5 B5
Neu Fahrland *Berlin* 5 B1
Neu Lindenberg *Berlin* 5 A4
Neubiberg *Munich* 21 B3
Neuenhagen *Berlin* 5 A4
Neuessling *Vienna* 32 A3
Neuhausen *Munich* 21 B2
Neuherberg *Munich* 21 A2
Neuhönow *Berlin* 5 A5
Neuilly-Plaisance *Paris* 24 A4
Neuilly-sur-Marne *Paris* 24 A4
Neuilly-sur-Seine *Paris* 24 A2
Neukagran *Vienna* 32 A2
Neukettenhof *Vienna* 32 B2
Neukölln *Berlin* 5 B3
Neuperlach *Munich* 21 B2
Neuried *Munich* 21 B1
Neustift am Walde *Vienna* 32 A1
Neusüssenbrunn *Vienna* 32 A2
Neuwaldegg *Vienna* 32 A1
Neve Ya'akov *Jerusalem* 13 A2
Neves *Rio de Janeiro* 25 B2
New Baghdād *Baghdad* 3 B2
New Barakpur *Kolkata* 14 A2
New Brighton *New York* 22 C1
New Canada *Johannesburg* 13 B1
New Canada Dam *Johannesburg* 13 B1
New Carrollton *Washington* 33 B4
New Cross *London* 15 B3
New Delhi *Delhi* 10 B2
New Dorp *New York* 22 C1
New Dorp Beach *New York* 22 C1
New Malden *London* 15 B2
New Milford *New York* 22 A1
New Mumbai = Navi Mumbai *Mumbai* 20 A2
New Territories *Hong Kong* 12 A1
New Toronto *Toronto* 31 B1
New Utrecht *New York* 22 C2
New York *New York* 22 B3
New York La Guardia ✈ (LGA) *New York* 22 B2
Newark B. *New York* 22 B1
Newbattle *Edinburgh* 11 B3
Newbury Park *London* 15 A4
Newcraighall *Edinburgh* 11 B3
Newham □ *London* 15 A4
Newhaven *Edinburgh* 11 B2
Newington *Edinburgh* 11 B2
Newlands *Johannesburg* 13 B1
Newlands *Wellington* 33 B1
Newport *Melbourne* 18 B1
Newton *Boston* 6 B1
Newtonbrook *Toronto* 31 A2
Newtongrange *Edinburgh* 11 B3
Newtonville *Boston* 6 A1
Newtown *Sydney* 29 B2
Ngaio *Wellington* 33 B1
Ngau Chi Wan *Hong Kong* 12 B2
Ngau Tau Kok *Hong Kong* 12 B2
Ngauranga *Wellington* 33 B1
Ngong Shuen Chau *Hong Kong* 12 B1
Ngua Kok Wan *Hong Kong* 12 A1
Nhava Sheva *Mumbai* 20 B2
Niāvarān *Tehran* 31 A2
Nibra *Kolkata* 14 B1
Nidāl *Baghdad* 3 B2
Niddrie *Edinburgh* 11 B3
Niddrie *Melbourne* 18 A1
Nieder Neuendorf *Berlin* 5 A2
Niederschöneweide *Berlin* 5 B3
Niederschönhausen *Berlin* 5 A3
Niemeyer *Rio de Janeiro* 25 B1
Nieuwendam *Amsterdam* 2 A2
Nihonbashi *Tokyo* 30 A3
Niipperi *Helsinki* 11 B1
Nikea *Athens* 2 B1
Nikolassee *Berlin* 5 B2
Nikolskiy *Moscow* 19 B1
Niles *Chicago* 9 A2
Nimta *Kolkata* 14 A2
Ninoy Aquino Int. ✈ (MNL) *Manila* 17 B2
Nippa *Tokyo* 30 B2
Nippori *Tokyo* 30 A3
Nishi *Osaka* 23 A1
Nishinari *Osaka* 23 B1
Nishinomiya *Osaka* 23 A1
Nishiyodogawa *Osaka* 23 A1
Niterói *Rio de Janeiro* 25 B2
Nockeby *Stockholm* 29 B1
Noel Park *London* 15 A3
Nogatino *Moscow* 19 B3
Nogent-sur-Marne *Paris* 24 A3
Noida *Delhi* 10 B2
Noisiel *Paris* 24 A4
Noisiel *Paris* 24 B4
Noisy-le-Grand *Paris* 24 A4
Noisy-le-Roi *Paris* 24 A1
Noisy-le-Sec *Paris* 24 A3
Nokkala *Helsinki* 11 C1
Nomentano *Rome* 26 B2
Nonakashinden *Tokyo* 30 A2
Nongminyundong Jiangxisuo *Guangzhou* 11 B2
Nonhyeon *Seoul* 27 B2
Nonthaburi *Bangkok* 3 A1
Noordgesig *Johannesburg* 13 B1
Noordzeekanaal *Amsterdam* 2 A1
Nord, Gare du *Paris* 24 A3
Nordmarka *Oslo* 23 A3
Nordrand-Siedlung *Vienna* 32 A2
Nordstrand *Oslo* 23 A3
Normandale *Wellington* 33 B2
Norridge *Chicago* 9 B2
Norrmalm *Stockholm* 29 A2
North Arlington *New York* 22 B1
North Bay Village *Miami* 18 A2
North Bergen *New York* 22 B1
North Bull I. *Dublin* 10 A3
North Cheam *London* 15 B2
North Cray *London* 15 B4
North Decatur *Atlanta* 3 B3
North Druid Hills *Atlanta* 3 B3
North Esk → *Edinburgh* 11 B2
North Gyle *Edinburgh* 11 B2
North Hackensack *New York* 22 A1
North Harbor *Manila* 17 B1
North Hd. *Sydney* 29 A2
North Hollywood *Los Angeles* 16 B2
North Lexington *Boston* 6 A1
North Miami *Miami* 18 A2
North Miami Beach *Miami* 18 A2
North Nazimabad *Karachi* 13 A2
North Pt. *Hong Kong* 12 B2
North Queensferry *Edinburgh* 11 A1
North Quincy *Boston* 6 B2
North Res. *Boston* 6 A2
North Riverside *Chicago* 9 B2
North Saugus *Boston* 6 A2
North Shore Channel → *Chicago* 9 B2
North Springfield *Washington* 33 C2
North Station *Boston* 6 A2
North Sydney *Sydney* 29 B2
North Woolwich *London* 15 A4
North York *Toronto* 31 A2
Northbridge *Sydney* 29 A2
Northbridge Park *Sydney* 29 A2
Northcliff *Johannesburg* 13 A1
Northcote *Melbourne* 18 A2
Northeastern University *Boston* 6 A2
Northern Virginia Regional Park ⌂ *Washington* 33 B3
Northlake *Chicago* 9 B1
Northmount *Toronto* 31 A2
Northolt *London* 15 A1
Northumberland Heath *London* 15 B5
Northwestern Station *Chicago* 9 B3
Northwestern University *Chicago* 9 A2
Northwood *London* 15 A1
Northwood Park *Toronto* 31 A1
Norwood *Johannesburg* 13 A2
Norwood Park *Chicago* 9 B2
Noryangjin *Seoul* 27 B1
Nossa Senhora do Ó *São Paulo* 27 B1
Nossegem *Brussels* 6 A3
Notre-Dame *Paris* 24 A3
Notre-Dame, Basilique *Montreal* 20 B2
Notre-Dame, Bois *Paris* 24 B4
Notre-Dame-de-Grace *Montreal* 20 B2
Notting Hill *London* 15 A2
Nova Milanese *Milan* 19 A2
Novate Milanese *Milan* 19 A1
Novaya Derevnya *St. Petersburg* 27 A1
Nové Město *Prague* 25 B2
Novoaleksandrovskoye *St. Petersburg* 27 B2
Novodevichy Convent *Moscow* 19 B2
Novogireyevo *Moscow* 19 B3
Novosaratovka *St. Petersburg* 27 B3
Nowe-Babice *Warsaw* 32 B1
Nowe Miasto *Warsaw* 32 B2
Nöykkiö *Helsinki* 11 B1
Nueva Atzacoalco *Mexico City* 18 B2
Nueva Pompeya *Buenos Aires* 7 C2
Nueva Tenochtitlán *Mexico City* 18 B2
Nuijala *Helsinki* 11 B1
Numabukuro *Tokyo* 30 A2
Nuñez *Buenos Aires* 7 B2
Nunhead *London* 15 B3
Ñuñoa *Santiago* 27 B2
Nusle *Prague* 25 B2
Nussdorf *Vienna* 32 A2
Nyanga *Cape Town* 8 A2
Nymphenburg *Munich* 21 B2
Nymphenburg, Schloss *Munich* 21 B2

O

O. R. Tambo Int. ✈ (JNB) *Johannesburg* 13 A2
Oak Grove *Atlanta* 3 A3
Oak Hill *Boston* 6 B1
Oak Lawn *Chicago* 9 C2
Oak Park *Chicago* 9 B2
Oak View *Washington* 33 A4
Oakdale *Atlanta* 3 A2
Oakland *San Francisco* 26 B3
Oakland *Washington* 33 B4
Oaklawn *Washington* 33 C4
Oakleigh *Melbourne* 18 B2
Oakton *Washington* 33 B2
Oakwood Beach *New York* 22 C1
Oatley *Sydney* 29 B1
Obalende *Lagos* 14 B2
Oba's Palace *Lagos* 14 B2
Oberföhring *Munich* 21 B2
Oberhaching *Munich* 21 B2
Oberlaa *Vienna* 32 B2
Oberlisse *Vienna* 32 A2
Obermenzing *Munich* 21 A1
Obermoos Schwaige *Munich* 21 A1
Oberschleissheim *Munich* 21 A2
Oberschöneweide *Berlin* 5 B4
Observatory *Johannesburg* 13 B2
Óbuda *Budapest* 7 A2
Obukhovo *St. Petersburg* 27 B2
Obvodnyy Kanal *St. Petersburg* 27 B1
Ocean Park *Hong Kong* 12 B2
Ochota *Warsaw* 32 B1
Ocoee *Orlando* 23 A1
Ōdana *Tokyo* 30 B2
Öden-Stockach *Munich* 21 B3
Odilampi *Helsinki* 11 B1
Odivelas *Lisbon* 16 A1
Odolany *Warsaw* 32 B1
Oeiras *Lisbon* 16 A1
Ofin *Lagos* 14 A3
Ogawa *Tokyo* 30 A1
Ogden Park *Chicago* 9 C2
Ogikubo *Tokyo* 30 A2
Ogogoro *Lagos* 14 B2
Ogoyo *Lagos* 14 B2
Ogudu *Lagos* 14 A2
O'Hare Int., Chicago ✈ (ORD) *Chicago* 9 B1
Ohariu Stream → *Wellington* 33 B1
O'Higgins, Parque *Santiago* 27 B2
Ōimachi *Tokyo* 30 B3
Ojota *Lagos* 14 A2
Okęcie *Warsaw* 32 B1
Okęcie, Warszawa ✈ (WAW) *Warsaw* 32 B1
Okelra *Lagos* 14 B2
Okeogbe *Lagos* 14 B2
Okhla *Delhi* 10 B2
Okhta → *St. Petersburg* 27 B2
Okkervil → *St. Petersburg* 27 B2
Okrzeszyn *Warsaw* 32 C2
Oksval *Oslo* 23 A3
Oktyabrskiy *Moscow* 19 B2
Okubo *Tokyo* 30 A3
Ōkura *Tokyo* 30 B1
Olari *Helsinki* 11 B1
Olaria *Rio de Janeiro* 25 B1
Old Admiralty *St. Petersburg* 27 B1
Old City *Jerusalem* 13 B2
Old City *Shanghai* 28 B1
Old City Hall *Toronto* 31 B2
Old Fort York *Toronto* 31 B2
Old Harbor *Boston* 6 B2
Old Town *Chicago* 9 B3
Old Town Hall = Altes Rathaus *Munich* 21 B2
Oldbawn *Dublin* 10 B1
Olgino *St. Petersburg* 27 A1
Olímpico, Estadio *Mexico City* 18 C1
Olivais *Lisbon* 16 A2
Olivar de los Padres *Mexico City* 18 B1
Olivar del Conde *Mexico City* 18 B1
Olives, Mt. of *Jerusalem* 13 B2
Olivia, L. *Orlando* 23 A1
Olivos *Buenos Aires* 7 B2
Olona → *Milan* 19 B1
Olympia, L. *Orlando* 23 A1
Olympic Stadium = Turner Field *Atlanta* 3 B2
Olympic Stadium *Helsinki* 11 B2
Olympique, Stade *Montreal* 20 A2
Ōmori *Tokyo* 30 B3
Onisigun *Lagos* 14 A2
Ontario Science Centre *Toronto* 31 A2
Ōokayama *Tokyo* 30 B3
Oostzaan *Amsterdam* 2 A2
Opa-Locka *Miami* 18 A1
Opa-Locka ✈ (OPF) *Miami* 18 A1
Opacz *Warsaw* 32 B1
Ophirton *Johannesburg* 13 B2
Oppegård *Oslo* 23 B3
Oppem *Brussels* 6 A1
Oppsal *Oslo* 23 A4
Ora *Jerusalem* 13 B1
Oradell *New York* 22 A1
Oradell Res. *New York* 22 A1
Orange Bowl Stadium *Miami* 18 B2
Orangi *Karachi* 13 A2
Ordrup *Copenhagen* 8 A3
Orech *Prague* 25 B1
Orient Heights *Boston* 6 A3
Orlando *Orlando* 23 A2
Orlando Dam *Johannesburg* 13 B1
Orlando East *Johannesburg* 13 B1
Orlando Executive ✈ *Orlando* 23 A2
Orlando Int. ✈ (MCO) *Orlando* 23 B3
Orlovista *Orlando* 23 A2
Orly *Paris* 24 B3
Orly, Paris ✈ (ORY) *Paris* 24 B3
Ormesson-sur-Marne *Paris* 24 B4
Ormond *Melbourne* 18 B2
Ormøya *Oslo* 23 A3
Orpington *London* 15 B4
Ortaköy *Istanbul* 12 B2
Ortica *Milan* 19 B2
Oruba *Lagos* 14 A2
Ōsaka *Osaka* 23 B2
Ōsaka Castle *Osaka* 23 A2
Ōsaka Harbour *Osaka* 23 B1
Ōsaka Itami Int. ✈ (ITM) *Osaka* 23 A1
Ōsaka Kansai ✈ (KIX) *Osaka* 23 B2
Ōsaki *Tokyo* 30 B3
Osasco *São Paulo* 27 B1
Osdorf *Berlin* 5 B3
Osdorp *Amsterdam* 2 A1
Oshodi *Lagos* 14 A2
Oslo *Oslo* 23 A3
Oslo ✈ (OSL) *Oslo* 23 A4
Ōsone *Tokyo* 30 B2
Osorun *Lagos* 14 B2
Ospitale *Milan* 19 A1
Ostankino *Moscow* 19 B2
Osterley *London* 15 B1
Osterley Park *London* 15 B1
Östermalm *Stockholm* 29 A2
Österskär *Stockholm* 29 A3
Ostia Malpasso *Rome* 26 C1
Ostiense *Rome* 26 B1
Østmarkkapellet *Oslo* 23 A4
Ostøya *Oslo* 23 A2
Ostre Aker *Oslo* 23 A3
Ōta *Tokyo* 30 B3
Otaniemi *Helsinki* 11 B1
Otari Open Air Museum *Wellington* 33 B1
Otsuka *Tokyo* 30 A3
Ottakring *Vienna* 32 A1
Ottávia *Rome* 26 B1
Otter *Cape Town* 8 B2
Ottobrunn *Munich* 21 B3
Ouderkerk *Amsterdam* 2 B2
Oulunkylä *Helsinki* 11 B2
Ourcq, Canal de l' *Paris* 24 A3
Outer Mission *San Francisco* 26 B2
Outremont *Montreal* 20 A2
Overijse *Brussels* 6 B3
Owhiro Bay *Wellington* 33 C1
Oworonsoki *Lagos* 14 A2
Oxgangs *Edinburgh* 11 B2
Oxon Hill *Washington* 33 C4
Oyodo *Osaka* 23 A1
Oyster B. *Sydney* 29 C1
Oyster Rock *Mumbai* 20 B1
Oyster Rocks *Karachi* 13 B2
Ozoir-la-Ferrière *Paris* 24 B4
Ozone Park *New York* 22 B2

P

Pacific Heights *San Francisco* 26 B2
Pacific Manor *San Francisco* 26 C2
Pacific Palisades *Los Angeles* 16 B1
Pacifica *San Francisco* 26 C2
Paco *Manila* 17 B1
Paco de Arcos *Lisbon* 16 A1
Paddington *London* 15 A2

INDEX TO CITY MAPS
Zwölfaxing 39

Soroksár Budapest 7 B2
Soroksari Duna → Budapest 7 B2
Sosenka → Moscow 19 B3
Sosnovka St. Petersburg 27 B2
Sŏul = Seoul Seoul 27 B2
Soundview New York 22 B2
South Beach New York 22 C1
South Bend Park Atlanta 3 B2
South Boston Boston 6 A2
South Decatur Atlanta 3 B3
South Deering Chicago 9 C3
South El Monte Los Angeles 16 B4
South Gate Los Angeles 16 C3
South Harbor Manila 17 B1
South Harrow London 15 A1
South Hd. Sydney 29 B2
South Hills Johannesburg 13 B2
South Hornchurch London 15 A5
South Lawn Washington 33 C3
South Miami Miami 18 B1
South Norwood London 15 B3
South of Market San Francisco 26 B2
South Ozone Park New York 22 B3
South Pasadena Los Angeles 16 B4
South Res. Boston 6 A2
South Ruislip London 15 A1
South San Francisco San Francisco 26 C2
South San Gabriel Los Angeles 16 B4
South Shore Chicago 9 C3
Southall London 15 A1
Southborough London 15 B4
Southend London 15 B3
Southern California, University of Los Angeles 16 B3
Southfields London 15 B2
Southwark □ London 15 B3
Southwest Museum Los Angeles 16 B3
Søvang Copenhagen 8 B3
Soweto Johannesburg 13 B1
Sowhānak Tehran 31 A3
Soya Tokyo 30 A4
Spandau Berlin 5 A1
Spånga Stockholm 29 A1
Spanish Monastery Miami 18 A2
Spectacle I. Boston 6 A3
Speicher-See Munich 21 A3
Speising Vienna 32 B1
Sphinx Cairo 7 B1
Spinaceto Rome 26 C1
Spit Junction Sydney 29 A2
Spořilov Prague 25 B3
Spot Pond Boston 6 A2
Spotswood Melbourne 18 B1
Springeberg Berlin 5 B5
Springfield Washington 33 C2
Squantum Boston 6 B2
Srednaya Rogatka St. Petersburg 27 C2
Śródmieście Warsaw 32 B2
Staaken Berlin 5 A1
Stabekk Oslo 23 A2
Stadlau Vienna 32 A2
Stadshuset Stockholm 29 B2
Stains Paris 24 A3
Stamford Hill London 15 A3
Stammersdorf Vienna 32 A2
Stanley Hong Kong 12 B2
Stanley Pen. Hong Kong 12 B2
Stanmore London 15 A2
Stapleton New York 22 C1
Staraya Derevnya St. Petersburg 27 B1
Staré Město Prague 25 B2
Stare Miasto Warsaw 32 B2
Starke, L. Orlando 23 A1
Staten Island Zoo New York 22 C1
Staten Islands Ferry Terminal New York 22 C1
Statenice Prague 25 B1
Stedelijk Museum Amsterdam 2 A2
Steele Creek Melbourne 18 A1
Steenokkerzeel Brussels 6 A2
Steer, L. Orlando 23 A2
Steglitz Berlin 5 B2
Stepaside Dublin 10 B2
Stephansdom Vienna 32 A2
Stepney London 15 A3
Sterling Park San Francisco 26 B2
Sticklinge udde Stockholm 29 A2
Stickney Chicago 9 C2
Stillorgan Dublin 10 B2
Stockholm Stockholm 29 B2
Stocksund Stockholm 29 A2
Stodůlky Prague 25 B1
Stoke Newington London 15 A3
Stokes Valley Wellington 33 B2
Stone Canyon Res. Los Angeles 16 B2
Stone Park Chicago 9 B1
Stonebridge London 15 A2
Stoneham Boston 6 A2
Stony Brook Res. Boston 6 B2
Stony Creek → Chicago 9 C2
Stora Värtan Stockholm 29 A2
Store Hareskov Copenhagen 8 A2
Store Magleby Copenhagen 8 B3
Storholmen Stockholm 29 A2
Stoyka St. Petersburg 27 B2
Straiton Edinburgh 11 B3
Strandfontein Cape Town 8 B2
Strašnice Prague 25 B2
Strasstrudering Munich 21 B3
Stratford London 15 A4
Strathfield Sydney 29 B1
Streatham London 15 B3
Streatham Vale London 15 B3
Strebersdorf Vienna 32 A2
Střešovice Prague 25 B2
Střížkov Prague 25 B2
Strombeek-Bever Brussels 6 A2
Stromovka Prague 25 B2
Studio City Los Angeles 16 B2
Stureby Stockholm 29 B2
Stuvsta Stockholm 29 B2
Subhepur Delhi 10 A2
Sucat Manila 17 C2
Suchdol Prague 25 B2
Sucy-en-Brie Paris 24 B4
Sue, L. Orlando 23 A2
Sugamo Tokyo 30 A3
Sugar Loaf Mt. = Açúcar, Pão de Rio de Janeiro 25 B2
Suge Tokyo 30 B2
Suginami Tokyo 30 A2
Sugō Tokyo 30 B2
Sui Sai Wan Hong Kong 12 B1
Suita Osaka 23 A2
Suitland Washington 33 B4
Sukchar Kolkata 14 A2
Sultanahme Camil Istanbul 12 B1
Sumida Tokyo 30 A3
Sumida → Tokyo 30 A3
Sumiyoshi Osaka 23 B2
Sumiyoshi Shrine Osaka 23 B1
Summerville Toronto 31 B1
Summit Chicago 9 C2
Sunamachi Tokyo 30 A4
Sunbury-on-Thames London 15 B1
Sundbyberg Stockholm 29 A1
Sundbyerne Copenhagen 8 B3
Sung Kong Hong Kong 12 B2
Sungei Kadut Industrial Estate Singapore 28 A2
Sungei Selatar Res. Singapore 28 A3
Sunset Park New York 22 C2
Sunter Jakarta 12 A2
Sunter, Kali → Jakarta 12 B2
Suomenlinna Helsinki 11 C2
Sur Bahr Jerusalem 13 B2
Sura Kolkata 14 B2
Suraksan Seoul 27 A2
Surbiton London 15 B2
Suresnes Paris 24 A2
Surfside Miami 18 A2
Surquillo Lima 14 B2
Surrey Hills Sydney 29 B2
Susaek Seoul 27 B1
Süssenbrunn Vienna 32 A2
Sutton Dublin 10 A3
Sutton London 15 B2
Suyu Seoul 27 B2
Suzukishinden Tokyo 30 A2
Svanemøllen Copenhagen 8 A3
Sveaborg = Suomenlinna Helsinki 11 C2
Sverdlov Moscow 19 B2
Svestad Oslo 23 B2
Svinö Helsinki 11 C1
Swanley London 15 B4
Swansea Toronto 31 B2
Swinburne I. New York 22 C1
Swords Dublin 10 A2
Sydenham Johannesburg 13 A2
Sydney Sydney 29 B2
Sydney, Univ. of Sydney 29 B2
Sydney Harbour Bridge Sydney 29 B2
Sydney Kingsford Smith ✈ (SYD) Sydney 29 B2
Sydstranden Copenhagen 8 B3
Sylvania Sydney 29 C1
Syon Park London 15 B2
Szczęśliwice Warsaw 32 B1
Széchnenyi-hegy Budapest 7 B1
Széphalom Budapest 7 A1

T

Taastrup Copenhagen 8 B1
Tabata Tokyo 30 A3
Tablada Buenos Aires 7 C1
Table B. Cape Town 8 A1
Table Mt. Cape Town 8 A1
Taboão da Serra São Paulo 27 B1
Täby Stockholm 29 A2
Tacuba Mexico City 18 B1
Tacubaya Mexico City 18 B1
Tafelbaai = Table B. Cape Town 8 A1
Taft Orlando 23 B2
Tagig → Manila 17 B2
Taguig Manila 17 B2
Tai Hang Hong Kong 12 B2
Tai Lo Shan Hong Kong 12 A2
Tai Po Tsai Hong Kong 12 A2
Tai Seng Singapore 28 A3
Tai Shui Hang Hong Kong 12 A2
Tai Tam B. Hong Kong 12 B2
Tai Tam Tuk Res. Hong Kong 12 B2
Tai Wai Hong Kong 12 A2
Tai Wan Tau Hong Kong 12 B2
Tai Wo Hau Hong Kong 12 A1
Tainaka Osaka 23 B2
Taishō Osaka 23 B1
Taita Wellington 33 B2
Tajrīsh Tehran 31 A2
Takaido Tokyo 30 A2
Takaishi Tokyo 30 B2
Takarazuka Osaka 23 A1
Takasago Tokyo 30 A4
Takatsu Tokyo 30 B2
Takeshita Tokyo 30 B2
Takinegawa Tokyo 30 A3
Takoma Park Washington 33 B3
Taksim Istanbul 12 B1
Talaide Lisbon 16 A1
Taliganga Kolkata 14 B2
Talipapa Manila 17 A2
Tallaght Dublin 10 B1
Tallkrogen Stockholm 29 B2
Tama Tokyo 30 B1
Tama → Tokyo 30 B2
Tama Kyūryō Tokyo 30 B2
Tamaden Tokyo 30 B2
Tamagawa-josui → Tokyo 30 A1
Taman Sari Jakarta 12 A1
Tamanduateí → São Paulo 27 B2
Tamboerskloof Cape Town 8 A1
Tambora Jakarta 12 A1
Tammisalo Helsinki 11 B3
Tammūh Cairo 7 B2
Tampines Singapore 28 A3
Tanah Abang Jakarta 12 B1
Tanah Kusir Jakarta 12 B1
Tangelo Park Orlando 23 B2
Tanjung Duren Jakarta 12 B1
Tanjung Priok Jakarta 12 A2
Tanum Oslo 23 A1
Tapada Lisbon 16 A1
Tapanila Helsinki 11 B3
Tapiales Buenos Aires 7 C1
Tapiola Helsinki 11 B1
Tapsia Kolkata 14 B2
Tara Mumbai 20 A1
Tarabya Istanbul 12 B2
Tårbæk Copenhagen 8 A3
Tarchomin Warsaw 32 B1
Tardeo Mumbai 20 B1
Targówek Warsaw 32 B2
Tårnby Copenhagen 8 B3
Tarqua Bay Lagos 14 B2
Tathong Channel Hong Kong 12 B2
Tathong Pt. Hong Kong 12 B2
Tatuapé São Paulo 27 B2
Taufkirchen Munich 21 B2
Tavares, I. dos Rio de Janeiro 25 A2
Tavros Athens 2 B2
Tawa Wellington 33 A1
Te Papa Museum Wellington 33 B1
Teaneck New York 22 A1
Tebet Jakarta 12 B2
Tecamachalco Mexico City 18 B1
Ted Williams Tunnel Boston 6 A2
Teddington London 15 B1
Tegel Berlin 5 A2
Tegel, Berlin ✈ (TXL) Berlin 5 A2
Tegeler See Berlin 5 A2
Tegelort Berlin 5 A2
Teheran = Tehrān Tehran 31 A2
Tehrān Tehran 31 A2
Tehrān Pārs Tehran 31 A3
Tei Tong Tsui Hong Kong 12 B2
Tejo, Rio → Lisbon 16 A2
Tekstilyshchik Moscow 19 B3
Telhal Lisbon 16 A1
Telok Blangah Singapore 28 B2
Teltow Berlin 5 B2
Teltow kanal Berlin 5 B3
Tempelhof Berlin 5 B3
Tempelhof, Berlin ✈ (THF) Berlin 5 B3
Temple City Los Angeles 16 B4
Temple Hills Washington 33 C4
Templeogue Dublin 10 B2
Temppeliaukio Church Helsinki 11 B2
Tenafly New York 22 A2
Tenayuca, Piramide de Mexico City 18 A1
Tengah → Singapore 28 A2
Tennoji Osaka 23 B2
Tepalcates Mexico City 18 B2
Tepeyac, Parque Nacional △ Mexico City 18 B2
Terrazzano Milan 19 A1
Terre des Hommes Montreal 20 A2
Terrugem Lisbon 16 A1
Tervuren Brussels 6 B3
Tervuren, Park van Brussels 6 B3
Tetuán Madrid 17 B1
Teufelsberg Berlin 5 B2
Thalkirchen Munich 21 B2
Thames Ditton London 15 B1
Thamesmead London 15 A4
Thana Cr. → Mumbai 20 A2
Thiais Paris 24 B3
Thisio Athens 2 B2
Thistletown Toronto 31 A1
Thomastown Melbourne 18 A2
Thompson I. Boston 6 B3
Thon Buri Bangkok 3 B1
Thornbury Melbourne 18 A2
Thorncliffe Toronto 31 A2
Thornhill Toronto 31 A2
Thornton Cape Town 8 A2
Thornton Heath London 15 B3
Threipmuir Res. Edinburgh 11 B2
Throgs Neck New York 22 B3
Tian'anmen Square Beijing 4 B2
Tiancun Beijing 4 B1
Tibet, L. Orlando 23 B1
Tibidabo Barcelona 4 A1
Tibradden Mt. Dublin 10 B2
Tiburon San Francisco 26 A2
Tiburtino Rome 26 B2
Ticomán Mexico City 18 A2
Tiefersee Berlin 5 B1
Tiejiangyin Beijing 4 C2
Tiergarten Berlin 5 A3
Tijgerhof Cape Town 8 A2
Tijuca Rio de Janeiro 25 B1
Tijuca, Pico da Rio de Janeiro 25 B1
Tijuca △ Rio de Janeiro 25 B1
Tikkurila Helsinki 11 B3
Tilak Nagar Delhi 10 B1
Tilanqiao Shanghai 28 B1
Timah, Bukit Singapore 28 A2
Timiryazev Park Moscow 19 B2
Tira Jerusalem 13 A1
Tirsa Cairo 7 B2
Tishrīyaa Baghdad 3 B2
Tiu Keng Leng Hong Kong 12 B2
Tizapán Mexico City 18 C1
Tlalnepantla → Mexico City 18 A1
Tlalpan Mexico City 18 C2
To Kwai Wan Hong Kong 12 B2
Toa Payoh Singapore 28 A3
Točná Prague 25 C2
Toco Hills Atlanta 3 B2
Todt Hill New York 22 C1
Tōkagi Tokyo 30 A4
Tokai Plantation Cape Town 8 B1
Tōkaichiba Tokyo 30 B2
Tōkyō Tokyo 30 B3
Tōkyō B. = Tōkyō-Wan Tokyo 30 B4
Tōkyō Disneyland Tokyo 30 B4
Tōkyō Haneda ✈ (HND) Tokyo 30 B3
Tōkyō Harbour Tokyo 30 B3
Tōkyō-Wan Tokyo 30 B4
Tolka → Dublin 10 A1
Tollygunge = Taliganga Kolkata 14 B2
Tolworth London 15 B2
Tomba di Nerone Rome 26 B1
Tommy Thompson Park Toronto 31 B3
Tondo Manila 17 B1
Tongbinggo Seoul 27 B1
Tongqiao Shanghai 28 A1
Toorak Melbourne 18 B2
Topanga State Park ⌂ Los Angeles 16 B1
Topkapı Istanbul 12 B1
Topkapı Palaca Istanbul 12 B1
Tor di Quinto Rome 26 B1
Tor Pignattara Rome 26 B2
Tor Sapienza Rome 26 B2
Torcy Paris 24 A4
Toronto Toronto 31 B2
Toronto, Univ. of Toronto 31 B2
Toronto City Centre ✈ (YTZ) Toronto 31 B2
Toronto Harbour Toronto 31 B2
Toronto I. Toronto 31 B2
Toronto Lester B. Pearson Int. ✈ (YYZ) Toronto 31 A1
Torre Lupara Rome 26 B2
Torre Nova Rome 26 B2
Torrellas → Barcelona 4 A1
Torrevécchia Rome 26 B1
Toshima Tokyo 30 A3
Toshimaen Tokyo 30 A2
Tottenham London 15 A3
Tottenham Melbourne 18 A1
Toussus-le-Noble Paris 24 B1
Toussus-le-Noble ✈ Paris 24 B1
Towchāl Cable Car Tehran 31 A2
Tower Hamlets □ London 15 A3
Tower of London London 15 A3
Towra Pt. Sydney 29 C2
Tøyen Oslo 23 A3
Toyonaka Osaka 23 A1
Trafaria Lisbon 16 A1
Traição, Cor. → São Paulo 27 B2
Tranegilde Copenhagen 8 B2
Trångsund Stockholm 29 B2
Trappenfelde Berlin 5 A4
Trastévere Rome 26 B1
Treasure I. San Francisco 26 B2
Třeboradice Prague 25 B3
Třebotov Prague 25 C1
Tremblay-en-France Paris 24 A4
Tremembe → São Paulo 27 A2
Tremont New York 22 A2
Trenno Milan 19 B1
Treptow Berlin 5 B3
Três Rios, Sa. dos Rio de Janeiro 25 B1
Trevi, Fontana di Rome 26 B1
Trezzano sul Naviglio Milan 19 B1
Trieste Rome 26 B2
Trinidad Washington 33 B4
Trinity Edinburgh 11 B2
Trinity College Dublin 10 A2
Trionfale Rome 26 B1
Triulzo Milan 19 B2
Troja Prague 25 B2
Trollbäcken Stockholm 29 B3
Trombay Mumbai 20 A2
Troparevo Moscow 19 C1
Trudeau, Montréal ✈ (YUL) Montreal 20 B1
Trudyashchikhsya, Ostrov St. Petersburg 27 B1
Tryvasshøgda Oslo 23 A3
Tseng Lan Shue Hong Kong 12 A2
Tseung Kwan Hong Kong 12 B2
Tsim Sha Tsui Hong Kong 12 B2
Tsing Yi Hong Kong 12 A1
Tsova Jerusalem 13 B1
Tsuen Wan Hong Kong 12 A1
Tsur Hadassa Jerusalem 13 B1
Tsurumi → Tokyo 30 B3
Tsz Wan Shan Hong Kong 12 A2
Tuas Singapore 28 B1
Tuchoměřice Prague 25 B1
Tuckahoe New York 22 A3
Tucuruvi São Paulo 27 A2
Tufello Rome 26 B2
Tufnell Park London 15 A3
Tufts University Boston 6 A2
Tughlakabad Delhi 10 B2
Tuindorp Amsterdam 2 A2
Tullamarine Melbourne 18 A1
Tulse Hill London 15 B3
Tung Lung Chau Hong Kong 12 B2
Tung O Hong Kong 12 B1
Tunis Baghdad 3 A2
Tuomarila Helsinki 11 B1
Tureberg Stockholm 29 A1
Turffontein Johannesburg 13 B2
Turkey L. Orlando 23 A2
Turkey Lake Park Orlando 23 A2
Turner Field Atlanta 3 B2
Turnham Green London 15 B2
Turnhouse Edinburgh 11 B1
Tuscolana, Via Rome 26 B2
Twelve Apostles Cape Town 8 A1
Twickenham London 15 B1
Twickenham Rugby Ground London 15 B1
Twin Peaks San Francisco 26 B2
Two Rock Mt. Dublin 10 B2
Tymon North Dublin 10 B1
Tysons Corner Washington 33 B2

U

U.S. Capitol Washington 33 B3
U.S. Cellular Field Chicago 9 C3
Ubeidiya Jerusalem 13 B2
Uberaba → São Paulo 27 B2
Ubin, Pulau Singapore 28 A3
Uccle Brussels 6 B2
Udelnaya St. Petersburg 27 A2
Udelnoe St. Petersburg 27 B1
Udlding Munich 21 A1
Ueno Tokyo 30 A3
Úholičky Prague 25 B1
Úhřiněves Prague 25 B3
Uithoorn Amsterdam 2 B1
Ujazdów Warsaw 32 B2
Újpalota Budapest 7 A2
Újpest Budapest 7 A2
Ukita Tokyo 30 A4
Ullerup Copenhagen 8 B3
Ullevål Oslo 23 A3
Ulriksdal Stockholm 29 A1
Ulyanka St. Petersburg 27 B1
Um Al-Khanazir Island Baghdad 3 B2
Umeda Osaka 23 A1
Ümraniye Istanbul 12 B2
Underground Atlanta Atlanta 3 B2
Underhill, L. Orlando 23 A3
Unětický potok → Prague 25 B2
Unhos Lisbon 16 A2
Unidad Santa Fe Mexico City 18 B1
Union City New York 22 B1
Union Port New York 22 B2
Union Station Toronto 31 B2
United Center Chicago 9 B2
United Nations Headquarters New York 22 B2
Universal Studios Los Angeles 16 B2
Universal Studios Orlando 23 B2
Universidad Madrid 17 B1
Universidad de Chile Santiago 27 B2
University Park Washington 33 B4
Unterbiberg Munich 21 B2
Unterföhring Munich 21 A3
Unterhaching Munich 21 B2
Unterlaa Vienna 32 B2
Untermenzing Munich 21 A1
Upper B. New York 22 C1
Upper Elmers End London 15 B3
Upper New York B. = Upper B. New York 22 C1
Upper Norwood London 15 B3
Upper Peirce Res. Singapore 28 A2
Upper Sydenham London 15 B3
Upper Tooting London 15 B3
Upton London 15 A4
Uptown Chicago 9 B2
Uran Mumbai 20 B2
Urayasu Tokyo 30 B4
Urbe ✈ Rome 26 B2
Urca Rio de Janeiro 25 B2
Uritsk St. Petersburg 27 C1
Úrőm Budapest 7 A2
Ursus Warsaw 32 B1
Ursvik Stockholm 29 A1
Usera Madrid 17 B1
Ushigome Tokyo 30 A3
Usina Rio de Janeiro 25 B1
Üsküdar Istanbul 12 B2
Ust-Slavyanka St. Petersburg 27 C3
Uteke Stockholm 29 A3
Utrata Warsaw 32 B2
Uttarpara Kolkata 14 B1
Utterslev Mose Copenhagen 8 A2

V

Vaclavské náměstí Prague 25 B2
Vadaul Mumbai 20 A2
Vaires-sur-Marne Paris 24 A4
Valby Copenhagen 8 B2
Valcannuta Rome 26 B1
Valdelatas Madrid 17 A1
Vale Washington 33 B1
Valenton Paris 24 B3
Valera Milan 19 A1
Vallcarca Barcelona 4 A1
Valldoreix Barcelona 4 A1
Vallecas Madrid 17 B2
Vallensbæk Copenhagen 8 B2
Vallensbæk Strand Copenhagen 8 B2
Vallentunasjön Stockholm 29 A2
Valleranello Rome 26 C1
Vallisaari Helsinki 11 C3
Vallvidrera Barcelona 4 A1
Valvidrera → Barcelona 4 A1
Van Gogh-museum Amsterdam 2 A2
Vanak Tehran 31 A2
Vanda = Vantaa Helsinki 11 B2
Vangede Copenhagen 8 A3
Vaniköy Istanbul 12 B2
Vanløse Copenhagen 8 A2
Vantaa Helsinki 11 B2
Vantaankoski Helsinki 11 B2
Vantaanpuisto Helsinki 11 B2
Vanves Paris 24 B2
Varedo Milan 19 A1
Varkiza Athens 2 C2
Vartiokylä Helsinki 11 B3
Vartiosaari Helsinki 11 B3
Vasamuseet Stockholm 29 B2
Vasco Cape Town 8 A2
Vasfanārd Tehran 31 B2
Vashi Mumbai 20 A2
Vasilyevskiy, Ostrov St. Petersburg 27 B1
Vatican City ■ Rome 26 B1
Vaucluse Sydney 29 B2
Vaucresson Paris 24 A1
Vaughan Toronto 31 A1
Vauhallan Paris 24 B2
Vaujours Paris 24 A4
Vauxhall London 15 B3
Vecsés Budapest 7 B3
Veleň Prague 25 A3
Veleslavin Prague 25 B2
Vélizy-Villacoublay Paris 24 B2
Velka-Chuchle Prague 25 B2
Velké Přílepy Prague 25 B1
Venda Seca Lisbon 16 A1
Venetian Islands Miami 18 B2
Venice Los Angeles 16 C2
Ventas Madrid 17 B1
Ventorro del Cano Madrid 17 B1
Venustiano Carranza Mexico City 18 B2
Verde → São Paulo 27 A1
Verdi Athens 2 A2
Verdugo Mts. Los Angeles 16 A2
Verdun Montreal 20 B2
Vérhalom Budapest 7 A2
Vermelho → São Paulo 27 B1
Vernon Los Angeles 16 B3
Verrières-le-Buisson Paris 24 B2
Versailles Buenos Aires 7 B1
Versailles Paris 24 B1
Veshnyaki Moscow 19 B3
Vesolyy Posolok St. Petersburg 27 B2
Vestra Helsinki 11 B1
Vestskoven Copenhagen 8 A2
Vicálvaro Madrid 17 B2
Vicente Lopez Buenos Aires 7 B2
Victoria Hong Kong 12 B2
Victoria, Mt. Wellington 33 B1
Victoria, Pont Montreal 20 B2
Victoria and Alfred Waterfront Cape Town 8 A1
Victoria Gardens Mumbai 20 B2
Victoria Harbour Hong Kong 12 B1
Victoria Island Lagos 14 B2
Victoria L. Johannesburg 13 B2
Victoria Lawn Tennis Courts Melbourne 18 B2
Victoria Park Singapore 28 B2
Victoria Peak Hong Kong 12 B1
Vienna = Wien Vienna 32 A2
Vienna Washington 33 B2
Vietnam Veterans Memorial Washington 33 B3
Vietnam War Museum Chicago 9 B3
View Park Los Angeles 16 B3
Vigário Geral Rio de Janeiro 25 A1
Vigentino Milan 19 B2
Viggbyholm Stockholm 29 A2
Vighignolo Milan 19 B1
Viikki Helsinki 11 B3
Vikhroli Mumbai 20 A2
Vila Guilherme São Paulo 27 B2
Vila Isabel Rio de Janeiro 25 B1
Vila Jaguára São Paulo 27 B1
Vila Madalena São Paulo 27 B1
Vila Maria São Paulo 27 B2
Vila Mariana São Paulo 27 B2
Vila Prudente São Paulo 27 B2
Viladecans Barcelona 4 B1
Vile Parle Mumbai 20 A2
Villa Adelina Buenos Aires 7 B1
Villa Ballester Buenos Aires 7 B1
Villa Barilari Buenos Aires 7 C2
Villa Bosch Buenos Aires 7 B1
Villa C. Colon Buenos Aires 7 C2
Villa Ciudadela Buenos Aires 7 B1
Villa de Guadalupe Mexico City 18 B2
Villa Devoto Buenos Aires 7 B1
Villa Diamante Buenos Aires 7 C2
Villa Dominico Buenos Aires 7 C3
Villa Lugano Buenos Aires 7 C2
Villa Lynch Buenos Aires 7 B1
Villa Madero Buenos Aires 7 C1
Villa Sáenz Pena Buenos Aires 7 B1
Villa Urquiza Buenos Aires 7 B2
Villaverde Madrid 17 B1
Villaverde Bajo Madrid 17 B1
Ville-d'Avray Paris 24 B2
Villecresnes Paris 24 B4
Villejuif Paris 24 B3
Villemomble Paris 24 A4
Villeneuve-la-Garenne Paris 24 A2
Villeneuve-le-Roi Paris 24 B3
Villeneuve-St-Georges Paris 24 B3
Villeparisis Paris 24 A4
Villevaudé Paris 24 A4
Villiers-le-Bâcle Paris 24 B1
Villiers-sur-Marne Paris 24 B4
Villinki Helsinki 11 C3
Villoresi, Canale Milan 19 A1
Vilvoorde Brussels 6 A2
Vimodrone Milan 19 A2
Vimont Montreal 20 A1
Vincennes Paris 24 A3
Vincennes, Bois de Paris 24 B3
Vineland Orlando 23 B1
Vinings Atlanta 3 A2
Vinohrady Prague 25 B2
Vinoř Prague 25 B3
Virányos Budapest 7 A1
Virgen del San Cristóbal Santiago 27 B2
Virginia, L. Orlando 23 A2
Virginia Gardens Miami 18 B1
Virginia Key Miami 18 B2
Viroflay Paris 24 B2
Vironas Athens 2 B2
Virum Copenhagen 8 A2
Visitacion Valley San Francisco 26 B2
Vista Alegre Lima 14 B3
Vista Alegre Santiago 27 C1
Vista Grove Atlanta 3 A3
Vitacura Santiago 27 B2
Vitinia Rome 26 C1
Vitry-sur-Seine Paris 24 B3
Vizcaya Museum and Gardens Miami 18 B2
Vladykino Moscow 19 A2
Vlezenbeek Brussels 6 B1
Vokovice Prague 25 B2
Volgelsdorf Berlin 5 B5
Volkhonka-Zil Moscow 19 C2
Vollen Oslo 23 B1
Volodarskoye St. Petersburg 27 B2
Volynkina-Derevnya St. Petersburg 27 B1
Vondelpark Amsterdam 2 A2
Vösendorf Vienna 32 B2
Voula Athens 2 C2
Vouliagmeni Athens 2 C2
Vredehoek Cape Town 8 A1
Vršovice Prague 25 B2
Vyborgskaya Storona St. Petersburg 27 B2
Vykhino Moscow 19 B3
Vyšehrad Prague 25 B2

W

Wachterhof Munich 21 B3
Wadala Mumbai 20 A2
Wadestown Wellington 33 B1
Wadi al-Arayis Jerusalem 13 B2
Wadi Fukin Jerusalem 13 B1
Waduk Pluit Jakarta 12 A1
Wah Fu Hong Kong 12 B1
Wahda Baghdad 3 B2
Währing Vienna 32 A2
Waidmannslust Berlin 5 A3
Wainuiomata Wellington 33 B2
Wainuiomata → Wellington 33 B2
Wakefield Boston 6 A2
Waldesruh Berlin 5 B4
Waldperlach Munich 21 B3
Waldtrudering Munich 21 B3
Walkinstown Dublin 10 B1
Wall Street New York 22 B1
Walt Disney World Orlando 23 B1
Walter D. Stone Memorial Zoo Boston 6 A2
Waltham Boston 6 A1
Waltham Forest □ London 15 A3
Walthamstow London 15 A3
Walton-on-Thames London 15 B1
Wambeek Brussels 6 A3
Wan Chai Hong Kong 12 B2
Wandsworth □ London 15 B2
Wannsee Berlin 5 B1
Wansdorf Berlin 5 A1
Wanstead London 15 A4
Wapping London 15 A3
Ward Dublin 10 A1
Ward I. Wellington 33 B2
Wards I. New York 22 B2
Warnberg Munich 21 B2
Warner Brothers Studios Los Angeles 16 B2
Warrāq el 'Arab Cairo 7 A2
Warringal Park Melbourne 18 A2
Warriston Edinburgh 11 B2
Warsaw = Warszawa Warsaw 32 B2
Warszawa Warsaw 32 B2
Warszawa ✈ (WAW) Warsaw 32 B1
Wartenberg Berlin 5 A4
Washington Washington 33 B3
Washington Heights New York 22 A2
Washington Park Chicago 9 C3
Washington Ronald Reagan National ✈ (DCA) Washington 33 B3
Wat Pho Bangkok 3 B1
Water of Leith → Edinburgh 11 B1
Watergraafsmeer Amsterdam 2 A2
Waterland Amsterdam 2 A2
Waterloo Brussels 6 B2
Waterloo Wellington 33 B2
Watermeal-Boitsfort Brussels 6 B2
Watertown Boston 6 A1
Watsonia Melbourne 18 A2
Waverley Boston 6 A1
Waverley Johannesburg 13 A2
Waverley Sydney 29 B2
Wawer Warsaw 32 B2
Wawrzyszew Warsaw 32 B1
Wazirabad Delhi 10 A2
Waziriya Baghdad 3 A2
Wazirpur Delhi 10 A2
Wealdstone London 15 A1
Wedding Berlin 5 A3
Weehawken New York 22 B1
Weesp Amsterdam 2 B3
Weidling Vienna 32 A1
Weidlingbach Vienna 32 A1
Weigongcun Beijing 4 B1
Weissensee Berlin 5 A3
Wellesley Hills Boston 6 B1
Welling London 15 B4
Wellington Boston 6 A2
Wellington Wellington 33 B1
Wellington Int. ✈ (WLE) Wellington 33 B1
Weltevreden Park Johannesburg 13 A1
Wembley London 15 A2
Wemmel Brussels 6 A1
Wemmer Pan Johannesburg 13 B2
Wenceslas Square = Vaclavské náměstí Prague 25 B2
Wendenschloss Berlin 5 B4
Wennington London 15 A5
Werneuchen Berlin 5 A5
West Don → Toronto 31 A2
West Drayton London 15 A1
West Ham London 15 A4
West Harrow London 15 A1
West Heath London 15 B4
West Hill Toronto 31 A3
West Hollywood Los Angeles 16 B2
West Lamma Channel Hong Kong 12 B1
West Los Angeles, University of Los Angeles 16 C2
West Medford Boston 6 A2
West Miami Miami 18 B1
West Molesey London 15 B1
West New York New York 22 B1
West of Twin Peaks San Francisco 26 B2
West Park Johannesburg 13 A1
West Rouge Toronto 31 A4
West Roxbury Boston 6 B2
West Springfield Washington 33 C2
West Town Chicago 9 B2
West Wharf Karachi 13 B1
Westchester Chicago 9 B1
Westchester Los Angeles 16 C2
Westchester New York 22 A2
Westcliff Johannesburg 13 B2
Westdene Johannesburg 13 B1
Westend Helsinki 11 C1
Wester Hailes Edinburgh 11 B2
Westerham Munich 21 B2
Western Addition San Francisco 26 B2
Westgate Washington 33 B3
Westlake Cape Town 8 B1
Westlake San Francisco 26 B2
Westminster London 15 A3
Westmount Montreal 20 B2
Weston Toronto 31 A1
Westwood Village Los Angeles 16 B2
Westzaan Amsterdam 2 A1
Wetton Cape Town 8 B2
Wexford Toronto 31 A3
Weybridge London 15 B1
Wezembeek-Oppem Brussels 6 A2
White Cloud Hill = Baiyun Hill Guangzhou 11 B2
White House, The Washington 33 B3
Whitechapel London 15 A3
Whitehall Dublin 10 A2
Whittier Los Angeles 16 C4
Whitton London 15 B1
Wieden Vienna 32 A2
Wien Vienna 32 A2
Wien-Schwechat ✈ (VIE) Vienna 32 B3
Wienerberg Vienna 32 B2
Wierzbno Warsaw 32 B2
Wijde Wormer Amsterdam 2 A2
Wilanów Warsaw 32 B2
Wilanówka → Warsaw 32 C2
Wilds, The Johannesburg 13 B2
Wilhelmshagen Berlin 5 B5
Wilket Creek Park Toronto 31 A2
Wilkieston Edinburgh 11 B1
Will Rogers State Historical Park ⌂ Los Angeles 16 B1
Willbrook Dublin 10 B2
Willesden London 15 A2
Willesden Green London 15 A2
Williamsbridge New York 22 A2
Williamsburg New York 22 B2
Williamsburg Orlando 23 B2
Williamstown Melbourne 18 B1
Willis, L. Orlando 23 B2
Willoughby Sydney 29 A2
Willow Springs Chicago 9 C1
Willowdale Toronto 31 A2
Wilmersdorf Berlin 5 B2
Wilmette Chicago 9 A2
Wilmington London 15 B5
Wimbledon London 15 B2
Wimbledon Common London 15 B2
Wimbledon Park London 15 B2
Wimbledon Tennis Ground London 15 B2
Winchester Boston 6 A2
Windermere Cape Town 8 A2
Windermere Orlando 23 B1
Windsor Johannesburg 13 A1
Windsor, Gare Montreal 20 B2
Windsor Hills Los Angeles 16 C2
Windy Arbour Dublin 10 B2
Winning Munich 21 B2
Wissous Paris 24 B2
Wittenau Berlin 5 A2
Witwatersrand, Univ. of Johannesburg 13 B2
Wlochy Warsaw 32 B1
Wo Mei Hong Kong 12 A2
Wo Yi Hop Hong Kong 12 A1
Woburn Boston 6 A2
Woburn Toronto 31 A3
Wola Warsaw 32 B1
Wolf Trap Farm Park Washington 33 B2
Wolgok Seoul 27 B2
Wolica Warsaw 32 C1
Wólka Węglowa Warsaw 32 B1
Wollaston Boston 6 B2
Woltersdorf Berlin 5 B5
Woluwe-St-Lambert Brussels 6 A2
Woluwe-St-Pierre Brussels 6 A2
Wong Chuk Hang Hong Kong 12 B2
Wong Chuk Wan Hong Kong 12 A2
Wong Chuk Yeung Hong Kong 12 A2
Wong Tai Sin Hong Kong 12 A2
Wood Green London 15 A3
Wood Ridge New York 22 A1
Woodbine Race Track Toronto 31 A1
Woodbridge Toronto 31 A1
Woodford London 15 A4
Woodford Bridge London 15 A4
Woodford Green London 15 A4
Woodhaven New York 22 B2
Woodhouselee Edinburgh 11 B2
Woodlands Singapore 28 A2
Woodmont Washington 33 B3
Woodside London 15 B3
Woodside New York 22 B2
Woodstock Cape Town 8 A1
Woollahra Sydney 29 B2
Woolooware B. Sydney 29 C1
Woolwich London 15 B4
World Trade Center, site of former New York 22 B1
Worli Mumbai 20 A1
Worth Chicago 9 C2
Wren's Nest Atlanta 3 B2
Wrigley Field Chicago 9 B3
Wuhlgarten Berlin 5 A4
Wujiaochang Shanghai 28 B2
Würm → Munich 21 B1
Würm-kanal Munich 21 A1
Wusong Shanghai 28 A1
Wyczółki Warsaw 32 C1
Wygoda Warsaw 32 B2
Wynberg Cape Town 8 B1

X

Xabregas Lisbon 16 A2
Xianggang = Hong Kong Hong Kong 12 B1
Xiaogang Park Guangzhou 11 B2
Xiaoping Guangzhou 11 A2
Xiasha chong Guangzhou 11 B1
Xichang Guangzhou 11 B2
Xicheng Beijing 4 B1
Xidan Beijing 4 B2
Xizhimen Beijing 4 B1
Xochimilco, Parque Ecológico Mexico City 18 C2
Xuanwu Beijing 4 B1
Xuhui Shanghai 28 B1

Y

Yaba Lagos 14 A2
Yaftābād Tehran 31 B1
Yahara Tokyo 30 A2
Yaho Tokyo 30 A1
Yakire Tokyo 30 A4
Yaksu Seoul 27 B2
Yamada Osaka 23 A2
Yamada Tokyo 30 B2
Yamato → Osaka 23 B1
Yan Kit Singapore 28 A3
Yanbu Guangzhou 11 B1
Yangcheon Seoul 27 B1
Yanghuayuan Beijing 4 C1
Yangjae Seoul 27 C2
Yangjiazhuang Shanghai 28 A1
Yangjing Shanghai 28 B2
Yangpu Shanghai 28 B2
Yangpu Park Shanghai 28 B2
Yannawa Bangkok 3 B2
Yarmūk Baghdad 3 B1
Yarra Bend Park Melbourne 18 A2
Yarraville Melbourne 18 A1
Yau Tong Hong Kong 12 B2
Yauza → Moscow 19 A3
Yeading London 15 A1
Yedikule Istanbul 12 C1
Yenikapı Istanbul 12 B1
Yeniköy Istanbul 12 B2
Yeongdeungpo Seoul 27 B1
Yeongdong Seoul 27 B2
Yeouido Seoul 27 B1
Yerba Buena I. San Francisco 26 B2
Yerres Paris 24 B4
Yerushalayim = Jerusalem Jerusalem 13 B2
Yiheyuan Beijing 4 A1
Yıldız Park Istanbul 12 B2
Yinhangzhen Shanghai 28 A2
Yishun Singapore 28 A3
Ylästö Helsinki 11 B2
Yodo → Osaka 23 A2
Yongdingmen Beijing 4 B2
Yongfucun Guangzhou 11 B2
Yongsan Seoul 27 B1
Yonkers New York 22 A2
York Toronto 31 A2
York Mills Toronto 31 A2
York University Toronto 31 A1
You'anmen Beijing 4 B1
Youngsfield Cape Town 8 B1
Yuanxiatian Guangzhou 11 A2
Yuexiu Park Guangzhou 11 B2
Yugo-Zarad Moscow 19 B2
Yuhalixqui, Volcan Mexico City 18 C2
Yung Shue Wan Hong Kong 12 B1
Yūsofābād Tehran 31 A2

Z

Zaandam Amsterdam 2 A1
Zaandijk Amsterdam 2 A1
Zaanstad Amsterdam 2 A1
Záběhlice Prague 25 B2
Zabki Warsaw 32 B2
Żacisze Warsaw 32 B2
Zahrā Baghdad 3 A1
Žalov Prague 25 A2
Załuski Warsaw 32 C1
Zamdorf Munich 21 B2
Zanevka St. Petersburg 27 B3
Zapote Manila 17 C1
Zaventem Brussels 6 A2
Zawady Warsaw 32 B2
Zāwiyet Abū Musallam Cairo 7 B1
Zawrā' Park Baghdad 3 B2
Zbraslav Prague 25 C2
Zbuzany Prague 25 B1
Zdiby Prague 25 B2
Zeekoevlei Cape Town 8 B2
Zehlendorf Berlin 5 B2
Zenne → Brussels 6 B1
Żerań Warsaw 32 B1
Zerzeń Warsaw 32 B2
Zeytinburnu Istanbul 12 C1
Zhabei Shanghai 28 B1
Zhdanov Moscow 19 B3
Zhenru Shanghai 28 B1
Zhernovka St. Petersburg 27 B2
Zhicun Guangzhou 11 B2
Zhongshan Park Shanghai 28 B1
Zhoucun Guangzhou 11 A2
Zhoujiadu Shanghai 28 B1
Zhoujiazhen Shanghai 28 B2
Zhulebino Moscow 19 B4
Zhushadi Guangzhou 11 A3
Zielona Warsaw 32 B3
Zielonka Warsaw 32 B2
Žižkov Prague 25 B2
Zličín Prague 25 B1
Zografou Athens 2 B2
Żoliborz Warsaw 32 B1
Zonnebloem Cape Town 8 A1
Zugliget Budapest 7 B1
Zugló Budapest 7 A2
Zuiderwoude Amsterdam 2 A3
Zumbi Rio de Janeiro 25 A1
Zunderdorp Amsterdam 2 A2
Zuvuvu → São Paulo 27 C1
Zwanenburg Amsterdam 2 A1
Zwölfaxing Vienna 32 B2

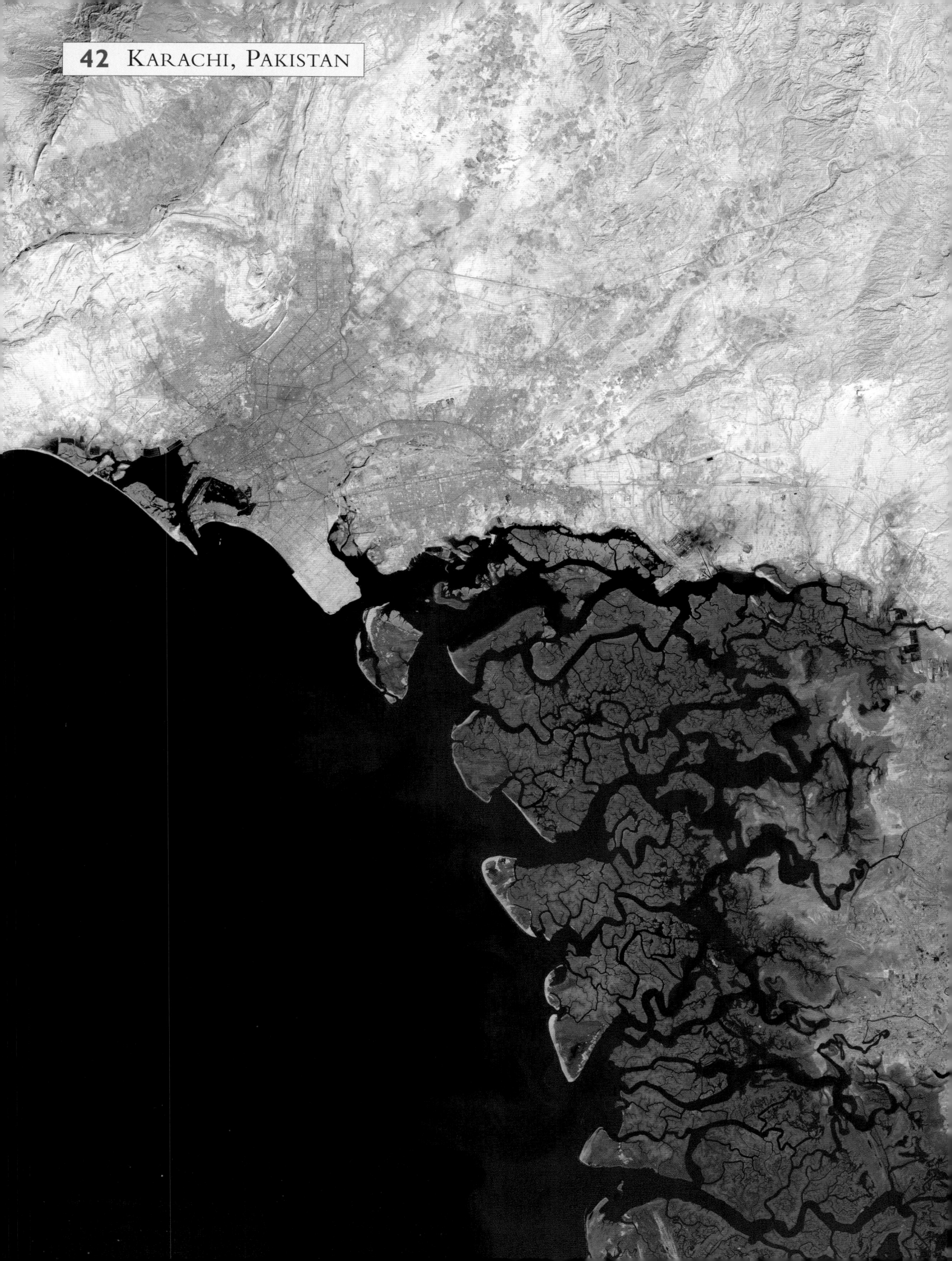

WORLD MAPS

SETTLEMENTS

■ PARIS   ◉ Rotterdam   ◉ Livorno   ◉ Brugge   ◎ Exeter   ◦ Torremolinos   ○ Oberammergau   ○ Thira

Settlement symbols and type styles vary according to the scale of each map and indicate the importance of towns on the map rather than specific population figures

● Vaduz   Capital cities have red infills   ∴   Ruins or archaeological sites

⬠   Urban agglomerations   ﹃   Wells in desert

ADMINISTRATION

———— International boundaries   ·········· Internal boundaries   PERU   Country names

- - - - · International boundaries (undefined or disputed)   ⬡ National parks   KENT   Administrative area names

International boundaries show the *de facto* situation where there are rival claims to territory

COMMUNICATIONS

———— Motorways, freeways and expressways   ———— Principal railways   LHR ⊕ Principal airports

———— Principal roads   - ＿ - Railways under construction   ⊕ Other airports

——— Other roads   ——— Other railways   ·········· Principal canals

+---← Road tunnels   +---← Railway tunnels   ⤬ Passes

PHYSICAL FEATURES

⌇ Perennial streams   ⬭ Intermittent lakes   ▲ 8850 Elevations in metres

- ⌇ - Intermittent streams   Swamps and marshes   ▼ 8500 Sea depths in metres

⬭ Perennial lakes   Permanent ice and glaciers   *1134* Height of lake surface above sea level in metres

⋰ Sand deserts

ELEVATION AND DEPTH TINTS

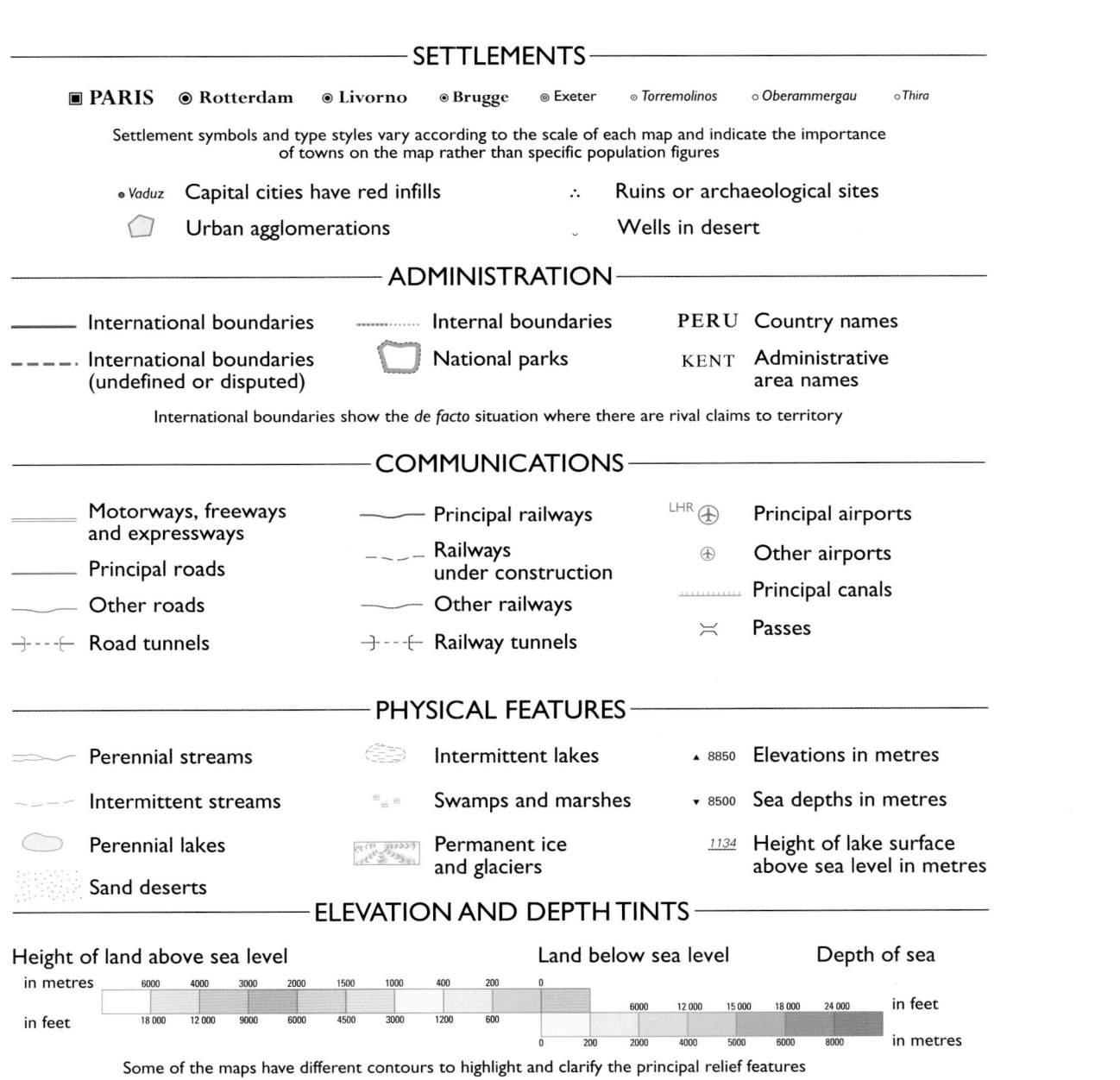

Height of land above sea level   Land below sea level   Depth of sea

| in metres | 6000 | 4000 | 3000 | 2000 | 1500 | 1000 | 400 | 200 | 0 | | | | | |
| in feet | 18 000 | 12 000 | 9000 | 6000 | 4500 | 3000 | 1200 | 600 | | | | | | |

| | 6000 | 12 000 | 15 000 | 18 000 | 24 000 | in feet |
| | 0 | 200 | 2000 | 4000 | 5000 | 6000 | 8000 | in metres |

Some of the maps have different contours to highlight and clarify the principal relief features

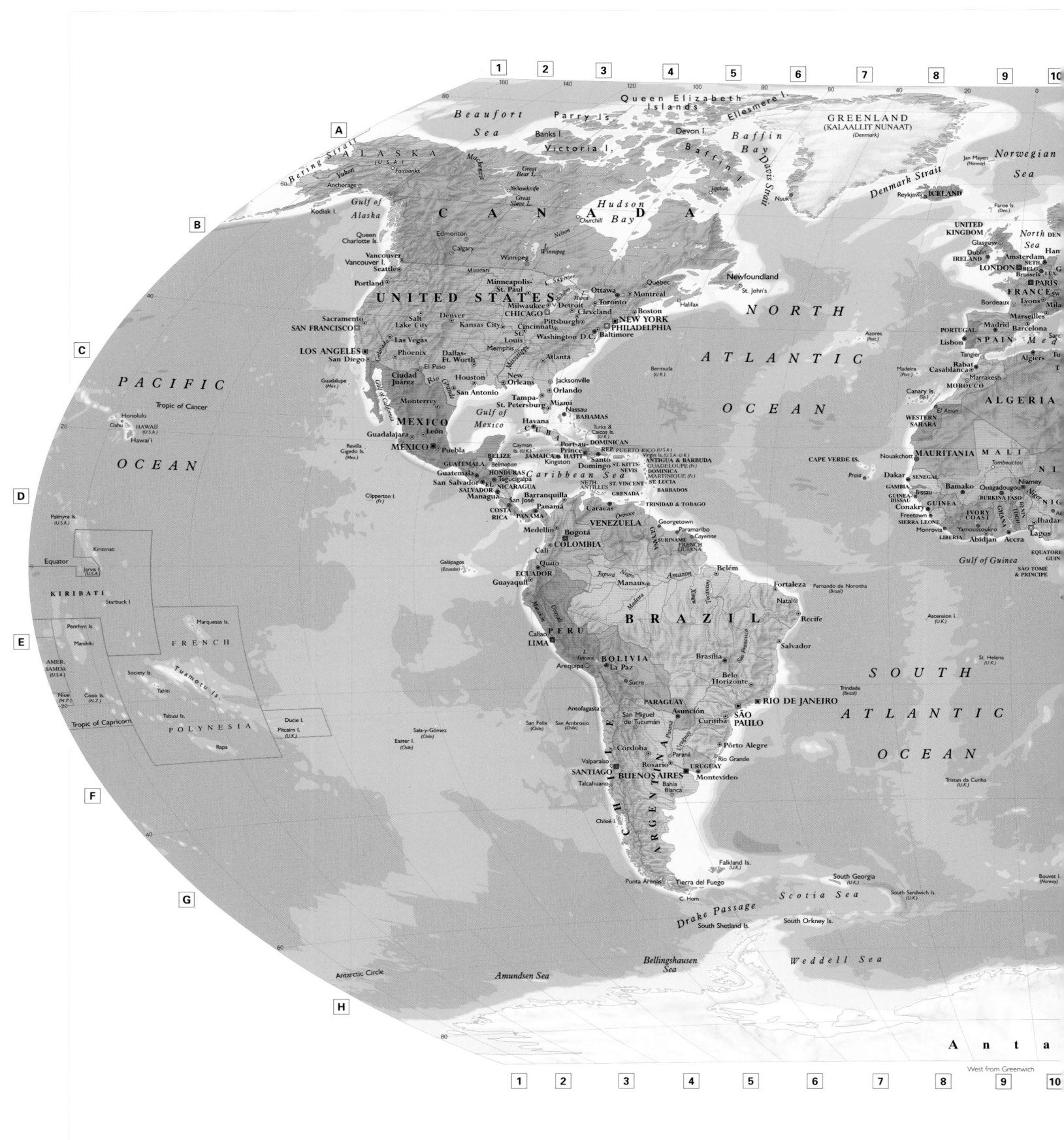

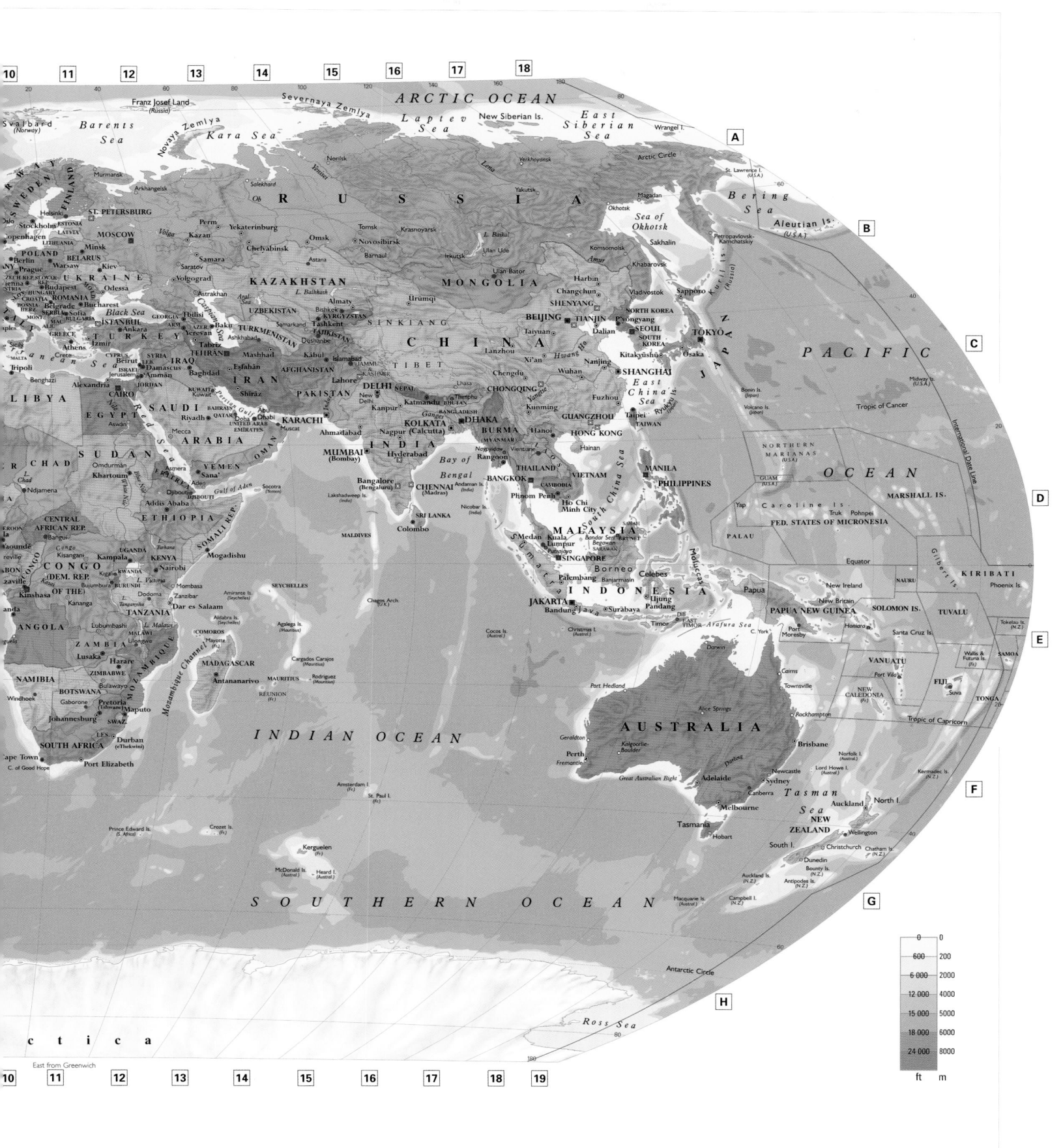

4 ARCTIC OCEAN

1:35 000 000

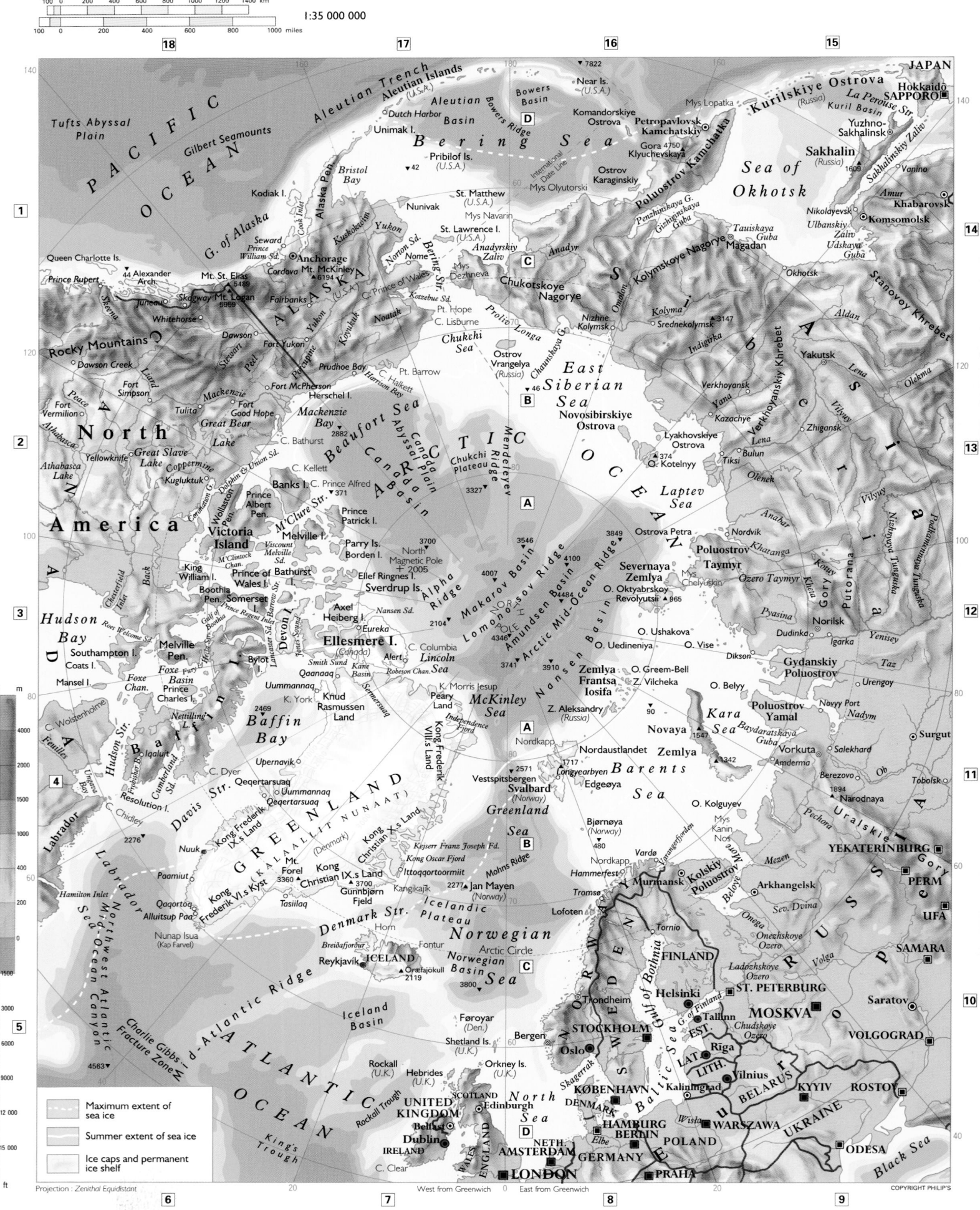

100 0 200 400 600 800 1000 1200 1400 km
100 0 200 400 600 800 1000 miles

Maximum extent of sea ice (dashed line)
Summer extent of sea ice
Ice caps and permanent ice shelf

Projection : Zenithal Equidistant

West from Greenwich   East from Greenwich

COPYRIGHT PHILIP'S

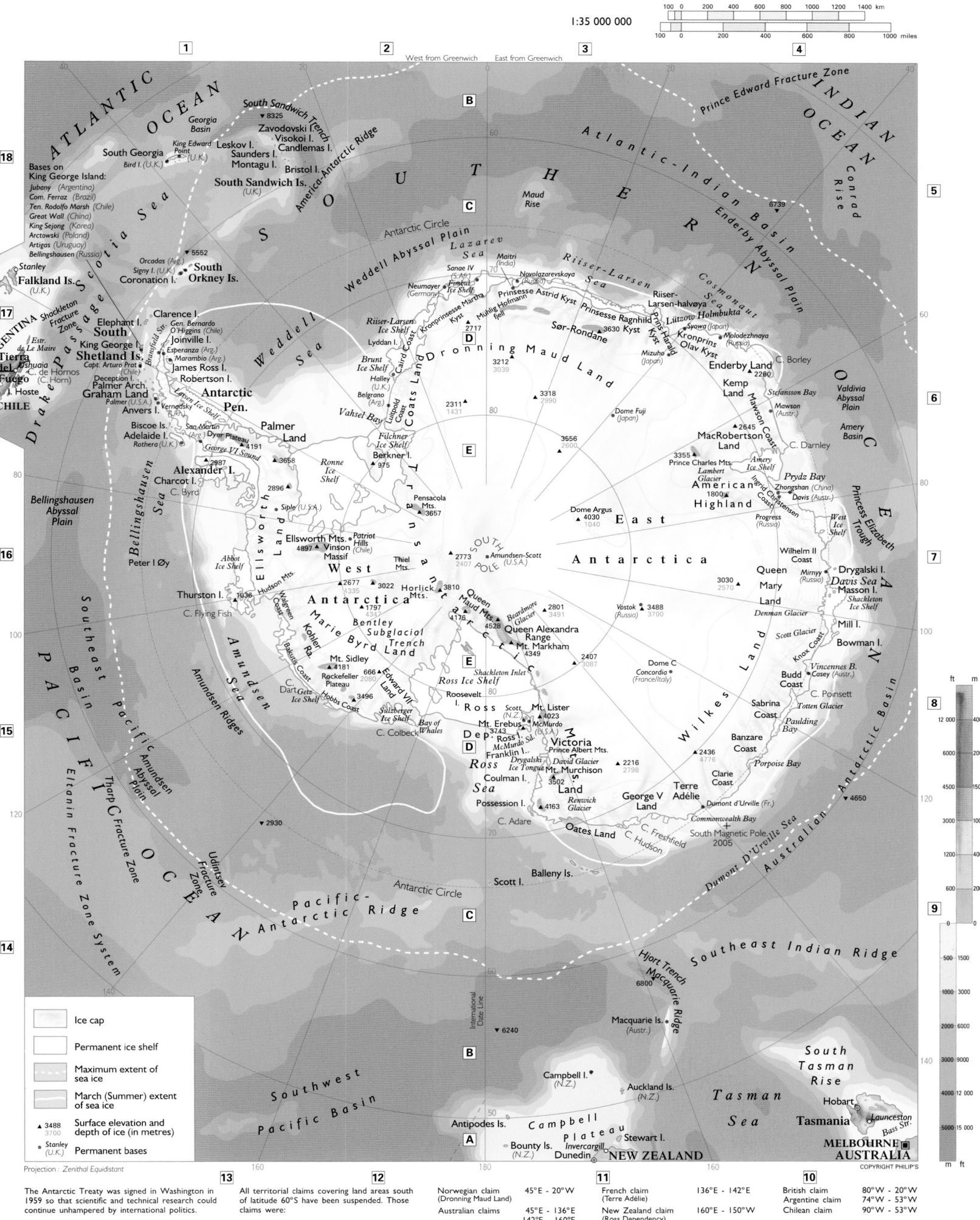

ANTARCTICA 5

1:35 000 000

100 0 200 400 600 800 1000 1200 1400 km
100 0 200 400 600 800 1000 miles

1 **2** West from Greenwich East from Greenwich **3** **4**

18

ATLANTIC OCEAN

Georgia Basin

South Sandwich Trench
▼8325
Zavodovski I.
Visokoi I.
Candlemas I.

South Georgia
King Edward Point (U.K.)
Bird I. (U.K.)

Leskov I.
Saunders I.
Montagu I.
Bristol I.

South Sandwich Is. (U.K.)

America-Antarctic Ridge

B

S O U T H E R N

Maud Rise

Atlantic-Indian Basin

Prince Edward Fracture Zone

INDIAN

OCEAN

Conrad Rise

5

Bases on King George Island:
Jubany (Argentina)
Com. Ferraz (Brazil)
Ten. Rodolfo Marsh (Chile)
Great Wall (China)
King Sejong (Korea)
Arctowski (Poland)
Artigas (Uruguay)
Bellingshausen (Russia)

C Antarctic Circle

Weddell Abyssal Plain

Lazarev Sea

Sanae IV (S.Afr.)
Maitri (India)
Neumayer (Germany)
Fimbul Ice Shelf
Novolazarevskaya (Russia)

Riiser-Larsen Sea

Enderby Abyssal Plain

Cosmonaut Sea

6739

18

Orcadas (Arg.)
▼5552
Signy I. (U.K.)

South Orkney Is.

Coronation I.

Prinsesse Martha Kyst
Kronprinsesse Martha Kyst
Prinsesse Astrid Kyst
Prinsesse Ragnhild Kyst

Riiser-Larsen-halvøya
Lützow Holmbukta
Syowa (Japan)
Molodezhnaya (Russia)

6

Stanley
Falkland Is. (U.K.)

Scotia Sea

Clarence I.
Gen. Bernardo O'Higgins (Chile)
Elephant I.

South Shetland Is.

Riiser-Larsen Ice Shelf
Lyddan I.

Coats Land
Caird Coast

Dronning Maud Land

2717

Muhlig Hofmann fjell
3212
3039

Sør-Rondane
3630
Kronprins Olav Kyst

Kronprins Harald Kyst
Kronprins Olav Kyst
Mizuho (Japan)

Enderby Land
C. Borley
2280

17

ARGENTINA
Shackleton Fracture Zone

King George I.
Capt. Arturo Prat (Chile)
James Ross I.
Robertson I.

Joinville I.
Esperanza (Arg.)
Marambio (Arg.)

Brunt Ice Shelf
Halley (U.K.)
Belgrano (Arg.)

3318
2990

Dome Fuji (Japan)

Kemp Land

Stefansson Bay

Valdivia Abyssal Plain

6

Estr. de Le Maire
Ushuaia
Tierra del Fuego
I. Hoste
C. de Hornos (C. Horn)

Deception I.
Palmer Arch.
Graham Land
Palmer (U.S.A.)
Anvers I.

Vahsel Bay

Filchner Ice Shelf

3656
2600

MacRobertson Land
2645

Mawson (Austr.)

Amery Basin

CHILE

Biscoe Is.
Adelaide I.
Rothera (U.K.)
San Martin (Arg.)
Dyer Plateau
4191

Vernadsky (U.K.)

Berkner I.
975

3355

Prince Charles Mts.
Lambert Glacier
1800

C. Darnley

Amery Ice Shelf

Prydz Bay
Zhongshan (China)
Davis (Austr.)

80

Drake Passage

Bellingshausen Abyssal Plain

George VI Sound
2987
Charcot I.
2896

Ronne Ice Shelf

3658

2311
1431

3810

American Highland

Progress (Russia)

Ingrid Christensen Coast

Princess Elizabeth Land

West Ice Shelf

80

16

Bellingshausen Sea

Peter I Øy

C. Byrd
Siple (U.S.A.)

Alexander I.

Pensacola Mts.
3657

SOUTH POLE
Amundsen-Scott (U.S.A.)
2773
2407

Dome Argus
4030
1040

East Antarctica

3030
2570

Queen Mary Land

Mirnyy (Russia)

Wilhelm II Coast

Davis Sea
Drygalski I.
Masson I.

Shackleton Ice Shelf

7

Thurston I.
1036
C. Flying Fish

Hudson Mts.

Ellsworth Mts.
4897
Vinson Massif

Patriot Hills (Chile)

Thiel Mts.

West Antarctica

Walgreen Coast

2677
4335

Horlick Mts.
3022

Queen Maud Mts.
4116

2801
3491

Vostok (Russia)
3488
3700

Mill I.

Bowman I.

7

15

Southeast Pacific Basin

Amundsen Abyssal Plain

Kohler Ra.
Bakutis Coast
Mt. Sidley
4181

Marie Byrd Land

Bentley Subglacial Trench

4347

Beardmore Glacier
4528

Queen Alexandra Range
Mt. Markham
4349

2407
3087

Dome C
Concordia (France/Italy)

Knox Coast

Budd Coast

Vincennes B.
Casey (Austr.)
C. Poinsett

Sabrina Coast

Totten Glacier
Paulding Bay

Wilkes Land

8

Amundsen Ridges

Dart C.
666
Rockefeller Plateau
2080
Getz Ice Shelf

Edward VII Land
3496

Shackleton Inlet

Ross Ice Shelf

Scott Glacier

Banzare Coast

8

Tharp Fracture Zone

Udintsev Fracture Zone

Hobbs Coast
Sulzberger Ice Shelf
C. Colbeck

Bay of Whales

Roosevelt I.

Ross Dep.

Scott (N.Z.)
Mt. Erebus
3743
McMurdo Sd.
Mt. Lister
4023
McMurdo (U.S.A.)

Victoria

Franklin I.
Drygalski Ice Tongue
David Glacier
Mt. Murchison
Coulman I.
3502

Prince Albert Mts.

2216
2798

Clarie Coast

Porpoise Bay

Australian-Antarctic Basin

4650

120

Eltanin Fracture Zone System

P A C I F I C   O C E A N

2930

Ross Sea

Possession I.

C. Adare

Renwick Glacier
4163

Land

2436
4776

George V Land

Terre Adélie

Dumont d'Urville (Fr.)
Commonwealth Bay
South Magnetic Pole
2005

Dumont D'Urville Sea

120

14

Antarctic Circle

Pacific-Antarctic Ridge

Oates Land

C. Hudson
C. Freshfield

Southeast Indian Ridge

Scott I.

Balleny Is.

Hjort Trench
Macquarie Ridge
6800

13 International Date Line

6240

Southwest Pacific Basin

Macquarie Is. (Austr.)

South Tasman Rise

B

Campbell I. (N.Z.)

Auckland Is. (N.Z.)

Tasman Sea

Hobart
Launceston
Bass Str.

Tasmania

A

Antipodes Is.
Bounty Is. (N.Z.)
Campbell Plateau
Stewart I.
Invercargill
Dunedin

NEW ZEALAND

MELBOURNE
AUSTRALIA

COPYRIGHT PHILIP'S

Projection: *Zenithal Equidistant*

Legend

| Ice cap |
| Permanent ice shelf |
| Maximum extent of sea ice |
| March (Summer) extent of sea ice |

▲ 3488 / 3700 Surface elevation and depth of ice (in metres)

● *Stanley (U.K.)* Permanent bases

ft / m
12 000 / 4000
6000 / 2000
4500 / 1500
3000 / 1000
1200 / 400
600 / 200
0 / 0
500 / 1500
1000 / 3000
2000 / 6000
3000 / 9000
4000 / 12 000
5000 / 15 000
m / ft

13 The Antarctic Treaty was signed in Washington in 1959 so that scientific and technical research could continue unhampered by international politics.

12 All territorial claims covering land areas south of latitude 60°S have been suspended. Those claims were:

11
Norwegian claim (Dronning Maud Land) 45°E - 20°W
Australian claims 45°E - 136°E, 142°E - 160°E
French claim (Terre Adélie) 136°E - 142°E
New Zealand claim (Ross Dependency) 160°E - 150°W

10
British claim 80°W - 20°W
Argentine claim 74°W - 53°W
Chilean claim 90°W - 53°W

1:20 000 000

100 0 100 200 300 400 500 600 700 800 km
100 0 100 200 300 400 500 miles

COPYRIGHT PHILIP'S

Seas, Oceans and Water Bodies

ATLANTIC OCEAN
Norwegian Sea
Barents Sea
White Sea
North Sea
Baltic Sea
Celtic Sea
Irish Sea
English Channel
Bay of Biscay
Mediterranean Sea
Ligurian Sea
Tyrrhenian Sea
Adriatic Sea
Ionian Sea
Aegean Sea
Sea of Crete
Black Sea
Sea of Azov
Caspian Sea
Caspian Depression
Sea of Marmara
Gulf of Bothnia
G. of Finland
G. of Riga
Gulf of Gdansk
Kattegat
Skagerrak
Str. of Otranto
Str. of Messina
Str. of Gibraltar
Str. of Bonifacio
Gulf of Lions
G. of Venice
G. of Taranto
Gulf of Antalya

Physical Features and Regions

West Siberian Lowlands
Ural Mountains
Kirgiziya Steppe
Obshchi Syrt
Timan Ridge
Northern Urals
Vychegda
Lapland
Scandinavia
Finland
Central Russian Uplands
Donets Basin
Ukraine
Caucasus
Transcaucasia
Pontine Mts.
Anatolia (Asia Minor)
Kurdistan
Armenia
Mesopotamia
Taurus
Volga Hts.
Valdai Hills
Kola Pen.
Kanin Pen.
North European Plain
Carpathians
Wallachia
Plain of Hungary
Transylvanian Alps
Sudeten
Moravian Hts.
Bohemian Forest
Erzgebirge
Black Forest
Vosges
Jura
Alps
Dinaric Alps
Balkans
Rhodope
Pindus
Peloponnese
Apennines
Gran Sasso
Sicily
Sardinia
Corsica
Elba
Malta
Massif Central
Pyrenees
Cantabrian Mts.
Old Castile
New Castile
Iberian Peninsula
Sierra Morena
Sierra Nevada
Andalusia
Plateau of the Shotts
Atlas
Africa
Mont Blanc
Monte Rosa
Matterhorn
Grossglockner
Harz
Jutland
Great Britain
Pennines
Grampian Mts.
Ben Nevis
Snowdon
British Isles
Ireland
Hebrides
Shetland Is.
Orkney Is.
Faeroes
Iceland
Rockall
Brittany
Channel Is.
Lundy
Vesterålen
Lofoten
North Cape
Gotland
Öland
Bornholm
Zealand
Funen
Åland
Balearic Is.
Majorca
Minorca
Ibiza
Cyprus
Rhodes
Crete
Cyclades
Dodecanese
Northern Sporades
Euboea
Lesbos
Khios
Samos
Calabria
Crimea

Rivers and Lakes

Ob
Pechora
Kama
Mezen
Volga
Kama Res.
Vychegda
N. Dvina
S. Dvina
Onega
L. Onega
L. Ladoga
Vyatka
Kolva
Belaya
Sura
Oka
Don
Desna
Dnieper
Dniester
W. Dvina
L. Ilmen
L. Peipus
L. Chudskoye
Vuoksa
Saimaa
Päijänne
L. Inari
L. Oulu
Torne
Ume
Klar
Glommen
Dal
Vänern
Vättern
Indals
Storsjön
Elbe
Oder
Vistula
W. Bug
Warta
Niemen
Rhine
Weser
Main
Danube
Inn
Drava
Sava
Drin
Morava
Tisza
Mures
Olt
Siret
Prut
Don
Donets
Volga
Ural
Kuban
Terek
Kura
Araks
Tigris
Euphrates
Asi
L. Urmia
L. Van
Rhône
Seine
Loire
Garonne
Ebro
Douro
Tagus
Guadiana
Guadalquivir
Po
L. Garda
L. Maggiore
L. Como
Tiber
Arno
Kremenchuk Res.
Tsimlyansk Res.
Kiev Res.
Rybinsk Res.
Kuybyshev Res.
Kakhovka Res.
Volgograd Res.
Kremenchuk Res.
Shannon
Trent
Thames
Severn
Mersey
L. Neagh
Dove
Tweed
Meuse
Moselle

Sea Areas (UK shipping forecast)

ROCKALL Sea areas named in weather forecasts

BAILEY
FAEROES
FAIR ISLE
VIKING
FORTIES
FORTH
CROMARTY
FISHER
GERMAN BIGHT
DOGGER
HUMBER
THAMES
DOVER
WIGHT
PORTLAND
PLYMOUTH
BISCAY
FINISTERRE
FITZROY
SOLE
LUNDY
FASTNET
SHANNON
ROCKALL
MALIN
HEBRIDES
BAILEY
SOUTH EAST ICELAND
NORTH UTSIRE
SOUTH UTSIRE
TYNE
LANDS END

Projection: Bonne

West from Greenwich   0   East from Greenwich

m
5000
4000
2000
1000
400
200
0
200
2000
4000
m

ft
15 000
12 000
6000
3000
1200
600
0
600
6000
12 000
ft

1:20 000 000

100 0 100 200 300 400 500 600 700 800 km
100 0 100 200 300 400 500 miles

COPYRIGHT PHILIP'S

ATLANTIC OCEAN

Norwegian Sea

North Sea

White Sea

Baltic Sea

Mediterranean Sea

Black Sea

Caspian Sea

Adriatic Sea

Tyrrhenian Sea

Ionian Sea

Aegean Sea

English Channel

Bay of Biscay

Gulf of Bothnia

ICELAND
Reykjavik

NORWAY
Oslo
Bergen
Stavanger
Trondheim
Narvik
Tromsø
Hammerfest

SWEDEN
Stockholm
Gothenburg
Uppsala
Örebro
Malmö

FINLAND
Helsinki
Turku
Tampere
Oulu
Vaasa

DENMARK
Copenhagen
Aalborg
Århus
Kiel

UNITED KINGDOM
LONDON
Birmingham
Manchester
Liverpool
Leeds
Sheffield
Glasgow
Edinburgh
Aberdeen
Dundee
Newcastle-upon-Tyne
Cardiff
Bristol
Plymouth
Southampton
SCOTLAND
ENGLAND
WALES

IRELAND
Dublin
Belfast
Cork

FRANCE
PARIS
Lyons
Marseilles
Toulouse
Bordeaux
Nantes
Lille
Rouen
Le Havre
Strasbourg
Dijon
St-Étienne
Nice
Grenoble
Toulon
Limoges
Brest

SPAIN
Madrid
Barcelona
Valencia
Seville
Málaga
Bilbao
Zaragoza
Córdoba
Granada
Murcia
Alicante
La Coruña
Valladolid
Vigo

PORTUGAL
Lisbon
Porto

GERMANY
Berlin
Hamburg
Munich
Cologne
Frankfurt am Main
Essen
Dortmund
Stuttgart
Düsseldorf
Bremen
Hannover
Leipzig
Dresden
Nürnberg
Bonn
Magdeburg
Halle
Chemnitz

NETHERLANDS
Amsterdam
The Hague
Rotterdam

BELGIUM
Brussels
Antwerp

LUX.
Luxembourg

SWITZERLAND
Bern
Zürich
Geneva
Basle

ITALY
Rome
Milan
Naples
Turin
Genoa
Florence
Bologna
Venice
Palermo
Catania
Messina
Trieste
Cagliari
Taranto
Bari

AUSTRIA
Vienna
Graz
Salzburg
Innsbruck
Linz

SLOVENIA
Ljubljana

CROATIA
Zagreb

BOSNIA-HERZ.
Sarajevo

SERBIA
Belgrade
Niš

MONTENEGRO
Podgorica

KOSOVO

MACEDONIA
Skopje

ALBANIA
Tirana

GREECE
Athens
Thessaloniki
Patra
Corfu

BULGARIA
Sofia
Plovdiv
Varna

ROMANIA
Bucharest
Cluj-Napoca
Timișoara
Brașov
Galați
Constanța
Ploiești

HUNGARY
Budapest
Debrecen
Miskolc

SLOVAK REP.
Bratislava

CZECH REP.
Prague
Ostrava

POLAND
Warsaw
Kraków
Łódź
Wrocław
Poznań
Gdańsk
Szczecin
Bydgoszcz
Katowice
Lublin
Białystok

BELARUS
Minsk

UKRAINE
Kiev
Kharkov
Dnepropetrovsk
Donetsk
Odessa
Lvov
Zaporozhye
Krivoy Rog
Nikolayev
Kherson
Mariupol
Zhytomyr
Chernigov

MOLDOVA
Kishinev

LITHUANIA
Vilnius
Kaunas

LATVIA
Riga

ESTONIA
Tallinn

R U S S I A
MOSCOW
ST. PETERSBURG
Nizhniy Novgorod
Kazan
Samara
Volgograd
Saratov
Rostov
Voronezh
Ufa
Perm
Ufa
Yaroslavl
Ivanovo
Tula
Kursk
Orel
Smolensk
Vologda
Kostroma
Kirov
Arkhangelsk
Murmansk
Tambov
Penza
Ulyanovsk
Rybinsk Res.
Kotlas
Vitebsk
Mahilyow
Gomel
Taganrog
Astrakhan
Krasnodar
Stavropol
Makhachkala

KARELIA
KOMI
UDMURTIA
TATARSTAN
BASHKORTOSTAN
MARI EL
CHUVASHIA
MORDOVIA
KALMYKIA
NORTH OSSETIA
CHECHENIA
INGUSHETIA
DAGESTAN
KARACHAI-CHERKESSIA
KABARDINO-BALKARIA
ADYGEA
CRIMEA

KAZAKHSTAN
Ural
Uralsk

GEORGIA
Tbilisi

ARMENIA
Yerevan

AZERBAIJAN
Baku

TURKEY
Ankara
Istanbul
İzmir
Adana
Bursa
Konya
Antalya
Kayseri
Samsun
Erzurum
Diyarbakır

SYRIA
Aleppo

IRAQ
Baghdad

IRAN
Tabriz

CYPRUS
Nicosia

CRETE
Rhodes

MOROCCO
Tangier
Ceuta
Melilla

ALGERIA
Algiers
Constantine
Annaba

TUNISIA
Tunis

MALTA
Valletta

Faroe Is. (Den.)
Shetland Is.
Orkney Is.
Hebrides
Channel Is.
Gotland
Corsica
Sardinia
Sicily
Balearic Is.
Majorca
Minorca
Ibiza

A f r i c a

Ob
Volga
Don
Dnieper
Dniester
Danube
Rhine
Elbe
Oder
Vistula
Loire
Seine
Garonne
Gironde
Rhône
Ebro
Tagus
Douro
Guadiana
Guadalquivir
Tigris
Euphrates
Ural
N. Dvina
W. Dvina
L. Onega
L. Ladoga
L. Chudskoye
Vänern
Vättern
Kattegat
Skagerrak
Str. of Gibraltar

Projection: Bonne
West from Greenwich East from Greenwich

■ LONDON Capital Cities

■ LONDON

1:6 000 000

50 0 25 50 75 100 125 150 175 km

50 0 25 50 75 100 125 miles

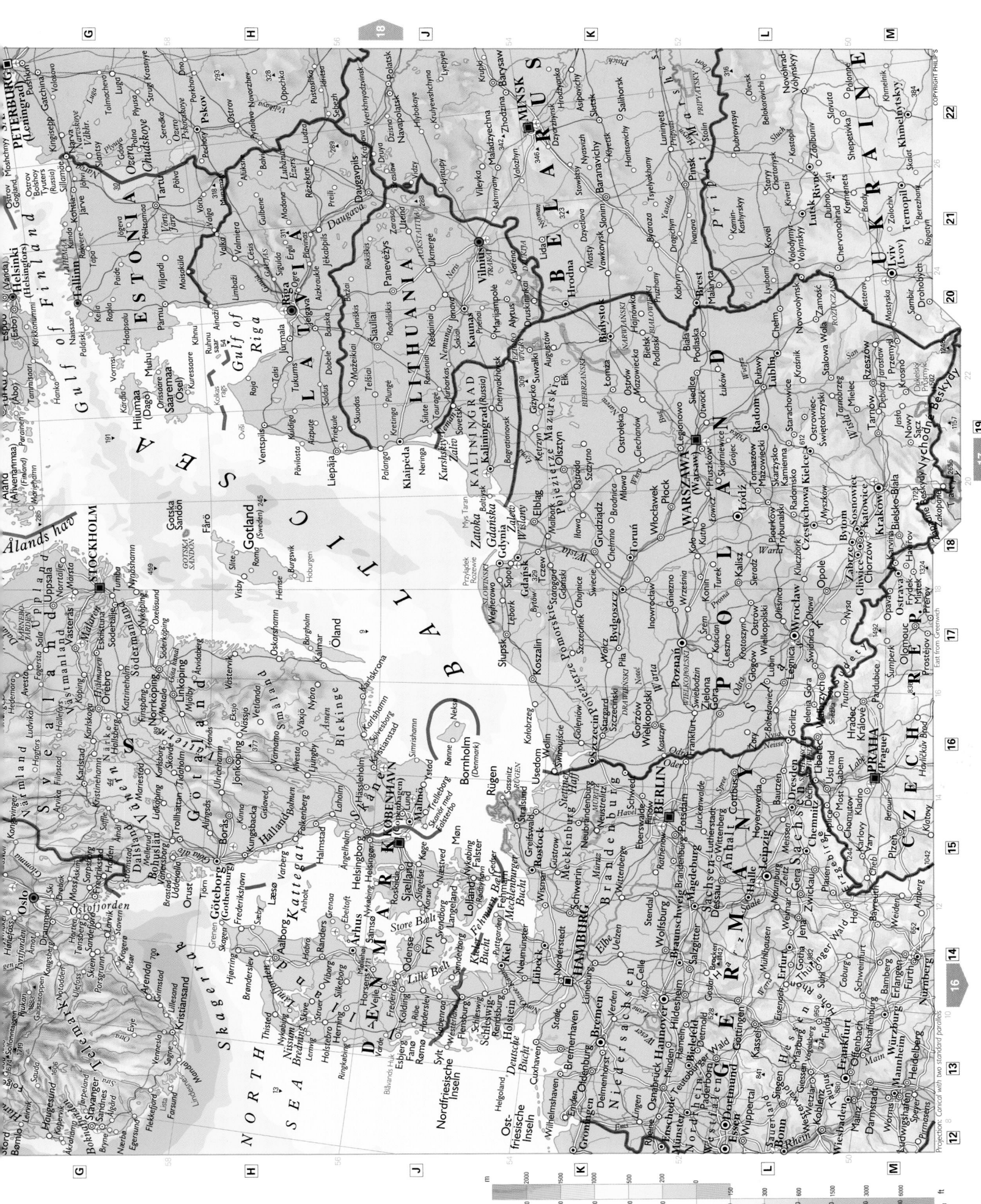

1:2 000 000

National Parks

Projection : Lambert's Conformal Conic

West from Greenwich

COPYRIGHT PHILIP'S

A T L A N T I C   O C E A N

N O R T H E R N   I R E L A N D

I R E L A N D

C E L T I C   S E A

I R I S H   S E A

St. George's Channel

North Channel

Firth of Clyde

SCOTLAND 11

1:2 000 000

Projection : Lambert's Conformal Conic

National Parks and Forest Parks in Scotland

Key to Scottish unitary authorities on map

1 CITY OF ABERDEEN	8 EAST RENFREWSHIRE
2 DUNDEE CITY	9 NORTH LANARKSHIRE
3 WEST DUNBARTONSHIRE	10 FALKIRK
4 EAST DUNBARTONSHIRE	11 CLACKMANNANSHIRE
5 CITY OF GLASGOW	12 WEST LOTHIAN
6 INVERCLYDE	13 CITY OF EDINBURGH
7 RENFREWSHIRE	14 MIDLOTHIAN

ORKNEY IS.
on same scale

SHETLAND IS.
on same scale

1:2 000 000

Key to English unitary authorities on map

25 HARTLEPOOL
26 DARLINGTON
27 STOCKTON-ON-TEES
28 MIDDLESBROUGH
29 REDCAR AND CLEVELAND
30 BLACKPOOL
31 BLACKBURN WITH DARWEN
32 HALTON
33 WARRINGTON
34 KINGSTON UPON HULL
35 NORTH EAST LINCOLNSHIRE
36 STOKE-ON-TRENT
37 TELFORD AND WREKIN
38 DERBY CITY
39 CITY OF NOTTINGHAM
40 LEICESTER CITY
41 RUTLAND
42 PETERBOROUGH
43 MILTON KEYNES
44 LUTON
45 NORTH SOMERSET
46 CITY OF BRISTOL
47 BATH AND NORTH EAST SOMERSET
48 SWINDON
49 READING
50 WOKINGHAM
51 WINDSOR AND MAIDENHEAD
52 SLOUGH
53 BRACKNELL FOREST
54 THURROCK
55 SOUTHEND-ON-SEA
56 MEDWAY
57 PLYMOUTH
58 TORBAY
59 POOLE
60 BOURNEMOUTH
61 SOUTHAMPTON
62 PORTSMOUTH
63 BRIGHTON AND HOVE

Key to Welsh unitary authorities on map

15 SWANSEA
16 NEATH PORT TALBOT
17 BRIDGEND
18 RHONDDA CYNON TAFF
19 MERTHYR TYDFIL
20 CAERPHILLY
21 BLAENAU GWENT
22 TORFAEN
23 CARDIFF
24 NEWPORT

N O R T H   S E A

I R I S H   S E A

North Channel

NORTHERN IRELAND

S C O T L A N D

Belfast

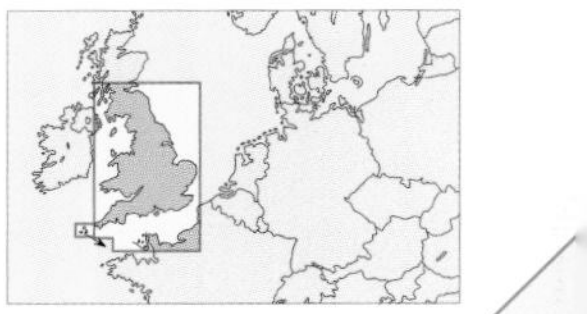

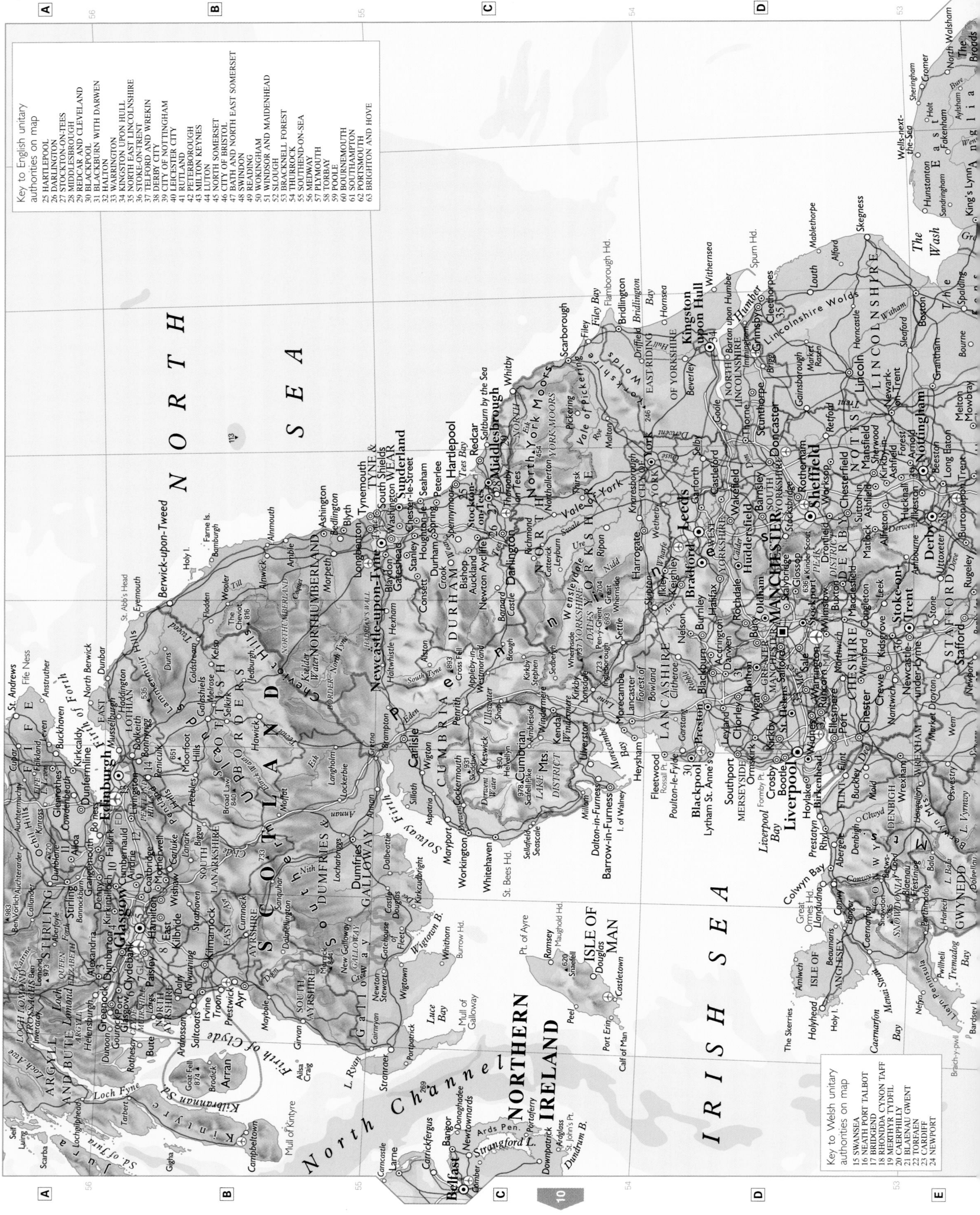

National Parks in England and Wales

Forest Parks in Scotland

East from Greenwich

West from Greenwich

Projection : Lambert's Conformal Conic

ISLES OF SCILLY
on same scale

CHANNEL ISLANDS
(U.K.)

1:5 000 000

50 0 25 50 75 100 125 150 175 km

50 0 25 50 75 100 125 miles

Projection: Conical with two standard parallels

East from Greenwich

COPYRIGHT PHILIP'S

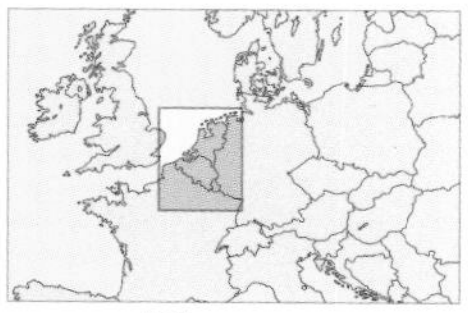

1:2 500 000

10 0 10 20 30 40 50 60 70 80 90 km
10 0 10 20 30 40 50 60 miles

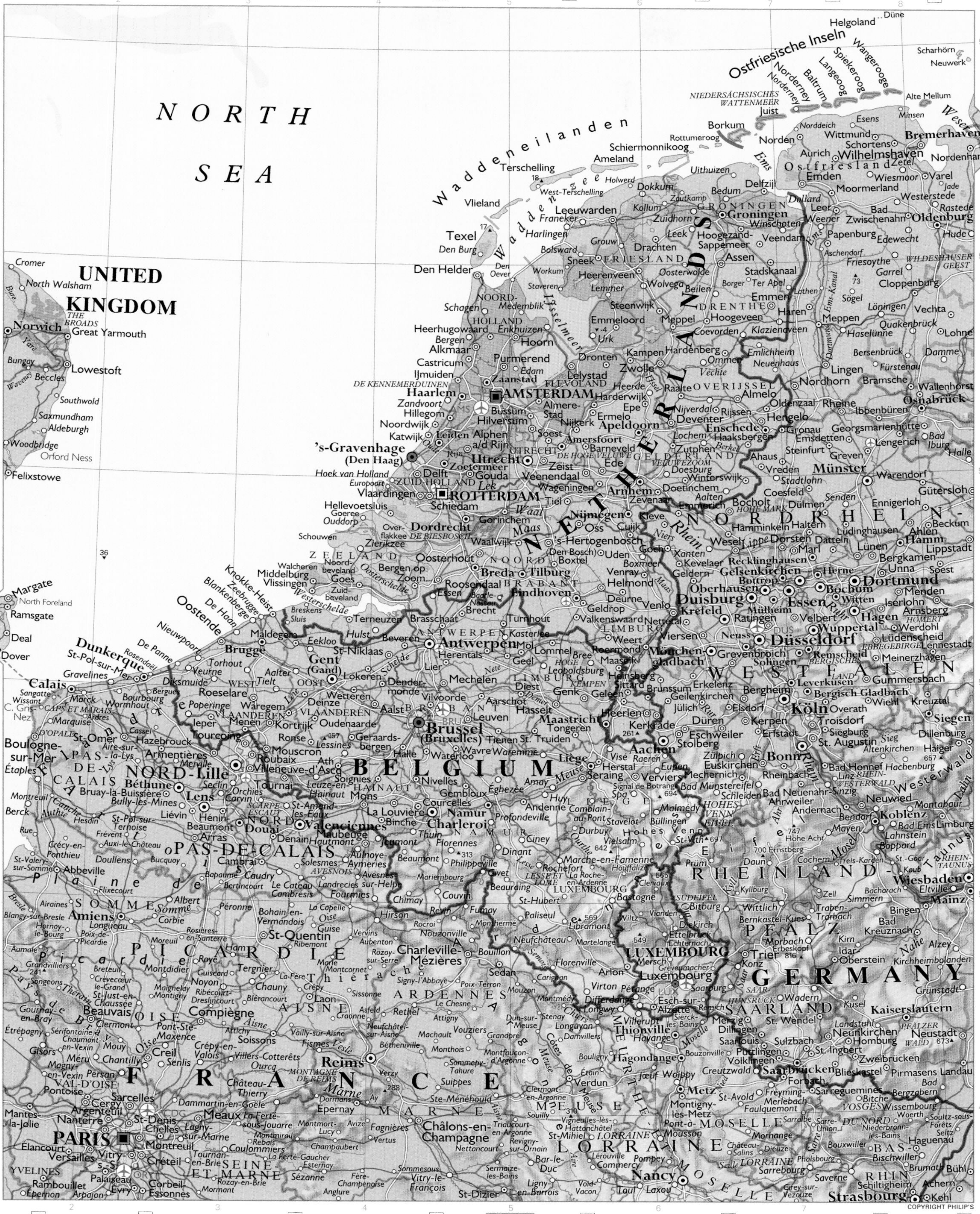

NORTH SEA

Waddeneilanden

NIEDERSÄCHSISCHES WATTENMEER

UNITED KINGDOM

THE BROADS

NETHERLANDS

GRONINGEN
FRIESLAND
DRENTHE
OVERIJSSEL
FLEVOLAND
NOORD-HOLLAND
ZUID-HOLLAND
ZEELAND
NOORD-BRABANT
LIMBURG

AMSTERDAM
's-Gravenhage (Den Haag)
ROTTERDAM
Utrecht
Haarlem

NORDRHEIN-WESTFALEN

Bremerhaven
Oldenburg
Münster
Dortmund
Düsseldorf
Köln
Bonn

BELGIUM

Brussel (Bruxelles)
Antwerpen
Gent (Gand)
Brugge
Liège
Namur
Charleroi

HAINAUT
VLAANDEREN
BRABANT

LUXEMBOURG

Luxembourg

GERMANY

RHEINLAND-PFALZ
SAARLAND
WESTFALEN

Wiesbaden
Mainz
Koblenz
Trier
Saarbrücken
Kaiserslautern

FRANCE

PARIS
Reims
Lille
Amiens
Nancy
Strasbourg

NORD
PAS-DE-CALAIS
PICARDIE
SOMME
AISNE
ARDENNES
LORRAINE
MOSELLE

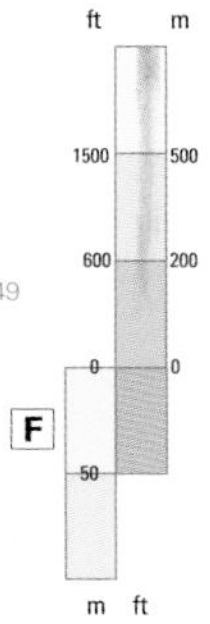

National Parks

Underlined towns give their name to the administrative area in which they stand.

COPYRIGHT PHILIP'S

1:5 000 000

50 0 25 50 75 100 125 150 175 km
50 0 25 50 75 100 125 miles

NORTH SEA

BALTIC SEA

DENMARK

UNITED KINGDOM

NETHERLANDS

BELGIUM

LUXEMBOURG

GERMANY

FRANCE

SWITZERLAND

ITALY

AUSTRIA

CZECH R

SLOVENIA

ADRIATIC SEA

Projection: Conical with two standard parallels

54

SŁOWIŃSKI
Zatoka   Baltiysk
Gdańska   Polessk (Russia)   Prienai   Vilnius
Wejherowo   Rumia   Gwardeysk   Gusev   Marijampolė   TRAKAI   LITHUANIA   Ashmyany   Smarhon   Maladzyechna   Barysaw   Krupki   Shklow   Mstsislaw
upsk   Lębork   Gdynia   Braniewo   Kaliningrad (Russia)   Bagrationovsk   Chernyakhovsk   Jeziono   Druskininkai   DZŪNIA   342   Zhodzina   Krychaw
Gdańsk   Sopot   Zalew   Kętrzyn   Giżycko   Suwałki   WIGRY   Lida   346   Valozhyn   MINSK   Cherven   Byrakaw   Mahilyow   B
329   Tczew   Elbląg   Wiślany   309   Valazhyn   Navahrudak   Dzyarzhynsk   S   Slawharad
Bytów   Starogard   Malbork   Olsztyn   Augustów   Hrodna   Nyoman   Navahrudak   Rahachow
omorskie   Gdański   Kwidzyn   Iława   Pojezierze Mazurski   323   Stowbtsy   Nyasvizh   Asipovichy   Babruysk   Zhlobin   Byarezina
Szczecinek   Chojnice   Świecie   Grudziądz   Brodnica   Działdowo   Szczytno   BIEBRZAŃSKI   Masty   Dzyatlava   Slutsk   Glusk   Aktsyabrski   Svyetlahorsk
Chełmno   Mława   NARWIAŃSKI   Vawkavysk   Slonim   Baranavichy   Klyetsk   Salihorsk   Pukh   Rechytsa
Bydgoszcz   Toruń   Rypin   Ciechanów   Ostrołęka   Ostrów   Łomża   Białystok   Pruzhany   Svislach   Lyakhavichy   Hantsavichy   Vasilevichy   Homyel   52
oznań   Inowrocław   Włocławek   Płock   Pułtusk   Mazowiecka   Hajnówka   BIAŁOWIESKI   Byaroza   Pinsk   Luninyets   Pripyats   Pyetrikaw   Kalinkavichy   Dobrush
Gniezno   Kutno   Legionowo   Mińsk   Siedlce   Bielsk   Sokołów   Pruzhany   Ivatsevichy   Tsyelyakhany   Loyew
Września   WARSZAWA   Mazowiecki   Podlaski   Biała   Drahichyn   Ivanava   M   a   r   s   h   Mazyr   Khoyniki
WIELKOPOLSKI   (Warsaw)   Pruszków   Otwock   Łuków   Podlaska   Brest   Kobryn   Yaselda   Pripyats (Pripet)   Davyd Haradok   316   Ovruch   Chornobyl
Śrem   Koło   Łowicz   Skierniewice   Międzyrzec   Malaryta   Zhabinka   Dragichyn   Stolin   PRIPYATSKY   Yelsk   (Chernobyl)   Oster
Kościan   Konin   Turek   Zyrardów   Grójec   Podlaski   Włodawa   Lyuboml   Kovel   Dubrovytsya   Olevsk   Ubort   Khoyniki
eszno   Kalisz   Łódź   Pilca   Radom   Puławy   Chełm   Kamin-   Staryy   Rozhyshche   Belokorovichi   Korosten   Kyyivs   C
Krotoszyn   Sieradz   Zduńska   Pabianice   Tomaszów   Lublin   Świdnik   Kashyrskyy   Chartoriysk   Kivertsi   Kostopil   Novohrad-   Radomyshl   Vdskh.   Dymer
Ostrów   Wieluń   Wola   Piotrków   Mazowiecki   Skarżysko-   Kraśnik   Novovolynsk   Volodymyr-   Lutsk   Rivne   Zdolbuniv   Volynskyy   Korostyshev   Irpin   KYYIV
Wielkopolski   Trybunalski   Kańskie   Kamienna   Starachowice   Volynskyy   Horokhiv   Dubno   Ostroh   Slavuta   Zhytomyr   (Kiev)   Vasylkiv
widnica   Olesnica   Wrocław   Kluczbork   Radomsko   Kielce   612   Ostrowiec-   Sandomierz   Zamość   Sokal   Chervonohrad   341   Berestechko   Kremenets   Shepetivka   Polonne   Pershotravensk   Fastiv
Dzierżoniów   Oława   Opole   Częstochowa   Świętokrzyski   Stalowa Wola   Rava-   Radekhiv   Brody   Kamyanka-   Berdychiv   Bila Tserkva   50
Kłodzko   Nysa   Tarnowskie   Myszków   Zawiercie   Pińczów   Tarnobrzeg   ROZTOCZAŃSKI   Ruska   Nesterov   Buzka   Kozyatyn   Skvyra   Tarashcha
1492   Racibórz   Góry   Bytom   Sosnowiec   Mielec   Yavoriv   Zolochiv   Zbarazh   Starokostyantyniv   Khmelnik   Tetiyev   Zhashkiv   E
umperk   Opava   Karviná   Gliwice   Chorzów   Katowice   Kraków   Tarnów   Rzeszów   Jarosław   Przemyśl   Mostyska   Lviv   U   K   R   A   I   N   Khmelnytskyy   Lipovets
Ostrava   Havířov   Zabrze   Tychy   Oświęcim   Bochnia   Dębica   Horodok   (Lvov)   384   Vinnytsya   D
ostějov   Frýdek-   Cieszyn   Bielsko-Biała   Żywiec   1725   Nowy   MAGURSKI   Jasło   Krosno   Sanok   Sambir   Drohobych   Khodoriv   Berezhany   Bar   270   Haysyn
škov   Místek   1324   Sącz   Targ   Zakopane   TATRAŃSKI   Bardejov   BIESZCZADZKI   Stryy   Rohatyn   Terebovlya   Horodok   Zhmerynka   327   Uman
Přerov   Żylina   Považská   GORCZAŃSKI   Nowy   2655   1157   1248   Boryslav   Skole   Kalush   Buchach   Skala-Podilska   Kamyanets-   Vapnyarka   Bershad
Zlín   Bystrica   Ružomberok   Poprad   Prešov   Humenné   Drohobych   Bolekhiv   Dnister   Chortkiv   Zalishchyky   Podilskyy   Mohyliv-   Bila Tserkva
Brno   Martin   Nizke   Tatry   2043   SLOVENSKÝ RAJ   Michalovce   Ivano-Frankivsk   Nadvirna   Horodenka   Khotyn   Podilskyy   48
donin   Bielé Karpaty   Trenčín   Banská Bystrica   1458   Košice   Uzhhorod   Volovets   Pechenizhyn   Kolomyya   Snyatyn   Novoselytsya   Lipcani   Okniţa   Balta
768   Prievidza   Zvolen   Slovenské Rudohorie   Chop   Mukacheve   Yaremcha   Storozhynets   Chernivtsi   Hlyboka   Drochia   Yampil   Ananyiv   19
Malé Karpaty   Nové   Levice   Lučenec   AGGTELEKI   1881   Berehove   Khust   Yasinya   Rakhiv   Rădăuţi   Dorohoi   Edineţ   Floreşti   Ribnita   Kotovsk   E
IEN   Bratislava   Zámky   Salgótarján   Ózd   Miskolc   Sátoraljaújhely   Chop   Vynohradiv   Tyachiv   Sighetu-   1565   Siret   Soroca   Dubăsari
enna   Nitra   BÜKK   Gyöngyös   Eger   Mezőkövesd   Nyíregyháza   Berehove   Marmatiei   Suceava   Botoşani   Făleşti   Orhei   STÎNGA
Bruck an   Komárno   Vác   Hatvan   Tisza   Carei   Baia Mare   Borşa   2303   Rădăuţi   Fălticeni   Ungheni   Dubăsari
der Leitha   Moson-   Esztergom   Dunakeszi   Jászberény   Pietrosul   Bistriţa   Vatra-Dornei   Paşcani   Chişinău   Vdkhr.
üsiedler   magyaróvár   Györ   Komárom   Karcag   Debrecen   HORTOBÁGYI   2102   Piatra   Roman   Iaşi   (Kishinev)   Tiraspol
Sopron   Tatabánya   BUDAPEST   Cegléd   Szolnok   Zalău   Dej   Reghin   1864   Bistriţa   Bacău   418   Huşi   Tighina   NISTRULUI
HUNGARY   Székesfehérvár   Érd   Kecskemét   Nagykőrös   Oradea   Cluj-Napoca   Turda   Târgu   Odorheiu   Miercurea-Ciuc   Bârlad   GĂGĂUZIA   Rozdilna   46
Ajka   Veszprém   709   Dunaújváros   Szolnok   KÖRÖS-MAROS   Salonta   1836   Mureş   1777   Secuiesc   Oneşti   Vaslui   Comrat   Dnister
BALATON   KISKUNSÁGI   Csongrád   Békéscsaba   Munţii Bihor   Secuiesc   Sfântu   Tecuci   Ciadâr-Lunga   Artsyz
laegerszeg   FELVIDÉKI   Balaton   Siófok   Kiskunfélegyháza   Szentes   Gyula   1380   Abrud   Aiud   Gheorghe   Bârlad   Cahul   Tatarbunary
Nagykanizsa   Kalocsa   Kiskőrös   Hódmezővásárhely   Makó   Arad   Deva   1848   Alba-Iulia   Sighişoara   1783   Focşani   Vulcaneşti   Bolhrad
Kaposvár   Szekszárd   Kiskunhalas   Szeged   Crişul Alb   Lugoj   Hunedoara   Sibiu   Mediaş   Sfântu   Ozero
rivnica   681   DUNA   Baja   Subotica   Senta   Mureş   Sânnicolau   Simeria   Gheorghe   Râmnicu Sărat   Galaţi   Reni   Sasyk
Pécs   DRÁVA   Mohács   Sombor   Kikinda   Mare   Timişoara   ROMANIA   Deva   Făgăraş   Braşov   Brăila   Vylkove
Bjelovar   Virovitica   Drava   984   Osijek   Novi Sad   Zrenjanin   Caransebeş   Vf. Peleaga   Carpaţii   Meridionali   Săcele   Buzău   Tulcea   Sulina
ATIA   Novska   Slavonski   Vojvodina   Petrovaradin   Vršac   Reşiţa   2509   Vulcan   Vf. Moldoveanu   Vf. Omul   Câmpina   DELTA   DUNĂREA
KOZARA   978   Brod   FRUŠKA   2518   Parângul Mare   Câmpulung   Vf. Moldoveanu   2543   Ploieşti   Babadag
anja Luka   Bosanska   GORA   Sremska   Pančevo   RETEZAT   Porta Orientalis   2507   Curtea de   Slobozia   Lacul
Gradiška   Sava   Mitrovica   Bela Crkva   1226   DOMOGLED-   Petroşani   Târgu-Jiu   Argeş   Ialomiţa   Razim
Doboj   Brčko   Zemun   VALEA CERNEI   Orşova   Portile   Drăgăşani   Piteşti   Târgoviste   F
Bijeljina   BEOGRAD   Smederevo   de Fier   Drobeta-   Slatina   Dâmboviţa   BUCUREŞTI   Feteşti   Năvodari
BOSNIA-   Tuzla   (Belgrade)   Požarevac   Turnu Severin   (Bucharest)   Călăraşi   Medgidia   DOBRIJ
1943   Travnik   Žepče   Sava   DERDAP   Craiova   Roşiori-   Olteniţa   Silistra   Constanţa
Zenica   Srebrenica   SERBIA   1366   Negotin   de-Vede   Alexandria   Giurgiu   Ruse   Mangalia   44
HERZEGOVINA   Han Pijesak   Valjevo   Kragujevac   Jagodina   Bor   Vidin   Băileşti   Caracal   Turnu   Zimnicea   Razgrad   Dobrich   G
13   2006   2112   Užice   Čačak   Zaječar   Corabia   Măgurele   Lom   Ruse   BULGARIA   Balchik
raglav   Cincar   Sarajevo   Višegrad   Kraljevo   Timok   Oryakhovo   COPYRIGHT PHILIP'S   Varna   Nos Kaliakra

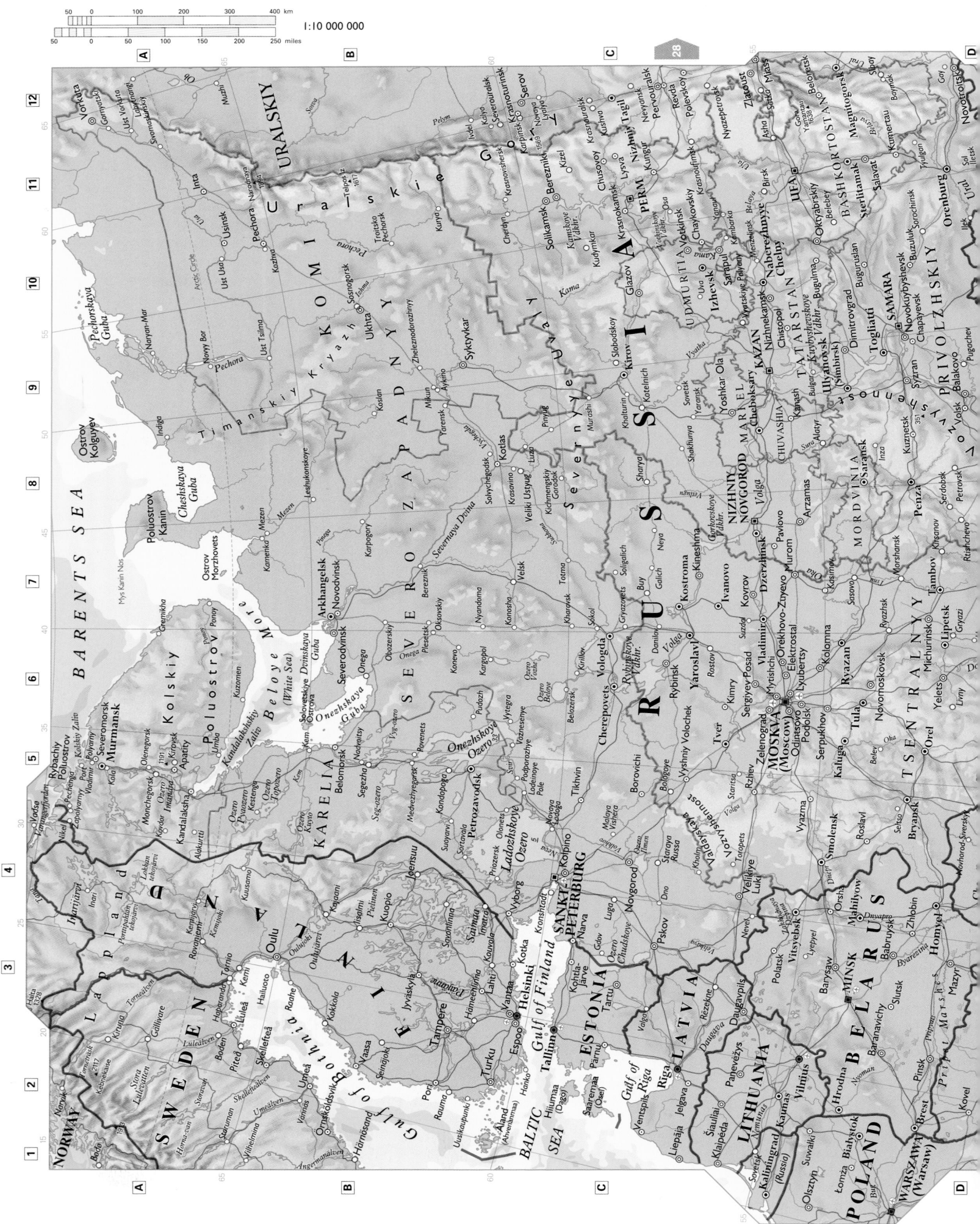

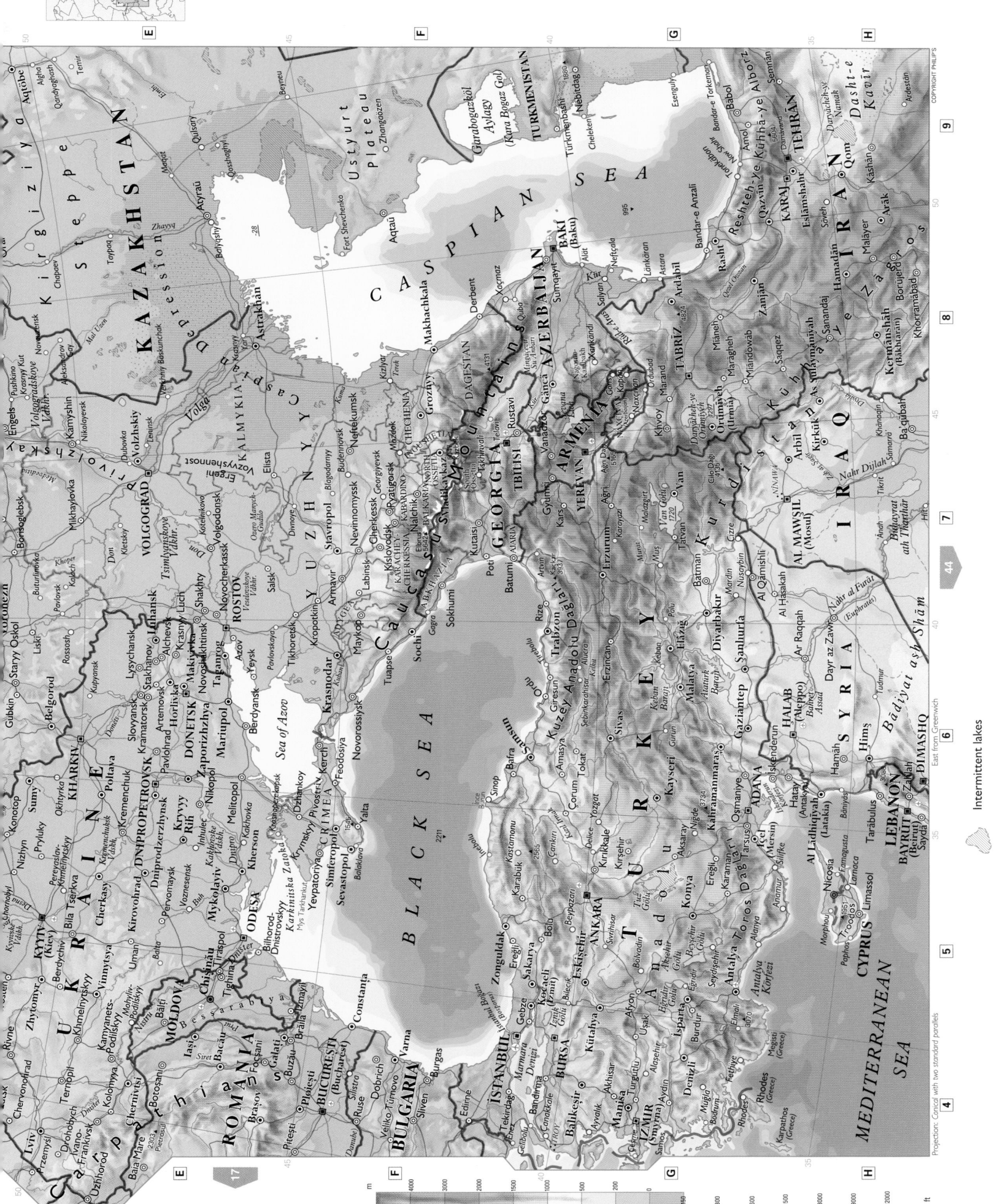

Intermittent lakes

COPYRIGHT PHILIP'S

Projection: Conical with two standard parallels

East from Greenwich

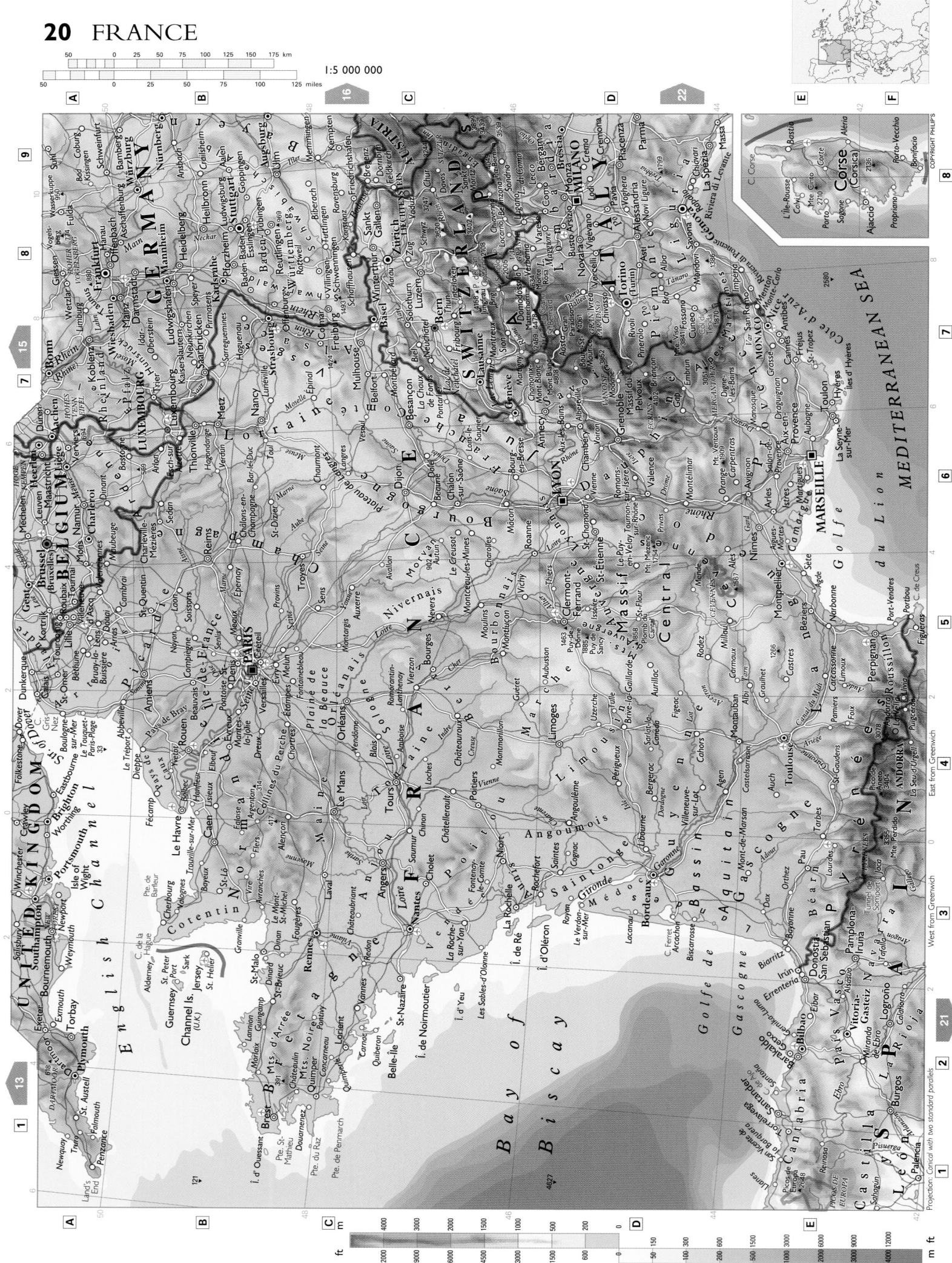

1:5 000 000

Projection: Conical with two standard parallels

1:5 000 000

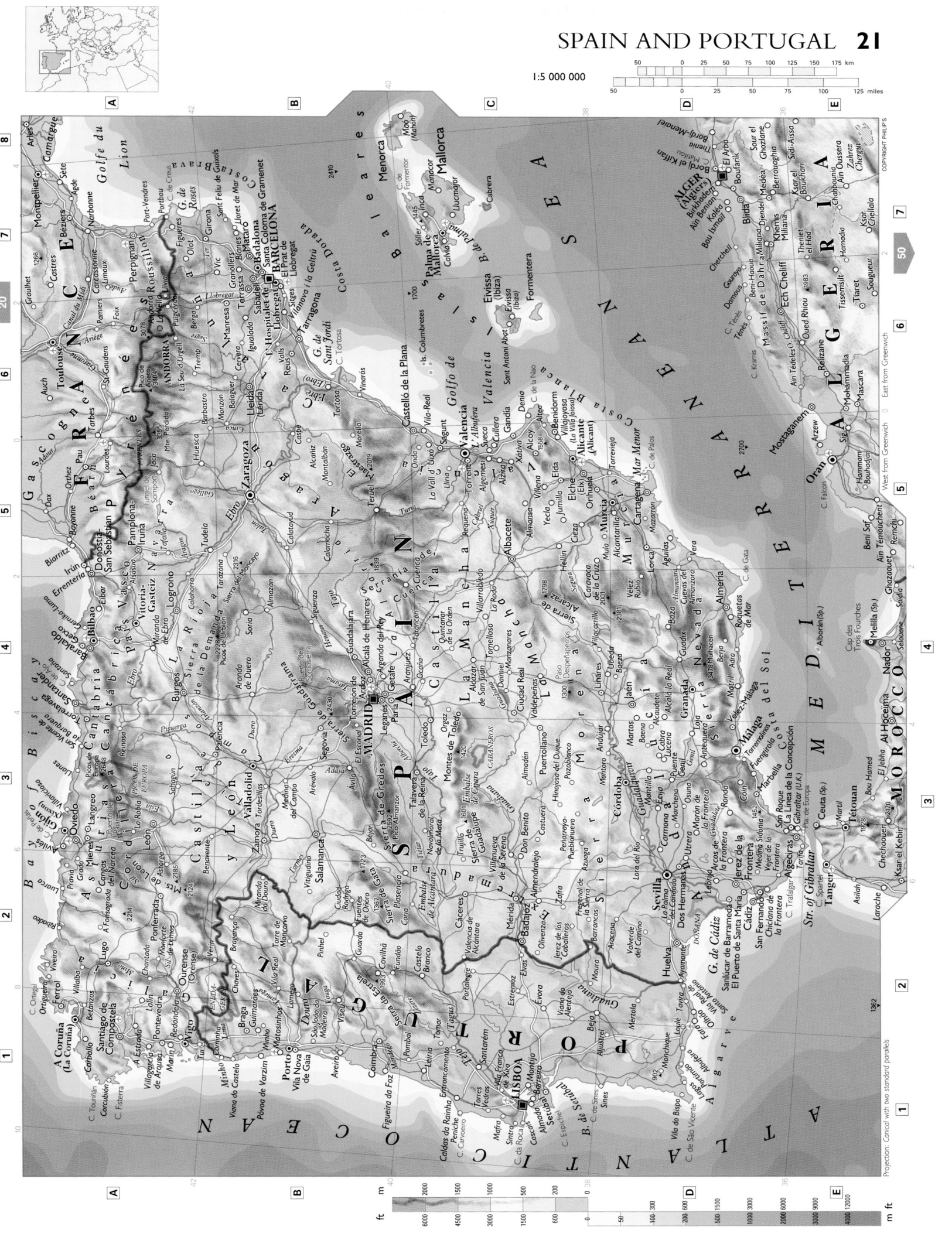

Projection: Conic with two standard parallels

Projection: Conical with two standard parallels

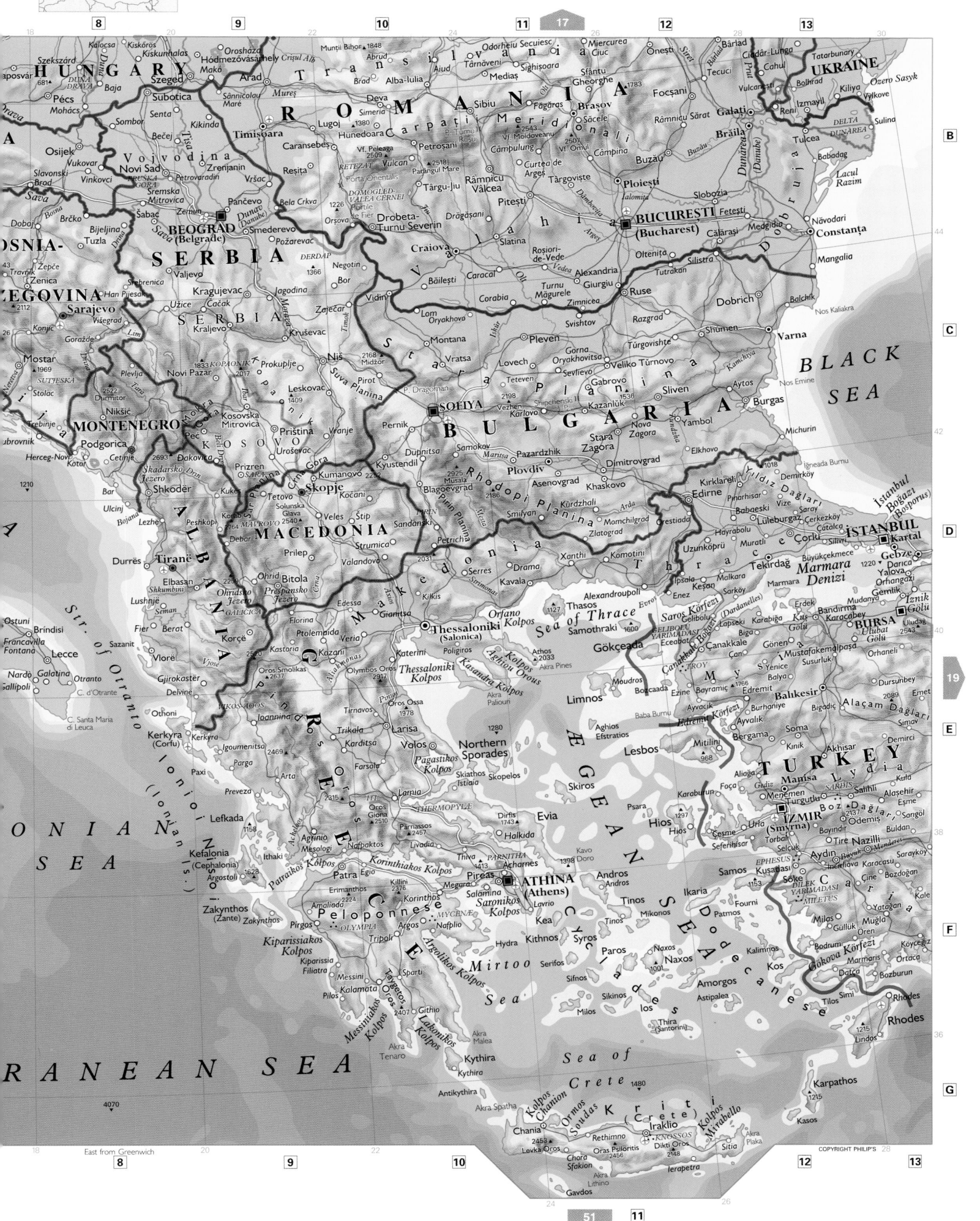

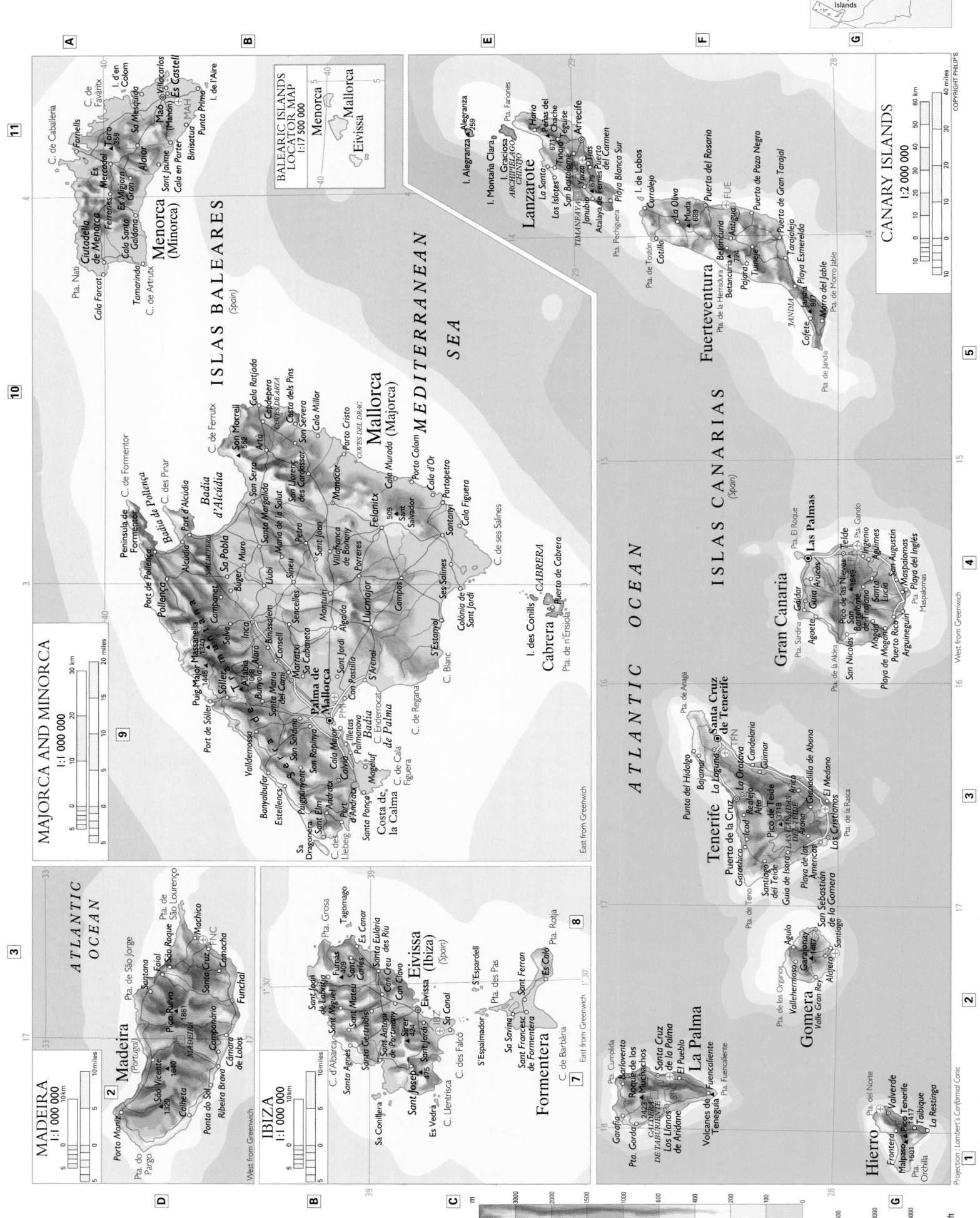

MENORCA (Minorca)

ISLAS BALEARES
(Spain)

MEDITERRANEAN SEA

Mallorca (Majorca)

BALEARIC ISLANDS
LOCATOR MAP
1:17 500 000

Menorca

Eivissa   Mallorca

MAJORCA AND MINORCA
1:1 000 000

CABRERA

Cabrera
Puerto de Cabrera

ATLANTIC OCEAN

ISLAS CANARIAS
(Spain)

CANARY ISLANDS
1:2 000 000

Lanzarote

Fuerteventura

Gran Canaria
Las Palmas

Tenerife
Santa Cruz de Tenerife

La Palma

Gomera

Hierro

MADEIRA
1:1 000 000

Madeira
(Portugal)

ATLANTIC OCEAN

Funchal

IBIZA
1:1 000 000

Eivissa (Ibiza)
(Spain)

Formentera

COPYRIGHT PHILIP'S

Projection: Lambert's Conformal Conic

1:47 000 000

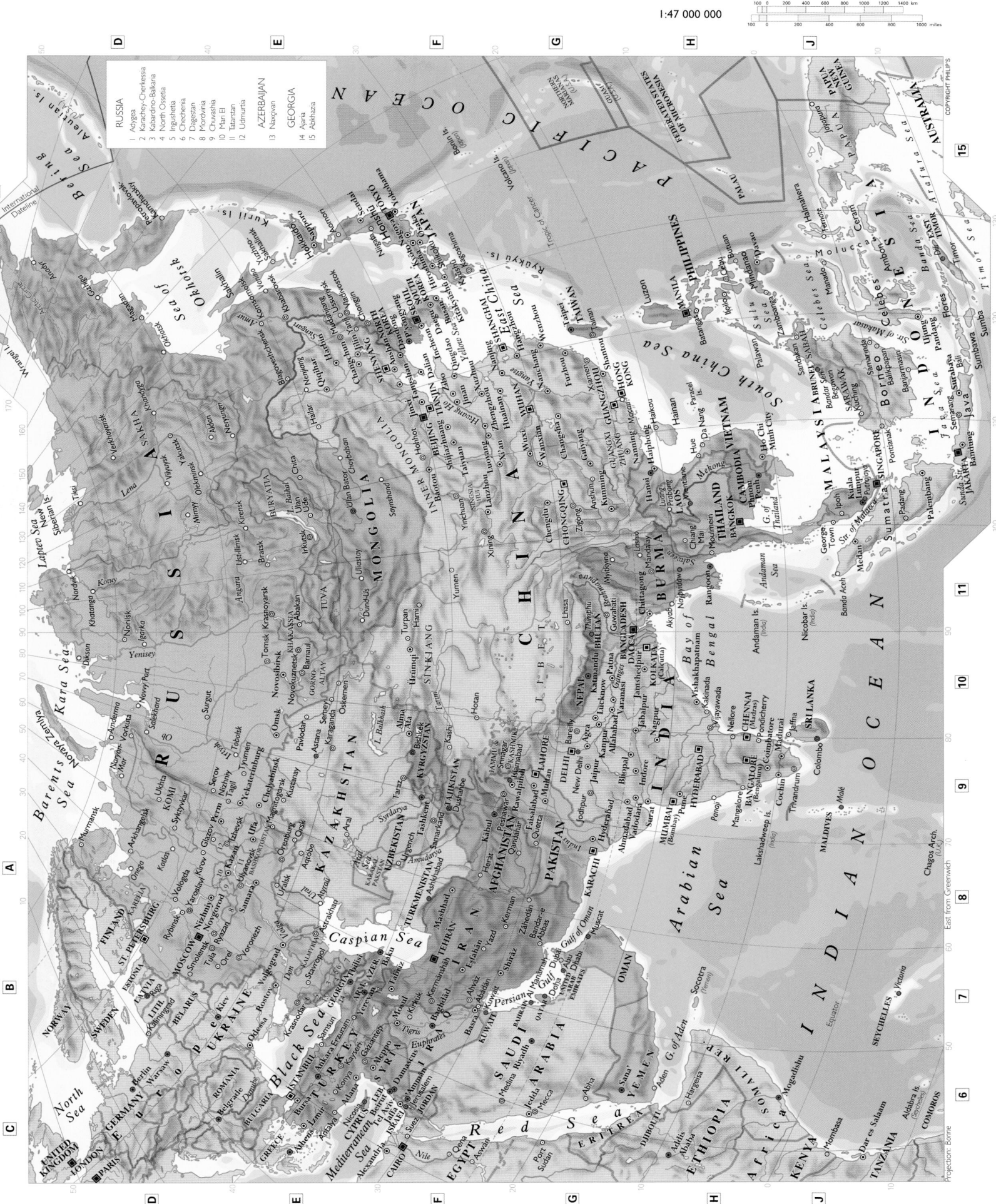

1:20 000 000

RUSSIA
1 Adygea
2 Karachey-Cherkessia
3 Kabardino-Balkaria
4 North Ossetia
5 Ingushetia
6 Chechenia
7 Dagestan
8 Mordvinia
9 Chuvashia
10 Mari El
11 Tatarstan
12 Udmurtia
13 Khakassia
AZERBAIJAN
14 Naxçivan
GEORGIA
15 Ajaria
16 Abkhazia
UKRAINE
17 Crimea

Projection: Conical Orthomorphic with two standard parallels

East from Greenwich

OCEAN

Severnaya Zemlya

Ostrov Shmidta
Mys Arkticheskiy
Ostrov Ushakova
Ostrov Pioner
Ostrov Komsomolets
781
965
Ostrov Oktyabrskoy Revolyutsii
Ostrov Bolshevik
Ostrov Pioner
Ostrov Sergeya Kirova
Proliv Vilkitskogo
Mys Chelyuskin
Ostrov Isachenko
Ostrov Petra

Poluostrov Taymyr
Byrranga Gory
1146
Oz. Taymyr
621
Nordvik

Laptev Sea

Novosibirskiye Ostrova
Ostrova Delonga
Ostrov Bennetta
Ostrov Genriyetty
Ostrov Zhannetty
Ostrov Zhokhova
Ostrov Faddeyevskiy
Ostrov Novaya Sibir
Ostrov Belkovskiy
Ostrov Kotelnyy
374
Ostrov Malyy Lyakhovskiy
Ostrov Bolshoy Lyakhovskiy
Ostrov Stolbovoy
Proliv Dmitriya Lapteva
Lyakhovskiye

East Siberian Sea

Ostrov Vrangelya
Mys Dezhneva (East C.)
Uelen
Bering Str.
Mys Shmidta
Proliv Longa
Ostrova Medvezhi

Chukchi Sea

St. Lawrence I. (U.S.A.)
International Date Line
Chaunskaya Guba
Pevek
Ostrov Ayon
1843
Mys Shelagskiy
Vankarem
Egvekinot
Ukolnoye
Anadyrskiy Zaliv
1194
Provideniya
Beringovskiy

Chukotskoye Nagorye
Bilibino
1853
Ust Chaun
Ambarchik
Chersky
Nizhne Kolymsk
Srednekolymsk
Markovo
Anadyr
Penzhino

Koryakskoye Nagorye
2453

Bering Sea

Poluostrov Kamchatka

Sredinnyy Khrebet

Khrebet Cherskogo
Verkhoyanskiy Khrebet
DALNEVOSTOCHNYY

Verkhoyansk
Batagay
2389
2295
Sangar
Sartang
2185
Deputatskiy
Druzhina
Khonuu
Zyryanka
Ust-Nera
3003
Pobeda
3147
Gora Chen
2682
Taskan
Omsukchan
Omolon
Oymyakon
Yogodnoye
Susuman
Palatka
Magadan
Ola

Yakutsk
Pokrovsk
Bestyakh
Namtsy
Nyurba
Verkhnevilyuysk
Vilyuysk
Sinsk
Olekminsk
Aldan
Tommot
Neryungri
Chulman
Nagornyy
Tynda

Khrebet Dzhugdzur
1906
2246

Ola
Okhotsk
Okhotskiy Perevoz
Ust-Maya
Nelkan
Ayan

Sea of Okhotsk

Udskaya Guba
Chumikan
Tuguri
Shantar

Sakhalin
Sakhalinskiy Zaliv
Nikolayevsk-na-Amur
Aleksandrovsk-Sakhalinskiy
Yuzhno-Sakhalinsk
Okha
Nogliki
Neftegorsk
Poronaysk
Dolinsk
Kholmsk
Korsakov

Kurilskiye Ostrova
Ostrov Paramushir
Ost-Kamchatsk
Petropavlovsk-Kamchatskiy
Yelizovo
Vilyuchinsk

Komsomolsk-na-Amur
Khabarovsk
Sikhote Alin
Sovetskaya Gavan
Vanino

HOKKAIDŌ
SAPPORO
Hakodate
Otaru

Honshū

RUSSIA

IRKUTSKIY

Yenisey
Achinsk
Krasnoyarsk
Kansk
Minusinsk
Abakan
Sayanogorsk
Bratsk
Ust-Ilimsk
Kirensk
Ust-Kut
Severobaykalsk
Magistralnyy
Taksimo
Chara
Ust-Nyukzha
Irkutsk
Angarsk
Ulan Ude
Chita
Nerchinsk
Shilka
Mogocha
Skovorodino
Zeya
Svobodnyy
Blagoveshchensk
Belogorsk
Birobidzhan

Ozero Baykal
Vostochnyy Sayan
2922
Zapadnyy Sayan
2028
Munku-Sardyk
3491
Hövsgöl Nuur

Amur

MONGOLIA
Ulaanbaatar
Hangayn Nuruu
3905
Hentiyn Nuruu
Choybalsan
Ondörhaan
Baruun-Urt

Altay (Aerhtai Shan)
4266
4885
Hami
Gaxun Nur
Gobi

CHINA
Dongbei (Manchuria)
QIQIHAR
DAQING
HARBIN
Jiamusi
Jixi
Mudanjiang
CHANGCHUN
JILIN
FUYU
FUSHUN
SHENYANG
ANSHAN
FUSHUN
CHIFENG
JINXI
BEIJING
TANGSHAN
DALIAN
BAOTOU
HOHHOT
Zhangjiakou
Chengde
Yingkou
Dandong

NORTH KOREA
PYONGYANG
Hamhŭng
Ch'ŏngjin
Wŏnsan
Namp'o

SOUTH KOREA
SEOUL
INCHEON
DAEJEON
DAEGU
BUSAN
GWANGJU
Vladivostok
Yanji

JAPAN
KYOTO
ŌSAKA
KOBE
Honshū
Sea of Japan (East Sea)

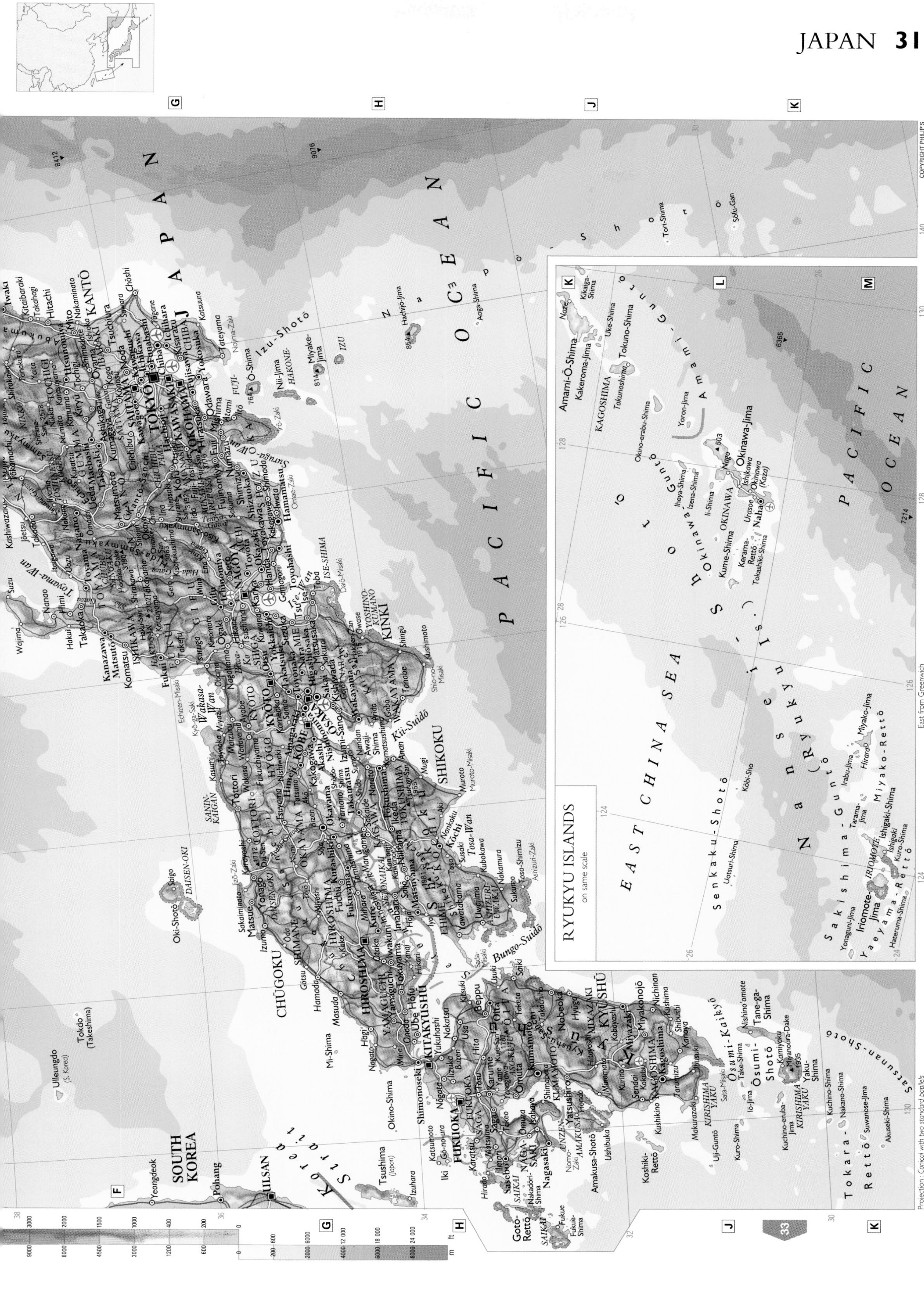

G H J K

8412
9016

8544
814 Miyake-Jima
HAKONE
FUJI
O-Shima
Nii-Jima
Izu
Izu-Shotō

KANTŌ
Chōshi
Katsuura
Nojima-Zaki
TOKYO
YOKOHAMA
CHIBA
KANAGAWA
SAITAMA
IBARAKI
Hitachi
Mito
Kitaibaraki
Iwaki

P A C I F I C   O C E A N

Aoga-Shima

J A P A N

NAGANO
NIIGATA
GUNMA
TOCHIGI
FUKUSHIMA
NAGOYA
GIFU
AICHI
SHIZUOKA
Hamamatsu
Omae-Zaki
Tō-Zaki

ISE-SHIMA
MIE
Tsu
Ise-Wan
Daiō-Misaki

KINKI
KUMANO
YOSHINO
WAKAYAMA
Shingū
Shio-no-Misaki
Kushimoto
Kii-Suidō

Kanazawa
Komatsu
Fukui
Matsue
KYOTO
OSAKA
KOBE
HYŌGO
SHIGA
NARA
Wakayama
Awaji-Shima

Toyama-Wan
Toyama
Takaoka
Nanao
Himi
Suzu
Wajima
ISHIKAWA
TOYAMA

Wakasa-Wan
Echizen-Misaki
Kyō-ga-Saki

Oki-Shotō
DAISEN-OKI
Saigo
Sakaiminato
Yonago
Tottori
Izumo
SHIMANE
Oda
Gotsu
Hamada
Masuda

SANIN-KAIGAN

CHŪGOKU
OKAYAMA
HIROSHIMA
YAMAGUCHI
Shimonoseki
KITAKYUSHU
FUKUOKA
Ube
Onoda
Mine
Hagi
Mi-Shima

SHIKOKU
TOKUSHIMA
KAGAWA
EHIME
KOCHI
Kōchi
Tosa-Wan
Muroto
Muroto-Misaki
Ashizuri-Zaki
Tosa-Shimizu
Sukumo
Nakamura
Kubokawa
Susaki
Uwajima

Bungo-Suidō
Sada-Misaki

KYUSHU
KUMAMOTO
MIYAZAKI
KAGOSHIMA
ŌITA
SAGA
NAGASAKI
Beppu
Nakatsu
Usa
Hita
Nobeoka
Hyūga
Miyakonojō
Nichinan
Kushima

UNZEN
AMAKUSA-SHOTŌ
Amakusa-Shoto
Ushibuka
Koshiki-Rettō

KIRISHIMA
YAKU
Ōsumi-Kaikyō
Ōsumi-Shotō
Tane-ga-Shima
Yaku-Shima
Nishino-omote

Tokara-Rettō
Nakano-Shima
Suwanose-Jima
Akuseki-Shima
Kuchino-Shima

Satsunan-Shotō

Goto-Rettō
SAIKAI
Nakadōri-Shima
Fukue-Shima
Fukue

SOUTH KOREA
Yeongdeok
Pohang
ULSAN
Ulleungdo (S. Korea)
Tokdo (Takeshima)

Tsushima (Japan)
Izuhara
Iki

Korea Strait

FUKUOKA
Nagasaki
Karatsu
Tosu
Kurume
Omuta
Yatsushiro
Minamata

RYUKYU ISLANDS
on same scale

K L M

E A S T   C H I N A   S E A

P A C I F I C   O C E A N

Amami-Ō-Shima
Naze
Kakeroma-Jima
Uke-Shima
Tokuno-Shima
KAGOSHIMA
Okino-erabu-Shima
Yoron-Jima
Iheya-Shima
Izena-Shima
Ii-Shima
OKINAWA
Okinawa-Jima (Koza)
Naha
Kume-Shima
Kerama-Rettō
Tokashiki-Shima

6365
7214
503
Nago
Ishikawa
Urasoe

N a n s e i - S h o t ō   (R y u k y u)

Kita-Daitō

Sakishima-Guntō
Miyako-Rettō
Miyako-Jima
Tarama-Jima
Irabu-Jima
Hirara
Ishigaki-Shima
Ishigaki
Kuro-Shima
Yaeyama-Rettō
Iriomote
IRIOMOTE
Uotsuri-Shima
Senkaku-Shotō
Yonaguni-Jima
Hateruma-Shima

Tori-Shima
Sōfu-Gan

COPYRIGHT PHILIP'S

East from Greenwich

Projection: Conical with two standard parallels

m ft
9000 3000
6000 2000
4500 1500
3000 1000
1200 400
600 200
0
200-600
2000 6000
4000 12 000
6000 18 000
9000 24 000

1:15 000 000

100 0 100 200 300 400 500 600 km
100 0 100 200 300 400 miles

Projection: Bonne

East from Greenwich

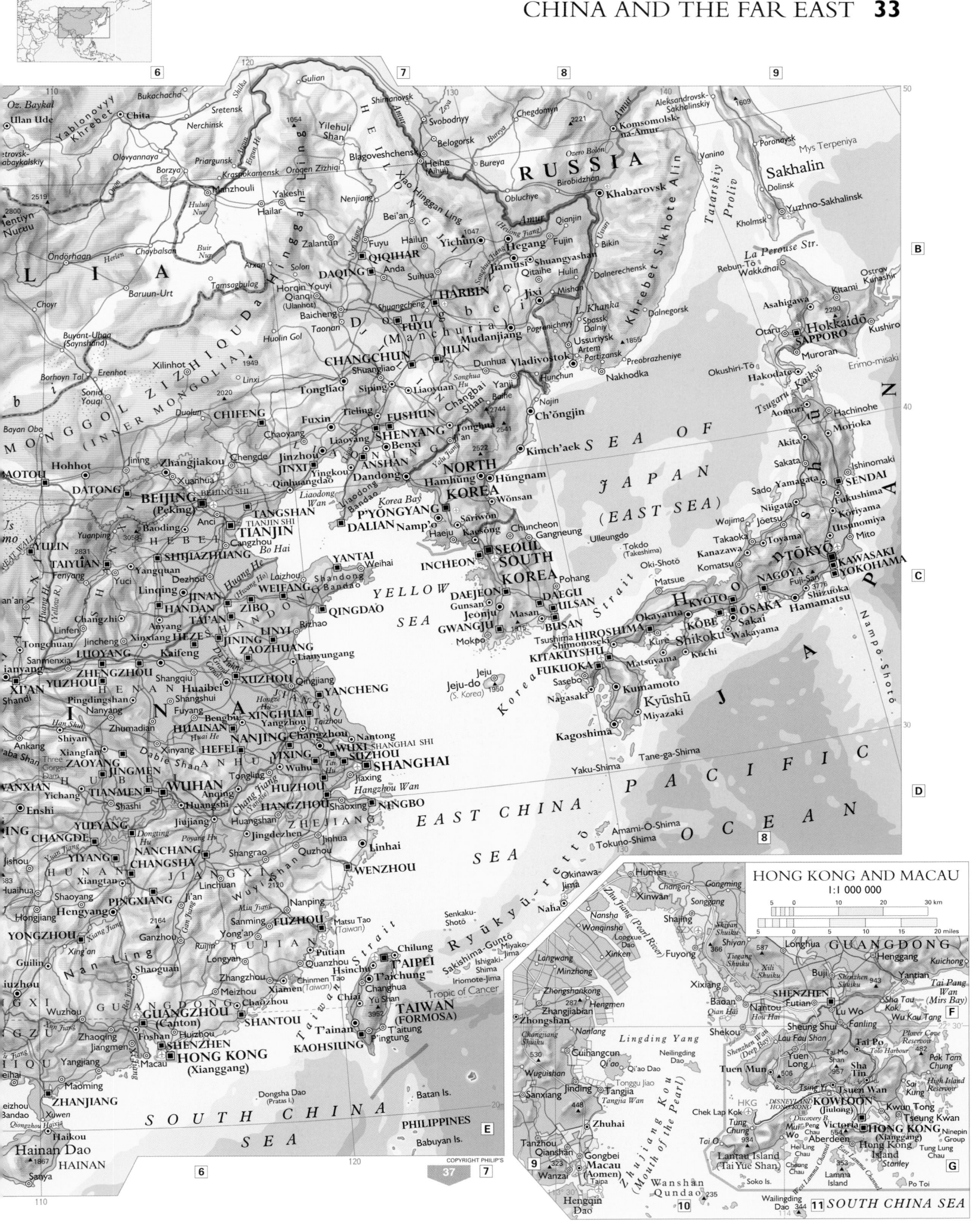

Map labels

RUSSIA

Oz. Baykal
Ulan Ude
Bukachacha
Gulian
Shimanovsk
Chegdomyn
2221
Komsomolsk-na-Amur
Aleksandrovsk-Sakhalinskiy
1609
Poronaysk
Mys Terpeniya

etrovsk-abaykalskiy
Chita
Sretensk
Nerchinsk
Shilka
1054
Yilehuli Shan
Svobodnyy
Belogorsk
Bureya
Amur
Vanino
Sakhalin
Dolinsk

Yablonovyy Khrebet
Olovyannaya
Priargunsk
Krasnokamensk
Orogen Zizhiqi
Blagoveshchensk
Heihe (Aihui)
Zeya
Birobidzhan
Obluchye
Khabarovsk
Kholmsk
Yuzhno-Sakhalinsk

2519
Manzhouli
Borzya
Hailar
Arxan
Solon
Qianjin
Amur (Heilong Jiang)
Amur
Kitami
Ostrov Kunashir

B

 Hentiyn Nuruu
2800
Ondörhaan
Herlen
Choybalsan
Hailar
Yakeshi
Nenjiang
Qiqihar
Daqing
Anda
Suihua
Jiamusi
Hegang
Qitaihe
Hulin
Dalnerechensk
Spassk-Dalniy
Vladivostok
La Perouse Str.
Rebun-To
Wakkanai
Asahigawa
2290
Hokkaidō
SAPPORO
Kushiro

LIA
Choyr
Baruun-Urt
Qinqi (Ulanhot)
Baicheng
Zalantun
Huolin Gol
Taonan
Shuangcheng
HARBIN
Mudanjiang
Jixi
Mishan
L. Khanka
Ussuriysk
Artem
Partizansk
Preobrazheniye
Muroran
Hakodate
Tsugaru-Kaikyō
Erimo-misaki

Buyant-Uhaa (Saynshand)
Xilinhot
1949
Changchun
Shuangliao
Fuyu
Jilin
Dunhua
Songhua Hu
Yanji
Ch'ongjin
Najin
Nakhodka
Okushiri-Tō
Aomori
Hachinohe
40

MONGGOL ZIZHIQU
Bayan Obo
Erenhot
Borhoyn Tal
Sonid Youqi
2020
Linxi
Duolun
Tongliao
Siping
Liaoyuan
Tonghua
Changbai Shan
2744
2541
Kimch'aek
SEA OF
Morioka
Akita
Sakata
Ishinomaki
SENDAI

Hohhot
Jining
Zhangjiakou
Xuanhua
Chengde
Chifeng
Fuxin
Tieling
Fushun
2522
Benxi
Shenyang
Liaoyang
T'an
NORTH KOREA
Hamhŭng
Hŭngnam
JAPAN (EAST SEA)
Sado
Yamagata
Fukushima
Niigata
Koriyama

BAOTOU
Datong
Yulin
Taiyuan
Yuanping
3058
Baoding
Beijing (Peking)
Beijing Shi
Tangshan
Anci
Tianjin Shi
Anshan
Yingkou
Qinhuangdao
Dandong
Liaodong Bandao
P'yongyang
Nampo
Wonsan
Haeju
Kaesong
Chuncheon
Gangneung
Ulleungdo
Tokdo (Takeshima)
Oki-Shotō
Matsue
Wajima
Jōetsu
Takaoka
Toyama
Kanazawa
Komatsu
TŌKYŌ
KAWASAKI
YOKOHAMA

C

Js mo
Yanquan
Yuci
Shijiazhuang
Cangzhou
Bo Hai
Yantai
Weihai
INCHEON
SEOUL
SOUTH KOREA
Pohang
NAGOYA
Fuji-San
3776
Shizuoka
Hamamatsu
KYŌTO
ŌSAKA
KŌBE
Sakai

an'an
Fenyang
Huang He (Yellow R.)
Shandong Bandao
Laizhou
Dezhou
Jinan
Weifang
Qingdao
YELLOW SEA
DAEJEON
Gunsan
Jeonju
DAEGU
ULSAN
Masan
BUSAN
Okayama
Kure
Wakayama
HIROSHIMA
Shikoku
Kōchi

Zibo
Handan
Linqing
Ta'an
Hanzhong
Anyang
Xinxiang
Heze
Jining
Linyi
Rizhao
GWANGJU
Mokpo
Tsushima
Shimonoseki
KITAKYUSHU
FUKUOKA
Matsuyama
Sasebo

LUOYANG
Kaifeng
Zhengzhou
Jincheng
Tongchuan
Sanmenxia
Changzhi
Linfen
HENAN
Lianyungang
Qingjiang
Jeju-do
Jeju
1950
(S. Korea)
Korea Strait
Nagasaki
Kumamoto
Kyūshū
Miyazaki

XI'AN
Shandi
YUZHOU
Pingdingshan
Nanyang
Shangqiu
Fuyang
Xuzhou
Yancheng
Kagoshima

ianyang
Xiangfan
Zhumadian
Bengbu
Xinghua
Yangzhou
Taizhou
Nantong
Tane-ga-Shima

aba Shan
Ankang
Shiyan
Dabie Shan
ANHUI
HUAINAN
Huaibei
Hefei
Yixing
WUXI
Shanghai Shi
Yaku-Shima
PACIFIC

JINGBE
ZAOYANG
JINGMEN
Tongling
Wuhu
SUZHOU
SHANGHAI
Jiaxing
D

ANXIAN
Yichang
Three Gorges Dam
TIANMEN
WUHAN
Huangshi
HANGZHOU
Shaoxing
NINGBO
Hangzhou Wan
EAST CHINA
OCEAN

ING
CHANGDE
YUEYANG
Dongting Hu
NANCHANG
Jiujiang
Huangshan
ZHEJIANG
Jingdezhen
Linhai
SEA
Amami-Ō-Shima
Tokuno-Shima

Jishou
YIYANG
CHANGSHA
Xiangtan
JIANGXI
Shangrao
Jinhua
Quzhou
WENZHOU
Okinawa-Jima
Naha

583
Huaihua
HUNAN
Shaoyang
PINGXIANG
Ji'an
Wuyi Shan
2120
Ryūkyū-rettō
Senkaku-Shotō
Ishigaki-Shima
Miyako-jima
Iriomote-Jima

Hongjiang
Hengyang
2164
Nanping
Matsu Tao (Taiwan)
Sakishima-Guntō

YONGZHOU
Guilin
Xing'an
Shaoguan
Ruijin
FUJIAN
Sanming
FUZHOU
Yong'an
Quanzhou
Putian
Chilung
Hsinchu
T'AIPEI
T'aichung
Changhua
Chiai
Tropic of Cancer

iuzhou
GXI
Wuzhou
GUANGDONG
Longyan
Zhangzhou
Xiamen (Taiwan)
Chinmen Tao
Yu Shan
3952
TAIWAN (FORMOSA)
T'ainan
T'aitung
P'ingtung

GZU
Zhaoqing
GUANGZHOU (Canton)
Foshan
SHANTOU
Chaozhou
Meizhou
Taiwan Strait
KAOHSIUNG

IIQU
Yangjiang
Maoming
SHENZHEN
HONG KONG (Xianggang)
Macau
Dongsha Dao (Pratas I.)
Batan Is.
PHILIPPINES
Babuyan Is.

ZHANJIANG
Bandao
Xuwen
Qiongzhou Haixia
Haikou
SOUTH CHINA
SEA
E

Hainan Dao
1867
HAINAN
Sanya

Inset map

HONG KONG AND MACAU
1:1 000 000

Humen
Changan
Gongming
Xinwan
Songgang
GUANGDONG

Zhu Jiang (Pearl River)
Shajing
Nansha
Wanqinsha
Longxue Dao
Xixiang
Baoan
Shenzhen
943
Longhua
Henggang
Kuichong

Nanfang
Minzhong
Zhongshankong
Nantou
Hou Hai
SHENZHEN
Futian
Lu Wo
Yantian
Tai Pang Wan (Mirs Bay)
F

Zhangjiaban
Zhongshan
Nanlang
Qian Hai
Shekou
Shenzhen Wan (Deep Bay)
Sheung Shui
Fanling
Sha Tau Kok
Wu Kau Tang

530
Cuihangcun
Qi'ao
Qi'ao Dao
Neilingding Dao
Lingding Yang
Lau Fau Shan
Tai Mo Shan
957
Sha Tin
Plover Cove Reservoir
482

Wuguishan
Changjiang Shuiku
448
Jinding
Tangjia Wan
Tanzhou
Tuen Mun
506
Tsing Yi
Tsuen Wan
High Island Reservoir

Sanxiang
323
Tonggu Jiao
Tangjia
Zhuhai
HKG
DISNEYLAND HONG KONG
554
KOWLOON (Jiulong)
Kwun Tong
Tseung Kwan

Macau (Aomen)
Taipa
Gongbei
Chek Lap Kok
Tai O
Tung Chung
934
Lantau Island (Tai Yue Shan)
Discovery B.
HONG KONG (Xianggang)
Victoria
Aberdeen
Hong Kong Island
Ninepin Group
G

Wanzai
Hengqin Dao
Wanshan Qundao
235
Soko Is.
353
Stanley
Cheung Chau
Lamma Island
Po Toi

Wailingding Dao
344
114
SOUTH CHINA SEA

1:6 000 000

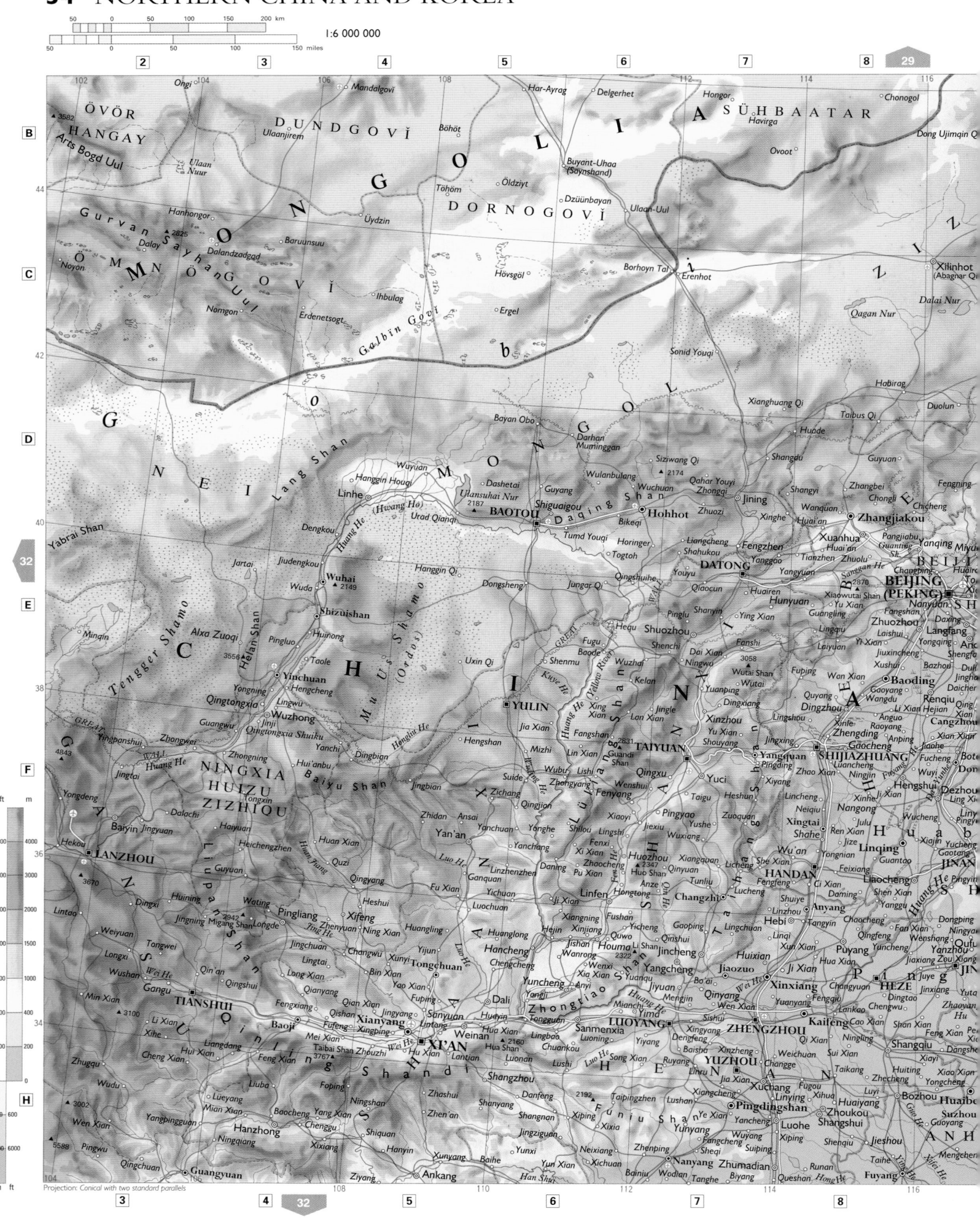

Sand deserts

B

C

30

D

E

JAPAN

(EAST SEA)

F

G

H

31

HORQIN Youyi Qianqi
(Ulanhot)

HARBIN

HEILONGJIANG

RUSSIA

Vladivostok

CHANGCHUN

JILIN

Manchuria

Changbai Shan

Paektu-san 2744

NORTH
KOREA

P'YŎNGYANG

SEA OF

Korea
Bay

DALIAN
(Lüda)

Bo Hai

SEOUL
SEONGNAM
INCHEON
SUWON

SOUTH
KOREA

DAEJEON

GWANGJU

BUSAN

YELLOW SEA

(Huang Hai)

Korea Strait

Tsushima
(Japan)

JAPAN

Jeju-do (S. Korea)

1:12 500 000

JAVA AND MADURA
1:7 500 000

```
50   0   50   100   150   200   250   300 km
50   0        50        100       150       200 miles
```

BALI
1:2 000 000

```
10   0   10        20        30 km
10   0        10        20 miles
```

Major labels (Luzon / Philippines):
Claveria, Bacarra, Laoag, C. Engaño, Bangued, Vigan, Tuao, Aparri, Tuguegarao, San Fernando, Bontoc, Baguio, Bolinao, Dagupan, Lingayen G., Angeles, San Fernando, Cabanatuan, Tarlac, San Jose, Baler, Mt. Pinatubo, Olongapo, Malolos, Quezon City, **MANILA**, Santa Cruz, Cavite, Batangas, Lipa, Lucena, Calapan, Mindoro, Calamian Group, Puerto Princesa

Visayan / Central Philippines:
Masbate, Samar, Catbalogan, Tacloban, Leyte, Cebu, Mandaue, Bacolod, Iloilo, Roxas, Panay, Negros, Dumaguete, Bohol, Butuan, Cagayan de Oro, Surigao, Siargao

Mindanao:
Dipolog, Ozamiz, Iligan, Malaybalay, Pagadian, Zamboanga, Cotabato, **DAVAO**, Digos, General Santos, Mati, Tinaca Pt., Sarangani B.

Sulawesi / Celebes:
Manado, Kotamobagu, Gorontalo, Palu, Toli-Toli, Luwuk, Poso, Kendari, Parepare, Makale, Palopo, Watampone, Mamuju, Sulawesi (Celebes)

Maluku / Halmahera:
Morotai, Tobelo, Ternate, Tidore, Halmahera, Ceram, Seram, Ambon, Buru, Namlea, Maluku, Banda Sea

Java and Madura:
Merak, Tangerang, **JAKARTA**, Bekasi, Bogor, Bandung, Cirebon, Tegal, Pekalongan, Semarang, Kudus, Pati, Rembang, Tuban, Bojonegoro, Gresik, Surabaya, Madura, Bangkalan, Pamekasan, Sumenep, Sukabumi, Tasikmalaya, Purwokerto, Cilacap, Yogyakarta, Surakarta, Madiun, Kediri, Malang, Probolinggo, Situbondo, Banyuwangi, Jember, Bali

Bali inset:
Singaraja, Banyuwangi, Negara, Denpasar, Tabanan, Klungkung, Bangli, Kuta, Nusa Penida, Lombok, Mataram, Ampenan, Bali, Jawa

Papua / Irian Jaya:
Manokwari, Sorong, Jazirah Doberai, Biak, Irian Jaya, Fakfak, Kaimana, Nabire, Pegunungan Maoke, Puncak Jaya, Wamena, Jayapura, Jayawijaya, Merauke, Papua New Guinea

Nusa Tenggara / lesser Sundas:
Flores, Ende, Maumere, Sumba, Waingapu, Kupang, Dili, EAST TIMOR, Alor, Wetar, Kepulauan Tanimbar, Kepulauan Kai, Kepulauan Aru, Dobo

Seas:
CELEBES SEA, SULU SEA, BANDA SEA, PACIFIC OCEAN, INDIAN OCEAN, ARAFURA SEA, BALI SEA, MOLUCCA SEA, CERAM SEA, FLORES SEA, SAWU SEA

1:10 000 000

50 0 100 200 300 400 km
50 0 50 100 150 200 250 miles

Projection: Conical with two standard parallels

Sand deserts

Intermittent lakes

continuation southwards on same scale

TURKMENISTAN

Meymaneh · Tokzar · SAMANGAN · TAKHAR · Wakhan
FĀRYĀB · SAR-E POL · BAGHLĀN · BADAKSHĀN · Hindu Kush · Karakoram
Herat · BADGHIS · GHOWR · PARVAN · KAPISA · NURISTAN · NORTH WEST FRONTIER · JAMMU & KASHMIR
AFGHANISTAN
BĀMĪĀN · KABUL · VARDAK · Jalālābād · PESHAWAR · Srinagar
DAY KUNDI · Ghazni · GHAZNĪ · PAKTIA · RAWALPINDI · Islamabad
FARĀH · ORŪZGĀN · ZĀBOL · PAKTĪKA · Attock · Jammu
Kandahār · KANDAHĀR · Toba Kakar · HIMACHAL PRADESH
HELMAND · Quetta · Loralai · MULTAN · Chandigarh · Shimla
IRAN · BALUCHISTAN · PAKISTAN · Dera Ghazi Khan · PUNJAB · LUDHIANA
Zāhedān · Kalat · FAISALABAD · LAHORE · Jullundur
Central Makran Range · Sukkur · Bikaner · Thar Desert · DELHI · New Delhi · Ghaziabad
Makran Coast Range · Larkana · SINDH · RAJASTHAN · JAIPUR · AGRA · KANPUR
KARACHI · HYDERABAD · Jodhpur · Udaipur · Kota · Gwalior · Jhansi

ARABIAN SEA
Tropic of Cancer

Mouths of the Indus · Rann of Kachchh · GUJARAT · MADHYA PRADESH
Gulf of Kachchh · AHMADABAD · Ujjain · BHOPAL · JABALPUR
Kathiawar · VADODARA (Baroda) · INDORE
Gulf of Khambhat · SURAT · Satpura Range
Diu · NASIK · Aurangabad · MAHARASHTRA · NAGPUR
MUMBAI (BOMBAY) · PUNE (Poona) · Solapur
ANDHRA PRADESH · HYDERABAD · Secunderabad
KARNATAKA · Belgaum · GOA

INDIAN OCEAN

Dharwad · Hubli · Kurnool · Chirala
GOA · Bellary · Nandyal · Ongole
KARNATAKA · Anantapur · Cuddapah · Nellore
BANGALORE (Bengaluru) · Tirupati · CHENNAI (Madras)
Mangalore · Mysore · Kolar · Vellore · Kanchipuram
Calicut (Kozhikode) · TAMIL NADU · Salem · Puducherry (Pondicherry)
COIMBATORE · Tiruchchirappalli · Thanjavur
COCHIN (Kochi) · MADURAI · Karaikal
Quilon (Kollam) · Tuticorin · Palk Strait
Trivandrum (Thiruvananthapuram) · Gulf of Mannar · Jaffna
Kanyakumari (C. Comorin) · Adam's Bridge

SRI LANKA
Anuradhapura · Trincomalee · Foul Pt.
Colombo · Kandy · Batticaloa
Moratuwa · Adam's Peak · Galle · Matara · Hambantota · Dondra Head

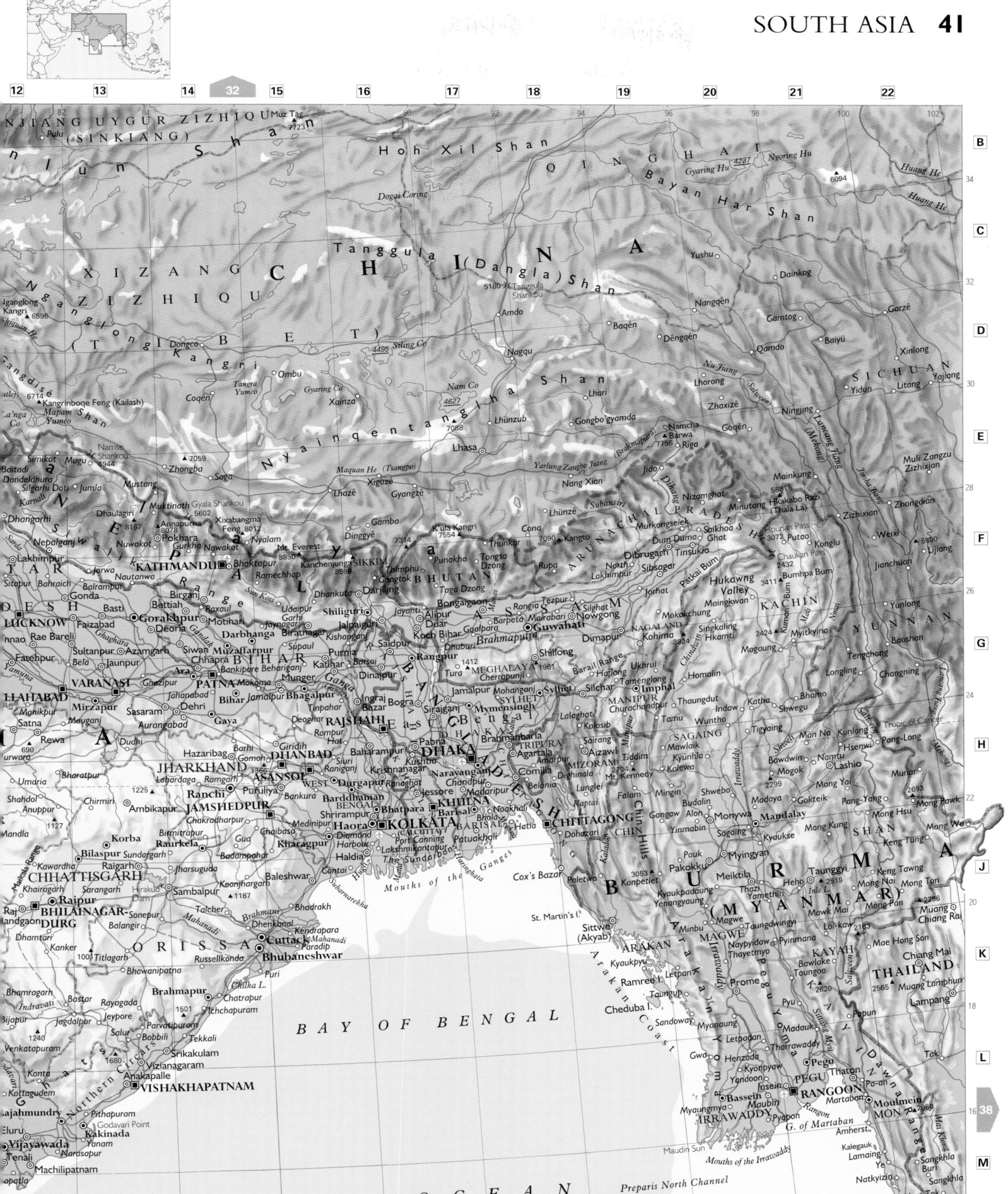

1:6 000 000

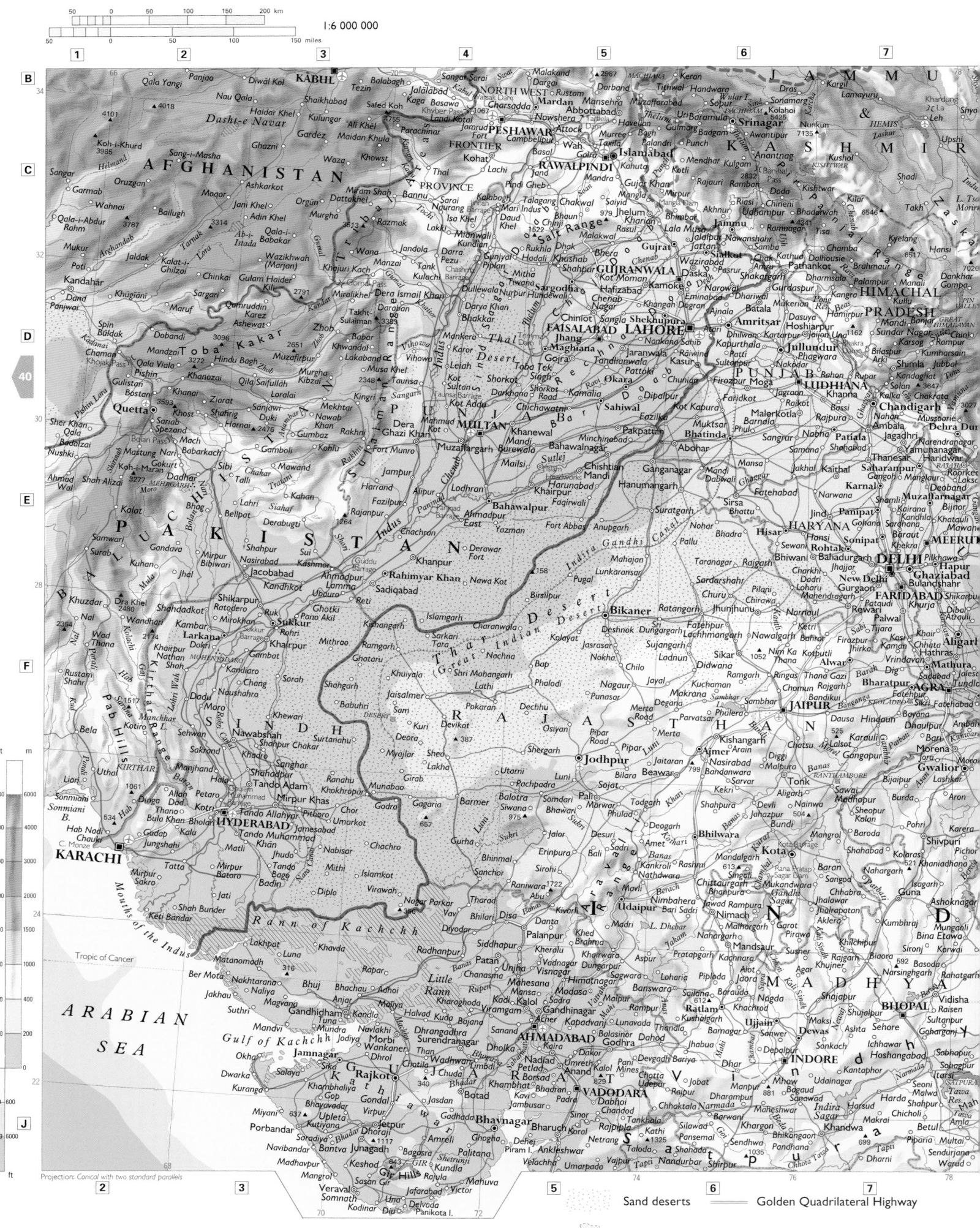

Projection: Conical with two standard parallels

Sand deserts

Golden Quadrilateral Highway

Intermittent lakes

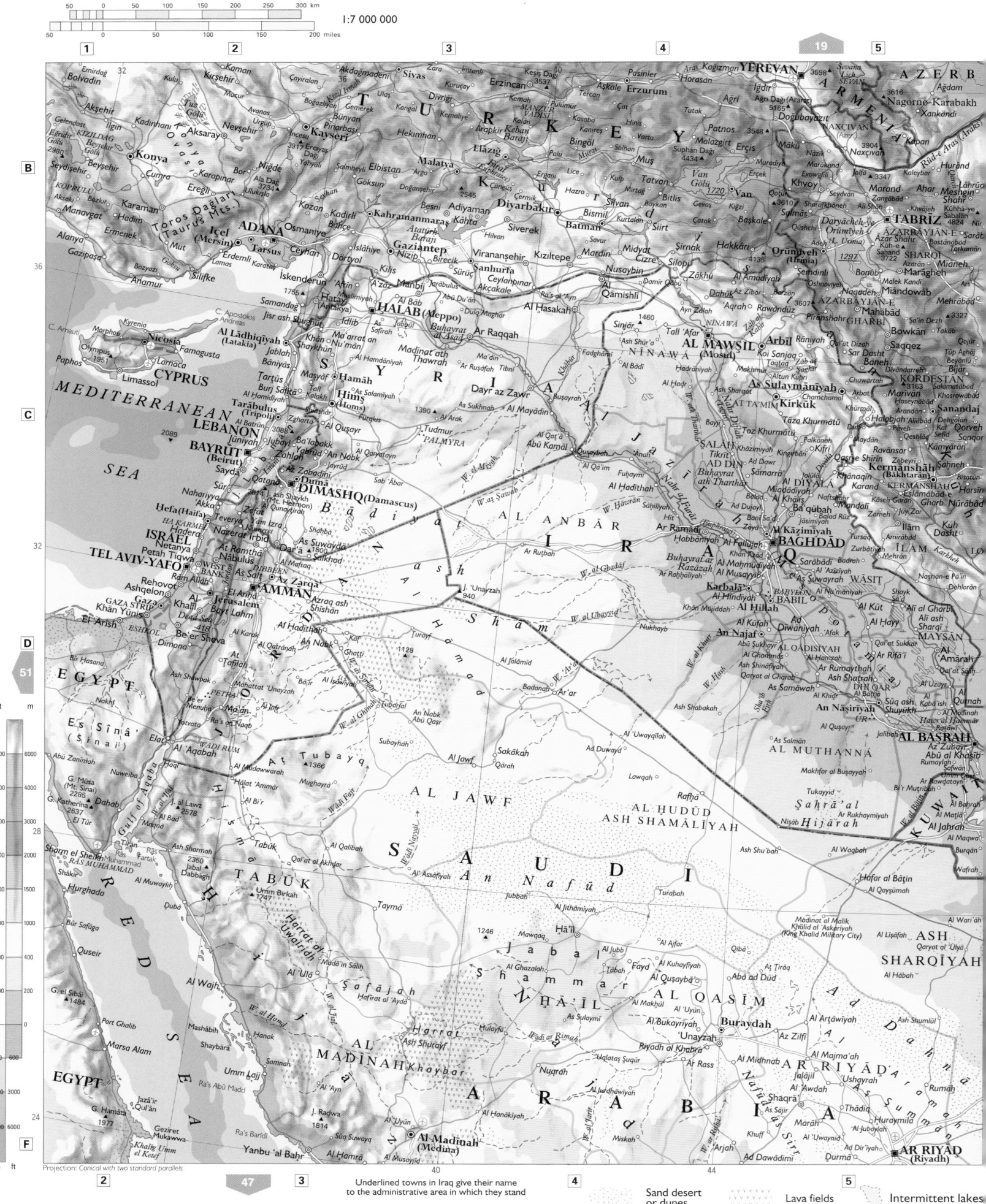

1:7 000 000

Projection: Conical with two standard parallels

Underlined towns in Iraq give their name to the administrative area in which they stand

Sand desert or dunes   Lava fields   Intermittent lakes

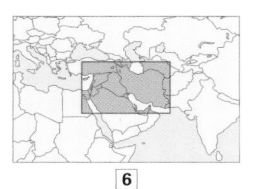

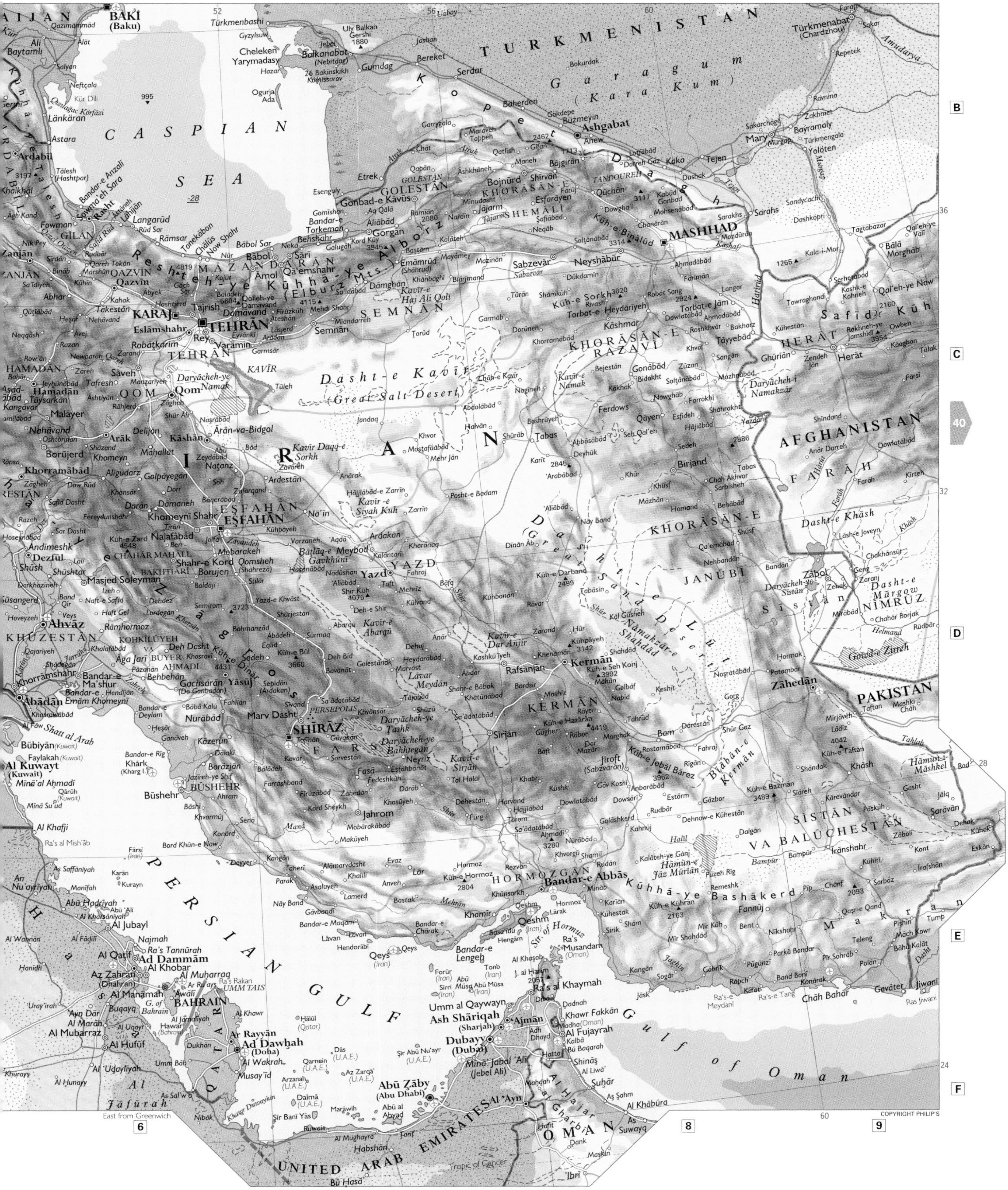

1:2 500 000

10 0 10 20 30 40 50 60 70 80 100 km
10 0 10 20 30 40 50 60 miles

| 1 | 2 | 3 | 4 | 44 | 5 | 6 |

CYPRUS

Paphos
Kivianes
Zyyi
Limassol
Akrotiri Bay
Episkopi Bay
C. Gata

M E D I T E R R A N E A N

S E A

2775

2089

Hims (Homs)
Al Hamidiyah
Shinshär
Furqlus
Tall Kalakh
Halbā
Al Minā'
ASH SHAMÁL
Al Hirmil
Al Qusayr
Tarābulus (Tripoli)
Zghartä
Qurnat as Sawdā 3088
HIMS
Al Batrūn
Bsharri
2616
Al Labwah
2464
Al Buray
Al Qāryatayn
Jubayl
Qartabā
Ibrāhîm
AL BIQA'
Bi'r Ghadīr
An Nabk
Jūniyah
Bikfayyā
2628
J. Sannīn
BAYRŪT (Beirut)
Alayh
Ash Shuwayfāt
Zahlah
Sirghāyā
Jayrūd
SYRIA
Ad Dāmūr
JABAL LUBNÁN
Az Zabadāni
Dumayr
Khān Abū Shāmat
1942 al Bārūk
DIMASHB
Saydā (Sidon)
Jazzīn
J. ash Shaykh (Mt. Hermon) 2814
Darayyā
DIMASHQ (Damascus)
DAM
Qatanā
Jaramānah
An Nabatīyah at Tahta
Marj 'Uyūn
Al Khiyām
Al Kiswah
Al Hājānah
AL JANŪB
Sūr (Tyre)
Al Mas'ada
'A'wai
Qatanā
Qiryat Shemona
Golan
1197
Al Qunaytirah
Buraq
Şafā
As Sanamayn
Nahariyya
Me'ona Haga lil
1208
Zefat
(Galilee)
Yām Kinneret (Sea of Galilee)
Fiq
Shaykh Miskin
DAR'Á
Izra
Shahbā
'Akko (Acre)
Mifraz Hefa
Qiryat
Karmi'el
HAZAFON
Teverya (Tiberias) -210
Sahem al Jawlān
W. al Harīr
J. al Duruz
Hefa (Haifa)
Qiryat Ata
Nazerat (Nazareth)
Taiyiba
Yarmūk
IRBID
Dar'ā
As Suwaydā
SUWAYDÁ
Dāliyat el Karmel
HA KARMEL
Afula
1247 Jarash
AJLŪN
Sahm al Jawlān
1800
Şalah
AL MAFRAQ
TEL MEGIDDO
Umm el Fahm
Jenin
Bet She'an
JARASH
Malah
CAESAREA
Pardes Hanna-Karkur
SHOMRON
Tūbās
'Ajlūn
At Ramthā
Buṣrá ash Shām
Şalkhad
Hadera
Tulkarm
SAMARIA
J. Umm ad Daraj
Irbid
Umm al Qittayn
ISRAEL
Netanya
Nablus
DIBEEN
Al Mafraq
HAMERKAZ
Ra'ananna
N. az Zarqā
AL MAFRAQ
Herzliyya
Kefar Sava
Petah Tiqwa
SHILO
AL BALQÁ
Benē Beraq
Ramat Gan
Az Zarqā
TEL AVIV-YAFO
Lod
WEST BANK
As Salt
'AMMÁN
Bat Yam
Holon
Ramla
Rām Allāh
Wādi as Sīr
Karama
Rishon le Ziyyon
Yavne
Rehovot
El Arīha (Jericho)
Nā'ūr
AMM
AZ ZARQÁ
Ashdod
Jerusalem (Yerushalayim) (Al Quds)
Ma'daba
Qiryat Mal'akhi
Bet Shemesh
MA'DABA
Azraq ash Shishan
Ashqelon
Qiryat Gat
Bayt Lahm (Bethlehem)
'AMMÁN
TEL LAKHISH
Al Khalīl (Hebron)
Dhibān
Gaza
N. Shiqma
Sederot
W. al Haydān
GAZA STRIP
Za Zāhirīyah
418
Al Hadithah
Khān Yūnis
Rafah
ESHKOL
'En Gedi
MASADA
Be'er Sheva (Beersheba)
Arad
Al Qatrānah
Al Karak
W. al Mujib
Bûr Sa'îd (Port Said)
Bûr Fu'ad
BÛR SA'ÎD
Khalīg el Tîna
Râs Burûn
Sabkhet el Bardawîl
Bîr el 'Abd
El Daheir
Bor Mashash
Sedom
AL KARAK
Ramani
Bîr el Garârât
En Boqeq
1305
Al Mazar
Qanṭara Suweis
Bîr Qatia
Bîr Lahfān
Dimona
HADAROM
333
W. al Hasā
W. Bā'ir
El Qanṭara
Bîr el Duweidar
Bîr Kaseiba
'Arîsh
Wâhid
Bîr Madkûr
SHAMÂL SÎNÎ
Abu 'Aweigila
Qezi'ot
JORDAN
At Tafilah
Ismâ'ilîya
Talâta
Muweilih
El Quseima
Sedé Boqér
AT TAFÎLAH
Dana
J. ash Shawmari
1072
ISMÂ'ÎLÎYA
Khamsa
El Buheirat el Murrat el Kubra (Great Bitter L.)
Bîr Hasana
Birein
892
Mizpe Ramon
Nijil
Mahattat 'Unayzah
Gineifa
G. Yi 'Allaq
1094
Bîr Beiḍa
Hamegev (Negev Desert)
Rujm Tal'at al Jamā'ah
1736
Ma'ān
E G Y P T
E S S Î N â'
(S i n a i)
Bîr el Thamâda
W. el Brûk
W. Chriaiya
El Agrûd
PETRA
Wādi Mūsa
Ma'ān
Mamarr Mitlâ
Bîr Gebeil Hisn
W. Mahashim
El Kuntilla
Ra's an Naqb
MA'ÁN
El Suweis (Suez)
Bûr Taufiq
Gebel el Tîh
948
G. el Kabrît
El Thamad
Yotvata?
Bî'r al Mâri
Adabiya
Uyûn Mûsa
Ain Sudr
Nakhl
Bîr Abu Muhammad
'En 'Avrona
1435
Al 'Aqabah
Ra's an Naqb
Mahattat ash Shidîyah
Gebel el Tîh
Bîr el Heisi
Elat
1592
J. Rum 1754
WADI RUM
Batn al Ghûl
Ghubbet el Bûs
Râs Sudr
El Wabeira
W. Girâfi
Bîr el Biarât
Al 'Aqabah
Rum
At Tubayq
SAUDI
Bîr Şandûq
1272
Râs Matarma
W. Abu Ga'da
J A N Û B S Î N Î
Bîr Tâba
1165
Haql
ARABIA
EL SUWEIS
Bîr Wuseit
Al Mudawwarah

Projection: Polyconic
East from Greenwich
COPYRIGHT PHILIP'S

==== 1974 Cease Fire Lines

1:15 000 000

100   0   100   200   300   400   500   600 km
100   0   100   200   300   400 miles

A **1** B **2** **44** **3** **45** **4** **45** **5** **6** **7**

LEBANON
BAYRŪT (Beirut)
DIMASHQ (Damascus)
SYRIA
Ḥerā
Ar Ramādī
Ba'qūbah
BAGHDAD
Khorramābād
Al Kūt
Dezfūl EŞFAHĀN
Khomeyni Shahr
Arāk
Kāshān
Khvor
Tabas
IRAN
Birjand
Farāh
AFGHANISTAN

ISRAEL
TEL AVIV-YAFO
Ashqelon
Jerusalem WEST BANK
Būr Sa'īd GAZA STRIP (Port Said)
Ismā'īliya
El Suweis (Suez)
AMMĀN
JORDAN
Jabal ad Durūz 1800
Ar Ruṭbah
Karbalā'
Al Ḥillah
An Najaf
IRAQ
Al 'Amārah
Ahvāz
Shahr-e Kord
Yazd
Anār
Rafsanjān
Kermān
Zābol

Elat
Al 'Aqabah
Ma'ān
Ar'ar
An Nāşirīyah
AL BAŞRAH (Basra)
Abādān
Khorramshahr
Marv Dasht
PERSEPOLIS
SHĪRĀZ
Kāzerūn
Sirjān
Bam
Zāhedān

G. Mûsa 2285
Sharm el Sheikh
Al Muwayliḥ
Dubā
Tabūk
2578
An Nafūd
Hafar al Bāṭin
Al Kuwayt
KUWAIT
Bûbiyān
Khārk
Būshehr
Deyyer
Jahrom
Neyrīz
Bandar-e Abbās
Qeshm
Īrānshahr

Hurghada
Būr Safāga
Al Wajh
Tamyā
Hā'il
Al Jubayl
Al Qaţīf
BAHRAIN
Al Manāmah
QATAR
Khamīr
Qeys
Str. of Hormuz
Ra's Musandam (Oman)
Gābrik
Jāsk

Qena
Quseir
THEBES KARNAK
El Uqsur (Luxor)
Isna
Idfū
Kôm Ombo
Aswân
Marsa Alam
Buraydah
'Unayzah
Ad Dammām
Az Zahrān (Dhahran)
Al Mubarraz
Al Hufūf
Ad Dawḥah (Doha)
Abū Zaby (Abu Dhabi)
Dubayy (Dubai)
Al Fujayrah
Al 'Ayn
Ash Shāriqah (Sharjah)
Gulf of Oman

EGYPT
Buḥeirat en Naser (L. Nasser)
Sharā'
AR RIYĀD (Riyadh)
As Sulaymānīyah
UNITED ARAB EMIRATES
Ruwais
Al 'Ubaylah
As Suwayq
As Sib
Maṭraḥ
Masqaţ (Muscat)
Nizwā
Izki
Şūr
Ra's al Ḥadd

SAUDI
Bīr Shalatein
Rābigh
Harad
'Ibrī
Khalūf
Maşīrah

ABU SIMBEL
Wadi Halfa
Halaib Triangle
Halaib
Yanbu 'al Baḥr
Al Madīnah (Medina)
Layla
ARABIA

Es Sahrâ en Nûbîya
Kosha
Delgo
Dongola
3rd Cataract
Muhammad Qol 2259
Ras Abu Shagara
Makkah (Mecca)
JIDDAH (Jedda)
At Tā'if 2565
Turabah
As Sulayyil
Rub' al Khālī (Empty Quarter)
Haymā'
Khalīj Maşīrah
OMAN

Kareima
4th Cataract
Ed Debba
Abu Hamed
Bûr Sûdân
Suakin
Al Qunfudhah
Al Līth

Dongola
5th Cataract
Berber
Atbara
Sinkat
Trinkitat
Nahr en Nîl (Nile)
Khamīs Mushayţ
Ash Sharawrah
Ra's al Madrakah

Wad Hamid
6th Cataract
Shendî
Nahr Atbara
Adarama
Haiya
Karora 2780
Nakfa
Abhā
Jīzān
Najrān
Salālah
Mirbāţ
J. al Hallānīyat

Omdurmân
EL KHARTÛM (Khartoum)
Kassalā
Khashm el Girba
ERITREA
Akordat
Asmera
Mitsiwa
Dahlak Kebir
Al Luḥayyah
Kamarān
Farasān
Ḥajjah
Shibām
Ḥadramawt
Ra's Fartak

El Obeid
Wâd Medanî
Gedaref
Aksum
Adwa
Adigrat
Mekele
116
SANA'
Dhamār
Ibb
Nişāb
2185
YEMEN
Ash Shiḥr
Sayḥūt
Al Mukallā

Ed Dueim
Umm Ruwaba
Singa
Nil el Azraq (Blue Nile)
Metema
Gonder
1830
Ras Dashen 4533
Danakil Desert
Al Ḥudaydah
Ta'izz 3200
Al Mukhā
J. Manār
Madinat ash Sha'b
Al' Adan (Aden)
Bāb el Mandeb
Gulf of Aden
'Abd al Kūrī (Yemen)
Bereeda
Ras Asir
Hadīboh 1503
Socotra (Yemen)

Jibalan Nubah
Nekemte
Lalibela
Debre Tabor
Bahir Dar
Debre Markos 4000
Dese
Aseb
Djibouti
DJIBOUTI
Tadjoura
Dikhil
L. Assal
Saylac
Berbera
Boosaaso
Karin
Xaafuun
Ras Xaafuun
El Gal

SUDAN
Ethiopian
Abay (Blue Nile)
Bure
L. Tana
Dire Dawa
Harer
HARGEISA
Burco (Burao)
Somaliland
Ceerigaabo
Qardho (Gardo)
Bender Beyla

Malakâl
Sobat
ADDIS ABEBA
Debre Zeyit
Awash
Jijiga
Las Anod (Laascaanood)
Garoowe
Puntland
Eyl

Sûdd
Bahr el Jebel (White Nile)
Metu
Dembidolo
Gore
ETHIOPIA
Highlands
Nazret
3381
Harar
Ogaden
Galaacyo
(Galcaio)

Pibor Post
Bôr
Tali Post
Jima
3686
Awasa
Batu 4307
Goba
Ginir
Imi
Kebri Dehar
Sina Dhago
INDIAN

Juba
Mongalla
Kapoeta
Elemi Triangle
Lokitaung
Yirga Alem
Arba Minch
L. Abaya
Dila
Kibre Mengist
L. Shamo
Negele
Shebele
Ferfer
Beledweyne (Belet Uen)
Dolo
Hobyo
Ceeldheere
OCEAN

Yei
Torit
Kajo Kaji 3187
1794
L. Turkana
Mega
Moyale
El Wak
Luuq (Lugh)
Baydhabo (Baidoa)
Jawhar (Giohar)

UGANDA
Arua
Gulu
Lira
Moroto
2749
3084
Turkwel
375
2752
South Horr
Marsabit
Wajir
Dif
Buurhakaba (Bur Acaba)
Wanleweyne (Uanle Uen)
MUQDISHO (Mogadishu)
Marka (Merca)

L. Albert
Pakwach
Soroti
Mt. Elgon
KENYA
3206
Kitale
Lodwar
Jamaame (Giamama)
Jilib (Gelib)

L. Kyoga
Mbale
Kismaayo (Chisimaio)
Equator

East from Greenwich
COPYRIGHT PHILIP'S

Projection: Sanson-Flamsteed's Sinusoidal
1 **2** **54** **3** **4** **5** **6**

Sand deserts

ft   m
12 000   4000
9000   3000
6000   2000
4500   1500
3000   1000
1200   400
600   200
0   0
200   600
1000   3000
2000   6000
4000   12 000
m   ft

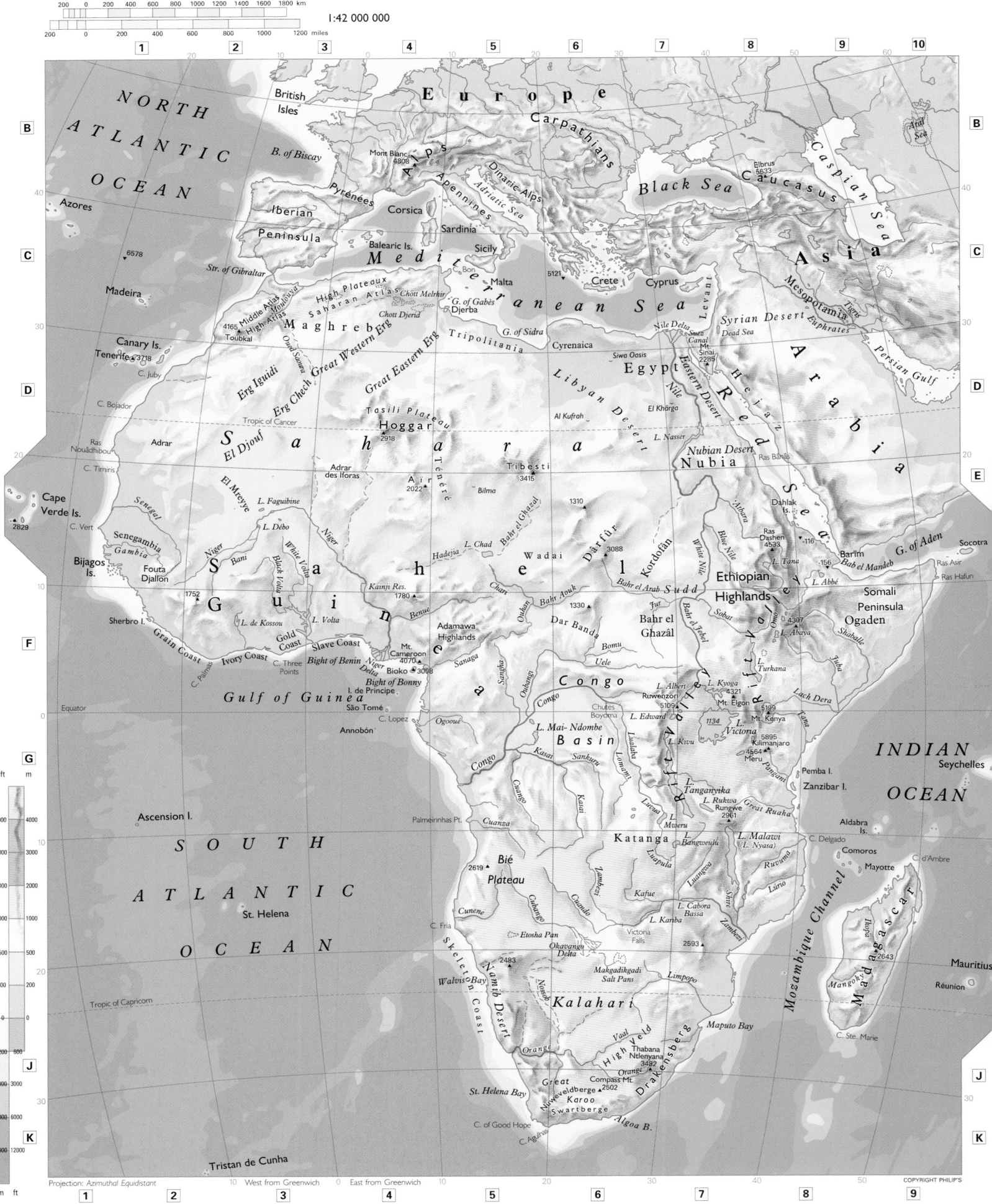

1:42 000 000

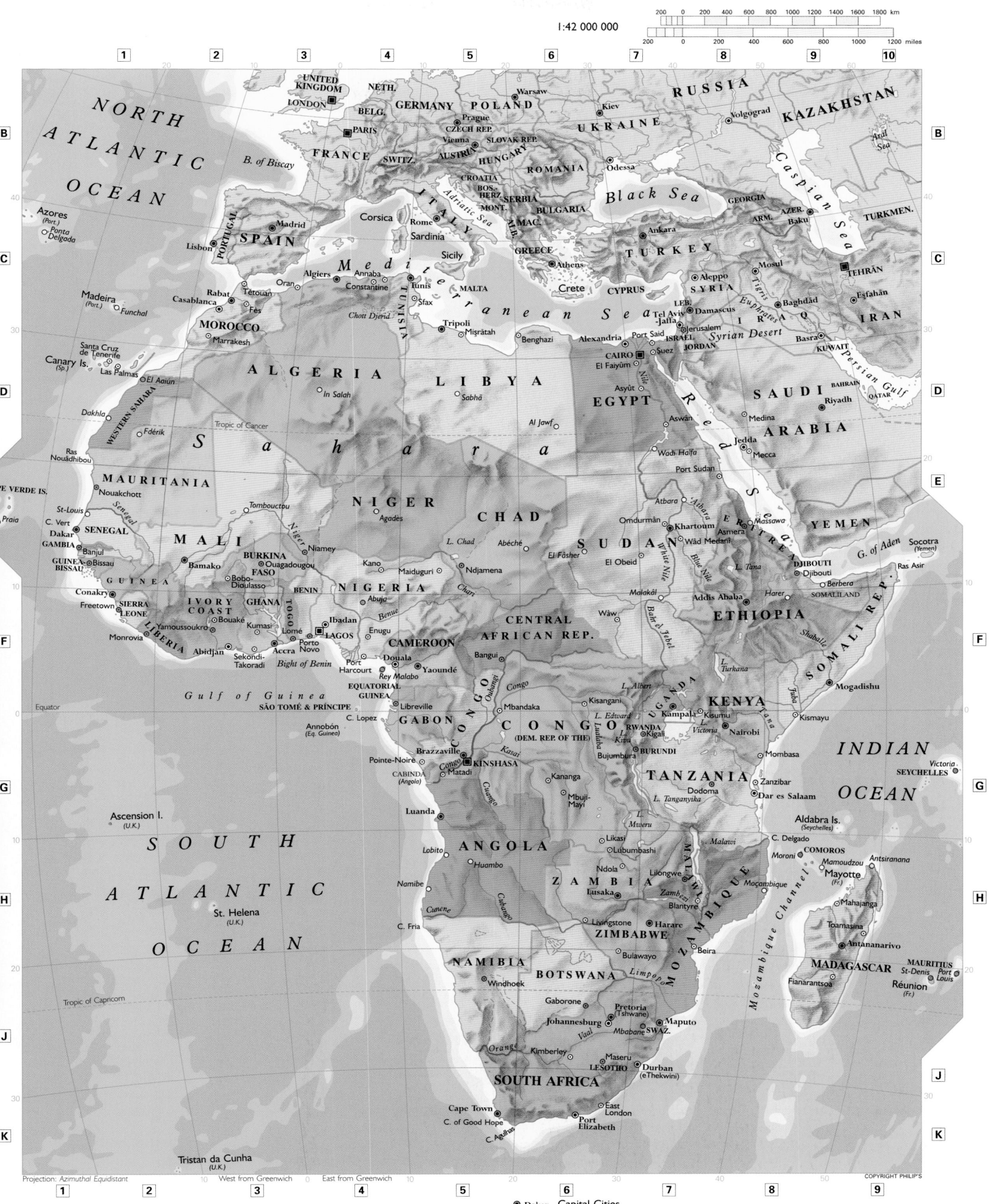

| | 200 | 0 | 200 | 400 | 600 | 800 | 1000 | 1200 | 1400 | 1600 | 1800 km |
| 200 | 0 | 200 | 400 | 600 | 800 | 1000 | 1200 miles |

NORTH ATLANTIC OCEAN

UNITED KINGDOM
LONDON
NETH.
BELG.
PARIS
FRANCE
B. of Biscay
GERMANY POLAND
Warsaw
Prague
CZECH REP.
Vienna SLOVAK REP.
SWITZ. AUSTRIA
HUNGARY
CROATIA
BOS.-
HERZ.
SERBIA
MONT.
MAC.
ROMANIA
BULGARIA
RUSSIA
Kiev
Volgograd
UKRAINE
Odessa
KAZAKHSTAN
Aral Sea

Azores
(Port.)
Ponta
Delgada
PORTUGAL
Lisbon
SPAIN
Madrid
Corsica
Rome
ITALY
Sardinia
Sicily
Adriatic Sea
Mediterranean
GREECE
Athens
Crete
Black Sea
GEORGIA
Ankara
TURKEY
ARM. AZER.
Baku
Caspian Sea
TURKMEN.

Madeira
(Port.)
Funchal
Santa Cruz
de Tenerife
Canary Is.
(Sp.)
Las Palmas
Rabat
Casablanca
Tétouan
Fes
MOROCCO
Marrakesh
Algiers
Oran
Annaba
Constantine
Chott Djerid
TUNISIA
Tunis
Sfax
MALTA
Tripoli
Mişrātah
Benghazi
Alexandria
CAIRO
El Faiyûm
Suez
Port Said
Tel Aviv-
Jaffa
ISRAEL
Jerusalem
JORDAN
Suez
LEB.
Damascus
SYRIA
Aleppo
Mosul
Euphrates
Baghdad
IRAQ
Eşfahān
TEHRĀN
IRAN
Basra
KUWAIT
Persian Gulf
Syrian Desert
Tigris

El Aaiún
Dakhla
WESTERN SAHARA
Ras
Nouâdhibou
Fdérik
Sahara
ALGERIA
LIBYA
In Salah
Sabhā
Al Jawf
EGYPT
Asyût
Aswân
Tropic of Cancer
Wadi Halfa
Port Sudan
SAUDI
ARABIA
Medina
Riyadh
Jedda
Mecca
BAHRAIN
QATAR
Red Sea

CAPE VERDE IS.
Praia
MAURITANIA
Nouakchott
St-Louis
C. Vert
Dakar
SENEGAL
GAMBIA
Banjul
GUINEA-
BISSAU
Bissau
GUINEA
Conakry
Freetown
SIERRA
LEONE
LIBERIA
Monrovia
Tombouctou
MALI
Bamako
BURKINA
FASO
Ouagadougou
Bobo-
Dioulasso
Niamey
Kano
IVORY
COAST
Yamoussoukro
Bouaké
Kumasi
GHANA
BENIN
TOGO
Abidjan
Accra
Lomé
Sekondi-
Takoradi
Porto
Novo
LAGOS
Ibadan
NIGERIA
Abuja
Enugu
Benue
Maiduguri
Ndjamena
Chari
NIGER
Agades
CHAD
Abéché
L. Chad
SUDAN
El Fâsher
El Obeid
Omdurmân
Khartoum
Wâd Medani
Atbara
White Nile
Blue Nile
ERITREA
Massawa
Asmera
L. Tana
DJIBOUTI
Djibouti
Berbera
YEMEN
G. of Aden
Socotra
(Yemen)
Ras Asir

Equator
BENIN
CAMEROON
Douala
Yaoundé
Rey Malabo
EQUATORIAL
GUINEA
SÃO TOMÉ & PRÍNCIPE
GABON
Libreville
C. Lopez
Annobón
(Eq. Guinea)
Port
Harcourt
Bight of Benin
Gulf of Guinea
CENTRAL
AFRICAN REP.
Bangui
Oubangui
Mbandaka
Congo
CONGO
CONGO
(DEM. REP. OF THE)
Kisangani
Wâw
Bahr el Jebel
Malakâl
Addis Ababa
ETHIOPIA
Harer
L. Turkana
Shabelle
SOMALILAND
SOMALI REP.
Mogadishu
UGANDA
Kampala
Kisumu
KENYA
Nairobi
L. Albert
L. Edward
RWANDA
Kigali
L. Kivu
BURUNDI
Bujumbura
L. Victoria
Juba
Kismayu
Mombasa

Ascension I.
(U.K.)
SOUTH ATLANTIC OCEAN
St. Helena
(U.K.)
Brazzaville
Pointe-Noire
CABINDA
(Angola)
KINSHASA
Matadi
Congo
Kasai
Kananga
Mbuji-
Mayi
Kwango
Luanda
Lobito
Namibe
ANGOLA
Huambo
Cunene
C. Fria
Cubango
TANZANIA
Dodoma
Zanzibar
Dar es Salaam
L. Tanganyika
L. Mweru
Likasi
Lubumbashi
Ndola
ZAMBIA
Lusaka
Livingstone
Zambezi
Malawi
L. Malawi
Lilongwe
Blantyre
MOZAMBIQUE
C. Delgado
COMOROS
Moroni
Mamoudzou
Mayotte
(Fr.)
Antsiranana
Mahajanga
Toamasina
Antananarivo
MADAGASCAR
Fianarantsoa
St-Denis
Réunion
(Fr.)
MAURITIUS
Port
Louis
INDIAN OCEAN
SEYCHELLES
Victoria
Aldabra Is.
(Seychelles)

NAMIBIA
Windhoek
BOTSWANA
Gaborone
Orange
Vaal
Kimberley
ZIMBABWE
Bulawayo
Harare
Beira
Limpopo
Moçambique
Mozambique Channel
Johannesburg
Pretoria
(Tshwane)
Maputo
Mbabane SWAZ.
Maseru
LESOTHO
Durban
(eThekwini)
SOUTH AFRICA
Tropic of Capricorn
Cape Town
C. of Good Hope
C. Agulhas
East
London
Port
Elizabeth

Tristan da Cunha
(U.K.)

● Dakar Capital Cities

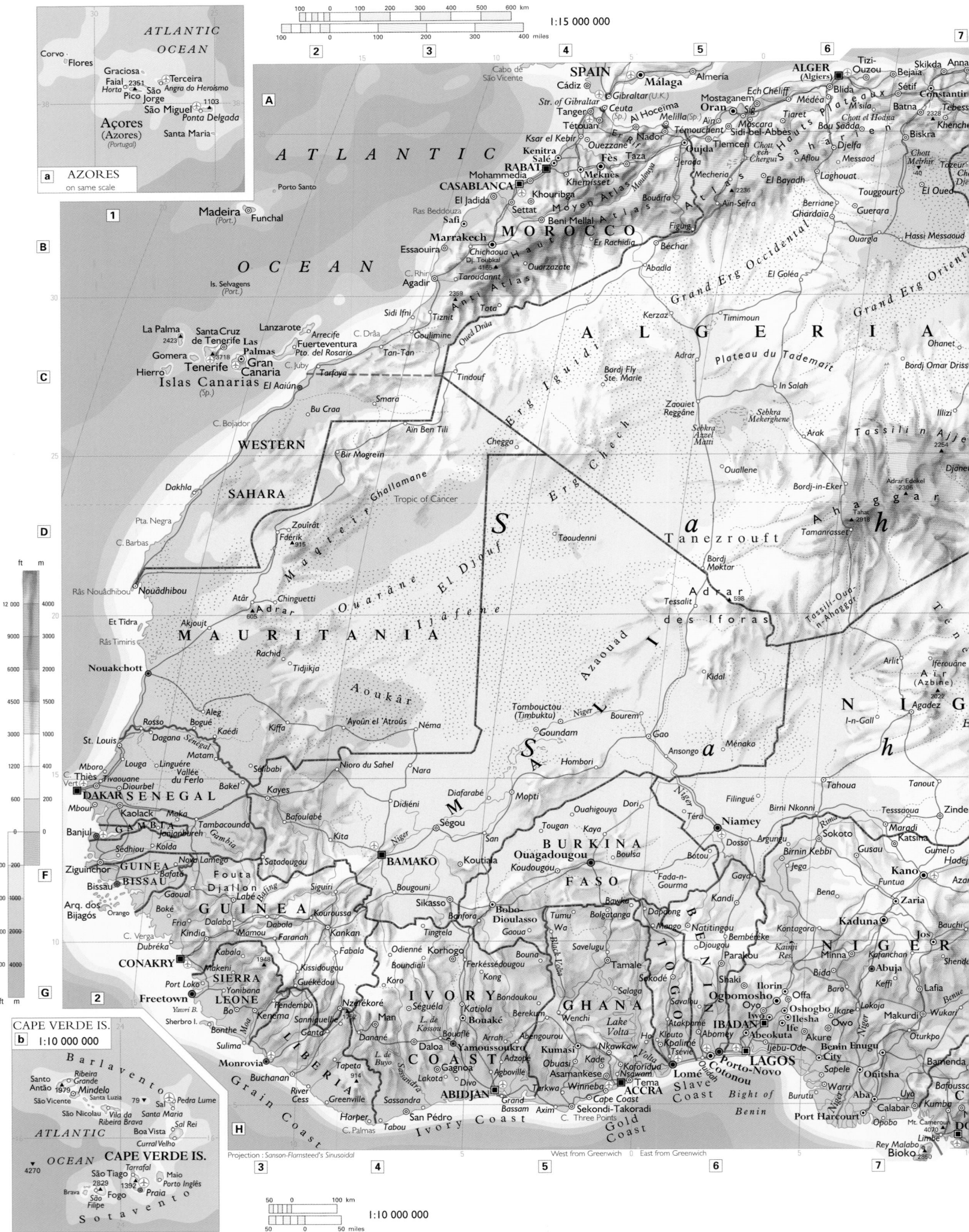

AZORES
on same scale

a

ATLANTIC OCEAN

Corvo Flores Graciosa
Faial ▲2351 São Terceira
Horta Pico Jorge Angra do Heroísmo
São Miguel ▲1103
Ponta Delgada Santa Maria

Açores
(Azores)
(Portugal)

1:15 000 000

100 0 100 200 300 400 500 600 km
100 0 100 200 300 400 miles

CAPE VERDE IS.
b 1:10 000 000

Barlavento
Santo Antão Ribeira Grande 1979
Mindelo Santa Luzia
São Vicente 79
São Nicolau Ribeira Brava Sal Pedra Lume
Santa Maria Sal Rei
Boa Vista

ATLANTIC OCEAN
4270 Tarrafal
São Tiago 2829 Maio
Brava 1392 Porto Inglês
São Fogo Praia
Filipe

CAPE VERDE IS.

Sotavento

1:10 000 000
50 0 100 km
50 0 50 miles

Projection : Sanson-Flamsteed's Sinusoidal   West from Greenwich   East from Greenwich

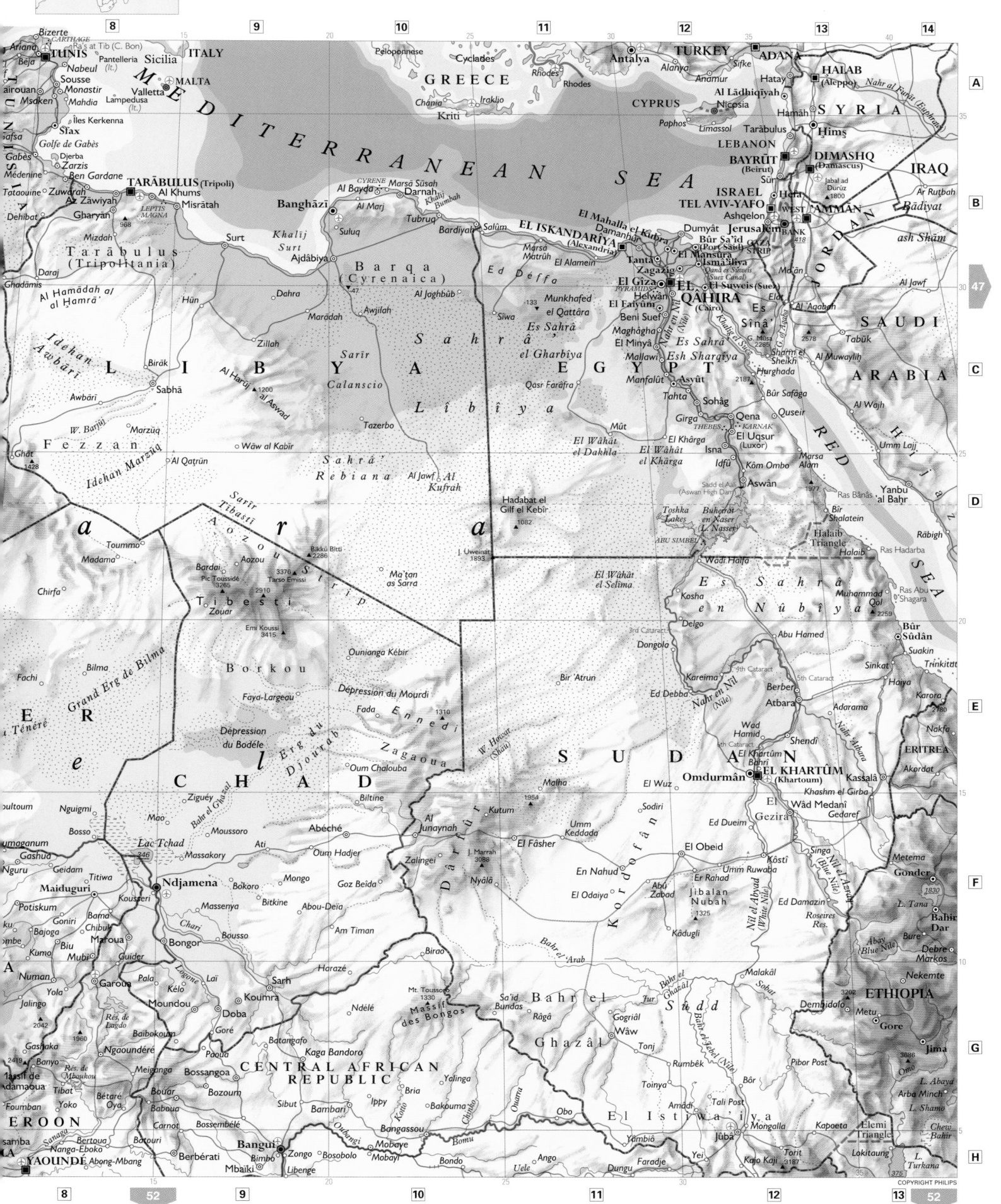

100 0 100 200 300 400 500 600 km

1:15 000 000

100 0 100 200 300 400 miles

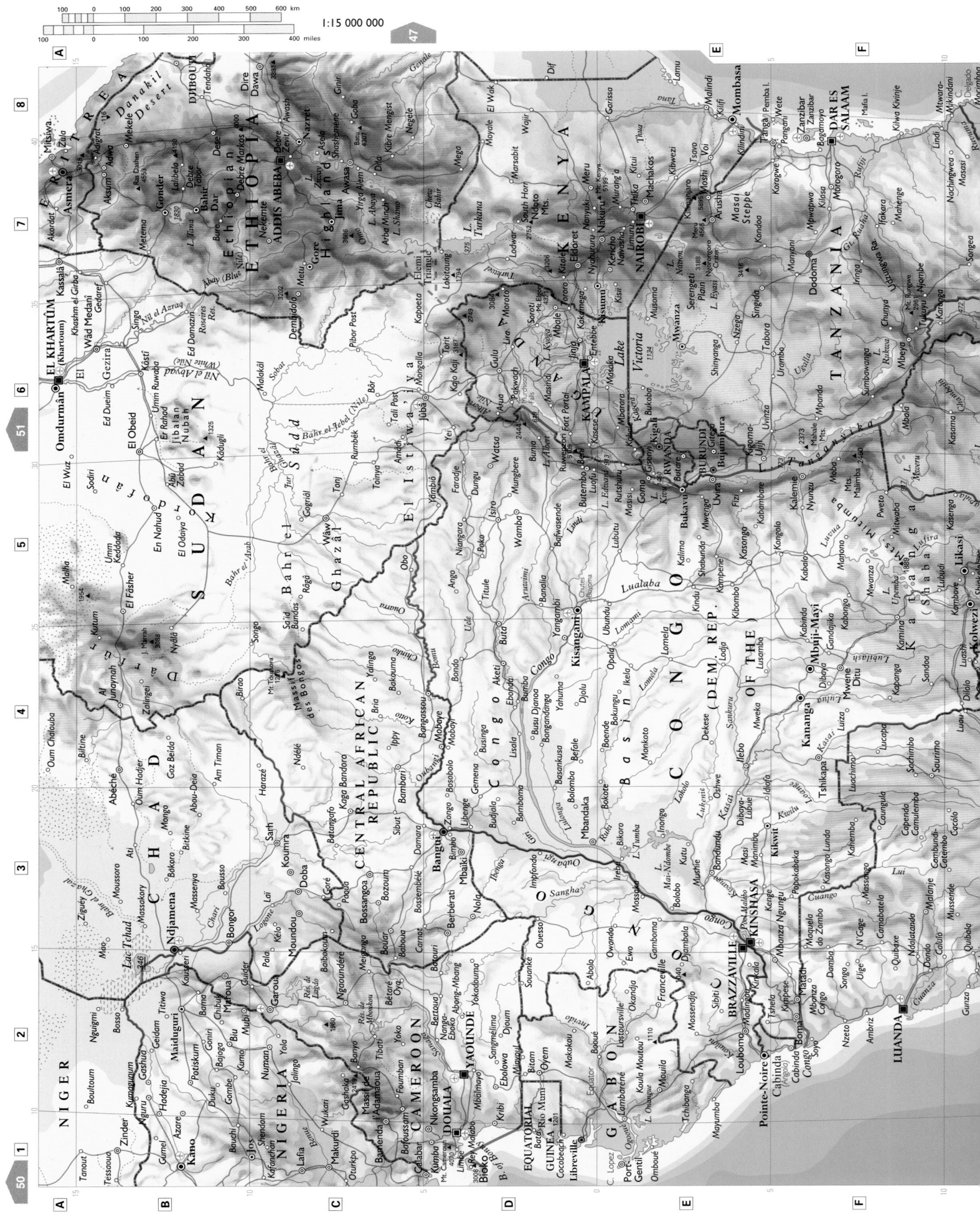

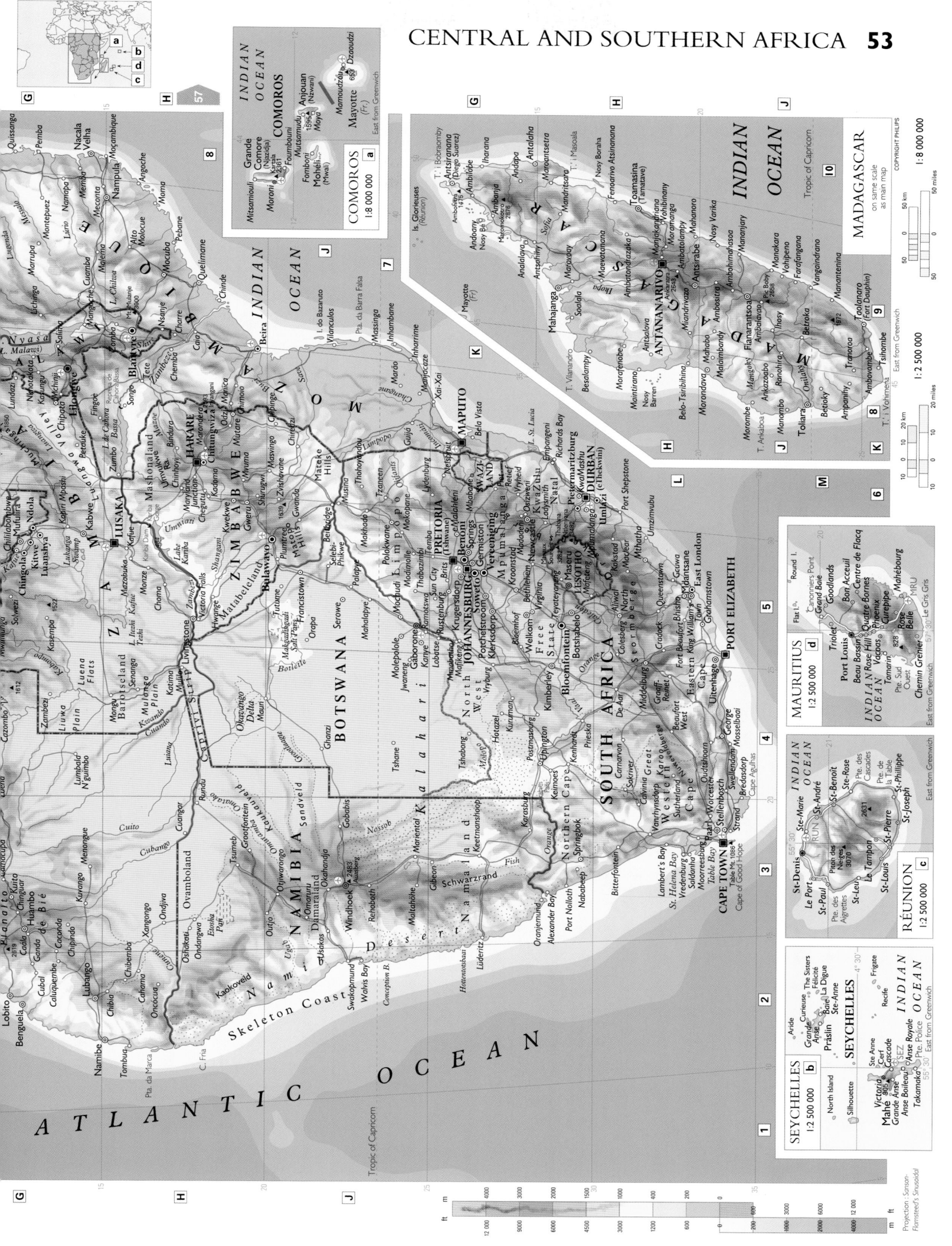

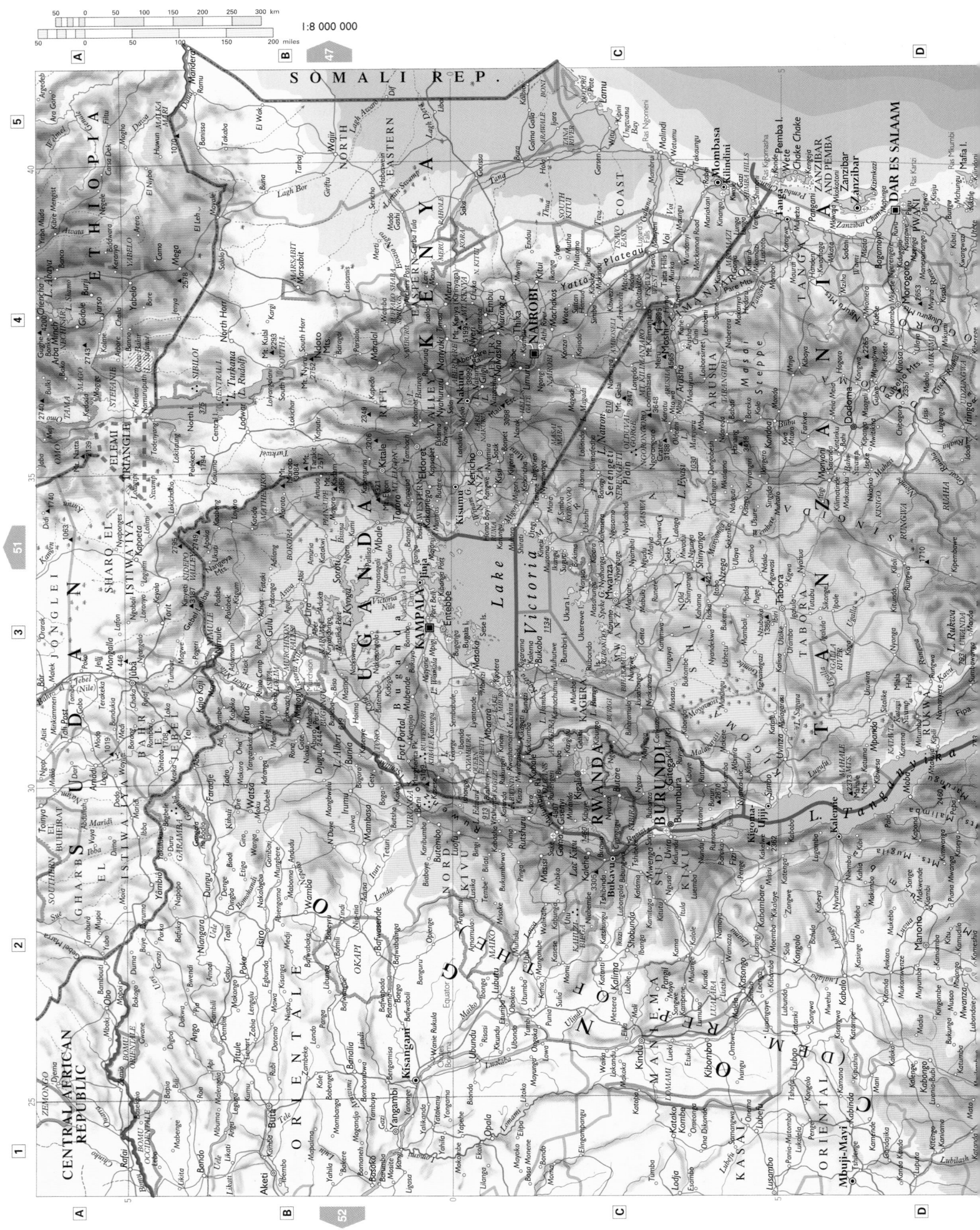

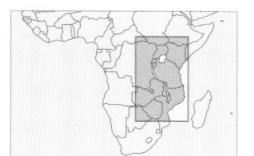

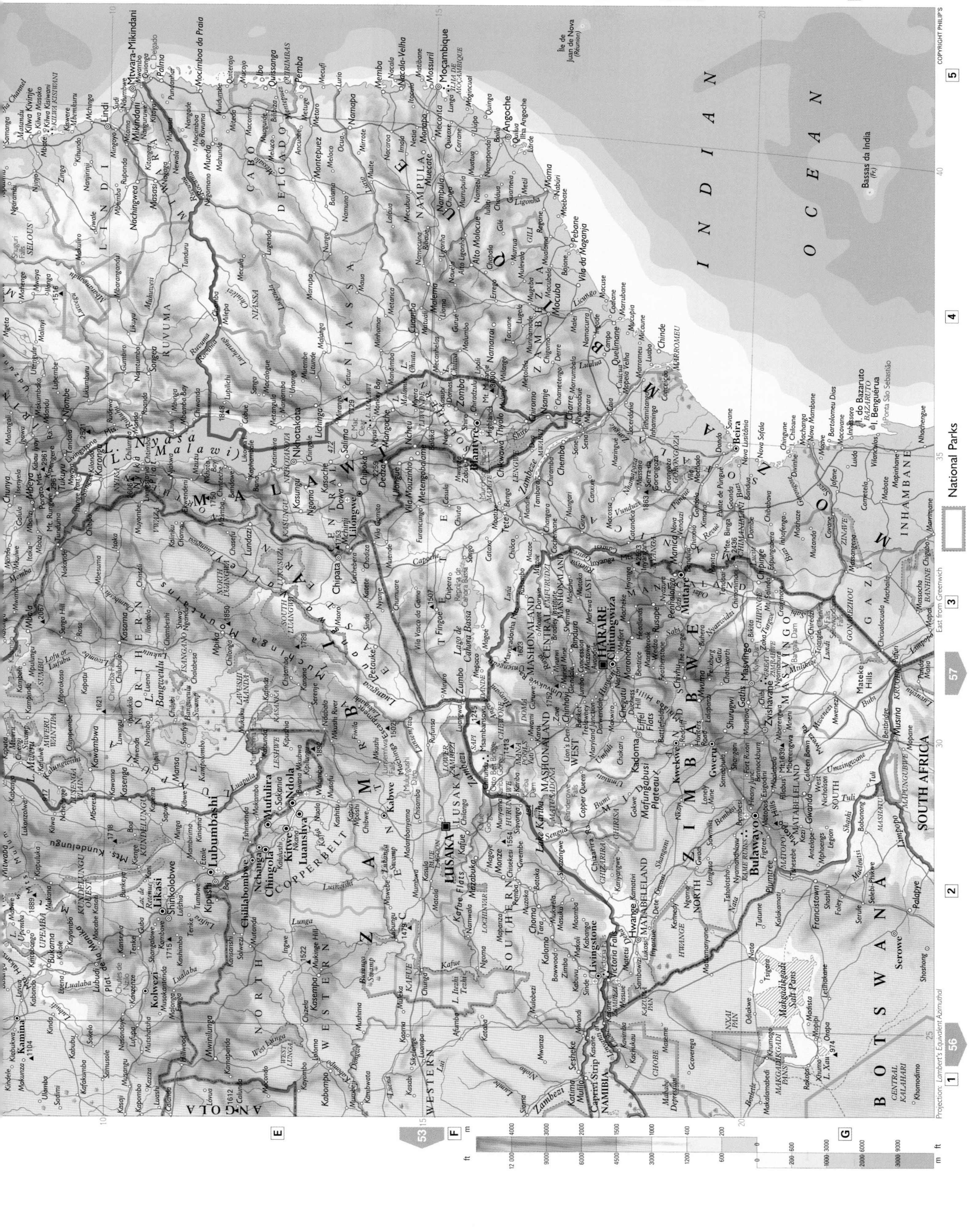

COPYRIGHT PHILIP'S

National Parks

Nature Reserves and
Game Reserves

∴ UNESCO World Heritage Sites

Projection: Lambert's Equivalent Azimuthal

East from Greenwich

1:8 000 000

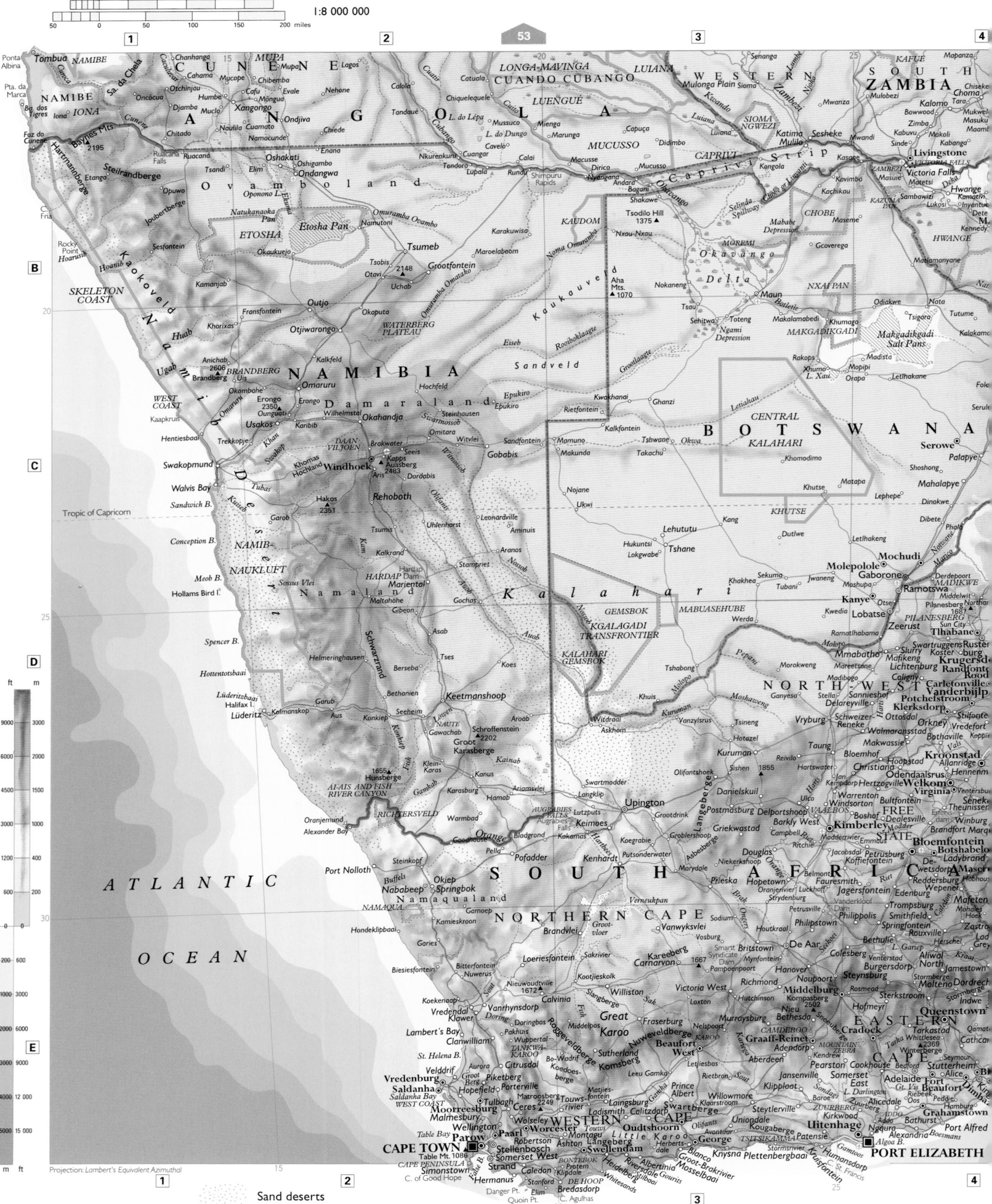

Sand deserts

National Parks

Nature Reserves and
Game Reserves

∴ UNESCO World Heritage Sites

MADAGASCAR
1:8 000 000

50   0   50   100   150 km

50   0   50   100 miles

COPYRIGHT PHILIP'S   East from Greenwich   Projection: Lambert's Equivalent Azimuthal

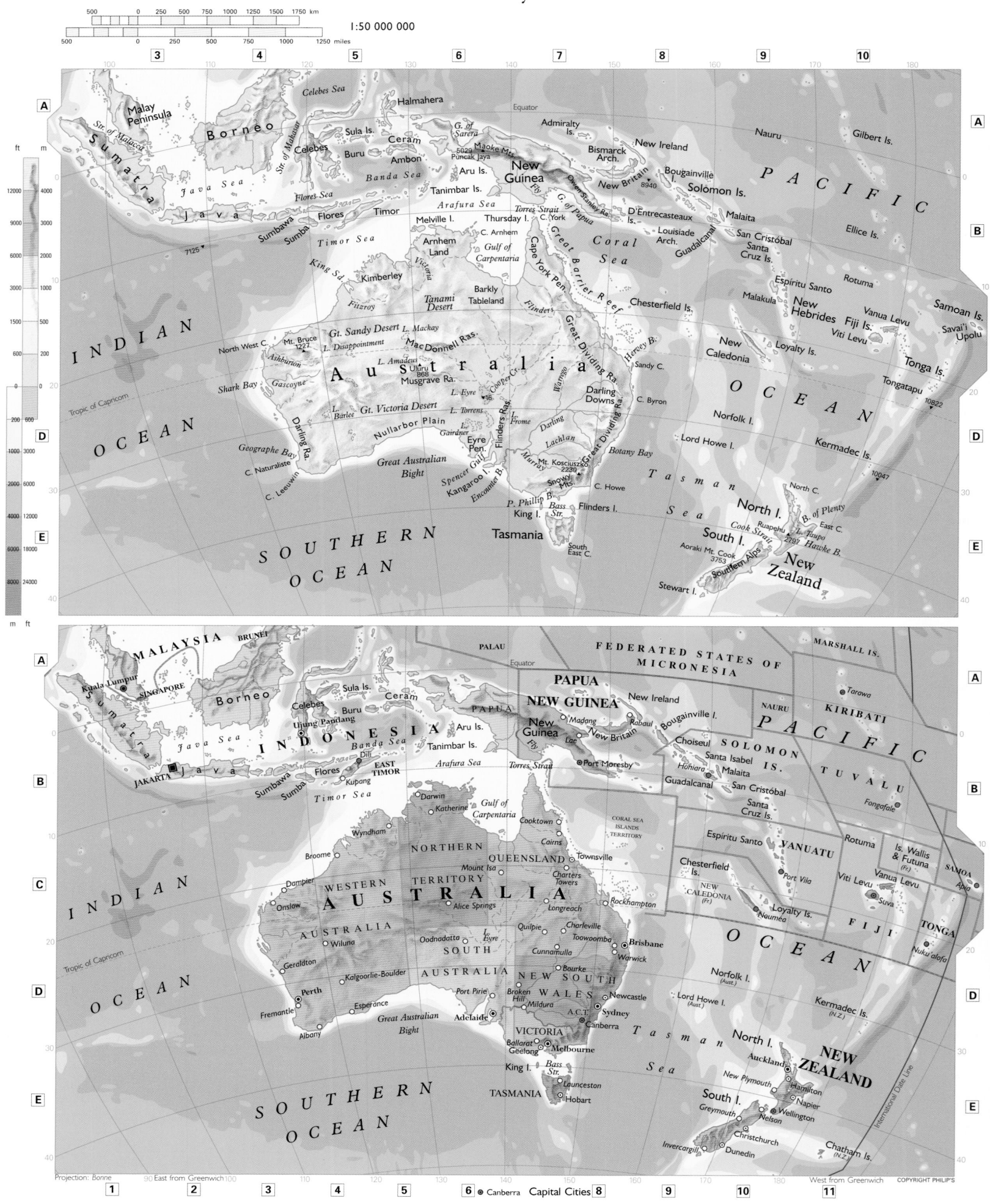

500 0 250 500 750 1000 1250 1500 1750 km
1:50 000 000
500 0 250 500 750 1000 1250 miles

Physical map (top):

INDIAN OCEAN

Malay Peninsula
Sumatra
Str. of Malacca
Java
Borneo
Celebes Sea
Str. of Makassar
Celebes
Sula Is.
Buru
Ceram
Ambon
Banda Sea
Halmahera
G. of Sarera
Maoke Mts.
5029 Puncak Jaya
Aru Is.
New Guinea
Admiralty Is.
New Ireland
Bismarck Arch.
New Britain 8940
Owen Stanley Ra.
D'Entrecasteaux Is.
Louisiade Arch.
Bougainville I.
Solomon Is.
Malaita
San Cristóbal
Santa Cruz Is.
Guadalcanal
Nauru
Gilbert Is.
PACIFIC
Ellice Is.
Samoan Is.
Savai'i
Upolu

Java Sea
Flores Sea
Sumbawa
Sumba
Flores
Timor
Timor Sea
7125
Melville I.
Arnhem Land
C. Arnhem
Gulf of Carpentaria
Tanimbar Is.
Arafura Sea
Torres Strait
Thursday I.
C. York
G. of Papua
Cape York Pen.
Great Barrier Reef
Coral Sea
Chesterfield Is.
Espíritu Santo
Malakula
New Hebrides
Rotuma
Vanua Levu
Fiji Is.
Viti Levu
Samoan Is.

King Sd.
Kimberley
Fitzroy
Tanami Desert
Barkly Tableland
Flinders
Hervey B.
New Caledonia
Loyalty Is.
Tonga Is.
Tongatapu
10822

North West C.
Mt. Bruce 1227
Ashburton
Gt. Sandy Desert
L. Mackay
L. Disappointment
MacDonnell Ras.
L. Amadeus
Uluru 868
Musgrave Ra.
Cooper Cr.
AUSTRALIA
Great Dividing Ra.
Warrego
Darling Downs
Sandy C.
C. Byron
Norfolk I.
Lord Howe I.
Kermadec Is.
10047

Shark Bay
Gascoyne
L. Barlee
Gt. Victoria Desert
L. Eyre 16
L. Torrens
L. Frome
Darling
Lachlan
Murray
Botany Bay

INDIAN OCEAN
Tropic of Capricorn
Geographe Bay
C. Naturaliste
C. Leeuwin
Darling Ra.
Nullarbor Plain
Gairdner
Eyre Pen.
Spencer Gulf
Kangaroo I.
Encounter B.
Great Australian Bight
Mt. Kosciuszko 2230
Snowy Mts.
C. Howe
Tasman Sea

P. Phillip B.
King I.
Bass Str.
Flinders I.
North C.
B. of Plenty
East C.
Ruapehu 2797
L. Taupo
Hawke B.

North I.
Cook Strait
South I.
Aoraki Mt. Cook 3753
Southern Alps
New Zealand
Stewart I.
South East C.

SOUTHERN OCEAN
Tasmania

ft m
12000 4000
9000 3000
6000 2000
3000 1000
1500 500
600 0
0
200 600
1000 3000
2000 6000
4000 12000
6000 18000
8000 24000
m ft

Political map (bottom):

MALAYSIA
BRUNEI
Kuala Lumpur
SINGAPORE
Sumatra
Borneo
Celebes
Ujung Pandang
Sula Is.
Buru
Ceram
PALAU
Equator
FEDERATED STATES OF MICRONESIA
MARSHALL IS.
PAPUA
NEW GUINEA
New Ireland
PAPUA
New Guinea
Madang
Rabaul
New Britain
Bougainville I.
Lae
Nauru
NAURU
Tarawa
KIRIBATI
PACIFIC

INDONESIA
Java Sea
JAKARTA
Java
Banda Sea
Dili
EAST TIMOR
Kupang
Flores
Sumbawa
Sumba
Timor Sea
Aru Is.
Tanimbar Is.
Arafura Sea
Torres Strait
Port Moresby
Fly
Choiseul
Santa Isabel
SOLOMON IS.
Honiara
Malaita
Guadalcanal
San Cristóbal
Santa Cruz Is.
TUVALU
Fongafale
SAMOA
Apia
Is. Wallis & Futuna (Fr.)

INDIAN OCEAN
Tropic of Capricorn
Darwin
Katherine
Gulf of Carpentaria
Cooktown
Cairns
Townsville
CORAL SEA ISLANDS TERRITORY
Espíritu Santo
VANUATU
Rotuma
Vanua Levu

Wyndham
Broome
NORTHERN TERRITORY
QUEENSLAND
Mount Isa
Charters Towers
Chesterfield Is.
Port Vila
NEW CALEDONIA (Fr.)
Viti Levu
Suva
FIJI

Dampier
Onslow
WESTERN AUSTRALIA
Alice Springs
Longreach
Rockhampton
Noumea
Loyalty Is.
TONGA
Nuku'alofa

Geraldton
Wiluna
Oodnadatta
L. Eyre
SOUTH AUSTRALIA
Quilpie
Charleville
Toowoomba
Cunnamulla
Warwick
Brisbane
OCEAN
Norfolk I. (Aust.)

Kalgoorlie-Boulder
Bourke
NEW SOUTH WALES
Lord Howe I. (Aust.)
Kermadec Is. (N.Z.)

Perth
Fremantle
Esperance
Port Pirie
Broken Hill
Mildura
A.C.T.
Newcastle
Sydney
Canberra
Tasman Sea
North I.
NEW ZEALAND

Albany
Great Australian Bight
Adelaide
VICTORIA
Ballarat
Geelong
Melbourne
King I.
Bass Str.
Launceston
Auckland
New Plymouth
Hamilton
Napier

SOUTHERN OCEAN
TASMANIA
Hobart
South I.
Greymouth
Nelson
Wellington
Christchurch
Dunedin
Invercargill
Chatham Is. (N.Z.)

Projection: Bonne
90 East from Greenwich 100
West from Greenwich
COPYRIGHT PHILIPS

Canberra Capital Cities

1:6 000 000

50   0   50   100   150   200 km
50   0   50   100   150 miles

FIJI a
on same scale

178 E   Kia   Udo Pt.   Ringgold Is.
Great Sea Reef   Naviaivi Bay   Rabi   *PACIFIC*
Yaqaga   Yadua   Buca   *OCEAN*
Yasawa Group   **Vanua Levu** ▲1031   Savusavu   Samoarna   Qamea
Yasawa   Nabouwalu   Savusavu Bay   Somosomo   **Taveuni**   Naitaba
Viwa   Naviti   Nacula   ▲1323   Rakiraki   Lawaki   Vanua Balavu
Vomo   Tavua   *Bligh Water*   Levuka Wakaya   Northern   *Lau*
Mananuca Group   Navai   **Viti Levu**   Korovou   **Ovalau**   Batiki Sawaleke   Lau   Vatu Vara   Mago   *Group*
Lautoka Malolo   Keiyasi   Yunidevo   Nausori   Nairai   Cicia
Sigatoka   Korolevu   **Suva**   Gau   *KORO*   Vanua Vatu   Lakeba   Oneata Moce
Vatulele   Beqa   *SEA*   Nayau   *Lakeba Passage*   Tubou   Moala   Southern   Ogea
FIJI   Yanuca   **Kadavu**   Totoya   *Lau*   Yagasa   Ogea Driki
Vatukoula   Vunisea   Matuku   *Group*   Cluster
178 E   East from Greenwich   180   West from Greenwich

SAMOA   Asau   Safune
Savai'i   Safotu   Saleilologa   *PACIFIC OCEAN*
▲1858   Sapapali'i   Apia   Falefa
Taga   Mulifanua   **AMERICAN SAMOA** (U.S.A.)
Manono   Falelatai   Siumu   Ofu   Olosega   Ta'u
OLE PUPU PU'E   **Upolu**   Tutuila   Pago Pago   Manu'a Is.
Safata Bay   Leone   Vaitogi   *AMERICAN SAMOA*

SAMOAN ISLANDS b
on same scale
172 W   West from Greenwich

TONGA c
on same scale

174 W   Fonualei   Toku
PACIFIC OCEAN   Vava'u   Neiafu
Late   Vava'u Group   Home Reef
Disney Reef
Ofolanga   Ha'ano
Tofua   Kao   Foa   Ha'apai
Lifuka   Group   Uiha
Fonuafo'ou   Nomuka   Oto Tolu   Group
Hunga Ha'apai   Nomuka Group   Mango   Tonumea
TONGA
Nuku'alofa   **Tongatapu**
Tongatapu Group   Eua
West from Greenwich

North Island

C. Reinga   North C.
C. Maria van Diemen   Ranguunu B.
Houhora Heads   Mangonui   Whangaroa Harb.
Ahipara B.   Okaihau   B. of Islands   C. Brett
Kaitaia   Waitangi
Tauroa Pt.   Rawene   Kaikohe
Hokianga Harbour   Kaikohe   Hikurangi
Waipoua Forest   **Whangarei**   Whangarei Harb.
Dargaville   Waipu   Bream Hd.   Bream B.   Little Barrier I.
Kaipara Harbour   Helensville   Hauraki Gulf   Great Barrier I.
Warkworth   C. Rodney   C. Colville   Cuvier I.
Takapuna   Coromandel   Whitianga
Manukau   **AUCKLAND**   Whangamata   Mayor I.
Waiuku   Papakura   Thames   Waihi   Tauranga Harb.
Pukekohe   Paeroa   **Tauranga**   *Bay of Plenty*   Whakaari (White I.)
Mercer   Waihi   Te Puke   *Runaway*
Waikato   Morrinsville   Whakatane   East C.
Hamilton   Te Aroha   Kawerau   Opotiki   Raukumara Ra.
Raglan   Cambridge   Putaruru   **Rotorua**   L. Rotorua   Te Kaha   ▲1752 Hikurangi
Kawhia Harbour   Te Awamutu   Kinleith   Matata   Waipiro
Waitomo   Otorohanga   Tokoroa   **UREWERA**   Motu   Tolaga Bay
Caves   Te Kuiti   Mangakino   Taupo   Waikaremoana   Ormond
Mokau   Ongarue   L. Taupo   Ruatahuna   **Gisborne**
North Taranaki Bight   Taumarunui   Rangitaiki   Nuhaka   Poverty Bay
New Plymouth   Waitara   **WHANGANUI**   Turangi   Kaimanawa Mts.   Wairoa   Waikokopu
Inglewood   Whangamomona   Taihape   Tarawera   Mahia Pen.
Mt. Taranaki or Mt. Egmont   **TONGARIRO** ▲2797
C. Egmont ▲2518   Ohakune   Waiouru   *Bay*   Hawke Bay
Opunake   Kapuni   Raetihi   *View*   **Napier**
Stratford   Eltham   Ruahine Ra.   C. Kidnappers
Hawera   Waverley   Hunterville   **Hastings**
South Taranaki Bight   Patea   Marton   Halcombe   Feilding   Waipawa
Wanganui   Bulls   Woodville   Waipukurau
Palmerston North   Dannevirke   Pahiatua
Foxton   Shannon   Levin   Eketahuna   C. Turnagain
Paraparaumu   Kapiti I.   Masterton
Otaki   Pelorus   Carterton
Upper Hutt   Featherston   Greytown   Martinborough   Wairarapa
Petone   **Lower Hutt**
Wellington   Eastbourne   C. Palliser

South Island

C. Farewell   Golden B.   D'Urville I.
Collingwood   **ABEL TASMAN**   Tasman B.
KAHURANGI   Takaka   Tasman Mts.   Motueka   Picton
Karamea   **Tasman Mts.**   **Nelson**   Havelock
Karamea Bight   Tadmor   Richmond   Wakefield   Blenheim
Seddonville   **Granity**   Murchison   **NELSON LAKES**   Renwick   Seddon
Westport   Lyell   Inangahua   Awatere   Ward
PAPAROA   Murchison   Mt. Travers ▲2337   ▲2885 Tapuae-o-Uenuku
Punakaiki   Reefton   Hanmer   **Spenser Mts.**   Clarence
Blackball   Grey   **Spenser Mts.**   Springs   Kaikoura
Runanga   Stillwater   Waiau
Greymouth   Hanmer Springs
Kumara   L. Brunner   Culverden
Hokitika   Waikari   Hurunui
Ross   **ARTHUR'S PASS**   Amberley   Pegasus Bay
Arthur's Pass   Oxford   Rangiora
Abut Hd.   Waimakariri   Kaiapoi   New Brighton
Coleridge   Springfield   **Christchurch**   *PACIFIC*
WESTLAND   Whitecliffs   Riccarton   Lyttelton   *OCEAN*
Westland Bight   Methven   Staveley   Lincoln   Banks Pen.
Mt. Cook   **Aoraki**   Canterbury Plains   Lake Ellesmere   Akaroa
▲3753   Mount Cook   Rakaia   Southbridge   Ellesmere
Southern Alps (Tiritiri o te Moana)   Tekapo   Ashburton   Rakaia   L. Ellesmere   Banks Pen.
Jackson B.   Okuru   Haast   MT. COOK   Ashburton Bight
MOUNT ASPIRING   Mt. Aspiring ▲3033   Fairlie   **Timaru**
Milford Sd.   Earnslaw   L. Wanaka   Pukaki   St. Andrews
Sutherland Falls ▲2819   Ohau   **Timaru**
Bligh Sound   Milford Sound   Wanaka   Twizel   Waimate
George Sound   **Queenstown**   Arrowtown   Kurow   Oamaru
Secretary I.   Cromwell   **Maheno**   Hampden
Doubtful Sd.   **FIORDLAND**   L. Kingston   Clyde   Naseby   Dunback
Breaksea Sd.   Manapouri   Alexandra   **Palmerston**
Resolution I.   L. Manapouri   Mossburn   Roxburgh   Waikouaiti
Dusky Sd.   **Southland**   Lumsden   Waipiata   Port Chalmers
Te Waewae Bay   Nightcaps   Lawrence   Mahinerangi   **Dunedin**
Orepuki   Winton   Milton   C. Saunders
Clifden   Tuatapere   Gore   Balclutha   Otago Harbour
Hedgehope   Mataura   Kaitangata
Riverton   **Invercargill**   Owaka
Invercargill   Tokanui   Nugget Pt.
Bluff   Foveaux Str.   Ruapuke I.
Solander I.   Halfmoon Bay
RAKIURA   Stewart I. (Rakiura)
South West C.   Port Pegasus

Projection: Conical with two standard parallels
166   168   East from Greenwich   170   172

TAHITI & MOOREA
1:1 000 000

Pte. Aroa
B. de Matavai   Pte. Vénus
Papetoai   Paopao   Mahina
Papeete   Arue   Papenoo   Tiarei
Pirae   **Tahiti** (France)
Mt. Tohiea ▲1207   Faaa   Hitiaa
Moorea (France)   Afareaitu   Mt. Aorai ▲2066   ▲ Mt. Orohena 2241
Haapiti   Pte. Nuupere   Faaone   Lac Vaihiria
Punaauia   Mt. Tetufera ▲1799   **Faaone**
PACIFIC   Paea   Isthme de Taravao
OCEAN   Paea   Afaahiti   Pte. Tatutaa
Maraa   Papara   Taravao
Atimaono   Mataiea   Vairao   ▲ Mt. Rooniu 1332
Pueu   Tautira
Teahupoo   **Presqu'île de Taiarapu**

149°45'W   149°30'W   West from Greenwich   149°15'W

COPYRIGHT PHILIP'S

10   0   10 km
10   0   10 miles
1:1 000 000

ft   m
9000   3000
6000   2000
3000   1000
1200   400
600   200
0   0
200   600
2000   6000
4000   12 000
6000   18 000
m   ft

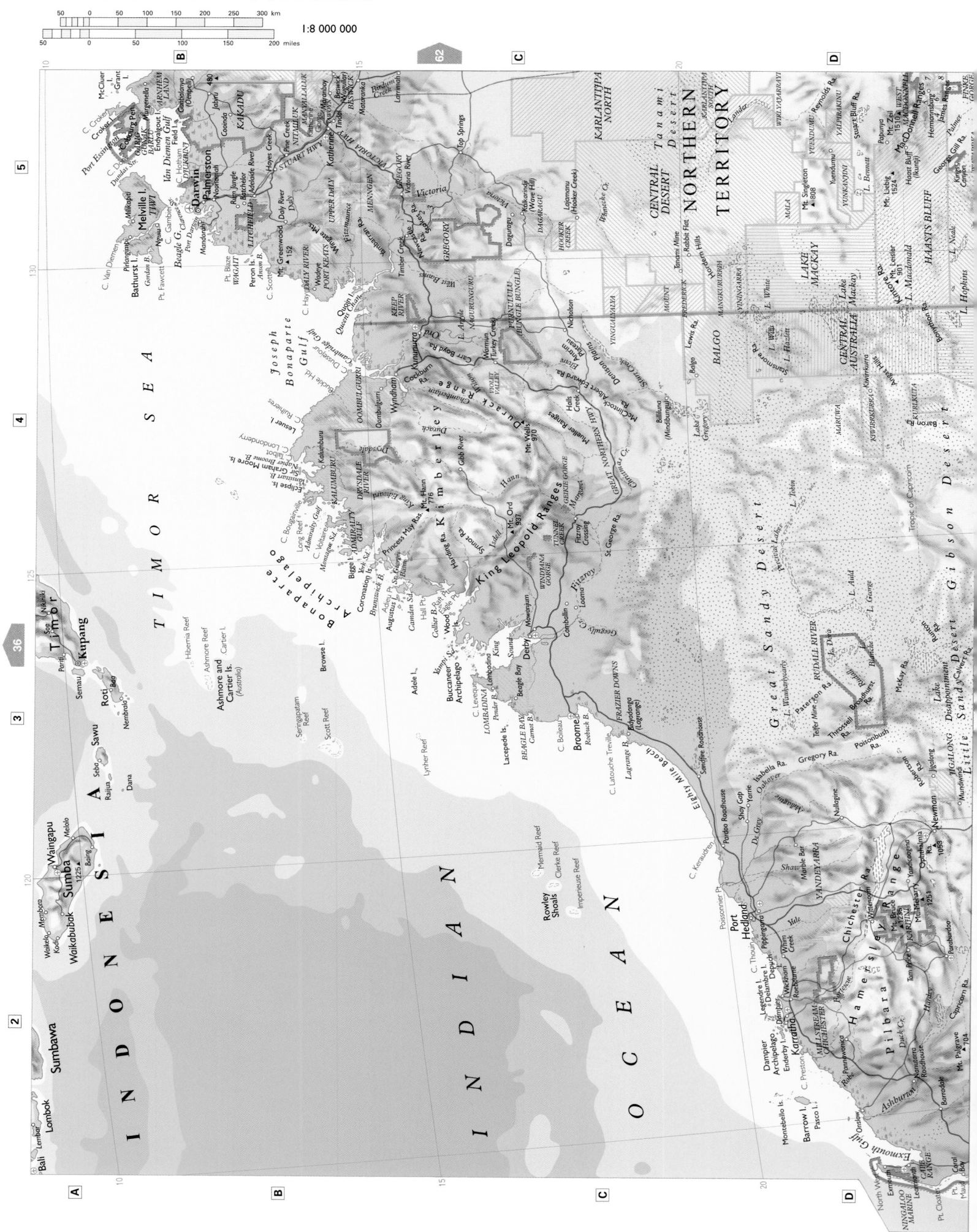

50 0 50 100 150 200 250 300 km

1:8 000 000

50 0 50 100 150 200 miles

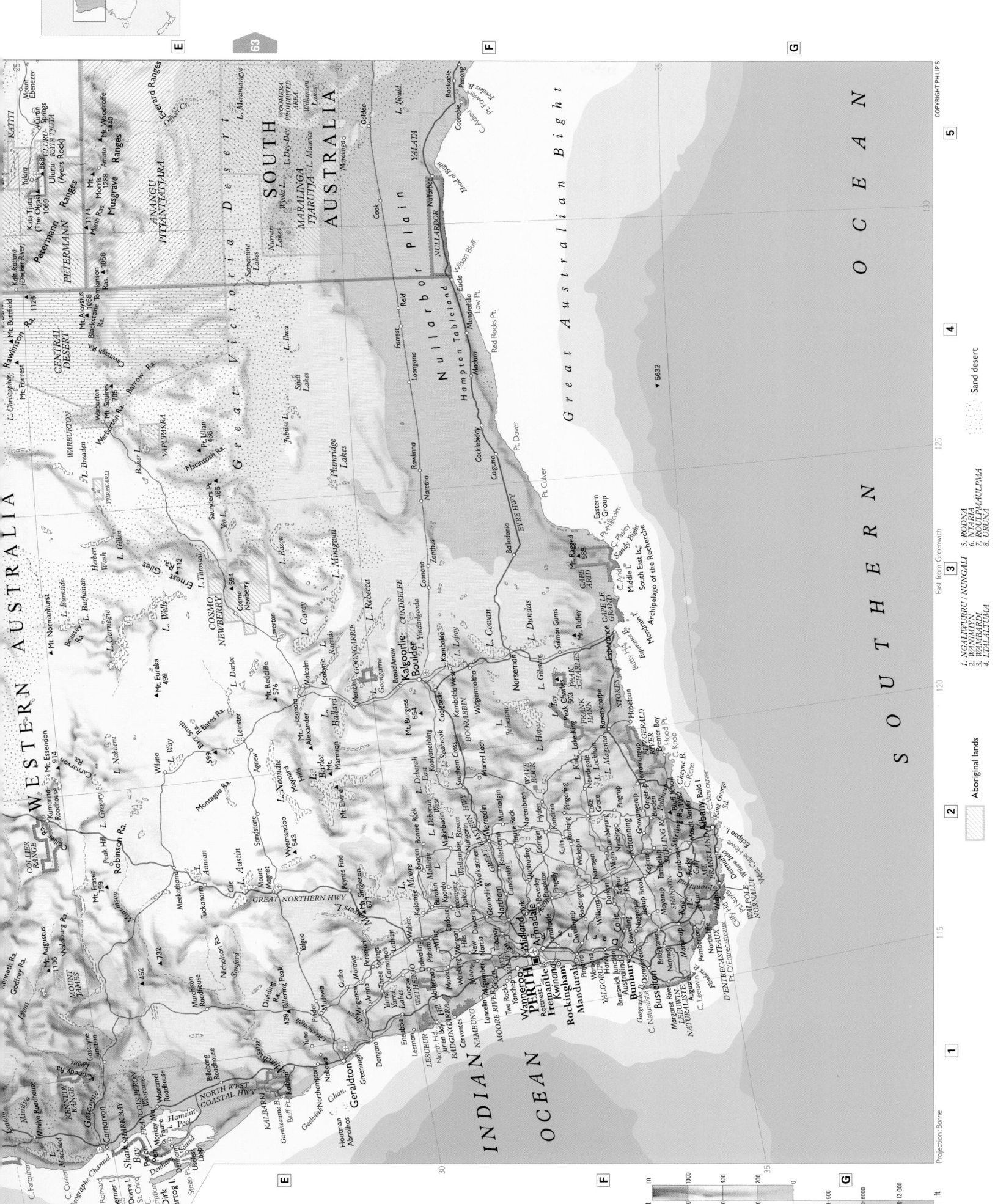

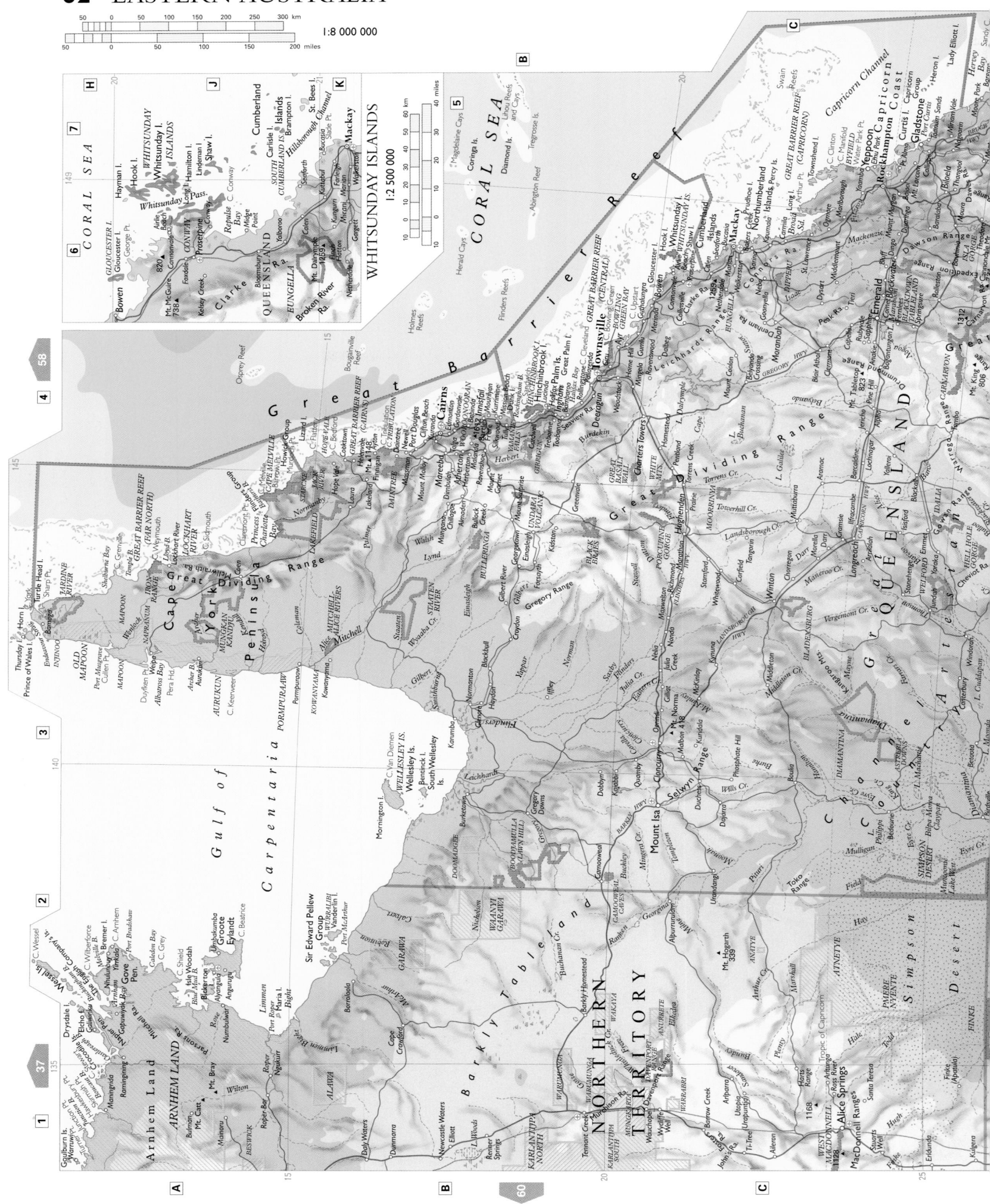

1:8 000 000

WHITSUNDAY ISLANDS
1:2 500 000

Aboriginal lands

Sand desert

East from Greenwich

on same scale

Projection: Bonne

TASMAN SEA

TASMANIA

NEW SOUTH WALES

SOUTH AUSTRALIA

VICTORIA

BRISBANE

SYDNEY

MELBOURNE

ADELAIDE

Canberra

6

7 150
8 160
9 170
10 180

1 90
2 100
3 110
4 120
5 140

B

RUSSIA

Moskva
Volga
Yekaterinburg
Tomsk
Novosibirsk
Ob'
Lena
Irkutsk
Oz. Baykal
Chita
Blagoveshchensk
Amur
Sea of Okhotsk
Okhotsk
Poluostrov Kamchatka
Shirshov Ridge
Komandorskiye Ostrova (Russia)
Near Is. (U.S.A.)
Andreanof Is. (U.S.A.)
Aleutian Basin
Bering Sea

KAZAKHSTAN
Astana (Aqmola)
Semey
Ulaanbaatar
Sakhalin
La Pérouse Str.
Kuril'skiye Ostrova (Russia)
Petropavlovsk-Kamchatskiy
7822
Aleutians
Aleutian Trench

Aral Sea
Balqash Köl
Khabarovsk
Kuril-Kamchatka Trench
10,542
Chinook Trough

C

Toshkent
Almaty
Ürümqi
MONGOLIA
Changchun
Harbin
Vladivostok
Hakodate
Sapporo
Emperor Trough
Northwest
Emperor Seamount Chain

KYRGYZSTAN
Altai
Shenyang
Sea of Japan
Pacific

D

TAJIKISTAN
Kabul
Srinagar
AFGHANISTAN
PAKISTAN
Lahore
Delhi
Kanpur
CHINA
Beijing
Tianjin
Taiyuan
Lanzhou
Kunlun Shan
XIZANG
Xi'an
Huang He
NORTH KOREA
Dalian
Qingdao
SOUTH KOREA
Seoul
Nagoya
Kyōto
Osaka
Kitakyūshū
Fuji-San 3776
Sendai
Tōkyō
Yokohama
JAPAN
Shatsky Rise
Midway Is. (U.S.A.)
Howa

Himalaya
8850
Mt Everest
Lhasa
NEPAL
Chongqing
Chang J.
Wuhan
Nanjing
Hangzhou
Shanghai
Shikoku
Kyūshū
Yellow Sea
Japan Trench
10,554
Lisianski I. (U.S.A.)

E

INDIA
Ganga
Brahmaputra
BANGLADESH
Kolkata (Calcutta)
Dhaka
Kanpur
Changsha
Kunming
Fuzhou
Taipei
East China Sea
Okinawa
Ryūkyū-rettō (Japan)
Iwo-Jima (Japan)
Ogasawara Gunto (Japan)
Minami-Tori-Shima (Japan)
Kazan-Rettō (Japan)
Mid-Pacific Mount

Hyderabad
Mandalay
BURMA
Irrawaddy
Guangzhou
Macau
Hong Kong
TAIWAN
Hanoi
Hainan
Philippine Sea
Kyushu-Palau Ridge
Shichito-Ozima-Ridge
Wake I. (U.S.A.)
P A

Bay of Bengal
Rangoon
Chennai (Madras)
Andaman Is. (India)
THAILAND
Bangkok
LAOS
Luzon
Paracel Is.
C. Engano
Manila
West Mariana Basin
NORTHERN MARIANAS (U.S.A.)
East Mariana Basin
MARSHALL IS.
Bikini Atoll

F

SRI LANKA
Nicobar Is. (India)
Phnom Penh
CAMBODIA
Thanh Pho Ho Chi Minh
VIETNAM
Mekong
South China Sea
G. of Thailand
Mindoro
Palawan
Samar
10,497
PHILIPPINES
Saipan
Tinian
GUAM (U.S.A.)
Challenger Deep 11,022
Mariana Trench
Micronesia
Enewetak Atoll
Ratak Chain
Ralik Chain
Kwajalein
Majuro

G

Colombo
Kuala Lumpur
MALAYSIA
PEN. MALAYSIA
Singapore
Sumatera
Sunda Ridge
Sulu Sea
Mindanao
Davao
Mindanao Trench
Celebes Sea
BRUNEI
SABAH
SARAWAK
4101
Sea
Koror
PALAU
Yap
Caroline Is.
Chuuk
FED. STATES OF MICRONESIA
West Caroline Basin
East Caroline Basin
Eauripik Rise
Pohnpei
Palikir
Jaluit I.
Melanesian Basin
Butaritari
Tarawa
Gilbert Is.
Howland I. (U.S.A.)
Baker I. (U.S.A.)
Pacific
Central

H

INDONESIA
Borneo
Palembang
Java Sea
Jakarta
Jawa
Surabaya
Sunda Island
Bali
Sumbawa
Flores
Sumba
Sulawesi
Ujung Pandang
Buru
Seram
Maluku
Halmahera
Banda Sea
Flores Sea
Java Trench
Selat Sunda
Puncak Jaya 5029
PAPUA
7440
Dili
EAST TIMOR
Timor
Arafura Sea
New Guinea
Lae
Admiralty Is.
Bismarck Arch.
New Ireland
PAPUA NEW GUINEA
New Britain
Rabaul
8940
Bougainville
Port Moresby
Solomon Rise
Melanesia
SOLOMON IS.
NAURU
Banaba
Phoenix Is.
Abariringa Enderbury
KIRIBATI
O
Pacific

Cocos Is. (Austral.)
Christmas I. (Austral.)
North Australian Basin
C. Arnhem
C. York
Torres Strait
Louisiade Arch.
Honiara
Guadalcanal
Santa Cruz I. 9165
Fongafale
TUVALU
Rotuma
Is. Wallis & Futuna (Fr.)
SAMOA
Apia
Tokelau I. (N.Z.)

L

INDIAN
Wharton Basin
North West C.
Broome
Exmouth Plateau
Darwin
Gulf of Carpentaria
Cairns
Townsville
Great Barrier Reef
Coral Sea Basin
Coral Sea
VANUATU
Île Chesterfield
Espiritu Santo
Port Vila
West Fiji Basin
Vanua Levu
Viti Levu
Suva
FIJI
7570
Nuku'alofa
TONGA
Tonga Trench
10,822

Ninety East Ridge
Mount Isa
Alice Springs
AUSTRALIA
L. Eyre
Rockhampton
NEW CALEDONIA (Fr.)
Nouméa
Îs. Loyauté
Middleton Basin
Brisbane
Norfolk Ridge
South Fiji Basin
Lord Howe Rise

OCEAN
Geraldton
Broken Ridge
Perth Basin
Naturaliste Plateau
Perth
Albany
Great Australian Bight
Adelaide
Murray
Mt. Kosciuszko 2230
Canberra
Sydney
Lord Howe I. (Austral.)
Norfolk I. (Austral.)
Kermadec Is. (N.Z.)
Kermadec Trench 10,047

M

Nouvelle Amsterdam (Fr.)
I. St. Paul (Fr.)
Mid-Indian Ridge
Melbourne
Bass Str.
Tasmania
Hobart
East Tasman Plateau
Tasman Sea
Aoraki Mt. Cook 3753
NEW ZEALAND
Auckland
Cook Strait
Wellington
Christchurch
Chatham Rise
Chatham Is. (N.Z.)
Louisville Ridge

SOUTHERN
Is. Crozet (Fr.)
Kerguelen (Fr.)
South Tasman Rise
South Tasman Basin
Dunedin
Invercargill
Bounty Is. (N.Z.)
Bounty Trough

N

Heard I. (Austral.)
OCEAN
Macquarie I. (Austral.)
Antipodes Is. (N.Z.)
Auckland Is. (N.Z.)
Campbell I. (N.Z.)
Campbell Plateau

ft m
12 000 4000
9000 3000
6000 2000
3000 1000
1500 500
600 200
0 0
200 600
1000 3000
2000 6000
4000 12 000
6000 18 000
8000 24 000
m ft

Projection: Mollweide's Homolographic

East from Greenwich

1 90
2 100
3 110
4 120
5 140
6
7 150
8 160
9 170
10 180

11 12 13 14
160 150 140 130
15
16 120 17 110 18 100 19 90 20 80 70 60 50 40 30 20

Arctic Circle

ALASKA
(U.S.A.)
Anchorage
5959

Bristol Bay
Juneau
Gulf of Alaska

R O C K Y

C A N A D A

Edmonton
L. Winnipeg
Newfoundland

B

Calgary
Winnipeg

Tufts
Abyssal
Plain

Vancouver
Vancouver I.
Victoria
Regina
St. Lawrence
Québec
St. John's

50
NORTH

C

Seattle
Portland
Boise

Snake

L. Superior
Montréal
Ottawa
Boston

Minneapolis
Missouri
L. Michigan
L. Huron
Toronto
Detroit
Buffalo
L. Ontario
L. Erie
Pittsburgh
New York
Philadelphia

40

ATLANTIC

D

Northeast
C. Mendocino
Mendocino Fracture Zone

Sacramento
San Francisco
Salt Lake City
Denver
Kansas City
St. Louis
Cincinnati
Baltimore
Washington D.C.

6741
Murray Fracture Zone
4418
UNITED STATES
Oklahoma City
Memphis
Atlanta
C. Hatteras

Pacific
Los Angeles
San Diego
Phoenix
Dallas
Houston
Jacksonville
Bermuda
(U.K.)

Ciudad Juárez
New Orleans
Tampa
Sargasso Sea

30

OCEAN

E

Molokai Fracture Zone
Golfo de California
San Antonio
Monterrey
Gulf of Mexico
Miami
BAHAMAS
West Indies

Tropic of Cancer
Basin
C. San Lucas
La Habana
CUBA
Florida Str.

Honolulu
Maui
Kauai
Oahu
HAWAIIAN IS.
(U.S.A.)
4205
Hilo
Hawaii
Guadalupe
(Mex.)
C. San Lucas
Guadalajara
Mérida
Canal de Yucatán
9200
HAITI
DOMINICAN REP.
Leeward Is.

20

F

Clarion Fracture Zone
Is. Revilla Gigedo
(Mex.)
Mexico
Puebla
7680
JAMAICA
Kingston
PUERTO RICO
(U.S.A.)

Johnston I.
(U.S.A.)
Acapulco
BELIZE
GUATEMALA
HONDURAS
Guatemala
Caribbean Sea
BARBADOS
Windward Is.

C I F I C
Middle America Trench
6662
San Salvador
EL SALVADOR
NICARAGUA
Managua
Barranquilla
Maracaibo

North West Christmas Ridge
I. Clipperton
(Fr.)
Guatemala Basin
COSTA RICA
San José
Colón
Panamá
PANAMA
Caracas
VENEZUELA

Palmyra I.
(U.S.A.)
Clipperton Fracture Zone
Cocos Ridge
I. del Coco
(Costa Rica)
Panama Basin
Medellín
Bogotá
G

Cooper Ridge
I. de Malpelo
(Colombia)
Cali
COLOMBIA

Teraina
Tabuaeran
Kiritimati

Equator
Galápagos Fracture Zone
Galápagos
(Ecuador)
Carnegie Ridge
Quito
ECUADOR

O C E A N
Jarvis I.
(U.S.A.)
Guayaquil
Iquitos
Amazonas

KIRIBATI
C. Paliñas
BRAZIL
H

Malden I.
Starbuck I.

Penrhyn
(Tongareva)
Trujillo
6369

Manihiki
Pukapuka
Manihiki
Vostok I.
Caroline I.
(Millennium I.)
Flint I.
Nuku Hiva
Îs. Marquises
Hiva Oa
Marquesas Fracture Zone
PERU
Lima
Cuzco
L. Titicaca
Nevado Ancohuma
6550

SAMOA
(U.S.A.)
Plateau
Yupanqui Basin
Mendaña
Fracture Zone
Arequipa
6866
La Paz

Suwarrow Is.
Îs. de la Société
Rangiroa
Bora Bora
Huahine
Îs. Tuamotu
Peru-Chile
Arica
BOLIVIA
J

Cook Is.
(N.Z.)
Raiatéa
Papeete
Tahiti
Iquique
Chile

Niue
(N.Z.)
Aitutaki
Atiu
FRENCH POLYNESIA
Îs. Gambier
Peru Basin
Antofagasta
PARAGUAY

Rarotonga
Mururoa
Tropic of Capricorn
Asunción

Mangaia
Îs. Tubuaï
Oeno I.
Henderson I.
Sala y Gómez Ridge
San Felix
(Chile)
8050
Trench
San Miguel de Tucumán
K

Pitcairn I.
(U.K.)
Ducie I.
Easter Fracture Zone
Sala-y-Gómez
(Chile)
San Ambrosio
(Chile)
Porto Alegre

Rapa
I. de Pascua
(Chile)
URUGUAY

Roggeveen Basin
Arch. de Juan Fernández
(Chile)
Córdoba
Aconcagua
6962
Rosario
L

Southwest
Challenger Fracture Zone
Valparaíso
Santiago
Buenos Aires
Montevideo
Río de la Plata

Pacific
Concepción
ARGENTINA
40

SOUTH
M

Basin
Menard Fracture Zone
ATLANTIC

Pacific-Antarctic Ridge
East Pacific Ridge
Chile Rise
OCEAN
6212
50

Southeast
Pacific Basin
Punta Arenas
Est. de Magallanes
Tierra del Fuego
C. de Hornos
Drake Passage
Falkland Is.
(U.K.)
South Georgia
(U.K.)
N

11 12 13 14 15 16 17 18 19 20
160 150 140 130 120 110 100 90 80 70 60 West from Greenwich 40

COPYRIGHT PHILIP'S

100 0   200   400   600   800 1000 1200 1400 km

1:35 000 000

100 0   200   400   600   800 1000 miles

Projection: Bonne

West from Greenwich

COPYRIGHT PHILIP'S

1:35 000 000

100 0 200 400 600 800 1000 1200 1400 km
100 0 200 400 600 800 1000 miles

RUSSIA
Asia
St. Lawrence I.
Bering Strait
Bering
Sea

ARCTIC OCEAN

International Date Line

GREENLAND
(Denmark)

Denmark Strait

ICELAND
Reykjavik

Queen Elizabeth Is.
Ellesmere I.

Beaufort
Sea

Baffin
Bay

Nuuk

ALASKA
(USA)
Yukon
Porcupine
Anchorage
Fairbanks
Kodiak I.
Gulf of Alaska
Juneau
Whitehorse
Juneau

NORTHWEST
Arctic Circle
YUKON
TERRITORY
Mackenzie
Great Bear
L.
Victoria I.

Baffin Island

Davis Strait

St. John's

TERRITORIES
Yellowknife
Great
Slave L.
Back
Dubawnt

NUNAVUT

Iqaluit

Hudson Strait

Skeena
BRITISH
COLUMBIA
Peace
Athabasca
CANADA
Churchill
Nelson
Hudson
Bay

NEWFOUNDLAND &
LABRADOR

Fraser
ALBERTA
Edmonton
Athabasca
SASKATCHEWAN
MANITOBA
L.
Winnipeg
Eastmain
QUÉBEC
St. Lawrence

St-Pierre
et Miquelon
(Fr.)

Victoria
Vancouver
WASHINGTON
Olympia
Seattle
Calgary
Saskatchewan
Regina
Winnipeg
ONTARIO
Québec
Montréal
PRINCE
EDWARD
I.
Charlottetown
NEW
BRUNSWICK
Fredericton
NOVA
SCOTIA
Halifax

Portland
Salem
OREGON
Columbia
Helena
MONTANA
Missouri
NORTH
DAKOTA
Bismarck
MINNESOTA
L. Superior
Ottawa
Toronto
L. Huron
L. Ontario
Buffalo
MAINE
Augusta
Concord
N.H.
Boston
MASS.
Providence

Boise
IDAHO
Snake
WYOMING
SOUTH
DAKOTA
Minneapolis-
St. Paul
WISCONSIN
Madison
MICHIGAN
Lansing
L. Michigan
Milwaukee
Detroit
Cleveland
Toledo
PA.
Erie
NEW YORK
Pittsburgh
Hartford
CONN.
NEW YORK
N.J.
PHILADELPHIA

Sacramento
Carson
City
Salt Lake
City
NEBRASKA
IOWA
CHICAGO
ILLINOIS
Indianapolis
INDIANA
Columbus
OHIO
Cincinnati
W.V.
Baltimore
MD.
DE.
Washington D.C.
Richmond
VIRGINIA

SAN FRANCISCO
San Jose
CALIFORNIA
NEVADA
UTAH
Denver
COLORADO
Lincoln
UNITED STATES
Kansas City
Topeka
St.
Louis
MISSOURI
Springfield
KENTUCKY
Nashville
TENNESSEE
NORTH
CAROLINA
Raleigh
Charlotte

Las Vegas
KANSAS
ARKANSAS
Memphis
Columbia
SOUTH
CAROLINA
Charleston

LOS ANGELES
Santa Fe
Albuquerque
ARIZONA
NEW MEXICO
OKLAHOMA
Oklahoma
City
Little Rock
Birmingham
MISSISSIPPI
ALABAMA
GEORGIA
Atlanta
Jacksonville

San Diego
Tijuana
Mexicali
Phoenix
Tucson
Dallas-
Ft. Worth
Jackson
Montgomery

El Paso
Colorado
TEXAS
Austin
Houston
Baton
Rouge
LOUISIANA
New
Orleans
Tallahassee
FLORIDA
Orlando

Guadalupe
(Mex.)
PACIFIC
OCEAN
Ciudad Juárez
Rio Grande
San Antonio
Tampa-
St. Petersburg
Miami
Nassau
BAHAMAS

NORTH
ATLANTIC
OCEAN

Bermuda
(U.K.)

Tropic of Cancer
Hermosillo
Culiacán
MEXICO
Monterrey
Torreón
Gulf of Mexico
Havana
CUBA
Florida Str.

Turks & Caicos Is.
(U.K.)

San Luis Potosí
Cayman Is.
(U.K.)
HAITI
Port-au-
Prince
DOMINICAN
REP.
Santo
Domingo
San Juan
PUERTO
RICO
(U.S.A.)

Revilla Gigedo Is.
(Mex.)
León
Guadalajara
MÉXICO
Toluca
Puebla
Mérida
JAMAICA
Kingston

Acapulco
BELIZE
Belmopan
Caribbean Sea

Maracaibo
VENEZUELA

GUATEMALA
Guatemala
HONDURAS
Tegucigalpa
Barranquilla
San Salvador
EL SALVADOR
NICARAGUA
Managua
L. Nicaragua
COSTA
RICA
San José
PANAMA
Panamá
COLOMBIA
Medellín
South
America

100 0 100 200 300 400 500 600 km
1:15 000 000
100 0 100 200 300 400 miles

Projection : Bonne

NORTHERN CANADA
continuation northwards on same
scale as main map

ARCTIC OCEAN

Sverdrup Islands

Queen Elizabeth Is.

GREENLAND (Denmark)

C. Columbia

Alert

Ellesmere Island

Eureka

Axel Heiberg

Amund Ringnes

Ellef Ringnes

Mackenzie King I.

Brock I.

Borden I.

Prince Patrick I.

Eglinton

Meighen

Meville I.

Cornwall

Grise Fiord

Jones Sound

Devon Island

C. Prince Alfred

Banks Island

McClure Strait

Viscount Melville Sound

Bathurst

Cornwallis I.

Resolute

Wellington Chan.

Lancaster Sound

NUNAVUT

NORTHWEST TERRITORIES

Holman

Victoria Island

M'Clintock Channel

Prince of Wales Island

Prince Somerset Island Albert Pen.

Arctic Bay

Nanisivik

Brodeur Peninsula

Bylot I.

Pond Inlet

Baffin Island

Devon I.

Lancaster Sound

Baffin Bay

Brodeur Peninsula

Arctic Bay

Nanisivik

Borden Pen.

Bylot I.

Pond Inlet

C. Adair

Clyde River

C. Raper

Baffin Island

Home B.

Fury and Hecla Str.

Igloolik

Hall Beach

Melville Peninsula

Prince Charles

Foxe Basin

Qikiqtarjuaq

Dyer

Cumberland Peninsula

Pangnirtung

Hoare B.

C. Mercy

Cumberland Sd.

Foxe Peninsula

Netilling L.

Iqaluit

Hall Peninsula

Meta Incognita Peninsula

Kimmirut

Frobisher Bay

Resolution I.

C. Chidley

Hudson Strait

Akpatok I.

Quaqtaq

Brodeur Peninsula

Simpson Pen.

Committee B.

Rae Isthmus

Repulse Bay

Chesterfield Inlet

NUNAVUT

Southampton I.

Coral Harbour

Coats I.

Mansel I.

Nottingham I.

Salisbury I.

Kingait

Salluit

Ivujivik

Kangiqsujuaq

Cratère du Nouveau Québec 657

Kangirsuk

Arnaud

Ungava Bay

Kangiqsualujjuaq

Hebron

Nain

Hopedale

C. Harrison

Rigolet

Cartwright

NEWFOUNDLAND & LABRADOR

Port Hope Simpson

Belle Isle

Str. of Belle Isle

C. Bauld

St. Anthony

Roes Welcome Sd.

Puvirnituq

Péninsule d'Ungava

L. Payne

Reuilles

Inukjuak

Mélèze

Caniapiscau

Baleine

George

Labrador Sea

Labrador

Smallwood Res.

North West River

Happy Valley-Goose Bay

Schefferville

Petitsikapau L.

Churchill Falls

Churchill

Labrador City

Fermont

Ashuanipi L.

Natashquan

St-Augustin

Baie Verte

Lewisporte

Deer Lake

Grand Falls-Windsor

Gander

Bonavista

Carbonear

St. John's

Newfoundland

Corner Brook

Stephenville

Channel-Port aux Basques

Marystown

Placentia

C. Race

Grand Banks

Hudson Bay

Tatnam

257

Sleeper Is.

King George Is.

Baker's Dozen Is.

Sanikiluaq

Belcher Is.

C. Henrietta Maria

Peawanuck

Winisk

Big Trout L.

Attawapiskat

Attawapiskat

Fort Albany

Albany

Moosonee

Akimiski I.

Charlton I.

Kuujjuarapik

Chisasibi

La Grande

Grande Baleine

Kanaaupscow

Wemindji

Eastmain

Waskaganish

Rupert

Moosonee

L. à l'Eau Claire

Pte. Louis XIV

James Bay

D A

L. Bienville

L. Minto

ONTARIO

St. Joseph

Ekwan

Attawapiskat

Winisk

Severn

Albany

Kenogami

Nakina

Greenstone

Nipigon

L. Nipigon

Marathon

Oba

Hearst

Kapuskasing

Cochrane

Timmins

Chapleau

Wawa

Missinaibi

Mattagami

L. Matagami

Abitibi L.

Amos

Val-d'Or

Rouyn-Noranda

Kirkland Lake

New Liskeard

QUÉBEC

Chibougamau

Mistassini L.

Rés. Gouin

Gagnon

Manicouagan

Mont-Laurier

Rés. Cabonga

Shawinigan

Trois-Rivières

La Tuque

Québec

Lévis

1190

Baie-Comeau

Port-Cartier

Sept-Îles

Havre-St-Pierre

Î. d'Anticosti

320

Gulf of St. Lawrence

Cabot Str.

Ray

C. North

Gaspé

Pén. de Gaspésie

Matane

Rimouski

Rivière-du-Loup

Edmundston

Miramichi

Bathurst

Campbellton

Î.s. de la Madeleine

PR. EDWARD I.

Summerside

Charlottetown

Northumberland Str.

ST-PIERRE et MIQUELON (Fr)

Cape Breton I.

Sydney

Glace Bay

Port Hawkesbury

Antigonish

New Glasgow

NOVA SCOTIA

Truro

Dartmouth

Halifax

Bridgewater

Liverpool

C. Sable

Sable I. (Nova Scotia)

6309

Lake Superior

Thunder Bay

Houghton 183

Ironwood

Marquette

MICHIGAN

Rhinelander

Menominee

Escanaba

Manistique

Petoskey

Traverse City

Cadillac

Lake Michigan

Green Bay

Appleton

Sheboygan

MILWAUKEE

Madison

Racine

Kenosha

Rockford

CHICAGO

Gary

South Bend

ILLINOIS

INDIANA

DETROIT

Windsor

Toledo

CLEVELAND

OHIO

Lake Huron

Georgian Bay

Manitoulin

Sault Ste. Marie

Sault Ste. Marie

Elliot Lake

Sudbury

North Bay

L. Nipissing

Parry Sound

Huntsville

OTTAWA

Hull

Pembroke

Outaouais

Cornwall

MONTRÉAL

Granby

Sherbrooke

St-Hyacinthe

Joliette

Drummondville

Thetford Mines

Woodstock

Fredericton

Saint John

B. of Fundy

Digby

Yarmouth

Kentville

Amherst

Moncton

NEW BRUNSWICK

Grand Falls

MAINE

Bangor

Augusta

Lewiston

Portland

VERMONT

NEW HAMPSHIRE

Montpelier

Concord

Manchester

Lowell

BOSTON

C. Cod

MASS.

Springfield

Hartford

CONN.

Providence

R.I.

New Haven

Bridgeport

NEW YORK

Newark

Allentown

Trenton

PENNSYLVANIA

Scranton

Binghamton

Elmira

Jamestown

Erie

L. Erie

Buffalo

Niagara Falls

Rochester

Syracuse

Albany

NEW YORK

Kingston

Belleville

Owen Sound

Barrie

Peterborough

Oshawa

TORONTO

Hamilton

L. Ontario

London

Kitchener

Sarnia

Flint

Lansing

Saginaw

Grand Rapids

St. Louis

Georgian Bay

Collingwood

Nakina

Kenogami

Wisconsin

Baffin Bay

174

175

177

West from Greenwich

COPYRIGHT PHILIP'S

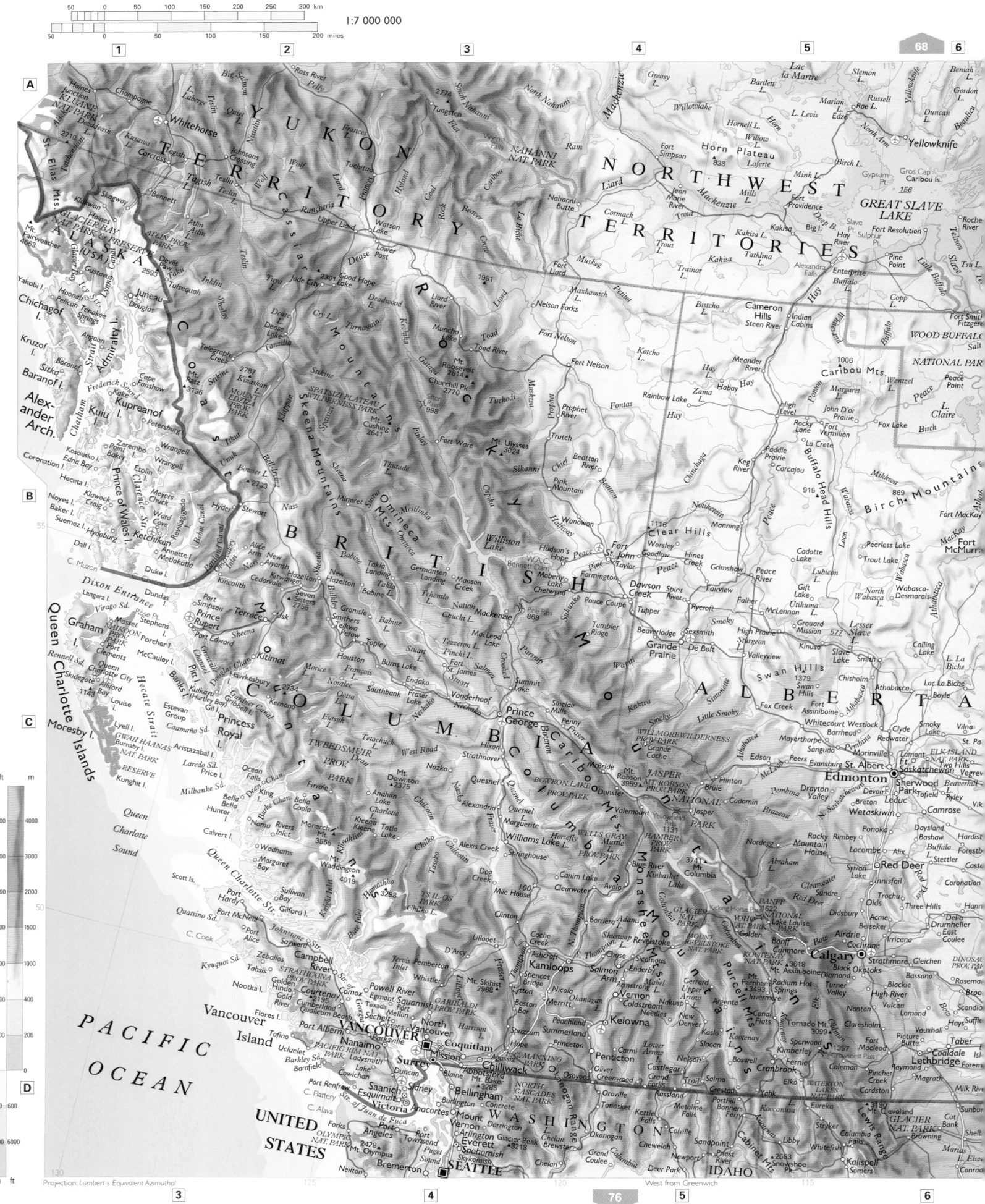

1:7 000 000

PACIFIC OCEAN

UNITED STATES

YUKON TERRITORY

NORTHWEST TERRITORIES

BRITISH COLUMBIA

ALBERTA

ALASKA (USA)

WASHINGTON

IDAHO

Projection: Lambert's Equivalent Azimuthal

West from Greenwich

National Parks

1:7 000 000

Projection: Lambert's Equivalent Azimuthal

100   0   100   200   300   400   500 km
1:12 000 000
100   0   50   100   150   200   250   300   350 miles

| 1 | 2 | 3 | 4 | 68 | 5 | 6 | 7 |

ALASKA
1:30 000 000   a
100   0   100   200   300   400   600 km
100   0   100   200   300   400 miles

Projection: Albers' Equal Area with two standard parallels

HAWAI'I   b
1:10 000 000
50   0   50   100 km
50   0   50   100 miles

West from Greenwich

ft   m
12 000   4000
9000   3000
6000   2000
4500   1500
3000   1000
1200   600
600   200
0   0
200   600
3000   2000
4000   6000
      12 000
m   ft

Tallahassee ⊛   U.S. state capitals

1:6 700 000

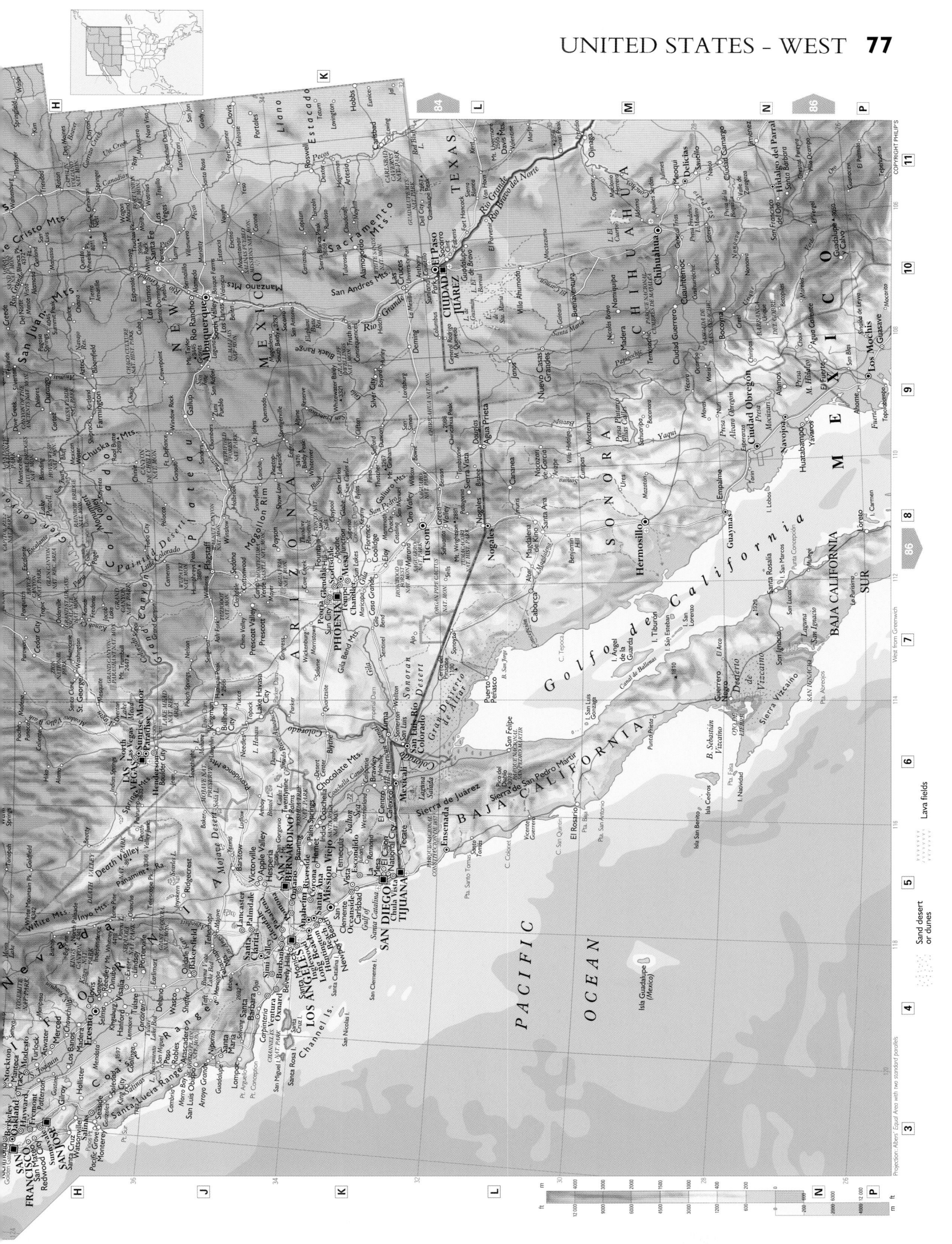

Sand desert or dunes

Lava fields

Projection: Albers Equal Area with two standard parallels

West from Greenwich

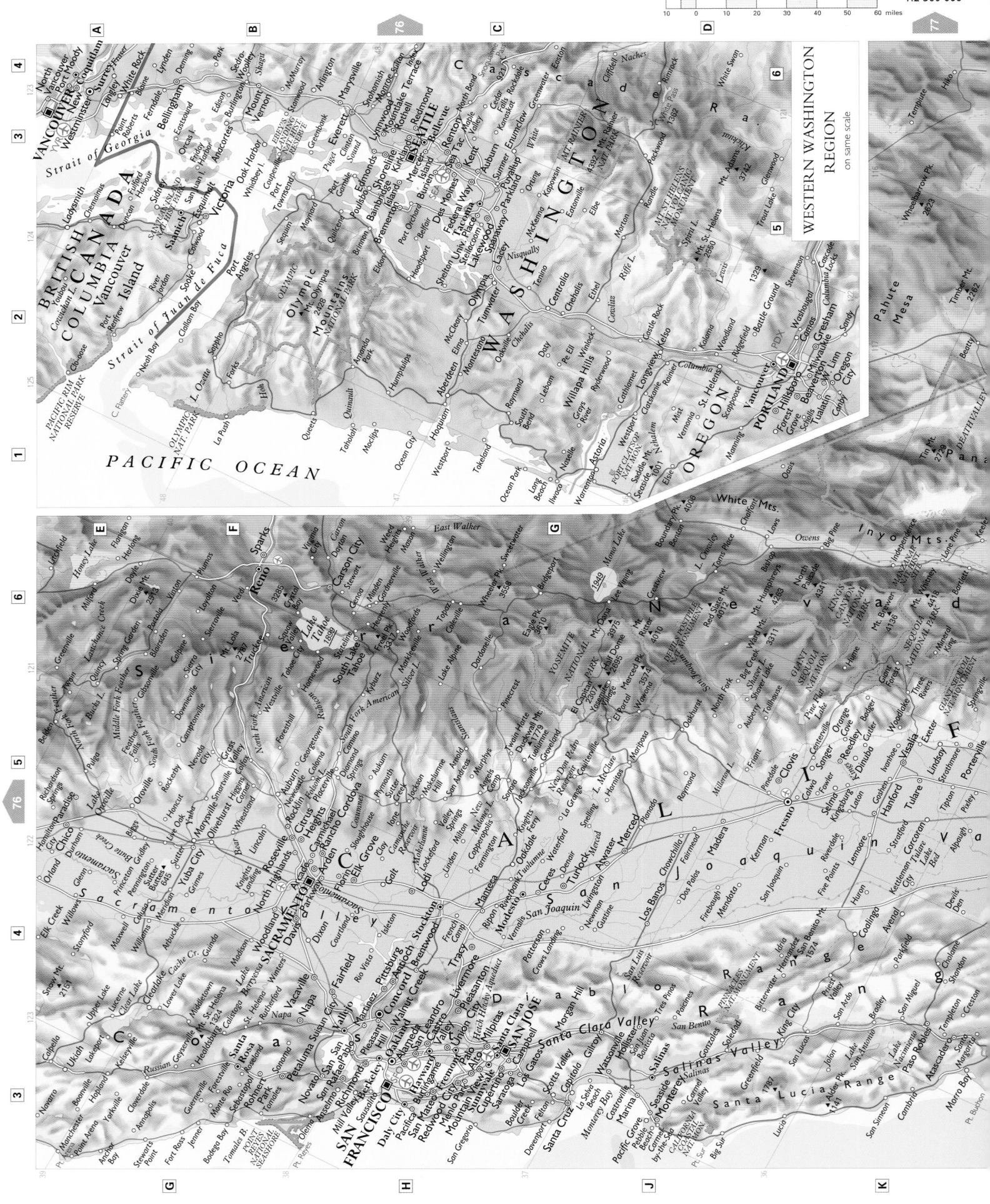

1:2 500 000

WESTERN WASHINGTON REGION
on same scale

PACIFIC OCEAN

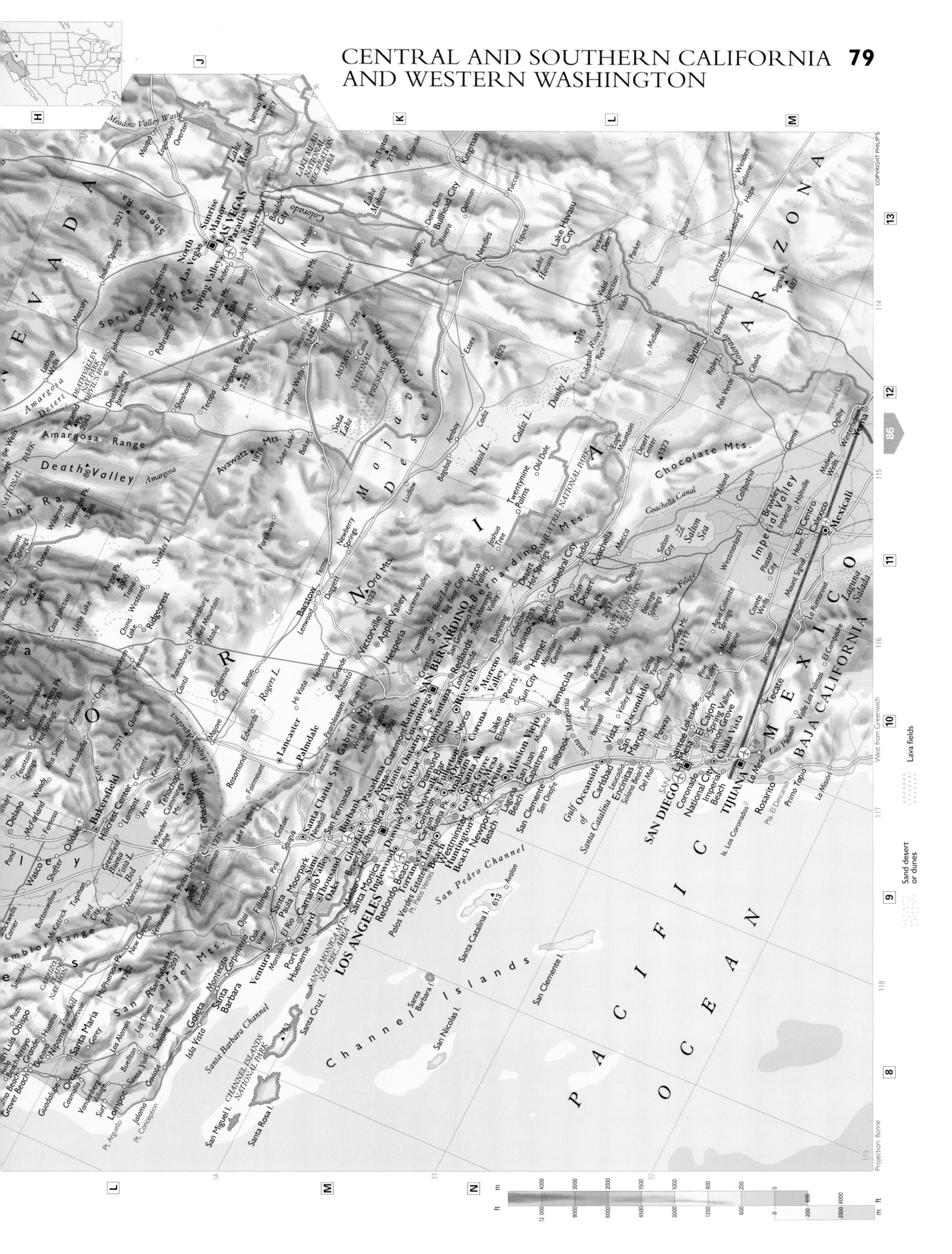

COPYRIGHT PHILIP'S

Projection: Bonne

West from Greenwich

Lava fields

Sand desert
or dunes

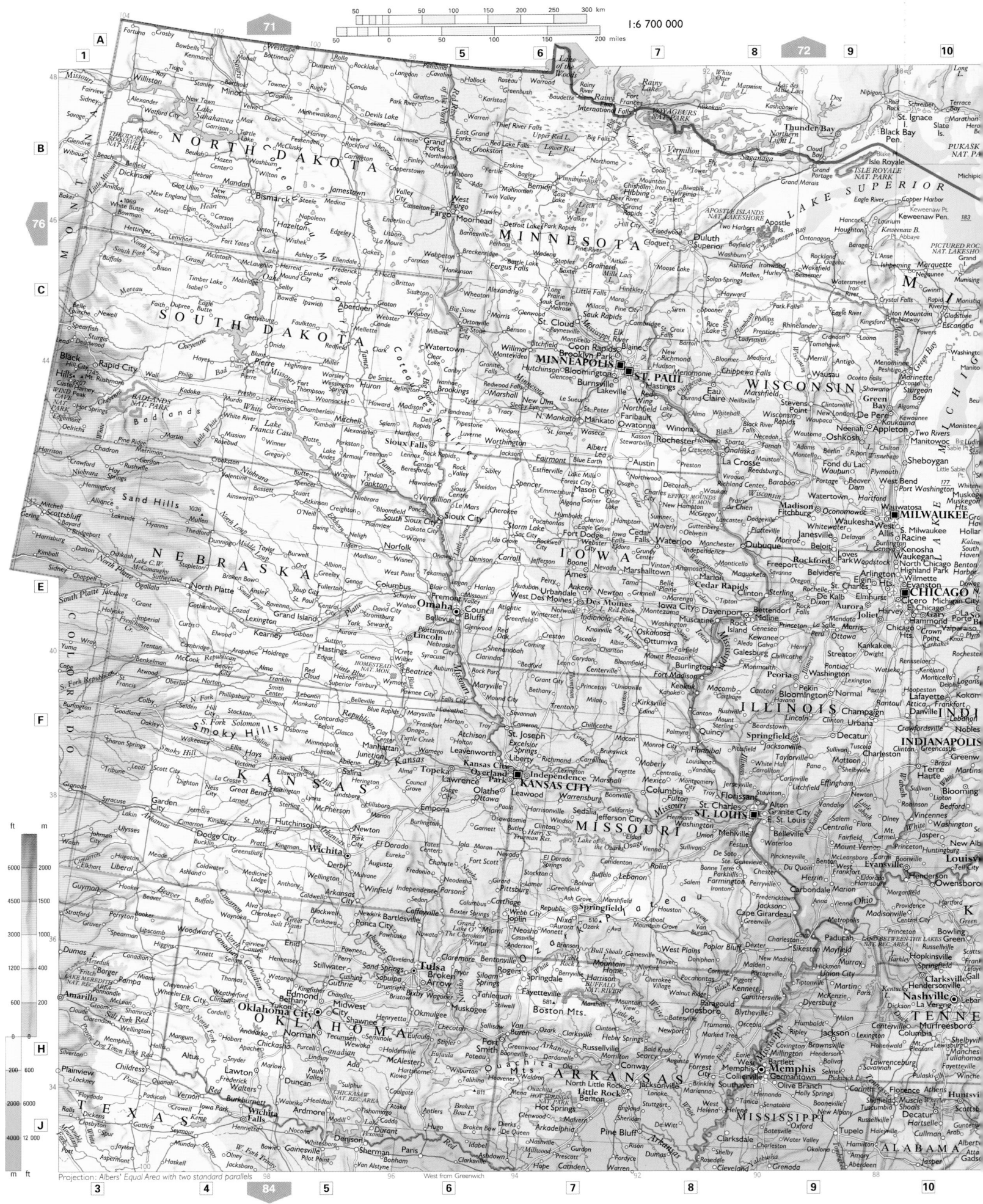

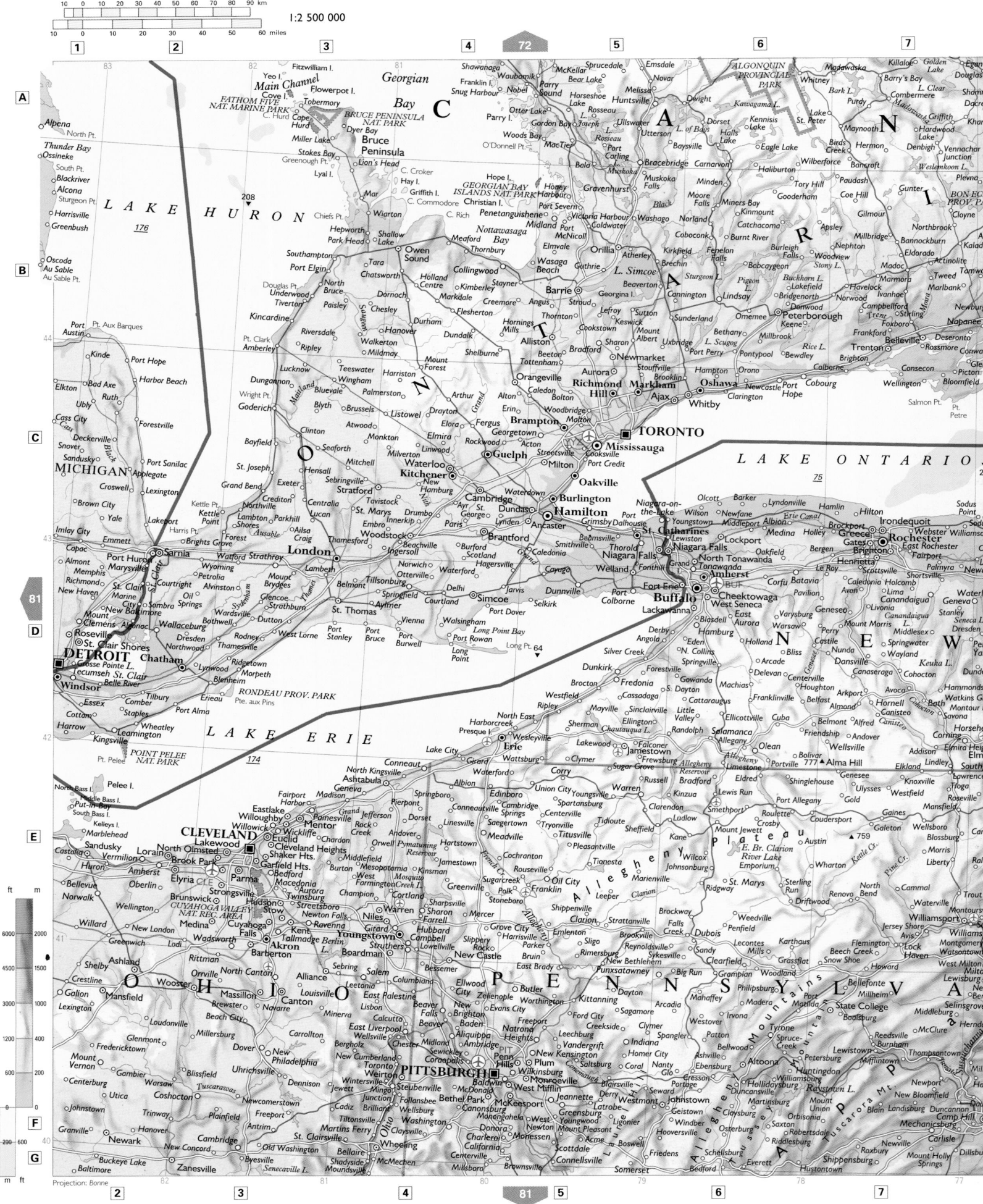

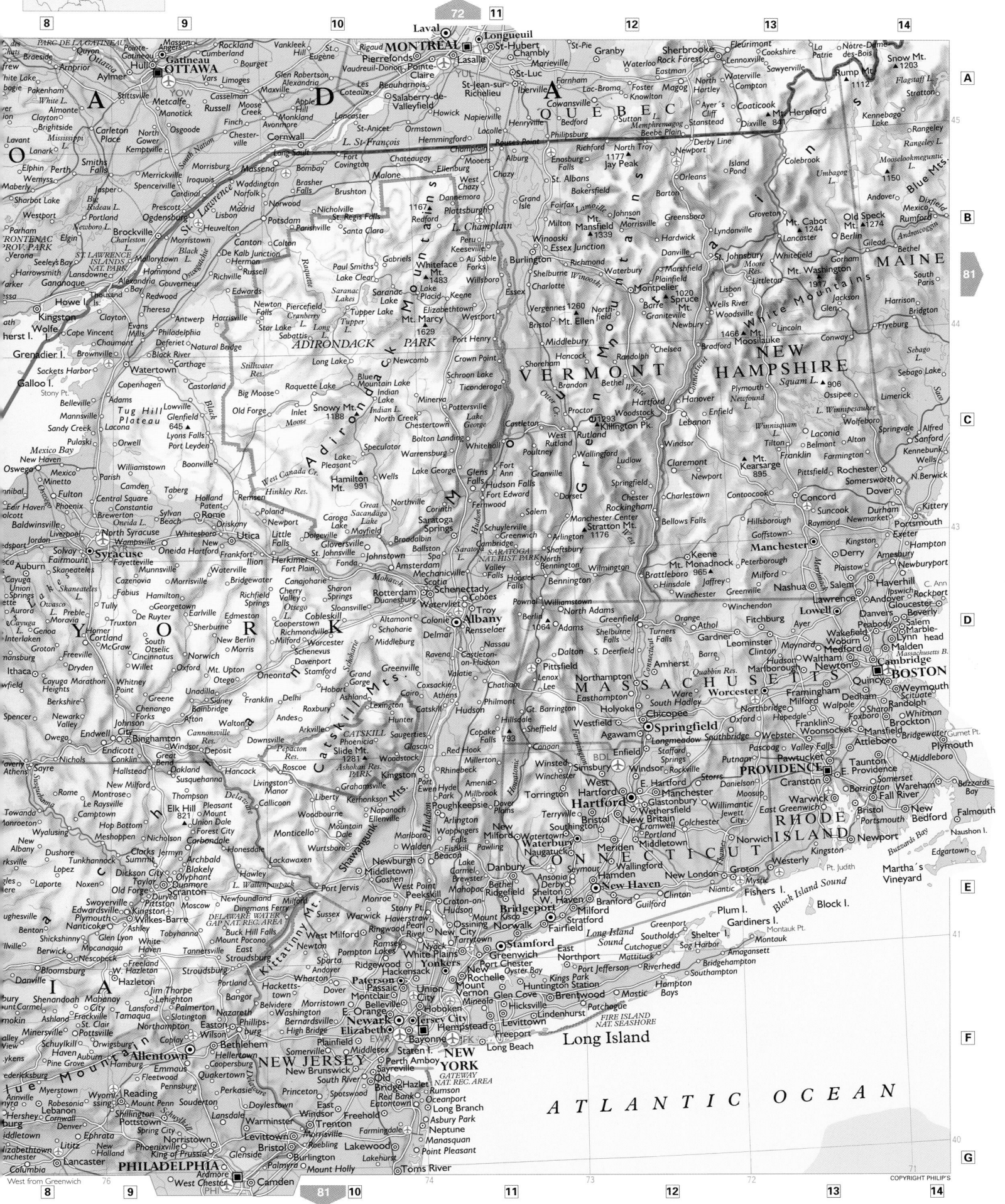

1:6 700 000

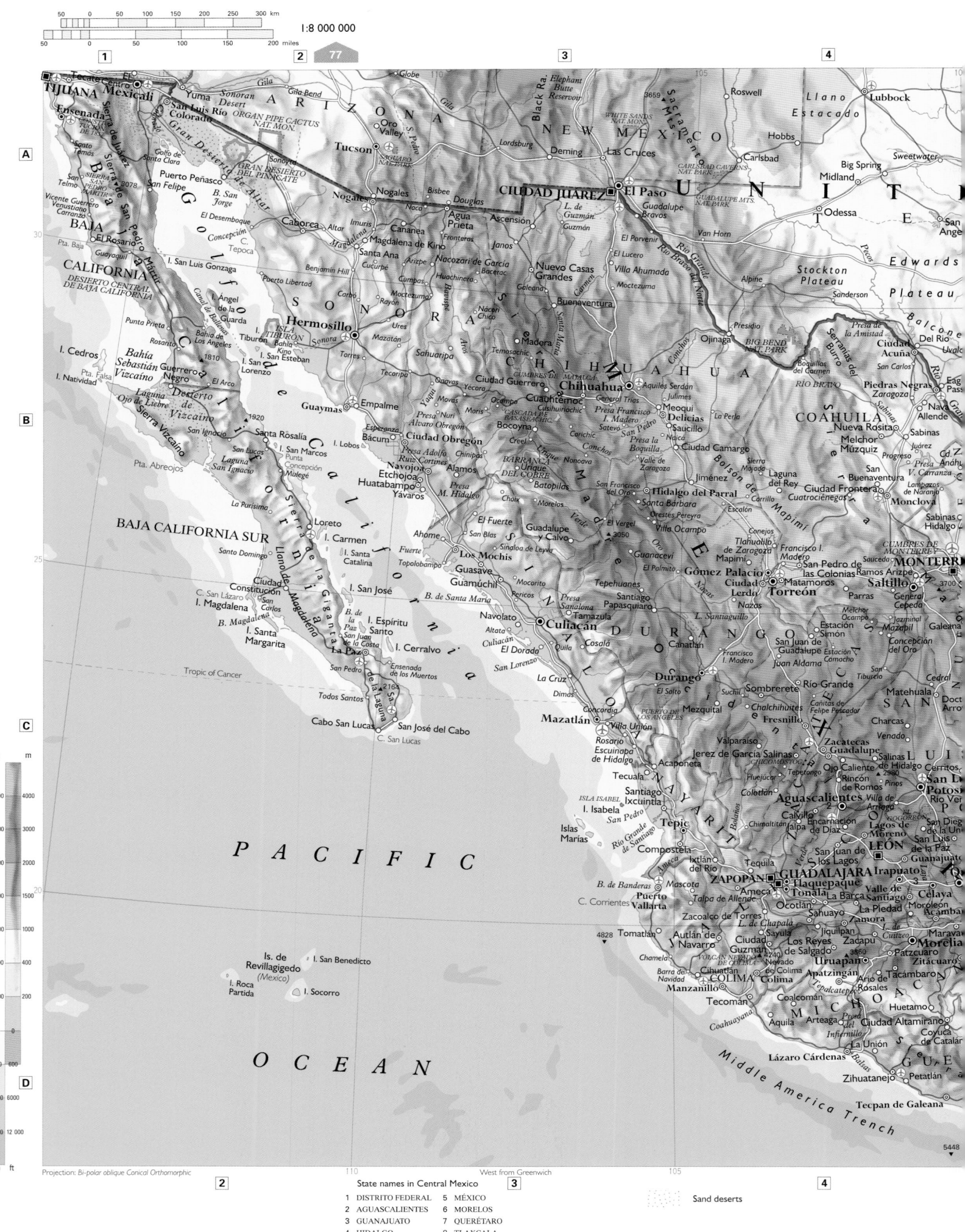

50   0   50   100 150 200 250 300 km
50   0   50   100 150 200 miles

1:8 000 000

1   **2**   **3**   **4**

ft   m
12 000   4000
9000   3000
6000   2000
4500   1500
3000   1000
1200   400
600   200
0   0
200   600
2000   6000
4000   12 000
m   ft

Projection: Bi-polar oblique Conical Orthomorphic

West from Greenwich

State names in Central Mexico

1 DISTRITO FEDERAL	5 MÉXICO
2 AGUASCALIENTES	6 MORELOS
3 GUANAJUATO	7 QUERÉTARO
4 HIDALGO	8 TLAXCALA

Sand deserts

5448

A
B
C
D

Tropic of Cancer

PACIFIC

OCEAN

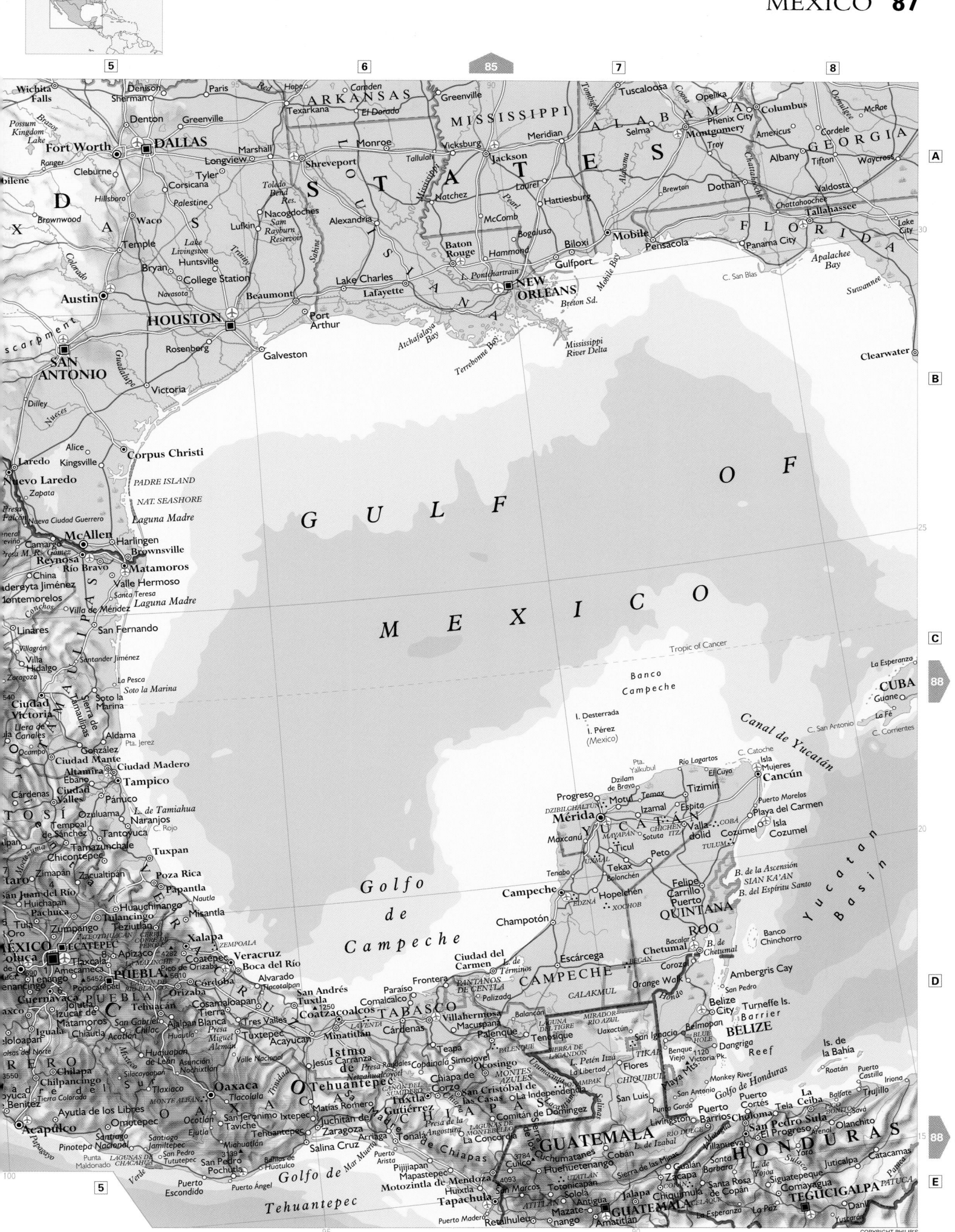

5   6   85   7   8

A

B

C
88

D
88

E

GULF   OF   MEXICO

Wichita Falls
Denison
Sherman
Paris
Hope
Camden
ARKANSAS
Greenville
Tuscaloosa
Opelika
Columbus
McRae
Possum Kingdom Lake
Denton
Greenville
El Dorado
Red
MISSISSIPPI
Phenix City
Montgomery
Americus
Cordele
Omulgee
Brazos
FORT WORTH
DALLAS
Marshall
Longview
Monroe
Vicksburg
Meridian
Selma
Troy
ALABAMA
Albany
Tifton
GEORGIA
Waycross
Valdosta
Ranger
Cleburne
Tyler
Corsicana
Shreveport
Tallulah
Jackson
Natchez
Laurel
Hattiesburg
Brewton
Dothan
Chattahoochee
Tallahassee
Lake City

bilene
Hillsboro
Palestine
Nacogdoches
Sam Rayburn Reservoir
Alexandria
McComb
Bogalusa
FLORIDA
Brownwood
Waco
Lufkin
Toledo Bend Res.
Pearl
Biloxi
Mobile
Pensacola
Panama City
Apalachee Bay
Suwannee
Temple
Lake Livingston
Baton Rouge
Hammond
Gulfport
C. San Blas
Bryan
Huntsville
Lake Charles
I. Pontchartrain
NEW ORLEANS
Mobile Bay
Austin
College Station
Beaumont
Lafayette
Breton Sd.
HOUSTON
Rosenberg
Port Arthur
Atchafalaya Bay
Mississippi River Delta
Clearwater
San Antonio
Galveston
Terrebonne Bay

CUBA
Guane
La Fé

GULF   OF   MEXICO

Banco Campeche

I. Desterrada
I. Pérez (Mexico)

Canal de Yucatán
C. San Antonio
C. Corrientes

Tropic of Cancer

Corpus Christi
PADRE ISLAND NAT. SEASHORE
Laguna Madre

Nuevo Laredo
Zapata
Presa Falcon
Nueva Ciudad Guerrero
Camargo
McAllen
Harlingen
Brownsville
Reynosa
Río Bravo
Matamoros
China
Valle Hermoso
dereyta Jiménez
Santa Teresa
Laguna Madre
ontemorelos
Villa de Méndez
Linares
San Fernando
Villagrán
Villa Hidalgo
Zaragoza
Ciudad Victoria
Llera de Canales
La Pesca
Soto la Marina
ampo
Sierra de Tamaulipas
Aldama
González
Pta. Jerez
Ciudad Mante
Ciudad Madero
Altamira
Tampico
Ebano
Ciudad Valles
Cárdenas
Páruco
L. de Tamiahua
C. Rojo
Ozuluama
Naranjos
Tantoyuca
Tamazunchale
Tampico
Chicontepec
Tuxpan
Zimapán
Zacualtipán
Poza Rica
Papantla
Nautla
Misantla

Río Lagartos
El Cuyo
Progreso
Dzilam de Bravo
Tizimín
Espita
Mérida
Motul
Temax
Valladolid
Cozumel
Maxcanú
Ticul
Sotuta
Peto
Tenabo
Tekax
Campeche
Hopelchén
Felipe Carrillo Puerto
Champotón
Escárcega
Chetumal

Golfo de Campeche

Ciudad del Carmen
Paraíso
Frontera
Comalcalco
Palizada
Villahermosa
Macuspana
Palenque

CAMPECHE
QUINTANA ROO
TABASCO

Belize City
Belize
Orange Walk
Corozal
Ambergris Cay
San Pedro

BELIZE
Belmopan

Veracruz
Boca del Río
Alvarado

GUATEMALA
HONDURAS
TEGUCIGALPA

Golfo de Tehuantepec

COPYRIGHT PHILIP'S

JAMAICA
1:3 000 000

50 0 50 100 150 200 250 300 km
50 0 50 100 150 200 miles
1:8 000 0

CARIBBEAN SEA

Montego Bay, Lucea, Falmouth, Runaway Bay, St. Ann's Bay, Galina Point, Negril, Cambridge, Wakefield, Ocho Rios, Port Maria, Annotto Bay, South Negril Pt., Maggotty, The Cockpit Country, Mount Denham 985▲, Dry Harbour Mountains, Moneague, Port Antonio, Savanna-la-Mar, Don Figueroa Mts., Linstead, Blue Mountains, John Crow Mts., Black River, Santa Cruz Mts., Mandeville, Spanish Town, Portmore, Blue Mountain 2256 Peak, Morant Point, Great Pedro Bluff, May Pen, KINGSTON, Morant Bay, Port Morant, Alligator Pond, Portland Bight, Portland Point

GULF OF MEXICO

I. Desterrada, I. Pérez (Mexico)

FLORIDA L. Okeechobee, West Palm Beach, West End, Little Abaco I., U.S.A., Cape Coral, Fort Myers, Boca Raton, Free port, Grand Bahama, Hope Town, Abaco I., Naples, The Everglades, Fort Lauderdale, Northwest Providence Channel, EVERGLADES NAT. PARK, C. Romano, MIAMI, Hialeah, Bimini Is., Berry Is., Nicolls Town, New Providence, Nassau, Eleuthera, BA, Dry Tortugas (U.S.A.), Key West, C. Sable, Florida Bay, Andros Town, Andros Island, Great Guana Cay, Great Exuma I., Exuma Sound

Straits of Florida, Florida Keys, Santaren Channel, Great Bahama Bank

LA HABANA (Havana), Guanabacoa, Santa Cruz del Norte, Matanzas, Cárdenas, Sagua la Grande, Cay Sal Bank, Canal Nicholás, Bahía Honda, Guanajay, Güines, Jovellanos, Colón, Santa Clara, Morón, Cayo Romano, Nuevitas, Arch. de Sabana, Arch. de Camagüey, CUBA, Pinar del Río, La Esperanza, Los Palacios, San Antonio de los Baños, Nueva Gerona, Cienfuegos, Trinidad 1140▲, Placetas, Sancti Spíritus, Ciego de Avila, Florida, Camagüey, Puerto Manatí, Guane, San Luis, La Fé, I. de la Juventud, Corrientes, G. de Batabanó, Pen. de Zapata, Tunas de Zaza, Golfo de Ana María, Arch. de Jardines de la Reina, Santa Cruz del Sur, Las Tunas, Gibara, Holguín, Manzanillo, Golfo de Guacanayabo, Bayamo, Sierra Maestra 1972▲, Santiago de Cuba

Yucatan Basin, Greater, Cayman Trench

Progreso, Dzilam de Bravo, Punta Yalkubul, Río Lagartos, El Cuyo, C. Catoche, Isla Mujeres, Motul, Temax, Tizimín, Cancún, Mérida, Izamal, Espita, Maxcanú, Sotuta, CHICHEN ITZA, Valladolid, Puerto Morelos, Playa del Carmen, Calkiní, Ticul, Tekax, MAYAPAN, Peto, Cozumel, Isla Cozumel, Campeche, Tenabo, Bolonchén, Hopelchén, Felipe Carrillo Puerto, B. de la Ascensión, SIAN KA'AN, B. del Espíritu Santo, Champotón, San José Carpizo, TULUM

Cayman Islands (U.K.), George Town, Grand Cayman, Cayman Brac, Little Cayman, C. Cruz

YUCATAN, MEXICO, QUINTANA ROO, Ciudad del Carmen, C. de Términos, Bacalar, PANTANOS DE CENTLA, Palizada, CAMPECHE, Balancán, CALAKMUL, Orange Walk, Chetumal, B. de Chetumal, Corozal, Banco Chinchorro

Misteriosa Bank, Is. Santanilla (Swan Islands) (Honduras)

Tenosique, MIRADOR-RIO AZUL, Uaxactún, Ambergris Cay, San Pedro, Ocosingo, SIERRA DE LACANDON, L. Petén Itzá, San Ignacio, Belmopan, Belize City, Turneffe Is., BELIZE, TIKAL, Flores, BLUE HOLE, Middlesex, Barrier, La Libertad, Benque Viejo 1120▲, Dangriga, Reef, Comitán de Domínguez, MONTES AZULES, GUATEMALA, CARACOL, CHIQUIBUL, Maya Mts. Victoria Peak, San Luis, Monkey River, Golfo de Honduras, Is. de la Bahía, Guanaja

Rosalind Bank, Banco Gorda, Serranilla Bank, Bajo Nuevo (Colombia)

LAGUNAS DE MONTE-BELLO, 3784▲, LAGUNA DEL TIGRE, Sebol, RIO DULCE, I. de Izabal, Puerto Barrios, Livingston, Puerto Cortés, Puerto Castilla, Roatán, Roatán, Utila, Camarón, Iriona, Punta Patuca, Brus Laguna, Cuilco, Cuchumatanes, Coban, Punta Gorda, San Pedro Sula, Tela, La Ceiba, Balfate, Trujillo, Savá, Sico, Auas, Laguna de Caratasca, Vol. Tajumulco 4211▲, Huehuetenango, PICO BONITO, El Progreso, Arenal, Olanchito, El Carbón, Puerto Lempira, Totonicapán, Sololá, ATITLAN, GUATEMALA, Santa Bárbara, Santa Rosa de Copán, Yoro, El Jaral, L. de Yojoa, Olancho, Catacamas, Coco (Segovia), Puerto Cabo Gracias á Dios, San Marcos, Antigua, Jalapa, COPAN, Chiquimula, 2849 2730, Zacapa, HONDURAS, Comayagua, Juticalpa, Leimus, Coatepeque, Retalhuleu, Mazatenango, Escuintla, La Esperanza, La Paz, TEGUCIGALPA, Yuscarán, Dirí, Danlí, Bonanza, Siuna, Mosquitia, Ahuachapán, Sonsonate, Santa Ana, Apopa, Cojutepeque, Nacaome, Choluteca, Somoto, Cord. Isabella, Siuna, SASLAYA, Puerto Cabezas, San José, Acajutla, Nueva San Salvador, SAN SALVADOR, Usulután, San Miguel, La Unión, Choluteca, El Sauce, Estelí, Jinotega, Matagalpa, Tuma, Prinzapolca, EL SALVADOR, G. de Fonseca, Puerto Morazán, El Progreso, Somoto, Muy Muy, San Pedro del Norte, Chinandega, NICARAGUA, La Barra, Corinto, León, Boaco, Siquia, Santo Domingo, Rama, El Bluff, La Paz Centro, L. de Managua, Tipitapa, Masaya, Juigalpa, Bluefields, MANAGUA, Granada, Diriamba, Jinotepe, Lago de Nicaragua, Cord. de Yolaina, Pta. Mono, Rivas, San Juan del Sur, B. de Salinas, Ometepe, B. de San Juan del Norte, GUANACASTE, San Carlos, Los Chiles, San Juan del Norte, SANTA ROSA, G. de Papagayo, La Cruz, San Juan, Liberia, Santa Cruz, Cañas, Nicoya, COSTA RICA, TORTUGUERO, Carmona, Puntarenas, Pen. de Nicoya, Alajuela, SAN JOSE, Cartago, Limón, Quepos, Pta. Mona, Santa Elena

C. Gracias a Dios, Pta. Gorda, Cayos Miskitos (Nicaragua)

I. de Providencia (Colombia), Cayos Roncador (Colombia), I. de San Andrés (Colombia), Is. del Maíz (Nicaragua), Cayos de Albuquerque (Colombia)

CARIBBEAN

PACIFIC OCEAN

Guatemala Trench

Bocas del Toro, Chiriquí, Almirante, Volcán Barú 3475▲, Bajo, Nombre de Dios, Portobelo, Panamá Canal, Colón, L. Gatún, Archipiélago de San Blas, Puerto Armuelles, David, Remedios, Santiago, Penonomé, Río Hato, Aguadulce, PANAMA, La Palma, Balboa, La Chorrera, Chepo, Chitré, Las Tablas, Golfo de Panamá, San Miguel, Chimán, El Real de Sta. Maria, Pta. Burica, Puerto Quepos, B. de Coronado, Ciudad Cortés, San Vito, La Concepción, AMISTAD, Buenos Aires, Golfito, G. Dulce, Pen. de Osa, CORCOVADO, Santiago, Soná, Golfo de Chiriquí, ISLA COIBA, I. de Coiba, I. de Cébaco, Pen. de Azuero, CERRO HOYA, Tonosí, Pocrí, Pta. Mala, Pedasí, Punta Mariato, I. Jicarón, Garachiné, Yaviza, DARIÉN, Jaqué, Golfo del Darién, Serranía del Darién, Golfo de Urabá, Monte

Isthmus of Panama, CARTAG, CARTA

GUADELOUPE

Pte. de la Grande Vigie, Port-Louis, Grande-Terre, Le Moule, La Désirade, Pointe Allègre, Petit-Canal, Ste-Rose, Pointe-à-Pitre, Ste-Anne, Pointe des Châteaux, Pointe-Noire, Basse-Terre, Le Gosier, Îles de la Petite Terre, Bouillante, GUADELOUPE (Fr.), Soufrière 1467▲, Capesterre-Belle-Eau, St-Louis, Marie-Galante, Basse-Terre, Trois-Rivières, 204▲, Capesterre, Îles des Saintes, Grand-Bourg, Pte. des Basses

MARTINIQUE

Cap St-Martin, Basse-Pointe, Le Prêcheur, Montagne Pelée 1463▲, Ste-Marie, Presqu'île de la Caravelle, St-Pierre, La Trinité, Le Robert, Schœlcher, Le François, Fort-de-France, Le Lamentin, Rivière-Salée, Le St-Esprit, MARTINIQUE (Fr.), Rivière-Pilote, Le Marin, Pte. d'Enfer

GUADELOUPE AND MARTINIQUE
1:2 000 000

10 0 10 20 30 40 50 60 km
10 0 10 20 30 40 miles

Projection: Bi-polar oblique Conical Orthomorphic

ATLANTIC OCEAN

PUERTO RICO
1:3 000 000
10 0 10 20 30 40 50 km
10 0 10 20 30 miles

PUERTO RICO (U.S.A.)

Pta. Agujereada
Isabela
Aguadilla
Barceloneta
Manati
Vega
Arecibo
Baja
Bayamón
Carolina
Rio Grande
SAN JUAN
Dewey
Mayagüez
San Sebastian
Adjuntas
Utuado
Caguas
Fajardo
Pta.
Puerca
Culebra
Vieques
Esperanza
San German
Mts. de
Uroyan
Yauco
Cordillera Central
1338 Cerro de Punta
Cayey
Coamo
Humacao
Yabucoa
Ponce
Guanica
Pta. Aguila
Guayama
I. Caja de Muertos

VIRGIN ISLANDS
1:2 000 000
10 0 10 20 30 km
10 0 10 20 miles

Rufling Pt.
The Settlement
Anegada
East Pt.
Virgin Islands (U.K.)
Jost Van
Dyke I.
Great
Camanoe
Virgin Is. (U.S.A.)
Hans
Lolik I.
Guana I.
521
Beef I.
Virgin Gorda
Spanish Town
Cruz Bay
Tortola
Road Town
Peter I.
Charlotte Amalie
St. Thomas I.
St. John I.

ST. LUCIA
1:1 000 000
5 0 5 10 km
5 0 5 10 miles

Cap Point
Pte. Hardy
Esperance Bay
Gros Islet
Gros Islet
Castries
Marquis
Girard
Anse la Raye
Canaries
Millet
Dennery
Soufrière
Soufrière Bay
750
Mt. Gimie
950
Trou Gras Pt.
Micoud
Petit Piton
Gros Piton Pt.
796
Vierge Pt.
Choiseul
Gros Piton
Laborie
Vieux Fort
ST. LUCIA
C. Moule à Chique

BARBADOS
1:1 000 000
5 0 5 10 km
5 0 5 10 miles

ATLANTIC OCEAN
Crab Hill
North Point
Fustic
Spring Hall
Boscobelle
Portland
245
Belleplaine
Speightstown
Bathsheba
Westmoreland
Mt. Hillaby
340
Martin's Bay
Alleynes Bay
Holetown
Jackson
Bridgefield
Massiah Street
Ragged Pt.
Black Rock
Ellerton
Six Cross Roads
Bridgetown
Ivy
Edey
The Crane
Carlisle Bay
Worthing
Oistins
St. Martins
Bay
South Point
Chancery Lane
BGI
BARBADOS
Hillcrest

AMAS

ATLANTIC OCEAN

Arthur's Town
New Bight
Cat I.
San Salvador I.
Conception I.
Rum Cay
Tropic of Cancer
Long I.
Clarence Town
Samana Cay
andy Cay
Crooked I.
Plana Cays
Albert Town
Snug Corner
Mayaguana I.
Cay Verde
Acklins I.
Mira por vos Cay
Cay Santa Domingo
Hogsty Reef
Little Inagua I.
Turks & Caicos Is. (U.K.)
anes
Caicos Is.
C. Lucrecia
INAGUA
Lake Rose
Cockburn Town
Moa
Great Inagua I.
Turks Is.
antilla
Matthew Town
Mouchoir Bank
Mayari
Silver Bank
Navidad Bank
Baracoa
Pta. de Maisi
Cap Haïtien
Monte Cristi
LA ISABELA
Puerto Rico Trench
Guantanamo
GUANTANAMO BAY (U.S.A.)
Jean Rabel
Port-de-Paix
Santiago de los Caballeros
San Francisco de Macoris
Milwaukee Deep 9200
Cap-à-Foux
Fort Liberté
Puerto Plata
La Vega
Nagua
Samana
Jamaica Channel
G. de la Gonâve
Gonaives
Cord. Central
3175
Sabana de la Mar
Hato Mayor
Bayamón
Anegada
Virgin Is.
Sombrero (U.K.)
î. de la Tortue
St-Marc
Hinche
Cerro Pico Duarte
HAITISES
Sánchez
Aguadilla
SAN JUAN
St. Thomas
Tortola
Road Town
Anguilla (U.K.)
HAITI
Azua
Higüey
C. Engano
Arecibo
Carolina
Virgin Gorda
Charlotte Amalie
St-Martin (Fr.)
PORT-AU-PRINCE
DOMINICAN REP.
San Pedro de Macoris
Fajardo
Virgin Is. (U.S.A.)
St-Barthélemy (Fr.)
Jérémie
î. de la Gonâve
San Juan
L. Enriquillo
SANTO DOMINGO
La Romana
Ponce
Culebra
Christiansted
St. Maarten (Neth.)
Saba (Neth.)
Barbuda
Marie Dame
Massif de la Hotte
2680
SIERRA DE BAORUCO
Mayagüez
Vieques
Guayama
St. Croix
St. Eustatius (Neth.)
1156
ANTIGUA & BARBUDA
Les Cayes
Aquin
Petit Goâve
Jacmel
Barahona
Compostela
B. de Yuma
PUERTO RICO (U.S.A.)
Frederiksted
ST. KITTS & NEVIS
St. John's
Pointe-à-Gravois
î. à Vache
Pedernales
San Cristóbal
I. Saona
Isla Mona
Mona Passage
Redonda
Antigua
Nevis
Montserrat
Soufrière
914 Hills (U.K.)
Guadeloupe Passage
I. Beata
C. Beata
Ste-Rose
Le Moule
La Désirade
Hispaniola
GUADELOUPE (Fr.)
1467
Pointe-à-Pitre

Greater Antilles / Lesser Antilles

Basse-Terre
Marie-Galante (Fr.)
Grand-Bourg
I. des Saintes (Fr.)
Dominica Passage
Portsmouth
1447
DOMINICA
Morne Diablotin
MORNE TROIS PITONS
Roseau
Martinique Passage
Mt. Pelée
1397
Ste-Marie
Le François
Fort-de-France
Rivière-Pilote
MARTINIQUE (Fr.)
St. Lucia Channel
Castries
ST. LUCIA
Soufrière
950
St. Vincent Passage
Soufrière 1234
St. Vincent
Speightstown
340
Kingstown
BARBADOS
Bequia
Bridgetown
Canouan
ST. VINCENT & THE GRENADINES
Carriacou
840
St. George's
GRENADA

CARIBBEAN SEA

Venezuelan Basin
Beata Ridge
Aves Ridge
Colombian Basin
Aves Channel
Windward Islands
Leeward Islands
Lesser Antilles
I. de Aves (Venezuela)
The Grenadines

ABC Islands / **Lesser Antilles**
Aruba (Neth.)
Oranjestad
Curaçao
Bonaire
NETH. ANTILLES
Willemstad
ARC. LOS ROQUES
I. Blanquilla (Ven.)
Is. Los Hermanos (Ven.)
Tobago
Pta. Gallinas
MACUIRA
C. San Román
Is. Las Aves (Ven.)
Is. Los Roques (Ven.)
I. Orchila (Ven.)
NUEVA ESPARTA
Is. Los Testigos (Ven.)
Scarborough
Port of Spain
940
Galera Point

COLOMBIA

Pta. Espada
Pen. de la Guajira
Golfo de Venezuela
I. La Tortuga (Ven.)
I. de Margarita
La Asunción
Porlamar
Pen. de Paria
Trinidad
Arima
Santa Marta
Ríohacha
Uribia
Paraguaná
Punta Cardón
Punta Fijo
MÉDANOS DE CORO
Puerto Cumarebo
CERRO EL COPEY
LAGUNA DE LA RESTINGA
Carupano
Rio Claro
TRINIDAD & TOBAGO
BARRAN-QUILLA
Ciénaga
ISLA DE SALAMANCA
GUAJIRA
San Rafael
Coro
La Vela
CUEVA DE LA QUEBRADA DEL TORO
Tucacas
Maiquetía
La Guaira
Vargas
CARACAS
Cumaná
Güiria
San Fernando
Serpent's Mouth
Baranoa
Soledad
TAYRONA
SA. NEVADA DE STA. MARTA
Mene de Mauroa
HENRI PITTIER
Puerto Cabello
C. Codera
Higuerote
Puerto La Cruz
Carioco
Caripito
ATLÁNTICO
Sabanalarga
Fundación
5775
Santa Rita
Baragua
CERRO SAROCHE
San Felipe
CARABOBO
Los Teques
Barcelona
MONAGAS
El Carmen
MAGDALENA
Plato
Valledupar
La Concepción
Cabimas
LARA
YARACUY
Rio Chico
MIRANDA
Aragua de Barcelona
Anaco
Maturín
MARIUSA
Sincé-lejo
Zambrano
CÉSAR
Villa del Rosario
Ciudad Ojeda
Lago de Maracaibo
Carora
VALENCIA
Villa de Cura
San Juan de los Morros
El Sombrero
Valle de la Pascua
Caicara
DELTA
Mompós
Machiques
TRUJILLO
El Toccuyo
Acarigua
CARONÍ
El Tigre
AMACURO
Magangué
PERIJÁ
Betijoque
Trujillo
DINIRA
PORTUGUESA
Calabozo
Pariaguan
Tucupita
Sincelejo
CIÉNAGAS DEL CATATUMBO
San Carlos del Zulia
Valera
Guanare
San Carlos
COJEDES
GUÁRICO
Santa Maria de Ipire
ANZOÁTEGUI
Ciudad Guayana
Sierra Imataca
MÉRIDA
Barinas
Guárico
AGUARO-GUARIQUITO
Soledad
El Pao
El Banco
CATATUMBO-BARI
NORTE DE SANTANDER
PARAMOS DEL BATALLON Y LA NEGRA
CORD. DE MÉRIDA
SA. NEVADA
Libertad
BARINAS
Ciudad de Nutrias
San Fernando de Apure
Ciudad Bolívar
El Callao
Ocaña
Bolívar
Simiti
TÁCHIRA
Santa Barbara
Achaguas
Apure
Embalse de Guri
Guasipati
Tumeremo
Cúcuta
ZAPO-CAIPAR
Bruzual
Mantecal
Mapire
Caicara

West from Greenwich

92

COPYRIGHT PHILIP'S

4000 3000 2000 1500 1000 600 400 200 ft
600 6000 12 000 18 000 24 000 ft
12 000 9000 6000 4500 3000 2000 1200 600 m
200 2000 4000 6000 8000 m

100 0   200   400   600   800   1000 1200 1400 km

1:35 000 000

100 0   200   400   600   800   1000 miles

NORTH ATLANTIC OCEAN

Tropic of Cancer

Bahamas

Yucatán Channel

Turks & Caicos Is.

Cuba

Greater Antilles

West Indies

Hispaniola

9200

Puerto Rico

Leeward Islands

Guadeloupe

Dominica

Martinique

St. Lucia

St. Vincent Barbados

Grenada

Tobago

Trinidad

Gulf of Campeche

Yucatán Peninsula

Isthmus of Tehuantepec

Central America

G. de Honduras

C. Gracias a Dios

Coco

L. Nicaragua

Guatemala Trench

Panama Canal

Isthmus of Panama

Gulf of Panamá

Caribbean Sea

Guajira Peninsula

Paraguana Peninsula

G. of Venezuela

Curaçao

Margarita

Lesser Antilles

Lesser Antilles

C. de la Aguja

5775

Sierra Nevada de Santa Marta

L. de Maracaibo

G. of Darién

I. del Coco

I. de Malpelo

Buenaventura B.

C. de San Francisco

Cordillera Occidental

Cordillera Central

Cordillera Oriental

Cauca

Magdalena

Cord. de Mérida

Apure

Meta

Orinoco

Embalse de Guri

Cuyuni

Llanos

Guiana Highlands

Angel Falls

Mt. Roraima 2772

Sierra Pacaraima

Pico de Neblina 3014

Casiquiare

Negro

Branco

Cowannyce Serra

Maroni

Oyapock

Devil's I.

C. Orange

I. de Maracá

Tumucumaque

Guaviare

Vaupés

Caquetá

Japurá

Putumayo

Napo

Marañón

Ucayali

Montaña

Amazon

Amazon

Amazon

Represa de Balbina

Marajó I.

Marajó B.

Equator

San Marcos B.

Juruá

Purus

Madeira

Roosevelt

Tapajós

Xingu

Tocantins

Araguaia

Tocantins

Itapicuru

Parnaíba

C. de São Roque

Galapagos Is.

1707

G. of Guayaquil

Pta. Pariñas

Pta. Negra

Sechura Desert

Cotopaxi 5897

Chimborazo 6267

Huascarán 6768

Amazon Basin

Sel

Basin

Caatinga

Plat. of Borborema

C. Branco

C. de São Roque

Madre de Dios

Beni

Mamoré

Guaporé

Sa. dos Parecis

Itonamas

Plateau of Mato Grosso

Represa de Sobradinho

São Francisco

Serra do Espinhaço

Brazilian Highlands

B. de Todos os Santos

Nevado Coropuna 6425

Chincha Alta

L. Titicaca 3812

Nevado Ancohuma 6550

Yungas

Altiplano (Bolivian Plateau)

L. de Poopó

Salar de Uyuni

Chaco Boreal

Chaco

Pilcomayo

Paraguay

Paranaíba

Grande

Paraná

Doce

Abrolhos Bank

Serra da Mantiqueira

Pico da Bandeira 2890

C. de São Tomé

PACIFIC

OCEAN

Tropic of Capricorn

San Félix

San Ambrosio

Pta. Tetas 8050

Atacama Desert

Cord. de Calalaste

Cerro Ojos del Salado 6863

Monte Pissis 6779

Cerro Bonete 6872

Salinas Grandes

Dulce

Salado

Chaco Austral

Gran Chaco

Bermejo

Pilcomayo

Rep. de Itaipú

Iguaçu Falls

Iguaçu

Paraná

Uruguay

Entre Ríos

Serra do Mar

C. Frio

I. de São Sebastião

C. Santa Marta Grande

Peru-Chile Trench

Arch. de Juan Fernández

Robinson Crusoe

Pta. Lengua da Vaca

Cerro Mercedario 6770 6960

Mt. Aconcagua

Sa. de Córdoba

L. Mar Chiquita

Negro

Paraná

Rio de la Plata

B. Samborombón

C. San Antonio

SOUTH

Pta. Lavapié

Salado

Salado

Pampas

Colorado

Bahía Blanca

L. dos Patos

L. Mirim

Chile Rise

Chiloé I.

Chonos Archipelago

Taitao Peninsula

G. of Penas

Wellington I.

Madre de Dios I.

Mte. San Valentín 4058

L. Buenos Aires

Chubut

Limay

Chico

Negro

San Matías G.

Valdés Peninsula

G. of San Jorge

C. Tres Puntas

Argentine Abyssal Plain

ATLANTIC OCEAN

6212

Patagonia

L. Viedma

L. Argentino

Magellan's Str.

Riesco I.

Santa Inés I.

Cockburn Chan.

Tierra del Fuego

Staten I.

C. Virgenes

West Falkland

Falkland Is.

705

East Falkland

South Georgia

Mt. Paget 2937

C. Horn

Beagle Chan.

Taitao Peninsula

ft   m

12000 4000

9000   3000

6000   2000

3000   1000

1500   600

600   200

0   0

200   600

1000   3000

2000   6000

4000   12000

6000   18000

8000   24000

m   ft

Projection: Lambert's Azimuthal Equal Area

West from Greenwich 50

COPYRIGHT PHILIP'S

1:35 000 000

■ LIMA   Capital Cities

West from Greenwich

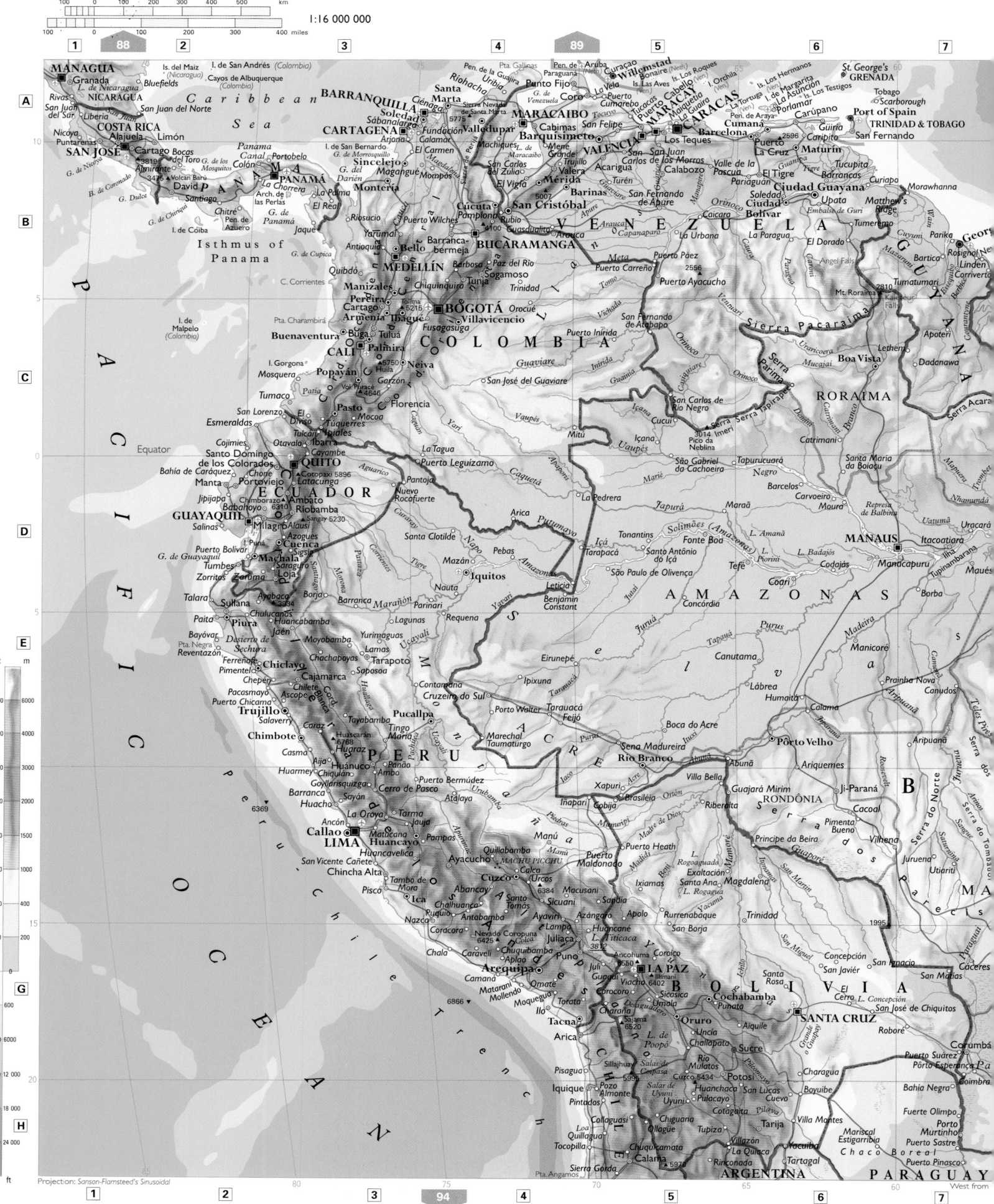

1:16 000 000

Projection: Sanson-Flamsteed's Sinusoidal

1:8 000 000

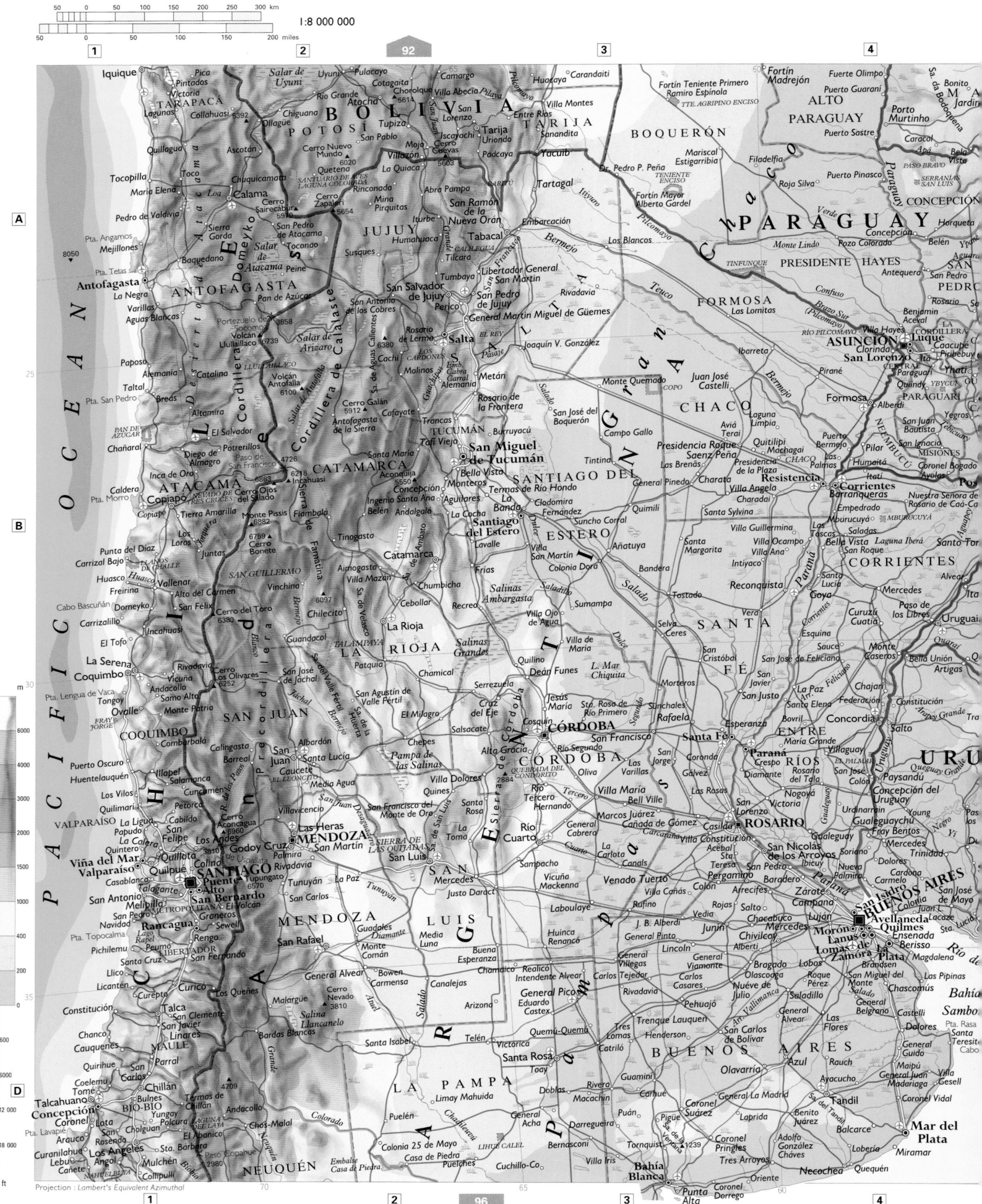

Projection : Lambert's Equivalent Azimuthal

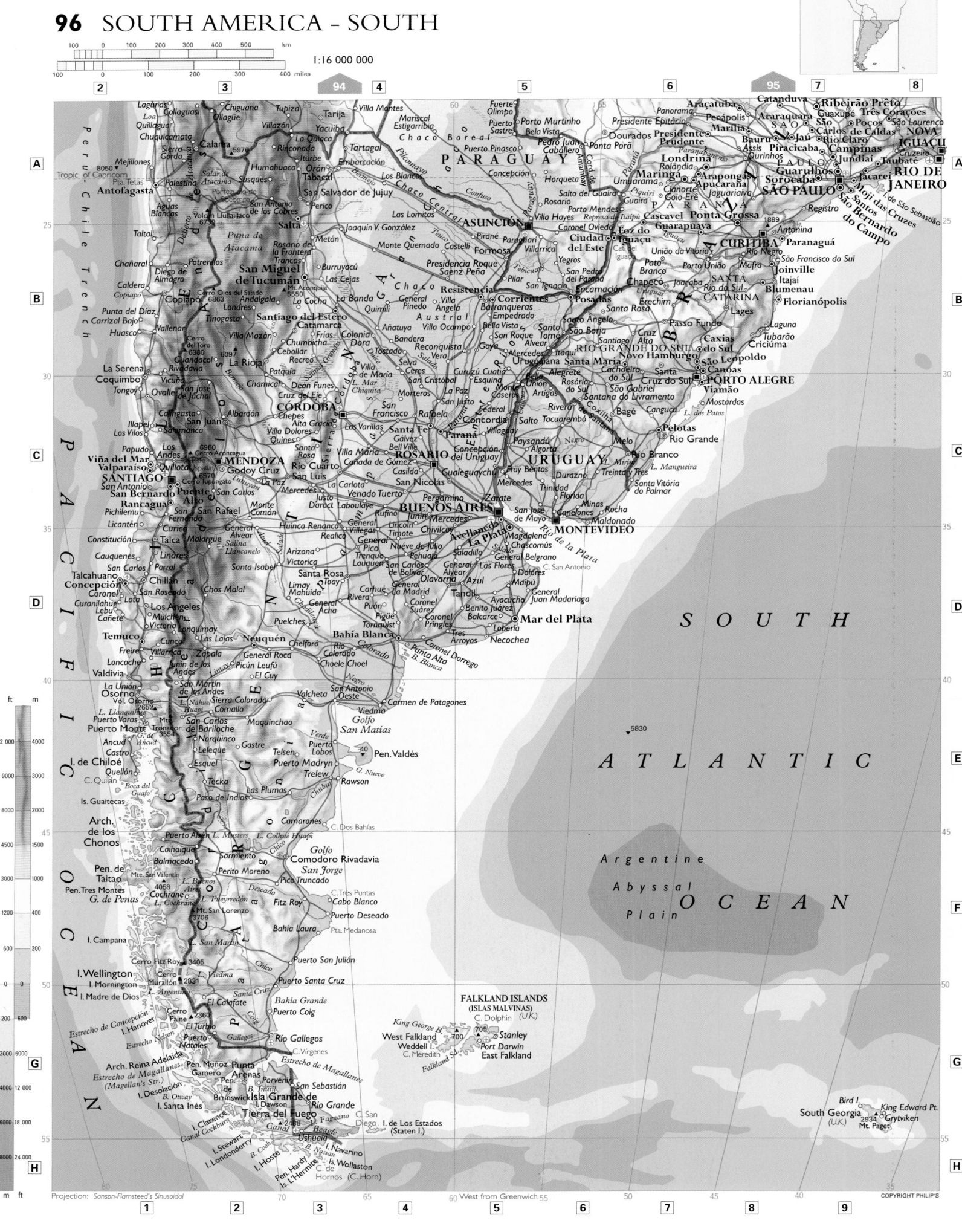

Projection: Sanson-Flamsteed's Sinusoidal

West from Greenwich

COPYRIGHT PHILIP'S

INDEX TO WORLD MAPS

The index contains the names of all the principal places and features shown on the World Maps. Each name is followed by an additional entry in italics giving the country or region within which it is located. The alphabetical order of names composed of two or more words is governed primarily by the first word, then by the second, and then by the country or region name that follows. This is an example of the rule:

Mīr Kūh *Iran*	26°22N 58°55E	**45** E8
Mīr Shahdād *Iran*	26°15N 58°29E	**45** E8
Mira *Italy*	45°26N 12°8E	**22** B5
Mira por vos Cay *Bahamas*	22°9N 74°30W	**89** B5

Physical features composed of a proper name (Erie) and a description (Lake) are positioned alphabetically by the proper name. The description is positioned after the proper name and is usually abbreviated:

Erie, L. *N. Amer.*	42°15N 81°0W	**82** D4

Where a description forms part of a settlement or administrative name, however, it is always written in full and put in its true alphabetical position:

Mount Morris *U.S.A.*	42°44N 77°52W	**82** D7

Names beginning with M' and Mc are indexed as if they were spelled Mac. Names beginning St. are alphabetized under Saint, but Sankt, Sint, Sant', Santa and San are all spelt in full and are alphabetized accordingly. If the same place name occurs two or more times in the index and all are in the same country, each is followed by the name of the administrative subdivision in which it is located.

The geographical co-ordinates which follow each name in the index give the latitude and longitude of each place. The first co-ordinate indicates latitude – the distance north or south of the Equator. The second co-ordinate indicates longitude – the distance east or west of the Greenwich Meridian. Both latitude and longitude are measured in degrees and minutes (there are 60 minutes in a degree).

The latitude is followed by N(orth) or S(outh) and the longitude by E(ast) or W(est).

The number in bold type which follows the geographical co-ordinates refers to the number of the map page where that feature or place will be found. This is usually the largest scale at which the place or feature appears.

The letter and figure that are immediately after the page number give the grid square on the map page, within which the feature is situated. The letter represents the latitude and the figure the longitude. A lower-case letter immediately after the page number refers to an inset map on that page.

In some cases the feature itself may fall within the specified square, while the name is outside. This is usually the case only with features that are larger than a grid square.

Rivers are indexed to their mouths or confluences, and carry the symbol ➔ after their names. The following symbols are also used in the index: ■ country, ☑ overseas territory or dependency, □ first-order administrative area, △ national park, ⌂ other park (provincial park, nature reserve or game reserve), ✈ (LHR) principal airport (and location identifier).

Abbreviations used in the index

A.C.T. – Australian Capital Territory
A.R. – Autonomous Region
Afghan. – Afghanistan
Afr. – Africa
Ala. – Alabama
Alta. – Alberta
Amer. – America(n)
Ant. – Antilles
Arch. – Archipelago
Ariz. – Arizona
Ark. – Arkansas
Atl. Oc. – Atlantic Ocean
B. – Baie, Bahía, Bay, Bucht, Bugt
B.C. – British Columbia
Bangla. – Bangladesh
Barr. – Barrage
Bos.-H. – Bosnia-Herzegovina
C. – Cabo, Cap, Cape, Coast
C.A.R. – Central African Republic
C. Prov. – Cape Province
Calif. – California
Cat. – Catarata
Cent. – Central
Chan. – Channel
Colo. – Colorado
Conn. – Connecticut
Cord. – Cordillera
Cr. – Creek
Czech. – Czech Republic
D.C. – District of Columbia
Del. – Delaware
Dem. – Democratic
Dep. – Dependency
Des. – Desert
Dét. – Détroit
Dist. – District
Dj. – Djebel
Dom. Rep. – Dominican Republic

E. – East
El Salv. – El Salvador
Eq. Guin. – Equatorial Guinea
Est. – Estrecho
Falk. Is. – Falkland Is.
Fd. – Fjord
Fla. – Florida
Fr. – French
G. – Golfe, Golfo, Gulf, Guba, Gebel
Ga. – Georgia
Gt. – Great, Greater
Guinea-Biss. – Guinea-Bissau
H.K. – Hong Kong
H.P. – Himachal Pradesh
Hants. – Hampshire
Harb. – Harbor, Harbour
Hd. – Head
Hts. – Heights
I.(s). – Île, Ilha, Insel, Isla, Island, Isle
Ill. – Illinois
Ind. – Indiana
Ind. Oc. – Indian Ocean
Ivory C. – Ivory Coast
J. – Jabal, Jebel
Jaz. – Jazīrah
Junc. – Junction
K. – Kap, Kapp
Kans. – Kansas
Kep. – Kepulauan
Ky. – Kentucky
L. – Lac, Lacul, Lago, Lagoa, Lake, Limni, Loch, Lough
La. – Louisiana
Ld. – Land
Liech. – Liechtenstein
Lux. – Luxembourg
Mad. P. – Madhya Pradesh
Madag. – Madagascar
Man. – Manitoba
Mass. – Massachusetts

Md. – Maryland
Me. – Maine
Medit. S. – Mediterranean Sea
Mich. – Michigan
Minn. – Minnesota
Miss. – Mississippi
Mo. – Missouri
Mont. – Montana
Mozam. – Mozambique
Mt.(s) – Mont, Montaña, Mountain
Mte. – Monte
Mti. – Monti
N. – Nord, Norte, North, Northern, Nouveau, Nahal, Nahr
N.B. – New Brunswick
N.C. – North Carolina
N. Cal. – New Caledonia
N. Dak. – North Dakota
N.H. – New Hampshire
N.I. – North Island
N.J. – New Jersey
N. Mex. – New Mexico
N.S. – Nova Scotia
N.S.W. – New South Wales
N.W.T. – North West Territory
N.Y. – New York
N.Z. – New Zealand
Nac. – Nacional
Nat. – National
Nebr. – Nebraska
Neths. – Netherlands
Nev. – Nevada
Nfld & L. – Newfoundland and Labrador
Nic. – Nicaragua
O. – Oued, Ouadi
Occ. – Occidentale
Okla. – Oklahoma
Ont. – Ontario
Or. – Orientale

Oreg. – Oregon
Os. – Ostrov
Oz. – Ozero
P. – Pass, Passo, Pasul, Pulau
P.E.I. – Prince Edward Island
Pa. – Pennsylvania
Pac. Oc. – Pacific Ocean
Papua N.G. – Papua New Guinea
Pass. – Passage
Peg. – Pegunungan
Pen. – Peninsula, Péninsule
Phil. – Philippines
Pk. – Peak
Plat. – Plateau
Prov. – Province, Provincial
Pt. – Point
Pta. – Ponta, Punta
Pte. – Pointe
Qué. – Québec
Queens. – Queensland
R. – Rio, River
R.I. – Rhode Island
Ra. – Range
Raj. – Rajasthan
Recr. – Recreational, Récréatif
Reg. – Region
Rep. – Republic
Res. – Reserve, Reservoir
Rhld-Pfz. – Rheinland-Pfalz
S. – South, Southern, Sur
Si. Arabia – Saudi Arabia
S.C. – South Carolina
S. Dak. – South Dakota
S.I. – South Island
S. Leone – Sierra Leone
Sa. – Serra, Sierra
Sask. – Saskatchewan
Scot. – Scotland
Sd. – Sound
Sev. – Severnaya
Sib. – Siberia

Sprs. – Springs
St. – Saint
Sta. – Santa
Ste. – Sainte
Sto. – Santo
Str. – Strait, Stretto
Switz. – Switzerland
Tas. – Tasmania
Tenn. – Tennessee
Terr. – Territory, Territoire
Tex. – Texas
Tg. – Tanjung
Trin. & Tob. – Trinidad & Tobago
U.A.E. – United Arab Emirates
U.K. – United Kingdom
U.S.A. – United States of America
Ut. P. – Uttar Pradesh
Va. – Virginia
Vdkhr. – Vodokhranilishche
Vdskh. – Vodoskhovyshche
Vf. – Vírful
Vic. – Victoria
Vol. – Volcano
Vt. – Vermont
W. – Wadi, West
W. Va. – West Virginia
Wall. & F. Is. – Wallis and Futuna Is.
Wash. – Washington
Wis. – Wisconsin
Wlkp. – Wielkopolski
Wyo. – Wyoming
Yorks. – Yorkshire

A

A Coruña Spain 43°20N 8°25W 21 A1
A Estrada Spain 42°43N 8°27W 21 A1
A Fonsagrada Spain 43°8N 7°4W 21 A2
Aabenraa Denmark 55°3N 9°25E 9 J13
Aachen Germany 50°45N 6°6E 16 C4
Aalborg Denmark 57°2N 9°54E 9 H13
Aalen Germany 48°51N 10°6E 16 D6
Aalst Belgium 50°56N 4°2E 15 D4
Aalten Neths. 51°56N 6°35E 15 C6
Aalter Belgium 51°5N 3°28E 15 C3
Äänekoski Finland 62°36N 25°44E 8 E21
Aarau Switz. 47°23N 8°4E 20 C8
Aare → Switz. 47°33N 8°14E 20 C8
Aarhus = Århus Denmark 56°8N 10°11E 9 H14
Aarschot Belgium 50°59N 4°49E 15 D4
Aba Dem. Rep. of the Congo 3°58N 30°17E 54 B3
Aba Nigeria 5°10N 7°19E 50 G7
Abaco I. Bahamas 26°25N 77°10W 88 A4
Ābādān Iran 30°22N 48°20E 45 D6
Ābādeh Iran 31°8N 52°40E 45 D7
Abadla Algeria 31°2N 2°45W 50 B5
Abaetetuba Brazil 1°40S 48°50W 93 D9
Abagnar Qi = Xilinhot China 43°52N 116°2E 34 C9
Abah, Tanjung Indonesia 8°46S 115°38E 37 K18
Abai Paraguay 25°58S 55°54W 95 B4
Abakan Russia 53°40N 91°10E 29 D10
Abancay Peru 13°35S 72°55W 92 F4
Abariringa Kiribati 2°50S 171°40W 64 H10
Abarqū Iran 31°10N 53°20E 45 D7
Abashiri Japan 44°0N 144°15E 30 B12
Abashiri-Wan Japan 44°0N 144°30E 30 C12
Ābay = Nîl el Azraq → Sudan 15°38N 32°31E 51 E12
Abay Kazakhstan 49°38N 72°53E 28 E8
Abaya, L. Ethiopia 6°30N 37°50E 47 F2
Abaza Russia 52°39N 90°6E 28 D9
'Abbāsābād Iran 33°34N 58°23E 45 C8
Abbay = Nîl el Azraq → Sudan 15°38N 32°31E 51 E12
Abbaye, Pt. U.S.A. 46°58N 88°8W 80 B9
Abbé, L. Ethiopia 11°8N 41°47E 47 E3
Abbeville France 50°6N 1°49E 20 A4
Abbeville Ala., U.S.A. 31°34N 85°15W 85 F12
Abbeville La., U.S.A. 29°58N 92°8W 84 G8
Abbeville S.C., U.S.A. 34°11N 82°23W 85 D13
Abbeyfeale Ireland 52°23N 9°18W 10 D2
Abbot Ice Shelf Antarctica 73°0S 92°0W 5 D16
Abbotsford Canada 49°5N 122°20W 70 D4
Abbottabad Pakistan 34°10N 73°15E 42 B5
ABC Islands = Netherlands Antilles ☑ W. Indies 12°15N 69°0W 92 A5
Abd al Kūrī Yemen 12°5N 52°20E 47 E5
Ābdar Iran 30°16N 55°19E 45 D7
'Abdolābād Iran 34°12N 56°30E 45 C8
Abdulpur Bangla. 24°15N 88°59E 43 G13
Abéché Chad 13°50N 20°35E 51 F10
Abel Tasman △ N.Z. 40°59S 173°3E 59 D4
Abengourou Ivory C. 6°42N 3°27W 50 G5
Åbenrå = Aabenraa Denmark 55°3N 9°25E 9 J13
Abeokuta Nigeria 7°3N 3°19E 50 G6
Aber Uganda 2°12N 32°25E 54 B3
Aberaeron U.K. 52°15N 4°15W 13 E3
Aberayron = Aberaeron U.K. 52°15N 4°15W 13 E3
Aberchirder U.K. 57°34N 2°37W 11 D6
Abercorn Australia 25°12S 151°5E 63 D5
Aberdare U.K. 51°43N 3°27W 13 F4
Aberdare △ Kenya 0°22S 36°44E 54 C4
Aberdare Ra. Kenya 0°15S 36°50E 54 C4
Aberdeen Australia 32°9S 150°56E 63 E5
Aberdeen Canada 52°20N 106°8W 71 C7
Aberdeen China 22°14N 114°8E 33 G11
Aberdeen S. Africa 32°28S 24°2E 56 E3
Aberdeen U.K. 57°9N 2°5W 11 D6
Aberdeen Idaho, U.S.A. 42°57N 112°50W 76 E7
Aberdeen Md., U.S.A. 39°31N 76°10W 81 F15
Aberdeen Miss., U.S.A. 33°49N 88°33W 85 E10
Aberdeen S. Dak., U.S.A. 45°28N 98°29W 80 C4
Aberdeen Wash., U.S.A. 46°59N 123°50W 78 D3
Aberdeen, City of ☑ U.K. 57°10N 2°10W 11 D6
Aberdeenshire ☑ U.K. 57°17N 2°36W 11 D6
Aberdovey = Aberdyfi U.K. 52°33N 4°3W 13 E3
Aberdyfi U.K. 52°33N 4°3W 13 E3
Aberfeldy U.K. 56°37N 3°51W 11 E5
Aberfoyle U.K. 56°11N 4°23W 11 E4
Abergavenny U.K. 51°49N 3°1W 13 F4
Abergele U.K. 53°17N 3°35W 12 D4
Abernathy U.S.A. 33°50N 101°51W 84 E4
Abert, L. U.S.A. 42°38N 120°14W 76 E3
Aberystwyth U.K. 52°25N 4°5W 13 E3
Abhā Si. Arabia 18°0N 42°34E 47 D3
Abhar Iran 36°9N 49°13E 45 B6
Abhayapuri India 26°24N 90°38E 43 F14
Abidjan Ivory C. 5°26N 3°58W 50 G5
Abilene Kans., U.S.A. 38°55N 97°13W 80 F5
Abilene Tex., U.S.A. 32°28N 99°43W 84 E5
Abingdon U.K. 51°40N 1°17W 13 F6
Abingdon U.S.A. 36°43N 81°59W 81 G13
Abington Reef Australia 18°0S 149°35E 62 B4
Abitau → Canada 59°53N 109°3W 71 B7
Abitibi → Canada 51°3N 80°55W 72 B3
Abitibi, L. Canada 48°40N 79°40W 72 C4
Abkhaz Republic = Abkhazia ☑ Georgia 43°12N 41°5E 19 F7
Abkhazia ☑ Georgia 43°12N 41°5E 19 F7
Abminga Australia 26°8S 134°51E 63 D1
Åbo = Turku Finland 60°30N 22°19E 9 F20
Abohar India 30°10N 74°10E 42 D6
Abomey Benin 7°10N 2°5E 50 G6

Abong-Mbang Cameroon 4°0N 13°8E 52 D2
Abou-Deïa Chad 11°20N 19°20E 51 F9
Aboyne U.K. 57°4N 2°47W 11 D6
Abra Pampa Argentina 22°43S 65°42W 94 A2
Abraham L. Canada 52°15N 116°35W 70 C5
Abreojos, Pta. Mexico 26°50N 113°40W 86 B2
Abrolhos, Banco dos Brazil 18°0S 38°0W 93 F11
Abrud Romania 46°19N 23°5E 17 E12
Absaroka Range U.S.A. 44°45N 109°50W 76 D9
Abu India 24°41N 72°50E 42 G5
Abū al Abyad U.A.E. 24°11N 53°50E 45 E7
Abū al Khaşīb Iraq 30°25N 48°0E 45 D6
Abū 'Alī Si. Arabia 27°20N 49°27E 45 E6
Abū 'Alī → Lebanon 34°25N 35°50E 46 A4
Abu Dhabi = Abū Ẓāby U.A.E. 24°28N 54°22E 45 E7
Abu Du'ān Syria 36°25N 38°15E 44 B3
Abu el Gaïn, W. → Egypt 29°35N 33°30E 46 F2
Abu Ga'da, W. → Egypt 29°15N 32°53E 46 F1
Abū Ḩadrīyah Si. Arabia 27°20N 48°58E 45 E6
Abu Hamed Sudan 19°32N 33°13E 51 E12
Abū Kamāl Syria 34°30N 41°0E 44 C5
Abū Madd, Ra's Si. Arabia 24°50N 37°7E 44 E3
Abū Mūsā U.A.E. 25°52N 55°3E 45 E7
Abū Qaşr Si. Arabia 30°21N 38°34E 44 D3
Abū Shagara, Ras Sudan 21°4N 37°19E 51 D13
Abu Simbel Egypt 22°18N 31°40E 51 D12
Abū Şukhayr Iraq 31°54N 44°30E 44 D5
Abū Zabad Sudan 12°25N 29°10E 51 F11
Abū Ẓāby U.A.E. 24°28N 54°22E 45 E7
Abū Zeydābād Iran 33°54N 51°45E 45 C6
Abuja Nigeria 9°5N 7°32E 50 G7
Abukuma-Gawa → Japan 38°6N 140°52E 30 E10
Abukuma-Sammyaku Japan 37°30N 140°45E 30 F10
Abunã Brazil 9°40S 65°20W 92 E5
Abunã → Brazil 9°41S 65°20W 92 E5
Aburo Dem. Rep. of the Congo 2°4N 30°53E 54 B3
Abut Hd. N.Z. 43°7S 170°15E 59 E3
Ābyek Iran 36°4N 50°33E 45 B6
Acadia △ U.S.A. 44°20N 68°13W 81 C19
Açailândia Brazil 4°57S 47°0W 93 D9
Acajutla El Salv. 13°36N 89°50W 88 D2
Acámbaro Mexico 20°2N 100°44W 86 D4
Acaponeta Mexico 22°30N 105°22W 86 C3
Acapulco Mexico 16°51N 99°55W 87 D5
Acaraí, Serra Brazil 1°50N 57°50W 92 C7
Acarigua Venezuela 9°33N 69°12W 92 B5
Acatlán Mexico 18°12N 98°3W 87 D5
Acayucán Mexico 17°57N 94°55W 87 D6
Accomac U.S.A. 37°43N 75°40W 81 G16
Accra Ghana 5°35N 0°6W 50 G5
Accrington U.K. 53°45N 2°22W 12 D5
Acebal Argentina 33°20S 60°50W 94 C3
Aceh ☑ Indonesia 4°15N 97°30E 36 D1
Achalpur India 21°22N 77°32E 40 J10
Acharnes Greece 38°5N 23°44E 23 E10
Acheloos → Greece 38°19N 21°7E 23 E9
Acheng China 45°30N 126°58E 35 B14
Acher India 23°10N 72°32E 42 H5
Achill Hd. Ireland 53°58N 10°15W 10 C1
Achill I. Ireland 53°58N 10°1W 10 C1
Achinsk Russia 56°20N 90°20E 29 D10
Acireale Italy 37°37N 15°10E 22 F6
Ackerman U.S.A. 33°19N 89°11W 85 E10
Acklins I. Bahamas 22°30N 74°0W 89 B5
Acme Canada 51°33N 113°30W 70 C6
Acme U.S.A. 40°8N 79°26W 82 F5
Aconcagua, Cerro Argentina 32°39S 70°0W 94 C2
Aconquija, Mt. Argentina 27°0S 66°0W 94 B2
Açores, Is. dos Atl. Oc. 38°0N 27°0W 50 a
Acornhoek S. Africa 24°37S 31°2E 57 C5
Acraman, L. Australia 32°2S 135°23E 63 E2
Acre = 'Akko Israel 32°55N 35°4E 46 C4
Acre ☑ Brazil 9°1S 71°0W 92 E4
Acre → Brazil 8°45S 67°22W 92 E5
Actinolite Canada 44°32N 77°19W 82 B7
Acton Canada 43°38N 80°3W 82 C4
Ad Dammām Si. Arabia 26°20N 50°5E 45 E6
Ad Dāmūr Lebanon 33°43N 35°27E 46 B4
Ad Dawādimī Si. Arabia 24°35N 44°15E 44 E5
Ad Dawḥah Qatar 25°15N 51°35E 45 E6
Ad Dawr Iraq 34°27N 43°47E 44 C4
Ad Dir'īyah Si. Arabia 24°44N 46°35E 44 E5
Ad Dīwānīyah Iraq 32°0N 45°0E 44 D5
Ad Dujayl Iraq 33°51N 44°14E 44 C5
Ad Duwayd Si. Arabia 30°15N 42°17E 44 D4
Ada Minn., U.S.A. 47°18N 96°31W 80 B5
Ada Okla., U.S.A. 34°46N 96°41W 84 D6
Adabiya Egypt 29°53N 32°28E 46 F1
Adair, C. Canada 71°30N 71°34W 69 B12
Adaja → Spain 41°32N 4°52W 21 B3
Adak I. U.S.A. 51°45N 176°45W 74 a
Adamaoua, Massif de l' Cameroon 7°20N 12°20E 51 G8
Adamawa Highlands = Adamaoua, Massif de l'
Adamello, Mte. Italy 46°9N 10°30E 20 C9
Adaminaby Australia 36°0S 148°45E 63 F4
Adams Mass., U.S.A. 42°38N 73°7W 83 D11
Adams N.Y., U.S.A. 43°49N 76°1W 83 C8
Adams Wis., U.S.A. 43°57N 89°49W 80 D9
Adams, Mt. U.S.A. 46°12N 121°30W 78 D5
Adam's Bridge Sri Lanka 9°15N 79°40E 40 Q11
Adam's Peak Sri Lanka 6°48N 80°30E 40 R12
Adana Turkey 37°0N 35°16E 44 B2
Adapazarı = Sakarya Turkey 40°48N 30°25E 19 F5
Adarama Sudan 17°10N 34°52E 51 E12

Adare, C. Antarctica 71°0S 171°0E 5 D11
Adaut Indonesia 8°8S 131°7E 37 F8
Adavale Australia 25°52S 144°32E 63 D3
Adda → Italy 45°8N 9°53E 20 D8
Addis Ababa = Addis Abeba Ethiopia 9°2N 38°42E 47 F2
Addis Abeba Ethiopia 9°2N 38°42E 47 F2
Addison U.S.A. 42°1N 77°14W 82 D7
Addo S. Africa 33°32S 25°45E 56 E4
Addo △ S. Africa 33°30S 25°50E 56 E4
Ādeh Iran 37°42N 45°11E 44 B5
Adel U.S.A. 31°8N 83°25W 85 F13
Adelaide Australia 34°52S 138°30E 63 E2
Adelaide S. Africa 32°42S 26°20E 56 E4
Adelaide I. Antarctica 67°15S 68°30W 5 C17
Adelaide Pen. Canada 68°15N 97°30W 68 C10
Adelaide River Australia 13°15S 131°7E 60 B5
Adelaide Village Bahamas 25°0N 77°31W 88 A4
Adelanto U.S.A. 34°35N 117°22W 79 L9
Adele I. Australia 15°32S 123°9E 60 C3
Adélie, Terre Antarctica 68°0S 140°0E 5 C10
Adelie Land = Adélie, Terre Antarctica 68°0S 140°0E 5 C10
Aden = Al 'Adan Yemen 12°45N 45°0E 47 E4
Aden, G. of Ind. Oc. 12°30N 47°30E 47 E4
Adendorp S. Africa 32°15S 24°30E 56 E3
Adh Dhayd U.A.E. 25°17N 55°53E 45 E7
Adhoi India 23°26N 70°32E 42 H4
Adi Indonesia 4°15S 133°30E 37 E8
Adieu, C. Australia 32°0S 132°10E 61 F5
Adieu Pt. Australia 15°14S 124°35E 60 C3
Adige → Italy 45°9N 12°20E 22 B5
Adigrat Ethiopia 14°20N 39°26E 47 E2
Adilabad India 19°33N 78°20E 40 K11
Adirondack △ U.S.A. 44°0N 74°20W 83 C10
Adirondack Mts. U.S.A. 44°0N 74°0W 83 C10
Adis Abeba = Addis Abeba Ethiopia 9°2N 38°42E 47 F2
Adjumani Uganda 3°0N 31°50E 54 B3
Adjuntas Puerto Rico 18°10N 66°43W 89 d
Adlavik Is. Canada 55°0N 58°40W 73 B8
Admiralty G. Australia 14°20S 125°55E 60 B4
Admiralty I. U.S.A. 57°30N 134°30W 70 B2
Admiralty Is. Papua N. G. 2°0S 147°0E 58 B7
Adolfo González Chaves Argentina 38°2S 60°5W 94 D3
Adolfo Ruiz Cortines, Presa Mexico 27°15N 109°6W 86 B3
Adonara Indonesia 8°15S 123°5E 37 F6
Adoni India 15°33N 77°18E 40 M10
Adour → France 43°32N 1°32E 20 E3
Adra India 23°30N 86°42E 43 H12
Adra Spain 36°43N 3°3W 21 D4
Adrano Italy 37°40N 14°50E 22 F6
Adrar Algeria 27°51N 0°11E 50 C6
Adrar Mauritania 20°30N 7°30W 50 D3
Adrar des Iforas Africa 19°40N 1°40E 50 E6
Adrian Mich., U.S.A. 41°54N 84°2W 81 E11
Adrian Tex., U.S.A. 35°16N 102°40W 84 D3
Adriatic Sea Medit. S. 43°0N 16°0E 22 C6
Adua Indonesia 1°45S 129°50E 37 E7
Adwa Ethiopia 14°15N 38°52E 47 E2
Adygea ☑ Russia 45°0N 40°0E 19 F7
Adzhar Republic = Ajaria ☑ Georgia 41°30N 42°0E 19 F7
Adzopé Ivory C. 6°7N 3°49W 50 G5
Ægean Sea Medit. S. 38°30N 25°0E 23 E11
Aerht'ai Shan Mongolia 46°40N 92°45E 32 B4
Afaahiti Tahiti 17°45S 149°17W 59 d
'Afak Iraq 32°4N 45°15E 44 C5
Afandou Greece 36°18N 28°12E 25 C10
Afareaitu Moorea 17°33S 149°47W 59 d
Afghanistan ■ Asia 33°0N 65°0E 40 C4
Aflou Algeria 34°7N 2°3E 50 B6
Africa 10°0N 20°0E 48 E6
'Afrīn Syria 36°32N 36°50E 44 B3
Afton N.Y., U.S.A. 42°14N 75°32W 83 D9
Afton Wyo., U.S.A. 42°44N 110°56W 76 E8
Afuá Brazil 0°15S 50°20W 93 D8
'Afula Israel 32°37N 35°17E 46 C4
Afyon Turkey 38°45N 30°33E 19 G5
Afyonkarahisar = Afyon Turkey 38°45N 30°33E 19 G5
Āgā Jarī Iran 30°42N 49°50E 45 D6
Agadès = Agadez Niger 16°58N 7°59E 50 E7
Agadez Niger 16°58N 7°59E 50 E7
Agadir Morocco 30°28N 9°55W 50 B4
Agaete Canary Is. 28°6N 15°44W 24 F4
Agalega Is. Mauritius 11°0S 57°0E 3 E12
Agar India 23°40N 76°2E 42 H7
Agartala India 23°50N 91°23E 41 H17
Agassiz Canada 49°14N 121°46W 70 D4
Agats Indonesia 5°33S 138°0E 37 F9
Agawam U.S.A. 42°5N 72°37W 83 D12
Agboville Ivory C. 5°55N 4°15W 50 G5
Ağdam Azerbaijan 40°0N 46°58E 44 B5
Agde France 43°19N 3°28E 20 E5
Agen France 44°12N 0°38E 20 D4
Āgh Kand Iran 37°15N 48°4E 45 B6
Aghia Deka Greece 35°3N 24°58E 25 D6
Aghia Ekaterinis, Akra Greece 39°50N 19°50E 25 A3
Aghia Galini Greece 35°6N 24°41E 25 D6
Aghia Varvara Greece 35°8N 25°1E 25 D7
Aghios Efstratios Greece 39°34N 24°58E 23 E11
Aghios Ioannis, Akra Greece 35°20N 25°40E 25 D7
Aghios Isidoros Greece 36°9N 27°51E 25 C9
Aghios Nikolaos Greece 35°11N 25°41E 25 D7
Aghios Stephanos Greece 39°46N 19°39E 25 A3
Aghiou Orous, Kolpos Greece 40°6N 24°0E 23 D11
Aginskoye Russia 51°6N 114°32E 29 D12
Agnew Australia 28°1S 120°31E 61 E3
Agori India 24°33N 82°57E 43 G10
Agra India 27°17N 77°58E 42 F7

Ağrı Turkey 39°44N 43°3E 19 G7
Agri → Italy 40°13N 16°44E 22 D7
Ağrı Dağı Turkey 39°50N 44°15E 44 B5
Ağrı Karakose = Ağri Turkey 39°44N 43°3E 19 G7
Agrigento Italy 37°19N 13°34E 22 F5
Agrinio Greece 38°37N 21°27E 23 E9
Agua Caliente Mexico 32°29N 116°59W 79 N10
Agua Caliente Springs U.S.A. 32°56N 116°19W 79 N10
Água Clara Brazil 20°25S 52°45W 93 H8
Agua Fria △ U.S.A. 34°14N 112°0W 77 J8
Agua Hechicera Mexico 32°28N 116°15W 79 N10
Agua Prieta Mexico 31°18N 109°34W 86 A3
Aguadilla Puerto Rico 18°26N 67°10W 89 d
Aguadulce Panama 8°15N 80°32W 88 E3
Aguanga U.S.A. 33°27N 116°51W 79 M10
Aguanish Canada 50°14N 62°2W 73 B7
Aguanish → Canada 50°13N 62°5W 73 B7
Aguapey → Argentina 29°7S 56°36W 94 B4
Aguaray Guazú → Paraguay 24°47S 57°19W 94 A4
Aguarico → Ecuador 0°59S 75°11W 92 D3
Aguaro-Guariquito △ Venezuela 8°20N 66°35W 89 E6
Aguas Blancas Chile 24°15S 69°55W 94 A2
Aguas Calientes, Sierra de Argentina 25°26S 66°40W 94 B2
Aguascalientes Mexico 21°53N 102°18W 86 C4
Aguascalientes ☑ Mexico 22°0N 102°20W 86 C4
Aguila, Punta Puerto Rico 17°57N 67°13W 89 d
Aguilares Argentina 27°26S 65°35W 94 B2
Aguilas Spain 37°23N 1°35W 21 D5
Agüimes Canary Is. 27°58N 15°27W 24 G4
Aguja, C. de la Colombia 11°18N 74°12W 90 B3
Agujereada, Pta. Puerto Rico 18°30N 67°8W 89 d
Agulhas, C. S. Africa 34°52S 20°0E 56 E3
Agulo Canary Is. 28°11N 17°12W 24 F2
Agung, Gunung Indonesia 8°20S 115°28E 37 J18
Agur Uganda 2°28N 32°55E 54 B3
Agusan → Phil. 9°0N 125°30E 37 C7
Aha Mts. Botswana 19°45S 21°0E 56 B3
Ahaggar Algeria 23°0N 6°30E 50 D7
Ahar Iran 38°35N 47°0E 44 B5
Ahipara B. N.Z. 35°5S 173°5E 59 A4
Ahiri India 19°30N 80°0E 40 K12
Ahmad Wal Pakistan 29°18N 65°58E 42 E1
Ahmadabad India 23°0N 72°40E 42 H5
Aḩmadābād Khorāsān, Iran 35°3N 60°50E 45 C9
Aḩmadābād Khorāsān, Iran 35°49N 59°42E 45 C9
Aḩmadī Iran 27°56N 56°42E 45 E8
Ahmadnagar India 19°7N 74°46E 40 K9
Ahmadpur East Pakistan 29°12N 71°10E 42 E4
Ahmadpur Lamma Pakistan 28°19N 70°3E 42 E4
Ahmedabad = Ahmadabad India 23°0N 72°40E 42 H5
Ahmednagar = Ahmadnagar India 19°7N 74°46E 40 K9
Ahome Mexico 25°55N 109°11W 86 B3
Ahoskie U.S.A. 36°17N 76°59W 85 C16
Ahram Iran 28°52N 51°16E 45 D6
Ahrax Pt. Malta 35°59N 14°22E 25 D1
Ahuachapán El Salv. 13°54N 89°52W 88 D2
Ahvāz Iran 31°20N 48°40E 45 D6
Ahvenanmaa = Åland Finland 60°15N 20°0E 9 F19
Ahwar Yemen 13°30N 46°40E 47 E4
Ai → 36°26N 90°14E 43 F14
Ai-Ais Namibia 27°54S 17°59E 56 D2
Ai-Ais and Fish River Canyon △ Namibia 24°45S 17°15E 56 C2
Aichi ☑ Japan 35°0N 137°15E 31 G8
Aigrettes, Pte. des Réunion 21°3S 55°13E 53 c
Aiguá Uruguay 34°13S 54°46W 95 C5
Aigues-Mortes France 43°35N 4°12E 20 E6
Aihui = Heihe China 50°10N 127°30E 33 A7
Aija Peru 9°50S 77°45W 92 E3
Aikawa Japan 38°2N 138°15E 30 E9
Aiken U.S.A. 33°34N 81°43W 85 E14
Aileron Australia 22°39S 133°20E 62 C1
Aillik Canada 55°11N 59°18W 73 A8
Ailsa Craig Canada 43°8N 81°33W 82 C3
Ailsa Craig U.K. 55°15N 5°6W 11 F3
Aim Russia 59°0N 133°55E 29 D14
Aimere Indonesia 8°45S 121°3E 37 F6
Aimogasta Argentina 28°33S 66°50W 94 B2
Aïn Ben Tili Mauritania 25°59N 9°27W 50 C4
Aïn Sefra Algeria 32°47N 0°37W 50 B5
Ain Sudr Egypt 29°50N 33°6E 46 F2
Aïn Témouchent Algeria 35°16N 1°8W 50 A5
Ainaži Latvia 57°50N 24°24E 9 H21
Ainsworth U.S.A. 42°33N 99°52W 80 D4
Aiquile Bolivia 18°10S 65°10W 92 G5
Air Niger 18°30N 8°0E 50 E7
Air Force I. Canada 67°58N 74°5W 69 C12
Air Hitam Malaysia 1°55N 103°11E 39 M4
Airdrie Canada 51°18N 114°2W 70 C6
Airdrie U.K. 55°52N 3°57W 11 F5
Aire → U.K. 53°43N 0°55W 12 D7
Aire, I. de l' Spain 39°48N 4°16E 24 B11
Airlie Beach Australia 20°16S 148°43E 62 J6
Aisne → France 49°26N 2°50E 20 B5
Ait India 25°54N 79°14E 43 G8
Aitkin U.S.A. 46°32N 93°42W 80 B7
Aitutaki Cook Is. 18°25S 159°45W 65 J12
Aiud Romania 46°19N 23°44E 17 E12
Aix-en-Provence France 43°32N 5°27E 20 E6
Aix-la-Chapelle = Aachen Germany 50°45N 6°6E 16 C4
Aix-les-Bains France 45°41N 5°53E 20 D6

Aizawl India 23°40N 92°44E 41 H18
Aizkraukle Latvia 56°36N 25°11E 9 H21
Aizpute Latvia 56°43N 21°40E 9 H19
Aizuwakamatsu Japan 37°30N 139°56E 30 F9
Ajaccio France 41°55N 8°40E 20 F8
Ajaigarh India 24°52N 80°16E 43 G9
Ajalpan Mexico 18°22N 97°15W 87 D5
Ajanta Ra. India 20°28N 75°50E 40 J9
Ajari Rep. = Ajaria ☑ Georgia 41°30N 42°0E 19 F7
Ajaria ☑ Georgia 41°30N 42°0E 19 F7
Ajax Canada 43°50N 79°1W 82 C5
Ajdābiyā Libya 30°54N 20°4E 51 B10
Ajka Hungary 47°4N 17°31E 17 E9
'Ajlūn Jordan 32°18N 35°47E 46 C4
'Ajlūn ☑ Jordan 32°18N 35°47E 46 C4
'Ajmān U.A.E. 25°25N 55°30E 45 E7
Ajmer India 26°28N 74°37E 42 F6
Ajnala India 31°50N 74°48E 42 D6
Ajo U.S.A. 32°22N 112°52W 77 K7
Ajo, C. de Spain 43°31N 3°35W 21 A4
Akabira Japan 43°33N 142°5E 30 C11
Akagera △ Rwanda 1°31S 30°33E 54 C3
Akamas Cyprus 35°3N 32°18E 25 D11
Akan △ Japan 43°20N 144°20E 30 C12
Akanthou Cyprus 35°22N 33°45E 25 D12
Akaroa N.Z. 43°49S 172°59E 59 E4
Akashi Japan 34°45N 134°58E 31 G7
Akbarpur Bihar, India 24°39N 83°58E 43 G10
Akbarpur Ut. P., India 26°25N 82°32E 43 F10
Akçakale Turkey 36°41N 38°56E 44 B3
Akçakoca Turkey 41°4N 31°6E 44 B1
Akelamo Indonesia 1°35N 129°40E 37 D7
Aketi Dem. Rep. of the Congo 2°38N 23°47E 52 D4
Akhisar Turkey 38°56N 27°48E 23 E12
Akhnur India 32°52N 74°45E 43 C6
Akhtyrka = Okhtyrka Ukraine 50°25N 35°0E 19 D5
Aki Japan 33°30N 133°54E 31 H6
Akimiski I. Canada 52°50N 81°30W 72 B3
Akincilar = Louroujina Cyprus 35°0N 33°28E 25 E12
Akita Japan 39°45N 140°7E 30 E10
Akita ☑ Japan 39°40N 140°30E 30 E10
Akjoujt Mauritania 19°45N 14°15W 50 E3
Akkeshi Japan 43°2N 144°51E 30 C12
'Akko Israel 32°55N 35°4E 46 C4
Aklavik Canada 68°12N 135°0W 68 C6
Aklera India 24°26N 76°32E 42 G7
Akō Japan 34°45N 134°24E 31 G7
Akola India 20°42N 77°2E 40 J10
Akordat Eritrea 15°30N 37°40E 47 D2
Akpatok I. Canada 60°25N 68°8W 69 C13
Åkrahamn Norway 59°15N 5°10E 9 G11
Akranes Iceland 64°19N 22°5W 8 D2
Akron Colo., U.S.A. 40°10N 103°13W 76 F12
Akron Ohio, U.S.A. 41°5N 81°31W 82 E3
Akrotiri Cyprus 34°36N 32°57E 25 E11
Akrotiri Bay Cyprus 34°35N 33°10E 25 E12
Aksai Chin China 35°15N 79°55E 43 B8
Aksaray Turkey 38°25N 34°2E 44 B2
Aksay = Aqsay Kazakhstan 51°11N 53°0E 19 D9
Akşehir Turkey 38°18N 31°30E 44 B1
Akşehir Gölü Turkey 38°30N 31°25E 19 G5
Aksu China 41°5N 80°10E 32 B3
Aksum Ethiopia 14°5N 38°40E 47 E2
Aktsyabrski Belarus 52°38N 28°53E 17 B15
Aktyubinsk = Aqtöbe Kazakhstan 50°17N 57°10E 19 D10
Akure Nigeria 7°15N 5°5E 50 G7
Akureyri Iceland 65°40N 18°6W 8 D4
Akuseki-Shima Japan 29°27N 129°37E 31 K4
Akyab = Sittwe Burma 20°18N 92°45E 41 J18
Al 'Adan Yemen 12°45N 45°0E 47 E4
Al Aḩsā = Hasa Si. Arabia 25°50N 49°0E 45 E6
Al Ajfar Si. Arabia 27°26N 43°0E 44 E4
Al Amādīyah Iraq 37°5N 43°30E 44 B4
Al 'Amārah Iraq 31°55N 47°15E 44 D5
Al Anbār ☑ Iraq 33°25N 42°0E 44 C4
Al 'Aqabah Jordan 29°31N 35°0E 46 F4
Al 'Aqabah ☑ Jordan 29°30N 35°0E 46 F4
Al Arak Syria 34°38N 38°35E 44 C3
Al 'Aramah Si. Arabia 25°30N 46°0E 44 E5
Al 'Arţāwīyah Si. Arabia 26°31N 45°20E 44 E5
Al 'Āşimah = 'Ammān ☑ Jordan 31°40N 36°30E 46 D5
Al 'Assāfīyah Si. Arabia 28°17N 38°59E 44 D3
Al 'Awdah Si. Arabia 25°45N 45°41E 44 E5
Al 'Ayn Si. Arabia 25°4N 38°6E 44 E3
Al 'Ayn U.A.E. 24°15N 55°45E 45 E7
Al 'Azīzīyah Iraq 32°54N 45°4E 44 C5
Al Bāb Syria 36°23N 37°29E 44 B3
Al Bad' Si. Arabia 28°28N 35°1E 44 D2
Al Bādī Iraq 35°56N 41°32E 44 C4
Al Baḩrah Kuwait 29°40N 47°52E 44 D5
Al Baḩral Mayyit = Dead Sea Asia 31°30N 35°30E 46 D4
Al Balqā' ☑ Jordan 32°5N 35°45E 46 C4
Al Bārūk, J. Lebanon 33°39N 35°40E 46 B4
Al Başrah Iraq 30°30N 47°50E 44 D5
Al Baţḩā Iraq 31°6N 45°53E 44 D5
Al Batrūn Lebanon 34°15N 35°40E 46 A4
Al Bayḑā Libya 32°50N 21°44E 51 B10
Al Biqā Lebanon 34°10N 36°10E 46 A5
Al Bi'r Si. Arabia 28°51N 36°16E 44 D3
Al Bukayriyah Si. Arabia 26°9N 43°40E 44 E4
Al Burayj Syria 34°15N 37°40E 46 A6
Al Faḑilī Si. Arabia 26°58N 49°10E 45 E6
Al Fallūjah Iraq 33°20N 43°55E 44 C4
Al Fāw Iraq 30°0N 48°30E 45 D6
Al Fujayrah U.A.E. 25°7N 56°18E 45 E8
Al Ghammās Iraq 31°45N 44°37E 44 D5
Al Ghazālah Si. Arabia 26°48N 41°19E 44 E4

Al Ḥadīthah Iraq 34°0N 41°13E 44 C4
Al Ḥadīthah Si. Arabia 31°28N 37°8E 46 D6
Al Ḥaḍr Iraq 35°35N 42°44E 44 C4
Al Ḥājānah Syria 33°20N 36°33E 46 B5
Al Hajar al Gharbī Oman 24°10N 56°15E 45 E8
Al Ḥāmad Si. Arabia 31°30N 39°30E 44 D3
Al Ḥamdānīyah Syria 35°25N 36°50E 44 C3
Al Ḥamīdīyah Syria 34°42N 35°57E 46 A4
Al Ḥammār Iraq 30°57N 46°51E 44 D5
Al Ḥamrā' Si. Arabia 24°2N 38°55E 44 E3
Al Ḥamzah Iraq 31°43N 44°58E 44 D5
Al Ḥanākīyah Si. Arabia 24°51N 40°31E 44 E4
Al Ḥarūj al Aswad Libya 27°0N 17°10E 51 C9
Al Ḥasakah Syria 36°35N 40°45E 44 B4
Al Ḥayy Iraq 32°5N 46°0E 44 C5
Al Ḥijarah Asia 30°0N 44°0E 44 D4
Al Ḥillah Iraq 32°30N 44°25E 44 C5
Al Ḥillah Si. Arabia 23°35N 46°50E 47 B4
Al Ḥindīyah Iraq 32°30N 44°10E 44 C5
Al Ḥirmil Lebanon 34°26N 36°24E 46 A5
Al Hoceïma Morocco 35°8N 3°58W 50 A5
Al Ḥudaydah Yemen 14°50N 43°0E 47 E3
Al Ḥudūd ash Shamālīyah □
   Si. Arabia 29°10N 42°30E 44 D4
Al Ḥufūf Si. Arabia 25°25N 49°45E 45 E6
Al Ḥumaydah Si. Arabia 29°14N 34°56E 44 D2
Al Ḥunayy Si. Arabia 25°58N 48°45E 45 E6
Al Īsāwīyah Si. Arabia 30°43N 37°59E 44 D3
Al Jafr Jordan 30°18N 36°14E 46 E5
Al Jāfūrah Si. Arabia 25°0N 50°15E 45 E7
Al Jaghbūb Libya 29°42N 24°38E 51 C10
Al Jahrah Kuwait 29°25N 47°40E 44 D5
Al Jalāmīd Si. Arabia 31°20N 40°6E 44 D4
Al Jamalīyah Qatar 25°37N 51°5E 45 E6
Al Janūb □ Lebanon 33°20N 35°20E 46 B4
Al Jawf Libya 24°10N 23°24E 51 D10
Al Jawf Si. Arabia 29°55N 39°40E 44 D3
Al Jawf Si. Arabia 29°30N 39°30E 44 D3
Al Jazair = Algeria ■
   Africa 28°30N 2°0E 50 C6
Al Jazirah Iraq 33°30N 44°0E 44 C5
Al Jithāmīyah Si. Arabia 27°41N 41°43E 44 E4
Al Jubayl Si. Arabia 27°0N 49°50E 45 E6
Al Jubaylah Si. Arabia 24°55N 46°25E 44 E5
Al Jubb Si. Arabia 27°11N 42°17E 44 E4
Al Junaynah Sudan 13°27N 22°45E 51 F10
Al Kabā'ish Iraq 30°58N 47°0E 44 D5
Al Karak Jordan 31°11N 35°42E 46 D4
Al Karak □ Jordan 31°0N 36°0E 46 E5
Al Kāẓimīyah Iraq 33°22N 44°18E 44 C5
Al Khābūrah Oman 23°57N 57°5E 45 F8
Al Khafji Si. Arabia 28°24N 48°29E 45 E6
Al Khalīl West Bank 31°32N 35°6E 46 D4
Al Khāliṣ Iraq 33°49N 44°32E 44 C5
Al Kharsānīyah
   Si. Arabia 27°13N 49°18E 45 E6
Al Khasab Oman 26°14N 56°15E 45 E8
Al Khawr Qatar 25°41N 51°30E 45 E6
Al Khiḍr Iraq 31°12N 45°33E 44 D5
Al Khiyām Lebanon 33°20N 35°36E 46 B4
Al Khobar Si. Arabia 26°17N 50°12E 45 E6
Al Khums Libya 32°40N 14°17E 51 B8
Al Kiswah Syria 33°23N 36°14E 46 B5
Al Kūfah Iraq 32°2N 44°24E 44 C5
Al Kufrah Libya 24°17N 23°15E 51 D10
Al Kuhayfīyah Si. Arabia 27°12N 43°3E 44 E4
Al Kūt Iraq 32°30N 46°0E 44 C5
Al Kuwayt Kuwait 29°30N 48°0E 44 D5
Al Labwah Lebanon 34°11N 36°20E 46 A5
Al Lādhiqīyah Syria 35°30N 35°45E 44 C2
Al Līth Si. Arabia 20°9N 40°15E 47 C3
Al Liwā' Oman 24°31N 56°36E 45 E8
Al Luḥayyah Yemen 15°45N 42°40E 47 D3
Al Madīnah Iraq 30°57N 47°16E 44 D5
Al Madīnah Si. Arabia 24°35N 39°52E 44 E3
Al Mafraq Jordan 32°17N 36°14E 46 C5
Al Mafraq □ Jordan 32°17N 36°14E 46 C5
Al Maghreb = Morocco ■
   N. Afr. 32°0N 5°50W 50 B4
Al Maḥmūdīyah Iraq 33°3N 44°21E 44 C5
Al Majma'ah Si. Arabia 25°57N 45°22E 44 E5
Al Makhruq, W. →
   Jordan 31°28N 37°0E 46 D6
Al Makḥūl Si. Arabia 26°37N 42°39E 44 E4
Al Manāmah Bahrain 26°10N 50°30E 45 E6
Al Maqwa' Kuwait 29°10N 47°59E 44 D5
Al Marāh Si. Arabia 25°35N 49°35E 45 E6
Al Marj Libya 32°25N 20°30E 51 B10
Al Maṭlā Kuwait 29°24N 47°40E 44 D5
Al Mawsil Iraq 36°15N 43°5E 44 B4
Al Mayādin Syria 35°1N 40°27E 44 C4
Al Mazār Jordan 31°4N 35°41E 46 D4
Al Midhnab Si. Arabia 25°50N 44°18E 44 E5
Al Minā' Lebanon 34°24N 35°49E 46 A4
Al Miqdādīyah Iraq 34°0N 45°0E 44 C5
Al Mubarraz Si. Arabia 25°30N 49°40E 45 E6
Al Mudawwarah Jordan 29°19N 36°0E 46 F5
Al Mughayrā' U.A.E. 24°5N 53°32E 45 E7
Al Muḥarraq Bahrain 26°15N 50°40E 45 E6
Al Mukallā Yemen 14°33N 49°2E 47 E4
Al Mukhā Yemen 13°18N 43°15E 47 E3
Al Musayjīd Si. Arabia 24°5N 39°5E 44 E3
Al Musayyib Iraq 32°40N 44°20E 44 C5
Al Muthanná □ Iraq 30°30N 45°0E 44 D5
Al Muwaylih Si. Arabia 27°40N 35°30E 44 E2
Al Qā'im Iraq 34°21N 41°7E 44 C4
Al Qalībah Si. Arabia 28°24N 37°42E 44 D3
Al Qāmishlī Syria 37°2N 41°14E 44 B4
Al Qaryatayn Syria 34°12N 37°13E 46 A6
Al Qaṭ'a Syria 34°40N 40°48E 44 C4
Al Qaṭīf Si. Arabia 26°35N 50°0E 45 E6
Al Qaṭrānah Jordan 31°12N 36°6E 46 D5
Al Qaṭrūn Libya 24°56N 15°3E 51 D9
Al Qayṣūmah Si. Arabia 28°20N 46°7E 44 D5
Al Quds = Jerusalem
   Israel/West Bank 31°47N 35°10E 46 D4

Al Qunayṭirah Syria 32°55N 35°45E 46 C4
Al Qunfudhah Si. Arabia 19°3N 41°4E 47 D3
Al Qurnah Iraq 31°1N 47°25E 44 D5
Al Quṣayr Egypt 30°39N 45°50E 44 D5
Al Quṣayr Syria 34°31N 36°34E 46 A5
Al Qutayfah Syria 33°44N 36°36E 46 B5
Al 'Ubaylah Si. Arabia 21°59N 50°57E 47 C5
Al 'Uḍaylīyah Si. Arabia 25°8N 49°18E 45 E6
Al 'Ulā Si. Arabia 26°35N 38°0E 44 E3
Al 'Uqayr Si. Arabia 25°40N 50°15E 45 E6
Al 'Uwaynid Si. Arabia 24°50N 46°0E 44 E5
Al 'Uwayqīlah Si. Arabia 30°30N 42°10E 44 D4
Al 'Uyūn Ḥijāz, Si. Arabia 24°33N 39°35E 44 E3
Al 'Uyūn Najd, Si. Arabia 26°30N 43°50E 44 E4
Al 'Uzayr Iraq 31°19N 47°25E 44 D5
Al Wajh Si. Arabia 26°10N 36°30E 44 E3
Al Wakrah Qatar 25°10N 51°40E 45 E6
Al Waqbah Si. Arabia 28°48N 45°33E 44 D5
Al Wari'āh Si. Arabia 27°51N 47°25E 44 E5
Al Yaman = Yemen ■
   Asia 15°0N 44°0E 47 E3
Ala Dağ Turkey 37°44N 35°9E 44 B3
Ala Tau Asia 45°30N 80°40E 28 E9
Ala Tau Shankou = Dzungarian
   Gate Asia 45°10N 82°0E 32 B3
Alabama □ U.S.A. 33°0N 87°0W 85 E11
Alabama → U.S.A. 31°8N 87°57W 85 F11
Alabaster U.S.A. 33°15N 86°49W 85 E11
Alaçam Dağları Turkey 39°18N 29°49E 23 E13
Alacant = Alicante Spain 38°23N 0°30W 21 C5
Alachua U.S.A. 29°47N 82°30W 85 G13
Alagoa Grande Brazil 7°3S 35°35W 93 E11
Alagoas □ Brazil 9°0S 36°0W 93 E11
Alagoinhas Brazil 12°7S 38°20W 93 F11
Alaior Spain 39°57N 4°8E 24 B11
Alajero Canary Is. 28°3N 17°13W 24 F2
Alajuela Costa Rica 10°2N 84°8W 88 D3
Alakamisy Madag. 21°19S 47°14E 57 C8
Alaknanda → India 30°8N 78°36E 43 D8
Alakurtti Russia 66°58N 30°25E 8 C24
Alamarvdasht Iran 27°37N 52°59E 45 E7
Alameda Calif., U.S.A. 37°46N 122°15W 78 H4
Alameda N. Mex.,
   U.S.A. 35°11N 106°37W 77 J10
Alamo U.S.A. 37°22N 115°10W 79 H11
Alamogordo U.S.A. 32°54N 105°57W 77 K11
Alamos Mexico 27°1N 108°56W 86 B3
Alamosa U.S.A. 37°28N 105°52W 77 H11
Åland Finland 60°15N 20°0E 9 F19
Ålands hav Europe 60°0N 19°30E 9 G18
Alania = North Ossetia □
   Russia 43°30N 44°30E 19 F7
Alanya Turkey 36°38N 32°0E 44 B1
Alaotra, Farihin' Madag. 17°30S 48°30E 57 B8
Alapayevsk Russia 57°52N 61°42E 28 D7
Alappuzha = Alleppey
   India 9°30N 76°28E 40 Q10
Alaró Spain 39°42N 2°47E 24 B9
Alarobia-Vohiposa
   Madag. 20°59S 47°9E 57 C8
Alaşehir Turkey 38°23N 28°30E 23 E13
Alaska □ U.S.A. 64°0N 154°0W 74 a
Alaska, G. of Pac. Oc. 58°0N 145°0W 74 a
Alaska Peninsula U.S.A. 56°0N 159°0W 74 a
Alaska Range U.S.A. 62°50N 151°0W 74 a
Älät Azerbaijan 39°58N 49°25E 45 B6
Alatau Shan = Ala Tau
   Asia 45°30N 80°40E 28 E9
Alatyr Russia 54°55N 46°35E 18 D8
Alausi Ecuador 2°0S 78°50W 92 D3
Alava, C. U.S.A. 48°10N 124°44W 76 B1
Alavo = Alavus Finland 62°35N 23°36E 8 E20
Alavus Finland 62°35N 23°36E 8 E20
Alawoona Australia 34°45S 140°30E 63 E3
'Alayh Lebanon 33°46N 35°33E 46 B4
Alazani → Azerbaijan 41°5N 46°40E 19 F8
Alba Italy 44°42N 8°2E 20 D8
Alba-Iulia Romania 46°8N 23°39E 17 E12
Albacete Spain 39°0N 1°50W 21 C5
Albacutya, L. Australia 35°45S 141°58E 63 F3
Albanel, L. Canada 50°55N 73°12W 72 B5
Albania ■ Europe 41°0N 20°0E 23 D9
Albany Australia 35°1S 117°58E 61 G2
Albany Ga., U.S.A. 31°35N 84°10W 85 F12
Albany N.Y., U.S.A. 42°39N 73°45W 83 D11
Albany Oreg., U.S.A. 44°38N 123°6W 76 D2
Albany Tex., U.S.A. 32°44N 99°18W 84 E5
Albany → Canada 52°17N 81°31W 72 B3
Albarca, C. d' Spain 39°4N 1°22E 24 B7
Albardón Argentina 31°20S 68°30W 94 C2
Albatross B. Australia 12°45S 141°30E 62 A3
Albemarle U.S.A. 35°21N 80°12W 85 D14
Albemarle Sd. U.S.A. 36°5N 76°0W 85 C16
Alberche → Spain 39°58N 4°46W 21 C3
Alberdi Paraguay 26°14S 58°20W 94 B4
Alberga → Australia 27°6S 135°33E 63 D2
Albert, L. Africa 1°30N 31°0E 54 B3
Albert, L. Australia 35°30S 139°10E 63 F2
Albert Edward Ra.
   Australia 18°17S 127°57E 60 C4
Albert Lea U.S.A. 43°39N 93°22W 80 D7
Albert Nile → Uganda 3°36N 32°2E 54 B3
Albert Town Bahamas 22°37N 74°33W 89 B5
Alberta □ Canada 54°40N 115°0W 70 C6
Alberti Argentina 35°1S 60°16W 94 D3
Albertinia S. Africa 34°11S 21°34E 56 E3
Alberton Canada 46°50N 64°0W 73 C7
Albertville France 45°40N 6°22E 20 D7
Albertville U.S.A. 34°16N 86°13W 85 D11
Albi France 43°56N 2°9E 20 E5
Albia U.S.A. 41°2N 92°48W 80 E7
Albina Suriname 5°37N 54°15W 93 B8
Albina, Ponta Angola 15°52S 11°44E 56 B1
Albion Mich., U.S.A. 42°15N 84°45W 81 D11
Albion Nebr., U.S.A. 41°42N 98°0W 80 E4
Albion Pa., U.S.A. 41°53N 80°22W 82 E4
Alborán Medit. S. 35°57N 3°0W 21 E4
Ålborg = Aalborg Denmark 57°2N 9°54E 9 H13

Alborz, Reshteh-ye Kūhhā-ye
   Iran 36°0N 52°0E 45 C7
Albufeira Portugal 37°5N 8°15W 21 D1
Albuquerque U.S.A. 35°5N 106°39W 77 J10
Albuquerque, Cayos de
   Caribbean 12°10N 81°50W 88 D3
Alburg U.S.A. 44°59N 73°18W 83 B11
Albury Australia 36°3S 146°56E 63 F4
Alcalá de Henares Spain 40°28N 3°22W 21 B4
Alcalá la Real Spain 37°27N 3°57W 21 D4
Álcamo Italy 37°59N 12°55E 22 F5
Alcañiz Spain 41°2N 0°8W 21 B5
Alcântara Brazil 2°20S 44°30W 93 D10
Alcántara, Embalse de
   Spain 39°44N 6°50W 21 C2
Alcantarilla Spain 37°59N 1°12W 21 D5
Alcaraz, Sierra de Spain 38°40N 2°20E 21 C4
Alcaudete Spain 37°35N 4°5W 21 D3
Alcázar de San Juan
   Spain 39°24N 3°12W 21 C4
Alchevsk Ukraine 48°30N 38°45E 19 E6
Alcira = Alzira Spain 39°9N 0°30W 21 C5
Alcova U.S.A. 42°34N 106°43W 76 E10
Alcoy Spain 38°43N 0°30W 21 C5
Alcúdia Spain 39°51N 3°7E 24 B10
Alcúdia, B. d' Spain 39°47N 3°15E 24 B10
Aldabra Is. Seychelles 9°22S 46°28E 49 G8
Aldama Mexico 22°55N 98°4E 44 C5
Aldan Russia 58°40N 125°30E 29 D13
Aldan → Russia 63°28N 129°35E 29 C13
Aldea, Pta. de la
   Canary Is. 28°0N 15°50W 24 G4
Aldeburgh U.K. 52°10N 1°37E 13 E9
Alder Pk. U.S.A. 35°53N 121°22W 78 K5
Alderney U.K. 49°42N 2°11W 13 H5
Aldershot U.K. 51°15N 0°44W 13 F7
Aledo U.S.A. 41°12N 90°45W 80 E8
Aleg Mauritania 17°3N 13°55W 50 E3
Alegranza Canary Is. 29°23N 13°32W 24 E6
Alegranza, I. Canary Is. 29°23N 13°32W 24 E6
Alegre Brazil 20°50S 41°30W 95 A7
Alegrete Brazil 29°40S 56°0W 95 B4
Aleksandriya = Oleksandriya
   Ukraine 50°37N 26°19E 17 C14
Aleksandrov Gay Russia 50°9N 48°34E 19 D8
Aleksandrovsk-Sakhalinskiy
   Russia 50°50N 142°20E 29 D15
Aleksandry, Zemlya
   Russia 80°25N 48°0E 28 A5
Além Paraíba Brazil 21°52S 42°41W 95 A7
Alemania Argentina 25°40S 65°30W 94 B2
Alemania Chile 25°10S 69°55W 94 B2
Alençon France 48°27N 0°4E 20 B4
Alenquer Brazil 1°56S 54°46W 93 D8
'Alenuihähä Channel
   U.S.A. 20°30N 156°0W 74 b
Aleppo = Ḥalab Syria 36°10N 37°15E 44 B3
Aléria France 42°5N 9°26E 20 E9
Alert Canada 83°2N 60°0W 69 A13
Alès France 44°9N 4°5E 20 D6
Alessándria Italy 44°54N 8°37E 20 D8
Ålesund Norway 62°28N 6°12E 8 E12
Aleutian Basin Pac. Oc. 57°0N 177°0E 64 B9
Aleutian Is. Pac. Oc. 52°0N 175°0W 74 a
Aleutian Trench Pac. Oc. 48°0N 180°0E 4 D17
Alexander, Mt.
   Australia 28°58S 120°16E 61 E3
Alexander Arch. U.S.A. 56°0N 136°0W 68 D6
Alexander Bay S. Africa 28°40S 16°30E 56 D2
Alexander City U.S.A. 32°56N 85°58W 85 E12
Alexander I., Antarctica 69°0S 70°0W 5 C17
Alexandra Australia 37°8S 145°40E 63 F4
Alexandra N.Z. 45°14S 169°25E 59 F2
Alexandra Falls Canada 60°29N 116°18W 70 A5
Alexandria = El Iskandarîya
   Egypt 31°13N 29°58E 51 B11
Alexandria B.C.,
   Canada 52°35N 122°27W 70 C4
Alexandria Ont.,
   Canada 45°19N 74°38W 83 A10
Alexandria Romania 43°57N 25°24E 17 G13
Alexandria S. Africa 33°38S 26°28E 56 E4
Alexandria U.K. 55°59N 4°35W 11 F4
Alexandria La., U.S.A. 31°18N 92°27W 84 F8
Alexandria Minn.,
   U.S.A. 45°53N 95°22W 80 C6
Alexandria S. Dak.,
   U.S.A. 43°39N 97°47W 80 D5
Alexandria Va., U.S.A. 38°49N 77°5W 81 F15
Alexandria Bay U.S.A. 44°20N 75°55W 83 B9
Alexandrina, L.
   Australia 35°25S 139°10E 63 F2
Alexandroupoli Greece 40°50N 25°54E 23 D11
Alexis → Canada 52°33N 56°8W 73 B8
Alexis Creek Canada 52°10N 123°20W 70 C4
Aleysk Russia 52°40N 83°0E 28 D9
Alfabia Spain 39°44N 2°44E 24 B9
Alfenas Brazil 21°20S 46°10W 95 A6
Alford Aberds., U.K. 57°14N 2°41W 11 D6
Alford Lincs., U.K. 53°15N 0°10E 12 D8
Alfred Maine, U.S.A. 43°29N 70°43W 83 C14
Alfred N.Y., U.S.A. 42°16N 77°48W 82 D7
Alfreton U.K. 53°6N 1°24W 12 D6
Algaida Spain 39°33N 2°53E 24 B9
Ålgård Norway 58°46N 5°53E 9 G11
Algarve Portugal 36°58N 8°20W 21 E1
Algeciras Spain 36°9N 5°28W 21 D3
Algemesí Spain 39°11N 0°27W 21 C5
Alger Algeria 36°42N 3°8E 50 A6
Algeria ■ Africa 28°30N 2°0E 50 C6
Algha Kazakhstan 49°53N 57°20E 19 E10
Alghero Italy 40°33N 8°19E 22 D3
Algiers = Alger Algeria 36°42N 3°8E 50 A6
Algoa B. S. Africa 33°50S 25°45E 56 E4
Algoma U.S.A. 44°36N 87°26W 80 C10
Algona U.S.A. 43°4N 94°14W 80 D6

Algonac U.S.A. 42°37N 82°32W 82 D2
Algonquin □ Canada 45°50N 78°30W 72 C4
Algorta Uruguay 32°25S 57°23W 96 C5
Alhambra U.S.A. 34°5N 118°7W 79 L8
Alhucemas = Al Hoceïma
   Morocco 35°8N 3°58W 50 A5
'Alī al Gharbī Iraq 32°30N 46°45E 44 C5
'Alī ash Sharqī Iraq 32°7N 46°44E 44 C5
'Alī Bayramlı Azerbaijan 39°59N 48°52E 45 B6
'Alī Khēl Afghan. 33°57N 69°43E 42 C3
'Alī Shāh Iran 38°9N 45°50E 44 B5
Alīābād Iran 36°40N 54°33E 45 B7
'Alīābād Khorāsān, Iran 35°4N 59°37E 45 C8
'Alīābād Kordestān, Iran 35°4N 46°58E 44 C5
'Alīābād Yazd, Iran 31°41N 53°49E 45 D7
Aliağa Turkey 38°47N 26°59E 23 E12
Aliakmonas → Greece 40°30N 22°36E 23 D10
Alicante Spain 38°23N 0°30W 21 C5
Alice S. Africa 32°48S 26°55E 56 E4
Alice U.S.A. 27°45N 98°5W 84 H5
Alice → Queens.,
   Australia 24°2S 144°50E 62 C3
Alice → Queens.,
   Australia 15°35S 142°20E 62 B3
Alice Arm Canada 55°29N 129°31W 70 B3
Alice Springs Australia 23°40S 133°50E 62 C1
Alicedale S. Africa 33°15S 26°4E 56 E4
Aliceville U.S.A. 33°8N 88°9W 85 E10
Aliganj India 27°30N 79°10E 43 F8
Aligarh Raj., India 25°55N 76°15E 42 G7
Aligarh Ut. P., India 27°55N 78°10E 42 F8
Alīgūdarz Iran 33°25N 49°45E 45 C6
Alimia Greece 36°16N 27°43E 25 C9
Alingsås Sweden 57°56N 12°31E 9 H15
Alipur Pakistan 29°25N 70°55E 42 E4
Alipur Duar India 26°30N 89°35E 41 F16
Aliquippa U.S.A. 40°37N 80°15W 82 F4
Alitus = Alytus Lithuania 54°24N 24°3E 9 J21
Aliwal North S. Africa 30°45S 26°45E 56 E4
Alix Canada 52°24N 113°11W 70 C6
Aljustrel Portugal 37°55N 8°10W 21 D1
Alkmaar Neths. 52°37N 4°45E 15 B4
All American Canal
   U.S.A. 32°45N 115°15W 77 K6
Allagash → U.S.A. 47°5N 69°3W 81 B19
Allah Dad Pakistan 25°38N 67°34E 42 G2
Allahabad India 25°25N 81°58E 43 G9
Allan Canada 51°53N 106°4W 71 C7
Allanridge S. Africa 27°45S 26°40E 56 D4
Allegany U.S.A. 42°6N 78°30W 82 D6
Allegheny → U.S.A. 40°27N 80°1W 82 F5
Allegheny Mts. U.S.A. 38°15N 80°10W 81 F13
Allegheny Plateau
   U.S.A. 41°30N 78°30W 81 E14
Allegheny Res. U.S.A. 41°50N 79°0W 82 E6
Allègre, Pte. Guadeloupe 16°22N 61°46W 88 b
Allen, Bog of Ireland 53°15N 7°0W 10 C5
Allen, L. Ireland 54°8N 8°4W 10 B3
Allendale U.S.A. 33°1N 81°18W 85 E14
Allende Mexico 28°20N 100°51W 86 B4
Allentown U.S.A. 40°37N 75°29W 83 F9
Alleppey India 9°30N 76°28E 40 Q10
Aller → Germany 52°56N 9°12E 16 B5
Alleynes B. Barbados 13°13S 59°39W 89 g
Alliance Nebr., U.S.A. 42°6N 102°52W 80 D2
Alliance Ohio, U.S.A. 40°55N 81°6W 82 F3
Allier → France 46°57N 3°4E 20 C5
Alliford Bay Canada 53°12N 131°58W 70 C2
Alligator Pond Jamaica 17°52N 77°34W 88 a
Alliston Canada 44°9N 79°52W 82 B5
Alloa U.K. 56°7N 3°47W 11 E5
Allora Australia 28°2S 152°0E 63 D5
Alluitsup Paa Greenland 60°30N 45°35W 4 C5
Alma Canada 48°35N 71°40W 73 C5
Alma Ga., U.S.A. 31°33N 82°28W 85 F13
Alma Kans., U.S.A. 39°1N 96°17W 80 F5
Alma Mich., U.S.A. 43°23N 84°39W 81 D11
Alma Nebr., U.S.A. 40°6N 99°22W 80 E4
Alma Wis., U.S.A. 44°20N 91°55W 80 C8
Alma Ata = Almaty
   Kazakhstan 43°15N 76°57E 28 E8
Alma Hill U.S.A. 42°2N 78°0W 82 D7
Almada Portugal 38°41N 9°8W 21 C1
Almada Australia 17°22S 144°40E 62 B3
Almadén Spain 38°49N 4°52W 21 C3
Almalyk = Olmaliq
   Uzbekistan 40°50N 69°35E 28 E7
Almanor, L. U.S.A. 40°14N 121°9W 76 F3
Almansa Spain 38°51N 1°5W 21 C5
Almanzor, Pico Spain 40°15N 5°18W 21 B3
Almanzora → Spain 37°14N 1°46W 21 D5
Almaty Kazakhstan 43°15N 76°57E 28 E8
Almazán Spain 41°30N 2°30W 21 B4
Almeirim Brazil 1°30S 52°34W 93 D8
Almelo Neths. 52°22N 6°42E 15 B6
Almendralejo Spain 38°41N 6°26W 21 C2
Almere-Stad Neths. 52°20N 5°15E 15 B5
Almería Spain 36°52N 2°27W 21 D4
Almirante Panama 9°10N 82°30W 88 E3
Almond U.S.A. 42°19N 77°44W 82 D7
Almont U.S.A. 42°55N 83°3W 82 D1
Almonte Canada 45°14N 76°12W 83 A8
Almora India 29°38N 79°40E 43 E8
Almyrou, Ormos Greece 35°23N 24°20E 25 D6
Alness U.K. 57°41N 4°16W 11 D4
Alnmouth U.K. 55°24N 1°37W 12 B6
Alnwick U.K. 55°24N 1°42W 12 B6
Aloi Uganda 2°16N 33°10E 54 B3
Alon Burma 22°12N 95°5E 41 H19
Alor Indonesia 8°15S 124°30E 37 F6
Alor Setar Malaysia 6°7N 100°22E 39 J3
Alot India 23°56N 75°40E 42 H6
Aloysius, Mt. Australia 26°0S 128°38E 61 E4
Alpaugh U.S.A. 35°53N 119°29W 78 K7
Alpena U.S.A. 45°4N 83°27W 81 C12
Alpha Australia 23°39S 146°37E 62 C4
Alpha Ridge Arctic 84°0N 118°0W 4 A2

Alphen aan den Rijn
   Neths. 52°7N 4°40E 15 B4
Alpine Ariz., U.S.A. 33°51N 109°9W 77 K9
Alpine Calif., U.S.A. 32°50N 116°46W 79 N10
Alpine Tex., U.S.A. 30°22N 103°40W 84 F3
Alps Europe 46°30N 9°30E 20 C8
Alpurrurulam Australia 20°59S 137°50E 62 C2
Alsace □ France 48°15N 7°25E 20 B7
Alsask Canada 51°21N 109°59W 71 C7
Alsasua Spain 42°54N 2°10W 21 A4
Alsek → U.S.A. 59°10N 138°12W 70 B1
Alsta Norway 65°58N 12°40E 8 D15
Alston U.K. 54°49N 2°25W 12 C5
Alta Norway 69°57N 23°10E 8 B20
Alta Gracia Argentina 31°40S 64°30W 94 C3
Alta Sierra U.S.A. 35°42N 118°33W 79 K8
Altaelva → Norway 69°54N 23°17E 8 B20
Altafjorden Norway 70°5N 23°5E 8 A20
Altai = Aerhtai Shan
   Mongolia 46°40N 92°45E 32 B4
Altai = Gorno-Altay □
   Russia 51°0N 86°0E 28 D9
Altamaha → U.S.A. 31°20N 81°20W 85 F14
Altamira Brazil 3°12S 52°10W 93 D8
Altamira Chile 25°47S 69°51W 94 B2
Altamira Mexico 22°24N 97°55W 87 C5
Altamont U.S.A. 42°42N 74°2W 83 D10
Altamura Italy 40°49N 16°33E 22 D7
Altanbulag Mongolia 50°16N 106°30E 32 A5
Altar Mexico 30°43N 111°44W 86 A2
Altar, Gran Desierto de
   Mexico 31°50N 114°10W 86 D2
Altata Mexico 24°40N 107°55W 86 C3
Altavista U.S.A. 37°6N 79°17W 81 G14
Altay China 47°48N 88°10E 32 B3
Altea Spain 38°38N 0°2W 21 C5
Altiplano Bolivia 17°0S 68°0W 92 G5
Alto Araguaia Brazil 17°15S 53°20W 93 G8
Alto Cuchumatanes =
   Cuchumatanes, Sierra de los
   Guatemala 15°35N 91°25W 88 C1
Alto del Carmen Chile 28°46S 70°30W 94 B1
Alto Ligonha Mozam. 15°30S 38°11E 55 F4
Alto Molocue Mozam. 15°50S 37°35E 55 F4
Alto Paraguay □
   Paraguay 21°0S 58°30W 94 A4
Alto Paraná □ Paraguay 25°30S 54°50W 95 B5
Alton Canada 43°54N 80°5W 82 C4
Alton U.K. 51°9N 0°59W 13 F7
Alton Ill., U.S.A. 38°53N 90°11W 80 F8
Alton N.H., U.S.A. 43°27N 71°13W 83 C13
Altona Canada 49°6N 97°33W 71 D9
Altoona U.S.A. 40°31N 78°24W 82 F6
Altun Kupri Iraq 35°45N 44°9E 44 C5
Altun Shan China 38°30N 88°0E 32 C3
Alturas U.S.A. 41°29N 120°32W 76 F3
Altus U.S.A. 34°38N 99°20W 84 D5
Alucra Turkey 40°22N 38°47E 19 F6
Alūksne Latvia 57°24N 27°3E 9 H22
Alunite U.S.A. 35°59N 114°55W 79 K12
Alusi Indonesia 7°35S 131°40E 37 F8
Alva U.S.A. 36°48N 98°40W 84 C5
Alvarado Mexico 18°46N 95°46W 87 D5
Alvarado U.S.A. 32°24N 97°13W 84 E6
Alvaro Obregón, Presa
   Mexico 27°52N 109°52W 86 B3
Alvear Argentina 29°5S 56°30W 94 B4
Alvesta Sweden 56°54N 14°35E 9 H16
Alvin U.S.A. 29°26N 95°15W 84 G7
Alvinston Canada 42°49N 81°52W 82 D3
Älvkarleby Sweden 60°34N 17°26E 9 F17
Alvord Desert U.S.A. 42°30N 118°25W 76 E4
Älvsbyn Sweden 65°40N 21°0E 8 D19
Alwar India 27°38N 76°34E 42 F7
Alxa Zuoqi China 38°50N 105°40E 34 E3
Alyangula Australia 13°55S 136°30E 62 A2
Alyata = Älät Azerbaijan 39°58N 49°25E 45 B6
Alyth U.K. 56°38N 3°13W 11 E5
Alytus Lithuania 54°24N 24°3E 9 J21
Alzada U.S.A. 45°2N 104°25W 76 D11
Alzamay Russia 55°33N 98°39E 29 D10
Alzira Spain 39°9N 0°30W 21 C5
Am Timan Chad 11°0N 20°10E 51 F10
Amadeus, L. Australia 24°54S 131°0E 61 D5
Amadi
   Dem. Rep. of the Congo 3°40N 26°40E 54 B2
Âmâdi Sudan 5°29N 30°25E 51 G12
Amadjuak L. Canada 65°0N 71°8W 69 C12
Amagansett U.S.A. 40°59N 72°9W 83 F12
Amagasaki Japan 34°42N 135°23E 31 G7
Amahai Indonesia 3°20S 128°55E 37 E7
Amaile Samoa 13°59S 171°22W 59 b
Amakusa-Shotō Japan 32°15N 130°10E 31 H5
Åmål Sweden 59°3N 12°42E 9 G15
Amaliada Greece 37°47N 21°22E 23 F9
Amalner India 21°5N 75°5E 40 J9
Amamapare Indonesia 4°53S 136°38E 37 E9
Amambaí Brazil 23°5S 55°13W 95 A4
Amambaí → Brazil 23°22S 53°56W 95 A5
Amambay □ Paraguay 23°0S 56°0W 95 A4
Amambay, Cordillera de
   S. Amer. 23°0S 55°45W 95 A4
Amami-Guntō Japan 27°16N 129°21E 31 L4
Amami-Ō-Shima Japan 28°16N 129°21E 31 K4
Amaná, L. Brazil 2°35S 64°40W 92 D6
Amanat → India 24°7N 84°4E 43 G11
Amanda Park U.S.A. 47°28N 123°55W 78 C3
Amankeldi Kazakhstan 50°10N 65°10E 28 D7
Amapá Brazil 2°5N 50°50W 93 C8
Amapá □ Brazil 1°40N 52°0W 93 C8
Amarante Brazil 6°14S 42°50W 93 E10
Amaranth Canada 50°36N 98°43W 71 C9
Amargosa → U.S.A. 36°14N 116°51W 79 J10
Amargosa Desert
   U.S.A. 36°40N 116°30W 79 J10
Amargosa Range
   U.S.A. 36°20N 116°45W 79 J10

Amari Greece 35°13N 24°40E 25 D6
Amarillo U.S.A. 35°13N 101°50W 84 D4
Amarkantak India 22°40N 81°45E 43 H9
Amaro, Mte. Italy 42°5N 14°5E 22 C6
Amarpur India 25°5N 87°0E 43 G12
Amarwara India 22°18N 79°10E 43 H8
Amasya Turkey 40°40N 35°50E 19 F6
Amata Australia 26°9S 131°9E 61 E5
Amatikulu S. Africa 29°3S 31°33E 57 D5
Amatitlán Guatemala 14°29N 90°38W 88 D1
Amay Belgium 50°33N 5°19E 15 D5
Amazon = Amazonas → S. Amer. 0°5S 50°0W 93 D8
Amazonas □ Brazil 5°0S 65°0W 92 E6
Amazonas → S. Amer. 0°5S 50°0W 93 D8
Ambah India 26°43N 78°13E 42 F8
Ambahakily Madag. 21°36S 43°41E 57 C7
Ambahita Madag. 24°1S 45°16E 57 C8
Ambala India 30°23N 76°56E 42 D7
Ambalavao Madag. 21°50S 46°56E 57 C8
Ambanja Madag. 13°40S 48°27E 57 A8
Ambararata Madag. 15°3S 48°33E 57 B8
Ambarchik Russia 69°40N 162°20E 29 C17
Ambarijeby Madag. 14°56S 47°41E 57 A8
Ambaro, Helodranon' Madag. 13°23S 48°38E 57 A8
Ambato Ecuador 1°5S 78°42W 92 D3
Ambato Madag. 13°24S 48°29E 57 A8
Ambato, Sierra de Argentina 28°25S 66°10W 94 B2
Ambato Boeny Madag. 16°28S 46°43E 57 B8
Ambatofinandrahana Madag. 20°33S 46°48E 57 C8
Ambatolampy Madag. 19°20S 47°35E 57 B8
Ambatomainty Madag. 17°41S 45°40E 57 B8
Ambatomanoina Madag. 18°18S 47°37E 57 B8
Ambatondrazaka Madag. 17°55S 48°28E 57 B8
Ambatosoratra Madag. 17°37S 48°31E 57 B8
Ambenja Madag. 15°17S 46°58E 57 B8
Amberg Germany 49°26N 11°52E 16 D6
Ambergris Cay Belize 18°0N 87°55W 87 D7
Amberley Canada 44°2N 81°42W 82 B3
Amberley N.Z. 43°9S 172°44E 59 E4
Ambikapur India 23°15N 83°15E 43 H10
Ambilobé Madag. 13°10S 49°3E 57 A8
Ambinanindrano Madag. 20°5S 48°23E 57 C8
Ambinanitelo Madag. 15°21S 49°35E 57 B8
Ambinda Madag. 16°25S 45°52E 57 B8
Amble U.K. 55°20N 1°36W 12 B6
Ambleside U.K. 54°26N 2°58W 12 C5
Ambo Peru 10°5S 76°10W 92 F3
Amboahangy Madag. 24°15S 46°22E 57 C8
Ambodifototra Madag. 16°59S 49°52E 57 B8
Ambodilazana Madag. 18°6S 49°10E 57 B8
Ambodiriana Madag. 17°55S 49°18E 57 B8
Ambohidratrimo Madag. 18°50S 47°26E 57 B8
Ambohidray Madag. 18°36S 48°18E 57 B8
Ambohimahamasina Madag. 21°56S 47°11E 57 C8
Ambohimahasoa Madag. 21°7S 47°13E 57 C8
Ambohimanga Madag. 20°52S 47°36E 57 C8
Ambohimitombo Madag. 20°43S 47°26E 57 C8
Ambohitra Madag. 12°30S 49°10E 57 A8
Amboise France 47°24N 1°2E 20 C4
Ambon Indonesia 3°43S 128°12E 37 E7
Ambondro Madag. 25°13S 45°44E 57 D8
Amboseli, L. Kenya 2°40S 37°10E 54 C4
Amboseli △ Kenya 2°37S 37°13E 54 C4
Ambositra Madag. 20°31S 47°25E 57 C8
Ambovombe Madag. 25°11S 46°5E 57 D8
Amboy U.S.A. 34°33N 115°45W 79 L11
Amboyna Cay S. China Sea 7°50N 112°50E 36 C4
Ambridge U.S.A. 40°36N 80°14W 82 F4
Ambriz Angola 7°48S 13°8E 52 F2
Amchitka I. U.S.A. 51°32N 179°0E 74 a
Amderma Russia 69°45N 61°30E 28 C7
Amdhi India 23°51N 81°27E 43 H9
Amdo China 32°20N 91°40E 41 C17
Ameca Mexico 20°33N 104°2W 86 C4
Ameca → Mexico 20°41N 105°18W 86 C3
Amecameca de Juárez Mexico 19°8N 98°46W 87 D5
Ameland Neths. 53°27N 5°45E 15 A5
Amenia U.S.A. 41°51N 73°33W 83 E11
America-Antarctica Ridge S. Ocean 59°0S 16°0W 5 B2
American Falls U.S.A. 42°47N 112°51W 76 E7
American Falls Res. U.S.A. 42°47N 112°52W 76 E7
American Fork U.S.A. 40°23N 111°48W 76 F8
American Highland Antarctica 73°0S 75°0E 5 D6
American Samoa ☑ Pac. Oc. 14°20S 170°0W 59 b
American Samoa △ Amer. Samoa 14°15S 170°28W 59 b
Americana Brazil 22°45S 47°20W 95 A6
Americus U.S.A. 32°4N 84°14W 85 E12
Amersfoort Neths. 52°9N 5°23E 15 B5
Amersfoort S. Africa 26°59S 29°53E 57 D4
Amery Basin S. Ocean 68°15S 74°30E 5 C6
Amery Ice Shelf Antarctica 69°30S 72°0E 5 C6
Ames U.S.A. 42°2N 93°37W 80 D7
Amesbury U.S.A. 42°51N 70°56W 83 D14
Amet India 25°18N 73°56E 42 G5
Amga Russia 60°50N 132°0E 29 C14
Amga → Russia 62°38N 134°32E 29 C14
Amgu Russia 45°45N 137°15E 30 B8
Amgun → Russia 52°56N 139°38E 29 D14
Amherst Canada 45°48N 64°8W 73 C7
Amherst Mass., U.S.A. 42°23N 72°31W 83 D12
Amherst N.Y., U.S.A. 42°59N 78°48W 82 D6
Amherst Ohio, U.S.A. 41°24N 82°14W 82 E2
Amherst I. Canada 44°8N 76°43W 83 B8
Amherstburg Canada 42°6N 83°6W 72 D3
Amiata, Mte. Italy 42°53N 11°37E 22 C4
Amidon U.S.A. 46°29N 103°19W 80 B2
Amiens France 49°54N 2°16E 20 B5
Aminuis Namibia 23°43S 19°21E 56 C2
Amīrābād Iran 33°20N 46°16E 44 C5
Amirante Is. Seychelles 6°0S 53°0E 26 J7
Amisk ⌓ Canada 56°43N 98°0W 71 B9
Amisk L. Canada 54°35N 102°15W 71 C8
Amistad, Presa de la Mexico 29°26N 101°3W 86 B4
Amistad ⌓ U.S.A. 29°32N 101°12W 84 G4
Amite U.S.A. 30°44N 90°30W 85 F9
Amla India 21°56N 78°7E 42 J8
Amlapura = Karangasem Indonesia 8°27S 115°37E 37 J18
Amlia I. U.S.A. 52°4N 173°30W 74 a
Amlwch U.K. 53°24N 4°20W 12 D3
'Ammān Jordan 31°57N 35°52E 46 D4
'Ammān □ Jordan 31°40N 36°30E 46 D5
'Ammān ✈ (AMM) Jordan 31°45N 36°2E 46 D5
Ammanford U.K. 51°48N 3°59W 13 F4
Ammassalik = Tasiilaq Greenland 65°40N 37°20W 4 C6
Ammochostos = Famagusta Cyprus 35°8N 33°55E 25 D12
Ammon U.S.A. 43°28N 111°58W 76 E8
Amnat Charoen Thailand 15°51N 104°38E 38 E5
Amnura Bangla. 24°37N 88°25E 43 G13
Āmol Iran 36°23N 52°20E 45 B7
Amorgos Greece 36°50N 25°57E 23 F11
Amory U.S.A. 33°59N 88°29W 85 E10
Amos Canada 48°35N 78°5W 72 C4
Åmot Norway 59°57N 9°54E 9 G13
Amoy = Xiamen China 24°25N 118°4E 33 D6
Ampanavoana Madag. 15°41S 50°22E 57 B9
Ampang Malaysia 3°8N 101°45E 39 L3
Ampangalana, Lakandranon' Madag. 22°48S 47°50E 57 C8
Ampanihy Madag. 24°40S 44°45E 57 C7
Amparafaravola Madag. 17°35S 48°13E 57 B8
Ampasinambo Madag. 20°31S 48°0E 57 C8
Ampasindava, Helodranon' Madag. 13°40S 48°15E 57 A8
Ampasindava, Saikanosy Madag. 13°42S 47°55E 57 A8
Ampenan Indonesia 8°34S 116°4E 37 K18
Amper → Germany 48°29N 11°55E 16 D6
Amphoe Kathu Thailand 7°55N 98°21E 39 a
Amphoe Thalang Thailand 8°1N 98°20E 39 a
Ampitsikinana Madag. 12°57S 49°49E 57 A8
Ampombiantambo Madag. 12°42S 48°57E 57 A8
Ampotaka Madag. 25°3S 44°41E 57 D7
Ampoza Madag. 22°20S 44°44E 57 C7
Amqui Canada 48°28N 67°27W 73 C6
Amravati India 20°55N 77°45E 40 J10
Amreli India 21°35N 71°17E 42 J4
Amritsar India 31°35N 74°57E 42 D6
Amroha India 28°53N 78°30E 43 E8
Amsterdam Neths. 52°23N 4°54E 15 B4
Amsterdam U.S.A. 42°56N 74°11W 83 D10
Amsterdam ✈ (AMS) Neths. 52°18N 4°45E 15 B4
Amsterdam, I. = Nouvelle Amsterdam, Î. Ind. Oc. 38°30S 77°30E 3 F13
Amstetten Austria 48°7N 14°51E 16 D8
Amudarya → Uzbekistan 43°58N 59°34E 28 E6
Amund Ringnes I. Canada 78°20N 96°25W 69 B10
Amundsen Abyssal Plain S. Ocean 65°0S 125°0W 5 C14
Amundsen Basin Arctic 87°30N 80°0E 4 A
Amundsen Gulf Canada 71°0N 124°0W 68 B7
Amundsen Ridges S. Ocean 69°15S 123°0W 5 C14
Amundsen-Scott Antarctica 90°0S 166°0E 5 E
Amundsen Sea Antarctica 72°0S 115°0W 5 D15
Amuntai Indonesia 2°28S 115°25E 36 E5
Amur → Russia 52°56N 141°10E 29 D15
Amurang Indonesia 1°5N 124°40E 37 D6
Amursk Russia 50°14N 136°54E 29 D14
Amyderya = Amudarya → Uzbekistan 43°58N 59°34E 28 E6
An Bien Vietnam 9°45N 105°0E 39 H5
An Hoa Vietnam 15°40N 108°5E 38 E7
An Nabatīyah at Tahta Lebanon 33°23N 35°27E 46 B4
An Nabk Si. Arabia 31°20N 37°20E 44 D3
An Nabk Syria 34°2N 36°44E 46 A5
An Nafūd Si. Arabia 28°15N 41°0E 44 D4
An Najaf Iraq 32°3N 44°15E 44 C5
An Nāşirīyah Iraq 31°0N 46°15E 44 D5
An Nhon Vietnam 13°55N 109°7E 38 F7
An Nu'ayrīyah Si. Arabia 27°30N 48°30E 45 E6
An Thoi, Dao Vietnam 9°58N 104°0E 39 H5
An Uaimh Ireland 53°39N 6°41W 10 C5
Anabar → Russia 73°8N 113°36E 29 B12
'Anabtā West Bank 32°19N 35°7E 46 C4
Anaconda U.S.A. 46°8N 112°57W 76 C7
Anacortes U.S.A. 48°30N 122°37W 78 B4
Anadarko U.S.A. 35°4N 98°15W 84 D5
Anadolu Turkey 39°0N 30°0E 19 G5
Anadyr Russia 64°35N 177°20E 29 C18
Anadyr → Russia 64°55N 176°5E 29 C18
Anadyrskiy Zaliv Russia 64°0N 180°0E 29 C19
Anaga, Pta. de Canary Is. 28°34N 16°9W 24 F3
'Ānah Iraq 34°25N 42°0E 44 C4
Anaheim U.S.A. 33°50N 117°55W 79 M9
Anahim Lake Canada 52°28N 125°18W 70 C3
Anakapalle India 17°42N 83°6E 41 L13
Anakie Australia 23°32S 147°45E 62 C4
Analalava Madag. 14°35S 48°0E 57 A8
Analavoka Madag. 22°23S 46°30E 57 C8
Analipsis Greece 39°36N 19°55E 25 A3
Anambar → Pakistan 30°15N 68°50E 42 D3
Anambas, Kepulauan Indonesia 3°20N 106°30E 36 D3
Anambas Is. = Anambas, Kepulauan Indonesia 3°20N 106°30E 36 D3
Anamosa U.S.A. 42°7N 91°17W 80 D8
Anamur Turkey 36°8N 32°58E 44 B2
Anan Japan 33°54N 134°40E 31 H7
Anand India 22°32N 72°59E 42 H5
Anantapur India 14°39N 77°42E 40 M10
Anantnag India 33°45N 75°10E 43 C6
Ananyiv Ukraine 47°44N 29°58E 17 E15
Anapodiaris → Greece 34°59N 25°20E 25 E7
Anápolis Brazil 16°15S 48°50W 93 G9
Anapu → Brazil 1°53S 50°53W 93 D8
Anār Iran 30°55N 55°13E 45 D7
Anārak Iran 33°25N 53°40E 45 C7
Anas → India 23°26N 74°0E 42 H5
Anatolia = Anadolu Turkey 39°0N 30°0E 19 G5
Anatsogno Madag. 23°33S 43°46E 57 C7
Añatuya Argentina 28°20S 62°50W 94 B3
Anaunethad L. Canada 60°55N 104°25W 71 A8
Anbyŏn N. Korea 39°1N 127°35E 35 E14
Ancaster Canada 43°13N 79°59W 82 C5
Anchor Bay U.S.A. 38°48N 123°34W 78 G3
Anchorage U.S.A. 61°13N 149°54W 68 C5
Anci China 39°20N 116°40E 34 E9
Ancohuma, Nevado Bolivia 16°0S 68°50W 92 G5
Ancón Peru 11°50S 77°10W 92 F3
Ancona Italy 43°38N 13°30E 22 C5
Ancud Chile 42°0S 73°50W 96 E2
Ancud, G. de Chile 42°0S 73°0W 96 E2
Anda China 46°24N 125°19E 33 B7
Andacollo Argentina 37°10S 70°42W 94 D1
Andacollo Chile 30°14S 71°6W 94 C1
Andaingo Madag. 18°12S 48°17E 57 B8
Andalgalá Argentina 27°40S 66°30W 94 B2
Åndalsnes Norway 62°35N 7°43E 8 E12
Andalucía □ Spain 37°35N 5°0W 21 D3
Andalusia = Andalucía □ Spain 37°35N 5°0W 21 D3
Andalusia U.S.A. 31°18N 86°29W 85 F11
Andaman Is. Ind. Oc. 12°30N 92°45E 27 G11
Andaman Sea Ind. Oc. 13°0N 96°0E 36 B1
Andamooka Australia 30°27S 137°9E 63 E2
Andapa Madag. 14°39S 49°39E 57 A8
Andara Namibia 18°2S 21°9E 56 B3
Andenes Norway 69°19N 16°18E 8 B17
Andenne Belgium 50°28N 5°5E 15 D5
Anderson Alaska, U.S.A. 64°25N 149°15W 74 a
Anderson Calif., U.S.A. 40°27N 122°18W 76 F2
Anderson Ind., U.S.A. 40°10N 85°41W 81 E11
Anderson Mo., U.S.A. 36°39N 94°27W 80 G6
Anderson S.C., U.S.A. 34°31N 82°39W 85 D13
Anderson → Canada 69°42N 129°0W 68 C7
Andes U.S.A. 42°12N 74°47W 83 D10
Andes, Cord. de los S. Amer. 20°0S 68°0W 92 H5
Andfjorden Norway 69°10N 16°20E 8 B17
Andhra Pradesh □ India 18°0N 79°0E 40 L11
Andijon Uzbekistan 41°10N 72°15E 28 E8
Andikíthira = Antikythira Greece 35°52N 23°15E 23 G10
Andilamena Madag. 17°1S 48°35E 57 B8
Andīmeshk Iran 32°27N 48°21E 45 C6
Andizhan = Andijon Uzbekistan 41°10N 72°15E 28 E8
Andoany Madag. 13°25S 48°16E 57 A8
Andohahela ⌓ Madag. 24°4S 46°44E 57 C8
Andong S. Korea 36°40N 128°43E 35 F15
Andongwei China 35°6N 119°20E 35 G10
Andorra ■ Europe 42°30N 1°30E 20 E4
Andorra La Vella Andorra 42°31N 1°32E 20 E4
Andover U.K. 51°12N 1°29W 13 F6
Andover Maine, U.S.A. 44°38N 70°45W 83 B14
Andover Mass., U.S.A. 42°40N 71°8W 83 D13
Andover N.J., U.S.A. 40°59N 74°45W 83 F10
Andover N.Y., U.S.A. 42°10N 77°48W 82 D7
Andover Ohio, U.S.A. 41°36N 80°34W 82 E4
Andøya Norway 69°10N 15°50E 8 B16
Andradina Brazil 20°54S 51°23W 93 H8
Andrahary Madag. 13°37S 49°17E 57 A8
Andramasina Madag. 19°11S 47°35E 57 B8
Andranopasy Madag. 21°17S 43°44E 57 C7
Andranovory Madag. 23°8S 44°10E 57 C7
Andratx Spain 39°39N 2°25E 24 B9
Andreanof Is. U.S.A. 51°30N 176°0W 74 a
Andrews S.C., U.S.A. 33°27N 79°34W 85 E15
Andrews Tex., U.S.A. 32°19N 102°33W 84 E3
Ándria Italy 41°13N 16°17E 22 D7
Andriamena Madag. 17°26S 47°30E 57 B8
Andriandampy Madag. 22°45S 45°41E 57 C8
Andriba Madag. 17°30S 46°58E 57 B8
Andringitra ⌓ Madag. 22°13S 46°5E 57 C8
Androka Madag. 24°58S 44°2E 57 C7
Andros Greece 37°50N 24°57E 23 F11
Andros I. Bahamas 24°30N 78°0W 88 B4
Andros Town Bahamas 24°43N 77°47W 88 B4
Androscoggin → U.S.A. 43°58N 69°52W 83 C14
Andselv Norway 69°4N 18°34E 8 B18
Andújar Spain 38°3N 4°5W 21 C3
Andulo Angola 11°25S 16°45E 52 G3
Anegada Br. Virgin Is. 18°45N 64°20W 89 e
Anegada Passage W. Indies 18°15N 63°45W 89 C7
Aneto, Pico de Spain 42°37N 0°40E 21 A6
Ang Mo Kio Singapore 1°23N 103°50E 39 d
Ang Thong Thailand 14°35N 100°31E 38 E3
Ang Thong, Ko Thailand 9°37N 99°41E 39 b
Ang Thong △ Thailand 9°40N 99°43E 39 H2
Angamos, Punta Chile 23°1S 70°32W 94 A1
Angara → Russia 58°5N 94°20E 29 D10
Angarsk Russia 52°30N 104°0E 29 D11
Angas Hills Australia 23°0S 127°50E 60 D4
Angaston Australia 34°30S 139°8E 63 E2
Ånge Sweden 62°31N 15°35E 8 E16
Ángel, Salto = Angel Falls Venezuela 5°57N 62°30W 92 B6
Ángel de la Guarda, I. Mexico 29°20N 113°25W 86 B2
Angel Falls Venezuela 5°57N 62°30W 92 B6
Angeles Phil. 15°9N 120°33E 37 A6
Ängelholm Sweden 56°15N 12°58E 9 H15
Angels Camp U.S.A. 38°4N 120°32W 78 G6
Ångermanälven → Sweden 64°0N 17°20E 8 E17
Ångermanland Sweden 63°36N 17°45E 8 E17
Angers Canada 45°31N 75°29W 83 A9
Angers France 47°30N 0°35W 20 C3
Ängesån → Sweden 66°16N 22°47E 8 C20
Angikuni L. Canada 62°12N 99°59W 71 A9
Angkor Cambodia 13°22N 103°50E 38 F4
Anglesey U.K. 53°17N 4°20W 12 D3
Anglesey, Isle of □ U.K. 53°16N 4°18W 12 D3
Angleton U.S.A. 29°10N 95°26W 84 G7
Anglisidhes Cyprus 34°51N 33°27E 25 E12
Angmagssalik = Tasiilaq Greenland 65°40N 37°20W 4 C6
Ango Dem. Rep. of the Congo 4°10N 26°5E 54 B2
Angoche Mozam. 16°8S 39°55E 55 F4
Angoche, I. Mozam. 16°20S 39°50E 55 F4
Angol Chile 37°56S 72°45W 94 D1
Angola Ind., U.S.A. 41°38N 85°0W 81 E11
Angola N.Y., U.S.A. 42°38N 79°2W 82 D5
Angola ■ Africa 12°0S 18°0E 53 G3
Angoulême France 45°39N 0°10E 20 D4
Angoumois France 45°50N 0°25E 20 D3
Angra do Heroismo Azores 38°39N 27°13W 50 a
Angra dos Reis Brazil 23°0S 44°10W 95 A7
Angtassom Cambodia 11°1N 104°41E 39 G5
Angu Dem. Rep. of the Congo 3°23N 24°30E 54 B1
Anguang China 45°15N 123°45E 35 B12
Anguilla ☑ W. Indies 18°14N 63°5W 89 C7
Anguo China 38°28N 115°15E 34 E8
Angurugu Australia 14°0S 136°25E 62 A2
Angus Canada 44°19N 79°53W 82 B5
Angus □ U.K. 56°46N 2°56W 11 E6
Angwa → Zimbabwe 16°0S 30°23E 57 B5
Anhanduí → Brazil 21°46S 52°9W 95 A5
Anholt Denmark 56°42N 11°33E 9 H14
Anhui □ China 32°0N 117°0E 33 C6
Anhwei = Anhui □ China 32°0N 117°0E 33 C6
Anichab Namibia 21°0S 14°46E 56 C1
Animas → U.S.A. 36°43N 108°13W 77 H9
Anivorano Madag. 18°44S 48°58E 57 B8
Anjalankoski Finland 60°45N 26°51E 8 F22
Anjar India 23°6N 70°10E 42 H4
Anjou France 47°20N 0°15W 20 C3
Anjouan Comoros Is. 12°15S 44°20E 53 a
Anjozorobe Madag. 18°22S 47°52E 57 B8
Anju N. Korea 39°36N 125°40E 35 E13
Ankaboa, Tanjona Madag. 21°58S 43°20E 57 C7
Ankang China 32°40N 109°1E 34 H5
Ankara Turkey 39°57N 32°54E 19 G5
Ankarafantsika ⌓ Madag. 16°8S 47°5E 57 B8
Ankaramena Madag. 21°57S 46°39E 57 C8
Ankaratra Madag. 19°25S 47°12E 53 H9
Ankasakasa Madag. 16°21S 44°52E 57 B7
Ankavandra Madag. 18°46S 45°18E 57 B8
Ankazoabo Madag. 22°18S 44°31E 57 C7
Ankazobe Madag. 18°20S 47°10E 57 B8
Ankeny U.S.A. 41°44N 93°36W 80 E7
Ankilimalinika Madag. 22°58S 43°45E 57 C7
Ankilizato Madag. 20°25S 45°1E 57 C8
Ankisabe Madag. 19°17S 46°29E 57 B8
Ankoro Dem. Rep. of the Congo 6°45S 26°55E 54 D2
Ankororoka Madag. 25°30S 45°11E 57 D8
Anlong Veng Cambodia 14°14N 104°5E 38 E5
Anmyeondo S. Korea 36°25N 126°25E 35 F14
Ann, C. U.S.A. 42°38N 70°35W 83 D14
Ann Arbor U.S.A. 42°17N 83°45W 81 D12
Anna U.S.A. 37°28N 89°15W 80 G9
Annaba Algeria 36°50N 7°46E 50 A7
Annalee → Ireland 54°2N 7°24W 10 B4
Annam Vietnam 16°0N 108°0E 38 E7
Annamitique, Chaîne Asia 17°0N 106°0E 38 D6
Annan U.K. 54°59N 3°16W 11 G5
Annan → U.K. 54°58N 3°16W 11 G5
Annapolis U.S.A. 38°59N 76°30W 81 F15
Annapolis Royal Canada 44°44N 65°32W 73 D6
Annapurna Nepal 28°34N 83°50E 43 E10
Annean, L. Australia 26°54S 118°14E 61 E2
Annecy France 45°55N 6°8E 20 D7
Annette I. U.S.A. 55°9N 131°28W 70 B2
Anning China 24°55N 102°26E 32 D5
Anniston U.S.A. 33°39N 85°50W 85 E12
Annobón Atl. Oc. 1°25S 5°36E 49 G4
Annotto B. Jamaica 18°17N 76°45W 88 a
Annville U.S.A. 40°20N 76°31W 83 F8
Anogia Greece 35°16N 24°52E 25 D6
Anorotsangana Madag. 13°56S 47°55E 57 A8
Anosibe Madag. 19°26S 48°13E 57 B8
Anping Hebei, China 38°15N 115°30E 34 E8
Anping Liaoning, China 41°5N 123°30E 35 D12
Anqing China 30°30N 117°3E 33 C6
Anqiu China 36°25N 119°10E 35 F10
Ansai China 36°50N 109°20E 34 F5
Ansan S. Korea 37°21N 126°52E 35 F14
Ansbach Germany 49°28N 10°34E 16 D6
Anse Boileau Seychelles 4°43S 55°29E 53 b
Anse Royale Seychelles 4°44S 55°31E 53 b
Anshan China 41°5N 122°58E 35 D12
Anshun China 26°18N 105°57E 32 D5
Ansley U.S.A. 41°18N 99°23W 80 E4
Anson U.S.A. 32°45N 99°54W 84 E5
Anson B. Australia 13°20S 130°6E 60 B5
Ansongo Mali 15°25N 0°35E 50 E6
Ansonia U.S.A. 41°21N 73°5W 83 E11
Anstruther U.K. 56°14N 2°41W 11 E6
Ansudu Indonesia 2°11S 139°22E 37 E9
Antabamba Peru 14°40S 73°0W 92 F4
Antakya = Hatay Turkey 36°14N 36°10E 44 B3
Antalaha Madag. 14°57S 50°20E 57 A9
Antalya Turkey 36°52N 30°45E 19 G5
Antalya Körfezi Turkey 36°15N 31°30E 19 G5
Antambohobe Madag. 22°20S 46°47E 57 C8
Antanambao-Manampotsy Madag. 19°29S 48°34E 57 B8
Antanambe Madag. 16°26S 49°52E 57 B8
Antananarivo Madag. 18°55S 47°31E 57 B8
Antananarivo □ Madag. 19°0S 47°0E 57 B8
Antanifotsy Madag. 19°39S 47°19E 57 B8
Antanimbaribe Madag. 21°30S 44°48E 57 C7
Antanimora Madag. 24°49S 45°40E 57 C8
Antarctic Pen. Antarctica 67°0S 60°0W 5 C18
Antarctica 90°0S 0°0 5 E3
Antelope Zimbabwe 21°2S 28°31E 55 G2
Antequera Paraguay 24°8S 57°7W 94 A4
Antequera Spain 37°5N 4°33W 21 D3
Antero, Mt. U.S.A. 38°41N 106°15W 76 G10
Antevamena Madag. 21°2S 44°8E 57 C7
Anthony Kans., U.S.A. 37°9N 98°2W 80 G4
Anthony N. Mex., U.S.A. 32°0N 106°36W 77 K10
Anti Atlas Morocco 30°0N 8°30W 50 C4
Anti-Lebanon = Sharqi, Al Jabal ash Lebanon 33°40N 36°10E 46 B5
Antibes France 43°34N 7°6E 20 E7
Anticosti, Î. d' Canada 49°30N 63°0W 73 C7
Antigo U.S.A. 45°9N 89°9W 80 C9
Antigonish Canada 45°38N 61°58W 73 C7
Antigua Canary Is. 28°24N 14°1W 24 F5
Antigua Guatemala 14°34N 90°41W 88 D1
Antigua W. Indies 17°0N 61°50W 89 C7
Antigua & Barbuda ■ W. Indies 17°20N 61°48W 89 C7
Antikythira Greece 35°52N 23°15E 23 G10
Antilla Cuba 20°40N 75°50W 88 B4
Antilles = West Indies Cent. Amer. 15°0N 65°0W 89 D7
Antioch U.S.A. 38°1N 121°48W 78 G5
Antioquia Colombia 6°40N 75°55W 92 B3
Antipodes Is. Pac. Oc. 49°45S 178°40E 64 M9
Antlers U.S.A. 34°14N 95°37W 84 D7
Antoetra Madag. 20°46S 47°20E 57 C8
Antofagasta Chile 23°50S 70°30W 94 A1
Antofagasta □ Chile 24°0S 69°0W 94 A2
Antofagasta de la Sierra Argentina 26°5S 67°20W 94 B2
Antofalla Argentina 25°30S 68°5W 94 B2
Antofalla, Salar de Argentina 25°40S 67°45W 94 B2
Anton U.S.A. 33°49N 102°10W 84 E3
Antongila, Helodrano Madag. 15°30S 49°50E 57 B8
Antonibé Madag. 15°7S 47°24E 57 B8
Antonibé, Presqu'île d' Madag. 14°55S 47°20E 57 A8
Antonina Brazil 25°26S 48°42W 95 B6
Antrim U.K. 54°43N 6°14W 10 B5
Antrim U.S.A. 40°7N 81°21W 82 F3
Antrim □ U.K. 54°56N 6°25W 10 B5
Antrim, Mts. of U.K. 55°3N 6°14W 10 A5
Antrim Plateau Australia 18°8S 128°20E 60 C4
Antsakabary Madag. 15°3S 48°56E 57 B8
Antsalova Madag. 18°40S 44°37E 57 B7
Antsenavolo Madag. 21°24S 48°3E 57 C8
Antsiafabositra Madag. 17°18S 46°57E 57 B8
Antsirabe Antananarivo, Madag. 19°55S 47°2E 57 B8
Antsirabe Antsiranana, Madag. 14°0S 49°59E 57 A8
Antsirabe Mahajanga, Madag. 15°57S 48°58E 57 B8
Antsiranana Madag. 12°25S 49°20E 57 A8
Antsiranana □ Madag. 12°16S 49°17E 57 A8
Antsohihy Madag. 14°50S 47°59E 57 A8
Antsohimbondrona Seranana Madag. 13°7S 48°48E 57 A8
Antu China 42°30N 128°20E 35 C15
Antwerp = Antwerpen Belgium 51°13N 4°25E 15 C4
Antwerp U.S.A. 44°12N 75°37W 83 B9
Antwerpen Belgium 51°13N 4°25E 15 C4
Antwerpen □ Belgium 51°15N 4°40E 15 C4
Anupgarh India 29°10N 73°10E 42 E5
Anuppur India 23°6N 81°41E 43 H9
Anuradhapura Sri Lanka 8°22N 80°28E 40 Q12
Anveh Iran 27°23N 54°11E 45 E7
Anvers = Antwerpen Belgium 51°13N 4°25E 15 C4
Anvers I. Antarctica 64°30S 63°40W 5 C17
Anxi China 40°30N 95°43E 32 B4
Anxious B. Australia 33°24S 134°45E 63 E1
Anyang China 36°5N 114°21E 34 F8
Anyang S. Korea 37°23N 126°55E 35 F14
Anyer Indonesia 6°4S 105°53E 37 G11
Anyi China 35°2N 111°2E 34 G6
Anza U.S.A. 33°35N 116°39W 79 M10
Anze China 36°10N 112°12E 34 F7
Anzhero-Sudzhensk Russia 56°10N 86°0E 28 D9
Ánzio Italy 41°27N 12°37E 22 D5
Ao Makham Thailand 7°50N 98°24E 39 a
Ao Phangnga △ Thailand 8°10N 98°32E 39 a
Aoga-Shima Japan 32°28N 139°46E 31 H9
Aoji N. Korea 42°31N 130°23E 35 C16
Aomen = Macau China 22°12N 113°33E 33 G10
Aomori Japan 40°45N 140°45E 30 D10
Aomori □ Japan 40°45N 140°40E 30 D10
Aonla India 28°16N 79°11E 43 E8
Aorai, Mt. Tahiti 17°34S 149°30W 59 d
Aoraki Mount Cook N.Z. 43°36S 170°9E 59 E3

Aoral, Phnum *Cambodia* 12°N 104°15E **39** G5
Aosta *Italy* 45°45N 7°20E **20** D7
Aotearoa = New Zealand ■
Oceania 40°S 176°0E **59** D6
Aoukâr *Mauritania* 17°40N 10°0W **50** E4
Aozou Strip *Chad* 22°N 19°0E **51** D9
Apá → *S. Amer.* 22°6S 58°2W **94** A4
Apache *U.S.A.* 34°54N 98°22W **84** D5
Apache Junction
U.S.A. 33°25N 111°33W **77** K8
Apalachee B. *U.S.A.* 30°0N 84°0W **85** G13
Apalachicola *U.S.A.* 29°43N 84°59W **85** G12
Apalachicola →
U.S.A. 29°43N 84°58W **85** G12
Apaporis → *Colombia* 1°23S 69°25W **92** D5
Aparados da Serra △
Brazil 29°10S 50°8W **95** B5
Aparri *Phil.* 18°22N 121°38E **37** A6
Apatity *Russia* 67°34N 33°22E **8** C25
Apatula = Finke
Australia 25°34S 134°35E **62** D1
Apatzingán *Mexico* 19°5N 102°21W **86** D4
Apeldoorn *Neths.* 52°13N 5°57E **15** B5
Apennines = Appennini
Italy 44°30N 10°0E **22** B4
Api *Nepal* 30°0N 80°57E **32** C3
Apia *Samoa* 13°50S 171°50W **59** b
Apiacás, Serra dos *Brazil* 9°50S 57°0W **92** E7
Apies → *S. Africa* 25°15S 28°8E **57** D4
Apizaco *Mexico* 19°25N 98°8W **87** D5
Aplao *Peru* 16°0S 72°40W **92** G4
Apo, Mt. *Phil.* 6°53N 125°14E **37** C7
Apolakia *Greece* 36°5N 27°48E **25** C9
Apolakia, Ormos *Greece* 36°5N 27°45E **25** C9
Apollonia = Marsá Susah
Libya 32°52N 21°59E **51** B10
Apollonia *Greece* 36°15N 27°58E **25** C9
Apolo *Bolivia* 14°30S 68°30W **92** F5
Apopa *El Salv.* 13°48N 89°10W **88** D2
Aporé → *Brazil* 19°27S 50°57W **93** G8
Apostle Is. *U.S.A.* 47°0N 90°40W **80** B8
Apostle Islands △ *U.S.A.* 46°55N 91°0W **80** B8
Apostolos Andreas, C.
Cyprus 35°42N 34°35E **25** D13
Apoteri *Guyana* 4°2N 58°32W **92** C7
Appalachian Mts. *U.S.A.* 38°0N 80°0W **81** G14
Appennini *Italy* 44°30N 10°0E **22** B4
Apple Hill *Canada* 45°13N 74°46W **83** A10
Apple Valley *U.S.A.* 34°32N 117°14W **79** L9
Appleby-in-Westmorland
U.K. 54°35N 2°29W **12** C5
Appledore *U.K.* 51°3N 4°13W **13** F3
Appleton *U.S.A.* 44°16N 88°25W **80** C9
Approuague →
Fr. Guiana 4°30N 51°57W **93** C8
Aprília *Italy* 41°36N 12°39E **22** D5
Apsley *Canada* 44°45N 78°6W **82** B6
Apucarana *Brazil* 23°55S 51°33W **95** A5
Apure → *Venezuela* 7°37N 66°25W **92** B5
Apurimac → *Peru* 12°17S 73°56W **92** F4
Āq Qālā *Iran* 37°10N 54°30E **45** B7
Aqaba = Al ʿAqabah
Jordan 29°31N 35°0E **46** F4
Aqaba, G. of *Red Sea* 28°15N 33°20E **44** D2
ʿAqabah, Khalīj al = Aqaba, G. of
Red Sea 29°0N 34°40E **44** D2
ʿAqdā *Iran* 32°26N 53°37E **45** C7
ʿAqrah *Iraq* 36°46N 43°45E **44** B4
Aqsay *Kazakhstan* 51°11N 53°0E **19** E10
Aqtaū *Kazakhstan* 43°39N 51°12E **19** F9
Aqtöbe *Kazakhstan* 50°17N 57°10E **19** D10
Aqtoghay *Kazakhstan* 46°57N 79°40E **28** E8
Aquidauana *Brazil* 20°30S 55°50W **93** H7
Aquila *Mexico* 18°36N 103°30W **86** D4
Aquiles Serdán *Mexico* 28°36N 105°53W **86** B3
Aquin *Haiti* 18°16N 73°24W **89** C5
Aquitain, Bassin *France* 44°0N 0°30W **20** D3
Ar Rachidiya = Er Rachidia
Morocco 31°58N 4°20W **50** B5
Ar Rafid *Syria* 32°57N 35°52E **46** C4
Ar Raḥḥālīyah *Iraq* 32°44N 43°23E **44** C4
Ar Ramādī *Iraq* 33°25N 43°20E **44** C4
Ar Ramthā *Jordan* 32°34N 36°0E **46** C5
Ar Raqqah *Syria* 35°59N 39°8E **44** C3
Ar Rass *Si. Arabia* 25°50N 43°40E **44** E4
Ar Rayyān *Qatar* 25°17N 51°25E **45** E6
Ar Rifāʿī *Iraq* 31°50N 46°10E **44** D5
Ar Riyāḍ *Si. Arabia* 24°41N 46°42E **44** E5
Ar Ruʿays *Qatar* 26°8N 51°12E **45** E6
Ar Rukhaymīyah *Iraq* 29°22N 45°38E **44** D5
Ar Rumaythah *Iraq* 31°31N 45°12E **44** D5
Ar Ruṣāfah *Syria* 35°45N 38°49E **44** C3
Ar Ruṭbah *Iraq* 33°0N 40°15E **44** C4
Ara *India* 25°35N 84°32E **43** G11
Arab *U.S.A.* 34°19N 86°30W **85** D11
ʿArab, Bahr el → *Sudan* 9°0N 29°30E **51** G11
Arab, Shatt al → *Asia* 29°57N 48°34E **45** D6
ʿArabābād *Iran* 33°2N 57°41E **45** C8
Arabia *Asia* 25°0N 45°0E **26** F6
Arabian Desert = Es Sahrâ' Esh
Sharqîya *Egypt* 27°30N 32°30E **51** C12
Arabian Gulf = Persian Gulf
Asia 27°0N 50°0E **45** E6
Arabian Sea *Ind. Oc.* 16°0N 65°0E **26** G8
Aracaju *Brazil* 10°55S 37°4W **93** F11
Aracati *Brazil* 4°30S 37°44W **93** D11
Araçatuba *Brazil* 21°10S 50°30W **95** A5
Aracena *Spain* 37°53N 6°38W **21** D2
Araçuaí *Brazil* 16°52S 42°4W **93** G10
Arad *Israel* 31°15N 35°12E **46** D4
Arad *Romania* 46°10N 21°20E **17** E11
Aradhippou *Cyprus* 34°57N 33°36E **25** E12
Arafura Sea *E. Indies* 9°0S 135°0E **58** B6
Aragón □ *Spain* 41°25N 0°40W **21** B5
Aragón → *Spain* 42°13N 1°44W **21** A5

Araguacema *Brazil* 8°50S 49°20W **93** E9
Araguaia → *Brazil* 5°21S 48°41W **93** E9
Araguaína *Brazil* 7°12S 48°12W **93** E9
Araguari *Brazil* 18°38S 48°11W **93** G9
Araguari → *Brazil* 1°15N 49°55W **93** C9
Arain *India* 26°27N 75°2E **42** F6
Arak *Algeria* 25°20N 3°45E **50** C6
Arāk *Iran* 34°0N 49°40E **45** C6
Arakan Coast *Burma* 19°0N 94°0E **41** K19
Arakan Yoma *Burma* 20°0N 94°40E **41** K19
Araks = Aras, Rūd-e →
Asia 40°5N 48°29E **44** B5
Aral *Kazakhstan* 46°41N 61°45E **28** E7
Aral Sea *Asia* 44°30N 60°0E **28** E7
Aral Tengizi = Aral Sea
Asia 44°30N 60°0E **28** E7
Aralsk = Aral *Kazakhstan* 46°41N 61°45E **28** E7
Aralskoye More = Aral Sea
Asia 44°30N 60°0E **28** E7
Aramac *Australia* 22°58S 145°14E **62** C4
Aran I. *Ireland* 55°0N 8°30W **10** A3
Aran Is. *Ireland* 53°6N 9°38W **10** C2
Aranda de Duero *Spain* 41°39N 3°42W **21** B4
Arandān *Iran* 35°23N 46°55E **44** C5
Aranjuez *Spain* 40°1N 3°40W **21** B4
Aranos *Namibia* 24°9S 19°7E **56** C2
Aransas Pass *U.S.A.* 27°55N 97°9W **84** H6
Aranyaprathet *Thailand* 13°41N 102°30E **38** F4
Arapahoe *U.S.A.* 40°18N 99°54W **80** E4
Arapey Grande →
Uruguay 30°55S 57°49W **94** C4
Arapgir *Turkey* 39°5N 38°30E **44** B3
Arapiraca *Brazil* 9°45S 36°39W **93** E11
Arapongas *Brazil* 23°29S 51°28W **95** A5
Ar'ar *Si. Arabia* 30°59N 41°2E **44** D4
Araranguá *Brazil* 29°0S 49°30W **95** B6
Araraquara *Brazil* 21°50S 48°0W **93** H9
Ararás, Serra das *Brazil* 25°0S 53°10W **95** B5
Ararat *Australia* 37°16S 142°58E **63** F3
Araria *India* 26°9N 87°33E **43** F12
Araripe, Chapada do
Brazil 7°20S 40°0W **93** E11
Araruama, L. de *Brazil* 22°53S 42°12W **95** A7
Aras, Rūd-e → *Asia* 40°5N 48°29E **44** B5
Arauca *Colombia* 7°0N 70°40W **92** B4
Arauca → *Venezuela* 7°24N 66°35W **92** B5
Arauco *Chile* 37°16S 73°25W **94** D1
Aravalli Range *India* 25°0N 73°30E **42** G5
Arawale △ *Kenya* 1°24S 40°9E **54** C5
Araxá *Brazil* 19°35S 46°55W **93** G9
Araya, Pen. de *Venezuela* 10°40N 64°0W **92** A6
Arba Minch *Ethiopia* 6°0N 37°30E **47** F2
Arbat *Iraq* 35°25N 45°35E **44** C5
Árbatax *Italy* 39°56N 9°42E **22** E3
Arbīl *Iraq* 36°15N 44°5E **44** B5
Arborfield *Canada* 53°6N 103°39W **71** C8
Arborg *Canada* 50°54N 97°13W **71** C9
Arbroath *U.K.* 56°34N 2°35W **11** E6
Arbuckle *U.S.A.* 39°1N 122°3W **78** F4
Arcachon *France* 44°40N 1°10W **20** D3
Arcade *U.S.A.* 42°32N 78°25W **82** D6
Arcadia *Fla., U.S.A.* 27°13N 81°52W **85** H14
Arcadia *La., U.S.A.* 32°33N 92°55W **84** E8
Arcadia *Pa., U.S.A.* 40°47N 78°51W **82** F6
Arcata *U.S.A.* 40°52N 124°5W **76** F1
Archangel = Arkhangelsk
Russia 64°38N 40°36E **18** B7
Archangelos *Greece* 36°13N 28°7E **25** C10
Archbald *U.S.A.* 41°30N 75°32W **83** E9
Archer → *Australia* 13°28S 141°41E **62** A3
Archer B. *Australia* 13°20S 141°30E **62** A3
Archer Bend = Mungkan
Kandju △ *Australia* 13°35S 142°52E **62** A3
Archers Post *Kenya* 0°35N 37°35E **54** B4
Arches △ *U.S.A.* 38°45N 109°25W **76** G9
Archipel-de-Mingan △
Canada 50°13N 63°10W **73** B7
Archipiélago Chinijo △
Canary Is. 29°20N 13°30W **24** E6
Archipiélago Los Roques △
Venezuela 11°50N 66°44W **89** D6
Arckaringa Cr. →
Australia 28°10S 135°22E **63** D2
Arco *U.S.A.* 43°38N 113°18W **76** E7
Arcos de la Frontera
Spain 36°45N 5°49W **21** D3
Arcot *India* 12°53N 79°20E **40** N11
Arctic Bay *Canada* 73°1N 85°7W **69** B11
Arctic Mid-Ocean Ridge
Arctic 87°0N 90°0E **4** A
Arctic Ocean *Arctic* 78°0N 160°0W **4** B18
Arctic Red River = Tsiigehtchic
Canada 67°15N 134°0W **68** C6
Arctowski *Antarctica* 62°30S 58°0W **5** C18
Arda → *Bulgaria* 41°40N 26°30E **23** D12
Ardabīl *Iran* 38°15N 48°18E **45** B6
Ardabīl □ *Iran* 38°15N 48°20E **45** B6
Ardakān = Sepīdān *Iran* 30°20N 52°5E **45** D7
Ardakān *Iran* 32°19N 53°59E **45** C7
Ardara *Ireland* 54°46N 8°25W **10** B3
Ardee *Ireland* 53°52N 6°33W **10** C5
Arden *Canada* 44°43N 76°56W **82** B8
Arden *Calif., U.S.A.* 38°36N 121°33W **78** G5
Arden *Nev., U.S.A.* 36°1N 115°14W **79** J11
Ardenne *Belgium* 49°50N 5°5E **15** E5
Ardennes = Ardenne
Belgium 49°50N 5°5E **15** E5
Arderin *Ireland* 53°2N 7°39W **10** C4
Ardestān *Iran* 33°20N 52°25E **45** C7
Ardfert *Ireland* 52°20N 9°47W **10** D2
Ardglass *U.K.* 54°16N 5°36W **10** B6
Ardivachar Pt. *U.K.* 57°23N 7°26W **11** D1
Ardlethan *Australia* 34°22S 146°53E **63** E4
Ardmore *Okla., U.S.A.* 34°10N 97°8W **84** D6
Ardmore *Pa., U.S.A.* 40°2N 75°17W **83** F9

Ardnamurchan, Pt. of
U.K. 56°43N 6°14W **11** E2
Ardnave Pt. *U.K.* 55°53N 6°20W **11** F2
Ardrossan *Australia* 34°26S 137°53E **63** E2
Ardrossan *U.K.* 55°39N 4°49W **11** F4
Ards Pen. *U.K.* 54°33N 5°34W **10** B6
Arecibo *Puerto Rico* 18°29N 66°43W **89** d
Areia Branca *Brazil* 5°0S 37°0W **93** E11
Arena, Pt. *U.S.A.* 38°57N 123°44W **78** G3
Arenal *Honduras* 15°21N 86°50W **88** C2
Arendal *Norway* 58°28N 8°46E **9** G13
Arequipa *Peru* 16°20S 71°30W **92** G4
Arévalo *Spain* 41°3N 4°43W **21** B3
Arezzo *Italy* 43°25N 11°53E **22** C4
Arga → *Spain* 42°18N 1°47W **21** A5
Arganda del Rey *Spain* 40°19N 3°26W **21** B4
Argenta *Canada* 50°11N 116°56W **70** C5
Argentan *France* 48°45N 0°1W **20** B3
Argentário, Mte. *Italy* 42°24N 11°9E **22** C4
Argentia *Canada* 47°18N 53°58W **73** C9
Argentina ■ *S. Amer.* 35°0S 66°0W **96** G3
Argentino, L. *Argentina* 50°10S 73°0W **96** G2
Argeş → *Romania* 44°5N 26°38E **17** F14
Arghandab → *Afghan.* 31°30N 64°15E **42** D1
Argirades *Greece* 39°27N 19°58E **25** B3
Argiroupoli *Greece* 35°17N 24°20E **25** D6
Argolikos Kolpos *Greece* 37°20N 22°52E **23** F10
Argos *Greece* 37°40N 22°43E **23** F10
Argostoli *Greece* 38°11N 20°29E **23** E9
Arguello, Pt. *U.S.A.* 34°35N 120°39W **79** L6
Arguineguín *Canary Is.* 27°46N 15°41W **24** G4
Argun → *Russia* 53°20N 121°28E **29** D13
Argungu *Nigeria* 12°40N 4°31E **50** F6
Argus Pk. *U.S.A.* 35°52N 117°26W **79** K9
Argyle, L. *Australia* 16°20S 128°40E **60** C4
Argyle → *U.K.* 56°6N 5°0W **11** E4
Argyll □ *U.K.* 56°13N 5°28W **11** E3
Argyll & Bute □ *U.K.* 56°13N 5°28W **11** E3
Århus *Denmark* 56°8N 10°11E **9** H14
Ariadnoye *Russia* 45°8N 134°25E **30** B7
Ariamsvlei *Namibia* 28°9S 19°51E **56** D2
Ariana *Tunisia* 36°52N 10°12E **51** A8
Arica *Chile* 18°32S 70°20W **92** G4
Arica *Colombia* 2°0S 71°50W **92** D4
Arico *Canary Is.* 28°9N 16°29W **24** F3
Arid, C. *Australia* 34°1S 123°10E **61** F3
Arida *Japan* 34°5N 135°8E **31** G7
Aride *Seychelles* 4°13S 55°40E **53** b
Ariège → *France* 43°30N 1°25E **20** E4
Arila, Akra *Greece* 39°43N 19°39E **25** A3
Arima *Trin. & Tob.* 10°38N 61°17W **89** D7
Arinos → *Brazil* 10°25S 58°20W **92** E7
Ario de Rosales *Mexico* 19°12N 101°43W **86** D4
Aripo, Mt. *Trin. & Tob.* 10°45N 61°15W **93** K15
Aripuanã *Brazil* 9°25S 60°30W **92** E6
Aripuanã → *Brazil* 5°7S 60°25W **92** E6
Ariquemes *Brazil* 9°55S 63°6W **92** E6
Arisaig *U.K.* 56°55N 5°51W **11** E3
Aristazabal I. *Canada* 52°40N 129°10W **70** C3
Arivonimamo *Madag.* 19°1S 47°11E **57** B8
Arizaro, Salar de
Argentina 24°40S 67°50W **94** A2
Arizona *Argentina* 35°45S 65°25W **94** D2
Arizpe *Mexico* 30°20N 110°10W **86** A2
'Arjah *Si. Arabia* 24°43N 44°17E **44** E5
Arjeplog *Sweden* 66°3N 17°54E **8** C17
Arjepluovve = Arjeplog
Sweden 66°3N 17°54E **8** C17
Arjona *Colombia* 10°14N 75°22W **92** A3
Arjuna *Indonesia* 7°49S 112°34E **37** G15
Arka *Russia* 60°15N 142°0E **29** C15
Arkadelphia *U.S.A.* 34°7N 93°4W **84** D8
Arkaig, L. *U.K.* 56°59N 5°10W **11** E3
Arkalyk = Arqalyk
Kazakhstan 50°13N 66°50E **28** D7
Arkansas □ *U.S.A.* 35°0N 92°30W **84** D8
Arkansas → *U.S.A.* 33°47N 91°4W **84** E9
Arkansas City *U.S.A.* 37°4N 97°2W **80** G5
Arkaroola *Australia* 30°20S 139°22E **63** E2
Arkhangelsk *Russia* 64°38N 40°36E **18** B7
Arki *India* 31°9N 76°58E **42** D7
Arklow *Ireland* 52°48N 6°10W **10** D5
Arkport *U.S.A.* 42°24N 77°42W **82** D7
Arkticheskiy, Mys
Russia 81°10N 95°0E **29** A10
Arkville *U.S.A.* 42°9N 74°37W **83** D10
Arlanza → *Spain* 42°3N 4°17W **21** A3
Arlanzón → *Spain* 42°3N 4°17W **21** A3
Arlbergrass *Austria* 47°9N 10°12E **16** E6
Arles *France* 43°41N 4°40E **20** E6
Arlington *S. Africa* 28°1S 27°53E **57** D4
Arlington *N.Y., U.S.A.* 41°42N 73°54W **83** E11
Arlington *Oreg., U.S.A.* 45°43N 120°12W **76** D3
Arlington *S. Dak., U.S.A.* 44°22N 97°8W **80** C5
Arlington *Tex., U.S.A.* 32°44N 97°6W **84** E6
Arlington *Va., U.S.A.* 38°53N 77°7W **81** F15
Arlington *Vt., U.S.A.* 43°5N 73°9W **83** C11
Arlington *Wash., U.S.A.* 48°12N 122°8W **78** B4
Arlington Heights
U.S.A. 42°5N 87°59W **80** D10
Arlit *Niger* 19°0N 7°38E **50** E7
Arlon *Belgium* 49°42N 5°49E **15** E5
Arlparra *Australia* 22°11S 134°30E **62** C1
Arltunga *Australia* 23°26S 134°41E **62** C1
Armadale *Australia* 32°9S 116°0E **61** F2
Armagh *U.K.* 54°21N 6°39W **10** B5
Armagh □ *U.K.* 54°18N 6°37W **10** B5
Armando Bermudez △
Dom. Rep. 19°3N 71°0W **89** C5
Armavir *Russia* 45°2N 41°7E **19** E7
Armenia *Colombia* 4°35N 75°45W **92** C3
Armenia ■ *Asia* 40°20N 45°0E **19** F7
Armenistís, Akra *Greece* 36°8N 27°42E **25** C9
Armidale *Australia* 30°30S 151°40E **63** E5
Armour *U.S.A.* 43°19N 98°21W **80** D4
Armstrong *B.C.,*
Canada 50°25N 119°10W **70** C5

Armstrong *Ont., Canada* 50°18N 89°4W **72** B2
Arnarfjörður *Iceland* 65°48N 23°40W **8** D2
Arnaud → *Canada* 59°59N 69°46W **69** D13
Arnauti, C. *Cyprus* 35°6N 32°17E **25** D11
Arnett *U.S.A.* 36°8N 99°46W **84** C5
Arnhem *Neths.* 51°58N 5°55E **15** C5
Arnhem, C. *Australia* 12°20S 137°30E **62** A2
Arnhem B. *Australia* 12°20S 136°10E **62** A2
Arnhem Land *Australia* 13°10S 134°30E **62** A1
Arno → *Italy* 43°41N 10°17E **22** C4
Arno Bay *Australia* 33°54S 136°34E **63** E2
Arnold *U.K.* 53°1N 1°7W **12** D6
Arnold *U.S.A.* 38°15N 120°21W **78** G6
Arnot *Canada* 55°56N 96°41W **71** B9
Arnøya *Norway* 70°9N 20°40E **8** A19
Arnprior *Canada* 45°26N 76°21W **83** A8
Arnsberg *Germany* 51°24N 8°5E **16** C5
Aroa, Pte. *Moorea* 17°28S 149°46W **59** d
Aroab *Namibia* 26°41S 19°39E **56** D2
Aron *India* 25°57N 77°56E **42** G6
Arona *Canary Is.* 28°6N 16°40W **24** F3
Aros → *Mexico* 29°9N 107°57W **86** B3
Arqalyk *Kazakhstan* 50°13N 66°50E **28** D7
Arrah = Ara *India* 25°35N 84°32E **43** G11
Arrah *Ivory C.* 6°40N 3°58W **50** G5
Arran *U.K.* 55°34N 5°12W **11** F3
Arras *France* 50°17N 2°46E **20** A5
Arrecife *Canary Is.* 28°57N 13°37W **24** F6
Arrecifes *Argentina* 34°6S 60°9W **94** C3
Arrée, Mts. d' *France* 48°26N 3°55W **20** B2
Arriaga *Mexico* 16°14N 93°54W **87** D6
Arrilalah *Australia* 23°43S 143°54E **62** C3
Arrino *Australia* 29°30S 115°40E **61** E2
Arrow, L. *Ireland* 54°3N 8°19W **10** B3
Arrowtown *N.Z.* 44°57S 168°50E **59** F2
Arroyo Grande *U.S.A.* 35°7N 120°35W **79** K6
Ars *Iran* 37°9N 47°46E **44** B5
Arsenault L. *Canada* 55°6N 108°32W **71** B7
Arsenev *Russia* 44°10N 133°15E **30** B6
Arta *Greece* 39°8N 21°2E **23** E9
Artà *Spain* 39°41N 3°21E **24** B10
Artà, Coves de *Spain* 39°40N 3°24E **24** B10
Arteaga *Mexico* 18°28N 102°25W **86** D4
Artem *Russia* 43°22N 132°13E **30** C6
Artemovsk *Russia* 54°45N 93°35E **29** D10
Artemovsk *Ukraine* 48°35N 38°0E **19** E6
Artesia = Mosomane
Botswana 24°2S 26°19E **56** C4
Artesia *U.S.A.* 32°51N 104°24W **77** K11
Arthur *Canada* 43°50N 80°32W **82** C4
Arthur → *Australia* 41°2S 144°40E **63** G3
Arthur Cr. → *Australia* 22°30S 136°25E **62** C2
Arthur Pt. *Australia* 22°7S 150°3E **62** C5
Arthur River *Australia* 33°20S 117°2E **61** F2
Arthur's Pass *N.Z.* 42°54S 171°35E **59** E3
Arthur's Pass △ *N.Z.* 42°53S 171°42E **59** E3
Arthur's Town *Bahamas* 24°38N 75°42W **89** B4
Artigas *Antarctica* 62°30S 58°0W **5** C18
Artigas *Uruguay* 30°20S 56°30W **94** C4
Artillery L. *Canada* 63°9N 107°52W **71** A7
Artois *France* 50°20N 2°30E **20** A5
Artrutx, C. de *Spain* 39°55N 3°49E **24** B10
Artsyz *Ukraine* 46°4N 29°26E **17** E15
Artux *China* 39°40N 76°10E **32** C2
Artvin *Turkey* 41°14N 41°44E **19** F7
Artyk *Russia* 64°12N 145°6E **29** C15
Aru, Kepulauan *Indonesia* 6°0S 134°30E **37** F8
Aru Is. = Aru, Kepulauan
Indonesia 6°0S 134°30E **37** F8
Arua *Uganda* 3°1N 30°58E **54** B3
Aruanã *Brazil* 14°54S 51°10W **93** F8
Aruba ☐ *W. Indies* 12°30N 70°0W **89** D6
Arucas *Canary Is.* 28°6N 15°28W **24** G4
Arué *Tahiti* 17°31S 149°30W **59** d
Arun → *Nepal* 26°55N 87°10E **43** F12
Arun → *U.K.* 50°49N 0°33W **13** G7
Arunachal Pradesh ☐
India 28°0N 95°0E **41** F19
Arusha *Tanzania* 3°20S 36°40E **54** C4
Arusha □ *Tanzania* 4°0S 36°30E **54** C4
Arusha → *Tanzania* 3°16S 36°47E **54** C4
Arusha Chini *Tanzania* 3°32S 37°20E **54** C4
Aruwimi →
Dem. Rep. of the Congo 1°13N 23°36E **54** B1
Arvada *Colo., U.S.A.* 39°48N 105°5W **76** G11
Arvada *Wyo., U.S.A.* 44°39N 106°8W **76** D10
Arvayheer *Mongolia* 46°15N 102°48E **32** B5
Arvi *Greece* 34°59N 25°28E **25** E7
Arviat *Canada* 61°6N 93°59W **71** A10
Arvidsjaur *Sweden* 65°35N 19°10E **8** D18
Arvika *Sweden* 59°40N 12°36E **9** G15
Arvin *U.S.A.* 35°12N 118°50W **79** K8
Arwal *India* 25°15N 84°41E **43** G11
Arxan *China* 47°11N 119°57E **33** B6
Arys *Kazakhstan* 42°26N 68°48E **28** E7
Arzamas *Russia* 55°27N 43°55E **18** C7
Arzanah *U.A.E.* 24°47N 52°34E **45** E7
Aş Şafā *Syria* 33°10N 37°0E **46** B6
Aş Saffānīyah *Si. Arabia* 27°55N 48°50E **45** E6
Aş Şafirah *Syria* 36°5N 37°21E **44** B3
Aş Şahm *Oman* 24°10N 56°53E **45** E8
As Sājir *Si. Arabia* 25°11N 44°36E **44** E5
As Salamīyah *Syria* 35°1N 37°2E **44** C3
As Salmān *Iraq* 30°30N 44°32E **44** D4
As Salt *Jordan* 32°2N 35°43E **46** C4
As Sal'w'a *Qatar* 24°23N 50°50E **45** E6
As Samāwah *Iraq* 31°15N 45°15E **44** D5
As Sanamayn *Syria* 33°3N 36°10E **46** B5
As Sohar = Şuḥār *Oman* 24°20N 56°40E **45** E8
As Sukhnah *Syria* 34°52N 38°52E **44** C3
As Sulaymānīyah *Iraq* 35°35N 45°29E **44** C5
As Sulaymī *Si. Arabia* 26°17N 41°21E **44** E4
As Sulayyil *Si. Arabia* 20°27N 45°34E **47** C4
As Summān *Si. Arabia* 25°0N 47°0E **44** E5
As Suwaydā *Syria* 32°40N 36°30E **46** C5
As Suwaydā □ *Syria* 32°45N 36°45E **46** C5
As Suwayq *Oman* 23°51N 57°26E **45** F8

Aş Şuwayrah *Iraq* 32°55N 45°0E **44** C5
Asab *Namibia* 25°30S 18°0E **56** D2
Asad, Buḥayrat al *Syria* 36°0N 38°15E **44** C3
Asahi-Gawa → *Japan* 34°36N 133°58E **31** G6
Asahigawa *Japan* 43°46N 142°22E **30** C11
Asaluyeh *Iran* 27°29N 52°37E **45** E7
Asamankese *Ghana* 5°50N 0°40W **50** G5
Asan → *India* 26°37N 78°24E **43** F8
Asansol *India* 23°40N 87°1E **43** H12
Asau *Samoa* 13°27S 172°33W **59** b
Asbesberge *S. Africa* 29°0S 23°0E **56** D3
Asbestos *Canada* 45°47N 71°58W **73** C5
Asbury Park *U.S.A.* 40°13N 74°1W **83** F10
Ascensión *Mexico* 31°6N 107°59W **86** A3
Ascensión, B. de la
Mexico 19°40N 87°30W **87** D7
Ascension I. *Atl. Oc.* 7°57S 14°23W **49** G2
Aschaffenburg *Germany* 49°58N 9°6E **16** D5
Aschersleben *Germany* 51°45N 11°29E **16** C6
Áscoli Piceno *Italy* 42°51N 13°34E **22** C5
Ascope *Peru* 7°46S 79°8W **92** E3
Ascotán *Chile* 21°45S 68°17W **94** A2
Aseb *Eritrea* 13°0N 42°40E **47** E3
Asela *Ethiopia* 8°0N 39°0E **47** F2
Asenovgrad *Bulgaria* 42°1N 24°51E **23** C11
Asgabat = Ashgabat
Turkmenistan 38°0N 57°50E **45** B8
Asgata *Cyprus* 34°46N 33°15E **25** E12
Ash Fork *U.S.A.* 35°13N 112°29W **77** J7
Ash Grove *U.S.A.* 37°19N 93°35W **80** G7
Ash Shabakah *Iraq* 30°49N 43°39E **44** D4
Ash Shamāl □ *Lebanon* 34°25N 36°0E **46** A5
Ash Shāmīyah *Iraq* 31°55N 44°35E **44** D5
Ash Shāriqah *U.A.E.* 25°23N 55°26E **45** E7
Ash Sharmah *Si. Arabia* 28°1N 35°16E **44** D2
Ash Sharqāt *Iraq* 35°27N 43°16E **44** C4
Ash Shaṭrah *Iraq* 31°30N 46°10E **44** D5
Ash Shawbak *Jordan* 30°32N 35°34E **46** D2
Ash Shiḥr *Yemen* 14°45N 49°36E **47** E4
Ash Shināfiyah *Iraq* 31°35N 44°39E **44** D5
Ash Shu'bah *Si. Arabia* 28°54N 44°44E **44** D5
Ash Shumlūl *Si. Arabia* 26°31N 47°20E **44** E5
Ash Shūr'a *Iraq* 35°58N 43°13E **44** C4
Ash Shurayf *Si. Arabia* 25°43N 39°14E **44** E3
Ash Shuwayfāt *Lebanon* 33°45N 35°30E **46** B4
Asha *Russia* 55°0N 57°16E **18** D10
Ashbourne *U.K.* 53°2N 1°43W **12** D6
Ashburn *U.S.A.* 31°43N 83°39W **85** F13
Ashburton *N.Z.* 43°53S 171°48E **59** E3
Ashburton → *Australia* 21°40S 114°56E **60** D1
Ashcroft *Canada* 50°40N 121°20W **70** C4
Ashdod *Israel* 31°49N 34°35E **46** D3
Ashdown *U.S.A.* 33°40N 94°8W **84** E7
Asheboro *U.S.A.* 35°43N 79°49W **85** D15
Ashern *Canada* 51°11N 98°21W **71** C9
Asherton *U.S.A.* 28°27N 99°46W **84** G5
Asheville *U.S.A.* 35°36N 82°33W **85** D13
Ashewat *Pakistan* 31°22N 68°32E **42** D3
Asheweig → *Canada* 54°17N 87°12W **72** B2
Ashford *Australia* 29°15S 151°3E **63** D5
Ashford *U.K.* 51°8N 0°53E **13** F8
Ashgabat *Turkmenistan* 38°0N 57°50E **45** B8
Ashibetsu *Japan* 43°31N 142°11E **30** C11
Ashikaga *Japan* 36°28N 139°29E **31** F9
Ashington *U.K.* 55°11N 1°33W **12** B6
Ashizuri-Uwakai △
Japan 32°56N 132°32E **31** H6
Ashizuri-Zaki *Japan* 32°44N 133°0E **31** H6
Ashkarkot *Afghan.* 33°3N 67°58E **42** C2
Ashkhabad = Ashgabat
Turkmenistan 38°0N 57°50E **45** B8
Ashkhāneh *Iran* 37°26N 56°55E **45** B8
Ashland *Kans., U.S.A.* 37°11N 99°46W **80** G4
Ashland *Ky., U.S.A.* 38°28N 82°38W **81** F12
Ashland *Maine, U.S.A.* 46°38N 68°24W **81** B19
Ashland *Ohio, U.S.A.* 40°52N 82°19W **82** F2
Ashland *Oreg., U.S.A.* 42°12N 122°43W **76** E2
Ashland *Pa., U.S.A.* 40°45N 76°22W **83** F8
Ashland *Va., U.S.A.* 37°46N 77°29W **81** G15
Ashland *Wis., U.S.A.* 46°35N 90°53W **80** B8
Ashley *N. Dak., U.S.A.* 46°2N 99°22W **80** B4
Ashley *Pa., U.S.A.* 41°12N 75°55W **83** E9
Ashmore and Cartier Is.
Ind. Oc. 12°15S 123°0E **60** B3
Ashmore Reef *Australia* 12°14S 123°5E **60** B3
Ashmyany *Belarus* 54°26N 25°52E **17** A13
Ashokan Res. *U.S.A.* 41°56N 74°13W **83** E10
Ashoknagar *India* 24°34N 77°43E **42** G7
Ashqelon *Israel* 31°42N 34°35E **46** D3
Ashta *India* 23°1N 76°43E **42** H7
Ashtabula *U.S.A.* 41°52N 80°47W **82** E4
Āshtiyān *Iran* 34°31N 50°0E **45** C6
Ashton *S. Africa* 33°50S 20°5E **56** E3
Ashton *U.S.A.* 44°4N 111°27W **76** D8
Ashuanipi, L. *Canada* 52°45N 66°15W **73** B6
Ashuapmushuan →
Canada 48°37N 72°20W **72** C5
Ashville *U.S.A.* 40°34N 78°33W **82** F6
Asia *Asia* 45°0N 75°0E **26** E9
Asia, Kepulauan
Indonesia 1°0N 131°13E **37** D8
Asifabad *India* 19°20N 79°24E **40** K11
Asinara *Italy* 41°4N 8°16E **22** D3
Asinara, G. dell' *Italy* 41°0N 8°30E **22** D3
Asino *Russia* 57°0N 86°0E **28** D9
Asipovichy *Belarus* 53°19N 28°33E **17** B15
'Asīr *Si. Arabia* 18°40N 42°30E **47** D3
Asir, Ras *Somali Rep.* 11°55N 51°10E **47** E5
Askham *S. Africa* 26°59N 20°47E **56** D3
Askim *Norway* 59°35N 11°10E **9** G14
Askja *Iceland* 65°3N 16°48W **8** D5
Asklipio *Greece* 36°4N 27°56E **25** C9
Askøyna *Norway* 60°29N 5°10E **8** F11
Asmara = Asmera
Eritrea 15°19N 38°55E **47** D2

Asmera Eritrea 15°19N 38°55E 47 D2
Åsnen Sweden 56°37N 14°45E 9 H16
Aso Kuju △ Japan 32°53N 131°6E 31 H5
Aspatria U.K. 54°47N 3°19W 12 C4
Aspen U.S.A. 39°11N 106°49W 76 G10
Aspermont U.S.A. 33°8N 100°14W 84 E4
Aspiring, Mt. N.Z. 44°23S 168°46E 59 F2
Asprokavos, Akra Greece 39°21N 20°6E 25 B4
Aspur India 23°58N 74°7E 42 H6
Asquith Canada 52°8N 107°13W 71 C7
Assab = Aseb Eritrea 13°0N 42°40E 47 E3
Assal, L. Djibouti 11°40N 42°26E 47 E3
Assam □ India 26°0N 93°0E 41 G18
Assateague Island ⌓ U.S.A. 38°15N 75°10W 81 F16
Asse Belgium 50°24N 4°10E 15 D4
Assen Neths. 53°0N 6°35E 15 A6
Assiniboia Canada 49°40N 105°59W 71 D7
Assiniboine → Canada 49°53N 97°8W 71 D9
Assiniboine, Mt. Canada 50°52N 115°39W 70 C5
Assis Brazil 22°40S 50°20W 95 A5
Assisi Italy 43°4N 12°37E 22 C5
Assynt, L. U.K. 58°10N 5°3W 11 C3
Astana Kazakhstan 51°10N 71°30E 32 A2
Āstāneh Iran 37°17N 49°59E 45 B6
Astara Azerbaijan 38°30N 48°50E 45 B6
Astarabad = Gorgān Iran 36°55N 54°30E 45 B7
Asterousia Greece 34°59N 25°3E 25 E7
Asti Italy 44°54N 8°12E 20 D8
Astipalea Greece 36°32N 26°22E 23 F12
Astorga Spain 42°29N 6°8W 21 A2
Astoria U.S.A. 46°11N 123°50W 78 D3
Astrakhan Russia 46°25N 48°5E 19 E8
Astrebla Downs Australia 24°12S 140°34E 62 C3
Asturias □ Spain 43°15N 6°0W 21 A3
Asunción Paraguay 25°10S 57°30W 94 B4
Asunción Nochixtlán Mexico 17°28N 97°14W 87 D5
Aswa → Uganda 3°43N 31°55E 54 B3
Aswa-Lolim ⌓ Uganda 2°43N 31°35E 54 B3
Aswân Egypt 24°4N 32°57E 51 D12
Aswan High Dam = Sadd el Aali Egypt 23°54N 32°54E 51 D12
Asyût Egypt 27°11N 31°4E 51 C12
At Ṭafīlah Jordan 30°45N 35°30E 46 E4
At Ṭafīlah □ Jordan 30°45N 35°30E 46 E4
Aṭ Ṭā'if Si. Arabia 21°5N 40°27E 47 C3
At Ta'mīm □ Iraq 35°30N 44°20E 44 C5
Aṭ Ṭirāq Si. Arabia 27°19N 44°33E 44 E5
Aṭ Ṭubayq Si. Arabia 29°30N 37°0E 44 D3
Aṭ Ṭunayb Jordan 31°48N 35°57E 46 D4
Atacama □ Chile 27°30S 70°0W 94 B2
Atacama, Desierto de Chile 24°0S 69°20W 94 A2
Atacama, Salar de Chile 23°30S 68°20W 94 A2
Atakpamé Togo 7°31N 1°13E 50 G6
Atalaya Peru 10°45S 73°50W 92 F4
Atalaya de Femes Canary Is. 28°56N 13°47W 24 F6
Atami Japan 35°5N 139°4E 31 G9
Atamyrat Turkmenistan 37°50N 65°12E 28 F7
Atapupu Indonesia 9°0S 124°51E 37 F6
Atâr Mauritania 20°30N 13°5W 50 D3
Atari Pakistan 30°56N 74°2E 42 D6
Atascadero U.S.A. 35°29N 120°40W 78 K6
Atasū Kazakhstan 48°30N 71°0E 28 E8
Atatürk Barajı Turkey 37°28N 38°30E 19 G6
Atauro E. Timor 8°10S 125°30E 37 F7
Ataviros Greece 36°12N 27°50E 25 C9
Atbara Sudan 17°42N 33°59E 51 E12
'Atbara, Nahr → Sudan 17°40N 33°56E 51 E12
Atbasar Kazakhstan 51°48N 68°20E 28 D7
Atchafalaya B. U.S.A. 29°25N 91°25W 84 G9
Atchison U.S.A. 39°34N 95°7W 80 F6
Āteshān Iran 35°35N 52°37E 45 C7
Ath Belgium 50°38N 3°47E 15 D3
Athabasca Canada 54°45N 113°20W 70 C6
Athabasca → Canada 58°40N 110°50W 71 B6
Athabasca, L. Canada 59°15N 109°15W 71 B7
Athabasca Sand Dunes ⌓ Canada 59°4N 108°43W 71 B7
Athboy Ireland 53°37N 6°56W 10 C5
Athenry Ireland 53°18N 8°44W 10 C3
Athens = Athina Greece 37°58N 23°43E 23 F10
Athens Ala., U.S.A. 34°48N 86°58W 85 D11
Athens Ga., U.S.A. 33°57N 83°23W 85 E13
Athens N.Y., U.S.A. 42°16N 73°49W 83 D11
Athens Ohio, U.S.A. 39°20N 82°6W 81 F12
Athens Pa., U.S.A. 41°57N 76°31W 83 E8
Athens Tenn., U.S.A. 35°27N 84°36W 85 D12
Athens Tex., U.S.A. 32°12N 95°51W 84 E7
Atherley Canada 44°37N 79°20W 82 B5
Atherton Australia 17°17S 145°30E 62 B4
Athi River Kenya 1°28S 36°58E 54 C4
Athienou Cyprus 35°3N 33°32E 25 D12
Athina Greece 37°58N 23°43E 23 F10
Athínai = Athina Greece 37°58N 23°43E 23 F10
Athlone Ireland 53°25N 7°56W 10 C4
Athna Cyprus 35°3N 33°47E 25 D12
Athol U.S.A. 42°36N 72°14W 83 D12
Atholl, Forest of U.K. 56°51N 3°50W 11 E5
Atholville Canada 47°59N 66°43W 73 C6
Athos Greece 40°9N 24°22E 23 D11
Athy Ireland 53°0N 7°0W 10 C5
Ati Chad 13°13N 18°20E 51 F9
Atiak Uganda 3°12N 32°2E 54 B3
Atik L. Canada 55°15N 96°0W 71 B9
Atikaki ⌓ Canada 51°30N 95°31W 71 C9
Atikameg → Canada 52°30N 82°46W 72 B3
Atikokan Canada 48°45N 91°37W 72 C1
Atikonak L. Canada 52°40N 64°32W 73 B7
Atimaono Tahiti 17°46S 149°28W 59 d
Atitlán △ Cent. Amer. 14°38N 91°10W 87 E6
Atiu Cook Is. 20°0S 158°10W 65 J12
Atka Russia 60°50N 151°48E 29 C16
Atka I. U.S.A. 52°7N 174°30W 74 a
Atkinson U.S.A. 42°32N 98°59W 80 D4
Atlanta Ga., U.S.A. 33°45N 84°23W 85 E12
Atlanta Tex., U.S.A. 33°7N 94°10W 84 E7
Atlantic U.S.A. 41°24N 95°1W 80 E6
Atlantic City U.S.A. 39°21N 74°27W 81 F16
Atlantic-Indian Basin Antarctica 60°0S 30°0E 5 B4
Atlantic Ocean 0°0 20°0W 2 D8
Atlas Mts. = Haut Atlas Morocco 32°30N 5°0W 50 B4
Atlin Canada 59°31N 133°41W 70 B2
Atlin, L. Canada 59°26N 133°45W 70 B2
Atlin ⌓ Canada 59°10N 134°30W 70 B2
Atmore U.S.A. 31°2N 87°29W 85 F11
Atoka U.S.A. 34°23N 96°8W 84 D6
Atolia U.S.A. 35°19N 117°37W 79 K9
Atrai → Bangla. 24°7N 89°22E 43 G13
Atrak = Atrek → Turkmenistan 37°35N 53°58E 45 B8
Atrauli India 28°2N 78°20E 42 E8
Atrek → Turkmenistan 37°35N 53°58E 45 B8
Atsuta Japan 43°24N 141°26E 30 C10
Attalla U.S.A. 34°1N 86°6W 85 D11
Attapu Laos 14°48N 106°50E 38 E6
Attawapiskat Canada 52°56N 82°24W 72 B3
Attawapiskat → Canada 52°57N 82°18W 72 B3
Attawapiskat L. Canada 52°18N 87°54W 72 B2
Attica Ind., U.S.A. 40°18N 87°15W 80 E10
Attica Ohio, U.S.A. 41°4N 82°53W 82 E2
Attikamagen L. Canada 55°0N 66°30W 73 B6
Attleboro U.S.A. 41°57N 71°17W 83 E13
Attock Pakistan 33°52N 72°20E 42 C5
Attopeu = Attapu Laos 14°48N 106°50E 38 E6
Attu I. U.S.A. 52°55N 172°55E 74 a
Attur India 11°35N 78°30E 40 P11
Atuel → Argentina 36°17S 66°50W 94 D2
Åtvidaberg Sweden 58°12N 16°0E 9 G17
Atwater U.S.A. 37°21N 120°37W 78 H6
Atwood Canada 43°40N 81°1W 82 C3
Atwood U.S.A. 39°48N 101°3W 80 F3
Atyraū Kazakhstan 47°5N 52°0E 19 E9
Au Sable U.S.A. 44°25N 83°20W 82 B1
Au Sable → U.S.A. 44°25N 83°20W 81 C12
Au Sable Forks U.S.A. 44°27N 73°41W 83 B11
Au Sable Pt. U.S.A. 44°20N 83°20W 82 B1
Auas Honduras 15°29N 84°20W 88 C3
Auasberg Namibia 22°37S 17°13E 56 C2
Aubagne France 43°17N 5°37E 20 E6
Aube → France 48°34N 3°43E 20 B5
Auberry U.S.A. 37°7N 119°29W 78 H7
Auburn Ala., U.S.A. 32°36N 85°29W 85 E12
Auburn Calif., U.S.A. 38°54N 121°4W 78 G5
Auburn Ind., U.S.A. 41°22N 85°4W 81 E11
Auburn Maine, U.S.A. 44°6N 70°14W 81 C18
Auburn N.Y., U.S.A. 42°56N 76°34W 83 D8
Auburn Nebr., U.S.A. 40°23N 95°51W 80 E6
Auburn Pa., U.S.A. 40°36N 76°6W 83 F8
Auburn Wash., U.S.A. 47°18N 122°14W 78 C4
Auburn Ra. Australia 25°15S 150°30E 63 D5
Auburndale U.S.A. 28°4N 81°48W 85 G14
Aubusson France 45°57N 2°11E 20 D5
Auch France 43°39N 0°36E 20 E4
Auchterarder U.K. 56°18N 3°41W 11 E5
Auchtermuchty U.K. 56°18N 3°13W 11 E5
Auckland N.Z. 36°52S 174°46E 59 B5
Auckland Is. Pac. Oc. 50°40S 166°5E 64 N8
Aude → France 43°13N 3°14E 20 E5
Auden Canada 50°14N 87°53W 72 B2
Audubon U.S.A. 41°43N 94°56W 80 E6
Augathella Australia 25°48S 146°35E 63 D4
Aughnacloy U.K. 54°25N 6°59W 10 B5
Aughrim Ireland 53°18N 8°19W 10 C3
Augrabies Falls S. Africa 28°35S 20°20E 56 D3
Augrabies Falls △ S. Africa 28°40S 20°22E 56 D3
Augsburg Germany 48°25N 10°52E 16 D6
Augusta Australia 34°19S 115°9E 61 F2
Augusta Italy 37°13N 15°13E 22 F6
Augusta Ark., U.S.A. 35°17N 91°22W 84 D9
Augusta Ga., U.S.A. 33°28N 81°58W 85 E14
Augusta Kans., U.S.A. 37°41N 96°59W 80 G5
Augusta Maine, U.S.A. 44°19N 69°47W 81 C19
Augusta Mont., U.S.A. 47°30N 112°24W 76 C7
Augustów Poland 53°51N 23°0E 17 B12
Augustus, Mt. Australia 24°20S 116°50E 61 D2
Augustus I. Australia 15°20S 124°30E 60 C3
Aujuittuq = Grise Fiord Canada 76°25N 82°57W 69 B11
Aukštaitija △ Lithuania 55°15N 26°0E 9 J22
Aukum U.S.A. 38°34N 120°43W 78 G6
Auld, L. Australia 22°25S 123°50E 60 D3
Ault U.S.A. 40°35N 104°44W 76 F11
Aunis France 46°5N 0°50W 20 C3
Aunu'u Amer. Samoa 14°20S 170°31W 59 b
Auponhia Indonesia 1°58S 125°27E 37 E7
Aur, Pulau Malaysia 2°35N 104°10E 39 L5
Auraiya India 26°28N 79°33E 43 F8
Aurangabad Bihar, India 24°45N 84°18E 43 G11
Aurangabad Maharashtra, India 19°50N 75°23E 40 K9
Aurich Germany 53°28N 7°28E 16 B4
Aurillac France 44°55N 2°26E 20 D5
Aurora Canada 44°0N 79°28W 82 C5
Aurora S. Africa 32°40S 18°29E 56 E2
Aurora Colo., U.S.A. 39°43N 104°49W 76 G11
Aurora Ill., U.S.A. 41°45N 88°19W 80 E9
Aurora Mo., U.S.A. 36°58N 93°43W 80 G7
Aurora N.Y., U.S.A. 42°45N 76°42W 83 D8
Aurora Nebr., U.S.A. 40°52N 98°0W 80 E5
Aurora Ohio, U.S.A. 41°21N 81°20W 82 E3
Aurukun Australia 13°20S 141°45E 62 A3
Aus Namibia 26°35S 16°12E 56 D2
Ausable → Canada 43°19N 81°46W 82 C3
Auschwitz = Oświęcim Poland 50°2N 19°11E 17 C10
Austin Minn., U.S.A. 43°40N 92°58W 80 D7
Austin Nev., U.S.A. 39°30N 117°4W 76 G5
Austin Pa., U.S.A. 41°38N 78°6W 82 E6
Austin Tex., U.S.A. 30°17N 97°45W 84 F6
Austin, L. Australia 27°40S 118°0E 61 E2
Austin I. Canada 61°10N 94°0W 71 A10
Austra Norway 65°8N 11°55E 8 D14
Austral Is. = Tubuaï, Îs. French Polynesia 25°0S 150°0W 65 K13
Austral Seamount Chain Pac. Oc. 24°0S 150°0W 65 K13
Australia ■ Oceania 23°0S 135°0E 58 D6
Australian-Antarctic Basin S. Ocean 60°0S 120°0E 5 C9
Australian Capital Territory □ Australia 35°30S 149°0E 63 F4
Australind Australia 33°17S 115°42E 61 F2
Austria ■ Europe 47°0N 14°0E 16 E8
Austvågøya Norway 68°20N 14°40E 8 B16
Autlán de Navarro Mexico 19°46N 104°22W 86 D4
Autun France 46°58N 4°17E 20 C6
Auvergne □ France 45°20N 3°15E 20 D5
Auvergne, Mts. d' France 45°20N 2°55E 20 D5
Auxerre France 47°48N 3°32E 20 C5
Av-Dovurak Russia 51°17N 91°35E 29 D10
Ava U.S.A. 36°57N 92°40W 80 G7
Avallon France 47°30N 3°53E 20 C5
Avalon U.S.A. 33°21N 118°20W 79 M8
Avalon Pen. Canada 47°30N 53°20W 73 C9
Avanos Turkey 38°43N 34°51E 44 B2
Avaré Brazil 23°4S 48°58W 95 A6
Avawatz Mts. U.S.A. 35°40N 116°30W 79 K10
Aveiro Brazil 3°10S 55°5W 93 D7
Aveiro Portugal 40°37N 8°38W 21 B1
Āvej Iran 35°40N 49°15E 45 C6
Avellaneda Argentina 34°40S 58°22W 94 C4
Avellino Italy 40°54N 14°47E 22 D6
Avenal U.S.A. 36°0N 120°8W 78 K6
Aversa Italy 40°58N 14°12E 22 D6
Avery U.S.A. 47°15N 115°49W 76 C6
Aves, I. de W. Indies 15°45N 63°55W 89 C7
Aves, Is. las Venezuela 12°0N 67°30W 89 D6
Avesta Sweden 60°9N 16°10E 9 F17
Aveyron → France 44°5N 1°16E 20 D4
Avezzano Italy 42°2N 13°25E 22 C5
Aviá Terai Argentina 26°45S 60°50W 94 B3
Aviemore U.K. 57°12N 3°50W 11 D5
Avignon France 43°57N 4°50E 20 E6
Ávila Spain 40°39N 4°43W 21 B3
Avila Beach U.S.A. 35°11N 120°44W 79 K6
Avilés Spain 43°35N 5°57W 21 A3
Avis U.S.A. 41°11N 77°19W 82 E7
Avoca U.S.A. 42°25N 77°25W 82 D7
Avoca → Australia 35°40S 143°43E 63 F3
Avoca → Ireland 52°48N 6°10W 10 D5
Avola Canada 51°45N 119°19W 70 C5
Avola Italy 36°56N 15°7E 22 F6
Avon U.S.A. 42°55N 77°45W 82 D7
Avon → Australia 31°40S 116°7E 61 F2
Avon → Bristol, U.K. 51°29N 2°41W 13 F5
Avon → Dorset, U.K. 50°44N 1°46W 13 G6
Avon → Warks., U.K. 52°0N 2°8W 13 E5
Avon Park U.S.A. 27°36N 81°31W 85 H14
Avondale Zimbabwe 17°43S 30°58E 55 F3
Avonlea Canada 50°0N 105°0W 71 D8
Avonmore Canada 45°10N 74°58W 83 A10
Avonmouth U.K. 51°30N 2°42W 13 F5
Avranches France 48°40N 1°20W 20 B3
Awa-Shima Japan 38°27N 139°14E 30 E9
A'waj → Syria 33°23N 36°20E 46 B5
Awaji-Shima Japan 34°30N 134°50E 31 G7
'Awālī Bahrain 26°0N 50°30E 45 E6
Awantipur India 33°55N 75°3E 43 C6
Awasa Ethiopia 7°2N 38°28E 47 F2
Awash Ethiopia 9°1N 40°10E 47 F3
Awatere → N.Z. 41°37S 174°10E 59 D5
Awbārī Libya 26°46N 12°57E 51 C8
Awbārī, Idehan Libya 27°10N 11°30E 51 C8
Awe, L. U.K. 56°17N 5°16W 11 E3
Awjilah Libya 29°8N 21°7E 51 C10
Axe → U.K. 50°42N 3°4W 13 F5
Axel Heiberg I. Canada 80°0N 90°0W 69 B11
Axim Ghana 4°51N 2°15W 50 H5
Axios → Greece 40°57N 22°35E 23 D10
Axminster U.K. 50°46N 3°0W 13 G4
Ayabaca Peru 4°40S 79°53W 92 D3
Ayabe Japan 35°20N 135°20E 31 G7
Ayacucho Argentina 37°5S 58°20W 94 D4
Ayacucho Peru 13°0S 74°0W 92 F4
Ayaguz = Ayaköz Kazakhstan 48°10N 80°10E 32 B3
Ayaköz Kazakhstan 48°10N 80°10E 32 B3
Ayamonte Spain 37°12N 7°24W 21 D2
Ayan Russia 56°30N 138°16E 29 D14
Ayaviri Peru 14°50S 70°35W 92 F4
Aydın Turkey 37°51N 27°51E 23 F12
Aydingkol Hu China 42°40N 89°15E 32 B3
Ayer U.S.A. 42°34N 71°35W 83 D13
Ayer Hitam Malaysia 5°24N 100°16E 39 c
Ayer's Cliff Canada 45°10N 72°3W 83 A12
Ayers Rock = Uluru Australia 25°23S 131°5E 61 E5
Ayeyarwady = Irrawaddy → Burma 15°50N 95°6E 41 M19
Ayia Napa Cyprus 34°59N 34°0E 25 E13
Áyia Phyla Cyprus 34°43N 33°1E 25 E12
Áyios Amvrósios Cyprus 35°20N 33°35E 25 D12
Áyios Seryios Cyprus 35°12N 33°53E 25 D12
Áyios Theodhoros Cyprus 35°22N 34°1E 25 D13
Aykhal Russia 66°0N 111°30E 29 C12
Aykino Russia 62°15N 49°56E 18 B8
Aylesbury U.K. 51°49N 0°49W 13 F7
Aylmer Canada 42°46N 80°59W 83 D4
Aylmer, L. Canada 64°5N 108°30W 68 C9
'Ayn, Wādī al Oman 22°15N 55°28E 45 F7
Ayn Dār Si. Arabia 25°55N 49°10E 45 E7
Ayn Zālah Iraq 36°45N 42°35E 44 B4
Ayolas Paraguay 27°10S 56°59W 94 B4
Ayon, Ostrov Russia 69°50N 169°0E 29 C17
'Ayoûn el 'Atroûs Mauritania 16°38N 9°37W 50 E4
Ayr Australia 19°35S 147°25E 62 B4
Ayr Canada 43°17N 80°27W 82 C4
Ayr U.K. 55°28N 4°38W 11 F4
Ayr → U.K. 55°28N 4°38W 11 F4
Ayre, Pt. of I. of Man 54°25N 4°21W 12 C3
Ayton Australia 15°56S 145°22E 62 B4
Aytos Bulgaria 42°42N 27°16E 23 C12
Ayu, Kepulauan Indonesia 0°35N 131°5E 37 D8
Ayutla Guatemala 14°40N 92°10W 88 D1
Ayutla de los Libres Mexico 16°54N 99°13W 87 D5
Ayvacık Turkey 39°36N 26°24E 23 E12
Ayvalık Turkey 39°20N 26°46E 23 E12
Az Zabadānī Syria 33°43N 36°5E 46 B5
Az Ẓāhirīyah West Bank 31°25N 34°58E 46 D3
Az Ẓahrān Si. Arabia 26°10N 50°7E 45 E6
Az Zarqā Jordan 32°5N 36°4E 46 C5
Az Zarqā' U.A.E. 24°53N 53°4E 45 E7
Az Zarqā □ Jordan 32°5N 36°4E 46 C5
Az Zāwiyah Libya 32°52N 12°56E 51 B8
Az Zībār Iraq 36°52N 44°4E 44 B5
Az Zilfī Si. Arabia 26°12N 44°52E 44 E5
Az Zubayr Iraq 30°26N 47°40E 44 D5
Azad Kashmir □ Pakistan 33°50N 73°50E 43 C5
Azamgarh India 26°5N 83°13E 43 F10
Azangaro Peru 14°55S 70°13W 92 F4
Azaouad Mali 19°0N 3°0W 50 E5
Āzār Shahr Iran 37°45N 45°59E 44 B5
Azarān Iran 37°25N 47°16E 44 B5
Azärbayjan = Azerbaijan ■ Asia 40°20N 48°0E 19 F8
Āzarbāyjān-e Gharbī □ Iran 37°0N 44°30E 44 B5
Āzarbāyjān-e Sharqī □ Iran 37°20N 47°0E 44 B5
Azare Nigeria 11°55N 10°10E 50 F8
A'zāz Syria 36°36N 37°4E 44 B3
Azbine = Aïr Niger 18°30N 8°0E 50 E7
Azerbaijan ■ Asia 40°20N 48°0E 19 F8
Azimganj India 24°14N 88°16E 43 G13
Azogues Ecuador 2°35S 78°0W 92 D3
Azores = Açores, Is. dos Atl. Oc. 38°0N 27°0W 50 a
Azov Russia 47°3N 39°25E 19 E6
Azov, Sea of Europe 46°0N 36°30E 19 E6
Azovskoye More = Azov, Sea of Europe 46°0N 36°30E 19 E6
Azraq ash Shīshān Jordan 31°50N 36°49E 46 D5
Aztec U.S.A. 36°49N 107°59W 77 H10
Azúa de Compostela Dom. Rep. 18°25N 70°44W 89 C5
Azuaga Spain 38°16N 5°39W 21 C3
Azuero, Pen. de Panama 7°30N 80°30W 88 E3
Azul Argentina 36°42S 59°43W 94 D4
Azusa U.S.A. 34°8N 117°52W 79 L9
Azzel Matti, Sebkra Algeria 26°10N 0°43E 50 C6

B

Ba Be △ Vietnam 22°25N 105°37E 38 A5
Ba Don Vietnam 17°45N 106°26E 38 D6
Ba Dong Vietnam 9°40N 106°33E 39 H6
Ba Ngoi = Cam Lam Vietnam 11°54N 109°10E 39 G7
Ba Tri Vietnam 10°2N 106°36E 39 G6
Ba Vi △ Vietnam 21°1N 105°22E 38 B5
Ba Xian = Bazhou China 39°8N 116°22E 34 E9
Baa Indonesia 10°50S 123°0E 37 F6
Baardheere Somali Rep. 2°20N 42°27E 47 G3
Baarle-Nassau Belgium 51°27N 4°56E 15 C4
Bab el Mandeb Red Sea 12°35N 43°25E 47 E3
Bābā, Koh-i- Afghan. 34°30N 67°0E 40 B5
Baba Burnu Turkey 39°29N 26°2E 23 E12
Bābā Kalū Iran 30°7N 50°49E 45 D6
Babadag Romania 44°53N 28°44E 17 F15
Babaeski Turkey 41°26N 27°6E 23 D12
Babahoyo Ecuador 1°40S 79°30W 92 D3
Babai = Sarju → India 27°21N 81°23E 43 F9
Babar Indonesia 8°0S 129°30E 37 F7
Babar Pakistan 31°7N 69°32E 42 D3
Babarkach Pakistan 29°45N 68°0E 42 E3
Babb U.S.A. 48°51N 113°27W 76 B7
Baberu India 25°33N 80°43E 43 G9
Babi Besar, Pulau Malaysia 2°25N 103°59E 39 L4
Bābil □ Iraq 32°30N 44°30E 44 C5
Babinda Australia 17°20S 145°56E 62 B4
Babine Canada 55°22N 126°37W 70 B3
Babine → Canada 55°45N 127°44W 70 B3
Babine L. Canada 54°48N 126°0W 70 C3
Babo Indonesia 2°30S 133°30E 37 E8
Bābol Iran 36°40N 52°50E 45 B7
Bābol Sar Iran 36°45N 52°45E 45 B7
Baboua C.A.R. 5°49N 14°58E 52 C2
Babruysk Belarus 53°10N 29°15E 17 B15
Babuhri India 26°49N 69°43E 42 F3
Babusar Pass Pakistan 35°12N 73°59E 43 B5
Babuyan Chan. Phil. 18°40N 121°30E 37 A6
Babylon Iraq 32°34N 44°22E 44 C5
Bac Can Vietnam 22°8N 105°49E 38 A5
Bac Giang Vietnam 21°16N 106°11E 38 B6
Bac Lieu Vietnam 9°17N 105°43E 39 H5
Bac Ninh Vietnam 21°13N 106°4E 38 B6
Bac Phan Vietnam 22°0N 105°0E 38 B5
Bac Quang Vietnam 22°30N 104°48E 38 A5
Bacabal Brazil 4°15S 44°45W 93 D10
Bacalar Mexico 18°43N 88°27W 87 D7
Bacan, Kepulauan Indonesia 0°35S 127°30E 37 E7
Bacarra Phil. 18°15N 120°37E 37 A6
Bacău Romania 46°35N 26°55E 17 E14
Bacerac Mexico 30°18N 108°50W 86 A3
Bach Long Vi, Dao Vietnam 20°10N 107°40E 38 B6
Bach Ma △ Vietnam 16°11N 107°49E 38 D6
Bachhwara India 25°35N 85°54E 43 G11
Back → Canada 65°10N 104°0W 68 C9
Bacolod Phil. 10°40N 122°57E 37 B6
Bacuk Malaysia 6°4N 102°25E 39 J4
Bácum Mexico 27°33N 110°5W 86 B2
Bād Iran 33°41N 52°1E 45 C7
Bad → U.S.A. 44°21N 100°22W 80 C3
Bad Axe U.S.A. 43°48N 83°0W 82 C2
Bad Ischl Austria 47°44N 13°38E 16 E7
Bad Kissingen Germany 50°11N 10°4E 16 C6
Bada Barabil India 22°7N 85°24E 43 H11
Badagara India 11°35N 75°40E 40 P9
Badain Jaran Shamo China 40°23N 102°0E 32 B5
Badajós, L. Brazil 3°15S 62°50W 92 D6
Badajoz Spain 38°50N 6°59W 21 C2
Badakhshān □ Afghan. 36°30N 71°0E 40 A7
Badalona Spain 41°26N 2°15E 21 B7
Badalzai Afghan. 29°50N 65°35E 42 E1
Badampahar India 22°10N 86°10E 41 H15
Badanah Si. Arabia 30°58N 41°30E 44 D4
Badarinath India 30°45N 79°30E 43 D8
Badas, Kepulauan Indonesia 0°45N 107°5E 36 D3
Baddo → Pakistan 28°0N 64°20E 40 F4
Bade Indonesia 7°10S 139°35E 37 F9
Baden Austria 48°1N 16°13E 16 D9
Baden U.S.A. 40°38N 80°14W 82 F4
Baden-Baden Germany 48°44N 8°13E 16 D5
Baden-Württemberg □ Germany 48°20N 8°40E 16 D5
Badgam India 34°1N 74°45E 43 B6
Badgastein Austria 47°7N 13°9E 16 E7
Badger Canada 49°0N 56°4W 73 C8
Badger U.S.A. 36°38N 119°1W 78 J7
Bādghīs □ Afghan. 35°0N 63°0E 40 B3
Badgingarra △ Australia 30°23S 115°22E 61 F2
Badin Pakistan 24°38N 68°54E 42 G3
Badlands U.S.A. 43°55N 102°30W 80 D2
Badlands △ U.S.A. 43°38N 102°56W 80 D2
Badrah Iraq 33°6N 45°58E 44 C5
Badrinath India 30°44N 79°29E 43 D8
Badulla Sri Lanka 7°1N 81°7E 40 R12
Badung, Selat Indonesia 8°40S 115°22E 37 K18
Baena Spain 37°37N 4°20W 21 D3
Baengnyeongdo S. Korea 37°57N 124°40E 35 F13
Baeza Spain 37°57N 3°25W 21 D4
Bafatá Guinea-Biss. 12°8N 14°40W 50 F3
Baffin B. N. Amer. 72°0N 64°0W 69 B13
Baffin I. Canada 68°0N 75°0W 69 C12
Bafing → Mali 13°49N 10°50W 50 F3
Bafliyūn Syria 36°37N 36°59E 44 B3
Bafoulabé Mali 13°50N 10°55W 50 F3
Bafoussam Cameroon 5°28N 10°25E 52 C2
Bāfq Iran 31°40N 55°25E 45 D7
Bafra Turkey 41°34N 35°54E 19 F6
Bāft Iran 29°15N 56°38E 45 D8
Bafwasende Dem. Rep. of the Congo 1°3N 27°5E 54 B2
Bagaha India 27°6N 84°5E 43 F11
Bagamoyo Tanzania 6°28S 38°55E 54 D4
Bagan Datoh Malaysia 3°59N 100°47E 39 L3
Bagan Serai Malaysia 5°1N 100°32E 39 K3
Baganga Phil. 7°34N 126°33E 37 C7
Bagani Namibia 18°7S 21°41E 56 B3
Bagansiapiapi Indonesia 2°12N 100°50E 36 D2
Bagasra India 21°30N 71°0E 42 J4
Bagaud India 22°19N 75°53E 42 H6
Bagdad U.S.A. 34°35N 115°53W 79 L11
Bagdarin Russia 54°26N 113°36E 29 D12
Bagé Brazil 31°20S 54°15W 95 C5
Bagenalstown = Muine Bheag Ireland 52°42N 6°58W 10 D5
Baggs U.S.A. 41°2N 107°39W 76 F10
Bagh Pakistan 33°59N 73°45E 43 C5
Baghain → India 25°32N 81°1E 43 G9
Baghdād Iraq 33°20N 44°23E 44 C5
Bagheria Italy 38°5N 13°30E 22 E5
Baghlān Afghan. 32°12N 68°46E 40 A6
Baghlān □ Afghan. 36°0N 68°30E 40 B6
Bagley U.S.A. 47°32N 95°24W 80 B6
Bago = Pegu Burma 17°20N 96°29E 41 L20
Bagodar India 24°5N 85°52E 43 G11
Bagrationovsk Russia 54°23N 20°39E 9 J19
Baguio Phil. 16°26N 120°34E 37 A6
Bah India 26°53N 78°36E 43 F8
Bahadurganj India 26°16N 87°49E 43 F12
Bahadurgarh India 28°40N 76°57E 42 E7
Bahama, Canal Viejo de W. Indies 22°10N 77°30W 88 B4
Bahamas ■ N. Amer. 24°0N 75°0W 89 B5
Bahār Iran 34°54N 48°26E 45 C6
Baharampur India 24°2N 88°27E 43 G13
Baharu Pandan = Pandan Malaysia 1°32N 103°46E 39 d
Bahawalnagar Pakistan 30°0N 73°15E 42 E5
Bahawalpur Pakistan 29°24N 71°40E 42 E4
Bäherden Turkmenistan 38°25N 57°26E 45 B8
Baheri India 28°45N 79°34E 43 E8
Bahgul → India 27°45N 79°36E 43 F8
Bahi Tanzania 5°58S 35°21E 54 D4
Bahi Swamp Tanzania 6°10S 35°0E 54 D4

Bahia = Salvador Brazil 13°0S 38°30W 93 F11
Bahia □ Brazil 12°0S 42°0W 93 F10
Bahía, Is. de la Honduras 16°45N 86°15W 88 C2
Bahía Blanca Argentina 38°35S 62°13W 94 D3
Bahía de Caráquez Ecuador 0°40S 80°27W 92 D2
Bahía Kino Mexico 28°47N 111°58W 86 B2
Bahía Laura Argentina 48°10S 66°30W 96 F3
Bahía Negra Paraguay 20°5S 58°5W 92 H7
Bahir Dar Ethiopia 11°37N 37°10E 47 E2
Bahmanzād Iran 31°15N 51°47E 45 D6
Bahraich India 27°38N 81°37E 43 F9
Bahrain ■ Asia 26°0N 50°35E 45 E6
Bahror India 27°51N 76°20E 42 F7
Bāhū Kalāt Iran 25°43N 61°25E 45 E9
Bai Bung, Mui = Ca Mau, Mui Vietnam 8°38N 104°44E 39 H5
Bai Duc Vietnam 18°3N 105°49E 38 C5
Bai Thuong Vietnam 19°54N 105°23E 38 C5
Baia Mare Romania 47°40N 23°35E 17 E12
Baião Brazil 2°40S 49°40W 93 D9
Baïbokoum Chad 7°46N 15°43E 51 G9
Baicheng China 45°38N 122°42E 35 B12
Baidoa = Baydhabo Somali Rep. 3°8N 43°30E 47 G3
Baie-Comeau Canada 49°12N 68°10W 73 C6
Baie-St-Paul Canada 47°28N 70°32W 73 C5
Baie Ste-Anne Seychelles 4°18S 55°45E 53 b
Baie-Trinité Canada 49°25N 67°20W 73 C6
Baie Verte Canada 49°55N 56°12W 73 C8
Baihar India 22°6N 80°33E 43 H9
Baihe China 32°50N 110°5E 34 H6
Ba'ījī Iraq 35°0N 43°30E 44 C4
Baijnath India 29°55N 79°37E 43 E8
Baikal, L. = Baykal, Oz. Russia 53°0N 108°0E 29 D11
Baikonur = Bayqongyr Kazakhstan 45°40N 63°20E 28 E7
Baikunthpur India 23°15N 82°33E 43 H10
Baile Atha Cliath = Dublin Ireland 53°21N 6°15W 10 C5
Băileşti Romania 44°1N 23°20E 17 F12
Bainbridge Ga., U.S.A. 30°55N 84°35W 85 F12
Bainbridge N.Y., U.S.A. 42°18N 75°29W 83 D9
Bainbridge Island U.S.A. 47°38N 122°32W 78 C4
Baing Indonesia 10°14S 120°34E 37 F6
Bainiu China 32°50N 112°15E 34 H7
Bā'ir Jordan 30°45N 36°55E 46 E5
Bairiki = Tarawa Kiribati 1°30N 173°0E 64 G9
Bairin Youqi China 43°30N 118°35E 35 C10
Bairin Zuoqi China 43°58N 119°15E 35 C10
Bairnsdale Australia 37°48S 147°36E 63 F4
Baisha China 34°20N 112°32E 34 G7
Baitadi Nepal 29°35N 80°25E 43 E9
Baiyin China 36°45N 104°14E 34 F3
Baiyu Shan China 37°15N 107°30E 34 F4
Baj Baj India 22°30N 88°5E 43 H13
Baja Hungary 46°12N 18°59E 17 E10
Baja, Pta. Mexico 29°58N 115°49W 86 B1
Baja California Mexico 31°10N 115°12W 86 A1
Baja California □ Mexico 30°0N 115°0W 86 B2
Baja California Sur □ Mexico 25°50N 111°50W 86 B2
Bajag India 22°40N 81°21E 43 H9
Bajamar Canary Is. 28°33N 16°20W 24 F3
Bajana India 23°7N 71°49E 42 H4
Bajatrejo Indonesia 8°29S 114°19E 37 J17
Bajera Indonesia 8°31S 115°2E 37 J18
Bājgīrān Iran 37°36N 58°24E 45 B8
Bajimba, Mt. Australia 29°17S 152°6E 63 D5
Bajo Boquete Panama 8°46N 82°27W 88 E3
Bajo Nuevo Caribbean 15°40N 78°50W 88 C4
Bajoga Nigeria 10°57N 11°20E 51 F8
Bajool Australia 23°40S 150°35E 62 C5
Bakel Senegal 14°56N 12°20W 50 F3
Baker Calif., U.S.A. 35°16N 116°4W 79 K10
Baker Mont., U.S.A. 46°22N 104°17W 76 C11
Baker, L. Canada 64°0N 96°0W 68 C10
Baker, Mt. U.S.A. 48°50N 121°49W 76 B3
Baker City U.S.A. 44°47N 117°50W 76 D5
Baker I. Pac. Oc. 0°10N 176°35W 64 G10
Baker I. U.S.A. 55°20N 133°40W 70 B2
Baker L. Australia 26°54S 126°5E 61 E4
Baker Lake Canada 64°20N 96°3W 68 C10
Bakers Creek Australia 21°13S 149°7E 62 C4
Bakers Dozen Is. Canada 56°45N 78°45W 72 A4
Bakersfield Calif., U.S.A. 35°23N 119°1W 79 K8
Bakersfield Vt., U.S.A. 44°45N 72°48W 83 B12
Bakharden = Bäherden Turkmenistan 38°25N 57°26E 45 B8
Bākhtarān = Kermānshāh Iran 34°23N 47°0E 44 C5
Bākhtarān = Kermānshāh □ Iran 34°0N 46°30E 44 C5
Bakı Azerbaijan 40°29N 49°56E 45 A6
Bakkafjörður Iceland 66°2N 14°48W 8 C6
Bakouma C.A.R. 5°40N 22°56E 52 C4
Bakswaho India 24°15N 79°18E 43 G8
Baku = Bakı Azerbaijan 40°29N 49°56E 45 A6
Bakutis Coast Antarctica 74°0S 120°0W 5 D15
Baky = Bakı Azerbaijan 40°29N 49°56E 45 A6
Bala Canada 45°1N 79°37W 82 A5
Bala U.K. 52°54N 3°36W 12 E4
Bala, L. U.K. 52°53N 3°37W 12 E4
Balabac I. Phil. 8°0N 117°0E 36 C5
Balabac Str. E. Indies 7°53N 117°5E 36 C5
Balabagh Afghan. 34°25N 70°12E 42 B4
Ba'labakk Lebanon 34°0N 36°10E 46 B5
Balabalangan, Kepulauan Indonesia 2°20S 117°30E 36 E5
Balad Iraq 34°0N 44°9E 44 C5
Balad Rūz Iraq 33°42N 45°5E 44 C5
Bālādeh Fārs, Iran 29°17N 51°56E 45 D6
Bālādeh Māzandaran, Iran 36°12N 51°48E 45 B6
Balaghat India 21°49N 80°12E 40 J12
Balaghat Ra. India 18°50N 76°30E 40 K10
Balaguer Spain 41°50N 0°50E 21 B6
Balaklava Ukraine 44°30N 33°30E 19 F5
Balakovo Russia 52°4N 47°55E 18 D8
Balamau India 27°10N 80°21E 43 F9
Balancán Mexico 17°48N 91°32W 87 D6
Balashov Russia 51°30N 43°10E 19 D7
Balasinor India 22°57N 73°23E 42 H5
Balasore = Baleshwar India 21°35N 87°3E 41 J15
Balaton Hungary 46°50N 17°40E 17 E9
Balbina, Represa de Brazil 2°0S 59°30W 92 D7
Balboa Panama 8°57N 79°34W 88 E4
Balbriggan Ireland 53°37N 6°11W 10 C5
Balcarce Argentina 38°0S 58°10W 94 D4
Balcarres Canada 50°50N 103°35W 71 C8
Balchik Bulgaria 43°28N 28°11E 23 C13
Balclutha N.Z. 46°15S 169°45E 59 G2
Balcones Escarpment U.S.A. 29°30N 99°15W 84 G5
Bald I. Australia 34°57S 118°27E 61 F2
Bald Knob U.S.A. 35°19N 91°34W 84 D9
Baldock L. Canada 56°33N 97°57W 71 B9
Baldwin Mich., U.S.A. 43°54N 85°51W 81 D11
Baldwin Pa., U.S.A. 40°21N 79°58W 82 F5
Baldwinsville U.S.A. 43°10N 76°20W 83 C8
Baldy Peak U.S.A. 33°54N 109°34W 77 K9
Baleares, Is. Spain 39°30N 3°0E 24 B10
Balearic Is. = Baleares, Is. Spain 39°30N 3°0E 24 B10
Baleine = Whale → Canada 58°15N 67°40W 73 A6
Baleine, Petite R. de la → Canada 56°0N 76°45W 72 A4
Baler Phil. 15°46N 121°34E 37 A6
Baleshare U.K. 57°31N 7°22W 11 D1
Baleshwar India 21°35N 87°3E 41 J15
Baley Russia 51°36N 116°37E 29 D12
Balfate Honduras 15°48N 86°25W 88 C2
Balgo Australia 20°9S 127°58E 60 D4
Bali Greece 35°25N 24°47E 25 D6
Bali India 25°11N 73°17E 42 G5
Bali Indonesia 8°20S 115°0E 37 J18
Bali □ Indonesia 8°20S 115°0E 37 J18
Bali, Selat Indonesia 8°18S 114°25E 37 J17
Bali Sea Indonesia 8°0S 115°0E 37 J17
Baliapal India 21°40N 87°17E 43 J12
Balige Indonesia 2°14N 99°7E 39 L2
Balik Pulau Malaysia 5°21N 100°14E 39 c
Balikeşir Turkey 39°39N 27°53E 23 E12
Balikpapan Indonesia 1°10S 116°55E 36 E5
Balimbing Phil. 5°5N 119°58E 37 C5
Baling Malaysia 5°41N 100°55E 39 K3
Balkan Mts. = Stara Planina Bulgaria 43°15N 23°0E 23 C10
Balkanabat Turkmenistan 39°30N 54°22E 45 B7
Balkhash = Balqash Kazakhstan 46°50N 74°50E 28 E8
Balkhash, Ozero = Balqash Köli Kazakhstan 46°0N 74°50E 28 E8
Ballachulish U.K. 56°41N 5°8W 11 E3
Balladonia Australia 32°27S 123°51E 61 F3
Ballaghaderreen Ireland 53°55N 8°34W 10 C3
Ballarat Australia 37°33S 143°50E 63 F3
Ballard, L. Australia 29°20S 120°40E 61 E3
Ballater U.K. 57°3N 3°3W 11 D5
Ballenas, Canal de Mexico 29°10N 113°29W 86 B2
Balleny Is. Antarctica 66°30S 163°0E 5 C11
Ballia India 25°46N 84°12E 43 G11
Ballina Australia 28°50S 153°31E 63 D5
Ballina Ireland 54°7N 9°9W 10 B2
Ballinasloe Ireland 53°20N 8°13W 10 C3
Ballinger U.S.A. 31°45N 99°57W 84 F5
Ballinrobe Ireland 53°38N 9°13W 10 C2
Ballinskelligs B. Ireland 51°48N 10°13W 10 E1
Ballston Spa U.S.A. 43°0N 73°51W 83 D11
Ballyboghil Ireland 53°32N 6°16W 10 C5
Ballybunion Ireland 52°31N 9°40W 10 D2
Ballycanew Ireland 52°37N 6°19W 10 D5
Ballycastle U.K. 55°12N 6°15W 10 A5
Ballyclare U.K. 54°46N 6°0W 10 B5
Ballydehob Ireland 51°34N 9°28W 10 E2
Ballygawley U.K. 54°27N 7°2W 10 B4
Ballyhaunis Ireland 53°46N 8°46W 10 C3
Ballyheige Ireland 52°23N 9°49W 10 D2
Ballymena U.K. 54°52N 6°17W 10 B5
Ballymoney U.K. 55°5N 6°31W 10 A5
Ballymote Ireland 54°5N 8°31W 10 B3
Ballynahinch U.K. 54°24N 5°54W 10 B6
Ballyquintin Pt. U.K. 54°20N 5°30W 10 B6
Ballyshannon Ireland 54°30N 8°11W 10 B3
Balmaceda Chile 46°0S 71°50W 96 F2
Balmertown Canada 51°4N 93°41W 71 C10
Balmoral Australia 37°15S 141°48E 63 F3
Balmorhea U.S.A. 30°59N 103°45W 84 F3
Balochistan = Baluchistan □ Pakistan 27°30N 65°0E 40 F4
Balonne → Australia 28°47S 147°56E 63 D4
Balotra India 25°50N 72°14E 42 G5
Balqash Kazakhstan 46°50N 74°50E 28 E8
Balqash Köli Kazakhstan 46°0N 74°50E 28 E8
Balrampur India 27°30N 82°20E 43 F10
Balranald Australia 34°38S 143°33E 63 E3
Balsas → Brazil 7°15S 44°35W 93 E9
Balsas → Mexico 17°55N 102°10W 86 D4
Balsas del Norte Mexico 18°0N 99°46W 87 D5
Balta Ukraine 48°2N 29°45E 17 D15
Bălţi Moldova 47°48N 27°58E 17 E14
Baltic Sea Europe 57°0N 19°0E 9 H18
Baltimore Ireland 51°29N 9°22W 10 E2
Baltimore Md., U.S.A. 39°17N 76°36W 81 F15
Baltimore Ohio, U.S.A. 39°51N 82°36W 82 G2
Baltinglass Ireland 52°56N 6°43W 10 D5
Baltit Pakistan 36°15N 74°40E 43 A6
Baltiysk Russia 54°41N 19°58E 9 J18
Baluchistan □ Pakistan 27°30N 65°0E 40 F4
Balurghat India 25°15N 88°44E 43 G13
Balvi Latvia 57°8N 27°15E 9 H22
Balya Turkey 39°44N 27°35E 23 E12
Balykchy Kyrgyzstan 42°26N 76°12E 32 B2
Bam Iran 29°7N 58°14E 45 D8
Bama Nigeria 11°33N 13°41E 51 F8
Bamaga Australia 10°50S 142°25E 62 A3
Bamaji L. Canada 51°9N 91°25W 72 B1
Bamako Mali 12°34N 7°55W 50 F4
Bambari C.A.R. 5°40N 20°35E 52 C4
Bambaroo Australia 18°50S 146°10E 62 B4
Bamberg Germany 49°54N 10°54E 16 D6
Bamberg U.S.A. 33°18N 81°2W 85 E14
Bambili Dem. Rep. of the Congo 3°40N 26°0E 54 B2
Bamburgh U.K. 55°37N 1°43W 12 B6
Bamenda Cameroon 5°57N 10°11E 52 C2
Bamfield Canada 48°45N 125°10W 70 D3
Bāmīān □ Afghan. 35°0N 67°0E 40 B5
Bamiancheng China 43°15N 124°2E 35 C13
Bampūr Iran 27°15N 60°21E 45 E9
Bampūr → Iran 27°24N 59°0E 45 E8
Ban Ao Tu Khun Thailand 8°9N 98°20E 39 a
Ban Ban Laos 19°31N 103°30E 38 C4
Ban Bang Hin Thailand 9°32N 98°35E 39 H2
Ban Bang Khu Thailand 7°57N 98°23E 39 a
Ban Bang Rong Thailand 8°3N 98°25E 39 a
Ban Bo Phut Thailand 9°33N 100°2E 39 b
Ban Chaweng Thailand 9°32N 100°3E 39 b
Ban Chiang Klang Thailand 19°25N 100°55E 38 C3
Ban Choho Thailand 15°2N 102°9E 38 E4
Ban Dan Lan Hoi Thailand 17°0N 99°35E 38 D2
Ban Don = Surat Thani Thailand 9°6N 99°20E 39 H2
Ban Don Vietnam 12°53N 107°48E 38 F6
Ban Don, Ao → Thailand 9°20N 99°25E 39 H2
Ban Dong Thailand 19°30N 100°59E 38 C3
Ban Hong Thailand 18°18N 98°50E 38 C2
Ban Hua Thanon Thailand 9°26N 100°1E 39 b
Ban Kantang Thailand 7°25N 99°31E 39 J2
Ban Karon Thailand 7°51N 98°18E 39 a
Ban Kata Thailand 7°50N 98°18E 39 a
Ban Keun Laos 18°22N 102°35E 38 C4
Ban Khai Thailand 12°46N 101°18E 38 F3
Ban Kheun Laos 20°13N 101°7E 38 B3
Ban Khlong Khian Thailand 8°10N 98°26E 39 a
Ban Khlong Kua Thailand 6°57N 100°8E 39 J3
Ban Khuan Thailand 8°20N 98°25E 39 a
Ban Khuan Mao Thailand 7°50N 99°37E 39 J2
Ban Ko Yai Chim Thailand 11°17N 99°26E 39 G2
Ban Laem Thailand 13°13N 99°59E 38 F2
Ban Lamai Thailand 9°28N 100°3E 39 b
Ban Lao Ngam Laos 15°28N 106°10E 38 E6
Ban Le Kathe Thailand 15°49N 98°53E 38 E2
Ban Lo Po Noi Thailand 8°1N 98°34E 39 a
Ban Mae Chedi Thailand 19°11N 99°31E 38 C2
Ban Mae Nam Thailand 9°34N 100°0E 39 b
Ban Mae Sariang Thailand 18°10N 97°56E 38 C1
Ban Mê Thuôt = Buon Ma Thuot Vietnam 12°40N 108°3E 38 F7
Ban Mi Thailand 15°3N 100°32E 38 E3
Ban Muong Mo Laos 19°4N 103°58E 38 C4
Ban Na Bo Thailand 9°19N 99°41E 39 b
Ban Na Mo Laos 17°7N 105°40E 38 D5
Ban Na San Thailand 8°53N 99°52E 39 H2
Ban Na Tong Laos 20°56N 101°47E 38 B3
Ban Nam Bac Laos 20°38N 102°20E 38 B4
Ban Nam Ma Laos 22°2N 101°37E 38 A3
Ban Ngang Laos 15°59N 106°11E 38 E6
Ban Nong Bok Laos 17°5N 104°48E 38 D5
Ban Nong Boua Laos 15°40N 106°33E 38 E6
Ban Nong Pling Thailand 15°40N 100°10E 38 E3
Ban Pak Chan Thailand 10°32N 98°51E 39 G2
Ban Patong Thailand 7°54N 98°18E 39 a
Ban Phai Thailand 16°4N 102°44E 38 D4
Ban Phak Chit Thailand 8°0N 98°24E 39 a
Ban Pong Thailand 13°50N 99°55E 38 F2
Ban Rawai Thailand 7°47N 98°20E 39 a
Ban Ron Phibun Thailand 8°9N 99°51E 39 H2
Ban Sakhu Thailand 8°4N 98°18E 39 a
Ban Sanam Chai Thailand 7°33N 100°25E 39 J3
Ban Sangkha Thailand 14°37N 103°52E 38 E4
Ban Tak Thailand 17°2N 99°4E 38 D2
Ban Tako Thailand 14°5N 102°40E 38 E4
Ban Tha Dua Thailand 17°59N 98°39E 38 D2
Ban Tha Nun Thailand 8°12N 98°18E 39 a
Ban Tha Rua Thailand 7°59N 98°22E 39 a
Ban Tha Yu Thailand 8°17N 98°22E 39 a
Ban Thahine Laos 14°12N 105°33E 38 E5
Ban Thong Krut Thailand 9°25N 99°57E 39 b
Ban Xien Kok Laos 20°54N 100°39E 38 B3
Ban Yen Nhan Vietnam 20°57N 106°2E 38 B6
Banaba Kiribati 0°45S 169°50E 64 H8
Banalia Dem. Rep. of the Congo 1°32N 25°5E 54 B2
Banam Cambodia 11°20N 105°17E 39 G5
Bananal, I. do Brazil 11°30S 50°30W 93 F8
Banaras = Varanasi India 25°22N 83°0E 43 G10
Banas → Gujarat, India 23°45N 71°25E 42 H4
Banas → Mad. P., India 24°15N 81°30E 43 G9
Bânâs, Ras Egypt 23°57N 35°59E 51 D13
Banbridge U.K. 54°22N 6°16W 10 B5
Banbury U.K. 52°4N 1°20W 13 E6
Banchory U.K. 57°3N 2°29W 11 D6
Bancroft Canada 45°3N 77°51W 82 A7
Band Bonī Iran 25°30N 59°33E 45 E8
Band Qīr Iran 31°39N 48°53E 45 D6
Banda Mad. P., India 24°3N 78°57E 43 G8
Banda Ut. P., India 25°30N 80°26E 43 G9
Banda, Kepulauan Indonesia 4°37S 129°50E 37 E7
Banda Aceh Indonesia 5°35N 95°20E 36 C1
Banda Banda, Mt. Australia 31°10S 152°28E 63 E5
Banda Elat Indonesia 5°40S 133°5E 37 F8
Banda Is. = Banda, Kepulauan Indonesia 4°37S 129°50E 37 E7
Banda Sea Indonesia 6°0S 130°0E 37 F8
Bandai-Asahi △ Japan 37°38N 140°5E 30 F10
Bandai-San Japan 37°36N 140°4E 30 F10
Bandān Iran 31°23N 60°44E 45 D9
Bandanaira Indonesia 4°32S 129°54E 37 E7
Bandanwara India 26°9N 74°38E 42 F6
Bandar = Machilipatnam India 16°12N 81°8E 41 L12
Bandar-e Abbās Iran 27°15N 56°15E 45 E8
Bandar-e Anzalī Iran 37°30N 49°30E 45 B6
Bandar-e Bushehr = Būshehr Iran 28°55N 50°55E 45 D6
Bandar-e Chārak Iran 26°45N 54°20E 45 E7
Bandar-e Deylam Iran 30°5N 50°10E 45 D6
Bandar-e Emām Khomeynı Iran 30°30N 49°5E 45 D6
Bandar-e Lengeh Iran 26°35N 54°58E 45 E7
Bandar-e Maqām Iran 26°56N 53°29E 45 E7
Bandar-e Ma'shur Iran 30°35N 49°10E 45 D6
Bandar-e Rīg Iran 29°29N 50°38E 45 D6
Bandar-e Torkeman Iran 37°0N 54°10E 45 B7
Bandar Lampung Indonesia 5°20S 105°10E 36 F3
Bandar Maharani = Muar Malaysia 2°3N 102°34E 39 L4
Bandar Penggaram = Batu Pahat Malaysia 1°50N 102°56E 39 M4
Bandar Seri Begawan Brunei 4°52N 115°0E 36 D5
Bandar Sri Aman = Sri Aman Malaysia 1°15N 111°32E 36 D4
Bandawe Malawi 11°58S 34°5E 55 E3
Bandeira, Pico da Brazil 20°26S 41°47W 95 A7
Bandera Argentina 28°55S 62°20W 94 B3
Banderas, B. de Mexico 20°40N 105°25W 86 C3
Bandhavgarh India 23°40N 81°2E 43 H9
Bandi → India 26°12N 75°47E 42 F6
Bandikui India 27°3N 76°34E 42 F7
Bandırma Turkey 40°20N 28°0E 23 D13
Bandjarmasin = Banjarmasin Indonesia 3°20S 114°35E 36 E4
Bandon Ireland 51°44N 8°44W 10 E3
Bandon → Ireland 51°43N 8°37W 10 E3
Bandula Mozam. 19°0S 33°7E 55 F3
Bandundu Dem. Rep. of the Congo 3°15S 17°22E 52 E3
Bandung Indonesia 6°54S 107°36E 37 G12
Bāneh Iran 35°59N 45°53E 44 C5
Banes Cuba 21°0N 75°42W 89 B4
Banff Canada 51°10N 115°34W 70 C5
Banff U.K. 57°40N 2°33W 11 D6
Banff △ Canada 51°30N 116°15W 70 C5
Bang Fai → Laos 16°57N 104°45E 38 D5
Bang Hieng → Laos 16°10N 105°10E 38 D5
Bang Krathum Thailand 16°34N 100°18E 38 D3
Bang Lamung Thailand 13°3N 100°56E 38 F3
Bang Mun Nak Thailand 16°2N 100°23E 38 D3
Bang Pa In Thailand 14°14N 100°35E 38 E3
Bang Rakam Thailand 16°45N 100°7E 38 D3
Bang Saphan Thailand 11°14N 99°28E 39 G2
Bang Thao Thailand 7°59N 98°18E 39 a
Bangaduni I. India 21°34N 88°52E 43 J13
Bangala Dam Zimbabwe 21°7S 31°25E 55 G3
Bangalore India 12°59N 77°40E 40 N10
Banganga → India 27°6N 77°25E 42 F6
Bangaon India 23°0N 88°47E 43 H13
Bangassou C.A.R. 4°55N 23°7E 52 D4
Banggai Indonesia 1°34S 123°30E 37 E6
Banggai, Kepulauan Indonesia 1°40S 123°30E 37 E6
Banggai Arch. = Banggai, Kepulauan Indonesia 1°40S 123°30E 37 E6
Banggi, Pulau Malaysia 7°17N 117°12E 36 C5
Banghāzī Libya 32°11N 20°3E 51 B10
Bangka Sulawesi, Indonesia 1°50N 125°5E 37 D7
Bangka Sumatera, Indonesia 2°0S 105°50E 36 E3
Bangka, Selat Indonesia 2°30S 105°30E 36 E3
Bangka-Belitung □ Indonesia 2°30S 107°0E 36 E3
Bangkalan Indonesia 7°2S 112°46E 37 G15
Bangkinang Indonesia 0°18N 101°5E 36 D2
Bangko Indonesia 2°5S 102°9E 36 E2
Bangkok Thailand 13°45N 100°35E 38 F3
Bangladesh ■ Asia 24°0N 90°0E 41 H17
Bangli Indonesia 8°27S 115°21E 37 J18
Bangong Co China 33°45N 78°43E 43 C8
Bangor Down, U.K. 54°40N 5°40W 10 B6
Bangor Gwynedd, U.K. 53°14N 4°8W 12 D3
Bangor Maine, U.S.A. 44°48N 68°46W 81 C19
Bangor Pa., U.S.A. 40°52N 75°13W 83 F9
Bangued Phil. 17°40N 120°37E 37 A6
Bangui C.A.R. 4°23N 18°35E 52 D3
Banguru Dem. Rep. of the Congo 0°30N 27°10E 54 B2
Bangweulu, L. Zambia 11°0S 30°0E 55 E3
Bangweulu Swamp Zambia 11°20S 30°15E 55 E3
Banhine △ Mozam. 22°49S 32°55E 57 C5
Baní Dom. Rep. 18°16N 70°22W 89 C5
Banī Sa'd Iraq 33°34N 44°32E 44 C5
Banihal Pass India 33°30N 75°12E 43 C6
Banissa Kenya 3°55N 40°19E 54 B4
Bāniyās Syria 35°10N 36°0E 44 C3
Banja Luka Bos.-H. 44°49N 17°11E 22 B7
Banjar India 31°38N 77°21E 42 D7
Banjar → India 22°36N 80°22E 43 H9
Banjarmasin Indonesia 3°20S 114°35E 36 E4
Banjul Gambia 13°28N 16°40W 50 F2
Banka India 24°53N 86°55E 43 G12
Banket Zimbabwe 17°27S 30°19E 55 F3
Bankipore India 25°35N 85°10E 41 G14
Banks I. B.C., Canada 53°20N 130°0W 70 C3
Banks I. N.W.T., Canada 73°15N 121°30W 68 B7
Banks Pen. N.Z. 43°45S 173°15E 59 E4
Banks Str. Australia 40°40S 148°10E 63 G4
Bankura India 23°11N 87°18E 43 H12
Banmankhi India 25°53N 87°11E 43 G12
Bann → Armagh, U.K. 54°30N 6°31W 10 B5
Bann → L'derry., U.K. 55°8N 6°41W 10 A5
Bannang Sata Thailand 6°16N 101°16E 39 J3
Banning U.S.A. 33°56N 116°53W 79 M10
Bannockburn Canada 44°39N 77°33W 82 B7
Bannockburn U.K. 56°5N 3°55W 11 E5
Bannockburn Zimbabwe 20°17S 29°48E 55 G2
Bannu Pakistan 33°0N 70°18E 40 C7
Bano India 22°40N 84°55E 43 H11
Bansgaon India 26°33N 83°21E 43 F10
Banská Bystrica Slovak Rep. 48°46N 19°14E 17 D10
Banswara India 23°32N 74°24E 42 H6
Bantaeng Indonesia 5°32S 119°56E 37 F5
Banten □ Indonesia 6°30S 106°0E 37 G11
Bantry Ireland 51°41N 9°27W 10 E2
Bantry B. Ireland 51°37N 9°44W 10 E2
Bantul Indonesia 7°55S 110°19E 37 G14
Bantva India 21°29N 70°12E 42 J4
Banyak, Kepulauan Indonesia 2°10N 97°10E 36 D1
Banyalbufar Spain 39°42N 2°31E 24 B9
Banyo Cameroon 6°52N 11°45E 52 C2
Banyumas Indonesia 7°32S 109°18E 37 G13
Banyuwangi Indonesia 8°13S 114°21E 37 J17
Banzare Coast Antarctica 68°0S 125°0E 5 C9
Bao Ha Vietnam 22°11N 104°21E 38 A5
Bao Lac Vietnam 22°57N 105°40E 38 A5
Bao Loc Vietnam 11°32N 107°48E 39 G6
Bao'an = Shenzhen China 22°32N 114°5E 33 F10
Baocheng China 33°12N 106°56E 34 H4
Baode China 39°1N 111°5E 34 E6
Baodi China 39°38N 117°20E 35 E9
Baoding China 38°50N 115°28E 34 E8
Baoji China 34°20N 107°5E 34 G4
Baoshan China 25°10N 99°5E 32 D4
Baotou China 40°32N 110°2E 34 D6
Baoying China 33°17N 119°20E 35 H10
Baoyou = Ledong China 18°41N 109°5E 38 C7
Bap India 27°23N 72°18E 42 F5
Bapatla India 15°55N 80°30E 41 M12
Bāqerābād Iran 33°2N 51°58E 45 C6
Ba'qūbah Iraq 33°45N 44°50E 44 C5
Baquedano Chile 23°20S 69°52W 94 A2
Bar Montenegro 42°8N 19°6E 23 C8
Bar Ukraine 49°4N 27°40E 17 D14
Bar Bigha India 25°21N 85°47E 43 G11
Bar Harbor U.S.A. 44°23N 68°13W 81 C19
Bar-le-Duc France 48°47N 5°10E 20 B6
Bara India 25°16N 81°43E 43 G9
Bara Banki India 26°55N 81°12E 43 F9
Barabai Indonesia 2°32S 115°34E 36 E5
Baraboo U.S.A. 43°28N 89°45W 80 D9
Baracoa Cuba 20°20N 74°30W 89 B5
Baradā → Syria 33°33N 36°34E 46 B5
Baradero Argentina 33°52S 59°29W 94 C4
Baraga U.S.A. 46°47N 88°30W 80 B9
Baragoi Kenya 1°47N 36°47E 54 B4
Barah → India 27°42N 77°5E 42 F6
Barahona Dom. Rep. 18°13N 71°7W 89 C5
Barail Range India 25°15N 93°20E 41 G18
Barakaldo Spain 43°18N 2°59W 21 A4
Barakar → India 24°7N 86°14E 43 G12
Barakot India 21°33N 84°59E 43 J11
Barakpur India 22°47N 88°21E 43 H13
Baralaba Australia 24°13S 149°50E 62 C4
Baralzon L. Canada 60°0N 98°3W 71 B9
Baramula India 34°15N 74°20E 43 B6
Baran India 25°9N 76°40E 42 G7
Baran → Pakistan 25°13N 68°17E 42 G3
Baranavichy Belarus 53°10N 26°0E 17 B14
Baranof U.S.A. 57°5N 134°50W 70 B2
Baranof I. U.S.A. 57°0N 135°0W 68 D6
Barapasi Indonesia 2°15S 137°5E 37 E9
Barasat India 22°46N 88°31E 43 H13
Barat Daya, Kepulauan Indonesia 7°30S 128°0E 37 F7
Barataria B. U.S.A. 29°20N 89°55W 85 G10
Barauda India 23°33N 75°15E 42 H6
Baraut India 29°13N 77°7E 42 E7
Barbacena Brazil 21°15S 43°56W 95 A7
Barbados ■ W. Indies 13°10N 59°30W 89 g
Barbària, C. de Spain 38°39N 1°24E 24 C7
Barbas, C. W. Sahara 22°20N 16°42W 50 D2
Barbastro Spain 42°2N 0°5E 21 A6
Barberton S. Africa 25°42S 31°2E 57 D5
Barberton U.S.A. 41°1N 81°39W 82 E3
Barbosa Colombia 5°57N 73°37W 92 B4
Barbourville U.S.A. 36°52N 83°53W 81 G12
Barbuda W. Indies 17°30N 61°40W 89 C7
Barcaldine Australia 23°43S 145°6E 62 C4
Barcellona Pozzo di Gotto Italy 38°9N 15°13E 22 E6
Barcelona Spain 41°22N 2°10E 21 B7
Barcelona Venezuela 10°10N 64°40W 92 A6
Barceloneta Puerto Rico 18°27N 66°32W 89 d
Barcelos Brazil 1°0S 63°0W 92 D6
Barcoo → Australia 25°30S 142°50E 62 D3
Bardaī Chad 21°25N 17°0E 51 D9
Bardas Blancas Argentina 35°49S 69°45W 94 D2
Bardawīl, Sabkhet el Egypt 31°10N 33°15E 46 D2
Barddhaman India 23°14N 87°39E 43 H12
Bardejov Slovak Rep. 49°18N 21°15E 17 D11
Bardera = Baardheere Somali Rep. 2°20N 42°27E 47 G3
Bardīyah Libya 31°45N 25°6E 51 B10
Bardsey I. U.K. 52°45N 4°47W 12 E3

Bardstown *U.S.A.* 37°49N 85°28W **81** G11
Bareilly *India* 28°22N 79°27E **43** E8
Barela *India* 23°6N 80°3E **43** H9
Barents Sea *Arctic* 73°0N 39°0E **4** B9
Barfleur, Pte. de *France* 49°42N 1°16W **20** B3
Bargara *Australia* 24°50S 152°25E **62** C5
Bargi Dam *India* 22°50N 80°0E **43** H9
Barguzin *Russia* 53°37N 109°37E **29** D11
Barh *India* 25°29N 85°46E **43** G11
Barhaj *India* 26°18N 83°44E **43** F10
Barharwa *India* 24°52N 87°47E **43** G12
Barhi *India* 24°15N 85°25E **43** G11
Bari *India* 26°39N 77°39E **42** F7
Bari *Italy* 41°8N 16°51E **22** D7
Bari Doab *Pakistan* 30°20N 73°0E **42** D5
Bari Sadri *India* 24°28N 74°30E **42** G6
Barīdī, Ra's *Si. Arabia* 24°17N 37°31E **44** E3
Barīm *Yemen* 12°39N 43°25E **48** E8
Barinas *Venezuela* 8°36N 70°15W **92** B4
Baring, C. *Canada* 70°0N 117°30W **68** C8
Baringo, L. *Kenya* 0°47N 36°16E **54** B4
Barisal *Bangla.* 22°45N 90°20E **41** H17
Barisal □ *Bangla.* 22°45N 90°20E **41** H17
Barisan, Pegunungan
  Indonesia 3°30S 102°15E **36** E2
Barito → *Indonesia* 4°0S 114°50E **36** E4
Baritú △ *Argentina* 23°43S 64°40W **94** A3
Barjūj, Wadi → *Libya* 25°26N 12°12E **51** C8
Bark L. *Canada* 45°27N 77°51W **82** A7
Barkakana *India* 23°37N 85°29E **43** H11
Barker *U.S.A.* 43°20N 78°33W **82** C6
Barkley, L. *U.S.A.* 37°1N 88°14W **85** C10
Barkley Sound *Canada* 48°50N 125°10W **70** D3
Barkly East *S. Africa* 30°58S 27°33E **56** E4
Barkly Homestead
  Australia 19°52S 135°50E **62** B2
Barkly Tableland
  Australia 17°50S 136°40E **62** B2
Barkly West *S. Africa* 28°5S 24°31E **56** D3
Barkol Kazak Zizhixian
  China 43°37N 93°2E **32** B4
Bârlad *Romania* 46°15N 27°38E **17** E14
Bârlad → *Romania* 45°38N 27°32E **17** F14
Barlee, L. *Australia* 29°15S 119°30E **61** E2
Barlee, Mt. *Australia* 24°38S 128°13E **61** D4
Barletta *Italy* 41°19N 16°17E **22** D7
Barlovento *Canary Is.* 28°48N 17°48W **24** F2
Barlovento *C. Verde Is.* 17°0N 25°0W **50** b
Barlow L. *Canada* 62°0N 103°0W **71** A8
Barmedman *Australia* 34°9S 147°21E **63** E4
Barmer *India* 25°45N 71°20E **42** G4
Barmera *Australia* 34°15S 140°28E **63** E3
Barmouth *U.K.* 52°44N 4°4W **12** E3
Barna → *India* 25°21N 83°3E **43** G10
Barnagar *India* 23°7N 75°19E **42** H6
Barnala *India* 30°23N 75°33E **42** D6
Barnard Castle *U.K.* 54°33N 1°55W **12** C6
Barnaul *Russia* 53°20N 83°40E **28** D9
Barnesville, Ga., *U.S.A.* 33°3N 84°9W **85** E12
Barnesville, Minn.,
  U.S.A. 46°43N 96°28W **80** B5
Barnet □ *U.K.* 51°38N 0°9W **13** F7
Barneveld *Neths.* 52°7N 5°36E **15** B5
Barnhart *U.S.A.* 31°8N 101°10W **84** F4
Barnsley *U.K.* 53°34N 1°27W **12** D6
Barnstable *U.S.A.* 41°42N 70°18W **81** E18
Barnstaple *U.K.* 51°5N 4°4W **13** F3
Barnstaple Bay = Bideford Bay
  U.K. 51°5N 4°20W **13** F3
Barnwell *U.S.A.* 33°15N 81°23W **85** E14
Baro *Nigeria* 8°35N 6°18E **50** G7
Baroda = Vadodara
  India 22°20N 73°10E **42** H5
Baroda *India* 25°29N 76°35E **42** G7
Baroe *S. Africa* 33°13S 24°33E **56** E3
Baron Ra. *Australia* 23°30S 127°45E **60** D4
Barotseland *Zambia* 15°0S 24°0E **53** H4
Barpeta *India* 26°20N 91°10E **41** F17
Barqa *Libya* 27°0N 23°0E **51** C10
Barques, Pt. Aux *U.S.A.* 44°4N 82°58W **82** C2
Barquísimeto *Venezuela* 10°4N 69°19W **92** A5
Barr Smith Range
  Australia 27°4S 120°20E **61** E3
Barra *Brazil* 11°5S 43°10W **93** F10
Barra *U.K.* 57°0N 7°29W **11** E1
Barra, Sd. of *U.K.* 57°4N 7°25W **11** D1
Barra de Navidad
  Mexico 19°12N 104°41W **86** D4
Barra do Corda *Brazil* 5°30S 45°10W **93** E9
Barra do Garças *Brazil* 15°54S 52°16W **93** G8
Barra do Piraí *Brazil* 22°30S 43°50W **95** A7
Barra Falsa, Pta. da
  Mozam. 22°58S 35°37E **57** C6
Barra Hd. *U.K.* 56°47N 7°40W **11** E1
Barra Mansa *Brazil* 22°35S 44°12W **95** A7
Barraba *Australia* 30°21S 150°35E **63** E5
Barrackpur = Barakpur
  India 22°47N 88°21E **43** H13
Barradale *Australia* 22°42S 114°58E **60** D1
Barraigh = Barra *U.K.* 57°0N 7°29W **11** E1
Barranca *Lima, Peru* 10°45S 77°50W **92** F3
Barranca *Loreto, Peru* 4°50S 76°50W **92** D3
Barranca del Cobre △
  Mexico 27°18N 107°40W **86** B3
Barrancabermeja
  Colombia 7°0N 73°50W **92** B4
Barrancas *Venezuela* 8°55N 62°5W **92** B6
Barrancos *Portugal* 38°10N 6°58W **21** C2
Barranqueras *Argentina* 27°30S 59°0W **94** B4
Barranquilla *Colombia* 11°0N 74°50W **92** A4
Barraute *Canada* 48°26N 77°38W **72** C4
Barre *Mass., U.S.A.* 42°25N 72°6W **83** D12
Barre *Vt., U.S.A.* 44°12N 72°30W **83** B12
Barreal *Argentina* 31°33S 69°28W **94** C2
Barreiras *Brazil* 12°8S 45°0W **93** F10
Barreirinhas *Brazil* 2°30S 42°50W **93** D10
Barreiro *Portugal* 38°39N 9°5W **21** C1

Barren, Nosy *Madag.* 18°25S 43°40E **57** B7
Barretos *Brazil* 20°30S 48°35W **93** H9
Barrhead *Canada* 54°10N 114°24W **70** C6
Barrie *Canada* 44°24N 79°40W **82** B5
Barrier Ra. *Australia* 31°0S 141°30E **63** E3
Barrier Reef *Belize* 17°9N 88°3W **87** D7
Barrière *Canada* 51°12N 120°7W **70** C4
Barrington *U.S.A.* 41°44N 71°18W **83** E13
Barrington L. *Canada* 56°55N 100°15W **71** B8
Barrington Tops
  Australia 32°6S 151°28E **63** E5
Barringun *Australia* 29°1S 145°41E **63** D4
Barron *U.S.A.* 45°24N 91°51W **80** C8
Barrow *U.S.A.* 71°18N 156°47W **74** a
Barrow → *Ireland* 52°25N 6°58W **10** D5
Barrow, Pt. *U.S.A.* 71°23N 156°29W **66** B4
Barrow Creek *Australia* 21°30S 133°55E **62** C1
Barrow I. *Australia* 20°45S 115°20E **60** D2
Barrow-in-Furness *U.K.* 54°7N 3°14W **12** C4
Barrow Pt. *Australia* 14°20S 144°40E **62** A3
Barrow Ra. *Australia* 26°0S 127°40E **61** E4
Barrow Str. *Canada* 74°20N 95°0W **4** B3
Barry *U.K.* 51°24N 3°16W **13** F4
Barry's Bay *Canada* 45°29N 77°41W **82** A7
Barsat *Pakistan* 36°10N 72°45E **43** A5
Barsi *India* 18°10N 75°50E **40** K9
Barsoi *India* 25°48N 87°57E **41** G15
Barstow *U.S.A.* 34°54N 117°1W **79** L9
Barthélemy, Col *Vietnam* 19°26N 104°6E **38** C5
Bartica *Guyana* 6°25N 58°40W **92** B7
Bartle Frere *Australia* 17°27S 145°50E **62** B4
Bartlesville *U.S.A.* 36°45N 95°59W **84** C7
Bartlett, Calif., *U.S.A.* 36°29N 118°2W **78** J8
Bartlett, Tenn., *U.S.A.* 35°12N 89°52W **85** D10
Bartlett, L. *Canada* 63°5N 118°20W **70** A5
Barton *U.S.A.* 44°45N 72°11W **83** B12
Barton upon Humber
  U.K. 53°41N 0°25W **12** D7
Bartow *U.S.A.* 27°54N 81°50W **85** H14
Barú, Volcan *Panama* 8°55N 82°35W **88** E3
Barumba
  Dem. Rep. of the Congo 1°3N 23°37E **54** B1
Baruun Urt *Mongolia* 46°46N 113°15E **29** E12
Baruunsuu *Mongolia* 43°43N 105°35E **34** C3
Barwani *India* 22°2N 74°57E **42** H6
Barysaw *Belarus* 54°17N 28°28E **17** A15
Barzān *Iraq* 36°55N 44°3E **44** B5
Bāsa'idū *Iran* 26°35N 55°20E **45** E7
Basal *Pakistan* 33°33N 72°13E **42** C5
Basankusa
  Dem. Rep. of the Congo 1°5N 19°50E **52** D3
Basarabeasca *Moldova* 46°21N 28°58E **17** E15
Basarabia = Bessarabiya
  Moldova 47°0N 28°10E **17** E15
Basawa *Afghan.* 34°15N 70°50E **42** B4
Bascuñán, C. *Chile* 28°52S 71°35W **94** B1
Basel *Switz.* 47°35N 7°35E **20** C7
Bashäkerd, Kühhä-ye
  Iran 26°42N 58°35E **45** E8
Bashaw *Canada* 52°35N 112°58W **70** C6
Bāshī *Iran* 28°41N 51°4E **45** D6
Bashkir Republic =
  Bashkortostan □
  Russia 54°0N 57°0E **18** D10
Bashkortostan □ *Russia* 54°0N 57°0E **18** D10
Basibasy *Madag.* 22°10S 43°40E **57** C7
Basilan *Phil.* 6°35N 122°0E **37** C6
Basilan Str. *Phil.* 6°50N 122°0E **37** C6
Basildon *U.K.* 51°34N 0°28E **13** F8
Basim = Washim *India* 20°3N 77°0E **40** J10
Basin *U.S.A.* 44°23N 108°2W **76** D9
Basingstoke *U.K.* 51°15N 1°5W **13** F6
Baskatong, Rés. *Canada* 46°46N 75°50W **72** C4
Basle = Basel *Switz.* 47°35N 7°35E **20** C7
Basoda *India* 23°52N 77°54E **42** H7
Basoko
  Dem. Rep. of the Congo 1°16N 23°40E **54** B1
Basque Provinces = País Vasco □
  Spain 42°50N 2°45W **21** A4
Basra = Al Başrah *Iraq* 30°30N 47°50E **44** D5
Bass Str. *Australia* 39°15S 146°30E **63** F4
Bassano *Canada* 50°48N 112°20W **70** C6
Bassano del Grappa *Italy* 45°46N 11°44E **22** B4
Bassas da India *Ind. Oc.* 22°0S 39°0E **53** J7
Basse-Pointe *Martinique* 14°52N 61°8W **88** c
Basse-Terre *Guadeloupe* 16°0N 61°44W **88** b
Basse Terre *Trin. & Tob.* 10°7N 61°19W **93** K15
Bassein *Burma* 16°45N 94°30E **41** L19
Basses, Pte. des
  Guadeloupe 15°52N 61°17W **88** b
Basseterre
  St. Kitts & Nevis 17°17N 62°43W **89** C7
Bassett *U.S.A.* 42°35N 99°32W **80** D4
Bassi *India* 30°44N 76°21E **42** D7
Bastak *Iran* 27°15N 54°25E **45** E7
Baştām *Iran* 36°29N 55°4E **45** B7
Bastar *India* 19°15N 81°40E **41** K12
Basti *India* 26°52N 82°55E **43** F10
Bastia *France* 42°40N 9°30E **20** E8
Bastogne *Belgium* 50°1N 5°43E **15** D5
Bastrop *La., U.S.A.* 32°47N 91°55W **84** E9
Bastrop *Tex., U.S.A.* 30°7N 97°19W **84** F6
Basuo = Dongfang
  China 18°50N 108°33E **38** C7
Bat Yam *Israel* 32°2N 34°44E **46** C3
Bata *Eq. Guin.* 1°57N 9°50E **52** D1
Bataan □ *Phil.* 14°40N 120°25E **37** B6
Batabanó *Cuba* 22°41N 82°18W **88** B3
Batabanó, G. de *Cuba* 22°30N 82°30W **88** B3
Batac *Phil.* 18°3N 120°34E **37** A6
Batagai *Russia* 67°38N 134°38E **29** C14
Batala *India* 31°48N 75°12E **42** D6
Batama
  Dem. Rep. of the Congo 0°30N 26°33E **54** B2
Batamay *Russia* 63°30N 129°15E **29** C13
Batang *Indonesia* 6°55S 109°45E **37** G13

Batangafo *C.A.R.* 7°25N 18°20E **52** C3
Batangas *Phil.* 13°35N 121°10E **37** B6
Batanta *Indonesia* 0°55S 130°40E **37** E8
Batatais *Brazil* 20°54S 47°37W **95** A6
Batavia *U.S.A.* 43°0N 78°11W **82** D6
Batchelor *Australia* 13°4S 131°1E **60** B5
Batdambang *Cambodia* 13°7N 103°12E **38** F4
Batemans B. *Australia* 35°40S 150°12E **63** F5
Batemans Bay *Australia* 35°44S 150°11E **63** F5
Bates Ra. *Australia* 27°27S 121°5E **61** E3
Batesburg-Leesville
  U.S.A. 33°54N 81°33W **85** E14
Batesville *Ark., U.S.A.* 35°46N 91°39W **84** D9
Batesville *Miss., U.S.A.* 34°19N 89°57W **85** D10
Batesville *Tex., U.S.A.* 28°58N 99°37W **84** G5
Bath *Canada* 44°11N 76°47W **83** B8
Bath *U.K.* 51°23N 2°22W **13** F5
Bath *Maine, U.S.A.* 43°55N 69°49W **81** D19
Bath *N.Y., U.S.A.* 42°20N 77°19W **82** D7
Bath & North East Somerset □
  U.K. 51°21N 2°27W **13** F5
Batheay *Cambodia* 11°59N 104°57E **39** G5
Bathsheba *Barbados* 13°13N 59°32W **89** g
Bathurst *Australia* 33°25S 149°31E **63** E4
Bathurst *Canada* 47°37N 65°43W **73** C6
Bathurst *S. Africa* 33°30S 26°50E **56** E4
Bathurst, C. *Canada* 70°34N 128°0W **68** B7
Bathurst B. *Australia* 14°16S 144°25E **62** A3
Bathurst Harb.
  Australia 43°15S 146°10E **63** G4
Bathurst I. *Australia* 11°30S 130°10E **60** B5
Bathurst I. *Canada* 76°0N 100°30W **69** B11
Bathurst Inlet *Canada* 66°50N 108°1W **68** C9
Batiki *Fiji* 17°48S 179°10E **59** a
Batlow *Australia* 35°31S 148°9E **63** F4
Batman *Turkey* 37°55N 41°5E **44** B4
Batn al Ghūl *Jordan* 29°36N 35°56E **46** F4
Batna *Algeria* 35°34N 6°15E **50** A7
Batoka *Zambia* 16°45S 27°15E **55** F2
Baton Rouge *U.S.A.* 30°27N 91°11W **84** F9
Batong, Ko *Thailand* 6°32N 99°12E **39** J2
Batopilas *Mexico* 27°1N 107°44W **86** B3
Batouri *Cameroon* 4°30N 14°25E **52** D2
Bâtsfjord *Norway* 70°38N 29°39E **8** A23
Battambang = Batdambang
  Cambodia 13°7N 103°12E **38** F4
Batticaloa *Sri Lanka* 7°43N 81°45E **40** R12
Battipáglia *Italy* 40°37N 14°58E **22** D6
Battle *U.K.* 50°55N 0°30E **13** G8
Battle → *Canada* 52°43N 108°15W **71** C7
Battle Creek *U.S.A.* 42°19N 85°11W **81** D11
Battle Ground *U.S.A.* 45°47N 122°32W **78** E4
Battle Harbour *Canada* 52°16N 55°35W **73** B8
Battle Lake *U.S.A.* 46°17N 95°43W **80** B6
Battle Mountain
  U.S.A. 40°38N 116°56W **76** F5
Battlefields *Zimbabwe* 18°37S 29°47E **55** F2
Battleford *Canada* 52°45N 108°15W **71** C7
Batu *Ethiopia* 6°55N 39°45E **47** F2
Batu *Malaysia* 3°15N 101°40E **39** L3
Batu, Kepulauan
  Indonesia 0°30S 98°25E **36** E1
Batu Ferringhi *Malaysia* 5°28N 100°15E **39** c
Batu Gajah *Malaysia* 4°28N 101°3E **39** K3
Batu Is. = Batu, Kepulauan
  Indonesia 0°30S 98°25E **36** E1
Batu Pahat *Malaysia* 1°50N 102°56E **39** M4
Batuata *Indonesia* 6°12S 122°42E **37** F6
Batugondang, Tanjung
  Indonesia 8°6S 114°29E **37** J17
Batumi *Georgia* 41°39N 41°44E **19** F7
Batur *Indonesia* 8°15S 115°25E **37** J18
Batur, Danau *Indonesia* 8°15S 115°24E **37** J18
Batur, Gunung
  Indonesia 8°14S 115°23E **37** J18
Batura Sar *Pakistan* 36°30N 74°31E **43** A6
Baturaja *Indonesia* 4°11S 104°15E **36** E2
Baturité *Brazil* 4°28S 38°45W **93** D11
Baturiti *Indonesia* 8°19S 115°11E **37** J18
Bau *Malaysia* 1°25N 110°9E **36** D4
Baubau *Indonesia* 5°25S 122°38E **37** F6
Baucau *E. Timor* 8°27S 126°27E **37** F7
Bauchi *Nigeria* 10°22N 9°48E **50** F7
Baudette *U.S.A.* 48°43N 94°36W **80** A6
Bauer, C. *Australia* 32°44S 134°4E **63** E1
Bauhinia *Australia* 24°35S 149°18E **62** C4
Baukau = Baucau
  E. Timor 8°27S 126°27E **37** F7
Bauld, C. *Canada* 51°38N 55°26W **69** D14
Bauru *Brazil* 22°10S 49°0W **95** A6
Bausi *India* 24°48N 87°1E **43** G12
Bauska *Latvia* 56°24N 24°15E **9** H21
Bautzen *Germany* 51°10N 14°26E **16** C8
Bavānāt *Iran* 30°28N 53°27E **45** D7
Bavaria = Bayern □
  Germany 48°50N 12°0E **16** D6
Bavispe → *Mexico* 29°15N 109°11W **86** B3
Bawdwin *Burma* 23°5N 97°20E **41** H20
Bawean *Indonesia* 5°46S 112°35E **36** F4
Bawku *Ghana* 11°3N 0°19W **50** F5
Bawlake *Burma* 19°11N 97°21E **41** K20
Baxter *U.S.A.* 31°47N 82°21W **85** F13
Baxter Springs *U.S.A.* 37°2N 94°44W **80** G6
Baxter State *U.S.A.* 46°5N 68°57W **81** B19
Bay City *Mich., U.S.A.* 43°36N 83°54W **81** D12
Bay City *Tex., U.S.A.* 28°59N 95°58W **84** G7
Bay Roberts *Canada* 47°36N 53°16W **73** C9
Bay St. Louis *U.S.A.* 30°19N 89°20W **85** F10
Bay Springs *U.S.A.* 31°59N 89°17W **85** F10
Bay View *N.Z.* 39°25S 176°50E **59** C6
Baya
  Dem. Rep. of the Congo 11°53S 27°25E **55** E2
Bayamo *Cuba* 20°20N 76°40W **88** B4

Bayamón *Puerto Rico* 18°24N 66°9W **89** d
Bayan Har Shan *China* 34°0N 98°0E **32** C4
Bayan Hot = Alxa Zuoqi
  China 38°50N 105°40E **34** E3
Bayan Lepas *Malaysia* 5°17N 100°16E **39** c
Bayan Obo *China* 41°52N 109°59E **34** D5
Bayan-Ovoo = Erdenetsogt
  Mongolia 42°55N 106°5E **34** C4
Bayana *India* 26°55N 77°18E **42** F7
Bayanaūyl *Kazakhstan* 50°45N 75°45E **28** D8
Bayandalay *Mongolia* 43°30N 103°29E **34** C2
Bayanhongor *Mongolia* 46°8N 102°43E **32** B5
Bayard *N. Mex., U.S.A.* 32°46N 108°8W **77** K9
Bayard *Nebr., U.S.A.* 41°45N 103°20W **80** E2
Baybay *Phil.* 10°40N 124°55E **37** B6
Baydaratskaya Guba
  Russia 69°0N 67°30E **28** C7
Baydhabo *Somali Rep.* 3°8N 43°30E **47** G3
Bayern □ *Germany* 48°50N 12°0E **16** D6
Bayeux *France* 49°17N 0°42W **20** B3
Bayfield *Canada* 43°34N 81°42W **82** C3
Bayfield *U.S.A.* 46°49N 90°49W **80** B8
Bayındır *Turkey* 38°13N 27°39E **23** E12
Baykal, Oz. *Russia* 53°0N 108°0E **29** D11
Baykan *Turkey* 38°7N 41°44E **44** B4
Baymak *Russia* 52°36N 58°19E **18** D10
Baynes Mts. *Namibia* 17°15S 13°0E **56** B1
Bayombong *Phil.* 16°30N 121°10E **37** A6
Bayonne *France* 43°30N 1°28W **20** E3
Bayonne *U.S.A.* 40°40N 74°6W **83** F10
Bayovar *Peru* 5°50S 81°0W **92** E2
Bayram-Ali = Bayramaly
  Turkmenistan 37°37N 62°10E **45** B9
Bayramaly *Turkmenistan* 37°37N 62°10E **45** B9
Bayramiç *Turkey* 39°48N 26°36E **23** E12
Bayreuth *Germany* 49°56N 11°35E **16** D6
Bayrūt *Lebanon* 33°53N 35°31E **46** B4
Bays, L. of *Canada* 45°15N 79°4W **82** A5
Baysville *Canada* 45°9N 79°7W **82** A5
Bayt Laḥm *West Bank* 31°43N 35°12E **46** D4
Baytown *U.S.A.* 29°43N 94°59W **84** G7
Bayun *Indonesia* 8°11S 115°16E **37** J18
Baza *Spain* 37°30N 2°47W **21** D4
Bazaruto, I. do *Mozam.* 21°40S 35°28E **57** C6
Bazaruto △ *Mozam.* 21°42S 35°26E **57** C6
Bazhou *China* 39°8N 116°22E **34** E9
Bazmān, Küh-e *Iran* 28°4N 60°1E **45** D9
Beach *U.S.A.* 46°58N 104°0W **80** B2
Beach City *U.S.A.* 40°39N 81°35W **82** F3
Beachport *Australia* 37°29S 140°0E **63** F3
Beachville *Canada* 43°5N 80°49W **82** C4
Beachy Hd. *U.K.* 50°44N 0°15E **13** G8
Beacon *Australia* 30°26S 117°52E **61** F2
Beacon *U.S.A.* 41°30N 73°58W **83** E11
Beaconsfield *Australia* 41°11S 146°48E **63** G4
Beagle, Canal *S. Amer.* 55°0S 68°30W **96** H3
Beagle Bay *Australia* 16°58S 122°40E **60** C3
Beagle G. *Australia* 12°15S 130°25E **60** B5
Bealanana *Madag.* 14°33S 48°44E **57** A8
Beals Cr. → *U.S.A.* 32°10N 100°51W **84** E4
Beamsville *Canada* 43°12N 79°28E **82** C5
Bear → *Calif., U.S.A.* 38°56N 121°36W **78** G5
Bear → *Utah, U.S.A.* 41°30N 112°8W **74** B4
Bear I. *Ireland* 51°38N 9°50W **10** E2
Bear L. *Canada* 55°8N 96°0W **71** B9
Bear L. *U.S.A.* 41°59N 111°21W **76** F8
Bear Lake *Canada* 45°27N 79°35W **82** A5
Beardmore *Canada* 49°36N 87°57W **72** C2
Beardmore Glacier
  Antarctica 84°30S 170°0E **5** E11
Beardstown *U.S.A.* 40°1N 90°26W **80** E8
Bearma → *India* 24°20N 79°51E **43** G8
Bearpaw Mts. *U.S.A.* 48°12N 109°30W **76** B9
Bearskin Lake *Canada* 53°58N 91°2W **72** B1
Beas → *India* 31°10N 74°59E **42** D6
Beata, C. *Dom. Rep.* 17°40N 71°30W **89** C5
Beata, I. *Dom. Rep.* 17°34N 71°31W **89** C5
Beatrice *U.S.A.* 40°16N 96°45W **80** E6
Beatrice *Zimbabwe* 18°15S 30°55E **55** F3
Beatrice, C. *Australia* 14°20S 136°55E **62** A2
Beatton → *Canada* 56°15N 120°45W **70** B4
Beatton River *Canada* 57°26N 121°20W **70** B4
Beatty *U.S.A.* 36°54N 116°46W **78** J10
Beau Bassin *Mauritius* 20°13S 57°27E **53** d
Beauce, Plaine de la
  France 48°10N 1°45E **20** B4
Beauceville *Canada* 46°13N 70°46W **73** C5
Beaudesert *Australia* 27°59S 153°0E **63** D5
Beaufort *Malaysia* 5°30N 115°40E **36** C5
Beaufort *N.C., U.S.A.* 34°43N 76°40W **85** D16
Beaufort *S.C., U.S.A.* 32°26N 80°40W **85** E14
Beaufort Sea *Arctic* 72°0N 140°0W **4** B1
Beaufort West *S. Africa* 32°18S 22°36E **56** E3
Beauharnois *Canada* 45°20N 73°52W **83** A11
Beaulieu → *Canada* 62°3N 113°11W **70** A6
Beauly *U.K.* 57°30N 4°28W **11** D4
Beauly → *U.K.* 57°29N 4°27N **11** D4
Beaumaris *U.K.* 53°16N 4°6W **12** D3
Beaumont *Belgium* 50°15N 4°14E **15** D4
Beaumont *U.S.A.* 30°5N 94°6W **84** F7
Beaune *France* 47°2N 4°50E **20** C6
Beaupré *Canada* 47°3N 70°54W **73** C5
Beauraing *Belgium* 50°7N 4°57E **15** D4
Beausejour *Canada* 50°5N 96°35W **71** C9
Beauvais *France* 49°25N 2°8E **20** B5
Beauval *Canada* 55°9N 107°37W **71** B7
Beaver *Okla., U.S.A.* 36°49N 100°31W **84** C4
Beaver *Pa., U.S.A.* 40°42N 80°19W **82** F4
Beaver *Utah, U.S.A.* 38°17N 112°38W **76** G7
Beaver → *B.C., Canada* 59°52N 124°20W **70** B4
Beaver → *Ont., Canada* 55°55N 87°48W **72** A2
Beaver → *Sask., Canada* 55°26N 107°45W **71** B7
Beaver City *U.S.A.* 40°8N 99°50W **80** E4
Beaver Creek *Canada* 63°0N 141°0W **68** C5

Beaver Dam *U.S.A.* 43°28N 88°50W **80** D9
Beaver Falls *U.S.A.* 40°46N 80°20W **82** F4
Beaver Hill L. *Canada* 54°5N 94°50W **71** C10
Beaver I. *U.S.A.* 45°40N 85°33W **81** C11
Beavercreek *U.S.A.* 39°43N 84°11W **81** F11
Beaverhill L. *Canada* 53°27N 112°32W **70** C6
Beaverlodge *Canada* 55°11N 119°29W **70** B5
Beaverstone → *Canada* 54°59N 89°25W **72** B2
Beaverton *Canada* 44°26N 79°9W **82** B5
Beaverton *U.S.A.* 45°29N 122°48W **78** E4
Beawar *India* 26°3N 74°18E **42** F6
Bebedouro *Brazil* 21°0S 48°25W **95** A6
Bebera, Tanjung
  Indonesia 8°44S 115°51E **37** K18
Beboa *Madag.* 17°22S 44°33E **57** B7
Bécancour *Canada* 46°20N 72°26W **81** B17
Beccles *U.K.* 52°27N 1°35E **13** E9
Bečej *Serbia* 45°36N 20°3E **23** B9
Béchar *Algeria* 31°38N 2°18W **50** B5
Beckley *U.S.A.* 37°47N 81°11W **81** G13
Beddouza, Ras *Morocco* 32°33N 9°9W **50** B4
Bedford *Canada* 45°7N 72°59W **83** A12
Bedford *S. Africa* 32°40S 26°10E **56** E4
Bedford *U.K.* 52°8N 0°28W **13** E7
Bedford *Ind., U.S.A.* 38°52N 86°29W **80** F10
Bedford *Iowa, U.S.A.* 40°40N 94°44W **80** E6
Bedford *Ohio, U.S.A.* 41°23N 81°32W **82** E3
Bedford *Pa., U.S.A.* 40°1N 78°30W **82** F6
Bedford *Va., U.S.A.* 37°20N 79°31W **81** G6
Bedford, C. *Australia* 15°14S 145°21E **62** B4
Bedfordshire □ *U.K.* 52°4N 0°28W **13** E7
Bedok *Singapore* 1°19N 103°56E **39** d
Bedourie *Australia* 24°30S 139°30E **62** C2
Bedum *Neths.* 53°18N 6°36E **15** A6
Beebe Plain *Canada* 45°1N 72°9W **83** A12
Beech Creek *U.S.A.* 41°5N 77°36W **82** E7
Beechy *Canada* 50°53N 107°24W **71** C7
Beef I. *Br. Virgin Is.* 18°26N 64°30W **89** e
Beenleigh *Australia* 27°43S 153°10E **63** D5
Be'er Menuḥa *Israel* 30°19N 35°8E **44** D2
Be'er Sheva *Israel* 31°15N 34°48E **46** D3
Beersheba = Be'er Sheva
  Israel 31°15N 34°48E **46** D3
Beestekraal *S. Africa* 25°23S 27°38E **57** D4
Beeston *U.K.* 52°56N 1°14W **12** E6
Beeton *Canada* 44°5N 79°47W **82** B5
Beeville *U.S.A.* 28°24N 97°45W **84** G6
Befale
  Dem. Rep. of the Congo 0°25N 20°45E **52** D4
Befandriana *Mahajanga,
  Madag.* 15°16S 48°32E **57** B8
Befandriana *Toliara,
  Madag.* 21°55S 44°0E **57** C7
Befasy *Madag.* 20°33S 44°23E **57** C7
Befotaka *Antsiranana,
  Madag.* 13°15S 48°16E **57** A8
Befotaka *Fianarantsoa,
  Madag.* 23°49S 47°0E **57** C8
Bega *Australia* 36°41S 149°51E **63** F4
Begusarai *India* 25°24N 86°9E **43** G12
Behābād *Iran* 32°24N 59°47E **45** C8
Behala *India* 22°30N 88°18E **43** H13
Behara *Madag.* 24°55S 46°20E **57** C8
Behbehān *Iran* 30°30N 50°15E **45** D6
Behm Canal *U.S.A.* 55°10N 131°0W **70** B2
Behshahr *Iran* 36°45N 53°35E **45** B7
Bei Jiang → *China* 23°2N 112°58E **33** G9
Bei'an *China* 48°10N 126°20E **33** B7
Beihai *China* 21°28N 109°6E **33** D5
Beijing *China* 39°53N 116°21E **34** E9
Beijing □ *China* 39°55N 116°20E **34** E9
Beilen *Neths.* 52°52N 6°27E **15** B6
Beilpajah *Australia* 32°54S 143°52E **63** E3
Beinn na Faoghla = Benbecula
  U.K. 57°26N 7°21W **11** D1
Beipiao *China* 41°52N 120°32E **35** D11
Beira *Mozam.* 19°50S 34°52E **55** F3
Beirut = Bayrūt *Lebanon* 33°53N 35°31E **46** B4
Beiseker *Canada* 51°23N 113°32W **70** C6
Beit Lekhem = Bayt Laḥm
  West Bank 31°43N 35°12E **46** D4
Beitaolaizhao *China* 44°58N 125°58E **35** B13
Beitbridge *Zimbabwe* 22°12S 30°0E **55** G3
Beizhen = Binzhou
  China 37°20N 118°2E **35** F10
Beizhen *China* 41°38N 121°54E **35** D11
Beizhengzhen *China* 44°31N 123°30E **35** B12
Beja *Portugal* 38°2N 7°53W **21** C2
Béja *Tunisia* 36°43N 9°12E **51** A7
Bejaïa *Algeria* 36°42N 5°2E **50** A7
Béjar *Spain* 40°23N 5°46W **21** B3
Bejestān *Iran* 34°30N 58°5E **45** C8
Bekaa Valley = Al Biqā
  Lebanon 34°10N 36°10E **46** A5
Békéscsaba *Hungary* 46°40N 21°5E **17** E11
Bekily *Madag.* 24°13S 45°19E **57** C8
Bekisopa *Madag.* 21°40S 45°54E **57** C8
Bekitro *Madag.* 24°33S 45°18E **57** C8
Bekodoka *Madag.* 16°58S 45°7E **57** B8
Bekok *Malaysia* 2°20N 103°7E **39** L4
Bekopaka *Madag.* 19°9S 44°48E **57** B7
Bekuli *Indonesia* 8°22S 114°13E **37** J17
Bela *India* 25°50N 82°0E **43** G10
Bela *Pakistan* 26°12N 66°20E **42** F2
Bela Bela *S. Africa* 24°51S 28°19E **57** C4
Bela Crkva *Serbia* 44°55N 21°27E **23** B9
Bela Vista *Brazil* 22°12S 56°20W **94** A4
Bela Vista *Mozam.* 26°10S 32°44E **57** D5
Belan → *India* 24°2N 81°45E **43** G9
Belarus ■ *Europe* 53°30N 27°0E **17** B14
Belau = Palau ■ *Palau* 7°30N 134°30E **58** A6
Belavenona *Madag.* 24°50S 47°4E **57** C8
Belawan *Indonesia* 3°33N 98°32E **36** D1
Belaya → *Russia* 54°40N 56°0E **18** C9
Belaya Tserkov = Bila Tserkva
  Ukraine 49°45N 30°10E **17** D16

Belaya Zemlya, Ostrova
  Russia 81°36N 62°18E **28** A7
Belcher Chan. Canada 77°15N 95°0W **69** B10
Belcher Is. Canada 56°15N 78°45W **72** A3
Belden U.S.A. 40°2N 121°17W **78** E5
Belebey Russia 54°7N 54°7E **18** D9
Beledweyne Somali Rep. 4°30N 45°5E **47** G4
Belém Brazil 1°20S 48°30W **93** D9
Belén Argentina 27°40S 67°5W **94** B2
Belén Paraguay 23°30S 57°6W **94** A4
Belen U.S.A. 34°40N 106°46W **77** J10
Belet Uen = Beledweyne
  Somali Rep. 4°30N 45°5E **47** G4
Belev Russia 53°50N 36°5E **18** D6
Belfair U.S.A. 47°27N 122°50W **78** C4
Belfast S. Africa 25°42S 30°2E **57** D5
Belfast U.K. 54°37N 5°56W **10** B6
Belfast Maine, U.S.A. 44°26N 69°1W **81** C19
Belfast N.Y., U.S.A. 42°21N 78°7W **82** D6
Belfast L. U.K. 54°40N 5°50W **10** B6
Belfield U.S.A. 46°53N 103°12W **80** B2
Belfort France 47°38N 6°50E **20** C7
Belfry U.S.A. 45°9N 109°1W **76** D9
Belgaum India 15°55N 74°35E **40** M9
Belgium ■ Europe 50°30N 5°0E **15** D4
Belgorod Russia 50°35N 36°35E **19** D6
Belgorod-Dnestrovskiy =
  Bilhorod-Dnistrovskyy
  Ukraine 46°11N 30°23E **19** E5
Belgrade = Beograd
  Serbia 44°50N 20°37E **23** B9
Belgrade U.S.A. 45°47N 111°11W **76** D8
Belgrano Antarctica 77°52S 34°37W **5** D1
Belhaven U.S.A. 35°33N 76°37W **85** D16
Beli Drim → Europe 42°6N 20°25E **23** C9
Belimbing Indonesia 8°24S 115°2E **37** J18
Belinyu Indonesia 1°35S 105°50E **36** E3
Beliton Is. = Belitung
  Indonesia 3°10S 107°50E **36** E3
Belitung Indonesia 3°10S 107°50E **36** E3
Belize ■ Cent. Amer. 17°0N 88°30W **87** D7
Belize City Belize 17°25N 88°10W **87** D7
Belkovskiy, Ostrov
  Russia 75°32N 135°44E **29** B14
Bell → Canada 49°48N 77°38W **72** C4
Bell I. Canada 50°46N 55°35W **73** B8
Bell-Irving → Canada 56°12N 129°5W **70** B3
Bell Peninsula Canada 63°50N 82°0W **69** C11
Bell Ville Argentina 32°40S 62°40W **94** C3
Bella Bella Canada 52°10N 128°10W **70** C3
Bella Coola Canada 52°25N 126°40W **70** C3
Bella Unión Uruguay 30°15S 57°40W **94** C4
Bella Vista Corrientes,
  Argentina 28°33S 59°0W **94** B4
Bella Vista Tucuman,
  Argentina 27°10S 65°25W **94** B2
Bellaire U.S.A. 40°1N 80°45W **82** F4
Bellary India 15°10N 76°56E **40** M10
Bellata Australia 29°53S 149°46E **63** D4
Belle Fourche U.S.A. 44°40N 103°51W **80** C2
Belle Fourche →
  U.S.A. 44°26N 102°18W **74** B6
Belle Glade U.S.A. 26°41N 80°40W **85** H14
Belle-Île France 47°20N 3°10W **20** C2
Belle Isle Canada 51°57N 55°25W **73** B8
Belle Isle, Str. of Canada 51°30N 56°30W **73** B8
Belle Plaine U.S.A. 41°54N 92°17W **80** E7
Belle River Canada 42°18N 82°43W **82** D2
Bellefontaine U.S.A. 40°22N 83°46W **81** E12
Bellefonte U.S.A. 40°55N 77°47W **82** F7
Belleoram Canada 47°31N 55°25W **73** C8
Belleplaine Barbados 13°15N 59°34W **89** g
Belleville Canada 44°10N 77°23W **82** B7
Belleville Ill., U.S.A. 38°31N 89°59W **80** F9
Belleville Kans., U.S.A. 39°50N 97°38W **80** F6
Belleville N.J., U.S.A. 40°47N 74°9W **83** F10
Belleville N.Y., U.S.A. 43°46N 76°10W **83** C8
Bellevue Idaho, U.S.A. 43°28N 114°16W **76** E6
Bellevue Nebr., U.S.A. 41°9N 95°54W **80** E6
Bellevue Ohio, U.S.A. 41°17N 82°51W **82** E2
Bellevue Wash., U.S.A. 47°37N 122°12W **78** C4
Bellin = Kangirsuk
  Canada 60°0N 70°0W **69** D13
Bellingen Australia 30°25S 152°50E **63** E5
Bellingham U.S.A. 48°46N 122°29W **78** B4
Bellingshausen Abyssal Plain
  S. Ocean 64°0S 90°0W **5** C16
Bellingshausen Sea
  Antarctica 66°0S 80°0W **5** C17
Bellinzona Switz. 46°11N 9°1E **20** C8
Bello Colombia 6°20N 75°33W **92** B3
Bellows Falls U.S.A. 43°8N 72°27W **83** C12
Bellpat Pakistan 29°0N 68°5E **42** E3
Belluno Italy 46°9N 12°13E **22** A5
Bellwood U.S.A. 40°36N 78°20W **82** F6
Belmont Canada 42°53N 81°5W **82** D3
Belmont S. Africa 29°28S 24°22E **56** D3
Belmont U.S.A. 42°14N 78°2W **82** D6
Belmonte Brazil 16°0S 39°0W **93** G11
Belmopan Belize 17°18N 88°30W **87** D7
Belmullet Ireland 54°14N 9°58W **10** B2
Belo Horizonte Brazil 19°55S 43°56W **93** G10
Belo-sur-Mer Madag. 20°42S 44°0E **57** C7
Belo-Tsiribihina Madag. 19°40S 44°30E **57** B7
Belogorsk Russia 51°0N 128°20E **29** D13
Beloha Madag. 25°10S 45°3E **57** D8
Beloit Kans., U.S.A. 39°28N 98°6W **80** F4
Beloit Wis., U.S.A. 42°31N 89°2W **80** D9
Belokorovichi Ukraine 51°7N 28°2E **17** C15
Belomorsk Russia 64°35N 34°54E **18** B5
Belonia India 23°15N 91°30E **41** H17
Beloretsk Russia 53°58N 58°24E **18** D10
Belorussia = Belarus ■
  Europe 53°30N 27°0E **17** B14
Belovo Russia 54°30N 86°0E **28** D9
Beloyarskiy Russia 63°42N 66°40E **28** C7
Beloye, Ozero Russia 60°10N 37°35E **18** B6

Beloye More Russia 66°30N 38°0E **8** C25
Belozersk Russia 60°1N 37°45E **18** B6
Belpre U.S.A. 39°17N 81°34W **81** F13
Belrain India 28°23N 80°55E **43** E9
Belt U.S.A. 47°23N 110°55W **76** C8
Beltana Australia 30°48S 138°25E **63** E2
Belterra Brazil 2°45S 55°0W **93** D8
Belton U.S.A. 31°3N 97°28W **84** F6
Belton L. U.S.A. 31°6N 97°28W **84** F6
Beltsy = Bălţi Moldova 47°48N 27°58E **17** E14
Belturbet Ireland 54°6N 7°26W **10** B4
Belukha Russia 49°50N 86°50E **28** E9
Beluran Malaysia 5°48N 117°35E **36** C5
Belvando → Australia 21°38S 146°50E **62** C4
Belyando Crossing
  Australia 21°32S 146°51E **62** C4
Belyy, Ostrov Russia 73°30N 71°0E **28** B8
Belyy Yar Russia 58°26N 84°39E **28** D9
Belzoni U.S.A. 33°11N 90°29W **85** E9
Bemaraha, Lembalemban' i
  Madag. 18°40S 44°45E **57** B7
Bemarivo Madag. 21°45S 44°45E **57** C7
Bemarivo → Antsiranana,
  Madag. 14°9S 50°9E **57** A9
Bemarivo → Mahajanga,
  Madag. 15°27S 47°40E **57** B8
Bemavo Madag. 21°33S 45°25E **57** C8
Bembéréke Benin 10°11N 2°43E **50** F6
Bembesi Zimbabwe 20°0S 28°58E **55** G2
Bembesi → Zimbabwe 18°57S 27°47E **55** F2
Bemetara India 21°42N 81°32E **43** J9
Bemidji U.S.A. 47°28N 94°53W **80** B6
Bemolanga Madag. 17°44S 45°6E **57** B8
Ben Iran 32°32N 50°45E **45** C6
Ben Cruachan U.K. 56°26N 5°8W **11** E3
Ben Dearg U.K. 57°47N 4°56W **11** D4
Ben En △ Vietnam 19°37N 105°30E **38** C5
Ben Gardane Tunisia 33°11N 11°11E **51** B8
Ben Hope U.K. 58°25N 4°36W **11** C4
Ben Lawers U.K. 56°32N 4°14W **11** E4
Ben Lomond N.S.W.,
  Australia 30°1S 151°43E **63** E5
Ben Lomond Tas.,
  Australia 41°38S 147°42E **63** G4
Ben Lomond U.K. 56°11N 4°38W **11** E4
Ben Lomond △
  Australia 41°33S 147°39E **63** G4
Ben Luc Vietnam 10°39N 106°29E **39** G6
Ben Macdhui U.K. 57°4N 3°40W **11** D5
Ben Mhor U.K. 57°15N 7°18W **11** D1
Ben More Argyll & Bute,
  U.K. 56°26N 6°1W **11** E2
Ben More Stirling, U.K. 56°23N 4°32W **11** E4
Ben More Assynt U.K. 58°8N 4°52W **11** C4
Ben Nevis U.K. 56°48N 5°1W **11** E3
Ben Quang Vietnam 17°3N 106°55E **38** D6
Ben Tre Vietnam 10°14N 106°23E **39** G6
Ben Vorlich U.K. 56°21N 4°14W **11** E4
Ben Wyvis U.K. 57°40N 4°35W **11** D4
Bena Nigeria 11°20N 5°50E **50** F7
Benalla Australia 36°30S 146°0E **63** F4
Benares = Varanasi
  India 25°22N 83°0E **43** G10
Benavente Spain 42°2N 5°43W **21** A3
Benavides U.S.A. 27°36N 98°25W **84** H5
Benbecula U.K. 57°26N 7°21W **11** D1
Benbonyathe Hill
  Australia 30°25S 139°11E **63** E2
Bend U.S.A. 44°4N 121°19W **76** D3
Bender Beyla Somali Rep. 9°30N 50°48E **47** F5
Bendery = Tighina
  Moldova 46°50N 29°30E **17** E15
Bendigo Australia 36°40S 144°15E **63** F3
Benē Beraq Israel 32°6N 34°51E **46** C3
Benenitra Madag. 23°27S 45°5E **57** C8
Benevento Italy 41°8N 14°45E **22** D6
Benga Mozam. 16°11S 33°40E **55** F3
Bengal, Bay of Ind. Oc. 15°0N 90°0E **41** M17
Bengaluru = Bangalore
  India 12°59N 77°40E **40** N10
Bengbu China 32°58N 117°20E **35** H9
Benghazi = Banghāzī
  Libya 32°11N 20°3E **51** B10
Bengkalis Indonesia 1°30N 102°10E **39** M4
Bengkulu Indonesia 3°50S 102°12E **36** E2
Bengkulu □ Indonesia 3°48S 102°16E **36** E2
Bengough Canada 49°25N 105°10W **71** D7
Benguela Angola 12°37S 13°25E **53** G2
Benguérua, I. Mozam. 21°58S 35°28E **57** C6
Beni Dem. Rep. of the Congo 0°30N 29°27E **54** B2
Beni → Bolivia 10°23S 65°24W **92** F5
Beni Mellal Morocco 32°21N 6°21W **50** B4
Beni Suef Egypt 29°5N 31°6E **51** C12
Beniah L. Canada 63°23N 112°17W **70** A6
Benidorm Spain 38°33N 0°9W **21** C5
Benin ■ Africa 10°0N 2°0E **50** G6
Benin, Bight of W. Afr. 5°0N 3°0E **50** H6
Benin City Nigeria 6°20N 5°31E **50** G7
Benito Juárez Argentina 37°40S 59°43W **94** D4
Benitses Greece 39°32N 19°55E **25** A3
Benjamin Aceval
  Paraguay 24°58S 57°34W **94** A4
Benjamin Constant
  Brazil 4°40S 70°15W **92** D4
Benjamin Hill Mexico 30°9N 111°7W **86** A2
Benkelman U.S.A. 40°3N 101°32W **80** E3
Bennett Canada 59°51N 135°0W **70** B2
Bennett, L. Australia 22°50S 131°2E **60** D5
Bennetta, Ostrov
  Russia 76°21N 148°56E **29** B15
Bennettsville U.S.A. 34°37N 79°41W **85** D15
Bennington N.H., U.S.A. 43°0N 71°55W **83** D11
Bennington Vt., U.S.A. 42°53N 73°12W **83** D11
Benom Malaysia 3°50N 102°6E **39** L4
Benoni S. Africa 26°11S 28°18E **57** D4

Benque Viejo Belize 17°5N 89°8W **87** D7
Benson Ariz., U.S.A. 31°58N 110°18W **77** L8
Benson Minn., U.S.A. 45°19N 95°36W **80** C6
Bent Iran 26°20N 59°31E **45** E8
Benteng Indonesia 6°10S 120°30E **37** F6
Bentinck I. Australia 17°3S 139°35E **62** B2
Bentley Subglacial Trench
  Antarctica 80°0S 115°0W **5** E15
Bento Gonçalves Brazil 29°10S 51°31W **95** B5
Benton Ark., U.S.A. 34°34N 92°35W **84** D8
Benton Calif., U.S.A. 37°48N 118°32W **78** H8
Benton Ill., U.S.A. 38°0N 88°55W **80** F9
Benton Pa., U.S.A. 41°12N 76°23W **83** E8
Benton Harbor U.S.A. 42°6N 86°27W **80** D10
Bentong Malaysia 3°31N 101°55E **39** L3
Bentonville U.S.A. 36°22N 94°13W **84** C7
Benue → Nigeria 7°48N 6°46E **50** G7
Benxi China 41°20N 123°48E **35** D12
Beo Indonesia 4°25N 126°50E **37** D7
Beograd Serbia 44°50N 20°37E **23** B9
Beolgyo S. Korea 34°51N 127°21E **35** G14
Beppu Japan 33°15N 131°30E **31** H5
Beqa Fiji 18°23S 178°8E **59** a
Beqaa Valley = Al Biqā
  Lebanon 34°10N 36°10E **46** A5
Ber Mota India 23°27N 68°34E **42** H3
Bera, Tasik Malaysia 3°5N 102°38E **39** L4
Berach → India 25°15N 75°2E **42** G6
Beraketa Madag. 23°7S 44°25E **57** C7
Berastagi Indonesia 3°11N 98°31E **39** L2
Berat Albania 40°43N 19°59E **23** D8
Berau, Teluk Indonesia 2°30S 132°30E **37** E8
Beravina Madag. 18°10S 45°14E **57** B8
Berber Sudan 18°0N 34°0E **51** E12
Berbera Somali Rep. 10°30N 45°2E **47** E4
Berbérati C.A.R. 4°15N 15°40E **52** D3
Berbice → Guyana 6°20N 57°32W **92** B7
Berdichev = Berdychiv
  Ukraine 49°57N 28°30E **17** D15
Berdsk Russia 54°47N 83°2E **28** D9
Berdyansk Ukraine 46°45N 36°50E **19** E6
Berdychiv Ukraine 49°57N 28°30E **17** D15
Berea U.S.A. 37°34N 84°17W **81** G11
Berebere Indonesia 2°25N 128°45E **37** D7
Bereeda Somali Rep. 11°45N 51°0E **47** E5
Berehove Ukraine 48°15N 22°35E **17** D12
Bereket Turkmenistan 39°16N 55°32E **45** B7
Berekum Ghana 7°29N 2°34W **50** G5
Berens → Canada 52°25N 97°2W **71** C9
Berens I. Canada 52°18N 97°18W **71** C9
Berens River Canada 52°25N 97°0W **71** C9
Beresford U.S.A. 43°5N 96°47W **80** D5
Berestechko Ukraine 50°22N 25°5E **17** C13
Berevo Mahajanga,
  Madag. 17°14S 44°17E **57** B7
Berevo Toliara, Madag. 19°44S 44°58E **57** B7
Berezhany Ukraine 49°26N 24°58E **17** D13
Berezina = Byarezina →
  Belarus 52°33N 30°14E **17** B16
Berezniki Russia 62°51N 42°40E **18** B7
Berezniki Russia 59°24N 56°46E **18** C10
Berezovo Russia 64°0N 65°0E **28** C7
Berga Spain 42°6N 1°48E **21** A6
Bergama Turkey 39°8N 27°11E **23** E12
Bérgamo Italy 45°41N 9°43E **20** D8
Bergen Neths. 52°40N 4°43E **15** B4
Bergen Norway 60°20N 5°20E **8** F11
Bergen U.S.A. 43°5N 77°57W **82** C7
Bergen op Zoom Neths. 51°28N 4°18E **15** C4
Bergerac France 44°51N 0°30E **20** D4
Bergholz U.S.A. 40°31N 80°53W **82** F4
Bergisch Gladbach
  Germany 50°59N 7°8E **15** D7
Bergville S. Africa 28°52S 29°18E **57** D4
Berhala, Selat Indonesia 1°0S 104°15E **36** E2
Berhampore = Baharampur
  India 24°2N 88°27E **43** G13
Berhampur = Brahmapur
  India 19°15N 84°54E **41** K14
Bering Sea Pac. Oc. 58°0N 171°0W **74** a
Bering Strait Pac. Oc. 65°30N 169°0W **74** a
Beringovskiy Russia 63°3N 179°19E **29** C18
Berisso Argentina 34°56S 57°50W **94** C4
Berja Spain 36°50N 2°56W **21** D4
Berkeley U.S.A. 37°51N 122°16W **78** H4
Berkner I. Antarctica 79°30S 50°0W **5** D18
Berkshire U.S.A. 42°19N 76°11W **83** D8
Berkshire Downs U.K. 51°33N 1°29W **13** F6
Berlin Germany 52°31N 13°23E **16** B7
Berlin Md., U.S.A. 38°20N 75°13W **81** F16
Berlin N.H., U.S.A. 44°28N 71°11W **83** B13
Berlin N.Y., U.S.A. 42°42N 73°23W **83** D11
Berlin Wis., U.S.A. 43°58N 88°57W **80** D9
Berlin L. U.S.A. 41°3N 81°0W **82** E4
Bermejo → Formosa,
  Argentina 26°51S 58°23W **94** B4
Bermejo → San Juan,
  Argentina 32°30S 67°30W **94** C2
Bermejo, Paso = Uspallata, P. de
  Argentina 32°37S 69°22W **94** C2
Bermen, L. Canada 53°35N 68°55W **73** B6
Bermuda ☑ Atl. Oc. 32°18N 64°45W **89** F13
Bern Switz. 46°57N 7°28E **20** C7
Bernalillo U.S.A. 35°18N 106°33W **77** J10
Bernardo de Irigoyen
  Argentina 26°15S 53°40W **95** B5
Bernardsville U.S.A. 40°43N 74°34W **83** F10
Bernasconi Argentina 37°55S 63°44W **94** D3
Bernburg Germany 51°47N 11°44E **16** C6
Berne = Bern Switz. 46°57N 7°28E **20** C7
Berneray U.K. 57°43N 7°11W **11** D1
Bernier I. Australia 24°50S 113°12E **61** D1
Bernina, Piz Switz. 46°20N 9°54E **20** C8
Beroha Madag. 21°40S 45°10E **57** C8
Beroun Czech Rep. 49°57N 14°5E **16** D8
Berri Australia 34°14S 140°35E **63** E3
Berriane Algeria 32°50N 3°46E **50** B6

Berry Australia 34°46S 150°43E **63** E5
Berry France 46°50N 2°0E **20** C5
Berry Is. Bahamas 25°40N 77°50W **88** A4
Berryessa, L. U.S.A. 38°31N 122°6W **78** G4
Berryville U.S.A. 36°22N 93°34W **84** C8
Bersba Namibia 26°0S 17°46E **56** D2
Bershad Ukraine 48°22N 29°31E **17** D15
Berthold U.S.A. 48°19N 101°44W **80** A3
Berthoud U.S.A. 40°19N 105°5W **76** F11
Bertoua Cameroon 4°30N 13°45E **52** D2
Bertraghboy B. Ireland 53°22N 9°54W **10** C2
Berwick U.S.A. 41°3N 76°14W **83** E8
Berwick-upon-Tweed
  U.K. 55°46N 2°0W **12** B6
Berwyn Mts. U.K. 52°54N 3°26W **12** E4
Besal Pakistan 35°4N 73°56E **43** B5
Besalampy Madag. 16°43S 44°29E **57** B7
Besançon France 47°15N 6°2E **20** C7
Besar Indonesia 2°40S 116°0E **36** E5
Besnard L. Canada 55°25N 106°0W **71** B7
Besni Turkey 37°41N 37°52E **44** B3
Besor, N. → Egypt 31°28N 34°22E **46** D3
Bessarabiya Moldova 47°0N 28°10E **17** E15
Bessarabka = Basarabeasca
  Moldova 46°21N 28°58E **17** E15
Bessemer Ala., U.S.A. 33°24N 86°58W **85** E11
Bessemer Mich., U.S.A. 46°29N 90°3W **80** B8
Bessemer Pa., U.S.A. 40°59N 80°30W **82** F4
Beswick Australia 14°34S 132°53E **60** B5
Bet She'an Israel 32°30N 35°30E **46** C4
Bet Shemesh Israel 31°44N 35°0E **46** D4
Betafo Madag. 19°50S 46°51E **57** B8
Betancuria Canary Is. 28°25N 14°3W **24** F5
Betanzos Spain 43°15N 8°12W **21** A1
Betanzos Peru 5°40N 14°5E **52** C2
Bétaré Oya Cameroon 19°11S 47°52E **57** B8
Betatao Madag. 18°11S 47°52E **57** B8
Bethal S. Africa 26°27S 29°28E **57** D4
Bethanien Namibia 26°31S 17°8E **56** D2
Bethany Canada 44°11N 78°34W **82** B6
Bethany Mo., U.S.A. 40°16N 94°2W **80** E6
Bethany Okla., U.S.A. 35°31N 97°38W **84** H6
Bethel Alaska, U.S.A. 60°48N 161°45W **74** a
Bethel Conn., U.S.A. 41°22N 73°25W **83** E11
Bethel Maine, U.S.A. 44°25N 70°47W **83** B14
Bethel Vt., U.S.A. 43°50N 72°38W **83** C12
Bethel Park U.S.A. 40°19N 80°2W **82** F4
Bethlehem = Bayt Lahm
  West Bank 31°43N 35°12E **46** D4
Bethlehem S. Africa 28°14S 28°18E **57** D4
Bethlehem U.S.A. 40°37N 75°23W **83** F9
Bethulie S. Africa 30°30S 25°59E **56** E4
Béthune France 50°30N 2°38E **20** A5
Betioky Madag. 23°48S 44°20E **57** C7
Betong Thailand 5°45N 101°5E **39** K3
Betoota Australia 25°45S 140°42E **62** D3
Betpaqdala Kazakhstan 45°45N 70°30E **32** B2
Betroka Madag. 23°16S 46°0E **57** C8
Betsiamites Canada 48°56N 68°40W **73** C6
Betsiamites → Canada 48°56N 68°38W **73** C6
Betsiboka → Madag. 16°3S 46°36E **57** B8
Bettendorf U.S.A. 41°32N 90°30W **80** E8
Bettiah India 26°48N 84°33E **43** F11
Betul India 21°58N 77°59E **40** J10
Betws-y-Coed U.K. 53°5N 3°48W **12** D4
Beulah Mich., U.S.A. 44°38N 86°6W **80** C10
Beulah N. Dak., U.S.A. 47°16N 101°47W **80** B3
Beveren Belgium 51°12N 4°16E **15** C4
Beverley Australia 32°9S 116°56E **61** F2
Beverley U.K. 53°51N 0°26W **12** D7
Beverly U.S.A. 42°33N 70°53W **83** D14
Beverly Hills Calif.,
  U.S.A. 34°5N 118°24W **79** L8
Beverly Hills Fla.,
  U.S.A. 28°55N 82°28W **85** G13
Bevoalavo Madag. 25°13S 45°26E **57** D7
Bewas → India 23°59N 79°21E **43** H8
Bexhill U.K. 50°51N 0°29E **13** G8
Beyānlū Iran 36°0N 47°51E **44** C5
Beyneu Kazakhstan 45°18N 55°9E **19** E10
Beypazarı Turkey 40°10N 31°56E **19** F5
Beyşehir Gölü Turkey 37°41N 31°33E **44** B1
Béziers France 43°20N 3°12E **20** E5
Bezwada = Vijayawada
  India 16°31N 80°39E **41** L12
Bhabua India 25°3N 83°37E **43** G10
Bhachau India 23°20N 70°16E **40** H7
Bhadar → Gujarat, India 22°17N 72°20E **42** H5
Bhadar → Gujarat, India 21°27N 69°47E **42** J3
Bhadarwah India 32°58N 75°46E **43** C6
Bhadgaon = Bhaktapur
  Nepal 27°38N 85°24E **43** F11
Bhadohi India 25°25N 82°34E **43** G10
Bhadra India 29°8N 75°14E **42** E6
Bhadrakh India 21°10N 86°30E **41** J15
Bhadran India 22°19N 72°6E **42** H5
Bhadravati India 13°49N 75°40E **40** N9
Bhag Pakistan 29°2N 67°49E **42** E2
Bhagalpur India 25°10N 87°0E **43** G12
Bhagirathi → Uttarakhand,
  India 30°8N 78°35E **43** D8
Bhagirathi → W. Bengal,
  India 23°25N 88°23E **43** H13
Bhakkar Pakistan 31°40N 71°5E **42** D4
Bhakra Dam India 31°30N 76°45E **42** D7
Bhaktapur Nepal 27°38N 85°24E **43** F11
Bhamo Burma 24°15N 97°15E **41** G20
Bhandara India 21°5N 79°42E **40** J11
Bhanpura India 24°31N 75°44E **42** G6
Bhanrer Ra. India 23°40N 79°45E **43** H8
Bhaptiahi India 26°19N 86°44E **43** F12
Bharat = India ■ Asia 20°0N 78°0E **40** K11
Bharatpur Chhattisgarh,
  India 23°44N 81°46E **43** H9
Bharatpur Raj., India 27°15N 77°30E **42** F7
Bharatpur Nepal 27°34N 84°10E **43** F11

Bharno India 23°14N 84°53E **43** H11
Bharuch India 21°47N 73°0E **40** J8
Bhatinda India 30°15N 74°57E **42** D6
Bhatpara India 22°50N 88°25E **43** H13
Bhattu India 29°36N 75°19E **42** E6
Bhaun Pakistan 32°55N 72°40E **42** C5
Bhaunagar = Bhavnagar
  India 21°45N 72°10E **40** J8
Bhavnagar India 21°45N 72°10E **40** J8
Bhawari India 25°42N 73°4E **42** G5
Bhayavadar India 21°51N 70°15E **42** J4
Bhera Pakistan 32°29N 72°57E **42** C5
Bhikangaon India 21°52N 75°57E **42** J6
Bhilai = Bhilainagar-Durg
  India 21°13N 81°26E **41** J12
Bhilainagar-Durg India 21°13N 81°26E **41** J12
Bhilsa = Vidisha India 23°28N 77°53E **42** H7
Bhilwara India 25°25N 74°38E **42** G6
Bhima → India 16°25N 77°17E **40** L10
Bhimbar Pakistan 32°59N 74°3E **43** C6
Bhind India 26°30N 78°46E **43** F8
Bhinga India 27°43N 81°56E **43** F9
Bhinmal India 25°0N 72°15E **42** G5
Bhisho S. Africa 32°50S 27°23E **57** E4
Bhiwandi India 19°20N 73°0E **40** K8
Bhiwani India 28°50N 76°9E **42** E7
Bhogava → India 22°26N 72°20E **42** H5
Bhola Bangla. 22°45N 90°35E **41** H17
Bholari Pakistan 25°19N 68°13E **42** G3
Bhopal India 23°20N 77°30E **42** H7
Bhubaneshwar India 20°15N 85°50E **41** J14
Bhuj India 23°15N 69°49E **42** H3
Bhumiphol Res. Thailand 17°20N 98°40E **38** D2
Bhusawal India 21°3N 75°46E **40** J9
Bhutan ■ Asia 27°25N 90°30E **41** F17
Biafra, B. of = Bonny, Bight of
  Africa 3°30N 9°20E **52** D1
Biak Indonesia 1°10S 136°6E **37** E9
Biała Podlaska Poland 52°4N 23°6E **17** B12
Biała Poland 54°2N 15°58E **16** A8
Białogard Poland 53°10N 23°10E **17** B12
Białystok Poland 23°56N 76°56E **42** H7
Biaora India 23°56N 76°56E **42** H7
Biārjmand Iran 36°6N 55°53E **45** B7
Biaro Indonesia 2°5N 125°26E **37** D7
Biarritz France 43°29N 1°33W **20** E3
Bias Indonesia 8°24S 115°36E **37** J18
Bibai Japan 43°19N 141°52E **30** C10
Bibby I. Canada 61°55N 93°0W **71** A10
Biberach Germany 48°5N 9°47E **16** D5
Bibungwa
  Dem. Rep. of the Congo 2°40S 28°15E **54** C2
Bicester U.K. 51°54N 1°9W **13** F6
Bicheno Australia 41°52S 148°18E **63** G4
Bichia India 22°27N 80°42E **43** H9
Bickerton I. Australia 13°45S 136°10E **62** A2
Bida Nigeria 9°3N 5°58E **50** G7
Bidar India 17°55N 77°35E **40** L10
Biddeford U.S.A. 43°30N 70°28W **81** D18
Bideford U.K. 51°1N 4°13W **13** F3
Bideford Bay U.K. 51°5N 4°20W **13** F3
Bidhuna India 26°49N 79°31E **43** F8
Bidokht Iran 34°20N 58°46E **45** C8
Bidor Malaysia 4°6N 101°15E **39** K3
Bidyadanga Australia 18°45S 121°43E **60** C3
Bié, Planalto de Angola 12°0S 16°0E **53** G3
Bieber U.S.A. 41°7N 121°8W **76** F3
Biel Switz. 47°8N 7°14E **20** C7
Bielefeld Germany 52°1N 8°33E **16** B5
Biella Italy 45°34N 8°3E **20** D8
Bielsk Podlaski Poland 52°47N 23°12E **17** B12
Bielsko-Biała Poland 49°50N 19°2E **17** D10
Bien Hoa Vietnam 10°57N 106°49E **39** G6
Bienne = Biel Switz. 47°8N 7°14E **20** C7
Bienville, L. Canada 55°5N 72°40W **72** A5
Biesiesfontein S. Africa 30°57S 17°58E **56** E2
Big → Canada 54°50N 58°55W **73** B8
Big B. Canada 55°43N 60°35W **73** A7
Big Bear City U.S.A. 34°16N 116°51W **79** L10
Big Bear Lake U.S.A. 34°15N 116°56W **79** L10
Big Belt Mts. U.S.A. 46°30N 111°25W **76** C8
Big Bend Swaziland 26°50S 31°58E **57** D5
Big Bend △ U.S.A. 29°20N 103°5W **84** G3
Big Black → U.S.A. 32°3N 91°4W **85** F9
Big Blue → U.S.A. 39°35N 96°34W **80** F5
Big Creek U.S.A. 37°11N 119°14W **78** H7
Big Cypress △ U.S.A. 26°0N 81°10W **85** H14
Big Desert Australia 35°45S 141°10E **63** F3
Big Falls U.S.A. 48°12N 93°48W **80** A7
Big Fork → U.S.A. 48°31N 93°43W **80** A7
Big Horn Mts. = Bighorn Mts.
  U.S.A. 44°25N 107°0W **76** D10
Big I. Canada 61°7N 116°45W **70** A5
Big Lake U.S.A. 31°12N 101°28W **84** F4
Big Moose U.S.A. 43°49N 74°58W **83** C10
Big Muddy Cr. →
  U.S.A. 48°8N 104°36W **76** B11
Big Pine U.S.A. 37°10N 118°17W **78** H8
Big Piney U.S.A. 42°32N 110°7W **76** E8
Big Quill L. Canada 51°55N 104°13W **71** C8
Big Rapids U.S.A. 43°42N 85°29W **81** D11
Big Rideau L. Canada 44°40N 76°15W **83** B8
Big River Canada 53°50N 107°0W **71** C7
Big Run U.S.A. 40°57N 78°55W **82** F6
Big Sable Pt. U.S.A. 44°3N 86°1W **80** C10
Big Salmon → Canada 61°52N 134°55W **70** A2
Big Sand L. Canada 57°45N 99°45W **71** B9
Big Sandy U.S.A. 48°11N 110°7W **76** B8
Big Sandy → U.S.A. 38°25N 82°36W **81** F12
Big Sandy Cr. = Sandy Cr. →
  U.S.A. 41°51N 109°47W **76** F9
Big Sandy Cr. →
  U.S.A. 38°7N 102°29W **76** G12
Big Sioux → U.S.A. 42°29N 96°27W **80** D5
Big South Fork △
  U.S.A. 36°27N 84°47W **85** C12
Big Spring U.S.A. 32°15N 101°28W **84** E4
Big Stone City U.S.A. 45°18N 96°28W **80** C5

Big Stone Gap *U.S.A.* 36°52N 82°47W **81** G12
Big Stone L. *U.S.A.* 45°18N 96°27W **80** C5
Big Sur *U.S.A.* 36°15N 121°48W **78** J5
Big Timber *U.S.A.* 45°50N 109°57W **76** D9
Big Trout L. *Canada* 53°40N 90°0W **72** B2
Big Trout Lake *Canada* 53°45N 90°0W **72** B2
Biğa *Turkey* 40°13N 27°14E **23** D12
Bigadiç *Turkey* 39°22N 28°7E **23** E13
Biggar *Canada* 52°4N 108°0W **71** C7
Biggar *U.K.* 55°38N 3°32W **11** F5
Bigge I. *Australia* 14°35S 125°10E **60** B4
Biggenden *Australia* 25°31S 152°4E **63** D5
Biggleswade *U.K.* 52°5N 0°14W **13** E7
Biggs *U.S.A.* 39°25N 121°43W **78** F2
Bighorn *U.S.A.* 46°10N 107°27W **76** C10
Bighorn → *U.S.A.* 46°10N 107°28W **76** C10
Bighorn Canyon △
   U.S.A. 45°10N 108°0W **76** D10
Bighorn L. *U.S.A.* 44°55N 108°15W **76** D9
Bighorn Mts. *U.S.A.* 44°30N 107°30W **76** D10
Bigstone L. *Canada* 53°42N 95°44W **71** C9
Bigwa *Tanzania* 7°10S 39°10E **54** D4
Bihać *Bos.-H.* 44°49N 15°57E **16** F8
Bihar *India* 25°5N 85°40E **43** G11
Bihar □ *India* 25°0N 86°0E **43** G12
Biharamulo *Tanzania* 2°25S 31°25E **54** C3
Biharamulo □ *Tanzania* 2°24S 31°25E **54** C3
Bihariganj *India* 25°44N 86°59E **43** G12
Bihor, Munţii *Romania* 46°29N 22°47E **17** E12
Bijagós, Arquipélago dos
   Guinea-Biss. 11°15N 16°10W **50** F2
Bijaipur *India* 26°2N 77°20E **42** F7
Bijapur *Chhattisgarh,*
   India 18°50N 80°50E **41** K12
Bijapur *Karnataka, India* 16°50N 75°55E **40** L9
Bījār *Iran* 35°52N 47°35E **44** C5
Bijawar *India* 24°38N 79°30E **43** G8
Bijeljina *Bos.-H.* 44°46N 19°14E **23** B8
Bijnor *India* 29°27N 78°11E **42** E8
Bikaner *India* 28°2N 73°18E **42** E5
Bikapur *India* 26°30N 82°7E **43** F10
Bikeqi *China* 40°43N 111°20E **34** D6
Bikfayyā *Lebanon* 33°55N 35°41E **46** B4
Bikin *Russia* 46°50N 134°20E **30** A7
Bikin → *Russia* 46°51N 134°2E **30** A7
Bikini Atoll *Marshall Is.* 12°0N 167°30E **64** F8
Bikita *Zimbabwe* 20°5S 31°41E **57** C5
Bikkū Bīttī *Libya* 22°0N 19°12E **51** D9
Bila Tserkva *Ukraine* 49°45N 30°10E **17** D16
Bilara *India* 26°14N 73°53E **42** F5
Bilaspur *Chhattisgarh,*
   India 22°2N 82°15E **43** H10
Bilaspur *Punjab, India* 31°19N 76°50E **42** D7
Bilauk Taungdan *Thailand* 13°0N 99°0E **38** F2
Bilbao *Spain* 43°16N 2°56W **21** A4
Bilbo = Bilbao *Spain* 43°16N 2°56W **21** A4
Bíldudalur *Iceland* 65°41N 23°36W **8** D2
Bílé Karpaty *Europe* 49°5N 18°0E **17** D9
Bilecik *Turkey* 40°5N 30°5E **19** F5
Bilgram *India* 27°11N 80°2E **43** F9
Bilhaur *India* 26°51N 80°5E **43** F9
Bilhorod-Dnistrovskyy
   Ukraine 46°11N 30°23E **19** E5
Bilibino *Russia* 68°3N 166°20E **29** C17
Bilibiza *Mozam.* 12°30S 40°20E **55** E5
Billabong Roadhouse
   Australia 27°25S 115°49E **61** E2
Billiluna *Australia* 19°37S 127°41E **60** C4
Billings *U.S.A.* 45°47N 108°30W **76** D9
Billiton Is. = Belitung
   Indonesia 3°10S 107°50E **36** E3
Bilma *Niger* 18°50N 13°30E **51** E8
Biloela *Australia* 24°24S 150°31E **62** C5
Biloxi *U.S.A.* 30°24N 88°53W **85** F10
Bilpa Morea Claypan
   Australia 25°0S 140°0E **62** D3
Biltine *Chad* 14°40N 20°50E **51** F10
Bima *Indonesia* 8°22S 118°49E **37** F5
Bimbo *C.A.R.* 4°15N 18°33E **52** D3
Bimini Is. *Bahamas* 25°42N 79°25W **88** A4
Bin Xian *Heilongjiang,*
   China 45°42N 127°32E **35** B14
Bin Xian *Shaanxi, China* 35°2N 108°4E **34** G5
Bina-Etawah *India* 24°13N 78°14E **42** G8
Binalbagan *Phil.* 10°12N 122°50E **37** B6
Binalong *Australia* 34°40S 148°39E **63** E4
Bīnālūd, Kūh-e *Iran* 36°30N 58°30E **45** B8
Binatang = Bintangau
   Malaysia 2°10N 111°40E **36** D4
Binche *Belgium* 50°26N 4°10E **15** D4
Bindki *India* 26°2N 80°36E **43** F9
Bindura *Zimbabwe* 17°18S 31°18E **55** F3
Bingara *Australia* 29°52S 150°36E **63** D5
Bingham *U.S.A.* 45°3N 69°53W **81** C19
Binghamton *U.S.A.* 42°6N 75°55W **83** D9
Bingöl *Turkey* 38°53N 40°29E **44** B4
Binh Dinh = An Nhon
   Vietnam 13°55N 109°7E **38** F7
Binh Khe *Vietnam* 13°57N 108°51E **38** F7
Binh Son *Vietnam* 15°20N 108°40E **38** E7
Binhai *China* 34°2N 119°49E **35** G10
Binisatua *Spain* 39°50N 4°11E **24** B11
Binissalem *Spain* 39°41N 2°50E **24** B9
Binjai *Indonesia* 3°20N 98°30E **36** D1
Binnaway *Australia* 31°28S 149°24E **63** E4
Binongko *Indonesia* 5°57S 124°2E **37** F6
Binscarth *Canada* 50°37N 101°17W **71** C8
Bintan *Indonesia* 1°0N 104°0E **36** D2
Bintangau *Malaysia* 2°10N 111°40E **36** D4
Bintulu *Malaysia* 3°10N 113°0E **36** D4
Bintuni *Indonesia* 2°7S 133°32E **37** E8
Binzert = Bizerte *Tunisia* 37°15N 9°50E **51** A7
Binzhou *China* 37°20N 118°2E **35** F10
Bío Bío □ *Chile* 37°35S 72°0W **94** D1
Biobío → *Chile* 36°49S 73°10W **94** D1
Bioko *Eq. Guin.* 3°30N 8°40E **52** D1
Bir *India* 19°4N 75°46E **40** K9

Bîr Abu Muḥammad
   Egypt 29°44N 34°14E **46** F3
Bi'r ad Dabbāghāt *Jordan* 30°26N 35°32E **46** E4
Bi'r al Butayyihāt *Jordan* 29°47N 35°20E **46** F4
Bi'r al Mārī *Jordan* 30°4N 35°33E **46** E4
Bi'r al Qaţţār *Jordan* 29°47N 35°32E **46** F4
Bîr Atrun *Sudan* 18°15N 26°40E **51** E11
Bîr Beiḍa *Egypt* 30°25N 34°29E **46** E3
Bîr el 'Abd *Egypt* 31°2N 33°0E **46** D2
Bîr el Biarât *Egypt* 29°30N 34°43E **46** F3
Bîr el Duweidar *Egypt* 30°56N 32°32E **46** E1
Bîr el Garârât *Egypt* 31°3N 33°34E **46** D2
Bîr el Heisi *Egypt* 29°22N 34°36E **46** F3
Bîr el Jafir *Egypt* 30°50N 32°41E **46** E1
Bîr el Mâlḥi *Egypt* 30°38N 33°19E **46** E2
Bîr el Thamâda *Egypt* 30°12N 33°27E **46** E2
Bîr Gebeil Ḥişn *Egypt* 30°2N 33°18E **46** E2
Bi'r Ghadîr *Syria* 34°6N 37°3E **46** A6
Bîr Ḥasana *Egypt* 30°29N 33°46E **46** E2
Bîr Kaseiba *Egypt* 31°0N 33°17E **46** E2
Bîr Lahfân *Egypt* 31°0N 33°51E **46** E2
Bîr Madkûr *Egypt* 30°44N 32°33E **46** E1
Bîr Mogreïn *Mauritania* 25°10N 11°25W **50** C3
Bi'r Muṭribah *Kuwait* 29°54N 47°17E **44** D5
Bîr Qaţia *Egypt* 30°58N 32°45E **46** E1
Bîr Shalatein *Egypt* 23°5N 35°25E **51** D13
Birāk *Libya* 27°31N 14°20E **51** C8
Biratnagar *Nepal* 26°27N 87°17E **43** F12
Birawa
   Dem. Rep. of the Congo 2°20S 28°48E **54** C2
Birch → *Canada* 58°28N 112°17W **70** B6
Birch Hills *Canada* 52°59N 105°25W **71** C7
Birch I. *Canada* 52°26N 99°54W **71** C9
Birch I. *N.W.T., Canada* 62°4N 116°33W **70** A5
Birch L. *Ont., Canada* 51°23N 92°18W **72** B1
Birch Mts. *Canada* 57°30N 113°10W **70** B6
Birch River *Canada* 52°24N 101°6W **71** C8
Birchip *Australia* 35°56S 142°55E **63** F3
Bird *Canada* 56°30N 94°13W **71** B10
Bird I. = Aves, I. de
   W. Indies 15°45N 63°55W **89** C7
Bird I. *S. Georgia* 54°0S 38°3W **96** G9
Birds Creek *Canada* 45°6N 77°52W **82** A7
Birdsville *Australia* 25°51S 139°20E **62** D2
Birdum Cr. → *Australia* 15°14S 133°0E **60** C5
Birecik *Turkey* 37°2N 38°0E **44** B3
Birein *Israel* 30°50N 34°28E **46** E3
Bireuen *Indonesia* 5°14N 96°39E **36** C1
Birigüi *Brazil* 21°18S 50°16W **95** A5
Bīrjand *Iran* 32°53N 59°13E **45** C8
Birkenhead *U.K.* 53°23N 3°2W **12** D4
Bîrlad = Bârlad
   Romania 46°15N 27°38E **17** E14
Birmingham *U.K.* 52°29N 1°52W **13** E6
Birmingham *U.S.A.* 33°31N 86°48W **85** E11
Birmingham Int. ✈ (BHX)
   U.K. 52°26N 1°45W **13** E6
Birmitrapur *India* 22°24N 84°46E **41** H14
Birni Nkonni *Niger* 13°55N 5°15E **50** F7
Birnin Kebbi *Nigeria* 12°32N 4°12E **50** F6
Birobidzhan *Russia* 48°50N 132°50E **29** E14
Birr *Ireland* 53°6N 7°54W **10** C4
Birrie → *Australia* 29°43S 146°37E **63** D4
Birsilpur *India* 28°11N 72°15E **42** E5
Birsk *Russia* 55°25N 55°30E **18** C10
Birtle *Canada* 50°30N 101°5W **71** C8
Birur *India* 13°30N 75°55E **40** N9
Birżai *Lithuania* 56°11N 24°45E **9** H21
Birzebbugga *Malta* 35°50N 14°32E **25** D2
Bisa *Indonesia* 1°15S 127°28E **37** E7
Bisalpur *India* 28°14N 79°48E **43** E8
Bisbee *U.S.A.* 31°27N 109°55W **77** L9
Biscarrosse *France* 44°29N 1°20W **20** D3
Biscay, B. of *Atl. Oc.* 45°0N 2°0W **20** D1
Biscayne B. *U.S.A.* 25°40N 80°12W **85** J14
Biscoe Is. *Antarctica* 66°0S 67°0W **5** C17
Biscotasing *Canada* 47°18N 82°9W **72** C3
Bishkek *Kyrgyzstan* 42°54N 74°46E **28** E8
Bishnupur *India* 23°8N 87°20E **43** H12
Bisho = Bhisho *S. Africa* 32°50S 27°23E **57** E4
Bishop *Calif., U.S.A.* 37°22N 118°24W **78** H8
Bishop *Tex., U.S.A.* 27°35N 97°48W **84** H6
Bishop Auckland *U.K.* 54°39N 1°40W **12** C6
Bishop's Falls *Canada* 49°2N 55°30W **73** C8
Bishop's Stortford *U.K.* 51°52N 0°10E **13** F8
Bisina, L. *Uganda* 1°38N 33°56E **54** B3
Biskra *Algeria* 34°50N 5°44E **50** B7
Bismarck *U.S.A.* 46°48N 100°47W **80** B3
Bismarck Arch.
   Papua N. G. 2°30S 150°0E **58** B7
Biso *Uganda* 1°44N 31°26E **54** B3
Bison *U.S.A.* 45°31N 102°28W **80** C2
Bīsotūn *Iran* 34°23N 47°26E **44** C5
Bissagos = Bijagós, Arquipélago
   dos *Guinea-Biss.* 11°15N 16°10W **50** F2
Bissau *Guinea-Biss.* 11°45N 15°45W **50** F2
Bistcho L. *Canada* 59°45N 118°50W **70** B5
Bistriţa *Romania* 47°9N 24°35E **17** E13
Bistriţa → *Romania* 46°30N 26°57E **17** E14
Biswan *India* 27°29N 81°2E **43** F9
Bitam *Gabon* 2°5N 11°25E **52** D2
Bitkine *Chad* 11°59N 18°13E **51** F9
Bitlis *Turkey* 38°20N 42°3E **44** B4
Bitola *Macedonia* 41°1N 21°20E **23** D9
Bitolj = Bitola *Macedonia* 41°1N 21°20E **23** D9
Bitter Creek *U.S.A.* 41°33N 108°33W **76** F9
Bitterfontein *S. Africa* 31°1S 18°32E **56** E2
Bitterroot → *U.S.A.* 46°52N 114°7W **76** C6
Bitterroot Range *U.S.A.* 46°0N 114°20W **76** C6
Bitterwater *U.S.A.* 36°23N 121°0W **78** J6
Biu *Nigeria* 10°40N 12°3E **51** F8
Biwa-Ko *Japan* 35°15N 136°10E **31** G8
Biwabik *U.S.A.* 47°32N 92°21W **80** B7
Bixby *U.S.A.* 35°57N 95°53W **84** D7
Biyang *China* 32°38N 113°21E **34** H7
Biysk *Russia* 52°40N 85°0E **28** D9
Bizana *S. Africa* 30°50S 29°52E **57** E4

Bizen *Japan* 34°43N 134°8E **31** G7
Bizerte *Tunisia* 37°15N 9°50E **51** A7
Bjargtangar *Iceland* 65°30N 24°30W **8** D1
Bjelovar *Croatia* 45°56N 16°49E **22** B7
Bjørneborg = Pori
   Finland 61°29N 21°48E **8** F19
Bjørnevatn *Norway* 69°40N 30°0E **8** B24
Bjørnøya *Arctic* 74°30N 19°0E **4** B8
Black = Da → *Vietnam* 21°15N 105°20E **38** B5
Black → *Canada* 44°42N 79°19W **82** B5
Black → *Ariz., U.S.A.* 33°44N 110°13W **77** K8
Black → *Ark., U.S.A.* 35°38N 91°20W **84** D9
Black → *La., U.S.A.* 31°16N 91°50W **84** F9
Black → *Mich., U.S.A.* 42°59N 82°27W **82** D2
Black → *N.Y., U.S.A.* 43°59N 76°4W **83** C8
Black → *Wis., U.S.A.* 43°57N 91°22W **80** D8
Black Bay Pen. *Canada* 48°38N 88°21W **72** C2
Black Birch L. *Canada* 56°53N 107°45W **71** B7
Black Braes △ *Australia* 19°10S 144°10E **62** B3
Black Canyon of the Gunnison △
   U.S.A. 38°40N 107°35W **76** G10
Black Diamond *Canada* 50°45N 114°14W **70** C6
Black Duck → *Canada* 56°51N 89°2W **72** A2
Black Forest = Schwarzwald
   Germany 48°30N 8°20E **16** D5
Black Forest *U.S.A.* 39°0N 104°43W **76** G11
Black Hd. *Ireland* 53°9N 9°16W **10** C2
Black Hills *U.S.A.* 44°0N 103°45W **80** D2
Black I. *Canada* 51°12N 96°30W **71** C9
Black L. *Canada* 59°12N 105°15W **71** B7
Black L. *Mich., U.S.A.* 45°28N 84°16W **81** C11
Black L. *N.Y., U.S.A.* 44°31N 75°36W **83** B9
Black Lake *Canada* 59°11N 105°20W **71** B7
Black Mesa *U.S.A.* 36°58N 102°58W **84** C3
Black Mt. = Mynydd Du
   U.K. 51°52N 3°50W **13** F4
Black Mts. *U.K.* 51°55N 3°7W **13** F4
Black Range *U.S.A.* 33°15N 107°50W **77** K10
Black River *Jamaica* 18°0N 77°50W **88** a
Black River *U.S.A.* 44°0N 75°47W **83** C9
Black River Falls *U.S.A.* 44°18N 90°51W **80** C8
Black Rock *Barbados* 13°7N 59°37W **89** g
Black Rock Desert
   U.S.A. 41°10N 118°50W **76** F4
Black Sea *Eurasia* 43°30N 35°0E **19** F6
Black Tickle *Canada* 53°28N 55°45W **73** B8
Black Volta → *Africa* 8°41N 1°33W **50** G5
Black Warrior → *U.S.A.* 32°32N 87°51W **85** E11
Blackall *Australia* 24°25S 145°45E **62** C4
Blackball *N.Z.* 42°22S 171°26E **59** E3
Blackbull *Australia* 17°55S 141°45E **62** B3
Blackburn *U.K.* 53°45N 2°29W **12** D5
Blackburn with Darwen □
   U.K. 53°45N 2°29W **12** D5
Blackdown Tableland △
   Australia 23°52S 149°7E **62** C4
Blackfoot *U.S.A.* 43°11N 112°21W **76** E7
Blackfoot → *U.S.A.* 46°52N 113°53W **76** C7
Blackfoot Res. *U.S.A.* 42°55N 111°39W **76** E8
Blackpool *U.K.* 53°49N 3°3W **12** D4
Blackpool □ *U.K.* 53°49N 3°3W **12** D4
Blackriver *U.S.A.* 44°46N 83°17W **82** B1
Blacks Harbour *Canada* 45°3N 66°49W **73** C6
Blackstairs Mt. *Ireland* 52°33N 6°48W **10** D5
Blackstone Ra. *Australia* 26°0S 128°30E **61** E4
Blacktown *Australia* 33°48S 150°55E **63** E5
Blackwater = West Road →
   Canada 53°18N 122°53W **70** C4
Blackwater *Australia* 23°35S 148°53E **62** C4
Blackwater → *Meath,*
   Ireland 53°39N 6°41W **10** C4
Blackwater → *Waterford,*
   Ireland 52°4N 7°52W **10** D4
Blackwater → *U.K.* 54°31N 6°35W **10** B5
Blackwell *U.S.A.* 36°48N 97°17W **84** C6
Blackwells Corner
   U.S.A. 35°37N 119°47W **79** K7
Bladensburg △
   Australia 22°30S 142°59E **62** C3
Blaenau Ffestiniog *U.K.* 53°0N 3°56W **12** E4
Blaenau Gwent □ *U.K.* 51°48N 3°12W **13** F4
Blagodarnoye = Blagodarnyy
   Russia 45°7N 43°37E **19** E7
Blagodarnyy *Russia* 45°7N 43°37E **19** E7
Blagoevgrad *Bulgaria* 42°2N 23°5E **23** C10
Blagoveshchensk
   Russia 50°20N 127°30E **29** D13
Blahkiuh *Indonesia* 8°31S 115°12E **37** J18
Blain *U.S.A.* 40°20N 77°31W **82** F7
Blaine *Minn., U.S.A.* 45°9N 93°13W **80** C7
Blaine *Wash., U.S.A.* 48°59N 122°45W **78** B4
Blaine Lake *Canada* 52°51N 106°52W **71** C7
Blair *U.S.A.* 41°33N 96°8W **80** E5
Blair Athol *Australia* 22°42S 147°31E **62** C4
Blair Atholl *U.K.* 56°46N 3°50W **11** E5
Blairgowrie *U.K.* 56°35N 3°21W **11** E5
Blairsden *U.S.A.* 39°47N 120°37W **78** F6
Blairsville *U.S.A.* 40°26N 79°16W **82** F5
Blake Pt. *U.S.A.* 48°11N 88°25W **80** A3
Blakely *Ga., U.S.A.* 31°23N 84°56W **85** F12
Blakely *Pa., U.S.A.* 41°28N 75°37W **83** E9
Blanc, C. *Spain* 39°21N 2°51E **24** B9
Blanc, Mont *Europe* 45°48N 6°50E **20** D7
Blanca, B. *Argentina* 39°10S 61°30W **96** D4
Blanca, Cord. *Peru* 9°10S 77°35W **92** E3
Blanca Peak *U.S.A.* 37°35N 105°29W **77** H11
Blanche, C. *Australia* 33°1S 134°9E **63** E1
Blanche, L. *S. Austral.,*
   Australia 29°15S 139°40E **63** D2
Blanche, L. *W. Austral.,*
   Australia 22°25S 123°17E **60** D3

Blanchisseuse
   Trin. & Tob. 10°48N 61°18W **93** K15
Blanco *S. Africa* 33°55S 22°23E **56** E3
Blanco *U.S.A.* 30°6N 98°25W **84** G5
Blanco → *Argentina* 30°20S 68°42W **94** C2
Blanco, C. *Costa Rica* 9°34N 85°8W **88** E2
Blanco, C. *U.S.A.* 42°51N 124°34W **76** E1
Blanda → *Iceland* 65°37N 20°9W **8** D3
Blandford Forum *U.K.* 50°51N 2°9W **13** G5
Blanding *U.S.A.* 37°37N 109°29W **77** H9
Blanes *Spain* 41°40N 2°48E **21** B7
Blankenberge *Belgium* 51°20N 3°9E **15** C3
Blanquilla *Venezuela* 11°51N 64°37W **89** D7
Blanquillo *Uruguay* 32°53S 55°37W **95** C4
Blantyre *Malawi* 15°45S 35°0E **55** F4
Blarney *Ireland* 51°56N 8°33W **10** E3
Blasdell *U.S.A.* 42°48N 78°50W **82** D6
Blatchley *U.N.* 37°37N 109°25E **15** C4
Blayais *France* 45°8N 0°40W **20** D3
Blaydon *U.K.* 54°58N 1°42W **12** C6
Blayney *Australia* 33°32S 149°14E **63** E4
Blaze, Pt. *Australia* 12°56S 130°11E **60** B5
Blekinge *Sweden* 56°25N 15°20E **9** H16
Blenheim *Canada* 42°20N 82°0W **82** D3
Blenheim *N.Z.* 41°38S 173°57E **59** D5
Bletchley *U.K.* 51°59N 0°44W **13** F7
Blida *Algeria* 36°30N 2°49E **50** A6
Bligh Sound *N.Z.* 44°47S 167°32E **59** F1
Bligh Water *Fiji* 17°0S 178°0E **59** a
Blind River *Canada* 46°10N 82°58W **72** C3
Bliss *Idaho, U.S.A.* 42°56N 114°57W **76** E6
Bliss *N.Y., U.S.A.* 42°34N 78°15W **82** D6
Blissfield *U.S.A.* 41°50N 83°52W **81** E12
Blitar *Indonesia* 8°5S 112°11E **37** H15
Blitta *Togo* 8°23N 1°6E **50** G6
Block I. *U.S.A.* 41°11N 71°35W **83** E13
Block Island Sd. *U.S.A.* 41°15N 71°40W **83** E13
Bloemfontein *S. Africa* 29°6S 26°7E **56** D4
Bloemhof *S. Africa* 27°38S 25°32E **56** D4
Blois *France* 47°35N 1°20E **20** C4
Blönduós *Iceland* 65°40N 20°12W **8** D3
Blongas *Indonesia* 8°53S 116°2E **37** K19
Bloodvein → *Canada* 51°47N 96°43W **71** C9
Bloody Foreland *Ireland* 55°10N 8°17W **10** A3
Bloomer *U.S.A.* 45°6N 91°29W **80** C8
Bloomfield *Canada* 43°59N 77°14W **82** C7
Bloomfield *Iowa, U.S.A.* 40°45N 92°25W **80** E7
Bloomfield *N. Mex.,*
   U.S.A. 36°43N 107°59W **77** H10
Bloomfield *Nebr., U.S.A.* 42°36N 97°39W **80** D5
Bloomington *Ill., U.S.A.* 40°28N 89°0W **80** E9
Bloomington *Ind.,*
   U.S.A. 39°10N 86°32W **80** F10
Bloomington *Minn.,*
   U.S.A. 44°50N 93°17W **80** C7
Bloomsburg *U.S.A.* 41°0N 76°27W **83** F8
Bloomsbury *Australia* 20°48S 148°38E **62** J6
Blora *Indonesia* 6°57S 111°25E **37** G14
Blossburg *U.S.A.* 41°41N 77°4W **82** E7
Blouberg *S. Africa* 23°8S 28°59E **57** C4
Blountstown *U.S.A.* 30°27N 85°3W **85** F12
Blue Earth *U.S.A.* 43°38N 94°6W **80** D7
Blue Hole △ *Belize* 17°24N 88°30W **88** C2
Blue Lagoon □ *Zambia* 15°28S 27°26E **55** F2
Blue Mesa Res. *U.S.A.* 38°28N 107°20W **76** G10
Blue Mountain Lake
   U.S.A. 43°51N 74°27W **83** C10
Blue Mountain Pk.
   Jamaica 18°3N 76°36W **88** a
Blue Mt. *U.S.A.* 40°30N 76°30W **83** F8
Blue Mts. *Jamaica* 18°3N 76°36W **88** a
Blue Mts. *Maine, U.S.A.* 44°50N 70°35W **83** B14
Blue Mts. *Oreg., U.S.A.* 45°0N 118°20W **76** D4
Blue Mud B. *Australia* 13°30S 136°0E **62** A2
Blue Nile = Nîl el Azraq →
   Sudan 15°38N 32°31E **51** E12
Blue Rapids *U.S.A.* 39°41N 96°39W **80** F5
Blue Ridge *U.S.A.* 36°40N 80°50W **81** G13
Blue River *Canada* 52°6N 119°18W **70** C5
Bluefield *U.S.A.* 37°15N 81°17W **81** G13
Bluefields *Nic.* 12°20N 83°50W **88** D3
Bluevale *Canada* 43°51N 81°15W **82** C3
Bluff *Australia* 23°35S 149°4E **62** C4
Bluff *N.Z.* 46°37S 168°20E **59** G2
Bluff *U.S.A.* 37°17N 109°33W **77** H9
Bluff Knoll *Australia* 34°24S 118°15E **61** F2
Bluff Pt. *Australia* 27°50S 114°5E **61** E1
Bluffton *U.S.A.* 40°44N 85°11W **81** E11
Blumenau *Brazil* 27°0S 49°0W **95** B6
Bly *U.S.A.* 42°24N 121°3W **76** E3
Blyde River Canyon △
   S. Africa 24°37S 31°2E **57** C5
Blyth *Canada* 43°44N 81°26W **82** C3
Blyth *U.K.* 55°8N 1°31W **12** B6
Blythe *U.S.A.* 33°37N 114°36W **79** M12
Blytheville *U.S.A.* 35°56N 89°55W **85** D10
Bo *S. Leone* 7°55N 11°50W **50** G3
Bo Duc *Vietnam* 11°58N 106°50E **39** G6
Bo Hai *China* 39°0N 119°0E **35** E10
Bo Xian = Bozhou
   China 33°55N 115°41E **34** H8
Boa Vista *Brazil* 2°48N 60°30W **92** C6
Boa Vista *C. Verde Is.* 16°0N 22°49W **50** b
Boaco *Nic.* 12°29N 85°35W **88** D2
Bo'ai *China* 35°10N 113°3E **34** G7
Boalsburg *U.S.A.* 40°46N 77°47W **82** F7
Boane *Mozam.* 26°6S 32°19E **57** D5
Boardman *U.S.A.* 41°2N 80°40W **82** E4
Bobadah *Australia* 32°19S 146°41E **63** E4
Bobbili *India* 18°35N 83°30E **41** K13
Bobcaygeon *Canada* 44°33N 78°33W **82** B6
Bobo-Dioulasso
   Burkina Faso 11°8N 4°13W **50** F5
Bóbr → *Poland* 52°4N 15°4E **16** B8
Bobraomby, Tanjon' i
   Madag. 12°40S 49°10E **57** A8
Bobruysk = Babruysk
   Belarus 53°10N 29°15E **17** B15

Boby, Pic *Madag.* 22°12S 46°55E **53** J9
Boca del Río *Mexico* 19°5N 96°4W **87** D5
Boca do Acre *Brazil* 8°50S 67°27W **92** E5
Boca Raton *U.S.A.* 26°21N 80°5W **85** H14
Bocas del Dragón
   Venezuela 11°0N 61°50W **93** K15
Bocas del Toro *Panama* 9°15N 82°20W **88** E3
Bochnia *Poland* 49°58N 20°27E **17** D11
Bocholt *Germany* 51°28N 7°13E **16** C4
Bochum *Germany* 51°28N 7°13E **16** C4
Bocoyna *Mexico* 27°52N 107°35W **86** B3
Boda *Dem. Rep. of the Congo* 0°24S 21°12E **52** E4
Bodaybo *Russia* 57°50N 114°0E **29** D12
Boddam *U.K.* 59°56N 1°17W **11** B7
Boddington *Australia* 32°50S 116°30E **61** F2
Bodega Bay *U.S.A.* 38°20N 123°3W **78** G3
Boden *Sweden* 65°50N 21°42E **8** D19
Bodensee *Europe* 47°35N 9°25E **20** C8
Bodhan *India* 18°40N 77°44E **40** K10
Bodmin *U.K.* 50°28N 4°43W **13** G3
Bodmin Moor *U.K.* 50°33N 4°36W **13** G3
Bodø *Norway* 67°17N 14°24E **8** C16
Bodrog → *Hungary* 48°11N 21°22E **17** D11
Bodrum *Turkey* 37°3N 27°30E **23** F12
Boende
   Dem. Rep. of the Congo 0°24S 21°12E **52** E4
Boerne *U.S.A.* 29°47N 98°44W **84** G5
Boesmans → *S. Africa* 33°42S 26°39E **56** E4
Bogalusa *U.S.A.* 30°47N 89°52W **85** F10
Bogan → *Australia* 30°20S 146°55E **63** D4
Bogan Gate *Australia* 33°7S 147°49E **63** E4
Bogantungan *Australia* 23°41S 147°17E **62** C4
Bogata *U.S.A.* 33°28N 95°13W **84** E7
Bogda Shan *China* 43°35N 90°0E **32** B3
Boggabilla *Australia* 28°36S 150°24E **63** D5
Boggabri *Australia* 30°45S 150°5E **63** E5
Boggeragh Mts. *Ireland* 52°2N 8°55W **10** D3
Boglan = Solhan *Turkey* 38°57N 41°3E **44** B4
Bogo *Phil.* 11°3N 124°0E **37** B6
Bogong, Mt. *Australia* 36°47S 147°17E **63** F4
Bogor *Indonesia* 6°36S 106°48E **37** G12
Bogotá *Colombia* 4°34N 74°0W **92** C4
Bogotol *Russia* 56°15N 89°50E **28** D9
Bogra *Bangla.* 24°51N 89°22E **41** G16
Boguchany *Russia* 58°40N 97°30E **29** D10
Bogué *Mauritania* 16°45N 14°10W **50** E3
Bohemian Forest = Böhmerwald
   Germany 49°8N 13°14E **16** D7
Böhmerwald *Germany* 49°8N 13°14E **16** D7
Bohol □ *Phil.* 9°50N 124°10E **37** C6
Bohol Sea *Phil.* 9°0N 124°0E **37** C6
Bohorok *Indonesia* 3°30N 98°12E **39** L2
Bohuslän *Sweden* 58°25N 12°0E **9** G15
Boi, Pta. do *Brazil* 23°55S 45°15W **95** A6
Boiaçu *Brazil* 0°27S 61°46W **92** D6
Boileau, C. *Australia* 17°40S 122°7E **60** C3
Boise *U.S.A.* 43°37N 116°13W **76** E5
Boise City *U.S.A.* 36°44N 102°31W **84** C3
Boissevain *Canada* 49°15N 100°5W **71** D8
Bojador, C. *W. Sahara* 26°0N 14°30W **50** C3
Bojana → *Albania* 41°52N 19°22E **23** D8
Bojnūrd *Iran* 37°30N 57°20E **45** B8
Bojonegoro *Indonesia* 7°11S 111°54E **37** G14
Bokaro *India* 23°46N 85°55E **43** H11
Boké *Guinea* 10°56N 14°17W **50** F3
Bokhara → *Australia* 29°55S 146°42E **63** D4
Boknafjorden *Norway* 59°14N 5°40E **9** G11
Bokor △ *Cambodia* 10°50N 104°1E **39** G5
Bokora △ *Uganda* 2°12N 31°32E **54** B3
Bokoro *Chad* 12°25N 17°14E **51** F9
Bokpyin *Burma* 11°18N 98°42E **39** G2
Bokungu
   Dem. Rep. of the Congo 0°35S 22°50E **52** E4
Bolan → *Pakistan* 28°38N 67°42E **42** E2
Bolan Pass *Pakistan* 29°50N 67°20E **40** E5
Bolaños → *Mexico* 21°12N 104°5W **86** C4
Bolbec *France* 49°30N 0°30E **20** B4
Boldājī *Iran* 31°56N 51°3E **45** D6
Bole *China* 45°11N 81°37E **32** B3
Bolekhiv *Ukraine* 49°0N 23°57E **17** D12
Bolesławiec *Poland* 51°17N 15°37E **16** C8
Bolgatanga *Ghana* 10°44N 0°53W **50** F5
Bolgrad = Bolhrad
   Ukraine 45°40N 28°32E **17** F15
Bolhrad *Ukraine* 45°40N 28°32E **17** F15
Bolívar *Mo., U.S.A.* 37°37N 93°25W **80** G7
Bolívar *N.Y., U.S.A.* 42°4N 78°10W **82** D6
Bolívar *Tenn., U.S.A.* 35°12N 89°0W **85** D10
Bolivia ■ *S. Amer.* 17°6S 64°0W **92** G6
Bolivian Plateau = Altiplano
   Bolivia 17°0S 68°0W **92** G5
Bollnäs *Sweden* 61°21N 16°24E **8** F17
Bollon *Australia* 28°2S 147°29E **63** D4
Bolmen *Sweden* 56°55N 13°40E **9** H15
Bolobo
   Dem. Rep. of the Congo 2°6S 16°20E **52** E3
Bologna *Italy* 44°29N 11°20E **22** B4
Bologoye *Russia* 57°55N 34°5E **18** C5
Bolomba
   Dem. Rep. of the Congo 0°35N 19°0E **52** D3
Bolonchén *Mexico* 20°11N 89°45W **87** D7
Boloven, Cao Nguyen
   Laos 15°10N 106°30E **38** E6
Bolpur *India* 23°40N 87°45E **43** H12
Bolsena, L. di *Italy* 42°36N 11°56E **22** C4
Bolshevik, Ostrov
   Russia 78°30N 102°0E **29** B11
Bolshoy Anyuy →
   Russia 68°30N 160°49E **29** C17
Bolshoy Begichev, Ostrov
   Russia 74°20N 112°30E **29** B12
Bolshoy Kamen *Russia* 43°7N 132°19E **30** C6
Bolshoy Kavkas = Caucasus
   Mountains *Eurasia* 42°50N 44°0E **19** F7
Bolshoy Lyakhovskiy, Ostrov
   Russia 73°35N 142°0E **29** B15
Bolshoy Tyuters, Ostrov
   Russia 59°51N 27°13E **9** G22

Bolsward *Neths.* 53°3N 5°32E **15 A5**
Bolt Head *U.K.* 50°12N 3°48W **13 G4**
Bolton *Canada* 43°54N 79°45W **82 C5**
Bolton *U.K.* 53°35N 2°26W **12 D5**
Bolton Landing *U.S.A.* 43°32N 73°35W **83 C11**
Bolu *Turkey* 40°45N 31°35E **19 F5**
Bolungavík *Iceland* 66°9N 23°15W **8 C2**
Bolvadin *Turkey* 38°45N 31°4E **44 B1**
Bolzano *Italy* 46°31N 11°22E **22 A4**
Bom Jesus da Lapa
  Brazil 13°15S 43°25W **93 F10**
Boma *Dem. Rep. of the Congo* 5°50S 13°4E **52 F2**
Bombala *Australia* 36°56S 149°15E **63 F4**
Bombay = Mumbai
  India 18°56N 72°50E **40 K8**
Bombay *U.S.A.* 44°56N 74°34W **83 B10**
Bombboma
  Venezuela 9°53N 61°37W **93 L15**
Bomboma
  Dem. Rep. of the Congo 2°25N 18°55E **52 D3**
Bombombwa
  Dem. Rep. of the Congo 1°40N 25°40E **54 B2**
Bomili
  Dem. Rep. of the Congo 1°45N 27°5E **54 B2**
Bømlo *Norway* 59°37N 5°13E **9 G11**
Bomokandi →
  Dem. Rep. of the Congo 3°39N 26°8E **54 B2**
Bomu → *C.A.R.* 4°40N 22°30E **52 D4**
Bon, C. = Ra's at Tib
  Tunisia 37°1N 11°2E **22 F4**
Bon Acceuil *Mauritius* 20°10S 57°39E **53 d**
Bon Echo △ *Canada* 44°55N 77°16W **82 B7**
Bon Sar Pa *Vietnam* 12°24N 107°35E **38 F6**
Bonāb *Iran* 36°35N 48°41E **45 B6**
Bonaigarh *India* 21°50N 84°57E **43 J11**
Bonaire *Neth. Ant.* 12°10N 68°15W **89 D6**
Bonampak *Mexico* 16°44N 91°5W **87 D6**
Bonang *Australia* 37°11S 148°41E **63 F4**
Bonanza *Nic.* 13°54N 84°35W **88 D3**
Bonaparte Arch.
  Australia 14°0S 124°30E **60 B3**
Bonar Bridge *U.K.* 57°54N 4°20W **11 D4**
Bonasse *Trin. & Tob.* 10°5N 61°54W **93 K15**
Bonaventure *Canada* 48°5N 65°32W **73 C6**
Bonavista *Canada* 48°40N 53°5W **73 C9**
Bonavista, C. *Canada* 48°42N 53°5W **73 C9**
Bonavista B. *Canada* 48°45N 53°25W **73 C9**
Bondo
  Dem. Rep. of the Congo 3°55N 23°53E **54 B1**
Bondoukou *Ivory C.* 8°2N 2°47W **50 G5**
Bondowoso *Indonesia* 7°55S 113°49E **37 G15**
Bone, Teluk *Indonesia* 4°10S 120°50E **37 E6**
Bonerate *Indonesia* 7°25S 121°5E **37 F6**
Bonerate, Kepulauan
  Indonesia 6°30S 121°10E **37 F6**
Bo'ness *U.K.* 56°1N 3°37W **11 E5**
Bonete, Cerro *Argentina* 27°55S 68°40W **94 B2**
Bong Son = Hoai Nhon
  Vietnam 14°28N 109°1E **38 E7**
Bongaigaon *India* 26°28N 90°34E **32 D4**
Bongandanga
  Dem. Rep. of the Congo 1°24N 21°3E **52 D4**
Bongor *Chad* 10°35N 15°20E **51 F9**
Bongos, Massif des *C.A.R.* 8°40N 22°25E **52 C4**
Bonham *U.S.A.* 33°35N 96°11W **84 E6**
Boni △ *Kenya* 1°35S 41°18E **54 C5**
Bonifacio *France* 41°24N 9°10E **20 F8**
Bonifacio, Bouches de
  Medit. S. 41°12N 9°15E **22 D3**
Bonin Is. = Ogasawara Gunto
  Pac. Oc. 27°0N 142°0E **27 F16**
Bonn *Germany* 50°46N 7°6E **16 C4**
Bonne Terre *U.S.A.* 37°55N 90°33W **80 G8**
Bonners Ferry *U.S.A.* 48°42N 116°19W **76 B5**
Bonney, L. *Australia* 37°50S 140°20E **63 F3**
Bonnie Rock *Australia* 30°29S 118°22E **61 F2**
Bonny, Bight of *Africa* 3°30N 9°20E **52 D1**
Bonnyrigg *U.K.* 55°53N 3°6W **11 F5**
Bonnyville *Canada* 54°20N 110°45W **71 C6**
Bonoi *Indonesia* 1°45S 137°41E **37 E9**
Bonsall *U.S.A.* 33°16N 117°14W **79 M9**
Bontang *Indonesia* 0°10N 117°30E **36 D5**
Bontebok △ *S. Africa* 34°5S 20°28E **56 E3**
Bonthe *S. Leone* 7°30N 12°33W **50 G3**
Bontoc *Phil.* 17°7N 120°58E **37 A6**
Bonython Ra. *Australia* 23°40S 128°45E **60 D4**
Boodjamulla △ *Australia* 18°15S 138°6E **62 B2**
Bookabie *Australia* 31°50S 132°41E **61 F5**
Booker *U.S.A.* 36°27N 100°32W **84 C4**
Booligal *Australia* 33°58S 144°53E **63 E3**
Böön Tsagaan Nuur
  Mongolia 45°35N 99°9E **32 B4**
Boonah *Australia* 27°58S 152°41E **63 D5**
Boone *Iowa, U.S.A.* 42°4N 93°53W **80 D7**
Boone *N.C., U.S.A.* 36°13N 81°41W **85 C14**
Booneville *Ark., U.S.A.* 35°8N 93°55W **84 D8**
Booneville *Miss., U.S.A.* 34°39N 88°34W **85 D10**
Boonville *Calif., U.S.A.* 39°1N 123°22W **78 F3**
Boonville *Ind., U.S.A.* 38°3N 87°16W **80 F10**
Boonville *Mo., U.S.A.* 38°58N 92°44W **80 F7**
Boonville *N.Y., U.S.A.* 43°29N 75°20W **83 C9**
Boorabbin △ *Australia* 31°30S 120°10E **61 F3**
Boorindal *Australia* 30°22S 146°11E **63 E4**
Boorowa *Australia* 34°28S 148°44E **63 E4**
Boosaaso *Somali Rep.* 11°12N 49°18E **47 E4**
Boothia, Gulf of *Canada* 71°0N 90°0W **69 B11**
Boothia Pen. *Canada* 71°0N 94°0W **68 B10**
Bootle *U.K.* 53°28N 3°1W **12 D4**
Booué *Gabon* 0°5S 11°55E **52 E2**
Boquilla, Presa de la
  Mexico 27°31N 105°30W **86 B3**
Boquillas del Carmen
  Mexico 29°11N 102°58W **86 B4**
Bôr *Serbia* 44°5N 22°7E **23 B10**
Bôr *Sudan* 6°10N 31°40E **51 G12**
Bor Mashash *Israel* 31°7N 34°50E **46 D3**
Bora Bora
  French Polynesia 16°30S 151°45W **65 J12**

Borah Peak *U.S.A.* 44°8N 113°47W **76 D7**
Borås *Sweden* 57°43N 12°56E **9 H15**
Borāzjān *Iran* 29°22N 51°10E **45 D6**
Borba *Brazil* 4°12S 59°34W **92 D7**
Borborema, Planalto da
  Brazil 7°0S 37°0W **90 D7**
Bord Khūn-e Now *Iran* 28°3N 51°28E **45 D6**
Borda, C. *Australia* 35°45S 136°34E **63 F2**
Bordeaux *France* 44°50N 0°36W **20 D3**
Borden *Australia* 34°3S 118°12E **61 F2**
Borden-Carleton *Canada* 46°18N 63°47W **73 C7**
Borden I. *Canada* 78°30N 111°30W **69 B8**
Borden Pen. *Canada* 73°0N 83°0W **69 B11**
Border Ranges △
  Australia 28°24S 152°56E **63 D5**
Borders = Scottish Borders □
  U.K. 55°35N 2°50W **11 F6**
Bordertown *Australia* 36°19S 140°45E **63 F3**
Borðeyri *Iceland* 65°12N 21°6W **8 D3**
Bordj Fly Ste. Marie
  Algeria 27°19N 2°32W **50 C5**
Bordj-in-Eker *Algeria* 24°9N 5°3E **50 D7**
Bordj Moktar *Algeria* 21°20N 0°56E **50 D6**
Bordj Omar Driss *Algeria* 28°10N 6°40E **50 C7**
Borehamwood *U.K.* 51°40N 0°15W **13 F7**
Borgarfjörður *Iceland* 65°33N 13°47W **8 D7**
Borgarnes *Iceland* 64°32N 21°55W **8 D3**
Børgefjellet *Norway* 65°20N 13°45E **8 D15**
Borger *Neths.* 52°54N 6°44E **15 B6**
Borger *U.S.A.* 35°39N 101°24W **84 D4**
Borgholm *Sweden* 56°52N 16°39E **9 H17**
Borhoyn Tal *Mongolia* 43°50N 111°58E **34 C6**
Borikhane *Laos* 18°33N 103°43E **38 C4**
Borisoglebsk *Russia* 51°27N 42°5E **19 D7**
Borisov = Barysaw
  Belarus 54°17N 28°28E **17 A15**
Borja *Peru* 4°20S 77°40W **92 D3**
Borkou *Chad* 18°15N 18°50E **51 E9**
Borkum *Germany* 53°34N 6°40E **16 B4**
Borlänge *Sweden* 60°29N 15°26E **9 F16**
Borley, C. *Antarctica* 66°15S 52°30E **5 C5**
Borneo *E. Indies* 1°0N 115°0E **36 D5**
Bornholm *Denmark* 55°10N 15°0E **9 J16**
Borogontsy *Russia* 62°42N 131°8E **29 C14**
Borohoro Shan *China* 44°6N 83°10E **32 B3**
Boron *U.S.A.* 35°0N 117°39W **79 L9**
Borongan *Phil.* 11°37N 125°26E **37 B7**
Borovichi *Russia* 58°25N 33°55E **18 C5**
Borrego Springs
  U.S.A. 33°15N 116°23W **79 M10**
Borrisokane *Ireland* 53°0N 8°7W **10 D3**
Borroloola *Australia* 16°4S 136°17E **62 B2**
Borşa *Romania* 47°41N 24°50E **17 E13**
Borsad *India* 22°25N 72°54E **42 H5**
Borth *U.K.* 52°29N 4°2W **13 E3**
Borūjerd *Iran* 33°55N 48°50E **45 C6**
Boryeong *S. Korea* 36°21N 126°36E **35 F14**
Boryslav *Ukraine* 49°18N 23°28E **17 D12**
Borzya *Russia* 50°24N 116°31E **29 D12**
Bosa *Italy* 40°18N 8°30E **22 D3**
Bosanska Gradiška
  Bos.-H. 45°10N 17°15E **22 B7**
Boscastle *U.K.* 50°41N 4°42W **13 G3**
Boscobelle *Barbados* 13°17N 59°35W **89 g**
Bose *China* 23°53N 106°35E **32 D5**
Boseong *S. Korea* 34°46N 127°5E **35 G14**
Boshan *China* 36°28N 117°49E **35 F9**
Boshof *S. Africa* 28°31S 25°13E **56 D4**
Boshrūyeh *Iran* 33°50N 57°30E **45 C8**
Bosna → *Bos.-H.* 45°4N 18°29E **23 B8**
Bosna i Hercegovina = Bosnia-
  Herzegovina ■ *Europe* 44°0N 18°0E **22 B7**
Bosnia-Herzegovina ■
  Europe 44°0N 18°0E **22 B7**
Bosnik *Indonesia* 1°5S 136°10E **37 E9**
Bosobolo
  Dem. Rep. of the Congo 4°15N 19°50E **52 D3**
Bosporus = İstanbul Boğazı
  Turkey 41°5N 29°3E **23 D13**
Bosque Farms *U.S.A.* 35°51N 106°42W **77 J10**
Bossangoa *C.A.R.* 6°35N 17°30E **52 C3**
Bossier City *U.S.A.* 32°31N 93°44W **84 E8**
Bosso *Niger* 13°43N 13°19E **51 F8**
Bostan *Pakistan* 30°26N 67°2E **42 D2**
Bostānābād *Iran* 37°50N 46°50E **44 B5**
Bosten Hu *China* 41°55N 87°40E **32 B3**
Boston *U.K.* 52°59N 0°2W **12 E7**
Boston *U.S.A.* 42°22N 71°3W **83 D13**
Boston Bar *Canada* 49°52N 121°30W **70 D4**
Boston Mts. *U.S.A.* 35°42N 93°15W **84 D8**
Boswell *Canada* 49°28N 116°45W **70 D5**
Boswell *U.S.A.* 40°10N 79°2W **82 F5**
Botad *India* 22°15N 71°40E **42 H4**
Botany B. *Australia* 33°58S 151°11E **58 B8**
Botene *Laos* 17°35N 101°12E **38 D3**
Bothaville *S. Africa* 27°23S 26°34E **56 D4**
Bothnia, G. of *Europe* 62°0N 20°0E **8 F19**
Bothwell *Australia* 42°20S 147°1E **63 G4**
Bothwell *Canada* 42°38N 81°52W **82 D3**
Botletle → *Botswana* 20°10S 23°15E **56 C3**
Botoşani *Romania* 47°42N 26°41E **17 E14**
Botou *Burkina Faso* 12°42N 1°59E **50 F6**
Botshabelo *S. Africa* 29°14S 26°44E **56 D4**
Botswana ■ *Africa* 22°0S 24°0E **56 C3**
Bottineau *U.S.A.* 48°50N 100°27W **80 A3**
Bottrop *Germany* 51°31N 6°58E **15 C6**
Botucatu *Brazil* 22°55S 48°30W **95 A6**
Botum Sakor △
  Cambodia 11°5N 103°15E **39 G4**
Botwood *Canada* 49°6N 55°23W **73 C8**
Bou Saâda *Algeria* 35°11N 4°9E **50 A6**
Bouaflé *Ivory C.* 7°1N 5°47W **50 G4**
Bouaké *Ivory C.* 7°40N 5°2W **50 G4**
Bouar *C.A.R.* 6°0N 15°40E **52 C3**
Bouârfa *Morocco* 32°32N 1°58W **50 B5**
Boucaut B. *Australia* 12°0S 134°25E **62 A1**
Bouctouche *Canada* 46°30N 64°45W **73 C7**

Bougainville, C. *Australia* 13°57S 126°4E **60 B4**
Bougainville I. *Papua N. G.* 6°0S 155°0E **58 B8**
Bougainville Reef
  Australia 15°30S 147°5E **62 B4**
Bougie = Bejaïa *Algeria* 36°42N 5°2E **50 A7**
Bougouni *Mali* 11°30N 7°20W **50 F4**
Bouillon *Belgium* 49°44N 5°3E **15 E5**
Boulder *Colo., U.S.A.* 40°1N 105°17W **76 F11**
Boulder *Mont., U.S.A.* 46°14N 112°7W **76 C7**
Boulder City *U.S.A.* 35°58N 114°49W **79 K12**
Boulder Creek *U.S.A.* 37°7N 122°7W **78 H4**
Boulder Dam = Hoover Dam
  U.S.A. 36°1N 114°44W **79 K12**
Boulia *Australia* 22°52S 139°51E **62 C2**
Boulogne-sur-Mer *France* 50°42N 1°36E **20 A4**
Boulsa *Burkina Faso* 12°39N 0°34W **50 F5**
Boultoum *Niger* 14°45N 10°25E **51 F8**
Bouma △ *Fiji* 16°50S 179°52E **59 a**
Boun Neua *Laos* 21°38N 101°54E **38 B3**
Boun Tai *Laos* 21°23N 101°58E **38 B3**
Boundary Peak *U.S.A.* 37°51N 118°21W **78 H8**
Boundiali *Ivory C.* 9°30N 6°20W **50 G4**
Bountiful *U.S.A.* 40°53N 111°52W **76 F8**
Bounty Is. *Pac. Oc.* 48°0S 178°30E **64 M9**
Bounty Trough *Pac. Oc.* 46°0S 178°0E **64 M9**
Bourbonnais *France* 46°28N 3°0E **20 C5**
Bourdel L. *Canada* 56°43N 74°10W **72 A5**
Bourem *Mali* 17°0N 0°24W **50 E5**
Bourg-en-Bresse *France* 46°13N 5°12E **20 C6**
Bourg-St-Maurice *France* 45°35N 6°46E **20 D7**
Bourgas = Burgas
  Bulgaria 42°33N 27°29E **23 C12**
Bourges *France* 47°9N 2°25E **20 C5**
Bourget *Canada* 45°26N 75°9W **83 A9**
Bourgogne □ *France* 47°0N 4°50E **20 C6**
Bourke *Australia* 30°8S 145°55E **63 E4**
Bourne *U.K.* 52°47N 0°22W **12 E7**
Bournemouth *U.K.* 50°43N 1°52W **13 G6**
Bournemouth □ *U.K.* 50°43N 1°52W **13 G6**
Bouse *U.S.A.* 33°56N 114°0W **79 M13**
Bousso *Chad* 10°34N 16°52E **51 F9**
Bouvet I. = Bouvetøya
  Antarctica 54°26S 3°24E **2 G10**
Bouvetøya *Antarctica* 54°26S 3°24E **2 G10**
Bovill *U.S.A.* 46°51N 116°24W **76 C5**
Bovril *Argentina* 31°21S 59°26W **94 C4**
Bow → *Canada* 49°57N 111°41W **70 C6**
Bow Island *Canada* 49°50N 111°23W **76 B8**
Bowbells *U.S.A.* 48°48N 102°15W **80 A2**
Bowdle *U.S.A.* 45°27N 99°39W **80 C4**
Bowelling *Australia* 33°25S 116°30E **61 F2**
Bowen *Argentina* 35°0S 67°31W **94 D2**
Bowen *Australia* 20°0S 148°16E **62 J6**
Bowen Mts. *Australia* 37°0S 147°50E **63 F4**
Bowers Basin *Pac. Oc.* 53°45N 176°0E **4 D16**
Bowers Ridge *Pac. Oc.* 54°0N 180°0E **4 D17**
Bowie *Ariz., U.S.A.* 32°19N 109°29W **77 K9**
Bowie *Tex., U.S.A.* 33°34N 97°51W **84 E6**
Bowkān *Iran* 36°31N 46°12E **44 B5**
Bowland, Forest of *U.K.* 54°0N 2°30W **12 D5**
Bowling Green *Ky.,
  U.S.A.* 36°59N 86°27W **80 G10**
Bowling Green *Ohio,
  U.S.A.* 41°23N 83°39W **81 E12**
Bowling Green, C.
  Australia 19°19S 147°25E **62 B4**
Bowling Green Bay △
  Australia 19°26S 146°57E **62 B4**
Bowman *U.S.A.* 46°11N 103°24W **80 B2**
Bowman I. *Antarctica* 65°0S 104°0E **5 C8**
Bowmanville = Clarington
  Canada 43°55N 78°41W **82 C6**
Bowmore *U.K.* 55°45N 6°17W **11 F2**
Bowral *Australia* 34°26S 150°27E **63 E5**
Bowraville *Australia* 30°37S 152°52E **63 E5**
Bowron → *Canada* 54°3N 121°50W **70 C4**
Bowron Lake △ *Canada* 53°10N 121°5W **70 C4**
Bowser L. *Canada* 56°30N 129°30W **70 B3**
Bowsman *Canada* 52°14N 101°12W **71 C8**
Bowwood *Zambia* 17°5S 26°20E **55 F2**
Box Cr. → *Australia* 34°10S 143°50E **63 E3**
Boxmeer *Neths.* 51°38N 5°56E **15 C5**
Boxtel *Neths.* 51°36N 5°20E **15 C5**
Boyce *U.S.A.* 31°23N 92°40W **84 F8**
Boyd L. *Canada* 52°46N 76°42W **72 B4**
Boyle *Canada* 54°35N 112°49W **70 C6**
Boyle *Ireland* 53°59N 8°18W **10 C3**
Boyne → *Ireland* 53°43N 6°15W **10 C5**
Boyne City *U.S.A.* 45°13N 85°1W **81 C11**
Boynton Beach *U.S.A.* 26°32N 80°4W **85 H14**
Boyolali *Indonesia* 7°32S 110°35E **37 G14**
Boyoma, Chutes
  Dem. Rep. of the Congo 0°35N 25°23E **54 B2**
Boysen Res. *U.S.A.* 43°25N 108°11W **76 E9**
Boyuibe *Bolivia* 20°25S 63°17W **92 G6**
Boyup Brook *Australia* 33°50S 116°23E **61 F2**
Boz Dağları *Turkey* 38°20N 28°0E **23 E13**
Bozburun *Turkey* 36°43N 28°4E **23 F13**
Bozcaada *Turkey* 39°49N 26°3E **23 E12**
Bozdoğan *Turkey* 37°40N 28°17E **23 F13**
Bozeman *U.S.A.* 45°41N 111°2W **76 D8**
Bozhou *China* 33°55N 115°41E **34 H8**
Bozoum *C.A.R.* 6°25N 16°35E **52 C3**
Bozyazı *Turkey* 36°6N 33°0E **44 B2**
Bra *Italy* 44°42N 7°51E **20 D7**
Brabant □ *Belgium* 50°46N 4°30E **15 D4**
Brabant L. *Canada* 55°58N 103°43W **71 B8**
Brač *Croatia* 43°20N 16°40E **22 C7**
Bracadale, L. *U.K.* 57°20N 6°30W **11 D2**
Bracciano, L. di *Italy* 42°7N 12°14E **22 C5**
Bracebridge *Canada* 45°2N 79°19W **82 A5**
Bräcke *Sweden* 62°45N 15°26E **8 E16**
Brackettville *U.S.A.* 29°19N 100°25W **84 G4**
Bracknell *U.K.* 51°25N 0°43W **13 F7**
Bracknell Forest □ *U.K.* 51°25N 0°44W **13 F7**

Brad *Romania* 46°10N 22°50E **17 E12**
Bradenton *U.S.A.* 27°30N 82°34W **85 H13**
Bradford *Canada* 44°7N 79°34W **82 B5**
Bradford *U.K.* 53°47N 1°45W **12 D6**
Bradford *Pa., U.S.A.* 41°58N 78°38W **82 E6**
Bradford *Vt., U.S.A.* 43°59N 72°9W **83 C12**
Bradley *Ark., U.S.A.* 33°6N 93°39W **84 E8**
Bradley *Calif., U.S.A.* 35°52N 120°48W **78 K6**
Bradley Institute
  Zimbabwe 17°7S 31°25E **55 F3**
Brady *U.S.A.* 31°9N 99°20W **84 F5**
Braeside *Canada* 45°28N 76°24W **83 A8**
Braga *Portugal* 41°35N 8°25W **21 B1**
Bragado *Argentina* 35°2S 60°27W **94 D3**
Bragança *Brazil* 1°0S 47°2W **93 D9**
Bragança *Portugal* 41°48N 6°50W **21 B2**
Bragança Paulista
  Brazil 22°55S 46°32W **95 A6**
Brahestad = Raahe
  Finland 64°40N 24°28E **8 D21**
Brahmanbaria *Bangla.* 23°58N 91°15E **41 H17**
Brahmani → *India* 20°39N 86°46E **41 J15**
Brahmapur *India* 19°15N 84°54E **41 K14**
Brahmaputra → *Asia* 23°40N 90°35E **43 H13**
Braich-y-pwll *U.K.* 52°47N 4°46W **12 E3**
Braidwood *Australia* 35°27S 149°49E **63 F4**
Brăila *Romania* 45°19N 27°59E **17 F14**
Brainerd *U.S.A.* 46°22N 94°12W **80 B7**
Braintree *U.K.* 51°53N 0°34E **13 F8**
Braintree *U.S.A.* 42°13N 71°0W **83 D14**
Brak → *S. Africa* 29°35S 22°55E **56 D3**
Brakwater *Namibia* 22°28S 17°3E **56 C2**
Brampton *Canada* 43°45N 79°45W **82 C5**
Brampton *U.K.* 54°57N 2°44W **12 C5**
Bramton I. *Australia* 20°50S 149°17E **62 J7**
Branco → *Brazil* 1°20S 61°50W **92 D6**
Brandberg *Namibia* 21°10S 14°33E **56 C1**
Brandberg △ *Namibia* 21°10S 14°30E **56 C1**
Brandenburg = Neubrandenburg
  Germany 53°33N 13°15E **16 B7**
Brandenburg *Germany* 52°25N 12°33E **16 B7**
Brandenburg □ *Germany* 52°50N 13°0E **16 B6**
Brandfort *S. Africa* 28°40S 26°30E **56 D4**
Brandon *Canada* 49°50N 99°57W **71 D9**
Brandon *U.K.* 52°27N 0°37E **13 E8**
Brandon Mt. *Ireland* 52°15N 10°15W **10 D1**
Brandsen *Argentina* 35°10S 58°15W **94 D4**
Brandvlei *S. Africa* 30°25S 20°30E **56 E3**
Branford *U.S.A.* 41°17N 72°49W **83 E12**
Braniewo *Poland* 54°25N 19°50E **17 A10**
Bransfield Str. *Antarctica* 63°0S 59°0W **5 C18**
Branson *U.S.A.* 36°39N 93°13W **80 G7**
Brantford *Canada* 43°10N 80°15W **82 C4**
Bras d'Or L. *Canada* 45°50N 60°50W **73 C7**
Brasher Falls *U.S.A.* 44°49N 74°47W **83 B10**
Brasil = Brazil ■ *S. Amer.* 12°0S 50°0W **93 F9**
Brasil, Planalto *Brazil* 18°0S 46°30W **90 E6**
Brasiléia *Brazil* 11°0S 68°45W **92 F5**
Brasília *Brazil* 15°47S 47°55W **93 G9**
Brasília Legal *Brazil* 3°49S 55°36W **93 D7**
Braslaw *Belarus* 55°38N 27°0E **9 J22**
Braşov *Romania* 45°38N 25°35E **17 F13**
Brasschaat *Belgium* 51°19N 4°27E **15 C4**
Brassey, Banjaran
  Malaysia 5°0N 117°15E **36 D5**
Brassey Ra. *Australia* 25°8S 122°15E **61 E3**
Brasstown Bald *U.S.A.* 34°53N 83°49W **85 D13**
Brastad *Sweden* 58°23N 11°30E **9 G14**
Bratislava *Slovak Rep.* 48°10N 17°7E **17 D9**
Bratsk *Russia* 56°10N 101°30E **29 D11**
Brattleboro *U.S.A.* 42°51N 72°34W **83 D12**
Braunau *Austria* 48°15N 13°3E **16 D7**
Braunschweig *Germany* 52°15N 10°31E **16 B6**
Braunton *U.K.* 51°7N 4°10W **13 F3**
Brava *C. Verde Is.* 15°0N 24°40W **50 b**
Bravo del Norte, Rio = Grande,
  Rio → *N. Amer.* 25°58N 97°9W **84 J6**
Brawley *U.S.A.* 32°59N 115°31W **79 N11**
Bray *Ireland* 53°13N 6°7W **10 C5**
Bray, Mt. *Australia* 14°0S 134°30E **62 A1**
Bray, Pays de *France* 49°46N 1°26E **20 B4**
Brazeau → *Canada* 52°55N 115°14W **70 C5**
Brazil *U.S.A.* 39°32N 87°8W **80 F10**
Brazil ■ *S. Amer.* 12°0S 50°0W **93 F9**
Brazilian Highlands = Brasil,
  Planalto *Brazil* 18°0S 46°30W **90 E6**
Brazo Sur → *S. Amer.* 25°21S 57°42W **94 B4**
Brazos → *U.S.A.* 28°53N 95°23W **84 G7**
Brazzaville *Congo* 4°9S 15°12E **52 E3**
Brčko *Bos.-H.* 44°54N 18°46E **23 B8**
Breaden, L. *Australia* 25°51S 125°28E **61 E4**
Breaksea Sd. *N.Z.* 45°35S 166°35E **59 F1**
Bream B. *N.Z.* 35°56S 174°28E **59 A5**
Bream Hd. *N.Z.* 35°51S 174°36E **59 A5**
Breas *Chile* 25°29S 70°24W **94 B1**
Brebes *Indonesia* 6°52S 109°3E **37 G13**
Brechin *Canada* 44°32N 79°10W **82 B5**
Brechin *U.K.* 56°44N 2°39W **11 E6**
Brecht *Belgium* 51°21N 4°38E **15 C4**
Breckenridge *Colo.,
  U.S.A.* 39°29N 106°3W **76 G10**
Breckenridge *Minn.,
  U.S.A.* 46°16N 96°35W **80 B5**
Breckenridge *Tex.,
  U.S.A.* 32°45N 98°54W **84 E5**
Breckland *U.K.* 52°30N 0°40E **13 E8**
Brecon *U.K.* 51°57N 3°23W **13 F4**
Brecon Beacons *U.K.* 51°53N 3°26W **13 F4**
Brecon Beacons △ *U.K.* 51°50N 3°30W **13 F4**
Breda *Neths.* 51°35N 4°45E **15 C4**
Bredasdorp *S. Africa* 34°33S 20°2E **56 E3**
Bree *Belgium* 51°8N 5°35E **15 C5**
Bregenz *Austria* 47°30N 9°45E **16 E5**
Breiðafjörður *Iceland* 65°15N 23°15W **8 D2**
Brejo *Brazil* 3°41S 42°47W **93 D10**
Bremen *Germany* 53°4N 8°47E **16 B5**

Bremer Bay *Australia* 34°21S 119°20E **61 F2**
Bremer I. *Australia* 12°5S 136°45E **62 A2**
Bremerhaven *Germany* 53°33N 8°36E **16 B5**
Bremerton *U.S.A.* 47°34N 122°37W **78 C4**
Brenham *U.S.A.* 30°10N 96°24W **84 F6**
Brennerpass *Austria* 47°2N 11°30E **16 E6**
Brent *U.S.A.* 32°56N 87°10W **85 E11**
Brentwood *U.K.* 51°37N 0°19E **13 F8**
Brentwood *Calif.,
  U.S.A.* 37°56N 121°42W **78 H5**
Brentwood *N.Y., U.S.A.* 40°47N 73°15W **83 F11**
Bréscia *Italy* 45°33N 10°15E **20 D9**
Breskens *Neths.* 51°23N 3°33E **15 C3**
Breslau = Wrocław *Poland* 51°5N 17°5E **17 C9**
Bressanone *Italy* 46°43N 11°39E **22 A4**
Bressay *U.K.* 60°9N 1°6W **11 A7**
Brest *Belarus* 52°10N 23°40E **17 B12**
Brest *France* 48°24N 4°31W **20 B1**
Brest-Litovsk = Brest
  Belarus 52°10N 23°40E **17 B12**
Bretagne □ *France* 48°10N 3°0W **20 B2**
Breton *Canada* 53°7N 114°28W **70 C6**
Breton Sd. *U.S.A.* 29°35N 89°15W **85 G10**
Brett, C. *N.Z.* 35°10S 174°20E **59 A5**
Brevard *U.S.A.* 35°14N 82°44W **85 D13**
Breves *Brazil* 1°40S 50°29W **93 D8**
Brewarrina *Australia* 30°0S 146°51E **63 E4**
Brewer *U.S.A.* 44°48N 68°46W **81 C19**
Brewer, Mt. *U.S.A.* 36°44N 118°28W **78 J8**
Brewster *N.Y., U.S.A.* 41°24N 73°36W **83 E11**
Brewster *Ohio, U.S.A.* 40°43N 81°36W **82 F3**
Brewster *Wash., U.S.A.* 48°6N 119°47W **76 B4**
Brewster, Kap = Kangikajik
  Greenland 70°7N 22°0W **4 B6**
Brewton *U.S.A.* 31°7N 87°4W **85 F11**
Breyten *S. Africa* 26°16S 30°0E **57 D5**
Bria *C.A.R.* 6°30N 21°58E **52 C4**
Briançon *France* 44°54N 6°39E **20 D7**
Bribie I. *Australia* 27°0S 153°10E **63 D5**
Bribri *Costa Rica* 9°38N 82°50W **88 E3**
Bridgefield *Barbados* 13°9N 59°36W **89 g**
Bridgehampton *U.S.A.* 40°56N 72°19W **83 F12**
Bridgend *U.K.* 51°30N 3°34W **13 F4**
Bridgend □ *U.K.* 51°36N 3°36W **13 F4**
Bridgenorth *Canada* 44°23N 78°23W **82 B6**
Bridgeport *Calif., U.S.A.* 38°15N 119°14W **78 G7**
Bridgeport *Conn.,
  U.S.A.* 41°11N 73°12W **83 E11**
Bridgeport *N.Y., U.S.A.* 43°10N 76°9W **83 C8**
Bridgeport *Nebr., U.S.A.* 41°40N 103°6W **80 E2**
Bridgeport *Tex., U.S.A.* 33°13N 97°45W **84 E6**
Bridger *U.S.A.* 45°18N 108°55W **76 D9**
Bridgeton *U.S.A.* 39°26N 75°14W **81 F16**
Bridgetown *Australia* 33°58S 116°7E **61 F2**
Bridgetown *Barbados* 13°6N 59°37W **89 g**
Bridgetown *Canada* 44°55N 65°18W **73 D6**
Bridgewater *Australia* 42°44S 147°14E **63 G4**
Bridgewater *Canada* 44°25N 64°31W **73 D7**
Bridgewater *Mass.,
  U.S.A.* 41°59N 70°58W **83 E14**
Bridgewater *N.Y.,
  U.S.A.* 42°53N 75°15W **83 D9**
Bridgewater, C.
  Australia 38°23S 141°23E **63 F3**
Bridgnorth *U.K.* 52°32N 2°25W **13 E5**
Bridgton *U.S.A.* 44°3N 70°42W **83 B14**
Bridgwater *U.K.* 51°8N 2°59W **13 F5**
Bridgwater B. *U.K.* 51°15N 3°15W **13 F4**
Bridlington *U.K.* 54°5N 0°12W **12 C7**
Bridlington B. *U.K.* 54°4N 0°10W **12 C7**
Bridport *Australia* 40°59S 147°23E **63 G4**
Bridport *U.K.* 50°44N 2°45W **13 G5**
Brig *Switz.* 46°18N 7°59E **20 C7**
Brigg *U.K.* 53°34N 0°28W **12 D7**
Brigham City *U.S.A.* 41°31N 112°1W **76 F7**
Bright *Australia* 36°42S 146°56E **63 F4**
Brighton *Australia* 35°5S 138°30E **63 F2**
Brighton *Canada* 44°2N 77°44W **82 B7**
Brighton *Trin. & Tob.* 10°13N 61°39W **93 K15**
Brighton *U.K.* 50°49N 0°7W **13 G7**
Brighton *U.S.A.* 43°8N 77°34W **82 C7**
Brightside *Canada* 45°7N 76°29W **83 A8**
Brilliant *U.S.A.* 40°15N 80°39W **82 F4**
Bríndisi *Italy* 40°39N 17°55E **23 D7**
Brinkley *U.S.A.* 34°53N 91°12W **84 D9**
Brinnon *U.S.A.* 47°41N 122°54W **78 C4**
Brion, Î. *Canada* 47°46N 61°26W **73 C7**
Brisay *Canada* 54°20N 70°31W **73 B5**
Brisbane *Australia* 27°25S 153°2E **63 D5**
Brisbane → *Australia* 27°24S 153°9E **63 D5**
Bristol *U.K.* 51°26N 2°35W **13 F5**
Bristol *Conn., U.S.A.* 41°40N 72°57W **83 E12**
Bristol *Pa., U.S.A.* 40°6N 74°51W **83 F10**
Bristol *R.I., U.S.A.* 41°40N 71°16W **83 E13**
Bristol *Tenn., U.S.A.* 36°36N 82°11W **85 C13**
Bristol *Vt., U.S.A.* 44°8N 73°4W **83 B11**
Bristol, City of □ *U.K.* 51°27N 2°36W **13 F5**
Bristol B. *U.S.A.* 58°0N 160°0W **74 a**
Bristol Channel *U.K.* 51°18N 4°30W **13 F3**
Bristol I. *Antarctica* 58°45S 28°0W **5 B1**
Bristol L. *U.S.A.* 34°28N 115°41W **77 J6**
Bristow *U.S.A.* 35°50N 96°23W **84 D6**
Britain = Great Britain
  Europe 54°0N 2°15W **6 E5**
British Columbia □
  Canada 55°0N 125°15W **70 C3**
British Indian Ocean Terr. =
  Chagos Arch. ☑ *Ind. Oc.* 6°0S 72°0E **26 J9**
British Isles *Europe* 54°0N 4°0W **14 D5**
British Virgin Is. ☑
  W. Indies 18°30N 64°30W **89 e**
Brits *S. Africa* 25°37S 27°48E **57 D4**
Britstown *S. Africa* 30°37S 23°30E **56 E3**
Britt *Canada* 45°46N 80°34W **72 C3**
Brittany = Bretagne □
  France 48°10N 3°0W **20 B2**
Britton *U.S.A.* 45°48N 97°45W **80 C5**

Brive-la-Gaillarde France 45°10N 1°32E 20 D4
Brixen = Bressanone
  Italy 46°43N 11°39E 22 A4
Brixham U.K. 50°23N 3°31W 13 G4
Brno Czech Rep. 49°10N 16°35E 17 D9
Broach = Bharuch India 21°47N 73°0E 40 J8
Broad → U.S.A. 34°1N 81°4W 85 D14
Broad Arrow Australia 30°23S 121°15E 61 F3
Broad B. U.K. 58°14N 6°18W 11 C2
Broad Haven Ireland 54°20N 9°55W 10 B2
Broad Law U.K. 55°30N 3°21W 11 F5
Broad Pk. = Faichan Kangri
  India 35°48N 76°34E 43 B7
Broad Sd. Australia 22°0S 149°45E 62 C4
Broadalbin U.S.A. 43°4N 74°12W 83 C10
Broadback → Canada 51°21N 78°52W 72 B4
Broadhurst Ra.
  Australia 22°30S 122°30E 60 D3
Broads, The U.K. 52°45N 1°30E 12 E9
Broadus U.S.A. 45°27N 105°25W 76 D11
Brochet, L. Canada 58°36N 101°35W 71 B8
Brock I. Canada 77°52N 114°19W 69 B8
Brocken Germany 51°47N 10°37E 16 C6
Brockport U.S.A. 43°13N 77°56W 82 C7
Brockton U.S.A. 42°5N 71°1W 83 D13
Brockville Canada 44°35N 75°41W 83 B9
Brockway Mont.,
  U.S.A. 47°18N 105°45W 76 C11
Brockway Pa., U.S.A. 41°15N 78°47W 82 E6
Brocton U.S.A. 42°23N 79°26W 82 D5
Brodeur Pen. Canada 72°30N 88°10W 69 B11
Brodick U.K. 55°35N 5°9W 11 F3
Brodnica Poland 53°15N 19°25E 17 B10
Brody Ukraine 50°5N 25°10E 17 C13
Brogan U.S.A. 44°15N 117°31W 76 D5
Broken Arrow U.S.A. 36°3N 95°48W 84 C7
Broken Bow Nebr.,
  U.S.A. 41°24N 99°38W 80 E4
Broken Bow Okla., U.S.A. 34°2N 94°44W 84 D7
Broken Bow Lake U.S.A. 34°9N 94°40W 84 D7
Broken Hill Australia 31°58S 141°29E 63 E3
Broken Ridge Ind. Oc. 30°0S 94°0E 64 L1
Broken River Ra.
  Australia 21°0S 148°22E 62 K6
Bromley □ U.K. 51°24N 0°2E 13 F8
Bromo Indonesia 7°55S 112°55E 37 G15
Bromsgrove U.K. 52°21N 2°2W 13 E5
Brønderslev Denmark 57°16N 9°57E 9 H13
Bronkhorstspruit
  S. Africa 25°46S 28°45E 57 D4
Brønnøysund Norway 65°28N 12°14E 8 D15
Brook Park U.S.A. 41°23N 81°48W 82 E4
Brookhaven U.S.A. 31°35N 90°26W 85 F9
Brookings Oreg., U.S.A. 42°3N 124°17W 76 E1
Brookings S. Dak.,
  U.S.A. 44°19N 96°48W 80 C5
Brooklin Canada 43°55N 78°55W 82 C6
Brooklyn Park U.S.A. 45°6N 93°23W 80 C7
Brooks Canada 50°35N 111°55W 70 C6
Brooks Range U.S.A. 68°0N 152°0W 74 a
Brooksville U.S.A. 28°33N 82°23W 85 G13
Brookton Australia 32°22S 117°0E 61 F2
Brookville U.S.A. 41°10N 79°5W 82 E5
Broom, L. U.K. 57°55N 5°15W 11 D3
Broome Australia 18°0S 122°15E 60 C3
Brora U.K. 58°0N 3°52W 11 C5
Brora → U.K. 58°0N 3°51W 11 C5
Brosna → Ireland 53°14N 7°58W 10 C4
Brothers U.S.A. 43°49N 120°36W 76 E3
Brough U.K. 54°32N 2°18W 12 C5
Brough Hd. U.K. 59°8N 3°20W 11 B5
Broughton Island = Qikiqtarjuaq
  Canada 67°33N 63°0W 69 C13
Brown, L. Australia 31°5S 118°15E 61 F2
Brown, Pt. Australia 32°32S 133°50E 63 E1
Brown City U.S.A. 43°13N 82°59W 82 C2
Brown Willy U.K. 50°35N 4°37W 13 G3
Brownfield U.S.A. 33°11N 102°17W 84 E3
Browning U.S.A. 48°34N 113°1W 76 B7
Brownsville Oreg.,
  U.S.A. 44°24N 122°59W 76 D2
Brownsville Pa., U.S.A. 40°1N 79°53W 82 F5
Brownsville Tenn.,
  U.S.A. 35°36N 89°16W 85 D10
Brownsville Tex., U.S.A. 25°54N 97°30W 84 J6
Brownville U.S.A. 44°0N 75°59W 83 C9
Brownwood U.S.A. 31°43N 98°59W 84 F5
Browse I. Australia 14°7S 123°33E 60 B3
Bruas Malaysia 4°30N 100°47E 39 K3
Bruay-la-Buissière France 50°29N 2°33E 20 A5
Bruce, Mt. Australia 22°37S 118°8E 60 D2
Bruce Pen. Canada 45°0N 81°30W 82 B3
Bruce Peninsula △
  Canada 45°14N 81°36W 82 A3
Bruce Rock Australia 31°52S 118°8E 61 F2
Bruck an der Leitha
  Austria 48°1N 16°47E 17 D9
Bruck an der Mur
  Austria 47°24N 15°16E 16 E8
Brue → U.K. 51°13N 2°59W 13 F5
Bruges = Brugge Belgium 51°13N 3°13E 15 C3
Brugge Belgium 51°13N 3°13E 15 C3
Bruin U.S.A. 41°3N 79°43W 82 E5
Brûk, W. al → Egypt 30°15N 33°50E 46 E2
Brûlé Canada 53°15N 117°58W 70 C5
Brûlé, L. Canada 53°35N 64°4W 73 B7
Brumado Brazil 14°14S 41°40W 93 F10
Brumunddal Norway 60°53N 10°56E 8 F14
Bruneau U.S.A. 42°53N 115°48W 76 E6
Bruneau → U.S.A. 42°56N 115°57W 76 E6
Brunei = Bandar Seri Begawan
  Brunei 4°52N 115°0E 36 D5
Brunei ■ Asia 4°50N 115°0E 36 D5
Brunner, L. N.Z. 42°37S 171°27E 59 E3
Brunssum Neths. 50°57N 5°59E 15 D5
Brunswick = Braunschweig
  Germany 52°15N 10°31E 16 B6

Brunswick Ga., U.S.A. 31°10N 81°30W 85 F14
Brunswick Maine,
  U.S.A. 43°55N 69°58W 81 D19
Brunswick Md., U.S.A. 39°19N 77°38W 81 F15
Brunswick Mo., U.S.A. 39°26N 93°8W 80 F7
Brunswick Ohio, U.S.A. 41°14N 81°51W 82 E3
Brunswick, Pen. de
  Chile 53°30S 71°30W 96 G2
Brunswick B. Australia 15°15S 124°50E 60 C3
Brunswick Junction
  Australia 33°15S 115°50E 61 F2
Brunt Ice Shelf Antarctica 75°30S 25°0W 5 D2
Brus Laguna Honduras 15°47N 84°35W 88 C3
Brush U.S.A. 40°15N 103°37W 76 F12
Brushton U.S.A. 44°50N 74°31W 83 B10
Brusque Brazil 27°5S 49°0W 95 B6
Brussel Belgium 50°51N 4°21E 15 D4
Brussel ✈ (BRU) Belgium 50°54N 4°29E 15 D5
Brussels = Brussel
  Belgium 50°51N 4°21E 15 D4
Brussels Canada 43°44N 81°15W 82 C3
Bruthen Australia 37°42S 147°50E 63 F4
Bruxelles = Brussel
  Belgium 50°51N 4°21E 15 D4
Bryan Ohio, U.S.A. 41°28N 84°33W 81 E11
Bryan Tex., U.S.A. 30°40N 96°22W 84 F6
Bryan, Mt. Australia 33°30S 139°5E 63 E2
Bryansk Russia 53°13N 34°25E 18 D4
Bryce Canyon △
  U.S.A. 37°30N 112°10W 77 H7
Bryne Norway 58°44N 5°38E 9 G11
Bryson City U.S.A. 35°26N 83°27W 85 D13
Bsharri Lebanon 34°15N 36°0E 46 A5
Bū Baqarah U.A.E. 25°35N 56°25E 45 E8
Bu Craa W. Sahara 26°45N 12°50W 50 C3
Bū Ḩasā U.A.E. 23°30N 53°20E 45 F7
Bua Fiji 16°48S 178°37E 59 a
Bua Yai Thailand 15°33N 102°26E 38 E4
Buan S. Korea 35°44N 126°44E 35 G14
Buapinang Indonesia 4°40S 121°30E 37 E6
Buanza Burundi 3°6S 29°23E 54 C2
Bubi → Zimbabwe 22°20S 31°7E 55 G3
Būbīyān Kuwait 29°45N 48°15E 45 D6
Buca Fiji 16°38S 179°52E 59 a
Bucaramanga Colombia 7°0N 73°0W 92 B4
Bucasia Australia 21°2S 149°10E 62 K7
Buccaneer Arch.
  Australia 16°7S 123°20E 60 C3
Buccoo Reef
  Trin. & Tob. 11°10N 60°51W 93 J16
Buchach Ukraine 49°5N 25°25E 17 D13
Buchan U.K. 57°32N 2°21W 11 D6
Buchan Ness U.K. 57°29N 1°46W 11 D7
Buchanan Canada 51°40N 102°45W 71 C8
Buchanan Liberia 5°57N 10°2W 50 G3
Buchanan, L. Queens.,
  Australia 21°35S 145°52E 62 C4
Buchanan, L. W. Austral.,
  Australia 25°33S 123°2E 61 E3
Buchanan, L. U.S.A. 30°45N 98°25W 84 F5
Buchanan Cr. →
  Australia 19°13S 136°33E 62 B2
Buchans Canada 48°50N 56°52W 73 C8
Bucharest = București
  Romania 44°27N 26°10E 17 F14
Bucheon S. Korea 37°28N 126°45E 35 F14
Buchon, Pt. U.S.A. 35°15N 120°54W 78 K6
Buck Hill Falls U.S.A. 41°11N 75°16W 83 E9
Buckeye Lake U.S.A. 39°55N 82°29W 82 G2
Buckhannon U.S.A. 39°0N 80°8W 81 F13
Buckhaven U.K. 56°11N 3°3W 11 E5
Buckhorn L. Canada 44°29N 78°23W 82 B6
Buckie U.K. 57°41N 2°58W 11 D6
Buckingham Canada 45°37N 75°24W 72 C4
Buckingham U.K. 51°59N 0°57W 13 F7
Buckingham B.
  Australia 12°10S 135°40E 62 A2
Buckinghamshire □
  U.K. 51°53N 0°55W 13 F7
Buckle Hd. Australia 14°26S 127°52E 60 B4
Buckleboo Australia 32°54S 136°12E 63 E2
Buckley U.K. 53°10N 3°5W 12 D4
Buckley → Australia 20°10S 138°49E 62 C2
Bucklin U.S.A. 37°33N 99°38W 80 G4
Bucks L. U.S.A. 39°54N 121°12W 78 F5
București Romania 44°27N 26°10E 17 F14
Bucyrus U.S.A. 40°48N 82°59W 81 E12
Budalin Burma 22°20N 95°10E 41 H19
Budapest Hungary 47°29N 19°3E 17 E10
Budaun India 28°5N 79°10E 43 E8
Budd Coast Antarctica 68°0S 112°0E 5 C8
Bude U.K. 50°49N 4°34W 13 G3
Budennovsk Russia 44°50N 44°10E 19 F7
Budge Budge = Baj Baj
  India 22°30N 88°5E 43 H13
Budgewoi Australia 33°13S 151°34E 63 E5
Budjala
  Dem. Rep. of the Congo 2°50N 19°40E 52 D3
Buellton U.S.A. 34°37N 120°12W 79 L6
Buena Esperanza
  Argentina 34°45S 65°15W 94 C2
Buena Park U.S.A. 33°52N 117°59W 79 M9
Buena Vista Colo.,
  U.S.A. 38°51N 106°8W 76 G10
Buena Vista Va., U.S.A. 37°44N 79°21W 81 G14
Buena Vista Lake Bed
  U.S.A. 35°12N 119°18W 79 K7
Buenaventura Colombia 3°53N 77°4W 92 C3
Buenaventura Mexico 29°51N 107°29W 86 B3
Buenos Aires Argentina 34°36S 58°22W 94 C4
Buenos Aires Costa Rica 9°10N 83°20W 88 E3
Buenos Aires □ Argentina 36°30S 60°0W 94 D4
Buenos Aires, L.
  Argentina 46°35S 72°30W 96 F2
Buffalo Mo., U.S.A. 37°39N 93°6W 80 G7
Buffalo N.Y., U.S.A. 42°53N 78°53W 82 D6
Buffalo Okla., U.S.A. 36°50N 99°38W 84 C5

Buffalo S. Dak., U.S.A. 45°35N 103°33W 80 C2
Buffalo Wyo., U.S.A. 44°21N 106°42W 76 D10
Buffalo → Canada 60°5N 115°5W 70 A5
Buffalo → S. Africa 28°43S 30°37E 57 D5
Buffalo △ Canada 36°14N 92°36W 84 C8
Buffalo Head Hills
  Canada 57°25N 115°55W 70 B5
Buffalo L. Alta., Canada 52°27N 112°54W 70 C6
Buffalo L. N.W.T.,
  Canada 60°12N 115°25W 70 A5
Buffalo Narrows
  Canada 55°51N 108°29W 71 B7
Buffalo Springs △ Kenya 0°32N 37°35E 54 B4
Buffels → S. Africa 29°36S 17°3E 56 D2
Buford U.S.A. 34°10N 84°0W 85 D12
Bug → Poland 52°31N 21°5E 17 B11
Bug → Buh → Ukraine 46°59N 31°58E 19 E5
Buga Colombia 4°0N 76°15W 92 C3
Bugala I. Uganda 0°40S 32°20E 54 C3
Buganda Uganda 0°0 31°30E 54 C3
Buganga Uganda 0°3S 32°0E 54 C3
Bugel, Tanjung Indonesia 6°26S 111°3E 37 G14
Bugibba Malta 35°57N 14°25E 25 D1
Bugsuk I. Phil. 8°12N 117°18E 36 C5
Bugulma Russia 54°33N 52°48E 18 D9
Bugungu Uganda 2°17N 31°50E 54 B3
Buguruslan Russia 53°39N 52°26E 18 D9
Buh → Ukraine 46°59N 31°58E 19 E5
Buhera Zimbabwe 19°18S 31°29E 57 B5
Buhl U.S.A. 42°36N 114°46W 76 E6
Builth Wells U.K. 52°9N 3°25W 13 E4
Buir Nur Mongolia 47°50N 117°42E 33 B6
Buji China 22°37N 114°5E 33 F11
Bujumbura Burundi 3°16S 29°18E 54 C2
Bukachacha Russia 52°55N 116°50E 29 D12
Bukama
  Dem. Rep. of the Congo 9°10S 25°50E 55 D2
Bukavu
  Dem. Rep. of the Congo 2°20S 28°52E 54 C2
Bukene Tanzania 4°15S 32°48E 54 C3
Bukhara = Buxoro
  Uzbekistan 39°48N 64°25E 28 F7
Bukhoro = Buxoro
  Uzbekistan 39°48N 64°25E 28 F7
Bukima Tanzania 1°50S 33°25E 54 C3
Bukit Badung Indonesia 8°49S 115°10E 37 K18
Bukit Kerajaan Malaysia 5°25N 100°15E 39 c
Bukit Mertajam Malaysia 5°22N 100°28E 39 c
Bukit Ni Malaysia 1°22N 104°12E 39 d
Bukit Panjang Singapore 1°23N 103°46E 39 d
Bukit Tengah Malaysia 5°22N 100°25E 39 c
Bukittinggi Indonesia 0°20S 100°20E 36 E2
Bukoba Tanzania 1°20S 31°49E 54 C3
Bukum, Pulau Singapore 1°14N 103°46E 39 d
Bukuya Uganda 0°40N 31°52E 54 B3
Būl, Kuh-e Iran 30°48S 52°45E 45 D7
Bula Indonesia 3°6S 130°30E 37 E8
Bulahdelah Australia 32°23S 152°13E 63 E5
Bulan Phil. 12°40N 123°52E 37 B6
Bulandshahr India 28°28N 77°51E 42 E7
Bulawayo Zimbabwe 20°7S 28°32E 55 G2
Buldan Turkey 38°2N 28°50E 23 E13
Bulgan Mongolia 48°45N 103°34E 32 B5
Bulgar Russia 54°57N 49°4E 18 D8
Bulgaria ■ Europe 42°35N 25°30E 23 C11
Buli, Teluk Indonesia 0°48N 128°25E 37 D7
Buliluyan, C. Phil. 8°20N 117°15E 36 C5
Bulim Singapore 1°22N 103°43E 39 d
Bulkley → Canada 55°15N 127°40W 70 B3
Bull Shoals L. U.S.A. 36°22N 92°35W 84 C8
Bulleringa △ Australia 17°39S 143°56E 62 B3
Bullhead City U.S.A. 35°8N 114°32W 79 K12
Büllingen Belgium 50°25N 6°16E 15 D6
Bullock Creek Australia 17°43S 144°31E 62 B3
Bulloo → Australia 28°43S 142°30E 63 D3
Bulloo L. Australia 28°43S 142°25E 63 D3
Bulls N.Z. 40°10S 175°24E 59 D5
Bulman Australia 13°39S 134°20E 62 A1
Bulnes Chile 36°42S 72°19W 94 D1
Bulsar = Valsad India 20°40N 72°58E 40 J8
Bultfontein S. Africa 28°18S 26°10E 56 D4
Bulukumba Indonesia 5°33S 120°11E 37 F6
Bulun Russia 70°37N 127°30E 29 B13
Bumba
  Dem. Rep. of the Congo 2°13N 22°30E 52 D4
Bumbah, Khalīj Libya 32°20N 23°15E 51 B10
Bumbiri I. Tanzania 1°40S 31°55E 54 C3
Bumhpa Bum Burma 26°51N 97°14E 41 F20
Bumi → Zimbabwe 17°0S 28°20E 55 F2
Buna Kenya 2°58N 39°30E 54 B4
Bunaken Indonesia 1°37N 124°46E 37 D6
Bunazi Tanzania 1°3S 31°23E 54 C3
Bunbury Australia 33°20S 115°35E 61 F2
Bunclody Ireland 52°39N 6°40W 10 D5
Buncrana Ireland 55°8N 7°27W 10 A4
Bundaberg Australia 24°54S 152°22E 63 C5
Bundey → Australia 21°46S 135°37E 62 C2
Bundjalung △ Australia 29°16S 153°21E 63 D5
Bundoran Ireland 54°28N 8°16W 10 B3
Bung Kan Thailand 18°23N 103°37E 38 C4
Bungay U.K. 52°27N 1°28E 13 E9
Bungil Cr. → Australia 27°5S 149°5E 63 D4
Bungle Bungle = Purnululu △
  Australia 17°20S 128°20E 60 C4
Bungo-Suidō Japan 33°0N 132°15E 31 H6
Bungoma Kenya 0°34N 34°34E 54 B3
Bungotakada Japan 33°35N 131°25E 31 H5
Bunia
  Dem. Rep. of the Congo 1°35S 30°20E 54 C3
Bunji Pakistan 35°45N 74°40E 43 B6
Bunkie U.S.A. 30°57N 92°11W 84 F8
Bunnell U.S.A. 29°28N 81°16W 85 G14
Buntok Indonesia 1°40S 114°58E 36 E4
Bunya Mts. △ Australia 26°51S 151°34E 63 D5

Bunyola Spain 39°41N 2°42E 24 B9
Bunyu Indonesia 3°35N 117°50E 36 D5
Buol Indonesia 1°15N 121°32E 37 D6
Buon Brieng Vietnam 13°9N 108°12E 38 F7
Buon Ma Thuot Vietnam 12°40N 108°3E 38 F7
Buong Long Cambodia 13°44N 106°59E 38 F6
Buorkhaya, Mys
  Russia 71°50N 132°40E 29 B14
Buqayq Si. Arabia 26°0N 49°45E 45 E6
Bur Acaba = Buurhakaba
  Somali Rep. 3°12N 44°20E 47 G3
Bûr Safâga Egypt 26°43N 33°57E 44 E2
Bûr Sa'îd Egypt 31°16N 32°18E 51 B12
Bûr Sûdân Sudan 19°32N 37°9E 51 E13
Bura Kenya 1°4S 39°58E 54 C4
Burakin Australia 30°31S 117°10E 61 F2
Burao = Burco Somali Rep. 9°32N 45°32E 47 F4
Burāq Syria 33°11N 36°29E 46 B5
Buraydah Si. Arabia 26°20N 43°59E 44 E4
Burbank U.S.A. 34°12N 118°18W 79 L8
Burco Somali Rep. 9°32N 45°32E 47 F4
Burda India 25°50N 77°35E 42 G6
Burdekin → Australia 19°38S 147°25E 62 B4
Burdur Turkey 37°45N 30°17E 19 G5
Burdwan = Barddhaman
  India 23°14N 87°39E 43 H12
Bure Ethiopia 10°40N 37°4E 47 E2
Bure → U.K. 52°38N 1°43E 12 E9
Bureya → Russia 49°27N 129°30E 29 E13
Burford Canada 43°7N 80°27W 82 C4
Burgas Bulgaria 42°33N 27°29E 23 C12
Burgeo Canada 47°37N 57°38W 73 C8
Burgersdorp S. Africa 31°0S 26°20E 56 E4
Burgess, Mt. Canada 30°50S 121°5E 61 F3
Burghead U.K. 57°43N 3°30W 11 D5
Burgos Spain 42°21N 3°41E 24 A4
Burgsvik Sweden 57°3N 18°19E 9 H18
Burgundy = Bourgogne □
  France 47°0N 4°50E 20 C6
Burhaniye Turkey 39°30N 26°58E 23 E12
Burhanpur India 21°18N 76°14E 40 J10
Burhi Gandak → India 25°20N 86°37E 43 G12
Burhner → India 22°43N 80°31E 43 H9
Burias I. Phil. 12°55N 123°5E 37 B6
Burica, Pta. Costa Rica 8°3N 82°51W 88 E3
Burien U.S.A. 47°28N 122°20W 78 C4
Burigi, L. Tanzania 2°2S 31°22E 54 C3
Burigi △ Tanzania 2°20S 31°6E 54 C3
Burin Canada 47°1N 55°14W 73 C8
Buriram Thailand 15°0N 103°0E 38 E4
Burkburnett U.S.A. 34°6N 98°34W 84 D5
Burke → Australia 23°12S 139°33E 62 C2
Burke Chan. Canada 52°10N 127°30W 70 C3
Burketown Australia 17°45S 139°33E 62 B2
Burkina Faso ■ Africa 12°0N 1°0W 50 F5
Burk's Falls Canada 45°37N 79°24W 72 C4
Burleigh Falls Canada 44°33N 78°12W 82 B6
Burley U.S.A. 42°32N 113°48W 76 E7
Burlingame U.S.A. 37°35N 122°21W 78 H4
Burlington Canada 43°18N 79°45E 82 C5
Burlington Colo.,
  U.S.A. 39°18N 102°16W 76 G12
Burlington Iowa, U.S.A. 40°49N 91°14W 80 E8
Burlington Kans., U.S.A. 38°12N 95°45W 80 F6
Burlington N.C., U.S.A. 36°6N 79°26W 85 C15
Burlington N.J., U.S.A. 40°4N 74°51W 83 F10
Burlington Vt., U.S.A. 44°29N 73°12W 83 B11
Burlington Wash.,
  U.S.A. 48°28N 122°20W 78 B4
Burlington Wis., U.S.A. 42°41N 88°17W 80 D9
Burma ■ Asia 21°0N 96°30E 41 J20
Burnaby I. Canada 52°25N 131°19W 70 C2
Burnet U.S.A. 30°45N 98°14W 84 F5
Burney U.S.A. 40°53N 121°40W 76 F3
Burnham U.S.A. 40°38N 77°34W 82 F7
Burnham-on-Sea U.K. 51°14N 3°0W 13 F5
Burnie Australia 41°4S 145°56E 63 G4
Burnley U.K. 53°47N 2°14W 12 D5
Burns U.S.A. 43°35N 119°3W 76 E4
Burns Junction U.S.A. 42°47N 117°51W 76 E5
Burns Lake Canada 54°14N 125°45W 70 C3
Burnside → Canada 66°51N 108°4W 68 C9
Burnside, L. Australia 25°22S 123°0E 61 E3
Burnsville U.S.A. 44°47N 93°17W 80 C7
Burnt River Canada 44°41N 78°42W 82 B6
Burntwood → Canada 56°8N 96°34W 71 B9
Burntwood L. Canada 55°22N 100°26W 71 B8
Burqān Kuwait 29°0N 47°57E 44 D5
Burqin China 47°43N 87°0E 32 B3
Burra Australia 33°40S 138°55E 63 E2
Burray U.K. 58°51N 2°54W 11 C6
Burren Ireland 53°9N 9°5W 10 C2
Burren △ Ireland 53°1N 8°58W 10 C3
Burren Junction
  Australia 30°7S 148°58E 63 E4
Burrinjuck Res. Australia 35°0S 148°36E 63 F4
Burro, Serranías del
  Mexico 28°56N 102°5W 86 B4
Burrow Hd. U.K. 54°41N 4°24W 11 G4
Burruyacú Argentina 26°30S 64°40W 94 B3
Burry Port U.K. 51°41N 4°15W 13 F3
Bursa Turkey 40°15N 29°5E 23 D13
Burstall Canada 50°39N 109°54W 71 C7
Burton Ohio, U.S.A. 41°28N 81°8W 82 E3
Burton, S.C., U.S.A. 32°26N 80°43W 85 E14
Burton, L. Canada 54°45N 78°20W 72 B4
Burton upon Trent U.K. 52°48N 1°38W 12 E6
Burtundy Australia 33°45N 142°15E 63 E3
Buru Indonesia 3°30S 126°30E 37 E7
Burûn, Râs Egypt 31°14N 33°7E 46 D2
Burundi ■ Africa 3°15S 30°0E 54 C3
Bururi Burundi 3°57S 29°37E 54 C2
Burutu Nigeria 5°20N 5°29E 50 G7
Burwell U.S.A. 41°47N 99°8W 80 E4
Burwick U.K. 58°45N 2°58W 11 C5
Bury U.K. 53°35N 2°17W 12 D5

Bury St. Edmunds U.K. 52°15N 0°43E 13 E8
Buryatia □ Russia 53°0N 110°0E 29 D11
Busan S. Korea 35°5N 129°0E 35 G15
Busango Swamp Zambia 14°15S 25°45E 55 E2
Buşayrah Syria 35°9N 40°26E 44 C4
Büshehr Iran 28°55N 50°55E 45 D6
Büshehr □ Iran 28°20N 51°45E 45 D6
Bushenyi Uganda 0°35S 30°10E 54 C3
Bushire = Büshehr Iran 28°55N 50°55E 45 D6
Businga
  Dem. Rep. of the Congo 3°16N 20°59E 52 D4
Buşra ash Shām Syria 32°30N 36°25E 46 C5
Busselton Australia 33°42S 115°15E 61 F2
Bussum Neths. 52°16N 5°10E 15 B5
Busto Arsízio Italy 45°37N 8°51E 20 D8
Busu Djanoa
  Dem. Rep. of the Congo 1°43N 21°23E 52 D4
Busuanga I. Phil. 12°10N 120°0E 37 B6
Busungbiu Indonesia 8°16S 114°58E 37 J17
Buta Dem. Rep. of the Congo 2°50N 24°53E 54 B1
Butare Rwanda 2°31S 29°52E 54 C2
Butaritari Kiribati 3°30N 174°0E 64 G9
Bute U.K. 55°48N 5°2W 11 F3
Bute Inlet Canada 50°40N 124°53W 70 C4
Butemba Uganda 1°9N 31°37E 54 B3
Butembo
  Dem. Rep. of the Congo 0°9N 29°18E 54 B2
Butere Kenya 0°13N 34°30E 54 B3
Butha Qi China 48°0N 122°32E 33 B7
Butiaba Uganda 1°50N 31°20E 54 B3
Butler Mo., U.S.A. 38°16N 94°20W 80 F6
Butler Pa., U.S.A. 40°52N 79°54W 82 F5
Buton Indonesia 5°0S 122°45E 37 E6
Butte Mont., U.S.A. 46°0N 112°32W 76 C7
Butte Nebr., U.S.A. 42°58N 98°51W 80 D4
Butte Creek → U.S.A. 39°12N 121°56W 78 F5
Butterworth = Gcuwa
  S. Africa 32°20S 28°11E 57 E4
Butterworth Malaysia 5°24N 100°23E 39 c
Buttevant Ireland 52°14N 8°40W 10 D3
Buttfield, Mt. Australia 24°45S 128°9E 61 E4
Button B. Canada 58°45N 94°23W 71 B10
Buttonwillow U.S.A. 35°24N 119°28W 79 K7
Butty Hd. Australia 33°54S 121°39E 61 F3
Butuan Phil. 8°57N 125°33E 37 C7
Butung = Buton Indonesia 5°0S 122°45E 37 E6
Buturlinovka Russia 50°50N 40°35E 19 D7
Buxa Duar India 27°45N 89°35E 43 F13
Buxar India 25°34N 83°58E 43 G10
Buxoro Uzbekistan 39°48N 64°25E 28 F7
Buxtehude Germany 53°28N 9°39E 16 B5
Buxton U.K. 53°16N 1°54W 12 D6
Buy Russia 58°28N 41°28E 18 C7
Buyant-Uhaa Mongolia 44°55N 110°11E 33 B6
Buyo, L. de Ivory C. 6°16N 7°10W 50 G4
Büyük Menderes →
  Turkey 37°28N 27°11E 23 F12
Büyükçekmece Turkey 41°2N 28°35E 23 D13
Buzău Romania 45°10N 26°50E 17 F14
Buzău → Romania 45°26N 27°44E 17 F14
Buzen Japan 33°35N 131°5E 31 H5
Buzi → Mozam. 19°50S 34°43E 55 F3
Büzmeýin Turkmenistan 38°3N 58°12E 45 B8
Buzuluk Russia 52°48N 52°12E 18 D9
Buzzards Bay U.S.A. 41°45N 70°37W 83 E14
Bwana Mkubwe
  Dem. Rep. of the Congo 13°8S 28°38E 55 E2
Bwindi △ Uganda 1°2S 29°42E 54 C2
Byarezina → Belarus 52°33N 30°14E 17 B16
Bydgoszcz Poland 53°10N 18°0E 17 B9
Byelorussia = Belarus ■
  Europe 53°30N 27°0E 17 B14
Byers U.S.A. 39°43N 104°14W 76 B11
Byesville U.S.A. 39°58N 81°32W 82 G3
Byfield △ Australia 22°52S 150°45E 62 C5
Byfleet □ U.K. 22°52S 150°45E 62 C5
Bykhaw Belarus 53°31N 30°14E 17 B16
Bykhov = Bykhaw
  Belarus 53°31N 30°14E 17 B16
Bylas U.S.A. 33°8N 110°7W 77 K8
Bylot Canada 58°25N 94°8W 71 B10
Bylot I. Canada 73°13N 78°34W 69 B12
Byrd, C. Antarctica 69°38S 76°7W 5 C17
Byrock Australia 30°40S 146°27E 63 E4
Byron, C. Australia 28°43S 153°38E 63 D5
Byron Bay Australia 28°43S 153°37E 63 D5
Byrranga, Gory Russia 75°0N 100°0E 29 B11
Byrranga Mts. = Byrranga, Gory
  Russia 75°0N 100°0E 29 B11
Byske Sweden 64°57N 21°11E 8 D19
Byskeälven → Sweden 64°57N 21°13E 8 D19
Bytom Poland 50°25N 18°54E 17 C10
Bytów Poland 54°10N 17°30E 17 A9
Byumba Rwanda 1°35S 30°4E 54 C3

C

C.W. McConaughy, L.
  U.S.A. 41°14N 101°40W 80 E3
Ca → Vietnam 18°45N 105°45E 38 C5
Ca Mau Vietnam 9°7N 105°8E 39 H5
Ca Mau, Mui Vietnam 8°38N 104°44E 39 H5
Ca Na Vietnam 11°20N 108°54E 39 G7
Caaguazú Paraguay 25°23S 57°5W 94 B4
Caála Angola 12°46S 15°30E 53 G3
Caamaño Sd. Canada 52°55N 129°25W 70 C3
Caazapá Paraguay 26°8S 56°19W 94 B4
Caazapá □ Paraguay 26°10S 56°0W 94 B4
Caballeria, C. de Spain 40°5N 4°5E 24 A11
Cabanatuan Phil. 15°30N 120°58E 37 A6
Cabano Canada 47°40N 68°56W 73 C6
Cabazon U.S.A. 33°55N 116°47W 79 M10
Cabedelo Brazil 7°0S 34°50W 93 E12
Cabildo Chile 32°30S 71°5W 94 C1
Cabimas Venezuela 10°23N 71°25W 92 A4

Cabinda Angola 5°33S 12°11E 52 F2
Cabinda □ Angola 5°0S 12°30E 52 F2
Cabinet Mts. U.S.A. 48°10N 115°50W 76 B6
Cabo Blanco Argentina 47°15S 65°47W 96 F3
Cabo Frio Brazil 22°51S 42°3W 95 A7
Cabo Pantoja Peru 1°0S 75°10W 92 D3
Cabo San Lucas Mexico 22°53N 109°54W 86 C3
Cabo Verde = Cape Verde Is. ■ Atl. Oc. 16°0N 24°0W 50 b
Cabonga, Réservoir Canada 47°20N 76°40W 72 C4
Cabool U.S.A. 37°7N 92°6W 80 G7
Caboolture Australia 27°5S 152°58E 63 D5
Cabora Bassa Dam = Cahora Bassa, Lago de Mozam. 15°20S 32°50E 55 F3
Caborca Mexico 30°37N 112°6W 86 A2
Cabot, Mt. U.S.A. 44°30N 71°25W 83 B13
Cabot Hd. Canada 45°14N 81°17W 82 A3
Cabot Str. Canada 47°15N 59°40W 73 C8
Cabra Spain 37°30N 4°28W 21 D3
Cabrera Spain 39°8N 2°57E 24 B9
Cabri Canada 50°35N 108°25W 71 C7
Cabriel → Spain 39°14N 1°3W 21 C5
Caçador Brazil 26°47S 51°0W 95 B5
Čačak Serbia 43°54N 20°20E 23 C9
Caçapava do Sul Brazil 30°30S 53°30W 95 C5
Cáceres Brazil 16°5S 57°40W 92 G7
Cáceres Spain 39°26N 6°23W 21 C2
Cache Bay Canada 46°22N 80°0W 72 C4
Cache Cr. → U.S.A. 38°42N 121°42W 78 G5
Cache Creek Canada 50°48N 121°19W 70 C4
Cachi Argentina 25°5S 66°10W 94 B2
Cachimbo, Serra do Brazil 9°30S 55°30W 93 E7
Cachinal de la Sierra Chile 24°58S 69°32W 94 A2
Cachoeira Brazil 12°30S 39°0W 93 F11
Cachoeira do Sul Brazil 30°3S 52°53W 95 C5
Cachoeiro de Itapemirim Brazil 20°51S 41°7W 95 A7
Cacoal Brazil 11°32S 61°18W 92 F6
Cacólo Angola 10°9S 19°21E 52 G3
Caconda Angola 13°48S 15°8E 53 G3
Caddo U.S.A. 34°7N 96°16W 84 D6
Cader Idris U.K. 52°42N 3°53W 13 E4
Cadereyta de Jiménez Mexico 25°36N 100°0W 86 B5
Cadibarrawirracanna, L. Australia 28°52S 135°27E 63 D2
Cadillac U.S.A. 44°15N 85°24W 81 C11
Cadiz Phil. 10°57N 123°15E 37 B6
Cádiz Spain 36°30N 6°20W 21 D2
Cadiz Calif., U.S.A. 34°30N 115°28W 79 L11
Cadiz Ohio, U.S.A. 40°22N 81°0W 82 F4
Cádiz, G. de Spain 36°40N 7°0W 21 D2
Cadiz L. U.S.A. 34°18N 115°24W 77 J6
Cadney Park Australia 27°55S 134°3E 63 D1
Cadomin Canada 53°2N 117°20W 70 C5
Cadotte Lake Canada 56°26N 116°23W 70 B5
Cadoux Australia 30°46S 117°7E 61 F2
Caen France 49°10N 0°22W 20 B3
Caernarfon U.K. 53°8N 4°16W 12 D3
Caernarfon B. U.K. 53°4N 4°40W 12 D3
Caernarvon = Caernarfon U.K. 53°8N 4°16W 12 D3
Caerphilly U.K. 51°35N 3°13W 13 F4
Caerphilly □ U.K. 51°37N 3°12W 13 F4
Caesarea Israel 32°30N 34°53E 46 C3
Caetité Brazil 13°50S 42°32W 93 F10
Cafayate Argentina 26°2S 66°0W 94 B2
Cafu Angola 16°30S 15°8E 56 B2
Cagayan de Oro Phil. 8°30N 124°40E 37 C6
Cagayan Is. Phil. 9°40N 121°16E 37 C5
Cágliari Italy 39°13N 9°7E 22 E3
Cágliari, G. di Italy 39°8N 9°11E 22 E3
Caguán → Colombia 0°8S 74°18W 92 D4
Caguas Puerto Rico 18°14N 66°2W 89 d
Caha Mts. Ireland 51°45N 9°40W 10 E2
Cahama Angola 16°17S 14°19E 56 B1
Caher Ireland 52°22N 7°56W 10 D4
Cahersiveen Ireland 51°56N 10°14W 10 E1
Cahora Bassa, L. de Mozam. 15°35S 32°0E 55 F3
Cahora Bassa, Lago de Mozam. 15°20S 32°50E 55 F3
Cahore Pt. Ireland 52°33N 6°12W 10 D5
Cahors France 44°27N 1°27E 20 D4
Cahul Moldova 45°50N 28°15E 17 F15
Cai Bau, Dao Vietnam 21°10N 107°27E 38 B6
Cai Nuoc Vietnam 8°56N 105°1E 39 H5
Caia Mozam. 17°51S 35°24E 55 F4
Caianda Angola 11°2S 23°31E 55 E1
Caibarién Cuba 22°30N 79°30W 88 B4
Caicara Venezuela 7°38N 66°10W 92 B5
Caicó Brazil 6°20S 37°0W 93 E11
Caicos Is. Turks & Caicos 21°40N 71°40W 89 B5
Caicos Passage W. Indies 22°45N 72°45W 89 B5
Caiguna Australia 32°16S 125°29E 61 F4
Caird Coast Antarctica 75°0S 25°0W 5 D1
Cairn Gorm U.K. 57°7N 3°39W 11 D5
Cairngorm Mts. U.K. 57°6N 3°42W 11 D5
Cairngorms △ U.K. 57°10N 3°50W 11 D5
Cairnryan U.K. 54°59N 5°1W 11 G3
Cairns Australia 16°57S 145°45E 62 B4
Cairns L. Canada 51°42N 94°30W 71 C10
Cairo = El Qâhira Egypt 30°2N 31°13E 51 B12
Cairo Ga., U.S.A. 30°52N 84°13W 85 F12
Cairo Ill., U.S.A. 37°0N 89°11W 80 G9
Cairo N.Y., U.S.A. 42°18N 74°0W 83 D10
Caithness U.K. 58°25N 3°35W 11 C5
Caithness, Ord of U.K. 58°8N 3°36W 11 C5
Caja de Muertos, I. Puerto Rico 17°54N 66°32W 89 d
Cajamarca Peru 7°5S 78°28W 92 E3
Cajazeiras Brazil 6°52S 38°30W 93 E11
Cala d'Or Spain 39°23N 3°14E 24 B10
Cala en Porter Spain 39°52N 4°8E 24 B11
Cala Figuera Spain 39°20N 3°10E 24 B10
Cala Figuera, C. de Spain 39°27N 2°31E 24 B9
Cala Forcat Spain 40°0N 3°47E 24 B10
Cala Major Spain 39°33N 2°37E 24 B9
Cala Mezquida = Sa Mesquida Spain 39°55N 4°16E 24 B11
Cala Millor Spain 39°35N 3°22E 24 B10
Cala Murada Spain 39°27N 3°17E 24 B10
Cala Ratjada Spain 39°43N 3°27E 24 B10
Cala Santa Galdana Spain 39°56N 3°58E 24 B10
Calabar Nigeria 4°57N 8°20E 50 H7
Calabogie Canada 45°18N 76°43W 83 A8
Calabozo Venezuela 9°0N 67°28W 92 B5
Calábria □ Italy 39°0N 16°30E 22 E7
Calahorra Spain 42°18N 1°59W 21 A5
Calais France 50°57N 1°56E 20 A4
Calais U.S.A. 45°11N 67°17W 81 C20
Calakmul ⌓ Mexico 18°14N 89°48W 87 D7
Calalaste, Cord. de Argentina 25°0S 67°0W 94 B2
Calama Brazil 8°0S 62°50W 92 E6
Calama Chile 22°30S 68°55W 94 A2
Calamar Colombia 10°15N 74°55W 92 A4
Calamian Group Phil. 11°50N 119°55E 37 B5
Calamocha Spain 40°50N 1°17W 21 B5
Calang Indonesia 4°37N 95°37E 36 D1
Calanscio, Sarîr Libya 27°30N 21°30E 51 C10
Calapan Phil. 13°25N 121°7E 37 B6
Călăraşi Romania 44°12N 27°20E 17 F14
Calatayud Spain 41°20N 1°40W 21 B5
Calauag Phil. 13°55N 122°15E 37 B6
Calavite, C. Phil. 13°26N 120°20E 37 B6
Calbayog Phil. 12°4N 124°38E 37 B6
Calca Peru 13°22S 72°0W 92 F4
Calcasieu L. U.S.A. 29°55N 93°18W 84 G8
Calcium U.S.A. 44°1N 75°50W 83 B9
Calcutta = Kolkata India 22°34N 88°21E 43 H13
Calcutta U.S.A. 40°40N 80°34W 82 F4
Caldas da Rainha Portugal 39°24N 9°8W 21 C1
Calder → U.K. 53°44N 1°22W 12 D6
Caldera Chile 27°5S 70°55W 94 B1
Caldera de Taburiente △ Canary Is. 28°43N 17°52W 24 F2
Caldwell Idaho, U.S.A. 43°40N 116°41W 76 E5
Caldwell Kans., U.S.A. 37°2N 97°37W 80 G5
Caldwell Tex., U.S.A. 30°32N 96°42W 84 F6
Caledon Canada 43°51N 79°51W 82 C5
Caledon S. Africa 34°14S 19°26E 56 E2
Caledon → S. Africa 30°31S 26°5E 56 E4
Caledon B. Australia 12°45S 137°0E 62 A2
Caledonia Canada 43°7N 79°58W 82 C5
Caledonia U.S.A. 42°58N 77°51W 82 D7
Calemba Angola 16°0S 15°44E 56 B2
Calen Australia 20°56S 148°48E 62 J6
Caletones Chile 34°6S 70°27W 94 C1
Calexico U.S.A. 32°40N 115°30W 79 N11
Calf of Man I. of Man 54°3N 4°48W 12 C3
Calgary Canada 51°0N 114°10W 70 C6
Calheta Madeira 32°44N 17°11W 24 D2
Calhoun U.S.A. 34°30N 84°57W 85 D12
Cali Colombia 3°25N 76°35W 92 C3
Calicut India 11°15N 75°43E 40 P9
Caliente U.S.A. 37°37N 114°31W 77 H6
California Mo., U.S.A. 38°38N 92°34W 80 F7
California Pa., U.S.A. 40°4N 79°54W 82 F5
California □ U.S.A. 37°30N 119°30W 78 H7
California, Baja, T.N. = Baja California □ Mexico 30°0N 115°0W 86 B2
California, Baja, T.S. = Baja California Sur □ Mexico 25°50N 111°50W 86 B2
California, G. de Mexico 27°0N 111°0W 86 B2
California City U.S.A. 35°10N 117°55W 79 K9
California Hot Springs U.S.A. 35°51N 118°41W 79 K8
Calilegua △ Argentina 25°36S 64°50W 94 B3
Calingasta Argentina 31°15S 69°30W 94 C2
Calipatria U.S.A. 33°8N 115°31W 79 M11
Calistoga U.S.A. 38°35N 122°35W 78 G4
Calitzdorp S. Africa 33°33S 21°42E 56 E3
Callabonna, L. Australia 29°40S 140°5E 63 D3
Callan Ireland 52°32N 7°24W 10 D4
Callander U.K. 56°15N 4°13W 11 E4
Callao Peru 12°3S 77°8W 92 F3
Callicoon U.S.A. 41°46N 75°3W 83 E9
Calling Lake Canada 55°15N 113°12W 70 B6
Calliope Australia 24°0S 151°16E 62 C5
Calma, Costa de la Spain 39°28N 2°26E 24 B9
Calne U.K. 51°26N 2°0W 13 F6
Calola Angola 16°25S 17°48E 56 B2
Caloundra Australia 26°45S 153°10E 63 D5
Calpella U.S.A. 39°14N 123°12W 78 F3
Calpine U.S.A. 39°40N 120°27W 78 F6
Calstock Canada 49°47N 84°9W 72 C3
Caltagirone Italy 37°14N 14°31E 22 F6
Caltanissetta Italy 37°29N 14°4E 22 F6
Calulo Angola 10°1S 14°56E 52 G2
Calvert → Australia 16°17S 137°44E 62 B2
Calvert I. Canada 51°30N 128°0W 70 C3
Calvert Ra. Australia 24°0S 122°30E 60 D3
Calvi France 42°34N 8°45E 20 E8
Calvià Spain 39°34N 2°31E 24 B9
Calvillo Mexico 21°51N 102°43W 86 C4
Calvinia S. Africa 31°28S 19°45E 56 E2
Calwa U.S.A. 36°42N 119°46W 78 J7
Cam → U.K. 52°21N 0°16E 13 E8
Cam Lam Vietnam 11°54N 109°10E 39 G7
Cam Pha Vietnam 21°7N 107°18E 38 B6
Cam Ranh Vietnam 11°54N 109°12E 39 G7
Cam Xuyen Vietnam 18°15N 106°0E 38 C6
Camabatela Angola 8°20S 15°26E 52 F3
Camacha Madeira 32°41N 16°49W 24 D3
Camacupa Angola 11°58S 17°22E 53 G3
Camagüey Cuba 21°20N 77°55W 88 B4
Camaná Peru 16°30S 72°50W 92 G4
Camanche Res. U.S.A. 38°14N 121°1W 78 G6
Camaquã Brazil 30°51S 51°49W 95 C5
Camaquã → Brazil 31°17S 51°47W 95 C5
Câmara de Lobos Madeira 32°39N 16°59W 24 D3
Camargo Mexico 26°19N 98°50W 87 B5
Camarillo U.S.A. 34°13N 119°2W 79 L7
Camarón, C. Honduras 16°0N 85°5W 88 C2
Camarones Argentina 44°50S 65°40W 96 E3
Camas U.S.A. 45°35N 122°24W 78 E4
Camas Valley U.S.A. 43°2N 123°40W 76 E2
Camballin Australia 17°59S 124°12E 60 C3
Cambará Brazil 23°2S 50°5W 95 A5
Cambay = Khambhat India 22°23N 72°33E 42 H5
Cambay, G. of = Khambhat, G. of India 20°45N 72°30E 40 J8
Cambodia ■ Asia 12°15N 105°0E 38 F5
Camborne U.K. 50°12N 5°19W 13 G2
Cambrai France 50°11N 3°14E 20 A5
Cambria U.S.A. 35°34N 121°5W 78 K5
Cambrian Mts. U.K. 52°3N 3°57W 13 E4
Cambridge Canada 43°23N 80°15W 82 C4
Cambridge Jamaica 18°18N 77°54W 88 a
Cambridge N.Z. 37°54S 175°29E 59 B5
Cambridge U.K. 52°12N 0°8E 13 E8
Cambridge Mass., U.S.A. 42°23N 71°7W 83 D13
Cambridge Minn., U.S.A. 45°34N 93°13W 80 C7
Cambridge N.Y., U.S.A. 43°2N 73°22W 83 C11
Cambridge Nebr., U.S.A. 40°17N 100°10W 80 E3
Cambridge Ohio, U.S.A. 40°2N 81°35W 82 F3
Cambridge Bay = Ikaluktutiak Canada 69°10N 105°0W 68 C9
Cambridge G. Australia 14°55S 128°15E 60 B4
Cambridge Springs U.S.A. 41°48N 80°4W 82 E4
Cambridgeshire □ U.K. 52°25N 0°7W 13 E7
Cambuci Brazil 21°35S 41°55W 95 A7
Cambundi-Catembo Angola 10°10S 17°35E 52 G3
Camden Australia 34°1S 150°43E 63 B5
Camden Ala., U.S.A. 31°59N 87°17W 85 F11
Camden Ark., U.S.A. 33°35N 92°50W 84 E8
Camden Maine, U.S.A. 44°13N 69°4W 81 C19
Camden N.J., U.S.A. 39°55N 75°7W 83 G9
Camden N.Y., U.S.A. 43°20N 75°45W 83 C9
Camden S.C., U.S.A. 34°16N 80°36W 85 D14
Camden Sd. Australia 15°27S 124°25E 60 C3
Camdenton U.S.A. 38°1N 92°45W 80 F7
Camelford U.K. 50°37N 4°42W 13 G3
Cameron Ariz., U.S.A. 35°53N 111°25W 77 J8
Cameron La., U.S.A. 29°48N 93°20W 84 G8
Cameron Mo., U.S.A. 39°44N 94°14W 80 F6
Cameron Tex., U.S.A. 30°51N 96°59W 84 F6
Cameron Highlands Malaysia 4°27N 101°22E 39 K3
Cameron Hills Canada 59°48N 118°0W 70 B5
Cameroon ■ Africa 6°0N 12°30E 51 G7
Cameroun, Mt. Cameroon 4°13N 9°10E 52 D1
Cametá Brazil 2°12S 49°30W 93 D9
Camiguin I. Phil. 18°56N 121°55E 37 C6
Camilla U.S.A. 31°14N 84°12W 85 F12
Caminha Portugal 41°50N 8°50W 21 B1
Camino U.S.A. 38°44N 120°41W 78 G6
Camira Creek Australia 29°15S 152°58E 63 D5
Cammal U.S.A. 41°24N 77°28W 82 E7
Camocim Brazil 2°55S 40°50W 93 D10
Camooweal Australia 19°56S 138°7E 62 B2
Camooweal Caves △ Australia 20°1S 138°11E 62 C2
Camopi Fr. Guiana 3°12N 52°17W 93 C8
Camp Hill U.S.A. 40°14N 76°55W 82 F8
Camp Nelson U.S.A. 36°8N 118°39W 79 J8
Camp Pendleton U.S.A. 33°13N 117°24W 79 M9
Camp Verde U.S.A. 34°34N 111°51W 77 J8
Camp Wood U.S.A. 29°40N 100°1W 84 G4
Campana Argentina 34°10S 58°55W 94 C4
Campana, I. Chile 48°20S 75°20W 96 F1
Campanário Madeira 32°39N 17°2W 24 D2
Campanet Spain 39°46N 2°58E 24 B9
Campánia □ Italy 41°0N 14°30E 22 D6
Campbell S. Africa 28°48S 23°44E 56 D3
Campbell Calif., U.S.A. 37°17N 121°57W 78 H5
Campbell Ohio, U.S.A. 41°5N 80°37W 82 E4
Campbell I. Pac. Oc. 52°30S 169°0E 64 N8
Campbell L. Canada 63°14N 106°55W 71 A7
Campbell Plateau S. Ocean 50°0S 170°0E 5 A11
Campbell River Canada 50°5N 125°20W 70 C3
Campbell Town Australia 41°52S 147°30E 63 G4
Campbellford Canada 44°18N 77°48W 82 B7
Campbellpur Pakistan 33°46N 72°26E 42 C5
Campbellsville U.S.A. 37°21N 85°20W 81 G11
Campbellton Canada 47°57N 66°43W 73 C6
Campbelltown Australia 34°4S 150°49E 63 E5
Campbeltown U.K. 55°26N 5°36W 11 F3
Campeche Mexico 19°51N 90°32W 87 D6
Campeche □ Mexico 19°0N 90°30W 87 D6
Campeche, Golfo de Mexico 19°30N 93°0W 87 D6
Camperdown Australia 38°14S 143°9E 63 F3
Camperville Canada 51°59N 100°9W 71 C8
Câmpina Romania 45°10N 25°45E 17 F13
Campina Grande Brazil 7°20S 35°47W 93 E11
Campinas Brazil 22°50S 47°0W 95 A6
Campo Grande Brazil 20°25S 54°40W 93 H8
Campo Maior Brazil 4°50S 42°12W 93 D10
Campo Mourão Brazil 24°3S 52°22W 95 A5
Campobasso Italy 41°34N 14°39E 22 D6
Campos Brazil 21°50S 41°20W 95 A7
Campos Spain 39°26N 3°1E 24 B10
Campos Belos Brazil 13°10S 47°3W 93 F9
Campos Novos Brazil 27°21S 51°50W 95 B5
Camptonville U.S.A. 39°27N 121°3W 78 F5
Camptown U.S.A. 41°44N 76°14W 83 E8
Câmpulung Romania 45°17N 25°3E 17 F13
Camrose Canada 53°0N 112°50W 70 C6
Camsell Portage Canada 59°37N 109°15W 71 B7
Çan Turkey 40°2N 27°3E 23 D12
Can Clavo Spain 38°57N 1°27E 24 C7
Can Creu Spain 38°58N 1°28E 24 C7
Can Gio Vietnam 10°25N 106°58E 39 G6
Can Pastilla Spain 39°32N 2°42E 24 B9
Can Tho Vietnam 10°2N 105°46E 39 G5
Canaan U.S.A. 42°2N 73°20W 83 D11
Canada ■ N. Amer. 60°0N 100°0W 68 D10
Canada Abyssal Plain Arctic 80°0N 140°0W 4 B18
Canada Basin Arctic 80°0N 145°0W 4 B18
Cañada de Gómez Argentina 32°40S 61°30W 94 C3
Canadian U.S.A. 35°55N 100°23W 84 D4
Canadian → U.S.A. 35°28N 95°3W 84 D7
Canadian Shield Canada 53°0N 75°0W 66 D12
Canajoharie U.S.A. 42°54N 74°35W 83 D10
Çanakkale Turkey 40°8N 26°24E 23 D12
Çanakkale Boğazı Turkey 40°17N 26°32E 23 D12
Canal Flats Canada 50°10N 115°48W 70 C5
Canalejas Argentina 35°15S 66°34W 94 D2
Canals Argentina 33°35S 62°53W 94 C3
Canandaigua U.S.A. 42°54N 77°17W 82 D7
Canandaigua L. U.S.A. 42°47N 77°19W 82 D7
Cananea Mexico 31°0N 110°18W 86 A2
Canarias, Is. Atl. Oc. 28°30N 16°0W 24 F4
Canaries St. Lucia 13°55N 61°4W 89 f
Canarreos, Arch. de los Cuba 21°35N 81°40W 88 B3
Canary Is. = Canarias, Is. Atl. Oc. 28°30N 16°0W 24 F4
Canaseraga U.S.A. 42°27N 77°45W 82 D7
Canatlán Mexico 24°31N 104°47W 86 C4
Canaveral, C. U.S.A. 28°27N 80°32W 85 G14
Canaveral ⌓ U.S.A. 28°28N 80°34W 85 G14
Canavieiras Brazil 15°39S 39°0W 93 G11
Canberra Australia 35°15S 149°8E 63 F4
Canby Calif., U.S.A. 41°27N 120°52W 76 F3
Canby Minn., U.S.A. 44°43N 96°16W 80 C5
Canby Oreg., U.S.A. 45°16N 122°42W 78 E4
Cancún Mexico 21°8N 86°44W 87 C7
Candelaria Argentina 27°29S 55°44W 95 B4
Candelaria Canary Is. 28°22N 16°22W 24 F3
Candelo Australia 36°47S 149°43E 63 F4
Candi Dasa Indonesia 8°30S 115°34E 37 J18
Candia = Iraklio Greece 35°20N 25°12E 25 D7
Candle L. Canada 53°50N 105°18W 71 C7
Candlemas I. Antarctica 57°3S 26°40W 5 B1
Cando U.S.A. 48°32N 99°12W 80 A4
Canea = Chania Greece 35°30N 24°4E 25 D6
Canelones Uruguay 34°32S 56°17W 95 C4
Cañete Chile 37°50S 73°30W 94 D1
Cangas del Narcea Spain 43°10N 6°32W 21 A2
Canguaretama Brazil 6°20S 35°5W 93 E11
Canguçu Brazil 31°22S 52°43W 95 C5
Canguçu, Serra do Brazil 31°20S 52°40W 95 C5
Cangzhou China 38°19N 116°52E 34 E9
Caniapiscau → Canada 56°40N 69°30W 73 A6
Caniapiscau, L. Canada 54°10N 69°55W 73 B6
Canicattì Italy 37°21N 13°51E 22 F5
Canim Lake Canada 51°47N 120°54W 70 C4
Canindeyu □ Paraguay 24°10S 55°0W 95 A5
Canisteo U.S.A. 42°16N 77°36W 82 D7
Canisteo → U.S.A. 42°7N 77°8W 82 D7
Cañitas de Felipe Pescador Mexico 23°36N 102°43W 86 C4
Çankırı Turkey 40°40N 33°37E 19 F5
Cankuzo Burundi 3°10S 30°31E 54 C3
Canmore Canada 51°7N 115°18W 70 C5
Cann River Australia 37°35S 149°7E 63 F4
Canna U.K. 57°3N 6°33W 11 D2
Cannanore India 11°53N 75°27E 40 P9
Cannes France 43°32N 7°1E 20 E7
Canning Town = Port Canning India 22°23N 88°40E 43 H13
Cannington Canada 44°20N 79°2W 82 B5
Cannock U.K. 52°41N 2°1W 13 E5
Cannonball → U.S.A. 46°26N 100°35W 80 B3
Cannondale Mt. Australia 25°13S 148°57E 62 D4
Cannonsville Res. U.S.A. 42°4N 75°22W 83 D9
Cannonvale Australia 20°17S 148°43E 62 J6
Canoas Brazil 29°56S 51°11W 95 B5
Canoe L. Canada 55°10N 108°15W 71 B7
Cañon City U.S.A. 38°27N 105°14W 76 G11
Cañón de Río Blanco △ Mexico 18°43N 97°15W 87 D5
Cañón del Sumidero △ Mexico 19°22N 96°24W 87 D5
Canonniers Pt. Mauritius 20°2S 57°32E 53 d
Canora Canada 51°40N 102°30W 71 C8
Canowindra Australia 33°35S 148°38E 63 E4
Canso Canada 45°20N 61°0W 73 C7
Cantabria □ Spain 43°10N 4°0W 21 A4
Cantabrian Mts. = Cantábrica, Cordillera Spain 43°0N 5°10W 21 A3
Cantábrica, Cordillera Spain 43°0N 5°10W 21 A3
Cantal, Plomb du France 45°3N 2°45E 20 D5
Canterbury Australia 25°23S 141°53E 62 D3
Canterbury U.K. 51°16N 1°6E 13 F9
Canterbury Bight N.Z. 44°16S 171°55E 59 F3
Canterbury Plains N.Z. 43°55S 171°22E 59 E3
Cantil U.S.A. 35°18N 117°58W 79 K9
Canton = Guangzhou China 23°6N 113°13E 33 D6
Canton Ga., U.S.A. 34°14N 84°29W 85 D12
Canton Ill., U.S.A. 40°33N 90°2W 80 E8
Canton Miss., U.S.A. 32°37N 90°2W 85 E9
Canton Mo., U.S.A. 40°8N 91°32W 80 E8
Canton N.Y., U.S.A. 44°36N 75°10W 83 B9
Canton Ohio, U.S.A. 40°48N 81°23W 82 F3
Canton Pa., U.S.A. 41°39N 76°51W 82 E8
Canton S. Dak., U.S.A. 43°18N 96°35W 80 D5
Canton L. U.S.A. 36°6N 98°35W 84 C5
Canudos Brazil 7°13S 58°5W 92 E7
Canumã → Brazil 3°55S 59°10W 92 D7
Canutama Brazil 6°30S 64°20W 92 E6
Canutillo U.S.A. 31°55N 106°36W 84 F1
Canvey U.K. 51°31N 0°37E 13 F8
Canyon U.S.A. 34°59N 101°55W 84 D4
Canyon De Chelly ⌓ U.S.A. 36°10N 109°20W 77 H9
Canyonlands △ U.S.A. 38°15N 110°0W 77 G9
Canyons of the Ancients ⌓ U.S.A. 37°30N 108°55W 77 H9
Canyonville U.S.A. 42°56N 123°17W 76 E2
Cao Bang Vietnam 22°40N 106°15E 38 A6
Cao He → China 40°10N 124°32E 35 D13
Cao Lanh Vietnam 10°27N 105°38E 39 G5
Cao Xian China 34°50N 115°35E 34 G8
Cap-aux-Meules Canada 47°23N 61°52W 73 C7
Cap-Chat Canada 49°6N 66°40W 73 C6
Cap-de-la-Madeleine Canada 46°22N 72°31W 72 C5
Cap-Haïtien Haiti 19°40N 72°20W 89 C5
Cap Pt. St. Lucia 14°7N 60°57W 89 f
Capac U.S.A. 43°1N 82°56W 82 C2
Capanaparo → Venezuela 7°1N 67°7W 92 B5
Cape → Australia 20°59S 146°51E 62 C4
Cape Arid △ Australia 33°58S 123°13E 61 F3
Cape Barren I. Australia 40°25S 148°15E 63 G4
Cape Breton Highlands △ Canada 46°50N 60°40W 73 C7
Cape Breton I. Canada 46°0N 60°30W 73 C7
Cape Charles U.S.A. 37°16N 76°1W 81 G15
Cape Coast Ghana 5°5N 1°15W 50 G5
Cape Cod ⌓ U.S.A. 41°56N 70°6W 81 E18
Cape Coral U.S.A. 26°33N 81°57W 85 H14
Cape Crawford Australia 16°41S 135°43E 62 B2
Cape Dorset = Kingait Canada 64°14N 76°32W 69 C12
Cape Fear → U.S.A. 33°53N 78°1W 85 E15
Cape Girardeau U.S.A. 37°19N 89°32W 80 G9
Cape Hatteras ⌓ U.S.A. 35°30N 75°28W 85 D17
Cape Le Grand △ Australia 33°54S 122°26E 61 F3
Cape Lookout ⌓ U.S.A. 35°45N 76°25W 85 D16
Cape May U.S.A. 38°56N 74°56W 81 F16
Cape May Point U.S.A. 38°56N 74°58W 81 F16
Cape Melville △ Australia 14°26S 144°28E 62 A3
Cape Peninsula △ S. Africa 34°20S 18°28E 56 E2
Cape Range △ Australia 22°3S 114°0E 60 D1
Cape St. George Canada 48°28N 59°14W 73 C8
Cape Tormentine Canada 46°8N 63°47W 73 C7
Cape Town S. Africa 33°55S 18°22E 56 E2
Cape Tribulation △ Australia 16°5S 145°25E 62 B4
Cape Verde Is. ■ Atl. Oc. 16°0N 24°0W 50 b
Cape Vincent U.S.A. 44°8N 76°20W 83 B8
Cape York Peninsula Australia 12°0S 142°30E 62 A3
Capela Brazil 10°30S 37°0W 93 F11
Capella Australia 23°2S 148°1E 62 C4
Capesterre-Belle-Eau Guadeloupe 16°4N 61°36W 88 b
Capesterre-de-Marie-Galante Guadeloupe 15°53N 61°14W 88 b
Capim → Brazil 1°40S 47°47W 93 D9
Capitan U.S.A. 33°35N 105°35W 77 K11
Capitán Arturo Prat Antarctica 63°0S 61°0W 5 C17
Capitol Reef △ U.S.A. 38°15N 111°10W 77 G8
Capitola U.S.A. 36°59N 121°57W 78 J5
Capoche → Mozam. 15°35S 33°0E 55 F3
Capraia Italy 43°2N 9°50E 20 E8
Capreol Canada 46°43N 80°56W 72 C3
Capri Italy 40°33N 14°14E 22 D6
Capricorn Coast Australia 23°16S 150°49E 62 C5
Capricorn Group Australia 23°30S 151°55E 62 C5
Capricorn Ra. Australia 23°20S 116°50E 60 D2
Caprivi Game ⌓ Namibia 17°55S 22°37E 56 B3
Caprivi Strip Namibia 18°0S 23°0E 56 B3
Captain's Flat Australia 35°35S 149°27E 63 F4
Capulin Volcano ⌓ U.S.A. 36°47N 103°58W 84 C3
Caquetá → Colombia 1°15S 69°15W 92 D5
Caracal Romania 44°8N 24°22E 17 F13
Caracas Venezuela 10°30N 66°55W 92 A5
Caracol Belize 16°45N 89°6E 88 C2
Caracol Mato Grosso do Sul, Brazil 22°18S 57°1W 94 A4
Caracol Piauí, Brazil 9°15S 43°22W 93 E10
Carajas Brazil 6°5S 50°23W 93 E8
Carajás, Serra dos Brazil 6°0S 51°30W 93 E8
Carangola Brazil 20°44S 42°5W 95 A7
Caransebeş Romania 45°28N 22°18E 17 F12
Caraquet Canada 47°48N 64°57W 73 C6
Caratasca, L. de Honduras 15°20N 83°40W 88 C3
Caratinga Brazil 19°50S 42°10W 93 G10
Caraúbas Brazil 5°43S 37°33W 93 E11
Caravaca de la Cruz Spain 38°8N 1°52W 21 C5
Caravelas Brazil 17°45S 39°15W 93 G11
Caraveli Peru 15°45S 73°25W 92 G4
Caravelle, Presqu'île de la Martinique 14°46N 60°48W 88 c
Caraz Peru 9°3S 77°47W 92 E3
Carazinho Brazil 28°16S 52°46W 95 B5
Carballo Spain 43°13N 8°41W 21 A1
Carberry Canada 49°50N 99°25W 71 D9
Carbó Mexico 29°42N 110°58W 86 B2

Carbonara, C. *Italy* 39°6N 9°31E **22** E3
Carbondale *Colo.,*
  U.S.A. 39°24N 107°13W **76** G10
Carbondale *Ill., U.S.A.* 37°44N 89°13W **80** G9
Carbondale *Pa., U.S.A.* 41°35N 75°30W **83** E9
Carbonear *Canada* 47°42N 53°13W **73** D9
Carbónia *Italy* 39°10N 8°30E **22** E3
Carcajou *Canada* 57°47N 117°6W **70** B5
Carcarana → *Argentina* 32°27S 60°48W **94** C3
Carcasse, C. *Haiti* 18°30N 74°28W **89** C5
Carcassonne *France* 43°13N 2°20E **20** E5
Carcross *Canada* 60°13N 134°45W **70** A2
Cardamon Hills *India* 9°30N 77°15E **40** Q10
Cardamon Mts. = Kravanh,
  Chuor Phnum
  Cambodia 12°0N 103°32E **39** G4
Cárdenas *Cuba* 23°0N 81°30W **88** B3
Cárdenas *San Luis Potosí,*
  Mexico 22°0N 99°38W **87** C5
Cárdenas *Tabasco,*
  Mexico 17°59N 93°22W **87** D6
Cardiff *U.K.* 51°29N 3°10W **13** F4
Cardiff □ *U.K.* 51°31N 3°12W **13** F4
Cardiff-by-the-Sea
  U.S.A. 33°1N 117°17W **79** M9
Cardigan *U.K.* 52°5N 4°40W **13** E3
Cardigan B. *U.K.* 52°30N 4°30W **13** E3
Cardinal *Canada* 44°47N 75°23W **83** B9
Cardona *Uruguay* 33°53S 57°18W **94** C4
Cardoso, Ilha do *Brazil* 25°8S 47°58W **95** B5
Cardston *Canada* 49°15N 113°20W **70** D6
Cardwell *Australia* 18°14S 146°2E **62** B4
Careen L. *Canada* 57°0N 108°11W **71** B7
Carei *Romania* 47°40N 22°29E **17** E12
Careme = Ciremay
  Indonesia 6°55S 108°27E **37** G13
Carey *U.S.A.* 43°19N 113°57W **76** E7
Carey, L. *Australia* 29°0S 122°15E **61** E3
Carey L. *Canada* 62°12N 102°55W **71** A8
Carhué *Argentina* 37°10S 62°50W **94** D3
Caria *Turkey* 37°20N 28°10E **23** F13
Cariacica *Brazil* 20°16S 40°25W **93** H10
Caribbean Sea *W. Indies* 15°0N 75°0W **89** D5
Cariboo Mts. *Canada* 53°0N 121°0W **70** C4
Caribou *U.S.A.* 46°52N 68°1W **81** B19
Caribou → *Man.,*
  Canada 59°20N 94°44W **71** B10
Caribou → *N.W.T.,*
  Canada 61°27N 125°45W **70** A3
Caribou I. *Canada* 47°22N 85°49W **72** C2
Caribou Is. *Canada* 61°55N 113°15W **70** A6
Caribou L. *Man., Canada* 59°21N 96°10W **71** B9
Caribou L. *Ont., Canada* 50°25N 89°5W **72** B2
Caribou Mts. *Canada* 59°12N 115°40W **70** B5
Caribou River △ *Canada* 59°35N 96°35W **71** B9
Carichíc *Mexico* 27°56N 107°3W **86** B3
Carinda *Australia* 30°28S 147°41E **63** E4
Carinhanha *Brazil* 14°15S 44°46W **93** F10
Carinhanha → *Brazil* 14°20S 43°47W **93** F10
Carinthia = Kärnten □
  Austria 46°52N 13°30E **16** E8
Caripito *Venezuela* 10°8N 63°6W **92** A6
Carleton, Mt. *Canada* 47°23N 66°53W **73** C6
Carleton Place *Canada* 45°8N 76°9W **83** A8
Carletonville *S. Africa* 26°23S 27°22E **56** D4
Carlin *U.S.A.* 40°43N 116°7W **76** F5
Carlingford L. *U.K.* 54°3N 6°9W **10** B5
Carlinville *U.S.A.* 39°17N 89°53W **80** F9
Carlisle *U.K.* 54°54N 2°56W **12** C5
Carlisle *U.S.A.* 40°12N 77°12W **82** F7
Carlisle B. *Barbados* 13°5N 59°37W **89** g
Carlisle I. *Australia* 20°49S 149°18E **62** J7
Carlos Casares *Argentina* 35°32S 61°20W **94** D3
Carlos Tejedor *Argentina* 35°25S 62°25W **94** D3
Carlow *Ireland* 52°50N 6°56W **10** D5
Carlow □ *Ireland* 52°43N 6°50W **10** D5
Carlsbad *Calif., U.S.A.* 33°10N 117°21W **79** M9
Carlsbad *N. Mex.,*
  U.S.A. 32°25N 104°14W **77** K11
Carlsbad Caverns △
  U.S.A. 32°10N 104°35W **77** K11
Carluke *U.K.* 55°45N 3°50W **11** F5
Carlyle *Canada* 49°40N 102°20W **71** D8
Carmacks *Canada* 62°5N 136°16W **68** C6
Carman *Canada* 49°30N 98°0W **71** D9
Carmarthen *U.K.* 51°52N 4°19W **13** F3
Carmarthen B. *U.K.* 51°40N 4°30W **13** F3
Carmarthenshire □ *U.K.* 51°55N 4°13W **13** F3
Carmaux *France* 44°3N 2°10E **20** D5
Carmel *U.S.A.* 41°26N 73°41W **83** E11
Carmel-by-the-Sea
  U.S.A. 36°33N 121°55W **78** J5
Carmel Valley *U.S.A.* 36°29N 121°43W **78** J5
Carmelo *Uruguay* 34°0S 58°20W **94** C4
Carmen *Paraguay* 27°13S 56°12W **95** B4
Carmen → *Mexico* 30°42N 106°29W **86** A3
Carmen, I. *Mexico* 25°57N 111°12W **86** B2
Carmen de Patagones
  Argentina 40°50S 63°0W **96** E4
Carmensa *Argentina* 35°15S 67°40W **94** D2
Carmi *Canada* 49°36N 119°8W **70** D5
Carmi *U.S.A.* 38°5N 88°10W **80** F9
Carmichael *U.S.A.* 38°38N 121°19W **78** G5
Carmila *Australia* 21°55S 149°24E **62** C4
Carmona *Costa Rica* 10°0N 85°15W **88** E2
Carmona *Spain* 37°28N 5°42W **21** D3
Carn Ban *U.K.* 57°7N 4°15W **11** D4
Carn Eige *U.K.* 57°17N 5°8W **11** D3
Carnamah *Australia* 29°41S 115°53E **61** E2
Carnarvon *Australia* 24°51S 113°42E **61** D1
Carnarvon *Canada* 45°3N 78°41W **82** A6
Carnarvon *S. Africa* 30°56S 22°8E **56** E3
Carnarvon △ *Australia* 24°54S 148°2E **62** C4
Carnarvon Ra. *Queens.,*
  Australia 25°15S 148°30E **62** D4
Carnarvon Ra. *W. Austral.,*
  Australia 25°20S 120°45E **61** E3

Carnation *U.S.A.* 47°39N 121°55W **78** C5
Carncastle *U.K.* 54°54N 5°53W **10** B6
Carndonagh *Ireland* 55°16N 7°15W **10** A4
Carnduff *Canada* 49°10N 101°50W **71** D8
Carnegie *U.S.A.* 40°24N 80°5W **82** F4
Carnegie, L. *Australia* 26°5S 122°30E **61** E3
Carnegie Ridge *Pac. Oc.* 1°0S 87°0W **65** H19
Carnic Alps = Karnische Alpen
  Europe 46°36N 13°0E **16** E7
Carniche Alpi = Karnische Alpen
  Europe 46°36N 13°0E **16** E7
Carnot *C.A.R.* 4°59N 15°56E **52** D3
Carnot, C. *Australia* 34°57S 135°38E **63** E2
Carnot B. *Australia* 17°20S 122°15E **60** C3
Carnoustie *U.K.* 56°30N 2°42W **11** E6
Carnsore Pt. *Ireland* 52°10N 6°22W **10** D5
Caro *U.S.A.* 43°29N 83°24W **81** D12
Caroga Lake *U.S.A.* 43°8N 74°28W **83** C10
Carol City *U.S.A.* 25°56N 80°14W **85** J14
Carolina *Brazil* 7°10S 47°30W **93** E9
Carolina *Puerto Rico* 18°23N 65°58W **89** d
Carolina *S. Africa* 26°5S 30°6E **57** D5
Caroline I. *Kiribati* 9°58S 150°13W **65** H12
Caroline Is. *Micronesia* 8°0N 150°0E **64** G6
Caroni → *Trin. & Tob.* 10°34N 61°23W **93** K15
Caroní → *Venezuela* 8°21N 62°43W **92** B6
Caronie = Nébrodi, Monti
  Italy 37°54N 14°35E **22** F6
Caroona *Australia* 31°24S 150°26E **63** E5
Carpathians *Europe* 49°30N 21°0E **17** D11
Carpații Meridionali
  Romania 45°30N 25°0E **17** F13
Carpentaria, G. of
  Australia 14°0S 139°0E **62** A2
Carpentras *France* 44°3N 5°2E **20** D6
Carpi *Italy* 44°47N 10°53E **22** B4
Carpinteria *U.S.A.* 34°24N 119°31W **79** L7
Carr Boyd Ra. *Australia* 16°15S 128°35E **60** C4
Carra, L. *Ireland* 53°41N 9°14W **10** C2
Carrabelle *U.S.A.* 29°51N 84°40W **85** G12
Carranza, Presa V.
  Mexico 27°20N 100°50W **86** B4
Carrara *Italy* 44°5N 10°6E **20** D9
Carrauntoohill *Ireland* 52°0N 9°45W **10** D2
Carrick-on-Shannon
  Ireland 53°57N 8°5W **10** C3
Carrick-on-Suir *Ireland* 52°21N 7°24W **10** D4
Carrickfergus *U.K.* 54°43N 5°49W **10** B6
Carrickmacross *Ireland* 53°59N 6°43W **10** C5
Carrieton *Australia* 32°25S 138°31E **63** E2
Carrillo *Mexico* 26°54N 103°55W **86** B4
Carrington *U.S.A.* 47°27N 99°8W **80** B4
Carrizal Bajo *Chile* 28°5S 71°20W **94** B1
Carrizalillo *Chile* 29°5S 71°30W **94** B1
Carrizo Cr. → *U.S.A.* 36°55N 103°55W **77** H12
Carrizo Plain △ *U.S.A.* 35°11N 119°47W **78** K7
Carrizo Springs *U.S.A.* 28°31N 99°52W **84** G5
Carrizozo *U.S.A.* 33°38N 105°53W **77** K11
Carroll *U.S.A.* 42°4N 94°52W **80** D6
Carrollton *Ga., U.S.A.* 33°35N 85°5W **85** E12
Carrollton *Ill., U.S.A.* 39°18N 90°24W **80** F8
Carrollton *Ky., U.S.A.* 38°41N 85°11W **81** F11
Carrollton *Mo., U.S.A.* 39°22N 93°30W **80** F7
Carrollton *Ohio, U.S.A.* 40°34N 81°5W **82** F3
Carron → *U.K.* 57°53N 4°22W **11** D4
Carron, L. *U.K.* 57°22N 5°35W **11** D3
Carrot → *Canada* 53°50N 101°17W **71** C8
Carrot River *Canada* 53°17N 103°35W **71** C8
Carruthers *Canada* 52°52N 109°16W **71** C7
Carson *Calif., U.S.A.* 33°49N 118°16W **79** M8
Carson *N. Dak., U.S.A.* 46°25N 101°34W **80** B3
Carson → *U.S.A.* 39°45N 118°40W **78** F8
Carson City *U.S.A.* 39°10N 119°46W **78** F7
Carson Sink *U.S.A.* 39°50N 118°25W **76** G4
Cartagena *Colombia* 10°25N 75°33W **92** A3
Cartagena *Spain* 37°38N 0°59W **21** D5
Cartago *Colombia* 4°45N 75°55W **92** C3
Cartago *Costa Rica* 9°50N 83°55W **88** E3
Cartersville *U.S.A.* 34°10N 84°48W **85** D12
Carterton *N.Z.* 41°2S 175°31E **59** D5
Carthage *Tunisia* 36°52N 10°20E **22** F4
Carthage *Ill., U.S.A.* 40°25N 91°8W **80** E8
Carthage *Mo., U.S.A.* 37°11N 94°19W **80** G6
Carthage *N.Y., U.S.A.* 43°59N 75°37W **81** D16
Carthage *Tex., U.S.A.* 32°9N 94°20W **84** E7
Cartier I. *Australia* 12°31S 123°29E **60** B3
Cartwright *Canada* 53°41N 56°58W **73** B8
Caruaru *Brazil* 8°15S 35°55W **93** E11
Carúpano *Venezuela* 10°39N 63°15W **92** A6
Caruthersville *U.S.A.* 36°11N 89°39W **80** G9
Carvoeiro *Brazil* 1°30S 61°59W **92** D6
Carvoeiro, C. *Portugal* 39°21N 9°24W **21** C1
Cary *U.S.A.* 35°47N 78°46W **85** D15
Casa de Piedra *Argentina* 38°55S 67°28W **94** D2
Casa de Piedra, Embalse
  Argentina 38°55S 67°28W **94** D2
Casa Grande *U.S.A.* 32°53N 111°45W **77** K8
Casa Nova *Brazil* 9°25S 41°5W **93** E10
Casablanca *Chile* 33°20S 71°25W **94** C1
Casablanca *Morocco* 33°36N 7°36W **50** B4
Cascada de Basaseachic △
  Mexico 28°9N 108°15W **86** B3
Cascade *Seychelles* 4°39S 55°29E **53** b
Cascade *Idaho, U.S.A.* 44°31N 116°2W **76** D5
Cascade *Mont., U.S.A.* 47°16N 111°42W **76** C8
Cascade Locks *U.S.A.* 45°40N 121°54W **78** E5
Cascade Ra. *U.S.A.* 47°0N 121°30W **78** D5
Cascade Res. *U.S.A.* 44°32N 116°3W **76** D5
Cascades, Pte. des *Réunion* 21°9S 55°51E **53** c
Cascais *Portugal* 38°41N 9°25W **21** C1
Cascavel *Brazil* 24°57S 53°28W **95** A5
Cáscina *Italy* 43°41N 10°33E **22** C4
Casco B. *U.S.A.* 43°45N 70°0W **81** D19
Caserta *Italy* 41°4N 14°20E **22** D6
Casey *Antarctica* 66°0S 76°0E **5** C8
Caseyr, Raas = Asir, Ras
  Somali Rep. 11°55N 51°10E **47** E5

Cashel *Ireland* 52°30N 7°53W **10** D4
Casiguran *Phil.* 16°22N 122°7E **37** A6
Casilda *Argentina* 33°10S 61°10W **94** C3
Casino *Australia* 28°52S 153°3E **63** D5
Casiquiare → *Venezuela* 2°1N 67°7W **92** C5
Casma *Peru* 9°30S 78°20W **92** E3
Casmalia *U.S.A.* 34°50N 120°32W **79** L6
Caspe *Spain* 41°14N 0°1W **21** B5
Casper *U.S.A.* 42°51N 106°19W **76** E10
Caspian Depression
  Eurasia 47°0N 48°0E **19** E8
Caspian Sea *Eurasia* 43°0N 50°0E **19** F9
Cass City *U.S.A.* 43°36N 83°10W **82** C1
Cass Lake *U.S.A.* 47°23N 94°37W **80** B6
Cassadaga *U.S.A.* 42°20N 79°19W **82** D5
Casselman *Canada* 45°19N 75°5W **83** A9
Casselton *U.S.A.* 46°54N 97°13W **80** B5
Cassiar Mts. *Canada* 59°30N 130°30W **70** B2
Cassino *Italy* 41°30N 13°49E **22** D5
Cassville *U.S.A.* 36°41N 93°52W **80** G7
Castaic *U.S.A.* 34°30N 118°38W **79** L8
Castalia *U.S.A.* 41°24N 82°49W **82** E2
Castanhal *Brazil* 1°18S 47°55W **93** D9
Castara *Trin. & Tob.* 11°17N 60°42W **93** J16
Castellammare di Stábia
  Italy 40°42N 14°29E **22** D6
Castelli *Argentina* 36°7S 57°47W **94** D4
Castelló de la Plana *Spain* 39°58N 0°3W **21** C5
Castelo *Brazil* 20°33S 41°14W **95** A7
Castelo Branco *Portugal* 39°50N 7°31W **21** C2
Castelsarrasin *France* 44°2N 1°7E **20** E4
Castelvetrano *Italy* 37°41N 12°47E **22** F5
Casterton *Australia* 37°30S 141°30E **63** F3
Castile *U.S.A.* 42°38N 78°3W **82** D6
Castilla-La Mancha □
  Spain 39°30N 3°30W **21** C4
Castilla y Leon □ *Spain* 42°0N 5°0W **21** B3
Castillos *Uruguay* 34°12S 53°52W **95** C5
Castle Dale *U.S.A.* 39°13N 111°1W **76** G8
Castle Douglas *U.K.* 54°56N 3°56W **11** G5
Castle Rock *Colo.,*
  U.S.A. 39°22N 104°51W **76** G11
Castle Rock *Wash.,*
  U.S.A. 46°17N 122°54W **78** D4
Castlebar *Ireland* 53°52N 9°18W **10** C2
Castlebay *U.K.* 56°57N 7°31W **11** E1
Castleblaney *Ireland* 54°7N 6°44W **10** B5
Castlederg *U.K.* 54°42N 7°35W **10** B4
Castleford *U.K.* 53°43N 1°21W **12** D6
Castlegar *Canada* 49°20N 117°40W **70** D5
Castlemaine *Australia* 37°2S 144°12E **63** F3
Castlemaine *Ireland* 52°10N 9°42W **10** D2
Castlepollard *Ireland* 53°41N 7°19W **10** C4
Castlerea *Ireland* 53°46N 8°29W **10** C3
Castlereagh →
  Australia 30°12S 147°32E **63** E4
Castlereagh B. *Australia* 12°10S 135°10E **62** A2
Castleton *U.S.A.* 43°37N 73°11W **83** C11
Castleton-on-Hudson
  U.S.A. 42°31N 73°45W **83** D11
Castletown *I. of Man* 54°5N 4°38W **12** C3
Castletown Bearhaven
  Ireland 51°39N 9°55W **10** E2
Castor *Canada* 52°15N 111°50W **70** C6
Castor → *Canada* 53°24N 78°58W **72** B4
Castorland *U.S.A.* 43°53N 75°31W **83** C9
Castres *France* 43°37N 2°13E **20** E5
Castricum *Neths.* 52°33N 4°40E **15** B4
Castries *St. Lucia* 14°2N 60°58W **89** f
Castro *Brazil* 24°45S 50°0W **95** A6
Castro *Chile* 42°30S 73°50W **96** E2
Castro Alves *Brazil* 12°46S 39°33W **93** F11
Castro Valley *U.S.A.* 37°41N 122°5W **78** H4
Castroville *U.S.A.* 36°46N 121°45W **78** J5
Castuera *Spain* 38°43N 5°37W **21** C3
Cat Ba, Dao *Vietnam* 20°50N 107°0E **38** B6
Cat Ba △ *Vietnam* 20°47N 107°3E **38** B6
Cat I. *Bahamas* 24°30N 75°30W **89** B4
Cat L. *Canada* 51°40N 91°50W **72** B1
Cat Lake *Canada* 51°40N 91°50W **72** B1
Cat Tien △ *Vietnam* 11°25N 107°17E **39** G6
Catacamas *Honduras* 14°54N 85°56W **88** D2
Cataguases *Brazil* 21°23S 42°39W **95** A7
Catalão *Brazil* 18°10S 47°57W **93** G9
Çatalca *Turkey* 41°8N 28°27E **23** D13
Catalina *Canada* 48°31N 53°4W **73** C9
Catalina *Chile* 25°13S 69°43W **94** B2
Catalina *U.S.A.* 32°30N 110°50W **77** K8
Catalonia = Cataluña □
  Spain 41°40N 1°15E **21** B6
Cataluña □ *Spain* 41°40N 1°15E **21** B6
Catamarca *Argentina* 28°30S 65°50W **94** B2
Catamarca □ *Argentina* 27°0S 65°50W **94** B2
Catanduanes □ *Phil.* 13°50N 124°20E **37** B6
Catanduva *Brazil* 21°5S 48°58W **95** A6
Catánia *Italy* 37°30N 15°6E **22** F6
Catanzaro *Italy* 38°54N 16°35E **22** E7
Catarman *Phil.* 12°28N 124°35E **37** B6
Catatumbo-Bari △
  Colombia 9°3N 73°12W **89** E5
Catchacoma *Canada* 44°44N 78°19W **82** B6
Cateel *Phil.* 7°47N 126°24E **37** C7
Catembe *Mozam.* 26°0S 32°33E **57** D5
Caterham *U.K.* 51°15N 0°4W **13** F7
Cathcart *S. Africa* 32°18S 27°10E **56** E4
Cathedral City *U.S.A.* 33°47N 116°28W **79** M10
Cathlamet *U.S.A.* 46°12N 123°23W **78** D3
Catlettsburg *U.S.A.* 38°25N 82°36W **81** F12
Catoche, C. *Mexico* 21°35N 87°5W **87** C7
Catriló *Argentina* 36°26S 63°24W **94** D3
Catrimani *Brazil* 0°27N 61°41W **92** C6
Catrimani → *Brazil* 0°28N 61°44W **92** C6
Catskill *U.S.A.* 42°14N 73°52W **83** D11
Catskill △ *U.S.A.* 42°8N 74°39W **83** D10
Catskill Mts. *U.S.A.* 42°10N 74°25W **83** D10
Catt, Mt. *Australia* 13°49S 134°23E **62** A1
Cattaraugus *U.S.A.* 42°20N 78°52W **82** D6

Catterick *U.K.* 54°23N 1°37W **12** C6
Catuala *Angola* 16°25S 19°2E **56** B2
Catuane *Mozam.* 26°48S 32°18E **57** D5
Catur *Mozam.* 13°45S 35°30E **55** E4
Cauca → *Colombia* 8°54N 74°28W **92** B4
Caucaia *Brazil* 3°40S 38°35W **93** D11
Caucasus Mountains
  Eurasia 42°50N 44°0E **19** F7
Caucete *Argentina* 31°38S 68°20W **94** C2
Caungula *Angola* 8°26S 18°38E **52** F3
Cauquenes *Chile* 36°0S 72°22W **94** D1
Caura → *Venezuela* 7°38N 64°53W **92** B6
Cauresi → *Mozam.* 17°8S 33°0E **55** F3
Causapscal *Canada* 48°19N 67°12W **73** C6
Cauvery → *India* 11°9N 78°52E **40** P11
Caux, Pays de *France* 49°38N 0°35E **20** B4
Cavalier *U.S.A.* 48°48N 97°37W **80** A5
Cavan *Ireland* 54°0N 7°22W **10** B4
Cavan □ *Ireland* 54°1N 7°16W **10** C4
Cave Creek *U.S.A.* 33°50N 111°57W **77** K8
Cavenagh Ra. *Australia* 26°12S 127°55E **61** E4
Cavendish *Australia* 37°31S 142°2E **63** F3
Caviana, I. *Brazil* 0°10S 50°10W **93** C8
Cavite *Phil.* 14°29N 120°54E **37** B6
Cawndilla L. *Australia* 32°30S 142°15E **63** E3
Cawnpore = Kanpur
  India 26°28N 80°20E **43** F9
Caxias *Brazil* 4°55S 43°20W **93** D10
Caxias do Sul *Brazil* 29°10S 51°10W **95** B5
Cay Sal Bank *Bahamas* 23°45N 80°0W **88** B4
Cayambe *Ecuador* 0°3N 78°8W **92** C3
Cayenne *Fr. Guiana* 5°5N 52°18W **93** B8
Cayey *Puerto Rico* 18°7N 66°10W **89** d
Cayman Brac
  Cayman Is. 19°43N 79°49W **88** C4
Cayman Is. ☑ *W. Indies* 19°40N 80°30W **88** C3
Cayman Trough
  Caribbean 19°0N 81°0W **66** H11
Cayuga *Canada* 42°59N 79°50W **82** D5
Cayuga *U.S.A.* 42°54N 76°44W **83** D8
Cayuga Heights *U.S.A.* 42°27N 76°29W **83** D8
Cayuga L. *U.S.A.* 42°41N 76°41W **83** D8
Cazenovia *U.S.A.* 42°56N 75°51W **83** D9
Cazombo *Angola* 11°54S 22°56E **53** G4
Ceanannus Mor *Ireland* 53°44N 6°53W **10** C5
Ceará = Fortaleza *Brazil* 3°45S 38°35W **93** D11
Ceará □ *Brazil* 5°0S 40°0W **93** E11
Ceará-Mirim *Brazil* 5°38S 35°25W **93** E11
Cébaco, I. de *Panama* 7°33N 81°9W **88** E3
Cebollar *Argentina* 29°10S 66°35W **94** B2
Cebu *Phil.* 10°18N 123°54E **37** B6
Cecil Plains *Australia* 27°30S 151°11E **63** D5
Cedar → *U.S.A.* 41°17N 91°21W **80** E8
Cedar City *U.S.A.* 37°41N 113°4W **77** H7
Cedar Creek Res. *U.S.A.* 32°11N 96°4W **84** E6
Cedar Falls *Iowa, U.S.A.* 42°32N 92°27W **80** D7
Cedar Falls *Wash.,*
  U.S.A. 47°25N 121°45W **78** C5
Cedar Key *U.S.A.* 29°8N 83°2W **85** G13
Cedar L. *Canada* 53°10N 100°0W **71** C9
Cedar Park *U.S.A.* 30°30N 97°49W **84** F6
Cedar Rapids *U.S.A.* 41°59N 91°40W **80** E8
Cedartown *U.S.A.* 34°1N 85°15W **85** D12
Cedarvale *Canada* 55°1N 128°22W **70** B3
Cedarville *S. Africa* 30°23S 29°3E **57** E4
Cedral *Mexico* 23°50N 100°45W **86** C4
Cedro *Brazil* 6°34S 39°3W **93** E11
Cedros, I. *Mexico* 28°12N 115°15W **86** B1
Cedros B. *Trin. & Tob.* 10°16N 61°54W **93** K15
Ceduna *Australia* 32°7S 133°46E **63** E1
Ceeldheere *Somali Rep.* 3°50N 47°8E **47** G4
Ceerigaabo *Somali Rep.* 10°35N 47°20E **47** E4
Cefalù *Italy* 38°2N 14°1E **22** E6
Ceglèd *Hungary* 47°11N 19°47E **17** E10
Cekik *Indonesia* 8°12S 114°27E **37** J17
Celaque △ *Honduras* 14°30N 88°43W **88** D2
Celaya *Mexico* 20°31N 100°37W **86** C4
Celebes = Sulawesi
  Indonesia 2°0S 120°0E **37** E6
Celebes Sea *Indonesia* 3°0N 123°0E **37** D6
Celina *U.S.A.* 40°33N 84°35W **81** E11
Celje *Slovenia* 46°16N 15°18E **16** E8
Celle *Germany* 52°37N 10°4E **16** B6
Celtic Sea *Atl. Oc.* 50°9N 9°34W **14** F2
Cenderwasih, Teluk
  Indonesia 3°0S 135°20E **37** E9
Center *N. Dak., U.S.A.* 47°7N 101°18W **80** B3
Center *Tex., U.S.A.* 31°48N 94°11W **84** F7
Centerburg *U.S.A.* 40°18N 82°42W **82** F2
Centerville *Calif., U.S.A.* 36°44N 119°30W **78** J7
Centerville *Iowa, U.S.A.* 40°44N 92°52W **80** E7
Centerville *Pa., U.S.A.* 40°3N 79°59W **82** F5
Centerville *Tenn.,*
  U.S.A. 35°47N 87°28W **85** D11
Centerville *Tex., U.S.A.* 31°16N 95°59W **84** F7
Central □ *Kenya* 0°30S 37°30E **54** C4
Central □ *Malawi* 13°30S 33°30E **55** E3
Central □ *Zambia* 14°25S 28°50E **55** E2
Central, Cordillera
  Colombia 5°0N 75°0W **92** C4
Central, Cordillera
  Costa Rica 10°10N 84°5W **88** D3
Central, Cordillera
  Dom. Rep. 19°15N 71°0W **89** C5
Central, Cordillera
  Puerto Rico 18°8N 66°35W **89** d
Central African Rep. ■
  Africa 7°0N 20°0E **51** G9
Central America *America* 12°0N 85°0W **66** H11
Central Butte *Canada* 50°48N 106°31W **71** C7
Central City *Colo.,*
  U.S.A. 39°48N 105°31W **76** G11
Central City *Ky., U.S.A.* 37°18N 87°7W **80** G10
Central City *Nebr., U.S.A.* 41°7N 98°0W **80** E4
Central I. *Kenya* 3°30N 36°0E **54** B4

Central Island △ *Kenya* 2°33N 36°1E **54** B4
Central Kalahari △
  Botswana 22°36S 23°58E **56** C3
Central Makran Range
  Pakistan 26°30N 64°15E **40** F4
Central Pacific Basin
  Pac. Oc. 8°0N 175°0W **64** G10
Central Patricia *Canada* 51°30N 90°9W **72** B1
Central Point *U.S.A.* 42°23N 122°55W **76** E2
Central Russian Uplands
  Europe 54°0N 36°0E **6** E13
Central Siberian Plateau
  Russia 65°0N 105°0E **26** B12
Central Square *U.S.A.* 43°17N 76°9W **83** C8
Centralia *Canada* 43°17N 81°28W **82** C3
Centralia *Ill., U.S.A.* 38°32N 89°8W **80** F9
Centralia *Mo., U.S.A.* 39°13N 92°8W **80** F7
Centralia *Wash., U.S.A.* 46°43N 122°58W **78** D4
Centre de Flacq *Mauritius* 20°12S 57°43E **53** d
Centreville *N.Y., U.S.A.* 42°28N 78°14W **82** D6
Centreville *Pa., U.S.A.* 41°44N 79°45W **82** E5
Cephalonia = Kefalonia
  Greece 38°15N 20°30E **23** E9
Cepu *Indonesia* 7°9S 111°35E **37** G14
Ceram = Seram *Indonesia* 3°10S 129°0E **37** E7
Ceram Sea = Seram Sea
  Indonesia 2°30S 128°30E **37** E7
Ceredigion □ *U.K.* 52°16N 4°15W **13** E3
Ceres *Argentina* 29°55S 61°55W **94** B3
Ceres *S. Africa* 33°21S 19°18E **56** E2
Ceres *U.S.A.* 37°35N 120°57W **78** H6
Cerf *Seychelles* 4°38S 55°40E **53** b
Cerignola *Italy* 41°17N 15°53E **22** D6
Cerigo = Kythira *Greece* 36°8N 23°0E **23** F10
Çerkezköy *Turkey* 41°17N 28°0E **23** D12
Cerralvo, I. *Mexico* 24°15N 109°55W **86** C3
Cerritos *Mexico* 22°25N 100°16W **86** C4
Cerro Chato *Uruguay* 33°6S 55°8W **95** C4
Cerro Cofre de Perote △
  Mexico 19°29N 97°8W **87** D5
Cerro Corá △ *Paraguay* 22°35S 56°2W **95** A4
Cerro el Copey △
  Venezuela 10°59N 63°53W **89** D7
Cerro Hoya △ *Panama* 7°17N 80°45W **88** E3
Cerro Saroche △
  Venezuela 10°8N 69°38W **89** D6
Cervantes *Australia* 30°31S 115°3E **61** F2
Cervera *Spain* 41°40N 1°16E **21** B6
Cesena *Italy* 44°8N 12°15E **22** B5
Cēsis *Latvia* 57°18N 25°15E **9** H21
Česká Rep. = Czech Rep. ■
  Europe 50°0N 15°0E **16** D8
České Budějovice
  Czech Rep. 48°55N 14°25E **16** D8
Českomoravská Vrchovina
  Czech Rep. 49°30N 15°40E **16** D8
Çeşme *Turkey* 38°20N 26°23E **23** E12
Cessnock *Australia* 32°50S 151°21E **63** E5
Cetinje *Montenegro* 42°23N 18°59E **23** C8
Cetraro *Italy* 39°31N 15°55E **22** E6
Ceuta *N. Afr.* 35°52N 5°18W **21** E3
Cévennes *France* 44°10N 3°50E **20** D5
Ceyhan *Turkey* 37°4N 35°47E **44** B2
Ceylanpınar *Turkey* 36°50N 40°2E **44** B4
Ceylon = Sri Lanka ■
  Asia 7°30N 80°50E **40** R12
Cha-am *Thailand* 12°48N 99°58E **38** F2
Chacabuco *Argentina* 34°40S 60°27W **94** C3
Chachapoyas *Peru* 6°15S 77°50W **92** E3
Chachoengsao *Thailand* 13°42N 101°5E **38** F3
Chachran *Pakistan* 28°55N 70°30E **42** E4
Chachro *Pakistan* 25°5N 70°15E **42** G4
Chaco □ *Argentina* 26°30S 61°0W **94** B3
Chaco □ *Paraguay* 26°0S 60°0W **94** B3
Chaco → *U.S.A.* 36°46N 108°39W **77** H9
Chaco △ *Argentina* 27°0S 59°30W **94** B4
Chaco Austral *S. Amer.* 27°0S 61°30W **96** B4
Chaco Boreal *S. Amer.* 22°0S 60°0W **92** H6
Chaco Central *S. Amer.* 24°0S 61°0W **96** A4
Chaco Culture △
  U.S.A. 36°3N 107°58W **77** H10
Chacon, C. *U.S.A.* 54°42N 132°0W **70** C2
Chad ■ *Africa* 15°0N 17°15E **51** F8
Chad, L. = Tchad, L.
  Chad 13°30N 14°30E **51** F8
Chadileuvú → *Argentina* 37°46S 66°0W **94** D2
Chadiza *Zambia* 14°45S 32°27E **55** E3
Chadron *U.S.A.* 42°50N 103°0W **80** D2
Chadyr-Lunga = Ciadâr-Lunga
  Moldova 46°3N 28°51E **17** E15
Chae Hom *Thailand* 18°43N 99°35E **38** C2
Chae Son △ *Thailand* 18°42N 99°20E **38** C2
Chaem → *Thailand* 18°11N 98°38E **38** C2
Chaeryŏng *N. Korea* 38°24N 125°36E **35** E13
Chagai Hills = Chāh Gay Hills
  Afghan. 29°30N 64°0E **40** E3
Chagda *Russia* 58°45N 130°38E **29** D14
Chagos Arch. ☑ *Ind. Oc.* 6°0S 72°0E **26** J9
Chagres △ *Panama* 9°28N 79°37W **88** E4
Chaguanas *Trin. & Tob.* 10°30N 61°26W **93** K15
Chāh Ākhvor *Iran* 32°41N 59°40E **45** C8
Chāh Bahar *Iran* 25°20N 60°40E **45** E9
Chāh-e-Kavīr *Iran* 34°29N 56°52E **45** C8
Chāh Gay Hills *Afghan.* 29°30N 64°0E **40** E3
Chahār Borjak *Afghan.* 30°17N 62°3E **40** D3
Chahār Maḩāll va Bakhtīarī □
  Iran 32°0N 49°0E **45** C6
Chai Badan *Thailand* 15°12N 101°8E **38** E3
Chai Wan *China* 22°16N 114°14E **33** G11
Chaibasa *India* 22°42N 85°49E **43** H11
Chainat *Thailand* 15°11N 100°8E **38** E3
Chaiya *Thailand* 9°23N 99°14E **39** H2
Chaiyaphum *Thailand* 15°48N 102°2E **38** E4
Chaj Doab *Pakistan* 32°15N 73°0E **42** C5
Chajari *Argentina* 30°42S 58°0W **94** C4
Chak Amru *Pakistan* 32°22N 75°11E **42** C6

Chakar → Pakistan 29°29N 68°2E **42** E3
Chakari Zimbabwe 18°5S 29°51E **57** B4
Chake Chake Tanzania 5°15S 39°45E **54** D4
Chakhānsūr Afghan. 31°10N 62°0E **40** D3
Chakonipau, L. Canada 56°18N 68°30W **73** A6
Chakradharpur India 22°45N 85°40E **43** H11
Chakrata India 30°42N 77°51E **42** D7
Chakwal Pakistan 32°56N 72°53E **42** C5
Chala Peru 15°48S 74°20W **92** G4
Chalchihuites Mexico 23°29N 103°53W **86** C4
Chalcis = Halkida
  Greece 38°27N 23°42E **23** E10
Chaleur B. Canada 47°55N 65°30W **73** C6
Chalfant U.S.A. 37°32N 118°21W **78** H8
Chalhuanca Peru 14°15S 73°15W **92** F4
Chalisgaon India 20°30N 75°10E **40** J9
Chalk River Canada 46°1N 77°27W **72** C4
Chalky Inlet N.Z. 46°3S 166°31E **59** G1
Challapata Bolivia 18°53S 66°50W **92** G5
Challenger Deep Pac. Oc. 11°30N 142°0E **64** F6
Challenger Fracture Zone
  Pac. Oc. 35°0S 105°0W **65** L17
Challis U.S.A. 44°30N 114°14W **76** D6
Chalmette U.S.A. 29°56N 89°57W **85** G10
Chalon-sur-Saône France 46°48N 4°50E **20** C6
Chalong Thailand 7°50N 98°22E **39** a
Châlons-en-Champagne
  France 48°58N 4°20E **20** B6
Chálten, Cerro = Fitz Roy, Cerro
  Argentina 49°17S 73°5W **96** F2
Chālūs Iran 36°38N 51°26E **45** B6
Cham, Cu Lao Vietnam 15°57N 108°30E **38** E7
Chama U.S.A. 36°54N 106°35W **77** H10
Chamaicó Argentina 35°3S 64°58W **94** D3
Chaman Pakistan 30°58N 66°25E **40** D5
Chamba India 32°35N 76°10E **42** C7
Chamba Tanzania 11°37S 37°0E **55** E4
Chambal → India 26°29N 79°15E **43** F8
Chamberlain U.S.A. 43°49N 99°20W **80** D4
Chamberlain →
  Australia 15°30S 127°54E **60** C4
Chamberlain L. U.S.A. 46°14N 69°19W **81** B19
Chambers U.S.A. 35°11N 109°26W **77** J9
Chambersburg U.S.A. 39°56N 77°40W **81** F15
Chambéry France 45°34N 5°55E **20** D6
Chambeshi → Zambia 11°53S 29°48E **52** G6
Chambly Canada 45°27N 73°17W **83** A11
Chambord Canada 48°25N 72°6W **73** C5
Chamchamal Iraq 35°32N 44°50E **44** C5
Chamela Mexico 19°32N 105°5W **86** D3
Chamical Argentina 30°22S 66°27W **94** C2
Chamkar Luong
  Cambodia 11°0N 103°45E **39** G4
Chamoli India 30°24N 79°21E **43** D8
Chamonix-Mont Blanc
  France 45°55N 6°51E **20** D7
Chamouchouane =
  Ashuapmushuan →
  Canada 48°37N 72°20W **72** C5
Champa India 22°2N 82°43E **43** H10
Champagne Canada 60°49N 136°30W **70** A1
Champagne France 48°40N 4°20E **20** B6
Champaign U.S.A. 40°7N 88°15W **80** E9
Champawat India 29°20N 80°6E **43** E9
Champdoré, L. Canada 55°55N 65°49W **73** A6
Champion U.S.A. 41°19N 80°51W **82** E4
Champlain U.S.A. 44°59N 73°27W **83** B11
Champlain, L. U.S.A. 44°40N 73°20W **83** B11
Champotón Mexico 19°21N 90°43W **87** D6
Champua India 22°5N 85°40E **43** H11
Chana Thailand 6°55N 100°44E **39** J3
Chañaral Chile 26°23S 70°40W **94** B1
Chanārān Iran 36°39N 59°6E **45** B8
Chanasma India 23°44N 72°5E **42** H5
Chancery Lane Barbados 13°3N 59°30W **89** g
Chanco Chile 35°44S 72°32W **94** D1
Chand India 21°57N 79°7E **43** J8
Chandan India 24°38N 86°40E **43** G12
Chandan Chauki India 28°33N 80°47E **43** E9
Chandannagar India 22°52N 88°24E **43** H13
Chandausi India 28°27N 78°49E **43** E8
Chandeleur Is. U.S.A. 29°55N 88°57W **85** G10
Chandeleur Sd. U.S.A. 29°55N 89°0W **85** G10
Chandigarh India 30°43N 76°47E **42** D7
Chandil India 22°58N 86°3E **43** H11
Chandler Australia 27°0S 133°19E **63** D1
Chandler Canada 48°18N 64°46W **73** C7
Chandler Ariz., U.S.A. 33°18N 111°50W **77** K8
Chandler Okla., U.S.A. 35°42N 96°53W **84** D6
Chandod India 21°59N 73°28E **42** J5
Chandpur Bangla. 23°8N 90°45E **41** H17
Chandrapur India 19°57N 79°25E **40** K11
Chānf Iran 26°38N 60°29E **45** E9
Chang Pakistan 26°59N 68°30E **42** F3
Chang, Ko Thailand 12°0N 102°23E **39** G4
Ch'ang Chiang = Chang Jiang →
  China 31°48N 121°10E **33** C7
Chang Jiang → China 31°48N 121°10E **33** C7
Changa India 33°53N 77°35E **43** C7
Changan India 22°48N 158°20E **43** C7
Changanacheri India 9°25N 76°31E **40** Q10
Changane → Mozam. 24°30S 33°30E **57** C5
Changbai China 41°25N 128°5E **35** D15
Changbai Shan China 42°20N 129°0E **35** C15
Changchiak'ou = Zhangjiakou
  China 40°48N 114°55E **34** D8
Ch'angchou = Changzhou
  China 31°47N 119°58E **33** C6
Changchun China 43°57N 125°17E **35** C13
Changchunling China 45°18N 125°27E **35** B13
Changde China 29°4N 111°35E **33** D6
Changdo-ri N. Korea 38°30N 127°40E **35** E14
Changhai = Shanghai
  China 31°15N 121°26E **33** C7
Changhua Taiwan 24°2N 120°30E **33** D7
Changhŭngni
  N. Korea 40°24N 128°19E **35** D15
Changi Singapore 1°23N 103°59E **39** d
Changi, Singapore ✈ (SIN)
  Singapore 1°23N 103°59E **39** M4
Changji China 44°1N 87°19E **32** B3
Changjiang China 19°20N 108°55E **38** C7
Changjiang Shuiku
  China 22°29N 113°27E **33** G10
Changjin N. Korea 40°23N 127°15E **35** D14
Changjin-ho N. Korea 40°30N 127°15E **35** D14
Changli China 39°40N 119°13E **35** E10
Changling China 44°20N 123°58E **35** B12
Changlun Malaysia 6°25N 100°26E **39** J3
Changping China 40°14N 116°12E **34** D9
Changsha China 28°12N 113°0E **33** D6
Changshan Qundao
  China 39°11N 122°32E **35** E12
Changson N. Korea 38°15N 125°6E **35** E13
Changwu China 35°10N 107°45E **34** G4
Changyi China 36°40N 119°30E **35** F10
Changyŏn N. Korea 38°15N 125°6E **35** E13
Changyuan China 35°15N 114°42E **34** G8
Changzhi China 36°10N 113°6E **34** F7
Changzhou China 31°47N 119°58E **33** C6
Chanhanga Angola 16°0S 14°8E **56** B1
Chania Greece 35°30N 24°4E **25** D6
Chania □ Greece 35°30N 24°4E **25** D6
Chanion, Kolpos Greece 35°33N 23°55E **25** D5
Channapatna India 12°40N 77°15E **40** N10
Channel Is. U.K. 49°19N 2°24W **13** H5
Channel Is. U.S.A. 33°40N 119°15W **79** M7
Channel Islands △
  U.S.A. 34°0N 119°24W **79** L7
Channel-Port aux Basques
  Canada 47°30N 59°9W **73** C8
Channel Tunnel Europe 51°0N 1°30E **13** F9
Channing U.S.A. 35°41N 102°20W **84** D3
Chantada Spain 42°36N 7°46W **21** A2
Chanthaburi Thailand 12°38N 102°12E **38** F4
Chantrey Inlet Canada 67°48N 96°20W **68** C10
Chanute U.S.A. 37°41N 95°27W **80** G6
Chao Phraya →
  Thailand 13°40N 100°31E **38** F3
Chao Phraya Lowlands
  Thailand 15°30N 100°0E **38** E3
Chaocheng China 36°4N 115°37E **34** F8
Chaoyang China 41°35N 120°22E **35** D11
Chaozhou China 23°42N 116°32E **33** D6
Chapaev Kazakhstan 50°25N 51°10E **19** D9
Chapais Canada 49°47N 74°51W **72** C5
Chapala Mozam. 15°50S 37°35E **55** F4
Chapala, L. de Mexico 20°15N 103°0W **86** C4
Chapayevsk Russia 53°0N 49°40E **18** D8
Chapecó Brazil 27°14S 52°41W **95** B5
Chapel Hill U.S.A. 35°55N 79°4W **85** D15
Chapleau Canada 47°50N 83°24W **72** C3
Chaplin Canada 50°28N 106°40W **71** C7
Chaplin L. Canada 50°22N 106°36W **71** C7
Chappell U.S.A. 41°6N 102°28W **80** E2
Chapra = Chhapra
  India 25°48N 84°44E **43** G11
Chara Russia 56°54N 118°20E **29** D12
Charadai Argentina 27°35S 59°55W **94** B4
Charagua Bolivia 19°45S 63°10W **92** G6
Charaka Greece 35°1N 25°7E **25** D7
Charambirá, Punta
  Colombia 4°16N 77°32W **92** C3
Charaña Bolivia 17°30S 69°25W **92** G5
Charanwala India 27°51N 72°10E **42** F5
Charata Argentina 27°13S 61°14W **94** B3
Charcas Mexico 23°8N 101°7W **86** C4
Charcot I. Antarctica 70°0S 70°0W **5** C17
Chard U.K. 50°52N 2°58W **13** G5
Chardon U.S.A. 41°35N 81°12W **82** E3
Chardzhou = Türkmenabat
  Turkmenistan 39°6N 63°34E **45** B9
Charente → France 45°57N 1°5W **20** D3
Chari → Chad 12°58N 14°31E **51** F8
Chārīkār Afghan. 35°0N 69°10E **40** B6
Chariton U.S.A. 41°1N 93°19W **80** E7
Chariton → U.S.A. 39°19N 92°58W **80** F7
Chärjew = Türkmenabat
  Turkmenistan 39°6N 63°34E **45** B9
Charkhari India 25°24N 79°45E **43** G8
Charkhi Dadri India 28°37N 76°17E **42** E7
Charleroi Belgium 50°24N 4°27E **15** D4
Charleroi U.S.A. 40°9N 79°57W **82** F5
Charles, C. U.S.A. 37°7N 75°58W **81** G16
Charles, Peak Australia 32°52S 121°11E **61** F3
Charles City U.S.A. 43°4N 92°41W **80** D7
Charles L. Canada 59°50N 110°33W **71** B6
Charles Town U.S.A. 39°17N 77°52W **81** F15
Charlesbourg Canada 46°51N 71°16W **81** B18
Charleston Ill., U.S.A. 39°30N 88°10W **80** F9
Charleston Miss., U.S.A. 34°1N 90°4W **85** D9
Charleston Mo., U.S.A. 36°55N 89°21W **80** G9
Charleston S.C., U.S.A. 32°46N 79°56W **85** E15
Charleston W. Va.,
  U.S.A. 38°21N 81°38W **81** F13
Charleston L. Canada 44°32N 76°0W **83** B9
Charleston Peak
  U.S.A. 36°16N 115°42W **79** J11
Charlestown Ireland 53°58N 8°48W **10** C3
Charlestown S. Africa 27°26S 29°53E **57** D4
Charlestown Ind.,
  U.S.A. 38°27N 85°40W **81** F11
Charlestown N.H.,
  U.S.A. 43°14N 72°25W **83** C12
Charlestown of Aberlour
  U.K. 57°28N 3°14W **11** D5
Charleville = Rath Luirc
  Ireland 52°21N 8°40W **10** D3
Charleville Australia 26°24S 146°15E **63** D4
Charleville-Mézières
  France 49°44N 4°40E **20** B6
Charlevoix U.S.A. 45°19N 85°16W **81** C11

Charlotte Mich., U.S.A. 42°34N 84°50W **81** D11
Charlotte N.C., U.S.A. 35°13N 80°50W **85** D14
Charlotte Vt., U.S.A. 44°19N 73°16W **83** B11
Charlotte Amalie
  U.S. Virgin Is. 18°21N 64°56W **89** e
Charlotte Harbor U.S.A. 26°57N 82°4W **85** H13
Charlotte L. Canada 52°12N 125°19W **70** C3
Charlottesville U.S.A. 38°2N 78°30W **81** F14
Charlottetown Nfld. & L.,
  Canada 52°46N 56°7W **73** B8
Charlottetown P.E.I.,
  Canada 46°14N 63°8W **73** C7
Charlotteville
  Trin. & Tob. 11°20N 60°33W **93** J16
Charlton Australia 36°16S 143°24E **63** F3
Charlton I. Canada 52°0N 79°20W **72** B4
Charny Canada 46°43N 71°15W **73** C5
Charolles France 46°27N 4°16E **20** C6
Charre Mozam. 17°13S 35°10E **55** F4
Charsadda Pakistan 34°7N 71°45E **42** B4
Charters Towers
  Australia 20°5S 146°13E **62** C4
Chartres France 48°29N 1°30E **20** B4
Chascomús Argentina 35°30S 58°0W **94** D4
Chase Canada 50°50N 119°41W **70** C5
Chasefu Zambia 11°55S 33°8E **55** E3
Chashma Barrage
  Pakistan 32°27N 71°20E **42** C4
Chāt Iran 37°59N 55°16E **45** B7
Châteaubriant France 47°43N 1°23W **20** C3
Chateaugay U.S.A. 44°56N 74°5W **83** B10
Châteauguay, L. Canada 56°26N 70°3W **73** A5
Châteaulin France 48°11N 4°8W **20** B1
Châteauroux France 46°50N 1°40E **20** C4
Châteaux, Pte. des
  Guadeloupe 16°15N 61°10W **88** b
Châtellerault France 46°50N 0°30E **20** C4
Chatham = Miramichi
  Canada 47°2N 65°28W **73** C6
Chatham Canada 42°24N 82°11W **82** D2
Chatham U.K. 51°22N 0°32E **13** F8
Chatham U.S.A. 42°21N 73°36W **83** D11
Chatham Is. Pac. Oc. 44°0S 176°40W **64** M10
Chatham Rise Pac. Oc. 43°0S 180°0E **64** M10
Chatmohar Bangla. 24°15N 89°15E **43** G13
Chatra India 24°12N 84°56E **43** G11
Chatrapur India 19°22N 85°2E **41** K14
Chats, L. des Canada 45°30N 76°20W **83** A8
Chatsu India 26°36N 75°57E **42** F6
Chatsworth Canada 44°27N 80°54W **82** B4
Chatsworth Zimbabwe 19°38S 31°13E **55** F3
Châttagâm = Chittagong
  Bangla. 22°19N 91°48E **41** H17
Chattahoochee U.S.A. 30°42N 84°51W **85** F12
Chattahoochee →
  U.S.A. 30°54N 84°57W **85** F12
Chattanooga U.S.A. 35°3N 85°19W **85** D12
Chatteris U.K. 52°28N 0°2E **13** E8
Chatturat Thailand 15°40N 101°51E **38** E3
Chau Doc Vietnam 10°42N 105°7E **39** G5
Chaukan Pass Burma 27°8N 97°10E **41** F20
Chaumont France 48°7N 5°8E **20** B6
Chaumont U.S.A. 44°4N 76°8W **83** B8
Chaunskaya G. Russia 69°0N 169°0E **29** C17
Chautauqua L. U.S.A. 42°10N 79°24W **82** D5
Chauvin Canada 52°45N 110°10W **71** C6
Chaves Brazil 0°15S 49°55W **93** D9
Chaves Portugal 41°45N 7°32W **21** B2
Chawang Thailand 8°25N 99°30E **39** H2
Chaykovskiy Russia 56°47N 54°9E **18** C9
Chazy U.S.A. 44°53N 73°26W **83** B11
Cheb Czech Rep. 50°9N 12°28E **16** C7
Cheboksary Russia 56°8N 47°12E **18** C8
Cheboygan U.S.A. 45°39N 84°29W **81** C11
Chech, Erg Africa 25°0N 2°15W **50** D5
Chechenia □ Russia 43°30N 45°29E **19** F8
Checheno-Ingush Republic =
  Chechenia □ Russia 43°30N 45°29E **19** F8
Chechnya = Chechenia □
  Russia 43°30N 45°29E **19** F8
Checotah U.S.A. 35°28N 95°31W **84** D7
Chedabucto B. Canada 45°25N 61°8W **73** C7
Cheduba I. Burma 18°45N 93°40E **41** K18
Cheektowaga U.S.A. 42°54N 78°45W **82** D6
Cheepie Australia 26°33S 145°1E **63** D4
Chegdomyn Russia 51°7N 133°1E **29** D14
Chegga Mauritania 25°27N 5°40W **50** C4
Chegutu Zimbabwe 18°10S 30°14E **55** F3
Chehalis U.S.A. 46°40N 122°58W **78** D4
Chehalis → U.S.A. 46°57N 123°50W **78** D3
Cheju = Jeju S. Korea 33°31N 126°32E **35** H14
Cheju-do = Jeju-do
  S. Korea 33°29N 126°34E **35** H14
Chekiang = Zhejiang □
  China 29°0N 120°0E **33** D7
Chela, Sa. da Angola 16°20S 13°20E **56** B1
Chelan U.S.A. 47°51N 120°1E **76** C4
Chelan, L. U.S.A. 48°11N 120°30W **76** B3
Cheleken = Hazar
  Turkmenistan 39°34N 53°16E **19** G9
Cheleken Yarymadasy
  Turkmenistan 39°30N 53°15E **45** B7
Chelforó Argentina 39°0S 66°33W **96** D3
Chelkar = Shalqar
  Kazakhstan 47°48N 59°39E **28** E6
Chelm Poland 51°8N 23°30E **17** C12
Chelmno Poland 53°20N 18°30E **17** B10
Chelmsford U.K. 51°44N 0°29E **13** F8
Chelsea Australia 38°5S 145°8E **63** F4
Chelsea U.S.A. 43°59N 72°27W **83** C12
Cheltenham U.K. 51°54N 2°4W **13** F5
Chelyabinsk Russia 55°10N 61°24E **28** D7
Chelyuskin, C. = Chelyuskin, Mys
  Russia 77°30N 103°0E **29** B11
Chelyuskin, Mys Russia 77°30N 103°0E **29** B11
Chemainus Canada 48°55N 123°42W **78** B3
Chemba Mozam. 17°9S 34°53E **53** H6

Chemin Grenier Mauritius 20°29S 57°28E **53** d
Chemnitz Germany 50°51N 12°54E **16** C7
Chemult U.S.A. 43°14N 121°47W **76** E3
Chen, Gora Russia 65°16N 141°50E **29** C15
Chenab → Pakistan 30°23N 71°2E **42** D4
Chenab Nagar Pakistan 31°45N 72°55E **42** D5
Chenango Forks U.S.A. 42°15N 75°51W **83** D9
Cheney U.S.A. 47°30N 117°35W **76** C5
Cheng Xian China 33°43N 105°42E **34** H3
Chengcheng China 35°8N 109°56E **34** G5
Chengchou = Zhengzhou
  China 34°45N 113°34E **34** G7
Chengde China 40°59N 117°58E **35** D9
Chengdu China 30°38N 104°2E **32** C5
Chenggu China 33°10N 107°21E **34** H4
Chengjiang China 24°39N 103°0E **32** D5
Chengmai China 19°50N 109°58E **38** C7
Ch'engtu = Chengdu
  China 30°38N 104°2E **32** C5
Chengwu China 34°58N 115°50E **34** G8
Chengyang China 36°18N 120°21E **35** F11
Chenjiagang China 34°23N 119°47E **35** G10
Chennai India 13°8N 80°19E **40** N12
Cheò, Eilean a' = Skye
  U.K. 57°15N 6°10W **11** D2
Cheom Ksan Cambodia 14°13N 104°56E **38** E5
Cheonan S. Korea 36°48N 127°9E **35** F14
Cheongdo S. Korea 35°38N 128°42E **35** G15
Cheongju S. Korea 36°39N 127°27E **35** F14
Cheorwon S. Korea 38°15N 127°10E **35** E14
Chepén Peru 7°15S 79°23W **92** E3
Chepes Argentina 31°20S 66°35W **94** C2
Chepo Panama 9°10N 79°6W **88** E4
Chepstow U.K. 51°38N 2°41W **13** F5
Chequamegon B. U.S.A. 46°39N 90°51W **80** B8
Cher → France 47°21N 0°29E **20** C4
Cheraw U.S.A. 34°42N 79°53W **85** D15
Cherbourg France 49°39N 1°40W **20** B3
Cherdyn Russia 60°24N 56°29E **18** B10
Cheremkhovo Russia 53°8N 103°1E **29** D11
Cherepovets Russia 59°5N 37°55E **18** C6
Chergui, Chott ech
  Algeria 34°21N 0°25E **50** B6
Cherikov = Cherykaw
  Belarus 53°32N 31°20E **17** B16
Cherkasy Ukraine 49°27N 32°4E **19** E5
Cherkessk Russia 44°15N 42°5E **19** F7
Cherlak Russia 54°15N 74°55E **28** D8
Chernaya Russia 70°30N 89°10E **29** B9
Chernigov = Chernihiv
  Ukraine 51°28N 31°20E **18** D5
Chernigovka Russia 44°19N 132°34E **30** B6
Chernihiv Ukraine 51°28N 31°20E **18** D5
Chernivtsi Ukraine 48°15N 25°52E **17** D13
Chernobyl = Chornobyl
  Ukraine 51°20N 30°15E **17** C16
Chernogorsk Russia 53°49N 91°18E **29** D10
Chernovtsy = Chernivtsi
  Ukraine 48°15N 25°52E **17** D13
Chernyakhovsk Russia 54°36N 21°48E **9** J19
Chernysheyskiy Russia 63°0N 112°30E **29** C12
Cherokee Iowa, U.S.A. 42°45N 95°33W **80** D6
Cherokee Okla., U.S.A. 36°45N 98°21W **84** C5
Cherokee Village U.S.A. 36°17N 91°31W **84** C9
Cherokees, Grand Lake O' The
  U.S.A. 36°28N 94°55W **84** C7
Cherrapunji India 25°17N 91°47E **41** G17
Cherry Valley U.S.A. 42°48N 74°45W **83** D10
Cherskiy Russia 68°45N 161°18E **29** C17
Cherskogo Khrebet
  Russia 65°0N 143°0E **29** C15
Chersonisos Greece 35°18N 25°22E **25** D7
Chersonisos Akrotiri
  Greece 35°30N 24°10E **25** D6
Cherven Belarus 53°45N 28°28E **17** B15
Chervonohrad Ukraine 50°25N 24°10E **17** C13
Cherwell → U.K. 51°44N 1°14W **13** F6
Cherykaw Belarus 53°32N 31°20E **17** B16
Chesapeake U.S.A. 36°49N 76°16W **81** G15
Chesapeake B. U.S.A. 38°0N 76°10W **81** F14
Cheshire □ U.K. 53°14N 2°30W **12** D5
Cheshskaya Guba Russia 67°20N 47°0E **18** A8
Cheshunt U.K. 51°43N 0°1W **13** F7
Chesil Beach U.K. 50°37N 2°33W **13** G5
Chesley Canada 44°17N 81°5W **82** B3
Chester U.K. 53°12N 2°53W **12** D5
Chester Calif., U.S.A. 40°19N 121°14W **76** F3
Chester Ill., U.S.A. 37°55N 89°49W **80** G9
Chester Mont., U.S.A. 48°31N 110°58W **76** B8
Chester Pa., U.S.A. 39°51N 75°22W **81** F16
Chester S.C., U.S.A. 34°43N 81°12W **85** D14
Chester Vt., U.S.A. 43°16N 72°36W **83** C12
Chester W. Va., U.S.A. 40°37N 80°34W **82** F4
Chester-le-Street U.K. 54°51N 1°34E **12** C6
Chesterfield U.K. 53°15N 1°25W **12** D6
Chesterfield, Îs. N. Cal. 19°52S 158°15E **58** C8
Chesterfield Inlet
  Canada 63°30N 90°45W **68** C10
Chesterton Ra.
  Australia 25°30S 147°27E **63** D4
Chesterton Range △
  Australia 26°16S 147°22E **63** D4
Chestertown U.S.A. 43°40N 73°48W **83** C11
Chesuncook L. U.S.A. 46°0N 69°21W **81** C19
Chéticamp Canada 46°37N 60°59W **73** C7
Chetumal Mexico 18°30N 88°20W **87** D7
Chetumal, B. de
  Cent. Amer. 18°40N 88°10W **87** D7
Chetwynd Canada 55°45N 121°36W **70** B4
Cheviot, The U.K. 55°29N 2°9W **12** B5
Cheviot Hills U.K. 55°20N 2°30W **12** B5
Cheviot Ra. Australia 25°20S 143°45E **62** D3
Chew Bahir Ethiopia 4°40N 36°50E **47** G2
Chewelah U.S.A. 48°17N 117°43W **76** B5
Chewore △ Zimbabwe 16°0S 29°52E **55** F2
Cheyenne Okla., U.S.A. 35°37N 99°40W **84** D5

Cheyenne Wyo., U.S.A. 41°8N 104°49W **76** F11
Cheyenne → U.S.A. 44°41N 101°18W **80** C3
Cheyenne Wells
  U.S.A. 38°49N 102°21W **76** G12
Cheyne B. Australia 34°35S 118°50E **61** F2
Chhabra India 24°40N 76°54E **42** G7
Chhaktala India 22°6N 74°11E **42** H6
Chhapra India 25°48N 84°44E **43** G11
Chhata India 27°42N 77°30E **42** F7
Chhatarpur Jharkhand,
  India 24°23N 84°11E **43** G11
Chhatarpur Mad. P.,
  India 24°55N 79°35E **43** G8
Chhattisgarh □ India 22°0N 82°0E **43** J10
Chhep Cambodia 13°45N 105°24E **38** F5
Chhindwara Mad. P.,
  India 23°3N 79°29E **43** H8
Chhindwara Mad. P.,
  India 22°2N 78°59E **43** H8
Chhlong Cambodia 12°15N 105°58E **39** F5
Chhota Tawa → India 22°14N 76°36E **42** H7
Chhoti Kali Sindh →
  India 24°2N 75°31E **42** G6
Chhuikhadan India 21°32N 80°59E **43** J9
Chhuk Cambodia 10°46N 104°28E **39** G5
Chi → Thailand 15°11N 104°43E **38** E5
Chiai Taiwan 23°29N 120°25E **33** D7
Chiamboni Somali Rep. 1°39S 41°35E **52** E8
Chiang Dao Thailand 19°22N 98°58E **38** C2
Chiang Kham Thailand 19°32N 100°18E **38** C3
Chiang Khan Thailand 17°52N 101°36E **38** D3
Chiang Khong Thailand 20°17N 100°24E **38** B3
Chiang Mai Thailand 18°47N 98°59E **38** C2
Chiang Rai Thailand 19°52N 99°50E **38** C2
Chiang Saen Thailand 20°16N 100°5E **38** B3
Chiapa → Mexico 16°42N 93°0W **87** D6
Chiapa de Corzo Mexico 16°42N 93°0W **87** D6
Chiapas □ Mexico 16°30N 92°30W **87** D6
Chiapas, Sa. Madre de
  Mexico 15°40N 93°0W **87** D6
Chiautla de Tapia
  Mexico 18°18N 98°36W **87** D5
Chiávari Italy 44°19N 9°19E **20** D8
Chiavenna Italy 46°19N 9°24E **20** C8
Chiba Japan 35°30N 140°7E **31** G10
Chiba □ Japan 35°30N 140°20E **31** G10
Chibabava Mozam. 20°17S 33°35E **57** C5
Chibemba Cunene, Angola 15°48S 14°8E **53** H2
Chibemba Huila, Angola 16°20S 15°20E **56** B2
Chibi Zimbabwe 20°18S 30°25E **57** C5
Chibia Angola 15°10S 13°42E **53** H2
Chibougamau Canada 49°56N 74°24W **72** C5
Chibougamau, L.
  Canada 49°50N 74°20W **72** C5
Chibuk Nigeria 10°52N 12°50E **51** F8
Chibuto Mozam. 24°40S 33°33E **57** C5
Chic-Chocs, Mts. Canada 48°55N 66°0W **73** C6
Chicacole = Srikakulam
  India 18°14N 83°58E **41** K13
Chicago U.S.A. 41°52N 87°38W **80** E10
Chicago Heights U.S.A. 41°30N 87°38W **80** E10
Chichagof I. U.S.A. 57°30N 135°30W **68** D6
Chichaoua Morocco 31°32N 8°44W **50** B4
Chichawatni Pakistan 30°32N 72°42E **42** D5
Chichén-Itzá Mexico 20°37N 88°35W **87** C7
Chicheng China 40°55N 115°55E **34** D8
Chichester U.K. 50°50N 0°47W **13** G7
Chichibu Japan 35°59N 139°10E **31** F9
Chichibu-Tama △
  Japan 35°52N 138°42E **31** G9
Ch'ich'ihaerh = Qiqihar
  China 47°26N 124°0E **33** B7
Chicholi India 22°1N 77°40E **42** H8
Chickasaw U.S.A. 34°26N 97°0W **84** D6
Chickasha U.S.A. 35°3N 97°58W **84** D6
Chiclana de la Frontera
  Spain 36°26N 6°9W **21** D2
Chiclayo Peru 6°42S 79°50W **92** E3
Chico U.S.A. 39°44N 121°50W **78** F5
Chico → Chubut, Argentina 44°0S 67°0W **96** E3
Chico → Santa Cruz,
  Argentina 50°0S 68°30W **96** G3
Chicomo Mozam. 24°31S 34°6E **57** C5
Chicomostoc Mexico 22°28N 102°46W **86** C4
Chicontepec Mexico 20°58N 98°10W **87** C5
Chicopee U.S.A. 42°9N 72°37W **83** D12
Chicoutimi Canada 48°28N 71°5W **73** C5
Chicualacuala Mozam. 22°6S 31°42E **57** C5
Chidambaram India 11°20N 79°45E **40** P11
Chidenguele Mozam. 24°55S 34°11E **57** C5
Chidley, C. Canada 60°23N 64°26W **69** C13
Chiducuane Mozam. 24°35S 34°25E **57** C5
Chiede Angola 17°15S 16°22E **56** B2
Chiefs Pt. Canada 44°41N 81°18W **82** B3
Chiem Hoa Vietnam 22°12N 105°17E **38** A5
Chiemsee Germany 47°53N 12°28E **16** E7
Chiengi Zambia 8°45S 29°10E **55** D2
Chiengmai = Chiang Mai
  Thailand 18°47N 98°59E **38** C2
Chiese → Italy 45°8N 10°25E **20** D9
Chieti Italy 42°21N 14°10E **22** C6
Chifeng China 42°18N 118°58E **35** C10
Chignecto B. Canada 45°30N 64°40W **73** C7
Chiguana Bolivia 21°0S 67°58W **94** A2
Chigwell U.K. 51°37N 0°6E **13** F8
Chihli, G. of = Bo Hai
  China 39°0N 119°0E **35** E10
Chihuahua Mexico 28°38N 106°5W **86** B3
Chihuahua □ Mexico 28°30N 106°0W **86** B3
Chiili = Shīeli Kazakhstan 44°20N 66°15E **28** E7
Chik Ballapur India 13°25N 77°45E **40** N10
Chikmagalur India 13°15N 75°45E **40** N9
Chikwawa Malawi 16°2S 34°50E **55** F3
Chilanga Zambia 15°33S 28°16E **55** F2
Chilapa Mexico 17°36N 99°10W **87** D5
Chilas Pakistan 35°25N 74°5E **43** B6

Chilaw *Sri Lanka* 7°30N 79°50E **40 R11**
Chilcotin → *Canada* 51°44N 122°23W **70 C4**
Childers *Australia* 25°15S 152°17E **63 D5**
Childress *U.S.A.* 34°25N 100°13W **84 D4**
Chile ■ *S. Amer.* 35°0S 72°0W **96 D2**
Chile Rise *Pac. Oc.* 38°0S 92°0W **65 L18**
Chilecito *Argentina* 29°10S 67°30W **94 B2**
Chilete *Peru* 7°10S 78°50W **92 E3**
Chililabombwe *Zambia* 12°18S 27°43E **55 E2**
Chilim *Pakistan* 35°5N 75°5E **43 B6**
Chilin = Jilin *China* 43°44N 126°30E **35 C14**
Chilka L. *India* 19°40N 85°25E **41 K14**
Chilko → *Canada* 52°0N 123°40W **70 C4**
Chilko L. *Canada* 51°20N 124°10W **70 C4**
Chillagoe *Australia* 17°7S 144°33E **62 B3**
Chillán *Chile* 36°40S 72°10W **94 D1**
Chillicothe *Ill., U.S.A.* 40°55N 89°29W **80 E9**
Chillicothe *Mo., U.S.A.* 39°48N 93°33W **80 F7**
Chillicothe *Ohio, U.S.A.* 39°20N 82°59W **81 F12**
Chilliwack *Canada* 49°10N 121°54W **70 D4**
Chilo *India* 27°25N 73°32E **42 F5**
Chiloane, I. *Mozam.* 20°40S 34°55E **57 C5**
Chiloé, I. de *Chile* 42°30S 73°50W **96 E2**
Chilpancingo *Mexico* 17°33N 99°30W **87 D5**
Chiltern Hills *U.K.* 51°40N 0°53W **13 F7**
Chilton *U.S.A.* 44°2N 88°10W **80 C9**
Chilubi *Zambia* 11°5S 29°58E **55 E2**
Chilubula *Zambia* 10°14S 30°51E **55 E3**
Chilumba *Malawi* 10°28S 34°12E **55 E3**
Chilung *Taiwan* 25°3N 121°45E **33 D7**
Chilwa, L. *Malawi* 15°15S 35°40E **55 F4**
Chimaltitán *Mexico* 21°35N 103°50W **86 C4**
Chimán *Panama* 8°45N 78°40W **88 E4**
Chimanimani *Zimbabwe* 19°48S 32°52E **57 B5**
Chimay *Belgium* 50°3N 4°20E **15 D4**
Chimayo *U.S.A.* 36°0N 105°56W **77 J11**
Chimbay *Uzbekistan* 42°57N 59°47E **28 E6**
Chimborazo *Ecuador* 1°29S 78°55W **92 D3**
Chimbote *Peru* 9°0S 78°35W **92 E3**
Chimkent = Shymkent
  Kazakhstan 42°18N 69°36E **28 E7**
Chimoio *Mozam.* 19°4S 33°30E **55 F3**
Chimpembe *Zambia* 9°31S 29°33E **55 D2**
Chin □ *Burma* 22°0N 93°0E **41 J18**
Chin Hills *Burma* 22°30N 93°30E **41 H18**
Chin Ling Shan = Qinling Shandi
  China 33°50N 108°10E **34 H5**
China *Mexico* 25°42N 99°14W **87 B5**
China ■ *Asia* 30°0N 110°0E **33 C6**
China, Great Plain of
  Asia 35°0N 115°0E **26 E13**
China Lake *U.S.A.* 35°44N 117°37W **79 K9**
Chinan = Jinan *China* 36°38N 117°1E **34 F9**
Chinandega *Nic.* 12°35N 87°12W **88 D2**
Chinati Peak *U.S.A.* 29°57N 104°29W **84 G2**
Chincha Alta *Peru* 13°25S 76°7W **92 F3**
Chinchaga → *Canada* 58°53N 118°20W **70 B5**
Chinchilla *Australia* 26°45S 150°38E **63 D5**
Chinchorro, Banco
  Mexico 18°35N 87°22W **87 D7**
Chinchou = Jinzhou
  China 41°5N 121°3E **35 D11**
Chincoteague *U.S.A.* 37°56N 75°23W **81 G16**
Chinde *Mozam.* 18°35S 36°30E **55 F4**
Chindwin → *Burma* 21°26N 95°15E **41 J19**
Chineni *India* 33°2N 75°15E **43 C6**
Chinga *Mozam.* 15°13S 38°35E **55 F4**
Chingola *Zambia* 12°31S 27°53E **55 E2**
Chingole *Malawi* 13°4S 34°17E **55 E3**
Ch'ingtao = Qingdao
  China 36°5N 120°20E **35 F11**
Chinguetti *Mauritania* 20°25N 12°24W **50 D3**
Chingune *Mozam.* 20°33S 34°58E **57 C5**
Chinhanguanine
  Mozam. 25°21S 32°30E **57 D5**
Chinhoyi *Zimbabwe* 17°20S 30°8E **55 F3**
Chini *India* 31°32N 78°15E **42 D8**
Chiniot *Pakistan* 31°45N 73°0E **42 D5**
Chínipas *Mexico* 27°23N 108°32W **86 B3**
Chinji *Pakistan* 32°42N 72°22E **42 C5**
Chinju = Jinju *S. Korea* 35°12N 128°2E **35 G15**
Chinko → *C.A.R.* 4°50N 23°53E **52 D4**
Chinle *U.S.A.* 36°9N 109°33W **77 H9**
Chinnampo = Namp'o
  N. Korea 38°52N 125°10E **35 E13**
Chino *Japan* 35°59N 138°9E **31 G9**
Chino *U.S.A.* 34°1N 117°41W **79 L9**
Chino Valley *U.S.A.* 34°45N 112°27W **77 J7**
Chinon *France* 47°10N 0°15E **20 C4**
Chinook *U.S.A.* 48°35N 109°14W **76 B9**
Chinook Trough
  Pac. Oc. 44°0N 175°0W **64 C10**
Chinsali *Zambia* 10°30S 32°2E **55 E3**
Chióggia *Italy* 45°13N 12°17E **22 B5**
Chíos = Hios *Greece* 38°27N 26°9E **23 E12**
Chipata *Zambia* 13°38S 32°28E **55 E3**
Chipindo *Angola* 13°49S 15°48E **53 G3**
Chipinge *Zimbabwe* 20°13S 32°28E **55 G3**
Chipinge □ *Zimbabwe* 20°14S 33°0E **55 G3**
Chipley *U.S.A.* 30°47N 85°32W **85 F12**
Chipman *Canada* 46°6N 65°53W **73 C6**
Chipoka *Malawi* 13°57S 34°28E **55 E3**
Chippenham *U.K.* 51°27N 2°6W **13 F5**
Chippewa → *U.S.A.* 44°25N 92°5W **80 C7**
Chippewa Falls *U.S.A.* 44°56N 91°24W **80 C8**
Chipping Norton *U.K.* 51°56N 1°32W **13 F6**
Chiputneticook Lakes
  N. Amer. 45°35N 67°35W **81 C20**
Chiquián *Peru* 10°10S 77°0W **92 F3**
Chiquibul → *Belize* 16°49N 88°52W **88 C2**
Chiquimula *Guatemala* 14°51N 89°37W **88 D2**
Chiquinquira *Colombia* 5°37N 73°50W **92 B4**
Chirala *India* 15°50N 80°26E **40 M12**
Chiramba *Mozam.* 16°55S 34°39E **55 F3**
Chirawa *India* 28°14N 75°42E **42 E6**
Chirchiq *Uzbekistan* 41°29N 69°35E **28 E7**
Chiredzi *Zimbabwe* 21°0S 31°38E **57 C5**

Chiricahua △ *U.S.A.* 32°0N 109°20W **77 K9**
Chiricahua Peak
  U.S.A. 31°51N 109°18W **77 L9**
Chiriquí, G. de *Panama* 8°0N 82°10W **88 E3**
Chiriquí, L. de *Panama* 9°10N 82°0W **88 E3**
Chirisa △ *Zimbabwe* 17°53S 28°15E **55 F2**
Chirivira Falls *Zimbabwe* 21°10S 32°12E **55 G3**
Chirmiri *India* 23°15N 82°20E **43 H10**
Chirripó Grande, Cerro
  Costa Rica 9°29N 83°29W **88 E3**
Chirundu *Zimbabwe* 16°3S 28°50E **57 B4**
Chisamba *Zambia* 14°55S 28°20E **55 E2**
Chisapani *Nepal* 28°37N 81°16E **43 E9**
Chisasibi *Canada* 53°50N 79°0W **72 B4**
Chisholm *Canada* 54°55N 114°10W **70 C6**
Chisholm *U.S.A.* 47°29N 92°53W **80 B7**
Chishtian Mandi
  Pakistan 29°50N 72°55E **42 E5**
Chisimaio = Kismaayo
  Somali Rep. 0°22S 42°32E **47 H3**
Chisimba Falls *Zambia* 10°12S 30°56E **55 E3**
Chișinău *Moldova* 47°2N 28°50E **17 E15**
Chisos Mts. *U.S.A.* 29°5N 103°15W **84 G3**
Chistopol *Russia* 55°25N 50°38E **18 C9**
Chita *Russia* 52°0N 113°35E **29 D12**
Chitipa *Malawi* 9°41S 33°19E **55 D3**
Chitose *Japan* 42°49N 141°39E **30 C10**
Chitral *Pakistan* 35°50N 71°56E **40 B7**
Chitré *Panama* 7°59N 80°27W **88 E3**
Chittagong *Bangla.* 22°19N 91°48E **41 H17**
Chittagong □ *Bangla.* 24°5N 91°0E **41 G17**
Chittaurgarh *India* 24°52N 74°38E **42 G6**
Chittoor *India* 13°15N 79°5E **40 N11**
Chitungwiza *Zimbabwe* 18°0S 31°6E **55 F3**
Chiusi *Italy* 43°1N 11°57E **22 C4**
Chivasso *Italy* 45°11N 7°53E **20 D7**
Chivhu *Zimbabwe* 19°2S 30°52E **55 F3**
Chivilcoy *Argentina* 34°55S 60°0W **94 C4**
Chiwanda *Tanzania* 11°23S 34°55E **55 E3**
Chizarira *Zimbabwe* 17°36S 27°45E **55 F2**
Chizarira △ *Zimbabwe* 17°44S 27°52E **55 F2**
Chizela *Zambia* 13°8S 25°0E **55 E2**
Chkalov = Orenburg
  Russia 51°45N 55°6E **18 D10**
Chloride *U.S.A.* 35°25N 114°12W **79 K12**
Cho Bo *Vietnam* 20°46N 105°10E **38 B5**
Cho-do *N. Korea* 38°30N 124°40E **35 E13**
Cho Phuoc Hai *Vietnam* 10°26N 107°18E **39 G6**
Choa Chu Kang *Singapore* 1°22N 103°41E **39 d**
Choba *Kenya* 2°30N 38°5E **54 B4**
Chobe △ *Botswana* 18°37S 24°23E **56 B4**
Chocolate Mts.
  U.S.A. 33°15N 115°15W **79 M11**
Choctawhatchee →
  U.S.A. 30°25N 86°8W **85 F11**
Choele Choel *Argentina* 39°11S 65°40W **96 D3**
Choiseul *St. Lucia* 13°47N 61°3W **89 f**
Choiseul *Solomon Is.* 7°0S 156°40E **58 B8**
Choix *Mexico* 26°43N 108°17W **86 B3**
Chojnice *Poland* 53°42N 17°32E **17 B9**
Chok Chai *Thailand* 14°44N 102°10E **38 E4**
Chōkai-San *Japan* 39°6N 140°3E **30 E10**
Choke Canyon Res.
  U.S.A. 28°30N 98°20W **84 G5**
Chokurdakh *Russia* 70°38N 147°55E **29 B15**
Cholame *U.S.A.* 35°44N 120°18W **78 K6**
Cholet *France* 47°4N 0°52W **20 C3**
Cholguan *Chile* 37°10S 72°3W **94 D1**
Choloma *Honduras* 15°37N 87°57W **88 C2**
Choluteca *Honduras* 13°20N 87°14W **88 D2**
Choluteca → *Honduras* 13°0N 87°20W **88 D2**
Chom Bung *Thailand* 13°37N 99°36E **38 F2**
Chom Thong *Thailand* 18°25N 98°41E **38 C2**
Choma *Zambia* 16°48S 26°59E **55 F2**
Chomolungma = Everest, Mt.
  Nepal 28°5N 86°58E **43 E12**
Chomun *India* 27°15N 75°40E **42 F6**
Chomutov *Czech Rep.* 50°28N 13°23E **16 C7**
Chon Buri *Thailand* 13°21N 101°1E **38 F3**
Chon Thanh *Vietnam* 11°24N 106°36E **39 G6**
Chone *Ecuador* 0°40S 80°0W **92 D3**
Chong Kai *Cambodia* 13°57N 103°35E **38 F4**
Chong Mek *Thailand* 15°10N 105°27E **38 E5**
Chong Phangan *Thailand* 9°39N 100°0E **39 b**
Chong Samui *Thailand* 9°21N 99°50E **39 b**
Ch'ŏngjin *N. Korea* 41°47N 129°50E **35 D15**
Chŏngju *N. Korea* 39°40N 125°5E **35 E13**
Chongli *China* 40°58N 115°15E **34 D8**
Chongqing *China* 29°35N 106°25E **32 D5**
Chongqing Shi □ *China* 30°0N 108°0E **32 C5**
Chonguene *Mozam.* 25°3S 33°49E **57 C5**
Chonos, Arch. de los *Chile* 45°0S 75°0W **96 F2**
Chop *Ukraine* 48°26N 22°12E **17 D12**
Chopim → *Brazil* 25°35S 53°5W **95 B5**
Chor *Pakistan* 25°31N 69°46E **42 G3**
Chora Sfakion *Greece* 35°15N 24°9E **25 D6**
Chorbat La *India* 34°42N 76°37E **43 B7**
Chorley *U.K.* 53°39N 2°38W **12 D5**
Chornobyl *Ukraine* 51°20N 30°15E **17 C16**
Chorolque, Cerro *Bolivia* 20°59S 66°5W **94 A2**
Chorregon *Australia* 22°40S 143°32E **62 C3**
Chorro el Indio △
  Venezuela 7°43N 72°9W **89 E5**
Chortkiv *Ukraine* 49°2N 25°46E **17 D13**
Chorzów *Poland* 50°18N 18°57E **17 C10**
Chos-Malal *Argentina* 37°20S 70°15W **94 D1**
Ch'osan *N. Korea* 40°50N 125°47E **35 D13**
Choszczno *Poland* 53°7N 15°25E **16 B8**
Choteau *U.S.A.* 47°49N 112°11W **76 C7**
Chotila *India* 22°23N 71°15E **42 H4**
Chotta Udepur *India* 22°19N 74°1E **42 H6**
Chowchilla *U.S.A.* 37°7N 120°16W **78 H6**
Choybalsan *Mongolia* 48°4N 114°30E **33 B6**
Choyr *Mongolia* 46°24N 108°30E **29 E11**
Christchurch *N.Z.* 43°33S 172°47E **59 E4**
Christchurch *U.K.* 50°44N 1°47W **13 G6**
Christian I. *Canada* 44°50N 80°12W **82 B4**

Christiana *S. Africa* 27°52S 25°8E **56 D4**
Christiansted
  U.S. Virgin Is. 17°45N 64°42W **89 C7**
Christie B. *Canada* 62°32N 111°10W **71 A6**
Christina → *Canada* 56°40N 111°3W **71 B6**
Christmas Cr. →
  Australia 18°29S 125°23E **60 C4**
Christmas I. = Kiritimati
  Kiribati 1°58N 157°27W **65 G12**
Christmas I. *Ind. Oc.* 10°30S 105°40E **64 J2**
Christopher, L.
  Australia 24°49S 127°42E **61 E4**
Chtimba *Malawi* 10°35S 34°13E **55 E3**
Chū = Shū *Kazakhstan* 43°36N 73°42E **28 E8**
Chu → *Vietnam* 19°53N 105°45E **38 C5**
Chu Lai *Vietnam* 15°28N 108°45E **38 E7**
Chuadanga *Bangla.* 23°38N 88°51E **43 H13**
Chuak, Ko *Thailand* 9°28N 99°41E **39 b**
Ch'uanchou = Quanzhou
  China 24°55N 118°34E **33 D6**
Chuankou *China* 34°20N 110°59E **34 G6**
Chubbuck *U.S.A.* 42°55N 112°28W **76 E7**
Chūbu □ *Japan* 36°45N 137°30E **31 F8**
Chubu-Sangaku △
  Japan 36°30N 137°40E **31 F8**
Chubut → *Argentina* 43°20S 65°5W **96 E3**
Chuchi L. *Canada* 55°12N 124°30W **70 B4**
Chuda *India* 22°29N 71°41E **42 H4**
Chudskoye, Ozero
  Russia 58°13N 27°30E **9 G22**
Chūgoku □ *Japan* 35°0N 133°0E **31 G6**
Chūgoku-Sanchi *Japan* 35°0N 133°0E **31 G6**
Chugwater *U.S.A.* 41°46N 104°50W **76 F11**
Chuka *Kenya* 0°20S 37°39E **54 C4**
Chukchi Plateau *Arctic* 78°0N 165°0W **4 B17**
Chukchi Sea *Russia* 68°0N 175°0W **29 C19**
Chukotskoye Nagorye
  Russia 68°0N 175°0E **29 C18**
Chula Vista *U.S.A.* 32°38N 117°5W **79 N9**
Chulucanas *Peru* 5°8S 80°10W **92 E2**
Chulym → *Russia* 57°43N 83°51E **28 D9**
Chum Phae *Thailand* 16°40N 102°6E **38 D4**
Chum Saeng *Thailand* 15°55N 100°15E **38 E3**
Chumar *India* 32°40N 78°35E **43 C8**
Chumbicha *Argentina* 29°0S 66°10W **94 B2**
Chumikan *Russia* 54°40N 135°10E **29 D14**
Chumphon *Thailand* 10°35N 99°14E **39 G2**
Chumuare *Mozam.* 14°31S 31°50E **55 E3**
Chuna → *Russia* 57°47N 94°37E **29 D10**
Chuncheon *S. Korea* 37°58N 127°44E **35 F14**
Chunchura *India* 22°53N 88°27E **43 H13**
Chunga *Zambia* 15°0S 26°2E **55 F2**
Chunggang-ŭp
  N. Korea 41°48N 126°48E **35 D14**
Chunghwa *N. Korea* 38°52N 125°47E **35 E13**
Chungju *S. Korea* 36°58N 127°58E **35 F14**
Chungking = Chongqing
  China 29°35N 106°25E **32 D5**
Chungt'iaoshan = Zhongtiao
  Shan *China* 35°0N 111°10E **34 G6**
Chunian *Pakistan* 30°57N 74°0E **42 D6**
Chunya *Tanzania* 8°30S 33°27E **55 D3**
Chunyang *China* 43°38N 129°23E **35 C15**
Chupara Pt.
  Trin. & Tob. 10°49N 61°22W **93 K15**
Chuquibamba *Peru* 15°47S 72°44W **92 G4**
Chuquicamata *Chile* 22°15S 69°0W **94 A2**
Chur *Switz.* 46°52N 9°32E **20 C8**
Churachandpur *India* 24°20N 93°40E **41 G18**
Church Stretton *U.K.* 52°32N 2°48W **13 E5**
Churchill → *Man.,*
  Canada 58°47N 94°11W **71 B10**
Churchill *Canada* 58°47N 94°12W **71 B10**
Churchill → *Nfld. & L.,*
  Canada 53°19N 60°10W **73 B7**
Churchill, C. *Canada* 58°46N 93°12W **71 B10**
Churchill Falls *Canada* 53°36N 64°19W **73 B7**
Churchill L. *Canada* 55°55N 108°20W **71 B7**
Churchill Pk. *Canada* 58°10N 125°10W **70 B3**
Churki *India* 23°50N 83°12E **43 H10**
Churu *India* 28°20N 74°50E **42 E6**
Churún Merú = Angel Falls
  Venezuela 5°57N 62°30W **92 B6**
Chushal *India* 33°40N 78°40E **43 C8**
Chuska Mts. *U.S.A.* 36°15N 108°50W **77 H9**
Chusovoy *Russia* 58°22N 57°50E **18 C10**
Chute-aux-Outardes
  Canada 49°7N 68°24W **73 C6**
Chuuk = Truk
  Micronesia 7°25N 151°46E **64 G7**
Chuvash Republic = Chuvashia □
  Russia 55°30N 47°0E **18 C8**
Chuvashia □ *Russia* 55°30N 47°0E **18 C8**
Chuwārtah *Iraq* 35°43N 45°34E **44 C5**
Chuy *Uruguay* 33°41S 53°27W **95 C5**
Ci Xian *China* 36°20N 114°25E **34 F8**
Ciadâr-Lunga *Moldova* 46°3N 28°51E **17 E15**
Cianjur *Indonesia* 6°49S 107°8E **37 G12**
Cianorte *Brazil* 23°37S 52°37W **95 A5**
Cibola *U.S.A.* 33°17N 114°42W **79 M12**
Cicero *U.S.A.* 41°51N 87°44W **80 E2**
Ciechanów *Poland* 52°52N 20°38E **17 B11**
Ciego de Ávila *Cuba* 21°50N 78°50W **88 B4**
Ciénaga *Colombia* 11°1N 74°15W **92 A4**
Cienfuegos *Cuba* 22°10N 80°30W **88 B3**
Cieszyn *Poland* 49°45N 18°35E **17 D10**
Cieza *Spain* 38°17N 1°23W **21 C5**
Cihuatlán *Mexico* 19°14N 104°35W **86 D4**
Cijara, Embalse de *Spain* 39°18N 4°52W **21 C3**
Cijulang *Indonesia* 7°42S 108°27E **37 G13**
Cilacap *Indonesia* 7°43S 109°0E **37 G13**
Cill Chainnigh = Kilkenny
  Ireland 52°39N 7°15W **10 D4**

Cilo Daǧı *Turkey* 37°28N 43°55E **19 G7**
Cima *U.S.A.* 35°14N 115°30W **79 K11**
Cimarron *Kans., U.S.A.* 37°48N 100°21W **80 G3**
Cimarron *N. Mex.,*
  U.S.A. 36°31N 104°55W **77 H11**
Cimarron → *U.S.A.* 36°10N 96°16W **84 C6**
Cimişlia *Moldova* 46°34N 28°44E **17 E15**
Cimone, Mte. *Italy* 44°12N 10°42E **22 B4**
Cinca → *Spain* 41°26N 0°21E **21 B6**
Cincar *Bos.-H.* 43°55N 17°5E **22 C7**
Cincinnati *U.S.A.* 39°9N 84°27W **81 F11**
Cincinnatus *U.S.A.* 42°33N 75°54W **83 D9**
Çine *Turkey* 37°37N 28°2E **23 F13**
Ciney *Belgium* 50°18N 5°5E **15 D5**
Cinto, Mte. *France* 42°24N 8°54E **20 E8**
Circle *Alaska, U.S.A.* 65°50N 144°4W **74 a**
Circle *Mont., U.S.A.* 47°25N 105°35W **76 C11**
Circleville *U.S.A.* 39°36N 82°57W **81 F12**
Cirebon *Indonesia* 6°45S 108°32E **37 G13**
Ciremay *Indonesia* 6°55S 108°27E **37 G13**
Cirencester *U.K.* 51°43N 1°57W **13 F6**
Cirium *Cyprus* 34°40N 32°53E **25 E11**
Cisco *U.S.A.* 32°23N 98°59W **84 E5**
Citlaltépetl = Orizaba, Pico de
  Mexico 18°58N 97°15W **87 D5**
Citrus Heights *U.S.A.* 38°42N 121°17W **78 G5**
Citrusdal *S. Africa* 32°35S 19°0E **56 E2**
Città del Vaticano = Vatican
  City ■ *Europe* 41°54N 12°27E **22 D5**
Città di Castello *Italy* 43°27N 12°14E **22 C5**
Ciudad Acuña *Mexico* 29°18N 100°55W **86 B4**
Ciudad Altamirano
  Mexico 18°20N 100°40W **86 D4**
Ciudad Anáhuac
  Mexico 27°14N 100°7W **86 B4**
Ciudad Bolívar *Venezuela* 8°5N 63°36W **92 B6**
Ciudad Camargo
  Mexico 27°40N 105°10W **86 B3**
Ciudad Cortés *Costa Rica* 8°55N 84°0W **88 E3**
Ciudad de México *Mexico* 19°24N 99°9W **87 D5**
Ciudad de Valles *Mexico* 22°0N 99°0W **87 C5**
Ciudad del Carmen
  Mexico 18°38N 91°50W **87 D6**
Ciudad del Este *Paraguay* 25°30S 54°50W **95 B5**
Ciudad Delicias = Delicias
  Mexico 28°13N 105°28W **86 B3**
Ciudad Frontera
  Mexico 26°56N 101°27W **86 B4**
Ciudad Guayana
  Venezuela 8°0N 62°30W **92 B6**
Ciudad Guerrero
  Mexico 28°33N 107°30W **86 B3**
Ciudad Guzmán
  Mexico 19°41N 103°29W **86 D4**
Ciudad Juárez *Mexico* 31°44N 106°29W **86 A3**
Ciudad Lerdo *Mexico* 25°32N 103°32W **86 B4**
Ciudad Madero *Mexico* 22°19N 97°50W **87 C5**
Ciudad Mante *Mexico* 22°44N 98°59W **87 C5**
Ciudad Obregón
  Mexico 27°29N 109°56W **86 B3**
Ciudad Real *Spain* 38°59N 3°55W **21 C4**
Ciudad Rodrigo *Spain* 40°35N 6°32W **21 B2**
Ciudad Victoria *Mexico* 23°44N 99°8W **87 C5**
Ciudadela *Spain* 40°0N 3°50E **24 B10**
Civitanova Marche *Italy* 43°18N 13°44E **22 C5**
Civitavécchia *Italy* 42°6N 11°48E **22 C4**
Cizre *Turkey* 37°19N 42°10E **44 B4**
Clackmannanshire □
  U.K. 56°10N 3°43W **11 E5**
Clacton-on-Sea *U.K.* 51°47N 1°11E **13 F9**
Claire, L. *Canada* 58°35N 112°5W **70 B6**
Clairton *U.S.A.* 40°18N 79°53W **82 F5**
Clallam Bay *U.S.A.* 48°15N 124°16W **78 B2**
Clanton *U.S.A.* 32°51N 86°38W **85 E11**
Clanwilliam *S. Africa* 32°11S 18°52E **56 E2**
Clara *Ireland* 53°21N 7°37W **10 C4**
Claraville *U.S.A.* 35°24N 118°20W **79 K8**
Clare *Australia* 33°50S 138°37E **63 E2**
Clare *U.S.A.* 43°49N 84°46W **81 D11**
Clare □ *Ireland* 52°45N 9°0W **10 D3**
Clare → *Ireland* 53°20N 9°2W **10 C2**
Clare I. *Ireland* 53°49N 10°0W **10 C1**
Claremont *Calif., U.S.A.* 34°6N 117°43W **79 L9**
Claremont *N.H., U.S.A.* 43°23N 72°20W **83 C12**
Claremont Pt. *Australia* 14°1S 143°41E **62 A3**
Claremore *U.S.A.* 36°19N 95°36W **84 C7**
Claremorris *Ireland* 53°45N 9°0W **10 C3**
Clarence → *Australia* 29°25S 153°22E **63 D5**
Clarence → *N.Z.* 42°10S 173°56E **59 E4**
Clarence, I. *Chile* 54°0S 72°0W **96 G2**
Clarence I. *Antarctica* 61°10S 54°0W **5 C18**
Clarence Str. *Australia* 12°0S 131°0E **60 B5**
Clarence Town *Bahamas* 23°6N 74°59W **89 B5**
Clarendon *Pa., U.S.A.* 41°47N 79°6W **82 E5**
Clarendon *Tex., U.S.A.* 34°56N 100°53W **84 D4**
Clarenville *Canada* 48°10N 54°1W **73 C9**
Claresholm *Canada* 50°2N 113°33W **70 D6**
Clarie Coast *Antarctica* 68°0S 135°0E **5 C9**
Clarinda *U.S.A.* 40°44N 95°2W **80 E6**
Clarington *Canada* 43°55N 78°41W **82 C6**
Clarion *Iowa, U.S.A.* 42°44N 93°44W **80 D7**
Clarion *Pa., U.S.A.* 41°13N 79°23W **82 E5**
Clarion → *U.S.A.* 41°7N 79°41W **82 E5**
Clarion Fracture Zone
  Pac. Oc. 20°0N 120°0W **66 H7**

Clarks Summit *U.S.A.* 41°30N 75°42W **83 E9**
Clarksburg *U.S.A.* 39°17N 80°30W **81 F13**
Clarksdale *U.S.A.* 34°12N 90°35W **85 D9**
Clarkston *U.S.A.* 46°25N 117°3W **76 C5**
Clarksville *Ark., U.S.A.* 35°28N 93°28W **84 D8**
Clarksville *Tenn.,*
  U.S.A. 36°32N 87°21W **85 C11**
Clarksville *Tex., U.S.A.* 33°37N 95°3W **84 E7**
Clatskanie *U.S.A.* 46°6N 123°12W **78 D3**
Claude *U.S.A.* 35°7N 101°22W **84 D4**
Claveria *Phil.* 18°37N 121°4E **37 A6**
Clay *U.S.A.* 38°17N 121°10W **78 G5**
Clay Center *U.S.A.* 39°23N 97°8W **80 F5**
Claypool *U.S.A.* 33°25N 110°51W **77 K8**
Claysburg *U.S.A.* 40°17N 78°27W **82 F6**
Claysville *U.S.A.* 40°7N 80°25W **82 F4**
Clayton *Canada* 45°37N 76°19W **83 A8**
Clayton *N. Mex.,*
  U.S.A. 36°27N 103°11W **77 H12**
Clayton *N.Y., U.S.A.* 44°14N 76°5W **83 B8**
Clear, C. *Ireland* 51°25N 9°32W **10 E2**
Clear I. *Ireland* 51°26N 9°30W **10 E2**
Clear L. *U.S.A.* 39°2N 122°47W **78 F4**
Clear Hills *Canada* 56°40N 119°30W **70 B5**
Clear I. *Ireland* 51°26N 9°30W **10 E2**
Clear L. *U.S.A.* 39°2N 122°47W **78 F4**
Clear Lake *Iowa, U.S.A.* 43°8N 93°23W **80 D7**
Clear Lake *S. Dak.,*
  U.S.A. 44°45N 96°41W **80 C5**
Clear Lake Res. *U.S.A.* 41°56N 121°5W **76 F3**
Clearfield *Pa., U.S.A.* 41°2N 78°27W **82 E6**
Clearfield *Utah, U.S.A.* 41°7N 112°2W **76 F7**
Clearlake *U.S.A.* 38°57N 122°38W **78 G4**
Clearwater *Canada* 51°38N 120°2W **70 C4**
Clearwater *U.S.A.* 27°59N 82°48W **85 H13**
Clearwater → *Alta.,*
  Canada 52°22N 114°57W **70 C6**
Clearwater → *Alta.,*
  Canada 56°44N 111°23W **71 B6**
Clearwater L. *Canada* 53°34N 99°49W **71 C9**
Clearwater Lake △
  Canada 54°0N 101°0W **71 C8**
Clearwater Mts. *U.S.A.* 46°5N 115°20W **76 C6**
Clearwater River △
  Canada 56°55N 109°10W **71 B7**
Cleburne *U.S.A.* 32°21N 97°23W **84 E6**
Clee Hills *U.K.* 52°26N 2°35W **13 E5**
Cleethorpes *U.K.* 53°33N 0°3W **12 D7**
Cleeve Cloud *U.K.* 51°56N 2°0W **13 F6**
Clemson *U.S.A.* 34°41N 82°50W **85 D13**
Clerke Reef *Australia* 17°22S 119°20E **60 C2**
Clermont *Australia* 22°49S 147°39E **62 C4**
Clermont *U.S.A.* 28°33N 81°46W **85 G14**
Clermont-Ferrand *France* 45°46N 3°4E **20 D5**
Clervaux *Lux.* 50°4N 6°2E **15 D6**
Clevedon *U.K.* 51°26N 2°52W **13 F5**
Cleveland *Miss., U.S.A.* 33°45N 90°43W **85 E9**
Cleveland *Ohio, U.S.A.* 41°29N 81°41W **82 E3**
Cleveland *Okla., U.S.A.* 36°19N 96°28W **84 C6**
Cleveland *Tenn., U.S.A.* 35°10N 84°53W **85 D12**
Cleveland *Tex., U.S.A.* 30°21N 95°5W **84 F7**
Cleveland, C. *Australia* 19°11S 147°1E **62 B4**
Cleveland, Mt. *U.S.A.* 48°56N 113°51W **76 B7**
Cleveland Heights
  U.S.A. 41°31N 81°33W **82 E3**
Clevelândia *Brazil* 26°24S 52°23W **95 B5**
Clew B. *Ireland* 53°50N 9°49W **10 C2**
Clewiston *U.S.A.* 26°45N 80°56W **85 H14**
Clifden *Ireland* 53°29N 10°1W **10 C1**
Clifden *N.Z.* 46°1S 167°42E **59 G1**
Cliffdell *U.S.A.* 46°56N 121°5W **78 D5**
Cliffy Hd. *Australia* 35°1S 116°29E **61 G2**
Clifton *Australia* 27°59S 151°53E **63 D5**
Clifton *Ariz., U.S.A.* 33°3N 109°18W **77 K9**
Clifton *Colo., U.S.A.* 39°7N 108°25W **76 G9**
Clifton *Tex., U.S.A.* 31°47N 97°35W **84 F6**
Clifton Beach *Australia* 16°46S 145°39E **62 B4**
Clinch → *U.S.A.* 35°53N 84°29W **85 D12**
Clingmans Dome
  U.S.A. 35°34N 83°30W **85 D13**
Clint *U.S.A.* 31°35N 106°14W **84 F1**
Clinton *B.C., Canada* 51°6N 121°35W **70 C4**
Clinton *Ont., Canada* 43°37N 81°32W **82 C3**
Clinton *N.Z.* 46°12S 169°23E **59 G2**
Clinton *Ark., U.S.A.* 35°36N 92°28W **84 D8**
Clinton *Conn., U.S.A.* 41°17N 72°32W **83 E12**
Clinton *Ill., U.S.A.* 40°9N 88°57W **80 E9**
Clinton *Ind., U.S.A.* 39°40N 87°24W **80 F10**
Clinton *Iowa, U.S.A.* 41°51N 90°12W **80 E8**
Clinton *Mass., U.S.A.* 42°25N 71°41W **83 D13**
Clinton *Miss., U.S.A.* 32°20N 90°20W **85 E9**
Clinton *Mo., U.S.A.* 38°22N 93°46W **80 F7**
Clinton *N.C., U.S.A.* 35°0N 78°22W **85 D15**
Clinton *Okla., U.S.A.* 35°31N 98°58W **84 D5**
Clinton *Tenn., U.S.A.* 36°6N 84°8W **85 C12**
Clinton *Wash., U.S.A.* 47°59N 122°21W **78 C4**
Clinton, C. *Australia* 22°30S 150°45E **62 C5**
Clinton Colden L.
  Canada 63°58N 107°27W **68 C9**
Clintonville *U.S.A.* 44°37N 88°46W **80 C9**
Clipperton, I. *Pac. Oc.* 10°18N 109°13W **65 F17**
Clipperton Fracture Zone
  Pac. Oc. 19°0N 122°0W **65 G16**
Clisham *U.K.* 57°58N 6°49W **11 D2**
Clitheroe *U.K.* 53°53N 2°22W **12 D5**
Clo-oose *Canada* 48°39N 124°49W **78 B2**
Cloates, Pt. *Australia* 22°43S 113°40E **60 D1**
Clocolan *S. Africa* 28°55S 27°34E **57 D4**
Clodomira *Argentina* 27°35S 64°14W **94 B3**
Clogher Hd. *Ireland* 53°48N 6°14W **10 C5**
Clonakilty *Ireland* 51°37N 8°53W **10 E3**
Clonakilty B. *Ireland* 51°35N 8°51W **10 E3**
Cloncurry *Australia* 20°40S 140°28E **62 C3**
Cloncurry → *Australia* 18°37S 140°40E **62 B3**
Clondalkin *Ireland* 53°19N 6°25W **10 C5**
Clones *Ireland* 54°11N 7°15W **10 B4**

Clonmel Ireland 52°21N 7°42W 10 D4
Cloquet U.S.A. 46°43N 92°28W 80 B7
Clorinda Argentina 25°16S 57°45W 94 B4
Cloud Bay Canada 48°5N 89°26W 72 C2
Cloud Peak U.S.A. 44°23N 107°11W 76 D10
Cloudcroft U.S.A. 32°58N 105°45W 77 K11
Cloverdale U.S.A. 38°48N 123°1W 78 G4
Clovis Calif., U.S.A. 36°49N 119°42W 78 J7
Clovis N. Mex., U.S.A. 34°24N 103°12W 77 J12
Cloyne Canada 44°49N 77°11W 82 B7
Cluj-Napoca Romania 46°47N 23°38E 17 E12
Clunes Australia 37°20S 143°45E 63 F3
Clutha → N.Z. 46°20S 169°49E 59 G2
Clwyd → U.K. 53°19N 3°31W 12 D4
Clyde Canada 54°9N 113°39W 70 C6
Clyde N.Z. 45°12S 169°20E 59 F2
Clyde U.S.A. 43°5N 76°52W 82 C8
Clyde → U.K. 55°55N 4°30W 11 F4
Clyde, Firth of U.K. 55°22N 5°1W 11 F3
Clyde Muirshiel △ U.K. 55°50N 4°40W 11 F4
Clyde River Canada 70°30N 68°30W 69 B13
Clydebank U.K. 55°54N 4°23N 11 F4
Clymer N.Y., U.S.A. 42°1N 79°37W 82 D5
Clymer Pa., U.S.A. 40°40N 79°1W 82 D5
Coachella U.S.A. 33°41N 116°10W 79 M10
Coachella Canal U.S.A. 32°43N 114°57W 79 N12
Coahoma U.S.A. 32°18N 101°18W 84 E4
Coahuayana → Mexico 18°41N 103°45W 86 D4
Coahuila □ Mexico 27°20N 102°0W 86 B4
Coal → Canada 59°39N 126°57W 70 B3
Coalane Mozam. 17°48S 37°2E 55 F4
Coalcomán Mexico 18°47N 103°9W 86 D4
Coaldale Canada 49°45N 112°35W 70 D6
Coalgate U.S.A. 34°32N 96°13W 84 D6
Coalinga U.S.A. 36°9N 120°21W 78 J6
Coalisland U.K. 54°33N 6°42W 10 B5
Coalville U.K. 52°44N 1°23W 12 E6
Coalville U.S.A. 40°55N 111°24W 76 F8
Coamo Puerto Rico 18°5N 66°22W 89 d
Coari Brazil 4°8S 63°7W 92 D6
Coast □ Kenya 2°40S 39°45E 54 C4
Coast Mts. Canada 55°0N 129°20W 70 C3
Coast Ranges U.S.A. 39°0N 123°0W 78 G4
Coatbridge U.K. 55°52N 4°6W 11 F4
Coatepec Mexico 19°27N 96°58W 87 D5
Coatepeque Guatemala 14°46N 91°55W 88 D1
Coatesville U.S.A. 39°59N 75°50W 81 F16
Coaticook Canada 45°10N 71°46W 83 A13
Coats I. Canada 62°30N 83°0W 69 C11
Coats Land Antarctica 77°0S 25°0W 5 D1
Coatzacoalcos Mexico 18°7N 94°25W 87 D6
Cobá Mexico 20°31N 87°45W 87 D7
Cobalt Canada 47°25N 79°42W 72 C4
Cobán Guatemala 15°30N 90°21W 88 C1
Cobar Australia 31°27S 145°48E 63 E4
Cóbh Ireland 51°51N 8°17W 10 E3
Cobija Bolivia 11°0S 68°50W 92 F5
Cobleskill U.S.A. 42°41N 74°29W 83 D10
Coboconk Canada 44°39N 78°48W 82 B6
Cobourg Canada 43°58N 78°10W 82 C6
Cobourg Pen. Australia 11°20S 132°15E 60 B5
Cobram Australia 35°54S 145°40E 63 F4
Cóbué Mozam. 12°0S 34°58E 55 E3
Coburg Germany 50°15N 10°58E 16 C6
Cocanada = Kakinada India 16°57N 82°11E 41 L13
Cochabamba Bolivia 17°26S 66°10W 92 G5
Cochemane Mozam. 17°0S 32°54E 55 F3
Cochin India 9°58N 76°20E 40 Q10
Cochin China = Nam-Phan Vietnam 10°30N 106°0E 39 G6
Cochran U.S.A. 32°23N 83°21W 85 E13
Cochrane Alta., Canada 51°11N 114°30W 70 C6
Cochrane Ont., Canada 49°0N 81°0W 72 C3
Cochrane Chile 47°15S 72°33W 96 F2
Cochrane → Canada 59°0N 103°40W 71 B8
Cochrane, L. Chile 47°10S 72°0W 96 F2
Cochranton U.S.A. 41°31N 80°3W 82 E4
Cockburn Australia 32°5S 141°0E 63 E3
Cockburn, Canal Chile 54°30S 72°0W 96 G2
Cockburn I. Canada 45°55N 83°22W 72 C3
Cockburn Ra. Australia 15°46S 128°0E 60 C4
Cockermouth U.K. 54°40N 3°22W 12 C4
Cocklebiddy Australia 32°0S 126°3E 61 F4
Cockpit Country, The Jamaica 18°15N 77°45W 88 a
Coco → Cent. Amer. 15°0N 83°8W 88 D3
Coco, I. del Pac. Oc. 5°25N 87°55W 65 G19
Cocoa U.S.A. 28°21N 80°44W 85 G14
Cocobeach Gabon 0°59N 9°34E 52 D1
Cocos B. Trin. & Tob. 10°25N 61°2W 93 K15
Cocos Is. Ind. Oc. 12°10S 96°55E 64 J1
Cocos Ridge Pac. Oc. 4°0N 88°0W 65 G19
Cod, C. U.S.A. 42°5N 70°10W 81 D18
Codajás Brazil 3°55S 62°0W 92 D6
Codó Brazil 4°30S 43°55W 93 D10
Cody U.S.A. 44°32N 109°3W 76 D9
Coe Hill Canada 44°52N 77°50W 82 B7
Coelemu Chile 36°30S 72°48W 94 D1
Coen Australia 13°52S 143°12E 62 A3
Coeur d'Alene U.S.A. 47°41N 116°46W 76 C5
Coeur d'Alene L. U.S.A. 47°32N 116°49W 76 C5
Coevorden Neths. 52°40N 6°44E 15 B6
Cofete Canary Is. 28°6N 14°23W 24 F5
Coffeyville U.S.A. 37°2N 95°37W 80 G6
Coffin B. Australia 34°38S 135°28E 63 E2
Coffin Bay Australia 34°37S 135°29E 63 E2
Coffin Bay △ Australia 34°34S 135°19E 63 E2
Coffin Bay Peninsula Australia 34°32S 135°15E 63 E2
Coffs Harbour Australia 30°16S 153°5E 63 E5
Cognac France 45°41N 0°20W 20 D3
Cohocton U.S.A. 42°30N 77°30W 82 D7
Cohocton → U.S.A. 42°9N 77°6W 82 D7

Cohoes U.S.A. 42°46N 73°42W 83 D11
Cohuna Australia 35°45S 144°15E 63 F3
Coiba, I. de Panama 7°30N 81°40W 88 E3
Coig → Argentina 51°0S 69°10W 96 G3
Coigeach, Rubha U.K. 58°6N 5°26W 11 C3
Coihaique Chile 45°30S 71°45W 96 F2
Coimbatore India 11°2N 76°59E 40 P10
Coimbra Brazil 19°55S 57°48W 92 G7
Coimbra Portugal 40°15N 8°27E 21 B1
Coín Spain 36°40N 4°48W 21 D3
Coipasa, Salar de Bolivia 19°26S 68°9W 92 G5
Cojimies Ecuador 0°20N 80°0W 92 C3
Cojutepequé El Salv. 13°41N 88°54W 88 D2
Cokeville U.S.A. 42°5N 110°57W 76 E8
Colac Australia 38°21S 143°35E 63 F3
Colatina Brazil 19°32S 40°37W 93 G10
Colbeck, C. Antarctica 77°6S 157°48W 5 D13
Colborne Canada 44°0N 77°53W 82 C7
Colby U.S.A. 39°24N 101°3W 80 F3
Colca → Peru 15°55S 72°43W 92 G4
Colchester U.K. 51°54N 0°55E 13 F8
Colchester U.S.A. 41°35N 72°20W 83 E12
Cold L. Canada 54°33N 110°5W 71 C7
Cold Lake Canada 54°27N 110°10W 71 C6
Coldstream Canada 50°13N 119°11W 70 C5
Coldstream U.K. 55°39N 2°15W 11 F6
Coldwater Canada 44°42N 79°40W 82 B5
Coldwater Kans., U.S.A. 37°16N 99°20W 80 G4
Coldwater Mich., U.S.A. 41°57N 85°0W 81 E11
Colebrook U.S.A. 44°54N 71°30W 83 B13
Coleman Canada 49°40N 114°30W 70 D6
Coleman U.S.A. 31°50N 99°26W 84 F5
Coleman → Australia 15°6S 141°38E 62 B3
Colenso S. Africa 28°44S 29°50E 57 D4
Coleraine Australia 37°36S 141°40E 63 F3
Coleraine U.K. 55°8N 6°41W 10 A5
Coleridge, L. N.Z. 43°17S 171°30E 59 E3
Colesberg S. Africa 30°45S 25°5E 56 E4
Coleville U.S.A. 38°34N 119°30W 78 G7
Colfax Calif., U.S.A. 39°6N 120°57W 78 F6
Colfax La., U.S.A. 31°31N 92°42W 84 F8
Colfax Wash., U.S.A. 46°53N 117°22W 76 C5
Colhué Huapi, L. Argentina 45°30S 69°0W 96 F3
Coligny S. Africa 26°17S 26°15E 57 D4
Colima Mexico 19°14N 103°43W 86 D4
Colima □ Mexico 19°10N 104°0W 86 D4
Colima, Nevado de Mexico 19°33N 103°38W 86 D4
Colina Chile 33°13S 70°45W 94 C1
Colinas Brazil 6°0S 44°10W 93 E10
Coll U.K. 56°39N 6°34W 11 E2
Collahuasi Chile 21°5S 68°45W 94 A2
Collarenebri Australia 29°33S 148°34E 63 D4
Colleen Bawn Zimbabwe 21°0S 29°12E 55 G2
Collie Australia 33°22S 116°8E 61 F2
Collier B. Australia 16°10S 124°15E 60 C3
Collier Ra. Australia 24°45S 119°10E 61 D2
Collier Range △ Australia 24°39S 119°7E 61 D2
Collierville U.S.A. 35°3N 89°40W 85 D10
Collingwood Canada 44°29N 80°13W 82 B4
Collingwood N.Z. 40°41S 172°40E 59 D4
Collins Canada 50°17N 89°27W 72 B2
Collins Bay Canada 44°14N 76°36W 83 B8
Collinsville Australia 20°30S 147°56E 62 C4
Collipulli Chile 37°55S 72°30W 94 D1
Collooney Ireland 54°11N 8°29W 10 B3
Colmar France 48°5N 7°20E 20 B7
Colo → Australia 33°25S 150°52E 63 E5
Cologne = Köln Germany 50°56N 6°57E 16 C4
Colom, I. d'en Spain 39°58N 4°16E 24 B11
Coloma U.S.A. 38°48N 120°53W 78 G6
Colomb-Béchar = Béchar Algeria 31°38N 2°18W 50 B5
Colombia ■ S. Amer. 3°45N 73°0W 92 C4
Colombian Basin S. Amer. 14°0N 76°0W 66 H12
Colombo Sri Lanka 6°56N 79°58E 40 R11
Colón B. Aires, Argentina 33°53S 61°7W 94 C3
Colón Entre Ríos, Argentina 32°12S 58°10W 94 C4
Colón Cuba 22°42N 80°54W 88 B3
Colón Panama 9°20N 79°54W 88 E4
Colón, Arch. de Ecuador 0°0 91°0W 90 D1
Colònia de Sant Jordi Spain 39°19N 2°59E 24 B9
Colonia del Sacramento Uruguay 34°25S 57°50W 94 C4
Colonia Dora Argentina 28°34S 62°59W 94 B3
Colonial Beach U.S.A. 38°15N 76°58W 81 F15
Colonie U.S.A. 42°43N 73°50W 83 D11
Colonsay Canada 51°59N 105°52W 71 C7
Colonsay U.K. 56°5N 6°12W 11 E2
Colorado □ U.S.A. 39°30N 105°30W 76 G11
Colorado → Argentina 39°50S 62°8W 96 D4
Colorado → N. Amer. 31°45N 114°40W 77 L6
Colorado → U.S.A. 28°36N 95°59W 84 G7
Colorado City U.S.A. 32°24N 100°52W 84 E4
Colorado Plateau U.S.A. 37°0N 111°0W 77 H8
Colorado River Aqueduct U.S.A. 33°50N 117°23W 79 L12
Colorado Springs U.S.A. 38°50N 104°49W 76 G11
Colotlán Mexico 22°6N 103°16W 86 C4
Colstrip U.S.A. 45°53N 106°38W 76 D10
Colton U.S.A. 44°33N 74°56W 83 B10
Columbia Ky., U.S.A. 37°6N 85°18W 81 G11
Columbia La., U.S.A. 32°6N 92°5W 84 E8
Columbia Miss., U.S.A. 31°15N 89°50W 85 F10
Columbia Mo., U.S.A. 38°57N 92°20W 80 F7
Columbia Pa., U.S.A. 40°2N 76°30W 83 F8
Columbia S.C., U.S.A. 34°0N 81°2W 85 D14
Columbia Tenn., U.S.A. 35°37N 87°2W 85 D11

Columbia → N. Amer. 46°15N 124°5W 78 D2
Columbia, C. Canada 83°6N 69°57W 69 A11
Columbia, District of □ U.S.A. 38°55N 77°0W 81 F15
Columbia, Mt. Canada 52°8N 117°20W 70 C5
Columbia Basin U.S.A. 46°45N 119°5W 76 C4
Columbia Falls U.S.A. 48°23N 114°11W 76 B6
Columbia Mts. Canada 52°0N 119°0W 70 C5
Columbia Plateau U.S.A. 44°0N 117°30W 76 E5
Columbiana U.S.A. 40°53N 80°42W 82 F4
Columbretes, Is. Spain 39°50N 0°50E 21 C6
Columbus Ga., U.S.A. 32°28N 84°59W 85 E12
Columbus Ind., U.S.A. 39°13N 85°55W 81 F11
Columbus Kans., U.S.A. 37°10N 94°50W 80 G6
Columbus Miss., U.S.A. 33°30N 88°25W 85 E10
Columbus Mont., U.S.A. 45°38N 109°15W 76 D9
Columbus N. Mex., U.S.A. 31°50N 107°38W 77 L10
Columbus Nebr., U.S.A. 41°26N 97°22W 80 E5
Columbus Ohio, U.S.A. 39°58N 83°0W 81 F12
Columbus Tex., U.S.A. 29°42N 96°33W 84 G6
Colusa U.S.A. 39°13N 122°1W 78 F4
Colville U.S.A. 48°33N 117°54W 76 B5
Colville → U.S.A. 70°25N 150°30W 74 a
Colville, C. N.Z. 36°29S 175°21E 59 B5
Colwood Canada 48°26N 123°29W 78 B3
Colwyn Bay U.K. 53°18N 3°44W 12 D4
Comácchio Italy 44°42N 12°11E 22 B5
Comalcalco Mexico 18°16N 93°13W 87 D6
Comallo Argentina 41°0S 70°5W 96 E2
Comanche U.S.A. 31°54N 98°36W 84 F5
Comandante Ferraz Antarctica 62°30S 58°0W 5 C18
Comayagua Honduras 14°25N 87°37W 88 D2
Combahee → U.S.A. 32°31N 80°31W 85 E14
Combarbalá Chile 31°11S 71°2W 94 C1
Combe Martin U.K. 51°12N 4°3W 13 F3
Comber Canada 42°14N 82°33W 82 D2
Comber U.K. 54°33N 5°45W 10 B6
Combermere Canada 45°22N 77°37W 82 A7
Comblain-au-Pont Belgium 50°29N 5°35E 15 D5
Comeragh Mts. Ireland 52°18N 7°34W 10 D4
Comet Australia 23°36S 148°38E 62 C4
Comilla Bangla. 23°28N 91°10E 41 H17
Comino Malta 36°1N 14°20E 25 C1
Comino, C. Italy 40°32N 9°49E 22 D3
Comitán de Domínguez Mexico 16°15N 92°8W 87 D6
Commerce Ga., U.S.A. 34°12N 83°28W 85 D13
Commerce Tex., U.S.A. 33°15N 95°54W 84 E7
Committee B. Canada 68°30N 86°30W 69 C11
Commodore, C. Canada 44°47N 80°54W 82 B4
Commonwealth B. Antarctica 67°0S 144°0E 5 C10
Commoron Cr. → Australia 28°22S 150°8E 63 D5
Communism Pk. = imeni Ismail Samani, Pik Tajikistan 39°0N 72°2E 28 F8
Como Italy 45°47N 9°5E 20 B8
Como, Lago di Italy 46°0N 9°11E 20 B8
Comodoro Rivadavia Argentina 45°50S 67°40W 96 F3
Comorin, C. = Kanyakumari India 8°3N 77°40E 40 Q10
Comoros ■ Ind. Oc. 12°10S 44°15E 53 a
Comox Canada 49°42N 124°55W 70 D4
Compiègne France 49°24N 2°50E 20 B5
Compostela Mexico 21°14N 104°55W 86 C4
Comprida, I. Brazil 24°50S 47°42W 95 A6
Compton Canada 45°14N 71°49W 83 A13
Compton U.S.A. 33°53N 118°13W 79 M8
Comrat Moldova 46°18N 28°40E 17 E15
Con Cuong Vietnam 19°2N 104°54E 38 C5
Con Dao △ Vietnam 8°42N 106°35E 39 H6
Con Son Vietnam 8°41N 106°37E 39 H6
Conakry Guinea 9°29N 13°49W 50 G3
Conara Australia 41°50S 147°26E 63 G4
Concarneau France 47°52N 3°56W 20 C2
Conceição Mozam. 18°47S 36°7E 55 F4
Conceição da Barra Brazil 18°35S 39°45W 93 G11
Conceição do Araguaia Brazil 8°0S 49°2W 93 E9
Concepción Argentina 27°20S 65°35W 94 B2
Concepción Bolivia 16°15S 62°8W 92 G6
Concepción Chile 36°50S 73°0W 94 D1
Concepción Mexico 18°15N 90°5W 87 D6
Concepción Paraguay 23°22S 57°26W 94 A4
Concepción □ Chile 37°0S 72°30W 94 D1
Concepción → Mexico 30°32N 113°2W 86 A2
Concepción, Est. de Chile 50°30S 74°55W 96 G2
Concepción, L. Bolivia 17°20S 61°20W 92 G6
Concepción, Pta. Mexico 26°53N 111°50W 86 B2
Concepción del Oro Mexico 24°38N 101°25W 86 C4
Concepción del Uruguay Argentina 32°35S 58°20W 94 C4
Conception, Pt. U.S.A. 34°27N 120°28W 79 L6
Conception B. Canada 47°45N 53°0W 73 C9
Conception I. Bahamas 23°52N 75°9W 89 B4
Concession Zimbabwe 17°27S 30°56E 55 F3
Conchas Dam U.S.A. 35°22N 104°11W 77 J11
Concho U.S.A. 34°28N 109°36W 77 J9
Concho → U.S.A. 31°34N 99°43W 84 F5
Conchos → Chihuahua, Mexico 29°35N 104°25W 86 B4
Conchos → Chihuahua, Mexico 27°29N 105°45W 86 B3
Conchos → Tamaulipas, Mexico 24°55N 97°38W 87 B5
Concord Calif., U.S.A. 37°59N 122°2W 78 H4

Concord N.C., U.S.A. 35°25N 80°35W 85 D14
Concord N.H., U.S.A. 43°12N 71°32W 83 C13
Concordia Antarctica 75°6S 123°23E 5 D17
Concordia Argentina 31°20S 58°2W 94 C4
Concórdia Amazonas, Brazil 4°36S 66°36W 92 D5
Concórdia Sta. Catarina, Brazil 27°14S 52°1W 95 B5
Concordia Mexico 23°17N 106°4W 86 C3
Concordia U.S.A. 39°34N 97°40W 80 F5
Concrete U.S.A. 48°32N 121°45W 76 B3
Condamine Australia 26°56S 150°9E 63 D5
Conde U.S.A. 45°9N 98°6W 80 C4
Condeúba Brazil 14°52S 42°0W 93 F10
Condobolin Australia 33°4S 147°6E 63 E4
Condon U.S.A. 45°14N 120°11W 76 D3
Conegliano Italy 45°53N 12°18E 22 B5
Conejera, I. = Conills, I. des Spain 39°11N 2°58E 24 B9
Conejos Mexico 26°14N 103°53W 86 B4
Conemaugh → U.S.A. 40°28N 79°19W 82 F5
Confuso → Paraguay 25°9S 57°34W 94 B4
Congleton U.K. 53°10N 2°13W 12 D5
Congo (Brazzaville) = Congo ■ Africa 1°0S 16°0E 52 E3
Congo (Kinshasa) = Congo, Dem. Rep. of the ■ Africa 3°0S 23°0E 52 E4
Congo ■ Africa 1°0S 16°0E 52 E3
Congo → Africa 6°4S 12°24E 52 F2
Congo, Dem. Rep. of the ■ Africa 3°0S 23°0E 52 E4
Congo Basin Africa 0°10S 24°30E 52 E4
Congonhas Brazil 20°30S 43°52W 95 A7
Congress U.S.A. 34°9N 112°51W 77 J7
Conills, I. des Spain 39°11N 2°58E 24 B9
Coniston Canada 46°29N 80°51W 72 C3
Conjeeveram = Kanchipuram India 12°52N 79°45E 40 N11
Conklin Canada 55°38N 111°5W 71 B6
Conklin U.S.A. 42°2N 75°49W 83 D9
Conn, L. Ireland 54°3N 9°15W 10 B2
Connacht □ Ireland 53°43N 9°12W 10 C2
Conneaut U.S.A. 41°57N 80°34W 82 E4
Conneautville U.S.A. 41°45N 80°22W 82 E4
Connecticut □ U.S.A. 41°30N 72°45W 83 E12
Connecticut → U.S.A. 41°16N 72°20W 83 E12
Connell U.S.A. 46°40N 118°52W 76 C4
Connellsville U.S.A. 40°1N 79°35W 82 F5
Connemara □ Ireland 53°29N 9°45W 10 C2
Connemara △ Ireland 53°32N 9°52W 10 C2
Connersville U.S.A. 39°39N 85°8W 81 F11
Connors Ra. Australia 21°40S 149°10E 62 C4
Conoename → Suriname 5°48N 55°55W 93 B7
Conquest Canada 51°32N 107°14W 71 C7
Conrad U.S.A. 48°10N 111°57W 76 B8
Conran, C. Australia 37°49S 148°44E 63 F4
Conroe U.S.A. 30°19N 95°27W 84 F7
Consecon Canada 44°0N 77°31W 82 C7
Conselheiro Lafaiete Brazil 20°40S 43°48W 95 A7
Consell Spain 39°40N 2°48E 24 B9
Consett U.K. 54°51N 1°50W 12 C6
Consort Canada 52°1N 110°46W 71 C6
Constance = Konstanz Germany 47°40N 9°10E 16 E5
Constance, L. = Bodensee Europe 47°35N 9°25E 20 C8
Constanța Romania 44°14N 28°38E 17 F15
Constantine Algeria 36°25N 6°42E 50 A7
Constitución Chile 35°20S 72°30W 94 D1
Constitución Uruguay 31°0S 57°50W 94 C4
Constitución de 1857 △ Mexico 32°4N 115°55W 86 A1
Consul Canada 49°20N 109°30W 71 D7
Contact U.S.A. 41°46N 114°45W 76 F6
Contai India 21°54N 87°46E 43 J12
Contamana Peru 7°19S 74°55W 92 E4
Contas → Brazil 14°17S 39°1W 93 F11
Contoocook U.S.A. 43°13N 71°45W 83 C13
Contra Costa Mozam. 25°9S 33°30E 57 D5
Contwoyto L. Canada 65°42N 110°50W 68 C8
Conway = Conwy U.K. 53°17N 3°50W 12 D4
Conway Australia 20°24S 148°41E 62 J6
Conway Canada 44°6N 76°54W 82 B8
Conway Ark., U.S.A. 35°5N 92°26W 84 D8
Conway N.H., U.S.A. 43°59N 71°7W 83 C13
Conway S.C., U.S.A. 33°51N 79°3W 85 E15
Conway, C. Australia 20°34S 148°46E 62 J6
Conway, L. Australia 28°17S 135°35E 63 D2
Conwy U.K. 53°17N 3°50W 12 D4
Conwy □ U.K. 53°10N 3°44W 12 D4
Conwy → U.K. 53°17N 3°50W 12 D4
Coober Pedy Australia 29°1S 134°43E 63 D1
Cooch Behar = Koch Bihar India 26°22N 89°29E 41 F16
Cooinda Australia 13°15S 130°5E 60 B5
Cook Australia 30°37S 130°25E 61 F5
Cook U.S.A. 47°51N 92°41W 80 B7
Cook, B. Chile 55°10S 70°0W 96 H3
Cook, C. Canada 50°8N 127°55W 70 C3
Cook, Mt. = Aoraki Mount Cook N.Z. 43°36S 170°9E 59 E3
Cook Inlet U.S.A. 60°0N 152°0W 68 C4
Cook Is. Pac. Oc. 17°0S 160°0W 65 J12
Cook Strait N.Z. 41°15S 174°29E 59 D5
Cookeville U.S.A. 36°10N 85°30W 85 C12
Cookhouse S. Africa 32°44S 25°47E 56 E4
Cooks Harbour Canada 51°36N 55°52W 73 B8
Cookshire Canada 45°25N 71°38W 83 A13
Cookstown Canada 44°11N 79°42W 82 B5
Cookstown U.K. 54°39N 6°45W 10 B5
Cooktown Australia 15°30S 145°16E 62 B4
Coolabah Australia 31°1S 146°43E 63 E4

Cooladdi Australia 26°37S 145°23E 63 D4
Coolah Australia 31°48S 149°41E 63 E4
Coolamon Australia 34°46S 147°8E 63 E4
Coolgardie Australia 30°55S 121°8E 61 F3
Coolidge U.S.A. 32°59N 111°31W 77 K8
Coolidge Dam U.S.A. 33°10N 110°32W 77 K8
Cooma Australia 36°12S 149°8E 63 F4
Coon Rapids U.S.A. 45°9N 93°19W 80 C7
Coonabarabran Australia 31°14S 149°18E 63 E4
Coonamble Australia 30°56S 148°27E 63 E4
Coonana Australia 31°0S 123°0E 61 F3
Coondapoor India 13°42N 74°40E 40 N9
Cooninnie, L. Australia 26°4S 139°59E 63 D2
Cooper U.S.A. 33°23N 95°42W 84 E7
Cooper Cr. → Australia 28°29S 137°46E 63 D2
Cooper Ridge Pac. Oc. 0°0N 150°30W 65 G12
Cooperstown N. Dak., U.S.A. 47°27N 98°8W 80 B4
Cooperstown N.Y., U.S.A. 42°42N 74°56W 83 D10
Coorabie Australia 31°54S 132°18E 61 F5
Coorong, The Australia 35°50S 139°20E 63 F2
Coorow Australia 29°53S 116°2E 61 E2
Cooroy Australia 26°22S 152°54E 63 D5
Coos Bay U.S.A. 43°22N 124°13W 76 E1
Coosa → U.S.A. 32°30N 86°16W 85 E11
Cootamundra Australia 34°36S 148°1E 63 E4
Cootehill Ireland 54°4N 7°5W 10 B4
Copahue Paso Argentina 37°49S 71°8W 94 D1
Copainalá Mexico 17°4N 93°18W 87 D6
Copake U.S.A. 42°7N 73°31W 83 D11
Copán Honduras 14°50N 89°9W 88 D2
Cope U.S.A. 39°40N 102°51W 76 G12
Copenhagen = København Denmark 55°40N 12°26E 9 J15
Copenhagen U.S.A. 43°54N 75°41W 83 C9
Copiapó Chile 27°30S 70°20W 94 B1
Copiapó → Chile 27°19S 70°56W 94 B1
Coplay U.S.A. 40°44N 75°29W 83 F9
Copo △ Argentina 25°53S 61°43W 94 B3
Copp L. Canada 60°14N 114°40W 70 A6
Copper Canyon = Barranca del Cobre △ Mexico 27°18N 107°40W 86 B3
Copper Harbor U.S.A. 47°28N 87°53W 80 B10
Copper Queen Zimbabwe 17°29S 29°18E 55 F2
Copperas Cove U.S.A. 31°8N 97°54W 84 F6
Copperbelt □ Zambia 13°15S 27°30E 55 E2
Coppermine = Kugluktuk Canada 67°50N 115°5W 68 C8
Coppermine → Canada 67°49N 116°4W 68 C8
Copperopolis U.S.A. 37°58N 120°38W 78 H6
Coquet → U.K. 55°20N 1°32W 12 B6
Coquille U.S.A. 43°11N 124°11W 76 E1
Coquimbo Chile 30°0S 71°20W 94 C1
Coquimbo □ Chile 31°0S 71°0W 94 C1
Coquitlam Canada 49°17N 122°45W 70 D4
Corabia Romania 43°48N 24°30E 17 G13
Coracora Peru 15°5S 73°45W 92 G4
Coraki Australia 28°59S 153°17E 63 D5
Coral U.S.A. 40°29N 79°10W 82 F5
Coral Bay Australia 23°8S 113°46W 60 D1
Coral Gables U.S.A. 25°43N 80°16W 85 J14
Coral Harbour Canada 64°8N 83°10W 69 C11
Coral Sea Pac. Oc. 15°0S 150°0E 58 C8
Coral Sea Basin Pac. Oc. 14°0S 152°0E 64 J7
Coral Sea Islands Terr. □ Australia 20°0S 155°0E 58 C8
Coral Springs U.S.A. 26°16N 80°16W 85 H14
Coraopolis U.S.A. 40°31N 80°10W 82 F4
Corato Italy 41°9N 16°25E 22 D7
Corbett △ India 29°20N 79°0E 43 E8
Corbin U.S.A. 36°57N 84°6W 81 G11
Corby U.K. 52°30N 0°41W 13 E7
Corcaigh = Cork Ireland 51°54N 8°29W 10 E3
Corcoran U.S.A. 36°6N 119°33W 78 J7
Corcovado △ Costa Rica 8°33N 83°35W 88 E3
Corcubión Spain 42°56N 9°12W 21 A1
Cordele U.S.A. 31°58N 83°47W 85 F13
Cordell U.S.A. 35°17N 98°59W 84 D5
Córdoba Argentina 31°20S 64°10W 94 C3
Córdoba Mexico 18°53N 96°56W 87 D5
Córdoba Spain 37°50N 4°50W 21 D3
Córdoba □ Argentina 31°22S 64°15W 94 C3
Córdoba, Sierra de Argentina 31°10S 64°25W 94 C3
Cordova U.S.A. 60°33N 145°45W 68 C5
Corella → Australia 19°34S 140°47E 62 B3
Corfield Australia 21°40S 143°21E 62 C3
Corfu = Kerkyra Greece 39°38N 19°50E 25 A3
Corfu, Str. of = Kerkyras, Notio Steno Greece 39°34N 20°0E 25 A4
Coria Spain 39°58N 6°33W 21 C2
Coringa Is. Australia 16°58S 149°58E 62 B4
Corinth = Korinthos Greece 37°56N 22°55E 23 F10
Corinth Miss., U.S.A. 34°56N 88°31W 85 D10
Corinth N.Y., U.S.A. 43°15N 73°49W 83 C11
Corinth, G. of = Korinthiakos Kolpos Greece 38°16N 22°30E 23 E10
Corinto Brazil 18°20S 44°30W 93 G10
Corinto Nic. 12°30N 87°10W 88 D2
Cork Ireland 51°54N 8°29W 10 E3
Cork □ Ireland 51°57N 8°40W 10 E3
Cork Harbour Ireland 51°47N 8°16W 10 E3
Çorlu Turkey 41°11N 27°49E 23 D12
Cormack L. Canada 60°56N 121°37W 70 A4
Cormorant Canada 54°14N 100°35W 71 C8
Cormorant L. Canada 54°15N 100°50W 71 C8
Corn Is. = Maíz, Is. del Nic. 12°15N 83°4W 88 D3
Cornélio Procópio Brazil 23°7S 50°40W 95 A5
Corner Brook Canada 48°57N 57°58W 73 C8
Cornești Moldova 47°21N 28°1E 17 E15
Corning Ark., U.S.A. 36°25N 90°35W 85 C9

Corning Calif., U.S.A.   39°56N 122°11W 76 G2
Corning Iowa, U.S.A.   40°59N 94°44W 80 E6
Corning N.Y., U.S.A.   42°9N 77°3W 82 D7
Cornwall Canada   45°2N 74°44W 83 A10
Cornwall U.K.   40°17N 76°25W 83 F8
Cornwall □ U.K.   50°26N 4°40W 13 G3
Cornwall I. Canada   77°37N 94°38W 69 B10
Cornwallis I. Canada   75°8N 95°0W 69 B10
Corny Pt. Australia   34°55S 137°0E 63 E2
Coro Venezuela   11°25N 69°41W 92 A5
Coroatá Brazil   4°8S 44°0W 93 D10
Corocoro Bolivia   17°15S 68°28W 92 G5
Coroico Bolivia   16°0S 67°50W 92 G5
Coromandel N.Z.   36°45S 175°31E 59 B5
Coromandel Coast India   12°30N 81°0E 40 N12
Corona Calif., U.S.A.   33°53N 117°34W 79 M9
Corona N. Mex., U.S.A.   34°15N 105°36W 77 J11
Coronado U.S.A.   32°41N 117°10W 79 N9
Coronado, B. de Costa Rica   9°0N 83°40W 88 E3
Coronados, Is. Los
  Mexico   32°26N 117°19W 79 N9
Coronation Canada   52°5N 111°27W 70 C6
Coronation Gulf Canada   68°25N 110°0W 68 C9
Coronation I. Antarctica   60°45S 46°0W 5 C18
Coronation Is. Australia   14°57S 124°56E 60 B3
Coronda Argentina   31°58S 60°56W 94 C3
Coronel Chile   37°0S 73°10W 94 D1
Coronel Bogado
  Paraguay   27°11S 56°18W 94 B4
Coronel Dorrego
  Argentina   38°40S 61°10W 94 D3
Coronel Oviedo
  Paraguay   25°24S 56°30W 94 B4
Coronel Pringles
  Argentina   38°0S 61°30W 94 D3
Coronel Suárez
  Argentina   37°30S 61°52W 94 D3
Coronel Vidal Argentina   37°28S 57°45W 94 D4
Coropuna, Nevado Peru   15°30S 72°41W 92 G4
Corowa Australia   35°58S 146°21E 63 F4
Corozal □ Belize   18°23N 88°23W 87 D7
Corozal Pt. Trin. & Tob.   10°45N 61°37W 93 K15
Corpus Argentina   27°10S 55°30W 95 B4
Corpus Christi U.S.A.   27°47N 97°24W 84 H6
Corpus Christi, L. U.S.A.   28°2N 97°52W 84 G6
Corralejo Canary Is.   28°43N 13°53W 24 F6
Corraun Pen. Ireland   53°54N 9°54W 10 C2
Corrib, L. Ireland   53°27N 9°16W 10 C2
Corrientes Argentina   27°30S 58°45W 94 B4
Corrientes □ Argentina   28°0S 57°0W 94 B4
Corrientes → Argentina   30°42S 59°38W 94 C4
Corrientes → Peru   3°43S 74°35W 92 D4
Corrientes, C. Colombia   5°30N 77°34W 92 B3
Corrientes, C. Cuba   21°43N 84°30W 88 B3
Corrientes, C. Mexico   20°25N 105°42W 86 C3
Corrigan U.S.A.   31°0N 94°52W 84 F7
Corrigin Australia   32°20S 117°53E 61 F2
Corriverton Guyana   5°55N 57°20W 92 B7
Corry U.S.A.   41°55N 79°39W 82 E5
Corse □ France   42°0N 9°0E 20 F8
Corse, C. France   43°1N 9°25E 20 E8
Corsica = Corse □ France   42°0N 9°0E 20 F8
Corsicana U.S.A.   32°6N 96°28W 84 E6
Corte France   42°19N 9°11E 20 E8
Cortés, Mar de = California, G. de
  Mexico   27°0N 111°0W 86 B2
Cortez U.S.A.   37°21N 108°35W 77 H9
Cortland N.Y., U.S.A.   42°36N 76°11W 83 D8
Cortland Ohio, U.S.A.   41°20N 80°44W 82 E4
Çorum Turkey   40°30N 34°57E 19 F5
Corumbá Brazil   19°0S 57°30W 92 G7
Corunna = A Coruña
  Spain   43°20N 8°25W 21 A1
Corvallis U.S.A.   44°34N 123°16W 76 D2
Corvette, L. de la Canada   53°25N 74°3W 72 B5
Corvo Azores   39°43N 31°8W 50 a
Corydon U.S.A.   40°46N 93°19W 80 E7
Cosalá Mexico   24°23N 106°41W 86 C3
Cosamaloapan de Carpio
  Mexico   18°22N 95°48W 87 D5
Cosenza Italy   39°18N 16°15E 22 E7
Coshocton U.S.A.   40°16N 81°51W 82 F3
Cosmo Newberry
  Australia   28°0S 122°54E 61 E3
Cosmonaut Sea S. Ocean   66°30S 40°0E 5 C5
Coso Junction U.S.A.   36°3N 117°57W 79 J9
Coso Pk. U.S.A.   36°13N 117°44W 79 J9
Cosquín Argentina   31°15S 64°30W 94 C3
Costa Blanca Spain   38°25N 0°10W 21 C5
Costa Brava Spain   41°30N 3°0E 21 B7
Costa Daurada Spain   41°12N 1°15E 21 B6
Costa del Sol Spain   36°30N 4°30W 21 D3
Costa dels Pins Spain   39°38N 3°26E 24 B10
Costa Mesa U.S.A.   33°38N 117°55W 79 M9
Costa Rica ■ Cent. Amer.   10°0N 84°0W 88 E3
Costa Smeralda Italy   41°5N 9°35E 22 D3
Cosumnes → U.S.A.   38°16N 121°26W 78 G5
Cotabato Phil.   7°14N 124°15E 37 C6
Cotagaita Bolivia   20°45S 65°40W 94 A2
Côte d'Azur France   43°25N 7°10E 20 E7
Côte-d'Ivoire = Ivory Coast ■
  Africa   7°30N 5°0W 50 G4
Coteau des Prairies
  U.S.A.   45°20N 97°50W 80 C5
Coteau du Missouri
  U.S.A.   47°0N 100°0W 80 B4
Cotentin France   49°15N 1°30W 20 B3
Cotillo Canary Is.   28°41N 14°1W 24 F5
Cotonou Benin   6°20N 2°25E 50 G6
Cotopaxi Ecuador   0°40S 78°30W 92 D3
Cotswold Hills U.K.   51°42N 2°10W 13 F5
Cottage Grove U.S.A.   43°48N 123°3W 76 E2
Cottam Canada   42°8N 82°45W 82 D2
Cottbus Germany   51°45N 14°20E 16 C8
Cottonwood U.S.A.   34°45N 112°1W 77 J7
Cotulla U.S.A.   28°26N 99°14W 84 G5

Coudersport U.S.A.   41°46N 78°1W 82 E6
Coudedic, C. du Australia   36°5S 136°40E 63 F2
Coulee City U.S.A.   47°37N 119°17W 76 C4
Coulman I. Antarctica   73°35S 170°0E 5 D11
Coulonge → Canada   45°52N 76°46W 72 C4
Coulterville U.S.A.   37°43N 120°12W 78 H6
Council U.S.A.   44°44N 116°26W 76 D5
Council Bluffs U.S.A.   41°16N 95°52W 80 E6
Council Grove U.S.A.   38°40N 96°29W 80 F5
Coupeville U.S.A.   48°13N 122°41W 78 B4
Courantyne → S. Amer.   5°55N 57°5W 92 B7
Courcelles Belgium   50°28N 4°22E 15 D4
Courdenay Canada   45°35N 77°35W 72 C4
Courland Canada   42°51N 80°38W 82 D3
Courtland U.S.A.   38°20N 121°34W 78 G5
Courtrai = Kortrijk
  Belgium   50°50N 3°17E 15 D3
Courtright Canada   42°49N 82°28W 82 D2
Coushatta U.S.A.   32°1N 93°21W 84 E8
Coutts Crossing
  Australia   29°49S 152°55E 63 D5
Couva Trin. & Tob.   10°25N 61°27W 93 K15
Couvin Belgium   50°3N 4°29E 15 D4
Cove I. Canada   45°17N 81°44W 82 A3
Coventry U.K.   52°25N 1°28W 13 E6
Covilhã Portugal   40°17N 7°31W 21 B2
Covington Ga., U.S.A.   33°36N 83°51W 85 E13
Covington Ky., U.S.A.   39°5N 84°30W 81 F11
Covington Tenn., U.S.A.   35°34N 89°39W 85 D10
Covington Va., U.S.A.   37°47N 79°59W 81 G8
Cowal, L. Australia   33°40S 147°25E 63 E4
Cowan L. Australia   31°45S 121°45E 61 F3
Cowan L. Canada   54°0N 107°15W 71 C7
Cowangie Australia   35°12S 141°26E 63 F3
Cowansville Canada   45°14N 72°46W 83 A12
Coward Springs
  Australia   29°24S 136°49E 63 D2
Cowcowing Lakes
  Australia   30°55S 117°20E 61 F2
Cowdenbeath U.K.   56°7N 3°21W 11 E5
Cowell Australia   33°39S 136°56E 63 E2
Cowes U.K.   50°45N 1°18W 13 G6
Cowichan L. Canada   48°53N 124°17W 78 B2
Cowlitz → U.S.A.   46°6N 122°55W 78 D4
Cowra Australia   33°49S 148°42E 63 E4
Coxilha Grande Brazil   28°18S 51°30W 95 B5
Coxim Brazil   18°30S 54°55W 93 G8
Cox's Bazar Bangla.   21°26N 91°59E 41 J17
Coyote Wells U.S.A.   32°44N 115°58W 79 N11
Coyuca de Benitez
  Mexico   17°2N 100°4W 87 D4
Coyuca de Catalán
  Mexico   18°20N 100°39W 86 D4
Cozad U.S.A.   40°52N 99°59W 80 E4
Cozumel Mexico   20°31N 86°55W 87 C7
Cozumel, Isla Mexico   20°30N 86°40W 87 C7
Crab Hill Barbados   13°19N 59°38W 89 g
Cracow = Kraków
  Poland   50°4N 19°57E 17 C10
Cracow Australia   25°17S 150°17E 63 D5
Cradle Mt.-Lake St. Clair △
  Australia   41°49S 147°56E 63 G4
Cradock Australia   32°6S 138°31E 63 E2
Cradock S. Africa   32°8S 25°36E 56 E4
Craig U.S.A.   40°31N 107°33W 76 F10
Craigavon U.K.   54°27N 6°23W 10 B5
Craigmore Zimbabwe   20°28S 32°50E 55 G3
Craik Canada   51°3N 105°49W 71 C7
Crailsheim Germany   49°8N 10°5E 16 D6
Craiova Romania   44°21N 23°48E 17 F12
Cramsie Australia   23°20S 144°15E 62 C3
Cranberry L. U.S.A.   44°11N 74°50W 83 B10
Cranberry Portage
  Canada   54°35N 101°23W 71 C8
Cranbrook Australia   34°18S 117°33E 61 F2
Cranbrook Canada   49°30N 115°46W 70 D5
Crandon U.S.A.   45°34N 88°54W 80 C9
Crane Oreg., U.S.A.   43°25N 118°35W 76 E4
Crane Tex., U.S.A.   31°24N 102°21W 84 F3
Crane, The Barbados   13°6N 59°27W 89 g
Cranston U.S.A.   41°47N 71°26W 83 E13
Crater L. U.S.A.   42°56N 122°6W 76 E2
Crater Lake △ U.S.A.   42°55N 122°10W 76 E2
Craters of the Moon △
  U.S.A.   43°25N 113°30W 76 E7
Crateús Brazil   5°10S 40°39W 93 E10
Crato Brazil   7°10S 39°25W 93 E11
Craven, L. Canada   54°20N 76°56W 72 B4
Crawford U.S.A.   42°41N 103°25W 80 D2
Crawfordsville U.S.A.   40°2N 86°54W 80 E10
Crawley U.K.   51°7N 0°11W 13 F7
Crazy Mts. U.S.A.   46°12N 110°20W 76 C8
Crean L. Canada   54°5N 106°9W 71 C7
Crediton Canada   43°17N 81°33W 82 C3
Crediton U.K.   50°47N 3°40W 13 G4
Cree → Canada   58°57N 105°47W 71 B7
Cree → U.K.   54°55N 4°25W 11 G4
Cree L. Canada   57°30N 106°30W 71 B7
Creekside U.S.A.   40°40N 79°11W 82 F5
Creel Mexico   27°45N 107°38W 86 B3
Creemore Canada   44°19N 80°6W 82 B4
Creighton Canada   54°45N 101°54W 71 C8
Creighton U.S.A.   42°28N 97°54W 80 D5
Crema Italy   45°22N 9°41E 20 D8
Cremona Italy   45°7N 10°2E 20 D8
Cres Croatia   44°58N 14°25E 16 F8
Crescent City U.S.A.   41°45N 124°12W 76 F1
Crespo Argentina   32°2S 60°19W 94 C3
Cresson U.S.A.   40°28N 78°36W 82 F6
Crestline Calif., U.S.A.   34°14N 117°18W 79 L9
Crestline Ohio, U.S.A.   40°47N 82°44W 82 F2
Creston Canada   49°10N 116°31W 70 D5
Creston Calif., U.S.A.   35°32N 120°33W 78 K6

Creston Iowa, U.S.A.   41°4N 94°22W 80 E6
Crestview Calif., U.S.A.   37°46N 118°58W 78 H8
Crestview Fla., U.S.A.   30°46N 86°34W 85 F11
Crete = Kriti Greece   35°15N 25°0E 25 D7
Crete U.S.A.   40°38N 96°58W 80 E5
Créteil France   48°47N 2°27E 20 B5
Creus, C. de Spain   42°20N 3°19E 21 A7
Creuse → France   47°0N 0°34E 20 C4
Crewe U.K.   53°6N 2°26E 12 D5
Crewkerne U.K.   50°53N 2°48W 13 G5
Crianlarich U.K.   56°24N 4°37W 11 E4
Criciúma Brazil   28°40S 49°23W 95 B6
Crieff U.K.   56°22N 3°50W 11 E5
Crimea □ Ukraine   45°30N 33°10E 19 E5
Crimean Pen. = Krymskyy
  Pivostriv Ukraine   45°0N 34°0E 19 F5
Crișul Alb → Romania   46°42N 21°17E 17 E11
Crișul Negru →
  Romania   46°42N 21°16E 17 E11
Crna → Macedonia   41°33N 21°59E 23 D9
Crna Gora = Montenegro ■
  Europe   42°40N 19°20E 23 C8
Crna Gora Macedonia   42°10N 21°30E 23 C9
Crna Reka = Crna →
  Macedonia   41°33N 21°59E 23 D9
Croagh Patrick Ireland   53°46N 9°40W 10 C2
Croatia ■ Europe   45°20N 16°0E 16 F9
Crocker, Banjaran
  Malaysia   5°40N 116°30E 36 C5
Crockett U.S.A.   31°19N 95°27W 84 F7
Crocodile = Umgwenya →
  Mozam.   25°14S 32°18E 57 D5
Crocodile Is. Australia   12°3S 134°58E 62 A1
Crohy Hd. Ireland   54°55N 8°26W 10 B3
Croix, L. la Canada   48°20N 92°15W 72 C1
Croker, C. Australia   10°58S 132°35E 60 B5
Croker, C. Canada   44°58N 80°59W 82 B4
Croker I. Australia   11°12S 132°32E 60 B5
Cromarty U.K.   57°40N 4°2W 11 D4
Cromer U.K.   52°56N 1°17E 12 E9
Cromwell N.Z.   45°3S 169°14E 59 F2
Cromwell U.S.A.   41°36N 72°39W 83 E12
Crook U.K.   54°43N 1°45W 12 C6
Crooked → Canada   54°50N 122°54W 70 C4
Crooked → U.S.A.   44°32N 121°16W 76 D3
Crooked I. Bahamas   22°50N 74°10W 89 B5
Crooked Island Passage
  Bahamas   22°55N 74°35W 89 B5
Crookston Minn., U.S.A.   47°47N 96°37W 80 B5
Crookston Nebr., U.S.A.   42°56N 100°45W 80 D3
Crookwell Australia   34°28S 149°24E 63 E4
Crosby N. Dak., U.S.A.   48°55N 103°18W 80 A2
Crosby Pa., U.S.A.   41°45N 78°23W 82 E6
Crosbyton U.S.A.   33°40N 101°14W 84 E4
Cross City U.S.A.   29°38N 83°7W 85 G13
Cross Fell U.K.   54°43N 2°28W 12 C5
Cross L. Canada   54°45N 97°30W 71 C9
Cross Lake Canada   54°37N 97°47W 71 C9
Cross Sound U.S.A.   58°0N 135°0W 68 D6
Crossett U.S.A.   33°8N 91°58W 84 E9
Crosshaven Ireland   51°47N 8°17W 10 E3
Crossmaglen U.K.   54°5N 6°36W 10 B5
Crossmolina Ireland   54°6N 9°20W 10 B2
Crossville U.S.A.   35°57N 85°2W 85 D12
Croswell U.S.A.   43°16N 82°37W 82 C2
Croton-on-Hudson
  U.S.A.   41°12N 73°55W 83 E11
Crotone Italy   39°5N 17°8E 22 E7
Crow → U.S.A.   59°41N 124°20W 70 B4
Crow Agency U.S.A.   45°36N 107°28W 76 D10
Crow Hd. Ireland   51°35N 10°9W 10 E1
Crowell U.S.A.   33°59N 99°43W 84 E5
Crowley U.S.A.   30°13N 92°22W 84 F8
Crowley, L. U.S.A.   37°35N 118°42W 78 H8
Crown Point Ind.,
  U.S.A.   41°25N 87°22W 80 E10
Crown Point N.Y.,
  U.S.A.   43°57N 73°26W 83 C11
Crown Pt. Trin. & Tob.   11°18N 60°51W 93 J16
Crownpoint U.S.A.   35°41N 108°9W 77 J9
Crows Landing U.S.A.   37°23N 121°6W 78 H5
Crows Nest Australia   27°16S 152°4E 63 D5
Crowsnest Pass Canada   49°40N 114°40W 70 D6
Croydon Australia   18°13S 142°14E 62 B3
Croydon □ U.K.   51°22N 0°5W 13 F7
Crozet, Is. Ind. Oc.   46°27S 52°0E 3 G12
Crusheen Ireland   52°57N 8°53W 10 D3
Cruz, C. Cuba   19°50N 77°50W 88 C4
Cruz Alta Brazil   28°45S 53°40W 95 B5
Cruz Bay U.S. Virgin Is.   18°20N 64°48W 89 e
Cruz del Eje Argentina   30°45S 64°50W 94 C3
Cruzeiro Brazil   22°33S 45°0W 95 A7
Cruzeiro do Oeste Brazil   23°46S 53°4W 95 A5
Cruzeiro do Sul Brazil   7°35S 72°35W 92 E4
Cry L. Canada   58°45N 129°0W 70 B3
Crystal Bay U.S.A.   39°15N 120°0W 78 F7
Crystal Brook Australia   33°21S 138°12E 63 E2
Crystal City U.S.A.   28°41N 99°50W 84 G5
Crystal Falls U.S.A.   46°5N 88°20W 80 B9
Crystal River U.S.A.   28°54N 82°35W 85 G13
Crystal Springs U.S.A.   31°59N 90°21W 85 F9
Csongrád Hungary   46°43N 20°12E 17 E11
Cu Lao Hon Vietnam   10°54N 108°18E 39 G7
Cua Rao Vietnam   19°16N 104°27E 38 C5
Cuácua → Mozam.   17°54S 37°0E 55 F4
Cuamato Angola   17°2S 15°7E 56 B2
Cuamba Mozam.   14°45S 36°22E 55 E4
Cuando → Angola   17°30S 23°15E 53 H4
Cuando Cubango □
  Angola   16°25S 20°0E 56 B3
Cuangar Angola   17°36S 18°39E 56 B2
Cuango = Kwango →
  Dem. Rep. of the Congo   3°14S 17°22E 52 E3
Cuanza → Angola   9°21S 13°9E 52 F2
Cuarto → Argentina   33°25S 63°2W 94 C3
Cuatrociénegas Mexico   26°59N 102°5W 86 B4

Cuauhtémoc Mexico   28°25N 106°52W 86 B3
Cuba N. Mex., U.S.A.   36°1N 107°4W 77 H10
Cuba N.Y., U.S.A.   42°13N 78°17W 82 D6
Cuba ■ W. Indies   22°0N 79°0W 88 B4
Cubango → Africa   18°50S 22°25E 56 B3
Cuc Phuong △ Vietnam   20°17N 105°38E 38 B5
Cuchumatanes, Sierra de los
  Guatemala   15°35N 91°25W 88 C1
Cuckfield U.K.   51°1N 0°8W 13 F7
Cucuí Brazil   1°12N 66°50W 92 C5
Cucurpé Mexico   30°20N 110°43W 86 A2
Cúcuta Colombia   7°54N 72°31W 92 B4
Cuddalore India   11°46N 79°45E 40 P11
Cuddapah India   14°30N 78°47E 40 M11
Cuddapan, L. Australia   25°45S 141°26E 62 D3
Cue Australia   27°25S 117°54E 61 E2
Cuenca Ecuador   2°50S 79°9W 92 D3
Cuenca Spain   40°5N 2°10W 21 B4
Cuenca, Serranía de
  Spain   39°55N 1°50W 21 C5
Cuernavaca Mexico   18°55N 99°15W 87 D5
Cuero U.S.A.   29°6N 97°17W 84 G6
Cueva de la Quebrada del Toro △
  Venezuela   10°46N 69°3W 89 D6
Cuevas del Almanzora
  Spain   37°18N 1°58W 21 D5
Cuevo Bolivia   20°15S 63°30W 92 H6
Cuiabá Brazil   15°30S 56°0W 93 G7
Cuiabá → Brazil   17°5S 56°36W 93 G7
Cuihangcun China   22°27N 113°32E 33 G10
Cuijk Neths.   51°44N 5°50E 15 C5
Cuilapa Guatemala   14°16N 90°29W 88 D1
Cuilco Guatemala   15°24N 91°58W 88 C1
Cuillin Hills U.K.   57°13N 6°15W 11 D2
Cuillin Sd. U.K.   57°4N 6°20W 11 D2
Cuilo = Kwilu →
  Dem. Rep. of the Congo   3°22S 17°22E 52 E3
Cuito → Angola   18°1S 20°48E 56 B3
Cuitzeo, L. de Mexico   19°55N 101°5W 86 D4
Cukai Malaysia   4°13N 103°25E 39 K4
Culbertson U.S.A.   48°9N 104°31W 76 B11
Culcairn Australia   35°41S 147°3E 63 F4
Culebra Puerto Rico   18°19N 65°18W 89 d
Culgoa → Australia   29°56S 146°20E 63 D4
Culgoa Flood Plain △
  Australia   28°58S 147°5E 63 D4
Culiacán Mexico   24°50N 107°23W 86 C3
Culiacán → Mexico   24°30N 107°42W 86 C3
Culik Indonesia   8°21S 115°37E 37 J18
Culion Phil.   11°54N 119°58E 37 B6
Cullarin Ra. Australia   34°30S 149°30E 63 E4
Cullen U.K.   57°42N 2°49W 11 D6
Cullen Pt. Australia   11°57S 141°54E 62 A3
Cullera Spain   39°9N 0°17W 21 C5
Cullman U.S.A.   34°11N 86°51W 85 D11
Cullompton U.K.   50°51N 3°24W 13 G4
Culpeper U.S.A.   38°30N 78°0W 81 F14
Culuene → Brazil   12°56S 52°51W 93 F8
Culver, Pt. Australia   32°54S 124°43E 61 F3
Culverden N.Z.   42°47S 172°49E 59 E4
Cumaná Venezuela   10°30N 64°5W 92 A6
Cumberland B.C.,
  Canada   49°40N 125°0W 70 D4
Cumberland Ont.,
  Canada   45°29N 75°24W 83 A9
Cumberland U.S.A.   39°39N 78°46W 81 F14
Cumberland → U.S.A.   37°9N 88°25W 80 G9
Cumberland, L. U.S.A.   36°52N 85°9W 81 G11
Cumberland Gap △
  U.S.A.   36°36N 83°40W 81 G12
Cumberland I. U.S.A.   30°50N 81°25W 85 F14
Cumberland Is.
  Australia   20°35S 149°10E 62 J7
Cumberland Island △
  U.S.A.   30°12N 81°24W 85 F14
Cumberland L. Canada   54°3N 102°18W 71 C8
Cumberland Pen. Canada   67°0N 64°0W 69 C13
Cumberland Plateau
  U.S.A.   36°0N 85°0W 85 D12
Cumberland Sd. Canada   65°30N 66°0W 69 C13
Cumbernauld U.K.   55°57N 3°58W 11 F5
Cumborah Australia   29°40S 147°45E 63 D4
Cumbria □ U.K.   54°42N 2°52W 12 C5
Cumbrian Mts. U.K.   54°30N 3°0W 12 C5
Cumbum India   15°40N 79°10E 40 M11
Cuminá → Brazil   1°30S 56°0W 93 D7
Cummings Mt. U.S.A.   35°2N 118°34W 79 K8
Cummins Australia   34°16S 135°43E 63 E2
Cumnock Australia   32°59S 148°46E 63 E4
Cumnock U.K.   55°28N 4°17W 11 F4
Cumpas Mexico   30°2N 109°48W 86 B3
Cumplida, Pta.
  Canary Is.   28°50N 17°48W 24 F2
Cunco Chile   38°55S 72°2W 96 D2
Cuncumén Chile   31°53S 70°38W 94 C1
Cunderdin Australia   31°37S 117°12E 61 F2
Cunene → Angola   17°20S 11°50E 56 B1
Cúneo Italy   44°23N 7°32E 20 D7
Çüngüş Turkey   38°13N 39°17E 44 B3
Cunillera, I. = Sa Conillera
  Spain   38°59N 1°13E 24 C7
Cunnamulla Australia   28°2S 145°38E 63 D4
Cupar Canada   50°57N 104°10W 71 C8
Cupar U.K.   56°19N 3°1W 11 E5
Cupertino U.S.A.   37°19N 122°2W 78 H4
Cupica, G. de Colombia   6°25N 77°30W 92 B3
Curaçao Neth. Ant.   12°10N 69°0W 89 D6
Curanilahue Chile   37°29S 73°28W 94 D1
Curaray → Peru   2°20S 74°5W 92 D4
Curepipe Mauritius   20°19S 57°31E 53 d
Curepto Chile   35°8S 72°1W 94 D1
Curiapo Venezuela   8°33N 61°5W 92 B6
Curicó Chile   34°55S 71°20W 94 C1
Curieuse Seychelles   4°15S 55°44E 53 b

Curitiba Brazil   25°20S 49°10W 95 B6
Curitibanos Brazil   27°18S 50°36W 95 B5
Currabubula Australia   31°16S 150°44E 63 E5
Currais Novos Brazil   6°13S 36°30W 93 E11
Curral Velho C. Verde Is.   16°8N 22°48W 50 b
Curralinho Brazil   1°45S 49°46W 93 D9
Currane, L. Ireland   51°49N 10°4W 10 E1
Currant U.S.A.   38°44N 115°28W 76 G6
Currawinya △ Australia   28°25S 144°18E 63 D4
Current → U.S.A.   36°15N 90°55W 84 C9
Currie Australia   39°56S 143°53E 63 F3
Currie U.S.A.   40°16N 114°45W 76 F6
Curtea de Argeș
  Romania   45°12N 24°42E 17 F13
Curtin Springs Australia   25°20S 131°45E 61 E5
Curtis U.S.A.   40°38N 100°31W 80 E3
Curtis Group Australia   39°30S 146°37E 63 F4
Curtis I. Australia   23°35S 151°10E 62 C5
Curuápanema → Brazil   2°25S 55°2W 93 D7
Curuçá Brazil   0°43S 47°50W 93 D9
Curuguaty Paraguay   24°31S 55°42W 95 A4
Curup Indonesia   4°26S 102°13E 36 E2
Cururupu Brazil   1°50S 44°50W 93 D10
Curuzú Cuatiá Argentina   29°50S 58°5W 94 B4
Curvelo Brazil   18°45S 44°27W 93 G10
Cusco = Cuzco Peru   13°32S 72°0W 92 F4
Cushendall U.K.   55°5N 6°4W 10 A5
Cushing U.S.A.   35°59N 96°46W 84 D6
Cushing, Mt. Canada   57°35N 126°57W 70 B3
Cusihuiriáchic Mexico   28°14N 106°50W 86 B3
Custer U.S.A.   43°46N 103°36W 80 D2
Cut Bank U.S.A.   48°38N 112°20W 76 B7
Cutchogue U.S.A.   41°1N 72°30W 83 F12
Cuthbert U.S.A.   31°46N 84°48W 85 F12
Cutler U.S.A.   36°31N 119°17W 78 J7
Cuttaburra → Australia   29°43S 144°22E 63 D3
Cuttack India   20°25N 85°57E 41 J14
Cuvier, C. Australia   23°14S 113°22E 61 D1
Cuvier I. N.Z.   36°27S 175°50E 59 B5
Cuxhaven Germany   53°51N 8°41E 16 B5
Cuyahoga Falls U.S.A.   41°8N 81°29W 82 E3
Cuyahoga Valley △
  U.S.A.   41°14N 81°33W 82 E3
Cuyo Phil.   10°51N 121°2E 37 B6
Cuyuni → Guyana   6°23N 58°41W 92 B7
Cuzco Bolivia   20°0S 66°50W 92 H5
Cuzco Peru   13°32S 72°0W 92 F4
Cwmbran U.K.   51°39N 3°2W 13 F4
Cyangugu Rwanda   2°29S 28°54E 54 C2
Cyclades Greece   37°0N 24°30E 23 F11
Cygnet Australia   43°8S 147°1E 63 G4
Cynthiana U.S.A.   38°23N 84°18W 81 F11
Cypress Hills Canada   49°40N 109°30W 71 D7
Cypress Hills △ Canada   49°40N 109°30W 71 D7
Cyprus ■ Asia   35°0N 33°0E 25 E12
Cyrenaica = Barqa Libya   27°0N 23°0E 51 C10
Cyrene Libya   32°53N 21°52E 51 B10
Czar Canada   52°27N 110°50W 71 C6
Czech Rep. ■ Europe   50°0N 15°0E 16 D8
Częstochowa Poland   50°49N 19°7E 17 C10

D

Da → Vietnam   21°15N 105°20E 38 B5
Da Hinggan Ling China   48°0N 121°0E 33 B7
Da Lat Vietnam   11°56N 108°25E 39 G7
Da Nang Vietnam   16°4N 108°13E 38 D7
Da Qaidam China   37°50N 95°15E 32 C4
Da Yunhe → Hopei,
  China   39°10N 117°10E 35 E9
Da Yunhe → Jiangsu,
  China   34°25N 120°5E 35 H11
Da'an China   45°30N 124°7E 35 B13
Daan Viljoen △ Namibia   22°2S 16°45E 56 C2
Daba Shan China   32°0N 109°0E 33 C5
Dabbagh, Jabal Si. Arabia   27°52N 35°45E 44 E2
Dabhoi India   22°10N 73°20E 42 H5
Dabo = Pasirkuning
  Indonesia   0°30S 104°33E 36 E2
Dabola Guinea   10°50N 11°5W 50 F3
Dabung Malaysia   5°23N 102°1E 39 K4
Dacca = Dhaka Bangla.   23°43N 90°26E 43 H14
Dacca = Dhaka □
  Bangla.   24°25N 90°25E 43 G14
Dachau Germany   48°15N 11°26E 16 D6
Dachigam △ India   34°10N 75°0E 42 B6
Dacre Canada   45°22N 76°57W 82 A8
Dadanawa Guyana   2°50N 59°30W 92 C7
Dade City U.S.A.   28°22N 82°11W 85 G13
Dadhar Pakistan   29°28N 67°39E 42 E2
Dadnah U.A.E.   25°32N 56°22E 45 E8
Dadra & Nagar Haveli □
  India   20°5N 73°0E 40 J8
Dadri = Charkhi Dadri
  India   28°37N 76°17E 42 E7
Dadu Pakistan   26°45N 67°45E 42 F2
Daegu S. Korea   35°50N 128°37E 35 G15
Daejeon S. Korea   36°20N 127°28E 35 F14
Daejeong S. Korea   33°8N 126°17E 35 H14
Daet Phil.   14°2N 122°55E 37 B6
Dafnes Greece   35°13N 25°3E 25 D7
Dagana Senegal   16°30N 15°35W 50 E2
Dagestan □ Russia   42°30N 47°0E 19 F8
Daggett U.S.A.   34°52N 116°52W 79 L10
Daghestan Republic =
  Dagestan □ Russia   42°30N 47°0E 19 F8
Dağlıq Qarabağ =
  Nagorno-Karabakh □
  Azerbaijan   39°55N 46°45E 44 B5
Dagö = Hiiumaa Estonia   58°50N 22°45E 9 G20
Dagu China   38°59N 117°40E 35 E9
Dagupan Phil.   16°3N 120°20E 37 A6
Daguragu Australia   17°33S 130°30E 60 C5
Dahab Egypt   28°31N 34°31E 44 D2
Dahlak Kebir Eritrea   15°50N 40°10E 47 D3
Dahlonega U.S.A.   34°32N 83°59W 85 D13

Dahod *India* 22°50N 74°15E **42** H6
Dahongliutan *China* 35°45N 79°20E **43** B8
Dahra *Libya* 29°30N 17°50E **51** C9
Dahûk *Iraq* 36°50N 43°1E **44** B3
Dai Hao *Vietnam* 18°1N 106°25E **38** C6
Dai-Sen *Japan* 35°22N 133°32E **31** G6
Dai Xian *China* 39°4N 112°58E **34** E7
Daicheng *China* 38°42N 116°38E **34** E9
Daikondi = Day Kundī □
Afghan. 34°0N 66°0E **40** C5
Daingean *Ireland* 53°18N 7°17W **10** C4
Daintree *Australia* 16°20S 145°20E **62** B4
Daintree △ *Australia* 16°8S 145°2E **62** B4
Daiō-Misaki *Japan* 34°15N 136°45E **31** G8
Daisen-Oki □ *Japan* 35°23N 133°30E **31** G6
Daisetsu-Zan *Japan* 43°30N 142°57E **30** C11
Daisetsu-Zan △ *Japan* 43°30N 142°55E **30** C11
Dajarra *Australia* 21°42S 139°30E **62** C2
Dajiawa *China* 37°9N 119°0E **35** F10
Dak Dam *Cambodia* 12°20N 107°21E **38** F6
Dak Nhe *Vietnam* 15°28N 107°48E **38** E6
Dak Pek *Vietnam* 15°4N 107°44E **38** E6
Dak Song *Vietnam* 12°19N 107°35E **39** F6
Dak Sui *Vietnam* 14°55N 107°43E **38** E6
Dakar *Senegal* 14°34N 17°29W **50** F2
Dakhla *W. Sahara* 23°50N 15°53W **50** D2
Dakhla, El Wâhât el
Egypt 25°30N 28°50E **51** C11
Dakor *India* 22°45N 73°11E **42** H5
Dakota City *U.S.A.* 42°25N 96°25W **80** D5
Đakovica *Serbia* 42°22N 20°26E **23** C9
Dalachi *China* 36°48N 105°0E **34** F3
Dalai Nur *China* 43°20N 116°45E **34** C9
Dālakī *Iran* 29°26N 51°17E **45** D6
Dalälven → *Sweden* 60°12N 16°43E **9** F17
Dalaman *Turkey* 36°41N 28°43E **23** F13
Dalandzadgad *Mongolia* 43°27N 104°30E **34** C3
Dalap-Uliga-Darrit = Majuro
Marshall Is. 7°9N 171°12E **64** G9
Dalarna *Sweden* 61°0N 14°0E **8** F16
Dālbandīn *Pakistan* 29°0N 64°23E **40** E4
Dalbeattie *U.K.* 54°56N 3°50W **11** G5
Dalbeg *Australia* 20°16S 147°18E **62** C4
Dalby *Australia* 27°10S 151°17E **63** D5
Dale City *U.S.A.* 38°38N 77°19W **81** F15
Dale Hollow L. *U.S.A.* 36°32N 85°27W **85** C12
Dalgān *Iran* 27°31N 59°19E **45** E8
Dalhart *U.S.A.* 36°4N 102°31W **84** C3
Dalhousie *Canada* 48°5N 66°26W **73** C6
Dalhousie *India* 32°38N 75°58E **42** C6
Dali *Shaanxi, China* 34°48N 109°58E **34** G5
Dali *Yunnan, China* 25°40N 100°10E **32** D5
Dalian *China* 38°50N 121°40E **35** E11
Daliang Shan *China* 28°0N 102°45E **32** D5
Daling He → *China* 40°55N 121°40E **35** D11
Dāliyat el Karmel *Israel* 32°43N 35°2E **46** C4
Dalkeith *U.K.* 55°54N 3°4W **11** F5
Dallas *Oreg., U.S.A.* 44°55N 123°19W **76** D2
Dallas *Tex., U.S.A.* 32°47N 96°48W **84** E6
Dalles, The *U.S.A.* 45°36N 121°10W **76** D3
Dalmā *U.A.E.* 24°30N 52°20E **45** E7
Dalmacija *Croatia* 43°20N 17°0E **22** C7
Dalmas, L. *Canada* 53°30N 71°50W **73** B5
Dalmatia = Dalmacija
Croatia 43°20N 17°0E **22** C7
Dalmau *India* 26°4N 81°2E **43** F9
Dalmellington *U.K.* 55°19N 4°23W **11** F4
Dalnegorsk *Russia* 44°32N 135°33E **30** B7
Dalnerechensk *Russia* 45°50N 133°40E **30** B6
Dalnevostochnyy □
Russia 67°0N 140°0E **29** C14
Daloa *Ivory C.* 7°0N 6°30W **50** G4
Dalry *U.K.* 55°42N 4°43W **11** F4
Dalrymple, L. *Australia* 20°40S 147°0E **62** C4
Dalrymple, Mt. *Australia* 21°1S 148°39E **62** K6
Dalsland *Sweden* 58°50N 12°15E **9** G15
Daltenganj *India* 24°0N 84°4E **43** H11
Dalton *Ga., U.S.A.* 34°46N 84°58W **85** D12
Dalton *Mass., U.S.A.* 42°28N 73°11W **83** D11
Dalton *Nebr., U.S.A.* 41°25N 102°58W **80** E2
Dalton-in-Furness *U.K.* 54°10N 3°11W **12** C4
Dalvík *Iceland* 65°58N 18°32W **8** D4
Dálvvadis = Jokkmokk
Sweden 66°35N 19°50E **8** C18
Dalwallinu *Australia* 30°17S 116°40E **61** F2
Daly → *Australia* 13°35S 130°19E **60** B5
Daly City *U.S.A.* 37°42N 122°27W **78** H4
Daly L. *Canada* 56°32N 105°39W **71** B7
Daly River *Australia* 13°46S 130°42E **60** B5
Daly Waters *Australia* 16°15S 133°24E **62** B1
Dam Doi *Vietnam* 8°50N 105°12E **39** H5
Dam Ha *Vietnam* 21°21N 107°36E **38** B6
Daman *India* 20°25N 72°57E **40** J8
Dāmaneh *Iran* 33°1N 50°29E **45** C6
Damanhûr *Egypt* 31°0N 30°30E **51** B12
Damant L. *Canada* 61°45N 105°5W **71** A7
Damanzhuang *China* 38°5N 116°35E **34** E9
Damar *Indonesia* 7°7S 128°40E **37** F7
Damara *C.A.R.* 4°58N 18°42E **52** D3
Damaraland *Namibia* 20°0S 15°0E **56** C2
Damascus = Dimashq
Syria 33°30N 36°18E **46** B5
Damāvand *Iran* 35°47N 52°0E **45** C7
Damāvand, Qolleh-ye
Iran 35°56N 52°10E **45** C7
Damba *Angola* 6°44S 15°20E **52** F3
Dâmbovita → *Romania* 44°12N 26°26E **17** F14
Dame Marie *Haiti* 18°36N 74°26W **89** C5
Dāmghān *Iran* 36°10N 54°17E **45** B7
Damiel *Spain* 39°4N 3°37W **21** C4
Damietta = Dumyât
Egypt 31°24N 31°48E **51** B12
Daming *China* 36°15N 115°6E **34** F8
Damīr Qābū *Syria* 36°58N 41°51E **44** B4
Dammam = Ad Dammām
Si. Arabia 26°20N 50°5E **45** E6
Damodar → *India* 23°17N 87°35E **43** H12

Damoh *India* 23°50N 79°28E **43** H8
Dampier *Australia* 20°41S 116°42E **60** D2
Dampier, Selat *Indonesia* 0°40S 131°0E **37** E8
Dampier Arch.
Australia 20°38S 116°32E **60** D2
Damrei, Chuor Phnum
Cambodia 11°30N 103°0E **39** G4
Damyang *S. Korea* 35°19N 126°59E **35** G14
Dana *Indonesia* 11°0S 122°52E **37** F6
Dana *Jordan* 30°41N 35°37E **46** E4
Dana, L. *Canada* 50°53N 77°20W **72** B4
Dana, Mt. *U.S.A.* 37°54N 119°12W **78** H7
Danakil Desert *Ethiopia* 12°45N 41°0E **47** E3
Danané *Ivory C.* 7°16N 8°9W **50** G4
Danau Poso *Indonesia* 1°52S 120°35E **37** E6
Danbury *U.S.A.* 41°24N 73°28W **83** E11
Danby L. *U.S.A.* 34°13N 115°5W **77** J6
Dand *Afghan.* 31°28N 65°32E **42** D1
Dande △ *Zimbabwe* 15°56S 30°16E **55** F3
Dandeldhura *Nepal* 29°20N 80°35E **43** E9
Dandeli *India* 15°5N 74°30E **40** M9
Dandenong *Australia* 38°0S 145°15E **63** F4
Dandong *China* 40°10N 124°20E **35** D13
Danfeng *China* 33°45N 110°25E **34** H6
Danger Is. = Pukapuka
Cook Is. 10°53S 165°49W **65** J11
Danger Pt. *S. Africa* 34°40S 19°17E **56** E2
Danginpuri *Indonesia* 8°40S 115°13E **37** K18
Dangla Shan = Tanggula Shan
China 32°40N 92°10E **32** C4
Dangrek, Phnom
Thailand 14°15N 105°0E **38** E5
Dangriga *Belize* 17°0N 88°13W **87** D7
Dangshan *China* 34°27N 116°22E **34** G9
Daniel *U.S.A.* 42°52N 110°4W **76** E8
Daniel's Harbour
Canada 50°13N 57°35W **73** B8
Danielskuil *S. Africa* 28°11S 23°33E **56** D3
Danielson *U.S.A.* 41°48N 71°53W **83** E13
Danilov *Russia* 58°16N 40°13E **18** C7
Daning *China* 36°28N 110°45E **34** F6
Dank *Oman* 23°33N 56°16E **45** F8
Dankhar Gompa *India* 32°10N 78°10E **42** C8
Danlí *Honduras* 14°4N 86°35W **88** D2
Danmark = Denmark ■
Europe 55°45N 10°0E **9** J14
Dannemora *U.S.A.* 44°43N 73°44W **83** B11
Dannevirke *N.Z.* 40°12S 176°8E **59** D6
Dannhauser *S. Africa* 28°0S 30°3E **57** D5
Dansville *U.S.A.* 42°34N 77°42W **82** D7
Danta *India* 24°11N 72°46E **42** G5
Dantan *India* 21°57N 87°20E **43** J12
Danube = Dunărea →
Europe 45°20N 29°40E **17** F15
Danvers *U.S.A.* 42°34N 70°56W **83** D14
Danville *Ill., U.S.A.* 40°8N 87°37W **80** E10
Danville *Ky., U.S.A.* 37°39N 84°46W **81** G11
Danville *Pa., U.S.A.* 40°58N 76°37W **83** F8
Danville *Va., U.S.A.* 36°36N 79°23W **81** G14
Danville *Vt., U.S.A.* 44°25N 72°9W **83** B12
Danzhou *China* 19°31N 109°33E **38** C7
Danzig = Gdańsk
Poland 54°22N 18°40E **17** A10
Dapaong *Togo* 10°55N 0°16E **50** F6
Daqing Shan *China* 40°40N 111°0E **34** D6
Daqq-e Sorkh, Kavīr
Iran 33°45N 52°50E **45** C7
Dar Banda *Africa* 8°0N 23°0E **48** F6
Dar el Beida = Casablanca
Morocco 33°36N 7°36W **50** B4
Dar es Salaam *Tanzania* 6°50S 39°12E **54** D4
Dar Mazār *Iran* 29°14N 57°20E **45** D8
Dar'ā *Syria* 32°36N 36°7E **46** C5
Dar'ā □ *Syria* 32°55N 36°10E **46** C5
Dārāb *Iran* 28°50N 54°30E **45** D7
Daraban *Pakistan* 31°44N 70°20E **42** D4
Daraina *Madag.* 13°12S 49°40E **57** A8
Daraj *Libya* 30°10N 10°28E **51** B8
Dārān *Iran* 32°59N 50°24E **45** C6
Dārayyā *Syria* 33°28N 36°15E **46** B5
Darband *Pakistan* 34°20N 72°50E **42** B5
Darband, Kūh-e *Iran* 31°34N 57°8E **45** D8
Darbhanga *India* 26°15N 85°55E **43** F11
D'Arcy *Canada* 50°33N 122°29W **70** C4
Dardanelle *Ark., U.S.A.* 35°13N 93°9W **84** D8
Dardanelle *Calif.,*
U.S.A. 38°20N 119°50W **78** G7
Dardanelles = Çanakkale Boğazı
Turkey 40°17N 26°32E **23** D12
Dārestān *Iran* 29°9N 58°42E **45** D8
Dârfûr *Sudan* 13°40N 24°0E **51** F10
Dargai *Pakistan* 34°25N 71°55E **42** B4
Dargaville *N.Z.* 35°57S 173°52E **59** A4
Darhan *Mongolia* 49°37N 106°21E **32** B5
Darhan Muminggan Lianheqi
China 41°40N 110°28E **34** D6
Darıca *Turkey* 40°45N 29°23E **23** D13
Darién, G. del *Colombia* 9°0N 77°0W **92** B3
Darién △ *Panama* 7°36N 77°57W **88** E4
Dariganga = Ovoot
Mongolia 45°21N 113°45E **34** B7
Darjeeling = Darjiling
India 27°3N 88°18E **43** F13
Darjiling *India* 27°3N 88°18E **43** F13
Darkan *Australia* 33°20S 116°43E **61** F2
Darkhana *Pakistan* 30°39N 72°11E **42** D5
Darkhazîneh *Iran* 31°54N 48°39E **45** D6
Darkot Pass *Pakistan* 36°45N 73°26E **43** A5
Darling → *Australia* 34°4S 141°54E **63** E3
Darling Downs
Australia 27°30S 150°30E **63** D5
Darling Ra. *Australia* 32°30S 116°20E **61** F2
Darlington *U.K.* 54°32N 1°33W **12** C6
Darlington *U.S.A.* 34°18N 79°52W **85** D15
Darlington □ *U.K.* 54°32N 1°33W **12** C6
Darlington, L. *S. Africa* 33°10S 25°9E **56** E4
Darlot, L. *Australia* 27°48S 121°35E **61** E3

Darłowo *Poland* 54°25N 16°25E **16** A9
Darmstadt *Germany* 49°51N 8°39E **16** D5
Darnah *Libya* 32°45N 22°45E **51** B10
Darnall *S. Africa* 29°23S 31°18E **57** D5
Darnley, C. *Antarctica* 68°0S 69°0E **5** C6
Darnley B. *Canada* 69°30N 123°30W **68** C7
Darr → *Australia* 23°39S 143°50E **62** C3
Darra Pezu *Pakistan* 32°19N 70°44E **42** C4
Darrequeira *Argentina* 37°42S 63°10W **94** D3
Darrington *U.S.A.* 48°15N 121°36W **76** B3
Dart → *U.K.* 50°24N 3°39W **13** G4
Dart, C. *Antarctica* 73°6S 126°20W **5** D14
Dartford *U.K.* 51°26N 0°13E **13** F8
Dartmoor *U.K.* 50°38N 3°57W **13** G4
Dartmoor △ *U.K.* 50°37N 3°59W **13** G4
Dartmouth *Canada* 44°40N 63°30W **73** D7
Dartmouth *U.K.* 50°21N 3°36W **13** G4
Dartmouth Res.
Australia 26°4S 145°18E **63** D4
Dartuch, C. = Artrutx, C. de
Spain 39°55N 3°49E **24** B10
Darvaza *Turkmenistan* 40°11N 58°24E **28** E6
Darvel, Teluk = Lahad Datu,
Telok *Malaysia* 4°50N 118°20E **37** D5
Darwen *U.K.* 53°42N 2°29W **12** D5
Darwendale *Zimbabwe* 17°41S 30°33E **57** B5
Darwha *India* 20°15N 77°45E **40** J10
Darwin *Australia* 12°25S 130°51E **60** B5
Darwin *U.S.A.* 36°15N 117°35W **79** J9
Darya Khan *Pakistan* 31°48N 71°6E **42** D4
Daryācheh-ye Bakhtegān
Iran 29°40N 53°50E **45** D7
Daryoi Amu = Amudarya →
Uzbekistan 43°58N 59°34E **28** E6
Dās *U.A.E.* 25°20N 53°30E **45** E7
Dashen, Ras *Ethiopia* 13°8N 38°26E **47** E2
Dashetai *China* 41°0N 109°5E **34** D5
Dashköpri *Turkmenistan* 36°16N 62°8E **45** B9
Dashoguz *Turkmenistan* 41°49N 59°58E **28** E6
Dasht → *Pakistan* 25°10N 61°40E **40** G2
Daska *Pakistan* 32°20N 74°20E **42** C6
Dasuya *India* 31°49N 75°38E **42** D6
Datça *Turkey* 36°46N 27°40E **23** F12
Datia *India* 25°39N 78°27E **43** G8
Datong *China* 40°6N 113°18E **34** D7
Dattakhel *Pakistan* 32°54N 69°46E **42** C3
Datu, Tanjung *Indonesia* 2°5N 109°39E **36** D3
Datu Piang *Phil.* 7°2N 124°30E **37** C6
Datuk, Tanjong = Datu, Tanjung
Indonesia 2°5N 109°39E **36** D3
Daud Khel *Pakistan* 32°53N 71°34E **42** C4
Daudnagar *India* 25°2N 84°24E **43** G11
Daugava → *Latvia* 57°4N 24°3E **9** H21
Daugavpils *Latvia* 55°53N 26°32E **9** J22
Daulpur *India* 26°45N 77°59E **42** F7
Dauphin *Canada* 51°9N 100°5W **71** C8
Dauphin *U.S.A.* 40°22N 76°56W **82** F8
Dauphin L. *Canada* 51°20N 99°45W **71** C9
Dauphiné *France* 45°15N 5°25E **20** D6
Dausa *India* 26°52N 76°20E **42** F7
Davangere *India* 14°25N 75°55E **40** M9
Davao *Phil.* 7°0N 125°40E **37** C7
Davao G. *Phil.* 6°30N 125°48E **37** C7
Dāvar Panāh = Sarāvān
Iran 27°25N 62°15E **45** E9
Davenport *Calif., U.S.A.* 37°1N 122°12W **78** H4
Davenport *Iowa, U.S.A.* 41°32N 90°35W **80** E8
Davenport *Wash., U.S.A.* 47°39N 118°9W **76** C4
Davenport Ra. *Australia* 20°28S 134°0E **62** C1
Davenport Range △
Australia 20°36S 134°22E **62** C1
Daventry *U.K.* 52°16N 1°10W **13** E6
David *Panama* 8°30N 82°30W **88** E3
David City *U.S.A.* 41°15N 97°8W **80** E5
David Glacier *Antarctica* 75°20S 162°0E **5** D21
David Gorodok = Davyd Haradok
Belarus 52°4N 27°8E **17** B14
Davidson *Canada* 51°16N 105°59W **71** C7
Davis *Antarctica* 68°34S 77°55E **5** C6
Davis *U.S.A.* 38°33N 121°44W **78** G5
Davis Dam *U.S.A.* 35°12N 114°34W **79** K12
Davis Inlet *Canada* 55°50N 60°59W **73** A7
Davis Mts. *U.S.A.* 30°50N 103°55W **84** F3
Davis Sea *Antarctica* 66°0S 92°0E **5** C7
Davis Str. *N. Amer.* 65°0N 58°0W **66** C14
Davlos *Cyprus* 35°25N 33°54E **25** D12
Davos *Switz.* 46°48N 9°49E **20** C8
Davy L. *Canada* 58°53N 108°18W **71** B7
Davyd Haradok *Belarus* 52°4N 27°8E **17** B14
Dawei = Tavoy *Burma* 14°2N 98°12E **38** E2
Dawes Ra. *Australia* 24°40S 150°40E **62** C5
Dawlish *U.K.* 50°35N 3°28W **13** G4
Dawna Ra. *Burma* 16°30N 98°30E **38** D2
Dawros Hd. *Ireland* 54°50N 8°33W **10** B3
Dawson *U.S.A.* 31°46N 84°27W **85** F12
Dawson, I. *Chile* 53°50S 70°50W **96** G2
Dawson B. *Canada* 52°53N 100°49W **71** C8
Dawson City *Canada* 64°10N 139°30W **68** C6
Dawson Creek *Canada* 55°45N 120°15W **70** B4
Dawson Inlet *Canada* 61°50N 93°25W **71** A10
Dawson Ra. *Australia* 24°30S 149°48E **62** C4
Dax *France* 43°44N 1°3W **20** E3
Daxian *China* 31°15N 107°23E **32** C5
Daxindian *China* 37°30N 120°50E **35** F11
Daxinggou *China* 43°25N 129°40E **35** C15
Daxue Shan *China* 30°30N 101°30E **32** C5
Day Kundī □ *Afghan.* 34°0N 66°0E **40** C5
Daylesford *Australia* 37°21S 144°9E **63** F3
Dayr az Zawr *Syria* 35°20N 40°5E **44** C4
Daysland *Canada* 52°50N 112°20W **70** C6
Dayton *Nev., U.S.A.* 39°14N 119°36W **78** F7
Dayton *Ohio, U.S.A.* 39°45N 84°12W **81** F11
Dayton *Pa., U.S.A.* 40°53N 79°15W **82** F5
Dayton *Tenn., U.S.A.* 35°30N 85°1W **85** D12
Dayton *Wash., U.S.A.* 46°19N 117°59W **76** C5
Dayton *Wyo., U.S.A.* 44°53N 107°16W **76** D10
Daytona Beach *U.S.A.* 29°13N 81°1W **85** G14

Dayville *U.S.A.* 44°28N 119°32W **76** D4
De Aar *S. Africa* 30°39S 24°0E **56** E3
De Biesbosch △ *Neths.* 51°45N 4°48E **15** C4
De Funiak Springs
U.S.A. 30°43N 86°7W **85** F11
De Grey → *Australia* 20°12S 119°12E **60** D2
De Haan *Belgium* 51°16N 3°2E **15** C3
De Hoge Veluwe △ *Neths.* 52°5N 5°46E **15** B5
De Hoop △ *S. Africa* 34°30S 20°28E **56** E3
De Kalb Junction *U.S.A.* 44°30N 75°16W **83** B9
De Kennemerduinen △
Neths. 52°27N 4°33E **15** B4
De Land *U.S.A.* 29°2N 81°18W **85** G14
De Leon *U.S.A.* 32°7N 98°32W **84** E5
De Panne *Belgium* 51°6N 2°34E **15** C2
De Pere *U.S.A.* 44°27N 88°4W **80** C9
De Queen *U.S.A.* 34°2N 94°21W **84** D7
De Quincy *U.S.A.* 30°27N 93°26W **84** F8
De Ruyters *U.S.A.* 42°45N 75°53W **83** D9
De Smet *U.S.A.* 44°23N 97°33W **80** C5
De Soto *U.S.A.* 38°8N 90°34W **80** F8
De Tour Village *U.S.A.* 46°0N 83°56W **81** B12
De Witt *U.S.A.* 34°18N 91°20W **84** D9
Dead Sea *Asia* 31°30N 35°30E **46** D4
Deadwood *U.S.A.* 44°23N 103°44W **80** C2
Deadwood L. *Canada* 59°10N 128°30W **70** B3
Deal *U.K.* 51°13N 1°25E **13** F9
Deal I. *Australia* 39°30S 147°20E **63** F4
Dealesville *S. Africa* 28°41S 25°44E **56** D4
Dean → *Canada* 52°49N 126°58W **70** C3
Dean, Forest of *U.K.* 51°45N 2°33W **13** F5
Dean Chan. *Canada* 52°30N 127°15W **70** C3
Deán Funes *Argentina* 30°20S 64°20W **94** C3
Dease → *Canada* 59°56N 128°32W **70** B3
Dease L. *Canada* 58°40N 130°5W **70** B2
Dease Lake *Canada* 58°25N 130°6W **70** B2
Death Valley *U.S.A.* 36°15N 116°50W **79** J10
Death Valley △ *U.S.A.* 36°29N 117°6W **79** J9
Death Valley Junction
U.S.A. 36°20N 116°25W **79** J10
Deba *India* 23°51N 90°33E **43** H14
Debar *Macedonia* 41°31N 20°30E **23** D9
Debden *Canada* 53°30N 106°50W **71** C7
Debica *Poland* 50°2N 21°25E **17** C11
Deborah East, L.
Australia 30°45S 119°30E **61** F2
Deborah West, L.
Australia 30°45S 119°5E **61** F2
Debre Markos *Ethiopia* 10°20N 37°40E **47** E2
Debre Tabor *Ethiopia* 11°50N 38°26E **47** E2
Debre Zebit *Ethiopia* 11°48N 38°30E **47** E2
Debrecen *Hungary* 47°33N 21°42E **17** E11
Decatur *Ala., U.S.A.* 34°36N 86°59W **85** D11
Decatur *Ga., U.S.A.* 33°46N 84°16W **85** D12
Decatur *Ill., U.S.A.* 39°51N 88°57W **80** F9
Decatur *Ind., U.S.A.* 40°50N 84°56W **81** E11
Decatur *Tex., U.S.A.* 33°14N 97°35W **84** E6
Deccan *India* 18°0N 79°0E **40** L11
Deception Bay *Australia* 27°10S 153°5E **63** D5
Deception I. *Antarctica* 63°0S 60°15W **5** C17
Deception L. *Canada* 56°33N 104°13W **71** B8
Dechhu *India* 26°46N 72°20E **42** F5
Děčín *Czech Rep.* 50°47N 14°12E **16** C8
Deckerville *U.S.A.* 43°32N 82°44W **82** C2
Decorah *U.S.A.* 43°18N 91°48W **80** D8
Dedéagach = Alexandroupoli
Greece 40°50N 25°54E **23** D11
Dedham *U.S.A.* 42°15N 71°10W **83** D13
Dedza *Malawi* 14°20S 34°20E **55** E3
Dee → *Aberds., U.K.* 57°9N 2°5W **11** D6
Dee → *Dumf. & Gall., U.K.* 54°51N 4°3W **11** G4
Dee → *Wales, U.K.* 53°22N 3°17W **12** D4
Deep B. *Canada* 61°15N 116°35W **70** A5
Deep Bay = Shenzhen Wan
China 22°27N 113°55E **33** G10
Deepwater *Australia* 29°25S 151°51E **63** D5
Deer → *Canada* 58°23N 94°13W **71** B10
Deer L. *Canada* 52°40N 94°20W **71** C10
Deer Lake *Nfld. & L.,*
Canada 49°11N 57°27W **73** C8
Deer Lake *Ont., Canada* 52°36N 94°20W **71** C10
Deer Lodge *U.S.A.* 46°24N 112°44W **76** C7
Deer Park *U.S.A.* 47°57N 117°28W **76** C5
Deer River *U.S.A.* 47°20N 93°48W **80** B7
Deeragun *Australia* 19°16S 146°33E **62** B4
Deerdepoort *S. Africa* 24°37S 26°27E **56** C4
Defiance *U.S.A.* 41°17N 84°22W **81** E11
Degana *India* 26°50N 74°20E **42** F6
Dégelis *Canada* 47°30N 68°35W **73** C6
Deggendorf *Germany* 48°50N 12°57E **16** D7
Degh → *Pakistan* 31°3N 73°21E **42** D5
Degirmenlik = Kythréa
Cyprus 35°15N 33°29E **25** D12
Deh Bīd *Iran* 30°39N 53°11E **45** D7
Deh Dasht *Iran* 30°47N 50°33E **45** D6
Deh-e Shīr *Iran* 31°29N 53°45E **45** D7
Dehaj *Iran* 30°42N 54°53E **45** D7
Dehak *Iran* 27°11N 62°37E **45** E9
Dehdez *Iran* 31°43N 50°17E **45** D6
Dehej *India* 21°44N 72°40E **42** J5
Dehestān *Iran* 28°30N 55°35E **45** D7
Dehgolān *Iran* 35°17N 47°25E **44** C5
Dehibat *Tunisia* 32°0N 10°47E **51** B8
Dehlorān *Iran* 32°41N 47°16E **45** C5
Dehnow-e Kūhestān
Iran 27°58N 58°32E **45** E8
Dehra Dun *India* 30°20N 78°4E **42** D8
Dehri *India* 24°50N 84°15E **43** G11
Dehui *China* 44°30N 125°40E **35** B13
Deinze *Belgium* 50°59N 3°32E **15** D3
Dej *Romania* 47°10N 23°52E **17** E12
Deka → *Zimbabwe* 18°4S 26°42E **56** B4
DeKalb *U.S.A.* 41°56N 88°46W **80** E9
Dekese
Dem. Rep. of the Congo 3°24S 21°24E **52** E4

Del Norte *U.S.A.* 37°41N 106°21W **77** H10
Del Rio *U.S.A.* 29°22N 100°54W **84** G4
Delambre I. *Australia* 20°26S 117°5E **60** D2
Delano *U.S.A.* 35°46N 119°15W **79** K7
Delano Peak *U.S.A.* 38°22N 112°22W **76** G7
Delareyville *S. Africa* 26°41S 25°26E **56** D4
Delaronde L. *Canada* 54°3N 107°3W **71** C7
Delavan *U.S.A.* 42°38N 88°39W **80** D9
Delaware *U.S.A.* 40°18N 83°4W **81** E12
Delaware □ *U.S.A.* 39°0N 75°20W **81** F16
Delaware → *U.S.A.* 39°15N 75°20W **83** G9
Delaware B. *U.S.A.* 39°0N 75°10W **81** F16
Delaware Water Gap △
U.S.A. 41°10N 74°55W **83** E10
Delay → *Canada* 56°56N 71°28W **73** A5
Delegate *Australia* 37°4S 148°56E **63** F4
Delevan *U.S.A.* 42°29N 78°29W **82** D6
Delft *Neths.* 52°1N 4°22E **15** B4
Delfzijl *Neths.* 53°20N 6°55E **15** A6
Delgado, C. *Mozam.* 10°45S 40°40E **55** E5
Delgerhet *Mongolia* 45°50N 110°30E **34** B6
Delgo *Sudan* 20°6N 30°40E **51** D12
Delhi *Canada* 42°51N 80°30W **82** D4
Delhi *India* 28°39N 77°13E **42** E7
Delhi *La., U.S.A.* 32°28N 91°30W **84** E9
Delhi *N.Y., U.S.A.* 42°17N 74°55W **83** D10
Delia *Canada* 51°38N 112°23W **70** C6
Delice *Turkey* 39°54N 34°2E **19** G5
Delicias *Mexico* 28°13N 105°28W **86** B3
Delījān *Iran* 33°59N 50°40E **45** C6
Déline *Canada* 65°11N 123°25W **68** C7
Delisle *Canada* 51°55N 107°8W **71** C7
Dell City *U.S.A.* 31°56N 105°12W **84** F2
Dell Rapids *U.S.A.* 43°50N 96°43W **80** D5
Delmar *U.S.A.* 42°37N 73°47W **83** D11
Delmenhorst *Germany* 53°3N 8°37E **16** B5
Delonga, Ostrova
Russia 76°40N 149°20E **29** B15
Deloraine *Australia* 41°30S 146°40E **63** G4
Deloraine *Canada* 49°15N 100°29W **71** D8
Delphi *U.S.A.* 40°36N 86°41W **80** E10
Delphos *U.S.A.* 40°51N 84°21W **81** E11
Delportshoop *S. Africa* 28°22S 24°20E **56** D3
Delray Beach *U.S.A.* 26°28N 80°4W **85** H14
Delta *Colo., U.S.A.* 38°44N 108°4W **76** G9
Delta *Utah, U.S.A.* 39°21N 112°35W **76** G7
Delta Dunărea △
Romania 45°15N 29°23E **17** F15
Delta Junction *U.S.A.* 64°2N 145°44W **68** C5
Deltona *U.S.A.* 28°54N 81°16W **85** G14
Delungra *Australia* 29°39S 150°51E **63** D5
Delvada *India* 20°46N 71°2E **42** J4
Delvinë *Albania* 39°59N 20°6E **23** E9
Demak *Indonesia* 6°53S 110°38E **37** G14
Demanda, Sierra de la
Spain 42°15N 3°0W **21** A4
Demavend = Damāvand,
Qolleh-ye *Iran* 35°56N 52°10E **45** C7
Dembia
Dem. Rep. of the Congo 3°33N 25°48E **54** B2
Dembidolo *Ethiopia* 8°34N 34°50E **47** F1
Demchok *India* 32°42N 79°29E **43** C8
Demer → *Belgium* 50°57N 4°42E **15** D4
Deming *N. Mex.,*
U.S.A. 32°16N 107°46W **77** K10
Deming *Wash., U.S.A.* 48°50N 122°13W **78** B4
Demini → *Brazil* 0°46S 62°56W **92** D6
Demirci *Turkey* 39°2N 28°38E **23** E13
Demirköy *Turkey* 41°49N 27°45E **23** D12
Demopolis *U.S.A.* 32°31N 87°50W **85** E11
Dempo *Indonesia* 4°2S 103°15E **36** E2
Den Bosch = 's-Hertogenbosch
Neths. 51°42N 5°17E **15** C5
Den Burg *Neths.* 53°3N 4°47E **15** A4
Den Chai *Thailand* 17°59N 100°4E **38** D3
Den Haag = 's-Gravenhage
Neths. 52°7N 4°17E **15** B4
Den Helder *Neths.* 52°57N 4°45E **15** B4
Den Oever *Neths.* 52°56N 5°2E **15** B5
Denair *U.S.A.* 37°32N 120°48W **78** H6
Denali = McKinley, Mt.
U.S.A. 63°4N 151°0W **74** a
Denau *Uzbekistan* 38°16N 67°54E **28** F7
Denbigh *Canada* 45°8N 77°15W **82** A7
Denbigh *U.K.* 53°12N 3°25W **12** D4
Denbighshire □ *U.K.* 53°8N 3°22W **12** D4
Dendang *Indonesia* 3°7S 107°56E **36** E3
Dendermonde *Belgium* 51°2N 4°5E **15** C4
Dengfeng *China* 34°25N 113°2E **34** G7
Dengkou *China* 40°18N 106°55E **34** D4
Denham *Australia* 25°56S 113°31E **61** E1
Denham, Mt. *Jamaica* 18°13N 77°32W **88** a
Denham Ra. *Australia* 21°55S 147°46E **62** C4
Denham Sd. *Australia* 25°45S 113°15E **61** E1
Denholm *Canada* 52°39N 108°1W **71** C7
Denia *Spain* 38°49N 0°8E **21** C6
Denial B. *Australia* 32°14S 133°32E **63** E1
Deniliquin *Australia* 35°30S 144°58E **63** F3
Denison *Iowa, U.S.A.* 42°1N 95°21W **80** D6
Denison *Tex., U.S.A.* 33°45N 96°33W **84** E6
Denison Plains *Australia* 18°35S 128°0E **60** C4
Denizli *Turkey* 37°42N 29°2E **23** F13
Denman Glacier
Antarctica 66°45S 99°25E **5** C7
Denmark *Australia* 34°59S 117°25E **61** F2
Denmark ■ *Europe* 55°45N 10°0E **9** J14
Denmark Str. *Atl. Oc.* 66°0N 30°0W **66** C17
Dennery *St. Lucia* 13°55N 60°54W **89** f
Dennison *U.S.A.* 40°24N 81°19W **82** F3
Denny *U.K.* 56°1N 3°55W **11** E5
Denpasar *Indonesia* 8°39S 115°13E **37** K18
Denpasar ✈ (DPS)
Indonesia 8°44S 115°10E **37** K18
Denton *Mont., U.S.A.* 47°19N 109°57W **76** C9
Denton *Tex., U.S.A.* 33°13N 97°8W **84** E6

D'Entrecasteaux, Pt.
Australia 34°50S 115°57E **61** F2

D'Entrecasteaux △
  Australia   34°20S 115°33E **61 F2**
D'Entrecasteaux Is.
  Papua N. G.   9°0S 151°0E **58 B8**
Denver Colo., U.S.A. 39°42N 104°59W **76 G11**
Denver Pa., U.S.A.   40°14N 76°8W **83 F8**
Denver City U.S.A.   32°58N 102°50W **84 E3**
Deoband India   29°42N 77°43E **42 E7**
Deogarh India   25°32N 73°54E **42 G5**
Deoghar India   24°30N 86°42E **43 G12**
Deolali India   19°58N 73°50E **40 K8**
Deoli = Devli India   25°50N 75°20E **42 G6**
Deora India   26°22N 70°55E **42 F4**
Deori India   23°24N 79°1E **43 H8**
Deoria India   26°31N 83°48E **43 F10**
Deosai Mts. Pakistan 35°40N 75°0E **43 B6**
Deosri India   26°46N 90°29E **43 F14**
Depalpur India   22°51N 75°33E **42 H6**
Deping China   37°25N 116°58E **35 F9**
Deposit U.S.A.   42°4N 75°25W **83 D9**
Depuch I. Australia   20°37S 117°44E **60 D2**
Deputatskiy Russia   69°18N 139°54E **29 C14**
Dera Ghazi Khan
  Pakistan   30°5N 70°43E **42 D4**
Dera Ismail Khan
  Pakistan   31°50N 70°50E **42 D4**
Derabugti Pakistan   29°2N 69°9E **42 E3**
Derawar Fort Pakistan 28°46N 71°20E **42 E4**
Derbent Russia   42°5N 48°15E **19 F8**
Derby Australia   17°18S 123°38E **60 C3**
Derby U.K.   52°56N 1°28W **12 E6**
Derby Conn., U.S.A.   41°19N 73°5W **83 E11**
Derby Kans., U.S.A.   37°33N 97°16W **80 G5**
Derby N.Y., U.S.A.   42°41N 78°58W **82 D6**
Derby □ U.K.   52°56N 1°28W **12 E6**
Derby Line U.S.A.   45°0N 72°6W **83 B12**
Derbyshire □ U.K.   53°11N 1°38W **12 E6**
Derdepoort S. Africa 24°38S 26°24E **56 C4**
Dereham U.K.   52°41N 0°57E **13 E8**
Derg → U.K.   54°44N 7°26W **10 B4**
Derg, L. Ireland   53°0N 8°20W **10 D3**
Deridder U.S.A.   30°51N 93°17W **84 F8**
Dermott U.S.A.   33°32N 91°26W **84 E9**
Derry = Londonderry
  U.K.   55°0N 7°20W **10 B4**
Derry = Londonderry □
  U.K.   55°0N 7°20W **10 B4**
Derry N.H., U.S.A.   42°53N 71°19W **83 D13**
Derry Pa., U.S.A.   40°20N 79°18W **82 F5**
Derryveagh Mts. Ireland 54°56N 8°11W **10 B3**
Derwent → Cumb., U.K. 54°39N 3°33W **12 C4**
Derwent → Derby, U.K. 52°57N 1°28W **12 E6**
Derwent → N. Yorks.,
  U.K.   53°45N 0°58W **12 D7**
Derwent Water U.K.   54°35N 3°9W **12 C4**
Des Moines Iowa, U.S.A. 41°35N 93°37W **80 E7**
Des Moines N. Mex.,
  U.S.A.   36°46N 103°50W **77 H12**
Des Moines Wash.,
  U.S.A.   47°24N 122°19W **78 C4**
Des Moines → U.S.A.   40°23N 91°25W **80 E8**
Desaguadero →
  Argentina   34°30S 66°46W **94 C2**
Desaguadero → Bolivia 16°35S 69°5W **92 G5**
Desar Malaysia   1°31N 104°17E **39 d**
Descanso, Pta. Mexico 32°21N 117°3W **79 N9**
Deschaillons-sur-St-Laurent
  Canada   46°32N 72°7W **73 C5**
Deschambault L.
  Canada   54°50N 103°30W **71 C8**
Deschutes → U.S.A.   45°38N 120°55W **76 D3**
Dese Ethiopia   11°5N 39°40E **47 E2**
Deseado → Argentina   47°45S 65°54W **96 F3**
Deseronto Canada   44°12N 77°3W **82 B7**
Desert Center U.S.A. 33°43N 115°24W **79 M11**
Desert Hot Springs
  U.S.A.   33°58N 116°30W **79 M10**
Deshnok India   27°48N 73°21E **42 F5**
Desierto Central de Baja
  California △ Mexico 29°40N 114°50W **86 B2**
Desna → Ukraine   50°33N 30°32E **17 C16**
Desolación, I. Chile 53°0S 74°0W **96 G2**
Despeñaperros, Paso
  Spain   38°24N 3°30W **21 C4**
Dessau Germany   51°51N 12°14E **16 C7**
Dessye = Dese Ethiopia 11°5N 39°40E **47 E2**
D'Estrees B. Australia 35°55S 137°45E **63 F2**
Desuri India   25°18N 73°35E **42 G5**
Det Udom Thailand   14°54N 105°5E **38 E5**
Dete Zimbabwe   18°38S 26°50E **56 B4**
Detmold Germany   51°56N 8°52E **16 C5**
Detour, Pt. U.S.A.   45°40N 86°40W **80 C10**
Detroit U.S.A.   42°19N 83°12W **82 D1**
Detroit Lakes U.S.A. 46°49N 95°51W **80 B6**
Deua △ Australia   35°32S 149°46E **63 F4**
Deurne Neths.   51°27N 5°49E **15 C5**
Deutsche Bucht Germany 54°15N 8°0E **16 A5**
Deutschland = Germany ■
  Europe   51°0N 10°0E **16 C6**
Deva Romania   45°53N 22°55E **17 F12**
Devakottai India   9°55N 78°45E **40 Q11**
Devaprayag India   30°13N 78°35E **43 D8**
Deventer Neths.   52°15N 6°10E **15 B6**
Deveron → U.K.   57°41N 2°32W **11 D6**
Devgadh Bariya India 22°40N 73°55E **42 H5**
Devikot India   26°42N 71°12E **42 F4**
Devils Den U.S.A.   36°24N 119°58W **78 K7**
Devils Hole = Death Valley △
  U.S.A.   36°29N 117°6W **79 J9**
Devils Lake U.S.A.   48°7N 98°52W **80 A4**
Devils Paw Canada   58°47N 134°0W **70 B2**
Devils Postpile △ U.S.A. 37°37N 119°5W **78 H7**
Devils Tower U.S.A.   44°35N 104°42W **76 D11**
Devils Tower △
  U.S.A.   44°48N 104°55W **76 D11**
Devine U.S.A.   29°8N 98°54W **84 G5**
Devizes U.K.   51°22N 1°58W **13 F6**

Devli India   25°50N 75°20E **42 G6**
Devon Canada   53°24N 113°44W **70 C6**
Devon □ U.K.   50°50N 3°40W **13 G4**
Devon I. Canada   75°10N 85°0W **69 B11**
Devonport Australia   41°10S 146°22E **63 G4**
Devonport N.Z.   36°49S 174°49E **59 B5**
Dewas India   22°59N 76°3E **42 H7**
Dewetsdorp S. Africa 29°33S 26°39E **56 D4**
Dewey Puerto Rico   18°18N 65°18W **89 d**
Dexter Maine, U.S.A. 45°1N 69°18W **81 C19**
Dexter Mo., U.S.A.   36°48N 89°57W **80 G9**
Dexter N. Mex., U.S.A. 33°12N 104°22W **77 K11**
Dey-Dey, L. Australia 29°12S 131°4E **61 E5**
Deyang China   31°3N 104°27E **32 C5**
Deyhūk Iran   33°15N 57°30E **45 C8**
Deyyer Iran   27°55N 51°55E **45 E6**
Dez → Iran   31°39N 48°52E **45 D6**
Dezadeash L. Canada   60°28N 136°58W **70 A1**
Dezfūl Iran   32°20N 48°30E **45 C6**
Dezhneva, Mys Russia 66°5N 169°40W **29 C19**
Dezhou China   37°26N 116°18E **34 F9**
Dhadhar → India   24°56N 85°24E **43 G11**
Dhahiriya = Aẕ Ẕāhirīyah
  West Bank   31°25N 34°58E **46 D3**
Dhahran = Aẕ Ẕahrān
  Si. Arabia   26°10N 50°7E **45 E6**
Dhak Pakistan   32°25N 72°33E **42 C5**
Dhaka Bangla.   23°43N 90°26E **43 H14**
Dhaka □ Bangla.   24°25N 90°25E **43 G14**
Dhali Cyprus   35°1N 33°25E **25 D12**
Dhamār Yemen   14°30N 44°20E **47 E3**
Dhampur India   29°19N 78°33E **43 E8**
Dhamtari India   20°42N 81°35E **41 J12**
Dhanbad India   23°50N 86°30E **43 H12**
Dhangarhi Nepal   28°55N 80°40E **43 E9**
Dhankuta Nepal   26°55N 87°40E **43 F12**
Dhanpuri India   23°13N 81°30E **43 H9**
Dhar India   22°35N 75°26E **42 H6**
Dharampur India   22°13N 75°18E **42 H6**
Dharamsala = Dharmsala
  India   32°16N 76°23E **42 C7**
Dharan Nepal   26°49N 87°17E **43 F12**
Dhariwal India   31°57N 75°19E **42 D6**
Dharla → Bangla.   25°46N 89°42E **43 G13**
Dharmapuri India   12°10N 78°10E **40 N11**
Dharmjaygarh India   22°28N 83°13E **43 H10**
Dharmsala India   32°16N 76°23E **42 C7**
Dharni India   21°33N 76°53E **42 J7**
Dharwad India   15°30N 75°4E **40 M9**
Dhasan → India   25°48N 79°24E **43 G8**
Dhaulagiri Nepal   28°39N 83°28E **43 E10**
Dhebar, L. India   24°10N 74°0E **42 G6**
Dheftera Cyprus   35°5N 33°16E **25 D12**
Dhenkanal India   20°45N 85°35E **41 J14**
Dherinia Cyprus   35°3N 33°57E **25 D12**
Dhī Qār □ Iraq   31°0N 46°15E **44 D5**
Dhiarrizos → Cyprus   34°41N 32°34E **25 E11**
Dhībān Jordan   31°30N 35°46E **46 D4**
Dhilwan India   31°31N 75°21E **42 D6**
Dhimarkhera India   23°28N 80°22E **43 H9**
Dhodhekánisos = Dodecanese
  Greece   36°35N 27°0E **23 F12**
Dholka India   22°44N 72°29E **42 H5**
Dhoraji India   21°45N 70°37E **42 J4**
Dhrangadhra India   22°59N 71°31E **42 H4**
Dhrol India   22°33N 70°25E **42 H4**
Dhuburi India   26°2N 89°59E **41 F16**
Dhule India   20°58N 74°50E **40 J9**
Di Linh Vietnam   11°35N 108°4E **39 G7**
Di Linh, Cao Nguyen
  Vietnam   11°30N 108°0E **39 G7**
Dia Greece   35°28N 25°14E **25 D7**
Diablo Range U.S.A.   37°20N 121°25W **78 J5**
Diafarabé Mali   14°9N 4°57W **50 F5**
Diamante Argentina   32°5S 60°40W **94 C3**
Diamante → Argentina 34°30S 66°46W **94 C2**
Diamantina Brazil   18°17S 43°40W **93 G10**
Diamantina →
  Australia   26°45S 139°10E **63 D2**
Diamantina △ Australia 23°33S 141°23E **62 C3**
Diamantino Brazil   14°30S 56°30W **93 F7**
Diamond Harbour
  India   22°11N 88°14E **43 H13**
Diamond Is. Australia 17°25S 151°5E **62 B5**
Diamond Mts. U.S.A.   39°40N 115°50W **76 G6**
Diamond Springs
  U.S.A.   38°42N 120°49W **78 G6**
Diaoyu Tai = Senkaku-Shotō
  E. China Sea   25°45N 123°30E **31 M1**
Dibā U.A.E.   25°45N 56°16E **45 E8**
Dibai India   28°13N 78°15E **42 E8**
Dibaya
  Dem. Rep. of the Congo 6°30S 22°57E **52 F4**
Dibaya-Lubue
  Dem. Rep. of the Congo 4°12S 19°54E **52 E3**
Dibbeen △ Jordan   32°20N 35°45E **46 C4**
D'Iberville, Lac Canada 55°55N 73°15W **72 A5**
Dibete Botswana   23°45S 26°32E **56 C4**
Dibrugarh India   27°29N 94°55E **41 F19**
Dickens U.S.A.   33°37N 100°50W **84 E4**
Dickinson U.S.A.   46°53N 102°47W **80 B2**
Dickson U.S.A.   36°5N 87°23W **85 C11**
Dickson City U.S.A.   41°28N 75°36W **83 E9**
Didiéni Mali   13°53N 8°6W **50 F4**
Didsbury Canada   51°35N 114°10W **70 C6**
Didwana India   27°23N 74°36E **42 F6**
Diefenbaker, L. Canada 51°0N 106°55W **71 C7**
Diego de Almagro Chile 26°22S 70°3W **94 B1**
Diego Suarez = Antsiranana
  Madag.   12°25S 49°20E **57 A8**
Diekirch Lux.   49°52N 6°10E **15 E6**
Dien Ban Vietnam   15°53N 108°16E **38 E7**
Dien Bien Vietnam   21°20N 103°0E **38 B4**
Dien Khanh Vietnam   12°15N 109°6E **38 F7**
Dieppe France   49°54N 1°4E **20 B4**
Dierks U.S.A.   34°7N 94°1W **84 D7**

Diest Belgium   50°58N 5°4E **15 D5**
Dif Somali Rep.   0°59N 40°58E **47 G3**
Differdange Lux.   49°31N 5°54E **15 E5**
Dig India   27°28N 77°20E **42 F7**
Digba
  Dem. Rep. of the Congo 4°25N 25°48E **54 B2**
Digby Canada   44°38N 65°50W **73 D6**
Diggi India   26°22N 75°26E **42 F6**
Dighinala Bangla.   23°15N 92°5E **41 H18**
Dighton U.S.A.   38°29N 100°28W **80 F3**
Digne-les-Bains France 44°5N 6°12E **20 D7**
Digos Phil.   6°45N 125°20E **37 C7**
Digranes Iceland   66°4N 14°44W **8 C6**
Digul → Indonesia   7°7S 138°42E **37 F9**
Dihang → Brahmaputra →
  Asia   23°40N 90°35E **43 H13**
Dijlah, Nahr → Asia   31°0N 47°25E **44 D5**
Dijon France   47°20N 5°3E **20 C6**
Dikhil Djibouti   11°8N 42°20E **47 E3**
Dikkil = Dikhil Djibouti 11°8N 42°20E **47 E3**
Diksmuide Belgium   51°2N 2°52E **15 C2**
Dikson Russia   73°40N 80°5E **28 B9**
Dikti Oros Greece   35°8N 25°30E **25 D7**
Dila Ethiopia   6°21N 38°22E **47 F2**
Dili E. Timor   8°39S 125°34E **37 F7**
Dilli = Delhi India   28°39N 77°13E **42 E7**
Dillingham U.S.A.   59°3N 158°28W **74 a**
Dillon Canada   55°56N 108°35W **71 B7**
Dillon Mont., U.S.A. 45°13N 112°38W **76 D7**
Dillon S.C., U.S.A.   34°25N 79°22W **85 D15**
Dillon → Canada   55°56N 108°56W **71 B7**
Dillsburg U.S.A.   40°7N 77°2W **82 F7**
Dilolo
  Dem. Rep. of the Congo 10°28S 22°18E **52 G4**
Dimapur India   25°54N 93°45E **32 D4**
Dimas Mexico   23°43N 106°47W **86 C3**
Dimashq Syria   33°30N 36°18E **46 B5**
Dimashq □ Syria   33°30N 36°30E **46 B5**
Dimbaza S. Africa   32°50S 27°14E **57 E4**
Dimboola Australia   36°28S 142°7E **63 F3**
Dîmbovița = Dâmbovița →
  Romania   44°12N 26°26E **17 F14**
Dimbulah Australia   17°8S 145°4E **62 B4**
Dimitrovgrad Bulgaria 42°5N 25°35E **23 C11**
Dimitrovgrad Russia   54°14N 49°39E **18 D8**
Dimitrovo = Pernik
  Bulgaria   42°35N 23°2E **23 C10**
Dimmitt U.S.A.   34°33N 102°19W **84 D3**
Dimona Israel   31°2N 35°1E **46 D4**
Dinagat Phil.   10°10N 125°40E **37 B7**
Dinajpur Bangla.   25°33N 88°43E **41 G16**
Dinan France   48°28N 2°2W **20 B2**
Dinān Āb Iran   32°4N 56°49E **45 C8**
Dinant Belgium   50°16N 4°55E **15 D4**
Dinapur India   25°38N 85°5E **43 G11**
Dīnār, Kūh-e Iran   30°42N 51°46E **45 D6**
Dinara Planina Croatia 44°0N 16°30E **22 C7**
Dinard France   48°38N 2°6W **20 B2**
Dinaric Alps = Dinara Planina
  Croatia   44°0N 16°30E **22 C7**
Dindigul India   10°25N 78°0E **40 P11**
Dindori India   22°57N 81°5E **43 H9**
Ding Xian = Dingzhou
  China   38°30N 114°59E **34 E8**
Dinga Pakistan   25°26N 67°10E **42 G2**
Ding'an China   19°42N 110°19E **38 C8**
Dingbian China   37°35N 107°32E **34 F4**
Dingle Ireland   52°9N 10°17W **10 D1**
Dingle B. Ireland   52°3N 10°20W **10 D1**
Dingmans Ferry U.S.A. 41°13N 74°55W **83 E10**
Dingo Australia   23°38S 149°19E **62 C4**
Dingtao China   35°5N 115°35E **34 G8**
Dingwall U.K.   57°36N 4°26W **11 D4**
Dingxi China   35°30N 104°33E **34 G3**
Dingxiang China   38°30N 112°58E **34 E7**
Dingzhou China   38°30N 114°59E **34 E8**
Dinh, Mui Vietnam   11°22N 109°1E **39 G7**
Dinh Lap Vietnam   21°33N 107°6E **38 B6**
Dinin → Ireland   52°43N 7°18W **10 D4**
Dinira △ Venezuela   9°57N 70°6W **89 E6**
Dinokwe Botswana   23°29S 26°37E **56 C4**
Dinorwic Canada   49°41N 92°30W **71 D10**
Dinosaur △ Canada   50°47N 111°30W **70 C6**
Dinosaur △ U.S.A.   40°30N 108°45W **76 F9**
Dinuba U.S.A.   36°32N 119°23W **78 J7**
Dionisiades Greece   35°20N 26°10E **25 D8**
Diourbel Senegal   14°39N 16°12W **50 F2**
Dipalpur Pakistan   30°40N 73°39E **42 D5**
Dipkarpaz = Rizokarpaso
  Cyprus   35°36N 34°23E **25 D13**
Diplo Pakistan   24°35N 69°35E **42 G3**
Dipolog Phil.   8°36N 123°20E **37 C6**
Dir Pakistan   35°8N 71°59E **40 B7**
Dire Dawa Ethiopia   9°35N 41°45E **47 F3**
Dirfis Oros Greece   38°40N 23°54E **23 E10**
Diriamba Nic.   11°51N 86°19W **88 D2**
Dirk Hartog I. Australia 25°50S 113°5E **61 E1**
Dirranbandi Australia 28°33S 148°17E **63 D4**
Disa India   24°18N 72°10E **42 G5**
Disappointment, C.
  U.S.A.   46°18N 124°5W **76 C1**
Disappointment, L.
  Australia   23°20S 122°40E **60 D3**
Disaster B. Australia 37°15S 149°58E **63 F4**
Discovery B. Australia 38°10S 140°40E **63 F3**
Discovery B. Australia 22°18N 114°1E **33 G11**
Disko = Qeqertarsuaq
  Greenland   69°45N 53°30W **66 C14**
Disney Reef Tonga   19°17S 174°7W **59 c**
Diss U.K.   52°23N 1°7E **13 E9**
Disteghil Sar Pakistan 36°20N 75°12E **43 A6**
District of Columbia □
  U.S.A.   38°55N 77°0W **81 F15**
Distrito Federal □ Brazil 15°45S 47°45W **93 G9**
Distrito Federal □
  Mexico   19°15N 99°10W **87 D5**

Diu India   20°45N 70°58E **42 J4**
Dīvāndarreh Iran   35°55N 47°2E **44 C5**
Divide U.S.A.   45°45N 112°45W **76 D7**
Dividing Ra. Australia 27°45S 116°0E **61 E2**
Divinópolis Brazil   20°10S 44°54W **93 H10**
Divnoye Russia   45°55N 43°21E **19 E7**
Divo Ivory C.   5°48N 5°15W **50 G4**
Dīwāl Kol Afghan.   34°23N 67°52E **42 B2**
Dixie Mt. U.S.A.   39°55N 120°16W **78 F6**
Dixon Calif., U.S.A. 38°27N 121°49W **78 G5**
Dixon Ill., U.S.A.   41°50N 89°29W **80 E9**
Dixon Entrance U.S.A. 54°30N 132°0W **68 D6**
Dixville Canada   45°4N 71°46W **83 A13**
Diyālā □ Iraq   33°45N 44°35E **44 C5**
Diyālā → Iraq   33°13N 44°30E **44 C5**
Diyarbakır Turkey   37°55N 40°18E **44 B4**
Diyodar India   24°8N 71°50E **42 G4**
Djakarta = Jakarta
  Indonesia   6°9S 106°52E **37 G12**
Djamba Angola   16°45S 13°58E **56 B1**
Djambala Congo   2°32S 14°30E **52 E2**
Djanet Algeria   24°35N 9°32E **50 D7**
Djawa = Jawa Indonesia 7°0S 110°0E **36 F3**
Djelfa Algeria   34°40N 3°15E **50 B6**
Djema C.A.R.   6°3N 25°15E **54 A2**
Djerba, Î. de Tunisia 33°50N 10°48E **51 B8**
Djerid, Chott Tunisia 33°42N 8°30E **50 B7**
Djibouti Djibouti   11°30N 43°5E **47 E3**
Djibouti ■ Africa   12°0N 43°0E **47 E3**
Djolu Dem. Rep. of the Congo 0°35N 22°5E **52 D4**
Djougou Benin   9°40N 1°45E **50 G6**
Djoum Cameroon   2°41N 12°35E **52 D2**
Djourab, Erg du Chad 16°40N 18°50E **51 E9**
Djugu
  Dem. Rep. of the Congo 1°55N 30°35E **54 B3**
Djukbinj △ Australia 12°11S 131°2E **60 B5**
Dmitriya Lapteva, Proliv
  Russia   73°0N 140°0E **29 B15**
Dnepr = Dnipro →
  Ukraine   46°30N 32°18E **19 E5**
Dneprodzerzhinsk =
  Dniprodzerzhynsk
  Ukraine   48°32N 34°37E **19 E5**
Dnepropetrovsk =
  Dnipropetrovsk
  Ukraine   48°30N 35°0E **19 E6**
Dnestr = Dnister →
  Europe   46°18N 30°17E **17 E16**
Dnieper = Dnipro →
  Ukraine   46°30N 32°18E **19 E5**
Dniester = Dnister →
  Europe   46°18N 30°17E **17 E16**
Dnipro → Ukraine   46°30N 32°18E **19 E5**
Dniprodzerzhynsk
  Ukraine   48°32N 34°37E **19 E5**
Dnipropetrovsk Ukraine 48°30N 35°0E **19 E6**
Dnister → Europe   46°18N 30°17E **17 E16**
Dno Russia   57°50N 29°58E **9 H23**
Dnyapro = Dnipro →
  Ukraine   46°30N 32°18E **19 E5**
Do Gonbadān = Gachsārān
  Iran   30°15N 50°45E **45 D6**
Doaktown Canada   46°33N 66°8W **73 C6**
Doan Hung Vietnam   21°30N 105°10E **38 B5**
Doany Madag.   14°21S 49°30E **57 A8**
Doba Chad   8°40N 16°50E **51 G9**
Dobandi Pakistan   31°13N 66°50E **42 D2**
Dobbyn Australia   19°44S 140°2E **62 B3**
Dobele Latvia   56°37N 23°16E **9 H20**
Doberai, Jazirah Indonesia 1°25S 133°0E **37 E8**
Doblas Argentina   37°5S 64°0W **94 D3**
Dobo Indonesia   5°45S 134°15E **37 F8**
Doboj Bos.-H.   44°46N 18°4E **23 B8**
Dobrich Bulgaria   43°37N 27°49E **23 C12**
Dobruja Europe   44°30N 28°15E **17 F15**
Dobrush Belarus   52°25N 31°22E **17 B16**
Doc, Mui Vietnam   17°58N 106°30E **38 D6**
Docker River = Kaltukatjara
  Australia   24°52S 129°5E **61 D4**
Doctor Arroyo Mexico 23°40N 100°11W **86 C4**
Doctor Pedro P. Peña
  Paraguay   22°27S 62°21W **94 A3**
Doda India   33°10N 75°34E **43 C6**
Doda, L. Canada   49°25N 75°13W **72 C4**
Dodecanese Greece   36°35N 27°0E **23 F12**
Dodekanisa = Dodecanese
  Greece   36°35N 27°0E **23 F12**
Dodge City U.S.A.   37°45N 100°1W **80 G3**
Dodge L. Canada   59°50N 105°36W **71 B7**
Dodgeville U.S.A.   42°58N 90°8W **80 D8**
Dodoma Tanzania   6°8S 35°45E **54 D4**
Dodoma □ Tanzania   6°0S 36°0E **54 D4**
Dodori □ Kenya   1°55S 41°5E **54 C5**
Dodsland Canada   51°50N 108°45W **71 C7**
Dodson U.S.A.   48°24N 108°15W **76 B9**
Doesburg Neths.   52°1N 6°9E **15 B6**
Doetinchem Neths.   51°59N 6°18E **15 C6**
Dog Creek Canada   51°35N 122°14W **70 C4**
Dog L., Man., Canada 51°2N 98°31W **71 C9**
Dog L., Ont., Canada 48°48N 89°30W **72 C2**
Dogran Pakistan   31°48N 73°35E **42 D5**
Doğubayazıt Turkey   39°31N 44°5E **44 B5**
Doha = Ad Dawḥah
  Qatar   25°15N 51°35E **45 E6**
Dohazari Bangla.   22°10N 92°5E **41 H18**
Dohrighat India   26°16N 83°31E **43 F10**
Doi Indonesia   2°14N 127°49E **37 D7**
Doi Inthanon △ Thailand 18°33N 98°34E **38 C2**
Doi Khuntan △ Thailand 18°33N 99°14E **38 C2**
Doi Luang Thailand   18°30N 101°0E **38 C3**
Doi Luang △ Thailand 18°20N 99°30E **38 C2**
Doi Saket Thailand   18°52N 99°9E **38 C2**
Doi Suthep △ Thailand 18°49N 98°54E **38 C2**
Dois Irmãos, Sa. Brazil 9°0S 42°30W **93 E10**
Dokkum Neths.   53°20N 5°59E **15 A5**
Dokri Pakistan   27°25N 68°7E **42 F3**

Dolak, Pulau Indonesia 8°0S 138°30E **37 F9**
Dolbeau Canada   48°53N 72°14W **73 C5**
Dole France   47°7N 5°31E **20 C6**
Dolgellau U.K.   52°45N 3°53W **12 E4**
Dolgelley = Dolgellau
  U.K.   52°45N 3°53W **12 E4**
Dolinsk Russia   47°21N 142°48E **29 E15**
Dollard Neths.   53°20N 7°10E **15 A7**
Dolo Ethiopia   4°11N 42°3E **47 G3**
Dolomites = Dolomiti
  Italy   46°23N 11°51E **22 A4**
Dolomiti Italy   46°23N 11°51E **22 A4**
Dolores Argentina   36°20S 57°40W **94 D4**
Dolores Uruguay   33°34S 58°15W **94 C4**
Dolores U.S.A.   37°28N 108°30W **77 H9**
Dolores → U.S.A.   38°49N 109°17W **76 G9**
Dolphin, C. Falk. Is. 51°10S 59°0W **96 G5**
Dolphin and Union Str.
  Canada   69°5N 114°45W **68 C8**
Dom Pedrito Brazil   31°0S 54°40W **95 C5**
Doma △ Zimbabwe   16°28S 30°12E **55 F3**
Domariaganj → India   26°17N 83°44E **43 F10**
Domasi Malawi   15°15S 35°22E **55 F4**
Dombarovskiy Russia   50°46N 59°32E **28 D6**
Dombås Norway   62°4N 9°8E **8 E13**
Dome Argus Antarctica 80°50S 76°30E **5 E12**
Dome C. Antarctica   75°12S 123°37E **5 D17**
Dome Fuji Antarctica 77°20S 39°45E **5 D5**
Domel I. = Letsôk-aw Kyun
  Burma   11°30N 98°25E **39 G2**
Domeyko Chile   29°0S 71°0W **94 B1**
Domeyko, Cordillera
  Chile   24°30S 69°0W **94 A2**
Dominador Chile   24°21S 69°20W **94 A2**
Dominica ■ W. Indies 15°20N 61°20W **89 C7**
Dominica Passage
  W. Indies   15°10N 61°20W **89 C7**
Dominican Rep. ■
  W. Indies   19°0N 70°30W **89 C5**
Domodóssola Italy   46°7N 8°17E **20 D8**
Domville, Mt. Australia 28°1S 151°15E **63 D5**
Don → Russia   47°4N 39°18E **19 E6**
Don → Aberds., U.K.   57°11N 2°5W **11 D6**
Don → S. Yorks., U.K. 53°41N 0°52W **12 D7**
Don, C. Australia   11°18S 131°46E **60 B5**
Don Benito Spain   38°53N 5°51W **21 C3**
Don Figuerero Mts.
  Jamaica   18°5N 77°36W **88 a**
Don Sak Thailand   9°18N 99°41E **39 b**
Dona Ana = Nhamaabué
  Mozam.   17°25S 35°5E **55 F4**
Donaghadee U.K.   54°39N 5°33W **10 B6**
Donaghmore Ireland   52°52N 7°36W **10 D4**
Donald Australia   36°23S 143°0E **63 F3**
Donaldsonville U.S.A. 30°6N 90°59W **84 F9**
Donalsonville U.S.A. 31°3N 84°53W **85 F12**
Donau = Dunărea →
  Europe   45°20N 29°40E **17 F15**
Donauwörth Germany   48°43N 10°47E **16 D6**
Doncaster U.K.   53°32N 1°6W **12 D6**
Dondo Angola   9°45S 14°25E **52 F2**
Dondo Mozam.   19°33S 34°46E **55 F3**
Dondo, Teluk Indonesia 0°50N 120°30E **37 D6**
Dondra Head Sri Lanka 5°55N 80°40E **40 S12**
Donegal Ireland   54°39N 8°5W **10 B3**
Donegal □ Ireland   54°53N 8°0W **10 B4**
Donegal B. Ireland   54°31N 8°49W **10 B3**
Donets → Russia   47°33N 40°55E **19 E7**
Donets Basin Ukraine 49°0N 38°0E **6 F13**
Donetsk Ukraine   48°0N 37°45E **19 E6**
Dong Ba Thin Vietnam 12°8N 109°13E **39 F7**
Dong Dang Vietnam   21°54N 106°42E **38 B6**
Dong Giam Vietnam   19°25N 105°31E **38 C5**
Dong Ha Vietnam   16°55N 107°8E **38 D6**
Dong Hene Vietnam   16°40N 105°18E **38 D5**
Dong Hoi Vietnam   17°29N 106°36E **38 D6**
Dong Khe Vietnam   22°26N 106°27E **38 A6**
Dong Ujimqin Qi China 45°32N 116°55E **34 B9**
Dong Van Vietnam   23°16N 105°22E **38 A5**
Dong Xoai Vietnam   11°32N 106°55E **39 G6**
Dongara Australia   29°14S 114°57E **61 E1**
Dongbei China   45°0N 125°0E **30 A5**
Dongchuan China   26°8N 103°1E **32 D5**
Dongco China   32°8N 84°50E **41 C14**
Dongfang China   18°50N 108°33E **38 C7**
Dongfeng China   42°40N 125°34E **35 C13**
Donggala Indonesia   0°30S 119°40E **37 E5**
Donggang China   39°52N 124°10E **35 E13**
Dongguan China   22°58N 113°44E **35 F10**
Dongguang China   37°50N 116°30E **34 F9**
Donghae S. Korea   37°29N 129°7E **35 F15**
Dongjingcheng China   44°5N 129°10E **35 B15**
Dongnae S. Korea   35°12N 129°13E **35 G15**
Dongning China   44°2N 131°5E **35 B16**
Dongola Sudan   19°9N 30°22E **51 E12**
Dongping China   35°55N 116°20E **34 G9**
Dongsheng China   39°50N 110°0E **34 E6**
Dongtai China   32°51N 120°21E **35 H11**
Dongting Hu China   29°18N 112°45E **33 D6**
Donington, C. Australia 34°45S 136°0E **63 E2**
Doniphan U.S.A.   36°37N 90°50W **80 G8**
Dønna Norway   66°6N 12°30E **8 C15**
Donna U.S.A.   26°9N 98°4W **84 H5**
Donnacona Canada   46°41N 71°41W **73 C5**
Donnelly's Crossing
  N.Z.   35°42S 173°38E **59 A4**
Donnybrook Australia 33°34S 115°48E **61 F2**
Donnybrook S. Africa 29°59S 29°48E **57 D4**
Donora U.S.A.   40°11N 79°52W **82 F5**
Donostia = Donostia-San
  Sebastián Spain   43°17N 1°58W **21 A5**
Donostia-San Sebastián
  Spain   43°17N 1°58W **21 A5**
Donwood Canada   44°19N 78°16W **82 B6**
Doon → U.K.   55°27N 4°39W **11 F4**
Dora, L. Australia   22°0S 123°0E **60 D3**
Dora Báltea → Italy   45°11N 8°3E **20 D8**
Doran L. Canada   61°13N 108°6W **71 A7**

Dorchester *U.K.*	50°42N 2°27W	**13** G5
Dorchester, C. *Canada*	65°27N 77°27W	**69** C12
Dordabis *Namibia*	22°52S 17°38E	**56** C2
Dordogne → *France*	45°2N 0°36W	**20** D3
Dordrecht *Neths.*	51°48N 4°39E	**15** C4
Dordrecht *S. Africa*	31°20S 27°3E	**56** E4
Doré L. *Canada*	54°46N 107°17W	**71** C7
Dori *Burkina Faso*	14°3N 0°2W	**50** F5
Doring → *S. Africa*	31°54S 18°39E	**56** E2
Doringbos *S. Africa*	31°59S 19°16E	**56** E2
Dorking *U.K.*	51°14N 0°19W	**13** F7
Dornbirn *Austria*	47°25N 9°45E	**16** E5
Dornie *U.K.*	57°17N 5°31W	**11** D3
Dornoch *Canada*	44°18N 80°51W	**82** B4
Dornoch *U.K.*	57°53N 4°2W	**11** D4
Dornoch Firth *U.K.*	57°51N 4°4W	**11** D4
Dornogovĭ □ *Mongolia*	44°0N 110°0E	**34** C6
Doro, Kavo *Greece*	38°9N 24°38E	**23** E11
Dorohoi *Romania*	47°56N 26°23E	**17** E14
Döröö Nuur *Mongolia*	48°0N 93°0E	**32** B4
Dorr *Iran*	33°17N 50°38E	**45** C6
Dorre I. *Australia*	25°13S 113°12E	**61** E1
Dorrigo *Australia*	30°20S 152°44E	**63** E5
Dorris *U.S.A.*	41°58N 121°55W	**76** F3
Dorset *Canada*	45°14N 78°54W	**82** A6
Dorset *Ohio, U.S.A.*	41°40N 80°40W	**82** E4
Dorset *Vt., U.S.A.*	43°15N 73°5W	**83** C11
Dorset □ *U.K.*	50°45N 2°26W	**13** G5
Dortmund *Germany*	51°30N 7°28E	**16** C4
Dörtyol *Turkey*	36°50N 36°13E	**44** B3
Doruma		
Dem. Rep. of the Congo	4°42N 27°33E	**54** B2
Dorŭneh *Iran*	35°10N 57°18E	**45** C8
Dos Bahías, C. *Argentina*	44°58S 65°32W	**96** E3
Dos Hermanas *Spain*	37°16N 5°55W	**21** D3
Dos Palos *U.S.A.*	36°59N 120°37W	**78** J6
Dosso *Niger*	13°0N 3°13E	**50** F6
Dothan *U.S.A.*	31°13N 85°24W	**85** F12
Doty *U.S.A.*	46°38N 123°17W	**78** D3
Douai *France*	50°21N 3°4E	**20** A5
Douala *Cameroon*	4°0N 9°45E	**52** D1
Douarnenez *France*	48°6N 4°21W	**20** B1
Double Island Pt.		
Australia	25°56S 153°11E	**63** D5
Double Mountain Fork →		
U.S.A.	33°16N 100°0W	**84** E4
Doubs → *France*	46°53N 5°1E	**20** C6
Doubtful Sd. *N.Z.*	45°20S 166°49E	**59** F1
Doubtless B. *N.Z.*	34°55S 173°26E	**59** A4
Douglas *Canada*	45°31N 76°56W	**82** A7
Douglas I. of Man	54°10N 4°28W	**12** C3
Douglas *S. Africa*	29°4S 23°46E	**56** D3
Douglas *Ariz., U.S.A.*	31°21N 109°33W	**77** L9
Douglas *Ga., U.S.A.*	31°31N 82°51W	**85** F13
Douglas *Wyo., U.S.A.*	42°45N 105°24W	**76** E11
Douglas Apsley △		
Australia	41°45S 148°11E	**63** G4
Douglas Chan. *Canada*	53°40N 129°20W	**70** C3
Douglas Pt. *Canada*	44°19N 81°37W	**82** B3
Douglasville *U.S.A.*	33°45N 84°45W	**85** E12
Dounreay *U.K.*	58°35N 3°44W	**11** C5
Dourada, Serra *Brazil*	13°10S 48°45W	**93** F9
Dourados *Brazil*	22°9S 54°50W	**95** A5
Dourados → *Brazil*	21°58S 54°18W	**95** A5
Dourados, Serra dos		
Brazil	23°30S 53°30W	**95** A5
Douro → *Europe*	41°8N 8°40W	**21** B1
Dove → *U.K.*	52°51N 1°36W	**12** E6
Dove Creek *U.S.A.*	37°46N 108°54W	**77** H9
Dover *Australia*	43°18S 147°2E	**63** G4
Dover *U.K.*	51°7N 1°19E	**13** F9
Dover *Del., U.S.A.*	39°10N 75°32W	**81** F16
Dover *N.H., U.S.A.*	43°12N 70°56W	**83** C14
Dover *N.J., U.S.A.*	40°53N 74°34W	**83** F10
Dover *Ohio, U.S.A.*	40°32N 81°29W	**82** F3
Dover, Pt. *Australia*	32°32S 125°32E	**61** F4
Dover, Str. of *Europe*	51°0N 1°30E	**13** G9
Dover-Foxcroft *U.S.A.*	45°11N 69°13W	**81** C19
Dover Plains *U.S.A.*	41°43N 73°35W	**83** E11
Dovey = Dyfi → *U.K.*	52°32N 4°3W	**13** E3
Dovrefjell *Norway*	62°15N 9°33E	**8** E13
Dow Rūd *Iran*	33°28N 49°4E	**45** C6
Dowa *Malawi*	13°38S 33°58E	**55** E3
Dowagiac *U.S.A.*	41°59N 86°6W	**80** E10
Dowerin *Australia*	31°12S 117°2E	**61** F2
Dowgha'i *Iran*	36°54N 58°32E	**45** B8
Dowlatābād *Kermān,*		
Iran	28°20N 56°40E	**45** D8
Dowlatābād *Khorāsān,*		
Iran	35°16N 59°29E	**45** C8
Down □ *U.K.*	54°23N 6°2W	**10** B5
Downey *Calif., U.S.A.*	33°56N 118°9W	**79** M8
Downey *Idaho, U.S.A.*	42°26N 112°7W	**76** E7
Downham Market *U.K.*	52°37N 0°23E	**13** E8
Downieville *U.S.A.*	39°34N 120°50W	**78** F6
Downpatrick *U.K.*	54°20N 5°43W	**10** B6
Downpatrick Hd. *Ireland*	54°20N 9°21W	**10** B2
Downsville *U.S.A.*	42°5N 75°0W	**83** D10
Downton, Mt. *Canada*	52°42N 124°52W	**70** C4
Dowsārī *Iran*	28°25N 57°59E	**45** D8
Doyle *U.S.A.*	40°2N 120°6W	**78** E6
Doylestown *U.S.A.*	40°21N 75°10W	**83** F9
Dozois, Rés. *Canada*	47°30N 77°5W	**72** C4
Dra Khel *Pakistan*	27°58N 66°45E	**42** F2
Drâa, C. *Morocco*	28°47N 11°0W	**50** C3
Drâa, Oued → *Morocco*	28°40N 11°0W	**50** C3
Drachten *Neths.*	53°7N 6°5E	**15** A6
Drăgăşani *Romania*	44°39N 24°17E	**17** F13
Dragoman, Prokhod		
Bulgaria	42°58N 22°53E	**23** C10
Dragon's Mouths = Bocas del		
Dragon *Venezuela*	11°0N 61°50W	**93** K15
Draguignan *France*	43°32N 6°27E	**20** E7
Drain *U.S.A.*	43°40N 123°19W	**76** E2
Drake *U.S.A.*	47°55N 100°23W	**80** B3
Drake Passage *S. Ocean*	58°0S 68°0W	**5** B17
Drakensberg *S. Africa*	31°0S 28°0E	**57** D4
Drama *Greece*	41°9N 24°10E	**23** D11
Drammen *Norway*	59°42N 10°12E	**9** G14
Drangajökull *Iceland*	66°9N 22°15W	**8** C2
Dras *India*	34°25N 75°48E	**43** B6
Drastis, Akra *Greece*	39°48N 19°40E	**25** A3
Drau = Drava →		
Croatia	45°33N 18°55E	**23** B8
Drava → *Croatia*	45°33N 18°55E	**23** B8
Drayton *Canada*	43°46N 80°40W	**82** C4
Drayton Valley *Canada*	53°12N 114°58W	**70** C6
Drenthe □ *Neths.*	52°52N 6°40E	**15** B6
Drepano, Akra *Greece*	35°28N 24°14E	**25** D6
Drepanum, C. *Cyprus*	34°54N 32°19E	**25** E11
Dresden *Canada*	42°35N 82°11W	**82** D2
Dresden *Germany*	51°3N 13°44E	**16** C7
Dresden *U.S.A.*	42°41N 76°57W	**82** D8
Dreux *France*	48°44N 1°23E	**20** B4
Driffield *U.K.*	54°0N 0°26W	**12** C7
Driftwood *U.S.A.*	41°20N 78°8W	**82** E6
Driggs *U.S.A.*	43°44N 111°6W	**76** E8
Drin → *Albania*	42°1N 19°38E	**23** C8
Drina → *Bos.-H.*	44°53N 19°21E	**23** B8
Drøbak *Norway*	59°39N 10°39E	**9** G14
Drobeta-Turnu Severin		
Romania	44°39N 22°41E	**17** F12
Drochia *Moldova*	48°2N 27°48E	**17** D14
Drogheda *Ireland*	53°43N 6°22W	**10** C5
Drogichin = Dragichyn		
Belarus	52°15N 25°8E	**17** B13
Drogobych = Drohobych		
Ukraine	49°20N 23°30E	**17** D12
Drohobych *Ukraine*	49°20N 23°30E	**17** D12
Droichead Atha = Drogheda		
Ireland	53°43N 6°22W	**10** C5
Droichead Nua *Ireland*	53°11N 6°48W	**10** C5
Droitwich *U.K.*	52°16N 2°8W	**13** E5
Drôme → *France*	44°46N 4°46E	**20** D6
Dromedary, C. *Australia*	36°17S 150°10E	**63** F5
Dromore *U.K.*	54°31N 7°28W	**10** B4
Dromore West *Ireland*	54°15N 8°52W	**10** B3
Dronfield *U.K.*	53°19N 1°27W	**12** D6
Dronning Maud Land		
Antarctica	72°30S 12°0E	**5** D3
Dronten *Neths.*	52°32N 5°43E	**15** B5
Druk Yul = Bhutan ■		
Asia	27°25N 90°30E	**41** F17
Drumbo *Canada*	43°16N 80°35W	**82** C4
Drumcliff *Ireland*	54°20N 8°29W	**10** B3
Drumheller *Canada*	51°25N 112°40W	**70** C6
Drummond *U.S.A.*	46°40N 113°9W	**76** C7
Drummond I. *U.S.A.*	46°1N 83°39W	**81** B12
Drummond Pt. *Australia*	34°9S 135°16E	**63** E2
Drummond Ra.		
Australia	23°45S 147°10E	**62** C4
Drummondville *Canada*	45°55N 72°25W	**72** C5
Drumright *U.S.A.*	35°59N 96°36W	**84** D6
Druskininkai *Lithuania*	54°3N 23°58E	**9** J20
Drut → *Belarus*	53°8N 30°5E	**17** B16
Druzhina *Russia*	68°14N 145°18E	**29** C15
Dry Harbour Mts.		
Jamaica	18°19N 77°24W	**88** a
Dry Tortugas *U.S.A.*	24°38N 82°55W	**85** F13
Dryden *Canada*	49°47N 92°50W	**71** D10
Dryden *U.S.A.*	42°30N 97°15W	**82** D8
Drygalski I. *Antarctica*	66°0S 92°0E	**5** C7
Drygalski Ice Tongue		
Antarctica	75°24S 163°30E	**5** D21
Drysdale → *Australia*	13°59S 126°51E	**60** B4
Drysdale I. *Australia*	11°41S 136°0E	**62** A2
Drysdale River △		
Australia	14°56S 127°2E	**60** B4
Du Gué → *Canada*	57°21N 70°45W	**72** A5
Du Quoin *U.S.A.*	38°1N 89°14W	**80** F9
Duanesburg *U.S.A.*	42°45N 74°11W	**83** D10
Duaringa *Australia*	23°42S 149°42E	**62** C4
Duarte, Pico *Dom. Rep.*	19°2N 70°59W	**89** D5
Dubai = Dubayy *U.A.E.*	25°18N 55°20E	**45** E7
Dubăsari *Moldova*	47°15N 29°10E	**17** E15
Dubăsari Vdkhr.		
Moldova	47°30N 29°0E	**17** E15
Dubawnt → *Canada*	64°33N 100°6W	**71** A8
Dubawnt L. *Canada*	63°8N 101°28W	**71** A8
Dubayy *U.A.E.*	25°18N 55°20E	**45** E7
Dubbo *Australia*	32°11S 148°35E	**63** E4
Dubele		
Dem. Rep. of the Congo	2°56N 29°35E	**54** B2
Dublin *Ireland*	53°21N 6°15W	**10** C5
Dublin *Ga., U.S.A.*	32°32N 82°54W	**85** E13
Dublin *Tex., U.S.A.*	32°5N 98°21W	**84** E5
Dublin □ *Ireland*	53°24N 6°20W	**10** C5
Dublin ✈ (DUB) *Ireland*	53°26N 6°15W	**10** C5
Dubno *Ukraine*	50°25N 25°45E	**17** C13
Dubois *Idaho, U.S.A.*	44°10N 112°14W	**76** D7
Dubois *Pa., U.S.A.*	41°7N 78°46W	**82** E6
Dubossary = Dubăsari		
Moldova	47°15N 29°10E	**17** E15
Dubossary Vdkhr. = Dubăsari		
Vdkhr. *Moldova*	47°30N 29°0E	**17** E15
Dubovka *Russia*	49°5N 44°50E	**19** E7
Dubrajpur *India*	23°48N 87°25E	**43** H12
Dubréka *Guinea*	9°46N 13°31W	**50** G3
Dubrovitsa = Dubrovytsya		
Ukraine	51°31N 26°35E	**17** C14
Dubrovnik *Croatia*	42°39N 18°6E	**23** C8
Dubrovytsya *Ukraine*	51°31N 26°35E	**17** C14
Dubuque *U.S.A.*	42°30N 90°41W	**80** D8
Duchesne *U.S.A.*	40°10N 110°24W	**76** F8
Duchess *Australia*	21°20S 139°50E	**62** C2
Ducie I. *Pac. Oc.*	24°40S 124°48W	**65** K15
Duck → *U.S.A.*	36°2N 87°52W	**85** C11
Duck Cr. → *Australia*	22°37S 116°53E	**60** D2
Duck Lake *Canada*	52°50N 106°16W	**71** C7
Duck Mountain		
Canada	51°45N 101°0W	**71** C8
Duckwall, Mt. *U.S.A.*	37°58N 120°7W	**78** H6
Dudhi *India*	24°15N 83°10E	**43** G10
Dudinka *Russia*	69°30N 86°13E	**29** C9
Dudley *U.K.*	52°31N 2°5W	**13** E5
Dudwa *India*	28°30N 80°41E	**43** E9
Dudwa △ *India*	28°30N 80°30E	**43** E9
Duero = Douro → *Europe*	41°8N 8°40W	**21** B1
Dufftown *U.K.*	57°27N 3°8W	**11** D5
Dugi Otok *Croatia*	44°0N 15°3E	**16** G8
Duisburg *Germany*	51°26N 6°45E	**16** C4
Duiwelskloof = Modjadjiskloof		
S. Africa	23°42S 30°10E	**57** C5
Dūkdamīn *Iran*	35°59N 57°43E	**45** C8
Dukelský Průsmyk		
Slovak Rep.	49°25N 21°42E	**17** D11
Dukhān *Qatar*	25°25N 50°50E	**45** E6
Duki *Pakistan*	30°14N 68°25E	**40** D6
Duku *Nigeria*	10°43N 10°43E	**51** F8
Dulce *U.S.A.*	36°56N 107°0W	**77** H10
Dulce → *Argentina*	30°32S 62°33W	**94** C3
Dulce, G. *Costa Rica*	8°40N 83°20W	**88** E3
Dulf *Iraq*	35°7N 45°51E	**44** C5
Duliu *China*	39°2N 116°55E	**34** E9
Dullewala *Pakistan*	31°50N 71°25E	**42** D4
Dullstroom *S. Africa*	25°27S 30°7E	**57** D5
Dulq Maghār *Syria*	36°22N 38°39E	**44** B3
Duluth *U.S.A.*	46°47N 92°6W	**80** B7
Dum Dum *India*	22°39N 88°26E	**43** H13
Dum Duma *India*	27°40N 95°40E	**41** F19
Dūmā *Syria*	33°34N 36°24E	**46** B5
Dumaguete *Phil.*	9°17N 123°15E	**37** C6
Dumai *Indonesia*	1°35N 101°28E	**36** D2
Dumaran *Phil.*	10°33N 119°50E	**37** B5
Dumas *Ark., U.S.A.*	33°53N 91°29W	**84** E9
Dumas *Tex., U.S.A.*	35°52N 101°58W	**84** D4
Dumayr *Syria*	33°39N 36°42E	**46** B5
Dumbarton *U.K.*	55°57N 4°33W	**11** F4
Dumbleyung *Australia*	33°17S 117°42E	**61** F2
Dumfries *U.K.*	55°4N 3°37W	**11** F5
Dumfries & Galloway □		
U.K.	55°9N 3°58W	**11** F5
Dumka *India*	24°12N 87°15E	**43** G12
Dumoine → *Canada*	46°13N 77°51W	**72** C4
Dumoine, L. *Canada*	46°55N 77°55W	**72** C4
Dumont d'Urville		
Antarctica	67°0S 110°0E	**5** C10
Dumont d'Urville Sea		
S. Ocean	63°30S 138°0E	**5** C9
Dumraon *India*	25°33N 84°8E	**43** G11
Dumyât *Egypt*	31°24N 31°48E	**51** B12
Dún Dealgan = Dundalk		
Ireland	54°1N 6°24W	**10** B5
Dún Laoghaire *Ireland*	53°17N 6°8W	**10** C5
Duna = Dunărea →		
Europe	45°20N 29°40E	**17** F15
Dunagiri *India*	30°31N 79°52E	**43** D8
Dunaj = Dunărea →		
Europe	45°20N 29°40E	**17** F15
Dunakeszi *Hungary*	47°37N 19°8E	**17** E10
Dunărea → *Europe*	45°20N 29°40E	**17** F15
Dunaújváros *Hungary*	46°58N 18°57E	**17** E10
Dunav = Dunărea →		
Europe	45°20N 29°40E	**17** F15
Dunay *Russia*	42°52N 132°22E	**30** C6
Dunback *N.Z.*	45°23S 170°36E	**59** F3
Dunbar *N.Z.*	56°0N 2°31W	**11** E6
Dunblane *U.K.*	56°11N 3°58W	**11** E5
Duncan *Canada*	48°45N 123°40W	**78** B3
Duncan *Ariz., U.S.A.*	32°43N 109°6W	**77** K9
Duncan *Okla., U.S.A.*	34°30N 97°57W	**84** D6
Duncan, L. *Canada*	53°29N 77°58W	**72** B4
Duncan L. *Canada*	62°51N 113°58W	**70** A6
Duncan Town *Bahamas*	22°15N 75°45W	**88** B4
Duncannon *U.S.A.*	40°23N 77°2W	**82** F7
Duncansby Head *U.K.*	58°38N 3°1W	**11** C5
Duncansville *U.S.A.*	40°25N 78°26W	**82** F6
Dundalk *Canada*	44°10N 80°24W	**82** B4
Dundalk *Ireland*	54°1N 6°24W	**10** B5
Dundalk Bay *Ireland*	53°55N 6°15W	**10** C5
Dundas = Uummannaq		
Greenland	77°28N 69°13W	**4** B4
Dundas *Canada*	43°17N 79°59W	**82** C5
Dundas, L. *Australia*	32°35S 121°50E	**61** F3
Dundas I. *Canada*	54°30N 130°50W	**70** C2
Dundas Str. *Australia*	11°15S 131°35E	**60** B5
Dundee *S. Africa*	28°11S 30°15E	**57** D5
Dundee *U.K.*	56°28N 2°59W	**11** E6
Dundee *U.S.A.*	42°32N 76°59W	**82** D8
Dundee City □ *U.K.*	56°30N 2°58W	**11** E6
Dundgovĭ □ *Mongolia*	45°10N 106°0E	**34** B4
Dundrum *U.K.*	54°16N 5°52W	**10** B6
Dundrum B. *U.K.*	54°13N 5°47W	**10** B6
Dunedin *N.Z.*	45°50S 170°33E	**59** F3
Dunedin *U.S.A.*	28°1N 82°46W	**85** G13
Dunfanaghy *Ireland*	55°11N 7°58W	**10** A4
Dunfermline *U.K.*	56°5N 3°27W	**11** E5
Dungannon *Canada*	43°51N 81°36W	**82** C3
Dungannon *U.K.*	54°31N 6°46W	**10** B5
Dungarpur *India*	23°52N 73°45E	**42** H5
Dungarvan *Ireland*	52°5N 7°37W	**10** D4
Dungarvan Harbour		
Ireland	52°4N 7°35W	**10** D4
Dungeness *U.K.*	50°54N 0°59E	**13** G8
Dunglow *Ireland*	54°57N 8°21W	**10** B3
Dungo, L. do *Angola*	17°15S 19°0E	**56** B2
Dungog *Australia*	32°22S 151°46E	**63** E5
Dungu		
Dem. Rep. of the Congo	3°40N 28°32E	**54** B2
Dungun *Malaysia*	4°45N 103°25E	**39** K4
Dunhua *China*	43°20N 128°14E	**35** C15
Dunhuang *China*	40°8N 94°36E	**32** B4
Dunk I. *Australia*	17°59S 146°29E	**62** B4
Dunkeld *U.K.*	33°25S 149°29E	**63** E4
Dunkeld *U.K.*	56°34N 3°35W	**11** E5
Dunkerque *France*	51°2N 2°20E	**20** A5
Dunkery Beacon *U.K.*	51°9N 3°36W	**13** F4
Dunkirk = Dunkerque		
France	51°2N 2°20E	**20** A5
Dunkirk *U.S.A.*	42°29N 79°20W	**82** D5
Dúnleary = Dún Laoghaire		
Ireland	53°17N 6°8W	**10** C5
Dunleer *Ireland*	53°50N 6°24W	**10** C5
Dunmanus B. *Ireland*	51°31N 9°50W	**10** E2
Dunmanway *Australia*	16°42S 133°25E	**62** B1
Dunmara *Australia*	41°25N 75°38W	**83** E9
Dunmore *U.S.A.*	52°9N 7°0W	**10** D5
Dunmore East *Ireland*	52°10N 10°35W	**10** D1
Dunmore Hd. *Ireland*		
Dunmore Town		
Bahamas	25°30N 76°39W	**88** A4
Dunn *U.S.A.*	35°19N 78°37W	**85** D15
Dunnellon *U.S.A.*	29°3N 82°28W	**85** G13
Dunnet Hd. *U.K.*	58°40N 3°21W	**11** C5
Dunning *U.S.A.*	41°50N 100°6W	**80** E4
Dunnville *Canada*	42°54N 79°36W	**82** D5
Dunolly *Australia*	36°51S 143°44E	**63** F3
Dunoon *U.K.*	55°57N 4°56W	**11** F4
Duns *U.K.*	55°47N 2°20W	**11** F6
Dunseith *U.S.A.*	48°50N 100°3W	**80** A3
Dunshaughlin *Ireland*	53°31N 6°33W	**10** C5
Dunsmuir *U.S.A.*	41°13N 122°16W	**76** F2
Dunstable *U.K.*	51°53N 0°32W	**13** F7
Dunstan Mts. *N.Z.*	44°53S 169°35E	**59** F2
Dunster *Canada*	53°8N 119°50W	**70** C5
Dunvegan *U.K.*	57°27N 6°35W	**11** D2
Dunvegan L. *Canada*	60°8N 107°10W	**71** A7
Duolun *China*	42°12N 116°28E	**34** C9
Duong Dong *Vietnam*	10°13N 103°58E	**39** G4
Dupree *U.S.A.*	45°4N 101°35W	**80** C3
Dupuyer *U.S.A.*	48°13N 112°30W	**76** B7
Duque de Caxias *Brazil*	22°46S 43°18W	**95** A7
Durack → *Australia*	15°33S 127°52E	**60** C4
Durack Ra. *Australia*	16°50S 127°40E	**60** C4
Durance → *France*	43°55N 4°45E	**20** E6
Durand *U.S.A.*	44°38N 91°58W	**80** C8
Durango *Mexico*	24°3N 104°39W	**86** C4
Durango *U.S.A.*	37°16N 107°53W	**77** H10
Durango □ *Mexico*	24°50N 105°20W	**86** C4
Durant *Miss., U.S.A.*	33°4N 89°51W	**85** E10
Durant *Okla., U.S.A.*	33°59N 96°25W	**84** E6
Durazno *Uruguay*	33°25S 56°31W	**94** C4
Durazzo = Durrës		
Albania	41°19N 19°28E	**23** D8
Durban *S. Africa*	29°49S 31°1E	**57** D5
Durbuy *Belgium*	50°21N 5°28E	**15** D5
Düren *Germany*	50°48N 6°29E	**16** C4
Durg = Bhilainagar-Durg		
India	21°13N 81°26E	**41** J12
Durgapur *India*	23°30N 87°20E	**43** H12
Durham *Canada*	44°10N 80°49W	**82** B4
Durham *U.K.*	54°47N 1°34W	**12** C6
Durham *Calif., U.S.A.*	39°39N 121°48W	**78** F5
Durham *N.C., U.S.A.*	35°59N 78°54W	**85** D15
Durham *N.H., U.S.A.*	43°8N 70°56W	**83** C14
Durham □ *U.K.*	54°42N 1°45W	**12** C6
Durma *Si. Arabia*	24°37N 46°8E	**44** E5
Durmitor *Montenegro*	43°10N 19°0E	**23** C8
Durness *U.K.*	58°34N 4°45W	**11** C4
Durrës *Albania*	41°19N 19°28E	**23** D8
Durrow *Ireland*	52°51N 7°24W	**10** D4
Dursey I. *Ireland*	51°36N 10°12W	**10** E1
Dursley *U.K.*	51°40N 2°21W	**13** F5
Dursunbey *Turkey*	39°35N 28°37E	**23** E13
Duru		
Dem. Rep. of the Congo	4°14N 28°50E	**54** B2
Durūz, Jabal ad *Jordan*	32°35N 36°40E	**46** C5
D'Urville, Tanjung		
Indonesia	1°28S 137°54E	**37** E9
D'Urville I. *N.Z.*	40°50S 173°55E	**59** D4
Duryea *U.S.A.*	41°20N 75°45W	**83** E9
Dushak *Turkmenistan*	37°13N 60°1E	**45** B9
Dushanbe *Tajikistan*	38°33N 68°48E	**28** F7
Dushore *U.S.A.*	41°31N 76°24W	**83** E8
Dusky Sd. *N.Z.*	45°47S 166°30E	**59** F1
Dussejour, C. *Australia*	14°45S 128°13E	**60** B4
Düsseldorf *Germany*	51°14N 6°47E	**16** C4
Dutch Harbor *U.S.A.*	53°53N 166°32W	**74** a
Dutlwe *Botswana*	23°58S 23°46E	**56** C3
Dutton *Canada*	42°39N 81°30W	**82** D3
Dutton → *Australia*	20°44S 143°10E	**62** C3
Dutywa *S. Africa*	32°8S 28°18E	**57** E4
Duwayhin, Khawr		
U.A.E.	24°20N 51°25E	**45** E6
Duyun *China*	26°18N 107°29E	**32** D5
Dvina, Severnaya →		
Russia	64°32N 40°30E	**18** B7
Dvinsk = Daugavpils		
Latvia	55°53N 26°32E	**9** J22
Dvinskaya Guba *Russia*	65°0N 39°0E	**18** B6
Dwarka *India*	22°18N 69°8E	**42** H3
Dwellingup *Australia*	32°43S 116°4E	**61** F2
Dwight *Canada*	45°20N 79°1W	**82** A5
Dwight *U.S.A.*	41°5N 88°26W	**80** E9
Dyatlovo = Dzyatlava		
Belarus	53°28N 25°28E	**17** B13
Dyce *U.K.*	57°13N 2°12W	**11** D6
Dyer, C. *Canada*	66°37N 61°16W	**69** C13
Dyer Bay *Canada*	45°10N 81°20W	**82** A3
Dyer Plateau *Antarctica*	70°45S 65°30W	**5** D17
Dyersburg *U.S.A.*	36°3N 89°23W	**85** C10
Dyfi → *U.K.*	52°32N 4°3W	**13** E3
Dymer *Ukraine*	50°47N 30°18E	**17** C16
Dysart *Australia*	22°32S 148°23E	**62** C4
Dzaoudzi *Mayotte*	12°47S 45°16E	**53** a
Dzavhan Gol → *Mongolia*	48°54N 93°23E	**32** B4
Dzerzhinsk *Russia*	56°14N 43°30E	**18** C7
Dzhalinda *Russia*	53°26N 124°0E	**29** D13
Dzhambul = Taraz		
Kazakhstan	42°54N 71°22E	**28** E8
Dzhankoy *Ukraine*	45°40N 34°20E	**19** E5
Dzhezkazgan = Zhezqazghan		
Kazakhstan	47°44N 67°40E	**28** E7
Dzhizak = Jizzax		
Uzbekistan	40°6N 67°50E	**28** E7
Dzhugdzur, Khrebet		
Russia	57°30N 138°0E	**29** D14
Dzhungarskiye Vorota =		
Dzungarian Gate *Asia*	45°10N 82°0E	**32** B3
Działdowo *Poland*	53°15N 20°15E	**17** B11
Dzibilchaltún *Mexico*	21°10N 89°35W	**87** C7
Dzierżoniów *Poland*	50°45N 16°39E	**17** C9
Dzilam de Bravo *Mexico*	21°24N 88°53W	**87** C7
Dzūkija △ *Lithuania*	54°10N 24°30E	**9** J21
Dzungarian Basin = Junggar		
Pendi *China*	44°30N 86°0E	**32** B3
Dzungarian Gate *Asia*	45°10N 82°0E	**32** B3
Dzüünharaa *Mongolia*	48°52N 106°28E	**32** B5
Dzüünmod *Mongolia*	47°45N 106°58E	**32** B5
Dzyarzhynsk *Belarus*	53°40N 27°1E	**17** B14
Dzyatlava *Belarus*	53°28N 25°28E	**17** B13

E

E.C. Manning △ *Canada*	49°5N 120°45W	**70** D4
Eabamet L. *Canada*	51°30N 87°46W	**72** B2
Eabametoong *Canada*	51°30N 87°46W	**72** B2
Eads *U.S.A.*	38°29N 102°47W	**76** G12
Eagar *U.S.A.*	34°6N 109°17W	**77** J9
Eagle *Alaska, U.S.A.*	64°47N 141°12W	**68** C5
Eagle *Colo., U.S.A.*	39°39N 106°50W	**76** G10
Eagle → *Canada*	53°36N 57°26W	**73** B8
Eagle Butte *U.S.A.*	45°0N 101°10W	**80** C3
Eagle Grove *U.S.A.*	42°40N 93°54W	**80** D7
Eagle L. *Canada*	49°42N 93°13W	**71** D10
Eagle L. *Calif., U.S.A.*	40°39N 120°45W	**76** F3
Eagle L. *Maine, U.S.A.*	46°20N 69°22W	**81** B19
Eagle Lake *Canada*	45°8N 78°29W	**82** A6
Eagle Lake *Maine, U.S.A.*	47°3N 68°36W	**81** B19
Eagle Lake *Tex., U.S.A.*	29°35N 96°20W	**84** G6
Eagle Mountain		
U.S.A.	33°49N 115°27W	**79** M11
Eagle Nest *U.S.A.*	36°33N 105°16W	**77** H11
Eagle Pass *U.S.A.*	28°43N 100°30W	**84** G4
Eagle Pk. *U.S.A.*	38°10N 119°25W	**78** G7
Eagle Pt. *Australia*	16°11S 124°23E	**60** C3
Eagle River *Mich., U.S.A.*	47°25N 88°18W	**80** B9
Eagle River *Wis., U.S.A.*	45°55N 89°15W	**80** C9
Eaglehawk *Australia*	36°44S 144°15E	**63** F3
Eagles Mere *U.S.A.*	41°25N 76°33W	**83** E8
Ealing □ *U.K.*	51°31N 0°20W	**13** F7
Ear Falls *Canada*	50°38N 93°13W	**71** C10
Earle *U.S.A.*	35°16N 90°28W	**85** D9
Earlimart *U.S.A.*	35°53N 119°16W	**79** K7
Earlville *U.S.A.*	42°44N 75°32W	**83** D9
Earn → *U.K.*	56°21N 3°18W	**11** E5
Earn, L. *U.K.*	56°23N 4°13W	**11** E4
Earnslaw, Mt. *N.Z.*	44°32S 168°27E	**59** F2
Earth *U.S.A.*	34°14N 102°24W	**84** D3
Easley *U.S.A.*	34°50N 82°36W	**85** D13
East Anglia *U.K.*	52°30N 1°0E	**13** E9
East Angus *Canada*	45°30N 71°40W	**73** C5
East Antarctica *Antarctica*	80°0S 90°0E	**5** D7
East Aurora *U.S.A.*	42°46N 78°37W	**82** D6
East Ayrshire □ *U.K.*	55°26N 4°11W	**11** F4
East Bengal *Bangla.*	24°0N 90°0E	**41** G17
East Beskids = Vychodné Beskydy		
Europe	49°20N 22°0E	**17** D11
East Brady *U.S.A.*	40°59N 79°37W	**82** F5
East Branch Clarion River L.		
U.S.A.	41°35N 78°35W	**82** E6
East C. = Dezhneva, Mys		
Russia	66°5N 169°40W	**29** C19
East C. *N.Z.*	37°42S 178°35E	**59** B7
East Caroline Basin		
Pac. Oc.	4°0N 146°45E	**64** G6
East Chicago *U.S.A.*	41°38N 87°27W	**80** E10
East China Sea *Asia*	30°0N 126°0E	**33** D7
East Coulee *Canada*	51°23N 112°27W	**70** C6
East Dereham = Dereham		
U.K.	52°41N 0°57E	**13** E8
East Dunbartonshire □		
U.K.	55°57N 4°13W	**11** F4
East Falkland *Falk. Is.*	51°30S 58°30W	**96** G5
East Grand Forks *U.S.A.*	47°56N 97°1W	**80** B5
East Greenwich *U.S.A.*	41°40N 71°27W	**83** E13
East Grinstead *U.K.*	51°7N 0°0	**13** F8
East Hartford *U.S.A.*	41°46N 72°39W	**83** E12
East Helena *U.S.A.*	46°35N 111°56W	**76** C8
East Indies *Asia*	0°0 120°0E	**26** J14
East Kilbride *U.K.*	55°47N 4°11W	**11** F4
East Lamma Channel		
China	22°14N 114°9E	**33** G11
East Lansing *U.S.A.*	42°44N 84°29W	**81** D11
East Liverpool *U.S.A.*	40°37N 80°35W	**82** F4
East London *S. Africa*	33°0S 27°55E	**57** E4
East Lothian □ *U.K.*	55°58N 2°44W	**11** F6
East Main = Eastmain		
Canada	52°10N 78°30W	**72** B4
East Mariana Basin		
Pac. Oc.	12°0N 153°0E	**64** F7
East Northport *U.S.A.*	40°53N 73°20W	**83** F11
East Orange *U.S.A.*	40°46N 74°12W	**83** F10
East Pacific Rise *Pac. Oc.*	15°0S 110°0W	**65** J17
East Palestine *U.S.A.*	40°50N 80°33W	**82** F4
East Pine *Canada*	55°48N 120°12W	**70** B4
East Point *Canada*	46°27N 61°58W	**73** C7
East Providence *U.S.A.*	41°49N 71°23W	**83** E13
East Pt. *Br. Virgin Is.*	18°40N 64°18W	**89** e
East Pt. *U.S.A.*	33°41N 84°27W	**85** E12
East Renfrewshire □		
U.K.	55°46N 4°21W	**11** F4
East Retford = Retford		
U.K.	53°19N 0°56W	**12** D7
East Riding of Yorkshire □		
U.K.	53°55N 0°30W	**12** D7
East Rochester *U.S.A.*	43°7N 77°29W	**82** C7
East St. Louis *U.S.A.*	38°37N 90°9W	**80** F8
East Schelde = Oosterschelde →		
Neths.	51°33N 4°0E	**15** C4
East Sea = Japan, Sea of		
Asia	40°0N 135°0E	**30** E7

East Siberian Sea *Russia* 73°0N 160°0E **29** B17
East Stroudsburg *U.S.A.* 41°1N 75°11W **83** E9
East Sussex □ *U.K.* 50°56N 0°19E **13** G8
East Tasman Plateau
 Pac. Oc. 43°30S 152°0E **64** M7
East Tawas *U.S.A.* 44°17N 83°29W **81** C12
East Timor ■ *Asia* 8°50S 126°0E **37** F7
East Toorale *Australia* 30°27S 145°28E **63** E4
East Walker → *U.S.A.* 38°52N 119°10W **78** G7
East Windsor *U.S.A.* 40°17N 74°34W **83** F10
Eastbourne *N.Z.* 41°19S 174°55E **59** D5
Eastbourne *U.K.* 50°46N 0°18E **13** G8
Eastend *Canada* 49°32N 108°50W **71** D7
Easter Fracture Zone
 Pac. Oc. 25°0S 115°0W **65** K16
Easter I. = Pascua, I. de
 Chile 27°7S 109°23W **65** K17
Eastern □ *Kenya* 0°0 38°30E **54** C4
Eastern Cape □ *S. Africa* 32°0S 26°0E **56** E4
Eastern Cr. → *Australia* 20°40S 141°35E **62** C3
Eastern Desert = Es Sahrâ' Esh
 Sharqîya *Egypt* 27°30N 32°30E **51** C12
Eastern Ghats *India* 14°0N 78°50E **40** N11
Eastern Group = Lau Group
 Fiji 17°0S 178°30W **59** a
Eastern Group *Australia* 33°30S 124°30E **61** F3
Eastern Transvaal =
 Mpumalanga □
 S. Africa 26°0S 30°0E **57** D5
Easterville *Canada* 53°8N 99°49W **71** C9
Easthampton *U.S.A.* 42°16N 72°40W **83** D12
Eastlake *U.S.A.* 41°40N 81°26W **82** E3
Eastland *U.S.A.* 32°24N 98°49W **84** E5
Eastleigh *U.K.* 50°58N 1°21W **13** G6
Eastmain *Canada* 52°10N 78°30W **72** B4
Eastmain → *Canada* 52°27N 78°26W **72** B4
Eastman *Canada* 45°18N 72°19W **83** A12
Eastman *U.S.A.* 32°12N 83°11W **85** E13
Easton *Md., U.S.A.* 38°47N 76°5W **81** F15
Easton *Pa., U.S.A.* 40°41N 75°13W **83** F9
Easton *Wash., U.S.A.* 47°14N 121°11W **78** C5
Eastport *U.S.A.* 44°56N 67°0W **81** C14
Eastsound *U.S.A.* 48°42N 122°55W **78** B4
Eaton *U.S.A.* 40°32N 104°42W **76** F11
Eatonia *Canada* 51°13N 109°25W **71** C7
Eatonton *U.S.A.* 33°20N 83°23W **85** E13
Eatontown *U.S.A.* 40°19N 74°4W **83** F10
Eatonville *U.S.A.* 46°52N 122°16W **78** D4
Eau Claire *U.S.A.* 44°49N 91°30W **80** C8
Eau Claire, L. à l' *Canada* 56°10N 74°25W **72** A5
Eauripik Rise *Pac. Oc.* 2°0N 142°0E **64** G6
Ebano *Mexico* 22°13N 98°24W **87** C5
Ebbw Vale *U.K.* 51°46N 3°12W **13** F4
Ebeltoft *Denmark* 56°12N 10°41E **9** H14
Ebenezer, Mt. *Australia* 25°6S 132°34E **61** E5
Ebensburg *U.S.A.* 40°29N 78°44W **82** F6
Eberswalde-Finow
 Germany 52°50N 13°49E **16** B7
Ebetsu *Japan* 43°7N 141°34E **30** C10
Ebey's Landing △
 U.S.A. 48°12N 122°41W **78** B4
Ebinur Hu *China* 44°55N 82°55E **32** B3
Ebolowa *Cameroon* 2°55N 11°10E **52** D2
Ebonda
 Dem. Rep. of the Congo 2°12N 22°21E **52** D4
Ebre = Ebro → *Spain* 40°43N 0°54E **21** B6
Ebro → *Spain* 40°43N 0°54E **21** B6
Ecatepec de Morelos
 Mexico 19°36N 99°3W **87** D5
Ecbatana = Hamadān
 Iran 34°52N 48°32E **45** C6
Eceabat *Turkey* 40°11N 26°21E **23** D12
Ech Chélif *Algeria* 36°10N 1°20E **50** A6
Echigo-Sammyaku
 Japan 36°50N 139°50E **31** F9
Echizen-Misaki *Japan* 35°59N 135°57E **31** G7
Echo Bay *N.W.T., Canada* 66°5N 117°55W **68** C8
Echo Bay *Ont., Canada* 46°29N 84°4W **72** C3
Echoing → *Canada* 55°51N 92°5W **72** B1
Echternach *Lux.* 49°49N 6°25E **15** E6
Echuca *Australia* 36°10S 144°45E **63** F3
Écija *Spain* 37°30N 5°10W **21** D3
Eclipse I. *Australia* 35°5S 117°58E **61** G2
Eclipse Is. *Australia* 13°54S 126°19E **60** B4
Eclipse Sd. *Canada* 72°38N 79°0W **69** B12
Ecuador ■ *S. Amer.* 2°0S 78°0W **92** D3
Ed Damazin *Sudan* 11°46N 34°21E **51** F12
Ed Dar el Beida = Casablanca
 Morocco 33°36N 7°36W **50** B4
Ed Debba *Sudan* 18°0N 30°51E **51** E12
Ed Déffa *Egypt* 30°40N 26°30E **51** B11
Ed Dueim *Sudan* 14°0N 32°10E **51** F12
Edam *Canada* 53°11N 108°46W **71** C7
Edam *Neths.* 52°31N 5°3E **15** B5
Eday *U.K.* 59°11N 2°47W **11** B6
Eddrachillis B. *U.K.* 58°17N 5°14W **11** C3
Eddystone *U.K.* 50°11N 4°16W **13** G3
Eddystone Pt. *Australia* 40°59S 148°20E **63** G4
Ede *Neths.* 52°4N 5°40E **15** B5
Edehon L. *Canada* 60°25N 97°15W **71** A9
Edekel, Adrar *Algeria* 23°56N 6°47E **50** D7
Eden *Australia* 37°3S 149°55E **63** F4
Eden *N.C., U.S.A.* 36°29N 79°53W **85** C15
Eden *N.Y., U.S.A.* 42°39N 78°55W **82** D6
Eden *Tex., U.S.A.* 31°13N 99°51W **84** F5
Eden → *U.K.* 54°57N 3°1W **12** C4
Edenburg *S. Africa* 29°43S 25°58E **56** D4
Edendale *S. Africa* 29°39S 30°18E **57** D5
Edenderry *Ireland* 53°21N 7°4W **10** C4
Edenton *U.S.A.* 36°4N 76°39W **85** C16
Edenville *S. Africa* 27°37S 27°34E **57** D4
Eder → *Germany* 51°12N 9°28E **16** C5
Edessa *Greece* 40°48N 22°5E **23** D10
Edfu = Idfû *Egypt* 24°55N 32°49E **51** D12
Edgar *U.S.A.* 40°22N 97°58W **80** E5
Edgartown *U.S.A.* 41°23N 70°31W **83** E14
Edge Hill *U.K.* 52°8N 1°26W **13** E6

Edgefield *U.S.A.* 33°47N 81°56W **85** E14
Edgeley *U.S.A.* 46°22N 98°43W **80** B4
Edgemont *U.S.A.* 43°18N 103°50W **80** D2
Edgeøya *Svalbard* 77°45N 22°30E **4** B9
Edgewater *U.S.A.* 40°48N 22°55E **23** D10
Édhessa = Edessa *Greece* 40°48N 22°55E **23** D10
Edievale *N.Z.* 45°49S 169°22E **59** F2
Edina *U.S.A.* 40°10N 92°11W **80** E7
Edinboro *U.S.A.* 41°52N 80°8W **82** E4
Edinburg *U.S.A.* 26°18N 98°10W **84** H5
Edinburgh *U.K.* 55°57N 3°13W **11** F5
Edinburgh ✈ (EDI) *U.K.* 55°54N 3°22W **11** F5
Edinburgh, City of □
 U.K. 55°57N 3°17W **11** F5
Edineţ *Moldova* 48°9N 27°18E **17** D14
Edirne *Turkey* 41°40N 26°34E **23** D12
Edison *U.S.A.* 48°33N 122°27W **78** B4
Edithburgh *Australia* 35°5S 137°43E **63** F2
Edmeston *U.S.A.* 42°42N 75°15W **83** D9
Edmond *U.S.A.* 35°39N 97°29W **84** D6
Edmonds *U.S.A.* 47°48N 122°22W **78** C4
Edmonton *Australia* 17°2S 145°46E **62** B4
Edmonton *Canada* 53°30N 113°30W **70** C6
Edmund L. *Canada* 54°45N 93°17W **72** B1
Edmundston *Canada* 47°23N 68°20W **73** C6
Edna *U.S.A.* 28°59N 96°39W **84** G6
Edremit *Turkey* 39°34N 27°0E **23** E12
Edremit Körfezi *Turkey* 39°30N 26°45E **23** E12
Edson *Canada* 53°35N 116°28W **70** C5
Eduardo Castex
 Argentina 35°50S 64°18W **94** D3
Edward → *Australia* 35°5S 143°30E **63** F3
Edward, L. *Africa* 0°25S 29°40E **54** C2
Edward VII Land
 Antarctica 80°0S 150°0W **5** E13
Edwards *Calif., U.S.A.* 34°50N 117°40W **79** L9
Edwards *N.Y., U.S.A.* 44°20N 75°15W **83** B9
Edwards Plateau
 U.S.A. 30°45N 101°20W **84** F4
Edwardsville *U.S.A.* 41°15N 75°56W **83** E9
Edzná *Mexico* 19°39N 90°19W **87** D6
Edzo *Canada* 62°49N 116°4W **70** A5
Eeklo *Belgium* 51°11N 3°33E **15** C3
Eesti = Estonia ■ *Europe* 58°30N 25°30E **9** G21
Effigy Mounds △ *U.S.A.* 43°5N 91°11W **80** D8
Effingham *U.S.A.* 39°7N 88°33W **80** F9
Égadi, Ísole *Italy* 37°55N 12°16E **22** F5
Egan Range *U.S.A.* 39°35N 114°55W **76** G6
Eganville *Canada* 45°32N 77°5W **82** A7
Eger = Cheb *Czech Rep.* 50°9N 12°28E **16** C7
Eger *Hungary* 47°53N 20°27E **17** E11
Egersund *Norway* 58°26N 6°1E **9** G12
Egg L. *Canada* 55°5N 105°30W **71** B7
Éghezée *Belgium* 50°35N 4°55E **15** D4
Egio *Greece* 38°15N 22°5E **23** E10
Eglinton I. *Canada* 75°48N 118°30W **69** B8
Egmont *Canada* 49°45N 123°56W **70** D4
Egmont, C. *N.Z.* 39°16S 173°45E **59** C4
Egmont, Mt. = Taranaki, Mt.
 N.Z. 39°17S 174°5E **59** C5
Egmont △ *N.Z.* 39°17S 174°4E **59** C5
Egra *India* 21°54N 87°32E **43** J12
Eğridir *Turkey* 37°52N 30°51E **19** G5
Eğridir Gölü *Turkey* 37°53N 30°50E **19** G5
Egvekinot *Russia* 66°19N 179°50W **29** C19
Egypt ■ *Africa* 28°0N 31°0E **51** C12
Ehime □ *Japan* 33°30N 132°40E **31** H6
Ehrenberg *U.S.A.* 33°36N 114°31W **79** M12
Eibar *Spain* 43°11N 2°28W **21** A4
Eidsvold *Australia* 25°25S 151°12E **63** D5
Eidsvoll *Norway* 60°19N 11°14E **9** F14
Eifel *Germany* 50°15N 6°50E **16** C4
Eiffel Flats *Zimbabwe* 18°20S 30°0E **55** F3
Eigg *U.K.* 56°54N 6°10W **11** E2
Eighty Mile Beach
 Australia 19°30S 120°40E **60** C3
Eil, L. *U.K.* 56°51N 5°16W **11** E3
Eildon, L. *Australia* 37°10S 146°0E **63** F4
Eilean Sar = Western Isles □
 U.K. 57°30N 7°10W **11** D1
Einasleigh *Australia* 18°32S 144°5E **62** B3
Einasleigh → *Australia* 17°30S 142°17E **62** B3
Eindhoven *Neths.* 51°26N 5°28E **15** C5
Eire = Ireland ■ *Europe* 53°50N 7°52W **10** C4
Eiríksjökull *Iceland* 64°46N 20°24W **8** D3
Eirunepé *Brazil* 6°35S 69°53W **92** E5
Eiseb → *Namibia* 20°33S 20°59E **56** C3
Eisenach *Germany* 50°58N 10°19E **16** C6
Eisenerz *Austria* 47°32N 14°54E **16** E8
Eivissa *Spain* 38°54N 1°26E **24** C7
Ejeda *Madag.* 24°20S 44°31E **57** C7
Ejutla *Mexico* 16°34N 96°44W **87** D5
Ekalaka *U.S.A.* 45°53N 104°33W **76** D11
Ekaterinburg = Yekaterinburg
 Russia 56°50N 60°30E **28** D7
Ekenäs = Tammisaari
 Finland 60°0N 23°26E **9** G20
Eketahuna *N.Z.* 40°38S 175°43E **59** D5
Ekibastuz *Kazakhstan* 51°50N 75°10E **28** D8
Ekoli *Dem. Rep. of the Congo* 0°23S 24°13E **54** C1
Eksjö *Sweden* 57°40N 14°58E **9** H16
Ekuma → *Namibia* 18°40S 16°2E **56** B2
Ekwan → *Canada* 53°12N 82°15W **72** B3
Ekwan Pt. *Canada* 53°16N 82°7W **72** B3
El Aaiún *W. Sahara* 27°9N 13°12W **50** C3
El Abanico *Chile* 37°20S 71°31W **94** D1
El 'Agrûd *Egypt* 30°14N 34°24E **46** E3
El 'Alamein *Egypt* 30°48N 28°58E **51** B11
El 'Aqaba, W. → *Egypt* 30°7N 33°54E **46** E2
El Arîḥâ *West Bank* 31°52N 35°27E **46** D4
El 'Arîsh *Egypt* 31°8N 33°50E **46** D2
El 'Arîsh, W. → *Egypt* 31°8N 33°47E **46** D2
El Asnam = Ech Chéliff
 Algeria 36°10N 1°20E **50** A6
El Bayadh *Algeria* 33°40N 1°1E **50** B6
El Bluff *Nic.* 11°59N 83°40W **88** D3
El Cajon *U.S.A.* 32°48N 116°58W **79** N10
El Calafate *Argentina* 50°19S 72°15W **96** G2

El Campo *U.S.A.* 29°12N 96°16W **84** G6
El Capitan *U.S.A.* 37°44N 119°38E **78** H7
El Carbón *Honduras* 15°25N 85°32W **88** C2
El Carmen *Colombia* 9°43N 75°8W **92** B3
El Centro *U.S.A.* 32°48N 115°34W **79** N11
El Cerro *Bolivia* 17°30S 61°40W **92** G6
El Compadre *Mexico* 32°20N 116°14W **79** N10
El Cuy *Argentina* 39°55S 68°25W **96** D3
El Cuyo *Mexico* 21°31N 87°41W **87** C7
El Daheir *Egypt* 31°0N 34°10E **46** D3
El Descanso *Mexico* 32°12N 116°58W **79** N10
El Diviso *Colombia* 1°22N 78°14W **92** C3
El Djouf *Mauritania* 20°0N 9°0W **50** D4
El Dorado *Ark., U.S.A.* 33°12N 92°40W **84** E8
El Dorado *Kans., U.S.A.* 37°49N 96°52W **80** G5
El Dorado *Venezuela* 6°55N 61°37W **92** B6
El Dorado Springs *U.S.A.* 37°52N 94°1W **80** G6
El Escorial *Spain* 40°35N 4°7E **21** B3
El Faiyûm *Egypt* 29°19N 30°50E **51** C12
El Fâsher *Sudan* 13°33N 25°26E **51** F11
El Ferrol = Ferrol *Spain* 43°29N 8°15W **21** A1
El Fuerte *Mexico* 26°25N 108°39W **86** B3
El Gal *Somali Rep.* 10°58N 50°20E **47** E5
El Geneina = Al Junaynah
 Sudan 13°27N 22°45E **51** F10
El Gezira □ *Sudan* 15°0N 33°0E **51** F12
El Gîza *Egypt* 30°0N 31°12E **51** C12
El Gogorrón △ *Mexico* 21°49N 100°57W **86** C4
El Goléa *Algeria* 30°30N 2°50E **50** B6
El Golfo de Santa Clara
 Mexico 31°42N 114°30W **86** A2
El Guácharo △ *Venezuela* 10°8N 63°21W **89** D7
El Guache △ *Venezuela* 9°45N 69°30W **89** E6
El Iskandarîya *Egypt* 31°13N 29°58E **51** B11
El Istiwa'iya *Sudan* 5°0N 28°0E **51** G11
El Jadida *Morocco* 33°11N 8°17W **50** B4
El Jardal *Honduras* 14°54N 88°50W **88** D2
El Kef □ *Tunisia* 36°0N 9°0E **51** A7
El Khârga *Egypt* 25°30N 30°33E **51** C12
El Khartûm *Sudan* 15°31N 32°35E **51** E12
El Khartûm Bahrî
 Sudan 15°40N 32°31E **51** E12
El Kuntilla *Egypt* 30°1N 34°45E **46** E3
El Leoncito △ *Argentina* 31°58S 69°10W **94** C2
El Lucero *Mexico* 30°37N 106°31W **86** A3
El Maestrazgo *Spain* 40°30N 0°25W **21** B5
El Mahalla el Kubra
 Egypt 31°0N 31°0E **51** B12
El Malpais △ *U.S.A.* 34°53N 108°0W **77** J10
El Mansûra *Egypt* 31°0N 31°19E **51** B12
El Medano *Canary Is.* 28°3N 16°32W **24** F3
El Milagro *Argentina* 30°59S 65°59W **94** C2
El Minyâ *Egypt* 28°7N 30°33E **51** C12
El Monte *U.S.A.* 34°4N 118°1W **79** L8
El Obeid *Sudan* 13°8N 30°10E **51** F12
El Odaiya *Sudan* 12°8N 28°12E **51** F11
El Oro *Mexico* 19°51N 100°7W **87** D4
El Oued *Algeria* 33°20N 6°58E **50** B7
El Palmar △ *Argentina* 32°10S 58°31W **94** C4
El Palmito, Presa
 Mexico 25°40N 105°30W **86** B3
El Paso *U.S.A.* 31°45N 106°29W **84** F1
El Pinacate y Gran Desierto de
 Altar = Gran Desierto del
 Pinacate △ *Mexico* 31°51N 113°32W **86** A2
El Portal *U.S.A.* 37°41N 119°47W **78** H7
El Porvenir *Mexico* 31°15N 105°51W **86** A3
El Prat de Llobregat *Spain* 41°19N 2°5E **21** B7
El Progreso *Honduras* 15°26N 87°51W **88** C2
El Pueblito *Mexico* 29°6N 105°7W **86** B3
El Pueblo *Canary Is.* 28°36N 17°47W **24** F2
El Puerto de Santa María
 Spain 36°36N 6°13W **21** D2
El Qâhira *Egypt* 30°2N 31°13E **51** B12
El Qantara *Egypt* 30°51N 32°20E **46** E1
El Quseima *Egypt* 30°40N 34°15E **46** E3
El Real de Santa María
 Panama 8°0N 77°40W **92** B3
El Reno *U.S.A.* 35°32N 97°57W **84** H6
El Rey △ *Argentina* 24°40S 64°34W **94** A3
El Rio *U.S.A.* 34°14N 119°10W **79** L7
El Roque, Pta. *Canary Is.* 28°10N 15°25W **24** F4
El Rosarito *Mexico* 28°38N 114°4W **86** B2
El Salto *Mexico* 23°47N 105°22W **86** C3
El Salvador ■ *Cent. Amer.* 13°50N 89°0W **88** D2
El Sauce *Nic.* 13°0N 86°40W **88** D2
El Sueco *Mexico* 29°54N 106°24W **86** B3
El Suweis *Egypt* 29°58N 32°31E **51** C12
El Tamarâni, W. → *Egypt* 30°7N 34°43E **46** E3
El Thamad *Egypt* 29°40N 34°28E **46** F3
El Tigre *Venezuela* 8°44N 64°15W **92** B6
El Tîh, Gebel *Egypt* 29°40N 33°50E **46** F2
El Tofo *Chile* 29°22S 71°18W **94** B1
El Tránsito *Chile* 28°52S 70°17W **94** B1
El Tûr *Egypt* 28°14N 33°36E **46** F2
El Turbio *Argentina* 51°45S 72°5W **96** G2
El Uqsur *Egypt* 25°41N 32°38E **51** C12
El Vergel *Mexico* 26°28N 106°22W **86** B3
El Vigía *Venezuela* 8°38N 71°39W **92** B4
El Wabeira *Egypt* 29°34N 33°6E **46** F2
El Wak *Kenya* 2°49N 40°56E **54** B5
El Wuz *Sudan* 15°5N 30°7E **51** E12
Elat *Israel* 29°30N 34°56E **46** F3
Elâzığ *Turkey* 38°37N 39°14E **44** B3
Elba *Italy* 42°46N 10°17E **22** C4
Elba *U.S.A.* 31°25N 86°4W **85** F11
Elbasan *Albania* 41°9N 20°9E **23** D9
Elbe *U.S.A.* 46°45N 122°10W **78** D4
Elbe → *Europe* 53°50N 9°0E **16** B5
Elbert, Mt. *U.S.A.* 39°7N 106°27W **76** G10
Elberton *U.S.A.* 34°7N 82°52W **85** D13
Elbeuf *France* 49°17N 1°2E **20** B4
Elbing = Elbląg *Poland* 54°10N 19°25E **17** A10
Elbistan *Turkey* 38°13N 37°12E **44** B3
Elbląg *Poland* 54°10N 19°25E **17** A10

Elbow *Canada* 51°7N 106°35W **71** C7
Elbrus *Russia* 43°21N 42°30E **19** F7
Elburz Mts. = Alborz, Reshteh-ye
 Kūhhā-ye *Iran* 36°0N 52°0E **45** C7
Elche *Spain* 38°15N 0°42W **21** C5
Elcho I. *Australia* 11°55S 135°45E **62** A2
Elda *Spain* 38°29N 0°47W **21** C5
Eldama Ravine *Kenya* 0°3N 35°43E **54** B4
Elde → *Germany* 53°7N 11°15E **16** B6
Eldon *Mo., U.S.A.* 38°21N 92°35W **80** F7
Eldon *Wash., U.S.A.* 47°33N 123°3W **78** C3
Eldora *U.S.A.* 42°22N 93°5W **80** D7
Eldorado *Argentina* 26°28S 54°43W **95** B5
Eldorado *Canada* 44°35N 77°31W **82** B7
Eldorado *Ill., U.S.A.* 37°49N 88°26W **80** G10
Eldorado *Tex., U.S.A.* 30°52N 100°36W **84** F4
Eldoret *Kenya* 0°30N 35°17E **54** B4
Eldred *U.S.A.* 41°58N 78°23W **82** E6
Elea, C. *Cyprus* 35°19N 34°4E **25** D13
Eleanora, Pk. *Australia* 32°57S 121°9E **61** F3
Elefantes → *Africa* 24°10S 32°40E **57** C5
Elektrostal *Russia* 55°41N 38°32E **18** C6
Elemi Triangle *Africa* 5°0N 35°20E **54** B4
Elephant Butte Res.
 U.S.A. 33°9N 107°11W **77** K10
Elephant I. *Antarctica* 61°0S 55°0W **5** C18
Eleuthera *Bahamas* 25°0N 76°20W **88** B4
Elgin *Canada* 44°36N 76°13W **83** B8
Elgin *U.K.* 57°39N 3°19W **11** D5
Elgin *Ill., U.S.A.* 42°2N 88°17W **80** D9
Elgin *N. Dak., U.S.A.* 46°24N 101°51W **80** B3
Elgin *Oreg., U.S.A.* 45°34N 117°55W **76** D5
Elgin *Tex., U.S.A.* 30°21N 97°22W **84** F6
Elgon, Mt. *Africa* 1°10N 34°30E **54** B3
Eliase *Indonesia* 8°21S 130°48E **37** F8
Elim *Namibia* 17°48S 15°31E **56** B2
Elim *S. Africa* 34°35S 19°45E **56** E2
Elista *Russia* 46°16N 44°14E **19** E7
Elizabeth *Australia* 34°42S 138°41E **63** E2
Elizabeth *U.S.A.* 40°39N 74°12W **83** F10
Elizabeth City *U.S.A.* 36°18N 76°14W **85** C16
Elizabethton *U.S.A.* 36°21N 82°13W **85** C13
Elizabethtown *Ky.,*
 U.S.A. 37°42N 85°52W **81** G11
Elizabethtown *N.Y.,*
 U.S.A. 44°13N 73°36W **83** B11
Elizabethtown *Pa., U.S.A.* 40°9N 76°36W **83** F8
Elk *Poland* 53°50N 22°21E **17** B12
Elk → *Canada* 49°11N 115°14W **70** D5
Elk → *U.S.A.* 34°46N 87°16W **85** D11
Elk City *U.S.A.* 35°25N 99°25W **84** D5
Elk Creek *U.S.A.* 39°36N 122°32W **78** F4
Elk Grove *U.S.A.* 38°25N 121°22W **78** G5
Elk Island △ *Canada* 53°35N 112°59W **70** C6
Elk Lake *Canada* 47°40N 80°25W **72** C3
Elk Point *Canada* 53°54N 110°55W **71** C6
Elk River *Idaho, U.S.A.* 46°47N 116°11W **76** C5
Elk River *Minn., U.S.A.* 45°18N 93°35W **80** C7
Elkedra → *Australia* 21°8S 136°22E **62** C2
Elkhart *Ind., U.S.A.* 41°41N 85°58W **81** E11
Elkhart *Kans., U.S.A.* 37°0N 101°54W **80** G3
Elkhorn *Canada* 49°59N 101°14W **71** D8
Elkhorn → *U.S.A.* 41°8N 96°19W **80** E5
Elkhovo *Bulgaria* 42°10N 26°35E **23** C12
Elkin *U.S.A.* 36°15N 80°51W **85** C14
Elkins *U.S.A.* 38°55N 79°51W **81** F14
Elkland *U.S.A.* 41°59N 77°19W **82** E7
Elko *Canada* 49°20N 115°10W **70** D5
Elko *U.S.A.* 40°50N 115°46W **76** F6
Elkton *U.S.A.* 43°49N 83°11W **82** C1
Ellas = Greece ■ *Europe* 40°0N 23°0E **23** E9
Ellef Ringnes I. *Canada* 78°30N 102°2W **69** B9
Ellen, Mt. *U.S.A.* 44°9N 72°56W **83** B12
Ellenburg *U.S.A.* 44°54N 73°48W **83** B11
Ellendale *U.S.A.* 46°0N 98°32W **80** B4
Ellensburg *U.S.A.* 46°59N 120°34W **78** C5
Ellenville *U.S.A.* 41°43N 74°24W **83** E10
Ellerton *Barbados* 13°7N 59°33W **89** g
Ellery, Mt. *Australia* 37°28S 148°47E **63** F4
Ellesmere, L. *N.Z.* 43°47S 172°28E **59** G4
Ellesmere I. *Canada* 79°30N 80°0W **69** B12
Ellesmere Port *U.K.* 53°17N 2°54W **12** D5
Ellice Is. = Tuvalu ■
 Pac. Oc. 8°0S 178°0E **58** B10
Ellicottville *U.S.A.* 42°17N 78°40W **82** D6
Ellington *U.S.A.* 42°13N 79°6W **82** D5
Elliot *Australia* 17°33S 133°32E **62** B1
Elliot *S. Africa* 31°22S 27°48E **57** E4
Elliot Lake *Canada* 46°25N 82°35W **72** C3
Elliotdale = Xhora
 S. Africa 31°55S 28°38E **57** E4
Ellis *U.S.A.* 38°56N 99°34W **80** F4
Elliston *Australia* 33°39S 134°53E **63** E1
Ellisville *U.S.A.* 31°36N 89°12W **85** F10
Ellon *U.K.* 57°22N 2°4W **11** D6
Ellore = Eluru *India* 16°48N 81°8E **41** L12
Ellsworth *Kans., U.S.A.* 38°44N 98°14W **80** F4
Ellsworth *Maine, U.S.A.* 44°33N 68°25W **81** C19
Ellsworth Land *Antarctica* 76°0S 89°0W **5** D16
Ellsworth Mts. *Antarctica* 78°30S 85°0W **5** D16
Ellwood City *U.S.A.* 40°52N 80°17W **82** F4
Elma *Canada* 49°52N 95°55W **71** D9
Elma *U.S.A.* 47°0N 123°25W **78** D3
Elmalı *Turkey* 36°44N 29°56E **19** G4
Elmhurst *U.S.A.* 41°53N 87°56W **80** E10
Elmira *Canada* 43°36N 80°33W **82** C4
Elmira *U.S.A.* 42°6N 76°48W **82** D8
Elmira Heights *U.S.A.* 42°8N 76°50W **82** D8
Elmore *Australia* 36°30S 144°37E **63** F3
Elmshorn *Germany* 53°43N 9°40E **16** B5
Elmvale *Canada* 44°35N 79°52W **82** B5
Elora *Canada* 43°41N 80°26W **82** C4
Elounda *Greece* 35°16N 25°42E **25** D7
Eloy *U.S.A.* 32°45N 111°33W **77** K8
Elphin *Canada* 44°55N 76°37W **83** B8
Elrose *Canada* 51°12N 108°0W **71** C7
Elsie *U.S.A.* 45°52N 123°36W **78** E3

Elsinore = Helsingør
 Denmark 56°2N 12°35E **9** H15
Eltanin Fracture Zone System
 S. Ocean 54°0S 130°0W **5** B14
Eltham *N.Z.* 39°26S 174°19E **59** C5
Eluru *India* 16°48N 81°8E **41** L12
Elvas *Portugal* 38°50N 7°10W **21** C2
Elverum *Norway* 60°53N 11°34E **8** F14
Elvire → *Australia* 17°51S 128°11E **60** C4
Elvire, Mt. *Australia* 29°22S 119°36E **61** E2
Elwell, L. = Tiber Res.
 U.S.A. 48°19N 111°6W **76** B8
Elwood *Ind., U.S.A.* 40°17N 85°50W **81** E11
Elwood *Nebr., U.S.A.* 40°36N 99°52W **80** E4
Elx = Elche *Spain* 38°15N 0°42W **21** C5
Ely *U.K.* 52°24N 0°16E **13** E8
Ely *Minn., U.S.A.* 47°55N 91°51W **80** B8
Ely *Nev., U.S.A.* 39°15N 114°54W **76** G6
Elyria *U.S.A.* 41°22N 82°7W **82** E2
eMalahleni *S. Africa* 25°51S 29°14E **57** D4
Emāmrūd *Iran* 36°30N 55°0E **45** B7
Embarcación *Argentina* 23°10S 64°0W **94** A3
Embetsu *Japan* 44°44N 141°47E **30** B10
Embi *Kazakhstan* 48°50N 58°8E **28** E6
Embi → *Kazakhstan* 46°55N 53°28E **19** E9
Embro *Canada* 43°9N 80°54W **82** C4
Embrun *France* 44°34N 6°30E **20** D7
Embu *Kenya* 0°32S 37°38E **54** C4
Emden *Germany* 53°21N 7°12E **16** B4
Emerald *Australia* 23°32S 148°10E **62** C4
Emerson *Canada* 49°0N 97°10W **71** D9
Emet *Turkey* 39°20N 29°15E **23** E13
Emi Koussi *Chad* 19°45N 18°55E **51** E9
Eminabad *Pakistan* 32°2N 74°8E **42** C6
Emine, Nos *Bulgaria* 42°40N 27°56E **23** C12
Emissi, Tarso *Chad* 21°27N 18°36E **51** D9
Emlenton *U.S.A.* 41°11N 79°43W **82** E5
Emmaus *S. Africa* 29°2S 25°15E **56** D4
Emmaus *U.S.A.* 40°32N 75°30W **83** F9
Emmeloord *Neths.* 52°44N 5°46E **15** B5
Emmen *Neths.* 52°48N 6°57E **15** B6
Emmet *Australia* 24°45S 144°30E **62** C3
Emmetsburg *U.S.A.* 43°7N 94°41W **80** D6
Emmett *Idaho, U.S.A.* 43°52N 116°30W **76** E5
Emmett *Mich., U.S.A.* 42°59N 82°46W **82** D2
Emmonak *U.S.A.* 62°47N 164°31W **74** a
Emo *Canada* 48°38N 93°50W **71** D10
Empalme *Mexico* 27°58N 110°51W **86** B2
Empangeni *S. Africa* 28°50S 31°52E **57** D5
Empedrado *Argentina* 28°0S 58°46W **94** B4
Emperor Seamount Chain
 Pac. Oc. 40°0N 170°0E **64** D9
Emperor Trough *Pac. Oc.* 43°0N 175°30E **64** C9
Emporia *Kans., U.S.A.* 38°25N 96°11W **80** F6
Emporia *Va., U.S.A.* 36°42N 77°32W **81** G15
Emporium *U.S.A.* 41°31N 78°14W **82** E6
Empress *Canada* 50°57N 110°0W **71** C7
Empty Quarter = Rub' al Khālī
 Si. Arabia 19°0N 48°0E **47** D4
Ems → *Germany* 53°20N 7°12E **16** B4
Emsdale *Canada* 45°32N 79°19W **82** A5
Emu *China* 43°40N 128°6E **35** C15
Emu Park *Australia* 23°13S 150°50E **62** C5
eMuziwezinto *S. Africa* 30°15S 30°45E **57** E5
'En 'Avrona *Israel* 29°43N 35°0E **46** F4
'En Boqeq *Israel* 31°12N 35°21E **46** D4
'En Gedi *Israel* 31°28N 35°25E **46** D4
En Nahud *Sudan* 12°45N 28°25E **51** F11
Ena *Japan* 35°25N 137°25E **31** G8
Enana *Namibia* 17°30S 16°23E **56** B2
Enard B. *U.K.* 58°5N 5°20W **11** C3
Enare = Inarijärvi *Finland* 69°0N 28°0E **8** B23
Enarotali *Indonesia* 3°55S 136°21E **37** E9
Encampment *U.S.A.* 41°12N 106°47W **76** F10
Encantadas, Serra *Brazil* 30°40S 53°0W **95** C5
Encarnación *Paraguay* 27°15S 55°50W **95** B4
Encarnación de Díaz
 Mexico 21°31N 102°14W **86** C4
Encinitas *U.S.A.* 33°3N 117°17W **79** M9
Encino *U.S.A.* 34°39N 105°28W **77** J11
Encounter B. *Australia* 35°45S 138°45E **63** F2
Endako *Canada* 54°6N 125°2W **70** C3
Endau Rompin △
 Malaysia 2°40N 103°15E **39** L4
Ende *Indonesia* 8°45S 121°40E **37** F6
Endeavour Str. *Australia* 10°45S 142°0E **62** A3
Enderbury I. *Kiribati* 3°8S 171°5W **64** H10
Enderby *Canada* 50°35N 119°10W **70** C5
Enderby Abyssal Plain
 S. Ocean 60°0S 40°0E **5** C5
Enderby I. *Australia* 20°35S 116°30E **60** D2
Enderby Land *Antarctica* 66°0S 53°0E **5** C5
Enderlin *U.S.A.* 46°38N 97°36W **80** B5
Enderrocat, C. *Spain* 39°28N 2°43E **24** B9
Endicott *U.S.A.* 42°6N 76°4W **83** D8
Endwell *U.S.A.* 42°6N 76°2W **83** D8
Endyalgout I. *Australia* 11°40S 132°35E **60** B5
Eneabba *Australia* 29°49S 115°16E **61** E2
Enewetak Atoll
 Marshall Is. 11°30N 162°15E **64** F8
Enez *Turkey* 40°45N 26°5E **23** D12
Enfer, Pte. d' *Martinique* 14°22N 60°54W **88** c
Enfield *Canada* 44°56N 63°32W **73** D7
Enfield *Conn., U.S.A.* 41°58N 72°36W **83** E12
Enfield *N.C., U.S.A.* 36°11N 77°41W **85** C16
Enfield *N.H., U.S.A.* 43°39N 72°9W **83** C12
Engadin *Switz.* 46°45N 10°10E **20** C9
Engaño, C. *Dom. Rep.* 18°30N 68°20W **89** C6
Engaño, C. *Phil.* 18°35N 122°23E **37** A6
Engaru *Japan* 44°3N 143°31E **30** B11
Engcobo = Ngcobo
 S. Africa 31°37S 28°0E **57** E4
Engels *Russia* 51°28N 46°6E **19** D8
Engemann L. *Canada* 58°0N 106°55W **71** B7
Enggano *Indonesia* 5°20S 102°40E **36** F2

England *U.S.A.* 34°33N 91°58W **84 D9**
England □ *U.K.* 53°0N 2°0W **13 E5**
Englee *Canada* 50°45N 56°5W **73 B8**
Englehart *Canada* 47°49N 79°52W **72 C4**
Englewood *U.S.A.* 39°38N 104°59W **76 G11**
English ➤ *Canada* 49°12N 91°5W **71 C10**
English Bazar = Ingraj Bazar
  India 24°58N 88°10E **43 G13**
English Channel *Europe* 50°0N 2°0W **13 G6**
English Company's Is., The
  Australia 11°50S 136°32E **62 A2**
English River *Canada* 49°14N 91°0W **72 C1**
Enid *U.S.A.* 36°24N 97°53W **84 C6**
Enkhuizen *Neths.* 52°42N 5°17E **15 B5**
Enna *Italy* 37°34N 14°16E **22 F6**
Ennadai L. *Canada* 60°58N 101°20W **71 A8**
Ennedi *Chad* 17°15N 22°0E **51 E10**
Enngonia *Australia* 29°21S 145°50E **63 D4**
Ennis *Ireland* 52°51N 8°59W **10 D3**
Ennis *Mont., U.S.A.* 45°21N 111°44W **76 D8**
Ennis *Tex., U.S.A.* 32°20N 96°38W **84 E6**
Enniscorthy *Ireland* 52°30N 6°34W **10 D5**
Enniskillen *U.K.* 54°21N 7°39W **10 B4**
Ennistimon *Ireland* 52°57N 9°17W **10 D2**
Enns ➤ *Austria* 48°14N 14°32E **16 D8**
Eno *Finland* 62°47N 30°10E **8 E24**
Enonekiö *Finland* 68°23N 23°37E **8 B20**
Enosburg Falls *U.S.A.* 44°55N 72°48W **83 B12**
Enriquillo, L. *Dom. Rep.* 18°20N 72°5W **89 C5**
Enschede *Neths.* 52°13N 6°53E **15 B6**
Ensenada *Argentina* 34°55S 57°55W **94 C4**
Ensenada *Mexico* 31°52N 116°37W **86 A1**
Ensenada de los Muertos
  Mexico 23°59N 109°51W **86 C2**
Ensiola, Pta. de n' *Spain* 39°7N 2°55E **24 B9**
Entebbe *Uganda* 0°4N 32°28E **54 B3**
Enterprise *Canada* 60°47N 115°45W **70 A5**
Enterprise *Ala., U.S.A.* 31°19N 85°51W **85 F12**
Enterprise *Oreg., U.S.A.* 45°25N 117°17W **76 D5**
Entre Ríos *Bolivia* 21°30S 64°25W **94 A3**
Entre Ríos □ *Argentina* 30°30S 58°30W **94 C4**
Entroncamento *Portugal* 39°28N 8°28W **21 C1**
Enugu *Nigeria* 6°30N 7°30E **50 G7**
Enumclaw *U.S.A.* 47°12N 121°59W **78 C5**
Eólie, Ís. *Italy* 38°30N 14°57E **22 E6**
Epe *Neths.* 52°21N 5°59E **15 B5**
Épernay *France* 49°3N 3°56E **20 B5**
Ephesus *Turkey* 37°55N 27°22E **23 F12**
Ephraim *U.S.A.* 39°22N 111°35W **76 G8**
Ephrata *Pa., U.S.A.* 40°11N 76°11W **83 F8**
Ephrata *Wash., U.S.A.* 47°19N 119°33W **76 C4**
Épinal *France* 48°10N 6°27E **20 B7**
Episkopi *Cyprus* 34°40N 32°54E **25 E11**
Episkopi *Greece* 35°20N 24°20E **25 D6**
Episkopi Bay *Cyprus* 34°35N 32°50E **25 E11**
Epsom *U.K.* 51°19N 0°16W **13 F7**
Epukiro *Namibia* 21°40S 19°9E **56 C2**
Equatoria = El Istiwa'iya
  Sudan 5°0N 28°0E **51 G11**
Equatorial Guinea ■ *Africa* 2°0N 8°0E **52 D1**
Er Rachidia *Morocco* 31°58N 4°20W **50 B5**
Er Rahad *Sudan* 12°45N 30°32E **51 F12**
Er Rif *Morocco* 35°1N 4°1W **50 A5**
Erāwadī Myit = Irrawaddy ➤
  Burma 15°50N 95°6E **41 M19**
Erāwadī Myitwanya = Irrawaddy,
  Mouths of the *Burma* 15°30N 95°0E **41 M19**
Erawan △ *Thailand* 14°25N 98°58E **38 E2**
Erbil = Arbīl *Iraq* 36°15N 44°5E **44 B5**
Erçek *Turkey* 38°39N 43°36E **44 B4**
Erciyaş Dağı *Turkey* 38°30N 35°30E **44 B2**
Érd *Hungary* 47°22N 18°56E **17 E10**
Erdao Jiang ➤ *China* 42°37N 128°0E **35 C14**
Erdek *Turkey* 40°23N 27°47E **23 D12**
Erdene = Ulaan-Uul
  Mongolia 44°13N 111°10E **34 B6**
Erdenet *Mongolia* 49°2N 104°5E **32 B5**
Erdenetsogt *Mongolia* 42°55N 106°5E **34 C4**
Erebus, Mt. *Antarctica* 77°35S 167°0E **5 D11**
Erechim *Brazil* 27°35S 52°15W **95 B5**
Ereğli *Konya, Turkey* 37°31N 34°4E **44 B2**
Ereğli *Zonguldak, Turkey* 41°15N 31°24E **19 F5**
Erenhot *China* 43°48N 112°2E **34 C7**
Eresma ➤ *Spain* 41°26N 4°45W **21 B3**
Erfenisdam *S. Africa* 28°30S 26°50E **56 D4**
Erfurt *Germany* 50°58N 11°2E **16 C6**
Ergani *Turkey* 38°17N 39°49E **44 B3**
Ergel *Mongolia* 43°8N 109°5E **34 C5**
Ergeni Vozvyshennost
  Russia 47°0N 44°0E **19 E7**
Ērgļi *Latvia* 56°54N 25°38E **9 H21**
Eriboll, L. *U.K.* 58°30N 4°42W **11 C4**
Érice *Italy* 38°2N 12°35E **22 E5**
Erie *U.S.A.* 42°8N 80°5W **82 D4**
Erie, L. *N. Amer.* 42°15N 81°0W **82 D4**
Erie Canal *U.S.A.* 43°5N 78°43W **82 C7**
Erieau *Canada* 42°16N 81°57W **82 D3**
Erikoussa *Greece* 39°53N 19°34E **25 A3**
Eriksdale *Canada* 50°52N 98°7W **71 C9**
Erimanthos *Greece* 37°57N 21°50E **23 F9**
Erimo-misaki *Japan* 41°50N 143°15E **30 D11**
Erin *Canada* 43°45N 80°7W **82 C4**
Erin Pt. *Trin. & Tob.* 10°3N 61°39W **93 K15**
Erinpura *India* 25°9N 73°3E **42 G5**
Eriskay *U.K.* 57°4N 7°18W **11 D1**
Eritrea ■ *Africa* 14°0N 38°30E **47 D2**
Erlangen *Germany* 49°36N 11°0E **16 D6**
Erldunda *Australia* 25°14S 133°12E **62 D1**
Ermelo *Neths.* 52°18N 5°35E **15 B5**
Ermelo *S. Africa* 26°31S 29°59E **57 D4**
Ermenek *Turkey* 36°38N 33°0E **44 B2**
Ermones *Greece* 39°37N 19°46E **25 A3**
Ernakulam *India* 9°59N 76°22E **40 Q10**
Erne ➤ *Ireland* 54°30N 8°16W **10 B3**
Erne, Lower L. *U.K.* 54°28N 7°47W **10 B4**
Erne, Upper L. *U.K.* 54°14N 7°32W **10 B4**
Ernest Giles Ra. *Australia* 27°0S 123°45E **61 E3**

Erode *India* 11°24N 77°45E **40 P10**
Eromanga *Australia* 26°40S 143°11E **63 D3**
Erongo *Namibia* 21°39S 15°58E **56 C2**
Erramala Hills *India* 15°30N 78°15E **40 M11**
Errentería *Spain* 43°19N 1°54W **21 A5**
Erri-Nundra △ *Australia* 37°28S 148°5E **63 F4**
Errigal *Ireland* 55°2N 8°6W **10 A3**
Erris Hd. *Ireland* 54°19N 10°0W **10 B1**
Erskine ➤ *U.S.A.* 47°40N 96°0W **80 B6**
Ertis = Irtysh ➤ *Russia* 61°4N 68°52E **28 C7**
Erwin *U.S.A.* 36°9N 82°25W **85 C13**
Erzgebirge *Germany* 50°27N 12°55E **16 C7**
Erzin *Russia* 50°15N 95°10E **29 D10**
Erzincan *Turkey* 39°46N 39°30E **44 B3**
Erzurum *Turkey* 39°57N 41°15E **44 B4**
Es Caló *Spain* 38°40N 1°30E **24 C8**
Es Canar *Spain* 39°2N 1°36E **24 B8**
Es Mercadal *Spain* 39°59N 4°5E **24 B11**
Es Migjorn Gran *Spain* 39°57N 4°3E **24 B11**
Es Sahrâ' Esh Sharqîya
  Egypt 27°30N 32°30E **51 C12**
Es Sînâ' *Egypt* 29°0N 34°0E **46 F3**
Es Vedrà *Spain* 38°52N 1°12E **24 C7**
Esambo
  Dem. Rep. of the Congo 3°48S 23°30E **54 C1**
Esan-Misaki *Japan* 41°40N 141°10E **30 D10**
Esashi *Hokkaidō, Japan* 44°56N 142°35E **30 B11**
Esashi *Hokkaidō, Japan* 41°52N 140°7E **30 D10**
Esbjerg *Denmark* 55°29N 8°29E **9 J13**
Esbo = Espoo *Finland* 60°12N 24°40E **9 F21**
Escalante *U.S.A.* 37°47N 111°36W **77 H8**
Escalante ➤ *U.S.A.* 37°24N 110°57W **77 H8**
Escalón *Mexico* 26°45N 104°20W **86 B4**
Escambia ➤ *U.S.A.* 30°32N 87°11W **85 F11**
Escanaba *U.S.A.* 45°45N 87°4W **80 C10**
Esch-sur-Alzette *Lux.* 49°32N 6°0E **15 E6**
Escondido *U.S.A.* 33°7N 117°5W **79 M9**
Escuinapa de Hidalgo
  Mexico 22°50N 105°50W **86 C3**
Escuintla *Guatemala* 14°20N 90°48W **88 D1**
Esenguly *Turkmenistan* 37°37N 53°59E **28 F6**
Esfahān *Iran* 32°39N 51°43E **45 C6**
Esfahān □ *Iran* 32°50N 51°50E **45 C6**
Esfarāyen *Iran* 37°4N 57°30E **45 B8**
Esfideh *Iran* 33°39N 59°46E **45 C8**
Esh Sham = Dimashq
  Syria 33°30N 36°18E **46 B5**
Esha Ness *U.K.* 60°29N 1°38W **11 A7**
Esher *U.K.* 51°21N 0°20W **13 F7**
Eshkol △ *Israel* 31°20N 34°30E **46 D3**
Eshowe *S. Africa* 28°50S 31°30E **57 D5**
Esigodini *Zimbabwe* 20°18S 28°56E **57 C4**
Esil = Ishim ➤ *Russia* 57°45N 71°10E **28 D8**
Esk ➤ *Dumf. & Gall., U.K.* 54°58N 3°2W **11 G5**
Esk ➤ *N. Yorks., U.K.* 54°30N 0°37W **12 C7**
Eskān *Iran* 26°48N 63°9E **45 E9**
Esker Siding *Canada* 53°53N 66°25W **73 B6**
Eskifjörður *Iceland* 65°3N 13°55W **8 D7**
Eskilstuna *Sweden* 59°22N 16°32E **9 G17**
Eskimo Point = Arviat
  Canada 61°6N 93°59W **71 A10**
Eskişehir *Turkey* 39°50N 30°30E **19 G5**
Esla ➤ *Spain* 41°29N 6°3W **21 B2**
Eslāmābād-e Gharb *Iran* 34°10N 46°30E **44 C5**
Eslāmshahr *Iran* 35°40N 51°10E **45 C6**
Eşme *Turkey* 38°23N 28°58E **23 E13**
Esmeraldas *Ecuador* 1°0N 79°40W **92 C3**
Esna = Isna *Egypt* 25°17N 32°30E **51 C12**
Esnagi L. *Canada* 48°36N 84°33W **72 C3**
España = Spain ■ *Europe* 39°0N 4°0W **21 B4**
Espanola *Canada* 46°15N 81°46W **72 C3**
Espanola *U.S.A.* 35°59N 106°5W **77 J10**
Esparza *Costa Rica* 9°59N 84°40W **88 E3**
Esperance *Australia* 33°45S 121°55E **61 F3**
Esperance B. *Australia* 33°48S 121°55E **61 F3**
Esperance Harbour
  St. Lucia 14°4N 60°55W **89 f**
Esperanza *Antarctica* 65°0S 55°0W **5 C18**
Esperanza *Argentina* 31°29S 61°3W **94 C3**
Esperanza *Puerto Rico* 18°6N 65°28W **89 d**
Espichel, C. *Portugal* 38°22N 9°16W **21 C1**
Espigão, Serra do *Brazil* 26°35S 50°30W **95 B5**
Espinazo, Sierra del = Espinhaço,
  Serra do *Brazil* 17°30S 43°30W **93 G10**
Espinhaço, Serra do
  Brazil 17°30S 43°30W **93 G10**
Espinilho, Serra do *Brazil* 28°30S 55°0W **95 B5**
Espírito Santo □ *Brazil* 20°0S 40°45W **93 H10**
Espíritu Santo *Vanuatu* 15°15S 166°50E **58 C9**
Espíritu Santo, B. del
  Mexico 19°20N 87°35W **87 D7**
Espíritu Santo, I.
  Mexico 24°30N 110°22W **86 C2**
Espita *Mexico* 21°1N 88°19W **87 C7**
Espoo *Finland* 60°12N 24°40E **9 F21**
Espungabera *Mozam.* 20°29S 32°45E **57 C5**
Esquel *Argentina* 42°55S 71°20W **96 E2**
Esquimalt *Canada* 48°26N 123°25W **78 B3**
Esquina *Argentina* 30°0S 59°30W **94 C4**
Essaouira *Morocco* 31°32N 9°42W **50 B4**
Essebie
  Dem. Rep. of the Congo 2°58N 30°40E **54 B3**
Essen *Belgium* 51°28N 4°28E **15 C4**
Essen *Germany* 51°28N 7°2E **16 C4**
Essendon, Mt. *Australia* 25°0S 120°29E **61 E3**
Essequibo ➤ *Guyana* 6°50S 58°30W **92 B7**
Essex *Canada* 42°10N 82°49W **82 D2**
Essex *Calif., U.S.A.* 34°44N 115°15W **79 L11**
Essex *N.Y., U.S.A.* 44°19N 73°21W **83 B11**
Essex □ *U.K.* 51°54N 0°27E **13 F8**
Essex Junction *U.S.A.* 44°29N 73°7W **83 B11**
Esslingen *Germany* 48°44N 9°18E **16 D5**
Estación Camacho
  Mexico 24°25N 102°18W **86 C4**
Estación Simón *Mexico* 24°42N 102°35W **86 C4**
Estados, I. de Los
  Argentina 54°40S 64°30W **96 G4**

Eştahbānāt *Iran* 29°8N 54°4E **45 D7**
Estância *Brazil* 11°16S 37°26W **93 F11**
Estancia *U.S.A.* 34°46N 106°4W **77 J10**
Estārm *Iran* 28°21N 58°21E **45 D8**
Estcourt *S. Africa* 29°0S 29°53E **57 D4**
Este △ *Dom. Rep.* 18°14N 68°42W **89 C6**
Esteli *Nic.* 13°9N 86°22W **88 D2**
Estellencs *Spain* 39°39N 2°29E **24 B9**
Esterhazy *Canada* 50°37N 102°5W **71 C8**
Estevan *Canada* 49°10N 102°59W **71 D8**
Estevan Group *Canada* 53°3N 129°38W **70 C3**
Estherville *U.S.A.* 43°24N 94°50W **80 D6**
Eston *Canada* 51°8N 108°40W **71 C7**
Estonia ■ *Europe* 58°30N 25°30E **9 G21**
Estreito *Brazil* 6°32S 47°25W **93 E9**
Estrela, Serra da *Portugal* 40°10N 7°45W **21 B2**
Estremoz *Portugal* 38°51N 7°39W **21 C2**
Estrondo, Serra do *Brazil* 7°20S 48°0W **93 E9**
Esztergom *Hungary* 47°47N 18°44E **17 E10**
Et Tîdra *Mauritania* 19°45N 16°20W **50 E2**
Etah *India* 27°35N 78°40E **43 F8**
Étampes *France* 48°26N 2°10E **20 B5**
Etanga *Namibia* 17°55S 13°0E **56 B1**
Etawah *India* 26°48N 79°6E **43 F8**
Etawney L. *Canada* 57°50N 96°50W **71 B9**
Etchojoa *Mexico* 26°55N 109°38W **86 B3**
eThekwini = Durban
  S. Africa 29°49S 31°1E **57 D5**
Ethel *U.S.A.* 46°32N 122°46W **78 D4**
Ethelbert *Canada* 51°32N 100°25W **71 C8**
Ethiopia ■ *Africa* 8°0N 40°0E **47 F3**
Ethiopian Highlands
  Ethiopia 10°0N 37°0E **47 F2**
Etive, L. *U.K.* 56°29N 5°10W **11 E3**
Etna *Italy* 37°50N 14°55E **22 F6**
Etoile
  Dem. Rep. of the Congo 11°33S 27°30E **55 E2**
Etosha △ *Namibia* 19°0S 16°0E **56 B2**
Etosha Pan *Namibia* 18°40S 16°30E **56 B2**
Etowah *U.S.A.* 35°20N 84°32W **85 D12**
Etrek *Turkmenistan* 37°36N 54°46E **45 B7**
Ettelbruck *Lux.* 49°51N 6°5E **15 E6**
Ettrick Water ➤ *U.K.* 55°31N 2°55W **11 F6**
Etuku
  Dem. Rep. of the Congo 3°42S 25°45E **54 C2**
Etzná-Tixmucuy = Edzná
  Mexico 19°39N 90°19W **87 D6**
Eua *Tonga* 21°22S 174°56W **59 c**
Euboea = Evia *Greece* 38°30N 24°0E **23 E11**
Eucla *Australia* 31°41S 128°52E **61 F4**
Euclid *U.S.A.* 41°34N 81°32W **82 E3**
Eucumbene, L. *Australia* 36°2S 148°40E **63 F4**
Eudora *U.S.A.* 33°7N 91°16W **84 E9**
Eufaula *Ala., U.S.A.* 31°54N 85°9W **85 F12**
Eufaula *Okla., U.S.A.* 35°17N 95°35W **84 D7**
Eufaula L. *U.S.A.* 35°18N 95°21W **84 D7**
Eugene *U.S.A.* 44°5N 123°4W **76 D2**
Eugowra *Australia* 33°22S 148°24E **63 E4**
Eulo *Australia* 28°10S 145°3E **63 D4**
Eungella △ *Australia* 20°57S 148°40E **62 C4**
Eunice *La., U.S.A.* 30°30N 92°25W **84 F8**
Eunice *N. Mex., U.S.A.* 32°26N 103°10W **77 K12**
Eupen *Belgium* 50°37N 6°3E **15 D6**
Euphrates = Furāt, Nahr al ➤
  Asia 31°0N 47°25E **44 D5**
Eureka *Canada* 80°0N 85°56W **69 B11**
Eureka *Calif., U.S.A.* 40°47N 124°9W **76 F1**
Eureka *Kans., U.S.A.* 37°49N 96°17W **80 G5**
Eureka *Mont., U.S.A.* 48°53N 115°3W **76 B6**
Eureka *Nev., U.S.A.* 39°31N 115°58W **76 G6**
Eureka *S. Dak., U.S.A.* 45°46N 99°38W **80 C4**
Eureka, Mt. *Australia* 26°35S 121°35E **61 E3**
Euroa *Australia* 36°44S 145°35E **63 F4**
Europa, Île *Ind. Oc.* 22°20S 40°22E **53 J8**
Europa, Picos de *Spain* 43°10N 4°49W **21 A3**
Europa, Pt. *Gib.* 36°3N 5°21W **21 D3**
Europe 50°0N 20°0E **6 E10**
Europoort *Neths.* 51°57N 4°10E **15 C4**
Eustis *U.S.A.* 28°51N 81°41W **85 G14**
Eutsuk L. *Canada* 53°20N 126°45W **70 C3**
Evale *Angola* 16°33S 15°44E **56 B2**
Evans *U.S.A.* 40°23N 104°41W **76 F11**
Evans, L. *Canada* 50°50N 77°0W **72 B4**
Evans City *U.S.A.* 40°46N 80°4W **82 F4**
Evans Head *Australia* 29°7S 153°27E **63 D5**
Evansburg *Canada* 53°36N 114°59W **70 C6**
Evanston *Ill., U.S.A.* 42°3N 87°40W **80 D10**
Evanston *Wyo., U.S.A.* 41°16N 110°58W **76 F8**
Evansville *U.S.A.* 37°58N 87°35W **80 G10**
Evaz *Iran* 27°46N 53°59E **45 E7**
Eveleth *U.S.A.* 47°28N 92°32W **80 B7**
Evensk *Russia* 62°12N 159°30E **29 C16**
Everard, L. *Australia* 31°30S 135°0E **63 E2**
Everard Ranges *Australia* 27°5S 132°28E **61 E5**
Everest, Mt. *Nepal* 28°5N 86°58E **43 E12**
Everett *Pa., U.S.A.* 40°1N 78°23W **82 F6**
Everett *Wash., U.S.A.* 47°59N 122°12W **78 C4**
Everglades, The *U.S.A.* 25°50N 81°0W **85 J14**
Everglades △ *U.S.A.* 25°30N 81°0W **85 J14**
Everglades City *U.S.A.* 25°52N 81°23W **85 J14**
Evergreen *Ala., U.S.A.* 31°26N 86°57W **85 F11**
Evergreen *Mont.,
  U.S.A.* 48°14N 114°17W **76 B6**
Evesham *U.K.* 52°6N 1°56W **13 E6**
Évora *Portugal* 38°33N 7°57W **21 C2**
Evowghlī *Iran* 38°43N 45°13E **44 B5**
Évreux *France* 49°3N 1°8E **20 B4**
Evros ➤ *Greece* 41°40N 26°34E **23 D12**
Évry *France* 48°38N 2°27E **20 B5**
Évvoia = Evia *Greece* 38°30N 24°0E **23 E11**
Ewe, L. *U.K.* 57°49N 5°38W **11 D3**
Ewing *U.S.A.* 42°16N 98°21W **80 D4**
Ewo *Congo* 0°48S 14°45E **52 E2**
Exaltación *Bolivia* 13°10S 65°20W **92 F5**
Excelsior Springs *U.S.A.* 39°20N 94°13W **80 F6**

Exe ➤ *U.K.* 50°41N 3°29W **13 G4**
Exeter *Canada* 43°21N 81°29W **82 C3**
Exeter *U.K.* 50°43N 3°31W **13 G4**
Exeter *Calif., U.S.A.* 36°18N 119°9W **78 J7**
Exeter *N.H., U.S.A.* 42°59N 70°57W **83 D14**
Exmoor *U.K.* 51°12N 3°45W **13 F4**
Exmoor △ *U.K.* 51°8N 3°42W **13 F4**
Exmouth *Australia* 21°54S 114°10E **60 D1**
Exmouth *U.K.* 50°37N 3°25W **13 G4**
Exmouth G. *Australia* 22°15S 114°15E **60 D1**
Exmouth Plateau *Ind. Oc.* 19°0S 114°0E **64 J3**
Expedition △ *Australia* 25°41S 149°7E **63 D4**
Expedition Ra. *Australia* 24°30S 149°12E **62 C4**
Extremadura □ *Spain* 39°30N 6°5W **21 C2**
Exuma Sound *Bahamas* 24°30N 76°20W **88 B4**
Eyasi, L. *Tanzania* 3°30S 35°0E **54 C4**
Eye *Pen. U.K.* 58°13N 6°10W **11 C2**
Eyemouth *U.K.* 55°52N 2°5W **11 F6**
Eyjafjörður *Iceland* 66°15N 18°30W **8 C4**
Eyl *Somali Rep.* 8°0N 49°50E **47 F4**
Eyre (North), L.
  Australia 28°30S 137°20E **63 D2**
Eyre (South), L.
  Australia 29°18S 137°25E **63 D2**
Eyre, L. *Australia* 29°30S 137°26E **58 D6**
Eyre Mts. *N.Z.* 45°25S 168°25E **59 F2**
Eyre Pen. *Australia* 33°30S 136°17E **63 E2**
Eysturoy *Færoe Is.* 62°13N 6°54W **8 E9**
Eyvān = Jūy Zar *Iran* 33°50N 46°18E **44 C5**
Eyvānkī *Iran* 35°24N 51°56E **45 C6**
Ezine *Turkey* 39°48N 26°20E **23 E12**
Ezouza ➤ *Cyprus* 34°44N 32°27E **25 E11**

F

F.Y.R.O.M. = Macedonia ■
  Europe 41°53N 21°40E **23 D9**
Faaa *Tahiti* 17°34S 149°35W **59 d**
Faaone *Tahiti* 17°40S 149°21W **59 d**
Fabala *Guinea* 9°44N 9°5W **50 G4**
Fabens *U.S.A.* 31°30N 106°10W **84 F1**
Fabius *U.S.A.* 42°50N 75°59W **83 D9**
Fabriano *Italy* 43°20N 12°54E **22 C5**
Fachi *Niger* 18°6N 11°34E **51 E8**
Fada *Chad* 17°13N 21°34E **51 E10**
Fada-n-Gourma
  Burkina Faso 12°10N 0°30E **50 F6**
Faddeyevskiy, Ostrov
  Russia 76°0N 144°0E **29 B15**
Fadghāmī *Syria* 35°53N 40°52E **44 C4**
Faenza *Italy* 44°17N 11°53E **22 B4**
Færoe Is. = Føroyar ☑
  Atl. Oc. 62°0N 7°0W **8 F9**
Făgăras *Romania* 45°48N 24°58E **17 F13**
Fagersta *Sweden* 60°1N 15°46E **9 F16**
Fagnano, L. *Argentina* 54°30S 68°0W **96 G3**
Fahliān *Iran* 30°11N 51°28E **45 D6**
Fahraj *Kermān, Iran* 29°0N 59°0E **45 D8**
Fahraj *Yazd, Iran* 31°46N 54°36E **45 D7**
Faial *Azores* 38°34N 28°42W **50 a**
Faial *Madeira* 32°47N 16°53W **24 D3**
Faichan Kangri *India* 35°48N 76°34E **43 B7**
Fair Haven *N.Y., U.S.A.* 43°18N 76°42W **83 C8**
Fair Haven *Vt., U.S.A.* 43°36N 73°16W **83 D17**
Fair Hd. *U.K.* 55°14N 6°9W **10 A5**
Fair Isle *U.K.* 59°32N 1°38W **14 B6**
Fair Oaks *U.S.A.* 38°39N 121°16W **78 G5**
Fairbanks *U.S.A.* 64°51N 147°43W **68 C5**
Fairbury *U.S.A.* 40°8N 97°11W **80 E5**
Fairfax *U.S.A.* 44°40N 73°1W **83 B11**
Fairfield *Ala., U.S.A.* 33°29N 86°55W **85 E11**
Fairfield *Calif., U.S.A.* 38°15N 122°3W **78 G4**
Fairfield *Idaho, U.S.A.* 43°21N 114°44W **76 E6**
Fairfield *Ill., U.S.A.* 38°23N 88°22W **80 F10**
Fairfield *Iowa, U.S.A.* 40°56N 91°57W **80 E8**
Fairfield *Tex., U.S.A.* 31°44N 96°10W **84 F6**
Fairford *Canada* 51°37N 98°38W **71 C9**
Fairhope *U.S.A.* 30°31N 87°54W **85 F11**
Fairlie *N.Z.* 44°5S 170°49E **59 F3**
Fairmead *U.S.A.* 37°5N 120°10W **78 H6**
Fairmont *Minn., U.S.A.* 43°39N 94°28W **80 D8**
Fairmont *W. Va., U.S.A.* 39°29N 80°9W **81 F13**
Fairmount *Calif., U.S.A.* 34°45N 118°26W **79 L8**
Fairmount *N.Y., U.S.A.* 43°5N 76°12W **83 C8**
Fairplay *U.S.A.* 39°15N 106°2W **76 G10**
Fairport *U.S.A.* 43°6N 77°27W **82 C7**
Fairport Harbor *U.S.A.* 41°45N 81°17W **82 E3**
Fairview *Canada* 56°5N 118°25W **70 B5**
Fairview *Mont., U.S.A.* 47°51N 104°3W **76 C11**
Fairview *Okla., U.S.A.* 36°16N 98°29W **84 C5**
Fairweather, Mt.
  U.S.A. 58°55N 137°32W **70 B1**
Faisalabad *Pakistan* 31°30N 73°5E **42 D5**
Faith *U.S.A.* 45°2N 102°2W **80 C2**
Faizabad *India* 26°45N 82°10E **43 F10**
Faizabad *Puerto Rico* 18°20N 65°39W **89 d**
Fajr, W. ➤ *Si. Arabia* 29°10N 38°10E **44 D3**
Fakenham *U.K.* 52°51N 0°51E **12 E8**
Fakfak *Indonesia* 2°55S 132°18E **37 E8**
Faku *China* 42°32N 123°21E **35 C12**
Falaise *France* 48°54N 0°12W **20 B3**
Falaise, Mui *Vietnam* 19°6N 105°45E **38 C5**
Falam *Burma* 23°0N 93°45E **41 H18**
Falcó, C. des *Spain* 38°50N 1°23E **24 C7**
Falcón, Presa *Mexico* 26°35N 99°10W **87 B5**
Falcon Lake *Canada* 49°42N 95°15W **71 D9**
Falcon Res. *U.S.A.* 26°34N 99°10W **84 M5**
Falconara Maríttima
  Italy 43°37N 13°24E **22 C5**
Falcone, C. del *Italy* 40°58N 8°12E **22 D3**
Falconer *U.S.A.* 42°7N 79°12W **82 D5**
Falefa *Samoa* 13°54S 171°31W **59 b**
Falelatai *Samoa* 13°51S 171°59W **59 b**
Falelima *Samoa* 13°32S 172°41W **59 b**
Faleshty = Fălești
  Moldova 47°32N 27°44E **17 E14**

Fălești *Moldova* 47°32N 27°44E **17 E14**
Falfurrias *U.S.A.* 27°14N 98°9W **84 H5**
Falher *Canada* 55°44N 117°15W **70 B5**
Falkenberg *Sweden* 56°54N 12°30E **9 H15**
Falkirk *U.K.* 56°0N 3°47W **11 F5**
Falkland □ *U.K.* 55°58N 3°49W **11 F5**
Falkland Is. □ *Atl. Oc.* 51°30S 59°0W **96 G5**
Falkland Sd. *Falk. Is.* 52°0S 60°0W **96 G5**
Fall River *U.S.A.* 41°43N 71°10W **83 E13**
Fallbrook *U.S.A.* 33°23N 117°15W **79 M9**
Fallon *U.S.A.* 39°28N 118°47W **76 G4**
Falls City *U.S.A.* 40°3N 95°36W **80 E6**
Falls Creek *U.S.A.* 41°9N 78°48W **82 E6**
Falmouth *Jamaica* 18°30N 77°40W **88 a**
Falmouth *U.K.* 50°9N 5°5W **13 G2**
Falmouth *U.S.A.* 41°33N 70°37W **83 E14**
Falsa, Pta. *Mexico* 27°51N 115°3W **86 B1**
False B. *S. Africa* 34°15S 18°40E **56 E2**
Falso, C. *Honduras* 15°12N 83°21W **88 C3**
Falster *Denmark* 54°45N 11°55E **9 J14**
Falsterbo *Sweden* 55°23N 12°50E **9 J15**
Fălticeni *Romania* 47°21N 26°20E **17 E14**
Falun *Sweden* 60°37N 15°37E **8 F16**
Famagusta *Cyprus* 35°8N 33°55E **25 D12**
Famagusta Bay *Cyprus* 35°15N 34°0E **25 D13**
Famatina, Sierra de
  Argentina 27°30S 68°0W **94 B2**
Family L. *Canada* 51°54N 95°27W **71 C9**
Fan, L. *Australia* 35°37N 119°12W **79 K7**
Fan Xian *China* 35°55N 115°38E **34 G8**
Fanad Hd. *Ireland* 55°17N 7°38W **10 A4**
Fandriana *Madag.* 20°14S 47°21E **57 C8**
Fang *Thailand* 19°55N 99°13E **38 C2**
Fangcheng *China* 33°18N 112°59E **34 H7**
Fangshan *China* 38°3N 111°25E **34 E6**
Fangzi *China* 36°33N 119°10E **35 F10**
Fanjakana *Madag.* 21°10S 46°53E **57 C8**
Fanjiatun *China* 43°40N 125°15E **35 C13**
Fanling *China* 22°30N 114°8E **33 F11**
Fannich, L. *U.K.* 57°38N 4°59W **11 D4**
Fannūj *Iran* 26°35N 59°38E **45 E8**
Fano *Denmark* 55°25N 8°25E **9 J13**
Fano *Italy* 43°50N 13°1E **22 C5**
Fanshi *China* 39°12N 113°20E **34 E7**
Fao = Al Fāw *Iraq* 30°0N 48°30E **45 D6**
Faqirwali *Pakistan* 29°27N 73°0E **42 E5**
Far East = Dalnevostochnyy □
  Russia 67°0N 140°0E **29 C14**
Far East *Asia* 40°0N 130°0E **26 E14**
Faradje
  Dem. Rep. of the Congo 3°50N 29°45E **54 B2**
Farafangana *Madag.* 22°49S 47°50E **57 C8**
Farāh *Afghan.* 32°20N 62°7E **40 C3**
Farāh □ *Afghan.* 32°25N 62°10E **40 C3**
Farahalana *Madag.* 14°26S 50°10E **57 A9**
Faranah *Guinea* 10°3N 10°45W **50 F3**
Farasān, Jazā'ir
  Si. Arabia 16°45N 41°55E **47 D3**
Farasan Is. = Farasān, Jazā'ir
  Si. Arabia 16°45N 41°55E **47 D3**
Faratsiho *Madag.* 19°24S 46°57E **57 B8**
Fareham *U.K.* 50°51N 1°11W **13 G6**
Farewell C. = Nunap Isua
  Greenland 59°48N 43°55W **66 D15**
Farewell, C. *N.Z.* 40°29S 172°43E **59 D4**
Farghona *Uzbekistan* 40°23N 71°19E **28 E8**
Fargo *U.S.A.* 46°53N 96°48W **80 B5**
Fār'iah, W. al ➤
  West Bank 32°12N 35°27E **46 C4**
Faribault *U.S.A.* 44°18N 93°16W **80 C7**
Faridabad *India* 28°26N 77°19E **42 E6**
Faridkot *India* 30°44N 74°45E **42 D6**
Faridpur *Bangla.* 23°15N 89°55E **43 H13**
Faridpur *India* 28°13N 79°33E **43 E8**
Farīmān *Iran* 35°40N 59°49E **45 C8**
Farina *Australia* 30°3S 138°15E **63 E2**
Fariones, Pta. *Canary Is.* 29°13N 13°28W **24 E6**
Farleigh *Australia* 21°4S 149°8E **62 K7**
Farmerville *U.S.A.* 32°47N 92°24W **84 E8**
Farmingdale *U.S.A.* 40°12N 74°10W **83 F10**
Farmington *Canada* 55°54N 120°30W **70 B4**
Farmington *Calif.,
  U.S.A.* 37°55N 120°59W **78 H6**
Farmington *Maine,
  U.S.A.* 44°40N 70°9W **81 C18**
Farmington *Mo., U.S.A.* 37°47N 90°25W **80 G8**
Farmington *N.H., U.S.A.* 43°24N 71°4W **83 C13**
Farmington *N. Mex.,
  U.S.A.* 36°44N 108°12W **77 H9**
Farmington *Utah,
  U.S.A.* 40°59N 111°53W **76 F8**
Farmington ➤ *U.S.A.* 41°51N 72°38W **83 E12**
Farmville *U.S.A.* 37°18N 78°24W **81 G14**
Farne Is. *U.K.* 55°38N 1°37W **12 B6**
Farnham *Canada* 45°17N 72°59W **83 A12**
Farnham, Mt. *Canada* 50°29N 116°30W **70 C5**
Faro *Brazil* 2°10S 56°39W **93 D7**
Faro *Canada* 62°11N 133°22W **68 C6**
Faro *Portugal* 37°2N 7°55W **21 D2**
Fårö *Sweden* 57°55N 19°5E **9 H18**
Farquhar, C. *Australia* 23°50S 113°36E **61 D1**
Farrars Cr. ➤ *Australia* 25°35S 140°43E **62 D3**
Farrāshband *Iran* 28°57N 52°5E **45 D7**
Farrell *U.S.A.* 41°13N 80°30W **82 E4**
Farrokhī *Iran* 33°50N 59°31E **45 C8**
Farruch, C. = Ferrutx, C. de
  Spain 39°47N 3°21E **24 B10**
Farrukhabad *India* 27°24N 79°34E **43 F8**
Fārs □ *Iran* 29°30N 55°0E **45 D7**
Fārsala *Greece* 39°17N 22°23E **23 E10**
Fārsi *Iran* 27°58N 50°11E **45 E6**
Farson *U.S.A.* 42°7N 109°26W **76 E9**
Farsund *Norway* 58°5N 6°55E **9 G12**
Fartak, Râs *Si. Arabia* 28°5N 34°34E **44 D2**
Fartak, Ra's *Yemen* 15°38N 52°15E **47 D5**

Fartura, Serra da *Brazil* 26°21S 52°52W **95** B5
Fārūj *Iran* 37°14N 58°14E **45** B8
Farvel, Kap = Nunap Isua
Greenland 59°48N 43°55W **66** D15
Farwell *U.S.A.* 34°23N 103°2W **84** D3
Fāryāb □ *Afghan.* 36°0N 65°0E **40** B4
Fasā *Iran* 29°0N 53°39E **45** D7
Fasano *Italy* 40°50N 17°22E **22** D7
Fastiv *Ukraine* 50°7N 29°57E **17** C15
Fastnet Rock *Ireland* 51°22N 9°37W **10** E2
Fastov = Fastiv *Ukraine* 50°7N 29°57E **17** C15
Fatagar, Tanjung
Indonesia 2°46S 131°57E **37** E8
Fatehabad *Haryana, India* 29°31N 75°27E **42** E6
Fatehabad *Ut. P., India* 27°1N 78°19E **42** F8
Fatehgarh *India* 27°25N 79°35E **43** F8
Fatehpur *Bihar, India* 24°38N 85°14E **43** G11
Fatehpur *Raj., India* 28°0N 74°40E **42** F6
Fatehpur *Ut. P., India* 25°56N 81°13E **43** G9
Fatehpur *Ut. P., India* 27°10N 81°13E **43** F9
Fatehpur Sikri *India* 27°6N 77°40E **42** F6
Fathom Five △ *Canada* 45°17N 81°40W **82** A3
Fatima *Canada* 47°24N 61°53W **73** C7
Faulkton *U.S.A.* 45°2N 99°8W **80** C4
Faure I. *Australia* 25°52S 113°50E **61** E1
Fauresmith *S. Africa* 29°44S 25°17E **56** D4
Fauske *Norway* 67°17N 15°25E **8** C16
Favara *Italy* 37°19N 13°39E **22** F5
Favāritx, C. de *Spain* 40°0N 4°15E **24** B11
Favignana *Italy* 37°56N 12°20E **22** F5
Fawcett, Pt. *Australia* 11°46S 130°2E **60** B5
Fawn → *Canada* 55°20N 87°35W **72** A2
Fawnskin *U.S.A.* 34°16N 116°56W **79** L10
Faxaflói *Iceland* 64°29N 23°0W **8** D2
Faya-Largeau *Chad* 17°58N 19°6E **51** E9
Fayd *Si. Arabia* 27°1N 42°52E **44** E4
Fayette *Ala., U.S.A.* 33°41N 87°50W **85** E11
Fayette *Mo., U.S.A.* 39°9N 92°41W **80** F7
Fayette *N.Y., U.S.A.* 42°48N 76°48W **83** D8
Fayetteville *Ark., U.S.A.* 36°4N 94°10W **84** C7
Fayetteville *N.C., U.S.A.* 35°3N 78°53W **85** D15
Fayetteville *N.Y., U.S.A.* 43°1N 76°0W **83** C9
Fayetteville *Tenn., U.S.A.* 35°9N 86°34W **85** D11
Faylakah *Kuwait* 29°27N 48°20E **45** D6
Fazilka *India* 30°27N 74°2E **42** D6
Fazilpur *Pakistan* 29°18N 70°29E **42** E4
Fdérik *Mauritania* 22°40N 12°45W **50** D3
Feakle *Ireland* 52°56N 8°40W **10** D3
Feale → *Ireland* 52°27N 9°37W **10** D2
Fear, C. *U.S.A.* 33°50N 77°58W **85** E16
Feather → *U.S.A.* 38°47N 121°36W **76** G3
Feather Falls *U.S.A.* 39°36N 121°16W **78** F5
Featherston *N.Z.* 41°6S 175°20E **59** D5
Featherstone *Zimbabwe* 18°42S 30°55E **55** F3
Fécamp *France* 49°45N 0°22E **20** B4
Fedala = Mohammedia
Morocco 33°44N 7°21W **50** B4
Federación *Argentina* 31°0S 57°55W **94** C4
Féderal *Argentina* 30°57S 58°48W **96** C5
Federal Way *U.S.A.* 47°18N 122°19W **78** C4
Fedeshkūh *Iran* 28°49N 53°50E **45** D7
Fehmarn *Germany* 54°27N 11°7E **16** A6
Fehmarn Bælt *Europe* 54°35N 11°20E **9** J14
Fehmarn Belt = Fehmarn Bælt
Europe 54°35N 11°20E **9** J14
Fei Xian *China* 35°18N 117°59E **35** G9
Feijó *Brazil* 8°9S 70°21W **92** E4
Feilding *N.Z.* 40°13S 175°35E **59** D5
Feira de Santana *Brazil* 12°15S 38°57W **93** F11
Feixiang *China* 36°30N 114°45E **34** F8
Felanitx *Spain* 39°28N 3°9E **24** B10
Feldkirch *Austria* 47°15N 9°37E **16** E5
Félicité *Seychelles* 4°19S 55°52E **53** b
Felipe Carrillo Puerto
Mexico 19°38N 88°3W **87** D7
Felixburg *Zimbabwe* 19°29S 30°51E **57** B5
Felixstowe *U.K.* 51°58N 1°23E **13** F9
Felton *U.S.A.* 37°3N 122°4W **78** H4
Femer Bælt = Fehmarn Bælt
Europe 54°35N 11°20E **9** J14
Femunden *Norway* 62°10N 11°53E **8** E14
Fen He → *China* 35°36N 110°42E **34** G6
Fenelon Falls *Canada* 44°32N 78°45W **82** B6
Feng Xian *Jiangsu, China* 34°43N 116°35E **34** G9
Feng Xian *Shaanxi,
China* 33°54N 106°40E **34** H4
Fengcheng *China* 40°28N 124°5E **35** D13
Fengfeng *China* 36°28N 114°8E **34** F8
Fengning *China* 41°10N 116°33E **34** D9
Fengqiu *China* 35°2N 114°25E **34** G8
Fengrun *China* 39°48N 118°8E **35** E10
Fengtai *China* 39°49N 116°14E **34** E9
Fengxiang *China* 34°29N 107°25E **34** G4
Fengyang *China* 32°51N 117°29E **35** H9
Fengzhen *China* 40°25N 113°2E **34** D7
Fenoarivo *Fianarantsoa,
Madag.* 21°43S 46°24E **57** C8
Fenoarivo *Fianarantsoa,
Madag.* 20°52S 46°53E **57** C8
Fenoarivo Afovoany
Madag. 18°26S 46°34E **57** B8
Fenoarivo Atsinanana
Madag. 17°22S 49°25E **57** B8
Fens, The *U.K.* 52°38N 0°2E **13** E7
Fenton *U.S.A.* 42°48N 83°42W **81** D12
Fenxi *China* 36°40N 111°31E **34** F6
Fenyang *China* 37°18N 111°48E **34** F6
Feodosiya *Ukraine* 45°2N 35°16E **19** E6
Ferbane *Ireland* 53°16N 7°50W **10** C4
Ferdows *Iran* 33°58N 58°2E **45** C8
Ferfer *Somali Rep.* 5°4N 45°9E **47** F4
Fergana = Farghona
Uzbekistan 40°23N 71°19E **28** E8
Fergus *Canada* 43°43N 80°24W **82** C4
Fergus Falls *U.S.A.* 46°17N 96°4W **80** B5
Ferland *Canada* 50°19N 88°27W **72** B2

Ferlo, Vallée du *Senegal* 15°15N 14°15W **50** E3
Fermanagh □ *U.K.* 54°21N 7°40W **10** B4
Fermo *Italy* 43°9N 13°43E **22** C5
Fermont *Canada* 52°47N 67°5W **73** B6
Fermoy *Ireland* 52°9N 8°16W **10** D3
Fernández *Argentina* 27°55S 63°50W **94** B3
Fernandina Beach
U.S.A. 30°40N 81°27W **85** F14
Fernando de Noronha
Brazil 4°0S 33°10W **93** D12
Fernando Póo = Bioko
Eq. Guin. 3°30N 8°40E **52** D1
Ferndale *Canada* 44°58N 81°17W **82** B3
Ferndale *U.S.A.* 48°51N 122°36W **78** B4
Fernie *Canada* 49°30N 115°5W **70** D5
Fernlees *Australia* 23°51S 148°7E **62** C4
Fernley *U.S.A.* 39°36N 119°15W **76** G4
Fernwood *U.S.A.* 43°16N 73°38W **83** C11
Ferozepore = Firozpur
India 30°55N 74°40E **42** D6
Ferrara *Italy* 44°50N 11°35E **22** B4
Ferreñafe *Peru* 6°42S 79°50W **92** E3
Ferrerías *Spain* 39°59N 4°1E **24** B11
Ferret, C. *France* 44°38N 1°15W **20** D3
Ferriday *U.S.A.* 31°38N 91°33W **84** F9
Ferrol *Spain* 43°29N 8°15W **21** A1
Ferron *U.S.A.* 39°5N 111°8W **76** G8
Ferrutx, C. de *Spain* 39°47N 3°21E **24** B10
Ferryland *Canada* 47°2N 52°53W **73** C9
Fertile *U.S.A.* 47°32N 96°17W **80** B5
Fès *Morocco* 34°0N 5°0W **50** B5
Fessenden *U.S.A.* 47°39N 99°38W **80** B4
Festus *U.S.A.* 38°13N 90°24W **80** F8
Fetești *Romania* 44°22N 27°51E **17** F14
Fethiye *Turkey* 36°36N 29°6E **19** G4
Fetlar *U.K.* 60°36N 0°52W **11** A8
Feuilles → *Canada* 58°47N 70°4W **69** D12
Fez = Fès *Morocco* 34°0N 5°0W **50** B5
Fezzan *Libya* 27°0N 13°0E **51** C8
Fiambalá *Argentina* 27°45S 67°37W **94** B2
Fianarantsoa *Madag.* 21°26S 47°5E **57** C8
Fianarantsoa □ *Madag.* 19°30S 47°0E **57** B8
Ficksburg *S. Africa* 28°51S 27°53E **57** D4
Field → *Australia* 23°48S 138°0E **62** C2
Field I. *Australia* 12°5S 132°23E **60** B5
Fier *Albania* 40°43N 19°33E **23** D8
Fife □ *U.K.* 56°16N 3°1W **11** E5
Fife △ *U.K.* 56°15N 3°15W **11** E5
Fife Ness *U.K.* 56°17N 2°35W **11** E6
Fifth Cataract *Sudan* 18°22N 33°50E **51** E12
Figeac *France* 44°37N 2°2E **20** D5
Figtree *Zimbabwe* 20°22S 28°20E **55** G2
Figueira da Foz *Portugal* 40°7N 8°54W **21** B1
Figueres *Spain* 42°18N 2°58E **21** A7
Figuig *Morocco* 32°5N 1°11W **50** B5
Fihaonana *Madag.* 18°36S 47°12E **57** B8
Fiherenana *Madag.* 18°29S 48°24E **57** B8
Fiherenana → *Madag.* 23°19S 43°37E **57** C7
Fiji ■ *Pac. Oc.* 17°20S 179°0E **59** a
Filabusi *Zimbabwe* 20°34S 29°20E **57** B4
Filadelfia *Paraguay* 22°21S 60°2W **94** A3
Filchner Ice Shelf *Antarctica* 79°0S 40°0W **5** D1
Filey *U.K.* 54°12N 0°18W **12** C7
Filey B. *U.K.* 54°12N 0°15W **12** C7
Filfla *Malta* 35°47N 14°24E **25** D1
Filiatra *Greece* 37°9N 21°35E **23** F9
Filingué *Niger* 14°21N 3°22E **50** F6
Filipstad *Sweden* 59°43N 14°9E **9** G16
Fillmore *Calif., U.S.A.* 34°24N 118°55W **79** L8
Fillmore *Utah, U.S.A.* 38°58N 112°20W **76** G7
Fimbul Ice Shelf *S. Ocean* 69°30S 1°0W **5** C2
Finch *Canada* 45°11N 75°7W **83** A9
Finch Hatton *Australia* 20°25S 148°39E **62** K6
Findhorn → *U.K.* 57°38N 3°38W **11** D5
Findlay *U.S.A.* 41°2N 83°39W **81** E12
Fine *U.S.A.* 44°14N 75°8W **83** B9
Finger L. *Canada* 53°33N 93°30W **72** B1
Finger Lakes *U.S.A.* 42°40N 76°30W **83** D8
Fíngoè *Mozam.* 14°55S 31°50E **55** E3
Finisterre, C. = Fisterra, C.
Spain 42°50N 9°19W **21** A1
Finke *Australia* 25°34S 134°35E **62** D1
Finke Gorge △ *Australia* 24°8S 132°49E **60** D5
Finland ■ *Europe* 63°0N 27°0E **8** E22
Finland, G. of *Europe* 60°0N 26°0E **9** G22
Finlay → *Canada* 57°0N 125°10W **70** B3
Finley *Australia* 35°38S 145°35E **63** F4
Finley *U.S.A.* 47°31N 97°50W **80** B5
Finn → *Ireland* 54°51N 7°28W **10** B4
Finnigan, Mt. *Australia* 15°49S 145°17E **62** B4
Finniss, C. *Australia* 33°8S 134°51E **63** E1
Finnmark *Norway* 69°37N 23°57E **8** B20
Finnsnes *Norway* 69°14N 18°0E **8** B18
Finspång *Sweden* 58°43N 15°47E **9** G16
Fiora → *Italy* 42°20N 11°34E **22** C4
Fiordland △ *N.Z.* 45°46S 167°0E **59** F1
Fiq *Syria* 32°46N 35°41E **46** C4
Firat = Furāt, Nahr al →
Asia 31°0N 47°25E **44** D5
Fire Island △ *U.S.A.* 40°38N 73°8W **83** F11
Firebag → *Canada* 57°45N 111°21W **71** B6
Firebaugh *U.S.A.* 36°52N 120°27W **78** J6
Firedrake L. *Canada* 61°25N 104°30W **71** A8
Firenze *Italy* 43°46N 11°15E **22** C4
Firk, Sha'ib → *Iraq* 30°59N 44°34E **44** D5
Firozabad *India* 27°10N 78°25E **43** F8
Firozpur *India* 30°55N 74°40E **42** D6
Firozpur-Jhirka *India* 27°48N 76°57E **42** F7
Firvale *Canada* 52°27N 126°13W **70** C3
Fish → *Namibia* 28°7S 17°10E **56** D2
Fish → *S. Africa* 31°30S 20°16E **56** E3
Fish River Canyon
Namibia 27°40S 17°35E **56** D2
Fisher B. *Canada* 51°35N 97°13W **71** C9
Fishers I. *U.S.A.* 41°15N 72°0W **83** E13

Fishguard *U.K.* 52°0N 4°58W **13** E3
Fishing L. *Canada* 52°10N 95°24W **71** C9
Fisterra, C. *Spain* 42°50N 9°19W **21** A1
Fitchburg *Mass., U.S.A.* 42°35N 71°48W **83** D13
Fitchburg *Wis., U.S.A.* 42°58N 89°28W **80** D9
Fitz Roy *Argentina* 47°0S 67°0W **96** F3
Fitz Roy, Cerro *Argentina* 49°17S 73°5W **96** F2
Fitzgerald *Canada* 59°51N 111°36W **70** B6
Fitzgerald *U.S.A.* 31°43N 83°15W **85** F13
Fitzgerald River △
Australia 33°53S 119°55E **61** F3
Fitzmaurice → *Australia* 14°45S 130°5E **60** B5
Fitzroy → *Queens.,
Australia* 23°32S 150°52E **62** C5
Fitzroy → *W. Austral.,
Australia* 17°31S 123°35E **60** C3
Fitzroy Crossing
Australia 18°9S 125°38E **60** C4
Fitzwilliam I. *Canada* 45°30N 81°45W **82** A3
Fiume = Rijeka *Croatia* 45°20N 14°21E **16** F8
Five Points *U.S.A.* 36°26N 120°6W **78** J6
Fizi *Dem. Rep. of the Congo* 4°17S 28°55E **54** C2
Flagstaff *U.S.A.* 35°12N 111°39W **77** J8
Flagstaff L. *U.S.A.* 45°12N 70°18W **83** A14
Flaherty I. *Canada* 56°15N 79°15W **72** A4
Flåm *Norway* 60°50N 7°7E **8** F12
Flambeau → *U.S.A.* 45°18N 91°14W **80** C8
Flamborough Hd. *U.K.* 54°7N 0°5W **12** C7
Flaming Gorge △
U.S.A. 41°10N 109°25W **76** F9
Flaming Gorge Res.
U.S.A. 41°10N 109°25W **76** F9
Flamingo, Teluk *Indonesia* 5°30S 138°0E **37** F9
Flanders = Flandre
Europe 50°50N 2°30E **15** B9
Flandre *Europe* 50°50N 2°30E **15** B9
Flandre-Occidentale = West-
Vlaanderen □ *Belgium* 51°0N 3°0E **15** D2
Flandre-Orientale = Oost-
Vlaanderen □ *Belgium* 51°5N 3°50E **15** C3
Flandreau *U.S.A.* 44°3N 96°36W **80** C5
Flanigan *U.S.A.* 40°10N 119°53W **78** E7
Flannan Is. *U.K.* 58°9N 7°52W **11** C1
Flåsjön *Sweden* 64°5N 15°40E **8** D16
Flat → *Canada* 61°33N 125°18W **70** A3
Flat I. *Mauritius* 19°53S 57°35E **53** d
Flathead L. *U.S.A.* 47°51N 114°8W **76** C6
Flattery, C. *Australia* 14°58S 145°21E **62** A4
Flattery, C. *U.S.A.* 48°23N 124°29W **78** B2
Flatwoods *U.S.A.* 38°31N 82°43W **81** F12
Fleetwood *U.K.* 53°55N 3°1W **12** D4
Fleetwood *U.S.A.* 40°27N 75°49W **83** F9
Flekkefjord *Norway* 58°18N 6°39E **9** G12
Flemington *U.S.A.* 41°7N 77°28W **82** E7
Flensburg *Germany* 54°47N 9°27E **16** A5
Flers *France* 48°47N 0°33W **20** B3
Flesherton *Canada* 44°16N 80°33W **82** B4
Flesko, Tanjung
Indonesia 0°29N 124°30E **37** D6
Fleurieu Pen. *Australia* 35°40S 138°5E **63** F2
Flevoland □ *Neths.* 52°30N 5°30E **15** B5
Flin Flon *Canada* 54°46N 101°53W **71** C8
Flinders → *Australia* 17°36S 140°36E **62** B3
Flinders B. *Australia* 34°19S 115°19E **61** F2
Flinders Group *Australia* 14°11S 144°15E **62** A3
Flinders I. *S. Austral.,
Australia* 33°44S 134°41E **63** E1
Flinders I. *Tas., Australia* 40°0S 148°0E **63** G4
Flinders Ranges
Australia 31°30S 138°30E **63** E2
Flinders Reefs *Australia* 17°37S 148°31E **62** B4
Flint *U.K.* 53°15N 3°8W **12** D4
Flint *U.S.A.* 43°1N 83°41W **81** D12
Flint → *U.S.A.* 30°57N 84°34W **85** F12
Flint I. *Kiribati* 11°26S 151°48W **65** J12
Flintshire □ *U.K.* 53°17N 3°17W **12** D4
Flodden *U.K.* 55°37N 2°8W **12** B5
Floodwood *U.S.A.* 46°56N 92°55W **80** B7
Flora *U.S.A.* 38°40N 88°29W **80** F9
Florala *U.S.A.* 31°0N 86°20W **85** F11
Florence = Firenze *Italy* 43°46N 11°15E **22** C4
Florence *Ala., U.S.A.* 34°48N 87°41W **85** D11
Florence *Ariz., U.S.A.* 33°2N 111°23W **77** K8
Florence *Colo., U.S.A.* 38°23N 105°8W **76** G11
Florence *Oreg., U.S.A.* 43°58N 124°7W **76** D1
Florence *S.C., U.S.A.* 34°12N 79°46W **85** D15
Florence, L. *Australia* 28°53S 138°9E **63** D2
Florencia *Colombia* 1°36N 75°36W **92** C3
Florennes *Belgium* 50°15N 4°35E **15** D4
Florenville *Belgium* 49°40N 5°19E **15** E5
Flores *Azores* 39°26N 31°13W **50** a
Flores *Guatemala* 16°59N 89°50W **88** C2
Flores *Indonesia* 8°35S 121°0E **37** F6
Flores I. *Canada* 49°20N 126°10W **70** D3
Flores Sea *Indonesia* 6°30S 120°0E **37** F6
Floreşti *Moldova* 47°53N 28°17E **17** E15
Floresville *U.S.A.* 29°8N 98°10W **84** G5
Floriano *Brazil* 6°50S 43°0W **93** E10
Florianópolis *Brazil* 27°30S 48°30W **95** B6
Florida *Cuba* 21°32N 78°14W **88** B4
Florida *Uruguay* 34°7S 56°10W **95** C4
Florida □ *U.S.A.* 28°0N 82°0W **85** G14
Florida, Straits of *U.S.A.* 25°0N 80°0W **88** B4
Florida Keys *U.S.A.* 24°40N 81°0W **85** J14
Florin *U.S.A.* 38°30N 121°24W **78** G5
Florina *Greece* 40°48N 21°26E **23** D9
Florissant *U.S.A.* 38°47N 90°19W **80** F8
Florø *Norway* 61°35N 5°1E **8** F11
Flower Station *Canada* 45°10N 76°41W **83** A8
Flowerpot I. *Canada* 45°18N 81°38W **82** A3
Floydada *U.S.A.* 33°59N 101°20W **84** E4
Fluk *Indonesia* 1°42S 127°44E **37** E7
Flushing = Vlissingen
Neths. 51°26N 3°34E **15** C3
Fly → *Papua N. G.* 8°25S 143°0E **58** B7

Flying Fish, C. *Antarctica* 72°6S 102°29W **5** D15
Foa *Tonga* 19°45S 174°18W **59** c
Foam Lake *Canada* 51°40N 103°32W **71** C8
Foça *Turkey* 38°39N 26°46E **23** E12
Fochabers *U.K.* 57°37N 3°6W **11** D5
Focșani *Romania* 45°41N 27°15E **17** F14
Fóggia *Italy* 41°27N 15°34E **22** D6
Fogo *Canada* 49°43N 54°17W **73** C9
Fogo *C. Verde Is.* 15°5N 24°20W **50** b
Fogo I. *Canada* 49°40N 54°5W **73** C9
Föhr *Germany* 54°43N 8°30E **16** A5
Foix *France* 42°58N 1°38E **20** E4
Folda *Nord-Trøndelag,
Norway* 64°32N 10°30E **8** D14
Folda *Nordland, Norway* 67°38N 14°50E **8** C16
Foley *Botswana* 21°34S 27°21E **56** C4
Foley *U.S.A.* 30°24N 87°41W **85** F11
Foleyet *Canada* 48°15N 82°25W **72** C3
Folgefonna *Norway* 60°3N 6°23E **9** F12
Foligno *Italy* 42°57N 12°42E **22** C5
Folkestone *U.K.* 51°5N 1°12E **13** F9
Folkston *U.S.A.* 30°50N 82°0W **85** F13
Follansbee *U.S.A.* 40°19N 80°35W **82** F4
Folsom L. *U.S.A.* 38°42N 121°9W **78** G5
Fomboni *Comoros Is.* 12°18S 43°46E **53** a
Fond-du-Lac *Canada* 59°19N 107°12W **71** B7
Fond du Lac *U.S.A.* 43°47N 88°27W **80** D9
Fond-du-Lac → *Canada* 59°17N 106°0W **71** B7
Fonda *U.S.A.* 42°57N 74°22W **83** D10
Fondi *Italy* 41°21N 13°25E **22** D5
Fongafale *Tuvalu* 8°31S 179°13E **58** B10
Fonsagrada = A Fonsagrada
Spain 43°8N 7°4W **21** A2
Fonseca, G. de
Cent. Amer. 13°10N 87°40W **88** D2
Fontainebleau *France* 48°24N 2°40E **20** B5
Fontana *U.S.A.* 34°6N 117°26W **79** L9
Fontas → *Canada* 58°14N 121°48W **70** B4
Fonte Boa *Brazil* 2°33S 66°0W **92** D5
Fontenay-le-Comte
France 46°28N 0°48W **20** C3
Fontenelle Res. *U.S.A.* 42°1N 110°3W **76** E8
Fontur *Iceland* 66°23N 14°32W **8** C6
Fonuafo'ou *Tonga* 20°19S 175°25W **59** c
Fonualei *Tonga* 18°1S 174°19W **59** c
Foochow = Fuzhou
China 26°5N 119°16E **33** D6
Foping *China* 33°41N 108°0E **34** H5
Forbes *Australia* 33°22S 148°5E **63** E4
Forbesganj *India* 26°17N 87°18E **43** F12
Ford City *Calif., U.S.A.* 35°9N 119°27W **79** K7
Ford City *Pa., U.S.A.* 40°46N 79°32W **82** F5
Førde *Norway* 61°27N 5°53E **8** F11
Fords Bridge *Australia* 29°41S 145°29E **63** D4
Fordyce *U.S.A.* 33°49N 92°25W **84** E8
Forel, Mt. *Greenland* 66°52N 36°55W **66** C16
Foremost *Canada* 49°26N 111°34W **70** D6
Forest *Canada* 43°6N 82°0W **82** C3
Forest *U.S.A.* 32°22N 89°29W **85** E10
Forest City *Iowa, U.S.A.* 43°16N 93°39W **80** D7
Forest City *N.C., U.S.A.* 35°20N 81°52W **85** D14
Forest City *Pa., U.S.A.* 41°39N 75°28W **83** E9
Forest Grove *U.S.A.* 45°31N 123°7W **78** E3
Forestburg *Canada* 52°35N 112°1W **70** C6
Foresthill *U.S.A.* 39°1N 120°49W **78** F6
Forestier Pen. *Australia* 43°0S 148°0E **63** G4
Forestville *Canada* 48°48N 69°2W **73** C6
Forestville *Calif., U.S.A.* 38°28N 122°54W **78** G4
Forestville *N.Y., U.S.A.* 42°28N 79°10W **82** D5
Forfar *U.K.* 56°39N 2°53W **11** E6
Forillon △ *Canada* 48°46N 64°12W **73** C7
Forks *U.S.A.* 47°57N 124°23W **78** C2
Forksville *U.S.A.* 41°29N 76°35W **83** E8
Forlì *Italy* 44°13N 12°3E **22** B5
Forman *U.S.A.* 46°7N 97°38W **80** B5
Formby Pt. *U.K.* 53°33N 3°6W **12** D4
Formentera *Spain* 38°43N 1°27E **24** C7
Formentor, C. de *Spain* 39°58N 3°13E **24** B10
Formentor, Pen. de
Spain 39°56N 3°11E **24** B10
Former Yugoslav Republic of
Macedonia = Macedonia ■
Europe 41°53N 21°40E **23** D9
Fórmia *Italy* 41°15N 13°37E **22** D5
Formosa = Taiwan ■
Asia 23°30N 121°0E **33** D7
Formosa *Argentina* 26°15S 58°10W **94** B4
Formosa *Brazil* 15°32S 47°20W **93** G9
Formosa □ *Argentina* 25°0S 60°0W **94** B4
Formosa, Serra *Brazil* 12°0S 55°0W **93** F8
Formosa B. = Ungwana B.
Kenya 2°45S 40°20E **54** C5
Fornells *Spain* 40°3N 4°7E **24** A11
Føroyar ☑ *Atl. Oc.* 62°0N 7°0W **8** f9
Forres *U.K.* 57°37N 3°37W **11** D5
Forrest *Australia* 30°51S 128°6E **61** F4
Forrest, Mt. *Australia* 24°48S 127°45E **61** D4
Forrest City *U.S.A.* 35°1N 90°47W **85** D9
Forsayth *Australia* 18°33S 143°34E **62** B3
Forssa *Finland* 60°49N 23°38E **8** F20
Forst *Germany* 51°45N 14°37E **16** C8
Forster *Australia* 32°12S 152°31E **63** E5
Forsyth *U.S.A.* 46°16N 106°41W **76** C10
Fort Abbas *Pakistan* 29°12N 72°52E **42** E5
Fort Albany *Canada* 52°15N 81°35W **72** B3
Fort Assiniboine
Canada 54°20N 114°45W **70** C6
Fort Augustus *U.K.* 57°9N 4°42W **11** D4
Fort Beaufort *S. Africa* 32°46S 26°40E **56** E4
Fort Benton *U.S.A.* 47°49N 110°40W **76** C8
Fort Bragg *U.S.A.* 39°26N 123°48W **76** G2
Fort Bridger *U.S.A.* 41°19N 110°23W **76** F8
Fort Chipewyan *Canada* 58°42N 111°8W **70** B6
Fort Clatsop *U.S.A.* 46°8N 123°53W **78** D3
Fort Collins *U.S.A.* 40°35N 105°5W **76** F11
Fort-Coulonge *Canada* 45°50N 76°45W **72** C4
Fort Covington *U.S.A.* 44°59N 74°29W **83** B10

Fort Dauphin = Taolanaro
Madag. 25°2S 47°0E **57** D8
Fort Davis *U.S.A.* 30°35N 103°54W **84** F3
Fort-de-France *Martinique* 14°36N 61°2W **88** c
Fort Defiance *U.S.A.* 35°45N 109°5W **77** J9
Fort Dodge *U.S.A.* 42°30N 94°11W **80** D6
Fort Edward *U.S.A.* 43°16N 73°35W **83** C11
Fort Erie *Canada* 42°54N 78°56W **82** D6
Fort Fairfield *U.S.A.* 46°46N 67°50W **81** B20
Fort Frances *Canada* 48°36N 93°24W **71** D10
Fort Franklin = Déline
Canada 65°11N 123°25W **68** C7
Fort Garland *U.S.A.* 37°26N 105°26W **77** H11
Fort George = Chisasibi
Canada 53°50N 79°0W **72** B4
Fort Good Hope *Canada* 66°14N 128°40W **68** C7
Fort Hancock *U.S.A.* 31°18N 105°51W **84** F2
Fort Hope = Eabametoong
Canada 51°30N 88°0W **72** B2
Fort Irwin *U.S.A.* 35°16N 116°41W **79** K10
Fort Kent *U.S.A.* 47°15N 68°36W **81** B19
Fort Klamath *U.S.A.* 42°42N 122°0W **76** E3
Fort Laramie *U.S.A.* 42°13N 104°31W **76** E11
Fort Lauderdale *U.S.A.* 26°7N 80°8W **85** H14
Fort Liard *Canada* 60°14N 123°30W **70** A4
Fort Liberté *Haiti* 19°42N 71°51W **89** C5
Fort Lupton *U.S.A.* 40°5N 104°49W **76** F11
Fort MacKay *Canada* 57°12N 111°41W **70** B6
Fort Macleod *Canada* 49°45N 113°30W **70** D6
Fort McMurray *Canada* 56°44N 111°7W **70** B6
Fort McPherson
Canada 67°30N 134°55W **68** C6
Fort Madison *U.S.A.* 40°38N 91°27W **80** E8
Fort Meade *U.S.A.* 27°45N 81°48W **85** H14
Fort Morgan *U.S.A.* 40°15N 103°48W **76** F12
Fort Myers *U.S.A.* 26°39N 81°52W **85** H14
Fort Nelson *Canada* 58°50N 122°44W **70** B4
Fort Nelson → *Canada* 59°32N 124°0W **70** B4
Fort Norman = Tulita
Canada 64°57N 125°30W **68** C7
Fort Payne *U.S.A.* 34°26N 85°43W **85** D12
Fort Peck *U.S.A.* 48°1N 106°27W **76** B10
Fort Peck Dam *U.S.A.* 48°0N 106°26W **76** C10
Fort Peck L. *U.S.A.* 48°0N 106°26W **76** C10
Fort Pierce *U.S.A.* 27°27N 80°20W **85** H14
Fort Pierre *U.S.A.* 44°21N 100°22W **80** C3
Fort Plain *U.S.A.* 42°56N 74°37W **83** D10
Fort Portal *Uganda* 0°40N 30°20E **54** B3
Fort Providence *Canada* 61°3N 117°40W **70** A5
Fort Qu'Appelle
Canada 50°45N 103°50W **71** C8
Fort Resolution *Canada* 61°10N 113°40W **70** A6
Fort Rixon *Zimbabwe* 20°2S 29°17E **55** G2
Fort Ross *U.S.A.* 38°32N 123°13W **78** G3
Fort Rupert = Waskaganish
Canada 51°30N 78°40W **72** B4
Fort St. James *Canada* 54°30N 124°10W **70** C4
Fort St. John *Canada* 56°15N 120°50W **70** B4
Fort Saskatchewan
Canada 53°40N 113°15W **70** C6
Fort Scott *U.S.A.* 37°50N 94°42W **80** G7
Fort Severn *Canada* 56°0N 87°40W **72** A2
Fort Shevchenko
Kazakhstan 44°35N 50°23E **19** F9
Fort Simpson *Canada* 61°45N 121°15W **70** A4
Fort Smith *Canada* 60°0N 111°51W **70** B6
Fort Smith *U.S.A.* 35°23N 94°25W **84** D7
Fort Stockton *U.S.A.* 30°53N 102°53W **84** F3
Fort Sumner *U.S.A.* 34°28N 104°15W **77** J11
Fort Thompson *U.S.A.* 44°3N 99°26W **80** C4
Fort Union *U.S.A.* 35°54N 105°1W **77** J11
Fort Valley *U.S.A.* 32°33N 83°53W **85** E13
Fort Vermilion *Canada* 58°24N 116°0W **70** B5
Fort Walton Beach
U.S.A. 30°25N 86°36W **85** F11
Fort Ware *Canada* 57°26N 125°41W **70** B3
Fort Wayne *U.S.A.* 41°4N 85°9W **81** E11
Fort William *U.K.* 56°49N 5°7W **11** E3
Fort Worth *U.S.A.* 32°43N 97°19W **84** E6
Fort Yates *U.S.A.* 46°5N 100°38W **80** B3
Fort Yukon *U.S.A.* 66°34N 145°16W **74** a
Fortaleza *Brazil* 3°45S 38°35W **93** D11
Forteau *Canada* 51°28N 56°58W **73** B8
Fortescue → *Australia* 21°0S 116°4E **60** D2
Forth → *U.K.* 56°9N 3°50W **11** E5
Forth, Firth of *U.K.* 56°5N 2°55W **11** E6
Fortrose *U.K.* 57°35N 4°9W **11** D4
Fortuna *Calif., U.S.A.* 40°36N 124°9W **76** F1
Fortuna *N. Dak., U.S.A.* 48°55N 103°47W **80** A2
Fortune *Canada* 47°4N 55°50W **73** C8
Fortune B. *Canada* 47°30N 55°22W **73** C8
Forūr *Iran* 26°17N 54°32E **45** E7
Fosen *Norway* 63°50N 10°20E **8** E14
Foshan *China* 23°4N 113°5E **33** D6
Fosnavåg *Norway* 62°22N 5°38E **8** E11
Fossano *Italy* 44°33N 7°43E **20** D7
Fossil *U.S.A.* 45°0N 120°9W **76** D3
Fossil Butte △ *U.S.A.* 41°50N 110°27W **76** F8
Foster *Canada* 45°17N 72°30W **83** A12
Foster → *Canada* 55°47N 105°49W **71** B7
Fosters Ra. *Australia* 21°35S 133°48E **62** C1
Fostoria *U.S.A.* 41°10N 83°25W **81** E12
Fotadrevo *Madag.* 24°3S 45°1E **57** C8
Fougères *France* 48°21N 1°14W **20** B3
Foul Pt. *Sri Lanka* 8°35N 81°18E **40** Q12
Foula *U.K.* 60°10N 2°5W **11** A6
Foulness I. *U.K.* 51°36N 0°55E **13** F8
Foulpointe *Madag.* 17°41S 49°31E **57** B8
Foumban *Cameroon* 5°45N 10°50E **52** C2
Foumbouni *Comoros Is.* 11°51S 43°29E **53** a
Fountain *U.S.A.* 38°41N 104°42W **76** G11
Fountain Hills *U.S.A.* 33°37N 111°43W **77** K8
Fountain Springs
U.S.A. 35°54N 118°51W **79** K8
Fouriesburg *S. Africa* 28°38S 28°14E **56** D4
Fourni *Greece* 37°36N 26°32E **23** F12
Fourth Cataract *Sudan* 18°47N 32°3E **51** E12

Fouta Djallon *Guinea* 11°20N 12°10W **50** F3
Foux, Cap-à- *Haiti* 19°43N 73°27W **89** C5
Foveaux Str. *N.Z.* 46°42S 168°10E **59** G2
Fowey *U.K.* 50°20N 4°39W **13** G3
Fowler *Calif., U.S.A.* 36°38N 119°41W **78** J7
Fowler *Colo., U.S.A.* 38°8N 104°2W **76** G11
Fowler, Pt. *Australia* 32°2S 132°3E **61** F5
Fowman *Iran* 37°13N 49°19E **45** B6
Fox → *Canada* 56°3N 93°18W **71** B10
Fox Creek *Canada* 54°24N 116°48W **70** C5
Fox Lake *Canada* 58°28N 114°31W **70** B6
Fox Valley *Canada* 50°30N 109°25W **71** C7
Foxboro *Canada* 44°14N 77°26W **82** B7
Foxboro *U.S.A.* 42°4N 71°16W **83** D13
Foxdale *Australia* 20°22S 148°35E **62** J6
Foxe Basin *Canada* 66°0N 77°0W **69** C12
Foxe Chan. *Canada* 65°0N 80°0W **69** C12
Foxe Pen. *Canada* 65°0N 76°0W **69** C12
Foxford *Ireland* 53°59N 9°7W **10** C2
Foxton *N.Z.* 40°29S 175°18E **59** D5
Foyle, Lough *U.K.* 55°7N 7°4W **10** A4
Foynes *Ireland* 52°37N 9°7W **10** D2
Foz do Cunene *Angola* 17°15S 11°48E **56** B1
Foz do Iguaçu *Brazil* 25°30S 54°30W **95** B5
Frackville *U.S.A.* 40°47N 76°14W **83** F8
Fraile Muerto *Uruguay* 32°31S 54°32W **95** C5
Framingham *U.S.A.* 42°18N 71°24W **83** D13
Franca *Brazil* 20°33S 47°30W **93** H9
Francavilla Fontana
Italy 40°32N 17°35E **23** D7
France ■ *Europe* 47°0N 3°0E **20** C5
Frances *Australia* 36°41S 140°55E **63** F3
Frances → *Canada* 60°16N 129°10W **70** A3
Frances L. *Canada* 61°23N 129°30W **70** A3
Franceville *Gabon* 1°40S 13°32E **52** E2
Franche-Comté □ *France* 46°50N 5°55E **20** C6
Francis Case, L. *U.S.A.* 43°4N 98°34W **80** D5
Francisco Beltrão *Brazil* 26°5S 53°4W **95** B5
Francisco Ignacio Madero
Coahuila, Mexico 25°48N 103°18W **86** B4
Francisco Ignacio Madero *Durango,*
Mexico 24°26N 104°18W **86** C4
Francisco Ignacio Madero, Presa
Mexico 28°10N 105°37W **86** B3
Francistown *Botswana* 21°7S 27°33E **57** C4
François *Canada* 47°35N 56°45W **73** C8
François L. *Canada* 54°0N 125°30W **70** C3
Francois Peron △
Australia 25°42S 113°33E **61** E1
Francs Pk. *U.S.A.* 43°58N 109°20W **76** E9
Franeker *Neths.* 53°12N 5°33E **15** A5
Frank Hann △ *Australia* 32°52S 120°19E **61** F3
Frankford *Canada* 44°12N 77°36W **82** B7
Frankford *S. Africa* 27°17S 28°30E **57** D4
Frankfort *Ind., U.S.A.* 40°17N 86°31W **80** E10
Frankfort *Kans., U.S.A.* 39°42N 96°25W **80** F6
Frankfort *Ky., U.S.A.* 38°12N 84°52W **81** F11
Frankfort *N.Y., U.S.A.* 43°2N 75°4W **83** C9
Frankfurt *Brandenburg,*
Germany 52°20N 14°32E **16** B8
Frankfurt *Hessen, Germany* 50°7N 8°41E **16** C5
Fränkische Alb *Germany* 49°10N 11°23E **16** D6
Frankland → *Australia* 35°0S 116°48E **61** G2
Franklin *Ky., U.S.A.* 36°43N 86°35W **80** G10
Franklin *La., U.S.A.* 29°48N 91°30W **84** G9
Franklin *Mass., U.S.A.* 42°5N 71°24W **83** D13
Franklin *N.H., U.S.A.* 43°27N 71°39W **83** C13
Franklin *N.Y., U.S.A.* 42°20N 75°9W **83** D9
Franklin *Nebr., U.S.A.* 40°6N 98°57W **80** E4
Franklin *Pa., U.S.A.* 41°24N 79°50W **82** E5
Franklin *Va., U.S.A.* 36°41N 76°56W **81** G15
Franklin *W. Va., U.S.A.* 38°39N 79°20W **81** F14
Franklin B. *Canada* 69°45N 126°0W **68** C7
Franklin D. Roosevelt L.
U.S.A. 48°18N 118°9W **76** B4
Franklin-Gordon Wild Rivers △
Australia 42°19S 145°51E **63** G4
Franklin I. *Antarctica* 76°10S 168°30E **5** D11
Franklin I. *Canada* 45°24N 80°20W **82** A4
Franklin L. *U.S.A.* 40°25N 115°22W **76** F6
Franklin Mts. *Canada* 65°0N 125°0W **68** B7
Franklin Str. *Canada* 72°0N 96°0W **68** B10
Franklinton *U.S.A.* 30°51N 90°9W **85** F9
Franklinville *U.S.A.* 42°20N 78°27W **82** D6
Frankston *Australia* 38°8S 145°8E **63** F4
Fransfontein *Namibia* 20°12S 15°1E **56** C2
Frantsa Iosifa, Zemlya
Russia 82°0N 55°0E **28** A6
Franz *Canada* 48°25N 84°30W **72** C3
Franz Josef Land = Frantsa Iosifa,
Zemlya *Russia* 82°0N 55°0E **28** A6
Fraser *U.S.A.* 42°32N 82°57W **82** D2
Fraser → *B.C., Canada* 49°7N 123°11W **78** A3
Fraser → *Nfld. & L.,*
Canada 56°39N 62°10W **73** A7
Fraser, Mt. *Australia* 25°35S 118°20E **61** E2
Fraser I. *Australia* 25°15S 153°10E **63** D5
Fraser Lake *Canada* 54°0N 124°50W **70** C4
Fraserburg *S. Africa* 31°55S 21°30E **56** E3
Fraserburgh *U.K.* 57°42N 2°1W **11** D6
Fraserdale *Canada* 49°55N 81°37W **72** C3
Fray Bentos *Uruguay* 33°10S 58°15W **94** C4
Fray Jorge △ *Chile* 30°42S 71°40W **94** C1
Fredericia *Denmark* 55°34N 9°45E **9** J13
Frederick *Md., U.S.A.* 39°25N 77°25W **81** F15
Frederick *Okla., U.S.A.* 34°23N 99°1W **84** D5
Frederick *S. Dak., U.S.A.* 45°50N 98°31W **80** C4
Fredericksburg *Pa.,*
U.S.A. 40°27N 76°26W **83** F8
Fredericksburg *Tex.,*
U.S.A. 30°16N 98°52W **84** F5
Fredericksburg *Va.,*
U.S.A. 38°18N 77°28W **81** F15
Fredericktown *Mo.,*
U.S.A. 37°34N 90°18W **80** G8
Fredericktown *Ohio,*
U.S.A. 40°29N 82°33W **82** F2

Frederico Westphalen
Brazil 27°22S 53°24W **95** B5
Fredericton *Canada* 45°57N 66°40W **73** C6
Fredericton Junction
Canada 45°41N 66°40W **73** C6
Frederikshåb = Paamiut
Greenland 62°0N 49°43W **4** C5
Frederikshamn = Hamina
Finland 60°34N 27°12E **8** F22
Frederikshavn *Denmark* 57°28N 10°31E **9** H14
Frederiksted
U.S. Virgin Is. 17°43N 64°53W **89** C7
Fredonia *Ariz., U.S.A.* 36°57N 112°32W **77** H7
Fredonia *Kans., U.S.A.* 37°32N 95°49W **80** G6
Fredonia *N.Y., U.S.A.* 42°26N 79°20W **82** D5
Fredrikstad *Norway* 59°13N 10°57E **9** G14
Free State □ *S. Africa* 28°30S 27°0E **56** D4
Freehold *U.S.A.* 40°16N 74°17W **83** F10
Freeland *U.S.A.* 41°1N 75°54W **83** E9
Freels, C. *Nfld. & L.,*
Canada 49°15N 53°30W **73** C9
Freels, C. *Nfld. & L.,*
Canada 46°37N 53°32W **73** C9
Freeman *Calif., U.S.A.* 35°35N 117°53W **79** K9
Freeman *S. Dak., U.S.A.* 43°21N 97°26W **80** D5
Freeport *Bahamas* 26°30N 78°47W **88** A4
Freeport *Ill., U.S.A.* 42°17N 89°36W **80** D9
Freeport *N.Y., U.S.A.* 40°39N 73°35W **83** F11
Freeport *Ohio, U.S.A.* 40°12N 81°15W **82** F3
Freeport *Pa., U.S.A.* 40°41N 79°41W **82** F5
Freeport *Tex., U.S.A.* 28°57N 95°21W **84** G7
Freetown *S. Leone* 8°30N 13°17W **50** G3
Freeville *U.S.A.* 42°30N 76°20W **83** D8
Frégate, L. de la *Canada* 53°15N 74°45W **72** B5
Fregenal de la Sierra
Spain 38°10N 6°39W **21** C2
Freibourg = Fribourg
Switz. 46°49N 7°9E **20** C7
Freiburg *Germany* 47°59N 7°51E **16** E4
Freire *Chile* 38°54S 72°38W **96** D2
Freirina *Chile* 28°30S 71°10W **94** B1
Freising *Germany* 48°24N 11°45E **16** D6
Freistadt *Austria* 48°30N 14°30E **16** D8
Fréjus *France* 43°25N 6°44E **20** E7
Fremantle *Australia* 32°7S 115°47E **61** F2
Fremont *Calif., U.S.A.* 37°32N 121°57W **78** H4
Fremont *Mich., U.S.A.* 43°28N 85°57W **81** D11
Fremont *Nebr., U.S.A.* 41°26N 96°30W **80** E5
Fremont *Ohio, U.S.A.* 41°21N 83°7W **81** E12
Fremont → *U.S.A.* 38°24N 110°42W **76** G8
French Camp *U.S.A.* 37°53N 121°16W **78** H5
French Cays = Plana Cays
Bahamas 22°38N 73°30W **89** B5
French Creek → *U.S.A.* 41°24N 79°50W **82** E5
French Guiana ☑ *S. Amer.* 4°0N 53°0W **93** C8
French Polynesia ☑
Pac. Oc. 20°0S 145°0W **65** J13
Frenchman Cr. →
N. Amer. 48°31N 107°10W **76** B10
Frenchman Cr. →
U.S.A. 40°14N 100°50W **80** E3
Fresco → *Brazil* 7°15S 51°30W **93** E8
Freshfield, C. *Antarctica* 68°25S 151°10E **5** C10
Fresnillo *Mexico* 23°10N 102°53W **86** C4
Fresno *U.S.A.* 36°44N 119°47W **78** J7
Fresno Res. *U.S.A.* 48°36N 109°57W **76** B9
Frew → *Australia* 20°0S 135°38E **62** C2
Frewsburg *U.S.A.* 42°3N 79°10W **82** D5
Freycinet ☑ *Australia* 42°11S 148°19E **63** G4
Freycinet Pen. *Australia* 42°10S 148°25E **63** G4
Fria *Guinea* 10°27N 13°38W **50** F3
Fria, C. *Namibia* 18°0S 12°0E **56** B1
Friant *U.S.A.* 36°59N 119°43W **78** J7
Frías *Argentina* 28°40S 65°5W **94** B2
Fribourg *Switz.* 46°49N 7°9E **20** C7
Friday Harbor *U.S.A.* 48°32N 123°1W **78** B3
Friedens *U.S.A.* 40°3N 78°59W **82** F6
Friedrichshafen *Germany* 47°39N 9°30E **16** E5
Friendship *U.S.A.* 42°12N 78°8W **82** D6
Friesland □ *Neths.* 53°5N 5°50E **15** A5
Frigate *Seychelles* 4°35S 55°56E **53** b
Frío → *U.S.A.* 28°26N 98°11W **84** G5
Frio, C. *Brazil* 22°50S 41°50W **90** F6
Friona *U.S.A.* 34°38N 102°43W **84** D3
Fritch *U.S.A.* 35°38N 101°36W **84** D4
Frobisher B. *Canada* 62°30N 66°0W **69** C13
Frobisher Bay = Iqaluit
Canada 63°44N 68°31W **69** C13
Frobisher L. *Canada* 56°20N 108°15W **71** B7
Frohavet *Norway* 64°0N 9°30E **8** E13
Frome *U.K.* 51°14N 2°19W **13** F5
Frome → *U.K.* 50°41N 2°6W **13** G5
Frome, L. *Australia* 30°45S 139°45E **63** E2
Front Range *U.S.A.* 40°25N 105°45W **74** C5
Front Royal *U.S.A.* 38°55N 78°12W **81** F14
Frontenac △ *Canada* 44°32N 76°30W **83** B8
Frontera *Canary Is.* 27°47N 17°59W **24** G2
Frontera *Mexico* 18°32N 92°38W **87** D6
Fronteras *Mexico* 30°56N 109°31W **86** A3
Frosinone *Italy* 41°38N 13°19E **22** D5
Frostburg *U.S.A.* 39°39N 78°56W **81** F14
Frostisen *Norway* 68°14N 17°10E **8** B17
Froya *Norway* 63°43N 8°40E **8** E13
Frunze = Bishkek
Kyrgyzstan 42°54N 74°46E **28** E8
Frutal *Brazil* 20°0S 49°0W **93** H9
Frýdek-Místek
Czech Rep. 49°40N 18°20E **17** D10
Fryeburg *U.S.A.* 44°1N 70°59W **83** B14
Fu Xian = Wafangdian
China 39°38N 121°58E **35** E11
Fu Xian *China* 36°0N 109°20E **34** G5
Fucheng *China* 37°50N 116°10E **34** F9
Fuchou = Fuzhou *China* 26°5N 119°16E **33** D6
Fuchū *Japan* 34°34N 133°14E **31** G6
Fuencaliente *Canary Is.* 28°28N 17°50W **24** F2
Fuencaliente, Pta.
Canary Is. 28°27N 17°51W **24** F2

Fuengirola *Spain* 36°32N 4°41W **21** D3
Fuentes de Oñoro *Spain* 40°33N 6°52W **21** B2
Fuerte → *Mexico* 25°54N 109°22W **86** B3
Fuerte Olimpo *Paraguay* 21°0S 57°51W **94** A4
Fuerteventura *Canary Is.* 28°30N 14°0W **24** F6
Fuerteventura ✈ (FUE)
Canary Is. 28°24N 13°52W **24** F6
Fufeng *China* 34°22N 108°0E **34** G5
Fugou *China* 34°3N 114°25E **34** G8
Fugu *China* 39°2N 111°3E **34** E6
Fuhai *China* 47°2N 87°25E **32** B3
Fuḥaymī *Iraq* 34°16N 42°10E **44** C4
Fuji *Japan* 35°9N 138°39E **31** G9
Fuji-Hakone-Izu △
Japan 35°15N 138°45E **31** G9
Fuji-San *Japan* 35°22N 138°44E **31** G9
Fuji-Yoshida *Japan* 35°30N 138°46E **31** G9
Fujian □ *China* 26°0N 118°0E **33** D6
Fujinomiya *Japan* 35°10N 138°40E **31** G9
Fujisawa *Japan* 35°22N 139°29E **31** G9
Fujiyama, Mt. = Fuji-San
Japan 35°22N 138°44E **31** G9
Fukagawa *Japan* 43°43N 142°2E **30** C11
Fukien = Fujian □ *China* 26°0N 118°0E **33** D6
Fukuchiyama *Japan* 35°19N 135°9E **31** G7
Fukue-Shima *Japan* 32°40N 128°45E **31** H4
Fukui *Japan* 36°5N 136°10E **31** F8
Fukui □ *Japan* 36°0N 136°12E **31** G8
Fukuoka *Japan* 33°39N 130°21E **31** H5
Fukuoka □ *Japan* 33°30N 131°0E **31** H5
Fukushima *Japan* 37°44N 140°28E **30** F10
Fukushima □ *Japan* 37°30N 140°15E **30** F10
Fukuyama *Japan* 34°35N 133°20E **31** G6
Fulaga *Fiji* 19°8S 178°33W **59** a
Fulda *U.S.A.* 43°52N 95°36W **80** D6
Fulda *Germany* 50°32N 9°40E **16** C5
Fulda → *Germany* 51°25N 9°39E **16** C5
Fulford Harbour
Canada 48°47N 123°27W **78** B3
Fullerton *Calif., U.S.A.* 33°53N 117°56W **79** M9
Fullerton *Nebr., U.S.A.* 41°22N 97°58W **80** E5
Fulongquan *China* 44°20N 124°42E **35** B13
Fulton *Mo., U.S.A.* 38°52N 91°57W **80** F8
Fulton *N.Y., U.S.A.* 43°19N 76°25W **83** C8
Funabashi *Japan* 35°45N 140°0E **31** G10
Funafuti = Fongafale
Tuvalu 8°31S 179°13E **58** B10
Funchal *Madeira* 32°38N 16°54W **24** D3
Funchal ✈ (FNC)
Madeira 32°42N 16°45W **24** D3
Fundación *Colombia* 10°31N 74°11W **92** A4
Fundão *Portugal* 40°8N 7°30W **21** B2
Fundy, B. of *Canada* 45°0N 66°0W **73** D6
Fundy △ *Canada* 45°35N 65°10W **73** C6
Funhalouro *Mozam.* 23°3S 34°25E **57** C5
Funing *Hebei, China* 39°53N 119°12E **35** E10
Funing *Jiangsu, China* 33°45N 119°50E **35** H10
Funiu Shan *China* 33°30N 112°20E **34** H7
Funtua *Nigeria* 11°30N 7°18E **50** F7
Fuping *Hebei, China* 38°48N 114°12E **34** E8
Fuping *Shaanxi, China* 34°42N 109°10E **34** G5
Furano *Japan* 43°21N 142°23E **30** C11
Furāt, Nahr al → *Asia* 31°0N 47°25E **44** D5
Fürg *Iran* 28°18N 55°13E **45** D7
Furnás *Spain* 39°3N 1°32E **24** B8
Furnas, Represa de
Brazil 20°50S 45°30W **95** A6
Furneaux Group
Australia 40°10S 147°50E **63** G4
Furqlus *Syria* 34°36N 37°8E **46** A6
Fürstenwalde *Germany* 52°22N 14°3E **16** B8
Fürth *Germany* 49°28N 10°59E **16** D6
Furukawa *Japan* 38°34N 140°58E **30** E10
Fury and Hecla Str.
Canada 69°56N 84°0W **69** C11
Fusagasugá *Colombia* 4°21N 74°22W **92** C4
Fushan *Shandong,*
China 37°30N 121°15E **35** F11
Fushan *Shanxi, China* 35°58N 111°51E **34** G6
Fushun *China* 41°50N 123°56E **35** D12
Fusong *China* 42°20N 127°15E **35** C14
Futian *China* 22°32N 114°4E **33** F11
Fuxin *China* 42°5N 121°48E **35** C11
Fuyang *China* 33°0N 115°48E **34** H8
Fuyang He → *China* 38°12N 117°0E **34** E9
Fuyong *China* 22°42N 113°49E **33** F10
Fuyu *Heilongjiang, China* 47°49N 124°27E **33** B7
Fuyu *Jilin, China* 45°12N 124°43E **35** B13
Fuyun *China* 47°0N 89°28E **32** B3
Fuzhou *China* 26°5N 119°16E **33** D6
Fylde *U.K.* 53°50N 2°58W **12** D5
Fyn *Denmark* 55°20N 10°30E **9** J14
Fyne, L. *U.K.* 55°59N 5°23W **11** F3

G

Gaalkacyo *Somali Rep.* 6°30N 47°30E **47** F4
Gabela *Angola* 11°0S 14°24E **52** G2
Gabès *Tunisia* 33°53N 10°2E **51** B8
Gabès, G. de *Tunisia* 34°0N 10°30E **51** B8
Gabon ■ *Africa* 0°10S 10°0E **52** E2
Gaborone *Botswana* 24°45S 25°57E **56** C4
Gabriels *U.S.A.* 44°26N 74°12W **83** B10
Găbrîk *Iran* 25°44N 58°28E **45** E8
Gabrovo *Bulgaria* 42°52N 25°19E **23** C11
Gāch Sār *Iran* 36°7N 51°19E **45** B6
Gachsārān *Iran* 30°15N 50°45E **45** D6
Gadag *India* 15°30N 75°45E **40** M9
Gadap *Pakistan* 25°5N 67°28E **42** G2
Gadarwara *India* 22°50N 78°50E **43** H8
Gadhada *India* 22°0N 71°35E **42** J4
Gadra *Pakistan* 25°40N 70°38E **42** G4
Gadsden *U.S.A.* 34°1N 86°1W **85** D11
Gadwal *India* 16°10N 77°50E **40** L10
Gaffney *U.S.A.* 35°5N 81°39W **85** D14
Gafsa *Tunisia* 34°24N 8°43E **50** B7

Gagaria *India* 25°43N 70°46E **42** G4
Găgăuzia □ *Moldova* 46°10N 28°40E **17** E15
Gagnoa *Ivory C.* 6°56N 5°16W **50** G4
Gagnon *Canada* 51°50N 68°5W **73** B6
Gagnon, L. *Canada* 62°3N 110°27W **71** A6
Gahini *Rwanda* 1°50S 30°30E **54** C3
Gahmar *India* 25°27N 83°49E **43** G10
Gai Xian = Gaizhou
China 40°22N 122°20E **35** D12
Gaidouronisi *Greece* 34°53N 25°41E **25** E7
Gail *U.S.A.* 32°46N 101°27W **84** E4
Gaillimh = Galway *Ireland* 53°17N 9°3W **10** C2
Gaines *U.S.A.* 41°46N 77°35W **82** E7
Gainesville *Fla., U.S.A.* 29°40N 82°20W **85** G13
Gainesville *Ga., U.S.A.* 34°18N 83°50W **85** D13
Gainesville *Mo., U.S.A.* 36°36N 92°26W **80** G7
Gainesville *Tex., U.S.A.* 33°38N 97°8W **84** E6
Gainsborough *U.K.* 53°24N 0°46W **12** D7
Gairdner, L. *Australia* 31°30S 136°0E **63** E2
Gairloch *U.K.* 57°43N 5°41W **11** D3
Gairloch, L. *U.K.* 57°43N 5°45W **11** D3
Gaizhou *China* 40°22N 122°20E **35** D12
Gaj → *Pakistan* 26°26N 67°21E **42** F2
Gaj → *Burma* 22°5N 94°5E **41** H19
Gakuch *Pakistan* 36°7N 73°45E **43** A5
Galán, Cerro *Argentina* 25°55S 66°52W **94** B2
Galana → *Kenya* 3°9S 40°8E **54** C5
Galápagos = Colón, Arch. de
Ecuador 0°0 91°0W **90** D1
Galapagos Fracture Zone
Pac. Oc. 3°0N 110°0W **65** G17
Galapagos Rise *Pac. Oc.* 15°0S 95°0W **65** J18
Galashiels *U.K.* 55°37N 2°49W **11** F6
Galatea *Cyprus* 35°25N 34°4E **25** D13
Galați *Romania* 45°27N 28°2E **17** F15
Galatina *Italy* 40°10N 18°10E **23** D8
Galax *U.S.A.* 36°40N 80°56W **81** G13
Galcaio = Gaalkacyo
Somali Rep. 6°30N 47°30E **47** F4
Galdhøpiggen *Norway* 61°38N 8°18E **8** F13
Galeana *Chihuahua,*
Mexico 30°7N 107°38W **86** A3
Galeana *Nuevo León,*
Mexico 24°50N 100°4W **86** A3
Galela *Indonesia* 1°50N 127°49E **37** D7
Galena *U.S.A.* 64°44N 156°56W **74** a
Galeota Pt. *Trin. & Tob.* 10°8N 60°59W **93** K16
Galera Pt. *Trin. & Tob.* 10°49N 60°54W **89** D7
Galesburg *U.S.A.* 40°57N 90°22W **80** E8
Galeton *U.S.A.* 41°44N 77°39W **82** E7
Galich *Russia* 58°22N 42°24E **18** C7
Galicia □ *Spain* 42°43N 7°45E **21** A2
Galilee = Hagalil *Israel* 32°53N 35°18E **46** C4
Galilee, L. *Australia* 22°20S 145°50E **62** C4
Galilee, Sea of = Yam Kinneret
Israel 32°45N 35°35E **46** C4
Galina Pt. *Jamaica* 18°24N 76°58W **88** a
Galinoporni *Cyprus* 35°31N 34°18E **25** D13
Galion *U.S.A.* 40°44N 82°47W **82** F2
Galiuro Mts. *U.S.A.* 32°30N 110°20W **77** K8
Galiwinku *Australia* 12°2S 135°34E **62** A2
Gallan Hd. *U.K.* 58°15N 7°2W **11** D1
Gallatin *U.S.A.* 36°24N 86°27W **85** C11
Galle *Sri Lanka* 6°5N 80°10E **40** R12
Gállego → *Spain* 41°39N 0°51W **21** B5
Gallegos → *Argentina* 51°35S 69°0W **96** G3
Galley Hd. *Ireland* 51°32N 8°55W **10** E3
Gallinas, Pta. *Colombia* 12°28N 71°40W **92** A4
Gallipoli = Gelibolu
Turkey 40°28N 26°43E **23** D12
Gallipoli *Italy* 40°3N 17°58E **23** D8
Gallipolis *U.S.A.* 38°49N 82°12W **81** F12
Gällivare *Sweden* 67°9N 20°40E **8** C19
Galloo I. *U.S.A.* 43°55N 76°25W **83** C8
Galloway *U.K.* 55°1N 4°29W **11** F4
Galloway, Mull of *U.K.* 54°39N 4°52W **11** G4
Galloway △ *U.K.* 55°3N 4°20W **11** F4
Gallup *U.S.A.* 35°32N 108°45W **77** J9
Galoya *Sri Lanka* 8°10N 80°55E **40** Q12
Galt *U.S.A.* 38°15N 121°18W **78** G5
Galty Mts. *Ireland* 52°22N 8°10W **10** D3
Galtymore *Ireland* 52°21N 8°11W **10** D3
Galugāh *Iran* 36°43N 53°48E **45** B7
Galva *U.S.A.* 41°10N 90°3W **80** E8
Galveston *U.S.A.* 29°18N 94°48W **84** G7
Galveston B. *U.S.A.* 29°36N 94°50W **84** G7
Gálvez *Argentina* 32°0S 61°14W **94** C3
Galway *Ireland* 53°17N 9°3W **10** C2
Galway □ *Ireland* 53°22N 9°1W **10** C2
Galway B. *Ireland* 53°13N 9°10W **10** C2
Gam → *Vietnam* 21°55N 105°12E **38** B5
Gamagōri *Japan* 34°50N 137°14E **31** G8
Gambat *Pakistan* 27°17N 68°26E **42** F3
Gambhir → *India* 26°58N 77°27E **42** F6
Gambia ■ *W. Afr.* 13°25N 16°0W **50** F2
Gambia → *W. Afr.* 13°28N 16°34W **50** F2
Gambier, C. *Australia* 11°56S 130°57E **60** B5
Gambier, Îs.
French Polynesia 23°8S 134°58W **65** K14
Gambier Is. *Australia* 35°3S 136°30E **63** F2
Gambo *Canada* 48°47N 54°13W **73** C9
Gamboli *Pakistan* 29°53N 68°24E **42** E3
Gamboma *Congo* 1°55S 15°52E **52** E3
Gamkab → *Namibia* 28°4S 17°54E **56** D2
Gamlakarleby = Kokkola
Finland 63°50N 23°8E **8** E20
Gammon → *Canada* 51°24N 95°44W **71** C9
Gammon Ranges △
Australia 30°38S 139°8E **63** E2
Gamtoos → *S. Africa* 33°58S 25°1E **56** E4
Gan Jiang → *China* 29°15N 116°0E **33** D6
Ganado *U.S.A.* 35°43N 109°33W **77** J9
Gananoque *Canada* 44°20N 76°10W **83** B8
Ganāveh *Iran* 29°35N 50°35E **45** D6
Gäncä *Azerbaijan* 40°45N 46°20E **19** F8

Gancheng *China* 18°51N 108°37E **38** C7
Gand = Gent *Belgium* 51°2N 3°42E **15** C3
Ganda *Angola* 13°3S 14°35E **53** G2
Gandajika
Dem. Rep. of the Congo 6°46S 23°58E **52** F4
Gandak → *India* 25°39N 85°13E **43** G11
Gandava *Pakistan* 28°32N 67°32E **42** E2
Gander *Canada* 48°58N 54°35W **73** C9
Gander L. *Canada* 48°58N 54°35W **73** C9
Ganderowe Falls
Zimbabwe 17°20S 29°10E **55** F2
Gandhi Sagar *India* 24°40N 75°40E **42** G6
Gandhinagar *India* 23°15N 72°45E **42** H5
Gandia *Spain* 38°58N 0°9W **21** C5
Gando, Pta. *Canary Is.* 27°55N 15°22W **24** G4
Ganedidalem = Gani
Indonesia 0°48S 128°14E **37** E7
Ganga → *India* 23°20N 90°30E **43** H14
Ganga Sagar *India* 21°38N 88°5E **43** J13
Gangan → *India* 28°38N 78°58E **43** E8
Ganganagar *India* 29°56N 73°56E **42** E5
Gangapur *India* 26°32N 76°49E **42** F7
Gangaw *Burma* 22°5N 94°5E **41** H19
Gangdisê Shan *China* 31°20N 81°0E **43** D9
Ganges = Ganga →
India 23°20N 90°30E **43** H14
Ganges *Canada* 48°51N 123°31W **70** D4
Ganges, Mouths of the
India 21°30N 90°0E **43** J14
Ganggyeong *S. Korea* 36°10N 127°0E **35** F14
Ganghwa *S. Korea* 37°45N 126°30E **35** F14
Gangneung *S. Korea* 37°45N 128°54E **35** F15
Gangoh *India* 29°46N 77°18E **42** E7
Gangotri *India* 30°50N 79°10E **43** D8
Gangotri △ *India* 30°50N 79°10E **43** D8
Gangseong *S. Korea* 38°24N 128°30E **35** E15
Gangtok *India* 27°20N 88°37E **41** F16
Gangu *China* 34°40N 105°15E **34** G3
Gangyao *China* 44°12N 126°37E **35** B14
Gani *Indonesia* 0°48S 128°14E **37** E7
Ganj *India* 27°45N 78°57E **43** F8
Gannett Peak *U.S.A.* 43°11N 109°39W **76** E9
Ganquan *China* 36°20N 109°20E **34** F5
Gansu □ *China* 36°0N 104°0E **34** G3
Ganta *Liberia* 7°15N 8°59W **50** G4
Gantheaume, C.
Australia 36°4S 137°32E **63** F2
Gantheaume B.
Australia 27°40S 114°10E **61** E1
Gantsevichi = Hantsavichy
Belarus 52°49N 26°30E **17** B14
Ganyem = Genyem
Indonesia 2°46S 140°12E **37** E10
Ganyu *China* 34°50N 119°8E **35** G10
Ganzhou *China* 25°51N 114°56E **33** D6
Gao *Mali* 16°15N 0°5W **50** E5
Gaomi *China* 36°20N 119°42E **35** F10
Gaoping *China* 35°45N 112°55E **34** G7
Gaotang *China* 36°50N 116°15E **34** F9
Gaoua *Burkina Faso* 10°20N 3°8W **50** F5
Gaoual *Guinea* 11°45N 13°25W **50** F3
Gaoxiong = Kaohsiung
Taiwan 22°35N 120°16E **33** D7
Gaoyang *China* 38°40N 115°45E **34** E8
Gaoyou Hu *China* 32°45N 119°20E **35** H10
Gaoyuan *China* 37°8N 117°58E **35** F9
Gap *France* 44°33N 6°5E **20** D7
Gapat → *India* 24°30N 82°28E **43** G10
Gapuwiyak *Australia* 12°25S 135°43E **62** A2
Gar *China* 32°10N 79°58E **32** C2
Gara, L. *Ireland* 53°57N 8°26W **10** C3
Garabogazköl Aylagy
Turkmenistan 41°0N 53°30E **19** F9
Garachico *Canary Is.* 28°22N 16°46W **24** F3
Garachiné *Panama* 8°0N 78°12W **88** E4
Garafia *Canary Is.* 28°48N 17°57W **24** F2
Garagum *Turkmenistan* 39°30N 60°0E **45** B8
Garah *Australia* 29°5S 149°38E **63** D4
Garajonay *Canary Is.* 28°7N 17°14W **24** F2
Garamba →
Dem. Rep. of the Congo 4°10N 29°40E **54** B2
Garanhuns *Brazil* 8°50S 36°30W **93** E11
Garautha *India* 25°34N 79°18E **43** G8
Garba Tula *Kenya* 0°30N 38°32E **54** B4
Garberville *U.S.A.* 40°6N 123°48W **76** F2
Garbiyang *India* 30°8N 80°54E **43** D9
Gard → *France* 43°51N 4°37E **20** E6
Garda, L. di *Italy* 45°40N 10°41E **22** B4
Garde L. *Canada* 62°50N 106°13W **71** A7
Garden City *Ga., U.S.A.* 32°6N 81°9W **85** E14
Garden City *Kans.,*
U.S.A. 37°58N 100°53W **80** G3
Garden City *Tex.,*
U.S.A. 31°52N 101°29W **84** F4
Garden Grove *U.S.A.* 33°47N 117°55W **79** M9
Gardēz *Afghan.* 33°37N 69°9E **42** C3
Gardiner *Maine, U.S.A.* 44°14N 69°47W **81** C19
Gardiner *Mont., U.S.A.* 45°2N 110°22W **76** D8
Gardiners I. *U.S.A.* 41°6N 72°6W **83** E12
Gardner *U.S.A.* 42°34N 71°59W **83** D13
Gardner Canal *Canada* 53°27N 128°8W **70** C3
Gardnerville *U.S.A.* 38°56N 119°45W **78** G7
Gardo = Qardho
Somali Rep. 9°30N 49°6E **47** F4
Garey *U.S.A.* 34°53N 120°19W **79** L6
Garfield *U.S.A.* 47°1N 117°9W **76** C5
Garforth *U.K.* 53°47N 1°24W **12** D6
Gargantua, C. *Canada* 47°36N 85°2W **81** B11
Gargett *Australia* 21°9S 148°46E **62** K6
Garibaldi △ *Canada* 49°50N 122°40W **70** D4
Gariep, L. *S. Africa* 30°40S 25°40E **56** E4
Garies *S. Africa* 30°32S 17°59E **56** E2
Garig Gunak Barlu △
Australia 11°26S 131°58E **60** B5
Garigliano → *Italy* 41°13N 13°45E **22** D5
Garissa *Kenya* 0°25S 39°40E **54** C4
Garland *Tex., U.S.A.* 32°54N 96°38W **84** E6

Garland *Utah, U.S.A.* 41°45N 112°10W **76** F7
Garmāb *Iran* 35°25N 56°45E **45** C8
Garmisch-Partenkirchen
Germany 47°30N 11°6E **16** E6
Garmsār *Iran* 35°20N 52°25E **45** C7
Garner *U.S.A.* 43°6N 93°36W **80** D7
Garnett *U.S.A.* 38°17N 95°14W **80** F6
Garo Hills *India* 25°30N 90°30E **43** G14
Garoe = Garoowe
Somali Rep. 8°25N 48°33E **47** F4
Garonne → *France* 45°2N 0°36W **20** D3
Garoowe *Somali Rep.* 8°25N 48°33E **47** F4
Garot *India* 24°19N 75°41E **42** G6
Garoua *Cameroon* 9°19N 13°21E **51** G8
Garrauli *India* 25°5N 79°22E **43** G8
Garrison *Mont., U.S.A.* 46°31N 112°49W **76** C7
Garrison *N. Dak., U.S.A.* 47°40N 101°25W **80** B3
Garrison Res. = Sakakawea, L.
U.S.A. 47°30N 101°25W **80** B3
Garron Pt. *U.K.* 55°3N 5°59W **10** A6
Garry → *U.K.* 56°44N 3°47W **11** E5
Garry, L. *Canada* 65°58N 100°18W **68** C9
Garrygala *Turkmenistan* 38°31N 56°29E **45** B8
Garsen *Kenya* 2°20S 40°5E **54** C5
Garson L. *Canada* 56°19N 110°2W **71** B6
Garstang *U.K.* 53°55N 2°46W **12** D5
Garu *India* 23°40N 84°14E **43** H11
Garub *Namibia* 26°37S 16°0E **56** D2
Garut *Indonesia* 7°14S 107°53E **37** G12
Garvie Mts. *N.Z.* 45°30S 168°50E **59** F2
Garwa = Garoua
Cameroon 9°19N 13°21E **51** G8
Garwa *India* 24°11N 83°47E **43** G10
Gary *U.S.A.* 41°36N 87°20W **80** E10
Garzê *China* 31°38N 100°1E **32** C5
Garzón *Colombia* 2°10N 75°40W **92** C3
Gas-San *Japan* 38°32N 140°1E **30** E10
Gasan Kuli = Esenguly
Turkmenistan 37°37N 53°59E **28** F6
Gascogne *France* 43°45N 0°20E **20** E4
Gascogne, G. de *Europe* 44°0N 2°0W **20** D2
Gascony = Gascogne
France 43°45N 0°20E **20** E4
Gascoyne → *Australia* 24°52S 113°37E **61** D1
Gascoyne Junction
Australia 25°2S 115°17E **61** E2
Gashaka *Nigeria* 7°20N 11°29E **51** G8
Gasherbrum *Pakistan* 35°40N 76°40E **43** B7
Gashua *Nigeria* 12°54N 11°0E **51** F8
Gasparillo *Trin. & Tob.* 10°18N 61°26W **93** K15
Gaspé *Canada* 48°52N 64°30W **73** C7
Gaspé, C. de *Canada* 48°48N 64°7W **73** C7
Gaspé Pen. = Gaspésie, Pén. de la
Canada 48°45N 65°40W **73** C6
Gaspésie, Pén. de la
Canada 48°45N 65°40W **73** C6
Gaspésie △ *Canada* 48°55N 66°10W **73** C6
Gasteiz = Vitoria-Gasteiz
Spain 42°50N 2°41W **21** A4
Gastonia *U.S.A.* 35°16N 81°11W **85** D14
Gastre *Argentina* 42°20S 69°15W **96** E3
Gata, C. *Cyprus* 34°34N 33°2E **25** E12
Gata, C. de *Spain* 36°41N 2°13W **21** D4
Gata, Sierra de *Spain* 40°20N 6°45W **21** B2
Gataga → *Canada* 58°35N 126°59W **70** B3
Gatchina *Russia* 59°35N 30°9E **9** G24
Gatehouse of Fleet *U.K.* 54°53N 4°12W **11** G4
Gates *U.S.A.* 43°9N 77°42W **82** C7
Gateshead *U.K.* 54°57N 1°35W **12** C6
Gatesville *U.S.A.* 31°26N 97°45W **84** F6
Gateway △ *U.S.A.* 40°38N 73°51W **83** F11
Gaths *Zimbabwe* 20°2S 30°32E **55** G3
Gatineau *Canada* 45°29N 75°39W **83** A9
Gatineau → *Canada* 45°27N 75°42W **72** C4
Gatineau △ *Canada* 45°40N 76°0W **72** C4
Gatton *Australia* 27°32S 152°17E **63** D5
Gatún, L. *Panama* 9°7N 79°56W **88** E4
Gatwick, London ✈ (LGW)
U.K. 51°10N 0°11W **13** F7
Gatyana *S. Africa* 32°16S 28°31E **57** E4
Gau *Fiji* 18°2S 179°18E **59** a
Gauer L. *Canada* 57°0N 97°50W **71** B9
Gauhati = Guwahati
India 26°10N 91°45E **41** F17
Gauja → *Latvia* 57°10N 24°16E **9** H21
Gaujas △ *Latvia* 57°10N 24°50E **9** H21
Gaula → *Norway* 63°21N 10°14E **8** E14
Gauri Phanta *India* 28°41N 80°36E **43** E9
Gaustatoppen *Norway* 59°48N 8°40E **9** G13
Gauteng □ *S. Africa* 26°0S 28°0E **57** D4
Gāv Koshī *Iran* 28°38N 57°12E **45** D8
Gāvakān *Iran* 29°37N 53°10E **45** D7
Gavāter *Iran* 25°10N 61°31E **45** E9
Gāvbandī *Iran* 27°12N 53°4E **45** E7
Gavdopoúla *Greece* 34°56N 24°0E **25** E6
Gávdos *Greece* 34°50N 24°5E **25** E6
Gaviota *U.S.A.* 34°29N 120°13W **79** L6
Gävkhūnī, Bāţlāq-e *Iran* 32°6N 52°52E **45** C7
Gävle *Sweden* 60°40N 17°9E **8** F17
Gawachab *Namibia* 27°4S 17°55E **56** D2
Gawilgarh Hills *India* 21°15N 76°45E **40** J10
Gawler *Australia* 34°30S 138°42E **63** E2
Gawler Ranges
Australia 32°30S 135°45E **63** E2
Gaxun Nur *China* 42°22N 100°30E **32** B5
Gay *Russia* 51°27N 58°27E **18** D10
Gaya *India* 24°47N 85°4E **43** G11
Gaya *Niger* 11°52N 3°28E **50** F6
Gaylord *U.S.A.* 45°2N 84°41W **81** C11
Gayndah *Australia* 25°35S 151°32E **63** D5
Gaysin = Haysyn
Ukraine 48°57N 29°25E **17** D15
Gayvoron = Hayvoron
Ukraine 48°22N 29°52E **17** D15
Gaza *Gaza Strip* 31°30N 34°28E **46** D3
Gaza □ *Mozam.* 23°10S 32°45E **57** C5
Gaza Strip ■ *Asia* 31°29N 34°25E **46** D3

Gazanjyk = Bereket
Turkmenistan 39°16N 55°32E **45** B7
Gāzbor *Iran* 28°5N 58°51E **45** D8
Gazi *Dem. Rep. of the Congo* 1°3N 24°30E **54** B1
Gaziantep *Turkey* 37°6N 37°23E **44** B3
Gazimağusa = Famagusta
Cyprus 35°8N 33°55E **25** D12
Gcoverega *Botswana* 19°8S 24°18E **56** B3
Gcuwa *S. Africa* 32°20S 28°11E **57** E4
Gdańsk *Poland* 54°22N 18°40E **17** A10
Gdańska, Zatoka
Poland 54°30N 19°20E **17** A10
Gdov *Russia* 58°48N 27°55E **9** G22
Gdynia *Poland* 54°35N 18°33E **17** A10
Gebe *Indonesia* 0°5N 129°25E **37** D7
Gebze *Turkey* 40°47N 29°25E **23** D13
Gedaref *Sudan* 14°2N 35°28E **51** F13
Gediz → *Turkey* 38°35N 26°48E **23** E12
Gedser *Denmark* 54°35N 11°55E **9** J14
Gedung, Pulau *Malaysia* 5°17N 100°23E **39** c
Geegully Cr. →
Australia 18°32S 123°41E **60** C3
Geel *Belgium* 51°10N 4°59E **15** C4
Geelong *Australia* 38°10S 144°22E **63** F3
Geelvink B. = Cenderawasih, Teluk
Indonesia 3°0S 135°20E **37** E9
Geelvink Chan. *Australia* 28°30S 114°0E **61** E1
Geesthacht *Germany* 53°26N 10°22E **16** B6
Geidam *Nigeria* 12°57N 11°57E **51** F8
Geikie → *Canada* 57°45N 103°52W **71** B8
Geikie Gorge △ *Australia* 18°3S 125°41E **60** C4
Geistown *U.S.A.* 40°18N 78°52W **82** F6
Geita *Tanzania* 2°48S 32°12E **54** C3
Gejiu *China* 23°20N 103°10E **32** D5
Gel, Meydān-e *Iran* 29°4N 54°50E **45** D7
Gela *Italy* 37°4N 14°15E **22** F6
Gelang Patah *Malaysia* 1°27N 103°35E **39** d
Gelderland □ *Neths.* 52°5N 6°10E **15** B6
Geldrop *Neths.* 51°25N 5°32E **15** C5
Geleen *Neths.* 50°57N 5°49E **15** D5
Gelib = Jilib *Somali Rep.* 0°29N 42°46E **47** G3
Gelibolu *Turkey* 40°28N 26°43E **23** D12
Gelsenkirchen *Germany* 51°32N 7°6E **16** C4
Gelugur *Malaysia* 5°22N 100°18E **39** c
Gemas *Malaysia* 2°37N 102°36E **39** L4
Gembloux *Belgium* 50°34N 4°43E **15** D4
Gemena
Dem. Rep. of the Congo 3°13N 19°48E **52** D3
Gemerek *Turkey* 39°15N 36°10E **44** B3
Gemlik *Turkey* 40°26N 29°9E **23** D13
Gemsbok △ *Botswana* 25°5S 21°1E **56** D3
Genadi *Greece* 36°2N 27°56E **25** C9
Genale → *Ethiopia* 6°2N 39°1E **47** F2
General Acha *Argentina* 37°20S 64°38W **94** D3
General Alvear *B. Aires,*
Argentina 36°0S 60°0W **94** D4
General Alvear *Mendoza,*
Argentina 35°0S 67°40W **94** D2
General Artigas
Paraguay 26°52S 56°16W **94** B4
General Belgrano
Argentina 36°35S 58°47W **94** D4
General Bernardo O'Higgins
Antarctica 63°0S 58°3W **5** C18
General Cabrera
Argentina 32°53S 63°52W **94** C3
General Cepeda *Mexico* 25°21N 101°22W **86** B4
General Guido *Argentina* 36°40S 57°50W **94** D4
General Juan Madariaga
Argentina 37°0S 57°0W **94** D4
General La Madrid
Argentina 37°17S 61°20W **94** D3
General MacArthur
Phil. 11°18N 125°28E **37** B7
General Martin Miguel de Güemes
Argentina 24°50S 65°0W **94** A3
General Pico *Argentina* 35°45S 63°50W **94** D3
General Pinedo
Argentina 27°15S 61°20W **94** B3
General Pinto *Argentina* 34°45S 61°50W **94** C3
General Roca *Argentina* 39°2S 67°35W **96** D3
General Santos *Phil.* 6°5N 125°14E **37** C7
General Treviño *Mexico* 26°14N 99°29W **87** B5
General Trías *Mexico* 28°21N 106°22W **86** B3
General Viamonte
Argentina 35°1S 61°3W **94** D3
General Villegas *Argentina* 35°5S 63°0W **94** D3
Genesee *Idaho, U.S.A.* 46°33N 116°56W **76** C5
Genesee *Pa., U.S.A.* 41°59N 77°54W **82** E7
Genesee → *U.S.A.* 43°16N 77°36W **82** C7
Geneseo *Ill., U.S.A.* 41°27N 90°9W **80** E8
Geneseo *N.Y., U.S.A.* 42°48N 77°49W **82** D7
Geneva = Genève *Switz.* 46°12N 6°9E **20** C7
Geneva *Ala., U.S.A.* 31°2N 85°52W **85** F12
Geneva *N.Y., U.S.A.* 42°52N 76°59W **82** D8
Geneva *Nebr., U.S.A.* 40°32N 97°36W **80** E5
Geneva *Ohio, U.S.A.* 41°48N 80°57W **82** E4
Geneva, L. = Léman, L.
Europe 46°26N 6°30E **20** C7
Genève *Switz.* 46°12N 6°9E **20** C7
Genil → *Spain* 37°42N 5°19W **21** D3
Genk *Belgium* 50°58N 5°32E **15** D5
Gennargentu, Mti. del
Italy 40°1N 9°19E **22** D3
Genoa = Génova *Italy* 44°25N 8°57E **20** D8
Genoa *Australia* 37°29S 149°35E **63** F4
Genoa *N.Y., U.S.A.* 42°40N 76°32W **82** D8
Genoa *Nebr., U.S.A.* 41°27N 97°44W **80** E5
Genoa *Nev., U.S.A.* 39°2N 119°50W **78** F7
Génova *Italy* 44°25N 8°57E **20** D8
Génova, G. di *Italy* 44°0N 9°0E **22** C3
Genriyetty, Ostrov
Russia 77°6N 156°30E **29** B16
Gent *Belgium* 51°2N 3°42E **15** C3
Genteng *Bali, Indonesia* 8°22S 114°9E **37** J17
Genteng *Jawa Barat,*
Indonesia 7°22S 106°24E **37** G12

Genyem *Indonesia* 2°46S 140°12E **37** E10
Geochang *S. Korea* 35°41N 127°55E **35** G14
Geographe B. *Australia* 33°30S 115°15E **61** F2
Geographe Chan.
Australia 24°30S 113°0E **61** D1
Georga, Zemlya *Russia* 80°30N 49°0E **28** A5
George *S. Africa* 33°58S 22°29E **56** E3
George → *Canada* 58°49N 66°10W **73** A6
George, L. *N.S.W.,*
Australia 35°10S 149°25E **63** F4
George, L. *S. Austral.,*
Australia 37°25S 140°0E **63** F3
George, L. *W. Austral.,*
Australia 22°45S 123°40E **60** D3
George, L. *Uganda* 0°5N 30°10E **54** B3
George, L. *Fla., U.S.A.* 29°17N 81°36W **85** G14
George, L. *N.Y., U.S.A.* 43°37N 73°33W **83** C11
George Gill Ra.
Australia 24°22S 131°45E **60** D5
George Pt. *Australia* 20°6S 148°36E **62** J6
George River = Kangiqsualujjuaq
Canada 58°30N 65°59W **69** D13
George Sound *N.Z.* 44°52S 167°25E **59** F1
George Town *Australia* 41°6S 146°49E **63** G4
George Town *Bahamas* 23°33N 75°47W **88** B4
George Town *Cayman Is.* 19°20N 81°24W **88** C3
George Town *Malaysia* 5°25N 100°20E **39** c
George V Land *Antarctica* 69°0S 148°0E **5** C10
George VI Sound
Antarctica 71°0S 68°0W **5** D17
George West *U.S.A.* 28°20N 98°7W **84** G5
Georgetown = Janjanbureh
Gambia 13°30N 14°47W **50** F3
Georgetown *Australia* 18°17S 143°33E **62** B3
Georgetown *Ont.,*
Canada 43°40N 79°56W **82** C5
Georgetown *P.E.I.,*
Canada 46°13N 62°24W **73** C7
Georgetown *Guyana* 6°50N 58°12W **92** B7
Georgetown *Calif.,*
U.S.A. 38°54N 120°50W **78** G6
Georgetown *Colo.,*
U.S.A. 39°42N 105°42W **76** G11
Georgetown *Ky., U.S.A.* 38°13N 84°33W **81** F11
Georgetown *N.Y.,*
U.S.A. 42°46N 75°44W **83** D9
Georgetown *Ohio,*
U.S.A. 38°52N 83°54W **81** F12
Georgetown *S.C.,*
U.S.A. 33°23N 79°17W **85** E15
Georgetown *Tex., U.S.A.* 30°38N 97°41W **84** F6
Georgia □ *U.S.A.* 32°50N 83°15W **85** E13
Georgia ■ *Asia* 42°0N 43°0E **19** F7
Georgia, Str. of *N. Amer.* 49°25N 124°0W **78** A3
Georgia Basin *S. Ocean* 50°45S 35°30W **5** B1
Georgian B. *Canada* 45°15N 81°0W **82** A4
Georgian Bay Islands △
Canada 44°53N 79°52W **82** B5
Georgiyevka *Kazakhstan* 49°19N 84°34E **28** E9
Georgina → *Australia* 23°30S 139°47E **62** C2
Georgina I. *Canada* 44°22N 79°17W **82** B5
Georgioupoli *Greece* 35°20N 24°15E **25** D6
Georgiyevsk *Russia* 44°12N 43°28E **19** F7
Gera *Germany* 50°53N 12°4E **16** C7
Geraardsbergen *Belgium* 50°45N 3°53E **15** D3
Geral, Serra *Brazil* 26°25S 50°0W **95** B6
Geral de Goiás, Serra
Brazil 12°0S 46°0W **93** F9
Geraldine *U.S.A.* 47°36N 110°16W **76** C8
Geraldton *Australia* 28°48S 114°32E **61** E1
Geraldton *Canada* 49°44N 86°59W **72** C2
Gereshk *Afghan.* 31°47N 64°35E **40** D4
Gerik *Malaysia* 5°50N 101°15E **39** K3
Gering *U.S.A.* 41°50N 103°40W **80** E2
Gerlach *U.S.A.* 40°39N 119°21W **76** F4
German Bight = Deutsche Bucht
Germany 54°15N 8°0E **16** A5
Germansen Landing
Canada 55°43N 124°40W **70** B4
Germantown *U.S.A.* 35°5N 89°49W **85** D10
Germany ■ *Europe* 51°0N 10°0E **16** C6
Germī *Iran* 39°1N 48°3E **45** B6
Germiston *S. Africa* 26°13S 28°10E **57** D4
Gernika-Lumo *Spain* 43°19N 2°40W **21** A4
Gero *Japan* 35°48N 137°14E **31** G8
Gerokgak *Indonesia* 8°11S 114°27E **37** J17
Gerona = Girona *Spain* 41°58N 2°46E **21** B7
Geropotamos → *Greece* 35°3N 24°50E **25** D6
Gerrard *Canada* 50°30N 117°17W **70** C5
Gertak Sanggul *Malaysia* 5°17N 100°12E **39** c
Gertak Sanggul, Tanjung
Malaysia 5°16N 100°11E **39** c
Gerung *Indonesia* 8°43S 116°7E **37** K19
Geser *Indonesia* 3°50S 130°54E **37** E8
Getafe *Spain* 40°18N 3°43W **21** B4
Gettysburg *Pa., U.S.A.* 39°50N 77°14W **81** F15
Gettysburg *S. Dak., U.S.A.* 45°1N 99°57W **80** C4
Getxo *Spain* 43°21N 2°59W **21** A4
Getz Ice Shelf *Antarctica* 75°0S 130°0W **5** D14
Geyser *U.S.A.* 47°16N 110°30W **76** C8
Geyserville *U.S.A.* 38°42N 122°54W **78** G4
Ghadāf, W. al → *Iraq* 32°56N 43°30E **44** C4
Ghadāmis *Libya* 30°11N 9°29E **51** B8
Ghaggar → *India* 29°30N 74°53E **42** E6
Ghaghara → *India* 25°45N 84°40E **43** G11
Ghaghat → *Bangla.* 25°19N 89°38E **43** G13
Ghagra *India* 23°17N 84°33E **43** H11
Ghagra → *India* 27°29N 81°9E **43** F9
Ghallamane *Mauritania* 23°15N 10°0W **50** D4
Ghana ■ *W. Afr.* 8°0N 1°0W **50** G5
Ghansor *India* 22°39N 80°1E **43** H9
Ghanzi *Botswana* 21°50S 21°34E **56** C3
Gharb Bahr el Ghazâl □
Sudan 7°30N 27°30E **48** F6
Ghardaïa *Algeria* 32°20N 3°37E **50** B6
Gharm *Tajikistan* 39°0N 70°20E **28** F8
Gharyān *Libya* 32°10N 13°0E **51** B8

Ghat *Libya* 24°59N 10°11E **51** D8
Ghatal *India* 22°40N 87°46E **43** H12
Ghatampur *India* 26°8N 80°13E **43** F9
Ghats, Eastern *India* 14°0N 78°50E **40** N11
Ghats, Western *India* 14°0N 75°0E **40** N9
Ghatsila *India* 22°36N 86°29E **43** H12
Ghawdex = Gozo *Malta* 36°3N 14°15E **25** C1
Ghazal, Bahr el → *Chad* 13°0N 15°47E **51** F9
Ghazâl, Bahr el →
Sudan 9°31N 30°25E **51** G12
Ghaziabad *India* 28°42N 77°26E **42** E7
Ghazipur *India* 25°38N 83°35E **43** G10
Ghaznī *Afghan.* 33°30N 68°28E **42** C3
Ghaznī □ *Afghan.* 32°10N 68°20E **40** C6
Ghent = Gent *Belgium* 51°2N 3°42E **15** C3
Gheorghe Gheorghiu-Dej = Oneşti
Romania 46°17N 26°47E **17** E14
Ghīnah, Wādī al →
Si. Arabia 30°27N 38°14E **44** D3
Ghizar → *Pakistan* 36°15N 73°43E **43** A5
Ghotaru *India* 27°20N 70°1E **42** F4
Ghotki *Pakistan* 28°5N 69°21E **42** E3
Ghowr □ *Afghan.* 34°0N 64°20E **40** C4
Ghughri *India* 22°39N 80°41E **43** H9
Ghugus *India* 19°58N 79°12E **40** K11
Ghulam Mohammad Barrage
Pakistan 25°30N 68°20E **42** G3
Ghūrīān *Afghan.* 34°17N 61°25E **40** B2
Gia Dinh *Vietnam* 10°49N 106°42E **39** G6
Gia Lai = Plei Ku
Vietnam 13°57N 108°0E **38** F7
Gia Nghia *Vietnam* 11°58N 107°42E **39** G6
Gia Ngoc *Vietnam* 14°50N 108°58E **38** E7
Gia Vuc *Vietnam* 14°42N 108°34E **38** E7
Giamama = Jamaame
Somali Rep. 0°4N 42°44E **47** G3
Gianitsa *Greece* 40°46N 22°24E **23** D10
Giant Forest *U.S.A.* 36°36N 118°43W **78** J8
Giant Sequoia △
U.S.A. 36°10N 118°35W **78** K8
Giants Causeway *U.K.* 55°16N 6°29W **10** A5
Gianyar *Indonesia* 8°32S 115°20E **37** K18
Giarabub = Al Jaghbūb
Libya 29°42N 24°38E **51** C10
Giarre *Italy* 37°43N 15°11E **22** F6
Gibara *Cuba* 21°9N 76°11W **88** B4
Gibb River *Australia* 16°26S 126°26E **60** C4
Gibbon *U.S.A.* 40°45N 98°51W **80** E4
Gibeon *Namibia* 25°9S 17°43E **56** D2
Gibraltar ☑ *Europe* 36°7N 5°22W **21** D3
Gibraltar, Str. of *Medit. S.* 35°55N 5°40W **21** E3
Gibraltar Range △
Australia 29°31S 152°19E **63** D5
Gibson Desert *Australia* 24°0S 126°0E **60** D4
Gibsons *Canada* 49°24N 123°32W **70** D4
Gibsonville *U.S.A.* 39°46N 120°54W **78** F6
Giddings *U.S.A.* 30°11N 96°56W **84** F6
Giebnegáisi = Kebnekaise
Sweden 67°53N 18°33E **8** C18
Giessen *Germany* 50°34N 8°41E **16** C5
Gifan *Iran* 37°54N 57°28E **45** B8
Gift Lake *Canada* 55°53N 115°49W **70** B5
Gifu *Japan* 35°30N 136°45E **31** G8
Gifu □ *Japan* 35°40N 137°0E **31** G8
Giganta, Sa. de la
Mexico 26°0N 111°39W **86** B2
Gigha *U.K.* 55°42N 5°44W **11** F3
Gíglio *Italy* 42°20N 10°52E **22** C4
Gíjón *Spain* 43°32N 5°42W **21** A3
Gil I. *Canada* 53°12N 129°15W **70** C3
Gila → *U.S.A.* 32°43N 114°33W **77** K6
Gila Bend *U.S.A.* 32°57N 112°43W **77** K7
Gila Bend Mts. *U.S.A.* 33°10N 113°0W **77** K7
Gila Cliff Dwellings △
U.S.A. 33°12N 108°16W **77** K9
Gīlān □ *Iran* 37°0N 50°0E **45** B6
Gilbert → *Australia* 16°35S 141°15E **62** B3
Gilbert Is. *Kiribati* 1°0N 172°0E **58** A10
Gilbert River *Australia* 18°9S 142°52E **62** B3
Gilbert Seamounts
Pac. Oc. 52°50N 150°10W **4** D18
Gilead *U.S.A.* 44°24N 70°59W **83** B14
Gilf el Kebîr, Hadabat el
Egypt 23°50N 25°50E **51** D11
Gilford I. *Canada* 50°40N 126°30W **70** C3
Gilgandra *Australia* 31°43S 148°39E **63** E4
Gilgil *Kenya* 0°30S 36°20E **54** C4
Gilgit *India* 35°50N 74°15E **43** B6
Gilgit → *Pakistan* 35°44N 74°37E **43** B6
Gili *Mozam.* 16°39S 38°27E **55** F4
Gilimanuk *Indonesia* 8°10S 114°26E **37** J17
Gillam *Canada* 56°20N 94°40W **71** B10
Gillen, L. *Australia* 26°11S 124°38E **61** E3
Gilles, L. *Australia* 32°50S 136°45E **63** E2
Gillette *U.S.A.* 44°18N 105°30W **76** D11
Gilliat *Australia* 20°40S 141°28E **62** C3
Gillingham *U.K.* 51°23N 0°33E **13** F8
Gilmer *U.S.A.* 32°44N 94°57W **84** E7
Gilmore, L. *Australia* 32°29S 121°37E **61** F3
Gilmour *Canada* 44°48N 77°37W **82** B7
Gilroy *U.S.A.* 37°1N 121°34W **78** H5
Gimcheon *S. Korea* 36°11N 128°4E **35** F15
Gimhae *S. Korea* 35°14N 128°53E **35** G15
Gimhwa *S. Korea* 38°17N 127°28E **35** E14
Gimie, Mt *St. Lucia* 13°54N 61°0W **89** f
Gimje *S. Korea* 35°48N 126°45E **35** G14
Gimli *Canada* 50°40N 97°0W **71** C9
Gin Gin *Australia* 25°0S 151°58E **63** D5
Gingin *Australia* 31°22S 115°43E **61** F2
Gingindlovu *S. Africa* 29°2S 31°30E **57** D5
Ginir *Ethiopia* 7°6N 40°40E **47** F3
Giofyros → *Greece* 35°20N 25°6E **25** D7
Giohar = Jawhar
Somali Rep. 2°48N 45°30E **47** G4
Giona, Oros *Greece* 38°38N 22°14E **23** E10
Gir △ *India* 21°0N 71°0E **42** J4

Gir Hills *India* 21°0N 71°0E **42** J4
Girab *India* 26°2N 70°38E **42** F4
Girâfi, W. → *Egypt* 29°58N 34°39E **46** F3
Girard *St. Lucia* 13°59N 60°57W **89** f
Girard *Kans., U.S.A.* 37°31N 94°51W **80** G6
Girard *Ohio, U.S.A.* 41°9N 80°42W **82** E4
Girard *Pa., U.S.A.* 42°0N 80°19W **82** E4
Girdle Ness *U.K.* 57°9N 2°3W **11** D6
Giresun *Turkey* 40°55N 38°30E **19** F6
Girga *Egypt* 26°17N 31°55E **51** C12
Giri → *India* 30°28N 77°41E **42** D7
Giridih *India* 24°10N 86°21E **43** G12
Giriftu *Kenya* 1°59N 39°46E **54** B4
Giriyondo *S. Africa* 23°15S 31°45E **57** C5
Girne = Kyrenia *Cyprus* 35°20N 33°20E **25** D12
Girona *Spain* 41°58N 2°46E **21** B7
Gironde → *France* 45°32N 1°7W **20** D3
Girraween △ *Australia* 28°46S 151°54E **63** D5
Girrigun △ *Australia* 18°15S 145°32E **62** B4
Giru *Australia* 19°30S 147°5E **62** B4
Girvan *U.K.* 55°14N 4°51W **11** F4
Gisborne *N.Z.* 38°39S 178°5E **59** C7
Gisenyi *Rwanda* 1°41S 29°15E **54** C2
Gislaved *Sweden* 57°19N 13°32E **9** H15
Gitega *Burundi* 3°26S 29°56E **54** C2
Githio *Greece* 36°46N 22°34E **23** F10
Giuba = Juba →
Somali Rep. 1°30N 42°35E **47** G3
Giurgiu *Romania* 43°52N 25°57E **17** G13
Giza = El Gîza *Egypt* 30°0N 31°12E **51** C12
Giza Pyramids *Egypt* 29°58N 31°9E **51** C12
Gizab *Afghan.* 33°22N 66°17E **42** C1
Gizhiga *Russia* 62°3N 160°30E **29** C17
Gizhiginskaya Guba
Russia 61°0N 158°0E **29** C16
Giżycko *Poland* 54°2N 21°48E **17** A11
Gjirokastër *Albania* 40°7N 20°10E **23** D8
Gjoa Haven *Canada* 68°38N 95°53W **68** C10
Gjøvik *Norway* 60°47N 10°43E **8** F14
Glace Bay *Canada* 46°11N 59°58W **73** C8
Glacier △ *Canada* 51°15N 117°30W **70** C5
Glacier △ *U.S.A.* 48°42N 113°48W **76** B7
Glacier Bay △ *U.S.A.* 58°45N 136°30W **70** B1
Glacier Peak *U.S.A.* 48°7N 121°7W **76** B3
Gladewater *U.S.A.* 32°33N 94°56W **84** E7
Gladstone *Queens.,*
Australia 23°52S 151°16E **62** C5
Gladstone *S. Austral.,*
Australia 33°15S 138°22E **63** E2
Gladstone *Canada* 50°13N 98°57W **71** C9
Gladstone *U.S.A.* 45°51N 87°1W **80** C10
Gladwin *U.S.A.* 43°59N 84°29W **81** D11
Glagah *Indonesia* 8°13S 114°18E **37** J17
Glåma = Glomma →
Norway 59°12N 10°57E **9** G14
Gláma *Iceland* 65°48N 23°0W **8** D2
Glamis *U.S.A.* 32°55N 115°5W **79** N11
Glamorgan, Vale of □
U.K. 51°28N 3°25W **13** F4
Glasco *Kans., U.S.A.* 39°22N 97°50W **80** F5
Glasco *N.Y., U.S.A.* 42°3N 73°57W **83** D11
Glasgow *U.K.* 55°51N 4°15W **11** F4
Glasgow *Ky., U.S.A.* 37°0N 85°55W **81** G11
Glasgow *Mont., U.S.A.* 48°12N 106°38W **76** B10
Glasgow, City of □ *U.K.* 55°51N 4°12W **11** F4
Glasgow Int. ✈ (GLA)
U.K. 55°51N 4°21W **11** F4
Glaslyn *Canada* 53°22N 108°21W **71** C7
Glastonbury *U.K.* 51°9N 2°43W **13** F5
Glastonbury *U.S.A.* 41°43N 72°37W **83** E12
Glazov *Russia* 58°9N 52°40E **18** C9
Gleichen *Canada* 50°52N 113°3W **70** C6
Gleiwitz = Gliwice
Poland 50°22N 18°41E **17** C10
Glen Affric *U.K.* 57°17N 5°1W **11** D3
Glen Canyon *U.S.A.* 37°15N 110°40W **77** H8
Glen Canyon △ *U.S.A.* 37°15N 111°0W **77** H8
Glen Canyon Dam
U.S.A. 36°57N 111°29W **77** H8
Glen Coe *U.K.* 56°40N 5°0W **11** E3
Glen Cove *U.S.A.* 40°51N 73°38W **83** F11
Glen Garry *U.K.* 57°3N 5°7W **11** D3
Glen Innes *Australia* 29°44S 151°44E **63** D5
Glen Lyon *U.S.A.* 41°10N 76°5W **83** E8
Glen Mor *U.K.* 57°9N 4°37W **11** D4
Glen More *U.K.* 57°8N 3°40W **11** D5
Glen Moriston *U.K.* 57°11N 4°52W **11** D4
Glen Robertson *Canada* 45°22N 74°30W **83** A10
Glen Spean *U.K.* 56°53N 4°40W **11** E4
Glen Ullin *U.S.A.* 46°49N 101°50W **80** B3
Glenallen *U.S.A.* 62°7N 145°33W **68** C5
Glenariff △ *Ireland* 55°2N 6°10W **10** A5
Glenbeigh *Ireland* 52°3N 9°58W **10** D2
Glencoe *Canada* 42°45N 81°43W **82** D3
Glencoe *S. Africa* 28°11S 30°11E **57** D5
Glencoe *U.S.A.* 44°46N 94°9W **80** C6
Glencolumbkille *Ireland* 54°43N 8°42W **10** B3
Glendale *Ariz., U.S.A.* 33°32N 112°11W **77** K7
Glendale *Calif., U.S.A.* 34°9N 118°15W **79** L8
Glendale *Zimbabwe* 17°22S 31°5E **55** F3
Glendive *U.S.A.* 47°7N 104°43W **76** C11
Glendo *U.S.A.* 42°30N 105°2W **76** E11
Glenelg → *Australia* 38°4S 140°59E **63** F3
Glenfield *U.S.A.* 43°43N 75°24W **83** C9
Glengad Hd. *Ireland* 55°19N 7°11W **10** A4
Glengarriff *Ireland* 51°45N 9°34W **10** E2
Glenmont *U.S.A.* 40°31N 82°6W **82** F2
Glenmorgan *Australia* 27°15S 149°45E **63** D4
Glenn *U.S.A.* 39°31N 122°1W **78** F4
Glennamaddy *Ireland* 53°37N 8°33W **10** C3
Glenns Ferry *U.S.A.* 42°57N 115°18W **76** E6
Glenora *Canada* 44°2N 77°3W **82** B7
Glenorchy *Australia* 42°49S 147°18E **63** G4
Glenore *Australia* 17°50S 141°12E **62** B3
Glenreagh *Australia* 30°2S 153°1E **63** E5

INDEX TO WORLD MAPS
Great Salt Plains L. 123

Glenrock U.S.A. 42°52N 105°52W 76 E11
Glenrothes U.K. 56°12N 3°10W 11 E5
Glens Falls U.S.A. 43°19N 73°39W 83 C11
Glenside U.S.A. 40°6N 75°9W 83 F9
Glenties Ireland 54°49N 8°16W 10 B3
Glenveagh △ Ireland 55°3N 8°1W 10 A3
Glenville U.S.A. 38°56N 80°50W 81 F13
Glenwood Canada 49°0N 54°58W 73 C9
Glenwood Ark., U.S.A. 34°20N 93°33W 84 D8
Glenwood Iowa, U.S.A. 41°3N 95°45W 80 E6
Glenwood Minn., U.S.A. 45°39N 95°23W 80 C6
Glenwood Wash., U.S.A. 46°1N 121°17W 78 D5
Glenwood Springs U.S.A. 39°33N 107°19W 76 G10
Glettinganes Iceland 65°30N 13°37W 8 D7
Glin Ireland 52°34N 9°17W 10 D2
Gliwice Poland 50°22N 18°41E 17 C10
Globe U.S.A. 33°24N 110°47W 77 K8
Głogów Poland 51°37N 16°5E 16 C9
Glomma → Norway 59°12N 10°57E 9 G14
Glorieuses, Îs. Ind. Oc. 11°30S 47°20E 57 A8
Glossop U.K. 53°27N 1°56W 12 D6
Gloucester Australia 32°0S 151°59E 63 E5
Gloucester U.K. 51°53N 2°15W 13 F5
Gloucester U.S.A. 42°37N 70°40W 83 D14
Gloucester I. Australia 20°0S 148°30E 62 J6
Gloucester Island △ Australia 20°2S 148°30E 62 J6
Gloucester Point U.S.A. 37°15N 76°30W 81 G15
Gloucestershire □ U.K. 51°46N 2°15W 13 F5
Gloversville U.S.A. 43°3N 74°21W 83 C10
Glovertown Canada 48°40N 54°3W 73 C9
Glusk Belarus 52°53N 28°41E 17 B15
Gmünd Austria 48°45N 15°0E 16 D8
Gmunden Austria 47°55N 13°48E 16 E7
Gniezno Poland 52°30N 17°35E 17 B9
Gnowangerup Australia 33°58S 117°59E 61 F2
Go Cong Vietnam 10°22N 106°40E 39 G6
Gō-no-ura Japan 33°44N 129°40E 31 H4
Goa India 15°33N 73°59E 40 M8
Goa □ India 15°33N 73°59E 40 M8
Goalen Hd. Australia 36°33S 150°4E 63 F5
Goalpara India 26°10N 90°40E 41 F17
Goaltor India 22°43N 87°10E 43 H12
Goalundo Ghat Bangla. 23°50N 89°47E 43 H13
Goat Fell U.K. 55°38N 5°11W 11 F3
Goba Ethiopia 7°1N 39°59E 47 F2
Goba Mozam. 26°15S 32°13E 57 D5
Gobabis Namibia 22°30S 19°0E 56 C2
Gobi Asia 44°0N 110°0E 34 C6
Gobō Japan 33°53N 135°10E 31 H7
Gochas Namibia 24°59S 18°55E 56 C2
Godalming U.K. 51°11N 0°36W 13 F7
Godavari → India 16°25N 82°18E 41 L13
Godavari Pt. India 17°0N 82°20E 41 L13
Godbout Canada 49°20N 67°38W 73 C6
Godda India 24°50N 87°13E 43 G12
Goderich Canada 43°45N 81°41W 82 C3
Godfrey Ra. Australia 24°0S 117°0E 61 D2
Godhavn = Qeqertarsuaq Greenland 69°15N 53°38W 4 C5
Godhra India 22°49N 73°40E 42 H5
Godoy Cruz Argentina 32°56S 68°52W 94 C2
Gods → Canada 56°22N 92°51W 72 A1
Gods L. Canada 54°40N 94°15W 72 B1
Gods River Canada 54°50N 94°5W 71 C10
Godthåb = Nuuk Greenland 64°10N 51°35W 67 C14
Goeie Hoop, Kaap die = Good Hope, C. of S. Africa 34°24S 18°30E 56 E2
Goéland, L. au Canada 49°50N 76°48W 72 C4
Goélands, L. aux Canada 55°27N 64°17W 73 A7
Goeree Neths. 51°50N 4°0E 15 C3
Goes Neths. 51°30N 3°55E 15 C3
Goffstown U.S.A. 43°1N 71°36W 83 C13
Gogama Canada 47°35N 81°43W 72 C3
Gogebic, L. U.S.A. 46°30N 89°35W 80 B9
Gogra = Ghaghara → India 25°45N 84°40E 43 G11
Gogriâl Sudan 8°30N 28°8E 51 G11
Gohana India 29°8N 76°42E 42 E7
Goharganj India 23°1N 77°41E 42 H7
Goi → India 22°4N 74°46E 42 H6
Goiânia Brazil 16°43S 49°20W 93 G9
Goiás Brazil 15°55S 50°10W 93 G8
Goiás □ Brazil 12°10S 48°0W 93 F9
Goio-Erê Brazil 24°12S 53°1W 95 A5
Gojō Japan 34°21N 135°42E 31 G7
Gojra Pakistan 31°10N 72°40E 42 D5
Gökçeada Turkey 40°10N 25°50E 23 D11
Gökova Körfezi Turkey 36°55N 27°50E 23 F12
Göksu → Turkey 36°19N 34°5E 44 B2
Gokteik Burma 22°26N 97°0E 41 H20
Gokurt Pakistan 29°40N 67°26E 42 E2
Gokwe Zimbabwe 18°7S 28°58E 57 B4
Gola India 28°3N 80°32E 43 E9
Golakganj India 26°8N 89°52E 43 F13
Golan Heights = Hagolan Syria 33°0N 35°45E 46 C4
Golāshkerd Iran 27°59N 57°16E 45 E8
Golchikha Russia 71°45N 83°30E 4 B12
Golconda U.S.A. 40°58N 117°30W 76 F5
Gold U.S.A. 41°52N 77°50W 82 E7
Gold Beach U.S.A. 42°25N 124°25W 76 E1
Gold Coast W. Afr. 4°0N 1°40W 50 H5
Gold Hill U.S.A. 42°26N 123°3W 76 E2
Gold River Canada 49°46N 126°3W 70 D3
Golden Canada 51°20N 116°59W 70 C5
Golden B. N.Z. 40°40S 172°50E 59 D4
Golden Gate U.S.A. 37°48N 122°29W 77 H2
Golden Gate Highlands △ S. Africa 28°40S 28°40E 57 D4
Golden Hinde Canada 49°40N 125°44W 70 D3
Golden Lake Canada 45°34N 77°21W 82 A7
Golden Spike ⌂ U.S.A. 41°37N 112°33W 76 F7
Golden Vale Ireland 52°33N 8°17W 10 D3
Goldendale U.S.A. 45°49N 120°50W 76 D3
Goldfield U.S.A. 37°42N 117°14W 77 H5
Goldsand L. Canada 57°2N 101°8W 71 B8
Goldsboro U.S.A. 35°23N 77°59W 85 D16
Goldsmith U.S.A. 31°59N 102°37W 84 F3
Goldthwaite U.S.A. 31°27N 98°34W 84 F5
Goleniów Poland 53°35N 14°50E 16 B8
Golestān □ Iran 37°20N 55°25E 45 B7
Golestānak Iran 30°36N 54°14E 45 D7
Goleta U.S.A. 34°27N 119°50W 79 L7
Golfito Costa Rica 8°41N 83°5W 88 E3
Golfo Aranci Italy 40°59N 9°38E 22 D3
Goliad U.S.A. 28°40N 97°23W 84 G6
Golpāyegān Iran 33°27N 50°18E 45 C6
Golra Pakistan 33°37N 72°56E 42 C5
Golspie U.K. 57°58N 3°59W 11 D5
Goma Dem. Rep. of the Congo 1°37S 29°10E 54 C2
Gomal Pass Pakistan 31°56N 69°20E 42 D3
Gomati → India 25°32N 83°11E 43 G10
Gombari Dem. Rep. of the Congo 2°45N 29°3E 54 B2
Gombe Nigeria 10°19N 11°2E 51 F8
Gombe → Tanzania 4°38S 31°40E 54 C3
Gomel = Homyel Belarus 52°28N 31°0E 17 B16
Gomera Canary Is. 28°7N 17°14W 24 F2
Gómez Palacio Mexico 25°34N 103°30W 86 B4
Gomīshān Iran 37°4N 54°6E 45 B7
Gomogomo Indonesia 6°39S 134°43E 37 F8
Gomoh India 23°52N 86°10E 43 H12
Gompa = Ganta Liberia 7°15N 8°59W 50 G4
Gonābād Iran 34°15N 58°45E 45 C8
Gonaïves Haiti 19°20N 72°42W 89 C5
Gonarezhou △ Zimbabwe 21°32S 31°55E 55 G3
Gonâve, G. de la Haiti 19°29N 72°42W 89 C5
Gonâve, Île de la Haiti 18°51N 73°3W 89 C5
Gonbad-e Kāvūs Iran 37°20N 55°25E 45 B7
Gonda India 27°9N 81°58E 43 F9
Gondal India 21°58N 70°52E 42 J4
Gonder Ethiopia 12°39N 37°30E 47 E2
Gondia India 21°23N 80°10E 40 J12
Gondola Mozam. 19°10S 33°37E 55 F3
Gönen Turkey 40°6N 27°39E 23 D12
Gongbei China 22°12N 113°32E 33 G10
Gonghe China 36°18N 100°32E 32 C5
Gongju S. Korea 36°27N 127°7E 35 F14
Gongming China 22°47N 113°53E 33 F10
Gongolgon Australia 30°21S 146°54E 63 E4
Gongzhuling China 43°30N 124°40E 35 C13
Goniri Nigeria 11°30N 12°15E 51 F8
Gonzales Calif., U.S.A. 36°30N 121°26W 78 J5
Gonzales Tex., U.S.A. 29°30N 97°27W 84 G6
González Mexico 22°48N 98°25W 87 C5
Good Hope, C. of S. Africa 34°24S 18°30E 56 E2
Good Hope Lake Canada 59°16N 129°18W 70 B3
Gooderham Canada 44°54N 78°21W 82 B6
Goodhouse S. Africa 28°57S 18°13E 56 D2
Gooding U.S.A. 42°56N 114°43W 76 E6
Goodland U.S.A. 39°21N 101°43W 80 F3
Goodlands Mauritius 20°2S 57°39E 53 d
Goodlow Canada 56°20N 120°8W 70 B4
Goodooga Australia 29°3S 147°28E 63 D4
Goodsprings U.S.A. 35°49N 115°27W 79 K11
Goole U.K. 53°42N 0°53W 12 D7
Goolgowi Australia 33°58S 145°41E 63 E4
Goomalling Australia 31°15S 116°49E 61 F2
Goomeri Australia 26°12S 152°6E 63 D5
Goonda Mozam. 19°48S 33°57E 55 F3
Goondiwindi Australia 28°30S 150°21E 63 D5
Goongarrie, L. Australia 30°3S 121°9E 61 F3
Goongarrie △ Australia 30°7S 121°30E 61 F3
Goonyella Australia 21°47S 147°58E 62 C4
Goose → Canada 53°20N 60°35W 73 B7
Goose Creek U.S.A. 32°59N 80°2W 85 E14
Goose L. U.S.A. 41°56N 120°26W 76 F3
Gop India 22°5N 69°50E 42 H3
Gopalganj India 26°28N 84°30E 43 F11
Göppingen Germany 48°42N 9°39E 16 D5
Gorakhpur India 26°47N 83°23E 43 F10
Goražde Bos.-H. 43°38N 18°58E 23 C8
Gorda, Pta. Canary Is. 28°45N 18°0W 24 F2
Gorda, Pta. Nic. 14°20N 83°10W 88 D3
Gordan B. Australia 11°35S 130°10E 60 B5
Gordon U.S.A. 42°48N 102°12W 80 D2
Gordon → Australia 42°27S 145°30E 63 G4
Gordon Bay Canada 45°12N 79°47W 82 A5
Gordon L. Alta., Canada 56°30N 110°25W 71 B6
Gordon L. N.W.T., Canada 63°5N 113°11W 70 A6
Gordonvale Australia 17°5S 145°50E 62 B4
Goré Chad 7°59N 16°31E 51 G9
Gore Ethiopia 8°12N 35°32E 47 F2
Gore N.Z. 46°5S 168°58E 59 G2
Gore Bay Canada 45°57N 82°28W 72 C3
Gorey Ireland 52°41N 6°18W 10 D5
Gorg Iran 29°29N 59°43E 45 D8
Gorgān Iran 36°55N 54°30E 45 B7
Gorgona, I. Colombia 3°0N 78°10W 92 C3
Gorham U.S.A. 44°23N 71°10W 83 B13
Goriganga → India 29°45N 80°23E 43 E9
Gorinchem Neths. 51°50N 4°59E 15 C4
Goris Armenia 39°31N 46°22E 19 G8
Gorízia Italy 45°56N 13°37E 22 B5
Gorkiy = Nizhniy Novgorod Russia 56°20N 44°0E 18 C7
Gorkovskoye Vdkhr. Russia 57°2N 43°4E 18 C7
Gorleston U.K. 52°35N 1°44E 13 E9
Görlitz Germany 51°9N 14°58E 16 C8
Gorlovka = Horlivka Ukraine 48°19N 38°5E 19 E6
Gorman U.S.A. 34°47N 118°51W 79 L8
Gorna Dzhumayo = Blagoevgrad Bulgaria 42°2N 23°5E 23 C10
Gorna Oryakhovitsa Bulgaria 43°7N 25°40E 23 C11
Gorno-Altay □ Russia 51°0N 86°0E 28 D9
Gorno-Altaysk Russia 51°50N 86°5E 28 D9
Gornozavodsk Russia 46°33N 141°50E 29 E15
Gornyatski Russia 67°32N 64°3E 18 A11
Gornyy Russia 44°57N 133°59E 30 B6
Gorodenka = Horodenka Ukraine 48°41N 25°29E 17 D13
Gorodok = Horodok Ukraine 49°46N 23°32E 17 D12
Gorokhov = Horokhiv Ukraine 50°30N 24°45E 17 C13
Goromonzi Zimbabwe 17°52S 31°22E 55 F3
Gorong, Kepulauan Indonesia 3°59S 131°25E 37 E8
Gorongosa △ Mozam. 18°50S 34°29E 57 B5
Gorongose → Mozam. 20°30S 34°40E 57 C5
Gorongoza Mozam. 18°44S 34°2E 55 F3
Gorongoza, Sa. da Mozam. 18°27S 34°2E 55 F3
Gorontalo Indonesia 0°35N 123°5E 37 D6
Gorontalo □ Indonesia 0°50N 122°20E 37 D6
Gort Ireland 53°3N 8°49W 10 C3
Gortis Greece 35°4N 24°58E 25 D6
Goryeong S. Korea 35°44N 128°15E 35 G15
Gorzów Wielkopolski Poland 52°43N 15°15E 16 B8
Gosford Australia 33°23S 151°18E 63 E5
Goshen Calif., U.S.A. 36°21N 119°25W 78 J7
Goshen Ind., U.S.A. 41°35N 85°50W 81 E11
Goshen N.Y., U.S.A. 41°24N 74°20W 83 E10
Goshogawara Japan 40°48N 140°27E 30 D10
Goslar Germany 51°54N 10°25E 16 C6
Gospič Croatia 44°35N 15°23E 16 F8
Gosport U.K. 50°48N 1°9W 13 G6
Gosse → Australia 19°32S 134°37E 62 B1
Göta älv → Sweden 57°42N 11°54E 9 H14
Göta kanal Sweden 58°30N 15°58E 9 G16
Götaland Sweden 57°30N 14°30E 9 H16
Göteborg Sweden 57°43N 11°59E 9 H14
Gotha Germany 50°56N 10°42E 16 C6
Gothenburg = Göteborg Sweden 57°43N 11°59E 9 H14
Gothenburg U.S.A. 40°56N 100°10W 80 E3
Gotland Sweden 57°30N 18°33E 9 H18
Gotō-Rettō Japan 32°55N 129°5E 31 H4
Gotska Sandön Sweden 58°24N 19°15E 9 G18
Gōtsu Japan 35°0N 132°14E 31 G6
Göttingen Germany 51°31N 9°55E 16 C5
Gottwaldov = Zlín Czech Rep. 49°14N 17°40E 17 D9
Goubangzi China 41°20N 121°52E 35 D11
Gouda Neths. 52°1N 4°42E 15 B4
Goudouras, Akra Greece 34°59N 26°6E 25 E8
Gouin, Rés. Canada 48°35N 74°40W 72 C5
Goulburn Australia 34°44S 149°44E 63 E4
Goulburn Is. Australia 11°40S 133°20E 62 A1
Goulimine Morocco 28°56N 10°0W 50 C3
Goundam Mali 16°27N 3°40W 50 E5
Gourits → S. Africa 34°21S 21°52E 56 E3
Gournes Greece 35°19N 25°16E 25 D7
Gourock U.K. 55°57N 4°49W 11 F4
Gouverneur U.S.A. 44°20N 75°28W 83 B9
Gouvia Greece 39°39N 19°50E 25 A3
Gove Peninsula Australia 12°17S 136°49E 62 A2
Governador Valadares Brazil 18°15S 41°57W 93 G10
Governor's Harbour Bahamas 25°10N 76°14W 88 A4
Govindgarh India 24°23N 81°18E 43 G9
Gowan Ra. Australia 25°0S 145°0E 62 D4
Gowanda U.S.A. 42°28N 78°56W 82 D6
Gower U.K. 51°35N 4°10W 13 F3
Gowna, L. Ireland 53°51N 7°34W 10 C4
Goya Argentina 29°10S 59°10W 94 B4
Goyder Lagoon Australia 27°3S 138°58E 63 D2
Goyllarisquizga Peru 10°31S 76°24W 92 F3
Goz Beïda Chad 12°10N 21°20E 51 F10
Gozo Malta 36°3N 14°15E 25 C1
Graaff-Reinet S. Africa 32°13S 24°32E 56 E3
Gračac Croatia 44°18N 15°57E 16 F8
Gracias a Dios, C. Honduras 15°0N 83°10W 88 D3
Graciosa Azores 39°4N 28°0W 50 a
Graciosa, I. Canary Is. 29°15N 13°32W 24 E6
Grado Spain 43°23N 6°4W 21 A2
Grady U.S.A. 34°49N 103°19W 77 J12
Grafham Water U.K. 52°19N 0°18W 13 E7
Grafton Australia 29°38S 152°58E 63 D5
Grafton N. Dak., U.S.A. 48°25N 97°25W 80 A5
Grafton W. Va., U.S.A. 39°21N 80°2W 81 F13
Graham Canada 49°20N 90°30W 72 C1
Graham U.S.A. 33°6N 98°35W 84 E5
Graham, Mt. U.S.A. 32°42N 109°52W 77 K9
Graham Bell, Ostrov = Greem-Bell, Ostrov Russia 81°0N 62°0E 28 A7
Graham I. Canada 53°40N 132°30W 70 C2
Graham Land Antarctica 65°0S 64°0W 5 C17
Grahamstown S. Africa 33°19S 26°31E 56 E4
Grahamsville U.S.A. 41°51N 74°33W 83 E10
Grain Coast W. Afr. 4°20N 10°0W 50 H3
Grajagan Indonesia 8°35S 114°13E 37 K17
Grajagan, Teluk Indonesia 8°40S 114°18E 37 K17
Grajaú Brazil 5°50S 46°4W 93 E9
Grajaú → Brazil 3°41S 44°48W 93 D10
Grampian U.S.A. 40°58N 78°37W 82 F6
Grampian Highlands = Grampian Mts. U.K. 56°50N 4°0W 11 E5
Grampian Mts. U.K. 56°50N 4°0W 11 E5
Grampians, The Australia 37°15S 142°20E 63 F3
Gran Canaria Canary Is. 27°55N 15°35W 24 G4
Gran Chaco S. Amer. 25°0S 61°0W 94 B3
Gran Desierto del Pinacate ⌂ Mexico 31°51N 113°32W 86 A2
Gran Paradiso Italy 45°33N 7°17E 20 D7
Gran Sasso d'Itália Italy 42°27N 13°42E 22 C5
Granada Nic. 11°58N 86°0W 88 D2
Granada Spain 37°10N 3°35W 21 D4
Granada U.S.A. 38°4N 102°19W 76 G12
Granadilla de Abona Canary Is. 28°7N 16°33W 24 F3
Granard Ireland 53°47N 7°30W 10 C4
Granbury U.S.A. 32°27N 97°47W 84 E6
Granby Canada 45°25N 72°45W 83 A12
Granby U.S.A. 40°5N 105°56W 76 F11
Grand → Canada 42°51N 79°34W 82 D5
Grand → Mo., U.S.A. 39°23N 93°7W 80 F7
Grand → S. Dak., U.S.A. 45°40N 100°45W 80 C3
Grand Bahama I. Bahamas 26°40N 78°30W 88 A4
Grand Baie Mauritius 20°0S 57°35E 53 d
Grand Bank Canada 47°6N 55°48W 73 C8
Grand Bassam Ivory C. 5°10N 3°49W 50 G5
Grand Bend Canada 43°18N 81°45W 82 C3
Grand-Bourg Guadeloupe 15°53N 61°19W 88 b
Grand Canal = Da Yunhe → China 39°10N 117°10E 35 E9
Grand Canyon U.S.A. 36°3N 112°9W 77 H7
Grand Canyon △ U.S.A. 36°15N 112°30W 77 H7
Grand Canyon-Parashant ⌂ U.S.A. 36°30N 113°45W 77 H7
Grand Cayman Cayman Is. 19°20N 81°20W 88 C3
Grand Coulee U.S.A. 47°57N 119°0W 76 C4
Grand Coulee Dam U.S.A. 47°57N 118°59W 76 C4
Grand Erg de Bilma Niger 18°30N 14°0E 51 E8
Grand Falls Canada 47°3N 67°44W 73 C6
Grand Falls-Windsor Canada 48°56N 55°40W 73 C8
Grand Forks Canada 49°0N 118°30W 70 D5
Grand Forks U.S.A. 47°55N 97°3W 80 B5
Grand Gorge U.S.A. 42°21N 74°29W 83 D10
Grand Haven U.S.A. 43°4N 86°13W 80 D10
Grand I. Mich., U.S.A. 46°31N 86°40W 80 B10
Grand I. N.Y., U.S.A. 43°0N 78°58W 82 D6
Grand Island U.S.A. 40°55N 98°21W 80 E4
Grand Isle La., U.S.A. 29°14N 90°0W 85 G9
Grand Isle Vt., U.S.A. 44°43N 73°18W 83 B11
Grand Junction U.S.A. 39°4N 108°33W 76 G9
Grand L. N.B., Canada 45°57N 66°7W 73 C6
Grand L. Nfld. & L., Canada 49°0N 57°30W 73 C8
Grand L. Nfld. & L., Canada 53°40N 60°30W 73 B7
Grand L. U.S.A. 29°55N 92°47W 84 G8
Grand Lake U.S.A. 40°15N 105°49W 76 F11
Grand Manan I. Canada 44°45N 66°52W 73 D6
Grand Marais Mich., U.S.A. 46°40N 85°59W 81 B11
Grand Marais Minn., U.S.A. 47°45N 90°25W 72 C1
Grand-Mère Canada 46°36N 72°40W 72 C5
Grand Portage U.S.A. 47°58N 89°41W 80 B9
Grand Prairie U.S.A. 32°44N 96°59W 84 E6
Grand Rapids Canada 53°12N 99°19W 71 C9
Grand Rapids Mich., U.S.A. 42°58N 85°40W 81 D11
Grand Rapids Minn., U.S.A. 47°14N 93°31W 80 B7
Grand St-Bernard, Col du Europe 45°50N 7°10E 20 D7
Grand Staircase-Escalante ⌂ U.S.A. 37°25N 111°33W 77 H8
Grand Teton U.S.A. 43°54N 110°50W 76 E8
Grand Teton △ U.S.A. 43°50N 110°50W 76 E8
Grand Union Canal U.K. 52°7N 0°53W 13 E7
Grande → Jujuy, Argentina 24°20S 65°2W 94 A2
Grande → Mendoza, Argentina 36°52S 69°45W 94 D2
Grande → Bolivia 15°51S 64°39W 92 G6
Grande → Bahia, Brazil 11°30S 44°30W 93 F10
Grande → Minas Gerais, Brazil 20°6S 51°4W 93 H8
Grande, B. Argentina 50°30S 68°20W 96 G3
Grande, Rio → N. Amer. 25°58N 97°9W 84 J6
Grande Anse Seychelles 4°18S 55°45E 53 b
Grande Baleine, R. de la → Canada 55°16N 77°47W 72 A4
Grande Cache Canada 53°53N 119°8W 70 C5
Grande Comore Comoros Is. 11°35S 43°20E 53 a
Grande-Entrée Canada 47°30N 61°40W 73 C7
Grande Prairie Canada 55°10N 118°50W 70 B5
Grande-Rivière Canada 48°26N 64°30W 73 C7
Grande-Terre Guadeloupe 16°20N 61°25W 88 b
Grande-Vallée Canada 49°14N 65°8W 73 C6
Grande Vigie, Pte. de la Guadeloupe 16°32N 61°27W 88 b
Grandfalls U.S.A. 31°20N 102°51W 84 F3
Grands-Jardins ⌂ Canada 47°41N 70°51W 73 C5
Grandview Canada 51°10N 100°42W 71 C8
Grandview U.S.A. 46°15N 119°54W 76 C4
Graneros Chile 34°5S 70°45W 94 C1
Grangemouth U.K. 56°1N 3°42W 11 E5
Granger U.S.A. 41°35N 109°58W 76 F9
Grangeville U.S.A. 45°56N 116°7W 76 D5
Granisle Canada 54°53N 126°13W 70 C3
Granite City U.S.A. 38°42N 90°8W 80 F8
Granite Falls U.S.A. 44°49N 95°33W 80 C6
Granite L. Canada 48°8N 57°5W 73 C8
Granite Mt. U.S.A. 33°5N 116°28W 79 M10
Granite Pk. U.S.A. 45°10N 109°48W 76 D9
Graniteville U.S.A. 44°8N 72°29W 83 B12
Granity N.Z. 41°39S 171°51E 59 D3
Granja Brazil 3°7S 40°50W 93 D10
Granollers Spain 41°39N 2°18E 21 B7
Grant U.S.A. 40°50N 101°43W 80 E3
Grant, Mt. U.S.A. 38°34N 118°48W 76 G4
Grant City U.S.A. 40°29N 94°25W 80 E6
Grant I. Australia 11°10S 132°52E 60 B5
Grant Range U.S.A. 38°30N 115°25W 76 G6
Grantham U.K. 52°55N 0°38W 12 E7
Grantown-on-Spey U.K. 57°20N 3°36W 11 D5
Grants U.S.A. 35°9N 107°52W 77 J10
Grants Pass U.S.A. 42°26N 123°19W 76 E2
Grantsville U.S.A. 40°36N 112°28W 76 F7
Granville France 48°50N 1°35W 20 B3
Granville N. Dak., U.S.A. 48°16N 100°47W 80 A3
Granville N.Y., U.S.A. 43°24N 73°16W 83 C11
Granville Ohio, U.S.A. 40°4N 82°31W 82 F2
Granville L. Canada 56°18N 100°30W 71 B8
Graskop S. Africa 24°56S 30°49E 57 C5
Grass → Canada 56°3N 96°33W 71 B9
Grass Range U.S.A. 47°2N 108°48W 76 C9
Grass River ⌂ Canada 54°40N 100°50W 71 C8
Grass Valley Calif., U.S.A. 39°13N 121°4W 78 F6
Grass Valley Oreg., U.S.A. 45°22N 120°47W 76 D3
Grasse France 43°38N 6°56E 20 E7
Grassflat U.S.A. 41°0N 78°6W 82 E6
Grasslands △ Canada 49°11N 107°38W 71 D7
Grassy Australia 40°3S 144°5E 63 G3
Graulhet France 43°45N 1°59E 20 E4
Gravelbourg Canada 49°50N 106°35W 71 D7
's-Gravenhage Neths. 52°7N 4°17E 15 B4
Gravenhurst Canada 44°52N 79°20W 82 B5
Gravesend Australia 29°35S 150°20E 63 D5
Gravesend U.K. 51°26N 0°22E 13 F8
Gravois, Pointe-à- Haiti 18°15N 73°56W 89 C5
Grayling U.S.A. 44°40N 84°43W 81 C11
Grays U.K. 51°28N 0°21E 13 F8
Grays Harbor U.S.A. 46°59N 124°1W 76 C1
Grays L. U.S.A. 43°4N 111°26W 76 E8
Grays River U.S.A. 46°21N 123°37W 78 D3
Graz Austria 47°4N 15°27E 16 E8
Greasy L. Canada 62°55N 122°12W 70 A4
Great Abaco I. = Abaco I. Bahamas 26°25N 77°10W 88 A4
Great Artesian Basin Australia 23°0S 144°0E 62 C3
Great Australian Bight Australia 33°30S 130°0E 61 F5
Great Bahama Bank Bahamas 23°15N 78°0W 88 B4
Great Barrier I. N.Z. 36°11S 175°25E 59 B5
Great Barrier Reef Australia 18°0S 146°50E 62 B4
Great Barrier Reef ⌂ Australia 20°0S 150°0E 62 B4
Great Barrington U.S.A. 42°12N 73°22W 83 D11
Great Basalt Wall △ Australia 19°52S 145°43E 62 B4
Great Basin U.S.A. 40°0N 117°0W 76 G5
Great Basin △ U.S.A. 38°56N 114°15W 76 G6
Great Bear → Canada 65°0N 124°0W 68 C7
Great Bear L. Canada 65°30N 120°0W 68 C8
Great Belt = Store Bælt Denmark 55°20N 11°0E 9 J14
Great Bend Kans., U.S.A. 38°22N 98°46W 80 F4
Great Bend Pa., U.S.A. 41°58N 75°45W 83 E9
Great Blasket I. Ireland 52°6N 10°32W 10 D1
Great Britain Europe 54°0N 2°15W 6 E5
Great Camanoe Br. Virgin Is. 18°30N 64°35W 89 e
Great Codroy Canada 47°51N 59°16W 73 C8
Great Divide, The = Great Dividing Ra. Australia 23°0S 146°0E 62 C4
Great Divide Basin U.S.A. 42°0N 108°0W 76 E9
Great Dividing Ra. Australia 23°0S 146°0E 62 C4
Great Driffield = Driffield U.K. 54°0N 0°26W 12 C7
Great Exuma I. Bahamas 23°30N 75°50W 88 B4
Great Falls U.S.A. 47°30N 111°17W 76 C8
Great Fish = Groot-Vis → S. Africa 33°28S 27°5E 56 E4
Great Guana Cay Bahamas 24°0N 76°20W 88 B4
Great Himalayan △ India 31°30N 77°30E 42 D7
Great Inagua I. Bahamas 21°0N 73°20W 89 B5
Great Indian Desert = Thar Desert India 28°0N 72°0E 42 F5
Great Karoo S. Africa 31°55S 21°0E 56 E3
Great Khingan Mts. = Da Hinggan Ling China 48°0N 121°0E 33 B7
Great Lake Australia 41°50S 146°40E 63 G4
Great Lakes N. Amer. 46°0N 84°0W 66 E11
Great Limpopo Transfrontier △ Africa 23°0S 31°45E 57 C5
Great Malvern U.K. 52°7N 2°18W 13 E5
Great Miami → U.S.A. 39°7N 84°49W 81 F11
Great Ormes Head U.K. 53°20N 3°52W 12 D4
Great Ouse → U.K. 52°48N 0°21E 12 E8
Great Palm I. Australia 18°45S 146°40E 62 B4
Great Pedro Bluff Jamaica 17°51N 77°44W 88 a
Great Pee Dee → U.S.A. 33°21N 79°10W 85 E15
Great Plains N. Amer. 47°0N 105°0W 66 E9
Great Ruaha → Tanzania 7°56S 37°52E 54 D4
Great Sacandaga L. U.S.A. 43°6N 74°16W 83 C10
Great Saint Bernard Pass = Grand St-Bernard, Col du Europe 45°50N 7°10E 20 D7
Great Salt Desert = Kavīr, Dasht-e Iran 34°30N 55°0E 45 C7
Great Salt L. U.S.A. 41°15N 112°40W 76 F7
Great Salt Lake Desert U.S.A. 40°50N 113°30W 76 F7
Great Salt Plains L. U.S.A. 36°45N 98°8W 84 C5

Great Sand Dunes △
   U.S.A. 37°48N 105°45W **77** H11
Great Sandy △ *Australia* 26°13S 153°2E **63** D5
Great Sandy Desert
   Australia 21°0S 124°0E **60** D3
Great Sandy Desert
   U.S.A. 43°35N 120°15W **74** B2
Great Sangi = Sangihe, Pulau
   Indonesia 3°35S 125°30E **37** D7
Great Sea Reef *Fiji* 16°15S 179°0E **59** a
Great Skellig *Ireland* 51°47N 10°33W **10** E1
Great Slave L. *Canada* 61°23N 115°38W **70** A5
Great Smoky Mts. △
   U.S.A. 35°40N 83°40W **85** D13
Great Stour = Stour →
   U.K. 51°18N 1°22E **13** F9
Great Victoria Desert
   Australia 29°30S 126°30E **61** E4
Great Wall *Antarctica* 62°30S 58°0W **5** C18
Great Wall *China* 38°30N 109°30E **34** E5
Great Whernside *U.K.* 54°10N 1°58W **12** C6
Great Yarmouth *U.K.* 52°37N 1°44E **13** E9
Great Zab = Zāb al Kabīr →
   Iraq 36°1N 43°24E **44** B4
Great Zimbabwe
   Zimbabwe 20°16S 30°54E **55** G3
Greater Antilles *W. Indies* 17°40N 74°0W **89** C5
Greater London □ *U.K.* 51°31N 0°6W **13** F7
Greater Manchester □
   U.K. 53°30N 2°15W **12** D5
Greater St. Lucia Wetlands △
   S. Africa 28°6S 32°27E **57** D5
Greater Sudbury = Sudbury
   Canada 46°30N 81°0W **72** C3
Greater Sunda Is. *Indonesia* 7°0S 112°0E **36** F4
Greco, C. *Cyprus* 34°57N 34°5E **25** E13
Gredos, Sierra de *Spain* 40°20N 5°0W **21** B3
Greece *U.S.A.* 43°13N 77°41W **82** C7
Greece ■ *Europe* 40°0N 23°0E **23** E9
Greeley *Colo., U.S.A.* 40°25N 104°42W **76** F11
Greeley *Nebr., U.S.A.* 41°33N 98°32W **80** E4
Greely Fd. *Canada* 80°30N 85°0W **69** A11
Greem-Bell, Ostrov *Russia* 81°0N 62°0E **28** A7
Green → *Ky., U.S.A.* 37°54N 87°30W **80** G2
Green → *Utah, U.S.A.* 38°11N 109°53W **76** G9
Green B. *U.S.A.* 45°0N 87°30W **80** C10
Green Bay *U.S.A.* 44°31N 88°0W **80** C1
Green C. *Australia* 37°13S 150°1E **63** F5
Green Cove Springs
   U.S.A. 29°59N 81°42W **85** G14
Green Lake *Canada* 54°17N 107°47W **71** C7
Green Mts. *U.S.A.* 43°45N 72°45W **83** C12
Green River *Utah,*
   U.S.A. 38°59N 110°10W **76** G8
Green River *Wyo.,*
   U.S.A. 41°32N 109°28W **76** F9
Green Valley *U.S.A.* 31°52N 110°56W **77** L8
Greenbank *U.S.A.* 48°6N 122°34W **78** B4
Greenbush *Mich., U.S.A.* 44°35N 83°19W **82** B1
Greenbush *Minn., U.S.A.* 48°42N 96°11W **80** A5
Greencastle *U.S.A.* 39°38N 86°52W **80** F10
Greene *U.S.A.* 42°20N 75°46W **83** D9
Greeneville *U.S.A.* 36°10N 82°50W **85** C13
Greenfield *Calif., U.S.A.* 36°19N 121°15W **78** J5
Greenfield *Calif., U.S.A.* 35°15N 119°0W **79** K8
Greenfield *Ind., U.S.A.* 39°47N 85°46W **81** F11
Greenfield *Iowa, U.S.A.* 41°18N 94°28W **80** E7
Greenfield *Mass.,*
   U.S.A. 42°35N 72°36W **83** D12
Greenfield *Mo., U.S.A.* 37°25N 93°51W **80** G7
Greenfield Park *Canada* 45°29N 73°28W **83** A11
Greenland ☑ *N. Amer.* 66°0N 45°0W **67** C15
Greenland Sea *Arctic* 73°0N 10°0W **4** B7
Greenock *U.K.* 55°57N 4°46W **11** F4
Greenore *Ireland* 54°2N 6°8W **10** B5
Greenore Pt. *Ireland* 52°14N 6°19W **10** D5
Greenough *Australia* 28°58S 114°43E **61** E1
Greenough → *Australia* 28°51S 114°38E **61** E1
Greenough Pt. *Canada* 44°58N 81°26W **82** B3
Greenport *U.S.A.* 41°6N 72°22W **83** E12
Greensboro *Ga., U.S.A.* 33°35N 83°11W **85** E13
Greensboro *N.C., U.S.A.* 36°4N 79°48W **85** C15
Greensboro *Vt., U.S.A.* 44°36N 72°18W **83** B12
Greensburg *Ind., U.S.A.* 39°20N 85°29W **81** F11
Greensburg *Kans.,*
   U.S.A. 37°36N 99°18W **80** G4
Greensburg *Pa., U.S.A.* 40°18N 79°33W **82** F5
Greenstone Pt. *U.K.* 57°55N 5°37W **11** D3
Greenvale *Australia* 18°59S 145°7E **62** B4
Greenville *Liberia* 5°1N 9°6W **50** G4
Greenville *Ala., U.S.A.* 31°50N 86°38W **85** F11
Greenville *Calif., U.S.A.* 40°8N 120°57W **78** E6
Greenville *Maine,*
   U.S.A. 45°28N 69°35W **81** C19
Greenville *Mich., U.S.A.* 43°11N 85°15W **81** D11
Greenville *Miss., U.S.A.* 33°24N 91°4W **85** E9
Greenville *Mo., U.S.A.* 37°8N 90°27W **80** G8
Greenville *N.C., U.S.A.* 35°37N 77°23W **85** D16
Greenville *N.H., U.S.A.* 42°46N 71°49W **83** D13
Greenville *N.Y., U.S.A.* 42°25N 74°1W **83** D10
Greenville *Ohio, U.S.A.* 40°6N 84°38W **81** E11
Greenville *Pa., U.S.A.* 41°24N 80°23W **82** E4
Greenville *S.C., U.S.A.* 34°51N 82°24W **85** D13
Greenville *Tex., U.S.A.* 33°8N 96°7W **84** E6
Greenwater Lake △
   Canada 52°32N 103°30W **71** C8
Greenwich *Conn., U.S.A.* 41°2N 73°38W **83** E11
Greenwich *N.Y., U.S.A.* 43°5N 73°30W **83** C11
Greenwich *Ohio, U.S.A.* 41°2N 82°31W **82** E2
Greenwich □ *U.K.* 51°29N 0°1E **13** F8
Greenwood *Canada* 49°10N 118°40W **70** D5
Greenwood *Ark., U.S.A.* 35°13N 94°16W **84** D7
Greenwood *Ind., U.S.A.* 39°37N 86°7W **80** F10
Greenwood *Miss., U.S.A.* 33°31N 90°11W **85** E9
Greenwood *S.C., U.S.A.* 34°12N 82°10W **85** D13
Greenwood, Mt.
   Australia 13°48S 130°4E **60** B5

Gregory *U.S.A.* 43°14N 99°26W **80** D4
Gregory → *Australia* 17°53S 139°17E **62** B2
Gregory, L. *S. Austral.,*
   Australia 28°55S 139°0E **63** D2
Gregory, L. *W. Austral.,*
   Australia 20°0S 127°40E **60** D4
Gregory → *Australia* 25°38S 119°58E **61** E2
Gregory △ *Australia* 15°38S 131°15E **60** C5
Gregory Downs
   Australia 18°35S 138°45E **62** B2
Gregory Ra. *Queens.,*
   Australia 19°30S 143°40E **62** B3
Gregory Ra. *W. Austral.,*
   Australia 21°20S 121°12E **60** D3
Greifswald *Germany* 54°5N 13°23E **16** A7
Greiz *Germany* 50°39N 12°10E **16** C7
Gremikha *Russia* 67°59N 39°47E **18** A6
Grenå *Denmark* 56°25N 10°53E **9** H14
Grenada *U.S.A.* 33°47N 89°49W **85** E10
Grenada ■ *W. Indies* 12°10N 61°40W **89** D7
Grenadier I. *U.S.A.* 44°3N 76°22W **83** B8
Grenadines, The
   St. Vincent 12°40N 61°20W **89** D7
Grenen *Denmark* 57°44N 10°40E **9** H14
Grenfell *Australia* 33°52S 148°8E **63** E4
Grenfell *Canada* 50°30N 102°56W **71** C8
Grenoble *France* 45°12N 5°42E **20** D6
Grenville, C. *Australia* 12°0S 143°13E **62** A3
Grenville Chan. *Canada* 53°40N 129°46W **70** C3
Gresham *U.S.A.* 45°30N 122°25W **78** E4
Gresik *Indonesia* 7°13S 112°38E **37** G15
Gretna *U.K.* 55°0N 3°3W **11** F5
Gretna *U.S.A.* 29°54N 90°3W **85** G9
Grevenmacher *Lux.* 49°41N 6°26E **15** E6
Grey → *Canada* 47°34N 57°6W **73** C8
Grey → *N.Z.* 42°27S 171°12E **59** E3
Grey Ra. *Australia* 27°0S 143°30E **63** D3
Greybull *U.S.A.* 44°30N 108°3W **76** D9
Greymouth *N.Z.* 42°29S 171°13E **59** E3
Greystones *Ireland* 53°9N 6°5W **10** C5
Greytown *N.Z.* 41°5S 175°29E **59** D5
Greytown *S. Africa* 29°1S 30°36E **57** D5
Gribbell I. *Canada* 53°23N 129°0W **70** C3
Gridley *U.S.A.* 39°22N 121°42W **78** F5
Griekwastad *S. Africa* 28°49S 23°15E **56** D3
Griffin *U.S.A.* 33°15N 84°16W **85** E12
Griffith *Australia* 34°18S 146°2E **63** E4
Griffith *Canada* 45°15N 77°10W **82** A7
Griffith I. *Canada* 44°50N 80°55W **82** B4
Grimaylov = Hrymayliv
   Ukraine 49°20N 26°5E **17** D14
Grimes *U.S.A.* 39°4N 121°54W **78** F5
Grimsay *U.K.* 57°29N 7°14W **11** D1
Grimsby *Canada* 43°12N 79°34W **82** C5
Grimsby *U.K.* 53°34N 0°5W **12** D7
Grímsey *Iceland* 66°33N 17°58W **8** C5
Grimshaw *Canada* 56°10N 117°40W **70** B5
Grimstad *Norway* 58°20N 8°35E **9** G13
Grinnell *U.S.A.* 41°45N 92°43W **80** E8
Gris-Nez, C. *France* 50°52N 1°35E **20** A4
Grise Fiord *Canada* 76°25N 82°57W **69** B11
Groais I. *Canada* 50°55N 55°35W **73** B8
Groblersdal *S. Africa* 25°15S 29°25E **57** D4
Grodno = Hrodna
   Belarus 53°42N 23°52E **17** B12
Grodzyanka = Hrodzyanka
   Belarus 53°31N 28°42E **17** B15
Groesbeck *U.S.A.* 31°31N 96°32W **84** F6
Grójec *Poland* 51°50N 20°58E **17** C11
Grong *Norway* 64°25N 12°8E **8** D15
Groningen *Neths.* 53°15N 6°35E **15** A6
Groningen □ *Neths.* 53°16N 6°40E **15** A6
Groom *U.S.A.* 35°12N 101°6W **84** D4
Groot → *S. Africa* 33°45S 24°36E **56** E3
Groot-Berg → *S. Africa* 32°47S 18°8E **56** E2
Groot-Brakrivier *S. Africa* 34°2S 22°18E **56** E3
Groot Karasberge
   Namibia 27°20S 18°40E **56** D2
Groot-Kei → *S. Africa* 32°41S 28°22E **57** E4
Groot-Vis → *S. Africa* 33°28S 27°5E **56** E4
Grootdrink *S. Africa* 28°33S 21°42E **56** D3
Groote Eylandt *Australia* 14°0S 136°40E **62** A2
Grootfontein *Namibia* 19°31S 18°6E **56** B2
Grootlaagte → *Africa* 20°55S 21°27E **56** C3
Grootvloer → *S. Africa* 30°0S 20°40E **56** E3
Gros C. *Canada* 61°59N 113°32W **70** A6
Gros Islet *St. Lucia* 14°5N 60°58W **89** f
Gros Morne △ *Canada* 49°40N 57°50W **73** C8
Gros Piton *St. Lucia* 13°49N 61°5W **89** f
Gros Piton Pt. *St. Lucia* 13°49N 61°5W **89** f
Grossa, Pta. *Spain* 39°6N 1°36E **24** B8
Grosse Point *U.S.A.* 42°23N 82°54W **82** D2
Grosser Arber *Germany* 49°6N 13°8E **16** D7
Grosseto *Italy* 42°46N 11°8E **22** C4
Grossglockner *Austria* 47°5N 12°40E **16** E7
Groswater B. *Canada* 54°20N 57°40W **73** B8
Groton *Conn., U.S.A.* 41°21N 72°5W **83** E12
Groton *N.Y., U.S.A.* 42°36N 76°22W **83** D8
Groton *S. Dak., U.S.A.* 45°27N 98°6W **80** C4
Grouard Mission *Canada* 55°33N 116°9W **70** B5
Groundhog → *Canada* 48°45N 82°58W **72** C3
Grouw *Neths.* 53°5N 5°51E **15** A5
Grove City *U.S.A.* 41°10N 80°5W **82** E4
Grove Hill *U.S.A.* 31°42N 87°47W **85** F11
Groveland *U.S.A.* 37°50N 120°14W **78** H6
Grover Beach *U.S.A.* 35°7N 120°37W **79** K6
Groves *U.S.A.* 29°57N 93°54W **84** G8
Groveton *U.S.A.* 44°36N 71°31W **83** B13
Groznyy *Russia* 43°20N 45°45E **19** F8
Grudziądz *Poland* 53°30N 18°47E **17** B10
Gruinard B. *U.K.* 57°56N 5°35W **11** D3
Grundy Center *U.S.A.* 42°22N 92°47W **80** D7
Gruver *U.S.A.* 36°16N 101°24W **84** C4
Gryazi *Russia* 52°30N 39°58E **18** D6
Gryazovets *Russia* 58°50N 40°10E **18** C7

Grytviken *S. Georgia* 54°19S 36°33W **96** G9
Gua *India* 22°18N 85°20E **43** H11
Gua Musang *Malaysia* 4°53N 101°58E **39** K3
Guacanayabo, G. de
   Cuba 20°40N 77°20W **88** B4
Guachípas → *Argentina* 25°40S 65°30W **94** B2
Guadalajara *Mexico* 20°40N 103°20W **86** C4
Guadalajara *Spain* 40°37N 3°12W **21** B4
Guadalcanal *Solomon Is.* 9°32S 160°12E **58** B9
Guadales *Argentina* 34°30S 67°55W **94** C2
Guadalete → *Spain* 36°35N 6°13W **21** D2
Guadalquivir → *Spain* 36°47N 6°22W **21** D2
Guadalupe = Guadeloupe ☑
   W. Indies 16°20N 61°40W **88** b
Guadalupe *Mexico* 32°4N 116°32W **79** N10
Guadalupe *Zacatecas,*
   Mexico 22°45N 102°31W **86** C4
Guadalupe *U.S.A.* 34°58N 120°34W **79** L6
Guadalupe → *U.S.A.* 28°27N 96°47W **84** G6
Guadalupe, Sierra de
   Spain 39°28N 5°30W **21** C3
Guadalupe Bravos
   Mexico 31°20N 106°10W **86** A3
Guadalupe I. *Pac. Oc.* 29°0N 118°50W **66** G8
Guadalupe Mts. △
   U.S.A. 31°40N 104°30W **84** F2
Guadalupe Peak *U.S.A.* 31°50N 104°52W **84** F2
Guadalupe y Calvo
   Mexico 26°6N 106°58W **86** B3
Guadarrama, Sierra de
   Spain 41°0N 4°0W **21** B4
Guadeloupe ☑ *W. Indies* 16°20N 61°40W **88** b
Guadeloupe △ *Guadeloupe* 16°10N 61°40W **88** b
Guadeloupe Passage
   W. Indies 16°50N 62°15W **89** C7
Guadiana → *Portugal* 37°14N 7°22W **21** D2
Guadix *Spain* 37°18N 3°11W **21** D4
Guafo, Boca del *Chile* 43°35S 74°0W **96** E2
Guaico *Trin. & Tob.* 10°35N 61°9W **93** K15
Guainía → *Colombia* 2°1N 67°7W **92** C5
Guaíra *Brazil* 24°5S 54°10W **95** A5
Guaíra *Paraguay* 25°45S 56°30W **94** B4
Guaitecas, Is. *Chile* 44°0S 74°30W **96** E2
Guajará-Mirim *Brazil* 10°50S 65°20W **92** F5
Guajira, Pen. de la
   Colombia 12°0N 72°0W **92** A4
Gualán *Guatemala* 15°8N 89°22W **88** C2
Gualeguay *Argentina* 33°10S 59°14W **94** C4
Gualeguaychú *Argentina* 33°3S 59°31W **94** C4
Gualequay → *Argentina* 33°19S 59°39W **94** C4
Guam ☑ *Pac. Oc.* 13°27N 144°45E **64** F6
Guaminí *Argentina* 37°1S 62°28W **94** D3
Guamúchil *Mexico* 25°28N 108°6W **86** B3
Guana I. *Br. Virgin Is.* 18°30N 64°30W **89** e
Guanabacoa *Cuba* 23°8N 82°18W **88** B3
Guanacaste, Cordillera de
   Costa Rica 10°40N 85°4W **88** D2
Guanacaste △
   Costa Rica 10°57N 85°30W **88** D2
Guanaceví *Mexico* 25°56N 105°57W **86** B3
Guanahani = San Salvador I.
   Bahamas 24°0N 74°40W **89** B5
Guanaja *Honduras* 16°30N 85°55W **88** C2
Guanajay *Cuba* 22°56N 82°42W **88** B3
Guanajuato *Mexico* 21°1N 101°15W **86** C4
Guanajuato □ *Mexico* 21°0N 101°0W **86** C4
Guandacol *Argentina* 29°30S 68°40W **94** B2
Guane *Cuba* 22°10N 84°7W **88** B3
Guangdong □ *China* 23°0N 113°0E **33** D6
Guangling *China* 39°47N 114°22E **34** E8
Guangrao *China* 37°5N 118°25E **35** F10
Guangwu *China* 37°48N 105°57E **34** F3
Guangxi Zhuangzu Zizhiqu □
   China 24°0N 109°0E **33** D5
Guangzhou *China* 23°6N 113°13E **33** D6
Guánica *Puerto Rico* 17°58N 66°55W **89** d
Guanipa → *Venezuela* 9°56N 62°26W **92** B6
Guannan *China* 34°8N 119°21E **35** G10
Guantánamo *Cuba* 20°10N 75°14W **89** B4
Guantánamo B. *Cuba* 19°59N 75°10W **89** C4
Guantao *China* 36°42N 115°25E **34** F8
Guanyun *China* 34°20N 119°18E **35** G10
Guápay = Grande →
   Bolivia 15°51S 64°39W **92** G6
Guápiles *Costa Rica* 10°10N 83°46W **88** D3
Guapo B. *Trin. & Tob.* 10°12N 61°41W **93** K15
Guaporé *Brazil* 28°51S 51°54W **95** B5
Guaporé → *Brazil* 11°55S 65°4W **92** F5
Guaqui *Bolivia* 16°41S 68°54W **92** G5
Guaramacal △ *Venezuela* 9°13N 70°12W **89** E5
Guarapari *Brazil* 20°40S 40°30W **95** A7
Guarapuava *Brazil* 25°20S 51°30W **95** B5
Guaratinguetá *Brazil* 22°49S 45°9W **95** A6
Guaratuba *Brazil* 25°53S 48°38W **95** B6
Guarda *Portugal* 40°32N 7°20W **21** B2
Guardafui, C. = Asir, Ras
   Somali Rep. 11°55N 51°10E **47** E5
Guárico □ *Venezuela* 8°40N 66°35W **92** B5
Guarujá *Brazil* 24°2S 46°25W **95** A6
Guarulhos *Brazil* 23°29S 46°33W **95** A6
Guasave *Mexico* 25°34N 108°27W **86** B3
Guasdualito *Venezuela* 7°15N 70°44W **92** B4
Guatemala *Guatemala* 14°40N 90°22W **88** D1
Guatemala ■
    15°40N 90°30W **88** C1
Guatemala Basin *Pac. Oc.* 11°0N 95°0W **65** F18
Guatemala Trench
   Pac. Oc. 14°0N 95°0W **66** H10
Guatopo △ *Venezuela* 10°5N 66°30W **89** D6
Guaturo Pt.
   Trin. & Tob. 10°19N 60°59W **93** K16
Guaviare → *Colombia* 4°3N 67°44W **92** C5
Guaxupé *Brazil* 21°10S 47°5W **95** A6
Guayaguayare
   Trin. & Tob. 10°8N 61°2W **93** K15
Guayama *Puerto Rico* 17°59N 66°7W **89** d
Guayaquil *Ecuador* 2°15S 79°52W **92** D3

Guayaquil *Mexico* 29°59N 115°4W **86** B1
Guayaquil, G. de *Ecuador* 3°10S 81°0W **92** D2
Guaymas *Mexico* 27°56N 110°54W **86** B2
Guba
   Dem. Rep. of the Congo 10°38S 26°27E **55** E2
Gubkin *Russia* 51°17N 37°32E **19** D6
Gubkinskiy *Russia* 64°27N 76°36E **28** C8
Gudbrandsdalen *Norway* 61°33N 10°10E **8** F14
Guddu Barrage *Pakistan* 28°30N 69°50E **42** E3
Gudur *India* 14°12N 79°55E **40** M11
Guékédou *Guinea* 8°40N 10°5W **50** G3
Guelmine = Goulimine
   Morocco 28°56N 10°0W **50** C3
Guelph *Canada* 43°35N 80°20W **82** C4
Guerara *Algeria* 32°51N 4°22E **50** B6
Guéret *France* 46°11N 1°51E **20** C4
Guerneville *U.S.A.* 38°30N 123°0W **78** G4
Guernica = Gernika-Lumo
   Spain 43°19N 2°40W **21** A4
Guernsey *U.K.* 49°26N 2°35W **13** H5
Guernsey *U.S.A.* 42°16N 104°45W **76** E11
Guerrero □ *Mexico* 17°40N 100°0W **87** D5
Gügher *Iran* 29°28N 56°27E **45** D8
Guhakolak, Tanjung
   Indonesia 6°50S 105°14E **37** G11
Guia *Canary Is.* 28°8N 15°38W **24** F4
Guia de Isora *Canary Is.* 28°12N 16°46W **24** F3
Guia Lopes da Laguna
   Brazil 21°26S 56°7W **95** A4
Guiana Highlands
   S. Amer. 5°10N 60°40W **90** C4
Guidónia-Montecélio
   Italy 42°1N 12°45E **22** C5
Guijá *Mozam.* 24°27S 33°0E **57** C5
Guildford *U.K.* 51°14N 0°34W **13** F7
Guilford *U.S.A.* 41°17N 72°41W **83** E12
Guilin *China* 25°18N 110°15E **33** D6
Guillaume-Delisle, L.
   Canada 56°15N 76°17W **72** A4
Güímar *Canary Is.* 28°18N 16°24W **24** F3
Guimarães *Portugal* 41°28N 8°24W **21** B1
Guimaras □ *Phil.* 10°35N 122°37E **37** B6
Guinda *U.S.A.* 38°50N 122°12W **78** G4
Guinea *Africa* 8°0N 8°0E **48** F4
Guinea ■ *W. Afr.* 10°20N 11°30W **50** F3
Guinea, Gulf of *Atl. Oc.* 3°0N 2°30E **49** F4
Guinea-Bissau ■ *Africa* 12°0N 15°0W **50** F3
Güines *Cuba* 22°50N 82°0W **88** B3
Guingamp *France* 48°34N 3°10W **20** B2
Güiria *Venezuela* 10°32N 62°18W **92** A6
Guiuan *Phil.* 11°5N 125°55E **37** B7
Guiyang *China* 26°32N 106°40E **32** D5
Guizhou □ *China* 27°0N 107°0E **32** D5
Gujar Khan *Pakistan* 33°16N 73°19E **42** C5
Gujarat □ *India* 23°20N 71°0E **42** H4
Gujranwala *Pakistan* 32°10N 74°12E **42** C6
Gujrat *Pakistan* 32°40N 74°2E **42** C6
Gulbarga *India* 17°20N 76°50E **40** L10
Gulbene *Latvia* 57°8N 26°52E **9** H22
Gulf, The = Persian Gulf
   Asia 27°0N 50°0E **45** E6
Gulf Islands △ *U.S.A.* 30°10N 87°10W **85** F11
Gulfport *U.S.A.* 30°22N 89°6W **85** F10
Gulgong *Australia* 32°20S 149°49E **63** E4
Gulistan *Pakistan* 30°30N 66°35E **42** D2
Gulja = Yining *China* 43°58N 81°10E **32** B3
Gull Lake *Canada* 50°10N 108°29W **71** C7
Güllük *Turkey* 37°14N 27°35E **23** F12
Gulmarg *India* 34°3N 74°25E **43** B6
Gülshat *Kazakhstan* 46°38N 74°21E **28** C8
Gulu *Uganda* 2°48N 32°17E **54** B3
Gulwe *Tanzania* 6°30S 36°25E **54** D4
Gumal → *Pakistan* 31°40N 71°50E **42** D4
Gumbaz *Pakistan* 30°2N 69°0E **42** D3
Gumel *Nigeria* 12°39N 9°22E **50** F7
Gumi *S. Korea* 36°10N 128°12E **35** F15
Gumla *India* 23°3N 84°33E **43** H11
Gumlu *Australia* 19°53S 147°41E **62** B4
Gumma □ *Japan* 36°30N 138°20E **31** F9
Gumzai *Indonesia* 5°28S 134°42E **37** F8
Guna *India* 24°40N 77°19E **42** G7
Gunbalanya *Australia* 12°20S 133°4E **60** B5
Gundabooka △
   Australia 30°30S 145°20E **63** E4
Gunisao → *Canada* 53°56N 97°53W **71** C9
Gunisao L. *Canada* 53°33N 96°15W **71** C9
Gunjyal *Pakistan* 32°20N 71°55E **42** C4
Gunnbjørn Fjeld
   Greenland 68°55N 29°47W **4** C6
Gunnedah *Australia* 30°59S 150°15E **63** E5
Gunnewin *Australia* 25°59S 148°33E **63** D4
Gunningbar Cr. →
   Australia 31°14S 147°6E **63** E4
Gunnison *Colo.,*
   U.S.A. 38°33N 106°56W **76** G10
Gunnison *Utah, U.S.A.* 39°9N 111°49W **76** G8
Gunnison → *U.S.A.* 39°4N 108°35W **76** G9
Gunpowder *Australia* 19°42S 139°22E **62** B2
Gunsan *S. Korea* 35°59N 126°45E **35** G14
Gunter *Canada* 44°52N 77°32W **82** B7
Guntersville *U.S.A.* 34°21N 86°18W **85** D11
Guntong *Malaysia* 4°36N 101°3E **39** K3
Guntur *India* 16°23N 80°30E **41** L12
Gunungapi *Indonesia* 6°45S 126°30E **37** F7
Gunungsitoli *Indonesia* 1°15N 97°30E **36** D1
Guo He → *China* 32°59N 117°10E **35** H9
Guoyang *China* 33°32N 116°12E **34** H9
Gupis *Pakistan* 36°15N 73°20E **43** A5
Gurbantünggüt Shamo
   China 45°8N 87°20E **32** B3
Gurdaspur *India* 32°5N 75°31E **42** C6
Gurdon *U.S.A.* 33°55N 93°9W **84** E8
Gurgaon *India* 28°27N 77°1E **42** E7
Gurgueia → *Brazil* 6°50S 43°24W **93** E10

Gurha *India* 25°12N 71°39E **42** G4
Guri, Embalse de
   Venezuela 7°50N 62°52W **92** B6
Gurkha *Nepal* 28°5N 84°40E **43** E11
Gurla Mandhata = Naimona'nyi
   Feng *Nepal* 30°26N 81°18E **43** D9
Gurley *Australia* 29°45S 149°48E **63** D4
Gurnet Point *U.S.A.* 42°1N 70°34W **83** D14
Guro *Mozam.* 17°26S 32°30E **55** F3
Gurué *Mozam.* 15°25S 36°58E **55** F4
Gurun *Malaysia* 5°49N 100°27E **39** K3
Gürün *Turkey* 38°43N 37°15E **19** G6
Gurupá *Brazil* 1°25S 51°35W **93** D8
Gurupá, I. Grande de
   Brazil 1°25S 51°45W **93** D8
Gurupi *Brazil* 11°43S 49°4W **93** F9
Gurupi → *Brazil* 1°13S 46°6W **93** D9
Guruwe *Zimbabwe* 16°40S 30°42E **57** B5
Gurvan Sayhan Uul
   Mongolia 43°50N 104°0E **32** B5
Guryev = Atyraū
   Kazakhstan 47°5N 52°0E **19** E9
Gusau *Nigeria* 12°12N 6°40E **50** F7
Gushan *China* 39°50N 123°35E **35** E12
Gushgy = Serhetabat
   Turkmenistan 35°20N 62°18E **45** C3
Gusinoozersk *Russia* 51°16N 106°27E **29** D11
Gustavus *U.S.A.* 58°25N 135°44W **70** B1
Gustine *U.S.A.* 37°16N 121°0W **78** H6
Güstrow *Germany* 53°47N 12°10E **16** B7
Gütersloh *Germany* 51°54N 8°24E **16** C5
Gutha *Australia* 28°58S 115°55E **61** E2
Guthalungra *Australia* 19°52S 147°50E **62** B4
Guthrie *Canada* 44°28N 79°32W **82** B5
Guthrie *Okla., U.S.A.* 35°53N 97°25W **84** D6
Guthrie *Tex., U.S.A.* 33°37N 100°19W **84** E4
Guttenberg *U.S.A.* 42°47N 91°6W **80** D8
Gutu *Zimbabwe* 19°41S 31°9E **57** B5
Guwahati *India* 26°10N 91°45E **41** F17
Guy Fawkes River △
   Australia 30°0S 152°20E **63** D5
Guyana ■ *S. Amer.* 5°0N 59°0W **92** C7
Guyane française = French
   Guiana ☑ *S. Amer.* 4°0N 53°0W **93** C8
Guyang *China* 41°0N 110°5E **34** D6
Guyenne *France* 44°30N 0°40E **20** D4
Guymon *U.S.A.* 36°41N 101°29W **84** C4
Guyra *Australia* 30°15S 151°40E **63** E5
Guyuan *Hebei, China* 41°37N 115°40E **34** D8
Guyuan *Ningxia Huizu,*
   China 36°0N 106°20E **34** F4
Güzelyurt = Morphou
   Cyprus 35°12N 32°59E **25** D11
Guzhen *China* 33°22N 117°18E **35** H9
Guzmán, L. de *Mexico* 31°20N 107°30W **86** A3
Gwa *Burma* 17°36N 94°34E **41** L19
Gwaai *Zimbabwe* 19°15S 27°45E **55** F2
Gwaai → *Zimbabwe* 17°59S 26°52E **55** F2
Gwabegar *Australia* 30°37S 148°59E **63** E4
Gwädar *Pakistan* 25°10N 62°18E **40** G3
Gwaii Haanas △
   Canada 52°21N 131°26W **70** C2
Gwalior *India* 26°12N 78°10E **42** F8
Gwanda *Zimbabwe* 20°55S 29°0E **55** G2
Gwane
   Dem. Rep. of the Congo 4°45N 25°48E **54** B2
Gwangju *S. Korea* 35°9N 126°54E **35** G14
Gwanju = Gwangju
   S. Korea 35°9N 126°54E **35** G14
Gweebarra B. *Ireland* 54°51N 8°23W **10** B3
Gweedore *Ireland* 55°3N 8°13W **10** A3
Gweru *Zimbabwe* 19°28S 29°45E **55** F2
Gwinn *U.S.A.* 46°19N 87°27W **80** B2
Gwydir → *Australia* 29°27S 149°48E **63** D4
Gwynedd □ *U.K.* 52°52N 4°10W **12** E3
Gyandzha = Gäncä
   Azerbaijan 40°45N 46°20E **19** F8
Gyaring Hu *China* 34°50N 97°40E **32** C4
Gydanskiy Poluostrov
   Russia 70°0N 78°0E **28** C8
Gyeongju *S. Korea* 35°51N 129°14E **35** G15
Gympie *Australia* 26°11S 152°38E **63** D5
Gyöngyös *Hungary* 47°48N 19°56E **17** E10
Győr *Hungary* 47°41N 17°40E **17** E9
Gypsum Pt. *Canada* 61°53N 114°35W **70** A6
Gypsumville *Canada* 51°45N 98°40W **71** C9
Gyula *Hungary* 46°38N 21°17E **17** E11
Gyumri *Armenia* 40°47N 43°50E **19** F7
Gyzylarbat = Serdar
   Turkmenistan 39°4N 56°23E **45** B8
Gyzyletrek = Etrek
   Turkmenistan 37°36N 54°46E **45** B7

H

Ha 'Arava → *Israel* 30°50N 35°20E **46** E4
Ha Coi *Vietnam* 21°26N 107°46E **38** B6
Ha Dong *Vietnam* 20°58N 105°46E **38** B5
Ha Giang *Vietnam* 22°50N 104°59E **38** A5
Ha Karmel △ *Israel* 32°45N 35°5E **46** C4
Ha Long, Vinh *Vietnam* 20°56N 107°3E **38** B6
Ha Tien *Vietnam* 10°23N 104°29E **39** G5
Ha Tinh *Vietnam* 18°20N 105°54E **38** C5
Ha Trung *Vietnam* 19°58N 105°50E **38** C5
Haaksbergen *Neths.* 52°9N 6°45E **15** B6
Ha'ano *Tonga* 19°41S 174°18W **59** c
Ha'apai Group *Tonga* 19°47S 174°27W **59** c
Haapsalu *Estonia* 58°56N 23°30E **9** G20
Haarlem *Neths.* 52°23N 4°39E **15** B4
Haast → *N.Z.* 43°50S 169°2E **59** E2
Haast Bluff *Australia* 23°22S 132°0E **60** D5
Hab → *Pakistan* 24°53N 66°41E **42** G2
Hab Nadi Chauki
   Pakistan 25°0N 66°50E **42** G2
Habahe *China* 48°3N 86°23E **32** B3

Habaswein Kenya 1°2N 39°30E 54 B4
Habay Canada 58°50N 118°44W 70 B5
Ḩabbānīyah Iraq 33°17N 43°29E 44 C4
Haboro Japan 44°22N 141°42E 30 B10
Ḩabshān U.A.E. 23°50N 53°37E 45 F7
Hachijō-Jima Japan 33°5N 139°45E 31 H9
Hachinohe Japan 40°30N 141°29E 30 D10
Hachiōji Japan 35°40N 139°20E 31 G9
Hackensack U.S.A. 40°52N 74°4W 83 F10
Hackettstown U.S.A. 40°51N 74°50W 83 F10
Hadali Pakistan 32°16N 72°11E 42 C5
Hadarba, Ras Sudan 22°4N 36°51E 51 D13
Hadarom □ Israel 31°0N 35°0E 46 E4
Ḩadd, Ra's al Oman 22°35N 59°50E 47 C6
Haddington U.K. 55°57N 2°47W 11 F6
Hadejia Nigeria 12°30N 10°5E 50 F7
Ḩadera Israel 32°27N 34°55E 46 C3
Ḩadera, N. → Israel 32°28N 34°52E 46 C3
Haderslev Denmark 55°15N 9°30E 9 J13
Hadhramaut = Ḩaḑramawt Yemen 15°30N 49°30E 47 D4
Hadībоh Yemen 12°39N 54°2E 47 E5
Hadong S. Korea 35°5N 127°44E 35 G14
Ḩaḑramawt Yemen 15°30N 49°30E 47 D4
Ḩadrānīyah Iraq 35°38N 43°14E 44 C4
Hadrian's Wall U.K. 55°0N 2°30W 12 B5
Hae, Ko Thailand 7°44N 98°22E 39 a
Haeju N. Korea 38°3N 125°45E 35 E13
Haenam S. Korea 34°34N 126°35E 35 G14
Haenertsburg S. Africa 24°0S 29°50E 57 C4
Haerhpin = Harbin China 45°48N 126°40E 35 B14
Hafar al Bāţin Si. Arabia 28°32N 45°52E 44 D5
Ḩafīrat al 'Aydā Si. Arabia 26°26N 39°12E 44 E3
Ḩafit Oman 23°59N 55°49E 45 F7
Hafizabad Pakistan 32°5N 73°40E 42 C5
Haflong India 25°10N 93°5E 41 G18
Haft Gel Iran 31°30N 49°32E 45 D6
Hagalil Israel 32°53N 35°18E 46 C4
Hagen Germany 51°21N 7°27E 16 C4
Hagerman U.S.A. 33°7N 104°20W 77 K11
Hagerman Fossil Beds ⌂ U.S.A. 42°48N 114°57W 76 E6
Hagerstown U.S.A. 39°39N 77°43W 81 F15
Hagersville Canada 42°58N 80°3W 82 D4
Hagfors Sweden 60°3N 13°45E 9 F15
Hagi Japan 34°30N 131°22E 31 G5
Hagolan Syria 33°0N 35°45E 46 C4
Hagondange France 49°16N 6°11E 20 B7
Hags Hd. Ireland 52°57N 9°28W 10 D2
Hague, C. de la France 49°44N 1°56W 20 B3
Hague, The = 's-Gravenhage Neths. 52°7N 4°17E 15 B4
Haguenau France 48°49N 7°47E 20 B7
Hai Duong Vietnam 20°56N 106°19E 38 B6
Haicheng China 40°50N 122°45E 35 D12
Haidar Khel Afghan. 33°58N 68°38E 42 C3
Haidarâbâd = Hyderabad India 17°22N 78°29E 40 L11
Haidargarh India 26°37N 81°22E 43 F9
Haifa = Ḩefa Israel 32°46N 35°0E 46 C4
Haikou China 20°1N 110°16E 38 B8
Ḩā'il Si. Arabia 27°28N 41°45E 44 E4
Ḩā'il □ Si. Arabia 26°40N 41°40E 44 E4
Hailar China 49°10N 119°38E 33 B6
Hailey U.S.A. 43°31N 114°19W 76 E6
Haileybury Canada 47°30N 79°38W 72 C4
Hailin China 44°37N 129°30E 35 B15
Hailuoto Finland 65°3N 24°45E 8 D21
Hainan □ China 19°0N 109°30E 38 C7
Hainan Dao China 19°0N 109°30E 38 C7
Hainan Str. = Qiongzhou Haixia China 20°10N 110°15E 38 B8
Hainaut □ Belgium 50°30N 4°0E 15 D4
Haines Alaska, U.S.A. 59°14N 135°26W 70 B1
Haines Oreg., U.S.A. 44°55N 117°56W 76 D5
Haines City U.S.A. 28°7N 81°38W 85 G14
Haines Junction Canada 60°45N 137°30W 70 A1
Haiphong Vietnam 20°47N 106°41E 38 B6
Haiti ■ W. Indies 19°0N 72°30W 89 C5
Haiya Sudan 18°20N 36°21E 51 E13
Haiyan China 36°53N 100°59E 32 C5
Haiyang China 36°47N 121°9E 35 F11
Haiyuan China 36°35N 105°52E 34 F3
Haizhou China 34°37N 119°7E 35 G10
Haizhou Wan China 34°50N 119°20E 35 G10
Haj Ali Qoli, Kavīr Iran 35°55N 54°50E 45 C7
Hajdúböszörmény Hungary 47°40N 21°30E 17 E11
Haji Ibrahim Iraq 36°40N 44°30E 44 B5
Hājjīābād Iran 33°37N 60°0E 45 C9
Hajipur India 25°45N 85°13E 43 G11
Ḩajjah Yemen 15°42N 43°36E 47 D3
Ḩājjīābād Iran 28°19N 55°55E 45 D7
Ḩājjīābād-e Zarrīn Iran 33°9N 54°51E 45 C7
Hajnówka Poland 52°47N 23°35E 17 B12
Hakansson, Mts. Dem. Rep. of the Congo 8°40S 25°45E 55 D2
Hakkâri Turkey 37°34N 43°44E 44 B4
Hakken-Zan Japan 34°10N 135°54E 31 G7
Hakodate Japan 41°45N 140°44E 30 D10
Hakos Namibia 23°13S 16°21E 56 C2
Haku-San Japan 36°9N 136°46E 31 F8
Haku-San △ Japan 36°15N 136°45E 31 F8
Hakui Japan 36°53N 136°47E 31 F8
Hala Pakistan 25°43N 68°20E 40 G6
Ḩalab Syria 36°10N 37°15E 44 B3
Ḩalabjah Iraq 35°10N 45°58E 44 C5
Halaib Sudan 22°12N 36°30E 51 D13
Halaib Triangle Africa 22°30N 35°20E 51 D13
Hālat 'Ammār Si. Arabia 29°10N 36°4E 44 D3
Halbā Lebanon 34°34N 36°6E 46 A5
Halberstadt Germany 51°54N 11°3E 16 C6
Halcombe N.Z. 40°8S 175°30E 59 D5
Halcon Phil. 13°0N 121°30E 37 B6
Halde Fjäll = Haltiatunturi Finland 69°17N 21°18E 8 B19
Halden Norway 59°9N 11°23E 9 G14
Haldia Bangla. 22°1N 88°3E 43 H13
Haldwani India 29°31N 79°30E 43 E8
Hale → Australia 24°56S 135°53E 62 C2
Halesowen U.K. 52°27N 2°3W 13 E5
Halesworth U.K. 52°20N 1°31E 13 E9
Haleyville U.S.A. 34°14N 87°37W 85 D11
Half Dome U.S.A. 37°44N 119°32E 78 H7
Halfmoon Bay N.Z. 46°50S 168°5E 59 G2
Halfway → Canada 56°12N 121°32W 70 B4
Halia India 24°50N 82°19E 43 G10
Haliburton Canada 45°3N 78°30W 82 A6
Halifax Australia 18°32S 146°22E 62 B4
Halifax Canada 44°38N 63°35W 73 D7
Halifax U.K. 53°43N 1°52W 12 D6
Halifax U.S.A. 40°25N 76°55W 82 F8
Halifax B. Australia 18°50S 147°0E 62 B4
Halifax I. Namibia 26°38S 15°4E 56 D2
Halīl → Iran 27°40N 58°30E 45 E8
Halkida Greece 38°27N 23°42E 23 E10
Halkirk U.K. 58°30N 3°29W 11 C5
Hall Beach = Sanirajak Canada 68°46N 81°12W 69 C11
Hall Pen. Canada 63°30N 66°0W 69 C13
Hall Pt. Australia 15°40S 124°23E 60 C3
Halland Sweden 57°8N 12°47E 9 H15
Hallāniyat, Jazā'ir al Oman 17°30N 55°58E 47 D6
Hallasan S. Korea 33°22N 126°32E 35 H14
Halle Belgium 50°44N 4°13E 15 D4
Halle Germany 51°30N 11°56E 16 C6
Hällefors Sweden 59°47N 14°31E 9 G16
Hallett Australia 33°25S 138°55E 63 E2
Hallettsville U.S.A. 29°27N 96°57W 84 G6
Halley Antarctica 75°35S 26°39W 5 D1
Hallim S. Korea 33°24N 126°15E 35 H14
Hallingdalselva → Norway 60°23N 9°35E 8 F13
Hallock U.S.A. 48°47N 96°57W 80 A5
Halls Creek Australia 18°16S 127°38E 60 C4
Halls Gap Australia 37°8S 142°34E 63 F3
Halls Lake Canada 45°7N 78°45W 82 A6
Hallsberg Sweden 59°5N 15°7E 9 G16
Hallstead U.S.A. 41°58N 75°45W 83 E9
Halmahera Indonesia 0°40N 128°0E 37 D7
Halmstad Sweden 56°41N 12°52E 9 H15
Hälsingborg = Helsingborg Sweden 56°3N 12°42E 9 H15
Hälsingland Sweden 61°40N 16°5E 8 F17
Halstead U.K. 51°57N 0°40E 13 F8
Haltiatunturi Finland 69°17N 21°18E 8 B19
Halton □ U.K. 53°22N 2°45W 12 D5
Haltwhistle U.K. 54°58N 2°26W 12 C5
Ḩālūl Qatar 25°40N 52°40E 45 E7
Halvad India 23°1N 71°11E 42 H4
Ḩalvān Iran 33°57N 56°15E 45 C8
Ham Tan Vietnam 10°40N 107°45E 39 G6
Ham Yen Vietnam 22°4N 105°3E 38 A5
Hamab Namibia 28°7S 19°16E 56 D2
Hamada Japan 34°56N 132°4E 31 G6
Hamadān Iran 34°52N 48°32E 45 C6
Hamadān □ Iran 35°0N 49°0E 45 C6
Ḩamāh Syria 35°5N 36°40E 44 C3
Hamamatsu Japan 34°45N 137°45E 31 G8
Hamar Norway 60°48N 11°7E 8 F14
Hamâta, Gebel Egypt 24°17N 35°0E 44 E2
Hambantota Sri Lanka 6°10N 81°10E 40 R12
Hamber ⌂ Canada 52°20N 118°0W 70 C5
Hamburg Germany 53°33N 9°59E 16 B5
Hamburg Ark., U.S.A. 33°14N 91°48W 84 E9
Hamburg N.Y., U.S.A. 42°43N 78°50W 82 D6
Hamburg Pa., U.S.A. 40°33N 75°59W 83 F9
Ḩamḑ, W. al → Si. Arabia 24°55N 36°20E 44 E3
Hamden U.S.A. 41°23N 72°54W 83 E12
Häme Finland 61°38N 25°10E 8 F21
Hämeenlinna Finland 61°0N 24°28E 8 F21
Hamelin Pool Australia 26°22S 114°20E 61 E1
Hameln Germany 52°6N 9°21E 16 B5
Hamerkaz □ Israel 32°15N 34°55E 46 C3
Hamersley Ra. Australia 22°0S 117°45E 60 D2
Hamhŭng N. Korea 39°54N 127°30E 35 E14
Hami China 42°55N 93°25E 32 B4
Hamilton Australia 37°45S 142°2E 63 F3
Hamilton Canada 43°15N 79°50W 82 C5
Hamilton N.Z. 37°47S 175°19E 59 B5
Hamilton U.K. 55°46N 4°2W 11 F4
Hamilton Ala., U.S.A. 34°9N 87°59W 85 D11
Hamilton Mont., U.S.A. 46°15N 114°10W 76 C6
Hamilton N.Y., U.S.A. 42°50N 75°33W 83 D9
Hamilton Ohio, U.S.A. 39°24N 84°34W 81 F11
Hamilton Tex., U.S.A. 31°42N 98°7W 84 F5
Hamilton → Queens., Australia 23°30S 139°47E 62 C2
Hamilton → S. Austral., Australia 26°40S 135°19E 63 D2
Hamilton City U.S.A. 39°45N 122°1W 78 F4
Hamilton I. Australia 20°21S 148°56E 62 J6
Hamilton Inlet Canada 54°0N 57°30W 73 B8
Hamilton Mt. U.S.A. 43°25N 74°22W 83 C10
Hamina Finland 60°34N 27°12E 8 F22
Hamirpur H.P., India 31°41N 76°31E 42 D7
Hamirpur Ut. P., India 25°57N 80°9E 43 G9
Hamju N. Korea 39°51N 127°26E 35 E14
Hamlet U.S.A. 34°53N 79°42W 85 D15
Hamley Bridge Australia 34°17S 138°35E 63 E2
Hamlin = Hameln Germany 52°6N 9°21E 16 B5
Hamlin N.Y., U.S.A. 43°17N 77°55W 82 C7
Hamlin Tex., U.S.A. 32°53N 100°8W 84 E4
Hamm Germany 51°40N 7°50E 16 C4
Ḩammār, Hawr al Iraq 30°50N 47°10E 44 D5
Hammerfest Norway 70°39N 23°41E 8 A20
Hammond Ind., U.S.A. 41°38N 87°30W 80 E10
Hammond La., U.S.A. 30°30N 90°28W 85 F9
Hammond N.Y., U.S.A. 44°27N 75°42W 83 B9
Hammondsport U.S.A. 42°25N 77°13W 82 D7
Hammonton U.S.A. 39°39N 74°48W 81 F16
Hampden N.Z. 45°18S 170°50E 59 F3
Hampshire □ U.K. 51°7N 1°23W 13 F6
Hampshire Downs U.K. 51°15N 1°10W 13 F6
Hampton N.B., Canada 45°32N 65°51W 73 C6
Hampton Ont., Canada 43°58N 78°45W 82 C6
Hampton Ark., U.S.A. 33°32N 92°28W 84 E8
Hampton Iowa, U.S.A. 42°45N 93°13W 80 D7
Hampton N.H., U.S.A. 42°57N 70°50W 83 D14
Hampton S.C., U.S.A. 32°52N 81°7W 85 E14
Hampton Va., U.S.A. 37°2N 76°21W 81 G15
Hampton Bays U.S.A. 40°53N 72°30W 83 F12
Hampton Tableland Australia 32°0S 127°0E 61 F4
Hamyang S. Korea 35°32N 127°42E 35 G14
Han Pijesak Bos.-H. 44°5N 18°57E 23 B8
Hanak Si. Arabia 25°32N 37°0E 44 E3
Hanamaki Japan 39°23N 141°7E 30 E10
Hanang Tanzania 4°30S 35°25E 54 C4
Hanau Germany 50°7N 8°56E 16 C5
Hanbogd = Ihbulag Mongolia 43°11N 107°10E 34 C4
Hancheng China 35°31N 110°25E 34 G6
Hancock Mich., U.S.A. 47°8N 88°35W 80 B9
Hancock N.Y., U.S.A. 41°57N 75°17W 83 E9
Hancock Vt., U.S.A. 43°55N 72°50W 83 C12
Handa Japan 34°53N 136°55E 31 G8
Handa I. U.K. 58°23N 5°11W 11 C3
Handan China 36°35N 114°28E 34 F8
Handeni Tanzania 5°25S 38°2E 54 D4
Handwara India 34°21N 74°20E 43 B6
Hanegev Israel 30°50N 35°0E 46 E4
Hanford U.S.A. 36°20N 119°39W 78 J7
Hanford Reach ⌂ U.S.A. 46°40N 119°30W 76 C4
Hang Chat Thailand 18°20N 99°21E 38 C2
Hang Dong Thailand 18°41N 98°55E 38 C2
Hangang → S. Korea 37°50N 126°30E 35 F14
Hangayn Nuruu Mongolia 47°30N 99°0E 32 B4
Hangchou = Hangzhou China 30°18N 120°11E 33 C7
Hanggin Houqi China 40°58N 107°4E 34 D4
Hanggin Qi China 39°52N 108°50E 34 E5
Hangu China 39°18N 117°53E 35 E9
Hangzhou China 30°18N 120°11E 33 C7
Hangzhou Wan China 30°15N 120°45E 33 C7
Hanh Mongolia 51°32N 100°35E 32 A5
Hanhongor Mongolia 43°55N 104°28E 34 C3
Hania = Chania Greece 35°30N 24°4E 25 D6
Ḩanīdh Si. Arabia 26°35N 48°38E 45 E6
Ḩanīsh Yemen 13°45N 42°46E 47 E3
Hankinson U.S.A. 46°4N 96°54W 80 B5
Hankö Finland 59°50N 22°57E 9 G20
Hanksville U.S.A. 38°22N 110°43W 76 G8
Hanle India 32°42N 79°4E 43 C8
Hanmer Springs N.Z. 42°32S 172°50E 59 E4
Hann → Australia 17°26S 126°17E 60 C4
Hann, Mt. Australia 15°45S 126°0E 60 C4
Hanna Canada 51°40N 111°54W 70 C6
Hanna U.S.A. 41°52N 106°34W 76 F10
Hannah B. Canada 51°40N 80°0W 72 B4
Hannibal Mo., U.S.A. 39°42N 91°22W 80 F8
Hannibal N.Y., U.S.A. 43°19N 76°35W 83 C8
Hannover Germany 52°22N 9°46E 16 B5
Hanoi Vietnam 21°5N 105°55E 38 B5
Hanover = Hannover Germany 52°22N 9°46E 16 B5
Hanover Canada 44°9N 81°2W 82 B3
Hanover S. Africa 31°4S 24°29E 56 E3
Hanover N.H., U.S.A. 43°42N 72°17W 83 C12
Hanover Ohio, U.S.A. 40°4N 82°16W 82 F2
Hanover Pa., U.S.A. 39°48N 76°59W 81 F15
Hanover, I. Chile 51°0S 74°50W 96 G2
Hans Lollik I. U.S. Virgin Is. 18°24N 64°53W 89 e
Hansdiha India 24°36N 87°5E 43 G12
Hansi H.P., India 32°27N 77°50E 42 C7
Hansi Haryana, India 29°10N 75°57E 42 E6
Hanson, L. Australia 31°0S 136°15E 63 E2
Hantsavichy Belarus 52°49N 26°30E 17 B14
Hanumangarh India 29°35N 74°19E 42 E6
Hanzhong China 33°10N 107°1E 34 H4
Hanzhuang China 34°33N 117°23E 35 G9
Haora India 22°34N 88°18E 43 H13
Haparanda Sweden 65°52N 24°8E 8 D21
Happy U.S.A. 34°45N 101°52W 84 D4
Happy Camp U.S.A. 41°48N 123°23W 76 F2
Happy Valley-Goose Bay Canada 53°15N 60°20W 73 B7
Hapsu N. Korea 41°13N 128°51E 35 D15
Hapur India 28°45N 77°45E 42 E7
Ḩaql Si. Arabia 29°10N 34°58E 46 F3
Har Indonesia 5°16S 133°14E 37 F8
Har-Ayrag Mongolia 45°47N 109°16E 34 B5
Har Hu China 38°20N 97°38E 32 C4
Har Us Nuur Mongolia 48°0N 92°0E 32 B4
Har Yehuda Israel 31°35N 34°57E 46 D3
Ḩaraḑ Si. Arabia 24°22N 49°0E 47 C4
Haramosh Pakistan 35°50N 74°54E 43 B6
Haranomachi Japan 37°38N 140°58E 30 F10
Harare Zimbabwe 17°43S 31°2E 55 F3
Harazé Chad 9°57N 20°48E 51 G10
Harbin China 45°48N 126°40E 35 B14
Harbor Beach U.S.A. 43°51N 82°39W 82 C2
Harborcreek U.S.A. 42°9N 79°57W 82 D5
Harbour Breton Canada 47°29N 55°50W 73 C8
Harbour Deep Canada 50°25N 56°32W 73 B8
Harda India 22°27N 77°5E 42 H7
Hardangerfjorden Norway 60°5N 6°0E 9 F12
Hardangervidda Norway 60°7N 7°20E 8 F12
Hardap ⌂ Namibia 24°29S 17°45E 56 C2
Hardap Dam Namibia 24°32S 17°50E 56 C2
Hardenberg Neths. 52°34N 6°37E 15 B6
Harderwijk Neths. 52°21N 5°38E 15 B5
Hardey → Australia 22°45S 116°8E 60 D2
Hardin U.S.A. 45°44N 107°37W 76 D10
Harding S. Africa 30°35S 29°55E 57 E4
Harding Ra. Australia 16°17S 124°55E 60 C3
Hardisty Canada 52°40N 111°18W 70 C6
Hardoi India 27°26N 80°6E 43 F9
Hardwar = Haridwar India 29°58N 78°9E 42 E8
Hardwick U.S.A. 44°30N 72°22W 83 B12
Hardwood Lake Canada 45°12N 77°26W 82 A7
Hardy, Pen. Chile 55°30S 68°20W 96 H3
Hardy, Pte. St. Lucia 14°6N 60°56W 89 f
Hare B. Canada 51°15N 55°45W 73 B8
Hareid Norway 62°22N 6°1E 8 E12
Harer Ethiopia 9°20N 42°8E 47 F3
Hargeisa Somali Rep. 9°30N 44°2E 47 F3
Hari → Indonesia 1°16S 104°5E 36 E2
Haria Canary Is. 29°8N 13°32W 24 E6
Haridwar India 29°58N 78°9E 42 E8
Harim, Jabal al Oman 25°58N 56°14E 45 E8
Haringhata → Bangla. 22°0N 89°58E 41 J16
Harīr, W. al → Syria 32°44N 35°59E 46 C4
Harīrūd → Asia 37°24N 60°38E 45 B9
Härjedalen Sweden 62°22N 13°5E 8 E15
Harlan Iowa, U.S.A. 41°39N 95°19W 80 E6
Harlan Ky., U.S.A. 36°51N 83°19W 81 G12
Harlech U.K. 52°52N 4°6W 12 E3
Harlem U.S.A. 48°32N 108°47W 76 B9
Harlingen Neths. 53°11N 5°25E 15 A5
Harlingen U.S.A. 26°12N 97°42W 84 H6
Harlow U.K. 51°46N 0°8E 13 F8
Harlowton U.S.A. 46°26N 109°50W 76 C9
Harnai Pakistan 30°6N 67°56E 42 D2
Harney Basin U.S.A. 43°0N 119°30W 76 E4
Harney L. U.S.A. 43°14N 119°8W 76 E4
Harney Peak U.S.A. 43°52N 103°32W 80 D2
Härnösand Sweden 62°38N 17°55E 8 E17
Haroldswick U.K. 60°48N 0°50W 11 A8
Harp L. Canada 55°5N 61°50W 73 A7
Harper Liberia 4°25N 7°43W 50 H4
Harrai India 22°37N 79°13E 43 H8
Harrand Pakistan 29°28N 70°3E 42 E4
Harricana → Canada 50°56N 79°32W 72 B4
Harriman U.S.A. 35°56N 84°33W 85 D12
Harrington Harbour Canada 50°31N 59°30W 73 B8
Harris U.K. 57°50N 6°55W 11 D2
Harris, L. Australia 31°10S 135°10E 63 E2
Harris, Sd. of U.K. 57°44N 7°6W 11 D1
Harris Pt. Canada 43°6N 82°9W 82 C2
Harrisburg Ill., U.S.A. 37°44N 88°32W 80 G9
Harrisburg Nebr., U.S.A. 41°33N 103°44W 80 E2
Harrisburg Pa., U.S.A. 40°16N 76°53W 82 F8
Harrismith S. Africa 28°15S 29°8E 57 D4
Harrison Ark., U.S.A. 36°14N 93°7W 84 C8
Harrison Maine, U.S.A. 44°7N 70°39W 83 B14
Harrison Nebr., U.S.A. 42°41N 103°53W 80 D2
Harrison, C. Canada 54°55N 57°55W 73 B8
Harrison L. Canada 49°33N 121°50W 70 D4
Harrisonburg U.S.A. 38°27N 78°52W 81 F14
Harrisonville U.S.A. 38°39N 94°21W 80 F6
Harriston Canada 43°57N 80°53W 82 C4
Harrisville Mich., U.S.A. 44°39N 83°17W 82 B1
Harrisville N.Y., U.S.A. 44°9N 75°19W 83 B9
Harrisville Pa., U.S.A. 41°8N 80°0W 82 E5
Harrodsburg U.S.A. 37°46N 84°51W 81 G11
Harrogate U.K. 54°0N 1°33W 12 C6
Harrow Canada 42°2N 82°55W 82 D2
Harrow □ U.K. 51°35N 0°21W 13 F7
Harrowsmith Canada 44°24N 76°40W 83 B8
Harry S. Truman Res. U.S.A. 38°16N 93°24W 80 F7
Harsīn Iran 34°18N 47°33E 44 C5
Harstad Norway 68°48N 16°30E 8 B17
Harsud India 22°6N 76°44E 42 H7
Hart U.S.A. 43°42N 86°22W 80 D10
Hart, L. Australia 31°10S 136°25E 63 E2
Hartbees → S. Africa 28°45S 20°32E 56 D3
Hartford Conn., U.S.A. 41°46N 72°41W 83 E12
Hartford Ky., U.S.A. 37°27N 86°55W 80 G10
Hartford S. Dak., U.S.A. 43°38N 96°57W 80 D5
Hartford Vt., U.S.A. 43°40N 72°20W 83 C12
Hartford Wis., U.S.A. 43°19N 88°22W 80 D9
Hartford City U.S.A. 40°27N 85°22W 81 E11
Hartland Canada 46°20N 67°32W 73 C6
Hartland Pt. U.K. 51°1N 4°32W 13 F3
Hartlepool U.K. 54°42N 1°13W 12 C6
Hartlepool □ U.K. 54°42N 1°17W 12 C6
Hartley Bay Canada 53°25N 129°15W 70 C3
Hartmannberge Namibia 17°0S 13°0E 56 B1
Hartney Canada 49°30N 100°35W 71 D8
Harts → S. Africa 28°24S 24°17E 56 D3
Harts Range Australia 23°6S 134°55E 62 C1
Hartselle U.S.A. 34°27N 86°56W 85 D11
Hartshorne U.S.A. 34°51N 95°34W 84 D7
Hartstown U.S.A. 41°33N 80°23W 82 E4
Hartsville U.S.A. 34°23N 80°4W 85 D14
Hartswater S. Africa 27°34S 24°43E 56 D3
Hartwell U.S.A. 34°21N 82°56W 85 D13
Harunabad Pakistan 29°35N 73°8E 42 E5
Harvand Iran 28°25N 55°43E 45 D7
Harvey Australia 33°5S 115°54E 61 F2
Harvey Ill., U.S.A. 41°36N 87°50W 80 E10
Harvey N. Dak., U.S.A. 47°47N 99°56W 80 B4
Harwich U.K. 51°56N 1°17E 13 F9
Haryana □ India 29°0N 76°10E 42 E7
Haryn → Belarus 52°7N 27°17E 17 B14
Harz Germany 51°38N 10°44E 16 C6
Hasa Si. Arabia 25°50N 49°0E 45 E6
Ḩasā, W. al → Jordan 31°4N 35°29E 46 D4
Ḩasanābād Iran 32°8N 52°44E 45 C7
Ḩasb, W. → Iraq 31°45N 44°17E 44 D5
Hasdo → India 21°44N 82°44E 43 J10
Hashimoto Japan 34°19N 135°37E 31 G7
Hashtjerd Iran 35°52N 50°40E 45 C6
Hashtpur = Tālesh Iran 37°58N 48°58E 45 B6
Haskell U.S.A. 33°10N 99°44W 84 E5
Haskovo = Khaskovo Bulgaria 41°56N 25°30E 23 D11
Haslemere U.K. 51°5N 0°43W 13 F7
Hasselt Belgium 50°56N 5°21E 15 D5
Hassi Messaoud Algeria 31°51N 6°1E 50 B7
Hässleholm Sweden 56°10N 13°46E 9 H15
Hastings N.Z. 39°39S 176°52E 59 C6
Hastings U.K. 50°51N 0°35E 13 G8
Hastings Mich., U.S.A. 42°39N 85°17W 81 D11
Hastings Minn., U.S.A. 44°44N 92°51W 80 C7
Hastings Nebr., U.S.A. 40°35N 98°23W 80 E4
Hastings Ra. Australia 31°15S 152°14E 63 E5
Hat Yai Thailand 7°1N 100°27E 39 J3
Hatanbulag = Ergel Mongolia 43°8N 109°5E 34 C5
Hatay Turkey 36°14N 36°10E 44 B3
Hatch U.S.A. 32°40N 107°9W 77 K10
Hatchet L. Canada 58°36N 103°40W 71 B8
Hateruma-Shima Japan 24°3N 123°47E 31 M1
Hatfield P.O. Australia 33°54S 143°49E 63 E3
Hatgal Mongolia 50°26N 100°9E 32 A5
Hathras India 27°36N 78°6E 42 F8
Hatia Bangla. 22°30N 91°5E 41 H17
Hato Mayor Dom. Rep. 18°46N 69°15W 89 C6
Hatta India 24°7N 79°36E 43 G8
Hatta U.A.E. 24°45N 56°4E 45 E8
Hattah Australia 34°48S 142°17E 63 E3
Hattah Kulkyne △ Australia 34°16S 142°33E 63 E3
Hatteras, C. U.S.A. 35°14N 75°32W 85 D17
Hattiesburg U.S.A. 31°20N 89°17W 85 F10
Hatvan Hungary 47°40N 19°45E 17 E10
Hau Duc Vietnam 15°20N 108°13E 38 E7
Haugesund Norway 59°23N 5°13E 9 G11
Haukipudas Finland 65°12N 25°20E 8 D21
Haultain → Canada 55°51N 106°46W 71 B7
Hauraki G. N.Z. 36°35S 175°5E 59 B5
Haut Atlas Morocco 32°30N 5°0W 50 B4
Hautes Fagnes = Hohes Venn Belgium 50°30N 6°5E 15 D6
Hauts Plateaux Algeria 35°0N 1°0E 50 B6
Havana = La Habana Cuba 23°8N 82°22W 88 B3
Havana U.S.A. 40°18N 90°4W 80 E8
Havant U.K. 50°51N 0°58W 13 G7
Havasor = Kığzı Turkey 38°18N 43°25E 44 B4
Havasu, L. U.S.A. 34°18N 114°28W 79 L12
Havel → Germany 52°50N 12°3E 16 B7
Havelian Pakistan 34°2N 73°10E 42 B5
Havelock Canada 44°26N 77°53W 82 B7
Havelock N.Z. 41°17S 173°48E 59 D4
Havelock U.S.A. 34°53N 76°54W 85 D16
Haverfordwest U.K. 51°48N 4°58W 13 F3
Haverhill U.K. 52°5N 0°28E 13 E8
Haverhill U.S.A. 42°47N 71°5W 83 D13
Haverstraw U.S.A. 41°12N 73°58W 83 E11
Havirga Mongolia 45°41N 113°5E 34 B7
Havířov Czech Rep. 49°46N 18°20E 17 D10
Havlíčkův Brod Czech Rep. 49°36N 15°33E 16 D8
Havre U.S.A. 48°33N 109°41W 76 B9
Havre-Aubert Canada 47°12N 61°56W 73 C7
Havre-St.-Pierre Canada 50°18N 63°33W 73 B7
Haw → U.S.A. 35°36N 79°3W 85 D15
Hawai'i U.S.A. 19°30N 155°30W 74 b
Hawai'i □ U.S.A. 19°30N 156°30W 74 b
Hawaiian Is. Pac. Oc. 20°30N 156°0W 74 b
Hawaiian Ridge Pac. Oc. 24°0N 165°0W 65 E11
Hawarden U.S.A. 43°0N 96°29W 80 D5
Hawea, L. N.Z. 44°28S 169°19E 59 F2
Hawera N.Z. 39°35S 174°19E 59 C5
Hawick U.K. 55°26N 2°47W 11 F6
Hawk Junction Canada 48°5N 84°38W 72 C3
Hawke B. N.Z. 39°25S 177°20E 59 C6
Hawker Australia 31°59S 138°22E 63 E2
Hawke's Bay Canada 50°36N 57°10W 73 B8
Hawkesbury Canada 45°37N 74°37W 72 C5
Hawkesbury I. Canada 53°37N 129°3W 70 C3
Hawkesbury Pt. Australia 11°55S 134°5E 62 A1
Hawkinsville U.S.A. 32°17N 83°28W 85 E13
Hawley Minn., U.S.A. 46°53N 96°19W 80 B5
Hawley Pa., U.S.A. 41°28N 75°11W 83 E9
Ḩawrān, W. → Iraq 33°58N 42°34E 44 C4
Hawsh Müssá Lebanon 33°45N 35°55E 46 B4
Hawthorne U.S.A. 38°32N 118°38W 76 G4
Hay Australia 34°30S 144°51E 63 E3
Hay → Australia 24°50S 138°0E 62 C2
Hay → Canada 60°50N 116°26W 70 A5
Hay, C. Australia 14°5S 129°29E 60 B4
Hay I. Canada 44°53N 80°58W 82 B4
Hay L. Canada 58°50N 118°50W 70 B5
Hay-on-Wye U.K. 52°5N 3°8W 13 E4
Hay River Canada 60°51N 115°44W 70 A5
Hay Springs U.S.A. 42°41N 102°41W 80 D2
Haya = Tehoru Indonesia 3°23S 129°30E 37 E7
Hayachine-San Japan 39°34N 141°29E 30 E10
Hayastan = Armenia ■ Asia 40°20N 45°0E 19 F7
Haydān, W. al → Jordan 31°29N 35°34E 46 D4
Hayden U.S.A. 40°30N 107°16W 76 F10
Haydon Australia 18°0S 141°30E 62 B3
Hayes U.S.A. 44°23N 101°1W 80 C3
Hayes → Canada 57°3N 92°12W 72 A1
Hayes Creek Australia 13°43S 131°22E 60 B5
Hayle U.K. 50°11N 5°26W 13 G2
Hayling I. U.K. 50°48N 0°59W 13 G7
Haymen I. Australia 20°3S 148°52E 62 J6
Hayrabolu Turkey 41°12N 27°5E 23 D12
Hays Canada 50°6N 111°48W 70 C6
Hays U.S.A. 38°53N 99°20W 80 F4
Haysyn Ukraine 48°57N 29°25E 17 D15
Hayvoron Ukraine 48°22N 29°52E 17 D15
Hayward Calif., U.S.A. 37°40N 122°4W 78 H4
Hayward Wis., U.S.A. 46°1N 91°29W 80 B8
Haywards Heath U.K. 51°0N 0°5W 13 G7
Hazafon □ Israel 32°40N 35°20E 46 C4
Hazar Turkmenistan 39°34N 53°16E 19 G9
Hazārān, Kūh-e Iran 29°35N 57°20E 45 D8

Hazard *U.S.A.* 37°15N 83°12W **81** G12
Hazaribag *India* 23°58N 85°26E **43** H11
Hazaribag Road *India* 24°12N 85°57E **43** G11
Hazelton *Canada* 55°20N 127°42W **70** B3
Hazelton *U.S.A.* 46°29N 100°17W **80** B3
Hazen *U.S.A.* 47°18N 101°38W **80** B3
Hazlehurst *Ga., U.S.A.* 31°52N 82°36W **85** F13
Hazlehurst *Miss., U.S.A.* 31°52N 90°24W **85** F9
Hazlet *U.S.A.* 40°25N 74°12W **83** F10
Hazleton *U.S.A.* 40°57N 75°59W **83** F9
Hazlett, L. *Australia* 21°30S 128°48E **60** D4
Hazro *Turkey* 38°15N 40°47E **44** B4
Head of Bight *Australia* 31°30S 131°25E **61** F5
Headlands *Zimbabwe* 18°15S 32°2E **55** F3
Healdsburg *U.S.A.* 38°37N 122°52W **78** G4
Healdton *U.S.A.* 34°14N 97°29W **84** D6
Healesville *Australia* 37°35S 145°30E **63** F4
Heany Junction *Zimbabwe* 20°6S 28°54E **57** C4
Heard I. *Ind. Oc.* 53°0S 74°0E **3** G13
Hearne *U.S.A.* 30°53N 96°36W **84** F6
Hearst *Canada* 49°40N 83°41W **72** C3
Heart → *U.S.A.* 46°46N 100°50W **80** B3
Heart's Content *Canada* 47°54N 53°27W **73** C9
Heath, Pte. *Canada* 49°8N 61°40W **73** C7
Heathrow, London ✈ (LHR)
  U.K. 51°28N 0°27W **13** F7
Heavener *U.S.A.* 34°53N 94°36W **84** D7
Hebbronville *U.S.A.* 27°18N 98°41W **84** H5
Hebei □ *China* 39°0N 116°0E **34** E9
Hebel *Australia* 28°58S 147°47E **63** D4
Heber *U.S.A.* 32°44N 115°32W **79** N11
Heber Springs *U.S.A.* 35°30N 92°2W **84** D8
Hebgen L. *U.S.A.* 44°52N 111°20W **76** D8
Hebi *China* 35°57N 114°7E **34** G8
Hebrides *U.K.* 57°30N 7°0W **6** D4
Hebrides, Sea of the *U.K.* 57°5N 7°0W **11** D2
Hebron = Al Khalīl
  West Bank 31°32N 35°6E **46** D4
Hebron *Canada* 58°5N 62°30W **69** D13
Hebron *N. Dak., U.S.A.* 46°54N 102°3W **80** B2
Hebron *Nebr., U.S.A.* 40°10N 97°35W **80** E5
Hecate Str. *Canada* 53°10N 130°30W **70** C2
Heceta I. *U.S.A.* 55°46N 133°40W **70** B2
Hechi *China* 24°40N 108°2E **32** D5
Hechuan *China* 30°2N 106°12E **32** C5
Hecla *U.S.A.* 45°53N 98°9W **80** C4
Hecla I. *Canada* 51°10N 96°43W **71** C9
Hede *Sweden* 62°23N 13°30E **8** E15
Hedemora *Sweden* 60°18N 15°58E **9** F16
Heerde *Neths.* 52°24N 6°2E **15** B6
Heerenveen *Neths.* 52°57N 5°55E **15** B5
Heerhugowaard *Neths.* 52°40N 4°51E **15** B4
Heerlen *Neths.* 50°55N 5°58E **15** D5
Ḥefa *Israel* 32°46N 35°0E **46** C4
Ḥefa □ *Israel* 32°40N 35°0E **46** C4
Hefei *China* 31°52N 117°18E **33** C6
Hegang *China* 47°20N 130°19E **33** B8
Hei Ling Chau *China* 22°15N 114°2E **33** G11
Heichengzhen *China* 36°24N 106°3E **34** F4
Heidelberg *Germany* 49°24N 8°42E **16** D5
Heidelberg *S. Africa* 34°6S 20°59E **56** E3
Heihe *China* 50°10N 127°30E **33** A7
Heilbron *S. Africa* 27°16S 27°59E **57** D4
Heilbronn *Germany* 49°9N 9°13E **16** D5
Heiligongjiang □ *China* 48°0N 126°0E **33** B7
Heilunkiang = Heilongjiang □
  China 48°0N 126°0E **33** B7
Heimaey *Iceland* 63°26N 20°17W **8** E3
Heinze Kyun *Burma* 14°25N 97°45E **38** E1
Heishan *China* 41°40N 122°5E **35** D12
Heishui *China* 42°8N 119°30E **35** C10
Hejaz = Ḥijāz *Si. Arabia* 24°0N 40°0E **44** E3
Hejian *China* 38°25N 116°5E **34** E9
Hejin *China* 35°35N 110°42E **34** G6
Hekımhan *Turkey* 38°50N 37°55E **44** B3
Hekla *Iceland* 63°56N 19°35W **8** E4
Hekou *China* 22°30N 103°59E **32** D5
Helan Shan *China* 38°30N 105°55E **34** E3
Helen Atoll *Pac. Oc.* 2°40N 132°0E **37** D8
Helena *Ark., U.S.A.* 34°32N 90°36W **85** D9
Helena *Mont., U.S.A.* 46°36N 112°2W **76** C7
Helendale *U.S.A.* 34°44N 117°19W **79** L9
Helensburgh *U.K.* 56°1N 4°43W **11** E4
Helensville *N.Z.* 36°41S 174°29E **59** B5
Helenvale *Australia* 15°43S 145°14E **62** B4
Helgeland *Norway* 66°7N 13°29E **8** C15
Helgoland *Germany* 54°10N 7°53E **16** A4
Heligoland = Helgoland
  Germany 54°10N 7°53E **16** A4
Heligoland B. = Deutsche Bucht
  Germany 54°15N 8°0E **16** A5
Hell Hole Gorge △
  Australia 25°31S 144°12E **62** D3
Hella *Iceland* 63°50N 20°24W **8** E3
Hellas = Greece ■ *Europe* 40°0N 23°0E **23** E9
Hellertown *U.S.A.* 40°35N 75°21W **83** F9
Hellespont = Çanakkale Boğazı
  Turkey 40°17N 26°32E **23** D12
Hellevoetsluis *Neths.* 51°50N 4°8E **15** C4
Hellín *Spain* 38°31N 1°40W **21** C5
Hells Canyon △ *U.S.A.* 45°30N 116°58W **76** D5
Hell's Gate △ *Kenya* 0°54S 36°19E **54** C4
Helmand □ *Afghan.* 31°20N 64°0E **40** D4
Helmand → *Afghan.* 31°12N 61°34E **40** D2
Helmeringhausen
  Namibia 25°54S 16°57E **56** D2
Helmond *Neths.* 51°29N 5°41E **15** C5
Helmsdale *U.K.* 58°7N 3°39W **11** C5
Helmsdale → *U.K.* 58°8N 3°43W **11** C5
Helong *China* 42°40N 129°0E **35** C15
Helper *U.S.A.* 39°41N 110°51W **76** G8
Helsingborg *Sweden* 56°3N 12°42E **9** H15
Helsingfors = Helsinki
  Finland 60°10N 24°55E **9** F21
Helsingør *Denmark* 56°2N 12°35E **9** H15
Helsinki *Finland* 60°10N 24°55E **9** F21

Helston *U.K.* 50°6N 5°17W **13** G2
Helvellyn *U.K.* 54°32N 3°1W **12** C4
Helwân *Egypt* 29°50N 31°20E **51** C12
Hemel Hempstead *U.K.* 51°44N 0°28W **13** F7
Hemet *U.S.A.* 33°45N 116°58W **79** M10
Hemingford *U.S.A.* 42°19N 103°4W **80** D2
Hemis △ *India* 34°10N 77°15E **42** B7
Hemmingford *Canada* 45°3N 73°35W **83** A11
Hempstead *N.Y., U.S.A.* 40°42N 73°37W **83** F11
Hempstead *Tex., U.S.A.* 30°6N 96°5W **84** F6
Hemse *Sweden* 57°15N 18°22E **9** H18
Henan □ *China* 34°0N 114°0E **34** H8
Henares → *Spain* 40°24N 3°30W **21** B4
Henashi-Misaki *Japan* 40°37N 139°51E **30** D9
Henderson *Argentina* 36°18S 61°43W **94** D3
Henderson *Ky., U.S.A.* 37°50N 87°35W **80** G10
Henderson *N.C., U.S.A.* 36°20N 78°25W **85** C15
Henderson *N.Y., U.S.A.* 43°50N 76°10W **83** C8
Henderson *Nev., U.S.A.* 36°2N 114°58W **79** J12
Henderson *Tenn.,*
  U.S.A. 35°26N 88°38W **85** D10
Henderson *Tex., U.S.A.* 32°9N 94°48W **84** E7
Henderson I. *Pac. Oc.* 24°22S 128°19W **65** K15
Hendersonville *N.C.,*
  U.S.A. 35°19N 82°28W **85** D13
Hendersonville *Tenn.,*
  U.S.A. 36°18N 86°37W **85** C11
Hendījān *Iran* 30°14N 49°43E **45** D6
Hendorābī *Iran* 26°40N 53°37E **45** E7
Hengcheng *China* 38°18N 106°28E **34** E4
Hengdaohezi *China* 44°52N 129°0E **35** B15
Hengelo *Neths.* 52°16N 6°48E **15** B6
Henggang *China* 22°39N 114°12E **33** F11
Hengmen *China* 22°33N 113°35E **33** F10
Hengqin Dao *China* 22°7N 113°34E **33** G10
Hengshan *China* 37°58N 109°5E **34** F5
Hengshui *China* 37°41N 115°40E **34** H8
Hengyang *China* 26°59N 112°22E **33** D6
Henley-on-Thames *U.K.* 51°32N 0°54W **13** F7
Henlopen, C. *U.S.A.* 38°48N 75°6W **81** F16
Hennenman *S. Africa* 27°59S 27°1E **56** D4
Hennessey *U.S.A.* 36°6N 97°54W **84** C6
Henri Pittier △
  Venezuela 10°26N 67°37W **89** D6
Henrietta *N.Y., U.S.A.* 43°4N 77°37W **82** C7
Henrietta *Tex., U.S.A.* 33°49N 98°12W **84** E5
Henrietta, Ostrov = Genriyetty,
  Ostrov *Russia* 77°6N 156°30E **29** B16
Henrietta Maria, C.
  Canada 55°9N 82°20W **72** A3
Henry *U.S.A.* 41°7N 89°22W **80** E9
Henryetta *U.S.A.* 35°27N 95°59W **84** D7
Henryville *Canada* 45°8N 73°11W **83** A11
Hensall *Canada* 43°26N 81°30W **82** C3
Hentiesbaai *Namibia* 22°8S 14°18E **56** C1
Hentiyn Nuruu
  Mongolia 48°30N 108°30E **33** B5
Henty *Australia* 35°30S 147°0E **63** F4
Henzada *Burma* 17°38N 95°26E **41** L19
Heppner *U.S.A.* 45°21N 119°33W **76** D4
Hepworth *Canada* 44°37N 81°9W **82** B3
Hequ *China* 39°20N 111°15E **34** E6
Heraðsflói *Iceland* 65°42N 14°12W **8** D6
Heraðsvötn → *Iceland* 65°45N 19°25W **8** D4
Heraklion = Iraklio
  Greece 35°20N 25°12E **25** D7
Herald Cays *Australia* 16°58S 149°9E **62** B4
Herāt *Afghan.* 34°20N 62°7E **40** B3
Herāt □ *Afghan.* 35°0N 62°0E **40** B3
Herbert *Canada* 50°30N 107°10W **71** C7
Herbert → *Australia* 18°31S 146°17E **62** B4
Herberton *Australia* 17°20S 145°25E **62** B4
Herbertsdale *S. Africa* 34°1S 21°46E **56** E3
Herceg-Novi *Montenegro* 42°30N 18°33E **23** C8
Herchmer *Canada* 57°22N 94°10W **71** B10
Herðubreið *Iceland* 65°11N 16°21W **8** D5
Hereford *U.K.* 52°4N 2°43W **13** E5
Hereford *U.S.A.* 34°49N 102°24W **84** D3
Herefordshire □ *U.K.* 52°8N 2°40W **13** E5
Herentals *Belgium* 51°12N 4°51E **15** C4
Herford *Germany* 52°7N 8°39E **16** B5
Herington *U.S.A.* 38°40N 96°57W **80** F5
Herkimer *U.S.A.* 43°2N 74°59W **83** D10
Herlong *U.S.A.* 40°8N 120°8W **78** E6
Herm *U.K.* 49°30N 2°28W **13** H5
Hermann *U.S.A.* 38°42N 91°27W **80** F8
Hermannsburg
  Australia 23°57S 132°45E **60** D5
Hermanus *S. Africa* 34°27S 19°12E **56** E2
Hermidale *Australia* 31°30S 146°42E **63** E4
Hermiston *U.S.A.* 45°51N 119°17W **76** D4
Hermon *Canada* 45°6N 77°37W **82** A7
Hermon *U.S.A.* 44°28N 75°14W **83** B9
Hermon, Mt. = Shaykh, J. ash
  Lebanon 33°25N 35°50E **46** B4
Hermosillo *Mexico* 29°10N 111°0W **86** B2
Hernád → *Hungary* 47°56N 21°8E **17** D11
Hernandarias *Paraguay* 25°20S 54°40W **95** B5
Hernandez *U.S.A.* 36°24N 120°46W **78** J6
Hernando *Argentina* 32°28S 63°40W **94** C3
Hernando *U.S.A.* 34°50N 90°0W **85** D10
Herndon *U.S.A.* 40°43N 76°51W **82** F8
Herne *Germany* 51°32N 7°14E **15** C7
Herne Bay *U.K.* 51°21N 1°8E **13** F9
Herning *Denmark* 56°8N 8°58E **9** H13
Heroica Caborca = Caborca
  Mexico 30°37N 112°6W **86** A2
Heroica Nogales = Nogales
  Mexico 31°19N 110°56W **86** A2
Heron Bay *Canada* 48°40N 86°25W **72** C2
Heron I. *Australia* 23°27S 151°55E **62** C5
Herradura, Pta. de la
  Canary Is. 28°26N 14°8W **24** F5
Herreid *U.S.A.* 45°50N 100°4W **80** C3
Herrin *U.S.A.* 37°48N 89°2W **80** G10
Herriot *Canada* 56°22N 101°16W **71** B8
Herschel I. *Canada* 69°35N 139°5W **4** C1

Hershey *U.S.A.* 40°17N 76°39W **83** F8
Herstal *Belgium* 50°40N 5°38E **15** D5
Hertford *U.K.* 51°48N 0°4W **13** F7
Hertfordshire □ *U.K.* 51°51N 0°5W **13** F7
's-Hertogenbosch *Neths.* 51°42N 5°17E **15** C5
Hertzogville *S. Africa* 28°9S 25°30E **56** D4
Hervey B. *Australia* 25°0S 152°52E **62** C5
Herzliyya *Israel* 32°10N 34°50E **46** C3
Ḥeşār *Fārs, Iran* 29°52N 50°16E **45** D6
Ḥeşār *Markazī, Iran* 35°50N 49°12E **45** C6
Heshui *China* 35°48N 108°0E **34** G5
Heshun *China* 37°22N 113°32E **34** F7
Hesperia *U.S.A.* 34°25N 117°18W **79** L9
Hesse = Hessen □
  Germany 50°30N 9°0E **16** C5
Hessen □ *Germany* 50°30N 9°0E **16** C5
Hetauda *Nepal* 27°25N 85°2E **42** F11
Hetch Hetchy Aqueduct
  U.S.A. 37°29N 122°19W **78** H5
Hettinger *U.S.A.* 46°0N 102°42W **80** B2
Heuksando *S. Korea* 34°40N 125°30E **35** G13
Heunghae *S. Korea* 36°12N 129°21E **35** F15
Heuvelton *U.S.A.* 44°37N 75°25W **83** B9
Hewitt *U.S.A.* 31°28N 97°12W **84** F6
Hexham *U.K.* 54°58N 2°4W **12** C5
Hexigten Qi *China* 43°18N 117°30E **35** C9
Ḥeydarābād *Iran* 30°33N 55°38E **45** D7
Heysham *U.K.* 54°3N 2°53W **12** C5
Heywood *Australia* 38°8S 141°37E **63** F3
Heze *China* 35°14N 115°20E **34** G8
Hi Vista *U.S.A.* 34°45N 117°46W **79** L9
Hialeah *U.S.A.* 25°51N 80°16W **85** J14
Hiawatha *U.S.A.* 39°51N 95°32W **80** F7
Hibbing *U.S.A.* 47°25N 92°56W **80** B7
Hibbs B. *Australia* 42°35S 145°15E **63** G4
Hibernia Reef *Australia* 12°0S 123°23E **60** B3
Hickman *U.S.A.* 36°34N 89°11W **80** G9
Hickory *U.S.A.* 35°44N 81°21W **85** D14
Hicks, Pt. *Australia* 37°49S 149°17E **63** F4
Hicks L. *Canada* 61°25N 100°0W **71** A9
Hicksville *U.S.A.* 40°46N 73°32W **83** F11
Hida-Gawa → *Japan* 35°26N 137°3E **31** G8
Hida-Sammyaku *Japan* 36°30N 137°40E **31** F8
Hidaka-Sammyaku
  Japan 42°35N 142°45E **30** C11
Hidalgo □ *Mexico* 20°30N 99°0W **87** C5
Hidalgo, Presa M.
  Mexico 26°30N 108°35W **86** B3
Hidalgo del Parral
  Mexico 26°56N 105°40W **86** B3
Hierro *Canary Is.* 27°44N 18°0W **24** G1
Higashiajima-San
  Japan 37°40N 140°10E **30** F10
Higashiōsaka *Japan* 34°39N 135°37E **31** G7
Higgins *U.S.A.* 36°7N 100°2W **84** C4
Higgins Corner *U.S.A.* 39°2N 121°5W **78** F5
High Bridge *U.S.A.* 40°40N 74°54W **83** F10
High Island Res. *China* 22°22N 114°21E **33** G11
High Level *Canada* 58°31N 117°8W **70** B5
High Point *U.S.A.* 35°57N 80°0W **85** D15
High Prairie *Canada* 55°30N 116°30W **70** B5
High River *Canada* 50°30N 113°50W **70** C6
High Tatra = Tatry
  Slovak Rep. 49°20N 20°0E **17** D11
High Veld *Africa* 27°0S 27°0E **48** J6
High Wycombe *U.K.* 51°37N 0°45W **13** F7
Highland □ *U.K.* 57°17N 4°21W **11** D4
Highland Park *U.S.A.* 42°11N 87°48W **80** D10
Highmore *U.S.A.* 44°31N 99°27W **80** C4
Highrock L. *Canada* 55°45N 100°30W **71** B8
Higüey *Dom. Rep.* 18°37N 68°42W **89** C6
Hiiumaa *Estonia* 58°50N 22°45E **9** G20
Hijo = Tagum *Phil.* 7°33N 125°53E **37** C7
Hikari *Japan* 33°58N 131°58E **31** H5
Hiko *U.S.A.* 37°32N 115°14W **78** H11
Hikone *Japan* 35°15N 136°10E **31** G8
Hikurangi *Gisborne, N.Z.* 37°55S 178°4E **59** C6
Hikurangi *Northland,*
  N.Z. 35°36S 174°17E **59** A5
Hildesheim *Germany* 52°9N 9°56E **16** B5
Hill → *Australia* 30°23S 115°3E **61** F2
Hill City *Idaho, U.S.A.* 43°18N 115°3W **76** E6
Hill City *Kans., U.S.A.* 39°22N 99°51W **80** F4
Hill City *Minn., U.S.A.* 46°59N 93°36W **80** B7
Hill City *S. Dak., U.S.A.* 43°56N 103°35W **80** D2
Hill Island L. *Canada* 60°30N 109°50W **71** A7
Hillaby, Mt. *Barbados* 13°12N 59°35W **89** g
Hillcrest *Barbados* 13°13N 59°31W **89** g
Hillcrest Center *U.S.A.* 35°23N 118°57W **79** K8
Hillegom *Neths.* 52°18N 4°35E **15** B4
Hillsboro *Kans., U.S.A.* 38°21N 97°12W **80** F5
Hillsboro *N. Dak., U.S.A.* 47°26N 97°3W **80** B5
Hillsboro *Ohio, U.S.A.* 39°12N 83°37W **81** F12
Hillsboro *Oreg., U.S.A.* 45°31N 122°59W **78** E4
Hillsboro *Tex., U.S.A.* 32°1N 97°8W **84** E6
Hillsborough *Grenada* 12°28N 61°28W **89** D7
Hillsborough *U.K.* 43°7N 71°54W **83** C13
Hillsborough Channel
  Australia 20°54S 149°15E **62** J7
Hillsdale *Mich., U.S.A.* 41°56N 84°38W **81** E11
Hillsdale *N.Y., U.S.A.* 42°11N 73°32W **83** D11
Hillsport *Canada* 49°27N 85°34W **72** C2
Hillston *Australia* 33°30S 145°31E **63** E4
Hilton Head Island
  U.S.A. 32°13N 80°45W **85** E14
Hilversum *Neths.* 52°14N 5°10E **15** B5
Himachal Pradesh □
  India 31°30N 77°0E **42** D7
Himalaya *Asia* 29°0N 84°0E **43** E11
Himalchuli *Nepal* 28°27N 84°38E **43** E11
Himatnagar *India* 23°37N 72°57E **42** H5
Himeji *Japan* 34°50N 134°40E **31** G7
Himi *Japan* 36°50N 136°55E **31** F8
Ḥimṣ *Syria* 34°40N 36°45E **46** A5
Ḥimṣ □ *Syria* 34°30N 37°0E **46** A6

Hinche *Haiti* 19°9N 72°1W **89** C5
Hinchinbrook I.
  Australia 18°20S 146°15E **62** B4
Hinchinbrook Island △
  Australia 18°14S 146°6E **62** B4
Hinckley *U.K.* 52°33N 1°22W **13** E6
Hinckley *U.S.A.* 46°1N 92°56W **80** B7
Hindaun *India* 26°44N 77°5E **42** F7
Hindmarsh, L. *Australia* 36°5S 141°55E **63** F3
Hindu Bagh *Pakistan* 30°56N 67°50E **42** D2
Hindu Kush *Asia* 36°0N 71°0E **40** B7
Hindupur *India* 13°49N 77°32E **40** N10
Hines Creek *Canada* 56°20N 118°40W **70** B5
Hinesville *U.S.A.* 31°51N 81°36W **85** F14
Hinganghat *India* 20°30N 78°52E **40** J11
Hingham *U.S.A.* 48°33N 110°25W **76** B8
Hingir *India* 21°57N 83°41E **43** J10
Hingoli *India* 19°41N 77°15E **40** K10
Hinna = Imi *Ethiopia* 6°28N 42°10E **47** F3
Hinnøya *Norway* 68°35N 15°50E **8** B16
Hinojosa del Duque *Spain* 38°30N 5°9W **21** C3
Hinsdale *U.S.A.* 42°47N 72°29W **83** D12
Hinthada = Henzada
  Burma 17°38N 95°26E **41** L19
Hinton *Canada* 53°26N 117°34W **70** C5
Hinton *U.S.A.* 37°40N 80°54W **81** G13
Hios *Greece* 38°27N 26°9E **23** E12
Hirado *Japan* 33°22N 129°33E **31** H4
Hirakud Dam *India* 21°32N 83°45E **41** J13
Hiran → *India* 23°6N 79°21E **43** H8
Hirapur *India* 24°22N 79°13E **43** G8
Hirara *Japan* 24°48N 125°17E **31** M2
Hiratsuka *Japan* 35°19N 139°21E **31** G9
Hiroo *Japan* 42°17N 143°19E **30** C11
Hirosaki *Japan* 40°34N 140°28E **30** D10
Hiroshima *Japan* 34°24N 132°30E **31** G6
Hiroshima □ *Japan* 34°50N 133°0E **31** G6
Hisar *India* 29°12N 75°45E **42** E6
Hisb, Sha'ib → = Ḥasb, W. →
  Iraq 31°45N 44°17E **44** D5
Ḥismá *Si. Arabia* 28°30N 36°0E **44** D3
Hispaniola *W. Indies* 19°0N 71°0W **89** C5
Ḥīt *Iraq* 33°38N 42°49E **44** C4
Hita *Japan* 33°20N 130°58E **31** H5
Hitachi *Japan* 36°36N 140°39E **31** F10
Hitchin *U.K.* 51°58N 0°16W **13** F7
Hitiaa *Tahiti* 17°36S 149°18W **59** d
Hitoyoshi *Japan* 32°13N 130°45E **31** H5
Hitra *Norway* 63°30N 8°45E **8** E13
Hiva Oa *French Polynesia* 9°45S 139°0W **65** H14
Hixon *Canada* 53°25N 122°35W **70** C4
Ḥiyyon, N. → *Israel* 30°25N 35°10E **46** E4
Hjalmar L. *Canada* 61°33N 109°25W **71** A7
Hjälmaren *Sweden* 59°18N 15°40E **9** G16
Hjørring *Denmark* 57°29N 9°59E **9** H13
Hjort Trench *S. Ocean* 58°0S 157°30E **5** B10
Hkakabo Razi *Burma* 28°25N 97°23E **41** E20
Hlobane *S. Africa* 27°42S 31°0E **57** D5
Hluhluwe *S. Africa* 28°1S 32°15E **57** D5
Hluhluwe △ *S. Africa* 22°10S 32°5E **57** D5
Hlyboka *Ukraine* 48°5S 25°56E **17** D13
Ho *Ghana* 6°37N 0°27E **50** G6
Ho Chi Minh City = Thanh Pho
  Ho Chi Minh *Vietnam* 10°58N 106°40E **39** G6
Ho Thuong *Vietnam* 19°32N 105°48E **38** C5
Hoa Binh *Vietnam* 20°50N 105°20E **38** B5
Hoa Da *Vietnam* 11°16N 108°40E **39** G7
Hoa Hiep *Vietnam* 11°34N 105°51E **39** G5
Hoai Nhon *Vietnam* 14°28N 109°1E **38** E7
Hoang Lien Son *Vietnam* 22°0N 104°0E **38** A4
Hoanib → *Namibia* 19°27S 12°46E **56** B2
Hoare B. *Canada* 65°17N 62°30W **69** C13
Hoarusib → *Namibia* 19°3S 12°36E **56** B2
Hobart *Australia* 42°50S 147°21E **63** G4
Hobart *U.S.A.* 35°1N 99°6W **84** D5
Hobbs *U.S.A.* 32°42N 103°8W **77** K12
Hobbs Coast *Antarctica* 74°50S 131°0W **5** D14
Hobe Sound *U.S.A.* 27°4N 80°8W **85** H14
Hoboken *U.S.A.* 40°44N 74°3W **83** F10
Hobro *Denmark* 56°39N 9°46E **9** H13
Hoburgen *Sweden* 56°55N 18°7E **9** H18
Hobyo *Somali Rep.* 5°25N 48°30E **47** F4
Hochfeld *Namibia* 21°28S 17°58E **56** C2
Hodaka-Dake *Japan* 36°17N 137°39E **31** F8
Hodeida = Al Ḥudaydah
  Yemen 14°50N 43°0E **47** E3
Hodgeville *Canada* 50°7N 106°58W **71** C7
Hodgson *Canada* 51°13N 97°36W **71** C9
Hódmezővásárhely
  Hungary 46°28N 20°22E **17** E11
Hodna, Chott el *Algeria* 35°26N 4°43E **50** A6
Hodonín *Czech Rep.* 48°50N 17°10E **17** D9
Hoek van Holland *Neths.* 52°0N 4°7E **15** C4
Hoengseong *S. Korea* 37°29N 127°59E **35** F14
Hoeryong *N. Korea* 42°30N 129°45E **35** C15
Hoeyang *N. Korea* 38°43N 127°36E **35** E14
Hof *Germany* 50°19N 11°55E **16** C6
Hofmeyr *S. Africa* 31°39S 25°50E **56** E4
Höfn *Iceland* 64°15N 15°13W **8** D6
Hofors *Sweden* 60°31N 16°15E **9** F17
Hofsjökull *Iceland* 64°49N 18°48W **8** D4
Hōfu *Japan* 34°3N 131°34E **31** G5
Hogan Group *Australia* 39°13S 147°1E **63** F4
Hogarth, Mt. *Australia* 21°48S 136°58E **62** C2
Hoge Kempen △ *Belgium* 51°6N 5°15E **15** C5
Hogsty Reef *Bahamas* 21°41N 73°48W **89** B5
Hoh → *U.S.A.* 47°45N 124°29W **78** C2
Hoh Xil Shan *China* 35°0N 89°0E **32** C3
Hohenwald *U.S.A.* 35°33N 87°33W **85** D11
Hoher Rhön = Rhön
  Germany 50°24N 9°58E **16** C5
Hohes Venn *Belgium* 50°30N 6°5E **15** D6
Hohhot *China* 40°52N 111°40E **34** D6
Hoi An *Vietnam* 15°30N 108°19E **38** E7
Hoi Xuan *Vietnam* 20°25N 105°9E **38** B5
Hoisington *U.S.A.* 38°31N 98°47W **80** F4
Hōjō *Japan* 33°58N 132°46E **31** H6

Hokianga Harbour
  N.Z. 35°31S 173°22E **59** A4
Hokitika *N.Z.* 42°42S 171°0E **59** E3
Hokkaidō □ *Japan* 43°30N 143°0E **30** C11
Hola *Kenya* 1°29S 40°2E **54** B4
Holakas *Greece* 35°57N 27°53E **25** D9
Holbrook *Australia* 35°42S 147°18E **63** F4
Holbrook *U.S.A.* 34°54N 110°10W **77** J8
Holcomb *U.S.A.* 42°54N 77°25W **82** D7
Holden *U.S.A.* 39°6N 112°16W **76** G7
Holdenville *U.S.A.* 35°5N 96°24W **84** D6
Holdrege *U.S.A.* 40°26N 99°23W **80** E4
Holetown *Barbados* 13°11N 59°38W **89** g
Holguín *Cuba* 20°50N 76°20W **88** B4
Hollams Bird I. *Namibia* 24°40S 14°30E **56** C1
Holland = Netherlands ■
  Europe 52°0N 5°30E **15** C5
Holland *Mich., U.S.A.* 42°47N 86°7W **80** D10
Holland *N.Y., U.S.A.* 42°38N 78°32W **82** D6
Holland Centre *Canada* 44°23N 80°47W **82** B4
Holland Patent *U.S.A.* 43°14N 75°15W **83** C9
Hollandale *U.S.A.* 33°10N 90°51W **85** E9
Holley *U.S.A.* 43°14N 78°2W **82** C6
Hollidaysburg *U.S.A.* 40°26N 78°24W **82** F6
Hollis *U.S.A.* 34°41N 99°55W **84** D5
Hollister *Calif., U.S.A.* 36°51N 121°24W **78** J5
Hollister *Idaho, U.S.A.* 42°21N 114°35W **76** E6
Holly Hill *U.S.A.* 29°16N 81°3W **85** G14
Holly Springs *U.S.A.* 34°46N 89°27W **85** D10
Hollywood *U.S.A.* 26°0N 80°8W **85** J14
Holman *Canada* 70°44N 117°44W **68** B8
Hólmavík *Iceland* 65°42N 21°40W **8** D3
Holmen *U.S.A.* 43°58N 91°15W **80** D8
Holmes Reefs *Australia* 16°27S 148°0E **62** B4
Holmsund *Sweden* 63°41N 20°20E **8** E19
Holroyd → *Australia* 14°10S 141°36E **62** A3
Holstebro *Denmark* 56°22N 8°37E **9** H13
Holsworthy *U.K.* 50°48N 4°22W **13** G3
Holton *Canada* 54°31N 57°12W **73** B8
Holton *U.S.A.* 39°28N 95°44W **80** F6
Holtville *U.S.A.* 32°49N 115°23W **79** N11
Holwerd *Neths.* 53°22N 5°54E **15** A5
Holy I., *Anglesey, U.K.* 53°17N 4°37W **12** D3
Holy I. *Northumberland,*
  U.K. 55°40N 1°47W **12** B6
Holyhead *U.K.* 53°18N 4°38W **12** D3
Holyoke *Colo., U.S.A.* 40°35N 102°18W **76** F12
Holyoke *Mass., U.S.A.* 42°12N 72°37W **83** D12
Holyrood *Canada* 47°27N 53°8W **73** C9
Homa Bay *Kenya* 0°36S 34°30E **54** C3
Homalin *Burma* 24°55N 95°0E **41** G19
Homand *Iran* 32°28N 59°37E **45** C8
Homathko → *Canada* 51°0N 124°56W **70** C4
Home B. *Canada* 68°40N 67°10W **69** C13
Home Hill *Australia* 19°43S 147°25E **62** B4
Home Reef *Tonga* 18°59S 174°47W **59** c
Homedale *U.S.A.* 43°37N 116°56W **76** E5
Homer *Alaska, U.S.A.* 59°39N 151°33W **68** D4
Homer *La., U.S.A.* 32°48N 93°4W **84** E8
Homer *N.Y., U.S.A.* 42°38N 76°10W **83** D8
Homer City *U.S.A.* 40°32N 79°10W **82** F5
Homestead *Australia* 20°20S 145°40E **62** C4
Homestead *U.S.A.* 25°28N 80°29W **85** J14
Homestead △ *U.S.A.* 40°17N 96°50W **80** E5
Homoine *Mozam.* 23°55S 35°8E **57** C6
Homs = Ḥimṣ *Syria* 34°40N 36°45E **46** A5
Homyel *Belarus* 52°28N 31°0E **17** B16
Hon Chong *Vietnam* 10°25N 104°30E **39** G5
Hon Hai *Vietnam* 10°0N 109°0E **39** H7
Hon Me *Vietnam* 19°23N 105°56E **38** C5
Honan = Henan □ *China* 34°0N 114°0E **34** H8
Honbetsu *Japan* 43°7N 143°37E **30** C11
Honcut *U.S.A.* 39°20N 121°32W **78** F5
Honda, Bahía *Cuba* 22°54N 83°10W **88** B3
Hondeklipbaai *S. Africa* 30°19S 17°17E **56** E2
Hondo *Japan* 32°27N 130°12E **31** H5
Hondo *U.S.A.* 29°21N 99°9W **84** G5
Hondo, Río → *Belize* 18°25N 88°21W **87** D7
Honduras ■ *Cent. Amer.* 14°40N 86°30W **88** D2
Honduras, G. de
  Caribbean 16°50N 87°0W **88** C2
Hønefoss *Norway* 60°10N 10°18E **9** F14
Honesdale *U.S.A.* 41°34N 75°16W **83** E9
Honey Harbour *Canada* 44°52N 79°49W **82** B5
Honey L. *U.S.A.* 40°15N 120°19W **78** E6
Honfleur *France* 49°25N 0°13E **20** B4
Hong Gai *Vietnam* 20°57N 107°5E **38** B6
Hong He → *China* 32°25N 115°35E **34** H8
Hong Kong □ *China* 22°11N 114°14E **33** G11
Hong Kong I. *China* 22°15N 114°12E **33** G11
Hong Kong Int. ✈ (HKG)
  China 22°19N 113°57E **33** G10
Hongcheon *S. Korea* 37°44N 127°53E **35** F14
Hongjiang *China* 27°7N 109°59E **33** D5
Hongliu He → *China* 38°0N 109°50E **34** F5
Hongor *Mongolia* 45°45N 112°50E **34** B7
Hongseong *S. Korea* 36°37N 126°38E **35** F14
Hongshui He → *China* 23°48N 109°30E **33** E5
Hongtong *China* 36°16N 111°40E **34** F6
Honguedo, Détroit d'
  Canada 49°15N 64°0W **73** C7
Hongwon *N. Korea* 40°0N 127°56E **35** E14
Hongze Hu *China* 33°15N 118°35E **35** H10
Honiara *Solomon Is.* 9°27S 159°57E **58** B8
Honiton *U.K.* 50°47N 3°11W **13** G4
Honjō *Japan* 39°23N 140°3E **30** E10
Honningsvåg *Norway* 70°59N 25°59E **8** A21
Honolulu *U.S.A.* 21°19N 157°52W **74** b
Honshū *Japan* 36°0N 138°0E **30** F9
Hood, Mt. *U.S.A.* 45°23N 121°42W **78** E5
Hood, Pt. *Australia* 34°23S 119°34E **61** F2
Hood River *U.S.A.* 45°43N 121°31W **78** E5
Hoodsport *U.S.A.* 47°24N 123°9W **78** C3
Hoogeveen *U.S.A.* 52°44N 6°28E **15** B6
Hoogezand-Sappemeer
  Neths. 53°9N 6°45E **15** A6

Hooghly = Hugli →
Hooghly-Chinsura = Chunchura
   India 22°53N 88°27E **43** H13
Hook Hd. *Ireland* 52°7N 6°56W **10** D5
Hook I. *Australia* 20°4S 149°0E **62** J6
Hook of Holland = Hoek van
   Holland *Neths.* 52°0N 4°7E **15** C4
Hooker *U.S.A.* 36°52N 101°13W **84** C4
Hooker Creek = Lajamanu
   Australia 18°23S 130°38E **60** C5
Hoonah *U.S.A.* 58°7N 135°27W **70** B1
Hooper Bay *U.S.A.* 61°32N 166°6W **74** a
Hoopeston *U.S.A.* 40°28N 87°40W **80** E10
Hoopstad *S. Africa* 27°50S 25°55E **56** D4
Hoorn *Neths.* 52°38N 5°4E **15** B5
Hoover *U.S.A.* 33°24N 86°49W **85** E11
Hoover Dam *U.S.A.* 36°1N 114°44W **79** K12
Hooversville *U.S.A.* 40°9N 78°55W **82** F6
Hop Bottom *U.S.A.* 41°42N 75°46W **83** E9
Hope *Canada* 49°25N 121°25W **70** D4
Hope *Ariz., U.S.A.* 33°43N 113°42W **79** M13
Hope *Ark., U.S.A.* 33°40N 93°36W **84** E8
Hope, L. *S. Austral.,*
   Australia 28°24S 139°18E **63** D2
Hope, L. *W. Austral.,*
   Australia 32°35S 120°15E **61** F3
Hope, Pt. *U.S.A.* 68°21N 166°47W **66** C3
Hope I. *Canada* 44°55N 80°11W **82** B4
Hope Town *Bahamas* 26°35N 76°57W **88** A4
Hope Vale *Australia* 15°16S 145°20E **62** B4
Hopedale *Canada* 55°28N 60°13W **73** A7
Hopedale *U.S.A.* 42°8N 71°33W **83** D13
Hopefield *S. Africa* 33°3S 18°22E **56** E2
Hopei = Hebei □ *China* 39°0N 116°0E **34** E9
Hopelchén *Mexico* 19°46N 89°51W **87** D7
Hopetoun *Vic., Australia* 35°42S 142°22E **63** F3
Hopetoun *W. Austral.,*
   Australia 33°57S 120°7E **61** F3
Hopetown *S. Africa* 29°34S 24°3E **56** D3
Hopewell *U.S.A.* 37°18N 77°17W **81** G15
Hopkins, L. *Australia* 24°15S 128°35E **60** D4
Hopkinsville *U.S.A.* 36°52N 87°29W **80** G10
Hopland *U.S.A.* 38°58N 123°7W **78** G3
Hoquiam *U.S.A.* 46°59N 123°53W **78** D3
Hordern Hills *Australia* 20°15S 130°0E **60** D5
Horinger *China* 40°28N 111°48E **34** D6
Horizontina *Brazil* 27°37S 54°19W **95** B5
Horlick Mts. *Antarctica* 84°0S 102°0W **5** E15
Horlivka *Ukraine* 48°19N 38°5E **19** E6
Hormak *Iran* 29°58N 60°51E **45** D9
Hormoz *Iran* 27°35N 55°0E **45** E7
Hormoz, Jaz.-ye *Iran* 27°8N 56°28E **45** E8
Hormozgān □ *Iran* 27°30N 56°0E **45** E8
Hormuz, Kūh-e *Iran* 27°27N 55°10E **45** E7
Hormuz, Str. of *The Gulf* 26°30N 56°30E **45** E8
Horn *Austria* 48°39N 15°40E **16** D8
Horn → *Canada* 61°30N 118°1W **70** A5
Horn, Cape = Hornos, C. de
   Chile 55°50S 67°30W **96** H3
Horn Head *Ireland* 55°14N 8°0W **10** A3
Horn I. *Australia* 10°37S 142°17E **62** A3
Horn Plateau *Canada* 62°15N 119°15W **70** A5
Hornavan *Sweden* 66°15N 17°30E **8** C17
Hornbeck *U.S.A.* 31°20N 93°24W **84** F8
Hornbrook *U.S.A.* 41°55N 122°33W **76** F2
Horncastle *U.K.* 53°13N 0°7W **12** D7
Hornell *U.S.A.* 42°20N 77°40W **82** D7
Hornell L. *Canada* 62°20N 119°25W **70** A5
Hornepayne *Canada* 49°14N 84°48W **72** C3
Hornings Mills *Canada* 44°9N 80°12W **82** B4
Hornitos *U.S.A.* 37°30N 120°14W **78** H6
Hornos, C. de *Chile* 55°50S 67°30W **96** H3
Hornsby *Australia* 33°42S 151°2E **63** B5
Hornsea *U.K.* 53°55N 0°11W **12** D7
Horobetsu = Noboribetsu
   Japan 42°24N 141°6E **30** C10
Horodenka *Ukraine* 48°41N 25°29E **17** D13
Horodok *Khmelnytskyy,*
   Ukraine 49°10N 26°34E **17** D14
Horodok *Lviv, Ukraine* 49°46N 23°32E **17** D12
Horokhiv *Ukraine* 50°30N 24°45E **17** C13
Horqin Youyi Qianqi
   China 46°5N 122°3E **35** A12
Horqueta *Paraguay* 23°15S 56°55W **94** A4
Horse Cr. → *U.S.A.* 41°57N 103°58W **76** F12
Horse I. *Canada* 53°20N 99°6W **71** C9
Horse Is. *Canada* 50°15N 55°50W **73** B8
Horsefly L. *Canada* 52°25N 121°0W **70** C4
Horseheads *U.S.A.* 42°10N 76°49W **82** D8
Horsens *Denmark* 55°52N 9°51E **9** J13
Horseshoe Lake *Canada* 45°17N 79°51W **82** A5
Horsham *Australia* 36°44S 142°13E **63** F3
Horsham *U.K.* 51°4N 0°20W **13** F7
Horta *Azores* 38°32N 28°38W **50** a
Horten *Norway* 59°25N 10°32E **9** G14
Horton *U.S.A.* 39°40N 95°32W **80** F6
Horton → *Canada* 69°56N 126°52W **68** C7
Horwood L. *Canada* 48°5N 82°20W **72** C3
Hoseynābād *Khuzestān,*
   Iran 32°45N 48°20E **45** C6
Hoseynābād *Kordestān,*
   Iran 35°33N 47°8E **44** C5
Hoshangabad *India* 22°45N 77°45E **42** H7
Hoshiarpur *India* 31°30N 75°58E **42** D6
Hospet *India* 15°15N 76°20E **40** M10
Hoste, I. *Chile* 55°0S 69°0W **96** H3
Hot *Thailand* 18°8N 98°29E **38** C2
Hot Creek Range
   U.S.A. 38°40N 116°20W **76** G5
Hot Springs *Ark., U.S.A.* 34°31N 93°3W **84** D8
Hot Springs *S. Dak.,*
   U.S.A. 43°26N 103°29W **80** D2
Hot Springs △ *U.S.A.* 34°31N 93°3W **84** D8
Hotagen *Sweden* 63°59N 14°12E **8** E16
Hotan *China* 37°25N 79°55E **32** C2
Hotan He → *China* 40°22N 80°56E **32** B3
Hotazel *S. Africa* 27°17S 22°58E **56** D3

Hotchkiss *U.S.A.* 38°48N 107°43W **76** G10
Hotham, C. *Australia* 12°2S 131°18E **60** B5
Hoting *Sweden* 64°8N 16°15E **8** D17
Hotte, Massif de la *Haiti* 18°30N 73°45W **89** C5
Hottentotsbaai *Namibia* 26°8S 14°59E **56** D1
Hou Hai *China* 22°32N 113°56E **33** F10
Houei Sai *Laos* 20°18N 100°26E **38** B3
Houffalize *Belgium* 50°8N 5°48E **15** D5
Houghton *Mich., U.S.A.* 47°7N 88°34W **80** B9
Houghton *N.Y., U.S.A.* 42°25N 78°10W **82** D6
Houghton L. *U.S.A.* 44°21N 84°44W **81** C11
Houghton-le-Spring
   U.K. 54°51N 1°28W **12** C6
Houhora Heads *N.Z.* 34°49S 173°9E **59** A4
Houlton *U.S.A.* 46°8N 67°51W **81** B20
Houma *U.S.A.* 29°36N 90°43W **85** G9
Housatonic → *U.S.A.* 41°10N 73°7W **83** E11
Houston *Canada* 54°25N 126°39W **70** C3
Houston *Mo., U.S.A.* 37°22N 91°58W **80** G8
Houston *Tex., U.S.A.* 29°45N 95°21W **84** G7
Hout = Mogwadi →
   S. Africa 23°4S 29°36E **57** C4
Houtkraal *S. Africa* 30°23S 24°5E **56** E3
Houtman Abrolhos
   Australia 28°43S 113°48E **61** E1
Hovd □ *Mongolia* 48°2N 91°37E **32** B4
Hove *U.K.* 50°50N 0°10W **13** G7
Hovenweep △ *U.S.A.* 37°20N 109°0W **77** H9
Hövsgöl *Mongolia* 43°37N 109°39E **34** C5
Hövsgöl Nuur *Mongolia* 51°0N 100°30E **32** A5
Howar, Wadi → *Sudan* 17°30N 27°8E **51** E11
Howard *Australia* 25°16S 152°32E **63** D5
Howard *Pa., U.S.A.* 41°1N 77°40W **82** F7
Howard *S. Dak., U.S.A.* 44°1N 97°32W **80** C5
Howe *U.S.A.* 43°48N 113°0W **76** E7
Howe, C. *Australia* 37°30S 150°0E **63** F5
Howe, West Cape
   Australia 35°8S 117°36E **61** G2
Howe I. *Canada* 44°16N 76°17W **83** B8
Howell *U.S.A.* 42°36N 83°56W **81** D12
Howick *Canada* 45°11N 73°51W **83** A11
Howick *S. Africa* 29°28S 30°14E **57** D5
Howick Group *Australia* 14°20S 145°30E **62** A4
Howitt, L. *Australia* 27°40S 138°40E **63** D2
Howland I. *Pac. Oc.* 0°48N 176°38W **64** G10
Howrah = Haora *India* 22°34N 88°18E **43** H13
Howth *Ireland* 53°23N 6°6W **10** C5
Howth Hd. *Ireland* 53°22N 6°4W **10** C5
Höxter *Germany* 51°46N 9°22E **16** C5
Hoy *U.K.* 58°50N 3°15W **11** C5
Høyanger *Norway* 61°13N 6°4E **8** F12
Hoyerswerda *Germany* 51°26N 14°14E **16** C8
Hoylake *U.K.* 53°24N 3°4W **12** D4
Hpa-an = Pa-an *Burma* 16°51N 97°40E **41** L20
Hpunan Pass *Burma* 27°30N 96°55E **41** F20
Hradec Králové
   Czech Rep. 50°15N 15°50E **16** C8
Hrodna *Belarus* 53°42N 23°52E **17** B12
Hrodzyanka *Belarus* 53°31N 28°42E **17** B15
Hron → *Slovak Rep.* 47°49N 18°45E **17** E10
Hrvatska = Croatia ■
   Europe 45°20N 16°0E **16** F9
Hrymayliv *Ukraine* 49°20N 26°5E **17** D14
Hsenwi *Burma* 23°22N 97°55E **41** H20
Hsiamen = Xiamen
   China 24°25N 118°4E **33** D6
Hsian = Xi'an *China* 34°15N 109°0E **34** G5
Hsinchu *Taiwan* 24°48N 120°58E **33** D7
Hsinhailien = Lianyungang
   China 34°40N 119°11E **35** G10
Hsüchou = Xuzhou
   China 34°18N 117°10E **35** G9
Hu Xian *China* 34°8N 108°42E **34** G5
Hua Hin *Thailand* 12°34N 99°58E **38** F2
Hua Xian *Henan, China* 35°30N 114°30E **34** G8
Hua Xian *Shaanxi, China* 34°30N 109°48E **34** G5
Huab → *Namibia* 20°52S 13°25E **56** B2
Huachinera *Mexico* 30°9N 108°55W **86** A3
Huacho *Peru* 11°10S 77°35W **92** F3
Huade *China* 41°55N 113°59E **34** D7
Huadian *China* 43°0N 126°40E **35** C14
Huahine, Î.
   French Polynesia 16°46S 150°58W **65** J12
Huai Hat △ *Thailand* 16°52N 104°17E **38** D5
Huai He → *China* 33°0N 118°30E **33** C6
Huai Nam Dang △
   Thailand 19°30N 98°30E **38** C2
Huai Yot *Thailand* 7°45N 99°37E **39** J2
Huai'an *Hebei, China* 40°30N 114°20E **34** D8
Huai'an *Jiangsu, China* 33°30N 119°10E **35** H10
Huaibei *China* 34°0N 116°48E **34** G9
Huaide = Gongzhuling
   China 43°30N 124°40E **35** C13
Huaidezhen *China* 43°48N 124°50E **35** C13
Huainan *China* 32°38N 116°58E **33** C6
Huairen *China* 39°48N 113°20E **34** E7
Huairou *China* 40°20N 116°35E **34** D9
Huaiyang *China* 33°40N 114°52E **34** H8
Huaiyin *China* 33°30N 119°2E **35** H10
Huaiyuan *China* 32°55N 117°10E **35** H9
Huajuapán de León
   Mexico 17°48N 97°46W **87** D5
Hualapai Peak *U.S.A.* 35°5N 113°54W **77** J7
Huallaga → *Peru* 5°15S 75°30W **92** E3
Huambo *Angola* 12°42S 15°54E **53** G3
Huan Jiang → *China* 34°28N 109°0E **34** G5
Huan Xian *China* 36°33N 107°7E **34** F4
Huancabamba *Peru* 5°10S 79°15W **92** E3
Huancane *Peru* 15°10S 69°44W **92** G5
Huancavelica *Peru* 12°50S 75°5W **92** F3
Huancayo *Peru* 12°5S 75°12W **92** F3
Huanchaca *Bolivia* 20°15S 66°40W **92** H5
Huang Hai = Yellow Sea
   China 35°0N 123°0E **35** G12
Huang He → *China* 37°55N 118°50E **35** F10
Huang Xian *China* 37°38N 120°30E **35** F11
Huangling *China* 35°34N 109°15E **34** G5

Huanglong *China* 35°30N 109°59E **34** G5
Huangshan *China* 29°42N 118°25E **33** D6
Huangshi *China* 30°10N 115°3E **33** C6
Huangsongdian *China* 43°45N 127°25E **35** C14
Huanren *China* 41°23N 125°20E **35** D13
Huantai *China* 36°58N 117°56E **35** F9
Huánuco *Peru* 9°55S 76°15W **92** E3
Huaraz *Peru* 9°30S 77°32W **92** E3
Huarmey *Peru* 10°5S 78°5W **92** F3
Huascarán, Nevado *Peru* 9°7S 77°37W **92** E3
Huasco *Chile* 28°30S 71°15W **94** B1
Huasco → *Chile* 28°27S 71°13W **94** B1
Huasna *U.S.A.* 35°6N 120°24W **79** K6
Huatabampo *Mexico* 26°50N 109°38W **86** B3
Huauchinango *Mexico* 20°12N 98°3W **87** C5
Huautla de Jiménez
   Mexico 18°8N 96°51W **87** D5
Huayin *China* 34°35N 110°5E **34** G6
Hubbard *Ohio, U.S.A.* 41°9N 80°34W **82** E4
Hubbard *Tex., U.S.A.* 31°51N 96°48W **84** F6
Hubbart Pt. *Canada* 59°21N 94°41W **71** B10
Hubei □ *China* 31°0N 112°0E **33** C6
Hubli *India* 15°22N 75°15E **40** M9
Huch'ang *N. Korea* 41°25N 127°2E **35** D14
Hucknall *U.K.* 53°3N 1°13W **12** D6
Huddersfield *U.K.* 53°39N 1°47W **12** D6
Hudiksvall *Sweden* 61°43N 17°10E **8** F17
Hudson *Canada* 50°6N 92°9W **72** B1
Hudson *Mass., U.S.A.* 42°23N 71°34W **83** D13
Hudson *N.Y., U.S.A.* 42°15N 73°46W **83** D11
Hudson *Wis., U.S.A.* 44°58N 92°45W **80** C7
Hudson *Wyo., U.S.A.* 42°54N 108°35W **76** E9
Hudson → *U.S.A.* 40°42N 74°2W **83** F10
Hudson, C. *Antarctica* 68°21S 153°45E **5** C20
Hudson Bay *Nunavut,*
   Canada 60°0N 86°0W **69** D11
Hudson Bay *Sask.,*
   Canada 52°51N 102°23W **71** C8
Hudson Falls *U.S.A.* 43°18N 73°35W **83** C11
Hudson Mts. *Antarctica* 74°32S 99°20W **5** D16
Hudson Str. *Canada* 62°0N 70°0W **69** B13
Hudson's Hope *Canada* 56°0N 121°54W **70** B4
Hue *Vietnam* 16°30N 107°35E **38** D6
Huehuetenango
   Guatemala 15°20N 91°28W **88** C1
Huejúcar *Mexico* 22°21N 103°13W **86** C4
Huelva *Spain* 37°18N 6°57W **21** D2
Huentelauquén *Chile* 31°38S 71°33W **94** C1
Huerta, Sa. de la
   Argentina 31°10S 67°30W **94** C2
Huesca *Spain* 42°8N 0°25W **21** A5
Huetamo *Mexico* 18°35N 100°53W **86** D4
Hugh → *Australia* 25°1S 134°1E **62** D1
Hughenden *Australia* 20°52S 144°10E **62** C3
Hughesville *U.S.A.* 41°14N 76°44W **83** E8
Hugli → *India* 21°56N 88°4E **43** J13
Hugo *Colo., U.S.A.* 39°8N 103°28W **76** G12
Hugo *Okla., U.S.A.* 34°1N 95°31W **84** D7
Hugoton *U.S.A.* 37°11N 101°21W **80** G3
Hui Xian = Huixian
   China 35°27N 113°12E **34** G7
Hui Xian *China* 33°50N 106°4E **34** H4
Hui'anbu *China* 37°28N 106°38E **34** F4
Huichapan *Mexico* 20°23N 99°39W **87** C5
Huichon *N. Korea* 40°10N 126°16E **35** D14
Huifa He → *China* 43°0N 127°50E **35** C14
Huila, Nevado del *Colombia* 3°0N 76°0W **92** C3
Huimin *China* 37°27N 117°28E **35** F9
Huinan *China* 42°40N 126°2E **35** C14
Huinca Renancó
   Argentina 34°51S 64°22W **94** C3
Huining *China* 35°38N 105°0E **34** G3
Huinong *China* 39°5N 106°35E **34** E4
Huiting *China* 34°5N 116°5E **34** G9
Huixian *China* 35°27N 113°12E **34** G7
Huixtla *Mexico* 15°9N 92°28W **87** D6
Huize *China* 26°24N 103°15E **32** D5
Hukawng Valley
   Burma 26°30N 96°30E **41** F20
Hukuntsi *Botswana* 23°58S 21°45E **56** C3
Ḥulayfā' *Si. Arabia* 25°58N 40°45E **44** E4
Hulin He → *China* 45°0N 122°10E **35** B12
Hull = Kingston upon Hull
   U.K. 53°45N 0°21W **12** D7
Hull *Canada* 45°26N 75°43W **83** A9
Hull → *U.K.* 53°44N 0°20W **12** D7
Hulst *Neths.* 51°17N 4°2E **15** C4
Hulun Nur *China* 49°0N 117°30E **33** B6
Huma, Tanjung *Malaysia* 5°29N 100°16E **39** c
Humacao *Puerto Rico* 18°9N 65°50W **89** d
Humahuaca *Argentina* 23°10S 65°25W **94** A2
Humaitá *Brazil* 7°35S 63°1W **92** E6
Humaitá *Paraguay* 27°2S 58°31W **94** B4
Humansdorp *S. Africa* 34°2S 24°46E **56** E3
Humbe *Angola* 16°40S 14°55E **56** B1
Humber → *U.K.* 53°42N 0°27W **12** D7
Humboldt *Canada* 52°15N 105°9W **71** C7
Humboldt *Iowa, U.S.A.* 42°44N 94°13W **80** D6
Humboldt *Tenn., U.S.A.* 35°50N 88°55W **85** D10
Humboldt → *U.S.A.* 39°59N 118°36W **76** G4
Humboldt Gletscher =
   Sermersuaq *Greenland* 79°30N 62°0W **4** B4
Hume *U.S.A.* 36°48N 118°54W **78** J8
Hume, L. *Australia* 36°0S 147°5E **63** F4
Humen *China* 22°49N 113°40E **33** F10
Humenné *Slovak Rep.* 48°55N 21°50E **17** D11
Humphreys, Mt.
   U.S.A. 37°17N 118°40W **78** H8
Humphreys Peak
   U.S.A. 35°21N 111°41W **77** J8
Humptulips *U.S.A.* 47°14N 123°57W **78** C3
Hūn *Libya* 29°2N 16°0E **51** C9
Hun Jiang → *China* 40°50N 125°38E **35** D13
Húnaflói *Iceland* 65°50N 20°50W **8** D3
Hunan □ *China* 27°30N 112°0E **33** D6
Hunchun *China* 42°52N 130°28E **35** C16
Hundewali *Pakistan* 31°55N 72°38E **42** D5

Hundred Mile House
   Canada 51°38N 121°18W **70** C4
Hunedoara *Romania* 45°40N 22°50E **17** F12
Hung Yen *Vietnam* 20°39N 106°4E **38** B6
Hunga Ha'apai *Tonga* 20°41S 175°7W **59** c
Hungary ■ *Europe* 47°20N 19°20E **17** E10
Hungary, Plain of *Europe* 47°0N 20°0E **6** F10
Hungerford *Australia* 28°58S 144°24E **63** D3
Hŭngnam *N. Korea* 39°49N 127°45E **35** E14
Hunjiang *China* 41°54N 126°26E **35** D14
Hunsberge *Namibia* 27°45S 17°12E **56** D2
Hunsrück *Germany* 49°56N 7°27E **16** D4
Hunstanton *U.K.* 52°56N 0°29E **12** E8
Hunter *U.S.A.* 42°13N 74°13W **83** D10
Hunter I. *Australia* 40°30S 144°45E **63** G3
Hunter I. *Canada* 51°55N 128°0W **70** C3
Hunter Ra. *Australia* 32°45S 150°15E **63** E5
Hunters Road *Zimbabwe* 19°9S 29°49E **55** F2
Hunterville *N.Z.* 39°56S 175°35E **59** C5
Huntingburg *U.S.A.* 38°18N 86°57W **80** F10
Huntingdon *U.K.* 52°20N 0°11W **13** E7
Huntingdon *U.S.A.* 40°30N 78°1W **82** F6
Huntington *Ind., U.S.A.* 40°53N 85°30W **81** E11
Huntington *N.Y.,*
   U.S.A. 40°52N 73°26W **83** F11
Huntington *Oreg.,*
   U.S.A. 44°21N 117°16W **76** D5
Huntington *Utah,*
   U.S.A. 39°20N 110°58W **76** G8
Huntington *W. Va.,*
   U.S.A. 38°25N 82°27W **81** F12
Huntington Beach
   U.S.A. 33°40N 118°5W **79** M9
Huntly *N.Z.* 37°34S 175°11E **59** B5
Huntly *U.K.* 57°27N 2°47W **11** D6
Huntsville *Canada* 45°20N 79°14W **82** A5
Huntsville *Ala., U.S.A.* 34°44N 86°35W **85** D11
Huntsville *Tex., U.S.A.* 30°43N 95°33W **84** F7
Hunyani → *Zimbabwe* 15°57S 30°39E **55** F3
Hunyuan *China* 39°42N 113°42E **34** E7
Hunza → *India* 35°54N 74°20E **43** B6
Huo Xian = Huozhou
   China 36°36N 111°42E **34** F6
Huong Khe *Vietnam* 18°13N 105°41E **38** C5
Huonville *Australia* 43°0S 147°5E **63** G4
Huozhou *China* 36°36N 111°42E **34** F6
Hupeh = Hubei □ *China* 31°0N 112°0E **33** C6
Ḥūr *Iran* 30°50N 57°7E **45** D8
Hurand *Iran* 38°51N 47°22E **44** B5
Ḥuraymīla *Si. Arabia* 25°8N 46°8E **44** E5
Hurd, C. *Canada* 45°13N 81°44W **82** A3
Hure Qi *China* 42°45N 121°45E **35** C11
Hurghada *Egypt* 27°15N 33°50E **51** C12
Hurley *N. Mex., U.S.A.* 32°42N 108°8W **77** K9
Hurley *Wis., U.S.A.* 46°27N 90°11W **80** B8
Huron *Calif., U.S.A.* 36°12N 120°6W **78** J6
Huron *Ohio, U.S.A.* 41°24N 82°33W **82** E2
Huron *S. Dak., U.S.A.* 44°22N 98°13W **80** C4
Huron, L. *U.S.A.* 44°30N 82°40W **82** B2
Huron East *Canada* 43°37N 81°18W **82** C3
Hurricane *U.S.A.* 37°11N 113°17W **77** H7
Hurungwe ☐ *Zimbabwe* 16°7S 29°5E **55** F2
Hurunui → *N.Z.* 42°54S 173°18E **59** E4
Húsavík *Iceland* 66°3N 17°21E **8** C5
Huşi *Romania* 46°41N 28°7E **17** E15
Hustadvika *Norway* 63°0N 7°0E **8** E12
Hustontown *U.S.A.* 40°3N 78°2W **82** F6
Hutchinson *Kans., U.S.A.* 38°5N 97°56W **80** F5
Hutchinson *Minn.,*
   U.S.A. 44°54N 94°22W **80** C6
Hutte Sauvage, L. de la
   Canada 56°15N 64°45W **73** A7
Hutton, Mt. *Australia* 25°51S 148°20E **63** D4
Huy *Belgium* 50°31N 5°15E **15** D5
Huzhou *China* 30°51N 120°8E **33** C7
Hvammstangi *Iceland* 65°24N 20°57W **8** D3
Hvar *Croatia* 43°11N 16°28E **22** C7
Hvítá → *Iceland* 64°30N 21°58W **8** D3
Hwacheon-Cheosuji
   S. Korea 38°5N 127°50E **35** E14
Hwang Ho = Huang He →
   China 37°55N 118°50E **35** F10
Hwange *Zimbabwe* 18°18S 26°30E **55** F2
Hwange △ *Zimbabwe* 19°0S 26°30E **56** B4
Hyannis *Mass., U.S.A.* 41°39N 70°17W **81** E18
Hyannis *Nebr., U.S.A.* 42°0N 101°46W **80** E3
Hyargas Nuur *Mongolia* 49°0N 93°0E **32** B4
Hydaburg *U.S.A.* 55°15N 132°50W **70** B2
Hyde Park *U.S.A.* 41°47N 73°56W **83** E11
Hyden *Australia* 32°24S 118°53E **61** F2
Hyder *U.S.A.* 55°55N 130°5W **70** B2
Hyderabad *India* 17°22N 78°29E **40** L11
Hyderabad *Pakistan* 25°23N 68°24E **42** G3
Hydra *Greece* 37°20N 23°28E **23** F10
Hyères *France* 43°8N 6°9E **20** E7
Hyères, Îs. d' *France* 43°0N 6°20E **20** E7
Hyesan *N. Korea* 41°20N 128°10E **35** D15
Hyland → *Canada* 59°52N 128°12W **70** B3
Hymia *India* 33°40N 78°2E **43** C8
Hyndman Peak *U.S.A.* 43°45N 114°8W **76** E6
Hyōgo □ *Japan* 35°15N 134°50E **31** G7
Hyrum *U.S.A.* 41°38N 111°51W **76** F8
Hysham *U.S.A.* 46°18N 107°14W **76** C10
Hythe *U.K.* 51°4N 1°5E **13** F9
Hyūga *Japan* 32°25N 131°35E **31** H5
Hyvinge = Hyvinkää
   Finland 60°38N 24°50E **8** F21
Hyvinkää *Finland* 60°38N 24°50E **8** F21

I

I-n-Gall *Niger* 16°51N 7°1E **50** E7
Iaco → *Brazil* 9°3S 68°34W **92** E5
Iakora *Madag.* 23°6S 46°40E **57** C8
Ialissos *Greece* 36°23N 28°10E **25** C10
Ialomiţa → *Romania* 44°42N 27°51E **17** F14
Iaşi *Romania* 47°10N 27°40E **17** E14

Ib → *India* 21°34N 83°48E **43** J10
Iba *Phil.* 15°22N 120°0E **37** A6
Ibadan *Nigeria* 7°22N 3°58E **50** G6
Ibagué *Colombia* 4°20N 75°20W **92** C3
Ibar → *Serbia* 43°43N 20°45E **23** C9
Ibaraki □ *Japan* 36°10N 140°10E **31** F10
Ibarra *Ecuador* 0°21N 78°7W **92** C3
Ibb *Yemen* 14°2N 44°10E **47** E3
Ibembo
   Dem. Rep. of the Congo 2°35N 23°35E **54** B1
Ibenga → *Congo* 2°19N 18°9E **52** D3
Ibera, L. *Argentina* 28°30S 57°9W **94** B4
Iberian Peninsula *Europe* 40°0N 5°0W **6** H5
Iberville *Canada* 45°19N 73°17W **83** A11
Ibiá *Brazil* 19°30S 46°30W **93** G9
Ibiapaba, Sa. da *Brazil* 4°0S 41°30W **93** D10
Ibicuí → *Brazil* 29°25S 56°47W **95** B4
Ibicuy *Argentina* 33°55S 59°10W **94** C4
Ibiза = Eivissa *Spain* 38°54N 1°26E **24** C7
Ibo *Mozam.* 12°22S 40°40E **55** E5
Ibonma *Indonesia* 3°29S 133°31E **37** E8
Ibotirama *Brazil* 12°13S 43°12W **93** F10
Ibrāhīm → *Lebanon* 34°4N 35°38E **46** A4
'Ibrī *Oman* 23°14N 56°30E **45** F8
Ibu *Indonesia* 1°35N 127°33E **37** D7
Ibusuki *Japan* 31°12N 130°40E **31** J5
Ica *Peru* 14°0S 75°48W **92** F3
Iça → *Brazil* 2°55S 67°58W **92** D5
Icacos Pt. *Trin. & Tob.* 10°3N 61°57W **93** K15
Içana *Brazil* 0°21N 67°19W **92** C5
Içana → *Brazil* 0°26N 67°19W **92** C5
İçel *Turkey* 36°51N 34°36E **44** B2
Iceland ■ *Europe* 64°45N 19°0W **8** D4
Iceland Basin *Atl. Oc.* 61°0N 19°0W **4** C7
Icelandic Plateau *Arctic* 64°0N 10°0W **4** C7
Ich'ang = Yichang
   China 30°40N 111°20E **33** C6
Ichchapuram *India* 19°10N 84°40E **41** K14
Icheon *S. Korea* 37°17N 127°27E **35** F14
Ichhawar *India* 23°1N 77°1E **42** H7
Ichihara *Japan* 35°28N 140°5E **31** G10
Ichikawa *Japan* 35°43N 139°54E **31** G9
Ichilo → *Bolivia* 15°57S 64°50W **92** G6
Ichinohe *Japan* 40°13N 141°17E **30** D10
Ichinomiya *Japan* 35°18N 136°48E **31** G8
Ichinoseki *Japan* 38°55N 141°8E **30** E10
Icod *Canary Is.* 28°22N 16°43W **24** F3
Icy C. *U.S.A.* 70°20N 161°52W **66** B3
Ida Grove *U.S.A.* 42°21N 95°28W **80** D6
Idabel *U.S.A.* 33°54N 94°50W **84** E7
Idaho □ *U.S.A.* 45°0N 115°0W **76** D6
Idaho City *U.S.A.* 43°50N 115°50W **76** E6
Idaho Falls *U.S.A.* 43°30N 112°2W **76** E7
Idalia △ *Australia* 24°45S 144°5E **62** C3
Idar-Oberstein *Germany* 49°43N 7°16E **16** D4
Idensalmi = Iisalmi
   Finland 63°32N 27°10E **8** E22
Idfû *Egypt* 24°55N 32°49E **51** D12
Ídhra = Hydra *Greece* 37°20N 23°28E **23** F10
Idi *Indonesia* 5°2N 97°37E **36** C1
Idi, Oros = Psiloritis, Oros
   Greece 35°15N 24°45E **25** D6
Idiofa
   Dem. Rep. of the Congo 4°55S 19°42E **52** E3
Idlib *Syria* 35°55N 36°36E **44** C3
Idria *U.S.A.* 36°25N 120°41W **78** J6
Idutywa = Dutywa
   S. Africa 32°8S 28°18E **57** E4
Ieper *Belgium* 50°51N 2°53E **15** D2
Ierapetra *Greece* 35°1N 25°44E **25** D7
Iesi *Italy* 43°31N 13°14E **22** C5
Ifakara *Tanzania* 8°8S 36°41E **52** F7
'Ifāl, W. al → *Si. Arabia* 28°7N 35°3E **44** D2
Ifanadiana *Madag.* 21°19S 47°39E **57** C8
Ife *Nigeria* 7°30N 4°31E **50** G6
Iffley *Australia* 18°53S 141°12E **62** B3
Iforas, Adrar des *Africa* 19°40N 1°40E **50** E6
Ifould, L. *Australia* 30°52S 132°6E **61** F5
Iganga *Uganda* 0°37N 33°28E **54** B3
Igarapava *Brazil* 20°3S 47°47W **93** H9
Igarka *Russia* 67°30N 86°33E **28** C9
Iggesund *Sweden* 61°39N 17°10E **8** F17
Iglésias *Italy* 39°19N 8°32E **22** E3
Igloolik = Iglulik
   Canada 69°20N 81°49W **69** C11
Iglulgaarjuk = Chesterfield Inlet
   Canada 63°30N 90°45W **68** C10
Iglulik *Canada* 69°20N 81°49W **69** C11
Ignace *Canada* 49°30N 91°40W **72** C1
İğneada Burnu *Turkey* 41°53N 28°2E **23** D13
Igoumenitsa *Greece* 39°32N 20°18E **23** E9
Igrim *Russia* 63°12N 64°30E **28** C7
Iguaçu → *Brazil* 25°36S 54°36W **95** B5
Iguaçu, Cat. del *Brazil* 25°41S 54°26W **95** B5
Iguaçu △ *Brazil* 25°30S 54°0W **95** B5
Iguaçu Falls = Iguaçu, Cat. del
   Brazil 25°41S 54°26W **95** B5
Iguala *Mexico* 18°21N 99°32W **87** D5
Igualada *Spain* 41°37N 1°37E **21** B6
Iguassu = Iguaçu →
   Brazil 25°36S 54°36W **95** B5
Iguatu *Brazil* 6°20S 39°18W **93** E11
Iguazú △ *Argentina* 25°42S 54°22W **95** B5
Iguidi, Erg *Africa* 27°0N 6°0W **50** C4
Iharana *Madag.* 13°25S 50°0E **57** A9
Ihbulag *Mongolia* 43°11N 107°10E **34** C4
Iheya-Shima *Japan* 27°4N 127°58E **31** L3
Ihosy *Madag.* 22°24S 46°8E **57** C8
Ihotry, Farihy *Madag.* 21°56S 43°41E **57** C7
Ii *Finland* 65°19N 25°22E **8** D21
Ii-Shima *Japan* 26°43N 127°47E **31** L3
Iida *Japan* 35°35N 137°50E **31** G8
Iijoki → *Finland* 65°20N 25°20E **8** D21
Iisalmi *Finland* 63°32N 27°10E **8** E22
Iiyama *Japan* 36°51N 138°22E **31** F9
Iizuka *Japan* 33°38N 130°42E **31** H5
Ijâfene *Mauritania* 20°40N 8°0W **50** D4

Ijebu-Ode *Nigeria* 6°47N 3°58E **50 G6**
IJmuiden *Neths.* 52°28N 4°35E **15 B4**
Ijo älv = Iijoki ➤
Finland 65°20N 25°20E **8 D21**
IJssel ➤ *Neths.* 52°35N 5°50E **15 B5**
IJsselmeer *Neths.* 52°45N 5°20E **15 B5**
Ijuí *Brazil* 28°23S 53°55W **95 B5**
Ijuí ➤ *Brazil* 27°58S 55°20W **95 B4**
Ikalamavony *Madag.* 21°9S 46°35E **57 C8**
Ikaluktutiak *Canada* 69°10N 105°00W **68 C9**
Ikanga *Kenya* 1°42S 38°4E **54 C4**
Ikare *Nigeria* 7°32N 5°40E **50 G7**
Ikaria *Greece* 37°35N 26°10E **23 F12**
Ikeda *Japan* 34°1N 133°48E **31 G6**
Ikela *Dem. Rep. of the Congo* 1°6S 23°6E **52 E4**
Iki *Japan* 33°45N 129°42E **31 H4**
Ikimba L. *Tanzania* 1°30S 31°20E **54 C3**
Ikongo *Madag.* 21°52S 47°27E **57 C8**
Ikopa ➤ *Madag.* 16°45S 46°40E **57 B8**
Ikorongo △ *Tanzania* 1°50S 34°53E **54 C3**
Ikparjuk = Arctic Bay
Canada 73°1N 85°7W **69 B11**
Iksan *S. Korea* 35°59N 127°0E **35 G14**
Ikungu *Tanzania* 1°33S 33°42E **54 C3**
Ikuntji = Haast Bluff
Australia 23°22S 132°0E **60 D5**
Ilagan *Phil.* 17°7N 121°53E **37 A6**
Ilaka *Madag.* 19°33S 48°52E **57 B8**
Īlām *Iran* 33°36N 46°36E **44 C5**
Ilam *Nepal* 26°58N 87°58E **43 F12**
Īlām □ *Iran* 33°0N 47°0E **44 C5**
Ilanskiy *Russia* 56°14N 96°3E **29 D10**
Iława *Poland* 53°36N 19°34E **17 B10**
Ile ➤ *Kazakhstan* 45°53N 77°10E **28 E8**
Île-à-la-Crosse *Canada* 55°27N 107°53W **71 B7**
Île-à-la-Crosse, Lac
Canada 55°40N 107°45W **71 B7**
Île-de-France □ *France* 49°0N 2°20E **20 B5**
Ilebo *Dem. Rep. of the Congo* 4°17S 20°55E **52 E4**
Ilek *Russia* 51°32N 53°21E **28 D6**
Ilek ➤ *Russia* 51°30N 53°22E **18 D9**
Ilesha *Nigeria* 7°37N 4°40E **50 G6**
Ilford *Canada* 56°4N 95°35W **71 B9**
Ilfracombe *Australia* 23°30S 144°30E **62 C3**
Ilfracombe *U.K.* 51°12N 4°8W **13 F3**
Ilha de Moçambique
Mozam. 15°4S 40°52E **55 F5**
Ilha Grande, Represa
Brazil 23°10S 53°5W **95 A5**
Ilha Grande △ *Brazil* 23°10S 53°20W **95 A5**
Ilhéus *Brazil* 14°49S 39°2W **93 F11**
Ili = Ile ➤ *Kazakhstan* 45°53N 77°10E **28 E8**
Iliamna L. *U.S.A.* 59°30N 155°0W **74 a**
Ilias, Profitis *Greece* 36°17N 27°56E **25 C9**
Iligan *Phil.* 8°12N 124°13E **37 C6**
Ilion *U.S.A.* 43°1N 75°2W **83 D9**
Ilkeston *U.K.* 52°58N 1°19W **12 E6**
Ilkley *U.K.* 53°56N 1°48W **12 D6**
Illampu = Ancohuma, Nevado
Bolivia 16°0S 68°50W **92 G5**
Illana B. *Phil.* 7°35N 123°45E **37 C6**
Illapel *Chile* 32°0S 71°10W **94 C1**
Iller ➤ *Germany* 48°23N 9°58E **16 D6**
Illetas *Spain* 39°32N 2°35E **24 B9**
Illimani, Nevado *Bolivia* 16°30S 67°50W **92 G5**
Illinois □ *U.S.A.* 40°15N 89°30W **80 E9**
Illinois ➤ *U.S.A.* 38°58N 90°28W **80 F8**
Illizi *Algeria* 26°31N 8°32E **50 C7**
Ilma, L. *Australia* 29°13S 127°46E **61 E4**
Ilmajoki *Finland* 62°44N 22°34E **8 E20**
Ilmen, Ozero *Russia* 58°15N 31°10E **18 C5**
Ilo *Peru* 17°40S 71°20W **92 G4**
Iloilo *Phil.* 10°45S 122°33E **37 B6**
Ilomantsi *Finland* 62°38N 30°57E **8 E24**
Ilorin *Nigeria* 8°30N 4°35E **50 G6**
Ilwaco *U.S.A.* 46°19N 124°3W **78 D2**
Ilwaki *Indonesia* 7°55S 126°30E **37 F7**
Imabari *Japan* 34°4N 133°0E **31 G6**
Imaloto ➤ *Madag.* 23°27S 45°13E **57 C8**
Imandra, Ozero *Russia* 67°30N 33°0E **8 C25**
Imanombo *Madag.* 24°26S 45°49E **57 C8**
Imari *Japan* 33°15N 129°52E **31 H4**
Imatra *Finland* 61°12N 28°48E **8 F23**
imeni 26 Bakinskikh Komissarov
= Neftçala *Azerbaijan* 39°19N 49°12E **45 B6**
imeni 26 Bakinskikh Komissarov
Turkmenistan 39°22N 54°10E **45 B7**
imeni Ismail Samani, Pik
Tajikistan 39°0N 72°2E **28 F8**
Imeri, Serra *Brazil* 0°50N 65°25W **92 C5**
Imerimandroso *Madag.* 17°26S 48°35E **57 B8**
Imfolozi △ *S. Africa* 28°18S 31°50E **57 D5**
Imi *Ethiopia* 6°28N 42°10E **47 F3**
Imlay *U.S.A.* 40°40N 118°9W **76 F4**
Imlay City *U.S.A.* 43°2N 83°5W **82 D1**
Immingham *U.K.* 53°37N 0°13W **12 D7**
Immokalee *U.S.A.* 26°25N 81°25W **85 H14**
Ímola *Italy* 44°20N 11°42E **22 B4**
Imperatriz *Brazil* 5°30S 47°29W **93 E9**
Impéria *Italy* 43°53N 8°3E **20 E8**
Imperial *Canada* 51°21N 105°28W **71 C7**
Imperial *Calif., U.S.A.* 32°51N 115°34W **79 N11**
Imperial *Nebr., U.S.A.* 40°31N 101°39W **80 E3**
Imperial Beach *U.S.A.* 32°35N 117°6W **79 N9**
Imperial Dam *U.S.A.* 32°55N 114°25W **79 N12**
Imperial Res. *U.S.A.* 32°53N 114°28W **79 N12**
Imperial Valley *U.S.A.* 33°0N 115°30W **79 N11**
Imperieuse Reef
Australia 17°36S 118°50E **60 C2**
Impfondo *Congo* 1°40N 18°0E **52 D3**
Imphal *India* 24°48N 93°56E **41 G18**
Īmroz = Gökçeada
Turkey 40°20N 25°50E **23 D11**
Imuris *Mexico* 30°47N 110°52W **86 A2**
Imuruan B. *Phil.* 10°40N 119°10E **37 B5**
In Salah *Algeria* 27°10N 2°32E **50 C6**
Ina *Japan* 35°50N 137°55E **31 G8**

Inagua △ *Bahamas* 21°5N 73°24W **89 B5**
Inangahua *N.Z.* 41°52S 171°59E **59 D3**
Inanwatan *Indonesia* 2°8S 132°10E **37 E8**
Iñapari *Peru* 11°0S 69°40W **92 F5**
Inari *Finland* 68°54N 27°1E **8 B22**
Inarijärvi *Finland* 69°0N 28°0E **8 B23**
Inawashiro-Ko *Japan* 37°29N 140°6E **30 F10**
Inca *Spain* 39°43N 2°54E **24 B9**
Inca de Oro *Chile* 26°45S 69°54W **94 B2**
Incahuasi *Argentina* 27°2S 68°18W **94 B2**
Incahuasi *Chile* 29°12S 71°5W **94 B1**
İnce Burun *Turkey* 42°7N 34°56E **19 F5**
İncesu *Turkey* 38°38N 35°11E **44 B2**
Incheon *S. Korea* 37°27N 126°40E **35 F14**
İncirliova *Turkey* 37°50N 27°41E **23 F12**
Incline Village *U.S.A.* 39°10N 119°58W **76 G4**
Incomáti ➤ *Mozam.* 25°46S 32°43E **57 D5**
Indalsälven ➤ *Sweden* 62°36N 17°30E **8 E17**
Indaw *Burma* 24°15N 96°5E **41 G20**
Independence *Calif.,*
U.S.A. 36°48N 118°12W **78 J8**
Independence *Iowa,*
U.S.A. 42°28N 91°54W **80 D8**
Independence *Kans.,*
U.S.A. 37°14N 95°42W **80 G6**
Independence *Ky.,*
U.S.A. 38°57N 84°33W **81 F11**
Independence *Mo., U.S.A.* 39°6N 94°25W **80 F6**
Independence Fjord
Greenland 82°10N 29°0W **4 A6**
Independence Mts.
U.S.A. 41°20N 116°0W **76 F5**
Index *U.S.A.* 47°50N 121°33W **78 C5**
India ■ *Asia* 20°0N 78°0E **40 K11**
Indian ➤ *U.S.A.* 27°59N 80°34W **85 H14**
Indian Cabins *Canada* 59°52N 117°40W **70 B5**
Indian Harbour *Canada* 54°27N 57°13W **73 B8**
Indian Head *Canada* 50°30N 103°41W **71 C8**
Indian L. *U.S.A.* 43°46N 74°16W **83 C10**
Indian Lake *U.S.A.* 43°47N 74°16W **83 C10**
Indian Springs *U.S.A.* 36°35N 115°40W **79 J11**
Indiana *U.S.A.* 40°37N 79°9W **82 F5**
Indiana □ *U.S.A.* 40°0N 86°0W **81 F11**
Indianapolis *U.S.A.* 39°46N 86°9W **80 F10**
Indianola *Iowa, U.S.A.* 41°22N 93°34W **80 E7**
Indianola *Miss., U.S.A.* 33°27N 90°39W **85 J9**
Indiga *Russia* 67°38N 49°9E **18 A8**
Indigirka ➤ *Russia* 70°48N 148°54E **29 B15**
Indio *U.S.A.* 33°43N 116°13W **79 M10**
Indira Gandhi Canal *India* 28°0N 72°0E **42 F5**
Indira Sagar *India* 22°15N 76°40E **42 H7**
Indo-China *Asia* 15°0N 102°0E **26 G12**
Indonesia ■ *Asia* 5°0S 115°0E **36 F5**
Indore *India* 22°42N 75°53E **42 H6**
Indramayu *Indonesia* 6°20S 108°19E **37 G13**
Indravati ➤ *India* 19°20N 80°20E **41 K12**
Indre □ *France* 47°16N 0°11E **20 C4**
Indulkana *Australia* 26°58S 133°5E **63 D1**
Indus ➤ *Pakistan* 24°20N 67°47E **42 G2**
Indus, Mouths of the
Pakistan 24°0N 68°0E **42 H3**
İnebolu *Turkey* 41°55N 33°40E **19 F5**
Infiernillo, Presa del
Mexico 18°35N 101°50W **86 D4**
Ingenio *Canary Is.* 27°55N 15°26W **24 G4**
Ingenio Santa Ana
Argentina 27°25S 65°40W **94 B2**
Ingersoll *Canada* 43°4N 80°55W **82 C4**
Ingham *Australia* 18°43S 146°10E **62 B4**
Ingleborough *U.K.* 54°10N 2°22W **12 C5**
Inglewood *Queens.,*
Australia 28°25S 151°2E **63 D5**
Inglewood *Vic., Australia* 36°29S 143°53E **63 F3**
Inglewood *N.Z.* 39°9S 174°14E **59 C5**
Inglewood *U.S.A.* 33°58N 118°21W **79 M8**
Ingólfshöfði *Iceland* 63°48N 16°39W **8 E5**
Ingolstadt *Germany* 48°46N 11°26E **16 D6**
Ingomar *U.S.A.* 46°35N 107°23W **76 C10**
Ingonish *Canada* 46°42N 60°18W **73 C7**
Ingraj Bazar *India* 24°58N 88°10E **43 G13**
Ingrid Christensen Coast
Antarctica 69°30S 76°0E **5 C6**
Ingulec = Inhulec
Ukraine 47°42N 33°14E **19 E5**
Ingushetia □ *Russia* 43°20N 44°50E **19 F8**
Ingwavuma *S. Africa* 27°9S 31°59E **57 D5**
Inhaca *Mozam.* 26°1S 32°57E **57 D5**
Inhafenga *Mozam.* 20°36S 33°53E **57 C5**
Inhambane *Mozam.* 23°54S 35°30E **57 C6**
Inhambane □ *Mozam.* 22°30S 34°20E **57 C5**
Inhaminga *Mozam.* 18°26S 35°0E **55 F4**
Inharrime *Mozam.* 24°30S 35°0E **57 C6**
Inharrime ➤ *Mozam.* 24°30S 35°0E **57 C6**
Inhulec *Ukraine* 47°42N 33°14E **19 E5**
Ining = Yining *China* 43°58N 81°10E **32 B3**
Inírida ➤ *Colombia* 3°55N 67°52W **92 C5**
Inishbofin *Ireland* 53°37N 10°13W **10 C1**
Inisheer *Ireland* 53°3N 9°32W **10 C2**
Inishfree B. *Ireland* 55°4N 8°23W **10 A3**
Inishkea North *Ireland* 54°9N 10°11W **10 B1**
Inishkea South *Ireland* 54°7N 10°12W **10 B1**
Inishmaan *Ireland* 53°5N 9°35W **10 C2**
Inishmore *Ireland* 53°8N 9°45W **10 C2**
Inishmurray I. *Ireland* 54°26N 8°39W **10 B3**
Inishowen Pen. *Ireland* 55°14N 7°15W **10 A4**
Inishshark *Ireland* 53°37N 10°16W **10 C1**
Inishturk *Ireland* 53°42N 10°7W **10 C1**
Inishvickillane *Ireland* 52°3N 10°37W **10 D1**
Injune *Australia* 25°53S 148°32E **63 D4**
Inklin ➤ *N. Amer.* 58°50N 133°10W **70 B2**
Inland Kaikoura Ra.
N.Z. 41°59S 173°41E **59 D4**
Inland Sea = Setonaikai
Japan 34°20N 133°30E **31 G6**
Inle L. *Burma* 20°30N 96°58E **41 J20**
Inlet *U.S.A.* 43°45N 74°48W **83 C10**
Inn ➤ *Austria* 48°35N 13°28E **16 D7**

Innamincka *Australia* 27°44S 140°46E **63 D3**
Inner Hebrides *U.K.* 57°0N 6°30W **11 E2**
Inner Mongolia = Nei Monggol
Zizhiqu □ *China* 42°0N 112°0E **34 D7**
Inner Sound *U.K.* 57°30N 5°55W **11 D3**
Innerkip *Canada* 43°13N 80°42W **82 C4**
Innetalling I. *Canada* 56°0N 79°0W **72 A4**
Innisfail *Australia* 17°33S 146°5E **62 B4**
Innisfail *Canada* 52°2N 113°57W **70 C6**
In'noshima *Japan* 34°19N 133°10E **31 G6**
Innsbruck *Austria* 47°16N 11°23E **16 E6**
Inny ➤ *Ireland* 53°30N 7°50W **10 C4**
Inongo
Dem. Rep. of the Congo 1°55S 18°30E **52 E3**
Inoucdjouac = Inukjuak
Canada 58°25N 78°15W **69 D12**
Inowrocław *Poland* 52°50N 18°12E **17 B10**
Inscription, C. *Australia* 25°29S 112°59E **61 E1**
Insein *Burma* 16°50N 96°5E **41 L20**
Inta *Russia* 66°5N 60°8E **18 A11**
Intendente Alvear
Argentina 35°12S 63°32W **94 D3**
Interlaken *Switz.* 46°41N 7°50E **20 C7**
Interlaken *U.S.A.* 42°37N 76°44W **83 D8**
International Falls
U.S.A. 48°36N 93°25W **80 A7**
Intiyaco *Argentina* 28°43S 60°5W **94 B3**
Inukjuak *Canada* 58°25N 78°15W **69 D12**
Inútil, B. *Chile* 53°30S 70°15W **96 G2**
Inuvik *Canada* 68°16N 133°40W **68 C6**
Inveraray *U.K.* 56°14N 5°5W **11 E3**
Inverbervie *U.K.* 56°51N 2°17W **11 E6**
Invercargill *N.Z.* 46°24S 168°24E **59 G2**
Inverclyde □ *U.K.* 55°55N 4°49W **11 F4**
Inverell *Australia* 29°45S 151°8E **63 D5**
Invergordon *U.K.* 57°41N 4°10W **11 D4**
Inverloch *Australia* 38°38S 145°45E **63 F4**
Invermere *Canada* 50°30N 116°2W **70 C5**
Inverness *Canada* 46°15N 61°19W **73 C7**
Inverness *U.K.* 57°29N 4°13W **11 D4**
Inverness *U.S.A.* 28°50N 82°20W **85 G13**
Inverurie *U.K.* 57°17N 2°23W **11 D6**
Investigator Group
Australia 34°45S 134°20E **63 E1**
Investigator Str.
Australia 35°30S 137°0E **63 F2**
Inya *Russia* 50°28N 86°37E **28 D9**
Inyanga *Zimbabwe* 18°12S 32°40E **55 F3**
Inyangani *Zimbabwe* 18°5S 32°50E **55 F3**
Inyantue *Zimbabwe* 18°33S 26°39E **56 B4**
Inyo Mts. *U.S.A.* 36°40N 118°0W **79 J9**
Inyokern *U.S.A.* 35°39N 117°49W **79 K9**
Inza *Russia* 53°55N 46°25E **18 D8**
Iō-Jima *Japan* 30°48N 130°18E **31 J5**
Ioannina *Greece* 39°42N 20°47E **23 E9**
Iola *U.S.A.* 37°55N 95°24W **80 G6**
Iona *U.K.* 56°20N 6°25W **11 E2**
Ione *U.S.A.* 38°21N 120°56W **78 G6**
Ionia *U.S.A.* 42°59N 85°4W **81 D11**
Ionian Is. = Ionioi Nisoi
Greece 38°40N 20°0E **23 E9**
Ionian Sea *Medit. S.* 37°30N 17°30E **23 E7**
Ionioi Nisoi *Greece* 38°40N 20°0E **23 E9**
Ios *Greece* 36°41N 25°20E **23 F11**
Iowa □ *U.S.A.* 42°18N 93°30W **80 D7**
Iowa ➤ *U.S.A.* 41°10N 91°1W **80 E8**
Iowa City *U.S.A.* 41°40N 91°32W **80 E9**
Iowa Falls *U.S.A.* 42°31N 93°16W **80 D7**
Iowa Park *U.S.A.* 33°57N 98°40W **84 E5**
Ipala *Tanzania* 4°30S 32°52E **54 C3**
Ipameri *Brazil* 17°44S 48°9W **93 G9**
Ipatinga *Brazil* 19°32S 42°30W **93 G10**
Ipiales *Colombia* 0°50N 77°37W **92 C3**
Ipin = Yibin *China* 28°45N 104°32E **32 D5**
Ipixuna *Brazil* 7°0S 71°40W **92 E4**
Ipoh *Malaysia* 4°35N 101°5E **39 K3**
Ippy *C.A.R.* 6°5N 21°7E **52 C4**
İpsala *Turkey* 40°55N 26°23E **23 D12**
Ipswich *Australia* 27°35S 152°40E **63 D5**
Ipswich *U.K.* 52°4N 1°10E **13 E9**
Ipswich *Mass., U.S.A.* 42°41N 70°50W **83 D14**
Ipswich *S. Dak., U.S.A.* 45°27N 99°2W **80 C4**
Ipu *Brazil* 4°23S 40°42W **93 D10**
Iqaluit *Canada* 63°44N 68°31W **69 C13**
Iquique *Chile* 20°19S 70°5W **92 H4**
Iquitos *Peru* 3°45S 73°10W **92 D4**
Irabu-Jima *Japan* 24°50N 125°10E **31 M2**
Iracoubo *Fr. Guiana* 5°30N 53°10W **93 B8**
Īrafshān *Iran* 26°42N 61°56E **45 E9**
Iráklio *Greece* 35°20N 25°12E **25 D7**
Iráklio □ *Greece* 35°10N 25°10E **25 D7**
Iráklion = Iráklio *Greece* 35°20N 25°12E **25 D7**
Irákliou, Kolpos *Greece* 35°23N 25°8E **25 D7**
Irala *Paraguay* 25°55S 54°35W **95 B5**
Iran ■ *Asia* 33°0N 53°0E **45 C7**
Iran, Pegunungan
Malaysia 2°20N 114°50E **36 D4**
Iran Ra. = Iran, Pegunungan
Malaysia 2°20N 114°50E **36 D4**
Īrānshahr *Iran* 27°15N 60°40E **45 E9**
Irapuato *Mexico* 20°41N 101°28W **86 C4**
Iraq ■ *Asia* 33°0N 44°0E **44 C5**
Irati *Brazil* 25°25S 50°38W **95 B5**
Irbid *Jordan* 32°35N 35°48E **46 C4**
Irbid □ *Jordan* 32°30N 35°0E **46 C5**
Irebu *Dem. Rep. of the Congo* 0°40S 17°46E **52 E3**
Ireland ■ *Europe* 53°50N 7°52W **10 C4**
Iri = Iksan *S. Korea* 35°59N 127°0E **35 G14**
Irian Jaya = Papua □
Indonesia 4°0S 137°0E **37 E9**
Irian Jaya Barat □
Indonesia 1°30S 132°50E **37 E8**
Iringa *Tanzania* 7°48S 35°43E **54 D4**
Iringa □ *Tanzania* 7°48S 35°43E **54 D4**
Iriomote *Japan* 24°29N 123°53E **31 M1**
Iriomote-Jima *Japan* 24°19N 123°48E **31 M1**
Iriona *Honduras* 15°57N 85°11W **88 C2**

Iriri ➤ *Brazil* 3°52S 52°37W **93 D8**
Irish Republic ■ *Europe* 53°50N 7°52W **10 C4**
Irish Sea *Europe* 53°38N 4°48W **12 D3**
Irkutsk *Russia* 52°18N 104°20E **29 D11**
Irma *Canada* 52°55N 111°14W **71 C6**
Irō-Zaki *Japan* 34°36N 138°51E **31 G9**
Iron Baron *Australia* 32°58S 137°11E **63 E2**
Iron Gate = Portile de Fier
Europe 44°44N 22°30E **17 F12**
Iron Knob *Australia* 32°46S 137°8E **63 E2**
Iron Mountain *U.S.A.* 45°49N 88°4W **80 C9**
Iron Range △ *Australia* 12°34S 143°18E **62 A3**
Iron River *U.S.A.* 46°6N 88°39W **80 C9**
Irondequoit *U.S.A.* 43°13N 77°35W **82 C7**
Ironton *Mo., U.S.A.* 37°36N 90°38W **80 G9**
Ironton *Ohio, U.S.A.* 38°32N 82°41W **81 F12**
Ironwood *U.S.A.* 46°27N 90°9W **80 B8**
Ironwood Forest △
U.S.A. 32°30N 111°28W **77 K8**
Iroquois *Canada* 44°51N 75°19W **83 B9**
Iroquois Falls *Canada* 48°46N 80°41W **72 C3**
Irpin *Ukraine* 50°50N 18°12E **17 C16**
Irrara Cr. ➤ *Australia* 29°35S 145°31E **63 D4**
Irrawaddy □ *Burma* 17°0N 95°0E **41 L19**
Irrawaddy ➤ *Burma* 15°50N 95°6E **41 M19**
Irrawaddy, Mouths of the
Burma 15°30N 95°0E **41 M19**
Irricana *Canada* 51°19N 113°37W **70 C6**
Irtysh ➤ *Russia* 61°4N 68°52E **28 C7**
Irumu
Dem. Rep. of the Congo 1°32N 29°53E **54 B2**
Irún *Spain* 43°20N 1°52W **21 A5**
Irunea = Pamplona-Iruña
Spain 42°48N 1°38W **21 A5**
Irvine *Canada* 49°57N 110°16W **71 D6**
Irvine *U.K.* 55°37N 4°41W **11 F4**
Irvine *Calif., U.S.A.* 33°41N 117°46W **79 M9**
Irvine *Ky., U.S.A.* 37°42N 83°58W **81 G12**
Irvinestown *U.K.* 54°28N 7°39W **10 B4**
Irving *U.S.A.* 32°48N 96°56W **84 E6**
Irvona *U.S.A.* 40°46N 78°33W **82 F6**
Irwin ➤ *Australia* 29°15S 114°54E **61 E1**
Irymple *Australia* 34°14S 142°8E **63 E3**
Isa Khel *Pakistan* 32°41N 71°17E **42 C4**
Isaac ➤ *Australia* 22°55S 149°20E **62 C4**
Isabel *U.S.A.* 45°24N 101°26W **80 C3**
Isabel, I. *Mexico* 21°51N 105°55W **86 C3**
Isabela *Phil.* 6°40N 121°59E **37 C6**
Isabela *Puerto Rico* 18°30N 67°2W **89 d**
Isabella, Cord. *Nic.* 13°30N 85°25W **88 D2**
Isabella Ra. *Australia* 21°0S 121°4E **60 D3**
Isachenko, Ostrov
Russia 77°13N 89°27E **29 B9**
Ísafjarðardjúp *Iceland* 66°10N 23°0W **8 C2**
Ísafjörður *Iceland* 66°5N 23°9W **8 C2**
Isagarh *India* 24°48N 77°51E **42 G7**
Isahaya *Japan* 32°52N 130°2E **31 H5**
Isaka *Tanzania* 3°56S 32°59E **54 C3**
Isalo △ *Madag.* 22°33S 45°16E **57 C8**
Isan ➤ *India* 26°51N 80°7E **43 F9**
Isana = Içana ➤ *Brazil* 0°26N 67°19W **92 C5**
Isangano □ *Zambia* 11°8S 30°35E **55 E3**
Isar ➤ *Germany* 48°48N 12°57E **16 D7**
Íschia *Italy* 40°44N 13°57E **22 D5**
Isdell ➤ *Australia* 16°27S 124°51E **60 C3**
Ise *Japan* 34°25N 136°45E **31 G8**
Ise-Shima △ *Japan* 34°25N 136°48E **31 G8**
Ise-Wan *Japan* 34°43N 136°43E **31 G8**
Iseramagazi *Tanzania* 4°37S 32°10E **54 C3**
Isère □ *France* 44°59N 4°51E **20 D6**
Isère ➤ *France* 44°59N 4°51E **20 D6**
Isérnia *Italy* 41°36N 14°14E **22 D6**
Isfahan = Eşfahān *Iran* 32°39N 51°43E **45 C6**
Ishigaki *Japan* 24°26N 124°10E **31 M2**
Ishigaki-Shima *Japan* 24°20N 124°10E **31 M2**
Ishikari-Gawa ➤
Japan 43°15N 141°23E **30 C10**
Ishikari-Sammyaku
Japan 43°30N 143°0E **30 C11**
Ishikari-Wan *Japan* 43°25N 141°1E **30 C10**
Ishikawa *Japan* 26°25N 127°49E **31 L3**
Ishikawa □ *Japan* 36°30N 136°30E **31 F8**
Ishim *Russia* 56°10N 69°30E **28 D7**
Ishim ➤ *Russia* 57°45N 71°10E **28 D8**
Ishinomaki *Japan* 38°32N 141°20E **30 E10**
Ishioka *Japan* 36°11N 140°16E **31 F10**
Ishkoman *Pakistan* 36°30N 73°50E **43 A5**
Ishpeming *U.S.A.* 46°29N 87°40W **80 B10**
Isil Kul *Russia* 54°55N 71°16E **28 D8**
Isiolo *Kenya* 0°24N 37°33E **54 B4**
Isiro *Dem. Rep. of the Congo* 2°53N 27°40E **54 B2**
Isisford *Australia* 24°15S 144°21E **62 C3**
İskenderun *Turkey* 36°32N 36°10E **44 B3**
İskenderun Körfezi
Turkey 36°40N 35°50E **19 G6**
Iskŭr ➤ *Bulgaria* 43°45N 24°25E **23 C11**
Iskut ➤ *Canada* 56°45N 131°49W **70 B2**
Isla ➤ *U.K.* 56°32N 3°20W **11 E5**
Isla Coiba △ *Panama* 7°33N 81°36W **88 E3**
Isla de Salamanca △
Colombia 10°59N 74°40W **89 D5**
Isla Gorge △ *Australia* 25°10S 149°57E **62 D4**
Isla Isabel △ *Mexico* 33°0N 44°0E **44 C5**
Isla Tiburón y San Esteban △
Mexico 29°0N 112°27W **86 B2**
Isla Vista *U.S.A.* 34°25N 119°53W **79 L7**
Islam Headworks
Pakistan 29°49N 72°33E **42 E5**
Islamabad *Pakistan* 33°40N 73°10E **42 C5**
Islamgarh *Pakistan* 27°51N 70°48E **42 F4**
Islamkot *Pakistan* 24°42N 70°13E **42 G4**
Islampur *India* 26°16N 88°12E **43 F13**
Islampur *Bihar, India* 25°9N 85°12E **43 G11**
Island = Iceland ■ *Europe* 64°45N 19°0W **8 D4**
Island L. *Canada* 53°47N 94°25W **71 C10**
Island Lagoon *Australia* 31°30S 136°40E **63 E2**
Island Pond *U.S.A.* 44°49N 71°53W **83 B13**
Islands, B. of *Canada* 49°11N 58°15W **73 C8**

Islands, B. of *N.Z.* 35°15S 174°6E **59 A5**
Islay *U.K.* 55°46N 6°10W **11 F2**
Isle ➤ *France* 44°55N 0°15W **20 D3**
Isle aux Morts *Canada* 47°35N 59°0W **73 C8**
Isle of Wight □ *U.K.* 50°41N 1°17W **13 G6**
Isle Royale △ *U.S.A.* 48°0N 88°54W **80 A10**
Isleton *U.S.A.* 38°10N 121°37W **78 G5**
Ismail = Izmayil
Ukraine 45°22N 28°46E **17 F15**
Ismâ'ilîya *Egypt* 30°37N 32°18E **51 B12**
Isna *Egypt* 25°17N 32°30E **51 C12**
Isoanala *Madag.* 23°50S 45°44E **57 C8**
Isogstalo *India* 34°15N 78°46E **43 B8**
Isparta *Turkey* 37°47N 30°30E **19 G5**
İspica *Italy* 36°47N 14°55E **22 F6**
Israel ■ *Asia* 32°0N 34°50E **46 D3**
Issoire *France* 45°32N 3°15E **20 D5**
Issyk-Kul = Balykchy
Kyrgyzstan 42°26N 76°12E **32 B2**
Issyk-Kul, Ozero = Ysyk-Köl
Kyrgyzstan 42°25N 77°15E **28 E8**
İstanbul *Turkey* 41°0N 28°58E **23 D13**
İstanbul Boğazı *Turkey* 41°5N 29°3E **23 D13**
Istiea *Greece* 38°57N 23°9E **23 E10**
Istokpoga, L. *U.S.A.* 27°23N 81°17W **85 H14**
Istra *Croatia* 45°10N 14°0E **16 F7**
Istres *France* 43°31N 4°59E **20 E6**
Istria = Istra *Croatia* 45°10N 14°0E **16 F7**
Itá *Paraguay* 25°29S 57°21W **94 B4**
Itaberaba *Brazil* 12°32S 40°18W **93 F10**
Itabira *Brazil* 19°37S 43°13W **93 G10**
Itabirito *Brazil* 20°15S 43°48W **95 A7**
Itabuna *Brazil* 14°48S 39°16W **93 F11**
Itacaunas ➤ *Brazil* 5°21S 49°8W **93 E9**
Itacoatiara *Brazil* 3°8S 58°25W **92 D7**
Itaipú, Represa de *Brazil* 25°30S 54°30W **95 B5**
Itaituba *Brazil* 4°10S 55°50W **93 D7**
Itajaí *Brazil* 27°50S 48°39W **95 B6**
Itajubá *Brazil* 22°24S 45°30W **95 A6**
Itaka *Tanzania* 8°50S 32°49E **55 D3**
Itala △ *S. Africa* 27°30S 31°7E **57 D5**
Italy ■ *Europe* 42°0N 13°0E **22 C5**
Itamaraju *Brazil* 17°4S 39°32W **93 G11**
Itampolo *Madag.* 24°41S 43°57E **57 C7**
Itandrano *Madag.* 21°47S 45°17E **57 C8**
Itapecuru Mirim *Brazil* 3°24S 44°20W **93 D10**
Itaperuna *Brazil* 21°10S 41°54W **95 A7**
Itapetininga *Brazil* 23°36S 48°7W **95 A6**
Itapeva *Brazil* 23°59S 48°59W **95 A6**
Itapicuru ➤ *Bahia,*
Brazil 11°47S 37°32W **93 F11**
Itapicuru ➤ *Maranhão,*
Brazil 2°52S 44°12W **93 D10**
Itapipoca *Brazil* 3°30S 39°35W **93 D11**
Itapuá □ *Paraguay* 26°40S 55°40W **95 B4**
Itaquari *Brazil* 20°20S 40°25W **95 A7**
Itaquí *Brazil* 29°8S 56°30W **94 B4**
Itararé *Brazil* 24°6S 49°23W **95 A6**
Itarsi *India* 22°36N 77°51E **42 H7**
Itati *Argentina* 27°16S 58°15W **94 B4**
Itatiaia △ *Brazil* 22°22S 44°38W **95 A7**
Itchen ➤ *U.K.* 50°55N 1°22W **13 G6**
Itezhi Tezhi, L. *Zambia* 15°30S 25°30E **55 F2**
Ithaca = Ithaki *Greece* 38°25N 20°40E **23 E9**
Ithaca *U.S.A.* 42°27N 76°30W **83 D8**
Ithaki *Greece* 38°25N 20°40E **23 E9**
Itiquira ➤ *Brazil* 17°18S 56°44W **93 G7**
Itiyuro ➤ *Argentina* 22°40S 63°50W **94 A3**
Itō *Japan* 34°58N 139°5E **31 G9**
Itoigawa *Japan* 37°2N 137°51E **31 F8**
Itonamas ➤ *Bolivia* 12°28S 64°24W **92 F6**
Ittoqqortoormiit *Greenland* 70°20N 23°0W **4 B6**
Itu *Brazil* 23°17S 47°15W **95 A6**
Itu Aba I. *S. China Sea* 10°23N 114°21E **36 B4**
Ituiutaba *Brazil* 19°0S 49°25W **93 G9**
Itumbiara *Brazil* 18°20S 49°10W **93 G9**
Ituna *Canada* 51°10N 103°24W **71 C8**
Itunge Port *Tanzania* 9°40S 33°55E **55 D3**
Iturbe *Argentina* 23°0S 65°25W **94 A2**
Ituri ➤
Dem. Rep. of the Congo 1°40N 27°1E **54 B2**
Iturup, Ostrov *Russia* 45°0N 148°0E **29 E15**
Ituxi ➤ *Brazil* 7°18S 64°51W **92 E6**
Itzehoe *Germany* 53°55N 9°31E **16 B5**
Ivahona *Madag.* 23°27S 46°10E **57 C8**
Ivaí ➤ *Brazil* 23°18S 53°42W **95 A5**
Ivalo *Finland* 68°38N 27°35E **8 B22**
Ivalojoki ➤ *Finland* 68°40N 27°40E **8 B22**
Ivanava *Belarus* 52°7N 25°29E **17 B13**
Ivanhoe *Australia* 32°56S 144°20E **63 E4**
Ivanhoe *Canada* 44°23N 77°28W **82 B7**
Ivanhoe *Calif., U.S.A.* 36°23N 119°13W **78 J7**
Ivanhoe *Minn., U.S.A.* 44°28N 96°15W **80 C5**
Ivano-Frankivsk
Ukraine 48°40N 24°40E **17 D13**
Ivanovo = Ivanava
Belarus 52°7N 25°29E **17 B13**
Ivanovo *Russia* 57°5N 41°0E **18 C7**
Ivato *Madag.* 20°37S 47°10E **57 C8**
Ivatsevichy *Belarus* 52°43N 25°21E **17 B13**
Ivdel *Russia* 60°42N 60°24E **18 B11**
Ivinheima ➤ *Brazil* 23°14S 53°42W **95 A5**
Ivinhema *Brazil* 22°10S 53°37W **95 A5**
Ivory Coast *W. Afr.* 4°20N 5°0W **50 H4**
Ivory Coast ■ *Africa* 7°30N 5°0W **50 G4**
Ivrea *Italy* 45°28N 7°52E **20 D7**
Ivujivik *Canada* 62°24N 77°55W **69 C12**
Ivybridge *U.K.* 50°23N 3°56W **13 G4**
Iwaizumi *Japan* 39°50N 141°45E **30 E10**
Iwaki *Japan* 37°3N 140°55E **31 F10**
Iwakuni *Japan* 34°15N 132°8E **31 G6**
Iwamizawa *Japan* 43°12N 141°46E **30 C10**
Iwanai *Japan* 42°58N 140°30E **30 C10**
Iwata *Japan* 34°42N 137°51E **31 G8**
Iwate □ *Japan* 39°30N 141°30E **30 E10**
Iwate-San *Japan* 39°51N 141°0E **30 E10**

Iwo *Nigeria* 7°39N 4°9E **50 G6**
Iwŏn *N. Korea* 40°19N 128°39E **35 D15**
Ixiamas *Bolivia* 13°50S 68°5W **92 F5**
Ixopo *S. Africa* 30°11S 30°5E **57 E5**
Ixtepec *Mexico* 16°34N 95°6W **87 D5**
Ixtlán del Río *Mexico* 21°2N 104°22W **86 C4**
Iyo *Japan* 33°45N 132°45E **31 H6**
Izabal, L. de *Guatemala* 15°30N 89°10W **88 C2**
Izamal *Mexico* 20°56N 89°1W **87 C7**
Izena-Shima *Japan* 26°56N 127°56E **31 L3**
Izhevsk *Russia* 56°51N 53°14E **18 C9**
Izhma *Russia* 65°19N 52°54E **18 A9**
Izmayil *Ukraine* 45°22N 28°46E **17 F15**
İzmir *Turkey* 38°25N 27°8E **23 E12**
İzmit = Kocaeli *Turkey* 40°45N 29°50E **19 F4**
İznik Gölü *Turkey* 40°27N 29°30E **23 D13**
Izra *Syria* 32°51N 36°15E **46 C5**
Izu-Shotō *Japan* 34°30N 140°0E **31 G10**
Izúcar de Matamoros
  Mexico 18°36N 98°28W **87 D5**
Izumi-Sano *Japan* 34°23N 135°18E **31 G7**
Izumo *Japan* 35°20N 132°46E **31 G6**
Izyaslav *Ukraine* 50°5N 26°50E **17 C14**

J

J.F.K. Int. ✈ (JFK)
  U.S.A. 40°38N 73°47W **83 F11**
J. Strom Thurmond L.
  U.S.A. 33°40N 82°12W **85 E13**
Jabalpur *India* 23°9N 79°58E **43 H8**
Jabbūl *Syria* 36°4N 37°30E **44 B3**
Jabiru *Australia* 12°40S 132°53E **60 B5**
Jablah *Syria* 35°20N 36°0E **44 C3**
Jablonec nad Nisou
  Czech Rep. 50°43N 15°10E **16 C8**
Jaboatão *Brazil* 8°7S 35°1W **93 E12**
Jaboticabal *Brazil* 21°15S 48°17W **95 A6**
Jaca *Spain* 42°35N 0°33W **21 A5**
Jacareí *Brazil* 23°20S 46°0W **95 A6**
Jacarèzinho *Brazil* 23°5S 49°58W **95 A6**
Jack River △ *Australia* 14°58S 144°19E **62 A3**
Jackman *U.S.A.* 45°37N 70°15W **81 C18**
Jacksboro *U.S.A.* 33°13N 98°10W **84 E5**
Jackson *Barbados* 13°7N 59°36W **89 g**
Jackson *Ala., U.S.A.* 31°31N 87°53W **85 F11**
Jackson *Calif., U.S.A.* 38°21N 120°46W **78 G6**
Jackson *Ky., U.S.A.* 37°33N 83°23W **81 G12**
Jackson *Mich., U.S.A.* 42°15N 84°24W **81 D11**
Jackson *Minn., U.S.A.* 43°37N 95°1W **80 D6**
Jackson *Miss., U.S.A.* 32°18N 90°12W **85 E9**
Jackson *Mo., U.S.A.* 37°23N 89°40W **80 G9**
Jackson *N.H., U.S.A.* 44°10N 71°11W **83 B13**
Jackson *Ohio, U.S.A.* 39°3N 82°39W **81 F12**
Jackson *Tenn., U.S.A.* 35°37N 88°49W **85 D10**
Jackson *Wyo., U.S.A.* 43°29N 110°46W **76 E8**
Jackson *B. N.Z.* 43°58S 168°42E **59 E2**
Jackson L. *U.S.A.* 43°52N 110°36W **76 E8**
Jacksons *N.Z.* 42°46S 171°32E **59 E3**
Jackson's Arm *Canada* 49°52N 56°47W **73 C8**
Jacksonville *Ala.,*
  U.S.A. 33°49N 85°46W **85 E12**
Jacksonville *Calif.,*
  U.S.A. 37°52N 120°24W **78 H6**
Jacksonville *Fla.,*
  U.S.A. 30°20N 81°39W **85 F14**
Jacksonville *Ill., U.S.A.* 39°44N 90°14W **80 F8**
Jacksonville *N.C.,*
  U.S.A. 34°45N 77°26W **85 D16**
Jacksonville *Tex., U.S.A.* 31°58N 95°17W **84 F7**
Jacksonville Beach
  U.S.A. 30°17N 81°24W **85 F14**
Jacmel *Haiti* 18°14N 72°32W **89 C5**
Jacob Lake *U.S.A.* 36°43N 112°13W **77 H7**
Jacobabad *Pakistan* 28°20N 68°29E **42 E3**
Jacobina *Brazil* 11°11S 40°30W **93 F10**
Jacques-Cartier, Dét. de
  Canada 50°0N 63°30W **73 C7**
Jacques-Cartier, Mt.
  Canada 48°57N 66°0W **73 C6**
Jacques-Cartier △
  Canada 47°15N 71°33W **73 C5**
Jacuí → *Brazil* 30°2S 51°15W **95 C5**
Jacumba *U.S.A.* 32°37N 116°11W **79 N10**
Jacundá → *Brazil* 1°57S 50°26W **93 D8**
Jade City *Canada* 59°15N 129°37W **70 B3**
Jaén *Peru* 5°25S 78°40W **92 E3**
Jaén *Spain* 37°44N 3°43W **21 D4**
Jafarabad *India* 20°52N 71°22E **42 J4**
Jaffa = Tel Aviv-Yafo
  Israel 32°4N 34°48E **46 C3**
Jaffa, C. *Australia* 36°58S 139°40E **63 F2**
Jaffna *Sri Lanka* 9°45N 80°2E **40 Q12**
Jaffrey *U.S.A.* 42°49N 72°2W **83 D12**
Jagadhri *India* 30°10N 77°20E **42 D7**
Jagadishpur *India* 25°30N 84°21E **43 G11**
Jagdalpur *India* 19°3N 82°0E **41 K13**
Jagersfontein *S. Africa* 29°44S 25°27E **56 D4**
Jaghīn → *Iran* 27°17N 57°13E **45 E8**
Jagodina *Serbia* 44°5N 21°15E **23 C9**
Jagraon *India* 30°50N 75°25E **42 D6**
Jagtial *India* 18°50N 79°0E **40 K11**
Jaguariaíva *Brazil* 24°10S 49°50W **95 A6**
Jaguaribe → *Brazil* 4°25S 37°45W **93 D11**
Jagüey Grande *Cuba* 22°35N 81°7W **88 B3**
Jahanabad *India* 25°13N 84°59E **43 G11**
Jahazpur *India* 25°37N 75°17E **42 G6**
Jahrom *Iran* 28°30N 53°31E **45 D7**
Jaijon *India* 31°21N 76°9E **42 D7**
Jailolo *Indonesia* 1°5N 127°30E **37 D7**
Jailolo, Selat *Indonesia* 0°5N 129°5E **37 D7**
Jaipur *India* 27°0N 75°50E **42 F6**
Jais *India* 26°15N 81°32E **43 F9**
Jaisalmer *India* 26°55N 70°54E **42 F4**
Jaisinghnagar *India* 23°38N 78°34E **43 H8**

Jaitaran *India* 26°12N 73°56E **42 F5**
Jaithari *India* 23°14N 78°37E **43 H8**
Jājarm *Iran* 36°58N 56°27E **45 B8**
Jakam → *India* 23°54N 74°13E **42 H6**
Jakarta *Indonesia* 6°9S 106°52E **37 G12**
Jakhal *India* 29°48N 75°50E **42 E6**
Jakhau *India* 23°13N 68°43E **42 H3**
Jakobstad = Pietarsaari
  Finland 63°40N 22°43E **8 E20**
Jal *U.S.A.* 32°7N 103°12W **77 K12**
Jalājil *Si. Arabia* 25°40N 45°27E **44 E5**
Jalālābād *Afghan.* 34°30N 70°29E **42 B4**
Jalalabad *India* 27°41N 79°42E **43 F8**
Jalalpur Jattan *Pakistan* 32°38N 74°11E **42 C6**
Jalapa *Guatemala* 14°39N 89°59W **88 D2**
Jalapa Enríquez = Xalapa
  Mexico 19°32N 96°55W **87 D5**
Jalasjärvi *Finland* 62°29N 22°47E **8 E20**
Jalaun *India* 26°8N 79°25E **43 F8**
Jaldhaka → *Bangla.* 26°16N 89°16E **43 F13**
Jalesar *India* 27°29N 78°19E **42 F8**
Jaleswar *Nepal* 26°38N 85°48E **43 F11**
Jalgaon *India* 21°0N 75°42E **40 J9**
Jalībah *Iraq* 30°35N 46°32E **44 D5**
Jalingo *Nigeria* 8°55N 11°25E **51 G8**
Jalisco □ *Mexico* 20°20N 103°40W **86 D4**
Jalkot *Pakistan* 35°14N 73°24E **43 B5**
Jalna *India* 19°48N 75°38E **40 K9**
Jalón → *Spain* 41°47N 1°4W **21 B5**
Jalor *India* 25°21N 72°37E **42 G5**
Jalpa *Mexico* 21°38N 102°58W **86 C4**
Jalpaiguri *India* 26°32N 88°46E **41 F16**
Jalpan *Mexico* 21°14N 99°29W **87 C5**
Jaluit I. *Marshall Is.* 6°0N 169°30E **64 G8**
Jalūlā *Iraq* 34°16N 45°10E **44 C5**
Jamaame *Somali Rep.* 0°4N 42°44E **47 G3**
Jamaica ■ *W. Indies* 18°10N 77°30W **88 a**
Jamalpur *Bangla.* 24°52N 89°56E **41 G16**
Jamalpur *India* 25°18N 86°28E **43 G12**
Jamalpurganj *India* 23°2N 87°59E **43 H13**
Jamanxim → *Brazil* 4°43S 56°18W **93 D7**
Jambewangi *Indonesia* 8°17S 114°7E **37 J17**
Jambi *Indonesia* 1°38S 103°30E **36 E2**
Jambi □ *Indonesia* 1°30S 102°30E **36 E2**
Jambongan, Pulau
  Malaysia 6°45N 117°20E **36 C5**
Jambusar *India* 22°3N 72°51E **42 H5**
James → *S. Dak., U.S.A.* 42°52N 97°18W **80 D6**
James → *Va., U.S.A.* 36°56N 76°27W **81 G15**
James B. *Canada* 54°0N 80°0W **72 B3**
James Ranges *Australia* 24°10S 132°30E **60 D5**
James Ross I. *Antarctica* 63°58S 57°50W **5 C18**
Jamesabad *Pakistan* 25°17N 69°15E **42 G3**
Jamestown *Australia* 33°10S 138°32E **63 E2**
Jamestown *S. Africa* 31°6S 26°45E **56 E4**
Jamestown *N. Dak.,*
  U.S.A. 46°54N 98°42W **80 B4**
Jamestown *N.Y., U.S.A.* 42°6N 79°14W **82 D5**
Jamestown *Pa., U.S.A.* 41°29N 80°27W **82 E4**
Jamīlābād *Iran* 34°24N 48°28E **45 C6**
Jamira → *India* 21°35N 88°28E **43 J13**
Jamkhandi *India* 16°30N 75°15E **40 L9**
Jammu *India* 32°43N 74°54E **42 C6**
Jammu & Kashmir □
  India 34°25N 77°0E **43 B7**
Jamnagar *India* 22°30N 70°6E **42 H4**
Jamni → *India* 25°13N 78°35E **43 G8**
Jampur *Pakistan* 29°39N 70°40E **42 E4**
Jamrud *Pakistan* 33°59N 71°24E **42 C4**
Jämsä *Finland* 61°53N 25°10E **8 F21**
Jamshedpur *India* 22°44N 86°12E **43 H12**
Jamtara *India* 23°59N 86°49E **43 H12**
Jämtland *Sweden* 63°31N 14°0E **8 E16**
Jan L. *Canada* 54°56N 102°55W **71 C8**
Jan Mayen *Arctic* 71°0N 9°0W **4 B7**
Janakpur *India* 26°42N 85°55E **43 F11**
Janaúba *Brazil* 15°48S 43°19W **93 G10**
Jand *Pakistan* 33°30N 72°6E **42 C5**
Jandaq *Iran* 34°3N 54°22E **45 C7**
Jandía *Canary Is.* 28°6N 14°21W **24 F5**
Jandía, Pta. de *Canary Is.* 28°3N 14°31W **24 F5**
Jandía △ *Canary Is.* 28°4N 14°19W **24 F5**
Jandola *Pakistan* 32°20N 70°9E **42 C4**
Jandowae *Australia* 26°45S 151°7E **63 D5**
Janesville *U.S.A.* 42°41N 89°1W **80 D9**
Jangamo *Mozam.* 24°6S 35°21E **57 C6**
Janghai *India* 25°33N 82°19E **43 G10**
Jangheung *S. Korea* 34°41N 126°52E **35 G14**
Janjanbureh *Gambia* 13°30N 14°47W **50 F3**
Janjgir *India* 22°1N 82°34E **43 J10**
Janjina *Madag.* 20°30S 45°50E **57 C8**
Janos *Mexico* 30°54N 108°10W **86 A3**
Januária *Brazil* 15°25S 44°25W **93 G10**
Janūb Sīnī □ *Egypt* 29°30N 33°50E **46 F2**
Janubio *Canary Is.* 28°56N 13°50W **24 F6**
Jaora *India* 23°40N 75°10E **42 H6**
Japan ■ *Asia* 36°0N 136°0E **31 G8**
Japan, Sea of *Asia* 40°0N 135°0E **30 E7**
Japan Trench *Pac. Oc.* 32°0N 142°0E **64 D6**
Japen = Yapen *Indonesia* 1°50S 136°0E **37 E9**
Japla *India* 24°33N 84°1E **43 G11**
Japurá → *Brazil* 3°8S 65°46W **92 D5**
Jaquarão *Brazil* 32°34S 53°23W **95 C5**
Jaqué *Panama* 7°27N 78°8W **88 E4**
Jarābulus *Syria* 36°49N 38°1E **44 B3**
Jarama → *Spain* 40°24N 3°32W **21 B4**
Jaranwala *Pakistan* 31°15N 73°26E **42 D5**
Jarash *Jordan* 32°17N 35°54E **46 C4**
Jarash □ *Jordan* 32°17N 35°54E **46 C4**
Jardim *Brazil* 21°28S 56°2W **94 A4**
Jardín América *Argentina* 27°3S 55°14W **95 B4**
Jardine River △ *Australia* 11°13S 142°21E **62 A3**
Jardines de la Reina, Arch. de los
  Cuba 20°50N 78°50W **88 B4**
Jargalang *China* 43°5N 122°55E **35 C12**
Jari → *Brazil* 1°9S 51°54W **93 D8**

Jarīr, W. al → *Si. Arabia* 25°38N 42°30E **44 E4**
Jaroslaw *Poland* 50°2N 22°42E **17 C12**
Jarrahdale *Australia* 32°24S 116°5E **61 F2**
Jarrahi → *Iran* 30°49N 48°48E **45 D6**
Jarres, Plaine des *Laos* 19°27N 103°10E **38 C4**
Jartai *China* 39°45N 105°48E **34 E3**
Jarud Qi *China* 44°28N 120°50E **35 B11**
Järvenpää *Finland* 60°29N 25°5E **8 F21**
Jarvis *Canada* 42°53N 80°6W **82 D4**
Jarvis I. *Pac. Oc.* 0°15S 160°5W **65 H12**
Jarwa *India* 27°38N 82°30E **43 F10**
Jasdan *India* 22°2N 71°12E **42 H4**
Jashpurnagar *India* 22°54N 84°9E **43 H11**
Jasidih *India* 24°31N 86°39E **43 G12**
Jāsimīyah *Iraq* 33°45N 44°41E **44 C5**
Jasin *Malaysia* 2°20N 102°26E **39 L4**
Jāsk *Iran* 25°38N 57°45E **45 E8**
Jaslo *Poland* 49°45N 21°30E **17 D11**
Jaso *India* 24°30N 80°29E **43 G9**
Jasper *Alta., Canada* 52°55N 118°5W **70 C5**
Jasper *Ont., Canada* 44°52N 75°57W **83 B9**
Jasper *Ala., U.S.A.* 33°50N 87°17W **85 E11**
Jasper *Fla., U.S.A.* 30°31N 82°57W **85 F13**
Jasper *Ind., U.S.A.* 38°24N 86°56W **80 F10**
Jasper *Tex., U.S.A.* 30°56N 94°1W **84 F7**
Jasper △ *Canada* 52°50N 118°8W **70 C5**
Jasrasar *India* 27°43N 73°49E **42 F5**
Jászberény *Hungary* 47°30N 19°55E **17 E10**
Jataí *Brazil* 17°58S 51°48W **93 G8**
Jati *Pakistan* 24°20N 68°19E **42 G3**
Jatibarang *Indonesia* 6°28S 108°18E **37 G13**
Jatiluwih *Indonesia* 8°23S 115°8E **37 J18**
Jatinegara *Indonesia* 6°13S 106°52E **37 G12**
Játiva = Xàtiva *Spain* 38°59N 0°32W **21 C5**
Jaú *Brazil* 22°10S 48°30W **95 A6**
Jauja *Peru* 11°45S 75°15W **92 F3**
Jaunpur *India* 25°46N 82°44E **43 G10**
Java = Jawa *Indonesia* 7°0S 110°0E **36 F3**
Java Sea *Indonesia* 4°35S 107°15E **36 E3**
Java Trench *Ind. Oc.* 9°0S 105°0E **36 F3**
Jawa *Indonesia* 7°0S 110°0E **36 F3**
Jawa Barat □ *Indonesia* 7°0S 107°0E **37 G12**
Jawa Tengah □ *Indonesia* 7°0S 110°0E **37 G14**
Jawa Timur □ *Indonesia* 8°0S 113°0E **37 G15**
Jawad *India* 24°36N 74°51E **42 G6**
Jawhar *Somali Rep.* 2°48N 45°30E **47 G4**
Jay Peak *U.S.A.* 44°55N 72°32W **83 B12**
Jaya, Puncak *Indonesia* 3°57S 137°17E **37 E9**
Jayanti *India* 26°45N 89°40E **41 F16**
Jayapura *Indonesia* 2°28S 140°38E **37 E10**
Jayawijaya, Pegunungan
  Indonesia 5°0S 139°0E **37 F9**
Jaynagar *India* 26°43N 86°9E **43 F12**
Jayrūd *Syria* 33°49N 36°44E **44 C4**
Jayton *U.S.A.* 33°15N 100°34W **84 E4**
Jāz Mūrīān, Hāmūn-e
  Iran 27°20N 58°55E **45 E8**
Jazīreh-ye Shīf *Iran* 29°4N 50°54E **45 D6**
Jazminal *Mexico* 24°52N 101°24W **86 C4**
Jazzīn *Lebanon* 33°31N 35°35E **46 B4**
Jean *U.S.A.* 35°47N 115°20W **79 K11**
Jean Marie River
  Canada 61°32N 120°38W **70 A4**
Jean-Rabel *Haiti* 19°50N 73°5W **89 C5**
Jeanerette *U.S.A.* 29°55N 91°40W **84 G9**
Jeanette, Ostrov = Zhannetty,
  Ostrov *Russia* 76°43N 158°0E **29 B16**
Jeannette *U.S.A.* 40°20N 79°36W **82 F5**
Jebäl Bärez, Kūh-e *Iran* 28°30N 58°20E **45 D8**
Jebel, Bahr el → *Sudan* 9°30N 30°25E **51 G12**
Jebel Ali = Minā’ Jabal ‘Alī
  U.A.E. 25°2N 55°8E **45 E7**
Jecheon *S. Korea* 37°8N 128°12E **35 F15**
Jedburgh *U.K.* 55°29N 2°33W **11 F6**
Jedda = Jiddah *Si. Arabia* 21°29N 39°10E **47 C2**
Jeddore L. *Canada* 48°3S 55°55W **73 C8**
Jędrzejów *Poland* 50°35N 20°15E **17 C11**
Jefferson *Iowa, U.S.A.* 42°1N 94°23W **80 D6**
Jefferson *Ohio, U.S.A.* 41°44N 80°46W **82 E4**
Jefferson *Tex., U.S.A.* 32°46N 94°21W **84 E7**
Jefferson, Mt. *Nev.,*
  U.S.A. 38°47N 116°56W **76 G5**
Jefferson, Mt. *Oreg.,*
  U.S.A. 44°41N 121°48W **76 D3**
Jefferson City *Mo.,*
  U.S.A. 38°34N 92°10W **80 F7**
Jefferson City *Tenn.,*
  U.S.A. 36°7N 83°30W **85 C13**
Jeffersontown *U.S.A.* 38°12N 85°35W **81 F11**
Jeffersonville *U.S.A.* 38°17N 85°44W **81 F11**
Jeffrey City *U.S.A.* 42°30N 107°49W **76 E10**
Jega *Nigeria* 12°15N 4°23E **50 F6**
Jeju *S. Korea* 33°31N 126°32E **35 H14**
Jeju-do *S. Korea* 33°29N 126°34E **35 H14**
Jēkabpils *Latvia* 56°29N 25°57E **9 H21**
Jekyll I. *U.S.A.* 31°4N 81°25W **85 F14**
Jelenia Góra *Poland* 50°50N 15°45E **16 C8**
Jelgava *Latvia* 56°41N 23°49E **9 H20**
Jemaja *Indonesia* 3°5N 105°45E **39 L4**
Jemaluang *Malaysia* 2°16N 103°52E **39 L4**
Jember *Indonesia* 8°11S 113°41E **37 H15**
Jena *Germany* 50°54N 11°35E **16 C6**
Jena *U.S.A.* 31°41N 92°8W **84 F8**
Jenīn *West Bank* 32°28N 35°18E **46 C4**
Jenkins *U.S.A.* 37°10N 82°38W **81 G12**
Jenner *U.S.A.* 38°27N 123°7W **78 G3**
Jennings *U.S.A.* 30°13N 92°40W **84 F8**
Jeong-eup *S. Korea* 35°35N 126°50E **35 G14**
Jeonju *S. Korea* 35°50N 127°4E **35 G14**
Jepara *Indonesia* 6°36S 110°40E **37 G14**
Jeparit *Australia* 36°8S 142°1E **63 F3**
Jequié *Brazil* 13°51S 40°5W **93 F10**
Jequitinhonha *Brazil* 16°30S 41°0W **93 G10**
Jequitinhonha →
  Brazil 15°51S 38°53W **93 G11**
Jerada *Morocco* 34°17N 2°10W **50 B5**
Jerantut *Malaysia* 3°56N 102°22E **39 L4**

Jerejak, Pulau *Malaysia* 5°19N 100°19E **39 c**
Jérémie *Haiti* 18°40N 74°10W **89 C5**
Jerez, Pta. *Mexico* 22°58N 97°40W **87 C5**
Jerez de García Salinas
  Mexico 22°39N 103°0W **86 C4**
Jerez de la Frontera *Spain* 36°41N 6°7W **21 D2**
Jerez de los Caballeros
  Spain 38°20N 6°45W **21 C2**
Jericho = El Arīḥā
  West Bank 31°52N 35°27E **46 D4**
Jericho *Australia* 23°38S 146°6E **62 C4**
Jerilderie *Australia* 35°20S 145°41E **63 F4**
Jermyn *U.S.A.* 41°32N 75°33W **83 E9**
Jerome *U.S.A.* 42°44N 114°31W **76 E6**
Jerramungup *Australia* 33°55S 118°52E **61 F2**
Jersey *U.K.* 49°11N 2°7W **13 H5**
Jersey City *U.S.A.* 40°42N 74°4W **83 F10**
Jersey Shore *U.S.A.* 41°12N 77°15W **82 E7**
Jerseyville *U.S.A.* 39°7N 90°20W **80 F8**
Jerusalem
  Israel/West Bank 31°47N 35°10E **46 D4**
Jervis B. *Australia* 35°8S 150°46E **63 F5**
Jervis Inlet *Canada* 50°0N 123°57W **70 C4**
Jesi = Iesi *Italy* 43°31N 13°14E **22 C5**
Jessore *Bangla.* 23°10N 89°10E **41 H16**
Jesup *U.S.A.* 31°36N 81°53W **85 F14**
Jesús Carranza *Mexico* 17°26N 95°2W **87 D5**
Jesús María *Argentina* 30°59S 64°5W **94 C3**
Jetmore *U.S.A.* 38°4N 99°54W **80 F4**
Jetpur *India* 21°45N 70°10E **42 J4**
Jevnaker *Norway* 60°15N 10°26E **9 F14**
Jewett *U.S.A.* 40°22N 81°2W **82 F3**
Jewett City *U.S.A.* 41°36N 71°59W **83 E13**
Jeypore *India* 18°50N 82°38E **41 K13**
Jha Jha *India* 24°46N 86°22E **43 G12**
Jhaarkand = Jharkhand □
  India 24°0N 85°50E **43 H11**
Jhabua *India* 22°46N 74°36E **42 H6**
Jhajjar *India* 28°37N 76°42E **42 E7**
Jhal *Pakistan* 28°17N 67°27E **42 E2**
Jhal Jhao *Pakistan* 26°20N 65°35E **40 F4**
Jhalawar *India* 24°40N 76°10E **42 G7**
Jhalida *India* 23°22N 85°58E **43 H11**
Jhalrapatan *India* 24°33N 76°10E **42 G7**
Jhang Maghiana
  Pakistan 31°15N 72°22E **42 D5**
Jhansi *India* 25°30N 78°36E **43 G8**
Jhargram *India* 22°27N 86°59E **43 H12**
Jharia *India* 23°45N 86°26E **43 H12**
Jharkhand □ *India* 24°0N 85°50E **43 H11**
Jharsuguda *India* 21°56N 84°5E **41 J14**
Jhelum *Pakistan* 33°0N 73°45E **42 C5**
Jhelum → *Pakistan* 31°20N 72°10E **42 D5**
Jhilmilli *India* 23°24N 82°51E **43 H10**
Jhudo *Pakistan* 24°58N 69°18E **42 G3**
Jhunjhunu *India* 28°10N 75°30E **42 E6**
Ji-Paraná *Brazil* 10°52S 62°57W **92 F6**
Ji Xian *Hebei, China* 37°35N 115°30E **34 F8**
Ji Xian *Henan, China* 35°22N 114°5E **34 G8**
Ji Xian *Shanxi, China* 36°7N 110°40E **34 F6**
Jia Xian *Henan, China* 33°59N 113°12E **34 H7**
Jia Xian *Shaanxi, China* 38°12N 110°28E **34 E6**
Jiaji = Qionghai *China* 19°15N 110°26E **38 C8**
Jiamusi *China* 46°40N 130°26E **33 B8**
Ji'an *Jiangxi, China* 27°6N 114°59E **33 D6**
Ji'an *Jilin, China* 41°5N 126°10E **35 D14**
Jianchang *China* 40°55N 120°35E **35 D11**
Jianchangying *China* 40°10N 118°50E **35 D10**
Jiangcheng *China* 22°36N 101°52E **32 D5**
Jiangmen *China* 22°32N 113°0E **33 D6**
Jiangsu □ *China* 33°0N 120°0E **35 H11**
Jiangxi □ *China* 27°30N 116°0E **33 D6**
Jiao Xian = Jiaozhou
  China 36°18N 120°1E **35 F11**
Jiaohe *Hebei, China* 38°2N 116°20E **34 E9**
Jiaohe *Jilin, China* 43°40N 127°22E **35 C14**
Jiaozhou *China* 36°18N 120°1E **35 F11**
Jiaozhou Wan *China* 36°5N 120°10E **35 F11**
Jiaozuo *China* 35°16N 113°12E **34 G7**
Jiawang *China* 34°28N 117°26E **35 G9**
Jiaxiang *China* 35°25N 116°20E **34 G9**
Jiaxing *China* 30°49N 120°45E **33 C7**
Jiayi = Chiai *Taiwan* 23°29N 120°25E **33 D7**
Jibuti = Djibouti ■ *Africa* 12°0N 43°0E **47 E3**
Jicarón, I. *Panama* 7°10N 81°50W **88 E3**
Jiddah *Si. Arabia* 21°29N 39°10E **47 C2**
Jido *India* 29°2N 94°58E **41 E19**
Jieshou *China* 33°18N 115°22E **34 H8**
Jiexiu *China* 37°2N 111°55E **34 F6**
Jigalong *Australia* 23°21S 120°47E **60 D3**
Jigni *India* 25°45N 79°25E **43 G8**
Jihlava *Czech Rep.* 49°28N 15°35E **16 D8**
Jihlava → *Czech Rep.* 48°55N 16°36E **17 D9**
Jijiga *Ethiopia* 9°20N 42°50E **47 F3**
Jilib *Somali Rep.* 0°29N 42°46E **47 G3**
Jilin *China* 43°44N 126°30E **35 C14**
Jilin □ *China* 44°0N 127°0E **35 C14**
Jilong = Chilung *Taiwan* 25°3N 121°45E **33 D7**
Jim Thorpe *U.S.A.* 40°52N 75°44W **83 F9**
Jima *Ethiopia* 7°40N 36°47E **47 F2**
Jimbaran, Teluk
  Indonesia 8°46S 115°9E **37 K18**
Jiménez *Mexico* 27°8N 104°54W **86 B4**
Jimo *China* 36°23N 120°30E **35 F11**
Jin Xian = Jinzhou *Hebei,*
  China 38°2N 115°2E **34 E8**
Jin Xian = Jinzhou *Liaoning,*
  China 38°55N 121°42E **35 E11**
Jinan *China* 36°38N 117°1E **34 F9**
Jinchang *China* 38°30N 102°10E **32 C5**
Jincheng *China* 35°29N 112°50E **34 G7**
Jind *India* 29°19N 76°22E **42 E7**
Jindabyne *Australia* 36°25S 148°35E **63 F4**
Jinding *China* 22°20N 113°33E **33 G10**

Jindo *S. Korea* 34°28N 126°15E **35 G14**
Jindřichův Hradec
  Czech Rep. 49°10N 15°2E **16 D8**
Jing He → *China* 34°27N 109°4E **34 G5**
Jingbian *China* 37°20N 108°30E **34 F5**
Jingchuan *China* 35°20N 107°20E **34 G4**
Jingdezhen *China* 29°20N 117°11E **33 D6**
Jinggu *China* 23°35N 100°41E **32 D5**
Jinghai *China* 38°55N 116°55E **34 E9**
Jingle *China* 38°20N 111°55E **34 E6**
Jingning *China* 35°30N 105°43E **34 G3**
Jingo Hu *China* 43°55N 128°55E **35 C15**
Jingtai *China* 37°10N 104°6E **34 F3**
Jingyang *China* 38°2N 114°8E **34 E8**
Jingyang *China* 34°30N 108°50E **34 G5**
Jingyu *China* 42°25N 126°45E **35 C14**
Jingziguan *China* 33°15N 111°0E **34 H6**
Jinhua *China* 29°8N 119°38E **33 D6**
Jining *Nei Monggol Zizhiqu,*
  China 41°5N 113°0E **34 D7**
Jining *Shandong, China* 35°22N 116°34E **34 G9**
Jinja *Uganda* 0°25N 33°12E **54 B3**
Jinjang *Malaysia* 3°13N 101°39E **39 L3**
Jinji *China* 37°58N 106°8E **34 F4**
Jinju *S. Korea* 35°12N 128°2E **35 G15**
Jinnah Barrage *Pakistan* 32°58N 71°33E **42 C4**
Jinotega *Nic.* 13°6N 85°59W **88 D2**
Jinotepe *Nic.* 11°50N 86°10W **88 D2**
Jinsha Jiang → *China* 28°50N 104°36E **32 D5**
Jinxi *China* 40°52N 120°50E **35 D11**
Jinxiang *China* 35°5N 116°22E **34 G9**
Jinzhou *Hebei, China* 38°2N 115°2E **34 E8**
Jinzhou *Liaoning, China* 41°5N 121°3E **35 D11**
Jiparaná → *Brazil* 8°3S 62°52W **92 E6**
Jipijapa *Ecuador* 1°0S 80°40W **92 D2**
Jiquilpan *Mexico* 19°59N 102°43W **86 D4**
Jirisan *S. Korea* 35°20N 127°44E **35 G14**
Jishan *China* 35°34N 110°58E **34 G6**
Jisr ash Shughūr *Syria* 35°49N 36°18E **44 C3**
Jitarning *Australia* 32°48S 117°57E **61 F2**
Jitra *Malaysia* 6°16N 100°25E **39 J3**
Jiu → *Romania* 43°47N 23°48E **17 F12**
Jiudengkou *China* 39°56N 106°40E **34 E4**
Jiujiang *China* 29°42N 115°58E **33 D6**
Jiulong = Kowloon
  China 22°19N 114°11E **33 G11**
Jiuquan *China* 39°50N 98°20E **32 C4**
Jiutai *China* 44°10N 125°50E **35 B13**
Jiuxincheng *China* 39°17N 115°59E **34 E8**
Jiwani *Pakistan* 25°1N 61°44E **40 G2**
Jixi *China* 45°20N 130°50E **35 B16**
Jiyang *China* 37°0N 117°12E **35 F9**
Jiyuan *China* 35°7N 112°57E **34 G7**
Jīzān *Si. Arabia* 17°0N 42°20E **47 D3**
Jize *China* 36°54N 114°56E **34 F8**
Jizl, Wādī al → *Si. Arabia* 25°39N 38°25E **44 E3**
Jizō-Zaki *Japan* 35°34N 133°20E **31 G6**
Jizzax *Uzbekistan* 40°6N 67°50E **28 E7**
Joaçaba *Brazil* 27°5S 51°31W **95 B5**
João Pessoa *Brazil* 7°10S 34°52W **93 E12**
Joaquín V. González
  Argentina 25°10S 64°0W **94 B3**
Jobat *India* 22°25N 74°34E **42 H6**
Jodhpur *India* 26°23N 73°8E **42 F5**
Jodiya *India* 22°42N 70°18E **42 H4**
Joensuu *Finland* 62°37N 29°49E **8 E23**
Jōetsu *Japan* 37°12N 138°10E **31 F9**
Jofane *Mozam.* 21°15S 34°18E **57 C5**
Jogbani *India* 26°25N 87°15E **43 F12**
Jõgeva *Estonia* 58°45N 26°24E **9 G22**
Jogjakarta = Yogyakarta
  Indonesia 7°49S 110°22E **37 G14**
Johannesburg *S. Africa* 26°11S 28°2E **57 D4**
Johannesburg *U.S.A.* 35°22N 117°38W **79 K9**
Johilla → *India* 23°37N 81°14E **43 H9**
John Crow Mts. *Jamaica* 18°5N 76°25W **88 a**
John Day *U.S.A.* 44°25N 118°57W **76 D4**
John Day → *U.S.A.* 45°44N 120°39W **76 D3**
John Day Fossil Beds △
  U.S.A. 44°33N 119°38W **76 D4**
John D'or Prairie
  Canada 58°30N 115°8W **70 B5**
John H. Kerr Res.
  U.S.A. 36°36N 78°18W **85 C15**
John o' Groats *U.K.* 58°38N 3°4W **11 C5**
Johnnie *U.S.A.* 36°25N 116°5W **79 J10**
John's Ra. *Australia* 21°55S 133°23E **62 C1**
Johnson *U.S.A.* 44°38N 72°41W **83 B12**
Johnson City *Kans.,*
  U.S.A. 37°34N 101°45W **80 G3**
Johnson City *N.Y., U.S.A.* 42°7N 75°58W **83 D9**
Johnson City *Tenn.,*
  U.S.A. 36°19N 82°21W **85 C13**
Johnson City *Tex., U.S.A.* 30°17N 98°25W **84 F5**
Johnsonburg *U.S.A.* 41°29N 78°41W **82 E6**
Johnsondale *U.S.A.* 35°58N 118°32W **79 K8**
Johnsons Crossing
  Canada 60°29N 133°18W **70 A2**
Johnston, L. *Australia* 32°25S 120°30E **61 F3**
Johnston Falls = Mambilima Falls
  Zambia 10°31S 28°45E **55 E2**
Johnstone Str. *Canada* 50°28N 126°0W **70 C3**
Johnstown *Ireland* 52°45N 7°33W **10 D4**
Johnstown *N.Y., U.S.A.* 43°0N 74°22W **83 C10**
Johnstown *Ohio, U.S.A.* 40°9N 82°41W **82 F2**
Johnstown *Pa., U.S.A.* 40°20N 78°55W **82 F6**
Johor, Selat *Asia* 1°28N 103°47E **39 d**
Johor Bahru *Malaysia* 1°28N 103°46E **39 d**
Jõhvi *Estonia* 59°22N 27°27E **9 G22**
Joinville *Brazil* 26°15S 48°55W **95 B6**
Joinville I. *Antarctica* 65°0S 55°30W **5 C18**
Jojutla *Mexico* 18°37N 99°11W **87 D5**
Jokkmokk *Sweden* 66°35N 19°50E **8 C18**
Jökulsá á Bru → *Iceland* 65°40N 14°16W **8 D6**

Jökulsá á Fjöllum ➤
  Iceland 66°10N 16°30W **8** C5
Jolfā Āzarbājān-e Sharqī,
  Iran 38°57N 45°38E **44** B5
Jolfā Eşfahan, Iran 32°58N 51°37E **45** C6
Joliet U.S.A. 41°32N 88°5W **80** E9
Joliette Canada 46°3N 73°24W **72** C5
Jolo Phil. 6°0N 121°0E **37** C6
Jolon U.S.A. 35°58N 121°9W **78** K5
Jombang Indonesia 7°33S 112°14E **37** G15
Jonava Lithuania 55°8N 24°12E **9** J21
Jones Sound Canada 76°0N 85°0W **69** B11
Jonesboro Ark., U.S.A. 35°50N 90°42W **85** D9
Jonesboro La., U.S.A. 32°15N 92°43W **84** E8
Joniškis Lithuania 56°13N 23°35E **9** H20
Jönköping Sweden 57°45N 14°8E **9** H16
Jonquière Canada 48°27N 71°14W **73** C5
Joplin U.S.A. 37°6N 94°31W **80** G6
Jora India 26°20N 77°49E **42** F6
Jordan Mont., U.S.A. 47°19N 106°55W **76** C10
Jordan N.Y., U.S.A. 43°4N 76°29W **83** C8
Jordan ■ Asia 31°0N 36°0E **46** E5
Jordan ➤ Asia 31°48N 35°32E **46** D4
Jordan Valley U.S.A. 42°59N 117°3W **76** E5
Jorhat India 26°45N 94°12E **41** F19
Jörn Sweden 65°4N 20°1E **8** D19
Jorong Indonesia 3°58S 114°56E **36** E4
Jørpeland Norway 59°3N 6°1E **9** G12
Jorquera ➤ Chile 28°3S 69°58W **94** B2
Jos Nigeria 9°53N 8°51E **50** G7
José Batlle y Ordóñez
  Uruguay 33°20S 55°10W **95** C4
Joseph, L. Canada 45°10N 79°44W **82** A5
Joseph Bonaparte G.
  Australia 14°35S 128°50E **60** B4
Joseph, L. Canada 52°45N 65°18W **73** B6
Joshinath India 30°34N 79°34E **43** D8
Joshinetsu-Kōgen △
  Japan 36°42N 138°32E **31** F9
Joshua Tree U.S.A. 34°8N 116°19W **79** L10
Joshua Tree △ U.S.A. 33°55N 116°0W **79** M10
Jost Van Dyke I.
  Br. Virgin Is. 18°29N 64°47W **89** e
Jostedalsbreen Norway 61°40N 6°59E **8** F12
Jotunheimen Norway 61°35N 8°25E **8** F13
Joubertberg Namibia 18°30S 14°0E **56** B1
Jourdanton U.S.A. 28°55N 98°33W **84** G5
Jovellanos Cuba 22°40N 81°10W **88** B3
Ju Xian China 36°35N 118°20E **35** F10
Juan Aldama Mexico 24°19N 103°21W **86** C4
Juan Bautista Alberdi
  Argentina 34°26S 61°48W **94** C3
Juan de Fuca, Str of.
  N. Amer. 48°15N 124°0W **78** B3
Juan de Nova Ind. Oc. 17°3S 43°45E **57** B7
Juan Fernández, Arch. de
  Pac. Oc. 33°50S 80°0W **90** G2
Juan José Castelli
  Argentina 25°27S 60°57W **94** B3
Juan L. Lacaze Uruguay 34°26S 57°25W **94** C4
Juankoski Finland 63°3N 28°19E **8** E23
Juárez Mexico 32°20N 115°57W **79** N11
Juárez Coahuila, Mexico 27°37N 100°44W **86** B4
Juárez, Sierra de Mexico 32°0N 116°0W **86** A1
Juàzeiro Brazil 9°30S 40°30W **93** E10
Juàzeiro do Norte Brazil 7°10S 39°18W **93** E11
Jubā Sudan 4°50N 31°35E **51** H12
Juba ➤ Somali Rep. 1°30N 42°35E **47** G3
Jubany Antarctica 62°30S 58°0W **5** C18
Jubayl Lebanon 34°5N 35°39E **46** A4
Jubbah Si. Arabia 28°2N 40°56E **44** D4
Jubbal India 31°5N 77°40E **42** D7
Jubbulpore = Jabalpur
  India 23°9N 79°58E **43** H8
Jubilee L. Australia 29°0S 126°50E **61** E4
Juby, C. Morocco 28°0N 12°59W **50** C3
Júcar = Xúquer ➤ Spain 39°5N 0°10W **21** C5
Júcaro Cuba 21°37N 78°51W **88** B4
Juchitán de Zaragoza
  Mexico 16°26N 95°1W **87** D5
Judea = Har Yehuda
  Israel 31°35N 34°57E **46** D3
Judith ➤ U.S.A. 47°44N 109°39W **76** C9
Judith, Pt. U.S.A. 41°22N 71°29W **83** E13
Judith Gap U.S.A. 46°41N 109°45W **76** C9
Jugoslavia = Serbia ■
  Europe 43°20N 20°0E **23** B9
Juigalpa Nic. 12°6N 85°26W **88** D2
Juiz de Fora Brazil 21°43S 43°19W **95** A7
Jujuy □ Argentina 23°20S 65°40W **94** A2
Julesburg U.S.A. 40°59N 102°16W **76** F12
Juli Peru 16°10S 69°25W **92** G5
Julia Cr. ➤ Australia 20°0S 141°11E **62** C3
Julia Creek Australia 20°39S 141°44E **62** C3
Juliaca Peru 15°25S 70°10W **92** G4
Julian U.S.A. 33°4N 116°38W **79** M10
Julian, L. Canada 54°25N 77°57W **72** B4
Julianatop Suriname 3°40N 56°30W **93** C7
Julianehåb = Qaqortoq
  Greenland 60°43N 46°0W **4** C5
Julimes Mexico 28°25N 105°27W **86** B3
Jullundur India 31°20N 75°40E **42** D6
Julu China 37°15N 115°2E **34** F8
Jumbo Zimbabwe 17°30S 30°58E **55** F3
Jumbo Pk. U.S.A. 36°12N 114°11W **79** J12
Jumentos Cays Bahamas 23°0N 75°40W **88** B4
Jumilla Spain 38°28N 1°19W **21** C5
Jumla Nepal 29°15N 82°13E **43** E10
Jumna = Yamuna ➤
  India 25°30N 81°53E **43** G9
Jumunjin S. Korea 37°55N 128°54E **35** F15
Junagadh India 21°30N 70°30E **42** J4
Junction Tex., U.S.A. 30°29N 99°46W **84** F5
Junction Utah, U.S.A. 38°14N 112°13W **77** G7
Junction B. Australia 11°52S 133°55E **62** A1
Junction City Kans.,
  U.S.A. 39°2N 96°50W **80** F5

Junction City Oreg.,
  U.S.A. 44°13N 123°12W **76** D2
Junction Pt. Australia 11°45S 133°50E **62** A1
Jundah Australia 24°46S 143°2E **62** C3
Jundiaí Brazil 24°30S 47°0W **95** A6
Juneau U.S.A. 58°18N 134°25W **70** B2
Junee Australia 34°53S 147°35E **63** E4
Jungfrau Switz. 46°32N 7°58E **20** C7
Junggar Pendi China 44°30N 86°0E **32** B3
Jungshahi Pakistan 24°52N 67°44E **42** G2
Juniata ➤ U.S.A. 40°24N 77°1W **82** F7
Junín Argentina 34°33S 60°57W **94** C3
Junín de los Andes
  Argentina 39°45S 71°0W **96** D2
Jūniyah Lebanon 33°59N 35°38E **46** B4
Juntas Chile 28°24S 69°58W **94** B2
Juntura U.S.A. 43°45N 118°5W **76** E4
Jur, Nahr el ➤ Sudan 8°45N 29°15E **51** G11
Jura = Jura, Mts. du
  Europe 46°40N 6°5E **20** C7
Jura U.K. 56°0N 5°50W **11** F3
Jura, Mts. du Europe 46°40N 6°5E **20** C7
Jura = Schwäbische Alb
  Germany 48°20N 9°30E **16** D5
Jura, Sd. of U.K. 55°57N 5°45W **11** F3
Jurbarkas Lithuania 55°4N 22°46E **9** J20
Jurien Bay Australia 30°18S 115°2E **61** F2
Jürmala Latvia 56°58N 23°34E **9** H20
Jurong Singapore 1°19N 103°42E **39** d
Juruá ➤ Brazil 2°37S 65°44W **92** D5
Juruena Brazil 13°0S 58°10W **92** F7
Juruena ➤ Brazil 7°20S 58°3W **92** E7
Juruti Brazil 2°9S 56°4W **93** D7
Justo Daract Argentina 33°52S 65°12W **94** C2
Jutaí ➤ Brazil 2°43S 66°57W **92** D5
Juticalpa Honduras 14°40N 86°12W **88** D2
Jutland = Jylland
  Denmark 56°25N 9°30E **9** H13
Juuka Finland 63°13N 29°17E **8** E23
Juventud, I. de la Cuba 21°40N 82°40W **88** B3
Jüy Zar Iran 33°50N 46°18E **44** C5
Juye China 35°22N 116°5E **34** G9
Jwaneng Botswana 24°45S 24°50E **53** J4
Jylland Denmark 56°25N 9°30E **9** H13
Jyväskylä Finland 62°14N 25°50E **8** E21

K

K2 Pakistan 35°58N 76°32E **43** B7
Kaakha = Kaka
  Turkmenistan 37°21N 59°36E **45** B8
Kaap Plateau S. Africa 28°30S 24°0E **56** D3
Kaapkruis Namibia 21°55S 13°57E **56** C1
Kaapstad = Cape Town
  S. Africa 33°55S 18°22E **56** E2
Kabaena Indonesia 5°15S 122°0E **37** F6
Kabala S. Leone 9°38N 11°37W **50** G3
Kabale Uganda 1°15S 30°0E **54** C3
Kabalo Dem. Rep. of the Congo 6°0S 27°0E **54** D2
Kabambare
  Dem. Rep. of the Congo 4°41S 27°39E **54** C2
Kabango
  Dem. Rep. of the Congo 8°35S 28°30E **55** D2
Kabanjahe Indonesia 3°6N 98°30E **36** D1
Kabarega Falls = Murchison Falls
  Uganda 2°15N 31°30E **54** B3
Kabarnet Kenya 0°30N 35°45E **54** B4
Kabasalan Phil. 7°47N 122°44E **37** C6
Kabat Indonesia 8°16S 114°19E **37** J17
Kabin Buri Thailand 13°57N 101°43E **38** F3
Kabinakagami L.
  Canada 48°54N 84°25W **72** C3
Kabinda
  Dem. Rep. of the Congo 6°19S 24°20E **52** F4
Kabompo Zambia 13°36S 24°14E **55** E1
Kabompo ➤ Zambia 14°11S 23°11E **53** G4
Kabondo
  Dem. Rep. of the Congo 8°58S 25°40E **55** D2
Kabongo
  Dem. Rep. of the Congo 7°22S 25°33E **54** D2
Kabrît, G. el Egypt 29°42N 33°16E **46** F2
Kabūd Gonbad Iran 37°5N 59°45E **45** B8
Kābul □ Afghan. 34°28N 69°11E **40** B6
Kābul ➤ Pakistan 33°55N 72°14E **42** C5
Kabunga
  Dem. Rep. of the Congo 1°38S 28°3E **54** C2
Kaburuang Indonesia 3°50N 126°30E **37** D7
Kabwe Zambia 14°30S 28°29E **55** E2
Kachchh, Gulf of India 22°50N 69°15E **42** H3
Kachchh, Rann of India 24°0N 70°0E **42** H4
Kachchhidhana India 21°44N 78°46E **43** J8
Kachebera Zambia 13°50S 32°50E **55** E3
Kachikau Botswana 18°8S 24°26E **56** B3
Kachin □ Burma 26°0N 97°30E **41** G20
Kachira, L. Uganda 0°40S 31°7E **54** C3
Kachīry Kazakhstan 53°10N 75°50E **28** D8
Kachnara India 23°50N 75°6E **42** H6
Kachot Cambodia 11°30N 103°3E **39** G4
Kaçkar Turkey 40°45N 41°10E **19** F7
Kadam, Mt. Uganda 1°45N 34°45E **54** B3
Kadan Kyun Burma 12°30N 98°20E **38** F2
Kadanai ➤ Afghan. 31°22N 65°45E **42** D1
Kadavu Fiji 19°0S 178°15E **59** a
Kadavu Passage Fiji 18°45S 178°0E **59** a
Kade Ghana 6°7N 0°56W **50** G5
Kadhimain = Al Kāzimīyah
  Iraq 33°22N 44°18E **44** C5
Kadi India 23°18N 72°23E **42** H5
Kadina Australia 33°55S 137°43E **63** E2
Kadipur India 26°10N 82°23E **43** F10
Kadirli Turkey 37°23N 36°5E **44** B3
Kadiyevka = Stakhanov
  Ukraine 48°35N 38°40E **19** E6

Kadoka U.S.A. 43°50N 101°31W **80** D3
Kadoma Zimbabwe 18°20S 29°52E **55** F2
Kaduna Nigeria 11°0N 29°45E **51** F11
Kaduna Nigeria 10°30N 7°21E **50** F7
Kaédi Mauritania 16°9N 13°28W **50** E3
Kaeng Khoï Thailand 14°35N 101°0E **38** E3
Kaeng Krachan △
  Thailand 12°57N 99°23E **38** F2
Kaeng Tana △ Thailand 15°31N 105°32E **38** E5
Kaesŏng N. Korea 37°58N 126°35E **35** F14
Kāf Si. Arabia 31°25N 37°29E **44** D3
Kafan = Kapan Armenia 39°18N 46°27E **44** B5
Kafanchan Nigeria 9°40N 8°20E **50** G7
Kafinda Zambia 12°32S 30°20E **55** E3
Kafue Zambia 15°46S 28°9E **55** F2
Kafue ➤ Zambia 15°30S 29°0E **53** H5
Kafue △ Zambia 15°12S 25°38E **55** F2
Kafue Flats Zambia 15°40S 27°25E **55** F2
Kafulwe Zambia 9°0S 29°1E **55** D2
Kaga Afghan. 34°14N 70°10E **42** B4
Kaga Bandoro C.A.R. 7°0N 19°10E **52** C3
Kagawa □ Japan 34°15N 134°0E **31** G7
Kagera □ Tanzania 2°0S 31°30E **54** C3
Kagera ➤ Uganda 0°57S 31°47E **54** C3
Kağızman Turkey 40°5N 43°10E **44** B4
Kagoshima Japan 31°35N 130°33E **31** J5
Kagoshima □ Japan 31°30N 130°30E **31** J5
Kagul = Cahul Moldova 45°50N 28°15E **17** F15
Kahak Iran 36°6N 49°46E **45** B6
Kahama Tanzania 4°8S 32°30E **54** C3
Kahan Pakistan 29°18N 68°54E **42** E3
Kahang Malaysia 2°12N 103°32E **39** L4
Kahayan ➤ Indonesia 3°40S 114°0E **36** E4
Kahe Tanzania 3°30S 37°25E **54** C4
Kahemba
  Dem. Rep. of the Congo 7°18S 18°55E **52** F3
Kahnūj Iran 27°55N 57°40E **45** E8
Kahoka U.S.A. 40°25N 91°44W **80** E8
Kaho'olawe U.S.A. 20°33N 156°37W **74** b
Kahramanmaraş Turkey 37°37N 36°53E **44** B3
Kâhta Turkey 37°46N 38°36E **44** B3
Kahului U.S.A. 20°54N 156°28W **74** b
Kahurangi △ N.Z. 41°10S 172°32E **59** D4
Kahuta Pakistan 33°35N 73°24E **42** C5
Kahuzi-Biega △
  Dem. Rep. of the Congo 1°50S 27°55E **54** C2
Kai, Kepulauan Indonesia 5°55S 132°45E **37** F8
Kai Besar Indonesia 5°35S 133°0E **37** F8
Kai Is. = Kai, Kepulauan
  Indonesia 5°55S 132°45E **37** F8
Kai Kecil Indonesia 5°45S 132°40E **37** F8
Kaiapoi N.Z. 43°24S 172°40E **59** E4
Kaiapoi N.Z. 43°24S 172°40E **59** E4
Kaidu He ➤ China 41°46N 86°31E **32** B3
Kaieteur Falls Guyana 5°1N 59°10E **92** B7
Kaifeng China 34°48N 114°21E **34** G8
Kaikohe N.Z. 35°25S 173°49E **59** A4
Kaikoura N.Z. 42°25S 173°43E **59** E4
Kailas = Kangrinboqe Feng
  China 31°0N 81°25E **43** D9
Kailu China 43°38N 121°18E **35** C11
Kailua U.S.A. 19°39N 155°59W **74** b
Kaimana Indonesia 3°39S 133°45E **37** E8
Kaimanawa Mts. N.Z. 39°15S 175°56E **59** C5
Kaimganj India 27°33N 79°24E **43** F8
Kaimur Hills India 24°30N 82°0E **43** G10
Kainab ➤ Namibia 28°32S 19°34E **56** D2
Kainji Res. Nigeria 10°1N 4°40E **50** F6
Kainuu Finland 64°30N 29°7E **8** D23
Kaipara Harbour N.Z. 36°25S 174°14E **59** B5
Kaipokok B. Canada 54°54N 59°47W **73** B8
Kaira India 22°45N 72°50E **42** H5
Kairana India 29°24N 77°15E **42** E7
Kaironi Indonesia 0°47S 133°40E **37** E8
Kairouan Tunisia 35°45N 10°5E **51** A8
Kaiserslautern Germany 49°26N 7°45E **16** D4
Kaitaia N.Z. 35°8S 173°17E **59** A4
Kaitangata N.Z. 46°17S 169°51E **59** G2
Kaithal India 29°48N 76°26E **42** E7
Kaitu ➤ Pakistan 33°10N 70°30E **42** C4
Kaiyuan Liaoning, China 42°28N 124°1E **35** C13
Kaiyuan Yunnan, China 23°40N 103°12E **32** D5
Kajaani Finland 64°17N 27°46E **8** D22
Kajabbi Australia 20°0S 140°1E **62** C3
Kajana = Kajaani
  Finland 64°17N 27°46E **8** D22
Kajang Malaysia 2°59N 101°48E **39** L3
Kajiado Kenya 1°53S 36°48E **54** C4
Kajo Kaji Sudan 3°58N 31°40E **51** H12
Kaka Turkmenistan 37°21N 59°36E **45** B8
Kakabeka Falls Canada 48°24N 89°37W **72** C2
Kakadu △ Australia 12°0S 132°3E **60** B5
Kakamas S. Africa 28°45S 20°33E **56** D3
Kakamega Kenya 0°20N 34°46E **54** B3
Kakanui Mts. N.Z. 45°10S 170°30E **59** F3
Kakdwip India 21°53N 88°11E **43** J13
Kake Japan 34°36N 132°19E **31** G6
Kake U.S.A. 56°59N 133°57W **70** B2
Kakegawa Japan 34°45N 138°1E **31** G9
Kakeroma-Jima Japan 28°8N 129°14E **31** K4
Kākhak Iran 34°9N 58°38E **45** C8
Kakhovka Ukraine 46°45N 33°30E **19** E5
Kakhovske Vdskh.
  Ukraine 47°5N 34°0E **19** E5
Kakinada India 16°57N 82°11E **41** L13
Kakisa Canada 60°56N 117°25W **70** A5
Kakisa ➤ Canada 61°3N 118°10W **70** A5
Kakogawa Japan 34°46N 134°51E **31** G7
Kakuma Kenya 3°35N 34°46E **54** B3
Kakwa ➤ Canada 54°37N 118°28W **70** C5
Kal Sefid Iran 34°52N 47°23E **44** C5
Kalaallit Nunaat = Greenland ☑
  N. Amer. 66°0N 45°0W **67** C15
Kalabagh Pakistan 33°0N 71°28E **42** C4
Kalabahi Indonesia 8°13S 124°31E **37** F6
Kalach Russia 50°22N 41°0E **19** D7

Kaladan ➤ Burma 20°20N 93°5E **41** J18
Kaladar Canada 44°37N 77°5W **82** B7
Kâdugli Sudan 11°0N 29°45E **51** F11
Kahalari Africa 24°0S 21°30E **56** C3
Kalahari Gemsbok △
  S. Africa 25°30S 20°30E **56** D3
Kalajoki Finland 64°12N 24°10E **8** D21
Kalakamati Botswana 20°40S 27°25E **57** C4
Kalakan Russia 55°15N 116°45E **29** D12
K'alak'unlun Shank'ou =
  Karakoram Pass Asia 35°33N 77°50E **43** B7
Kalam Pakistan 35°34N 72°30E **43** B5
Kalama
  Dem. Rep. of the Congo 2°52S 28°35E **54** C2
Kalama U.S.A. 46°1N 122°51W **78** E4
Kalamata Greece 37°3N 22°10E **23** F10
Kalamazoo U.S.A. 42°17N 85°35W **81** D11
Kalamazoo ➤ U.S.A. 42°40N 86°10W **80** D10
Kalan Turkey 39°7N 39°32E **44** B3
Kalannie Australia 30°22S 117°5E **61** F2
Kalāntarī Iran 32°10N 54°8E **45** C7
Kalao Indonesia 7°21S 121°0E **37** F6
Kalaotoa Indonesia 7°20S 121°50E **37** F6
Kalasin Thailand 16°26N 103°30E **38** D4
Kālat Iran 25°29N 59°22E **45** E9
Kalat Pakistan 29°8N 66°31E **40** E5
Kalāteh Iran 36°33N 55°41E **45** B7
Kalāteh-ye Ganj Iran 27°31N 57°55E **45** E8
Kalbā U.A.E. 25°5N 56°22E **45** E8
Kalbarri Australia 27°40S 114°10E **61** E1
Kalbarri △ Australia 27°51S 114°30E **61** E1
Kalce Slovenia 45°54N 14°13E **16** F8
Kale Turkey 37°27N 28°49E **23** F13
Kalegauk Kyun Burma 15°33N 97°35E **38** E1
Kalehe
  Dem. Rep. of the Congo 2°6S 28°50E **54** C2
Kalema Tanzania 1°12S 31°55E **54** C3
Kalemie
  Dem. Rep. of the Congo 5°55S 29°9E **54** D2
Kalewa Burma 23°10N 94°15E **41** H19
Kaleybar Iran 38°47N 47°2E **44** B5
Kalgoorlie-Boulder
  Australia 30°40S 121°22E **61** F3
Kali ➤ India 27°6N 79°55E **43** F8
Kali Sindh ➤ India 25°32N 76°17E **42** G6
Kaliakra, Nos Bulgaria 43°21N 28°30E **23** C13
Kalianda Indonesia 5°50S 105°45E **36** F3
Kalima
  Dem. Rep. of the Congo 2°33S 26°32E **54** C2
Kalimantan Indonesia 0°0 114°0E **36** E4
Kalimantan Barat □
  Indonesia 0°0 110°30E **36** E4
Kalimantan Selatan □
  Indonesia 2°30S 115°30E **36** E5
Kalimantan Tengah □
  Indonesia 2°0S 113°30E **36** E4
Kalimantan Timur □
  Indonesia 1°30N 116°30E **36** D5
Kálimnos Greece 37°0N 27°0E **23** F12
Kalimpong India 27°4N 88°35E **43** F13
Kaliningrad Russia 54°42N 20°32E **9** J19
Kalinkavichy Belarus 52°12N 29°20E **17** B15
Kalinkovichi = Kalinkavichy
  Belarus 52°12N 29°20E **17** B15
Kaliro Uganda 0°56N 33°30E **54** B3
Kalispell U.S.A. 48°12N 114°19W **76** B6
Kalisz Poland 51°45N 18°8E **17** C10
Kaliua Tanzania 5°5S 31°48E **54** D3
Kalix ➤ Sweden 65°50N 23°11E **8** D20
Kalix Sweden 65°53N 23°12E **8** D20
Kalixälven ➤ Sweden 65°50N 23°11E **8** D20
Kalka India 30°46N 76°57E **42** D7
Kalkarindji Australia 17°30S 130°47E **60** C5
Kalkaska U.S.A. 44°44N 85°11W **81** C11
Kalkfeld Namibia 20°57S 16°14E **56** C2
Kalkfontein Botswana 22°4S 20°57E **56** C3
Kalkrand Namibia 24°1S 17°35E **56** C2
Kallavesi Finland 62°58N 27°30E **8** E22
Kallsjön Sweden 63°38N 13°0E **8** E15
Kalmar Sweden 56°40N 16°20E **9** H17
Kalmykia □ Russia 46°5N 46°1E **19** E8
Kalmykovo Kazakhstan 49°0N 51°47E **19** E9
Kalna India 23°13N 88°25E **43** H13
Kalnai India 22°46N 83°30E **43** H10
Kalocsa Hungary 46°32N 19°0E **17** E10
Kalokhorio Cyprus 34°51N 33°2E **25** E12
Kaloko
  Dem. Rep. of the Congo 6°47S 25°48E **54** D2
Kalol Gujarat, India 22°37N 73°31E **42** H5
Kalol Gujarat, India 23°15N 72°33E **42** H5
Kalomo Zambia 17°0S 26°30E **55** F2
Kalpi India 26°8N 79°47E **43** F8
Kaltukatjara Australia 24°52S 129°5E **61** D4
Kalu Pakistan 25°5N 67°39E **42** G2
Kaluga Russia 54°35N 36°10E **18** D6
Kalulushi Zambia 12°50S 28°3E **55** E2
Kalumburu Australia 13°55S 126°35E **60** B4
Kalush Ukraine 49°3N 24°23E **17** D13
Kalutara Sri Lanka 6°35N 80°0E **40** R12
Kalya Russia 60°15N 59°59E **18** B10
Kalyan India 19°15N 73°9E **40** K8

Kambolé Zambia 8°47S 30°48E **55** D3
Kambos Cyprus 35°2N 32°44E **25** D11
Kambove
  Dem. Rep. of the Congo 10°51S 26°33E **55** E2
Kamchatka, Poluostrov
  Russia 57°0N 160°0E **29** D17
Kamchatka Pen. = Kamchatka,
  Poluostrov Russia 57°0N 160°0E **29** D17
Kamchiya ➤ Bulgaria 43°4N 27°44E **23** C12
Kame Ruins Zimbabwe 20°7S 28°25E **55** G2
Kamen Russia 53°50N 81°30E **28** D9
Kamen-Rybolov Russia 44°46N 132°2E **30** B6
Kamenjak, Rt Croatia 44°47N 13°55E **16** F7
Kamenka Russia 65°58N 44°0E **18** A7
Kamenka Bugskaya =
  Kamyanka-Buzka
  Ukraine 50°8N 24°16E **17** C13
Kamensk Uralskiy Russia 56°25N 62°2E **28** D7
Kamenskoye Russia 62°45N 165°30E **29** C17
Kameoka Japan 35°0N 135°35E **31** G7
Kamet India 30°55N 79°35E **43** D8
Kamiah U.S.A. 46°14N 116°2W **76** C5
Kamieskroon S. Africa 30°9S 17°56E **56** E2
Kamilukuak L. Canada 62°22N 101°40W **71** A8
Kamin-Kashyrskyy
  Ukraine 51°39N 24°56E **17** C13
Kamina
  Dem. Rep. of the Congo 8°45S 25°0E **55** D2
Kaminak L. Canada 62°10N 95°0W **71** A10
Kaministiquia Canada 48°32N 89°35W **72** C2
Kaminoyama Japan 38°9N 140°17E **30** E10
Kamiros Greece 36°20N 27°56E **25** C9
Kamituga
  Dem. Rep. of the Congo 3°2S 28°10E **54** C2
Kamla ➤ India 25°35N 86°36E **43** G12
Kamloops Canada 50°40N 120°20W **70** C4
Kamo Japan 37°39N 139°3E **30** F9
Kamoke Pakistan 32°4N 74°4E **42** C6
Kampala Uganda 0°20N 32°32E **54** B3
Kampar Malaysia 4°18N 101°9E **39** K3
Kampar ➤ Indonesia 0°30N 103°8E **36** D2
Kampen Neths. 52°33N 5°53E **15** B5
Kampene
  Dem. Rep. of the Congo 3°36S 26°40E **52** E5
Kamphaeng Phet
  Thailand 16°28N 99°30E **38** D2
Kampolombo, L. Zambia 11°37S 29°42E **55** E2
Kampong Chhnang
  Cambodia 12°20N 104°35E **39** F5
Kampong Pengerang
  Malaysia 1°22N 104°7E **39** d
Kampong Punggai
  Malaysia 1°27N 104°18E **39** d
Kampong Saom
  Cambodia 10°38N 103°30E **39** G4
Kampong Saom, Chaak
  Cambodia 10°50N 103°32E **39** G4
Kampong Tanjong Langsat
  Malaysia 1°28N 104°1E **39** d
Kampong Telok Ramunia
  Malaysia 1°22N 104°15E **39** d
Kampot Cambodia 10°36N 104°10E **39** G5
Kampuchea = Cambodia ■
  Asia 12°15N 105°0E **38** F5
Kampung Air Putih
  Malaysia 4°15N 103°10E **39** K4
Kampung Jerangau
  Malaysia 4°50N 103°10E **39** K4
Kampung Raja Malaysia 5°45N 102°35E **39** K4
Kampungbaru = Tolitoli
  Indonesia 1°5N 120°50E **37** D6
Kamrau, Teluk Indonesia 3°30S 133°36E **37** E8
Kamsack Canada 51°34N 101°54W **71** C8
Kamskoye Vdkhr.
  Russia 58°41N 56°7E **18** C10
Kamuchawie L.
  Canada 56°18N 101°59W **71** B8
Kamuela U.S.A. 20°1N 155°41W **74** b
Kamui-Misaki Japan 43°20N 140°21E **30** C10
Kamyanets-Podilskyy
  Ukraine 48°45N 26°40E **17** D14
Kamyanka-Buzka
  Ukraine 50°8N 24°16E **17** C13
Kāmyārān Iran 34°47N 46°56E **44** C5
Kamyshin Russia 50°10N 45°24E **19** D8
Kanaaupscow Canada 53°39N 77°9W **69** D12
Kanaaupscow ➤ Canada 54°2N 76°30W **72** B4
Kanab U.S.A. 37°3N 112°32W **77** H7
Kanab Cr. ➤ U.S.A. 36°24N 112°38W **77** H7
Kanacea Lau Group, Fiji 17°15S 179°6W **59** a
Kanacea Taveuni, Fiji 16°59S 179°56E **59** a
Kanagi Japan 40°54N 140°27E **30** D10
Kanairiktok ➤ Canada 55°2N 60°18W **73** A7
Kananga
  Dem. Rep. of the Congo 5°55S 22°18E **52** F4
Kanash Russia 55°30N 47°32E **18** C8
Kanaskat U.S.A. 47°19N 121°54W **78** C5
Kanastraíon, Ákra = Paliouri,
  Akra Greece 39°57N 23°45E **23** E10
Kanawha ➤ U.S.A. 38°50N 82°9W **81** F12
Kanazawa Japan 36°30N 136°38E **31** F8
Kanchanaburi Thailand 14°2N 99°31E **38** E2
Kanchipuram India 12°52N 79°45E **40** N11
Kanchenjunga Nepal 27°50N 88°10E **43** F13
Kandaghat India 30°59N 77°7E **42** D7
Kandahār Afghan. 31°32N 65°43E **40** D4
Kandalaksha Russia 67°9N 32°30E **8** C25
Kandalakshskiy Zaliv
  Russia 66°0N 35°0E **18** A6
Kandangan Indonesia 2°50S 115°20E **36** E5
Kandanghaur Indonesia 6°21S 108°6E **37** G13
Kandanos Greece 35°19N 23°44E **25** D5
Kandavu = Kadavu Fiji 19°0S 178°15E **59** a
Kandavu Passage = Kadavu
  Passage Fiji 18°45S 178°0E **59** a
Kandhkot Pakistan 28°16N 69°8E **42** E3

Kandhla India 29°18N 77°19E 42 E7
Kandi Benin 11°7N 2°55E 50 F6
Kandi India 23°58N 88°5E 43 H13
Kandiaro Pakistan 27°4N 68°13E 42 F3
Kandla India 23°0N 70°10E 42 H4
Kandos Australia 32°45S 149°58E 63 E4
Kandreho Madag. 17°29S 46°6E 57 B8
Kandy Sri Lanka 7°18N 80°43E 40 R12
Kane U.S.A. 41°40N 78°49W 82 E6
Kane Basin Greenland 79°1N 70°0W 66 B12
Käne'ohe U.S.A. 21°25N 157°48W 74 b
Kang Botswana 23°41S 22°50E 56 C3
Kang Krung △ Thailand 9°30N 98°50E 39 H2
Kangān Fārs, Iran 27°50N 52°3E 45 E7
Kangān Hormozgān, Iran 25°48N 57°28E 45 E8
Kangar Malaysia 6°27N 100°12E 39 J3
Kangaroo I. Australia 35°45S 137°0E 63 F2
Kangaroo Mts.
   Australia 23°29S 141°51E 62 C3
Kangasala Finland 61°28N 24°4E 8 F21
Kangāvar Iran 34°40N 48°0E 45 C6
Kangdong N. Korea 39°9N 126°5E 35 E14
Kangean, Kepulauan
   Indonesia 6°55S 115°23E 36 F5
Kangean Is. = Kangean,
   Kepulauan Indonesia 6°55S 115°23E 36 F5
Kanggye N. Korea 41°0N 126°35E 35 D14
Kangiqliniq = Rankin Inlet
   Canada 62°30N 93°0W 68 C10
Kangiqsualujjuaq
   Canada 58°30N 65°59W 69 D13
Kangiqsujuaq Canada 61°30N 72°0W 69 C12
Kangiqtugaapik = Clyde River
   Canada 70°30N 68°30W 69 B13
Kangirsuk Canada 60°0N 70°0W 69 D14
Kangkar Chemaran
   Malaysia 1°34N 104°12E 39 d
Kangkar Sungai Tiram
   Malaysia 1°35N 103°55E 39 d
Kangkar Teberau
   Malaysia 1°32N 103°51E 39 d
Kangping China 42°43N 123°18E 35 C12
Kangra India 32°6N 76°16E 42 C7
Kangrinboqe Feng China 31°0N 81°25E 43 D9
Kangto China 27°50N 92°35E 41 F18
Kanha △ India 22°15N 80°40E 43 H9
Kanhar → India 24°28N 83°8E 43 G10
Kaniama
   Dem. Rep. of the Congo 7°30S 24°12E 54 D1
Kaniapiskau = Caniapiscau →
   Canada 56°40N 69°30W 73 A6
Kaniapiskau, L. = Caniapiscau, L.
   Canada 54°10N 69°55W 73 B6
Kanin, Poluostrov Russia 68°0N 45°0E 18 A8
Kanin Nos, Mys Russia 68°39N 43°32E 18 A7
Kanin Pen. = Kanin, Poluostrov
   Russia 68°0N 45°0E 18 A8
Kaniva Australia 36°22S 141°18E 63 F3
Kanjut Sar Pakistan 36°7N 75°25E 43 A6
Kankaanpää Finland 61°44N 22°50E 8 F20
Kankakee U.S.A. 41°7N 87°52W 80 E10
Kankakee → U.S.A. 41°23N 88°15W 80 E9
Kankan Guinea 10°23N 9°15W 50 F4
Kankendy = Xankändi
   Azerbaijan 39°52N 46°49E 44 B5
Kanker India 20°10N 81°40E 41 J12
Kankroli India 25°4N 73°53E 42 G5
Kannapolis U.S.A. 35°30N 80°37W 85 D14
Kannauj India 27°3N 79°56E 43 F8
Kannod India 22°45N 76°40E 40 H10
Kano Nigeria 12°2N 8°30E 50 F7
Kan'onji Japan 34°7N 133°39E 31 G6
Kanowit Malaysia 2°14N 112°20E 36 D4
Kanoya Japan 31°25N 130°50E 31 J5
Kanpetlet Burma 21°10N 93°59E 41 J18
Kanpur India 26°28N 80°20E 43 F9
Kansas □ U.S.A. 38°30N 99°0W 80 F4
Kansas → U.S.A. 39°7N 94°37W 80 F6
Kansas City Kans., U.S.A. 39°7N 94°38W 80 F6
Kansas City Mo., U.S.A. 39°6N 94°35W 80 F6
Kansenia
   Dem. Rep. of the Congo 10°20S 26°0E 55 E2
Kansk Russia 56°20N 95°37E 29 D10
Kansu = Gansu □ China 36°0N 104°0E 34 G3
Kantaphor India 22°35N 76°34E 42 H7
Kantharalak Thailand 14°39N 104°39E 38 E5
Kantli → India 28°20N 75°30E 42 E6
Kantō □ Japan 36°15N 139°30E 31 F9
Kantō-Sanchi Japan 35°59N 138°50E 31 G9
Kanturk Ireland 52°11N 8°54W 10 D3
Kanuma Japan 36°34N 139°42E 31 F9
Kanus Namibia 27°50S 18°39E 56 D2
Kanyakumari India 8°3N 77°40E 40 Q10
Kanye Botswana 24°55S 25°28E 56 C4
Kanzenze
   Dem. Rep. of the Congo 10°30S 25°12E 55 E2
Kanzi, Ras Tanzania 7°1S 39°33E 54 D4
Kao Tonga 19°40S 175°1W 59 c
Kao Phara Thailand 8°3N 98°22E 39 a
Kaohsiung Taiwan 22°35N 120°16E 33 D7
Kaokoveld Namibia 19°15S 14°30E 56 B1
Kaolack Senegal 14°5N 16°8W 50 F2
Kaoshan China 44°38N 124°50E 35 B13
Kapaa U.S.A. 22°5N 159°19W 74 b
Kapadvanj India 23°5N 73°0E 42 H5
Kapan Armenia 39°18N 46°27E 44 B5
Kapanga
   Dem. Rep. of the Congo 8°30S 22°40E 52 F4
Kapchagai = Qapshaghay
   Kazakhstan 43°51N 77°14E 28 E8
Kapedo Kenya 1°10N 36°6E 54 B4
Kapela = Velika Kapela
   Croatia 45°10N 15°5E 16 F8
Kapema
   Dem. Rep. of the Congo 10°45S 28°22E 55 E2
Kapenguria Kenya 1°14N 35°7E 54 B4

Kapfenberg Austria 47°26N 15°18E 16 E8
Kapiri Mposhi Zambia 13°59S 28°43E 55 E2
Kāpīsā □ Afghan. 35°0N 69°20E 40 B6
Kapiskau → Canada 52°47N 81°55W 72 B3
Kapit Malaysia 2°0N 112°55E 36 D4
Kapiti I. N.Z. 40°50S 174°56E 59 D5
Kaplan U.S.A. 30°0N 92°17W 84 F8
Kapoe Thailand 9°34N 98°32E 39 H2
Kapoeta Sudan 4°50N 33°35E 51 H12
Kaposvár Hungary 46°25N 17°47E 17 E9
Kapowsin U.S.A. 46°59N 122°13W 78 D4
Kapps Namibia 22°32S 17°18E 56 C2
Kapsabet Kenya 0°12N 35°6E 54 B4
Kapsan N. Korea 41°4N 128°19E 35 D15
Kapsukas = Marijampolė
   Lithuania 54°33N 23°19E 9 J20
Kaptai L. Bangla. 22°40N 92°20E 41 H18
Kapuas → Indonesia 0°25S 109°20E 36 E3
Kapuas Hulu, Pegunungan
   Malaysia 1°30N 113°30E 36 D4
Kapuas Hulu Ra. = Kapuas Hulu,
   Pegunungan Malaysia 1°30N 113°30E 36 D4
Kapulo
   Dem. Rep. of the Congo 8°18S 29°15E 55 D2
Kapunda Australia 34°20S 138°56E 63 E2
Kapuni N.Z. 39°29S 174°8E 59 C5
Kapurthala India 31°23N 75°25E 42 D6
Kapuskasing Canada 49°25N 82°30W 72 C3
Kapuskasing → Canada 49°49N 82°0W 72 C3
Kaputar, Mt. Australia 30°15S 150°10E 63 E5
Kaputir Kenya 2°5N 35°28E 54 B4
Kara Russia 69°10N 65°0E 28 C7
Kara Bogaz Gol, Zaliv =
   Garabogazköl Aylagy
   Turkmenistan 41°0N 53°30E 19 F9
Kara-Kala = Garrygala
   Turkmenistan 38°31N 56°29E 45 B8
Kara Kalpak Republic =
   Qoraqalpoghistan □
   Uzbekistan 43°0N 58°0E 28 E6
Kara Kum = Garagum
   Turkmenistan 39°30N 60°0E 45 B8
Kara Sea Russia 75°0N 70°0E 28 B8
Karabiğa Turkey 40°23N 27°17E 23 D12
Karabük Turkey 41°12N 32°37E 19 F5
Karaburun Turkey 38°41N 26°28E 23 E12
Karabutak = Qarabutaq
   Kazakhstan 49°59N 60°14E 28 E7
Karacabey Turkey 40°12N 28°21E 23 D13
Karacasu Turkey 37°43N 28°35E 23 F13
Karachey-Cherkessia □
   Russia 43°40N 41°30E 19 F7
Karachi Pakistan 24°50N 67°0E 42 G2
Karad India 17°15N 74°10E 40 L9
Karaganda = Qaraghandy
   Kazakhstan 49°50N 73°10E 28 E8
Karagayly = Qaraghayly
   Kazakhstan 49°26N 76°0E 28 E8
Karaginskiy, Ostrov
   Russia 58°45N 164°0E 29 D17
Karagiye, Vpadina
   Kazakhstan 43°27N 51°45E 19 F9
Karagiye Depression = Karagiye,
   Vpadina Kazakhstan 43°27N 51°45E 19 F9
Karagola Road India 25°29N 87°23E 43 G12
Karaikal India 10°59N 79°50E 40 P11
Karaikkudi India 10°5N 78°45E 40 P11
Karaj Iran 35°48N 51°0E 45 C6
Karak Malaysia 3°25N 102°2E 39 L4
Karakalpakstan =
   Qoraqalpoghistan □
   Uzbekistan 43°0N 58°0E 28 E6
Karakelong Indonesia 4°35N 126°50E 37 D7
Karakitang Indonesia 3°14N 125°28E 37 D7
Karakol Kyrgyzstan 42°30N 78°20E 32 B2
Karakoram Pass Asia 35°33N 77°50E 43 B7
Karakoram Ra. Pakistan 35°30N 77°0E 43 B7
Karakuwisa Namibia 18°56S 19°40E 56 B2
Karalon Russia 57°5N 115°50E 29 D12
Karama Jordan 31°57N 35°35E 46 D4
Karaman Turkey 37°14N 33°13E 44 B2
Karamay China 45°30N 84°58E 32 B3
Karambu Indonesia 3°53S 116°6E 36 E5
Karamea Bight N.Z. 41°22S 171°40E 59 D3
Karamnasa → India 25°31N 83°52E 43 G10
Karān Si. Arabia 27°43N 49°49E 45 E6
Karand Iran 34°16N 46°15E 44 C5
Karanganyar Indonesia 7°38S 109°37E 37 G13
Karangasem Indonesia 8°27S 115°37E 37 J18
Karanjia India 21°47N 85°58E 43 J11
Karasburg Namibia 28°0S 18°44E 56 D2
Karasino Russia 66°50N 86°50E 28 C9
Karasjok Norway 69°27N 25°30E 8 B21
Karasuk Russia 53°44N 78°2E 28 D8
Karasuyama Japan 36°39N 140°9E 31 F10
Karatau, Khrebet = Qarataü
   Kazakhstan 43°30N 69°30E 28 E7
Karatax Shan China 35°57N 81°0E 32 C3
Karatsu Japan 33°26N 129°58E 31 H5
Karaul Russia 70°6N 82°15E 28 B9
Karauli India 26°30N 77°4E 42 F7
Karavostasi Cyprus 35°8N 32°50E 25 D11
Karawang Indonesia 6°30S 107°15E 37 G12
Karawanken Europe 46°30N 14°40E 16 E8
Karayazı Turkey 39°41N 42°9E 19 G7
Karazhal = Qarazhal
   Kazakhstan 48°2N 70°49E 28 E8
Karbalā' Iraq 32°36N 44°3E 44 C5
Karcag Hungary 47°19N 20°57E 17 E11
Karcha → Pakistan 34°45N 76°10E 43 B7
Karchana India 25°17N 81°56E 43 G9
Karditsa Greece 39°23N 21°54E 23 E9
Kärdla Estonia 59°0N 22°45E 9 G20
Kareeberge S. Africa 30°59S 21°50E 56 E3
Kareha → India 25°44N 86°21E 43 G12
Kareima Sudan 18°30N 31°49E 51 E12
Karelia □ Russia 65°30N 32°30E 8 D25

Karelian Republic = Karelia □
   Russia 65°30N 32°30E 8 D25
Karera India 25°32N 78°9E 42 G8
Kārevāndar Iran 27°53N 60°44E 45 E9
Kargasok Russia 59°3N 80°53E 28 D9
Kargat Russia 55°10N 80°15E 28 D9
Kargi Kenya 2°31N 37°34E 54 B4
Kargil India 34°32N 76°12E 43 B7
Kargopol Russia 61°30N 38°58E 18 B6
Karhal India 27°1N 78°57E 43 F8
Kariān Iran 26°57N 57°14E 45 E8
Karianga Madag. 22°25S 47°22E 57 C8
Kariba Zimbabwe 16°28S 28°50E 55 F2
Kariba, L. Zimbabwe 16°40S 28°25E 55 F2
Kariba Dam Zimbabwe 16°30S 28°35E 55 F2
Kariba Gorge Zambia 16°30S 28°50E 55 F2
Karibib Namibia 22°0S 15°56E 56 C2
Karijini △ Australia 23°8S 118°15E 60 D2
Karimata, Kepulauan
   Indonesia 1°25S 109°0E 36 E3
Karimata, Selat Indonesia 2°0S 108°40E 36 E3
Karimata Is. = Karimata,
   Kepulauan Indonesia 1°25S 109°0E 36 E3
Karimnagar India 18°26N 79°10E 40 K11
Karimun Kecil, Pulau
   Indonesia 1°8N 103°22E 39 d
Karimunjawa, Kepulauan
   Indonesia 5°50S 110°30E 36 F4
Karin Somali Rep. 10°50N 45°52E 47 E4
Karīt Iran 33°29N 56°55E 45 C8
Kariya Japan 34°58N 137°1E 31 G8
Kariyangwe Zimbabwe 18°0S 27°38E 57 B4
Karjala Finland 62°0N 30°25E 8 F24
Karkaralinsk = Qarqaraly
   Kazakhstan 49°26N 75°30E 28 E8
Karkheh → Iran 31°2N 47°29E 44 D5
Karkinitska Zatoka
   Ukraine 45°56N 33°0E 19 E5
Karkinitskiy Zaliv = Karkinitska
   Zatoka Ukraine 45°56N 33°0E 19 E5
Karkuk = Kirkūk Iraq 35°30N 44°21E 44 C5
Karleby = Kokkola
   Finland 63°50N 23°8E 8 E20
Karlovac Croatia 45°31N 15°36E 16 F8
Karlovo Bulgaria 42°38N 24°47E 23 C11
Karlovy Vary Czech Rep. 50°13N 12°51E 16 C7
Karlsbad = Karlovy Vary
   Czech Rep. 50°13N 12°51E 16 C7
Karlsena, Mys Russia 77°0N 67°42E 28 B7
Karlshamn Sweden 56°10N 14°51E 9 H16
Karlskoga Sweden 59°28N 14°33E 9 G16
Karlskrona Sweden 56°10N 15°35E 9 H16
Karlsruhe Germany 49°0N 8°23E 16 D5
Karlstad Sweden 59°23N 13°30E 9 G15
Karlstad U.S.A. 48°35N 96°31W 80 A5
Karmi'el Israel 32°55N 35°18E 46 C4
Karnak Egypt 25°43N 32°39E 51 C12
Karnal India 29°42N 77°2E 42 E7
Karnali → Nepal 28°45N 81°16E 43 E9
Karnaphuli Res. = Kaptai L.
   Bangla. 22°40N 92°20E 41 H18
Karnaprayag India 30°16N 79°15E 43 D8
Karnataka □ India 13°15N 77°0E 40 N10
Karnes City U.S.A. 28°53N 97°54W 84 G6
Karnische Alpen Europe 46°36N 13°0E 16 E7
Kärnten □ Austria 46°52N 13°30E 16 E8
Karoi Zimbabwe 16°48S 29°45E 55 F2
Karon, Ao Thailand 7°51N 98°17E 39 a
Karonga Malawi 9°57S 33°55E 55 D3
Karoo △ S. Africa 32°18S 22°27E 56 E3
Karoonda Australia 35°1S 139°59E 63 F2
Karor Pakistan 31°15N 70°59E 42 D4
Karora Sudan 17°44N 38°15E 51 E13
Karpasia Cyprus 35°32N 34°15E 25 D13
Karpathos Greece 35°37N 27°10E 23 G12
Karpinsk Russia 59°45N 60°1E 18 C11
Karpogory Russia 64°0N 44°27E 18 B7
Karpuz Burnu = Apostolos
   Andreas, C. Cyprus 35°42N 34°35E 25 D13
Karratha Australia 20°53S 116°40E 60 D2
Kars Turkey 40°40N 43°5E 19 F7
Karsakpay Kazakhstan 47°55N 66°40E 28 E7
Karshi = Qarshi
   Uzbekistan 38°53N 65°48E 28 F7
Karsiyang India 26°56N 88°18E 43 F13
Karsog India 31°23N 77°12E 42 D7
Kartala Comoros Is. 11°45S 43°21E 53 a
Kartaly Russia 53°3N 60°40E 28 D7
Kartapur India 31°27N 75°32E 42 D6
Karthaus U.S.A. 41°8N 78°9W 82 E6
Karufa Indonesia 3°50S 133°20E 37 E8
Karuma △ Uganda 2°5N 32°15E 54 B3
Karumba Australia 17°31S 140°50E 62 B3
Karumo Tanzania 2°25S 32°50E 54 C3
Karumwa Tanzania 3°12S 32°38E 54 C3
Kārūn → Iran 30°26N 48°10E 45 D6
Karungu Kenya 0°50S 34°10E 54 C3
Karviná Czech Rep. 49°53N 18°31E 17 D10
Karwan → India 27°26N 78°4E 42 F8
Karwar India 14°55N 74°13E 40 M9
Karwi India 25°12N 80°57E 43 G9
Karymskoye Russia 51°36N 114°21E 29 D12
Kasache Malawi 13°25S 34°20E 55 E3
Kasai →
   Dem. Rep. of the Congo 3°30S 16°10E 52 E3
Kasai-Oriental □
   Dem. Rep. of the Congo 5°0S 24°30E 54 D1
Kasaji
   Dem. Rep. of the Congo 10°25S 23°27E 55 E1
Kasama Zambia 10°16S 31°9E 55 E3
Kasan N. Korea 41°18N 126°55E 35 D14
Kasandra Kolpos Greece 40°5S 23°30E 23 D10
Kasane Namibia 17°34S 24°50E 56 B3
Kasanga Tanzania 8°30S 31°10E 55 D3
Kasanka △ Zambia 11°34S 30°15E 55 E3
Kasaragod India 12°30N 74°58E 40 N9
Kasba L. Canada 60°20N 102°10W 71 A8

Kāseh Garān Iran 34°5N 46°2E 44 C5
Kasempa Zambia 13°30S 25°44E 55 E2
Kasenga
   Dem. Rep. of the Congo 10°20S 28°45E 55 E2
Kasese Uganda 0°13N 30°3E 54 B3
Kasewa Zambia 14°28S 28°53E 55 E2
Kasganj India 27°48N 78°42E 43 F8
Kashabowie Canada 48°40N 90°26W 72 C1
Kashaf Iran 35°58N 61°7E 45 C9
Kāshān Iran 34°5N 51°30E 45 C6
Kashechewan Canada 52°18N 81°37W 72 B3
Kashgar = Kashi China 39°30N 76°2E 32 C2
Kashi China 39°30N 76°2E 32 C2
Kashimbo
   Dem. Rep. of the Congo 11°12S 26°19E 55 E2
Kashipur India 29°15N 79°0E 43 E8
Kashiwazaki Japan 37°22N 138°33E 31 F9
Kashk-e Kohneh
   Afghan. 34°55N 62°30E 40 B3
Kashkū'īyeh Iran 30°31N 55°40E 45 D7
Kāshmar Iran 35°16N 58°26E 45 C8
Kashmir Asia 34°0N 76°0E 43 C7
Kashmor Pakistan 28°28N 69°32E 42 E3
Kashun Noerh = Gaxun Nur
   China 42°22N 100°30E 32 B5
Kasiari India 22°8N 87°14E 43 H12
Kasimov Russia 54°55N 41°20E 18 D7
Kasinge
   Dem. Rep. of the Congo 6°15S 26°58E 54 D2
Kasiruta Indonesia 0°25S 127°12E 37 E7
Kaskaskia → U.S.A. 37°58N 89°57W 80 G9
Kaskattama → Canada 57°3N 90°4W 71 B10
Kaskinen Finland 62°22N 21°15E 8 E19
Kaskö = Kaskinen
   Finland 62°22N 21°15E 8 E19
Kaslo Canada 49°55N 116°55W 70 D5
Kasmere L. Canada 59°34N 101°10W 71 B8
Kasongo
   Dem. Rep. of the Congo 4°30S 26°33E 54 C2
Kasongo Lunda
   Dem. Rep. of the Congo 6°35S 16°49E 52 F3
Kasos Greece 35°20N 26°55E 23 G12
Kassalâ Sudan 15°30N 36°0E 51 E13
Kassel Germany 51°18N 9°26E 16 C5
Kassiopi Greece 39°48N 19°53E 25 A3
Kasson U.S.A. 44°2N 92°45W 80 C7
Kastamonu Turkey 41°25N 33°43E 19 F5
Kasteli Greece 35°29N 23°38E 25 D5
Kastelli Greece 35°12N 25°20E 25 D7
Kasterlee Belgium 51°15N 4°59E 15 C4
Kastoria Greece 40°30N 21°19E 23 D9
Kasulu Tanzania 4°37S 30°5E 54 C3
Kasumi Japan 35°38N 134°38E 31 G7
Kasungu Malawi 13°0S 33°29E 55 E3
Kasungu △ Malawi 12°53S 33°9E 55 E3
Kasur Pakistan 31°5N 74°25E 42 D6
Kata, Ao Thailand 7°48N 98°18E 39 a
Kata Archanes Greece 35°15N 25°10E 25 D7
Kata Tjuta Australia 25°20S 130°50E 61 E5
Kataba Zambia 16°5S 25°10E 55 F2
Katahdin, Mt. U.S.A. 45°54N 68°56W 81 C19
Katako Kombe
   Dem. Rep. of the Congo 3°25S 24°20E 54 C1
Katale Tanzania 4°52S 31°7E 54 C3
Katanda Katanga,
   Dem. Rep. of the Congo 7°52S 24°13E 54 D1
Katanda Nord-Kivu,
   Dem. Rep. of the Congo 0°55S 29°21E 54 C2
Katanga □
   Dem. Rep. of the Congo 8°0S 25°0E 54 D2
Katangi India 21°56N 79°50E 40 J11
Katanning Australia 33°40S 117°33E 61 F2
Katavi △ Tanzania 6°51S 31°3E 54 D3
Katavi Swamp Tanzania 6°50S 31°10E 54 D3
Katerini Greece 40°18N 22°37E 23 D10
Katghora India 22°30N 82°33E 43 H10
Katha Burma 24°10N 96°30E 41 G20
Katherîna, Gebel Egypt 28°30N 33°57E 44 D2
Katherine Australia 14°27S 132°20E 60 B5
Katherine Gorge
   Australia 14°18S 132°28E 60 B5
Kathi India 21°47N 74°3E 42 J6
Kathiawar India 22°20N 71°0E 42 H4
Kathikas Cyprus 34°55N 32°25E 25 E11
Kathmandu Nepal 27°45N 85°20E 43 F11
Kathua India 32°23N 75°34E 42 C6
Katihar India 25°34N 87°36E 43 G12
Katima Mulilo Namibia 17°28S 24°13E 56 B3
Katimbira Malawi 12°40S 34°0E 55 E3
Katingan = Mendawai →
   Indonesia 3°30S 113°0E 36 E4
Katiola Ivory C. 8°10N 5°10W 50 G4
Katmandu = Kathmandu
   Nepal 27°45N 85°20E 43 F11
Katni India 23°51N 80°24E 43 H9
Kato Chorio Greece 35°3N 25°47E 25 D7
Kato Korakiana Greece 39°42N 19°45E 25 A3
Káto Pyrgos Cyprus 35°11N 32°41E 25 D11
Katompe
   Dem. Rep. of the Congo 6°2S 26°23E 54 D2
Katong Singapore 1°18N 103°53E 39 d
Katonga → Uganda 0°34N 31°50E 54 B3
Katoomba Australia 33°41S 150°19E 63 E5
Katowice Poland 50°17N 19°5E 17 C10
Katrine, L. U.K. 56°15N 4°30W 11 E4
Katrineholm Sweden 59°9N 16°12E 9 G17
Katsepe Madag. 15°45S 46°15E 57 B8
Katsina Nigeria 13°0N 7°32E 50 F7
Katsumoto Japan 33°51N 129°42E 31 H4
Katsuura Japan 35°10N 140°20E 31 G10
Katsuyama Japan 36°3N 136°30E 31 F8
Kattavia Greece 35°57N 27°46E 25 D9
Kattegat Denmark 56°40N 11°20E 9 H14
Katumba
   Dem. Rep. of the Congo 7°40S 25°17E 54 D2
Katwa India 23°30N 88°5E 43 H13
Katwijk Neths. 52°12N 4°24E 15 B4

Kaua'i U.S.A. 22°3N 159°30W 74 b
Kauai Channel U.S.A. 21°45N 158°50W 74 b
Kaudom △ Namibia 18°45S 20°51E 56 B3
Kaukauna U.S.A. 32°35N 96°19W 84 E6
Kauhajoki Finland 62°25N 22°10E 8 E20
Kaukauna U.S.A. 44°17N 88°17W 80 C9
Kaukauveld Namibia 20°0S 20°15E 56 C3
Kaunakakai U.S.A. 21°6N 157°1W 74 b
Kaunas Lithuania 54°54N 23°54E 9 J20
Kaunia Bangla. 25°46N 89°26E 43 G13
Kautokeino Norway 69°0N 23°4E 8 B20
Kauwapur India 27°31N 82°18E 43 F10
Kavacha Russia 60°16N 169°51E 29 C17
Kavala Greece 40°57N 24°28E 23 D11
Kavalerovo Russia 44°15N 135°4E 30 B7
Kavali India 14°55N 80°1E 40 M12
Kavār Iran 29°11N 52°44E 45 D7
Kavi India 22°12N 72°38E 42 H5
Kavimba Botswana 18°2S 24°38E 56 B3
Kavīr, Dasht-e Iran 34°30N 55°0E 45 C7
Kavīr △ Iran 34°40N 52°0E 45 C7
Kavos Greece 39°23N 20°3E 25 B4
Kaw Fr. Guiana 4°30N 52°15W 93 C8
Kawagama L. Canada 45°18N 78°45W 82 A6
Kawagoe Japan 35°55N 139°29E 31 G9
Kawaguchi Japan 35°52N 139°45E 31 G9
Kawambwa Zambia 9°48S 29°3E 55 D2
Kawanoe Japan 34°1N 133°34E 31 G6
Kawardha India 22°0N 81°17E 43 J9
Kawasaki Japan 35°31N 139°43E 31 G9
Kawasi Indonesia 1°38S 127°28E 37 E7
Kawawachikamach
   Canada 54°48N 66°50W 73 B6
Kawerau N.Z. 38°7S 176°42E 59 C6
Kawhia N.Z. 38°4S 174°49E 59 C5
Kawhia Harbour N.Z. 38°5S 174°51E 59 C5
Kawio, Kepulauan
   Indonesia 4°30N 125°30E 37 D7
Kawthaung Burma 10°5N 98°36E 39 H2
Kawthoolei = Kayin □
   Burma 18°0N 97°30E 41 L20
Kawthule = Kayin □
   Burma 18°0N 97°30E 41 L20
Kaya Burkina Faso 13°4N 1°10W 50 F5
Kayah □ Burma 19°15N 97°15E 41 K20
Kayan → Indonesia 2°55N 117°35E 36 D5
Kaycee U.S.A. 43°43N 106°38W 76 E10
Kayeli Indonesia 3°20S 127°10E 37 E7
Kayenta U.S.A. 36°44N 110°15W 77 H8
Kayes Mali 14°25N 11°30W 50 F3
Kayin □ Burma 18°0N 97°30E 41 L20
Kayoa Indonesia 0°1N 127°28E 37 D7
Kayomba Zambia 13°11S 24°2E 55 E1
Kayseri Turkey 38°45N 35°30E 44 B2
Kaysville U.S.A. 41°2N 111°56W 76 F8
Kazachye Russia 70°52N 135°58E 29 B14
Kazakhstan ■ Asia 50°0N 70°0E 28 E8
Kazan Russia 55°50N 49°10E 18 C8
Kazan → Canada 64°2N 95°29W 71 A9
Kazan-Rettō Pac. Oc. 25°0N 141°0E 64 E6
Kazanlŭk Bulgaria 42°38N 25°20E 23 C11
Kazatin = Kozyatyn
   Ukraine 49°45N 28°50E 17 D15
Kāzerūn Iran 29°38N 51°40E 45 D6
Kazi Magomed = Qazimämmäd
   Azerbaijan 40°3N 49°0E 45 A6
Kazuma Pan △
   Zimbabwe 18°20S 25°48E 55 F2
Kazuno Japan 40°10N 140°45E 30 D10
Kazym → Russia 63°54N 65°50E 28 C7
Kea Greece 37°35N 24°22E 23 F11
Keady U.K. 54°15N 6°42W 10 B5
Kearney U.S.A. 40°42N 99°5W 80 E4
Kearny U.S.A. 33°3N 110°55W 77 K8
Kearsarge, Mt. U.S.A. 43°22N 71°50W 83 C13
Keban Turkey 38°50N 38°50E 19 G6
Keban Baraji Turkey 38°41N 38°33E 44 B3
Kebnekaise Sweden 67°53N 18°33E 8 C18
Kebri Dehar Ethiopia 6°45N 44°17E 47 F3
Kebumen Indonesia 7°42S 109°40E 37 G13
Kechika → Canada 59°41N 127°12W 70 B3
Kecskemét Hungary 46°57N 19°42E 17 E10
Kėdainiai Lithuania 55°15N 24°2E 9 J21
Kedarnath India 30°44N 79°4E 43 D8
Kedgwick Canada 47°40N 67°20W 73 C6
Kediri Indonesia 7°51S 112°1E 37 G15
Kedros Oros Greece 35°11N 24°37E 25 D6
Keeler U.S.A. 36°29N 117°52W 78 J9
Keeley L. Canada 54°54N 108°8W 71 C7
Keeling Is. = Cocos Is.
   Ind. Oc. 12°10S 96°55E 64 J1
Keelung = Chilung
   Taiwan 25°3N 121°45E 33 D7
Keene Canada 44°15N 78°10W 82 B6
Keene Calif., U.S.A. 35°13N 118°33W 79 K8
Keene N.H., U.S.A. 42°56N 72°17W 83 D12
Keene N.Y., U.S.A. 44°16N 73°46W 83 B11
Keep River △ Australia 15°49S 129°8E 60 C4
Keeper Hill Ireland 52°45N 8°16W 10 D3
Keerweer, C. Australia 14°0S 141°32E 62 A3
Keeseville U.S.A. 44°29N 73°30W 83 B11
Keetmanshoop Namibia 26°35S 18°8E 56 D2
Keewatin U.S.A. 49°46N 94°34W 71 D10
Keewatin → Canada 56°29N 100°46W 71 B8
Kefalonia Greece 38°15N 20°30E 23 E9
Kefamenanu Indonesia 9°28S 124°29E 37 F6
Kefar Sava Israel 32°11N 34°54E 46 C3
Keffi Nigeria 8°55N 7°43E 50 G7
Keflavík Iceland 64°2N 22°35W 8 D2
Keg River Canada 57°54N 117°55W 70 B5
Kegaska Canada 50°9N 61°18W 73 B7
Kehancha Kenya 1°11S 34°37E 54 C3
Keighley U.K. 53°52N 1°54W 12 D6
Keila Estonia 59°18N 24°25E 9 G21
Keimoes S. Africa 28°41S 20°59E 56 D3
Keitele Finland 63°10N 26°20E 8 E22
Keith Australia 36°6S 140°20E 63 F3

Keith *U.K.* 57°32N 2°57W **11** D6
Keiyasi *Fiji* 17°53S 177°46E **59** a
Keizer *U.S.A.* 44°57N 123°1W **76** D2
Kejimkujik △ *Canada* 44°25N 65°25W **73** D6
Kejserr Franz Joseph Fd.
  Greenland 73°30N 24°30W **4** B6
Kekri *India* 26°0N 75°10E **42** G6
Kelan *China* 38°43N 111°31E **34** E6
Kelang = Klang *Malaysia* 3°2N 101°26E **39** L3
Kelantan ⇀ *Malaysia* 6°13N 102°14E **39** J4
Kelkit ⇀ *Turkey* 40°45N 36°32E **19** F6
Kellerberrin *Australia* 31°36S 117°38E **61** F2
Kellett, C. *Canada* 72°0N 126°0W **69** B7
Kelleys I. *U.S.A.* 41°36N 82°42W **82** E2
Kellogg *U.S.A.* 47°32N 116°7W **76** C5
Kells = Ceanannus Mor
  Ireland 53°44N 6°53W **10** C5
Kélo *Chad* 9°10N 15°45E **51** G9
Kelokedhara *Cyprus* 34°48N 32°39E **25** E11
Kelowna *Canada* 49°50N 119°25W **70** D5
Kelsey Creek *Australia* 20°26S 148°31E **62** J6
Kelseyville *U.S.A.* 38°59N 122°50W **78** G4
Kelso *N.Z.* 45°54S 169°15E **59** F2
Kelso *U.K.* 55°36N 2°26W **11** F6
Kelso *U.S.A.* 46°9N 122°54W **78** D4
Keluang = Kluang
  Malaysia 2°3N 103°18E **39** L4
Kelvington *Canada* 52°10N 103°30W **71** C8
Kem *Russia* 65°0N 34°38E **18** B5
Kem ⇀ *Russia* 64°57N 34°41E **18** B5
Kema *Indonesia* 1°22N 125°8E **37** D7
Kemah *Turkey* 39°32N 39°5E **44** B3
Kemaman *Malaysia* 4°12N 103°18E **39** K4
Kemano *Canada* 53°35N 128°0W **70** C3
Kemasik *Malaysia* 4°25N 103°27E **39** K4
Kemerovo *Russia* 55°20N 86°5E **28** D9
Kemi *Finland* 65°44N 24°34E **8** D21
Kemi älv = Kemijoki ⇀
  Finland 65°47N 24°32E **8** D21
Kemi träsk = Kemijärvi
  Finland 66°43N 27°22E **8** C22
Kemijärvi *Finland* 66°43N 27°22E **8** C22
Kemijoki ⇀ *Finland* 65°47N 24°32E **8** D21
Kemmerer *U.S.A.* 41°48N 110°32W **76** F8
Kemmuna = Comino
  Malta 36°1N 14°20E **25** C1
Kemp, L. *U.S.A.* 33°46N 99°9W **84** E5
Kemp Land *Antarctica* 69°0S 55°0E **5** C5
Kempas *Malaysia* 1°33N 103°42E **39** d
Kempsey *Australia* 31°1S 152°50E **63** E5
Kempt, L. *Canada* 47°25N 74°22W **72** C5
Kempten *Germany* 47°45N 10°17E **16** E6
Kempton *Australia* 42°31S 147°12E **63** G4
Kemptville *Canada* 45°0N 75°38W **83** B9
Ken ⇀ *India* 25°13N 80°27E **43** G9
Kenai *U.S.A.* 60°33N 151°16W **68** C4
Kendai *India* 22°45N 82°37E **43** H10
Kendal *Indonesia* 6°56S 110°14E **37** G14
Kendal *U.K.* 54°20N 2°44W **12** C5
Kendall *Australia* 31°35S 152°44E **63** E5
Kendall *U.S.A.* 25°40N 80°19W **85** J14
Kendall ⇀ *Australia* 14°4S 141°35E **62** A3
Kendallville *U.S.A.* 41°27N 85°16W **81** E11
Kendari *Indonesia* 3°50S 122°30E **37** E6
Kendawangan *Indonesia* 2°32S 110°17E **36** E4
Kendi, Pulau *Malaysia* 5°13N 100°11E **39** c
Kendrapara *India* 20°35N 86°30E **41** J15
Kendrew *S. Africa* 32°32S 24°30E **56** E3
Kene Thao *Laos* 17°44N 101°10E **38** D3
Kenedy *U.S.A.* 28°49N 97°51W **84** G6
Kenema *S. Leone* 7°50N 11°14W **50** G3
Keng Kok *Laos* 16°26N 105°12E **38** D5
Keng Tawng *Burma* 20°45N 98°18E **41** J21
Keng Tung *Burma* 21°0N 99°30E **41** J21
Kengeja *Tanzania* 5°26S 39°45E **54** D4
Kenhardt *S. Africa* 29°19S 21°12E **56** D3
Kenitra *Morocco* 34°15N 6°40W **50** B4
Kenli *China* 37°30N 118°20E **35** F10
Kenmare *Ireland* 51°53N 9°36W **10** E2
Kenmare *U.S.A.* 48°41N 102°5W **80** A2
Kenmare River *Ireland* 51°48N 9°51W **10** E2
Kennebago Lake *U.S.A.* 45°4N 70°40W **83** A14
Kennebec *U.S.A.* 43°54N 99°52W **80** D4
Kennebec ⇀ *U.S.A.* 43°45N 69°46W **81** D19
Kennebunk *U.S.A.* 43°23N 70°33W **83** C14
Kennedy *Zimbabwe* 18°52S 27°10E **56** B4
Kennedy Ra. *Australia* 24°45S 115°10E **61** D2
Kennedy Range △
  Australia 24°34S 115°2E **61** D2
Kenner *U.S.A.* 29°59N 90°14W **85** G9
Kennet ⇀ *U.K.* 51°27N 0°57W **13** F7
Kenneth Ra. *Australia* 23°50S 117°8E **61** D2
Kennett *U.S.A.* 36°14N 90°3W **80** G8
Kennewick *U.S.A.* 46°12N 119°7W **76** C4
Kennisis Lake *Canada* 45°13N 78°36W **82** A6
Kenogami ⇀ *Canada* 51°6N 84°28W **72** B3
Kenora *Canada* 49°47N 94°29W **71** D10
Kenosha *U.S.A.* 42°35N 87°49W **80** D10
Kensington *Canada* 46°28N 63°34W **73** C7
Kent *Ohio, U.S.A.* 41°9N 81°22W **82** E3
Kent *Tex., U.S.A.* 31°4N 104°13W **84** F2
Kent *Wash., U.S.A.* 47°22N 122°14W **78** C4
Kent □ *U.K.* 51°12N 0°40E **13** F8
Kent Group *Australia* 39°30S 147°20E **63** F4
Kent Pen. *Canada* 68°30N 107°0W **68** C9
Kentaū *Kazakhstan* 43°32N 68°36E **28** E7
Kentland *U.S.A.* 40°46N 87°27W **81** E10
Kenton *U.S.A.* 40°39N 83°37W **81** E12
Kentucky □ *U.S.A.* 37°0N 84°0W **81** G11
Kentucky ⇀ *U.S.A.* 38°41N 85°11W **81** F11
Kentucky L. *U.S.A.* 37°1N 88°16W **80** G9
Kentville *Canada* 45°6N 64°29W **73** C7
Kentwood *U.S.A.* 30°56N 90°31W **85** F9
Kenya ■ *Africa* 1°0N 38°0E **54** B4
Kenya, Mt. *Kenya* 0°10S 37°18E **54** C4
Kenyir, Tasik *Malaysia* 5°1N 102°54E **39** K4
Keo Neua, Deo *Vietnam* 18°23N 105°10E **38** C5

Keokuk *U.S.A.* 40°24N 91°24W **80** E8
Keoladeo △ *India* 27°0N 77°20E **42** F7
Keonjhargarh *India* 21°28N 85°35E **43** J11
Kep *Cambodia* 10°29N 104°19E **38** G5
Kep *Vietnam* 21°24N 106°16E **38** B6
Kepala Batas *Malaysia* 5°31N 100°26E **39** c
Kepi *Indonesia* 6°32S 139°19E **37** F9
Kerala □ *India* 11°0N 76°15E **40** P10
Kerama-Rettō *Japan* 26°5N 127°15E **31** L3
Keran *Pakistan* 34°35N 73°59E **43** B5
Kerang *Australia* 35°40S 143°55E **63** F3
Keraudren, C. *Australia* 19°58S 119°45E **60** C2
Kerch *Ukraine* 45°20N 36°20E **19** E6
Kerguelen *Ind. Oc.* 49°15S 69°10E **3** G13
Kericho *Kenya* 0°22S 35°15E **54** C4
Kerinci *Indonesia* 1°40S 101°15E **36** E2
Kerki = Atamyrat
  Turkmenistan 37°50N 65°12E **28** F7
Kerkrade *Neths.* 50°53N 6°4E **15** D6
Kerkyra *Greece* 39°38N 19°50E **25** A3
Kerkyras, Notio Steno
  Greece 39°34N 20°0E **25** A4
Kermadec Is. *Pac. Oc.* 30°0S 178°15W **58** E11
Kermadec Trench
  Pac. Oc. 30°30S 176°0W **64** L10
Kerman *Iran* 30°15N 57°1E **45** D8
Kerman *U.S.A.* 36°43N 120°4W **78** J6
Kermān □ *Iran* 30°0N 57°0E **45** D8
Kermān, Bīābān-e *Iran* 28°45N 59°45E **45** D8
Kermānshāh *Iran* 34°23N 47°0E **44** C5
Kermānshāh □ *Iran* 34°0N 46°30E **44** C5
Kermit *U.S.A.* 31°52N 103°6W **84** F3
Kern ⇀ *U.S.A.* 35°16N 119°18W **79** K7
Kernow = Cornwall □
  U.K. 50°26N 4°40W **13** G3
Kernville *U.S.A.* 35°45N 118°26W **79** K8
Keroh *Malaysia* 5°43N 101°1E **39** K3
Kerrera *U.K.* 56°24N 5°33W **11** E3
Kerrobert *Canada* 51°56N 109°8W **71** C7
Kerrville *U.S.A.* 30°3N 99°8W **84** F5
Kerry □ *Ireland* 52°7N 9°35W **10** D2
Kerry Hd. *Ireland* 52°25N 9°56W **10** D2
Kerulen ⇀ *Asia* 48°48N 117°0E **33** B6
Kerzaz *Algeria* 29°29N 1°37W **50** C5
Kesagami ⇀ *Canada* 51°40N 79°45W **72** B4
Kesagami L. *Canada* 50°23N 80°15W **72** B4
Keşan *Turkey* 40°49N 26°38E **23** D12
Keshit *Iran* 29°43N 58°17E **45** D8
Kestell *S. Africa* 28°17S 28°42E **57** D4
Kestenga *Russia* 65°50N 31°45E **8** D24
Keswick *U.K.* 54°36N 3°8W **12** C4
Ket ⇀ *Russia* 58°55N 81°32E **28** D9
Ketapang *Bali, Indonesia* 8°9S 114°23E **37** J17
Ketapang *Kalimantan,*
  Indonesia 1°55S 110°0E **36** E4
Ketchikan *U.S.A.* 55°21N 131°39W **70** B2
Ketchum *U.S.A.* 43°41N 114°22W **76** E6
Ketef, Khalig Umm el
  Egypt 23°40N 35°35E **44** F2
Keti Bandar *Pakistan* 24°8N 67°27E **42** G2
Ketri *India* 28°1N 75°50E **42** E6
Kętrzyn *Poland* 54°7N 21°22E **17** A11
Kettering *U.K.* 52°24N 0°43W **13** E7
Kettering *U.S.A.* 39°41N 84°10W **81** F11
Kettle ⇀ *Canada* 56°40N 89°34W **71** B11
Kettle Falls *U.S.A.* 48°37N 118°3W **76** B4
Kettle Point *Canada* 43°10N 82°1W **82** C2
Kettle Pt. *Canada* 43°13N 82°1W **82** C2
Kettleman City *U.S.A.* 36°1N 119°58W **78** J7
Keuka L. *U.S.A.* 42°30N 77°9W **82** D7
Keuruu *Finland* 62°16N 24°41E **8** E21
Kewanee *U.S.A.* 41°14N 89°56W **80** E9
Kewaunee *U.S.A.* 44°27N 87°31W **80** C10
Keweenaw B. *U.S.A.* 47°0N 88°15W **80** B9
Keweenaw Pen. *U.S.A.* 47°15N 88°15W **80** B9
Keweenaw Pt. *U.S.A.* 47°25N 87°43W **80** B10
Key, L. *Ireland* 54°0N 8°15W **10** C3
Key Lake Mine *Canada* 57°5N 105°32W **71** B7
Key Largo *U.S.A.* 25°5N 80°27W **85** J14
Key West *U.S.A.* 24°33N 81°48W **88** B3
Keynsham *U.K.* 51°24N 2°29W **13** F5
Keyser *U.S.A.* 39°26N 78°59W **81** F14
Kezhma *Russia* 58°59N 101°9E **29** D11
Kezi *Zimbabwe* 20°58S 28°32E **57** C4
Kgalagadi Transfrontier □
  Africa 25°10S 21°0E **56** D3
Khabarovsk *Russia* 48°30N 135°5E **29** E14
Khabr *Iran* 28°51N 56°22E **45** D8
Khābūr ⇀ *Syria* 35°17N 40°35E **44** C4
Khachmas = Xaçmaz
  Azerbaijan 41°31N 48°42E **19** F8
Khachrod *India* 23°25N 75°20E **42** H6
Khadro *Pakistan* 26°11N 68°50E **42** F3
Khadzhilyangar = Dahongliutan
  China 35°45N 79°20E **43** B8
Khaga *India* 25°47N 81°7E **43** G9
Khagaria *India* 25°30N 86°32E **43** G12
Khaipur *Pakistan* 29°34N 72°17E **42** E5
Khair *India* 27°57N 77°46E **42** F7
Khairabad *India* 27°33N 80°47E **43** F9
Khairagarh *India* 21°27N 81°2E **43** J9
Khairpur *Pakistan* 27°32N 68°49E **42** F3
Khairpur Nathan Shah
  Pakistan 27°6N 67°44E **42** F2
Khairwara *India* 23°58N 73°38E **42** H5
Khaisor = *Pakistan* 31°17N 68°59E **42** D3
Khajuri Kach *Pakistan* 32°4N 69°51E **42** C3
Khakassia □ *Russia* 53°0N 90°0E **28** D9
Khakhea *Botswana* 24°48S 23°22E **56** C3
Khalafābād *Iran* 30°54N 49°24E **45** D6
Khalilabad *India* 26°48N 83°5E **43** F10
Khalīlī *Iran* 27°38N 53°17E **45** E7
Khalkhāl *Iran* 37°37N 48°32E **45** B6
Khalkis = Halkida
  Greece 38°27N 23°42E **23** E10
Khalmer Yu *Russia* 67°58N 65°1E **28** C7

Khalturin *Russia* 58°40N 48°50E **18** C8
Khalūf *Oman* 20°30N 58°13E **47** C6
Kham Keut *Laos* 18°15N 104°43E **38** C5
Khamaria *India* 23°5N 80°48E **43** H9
Khambhaliya *India* 22°14N 69°41E **42** H3
Khambhat *India* 22°23N 72°33E **42** H5
Khambhat, G. of *India* 20°45N 72°30E **40** J8
Khamir *Iran* 26°57N 55°36E **45** E7
Khamir *Yemen* 16°2N 44°0E **47** D3
Khamīs Mushayṭ
  Si. Arabia 18°18N 42°44E **47** D3
Khamsa *Egypt* 30°27N 32°23E **46** E1
Khān ⇀ *Namibia* 22°37S 14°56E **56** C2
Khān Abū Shāmat *Syria* 33°39N 36°53E **46** B5
Khān Azād *Iraq* 33°7N 44°22E **44** C5
Khān Mujiddah *Iraq* 32°21N 43°48E **44** C4
Khān Shaykhūn *Syria* 35°26N 36°38E **44** C3
Khan Tengri, Pik *Asia* 42°12N 80°10E **32** B3
Khān Yūnis *Gaza Strip* 31°21N 34°18E **46** D3
Khanai *Pakistan* 30°30N 67°8E **42** D2
Khānaqīn *Iraq* 34°23N 45°25E **44** C5
Khānbāghī *Iran* 36°10N 55°25E **45** B7
Khandwa *India* 21°49N 76°22E **40** J10
Khandyga *Russia* 62°42N 135°35E **29** C14
Khanewal *Pakistan* 30°20N 71°55E **42** D4
Khangah Dogran
  Pakistan 31°50N 73°37E **42** D5
Khanh Duong *Vietnam* 12°44N 108°44E **38** F7
Khania = Chania *Greece* 35°30N 24°4E **25** D6
Khaniadhana *India* 25°1N 78°8E **42** G8
Khanka, L. *Asia* 45°0N 132°24E **30** B6
Khankendy = Xankändi
  Azerbaijan 39°52N 46°49E **44** B5
Khanna *India* 30°42N 76°16E **42** D7
Khanozai *Pakistan* 30°37N 67°19E **42** D2
Khanpur *Pakistan* 28°42N 70°35E **42** E4
Khanty-Mansiysk *Russia* 61°0N 69°0E **28** C7
Khao Laem △ *Thailand* 14°56N 98°31E **38** E2
Khao Laem Res. *Thailand* 14°50N 98°30E **38** E2
Khao Lak △ *Thailand* 8°38N 98°18E **39** H2
Khao Luang △ *Thailand* 8°34N 99°42E **39** H2
Khao Phlu *Thailand* 9°29N 99°59E **39** b
Khao Pu-Khao Ya △
  Thailand 7°26N 99°57E **39** J2
Khao Sam Roi Yot △
  Thailand 12°13N 99°57E **39** F2
Khao Sok △ *Thailand* 8°55N 98°38E **39** H2
Khao Yai △ *Thailand* 14°21N 101°29E **38** E3
Khaoen Si Nakarin △
  Thailand 14°47N 99°0E **38** E2
Khapalu *Pakistan* 35°10N 76°20E **43** B7
Khapcheranga *Russia* 49°42N 112°24E **29** E12
Khaptao △ *Nepal* 29°20N 81°10E **43** E9
Kharaghoda *India* 23°11N 71°46E **42** H4
Kharagpur *India* 22°20N 87°25E **43** H12
Kharan Kalat *Pakistan* 28°34N 65°21E **40** E4
Kharānaq *Iran* 32°20N 54°45E **45** C7
Kharda *India* 18°40N 75°34E **40** K9
Khardung La *India* 34°20N 77°43E **43** B7
Kharg = Khārk, Jazīreh-ye
  Iran 29°15N 50°28E **45** D6
Khārga, El Wâhat el
  Egypt 25°10N 30°35E **51** C12
Khargon *India* 21°45N 75°40E **40** J9
Khari ⇀ *India* 25°54N 74°31E **42** G6
Kharian *Pakistan* 32°49N 73°52E **42** C5
Khārk, Jazīreh-ye *Iran* 29°15N 50°28E **45** D6
Kharkiv *Ukraine* 49°58N 36°20E **19** E6
Kharkov = Kharkiv
  Ukraine 49°58N 36°20E **19** E6
Kharovsk *Russia* 59°56N 40°13E **18** C7
Kharsawangarh *India* 22°48N 85°50E **43** H11
Kharta *Turkey* 40°55N 29°7E **23** D13
Khartoum = El Khartûm
  Sudan 15°31N 32°35E **51** E12
Khartum *Canada* 45°15N 77°5W **82** A7
Khasan *Russia* 42°25N 130°40E **30** C5
Khāsh *Iran* 28°15N 61°15E **45** D9
Khashm el Girba *Sudan* 14°59N 35°58E **51** F13
Khaskovo *Bulgaria* 41°56N 25°30E **23** D11
Khatanga *Russia* 72°0N 102°20E **29** B11
Khatanga ⇀ *Russia* 72°55N 106°0E **29** B11
Khatauli *India* 29°17N 77°43E **42** E7
Khatra *India* 22°59N 86°51E **43** H12
Khātūnābād *Iran* 30°1N 55°25E **45** D7
Khatyrka *Russia* 62°3N 175°15E **29** C18
Khavda *India* 23°51N 69°43E **42** H3
Khawr Fakkān *U.A.E.* 25°21N 56°22E **45** E8
Khaybar, Ḥarrat
  Si. Arabia 25°45N 40°0E **44** E4
Khāzimiyah *Iraq* 34°46N 43°37E **44** C4
Khe Bo *Vietnam* 19°8N 104°41E **38** C5
Khe Long *Vietnam* 21°29N 104°46E **38** B5
Khe Sanh *Vietnam* 16°37N 106°45E **38** D6
Khed Brahma *India* 24°7N 73°5E **42** G5
Khekra *India* 28°52N 77°20E **42** E7
Khemarak Phouminville = Krong
  Kaoh Kong *Cambodia* 11°37N 102°59E **39** G4
Khemisset *Morocco* 33°50N 6°1W **50** B4
Khemmarat *Thailand* 16°10N 105°15E **38** D5
Khenāmān *Iran* 30°27N 56°29E **45** D8
Khenchela *Algeria* 35°28N 7°11E **50** A7
Khersān ⇀ *Iran* 31°33N 50°22E **45** D6
Kherson *Ukraine* 46°35N 32°35E **19** E5
Kheta ⇀ *Russia* 71°54N 102°6E **29** B11
Khewari *Pakistan* 26°36N 68°52E **42** F3
Khilchipur *India* 24°2N 76°34E **42** G7
Khilok *Russia* 51°30N 110°45E **29** D11
Khios = Hios *Greece* 38°27N 26°9E **23** E12
Khirsadoh *India* 22°11N 78°47E **43** H8
Khiuma = Hiiumaa
  Estonia 58°50N 22°45E **9** G20
Khiva *Uzbekistan* 41°30N 60°18E **28** E7
Khlong Khlung *Thailand* 16°12N 99°43E **38** D2
Khmelnik *Ukraine* 49°33N 27°58E **17** D14
Khmelnytskyy *Ukraine* 49°23N 27°0E **17** D14
Khmer Rep. = Cambodia ■
  Asia 12°15N 105°0E **38** F5

Khoai, Hon *Vietnam* 8°26N 104°50E **39** H5
Khodoriv *Ukraine* 49°24N 24°19E **17** D13
Khodzent = Khüjand
  Tajikistan 40°17N 69°37E **28** E7
Khojak Pass *Afghan.* 30°51N 66°34E **42** D2
Khok Kloi *Thailand* 8°17N 98°19E **39** a
Khok Pho *Thailand* 6°43N 101°6E **39** J3
Khok Samrong *Thailand* 15°3N 100°43E **38** E3
Kholm *Russia* 57°10N 31°15E **18** C5
Kholmsk *Russia* 47°40N 142°5E **29** E15
Khomas Hochland
  Namibia 22°40S 16°0E **56** C2
Khomeyn *Iran* 33°40N 50°7E **45** C6
Khomeynī Shahr *Iran* 32°41N 51°31E **45** C6
Khomodino *Botswana* 22°46S 23°52E **56** C3
Khon Kaen *Thailand* 16°30N 102°47E **38** D4
Khong ⇀ *Cambodia* 13°32N 105°58E **38** F5
Khong Sedone *Laos* 15°34N 105°49E **38** E5
Khonuu *Russia* 66°30N 143°12E **29** C15
Khoper ⇀ *Russia* 49°30N 42°20E **19** D7
Khorāsān □ *Iran* 34°0N 58°0E **45** C8
Khorat = Nakhon Ratchasima
  Thailand 14°59N 102°12E **38** E4
Khorat, Cao Nguyen
  Thailand 15°30N 102°50E **38** E4
Khorixas *Namibia* 20°16S 14°59E **56** C1
Khorramābād *Khorāsān,*
  Iran 35°6N 57°57E **45** C8
Khorramābād *Lorestān,*
  Iran 33°30N 48°25E **45** C6
Khorrāmshahr *Iran* 30°29N 48°15E **45** D6
Khorugh *Tajikistan* 37°30N 71°36E **28** F8
Khosravī *Iran* 30°48N 51°28E **45** D6
Khosrowābād *Khuzestan,*
  Iran 30°10N 48°25E **45** D6
Khosrowābād *Kordestān,*
  Iran 35°31N 47°38E **44** C5
Khost *Pakistan* 30°13N 67°35E **42** D2
Khosūyeh *Iran* 28°32N 54°26E **45** D7
Khotyn *Ukraine* 48°31N 26°27E **17** D14
Khouribga *Morocco* 32°58N 6°57W **50** B4
Khowst *Afghan.* 33°22N 69°58E **40** C6
Khowst □ *Afghan.* 33°20N 70°0E **40** C6
Khoyniki *Belarus* 51°54N 29°55E **17** C15
Khrysokhou B. *Cyprus* 35°6N 32°25E **25** D11
Khu Khan *Thailand* 14°42N 104°12E **38** E5
Khuan Wa *Thailand* 7°53N 98°17E **39** a
Khudzhand = Khüjand
  Tajikistan 40°17N 69°37E **28** E7
Khuff *Si. Arabia* 24°55N 44°53E **44** E5
Khūgīānī *Afghan.* 31°34N 66°32E **42** D2
Khuis *Botswana* 26°40S 21°49E **56** D3
Khuiyala *India* 27°9N 70°25E **42** F4
Khŭjand *Tajikistan* 40°17N 69°37E **28** E7
Khujner *India* 23°47N 76°36E **42** H7
Khulna *Bangla.* 22°45N 89°34E **41** H16
Khulna □ *Bangla.* 22°25N 89°35E **41** H16
Khumago *Botswana* 20°26S 24°32E **56** C3
Khunjerab △ *Pakistan* 36°40N 75°30E **43** A6
Khunjerab Pass = Kinjirap Daban
  Asia 36°40N 75°25E **40** A9
Khūnsorkh *Iran* 27°9N 56°7E **45** E8
Khunti *India* 23°5N 85°17E **43** H11
Khūr *Iran* 32°55N 58°18E **45** C8
Khurai *India* 24°3N 78°23E **42** G8
Khurayṣ *Si. Arabia* 25°6N 48°2E **45** E6
Khurja *India* 28°15N 77°58E **42** E7
Khūrmāl *Iraq* 35°18N 46°2E **44** C5
Khurr, Wādī al *Iraq* 32°3N 43°52E **44** C4
Khūsf *Iran* 32°46N 58°53E **45** C8
Khushab *Pakistan* 32°20N 72°20E **42** C5
Khust *Ukraine* 48°10N 23°18E **17** D12
Khutse △ *Botswana* 23°31S 24°12E **56** C3
Khuzdar *Pakistan* 27°52N 66°30E **42** F2
Khūzestān □ *Iran* 31°0N 49°0E **45** D6
Khvāf *Iran* 34°33N 60°8E **45** C9
Khvājeh *Iran* 38°9N 46°35E **44** B5
Khvānsār *Iran* 29°56N 54°8E **45** D7
Khvor *Iran* 33°45N 55°0E **45** C7
Khvorgū *Iran* 27°34N 56°27E **45** E8
Khvormūj *Iran* 28°40N 51°30E **45** D6
Khvoy *Iran* 38°35N 45°0E **44** B5
Khyber Pass *Afghan.* 34°10N 71°8E **42** B4
Kia *Fiji* 16°16S 179°8E **59** a
Kiabukwa
  Dem. Rep. of the Congo 8°40S 24°48E **55** D1
Kiama *Australia* 34°40S 150°50E **63** E5
Kiamba *Phil.* 6°2N 124°46E **37** C6
Kiambi
  Dem. Rep. of the Congo 7°15S 28°0E **54** D2
Kiambu *Kenya* 1°8S 36°50E **54** C4
Kiangara *Madag.* 17°58S 47°2E **57** B8
Kiangsi = Jiangxi □
  China 27°30N 116°0E **33** D6
Kiangsu = Jiangsu □
  China 33°0N 120°0E **35** H11
Kibale △ *Uganda* 0°16N 30°18E **54** B3
Kibanga Port *Uganda* 0°10N 32°58E **54** B3
Kibara *Tanzania* 2°8S 33°30E **54** C3
Kibare, Mts.
  Dem. Rep. of the Congo 8°25S 27°10E **54** D2
Kibira *Burundi* 3°30S 30°24E **54** C2
Kibombo *Tanzania* 3°57S 25°53E **54** C2
Kibondo *Tanzania* 3°35S 30°45E **54** C3
Kibre Mengist *Ethiopia* 5°54N 38°59E **47** F2
Kibris = Cyprus ■ *Asia* 35°0N 33°0E **25** E12
Kibumbu *Burundi* 3°32S 29°45E **54** C2
Kibuye *Burundi* 3°39S 29°59E **54** C2
Kibuye *Rwanda* 2°3S 29°21E **54** C2
Kibwesa *Tanzania* 6°30S 29°58E **54** D2
Kibwezi *Kenya* 2°27S 37°57E **54** C4
Kichha *India* 28°53N 79°30E **43** E8
Kichha ⇀ *India* 28°41N 79°18E **43** E8
Kichmengskiy Gorodok
  Russia 59°59N 45°48E **18** B8

Kicking Horse Pass
  Canada 51°28N 116°16W **70** C5
Kidal *Mali* 18°26N 1°22E **50** E6
Kidderminster *U.K.* 52°24N 2°15W **13** E5
Kidepo Valley △ *Uganda* 3°52N 33°50E **54** B3
Kidete *Tanzania* 6°25S 37°17E **54** D4
Kidnappers, C. *N.Z.* 39°38S 177°5E **59** C6
Kidsgrove *U.K.* 53°5N 2°14W **12** D5
Kidston *Australia* 18°52S 144°8E **62** B3
Kidugallo *Tanzania* 6°49S 38°15E **54** D4
Kiel *Germany* 54°19N 10°8E **16** A6
Kiel Canal = Nord-Ostsee-Kanal
  Germany 54°12N 9°32E **16** A5
Kielce *Poland* 50°52N 20°42E **17** C11
Kielder Water *U.K.* 55°11N 2°31W **12** B5
Kieler Bucht *Germany* 54°35N 10°25E **16** A6
Kien Binh *Vietnam* 9°55N 105°19E **39** H5
Kien Tan *Vietnam* 10°7N 105°17E **39** G5
Kienge
  Dem. Rep. of the Congo 10°30S 27°30E **55** E2
Kiev = Kyyiv *Ukraine* 50°30N 30°28E **17** C16
Kiffa *Mauritania* 16°37N 11°24W **50** E3
Kifrī *Iraq* 34°45N 45°0E **44** C5
Kigali *Rwanda* 1°59S 30°4E **54** C3
Kigarama *Tanzania* 1°1S 31°50E **54** C3
Kigezi △ *Uganda* 0°34S 29°55E **54** C2
Kigoma □ *Tanzania* 5°0S 30°0E **54** D3
Kigoma-Ujiji *Tanzania* 4°55S 29°36E **54** C2
Kigomasha, Ras *Tanzania* 4°58S 38°58E **54** C4
Kiǧzı *Turkey* 38°18N 43°25E **44** B4
Kihnu *Estonia* 58°9N 24°1E **9** G21
Kii-Sanchi *Japan* 34°20N 136°0E **31** G8
Kii-Suidō *Japan* 33°40N 134°45E **31** H7
Kiira Dam *Uganda* 0°25N 33°0E **54** B3
Kikaiga-Shima *Japan* 28°19N 129°59E **31** K4
Kikinda *Serbia* 45°50N 20°30E **23** B9
Kikládhes = Cyclades
  Greece 37°0N 24°30E **23** F11
Kikwit
  Dem. Rep. of the Congo 5°0S 18°45E **52** E3
Kilar *India* 33°6N 76°25E **42** C7
Kīlauea Caldera *U.S.A.* 19°25N 155°17W **74** b
Kilbeggan *Ireland* 53°22N 7°30W **10** C4
Kilbrannan Sd. *U.K.* 55°37N 5°26W **11** F3
Kilchu *N. Korea* 40°57N 129°25E **35** D15
Kilcoy *Australia* 26°59S 152°30E **63** D5
Kildare *Ireland* 53°9N 6°55W **10** C5
Kildare □ *Ireland* 53°10N 6°50W **10** C5
Kildinstroy *Russia* 68°48N 33°6E **8** B25
Kilfinnane *Ireland* 52°21N 8°28W **10** D3
Kilgarvan *Ireland* 51°54N 9°27W **10** E2
Kilgore *U.S.A.* 32°23N 94°53W **84** E7
Kilgoris *Kenya* 1°0S 34°53E **54** C3
Kilifi *Kenya* 3°40S 39°48E **54** C4
Kilimanjaro *Tanzania* 3°7S 37°20E **54** C4
Kilimanjaro □ *Tanzania* 4°0S 38°0E **54** C4
Kilindini *Kenya* 4°4S 39°40E **54** C4
Kilis *Turkey* 36°42N 37°6E **44** B3
Kiliya *Ukraine* 45°28N 29°16E **17** F15
Kilkee *Ireland* 52°41N 9°39W **10** D2
Kilkeel *U.K.* 54°4N 6°0W **10** B5
Kilkenny *Ireland* 52°39N 7°15W **10** D4
Kilkenny □ *Ireland* 52°35N 7°15W **10** D4
Kilkieran B. *Ireland* 53°20N 9°41W **10** C2
Kilkis *Greece* 40°58N 22°57E **23** D10
Killala *Ireland* 54°13N 9°12W **10** B2
Killala B. *Ireland* 54°16N 9°8W **10** B2
Killaloe *Canada* 45°33N 77°25W **82** A7
Killaloe *Ireland* 52°48N 8°28W **10** D3
Killarney *Australia* 28°20S 152°18E **63** D5
Killarney *Canada* 45°55N 81°30W **72** C3
Killarney *Ireland* 52°4N 9°30W **10** D2
Killarney △ *Ireland* 52°0N 9°33W **10** D2
Killary Harbour *Ireland* 53°38N 9°52W **10** C2
Killdeer *U.S.A.* 47°22N 102°45W **80** B2
Killeen *U.S.A.* 31°7N 97°44W **84** F6
Killin *U.K.* 56°28N 4°19W **11** E4
Killiney *Ireland* 53°15N 6°7W **10** C5
Killington Pk. *U.S.A.* 43°36N 72°49W **83** C12
Killini *Greece* 37°54N 22°25E **23** F10
Killorglin *Ireland* 52°6N 9°47W **10** D2
Killybegs *Ireland* 54°38N 8°26W **10** B3
Kilmarnock *U.K.* 55°37N 4°29W **11** F4
Kilmore *Australia* 37°25S 144°53E **63** F3
Kilmore Quay *Ireland* 52°10N 6°36W **10** D5
Kilondo *Tanzania* 9°45S 34°20E **55** D3
Kilosa *Tanzania* 6°48S 37°0E **54** D4
Kilrush *Ireland* 52°38N 9°29W **10** D2
Kilwa Kisiwani *Tanzania* 8°58S 39°32E **55** D4
Kilwa Kivinje *Tanzania* 8°45S 39°25E **55** D4
Kilwa Masoko *Tanzania* 8°55S 39°30E **55** D4
Kilwinning *U.K.* 55°39N 4°43W **11** F4
Kim *U.S.A.* 37°15N 103°21W **77** H12
Kimaam *Indonesia* 7°58S 138°53E **37** F9
Kimamba *Tanzania* 6°45S 37°10E **54** D4
Kimba *Australia* 33°8S 136°23E **63** E2
Kimball *Nebr., U.S.A.* 41°14N 103°40W **80** E2
Kimball *S. Dak., U.S.A.* 43°45N 98°57W **80** D4
Kimberley *Australia* 16°20S 127°0E **60** C4
Kimberley *B.C., Canada* 49°40N 115°59W **70** D5
Kimberley *Ont., Canada* 44°23N 80°32W **82** B4
Kimberley *S. Africa* 28°43S 24°46E **56** D3
Kimberly *U.S.A.* 42°32N 114°22W **76** E6
Kimch'aek *N. Korea* 40°40N 129°10E **35** D15
Kimchŏn = Gimcheon
  S. Korea 35°14N 128°53E **35** G15
Kimmirut *Canada* 62°50N 69°50W **69** C13
Kimpese
  Dem. Rep. of the Congo 5°35S 14°26E **52** F2
Kimry *Russia* 56°55N 37°15E **18** C6
Kinabalu, Gunung
  Malaysia 6°3N 116°14E **36** C5
Kinaskan L. *Canada* 57°38N 130°8W **70** B2
Kinbasket L. *Canada* 52°0N 118°10W **70** C5
Kincardine *Canada* 44°10N 81°40W **82** B3
Kincolith *Canada* 55°0N 129°57W **70** C3

Kinda Dem. Rep. of the Congo 9°18S 25°4E 55 D2
Kinde U.S.A. 43°56N 83°0W 82 C2
Kinder Scout U.K. 53°24N 1°52W 12 D6
Kindersley Canada 51°30N 109°10W 71 C7
Kindia Guinea 10°0N 12°52W 50 F3
Kindu
  Dem. Rep. of the Congo 2°55S 25°50E 54 C2
Kineshma Russia 57°30N 42°5E 18 C7
Kinesi Tanzania 1°25S 33°50E 54 C3
King, L. Australia 33°10S 119°35E 61 F2
King, Mt. Australia 25°10S 147°30E 62 D4
King City U.S.A. 36°13N 121°8W 78 J5
King C. → Australia 24°35S 139°30E 62 C2
King Edward →
  Australia 14°14S 126°35E 60 B4
King Edward Point
  S. Georgia 54°17S 36°30W 96 G9
King Frederick VI Land = Kong
  Frederik VI Kyst
  Greenland 63°0N 43°0W 4 C5
King George B. Falk. Is. 51°30S 60°30W 96 G4
King George I. Antarctica 60°0S 60°0W 5 C18
King George Is. Canada 57°20N 80°30W 69 D11
King George Sd. Australia 35°5S 118°0E 61 G2
King I. = Kadan Kyun
  Burma 12°30N 98°20E 38 F2
King I. Australia 39°50S 144°0E 63 F3
King I. Canada 52°10N 127°40W 70 C3
King Khalid Military City =
  Madinat al Malik Khālid al
  Askarīyah Si. Arabia 27°54N 45°31E 44 E5
King Leopold Ranges
  Australia 17°30S 125°45E 60 C4
King of Prussia U.S.A. 40°5N 75°23W 83 F9
King Sd. Australia 16°50S 123°20E 60 C3
King Sejong Antarctica 62°30S 58°0W 5 C18
King William I. Canada 69°10N 97°25W 68 C10
King William's Town
  S. Africa 32°51S 27°22E 56 E4
Kingait Canada 64°14N 76°32W 69 C12
Kingaok = Bathurst Inlet
  Canada 66°50N 108°1W 68 C9
Kingaroy Australia 26°32S 151°51E 63 D5
Kingfisher U.S.A. 35°52N 97°56W 84 D6
Kingirbān Iraq 34°40N 44°54E 44 C5
Kingisepp = Kuressaare
  Estonia 58°15N 22°30E 9 G20
Kingisepp Russia 59°25N 28°40E 9 G23
Kingman Ariz., U.S.A. 35°12N 114°4W 79 K12
Kingman Kans., U.S.A. 37°39N 98°7W 80 G4
Kingoonya Australia 30°55S 135°19E 63 E2
Kingri Pakistan 30°27N 69°49E 42 D3
Kings → U.S.A. 36°3N 119°50W 78 J7
Kings Canyon Australia 24°15S 131°34E 60 D5
Kings Canyon △
  U.S.A. 36°50N 118°40W 78 J8
King's Lynn U.K. 52°45N 0°24E 12 E8
Kings Park U.S.A. 40°53N 73°16W 83 F11
Kings Peak U.S.A. 40°46N 110°23W 76 F8
Kingsbridge U.K. 50°17N 3°47W 13 G4
Kingsburg U.S.A. 36°31N 119°33W 78 J7
Kingscote Australia 35°40S 137°38E 63 F2
Kingscourt Ireland 53°55N 6°48W 10 C5
Kingsland U.S.A. 30°48N 81°41W 85 F14
Kingsport U.S.A. 36°33N 82°33W 85 C13
Kingston Canada 44°14N 76°30W 83 B8
Kingston Jamaica 18°0N 76°50W 88 a
Kingston N.Z. 45°20S 168°43E 59 F2
Kingston N.H., U.S.A. 42°56N 71°3W 83 D13
Kingston N.Y., U.S.A. 41°56N 73°59W 83 E11
Kingston Pa., U.S.A. 41°16N 75°54W 83 E9
Kingston R.I., U.S.A. 41°29N 71°30W 83 E13
Kingston Pk. U.S.A. 35°44N 115°55W 79 K11
Kingston South East
  Australia 36°51S 139°55E 63 F2
Kingston upon Hull U.K. 53°45N 0°21W 12 D7
Kingston upon Hull □
  U.K. 53°45N 0°21W 12 D7
Kingston-upon-Thames □
  U.K. 51°24N 0°17W 13 F7
Kingstown St. Vincent 13°10N 61°10W 89 D7
Kingstree U.S.A. 33°40N 79°50W 85 E15
Kingsville Canada 42°2N 82°45W 82 D2
Kingsville U.S.A. 27°31N 97°52W 84 H6
Kingussie U.K. 57°6N 4°2W 11 D4
Kingwood U.S.A. 30°2N 95°6W 84 F7
Kınık Turkey 39°6N 27°24E 23 E12
Kinistino Canada 52°57N 105°2W 71 C7
Kinjiup Daban Asia 36°0N 75°25E 43 A9
Kinkala Congo 4°18S 14°49E 52 E2
Kinki □ Japan 33°45N 136°0E 31 H8
Kinleith N.Z. 38°20S 175°56E 59 C5
Kinlochleven U.K. 56°43N 5°0W 11 E4
Kinmount Canada 44°48N 78°45W 82 B6
Kinna Sweden 57°32N 12°42E 9 H15
Kinnairds Hd. U.K. 57°43N 2°1W 11 D6
Kino Nuevo Mexico 28°52N 112°3W 86 B2
Kinoje → Canada 52°8N 81°25W 72 B3
Kinomoto Japan 35°30N 136°13E 31 G8
Kinoni Uganda 0°41S 30°28E 54 C3
Kinoosao Canada 57°5N 102°1W 71 B8
Kinross U.K. 56°13N 3°25W 11 E5
Kinsale Ireland 51°42N 8°31W 10 E3
Kinsale, Old Hd. of
  Ireland 51°37N 8°33W 10 E3
Kinsha = Chang Jiang →
  China 31°48N 121°10E 33 C7
Kinshasa
  Dem. Rep. of the Congo 4°20S 15°15E 52 E3
Kinsley U.S.A. 37°55N 99°25W 80 G4
Kinsman U.S.A. 41°26N 80°35W 82 E4
Kinston U.S.A. 35°16N 77°35W 85 D16
Kintamani Indonesia 8°14S 115°19E 37 J18
Kintore U.K. 57°14N 2°20W 11 D6
Kintore Ra. Australia 23°15S 128°47E 60 D4
Kintyre U.K. 55°30N 5°35W 11 F3

Kintyre, Mull of U.K. 55°17N 5°47W 11 F3
Kinushseo → Canada 55°15N 83°45W 72 A3
Kinuso Canada 55°20N 115°25W 70 B5
Kinvarra Ireland 53°8N 8°56W 10 C3
Kinyangiri Tanzania 4°25S 34°37E 54 C3
Kinyeti Sudan 3°57N 32°54E 54 B3
Kinzua U.S.A. 41°52N 78°58W 82 E6
Kiosk Canada 46°6N 78°53W 72 C4
Kipahigan L. Canada 55°20N 101°55W 71 B8
Kipanga Tanzania 6°15S 35°20E 54 D4
Kiparissia Greece 37°15N 21°40E 23 F9
Kiparissiakos Kolpos
  Greece 37°25N 21°25E 23 F9
Kipawa, L. Canada 46°50N 79°0W 72 C4
Kipembawe Tanzania 7°38S 33°27E 54 D3
Kipengere Ra. Tanzania 9°12S 34°15E 55 D3
Kipili Tanzania 7°28S 30°32E 54 D3
Kipini Kenya 2°30S 40°32E 54 C5
Kipling Canada 50°6N 102°38W 71 C8
Kippure Ireland 53°11N 6°21W 10 C5
Kipushi
  Dem. Rep. of the Congo 11°48S 27°12E 55 E2
Kiranomena Madag. 18°17S 46°2E 57 B8
Kirensk Russia 57°50N 107°55E 29 D11
Kirghiz Range Asia 42°40N 73°40E 32 B2
Kirghizia = Kyrgyzstan ■
  Asia 42°0N 75°0E 28 E8
Kirgiziya Steppe Eurasia 50°0N 55°0E 19 E10
Kiribati ■ Pac. Oc. 3°0S 180°0E 58 B10
Kırıkkale Turkey 39°51N 33°32E 19 G5
Kirillov Russia 59°49N 38°24E 18 C6
Kirin = Jilin China 43°44N 126°30E 35 C14
Kirinyaga = Kenya, Mt.
  Kenya 0°10S 37°18E 54 C4
Kirirom △ Cambodia 11°18N 104°5E 39 G5
Kirishima Yaku △
  Japan 31°24N 130°50E 31 J5
Kiritimati Kiribati 1°58N 157°27W 65 G12
Kirkby U.K. 53°30N 2°54W 12 D5
Kirkby-in-Ashfield U.K. 53°6N 1°14W 12 D6
Kirkby Lonsdale U.K. 54°12N 2°36W 12 C5
Kirkby Stephen U.K. 54°29N 2°21W 12 C5
Kirkcaldy U.K. 56°7N 3°9W 11 E5
Kirkcudbright U.K. 54°50N 4°2W 11 G4
Kirkee India 18°34N 73°56E 40 K8
Kirkenes Norway 69°40N 30°5E 8 B24
Kirkfield Canada 44°34N 78°59W 82 B6
Kirkintilloch U.K. 55°56N 4°8W 11 F4
Kirkjubæjarklaustur
  Iceland 63°47N 18°4W 8 E4
Kirkkonummi Finland 60°8N 24°26E 9 F21
Kirkland U.S.A. 47°40N 122°12W 78 C4
Kirkland Lake Canada 48°9N 80°2W 72 C3
Kırklareli Turkey 41°44N 27°15E 23 D12
Kirksville U.S.A. 40°12N 92°35W 80 E7
Kirkük Iraq 35°30N 44°21E 44 C5
Kirkwall U.K. 58°59N 2°58W 11 C6
Kirkwood S. Africa 33°22S 25°15E 56 E4
Kirov Russia 58°35N 49°40E 18 C8
Kirovabad = Gäncä
  Azerbaijan 40°45N 46°20E 19 F8
Kirovograd = Kirovohrad
  Ukraine 48°35N 32°20E 19 E5
Kirovohrad Ukraine 48°35N 32°20E 19 E5
Kirovsk Russia 67°32N 33°41E 18 A5
Kirovskiy Kamchatka,
  Russia 54°27N 155°42E 29 D16
Kirovskiy Primorsk,
  Russia 45°7N 133°30E 30 B6
Kirriemuir U.K. 56°41N 3°1W 11 E5
Kirsanov Russia 52°35N 42°40E 18 D7
Kırşehir Turkey 39°14N 34°5E 44 B2
Kirthar △ Pakistan 25°45N 67°30E 42 F2
Kirthar Range Pakistan 27°0N 67°0E 42 F2
Kirtland U.S.A. 36°44N 108°21W 77 H9
Kiruna Sweden 67°52N 20°15E 8 C19
Kirundu
  Dem. Rep. of the Congo 0°50S 25°35E 54 C2
Kiryū Japan 36°24N 139°20E 31 F9
Kisaga Tanzania 4°30S 34°23E 54 C3
Kisanga
  Dem. Rep. of the Congo 2°30N 26°35E 54 B2
Kisangani
  Dem. Rep. of the Congo 0°35N 25°15E 54 B2
Kisar Indonesia 8°5S 127°10E 37 F7
Kisarawe Tanzania 6°53S 39°0E 54 D4
Kisarazu Japan 35°23N 139°55E 31 G9
Kiselevsk Russia 54°0N 86°39E 28 D9
Kishanganga →
  Pakistan 34°18N 73°28E 43 B5
Kishanganj India 26°3N 88°14E 43 F13
Kishangarh Raj., India 26°34N 74°52E 42 F6
Kishangarh Raj., India 27°50N 70°30E 42 F4
Kishinev = Chişinău
  Moldova 47°2N 28°50E 17 E15
Kishiwada Japan 34°28N 135°22E 31 G7
Kishtwar India 33°20N 75°48E 42 C6
Kisigo → Tanzania 6°27S 34°17E 54 D3
Kisii Kenya 0°40S 34°45E 54 C3
Kisiju Tanzania 7°23S 39°19E 54 D4
Kisizi Uganda 1°0S 29°58E 54 C2
Kiskőrös Hungary 46°37N 19°20E 17 E10
Kiskunfélegyháza
  Hungary 46°42N 19°53E 17 E10
Kiskunhalas Hungary 46°28N 19°37E 17 E10
Kislovodsk Russia 43°50N 42°45E 19 F7
Kismaayo Somali Rep. 0°22S 42°32E 47 H3
Kiso-Gawa → Japan 35°20N 136°45E 31 G8
Kiso-Sammyaku Japan 35°45N 137°45E 31 G8
Kisofukushima Japan 35°52N 137°43E 31 G8
Kisoro Uganda 1°17S 29°48E 54 C2
Kissamos = Kasteli
  Greece 35°29N 23°38E 25 D5
Kissamos, Kolpos Greece 35°30N 23°38E 25 D5
Kissidougou Guinea 9°5N 10°5W 50 G3

Kissimmee U.S.A. 28°18N 81°24W 85 G14
Kissimmee → U.S.A. 27°9N 80°52W 85 H14
Kississing L. Canada 55°10N 101°20W 71 B8
Kisumu Kenya 0°3S 34°45E 54 C3
Kiswani Tanzania 4°5S 37°57E 54 C4
Kiswere Tanzania 9°27S 39°30E 54 D4
Kit Carson U.S.A. 38°46N 102°48W 76 G12
Kita Mali 13°5N 9°25W 50 F4
Kitaibaraki Japan 36°50N 140°45E 31 F10
Kitakami Japan 39°20N 141°10E 30 E10
Kitakami-Gawa →
  Japan 38°25N 141°19E 30 E10
Kitakami-Sammyaku
  Japan 39°30N 141°30E 30 E10
Kitakata Japan 37°39N 139°52E 30 F9
Kitakyūshū Japan 33°50N 130°50E 31 H5
Kitale Kenya 1°0N 35°0E 54 B4
Kitami Japan 43°48N 143°54E 30 C11
Kitami-Sammyaku
  Japan 44°22N 142°43E 30 B11
Kitangiri, L. Tanzania 4°5S 34°20E 54 C3
Kitaya Tanzania 10°38S 40°8E 55 E5
Kitchener Canada 43°27N 80°29W 82 C4
Kitee Finland 62°5N 30°8E 8 E24
Kitega = Gitega Burundi 3°26S 29°56E 54 C2
Kitengo
  Dem. Rep. of the Congo 7°26S 24°8E 54 D1
Kitgum Uganda 3°17N 32°52E 54 B3
Kithira = Kythira Greece 36°8N 23°0E 23 F10
Kithnos Greece 37°26N 24°27E 23 F11
Kiti Cyprus 34°50N 33°34E 25 E12
Kiti, C. Cyprus 34°48N 33°36E 25 E12
Kitimat Canada 54°3N 128°38W 70 C3
Kitinen → Finland 67°14N 27°27E 8 C22
Kitsuki Japan 33°25N 131°37E 31 H5
Kittakittaooloo, L.
  Australia 28°3S 138°14E 63 D2
Kittanning U.S.A. 40°49N 79°31W 82 F5
Kittatinny Mt. U.S.A. 41°19N 74°39W 83 F10
Kittery U.S.A. 43°5N 70°45W 83 C14
Kittilä Finland 67°40N 24°51E 8 C21
Kitui Kenya 1°17S 38°0E 54 C4
Kitwanga Canada 55°6N 128°4W 70 B3
Kitwe Zambia 12°54S 28°13E 55 E2
Kivarli India 24°33N 72°46E 42 G5
Kivertsi Ukraine 50°50N 25°28E 17 C13
Kividhes Cyprus 34°46N 32°51E 25 E11
Kivu, L.
  Dem. Rep. of the Congo 1°48S 29°0E 54 C2
Kiwirrkurra Australia 22°49S 127°45E 60 D4
Kiyev = Kyyiv Ukraine 50°30N 30°28E 17 C16
Kiyevskoye Vdkhr. = Kyyivske
  Vdskh. Ukraine 51°0N 30°25E 17 C16
Kizel Russia 59°3N 57°40E 18 C10
Kiziguru Rwanda 1°46S 30°23E 54 C3
Kızıl Irmak → Turkey 41°44N 35°58E 19 F6
Kizil Jilga China 35°26N 78°50E 43 B8
Kızıldağ △ Turkey 38°5N 31°20E 44 B1
Kızıltepe Turkey 37°12N 40°35E 44 B4
Kizimkazi Tanzania 6°28S 39°30E 54 D4
Kizlyar Russia 43°51N 46°40E 19 F8
Kizyl-Arvat = Serdar
  Turkmenistan 39°4N 56°23E 45 B8
Kjölur Iceland 64°50N 19°25E 8 D4
Kladno Czech Rep. 50°10N 14°7E 16 C8
Klaeng Thailand 12°47N 101°39E 38 F3
Klagenfurt Austria 46°38N 14°20E 16 E8
Klaipėda Lithuania 55°43N 21°10E 9 J19
Klaksvík Færoe Is. 62°14N 6°35W 8 E9
Klamath → U.S.A. 41°33N 124°5W 76 F1
Klamath Falls U.S.A. 42°13N 121°46W 76 E3
Klamath Mts. U.S.A. 41°50N 123°20W 76 F2
Klamono Indonesia 1°8S 131°30E 37 E8
Klang Malaysia 3°2N 101°26E 39 L3
Klappan → Canada 58°0N 129°43W 70 B3
Klarälven → Sweden 59°23N 13°32E 9 G15
Klatovy Czech Rep. 49°23N 13°18E 16 D7
Klawer S. Africa 31°44S 18°36E 56 E2
Klazienaveen Neths. 52°44N 7°0E 15 B6
Kleena Kleene Canada 52°0N 124°59W 70 C4
Klein-Karas Namibia 27°33S 18°7E 56 D2
Klerksdorp S. Africa 26°53S 26°38E 56 D4
Kletsk = Klyetsk Belarus 53°5N 26°45E 17 B14
Kletskiy Russia 49°16N 43°11E 19 E7
Klickitat U.S.A. 45°49N 121°9W 76 D3
Klickitat → U.S.A. 45°42N 121°17W 78 E5
Klidhes Cyprus 35°42N 34°36E 25 D13
Klinaklini → Canada 51°21N 125°40W 70 C3
Klip → S. Africa 27°3S 29°3E 57 D4
Klipdale S. Africa 34°19S 19°57E 56 E2
Klipplaat S. Africa 33°1S 24°22E 56 E3
Klodzko Poland 50°28N 16°38E 17 C9
Klong Wang Chao △
  Thailand 16°20N 99°9E 38 D2
Klouto Togo 6°57N 0°44E 50 G6
Kluane △ Canada 60°45N 139°30W 70 A1
Kluane L. Canada 61°15N 138°40W 68 C6
Kluang Malaysia 2°3N 103°18E 39 L4
Kluczbork Poland 50°58N 18°12E 17 C10
Klukwan U.S.A. 59°24N 135°54W 70 B1
Klungkung Indonesia 8°32S 115°24E 37 K18
Klyetsk Belarus 53°5N 26°45E 17 B14
Klyuchevskaya, Gora
  Russia 55°50N 160°30E 29 D17
Klyuchi Russia 56°18N 160°51E 29 D17
Knaresborough U.K. 54°1N 1°28W 12 C6
Knee L. Man., Canada 55°3N 94°45W 72 A1
Knee L. Sask., Canada 55°51N 107°0W 71 B7
Knight Inlet Canada 50°45N 125°40W 70 C3
Knighton U.K. 52°21N 3°3W 13 E4
Knights Ferry U.S.A. 37°50N 120°40W 78 H6
Knights Landing
  U.S.A. 38°48N 121°43W 78 G5
Knob, C. Australia 34°32S 119°16E 61 F2
Knock Ireland 53°48N 8°55W 10 C3
Knockmealdown Mts.
  Ireland 52°14N 7°56W 10 D4

Knokke-Heist Belgium 51°21N 3°17E 15 C3
Knossos Greece 35°16N 25°10E 25 D7
Knowlton Canada 45°13N 72°31W 83 A12
Knox U.S.A. 41°18N 86°37W 80 E10
Knox Coast Antarctica 66°30S 108°0E 5 C8
Knoxville Iowa, U.S.A. 41°19N 93°6W 80 E7
Knoxville Pa., U.S.A. 41°57N 77°27W 82 E7
Knoxville Tenn., U.S.A. 35°58N 83°55W 85 D13
Knud Rasmussen Land
  Greenland 78°0N 60°0W 4 A5
Knysna S. Africa 34°2S 23°2E 56 E3
Ko Kha Thailand 18°11N 99°24E 38 C2
Ko Tarutao △ Thailand 6°31N 99°26E 38 c
Ko Yao Thailand 8°7N 98°35E 39 a
Koartac = Quaqtaq
  Canada 60°55N 69°40W 69 C13
Koba Indonesia 6°37S 134°37E 37 F8
Kobarid Slovenia 46°15N 13°30E 16 E7
Kobayashi Japan 31°56N 130°59E 31 J5
Kōbe Japan 34°41N 135°13E 31 G7
København Denmark 55°40N 12°26E 9 J15
Kōbi-Sho Japan 25°56N 123°41E 31 M1
Koblenz Germany 50°21N 7°36E 16 C4
Kobryn Belarus 52°15N 24°22E 17 B13
Kocaeli Turkey 40°45N 29°50E 19 F4
Kočani Macedonia 41°55N 22°25E 23 D10
Koch Bihar India 26°22N 89°29E 41 F16
Kochas India 25°15N 83°56E 43 G10
Kochi = Cochin India 9°58N 76°20E 40 Q10
Kōchi Japan 33°30N 133°35E 31 H6
Kōchi □ Japan 33°40N 133°30E 31 H6
Kochiu = Gejiu China 23°20N 103°10E 32 D5
Kodarma India 24°28N 85°36E 43 G11
Kodiak U.S.A. 57°47N 152°24W 74 a
Kodiak I. U.S.A. 57°30N 152°45W 74 a
Kodinar India 20°46N 70°46E 42 J4
Kodinsk Russia 58°40N 99°0E 29 D11
Koedoesberge S. Africa 32°40S 20°11E 56 E3
Koes Namibia 26°0S 19°15E 56 D2
Koffiefontein S. Africa 29°30S 25°0E 56 D4
Kofiau Indonesia 1°11S 129°50E 37 E7
Koforidua Ghana 6°3N 0°17W 50 G5
Kōfu Japan 35°40N 138°30E 31 G9
Koga Japan 36°11N 139°43E 31 F9
Kogaluc → Canada 56°12N 61°44W 73 A7
Køge Denmark 55°27N 12°11E 9 J15
Kogon Uzbekistan 39°43N 64°33E 28 F7
Koh-i-Khurd Afghan. 33°30N 65°59E 42 C1
Koh-i-Maran Pakistan 29°18N 66°50E 42 E2
Kohat Pakistan 33°40N 71°29E 42 C4
Kohima India 25°35N 94°10E 41 G19
Kohkīlūyeh va Būyer Aḥmadi □
  Iran 31°30N 50°30E 45 D6
Kohler Ra. Antarctica 77°0S 110°0W 5 D15
Kohlu Pakistan 29°54N 69°15E 42 E3
Kohtla-Järve Estonia 59°20N 27°20E 9 G22
Koi Sanjaq Iraq 36°5N 44°38E 44 B5
Koillismaa Finland 65°44N 28°36E 8 D23
Koin N. Korea 40°28N 126°18E 35 D14
Kojō N. Korea 38°58N 127°58E 35 E14
Kojonup Australia 33°48S 117°10E 61 F2
Kojūr Iran 36°23N 51°43E 45 B6
Kokand = Qŭqon
  Uzbekistan 40°31N 70°56E 28 E8
Kokas Indonesia 2°42S 132°26E 37 E8
Kokchetav = Kökshetaū
  Kazakhstan 53°20N 69°25E 28 D7
Kokemäenjoki →
  Finland 61°32N 21°44E 8 F19
Kokkola Finland 63°50N 23°8E 8 E20
Koko Kyunzu Burma 14°10N 93°25E 41 M18
Kokomo U.S.A. 40°29N 86°8W 80 E10
Koksan N. Korea 38°46N 126°40E 35 E14
Kökshetaū Kazakhstan 53°20N 69°25E 28 D7
Koksoak → Canada 58°30N 68°10W 69 D13
Kokstad S. Africa 30°32S 29°29E 57 E4
Kokubu Japan 31°44N 130°46E 31 J5
Kola Indonesia 5°35S 134°30E 37 F8
Kola Russia 68°45N 33°8E 18 A5
Kola Pen. = Kolskiy Poluostrov
  Russia 67°30N 38°0E 18 A6
Kolachi → Pakistan 27°8N 67°2E 42 F2
Kolahoi India 34°12N 75°22E 43 B6
Kolaka Indonesia 4°3S 121°46E 37 E6
Kolar India 13°12N 78°15E 40 N11
Kolar Gold Fields India 12°58N 78°16E 40 N11
Kolaras India 25°14N 77°36E 42 G6
Kolari Finland 67°20N 23°48E 8 C20
Kolayat India 27°50N 72°50E 42 F5
Kolda Senegal 12°55N 14°57W 50 F3
Kolding Denmark 55°30N 9°29E 9 J13
Kolepom = Dolak, Pulau
  Indonesia 8°0S 138°30E 37 F9
Kolguyev, Ostrov Russia 69°20N 48°30E 18 A8
Kolhapur India 16°43N 74°15E 40 L9
Kolimbia Greece 36°15N 28°10E 25 C10
Kolín Czech Rep. 50°2N 15°9E 16 C8
Kolkas rags Latvia 57°46N 22°37E 9 H20
Kolkata India 22°34N 88°21E 43 H13
Kollam = Quilon India 8°50N 76°38E 40 Q10
Kollum Neths. 53°17N 6°10E 15 A6
Köln Germany 50°56N 6°57E 16 C4
Koło Poland 52°14N 18°40E 17 B10
Kołobrzeg Poland 54°10N 15°35E 16 A8
Kolomna Russia 55°8N 38°45E 18 C6
Kolomyya Ukraine 48°31N 25°2E 17 D13
Kolonodale Indonesia 2°3S 121°25E 37 E6
Kolosib India 24°15N 92°45E 41 G18
Kolpashevo Russia 58°20N 83°5E 28 D9
Kolpino Russia 59°44N 30°39E 18 C5
Kolskiy Poluostrov
  Russia 67°30N 38°0E 18 A6
Kolskiy Zaliv Russia 69°23N 34°0E 8 B26
Kolwezi
  Dem. Rep. of the Congo 10°40S 25°25E 55 E2
Kolyma → Russia 69°30N 161°0E 29 C17

Kolymskoye Nagorye
  Russia 63°0N 157°0E 29 C16
Kôm Ombo Egypt 24°25N 32°52E 51 D12
Komandorskiye Is. =
  Komandorskiye Ostrova
  Russia 55°0N 167°0E 29 D17
Komandorskiye Ostrova
  Russia 55°0N 167°0E 29 D17
Kómárno Slovak Rep. 47°49N 18°5E 17 E10
Komatipoort S. Africa 25°25S 31°55E 57 D5
Komatou Yialou Cyprus 35°25N 34°8E 25 D13
Komatsu Japan 36°25N 136°30E 31 F8
Komatsushima Japan 34°0N 134°35E 31 H7
Komi □ Russia 64°0N 55°0E 18 B10
Kommunarsk = Alchevsk
  Ukraine 48°30N 38°45E 19 E6
Kommunizma, Pik = imeni Ismail
  Samani, Pik Tajikistan 39°0N 72°2E 28 F8
Komodo Indonesia 8°37S 119°20E 37 F5
Komoran, Pulau
  Indonesia 8°18S 138°45E 37 F9
Komoro Japan 36°19N 138°26E 31 F9
Komotini Greece 41°9N 25°26E 23 D11
Kompasberg S. Africa 31°45S 24°32E 56 E3
Kompong Cham
  Cambodia 12°0N 105°30E 39 G5
Kompong Chhnang = Kampong
  Chhnang Cambodia 12°20N 104°35E 39 G5
Kompong Chikreng
  Cambodia 13°5N 104°18E 38 F5
Kompong Kleang
  Cambodia 13°6N 104°8E 38 F5
Kompong Luong
  Cambodia 11°49N 104°48E 39 G5
Kompong Pranak
  Cambodia 13°35N 104°55E 38 F5
Kompong Som = Kampong Saom
  Cambodia 10°38N 103°30E 39 G4
Kompong Som, Chhung =
  Kampong Saom, Chaak
  Cambodia 10°50N 103°32E 39 G4
Kompong Speu
  Cambodia 11°26N 104°32E 39 G5
Kompong Sralau
  Cambodia 14°5N 105°46E 38 E5
Kompong Thom
  Cambodia 12°35N 104°51E 38 F5
Kompong Trabeck
  Cambodia 13°6N 105°14E 38 F5
Kompong Trabeck
  Cambodia 11°9N 105°28E 39 G5
Kompong Trach
  Cambodia 11°25N 105°48E 39 G5
Kompong Tralach
  Cambodia 11°54N 104°47E 39 G5
Komrat = Comrat
  Moldova 46°18N 28°40E 17 E15
Komsberg S. Africa 32°40S 20°45E 56 E3
Komsomolets, Ostrov
  Russia 80°30N 95°0E 29 A10
Komsomolsk-na-Amure
  Russia 50°30N 137°0E 33 A8
Kon Tum Vietnam 14°24N 108°0E 38 E7
Kon Tum, Plateau du
  Vietnam 14°30N 108°30E 38 E7
Konar □ Afghan. 34°30N 71°3E 40 B7
Konārī Iran 28°13N 51°36E 45 D6
Konch India 26°0N 79°10E 43 G8
Konde Tanzania 4°57S 39°45E 54 C4
Kondinin Australia 32°34S 118°8E 61 F2
Kondoa Tanzania 4°55S 35°50E 54 C4
Kondopaga Russia 62°12N 34°17E 18 B5
Kondratyevo Russia 57°22N 98°15E 29 D10
Köneürgench
  Turkmenistan 42°19N 59°10E 28 E6
Konevo Russia 62°8N 39°20E 18 B6
Kong = Khong →
  Cambodia 13°32N 105°58E 38 F5
Kong Ivory C. 8°54N 4°36W 50 G5
Kong, Koh Cambodia 11°20N 103°0E 39 G4
Kong Christian IX Land
  Greenland 68°0N 36°0W 4 C6
Kong Christian X Land
  Greenland 74°0N 29°0W 4 B6
Kong Frederik IX Land
  Greenland 67°0N 52°0W 4 C5
Kong Frederik VI Kyst
  Greenland 63°0N 43°0W 4 C5
Kong Frederik VIII Land
  Greenland 78°30N 26°0W 4 B6
Kong Oscar Fjord
  Greenland 72°20N 24°0W 4 B6
Konglu Burma 27°13N 97°57E 41 F20
Kongola Namibia 17°45S 23°20E 56 B3
Kongolo Kasai-Or.,
  Dem. Rep. of the Congo 5°26S 24°49E 54 D1
Kongolo Katanga,
  Dem. Rep. of the Congo 5°22S 27°0E 54 D2
Kongsberg Norway 59°39N 9°39E 9 G13
Kongsvinger Norway 60°12N 12°2E 9 F15
Kongur Shan China 38°34N 75°18E 32 C2
Kongwa Tanzania 6°11S 36°26E 54 D4
Koni
  Dem. Rep. of the Congo 10°40S 27°11E 55 E2
Koni, Mts.
  Dem. Rep. of the Congo 10°36S 27°10E 55 E2
Konin Poland 52°12N 18°15E 17 B10
Konjic Bos.-H. 43°42N 17°58E 23 C7
Konkiep Namibia 26°49S 17°15E 56 D2
Kōnosu Japan 36°3N 139°31E 31 F9
Konotop Ukraine 51°12N 33°7E 19 D5
Konqi He → China 41°0N 86°0E 32 B3
Końskie Poland 51°15N 20°23E 17 C11
Konstanz Germany 47°40N 9°10E 16 E5
Kont Iran 26°55N 61°50E 45 E9

Kontagora *Nigeria* 10°23N 5°27E **50** F7
Kontiolahti *Finland* 62°46N 29°50E **8** E23
Kontokali *Greece* 39°38N 19°51E **25** A3
Konya *Turkey* 37°52N 32°35E **44** B2
Konza *Kenya* 1°45S 37°7E **54** C4
Koocanusa, L. *Canada* 49°20N 115°15W **76** B6
Kookynie *Australia* 29°17S 121°22E **61** E3
Koolyanobbing
Australia 30°48S 119°36E **61** F2
Koonibba *Australia* 31°54S 133°25E **63** E1
Koorawatha *Australia* 34°2S 148°33E **63** E4
Koorda *Australia* 30°48S 117°35E **61** F2
Kooskia *U.S.A.* 46°9N 115°59W **76** C6
Kootenay → *U.S.A.* 49°19N 117°39W **70** D5
Kootenay △ *Canada* 51°0N 116°0W **76** C5
Kootenay L. *Canada* 49°45N 116°50W **76** B5
Kootjieskolk *S. Africa* 31°15S 20°21E **56** E3
Kopaonik *Serbia* 43°10N 20°50E **23** C9
Kópavogur *Iceland* 64°6N 21°55W **8** D3
Koper *Slovenia* 45°31N 13°44E **16** F7
Kopervik *Norway* 59°17N 5°17E **9** G11
Kopet Dagh *Asia* 38°0N 58°0E **45** B8
Kopi *Australia* 33°24S 135°40E **63** E2
Köping *Sweden* 59°31N 16°3E **9** G17
Koppeh Dāgh = Kopet Dagh
Asia 38°0N 58°0E **45** B8
Koppies *S. Africa* 27°20S 27°30E **57** D4
Koprivnica *Croatia* 46°12N 16°45E **22** A7
Köprülü △ *Turkey* 37°20N 31°5E **44** B1
Kopychyntsi *Ukraine* 49°7N 25°58E **17** D13
Kora △ *Kenya* 0°14S 38°44E **54** C4
Korab *Macedonia* 41°44N 20°40E **23** D9
Koral *India* 21°50N 73°12E **42** J5
Korba *India* 22°20N 82°45E **43** H10
Korbu, G. *Malaysia* 4°41N 101°18E **39** K3
Korçë *Albania* 40°37N 20°50E **23** D9
Korčula *Croatia* 42°56N 16°57E **22** C7
Kord Kūy *Iran* 36°48N 54°7E **45** B7
Kord Sheykh *Iran* 28°31N 52°53E **45** D7
Kordestān □ *Iran* 36°0N 47°0E **44** C5
Kordofân *Sudan* 13°0N 29°0E **51** F11
Korea, North ■ *Asia* 40°0N 127°0E **35** E14
Korea, South ■ *Asia* 36°0N 128°0E **35** G15
Korea Bay *Korea* 39°0N 124°0E **35** E13
Korea Strait *Asia* 34°0N 129°30E **35** H15
Korets *Ukraine* 50°40N 27°5E **17** C14
Korhogo *Ivory C.* 9°29N 5°28W **50** G4
Korinthiakos Kolpos
Greece 38°16N 22°30E **23** E10
Korinthos *Greece* 37°56N 22°55E **23** F10
Korissia, L. *Greece* 39°27N 19°53E **25** B3
Kōriyama *Japan* 37°24N 140°23E **30** F10
Korla *China* 41°45N 86°4E **32** B3
Kormakiti, C. *Cyprus* 35°23N 32°56E **25** D11
Kornešty = Cornești
Moldova 47°21N 28°1E **17** E15
Koro *Fiji* 17°19S 179°23E **59** a
Koro *Ivory C.* 8°32N 7°30W **50** G4
Koro Sea *Fiji* 17°30S 179°45W **59** a
Korogwe *Tanzania* 5°5S 38°25E **54** D4
Korolevu *Fiji* 18°12S 177°46E **59** a
Koronadal *Phil.* 6°12N 125°1E **37** C6
Koror *Palau* 7°20N 134°28E **64** G5
Körös → *Hungary* 46°43N 20°12E **17** E11
Korosten *Ukraine* 50°54N 28°36E **17** C15
Korostyshev *Ukraine* 50°19N 29°4E **17** C15
Korovou *Fiji* 17°47S 178°32E **59** a
Koroyanitu △ *Fiji* 17°40S 177°35E **59** a
Korraraika, Helodranon' i
Madag. 17°45S 43°57E **57** B7
Korsakov *Russia* 46°36N 142°42E **29** E15
Korshunovo *Russia* 58°37N 110°10E **29** D12
Korsør *Denmark* 55°20N 11°9E **9** J14
Kortrijk *Belgium* 50°50N 3°17E **15** D3
Korwai *India* 24°7N 78°5E **42** G8
Koryakskoye Nagorye
Russia 61°0N 171°0E **29** C18
Kos *Greece* 36°50N 27°15E **23** F12
Kosan *N. Korea* 38°52N 127°25E **35** E14
Koschagyl *Kazakhstan* 46°40N 54°0E **19** E9
Kościan *Poland* 52°5N 16°40E **17** B9
Kosciusko *U.S.A.* 33°4N 89°35W **85** E10
Kosciuszko, Mt.
Australia 36°27S 148°16E **63** F4
Kosha *Sudan* 20°50N 30°30E **51** D12
K'oshih = Kashi *China* 39°30N 76°2E **32** C2
Koshiki-Rettō *Japan* 31°45N 129°49E **31** J4
Kosi *India* 27°48N 77°29E **42** F7
Kosi → *India* 28°41N 78°57E **43** E8
Košice *Slovak Rep.* 48°42N 21°15E **17** D11
Koskinou *Greece* 36°23N 28°13E **25** C10
Koslan *Russia* 63°34N 49°14E **18** B8
Košong *N. Korea* 38°40N 128°22E **35** E15
Kosovo □ *Serbia* 42°30N 21°0E **23** C9
Kosovska Mitrovica
Serbia 42°54N 20°52E **23** C9
Kossou, L. de *Ivory C.* 6°59N 5°31W **50** G4
Koster *S. Africa* 25°52S 26°54E **56** D4
Kôsti *Sudan* 13°8N 32°43E **51** F12
Kostopil *Ukraine* 50°51N 26°22E **17** C14
Kostroma *Russia* 57°50N 40°58E **18** C7
Kostrzyn *Poland* 52°35N 14°39E **16** B8
Koszalin *Poland* 54°11N 16°8E **16** A9
Kot Addu *Pakistan* 30°30N 71°0E **42** D4
Kot Kapura *India* 30°35N 74°50E **42** D6
Kot Moman *Pakistan* 32°13N 73°0E **42** C5
Kot Sultan *Pakistan* 30°46N 70°56E **42** D4
Kota *India* 25°14N 75°49E **42** G6
Kota Barrage *India* 25°6N 75°51E **42** G6
Kota Belud *Malaysia* 6°21N 116°26E **36** C5
Kota Bharu *Malaysia* 6°7N 102°14E **39** J4
Kota Kinabalu *Malaysia* 6°0N 116°4E **36** C5
Kota Tinggi *Malaysia* 1°44N 103°53E **39** M4
Kotabaru *Indonesia* 3°20S 116°20E **36** E5
Kotabumi *Indonesia* 4°49S 104°54E **36** E2
Kotamobagu *Indonesia* 0°57N 124°31E **37** D6

Kotapinang *Indonesia* 1°53N 100°5E **39** M3
Kotcho L. *Canada* 59°7N 121°12W **70** B4
Kotdwara *India* 29°45N 78°32E **43** E8
Kotelnich *Russia* 58°22N 48°24E **18** C8
Kotelnikovo *Russia* 47°38N 43°8E **19** E7
Kotelnyy, Ostrov
Russia 75°10N 139°0E **29** B14
Kothari → *India* 25°20N 75°4E **42** G6
Kothi *Chhattisgarh, India* 23°21N 82°3E **43** H10
Kothi *Mad. P., India* 24°45N 80°40E **43** G9
Kotiro *Pakistan* 26°17N 67°13E **42** F2
Kotka *Finland* 60°28N 26°58E **8** F22
Kotlas *Russia* 61°17N 46°43E **18** B8
Kotli *Pakistan* 33°30N 73°55E **42** C5
Kotma *India* 23°12N 81°58E **43** H9
Kotor *Montenegro* 42°25N 18°47E **23** C8
Kotovsk *Ukraine* 47°45N 29°35E **17** E15
Kotputli *India* 27°43N 76°12E **42** F7
Kotri *Pakistan* 25°22N 68°22E **42** G3
Kotto → *C.A.R.* 4°14N 22°2E **52** D4
Kotturu *India* 14°45N 76°10E **40** M10
Kotu Group *Tonga* 20°0S 174°45W **59** c
Kotuy → *Russia* 71°54N 102°6E **29** B11
Kotzebue *U.S.A.* 66°53N 162°39W **74** a
Kotzebue Sound *U.S.A.* 66°20N 163°0W **66** C3
Kouchibouguac △
Canada 46°50N 65°0W **73** C6
Koudougou *Burkina Faso* 12°10N 2°20W **50** F5
Koufonisi *Greece* 34°56N 26°8E **25** E8
Kougaberge *S. Africa* 33°48S 23°50E **56** E3
Kouilou → *Gabon* 4°10S 12°5E **52** E2
Koula Moutou *Gabon* 1°15S 12°25E **52** E2
Koulen = Kulen
Cambodia 13°50N 104°40E **38** F5
Kouloura *Greece* 39°42N 19°54E **25** A3
Koumala *Australia* 21°38S 149°15E **62** C4
Koumra *Chad* 8°50N 17°35E **51** G9
Kountze *U.S.A.* 30°22N 94°19W **84** F7
Kouris → *Cyprus* 34°38N 32°54E **25** E11
Kourou *Fr. Guiana* 5°9N 52°39W **93** B8
Kouroussa *Guinea* 10°45N 9°45W **50** F4
Kousséri *Cameroon* 12°0N 14°55E **51** F8
Koutiala *Mali* 12°25N 5°23W **50** F4
Kouvola *Finland* 60°52N 26°43E **8** F22
Kovdor *Russia* 67°34N 30°24E **8** C24
Kovel *Ukraine* 51°11N 24°38E **17** C13
Kovrov *Russia* 56°25N 41°25E **18** C7
Kowanyama *Australia* 15°29S 141°44E **62** B3
Kowloon *China* 22°19N 114°11E **33** G11
Kowŏn *N. Korea* 39°26N 127°14E **35** E14
Koyampattur = Coimbatore
India 11°2N 76°59E **40** P10
Köyceğiz *Turkey* 36°57N 28°40E **23** F13
Koyukuk → *U.S.A.* 64°55N 157°32W **66** C4
Koza = Okinawa *Japan* 26°19N 127°46E **31** L3
Kozan *Turkey* 37°26N 35°50E **44** B2
Kozani *Greece* 40°19N 21°47E **23** D9
Kozhikode = Calicut
India 11°15N 75°43E **40** P9
Kozhva *Russia* 65°10N 57°0E **18** A10
Kozyatyn *Ukraine* 49°45N 28°50E **17** D15
Kozyrevsk *Russia* 56°3N 159°51E **29** D16
Kpalimé *Togo* 6°57N 0°44E **50** G6
Kra, Isthmus of = Kra, Kho Khot
Thailand 10°15N 99°30E **39** G2
Kra, Kho Khot *Thailand* 10°15N 99°30E **39** G2
Kra Buri *Thailand* 10°22N 98°46E **39** G2
Kraai → *S. Africa* 30°40S 26°45E **56** E4
Krabi *Thailand* 8°4N 98°55E **39** H2
Kracheh *Cambodia* 12°32N 106°10E **38** F6
Kragan *Indonesia* 6°43S 111°38E **37** G14
Kragerø *Norway* 58°52N 9°25E **9** G13
Kragujevac *Serbia* 44°2N 20°56E **23** B9
Krakatau = Rakata, Pulau
Indonesia 6°10S 105°20E **36** F3
Krakatoa = Rakata, Pulau
Indonesia 6°10S 105°20E **36** F3
Krakor *Cambodia* 12°32N 104°12E **38** F5
Kraków *Poland* 50°4N 19°57E **17** C10
Kralanh *Cambodia* 13°35N 103°25E **38** F4
Kraljevo *Serbia* 43°44N 20°41E **23** C9
Kramatorsk *Ukraine* 48°50N 37°30E **19** E6
Kramfors *Sweden* 62°55N 17°48E **8** E17
Kranj *Slovenia* 46°16N 14°22E **16** E8
Krankskop *S. Africa* 28°0S 30°47E **57** D5
Krasavino *Russia* 60°58N 46°29E **18** B8
Kraskino *Russia* 42°44N 130°48E **30** C5
Kraśnik *Poland* 50°55N 22°15E **17** C12
Krasnoarmeysk *Russia* 51°0N 45°42E **28** D5
Krasnodar *Russia* 45°5N 39°0E **19** E6
Krasnokamensk *Russia* 50°3N 118°0E **29** D12
Krasnokamsk *Russia* 58°4N 55°48E **18** C10
Krasnoperekopsk *Ukraine* 46°0N 33°54E **19** E5
Krasnorechenskiy
Russia 44°41N 135°14E **30** B7
Krasnoselkup *Russia* 65°20N 82°10E **28** C9
Krasnoturinsk *Russia* 59°46N 60°12E **18** C11
Krasnoufimsk *Russia* 56°36N 57°38E **18** C10
Krasnouralsk *Russia* 58°21N 60°3E **18** C11
Krasnovishersk *Russia* 60°23N 57°3E **18** B10
Krasnoyarsk *Russia* 56°8N 93°0E **29** D10
Krasnyy Kut *Russia* 50°50N 47°0E **19** D8
Krasnyy Luch *Ukraine* 48°13N 39°0E **19** E6
Krasnyy Yar *Russia* 46°43N 48°23E **19** E8
Kratie = Kracheh
Cambodia 12°32N 106°10E **38** F6
Krau *Indonesia* 3°19S 140°5E **37** E10
Kravanh, Chuor Phnum
Cambodia 12°0N 103°32E **39** G4
Krefeld *Germany* 51°20N 6°33E **16** C4
Kremen *Croatia* 44°28N 15°53E **16** F8
Kremenchuk *Ukraine* 49°5N 33°25E **19** E5
Kremenchuksk Vdskh.
Ukraine 49°20N 32°30E **19** E5
Kremenets *Ukraine* 50°8N 25°43E **17** C13
Kremmling *U.S.A.* 40°4N 106°24W **76** F10
Krems *Austria* 48°25N 15°36E **16** D8

Kretinga *Lithuania* 55°53N 21°15E **9** J19
Kribi *Cameroon* 2°57N 9°56E **52** D1
Krichev = Krychaw
Belarus 53°40N 31°41E **17** B16
Kril'on, Mys *Russia* 45°53N 142°5E **30** B11
Krios, Akra *Greece* 35°13N 23°34E **25** D5
Krishna → *India* 15°57N 80°59E **41** M12
Krishnanagar *India* 23°24N 88°33E **43** H13
Kristiansand *Norway* 58°8N 8°1E **9** G13
Kristianstad *Sweden* 56°2N 14°9E **9** H16
Kristiansund *Norway* 63°7N 7°45E **8** E12
Kristiinankaupunki
Finland 62°16N 21°21E **8** E19
Kristinehamn *Sweden* 59°18N 14°7E **9** G16
Kristinestad =
Kristiinankaupunki
Finland 62°16N 21°21E **8** E19
Kriti *Greece* 35°15N 25°0E **25** D7
Kritsa *Greece* 35°10N 25°41E **25** D7
Krivoy Rog = Kryvyy Rih
Ukraine 47°51N 33°20E **19** E5
Krk *Croatia* 45°8N 14°40E **16** F8
Krokodil = Umgwenya →
Mozam. 25°14S 32°18E **57** D5
Krong Kaoh Kong
Cambodia 11°37N 102°59E **39** G4
Kronprins Olav Kyst
Antarctica 69°0S 42°0E **5** C5
Kronprinsesse Märtha Kyst
Antarctica 73°30S 10°0W **5** D2
Kronshtadt *Russia* 59°57N 29°51E **18** B4
Kroonstad *S. Africa* 27°43S 27°19E **56** D4
Kropotkin *Russia* 45°28N 40°28E **19** E7
Krosno *Poland* 49°42N 21°46E **17** D11
Krotoszyn *Poland* 51°42N 17°23E **17** C9
Krousonas *Greece* 35°13N 24°59E **25** D6
Kruger △ *S. Africa* 24°50S 26°10E **57** C5
Krugersdorp *S. Africa* 26°5S 27°46E **57** D4
Kruisfontein *S. Africa* 33°59S 24°43E **56** E3
Krung Thep = Bangkok
Thailand 13°45N 100°35E **38** F3
Krupki *Belarus* 54°19N 29°8E **17** A15
Kruševac *Serbia* 43°35N 21°28E **23** C9
Krychaw *Belarus* 53°40N 31°41E **17** B16
Krymskiy Poluostrov = Krymskyy
Pivostriv *Ukraine* 45°0N 34°0E **19** F5
Krymskyy Pivostriv
Ukraine 45°0N 34°0E **19** F5
Kryvyy Rih *Ukraine* 47°51N 33°20E **19** E5
Ksar es Souk = Er Rachidia
Morocco 31°58N 4°20W **50** B5
Ksar el Kebir *Morocco* 35°0N 6°0W **50** B4
Kuah *Malaysia* 6°19N 99°51E **39** J2
Kuala Belait *Malaysia* 4°35N 114°11E **36** D4
Kuala Berang *Malaysia* 5°5N 103°1E **39** K4
Kuala Dungun = Dungun
Malaysia 4°45N 103°25E **39** K4
Kuala Kangsar *Malaysia* 4°46N 100°56E **39** K3
Kuala Kelawang *Malaysia* 2°56N 102°5E **39** L4
Kuala Kerai *Malaysia* 5°30N 102°12E **39** K4
Kuala Kerian *Malaysia* 5°10N 100°25E **39** c
Kuala Kubu Bharu
Malaysia 3°34N 101°39E **39** L3
Kuala Lipis *Malaysia* 4°10N 102°3E **39** K4
Kuala Lumpur *Malaysia* 3°9N 101°41E **39** L3
Kuala Nerang *Malaysia* 6°16N 100°37E **39** J3
Kuala Pilah *Malaysia* 2°45N 102°15E **39** L4
Kuala Rompin *Malaysia* 2°49N 103°29E **39** L4
Kuala Selangor *Malaysia* 3°20N 101°15E **39** L3
Kuala Sepetang
Malaysia 4°49N 100°28E **39** K3
Kuala Terengganu
Malaysia 5°20N 103°8E **39** K4
Kualajelai *Indonesia* 2°58S 110°46E **36** E4
Kualakapuas *Indonesia* 2°55S 114°20E **36** E4
Kualakurun *Indonesia* 1°10S 113°50E **36** E4
Kualapembuang
Indonesia 3°14S 112°38E **36** E4
Kualasimpang *Indonesia* 4°17N 98°3E **36** D1
Kuancheng *China* 40°37N 118°30E **35** D10
Kuandang *Indonesia* 0°56N 122°57E **37** D6
Kuandian *China* 40°45N 124°45E **35** D13
Kuangchou = Guangzhou
China 23°6N 113°13E **33** D6
Kuantan *Malaysia* 3°49N 103°20E **39** L4
Kuba = Quba *Azerbaijan* 41°21N 48°32E **19** F8
Kuban → *Russia* 45°20N 37°30E **19** E6
Kubokawa *Japan* 33°12N 133°8E **31** H6
Kubu *Indonesia* 8°16S 115°35E **37** J18
Kubutambahan
Indonesia 8°5S 115°10E **37** J18
Kucar, Tanjung
Indonesia 8°39S 114°34E **37** K18
Kuchaman *India* 27°13N 74°47E **42** F6
Kuchinda *India* 21°44N 84°21E **43** J11
Kuching *Malaysia* 1°33N 110°25E **36** D4
Kuchino-eruba-Jima
Japan 30°28N 130°12E **31** J5
Kuchino-Shima *Japan* 29°57N 129°55E **31** K4
Kuchinotsu *Japan* 32°36N 130°11E **31** H5
Kucing = Kuching
Malaysia 1°33N 110°25E **36** D4
Kud → *Pakistan* 26°5N 66°20E **42** F2
Kuda *India* 23°10N 71°15E **42** H4
Kudat *Malaysia* 6°55N 116°55E **36** C5
Kudus *Indonesia* 6°48S 110°51E **37** G14
Kudymkar *Russia* 59°1N 54°39E **18** C9
Kueiyang = Guiyang
China 26°32N 106°40E **32** D5
Kufra Oasis = Al Kufrah
Libya 24°17N 23°15E **51** D10
Kufstein *Austria* 47°35N 12°11E **16** E7
Kugaaruk = Pelly Bay
Canada 68°38N 89°50W **69** C11
Kugaaruk = Pelly Bay
Canada 68°38N 89°50W **69** C11
Kugluktuk *Canada* 67°50N 115°5W **68** C8
Kugong I. *Canada* 56°18N 79°50W **72** A4

Küh-e-Jebāl Bārez *Iran* 29°0N 58°0E **45** D8
Kūhak *Iran* 27°12N 63°10E **45** E9
Kuhan *Pakistan* 28°19N 67°14E **42** E2
Kūhbonān *Iran* 31°23N 56°19E **45** D8
Kühestak *Iran* 26°47N 57°2E **45** E8
Kuhin *Iran* 36°22N 49°40E **45** B6
Kūhīrī *Iran* 26°55N 61°2E **45** E9
Kuhmo *Finland* 64°7N 29°31E **8** D23
Kuhmoinen *Finland* 61°28N 25°10E **9** F21
Kühpāyeh *Eşfahan, Iran* 32°44N 52°20E **45** C7
Kühpāyeh *Kermān, Iran* 30°35N 57°15E **45** D8
Kührān, Küh-e *Iran* 26°46N 58°12E **45** E8
Kui Buri *Thailand* 12°3N 99°52E **39** F2
Kuichong *China* 22°38N 114°25E **33** F11
Kuiseb → *Namibia* 22°59S 14°31E **56** C1
Kuito *Angola* 12°22S 16°55E **53** G3
Kuiu I. *U.S.A.* 57°45N 134°10W **70** B2
Kujang *N. Korea* 39°57N 126°1E **35** E14
Kuji *Japan* 40°11N 141°46E **30** D10
Kujū-San *Japan* 33°5N 131°15E **31** H5
Krivoy Rog → *Ukraine* 47°51N 33°20E **19** E5
Kukës *Albania* 42°5N 20°27E **23** C9
Kukup *Malaysia* 1°20N 103°27E **39** d
Kukup, Pulau *Malaysia* 1°18N 103°25E **39** d
Kula *Turkey* 38°32N 28°40E **23** E13
K'ula Shan *Bhutan* 28°14N 90°36E **32** C4
Kulachi *Pakistan* 31°56N 70°27E **42** D4
Kulai *Malaysia* 1°44N 103°35E **39** M4
Kulasekarappattinam
India 8°20N 78°5E **40** Q11
Kuldīga *Latvia* 56°58N 21°59E **9** H19
Kulen *Cambodia* 13°50N 104°40E **38** F5
Kulgam *India* 33°36N 75°2E **43** C6
Kulgera *Australia* 25°50S 133°18E **62** D1
Kulim *Malaysia* 5°22N 100°34E **39** K3
Kulin *Australia* 32°40S 118°2E **61** F2
Kulkayu = Hartley Bay
Canada 53°25N 129°15W **70** C3
Kullu *India* 31°58N 77°6E **42** D7
Kulob *Tajikistan* 37°55N 69°50E **28** F7
Kulsary = Qulsary
Kazakhstan 46°59N 54°1E **19** E9
Kulti *India* 23°43N 86°50E **43** H12
Kulunda *Russia* 52°35N 78°57E **28** D8
Kulungar *Afghan.* 34°0N 69°2E **42** C3
Kŭlvand *Iran* 31°21N 54°35E **45** D7
Kulwin *Australia* 35°2S 142°42E **63** F3
Kulyab = Kŭlob
Tajikistan 37°55N 69°50E **28** F7
Kuma → *Russia* 44°55N 47°0E **19** F8
Kumaganum *Nigeria* 13°8N 10°38E **51** F8
Kumagaya *Japan* 36°9N 139°22E **31** F9
Kumai *Indonesia* 2°44S 111°43E **36** E4
Kumamba, Kepulauan
Indonesia 1°36S 138°45E **37** E9
Kumamoto *Japan* 32°45N 130°45E **31** H5
Kumamoto □ *Japan* 32°55N 130°55E **31** H5
Kumanovo *Macedonia* 42°9N 21°42E **23** C9
Kumara *N.Z.* 42°37S 171°12E **59** E3
Kumarina Roadhouse
Australia 24°41S 119°32E **61** D2
Kumasi *Ghana* 6°41N 1°38W **50** G5
Kumba *Cameroon* 4°36N 9°24E **52** D1
Kumbakonam *India* 10°58N 79°25E **40** P11
Kumbarilla *Australia* 27°15S 150°55E **63** D5
Kumbhraj *India* 24°22N 77°3E **42** G7
Kumbia *Australia* 26°41S 151°39E **63** D5
Kŭmch'ŏn *N. Korea* 38°10N 126°29E **35** E14
Kumdok *India* 33°32N 78°10E **43** C8
Kume-Shima *Japan* 26°20N 126°47E **31** L3
Kumertau *Russia* 52°45N 55°57E **18** D10
Kumharsain *India* 31°19N 77°27E **42** D7
Kumi *Uganda* 1°30N 33°58E **54** B3
Kumo *Nigeria* 10°1N 11°12E **51** F8
Kumo älv = Kokemäenjoki →
Finland 61°32N 21°44E **8** F19
Kumon Bum *Burma* 26°30N 97°15E **41** F20
Kumtag Shamo *China* 39°40N 92°0E **32** C4
Kunashir, Ostrov *Russia* 44°0N 146°0E **29** E15
Kunda *Estonia* 59°30N 26°34E **9** G22
Kunda *India* 25°43N 81°31E **43** G9
Kundar → *Pakistan* 31°56N 69°19E **42** D3
Kundelungu △
Dem. Rep. of the Congo 10°30S 27°40E **55** E2
Kundelungu Ouest △
Dem. Rep. of the Congo 9°55S 27°17E **55** D2
Kundian *Pakistan* 32°27N 71°28E **42** C4
Kundla *India* 21°21N 71°25E **42** J4
Kung, Ao *Thailand* 8°5N 98°24E **39** a
Kunga → *Bangla.* 21°46N 89°30E **43** J13
Kunghit I. *Canada* 52°6N 131°3W **70** C2
Kungrad = Qŭnghirot
Uzbekistan 43°2N 58°50E **28** E6
Kungsbacka *Sweden* 57°30N 12°5E **9** H15
Kungur *Russia* 57°25N 56°57E **18** C10
Kungurri *Australia* 21°4S 148°45E **62** K6
Kuningan *Indonesia* 6°59S 108°29E **37** G13
Kunlong *Burma* 23°20N 98°50E **41** H21
Kunlun Shan *Asia* 36°0N 86°30E **32** C3
Kunming *China* 25°1N 102°41E **32** D5
Kununurra *Australia* 15°40S 128°50E **60** C4
Kunwari → *India* 26°26N 79°11E **43** F8
Kunya-Urgench = Köneürgench
Turkmenistan 42°19N 59°10E **28** E6
Kuopio *Finland* 62°53N 27°35E **8** E22
Kupa → *Croatia* 45°28N 16°24E **16** F9
Kupang *Indonesia* 10°19S 123°39E **37** F6
Kupreanof I. *U.S.A.* 56°50N 133°30W **70** B2
Kupyansk-Uzlovoi
Ukraine 49°40N 37°43E **19** E6
Kuqa *China* 41°35N 82°30E **32** B3
Kür → *Azerbaijan* 39°29N 49°15E **45** B6
Kür Dili *Azerbaijan* 39°3N 49°13E **45** B6
Kura = Kür →
Azerbaijan 39°29N 49°15E **45** B6
Kuranda *Australia* 16°48S 145°35E **62** B4
Kurashiki *Japan* 34°40N 133°50E **31** G6

Kurayn *Si. Arabia* 27°39N 49°50E **45** E6
Kurayoshi *Japan* 35°26N 133°50E **31** G6
Kürchatov *Kazakhstan* 50°45N 78°32E **28** D8
Kürdzhali *Bulgaria* 41°38N 25°21E **23** D11
Kure *Japan* 34°14N 132°32E **31** G6
Kuressaare *Estonia* 58°15N 22°30E **9** G20
Kurgan *Russia* 55°26N 65°18E **28** D7
Kuri *India* 26°37N 70°43E **42** F4
Kuria Maria Is. = Hallāniyat,
Jazā'ir al *Oman* 17°30N 55°58E **47** D6
Kuridala *Australia* 21°16S 140°29E **62** C3
Kurigram *Bangla.* 25°49N 89°39E **41** G16
Kurikka *Finland* 62°36N 22°24E **8** E20
Kuril Basin *Pac. Oc.* 47°0N 150°0E **4** E15
Kuril Is. = Kurilskiye Ostrova
Russia 45°0N 150°0E **29** E16
Kuril-Kamchatka Trench
Pac. Oc. 44°0N 153°0E **64** C7
Kurilsk *Russia* 45°14N 147°53E **29** E15
Kurilskiye Ostrova
Russia 45°0N 150°0E **29** E16
Kurino *Japan* 31°57N 130°43E **31** J5
Kurinskaya Kosa = Kür Dili
Azerbaijan 39°3N 49°13E **45** B6
Kurnool *India* 15°45N 78°0E **40** M11
Kuro-Shima *Kagoshima,
Japan* 30°50N 129°57E **31** J4
Kuro-Shima *Okinawa,
Japan* 24°14N 124°1E **31** M2
Kurow *N.Z.* 44°44S 170°29E **59** F3
Kurram → *Pakistan* 32°36N 71°20E **42** C4
Kurri Kurri *Australia* 32°50S 151°28E **63** E5
Kurrimine *Australia* 17°47S 146°6E **62** B4
Kurshskiy Zaliv *Russia* 55°9N 21°6E **9** J19
Kursk *Russia* 51°42N 36°11E **18** D6
Kuruçay *Turkey* 39°39N 38°29E **44** B3
Kuruktag *China* 41°0N 89°0E **32** B3
Kuruman *S. Africa* 27°28S 23°28E **56** D3
Kuruman → *S. Africa* 26°56S 20°39E **56** D3
Kurume *Japan* 33°15N 130°30E **31** H5
Kurunegala *Sri Lanka* 7°30N 80°23E **40** R12
Kurya *Russia* 61°42N 57°9E **18** B10
Kus Gölü *Turkey* 40°10N 27°55E **23** D12
Kuşadası *Turkey* 37°52N 27°15E **23** F12
Kusamba *Indonesia* 8°34S 115°27E **37** K18
Kusatsu *Japan* 36°37N 138°36E **31** F9
Kusawa L. *Canada* 60°20N 136°13W **70** A1
Kushalgarh *India* 23°10N 74°27E **42** H6
Kushikino *Japan* 31°44N 130°16E **31** J5
Kushima *Japan* 31°29N 131°14E **31** J5
Kushimoto *Japan* 33°28N 135°47E **31** H7
Kushiro *Japan* 43°0N 144°25E **30** C12
Kushiro-Gawa →
Japan 42°59N 144°23E **30** C12
Kushiro Shitsugen △
Japan 43°9N 144°26E **30** C12
Kūshk *Iran* 28°46N 56°51E **45** D8
Kushka = Serhetabat
Turkmenistan 35°20N 62°18E **45** C9
Kushol *India* 33°40N 76°36E **43** C7
Kushtia *Bangla.* 23°55N 89°5E **41** H16
Kushva *Russia* 58°18N 59°45E **18** C10
Kuskokwim → *U.S.A.* 60°5N 162°25W **66** C3
Kuskokwim B. *U.S.A.* 59°45N 162°25W **74** a
Kusmi *India* 23°17N 83°55E **43** H10
Kusŏng *N. Korea* 39°59N 125°15E **35** E13
Kussharo-Ko *Japan* 43°38N 144°21E **30** C12
Kustanay = Qostanay
Kazakhstan 53°10N 63°35E **28** D7
Kut, Ko *Thailand* 11°40N 102°35E **39** G4
Kuta *Indonesia* 8°43S 115°11E **37** K18
Kütahya *Turkey* 39°30N 30°2E **19** G5
Kutaisi *Georgia* 42°19N 42°40E **19** F7
Kutaraja = Banda Aceh
Indonesia 5°35N 95°20E **36** C1
Kutch, Gulf of = Kachchh, Gulf of
India 22°50N 69°15E **42** H3
Kutch, Rann of = Kachchh, Rann
of *India* 24°0N 70°0E **42** H4
Kutiyana *India* 21°36N 70°2E **42** J4
Kutno *Poland* 52°15N 19°23E **17** B10
Kutse *Botswana* 21°7S 22°16E **56** C3
Kuttabul *Australia* 21°1S 148°54E **62** K6
Kutu *Dem. Rep. of the Congo* 2°40S 18°11E **52** E3
Kutum *Sudan* 14°10N 24°40E **51** F10
Kuujjuaq *Canada* 58°6N 68°15W **69** D13
Kuujjuarapik *Canada* 55°20N 77°35W **72** A4
Kuusamo *Finland* 65°57N 29°8E **8** D23
Kuusankoski *Finland* 60°55N 26°38E **8** F22
Kuwait = Al Kuwayt
Kuwait 29°30N 48°0E **44** D5
Kuwait ■ *Asia* 29°30N 47°30E **44** D5
Kuwana *Japan* 35°5N 136°43E **31** G8
Kuwana → *India* 26°25N 83°15E **43** F10
Kuybyshev = Samara
Russia 53°8N 50°6E **18** D9
Kuybyshev *Russia* 55°27N 78°19E **28** D8
Kuybyshevskoye Vdkhr.
Russia 55°2N 49°30E **18** C8
Kuye He → *China* 38°23N 110°46E **34** E6
Kūyeh *Iran* 38°45N 47°57E **44** B5
Kuyto, Ozero *Russia* 65°6N 31°20E **8** D24
Kuyumba *Russia* 60°58N 96°59E **29** C10
Kuzey Anadolu Dağları
Turkey 41°30N 35°0E **19** F6
Kuznetsk *Russia* 53°12N 46°40E **18** D8
Kuzomen *Russia* 66°22N 36°50E **18** A6
Kvænangen *Norway* 70°5N 21°15E **8** A19
Kvaløya *Norway* 69°40N 18°30E **8** B18
Kvarner *Croatia* 44°50N 14°10E **16** F8
Kvarnerič *Croatia* 44°43N 14°37E **16** F8
Kwabhaca *S. Africa* 30°51S 29°0E **57** E4
Kwajalein *Marshall Is.* 9°5N 167°20E **64** G8
Kwakhanai *Botswana* 21°39S 21°16E **56** C3
Kwakoegron *Suriname* 5°12N 55°25W **93** B7
Kwale *Kenya* 4°15S 39°31E **54** C4
KwaMashu *S. Africa* 29°45S 30°58E **57** D5

Kwando → Africa 18°27S 23°32E 56 B3
Kwangchow = Guangzhou
  China 23°6N 113°13E 33 D6
Kwango →
  Dem. Rep. of the Congo 3°14S 17°22E 52 E3
Kwangsi-Chuang = Guangxi
  Zhuangzu Zizhiqu □
  China 24°0N 109°0E 33 D5
Kwangtung = Guangdong □
  China 23°0N 113°0E 33 D6
Kwataboahegan →
  Canada 51°9N 80°50W 72 B3
Kwatisore Indonesia 3°18S 134°50E 37 E8
KwaZulu Natal □ S. Africa 29°0S 30°0E 57 D5
Kweichow = Guizhou □
  China 27°0N 107°0E 32 D5
Kwekwe Zimbabwe 18°58S 29°48E 55 F2
Kwidzyn Poland 53°44N 18°55E 17 B10
Kwilu →
  Dem. Rep. of the Congo 3°22S 17°22E 52 E3
Kwinana Australia 32°15S 115°47E 61 F2
Kwoka Indonesia 0°31S 132°27E 37 E8
Kwun Tong China 22°19N 114°13E 33 G11
Kyabra Cr. → Australia 25°36S 142°55E 63 D3
Kyabram Australia 36°19S 145°4E 63 F4
Kyaikto Burma 17°20N 97°3E 38 D1
Kyakhta Russia 50°30N 106°25E 29 D11
Kyambura △ Uganda 0°7S 30°9E 54 C3
Kyancutta Australia 33°8S 135°33E 63 E2
Kyaukpadaung Burma 20°52N 95°8E 41 J19
Kyaukpyu Burma 19°28N 93°30E 41 K18
Kyaukse Burma 21°36N 96°10E 41 J20
Kyburz U.S.A. 38°47N 120°18W 78 G6
Kyelang India 32°35N 77°2E 42 C7
Kyenjojo Uganda 0°40N 30°37E 54 B3
Kyle Canada 50°50N 108°2W 71 C7
Kyle Dam Zimbabwe 20°15S 31°0E 55 G3
Kyle of Lochalsh U.K. 57°17N 5°44W 11 D3
Kymijoki → Finland 60°30N 26°55E 8 F22
Kymmene älv = Kymijoki →
  Finland 60°30N 26°55E 8 F22
Kyneton Australia 37°10S 144°29E 63 F3
Kynuna Australia 21°37S 141°55E 62 C3
Kyō-ga-Saki Japan 35°45N 135°15E 31 G7
Kyoga, L. Uganda 1°35N 33°0E 54 B3
Kyogle Australia 28°40S 153°0E 63 D5
Kyōngju = Gyeongju
  S. Korea 35°51N 129°14E 35 G15
Kyŏngsŏng N. Korea 41°35N 129°36E 35 D15
Kyonpyaw Burma 17°12N 95°10E 41 L19
Kyōto Japan 35°0N 135°45E 31 G7
Kyōto □ Japan 35°15N 135°45E 31 G7
Kyparissovouno Cyprus 35°19N 33°10E 25 D12
Kypros = Cyprus ■ Asia 35°0N 33°0E 25 D12
Kyrenia Cyprus 35°20N 33°20E 25 D12
Kyrgyzstan ■ Asia 42°0N 75°0E 28 E8
Kyro älv = Kyrönjoki →
  Finland 63°14N 21°45E 8 E19
Kyrönjoki → Finland 63°14N 21°45E 8 E19
Kystatyam Russia 67°20N 123°10E 29 C13
Kythira Greece 36°8N 23°0E 23 F10
Kythréa Cyprus 35°15N 33°29E 25 D12
Kyunhla Burma 23°25N 95°15E 41 H19
Kyuquot Sound Canada 50°2N 127°22W 70 D3
Kyūshū Japan 33°0N 131°0E 31 H5
Kyūshū □ Japan 33°0N 131°0E 31 H5
Kyushu-Palau Ridge
  Pac. Oc. 20°0N 136°0E 64 E5
Kyūshū-Sanchi Japan 32°35N 131°17E 31 H5
Kyustendil Bulgaria 42°16N 22°41E 23 C10
Kyusyur Russia 70°19N 127°30E 29 B13
Kyyiv Ukraine 50°30N 30°28E 17 C16
Kyyivske Vdskh.
  Ukraine 51°0N 30°25E 17 C16
Kyzyl Russia 51°50N 94°30E 32 A4
Kyzyl Kum Uzbekistan 42°30N 65°0E 28 E7
Kyzyl Kyya Kyrgyzstan 40°16N 72°8E 28 E8
Kyzyl Orda = Qyzylorda
  Kazakhstan 44°48N 65°28E 28 E7

L

La Alcarria Spain 40°31N 2°45W 21 B4
La Amistad △ Cent. Amer. 9°28N 83°18W 88 E3
La Asunción Venezuela 11°2N 63°53W 92 A6
La Baie Canada 48°19N 70°53W 73 C5
La Banda Argentina 27°45S 64°10W 94 B3
La Barca Mexico 20°17N 102°34W 86 C4
La Barge U.S.A. 42°16N 110°12W 76 E8
La Barra Nic. 12°54N 83°33W 88 D3
La Belle U.S.A. 26°46N 81°26W 85 H14
La Biche → Canada 59°57N 123°50W 70 B4
La Biche, L. Canada 54°50N 112°3W 70 C6
La Brea Trin. & Tob. 10°15N 61°37W 93 K15
La Calera Chile 32°50S 71°10W 94 C1
La Campana △ Chile 32°58S 71°14W 94 C1
La Canal = Sa Canal
  Spain 38°51N 1°23E 24 C7
La Carlota Argentina 33°30S 63°20W 94 C3
La Ceiba Honduras 15°40N 86°50W 88 C2
La Chaux-de-Fonds Switz. 47°7N 6°50E 20 C7
La Chorrera Panama 8°53N 79°47W 88 E4
La Cocha Argentina 27°50S 65°40W 94 B2
La Concepción Panama 8°31N 82°37W 88 E3
La Concordia Mexico 16°5N 92°38W 87 D6
La Coruña = A Coruña
  Spain 43°20N 8°25W 21 A1
La Crescent U.S.A. 43°50N 91°18W 80 D8
La Crete Canada 58°11N 116°24W 70 B5
La Crosse Kans., U.S.A. 38°32N 99°18W 80 F4
La Crosse Wis., U.S.A. 43°48N 91°15W 80 D8
La Cruz Costa Rica 11°4N 85°39W 88 D2
La Cruz Mexico 23°55N 106°54W 86 C3
La Désirade Guadeloupe 16°18N 61°3W 88 b
La Digue Seychelles 4°20S 55°51E 53 b

La Esperanza Cuba 22°46N 83°44W 88 B3
La Esperanza Honduras 14°15N 88°10W 88 D2
La Estrada = A Estrada
  Spain 42°43N 8°27W 21 A1
La Fayette U.S.A. 34°42N 85°17W 85 D12
La Follette U.S.A. 36°23N 84°7W 85 C12
La Grande U.S.A. 45°20N 118°5W 76 D4
La Grande → Canada 53°50N 79°0W 72 B5
La Grande 3, Rés.
  Canada 53°40N 75°10W 72 B4
La Grande 4, Rés. Canada 54°0N 73°15W 72 B5
La Grange Calif., U.S.A. 37°42N 120°27W 78 H6
La Grange Ga., U.S.A. 33°2N 85°2W 85 E12
La Grange Ky., U.S.A. 38°25N 85°22W 81 F11
La Grange Tex., U.S.A. 29°54N 96°52W 84 G6
La Guaira Venezuela 10°36N 66°56W 92 A5
La Habana Cuba 23°8N 82°22W 88 B3
La Independencia Mexico 16°15N 92°1W 87 D6
La Isabela Dom. Rep. 19°58N 71°2W 89 B5
La Junta U.S.A. 37°59N 103°33W 76 H12
La Laguna Canary Is. 28°28N 16°18W 24 F3
La Libertad = Puerto Libertad
  Mexico 29°55N 112°43W 86 B2
La Libertad Guatemala 16°47N 90°7W 88 C1
La Ligua Chile 32°30S 71°16W 94 C1
La Línea de la Concepción
  Spain 36°15N 5°23W 21 D3
La Loche Canada 56°29N 109°26W 71 B7
La Louvière Belgium 50°27N 4°10E 15 D4
La Lune Trin. & Tob. 10°3N 61°22W 93 K15
La Malbaie Canada 47°40N 70°10W 73 C5
La Malinche △ Mexico 19°15N 98°3W 87 D5
La Mancha Spain 39°10N 2°54W 21 C4
La Martre, L. Canada 63°15N 117°55W 70 A5
La Mesa Mexico 32°30N 116°57W 79 N10
La Mesa U.S.A. 32°46N 117°1W 79 N9
La Mesilla U.S.A. 32°16N 106°48W 77 K10
La Misión Mexico 32°6N 116°53W 86 A1
La Moure U.S.A. 46°21N 98°18W 80 B4
La Negra Chile 23°46S 70°18W 94 A1
La Oliva Canary Is. 28°36N 13°57W 24 F6
La Orotava Canary Is. 28°22N 16°31W 24 F3
La Oroya Peru 11°32S 75°54W 92 F3
La Palma Canary Is. 28°40N 17°50W 24 F2
La Palma Panama 8°15N 78°0W 88 E4
La Palma del Condado
  Spain 37°21N 6°38W 21 D2
La Paloma Chile 30°35S 71°0W 94 C1
La Pampa □ Argentina 36°50S 66°0W 94 D2
La Paragua Venezuela 6°50N 63°20W 92 B6
La Paz Entre Ríos,
  Argentina 30°50S 59°45W 94 C4
La Paz San Luis,
  Argentina 33°30S 67°20W 94 C2
La Paz Bolivia 16°20S 68°10W 92 G5
La Paz Honduras 14°20N 87°47W 88 D2
La Paz Mexico 24°10N 110°18W 86 C2
La Paz Centro Nic. 12°20N 86°41W 88 D2
La Pedrera Colombia 1°18S 69°43W 92 D5
La Pérade Canada 46°35N 72°12W 73 C5
La Perla Mexico 28°18N 104°32W 86 B4
La Perouse Str. Asia 45°40N 142°0E 30 B11
La Pesca Mexico 23°46N 97°47W 87 C5
La Piedad Mexico 20°21N 102°0W 86 C4
La Pine U.S.A. 43°40N 121°30W 76 E3
La Plata Argentina 35°0S 57°55W 94 D4
La Pocatière Canada 47°22N 70°2W 73 C5
La Porte U.S.A. 39°40N 95°1W 84 G7
La Purísima Mexico 26°10N 112°4W 86 B2
La Push U.S.A. 47°55N 124°38W 78 C2
La Quiaca Argentina 22°5S 65°35W 94 A2
La Restinga Canary Is. 27°38N 17°59W 24 G2
La Rioja Argentina 29°20S 67°0W 94 B2
La Rioja □ Argentina 29°30S 67°0W 94 B2
La Rioja □ Spain 42°20N 2°20W 21 A4
La Robla Spain 42°50N 5°41W 21 A3
La Roche-en-Ardenne
  Belgium 50°11N 5°35E 15 D5
La Roche-sur-Yon France 46°40N 1°25W 20 C3
La Rochelle France 46°10N 1°9W 20 C3
La Roda Spain 39°13N 2°15W 21 C4
La Romaine Canada 50°13N 60°40W 73 B7
La Romana Dom. Rep. 18°27N 68°57W 89 C6
La Ronge Canada 55°5N 105°20W 71 B7
La Rumorosa Mexico 32°34N 116°6W 79 N10
La Sabina = Sa Savina
  Spain 38°44N 1°25E 24 C7
La Salle U.S.A. 41°20N 89°6W 80 E9
La Santa Canary Is. 29°5N 13°40W 24 E6
La Sarre Canada 48°45N 79°15W 72 C4
La Scie Canada 49°57N 55°36W 73 C8
La Selva Beach U.S.A. 36°56N 121°51W 78 J5
La Serena Chile 29°55S 71°10W 94 B1
La Seu d'Urgell Spain 42°22N 1°23E 21 A6
La Seyne-sur-Mer France 43°7N 5°52E 20 E6
La Soufrière St. Vincent 13°20N 61°11W 89 D7
La Spézia Italy 44°7N 9°50E 20 D8
La Tagua Colombia 0°3N 74°40W 92 C4
La Tortuga Venezuela 11°0N 65°22W 89 D6
La Trinité Martinique 14°43N 60°58W 88 c
La Tuque Canada 47°30N 72°50W 72 C5
La Unión Chile 40°10S 73°0W 96 E2
La Unión El Salv. 13°20N 87°50W 88 D2
La Unión Mexico 17°58N 101°49W 86 D4
La Urbana Venezuela 7°8N 66°56W 92 B5
La Vache Pt.
  Trin. & Tob. 10°47N 61°28W 93 K15
La Vall d'Uixó Spain 39°49N 0°15W 21 C5
La Vega Dom. Rep. 19°20N 70°30W 89 C5
La Vela de Coro
  Venezuela 11°27N 69°34W 92 A5
La Venta Mexico 18°8N 94°3W 87 D6
La Vergne U.S.A. 36°1N 86°35W 85 C11
La Villa Joiosa = Villajoyosa
  Spain 38°30N 0°12W 21 C5
Laascaanood Somali Rep. 8°26N 47°19E 47 F4

Labasa Fiji 16°30S 179°27E 59 a
Labdah = Leptis Magna
  Libya 32°40N 14°12E 51 B8
Labe = Elbe → Europe 53°50N 9°0E 16 B5
Labé Guinea 11°24N 12°16W 50 F3
Laberge, L. Canada 61°11N 135°12W 70 A1
Labinsk Russia 44°40N 40°48E 19 F7
Labis Malaysia 2°22N 103°2E 39 L4
Laborie St. Lucia 13°45N 61°2W 89 f
Laboulaye Argentina 34°10S 63°30W 94 C3
Labrador Canada 53°20N 61°0W 73 B7
Labrador City Canada 52°57N 66°55W 73 B6
Labrador Sea Atl. Oc. 57°0N 54°0W 69 D14
Lábrea Brazil 7°15S 64°51W 92 E6
Labuan Malaysia 5°20N 115°14E 36 C5
Labuan, Pulau Malaysia 5°21N 115°13E 36 C5
Labuha Indonesia 0°30S 127°30E 37 E7
Labuhan Indonesia 6°22S 105°50E 37 G11
Labuhanbajo Indonesia 8°28S 119°54E 37 F6
Labuhanbilik Indonesia 2°31N 100°10E 39 L3
Labuk, Telok Malaysia 6°10N 117°50E 36 C5
Labyrinth, L. Australia 30°40S 135°11E 63 E2
Labytnangi Russia 66°39N 66°21E 28 C7
Lac-Bouchette Canada 48°16N 72°11W 73 C5
Lac Brochet Canada 57°53N 101°40W 71 B8
Lac Édouard Canada 47°40N 72°16W 72 C5
Lac La Biche Canada 54°45N 111°58W 70 C6
Lac la Martre = Wha Ti
  Canada 63°8N 117°16W 68 C8
Lac La Ronge △ Canada 55°9N 104°41W 71 B7
Lac-Mégantic Canada 45°35N 70°53W 73 C5
Lac Thien Vietnam 12°25N 108°11E 38 F7
Lacanau France 44°58N 1°5W 20 D3
Lacantún → Mexico 16°36N 90°39W 87 D6
Laccadive Is. = Lakshadweep Is.
  India 10°0N 72°30E 3 D13
Lacepede B. Australia 36°40S 139°40E 63 F2
Lacepede Is. Australia 16°55S 122°0E 60 C3
Lacerdónia Mozam. 18°3S 35°35E 55 F4
Lacey U.S.A. 47°7N 122°49W 78 C4
Lachania Greece 35°58N 27°54E 25 D9
Lachhmangarh India 27°50N 75°4E 42 F6
Lachi Pakistan 33°25N 71°20E 42 C4
Lachine Canada 45°26N 73°42W 72 C5
Lachlan → Australia 34°22S 143°55E 63 E3
Lachute Canada 45°39N 74°21W 72 C5
Lackagh Hills Ireland 54°16N 8°10W 10 B3
Lackawanna U.S.A. 42°50N 78°50W 82 D6
Lackawaxen U.S.A. 41°29N 74°59W 83 E10
Lacolle Canada 45°5N 73°22W 83 A11
Lacombe Canada 52°30N 113°44W 70 C6
Lacona U.S.A. 43°39N 76°10W 83 C8
Laconia U.S.A. 43°32N 71°28W 83 C13
Ladakh Ra. India 34°0N 78°0E 43 C8
Ladismith S. Africa 33°28S 21°15E 56 E3
Lādīz Iran 28°55N 61°15E 45 D9
Ladnun India 27°38N 74°25E 42 F6
Ladoga, L. = Ladozhskoye Ozero
  Russia 61°15N 30°30E 8 F24
Ladozhskoye Ozero
  Russia 61°15N 30°30E 8 F24
Lady Elliott I. Australia 24°7S 152°42E 62 C5
Lady Grey S. Africa 30°43S 27°13E 56 E4
Ladybrand S. Africa 29°9S 27°29E 56 D4
Ladysmith Canada 49°0N 123°49W 78 B3
Ladysmith S. Africa 28°32S 29°46E 57 D4
Ladysmith U.S.A. 45°28N 91°12W 80 C8
Lae Papua N. G. 6°40S 147°2E 58 B7
Laem Hin Khom Thailand 9°25N 99°56E 39 b
Laem Khat Thailand 8°6N 98°26E 39 a
Laem Nga Thailand 7°55N 98°27E 39 a
Laem Ngop Thailand 12°10N 102°26E 39 F4
Laem Phan Wa Thailand 7°47N 98°25E 39 a
Laem Pho Thailand 6°55N 101°19E 39 J3
Laem Phrom Thep Thailand 7°45N 98°19E 39 a
Laem Riang Thailand 8°7N 98°27E 39 a
Laem Sam Rong Thailand 9°35N 100°4E 39 b
Laem Son Thailand 7°59N 98°16E 39 a
Laem Yamu Thailand 7°59N 98°26E 39 a
Laerma Greece 36°9N 27°57E 25 C9
Læsø Denmark 57°15N 11°5E 9 H14
Lafayette Ind., U.S.A. 40°25N 86°54W 80 E10
Lafayette La., U.S.A. 30°14N 92°1W 84 F8
Lafayette Tenn., U.S.A. 36°31N 86°2W 85 C11
Laferte → Canada 61°53N 117°44W 70 A5
Lafia Nigeria 8°30N 8°34E 50 G7
Lafleche Canada 49°45N 106°40W 71 D7
Lagan → U.K. 54°36N 5°55W 10 B6
Lagarfljót → Iceland 65°40N 14°18W 8 D6
Lagdo, Rés. de Cameroon 8°40N 14°0E 51 G8
Lågen → Oppland, Norway 61°8N 10°25E 8 F14
Lågen → Vestfold, Norway 59°3N 10°3E 9 G14
Lages Brazil 27°48S 50°20W 95 B5
Lagos Nigeria 6°25N 3°27E 50 G6
Lagos Portugal 37°5N 8°41W 21 D1
Lagos de Moreno
  Mexico 21°21N 101°55W 86 C4
Lagrange = Bidyadanga
  Australia 18°45S 121°43E 60 C3
Lagrange B. Australia 18°38S 121°42E 60 C3
Laguna Brazil 28°30S 48°50W 95 B6
Laguna U.S.A. 35°2N 107°25W 77 J10
Laguna, Sa. de la
  Mexico 23°35N 109°55W 86 C3
Laguna Beach U.S.A. 33°33N 117°47W 79 M9
Laguna de la Restinga △
  Venezuela 10°58N 64°0W 89 D6
Laguna de Lachuá △
  Guatemala 15°55N 90°40W 88 C1
Laguna del Laja △ Chile 37°25S 71°20W 94 D1
Laguna del Tigre △
  Guatemala 17°32N 90°56W 88 C1
Laguna Limpia
  Argentina 26°32S 59°45W 94 B4

Lagunas Chile 21°0S 69°45W 94 A2
Lagunas Peru 5°10S 75°35W 92 E3
Lagunas de Chacahua △
  Mexico 16°0N 97°43W 87 D5
Lagunas de Montebello △
  Mexico 16°4N 91°42W 87 D6
Lahad Datu Malaysia 5°0N 118°20E 37 D5
Lahad Datu, Telok
  Malaysia 4°50N 118°20E 37 D5
Lahan Sai Thailand 14°25N 102°52E 38 E4
Lahanam Laos 16°16N 105°16E 38 D5
Lahar India 26°12N 78°57E 43 F8
Laharpur India 27°43N 80°56E 43 F9
Lahat Indonesia 3°45S 103°30E 36 E2
Lahewa Indonesia 1°22N 97°12E 36 D1
Lāhījān Iran 37°10N 50°6E 45 B6
Lahn → Germany 50°19N 7°37E 16 C4
Laholm Sweden 56°30N 13°2E 9 H15
Lahore Pakistan 31°32N 74°22E 42 D6
Lahri Pakistan 29°11N 68°13E 42 E3
Lāhrūd Iran 38°30N 47°52E 44 B5
Lahti Finland 60°58N 25°40E 8 F21
Lahtis = Lahti Finland 60°58N 25°40E 8 F21
Laï Chad 9°25N 16°18E 51 G9
Lai Chau Vietnam 22°5N 103°3E 38 A4
Laila = Layla Si. Arabia 22°10N 46°40E 47 C4
Laingsburg S. Africa 33°9S 20°52E 56 E3
Lainioälven → Sweden 67°35N 22°40E 8 C20
Lairg U.K. 58°2N 4°24W 11 C4
Laisamis Kenya 1°36N 37°48E 54 B4
Laishui China 39°23N 115°45E 34 E8
Laiwu China 36°15N 117°40E 35 F9
Laixi China 36°50N 120°31E 35 F11
Laiyang China 36°59N 120°45E 35 F11
Laiyuan China 39°20N 114°40E 34 E8
Laizhou China 37°8N 119°57E 35 F10
Laizhou Wan China 37°30N 119°30E 35 F10
Laja → Mexico 20°55N 100°46W 86 C4
Lajamanu Australia 18°23S 130°38E 60 C5
Lak Sao Laos 18°11N 104°59E 38 C5
Lakaband Pakistan 31°2N 69°15E 42 D3
Lake U.S.A. 44°33N 110°24W 76 D8
Lake Alpine U.S.A. 38°29N 120°0W 78 G7
Lake Andes U.S.A. 43°9N 98°32W 80 D4
Lake Arthur U.S.A. 30°5N 92°41W 84 F8
Lake Bindegolly △
  Australia 28°0S 144°12E 63 D3
Lake Cargelligo
  Australia 33°15S 146°22E 63 E4
Lake Charles U.S.A. 30°14N 93°13W 84 F8
Lake City Colo., U.S.A. 38°2N 107°19W 76 G10
Lake City Fla., U.S.A. 30°11N 82°38W 85 F13
Lake City Mich., U.S.A. 44°20N 85°13W 81 C11
Lake City Minn., U.S.A. 44°27N 92°16W 80 C7
Lake City Pa., U.S.A. 42°1N 80°21W 82 D4
Lake City S.C., U.S.A. 33°52N 79°45W 85 E15
Lake Cowichan Canada 48°49N 124°3W 70 D4
Lake District △ U.K. 54°30N 3°21W 12 C4
Lake Elsinore U.S.A. 33°38N 117°20W 79 M9
Lake Eyre △ Australia 28°40S 137°31E 63 D2
Lake Gairdner △
  Australia 31°41S 135°51E 63 E2
Lake George U.S.A. 43°26N 73°43W 83 C11
Lake Grace Australia 33°7S 118°28E 61 F2
Lake Harbour = Kimmirut
  Canada 62°50N 69°50W 69 C13
Lake Havasu City
  U.S.A. 34°27N 114°22W 79 L12
Lake Hughes U.S.A. 34°41N 118°26W 79 L8
Lake Isabella U.S.A. 35°38N 118°28W 79 K8
Lake Jackson U.S.A. 29°3N 95°27W 84 G7
Lake King Australia 33°5S 119°45E 61 F2
Lake Lenore Canada 52°24N 104°59W 71 C8
Lake Louise Canada 51°30N 116°10W 70 C5
Lake Malawi △ Malawi 14°2S 34°53E 55 E3
Lake Mburo △ Uganda 0°33S 30°56E 54 C3
Lake Mead △ U.S.A. 36°30N 114°22W 79 K12
Lake Meredith △
  U.S.A. 35°50N 101°50W 84 D4
Lake Mills U.S.A. 43°25N 93°32W 80 D7
Lake Nakuru △ Kenya 0°21S 36°5E 54 C4
Lake Placid U.S.A. 44°17N 73°59W 83 B11
Lake Pleasant U.S.A. 43°28N 74°25W 83 C10
Lake Providence U.S.A. 32°48N 91°10W 84 E9
Lake Roosevelt △
  U.S.A. 48°5N 118°14W 76 B4
Lake St. Peter Canada 45°18N 78°2W 82 A6
Lake Superior △ Canada 47°45N 84°45W 72 C3
Lake Torrens △
  Australia 30°55S 137°40E 63 E2
Lake Village U.S.A. 33°20N 91°17W 84 E9
Lake Wales U.S.A. 27°54N 81°35W 85 H14
Lake Worth U.S.A. 26°37N 80°3W 85 H14
Lakeba Fiji 18°13S 178°47E 59 a
Lakeba Passage Fiji 18°0S 178°45W 59 a
Lakefield Canada 44°25N 78°16W 82 B6
Lakefield △ Australia 15°24S 144°26E 62 B3
Lakehurst U.S.A. 40°1N 74°19W 83 F10
Lakeland Australia 15°49S 144°57E 62 B3
Lakeland U.S.A. 28°3N 81°57W 85 G14
Lakemba = Lakeba Fiji 18°13S 178°47W 59 a
Lakeport Calif., U.S.A. 39°3N 122°55W 78 F4
Lakeport Mich., U.S.A. 43°7N 82°30W 82 C2
Lakes Entrance Australia 37°50S 148°0E 63 F4
Lakeside Calif., U.S.A. 32°52N 116°55W 79 N10
Lakeside Nebr., U.S.A. 42°3N 102°26W 80 D2
Lakeview U.S.A. 42°11N 120°21W 76 E3
Lakeville U.S.A. 44°39N 93°14W 80 C7
Lakewood Colo., U.S.A. 39°42N 105°4W 76 G11
Lakewood N.J., U.S.A. 40°6N 74°13W 83 F10
Lakewood N.Y., U.S.A. 42°6N 79°19W 82 D5
Lakewood Ohio, U.S.A. 41°28N 81°47W 82 E3
Lakewood Wash.,
  U.S.A. 47°11N 122°32W 78 C4
Lakha India 26°9N 70°54E 42 F4
Lakhimpur India 27°57N 80°46E 43 F9
Lakhisarai India 25°11N 86°5E 43 G12

Lakhnadon India 22°36N 79°36E 43 H8
Lakhnau = Lucknow
  India 26°50N 81°0E 43 F9
Lakhonpheng Laos 15°54N 105°34E 38 E5
Lakhpat India 23°48N 68°47E 42 H3
Lakin U.S.A. 37°57N 101°15W 80 G3
Lakitusaki → Canada 54°21N 82°25W 72 B3
Lakki Greece 35°24N 23°57E 25 D5
Lakki Pakistan 32°36N 70°55E 42 C4
Lakonikos Kolpos
  Greece 36°40N 22°40E 23 F10
Lakor Indonesia 8°15S 128°17E 37 F7
Lakota Ivory C. 5°50N 5°30W 50 G4
Lakota U.S.A. 48°2N 98°21W 80 A4
Laksar India 29°46N 78°3E 42 E8
Laksefjorden Norway 70°45N 26°50E 8 A22
Lakselv Norway 70°2N 25°0E 8 A21
Lakshadweep Is. India 10°0N 72°30E 3 D13
Lakshmanpur India 22°58N 83°3E 43 H10
Lakshmikantapur India 22°5N 88°20E 43 H13
Lala Musa Pakistan 32°40N 73°57E 42 C5
Lalaghat India 24°30N 92°40E 41 G18
Lalago Tanzania 3°28S 33°58E 54 C3
Lalapanzi Zimbabwe 19°20S 30°15E 55 F3
L'Albufera Spain 39°20N 0°27W 21 C5
Lalganj India 25°52N 85°13E 43 G11
Lalgola India 24°25N 88°15E 43 G13
Lālī Iran 32°21N 49°6E 45 C6
Lalibela Ethiopia 12°3N 39°0E 47 E2
Lalin China 45°12N 127°0E 35 B14
Lalín Spain 42°40N 8°5W 21 A1
Lalin He → China 45°32N 125°40E 35 B13
Lalitapur Nepal 27°40N 85°20E 43 F11
Lalitpur India 24°42N 78°28E 43 G8
Lalkua India 29°5N 79°31E 43 E8
Lalsot India 26°34N 76°20E 42 F7
Lam Pao Res. Thailand 16°50N 103°15E 38 D4
Lamae Malaysia 9°51N 99°5E 39 H2
Lamaing Burma 15°25N 97°53E 38 E1
Lamar Colo., U.S.A. 38°5N 102°37W 76 G12
Lamar Mo., U.S.A. 37°30N 94°16W 80 G6
Lamas Peru 6°28S 76°31W 92 E3
Lamayuru India 34°18N 76°46E 43 B7
Lamayuru Jammu & Kashmir,
  India 34°25N 76°56E 43 B7
Lambaréné Gabon 0°41S 10°12E 52 E2
Lambasa = Labasa Fiji 16°30S 179°27E 59 a
Lambay I. Ireland 53°29N 6°1W 10 C5
Lambert's Bay S. Africa 32°5S 18°17E 56 E2
Lambeth Canada 42°54N 81°18W 82 D3
Lambomakondro
  Madag. 22°41S 44°44E 57 C7
Lambton Shores Canada 43°10N 81°56W 82 C3
Lame Deer U.S.A. 45°37N 106°40W 76 D10
Lamego Portugal 41°5N 7°52W 21 B2
Lamèque Canada 47°45N 64°38W 73 C7
Lameroo Australia 35°19S 140°33E 63 F3
Lamesa U.S.A. 32°44N 101°58W 84 E4
Lamia Greece 38°55N 22°26E 23 E10
Lamington △ Australia 28°13S 153°12E 63 D5
Lamma I. China 22°12N 114°7E 33 G11
Lammermuir Hills U.K. 55°50N 2°40W 11 F6
Lamoille → U.S.A. 44°38N 73°13W 83 B11
Lamon B. Phil. 14°30N 122°20E 37 B6
Lamont Canada 53°46N 112°50W 70 C6
Lamont Calif., U.S.A. 35°15N 118°55W 79 K8
Lamont Wyo., U.S.A. 42°13N 107°29W 76 E10
Lampa Peru 15°22S 70°22W 92 G4
Lampang Thailand 18°16N 99°32E 38 C2
Lampasas U.S.A. 31°4N 98°11W 84 F5
Lampazos de Naranjo
  Mexico 27°1N 100°31W 86 B4
Lampedusa Medit. S. 35°36N 12°40E 22 G5
Lampeter U.K. 52°7N 4°4W 13 E3
Lampione Medit. S. 35°33N 12°20E 22 G5
Lampman Canada 49°25N 102°50W 71 D8
Lampung □ Indonesia 5°30S 104°30E 36 F2
Lamta India 22°8N 80°7E 43 H9
Lamu Kenya 2°16S 40°55E 54 C5
Lamy U.S.A. 35°29N 105°53W 77 J11
Lan Xian China 38°15N 111°35E 34 E6
Läna'i U.S.A. 20°50N 156°55W 74 b
Lanak La China 34°27N 79°32E 43 B8
Lanak'o Shank'ou = Lanak La
  China 34°27N 79°32E 43 B8
Lanark Canada 45°1N 76°22W 83 A8
Lanark U.K. 55°40N 3°47W 11 F5
Lanbi Kyun Burma 10°50N 98°20E 39 G2
Lancang Jiang →
  China 21°40N 101°10E 32 D5
Lancashire □ U.K. 53°50N 2°48W 12 D5
Lancaster Canada 45°10N 74°30W 83 A10
Lancaster U.K. 54°3N 2°48W 12 C5
Lancaster Calif., U.S.A. 34°42N 118°8W 79 L8
Lancaster Ky., U.S.A. 37°37N 84°35W 81 G11
Lancaster N.H., U.S.A. 44°29N 71°34W 83 B13
Lancaster Ohio, U.S.A. 39°43N 82°36W 81 F12
Lancaster Pa., U.S.A. 40°2N 76°19W 83 F8
Lancaster S.C., U.S.A. 34°43N 80°46W 85 D14
Lancaster Wis., U.S.A. 42°51N 90°43W 80 D8
Lancaster Sd. Canada 74°13N 84°0W 69 B11
Lancelin Australia 31°0S 115°18E 61 F2
Lanchow = Lanzhou
  China 36°1N 103°52E 34 F2
Lanciano Italy 42°14N 14°23E 22 C6
Lanco Chile 39°51S 72°47W 96 D2
Land Between the Lakes △
  U.S.A. 36°25N 88°0W 85 C11
Landeck Austria 47°9N 10°34E 16 E6
Lander U.S.A. 42°50N 108°44W 76 E9
Lander → Australia 22°0S 132°0E 60 D5
Landes France 44°0N 1°0W 20 D3
Landi Kotal Pakistan 34°7N 71°6E 42 B4
Landisburg U.S.A. 40°21N 77°19W 82 F7
Land's End U.K. 50°4N 5°44W 13 G2
Landmannalaugar Iceland 63°59N 19°4W 8 E4
Landsborough Cr. →
  Australia 22°28S 144°35E 62 C3

Landshut Germany 48°34N 12°8E 16 D7
Lanesboro U.S.A. 41°57N 75°34W 83 E9
Lanett U.S.A. 32°52N 85°12W 85 E12
Lang Shan China 41°0N 106°30E 34 D4
Lang Son Vietnam 21°52N 106°42E 38 B6
Lang Suan Thailand 9°57N 99°4E 39 H2
La'nga Co China 30°45N 81°15E 43 D9
Langar Iran 35°23N 60°25E 45 C9
Langara I. Canada 54°14N 133°1W 70 C2
Langarūd Iran 37°11N 50°8E 45 B6
Langdon U.S.A. 48°45N 98°22W 80 A4
Langeberg S. Africa 33°55S 21°0E 56 E3
Langeberge S. Africa 28°15S 22°33E 56 D3
Langeland Denmark 54°56N 10°48E 9 J14
Langenburg Canada 50°51N 101°43W 71 C8
Langholm U.K. 55°9N 3°0W 11 F5
Langjökull Iceland 64°39N 20°12W 8 D3
Langkawi, Pulau Malaysia 6°25N 99°45E 39 J2
Langklip S. Africa 28°12S 20°20E 56 D3
Langkon Malaysia 6°30N 116°40E 36 C5
Langley Canada 49°7N 122°39W 78 A4
Langøya Norway 68°45N 14°50E 8 B16
Langreo Spain 43°18N 5°40W 21 A3
Langres France 47°52N 5°20E 20 C6
Langres, Plateau de France 47°45N 5°3E 20 C6
Langsa Indonesia 4°30N 97°57E 36 D1
Langtang △ Nepal 28°10N 85°30E 43 E11
Langtry U.S.A. 29°49N 101°34W 84 G4
Langu Thailand 6°53N 99°47E 39 J2
Languedoc France 43°58N 3°55E 20 E5
Langwang China 22°38N 113°27E 33 F9
Langxiangzhen China 39°43N 116°8E 34 E9
Lanigan Canada 51°51N 105°2W 71 C7
Lankao China 34°48N 114°50E 34 G8
Länkäran Azerbaijan 38°48N 48°52E 45 B6
Lannion France 48°46N 3°29W 20 B2
L'Annonciation Canada 46°25N 74°55W 72 C5
Lansdale U.S.A. 40°14N 75°17W 83 F9
Lansdowne Australia 31°48S 152°30E 63 E5
Lansdowne Canada 44°24N 76°1W 83 B8
Lansdowne India 29°50N 78°41E 43 E8
Lansdowne House = Neskantaga Canada 52°14N 87°53W 72 B2
L'Anse U.S.A. 46°45N 88°27W 80 B9
L'Anse au Loup Canada 51°32N 56°50W 73 B8
L'Anse aux Meadows Canada 51°36N 55°32W 73 B8
L'Anse la Raye St. Lucia 13°55N 61°3W 89 f
Lansford U.S.A. 40°50N 75°53W 83 F9
Lansing U.S.A. 42°44N 84°33W 81 D11
Lanta Yai, Ko Thailand 7°35N 99°3E 39 J2
Lantau I. China 22°15N 113°56E 33 G10
Lantian China 34°11N 109°20E 34 G5
Lanus Argentina 34°42S 58°23W 94 C4
Lanusei Italy 39°52N 9°34E 22 E3
Lanzarote Canary Is. 29°0N 13°40W 24 F6
Lanzarote ✈ (ACE) Canary Is. 28°57N 13°40W 24 F6
Lanzhou China 36°1N 103°52E 34 F2
Lao Bao Laos 16°35N 106°30E 38 D6
Lao Cai Vietnam 22°30N 103°57E 38 A4
Laoag Phil. 18°7N 120°34E 37 A6
Laoang Phil. 12°32N 125°8E 37 B7
Laoha He → China 43°25N 120°35E 35 C11
Laois □ Ireland 52°57N 7°36W 10 D4
Laon France 49°33N 3°35E 20 B5
Laona U.S.A. 45°34N 88°40W 80 C9
Laos ■ Asia 17°45N 105°0E 38 D5
Lapa Brazil 25°46S 49°44W 95 B6
Lapeer U.S.A. 43°3N 83°19W 81 D12
Lapithos Cyprus 35°21N 33°11E 25 D12
Lapland = Lappland Europe 68°7N 24°0E 8 B21
LaPorte Ind., U.S.A. 41°36N 86°43W 80 E10
Laporte Pa., U.S.A. 41°25N 76°30W 83 E8
Lappeenranta Finland 61°3N 28°12E 8 F23
Lappland Europe 68°7N 24°0E 8 B21
Lappo = Lapua Finland 62°58N 23°0E 8 E20
Laprida Argentina 37°34S 60°45W 94 D3
Lâpseki Turkey 40°20N 26°41E 23 D12
Laptev Sea Russia 76°0N 125°0E 29 B13
Lapua Finland 62°58N 23°0E 8 E20
L'Áquila Italy 42°22N 13°22E 22 C5
Lār Iran 27°40N 54°14E 45 E7
Laramie U.S.A. 41°19N 105°35W 76 F11
Laramie Mts. U.S.A. 42°0N 105°30W 76 F11
Laranjeiras do Sul Brazil 25°23S 52°23W 95 B5
Larantuka Indonesia 8°21S 122°55E 37 F6
Larat Indonesia 7°0S 132°0E 37 F8
Larde Mozam. 16°28S 39°43E 55 F4
Larder Lake Canada 48°5N 79°40W 72 C4
Lardos Greece 36°6N 28°1E 25 C10
Lardos, Akra = Lindos, Akra Greece 36°4N 28°10E 25 C10
Lardos, Ormos Greece 36°4N 28°2E 25 C10
Lare Kenya 0°20N 37°56E 54 C4
Laredo U.S.A. 27°30N 99°30W 84 H5
Laredo Sd. Canada 52°30N 128°53W 70 C3
Largo U.S.A. 27°54N 82°47W 85 H13
Largs U.K. 55°47N 4°52W 11 F4
Lariang Indonesia 1°26S 119°17E 37 E5
Larimore U.S.A. 47°54N 97°38W 80 B5
Larisa Greece 39°36N 22°27E 23 E10
Larkana Pakistan 27°32N 68°18E 42 F3
Larnaca Cyprus 34°55N 33°38E 25 E12
Larnaca Bay Cyprus 34°53N 33°45E 25 E12
Larne U.K. 54°51N 5°51W 10 B6
Larned U.S.A. 38°11N 99°6W 80 F4
Larose U.S.A. 29°34N 90°23W 85 G9
Larrimah Australia 15°35S 133°12E 60 C5
Larsen Ice Shelf Antarctica 67°0S 62°0W 5 C17
Larvik Norway 59°4N 10°2E 9 G14
Las Animas U.S.A. 38°4N 103°13W 76 G12
Las Anod = Laascaanood Somali Rep. 8°26N 47°19E 47 F4
Las Brenãs Argentina 27°5S 61°7W 94 B3
Las Cañadas del Teide △ Canary Is. 28°15N 16°37W 24 F3
Las Cejas Argentina 26°53S 64°44W 96 B4
Las Chimeneas Mexico 32°8N 116°5W 79 N10
Las Cruces U.S.A. 32°19N 106°47W 77 K10
Las Flores Argentina 36°10S 59°7W 94 D4
Las Heras Argentina 32°51S 68°49W 94 C2
Las Lajas Argentina 38°30S 70°25W 96 D2
Las Lomitas Argentina 24°43S 60°35W 94 A3
Las Palmas Argentina 27°8S 58°45W 94 B4
Las Palmas Canary Is. 28°7N 15°26W 24 F4
Las Palmas → Mexico 32°31N 116°58W 79 N10
Las Palmas ✈ (LPA) Canary Is. 27°55N 15°25W 24 G4
Las Piedras Uruguay 34°44S 56°14W 95 C4
Las Pipinas Argentina 35°30S 57°19W 94 D4
Las Plumas Argentina 43°40S 67°15W 96 E3
Las Rosas Argentina 32°30S 61°35W 94 C3
Las Tablas Panama 7°49N 80°14W 88 E3
Las Toscas Argentina 28°21S 59°18W 94 B4
Las Truchas Mexico 17°57N 102°13W 86 D4
Las Tunas Cuba 20°58N 76°59W 88 B4
Las Varillas Argentina 31°50S 62°50W 94 C3
Las Vegas N. Mex., U.S.A. 35°36N 105°13W 77 J11
Las Vegas Nev., U.S.A. 36°10N 115°8W 79 J11
Las Vegas McCarran Int. ✈ (LAS) U.S.A. 36°5N 115°9W 79 J11
Lascano Uruguay 33°35S 54°12W 95 C5
Lash-e Joveyn Afghan. 31°45N 61°30E 40 D2
Lashburn Canada 53°10N 109°40W 71 C7
Lashio Burma 22°56N 97°45E 41 H20
Lashkar India 26°10N 78°10E 42 F8
Lasithi Greece 35°11N 25°31E 25 D7
Lasithi □ Greece 35°5N 25°50E 25 D7
Lāsjerd Iran 35°24N 53°4E 45 C7
Lassen Pk. U.S.A. 40°29N 121°30W 76 F3
Lassen Volcanic △ U.S.A. 40°30N 121°20W 76 F3
Last Mountain L. Canada 51°5N 105°14W 71 C7
Lastchance Cr. → U.S.A. 40°2N 121°15W 78 E5
Lastoursville Gabon 0°55S 12°38E 52 E2
Lastovo Croatia 42°46N 16°55E 22 C7
Lat Yao Thailand 15°45N 99°48E 38 E2
Latacunga Ecuador 0°50S 78°35W 92 D3
Latakia = Al Lādhiqīyah Syria 35°30N 35°45E 44 C2
Latchford Canada 47°20N 79°50W 72 C4
Late Tonga 18°48S 174°39W 59 c
Latehar India 23°45N 84°30E 43 H11
Latham Australia 29°44S 116°20E 61 E2
Lathi India 27°43N 71°23E 42 F4
Lathrop Wells U.S.A. 36°39N 116°24W 79 J10
Latina Italy 41°28N 12°52E 22 D5
Latium = Lazio □ Italy 42°10N 12°30E 22 C5
Laton U.S.A. 36°26N 119°41W 78 J7
Latouche Treville, C. Australia 18°27S 121°49E 60 C3
Latrobe Australia 41°14S 146°30E 63 G4
Latrobe U.S.A. 40°19N 79°23W 82 F5
Latvia ■ Europe 56°50N 24°0E 9 H21
Lau Fau Shan China 22°28N 113°59E 33 G10
Lau Group Fiji 17°0S 178°30W 59 a
Lauchhammer Germany 51°29N 13°47E 16 C7
Laughlin U.S.A. 35°10N 114°34W 77 J6
Laukaa Finland 62°24N 25°56E 8 E21
Launceston Australia 41°24S 147°8E 63 G4
Launceston U.K. 50°38N 4°22W 13 G3
Laune → Ireland 52°7N 9°47W 10 D2
Launglon Bok Burma 13°50N 97°54E 38 F1
Laura Australia 15°32S 144°32E 62 B3
Laurel Miss., U.S.A. 31°41N 89°8W 85 F10
Laurel Mont., U.S.A. 45°40N 108°46W 76 D9
Laurel Hill U.S.A. 40°14N 79°6W 82 F5
Laurencekirk U.K. 56°50N 2°28W 11 E6
Laurens U.S.A. 34°30N 82°1W 85 D13
Laurentian Plateau Canada 52°0N 70°0W 73 B6
Lauria Italy 40°2N 15°50E 22 E6
Laurie L. Canada 56°35N 101°57W 71 B8
Laurinburg U.S.A. 34°47N 79°28W 85 D15
Laurium U.S.A. 47°14N 88°27W 80 B9
Lausanne Switz. 46°32N 6°38E 20 C7
Laut Indonesia 4°45N 108°0E 36 D3
Laut, Pulau Indonesia 3°40S 116°10E 36 E5
Laut Kecil, Kepulauan Indonesia 4°45S 115°40E 36 E5
Lautoka Fiji 17°37S 177°27E 59 a
Lava Beds ⌂ U.S.A. 41°40N 121°30W 76 F3
Lavagh More Ireland 54°46N 8°6W 10 B3
Laval France 48°4N 0°48W 20 B3
Laval-des-Rapides Canada 45°33N 73°42W 72 C5
Lavalle Argentina 28°15S 65°15W 94 B2
Lāvān Iran 26°48N 53°22E 45 E7
Lavant Canada 45°3N 76°42W 83 A8
Lāvar Meydān Iran 30°20N 54°30E 45 D7
Laverton Australia 28°44S 122°29E 61 E3
Lavras Brazil 21°20S 45°0W 95 A7
Lavrio Greece 37°40N 24°4E 23 F11
Lavris Greece 35°25N 24°40E 25 D6
Lavumisa Swaziland 27°20S 31°55E 57 D5
Lavushi Manda △ Zambia 12°46S 31°0E 55 E3
Lawaki Fiji 17°40S 178°35E 59 a
Lawas Malaysia 4°55N 115°25E 36 D5
Lawele Indonesia 5°13S 122°57E 37 F6
Lawn Hill = Boodjamulla △ Australia 18°15S 138°6E 62 B2
Lawqah Si. Arabia 29°49N 42°45E 44 D4
Lawrence N.Z. 45°55S 169°41E 59 F2
Lawrence Ind., U.S.A. 39°50N 86°2W 80 F10
Lawrence Kans., U.S.A. 38°58N 95°14W 80 F6
Lawrence Mass., U.S.A. 42°43N 71°10W 83 D13
Lawrenceburg Ind., U.S.A. 39°6N 84°52W 81 F11
Lawrenceburg Tenn., U.S.A. 35°14N 87°20W 85 D11
Lawrenceville Ga., U.S.A. 33°57N 83°59W 85 E13
Lawrenceville Pa., U.S.A. 41°59N 77°8W 82 E7
Laws U.S.A. 37°24N 118°20W 78 H8
Lawton U.S.A. 34°37N 98°25W 84 D5
Lawu Indonesia 7°40S 111°13E 37 G14
Laxford, L. U.K. 58°24N 5°6W 11 C3
Layla Si. Arabia 22°10N 46°40E 47 C4
Laylān Iraq 35°18N 44°31E 44 C5
Layton U.S.A. 41°4N 111°58W 76 F8
Laytonville U.S.A. 39°41N 123°29W 76 G2
Lazarev Russia 52°13N 141°30E 29 D15
Lazarev Sea S. Ocean 67°30S 3°0W 5 C2
Lazarivo Madag. 23°54S 44°59E 57 C8
Lázaro Cárdenas Mexico 17°55N 102°11W 86 D4
Lazio □ Italy 42°10N 12°30E 22 C5
Lazo Russia 43°25N 133°55E 30 C6
Le Bic Canada 48°20N 68°41W 73 C6
Le Creusot France 46°48N 4°24E 20 C6
Le François Martinique 14°38N 60°57W 88 c
Le Gosier Guadeloupe 16°14N 61°29W 88 b
Le Gris Gris Mauritius 20°31S 57°32E 53 d
Le Havre France 49°30N 0°5E 20 B4
Le Lamentin Martinique 14°35N 61°2W 88 c
Le Mans France 48°0N 0°10E 20 C4
Le Marin Martinique 14°27N 60°55W 88 c
Le Mars U.S.A. 42°47N 96°10W 80 D5
Le Mont-St-Michel France 48°40N 1°30W 20 B3
Le Moule Guadeloupe 16°20N 61°22W 88 b
Le Moyne, L. Canada 56°45N 68°47W 73 A6
Le Port Réunion 20°56S 55°18E 53 c
Le Prêcheur Martinique 14°50N 61°12W 88 c
Le Puy-en-Velay France 45°3N 3°52E 20 D5
Le Raysville U.S.A. 41°50N 76°10W 83 E8
Le Robert Martinique 14°40N 60°56W 88 c
Le Roy U.S.A. 42°58N 77°59W 82 D7
Le St-Esprit Martinique 14°34N 60°56W 88 c
Le Sueur U.S.A. 44°28N 93°55W 80 C7
Le Tampon Réunion 21°16S 55°32E 53 c
Le Thuy Vietnam 17°14N 106°49E 38 D6
Le Touquet-Paris-Plage France 50°30N 1°36E 20 A4
Le Tréport France 50°3N 1°20E 20 A4
Le Verdon-sur-Mer France 45°33N 1°4W 20 D3
Lea → U.K. 51°31N 0°1E 13 F8
Leach Cambodia 12°21N 103°46E 39 F4
Lead U.S.A. 44°21N 103°46W 80 C2
Leader Canada 50°50N 109°30W 71 C7
Leadville U.S.A. 39°15N 106°18W 76 G10
Leaf → U.S.A. 30°59N 88°44W 85 F10
Leaf Rapids Canada 56°30N 99°59W 71 B9
Leamington Canada 42°3N 82°36W 82 D2
Leamington U.S.A. 39°32N 112°17W 76 G7
Leamington Spa = Royal Leamington Spa U.K. 52°18N 1°31W 13 E6
Leandro Norte Alem Argentina 27°34S 55°15W 95 B4
Leane, L. Ireland 52°2N 9°32W 10 D2
Learmonth Australia 22°13S 114°10E 60 D1
Leask Canada 53°5N 106°45W 71 C7
Leatherhead U.K. 51°18N 0°20W 13 F7
Leavenworth Kans., U.S.A. 39°19N 94°55W 80 F6
Leavenworth Wash., U.S.A. 47°36N 120°40W 76 C3
Leawood U.S.A. 38°58N 94°37W 80 F6
Lebak Phil. 6°32N 124°5E 37 C6
Lebam U.S.A. 46°34N 123°33W 78 D3
Lebanon Ind., U.S.A. 40°3N 86°28W 80 E10
Lebanon Kans., U.S.A. 39°49N 98°33W 80 F4
Lebanon Ky., U.S.A. 37°34N 85°15W 81 G11
Lebanon Mo., U.S.A. 37°41N 92°40W 80 G7
Lebanon N.H., U.S.A. 43°39N 72°15W 83 C12
Lebanon Oreg., U.S.A. 44°32N 122°55W 76 D2
Lebanon Pa., U.S.A. 40°20N 76°26W 83 F8
Lebanon Tenn., U.S.A. 36°12N 86°18W 85 C11
Lebanon ■ Asia 34°0N 36°0E 46 B5
Lebec U.S.A. 34°51N 118°52W 79 L8
Lebel-sur-Quévillon Canada 49°3N 76°59W 72 C4
Lebomboberge S. Africa 24°30S 32°0E 57 C5
Lębork Poland 54°33N 17°46E 17 A9
Lebrija Spain 36°53N 6°5W 21 D2
Lebu Chile 37°40S 73°47W 94 D1
Lecce Italy 40°23N 18°11E 23 D8
Lecco Italy 45°51N 9°23E 20 D8
Lech → Germany 48°43N 10°56E 16 D6
Lecontes Mills U.S.A. 41°5N 78°17W 82 E6
Łęczyca Poland 52°5N 19°15E 17 B10
Ledong China 18°41N 109°5E 38 C7
Leduc Canada 53°15N 113°30W 70 C6
Lee U.S.A. 42°19N 73°15W 83 D11
Lee → Ireland 51°53N 8°56W 10 E3
Lee Vining U.S.A. 37°58N 119°7W 78 H7
Leech L. U.S.A. 47°10N 94°24W 80 B6
Leechburg U.S.A. 40°37N 79°36W 82 F5
Leeds U.K. 53°48N 1°33W 12 D6
Leeds U.S.A. 33°33N 86°33W 85 E11
Leek Neths. 53°10N 6°24E 15 A6
Leek U.K. 53°7N 2°1W 12 D5
Leeman Australia 29°57S 114°58E 61 E1
Leeper U.S.A. 41°22N 79°18W 82 E5
Leer Germany 53°13N 7°26E 16 B4
Leesburg U.S.A. 28°49N 81°53W 85 G14
Leesville U.S.A. 31°8N 93°16W 84 F8
Leeton Australia 34°33S 146°23E 63 E4
Leetonia U.S.A. 40°53N 80°45W 82 F4
Leeu Gamka S. Africa 32°47S 21°59E 56 E3
Leeuwarden Neths. 53°15N 5°48E 15 A5
Leeuwin, C. Australia 34°20S 115°9E 61 F2
Leeuwin Naturaliste △ Australia 34°6S 115°3E 61 F2
Leeward Is. Atl. Oc. 16°30N 63°30W 89 C7
Lefka Cyprus 35°6N 32°51E 25 D11
Lefkada Greece 38°40N 20°43E 23 E9
Lefkimi Greece 39°25N 20°3E 25 B4
Lefkimis, Akra Greece 39°29N 20°4E 25 B4
Lefkoniko Cyprus 35°18N 33°44E 25 D12
Lefroy Canada 44°16N 79°34W 82 B5
Lefroy, L. Australia 31°21S 121°40E 61 F3
Leganés Spain 40°19N 3°45W 21 B4
Legazpi Phil. 13°10N 123°45E 37 B6
Legendre I. Australia 20°22S 116°55E 60 D2
Leghorn = Livorno Italy 43°33N 10°19E 22 C4
Legionowo Poland 52°25N 20°50E 17 B11
Legnago Italy 45°11N 11°18E 22 B4
Legnica Poland 51°12N 16°10E 16 C9
Leh India 34°9N 77°35E 43 B7
Lehigh Acres U.S.A. 26°36N 81°39W 85 H14
Lehighton U.S.A. 40°50N 75°43W 83 F9
Lehututu Botswana 23°54S 21°55E 56 C3
Leiah Pakistan 30°58N 70°58E 42 D4
Leicester U.K. 52°38N 1°8W 13 E6
Leicester City □ U.K. 52°38N 1°8W 13 E6
Leicestershire □ U.K. 52°41N 1°17W 13 E6
Leichhardt → Australia 17°35S 139°48E 62 B2
Leichhardt Ra. Australia 20°46S 147°40E 62 C4
Leiden Neths. 52°9N 4°30E 15 B4
Leie → Belgium 51°2N 3°45E 15 C3
Leimus Nic. 14°40N 84°3W 88 D3
Leine → Germany 52°43N 9°36E 16 B5
Leinster Australia 27°51S 120°36E 61 E3
Leinster □ Ireland 53°3N 7°8W 10 C4
Leinster, Mt. Ireland 52°37N 6°46W 10 D5
Leipzig Germany 51°18N 12°22E 16 C7
Leiria Portugal 39°46N 8°53W 21 C1
Leirvik Norway 59°47N 5°28E 9 G11
Leisler, Mt. Australia 23°23S 129°20E 60 D4
Leith U.K. 55°59N 3°11W 11 F5
Leith Hill U.K. 51°11N 0°22W 13 F7
Leitrim Ireland 54°0N 8°5W 10 B3
Leitrim □ Ireland 54°8N 8°0W 10 B4
Leizhou Bandao China 21°0N 110°0E 33 D6
Lek → Neths. 51°54N 4°35E 15 C4
Leka Norway 65°5N 11°35E 8 D14
Leland Mich., U.S.A. 45°1N 85°45W 81 C11
Leland Miss., U.S.A. 33°24N 90°54W 85 E9
Leleque Argentina 42°28S 71°0W 96 E2
Lelystad Neths. 52°30N 5°25E 15 B5
Léman, L. Europe 46°26N 6°30E 20 C7
Lembar Indonesia 8°45S 116°4E 37 K19
Lembuak Indonesia 8°36S 116°11E 37 K19
Lemera Dem. Rep. of the Congo 3°0S 28°55E 54 C2
Lemhi Ra. U.S.A. 44°0N 113°0W 76 D7
Lemmer Neths. 52°51N 5°43E 15 B5
Lemmon U.S.A. 45°57N 102°10W 80 C2
Lemon Grove U.S.A. 32°44N 117°1W 79 N9
Lemoore U.S.A. 36°18N 119°46W 78 J7
Lemvig Denmark 56°33N 8°20E 9 H13
Lena → Russia 72°52N 126°40E 29 B13
Lenadoon Pt. Ireland 54°18N 9°3W 10 B2
Lenggong Malaysia 5°6N 100°58E 39 K3
Lengua de Vaca, Pta. Chile 30°14S 71°38W 94 C1
Lengwe △ Malawi 16°14S 34°45E 55 F3
Leninogorsk Kazakhstan 50°20N 83°30E 28 D9
Leninsk Russia 48°40N 45°15E 19 E8
Leninsk-Kuznetskiy Russia 54°44N 86°10E 28 D9
Lenkoran = Länkäran Azerbaijan 38°48N 48°52E 45 B6
Lenmalu Indonesia 1°45S 130°15E 37 E8
Lennox U.S.A. 43°21N 96°53W 80 D5
Lennoxville Canada 45°22N 71°51W 83 A13
Lenoir U.S.A. 35°55N 81°32W 85 D14
Lenoir City U.S.A. 35°48N 84°16W 85 D12
Lenore L. Canada 52°30N 104°59W 71 C8
Lenox U.S.A. 42°22N 73°17W 83 D11
Lens France 50°26N 2°50E 20 A5
Lensk Russia 60°48N 114°55E 29 C12
Lentas Greece 34°56N 24°56E 25 E6
Lentini Italy 37°17N 15°0E 22 F6
Lenwood U.S.A. 34°53N 117°7W 79 L9
Lenya Burma 11°33N 98°57E 39 G2
Leoben Austria 47°22N 15°5E 16 E8
Leodhas = Lewis U.K. 58°9N 6°40W 11 C2
Leola U.S.A. 45°43N 98°56W 80 C4
Leominster U.K. 52°14N 2°43W 13 E5
Leominster U.S.A. 42°32N 71°46W 83 D13
León Mexico 21°6N 101°41W 86 C4
León Nic. 12°20N 86°51W 88 D2
León Spain 42°38N 5°34W 21 A3
Leon U.S.A. 40°44N 93°45W 80 E7
Leon → U.S.A. 31°14N 97°28W 84 F6
León, Montes de Spain 42°30N 6°18W 21 A2
Leonardtown U.S.A. 38°17N 76°38W 81 F15
Leonardville Namibia 23°29S 18°49E 56 C2
Leone Amer. Samoa 14°23S 170°48W 59 b
Leongatha Australia 38°30S 145°58E 63 F4
Leonora Australia 28°49S 121°19E 61 E3
Leopoldina Brazil 21°28S 42°40W 95 A7
Leopoldsburg Belgium 51°7N 5°13E 15 C5
Leoti U.S.A. 38°29N 101°21W 80 F3
Leova Moldova 46°28N 28°15E 17 E15
Leoville Canada 53°39N 107°33W 71 C7
Lepel = Lyepyel Belarus 54°50N 28°40E 9 J23
Lépo, L. do Angola 17°0S 19°0E 56 B2
Leppävirta Finland 62°29N 27°46E 8 E22
Leptis Magna Libya 32°40N 14°12E 51 B8
Leribe Lesotho 28°51S 28°3E 57 D4
Lérida = Lleida Spain 41°37N 0°39E 21 B6
Lerwick U.K. 60°9N 1°9W 11 A7
Les Cayes Haiti 18°15N 73°46W 89 C5
Les Coteaux Canada 45°15N 74°13W 83 A10
Les Escoumins Canada 48°21N 69°24W 73 C6
Les Sables-d'Olonne France 46°30N 1°45W 20 C3
Lesbos Greece 39°10N 26°20E 23 E12
Leshan China 29°33N 103°41E 32 D5
Leshukonskoye Russia 64°54N 45°46E 18 B8
Leshwe ⌂ Dem. Rep. of the Congo 12°45S 29°30E 55 E2
Leskov I. Antarctica 56°0S 28°0W 5 B1
Leskovac Serbia 43°0N 21°58E 23 C9
Lesopilnoye Russia 46°44N 134°20E 30 A7
Lesotho ■ Africa 29°40S 28°0E 57 D4
Lesozavodsk Russia 45°30N 133°29E 30 B6
Lesse → Belgium 50°15N 4°54E 15 D4
Lesse et Lomme ⌂ Belgium 50°8N 5°9E 15 D5
Lesser Antilles W. Indies 15°0N 61°0W 89 D7
Lesser Slave L. Canada 55°30N 115°25W 70 B5
Lesser Sunda Is. Indonesia 8°0S 120°0E 37 F6
Lessines Belgium 50°42N 3°50E 15 D3
Lester B. Pearson Int., Toronto ✈ (YYZ) Canada 43°46N 79°35W 82 C5
Lestock Canada 51°19N 103°59W 71 C8
Lesuer I. Australia 13°50S 127°17E 60 B4
Lesueur △ Australia 30°11S 115°10E 61 F2
Lésvos = Lesbos Greece 39°10N 26°20E 23 E12
Leszno Poland 51°50N 16°30E 17 C9
Letaba S. Africa 23°59S 31°50E 57 C5
Letchworth U.K. 51°59N 0°13W 13 F7
Lethbridge Canada 49°45N 112°45W 70 D6
Lethem Guyana 3°20N 59°50W 92 C7
Leti, Kepulauan Indonesia 8°10S 128°0E 37 F7
Leti Is. = Leti, Kepulauan Indonesia 8°10S 128°0E 37 F7
Letiahau → Botswana 21°16S 24°0E 56 C3
Leticia Colombia 4°9S 70°0W 92 D5
Leting China 39°23N 118°55E 35 E10
Letjiesbos S. Africa 32°34S 22°16E 56 E3
Letlhakane Botswana 21°27S 25°30E 56 C4
Letlhakeng Botswana 24°0S 24°59E 56 C3
Letpadan Burma 17°45N 95°45E 41 L19
Letpan Burma 19°28N 94°10E 41 K19
Letsôk-aw Kyun Burma 11°30N 98°25E 39 G2
Letterkenny Ireland 54°57N 7°45W 10 B4
Leucadia U.S.A. 33°4N 117°18W 79 M9
Leuchars U.K. 56°24N 2°53W 11 E6
Leuser, G. Indonesia 3°46N 97°12E 36 D1
Leuven Belgium 50°52N 4°42E 15 D4
Leuze-en-Hainaut Belgium 50°36N 3°37E 15 D3
Levanger Norway 63°45N 11°19E 8 E14
Levelland U.S.A. 33°35N 102°23W 84 E3
Leven U.K. 56°12N 3°0W 11 E6
Leven, L. U.K. 56°12N 3°22W 11 E5
Leven, Toraka Madag. 12°30S 47°45E 57 A8
Leveque C. Australia 16°20S 123°0E 60 C3
Levice Slovak Rep. 48°13N 18°35E 17 D10
Levin N.Z. 40°37S 175°18E 59 D5
Lévis Canada 46°48N 71°9W 73 C5
Levis, L. Canada 62°37N 117°58W 70 A5
Levittown N.Y., U.S.A. 40°44N 73°31W 83 F11
Levittown Pa., U.S.A. 40°9N 74°51W 83 F10
Levka Oros Greece 35°18N 24°3E 25 D6
Levkás = Lefkada Greece 38°40N 20°43E 23 E9
Levkôsia = Nicosia Cyprus 35°10N 33°25E 25 D12
Levskigrad = Karlovo Bulgaria 42°38N 24°47E 23 C11
Levuka Fiji 17°34S 179°0E 59 a
Lewes U.K. 50°52N 0°1E 13 G8
Lewes U.S.A. 38°46N 75°9W 81 F16
Lewis U.K. 58°9N 6°40W 11 C2
Lewis → U.S.A. 45°51N 122°48W 78 E4
Lewis, Butt of U.K. 58°31N 6°16W 11 C2
Lewis Ra. Australia 20°3S 128°50E 60 D4
Lewis Range U.S.A. 48°5N 113°5W 76 B7
Lewis Run U.S.A. 41°52N 78°40W 82 E6
Lewisburg Pa., U.S.A. 40°58N 76°54W 82 F8
Lewisburg Tenn., U.S.A. 35°27N 86°48W 85 D11
Lewisburg W. Va., U.S.A. 37°48N 80°27W 81 G13
Lewisporte Canada 49°15N 55°3W 73 C8
Lewiston Idaho, U.S.A. 46°25N 117°1W 76 C5
Lewiston Maine, U.S.A. 44°6N 70°13W 81 C18
Lewiston N.Y., U.S.A. 43°11N 79°3W 82 C5
Lewistown Mont., U.S.A. 47°4N 109°26W 76 C9
Lewistown Pa., U.S.A. 40°36N 77°34W 82 F7
Lexington Ill., U.S.A. 40°39N 88°47W 80 E9
Lexington Ky., U.S.A. 38°3N 84°30W 81 F11
Lexington Mich., U.S.A. 43°16N 82°32W 82 C2
Lexington Mo., U.S.A. 39°11N 93°52W 80 F7
Lexington N.C., U.S.A. 35°49N 80°15W 85 D14
Lexington N.Y., U.S.A. 42°15N 74°22W 83 D10
Lexington Nebr., U.S.A. 40°47N 99°45W 80 E4
Lexington Ohio, U.S.A. 40°41N 82°35W 82 F2
Lexington Tenn., U.S.A. 35°39N 88°24W 85 D10
Lexington Va., U.S.A. 37°47N 79°27W 81 G14
Lexington Park U.S.A. 38°16N 76°27W 81 F15
Leyburn U.K. 54°19N 1°48W 12 C6
Leyland U.K. 53°42N 2°43W 12 D5
Leyte □ Phil. 11°0N 125°0E 37 B7
Lezhë Albania 41°47N 19°39E 23 D8
Lhasa China 29°25N 90°58E 32 D4
Lhazê China 29°5N 87°38E 32 D3
L'Hermite, I. Chile 55°50S 68°0W 96 H3
Lhokkruet Indonesia 4°55N 95°24E 36 D1
Lhokseumawe Indonesia 5°10N 97°10E 36 C1
L'Hospitalet de Llobregat Spain 41°21N 2°6E 21 B7
Li Thailand 17°48N 98°57E 38 D2
Li Xian Gansu, China 34°10N 105°5E 34 G3
Li Xian Hebei, China 38°30N 115°35E 34 E8
Liancourt Rocks = Tokdo Asia 37°15N 131°52E 31 F5
Lianga Phil. 8°38N 126°6E 37 C7
Liangcheng Nei Monggol Zizhiqu, China 40°28N 112°25E 34 D7
Liangcheng Shandong, China 35°32N 119°37E 35 G10
Liangdang China 33°56N 106°18E 34 H4
Liangpran Indonesia 1°4N 114°23E 36 D4
Lianshanguan China 40°53N 123°43E 35 D12
Lianshui China 33°42N 119°20E 35 H10

Lianyungang China 34°40N 119°11E 35 G10
Liao He → China 41°0N 121°50E 35 D11
Liaocheng China 36°28N 115°58E 34 F8
Liaodong Bandao China 40°0N 122°30E 35 E12
Liaodong Wan China 40°20N 121°10E 35 D11
Liaoning □ China 41°40N 122°30E 35 D12
Liaotung, G. of = Liaodong Wan
 China 40°20N 121°10E 35 D11
Liaoyang China 41°15N 122°58E 35 D12
Liaoyuan China 42°58N 125°2E 35 C13
Liaozhong China 41°23N 122°50E 35 D12
Liapades Greece 39°42N 19°40E 25 A3
Liard → Canada 61°51N 121°18W 70 A4
Liard River Canada 59°25N 126°5W 70 B3
Liari Pakistan 25°37N 66°30E 42 G2
Libau = Liepāja Latvia 56°30N 21°0E 9 H19
Libby U.S.A. 48°23N 115°33W 76 B6
Libenge
 Dem. Rep. of the Congo 3°40N 18°55E 52 D3
Liberal U.S.A. 37°3N 100°55W 80 G3
Liberec Czech Rep. 50°47N 15°7E 16 C8
Liberia Costa Rica 10°40N 85°30W 88 D2
Liberia ■ W. Afr. 6°30N 9°30W 50 G4
Libertador □ Chile 34°15S 70°45W 94 C1
Liberty Mo., U.S.A. 39°15N 94°25W 80 F6
Liberty N.Y., U.S.A. 41°48N 74°45W 83 E10
Liberty Pa., U.S.A. 41°34N 77°6W 82 E7
Liberty Tex., U.S.A. 30°3N 94°48W 84 F7
Liberty-Newark Int. ✈ (EWR)
 U.S.A. 40°42N 74°10W 83 F10
Lībīya, Sahrā' Africa 25°0N 25°0E 51 C10
Libobo, Tanjung
 Indonesia 0°54S 128°28E 37 E7
Libode S. Africa 31°33S 29°2E 57 E4
Libong, Ko Thailand 7°15N 99°23E 39 J2
Libourne France 44°55N 0°14W 20 D3
Libramont Belgium 49°55N 5°23E 15 E5
Libreville Gabon 0°25N 9°26E 52 D1
Libya ■ N. Afr. 27°0N 17°0E 51 C9
Libyan Desert = Lībīya, Sahrā'
 Africa 25°0N 25°0E 51 C10
Libyan Plateau = Ed Déffa
 Egypt 30°40N 26°30E 51 B11
Licantén Chile 35°55S 72°0W 94 D1
Licata Italy 37°6N 13°56E 22 F5
Licheng China 36°28N 113°20E 34 F7
Lichfield U.K. 52°41N 1°49W 13 E6
Lichinga Mozam. 13°13S 35°11E 55 E4
Lichtenburg S. Africa 26°8S 26°8E 56 D4
Licking → U.S.A. 39°6N 84°30W 81 F11
Licungo → Mozam. 17°40S 37°15E 55 F4
Lida Belarus 53°53N 25°15E 17 B13
Lidköping Sweden 58°31N 13°7E 9 G15
Liebig, Mt. Australia 23°18S 131°22E 60 D5
Liechtenstein ■ Europe 47°8N 9°35E 20 C8
Liège Belgium 50°38N 5°35E 15 D5
Liège □ Belgium 50°32N 5°35E 15 D5
Liegnitz = Legnica
 Poland 51°12N 16°10E 16 C9
Lieksa Finland 63°18N 30°2E 8 E24
Lienart
 Dem. Rep. of the Congo 3°3N 25°31E 54 B2
Lienyünchiangshih =
 Lianyungang China 34°40N 119°11E 35 G10
Lienz Austria 46°50N 12°46E 16 E7
Liepāja Latvia 56°30N 21°0E 9 H19
Lier Belgium 51°7N 4°34E 15 C4
Lietuva = Lithuania ■
 Europe 55°30N 24°0E 9 J21
Lièvre → Canada 45°31N 75°26W 72 C4
Liffey → Ireland 53°21N 6°13W 10 C5
Lifford Ireland 54°51N 7°29W 10 B4
Lifudzin Russia 44°21N 134°58E 30 B7
Lightning Ridge
 Australia 29°22S 148°0E 63 D4
Ligonha → Mozam. 16°54S 39°9E 55 F4
Ligonier U.S.A. 40°15N 79°14W 82 F5
Liguria □ Italy 44°30N 8°50E 20 D8
Ligurian Sea Medit. S. 43°20N 9°0E 22 C3
Lihou Reefs and Cays
 Australia 17°25S 151°40E 62 B5
Lihue U.S.A. 21°59N 159°23W 74 b
Lihué Calel △ Argentina 38°0S 65°10W 94 D2
Lijiang China 26°55N 100°20E 32 D5
Likasi
 Dem. Rep. of the Congo 10°55S 26°48E 55 E2
Likoma I. Malawi 12°3S 34°45E 55 E3
Likumburu Tanzania 9°43S 35°8E 55 D4
L'Île-Rousse France 42°38N 8°57E 20 E8
Lille France 50°38N 3°3E 20 A5
Lille Bælt Denmark 55°20N 9°45E 9 J13
Lillehammer Norway 61°8N 10°30E 8 F14
Lillesand Norway 58°15N 8°23E 9 G13
Lillian Pt. Australia 27°40S 126°6E 61 E4
Lilloet Canada 50°44N 121°57W 70 C4
Lillooet → Canada 49°15N 121°57W 70 D4
Lilongwe Malawi 14°0S 33°48E 55 E3
Liloy Phil. 8°4N 122°39E 37 C6
Lim → Europe 43°45N 19°15E 23 C8
Lim Chu Kang Singapore 1°26N 103°43E 39 d
Lima Indonesia 3°39S 127°58E 37 E7
Lima Peru 12°3S 77°2W 92 F3
Lima Mont., U.S.A. 44°38N 112°36W 76 D7
Lima N.Y., U.S.A. 42°54N 77°36W 82 D7
Lima Ohio, U.S.A. 40°44N 84°6W 81 E11
Lima → Portugal 41°41N 8°50W 21 B1
Liman Indonesia 7°48S 111°45E 37 G14
Limassol Cyprus 34°42N 33°1E 25 E12
Limavady U.K. 55°3N 6°56W 10 A5
Limay → Argentina 39°0S 68°0W 96 D3
Limay Mahuida
 Argentina 37°10S 66°45W 94 D2
Limbang Brunei 4°42N 115°6E 36 D5
Limbaži Latvia 57°31N 24°42E 9 H21
Limbdi India 22°34N 71°51E 42 H4
Limbe Cameroon 4°1N 9°10E 52 D1
Limburg Germany 50°22N 8°4E 16 C5

Limburg □ Belgium 51°2N 5°25E 15 C5
Limburg □ Neths. 51°20N 5°55E 15 C5
Limeira Brazil 22°35S 47°28W 95 A6
Limerick Ireland 52°40N 8°37W 10 D3
Limerick U.S.A. 43°41N 70°48W 83 C14
Limerick □ Ireland 52°30N 8°50W 10 D3
Limestone U.S.A. 42°2N 78°38W 82 D6
Limestone → Canada 56°31N 94°7W 71 B10
Limfjorden Denmark 56°55N 9°0E 9 H13
Limia = Lima → Portugal 41°41N 8°50W 21 B1
Limingen Norway 64°48N 13°35E 8 D15
Limmen Bight Australia 14°40S 135°35E 62 A2
Limmen Bight →
 Australia 15°7S 135°44E 62 B2
Limnos Greece 39°50N 25°5E 23 E11
Limoges Canada 45°20N 75°16W 83 A9
Limoges France 45°50N 1°15E 20 D4
Limón Costa Rica 10°0N 83°2W 88 E3
Limon U.S.A. 39°16N 103°41W 76 G12
Limousin □ France 45°30N 1°30E 20 D4
Limoux France 43°4N 2°12E 20 E5
Limpopo → S. Africa 24°5S 29°0E 57 C4
Limpopo → Africa 25°5S 33°30E 57 D5
Limuru Kenya 1°2S 36°35E 54 C4
Lin Xian China 37°57N 110°58E 34 F6
Linares Chile 35°50S 71°40W 94 D1
Linares Mexico 24°52N 99°34W 87 C5
Linares Spain 38°10N 3°40W 21 C4
Lincang China 23°58N 100°1E 32 D5
Lincheng China 37°25N 114°30E 34 F8
Lincoln = Beamsville
 Canada 43°12N 79°28W 82 C5
Lincoln Argentina 34°55S 61°30W 94 C3
Lincoln N.Z. 43°38S 172°30E 59 E4
Lincoln U.K. 53°14N 0°32W 12 D7
Lincoln Calif., U.S.A. 38°54N 121°17W 78 G5
Lincoln Ill., U.S.A. 40°9N 89°22W 80 E9
Lincoln Kans., U.S.A. 39°3N 98°9W 80 F4
Lincoln Maine, U.S.A. 45°22N 68°30W 81 C19
Lincoln N.H., U.S.A. 44°3N 71°40W 83 B13
Lincoln N. Mex.,
 U.S.A. 33°30N 105°23W 77 K11
Lincoln Nebr., U.S.A. 40°49N 96°41W 80 E5
Lincoln City U.S.A. 44°57N 124°1W 76 D1
Lincoln Hav = Lincoln Sea
 Arctic 84°0N 55°0W 66 A14
Lincoln Sea Arctic 84°0N 55°0W 66 A14
Lincolnshire □ U.K. 53°14N 0°32W 12 D7
Lincolnshire Wolds U.K. 53°26N 0°13W 12 D7
Lincolnton U.S.A. 35°29N 81°16W 85 D14
Lind U.S.A. 46°58N 118°37W 76 C4
Linda U.S.A. 39°8N 121°34W 78 F5
Lindeman I. Australia 20°27S 149°3E 62 J7
Linden Guyana 6°0N 58°10W 92 B7
Linden Ala., U.S.A. 32°18N 87°48W 85 E11
Linden Calif., U.S.A. 38°1N 121°5W 78 G5
Linden Tex., U.S.A. 33°1N 94°22W 84 E7
Lindenhurst U.S.A. 40°41N 73°23W 83 F11
Lindesnes Norway 57°58N 7°3E 9 H12
Lindi Tanzania 9°58S 39°38E 55 D4
Lindi □ Tanzania 9°40S 38°30E 55 D4
Lindi →
 Dem. Rep. of the Congo 0°33N 25°5E 54 B2
Lindley U.S.A. 42°1N 77°8W 82 D7
Lindos Greece 36°6N 28°4E 25 C10
Lindos, Akra Greece 36°4N 28°10E 25 C10
Lindsay Canada 44°22N 78°43W 82 B6
Lindsay Calif., U.S.A. 36°12N 119°5W 78 J7
Lindsay Okla., U.S.A. 34°50N 97°38W 84 D6
Lindsborg U.S.A. 38°35N 97°40W 80 F5
Line Islands Pac. Oc. 7°0N 160°0W 65 H12
Linesville U.S.A. 41°39N 80°26W 82 E4
Linfen China 36°3N 111°30E 34 F6
Ling Xian China 37°22N 116°30E 34 F9
Lingao China 19°56N 109°42E 38 C7
Lingayen Phil. 16°1N 120°14E 37 A6
Lingayen G. Phil. 16°10N 120°15E 37 A6
Lingbi China 33°33N 117°33E 35 H9
Lingchuan China 35°45N 113°12E 34 G7
Lingding Yang China 22°25N 113°44E 33 G10
Lingen Germany 52°31N 7°19E 16 B4
Lingga Indonesia 0°12S 104°37E 36 E2
Lingga, Kepulauan
 Indonesia 0°10S 104°30E 36 E2
Lingga Arch. = Lingga,
 Kepulauan Indonesia 0°10S 104°30E 36 E2
Lingle U.S.A. 42°8N 104°21W 76 E11
Lingqiu China 39°28N 114°22E 34 E8
Lingshi China 36°48N 111°48E 34 F6
Lingshou China 38°20N 114°20E 34 E8
Lingshui China 18°27N 110°0E 38 C8
Lingtai China 35°0N 107°40E 34 G4
Linguère Senegal 15°25N 15°5W 50 E2
Lingwu China 38°6N 106°20E 34 E4
Lingyuan China 41°10N 119°15E 35 D10
Linhai China 28°50N 121°8E 33 D7
Linhares Brazil 19°25S 40°4W 93 G10
Linhe China 40°48N 107°20E 34 D4
Linjiang China 41°50N 127°0E 35 D14
Linköping Sweden 58°28N 15°36E 9 G16
Linkou China 45°15N 130°18E 35 B16
Linnhe, L. U.K. 56°36N 5°25W 11 E3
Linosa Medit. S. 35°51N 12°50E 22 G5
Linqi China 35°45N 113°52E 34 G7
Linqing China 36°50N 115°42E 34 F8
Linqu China 36°25N 118°30E 35 F10
Linru China 34°11N 112°52E 34 G7
Lins Brazil 21°40S 49°44W 95 A6
Linstead Jamaica 18°8N 77°2W 88 a
Linta → Madag. 25°2S 44°5E 57 D7
Linton Ind., U.S.A. 39°2N 87°10W 80 F10
Linton N. Dak., U.S.A. 46°16N 100°14W 80 B3
Lintong China 34°20N 109°10E 34 G5
Linwood Canada 43°35N 80°43W 82 C4
Linxi China 43°36N 118°2E 35 C10
Linxia China 35°36N 103°10E 32 C5
Linyanti → Africa 17°50S 25°5E 56 B4

Linyi China 35°5N 118°21E 35 G10
Linz Austria 48°18N 14°18E 16 D8
Linzhenzhen China 36°30N 109°59E 34 F5
Linzi China 36°50N 118°0E 35 F10
Lion, G. du France 43°10N 4°0E 20 E6
Lionárisso Cyprus 35°28N 34°8E 25 D13
Lions, G. of = Lion, G. du
 France 43°10N 4°0E 20 E6
Lion's Den Zimbabwe 17°15S 30°5E 55 F3
Lion's Head Canada 44°58N 81°15W 82 B3
Lipa Phil. 13°57N 121°10E 37 B6
Lipali Mozam. 15°50S 35°50E 55 F4
Lípari Italy 38°26N 14°58E 22 E6
Lípari, Is. = Eólie, Ís.
 Italy 38°30N 14°57E 22 E6
Lipcani Moldova 48°14N 26°48E 17 D14
Liperi Finland 62°31N 29°24E 8 E23
Lipetsk Russia 52°37N 39°35E 18 D6
Lipkany = Lipcani
 Moldova 48°14N 26°48E 17 D14
Lipovets Ukraine 49°12N 29°1E 17 D15
Lippe → Germany 51°39N 6°36E 16 C4
Lipscomb U.S.A. 36°14N 100°16W 84 C4
Liptrap, C. Australia 38°50S 145°55E 63 F4
Lira Uganda 2°17N 32°57E 54 B3
Liria = Lliria Spain 39°37N 0°35W 21 C5
Lisala
 Dem. Rep. of the Congo 2°12N 21°38E 52 D4
Lisboa Portugal 38°42N 9°8W 21 C1
Lisbon = Lisboa Portugal 38°42N 9°8W 21 C1
Lisbon N. Dak., U.S.A. 46°27N 97°41W 80 B5
Lisbon N.H., U.S.A. 44°13N 71°55W 83 B13
Lisbon N.Y., U.S.A. 44°43N 75°19W 83 B9
Lisbon Ohio, U.S.A. 40°46N 80°46W 82 F4
Lisbon Falls U.S.A. 44°0N 70°4W 81 D18
Lisburn U.K. 54°31N 6°3W 10 B5
Lisburne, C. U.S.A. 68°53N 166°13W 4 C17
Liscannor B. Ireland 52°55N 9°24W 10 D2
Lisdoonvarna Ireland 53°2N 9°18W 10 C2
Lishi China 37°31N 111°8E 34 F6
Lishu China 43°20N 124°18E 35 C13
Lisianski I. U.S.A. 26°2N 174°0W 64 E10
Lisichansk = Lysychansk
 Ukraine 48°55N 38°30E 19 E6
Lisieux France 49°10N 0°12E 20 B4
Liski Russia 51°3N 39°30E 19 D6
Lismore Australia 28°44S 153°21E 63 D5
Lismore Ireland 52°8N 7°55W 10 D4
Lista Norway 58°7N 6°39E 9 G12
Lister, Mt. Antarctica 78°0S 162°0E 5 D11
Liston Australia 28°39S 152°6E 63 D5
Listowel Canada 43°44N 80°58W 82 C4
Listowel Ireland 52°27N 9°29W 10 D2
Litani → Lebanon 33°20N 35°15E 46 B4
Litchfield Calif., U.S.A. 40°24N 120°23W 78 E6
Litchfield Conn., U.S.A. 41°45N 73°11W 83 E11
Litchfield Ill., U.S.A. 39°11N 89°39W 80 F9
Litchfield Minn., U.S.A. 45°8N 94°32W 80 C6
Litchfield △ Australia 13°14S 131°1E 60 B5
Lithgow Australia 33°25S 150°8E 63 E5
Lithino, Akra Greece 34°55S 24°44E 25 E6
Lithuania ■ Europe 55°30N 24°0E 9 J21
Lititz U.S.A. 40°9N 76°18W 83 F8
Litoměřice Czech Rep. 50°33N 14°10E 16 C8
Little Abaco Bahamas 26°50N 77°30W 88 A4
Little Barrier I. N.Z. 36°12S 175°8E 59 B5
Little Bighorn Battlefield △
 U.S.A. 45°34N 107°25W 76 D10
Little Blue → U.S.A. 39°42N 96°41W 80 F5
Little Buffalo → Canada 61°0N 113°46W 70 A6
Little Cayman Cayman Is. 19°41N 80°3W 88 C3
Little Churchill →
 Canada 57°30N 95°22W 71 B9
Little Colorado →
 U.S.A. 36°12N 111°48W 77 H8
Little Current Canada 45°55N 82°0W 72 C3
Little Current → Canada 50°57N 84°36W 72 B3
Little Falls Minn., U.S.A. 45°59N 94°22W 80 C6
Little Falls N.Y., U.S.A. 43°3N 74°51W 83 C10
Little Fork → U.S.A. 48°31N 93°35W 80 A7
Little Grand Rapids
 Canada 52°0N 95°29W 71 C9
Little Humboldt →
 U.S.A. 41°1N 117°43W 76 F5
Little Inagua I. Bahamas 21°40N 73°50W 89 B5
Little Karoo S. Africa 33°45S 21°0E 56 E3
Little Khingan Mts. = Xiao
 Hinggan Ling China 49°0N 127°0E 33 B7
Little Lake U.S.A. 35°56N 117°55W 79 K9
Little Laut Is. = Laut Kecil,
 Kepulauan Indonesia 4°45S 115°40E 36 E5
Little Mecatina = Petit-
 Mécatina → Canada 50°40N 59°30W 73 B8
Little Minch U.K. 57°35N 6°45W 11 D2
Little Missouri →
 U.S.A. 47°36N 102°25W 80 B2
Little Ouse → U.K. 52°22N 1°12E 13 E9
Little Rann India 23°25N 71°25E 42 H4
Little Red → U.S.A. 35°11N 91°27W 84 D9
Little River N.Z. 43°45S 172°49E 59 E4
Little Rock U.S.A. 34°45N 92°17W 84 D8
Little Ruaha → Tanzania 7°57S 37°53E 54 D4
Little Sable Pt. U.S.A. 43°38N 86°33W 80 D10
Little Sioux → U.S.A. 41°48N 96°4W 80 E5
Little Smoky →
 Canada 54°44N 117°11W 70 C5
Little Snake → U.S.A. 40°27N 108°26W 76 F9
Little Tobago
 Trin. & Tob. 11°18N 60°30W 93 J16
Little Valley U.S.A. 42°15N 78°48W 82 D6
Little Wabash → U.S.A. 37°55N 88°5W 80 G9
Little White → U.S.A. 43°40N 100°40W 80 D3
Little Zab = Zāb aş Şaghīr →
 Iraq 35°17N 43°29E 44 C4
Littlefield U.S.A. 33°55N 102°20W 84 E3
Littlehampton U.K. 50°49N 0°32W 13 G7

Littleton U.S.A. 44°18N 71°46W 83 B13
Liu He → China 40°55N 121°35E 35 D11
Liuba China 33°38N 106°55E 34 H4
Liugou China 40°57N 118°15E 35 D10
Liuhe China 42°17N 125°43E 35 C13
Liukang Tenggaja = Sabalana,
 Kepulauan Indonesia 6°45S 118°50E 37 F5
Liuli Tanzania 11°3S 34°38E 55 E3
Liupanshui China 26°38N 104°48E 32 D5
Liuwa Plain Zambia 14°20S 22°30E 53 G4
Liuzhou China 24°22N 109°22E 33 D5
Liuzhuang China 33°12N 120°18E 35 H11
Livadhia Cyprus 34°57N 33°38E 25 E12
Livadia Greece 38°27N 22°54E 23 E10
Live Oak Calif., U.S.A. 39°17N 121°40W 78 F5
Live Oak Fla., U.S.A. 30°18N 82°59W 85 F13
Lively Canada 46°26N 81°9W 81 E13
Liveras Cyprus 35°23N 32°57E 25 D11
Livermore U.S.A. 37°41N 121°47W 78 H5
Livermore, Mt. U.S.A. 30°38N 104°11W 84 F2
Livermore Falls U.S.A. 44°29N 70°11W 81 C18
Liverpool Australia 33°54S 150°58E 63 B5
Liverpool Canada 44°5N 64°41W 73 D7
Liverpool U.K. 53°25N 3°0W 12 D4
Liverpool U.S.A. 43°6N 76°13W 83 C8
Liverpool Bay U.K. 53°30N 3°20W 12 D4
Liverpool Ra. Australia 31°50S 150°30E 63 E5
Livingston Guatemala 15°50N 88°50W 88 C2
Livingston U.K. 55°54N 3°30W 11 F5
Livingston Ala., U.S.A. 32°35N 88°11W 85 E10
Livingston Calif., U.S.A. 37°23N 120°43W 78 H6
Livingston Mont.,
 U.S.A. 45°40N 110°34W 76 D8
Livingston S.C., U.S.A. 33°38N 81°7W 85 E14
Livingston Tenn.,
 U.S.A. 36°23N 85°19W 85 C12
Livingston Tex., U.S.A. 30°43N 94°56W 84 F7
Livingston, L. U.S.A. 30°50N 95°10W 84 F7
Livingston Manor
 U.S.A. 41°54N 74°50W 83 E10
Livingstone Zambia 17°46S 25°52E 55 F2
Livingstone Mts. Tanzania 9°40S 34°20E 55 D3
Livingstonia Malawi 10°38S 34°5E 55 E3
Livny Russia 52°30N 37°30E 18 D6
Livonia Mich., U.S.A. 42°23N 83°23W 81 D12
Livonia N.Y., U.S.A. 42°49N 77°40W 82 D7
Livorno Italy 43°33N 10°19E 22 C4
Livramento Brazil 30°55S 55°30W 95 C4
Liwale Tanzania 9°48S 37°58E 55 D4
Liwonde △ Malawi 14°48S 35°20E 55 E4
Lizard I. Australia 14°42S 145°30E 62 A4
Lizard Pt. U.K. 49°57N 5°13E 13 H2
Ljubljana Slovenia 46°4N 14°33E 16 E8
Ljungan → Sweden 62°18N 17°23E 8 E17
Ljungby Sweden 56°49N 13°55E 9 H15
Ljusdal Sweden 61°46N 16°3E 8 F17
Ljusnan → Sweden 61°12N 17°8E 8 F17
Ljusne Sweden 61°13N 17°7E 8 F17
Llancanelo, Salina
 Argentina 35°40S 69°8W 94 D2
Llandeilo U.K. 51°53N 3°59W 13 F4
Llandovery U.K. 51°59N 3°48W 13 F4
Llandrindod Wells U.K. 52°14N 3°22W 13 E4
Llandudno U.K. 53°19N 3°50W 12 D4
Llanelli U.K. 51°41N 4°10W 13 F3
Llanes Spain 43°25N 4°50W 21 A3
Llangollen U.K. 52°58N 3°11W 12 E4
Llanidloes U.K. 52°27N 3°31W 13 E4
Llano U.S.A. 30°45N 98°41W 84 F5
Llano → U.S.A. 30°39N 98°26W 84 F5
Llano Estacado U.S.A. 33°30N 103°0W 84 E3
Llanos S. Amer. 5°0N 71°35W 92 C4
Llanos de la Chata △ Chile 28°8S 71°1W 94 B1
Llanquihue, L. Chile 41°10S 72°50W 96 E1
Llanwrtyd Wells U.K. 52°7N 3°38W 13 E4
Llebeig, C. des Spain 39°33N 2°18E 24 B9
Lleida Spain 41°37N 0°39E 21 B6
Llentrisca, C. Spain 38°52N 1°12E 24 C7
Llera de Canales Mexico 23°19N 99°1W 87 C5
Lleyn Peninsula U.K. 52°51N 4°36W 12 E3
Llico Chile 34°46S 72°5W 94 C1
Lliria Spain 39°37N 0°35W 21 C5
Llobregat → Spain 41°19N 2°9E 21 B7
Lloret de Mar Spain 41°41N 2°53E 21 B7
Lloseta Spain 39°43N 2°52E 24 B9
Lloyd B. Australia 12°45S 143°27E 62 A3
Lloyd L. Canada 57°22N 108°57W 71 B7
Lloydminster Canada 53°17N 110°0W 71 C7
Llubí Spain 39°42N 3°0E 24 B10
Llucmajor Spain 39°29N 2°53E 24 B9
Llullaillaco, Volcán
 S. Amer. 24°43S 68°30W 94 A2
Llullaillaco △ Chile 24°50S 68°51W 94 A2
Lo → Vietnam 21°18N 105°25E 38 B5
Loa U.S.A. 38°24N 111°39W 76 G8
Loa → Chile 21°26S 70°41W 94 A1
Loaita I. S. China Sea 10°41N 114°25E 36 B4
Loange →
 Dem. Rep. of the Congo 4°17S 20°2E 52 E4
Lobatse Botswana 25°12S 25°40E 56 D4
Lobería Argentina 38°10S 58°40W 94 D4
Lobito Angola 12°18S 13°35E 53 G2
Lobos Argentina 35°10S 59°0W 94 D4
Lobos, I. Mexico 27°20N 110°36W 86 B2
Lobos, I. de Canary Is. 28°45N 13°50W 24 F6
Loc Binh Vietnam 21°46N 106°54E 38 B6
Loc Ninh Vietnam 11°50N 106°34E 39 G6
Locarno Switz. 46°10N 8°47E 20 C8
Loch Baghasdail = Lochboisdale
 U.K. 57°9N 7°20W 11 D1
Loch Garman = Wexford
 Ireland 52°20N 6°28W 10 D5
Loch Lomond and the
 Trossachs △ U.K. 56°10N 4°40W 11 E4
Loch Nam Madadh = Lochmaddy
 U.K. 57°36N 7°10W 11 D1
Lochaber U.K. 56°59N 5°1W 11 E3

Locharbriggs U.K. 55°7N 3°35W 11 F5
Lochboisdale U.K. 57°9N 7°20W 11 D1
Loche, L. La Canada 56°30N 109°30W 71 B7
Lochem Neths. 52°9N 6°26E 15 B6
Loches France 47°7N 1°0E 20 C4
Lochgilphead U.K. 56°2N 5°26W 11 E3
Lochinvar △ Zambia 15°55S 27°15E 55 F2
Lochinver U.K. 58°9N 5°14W 11 C3
Lochmaddy U.K. 57°36N 7°10W 11 D1
Lochnagar Australia 23°33S 145°38E 62 C4
Lochnagar U.K. 56°57N 3°15W 11 E5
Lochy, L. U.K. 57°0N 4°53W 11 E4
Lock Australia 33°34S 135°46E 63 E2
Lock Haven U.S.A. 41°8N 77°28W 82 E7
Lockeford U.S.A. 38°10N 121°9W 78 G5
Lockeport Canada 43°47N 65°4W 73 D6
Lockerbie U.K. 55°7N 3°21W 11 F5
Lockhart U.S.A. 29°53N 97°40W 84 G6
Lockhart, L. Australia 33°15S 119°3E 61 F2
Lockhart River
 Australia 12°58S 143°30E 62 A3
Lockney U.S.A. 34°7N 101°27W 84 D4
Lockport U.S.A. 43°10N 78°42W 82 C6
Lod Israel 31°57N 34°54E 46 D3
Lodeinoye Pole Russia 60°44N 33°33E 18 B5
Lodge Bay Canada 52°14N 55°51W 73 B8
Lodge Grass U.S.A. 45°19N 107°22W 76 D10
Lodhran Pakistan 29°32N 71°30E 42 E4
Lodi Italy 45°19N 9°30E 20 D8
Lodi Calif., U.S.A. 38°8N 121°16W 78 G5
Lodi Ohio, U.S.A. 41°2N 82°0W 82 E3
Lodja
 Dem. Rep. of the Congo 3°30S 23°23E 54 C1
Lodwar Kenya 3°7N 35°36E 54 B4
Łódź Poland 51°45N 19°27E 17 C10
Loei Thailand 17°29N 101°35E 38 D3
Loengo
 Dem. Rep. of the Congo 4°48S 26°30E 54 C2
Loeriesfontein S. Africa 31°0S 19°26E 56 E2
Lofoten Norway 68°30N 14°0E 8 B16
Logan Iowa, U.S.A. 41°39N 95°47W 80 E6
Logan Ohio, U.S.A. 39°32N 82°25W 81 F12
Logan Utah, U.S.A. 41°44N 111°50W 76 F8
Logan W. Va., U.S.A. 37°51N 81°59W 81 G13
Logan, Mt. Canada 60°34N 140°23W 68 C5
Logandale U.S.A. 36°36N 114°29W 79 J12
Logansport Ind., U.S.A. 40°45N 86°22W 80 E10
Logansport La., U.S.A. 31°58N 94°0W 84 F8
Logone → Chad 12°6N 15°2E 51 F9
Logroño Spain 42°28N 2°27W 21 A4
Lohardaga India 23°27N 84°45E 43 H11
Loharia India 23°45N 74°14E 42 H6
Loharu India 28°27N 75°49E 42 E6
Lohri Wah → Pakistan 27°27N 67°37E 42 F2
Loi-kaw Burma 19°40N 97°17E 41 K20
Loimaa Finland 60°50N 23°5E 8 F20
Loir → France 47°33N 0°32W 20 C3
Loire → France 47°16N 2°10W 20 C2
Loja Ecuador 3°59S 79°16W 92 D3
Loja Spain 37°10N 4°9W 21 D3
Loji = Kawasi Indonesia 1°38S 127°28E 37 E7
Lokandu
 Dem. Rep. of the Congo 2°30S 25°45E 54 C2
Lokeren Belgium 51°6N 3°59E 15 C3
Lokgwabe Botswana 24°10S 21°50E 56 C3
Lokichar Kenya 2°23N 35°39E 54 B4
Lokichokio Kenya 4°19N 34°13E 54 B3
Lokitaung Kenya 4°12N 35°48E 54 B4
Lokkan tekojärvi
 Finland 67°55N 27°35E 8 C22
Lokoja Nigeria 7°47N 6°45E 50 G7
Lokolo →
 Dem. Rep. of the Congo 1°43S 18°23E 52 E3
Lola, Mt. U.S.A. 39°26N 120°22W 78 F6
Lolgorien Kenya 1°14S 34°48E 54 C3
Loliondo Tanzania 2°2S 35°39E 54 C4
Lolland Denmark 54°45N 11°30E 9 J14
Lolo U.S.A. 46°45N 114°5W 76 C6
Loma U.S.A. 47°56N 110°30W 76 C8
Loma Linda U.S.A. 34°3N 117°16W 79 L9
Lomaloma Fiji 17°17S 178°59W 59 a
Lomami →
 Dem. Rep. of the Congo 0°46N 24°16E 54 B1
Lomas de Zamora
 Argentina 34°45S 58°24W 94 C4
Lombadina Australia 16°31S 122°54E 60 C3
Lombárdia □ Italy 45°40N 9°30E 20 D8
Lombardy = Lombárdia □
 Italy 45°40N 9°30E 20 D8
Lomblen Indonesia 8°30S 123°32E 37 F6
Lombok Indonesia 8°45S 116°30E 37 K19
Lombok, Selat Indonesia 8°30S 115°50E 37 K18
Lomé Togo 6°9N 1°20E 50 G6
Lomela
 Dem. Rep. of the Congo 2°19S 23°15E 52 E4
Lomela →
 Dem. Rep. of the Congo 0°15S 20°40E 52 E4
Lommel Belgium 51°14N 5°19E 15 C5
Lomond Canada 50°24N 112°36W 70 C6
Lomond, L. U.K. 56°8N 4°38W 11 E4
Lomonosov Ridge Arctic 88°0N 140°0E 4 A
Lomphat Cambodia 13°30N 106°59E 38 F6
Lompobatang Indonesia 5°24S 119°56E 37 F5
Lompoc U.S.A. 34°38N 120°28W 79 L6
Łomża Poland 53°10N 22°2E 17 B12
Lon, Ko Thailand 7°47N 98°23E 39 a
Loncoche Chile 39°20S 72°50W 96 D2
Londa India 15°30N 74°30E 40 M9
Londiani Kenya 0°10S 35°33E 54 C4
London Canada 42°59N 81°15W 82 D3
London U.K. 51°30N 0°3W 13 F7
London Ky., U.S.A. 37°8N 84°5W 81 G11
London Ohio, U.S.A. 39°53N 83°27W 81 F12
London, Greater □ U.K. 51°36N 0°5W 13 F7

London Gatwick ✈ (LGW)
  U.K. 51°10N 0°11W 13 F7
London Heathrow ✈ (LHR)
  U.K. 51°28N 0°27W 13 F7
London Stansted ✈ (STN)
  U.K. 51°54N 0°14E 13 F8
Londonderry U.K. 55°0N 7°20W 10 B4
Londonderry □ U.K. 55°0N 7°20W 10 B4
Londonderry, C.
  Australia 13°45S 126°55E 60 B4
Londres Argentina 27°43S 67°7W 96 B3
Londrina Brazil 23°18S 51°10W 95 A5
Lone Pine U.S.A. 36°36N 118°4W 78 J8
Lonely Mine Zimbabwe 35°30S 28°49E 57 B4
Long B. U.S.A. 33°35N 78°45W 85 E15
Long Beach Calif.,
  U.S.A. 33°46N 118°11W 79 M8
Long Beach N.Y.,
  U.S.A. 40°35N 73°39W 83 F11
Long Beach Wash.,
  U.S.A. 46°21N 124°3W 78 D2
Long Branch U.S.A. 40°18N 74°0W 83 F11
Long Creek U.S.A. 44°43N 119°6W 76 D4
Long Eaton U.K. 52°53N 1°15W 12 E6
Long I. Australia 20°22S 148°51E 62 J6
Long I. Bahamas 23°20N 75°10W 89 B4
Long I. Canada 54°50N 79°20W 72 B4
Long I. Ireland 51°30N 9°34W 10 E2
Long I. U.S.A. 40°45N 73°30W 83 F11
Long Island Sd. U.S.A. 41°10N 73°0W 83 E12
Long L. Canada 49°30N 86°50W 72 C2
Long L. U.S.A. 44°0N 74°23W 83 C10
Long Lake U.S.A. 43°58N 74°25W 83 C10
Long Point Canada 42°34N 80°25W 82 D4
Long Point B. Canada 42°40N 80°10W 82 D4
Long Prairie U.S.A. 45°59N 94°52W 80 C6
Long Prairie → U.S.A. 46°20N 94°36W 80 B6
Long Pt. Ont., Canada 42°35N 80°2W 82 D4
Long Pt. Ont., Canada 43°56N 76°53W 83 C8
Long Range Mts.
  Canada 49°30N 57°30W 73 C8
Long Reef Australia 14°1S 125°48E 60 B4
Long Sault Canada 45°2N 74°53W 83 A10
Long Str. = Longa, Proliv
  Russia 70°0N 175°0E 29 C18
Long Thanh Vietnam 10°47N 106°57E 39 G6
Long Xian China 34°55N 106°55E 34 G4
Long Xuyen Vietnam 10°19N 105°28E 39 G5
Longa, Proliv Russia 70°0N 175°0E 29 C18
Longbenton U.K. 55°1N 1°31W 12 B6
Longboat Key U.S.A. 27°23N 82°39W 85 H13
Longde China 35°30N 106°20E 34 G4
Longford Australia 41°32S 147°3E 63 G4
Longford Ireland 53°43N 7°49W 10 C4
Longford □ Ireland 53°42N 7°45W 10 C4
Longhua Guangdong,
  China 22°39N 114°0E 33 F11
Longhua Hebei, China 41°18N 117°45E 35 D9
Longido Tanzania 2°43S 36°42E 54 C4
Longiram Indonesia 0°5S 115°45E 36 E5
Longkou China 37°40N 120°18E 35 F11
Longlac Canada 49°45N 86°25W 72 C2
Longmeadow U.S.A. 42°3N 72°34W 83 D12
Longmont U.S.A. 40°10N 105°6W 76 F11
Longnawan Indonesia 1°51N 114°55E 36 D4
Longreach Australia 23°28S 144°14E 62 C3
Longueuil Canada 45°31N 73°29W 83 A11
Longview Tex., U.S.A. 32°30N 94°44W 84 E7
Longview Wash., U.S.A. 46°8N 122°57W 78 D4
Longxi China 34°53N 104°40E 34 G3
Longxue Dao China 22°41N 113°38E 33 F10
Longyearbyen Svalbard 78°13N 15°40E 4 B8
Lonoke U.S.A. 34°47N 91°54W 84 D9
Lonquimay Chile 38°26S 71°14W 96 D2
Lons-le-Saunier France 46°40N 5°31E 20 C6
Looe U.K. 50°22N 4°28W 13 G3
Lookout, C. Canada 55°18N 83°56W 72 A3
Lookout, C. U.S.A. 34°35N 76°32W 85 D16
Loolmalasin Tanzania 3°0S 35°53E 54 C4
Loon → Alta., Canada 57°8N 115°3W 70 B5
Loon → Man., Canada 55°53N 101°59W 71 B8
Loon Lake Canada 54°2N 109°10W 71 C7
Loongana Australia 30°52S 127°5E 61 F4
Loop Hd. Ireland 52°34N 9°56W 10 D2
Lop China 37°3N 80°11E 32 C3
Lop Buri Thailand 14°48N 100°37E 38 E3
Lop Nor = Lop Nur
  China 40°20N 90°10E 32 B4
Lop Nur China 40°20N 90°10E 32 B4
Lopatina, Gora Russia 50°47N 143°10E 29 D15
Lopatka, Mys Russia 50°52N 156°40E 29 D16
Lopez U.S.A. 41°27N 76°20W 83 E8
Lopez, C. Gabon 0°47S 8°40E 52 E1
Lopphavet Norway 70°27N 21°15E 8 A19
Lora → Afghan. 31°35N 66°32E 40 D4
Lora, Hāmūn-i- Pakistan 29°38N 64°58E 40 E4
Lora Cr. → Australia 28°10S 135°22E 63 D2
Lora del Río Spain 37°39N 5°33W 21 D3
Lorain U.S.A. 41°28N 82°11W 82 E2
Loralai Pakistan 30°20N 68°41E 42 D3
Lorca Spain 37°41N 1°42W 21 D5
Lord Howe I. Pac. Oc. 31°33S 159°6E 58 E8
Lord Howe Rise Pac. Oc. 30°0S 162°30E 64 L8
Lordsburg U.S.A. 32°21N 108°43W 77 K9
Lorestān □ Iran 33°30N 48°40E 45 C6
Loreto Brazil 7°5S 45°10W 93 E9
Loreto Mexico 26°0N 111°21W 86 B2
Lorient France 47°45N 3°23W 20 C2
Lormi India 22°17N 81°41E 43 H9
Lorn U.K. 56°26N 5°10W 11 E3
Lorn, Firth of U.K. 56°20N 5°40W 11 E3
Lorne Australia 38°33S 143°59E 63 F3
Lorovouno Cyprus 35°8N 32°36E 25 D11
Lorraine □ France 48°53N 6°0E 20 B7
Los Alamos Calif.,
  U.S.A. 34°44N 120°17W 79 L6

Los Alamos N. Mex.,
  U.S.A. 35°53N 106°19W 77 J10
Los Altos U.S.A. 37°23N 122°7W 78 H4
Los Andes Chile 32°50S 70°40W 94 C1
Los Angeles Chile 37°28S 72°23W 94 D1
Los Angeles U.S.A. 34°4N 118°15W 79 M8
Los Angeles, Bahia de
  Mexico 28°56N 113°34W 86 B2
Los Angeles Aqueduct
  U.S.A. 35°22N 118°5W 79 K9
Los Angeles Int. ✈ (LAX)
  U.S.A. 33°57N 118°25W 79 M8
Los Banos U.S.A. 37°4N 120°51W 78 H6
Los Blancos Argentina 23°40S 62°30W 94 A3
Los Cardones △ Argentina 25°8S 65°50W 94 C1
Los Chiles Costa Rica 11°2N 84°43W 88 D3
Los Cristianos Canary Is. 28°3N 16°42W 24 F3
Los Gatos U.S.A. 37°14N 121°59W 78 H5
Los Haïtises △ Dom. Rep. 19°4N 69°36W 89 C6
Los Hermanos Is.
  Venezuela 11°45N 64°25W 89 D7
Los Islotes Canary Is. 29°4N 13°44W 24 E6
Los Llanos de Aridane
  Canary Is. 28°38N 17°54W 24 F2
Los Loros Chile 27°50S 70°6W 94 B1
Los Lunas U.S.A. 34°48N 106°44W 77 J10
Los Mochis Mexico 25°45N 108°57W 86 B3
Los Olivos U.S.A. 34°40N 120°7W 79 L6
Los Palacios Cuba 22°35N 83°15W 88 B3
Los Queñes Chile 35°1S 70°48W 94 D1
Los Reyes de Salgado
  Mexico 19°35N 102°29W 86 D4
Los Roques Is. Venezuela 11°50N 66°45W 89 D6
Los Teques Venezuela 10°21N 67°2W 92 A5
Los Testigos, Is. Venezuela 11°23N 63°6W 92 A6
Los Vilos Chile 32°10S 71°30W 94 C1
Lošinj Croatia 44°30N 14°30E 16 F8
Loskop Dam S. Africa 25°23S 29°20E 57 D4
Lossiemouth U.K. 57°42N 3°17W 11 D5
Lostwithiel U.K. 50°24N 4°41W 13 G3
Lot → France 44°18N 0°20E 20 D4
Lota Chile 37°5S 73°10W 94 D1
Lotfābād Iran 37°32N 59°20E 45 B8
Lothair S. Africa 26°22S 30°27E 57 D5
Lotta → Europe 68°42N 31°6E 8 B24
Loubomo Congo 4°9S 12°47E 52 E2
Loudonville U.S.A. 40°38N 82°14W 82 F2
Louga Senegal 15°45N 16°5W 50 E2
Loughborough U.K. 52°47N 1°11W 12 E6
Lougheed I. Canada 77°26N 105°6W 69 B9
Loughrea Ireland 53°12N 8°33W 10 C3
Loughros More B. Ireland 54°48N 8°32W 10 B3
Louis Trichardt S. Africa 23°1S 29°43E 57 C4
Louis XIV, Pte. Canada 54°37N 79°45W 72 B4
Louisa U.S.A. 38°7N 82°36W 81 F12
Louisbourg Canada 45°55N 60°0W 73 C8
Louisburgh Ireland 53°46N 9°49W 10 C2
Louise I. Canada 52°55N 131°50W 70 C2
Louiseville Canada 46°20N 72°56W 72 C5
Louisiade Arch.
  Papua N. G. 11°10S 153°0E 58 C8
Louisiana U.S.A. 39°27N 91°3W 80 F8
Louisiana □ U.S.A. 30°50N 92°0W 84 F9
Louisville Ky., U.S.A. 38°15N 85°46W 81 F11
Louisville Miss., U.S.A. 33°7N 89°3W 85 E10
Louisville Ohio, U.S.A. 40°50N 81°16W 82 F3
Louisville Ridge
  Pac. Oc. 31°0S 172°30W 64 L10
Loulé Portugal 37°9N 8°0W 21 D1
Loup City U.S.A. 41°17N 98°58W 80 E4
Loups Marins, Lacs des
  Canada 56°30N 73°45W 72 A5
Lourdes France 43°6N 0°3W 20 E3
Lourdes-de-Blanc-Sablon
  Canada 51°24N 57°12W 73 B8
Louroujina Cyprus 35°0N 33°28E 25 E12
Louth Australia 30°30S 145°8E 63 E4
Louth Ireland 53°58N 6°32W 10 C5
Louth U.K. 53°22N 0°1W 12 D7
Louth □ Ireland 53°56N 6°34W 10 C5
Louvain = Leuven
  Belgium 50°52N 4°42E 15 D4
Louwsburg S. Africa 27°37S 31°7E 57 D5
Lovech Bulgaria 43°8N 24°42E 23 C11
Loveland U.S.A. 40°24N 105°5W 76 F11
Lovell U.S.A. 44°50N 108°24W 76 D9
Lovelock U.S.A. 40°11N 118°28W 76 F4
Loviisa Finland 60°28N 26°12E 8 F22
Loving U.S.A. 32°17N 104°6W 77 K11
Lovington U.S.A. 32°57N 103°21W 77 K12
Lovisa = Loviisa Finland 60°28N 26°12E 8 F22
Low, L. Canada 52°29N 76°17W 72 B4
Low Pt. Australia 32°25S 127°25E 61 F4
Low Tatra = Nízké Tatry
  Slovak Rep. 48°55N 19°30E 17 D10
Lowa
  Dem. Rep. of the Congo 1°25S 25°47E 54 C2
Lowa →
  Dem. Rep. of the Congo 1°24S 25°51E 54 C2
Lowell U.S.A. 42°38N 71°19W 83 D13
Lowellville U.S.A. 41°2N 80°32W 82 E4
Löwen → Namibia 26°51S 18°17E 56 D2
Lower Alkali L. U.S.A. 41°16N 120°2W 76 F3
Lower Arrow L. Canada 49°40N 118°5W 70 D5
Lower California = Baja California
  Mexico 31°10N 115°12W 86 A1
Lower Hutt N.Z. 41°10S 174°55E 59 D5
Lower Lake U.S.A. 38°55N 122°37W 78 G4
Lower Manitou L.
  Canada 49°15N 93°0W 71 D10
Lower Post Canada 59°58N 128°30W 70 B3
Lower Red L. U.S.A. 47°58N 95°0W 80 B6
Lower Saxony = Niedersachsen □
  Germany 52°50N 9°0E 16 B5
Lower Tunguska = Tunguska,
  Nizhnyaya → Russia 65°48N 88°4E 29 C9
Lower Zambezi △ Zambia 15°25S 29°40E 55 F2

Lowestoft U.K. 52°29N 1°45E 13 E9
Lowgar □ Afghan. 34°0N 69°0E 40 B6
Łowicz Poland 52°6N 19°55E 17 B10
Lowville U.S.A. 43°47N 75°29W 83 C9
Loxton Australia 34°28S 140°31E 63 E3
Loxton S. Africa 31°30S 22°22E 56 E3
Loyalton U.S.A. 39°41N 120°14W 78 F6
Loyalty Is. = Loyauté, Îs.
  N. Cal. 20°50S 166°30E 58 D9
Loyang = Luoyang
  China 34°40N 112°26E 34 G7
Loyauté, Îs. N. Cal. 20°50S 166°30E 58 D9
Loyev = Loyew Belarus 51°56N 30°46E 17 C16
Loyew Belarus 51°56N 30°46E 17 C16
Loyoro Uganda 3°22N 34°14E 54 B3
Lu Wo China 22°33N 114°6E 33 F11
Luachimo Angola 7°23S 20°48E 52 F4
Luajan → India 24°44N 85°1E 43 G11
Lualaba →
  Dem. Rep. of the Congo 0°26N 25°20E 54 B2
Luampa Zambia 15°4S 24°20E 55 F1
Luan Chau Vietnam 21°38N 103°24E 38 B4
Luan He → China 39°20N 119°5E 35 E10
Luan Xian China 39°40N 118°40E 35 E10
Luancheng China 37°53N 114°40E 34 F8
Luanda Angola 8°50S 13°15E 52 F2
Luang, Thale Thailand 7°30N 100°15E 39 J3
Luang Prabang Laos 19°52N 102°10E 38 C4
Luangwa Zambia 15°35S 30°16E 55 F3
Luangwa → Zambia 14°25S 30°25E 55 E3
Luangwa Valley Zambia 13°30S 31°30E 55 E3
Luanne China 40°55N 117°40E 35 D9
Luanping China 40°53N 117°23E 35 D9
Luanshya Zambia 13°3S 28°28E 55 E2
Luapula □ Zambia 11°0S 29°0E 55 E2
Luapula → Africa 9°26S 28°33E 55 D2
Luarca Spain 43°32N 6°32W 21 A2
Luashi
  Dem. Rep. of the Congo 10°50S 23°36E 55 E1
Luau Angola 10°40S 22°10E 52 G4
Lubana, Ozero = Lubānas Ezers
  Latvia 56°45N 27°0E 9 H22
Lubānas Ezers Latvia 56°45N 27°0E 9 H22
Lubang Is. Phil. 13°50N 120°12E 37 B6
Lubango Angola 14°55S 13°30E 53 G2
Lubao
  Dem. Rep. of the Congo 5°17S 25°42E 54 D2
Lubbock U.S.A. 33°35N 101°51W 84 E4
Lübeck Germany 53°52N 10°40E 16 B6
Lubefu
  Dem. Rep. of the Congo 4°47S 24°27E 54 C1
Lubefu →
  Dem. Rep. of the Congo 4°10S 23°0E 54 C1
Lubero = Luofu
  Dem. Rep. of the Congo 0°1S 29°15E 54 C2
Lubicon L. Canada 56°23N 115°56W 70 B5
Lubilash →
  Dem. Rep. of the Congo 6°2S 23°45E 52 F4
Lubin Poland 51°24N 16°11E 16 C9
Lublin Poland 51°12N 22°38E 17 C12
Lubnān = Lebanon ■ Asia 34°0N 36°0E 46 B5
Lubnān, Jabal Lebanon 33°45N 35°40E 46 B4
Lubny Ukraine 50°3N 32°58E 28 D4
Lubongola
  Dem. Rep. of the Congo 2°35S 27°50E 54 C2
Lubudi
  Dem. Rep. of the Congo 9°57S 25°58E 52 F5
Lubudi →
  Dem. Rep. of the Congo 9°0S 25°35E 55 D2
Lubuklinggau Indonesia 3°15S 102°55E 36 E2
Lubuksikaping Indonesia 0°10N 100°15E 36 D2
Lubumbashi
  Dem. Rep. of the Congo 11°40S 27°28E 55 E2
Lubunda
  Dem. Rep. of the Congo 5°12S 26°41E 54 D2
Lubungu Zambia 14°35S 26°24E 55 E2
Lubutu
  Dem. Rep. of the Congo 0°45S 26°30E 54 C2
Luc An Chau Vietnam 22°6N 104°43E 38 A5
Lucan Canada 43°11N 81°24W 82 C3
Lucania, Mt. Canada 61°1N 140°27W 68 C5
Lucas Channel = Main Channel
  Canada 45°21N 81°45W 82 A3
Lucca Italy 43°50N 10°29E 22 C4
Luce Bay U.K. 54°45N 4°48W 11 G4
Lucea Jamaica 18°27N 78°10W 88 a
Lucedale U.S.A. 30°56N 88°35W 85 F10
Lucena Phil. 13°56N 121°37E 37 B6
Lucena Spain 37°27N 4°31W 21 D3
Lučenec Slovak Rep. 48°18N 19°42E 17 D10
Lucerne = Luzern Switz. 47°3N 8°18E 20 C8
Lucerne U.S.A. 39°6N 122°48W 78 F4
Lucerne Valley U.S.A. 34°27N 116°57W 79 L10
Lucero Mexico 30°49N 106°30W 86 A3
Lucheng China 36°20N 113°11E 34 F7
Lucheringo → Mozam. 11°43S 36°17E 55 E4
Lucia U.S.A. 36°2N 121°33W 78 J5
Lucinda Australia 18°32S 146°20E 62 B4
Luckenwalde Germany 52°5N 13°10E 16 B7
Luckhoff S. Africa 29°44S 24°43E 56 D3
Lucknow Canada 43°57N 81°31W 82 C3
Lucknow India 26°50N 81°0E 43 F9
Lüda = Dalian China 38°50N 121°40E 35 E11
Lüderitz Namibia 26°41S 15°8E 56 D2
Lüderitzbaai Namibia 26°36S 15°8E 56 D2
Ludhiana India 30°57N 75°56E 42 D6
Ludington U.S.A. 43°57N 86°27W 80 D10
Ludlow U.K. 52°22N 2°42W 13 E5
Ludlow Calif., U.S.A. 34°43N 116°10W 79 L10
Ludlow Pa., U.S.A. 41°43N 78°56W 82 E6
Ludlow Vt., U.S.A. 43°24N 72°42W 83 C12
Ludvika Sweden 60°8N 15°14E 9 F16
Ludwigsburg Germany 48°53N 9°11E 16 D5
Ludwigshafen Germany 49°29N 8°26E 16 D5
Lueki
  Dem. Rep. of the Congo 3°20S 25°48E 54 C2
Luena
  Dem. Rep. of the Congo 9°28S 25°43E 55 D2

Luena Zambia 10°40S 30°25E 55 E3
Luena Flats Zambia 14°47S 23°17E 53 G4
Luenha = Ruenya →
  Africa 16°24S 33°48E 55 F3
Lüeyang China 33°22N 106°10E 34 H4
Lufira →
  Dem. Rep. of the Congo 9°30S 27°0E 55 D2
Lufkin U.S.A. 31°21N 94°44W 84 F7
Lufupa
  Dem. Rep. of the Congo 10°37S 24°56E 55 E1
Luga Russia 58°40N 29°55E 9 G23
Lugano Switz. 46°1N 8°57E 20 C8
Lugansk = Luhansk
  Ukraine 48°38N 39°15E 19 E6
Lugard's Falls Kenya 3°6S 38°41E 54 C4
Lugela Mozam. 16°25S 36°43E 55 F4
Lugenda → Mozam. 11°25S 38°33E 55 E4
Lugh Ganana = Luuq
  Somali Rep. 3°48N 42°34E 47 G3
Lugnaquillia Ireland 52°58N 6°28E 10 D5
Lugo Italy 44°25N 11°54E 22 B4
Lugo Spain 43°2N 7°35W 21 A2
Lugoj Romania 45°42N 21°57E 17 F11
Lugovoy = Qulan
  Kazakhstan 42°55N 72°43E 28 E8
Luhansk Ukraine 48°38N 39°15E 19 E6
Lui → Angola 8°21S 17°33E 52 F3
Luiana Angola 17°25S 22°59E 56 B3
Luiana → Angola 17°24S 23°3E 53 H4
Luichow Pen. = Leizhou Bandao
  China 21°0N 110°0E 33 D6
Luimneach = Limerick
  Ireland 52°40N 8°37W 10 D3
Luing U.K. 56°14N 5°39W 11 E3
Luís Correia Brazil 3°0S 41°35W 93 D10
Luitpold Coast Antarctica 78°30S 32°0W 5 D1
Luiza Dem. Rep. of the Congo 7°40S 22°30E 52 F4
Luizi Dem. Rep. of the Congo 6°0S 27°25E 54 D2
Luján Argentina 34°45S 59°5W 94 C4
Lukanga Swamp Zambia 14°30S 27°40E 55 E2
Lukenie →
  Dem. Rep. of the Congo 3°0S 18°50E 52 E3
Lukolela
  Dem. Rep. of the Congo 5°23S 24°32E 54 D1
Lukosi Zimbabwe 18°30S 26°30E 55 F2
Łuków Poland 51°55N 22°23E 17 C12
Lukusuzi △ Zambia 12°43S 32°36E 55 E3
Luleå Sweden 65°35N 22°10E 8 D20
Luleälven → Sweden 65°35N 22°10E 8 D20
Lüleburgaz Turkey 41°23N 27°22E 23 D12
Luling U.S.A. 29°41N 97°39W 84 G6
Lulong China 39°53N 118°51E 35 E10
Lulonga →
  Dem. Rep. of the Congo 1°0N 18°10E 52 D3
Lulua →
  Dem. Rep. of the Congo 4°30S 20°30E 52 E4
Luma Amer. Samoa 14°16S 169°33W 59 b
Lumajang Indonesia 8°8S 113°13E 37 H15
Lumbala N'guimbo
  Angola 14°18S 21°18E 53 G4
Lumberton U.S.A. 34°37N 79°0W 85 D15
Lumsden Canada 50°39N 104°52W 71 C8
Lumsden N.Z. 45°44S 168°27E 59 F2
Lumut Malaysia 4°13N 100°37E 39 K3
Lumut, Tanjung
  Indonesia 3°50S 105°58E 36 E3
Luna India 23°43N 69°16E 42 H3
Lunavada India 23°8N 73°37E 42 H5
Lund Sweden 55°44N 13°12E 9 J15
Lundazi Zambia 12°20S 33°7E 55 E3
Lundi → Zimbabwe 21°43S 32°34E 55 G3
Lundu Malaysia 1°40N 109°50E 36 D3
Lundy U.K. 51°10N 4°41W 13 F3
Lune → U.K. 54°0N 2°51W 12 C5
Lüneburg Germany 53°15N 10°24E 16 B6
Lüneburg Heath = Lüneburger
  Heide Germany 53°10N 10°12E 16 B6
Lüneburger Heide
  Germany 53°10N 10°12E 16 B6
Lunenburg Canada 44°22N 64°18W 73 D7
Lunéville France 48°36N 6°30E 20 B7
Lunga → Zambia 14°34S 26°25E 55 E2
Lunga Lunga Kenya 4°33S 39°7E 54 C4
Lunglei India 22°55N 92°45E 41 H18
Luni India 26°0N 73°6E 42 G5
Luni → India 24°41N 71°14E 42 G4
Luninets = Luninyets
  Belarus 52°15N 26°50E 17 B14
Luning U.S.A. 38°30N 118°11W 76 G4
Luninyets Belarus 52°15N 26°50E 17 B14
Lunkaransar India 28°29N 73°44E 42 E5
Lunsemfwa → Zambia 14°54S 30°12E 55 E2
Lunsemfwa Falls Zambia 14°30S 29°6E 55 E2
Luo He → China 34°35N 110°20E 34 G6
Luochuan China 35°45N 109°26E 34 G5
Luofu
  Dem. Rep. of the Congo 0°1S 29°15E 54 C2
Luohe China 33°32N 114°2E 34 H8
Luonan China 34°5N 110°10E 34 G6
Luoning China 34°35N 111°40E 34 G6
Luoyang China 34°40N 112°26E 34 G7
Luozigou China 43°42N 130°18E 35 C16
Lupilichi Mozam. 11°47S 35°13E 55 E4
Luque Paraguay 25°19S 57°25W 94 B4
Luquillo, Sierra de
  Puerto Rico 18°20N 65°47W 89 d
Luray U.S.A. 38°40N 78°28W 81 F14
Lurgan U.K. 54°28N 6°19W 10 B5
Lusaka Zambia 15°28S 28°16E 55 F2
Lusaka □ Zambia 15°30S 29°0E 55 F2
Lusambo
  Dem. Rep. of the Congo 4°58S 23°28E 54 C1
Lusangaye
  Dem. Rep. of the Congo 4°54S 26°0E 54 C2
Luseland Canada 52°5N 109°24W 71 C7
Lusenga Plain △ Zambia 9°22S 29°14E 55 D2
Lushan China 33°45N 112°55E 34 H7

Lushi China 34°3N 111°3E 34 G6
Lushnjë Albania 40°55N 19°41E 23 D8
Lushoto Tanzania 4°47S 38°20E 54 C4
Lüshun China 38°45N 121°15E 35 E11
Lusk U.S.A. 42°46N 104°27W 76 E11
Lūt, Dasht-e Iran 31°30N 58°0E 45 D8
Luta = Dalian China 38°50N 121°40E 35 E11
Lutherstadt Wittenberg
  Germany 51°53N 12°39E 16 C7
Luton U.K. 51°53N 0°24W 13 F7
Luton □ U.K. 51°53N 0°24W 13 F7
Lutsel K'e Canada 62°24N 110°44E 71 A6
Lutsk Ukraine 50°50N 25°15E 17 C13
Lutto = Lotta → Europe 68°42N 31°6E 8 B24
Lützow Holmbukta
  Antarctica 69°10S 37°30E 5 C4
Lutzputs S. Africa 28°3S 20°40E 56 D3
Luuq Somali Rep. 3°48N 42°34E 47 G3
Luverne Ala., U.S.A. 31°43N 86°16W 85 F11
Luverne Minn., U.S.A. 43°39N 96°13W 80 D5
Luvua
  Dem. Rep. of the Congo 8°48S 25°17E 55 D2
Luvua →
  Dem. Rep. of the Congo 6°50S 27°30E 54 D2
Luvuvhu → S. Africa 22°25S 31°18E 57 C5
Luwegu → Tanzania 8°31S 37°23E 55 D4
Luwuk Indonesia 0°56S 122°47E 37 E6
Luxembourg Lux. 49°37N 6°9E 15 E6
Luxembourg □ Belgium 49°58N 5°30E 15 E5
Luxembourg ■ Europe 49°45N 6°0E 15 E5
Luxembourg ✈ (LUX)
  Lux. 49°37N 6°10E 15 E6
Luxi China 24°27N 98°36E 34 E6
Luxor = El Uqsur Egypt 25°41N 32°38E 51 C12
Luyi China 33°50N 115°35E 34 H8
Luza Russia 60°39N 47°10E 18 B8
Luzern Switz. 47°3N 8°18E 20 C8
Luzhou China 28°52N 105°20E 32 D5
Luziânia Brazil 16°20S 48°0W 93 G9
Luzon Phil. 16°0N 121°0E 37 A6
Lviv Ukraine 49°50N 24°0E 17 D13
Lvov = Lviv Ukraine 49°50N 24°0E 17 D13
Lyakhavichy Belarus 53°2N 26°32E 17 B14
Lyakhovskiye, Ostrova
  Russia 73°40N 141°0E 29 B15
Lyal I. Canada 44°57N 81°24W 82 B3
Lybster U.K. 58°18N 3°15W 11 C5
Lycksele Sweden 64°38N 18°40E 8 D18
Lydda = Lod Israel 31°57N 34°54E 46 D3
Lyddan I. Antarctica 74°0S 21°0W 5 D2
Lydenburg S. Africa 25°10S 30°29E 57 D5
Lydia Turkey 38°48N 28°19E 23 E13
Lyell N.Z. 41°48S 172°4E 59 D4
Lyell I. Canada 52°40N 131°35W 70 C2
Lyepyel Belarus 54°50N 28°40E 9 J2
Lykens U.S.A. 40°34N 76°42W 83 F8
Lyman U.S.A. 41°20N 110°18W 76 F8
Lyme B. U.K. 50°42N 2°53W 13 G4
Lyme Regis U.K. 50°43N 2°57W 13 G5
Lymington U.K. 50°45N 1°32W 13 G6
Łyna → Poland 54°37N 21°14E 17 A11
Lynchburg U.S.A. 37°25N 79°9W 81 G14
Lynd → Australia 16°28S 143°18E 62 B3
Lynd Ra. Australia 25°30S 149°20E 63 D4
Lynden Canada 43°14N 80°9W 82 C4
Lynden U.S.A. 48°57N 122°27W 78 B4
Lyndhurst Australia 30°15S 138°18E 63 E2
Lyndon → Australia 23°29S 114°6E 61 D1
Lyndonville N.Y., U.S.A. 43°20N 78°23W 82 C6
Lyndonville Vt., U.S.A. 44°31N 72°1W 83 B12
Lyngen Norway 69°45N 20°30E 8 B19
Lynher Reef Australia 15°27S 121°55E 60 C3
Lynn U.S.A. 42°28N 70°57W 83 D14
Lynn Haven U.S.A. 30°15N 85°39W 85 F12
Lynn Lake Canada 56°51N 101°3W 71 B8
Lynnwood U.S.A. 47°49N 122°18W 78 C4
Lynton U.K. 51°13N 3°50W 13 F4
Lyntupy Belarus 55°4N 26°23E 9 J22
Lynx L. Canada 62°25N 106°15W 71 A7
Lyon France 45°46N 4°50E 20 D6
Lyonnais France 45°45N 4°15E 20 D6
Lyons = Lyon France 45°46N 4°50E 20 D6
Lyons Ga., U.S.A. 32°12N 82°19W 85 E13
Lyons Kans., U.S.A. 38°21N 98°12W 80 F4
Lyons N.Y., U.S.A. 43°5N 77°0W 82 C7
Lyons → Australia 25°2S 115°9E 61 E2
Lyons Falls U.S.A. 43°37N 75°22W 83 C9
Lys = Leie → Belgium 51°2N 3°45E 15 C3
Lysi Cyprus 35°6N 33°41E 25 D12
Lysva Russia 58°7N 57°49E 18 C10
Lysychansk Ukraine 48°55N 38°30E 19 E6
Lytham St. Anne's U.K. 53°45N 3°0W 12 D4
Lyttelton N.Z. 43°35S 172°44E 59 E4
Lytton Canada 50°13N 121°31W 70 C4
Lyubertsy Russia 55°40N 37°51E 18 C6
Lyuboml Ukraine 51°11N 24°4E 17 C13

M

Ma → Vietnam 19°47N 105°56E 38 C5
Ma'adaba Jordan 30°43N 35°47E 46 E4
Maamba Zambia 17°17S 26°28E 56 B4
Ma'ān Jordan 30°12N 35°44E 46 E4
Ma'ān □ Jordan 30°0N 36°0E 46 F5
Maanselkä Finland 63°52N 28°32E 8 D23
Ma'anshan China 31°44N 118°29E 33 C6
Maarianhamina = Mariehamn
  Finland 60°5N 19°55E 9 F18
Ma'arrat an Nu'mān
  Syria 35°43N 36°43E 44 C3
Maas → Neths. 51°45N 4°32E 15 C4
Maaseik Belgium 51°6N 5°45E 15 C5
Maasin Phil. 10°8N 124°50E 37 B6
Maastricht Neths. 50°50N 5°40E 15 D5
Maave Mozam. 21°4S 34°47E 57 C5
Mababe Depression
  Botswana 18°50S 24°15E 56 B3

Mabalane *Mozam.* 23°37S 32°31E **57** C5
Mabel L. *Canada* 50°35N 118°43W **70** C5
Mabenge *Dem. Rep. of the Congo* 4°15N 24°12E **54** B1
Maberly *Canada* 44°50N 76°32W **83** B8
Mablethorpe *U.K.* 53°20N 0°15E **12** D8
Maboma *Dem. Rep. of the Congo* 2°30N 28°10E **54** B2
Mabuasehube ⌂ *Botswana* 25°5S 21°10E **56** D3
Mac Bac *Vietnam* 9°46N 106°7E **39** H6
Macachín *Argentina* 37°10S 63°43W **94** D3
Macaé *Brazil* 22°20S 41°43W **95** A7
McAlester *U.S.A.* 34°56N 95°46W **84** D7
McAllen *U.S.A.* 26°12N 98°14W **84** H5
MacAlpine L. *Canada* 66°32N 102°45W **68** C9
Macamic *Canada* 48°45N 79°0W **72** C4
Macao = Macau *China* 22°12N 113°33E **33** G10
Macapá *Brazil* 0°5N 51°4W **93** C8
Macarao △ *Venezuela* 10°22N 67°7W **89** D6
McArthur → *Australia* 15°54S 136°40E **62** B2
McArthur, Port *Australia* 16°4S 136°23E **62** B2
Macau *Brazil* 5°15S 36°40W **93** E11
Macau *China* 22°12N 113°33E **33** G10
McBride *Canada* 53°20N 120°19W **70** C4
McCall *U.S.A.* 44°55N 116°6W **76** D5
McCamey *U.S.A.* 31°8N 102°14W **84** F3
McCammon *U.S.A.* 42°39N 112°12W **76** E7
McCarran Int., Las Vegas ✈ **(LAS)** *U.S.A.* 36°5N 115°9W **79** J11
McCauley I. *Canada* 53°40N 130°15W **70** C2
McCleary *U.S.A.* 47°3N 123°16W **78** C3
Macclenny *U.S.A.* 30°17N 82°7W **85** F13
Macclesfield *U.K.* 53°15N 2°8W **12** D5
M'Clintock Chan. *Canada* 72°0N 102°0W **68** B9
McClintock Ra. *Australia* 18°44S 127°38E **60** C4
McCloud *U.S.A.* 41°15N 122°8W **76** F2
McCluer I. *Australia* 11°5S 133°0E **60** B5
McClure *U.S.A.* 40°42N 77°19W **82** F7
McClure, L. *U.S.A.* 37°35N 120°16W **78** H6
M'Clure Str. *Canada* 75°0N 119°0W **69** B8
McClusky *U.S.A.* 47°29N 100°27W **80** B3
McComb *U.S.A.* 31°15N 90°27W **85** F9
McCook *U.S.A.* 40°12N 100°38W **80** E3
McCreary *Canada* 50°47N 99°29W **71** C9
McCullough Mt. *U.S.A.* 35°35N 115°13W **79** K11
McCusker → *Canada* 55°32N 108°39W **71** B7
McDermitt *U.S.A.* 41°59N 117°43W **76** F5
McDonald *U.S.A.* 40°22N 80°14W **82** F4
Macdonald, L. *Australia* 23°30S 129°0E **60** D4
McDonald Is. *Ind. Oc.* 53°0S 73°0E **3** G13
MacDonnell Ranges *Australia* 23°40S 133°0E **60** D5
MacDowell L. *Canada* 52°15N 92°45W **72** B1
Macduff *U.K.* 57°40N 2°31W **11** D6
Macedonia *U.S.A.* 41°19N 81°31W **82** E3
Macedonia □ *Greece* 40°39N 22°0E **23** D10
Macedonia ■ *Europe* 41°53N 21°40E **23** D9
Maceió *Brazil* 9°40S 35°41W **93** E11
Macerata *Italy* 43°18N 13°27E **22** C5
McFarland *U.S.A.* 35°41N 119°14W **79** K7
McFarlane → *Canada* 59°12N 107°58W **71** B7
Macfarlane, L. *Australia* 32°0S 136°40E **63** E2
McGehee *U.S.A.* 33°38N 91°24W **84** E9
McGill *U.S.A.* 39°23N 114°47W **76** G6
Macgillycuddy's Reeks *Ireland* 51°58N 9°45W **10** E2
McGraw *U.S.A.* 42°36N 76°8W **83** D8
McGregor *U.S.A.* 43°1N 91°11W **80** D8
McGregor Ra. *Australia* 27°0S 142°45E **63** D3
McGuire, Mt. *Australia* 20°18S 148°23E **62** J6
Mach *Pakistan* 29°50N 67°20E **42** E2
Māch Kowr *Iran* 25°48N 61°28E **45** E9
Machado = Jiparaná → *Brazil* 8°3S 62°52W **92** E6
Machagai *Argentina* 26°56S 60°2W **94** B3
Machakos *Kenya* 1°30S 37°15E **54** C4
Machala *Ecuador* 3°20S 79°57W **92** D3
Machanga *Mozam.* 20°59S 35°0E **57** C6
Machattie, L. *Australia* 24°50S 139°48E **62** C2
Machava *Mozam.* 25°54S 32°28E **57** D5
Machece *Mozam.* 19°15S 35°32E **55** F4
Macheke *Zimbabwe* 18°5S 31°51E **57** B5
Machhu → *India* 23°6N 70°46E **42** H4
Machiara △ *Pakistan* 34°40N 73°30E **42** B5
Machias *Maine, U.S.A.* 44°43N 67°28W **81** C20
Machias *N.Y., U.S.A.* 42°25N 78°29W **82** D6
Machichi → *Canada* 57°3N 92°6W **71** B10
Machico *Madeira* 32°43N 16°44W **24** D3
Machilipatnam *India* 16°12N 81°8E **41** L12
Machiques *Venezuela* 10°4N 72°34W **92** A4
Machu Picchu *Peru* 13°8S 72°30W **92** F4
Machynlleth *U.K.* 52°35N 3°50W **13** E4
Macia *Mozam.* 25°2S 33°8E **57** D5
McIlwraith Ra. *Australia* 13°50S 143°20E **62** A3
McInnes L. *Canada* 52°13N 93°45W **71** C10
McIntosh *U.S.A.* 45°55N 101°21W **80** C3
McIntosh L. *Canada* 55°45N 105°0W **71** B8
Macintosh Ra. *Australia* 27°39S 125°32E **61** E4
Macintyre → *Australia* 28°37S 150°47E **63** D5
Mackay *Australia* 21°8S 149°11E **62** K7
Mackay *U.S.A.* 43°55N 113°37W **76** E7
MacKay → *Canada* 57°10N 111°38W **70** B6
Mackay, L. *Australia* 22°30S 129°0E **60** D4
McKay Ra. *Australia* 23°0S 122°30E **60** D3
McKeesport *U.S.A.* 40°20N 79°51W **82** F5
McKellar *Canada* 45°30N 79°55W **82** A5
McKenna *U.S.A.* 46°56N 122°33W **78** D4
Mackenzie *Canada* 55°20N 123°5W **70** B4
McKenzie *U.S.A.* 36°8N 88°31W **85** C10
Mackenzie → *Australia* 23°38S 149°46E **62** C4
Mackenzie → *Canada* 69°10N 134°20W **68** C6
McKenzie → *U.S.A.* 44°7N 123°6W **76** D2
Mackenzie Bay *Canada* 69°0N 137°30W **66** C6
Mackenzie City = Linden *Guyana* 6°0N 58°10W **92** B7
Mackenzie King I. *Canada* 77°45N 111°0W **69** B8
Mackenzie Mts. *Canada* 64°0N 130°0W **68** C7
Mackinaw City *U.S.A.* 45°47N 84°44W **81** C11
McKinlay *Australia* 21°16S 141°18E **62** C3
McKinlay → *Australia* 20°50S 141°28E **62** C3
McKinley, Mt. *U.S.A.* 63°4N 151°0W **74** a
McKinley Sea *Arctic* 82°0N 0°0 **4** A7
McKinney *U.S.A.* 33°12N 96°37W **84** E6
Mackinnon Road *Kenya* 3°40S 39°1E **54** C4
McKittrick *U.S.A.* 35°18N 119°37W **79** K7
Macklin *Canada* 52°20N 109°56W **71** C7
Macksville *Australia* 30°40S 152°56E **63** E5
McLaughlin *U.S.A.* 45°49N 100°49W **80** C3
Maclean *Australia* 29°26S 153°16E **63** D5
McLean *U.S.A.* 35°14N 100°36W **84** D4
McLeansboro *U.S.A.* 38°6N 88°32W **80** F9
Maclear *S. Africa* 31°2S 28°23E **57** E4
Maclear, C. *Malawi* 13°58S 34°49E **55** E3
Macleay → *Australia* 30°56S 153°0E **63** E5
McLennan *Canada* 55°42N 116°50W **70** B5
McLeod → *Canada* 54°9N 115°44W **70** C5
McLeod, L. *Australia* 24°9S 113°47E **61** D1
MacLeod B. *Canada* 62°53N 110°0W **71** A7
MacLeod Lake *Canada* 54°58N 123°0W **70** C4
McLoughlin, Mt. *U.S.A.* 42°27N 122°19W **76** E2
McMechen *U.S.A.* 39°57N 80°44W **82** G4
McMinnville *Oreg., U.S.A.* 45°13N 123°12W **76** D2
McMinnville *Tenn., U.S.A.* 35°41N 85°46W **85** D12
McMurdo *Antarctica* 77°0S 140°0E **5** D11
McMurdo Sd. *Antarctica* 77°0S 170°0E **5** D11
McMurray = Fort McMurray *Canada* 56°44N 111°7W **70** B6
McMurray *U.S.A.* 48°19N 122°14W **78** B4
Macodoene *Mozam.* 23°32S 35°5E **57** C6
Macomb *U.S.A.* 40°27N 90°40W **80** E8
Mâcon *France* 46°19N 4°50E **20** C6
Macon *Ga., U.S.A.* 32°51N 83°38W **85** E13
Macon *Miss., U.S.A.* 33°7N 88°34W **85** E10
Macon *Mo., U.S.A.* 39°44N 92°28W **80** F7
Macossa *Mozam.* 17°55S 33°56E **55** F3
Macoun L. *Canada* 56°32N 103°40W **71** B8
Macovane *Mozam.* 21°30S 35°2E **57** C6
McPherson *U.S.A.* 38°22N 97°40W **80** F5
McPherson Pk. *U.S.A.* 34°53N 119°53W **79** L7
McPherson Ra. *Australia* 28°15S 153°15E **63** D5
Macquarie → *Australia* 30°7S 147°24E **63** E4
Macquarie Harbour *Australia* 42°15S 145°23E **63** G4
Macquarie Is. *Pac. Oc.* 54°36S 158°55E **64** N7
Macquarie Ridge *S. Ocean* 57°0S 159°0E **5** B10
MacRobertson Land *Antarctica* 71°0S 64°0E **5** D6
Macroom *Ireland* 51°54N 8°57W **10** E3
MacTier *Canada* 45°8N 79°47W **82** A5
Macubela *Mozam.* 16°53S 37°49E **55** F4
Macuira △ *Colombia* 12°9N 71°21W **89** D5
Macuiza *Mozam.* 18°7S 34°29E **55** F3
Macumba → *Australia* 27°52S 137°12E **63** D2
Macuro *Venezuela* 10°42N 61°55W **93** K15
Macusani *Peru* 14°4S 70°29W **92** F4
Macuse *Mozam.* 17°45S 37°10E **55** F4
Macuspana *Mexico* 17°46N 92°36W **87** D6
Macusse *Angola* 17°48S 20°23E **56** B3
Ma'dabā □ *Jordan* 31°43N 35°47E **46** D4
Madadeni *S. Africa* 27°43S 30°3E **57** D5
Madagascar ■ *Africa* 20°0S 47°0E **57** C8
Madā'in Sālih *Si. Arabia* 26°46N 37°57E **44** E3
Madama *Niger* 22°0N 13°40E **51** D8
Madame, I. *Canada* 45°30N 60°58W **73** C7
Madang *Papua N. G.* 5°12S 145°49E **58** B7
Madaripur *Bangla.* 23°19N 90°15E **41** H17
Madauk *Burma* 17°56N 96°52E **41** L20
Madawaska *Canada* 45°30N 78°0W **82** A7
Madawaska → *Canada* 45°27N 76°21W **82** A7
Madaya *Burma* 22°12N 96°10E **41** H20
Maddalena *Italy* 41°16N 9°23E **22** D3
Madeira *Atl. Oc.* 32°50N 17°0W **24** D3
Madeira → *Brazil* 3°22S 58°45W **92** D7
Madeleine, Îs. de la *Canada* 47°30N 61°40W **73** C7
Madera *Mexico* 29°12N 108°7W **86** B3
Madera *Calif., U.S.A.* 36°57N 120°3W **78** J6
Madera *Pa., U.S.A.* 40°49N 78°26W **82** F6
Madha *India* 18°0N 75°30E **40** L9
Madhavpur *India* 21°15N 69°58E **42** J3
Madhepura *India* 26°11N 86°23E **43** F12
Madhubani *India* 26°21N 86°7E **43** F12
Madhupur *India* 24°16N 86°39E **43** G12
Madhya Pradesh □ *India* 22°50N 78°0E **42** J8
Madidi → *Bolivia* 12°32S 66°52W **92** F5
Madikeri *India* 12°30N 75°45E **40** N9
Madikwe ⌂ *S. Africa* 27°38S 32°15E **57** D5
Madill *U.S.A.* 34°6N 96°46W **84** D6
Madimba *Dem. Rep. of the Congo* 4°58S 15°5E **52** E3
Ma'din *Syria* 35°45N 39°36E **44** C3
Madinat al Malik Khālid al Askarīyah *Si. Arabia* 27°54N 45°31E **44** E5
Madingou *Congo* 4°10S 13°33E **52** E2
Madirovalo *Madag.* 16°26S 46°32E **57** B8
Madison *Calif., U.S.A.* 38°41N 121°59W **78** G5
Madison *Fla., U.S.A.* 30°28N 83°25W **85** F13
Madison *Ind., U.S.A.* 38°44N 85°23W **81** F11
Madison *Nebr., U.S.A.* 41°50N 97°27W **80** E5
Madison *Ohio, U.S.A.* 41°46N 81°3W **82** E3
Madison *S. Dak., U.S.A.* 44°0N 97°7W **80** C5
Madison *Wis., U.S.A.* 43°4N 89°24W **80** D9
Madison → *U.S.A.* 45°56N 111°31W **76** D8
Madison Heights *U.S.A.* 37°25N 79°8W **81** G14
Madisonville *Ky., U.S.A.* 37°20N 87°30W **80** G10
Madisonville *Tex., U.S.A.* 30°57N 95°55W **84** F7
Madista *Botswana* 21°15S 25°6E **56** C4
Madiun *Indonesia* 7°38S 111°32E **37** G14
Mado Gashi *Kenya* 0°44N 39°10E **54** B4
Madoc *Canada* 44°30N 77°28W **82** B7
Madona *Latvia* 56°53N 26°5E **9** H22
Madrakah, Ra's al *Oman* 19°0N 57°50E **47** D6
Madras = Chennai *India* 13°8N 80°19E **40** N12
Madras = Tamil Nadu □ *India* 11°0N 77°0E **40** P10
Madras *U.S.A.* 44°38N 121°8W **76** D3
Madre, L. *U.S.A.* 25°15N 97°30W **84** J6
Madre, Sierra *Phil.* 17°0N 122°0E **37** A6
Madre de Dios → *Bolivia* 10°59S 66°8W **92** F5
Madre de Dios, I. *Chile* 50°20S 75°10W **96** G1
Madre del Sur, Sierra *Mexico* 17°30N 100°0W **87** D5
Madre Occidental, Sierra *Mexico* 27°0N 107°0W **86** B3
Madre Oriental, Sierra *Mexico* 25°0N 100°0W **86** C5
Madri *India* 24°16N 73°32E **42** G5
Madrid *Spain* 40°24N 3°42W **21** B4
Madrid *U.S.A.* 44°45N 75°8W **83** B9
Madura *Australia* 31°55S 127°0E **61** F4
Madura *Indonesia* 7°30S 114°0E **37** G15
Madura, Selat *Indonesia* 7°30S 113°20E **37** G15
Madurai *India* 9°55N 78°10E **40** Q11
Madurantakam *India* 12°30N 79°50E **40** N11
Mae Chan *Thailand* 20°9N 99°52E **38** B2
Mae Hong Son *Thailand* 19°16N 97°56E **38** C2
Mae Khlong → *Thailand* 13°24N 100°0E **38** F3
Mae Phrik *Thailand* 17°27N 99°7E **38** D2
Mae Ping △ *Thailand* 17°37N 98°51E **38** D2
Mae Ramat *Thailand* 16°58N 98°31E **38** D2
Mae Rim *Thailand* 18°54N 98°57E **38** C2
Mae Sai *Thailand* 20°20N 99°55E **38** B2
Mae Sot *Thailand* 16°43N 98°34E **38** D2
Mae Suai *Thailand* 19°39N 99°33E **38** C2
Mae Tha *Thailand* 18°28N 99°8E **38** C2
Mae Wong △ *Thailand* 15°54N 99°12E **38** E2
Mae Yom △ *Thailand* 18°43N 100°15E **38** C3
Maebashi *Japan* 36°24N 139°4E **31** F9
Maesteg *U.K.* 51°36N 3°40W **13** F4
Maestra, Sierra *Cuba* 20°15N 77°0W **88** B4
Maevatanana *Madag.* 16°56S 46°49E **57** B8
Mafeking = Mafikeng *S. Africa* 25°50S 25°38E **56** D4
Mafeking *Canada* 52°40N 101°10W **71** C8
Mafeteng *Lesotho* 29°51S 27°15E **56** D4
Maffra *Australia* 37°53S 146°58E **63** F4
Mafia I. *Tanzania* 7°45S 39°50E **54** D4
Mafikeng *S. Africa* 25°50S 25°38E **56** D4
Mafra *Brazil* 26°10S 49°55W **95** B6
Mafra *Portugal* 38°55N 9°20W **21** C1
Mafungabusi Plateau *Zimbabwe* 18°30S 29°8E **55** F2
Magadan *Russia* 59°38N 150°50E **29** D16
Magadi *Kenya* 1°54S 36°19E **54** C4
Magadi, L. *Kenya* 1°54S 36°19E **54** C4
Magaliesburg *S. Africa* 26°0S 27°32E **57** D4
Magallanes, Estrecho de *Chile* 52°30S 75°0W **96** G2
Magangué *Colombia* 9°14N 74°45W **92** B4
Magdagachi *Russia* 53°27N 125°48E **29** D13
Magdalen Is. = Madeleine, Îs. de la *Canada* 47°30N 61°40W **73** C7
Magdalena *Argentina* 35°5S 57°30W **94** D4
Magdalena *Bolivia* 13°13S 63°57W **92** F6
Magdalena *U.S.A.* 34°7N 107°15W **77** J10
Magdalena → *Colombia* 11°6N 74°51W **92** A4
Magdalena → *Mexico* 30°40N 112°25W **86** A2
Magdalena, B. *Mexico* 24°35N 112°0W **86** C2
Magdalena, I. *Mexico* 24°40N 112°15W **86** C2
Magdalena, Llano de *Mexico* 25°0N 111°25W **86** C2
Magdalena de Kino *Mexico* 30°38N 110°57W **86** A2
Magdeburg *Germany* 52°7N 11°38E **16** B6
Magdelaine Cays *Australia* 16°33S 150°18E **62** B5
Magee *U.S.A.* 31°52N 89°44W **85** F10
Magelang *Indonesia* 7°29S 110°13E **37** G14
Magellan's Str. = Magallanes, Estrecho de *Chile* 52°30S 75°0W **96** G2
Magenta, L. *Australia* 33°30S 119°2E **61** F2
Magerøya *Norway* 71°3N 25°40E **8** A21
Maggiore, Lago *Italy* 45°57N 8°39E **20** D8
Maggotty *Jamaica* 18°9N 77°46W **88** a
Maghâgha *Egypt* 28°38N 30°50E **51** C12
Magherafelt *U.K.* 54°45N 6°37W **10** B5
Maghreb *N. Afr.* 32°0N 4°0W **50** B5
Magistralnyy *Russia* 56°16N 107°36E **29** D11
Magnetic Pole (North) *Canada* 82°42N 114°24W **69** B9
Magnetic Pole (South) *Antarctica* 64°8S 138°8E **5** C9
Magnitogorsk *Russia* 53°27N 59°4E **18** D10
Magnolia *Ark., U.S.A.* 33°16N 93°14W **84** E8
Magnolia *Miss., U.S.A.* 31°9N 90°28W **85** F9
Mago *Fiji* 17°26S 179°8W **59** a
Magog *Canada* 45°18N 72°9W **83** A12
Magoro *Uganda* 1°45N 34°12E **54** B3
Magoša = Famagusta *Cyprus* 35°8N 33°55E **25** D12
Magoulades *Greece* 39°45N 19°42E **25** A3
Magoye *Zambia* 16°1S 27°30E **55** F2
Magpie, L. *Canada* 51°0N 64°41W **73** B7
Magrath *Canada* 49°25N 112°50W **70** D6
Maguarinho, C. *Brazil* 0°15S 48°30W **93** D9
Magude *Mozam.* 25°2S 32°40E **57** D5
Mağusa = Famagusta *Cyprus* 35°8N 33°55E **25** D12
Maguse L. *Canada* 61°37N 95°10W **71** A9
Maguse Pt. *Canada* 61°20N 93°50W **71** A10
Magvana *India* 23°13N 69°22E **42** H3
Magwe *Burma* 20°10N 95°0E **41** J19
Magyarorszag = Hungary ■ *Europe* 47°20N 19°20E **17** E10
Maha Sarakham *Thailand* 16°12N 103°16E **38** D4
Mahābād *Iran* 36°50N 45°45E **44** B5
Mahabharat Lekh *Nepal* 28°30N 82°0E **43** E10
Mahabo *Madag.* 20°23S 44°40E **57** C7
Mahadeo Hills *India* 22°20N 78°30E **43** H8
Mahaffey *U.S.A.* 40°53N 78°44W **82** F6
Mahagi *Dem. Rep. of the Congo* 2°20N 31°0E **54** B3
Mahajamba → *Madag.* 15°33S 47°8E **57** B8
Mahajamba, Helodranon' i *Madag.* 15°24S 47°5E **57** B8
Mahajan *India* 28°48N 73°56E **42** E5
Mahajanga *Madag.* 15°40S 46°25E **57** B8
Mahajanga □ *Madag.* 17°0S 47°0E **57** B8
Mahajilo → *Madag.* 19°42S 45°22E **57** B8
Mahakam → *Indonesia* 0°35S 117°17E **36** E5
Mahalapye *Botswana* 23°1S 26°51E **56** C4
Mahale Mts. *Tanzania* 6°20S 30°0E **54** D3
Mahale Mts. △ *Tanzania* 6°10S 29°50E **54** D2
Maḩallāt *Iran* 33°55N 50°30E **45** C6
Māhān *Iran* 30°5N 57°18E **45** D8
Mahan → *India* 23°30N 82°50E **43** H10
Mahanadi → *India* 20°20N 86°25E **41** J15
Mahananda → *India* 25°12N 87°52E **43** G12
Mahanoro *Madag.* 19°54S 48°48E **57** B8
Mahanoy City *U.S.A.* 40°49N 76°9W **83** F8
Maharashtra □ *India* 20°30N 75°30E **40** J9
Mahasham, W. → *Egypt* 30°15N 34°10E **46** E3
Mahasoa *Madag.* 22°12S 46°6E **57** C8
Mahasolo *Madag.* 19°7S 46°22E **57** B8
Mahattat ash Shīdīyah *Jordan* 29°55N 35°55E **46** F4
Mahattat 'Unayzah *Jordan* 30°30N 35°47E **46** E4
Mahavavy → *Madag.* 15°57S 45°54E **57** B8
Mahaxay *Laos* 17°22N 105°12E **38** D5
Mahbubnagar *India* 16°45N 77°59E **40** L10
Maḩḑah *Oman* 24°24N 55°59E **45** E7
Mahdia *Tunisia* 35°28N 11°0E **51** A8
Mahe *India* 33°10N 78°32E **43** C8
Mahé *Seychelles* 5°0S 55°30E **53** b
Mahé ✈ **(SEZ)** *Seychelles* 4°40S 55°31E **53** b
Mahébourg *Mauritius* 20°24S 57°42E **53** d
Mahendragarh *India* 28°17N 76°14E **42** E7
Mahendranagar *Nepal* 28°55N 80°20E **43** E9
Mahenge *Tanzania* 8°45S 36°41E **55** D4
Maheno *N.Z.* 45°10S 170°50E **59** F3
Mahesana *India* 23°39N 72°26E **42** H5
Maheshwar *India* 22°11N 75°35E **42** H6
Mahgawan *India* 26°29N 78°37E **43** F8
Mahi → *India* 22°15N 72°55E **42** H5
Mahia Pen. *N.Z.* 39°9S 177°55E **59** C6
Mahilyow *Belarus* 53°55N 30°18E **17** B16
Mahina *Tahiti* 17°30S 149°27W **59** d
Mahinerangi, L. *N.Z.* 45°50S 169°56E **59** F2
Mahmud Kot *Pakistan* 30°16N 71°0E **42** D4
Mahnomen *U.S.A.* 47°19N 95°58W **80** B6
Mahoba *India* 25°15N 79°55E **43** G8
Mahón = Maó *Spain* 39°53N 4°16E **24** B11
Mahone Bay *Canada* 44°27N 64°23W **73** D7
Mahopac *U.S.A.* 41°22N 73°45W **83** E11
Mahuva *India* 21°5N 71°48E **42** J4
Mai-Ndombe, L. *Dem. Rep. of the Congo* 2°0S 18°20E **52** E3
Mai Thon, Ko *Thailand* 7°40N 98°28E **39** a
Maicuru → *Brazil* 2°14S 54°17W **93** D8
Maidan Khula *Afghan.* 33°36N 69°50E **42** C3
Maidenhead *U.K.* 51°31N 0°42W **13** F7
Maidstone *Canada* 53°5N 109°20W **71** C7
Maidstone *U.K.* 51°16N 0°32E **13** F8
Maiduguri *Nigeria* 12°0N 13°20E **51** F8
Maihar *India* 24°16N 80°45E **43** G9
Maijdi *Bangla.* 22°48N 91°10E **41** H17
Maikala Ra. *India* 22°0N 81°0E **41** J12
Maiko △ *Dem. Rep. of the Congo* 0°30S 27°50E **54** C2
Mailani *India* 28°17N 80°21E **43** E9
Mailsi *Pakistan* 29°48N 72°15E **42** E5
Main → *Germany* 50°0N 8°18E **16** C5
Main → *U.K.* 54°48N 6°18W **10** B5
Main Channel *Canada* 45°21N 81°45W **82** A3
Main Range △ *Australia* 28°11S 152°27E **63** D5
Main Ridge *Trin. & Tob.* 11°16N 60°40W **93** J16
Maine *France* 48°20N 0°15W **20** C3
Maine □ *U.S.A.* 45°20N 69°0W **81** C19
Maine → *Ireland* 52°9N 9°45W **10** D2
Maine, G. of *U.S.A.* 43°0N 68°30W **81** D19
Maingkwan *Burma* 26°15N 96°37E **41** F20
Mainit, L. *Phil.* 9°31N 125°30E **37** C7
Mainland *Orkney, U.K.* 58°59N 3°8W **11** C5
Mainland *Shet., U.K.* 60°15N 1°22W **11** A7
Mainoru *Australia* 14°0S 134°6E **62** A1
Mainpuri *India* 27°18N 79°4E **43** F8
Maintirano *Madag.* 18°3S 44°1E **57** B7
Mainz *Germany* 50°1N 8°14E **16** C5
Maio *C. Verde Is.* 15°10N 23°10W **50** b
Maipú *Argentina* 36°52S 57°50W **94** D4
Maiquetía *Venezuela* 10°36N 66°57W **92** A5
Mairabari *India* 26°30N 92°22E **41** F18
Maisi *Cuba* 20°17N 74°9W **89** B5
Maisi, Pta. de *Cuba* 20°10N 74°10W **89** B5
Maitland *N.S.W., Australia* 32°33S 151°36E **63** E5
Maitland *S. Austral., Australia* 34°23S 137°40E **63** E2
Maitland → *Canada* 43°45N 81°43W **82** C3
Maitri *Antarctica* 70°0S 3°0W **5** D3
Maíz, Is. del *Nic.* 12°15N 83°4W **88** D3
Maizuru *Japan* 35°25N 135°22E **31** G7
Majalengka *Indonesia* 6°50S 108°13E **37** G13
Majene *Indonesia* 3°38S 118°57E **37** E5
Majete ⌂ *Malawi* 15°54S 34°34E **55** F3
Majorca = Mallorca *Spain* 39°30N 3°0E **24** B10
Majuro *Marshall Is.* 7°9N 171°12E **64** G9
Maka *Senegal* 13°40N 14°10W **50** F3
Makaha *Zimbabwe* 17°20S 32°39E **57** B5
Makalamabedi *Botswana* 20°19S 23°51E **56** C3
Makale *Indonesia* 3°6S 119°51E **37** E5
Makalu-Barun △ *Nepal* 27°45N 87°10E **43** F12
Makamba *Burundi* 4°8S 29°49E **54** C2
Makarikari = Makgadikgadi Salt Pans *Botswana* 20°40S 25°45E **56** C4
Makarov Basin *Arctic* 87°0N 150°0W **4** A
Makarovo *Russia* 57°40N 107°45E **29** D11
Makasar = Ujung Pandang *Indonesia* 5°10S 119°20E **37** F5
Makasar, Selat *Indonesia* 1°0S 118°20E **37** E5
Makasar, Str. of = Makasar, Selat *Indonesia* 1°0S 118°20E **37** E5
Makat = Maqat *Kazakhstan* 47°39N 53°19E **19** E9
Makedonija = Macedonia ■ *Europe* 41°53N 21°40E **23** D9
Makeni *S. Leone* 8°55N 12°5W **50** G3
Makeyevka = Makiyivka *Ukraine* 48°0N 38°0E **19** E6
Makgadikgadi △ *Botswana* 20°27S 24°47E **56** C3
Makgadikgadi Salt Pans *Botswana* 20°40S 25°45E **56** C4
Makhachkala *Russia* 43°0N 47°30E **19** F8
Makhado = Louis Trichardt *S. Africa* 23°1S 29°43E **57** C4
Makham, Ao *Thailand* 7°51N 98°25E **39** a
Makhfar al Buşayyah *Iraq* 30°0N 46°10E **44** D5
Makhmūr *Iraq* 35°46N 43°35E **44** C4
Makian *Indonesia* 0°20N 127°20E **37** D7
Makindu *Kenya* 2°18S 37°50E **54** C4
Makīnsk *Kazakhstan* 52°37N 70°26E **28** D8
Makira = San Cristóbal *Solomon Is.* 10°30S 161°0E **58** C9
Makiyivka *Ukraine* 48°0N 38°0E **19** E6
Makkah *Si. Arabia* 21°30N 39°54E **47** C2
Makkovik *Canada* 55°10N 59°10W **73** A8
Makó *Hungary* 46°14N 20°33E **17** E11
Makogai *Fiji* 17°28S 179°0E **59** a
Makokou *Gabon* 0°40N 12°50E **52** D2
Makongo *Dem. Rep. of the Congo* 3°25N 26°17E **54** B2
Makoro *Dem. Rep. of the Congo* 3°10N 29°59E **54** B2
Makrai *India* 22°2N 77°0E **42** H7
Makran Coast Range *Pakistan* 25°40N 64°0E **40** G4
Makrana *India* 27°2N 74°46E **42** F6
Makrigialos *Greece* 35°2N 25°59E **25** D7
Mākū *Iran* 39°15N 44°31E **44** B5
Makunda *Botswana* 22°30S 20°7E **56** C3
Makurazaki *Japan* 31°15N 130°20E **31** J5
Makurdi *Nigeria* 7°43N 8°35E **50** G7
Makūyeh *Iran* 28°7N 53°9E **45** D7
Makwassie *S. Africa* 27°17S 26°0E **56** D4
Makwiro *Zimbabwe* 17°58S 30°25E **57** B5
Mal B. *Ireland* 52°50N 9°30W **10** D2
Mala, Pta. *Panama* 7°28N 80°2W **88** E3
Malabar Coast *India* 11°0N 75°0E **40** P9
Malacca, Straits of *Indonesia* 3°0N 101°0E **39** L3
Malad City *U.S.A.* 42°12N 112°15W **76** E7
Maladzyechna *Belarus* 54°20N 26°50E **17** A14
Málaga *Spain* 36°43N 4°23W **21** D3
Malagarasi *Tanzania* 5°5S 30°50E **54** D3
Malagarasi → *Tanzania* 5°12S 29°47E **54** D2
Malagasy Rep. = Madagascar ■ *Africa* 20°0S 47°0E **57** C8
Malahide *Ireland* 53°26N 6°9W **10** C5
Malaimbandy *Madag.* 20°20S 45°36E **57** C8
Malaita *Solomon Is.* 9°0S 161°0E **58** B9
Malakâl *Sudan* 9°33N 31°40E **51** G12
Malakand *Pakistan* 34°40N 71°55E **42** B4
Malakula *Vanuatu* 16°15S 167°30E **58** C9
Malakwal *Pakistan* 32°34N 73°13E **42** C5
Malamala *Indonesia* 3°21S 120°55E **37** E6
Malanda *Australia* 17°22S 145°35E **62** B4
Malang *Indonesia* 7°59S 112°45E **37** G15
Malanga *Mozam.* 13°28S 36°7E **55** E4
Malangen *Norway* 69°24N 18°37E **8** B18
Malanje *Angola* 9°36S 16°17E **52** F3
Mälaren *Sweden* 59°30N 17°10E **9** G17
Malargüe *Argentina* 35°32S 69°30W **94** D2
Malartic *Canada* 48°9N 78°9W **72** C4
Malaryta *Belarus* 51°50N 24°3E **17** C13
Malatya *Turkey* 38°25N 38°20E **44** B3
Malawi ■ *Africa* 11°55S 34°0E **55** E3
Malawi, L. *Africa* 12°30S 34°30E **55** E3
Malay Pen. *Asia* 7°25N 100°0E **39** J3
Malaya Vishera *Russia* 58°55N 32°25E **18** C5
Malaybalay *Phil.* 8°5N 125°7E **37** C7
Malāyer *Iran* 34°19N 48°51E **45** C6
Malaysia ■ *Asia* 5°0N 110°0E **39** K4
Malazgirt *Turkey* 39°10N 42°33E **44** B4
Malbon *Australia* 21°5S 140°17E **62** C3
Malbooma *Australia* 30°41S 134°11E **63** E1
Malbork *Poland* 54°3N 19°1E **17** B10
Malcolm *Australia* 28°51S 121°25E **61** E3
Malcolm, Pt. *Australia* 33°48S 123°45E **61** F3
Maldah *India* 25°2N 88°9E **43** G13
Maldegem *Belgium* 51°14N 3°26E **15** C3
Malden *Mass., U.S.A.* 42°26N 71°3W **83** D13
Malden *Mo., U.S.A.* 36°34N 89°57W **80** G9
Malden I. *Kiribati* 4°3S 155°1W **65** H12
Maldives ■ *Ind. Oc.* 5°0N 73°0E **26** H9
Maldon *U.K.* 51°44N 0°42E **13** F8
Maldonado *Uruguay* 34°59S 55°0W **95** C5
Maldonado, Pta. *Mexico* 16°20N 98°33W **87** D5
Malé Karpaty *Slovak Rep.* 48°30N 17°20E **17** D9

Maleas, Akra Greece 36°28N 23°7E 23 F10
Malebo, Pool Africa 4°17S 15°20E 52 E3
Malegaon India 20°30N 74°38E 40 J9
Malei Mozam. 17°12S 36°58E 55 F4
Malek Kandī Iran 37°9N 46°6E 44 B5
Malela
Dem. Rep. of the Congo 4°22S 26°8E 54 C2
Malema Mozam. 14°57S 37°20E 55 E4
Maleme Greece 35°31N 23°49E 25 D5
Malerkotla India 30°32N 75°58E 42 D6
Males Greece 35°6N 25°35E 25 D7
Malgomaj Sweden 64°40N 16°30E 8 D17
Malha Sudan 15°8N 25°10E 51 E11
Malhargarh India 24°17N 74°59E 42 G6
Malheur → U.S.A. 44°4N 116°59W 76 D5
Malheur L. U.S.A. 43°20N 118°48W 76 E4
Mali
Mali ■ Africa 17°0N 3°0W 50 E5
Mali → Burma 25°42N 97°30E 41 G20
Mali Kyun Burma 13°0N 98°20E 38 F2
Malia Greece 35°17N 25°32E 25 D7
Malia, Kolpos Greece 35°19N 25°27E 25 D7
Malibu U.S.A. 34°2N 118°41W 79 L8
Maliku Indonesia 0°39S 123°16E 37 E6
Malili Indonesia 2°42S 121°6E 37 E6
Malimba, Mts.
Dem. Rep. of the Congo 7°30S 29°30E 54 D2
Malin Hd. Ireland 55°23N 7°23W 10 A4
Malin Pen. Ireland 55°20N 7°17W 10 A4
Malindi Kenya 3°12S 40°5E 54 C5
Malines = Mechelen
Belgium 51°2N 4°29E 15 C4
Malino Indonesia 1°0N 121°0E 37 D6
Malinyi Tanzania 8°56S 36°0E 55 D4
Malita Phil. 6°19N 125°39E 37 C7
Maliwun Burma 10°17N 98°40E 39 G2
Maliya India 23°5N 70°46E 42 H4
Malka Mari △ Kenya 4°11N 40°46E 54 B5
Malkara Turkey 40°53N 26°53E 23 D12
Mallacoota Inlet
Australia 37°34S 149°40E 63 F4
Mallaig U.K. 57°0N 5°50W 11 D3
Mallawan India 27°4N 80°12E 43 F9
Mallawi Egypt 27°44N 30°44E 51 C12
Mallicolo = Malakula
Vanuatu 16°15S 167°30E 58 C9
Mallorca Spain 39°30N 3°0E 24 B10
Mallorytown Canada 44°29N 75°53W 83 B9
Mallow Ireland 52°8N 8°39W 10 D3
Malmberget Sweden 67°11N 20°40E 8 C19
Malmédy Belgium 50°25N 6°2E 15 D6
Malmesbury S. Africa 33°28S 18°41E 56 E2
Malmivaara = Malmberget
Sweden 67°11N 20°40E 8 C19
Malmö Sweden 55°36N 12°59E 9 J15
Malolo Fiji 17°45S 177°11E 59 a
Malolos Phil. 14°50N 120°49E 37 B6
Malolotja △ Swaziland 26°4S 31°6E 57 D5
Malombe L. Malawi 14°40S 35°15E 55 E4
Malone U.S.A. 44°51N 74°18W 83 B10
Måløy Norway 61°57N 5°6E 8 F11
Malpaso Canary Is. 27°43N 18°3W 24 G1
Malpaso, Presa =
Netzahualcóyotl, Presa
Mexico 17°8N 93°35W 87 D6
Malpelo, I. de Colombia 4°3N 81°35W 92 C2
Malpur India 23°21N 73°27E 42 H5
Malpura India 26°17N 75°23E 42 F6
Malta Idaho, U.S.A. 42°18N 113°22W 76 E7
Malta Mont., U.S.A. 48°21N 107°52W 76 B10
Malta ■ Europe 35°55N 14°26E 25 D2
Maltahöhe Namibia 24°55S 17°0E 56 C2
Malton Canada 43°42N 79°38W 82 C5
Malton U.K. 54°8N 0°49W 12 C7
Maluku Indonesia 1°0S 127°0E 37 E7
Maluku □ Indonesia 3°0S 128°0E 37 E7
Maluku Sea = Molucca Sea
Indonesia 0°0 125°0E 37 E6
Malvan India 16°2N 73°30E 40 M8
Malvern U.S.A. 34°22N 92°49W 84 D8
Malvern Hills U.K. 52°0N 2°19W 13 E5
Malvinas, Is. = Falkland Is. ☑
Atl. Oc. 51°30S 59°0W 96 G5
Malya Tanzania 3°5S 33°38E 54 C3
Malyn Ukraine 50°46N 29°3E 17 C15
Malyy Lyakhovskiy, Ostrov
Russia 74°7N 140°36E 29 B15
Malyy Taymyr, Ostrov
Russia 78°6N 107°15E 29 B11
Mama Russia 58°18N 112°54E 29 D12
Mamanguape Brazil 6°50S 35°4W 93 E11
Mamanuca Group Fiji 17°35S 177°5E 59 a
Mamarr Mitlâ Egypt 30°2N 32°54E 46 E1
Mamasa Indonesia 2°55S 119°20E 37 E5
Mambasa
Dem. Rep. of the Congo 1°22N 29°3E 54 B2
Mamberamo → Indonesia 2°0S 137°50E 37 E9
Mambilima Falls Zambia 10°31S 28°45E 55 E2
Mambirima
Dem. Rep. of the Congo 11°25S 27°33E 55 E2
Mambo Tanzania 4°52S 38°22E 54 C4
Mambrui Kenya 3°5S 40°5E 54 C5
Mamburao Phil. 13°13N 120°39E 37 B6
Mameigwess L. Canada 52°35N 87°50W 72 B2
Mammoth U.S.A. 32°43N 110°39W 77 K8
Mammoth Cave △
U.S.A. 37°8N 86°13W 80 G10
Mamoré → Bolivia 10°23S 65°53W 92 F5
Mamou Guinea 10°15N 12°0W 50 F3
Mamoudzou Mayotte 12°48S 45°14E 53 a
Mampikony Madag. 16°6S 47°38E 57 B8
Mamuju Indonesia 2°41S 118°50E 37 E5
Mamuno Botswana 22°16S 20°1E 56 C3
Man Ivory C. 7°30N 7°40W 50 G4
Man, I. of U.K. 54°15N 4°30W 12 C3
Man-Bazar India 23°4N 86°39E 43 H12
Man Na Burma 23°27N 97°19E 41 H20
Mana → Fr. Guiana 5°45N 53°55W 93 B8

Mana Pools △ Zimbabwe 15°56S 29°25E 55 F2
Manaar, G. of = Mannar, G. of
Asia 8°30N 79°0E 40 Q11
Manacapuru Brazil 3°16S 60°37W 92 D6
Manacor Spain 39°34N 3°13E 24 B10
Manado Indonesia 1°29N 124°51E 37 D6
Managua Nic. 12°6N 86°20W 88 D2
Managua, L. de Nic. 12°20N 86°30W 88 D2
Manakara Madag. 22°8S 48°1E 57 C8
Manali India 32°16N 77°10E 42 C7
Manama = Al Manāmah
Bahrain 26°10N 50°30E 45 E6
Manambao → Madag. 17°35S 44°0E 57 B7
Manambato Madag. 13°43S 49°7E 57 A8
Manambolosy Madag. 16°2S 49°40E 57 B8
Mananara → Madag. 16°10S 49°46E 57 B8
Mananara Madag. 23°21S 47°42E 57 C8
Mananara △ Madag. 16°14S 49°45E 57 B8
Mananjary Madag. 21°13S 48°20E 57 C8
Manantenina Madag. 24°17S 47°19E 57 C8
Manaos = Manaus Brazil 3°0S 60°0W 92 D7
Manapire → Venezuela 7°42N 66°7W 92 B5
Manapouri N.Z. 45°34S 167°39E 59 F1
Manapouri, L. N.Z. 45°32S 167°32E 59 F1
Manār, Jabal Yemen 14°2N 44°17E 47 E3
Manaravolo Madag. 23°59S 45°39E 57 C8
Manas China 44°17N 85°56E 32 B3
Manas → India 26°12N 90°40E 41 F17
Manas He → China 45°38N 85°12E 32 B3
Manaslu Nepal 28°33N 84°33E 43 E11
Manasquan U.S.A. 40°8N 74°3W 83 F10
Manassa U.S.A. 37°11N 105°56W 77 H11
Manatí Puerto Rico 18°26N 66°29W 89 d
Manaung Burma 18°45N 93°40E 41 K18
Manaus Brazil 3°0S 60°0W 92 D7
Manawan L. Canada 55°24N 103°14W 71 B8
Manbij Syria 36°31N 37°57E 44 B3
Manchegorsk Russia 67°54N 32°58E 28 C4
Manchester U.K. 53°29N 2°12W 12 D5
Manchester Calif.,
U.S.A. 38°58N 123°41W 78 G3
Manchester Conn.,
U.S.A. 41°47N 72°31W 83 E12
Manchester Ga., U.S.A. 32°51N 84°37W 85 E12
Manchester Iowa, U.S.A. 42°29N 91°27W 80 D8
Manchester Ky., U.S.A. 37°9N 83°46W 81 G12
Manchester N.H.,
U.S.A. 42°59N 71°28W 83 D13
Manchester N.Y., U.S.A. 42°56N 77°16W 82 D7
Manchester Pa., U.S.A. 40°4N 76°43W 83 F8
Manchester Tenn.,
U.S.A. 35°29N 86°5W 85 D11
Manchester Vt., U.S.A. 43°10N 73°5W 83 C11
Manchester Int. ✈ (MAN)
U.K. 53°21N 2°17W 12 D5
Manchester L. Canada 61°28N 107°29W 71 A7
Manchhar L. Pakistan 26°25N 67°39E 42 F2
Manchuria = Dongbei
China 45°0N 125°0E 30 A5
Manchurian Plain China 47°0N 124°0E 26 D14
Mand → India 21°42N 83°15E 43 J10
Mand → Iran 28°20N 52°30E 45 D7
Manda Ludewe, Tanzania 10°30S 34°40E 55 E3
Manda Mbeya, Tanzania 7°58S 32°29E 54 D3
Manda Mbeya, Tanzania 8°30S 32°49E 55 D3
Mandabé Madag. 21°0S 44°55E 57 C7
Mandaguari Brazil 23°32S 51°42W 95 A5
Mandah = Töhöm
Mongolia 44°27N 108°2E 34 B5
Mandal Norway 58°2N 7°25E 9 G12
Mandala, Puncak
Indonesia 4°44S 140°20E 37 E10
Mandalay Burma 22°0N 96°4E 41 J20
Mandale = Mandalay
Burma 22°0N 96°4E 41 J20
Mandalgarh India 25°12N 75°6E 42 G6
Mandalgovĭ Mongolia 45°45N 106°10E 34 B4
Mandalī Iraq 33°43N 45°28E 44 C5
Mandan U.S.A. 46°50N 100°54W 80 B3
Mandar, Teluk Indonesia 3°35S 119°15E 37 E5
Mandaue Phil. 10°20N 123°56E 37 B6
Mandera Kenya 3°55N 41°53E 54 B5
Mandeville Jamaica 18°2N 77°31W 88 a
Mandi India 31°39N 76°58E 42 D7
Mandi Burewala Pakistan 30°9N 72°41E 42 D5
Mandi Dabwali India 29°58N 74°42E 42 E6
Mandimba Mozam. 14°20S 35°40E 55 E4
Mandioli Indonesia 0°40S 127°20E 37 E7
Mandla India 22°39N 80°30E 43 H9
Mandorah Australia 12°32S 130°42E 60 B5
Mandoto Madag. 19°34S 46°17E 57 B8
Mandra Pakistan 33°23N 73°12E 42 C5
Mandrare → Madag. 25°10S 46°30E 57 D8
Mandritsara Madag. 15°50S 48°49E 57 B8
Mandsaur India 24°3N 75°8E 42 G6
Mandurah Australia 32°36S 115°48E 61 F2
Mandvi India 22°51N 69°22E 42 H3
Mandya India 12°30N 77°0E 40 N10
Mandzai Pakistan 30°55N 67°6E 42 D2
Maneh Iran 37°39N 57°7E 45 B8
Manera Madag. 22°55S 44°20E 57 C7
Maneroo Cr. →
Australia 23°21S 143°53E 62 C3
Manfalût Egypt 27°20N 30°52E 51 C12
Manfredónia Italy 41°38N 15°55E 22 D6
Mangabeiras, Chapada das
Brazil 10°0S 46°30W 93 F9
Mangai Cook Is. 21°55S 157°55W 65 K12
Mangalia Romania 43°50N 28°35E 17 G15
Mangalore India 12°55N 74°47E 40 N9
Mangan India 27°31N 88°32E 43 F13
Mangawan India 24°41N 81°33E 43 G9
Mangaweka N.Z. 39°48S 175°47E 59 C5
Mangaung Indonesia 2°50S 108°10E 36 E3
Manggawitu Indonesia 4°8S 133°32E 37 E8

Mangghystaü Tübegi
Kazakhstan 44°30N 52°30E 28 E6
Manggis Indonesia 8°29S 115°31E 37 J18
Mangindrano Madag. 14°17S 48°58E 57 A8
Mangkalihat, Tanjung
Indonesia 1°2N 118°59E 37 D5
Mangla Pakistan 33°7N 73°39E 42 C5
Mangla Dam Pakistan 33°9N 73°44E 43 C5
Manglaur India 29°44N 77°49E 42 E7
Mangnai Zhen China 37°52N 91°43E 32 C4
Mangnai China 38°24N 90°14E 32 C4
Mango Togo 10°20N 0°30E 50 F6
Mango Tonga 20°17S 174°29W 59 c
Mangoche Malawi 14°25S 35°16E 55 E4
Mangoky → Madag. 21°29S 43°41E 57 C7
Mangole Indonesia 1°50S 125°55E 37 E6
Mangombe
Dem. Rep. of the Congo 1°20S 26°48E 54 C2
Mangonui N.Z. 35°1S 173°32E 59 A4
Mangoro → Madag. 20°0S 48°45E 57 B8
Mangrol Mad. P., India 21°7N 70°7E 42 J4
Mangrol Raj., India 25°20N 76°31E 42 G6
Mangueira, L. da Brazil 33°0S 52°50W 95 C5
Mangum U.S.A. 34°53N 99°30W 84 D5
Manguri Australia 28°58S 134°22E 63 A1
Mangyshlak, Poluostrov =
Mangghystaü Tübegi
Kazakhstan 44°30N 52°30E 28 E6
Manhattan U.S.A. 39°11N 96°35W 80 F5
Manhiça Mozam. 25°23S 32°49E 57 D5
Mania → Madag. 19°42S 45°22E 57 B8
Manica Mozam. 18°58S 32°59E 57 B5
Manica □ Mozam. 19°10S 33°45E 57 B5
Manicaland □ Zimbabwe 19°0S 32°30E 55 F3
Manicoré Brazil 5°48S 61°16W 92 E6
Manicouagan →
Canada 49°30N 68°30W 73 C6
Manicouagan, Rés.
Canada 51°5N 68°40W 73 B6
Maniema □
Dem. Rep. of the Congo 3°0S 26°0E 54 C2
Manīfah Si. Arabia 27°44N 49°0E 45 E6
Manifold, C. Australia 22°41S 150°50E 62 C5
Manigotagan Canada 51°6N 96°18W 71 C9
Manigotagan → Canada 51°7N 96°20W 71 C9
Manihari India 25°21N 87°38E 43 G12
Manihiki Cook Is. 10°24S 161°1W 65 J11
Manihiki Plateau
Pac. Oc. 11°0S 164°0W 65 J11
Manika, Plateau de la
Dem. Rep. of the Congo 10°0S 25°5E 55 E2
Manikpur India 25°4N 81°7E 43 G9
Manila Phil. 14°35N 120°58E 37 B6
Manila U.S.A. 40°59N 109°43W 76 F9
Manila B. Phil. 14°40N 120°35E 37 B6
Manilla Australia 30°45S 150°43E 63 E5
Maningrida Australia 12°3S 134°13E 62 A1
Manipur □ India 25°0N 94°0E 41 G19
Manipur → Burma 23°45N 94°20E 41 H19
Manisa Turkey 38°38N 27°30E 23 E12
Manistee U.S.A. 44°15N 86°19W 80 C10
Manistee → U.S.A. 44°15N 86°21W 80 C10
Manistique U.S.A. 45°57N 86°15W 80 C10
Manitoba □ Canada 53°30N 97°0W 71 B9
Manitoba, L. Canada 51°0N 98°45W 71 C9
Manitou Canada 49°15N 98°32W 71 D9
Manitou, L. Canada 50°55N 65°17W 73 B6
Manitou Is. U.S.A. 45°8N 86°0W 80 C10
Manitou L. Canada 52°43N 109°43W 71 C7
Manitou Springs
U.S.A. 38°52N 104°55W 76 G11
Manitoulin I. Canada 45°40N 82°30W 72 C3
Manitouwadge Canada 49°8N 85°48W 72 C2
Manitowoc U.S.A. 44°5N 87°40W 80 C10
Manizales Colombia 5°5N 75°32W 92 B3
Manja Madag. 21°26S 44°20E 57 C7
Manjacaze Mozam. 24°45S 34°0E 57 C5
Manjakandriana Madag. 18°55S 47°47E 57 B8
Manjhand Pakistan 25°50N 68°10E 42 G3
Manjimup Australia 34°15S 116°6E 61 F2
Manjra → India 18°49N 77°52E 40 K10
Mankato Kans., U.S.A. 39°47N 98°13W 80 F4
Mankato Minn., U.S.A. 44°10N 94°0W 80 C6
Mankayane Swaziland 26°40S 31°4E 57 D5
Mankera Pakistan 31°23N 71°26E 42 D4
Mankota Canada 49°25N 107°5W 71 D7
Manlay = Üydzin
Mongolia 44°9N 107°0E 34 B4
Manmad India 20°18N 74°28E 40 J9
Mann Ranges Australia 26°6S 130°5E 61 E5
Manna Indonesia 4°25S 102°55E 36 E2
Mannahill Australia 32°25S 140°0E 63 E3
Mannar Sri Lanka 9°1N 79°54E 40 Q11
Mannar, G. of Asia 8°30N 79°0E 40 Q11
Mannar I. Sri Lanka 9°5N 79°45E 40 Q11
Mannheim Germany 49°29N 8°29E 16 D5
Manning Canada 56°53N 117°39W 70 B5
Manning Oreg., U.S.A. 45°45N 123°13W 78 E3
Manning S.C., U.S.A. 33°42N 80°13W 85 E14
Mannum Australia 34°50S 139°20E 63 E2
Manoharpur India 22°23N 85°12E 43 H11
Manokwari Indonesia 0°54S 134°0E 37 E8
Manombo Madag. 22°57S 43°28E 57 C7
Manono
Dem. Rep. of the Congo 7°15S 27°25E 54 D2
Manono Samoa 13°50S 172°5W 59 b
Manorhamilton Ireland 54°18N 8°10W 10 B3
Manosque France 43°49N 5°47E 20 E6
Manotick Canada 45°13N 75°41W 83 A9
Manouane → Canada 49°30N 71°10W 73 C5
Manouane, L. Canada 50°45N 70°45W 73 B5
Manp'o N. Korea 41°6N 126°24E 35 D14
Manpojin = Manp'o
N. Korea 41°6N 126°24E 35 D14
Manpur Chhattisgarh,
India 23°17N 83°35E 43 H10
Manpur Mad. P., India 22°26N 75°37E 42 H6

Manresa Spain 41°48N 1°50E 21 B6
Mansa Gujarat, India 23°27N 72°45E 42 H5
Mansa Punjab, India 30°0N 75°27E 42 E6
Mansa Zambia 11°13S 28°55E 55 E2
Mansehra Pakistan 34°20N 73°15E 42 B5
Mansel I. Canada 62°0N 80°0W 69 C12
Mansfield Australia 37°4S 146°6E 63 F4
Mansfield U.K. 53°9N 1°11W 12 D6
Mansfield La., U.S.A. 32°2N 93°43W 84 E8
Mansfield Mass., U.S.A. 42°2N 71°13W 83 D13
Mansfield Ohio, U.S.A. 40°45N 82°31W 82 F2
Mansfield Pa., U.S.A. 41°48N 77°5W 82 E7
Mansfield Tex., U.S.A. 32°33N 97°8W 84 E6
Mansfield, Mt. U.S.A. 44°33N 72°49W 83 B12
Manson Creek Canada 55°37N 124°32W 70 B4
Manta Ecuador 1°0S 80°40W 92 D2
Mantalingajan, Mt.
Phil. 8°55N 117°45E 36 C5
Mantare Tanzania 2°42S 33°13E 54 C3
Manteca U.S.A. 37°48N 121°13W 78 H5
Manteo U.S.A. 35°55N 75°40W 85 D17
Mantes-la-Jolie France 48°58N 1°41E 20 B4
Manthani India 18°40N 79°35E 40 K11
Manti U.S.A. 39°16N 111°38W 76 G8
Mantiqueira, Serra da
Brazil 22°0S 44°0W 95 A7
Manton U.S.A. 44°25N 85°24W 81 C11
Mántova Italy 45°9N 10°48E 22 B4
Mänttä Finland 62°3N 24°40E 8 E21
Mantua = Mántova Italy 45°9N 10°48E 22 B4
Manú Peru 12°10S 70°51W 92 F4
Manú → Peru 12°16S 70°55W 92 F4
Manu'a Is. Amer. Samoa 14°13S 169°35W 59 b
Manuel Alves → Brazil 11°19S 48°28W 93 F9
Manui Indonesia 3°35S 123°5E 37 E6
Manukau N.Z. 37°0S 174°52E 59 B5
Manuripi → Bolivia 11°6S 67°36W 92 F5
Many U.S.A. 31°34N 93°29W 84 F8
Manyani Kenya 3°5S 38°30E 54 C4
Manyara, L. Tanzania 3°40S 35°50E 54 C4
Manych-Gudilo, Ozero
Russia 46°24N 42°38E 19 E7
Manyonga → Tanzania 4°10S 34°15E 54 C3
Manyoni Tanzania 5°45S 34°55E 54 D3
Manzai Pakistan 32°12N 70°15E 42 C4
Manzanar △ U.S.A. 36°44N 118°9W 78 J7
Manzanares Spain 39°2N 3°22W 21 C4
Manzanillo Cuba 20°20N 77°31W 88 B4
Manzanillo Mexico 19°3N 104°20W 86 D4
Manzano Mts. U.S.A. 34°40N 106°20W 77 J10
Manzariyeh Iran 34°53N 50°50E 45 C6
Manzhouli China 49°35N 117°25E 33 B6
Manzini Swaziland 26°30S 31°25E 57 D5
Manzur Vadisi △ Turkey 39°10N 39°30E 44 B3
Mao Chad 14°4N 15°19E 51 F8
Maó Spain 39°53N 4°16E 24 B11
Maoke, Pegunungan
Indonesia 3°40S 137°30E 37 E9
Maolin China 43°58N 123°30E 35 C12
Maoming China 21°50N 110°54E 33 D6
Maoxing China 45°28N 124°40E 35 B13
Mapam Yumco China 30°45N 81°28E 43 D9
Mapastepec Mexico 15°26N 92°54E 87 D6
Maphrao, Ko Thailand 7°56N 98°26E 39 a
Mapia, Kepulauan
Indonesia 0°50N 134°20E 37 D8
Mapimí Mexico 25°49N 103°51W 86 B4
Mapimí, Bolsón de
Mexico 27°0N 104°15W 86 B4
Mapinga Tanzania 6°40S 39°12E 54 D4
Mapinhane Mozam. 22°20S 35°0E 57 C6
Maple Creek Canada 49°55N 109°29W 71 D7
Maple Valley U.S.A. 47°25N 122°3W 78 C4
Mapleton U.S.A. 44°2N 123°52W 76 D2
Mapuera → Brazil 1°5S 57°2W 92 D7
Mapulanguene Mozam. 24°29S 32°6E 57 C5
Mapungubwe △
S. Africa 22°12S 29°22E 55 G2
Maputo Mozam. 25°58S 32°32E 57 D5
Maputo □ Mozam. 26°0S 32°25E 57 D5
Maputo, B. de Mozam. 25°50S 32°45E 57 D5
Maputo → Mozam. 26°23S 32°48E 57 D5
Maqat Kazakhstan 47°39N 53°19E 19 E9
Maqèn China 34°24N 100°6E 32 C5
Maqiaohe China 44°40N 130°30E 35 B16
Maqnā Si. Arabia 28°25N 34°50E 44 D2
Maqteïr Mauritania 21°50N 11°40W 50 D3
Maquan He = Brahmaputra →
Asia 23°40N 90°35E 43 H13
Maquela do Zombo Angola 6°0S 15°15E 52 F3
Maquinchao Argentina 41°15S 68°50W 96 E3
Maquoketa U.S.A. 42°4N 90°40W 80 D8
Mar Canada 44°49N 81°12W 82 B3
Mar, Serra do Brazil 25°30S 49°0W 95 B6
Mar Chiquita, L.
Argentina 30°40S 62°50W 94 C3
Mar del Plata Argentina 38°0S 57°30W 94 D4
Mar Menor Spain 37°40N 0°45W 21 D5
Mara Tanzania 1°30S 34°32E 54 C3
Mara □ Tanzania 1°45S 34°20E 54 C3
Maraä Brazil 1°52S 65°25W 92 D5
Maraa Tahiti 17°46S 149°34W 59 d
Maraboon, L. Australia 23°41S 148°0E 62 C4
Maracá, I. de Brazil 2°10N 50°30W 93 C8
Maracaibo Venezuela 10°40N 71°37W 92 A4
Maracaibo, L. de
Venezuela 9°40N 71°30W 92 B4
Maracaju Brazil 21°38S 55°9W 95 A4
Maracas Bay Village
Trin. & Tob. 10°46N 61°28W 93 K15
Maracay Venezuela 10°15N 67°28W 92 A5
Marādah Libya 29°15N 19°15E 51 C9
Maradi Niger 13°29N 7°20E 50 F7
Marāgheh Iran 37°30N 46°12E 44 B5

Marāh Si. Arabia 25°0N 45°35E 44 E5
Marajó, I. de Brazil 1°0S 49°30W 93 D9
Marākand Iran 38°51N 45°16E 44 B5
Marakele △ S. Africa 32°14S 25°27E 57 E4
Maralal Kenya 1°0N 36°38E 54 B4
Maralinga Australia 30°13S 131°32E 61 F5
Marambio Antarctica 64°0S 57°0W 5 C18
Maran Malaysia 3°35N 102°45E 39 L4
Marana U.S.A. 32°27N 111°13W 77 K8
Maranboy Australia 14°40S 132°39E 60 B5
Marand Iran 38°30N 45°45E 44 B5
Marang Malaysia 5°12N 103°13E 39 K4
Maranguape Brazil 3°55S 38°50W 93 D11
Maranhão = São Luís
Brazil 2°39S 44°15W 93 D10
Maranhão □ Brazil 5°0S 46°0W 93 E9
Maranoa → Australia 27°50S 148°37E 63 D4
Marañón → Peru 4°30S 73°35W 92 D4
Marão Mozam. 24°18S 34°2E 57 C5
Maras = Kahramanmaraş
Turkey 37°37N 36°53E 44 B3
Marathasa Cyprus 34°59N 32°51E 25 E11
Marathon Australia 20°51S 143°32E 62 C3
Marathon Canada 48°44N 86°23W 72 C2
Marathon N.Y., U.S.A. 42°27N 76°2W 83 D8
Marathon Tex., U.S.A. 30°12N 103°15W 84 F3
Marathóvouno Cyprus 35°13N 33°37E 25 D12
Maratua Indonesia 2°10N 118°35E 37 D5
Maraval Trin. & Tob. 10°42N 61°31W 93 K15
Maravatío Mexico 19°54N 100°27W 86 D4
Marāwih U.A.E. 24°18N 53°18E 45 E7
Marbella Spain 36°30N 4°57W 21 D3
Marble Bar Australia 21°9S 119°44E 60 D2
Marble Falls U.S.A. 30°35N 98°16W 84 F5
Marblehead Mass.,
U.S.A. 42°29N 70°51W 83 D14
Marblehead Ohio, U.S.A. 41°32N 82°44W 82 E2
Marburg Germany 50°47N 8°46E 16 C5
Marca, Pta. Da Angola 16°31S 11°43E 52 H2
March U.K. 52°33N 0°5E 13 E8
Marche France 46°5N 1°20E 20 C4
Marche-en-Famenne
Belgium 50°14N 5°19E 15 D5
Marchena Spain 37°18N 5°23W 21 D3
Marco Island U.S.A. 25°58N 81°44W 85 J14
Marcos Juárez Argentina 32°42S 62°5W 94 C3
Marcus I. = Minami-Tori-Shima
Pac. Oc. 24°20N 153°58E 64 E7
Marcy, Mt. U.S.A. 44°7N 73°56W 83 B11
Mardan Pakistan 34°20N 72°0E 42 B5
Mardin Turkey 37°20N 40°43E 44 B4
Maree, L. U.K. 57°40N 5°26W 11 D3
Mareeba Australia 16°59S 145°28E 62 B4
Mareetsane S. Africa 26°9S 25°25E 56 D4
Marek = Stanke Dimitrov
Bulgaria 42°17N 23°9E 23 C10
Marengo U.S.A. 41°48N 92°4W 80 E7
Marerano Madag. 21°23S 44°52E 57 C7
Marfa U.S.A. 30°19N 104°1W 84 F2
Marfa Pt. Malta 35°59N 14°19E 25 D1
Margaret → Australia 18°9S 125°41E 60 C4
Margaret Bay Canada 51°20N 127°35W 70 C3
Margaret L. Canada 58°56N 115°25W 70 B5
Margaret River Australia 33°57S 115°4E 61 F2
Margarita, I. de Venezuela 11°0N 64°0W 92 A6
Margaritovo Russia 43°25N 134°45E 30 C7
Margate S. Africa 30°50S 30°20E 57 E5
Margate U.K. 51°23N 1°23E 13 F9
Margherita Pk. Uganda 0°22N 29°51E 54 B3
Marghilon Uzbekistan 40°27N 71°42E 28 E8
Mārgow, Dasht-e
Afghan. 30°40N 62°30E 40 D3
Marguerite Canada 52°30N 122°25W 70 C4
Mari El □ Russia 56°30N 48°0E 18 C8
Mari Indus Pakistan 32°57N 71°34E 42 C4
Mari Republic = Mari El □
Russia 56°30N 48°0E 18 C8
María de la Salut Spain 39°40N 3°5E 24 B10
María Elena Chile 22°18S 69°40W 94 A2
María Grande Argentina 31°45S 59°55W 94 C4
Maria I. N. Terr.,
Australia 14°52S 135°45E 62 A2
Maria I. Tas., Australia 42°35S 148°0E 63 G4
Maria Island △ Australia 42°38S 148°5E 63 G4
Maria van Diemen, C.
N.Z. 34°29S 172°40E 59 A4
Mariakani Kenya 3°50S 39°27E 54 C4
Mariala △ Australia 25°57S 145°2E 63 D4
Marian Australia 21°9S 148°57E 62 K6
Marian L. Canada 63°0N 116°15W 70 A5
Mariana Trench Pac. Oc. 13°0N 145°0E 64 F6
Marianna Ark., U.S.A. 34°46N 90°46W 85 D9
Marianna Fla., U.S.A. 30°46N 85°14W 85 F12
Marias → U.S.A. 47°56N 110°30W 76 C8
Marías, Islas Mexico 21°25N 106°28W 86 C3
Mariato, Punta Panama 7°12N 80°52W 88 E3
Maribor Slovenia 46°36N 15°40E 16 E8
Marico → Africa 23°35S 26°57E 56 C4
Maricopa Ariz., U.S.A. 33°4N 112°3W 77 K7
Maricopa Calif., U.S.A. 35°4N 119°24W 79 K7
Marié → Brazil 0°27S 66°26W 92 D5
Marie Byrd Land
Antarctica 79°30S 125°0W 5 D14
Marie-Galante
Guadeloupe 15°56N 61°16W 88 b
Mariecourt = Kangiqsujuaq
Canada 61°30N 72°0W 69 C12
Mariehamn Finland 60°5N 19°55E 9 F18
Mariembourg Belgium 50°6N 4°31E 15 D4
Mariental Namibia 24°36S 18°0E 56 C2
Marienville U.S.A. 41°28N 79°8W 82 E5
Mariestad Sweden 58°43N 13°50E 9 G15
Marietta Ga., U.S.A. 33°57N 84°33W 85 E12
Marietta Ohio, U.S.A. 39°25N 81°27W 81 F13
Marieville Canada 45°26N 73°10W 83 A11
Marijampolė Lithuania 54°33N 23°19E 9 J20

Marília Brazil 22°13S 50°0W 95 A6
Marín Spain 42°23N 8°42W 21 A1
Marina U.S.A. 36°41N 121°48W 78 J5
Marinduque Phil. 13°25N 122°0E 37 B6
Marine City U.S.A. 42°43N 82°30W 82 D2
Marinette U.S.A. 45°6N 87°38W 80 C10
Maringá Brazil 23°26S 52°2W 95 A5
Marion Ala., U.S.A. 32°38N 87°19W 85 E11
Marion Ill., U.S.A. 37°44N 88°56W 80 G9
Marion Ind., U.S.A. 40°32N 85°40W 81 E11
Marion Iowa, U.S.A. 42°2N 91°36W 80 D8
Marion Kans., U.S.A. 38°21N 97°1W 80 F5
Marion N.C., U.S.A. 35°41N 82°1W 85 D13
Marion Ohio, U.S.A. 40°35N 83°8W 81 E12
Marion S.C., U.S.A. 34°11N 79°24W 85 D15
Marion Va., U.S.A. 36°50N 81°31W 81 G13
Marion, L., U.S.A. 33°28N 80°10W 85 E14
Mariposa U.S.A. 37°29N 119°58W 78 H7
Mariscal Estigarribia Paraguay 22°3S 60°40W 94 A3
Maritime Alps = Maritimes, Alpes Europe 44°10N 7°10E 20 D7
Maritimes, Alpes Europe 44°10N 7°10E 20 D7
Maritsa = Evros → Greece 41°40N 26°34E 23 D12
Maritsa Greece 36°22N 28°8E 25 C10
Mariupol Ukraine 47°5N 37°31'E 19 E6
Mariusa △ Venezuela 9°24N 61°27W 89 E7
Marīvān Iran 35°30N 46°25E 44 C5
Marj 'Uyūn Lebanon 33°21N 35°34E 46 B4
Marka Somali Rep. 1°48N 44°50E 47 G3
Markam China 29°42N 98°38E 32 D4
Markdale Canada 44°19N 80°39W 82 B4
Marked Tree U.S.A. 35°32N 90°25W 85 D9
Market Drayton U.K. 52°54N 2°29W 12 E5
Market Harborough U.K. 52°29N 0°55W 13 E7
Market Rasen U.K. 53°24N 0°20W 12 D7
Markham Canada 43°52N 79°16W 82 C5
Markham, Mt. Antarctica 83°0S 164°0E 5 E11
Markleeville U.S.A. 38°42N 119°47W 78 G7
Markovo Russia 64°40N 170°24E 29 C17
Marks Russia 51°45N 46°50E 18 D8
Marksville U.S.A. 31°8N 92°4W 84 F8
Marla Australia 27°19S 133°33E 63 D1
Marlbank Canada 44°26N 77°6W 82 B7
Marlboro U.S.A. 41°36N 73°59W 83 E11
Marlborough Australia 22°46S 149°52E 62 C4
Marlborough U.K. 51°25N 1°43W 13 F6
Marlborough □ N.Z. 42°21N 71°33W 83 D13
Marlborough Downs U.K. 51°27N 1°53W 13 F6
Marlin U.S.A. 31°18N 96°54W 84 F6
Marlow U.K. 51°34N 0°46W 13 F7
Marlow U.S.A. 34°39N 97°58W 84 D6
Marmagao India 15°25N 73°56E 40 M8
Marmara Turkey 40°35N 27°34E 23 D12
Marmara, Sea of = Marmara Denizi Turkey 40°45N 28°15E 23 D13
Marmara Denizi Turkey 40°45N 28°15E 23 D13
Marmaris Turkey 36°50N 28°14E 23 F13
Marmion, Mt. Australia 29°16S 119°50E 61 E2
Marmion L. Canada 48°55N 91°20W 72 C1
Marmolada, Mte. Italy 46°26N 11°51E 22 A4
Marmora Canada 44°28N 77°41W 82 B7
Marne → France 48°47N 2°29E 20 B5
Maroala Madag. 15°23S 47°59E 57 B8
Maroantsetra Madag. 15°26S 49°44E 57 B8
Maroelaboom Namibia 19°15S 18°53E 56 B2
Marofandilia Madag. 20°7S 44°34E 57 C7
Marojejy △ Madag. 14°26S 49°21E 57 A8
Marolambo Madag. 20°2S 48°7E 57 C8
Maromandia Madag. 14°13S 48°5E 57 A8
Maromokotro Madag. 14°0S 49°0E 57 A8
Marondera Madag. 18°5S 31°42E 55 F3
Maroni → Fr. Guiana 5°30N 54°0W 93 B8
Maroochydore Australia 26°29S 153°5E 63 D5
Maroona Australia 37°27S 142°54E 63 F3
Marosakoa Madag. 15°26S 46°38E 57 B8
Maroseranana Madag. 18°32S 48°51E 57 B8
Marotandrano Madag. 16°10S 48°50E 57 B8
Marotaolano Madag. 12°47S 49°15E 57 A8
Maroua Cameroon 10°40N 14°20E 51 F8
Marovato Madag. 15°48S 48°5E 57 B8
Marovoay Madag. 16°6S 46°39E 57 B8
Marquard S. Africa 28°40S 27°28E 56 D4
Marquesas Fracture Zone Pac. Oc. 9°0S 125°0W 65 H15
Marquesas Is. = Marquises, Îs. French Polynesia 9°30S 140°0W 65 H14
Marquette U.S.A. 46°33N 87°24W 80 B10
Marquis St. Lucia 14°2N 60°54W 89 f
Marquises, Îs. French Polynesia 9°30S 140°0W 65 H14
Marra, Djebel Sudan 13°10N 24°22E 51 F10
Marracuene Mozam. 25°45S 32°35E 57 D5
Marrakech Morocco 31°9N 8°0W 50 B4
Marrawah Australia 40°55S 144°42E 63 G3
Marree Australia 29°39S 138°1E 63 D2
Marrero U.S.A. 29°53N 90°6W 85 G9
Marrimane Mozam. 22°58S 33°32E 57 C5
Marromeu Mozam. 18°15S 36°25E 55 F4
Marromeu △ Mozam. 19°0S 36°0E 57 B6
Marrowie Cr. → Australia 33°23S 145°40E 63 E4
Marrubane Mozam. 18°0S 37°0E 55 F4
Marrupa Mozam. 13°8S 37°30E 55 E4
Mars Hill U.S.A. 46°31N 67°52W 81 B20
Marsá 'Alam Egypt 25°5N 34°54E 47 B1
Marsá Matrûh Egypt 31°19N 27°9E 51 B11
Marsá Susah Libya 32°52N 21°59E 51 B10
Marsabit Kenya 2°18N 38°0E 54 B4
Marsabit △ Kenya 2°23S 37°56E 54 C4
Marsala Italy 37°48N 12°26E 22 F5
Marsalforn Malta 36°4N 14°16E 25 C1
Marsden Australia 33°47S 147°32E 63 E4
Marseille France 43°18N 5°23E 20 E6

Marseilles = Marseille France 43°18N 5°23E 20 E6
Marsh I. U.S.A. 29°34N 91°53W 84 G9
Marshall Ark., U.S.A. 35°55N 92°38W 84 D8
Marshall Mich., U.S.A. 42°16N 84°58W 81 D11
Marshall Minn., U.S.A. 44°27N 95°47W 80 C6
Marshall Mo., U.S.A. 39°7N 93°12W 80 F7
Marshall Tex., U.S.A. 32°33N 94°23W 84 E7
Marshall → Australia 22°59S 136°59E 62 C2
Marshall Is. ■ Pac. Oc. 9°0N 171°0E 58 A10
Marshalltown U.S.A. 42°3N 92°55W 80 D7
Marshbrook Zimbabwe 18°33S 31°9E 57 B5
Marshfield Mo., U.S.A. 37°15N 92°54W 80 G7
Marshfield Vt., U.S.A. 44°20N 72°20W 83 B12
Marshfield Wis., U.S.A. 44°40N 90°10W 80 C8
Marshūn Iran 36°19N 49°23E 45 B6
Märsta Sweden 59°37N 17°52E 9 G17
Mart U.S.A. 31°33N 96°50W 84 F6
Martaban Burma 16°30N 97°35E 41 L20
Martaban, G. of Burma 16°5N 96°30E 41 L20
Martapura Kalimantan, Indonesia 3°22S 114°47E 36 E4
Martapura Sumatera, Indonesia 4°19S 104°22E 36 E2
Marte R. Gómez, Presa Mexico 26°10N 99°0W 87 B5
Martelange Belgium 49°49N 5°43E 15 E5
Martha's Vineyard U.S.A. 41°25N 70°38W 83 E14
Martigny Switz. 46°6N 7°3E 20 C7
Martigues France 43°24N 5°4E 20 E6
Martin Slovak Rep. 49°6N 18°58E 17 D10
Martin S. Dak., U.S.A. 43°11N 101°44W 80 D3
Martin Tenn., U.S.A. 36°21N 88°51W 85 C10
Martin L. U.S.A. 32°41N 85°55W 85 E12
Martina Franca Italy 40°42N 17°20E 22 D7
Martinborough N.Z. 41°14S 175°29E 59 D5
Martinez Calif., U.S.A. 38°1N 122°8W 78 G4
Martinez Ga., U.S.A. 33°31N 82°5W 85 E13
Martinique ☑ W. Indies 14°40N 61°0W 88 c
Martinique Passage W. Indies 15°15N 61°0W 89 C7
Martinópolis Brazil 22°11S 51°12W 95 A5
Martin's Bay Barbados 13°12N 59°29W 89 g
Martins Ferry U.S.A. 40°6N 80°44W 82 F4
Martinsburg Pa., U.S.A. 40°19N 78°20W 82 F6
Martinsburg W. Va., U.S.A. 39°27N 77°58W 81 F15
Martinsville Ind., U.S.A. 39°26N 86°25W 80 F10
Martinsville Va., U.S.A. 36°41N 79°52W 81 G14
Marton N.Z. 40°4S 175°23E 59 D5
Martos Spain 37°44N 3°58W 21 D4
Marudi Malaysia 4°11N 114°19E 36 D4
Maruf Afghan. 31°30N 67°6E 40 D5
Marugame Japan 34°15N 133°40E 31 G6
Marunga Angola 17°28S 20°2E 56 B3
Marungu, Mts. Dem. Rep. of the Congo 7°30S 30°0E 54 D3
Marv Dasht Iran 29°50N 52°40E 45 D7
Marvast Iran 30°30N 54°15E 45 D7
Marvel Loch Australia 31°28S 119°29E 61 F2
Marwar India 25°43N 73°45E 42 G5
Mary Turkmenistan 37°40N 61°50E 45 B9
Maryborough = Port Laoise Ireland 53°2N 7°18W 10 C4
Maryborough Queens., Australia 25°31S 152°37E 63 D5
Maryborough Vic., Australia 37°3S 143°44E 63 F3
Maryfield Canada 49°50N 101°35W 71 D8
Maryland □ U.S.A. 39°0N 76°30W 81 F15
Maryland Junction Zimbabwe 17°45S 30°31E 55 F3
Maryport U.K. 54°44N 3°28W 12 C4
Mary's Harbour Canada 52°18N 55°51W 73 B8
Marystown Canada 47°10N 55°10W 73 C8
Marysville Calif., U.S.A. 39°9N 121°35W 78 F5
Marysville Kans., U.S.A. 39°51N 96°39W 80 F5
Marysville Mich., U.S.A. 42°54N 82°29W 82 D2
Marysville Ohio, U.S.A. 40°14N 83°22W 81 E12
Marysville Wash., U.S.A. 48°3N 122°11W 78 B4
Maryville Mo., U.S.A. 40°21N 94°52W 80 E6
Maryville Tenn., U.S.A. 35°46N 83°58W 85 D13
Marzūq Libya 25°53N 13°57E 51 C8
Marzūq, Idehān Libya 24°50N 13°51E 51 D8
Masada Israel 31°15N 35°20E 46 D4
Masahunga Tanzania 2°6S 33°18E 54 C3
Masai Malaysia 1°29N 103°55E 39 d
Masai Mara △ Kenya 1°25S 35°5E 54 C4
Masai Steppe Tanzania 4°30S 36°30E 54 C4
Masaka Uganda 0°21S 31°45E 54 C3
Masalembo, Kepulauan Indonesia 5°35S 114°30E 36 F4
Masalima, Kepulauan Indonesia 5°4S 117°5E 36 F5
Masamba Indonesia 2°30S 120°15E 37 E6
Masan S. Korea 35°11N 128°32E 35 G15
Masandam, Ra's Oman 26°30N 56°30E 45 E8
Masasi Tanzania 10°45S 38°52E 55 E4
Masaya Nic. 12°0N 86°7W 88 D2
Masbate Phil. 12°21N 123°36E 37 B6
Mascara Algeria 35°26N 0°6E 50 A6
Mascota Mexico 20°32N 104°49W 86 C4
Masela Indonesia 8°9S 129°51E 37 F7
Maseru Lesotho 29°18S 27°30E 56 D4
Mashaba Zimbabwe 20°2S 30°29E 55 G3
Mashābih Si. Arabia 25°35N 36°30E 44 E3
Mashatu △ Botswana 22°5S 29°5E 57 C4
Masherbrum Pakistan 35°38N 76°18E 43 B7
Mashhad Iran 36°20N 59°35E 45 B8
Mashīz Iran 29°56N 56°37E 45 D8
Māshkel, Hāmūn-i- Pakistan 28°20N 62°56E 45 D9
Mashki Chāh Pakistan 29°5N 62°30E 40 E3
Mashonaland Zimbabwe 16°30S 31°0E 53 H6
Mashonaland Central □ Zimbabwe 17°30S 31°0E 57 B5

Mashonaland East □ Zimbabwe 18°0S 32°0E 57 B5
Mashonaland West □ Zimbabwe 17°30S 29°30E 57 B4
Mashrakh India 26°7N 84°48E 43 F11
Masi Manimba Dem. Rep. of the Congo 4°40S 17°54E 52 E3
Masindi Uganda 1°40N 31°43E 54 B3
Masindi Port Uganda 1°43N 32°2E 54 B3
Maşīrah Oman 21°0N 58°50E 47 C6
Maşīrah, Khalīj Oman 20°10N 58°10E 47 C6
Masisi Dem. Rep. of the Congo 1°23S 28°49E 54 C2
Masjed Soleyman Iran 31°55N 49°18E 45 D6
Mask, L. Ireland 53°36N 9°22W 10 C2
Maskin Oman 23°44N 56°52E 45 F8
Masoala, Tanjon' i Madag. 15°59S 50°13E 57 B9
Masoala △ Madag. 15°30S 50°12E 57 B9
Masoarivo Madag. 19°3S 44°19E 57 B7
Masohi = Amahai Indonesia 3°20S 128°55E 37 E7
Masomeloka Madag. 20°17S 48°37E 57 C8
Mason Nev., U.S.A. 38°56N 119°8W 78 G7
Mason Tex., U.S.A. 30°45N 99°14W 84 F5
Mason City U.S.A. 43°9N 93°12W 80 D7
Maspalomas Canary Is. 27°46N 15°35W 24 G4
Maspalomas, Pta. Canary Is. 27°43N 15°36W 24 G4
Masqat Oman 23°37N 58°36E 47 C6
Massa Italy 44°1N 10°9E 20 D9
Massachusetts □ U.S.A. 42°30N 72°0W 83 D13
Massachusetts B. U.S.A. 42°25N 70°50W 83 D14
Massakory Chad 13°0N 15°49E 51 F9
Massanella Spain 39°48N 2°51E 24 B9
Massangena Mozam. 21°34S 33°0E 57 C5
Massango Angola 8°2S 16°21E 52 F3
Massawa = Mitsiwa Eritrea 15°35N 39°25E 47 D2
Massena U.S.A. 44°56N 74°54W 83 B10
Massénya Chad 11°21N 16°9E 51 F9
Masset Canada 54°2N 132°10W 70 C2
Massiah Street Barbados 13°9N 59°29W 89 g
Massif Central France 44°55N 3°0E 20 D5
Massillon U.S.A. 40°48N 81°32W 82 F3
Massinga Mozam. 23°15S 35°22E 57 C6
Massingir Mozam. 23°51S 32°4E 57 C5
Masson-Angers Canada 45°32N 75°25W 83 A9
Masson I. Antarctica 66°10S 93°20E 5 C7
Mastanli = Momchilgrad Bulgaria 41°33N 25°23E 23 D11
Masterton N.Z. 40°56S 175°39E 59 D5
Mastic U.S.A. 40°47N 72°54W 83 F12
Mastuj Pakistan 36°20N 72°36E 43 A5
Mastung Pakistan 29°50N 66°56E 40 E5
Masty Belarus 53°27N 24°38E 17 B13
Masuda Japan 34°40N 131°51E 31 G5
Masurian Lakes = Mazurski, Pojezierze Poland 53°50N 21°0E 17 B11
Masvingo Zimbabwe 20°8S 30°49E 55 G3
Masvingo □ Zimbabwe 21°0S 31°30E 55 G3
Maswa △ Tanzania 2°58S 34°19E 54 C3
Maşyāf Syria 35°4N 36°20E 44 C3
Mata-au = Clutha → N.Z. 46°20S 169°49E 59 G2
Matabeleland Zimbabwe 18°0S 27°0E 53 H5
Matabeleland North □ Zimbabwe 19°0S 28°0E 55 F2
Matabeleland South □ Zimbabwe 21°0S 29°0E 55 G2
Matachewan Canada 47°56N 80°39W 72 C3
Matadi Dem. Rep. of the Congo 5°52S 13°31E 52 F2
Matagalpa Nic. 13°0N 85°58W 88 D2
Matagami Canada 49°45N 77°34W 72 C4
Matagami, L. Canada 49°50N 77°40W 72 C4
Matagorda B. U.S.A. 28°40N 96°12W 84 G6
Matagorda I. U.S.A. 28°15N 96°30W 84 G6
Mataiea Tahiti 17°46S 149°25W 59 d
Matak Indonesia 3°18N 106°16E 36 D3
Matala Greece 34°59N 24°45E 25 E6
Matam Senegal 15°34N 13°17W 50 E3
Matamoros Campeche, Mexico 18°50N 90°50W 87 D6
Matamoros Coahuila, Mexico 25°32N 103°15W 86 B4
Matamoros Tamaulipas, Mexico 25°53N 97°30W 87 B5
Ma'tan as Sarra Libya 21°45N 22°0E 51 D10
Matandu → Tanzania 8°45S 34°19E 55 D3
Matane Canada 48°50N 67°33W 73 C6
Matanomadh India 23°33N 68°57E 42 H3
Matanzas Cuba 23°0N 81°40W 88 B3
Matapa Botswana 23°11S 24°39E 56 C3
Matapan, C. = Tenaro, Akra Greece 36°22N 22°27E 23 F10
Matapédia Canada 48°0N 66°59W 73 C6
Matapo □ Zimbabwe 20°30S 29°40E 55 G2
Matara Sri Lanka 5°58N 80°30E 40 S12
Mataram Indonesia 8°35S 116°7E 37 K19
Matarani Peru 17°0S 72°10W 92 G4
Mataranka Australia 14°55S 133°4E 60 B5
Matarma, Râs Egypt 30°27N 32°44E 46 E1
Mataró Spain 41°32N 2°29E 21 B7
Matatiele S. Africa 30°20S 28°49E 57 E4
Mataura N.Z. 46°11S 168°51E 59 G2
Matavai, B. de Tahiti 17°30S 149°23W 59 d
Matehuala Mexico 23°39N 100°39W 86 C4
Mateke Hills Zimbabwe 21°48S 31°0E 55 G3
Matelot Trin. & Tob. 10°50N 61°7W 93 K15
Matera Italy 40°40N 16°36E 22 D7
Matetsi Zimbabwe 18°12S 26°0E 55 F2
Matheniko △ Uganda 2°49N 34°27E 54 B3
Mathis U.S.A. 28°6N 97°50W 84 G6
Mathraki Greece 39°48N 19°31E 25 A3
Mathura India 27°30N 77°40E 42 F7

Mati Phil. 6°55N 126°15E 37 C7
Matiali India 26°56N 88°49E 43 F13
Matiane Mozam. 14°49S 40°45E 55 E5
Matibane Mozam. 14°49S 40°45E 55 E5
Matiri Ra. N.Z. 41°38S 172°20E 59 D4
Matla → India 21°40N 88°40E 43 J13
Matlamanyane Botswana 19°33S 25°57E 56 B4
Matli Pakistan 25°2N 68°39E 42 G3
Matlock U.K. 53°9N 1°33W 12 D6
Mato Grosso □ Brazil 14°0S 55°0W 93 F8
Mato Grosso, Planalto do Brazil 15°0S 55°0W 93 G8
Mato Grosso do Sul □ Brazil 18°0S 55°0W 93 G8
Matobo = Matapo △ Zimbabwe 20°30S 29°40E 55 G2
Matochkin Shar, Proliv Russia 73°23N 55°12E 28 B6
Matopo Hills Zimbabwe 20°36S 28°20E 55 G2
Matopos Zimbabwe 20°20S 28°29E 55 G2
Matosinhos Portugal 41°11N 8°42W 21 B1
Matroosberg S. Africa 33°23S 19°40E 56 E2
Matruḥ Oman 23°37N 58°30E 47 C6
Matsue Japan 35°25N 133°10E 31 G6
Matsum, Ko Thailand 9°22N 99°59E 39 b
Matsumae Japan 41°26N 140°7E 30 D10
Matsumoto Japan 36°15N 138°0E 31 F9
Matsusaka Japan 34°34N 136°32E 31 G8
Matsuura Japan 33°20N 129°49E 31 H4
Matsuyama Japan 33°45N 132°45E 31 H6
Mattagami → Canada 50°43N 81°29W 72 B3
Mattancheri India 9°50N 76°15E 40 Q10
Mattawa Canada 46°20N 78°45W 72 C4
Matterhorn Switz. 45°58N 7°39E 20 D7
Matthew Town Bahamas 20°57N 73°40W 89 B5
Matthews Ridge Guyana 7°37N 60°10W 92 B6
Mattice Canada 49°40N 83°20W 72 C3
Mattituck U.S.A. 40°59N 72°32W 83 F12
Mattō Japan 36°31N 136°34E 31 F8
Mattoon U.S.A. 39°29N 88°23W 80 F9
Matuba Mozam. 24°28S 32°49E 57 C5
Matucana Peru 11°55S 76°25W 92 F3
Matuku Fiji 19°10S 179°44E 59 a
Matūn = Khowst Afghan. 33°22N 69°58E 42 C3
Matura B. Trin. & Tob. 10°39N 61°1W 93 K15
Maturín Venezuela 9°45N 63°11W 92 B6
Matusadona △ Zimbabwe 16°58S 28°42E 55 F2
Mau Mad. P., India 26°17N 78°41E 43 F8
Mau U. P., India 25°56N 83°33E 43 G10
Mau U. P., India 25°17N 81°23E 43 G9
Mau Escarpment Kenya 0°40S 36°0E 54 C4
Mau Ranipur India 25°16N 79°8E 43 G8
Maua Kenya 0°14N 37°56E 54 B4
Maubeuge France 50°17N 3°57E 20 A6
Maubin Burma 16°44N 95°39E 41 L19
Maud, Pt. Australia 23°6S 113°45E 60 D1
Maud Rise S. Ocean 66°0S 3°0E 5 C3
Maude Australia 34°29S 144°18E 63 E3
Maudin Sun Burma 16°0N 94°30E 41 M19
Maués Brazil 3°20S 57°45W 92 D7
Mauganj India 24°50N 81°55E 43 G9
Maughold Hd. I. of Man 54°18N 4°18W 12 C3
Maulamyaing = Moulmein Burma 16°30N 97°40E 41 L20
Maule □ Chile 36°5S 72°30W 94 D1
Maumee U.S.A. 41°34N 83°39W 81 E12
Maumee → U.S.A. 41°42N 83°28W 81 E12
Maumere Indonesia 8°38S 122°13E 37 F6
Maun Botswana 20°0S 23°26E 56 C3
Mauna Kea U.S.A. 19°50N 155°28W 74 b
Mauna Loa U.S.A. 19°30N 155°35W 74 b
Maungmagan Kyunzu Burma 14°0N 97°48E 38 E1
Maungu Kenya 3°33S 38°45E 54 C4
Maupin U.S.A. 45°11N 121°5W 76 D3
Maurepas, L. U.S.A. 30°15N 90°30W 85 F9
Maurice, L. Australia 29°30S 131°0E 61 E5
Mauricie △ Canada 46°45N 73°0W 72 C5
Mauritania ■ Africa 20°50N 10°0W 50 E3
Mauritius ■ Ind. Oc. 20°0S 57°0E 53 d
Mauston U.S.A. 43°48N 90°5W 80 D8
Mavli India 24°45N 73°55E 42 G5
Mavuradonha Mts. Zimbabwe 16°30S 31°30E 55 F3
Mawa Dem. Rep. of the Congo 2°45N 26°40E 54 B2
Mawai India 22°30N 81°4E 43 H9
Mawana India 29°6N 77°58E 42 E7
Mawand Pakistan 29°33N 68°38E 42 E3
Mawjib, W. al → Jordan 31°28N 35°36E 46 D4
Mawk Mai Burma 20°14N 97°37E 41 J20
Mawlaik Burma 23°40N 94°26E 41 H19
Mawlamyine = Moulmein Burma 16°30N 97°40E 41 L20
Mawqaq Si. Arabia 27°25N 41°8E 44 E4
Mawson Base Antarctica 67°30S 62°53E 5 C6
Mawson Coast Antarctica 68°30S 63°0E 5 C6
Max U.S.A. 47°49N 101°18W 80 B3
Maxcanú Mexico 20°35N 89°59W 87 C6
Maxesibeni S. Africa 30°49S 29°23E 57 E4
Maxhamish L. Canada 59°50N 123°17W 70 B4
Maxixe Mozam. 23°54S 35°17E 57 C6
Maxville Canada 45°17N 74°51W 83 A10
Maxwell U.S.A. 39°17N 122°11W 78 F4
Maxwelton Australia 20°43S 142°41E 62 C3
May, C. U.S.A. 38°56N 74°58W 81 F16
May Pen Jamaica 17°58N 77°15W 88 a
Maya → Russia 60°28N 134°28E 29 D14
Maya Mts. Belize 16°30N 89°0W 87 D7
Mayaguana Bahamas 22°30N 72°44W 89 B5
Mayagüez Puerto Rico 18°12N 67°9W 89 d
Mayamey Iran 36°24N 55°42E 45 B7

Mayanup Australia 33°57S 116°27E 61 F2
Mayapán Mexico 20°29N 89°11W 87 C7
Mayarí Cuba 20°40N 75°41W 89 B4
Mayaro B. Trin. & Tob. 10°14N 60°59W 93 K16
Maybell U.S.A. 40°31N 108°5W 76 F9
Maybole U.K. 55°21N 4°42W 11 F4
Maydān Iraq 34°55N 45°37E 44 C5
Maydena Australia 42°45S 146°30E 63 G4
Mayenne France 47°30N 0°32W 20 C3
Mayenne → France 47°30N 0°32W 20 C3
Mayer U.S.A. 34°24N 112°14W 77 J7
Mayerthorpe Canada 53°57N 115°8W 70 C5
Mayfield Ky., U.S.A. 36°44N 88°38W 80 G9
Mayfield N.Y., U.S.A. 43°6N 74°16W 83 C10
Mayhill U.S.A. 32°53N 105°29W 77 K11
Maykop Russia 44°35N 40°10E 19 F7
Maymyo Burma 22°2N 96°28E 38 A1
Maynard Mass., U.S.A. 42°26N 71°27W 83 D13
Maynard Wash., U.S.A. 47°59N 122°55W 78 C4
Maynard Hills Australia 28°28S 119°49E 61 E2
Mayne → Australia 23°40S 141°55E 62 C3
Maynooth Canada 45°13N 77°56W 82 A7
Maynooth Ireland 53°23N 6°34W 10 C5
Mayo Canada 63°38N 135°57W 68 C6
Mayo □ Ireland 53°53N 9°3W 10 C2
Mayon Volcano Phil. 13°15N 123°41E 37 B6
Mayor I. N.Z. 37°16S 176°17E 59 B6
Mayotte ☑ Ind. Oc. 12°50S 45°10E 53 a
Maysān □ Iraq 31°55N 47°15E 44 D5
Maysville U.S.A. 38°39N 83°46W 81 F12
Mayu Indonesia 1°30N 126°30E 37 D7
Mayville N. Dak., U.S.A. 47°30N 97°20W 80 B5
Mayville N.Y., U.S.A. 42°15N 79°30W 82 D5
Mazabuka Zambia 15°52S 27°44E 55 F2
Mazagán = El Jadida Morocco 33°11N 8°17W 50 B4
Mazagão Brazil 0°7S 51°16W 93 D8
Mazán Peru 3°30S 73°0W 92 D4
Māzandarān □ Iran 36°30N 52°0E 45 B7
Mazapil Mexico 24°39N 101°34W 86 C4
Mazar China 36°32N 77°1E 32 C2
Mazara del Vallo Italy 37°39N 12°35E 22 F5
Mazarrón Spain 37°38N 1°19W 21 D5
Mazaruni → Guyana 6°25N 58°35W 92 B7
Mazatán Mexico 29°0N 110°8W 86 B2
Mazatenango Guatemala 14°35N 91°30W 88 D1
Mazatlán Mexico 23°13N 106°25W 86 C3
Mažeikiai Lithuania 56°20N 22°20E 9 H20
Māzhān Iran 32°30N 59°0E 45 C8
Mazīnān Iran 36°19N 56°56E 45 B8
Mazoe Mozam. 16°42S 33°7E 55 F3
Mazoe → Mozam. 16°20S 33°30E 55 F3
Mazowe Zimbabwe 17°28S 30°58E 55 F3
Mazurski, Pojezierze Poland 53°50N 21°0E 17 B11
Mazyr Belarus 51°59N 29°15E 17 B15
Mba Fiji 17°33S 177°41E 59 a
Mbabane Swaziland 26°18S 31°6E 57 D5
Mbaïki C.A.R. 3°53N 18°1E 52 D3
Mbala Zambia 8°46S 31°24E 55 D3
Mbalabala Zimbabwe 20°27S 29°3E 57 C4
Mbale Uganda 1°8N 34°12E 54 B3
Mbalmayo Cameroon 3°33N 11°33E 52 D2
Mbamba Bay Tanzania 11°13S 34°49E 55 E3
Mbandaka Dem. Rep. of the Congo 0°1N 18°18E 52 D3
Mbanza Congo Angola 6°18S 14°16E 52 F2
Mbanza Ngungu Dem. Rep. of the Congo 5°12S 14°53E 52 F2
Mbarangandu Tanzania 10°11S 36°48E 55 D4
Mbarara Uganda 0°35S 30°40E 54 C3
Mbengga = Beqa Fiji 18°23S 178°8E 59 a
Mbenkuru → Tanzania 9°25S 39°50E 55 D4
Mberengwa Zimbabwe 20°29S 29°57E 55 G2
Mberengwa, Mt. Zimbabwe 20°37S 29°55E 55 G2
Mbesuma Zambia 10°0S 32°2E 55 E3
Mbeya Tanzania 8°54S 33°29E 55 D3
Mbeya □ Tanzania 8°15S 33°30E 54 D3
Mbhashe → S. Africa 32°15S 28°54E 57 E4
Mbinga Tanzania 10°50S 35°0E 55 E4
Mbini = Río Muni Eq. Guin. 1°30N 10°0E 52 D2
Mbour Senegal 14°22N 16°54W 50 F2
Mbuji-Mayi Dem. Rep. of the Congo 6°9S 23°40E 54 D1
Mbulu Tanzania 3°45S 35°30E 54 C4
Mburucuyá Argentina 28°1S 58°14W 94 B4
Mburucuyá △ Argentina 28°1S 58°12W 94 B4
Mchinja Tanzania 9°44S 39°45E 55 D4
Mchinji Malawi 13°47S 32°58E 55 E3
Mdantsane S. Africa 32°56S 27°46E 57 E4
Mead, L. U.S.A. 36°0N 114°44W 79 J12
Meade U.S.A. 37°17N 100°20W 80 G3
Meadow Lake Canada 54°10N 108°26W 71 C7
Meadow Lake △ Canada 54°27N 109°0W 71 C7
Meadow Valley Wash → U.S.A. 36°40N 114°34W 79 J12
Meadville U.S.A. 41°39N 80°9W 82 E4
Meaford Canada 44°36N 80°35W 82 B4
Mealpaeg L. Canada 48°20N 56°30W 73 C8
Mealy Mts. Canada 53°10N 58°0W 73 B8
Meander River Canada 59°2N 117°42W 70 B5
Meares, C. U.S.A. 45°37N 124°0W 76 D1
Mearim → Brazil 3°4S 44°35W 93 D10
Meath □ Ireland 53°40N 6°57W 10 C5
Meath Park Canada 53°27N 105°22W 71 C7
Meaux France 48°58N 2°50E 20 B5
Mebechi-Gawa → Japan 40°31N 141°31E 30 D10
Mebulu, Tanjung Indonesia 8°50S 115°5E 37 K18
Mecanhelas Mozam. 15°12S 35°54E 55 F4
Mecca = Makkah Si. Arabia 21°30N 39°54E 47 C2
Mecca U.S.A. 33°34N 116°5W 79 M10
Mechanicsburg U.S.A. 40°13N 77°1W 82 F8
Mechanicville U.S.A. 42°54N 73°41W 83 D11

Mechelen *Belgium* 51°2N 4°29E **15** C4
Mecheria *Algeria* 33°35N 0°18W **50** B5
Mecklenburg *Germany* 53°33N 11°40E **16** B7
Mecklenburger Bucht
  Germany 54°20N 11°40E **16** A6
Meconta *Mozam.* 14°59S 39°50E **55** E4
Medan *Indonesia* 3°40N 98°38E **36** D1
Médanos de Coro △
  Venezuela 11°35N 69°44W **89** D6
Medanosa, Pta. *Argentina* 48°8S 66°0W **96** F3
Médéa *Algeria* 36°12N 2°50E **50** A6
Medellín *Colombia* 6°15N 75°35W **92** B3
Medelpad *Sweden* 62°33N 16°30E **8** E17
Medemblik *Neths.* 52°46N 5°8E **15** B5
Medford *Mass., U.S.A.* 42°25N 71°7W **83** D13
Medford *Oreg., U.S.A.* 42°19N 122°52W **76** E2
Medford *Wis., U.S.A.* 45°9N 90°20W **80** C8
Medgidia *Romania* 44°15N 28°19E **17** F15
Media Agua *Argentina* 31°58S 68°25W **94** C2
Media Luna *Argentina* 34°45S 66°44W **94** C2
Medianeira *Brazil* 25°17S 54°5W **95** B5
Mediaş *Romania* 46°9N 24°22E **17** E13
Medicine Bow *U.S.A.* 41°54N 106°12W **76** F10
Medicine Bow Mts.
  U.S.A. 40°40N 106°0W **76** F10
Medicine Bow Pk.
  U.S.A. 41°21N 106°19W **76** F10
Medicine Hat *Canada* 50°0N 110°45W **71** D6
Medicine Lake *U.S.A.* 48°30N 104°30W **76** B11
Medicine Lodge *U.S.A.* 37°17N 98°35W **80** G4
Medina = Al Madīnah
  St. Arabia 24°35N 39°52E **44** E3
Medina *N. Dak., U.S.A.* 46°54N 99°18W **80** B4
Medina *N.Y., U.S.A.* 43°13N 78°23W **82** C6
Medina *Ohio, U.S.A.* 41°8N 81°52W **82** E3
Medina → *U.S.A.* 29°16N 98°29W **84** G5
Medina del Campo *Spain* 41°18N 4°55W **21** B3
Medina L. *U.S.A.* 29°32N 98°56W **84** G5
Medina Sidonia *Spain* 36°28N 5°57W **21** D3
Medinipur *India* 22°25N 87°21E **43** H12
Mediterranean Sea *Europe* 35°0N 15°0E **6** H7
Médoc *France* 45°10N 0°50W **20** D3
Medveditsa → *Russia* 49°35N 42°41E **19** E7
Medvezhi, Ostrava
  Russia 71°0N 161°0E **29** B17
Medvezhyegorsk *Russia* 63°0N 34°25E **18** B5
Medway □ *U.K.* 51°25N 0°32E **13** F8
Medway → *U.K.* 51°27N 0°46E **13** F8
Meekatharra *Australia* 26°32S 118°29E **61** E2
Meeker *U.S.A.* 40°2N 107°55W **76** F10
Meerut *India* 29°1N 77°42E **42** E7
Meeteetse *U.S.A.* 44°9N 108°52W **76** D9
Mega *Ethiopia* 3°57N 38°19E **47** G2
Megara *Greece* 37°58N 23°22E **23** F10
Megasini *India* 21°38N 86°21E **43** J12
Meghalaya □ *India* 25°50N 91°0E **41** G17
Meghna → *Bangla.* 22°50N 90°50E **41** H17
Megion *Russia* 61°3N 76°6E **28** C8
Mégiscane, L. *Canada* 48°35N 75°55W **72** C4
Meharry, Mt. *Australia* 22°59S 118°35E **60** D2
Mehlville *U.S.A.* 38°31N 90°19W **80** F8
Mehndawal *India* 26°58N 83°5E **43** F10
Mehr Jān *Iran* 33°50N 55°6E **45** C7
Mehrābād *Iran* 36°53N 47°55E **44** B5
Mehrān *Iran* 33°7N 46°10E **44** C5
Mehrān → *Iran* 26°45N 55°26E **45** E7
Mehrgarh *Pakistan* 29°30N 67°30E **42** E2
Mehrīz *Iran* 31°35N 54°28E **45** D7
Mei Xian *China* 34°18N 107°55E **34** G4
Meighen I. *Canada* 80°0N 99°30W **69** B10
Meihekou *China* 42°32N 125°40E **35** C13
Meiktila *Burma* 20°53N 95°54E **41** J19
Meissen *Germany* 51°9N 13°29E **16** C7
Meizhou *China* 24°16N 116°6E **33** D6
Meja *India* 25°9N 82°7E **43** G10
Mejillones *Chile* 23°10S 70°30W **94** A1
Mekele *Ethiopia* 13°33N 39°30E **47** E2
Mekerghene, Sebkra
  Algeria 26°21N 1°30E **50** C6
Mekhtar *Pakistan* 30°30N 69°15E **40** D6
Meknès *Morocco* 33°57N 5°33W **50** B4
Mekong → *Asia* 9°30N 106°15E **39** H6
Mekongga *Indonesia* 3°39S 121°15E **37** E6
Mekvari = Kür →
  Azerbaijan 39°29N 49°15E **19** G8
Melagiri Hills *India* 12°20N 77°30E **40** N10
Melaka *Malaysia* 2°15N 102°15E **39** L4
Melalap *Malaysia* 5°10N 116°5E **36** C5
Melambes *Greece* 35°8N 24°40E **25** D6
Melanesia *Pac. Oc.* 4°0S 155°0E **64** H7
Melanesian Basin *Pac. Oc.* 0°5N 160°35E **64** G8
Melaya *Indonesia* 8°17S 114°30E **37** J17
Melbourne *Australia* 37°48S 144°58E **63** F4
Melbourne *U.S.A.* 28°5N 80°37W **85** G14
Melchor Múzquiz
  Mexico 27°53N 101°31W **86** B4
Melchor Ocampo
  Mexico 24°51N 101°39W **86** C4
Mélèzes → *Canada* 57°40N 69°29W **72** A5
Melfort *Canada* 52°50N 104°37W **71** C8
Melfort *Zimbabwe* 18°0S 31°25E **55** F3
Melhus *Norway* 63°17N 10°18E **8** E14
Melilla *N. Afr.* 35°21N 2°57W **21** E4
Melipilla *Chile* 33°42S 71°15W **94** C1
Melissa *Canada* 45°24N 79°14W **82** A5
Melita *Canada* 49°15N 101°0W **71** D8
Melitopol *Ukraine* 46°50N 35°22E **19** E6
Melk *Austria* 48°13N 15°20E **16** D8
Mellansel *Sweden* 63°26N 18°19E **8** E18
Mellerud *Sweden* 58°41N 12°28E **9** G15
Mellette *U.S.A.* 45°9N 98°30W **80** C4
Mellieha *Malta* 35°57N 14°22E **25** D1
Melo *Uruguay* 32°20S 54°10W **95** C5
Melolo *Indonesia* 9°53S 120°40E **37** F6
Melouprey *Cambodia* 13°48N 105°16E **38** F5

Melrhir, Chott *Algeria* 34°13N 6°30E **50** B7
Melrose *Australia* 32°42S 146°57E **63** E4
Melrose *U.K.* 55°36N 2°43W **11** F6
Melrose *Minn., U.S.A.* 45°40N 94°49W **80** C6
Melrose *N. Mex.,*
  U.S.A. 34°26N 103°38W **77** J12
Melstone *U.S.A.* 46°36N 107°52W **76** C10
Melton Mowbray *U.K.* 52°47N 0°54W **12** E7
Melun *France* 48°32N 2°39E **20** B5
Melville *Canada* 50°55N 102°50W **71** C8
Melville, C. *Australia* 14°11S 144°30E **62** A3
Melville, L. *Canada* 53°30N 60°0W **73** B8
Melville B. *Australia* 12°0S 136°45E **62** A2
Melville I. *Australia* 11°30S 131°0E **60** B5
Melville I. *Canada* 75°30N 112°0W **69** B8
Melville Pen. *Canada* 68°0N 84°0W **69** C11
Melvin, Lough *Ireland* 54°26N 8°10W **10** B3
Memba *Mozam.* 14°11S 40°30E **55** E5
Memboro *Indonesia* 9°30S 119°30E **37** F5
Memel = Klaipėda
  Lithuania 55°43N 21°10E **9** J19
Memel *S. Africa* 27°38S 29°36E **57** D4
Memmingen *Germany* 47°58N 10°10E **16** E6
Mempawah *Indonesia* 0°30N 109°5E **36** D3
Memphis *Mich., U.S.A.* 42°54N 82°46W **82** D2
Memphis *Tenn., U.S.A.* 35°8N 90°2W **85** D9
Memphis *Tex., U.S.A.* 34°44N 100°33W **84** D4
Memphrémagog, L.
  N. Amer. 45°8N 72°17W **83** B12
Mena *U.S.A.* 34°35N 94°15W **84** D7
Menai Strait *U.K.* 53°11N 4°13W **12** D3
Ménaka *Mali* 15°59N 2°18E **50** E6
Menan = Chao Phraya →
  Thailand 13°40N 100°31E **38** F3
Menarandra → *Madag.* 25°17S 44°30E **57** D7
Menard *U.S.A.* 30°55N 99°47W **84** F5
Menard Fracture Zone
  Pac. Oc. 43°0S 97°0W **65** M18
Mendaña Fracture Zone
  Pac. Oc. 16°0S 91°0W **65** J18
Mendawai → *Indonesia* 3°30S 113°0E **36** E4
Mende *France* 44°31N 3°30E **20** D5
Mendeleyev Ridge *Arctic* 80°0N 178°0W **4** B17
Mendhar *India* 33°35N 74°10E **43** C6
Mendocino *U.S.A.* 39°19N 123°48W **76** G2
Mendocino, C. *U.S.A.* 40°26N 124°25W **76** F1
Mendocino Fracture Zone
  Pac. Oc. 40°0N 142°0W **65** D13
Mendota *Calif., U.S.A.* 36°45N 120°23W **78** J6
Mendota *Ill., U.S.A.* 41°33N 89°7W **80** E9
Mendoyo *Indonesia* 8°23S 114°42E **37** J17
Mendoza *Argentina* 32°50S 68°52W **94** C2
Mendoza □ *Argentina* 33°0S 69°0W **94** C2
Mene Grande *Venezuela* 9°49N 70°56W **92** B4
Menemen *Turkey* 38°34N 27°3E **23** E12
Menen *Belgium* 50°47N 3°7E **15** D3
Menggala *Indonesia* 4°30S 105°15E **36** E3
Mengjin *China* 34°55N 112°45E **34** G7
Mengyin *China* 35°40N 117°58E **35** G9
Mengzi *China* 23°20N 103°22E **32** D5
Menihek *Canada* 54°28N 56°36W **73** B6
Menihek L. *Canada* 54°0N 67°0W **73** B6
Menin = Menen *Belgium* 50°47N 3°7E **15** D3
Menindee *Australia* 32°20S 142°25E **63** E3
Menindee L. *Australia* 32°20S 142°25E **63** E3
Meningie *Australia* 35°50S 139°18E **63** F2
Menjangan, Pulau
  Indonesia 8°7S 114°31E **37** J17
Menlo Park *U.S.A.* 37°27N 122°12W **78** H4
Menominee *U.S.A.* 45°6N 87°37W **80** C10
Menominee → *U.S.A.* 45°6N 87°35W **80** C10
Menomonie *U.S.A.* 44°53N 91°55W **80** C8
Menongue *Angola* 14°48S 17°52E **53** G3
Menorca *Spain* 40°0N 4°0E **24** B11
Mentakab *Malaysia* 3°29N 102°21E **39** L4
Mentawai, Kepulauan
  Indonesia 2°0S 99°0E **36** E1
Menton *France* 43°50N 7°29E **20** E7
Mentor *U.S.A.* 41°40N 81°21W **82** E3
Menzelinsk *Russia* 55°47N 53°11E **18** C9
Menzies *Australia* 29°40S 121°2E **61** E3
Meob B. *Namibia* 24°25S 14°34E **56** C1
Me'ona *Israel* 33°1N 35°15E **46** B4
Meoqui *Mexico* 28°17N 105°29W **86** B3
Meppel *Neths.* 52°42N 6°12E **15** B6
Merak *Indonesia* 6°10N 106°26E **37** F12
Meramangye, L.
  Australia 28°25S 132°13E **61** E5
Meran = Merano *Italy* 46°40N 11°9E **22** A4
Merano *Italy* 46°40N 11°9E **22** A4
Merauke *Indonesia* 8°29S 140°24E **37** F10
Merbein *Australia* 34°10S 142°2E **63** E3
Merbuk, Gunung
  Indonesia 8°13S 114°39E **37** J17
Merca = Marka
  Somali Rep. 1°48N 44°50E **47** G3
Merced *U.S.A.* 37°18N 120°29W **78** H6
Merced → *U.S.A.* 37°21N 120°59W **78** H6
Merced Pk. *U.S.A.* 37°36N 119°24W **78** H7
Mercedes *B. Aires,*
  Argentina 34°40S 59°30W **94** C4
Mercedes *Corrientes,*
  Argentina 29°10S 58°5W **94** B4
Mercedes *San Luis,*
  Argentina 33°40S 65°21W **94** C2
Mercedes *Uruguay* 33°12S 58°0W **94** C4
Merceditas *Chile* 28°20S 70°35W **94** B1
Mercer *N.Z.* 37°16S 175°5E **59** B5
Mercer *U.S.A.* 41°14N 80°15W **82** E4
Mercer Island *U.S.A.* 47°34N 122°13W **78** C4
Mercury *U.S.A.* 36°40N 115°59W **79** J11
Mercy, C. *Canada* 65°0N 63°30W **69** C13
Mere *U.K.* 51°6N 2°16W **13** F5
Meredith, C. *Falk. Is.* 52°15S 60°40W **96** G4
Meredith, L. *U.S.A.* 35°43N 101°33W **84** D4

Mergui *Burma* 12°26N 98°34E **38** F2
Mergui Arch. = Myeik Kyunzu
  Burma 11°30N 97°30E **39** G1
Mérida *Mexico* 20°58N 89°37W **87** C7
Mérida *Spain* 38°55N 6°25W **21** C2
Mérida *Venezuela* 8°24N 71°8W **92** B4
Mérida, Cord. de *Venezuela* 9°0N 71°0W **92** B4
Meriden *U.K.* 52°26N 1°38W **13** E6
Meriden *U.S.A.* 41°32N 72°48W **83** E12
Meridian *Calif., U.S.A.* 39°9N 121°55W **78** F5
Meridian *Idaho, U.S.A.* 43°37N 116°24W **76** E5
Meridian *Miss., U.S.A.* 32°22N 88°42W **85** E10
Merinda *Australia* 20°2S 148°11E **62** C4
Merir *Pac. Oc.* 4°10N 132°30E **37** D8
Merirumã *Brazil* 1°15N 54°50W **93** C8
Merkel *U.S.A.* 32°28N 100°1W **84** E4
Mermaid Reef *Australia* 17°6S 119°36E **60** C2
Merredin *Australia* 31°28S 118°18E **61** F2
Merrick *U.K.* 55°8N 4°28W **11** F4
Merrickville *Canada* 44°55N 75°50W **83** B9
Merrill *Oreg., U.S.A.* 42°1N 121°36W **76** E3
Merrill *Wis., U.S.A.* 45°11N 89°41W **80** C9
Merrimack → *U.S.A.* 42°49N 70°49W **83** D14
Merriman *U.S.A.* 42°55N 101°42W **80** D3
Merritt *Canada* 50°10N 120°45W **70** C4
Merritt Island *U.S.A.* 28°21N 80°42W **85** G14
Merriwa *Australia* 32°6S 150°22E **63** E5
Merry I. *Canada* 55°29N 77°31W **72** A4
Merryville *U.S.A.* 30°45N 93°33W **84** F8
Mersch *Lux.* 49°44N 6°7E **15** E6
Mersea I. *U.K.* 51°47N 0°58E **13** F8
Merseburg *Germany* 51°22N 11°59E **16** C6
Mersey → *U.K.* 53°25N 3°1W **12** D4
Merseyside □ *U.K.* 53°31N 3°2W **12** D4
Mersin = İçel *Turkey* 36°51N 34°36E **44** B5
Mersing *Malaysia* 2°25N 103°50E **39** L4
Merta *India* 26°39N 74°4E **42** F6
Merta Road *India* 26°43N 73°55E **42** F5
Merthyr Tydfil *U.K.* 51°45N 3°22W **13** F4
Merthyr Tydfil □ *U.K.* 51°46N 3°21W **13** F4
Merti *Kenya* 1°4N 38°40E **54** B4
Mértola *Portugal* 37°40N 7°40W **21** D2
Mertzon *U.S.A.* 31°16N 100°49W **84** F4
Meru *Kenya* 0°3N 37°40E **54** B4
Meru *Tanzania* 3°15S 36°46E **54** C4
Meru △ *Kenya* 0°5N 38°10E **54** B4
Mesa *U.S.A.* 33°25N 111°50W **77** K8
Mesa Verde △ *U.S.A.* 37°11N 108°29W **77** H9
Mesanagros *Greece* 36°1N 27°49E **25** C9
Mesaoría *Cyprus* 35°12N 33°14E **25** D12
Mesgouez, L. *Canada* 51°20N 75°0W **72** B5
Meshed = Mashhad *Iran* 36°20N 59°35E **45** B8
Meshgīn Shahr *Iran* 38°30N 47°45E **44** B5
Meshoppen *U.S.A.* 41°36N 76°3W **83** E8
Mesilinka → *Canada* 56°6N 124°30W **70** B4
Mesologi *Greece* 38°21N 21°28E **23** E9
Mesongi *Greece* 39°29N 19°56E **25** B3
Mesopotamia = Al Jazirah
  Iraq 33°30N 44°0E **44** C5
Mesopotamia *U.S.A.* 41°27N 80°57W **82** E4
Mesquite *U.S.A.* 36°48N 114°4W **77** H6
Messaad *Algeria* 34°8N 3°30E **50** B6
Messalo → *Mozam.* 12°25S 39°15E **55** E4
Messara, Kolpos *Greece* 35°6N 24°47E **25** D6
Messina = Musina
  S. Africa 22°20S 30°5E **57** C5
Messina *Italy* 38°11N 15°34E **22** E6
Messina, Str. di *Italy* 38°15N 15°35E **22** F6
Messini *Greece* 37°4N 22°1E **23** F10
Messiniakos Kolpos
  Greece 36°45N 22°5E **23** F10
Mesta → *Bulgaria* 40°54N 24°49E **23** D11
Meta → *S. Amer.* 6°12N 67°28W **92** B5
Meta Incognita Pen.
  Canada 62°45N 68°30W **69** C13
Metabetchouan *Canada* 48°26N 71°52W **73** C5
Metairie *U.S.A.* 29°59N 90°9W **85** G9
Metaline Falls *U.S.A.* 48°52N 117°22W **76** B5
Metán *Argentina* 25°30S 65°0W **94** B3
Metangula *Mozam.* 12°40S 34°50E **55** E3
Metcalfe *Canada* 45°14N 75°28W **83** A9
Metema *Ethiopia* 12°58N 36°12E **47** E2
Metengobalame *Mozam.* 14°49S 34°30E **55** E3
Methven *N.Z.* 43°38S 171°40E **59** E3
Metil *Mozam.* 16°24S 39°0E **55** F4
Metlakatla *U.S.A.* 55°8N 131°35W **68** D6
Metropolis *U.S.A.* 37°9N 88°44W **80** G9
Metropolitana □ *Chile* 33°30S 70°50W **94** C1
Metu *Ethiopia* 8°18N 35°35E **47** F2
Metz *France* 49°8N 6°10E **20** B7
Meulaboh *Indonesia* 4°11N 96°3E **36** D1
Meureudu *Indonesia* 5°19N 96°10E **36** C1
Meuse → *Europe* 50°45N 5°41E **15** D5
Meuse □ *France* 49°5N 5°25E **15** D6
Mexia *U.S.A.* 31°41N 96°29W **84** F6
Mexiana, I. *Brazil* 0°0 49°30W **93** D9
Mexicali *Mexico* 32°40N 115°30W **79** N11
Mexican Plateau *Mexico* 25°0N 104°0W **66** G9
Mexican Water *U.S.A.* 36°57N 109°32W **77** H9
México *Mexico* 19°24N 99°9W **87** D5
Mexico *Maine, U.S.A.* 44°34N 70°33W **83** B14
Mexico *Mo., U.S.A.* 39°10N 91°53W **80** F8
Mexico *N.Y., U.S.A.* 43°28N 76°14W **83** C8
Mexico *Tex., U.S.A.* 32°0N 102°3W **84** F3
Mexico ■ *Cent. Amer.* 25°0N 105°0W **86** C4
México, Ciudad de
  Mexico 19°24N 99°9W **87** D5
Mexico, G. of *Cent. Amer.* 25°0N 90°0W **87** C7
Mexico B. *U.S.A.* 43°35N 76°20W **83** C8
Meydān-e Naftūn *Iran* 31°56N 49°18E **45** D6
Meydani, Ra's-e *Iran* 25°24N 59°6E **45** E8
Meyers Chuck *U.S.A.* 55°45N 132°15W **70** B2
Meymaneh *Afghan.* 35°53N 64°38E **40** B4
Mezen *Russia* 65°50N 44°20E **18** A7
Mezen → *Russia* 65°44N 44°22E **18** A7
Mézenc, Mt. *France* 44°54N 4°11E **20** D6
Mezhdurechensk *Russia* 53°41N 88°3E **28** D9
Mezhdurechenskiy
  Russia 59°36N 65°56E **28** D7

Mezőkövesd *Hungary* 47°49N 20°35E **17** E11
Mezőtúr *Hungary* 47°1N 20°41E **17** E11
Mezquital *Mexico* 23°29N 104°23W **86** C4
Mfolozi → *S. Africa* 28°25S 32°26E **57** D5
Mgeta *Tanzania* 8°22S 36°6E **55** D4
Mhlaba Hills *Zimbabwe* 17°6S 119°36E **60** C2
Mhow *India* 22°33N 75°50E **42** H6
Miahuatlán *Mexico* 16°20N 96°36W **87** D5
Miami *Fla., U.S.A.* 25°46N 80°11W **85** J14
Miami *Okla., U.S.A.* 36°53N 94°53W **84** C7
Miami *Tex., U.S.A.* 35°42N 100°38W **84** D4
Miami Beach *U.S.A.* 25°47N 80°7W **85** J14
Mian Xian *China* 33°10N 106°32E **34** H4
Mianchi *China* 34°48N 111°48E **34** G6
Miāndarreh *Iran* 35°37N 53°39E **45** C7
Miāndowāb *Iran* 37°0N 46°5E **44** B5
Miandrivazo *Madag.* 19°31S 45°29E **57** B8
Miāneh *Iran* 37°30N 47°40E **44** B5
Mianwali *Pakistan* 32°38N 71°28E **42** C4
Mianyang *China* 31°22N 104°47E **32** C5
Miarinarivo *Antananarivo,*
  Madag. 18°57S 46°55E **57** B8
Miarinarivo *Toamasina,*
  Madag. 16°38S 48°15E **57** B8
Miarivaratra *Madag.* 20°13S 47°31E **57** C8
Miass *Russia* 54°59N 60°6E **18** D11
Mica *S. Africa* 24°10S 30°48E **57** C5
Michalovce *Slovak Rep.* 48°47N 21°58E **17** D11
Michigan □ *U.S.A.* 44°0N 85°0W **81** C11
Michigan, L. *U.S.A.* 44°0N 87°0W **80** D10
Michigan City *U.S.A.* 41°43N 86°54W **80** E10
Michipicoten I. *Canada* 47°40N 85°40W **72** C2
Michoacán □ *Mexico* 19°0N 101°50W **86** D4
Michurin *Bulgaria* 42°9N 27°51E **23** C12
Michurinsk *Russia* 52°58N 40°27E **18** D7
Micoud *St. Lucia* 13°49N 60°54W **89** f
Micronesia *Pac. Oc.* 11°0N 160°0E **64** G7
Micronesia, Federated States of ■
  Pac. Oc. 9°0N 150°0E **58** A8
Mid-Pacific Seamounts
  Pac. Oc. 10°0N 177°0W **64** F10
Midai *Indonesia* 3°0N 107°47E **36** D3
Midale *Canada* 49°25N 103°20W **71** D8
Middelburg *Neths.* 51°30N 3°36E **15** C3
Middelburg *Eastern Cape,*
  S. Africa 31°30S 25°0E **56** E4
Middelburg *Mpumalanga,*
  S. Africa 25°49S 29°28E **57** D4
Middelpos *S. Africa* 31°55S 20°13E **56** E3
Middelwit *S. Africa* 24°51S 27°3E **56** C4
Middle Alkali L. *U.S.A.* 41°27N 120°5W **76** F3
Middle America Trench =
  Guatemala Trench
  Pac. Oc. 10°0N 95°0W **66** H10
Middle Bass I. *U.S.A.* 41°41N 82°48W **82** E2
Middle East *Asia* 35°0N 40°0E **26** E5
Middle Fork Feather →
  U.S.A. 38°33N 121°30W **78** F5
Middle I. *Australia* 34°6S 123°11E **61** F3
Middle Loup → *U.S.A.* 41°17N 98°24W **80** E4
Middleboro *U.S.A.* 41°54N 70°55W **83** E14
Middleburg *Fla., U.S.A.* 30°4N 81°52W **85** F14
Middleburg *Pa., U.S.A.* 40°47N 77°3W **82** F7
Middleburgh *U.S.A.* 42°36N 74°20W **83** D10
Middlebury *U.S.A.* 44°1N 73°10W **83** B11
Middlefield *U.S.A.* 41°27N 81°4W **82** E3
Middlemount *Australia* 22°50S 148°40E **62** C4
Middleport *N.Y., U.S.A.* 43°13N 78°29W **82** C6
Middleport *Ohio, U.S.A.* 39°0N 82°3W **81** F12
Middlesboro *U.S.A.* 36°36N 83°43W **81** G12
Middlesbrough *U.K.* 54°35N 1°13W **12** C6
Middlesbrough □ *U.K.* 54°28N 1°13W **12** C6
Middlesex *Belize* 17°2N 88°31W **88** C2
Middlesex *N.J., U.S.A.* 40°36N 74°30W **83** F10
Middlesex *N.Y., U.S.A.* 42°42N 77°16W **82** D7
Middleton *Australia* 22°22S 141°32E **62** C3
Middleton *Canada* 44°57N 65°4W **73** D6
Middleton Cr. →
  Australia 22°35S 141°51E **62** C3
Middletown *U.K.* 54°17N 6°51W **10** B5
Middletown *Calif.,*
  U.S.A. 38°45N 122°37W **78** G4
Middletown *Conn.,*
  U.S.A. 41°34N 72°39W **83** E12
Middletown *N.Y.,*
  U.S.A. 41°27N 74°25W **83** E10
Middletown *Ohio,*
  U.S.A. 39°31N 84°24W **81** F11
Middletown *Pa., U.S.A.* 40°12N 76°44W **83** F8
Midge Point *Australia* 20°39S 148°43E **62** J6
Midhurst *Canada* 44°26N 79°43W **82** B5
Midhurst *U.K.* 50°59N 0°44W **13** G7
Midi, Canal du → *France* 43°45N 1°21E **20** E4
Midland *Australia* 31°54S 116°1E **61** F2
Midland *Canada* 44°45N 79°50W **82** B5
Midland *Calif., U.S.A.* 33°52N 114°48W **79** M12
Midland *Mich., U.S.A.* 43°37N 84°14W **81** D11
Midland *Pa., U.S.A.* 40°39N 80°27W **82** F4
Midland *Tex., U.S.A.* 32°0N 102°3W **84** F3
Midlands □ *Zimbabwe* 19°40S 29°0E **55** F2
Midleton *Ireland* 51°55N 8°10W **10** E3
Midlothian □ *U.K.* 55°51N 3°5W **11** F5
Midongy, Tangorombohitr' i
  Madag. 23°30S 47°0E **57** C8
Midongy Atsimo *Madag.* 23°35S 47°1E **57** C8
Midway Is. *Pac. Oc.* 28°13N 177°22W **64** E10
Midway Wells *U.S.A.* 32°41N 115°7W **79** N11
Midwest *Wyo., U.S.A.* 43°25N 106°16W **76** E10
Midwest City *U.S.A.* 35°27N 97°24W **84** H6
Midyat *Turkey* 37°25N 41°23E **44** B4
Midzŏr *Bulgaria* 43°24N 22°40E **23** C10
Mie □ *Japan* 34°30N 136°10E **31** G8
Międzychód *Poland* 52°35N 15°53E **16** B8
Międzyrzec Podlaski
  Poland 51°58N 22°45E **17** C12
Mielec *Poland* 50°15N 21°25E **17** C11

Mienga *Angola* 17°12S 19°48E **56** B2
Miercurea-Ciuc
  Romania 46°21N 25°48E **17** E13
Mieres *Spain* 43°18N 5°48W **21** A3
Mifflintown *U.S.A.* 40°34N 77°24W **82** F7
Mifraz Ḥefa *Israel* 32°52N 35°0E **46** C4
Migori *Kenya* 1°4S 34°28E **54** C3
Miguel Alemán, Presa
  Mexico 18°15N 96°32W **87** D5
Mihara *Japan* 34°24N 133°5E **31** G6
Mikese *Tanzania* 6°48S 37°55E **54** D4
Mikhaylovgrad = Montana
  Bulgaria 43°27N 23°16E **23** C10
Mikhaylovka *Russia* 50°3N 43°5E **19** D7
Mikines *Greece* 37°43N 22°46E **23** F10
Mikkeli *Finland* 61°43N 27°15E **8** F22
Mikkwa → *Canada* 58°25N 114°46W **70** B6
Míkonos = Mykonos
  Greece 37°30N 25°25E **23** F11
Mikumi *Tanzania* 7°26S 37°0E **54** D4
Mikumi △ *Tanzania* 7°35S 37°15E **54** D4
Mikun *Russia* 62°20N 50°0E **18** B9
Milaca *U.S.A.* 45°45N 93°39W **80** C7
Milagro *Ecuador* 2°11S 79°36W **92** D3
Milan = Milano *Italy* 45°28N 9°10E **20** D8
Milan *Mo., U.S.A.* 40°12N 93°7W **80** E7
Milan *Tenn., U.S.A.* 35°55N 88°46W **85** D10
Milange *Mozam.* 16°3S 35°45E **55** F4
Milano *Italy* 45°28N 9°10E **20** D8
Milanoa *Madag.* 13°35S 49°47E **57** A8
Milâs *Turkey* 37°20N 27°50E **23** F12
Milatos *Greece* 35°18N 25°34E **25** D7
Milazzo *Italy* 38°13N 15°15E **22** E6
Milbank *U.S.A.* 45°13N 96°38W **80** C5
Milbanke Sd. *Canada* 52°19N 128°33W **70** C3
Milden *Canada* 51°29N 107°32W **71** C7
Mildenhall *U.K.* 52°21N 0°32E **13** E8
Mildmay *Canada* 44°3N 81°7W **82** B3
Mildura *Australia* 34°13S 142°9E **63** E3
Miles *Australia* 26°40S 150°9E **63** D5
Miles City *U.S.A.* 46°25N 105°51W **76** C11
Milestone *Canada* 49°59N 104°31W **71** D8
Miletus *Turkey* 37°30N 27°18E **23** F12
Milford *Calif., U.S.A.* 40°10N 120°22W **78** E6
Milford *Conn., U.S.A.* 41°14N 73°3W **83** E11
Milford *Del., U.S.A.* 38°55N 75°26W **81** F16
Milford *Mass., U.S.A.* 42°8N 71°31W **83** D13
Milford *N.H., U.S.A.* 42°50N 71°39W **83** D13
Milford *N.Y., U.S.A.* 42°35N 74°56W **83** D10
Milford *Pa., U.S.A.* 41°19N 74°48W **83** E10
Milford *Utah, U.S.A.* 38°24N 113°1W **76** G7
Milford Haven *U.K.* 51°42N 5°7W **13** F2
Milford Sd. *N.Z.* 44°41S 167°47E **59** F1
Milford Sound *N.Z.* 44°41S 167°55E **59** F1
Milh, Baḥr al = Razāzah,
  Buḥayrat ar *Iraq* 32°40N 43°35E **44** C4
Milikapiti *Australia* 11°26S 130°40E **60** B5
Miling *Australia* 30°30S 116°17E **61** F2
Milk → *U.S.A.* 48°4N 106°19W **76** B10
Milk River *Canada* 49°10N 112°5W **70** D6
Mill → *U.S.A.* 42°57N 83°23W **82** D1
Mill I. *Antarctica* 66°0S 101°30E **5** C8
Mill Valley *U.S.A.* 37°54N 122°32W **78** H4
Millau *France* 44°8N 3°4E **20** D5
Millbridge *Canada* 44°41N 77°36W **82** B7
Millbrook *Canada* 44°10N 78°29W **82** B6
Millbrook *Ala., U.S.A.* 32°29N 86°22W **85** E11
Millbrook *N.Y., U.S.A.* 41°47N 73°42W **83** E11
Mille Lacs, L. des *Canada* 48°45N 90°35W **72** C1
Mille Lacs L. *U.S.A.* 46°15N 93°39W **80** B7
Milledgeville *U.S.A.* 33°5N 83°14W **85** E13
Millen *U.S.A.* 32°48N 81°57W **85** E14
Millennium I. = Caroline I.
  Kiribati 9°58S 150°13W **65** H12
Miller *U.S.A.* 44°31N 98°59W **80** C4
Miller Lake *Canada* 45°6N 81°26W **82** A3
Millersburg *Ohio, U.S.A.* 40°33N 81°55W **82** F3
Millersburg *Pa., U.S.A.* 40°32N 76°58W **82** F8
Millerton *U.S.A.* 41°57N 73°31W **83** E11
Millerton L. *U.S.A.* 37°1N 119°41W **78** J7
Millet *St. Lucia* 13°55N 60°59W **89** f
Millheim *U.S.A.* 40°54N 77°29W **82** F7
Millicent *Australia* 37°34S 140°21E **63** F3
Millington *U.S.A.* 35°20N 89°53W **85** D10
Millinocket *U.S.A.* 45°39N 68°43W **81** C19
Millmerran *Australia* 27°53S 151°16E **63** D5
Millom *U.K.* 54°13N 3°16W **12** C4
Mills L. *Canada* 61°30N 118°20W **70** A5
Millsboro *U.S.A.* 40°0N 80°0W **82** G5
Millstream Chichester △
  Australia 21°35S 117°6E **60** D2
Millstreet *Ireland* 52°4N 9°4W **10** D2
Milltown Malbay *Ireland* 52°52N 9°24W **10** D2
Millville *N.J., U.S.A.* 39°24N 75°2W **81** F16
Millville *Pa., U.S.A.* 41°7N 76°32W **83** E8
Millwood L. *U.S.A.* 33°42N 93°58W **84** E8
Milne → *Australia* 21°10S 137°33E **62** C2
Milo *U.S.A.* 45°15N 68°59W **81** C19
Milon, Akra *Greece* 36°15N 28°11E **25** C10
Milos *Greece* 36°44N 24°25E **23** F11
Milparinka *Australia* 29°46S 141°57E **63** D3
Milpitas *U.S.A.* 37°26N 121°55W **78** H5
Milton *N.S., Canada* 44°4N 64°45W **73** D7
Milton *Ont., Canada* 43°31N 79°53W **82** C5
Milton *N.Z.* 46°7S 169°59E **59** G2
Milton *Calif., U.S.A.* 38°3N 120°51W **78** G6
Milton *Fla., U.S.A.* 30°38N 87°3W **85** F11
Milton *Pa., U.S.A.* 41°1N 76°51W **82** F8
Milton *Vt., U.S.A.* 44°38N 73°7W **83** B11
Milton-Freewater
  U.S.A. 45°56N 118°23W **76** D4
Milton Keynes *U.K.* 52°1N 0°44W **13** E7
Milton Keynes □ *U.K.* 52°1N 0°44W **13** E7
Milverton *Canada* 43°34N 80°55W **82** C4
Milwaukee *U.S.A.* 43°2N 87°54W **80** D2
Milwaukee Deep *Atl. Oc.* 19°50N 68°0W **89** C6
Milwaukie *U.S.A.* 45°26N 122°38W **78** E4
Min Jiang → *Fujian,*
  China 26°0N 119°35E **33** D6

Min Jiang → *Sichuan,*
  China 28°45N 104°40E **32** D5
Min Xian *China* 34°25N 104°5E **34** G3
Mīnā' Jabal 'Alī *U.A.E.* 25°2N 55°8E **45** E7
Mina Pirquitas
  Argentina 22°40S 66°30W **94** A2
Mīnā Su'ud *Si. Arabia* 28°45N 48°28E **45** D6
Mīnā'al Aḥmadī *Kuwait* 29°5N 48°10E **45** D6
Minago → *Canada* 54°33N 98°59W **71** C9
Minaki *Canada* 49°59N 94°40W **71** D10
Minamata *Japan* 32°10N 130°30E **31** H5
Minami-Arapusa △
  Japan 35°30N 138°9E **31** G9
Minami-Tori-Shima
  Pac. Oc. 24°20N 153°58E **64** E7
Minas *Uruguay* 34°20S 55°10W **95** C4
Minas, Sierra de las
  Guatemala 15°9N 89°31W **88** C2
Minas Basin *Canada* 45°20N 64°12W **73** C7
Minas Gerais □ *Brazil* 18°50S 46°0W **93** G9
Minatitlán *Mexico* 17°59N 94°31W **87** D6
Minbu *Burma* 20°10N 94°52E **41** J19
Minchinabad *Pakistan* 30°10N 73°34E **42** D5
Mindanao *Phil.* 8°0N 125°0E **37** C7
Mindanao Sea = Bohol Sea
  Phil. 9°0N 124°0E **37** C6
Mindanao Trench
  Pac. Oc. 12°0N 126°6E **37** B7
Mindelo *C. Verde Is.* 16°24N 25°0W **50** b
Minden *Canada* 44°55N 78°43W **82** B6
Minden *Germany* 52°17N 8°55E **16** B5
Minden *La., U.S.A.* 32°37N 93°17W **84** E8
Minden *Nev., U.S.A.* 38°57N 119°46W **78** G7
Mindibungu = Billiluna
  Australia 19°37S 127°41E **60** C4
Mindiptana *Indonesia* 5°55S 140°22E **37** F10
Mindoro *Phil.* 13°0N 121°0E **37** B6
Mindoro Str. *Phil.* 12°30N 120°30E **37** B6
Mine *Japan* 34°12N 131°7E **31** G5
Minehead *U.K.* 51°12N 3°29W **13** F4
Mineola *N.Y., U.S.A.* 40°44N 73°38W **83** F11
Mineola *Tex., U.S.A.* 32°40N 95°29W **84** E7
Mineral King *U.S.A.* 36°27N 118°36W **78** J8
Mineral Wells *U.S.A.* 32°48N 98°7W **84** E5
Miners Bay *Canada* 44°49N 78°46W **82** B6
Minersville *U.S.A.* 40°41N 76°16W **83** F8
Minerva *N.Y., U.S.A.* 43°47N 73°59W **83** C11
Minerva *Ohio, U.S.A.* 40°44N 81°6W **82** F3
Minetto *U.S.A.* 43°24N 76°28W **83** C8
Minfeng *China* 37°4N 82°46E **32** C3
Mingäçevir Su Anbarı
  Azerbaijan 40°57N 46°50E **19** F8
Mingan *Canada* 50°20N 64°0W **73** B7
Mingechaurskoye Vdkhr. =
  Mingäçevir Su Anbarı
  Azerbaijan 40°57N 46°50E **19** F8
Mingela *Australia* 19°52S 146°38E **62** B4
Mingenew *Australia* 29°12S 115°21E **61** E2
Mingera Cr. →
  Australia 20°38S 137°45E **62** C2
Mingin *Burma* 22°50N 94°30E **41** H19
Mingo Junction *U.S.A.* 40°19N 80°37W **82** F4
Mingora *Pakistan* 34°48N 72°22E **43** B5
Mingteke Daban = Mintaka Pass
  Pakistan 37°0N 74°58E **43** A6
Mingyuegue *China* 43°2N 128°50E **35** C15
Minho = Miño → *Spain* 41°52N 8°40W **21** A2
Minho *Portugal* 41°25N 8°20W **21** B1
Minidoka *U.S.A.* 42°45N 113°29W **76** E7
Minigwal, L. *Australia* 29°31S 123°14E **61** E3
Minilya → *Australia* 23°45S 114°0E **61** D1
Minilya Roadhouse
  Australia 23°55S 114°0E **61** D1
Minipi L. *Canada* 52°25S 60°45W **73** B7
Mink L. *Canada* 61°54N 117°40W **70** A5
Minna *Nigeria* 9°37N 6°30E **50** G7
Minneapolis *Kans., U.S.A.* 39°8N 97°42W **80** F5
Minneapolis *Minn.,*
  U.S.A. 44°57N 93°16W **80** C7
Minnedosa *Canada* 50°14N 99°50W **71** C9
Minnesota □ *U.S.A.* 46°0N 94°15W **80** B6
Minnesota → *U.S.A.* 44°54N 93°9W **80** C7
Minnewaukan *U.S.A.* 48°4N 99°15W **80** A4
Minnipa *Australia* 32°51S 135°9E **63** E2
Minnitaki L. *Canada* 49°57N 92°10W **72** C1
Mino *Japan* 35°32N 136°55E **31** G8
Miño → *Spain* 41°52N 8°40W **21** A2
Minorca = Menorca *Spain* 40°0N 4°0E **24** B11
Minot *U.S.A.* 48°14N 101°18W **80** A3
Minqin *China* 38°38N 103°20E **34** E2
Minsk *Belarus* 53°52N 27°30E **17** B14
Mińsk Mazowiecki
  Poland 52°10N 21°33E **17** B11
Mintabie *Australia* 27°15S 133°7E **63** D1
Mintaka Pass *Pakistan* 37°0N 74°58E **43** A6
Minto *Canada* 46°5N 66°5W **73** C6
Minto, L. *Canada* 57°13N 75°0W **72** A5
Minton *Canada* 49°10N 104°35W **71** D8
Minturn *U.S.A.* 39°35N 106°26W **76** G10
Minudasht *Iran* 37°17N 56°7E **45** B8
Minusinsk *Russia* 53°43N 91°20E **29** D10
Minutang *India* 28°15N 96°30E **41** E20
Minvoul *Gabon* 2°9N 12°8E **52** D2
Minzhong *China* 22°37N 113°30E **33** F10
Miquelon *Canada* 49°25N 76°27W **72** C4
Miquelon *St-P. & M.* 47°8N 56°22W **73** C8
Mīr Kūh *Iran* 26°22N 58°55E **45** E8
Mīr Shahdād *Iran* 26°15N 58°29E **45** E8
Mira *Italy* 45°26N 12°8E **22** B5
Mira por vos Cay
  Bahamas 22°9N 74°30W **89** B5
Mirabello, Kolpos *Greece* 35°10N 25°50E **25** D7
Mirador-Río Azul △
  Guatemala 17°45N 89°50W **88** C2
Miraj *India* 16°50N 74°45E **40** L9
Miram Shah *Pakistan* 33°0N 70°2E **42** C4
Miramar *Argentina* 38°15S 57°50W **94** D4

Miramar *Mozam.* 23°50S 35°35E **57** C6
Miramichi *Canada* 47°2N 65°28W **73** C6
Miramichi B. *Canada* 47°15N 65°0W **73** C7
Miranda *Brazil* 20°10S 56°15W **93** H7
Miranda → *Brazil* 19°25S 57°20W **92** G7
Miranda de Ebro *Spain* 42°41N 2°57W **21** A4
Miranda do Douro
  Portugal 41°30N 6°16W **21** B2
Mirandópolis *Brazil* 21°9S 51°6W **95** A5
Mirango *Malawi* 13°32S 34°58E **55** E3
Mirani *Australia* 21°8S 148°53E **62** K6
Mirassol *Brazil* 20°46S 49°28W **95** A6
Mirbāṭ *Oman* 17°0N 54°45E **47** D5
Mires *Greece* 35°4N 24°56E **25** D6
Miri *Malaysia* 4°23N 113°59E **36** D4
Miriam Vale *Australia* 24°20S 151°33E **62** C5
Mirim, L. *S. Amer.* 32°45S 52°50W **95** C5
Mirnyy *Antarctica* 66°50S 92°30E **5** C14
Mirnyy *Russia* 62°33N 113°53E **29** C12
Mirokhan *Pakistan* 27°46N 68°6E **42** F3
Mirond L. *Canada* 55°6N 102°47W **71** B8
Mirpur *Pakistan* 33°32N 73°56E **43** C5
Mirpur Batoro *Pakistan* 24°44N 68°16E **42** G3
Mirpur Bibiwari *Pakistan* 28°33N 67°44E **42** E2
Mirpur Khas *Pakistan* 25°30N 69°0E **42** G3
Mirpur Sakro *Pakistan* 24°33N 67°41E **42** G2
Mirs Bay = Tai Pang Wan
  China 22°33N 114°24E **33** F11
Mirtağ *Turkey* 38°23N 41°56E **44** B4
Mirtoo Sea *Greece* 37°0N 23°20E **23** F10
Miryang *S. Korea* 35°31N 128°44E **35** G15
Mirzapur *India* 25°10N 82°34E **43** G10
Mirzapur-cum-Vindhyachal =
  Mirzapur *India* 25°10N 82°34E **43** G10
Misantla *Mexico* 19°56N 96°50W **87** D5
Misawa *Japan* 40°41N 141°24E **30** D10
Miscou I. *Canada* 47°57N 64°31W **73** C7
Mish'āb, Ra's al
  Si. Arabia 28°15N 48°43E **45** D6
Mishan *China* 45°37N 131°48E **30** B5
Mishawaka *U.S.A.* 41°40N 86°11W **80** E10
Mishima *Japan* 35°10N 138°52E **31** G9
Misión *Mexico* 32°6N 116°53W **79** N10
Misiones □ *Argentina* 27°0S 55°0W **95** B5
Misiones □ *Paraguay* 27°0S 56°0W **94** B4
Miskah *Si. Arabia* 24°49N 42°56E **44** E4
Miskitos, Cayos *Nic.* 14°26N 82°50W **88** D3
Miskolc *Hungary* 48°7N 20°50E **17** D11
Misoke
  Dem. Rep. of the Congo 0°42S 28°2E **54** C2
Misool *Indonesia* 1°52S 130°10E **37** E8
Miṣr = Egypt ■ *Africa* 28°0N 31°0E **51** C12
Miṣrātah *Libya* 32°24N 15°3E **51** B9
Missanabie *Canada* 48°20N 84°6W **72** C3
Missinaibi → *Canada* 50°43N 81°29W **72** B3
Missinaibi L. *Canada* 48°23N 83°40W **72** C3
Mission *Canada* 49°10N 122°15W **70** D4
Mission *S. Dak., U.S.A.* 43°18N 100°39W **80** D3
Mission *Tex., U.S.A.* 26°13N 98°20W **84** H5
Mission Beach *Australia* 17°53S 146°6E **62** B4
Mission Viejo *U.S.A.* 33°36N 117°40W **79** M9
Missisa L. *Canada* 52°20N 85°7W **72** B2
Missisicabi → *Canada* 51°14N 79°31W **72** B4
Mississagi → *Canada* 46°15N 83°9W **72** C3
Mississauga *Canada* 43°32N 79°35W **82** C5
Mississippi □ *U.S.A.* 33°0N 90°0W **85** E10
Mississippi → *U.S.A.* 29°9N 89°15W **85** G10
Mississippi L. *Canada* 45°5N 76°10W **83** A8
Mississippi River Delta
  U.S.A. 29°10N 89°15W **85** G10
Mississippi Sd. *U.S.A.* 30°20N 89°0W **85** F10
Missoula *U.S.A.* 46°52N 114°1W **76** C6
Missouri □ *U.S.A.* 38°25N 92°30W **80** F7
Missouri → *U.S.A.* 38°49N 90°7W **80** F8
Missouri City *U.S.A.* 29°37N 95°32W **84** G7
Missouri Valley *U.S.A.* 41°34N 95°53W **80** E6
Mist *U.S.A.* 45°59N 123°15W **78** E3
Mistassibi → *Canada* 48°53N 72°13W **73** B5
Mistassini *Canada* 48°53N 72°12W **73** C5
Mistassini → *Canada* 48°42N 72°20W **73** C5
Mistassini, L. *Canada* 51°0N 73°30W **72** B5
Mistastin L. *Canada* 55°57N 63°20W **73** A7
Mistinibi, L. *Canada* 55°56N 64°17W **73** A7
Mistissini *Canada* 48°53N 72°12W **73** C5
Misty L. *Canada* 58°53N 101°40W **71** B8
Misurata = Miṣrātah
  Libya 32°24N 15°3E **51** B9
Mitchell *Australia* 26°29S 147°58E **63** D4
Mitchell *Canada* 43°28N 81°12W **82** C3
Mitchell *Nebr., U.S.A.* 41°57N 103°49W **80** E2
Mitchell *Oreg., U.S.A.* 44°34N 120°9W **76** D3
Mitchell *S. Dak., U.S.A.* 43°43N 98°2W **80** D4
Mitchell → *Australia* 15°12S 141°35E **62** B3
Mitchell, Mt. *U.S.A.* 35°46N 82°16W **85** D13
Mitchell-Alice Rivers △
  Australia 15°28S 142°5E **62** B3
Mitchell Ra. *Australia* 12°49S 135°36E **62** A2
Mitchelstown *Ireland* 52°15N 8°16W **10** D3
Mitha Tiwana *Pakistan* 32°13N 72°6E **42** C5
Mithi *Pakistan* 24°44N 69°48E **42** G3
Mithrao *Pakistan* 27°28N 69°40E **42** F3
Mitilíni *Greece* 39°6N 26°35E **23** E12
Mitla Pass = Mamarr Mitlā
  Egypt 30°2N 32°54E **46** E1
Mito *Japan* 36°20N 140°30E **31** F10
Mitrovica = Kosovska Mitrovica
  Serbia 42°54N 20°52E **23** C9
Mitsamiouli *Comoros Is.* 11°20S 43°16E **53** a
Mitsinjo *Madag.* 16°1S 45°52E **57** B8
Mitsiwa *Eritrea* 15°35N 39°25E **47** D2
Mitsukaidō *Japan* 36°1N 139°59E **31** F9
Mittagong *Australia* 34°28S 150°29E **63** E5
Mittimatalik = Pond Inlet
  Canada 72°40N 77°0W **69** B12
Mitú *Colombia* 1°15N 70°13W **92** C4
Mitumba *Tanzania* 7°8S 31°2E **54** D3

Mitumba, Mts.
  Dem. Rep. of the Congo 7°0S 27°30E **54** D2
Mitwaba
  Dem. Rep. of the Congo 8°2S 27°17E **55** D2
Mityana *Uganda* 0°23N 32°2E **54** B3
Mixteco → *Mexico* 18°11N 98°30W **87** D5
Miyagi □ *Japan* 38°15N 140°45E **30** E10
Miyake-Jima *Japan* 34°5N 139°30E **31** G9
Miyako *Japan* 39°40N 141°59E **30** E10
Miyako-Jima *Japan* 24°45N 125°20E **31** M2
Miyako-Rettō *Japan* 24°24N 125°0E **31** M2
Miyakonojō *Japan* 31°40N 131°5E **31** J5
Miyani *India* 21°50N 69°26E **42** J3
Miyanoura-Dake *Japan* 30°20N 130°31E **31** J5
Miyazaki *Japan* 31°56N 131°30E **31** J5
Miyazaki □ *Japan* 32°30N 131°30E **31** H5
Miyazu *Japan* 35°35N 135°10E **31** G7
Miyet, Bahr el = Dead Sea
  Asia 31°30N 35°30E **46** D4
Miyoshi *Japan* 34°48N 132°51E **31** G6
Miyun *China* 40°28N 116°50E **34** D9
Miyun Shuiku *China* 40°30N 117°0E **35** D9
Mizdah *Libya* 31°30N 13°0E **51** B8
Mizen Hd. *Cork, Ireland* 51°27N 9°50W **10** E2
Mizen Hd. *Wicklow, Ireland* 52°51N 6°4W **10** D5
Mizhi *China* 37°47N 110°12E **34** F6
Mizoram □ *India* 23°30N 92°40E **41** H18
Mizpe Ramon *Israel* 30°34N 34°49E **46** E3
Mizuho *Antarctica* 70°30S 41°0E **5** D5
Mizusawa *Japan* 39°8N 141°8E **30** E10
Mjölby *Sweden* 58°20N 15°10E **9** G16
Mjøsa *Norway* 60°40N 11°0E **8** F14
Mkata *Tanzania* 5°45S 38°20E **54** D4
Mkhaya △ *Swaziland* 26°34S 31°45E **57** D5
Mkhuze △ *S. Africa* 27°27S 29°30E **57** D4
Mkokotoni *Tanzania* 5°55S 39°15E **54** D4
Mkomazi *Tanzania* 4°40S 38°7E **54** C4
Mkomazi → *S. Africa* 30°12S 30°50E **57** E5
Mkomazi △ *Tanzania* 4°45S 30°2E **54** C3
Mkulwe *Tanzania* 8°37S 32°20E **55** D3
Mkumbi, Ras *Tanzania* 7°38S 39°55E **54** D4
Mkushi *Zambia* 14°25S 29°15E **55** E2
Mkushi River *Zambia* 13°32S 29°45E **55** E2
Mkuze *S. Africa* 27°10S 32°0E **57** D5
Mladá Boleslav
  Czech Rep. 50°27N 14°53E **16** C8
Mlala Hills *Tanzania* 6°50S 31°40E **54** D3
Mlange = Mulanje, Mt.
  Malawi 16°2S 35°33E **55** F4
Mława *Poland* 53°9N 20°25E **17** B11
Mlawula △ *Swaziland* 26°12S 32°2E **57** D5
Mljet *Croatia* 42°43N 17°30E **22** C7
Mmabatho *S. Africa* 25°49S 25°30E **56** D4
Mo i Rana *Norway* 66°20N 14°7E **8** C16
Moa *Australia* 20°40N 74°56W **89** B4
Moa *Indonesia* 8°0S 128°0E **37** F7
Moa → *S. Leone* 6°59N 11°36W **50** G3
Moab *U.S.A.* 38°35N 109°33W **76** G9
Moala *Fiji* 18°36S 179°53E **59** a
Moama *Australia* 36°7S 144°46E **63** F3
Moamba *Mozam.* 25°36S 32°15E **57** D5
Moapa *U.S.A.* 36°40N 114°37W **79** J12
Moate *Ireland* 53°24N 7°44W **10** C4
Moba *Dem. Rep. of the Congo* 7°0S 29°48E **54** D2
Mobārakābād *Iran* 28°24N 53°20E **45** D7
Mobaye *C.A.R.* 4°25N 21°5E **52** D4
Mobayi
  Dem. Rep. of the Congo 4°15N 21°8E **52** D4
Moberly *U.S.A.* 39°25N 92°26W **80** F7
Moberly Lake *Canada* 55°50N 121°44W **70** B4
Mobile *U.S.A.* 30°41N 88°3W **85** F10
Mobile B. *U.S.A.* 30°30N 88°0W **85** F11
Moc Chau *Vietnam* 20°50N 104°38E **38** B5
Moc Hoa *Vietnam* 10°46N 105°56E **39** G5
Mocabe Kasari
  Dem. Rep. of the Congo 9°58S 26°12E **55** D2
Moçambique = Mozambique ■
  Africa 19°0S 35°0E **55** F4
Moçambique *Mozam.* 15°3S 40°42E **55** F5
Mocanaqua *U.S.A.* 41°9N 76°8W **83** E8
Moce *Fiji* 18°40S 178°29W **59** a
Mochima △ *Venezuela* 10°30N 64°5W **89** D7
Mochos *Greece* 35°16N 25°27E **25** D7
Mochudi *Botswana* 24°27S 26°7E **56** C4
Mocimboa da Praia
  Mozam. 11°25S 40°20E **55** E5
Moclips *U.S.A.* 47°14N 124°13W **78** C2
Mocoa *Colombia* 1°7N 76°35W **92** C3
Mococa *Brazil* 21°28S 47°0W **95** A6
Mocorito *Mexico* 25°29N 107°55W **86** B3
Moctezuma *Mexico* 29°48N 109°42W **86** B3
Moctezuma → *Mexico* 21°59N 98°34W **87** C5
Mocuba *Mozam.* 16°54S 36°57E **55** F4
Modane *France* 45°12N 6°40E **20** D7
Modasa *India* 23°30N 73°21E **42** H5
Modder → *S. Africa* 29°2S 24°37E **56** D3
Modderrivier *S. Africa* 29°2S 24°38E **56** D3
Módena *Italy* 44°40N 10°55E **22** B4
Modena *U.S.A.* 37°48N 113°56W **77** H7
Modesto *U.S.A.* 37°39N 121°0W **78** H6
Módica *Italy* 36°52N 14°46E **22** F6
Modimolle *S. Africa* 24°42S 28°22E **57** C4
Modjadjiskloof *S. Africa* 23°42S 30°10E **57** C5
Moe *Australia* 38°12S 146°19E **63** F4
Moebase *Mozam.* 17°3S 38°41E **55** F4
Moenkopi *U.S.A.* 36°7N 111°13W **77** H8
Moengo *Suriname* 5°45N 54°20W **93** B8
Moffat *U.K.* 55°21N 3°27W **11** F5
Moga *India* 30°48N 75°8E **42** D6
Mogadishu = Muqdisho
  Somali Rep. 2°2N 45°25E **47** G4
Mogador = Essaouira
  Morocco 31°32N 9°42W **50** B4
Mogalakwena →
  S. Africa 22°38S 28°40E **57** C4
Mogami-Gawa →
  Japan 38°45N 140°0E **30** E10

Mogán *Canary Is.* 27°53N 15°43W **24** G4
Mogaung *Burma* 25°20N 97°0E **41** G20
Mogi das Cruzes *Brazil* 23°31S 46°11W **95** A6
Mogi-Guaçu → *Brazil* 20°53S 48°10W **95** A6
Mogi-Mirim *Brazil* 22°29S 47°0W **95** A6
Mogilev = Mahilyow
  Belarus 53°55N 30°18E **17** B16
Mogilev-Podolskiy = Mohyliv-
  Podilskyy *Ukraine* 48°26N 27°48E **17** D14
Mogincual *Mozam.* 15°35S 40°25E **55** F5
Mogocha *Russia* 53°40N 119°50E **29** D12
Mogok *Burma* 23°0N 96°40E **41** H20
Mogollon Rim *U.S.A.* 34°10N 110°50W **77** J8
Mogumber *Australia* 31°2S 116°3E **61** F2
Mogwadi → *S. Africa* 23°4S 29°36E **57** C4
Mohács *Hungary* 45°58N 18°41E **17** F10
Mohales Hoek *Lesotho* 30°7S 27°26E **56** E4
Mohall *U.S.A.* 48°46N 101°31W **80** A3
Moḥammadābād *Iran* 37°52N 59°5E **45** B8
Mohammedia *Morocco* 33°44N 7°21W **50** B4
Mohana → *India* 24°43N 85°0E **43** G11
Mohanlalganj *India* 26°41N 80°58E **43** F9
Mohave, L. *U.S.A.* 35°12N 114°34W **79** K12
Mohawk → *U.S.A.* 42°47N 73°41W **83** D11
Mohéli *Comoros* 12°20S 43°40E **53** a
Mohenjodaro *Pakistan* 27°19N 68°7E **42** F3
Moher, Cliffs of *Ireland* 52°58N 9°27W **10** D2
Mohicanville Res. *U.S.A.* 40°45N 82°9W **82** F2
Mohns Ridge *Arctic* 72°30N 5°0W **4** B7
Mohoro *Tanzania* 8°6S 39°8E **54** D4
Mohsenābād *Iran* 36°40N 59°35E **45** B8
Mohyliv-Podilskyy
  Ukraine 48°26N 27°48E **17** D14
Moidart, L. *U.K.* 56°47N 5°52W **11** E3
Moira → *Canada* 44°21N 77°24W **82** B7
Moisaküla *Estonia* 58°3N 25°12E **9** G21
Moisie *Canada* 50°12N 66°1W **73** B6
Moisie → *Canada* 50°14N 66°5W **73** B6
Mojave *U.S.A.* 35°3N 118°10W **79** K8
Mojave → *U.S.A.* 35°7N 115°32W **79** K11
Mojave Desert *U.S.A.* 35°0N 116°30W **79** L10
Mojo *Bolivia* 21°48S 65°33W **94** A2
Mojokerto *Indonesia* 7°28S 112°26E **37** G15
Mokai *N.Z.* 38°32S 175°56E **59** C5
Mokambo
  Dem. Rep. of the Congo 12°25S 28°20E **55** E2
Mokameh *India* 25°24N 85°55E **43** G11
Mokau *N.Z.* 38°42S 174°39E **59** C5
Mokelumne → *U.S.A.* 38°13N 121°28W **78** G5
Mokelumne Hill
  U.S.A. 38°18N 120°43W **78** G6
Mokhotlong *Lesotho* 29°22S 29°2E **57** D4
Mokokchung *India* 26°15N 94°30E **41** F19
Mokolo → *S. Africa* 23°14S 27°43E **57** C4
Mokopane *S. Africa* 24°10S 28°55E **57** C4
Mokpo *S. Korea* 34°50N 126°25E **35** G14
Mokra Gora *Europe* 42°50N 20°30E **23** C9
Mol *Belgium* 51°11N 5°5E **15** C5
Molchanovo *Russia* 57°40N 83°50E **28** D9
Mold *U.K.* 53°9N 3°8W **12** D4
Moldavia = Moldova ■
  Europe 47°0N 28°0E **17** E15
Moldavia *Romania* 46°30N 27°0E **17** E14
Molde *Norway* 62°45N 7°9E **8** E12
Moldova ■ *Europe* 47°0N 28°0E **17** E15
Moldoveanu, Vf.
  Romania 45°36N 24°45E **17** F13
Mole → *U.K.* 51°24N 0°21W **13** F7
Mole Creek *Australia* 41°34S 146°24E **63** G4
Molepolole *Botswana* 24°28S 25°28E **56** C4
Molfetta *Italy* 41°12N 16°36E **22** D7
Moline *U.S.A.* 41°30N 90°31W **80** E8
Molinos *Argentina* 25°28S 66°15W **94** B2
Moliro
  Dem. Rep. of the Congo 8°12S 30°30E **54** D3
Mollendo *Peru* 17°0S 72°0W **92** G4
Mollerin, L. *Australia* 30°30S 117°35E **61** F2
Molo *Kenya* 0°35S 35°44E **54** C4
Molodechno = Maladzyechna
  Belarus 54°20N 26°50E **17** A14
Molodezhnaya *Antarctica* 67°40S 45°51E **5** C9
Moloka'i *U.S.A.* 21°8N 157°0W **74** b
Molokai Fracture Zone
  Pac. Oc. 28°0N 125°0W **65** E15
Molong *Australia* 33°5S 148°54E **63** E4
Molopo → *Africa* 28°30S 20°12E **56** D3
Molson L. *Canada* 54°22N 96°40W **71** C9
Molteno *S. Africa* 31°22S 26°22E **56** E4
Molu *Indonesia* 6°45S 131°40E **37** F8
Molucca Sea *Indonesia* 0°0 125°0E **37** E6
Moluccas = Maluku
  Indonesia 1°0S 127°0E **37** E7
Moma
  Dem. Rep. of the Congo 1°35S 23°52E **54** C1
Moma *Mozam.* 16°47S 39°4E **55** F4
Mombasa *Kenya* 4°3S 39°40E **54** C4
Mombetsu *Japan* 44°21N 143°22E **30** B11
Momchilgrad *Bulgaria* 41°33N 25°23E **23** D11
Momi *Dem. Rep. of the Congo* 1°42S 27°0E **54** C2
Mompós *Colombia* 9°14N 74°26W **92** B4
Møn *Denmark* 54°57N 12°20E **9** J15
Mon □ *Burma* 16°0N 97°30E **41** L20
Mona, Canal de la = Mona
  Passage *W. Indies* 18°30N 67°45W **89** C6
Mona, Isla *Puerto Rico* 18°5N 67°54W **89** C6
Mona, Pta. *Costa Rica* 9°37N 82°36W **88** E3
Mona Passage *W. Indies* 18°30N 67°45W **89** C6
Monaca *U.S.A.* 40°41N 80°17W **82** F4
Monaco ■ *Europe* 43°46N 7°23E **20** E7
Monadhliath Mts. *U.K.* 57°10N 4°4W **11** D4
Monadnock, Mt. *U.S.A.* 42°52N 72°7W **83** D12
Monaghan *Ireland* 54°15N 6°57W **10** B5
Monaghan □ *Ireland* 54°11N 6°56W **10** B5
Monahans *U.S.A.* 31°36N 102°54W **84** F3
Monar, L. *U.K.* 57°26N 5°8W **11** D3
Monarch Mt. *Canada* 51°55N 125°57W **70** C3

Monashee Mts. *Canada* 51°0N 118°43W **70** C5
Monasterevin *Ireland* 53°8N 7°4W **10** C4
Monastir = Bitola
  Macedonia 41°1N 21°20E **23** D9
Monastir *Tunisia* 35°50N 10°49E **51** A8
Moncayo, Sierra del
  Spain 41°48N 1°50W **21** B5
Monchegorsk *Russia* 67°54N 32°58E **8** C25
Mönchengladbach
  Germany 51°11N 6°27E **16** C4
Monchique *Portugal* 37°19N 8°38W **21** D1
Moncks Corner *U.S.A.* 33°12N 80°1W **85** E14
Monclova *Mexico* 26°54N 101°25W **86** B4
Moncton *Canada* 46°7N 64°51W **73** C7
Mondego → *Portugal* 40°9N 8°52W **21** B1
Mondeodo *Indonesia* 3°34S 122°9E **37** E6
Mondovì *Italy* 44°23N 7°49E **20** D7
Mondrain I. *Australia* 34°9S 122°14E **61** F3
Moneague *Jamaica* 18°16N 77°7W **88** a
Moneron, Ostrov
  Russia 46°15N 141°16E **30** A10
Monessen *U.S.A.* 40°9N 79°54W **82** F5
Monett *U.S.A.* 36°55N 93°55W **80** G7
Moneymore *U.K.* 54°41N 6°40W **10** B5
Monforte de Lemos *Spain* 42°31N 7°33W **21** A2
Mong Cai *Vietnam* 21°27N 107°54E **38** B6
Mong Hsu *Burma* 21°54N 98°30E **41** J21
Mong Kung *Burma* 21°35N 97°35E **41** J20
Mong Nai *Burma* 20°32N 97°46E **41** J20
Mong Pawk *Burma* 22°4N 99°16E **41** H21
Mong Ton *Burma* 20°17N 98°45E **41** J21
Mong Wa *Burma* 21°26N 100°27E **41** J22
Mong Yai *Burma* 22°21N 98°3E **41** H21
Mongalla *Sudan* 5°8N 31°42E **51** G12
Mongers, L. *Australia* 29°25S 117°5E **61** E2
Monghyr = Munger
  India 25°23N 86°30E **43** G12
Mongibello = Etna *Italy* 37°50N 14°55E **22** F6
Mongo *Chad* 12°14N 18°43E **51** F9
Mongolia ■ *Asia* 47°0N 103°0E **32** B5
Mongolia, Plateau of
  Asia 45°0N 105°0E **26** D12
Mongu *Zambia* 15°16S 23°12E **53** H4
Môngua *Angola* 16°43S 15°20E **56** B2
Monifieth *U.K.* 56°30N 2°48W **11** E6
Monkey Bay *Malawi* 14°7S 35°1E **55** E4
Monkey Mia *Australia* 25°48S 113°43E **61** E1
Monkey River *Belize* 16°22N 88°29W **87** D7
Monkland *Canada* 45°11N 74°52W **83** A10
Monkoto
  Dem. Rep. of the Congo 1°38S 20°35E **54** C4
Monkton *Canada* 43°35N 81°5W **82** C3
Monmouth *U.K.* 51°48N 2°42W **13** F5
Monmouth *Ill., U.S.A.* 40°55N 90°39W **80** E8
Monmouth *Oreg.,*
  U.S.A. 44°51N 123°14W **76** D2
Monmouthshire □ *U.K.* 51°48N 2°54W **13** F5
Mono, Pta. *Nic.* 12°0N 83°30W **88** D3
Mono L. *U.S.A.* 38°1N 119°1W **78** H7
Monolith *U.S.A.* 35°7N 118°22W **79** K8
Monolithos *Greece* 36°7N 27°45E **25** C9
Monongahela *U.S.A.* 40°12N 79°56W **82** F5
Monópoli *Italy* 40°57N 17°18E **22** D7
Monos I. *Trin. & Tob.* 10°42N 61°44W **93** K15
Monroe *Ga., U.S.A.* 33°47N 83°43W **85** E13
Monroe *La., U.S.A.* 32°30N 92°7W **84** E8
Monroe *Mich., U.S.A.* 41°55N 83°24W **81** E12
Monroe *N.C., U.S.A.* 34°59N 80°33W **85** D14
Monroe *N.Y., U.S.A.* 41°20N 74°11W **83** E10
Monroe *Utah, U.S.A.* 38°38N 112°7W **76** G7
Monroe *Wash., U.S.A.* 47°51N 121°58W **78** C5
Monroe *Wis., U.S.A.* 42°36N 89°38W **80** D9
Monroe City *U.S.A.* 39°39N 91°44W **80** F8
Monroeton *U.S.A.* 41°43N 76°29W **83** E8
Monroeville *Ala.,*
  U.S.A. 31°31N 87°20W **85** F11
Monroeville *Pa., U.S.A.* 40°26N 79°45W **82** F5
Monrovia *Liberia* 6°18N 10°47W **50** G3
Mons *Belgium* 50°27N 3°58E **15** D3
Monse *Indonesia* 4°7S 123°15E **37** E6
Mont-de-Marsan *France* 43°54N 0°31W **20** E3
Mont-Joli *Canada* 48°37N 68°10W **73** C6
Mont-Laurier *Canada* 46°35N 75°30W **72** C4
Mont-Louis *Canada* 49°15N 65°44W **73** C6
Mont-St-Michel, Le
  France 48°40N 1°30W **20** B3
Mont-Tremblant △
  Canada 46°30N 74°30W **72** C5
Montagne d'Ambre △
  Madag. 12°37S 49°8E **57** A8
Montagu *S. Africa* 33°45S 20°8E **56** E3
Montagu I. *Antarctica* 58°25S 26°20W **5** B1
Montague *Canada* 46°10N 62°39W **73** C7
Montague, I. *Mexico* 31°45N 114°48W **86** A2
Montague Ra. *Australia* 27°15S 119°30E **61** E2
Montague Sd. *Australia* 14°28S 125°20E **60** B4
Montalbán *Spain* 40°50N 0°45W **21** B5
Montalvo *U.S.A.* 34°15N 119°12W **79** L7
Montana *Bulgaria* 43°27N 23°16E **23** C10
Montana *Peru* 6°0S 73°0W **92** E4
Montana □ *U.S.A.* 47°0N 110°0W **76** C9
Montaña Clara, I.
  Canary Is. 29°17N 13°33W **24** E6
Montargis *France* 48°0N 2°43E **20** C5
Montauban *France* 44°2N 1°21E **20** D4
Montauk *U.S.A.* 41°3N 71°57W **83** E13
Montauk Pt. *U.S.A.* 41°4N 71°51W **83** E13
Montbéliard *France* 47°31N 6°48E **20** C7
Montceau-les-Mines
  France 46°40N 4°23E **20** C6
Montclair *U.S.A.* 40°49N 74°12W **83** F10
Monte Alegre *Brazil* 2°0S 54°0W **93** D8
Monte Azul *Brazil* 15°9S 42°53W **93** G10
Monte-Carlo *Monaco* 43°44N 7°25E **20** E7
Monte Caseros
  Argentina 30°10S 57°50W **94** C4

Monte Comán *Argentina* 34°40S 67°53W **94** C2
Monte Cristi *Dom. Rep.* 19°52N 71°39W **89** C5
Monte Lindo →
   Paraguay 23°56S 57°12W **94** A4
Monte Patria *Chile* 30°42S 70°58W **94** C1
Monte Quemado
   Argentina 25°53S 62°41W **94** B3
Monte Rio *U.S.A.* 38°28N 123°0W **78** G4
Monte Santu, C. di *Italy* 40°5N 9°44E **22** D3
Monte Vista *U.S.A.* 37°35N 106°9W **77** H10
Monteagudo *Argentina* 27°14S 54°8W **95** B5
Montebello *Canada* 45°40N 74°55W **72** C5
Montebello Is. *Australia* 20°30S 115°45E **60** D2
Montecarlo *Argentina* 26°34S 54°47W **95** B5
Montecito *U.S.A.* 34°26N 119°40W **79** L7
Montecristo *Italy* 42°20N 10°19E **22** C4
Montego Bay *Jamaica* 18°28N 77°55W **88** a
Montélimar *France* 44°33N 4°45E **20** D6
Montello *U.S.A.* 43°48N 89°20W **80** D9
Montemorelos *Mexico* 25°12N 99°49W **87** B5
Montenegro *Brazil* 29°39S 51°29W **95** B5
Montenegro ☐ *Europe* 42°40N 19°20E **23** C8
Montepuez *Mozam.* 13°8S 38°59E **55** E4
Montepuez → *Mozam.* 12°32S 40°27E **55** E5
Monterey *U.S.A.* 36°37N 121°55W **78** J5
Monterey B. *U.S.A.* 36°45N 122°0W **78** J5
Montería *Colombia* 8°46N 75°53W **92** B3
Monteros *Argentina* 27°11S 65°30W **94** B3
Monterrey *Mexico* 25°40N 100°19W **86** B4
Montes Azules ∆ *Mexico* 16°21N 91°3W **87** D6
Montes Claros *Brazil* 16°30S 43°50W **93** G10
Montesano *U.S.A.* 46°59N 123°36W **78** D3
Montesilvano *Italy* 42°29N 14°8E **22** C6
Montevideo *Uruguay* 34°50S 56°11W **95** C4
Montevideo *U.S.A.* 44°57N 95°43W **80** C6
Montezuma *U.S.A.* 41°35N 92°32W **80** E7
Montezuma Castle △
   U.S.A. 34°39N 111°45W **77** J8
Montgomery *U.K.* 52°34N 3°8W **13** E4
Montgomery Ala.,
   U.S.A. 32°23N 86°19W **85** E11
Montgomery Pa., *U.S.A.* 41°10N 76°53W **82** E8
Montgomery W. Va.,
   U.S.A. 38°11N 81°19W **81** F13
Montgomery City
   U.S.A. 38°59N 91°30W **80** F8
Monticello Ark., *U.S.A.* 33°38N 91°47W **84** E9
Monticello Fla., *U.S.A.* 30°33N 83°52W **85** F13
Monticello Ind., *U.S.A.* 40°45N 86°46W **80** E10
Monticello Iowa, *U.S.A.* 42°15N 91°12W **80** D8
Monticello Ky., *U.S.A.* 36°50N 84°51W **81** G11
Monticello Minn., *U.S.A.* 45°18N 93°48W **80** C7
Monticello Miss., *U.S.A.* 31°33N 90°7W **85** F9
Monticello N.Y., *U.S.A.* 41°39N 74°42W **83** E10
Monticello Utah, *U.S.A.* 37°52N 109°21W **77** H9
Montijo *Portugal* 38°41N 8°54W **21** C1
Montilla *Spain* 37°36N 4°40W **21** D3
Montluçon *France* 46°22N 2°36E **20** C5
Montmagny *Canada* 46°58N 70°34W **73** C5
Montmartre *Canada* 50°14N 103°27W **71** C8
Montmorillon *France* 46°26N 0°50E **20** C4
Monto *Australia* 24°52S 151°6E **62** C5
Montongbuwoh
   Indonesia 8°33S 116°4E **37** K19
Montoro *Spain* 38°1N 4°27W **21** C3
Montour Falls *U.S.A.* 42°21N 76°51W **82** D8
Montoursville *U.S.A.* 41°15N 76°55W **82** E8
Montpelier Idaho,
   U.S.A. 42°19N 111°18W **76** E8
Montpelier Vt., *U.S.A.* 44°16N 72°35W **83** B12
Montpellier *France* 43°37N 3°52E **20** E5
Montréal *Canada* 45°30N 73°33W **83** A11
Montreal → *Canada* 47°14N 84°39W **72** C3
Montréal L. *Canada* 54°20N 105°45W **71** C7
Montreal Lake *Canada* 54°3N 105°46W **71** C7
Montreux *Switz.* 46°26N 6°55E **20** C7
Montrose *U.K.* 56°44N 2°27W **11** E6
Montrose Colo., *U.S.A.* 38°29N 107°53W **76** G10
Montrose Pa., *U.S.A.* 41°50N 75°53W **83** E9
Monts, Pte. des *Canada* 49°20N 67°12W **73** C6
Montserrat ☑ *W. Indies* 16°40N 62°10W **89** C7
Montuiri *Spain* 39°34N 2°59E **24** B9
Monywa *Burma* 22°7N 95°11E **41** H19
Monza *Italy* 45°35N 9°16E **20** D8
Monze *Zambia* 16°17S 27°29E **55** F2
Monze, C. *Pakistan* 24°47N 66°37E **42** G2
Monzón *Spain* 41°52N 0°10E **21** B6
Mooers *U.S.A.* 44°58N 73°35W **83** B11
Mooi → *S. Africa* 28°45S 30°34E **57** D5
Mooi River *S. Africa* 29°13S 29°50E **57** D4
Moomba *Australia* 28°6S 140°12E **63** A3
Moonah → *Australia* 22°3S 138°33E **62** C2
Moonda, L. *Australia* 25°52S 140°25E **62** D3
Moonie *Australia* 27°46S 150°20E **63** D5
Moonie → *Australia* 29°19S 148°43E **63** D4
Moonta *Australia* 34°6S 137°32E **63** E2
Moora *Australia* 30°37S 115°58E **61** F2
Moorcroft *U.S.A.* 44°16N 104°57W **76** D11
Moore → *Australia* 31°22S 115°30E **61** F2
Moore, L. *Australia* 29°50S 117°35E **61** E2
Moore Falls *Canada* 44°48N 78°48W **82** B6
Moore Park *Australia* 24°43S 152°17E **62** C5
Moore Res. *U.S.A.* 44°20N 71°53W **83** B13
Moore River ∆ *Australia* 31°7S 115°52E **61** F2
Moorea *French Polynesia* 17°30S 149°50W **59** d
Moorefield *U.S.A.* 39°4N 78°58W **81** F14
Moorfoot Hills *U.K.* 55°44N 3°8W **11** F5
Moorhead *U.S.A.* 46°53N 96°45W **80** B5
Moorpark *U.S.A.* 34°17N 118°53W **79** L8
Mooreesburg *S. Africa* 33°6S 18°38E **56** E2
Moorrinya ∆ *Australia* 21°42S 144°58E **62** C3
Moose → *Canada* 51°20N 80°25W **72** B3
Moose → *Canada* 43°38N 75°24W **83** C9
Moose Creek *Canada* 45°15N 74°58W **83** A10
Moose Factory *Canada* 51°16N 80°32W **72** B3
Moose Jaw *Canada* 50°24N 105°30W **71** C7
Moose Jaw → *Canada* 50°34N 105°18W **71** C7

Moose Lake *Canada* 53°46N 100°8W **71** C8
Moose Lake *U.S.A.* 46°27N 92°46W **80** B7
Moose Mountain △
   Canada 49°48N 102°25W **71** D8
Moosehead L. *U.S.A.* 45°38N 69°40W **81** C19
Mooselookmeguntic L.
   U.S.A. 44°55N 70°49W **83** B14
Moosilauke, Mt. *U.S.A.* 44°3N 71°40W **83** B13
Moosomin *Canada* 50°9N 101°40W **71** C8
Moosonee *Canada* 51°17N 80°39W **72** B3
Moosup *U.S.A.* 41°43N 71°53W **83** E13
Mopane *S. Africa* 22°37S 29°52E **57** C4
Mopeia Velha *Mozam.* 17°30S 35°40E **55** F4
Mopipi *Botswana* 21°6S 24°55E **56** C3
Mopoi *C.A.R.* 5°6N 26°54E **54** A2
Mopti *Mali* 14°30N 4°0W **50** F5
Moqor *Afghan.* 32°50N 67°42E **42** C2
Moquegua *Peru* 17°15S 70°46W **92** G4
Mora *Sweden* 61°2N 14°38E **8** F16
Mora Minn., *U.S.A.* 45°53N 93°18W **80** C7
Mora N. Mex., *U.S.A.* 35°58N 105°20W **77** J11
Moradabad *India* 28°50N 78°50E **43** E8
Morafenobe *Madag.* 17°50S 44°53E **57** B7
Moramanga *Madag.* 18°56S 48°12E **57** B8
Moran Kans., *U.S.A.* 37°55N 95°10W **80** G6
Moran Wyo., *U.S.A.* 43°50N 110°31W **76** E8
Moranbah *Australia* 22°1S 148°6E **62** C4
Morant Bay *Jamaica* 17°53N 76°25W **88** a
Morant Cays *Jamaica* 17°22N 76°0W **88** C4
Morant Pt. *Jamaica* 17°55N 76°12W **88** a
Morar *India* 26°14N 78°14E **42** F8
Morar, L. *U.K.* 56°57N 5°40W **11** E3
Moratuwa *Sri Lanka* 6°45N 79°55E **40** R11
Morava → *Serbia* 44°36N 21°4E **23** B9
Morava → *Slovak Rep.* 48°10N 16°59E **17** D9
Moravia *U.S.A.* 42°43N 76°25W **83** D8
Moravian Hts. = Českomoravská
   Vrchovina *Czech Rep.* 49°30N 15°40E **16** D8
Morawa *Australia* 29°13S 116°0E **61** E2
Morawhanna *Guyana* 8°30N 59°40W **92** B7
Moray ☐ *U.K.* 57°31N 3°18W **11** D5
Moray Firth *U.K.* 57°40N 3°52W **11** D5
Morbi *India* 22°50N 70°42E **42** H4
Morden *Canada* 49°15N 98°10W **71** D9
Mordovian Republic =
   Mordvinia ☐ *Russia* 54°20N 44°30E **18** D7
Mordvinia ☐ *Russia* 54°20N 44°30E **18** D7
Moreau → *U.S.A.* 45°18N 100°43W **80** C3
Morebeng *S. Africa* 23°30S 29°55E **57** C4
Morecambe *U.K.* 54°5N 2°52W **12** C5
Morecambe B. *U.K.* 54°7N 3°0W **12** C5
Moree *Australia* 29°28S 149°54E **63** D4
Morehead *U.S.A.* 38°11N 83°26W **81** F12
Morehead City *U.S.A.* 34°43N 76°43W **85** H7
Morel → *India* 26°13N 76°36E **42** F7
Morelia *Mexico* 19°42N 101°7W **86** D4
Morella *Australia* 23°0S 143°52E **62** C3
Morella *Spain* 40°35N 0°5W **21** B5
Morelos *Mexico* 26°42N 107°40W **86** B3
Morelos ☐ *Mexico* 18°45N 99°0W **87** D5
Moremi △ *Botswana* 19°18S 23°10E **56** B3
Morena *India* 26°30N 78°4E **42** F8
Morena, Sierra *Spain* 38°20N 4°0W **21** C3
Moreno Valley *U.S.A.* 33°56N 117°14W **79** M10
Moresby I. *Canada* 52°30N 131°40W **70** C2
Moreton I. *Australia* 27°10S 153°25E **63** D5
Moreton Island △
   Australia 27°2S 153°24E **63** D5
Morgan *U.S.A.* 41°2N 111°41W **76** F8
Morgan City *U.S.A.* 29°42N 91°12W **84** G9
Morgan Hill *U.S.A.* 37°8N 121°39W **78** H5
Morganfield *U.S.A.* 37°41N 87°55W **80** G10
Morganton *U.S.A.* 35°45N 81°41W **85** D14
Morgantown *U.S.A.* 39°38N 79°57W **81** F14
Morgenzon *S. Africa* 26°45S 29°36E **57** D4
Morghak *Iran* 29°7N 57°54E **45** D8
Morhar → *India* 25°29N 85°11E **43** G11
Mori *Japan* 42°6N 140°35E **30** C10
Moriarty *U.S.A.* 34°59N 106°3W **77** J10
Morice L. *Canada* 53°50N 127°40W **70** C3
Morinville *Canada* 53°49N 113°41W **70** C6
Morioka *Japan* 39°45N 141°8E **30** E10
Moris *Mexico* 28°10N 108°32W **86** B3
Morlaix *France* 48°36N 3°52W **20** B2
Mornington *Australia* 38°15S 145°5E **63** F4
Mornington, I. *Chile* 49°50S 75°30W **96** F1
Mornington I. *Australia* 16°30S 139°30E **62** B2
Moro *Pakistan* 26°40N 68°0E **42** F2
Moro → *Pakistan* 29°42N 67°22E **42** E2
Moro G. *Phil.* 6°30N 123°0E **37** C6
Morocco ■ *N. Afr.* 32°0N 5°50W **50** B4
Morogoro *Tanzania* 6°50S 37°40E **54** D4
Morogoro ☐ *Tanzania* 8°0S 37°0E **54** D4
Moroleón *Mexico* 20°8N 101°12W **86** C4
Morombe *Madag.* 21°45S 43°22E **57** C7
Moron *Argentina* 34°39S 58°37W **94** C4
Morón *Cuba* 22°8N 78°39W **88** B4
Mörön *Mongolia* 49°38N 100°9E **32** B4
Morón de la Frontera
   Spain 37°6N 5°28W **21** D3
Morona → *Peru* 4°40S 77°10W **92** D3
Morondava *Madag.* 20°17S 44°17E **57** C7
Morongo Valley *U.S.A.* 34°3N 116°37W **79** L10
Moroni *Comoros Is.* 11°40S 43°16E **53** a
Moroni *U.S.A.* 39°32N 111°35W **76** G8
Morotai *Indonesia* 2°10N 128°30E **37** D7
Moroto *Uganda* 2°28N 34°42E **54** B3
Moroto, Mt. *Uganda* 2°30N 34°43E **54** B3
Morpeth *Canada* 42°23N 81°50W **82** D3
Morpeth *U.K.* 55°10N 1°41W **12** B6
Morphou *Cyprus* 35°12N 32°59E **25** D11
Morphou Bay *Cyprus* 35°15N 32°50E **25** D11
Morrilton *U.S.A.* 35°9N 92°44W **84** D8
Morrinhos *Brazil* 17°45S 49°10W **93** G9
Morrinsville *N.Z.* 37°40S 175°32E **59** B5
Morris *Canada* 49°25N 97°22W **71** D9
Morris Ill., *U.S.A.* 41°22N 88°26W **80** E9

Morris Minn., *U.S.A.* 45°35N 95°55W **80** C6
Morris N.Y., *U.S.A.* 42°33N 75°15W **83** D9
Morris Pa., *U.S.A.* 41°35N 77°17W **82** E7
Morris, Mt. *Australia* 26°9S 131°4E **61** E5
Morris Jesup, Kap
   Greenland 83°40N 34°0W **66** A16
Morrisburg *Canada* 44°55N 75°7W **83** B9
Morristown Ariz.,
   U.S.A. 33°51N 112°37W **77** K7
Morristown N.J., *U.S.A.* 40°48N 74°29W **83** F10
Morristown N.Y., *U.S.A.* 44°35N 75°39W **83** B9
Morristown Tenn.,
   U.S.A. 36°13N 83°18W **85** C13
Morrisville N.Y., *U.S.A.* 42°53N 75°35W **83** D9
Morrisville Pa., *U.S.A.* 40°13N 74°47W **83** F10
Morrisville Vt., *U.S.A.* 44°34N 72°36W **83** B12
Morro, Pta. *Chile* 27°6S 71°0W **94** B1
Morro Bay *U.S.A.* 35°22N 120°51W **78** K6
Morro del Jable *Canary Is.* 28°3N 14°23W **24** F5
Morro Jable, Pta. de
   Canary Is. 28°2N 14°20W **24** F5
Morrocoy △ *Venezuela* 10°48N 68°13W **89** D6
Morrosquillo, G. de
   Colombia 9°35N 75°40W **88** E4
Morrumbene *Mozam.* 23°31S 35°16E **57** C6
Morshansk *Russia* 53°28N 41°50E **18** D7
Morteros *Argentina* 30°50S 62°0W **94** C3
Mortlach *Canada* 50°27N 106°4W **71** C7
Mortlake *Australia* 38°5S 142°50E **63** F3
Morton Tex., *U.S.A.* 33°44N 102°46W **84** E3
Morton Wash., *U.S.A.* 46°34N 122°17W **78** D4
Moruga *Trin. & Tob.* 10°4N 61°16W **93** K15
Morundah *Australia* 34°57S 146°19E **63** E4
Moruya *Australia* 35°58S 150°3E **63** F5
Morvan *France* 47°5N 4°3E **20** C6
Morven *Australia* 26°22S 147°5E **63** D4
Morvern *U.K.* 56°38N 5°44W **11** E3
Morwell *Australia* 38°10S 146°22E **63** F4
Morzhovets, Ostrov
   Russia 66°44N 42°35E **18** A7
Moscos Is. *Burma* 14°0N 97°30E **38** F1
Moscow = Moskva
   Russia 55°45N 37°37E **18** C6
Moscow Idaho, *U.S.A.* 46°44N 117°0W **76** C5
Moscow Pa., *U.S.A.* 41°20N 75°31W **83** E9
Mosel → *Europe* 50°22N 7°36E **20** A7
Moselle = Mosel →
   Europe 50°22N 7°36E **20** A7
Moses Lake *U.S.A.* 47°8N 119°17W **76** C4
Mosgiel *N.Z.* 45°53S 170°21E **59** F3
Moshaweng → *S. Africa* 26°35S 22°50E **56** D3
Moshchnyy, Ostrov
   Russia 60°1N 27°50E **9** F22
Moshi *Tanzania* 3°22S 37°18E **54** C4
Moshupa *Botswana* 24°46S 25°29E **56** C4
Mosjøen *Norway* 65°51N 13°12E **8** D15
Moskenesøya *Norway* 67°58N 13°0E **8** C15
Moskenstraumen
   Norway 67°47N 12°45E **8** C15
Moskva *Russia* 55°45N 37°37E **18** C6
Mosomane *Botswana* 24°2S 26°19E **56** C4
Mosonmagyaróvár
   Hungary 47°52N 17°18E **17** E9
Mosquera *Colombia* 2°35N 78°24W **92** C3
Mosquero *U.S.A.* 35°47N 103°58W **77** J12
Mosquitia *Honduras* 15°20N 84°10W **88** C3
Mosquito Coast = Mosquitia
   Honduras 15°20N 84°10W **88** C3
Mosquito Creek L.
   U.S.A. 41°18N 80°46W **82** E4
Mosquito L. *Canada* 62°35N 103°20W **71** A8
Mosquitos, G. de los
   Panama 9°15N 81°10W **88** E3
Moss *Norway* 59°27N 10°40E **9** G14
Moss Vale *Australia* 34°32S 150°25E **63** E5
Mossbank *Canada* 49°56N 105°56W **71** D7
Mossburn *N.Z.* 45°41S 168°15E **59** F2
Mosselbaai *S. Africa* 34°11S 22°8E **56** E3
Mossendjo *Congo* 2°55S 12°42E **52** E2
Mossgiel *Australia* 33°15S 144°5E **63** E3
Mossman *Australia* 16°21S 145°15E **62** B4
Mossoró *Brazil* 5°10S 37°15W **93** E11
Mossuril *Mozam.* 14°58S 40°42E **55** E5
Most *Czech Rep.* 50°31N 13°38E **16** C7
Mosta *Malta* 35°55N 14°26E **25** C1
Mostaganem *Algeria* 35°54N 0°5E **50** A6
Mostar *Bos.-H.* 43°22N 17°50E **23** C7
Mostardas *Brazil* 31°2S 50°51W **95** C5
Mostiska = Mostyska
   Ukraine 49°48N 23°4E **17** D12
Mosty = Masty *Belarus* 53°27N 24°38E **17** B13
Mostyska *Ukraine* 49°48N 23°4E **17** D12
Mosul = Al Mawşil *Iraq* 36°15N 43°5E **44** B4
Motagua → *Guatemala* 15°44N 88°14W **88** C2
Motala *Sweden* 58°32N 15°1E **9** G16
Motaze *Mozam.* 24°48S 32°52E **57** C5
Moth *India* 25°43N 78°57E **43** G8
Motherwell *U.K.* 55°47N 3°58W **11** F5
Motihari *India* 26°30N 84°55E **43** F11
Motozintla de Mendoza
   Mexico 15°22N 92°14W **87** D6
Motril *Spain* 36°31N 3°37W **21** D4
Mott *U.S.A.* 46°23N 102°20W **80** B2
Motueka *N.Z.* 41°7S 173°1E **59** D4
Motueka → *N.Z.* 41°5S 173°1E **59** D4
Motul *Mexico* 21°6N 89°17W **87** C7
Mouchalagane →
   Canada 50°56N 68°41W **73** B6
Moudros *Greece* 39°50N 25°18E **23** E11
Mouila *Gabon* 1°50S 11°0E **52** E2
Moulamein *Australia* 35°3S 144°1E **63** F3
Moule à Chique, C.
   St. Lucia 13°43N 60°57W **89** f
Mouliana *Greece* 35°10N 25°59E **25** D7
Moulins *France* 46°35N 3°19E **20** C5
Moulmein *Burma* 16°30N 97°40E **41** L20

Moulouya, O. → *Morocco* 35°5N 2°25W **50** B5
Moultrie *U.S.A.* 31°11N 83°47W **85** F13
Moultrie, L. *U.S.A.* 33°20N 80°5W **85** E14
Mound City Mo., *U.S.A.* 40°7N 95°14W **80** E6
Mound City S. Dak.,
   U.S.A. 45°44N 100°4W **80** C3
Moundou *Chad* 8°40N 16°10E **51** G9
Moundsville *U.S.A.* 39°55N 80°44W **82** G4
Moung *Cambodia* 12°46N 103°27E **38** F4
Mount Airy *U.S.A.* 36°31N 80°37W **85** C14
Mount Albert *Canada* 44°8N 79°19W **82** B5
Mount Aspiring △ *N.Z.* 44°19S 168°47E **59** F2
Mount Barker S. Austral.,
   Australia 35°5S 138°52E **63** F2
Mount Barker W. Austral.,
   Australia 34°38S 117°40E **61** F2
Mount Bellew Bridge
   Ireland 53°28N 8°31W **10** C3
Mount Brydges *Canada* 42°54N 81°29W **82** D3
Mount Burr *Australia* 37°34S 140°26E **63** F3
Mount Carmel = Ha Karmel △
   Israel 32°45N 35°5E **46** C4
Mount Carmel Ill.,
   U.S.A. 38°25N 87°46W **80** F10
Mount Carmel Pa.,
   U.S.A. 40°47N 76°26W **83** F8
Mount Clemens *U.S.A.* 42°35N 82°53W **82** D2
Mount Coolon *Australia* 21°25S 147°25E **62** C4
Mount Darwin *Zimbabwe* 16°47S 31°38E **55** F3
Mount Desert I. *U.S.A.* 44°21N 68°20W **81** C19
Mount Dora *U.S.A.* 28°48N 81°38W **85** G14
Mount Edziza △
   Canada 57°30N 130°45W **70** B2
Mount Elgon △ E. Afr. 1°4N 34°42E **54** B3
Mount Field △ *Australia* 42°39S 146°35E **63** G4
Mount Fletcher S. Africa 30°40S 28°30E **57** E4
Mount Forest *Canada* 43°59N 80°43W **82** C4
Mount Frankland △
   Australia 31°47S 116°37E **60** F2
Mount Gambier
   Australia 37°50S 140°46E **63** F3
Mount Garnet *Australia* 17°37S 145°6E **62** B4
Mount Holly *U.S.A.* 39°59N 74°47W **83** G10
Mount Holly Springs
   U.S.A. 40°7N 77°12W **82** F7
Mount Hope N.S.W.,
   Australia 32°51S 145°51E **63** E4
Mount Hope S. Austral.,
   Australia 34°7S 135°23E **63** E2
Mount Isa *Australia* 20°42S 139°26E **62** C2
Mount Jewett *U.S.A.* 41°44N 78°39W **82** E6
Mount Kaputar △
   Australia 30°16S 150°10E **63** E5
Mount Kenya △ *Kenya* 0°7S 37°21E **54** C4
Mount Kilimanjaro △
   Tanzania 3°2S 37°19E **54** C4
Mount Kisco *U.S.A.* 41°12N 73°44W **83** E11
Mount Laguna *U.S.A.* 32°52N 116°25W **79** N10
Mount Larcom
   Australia 23°48S 150°59E **62** C5
Mount Lofty Ranges
   Australia 34°35S 139°5E **63** E2
Mount Magnet *Australia* 28°2S 117°47E **61** E2
Mount Maunganui
   N.Z. 37°40S 176°14E **59** B6
Mount Molloy *Australia* 16°42S 145°20E **62** B4
Mount Morgan
   Australia 23°40S 150°25E **62** C5
Mount Morris *U.S.A.* 42°44N 77°52W **82** D7
Mount Pearl *Canada* 47°31N 52°47W **73** C9
Mount Penn *U.S.A.* 40°20N 75°54W **83** F9
Mount Perry *Australia* 25°13S 151°42E **63** D5
Mount Pleasant Iowa,
   U.S.A. 40°58N 91°33W **80** E8
Mount Pleasant Mich.,
   U.S.A. 43°36N 84°46W **81** D11
Mount Pleasant Pa.,
   U.S.A. 40°9N 79°33W **82** F5
Mount Pleasant S.C.,
   U.S.A. 32°47N 79°52W **85** E15
Mount Pleasant Tenn.,
   U.S.A. 35°32N 87°12W **85** D11
Mount Pleasant Tex.,
   U.S.A. 33°9N 94°58W **84** E7
Mount Pleasant Utah,
   U.S.A. 39°33N 111°27W **76** G8
Mount Pocono *U.S.A.* 41°7N 75°22W **83** E9
Mount Rainier △
   U.S.A. 46°55N 121°50W **78** D5
Mount Revelstoke △
   Canada 51°5N 118°30W **70** C5
Mount Robson △ *Canada* 53°0N 119°0W **70** C5
Mount St. Helens △
   U.S.A. 46°14N 122°11W **78** D4
Mount Selinda *Zimbabwe* 20°24S 32°43E **57** C5
Mount Shasta *U.S.A.* 41°19N 122°19W **76** F2
Mount Signal *U.S.A.* 32°39N 115°37W **79** N11
Mount Sterling Ill.,
   U.S.A. 39°59N 90°45W **80** F8
Mount Sterling Ky.,
   U.S.A. 38°4N 83°56W **81** F12
Mount Surprise
   Australia 18°10S 144°17E **62** B3
Mount Union *U.S.A.* 40°23N 77°53W **82** F7
Mount Upton *U.S.A.* 42°26N 75°23W **83** D9
Mount Vernon Ill.,
   U.S.A. 38°19N 88°55W **80** F9
Mount Vernon Ind.,
   U.S.A. 37°56N 87°54W **80** G10
Mount Vernon N.Y.,
   U.S.A. 40°54N 73°49W **83** F11
Mount Vernon Ohio,
   U.S.A. 40°23N 82°29W **82** F2
Mount Vernon Wash.,
   U.S.A. 48°25N 122°20W **78** B4
Mount William △
   Australia 40°56S 148°14E **63** G4

Morris, Mt. 45°40N 3°23W **13** F4

Mountain Ash *U.K.* 51°40N 3°23W **13** F4
Mountain Center
   U.S.A. 33°42N 116°44W **79** M10
Mountain City Nev.,
   U.S.A. 41°50N 115°58W **76** F6
Mountain City Tenn.,
   U.S.A. 36°29N 81°48W **85** C14
Mountain Dale *U.S.A.* 41°41N 74°32W **83** E10
Mountain Grove *U.S.A.* 37°8N 92°16W **80** G7
Mountain Home Ark.,
   U.S.A. 36°20N 92°23W **84** C8
Mountain Home Idaho,
   U.S.A. 43°8N 115°41W **76** E6
Mountain Iron *U.S.A.* 47°32N 92°37W **80** B7
Mountain Pass *U.S.A.* 35°29N 115°35W **79** K11
Mountain View Ark.,
   U.S.A. 35°52N 92°7W **84** D8
Mountain View Calif.,
   U.S.A. 37°23N 122°5W **78** H4
Mountain View Hawai'i,
   U.S.A. 19°33N 155°7W **74** b
Mountain Zebra △
   S. Africa 32°14S 25°27E **56** E4
Mountainair *U.S.A.* 34°31N 106°15W **77** J10
Mountlake Terrace
   U.S.A. 47°47N 122°18W **78** C4
Mountmellick *Ireland* 53°7N 7°20W **10** C4
Mountrath *Ireland* 53°0N 7°28W **10** D4
Moura *Australia* 24°35S 149°58E **62** C4
Moura *Brazil* 1°32S 61°38W **92** D6
Moura *Portugal* 38°7N 7°30W **21** C2
Mourdi, Dépression du
   Chad 18°10N 23°0E **51** E10
Mourilyan *Australia* 17°35S 146°3E **62** B4
Mourne → *U.K.* 54°52N 7°26W **10** B4
Mourne Mts. *U.K.* 54°10N 6°0W **10** B5
Mournies *Greece* 35°29N 24°1E **25** D6
Mouscron *Belgium* 50°45N 3°12E **15** D3
Moussoro *Chad* 13°41N 16°35E **51** F9
Moutong *Indonesia* 0°28N 121°13E **37** D6
Movas *Mexico* 28°10N 109°25W **86** B3
Moville *Ireland* 55°11N 7°3W **10** A4
Mowandjum *Australia* 17°22S 123°40E **60** C3
Moy → *Ireland* 54°8N 9°8W **10** B2
Moya *Comoros Is.* 12°18S 44°18E **53** a
Moyale *Kenya* 3°30N 39°0E **54** G4
Moyen Atlas *Morocco* 33°0N 5°0W **50** B4
Moyo *Indonesia* 8°10S 117°40E **36** F5
Moyobamba *Peru* 6°0S 77°0W **92** E3
Moyyero → *Russia* 68°44N 103°42E **29** C11
Moyynqum *Kazakhstan* 44°12N 71°0E **32** C2
Moyynty *Kazakhstan* 47°10N 73°18E **28** E8
Mozambique = Moçambique
   Mozam. 15°3S 40°42E **55** F5
Mozambique ■ *Africa* 19°0S 35°0E **55** F4
Mozambique Chan.
   Africa 17°30S 42°30E **57** B7
Mozdok *Russia* 43°45N 44°48E **19** F7
Mozdūrān *Iran* 36°9N 60°35E **45** B9
Mozhnābād *Iran* 34°7N 60°6E **45** C9
Mozyr = Mazyr *Belarus* 51°59N 29°15E **17** B15
Mpanda *Tanzania* 6°23S 31°1E **54** D3
Mphoengs *Zimbabwe* 21°10S 27°51E **57** C4
Mpika *Zambia* 11°51S 31°25E **55** E3
Mpulungu *Zambia* 8°51S 31°5E **55** D3
Mpumalanga *S. Africa* 29°50S 30°33E **57** D5
Mpumalanga ☐ *S. Africa* 26°0S 30°0E **57** D5
Mpwapwa *Tanzania* 6°23S 36°30E **54** D4
Mqanduli *S. Africa* 31°49S 28°45E **57** E4
Msaken *Tunisia* 35°49N 10°33E **51** A8
Msambansovu *Zimbabwe* 15°50S 30°3E **55** F3
M'sila → *Algeria* 35°30N 4°29E **50** A6
Msoro *Zambia* 13°35S 31°50E **55** E3
Mstislavl = Mstsislaw
   Belarus 54°0N 31°50E **17** A16
Mstsislaw *Belarus* 54°0N 31°50E **17** A16
Mtama *Tanzania* 10°17S 39°21E **55** E4
Mtamvuna = Mthamvuna →
   S. Africa 31°6S 30°12E **57** E5
Mthamvuna → *S. Africa* 31°6S 30°12E **57** E5
Mthatha *S. Africa* 31°36S 28°49E **57** E4
Mtilikwe → *Zimbabwe* 21°9S 31°30E **55** G3
Mtito Andei *Kenya* 2°41S 38°10E **54** C4
Mtubatuba *S. Africa* 28°30S 32°8E **57** D5
Mtwalume *S. Africa* 30°30S 30°38E **57** E5
Mtwara-Mikindani
   Tanzania 10°20S 40°20E **55** E5
Mu Gia, Deo *Vietnam* 17°40N 105°47E **38** D5
Mu Ko Chang △
   Thailand 11°59N 102°22E **39** G4
Mu Us Shamo *China* 39°0N 109°0E **34** E5
Muang Chiang Rai = Chiang Rai
   Thailand 19°52N 99°50E **38** C2
Muang Khong *Laos* 14°7N 105°51E **38** E5
Muang Lamphun
   Thailand 18°40N 99°2E **38** C2
Muang Mai *Thailand* 8°5N 98°21E **39** a
Muang Pak Beng *Laos* 19°54N 101°8E **38** C3
Muar *Malaysia* 2°3N 102°34E **39** L4
Muarabungo *Indonesia* 1°28S 102°52E **36** E2
Muaraenim *Indonesia* 3°40S 103°50E **36** E2
Muarajuloi *Indonesia* 0°12S 114°3E **36** E4
Muarakaman *Indonesia* 0°2S 116°45E **36** E5
Muaratembesi *Indonesia* 1°42S 103°8E **36** E2
Muaratewe *Indonesia* 0°58S 114°52E **36** E4
Mubarraz = Al Mubarraz
   Si. Arabia 25°30N 49°40E **45** E6
Mubende *Uganda* 0°33N 31°22E **54** B3
Mubi *Nigeria* 10°18N 13°16E **51** F8
Mucajaí → *Brazil* 2°25N 60°52W **92** C6
Muchachos, Roque de los
   Canary Is. 28°44N 17°52W **24** F2
Muchinga Mts. *Zambia* 11°30S 31°30E **55** E3
Muck *U.K.* 56°50N 6°15W **11** E2
Muckadilla *Australia* 26°35S 148°23E **63** D4

Muckle Flugga *U.K.* 60°51N 0°54W **11** A8
Mucuri *Brazil* 18°0S 39°36W **93** G11
Mucusso *Angola* 18°1S 21°25E **56** B3
Muda *Canary Is.* 28°34N 13°57W **24** F6
Mudanjiang *China* 44°38N 129°30E **35** B15
Mudanya *Turkey* 40°25N 28°50E **23** D13
Muddy Cr. → *U.S.A.* 38°24N 110°42W **76** G8
Mudgee *Australia* 32°32S 149°31E **63** E4
Mudjatik → *Canada* 56°1N 107°36W **71** B7
Muecate *Mozam.* 14°55S 39°40E **55** E4
Mueda *Mozam.* 11°36S 39°28E **55** E4
Mueller Ranges
  Australia 18°18S 126°46E **60** C4
Muende *Mozam.* 14°28S 33°0E **55** E3
Muerto, Mar *Mexico* 16°10N 94°10W **87** D6
Mufulira *Zambia* 12°32S 28°15E **55** E2
Mufumbiro Range *Africa* 1°25S 29°30E **54** C2
Mughal Sarai *India* 25°18N 83°7E **43** G10
Mughayrā *Si. Arabia* 29°17N 37°41E **44** D3
Mugi *Japan* 33°40N 134°25E **31** H7
Mugila, Mts.
  Dem. Rep. of the Congo 7°0S 28°50E **54** D2
Muğla *Turkey* 37°15N 28°22E **23** F13
Mugu *Nepal* 29°45N 82°30E **43** E10
Muhammad, Râs *Egypt* 27°44N 34°16E **44** E2
Muhammad Qol *Sudan* 20°53N 37°9E **51** D13
Muhammadabad *India* 26°4N 83°25E **43** F10
Muhesi → *Tanzania* 7°0S 35°50E **54** D4
Mühlhausen *Germany* 51°12N 10°27E **16** C6
Mühlig Hofmann fjell
  Antarctica 72°30S 5°0E **5** D3
Muhos *Finland* 64°47N 25°59E **8** D21
Muhu *Estonia* 58°36N 23°11E **9** G20
Muhutwe *Tanzania* 1°35S 31°45E **54** C3
Mui Wo *China* 22°16N 113°59E **33** G10
Muine Bheag *Ireland* 52°42N 6°58W **10** D5
Muir, L. *Australia* 34°30S 116°40E **61** F2
Muir of Ord *U.K.* 57°32N 4°28W **11** D4
Mujeres, I. *Mexico* 21°13N 86°43W **88** B2
Mujnak = Muynak
  Uzbekistan 43°44N 59°10E **28** E6
Muka, Tanjung *Malaysia* 5°28N 100°11E **39** c
Mukacheve *Ukraine* 48°27N 22°45E **17** D12
Mukachevo = Mukacheve
  Ukraine 48°27N 22°45E **17** D12
Mukah *Malaysia* 2°55N 112°5E **36** D4
Mukandwara *India* 24°49N 75°59E **42** G6
Mukawwa, Geziret
  Egypt 23°55N 35°53E **44** F2
Mukdahan *Thailand* 16°32N 104°43E **38** D5
Mukden = Shenyang
  China 41°48N 123°27E **35** D12
Mukerian *India* 31°57N 75°37E **42** D6
Mukinbudin *Australia* 30°55S 118°5E **61** F2
Mukishi
  Dem. Rep. of the Congo 8°30S 24°44E **55** D1
Mukomuko *Indonesia* 2°30S 101°10E **36** E2
Mukomwenze
  Dem. Rep. of the Congo 6°49S 27°15E **54** D2
Muktsar *India* 30°30N 74°30E **42** D6
Mukur = Moqor *Afghan.* 32°50N 67°42E **42** C2
Mukutuwa → *Canada* 53°10N 97°24W **71** C9
Mukwela *Zambia* 17°0S 26°40E **55** F2
Mula *Spain* 38°3N 1°33W **21** C5
Mula → *Pakistan* 27°57N 67°36E **42** F2
Mulange
  Dem. Rep. of the Congo 3°40S 27°10E **54** C2
Mulanje, Mt. *Malawi* 16°2S 35°33E **55** F4
Mulchén *Chile* 37°45S 72°20W **94** D1
Mulde → *Germany* 51°53N 12°15E **16** C7
Mule Creek Junction
  U.S.A. 43°23N 104°13W **76** E11
Muleba *Tanzania* 1°50S 31°37E **54** C3
Mulegé *Mexico* 26°53N 111°59W **86** B2
Muleshoe *U.S.A.* 34°13N 102°43W **84** D3
Mulgrave *Canada* 45°38N 61°31W **73** C7
Mulhacén *Spain* 37°4N 3°20W **21** D4
Mulhouse *France* 47°40N 7°20E **20** C7
Mulifanua *Samoa* 13°50S 171°59W **59** b
Muling *China* 44°35N 130°10E **35** B16
Mull *U.K.* 56°25N 5°56W **11** E3
Mull, Sound of *U.K.* 56°30N 5°50W **11** E3
Mullaittivu *Sri Lanka* 9°15N 80°49E **40** Q12
Mullen *U.S.A.* 42°3N 101°1W **80** D3
Mullens *U.S.A.* 37°35N 81°23W **81** G13
Muller, Pegunungan
  Indonesia 0°30N 113°30E **36** D4
Mullet Pen. *Ireland* 54°13N 10°2W **10** B1
Mullewa *Australia* 28°29S 115°30E **61** E2
Mulligan → *Australia* 25°0S 139°0E **62** D2
Mullingar *Ireland* 53°31N 7°21W **10** C4
Mullins *U.S.A.* 34°12N 79°15W **85** D15
Mullumbimby *Australia* 28°30S 153°30E **63** D5
Mulobezi *Zambia* 16°45S 25°7E **55** F2
Mulonga Plain *Zambia* 16°20S 22°40E **53** H4
Mulroy B. *Ireland* 55°15N 7°46W **10** A4
Multan *Pakistan* 30°15N 71°36E **42** D4
Mulumbe, Mts.
  Dem. Rep. of the Congo 8°40S 27°30E **55** D2
Mulungushi Dam
  Zambia 14°48S 28°48E **55** E2
Mulvane *U.S.A.* 37°29N 97°15W **80** G5
Mumbai *India* 18°56N 72°50E **40** K8
Mumbwa *Zambia* 15°0S 27°0E **55** F2
Mumias *Kenya* 0°20N 34°29E **54** C3
Mun → *Thailand* 15°19N 105°30E **38** E5
Muna *Indonesia* 5°0S 122°30E **37** F6
Munabao *India* 25°45N 70°17E **42** G4
Munamagi *Estonia* 57°43N 27°4E **9** H22
Muncan *Indonesia* 8°34S 115°11E **37** K18
Muncar *Indonesia* 8°26S 114°20E **37** J17
München *Germany* 48°8N 11°34E **16** D6
Munchen-Gladbach =
  Mönchengladbach
  Germany 51°11N 6°27E **16** C4
Muncho Lake *Canada* 59°0N 125°50W **70** B3
Munch'ŏn *N. Korea* 39°14N 127°19E **35** E14

Muncie *U.S.A.* 40°12N 85°23W **81** E11
Muncoonie L. West
  Australia 25°12S 138°40E **62** D2
Mundabbera *Australia* 25°36S 151°18E **63** D5
Munday *U.S.A.* 33°27N 99°38W **84** E5
Münden *Germany* 51°25N 9°38E **16** C5
Mundiwindi *Australia* 23°47S 120°9E **60** D3
Mundo Novo *Brazil* 11°50S 40°29W **93** F10
Mundra *India* 22°54N 69°48E **42** H3
Mundrabilla *Australia* 31°52S 127°51E **61** F4
Mungallala *Australia* 26°28S 147°34E **63** D4
Mungallala Cr. →
  Australia 28°53S 147°5E **63** D4
Mungana *Australia* 17°8S 144°27E **62** B3
Mungaoli *India* 24°24N 78°7E **42** G8
Mungari *Mozam.* 17°12S 33°30E **55** F3
Mungbere
  Dem. Rep. of the Congo 2°36N 28°28E **54** B2
Mungeli *India* 22°4N 81°41E **43** H9
Munger *India* 25°23N 86°30E **43** G12
Mungeranie *Australia* 28°1S 138°39E **63** A2
Mungkan Kandju △
  Australia 13°35S 142°52E **62** A3
Munich = München
  Germany 48°8N 11°34E **16** D6
Munising *U.S.A.* 46°25N 86°40W **80** B10
Munku-Sardyk *Russia* 51°45N 100°20E **29** D11
Munnsville *U.S.A.* 42°58N 75°35W **83** D9
Muñoz Gamero, Pen.
  Chile 52°30S 73°5W **96** G2
Munroe L. *Canada* 59°13N 98°35W **71** B9
Münster *Germany* 51°58N 7°37E **16** C4
Munster □ *Ireland* 52°18N 8°44W **10** D3
Muntadgin *Australia* 31°45S 118°33E **61** F2
Muntok *Indonesia* 2°5S 105°10E **36** E3
Munyama *Zambia* 16°5S 28°31E **55** F2
Muong Beng *Laos* 20°23N 101°46E **38** B3
Muong Boum *Vietnam* 22°24N 102°48E **38** A4
Muong Et *Laos* 20°49N 104°1E **38** B5
Muong Hai *Laos* 21°3N 101°49E **38** B3
Muong Hiem *Laos* 20°5N 103°22E **38** B4
Muong Houn *Laos* 20°8N 101°23E **38** B3
Muong Hung *Vietnam* 20°56N 103°53E **38** B4
Muong Kau *Laos* 15°6N 105°47E **38** E5
Muong Khao *Laos* 19°38N 103°32E **38** C4
Muong Khoua *Laos* 21°5N 102°31E **38** B4
Muong Liep *Laos* 18°29N 101°40E **38** C3
Muong May *Laos* 14°49N 106°56E **38** E6
Muong Ngeun *Laos* 20°36N 101°3E **38** B3
Muong Ngoi *Laos* 20°43N 102°41E **38** B4
Muong Nhie *Vietnam* 22°12N 102°28E **38** A4
Muong Nong *Laos* 16°22N 106°30E **38** D6
Muong Ou Tay *Laos* 22°7N 101°48E **38** A3
Muong Oua *Laos* 18°18N 101°20E **38** C3
Muong Peun *Laos* 20°13N 103°52E **38** B4
Muong Phalane *Laos* 16°39N 105°34E **38** D5
Muong Phieng *Laos* 19°6N 101°32E **38** C3
Muong Phine *Laos* 16°32N 106°2E **38** D6
Muong Sai *Laos* 20°42N 101°59E **38** B3
Muong Saiapoun *Laos* 18°24N 101°31E **38** C3
Muong Sen *Vietnam* 19°24N 104°8E **38** C5
Muong Sing *Laos* 21°11N 101°9E **38** B3
Muong Son *Laos* 20°27N 103°19E **38** B4
Muong Soui *Laos* 19°33N 102°52E **38** C4
Muong Va *Laos* 21°53N 102°19E **38** B4
Muong Xia *Vietnam* 20°19N 104°50E **38** B5
Muonio *Finland* 67°57N 23°40E **8** C20
Muonio älv = Muonionjoki →
  Finland 67°11N 23°34E **8** C20
Muonioälven = Muonionjoki →
  Finland 67°11N 23°34E **8** C20
Muonionjoki → *Finland* 67°11N 23°34E **8** C20
Muping *China* 37°22N 121°36E **35** F11
Muqdisho *Somali Rep.* 2°2N 45°25E **47** G4
Mur → *Austria* 46°18N 16°52E **17** E9
Murakami *Japan* 38°14N 139°29E **30** E9
Murallón, Cerro *Chile* 49°48S 73°30W **96** F2
Muranda *Rwanda* 1°52S 29°20E **54** C2
Murang'a *Kenya* 0°45S 37°9E **54** C4
Murashi *Russia* 59°30N 49°0E **18** C8
Murat → *Turkey* 38°46N 40°0E **19** G7
Muratlı *Turkey* 41°10N 27°29E **23** D12
Murayama *Japan* 38°30N 140°25E **30** E10
Murchison → *Australia* 27°45S 114°0E **61** E1
Murchison, Mt.
  Antarctica 73°25S 166°20E **5** D11
Murchison Falls *Uganda* 2°15N 31°30E **54** B3
Murchison Falls △
  Uganda 2°17N 31°48E **54** B3
Murchison Ra. *Australia* 20°0S 134°10E **62** C1
Murchison Rapids
  Malawi 15°55S 34°35E **55** F3
Murchison Roadhouse
  Australia 27°39S 114°14E **61** E1
Murcia *Spain* 38°5N 1°10W **21** D5
Murcia □ *Spain* 37°50N 1°30W **21** D5
Murdo *U.S.A.* 43°53N 100°43W **80** D3
Murdoch Pt. *Australia* 14°37S 144°55E **62** A3
Mureş → *Romania* 46°15N 20°13E **17** E11
Mureşul = Mureş →
  Romania 46°15N 20°13E **17** E11
Murewa *Zimbabwe* 17°39S 31°47E **57** B5
Murfreesboro *N.C.*,
  U.S.A. 36°27N 77°6W **85** C16
Murfreesboro *Tenn.*,
  U.S.A. 35°51N 86°24W **85** D11
Murgap *Tajikistan* 38°10N 74°2E **28** F8
Murgap → *Turkmenistan* 38°18N 61°12E **45** B9
Murgenella *Australia* 11°34S 132°56E **60** B5
Murgha Kibzai *Pakistan* 30°44N 69°25E **42** D3
Murghob = Murgap
  Tajikistan 38°10N 74°2E **28** F8
Murgon *Australia* 26°15S 151°54E **63** D5
Muri *India* 23°22N 85°52E **43** H11
Muria *Indonesia* 6°36S 110°53E **37** G14
Muriaé *Brazil* 21°8S 42°23W **95** A7

Muriel Mine *Zimbabwe* 17°14S 30°40E **55** F3
Müritz *Germany* 53°25N 12°42E **16** B7
Murliganj *India* 25°54N 86°59E **43** G12
Murmansk *Russia* 68°57N 33°10E **8** B25
Murmashi *Russia* 68°47N 32°42E **8** B25
Muro *Spain* 39°44N 3°3E **24** B10
Murom *Russia* 55°35N 42°3E **18** C7
Muroran *Japan* 42°25N 141°0E **30** C10
Muroto *Japan* 33°18N 134°9E **31** H7
Muroto-Misaki *Japan* 33°15N 134°10E **31** H7
Murphy *U.S.A.* 43°13N 116°33W **76** E5
Murphys *U.S.A.* 38°8N 120°28W **78** G6
Murray *Ky., U.S.A.* 36°37N 88°19W **80** G9
Murray *Utah, U.S.A.* 40°40N 111°53W **76** F8
Murray → *Australia* 35°20S 139°22E **63** F2
Murray, L. → *Australia* 34°3N 81°13W **85** D14
Murray Bridge *Australia* 35°6S 139°14E **63** F2
Murray Fracture Zone
  Pac. Oc. 35°0N 130°0W **65** D14
Murray Harbour *Canada* 46°0N 62°28W **73** C7
Murray River △
  Australia 34°23S 140°32E **63** E3
Murraysburg *S. Africa* 31°58S 23°47E **56** E3
Murree *Pakistan* 33°56N 73°28E **42** C5
Murrieta *U.S.A.* 33°33N 117°13W **79** M9
Murrumbidgee →
  Australia 34°43S 143°12E **63** E3
Murrumburrah
  Australia 34°32S 148°22E **63** E4
Murrurundi *Australia* 31°42S 150°51E **63** E5
Murshidabad *India* 24°11N 88°19E **43** G13
Murtle L. *Canada* 52°8N 119°38W **70** C5
Murtoa *Australia* 36°35S 142°28E **63** F3
Murungu *Tanzania* 4°12S 31°10E **54** C3
Mururoa
  French Polynesia 21°52S 138°55W **65** K14
Murwara *India* 23°46N 80°28E **43** H9
Murwillumbah
  Australia 28°18S 153°27E **63** D5
Mürzzuschlag *Austria* 47°36N 15°41E **16** E8
Muş *Turkey* 38°45N 41°30E **44** B4
Mûsa, Gebel *Egypt* 28°33N 33°59E **44** D2
Musa Khel *Pakistan* 30°59N 69°52E **42** D3
Mûsa Qal'eh *Afghan.* 32°20N 64°50E **40** C4
Musafirkhana *India* 26°22N 81°48E **43** F9
Musala *Bulgaria* 42°13N 23°37E **23** C10
Musala *Indonesia* 1°41N 98°28E **36** D1
Musan *N. Korea* 42°12N 129°12E **35** C15
Musangu
  Dem. Rep. of the Congo 10°28S 23°55E **55** E1
Musasa *Tanzania* 3°25S 31°30E **54** C3
Musay'īd *Qatar* 25°0N 51°33E **45** E6
Muscat = Masqaţ *Oman* 23°37N 58°36E **47** C6
Muscatine *U.S.A.* 41°25N 91°3W **80** E8
Muscle Shoals *U.S.A.* 34°45N 87°40W **85** D11
Musengezi = Unsengedsi →
  Zimbabwe 15°43S 31°14E **55** F3
Musgrave Harbour
  Canada 49°27N 53°58W **73** C9
Musgrave Ranges
  Australia 26°0S 132°0E **61** E5
Mushie
  Dem. Rep. of the Congo 2°56S 16°55E **52** E3
Musi → *Indonesia* 2°20S 104°56E **36** E2
Musina *S. Africa* 22°20S 30°5E **57** C5
Muskeg → *Canada* 60°20N 123°20W **70** A4
Muskegon *U.S.A.* 43°14N 86°16W **80** D10
Muskegon → *U.S.A.* 43°14N 86°21W **80** D10
Muskegon Heights
  U.S.A. 43°12N 86°16W **80** D10
Muskogee *U.S.A.* 35°45N 95°22W **84** D7
Muskoka, L. *Canada* 45°0N 79°25W **82** B5
Muskoka Falls *Canada* 44°59N 79°17E **82** B5
Muskwa → *Canada* 58°47N 122°48W **70** B4
Muslīmiyah *Syria* 36°19N 37°12E **44** B3
Musofu *Zambia* 13°30S 29°0E **55** E2
Musoma *Tanzania* 1°30S 33°48E **54** C3
Musquaro, L. *Canada* 50°38N 61°5W **73** B7
Musquodoboit Harbour
  Canada 44°50N 63°9W **73** D7
Musselburgh *U.K.* 55°57N 3°2W **11** F5
Musselshell → *U.S.A.* 47°21N 107°57W **76** C10
Mussende *Angola* 10°32S 16°5E **52** G3
Mussoorie *India* 30°27N 78°6E **42** D8
Mussuco *Angola* 17°2S 19°3E **56** B2
Mustafakemalpaşa
  Turkey 40°2N 28°24E **23** D13
Mustang *Nepal* 29°10N 83°55E **43** E10
Musters, L. *Argentina* 45°20S 69°25W **96** F3
Musudan *N. Korea* 40°50N 129°43E **35** D15
Muswellbrook *Australia* 32°16S 150°56E **63** E5
Mût *Egypt* 25°28N 28°58E **51** C11
Mut *Turkey* 36°40N 33°28E **44** B2
Mutanda *Mozam.* 21°0S 33°34E **57** C5
Mutanda *Zambia* 12°24S 26°13E **55** E2
Mutare *Zimbabwe* 18°58S 32°38E **55** F3
Mutawintji △ *Australia* 31°10S 142°30E **63** E3
Mutha *Kenya* 1°48S 38°26E **54** C4
Muting *Indonesia* 7°23S 140°20E **37** F10
Mutki = Mirtağ *Turkey* 38°23N 41°56E **44** B4
Mutoko *Zimbabwe* 17°24S 32°13E **57** B5
Mutomo *Kenya* 1°27N 32°12E **54** B3
Mutoray *Russia* 60°56N 101°0E **29** C11
Mutsamudu *Comoros Is.* 12°10S 44°25E **53** a
Mutshatsha
  Dem. Rep. of the Congo 10°35S 24°20E **55** E1
Mutsu *Japan* 41°5N 140°55E **30** D10
Mutsu-Wan *Japan* 41°5N 140°55E **30** D10
Muttaburra *Australia* 22°38S 144°29E **62** C3
Mutton I. *Ireland* 52°49N 9°32W **10** D2
Mutuáli *Mozam.* 14°55S 37°0E **55** E4
Muweilih *Egypt* 30°42N 34°19E **46** E3
Muy Muy *Nic.* 12°39N 85°36W **88** D2
Muyinga *Burundi* 3°14S 30°33E **54** C3
Muynak *Uzbekistan* 43°44N 59°10E **28** E6
Muyunkum, Peski = Moyynqum
  Kazakhstan 44°12N 71°0E **32** B2

Muz Tag *China* 36°25N 87°25E **32** C3
Muzaffarabad *Pakistan* 34°25N 73°30E **43** B5
Muzaffargarh *Pakistan* 30°5N 71°14E **42** D4
Muzaffarnagar *India* 29°26N 77°40E **42** E7
Muzaffarpur *India* 26°7N 85°23E **43** F11
Muzhi *Russia* 65°25N 64°40E **18** A11
Muztag-Ata *China* 38°17N 75°7E **32** C2
Muztagh-Ata *China* 38°17N 75°7E **32** C2
Mvuma *Zimbabwe* 19°16S 30°30E **55** F3
Mvurwi *Zimbabwe* 17°0S 30°57E **55** F3
Mwabvi △ *Malawi* 16°42S 35°0E **55** F3
Mwadui *Tanzania* 3°26S 33°32E **54** C3
Mwali = Mohéli
  Comoros Is. 12°20S 43°40E **53** a
Mwambo *Tanzania* 10°30S 40°22E **55** E5
Mwandi *Zambia* 17°30S 24°51E **55** F1
Mwanza
  Dem. Rep. of the Congo 7°55S 26°43E **54** D2
Mwanza *Tanzania* 2°30S 32°58E **54** C3
Mwanza *Zambia* 16°58S 24°28E **55** F1
Mwanza □ *Tanzania* 2°0S 33°0E **54** C3
Mwaya *Tanzania* 9°32S 33°55E **55** D3
Mweelrea *Ireland* 53°39N 9°49W **10** C2
Mweka
  Dem. Rep. of the Congo 4°50S 21°34E **52** E4
Mwene-Ditu
  Dem. Rep. of the Congo 6°35S 22°27E **52** F4
Mwenezi *Zimbabwe* 21°15S 30°48E **55** G3
Mwenezi → *Mozam.* 22°40S 31°50E **55** G3
Mwenga
  Dem. Rep. of the Congo 3°1S 28°28E **54** C2
Mweru, L. *Zambia* 9°0S 28°40E **55** D2
Mweru Wantipa △
  Zambia 8°39S 29°25E **55** D2
Mweza Range *Zimbabwe* 21°0S 30°0E **55** G3
Mwilambwe
  Dem. Rep. of the Congo 8°7S 25°5E **54** D2
Mwimbi *Tanzania* 8°38S 31°39E **55** D3
Mwingi *Kenya* 0°56S 38°4E **54** C4
Mwinilunga *Zambia* 11°43S 24°25E **55** E1
My Tho *Vietnam* 10°29N 106°23E **39** G6
Myajlar *India* 26°15N 70°20E **42** F4
Myanaung *Burma* 18°18N 95°22E **41** K19
Myanmar = Burma ■
  Asia 21°0N 96°30E **41** J20
Myaungmya *Burma* 16°30N 94°40E **41** L19
Mycenæ = Mikines
  Greece 37°43N 22°46E **23** F10
Myeik Kyunzu *Burma* 11°30N 97°30E **39** G1
Myerstown *U.S.A.* 40°22N 76°19W **83** F8
Myingyan *Burma* 21°30N 95°20E **41** J19
Myitkyina *Burma* 25°24N 97°26E **41** G20
Mykines *Færoe Is.* 62°7N 7°35W **8** E9
Mykolayiv *Ukraine* 46°58N 32°0E **19** E5
Mykonos *Greece* 37°30N 25°25E **23** F11
Mymensingh *Bangla.* 24°45N 90°24E **41** G17
Mynydd Du *U.K.* 51°52N 3°50W **13** F4
Mýrdalsjökull *Iceland* 63°40N 19°6W **8** E4
Myrtle Beach *U.S.A.* 33°42N 78°53W **85** E15
Myrtle Creek *U.S.A.* 43°1N 123°17W **76** E2
Myrtle Point *U.S.A.* 43°4N 124°8W **76** E1
Myrtou *Cyprus* 35°18N 33°4E **25** D12
Mysia *Turkey* 39°50N 27°0E **23** E12
Mysore = Karnataka □
  India 13°15N 77°0E **40** N10
Mysore *India* 12°17N 76°41E **40** N10
Mystic *U.S.A.* 41°21N 71°58W **83** E13
Myszków *Poland* 50°45N 19°22E **17** C10
Mytishchi *Russia* 55°50N 37°50E **18** C6
Mývatn *Iceland* 65°36N 17°0W **8** D5
Mzimba *Malawi* 11°55S 33°39E **55** E3
Mzimkulu → *S. Africa* 30°44S 30°28E **57** E5
Mzimvubu → *S. Africa* 31°38S 29°33E **57** E4
Mzuzu *Malawi* 11°30S 33°55E **55** E3

N

Na Hearadh = Harris
  U.K. 57°50N 6°55W **11** D2
Na Noi *Thailand* 18°19N 100°43E **38** C3
Na Phao *Laos* 17°35N 105°44E **38** D5
Na Sam *Vietnam* 22°3N 106°37E **38** A6
Na San *Vietnam* 21°12N 104°2E **38** B5
Na Thon *Thailand* 9°32N 99°56E **39** b
Naab → *Germany* 49°1N 12°2E **16** D6
Naantali *Finland* 60°29N 22°2E **9** F20
Naas *Ireland* 53°12N 6°40W **10** C5
Nababeep *S. Africa* 29°36S 17°46E **56** D2
Nabadwip = Navadwip
  India 23°34N 88°20E **43** H13
Nabawa *Australia* 28°30S 114°48E **61** E1
Nabberu, L. *Australia* 25°50S 120°30E **61** E3
Naberezhnyye Chelny
  Russia 55°42N 52°19E **18** C9
Nabeul *Tunisia* 36°30N 10°44E **51** A8
Nabha *India* 30°26N 76°14E **42** D7
Nabīd *Iran* 29°40N 57°38E **45** D8
Nabire *Indonesia* 3°15S 135°26E **37** E9
Nabisar *Pakistan* 25°8N 69°40E **42** G3
Nabisipi → *Canada* 50°14N 62°13W **73** B7
Nabiswera *Uganda* 1°27N 32°15E **54** B3
Nāblus = Nābulus
  West Bank 32°14N 35°15E **46** C4
Naboomspruit *S. Africa* 24°32S 28°40E **57** C4
Nābulus *West Bank* 32°14N 35°15E **46** C4
Nacala *Mozam.* 14°32S 40°34E **55** E5
Nacala-Velha *Mozam.* 14°32S 40°34E **55** E5
Nacaome *Honduras* 13°31N 87°30W **88** D2
Nacaroa *Mozam.* 14°22S 39°56E **55** E4
Naches *U.S.A.* 46°44N 120°42W **76** C3
Naches → *U.S.A.* 46°38N 120°31W **78** D6
Nachicapau, L. *Canada* 56°40N 68°5W **73** A6
Nachingwea *Tanzania* 10°23S 38°49E **55** E4
Nachna *India* 27°34N 71°41E **42** F4
Nacimiento, L. *U.S.A.* 35°46N 120°53W **78** K6
Naco *Mexico* 31°19N 109°56W **86** A3

Nacogdoches *U.S.A.* 31°36N 94°39W **84** F7
Nácori Chico *Mexico* 29°40N 108°57W **86** B3
  Mexico 30°25N 109°38W **86** A3
Nacozari de García
  Mexico 30°25N 109°38W **86** A3
Nacula *Fiji* 16°54S 177°27E **59** a
Nådendal = Naantali
  Finland 60°29N 22°2E **9** F20
Nadi *Fiji* 17°42S 177°20E **59** a
Nadiad *India* 22°41N 72°56E **42** H5
Nador *Morocco* 35°14N 2°58W **50** B5
Nadur *Malta* 36°2N 14°18E **25** C1
Nadūshan *Iran* 32°2N 53°35E **45** C7
Nadvirna *Ukraine* 48°37N 24°30E **17** D13
Nadvoitsy *Russia* 63°52N 34°14E **18** B5
Nadvornaya = Nadvirna
  Ukraine 48°37N 24°30E **17** D13
Nadym *Russia* 65°35N 72°42E **28** C8
Nadym → *Russia* 66°12N 72°0E **28** C8
Nærbø *Norway* 58°40N 5°39E **9** G11
Næstved *Denmark* 55°13N 11°44E **9** J14
Nafpaktos *Greece* 38°24N 21°50E **23** E9
Nafplio *Greece* 37°33N 22°50E **23** F10
Naft-e Safīd *Iran* 31°40N 49°17E **45** D6
Naftshahr *Iran* 34°0N 45°30E **44** C5
Nafud Desert = An Nafūd
  Si. Arabia 28°15N 41°0E **44** D4
Naga *Phil.* 13°38N 123°15E **37** B6
Nagagami *Canada* 50°23N 84°20W **72** B3
Nagahama *Japan* 35°23N 136°16E **31** G8
Nagai *Japan* 38°6N 140°2E **30** E10
Nagaland □ *India* 26°0N 94°30E **41** G19
Nagano *Japan* 36°40N 138°10E **31** F9
Nagano □ *Japan* 36°15N 138°0E **31** F9
Nagaoka *Japan* 37°27N 138°51E **31** F9
Nagappattinam *India* 10°46N 79°51E **40** P11
Nagar → *Bangla.* 24°27N 89°12E **43** G13
Nagar Parkar *Pakistan* 24°28N 70°46E **42** G4
Nagasaki *Japan* 32°47N 129°50E **31** H4
Nagasaki □ *Japan* 32°50N 129°40E **31** H4
Nagato *Japan* 34°19N 131°5E **31** G5
Nagaur *India* 27°15N 73°45E **42** F5
Nagda *India* 23°27N 75°25E **42** H6
Nagercoil *India* 8°12N 77°26E **40** Q10
Nagina *India* 29°30N 78°30E **43** E8
Nāgīneh *Iran* 34°20N 57°15E **45** C8
Nagir *Pakistan* 36°12N 74°42E **43** A6
Nagles Mts. *Ireland* 52°8N 8°30W **10** D3
Nagod *India* 24°34N 80°36E **43** G9
Nagoorin *Australia* 24°17S 151°15E **62** C5
Nagorno-Karabakh □
  Azerbaijan 39°55N 46°45E **44** B5
Nagornyy *Russia* 55°58N 124°57E **29** D13
Nagoya *Japan* 35°10N 136°50E **31** G8
Nagpur *India* 21°8N 79°10E **40** J11
Nagua *Dom. Rep.* 19°23N 69°50W **89** C6
Naguabo *Puerto Rico* 18°13N 65°44W **89** d
Nagykanizsa *Hungary* 46°28N 17°0E **17** E9
Nagykőrös *Hungary* 47°5N 19°48E **17** E10
Naha *Japan* 26°13N 127°42E **31** L3
Nahan *India* 30°33N 77°18E **42** D7
Nahanni △ *Canada* 61°36N 125°41W **70** A4
Nahanni Butte *Canada* 61°2N 123°31W **70** A4
Nahargarh *Mad. P., India* 24°10N 75°14E **42** G6
Nahargarh *Raj., India* 24°55N 76°50E **42** G7
Nahariyya *Israel* 33°1N 35°5E **44** C2
Nahāvand *Iran* 34°10N 48°22E **45** C6
Nahuel Huapi, L.
  Argentina 41°0S 71°32W **96** E2
Nahuelbuta △ *Chile* 37°44S 72°57W **94** D1
Nai Yong *Thailand* 8°14N 98°22E **39** a
Naicá *Mexico* 27°53N 105°31W **86** B3
Naicam *Canada* 52°30N 104°30W **71** C8
Naikoon △ *Canada* 53°55N 131°55W **70** C2
Naimisharanya *India* 27°21N 80°30E **43** F9
Naimona'nyi Feng *Nepal* 30°26N 81°18E **43** D9
Nain *Canada* 56°34N 61°40W **73** A7
Nā'īn *Iran* 32°54N 53°0E **45** C7
Naini Tal *India* 29°30N 79°30E **43** E8
Nainpur *India* 22°30N 80°10E **43** H9
Nainwa *India* 25°46N 75°51E **42** G6
Nairai *Fiji* 17°49S 179°15E **59** a
Nairn *U.K.* 57°35N 3°53W **11** D5
Nairobi *Kenya* 1°17S 36°48E **54** C4
Nairobi △ *Kenya* 1°22S 36°50E **54** C4
Naissaar *Estonia* 59°34N 24°29E **9** G21
Naitaba *Fiji* 17°0S 179°16W **59** a
Naivasha *Kenya* 0°40S 36°30E **54** C4
Naivasha, L. *Kenya* 0°48S 36°20E **54** C4
Najaf = An Najaf *Iraq* 32°3N 44°15E **44** C5
Najafābād *Iran* 32°40N 51°15E **45** C6
Najd *Si. Arabia* 26°30N 42°0E **47** B3
Najibabad *India* 29°40N 78°20E **42** E8
Najin *N. Korea* 42°12N 130°15E **35** C16
Najmah *Si. Arabia* 26°42N 50°6E **45** E6
Najrān *Si. Arabia* 17°34N 44°18E **47** D3
Naju *S. Korea* 35°3N 126°43E **35** G14
Nakadōri-Shima *Japan* 32°57N 129°4E **31** H4
Nakalagba
  Dem. Rep. of the Congo 2°50N 27°58E **54** B2
Nakaminato *Japan* 36°21N 140°36E **31** F10
Nakamura *Japan* 32°59N 132°56E **31** H6
Nakano *Japan* 36°45N 138°22E **31** F9
Nakano-Shima *Japan* 29°51N 129°52E **31** K4
Nakashibetsu *Japan* 43°33N 144°59E **30** C12
Nakfa *Eritrea* 16°40N 38°32E **47** D2
Nakha Yai, Ko *Thailand* 8°3N 98°28E **39** a
Nakhichevan = Naxçıvan
  Azerbaijan 39°12N 45°15E **44** B5
Nakhichevan Rep. = Naxçıvan □
  Azerbaijan 39°25N 45°26E **44** B5
Nakhl *Egypt* 29°55N 33°43E **46** F2
Nakhl-e Taqī *Iran* 27°28N 52°36E **45** E7
Nakhodka *Russia* 42°53N 132°54E **30** C6
Nakhon Nayok
  Thailand 14°12N 101°13E **38** E3
Nakhon Pathom
  Thailand 13°49N 100°3E **38** F3

Nakhon Phanom
  Thailand 17°23N 104°43E **38 D5**
Nakhon Ratchasima
  Thailand 14°59N 102°12E **38 E4**
Nakhon Sawan
  Thailand 15°35N 100°10E **38 E3**
Nakhon Si Thammarat
  Thailand 8°29N 100°0E **39 H3**
Nakhon Thai *Thailand* 17°5N 100°44E **38 D3**
Nakhtarana *India* 23°20N 69°15E **42 H3**
Nakina *Canada* 50°10N 86°40W **72 B2**
Nakodar *India* 31°8N 75°31E **42 D6**
Naktong → *S. Korea* 35°7N 128°57E **35 G15**
Nakuru *Kenya* 0°15S 36°4E **54 C4**
Nakuru, L. *Kenya* 0°23S 36°5E **54 C4**
Nakusp *Canada* 50°20N 117°45W **70 C5**
Nal *Pakistan* 27°40N 66°12E **42 F2**
Nal → *Pakistan* 25°20N 65°30E **42 G1**
Nalázi *Mozam.* 24°3S 33°20E **57 C5**
Nalchik *Russia* 43°30N 43°33E **19 F7**
Nalgonda *India* 17°6N 79°15E **40 L11**
Nalhati *India* 24°17N 87°52E **43 G12**
Naliya *India* 23°16N 68°50E **42 H3**
Nallamalai Hills *India* 15°30N 78°50E **40 M11**
Nalubaale Dam *Uganda* 0°30N 33°5E **54 B3**
Nam Can *Vietnam* 8°46N 104°59E **39 H5**
Nam Co *China* 30°30N 90°45E **32 C4**
Nam Dinh *Vietnam* 20°25N 106°5E **38 B6**
Nam Du, Hon *Vietnam* 9°41N 104°21E **39 H5**
Nam Nao △ *Thailand* 17°5N 101°30E **38 D3**
Nam Ngum Res. *Laos* 18°35N 102°34E **38 C4**
Nam-Phan *Vietnam* 10°30N 106°0E **39 G6**
Nam Phong *Thailand* 16°42N 102°52E **38 D4**
Nam Tha *Laos* 20°58N 101°30E **38 B3**
Nam Tok *Thailand* 14°21N 99°4E **38 E2**
Namacunde *Angola* 17°18S 15°50E **56 B2**
Namacurra *Mozam.* 17°30S 36°50E **57 B6**
Namak, Daryācheh-ye
  Iran 34°30N 52°0E **45 C7**
Namak, Kavir-e *Iran* 34°30N 57°30E **45 C8**
Namakzār, Daryācheh-ye
  Iran 34°0N 60°30E **45 C9**
Namaland *Namibia* 26°0S 17°0E **56 C2**
Namanga *Kenya* 2°33S 36°47E **54 C4**
Namangan *Uzbekistan* 41°0N 71°40E **28 E8**
Namapa *Mozam.* 13°43S 39°50E **55 E4**
Namaqualand *S. Africa* 30°0S 17°25E **56 E2**
Namasagali *Uganda* 1°2N 33°0E **54 B3**
Namber *Indonesia* 1°2S 134°49E **37 E8**
Nambour *Australia* 26°32S 152°58E **63 D5**
Nambouwalu = Nabouwalu
  Fiji 17°0S 178°45E **59 a**
Nambucca Heads
  Australia 30°37S 153°0E **63 E5**
Nambung △ *Australia* 30°30S 115°5E **61 F2**
Namcha Barwa *China* 29°40N 95°10E **32 D4**
Namche Bazar *Nepal* 27°51N 86°47E **43 F12**
Namchonjöm = Nam-ch'on
  N. Korea 38°15N 126°26E **35 E14**
Namecunda *Mozam.* 14°54S 37°37E **55 E4**
Namenalala *Fiji* 17°8S 179°9E **59 a**
Nameponda *Mozam.* 15°50S 39°50E **55 F4**
Nametil *Mozam.* 15°40S 39°21E **55 F4**
Namew L. *Canada* 54°14N 101°56W **71 C8**
Namgia *India* 31°48N 78°40E **43 D8**
Namib Desert *Namibia* 22°30S 15°0E **56 C2**
Namib-Naukluft △
  Namibia 24°40S 15°16E **56 C2**
Namibe *Angola* 15°7S 12°11E **53 H2**
Namibe □ *Angola* 16°35S 12°30E **56 B1**
Namibia ■ *Africa* 22°0S 18°9E **56 C2**
Namibwoestyn = Namib Desert
  Namibia 22°30S 15°0E **56 C2**
Namlea *Indonesia* 3°18S 127°5E **37 E7**
Namoi → *Australia* 30°12S 149°30E **63 E4**
Nampa *U.S.A.* 43°34N 116°34W **76 E5**
Nampo *N. Korea* 38°52N 125°10E **35 E13**
Nampō-Shotō *Japan* 32°0N 140°0E **31 J10**
Nampula *Mozam.* 15°6S 39°15E **55 F4**
Namrole *Indonesia* 3°46S 126°46E **37 E7**
Namse Shankou *China* 30°0N 82°25E **43 E10**
Namsen → *Norway* 64°28N 11°37E **8 D14**
Namsos *Norway* 64°29N 11°30E **8 D14**
Namtok Chat Trakan △
  Thailand 17°17N 100°40E **38 D3**
Namtok Mae Surin △
  Thailand 18°55N 98°2E **38 C2**
Namtsy *Russia* 62°43N 129°37E **29 C13**
Namtu *Burma* 23°5N 97°28E **41 H20**
Namtumbo *Tanzania* 10°30S 36°4E **55 E4**
Namu *Canada* 51°52N 127°50W **70 C3**
Namuka-i-Lau *Fiji* 18°53S 178°37W **59 a**
Namur *Belgium* 50°27N 4°52E **15 D4**
Namur □ *Belgium* 50°17N 5°0E **15 D4**
Namuruputh *Kenya* 4°34N 35°57E **54 B4**
Namutoni *Namibia* 18°49S 16°55E **56 B2**
Namwala *Zambia* 15°44S 26°30E **55 F2**
Namwon *S. Korea* 35°23N 127°23E **35 G14**
Namyang *N. Korea* 42°57N 129°52E **35 C15**
Nan *Thailand* 18°48N 100°46E **38 C3**
Nan → *Thailand* 15°42N 100°9E **38 E3**
Nan-ch'ang = Nanchang
  China 28°42N 115°55E **33 D6**
Nanaimo *Canada* 49°10N 124°0W **70 D4**
Nanam *N. Korea* 41°44N 129°40E **35 D15**
Nanango *Australia* 26°40S 152°0E **63 D5**
Nanao *Japan* 37°0N 137°0E **31 F8**
Nanchang *China* 28°42N 115°55E **33 D6**
Nanching = Nanjing
  China 32°2N 118°47E **33 C6**
Nanchong *China* 30°43N 106°2E **32 C5**
Nancy *France* 48°42N 6°12E **20 B7**
Nanda Devi *India* 30°23N 79°59E **43 D8**
Nanda Devi △ *India* 30°30N 79°50E **43 D8**
Nanda Kot *India* 30°17N 80°5E **43 D9**
Nandan *Japan* 34°10N 134°42E **31 G7**

Nanded *India* 19°10N 77°20E **40 K10**
Nandewar Ra. *Australia* 30°15S 150°35E **63 E5**
Nandi = Nadi *Fiji* 17°42S 177°20E **59 a**
Nandigram *India* 22°1N 87°58E **43 H12**
Nandurbar *India* 21°20N 74°15E **40 J9**
Nang Rong *Thailand* 14°38N 102°48E **38 E4**
Nanga-Eboko *Cameroon* 4°41N 12°22E **52 D2**
Nanga Parbat *Pakistan* 35°10N 74°35E **43 B6**
Nangade *Mozam.* 11°5S 39°36E **55 E4**
Nangapinoh *Indonesia* 0°20S 111°44E **36 E4**
Nangarhār □ *Afghan.* 34°20N 70°0E **40 B7**
Nangatayap *Indonesia* 1°32S 110°34E **36 E4**
Nangeya Mts. *Uganda* 3°30N 33°30E **54 B3**
Nangong *China* 37°23N 115°22E **34 F8**
Nanhuang *China* 36°58N 121°48E **35 F11**
Nanjeko *Zambia* 15°31S 23°30E **55 F1**
Nanjing *China* 32°2N 118°47E **33 C6**
Nanjirinji *Tanzania* 9°41S 39°5E **55 D4**
Nankana Sahib *Pakistan* 31°27N 73°38E **42 D5**
Nanking = Nanjing
  China 32°2N 118°47E **33 C6**
Nankoku *Japan* 33°39N 133°44E **31 H6**
Nanlang *China* 22°30N 113°32E **33 G10**
Nanning *China* 22°48N 108°20E **32 D5**
Nannup *Australia* 33°59S 115°48E **61 F2**
Nanpara *India* 27°52N 81°33E **43 F9**
Nanpi *China* 38°2N 116°45E **34 E9**
Nanping *China* 26°38N 118°10E **33 D6**
Nanripe *Mozam.* 13°52S 38°52E **55 E4**
Nansei-Shotō = Ryūkyū-rettō
  Japan 26°0N 126°0E **31 M3**
Nansen Basin *Arctic* 84°0N 50°0E **4 A10**
Nansen Sd. *Canada* 81°0N 91°0W **69 A10**
Nansha *China* 22°45N 113°34E **33 F10**
Nanshan I. *S. China Sea* 10°45N 115°49E **36 B5**
Nansio *Tanzania* 2°3S 33°4E **54 C3**
Nantes *France* 47°12N 1°33W **20 C3**
Nanticoke *U.S.A.* 41°12N 76°0W **83 E8**
Nanton *Canada* 50°21N 113°46W **70 C6**
Nantong *China* 32°1N 120°52E **33 C7**
Nantou *China* 22°32N 113°55E **33 F10**
Nantucket *U.S.A.* 41°17N 70°6W **81 E18**
Nantucket I. *U.S.A.* 41°16N 70°5W **81 E18**
Nantwich *U.K.* 53°4N 2°31W **12 D5**
Nanty Glo *U.S.A.* 40°28N 78°50W **82 F6**
Nanuku Passage *Fiji* 16°45S 179°15W **59 a**
Nanuque *Brazil* 17°50S 40°21W **93 G10**
Nanusa, Kepulauan
  Indonesia 4°45N 127°1E **37 D7**
Nanutarra Roadhouse
  Australia 22°32S 115°30E **60 D2**
Nanyang *China* 33°11N 112°30E **34 H7**
Nanyuki *Kenya* 0°2N 37°4E **54 B4**
Nao, C. de la *Spain* 38°44N 0°14E **21 C6**
Naococane, L. *Canada* 52°50N 70°45W **73 B5**
Napa *U.S.A.* 38°18N 122°17W **78 G4**
Napa → *U.S.A.* 38°10N 122°19W **78 G4**
Napanee *Canada* 44°15N 77°0W **82 B8**
Napanoch *U.S.A.* 41°44N 74°22W **83 E10**
Nape *Laos* 18°18N 105°6E **38 C5**
Nape Pass = Keo Neua, Deo
  Vietnam 18°23N 105°10E **38 C5**
Napier *N.Z.* 39°30S 176°56E **59 C6**
Napier Broome B.
  Australia 14°2S 126°37E **60 B4**
Napier Pen. *Australia* 12°4S 135°43E **62 A2**
Napierville *Canada* 45°11N 73°25W **83 A11**
Naples = Nápoli *Italy* 40°50N 14°15E **22 D6**
Naples *U.S.A.* 26°8N 81°48W **85 H14**
Napo → *Peru* 3°20S 72°40W **92 D4**
Napo → *N. Dak., U.S.A.* 46°30N 99°46W **80 B4**
Napoleon *Ohio, U.S.A.* 41°23N 84°8W **81 E11**
Nápoli *Italy* 40°50N 14°15E **22 D6**
Napopo
  Dem. Rep. of the Congo 4°15N 28°0E **54 B2**
Naqadeh *Iran* 36°57N 45°23E **44 B5**
Naqb, Ra's an *Jordan* 29°48N 35°44E **46 F4**
Naqqāsh *Iran* 35°40N 49°6E **45 C6**
Nara *Japan* 34°40N 135°49E **31 G7**
Nara *Mali* 15°10N 7°20W **50 E4**
Nara □ *Japan* 34°30N 136°0E **31 G8**
Nara Canal *Pakistan* 24°30N 69°20E **42 G3**
Nara Visa *U.S.A.* 35°37N 103°6W **77 J12**
Naracoorte *Australia* 36°58S 140°45E **63 F3**
Naradhan *Australia* 33°34S 146°17E **63 E4**
Naraini *India* 25°11N 80°29E **43 G9**
Naranjos *Mexico* 21°21N 97°41W **87 C5**
Narasapur *India* 16°26N 81°40E **41 L12**
Narathiwat *Thailand* 6°30N 101°48E **39 J3**
Narayanganj *Bangla.* 23°40N 90°33E **41 H17**
Narayanpet *India* 16°45N 77°30E **40 L10**
Narbonne *France* 43°11N 3°0E **20 E5**
Nardīn *Iran* 37°3N 55°59E **45 B7**
Nardò *Italy* 40°11N 18°2E **23 D8**
Narembeen *Australia* 32°7S 118°24E **61 F2**
Narendranagar *India* 30°10N 78°18E **42 D8**
Nares Str. *Arctic* 80°0N 70°0W **66 A13**
Naretha *Australia* 31°0S 124°45E **61 F3**
Narew → *Poland* 52°26N 20°41E **17 B11**
Nari → *Pakistan* 29°40N 68°0E **42 E2**
Narin *Afghan.* 36°5N 69°0E **40 A6**
Narindra, Helodranon' i
  Madag. 14°55S 47°30E **57 A8**
Nariva Swamp
  Trin. & Tob. 10°26N 61°4W **93 K15**
Narmada → *India* 21°38N 72°36E **42 J5**
Narnaul *India* 28°5N 76°11E **42 E7**
Narodnaya *Russia* 65°5N 59°58E **18 A10**
Narok *Kenya* 1°55S 35°52E **54 C4**
Narooma *Australia* 36°14S 150°4E **63 F5**
Narowal *Pakistan* 32°6N 74°52E **42 C6**
Narrabri *Australia* 30°19S 149°46E **63 E4**
Narran → *Australia* 28°37S 148°12E **63 D4**
Narrandera *Australia* 34°42S 146°31E **63 E4**

Narrogin *Australia* 32°58S 117°14E **61 F2**
Narromine *Australia* 32°12S 148°12E **63 E4**
Narrow Hills △ *Canada* 54°0N 104°37W **71 C8**
Narsimhapur *India* 22°54N 79°14E **43 H8**
Narsinghgarh *India* 23°45N 76°40E **42 H7**
Naruto *Japan* 34°11N 134°37E **31 G7**
Narva *Estonia* 59°23N 28°12E **18 C4**
Narva → *Russia* 59°27N 28°2E **9 G23**
Narva Bay = Narva Laht
  Estonia 59°35N 27°35E **9 G22**
Narva Laht *Estonia* 59°35N 27°35E **9 G22**
Narvik *Norway* 68°28N 17°26E **8 B17**
Narwana *India* 29°39N 76°6E **42 E7**
Naryan-Mar *Russia* 67°42N 53°12E **18 A9**
Narym *Russia* 59°0N 81°30E **28 D9**
Naryn *Kyrgyzstan* 41°26N 75°58E **28 E8**
Naryn Qum *Kazakhstan* 47°30N 49°0E **19 E8**
Nasa *Norway* 66°29N 15°23E **8 C16**
Nasau *Fiji* 17°19S 179°27E **59 a**
Nasca = Nazca *Peru* 14°50S 74°57W **92 F4**
Naseby *N.Z.* 45°1S 170°10E **59 F3**
Naselle *U.S.A.* 46°22N 123°49W **78 D3**
Naser, Buheirat en
  Egypt 23°0N 32°30E **51 D12**
Nashua *Mont., U.S.A.* 48°8N 106°22W **76 B10**
Nashua *N.H., U.S.A.* 42°45N 71°28W **83 D13**
Nashville *Ark., U.S.A.* 33°57N 93°51W **84 E8**
Nashville *Ga., U.S.A.* 31°12N 83°15W **85 F13**
Nashville *Tenn., U.S.A.* 36°10N 86°47W **85 C11**
Nasik *India* 19°58N 73°50E **40 K8**
Nasirabad *India* 26°15N 74°45E **42 F6**
Nasirabad *Pakistan* 28°23N 68°24E **42 E3**
Nasiri = Ahvāz *Iran* 31°20N 48°40E **45 D6**
Nasiriyah = An Nāşirīyah
  Iraq 31°0N 46°15E **44 D5**
Naskaupi → *Canada* 53°47N 60°51W **73 B7**
Naşrābād *Iran* 34°8N 51°26E **45 C6**
Nasriān-e Pā'īn *Iran* 32°52N 46°52E **44 C5**
Nass → *Canada* 55°0N 129°40W **70 C3**
Nassau *Bahamas* 25°5N 77°20W **88 A4**
Nassau *U.S.A.* 42°31N 73°37W **83 D11**
Nassau, B. *Chile* 55°20S 68°0W **96 H3**
Nasser, L. = Naser, Buheirat en
  Egypt 23°0N 32°30E **51 D12**
Nässjö *Sweden* 57°39N 14°42E **9 H16**
Nastapoka → *Canada* 56°55N 76°33W **72 A4**
Nastapoka, Is. *Canada* 56°55N 76°50W **72 A4**
Nata *Botswana* 20°12S 26°12E **56 C4**
Nata → *Botswana* 20°14S 26°10E **56 C4**
Natal *Brazil* 5°47S 35°13W **93 E11**
Natal *Indonesia* 0°35N 99°7E **36 D1**
Natal Drakensberg △
  S. Africa 29°27S 29°30E **57 D4**
Nataŋnz *Iran* 33°30N 51°55E **45 C6**
Natashquan *Canada* 50°14N 61°46W **73 B7**
Natashquan → *Canada* 50°7N 61°50W **73 B7**
Natchez *U.S.A.* 31°34N 91°24W **84 F9**
Natchitoches *U.S.A.* 31°46N 93°5W **84 F8**
Natewa B. *Fiji* 16°35S 179°40E **59 a**
Nathalia *Australia* 36°1S 145°13E **63 F4**
Nathdwara *India* 24°55N 73°50E **42 G5**
Nati, Pta. *Spain* 40°3N 3°50E **24 A10**
Natimuk *Australia* 36°42S 142°0E **63 F3**
Nation → *Canada* 55°30N 123°32W **70 B4**
National City *U.S.A.* 32°40N 117°5W **79 N9**
Natitingou *Benin* 10°20N 1°26E **50 F6**
Natividad, I. *Mexico* 27°52N 115°11W **86 B1**
Natkyizin *Burma* 14°57N 97°59E **38 E1**
Natron, L. *Tanzania* 2°20S 36°0E **54 C4**
Natrona Heights *U.S.A.* 40°37N 79°44W **82 F5**
Natukanaoka Pan
  Namibia 18°40S 15°45E **56 B2**
Natuna Besar, Kepulauan
  Indonesia 4°0N 108°15E **36 D3**
Natuna Is. = Natuna Besar,
  Kepulauan *Indonesia* 4°0N 108°15E **36 D3**
Natuna Selatan, Kepulauan
  Indonesia 2°45N 109°0E **36 D3**
Natural Bridge *U.S.A.* 44°5N 75°30W **83 B9**
Natural Bridges △
  U.S.A. 37°36N 110°0W **77 H9**
Naturaliste, C. *Tas.*,
  Australia 40°50S 148°15E **63 G4**
Naturaliste, C. *W. Austral.*,
  Australia 33°32S 115°0E **61 F2**
Naturaliste Plateau
  Ind. Oc. 34°0S 112°0E **64 L3**
Nau Qala *Afghan.* 34°5N 68°5E **42 B3**
Naugatuck *U.S.A.* 41°30N 73°3W **83 E11**
Naujaat = Repulse Bay
  Canada 66°30N 86°30W **69 C11**
Naumburg *Germany* 51°9N 11°47E **16 C6**
Nauru ■ *Pac. Oc.* 1°0S 166°0E **58 B9**
Naushahra = Nowshera
  Pakistan 34°0N 72°0E **40 C8**
Naushahro *Pakistan* 26°50N 68°7E **42 F3**
Naushon I. *U.S.A.* 41°29N 70°45W **83 E14**
Nausori *Fiji* 18°2S 178°32E **59 a**
Nauta *Peru* 4°31S 73°35W **92 D4**
Nautanwa *India* 27°20N 83°25E **43 F10**
Naute △ *Namibia* 26°55S 17°57E **56 D2**
Nautla *Mexico* 20°13N 96°47W **87 C5**
Nava *Mexico* 28°25N 100°45W **86 B4**
Navadwip *India* 23°34N 88°20E **43 H13**
Navahrudak *Belarus* 53°40N 25°50E **17 B13**
Navajo Res. *U.S.A.* 36°48N 107°36W **77 H10**
Navalmoral de la Mata
  Spain 39°52N 5°33W **21 C3**
Navan = An Uaimh
  Ireland 53°39N 6°41W **10 C5**
Navarin, Mys *Russia* 62°15N 179°5E **29 C18**
Navarino, I. *Chile* 55°0S 67°40W **96 H3**
Navarra □ *Spain* 42°40N 1°40W **21 A5**
Navarre *U.S.A.* 40°43N 81°31W **82 F3**
Navarro *U.S.A.* 39°11N 123°45W **78 F3**
Navasota *U.S.A.* 30°23N 96°5W **84 F6**
Navassa I. *W. Indies* 18°30N 75°0W **89 C5**

Naver → *U.K.* 58°32N 4°14W **11 C4**
Navibandar *India* 21°26N 69°48E **42 J3**
Navidad *Chile* 33°57S 71°50W **94 C1**
Naviraí *Brazil* 23°8S 54°13W **95 A5**
Naviti *Fiji* 17°7S 177°15E **59 a**
Navlakhi *India* 22°58N 70°28E **42 H4**
Navoi *Uzbekistan* 40°9N 65°22E **28 E7**
Navojoa *Mexico* 27°6N 109°26W **86 B3**
Navolato *Mexico* 24°47N 107°42W **86 C3**
Navsari *India* 20°57N 72°59E **40 J8**
Navua *Fiji* 18°12S 178°11E **59 a**
Nawa Kot *Pakistan* 28°21N 71°24E **42 E4**
Nawab Khan *Pakistan* 30°17N 69°12E **42 D3**
Nawabganj *Ut. P., India* 26°56N 81°14E **43 F9**
Nawabganj *Ut. P., India* 28°32N 79°40E **43 E8**
Nawabshah *Pakistan* 26°15N 68°25E **42 F3**
Nawada *India* 24°50N 85°33E **43 G11**
Nawakot *Nepal* 27°55N 85°10E **43 F11**
Nawalgarh *India* 27°50N 75°15E **42 F6**
Nawanshahr *India* 32°33N 74°48E **43 C6**
Nawar, Dasht-i- *Afghan.* 33°52N 68°0E **42 C3**
Nawoiy = Navoi
  Uzbekistan 40°9N 65°22E **28 E7**
Naxçıvan *Azerbaijan* 39°12N 45°15E **44 B5**
Naxçıvan □ *Azerbaijan* 39°25N 45°26E **44 B5**
Naxos *Greece* 37°8N 25°25E **23 F11**
Nay, Mui *Vietnam* 12°55N 109°23E **36 B3**
Nāy Band *Būshehr, Iran* 27°20N 52°40E **45 E7**
Nāy Band *Khorāsān, Iran* 32°20N 57°34E **45 C8**
Nayakhan *Russia* 61°56N 159°0E **29 C16**
Nayarit □ *Mexico* 22°0N 105°0W **86 C4**
Nayau *Fiji* 18°6S 178°10E **59 a**
Nayoro *Japan* 44°21N 142°28E **30 B11**
Naypyidaw *Burma* 19°44N 96°12E **38 C1**
Nayyāl, W. → *Si. Arabia* 28°35N 39°4E **44 D3**
Nazaré *Brazil* 13°2S 39°0W **93 F11**
Nazareth = Nazerat
  Israel 32°42N 35°17E **46 C4**
Nazareth *U.S.A.* 40°44N 75°19W **83 F9**
Nazarovo *Russia* 57°2N 90°40E **29 D10**
Nazas *Mexico* 25°14N 104°8W **86 B4**
Nazas → *Mexico* 25°12N 104°12W **86 B4**
Nazca *Peru* 14°50S 74°57W **92 F4**
Nazca Ridge *Pac. Oc.* 20°0S 80°0W **65 K19**
Naze *Japan* 28°22N 129°27E **31 K4**
Naze, The *U.K.* 51°53N 1°18E **13 F9**
Nazerat *Israel* 32°42N 35°17E **46 C4**
Nāzik *Iran* 39°1N 45°4E **44 B5**
Nazilli *Turkey* 37°55N 28°15E **23 F13**
Nazko *Canada* 53°1N 123°37W **70 C4**
Nazko → *Canada* 53°7N 123°34W **70 C4**
Nazret *Ethiopia* 8°32N 39°22E **47 F2**
Nchanga *Zambia* 12°30S 27°49E **55 E2**
Ncheu *Malawi* 14°50S 34°47E **55 E3**
Ndala *Tanzania* 4°45S 33°15E **54 C3**
Ndalatando *Angola* 9°12S 14°48E **52 F2**
Ndareda *Tanzania* 4°12S 35°30E **54 C4**
Ndélé *C.A.R.* 8°25N 20°36E **52 C4**
Ndjamena *Chad* 12°10N 14°59E **51 F8**
Ndola *Zambia* 13°0S 28°34E **55 E2**
Ndomo → *S. Africa* 26°52S 32°15E **57 D5**
Ndoto Mts. *Kenya* 2°0N 37°0E **54 B4**
Nduguti *Tanzania* 4°18S 34°41E **54 C3**
Neagh, Lough *U.K.* 54°37N 6°25E **10 B5**
Neah Bay *U.S.A.* 48°22N 124°37W **78 B2**
Neale, L. *Australia* 24°15S 130°0E **60 D5**
Neales → *Australia* 28°8S 136°47E **63 D2**
Neapoli *Greece* 35°15N 25°37E **25 D7**
Near Is. *U.S.A.* 52°30N 174°0E **74 a**
Neath *U.K.* 51°39N 3°48W **13 F4**
Neath Port Talbot □
  U.K. 51°42N 3°45W **13 F4**
Nebine Cr. → *Australia* 29°27S 146°56E **63 D4**
Nebitdag = Balkanabat
  Turkmenistan 39°30N 54°22E **45 B7**
Nebo *Australia* 21°42S 148°42E **62 C4**
Nebraska □ *U.S.A.* 41°30N 99°30W **80 E4**
Nebraska City *U.S.A.* 40°41N 95°52W **80 E7**
Nébrodi, Monti *Italy* 37°54N 14°35E **22 F6**
Necedah *U.S.A.* 44°2N 90°4W **80 C8**
Nechako → *Canada* 53°55N 122°42W **70 C4**
Neches → *U.S.A.* 29°58N 93°51W **84 G8**
Neckar → *Germany* 49°27N 8°29E **16 D5**
Necochea *Argentina* 38°30S 58°50W **94 D4**
Nederland = Netherlands ■
  Europe 52°0N 5°30E **15 C5**
Nederland *U.S.A.* 29°58N 93°59W **84 G8**
Needles *Canada* 49°53N 118°7W **70 D5**
Needles *U.S.A.* 34°51N 114°37W **79 L12**
Needles, The *U.K.* 50°39N 1°35W **13 G6**
Neembucú □ *Paraguay* 27°0S 58°0W **94 B4**
Neemuch = Nimach
  India 24°30N 74°56E **42 G6**
Neenah *U.S.A.* 44°11N 88°28W **80 C9**
Neepawa *Canada* 50°15N 99°30W **71 C9**
Neftçala *Azerbaijan* 39°19N 49°12E **45 B6**
Neftegorsk *Russia* 53°1N 142°58E **29 D15**
Neftekumsk *Russia* 44°46N 44°50E **19 F7**
Nefteyugansk *Russia* 61°5N 72°42E **28 C8**
Nefyn *U.K.* 52°56N 4°31W **12 E3**
Negapatam = Nagappattinam
  India 10°46N 79°51E **40 P11**
Negara *Indonesia* 8°22S 114°37E **37 J17**
Negaunee *U.S.A.* 46°30N 87°36W **80 B10**
Negele *Ethiopia* 5°20N 39°36E **47 F2**
Negev Desert = Hanegev
  Israel 30°50N 35°0E **46 E4**
Negombo *Sri Lanka* 7°12N 79°50E **40 R11**
Negotin *Serbia* 44°16N 22°37E **23 B10**
Negra, Pta. *Mauritania* 22°54N 16°18E **50 D2**
Negra, Pta. *Peru* 6°6S 81°10W **92 E2**
Negrais, C. = Maudin Sun
  Burma 16°0N 94°30E **41 M19**
Negril *Jamaica* 18°22N 78°20W **88 a**
Negro → *Argentina* 41°2S 62°47W **96 E4**
Negro → *Brazil* 3°0S 60°0W **92 D7**
Negro → *Uruguay* 33°24S 58°22W **94 C4**

Negros *Phil.* 9°30N 122°40E **37 C6**
Neguac *Canada* 47°15N 65°5W **73 C6**
Nehalem → *U.S.A.* 45°40N 123°56W **78 E3**
Nehāvand *Iran* 35°56N 49°31E **45 C6**
Nehbandān *Iran* 31°35N 60°5E **45 D9**
Nei Monggol Zizhiqu □
  China 42°0N 112°0E **34 D7**
Neiafu *Tonga* 18°39S 173°59W **59 c**
Neiges, Piton des *Réunion* 21°5S 55°29E **53 c**
Neijiang *China* 29°35N 104°55E **32 D5**
Neillsville *U.S.A.* 44°34N 90°36W **80 C8**
Neilton *U.S.A.* 47°25N 123°53W **76 C2**
Neiqiu *China* 37°15N 114°30E **34 F8**
Neiva *Colombia* 2°56N 75°18W **92 C3**
Neixiang *China* 33°10N 111°52E **34 H6**
Nejanilini L. *Canada* 59°33N 97°48W **71 B9**
Nejd = Najd *Si. Arabia* 26°30N 42°0E **47 B3**
Nekā *Iran* 36°39N 53°19E **45 B7**
Nekemte *Ethiopia* 9°4N 36°30E **47 F2**
Nekso *Denmark* 55°4N 15°8E **9 J16**
Nelia *Australia* 20°39S 142°12E **62 C3**
Neligh *U.S.A.* 42°8N 98°2W **80 D4**
Nelkan *Russia* 57°40N 136°4E **29 D14**
Nellore *India* 14°27N 79°59E **40 M11**
Nelson *Canada* 49°30N 117°20W **70 D5**
Nelson *N.Z.* 41°18S 173°16E **59 D4**
Nelson *U.K.* 53°50N 2°13W **12 D5**
Nelson *Ariz., U.S.A.* 35°31N 113°19W **77 J7**
Nelson *Nev., U.S.A.* 35°42N 114°49W **79 K12**
Nelson → *Canada* 54°33N 98°2W **71 C9**
Nelson, C. *Australia* 38°26S 141°32E **63 F3**
Nelson, Estrecho *Chile* 51°30S 75°0W **96 G2**
Nelson Forks *Canada* 59°30N 124°0W **70 B4**
Nelson House *Canada* 55°47N 98°51W **71 B9**
Nelson L. *Canada* 55°48N 100°7W **71 B8**
Nelson Lakes △ *N.Z.* 41°55S 172°44E **59 D4**
Nelspoort *S. Africa* 32°7S 23°0E **56 E3**
Nelspruit *S. Africa* 25°29S 30°59E **57 D5**
Néma *Mauritania* 16°40N 7°15W **50 E4**
Neman → = Nemunas →
  Lithuania 55°25N 21°10E **9 J19**
Nemeiben L. *Canada* 55°20N 105°20W **71 B7**
Nemiscau *Canada* 51°18N 76°54W **72 B4**
Nemiscau, L. *Canada* 51°25N 76°40W **72 B4**
Nemunas → *Lithuania* 55°25N 21°10E **9 J19**
Nemuro *Japan* 43°20N 145°35E **30 C12**
Nemuro-Kaikyō *Japan* 43°30N 145°30E **30 C12**
Nen Jiang → *China* 45°28N 124°30E **35 B13**
Nenagh *Ireland* 52°52N 8°11W **10 D3**
Nenasi *Malaysia* 3°9N 103°23E **39 L4**
Nene → *U.K.* 52°49N 0°11E **13 E8**
Nenjiang *China* 49°10N 125°10E **33 B7**
Neno *Malawi* 15°25S 34°40E **55 F3**
Neodesha *U.S.A.* 37°25N 95°41W **80 G6**
Neora Valley △ *India* 27°0N 88°45E **43 F13**
Neosho *U.S.A.* 36°52N 94°22W **80 G6**
Neosho → *U.S.A.* 36°48N 95°18W **84 C7**
Nepal ■ *Asia* 28°0N 84°30E **43 F11**
Nepalganj *Nepal* 28°5N 81°40E **43 E9**
Nepalganj Road *India* 28°1N 81°41E **43 E9**
Nephi *U.S.A.* 39°43N 111°50W **76 G8**
Nephin *Ireland* 54°1N 9°22W **10 B2**
Nephin Beg Range *Ireland* 54°0N 9°40W **10 C2**
Neptune *U.S.A.* 40°13N 74°2W **83 F10**
Nerang *Australia* 27°58S 153°20E **63 D5**
Nerastro, Sarīr *Libya* 24°20N 20°37E **51 D10**
Nerchinsk *Russia* 52°0N 116°39E **29 D12**
Néret, L. *Canada* 54°45N 70°44W **73 B5**
Neretva → *Croatia* 43°1N 17°27E **23 C7**
Neringa *Lithuania* 55°20N 21°5E **9 J19**
Neris → *Lithuania* 55°8N 24°16E **9 J21**
Neryungri *Russia* 57°38N 124°28E **29 D13**
Nescopeck *U.S.A.* 41°3N 76°12W **83 E8**
Neskantaga *Canada* 52°14N 87°53W **72 B2**
Ness, L. *U.K.* 57°15N 4°32W **11 D4**
Ness City *U.S.A.* 38°27N 99°54W **80 F4**
Nesterov *Ukraine* 50°4N 23°58E **17 C12**
Nesvizh = Nyasvizh
  Belarus 53°14N 26°38E **17 B14**
Netanya *Israel* 32°20N 34°51E **46 C3**
Netarhat *India* 23°29N 84°16E **43 H11**
Nete → *Belgium* 51°7N 4°14E **15 C4**
Netherdale *Australia* 21°10S 148°33E **62 K6**
Netherlands ■ *Europe* 52°0N 5°30E **15 C5**
Netherlands Antilles ☑
  W. Indies 12°15N 69°0W **92 A5**
Netrang *India* 21°39N 73°21E **42 J5**
Nettilling L. *Canada* 66°30N 71°0W **69 C12**
Netzahualcóyotl, Presa
  Mexico 17°8N 93°35W **87 D6**
Neubrandenburg
  Germany 53°33N 13°15E **16 B7**
Neuchâtel *Switz.* 47°0N 6°55E **20 C7**
Neuchâtel, Lac de *Switz.* 46°53N 6°50E **20 C7**
Neufchâteau *Belgium* 49°50N 5°25E **15 E5**
Neumayer *Antarctica* 71°0S 68°30W **5 D17**
Neumünster *Germany* 54°4N 9°58E **16 A5**
Neunkirchen *Germany* 49°20N 7°9E **16 D4**
Neuquén *Argentina* 38°55S 68°0W **96 D3**
Neuruppin *Germany* 52°55N 12°48E **16 B7**
Neuse → *U.S.A.* 35°6N 76°29W **85 D16**
Neusiedler See *Austria* 47°50N 16°47E **17 E9**
Neva → *Russia* 59°56N 30°20E **18 C5**
Nevada *Iowa, U.S.A.* 42°1N 93°27W **80 D7**
Nevada *Mo., U.S.A.* 37°51N 94°22W **80 G6**
Nevada □ *U.S.A.* 39°0N 117°0W **76 G5**
Nevada City *U.S.A.* 39°16N 121°1W **78 F6**
Nevado, Cerro *Argentina* 35°30S 68°32W **94 D2**
Nevado de Colima = Volcán de
  Colima △ *Mexico* 19°30N 103°40W **86 D4**
Nevado de Tres Cruces △
  Chile 27°13S 69°5W **94 B2**
Nevel *Russia* 56°0N 29°55E **18 C4**

Nevelsk *Russia* 46°40N 141°51E **29** E15
Nevers *France* 47°0N 3°9E **20** C5
Nevertire *Australia* 31°50S 147°44E **63** E4
Neville *Canada* 49°58N 107°39W **71** D7
Nevinnomyssk *Russia* 44°40N 42°0E **19** F7
Nevis *St. Kitts & Nevis* 17°0N 62°30W **89** C7
Nevşehir *Turkey* 38°33N 34°40E **44** B2
Nevyansk *Russia* 57°30N 60°13E **18** C11
New → *U.S.A.* 38°10N 81°12W **81** F13
New Aiyansh *Canada* 55°12N 129°4W **70** B3
New Albany *Ind.,*
 U.S.A. 38°18N 85°49W **81** F11
New Albany *Miss.,*
 U.S.A. 34°29N 89°0W **85** D10
New Albany *Pa., U.S.A.* 41°36N 76°27W **83** E8
New Amsterdam *Guyana* 6°15N 57°36W **92** B7
New Angledool *Australia* 29°5S 147°55E **63** D4
New Baltimore *U.S.A.* 42°41N 82°44W **82** D2
New Bedford *U.S.A.* 41°38N 70°56W **83** E14
New Berlin *N.Y., U.S.A.* 42°37N 75°20W **83** D9
New Berlin *Wis., U.S.A.* 40°50N 76°57W **82** F8
New Bern *U.S.A.* 35°7N 77°3W **85** D16
New Bethlehem *U.S.A.* 41°0N 79°20W **82** F5
New Bight *Bahamas* 24°19N 75°24W **89** B4
New Bloomfield *U.S.A.* 40°25N 77°11W **82** F7
New Boston *U.S.A.* 33°28N 94°25W **84** E7
New Braunfels *U.S.A.* 29°42N 98°8W **84** G5
New Brighton *N.Z.* 43°29S 172°43E **59** E4
New Brighton *U.S.A.* 40°42N 80°19W **82** F4
New Britain *Papua N. G.* 5°50S 150°20E **58** B8
New Britain *U.S.A.* 41°40N 72°47W **83** E12
New Brunswick *U.S.A.* 40°30N 74°27W **83** F10
New Brunswick □
 Canada 46°50N 66°30W **73** C6
New Caledonia ☑ *Pac. Oc.* 21°0S 165°0E **58** D9
New Caledonia Trough
 Pac. Oc. 30°0S 165°0E **64** L8
New Castile = Castilla-La
 Mancha □ *Spain* 39°30N 3°30W **21** C4
New Castle *Ind., U.S.A.* 39°55N 85°22W **81** F11
New Castle *Pa., U.S.A.* 41°0N 80°21W **82** F4
New City *U.S.A.* 41°9N 73°59W **83** E11
New Concord *U.S.A.* 39°59N 81°54W **82** G3
New Cumberland
 U.S.A. 40°30N 80°36W **82** F4
New Cuyama *U.S.A.* 34°57N 119°38W **79** L7
New Delhi *India* 28°36N 77°11E **42** E7
New Denver *Canada* 50°0N 117°25W **70** D5
New Don Pedro Res.
 U.S.A. 37°43N 120°24W **78** H6
New England *U.S.A.* 43°0N 71°0W **75** B12
New England *N. Dak.,*
 U.S.A. 46°32N 102°52W **80** B2
New England Ra.
 Australia 30°20S 151°45E **63** E5
New Forest △ *U.K.* 50°53N 1°34W **13** G6
New Galloway *U.K.* 55°5N 4°9W **11** F4
New Glasgow *Canada* 45°35N 62°36W **73** C7
New Guinea *Oceania* 4°0S 136°0E **58** B6
New Hamburg *Canada* 43°23N 80°42W **82** C4
New Hampshire □
 U.S.A. 44°0N 71°30W **83** C13
New Hampton *U.S.A.* 43°3N 92°19W **80** D7
New Hanover *S. Africa* 29°22S 30°31E **57** D5
New Hartford *U.S.A.* 43°4N 75°18W **83** D9
New Haven *Conn.,*
 U.S.A. 41°18N 72°55W **83** E12
New Haven *Mich.,*
 U.S.A. 42°44N 82°48W **82** D2
New Haven *N.Y., U.S.A.* 43°28N 76°18W **83** C8
New Hazelton *Canada* 55°20N 127°30W **70** B3
New Hebrides = Vanuatu ■
 Pac. Oc. 15°0S 168°0E **58** C9
New Holland *U.S.A.* 40°6N 76°5W **83** F8
New Iberia *U.S.A.* 30°1N 91°49W **84** F9
New Ireland *Papua N. G.* 3°20S 151°50E **58** B8
New Jersey □ *U.S.A.* 40°0N 74°30W **81** F16
New Kensington *U.S.A.* 40°34N 79°46W **82** F5
New Lexington *U.S.A.* 39°43N 82°13W **81** F12
New Liskeard *Canada* 47°31N 79°41W **72** C4
New London *Conn.,*
 U.S.A. 41°22N 72°6W **83** E12
New London *Ohio, U.S.A.* 41°5N 82°24W **82** E2
New London *Wis.,*
 U.S.A. 44°23N 88°45W **80** C9
New Madrid *U.S.A.* 36°36N 89°32W **80** G9
New Martinsville
 U.S.A. 39°39N 80°52W **81** F13
New Meadows *U.S.A.* 44°58N 116°18W **76** D5
New Melones L. *U.S.A.* 37°57N 120°31W **78** H6
New Mexico □ *U.S.A.* 34°30N 106°0W **77** J11
New Milford *Conn.,*
 U.S.A. 41°35N 73°25W **83** E11
New Milford *Pa., U.S.A.* 41°52N 75°44W **83** E9
New Moore I. *Ind. Oc.* 21°37N 89°10E **43** J13
New Norcia *Australia* 30°57S 116°13E **61** F2
New Norfolk *Australia* 42°46S 147°2E **63** G4
New Orleans *U.S.A.* 29°57N 90°4W **85** G9
New Philadelphia
 U.S.A. 40°30N 81°27W **82** F3
New Plymouth *N.Z.* 39°4S 174°5E **59** C5
New Plymouth *U.S.A.* 43°58N 116°49W **76** E5
New Port Richey
 U.S.A. 28°16N 82°43W **85** G13
New Providence
 Bahamas 25°25N 78°35W **88** A4
New Quay *U.K.* 52°13N 4°21W **13** E3
New Radnor *U.K.* 52°15N 3°9W **13** E4
New Richmond *Canada* 48°15N 65°45W **73** C6
New Richmond *U.S.A.* 45°7N 92°32W **80** C7
New River Gorge △
 U.S.A. 38°0N 81°5W **81** G13
New Roads *U.S.A.* 30°42N 91°26W **84** F9
New Rochelle *U.S.A.* 40°55N 73°46W **83** F11
New Rockford *U.S.A.* 47°41N 99°8W **80** B4
New Romney *U.K.* 50°59N 0°57E **13** G8
New Ross *Ireland* 52°23N 6°57W **10** D5

New Salem *U.S.A.* 46°51N 101°25W **80** B3
New Scone = Scone *U.K.* 56°25N 3°24W **11** E5
New Siberian I. = Novaya Sibir,
 Ostrov Russia 75°10N 150°0E **29** B16
New Siberian Is. = Novosibirskiye
 Ostrova Russia 75°0N 142°0E **29** B15
New Smyrna Beach
 U.S.A. 29°1N 80°56W **85** G14
New South Wales □
 Australia 33°0S 146°0E **63** E4
New Tecumseth = Alliston
 Canada 44°9N 79°52W **82** B5
New Town *U.S.A.* 47°59N 102°30W **80** B2
New Tredegar *U.K.* 51°44N 3°16W **13** F4
New Ulm *U.S.A.* 44°19N 94°28W **80** C6
New Waterford *Canada* 46°13N 60°4W **73** C7
New Westminster
 Canada 49°13N 122°55W **78** A4
New York *U.S.A.* 40°43N 74°0W **83** F11
New York □ *U.S.A.* 43°0N 75°0W **83** D9
New York J.F. Kennedy Int. ✈
 (JFK) *U.S.A.* 40°38N 73°47W **83** F11
New Zealand ■ *Oceania* 40°0S 176°0E **59** D6
Newaj → *India* 24°24N 76°49E **42** G7
Newala *Tanzania* 10°58S 39°18E **55** E4
Newark *Del., U.S.A.* 39°41N 75°46W **81** F16
Newark *N.J., U.S.A.* 40°44N 74°10W **83** F10
Newark *N.Y., U.S.A.* 43°3N 77°6W **82** C7
Newark *Ohio, U.S.A.* 40°3N 82°24W **82** F2
Newark Liberty Int. ✈ (EWR)
 U.S.A. 40°42N 74°10W **83** F10
Newark-on-Trent *U.K.* 53°5N 0°48W **12** D7
Newark Valley *U.S.A.* 42°14N 76°11W **83** D8
Newberg *U.S.A.* 45°18N 122°58W **76** D2
Newberry *Mich., U.S.A.* 46°21N 85°30W **81** B11
Newberry *S.C., U.S.A.* 34°17N 81°37W **85** D14
Newberry Springs
 U.S.A. 34°50N 116°41W **79** L10
Newboro L. *Canada* 44°38N 76°20W **83** B8
Newbridge = Droichead Nua
 Ireland 53°11N 6°48W **10** C5
Newburgh *Canada* 44°19N 76°52W **82** B8
Newburgh *U.S.A.* 41°30N 74°1W **83** E10
Newbury *U.K.* 51°24N 1°20W **13** F6
Newbury *N.H., U.S.A.* 43°19N 72°3W **83** B12
Newbury *Vt., U.S.A.* 44°5N 72°4W **83** B12
Newburyport *U.S.A.* 42°49N 70°53W **83** D14
Newcastle *Australia* 33°0S 151°46E **63** E5
Newcastle *N.B., Canada* 47°1N 65°38W **73** C6
Newcastle *Ont., Canada* 43°55N 78°35W **72** D4
Newcastle *S. Africa* 27°45S 29°58E **57** D4
Newcastle *U.K.* 54°13N 5°54W **10** B6
Newcastle *Calif., U.S.A.* 38°53N 121°8W **78** G5
Newcastle *Wyo.,*
 U.S.A. 43°50N 104°11W **76** E11
Newcastle Emlyn *U.K.* 52°2N 4°28W **13** E3
Newcastle Ra. *Australia* 15°45S 130°15E **60** C5
Newcastle-under-Lyme
 U.K. 53°1N 2°14W **12** D5
Newcastle-upon-Tyne
 U.K. 54°58N 1°36W **12** C6
Newcastle Waters
 Australia 17°30S 133°28E **62** B1
Newcastle West *Ireland* 52°27N 9°3W **10** D2
Newcomb *U.S.A.* 43°58N 74°10W **83** C10
Newcomerstown *U.S.A.* 40°16N 81°36W **82** F3
Newdegate *Australia* 33°6S 119°0E **61** F2
Newell *Australia* 16°20S 145°16E **62** B4
Newell *U.S.A.* 44°43N 103°25W **80** C2
Newfane *U.S.A.* 43°17N 78°43W **82** C6
Newfield *U.S.A.* 42°18N 76°33W **83** D8
Newfound L. *U.S.A.* 43°40N 71°47W **83** C13
Newfoundland *Canada* 49°0N 58°0W **73** C8
Newfoundland *U.S.A.* 41°18N 75°19W **83** E9
Newfoundland & Labrador □
 Canada 53°0N 58°0W **73** B8
Newhaven *U.K.* 50°47N 0°3E **13** G8
Newkirk *U.S.A.* 36°53N 97°3W **84** C6
Newlyn *U.K.* 50°6N 5°34W **13** G2
Newman *Australia* 23°18S 119°45E **60** D2
Newman *U.S.A.* 37°19N 121°1W **78** H5
Newmarket *Canada* 44°3N 79°28W **82** B5
Newmarket *Ireland* 52°13N 9°0W **10** D2
Newmarket *U.K.* 52°15N 0°25E **13** E8
Newmarket *U.S.A.* 43°5N 70°56W **83** C14
Newnan *U.S.A.* 33°23N 84°48W **85** E12
Newport *Ireland* 53°53N 9°33W **10** C2
Newport *I. of W., U.K.* 50°42N 1°17W **13** G6
Newport *Newport, U.K.* 51°35N 3°0W **13** F5
Newport *Ark., U.S.A.* 35°37N 91°16W **84** D9
Newport *Ky., U.S.A.* 39°5N 84°29W **81** F11
Newport *N.H., U.S.A.* 43°22N 72°10W **83** C12
Newport *N.Y., U.S.A.* 43°11N 75°1W **83** C9
Newport *Oreg., U.S.A.* 44°39N 124°3W **76** D1
Newport *Pa., U.S.A.* 40°29N 77°8W **82** F7
Newport *R.I., U.S.A.* 41°29N 71°19W **83** E13
Newport *Tenn., U.S.A.* 35°58N 83°11W **85** D13
Newport *Vt., U.S.A.* 44°56N 72°13W **83** B12
Newport *Wash., U.S.A.* 48°11N 117°3W **76** B5
Newport □ *U.K.* 51°33N 3°1W **13** F4
Newport Beach *U.S.A.* 33°37N 117°56W **79** M9
Newport News *U.S.A.* 36°58N 76°25W **81** G15
Newport Pagnell *U.K.* 52°5N 0°43W **13** E7
Newquay *U.K.* 50°25N 5°6W **13** G2
Newry *U.K.* 54°11N 6°21W **10** B5
Newton *Ill., U.S.A.* 38°59N 88°10W **80** F9
Newton *Iowa, U.S.A.* 41°42N 93°3W **80** E7
Newton *Kans., U.S.A.* 38°3N 97°21W **80** F5
Newton *Mass., U.S.A.* 42°21N 71°12W **83** D13
Newton *Miss., U.S.A.* 32°19N 89°10W **85** D10
Newton *N.C., U.S.A.* 35°40N 81°13W **85** D14
Newton *N.J., U.S.A.* 41°3N 74°45W **83** E10
Newton *Tex., U.S.A.* 30°51N 93°46W **84** F8
Newton Abbot *U.K.* 50°32N 3°37W **13** G4
Newton Aycliffe *U.K.* 54°37N 1°34W **12** C6
Newton Falls *N.Y.,*
 U.S.A. 44°12N 74°59W **83** B10

Newton Falls *Ohio,*
 U.S.A. 41°11N 80°59W **82** E4
Newton Stewart *U.K.* 54°57N 4°30W **11** G4
Newtonmore *U.K.* 57°4N 4°8W **11** D4
Newtown *U.K.* 52°31N 3°19W **13** E4
Newtownabbey *U.K.* 54°40N 5°56W **10** B6
Newtownards *U.K.* 54°36N 5°42W **10** B6
Newtownbarry = Bunclody
 Ireland 52°39N 6°40W **10** D5
Newtownstewart *U.K.* 54°43N 7°23W **10** B4
Newville *U.S.A.* 40°10N 77°24W **82** F7
Neya *Russia* 58°21N 43°49E **18** C7
Neyrīz *Iran* 29°15N 54°19E **45** D7
Neyshābūr *Iran* 36°10N 58°50E **45** B8
Nezhin = Nizhyn *Ukraine* 51°5N 31°55E **19** D5
Nezperce *U.S.A.* 46°14N 116°14W **76** C5
Ngabang *Indonesia* 0°23N 109°55E **36** D3
Ngabordamlu, Tanjung
 Indonesia 6°56S 134°11E **37** F8
N'Gage *Angola* 7°46S 15°15E **52** F3
Ngami Depression
 Botswana 20°30S 22°46E **56** C3
Ngamo *Zimbabwe* 19°3S 27°32E **55** F2
Nganglong Kangri *China* 33°0N 81°0E **43** C9
Ngao *Thailand* 18°46N 99°59E **38** C2
Ngaoundéré *Cameroon* 7°15N 13°35E **52** C2
Ngapara *N.Z.* 44°57S 170°46E **59** F3
Ngara *Tanzania* 2°29S 30°40E **54** C3
Ngawi *Indonesia* 7°24S 111°26E **37** G14
Ngcobo *S. Africa* 31°37S 28°0E **57** E4
Nghia Lo *Vietnam* 21°33N 104°28E **38** B5
Ngoma *Malawi* 13°8S 33°45E **55** E3
Ngomahura *Zimbabwe* 20°26S 30°43E **55** G3
Ngomba *Tanzania* 8°20S 32°53E **55** D3
Ngomeni, Ras *Kenya* 2°59S 40°14E **54** C5
Ngong *Kenya* 1°22S 36°39E **54** C4
Ngoring Hu *China* 34°55N 97°5E **32** C4
Ngorongoro *Tanzania* 3°11S 35°32E **54** C4
Ngorongoro → *Tanzania* 2°40S 35°30E **54** C4
Ngozi *Burundi* 2°54S 29°50E **54** C2
Ngudu *Tanzania* 2°58S 33°25E **54** C3
Nguigmi *Niger* 14°20N 13°20E **51** F8
Nguiu *Australia* 11°46S 130°38E **60** B5
Ngukurr *Australia* 14°44S 134°44E **62** A1
Ngunga *Tanzania* 3°37S 33°37E **54** C3
Nguru *Nigeria* 12°56N 10°29E **51** F8
Nguru Mts. *Tanzania* 6°0S 37°30E **54** D4
Ngusi *Malawi* 14°0S 34°50E **55** E3
Nguyen Binh *Vietnam* 22°39N 105°56E **38** A5
Nha Trang *Vietnam* 12°16N 109°10E **39** F7
Nhacoongo *Mozam.* 24°18S 35°14E **57** C6
Nhamaabué *Mozam.* 17°25S 35°5E **55** F4
Nhamundá → *Brazil* 2°12S 56°41W **93** D7
Nhangulaze, L. *Mozam.* 24°0S 34°30E **57** C5
Nhill *Australia* 36°18S 141°40E **63** F3
Nho Quan *Vietnam* 20°18N 105°45E **38** B5
Nhulunbuy *Australia* 12°10S 137°20E **62** A2
Nia-nia
 Dem. Rep. of the Congo 1°30N 27°40E **54** B2
Niagara Falls *Canada* 43°7N 79°5W **82** C5
Niagara Falls *U.S.A.* 43°5N 79°4W **82** C6
Niagara-on-the-Lake
 Canada 43°15N 79°4W **82** C5
Niah *Malaysia* 3°58N 113°46E **36** D4
Niamey *Niger* 13°27N 2°6E **50** F6
Niangara
 Dem. Rep. of the Congo 3°42N 27°50E **54** B2
Niantic *U.S.A.* 41°20N 72°11W **83** E12
Nias *Indonesia* 1°0N 97°30E **36** D1
Niassa □ *Mozam.* 13°30S 36°0E **55** E4
Niassa △ *Mozam.* 12°4S 36°57E **55** E4
Nibāk *Si. Arabia* 24°25N 50°50E **45** E7
Nicaragua ■
 Cent. Amer. 11°40N 85°30W **88** D2
Nicaragua, L. de *Nic.* 12°0N 85°30W **88** D2
Nicastro *Italy* 38°59N 16°19E **22** E7
Nice *France* 43°42N 7°14E **20** E7
Niceville *U.S.A.* 30°31N 86°30W **85** F11
Nichicun, L. *Canada* 53°5N 71°0W **73** B5
Nichinan *Japan* 31°38N 131°23E **31** J5
Nicholás, Canal *W. Indies* 23°30N 80°5W **88** B3
Nicholasville *U.S.A.* 37°53N 84°34W **81** G11
Nichols *U.S.A.* 42°1N 76°22W **83** D8
Nicholson *Australia* 18°2S 128°54E **60** C4
Nicholson *U.S.A.* 41°37N 75°47W **83** E9
Nicholson → *Australia* 17°31S 139°36E **62** B2
Nicholson L. *Canada* 62°40N 102°40W **71** A8
Nicholson Ra. *Australia* 27°15S 116°45E **61** E2
Nicholville *U.S.A.* 44°41N 74°39W **83** B10
Nicobar Is. *Ind. Oc.* 8°0N 93°30E **27** J13
Nicola *Canada* 50°12N 120°40W **70** C4
Nicolls Town *Bahamas* 25°8N 78°0W **88** A4
Nicosia *Cyprus* 35°10N 33°25E **25** D12
Nicoya *Costa Rica* 10°9N 85°27W **88** D2
Nicoya, G. de *Costa Rica* 10°0N 85°0W **88** E3
Nicoya, Pen. de
 Costa Rica 9°45N 85°40W **88** E2
Nidd → *U.K.* 53°59N 1°23W **12** D6
Niedersachsen □ *Germany* 52°50N 9°0E **16** B5
Niekerkshoop *S. Africa* 29°19S 22°51E **56** D3
Niemba
 Dem. Rep. of the Congo 5°58S 28°24E **54** D2
Niemen = Nemunas →
 Lithuania 55°25N 21°10E **9** J19
Nienburg *Germany* 52°39N 9°13E **16** B5
Nieu Bethesda *S. Africa* 31°51S 24°34E **56** E3
Nieuw Amsterdam
 Suriname 5°53N 55°5W **93** B7
Nieuw Nickerie *Suriname* 6°0N 56°59W **93** B7
Nieuwoudtville *S. Africa* 31°23S 19°7E **56** E2
Nieuwpoort *Belgium* 51°8N 2°45E **15** C2
Nieves, Pico de las
 Canary Is. 27°57N 15°35W **24** G4
Niğde *Turkey* 37°58N 34°40E **44** B2
Nigel *S. Africa* 26°27S 28°25E **57** D4
Niger ■ *W. Afr.* 17°30N 10°0E **50** E7
Niger → *W. Afr.* 5°33N 6°33E **50** G7
Nigeria ■ *W. Afr.* 8°30N 8°0E **50** G7

Nighasin *India* 28°14N 80°52E **43** E9
Nightcaps *N.Z.* 45°57S 168°2E **59** F2
Nihon = Japan ■ *Asia* 36°0N 136°0E **31** G8
Nii-Jima *Japan* 34°20N 139°15E **31** G9
Niigata *Japan* 37°58N 139°0E **30** F9
Niigata □ *Japan* 37°15N 138°45E **31** F9
Niihama *Japan* 33°55N 133°16E **31** H6
Ni'ihau *U.S.A.* 21°54N 160°9W **74** b
Niimi *Japan* 34°59N 133°28E **31** G6
Niitsu *Japan* 37°48N 139°7E **30** F9
Nijil *Jordan* 30°32N 35°33E **46** E4
Nijkerk *Neths.* 52°13N 5°30E **15** B5
Nijmegen *Neths.* 51°50N 5°52E **15** C5
Nijverdal *Neths.* 52°22N 6°28E **15** B6
Nīk Pey *Iran* 36°50N 48°10E **45** B6
Nikel *Russia* 69°24N 30°13E **8** B24
Nikiniki *Indonesia* 9°49S 124°30E **37** F6
Nikkō *Japan* 36°45N 139°35E **31** F9
Nikkō △ *Japan* 36°56N 139°37E **31** F9
Nikolayev = Mykolayiv
 Ukraine 46°58N 32°0E **19** E5
Nikolayevsk *Russia* 50°0N 45°35E **19** E8
Nikolayevsk-na-Amur
 Russia 53°8N 140°44E **29** D15
Nikolskoye *Russia* 55°12N 166°0E **29** D17
Nikopol *Ukraine* 47°35N 34°25E **19** E5
Nīkshahr *Iran* 26°15N 60°10E **45** E9
Nikšić *Montenegro* 42°50N 18°57E **23** C8
Nīl, Nahr en → *Africa* 30°10N 31°6E **51** B12
Nīl el Abyad → *Sudan* 15°38N 32°31E **51** E12
Nīl el Azraq → *Sudan* 15°38N 32°31E **51** E12
Nila *Indonesia* 6°44S 129°31E **37** F7
Niland *U.S.A.* 33°14N 115°31W **79** M11
Nile = Nīl, Nahr en →
 Africa 30°10N 31°6E **51** B12
Niles *Mich., U.S.A.* 41°50N 86°15W **80** E10
Niles *Ohio, U.S.A.* 41°11N 80°46W **82** E4
Nim Ka Thana *India* 27°44N 75°48E **42** F6
Nimach *India* 24°30N 74°56E **42** G6
Nimbahera *India* 24°37N 74°45E **42** G6
Nîmes *France* 43°50N 4°23E **20** E6
Nimfaíon, Ákra = Pines, Akra
 Greece 40°5N 24°20E **23** D11
Nimmitabel *Australia* 36°29S 149°15E **63** F4
Nīnawá *Iraq* 36°25N 43°10E **44** B4
Nīnawá □ *Iraq* 36°15N 43°0E **44** B4
Nindigully *Australia* 28°21S 148°50E **63** D4
Ninepin Group *China* 22°16N 114°21E **33** G11
Nineveh = Nīnawá *Iraq* 36°25N 43°10E **44** B4
Ning Xian *China* 35°30N 107°58E **34** G4
Ningaloo → *Australia* 22°23S 113°32E **60** D1
Ning'an *China* 44°22N 129°20E **35** B15
Ningbo *China* 29°51N 121°28E **33** D7
Ningcheng *China* 41°32N 119°53E **35** D10
Ningjin *China* 37°35N 114°57E **34** F8
Ningjing Shan *China* 30°0N 98°20E **32** C4
Ningling *China* 34°25N 115°22E **34** G8
Ningpo = Ningbo *China* 29°51N 121°28E **33** D7
Ningqiang *China* 32°47N 106°15E **34** H4
Ningshan *China* 33°21N 108°21E **34** H5
Ningsia Hui A.R. = Ningxia Huizu
 Zizhiqu □ *China* 38°0N 106°0E **34** F4
Ningxia Huizu Zizhiqu □
 China 38°0N 106°0E **34** F4
Ningyang *China* 35°47N 116°45E **34** G9
Ninh Binh *Vietnam* 20°15N 105°55E **38** B5
Ninh Giang *Vietnam* 20°44N 106°24E **38** B6
Ninh Hoa *Vietnam* 12°30N 109°7E **38** F7
Ninh Ma *Vietnam* 12°48N 109°21E **38** F7
Ninove *Belgium* 50°51N 4°2E **15** D4
Nioaque *Brazil* 21°5S 55°50W **94** A4
Niobrara *U.S.A.* 42°45N 98°2W **80** D4
Niobrara → *U.S.A.* 42°46N 98°3W **80** D4
Nioro du Sahel *Mali* 15°15N 9°30W **50** E4
Niort *France* 46°19N 0°29W **20** C3
Nipawin *Canada* 53°20N 104°0W **71** C8
Nipigon *Canada* 49°0N 88°17W **72** C2
Nipigon, L. *Canada* 49°50N 88°30W **72** C2
Nipishish L. *Canada* 54°12N 60°45W **73** B7
Nipissing, L. *Canada* 46°20N 80°0W **72** C4
Nipomo *U.S.A.* 35°3N 120°29W **79** K6
Nippon = Japan ■ *Asia* 36°0N 136°0E **31** G8
Nipton *U.S.A.* 35°28N 115°16W **79** K11
Niquelândia *Brazil* 14°33S 48°23W **93** F9
Nīr *Iran* 38°2N 47°59E **44** B5
Nirasaki *Japan* 35°42N 138°27E **31** G9
Nirmal *India* 19°3N 78°20E **40** K11
Nirmali *India* 26°20N 86°35E **43** F12
Niš *Serbia* 43°19N 21°58E **23** C9
Nişāb *Si. Arabia* 29°11N 44°43E **44** D5
Nişāb *Yemen* 14°25N 46°29E **47** E4
Nishinomiya *Japan* 34°45N 135°20E **31** G7
Nishino'omote *Japan* 30°43N 130°59E **31** J5
Nishiwaki *Japan* 34°59N 134°58E **31** G7
Niskibi → *Canada* 56°29N 88°9W **72** A2
Nisqually → *U.S.A.* 47°7N 122°42W **78** C4
Nissaki *Greece* 39°43N 19°52E **25** A3
Nissum Bredning
 Denmark 56°40N 8°20E **9** H13
Nistru = Dnister →
 Europe 46°18N 30°17E **17** E16
Nisutlin → *Canada* 60°14N 132°34W **70** A2
Nitchequon *Canada* 53°10N 70°58W **73** B5
Niterói *Brazil* 22°53S 43°7W **95** A7
Nith → *Canada* 43°12N 80°23E **82** C4
Nith → *U.K.* 55°14N 3°33W **11** F5
Nitmiluk △ *Australia* 14°6S 132°15E **60** B5
Nitra *Slovak Rep.* 48°19N 18°4E **17** D10
Nitra → *Slovak Rep.* 47°46N 18°10E **17** E10
Niue *Pac. Oc.* 19°2S 169°54W **65** J11
Niut *Indonesia* 0°55N 110°6E **36** D4
Niuzhuang *China* 40°58N 122°28E **35** D12
Nivala *Finland* 63°56N 24°57E **8** E21
Nivelles *Belgium* 50°35N 4°20E **15** D4
Nivernais *France* 47°15N 3°30E **20** C5
Niverville *Canada* 49°36N 97°3W **71** D9
Niwas *India* 23°3N 80°26E **43** H9

Nixa *U.S.A.* 37°3N 93°18W **80** G7
Nixon *U.S.A.* 29°16N 97°46W **84** G6
Nizamabad *India* 18°45N 78°7E **40** K11
Nizamghat *India* 28°20N 95°45E **41** E19
Nizhne Kolymsk
 Russia 68°34N 160°55E **29** C17
Nizhnekamsk *Russia* 55°38N 51°49E **18** C9
Nizhneudinsk *Russia* 54°54N 99°3E **29** D10
Nizhnevartovsk *Russia* 60°56N 76°38E **28** C8
Nizhniy Bestyakh
 Russia 61°57N 129°54E **29** C13
Nizhniy Novgorod *Russia* 56°20N 44°0E **18** C7
Nizhniy Tagil *Russia* 57°55N 59°57E **18** C10
Nizhyn *Ukraine* 51°5N 31°55E **19** D5
Nizip *Turkey* 37°5N 37°50E **44** B3
Nizké Tatry *Slovak Rep.* 48°55N 19°30E **17** D10
Nizwá *Oman* 22°56N 57°32E **47** C6
Njakwa *Malawi* 11°1S 33°56E **55** E3
Njanji *Zambia* 14°25S 31°46E **55** E3
Njazidja = Grande Comore
 Comoros Is. 11°35S 43°20E **53** a
Njinjo *Tanzania* 8°48S 38°54E **55** D4
Njombe *Tanzania* 9°20S 34°50E **55** D3
Njombe → *Tanzania* 6°56S 35°6E **54** D4
Nkana *Zambia* 12°50S 28°8E **55** E2
Nkandla *S. Africa* 28°37S 31°5E **57** D5
Nkawkaw *Ghana* 6°36N 0°49W **50** G5
Nkayi *Zimbabwe* 19°41S 29°20E **55** F2
Nkhotakota *Malawi* 12°56S 34°15E **55** E3
Nkhotakota △ *Malawi* 12°50S 34°0E **55** E3
Nkongsamba *Cameroon* 4°55N 9°55E **52** D1
Nkurenkuru *Namibia* 17°42S 18°32E **56** B2
Nmai → *Burma* 25°30N 97°25E **41** G20
Noakhali = Maijdi
 Bangla. 22°48N 91°10E **41** H17
Nobel *Canada* 45°25N 80°6W **82** A4
Nobeoka *Japan* 32°36N 131°41E **31** H5
Noblesville *U.S.A.* 40°3N 86°1W **80** E10
Noboribetsu *Japan* 42°24N 141°6E **30** C10
Noccundra *Australia* 27°50S 142°36E **63** D3
Nocera Inferiore *Italy* 40°44N 14°38E **22** D6
Nocona *U.S.A.* 33°47N 97°44W **84** E6
Noda *Japan* 35°56N 139°52E **31** G9
Nogales *Mexico* 31°19N 110°56W **86** A2
Nogales *U.S.A.* 31°21N 110°56W **77** L8
Nōgata *Japan* 33°48N 130°44E **31** H5
Noggerup *Australia* 33°32S 116°5E **61** F2
Noginsk *Russia* 64°30N 90°50E **29** C10
Nogliki *Russia* 51°50N 143°10E **29** D15
Nogoa → *Australia* 23°40S 147°55E **62** C4
Nogoyá *Argentina* 32°24S 59°48W **94** C4
Nohar *India* 29°11N 74°49E **42** E6
Nohta *India* 23°40N 79°34E **43** H8
Noires, Mts. *France* 48°11N 3°40W **20** B2
Noirmoutier, Î. de *France* 46°58N 2°10W **20** C2
Nojane *Botswana* 23°15S 20°14E **56** C3
Nojima-Zaki *Japan* 34°54N 139°53E **31** G9
Nok Kundi *Pakistan* 28°50N 62°45E **40** E3
Nok Ta Phao, Ko *Thailand* 9°23N 99°59E **39** b
Nokaneng *Botswana* 19°40S 22°17E **56** B3
Nokia *Finland* 61°30N 23°30E **8** F20
Nokomis *Canada* 51°35N 105°0W **71** C8
Nokomis L. *Canada* 57°0N 103°0W **71** B8
Nola *C.A.R.* 3°35N 16°4E **52** D3
Noma Omuramba →
 Namibia 18°52S 20°53E **56** B3
Nombre de Dios *Panama* 9°34N 79°28W **88** E4
Nome *U.S.A.* 64°30N 165°25W **74** a
Nomo-Zaki *Japan* 32°35N 129°44E **31** H4
Nomuka *Tonga* 20°17S 174°48W **59** c
Nomuka Group *Tonga* 20°20S 174°48W **59** c
Nonacho L. *Canada* 61°42N 109°40W **71** A7
Nonda *Australia* 20°40S 142°28E **62** C3
Nong Chang *Thailand* 15°23N 99°51E **38** E2
Nong Het *Laos* 19°29N 103°59E **38** C4
Nong Khai *Thailand* 17°50N 102°46E **38** D4
Nong'an *China* 44°25N 125°5E **35** B13
Nongoma *S. Africa* 27°58S 31°35E **57** D5
Nongsa *Indonesia* 1°11N 104°8E **39** d
Nonoava *Mexico* 27°28N 106°44W **86** B3
Nonsan *S. Korea* 36°12N 127°5E **35** F14
Nonthaburi *Thailand* 13°50N 100°29E **38** F3
Noonamah *Australia* 12°40S 131°4E **60** B5
Noondie, L. *Australia* 28°30S 119°30E **61** E2
Noord Brabant □ *Neths.* 51°40N 5°0E **15** C5
Noord Holland □ *Neths.* 52°30N 4°45E **15** B4
Noordbeveland *Neths.* 51°35N 3°50E **15** C3
Noordoostpolder *Neths.* 52°45N 5°45E **15** B5
Noordwijk *Neths.* 52°14N 4°26E **15** B4
Noosa Heads *Australia* 26°25S 153°6E **63** D5
Nootka I. *Canada* 49°32N 126°42W **70** D3
Nopiming △ *Canada* 50°30N 95°37W **71** C9
Noralee *Canada* 53°59N 126°26W **70** C3
Noranda = Rouyn-Noranda
 Canada 48°20N 79°0W **72** C4
Norco *U.S.A.* 33°56N 117°33W **79** M9
Nord-Kivu □
 Dem. Rep. of the Congo 1°0S 29°0E **54** C2
Nord-Ostsee-Kanal
 Germany 54°12N 9°32E **16** A5
Nordaustlandet *Svalbard* 79°14N 23°0E **4** B9
Nordegg *Canada* 52°29N 116°5W **70** C5
Norderney *Germany* 53°42N 7°9E **16** B4
Norderstedt *Germany* 53°42N 10°1E **16** B5
Nordfjord *Norway* 61°55N 5°30E **8** F11
Nordfriesische Inseln
 Germany 54°40N 8°20E **16** A5
Nordhausen *Germany* 51°30N 10°47E **16** C6
Norðoyar *Føroe Is.* 62°17N 6°35W **8** E9
Nordkapp *Norway* 71°10N 25°50E **8** A21
Nordkapp *Svalbard* 80°31N 20°0E **4** A9
Nordkinnhalvøya
 Norway 70°55N 27°40E **8** A22
Nordrhein-Westfalen □
 Germany 51°45N 7°30E **16** C4
Nordvik *Russia* 74°2N 111°32E **29** B12
Nore → *Ireland* 52°25N 6°58W **10** D4
Noreland *Canada* 44°43N 78°48W **82** B6

Norfolk = Simcoe Canada 42°50N 80°23W 82 D4
Norfolk N.Y., U.S.A. 44°48N 74°59W 83 B10
Norfolk Nebr., U.S.A. 42°2N 97°25W 80 D5
Norfolk Va., U.S.A. 36°50N 76°17W 81 G15
Norfolk □ U.K. 52°39N 0°54E 13 E8
Norfolk Broads △ U.K. 52°45N 1°30E 13 E9
Norfolk I. Pac. Oc. 28°58S 168°3E 58 D9
Norfolk Ridge Pac. Oc. 29°0S 168°0E 64 K8
Norfork L. U.S.A. 36°15N 92°14W 84 C8
Norge = Norway ■ Europe 63°0N 11°0E 8 E14
Norilsk Russia 69°20N 88°6E 29 C9
Norma, Mt. Australia 20°55S 140°42E 62 C3
Normal U.S.A. 40°31N 88°59W 80 E9
Norman U.S.A. 35°13N 97°26W 84 D6
Norman → Australia 19°18S 141°51E 62 B3
Norman Wells Canada 65°17N 126°51W 68 C7
Normanby → Australia 14°23S 144°10E 62 A3
Normandie France 48°45N 0°10E 20 B4
Normandin Canada 48°49N 72°31W 72 C5
Normandy = Normandie France 48°45N 0°10E 20 B4
Normanhurst, Mt. Australia 25°4S 122°30E 61 E3
Normanton Australia 17°40S 141°10E 62 B3
Normétal Canada 49°0N 79°22W 72 C4
Norquay Canada 51°53N 102°5W 71 C8
Norquinco Argentina 41°51S 70°55W 96 E2
Norrbottens län □ Sweden 66°50N 20°0E 8 C19
Norris Point Canada 49°31N 57°53W 73 C8
Norristown U.S.A. 40°7N 75°21W 83 F9
Norrköping Sweden 58°37N 16°11E 9 G17
Norrland Sweden 62°15N 15°45E 8 E16
Norrtälje Sweden 59°46N 18°42E 9 G18
Norseman Australia 32°8S 121°43E 61 F3
Norsk Russia 52°30N 130°5E 29 D14
Norte, Pta. del Canary Is. 27°51N 17°57W 24 G2
Norte, Serra do Brazil 11°20S 59°0W 92 F7
North, C. Canada 47°2N 60°20W 73 C7
North Adams U.S.A. 42°42N 73°7W 83 D11
North America 40°0N 100°0W 66 F10
North Arm Canada 62°0N 114°30W 70 A5
North Augusta U.S.A. 33°30N 81°59W 85 E14
North Australian Basin Ind. Oc. 14°30S 116°30E 64 J3
North Ayrshire □ U.K. 55°45N 4°44W 11 F4
North Bass I. U.S.A. 41°40N 82°56W 82 E2
North Battleford Canada 52°50N 108°17W 71 C7
North Bay Canada 46°20N 79°30W 72 C4
North Belcher Is. Canada 56°50N 79°50W 72 A4
North Bend Oreg., U.S.A. 43°24N 124°14W 76 E1
North Bend Pa., U.S.A. 41°20N 77°42W 82 E7
North Bend Wash., U.S.A. 47°30N 121°47W 78 C5
North Bennington U.S.A. 42°56N 73°15W 83 D11
North Berwick U.K. 56°4N 2°42W 11 E6
North Berwick U.S.A. 43°18N 70°44W 83 C14
North Bruce Canada 44°22N 81°26W 82 B3
North C. Canada 47°5N 64°0W 73 C7
North C. N.Z. 34°23S 173°4E 59 A4
North Canadian → U.S.A. 35°22N 95°37W 84 D7
North Canton U.S.A. 40°53N 81°24W 82 F3
North Cape = Nordkapp Norway 71°10N 25°50E 8 A21
North Caribou L. Canada 52°50N 90°40W 72 B1
North Carolina □ U.S.A. 35°30N 80°0W 85 D15
North Cascades △ U.S.A. 48°45N 121°10W 76 B3
North Channel Canada 46°0N 83°0W 72 C3
North Channel U.K. 55°13N 5°52W 11 F3
North Charleston U.S.A. 32°53N 79°58W 85 E15
North Chicago U.S.A. 42°19N 87°51W 80 D10
North Collins U.S.A. 42°35N 78°56W 82 D6
North Creek U.S.A. 43°42N 73°59W 83 C11
North Dakota □ U.S.A. 47°30N 100°15W 80 B3
North Downs U.K. 51°19N 0°21E 13 F8
North East U.S.A. 42°13N 79°50W 82 D5
North East Frontier Agency = Arunachal Pradesh □ India 28°0N 95°0E 41 F19
North East Lincolnshire □ U.K. 53°34N 0°2W 12 D7
North Eastern □ Kenya 1°30N 40°0E 54 B5
North Esk → U.K. 56°46N 2°24W 11 E6
North European Plain Europe 55°0N 25°0E 6 E10
North Foreland U.K. 51°22N 1°28E 13 F9
North Fork U.S.A. 37°14N 119°21W 78 H7
North Fork American → U.S.A. 38°57N 120°59W 78 G5
North Fork Feather → U.S.A. 38°33N 121°30W 78 F5
North Fork Grand → U.S.A. 45°47N 102°16W 80 C2
North Fork Red → U.S.A. 34°24N 99°14W 84 D5
North Frisian Is. = Nordfriesische Inseln Germany 54°40N 8°20E 16 A5
North Gower Canada 45°8N 75°43W 83 A9
North Hd. Australia 30°14S 114°59E 61 F1
North Henik L. Canada 61°45N 97°40W 71 A9
North Highlands U.S.A. 38°40N 121°23W 78 G5
North Horr Kenya 3°20N 37°8E 54 B4
North I. Kenya 4°5N 36°5E 54 B4
North I. N.Z. 38°0S 175°0E 59 C5
North I. Seychelles 4°25S 55°13E 53 b
North Kingsville U.S.A. 41°54N 80°42W 82 E4
North Kitui ⌓ Kenya 0°15S 38°29E 54 C4
North Knife → Canada 58°53N 94°45W 71 B10
North Koel → India 24°45N 83°50E 43 G10
North Korea ■ Asia 40°0N 127°0E 35 E14
North Lakhimpur India 27°14N 94°7E 41 F19
North Lanarkshire □ U.K. 55°52N 3°56W 11 F5
North Las Vegas U.S.A. 36°11N 115°7W 79 J11
North Lincolnshire □ U.K. 53°36N 0°30W 12 D7
North Little Rock U.S.A. 34°45N 92°16W 84 D8
North Loup → U.S.A. 41°17N 98°24W 80 E4
North Luangwa △ Zambia 11°49S 32°9E 55 E3
North Magnetic Pole Canada 82°42N 114°24W 69 B9
North Mankato U.S.A. 44°10N 94°2W 80 C6
North Minch U.K. 58°5N 5°55W 11 C3
North Moose L. Canada 54°4N 100°12W 71 C8
North Myrtle Beach U.S.A. 33°48N 78°42W 85 E15
North Nahanni → Canada 62°15N 123°20W 70 A4
North Olmsted U.S.A. 41°25N 81°56W 82 E3
North Ossetia □ Russia 43°30N 44°30E 19 F7
North Pagai, I. = Pagai Utara, Pulau Indonesia 2°35S 100°0E 36 E2
North Palisade U.S.A. 37°6N 118°31W 78 H8
North Platte U.S.A. 41°8N 100°46W 80 E3
North Platte → U.S.A. 41°7N 100°42W 80 E3
North Pole Arctic 90°0N 0°0 4 A
North Portal Canada 49°0N 102°33W 71 D8
North Powder U.S.A. 45°2N 117°55W 76 D5
North Pt. Barbados 13°20N 59°37W 89 g
North Pt. Trin. & Tob. 11°21N 60°31W 93 J16
North Pt. U.S.A. 45°2N 83°16W 82 A1
North Rhine Westphalia = Nordrhein-Westfalen □ Germany 51°45N 7°30E 16 C4
North River Canada 53°49N 57°6W 73 B8
North Ronaldsay U.K. 59°22N 2°26W 11 B6
North Saskatchewan → Canada 53°15N 105°5W 71 C7
North Sea Europe 56°0N 4°0E 6 D6
North Seal → Canada 58°50N 98°7W 71 B9
North Somerset □ U.K. 51°24N 2°45W 13 F5
North Sydney Canada 46°12N 60°15W 73 C7
North Syracuse U.S.A. 43°8N 76°7W 83 C8
North Taranaki Bight N.Z. 38°50S 174°15E 59 C5
North Thompson → Canada 50°40N 120°20W 70 C4
North Tonawanda U.S.A. 43°2N 78°53W 82 C6
North Troy U.S.A. 45°0N 72°24W 83 B12
North Twin I. Canada 53°20N 80°0W 72 B4
North Tyne → U.K. 55°0N 2°8W 12 B5
North Uist U.K. 57°40N 7°15W 11 D1
North Vancouver Canada 49°19N 123°4W 78 A3
North Vernon U.S.A. 39°0N 85°38W 81 F11
North Wabasca L. Canada 56°0N 113°55W 70 B6
North Walsham U.K. 52°50N 1°22E 12 E9
North West = Severo-Zapadnyy □ Russia 65°0N 40°0E 28 C4
North-West □ S. Africa 27°0S 25°0E 56 D4
North West C. Australia 21°45S 114°9E 60 D1
North West Frontier □ Pakistan 34°0N 72°0E 42 C4
North West Highlands U.K. 57°33N 4°58W 11 D4
North West River Canada 53°30N 60°10W 73 B7
North Western □ Zambia 13°30S 25°30E 55 E2
North Wildwood U.S.A. 39°0N 74°48W 81 F16
North York Moors U.K. 54°23N 0°53W 12 C7
North York Moors △ U.K. 54°27N 0°51W 12 C7
North Yorkshire □ U.K. 54°15N 1°25W 12 C6
Northallerton U.K. 54°20N 1°26W 12 C6
Northam Australia 31°35S 116°42E 61 F2
Northam S. Africa 24°56S 27°18E 56 C4
Northampton Australia 28°27S 114°33E 61 E1
Northampton U.K. 52°15N 0°53W 13 E7
Northampton Mass., U.S.A. 42°19N 72°38W 83 D12
Northampton Pa., U.S.A. 40°41N 75°30W 83 F9
Northamptonshire □ U.K. 52°16N 0°55W 13 E7
Northbridge U.S.A. 42°9N 71°39W 83 D13
Northbrook Canada 44°44N 77°9W 82 B7
Northcliffe Australia 34°39S 116°7E 61 F2
Northeast Pacific Basin Pac. Oc. 32°0N 145°0W 65 D13
Northeast Providence Chan. W. Indies 26°0N 76°0W 88 A4
Northern = Limpopo □ S. Africa 24°5S 29°0E 57 C4
Northern □ Malawi 11°0S 34°0E 55 E3
Northern □ Zambia 10°30S 31°0E 55 E3
Northern Areas □ Pakistan 36°30N 73°0E 43 A5
Northern Cape □ S. Africa 30°0S 20°0E 56 D3
Northern Circars India 17°30N 82°30E 41 L13
Northern Indian L. Canada 57°20N 97°20W 71 B9
Northern Ireland □ U.K. 54°45N 7°0W 10 B5
Northern Lau Group Fiji 17°30S 178°59W 59 a
Northern Light L. Canada 48°15N 90°39W 72 C1
Northern Marianas ☒ Pac. Oc. 17°0N 145°0E 64 F6
Northern Province □ S. Africa 24°0S 29°0E 57 C4
Northern Range Trin. & Tob. 10°46N 61°15W 93 K15
Northern Sporades Greece 39°15N 23°30E 23 E10
Northern Territory □ Australia 20°0S 133°0E 60 D5
Northfield Minn., U.S.A. 44°27N 93°9W 80 C7
Northfield Vt., U.S.A. 44°9N 72°40W 83 B12
Northgate Canada 49°0N 102°16W 71 D8
Northland □ N.Z. 35°30S 173°30E 59 A4
Northome U.S.A. 47°52N 94°17W 80 B6
Northport Ala., U.S.A. 33°14N 87°35W 85 E11
Northport Wash., U.S.A. 48°55N 117°48W 76 B5
Northumberland □ U.K. 55°12N 2°0W 12 B6
Northumberland, C. Australia 38°5S 140°40E 63 F3
Northumberland Is. Australia 21°30S 149°50E 62 C4
Northumberland Str. Canada 46°20N 64°0W 73 C7
Northville U.S.A. 43°13N 74°11W 83 C10
Northwest Pacific Basin Pac. Oc. 32°0N 165°0E 64 D8
Northwest Providence Channel W. Indies 26°0N 78°0W 88 A4
Northwest Territories □ Canada 63°0N 118°0W 68 C8
Northwich U.K. 53°15N 2°31W 12 D5
Northwood Iowa, U.S.A. 43°27N 93°13W 80 D7
Northwood N. Dak., U.S.A. 47°44N 97°34W 80 B5
Norton U.S.A. 39°50N 99°53W 80 F4
Norton Zimbabwe 17°52S 30°40E 55 F3
Norton Sd. U.S.A. 63°50N 164°0W 74 a
Norwalk Calif., U.S.A. 33°54N 118°4W 79 M8
Norwalk Conn., U.S.A. 41°7N 73°22W 83 E11
Norwalk Iowa, U.S.A. 41°29N 93°41W 80 E7
Norwalk Ohio, U.S.A. 41°15N 82°37W 82 E2
Norway Maine, U.S.A. 44°13N 70°32W 81 C18
Norway Mich., U.S.A. 45°47N 87°55W 80 C10
Norway ■ Europe 63°0N 11°0E 8 E14
Norway House Canada 53°59N 97°50W 71 C9
Norwegian B. Canada 77°30N 90°0W 69 B11
Norwegian Basin Atl. Oc. 68°0N 2°0W 4 C7
Norwegian Sea Atl. Oc. 66°0N 1°0E 6 B6
Norwich Canada 42°59N 80°36W 82 D4
Norwich U.K. 52°38N 1°18E 13 E9
Norwich Conn., U.S.A. 41°31N 72°5W 83 E12
Norwich N.Y., U.S.A. 42°32N 75°32W 83 D9
Norwood Canada 44°23N 77°59W 82 B7
Norwood U.S.A. 44°45N 75°0W 83 B10
Nosappu-Misaki Japan 45°26N 141°39E 30 C12
Noshiro Japan 40°12N 140°0E 30 D10
Noşratābād Iran 29°55N 60°0E 45 D8
Noss Hd. U.K. 58°28N 3°3W 11 C5
Nossob → S. Africa 26°55S 20°45E 56 D3
Nosy Barren Madag. 18°25S 43°40E 53 H8
Nosy Bé Madag. 13°25S 48°15E 53 G9
Nosy Boraha Madag. 16°50S 49°55E 57 B8
Nosy Lava Madag. 14°33S 47°36E 57 A8
Nosy Varika Madag. 20°35S 48°32E 57 C8
Noteć → Poland 52°44N 15°26E 16 B8
Notikewin → Canada 57°2N 117°38W 70 B5
Notodden Norway 59°35N 9°17E 9 G13
Notre Dame B. Canada 49°45N 55°30W 73 C8
Notre-Dame-de-Koartac = Quaqtaq Canada 60°55N 69°40W 69 C13
Notre-Dame-des-Bois Canada 45°24N 71°4W 83 A13
Notre-Dame-d'Ivugivic = Ivujivik Canada 62°24N 77°55W 69 C12
Notre-Dame-du-Nord Canada 47°36N 79°30W 72 C4
Nottawasaga B. Canada 44°35N 80°15W 82 B4
Nottaway → Canada 51°22N 78°55W 72 B4
Nottingham U.K. 52°58N 1°10W 12 E6
Nottingham, City of □ U.K. 52°58N 1°10W 12 E6
Nottingham I. Canada 63°20N 77°55W 69 C12
Nottinghamshire □ U.K. 53°10N 1°3W 12 D6
Nottoway → U.S.A. 36°33N 76°55W 81 G15
Notwane → Botswana 23°35S 26°58E 56 C4
Nouâdhibou Mauritania 20°54N 17°0W 50 D2
Nouâdhibou, Râs Mauritania 20°50N 17°0W 50 D2
Nouakchott Mauritania 18°9N 15°58W 50 E2
Nouméa N. Cal. 22°17S 166°30E 58 D9
Noupoort S. Africa 31°10S 24°57E 56 E3
Nouveau Comptoir = Wemindji Canada 53°0N 78°49W 72 B4
Nouvelle Amsterdam, Î. Ind. Oc. 38°30S 77°30E 3 F13
Nouvelle-Calédonie = New Caledonia ☒ Pac. Oc. 21°0S 165°0E 58 D9
Nova Esperança Brazil 23°8S 52°24W 95 A5
Nova Friburgo Brazil 22°16S 42°30W 95 A7
Nova Iguaçu Brazil 22°45S 43°28W 95 A7
Nova Iorque Brazil 7°0S 44°5W 93 E10
Nova Lamego Guinea-Biss. 12°19N 14°11W 50 F3
Nova Lima Brazil 19°59S 43°51W 93 G10
Nova Lusitânia Mozam. 19°50S 34°34E 55 F3
Nova Mambone Mozam. 21°0S 35°3E 57 C6
Nova Scotia □ Canada 45°10N 63°0W 73 C7
Nova Sofala Mozam. 20°7S 34°42E 57 C5
Nova Venécia Brazil 18°45S 40°24W 93 G10
Nova Zagora Bulgaria 42°32N 26°1E 23 C11
Novar Canada 45°27N 79°15W 82 A5
Novara Italy 45°28N 8°38E 20 D8
Novato U.S.A. 38°6N 122°35W 78 G4
Novaya Ladoga Russia 60°7N 32°16E 18 B5
Novaya Lyalya Russia 59°4N 60°45E 18 C11
Novaya Sibir, Ostrov Russia 75°10N 150°0E 29 B16
Novaya Zemlya Russia 75°0N 56°0E 28 B6
Nové Zámky Slovak Rep. 48°2N 18°8E 17 D10
Novgorod Russia 58°30N 31°25E 18 C5
Novgorod-Severskiy = Novhorod-Siverskyy Ukraine 52°2N 33°10E 18 D5
Novhorod-Siverskyy Ukraine 52°2N 33°10E 18 D5
Novi Lígure Italy 44°46N 8°47E 20 D8
Novi Pazar Serbia 43°12N 20°28E 23 C9
Novi Sad Serbia 45°18N 19°52E 23 B8
Novo Hamburgo Brazil 29°37S 51°7W 95 B5
Novo Mesto Slovenia 45°47N 15°12E 22 B6
Novoaltaysk Russia 53°30N 84°0E 28 D9
Novocherkassk Russia 47°27N 40°15E 19 E7
Novodvinsk Russia 64°25N 40°42E 28 C5
Novogrudok = Navahrudak Belarus 53°40N 25°50E 17 B13
Novohrad-Volynskyy Ukraine 50°34N 27°35E 17 C14
Novokachalinsk Russia 45°5N 132°0E 30 B5
Novokuybyshevsk Russia 53°7N 49°58E 18 D8
Novokuznetsk Russia 53°45N 87°10E 28 D9
Novolazarevskaya Antarctica 71°0S 12°0E 5 D3
Novomoskovsk Russia 54°5N 38°15E 18 D6
Novorossiysk Russia 44°43N 37°46E 19 F6
Novorybnoye Russia 72°50N 105°50E 29 B11
Novoselytsya Ukraine 48°14N 26°15E 17 D14
Novoshakhtinsk Russia 47°46N 39°58E 19 E6
Novosibirsk Russia 55°0N 83°5E 28 D9
Novosibirskiye Ostrova Russia 75°0N 142°0E 29 B15
Novotroitsk Russia 51°10N 58°15E 18 D10
Novouzensk Russia 50°32N 48°17E 19 D8
Novovolynsk Ukraine 50°45N 24°4E 17 C13
Novska Croatia 45°19N 17°0E 22 B7
Novyy Urengoy Russia 65°48N 76°52E 28 C8
Novyy Bor Russia 66°43N 52°19E 18 A9
Novyy Port Russia 67°40N 72°30E 28 C8
Nowa Sól Poland 51°48N 15°44E 16 C8
Nowata U.S.A. 36°42N 95°38W 84 C7
Nowbarān Iran 35°8N 49°42E 45 C6
Nowghāb Iran 33°53N 59°4E 45 C8
Nowgong Assam, India 26°20N 92°50E 41 F18
Nowgong Mad. P., India 25°4N 79°27E 43 G8
Nowra Australia 34°53S 150°35E 63 E5
Nowshera Pakistan 34°0N 72°0E 40 C8
Nowy Sącz Poland 49°40N 20°41E 17 D11
Nowy Targ Poland 49°29N 20°2E 17 D11
Nowy Tomyśl Poland 52°19N 16°10E 16 B9
Noxen U.S.A. 41°25N 76°4W 83 E8
Noyabr'sk Russia 64°34N 76°21E 28 C8
Noyon France 49°34N 2°59E 20 B5
Noyon Mongolia 43°2N 102°4E 34 C2
Nqutu S. Africa 28°13S 30°32E 57 D5
Nsanje Malawi 16°55S 35°12E 55 F4
Nsawam Ghana 5°50N 0°24W 50 G5
Nsomba Zambia 10°45S 29°51E 55 E2
Nu Jiang → China 29°58N 97°25E 32 D4
Nu Shan China 26°0N 99°20E 32 D4
Nuba Mts. = Nubah, Jibalan Sudan 12°0N 31°0E 51 F12
Nubah, Jibalan Sudan 12°0N 31°0E 51 F12
Nubia Africa 21°0N 32°0E 48 D7
Nubian Desert = Nûbîya, Es Sahrâ en Sudan 21°30N 33°30E 51 D12
Nûbîya, Es Sahrâ en Sudan 21°30N 33°30E 51 D12
Nuboai Indonesia 2°10S 136°30E 37 E9
Nubra → India 34°35N 77°35E 43 B7
Nueces → U.S.A. 27°51N 97°30W 84 H6
Nueltin L. Canada 60°30N 99°30W 71 A9
Nuestra Señora del Rosario de Caá-Catí Argentina 27°45S 57°36W 94 B4
Nueva Ciudad Guerrero Mexico 26°34N 99°12W 87 B5
Nueva Gerona Cuba 21°53N 82°49W 88 B3
Nueva Palmira Uruguay 33°52S 58°20W 94 C4
Nueva Rosita Mexico 27°57N 101°13W 86 B4
Nueva San Salvador El Salv. 13°40N 89°18W 88 D2
Nuéve de Julio Argentina 35°30S 61°0W 94 D3
Nuevitas Cuba 21°30N 77°20W 88 B4
Nuevo, G. Argentina 43°0S 64°30W 96 E4
Nuevo Casas Grandes Mexico 30°25N 107°55W 86 A3
Nuevo Laredo Mexico 27°30N 99°31W 87 B5
Nuevo León □ Mexico 25°20N 100°0W 86 C5
Nuevo Rocafuerte Ecuador 0°55S 75°27W 92 D3
Nugget Pt. N.Z. 46°27S 169°50E 59 G2
Nuhaka N.Z. 39°3S 177°45E 59 C6
Nukey Bluff Australia 32°26S 135°29E 63 E2
Nukhayb Iraq 32°4N 42°3E 44 C4
Nuku Hiva French Polynesia 8°54S 140°6W 65 H13
Nuku'alofa Tonga 21°10S 175°12W 59 c
Nukus Uzbekistan 42°27N 59°41E 28 E6
Nullagine Australia 21°53S 120°7E 60 D3
Nullagine → Australia 21°20S 120°20E 60 D3
Nullarbor Australia 31°28S 130°55E 61 F5
Nullarbor △ Australia 32°39S 130°0E 61 F5
Nullarbor Plain Australia 31°10S 129°0E 61 F4
Numalla, L. Australia 28°43S 144°20E 63 D3
Numan Nigeria 9°29N 12°3E 51 G8
Numata Japan 36°45N 139°4E 31 F9
Numaykoos Lake ⌓ Canada 57°52N 95°58W 71 B9
Numazu Japan 35°7N 138°51E 31 G9
Numbulwar Australia 14°15S 135°45E 62 A2
Numfoor Indonesia 1°0S 134°50E 37 E8
Numurkah Australia 36°5S 145°26E 63 F4
Nunaksaluk I. Canada 55°49N 60°20W 73 A7
Nunap Isua Greenland 59°48N 43°55W 66 D15
Nunavut □ Canada 66°0N 85°0W 69 C11
Nunda U.S.A. 42°35N 77°56W 82 D7
Nuneaton U.K. 52°32N 1°27W 13 E6
Nungarin Australia 31°12S 118°6E 61 F2
Nungo Mozam. 13°23S 37°43E 55 E4
Nungwe Tanzania 2°48S 32°2E 54 C3
Nunivak I. U.S.A. 60°10N 166°30W 74 a
Nunkun India 33°57N 76°2E 43 C7
Núoro Italy 40°20N 9°20E 22 D3
Nūr Iran 36°33N 52°1E 45 B7
Nūrābād Hormozgān, Iran 27°47N 57°12E 45 E8
Nūrābād Lorestān, Iran 34°4N 47°58E 44 C5
Nuremberg = Nürnberg Germany 49°27N 11°3E 16 D6
Nuri Mexico 28°5N 109°22W 86 B3
Nuriootpa Australia 34°27S 139°0E 63 E2
Nuristān □ Afghan. 35°20N 71°0E 40 B7
Nurmes Finland 63°33N 29°10E 8 E23
Nürnberg Germany 49°27N 11°3E 16 D6
Nurpur Pakistan 31°53N 71°54E 42 D4
Nurran, L. = Terewah, L. Australia 29°52S 147°35E 63 D4
Nurrari Lakes Australia 29°1S 130°5E 61 E5
Nusa Barung Indonesia 8°30S 113°30E 37 H15
Nusa Dua Indonesia 8°48S 115°14E 37 K18
Nusa Kambangan Indonesia 7°40S 108°10E 37 G13
Nusa Tenggara Barat □ Indonesia 8°50S 117°30E 36 F5
Nusa Tenggara Timur □ Indonesia 9°30S 122°0E 37 F6
Nusaybin Turkey 37°3N 41°10E 19 G7
Nushki Pakistan 29°35N 66°0E 42 E2
Nuuk Greenland 64°10N 51°35W 67 C14
Nuupere, Pte. Moorea 17°36S 149°47W 59 d
Nuwakot Nepal 28°10N 83°55E 43 E10
Nuwayb'ī, W. an → Si. Arabia 29°18N 34°57E 46 F3
Nuweiba' Egypt 28°59N 34°39E 44 D2
Nuwerus S. Africa 31°8S 18°24E 56 E2
Nuweveldberge S. Africa 32°10S 21°45E 56 E3
Nuyts, Pt. Australia 35°4S 116°38E 61 G2
Nuyts Arch. Australia 32°35S 133°20E 63 E1
Nxai Pan △ Botswana 19°50S 24°46E 56 B3
Nxau-Nxau Botswana 18°57S 21°4E 56 B3
Nyabing Australia 33°33S 118°9E 61 F2
Nyack U.S.A. 41°5N 73°55W 83 E11
Nyagan Russia 62°30N 65°38E 28 C7
Nyahanga Tanzania 2°20S 33°37E 54 C3
Nyahua Tanzania 5°25S 33°23E 54 D3
Nyahururu Kenya 0°2N 36°27E 54 B4
Nyainqêntanglha Shan China 30°0N 90°0E 32 D3
Nyakanazi Tanzania 3°2S 31°10E 54 C3
Nyâlâ Sudan 12°2N 24°58E 51 F10
Nyamandhlovu Zimbabwe 19°55S 28°16E 55 F2
Nyambiti Tanzania 2°48S 33°27E 54 C3
Nyamira Kenya 0°36S 34°52E 54 B4
Nyamwaga Tanzania 1°27S 34°33E 54 C3
Nyandekwa Tanzania 3°57S 32°32E 54 C3
Nyandoma Russia 61°40N 40°12E 18 B7
Nyanga △ Zimbabwe 18°17S 32°46E 55 F3
Nyangana Namibia 18°0S 20°40E 56 B3
Nyanguge Tanzania 2°30S 33°12E 54 C3
Nyanza Rwanda 2°20S 29°42E 54 C2
Nyanza □ Kenya 0°10S 34°15E 54 C3
Nyanza-Lac Burundi 4°21S 29°36E 54 C2
Nyasa, L. = Malawi, L. Africa 12°30S 34°30E 55 E3
Nyasvizh Belarus 53°14N 26°38E 17 B14
Nyazepetrovsk Russia 56°3N 59°36E 18 C10
Nyazura Zimbabwe 18°40S 32°16E 55 F3
Nyazwidzi → Zimbabwe 20°0S 31°17E 55 G3
Nybro Sweden 56°44N 15°55E 9 H16
Nyda Russia 66°40N 72°58E 28 C8
Nyeri Kenya 0°23S 36°56E 54 C4
Nyika △ Malawi 10°30S 33°53E 55 E3
Nyíregyháza Hungary 47°58N 21°47E 17 E11
Nyiru, Mt. Kenya 2°8N 36°50E 54 B4
Nykarleby = Uusikaarlepyy Finland 63°32N 22°31E 8 E20
Nykøbing Nordjylland, Denmark 56°48N 8°51E 9 H13
Nykøbing Sjælland, Denmark 54°56N 11°52E 9 J14
Nykøbing Sjælland, Denmark 55°55N 11°40E 9 J14
Nyköping Sweden 58°45N 17°1E 9 G17
Nylstroom = Modimolle S. Africa 24°42S 28°22E 57 C4
Nymagee Australia 32°7S 146°20E 63 E4
Nymboida △ Australia 29°38S 152°26E 63 D5
Nynäshamn Sweden 58°54N 17°57E 9 G17
Nyngan Australia 31°30S 147°8E 63 E4
Nyoma Rap India 33°10N 78°40E 43 C8
Nyoman = Nemunas → Lithuania 55°25N 21°10E 9 J19
Nysa Poland 50°30N 17°22E 17 C9
Nysa → Europe 52°4N 14°46E 16 B8
Nyslott = Savonlinna Finland 61°52N 28°53E 8 F23
Nyssa U.S.A. 43°53N 117°0W 76 E5
Nystad = Uusikaupunki Finland 60°47N 21°25E 8 F19
Nyunzu Dem. Rep. of the Congo 5°57S 27°58E 54 D2
Nyurba Russia 63°17N 118°28E 29 C12
Nzega Tanzania 4°10S 33°12E 54 C3
Nzérékoré Guinea 7°49N 8°48W 50 G4
Nzeto Angola 7°10S 12°52E 52 F2
Nzilo, Chutes de Dem. Rep. of the Congo 10°18S 25°27E 55 E2
Nzubuka Tanzania 4°45S 32°50E 54 C3
Nzwani = Anjouan Comoros Is. 12°15S 44°20E 53 a

O

O Le Pupū Pu'e △ Samoa 13°59S 171°43W 59 b
Ō-Shima Hokkaidō, Japan 41°30N 139°22E 30 D9
Ō-Shima Shizuoka, Japan 34°44N 139°24E 31 G9
Oa, Mull of U.K. 55°35N 6°20W 11 F2

Oacoma *U.S.A.* 43°48N 99°24W **80** D4
Oahe, L. *U.S.A.* 44°27N 100°24W **80** C3
Oahe Dam *U.S.A.* 44°27N 100°24W **80** C3
O'ahu *U.S.A.* 21°28N 157°58W **74** b
Oak Harbor *U.S.A.* 48°18N 122°39W **78** B4
Oak Hill *U.S.A.* 37°59N 81°9W **81** G13
Oak Island *U.S.A.* 33°55N 78°10W **85** E15
Oak Ridge *U.S.A.* 36°1N 84°16W **85** C12
Oak View *U.S.A.* 34°24N 119°18W **79** L7
Oakan-Dake *Japan* 43°27N 144°10E **30** C12
Oakdale *Calif., U.S.A.* 37°46N 120°51W **78** H6
Oakdale *La., U.S.A.* 30°49N 92°40W **84** F8
Oakes *U.S.A.* 46°8N 98°6W **80** B4
Oakesdale *U.S.A.* 47°8N 117°15W **76** C5
Oakey *Australia* 27°25S 151°43E **63** D5
Oakfield *U.S.A.* 43°4N 78°16W **82** C6
Oakham *U.K.* 52°40N 0°43W **13** E7
Oakhurst *U.S.A.* 37°19N 119°40W **78** H7
Oakland *Calif., U.S.A.* 37°48N 122°18W **78** H4
Oakland *Pa., U.S.A.* 41°57N 75°36W **83** E9
Oakley *Idaho, U.S.A.* 42°15N 113°53W **76** E7
Oakley *Kans., U.S.A.* 39°8N 100°51W **80** F3
Oakover → *Australia* 21°0S 120°40E **60** D3
Oakridge *U.S.A.* 43°45N 122°28W **76** E2
Oakville *Canada* 43°27N 79°41W **82** C5
Oakville *U.S.A.* 46°51N 123°14W **78** D3
Oamaru *N.Z.* 45°5S 170°59E **59** F3
Oasis *Calif., U.S.A.* 37°29N 117°55W **78** H9
Oasis *Calif., U.S.A.* 33°28N 116°6W **79** M10
Oates Land *Antarctica* 69°0S 160°0E **5** C11
Oatlands *Australia* 42°17S 147°21E **63** G4
Oatman *U.S.A.* 35°1N 114°19W **79** K12
Oaxaca *Mexico* 17°3N 96°43W **87** D5
Oaxaca □ *Mexico* 17°0N 96°30W **87** D5
Ob → *Russia* 66°45N 69°30E **28** C7
Oba *Canada* 49°4N 84°7W **72** C3
Obama *Japan* 35°30N 135°45E **31** G7
Oban *U.K.* 56°25N 5°29W **11** E3
Oberá *Argentina* 27°21S 55°2W **95** B4
Oberhausen *Germany* 51°28N 6°51E **16** C4
Oberlin *Kans., U.S.A.* 39°49N 100°32W **80** F3
Oberlin *La., U.S.A.* 30°37N 92°46W **84** F8
Oberlin *Ohio, U.S.A.* 41°18N 82°13W **82** E2
Oberon *Australia* 33°45S 149°52E **63** E4
Obi, Kepulauan *Indonesia* 1°23S 127°45E **37** E7
Óbidos *Brazil* 1°50S 55°30W **93** D7
Obihiro *Japan* 42°56N 143°12E **30** C11
Obilatu *Indonesia* 1°25S 127°20E **37** E7
Obluchye *Russia* 49°1N 131°4E **29** E14
Obo *C.A.R.* 5°20N 26°32E **54** A2
Oboyan *Russia* 51°15N 36°21E **28** D4
Obozerskaya = Obozerskiy
Russia 63°34N 40°21E **18** B7
Obozerskiy *Russia* 63°34N 40°21E **18** B7
Observatory Inlet
Canada 55°10N 129°54W **70** B3
Obshchi Syrt *Russia* 52°0N 53°0E **6** E16
Obskaya Guba *Russia* 69°0N 73°0E **28** C8
Obuasi *Ghana* 6°17N 1°40W **50** G5
Ocala *U.S.A.* 29°11N 82°8W **85** G13
Ocampo *Chihuahua,*
Mexico 28°11N 108°23W **86** B3
Ocampo *Tamaulipas,*
Mexico 22°50N 99°20W **87** C5
Ocaña *Spain* 39°55N 3°30W **21** C4
Occidental, Cordillera
Colombia 5°0N 76°0W **92** C3
Occidental, Grand Erg
Algeria 30°20N 1°0E **50** B6
Ocean City *Md., U.S.A.* 38°20N 75°5W **81** F16
Ocean City *N.J., U.S.A.* 39°17N 74°35W **81** F16
Ocean City *Wash.,*
U.S.A. 47°4N 124°10W **78** C2
Ocean Falls *Canada* 52°18N 127°48W **70** C3
Ocean I. = Banaba
Kiribati 0°45S 169°50E **64** H8
Ocean Park *U.S.A.* 46°30N 124°3W **78** D2
Oceano *U.S.A.* 35°6N 120°37W **79** K6
Oceanport *U.S.A.* 40°19N 74°3W **83** F10
Oceanside *U.S.A.* 33°12N 117°23W **79** M9
Ochil Hills *U.K.* 56°14N 3°40W **11** E5
Ocho Rios *Jamaica* 18°24N 77°6W **88** a
Ocilla *U.S.A.* 31°36N 83°15W **85** F13
Ocmulgee → *U.S.A.* 31°58N 82°33W **85** F13
Ocniţa *Moldova* 48°25N 27°30E **17** D14
Oconee → *U.S.A.* 31°58N 82°33W **85** F13
Oconomowoc *U.S.A.* 43°7N 88°30W **80** D9
Oconto *U.S.A.* 44°53N 87°52W **80** C10
Oconto Falls *U.S.A.* 44°52N 88°9W **80** C9
Ocosingo *Mexico* 16°53N 92°6W **87** D6
Ocotal *Nic.* 13°41N 86°31W **88** D2
Ocotlán *Jalisco, Mexico* 20°21N 102°46W **86** C4
Ocotlán *Oaxaca, Mexico* 16°48N 96°40W **87** D5
Ōda *Japan* 35°11N 132°30E **31** G6
Ódáðahraun *Iceland* 65°5N 17°0W **8** D5
Ŏdaejin *N. Korea* 41°34N 129°40E **30** D4
Odate *Japan* 40°16N 140°34E **30** D10
Odawara *Japan* 35°20N 139°6E **31** G9
Odda *Norway* 60°3N 6°35E **9** F12
Odei → *Canada* 56°6N 96°54W **71** B9
Ödemiş *Turkey* 38°15N 28°0E **23** E13
Odendaalsrus *S. Africa* 27°48S 26°45E **56** D4
Odense *Denmark* 55°22N 10°23E **9** J14
Oder → *Europe* 53°33N 14°38E **16** B8
Odesa *Ukraine* 46°30N 30°45E **19** E5
Odessa = Odesa *Ukraine* 46°30N 30°45E **19** E5
Odessa *Canada* 44°17N 76°43W **83** B8
Odessa *Tex., U.S.A.* 31°52N 102°23W **84** F3
Odessa *Wash., U.S.A.* 47°20N 118°41W **76** C4
Odiakwe *Botswana* 20°12S 25°17E **56** C4
Odienné *Ivory C.* 9°30N 7°34W **50** G4
Odintsovo *Russia* 55°40N 37°16E **18** C6
O'Donnell *U.S.A.* 32°58N 101°50W **84** E4
O'Donnell Pt. *Canada* 45°5N 80°5W **82** A4
Odorheiu Secuiesc
Romania 46°21N 25°21E **17** E13
Odra = Oder → *Europe* 53°33N 14°38E **16** B8
Odzi *Zimbabwe* 19°0S 32°20E **57** B5
Odzi → *Zimbabwe* 19°45S 32°23E **57** B5
Oeiras *Brazil* 7°0S 42°8W **93** E10
Oelrichs *U.S.A.* 43°11N 103°14W **80** D2
Oelwein *U.S.A.* 42°41N 91°55W **80** D8
Oeno I. *Pac. Oc.* 24°0S 131°0W **65** K14
Oenpelli = Gunbalanya
Australia 12°20S 133°4E **60** B5
Ofanto → *Italy* 41°22N 16°13E **22** D7
Offa *Nigeria* 8°13N 4°42E **50** G6
Offaly □ *Ireland* 53°15N 7°30W **10** C4
Offenbach *Germany* 50°6N 8°44E **16** C5
Offenburg *Germany* 48°28N 7°56E **16** D4
Officer Cr. → *Australia* 27°46S 132°30E **61** E5
Ofolanga *Tonga* 19°38S 174°27W **59** c
Ofotfjorden *Norway* 68°27N 17°0E **8** B17
Ofu *Amer. Samoa* 14°11S 169°41W **59** b
Ōfunato *Japan* 39°4N 141°43E **30** E10
Oga *Japan* 39°55N 139°50E **30** E9
Oga-Hantō *Japan* 39°58N 139°47E **30** E9
Ogaden *Ethiopia* 7°30N 45°30E **47** F3
Ōgaki *Japan* 35°21N 136°37E **31** G8
Ogallala *U.S.A.* 41°8N 101°43W **80** E3
Ogasawara Gunto
Pac. Oc. 27°0N 142°0E **27** F16
Ogbomosho *Nigeria* 8°1N 4°11E **50** G6
Ogden *U.S.A.* 41°13N 111°58W **76** F8
Ogdensburg *U.S.A.* 44°42N 75°30W **83** B9
Ogea Driki *Fiji* 19°12S 178°27W **59** a
Ogea Levu *Fiji* 19°8S 178°24W **59** a
Ogeechee → *U.S.A.* 31°50N 81°3W **85** F14
Ogilby *U.S.A.* 32°49N 114°50W **79** N12
Oglio → *Italy* 45°2N 10°39E **22** B4
Ogmore *Australia* 22°37S 149°35E **62** C4
Ogoki *Canada* 51°38N 85°58W **72** B2
Ogoki → *Canada* 51°38N 85°57W **72** B2
Ogoki L. *Canada* 50°50N 87°10W **72** B2
Ogoki Res. *Canada* 50°45N 88°15W **72** B2
Ogooué → *Gabon* 1°0S 9°0E **52** E1
Ogowe = Ogooué → *Gabon* 1°0S 9°0E **52** E1
Ogre *Latvia* 56°49N 24°36E **9** H21
Ogurchinskiy, Ostrov
Turkmenistan 38°55N 53°2E **45** B7
Ohai *N.Z.* 45°55S 168°0E **59** F2
Ohakune *N.Z.* 39°24S 175°24E **59** C5
Ohata *Japan* 41°24N 141°10E **30** D10
Ohau, L. *N.Z.* 44°15S 169°53E **59** F2
Ohio □ *U.S.A.* 40°15N 82°45W **82** F2
Ohio → *U.S.A.* 36°59N 89°8W **80** G9
Ohře → *Czech Rep.* 50°30N 14°10E **16** C8
Ohrid *Macedonia* 41°8N 20°52E **23** D9
Ohridsko Jezero
Macedonia 41°8N 20°52E **23** D9
Ohrigstad *S. Africa* 24°39S 30°36E **57** C5
Oiapoque *Brazil* 3°50N 51°50W **93**
Oikou *China* 38°35N 117°42E **35** E9
Oil City *U.S.A.* 41°26N 79°42W **82** E5
Oil Springs *Canada* 42°47N 82°7W **82** D2
Oildale *U.S.A.* 35°25N 119°1W **79** K7
Oise → *France* 49°0N 2°4E **20** B5
Oistins *Barbados* 13°4N 59°33W **89** g
Oistins B. *Barbados* 13°4N 59°33W **89** g
Ōita *Japan* 33°14N 131°36E **31** H5
Ōita □ *Japan* 33°15N 131°30E **31** H5
Oiticica *Brazil* 5°3S 41°5W **93** E10
Ojai *U.S.A.* 34°27N 119°15W **79** L7
Ojinaga *Mexico* 29°34N 104°25W **86** B4
Ojiya *Japan* 37°18N 138°48E **31** F9
Ojo Caliente *Mexico* 21°53N 102°15W **86** C4
Ojos del Salado, Cerro
Argentina 27°0S 68°40W **94** B2
Oka → *Russia* 56°20N 43°59E **18** C7
Okaba *Indonesia* 8°6S 139°42E **37** F9
Okahandja *Namibia* 22°0S 16°59E **56** C2
Okanagan L. *Canada* 50°0N 119°30W **70** D5
Okandja *Gabon* 0°35S 13°45E **52** E2
Okanogan *U.S.A.* 48°22N 119°35W **76** B4
Okanogan → *U.S.A.* 48°6N 119°44W **76** B4
Okanogan Range
N. Amer. 49°0N 119°55W **70** D5
Okapi △
Dem. Rep. of the Congo 2°30N 27°20E **54** B2
Okaputa *Namibia* 20°5S 17°0E **56** C2
Okara *Pakistan* 30°50N 73°31E **42** D5
Okaukuejo *Namibia* 19°10S 16°0E **56** B2
Okavango Delta
Botswana 18°45S 22°45E **56** B3
Okavango Swamp = Okavango
Delta *Botswana* 18°45S 22°45E **56** B3
Okaya *Japan* 36°5N 138°10E **31** F9
Okayama *Japan* 34°40N 133°54E **31** G6
Okayama □ *Japan* 35°0N 133°50E **31** G6
Okazaki *Japan* 34°57N 137°10E **31** G8
Okeechobee *U.S.A.* 27°15N 80°50W **85** H14
Okeechobee, L. *U.S.A.* 27°0N 80°50W **85** H14
Okefenokee ⌂ *U.S.A.* 30°45N 82°18W **85** F13
Okefenokee Swamp
U.S.A. 30°40N 82°20W **85** F13
Okehampton *U.K.* 50°44N 4°0W **13** G4
Okha *India* 22°27N 69°4E **42** H3
Okha *Russia* 53°40N 143°0E **29** D15
Okhotsk *Russia* 59°20N 143°10E **29** D15
Okhotsk, Sea of *Asia* 55°0N 145°0E **29** D15
Okhotskiy Perevoz
Russia 61°52N 135°35E **29** C14
Okhtyrka *Ukraine* 50°25N 35°0E **19** D5
Oki-Shotō *Japan* 36°5N 133°15E **31** F6
Okiep *S. Africa* 29°39S 17°53E **56** D2
Okinawa *Japan* 26°19N 127°46E **31** L3
Okinawa □ *Japan* 26°40N 128°0E **31** L4
Okinawa-Guntō *Japan* 26°40N 128°0E **31** L4
Okinawa-Jima *Japan* 26°32N 128°0E **31** L4
Okino-erabu-Shima
Japan 27°21N 128°33E **31** L4
Oklahoma □ *U.S.A.* 35°20N 97°30W **84** D6
Oklahoma City *U.S.A.* 35°30N 97°30W **84** D6
Okmulgee *U.S.A.* 35°37N 95°58W **84** D7
Oknitsa = Ocniţa
Moldova 48°25N 27°30E **17** D14
Okolo *Uganda* 2°37N 31°8E **54** B3
Okolona *U.S.A.* 34°0N 88°45W **85** E10
Okombahe *Namibia* 21°23S 15°22E **56** C2
Okotoks *Canada* 50°43N 113°58W **70** C6
Oksibil *Indonesia* 4°59S 140°35E **37** E10
Oksovskiy *Russia* 62°33N 39°57E **18** B6
Oktyabrsk = Qandyaghash
Kazakhstan 49°28N 57°25E **19** E10
Oktyabrskiy = Aktsyabrski
Belarus 52°38N 28°53E **17** B15
Oktyabrskiy *Bashkortostan,*
Russia 54°28N 53°28E **18** D9
Oktyabrskiy *Kamchatka,*
Russia 52°39N 156°14E **29** D16
Oktyabrskoy Revolyutsii, Ostrov
Russia 79°30N 97°0E **29** B10
Okuru *N.Z.* 43°55S 168°55E **59** E2
Okushiri-Tō *Japan* 42°15N 139°30E **30** C9
Okwa → *Botswana* 22°30S 23°0E **56** C3
Ola *Russia* 59°35N 151°17E **29** D16
Ola *U.S.A.* 35°2N 93°13W **84** D8
Ólafsfjörður *Iceland* 66°4N 18°39W **8** C4
Ólafsvík *Iceland* 64°53N 23°43W **8** D2
Olancha *U.S.A.* 36°17N 118°1W **79** J8
Olancha Pk. *U.S.A.* 36°16N 118°7W **79** J8
Olanchito *Honduras* 15°30N 86°30W **88** C2
Öland *Sweden* 56°45N 16°38E **9** H17
Olary *Australia* 32°18S 140°19E **63** E3
Olascoaga *Argentina* 35°15S 60°39W **94** D3
Olathe *U.S.A.* 38°53N 94°49W **80** F6
Olavarría *Argentina* 36°55S 60°20W **94** D3
Oława *Poland* 50°57N 17°20E **17** C9
Ólbia *Italy* 40°55N 9°31E **22** D3
Olcott *U.S.A.* 43°20N 78°42W **82** C6
Old Bahama Chan. = Bahama,
Canal Viejo de
W. Indies 22°10N 77°30W **88** B4
Old Baldy Pk. = San Antonio, Mt.
U.S.A. 34°17N 117°38W **79** L9
Old Bridge *U.S.A.* 40°25N 74°22W **83** F10
Old Castile = Castilla y Leon □
Spain 42°0N 5°0W **21** B3
Old Crow *Canada* 67°30N 139°55W **68** C6
Old Dale *U.S.A.* 34°8N 115°47W **79** L11
Old Forge *N.Y., U.S.A.* 43°43N 74°58W **83** C10
Old Forge *Pa., U.S.A.* 41°22N 75°45W **83** E9
Old Perlican *Canada* 48°5N 53°1W **73** C9
Old Shinyanga *Tanzania* 3°33S 33°27E **54** C3
Old Speck Mt. *U.S.A.* 44°34N 70°57W **83** B14
Old Town *U.S.A.* 44°56N 68°39W **81** C19
Old Washington *U.S.A.* 40°2N 81°27W **82** F3
Old Wives L. *Canada* 50°5N 106°0W **71** C7
Oldbury *U.K.* 51°38N 2°33W **13** F5
Oldcastle *Ireland* 53°46N 7°10W **10** C4
Oldeani *Tanzania* 3°22S 35°35E **54** C4
Oldenburg *Germany* 53°9N 8°13E **16** B5
Oldenzaal *Neths.* 52°19N 6°53E **15** B6
Oldham *U.K.* 53°33N 2°7W **12** D5
Oldman → *Canada* 49°57N 111°42W **70** D6
Oldmeldrum *U.K.* 57°20N 2°19W **11** D6
Olds *Canada* 51°50N 114°10W **70** C6
Olduvai Gorge *Tanzania* 2°57S 35°23E **54** C4
Oldziyt *Mongolia* 44°40N 109°1E **34** B5
Olean *U.S.A.* 42°5N 78°26W **82** D6
Olekma → *Russia* 60°22N 120°42E **29** C13
Olekminsk *Russia* 60°25N 120°30E **29** C13
Oleksandriya *Ukraine* 50°37N 26°19E **17** C14
Olema *U.S.A.* 38°3N 122°47W **78** G4
Olenegorsk *Russia* 68°9N 33°18E **8** B25
Olenek *Russia* 68°28N 112°18E **29** C12
Olenek → *Russia* 73°0N 120°10E **29** B13
Oléron, Î. d' *France* 45°55N 1°15W **20** D3
Oleśnica *Poland* 51°13N 17°22E **17** C9
Olevsk *Ukraine* 51°12N 27°39E **17** C14
Olga, L. *Canada* 49°47N 77°15W **72** C4
Olgas, The = Kata Tjuta
Australia 25°20S 130°50E **61** E5
Ölgiy *Mongolia* 48°56N 89°57E **32** B3
Olhão *Portugal* 37°3N 7°48W **21** D2
Olifants = Elefantes →
Africa 24°10S 32°40E **57** C5
Olifants → *Namibia* 25°30S 19°30E **56** C2
Olifantshoek *S. Africa* 27°57S 22°42E **56** D3
Ólimbos, Óros = Olymbos Oros
Greece 40°6N 22°23E **23** D10
Olímpia *Brazil* 20°44S 48°54W **95** A6
Olinda *Brazil* 8°1S 34°51W **93** E12
Oliva *Argentina* 32°0S 63°38W **94** C3
Olivares, Cerro los
Argentina 30°18S 69°55W **94** C2
Olive Branch *U.S.A.* 34°57N 89°49W **85** D10
Olivehurst *U.S.A.* 39°6N 121°34W **78** F5
Olivenza *Spain* 38°41N 7°9W **21** C2
Oliver *Canada* 49°13N 119°37W **70** D5
Oliver L. *Canada* 56°56N 103°22W **71** B8
Ollagüe *Chile* 21°15S 68°10W **94** A2
Olmaliq *Uzbekistan* 40°50N 69°35E **28** E7
Olney *Ill., U.S.A.* 38°44N 88°5W **80** F9
Olney *Tex., U.S.A.* 33°22N 98°45W **84** E5
Oloitokitok *Kenya* 2°56S 37°30E **54** C4
Olomane → *Canada* 50°14N 60°37W **73** B7
Olomouc *Czech Rep.* 49°38N 17°12E **17** D9
Olonets *Russia* 61°0N 32°54E **18** B5
Olongapo *Phil.* 14°50N 120°18E **37** B6
Olosega *Amer. Samoa* 14°10S 169°37W **59** b
Olosenga = Swains I.
Amer. Samoa 11°11S 171°4W **65** J11
Olot *Spain* 42°11N 2°30E **21** A7
Olovyannaya *Russia* 50°58N 115°35E **29** D12
Oloy → *Russia* 66°29N 159°29E **29** C16
Olsztyn *Poland* 53°48N 20°29E **17** B11
Olt → *Romania* 43°43N 24°51E **17** G13
Olteniţa *Romania* 44°7N 26°42E **17** F14
Olton *U.S.A.* 34°11N 102°8W **84** D3
Olymbos *Cyprus* 35°21N 33°45E **25** D12
Olymbos Oros *Greece* 40°6N 22°23E **23** D10
Olympia *Greece* 37°39N 21°39E **23** F9
Olympia *U.S.A.* 47°3N 122°53W **78** D4
Olympic △ *U.S.A.* 47°45N 123°43W **78** C3
Olympic Dam *Australia* 30°30S 136°55E **63** E2
Olympic Mts. *U.S.A.* 47°55N 123°45W **78** C3
Olympus *Cyprus* 34°56N 32°52E **25** E11
Olympus, Mt. = Olymbos Oros
Greece 40°6N 22°23E **23** D10
Olympus, Mt. = Uludağ
Turkey 40°4N 29°13E **23** D13
Olympus, Mt. *U.S.A.* 47°48N 123°43W **78** C3
Olyphant *U.S.A.* 41°27N 75°36W **83** E9
Olyutorskiy, Mys
Russia 59°55N 170°27E **29** D18
Om → *Russia* 54°59N 73°22E **28** D8
Om Koi *Thailand* 17°48N 98°22E **38** D2
Ōma *Japan* 41°45N 141°5E **30** D10
Ōmachi *Japan* 36°30N 137°50E **31** F8
Omae-Zaki *Japan* 34°36N 138°14E **31** G9
Ōmagari *Japan* 39°27N 140°29E **30** E10
Omagh *U.K.* 54°36N 7°19W **10** B4
Omagh □ *U.K.* 54°35N 7°15W **10** B4
Omaha *U.S.A.* 41°17N 95°58W **80** E6
Omak *U.S.A.* 48°25N 119°31W **76** B4
Omalos *Greece* 35°19N 23°55E **25** D5
Oman ■ *Asia* 23°0N 58°0E **47** C6
Oman, G. of *Asia* 24°30N 58°30E **45** E8
Omaruru *Namibia* 21°26S 16°0E **56** C2
Omaruru → *Namibia* 22°7S 14°15E **56** C1
Omate *Peru* 16°45S 71°0W **92** G4
Ombai, Selat *Indonesia* 8°30S 124°50E **37** F6
Omboué *Gabon* 1°35S 9°15E **52** E1
Ombrone → *Italy* 42°42N 11°5E **22** C4
Omdurmân *Sudan* 15°40N 32°28E **51** E12
Omemee *Canada* 44°18N 78°33W **82** B6
Omeonga
Dem. Rep. of the Congo 3°40S 24°22E **54** C1
Ometepe, I. de *Nic.* 11°32N 85°35W **88** D2
Ometepec *Mexico* 16°41N 98°25W **87** D5
Ominato *Japan* 41°17N 141°10E **30** D10
Omineca → *Canada* 56°3N 124°16W **70** B4
Omineca Mts. *Canada* 56°30N 125°30W **70** B3
Omitara *Namibia* 22°16S 18°2E **56** C2
Ōmiya = Saitama *Japan* 35°54N 139°38E **31** G9
Ommen *Neths.* 52°31N 6°26E **15** B6
Ömnögovĭ □ *Mongolia* 43°15N 104°0E **34** C3
Omo → *Ethiopia* 6°25N 36°10E **47** F2
Omodhos *Cyprus* 34°51N 32°48E **25** E11
Omolon → *Russia* 68°42N 158°36E **29** C16
Omono-Gawa → *Japan* 39°46N 140°3E **30** E10
Ompha *Canada* 45°0N 76°50W **83** B8
Omsk *Russia* 55°0N 73°12E **28** D8
Omsukchan *Russia* 62°32N 155°48E **29** C16
Ōmu *Japan* 44°34N 142°58E **30** B11
Omul, Vf. *Romania* 45°27N 25°29E **17** F13
Ōmura *Japan* 32°56N 129°57E **31** H4
Omuramba Omatako →
Namibia 17°45S 20°25E **56** B2
Omuramba Ovambo →
Namibia 18°45S 16°59E **56** B2
Ōmuta *Japan* 33°5N 130°26E **31** H5
Onaga *U.S.A.* 39°29N 96°10W **80** F5
Onalaska *U.S.A.* 43°53N 91°14W **80** D8
Onancock *U.S.A.* 37°43N 75°45W **81** G16
Onang *Indonesia* 3°2S 118°49E **37** E5
Onangue, L. *Gabon* 0°57S 10°4E **52** E2
Onaping L. *Canada* 47°3N 81°30W **72** C3
Onavas *Mexico* 28°31N 109°35W **86** B3
Onawa *U.S.A.* 42°2N 96°6W **80** D5
Oncócua *Angola* 16°30S 13°25E **56** B1
Onda *Spain* 39°55N 0°17W **21** C5
Ondangwa *Namibia* 17°57S 16°4E **56** B2
Ondjiva *Angola* 16°48S 15°50E **56** B2
Öndörshil *Mongolia* 45°13N 108°5E **34** B5
Öndverðarnes *Iceland* 64°52N 24°0W **8** D2
One Tree *Australia* 34°11S 144°43E **63** E3
Oneata *Fiji* 18°26S 178°25W **59** a
Onega *Russia* 64°0N 38°10E **18** B6
Onega → *Russia* 63°58N 38°2E **18** B6
Onega, G. of = Onezhskaya Guba
Russia 64°24N 36°38E **18** B6
Onega, L. = Onezhskoye Ozero
Russia 61°44N 35°22E **18** B6
Oneida *U.S.A.* 43°6N 75°39W **83** C9
Oneida L. *U.S.A.* 43°12N 75°54W **83** C9
O'Neill *U.S.A.* 42°27N 98°39W **80** D4
Onekotan, Ostrov
Russia 49°25N 154°45E **29** E16
Onema
Dem. Rep. of the Congo 4°35S 24°30E **54** C1
Oneonta *U.S.A.* 42°27N 75°4W **83** D9
Oneşti *Romania* 46°17N 26°47E **17** E14
Onezhskaya Guba
Russia 64°24N 36°38E **18** B6
Onezhskoye Ozero
Russia 61°44N 35°22E **18** B6
Ongarue *N.Z.* 38°42S 175°19E **59** C5
Ongea Levu = Ogea Levu
Fiji 19°8S 178°24W **59** a
Ongers → *S. Africa* 31°4S 23°13E **56** E3
Ongerup *Australia* 33°58S 118°28E **61** F2
Ongjin *N. Korea* 37°56N 125°21E **35** F13
Ongkharak *Thailand* 14°8N 101°1E **38** E3
Ongniud Qi *China* 43°0N 118°38E **35** C10
Ongoka
Dem. Rep. of the Congo 1°20S 26°0E **54** C2
Ongole *India* 15°33N 80°2E **40** M12
Ongon = Havirga
Mongolia 45°41N 113°5E **34** B7
Onida *U.S.A.* 44°42N 100°4W **80** C3
Onilahy → *Madag.* 23°34S 43°45E **57** C7
Onitsha *Nigeria* 6°6N 6°42E **50** G7
Ono *Fiji* 18°55S 178°29E **59** a
Onoda *Japan* 33°59N 131°11E **31** G5
Onslow *Australia* 21°40S 115°12E **60** D2
Onslow B. *U.S.A.* 34°20N 77°15W **85** D16
Ontake-San *Japan* 35°53N 137°29E **31** G8
Ontario *Calif., U.S.A.* 34°4N 117°39W **79** L9
Ontario *Oreg., U.S.A.* 44°2N 116°58W **76** D5
Ontario □ *Canada* 48°0N 83°0W **72** B2
Ontario, L. *N. Amer.* 43°20N 78°0W **82** C7
Ontonagon *U.S.A.* 46°52N 89°19W **80** B9
Onyx *U.S.A.* 35°41N 118°14W **79** K8
Oodnadatta *Australia* 27°33S 135°30E **63** D2
Ooldea *Australia* 30°27S 131°50E **61** F5
Oombulgurri *Australia* 15°15S 127°45E **60** C4
Oorindi *Australia* 20°40S 141°1E **62** C3
Oost-Vlaanderen □
Belgium 51°5N 3°50E **15** C3
Oostende *Belgium* 51°15N 2°54E **15** C2
Oosterhout *Neths.* 51°39N 4°47E **15** C4
Oosterschelde → *Neths.* 51°33N 4°0E **15** C4
Oosterwolde *Neths.* 53°0N 6°17E **15** B6
Ootacamund = Udagamandalam
India 11°30N 76°44E **40** P10
Ootsa L. *Canada* 53°50N 126°2W **70** C3
Op Luang △ *Thailand* 18°12N 98°32E **38** C2
Opala
Dem. Rep. of the Congo 0°40S 24°20E **54** C1
Opanake *Sri Lanka* 6°35N 80°40E **40** R12
Opasatika *Canada* 49°30N 82°50W **72** C3
Opasquia ⌂ *Canada* 53°33N 93°5W **72** B1
Opava *Czech Rep.* 49°57N 17°58E **17** D9
Opelika *U.S.A.* 32°39N 85°23W **85** E12
Opelousas *U.S.A.* 30°32N 92°5W **84** F8
Opémisca, L. *Canada* 49°56N 74°52W **72** C5
Opheim *U.S.A.* 48°51N 106°24W **76** B10
Ophthalmia Ra.
Australia 23°15S 119°30E **60** D2
Opinaca → *Canada* 52°15N 78°2W **72** B4
Opinaca, Rés. *Canada* 52°39N 76°20W **72** B4
Opinnagau → *Canada* 54°12N 82°25W **72** B3
Opiscotéo, L. *Canada* 53°10N 68°10W **73** B6
Opobo *Nigeria* 4°35N 7°34E **50** H7
Opole *Poland* 50°42N 17°58E **17** C9
Oponono L. *Namibia* 18°8S 15°45E **56** B2
Oporto = Porto *Portugal* 41°8N 8°40W **21** B1
Opotiki *N.Z.* 38°1S 177°19E **59** C6
Opp *U.S.A.* 31°17N 86°16W **85** F11
Oppdal *Norway* 62°35N 9°41E **8** E13
Opportunity *U.S.A.* 47°39N 117°15W **76** C5
Opua *N.Z.* 35°19S 174°9E **59** A5
Opunake *N.Z.* 39°26S 173°52E **59** C4
Opuwo *Namibia* 18°3S 13°45E **56** B1
Ora *Cyprus* 34°51N 33°12E **25** E12
Oracle *U.S.A.* 32°37N 110°46W **77** K8
Oradea *Romania* 47°2N 21°58E **17** E11
Öræfajökull *Iceland* 64°2N 16°39W **8** D5
Orai *India* 25°58N 79°30E **43** G8
Oral = Zhayyq →
Kazakhstan 47°0N 51°48E **19** E9
Oral *Kazakhstan* 51°20N 51°20E **19** D9
Oran *Algeria* 35°45N 0°39W **50** A5
Orange *Australia* 33°15S 149°7E **63** E4
Orange *France* 44°8N 4°47E **20** D6
Orange *Calif., U.S.A.* 33°47N 117°51W **79** M9
Orange *Mass., U.S.A.* 42°35N 72°19W **83** D12
Orange *Tex., U.S.A.* 30°6N 93°44W **84** F8
Orange *Va., U.S.A.* 38°15N 78°7W **81** F14
Orange → *S. Africa* 28°41S 16°28E **56** D2
Orange, C. *Brazil* 4°20N 51°30W **93** C8
Orange Cove *U.S.A.* 36°38N 119°19W **78** J7
Orange Free State = Free State □
S. Africa 28°30S 27°0E **56** D4
Orange Grove *U.S.A.* 27°58N 97°56W **84** H6
Orange Walk *Belize* 18°6N 88°33W **87** D7
Orangeburg *U.S.A.* 33°30N 80°52W **85** E14
Orangeville *Canada* 43°55N 80°5W **82** C4
Orango *Guinea-Biss.* 11°5N 16°0W **50** F2
Oranienburg *Germany* 52°45N 13°14E **16** B7
Oranje = Orange →
S. Africa 28°41S 16°28E **56** D2
Oranjemund *Namibia* 28°38S 16°29E **56** D2
Oranjerivier *S. Africa* 29°40S 24°12E **56** D3
Oranjestad *Aruba* 12°32N 70°2W **89** D5
Orapa *Botswana* 21°15S 25°30E **53** J5
Oras *Phil.* 12°9N 125°28E **37** B7
Orbetello *Italy* 42°27N 11°13E **22** C4
Orbisonia *U.S.A.* 40°15N 77°54W **82** F7
Orbost *Australia* 37°40S 148°29E **63** F4
Orcadas *Antarctica* 60°44S 44°37W **5** C18
Orcas I. *U.S.A.* 48°42N 122°56W **78** B4
Orchard City *U.S.A.* 38°50N 107°58W **76** G10
Orchard Homes *U.S.A.* 46°55N 114°4W **76** C6
Orchila, I. *Venezuela* 11°48N 66°10W **89** D6
Orchilla, Pta. *Canary Is.* 27°42N 18°10W **24** G1
Orcutt *U.S.A.* 34°52N 120°27W **79** L6
Ord *U.S.A.* 41°36N 98°56W **80** E4
Ord → *Australia* 15°33S 128°15E **60** C4
Ord, Mt. *Australia* 17°20S 125°34E **60** C4
Ord Mts. *U.S.A.* 34°39N 116°45W **79** L10
Orderville *U.S.A.* 37°17N 112°38W **77** H7
Ordos = Mu Us Shamo
China 39°0N 109°0E **34** E5
Ordu *Turkey* 40°55N 37°53E **19** F6
Ordway *U.S.A.* 38°13N 103°46W **76** G12
Ore *Dem. Rep. of the Congo* 3°17N 29°30E **54** B2
Ore Mts. = Erzgebirge
Germany 50°27N 12°55E **16** C7
Örebro *Sweden* 59°20N 15°18E **9** G16
Oregon *U.S.A.* 42°1N 89°20W **80** D9
Oregon □ *U.S.A.* 44°0N 121°0W **76** E3
Oregon City *U.S.A.* 45°21N 122°36W **78** E4
Oregon Dunes ⌂
U.S.A. 43°40N 124°10W **76** E1
Orekhovo-Zuyevo
Russia 55°50N 38°55E **18** C6
Orel *Russia* 52°57N 36°3E **18** D6
Orem *U.S.A.* 40°19N 111°42W **76** F8
Ören *Turkey* 37°3N 27°57E **23** F12
Orenburg *Russia* 51°45N 55°6E **18** D10
Orense = Ourense *Spain* 42°19N 7°55W **21** A2
Orepuki *N.Z.* 46°19S 167°46E **59** G1

Orestes Pereyra *Mexico* 26°30N 105°39W **86 B3**
Orestiada *Greece* 41°30N 26°33E **23 D12**
Orfanos Kolpos *Greece* 40°33N 24°0E **23 D11**
Orford Ness *U.K.* 52°5N 1°35E **13 E9**
Organ Pipe Cactus △
　U.S.A. 32°0N 112°52W **77 K7**
Organos, Pta. de los
　Canary Is. 28°12N 17°17W **24 F2**
Orgaz *Spain* 39°39N 3°53W **21 C4**
Orgeyev = Orhei
　Moldova 47°24N 28°50E **17 E15**
Orhaneli *Turkey* 39°54N 28°59E **23 D12**
Orhangazi *Turkey* 40°29N 29°18E **23 D13**
Orhei *Moldova* 47°24N 28°50E **17 E15**
Orhon Gol ➔ *Mongolia* 50°21N 106°0E **32 A5**
Oriental, Cordillera
　Colombia 6°0N 73°0W **92 B4**
Oriental, Grand Erg *Algeria* 30°0N 6°30E **50 B7**
Orientale □
　Dem. Rep. of the Congo 2°20N 26°0E **54 B2**
Oriente *Argentina* 38°44S 60°37W **94 D3**
Orihuela *Spain* 38°7N 0°55W **21 C5**
Orillia *Canada* 44°40N 79°24W **82 B5**
Orinoco ➔ *Venezuela* 9°15N 61°30W **92 B6**
Orion *Canada* 49°27N 110°49W **71 D6**
Oriskany *U.S.A.* 43°10N 75°20W **83 C9**
Orissa □ *India* 20°0N 84°0E **41 K14**
Orissaare *Estonia* 58°34N 23°5E **9 G20**
Oristano *Italy* 39°54N 8°36E **22 E3**
Oristano, G. di *Italy* 39°50N 8°29E **22 E3**
Orizaba *Mexico* 18°51N 97°6W **87 D5**
Orizaba, Pico de *Mexico* 18°58N 97°15W **87 D5**
Orkanger *Norway* 63°18N 9°52E **8 E13**
Orkla ➔ *Norway* 63°18N 9°51E **8 E13**
Orkney *S. Africa* 26°58S 26°40E **56 D4**
Orkney □ *U.K.* 59°2N 3°13W **11 B5**
Orkney Is. *U.K.* 59°0N 3°0W **11 B6**
Orland *U.S.A.* 39°45N 122°12W **78 F4**
Orlando *U.S.A.* 28°32N 81°22W **85 G14**
Orléanais *France* 48°0N 2°0E **20 C5**
Orléans *France* 47°54N 1°52E **20 C4**
Orleans *U.S.A.* 44°49N 72°12W **83 B12**
Orléans, Î. d' *Canada* 46°54N 70°58W **73 C5**
Ormara *Pakistan* 25°16N 64°33E **40 G4**
Ormoc *Phil.* 11°0N 124°37E **37 B6**
Ormond *N.Z.* 38°33S 177°56E **59 C6**
Ormond Beach *U.S.A.* 29°17N 81°3W **85 G14**
Ormskirk *U.K.* 53°35N 2°54W **12 D5**
Ormstown *Canada* 45°8N 74°0W **83 A11**
Örnsköldsvik *Sweden* 63°17N 18°40E **8 E18**
Oro *N. Korea* 40°1N 127°27E **35 D14**
Oro ➔ *Mexico* 25°35N 105°2W **86 B3**
Oro Grande *U.S.A.* 34°36N 117°20W **79 L9**
Oro Valley *U.S.A.* 32°26N 110°58W **77 K8**
Orocué *Colombia* 4°48N 71°20W **92 C4**
Orohena, Mt. *Tahiti* 17°37S 149°28W **59 d**
Orol Dengizi = Aral Sea
　Asia 44°30N 60°0E **28 E7**
Oromocto *Canada* 45°54N 66°29W **73 C6**
Orono *Canada* 43°59N 78°37W **82 C6**
Orono *U.S.A.* 44°53N 68°40W **81 C19**
Oronsay *U.K.* 56°1N 6°15W **11 E2**
Oroqen Zizhiqi *China* 50°34N 123°43E **33 A7**
Oroquieta *Phil.* 8°32N 123°44E **37 C6**
Orosei *Italy* 40°23N 9°42E **22 D3**
Orosháza *Hungary* 46°32N 20°42E **17 E11**
Orotukan *Russia* 62°16N 151°42E **29 C16**
Oroville *Calif., U.S.A.* 39°31N 121°33W **78 F5**
Oroville *Wash., U.S.A.* 48°56N 119°26W **76 B4**
Oroville, L. *U.S.A.* 39°33N 121°29W **78 F5**
Orroroo *Australia* 32°43S 138°38E **63 E2**
Orrville *U.S.A.* 40°50N 81°46W **82 F3**
Orsha *Belarus* 54°30N 30°25E **18 D5**
Orsk *Russia* 51°12N 58°34E **28 D6**
Orşova *Romania* 44°41N 22°25E **17 F12**
Ortaca *Turkey* 36°49N 28°45E **23 F13**
Ortegal, C. *Spain* 43°43N 7°52W **21 A2**
Orthez *France* 43°29N 0°48W **20 E3**
Ortigueira *Spain* 43°40N 7°50W **21 A2**
Orting *U.S.A.* 47°6N 122°12W **78 C4**
Ortles *Italy* 46°31N 10°33E **20 C9**
Ortón ➔ *Bolivia* 10°50S 67°0W **92 F5**
Ortonville *U.S.A.* 45°19N 96°27W **80 C5**
Örümiyeh *Iran* 37°40N 45°0E **44 B5**
Orümïyeh, Daryācheh-ye
　Iran 37°50N 45°30E **44 B5**
Oruro *Bolivia* 18°0S 67°9W **92 G5**
Orust *Sweden* 58°10N 11°40E **9 G14**
Oruzgān □ *Afghan.* 33°0N 66°0E **40 C5**
Orvieto *Italy* 42°43N 12°7E **22 C5**
Orwell *N.Y., U.S.A.* 43°35N 75°50W **83 C9**
Orwell *Ohio, U.S.A.* 41°32N 80°52W **82 E4**
Orwell ➔ *U.K.* 51°59N 1°18E **13 F9**
Orwigsburg *U.S.A.* 40°38N 76°6W **83 F8**
Oryakhovo *Bulgaria* 43°40N 23°57E **23 C10**
Osa *Russia* 57°17N 55°26E **18 C10**
Osa, Pen. de *Costa Rica* 8°0N 84°0W **88 E3**
Osage *U.S.A.* 43°17N 92°49W **80 D7**
Osage ➔ *U.S.A.* 38°36N 91°57W **80 F8**
Osage City *U.S.A.* 38°38N 95°50W **80 F6**
Ōsaka *Japan* 34°42N 135°30E **31 G7**
Osan *S. Korea* 37°11N 127°4E **35 F14**
Osawatomie *U.S.A.* 38°31N 94°57W **80 F7**
Osborne *U.S.A.* 39°26N 98°42W **80 F4**
Osceola *Ark., U.S.A.* 35°42N 89°58W **85 D10**
Osceola *Iowa, U.S.A.* 41°2N 93°46W **80 E7**
Oscoda *U.S.A.* 44°26N 83°20W **82 B1**
Ösel = Saaremaa *Estonia* 58°30N 22°30E **9 G20**
Osgoode *Canada* 45°8N 75°36W **83 A9**
Osh *Kyrgyzstan* 40°37N 72°49E **32 B2**
Oshakati *Namibia* 17°45S 15°40E **53 H3**
Oshawa *Canada* 43°50N 78°50W **82 C6**
Oshigambo *Namibia* 17°45S 16°5E **56 B2**
Oshkosh *Nebr., U.S.A.* 41°24N 102°21W **80 E2**
Oshkosh *Wis., U.S.A.* 44°1N 88°33W **80 C9**
Oshmyany = Ashmyany
　Belarus 54°26N 25°52E **17 A13**

Oshnovïyeh *Iran* 37°2N 45°6E **44 B5**
Oshogbo *Nigeria* 7°48N 4°37E **50 G6**
Oshtorīnān *Iran* 34°1N 48°38E **45 C6**
Oshwe
　Dem. Rep. of the Congo 3°25S 19°28E **52 E3**
Osijek *Croatia* 45°34N 18°41E **23 B8**
Osipovichi = Asipovichy
　Belarus 53°19N 28°33E **17 B15**
Osiyan *India* 26°43N 72°55E **42 F5**
Osizweni *S. Africa* 27°49S 30°7E **57 D5**
Oskaloosa *U.S.A.* 41°18N 92°39W **80 E7**
Oskarshamn *Sweden* 57°15N 16°27E **9 H17**
Oskélanéo *Canada* 48°5N 75°15W **72 C4**
Öskemen *Kazakhstan* 50°0N 82°36E **28 E9**
Oslo *Norway* 59°54N 10°43E **9 G14**
Oslofjorden *Norway* 59°20N 10°35E **9 G14**
Osmanabad *India* 18°5N 76°10E **40 K10**
Osmaniye *Turkey* 37°5N 36°10E **44 B3**
Osnabrück *Germany* 52°17N 8°3E **16 B5**
Osório *Brazil* 29°53S 50°17W **95 B5**
Osorno *Chile* 40°25S 73°0W **96 E2**
Osorno, Vol. *Chile* 41°0S 72°30W **96 D2**
Osoyoos *Canada* 49°0N 119°30W **70 D5**
Ospika ➔ *Canada* 56°20N 124°0W **70 B4**
Osprey Reef *Australia* 13°52S 146°36E **62 A4**
Oss *Neths.* 51°46N 5°32E **15 C5**
Ossa, Mt. *Australia* 41°52S 146°3E **63 G4**
Ossa, Oros *Greece* 39°47N 22°42E **23 E10**
Ossabaw I. *U.S.A.* 31°50N 81°5W **85 F14**
Ossining *U.S.A.* 41°10N 73°55W **83 E11**
Ossipee *U.S.A.* 43°41N 71°7W **83 C13**
Ossokmanuan L. *Canada* 53°25N 65°0W **73 B7**
Ossora *Russia* 59°20N 163°13E **29 D17**
Ostend = Oostende
　Belgium 51°15N 2°54E **15 C2**
Oster *Ukraine* 50°57N 30°53E **17 C16**
Österbotten = Pohjanmaa
　Finland 62°58N 22°50E **8 E20**
Osterburg *U.S.A.* 40°16N 78°31W **82 F6**
Österdalälven *Sweden* 61°30N 13°45E **8 F15**
Österdalen *Norway* 61°40N 10°50E **8 F14**
Östermyra = Seinäjoki
　Finland 62°40N 22°51E **8 E20**
Österreich = Austria ■
　Europe 47°0N 14°0E **16 E8**
Östersund *Sweden* 63°10N 14°38E **8 E16**
Ostfriesische Inseln
　Germany 53°42N 7°0E **16 B4**
Ostrava *Czech Rep.* 49°51N 18°18E **17 D10**
Ostróda *Poland* 53°42N 19°58E **17 B10**
Ostroh *Ukraine* 50°20N 26°30E **17 C14**
Ostrołęka *Poland* 53°4N 21°32E **17 B11**
Ostrów Mazowiecka
　Poland 52°50N 21°51E **17 B11**
Ostrów Wielkopolski
　Poland 51°36N 17°44E **17 C9**
Ostrowiec-Świętokrzyski
　Poland 50°55N 21°22E **17 C11**
Ostuni *Italy* 40°44N 17°35E **23 D7**
Ōsumi-Kaikyō *Japan* 30°55N 131°0E **31 J5**
Ōsumi-Shotō *Japan* 30°30N 130°0E **31 J5**
Osuna *Spain* 37°14N 5°8W **21 D3**
Oswegatchie ➔ *U.S.A.* 44°42N 75°30W **83 B9**
Oswego *U.S.A.* 43°27N 76°31W **83 C8**
Oswego ➔ *U.S.A.* 43°27N 76°30W **83 C8**
Oswestry *U.K.* 52°52N 3°3W **12 E4**
Oświęcim *Poland* 50°2N 19°11E **17 C10**
Otago □ *N.Z.* 45°15S 170°0E **59 F2**
Otago Harbour *N.Z.* 45°47S 170°42E **59 F3**
Otahe B. *Trin. & Tob.* 10°15N 61°30W **93 K15**
Ōtake *Japan* 34°12N 132°13E **31 G6**
Otaki *N.Z.* 40°45S 175°10E **59 D5**
Otaru *Japan* 43°10N 141°0E **30 C10**
Otaru-Wan = Ishikari-Wan
　Japan 43°25N 141°1E **30 C10**
Otavalo *Ecuador* 0°13N 78°20W **92 C3**
Otavi *Namibia* 19°40S 17°24E **56 B2**
Otchinjau *Angola* 16°30S 13°56E **56 B1**
Otego *U.S.A.* 42°23N 75°10W **83 D9**
Otelnuk, L. *Canada* 56°9N 68°12W **73 A6**
Othello *U.S.A.* 46°50N 119°10W **76 C4**
Otish, Mts. *Canada* 52°22N 70°30W **73 B5**
Otjiwarongo *Namibia* 20°30S 16°33E **56 C2**
Oto Tolu Group *Tonga* 20°21S 174°32W **59 c**
Otoineppu *Japan* 44°44N 142°16E **30 B11**
Otorohanga *N.Z.* 38°12S 175°14E **59 C5**
Otra ➔ *Norway* 58°9N 8°1E **9 G13**
Otranto *Italy* 40°9N 18°28E **23 D8**
Otranto, C. d' *Italy* 40°7N 18°30E **23 D8**
Otranto, Str. of *Italy* 40°15N 18°40E **23 D8**
Otse *S. Africa* 25°2S 25°45E **56 D4**
Otsego L. *U.S.A.* 42°45N 74°53W **83 D10**
Ōtsu *Japan* 35°0N 135°50E **31 G7**
Ōtsuki *Japan* 35°36N 138°57E **31 G9**
Ottawa = Outaouais ➔
　Canada 45°27N 74°8W **72 C5**
Ottawa *Canada* 45°26N 75°42W **83 A9**
Ottawa *Ill., U.S.A.* 41°21N 88°51W **80 E9**
Ottawa *Kans., U.S.A.* 38°37N 95°16W **80 F6**
Ottawa Is. *Canada* 59°35N 80°10W **69 D11**
Otter Cr. ➔ *U.S.A.* 44°13N 73°17W **83 B11**
Otter Lake *Canada* 45°17N 79°56W **82 A5**
Otterville *Canada* 42°55N 80°36W **82 D4**
Ottery St. Mary *U.K.* 50°44N 3°17W **13 G4**
Otto Beit Bridge
　Zimbabwe 15°59S 28°56E **55 F2**
Ottosdal *S. Africa* 26°46S 25°59E **56 D4**
Ottumwa *U.S.A.* 41°1N 92°25W **80 E7**
Oturkpo *Nigeria* 7°16N 8°8E **50 G7**
Otway, B. *Chile* 53°30S 74°0W **96 G2**
Otway, C. *Australia* 38°52S 143°30E **63 F3**
Otwock *Poland* 52°5N 21°20E **17 B11**
Ou ➔ *Laos* 20°4N 102°13E **38 B4**
Ou Neua *Laos* 22°18N 101°48E **38 A3**
Ou-Sammyaku *Japan* 39°20N 140°35E **30 E10**

Ouachita ➔ *U.S.A.* 31°38N 91°49W **84 F9**
Ouachita, L. *U.S.A.* 34°34N 93°12W **84 D8**
Ouachita Mts. *U.S.A.* 34°30N 94°30W **84 D7**
Ouagadougou
　Burkina Faso 12°25N 1°30W **50 F5**
Ouahigouya *Burkina Faso* 13°31N 2°25W **50 F5**
Ouahran = Oran *Algeria* 35°45N 0°39W **50 A5**
Ouallene *Algeria* 24°41N 1°11E **50 D6**
Ouarâne *Mauritania* 21°0N 10°30W **50 D3**
Ouargla *Algeria* 31°59N 5°16E **50 B7**
Ouarra ➔ *C.A.R.* 5°5N 24°26E **52 C4**
Ouarzazate *Morocco* 30°55N 6°50W **50 B4**
Oubangi ➔
　Dem. Rep. of the Congo 0°30S 17°50E **52 E3**
Ouddorp *Neths.* 51°50N 3°57E **15 C3**
Oude Rijn ➔ *Neths.* 52°12N 4°24E **15 B4**
Oudenaarde *Belgium* 50°50N 3°37E **15 D3**
Oudtshoorn *S. Africa* 33°35S 22°14E **56 E3**
Ouessa *Congo* 1°37N 16°5E **52 D3**
Ouessant, Î. d' *France* 48°28N 5°6W **20 B1**
Ouesso *Congo* 1°37N 16°5E **52 D3**
Ouest, Pte. de l' *Canada* 49°52N 64°40W **73 C7**
Ouezzane *Morocco* 34°51N 5°35W **50 B4**
Oughter, L. *Ireland* 54°1N 7°28W **10 B4**
Oughterard *Ireland* 53°26N 9°18W **10 C2**
Ouidah *Benin* 6°25N 2°0E **50 G6**
Oujda *Morocco* 34°41N 1°55W **50 B5**
Oulainen *Finland* 64°17N 24°47E **8 D21**
Oulu *Finland* 65°1N 25°29E **8 D21**
Oulujärvi *Finland* 64°25N 27°15E **8 D22**
Oulujoki ➔ *Finland* 65°1N 25°30E **8 D21**
Oum Chalouba *Chad* 15°48N 20°46E **51 E10**
Oum Hadjer *Chad* 13°18N 19°41E **51 F9**
Ounasjoki ➔ *Finland* 66°31N 25°40E **8 C21**
Ounguati *Namibia* 22°0S 15°46E **56 C2**
Ounianga Kébir *Chad* 19°4N 20°29E **51 E10**
Our ➔ *Lux.* 49°55N 6°5E **15 E6**
Ouray *U.S.A.* 38°1N 107°40W **77 G10**
Ourense *Spain* 42°19N 7°55W **21 A2**
Ouricuri *Brazil* 7°53S 40°5W **93 E10**
Ourinhos *Brazil* 23°0S 49°54W **95 A6**
Ouro Fino *Brazil* 22°16S 46°25W **95 A6**
Ouro Prêto *Brazil* 20°20S 43°30W **95 A7**
Ourthe ➔ *Belgium* 50°29N 5°35E **15 D5**
Ouse ➔ *E. Sussex, U.K.* 50°47N 0°4E **13 G8**
Ouse ➔ *N. Yorks., U.K.* 53°44N 0°55W **12 D7**
Outaouais ➔ *Canada* 45°27N 74°8W **72 C5**
Outardes ➔ *Canada* 49°24N 69°30W **73 C6**
Outer Hebrides *U.K.* 57°30N 7°40W **11 D1**
Outjo *Namibia* 20°5S 16°7E **56 C2**
Outlook *Canada* 51°30N 107°0W **71 C7**
Outokumpu *Finland* 62°43N 29°1E **8 E23**
Ouyen *Australia* 35°1S 142°22E **63 F3**
Ovalau *Fiji* 17°40S 178°48E **59 a**
Ovalle *Chile* 30°33S 71°18W **94 C1**
Ovamboland *Namibia* 18°30S 16°0E **56 B2**
Overflakkee *Neths.* 51°44N 4°10E **15 C4**
Overijssel □ *Neths.* 52°25N 6°35E **15 B6**
Overland Park *U.S.A.* 38°58N 94°40W **80 F7**
Overton *U.S.A.* 36°33N 114°27W **79 J12**
Övertorneå *Sweden* 66°23N 23°38E **8 C20**
Ovid *U.S.A.* 42°41N 76°49W **83 D8**
Oviedo *Spain* 43°25N 5°50W **21 A3**
Oviši *Latvia* 57°33N 21°44E **9 H19**
Ovoot *Mongolia* 45°21N 113°45E **34 B7**
Övör Hangay □
　Mongolia 45°0N 102°30E **34 B2**
Øvre Ardal *Norway* 61°19N 7°48E **8 F12**
Ovruch *Ukraine* 51°25N 28°45E **17 C15**
Owaka *N.Z.* 46°27S 169°40E **59 G2**
Owambo = Ovamboland
　Namibia 18°30S 16°0E **56 B2**
Owasco L. *U.S.A.* 42°50N 76°31W **83 D8**
Owase *Japan* 34°7N 136°12E **31 G8**
Owatonna *U.S.A.* 44°5N 93°14W **80 C7**
Owbeh *Afghan.* 34°28N 63°10E **40 B3**
Owego *U.S.A.* 42°6N 76°16W **83 D8**
Owen Falls Dam = Nalubaale
　Dam *Uganda* 0°30N 33°5E **54 B3**
Owen Sound *Canada* 44°35N 80°55W **82 B4**
Owen Stanley Ra.
　Papua N. G. 8°30S 147°0E **58 B7**
Oweniny ➔ *Ireland* 54°8N 9°50W **10 B2**
Owens ➔ *U.S.A.* 36°32N 117°59W **78 J9**
Owens L. *U.S.A.* 36°26N 117°57W **79 J9**
Owensboro *U.S.A.* 37°46N 87°7W **80 G10**
Owl ➔ *Canada* 57°51N 92°44W **71 B10**
Owo *Nigeria* 7°10N 5°39E **50 G7**
Owosso *U.S.A.* 43°0N 84°10W **81 D11**
Owyhee *U.S.A.* 41°57N 116°6W **76 F5**
Owyhee ➔ *U.S.A.* 43°49N 117°2W **76 E5**
Owyhee, L. *U.S.A.* 43°38N 117°14W **76 E5**
Ox Mts. = Slieve Gamph
　Ireland 54°6N 9°0W **10 B3**
Oxarfjörður *Iceland* 66°15N 16°45W **8 C5**
Oxbow *Canada* 49°14N 102°10W **71 D8**
Oxelösund *Sweden* 58°43N 17°5E **9 G17**
Oxford *N.Z.* 43°18S 172°11E **59 E4**
Oxford *U.K.* 51°46N 1°15W **13 F6**
Oxford *Mass., U.S.A.* 42°7N 71°52W **83 D13**
Oxford *Miss., U.S.A.* 34°22N 89°31W **85 D10**
Oxford *N.C., U.S.A.* 36°19N 78°35W **85 G15**
Oxford *N.Y., U.S.A.* 42°27N 75°36W **83 D9**
Oxford *Ohio, U.S.A.* 39°31N 84°45W **81 F11**
Oxford L. *Canada* 54°51N 95°37W **71 C9**
Oxfordshire □ *U.K.* 51°48N 1°16W **13 F6**
Oxnard *U.S.A.* 34°12N 119°11W **79 L7**
Oxus = Amudarya ➔
　Uzbekistan 43°58N 59°34E **28 E6**
Oya *Malaysia* 2°55N 111°55E **36 D4**
Oyama *Japan* 36°18N 139°48E **31 F9**
Oyem *Gabon* 1°34N 11°31E **52 D2**
Oyen *Canada* 51°22N 110°28W **71 C6**
Oykel ➔ *U.K.* 57°56N 4°26W **11 D4**
Oymyakon *Russia* 63°25N 142°44E **29 C15**
Oyo *Nigeria* 7°46N 3°56E **50 G6**
Oyster Bay *U.S.A.* 40°52N 73°32W **83 F11**
Ōyūbari *Japan* 43°1N 142°5E **30 C11**
Ozamiz *Phil.* 8°15N 123°50E **37 C6**

Ozark *Ala., U.S.A.* 31°28N 85°39W **85 F12**
Ozark *Ark., U.S.A.* 35°29N 93°50W **84 D8**
Ozark *Mo., U.S.A.* 37°1N 93°12W **80 G7**
Ozark Plateau *U.S.A.* 37°20N 91°40W **80 G8**
Ozarks, L. of the *U.S.A.* 38°12N 92°38W **80 F7**
Ozd *Hungary* 48°14N 20°15E **17 D11**
Ozernovskiy *Russia* 51°30N 156°31E **29 D16**
Ozernyy *Russia* 53°53N 52°42E **18 D9**
Ozette, L. *U.S.A.* 48°6N 124°38W **78 B2**
Ozieri *Italy* 40°35N 9°0E **22 D3**
Ozona *U.S.A.* 30°43N 101°12W **84 F4**
Ozuluama *Mexico* 21°40N 97°51W **87 C5**

P

Pa-an *Burma* 16°51N 97°40E **41 L20**
Pa Mong Dam *Thailand* 18°0N 102°22E **38 D4**
Pa Sak ➔ *Thailand* 15°30N 101°0E **38 E3**
Paamiut *Greenland* 62°0N 49°43W **4 C5**
Paarl *S. Africa* 33°45S 18°56E **56 E2**
Pab Hills *Pakistan* 26°30N 66°45E **42 F2**
Pabbay *U.K.* 57°46N 7°14W **11 D1**
Pabianice *Poland* 51°40N 19°20E **17 C10**
Pabna *Bangla.* 24°1N 89°18E **41 G16**
Pabo *Uganda* 3°1N 32°10E **54 B3**
Pacaja ➔ *Brazil* 1°56S 50°50W **93 D8**
Pacaraima, Sa. *S. Amer.* 4°0N 62°30W **92 C6**
Pacasmayo *Peru* 7°20S 79°35W **92 E3**
Pachitea ➔ *Peru* 8°46S 74°33W **92 E4**
Pachmarhi *India* 22°28N 78°26E **43 H8**
Pachnes *Greece* 35°16N 24°4E **25 D6**
Pachpadra *India* 25°58N 72°10E **42 G5**
Pachuca *Mexico* 20°7N 98°44W **87 C5**
Pacific Antarctic Ridge
　Pac. Oc. 43°0S 115°0W **5 B13**
Pacific Grove *U.S.A.* 36°38N 121°56W **78 J5**
Pacific Ocean 10°0N 140°0W **65 G14**
Pacific Rim △ *Canada* 48°40N 124°45W **78 B2**
Pacifica *U.S.A.* 37°37N 122°27W **78 H4**
Pacitan *Indonesia* 8°12S 111°7E **37 H14**
Packwood *U.S.A.* 46°36N 121°40W **78 D5**
Padaido, Kepulauan
　Indonesia 1°15S 136°30E **37 E9**
Padang *Riau, Indonesia* 1°30N 102°30E **39 M4**
Padang *Sumatera Barat,*
　Indonesia 1°0S 100°20E **36 E2**
Padang Endau *Malaysia* 2°40N 103°38E **39 L4**
Padangpanjang
　Indonesia 0°40S 100°20E **36 E2**
Padangsidempuan
　Indonesia 1°30N 99°15E **36 D1**
Paderborn *Germany* 51°42N 8°45E **16 C5**
Padma *India* 24°12N 85°22E **43 G11**
Pádova *Italy* 45°25N 11°53E **22 B4**
Padra *India* 22°15N 73°7E **42 H5**
Padrauna *India* 26°54N 83°59E **43 F10**
Padre I. *U.S.A.* 27°10N 97°25W **84 M6**
Padre Island △ *U.S.A.* 27°0N 97°25W **84 H6**
Padstow *U.K.* 50°33N 4°58W **13 G3**
Padua = Pádova *Italy* 45°25N 11°53E **22 B4**
Paducah *Ky., U.S.A.* 37°5N 88°37W **80 G9**
Paducah *Tex., U.S.A.* 34°1N 100°18W **84 D4**
Paea *Tahiti* 17°41S 149°35W **59 d**
Paeroa *N.Z.* 37°23S 175°41E **59 B5**
Pafúri *Mozam.* 22°28S 31°17E **57 C5**
Pag *Croatia* 44°25N 15°3E **16 F8**
Pagadian *Phil.* 7°55N 123°30E **37 C6**
Pagai Selatan, Pulau
　Indonesia 3°0S 100°15E **36 E2**
Pagai Utara, Pulau
　Indonesia 2°35S 100°0E **36 E2**
Pagalu = Annobón *Atl. Oc.* 1°25S 5°36E **49 G4**
Pagara *India* 24°22N 80°1E **43 G9**
Pagastikos Kolpos
　Greece 39°15N 23°0E **23 E10**
Pagatan *Indonesia* 3°33S 115°59E **36 E5**
Page *U.S.A.* 36°57N 111°27W **77 H8**
Paget, Mt. *S. Georgia* 54°26S 36°31W **96 G9**
Pago Pago *Amer. Samoa* 14°16S 170°43W **59 b**
Pagosa Springs *U.S.A.* 37°16N 107°1W **77 H10**
Pagwa River *Canada* 50°2N 85°14W **72 B2**
Pāhala *U.S.A.* 19°12N 155°29W **74 b**
Pahang ➔ *Malaysia* 3°30N 103°9E **39 L4**
Pahiatua *N.Z.* 40°27S 175°50E **59 D5**
Pahokee *U.S.A.* 26°50N 80°40W **85 H14**
Pahrump *U.S.A.* 36°12N 115°59W **79 J11**
Pahute Mesa *U.S.A.* 37°20N 116°45W **78 H10**
Pai *Thailand* 19°19N 98°27E **38 C2**
Paicines *U.S.A.* 36°44N 121°17W **78 J5**
Paide *Estonia* 58°53N 25°33E **9 G21**
Paignton *U.K.* 50°26N 3°35W **13 G4**
Päijänne *Finland* 61°30N 25°30E **9 F21**
Pailani *India* 25°45N 80°26E **43 G9**
Pailin *Cambodia* 12°46N 102°36E **38 F4**
Painan *Indonesia* 1°21S 100°34E **36 E2**
Painesville *U.S.A.* 41°43N 81°15W **82 E3**
Paint Hills = Wemindji
　Canada 53°0N 78°49W **72 B4**
Paint L. *Canada* 55°28N 97°57W **71 B9**
Painted Desert *U.S.A.* 36°0N 111°0W **77 H8**
Paintsville *U.S.A.* 37°49N 82°48W **81 G12**
País Vasco □ *Spain* 42°50N 2°45W **21 A4**
Paisley *Canada* 44°18N 81°16W **82 B3**
Paisley *U.K.* 55°50N 4°25W **11 F4**
Paisley *U.S.A.* 42°42N 120°32W **76 E3**
Paita *Peru* 5°11S 81°9W **92 E2**
Pajares, Puerto de *Spain* 43°0N 5°46W **21 A3**
Pak Lay *Laos* 18°15N 101°27E **38 C3**
Pak Phanang *Thailand* 8°21N 100°12E **39 H3**
Pak Sane *Laos* 18°22N 103°39E **38 C4**
Pak Song *Laos* 15°11N 106°14E **38 E6**
Pak Suong *Laos* 19°58N 102°18E **38 C4**
Pak Tam Chung *China* 22°24N 114°19E **33 G11**
Pakaur *India* 24°38N 87°51E **43 G12**
Pakch'ŏn *N. Korea* 39°44N 125°35E **35 E13**
Pakenham *Canada* 45°18N 76°18W **83 A8**

Pakhuis *S. Africa* 32°9S 19°5E **56 E2**
Pakistan ■ *Asia* 30°0N 70°0E **42 E4**
Pakkading *Laos* 18°19N 103°59E **38 C4**
Pakokku *Burma* 21°20N 95°0E **41 J19**
Pakowki L. *Canada* 49°20N 111°0W **71 D6**
Pakpattan *Pakistan* 30°25N 73°27E **42 D5**
Paktīā □ *Afghan.* 33°30N 69°15E **40 C6**
Paktīkā □ *Afghan.* 32°30N 69°0E **40 C6**
Pakwach *Uganda* 2°28N 31°27E **54 B3**
Pakxe *Laos* 15°5N 105°52E **38 E5**
Pal Lahara *India* 21°27N 85°11E **43 J11**
Pala *Chad* 9°25N 15°5E **51 G9**
Pala *Dem. Rep. of the Congo* 6°45S 29°30E **54 D2**
Pala *U.S.A.* 33°22N 117°5W **79 M9**
Palabek *Uganda* 3°22N 32°33E **54 B3**
Palacios *U.S.A.* 28°42N 96°13W **84 G6**
Palagruža *Croatia* 42°24N 16°15E **22 C7**
Palam *India* 19°0N 77°0E **40 K10**
Palampur *India* 32°10N 76°30E **42 C7**
Palana *Australia* 39°45S 147°55E **63 F4**
Palana *Russia* 59°10N 159°59E **29 D16**
Palanan *Phil.* 17°8N 122°29E **37 A6**
Palanan Pt. *Phil.* 17°17N 122°30E **37 A6**
Palandri *Pakistan* 33°42N 73°40E **43 C5**
Palanga *Lithuania* 55°58N 21°3E **9 J19**
Palangkaraya *Indonesia* 2°16S 113°56E **36 E4**
Palani Hills *India* 10°14N 77°33E **40 P10**
Palanpur *India* 24°10N 72°25E **42 G5**
Palapye *Botswana* 22°30S 27°7E **56 C4**
Palas *Pakistan* 35°4N 73°14E **43 B5**
Palasponga *India* 21°47N 85°34E **43 J11**
Palatka *Russia* 60°6N 150°54E **29 C16**
Palatka *U.S.A.* 29°39N 81°38W **85 G14**
Palau ■ *Palau* 7°30N 134°30E **58 A6**
Palauk *Burma* 13°10N 98°40E **38 F2**
Palawan *Phil.* 9°30N 118°30E **36 C5**
Palayankottai *India* 8°45N 77°45E **40 Q10**
Paldiski *Estonia* 59°23N 24°9E **9 G21**
Palekastro *Greece* 35°12N 26°15E **25 D8**
Paleleh *Indonesia* 1°10N 121°50E **37 D6**
Palembang *Indonesia* 3°0S 104°50E **36 E2**
Palencia *Spain* 42°1N 4°34W **21 A3**
Palenque *Mexico* 17°29N 92°1W **87 D6**
Paleochora *Greece* 35°16N 23°39E **25 D5**
Paleokastritsa *Greece* 39°40N 19°41E **25 A3**
Paleometokho *Cyprus* 35°7N 33°11E **25 D12**
Palermo *Italy* 38°7N 13°22E **22 E5**
Palermo *U.S.A.* 39°26N 121°33W **76 G3**
Palestina *Chile* 23°50S 69°47W **94 A3**
Palestine *Asia* 32°0N 35°0E **46 D4**
Palestine *U.S.A.* 31°46N 95°38W **84 F7**
Paletwa *Burma* 21°10N 92°50E **41 J18**
Palghat *India* 10°46N 76°42E **40 P10**
Palgrave, Mt. *Australia* 23°22S 115°58E **60 D2**
Pali *India* 25°50N 73°20E **42 G5**
Palikir *Micronesia* 6°55N 158°9E **64 G7**
Palioúri, Ákra *Greece* 39°57N 23°45E **23 E10**
Palisades Res. *U.S.A.* 43°20N 111°12W **76 E8**
Paliseul *Belgium* 49°54N 5°8E **15 E5**
Palitana *India* 21°32N 71°49E **42 J4**
Palizada *Mexico* 18°15N 92°5W **87 D6**
Palk Bay *Asia* 9°30N 79°15E **40 Q11**
Palk Strait *Asia* 10°0N 79°45E **40 Q11**
Palkānah *Iraq* 35°49N 44°26E **44 C5**
Palkot *India* 22°51N 84°39E **43 H11**
Pallanza = Verbánia *Italy* 45°56N 8°33E **20 D8**
Pallarenda *Australia* 19°12S 146°46E **62 B4**
Pallinup ➔ *Australia* 34°27S 118°50E **61 F2**
Pallisa *Uganda* 1°12N 33°43E **54 B3**
Pallu *India* 28°59N 74°14E **42 E6**
Palm Bay *U.S.A.* 28°2N 80°35W **85 G14**
Palm Beach *U.S.A.* 26°43N 80°2W **85 H14**
Palm Coast *U.S.A.* 29°35N 81°12W **85 G14**
Palm Desert *U.S.A.* 33°43N 116°22W **79 M10**
Palm Is. *Australia* 18°40S 146°35E **62 B4**
Palm Springs *U.S.A.* 33°50N 116°33W **79 M10**
Palma *Mozam.* 10°46S 40°29E **55 E5**
Palma, B. de *Spain* 39°30N 2°39E **24 B9**
Palma de Mallorca *Spain* 39°35N 2°39E **24 B9**
Palma Nova = Palmanova
　Spain 39°32N 2°34E **24 B9**
Palma Soriano *Cuba* 20°15N 76°0W **88 B4**
Palmanova *Spain* 39°32N 2°34E **24 B9**
Palmares *Brazil* 8°41S 35°28W **93 E11**
Palmas *Brazil* 26°29S 52°0W **95 B5**
Palmas, C. *Liberia* 4°27N 7°46W **50 H4**
Pálmas, G. di *Italy* 39°0N 8°30E **22 E3**
Palmdale *U.S.A.* 34°35N 118°7W **79 L8**
Palmeira das Missões
　Brazil 27°55S 53°17W **95 B5**
Palmeira dos Índios
　Brazil 9°25S 36°37W **93 E11**
Palmer *Antarctica* 64°35S 65°0W **5 C17**
Palmer *U.S.A.* 61°36N 149°7W **68 B5**
Palmer ➔ *Australia* 16°0S 142°26E **62 B3**
Palmer Arch. *Antarctica* 64°15S 65°0W **5 C17**
Palmer Lake *U.S.A.* 39°7N 104°55W **76 G11**
Palmer Land *Antarctica* 73°0S 63°0W **5 D18**
Palmerston *Australia* 12°31S 130°59E **60 B5**
Palmerston *Canada* 43°50N 80°51W **82 C4**
Palmerston *N.Z.* 45°29S 170°43E **59 F3**
Palmerston North *N.Z.* 40°21S 175°39E **59 D5**
Palmerton *U.S.A.* 40°48N 75°37W **83 F9**
Palmetto *U.S.A.* 27°31N 82°34W **85 H13**
Palmi *Italy* 38°21N 15°51E **22 E6**
Palmira *Argentina* 32°59S 68°34W **94 C2**
Palmira *Colombia* 3°32N 76°16W **92 C3**
Palmyra = Tudmur
　Syria 34°36N 38°15E **44 C3**
Palmyra *N.J., U.S.A.* 39°48N 91°32W **80 F8**
Palmyra *N.J., U.S.A.* 40°0N 75°1W **83 G9**
Palmyra *N.Y., U.S.A.* 43°5N 77°18W **82 C7**
Palmyra *Mo., U.S.A.* 40°18N 76°36W **83 F8**
Palmyra Is. *Pac. Oc.* 5°52N 162°5W **65 G11**
Palo Alto *U.S.A.* 37°27N 122°10W **78 H4**
Palo Seco *Trin. & Tob.* 10°4N 61°36W **93 K15**
Palo Verde *U.S.A.* 33°26N 114°44W **79 M12**

Palo Verde △ *Costa Rica* 10°21N 85°21W **88** D2
Palomar Mt. *U.S.A.* 33°22N 116°50W **79** M10
Palopo *Indonesia* 3°0S 120°16E **37** E6
Palos, C. de *Spain* 37°38N 0°40W **21** D5
Palos Verdes, Pt.
  U.S.A. 33°46N 118°25W **79** M8
Palos Verdes Estates
  U.S.A. 33°48N 118°23W **79** M8
Palu *Indonesia* 1°0S 119°52E **37** E5
Palu *Turkey* 38°45N 40°0E **44** B3
Palwal *India* 28°8N 77°19E **42** E7
Pamanukan *Indonesia* 6°16S 107°49E **37** G12
Pamekasan *Indonesia* 7°10S 113°28E **37** G15
Pamenang *Indonesia* 8°24S 116°6E **37** J19
Pamiers *France* 43°7N 1°39E **20** E4
Pamir *Tajikistan* 37°40N 73°0E **28** F8
Pamlico → *U.S.A.* 35°20N 76°28W **85** D16
Pamlico Sd. *U.S.A.* 35°20N 76°0W **85** D17
Pampa *U.S.A.* 35°32N 100°58W **84** D4
Pampa de las Salinas
  Argentina 32°1S 66°58W **94** C2
Pampanua *Indonesia* 4°16S 120°8E **37** E6
Pampas *Argentina* 35°0S 63°0W **94** D3
Pampas *Peru* 12°20S 74°50W **92** F4
Pamplona *Colombia* 7°23N 72°39W **92** B4
Pamplona-Iruña *Spain* 42°48N 1°38W **21** A5
Pampoenpoort *S. Africa* 31°3S 22°40E **56** E3
Pan de Azúcar *Chile* 24°5S 68°10W **94** A2
Pan de Azúcar △ *Chile* 26°0S 70°40W **94** B1
Pana *U.S.A.* 39°23N 89°5W **80** F9
Panaca *U.S.A.* 37°47N 114°23W **77** H6
Panaitan *Indonesia* 6°36S 105°12E **37** G11
Panaji *India* 15°25N 73°50E **40** M8
Panamá *Panama* 9°0N 79°25W **88** E4
Panama ■ *Cent. Amer.* 8°48N 79°55W **88** E4
Panamá, G. de *Panama* 8°4N 79°20W **88** E4
Panama, Isthmus of
  Cent. Amer. 9°0N 79°0W **66** J12
Panama Basin *Pac. Oc.* 5°0N 83°30W **65** G19
Panama Canal *Panama* 9°10N 79°37W **88** E4
Panama City *U.S.A.* 30°10N 85°40W **85** F12
Panamint Range
  U.S.A. 36°20N 117°20W **79** J9
Panamint Springs
  U.S.A. 36°20N 117°28W **79** J9
Panão *Peru* 9°55S 75°55W **92** E3
Panare *Thailand* 6°51N 101°30E **39** J3
Panay *Phil.* 11°10N 122°30E **37** B6
Panay G. *Phil.* 11°0N 122°30E **37** B6
Panayarvi △ *Russia* 66°16N 30°10E **8** C24
Pančevo *Serbia* 44°52N 20°41E **23** B9
Panda *Mozam.* 24°2S 34°45E **57** C5
Pandan *Malaysia* 1°32N 103°46E **39** d
Pandan *Phil.* 11°45N 122°10E **37** B6
Pandan, Selat *Singapore* 1°15N 103°44E **39** d
Pandan Tampoi = Tampoi
  Malaysia 1°30N 103°39E **39** d
Pandegelang *Indonesia* 6°25S 106°5E **37** G12
Pandhana *India* 21°42N 76°13E **42** J7
Pandharpur *India* 17°41N 75°20E **40** L9
Pando *Uruguay* 34°44S 56°0W **95** C4
Pando, L. = Hope, L.
  Australia 28°24S 139°18E **63** D2
Pandokratoras *Greece* 39°45N 19°50E **25** A3
Pandora *Costa Rica* 9°43N 83°3W **88** E3
Panevėžys *Lithuania* 55°42N 24°25E **9** J21
Pang-Long *Burma* 23°11N 98°45E **41** H21
Pang Sida △ *Thailand* 14°5N 102°17E **38** E4
Pang-Yang *Burma* 22°7N 98°48E **41** H21
Panga
  Dem. Rep. of the Congo 1°52N 26°18E **54** B2
Pangalanes, Canal des =
  Ampangalana, Lakandranon'
  Madag. 22°48S 47°50E **57** C8
Pangani *Tanzania* 5°25S 38°58E **54** D4
Pangani → *Tanzania* 5°26S 38°58E **54** D4
Pangfou = Bengbu
  China 32°58N 117°20E **35** H9
Pangil
  Dem. Rep. of the Congo 3°10S 26°35E **54** C2
Pangkah, Tanjung
  Indonesia 6°51S 112°33E **37** G15
Pangkajene *Indonesia* 4°46S 119°34E **37** E5
Pangkalanbrandan
  Indonesia 4°1N 98°20E **36** D1
Pangkalanbuun
  Indonesia 2°41S 111°37E **36** E4
Pangkalpinang *Indonesia* 2°0S 106°0E **36** E3
Pangkor, P. *Malaysia* 4°13N 100°34E **39** K3
Pangody *Russia* 65°52N 74°27E **28** C8
Panguitch *U.S.A.* 37°50N 112°26W **77** H7
Pangutaran Group *Phil.* 6°18N 120°34E **37** C6
Panhandle *U.S.A.* 35°21N 101°23W **84** D4
Pani Mines *India* 22°29N 73°50E **42** H5
Pania-Mutombo
  Dem. Rep. of the Congo 5°11S 23°51E **54** D1
Panikota I. *India* 20°46N 71°21E **42** J4
Panipat *India* 29°25N 77°2E **42** E7
Panjal Range = Pir Panjal Range
  India 32°30N 76°50E **42** C7
Panjang, Hon *Vietnam* 9°20N 103°28E **39** H4
Panjgur *Pakistan* 27°0N 64°5E **40** F4
Panjim = Panaji *India* 15°25N 73°50E **40** M8
Panjin *China* 41°3N 122°2E **35** D12
Panjnad → *Pakistan* 28°57N 70°30E **42** E4
Panjnad Barrage
  Pakistan 29°22N 71°15E **42** E4
Panjwai *Afghan.* 31°26N 65°27E **42** D1
Panmunjŏm *N. Korea* 37°59N 126°38E **35** F14
Panna *India* 24°40N 80°15E **43** G9
Panna △ *India* 24°40N 80°0E **43** G8
Panna Hills *India* 24°40N 81°15E **43** G9
Pannawonica *Australia* 21°39S 116°19E **60** D2
Panngga, Tanjung
  Indonesia 8°54S 116°2E **37** K19
Pannirtuuq = Pangnirtung
  Canada 66°8N 65°43W **69** C13

Pano Akil *Pakistan* 27°51N 69°7E **42** F3
Pano Lefkara *Cyprus* 34°53N 33°20E **25** E12
Pano Panayia *Cyprus* 34°55N 32°38E **25** E11
Panorama *Brazil* 21°21S 51°51W **95** A5
Panormos *Greece* 35°25N 24°41E **25** D6
Pansemal *India* 21°39N 74°42E **42** J6
Panshan = Panjin *China* 41°3N 122°2E **35** D12
Panshi *China* 42°58N 126°5E **35** C14
Pantanal *Brazil* 17°30S 57°40W **92** H7
Pantanos de Centla △
  Mexico 18°25N 92°25W **87** D6
Pantar *Indonesia* 8°28S 124°10E **37** F6
Pante Macassar *E. Timor* 9°30S 123°58E **37** F6
Pantelleria *Italy* 36°50N 11°57E **22** F4
Pánuco *Mexico* 22°3N 98°10W **87** C5
Panzhihua *China* 26°33N 101°44E **32** D5
Paola *Malta* 35°52N 14°30E **25** D2
Paola *U.S.A.* 38°35N 94°53W **80** F6
Paonia *U.S.A.* 38°52N 107°36W **76** G10
Paopao *Moorea* 17°30S 149°49W **59** d
Paoting = Baoding
  China 38°50N 115°28E **34** E8
Paot'ou = Baotou *China* 40°32N 110°2E **34** D6
Paoua *C.A.R.* 7°9N 16°20E **52** C3
Pápa *Hungary* 47°22N 17°30E **17** E9
Papa Stour *U.K.* 60°20N 1°42W **11** A7
Papa Westray *U.K.* 59°20N 2°55W **11** B6
Papagayo → *Mexico* 16°46N 99°43W **87** D5
Papagayo, G. de
  Costa Rica 10°30N 85°50W **88** D2
Papakura *N.Z.* 37°4S 174°59E **59** B5
Papantla *Mexico* 20°27N 97°19W **87** C5
Papar *Malaysia* 5°45N 116°0E **36** C5
Papara *Tahiti* 17°43S 149°31W **59** d
Paparoa △ *N.Z.* 42°7S 171°26E **59** E3
Papeete *Tahiti* 17°32S 149°34W **59** d
Papenoo *Tahiti* 17°30S 149°25W **59** d
Papenoo → *Tahiti* 17°30S 149°25W **59** d
Papetoai *Moorea* 17°29S 149°52W **59** d
Paphos *Cyprus* 34°46N 32°25E **25** E11
Papoose *Chile* 25°0S 70°30W **94** B1
Papoutsa *Cyprus* 34°54N 33°4E **25** E12
Papua □ *Indonesia* 4°0S 137°0E **37** E9
Papua, G. of *Papua N. G.* 9°0S 144°50E **58** B7
Papua New Guinea ■
  Oceania 8°0S 145°0E **58** B7
Papudo *Chile* 32°29S 71°27W **94** C1
Papun *Burma* 18°2N 97°30E **41** K20
Papunya *Australia* 23°15S 131°54E **60** D5
Pará = Belém *Brazil* 1°20S 48°30W **93** D9
Pará □ *Brazil* 3°20S 52°0W **93** D8
Paraburdoo *Australia* 23°14S 117°32E **60** D2
Paracatu *Brazil* 17°10S 46°50W **93** G9
Paracel Is. *S. China Sea* 15°50N 112°0E **36** A4
Parachilna *Australia* 31°10S 138°21E **63** E2
Parachinar *Pakistan* 33°55N 70°5E **42** C4
Paradip *India* 20°15N 86°35E **41** J15
Paradise *Calif., U.S.A.* 39°46N 121°37W **78** F5
Paradise *Nev., U.S.A.* 36°5N 115°8W **79** J11
Paradise → *Canada* 53°27N 57°19W **73** B8
Paradise Hill *Canada* 53°32N 109°28W **71** C7
Paradise River *Canada* 53°27N 57°17W **73** B8
Paradise Valley *U.S.A.* 41°30N 117°32W **76** F5
Paradisi *Greece* 36°18N 28°7E **25** C10
Parado *Indonesia* 8°42S 118°30E **37** F5
Paragould *U.S.A.* 36°3N 90°29W **85** C9
Paragua → *Venezuela* 6°55N 62°55W **92** B6
Paraguaçú → *Brazil* 12°45S 38°54W **93** F11
Paraguaçú Paulista
  Brazil 22°22S 50°35W **95** A5
Paraguaná, Pen. de
  Venezuela 12°0N 70°0W **92** A5
Paraguarí *Paraguay* 25°36S 57°0W **94** B4
Paraguarí □ *Paraguay* 26°0S 57°10W **94** B4
Paraguay ■ *S. Amer.* 23°0S 57°0W **94** A4
Paraguay → *Paraguay* 27°18S 58°38W **94** B4
Paraíba = João Pessoa
  Brazil 7°10S 34°52W **93** E12
Paraíba □ *Brazil* 7°0S 36°0W **93** E11
Paraíba do Sul → *Brazil* 21°37S 41°3W **95** A7
Parainen *Finland* 60°18N 22°18E **9** F20
Paraíso *Mexico* 18°24N 93°14W **87** D6
Parak *Iran* 27°38N 52°25E **45** E7
Parakou *Benin* 9°25N 2°40E **50** G6
Paralimni *Cyprus* 35°2N 33°58E **25** D12
Paramaribo *Suriname* 5°50N 55°10W **93** B7
Páramos del Batallón y La
  Negra △ *Venezuela* 8°2N 71°55W **89** E5
Paramushir, Ostrov
  Russia 50°24N 156°0E **29** D16
Paran → *Israel* 30°20N 35°10E **46** E4
Paraná *Argentina* 31°45S 60°30W **94** C3
Paraná *Brazil* 12°30S 47°48W **93** F9
Paraná □ *Brazil* 24°30S 51°0W **95** A5
Paraná → *Argentina* 33°43S 59°15W **94** C4
Paranaguá *Brazil* 25°30S 48°30W **95** B6
Paranaíba *Brazil* 19°40S 51°11W **93** G8
Paranaíba → *Brazil* 20°6S 51°4W **93** H8
Paranapanema → *Brazil* 22°40S 53°9W **95** A5
Paranapiacaba, Serra do
  Brazil 24°31S 48°35W **95** A6
Paranavaí *Brazil* 23°4S 52°56W **95** A5
Paraparaumu *N.Z.* 40°57S 175°3E **59** D5
Parbati → *Mad. P., India* 25°50N 76°30E **42** G7
Parbati → *Raj., India* 26°54N 77°53E **42** F7
Parbhani *India* 19°8N 76°52E **40** K10
Parchim *Germany* 53°26N 11°52E **16** B6
Pardes Hanna-Karkur
  Israel 32°28N 34°57E **46** C3
Pardo → *Bahia, Brazil* 15°40S 39°0W **93** G11
Pardo → *Mato Grosso,
  Brazil* 21°46S 52°9W **95** A5

Pardoo Roadhouse
  Australia 20°6S 119°3E **60** D2
Pardubice *Czech Rep.* 50°3N 15°45E **16** C8
Pare *Indonesia* 7°43S 112°12E **37** G15
Pare Mts. *Tanzania* 4°0S 37°45E **54** C4
Parecis, Serra dos *Brazil* 13°0S 60°0W **92** F7
Paren *Russia* 62°30N 163°15E **29** C17
Parent *Canada* 47°55N 74°35W **72** C5
Parent, L. *Canada* 48°31N 77°1W **72** C4
Parepare *Indonesia* 4°0S 119°40E **37** E5
Parga *Greece* 39°15N 20°29E **23** E9
Pargas = Parainen
  Finland 60°18N 22°18E **9** F20
Pargo, Pta. do *Madeira* 32°49N 17°17W **24** D2
Parham *Canada* 44°39N 76°43W **83** B8
Paria → *U.S.A.* 36°52N 111°36W **77** H8
Paria, G. de *Venezuela* 10°20N 62°0W **93** K14
Pariaguán *Venezuela* 8°51N 64°34W **92** B6
Paricutín, Cerro
  Mexico 19°28N 102°15W **86** D4
Parigi *Indonesia* 0°50S 120°5E **37** E6
Parika *Guyana* 6°50N 58°20W **92** B7
Parikkala *Finland* 61°33N 29°31E **8** F23
Parima, Serra *Brazil* 2°30N 64°0W **92** C6
Parinari *Peru* 4°35S 74°25W **92** D4
Pariñas, Pta. *S. Amer.* 4°30S 82°0W **90** D2
Parintins *Brazil* 2°40S 56°50W **93** D7
Pariparit Kyun *Burma* 14°55N 93°45E **41** M18
Paris *Canada* 43°12N 80°25W **82** C4
Paris *France* 48°53N 2°20E **20** B5
Paris *Idaho, U.S.A.* 42°14N 111°24W **76** E8
Paris *Ky., U.S.A.* 38°13N 84°15W **81** F11
Paris *Tenn., U.S.A.* 36°18N 88°19W **85** C10
Paris *Tex., U.S.A.* 33°40N 95°33W **84** E7
Parish *U.S.A.* 43°25N 76°8W **83** C8
Parishville *U.S.A.* 44°38N 74°49W **83** B10
Park *U.S.A.* 48°45N 122°18W **78** B4
Park City *U.S.A.* 37°48N 97°20W **80** G5
Park Falls *U.S.A.* 45°56N 90°27W **80** C8
Park Head *Canada* 44°36N 81°9W **82** B3
Park Hills *U.S.A.* 37°51N 90°51W **80** G9
Park Range *U.S.A.* 40°41N 106°41W **76** F10
Park Rapids *U.S.A.* 46°55N 95°4W **80** B6
Park River *U.S.A.* 48°24N 97°45W **80** A5
Park Rynie *S. Africa* 30°25S 30°45E **57** E5
Parkā Bandar *Iran* 25°55N 59°35E **45** E8
Parkano *Finland* 62°1N 23°0E **8** E20
Parker *Ariz., U.S.A.* 34°9N 114°17W **79** L12
Parker *Pa., U.S.A.* 41°5N 79°41W **82** E5
Parker Dam *U.S.A.* 34°18N 114°8W **79** L12
Parkersburg *U.S.A.* 39°16N 81°34W **81** F13
Parkes *Australia* 33°9S 148°11E **63** E4
Parkfield *U.S.A.* 35°54N 120°26W **78** K6
Parkhill *Canada* 43°15N 81°38W **82** C3
Parkland *Canada* 47°9N 122°26W **78** C4
Parkston *U.S.A.* 43°24N 97°59W **80** D5
Parksville *Canada* 49°20N 124°21W **70** D4
Parkway *U.S.A.* 38°32N 121°26W **78** G5
Parla *Spain* 40°14N 3°46W **21** B4
Parma *Italy* 44°48N 10°20E **20** D9
Parma *Idaho, U.S.A.* 43°47N 116°57W **76** E5
Parma *Ohio, U.S.A.* 41°24N 81°43W **82** E3
Parnaguá *Brazil* 10°10S 44°38W **93** F10
Parnaíba *Brazil* 2°54S 41°47W **93** D10
Parnaíba → *Brazil* 3°0S 41°50W **93** D10
Parnassos *Greece* 38°35N 22°30E **23** E10
Pärnu *Estonia* 58°28N 24°33E **9** G21
Paro Dzong *Bhutan* 27°30N 89°32E **43** F13
Paroo → *Australia* 31°28S 143°32E **63** E3
Paroo-Darling △
  Australia 31°32S 144°0E **63** E3
Paros *Greece* 37°5N 25°12E **23** F11
Parowan *U.S.A.* 37°51N 112°50W **77** H7
Parral *Chile* 36°10S 71°52W **94** D1
Parramatta *Australia* 33°48S 151°1E **63** B5
Parras *Mexico* 25°25N 102°11W **86** B4
Parrett → *U.K.* 51°12N 3°1W **13** F4
Parris I. *U.S.A.* 32°20N 80°41W **85** E14
Parrsboro *Canada* 45°30N 64°25W **73** C7
Parry I. *Canada* 45°18N 80°10W **82** A4
Parry Is. *Canada* 77°0N 110°0W **69** B9
Parry Sound *Canada* 45°20N 80°0W **82** A5
Parsaloi *Kenya* 1°16N 36°51E **54** B4
Parsnip → *Canada* 55°10N 123°2W **70** B4
Parsons *U.S.A.* 37°20N 95°16W **80** G6
Parsons Ra. *Australia* 13°30S 135°15E **62** A2
Partinico *Italy* 38°3N 13°7E **22** E5
Partridge I. *Canada* 55°59N 87°37W **72** A2
Partry Mts. *Ireland* 53°40N 9°28W **10** C2
Paru → *Brazil* 1°33S 52°38W **93** D8
Parvān □ *Afghan.* 35°0N 69°0E **40** B6
Parvatipuram *India* 18°50N 83°25E **41** K13
Parvatsar *India* 26°52N 74°49E **42** F6
Parys *S. Africa* 26°52S 27°29E **56** D4
Pas, Pta. des *Spain* 38°46N 1°26E **24** C7
Pas, The *Canada* 53°45N 101°15W **71** C8
Pasadena *Canada* 49°1N 57°36W **73** C8
Pasadena *Calif., U.S.A.* 34°9N 118°8W **79** L8
Pasadena *Tex., U.S.A.* 29°43N 95°13W **84** G7
Pasaje → *Argentina* 25°39S 63°56W **94** B3
Pasar *Indonesia* 8°27S 114°54E **37** J17
Pascagoula *U.S.A.* 30°21N 88°33W **85** F10
Pascagoula → *U.S.A.* 30°23N 88°37W **85** F10
Pașcani *Romania* 47°14N 26°45E **17** E14
Pasco *U.S.A.* 46°14N 119°6W **76** C4
Pasco, Cerro de *Peru* 10°45S 76°10W **92** F3
Pasco I. *Australia* 20°57S 115°20E **60** D2
Pascoag *U.S.A.* 41°57N 71°42W **83** E13
Pascua, I. de *Chile* 27°7S 109°23W **65** K17
Pasfield L. *Canada* 58°24N 105°20W **71** B7
Pasir Mas *Malaysia* 6°2N 102°8E **39** J4
Pasir Panjang *Singapore* 1°17N 103°46E **39** d
Pasir Putih *Malaysia* 5°50N 102°24E **39** K4
Pasirian *Indonesia* 8°13S 113°8E **37** H15
Pasirkuning *Indonesia* 0°30S 104°33E **36** E2
Paskūh *Iran* 27°34N 61°39E **45** E9

Pasley, C. *Australia* 33°52S 123°35E **61** F3
Pašman *Croatia* 43°58N 15°20E **16** G8
Pasni *Pakistan* 25°15N 63°27E **40** G3
Paso Bravo △ *Paraguay* 22°32S 57°5W **94** A4
Paso Cantinela
  Mexico 32°33N 115°47W **79** N11
Paso de Indios *Argentina* 43°55S 69°0W **96** E3
Paso de los Libres
  Argentina 29°44S 57°10W **94** B4
Paso de los Toros
  Uruguay 32°45S 56°30W **94** C4
Paso Robles *U.S.A.* 35°38N 120°41W **78** K6
Paspébiac *Canada* 48°3N 65°17W **73** C6
Pasrur *Pakistan* 32°16N 74°43E **42** C6
Passage West *Ireland* 51°52N 8°21W **10** E3
Passaic *U.S.A.* 40°51N 74°7W **83** F10
Passau *Germany* 48°34N 13°28E **16** D7
Passero, C. *Italy* 36°41N 15°10E **22** F6
Passo Fundo *Brazil* 28°10S 52°20W **95** B5
Passos *Brazil* 20°45S 46°37W **93** H9
Pastavy *Belarus* 55°4N 26°50E **9** J22
Pastaza → *Peru* 4°50S 76°52W **92** D3
Pasto *Colombia* 1°13N 77°17W **92** C3
Pasuruan *Indonesia* 7°40S 112°44E **37** G15
Patagonia *Argentina* 45°0S 69°0W **96** F3
Patagonia *U.S.A.* 31°33N 110°45W **77** L8
Patambar *Iran* 25°34N 60°17E **45** D9
Patan = Lalitapur *Nepal* 27°40N 85°20E **43** F11
Patan *India* 23°54N 72°14E **42** H5
Patani *Indonesia* 0°20N 128°50E **37** D7
Pataudi *India* 28°18N 76°48E **42** E7
Patchewollock *Australia* 35°22S 142°12E **63** F3
Patchogue *U.S.A.* 40°46N 73°1W **83** F11
Pate *Kenya* 2°10S 41°0E **54** C5
Patea *N.Z.* 39°45S 174°30E **59** C5
Patensie *S. Africa* 33°46S 24°49E **56** E3
Paternò *Italy* 37°34N 14°54E **22** F6
Pateros *U.S.A.* 48°3N 119°54W **76** B4
Paterson *U.S.A.* 40°54N 74°9W **83** F10
Paterson Ra. *Australia* 21°45S 122°10E **60** D3
Pathankot *India* 32°18N 75°45E **42** C6
Pathein = Bassein
  Burma 16°45N 94°30E **41** L19
Pathfinder Res. *U.S.A.* 42°28N 106°51W **76** E10
Pathiu *Thailand* 10°42N 99°19E **39** G2
Pathum Thani *Thailand* 14°1N 100°32E **38** E3
Pati *Indonesia* 6°45S 111°1E **37** G14
Patía → *Colombia* 2°13N 78°40W **92** C3
Patiala *Punjab, India* 30°23N 76°26E **42** D7
Patiala *Ut. P., India* 27°43N 79°1E **43** F8
Patkai Bum *India* 27°0N 95°30E **41** F19
Patmos *Greece* 37°21N 26°36E **23** F12
Patna *India* 25°35N 85°12E **43** G11
Pato Branco *Brazil* 26°13S 52°40W **95** B5
Patonga *Uganda* 2°45N 33°15E **54** B3
Patos *Brazil* 6°55S 37°16W **93** E11
Patos, L. dos *Brazil* 31°20S 51°0W **95** C5
Patos, Río de los →
  Argentina 31°18S 69°25W **94** C2
Patos de Minas *Brazil* 18°35S 46°32W **93** G9
Patquía *Argentina* 30°2S 66°55W **94** C2
Patra *Greece* 38°14N 21°47E **23** E9
Patraikos Kolpos *Greece* 38°17N 21°30E **23** E9
Patras = Patra *Greece* 38°14N 21°47E **23** E9
Patriot Hills *Antarctica* 82°20S 81°25W **5** E16
Patrocínio *Brazil* 18°57S 47°0W **93** G9
Pattani *Thailand* 6°48N 101°15E **39** J3
Pattaya *Thailand* 12°52N 100°55E **38** F3
Patten *U.S.A.* 46°0N 68°38W **81** B19
Patterson *Calif., U.S.A.* 37°28N 121°8W **78** H5
Patterson *La., U.S.A.* 29°42N 91°18W **84** G9
Patterson, Mt. *U.S.A.* 38°29N 119°20W **78** G7
Patti *Punjab, India* 31°17N 74°54E **42** D6
Patti *Ut. P., India* 25°55N 82°12E **43** G10
Pattoki *Pakistan* 31°5N 73°52E **42** D5
Patton *U.S.A.* 40°38N 78°39W **82** F6
Patuakhali *Bangla.* 22°20N 90°25E **41** H17
Patuanak *Canada* 55°55N 107°43W **71** B7
Patuca → *Honduras* 15°50N 84°18W **88** C3
Patuca, Punta *Honduras* 15°49N 84°14W **88** C3
Patuca → *Honduras* 14°30N 85°30W **88** D2
Patvinsuo △ *Finland* 63°7N 30°45E **8** E24
Pátzcuaro *Mexico* 19°31N 101°38W **86** D4
Pau *France* 43°19N 0°25W **20** E3
Paudash *Canada* 44°59N 77°58W **82** B7
Pauk *Burma* 21°27N 94°30E **41** J19
Paul I. *Canada* 56°30N 61°20W **73** A7
Paul Smiths *U.S.A.* 44°26N 74°15W **83** B10
Paulatuk *Canada* 69°25N 124°0W **68** C7
Paulding Bay *S. Ocean* 66°0S 118°0E **5** C8
Paulistana *Brazil* 8°9S 41°9W **93** E10
Paulo Afonso *Brazil* 9°21S 38°15W **93** E11
Paulpietersburg *S. Africa* 27°23S 30°50E **57** D5
Pauls Valley *U.S.A.* 34°44N 97°13W **84** D6
Pauma Valley *U.S.A.* 33°16N 116°58W **79** M10
Pauri *India* 30°9N 78°47E **43** D8
Pāveh *Iran* 35°3N 46°22E **44** C5
Pavia *Italy* 45°7N 9°8E **20** D8
Pavilion *U.S.A.* 42°52N 78°1W **82** D6
Pāvilosta *Latvia* 56°53N 21°14E **9** H19
Pavlodar *Kazakhstan* 52°33N 77°0E **28** D8
Pavlograd = Pavlohrad
  Ukraine 48°30N 35°52E **19** E6
Pavlohrad *Ukraine* 48°30N 35°52E **19** E6
Pavlovo *Russia* 55°58N 43°5E **18** C7
Pavlovsk *Russia* 50°26N 40°5E **19** D7
Pavlovskaya *Russia* 46°17N 39°47E **19** E6
Pawai, Pulau *Singapore* 1°11N 103°44E **39** d
Pawayan *India* 28°4N 80°6E **43** E9
Pawhuska *U.S.A.* 36°40N 96°20W **84** C6
Pawling *U.S.A.* 41°34N 73°36W **83** E11
Pawnee *U.S.A.* 36°20N 96°48W **84** C6
Pawnee City *U.S.A.* 40°7N 96°9W **80** E5
Pawtucket *U.S.A.* 41°53N 71°23W **83** E13
Paxi *Greece* 39°14N 20°12E **23** E9

Paximadia *Greece* 35°0N 24°35E **25** E6
Paxton *U.S.A.* 40°27N 88°6W **80** E9
Payakumbuh *Indonesia* 0°20S 100°35E **36** E2
Payette *U.S.A.* 44°5N 116°56W **76** D5
Payne Bay = Kangirsuk
  Canada 60°0N 70°0W **69** D13
Payne L. *Canada* 59°30N 74°30W **69** D12
Paynes Find *Australia* 29°15S 117°42E **61** E2
Paynesville *U.S.A.* 45°23N 94°43W **80** C6
Paysandú *Uruguay* 32°19S 58°8W **94** C4
Payson *Ariz., U.S.A.* 34°14N 111°20W **77** J8
Payson *Utah, U.S.A.* 40°3N 111°44W **76** F8
Paz → *Guatemala* 13°44N 90°10W **88** D1
Paz, B. de la *Mexico* 24°9N 110°25W **86** C2
Pāzanān *Iran* 30°35N 49°59E **45** D6
Pazardzhik *Bulgaria* 42°12N 24°20E **23** C11
Pe Ell *U.S.A.* 46°34N 123°18W **78** D3
Peabody *U.S.A.* 42°31N 70°56W **83** D14
Peace → *Canada* 59°0N 111°25W **70** B6
Peace Point *Canada* 59°7N 112°27W **70** B6
Peace River *Canada* 56°15N 117°18W **70** B5
Peach Springs *U.S.A.* 35°32N 113°25W **77** J7
Peachland *Canada* 49°47N 119°45W **70** D5
Peachtree City *U.S.A.* 33°25N 84°35W **85** E12
Peak, The = Kinder Scout
  U.K. 53°24N 1°52W **12** D6
Peak Charles △
  Australia 32°42S 121°10E **61** F3
Peak District △ *U.K.* 53°24N 1°46W **12** D6
Peak Hill *N.S.W.,
  Australia* 32°47S 148°11E **63** E4
Peak Hill *W. Austral.,
  Australia* 25°35S 118°43E **61** E2
Peak Ra. *Australia* 22°50S 148°20E **62** C4
Peake Cr. → *Australia* 28°2S 136°7E **63** D2
Peale, Mt. *U.S.A.* 38°26N 109°14W **76** G9
Pearblossom *U.S.A.* 34°30N 117°55W **79** L9
Pearl → *U.S.A.* 30°11N 89°32W **85** F10
Pearl City *U.S.A.* 21°24N 157°59W **74** b
Pearl Harbor *U.S.A.* 21°21N 157°57W **74** b
Pearl River *U.S.A.* 41°4N 74°2W **83** E10
Pearsall *U.S.A.* 28°54N 99°6W **84** G5
Pearson Int. Toronto ✈ (YYZ)
  Canada 43°46N 79°35W **82** C5
Peary Land *Greenland* 82°40N 33°0W **4** A6
Pease → *U.S.A.* 34°12N 99°2W **84** D5
Peawanuck *Canada* 55°15N 85°12W **72** A2
Pebane *Mozam.* 17°10S 38°8E **55** F4
Pebas *Peru* 3°10S 71°46W **92** D4
Pebble Beach *U.S.A.* 36°34N 121°57W **78** J5
Peč *Serbia* 42°40N 20°17E **23** C9
Pechenga *Russia* 69°29N 31°4E **8** B24
Pechenizhyn *Ukraine* 48°30N 24°48E **17** D13
Pechiguera, Pta.
  Canary Is. 28°51N 13°53W **24** F6
Pechora *Russia* 65°10N 57°11E **18** A10
Pechora → *Russia* 68°13N 54°15E **18** A9
Pechorskaya Guba *Russia* 68°40N 54°0E **18** A9
Pechory *Russia* 57°48N 27°40E **9** H22
Pecos *N. Mex., U.S.A.* 35°35N 105°41W **77** J11
Pecos *Tex., U.S.A.* 31°26N 103°30W **84** F3
Pecos → *U.S.A.* 29°42N 101°22W **84** G4
Pécs *Hungary* 46°5N 18°15E **17** E10
Pedasí *Panama* 7°32N 80°2W **88** E3
Pedder, L. *Australia* 42°55S 146°10E **63** G4
Peddie *S. Africa* 33°14S 27°7E **57** E4
Pedernales *Dom. Rep.* 18°2N 71°44W **89** C5
Pedernales → *Venezuela* 9°45N 62°40W **89** E7
Pedieos → *Cyprus* 35°10N 33°54E **25** D12
Pedirka *Australia* 26°40S 135°14E **63** D2
Pedirka Desert *Australia* 26°45S 134°11E **63** A1
Pedra Azul *Brazil* 16°2S 41°17W **93** G10
Pedra Lume *C. Verde Is.* 16°40N 22°52W **50** b
Pedreiras *Brazil* 4°32S 44°40W **93** D10
Pedro Afonso *Brazil* 9°0S 48°10W **93** E9
Pedro Cays *Jamaica* 17°5N 77°48W **88** C4
Pedro de Valdivia *Chile* 22°55S 69°38W **94** A2
Pedro Juan Caballero
  Paraguay 22°30S 55°40W **95** A4
Pee Dee = Great Pee Dee →
  U.S.A. 33°21N 79°10W **85** E15
Peebinga *Australia* 34°52S 140°57E **63** E3
Peebles *U.K.* 55°40N 3°11W **11** F5
Peekskill *U.S.A.* 41°17N 73°55W **83** E11
Peel *I. of Man* 54°13N 4°40W **12** C3
Peel → *Australia* 30°50S 150°29E **63** E5
Peel → *Canada* 67°0N 135°0W **68** C6
Peel Sd. *Canada* 73°0N 96°0W **68** B10
Peera Peera Poolanna L.
  Australia 26°30S 138°0E **63** D2
Peerless Lake *Canada* 56°37N 114°40W **70** B6
Peers *Canada* 53°40N 116°0W **70** C5
Pegasus Bay *N.Z.* 43°20S 173°10E **59** E4
Pegu *Burma* 17°20N 96°29E **41** L20
Pegu Yoma *Burma* 19°0N 96°0E **41** K20
Pehuajó *Argentina* 35°45S 62°0W **94** D3
Pei Xian = Pizhou
  China 34°44N 116°55E **34** G9
Peine *Chile* 23°45S 68°8W **94** A2
Peine *Germany* 52°19N 10°14E **16** B6
Peip'ing = Beijing *China* 39°53N 116°21E **34** E9
Peipus, L. = Chudskoye, Ozero
  Russia 58°13N 27°30E **9** G22
Peixe *Brazil* 12°0S 48°40W **93** F9
Peixe → *Brazil* 21°31S 51°58W **93** H8
Pekalongan *Indonesia* 6°53S 109°40E **37** G13
Pekan *Malaysia* 3°30N 103°25E **39** L4
Pekan Nenas *Malaysia* 1°31N 103°31E **39** d
Pekanbaru *Indonesia* 0°30N 101°15E **36** D2
Pekin *U.S.A.* 40°35N 89°40W **80** E9
Peking = Beijing *China* 39°53N 116°21E **34** E9
Pekutatan *Indonesia* 8°25S 114°49E **37** J17
Pelabuhan Klang
  Malaysia 3°0N 101°23E **39** L3
Pelabuhan Ratu, Teluk
  Indonesia 7°5S 106°30E **37** G12
Pelabuhanratu *Indonesia* 7°0S 106°32E **37** G12
Pelagie, Is. *Italy* 35°39N 12°33E **22** G5

Pelaihari *Indonesia* 3°55S 114°45E **36** E4
Peleaga, Vf. *Romania* 45°22N 22°55E **17** F12
Pelée, Mt. *Martinique* 14°48N 61°10W **88** c
Pelee, Pt. *Canada* 41°54N 82°31W **72** D3
Pelee I. *Canada* 41°47N 82°40W **82** E2
Pelekech *Kenya* 3°52N 35°8E **54** B4
Peleng *Indonesia* 1°20S 123°30E **37** E6
Pelentong *Malaysia* 1°32N 103°49E **39** d
Pelican *U.S.A.* 57°58N 136°14W **70** B1
Pelican L. *Canada* 52°28N 100°20W **71** C8
Pelican Narrows
  Canada 55°10N 102°56W **71** B8
Pelješac *Croatia* 42°55N 17°25E **22** C7
Pelkosenniemi *Finland* 67°6N 27°28E **8** C22
Pella *S. Africa* 29°1S 19°6E **56** D2
Pella *U.S.A.* 41°25N 92°55W **80** E7
Pello *Finland* 66°47N 23°59E **8** C20
Pelly → *Canada* 62°47N 137°19W **70** A1
Pelly Bay *Canada* 68°38N 89°50W **69** C11
Peloponnese □ *Greece* 37°10N 22°0E **23** F10
Pelorus Sd. *N.Z.* 40°59S 173°59E **59** D4
Pelotas *Brazil* 31°42S 52°23W **95** C5
Pelotas → *Brazil* 27°28S 51°55W **95** B5
Pelvoux, Massif du
  France 44°52N 6°20E **20** D7
Pemalang *Indonesia* 6°53S 109°23E **37** G13
Pemanggil, Pulau
  Malaysia 2°37N 104°21E **39** L5
Pematangsiantar *Indonesia* 2°57N 99°5E **36** D1
Pemba *Mozam.* 12°58S 40°30E **55** E5
Pemba *Zambia* 16°30S 27°28E **55** F2
Pemba Channel *Tanzania* 5°0S 39°37E **54** D4
Pemba I. *Tanzania* 5°0S 39°45E **54** D4
Pemberton *Australia* 34°30S 116°0E **61** F2
Pemberton *Canada* 50°25N 122°50W **70** C4
Pembina → *Canada* 54°45N 114°17W **70** C6
Pembroke *Canada* 45°50N 77°7W **72** C4
Pembroke *U.K.* 51°41N 4°55W **13** F3
Pembrokeshire □ *U.K.* 51°52N 4°56W **13** F3
Pembrokeshire Coast △
  U.K. 51°50N 5°2W **13** F2
Pen-y-Ghent *U.K.* 54°10N 2°14W **12** C5
Penal *Trin. & Tob.* 10°9N 61°29W **93** K15
Penang = Pinang
  Malaysia 5°25N 100°15E **39** c
Penápolis *Brazil* 21°30S 50°0W **95** A6
Peñarroya-Pueblonuevo
  Spain 38°19N 5°16W **21** C3
Penarth *U.K.* 51°26N 3°11W **13** F4
Peñas, C. de *Spain* 43°42N 5°52W **21** A3
Peñas, G. de *Chile* 47°0S 75°0W **96** F2
Peñas del Chache
  Canary Is. 29°6N 13°33W **24** E6
Pench △ *India* 21°45N 79°20E **43** J8
Penchʼi = Benxi *China* 41°20N 123°48E **35** D7
Pend Oreille → *U.S.A.* 49°4N 117°37W **76** B5
Pend Oreille, L. *U.S.A.* 48°10N 116°21W **76** B5
Pendembu *S. Leone* 9°7N 11°14W **50** G3
Pender B. *Australia* 16°45S 122°42E **60** C3
Pendleton *U.S.A.* 45°40N 118°47W **76** D4
Pendra *India* 22°46N 81°57E **43** H9
Penedo *Brazil* 10°15S 36°36W **93** F11
Penelokan *Indonesia* 8°17S 115°22E **37** J17
Penetanguishene
  Canada 44°50N 79°55W **82** B5
Penfield *U.S.A.* 41°13N 78°35W **82** E6
Peng Chau *China* 22°17N 114°2E **33** G11
Pengalengan *Indonesia* 7°9S 107°30E **37** G12
Penge *Kasai-Or.,*
  Dem. Rep. of the Congo 5°30S 24°33E **54** D1
Penge *Sud-Kivu,*
  Dem. Rep. of the Congo 4°27S 28°25E **54** C2
Penglai *China* 37°48N 120°42E **35** F11
Penguin *Australia* 41°8S 146°6E **63** G4
Penhalonga *Zimbabwe* 18°52S 32°40E **55** F3
Peniche *Portugal* 39°19N 9°22W **21** C1
Penicuik *U.K.* 55°50N 3°13W **11** F5
Penida, Nusa *Indonesia* 8°45S 115°30E **37** K18
Peninsular Malaysia □
  Malaysia 4°0N 102°0E **39** L4
Penitente, Serra do *Brazil* 8°45S 46°20W **93** E9
Penkridge *U.K.* 52°44N 2°6W **12** E5
Penmarch, Pte. de *France* 47°48N 4°22W **20** C1
Penn Hills *U.S.A.* 40°28N 79°52W **82** F5
Penn Yan *U.S.A.* 42°40N 77°3W **82** D7
Pennant *Canada* 50°32N 108°14W **71** C7
Penner → *India* 14°35N 80°10E **40** M12
Pennines *U.K.* 54°45N 2°27W **12** C5
Pennington *U.S.A.* 39°15N 121°47W **78** F5
Pennsburg *U.S.A.* 40°23N 75°29W **83** F9
Pennsylvania □ *U.S.A.* 40°45N 77°30W **81** E15
Penny *Canada* 53°51N 121°20W **70** C4
Penny Str. *Canada* 76°30N 97°0W **69** B8
Penobscot → *U.S.A.* 44°30N 68°48W **81** C19
Penobscot B. *U.S.A.* 44°35N 68°50W **81** C19
Penola *Australia* 37°25S 140°48E **63** F3
Penong *Australia* 31°56S 133°1E **61** F5
Penonomé *Panama* 8°31N 80°21W **88** E3
Penrhyn *Cook Is.* 9°0S 158°0W **65** H12
Penrith *Australia* 33°43S 150°38E **63** E5
Penrith *U.K.* 54°40N 2°45W **12** C5
Penryn *U.K.* 50°9N 5°7W **13** G2
Pensacola *U.S.A.* 30°25N 87°13W **85** F11
Pensacola Mts. *Antarctica* 84°0S 40°0W **5** E1
Pense *Canada* 50°25N 104°59W **71** C8
Penshurst *Australia* 37°49S 142°20E **63** F3
Penticton *Canada* 49°30N 119°38W **70** D5
Pentland *Australia* 20°32S 145°25E **62** C4
Pentland Firth *U.K.* 58°43N 3°10W **11** C5
Pentland Hills *U.K.* 55°48N 3°25W **11** F5
Penza *Russia* 53°15N 45°5E **18** D8
Penzance *U.K.* 50°7N 5°33W **13** G2
Penzhino *Russia* 63°30N 167°55E **29** C17
Penzhinskaya Guba
  Russia 61°30N 163°0E **29** C17
Peoria *Ariz., U.S.A.* 33°43N 112°14W **77** K7

Peoria *Ill., U.S.A.* 40°42N 89°36W **80** E9
Pepacton Res. *U.S.A.* 42°5N 74°58W **83** D10
Pera Hd. *Australia* 12°55S 141°37E **62** A3
Perabumulih *Indonesia* 3°27S 104°15E **36** E2
Perak → *Malaysia* 4°0N 100°50E **39** K3
Perama *Kerkyra, Greece* 39°34N 19°54E **25** A3
Perama *Kriti, Greece* 35°20N 24°40E **25** D6
Perancak *Indonesia* 8°24S 114°37E **37** J17
Peräpohjola *Finland* 66°16N 26°10E **8** C22
Percé *Canada* 48°31N 64°13W **73** C7
Perche, Collines du
  France 48°30N 0°40E **20** B4
Percival Lakes *Australia* 21°25S 125°0E **60** D4
Percy Is. *Australia* 21°39S 150°16E **62** C5
Perdido, Mte. *Spain* 42°40N 0°5E **21** A6
Perdu, Mt. = Perdido, Mte.
  Spain 42°40N 0°5E **21** A6
Pereira *Colombia* 4°49N 75°43W **92** C3
Perenjori *Australia* 29°26S 116°16E **61** E2
Pereyaslav-Khmelnytskyy
  Ukraine 50°3N 31°28E **19** D5
Pérez, I. *Mexico* 22°24N 89°42W **87** C7
Pergamino *Argentina* 33°52S 60°30W **94** C3
Pergau → *Malaysia* 5°23N 102°2E **39** K3
Perham *U.S.A.* 46°36N 95°34W **80** B6
Perhentian, Kepulauan
  Malaysia 5°54N 102°42E **39** K4
Péribonka → *Canada* 48°45N 72°5W **73** C5
Péribonka, L. *Canada* 50°1N 71°10W **73** B5
Perico *Argentina* 24°20S 65°5W **94** A2
Pericos *Mexico* 25°3N 107°42W **86** B3
Périgueux *France* 45°10N 0°42E **20** D4
Perijá, Sierra de *Colombia* 9°30N 73°3W **92** B4
Perijá △ *Venezuela* 9°30N 72°55W **89** E5
Peristerona → *Cyprus* 35°8N 33°5E **25** D12
Perito Moreno *Argentina* 46°36S 70°56W **96** F2
Perkasie *U.S.A.* 40°22N 75°18W **83** F9
Perlas, Arch. de las
  Panama 8°41N 79°7W **88** E4
Perlas, Punta de *Nic.* 12°30N 83°30W **88** D3
Perm *Russia* 58°0N 56°10E **18** C10
Pernambuco = Recife
  Brazil 8°0S 35°0W **93** E12
Pernambuco □ *Brazil* 8°0S 37°0W **93** E11
Pernatty Lagoon
  Australia 31°30S 137°12E **63** E2
Pernik *Bulgaria* 42°35N 23°2E **23** C10
Peron Is. *Australia* 13°9S 130°4E **60** B5
Peron Pen. *Australia* 26°0S 113°10E **61** E1
Perow *Canada* 54°35N 126°10W **70** C3
Perpignan *France* 42°42N 2°53E **20** E5
Perris *U.S.A.* 33°47N 117°14W **79** M9
Perry *Fla., U.S.A.* 30°7N 83°35W **85** F13
Perry *Ga., U.S.A.* 32°28N 83°44W **85** E13
Perry *Iowa, U.S.A.* 41°51N 94°6W **80** E6
Perry *N.Y., U.S.A.* 42°42N 78°0W **82** D7
Perry *Okla., U.S.A.* 36°17N 97°14W **84** C6
Perryton *U.S.A.* 36°24N 100°48W **84** C4
Perryville *U.S.A.* 37°43N 89°52W **80** G10
Persepolis *Iran* 29°55N 52°50E **45** D7
Pershotravensk *Ukraine* 50°13N 27°40E **17** C14
Persia = Iran ■ *Asia* 33°0N 53°0E **45** C7
Persian Gulf *Asia* 27°0N 50°0E **45** E6
Perth *Australia* 31°57S 115°52E **61** F2
Perth *Canada* 44°55N 76°15W **83** B8
Perth *U.K.* 56°24N 3°26W **11** E5
Perth & Kinross □ *U.K.* 56°45N 3°55W **11** E5
Perth-Andover *Canada* 46°44N 67°42W **73** C6
Perth Amboy *U.S.A.* 40°30N 74°15W **83** F10
Perth Basin *Ind. Oc.* 30°0S 108°0E **64** L2
Peru *Ind., U.S.A.* 40°45N 86°4W **80** E10
Peru *N.Y., U.S.A.* 44°35N 73°32W **83** B11
Peru ■ *S. Amer.* 4°0S 75°0W **92** D4
Peru Basin *Pac. Oc.* 20°0S 95°0W **65** J18
Peru-Chile Trench
  Pac. Oc. 20°0S 72°0W **92** G3
Perúgia *Italy* 43°7N 12°23E **22** C5
Pervomaysk *Ukraine* 48°10N 30°46E **19** E5
Pervouralsk *Russia* 56°59N 59°59E **18** C10
Pésaro *Italy* 43°54N 12°55E **22** C5
Pescara *Italy* 42°28N 14°13E **22** C6
Peshawar *Pakistan* 34°2N 71°37E **42** B4
Peshkopi *Albania* 41°41N 20°25E **23** D9
Peshtigo *U.S.A.* 45°3N 87°45W **80** C10
Pesqueira *Brazil* 8°20S 36°42W **93** E11
Petah Tiqwa *Israel* 32°6N 34°53E **46** C3
Petaling Jaya *Malaysia* 3°4N 101°42E **39** L3
Petaloudes *Greece* 36°18N 28°5E **25** C10
Pétange *Lux.* 49°33N 5°55E **15** E5
Petatlán *Mexico* 17°31N 101°16W **86** D4
Petauke *Zambia* 14°14S 31°20E **55** E3
Petawawa *Canada* 45°54N 77°17W **72** C4
Petén Itzá, L. *Guatemala* 16°58N 89°50W **88** C2
Peter I. *Br. Virgin Is.* 18°22N 64°35W **89** e
Peter I. Øy *Antarctica* 69°0S 91°0W **5** C16
Peter Pond L. *Canada* 55°55N 108°44W **71** B7
Peterbell *Canada* 48°36N 83°21W **72** C3
Peterborough *Australia* 32°58S 138°51E **63** E2
Peterborough *Canada* 44°20N 78°20W **82** B6
Peterborough *U.K.* 52°35N 0°15W **13** E7
Peterborough *U.S.A.* 42°53N 71°57W **83** D13
Peterborough □ *U.K.* 52°35N 0°15W **13** E7
Peterculter *U.K.* 57°6N 2°16W **11** D6
Peterhead *U.K.* 57°31N 1°48W **11** D7
Petermann Ranges
  Australia 26°0S 130°30E **61** E5
Petersburg *Alaska,*
  U.S.A. 56°48N 132°58W **68** D6
Petersburg *Pa., U.S.A.* 40°34N 78°3W **82** F6
Petersburg *Va., U.S.A.* 37°14N 77°24W **81** G15
Petersburg *W. Va., U.S.A.* 39°1N 79°5W **81** F14
Petersfield *U.K.* 51°1N 0°56W **13** F7
Petit-Canal *Guadeloupe* 16°25N 61°31W **88** b

Petit Goâve *Haiti* 18°27N 72°51W **89** C5
Petit Lac Manicouagan
  Canada 51°25N 67°40W **73** B6
Petit-Mécatina →
  Canada 50°40N 59°30W **73** B8
Petit-Mécatina, Î. du
  Canada 50°30N 59°25W **73** B8
Petit Piton *St. Lucia* 13°51N 61°5W **89** f
Petit-Saguenay *Canada* 48°15N 70°4W **73** C5
Petitcodiac *Canada* 45°57N 65°11W **73** C6
Petite Terre, Îles de la
  Guadeloupe 16°13N 61°9W **88** b
Petitot → *Canada* 60°14N 123°29W **70** A4
Petitsikapau L. *Canada* 54°37N 66°25W **73** B6
Petlad *India* 22°30N 72°45E **42** H5
Peto *Mexico* 20°8N 88°55W **87** C7
Petone *N.Z.* 41°13S 174°53E **59** D5
Petorca *Chile* 32°15S 70°56W **94** C1
Petoskey *U.S.A.* 45°22N 84°57W **81** C11
Petra *Jordan* 30°20N 35°22E **46** E4
Petra *India* 39°37N 3°6E **24** B10
Petra, Ostrova *Russia* 76°15N 118°30E **29** B12
Petra Velikogo, Zaliv
  Russia 42°40N 132°0E **30** C6
Petre, Pt. *Canada* 43°50N 77°9W **82** C7
Petrich *Bulgaria* 41°24N 23°13E **23** D10
Petrified Forest △ *U.S.A.* 35°0N 109°30W **77** J9
Petrikov = Pyetrikaw
  Belarus 52°11N 28°29E **17** B15
Petrolândia *Brazil* 9°5S 38°20W **93** E11
Petrolia *Canada* 42°54N 82°9W **82** D2
Petrolina *Brazil* 9°24S 40°30W **93** E10
Petropavl *Kazakhstan* 54°53N 69°13E **28** D7
Petropavlovsk = Petropavl
  Kazakhstan 54°53N 69°13E **28** D7
Petropavlovsk-Kamchatskiy
  Russia 53°3N 158°43E **29** D16
Petrópolis *Brazil* 22°33S 43°9W **95** A7
Petroşani *Romania* 45°28N 23°20E **17** F12
Petrovaradin *Serbia* 45°16N 19°55E **23** B8
Petrovsk *Russia* 52°22N 45°19E **18** D8
Petrovsk-Zabaykalskiy
  Russia 51°20N 108°55E **29** D11
Petrozavodsk *Russia* 61°41N 34°20E **18** B5
Petrus Steyn *S. Africa* 27°38S 28°8E **57** D4
Petrusburg *S. Africa* 29°4S 25°26E **56** D4
Peumo *Chile* 34°21S 71°12W **94** C1
Peureulak *Indonesia* 4°48N 97°45E **36** D1
Pevek *Russia* 69°41N 171°19E **29** C18
Pforzheim *Germany* 48°52N 8°41E **16** D5
Pha Taem △ *Thailand* 15°32N 105°30E **38** E5
Phaestos *Greece* 35°2N 24°50E **25** D6
Phagwara *India* 31°10N 75°40E **42** D6
Phala *Botswana* 23°45S 26°50E **56** C4
Phalera = Phulera *India* 26°52N 75°16E **42** F6
Phalodi *India* 27°12N 72°24E **42** F5
Phaluai, Ko *Thailand* 9°32N 99°41E **39** b
Phan *Thailand* 19°28N 99°43E **38** C2
Phan Rang *Vietnam* 11°34N 109°0E **39** G7
Phan Ri = Hoa Da
  Vietnam 11°16N 108°40E **39** G7
Phan Si Pan *Vietnam* 22°18N 103°46E **38** A4
Phan Thiet *Vietnam* 11°1N 108°9E **39** G7
Phanat Nikhom
  Thailand 13°27N 101°11E **38** F3
Phangan, Ko *Thailand* 9°45N 100°0E **39** H3
Phangnga *Thailand* 8°28N 98°30E **39** H2
Phangnga, Ao *Thailand* 8°16N 98°33E **39** a
Phanom Sarakham
  Thailand 13°45N 101°21E **38** F3
Phaphund *India* 26°36N 79°28E **43** F8
Pharenda *India* 27°5N 83°17E **43** F10
Pharr *U.S.A.* 26°12N 98°11W **84** H5
Phatthalung *Thailand* 7°39N 100°6E **39** J3
Phayao *Thailand* 19°11N 99°55E **38** C2
Phelps *U.S.A.* 42°58N 77°3W **82** D7
Phelps L. *Canada* 59°15N 103°15W **71** B8
Phenix City *U.S.A.* 32°28N 85°0W **85** E12
Phet Buri *Thailand* 13°1N 99°55E **38** F2
Phetchabun *Thailand* 16°25N 101°8E **38** D3
Phetchabun, Thiu Khao
  Thailand 16°0N 101°20E **38** E3
Phetchaburi = Phet Buri
  Thailand 13°1N 99°55E **38** F2
Phi Phi, Ko *Thailand* 7°45N 98°46E **39** J2
Phiafay *Laos* 14°48N 106°0E **38** E6
Phibun Mangsahan
  Thailand 15°14N 105°14E **38** E5
Phichai *Thailand* 17°22N 100°10E **38** D3
Phichit *Thailand* 16°26N 100°22E **38** D3
Philadelphia *Miss.,*
  U.S.A. 32°46N 89°7W **85** E10
Philadelphia *N.Y., U.S.A.* 44°9N 75°43W **83** B9
Philadelphia *Pa., U.S.A.* 39°57N 75°9W **83** G9
Philip *U.S.A.* 44°2N 101°40W **80** C3
Philippeville *Belgium* 50°12N 4°33E **15** D4
Philippi *U.S.A.* 39°9N 80°3W **81** F13
Philippi L. *Australia* 24°20S 138°55E **62** C2
Philippine Basin *Pac. Oc.* 17°0N 132°0E **64** F5
Philippine Sea *Pac. Oc.* 18°0N 125°0E **64** F4
Philippine Trench = Mindanao
  Trench *Pac. Oc.* 12°0N 126°6E **37** B7
Philippines ■ *Asia* 12°0N 123°0E **37** B6
Philippolis *S. Africa* 30°15S 25°16E **56** E4
Philippopolis = Plovdiv
  Bulgaria 42°8N 24°44E **23** C11
Philipsburg *Canada* 45°2N 73°5W **83** A11
Philipsburg *Mont.,*
  U.S.A. 46°20N 113°18W **76** C7
Philipsburg *Pa., U.S.A.* 40°54N 78°13W **82** F6
Philipstown = Daingean
  Ireland 53°18N 7°17W **10** C4
Philipstown *S. Africa* 30°28S 24°30E **56** E3
Phillip I. *Australia* 38°30S 145°12E **63** F4
Phillips *U.S.A.* 45°42N 90°24W **80** C8
Phillipsburg *Kans.,*
  U.S.A. 39°45N 99°19W **80** F4

Phillipsburg *N.J., U.S.A.* 40°42N 75°12W **83** F9
Philmont *U.S.A.* 42°15N 73°39W **83** D11
Philomath *U.S.A.* 44°32N 123°22W **76** D2
Phimai *Thailand* 15°13N 102°30E **38** E4
Phitsanulok *Thailand* 16°50N 100°12E **38** D3
Phnom Dangrek
  Thailand 14°20N 104°0E **38** E5
Phnom Kulen △
  Cambodia 13°38N 104°15E **38** F5
Phnom Penh *Cambodia* 11°33N 104°55E **39** G5
Phnom Penh = Phnom Penh
  Cambodia 11°33N 104°55E **39** G5
Phoenicia *U.S.A.* 42°5N 74°14W **83** D10
Phoenix *Mauritius* 20°17S 57°30E **53** d
Phoenix *Ariz., U.S.A.* 33°26N 112°4W **77** K7
Phoenix *N.Y., U.S.A.* 43°14N 76°18W **83** C8
Phoenix Is. *Kiribati* 3°30S 172°0W **64** H10
Phoenixville *U.S.A.* 40°8N 75°31W **83** F9
Phon *Thailand* 15°49N 102°36E **38** E4
Phon Tiou *Laos* 17°53N 104°37E **38** D5
Phong → *Thailand* 16°23N 102°56E **38** D4
Phong Saly *Laos* 21°42N 102°9E **38** A4
Phong Tho *Vietnam* 22°32N 103°21E **38** A4
Phonhong *Laos* 18°30N 102°25E **38** C4
Phonum *Thailand* 8°49N 98°48E **39** H2
Phosphate Hill *Australia* 21°53S 139°58E **62** C2
Photharam *Thailand* 13°41N 99°51E **38** F2
Phra Nakhon Si Ayutthaya
  Thailand 14°25N 100°30E **38** E3
Phra Thong, Ko *Thailand* 9°5N 98°17E **39** H2
Phrae *Thailand* 18°7N 100°9E **38** C3
Phrom Phiram *Thailand* 17°2N 100°12E **38** D3
Phu Bia *Laos* 19°10N 103°0E **38** C4
Phu Chong-Na Yoi △
  Thailand 14°25N 105°30E **38** E5
Phu Dien *Vietnam* 18°58N 105°31E **38** C5
Phu Hin Rang Kla △
  Thailand 17°0N 100°59E **38** D3
Phu Kradung △ *Thailand* 17°0N 101°44E **38** D3
Phu Loi *Laos* 20°14N 103°14E **38** B4
Phu Luang △ *Thailand* 17°15N 101°29E **38** D3
Phu Ly *Vietnam* 20°35N 105°50E **38** B5
Phu Phan △ *Thailand* 17°0N 103°56E **38** D4
Phu Quoc, Dao *Vietnam* 10°20N 104°0E **39** G4
Phu Tho *Vietnam* 21°24N 105°13E **38** B5
Phu Wiang △ *Thailand* 16°39N 102°23E **38** D4
Phuc Yen *Vietnam* 21°16N 105°45E **38** B5
Phuket *Thailand* 7°53N 98°24E **39** a
Phuket, Ko *Thailand* 8°0N 98°22E **39** a
Phul *India* 30°19N 75°14E **42** D6
Phulad *India* 25°38N 73°49E **42** G5
Phulchari *Bangla.* 25°11N 89°37E **43** G13
Phulera *India* 26°52N 75°16E **42** F6
Phulpur *India* 25°31N 82°49E **43** G10
Phun Phin *Thailand* 9°7N 99°12E **39** H2
Phuntsholing *Bhutan* 26°51N 89°23E **43** F13
Piacenza *Italy* 45°1N 9°40E **20** D8
Piai, Tanjung *Malaysia* 1°17N 103°30E **39** d
Pian Cr. → *Australia* 30°2S 148°12E **63** E4
Pian-Upe △ *Uganda* 1°44N 34°20E **54** B3
Pianosa *Italy* 42°35N 10°5E **22** C4
Piapot *Canada* 49°59N 109°8W **71** D7
Piatra Neamţ *Romania* 46°56N 26°21E **17** E14
Piauí □ *Brazil* 7°0S 43°0W **93** E10
Piauí → *Brazil* 6°38S 42°42W **93** E10
Piave → *Italy* 45°32N 12°44E **22** B5
Pibor Post *Sudan* 6°47N 33°3E **51** G12
Picardie □ *France* 49°50N 3°0E **20** B5
Picardy = Picardie □
  France 49°50N 3°0E **20** B5
Picayune *U.S.A.* 30°32N 89°41W **85** F10
Pichhor *India* 25°58N 78°20E **43** G8
Pichilemu *Chile* 34°22S 72°0W **94** C1
Pichor *India* 25°11N 78°11E **42** G8
Pickerel L. *Canada* 48°40N 91°25W **72** C1
Pickering *U.S.A.* 54°15N 0°46W **12** C7
Pickering, Vale of *U.K.* 54°14N 0°45W **12** C7
Pickle Lake *Canada* 51°30N 90°12W **72** B1
Pickwick L. *U.S.A.* 35°4N 88°15W **85** D10
Picton *Australia* 34°12S 150°34E **63** E5
Picton *Canada* 44°1N 77°9W **82** B7
Picton *N.Z.* 41°18S 174°3E **59** D5
Pictou *Canada* 45°41N 62°42W **73** C7
Picture Butte *Canada* 49°55N 112°45W **70** D6
Pictured Rocks △
  U.S.A. 46°30N 86°30W **80** B10
Picún Leufú *Argentina* 39°30S 69°5W **96** D3
Pidurutalagala *Sri Lanka* 7°10N 80°50E **40** R12
Piedmont = Piemonte □
  Italy 45°0N 8°0E **20** D7
Piedmont *Ala., U.S.A.* 33°55N 85°37W **85** E12
Piedmont *S.C., U.S.A.* 34°42N 82°28W **75** D10
Piedras Negras *Mexico* 28°42N 100°31W **86** B4
Pieksämäki *Finland* 62°18N 27°10E **8** E22
Pielinen *Finland* 63°15N 29°40E **8** E23
Piemonte □ *Italy* 45°0N 8°0E **20** D7
Pienaarsrivier *S. Africa* 25°15S 28°18E **57** D4
Piercefield *U.S.A.* 44°13N 74°35W **83** B10
Pierceland *Canada* 54°20N 109°46W **71** C7
Pierpont *U.S.A.* 41°45N 80°34W **82** E4
Pierre *U.S.A.* 44°22N 100°21W **80** C3
Pierrefonds *Canada* 45°29N 73°51W **83** A11
Pierreville *Trin. & Tob.* 10°16N 61°0W **93** K16
Piet Retief *S. Africa* 27°1S 30°50E **57** D5
Pietarsaari *Finland* 63°40N 22°43E **8** E20
Pietermaritzburg
  S. Africa 29°35S 30°25E **57** D5
Pietersburg = Polokwane
  S. Africa 23°54S 29°25E **57** C4
Pietrosul, Vf. *Maramureş,*
  Romania 47°35N 24°43E **17** E13
Pietrosul, Vf. *Suceava,*
  Romania 47°12N 25°18E **17** E13

Pigeon L. *Canada* 44°27N 78°30W **82** B6
Piggott *U.S.A.* 36°23N 90°11W **85** C9
Pigüe *Argentina* 37°36S 62°25W **94** D3
Pihani *India* 27°36N 80°15E **43** F9
Pihlajavesi *Finland* 61°45N 28°45E **8** F23
Pijijiapan *Mexico* 15°42N 93°14W **87** D6
Pikangikum *Canada* 51°49N 94°0W **71** C10
Pikes Peak *U.S.A.* 38°50N 105°3W **76** G11
Piketberg *S. Africa* 32°55S 18°40E **56** E2
Pikeville *U.S.A.* 37°29N 82°31W **81** G12
Pikou *China* 39°18N 122°22E **35** E12
Pikwitonei *Canada* 55°35N 97°9W **71** B9
Piła *Poland* 53°10N 16°48E **17** B9
Pilanesberg △ *S. Africa* 25°15S 27°4E **56** D4
Pilani *India* 28°22N 75°33E **42** E6
Pilar *Paraguay* 26°50S 58°20W **94** B4
Pilaya → *Bolivia* 20°55S 64°4W **92** H6
Pilbara *Australia* 23°35S 117°25E **60** D2
Pilcomayo → *Paraguay* 25°21S 57°42W **94** B4
Pilgrim's Rest *S. Africa* 24°55S 30°44E **57** C5
Pilibhit *India* 28°40N 79°50E **43** E8
Pilica → *Poland* 51°52N 21°17E **17** C11
Pilipinas = Philippines ■
  Asia 12°0N 123°0E **37** B6
Pilkhawa *India* 28°43N 77°42E **42** E7
Pilliga *Australia* 30°21S 148°54E **63** E4
Pílos *Greece* 36°55N 21°42E **23** F9
Pilot Mound *Canada* 49°15N 98°54W **71** D9
Pilot Point *U.S.A.* 33°24N 96°58W **84** E6
Pilot Rock *U.S.A.* 45°29N 118°50W **76** D4
Pima *U.S.A.* 32°54N 109°50W **77** K9
Pimba *Australia* 31°18S 136°46E **63** E2
Pimenta Bueno *Brazil* 11°35S 61°10W **92** F6
Pimentel *Peru* 6°45S 79°55W **92** E3
Pin Valley △ *India* 31°50N 77°50E **42** D7
Pinang *Malaysia* 5°25N 100°15E **39** c
Pinar, C. des *Spain* 39°53N 3°12E **24** B10
Pinar del Río *Cuba* 22°26N 83°40W **88** B3
Pınarhisar *Turkey* 41°37N 27°30E **23** D12
Pinatubo, Mt. *Phil.* 15°8N 120°21E **37** A6
Pinawa *Canada* 50°9N 95°50W **71** C9
Pincher Creek *Canada* 49°30N 113°57W **70** D6
Pinchi L. *Canada* 54°38N 124°30W **70** C4
Pinckneyville *U.S.A.* 38°5N 89°23W **80** F9
Pińczów *Poland* 50°32N 20°32E **17** C11
Pindar *Australia* 28°30S 115°47E **61** E2
Pindi Gheb *Pakistan* 33°14N 72°21E **42** C5
Pindos Oros *Greece* 40°0N 21°0E **23** E9
Pindus Mts. = Pindos Oros
  Greece 40°0N 21°0E **23** E9
Pine → *B.C., Canada* 56°8N 120°43W **70** B4
Pine → *Sask., Canada* 58°50N 105°38W **71** B7
Pine Bluff *U.S.A.* 34°13N 92°1W **84** D9
Pine Bluffs *U.S.A.* 41°11N 104°4W **76** F11
Pine City *U.S.A.* 45°50N 92°59W **80** C7
Pine Cr. → *U.S.A.* 41°10N 77°16W **82** E7
Pine Creek *Australia* 13°50S 131°50E **60** B5
Pine Falls *Canada* 50°34N 96°11W **71** C9
Pine Flat L. *U.S.A.* 36°50N 119°20W **78** J7
Pine Grove *U.S.A.* 40°33N 76°23W **83** F8
Pine Hill *Australia* 23°38S 146°57E **62** C4
Pine Pass *Canada* 55°25N 122°42W **70** B4
Pine Point *Canada* 60°50N 114°28W **70** A6
Pine Ridge *U.S.A.* 43°2N 102°33W **80** D2
Pine River *Canada* 51°45N 100°30W **71** C8
Pine River *U.S.A.* 46°43N 94°24W **80** B6
Pine Valley *U.S.A.* 32°50N 116°32W **79** N10
Pinecrest *U.S.A.* 38°12N 120°1W **78** G6
Pinedale *Calif., U.S.A.* 36°50N 119°48W **78** J7
Pinedale *Wyo., U.S.A.* 42°52N 109°52W **76** E9
Pinega → *Russia* 64°30N 44°19E **18** B8
Pinehouse L. *Canada* 55°32N 106°35W **71** B7
Pineimuta → *Canada* 52°8N 88°33E **72** B2
Pinerolo *Italy* 44°53N 7°21E **20** D7
Pines, Akra *Greece* 40°5N 24°20E **23** D11
Pinetop-Lakeside *U.S.A.* 34°8N 109°56W **77** J9
Pinetown *S. Africa* 29°48S 30°54E **57** D5
Pineville *U.S.A.* 31°19N 92°26W **84** F8
Ping → *Thailand* 15°42N 100°9E **38** E3
Pingaring *Australia* 32°40S 118°32E **61** F2
Pingding *China* 37°47N 113°38E **34** F7
Pingdingshan *China* 33°43N 113°27E **34** H7
Pingdong *Taiwan* 22°39N 120°30E **33** D7
Pingdu *China* 36°42N 119°59E **35** F10
Pingelly *Australia* 32°32S 117°5E **61** F2
Pingliang *China* 35°35N 106°31E **34** G4
Pinglu *China* 39°31N 112°30E **34** E7
Pingluo *China* 38°52N 106°30E **34** E4
Pingquan *China* 41°1N 118°37E **35** D10
Pingrup *Australia* 33°32S 118°29E **61** F2
Pʼingtung *Taiwan* 22°38N 120°30E **33** D7
Pingwu *China* 32°25N 104°30E **34** H3
Pingxiang *China* 22°6N 106°46E **32** D5
Pingyao *China* 37°12N 112°10E **34** F7
Pingyi *China* 35°30N 117°35E **35** G9
Pingyin *China* 36°20N 116°25E **34** F9
Pingyuan *China* 37°10N 116°22E **34** F9
Pinhal *Brazil* 22°10S 46°46W **95** A6
Pinheiro *Brazil* 2°31S 45°5W **93** D9
Pinheiro Machado
  Brazil 31°34S 53°23W **95** C5
Pinhel *Portugal* 40°50N 7°1W **21** B2
Pini *Indonesia* 0°10N 98°40E **36** D1
Pinios → *Greece* 39°55N 22°41E **23** E10
Pinjarra *Australia* 32°37S 115°52E **61** F2
Pink Mountain *Canada* 57°3N 122°52W **70** B4
Pinnacles △ *U.S.A.* 36°25N 121°12W **78** J5
Pinnaroo *Australia* 35°17S 140°53E **63** F3
Pinon Hills *U.S.A.* 34°26N 117°39W **79** L9
Pinos *Mexico* 22°18N 101°34W **86** C4
Pinos, Mt. *U.S.A.* 34°49N 119°8W **79** L7
Pinos Pt. *U.S.A.* 36°38N 121°57W **77** H3
Pinrang *Indonesia* 3°46S 119°41E **37** E5
Pins, Pte. aux *Canada* 42°15N 81°51W **82** D3
Pinsk *Belarus* 52°10N 26°1E **17** B14
Pintados *Chile* 20°35S 69°40W **92** H5
Pinyug *Russia* 60°5N 48°0E **18** B8

Pioche *U.S.A.* 37°56N 114°27W **77** H6
Piombino *Italy* 42°55N 10°32E **22** C4
Pioner, Ostrov *Russia* 79°50N 92°0E **29** B10
Piopiotaki = Milford Sd.
  N.Z. 44°41S 167°47E **59** F1
Piorini, L. *Brazil* 3°15S 62°35W **92** D6
Piotrków Trybunalski
  Poland 51°23N 19°43E **17** C10
Pīp *Iran* 26°45N 60°10E **45** E9
Pipar *India* 26°25N 73°31E **42** F5
Pipar Road *India* 26°27N 73°27E **42** F5
Piparia *Mad. P., India* 22°45N 78°23E **43** H8
Piparia *Mad. P., India* 21°49N 77°37E **42** J7
Pipestone *U.S.A.* 44°0N 96°19W **80** D5
Pipestone → *Canada* 52°53N 89°23W **72** B2
Pipestone Cr. →
  Canada 49°38N 100°15W **71** D8
Piplan *Pakistan* 32°17N 71°21E **42** C4
Piploda *India* 23°37N 74°56E **42** H6
Pipmuacan, Rés. *Canada* 49°45N 70°30W **73** C5
Pippingarra *Australia* 20°27S 118°42E **60** D2
Piqua *U.S.A.* 40°9N 84°15W **81** E11
Piquiri → *Brazil* 24°3S 54°14W **95** A5
Pir Panjal Range *India* 32°30N 76°50E **42** C7
Pīr Sohrāb *Iran* 25°44N 60°54E **45** E9
Piracicaba *Brazil* 22°45S 47°40W **95** A6
Piracuruca *Brazil* 3°50S 41°50W **93** D10
Pirae *Tahiti* 17°31S 149°32W **59** d
Piræus = Piraeus *Greece* 37°57N 23°42E **23** F10
Piraiévs = Piraeus *Greece* 37°57N 23°42E **23** F10
Pirajuí *Brazil* 21°59S 49°29W **95** A6
Piram I. *India* 21°36N 72°21E **42** J5
Pirané *Argentina* 25°42S 59°6W **94** B4
Pīrānshahr *Iran* 36°41N 45°8E **44** B5
Pirapora *Brazil* 17°20S 44°56W **93** G10
Pirawa *India* 24°10N 76°2E **42** G7
Pireas *Greece* 37°57N 23°42E **23** F10
Pirgos *Greece* 37°40N 21°27E **23** F9
Piribebuy *Paraguay* 25°26S 57°2W **94** B4
Pirimapun *Indonesia* 6°20S 138°24E **37** F9
Pirin Planina *Bulgaria* 41°40N 23°30E **23** D10
Pirineos = Pyrénées
  Europe 42°45N 0°18E **20** E4
Piripiri *Brazil* 4°15S 41°46W **93** D10
Pirlangimpi *Australia* 11°24S 130°26E **60** B5
Pirmasens *Germany* 49°12N 7°36E **16** D4
Pirot *Serbia* 43°9N 22°33E **23** C10
Piru *Indonesia* 3°4S 128°12E **37** E7
Piru *U.S.A.* 34°25N 118°48W **79** L8
Pisa *Italy* 43°43N 10°23E **22** C4
Pisagua *Chile* 19°40S 70°15W **92** G4
Pisco *Peru* 13°50S 76°12W **92** F3
Písek *Czech Rep.* 49°19N 14°10E **16** D8
Pishan *China* 37°30N 78°33E **32** C2
Pīshīn *Iran* 26°6N 61°47E **45** E9
Pishin *Pakistan* 30°35N 67°0E **42** D2
Pishin Lora → *Pakistan* 29°9N 64°5E **42** E1
Pising *Indonesia* 5°8S 121°53E **37** F6
Pismo Beach *U.S.A.* 35°9N 120°38W **79** K6
Pissis, Cerro *Argentina* 27°45S 68°48W **94** B3
Pissouri *Cyprus* 34°40N 32°42E **25** E11
Pistóia *Italy* 43°55N 10°54E **22** C4
Pistol B. *Canada* 62°25N 92°37W **71** A10
Pisuerga → *Spain* 41°33N 4°52W **21** B3
Pit → *U.S.A.* 40°47N 122°6W **76** F2
Pitarpunga L. *Australia* 34°24S 143°30E **63** E3
Pitcairn I. *Pac. Oc.* 25°5S 130°5W **65** K14
Pitch L. *Trin. & Tob.* 10°12N 61°39W **93** K15
Piteå *Sweden* 65°20N 21°25E **8** D19
Piteälven → *Sweden* 65°20N 21°25E **8** D19
Pitești *Romania* 44°52N 24°54E **17** F13
Pithapuram *India* 17°10N 82°15E **41** L13
Pithara *Australia* 30°20S 116°35E **61** F2
Pithoragarh *India* 29°35N 80°13E **43** E9
Pithoro *Pakistan* 25°31N 69°23E **42** G3
Pitlochry *U.K.* 56°42N 3°44W **11** E5
Pitsilia *Cyprus* 34°55N 33°0E **25** E12
Pitt I. *Canada* 53°30N 129°50W **70** C3
Pittsburg *Calif., U.S.A.* 38°2N 121°53W **78** G5
Pittsburg *Kans., U.S.A.* 37°25N 94°42W **80** G6
Pittsburg *Tex., U.S.A.* 33°0N 94°59W **84** E7
Pittsburgh *U.S.A.* 40°26N 79°58W **82** F5
Pittsfield *Ill., U.S.A.* 39°36N 90°49W **80** F8
Pittsfield *Maine, U.S.A.* 44°47N 69°23W **81** C19
Pittsfield *Mass., U.S.A.* 42°27N 73°15W **83** D11
Pittsfield *N.H., U.S.A.* 43°18N 71°20W **83** C13
Pittston *U.S.A.* 41°19N 75°47W **83** E9
Pittsworth *Australia* 27°41S 151°37E **63** D5
Pituri → *Australia* 22°35S 138°30E **62** C2
Piura *Peru* 5°15S 80°38W **92** E2
Pixley *U.S.A.* 35°58N 119°18W **78** K7
Pizhou *China* 34°44N 116°55E **34** G9
Placentia *Canada* 47°20N 54°0W **73** C9
Placentia B. *Canada* 47°0N 54°40W **73** C9
Placerville *U.S.A.* 38°44N 120°48W **78** G6
Placetas *Cuba* 22°15N 79°44W **88** B4
Plainfield *N.J., U.S.A.* 40°37N 74°25W **83** F10
Plainfield *Ohio, U.S.A.* 40°13N 81°43W **82** F3
Plainfield *Vt., U.S.A.* 44°17N 72°26W **83** B12
Plains *Mont., U.S.A.* 47°28N 114°53W **76** C6
Plains *Tex., U.S.A.* 33°11N 102°50W **84** E3
Plainview *Nebr., U.S.A.* 42°21N 97°47W **80** D5
Plainview *Tex., U.S.A.* 34°11N 101°43W **84** D4
Plainwell *U.S.A.* 42°27N 85°38W **81** D11
Plaistow *U.S.A.* 42°50N 71°6W **83** D13
Plaka, Ákra *Greece* 35°11N 26°19E **25** D8
Plana Cays *Bahamas* 22°38N 73°30W **89** B5
Planada *U.S.A.* 37°16N 120°19W **78** H6
Plano *U.S.A.* 33°1N 96°42W **84** E6
Plant City *U.S.A.* 28°1N 82°7W **85** G13
Plaquemine *U.S.A.* 30°17N 91°14W **84** F9
Plasencia *Spain* 40°3N 6°8W **21** B2
Plaster City *U.S.A.* 32°47N 115°51W **79** N11
Plaster Rock *Canada* 46°53N 67°22W **73** C6
Plastun *Russia* 44°45N 136°19E **30** B8
Plata, Río de la →
  S. Amer. 34°45N 57°30W **94** C4

Plátani → *Italy* 37°23N 13°16E **22** F5
Platanos *Greece* 35°28N 23°33E **25** D5
Platte *U.S.A.* 43°23N 98°51W **80** D4
Platte → *Mo., U.S.A.* 39°16N 94°50W **80** F6
Platte → *Nebr., U.S.A.* 41°4N 95°53W **80** E6
Platteville *U.S.A.* 42°44N 90°29W **80** D8
Plattsburgh *U.S.A.* 44°42N 73°28W **83** B11
Plattsmouth *U.S.A.* 41°1N 95°53W **80** E6
Plauen *Germany* 50°30N 12°8E **16** C7
Plavinas *Latvia* 56°35N 25°46E **9** H21
Playa Blanca *Canary Is.* 28°55N 13°37W **24** F6
Playa Blanca Sur
  Canary Is. 28°51N 13°50W **24** F6
Playa de las Americas
  Canary Is. 28°5N 16°43W **24** F3
Playa de Mogán
  Canary Is. 27°48N 15°47W **24** G4
Playa del Carmen *Mexico* 20°37N 87°4W **87** C7
Playa del Inglés
  Canary Is. 27°45N 15°33W **24** G4
Playa Esmeralda
  Canary Is. 28°8N 14°16W **24** F5
Playgreen L. *Canada* 54°0N 98°15W **71** C9
Pleasant Bay *Canada* 46°51N 60°48W **73** C7
Pleasant Hill *U.S.A.* 37°57N 122°4W **78** H4
Pleasant Mount *U.S.A.* 41°44N 75°26W **83** E9
Pleasanton *Calif.,
  U.S.A.* 37°39N 121°52W **78** H5
Pleasanton *Tex., U.S.A.* 28°58N 98°29W **84** G5
Pleasantville *N.J.,
  U.S.A.* 39°24N 74°32W **81** F16
Pleasantville *Pa., U.S.A.* 41°35N 79°34W **82** E5
Plei Ku *Vietnam* 13°57N 108°0E **38** F7
Plenty → *Australia* 23°25S 136°31E **62** C2
Plenty, B. of *N.Z.* 37°45S 177°0E **59** B6
Plentywood *U.S.A.* 48°47N 104°34W **76** B11
Plesetsk *Russia* 62°43N 40°20E **18** B7
Plessisville *Canada* 46°14N 71°47W **73** C5
Plétipi, L. *Canada* 51°44N 70°6W **73** B5
Pleven *Bulgaria* 43°26N 24°37E **23** C11
Plevlja *Montenegro* 43°21N 19°21E **23** C8
Plevna *Canada* 44°58N 76°59W **82** B8
Plock *Poland* 52°32N 19°40E **17** B10
Plöckenstein *Germany* 48°46N 13°51E **16** D7
Ploiești *Romania* 44°57N 26°5E **17** F14
Plonge, Lac la *Canada* 55°8N 107°20W **71** B7
Plovdiv *Bulgaria* 42°8N 24°44E **23** C11
Plover Cove Res. *China* 22°28N 114°15E **33** G11
Plum *U.S.A.* 40°29N 79°47W **82** F5
Plum I. *U.S.A.* 41°11N 72°12W **83** E12
Plumas *U.S.A.* 39°45N 120°4W **78** F6
Plummer *U.S.A.* 47°20N 116°53W **76** C5
Plumtree *Zimbabwe* 20°27S 27°55E **55** G2
Plunge *Lithuania* 55°53N 21°59E **9** J19
Plymouth *Trin. & Tob.* 11°14N 60°48W **93** J16
Plymouth *U.K.* 50°22N 4°10W **13** G3
Plymouth *Calif., U.S.A.* 38°29N 120°51W **78** G6
Plymouth *Ind., U.S.A.* 41°21N 86°19W **80** E10
Plymouth *Mass., U.S.A.* 41°57N 70°40W **83** E14
Plymouth *N.C., U.S.A.* 35°52N 76°43W **85** D16
Plymouth *N.H., U.S.A.* 43°46N 71°41W **83** C13
Plymouth *Pa., U.S.A.* 41°14N 75°57W **83** E9
Plymouth *Wis., U.S.A.* 43°45N 87°59W **80** D10
Plympton-Wyoming = Wyoming
  Canada 42°57N 82°7W **82** D2
Plynlimon = Pumlumon Fawr
  U.K. 52°28N 3°46W **13** E4
Plyusa *Russia* 58°28N 29°27E **9** G23
Plzeň *Czech Rep.* 49°45N 13°22E **16** D7
Po → *Italy* 44°57N 12°4E **22** B5
Po Hai = Bo Hai *China* 39°0N 119°0E **35** E10
Po Toi *China* 22°10N 114°16E **33** G11
Pobeda *Russia* 65°12N 146°12E **29** C15
Pobedy, Pik *Kyrgyzstan* 42°0N 79°58E **32** B2
Pocahontas *Ark., U.S.A.* 36°16N 90°58W **85** C9
Pocahontas *Iowa, U.S.A.* 42°44N 94°40W **80** D6
Pocatello *U.S.A.* 42°52N 112°27W **76** E7
Pocomoke City *U.S.A.* 38°5N 75°34W **81** F16
Poços de Caldas *Brazil* 21°50S 46°33W **95** A6
Podgorica *Montenegro* 42°30N 19°19E **23** C8
Podilska Vysochyna
  Ukraine 49°0N 28°0E **17** D14
Podolsk *Russia* 55°25N 37°30E **18** C6
Podporozhye *Russia* 60°55N 34°2E **18** B5
Pofadder *S. Africa* 29°10S 19°22E **56** D2
Pogranichnyy *Russia* 44°25N 131°24E **30** C5
Poh *Indonesia* 0°46S 122°51E **37** E6
Pohang *S. Korea* 36°1N 129°23E **35** F15
Pohjanmaa *Finland* 62°58N 22°50E **8** E20
Pohnpei *Micronesia* 6°55N 158°10E **64** G7
Pohri *India* 25°32N 77°22E **42** G6
Poinsett, C. *Antarctica* 65°42S 113°18E **5** C8
Point Arena *U.S.A.* 38°55N 123°41W **78** G3
Point Baker *U.S.A.* 56°21N 133°37W **70** B2
Point Fortin
  Trin. & Tob. 10°10N 61°42W **93** K15
Point Hope *U.S.A.* 68°21N 166°47W **74** a
Point L. *Canada* 65°15N 113°4W **68** C8
Point Lisas Industrial Estate
  Trin. & Tob. 10°24N 61°29W **93** K15
Point Pedro *Sri Lanka* 9°50N 80°15E **40** Q12
Point Pelee △ *Canada* 41°57N 82°31W **82** E2
Point Pleasant *N.J.,
  U.S.A.* 40°5N 74°4W **83** F10
Point Pleasant *W. Va.,
  U.S.A.* 38°51N 82°8W **81** F12
Point Reyes △ *U.S.A.* 38°10N 122°55W **78** G2
Pointe-à-Pitre *Guadeloupe* 16°10N 61°32W **88** b
Pointe-au-Pic = La Malbaie
  Canada 47°40N 70°10W **73** C5
Pointe-Claire *Canada* 45°26N 73°50W **83** A11
Pointe-Gatineau *Canada* 45°27N 75°41W **83** A9
Pointe-Noire *Congo* 4°48S 11°53E **52** E2
Pointe-Noire *Guadeloupe* 16°14N 61°47W **88** b
Poipet *Cambodia* 13°39N 102°33E **38** F4
Poisonbush Ra.
  Australia 22°30S 121°30E **60** D3

Poissonnier Pt.
  Australia 19°57S 119°10E **60** C2
Poitiers *France* 46°35N 0°20E **20** C4
Poitou *France* 46°40N 0°10W **20** C3
Pojoaque *U.S.A.* 35°54N 106°1W **77** J10
Pokaran *India* 27°0N 71°50E **42** F4
Pokataroo *Australia* 29°30S 148°36E **63** D4
Pokhara *Nepal* 28°14N 83°58E **43** E10
Poko *Dem. Rep. of the Congo* 3°7N 26°52E **54** B2
Pokrovsk *Russia* 61°29N 129°0E **29** C13
Pola = Pula *Croatia* 44°54N 13°57E **16** F7
Polacca *U.S.A.* 35°50N 110°23W **77** J8
Polan *Iran* 25°30N 61°10E **45** E9
Poland *U.S.A.* 43°13N 75°3W **83** C9
Poland ■ *Europe* 52°0N 20°0E **17** C10
Polar Bear △ *Canada* 55°0N 83°45W **72** A2
Polatsk *Belarus* 55°30N 28°50E **9** J23
Polcura *Chile* 37°17S 71°43W **94** D1
Polesye = Pripet Marshes
  Europe 52°10N 28°10E **17** B15
Polevskoy *Russia* 56°26N 60°11E **18** C11
Police *Poland* 53°33N 14°33E **16** B8
Police, Pte. *Seychelles* 4°51S 55°32E **53** b
Poligiros *Greece* 40°23N 23°25E **23** D10
Polillo Is. *Phil.* 14°56N 122°0E **37** B6
Polis *Cyprus* 35°2N 32°26E **25** D11
Polk *U.S.A.* 41°22N 79°56W **82** E5
Pollachi *India* 10°35N 77°0E **40** P10
Pollença *Spain* 39°54N 3°1E **24** B10
Pollença, B. de *Spain* 39°53N 3°8E **24** B10
Polnovat *Russia* 63°50N 65°54E **28** C7
Polokwane *S. Africa* 23°54S 29°25E **57** C4
Polokwane → *S. Africa* 22°25S 30°5E **57** C5
Polonne *Ukraine* 50°6N 27°30E **17** C14
Polonnoye = Polonne
  Ukraine 50°6N 27°30E **17** C14
Polson *U.S.A.* 47°41N 114°9W **76** C6
Poltava *Ukraine* 49°35N 34°35E **19** E5
Põltsamaa *Estonia* 58°39N 25°58E **9** G21
Polunochnoye *Russia* 60°52N 60°25E **28** C7
Põlva *Estonia* 58°3N 27°3E **9** G22
Polyarny *Russia* 69°8N 33°20E **8** B25
Polyarnyye Zori *Russia* 67°22N 32°30E **8** C25
Polynesia *Pac. Oc.* 10°0S 162°0W **65** F11
Polynésie française = French
  Polynesia ☑ *Pac. Oc.* 20°0S 145°0W **65** J13
Pombal *Portugal* 39°55N 8°40W **21** C1
Pombia *Greece* 35°0N 24°51E **25** E6
Pomene *Mozam.* 22°53S 35°33E **57** C6
Pomeroy *Ohio, U.S.A.* 39°2N 82°2W **81** F12
Pomeroy *Wash., U.S.A.* 46°28N 117°36W **76** C5
Pomézia *Italy* 41°40N 12°30E **22** D5
Pomona *Australia* 26°22S 152°52E **63** D5
Pomona *U.S.A.* 34°4N 117°45W **79** L9
Pomorskie, Pojezierze
  Poland 53°40N 16°37E **17** B9
Pomos *Cyprus* 35°9N 32°33E **25** D11
Pomos, C. *Cyprus* 35°10N 32°33E **25** D11
Pompano Beach *U.S.A.* 26°14N 80°7W **85** H14
Pompeys Pillar *U.S.A.* 45°59N 107°57W **76** D10
Pompeys Pillar △
  U.S.A. 46°0N 108°0W **76** D10
Pompton Lakes *U.S.A.* 41°0N 74°17W **83** F10
Ponape = Pohnpei
  Micronesia 6°55N 158°10E **64** G7
Ponask L. *Canada* 54°0N 92°41W **72** B1
Ponca *U.S.A.* 42°34N 96°43W **80** D5
Ponca City *U.S.A.* 36°42N 97°5W **84** C6
Ponce *Puerto Rico* 18°1N 66°37W **89** d
Ponchatoula *U.S.A.* 30°26N 90°26W **85** F9
Poncheville, L. *Canada* 50°10N 76°55W **72** B4
Pond *U.S.A.* 35°43N 119°20W **79** K7
Pond Inlet *Canada* 72°40N 77°0W **69** B12
Pondicherry = Puducherry
  India 11°59N 79°50E **40** P11
Ponds, I. of *Canada* 53°27N 55°52W **73** B8
Ponferrada *Spain* 42°32N 6°35W **21** A2
Ponnani *India* 10°45N 75°59E **40** P9
Ponoka *Canada* 52°42N 113°40W **70** C6
Ponorogo *Indonesia* 7°52S 111°27E **37** G14
Ponoy *Russia* 67°0N 41°13E **18** A7
Ponoy → *Russia* 66°59N 41°17E **18** A7
Ponta Delgada *Azores* 37°44N 25°40W **50** a
Ponta do Sol *Madeira* 32°42N 17°7W **24** D2
Ponta Grossa *Brazil* 25°7S 50°10W **95** B5
Ponta Porã *Brazil* 22°20S 55°35W **95** A4
Pontarlier *France* 46°54N 6°20E **20** C7
Pontchartrain, L. *U.S.A.* 30°5N 90°5W **85** F9
Ponte do Pungué
  Mozam. 19°30S 34°33E **55** F3
Ponte Nova *Brazil* 20°25S 42°54W **95** A7
Ponteix *Canada* 49°46N 107°29W **71** D7
Pontevedra *Spain* 42°26N 8°40W **21** A1
Pontiac *Ill., U.S.A.* 40°53N 88°38W **80** E9
Pontiac *Mich., U.S.A.* 42°38N 83°18W **81** D12
Pontian Kechil *Malaysia* 1°29N 103°23E **39** d
Pontianak *Indonesia* 0°3S 109°15E **36** E3
Pontine Is. = Ponziane, Ísole
  Italy 40°55N 12°57E **22** D5
Pontine Mts. = Kuzey Anadolu
  Dağları *Turkey* 41°30N 35°0E **19** F6
Pontivy *France* 48°5N 2°58W **20** B2
Pontoise *France* 49°3N 2°5E **20** B5
Ponton → *Canada* 58°27N 116°11W **70** B5
Pontypool *Canada* 44°6N 78°38W **82** B6
Pontypool *U.K.* 51°42N 3°2W **13** F4
Ponziane, Ísole *Italy* 40°55N 12°57E **22** D5
Poochera *Australia* 32°43S 134°51E **63** E1
Poole *U.K.* 50°43N 1°59W **13** G6
Poole □ *U.K.* 50°43N 1°59W **13** G6
Poona = Pune *India* 18°29N 73°57E **40** K8
Pooncarie *Australia* 33°22S 142°31E **63** E3
Poopelloe L. *Australia* 31°40S 144°0E **63** E3
Poopó, L. de *Bolivia* 18°30S 67°35W **92** G5
Popayán *Colombia* 2°27N 76°36W **92** C3
Poperinge *Belgium* 50°51N 2°42E **15** D2
Popilta L. *Australia* 33°10S 141°42E **63** E3

Popio L. *Australia* 33°10S 141°52E **63** E3
Poplar *U.S.A.* 48°7N 105°12W **76** B11
Poplar → *Canada* 53°0N 97°19W **71** C9
Poplar Bluff *U.S.A.* 36°46N 90°24W **80** G8
Poplarville *U.S.A.* 30°51N 89°32W **85** F10
Popocatépetl, Volcán
  Mexico 19°2N 98°38W **87** D5
Popokabaka
  Dem. Rep. of the Congo 5°41S 16°40E **52** F3
Poprad *Slovak Rep.* 49°3N 20°18E **17** D11
Porali → *Pakistan* 25°58N 66°26E **42** G2
Porbandar *India* 21°44N 69°43E **42** J3
Porcher I. *Canada* 53°50N 130°30W **70** C2
Porcupine → *Canada* 59°11N 104°46W **71** B8
Porcupine → *U.S.A.* 66°34N 145°19W **74** a
Porcupine Gorge △
  Australia 20°22S 144°26E **62** C3
Pordenone *Italy* 45°57N 12°39E **22** B5
Pori *Finland* 61°29N 21°48E **8** F19
Porkhov *Russia* 57°45N 29°38E **9** H23
Porlamar *Venezuela* 10°57N 63°51W **92** A6
Pormpuraaw *Australia* 14°59S 141°26E **62** A3
Poronaysk *Russia* 49°13N 143°0E **29** E15
Poroshiri-Dake *Japan* 42°41N 142°52E **30** C11
Poroto Mts. *Tanzania* 9°0S 33°30E **55** D3
Porpoise B. *Antarctica* 66°0S 127°0E **5** C9
Porreres *Spain* 39°31N 3°2E **24** B10
Porsangerfjorden
  Norway 70°40N 25°40E **8** A21
Porsgrunn *Norway* 59°10N 9°40E **9** G13
Port Alberni *Canada* 49°14N 124°50W **78** A2
Port Alfred *S. Africa* 33°36S 26°55E **56** E4
Port Alice *Canada* 50°20N 127°25W **70** C3
Port Allegany *U.S.A.* 41°48N 78°17W **82** E6
Port Allen *U.S.A.* 30°27N 91°12W **84** F9
Port Alma *Australia* 23°38S 150°53E **62** C5
Port Alma *Canada* 42°10N 82°14W **82** D2
Port Angeles *U.S.A.* 48°7N 123°27W **78** B3
Port Antonio *Jamaica* 18°10N 76°26W **88** a
Port Aransas *U.S.A.* 27°50N 97°4W **84** H6
Port Arthur *Australia* 43°7S 147°50E **63** G4
Port Arthur *U.S.A.* 29°54N 93°56W **84** G8
Port au Choix *Canada* 50°43N 57°22W **73** B8
Port au Port B. *Canada* 48°40N 58°50W **73** C8
Port-au-Prince *Haiti* 18°40N 72°20W **89** C5
Port Augusta *Australia* 32°30S 137°50E **63** E2
Port Austin *U.S.A.* 44°3N 83°1W **82** B2
Port Bell *Uganda* 0°18N 32°35E **54** B3
Port Bergé Vaovao
  Madag. 15°33S 47°40E **57** B8
Port Blandford *Canada* 48°20N 54°10W **73** C9
Port Bradshaw
  Australia 12°30S 137°20E **62** A2
Port Broughton
  Australia 33°37S 137°56E **63** E2
Port Bruce *Canada* 42°39N 81°0W **82** D4
Port Burwell *Canada* 42°40N 80°48W **82** D4
Port Canning *India* 22°23N 88°40E **43** H13
Port Carling *Canada* 45°7N 79°35W **82** A5
Port-Cartier *Canada* 50°2N 66°50W **73** B6
Port Chalmers *N.Z.* 45°49S 170°30E **59** F3
Port Charlotte *U.S.A.* 26°59N 82°6W **85** H13
Port Chester *U.S.A.* 41°0N 73°40W **83** F11
Port Clements *Canada* 53°40N 132°10W **70** C2
Port Clinton *U.S.A.* 41°31N 82°56W **81** E12
Port Colborne *Canada* 42°50N 79°10W **82** D5
Port Coquitlam *Canada* 49°15N 122°45W **78** A4
Port Credit *Canada* 43°33N 79°35W **82** C5
Port Curtis *Australia* 23°57S 151°20E **62** C5
Port d'Alcúdia *Spain* 39°50N 3°7E **24** B10
Port Dalhousie *Canada* 43°13N 79°16W **82** C5
Port d'Andratx *Spain* 39°32N 2°23E **24** B9
Port Darwin *Australia* 12°24S 130°45E **60** B5
Port Darwin *Falk. Is.* 51°50S 59°0W **96** G5
Port Davey *Australia* 43°16S 145°55E **63** G4
Port-de-Paix *Haiti* 19°50N 72°50W **89** C5
Port Dickson *Malaysia* 2°30N 101°49E **39** L3
Port Douglas *Australia* 16°30S 145°30E **62** B4
Port Dover *Canada* 42°47N 80°12W **82** D4
Port Edward *Canada* 54°12N 130°10W **70** C2
Port Elgin *Canada* 44°25N 81°25W **82** B3
Port Elizabeth *S. Africa* 33°58S 25°40E **56** E4
Port Ellen *U.K.* 55°38N 6°11W **11** F2
Port Erin *I. of Man* 54°5N 4°45W **12** C3
Port Essington *Australia* 11°15S 132°10E **60** B5
Port Ewen *U.S.A.* 41°54N 73°59W **83** E11
Port Fairy *Australia* 38°22S 142°12E **63** F3
Port Gamble *U.S.A.* 47°51N 122°34W **78** C4
Port-Gentil *Gabon* 0°40S 8°50E **52** E1
Port Germein *Australia* 33°1S 138°1E **63** E2
Port Ghalib *Egypt* 25°20N 34°50E **44** E2
Port Gibson *U.S.A.* 31°58N 90°59W **84** F9
Port Glasgow *U.K.* 55°56N 4°41W **11** F4
Port Harcourt *Nigeria* 4°40N 7°10E **50** H7
Port Hardy *Canada* 50°41N 127°30W **70** C3
Port Harrison = Inukjuak
  Canada 58°25N 78°15W **69** D12
Port Hawkesbury
  Canada 45°36N 61°22W **73** C7
Port Hedland *Australia* 20°25S 118°35E **60** D2
Port Henry *U.S.A.* 44°3N 73°28W **83** B11
Port Hood *Canada* 46°0N 61°32W **73** C7
Port Hope *Canada* 43°56N 78°20W **82** C6
Port Hope *U.S.A.* 43°57N 82°43W **82** C2
Port Hope Simpson
  Canada 52°33N 56°18W **73** B8
Port Hueneme *U.S.A.* 34°7N 119°12W **79** L7
Port Huron *U.S.A.* 42°58N 82°26W **82** D2
Port Jefferson *U.S.A.* 40°57N 73°3W **83** F11
Port Jervis *U.S.A.* 41°22N 74°41W **83** E10
Port Kelang = Pelabuhan Klang
  Malaysia 3°0N 101°23E **39** L3
Port Kenny *Australia* 33°10S 134°41E **63** E1
Port Laoise *Ireland* 52°15N 7°8W **10** D4

Port Laoise *Ireland* 53°2N 7°18W **10** C4
Port Lavaca *U.S.A.* 28°37N 96°38W **84** G6
Port Leyden *U.S.A.* 43°35N 75°21W **83** C9
Port Lincoln *Australia* 34°42S 135°52E **63** E2
Port Loko *S. Leone* 8°48N 12°46W **50** G3
Port-Louis *Guadeloupe* 16°28N 61°32W **88** b
Port Louis *Mauritius* 20°10S 57°30E **53** d
Port MacDonnell
  Australia 38°5S 140°48E **63** F3
Port McNeill *Canada* 50°35N 127°6W **70** C3
Port Macquarie
  Australia 31°25S 152°25E **63** E5
Port Maria *Jamaica* 18°22N 76°54W **88** a
Port Matilda *U.S.A.* 40°48N 78°3W **82** F6
Port McNicoll *Canada* 44°44N 79°48W **82** B5
Port Mellon *Canada* 49°32N 123°31W **70** D4
Port-Menier *Canada* 49°51N 64°15W **73** C7
Port Moody *Canada* 49°17N 122°51W **78** A4
Port Morant *Jamaica* 17°54N 76°19W **88** a
Port Moresby *Papua N. G.* 9°24S 147°8E **58** B7
Port Musgrave
  Australia 11°55S 141°50E **62** A3
Port Neches *U.S.A.* 30°0N 93°59W **84** G8
Port Nolloth *S. Africa* 29°17S 16°52E **56** D2
Port Nouveau-Québec =
  Kangiqsualujjuaq
  Canada 58°30N 65°59W **69** D13
Port of Climax *Canada* 49°10N 108°20W **71** D7
Port of Coronach
  Canada 49°7N 105°31W **71** D7
Port of Spain
  Trin. & Tob. 10°40N 61°31W **89** D7
Port Orange *U.S.A.* 29°9N 80°59W **85** G14
Port Orchard *U.S.A.* 47°32N 122°38W **78** C4
Port Orford *U.S.A.* 42°45N 124°30W **76** E1
Port Pegasus *N.Z.* 47°12S 167°41E **59** G1
Port Perry *Canada* 44°6N 78°56W **82** B6
Port Phillip B. *Australia* 38°10S 144°50E **63** F3
Port Pirie *Australia* 33°10S 138°1E **63** E2
Port Renfrew *Canada* 48°30N 124°20W **78** B2
Port Roper *Australia* 14°45S 135°25E **62** A2
Port Rowan *Canada* 42°40N 80°30W **82** D4
Port Safaga = Bûr Safâga
  Egypt 26°43N 33°57E **44** E2
Port Said = Bûr Sa'îd
  Egypt 31°16N 32°18E **51** B12
Port St. Joe *U.S.A.* 29°49N 85°18W **85** G12
Port St. Johns = Umzimvubu
  S. Africa 31°38S 29°33E **57** E4
Port St. Lucie *U.S.A.* 27°18N 80°21W **85** H14
Port Sanilac *U.S.A.* 43°26N 82°33W **82** C2
Port Severn *Canada* 44°48N 79°43W **82** B5
Port Shepstone *S. Africa* 30°44S 30°28E **57** E5
Port Simpson *Canada* 54°30N 130°20W **70** C2
Port Stanley = Stanley
  Falk. Is. 51°40S 59°51W **96** G5
Port Stanley *Canada* 42°40N 81°10W **82** D3
Port Sudan = Bûr Sûdân
  Sudan 19°32N 37°9E **51** E13
Port Sulphur *U.S.A.* 29°29N 89°42W **85** G10
Port Talbot *U.K.* 51°35N 3°47W **13** F4
Port Townsend *U.S.A.* 48°7N 122°45W **78** B4
Port-Vendres *France* 42°32N 3°8E **20** E5
Port Vila *Vanuatu* 17°45S 168°18E **58** C9
Port Vladimir *Russia* 69°25N 33°6E **8** B25
Port Wakefield *Australia* 34°12S 138°10E **63** E2
Port Washington
  U.S.A. 43°23N 87°53W **80** D10
Porta Orientalis *Romania* 45°6N 22°18E **17** F12
Portacloy *Ireland* 54°20N 9°46W **10** B2
Portadown *U.K.* 54°25N 6°27W **10** B5
Portaferry *U.K.* 54°23N 5°33W **10** B6
Portage *Wis., U.S.A.* 43°33N 89°28W **80** D9
Portage la Prairie
  Canada 49°58N 98°18W **71** D9
Portageville *U.S.A.* 36°26N 89°42W **80** G9
Portalegre *Portugal* 39°19N 7°25E **21** C2
Portales *U.S.A.* 34°11N 103°20W **77** J12
Portarlington *Ireland* 53°9N 7°14W **10** C4
Portbou *Spain* 42°25N 3°9E **21** A7
Porter L. *N.W.T., Canada* 61°41N 108°5W **71** A7
Porter L. *Sask., Canada* 56°20N 107°20W **71** B7
Porterville *S. Africa* 33°0S 19°0E **56** E2
Porterville *U.S.A.* 36°4N 119°1W **78** J8
Porthcawl *U.K.* 51°29N 3°42W **13** F4
Porthill *U.S.A.* 48°59N 116°30W **76** B5
Porthmadog *U.K.* 52°55N 4°8W **12** E3
Portile de Fier *Europe* 44°44N 22°30E **17** F12
Portimão *Portugal* 37°8N 8°32W **21** D1
Portishead *U.K.* 51°29N 2°46W **13** F5
Portknockie *U.K.* 57°42N 2°51W **11** D6
Portland *N.S.W.,
  Australia* 33°20S 150°0E **63** E5
Portland *Vic., Australia* 38°20S 141°35E **63** F3
Portland *Canada* 44°42N 76°12W **83** B8
Portland *Conn., U.S.A.* 41°34N 72°38W **83** E12
Portland *Maine, U.S.A.* 43°39N 70°16W **81** D18
Portland *Mich., U.S.A.* 42°52N 84°54W **81** D11
Portland *Oreg., U.S.A.* 45°32N 122°37W **78** E4
Portland *Pa., U.S.A.* 40°55N 75°6W **83** F9
Portland *Tex., U.S.A.* 27°53N 97°20W **84** H6
Portland, I. of *U.K.* 50°33N 2°26W **13** G5
Portland B. *Australia* 38°15S 141°45E **63** F3
Portland Bight *Jamaica* 17°52N 77°5W **88** a
Portland Bill *U.K.* 50°31N 2°28W **13** G5
Portland Canal *U.S.A.* 55°56N 130°0W **70** B2
Portland Int. ✈ (PDX)
  U.S.A. 45°35N 122°36W **78** E4
Portland Pt. *Jamaica* 17°42N 77°11W **88** a
Portmadoc = Porthmadog
  U.K. 52°55N 4°8W **12** E3
Portmore *Jamaica* 17°53N 76°53W **88** a
Porto *France* 42°16N 8°42E **20** E8
Porto *Portugal* 41°8N 8°40W **21** B1
Pôrto Alegre *Brazil* 30°5S 51°10W **95** C5
Porto Colom *Spain* 39°26N 3°15E **24** B10

154 Porto Cristo
INDEX TO WORLD MAPS

Porto Cristo *Spain* 39°33N 3°20E **24** B10
Porto de Moz *Brazil* 1°41S 52°13W **93** D8
Porto Empédocle *Italy* 37°17N 13°32E **22** F5
Porto Esperança *Brazil* 19°37S 57°29W **92** G7
Porto Franco *Brazil* 6°20S 47°24W **93** E9
Porto Inglês *C. Verde Is.* 15°21N 23°10W **50** b
Porto Mendes *Brazil* 24°30S 54°15W **95** A5
Porto Moniz *Madeira* 32°52N 17°11W **24** D2
Porto Murtinho *Brazil* 21°45S 57°55W **92** H7
Porto Nacional *Brazil* 10°40S 48°30W **93** F9
Porto-Novo *Benin* 6°23N 2°42E **50** G6
Porto Primavera, Represa *Brazil* 22°10S 52°45W **95** A5
Porto Santo, I. de *Madeira* 33°45N 16°25W **50** B2
Porto São José *Brazil* 22°43S 53°10W **95** A5
Porto Seguro *Brazil* 16°26S 39°5W **93** G11
Porto Tórres *Italy* 40°50N 8°24E **22** D3
Porto União *Brazil* 26°10S 51°10W **95** B5
Porto-Vecchio *France* 41°35N 9°16E **20** F8
Pôrto Velho *Brazil* 8°46S 63°54W **92** E6
Porto Walter *Brazil* 8°15S 72°40W **92** E4
Portobelo *Panama* 9°35N 79°42W **88** E4
Portoferráio *Italy* 42°48N 10°20E **22** C4
Portola *U.S.A.* 39°49N 120°28W **78** F6
Portopetro *Spain* 39°22N 3°13E **24** B10
Portoscuso *Italy* 39°12N 8°24E **22** E3
Portoviejo *Ecuador* 1°7S 80°28W **92** D2
Portpatrick *U.K.* 54°51N 5°7W **11** G3
Portree *U.K.* 57°25N 6°12W **11** D2
Portrush *U.K.* 55°12N 6°40W **10** A5
Portsmouth *Dominica* 15°34N 61°27W **89** C7
Portsmouth *U.K.* 50°48N 1°6W **13** G6
Portsmouth *N.H., U.S.A.* 43°5N 70°45W **83** C14
Portsmouth *Ohio, U.S.A.* 38°44N 82°57W **81** F12
Portsmouth *R.I., U.S.A.* 41°36N 71°15W **83** E13
Portsmouth *Va., U.S.A.* 36°58N 76°23W **81** G15
Portsmouth □ *U.K.* 50°48N 1°6W **13** G6
Portsoy *U.K.* 57°41N 2°41W **11** D6
Portstewart *U.K.* 55°11N 6°43W **10** A5
Porttipahdan tekojärvi *Finland* 68°5N 26°40E **8** B22
Portugal ■ *Europe* 40°0N 8°0W **21** C1
Portumna *Ireland* 53°6N 8°14W **10** C3
Portville *U.S.A.* 42°3N 78°20W **82** D6
Porvenir *Chile* 53°10S 70°16W **96** G2
Posadas *Argentina* 27°30S 55°50W **95** B4
Posht-e Badam *Iran* 33°2N 55°23E **45** C7
Poso *Indonesia* 1°20S 120°55E **37** E6
Posse *Brazil* 14°4S 46°18W **93** F9
Possession I. *Antarctica* 72°4S 172°0E **5** D11
Possum Kingdom L. *U.S.A.* 32°52N 98°26W **84** E5
Post *U.S.A.* 33°12N 101°23W **84** E4
Post Falls *U.S.A.* 47°43N 116°57W **76** C5
Postavy = Pastavy *Belarus* 55°4N 26°50E **9** J22
Poste-de-la-Baleine = Kuujjuarapik *Canada* 55°20N 77°35W **72** A4
Postmasburg *S. Africa* 28°18S 23°5E **56** D3
Postojna *Slovenia* 45°46N 14°12E **16** F8
Poston *U.S.A.* 34°0N 114°24W **79** M12
Postville *Canada* 54°54N 59°47W **73** B8
Posyet *Russia* 42°39N 130°48E **30** C5
Potchefstroom *S. Africa* 26°41S 27°7E **56** D4
Poteau *U.S.A.* 35°3N 94°37W **84** D7
Poteet *U.S.A.* 29°2N 98°35W **84** G5
Potenza *Italy* 40°38N 15°48E **22** D6
Poteriteri, L. *N.Z.* 46°5S 167°10E **59** G1
Potgietersrus = Mokopane *S. Africa* 24°10S 28°55E **57** C4
Poti *Georgia* 42°10N 41°38E **19** F7
Potiskum *Nigeria* 11°39N 11°2E **51** F8
Potomac → *U.S.A.* 38°0N 76°23W **81** F14
Potosí *Bolivia* 19°38S 65°50W **92** G5
Potosi Mt. *U.S.A.* 35°57N 115°29W **79** K11
Pototan *Phil.* 10°54N 122°38E **37** B6
Potrerillos *Chile* 26°30S 69°30W **94** B2
Potsdam *Germany* 52°23N 13°4E **16** B7
Potsdam *U.S.A.* 44°40N 74°59W **83** B10
Pottersville *U.S.A.* 43°43N 73°50W **83** C11
Pottstown *U.S.A.* 40°15N 75°39W **83** F9
Pottsville *U.S.A.* 40°41N 76°12W **83** F8
Pottuvil *Sri Lanka* 6°55N 81°50E **40** R12
Pouce Coupé *Canada* 55°40N 120°10W **70** B4
Poughkeepsie *U.S.A.* 41°42N 73°56W **83** E11
Poulaphouca Res. *Ireland* 53°8N 6°30W **10** C5
Poulsbo *U.S.A.* 47°44N 122°38W **78** C4
Poultney *U.S.A.* 43°31N 73°14W **83** C11
Poulton-le-Fylde *U.K.* 53°51N 2°58W **12** D5
Pouso Alegre *Brazil* 22°14S 45°57W **95** A6
Pouthisat *Cambodia* 12°34N 103°50E **38** F4
Považská Bystrica *Slovak Rep.* 49°8N 18°27E **17** D10
Povenets *Russia* 62°50N 34°50E **18** B5
Poverty B. *N.Z.* 38°43S 178°2E **59** C7
Póvoa de Varzim *Portugal* 41°25N 8°46W **21** B1
Povorotnyy, Mys *Russia* 42°40N 133°2E **30** C6
Povungnituk = Puvirnituq *Canada* 60°2N 77°10W **69** C12
Powassan *Canada* 46°5N 79°25W **72** C4
Poway *U.S.A.* 32°58N 117°2W **79** N9
Powder → *U.S.A.* 46°45N 105°26W **76** C11
Powder River *U.S.A.* 43°2N 106°59W **76** E10
Powell *U.S.A.* 44°45N 108°46W **76** D9
Powell, L. *U.S.A.* 36°57N 111°29W **77** H8
Powell River *Canada* 49°50N 124°35W **70** D4
Powers *U.S.A.* 45°41N 87°32W **80** C10
Pownal *U.S.A.* 42°45N 73°14W **83** D11
Powys □ *U.K.* 52°20N 3°20W **13** E4
Poyang Hu *China* 29°5N 116°20E **33** D6
Poyarkovo *Russia* 49°36N 128°41E **29** E13
Poza Rica *Mexico* 20°33N 97°27W **87** C5
Požarevac *Serbia* 44°35N 21°18E **23** B9
Poznań *Poland* 52°25N 16°55E **17** B9
Pozo *U.S.A.* 35°20N 120°24W **79** K6
Pozo Almonte *Chile* 20°10S 69°50W **92** H5
Pozo Colorado *Paraguay* 23°30S 58°45W **94** A4
Pozoblanco *Spain* 38°23N 4°51W **21** C3
Pozzuoli *Italy* 40°49N 14°7E **22** D6
Prachin Buri *Thailand* 14°0N 101°25E **38** F3
Prachuap Khiri Khan *Thailand* 11°49N 99°48E **39** G2
Prado *Brazil* 17°20S 39°13W **93** G11
Prague = Praha *Czech Rep.* 50°4N 14°25E **16** C8
Praha *Czech Rep.* 50°4N 14°25E **16** C8
Praia *C. Verde Is.* 15°2N 23°34W **50** b
Prainha *Brazil* 1°45S 53°30W **93** D8
Prainha Nova *Brazil* 7°10S 60°30W **92** E6
Prairie *Australia* 20°50S 144°35E **62** C3
Prairie City *U.S.A.* 44°28N 118°43W **76** D4
Prairie Dog Town Fork Red → *U.S.A.* 34°34N 99°58W **84** D5
Prairie du Chien *U.S.A.* 43°3N 91°9W **80** D8
Prairies, L. of the *Canada* 51°16N 101°32W **71** C8
Pran Buri *Thailand* 12°23N 99°55E **38** F2
Prapat *Indonesia* 2°41N 98°58E **36** D1
Praslin *Seychelles* 4°18S 55°45E **53** b
Prasonisi, Akra *Greece* 35°42N 27°46E **25** D9
Prata *Brazil* 19°25S 48°54W **93** G9
Pratabpur *India* 23°28N 83°15E **43** H10
Pratapgarh *Raj., India* 24°2N 74°40E **42** G6
Pratapgarh *Ut. P., India* 25°56N 81°59E **43** G9
Prato *Italy* 43°53N 11°6E **22** C4
Pratt *U.S.A.* 37°39N 98°44W **80** G4
Prattville *U.S.A.* 32°28N 86°29W **85** E11
Pravia *Spain* 43°30N 6°12W **21** A2
Praya *Indonesia* 8°39S 116°17E **36** F5
Preble *U.S.A.* 42°44N 76°8W **83** D8
Precipice △ *Australia* 25°18S 150°5E **63** D5
Precordillera *Argentina* 30°0S 69°1W **94** C2
Preeceville *Canada* 51°57N 102°40W **71** C8
Preiļi *Latvia* 56°18N 26°43E **9** H22
Premont *U.S.A.* 27°22N 98°7W **84** H5
Prentice *U.S.A.* 45°33N 90°17W **80** C8
Preobrazheniye *Russia* 42°54N 133°54E **30** C6
Preparis North Channel *Ind. Oc.* 15°27N 94°5E **41** M18
Preparis South Channel *Ind. Oc.* 14°33N 93°30E **41** M18
Přerov *Czech Rep.* 49°28N 17°27E **17** D9
Prescott *Canada* 44°45N 75°30W **83** B9
Prescott *Ariz., U.S.A.* 34°33N 112°28W **77** J7
Prescott *Ark., U.S.A.* 33°48N 93°23W **84** E8
Prescott Valley *U.S.A.* 34°40N 112°18W **77** J7
Preservation Inlet *N.Z.* 46°8S 166°35E **59** G1
Presho *U.S.A.* 43°54N 100°3W **80** D3
Presidencia de la Plaza *Argentina* 27°0S 59°50W **94** B4
Presidencia Roque Saenz Peña *Argentina* 26°45S 60°30W **94** B3
Presidente Epitácio *Brazil* 21°56S 52°6W **93** H8
Presidente Hayes □ *Paraguay* 24°0S 59°0W **94** A4
Presidente Prudente *Brazil* 22°5S 51°25W **95** A5
Presidio *Mexico* 29°29N 104°23W **86** B4
Presidio *U.S.A.* 29°34N 104°22W **84** G2
Prešov *Slovak Rep.* 49°0N 21°15E **17** D11
Prespa, L. = Prespansko Jezero *Macedonia* 40°55N 21°0E **23** D9
Prespansko Jezero *Macedonia* 40°55N 21°0E **23** D9
Presque I. *U.S.A.* 42°10N 80°6W **82** D4
Presque Isle *U.S.A.* 46°41N 68°1W **81** B19
Prestatyn *U.K.* 53°20N 3°24W **12** D4
Presteigne *U.K.* 52°17N 3°0W **13** E5
Preston *Canada* 43°23N 80°21W **82** C4
Preston *U.K.* 53°46N 2°42W **12** D5
Preston *Idaho, U.S.A.* 42°6N 111°53W **76** E8
Preston *Minn., U.S.A.* 43°40N 92°5W **80** D7
Preston, C. *Australia* 20°51S 116°12E **60** D2
Prestonsburg *U.S.A.* 37°40N 82°47W **81** G12
Prestwick *U.K.* 55°29N 4°37W **11** F4
Pretoria *S. Africa* 25°44S 28°12E **57** D4
Preveza *Greece* 38°57N 20°45E **23** E9
Prey Veng *Cambodia* 11°35N 105°29E **39** G5
Pribilof Is. *U.S.A.* 57°0N 170°0W **74** a
Příbram *Czech Rep.* 49°41N 14°2E **16** D8
Price *U.S.A.* 39°36N 110°49W **76** G8
Price I. *Canada* 52°23N 128°41W **70** C3
Prichard *U.S.A.* 30°44N 88°5W **85** F10
Priekule *Latvia* 56°26N 21°35E **9** H19
Prienai *Lithuania* 54°38N 23°57E **9** J20
Prieska *S. Africa* 29°40S 22°42E **56** D3
Priest L. *U.S.A.* 48°35N 116°52W **76** B5
Priest River *U.S.A.* 48°11N 116°55W **76** B5
Priest Valley *U.S.A.* 36°10N 120°39W **78** J6
Prievidza *Slovak Rep.* 48°46N 18°36E **17** D10
Prikaspiyskaya Nizmennost = Caspian Depression *Eurasia* 47°0N 48°0E **19** E8
Prilep *Macedonia* 41°21N 21°32E **23** D9
Priluki = Pryluky *Ukraine* 50°30N 32°24E **19** D5
Prime Seal I. *Australia* 40°3S 147°43E **63** G4
Primo Tapia *Mexico* 32°16N 116°54W **79** N10
Primorskiy Kray □ *Russia* 45°0N 135°0E **30** B7
Primrose L. *Canada* 54°55N 109°45W **71** C7
Prince Albert *Canada* 53°15N 105°50W **71** C7
Prince Albert *S. Africa* 33°12S 22°2E **56** E3
Prince Albert △ *Canada* 54°0N 106°25W **71** C7
Prince Albert Mts. *Antarctica* 76°0S 161°30E **5** D11
Prince Albert Pen. *Canada* 72°30N 116°0W **68** B8
Prince Albert Sd. *Canada* 70°25N 115°0W **68** B8
Prince Alfred, C. *Canada* 74°20N 124°40W **69** B7
Prince Charles I. *Canada* 67°47N 76°12W **69** C12
Prince Charles Mts. *Antarctica* 72°0S 67°0E **5** D6
Prince Edward Fracture Zone *Ind. Oc.* 46°0S 35°0E **5** A4
Prince Edward I. □ *Canada* 46°20N 63°20W **73** C7
Prince Edward Is. *Ind. Oc.* 46°35S 38°0E **3** G11
Prince George *Canada* 53°55N 122°50W **70** C4
Prince Gustaf Adolf Sea *Canada* 78°30N 107°0W **69** B9
Prince of Wales, C. *U.S.A.* 65°36N 168°5W **66** C3
Prince of Wales I. *Australia* 10°40S 142°10E **62** A3
Prince of Wales I. *Canada* 73°0N 99°0W **68** B10
Prince of Wales I. *U.S.A.* 55°47N 132°50W **68** D6
Prince Patrick I. *Canada* 77°0N 120°0W **69** B8
Prince Regent Inlet *Canada* 73°0N 90°0W **4** B3
Prince Rupert *Canada* 54°20N 130°20W **70** C2
Princes Town *Trin. & Tob.* 10°16N 61°23W **93** K15
Princess Charlotte B. *Australia* 14°25S 144°0E **62** A3
Princess Elizabeth Trough *S. Ocean* 64°10S 83°0E **5** C7
Princess May Ranges *Australia* 15°30S 125°30E **60** C4
Princess Royal I. *Canada* 53°0N 128°40W **70** C3
Princeton *Canada* 49°27N 120°30W **70** D4
Princeton *Calif., U.S.A.* 39°24N 122°1W **78** F4
Princeton *Ill., U.S.A.* 41°23N 89°28W **80** E9
Princeton *Ind., U.S.A.* 38°21N 87°34W **80** F10
Princeton *Ky., U.S.A.* 37°7N 87°53W **80** G10
Princeton *Mo., U.S.A.* 40°24N 93°35W **80** E7
Princeton *N.J., U.S.A.* 40°21N 74°39W **83** F10
Princeton *W. Va., U.S.A.* 37°22N 81°6W **81** G13
Príncipe *São Tomé & Príncipe* 1°37N 7°25E **48** F4
Principe da Beira *Brazil* 12°20S 64°30W **92** F6
Prineville *U.S.A.* 44°18N 120°51W **76** D3
Prins Harald Kyst *Antarctica* 70°0S 35°1E **5** D4
Prinsesse Astrid Kyst *Antarctica* 70°45S 12°30E **5** D3
Prinsesse Ragnhild Kyst *Antarctica* 70°15S 27°30E **5** D4
Prinzapolca *Nic.* 13°20N 83°35W **88** D3
Priozersk *Russia* 61°2N 30°7E **8** F24
Pripet = Prypyat → *Europe* 51°20N 30°15E **17** C16
Pripet Marshes *Europe* 52°10N 28°10E **17** B15
Pripyat Marshes = Pripet Marshes *Europe* 52°10N 28°10E **17** B15
Pripyats = Prypyat → *Europe* 51°20N 30°15E **17** C16
Priština *Serbia* 42°40N 21°13E **23** C9
Privas *France* 44°45N 4°37E **20** D6
Privolzhskaya Vozvyshennost *Russia* 51°0N 46°0E **19** D8
Privolzhskiy □ *Russia* 56°0N 50°0E **28** D6
Prizren *Serbia* 42°13N 20°45E **23** C9
Probolinggo *Indonesia* 7°46S 113°13E **37** G15
Proctor *U.S.A.* 43°40N 73°2W **83** C11
Proddatur *India* 14°45N 78°30E **40** M11
Prodhromos *Cyprus* 34°57N 32°50E **25** E11
Profilia *Greece* 36°5N 27°51E **25** C9
Profondeville *Belgium* 50°23N 4°52E **15** D4
Progreso *Coahuila, Mexico* 27°28N 100°59W **86** B4
Progreso *Yucatán, Mexico* 21°20N 89°40W **87** C7
Progress *Antarctica* 66°22S 76°22E **5** C12
Progress *Russia* 49°45N 129°37E **29** E13
Prokopyevsk *Russia* 54°0N 86°45E **28** D9
Prokuplje *Serbia* 43°16N 21°36E **23** C9
Prome *Burma* 18°49N 95°13E **41** K19
Prophet → *Canada* 58°48N 122°40W **70** B4
Prophet River *Canada* 58°6N 122°43W **70** B4
Propriá *Brazil* 10°13S 36°51W **93** F11
Propriano *France* 41°41N 8°52E **20** F8
Proserpine *Australia* 20°21S 148°36E **62** J6
Prosna → *Poland* 52°6N 17°44E **17** B9
Prospect *U.S.A.* 43°18N 75°9W **83** C9
Prosser *U.S.A.* 46°12N 119°46W **76** C4
Prostějov *Czech Rep.* 49°30N 17°9E **17** D9
Proston *Australia* 26°8S 151°32E **63** D5
Provence *France* 43°40N 5°46E **20** E6
Providence *Ky., U.S.A.* 37°24N 87°46W **80** G10
Providence *R.I., U.S.A.* 41°49N 71°24W **83** E13
Providence Bay *Canada* 45°41N 82°15W **72** C3
Providence Mts. *U.S.A.* 35°10N 115°15W **79** K11
Providencia, I. de *Colombia* 13°25N 81°26W **88** D3
Provideniya *Russia* 64°23N 173°18W **29** C19
Provincetown *U.S.A.* 42°3N 70°11W **81** D18
Provins *France* 48°33N 3°15E **20** B5
Provo *U.S.A.* 40°14N 111°39W **76** F8
Provost *Canada* 52°25N 110°20W **71** C6
Prudhoe Bay *U.S.A.* 70°18N 148°22W **74** a
Prudhoe I. *Australia* 21°19S 149°41E **62** C4
Prud'homme *Canada* 52°20N 105°54W **71** C7
Pruszków *Poland* 52°9N 20°49E **17** B11
Prut → *Romania* 45°28N 28°10E **17** F15
Pruzhany *Belarus* 52°33N 24°28E **17** B13
Prydz B. *Antarctica* 69°0S 74°0E **5** C6
Pryluky *Ukraine* 50°30N 32°24E **19** D5
Pryor *U.S.A.* 36°19N 95°19W **84** C7
Prypyat → *Europe* 51°20N 30°15E **17** C16
Przemyśl *Poland* 49°50N 22°45E **17** D12
Przhevalsk = Karakol *Kyrgyzstan* 42°30N 78°20E **32** B2
Psara *Greece* 38°37N 25°38E **23** E11
Psiloritis, Oros *Greece* 35°15N 24°45E **25** D6
Psira *Greece* 35°12N 25°52E **25** D7
Pskov *Russia* 57°50N 28°25E **9** H23
Ptich = Ptsich → *Belarus* 52°9N 28°52E **17** B15
Ptichia = Vidos *Greece* 39°38N 19°55E **25** A3
Ptolemaida *Greece* 40°30N 21°43E **23** D9
Ptsich → *Belarus* 52°9N 28°52E **17** B15
Pu Xian *China* 36°24N 111°6E **34** F6
Pua *Thailand* 19°11N 100°55E **38** C3
Puán *Argentina* 37°30S 62°45W **94** D3
Pu'apu'a *Samoa* 13°34S 172°9W **59** b
Pucallpa *Peru* 8°25S 74°30W **92** E4
Puch'on = Bucheon *S. Korea* 37°28N 126°45E **35** F14
Pudasjärvi *Finland* 65°23N 26°53E **8** D22
Pudozh *Russia* 61°48N 36°32E **18** B6
Puducherry *India* 11°59N 79°50E **40** P11
Pudukkottai *India* 10°28N 78°47E **40** P11
Puebla *Mexico* 19°3N 98°12W **87** D5
Puebla □ *Mexico* 18°50N 98°0W **87** D5
Pueblo *U.S.A.* 38°16N 104°37W **76** G11
Puelches *Argentina* 38°5S 65°51W **94** D2
Puelén *Argentina* 37°32S 67°38W **94** D2
Puente Alto *Chile* 33°32S 70°35W **94** C1
Puente-Genil *Spain* 37°22N 4°47W **21** D3
Puerca, Pta. *Puerto Rico* 18°13N 65°36W **89** d
Puerco → *U.S.A.* 34°22N 107°50W **77** J10
Puerto Aisén *Chile* 45°27S 73°0W **96** F2
Puerto Ángel *Mexico* 15°40N 96°29W **87** D5
Puerto Arista *Mexico* 15°56N 93°48W **87** D6
Puerto Armuelles *Panama* 8°20N 82°51W **88** E3
Puerto Ayacucho *Venezuela* 5°40N 67°35W **92** B5
Puerto Barrios *Guatemala* 15°40N 88°32W **88** C2
Puerto Bermejo *Argentina* 26°55S 58°34W **94** B4
Puerto Bermúdez *Peru* 10°20S 74°58W **92** F4
Puerto Bolívar *Ecuador* 3°19S 79°55W **92** D3
Puerto Cabello *Venezuela* 10°28N 68°1W **92** A5
Puerto Cabezas *Nic.* 14°0N 83°30W **88** D3
Puerto Cabo Gracias á Dios *Nic.* 15°0N 83°10W **88** D3
Puerto Carreño *Colombia* 6°12N 67°22W **92** B5
Puerto Castilla *Honduras* 16°0N 86°0W **88** C2
Puerto Chicama *Peru* 7°45S 79°20W **92** E3
Puerto Coig *Argentina* 50°54S 69°15W **96** G3
Puerto Cortés *Honduras* 15°51N 88°0W **88** C2
Puerto Cumarebo *Venezuela* 11°29N 69°30W **92** A5
Puerto de Alcudia = Port d'Alcúdia *Spain* 39°50N 3°7E **24** B10
Puerto de Cabrera *Spain* 39°8N 2°56E **24** B9
Puerto de Gran Tarajal *Canary Is.* 28°13N 14°1W **24** F5
Puerto de la Cruz *Canary Is.* 28°24N 16°32W **24** F3
Puerto de los Angeles △ *Mexico* 23°39N 105°45W **86** C3
Puerto de Pozo Negro *Canary Is.* 28°19N 13°55W **24** F6
Puerto de Sóller = Port de Sóller *Spain* 39°48N 2°42E **24** B9
Puerto del Carmen *Canary Is.* 28°55N 13°38W **24** F6
Puerto del Rosario *Canary Is.* 28°30N 13°52W **24** F6
Puerto Deseado *Argentina* 47°55S 66°0W **96** F3
Puerto Escondido *Mexico* 15°50N 97°3W **87** D5
Puerto Heath *Bolivia* 12°34S 68°39W **92** F5
Puerto Inírida *Colombia* 3°53N 67°52W **92** C5
Puerto Juárez *Mexico* 21°11N 86°49W **87** C7
Puerto La Cruz *Venezuela* 10°13N 64°38W **92** A6
Puerto Leguízamo *Colombia* 0°12S 74°46W **92** D4
Puerto Lempira *Honduras* 15°16N 83°46W **88** C3
Puerto Libertad *Mexico* 29°55N 112°43W **86** B2
Puerto Limón *Colombia* 3°23N 73°30W **92** C4
Puerto Lobos *Argentina* 42°0S 65°3W **96** E3
Puerto Madryn *Argentina* 42°48S 65°4W **96** E3
Puerto Maldonado *Peru* 12°30S 69°10W **92** F5
Puerto Manatí *Cuba* 21°22N 76°50W **88** B4
Puerto Montt *Chile* 41°28S 73°0W **96** E2
Puerto Morazán *Nic.* 12°51N 87°11W **88** D2
Puerto Morelos *Mexico* 20°50N 86°52W **87** C7
Puerto Natales *Chile* 51°45S 72°15W **96** G2
Puerto Oscuro *Chile* 31°24S 71°35W **94** C1
Puerto Padre *Cuba* 21°13N 76°35W **88** B4
Puerto Páez *Venezuela* 6°13N 67°28W **92** B5
Puerto Peñasco *Mexico* 31°20N 113°33W **86** A2
Puerto Pinasco *Paraguay* 22°36S 57°50W **94** A4
Puerto Plata *Dom. Rep.* 19°48N 70°45W **89** C5
Puerto Pollensa = Port de Pollença *Spain* 39°54N 3°4E **24** B10
Puerto Princesa *Phil.* 9°46N 118°45E **37** C5
Puerto Quepos *Costa Rica* 9°29N 84°6W **88** E3
Puerto Rico *Canary Is.* 27°47N 15°42W **24** G4
Puerto Rico ☑ *W. Indies* 18°15N 66°45W **89** d
Puerto Rico Trench *Atl. Oc.* 19°50N 66°0W **89** C6
Puerto San Julián *Argentina* 49°18S 67°43W **96** F3
Puerto Santa Cruz *Argentina* 50°0S 68°32W **96** G3
Puerto Sastre *Paraguay* 22°2S 57°55W **94** A4
Puerto Suárez *Bolivia* 18°58S 57°52W **92** G7
Puerto Vallarta *Mexico* 20°37N 105°15W **86** C3
Puerto Varas *Chile* 41°19S 72°59W **96** E2
Puerto Wilches *Colombia* 7°21N 73°54W **92** B4
Puertollano *Spain* 38°43N 4°7W **21** C3
Pueu *Tahiti* 17°44S 149°13W **59** d
Pueyrredón, L. *Argentina* 47°20S 72°0W **96** F2
Puffin I. *Ireland* 51°50N 10°24W **10** E1
Pugachev *Russia* 52°0N 48°49E **18** D8
Pugal *India* 28°30N 72°48E **42** E5
Puge *Tanzania* 4°45S 33°11E **54** C3
Puget Sound *U.S.A.* 47°50N 122°30W **76** C2
Pugŏdong *N. Korea* 42°5N 130°0E **35** C16
Pugu *Tanzania* 6°55S 39°4E **54** D4
Pūgūnzī *Iran* 25°49N 59°10E **45** E8
Puig Major *Spain* 39°48N 2°47E **24** B9
Puigcerdà *Spain* 42°24N 1°50E **21** A6
Puigpunyent *Spain* 39°38N 2°32E **24** B9
Pujon-ho *N. Korea* 40°35N 127°35E **35** D14
Pukaki, L. *N.Z.* 44°4S 170°1E **59** F3
Pukapuka *Cook Is.* 10°53S 165°49W **65** J11
Pukaskwa △ *Canada* 48°20N 86°0W **72** C2
Pukatawagan *Canada* 55°45N 101°20W **71** B8
Pukchin *N. Korea* 40°12N 125°45E **35** D13
Pukch'ŏng *N. Korea* 40°14N 128°10E **35** D15
Pukekohe *N.Z.* 37°12S 174°55E **59** B5
Pukhrayan *India* 26°14N 79°51E **43** F8
Pula *Croatia* 44°54N 13°57E **16** F7
Pulacayo *Bolivia* 20°25S 66°41W **92** H5
Pulai *Malaysia* 1°20N 103°31E **39** d
Pulandian *China* 39°25N 121°58E **35** E11
Pulaski *N.Y., U.S.A.* 43°34N 76°8W **83** C8
Pulaski *Tenn., U.S.A.* 35°12N 87°2W **85** D11
Pulaski *Va., U.S.A.* 37°3N 80°47W **81** G13
Pulau → *Indonesia* 5°50S 138°15E **37** F9
Puławy *Poland* 51°23N 21°59E **17** C11
Pulga *U.S.A.* 39°48N 121°29W **78** F5
Pulicat L. *India* 13°40N 80°15E **40** N12
Pullman *U.S.A.* 46°44N 117°10W **76** C5
Pulog, Mt. *Phil.* 16°40N 120°50E **37** A6
Pułtusk *Poland* 52°43N 21°6E **17** B11
Pumlumon Fawr *U.K.* 52°28N 3°46W **13** E4
Puná, I. *Ecuador* 2°55S 80°5W **92** D2
Punaauia *Tahiti* 17°37S 149°34W **59** d
Punakaiki *N.Z.* 42°7S 171°20E **59** E3
Punakha Dzong *Bhutan* 27°42N 89°52E **41** F16
Punasar *India* 27°6N 73°6E **42** F5
Punata *Bolivia* 17°32S 65°50W **92** G5
Punch *India* 33°48N 74°4E **43** C6
Punch → *Pakistan* 33°12N 73°40E **42** C5
Punda Maria *S. Africa* 22°40S 31°5E **57** C5
Pune *India* 18°29N 73°57E **40** K8
P'ungsan *N. Korea* 40°50N 128°9E **35** D15
Pungue, Ponte de *Mozam.* 19°0S 34°0E **55** F3
Punjab □ *India* 31°0N 76°0E **42** D7
Punjab □ *Pakistan* 32°0N 72°30E **42** E6
Puno *Peru* 15°55S 70°3W **92** G4
Punpun → *India* 25°31N 85°18E **43** G11
Punta, Cerro de *Puerto Rico* 18°10N 66°37W **89** d
Punta Alta *Argentina* 38°53S 62°4W **96** D4
Punta Arenas *Chile* 53°10S 71°0W **96** G2
Punta del Díaz *Chile* 28°0S 70°45W **94** B1
Punta del Hidalgo *Canary Is.* 28°33N 16°19W **24** F3
Punta Gorda *Belize* 16°10N 88°45W **87** D7
Punta Gorda *U.S.A.* 26°56N 82°3W **85** H13
Punta Prieta *Mexico* 28°58N 114°17W **86** B2
Punta Prima *Spain* 39°48N 4°16E **24** B11
Puntarenas *Costa Rica* 10°0N 84°50W **88** E3
Puntland *Somali Rep.* 8°0N 49°0E **47** F4
Punto Fijo *Venezuela* 11°50N 70°13W **92** A4
Punxsatawney *U.S.A.* 40°57N 78°59W **82** F6
Pupuan *Indonesia* 8°19S 115°0E **37** J18
Puquio *Peru* 14°45S 74°10W **92** F4
Pur → *Russia* 67°31N 77°55E **28** C8
Puracé, Vol. *Colombia* 2°21N 76°23W **92** C3
Puralia = Puruliya *India* 23°17N 86°24E **43** H12
Puranpur *India* 28°31N 80°9E **43** E9
Purbeck, Isle of *U.K.* 50°39N 1°59W **13** G5
Purcell *U.S.A.* 35°1N 97°22W **84** D6
Purcell Mts. *Canada* 49°55N 116°15W **70** D5
Purdy *Canada* 45°19N 77°44W **82** A7
Puri *India* 19°50N 85°58E **41** K14
Purmerend *Neths.* 52°32N 4°58E **15** B4
Purnia *India* 25°45N 87°31E **43** G12
Purnululu △ *Australia* 17°20S 128°20E **60** C4
Pursat = Pouthisat *Cambodia* 12°34N 103°50E **38** F4
Purukcahu *Indonesia* 0°35S 114°35E **36** E4
Puruliya *India* 23°17N 86°24E **43** H12
Purus → *Brazil* 3°42S 61°28W **92** D6
Puruvesi *Finland* 61°50N 29°30E **8** F23
Purvis *U.S.A.* 31°9N 89°25W **85** F10
Purwa *India* 26°28N 80°47E **43** F9
Purwakarta *Indonesia* 6°35S 107°29E **37** G12
Purwo, Tanjung *Indonesia* 8°44S 114°21E **37** K18
Purwodadi *Indonesia* 7°7S 110°55E **37** G14
Purwokerto *Indonesia* 7°25S 109°14E **37** G13
Puryŏng *N. Korea* 42°5N 129°43E **35** C15
Pusa *India* 25°59N 85°41E **43** G11
Pusan = Busan *S. Korea* 35°5N 129°0E **35** G15
Pushkin *Russia* 59°45N 30°25E **9** G24
Pushkino *Russia* 51°16N 47°0E **19** D8
Put-in-Bay *U.S.A.* 41°39N 82°49W **82** E2
Putahow L. *Canada* 59°54N 100°40W **71** B8
Putao *Burma* 27°28N 97°30E **41** F20
Putaruru *N.Z.* 38°2S 175°50E **59** C5
Putignano *Italy* 40°51N 17°7E **22** D7
Puting, Tanjung *Indonesia* 3°31S 111°46E **36** E4
Putnam *U.S.A.* 41°55N 71°55W **83** E13
Putorana, Gory *Russia* 69°0N 95°0E **29** C10
Putrajaya *Malaysia* 2°55N 101°40E **39** L3
Puttalam *Sri Lanka* 8°1N 79°55E **40** Q11
Puttgarden *Germany* 54°30N 11°10E **16** A6
Putumayo → *S. Amer.* 3°7S 67°58W **92** D5
Putussibau *Indonesia* 0°50N 112°56E **36** D4
Puvirnituq *Canada* 60°2N 77°10W **69** C12
Puy-de-Dôme *France* 45°46N 2°57E **20** D5
Puyallup *U.S.A.* 47°12N 122°18W **78** C4
Puyang *China* 35°40N 115°1E **34** G8
Pūzeh Rīg *Iran* 27°20N 58°40E **45** E8
Pwani □ *Tanzania* 7°0S 39°0E **54** D4
Pweto *Dem. Rep. of the Congo* 8°25S 28°51E **55** D2

Pwllheli *U.K.* 52°53N 4°25W **12 E3**
Pyaozero, Ozero *Russia* 66°5N 30°58E **8 C24**
Pyapon *Burma* 16°20N 95°40E **41 L19**
Pyasina → *Russia* 73°30N 87°0E **29 B9**
Pyatigorsk *Russia* 44°2N 43°6E **19 F7**
Pyè = Prome *Burma* 18°49N 95°13E **41 K19**
Pyeongtaek *S. Korea* 37°1N 127°4E **35 F14**
Pyetrikaw *Belarus* 52°11N 28°29E **17 B15**
Pyhäjoki *Finland* 64°28N 24°14E **8 D21**
Pyinmana *Burma* 19°45N 96°12E **41 K20**
Pyla, C. *Cyprus* 34°56N 33°51E **25 E12**
Pymatuning Res. *U.S.A.* 41°30N 80°28W **82 E4**
Pyŏktong *N. Korea* 40°50N 125°50E **35 D13**
Pyŏnggang *N. Korea* 38°24N 127°17E **35 E14**
P'yŏngsong *N. Korea* 39°14N 125°52E **35 E13**
P'yŏngyang *N. Korea* 39°0N 125°30E **35 E13**
Pyote *U.S.A.* 31°32N 103°8W **84 F3**
Pyramid L. *U.S.A.* 40°1N 119°35W **76 F4**
Pyramid Pk. *U.S.A.* 36°25N 116°37W **79 J10**
Pyramids *Egypt* 29°58N 31°9E **51 C12**
Pyrénées *Europe* 42°45N 0°18E **20 E4**
Pyu *Burma* 18°30N 96°28E **41 K20**

Q

Qaanaaq *Greenland* 77°40N 69°0W **4 B4**
Qachasnek *S. Africa* 30°6S 28°42E **57 E4**
Qa'el Jafr *Jordan* 30°20N 36°25E **46 E5**
Qa'emābād *Iran* 31°44N 60°2E **45 D9**
Qā'emshahr *Iran* 36°30N 52°53E **45 B7**
Qagan Nur *China* 43°30N 114°55E **34 C8**
Qahar Youyi Zhongqi *China* 41°12N 112°40E **34 D7**
Qahremānshahr = Kermānshāh *Iran* 34°23N 47°0E **44 C5**
Qaidam Pendi *China* 37°0N 95°0E **32 C4**
Qajarīyeh *Iran* 31°1N 48°22E **45 D6**
Qala, Ras il *Malta* 36°2N 14°20E **25 C1**
Qala-i-Jadid = Spīn Būldak *Afghan.* 31°1N 66°25E **42 D2**
Qala Point = Qala, Ras il *Malta* 36°2N 14°20E **25 C1**
Qala Viala *Pakistan* 30°49N 67°17E **42 D2**
Qala Yangi *Afghan.* 34°20N 66°30E **42 B2**
Qal'at al Akhḍar *Si. Arabia* 28°4N 37°9E **44 E3**
Qal'at Dīzah *Iraq* 36°11N 45°7E **44 B5**
Qal'at Şāliḥ *Iraq* 31°31N 47°16E **44 D5**
Qal'at Sukkar *Iraq* 31°51N 46°5E **44 D5**
Qamani'tuaq = Baker Lake *Canada* 64°20N 96°3W **68 C10**
Qamdo *China* 31°15N 97°6E **32 C4**
Qamea *Fiji* 16°45S 179°45W **59 a**
Qamruddin Karez *Pakistan* 31°45N 68°20E **42 D3**
Qandahār = Kandahār *Afghan.* 31°32N 65°43E **40 D4**
Qandahār = Kandahār □ *Afghan.* 31°0N 65°0E **40 D4**
Qandyaghash *Kazakhstan* 49°28N 57°25E **19 E10**
Qapān *Iran* 37°40N 55°47E **45 B7**
Qapshaghay *Kazakhstan* 43°51N 77°14E **28 E8**
Qaqortoq *Greenland* 60°43N 46°0W **4 C5**
Qara Qash → *China* 35°0N 78°30E **43 B8**
Qarabutaq *Kazakhstan* 49°59N 60°14E **28 E7**
Qaraghandy *Kazakhstan* 49°50N 73°10E **28 E8**
Qaraghayly *Kazakhstan* 49°26N 76°0E **28 E8**
Qārah *Si. Arabia* 29°55N 40°3E **44 D4**
Qaratau *Kazakhstan* 43°30N 69°30E **28 E7**
Qaratau *Zhambyl, Kazakhstan* 43°10N 70°28E **28 E8**
Qarazhal *Kazakhstan* 48°2N 70°49E **28 E8**
Qardho *Somali Rep.* 9°30N 49°6E **47 F4**
Qareh → *Iran* 39°25N 47°22E **44 B5**
Qareh Tekān *Iran* 36°38N 49°29E **45 B6**
Qarnein *U.A.E.* 24°56N 52°52E **45 E7**
Qarqan He → *China* 39°30N 88°30E **32 C3**
Qarqaraly *Kazakhstan* 49°26N 75°30E **28 E8**
Qarshi *Uzbekistan* 38°53N 65°48E **28 F7**
Qartabā *Lebanon* 34°4N 35°50E **46 A4**
Qārūh *Kuwait* 28°49N 48°46E **45 D6**
Qaryat al Gharab *Iraq* 31°27N 44°48E **44 D5**
Qaryat al 'Ulyā *Si. Arabia* 27°33N 47°42E **44 E5**
Qasr 'Amra *Jordan* 31°48N 36°35E **44 D3**
Qaşr-e Qand *Iran* 26°15N 60°45E **45 E9**
Qaşr-e Shīrīn *Iran* 34°31N 45°35E **44 C5**
Qasr Farâfra *Egypt* 27°0N 28°1E **51 C11**
Qatanā *Syria* 33°26N 36°4E **46 B5**
Qatar ■ *Asia* 25°30N 51°15E **45 E6**
Qaţlīsh *Iran* 37°50N 57°19E **45 B8**
Qattâra, Munkhafed el *Egypt* 29°30N 27°30E **51 C11**
Qattâra Depression = Qattâra, Munkhafed el *Egypt* 29°30N 27°30E **51 C11**
Qausuittuq = Resolute *Canada* 74°42N 94°54W **69 B10**
Qawām al Ḥamzah = Al Ḥamzah *Iraq* 31°43N 44°58E **44 D5**
Qāyen *Iran* 33°40N 59°10E **45 C8**
Qazaqstan = Kazakhstan ■ *Asia* 50°0N 70°0E **28 E8**
Qazimämmäd *Azerbaijan* 40°3N 49°0E **45 A6**
Qazvīn *Iran* 36°15N 50°0E **45 B6**
Qazvīn □ *Iran* 36°15N 50°0E **45 B6**
Qena *Egypt* 26°10N 32°43E **51 C12**
Qeqertarsuaq *Greenland* 69°15N 53°38W **4 C5**
Qeqertarsuaq *Greenland* 69°45N 53°30W **66 C14**
Qeshlāq *Iran* 34°55N 46°28E **44 C5**
Qeshm *Iran* 26°55N 56°10E **45 E8**
Qeys *Iran* 26°32N 53°58E **45 E7**
Qezel Owzen → *Iran* 36°45N 49°22E **45 B6**
Qezi'ot *Israel* 30°52N 34°26E **46 E3**
Qi Xian *China* 34°40N 114°48E **34 G8**
Qian Gorlos *China* 45°5N 124°42E **35 B13**
Qian Hai *China* 22°32N 113°54E **33 F10**

Qian Xian *China* 34°31N 108°15E **34 G5**
Qianshan *China* 22°15N 113°31E **33 G10**
Qianyang *China* 34°40N 107°8E **34 G4**
Qi'ao *China* 22°25N 113°39E **33 G10**
Qi'ao Dao *China* 22°25N 113°38E **33 G10**
Qiemo *China* 38°8N 85°32E **32 C3**
Qijiaojing *China* 43°28N 91°36E **32 B4**
Qikiqtarjuaq *Canada* 67°33N 63°0W **69 C13**
Qila Saifullāh *Pakistan* 30°45N 68°17E **42 D3**
Qilian Shan *China* 38°30N 96°0E **32 C4**
Qin He → *China* 35°1N 113°22E **34 G7**
Qin Ling = Qinling Shandi *China* 33°50N 108°10E **34 H5**
Qin'an *China* 34°48N 105°40E **34 G3**
Qing Xian *China* 38°35N 116°45E **34 E9**
Qingcheng *China* 37°15N 117°40E **35 F9**
Qingdao *China* 36°5N 120°20E **35 F11**
Qingfeng *China* 35°52N 115°8E **34 G8**
Qinghai □ *China* 36°0N 98°0E **32 C4**
Qinghai Hu *China* 36°40N 100°10E **32 C5**
Qinghecheng *China* 41°28N 124°15E **35 D13**
Qinghemen *China* 41°48N 121°25E **35 D11**
Qingjian *China* 37°8N 110°8E **34 F6**
Qingjiang = Huaiyin *China* 33°30N 119°2E **35 H10**
Qingshui *China* 34°48N 106°8E **34 G4**
Qingshuihe *China* 39°55N 111°35E **34 E6**
Qingtongxia Shuiku *China* 37°50N 105°58E **34 F3**
Qingxu *China* 37°34N 112°22E **34 F7**
Qingyang *China* 36°2N 107°55E **34 F4**
Qingyuan *China* 42°10N 124°55E **35 C13**
Qingyun *China* 37°45N 117°20E **35 F9**
Qinhuangdao *China* 39°56N 119°30E **35 E10**
Qinling Shandi *China* 33°50N 108°10E **34 H5**
Qinshui *China* 35°40N 112°8E **34 G7**
Qinyang = Jiyuan *China* 35°7N 112°57E **34 G7**
Qinyuan *China* 36°29N 112°20E **34 F7**
Qinzhou *China* 21°58N 108°38E **32 D5**
Qionghai *China* 19°15N 110°26E **38 C8**
Qiongzhou Haixia *China* 20°10N 110°15E **38 B8**
Qiqihar *China* 47°26N 124°0E **33 B7**
Qira *China* 37°0N 80°48E **32 C3**
Qiraiya, W. → *Egypt* 30°27N 34°0E **46 E3**
Qiryat Ata *Israel* 32°47N 35°6E **46 C4**
Qiryat Gat *Israel* 31°32N 34°46E **46 D3**
Qiryat Mal'akhi *Israel* 31°44N 34°44E **46 D3**
Qiryat Shemona *Israel* 33°13N 35°35E **46 B4**
Qiryat Yam *Israel* 32°51N 35°4E **46 C4**
Qishan *China* 34°25N 107°38E **34 G4**
Qitai *China* 44°2N 89°35E **32 B3**
Qitaihe *China* 45°48N 130°51E **30 B5**
Qixia *China* 37°17N 120°52E **35 F11**
Qızılağac Körfäzi *Azerbaijan* 39°9N 49°0E **45 B6**
Qojūr *Iran* 36°12N 47°55E **44 B5**
Qom *Iran* 34°40N 51°0E **45 C6**
Qom □ *Iran* 34°40N 51°0E **45 C6**
Qomolangma Feng = Everest, Mt. *Nepal* 28°5N 86°58E **43 E12**
Qomsheh *Iran* 32°0N 51°55E **45 D6**
Qoqek = Tacheng *China* 46°40N 82°58E **32 B3**
Qoqon = Qŭqon *Uzbekistan* 40°31N 70°56E **28 E8**
Qoraqalpoghistan □ *Uzbekistan* 43°0N 58°0E **28 E6**
Qorveh *Iran* 35°10N 47°48E **44 C5**
Qostanay *Kazakhstan* 53°10N 63°35E **28 D7**
Quabbin Res. *U.S.A.* 42°20N 72°20W **83 D12**
Quairading *Australia* 32°0S 117°21E **61 F2**
Quakertown *U.S.A.* 40°26N 75°21W **83 F9**
Qualicum Beach *Canada* 49°22N 124°26W **70 D4**
Quambatook *Australia* 35°49S 143°34E **63 F3**
Quambone *Australia* 30°57S 147°53E **63 E4**
Quamby *Australia* 20°22S 140°17E **62 C3**
Quan Long = Ca Mau *Vietnam* 9°7N 105°8E **39 H5**
Quanah *U.S.A.* 34°18N 99°44W **84 D5**
Quang Ngai *Vietnam* 15°13N 108°58E **38 E7**
Quang Tri *Vietnam* 16°45N 107°13E **38 D6**
Quang Yen *Vietnam* 20°56N 106°52E **38 B6**
Quanzhou *China* 24°55N 118°34E **33 D6**
Qu'Appelle → *Canada* 50°33N 103°53W **71 C8**
Quaqtaq *Canada* 60°55N 69°40W **69 C13**
Quaraí *Brazil* 30°15N 56°20W **94 C4**
Quartu Sant'Élena *Italy* 39°15N 9°10E **22 E3**
Quartzsite *U.S.A.* 33°40N 114°13W **79 M12**
Quatre Bornes *Mauritius* 20°15S 57°28E **53 d**
Quatsino Sd. *Canada* 50°25N 127°58W **70 C3**
Quba *Azerbaijan* 41°21N 48°32E **19 F8**
Qūchān *Iran* 37°10N 58°27E **45 B8**
Queanbeyan *Australia* 35°17S 149°14E **63 F4**
Québec *Canada* 46°52N 71°13W **73 C5**
Québec □ *Canada* 48°0N 74°0W **73 C5**
Quebrada del Condorito △ *Argentina* 31°49S 64°40W **94 C3**
Queen Alexandra Ra. *Antarctica* 85°0S 170°0E **5 E11**
Queen Charlotte City *Canada* 53°15N 132°2W **70 C2**
Queen Charlotte Is. *Canada* 53°20N 132°10W **70 C2**
Queen Charlotte Sd. *Canada* 51°0N 128°0W **70 C3**
Queen Charlotte Strait *Canada* 50°45N 127°10W **70 C3**
Queen Elizabeth △ *Uganda* 0°0 30°0E **54 C3**
Queen Elizabeth △ *U.K.* 56°7N 4°30W **11 E4**
Queen Elizabeth Is. *Canada* 76°0N 95°0W **69 B10**
Queen Mary Land *Antarctica* 70°0S 95°0E **5 D7**
Queen Maud G. *Canada* 68°15N 102°30W **68 C9**
Queen Maud Land = Dronning Maud Land *Antarctica* 72°30S 12°0E **5 D3**

Queen Maud Mts. *Antarctica* 86°0S 160°0W **5 E13**
Queens Channel *Australia* 15°0S 129°30E **60 C4**
Queenscliff *Australia* 38°16S 144°39E **63 F3**
Queensland □ *Australia* 22°0S 142°0E **62 C3**
Queenstown *Australia* 42°4S 145°35E **63 G4**
Queenstown *N.Z.* 45°1S 168°40E **59 F2**
Queenstown *Singapore* 1°18N 103°48E **37 d**
Queenstown *S. Africa* 31°52S 26°52E **56 E4**
Queets *U.S.A.* 47°32N 124°19W **78 C2**
Queguay Grande → *Uruguay* 32°9S 58°9W **94 C4**
Queimadas *Brazil* 11°0S 39°38W **93 F11**
Quelimane *Mozam.* 17°53S 36°58E **55 F4**
Quellón *Chile* 43°7S 73°37W **96 E2**
Quelpart = Jeju-do *S. Korea* 33°29N 126°34E **35 H14**
Quemado *N. Mex., U.S.A.* 34°20N 108°30W **77 J9**
Quemado *Tex., U.S.A.* 28°56N 100°37W **84 G4**
Quemú-Quemú *Argentina* 36°3S 63°36W **94 D3**
Quequén *Argentina* 38°30S 58°30W **94 D4**
Querétaro *Mexico* 20°36N 100°23W **86 C4**
Querétaro □ *Mexico* 21°0N 99°55W **86 C5**
Queshan *China* 32°55N 114°2E **34 H8**
Quesnel *Canada* 53°0N 122°30W **70 C4**
Quesnel → *Canada* 52°58N 122°29W **70 C4**
Quesnel L. *Canada* 52°30N 121°20W **70 C4**
Questa *U.S.A.* 36°42N 105°36W **77 H11**
Quetico △ *Canada* 48°30N 91°45W **72 C1**
Quetta *Pakistan* 30°15N 66°55E **42 D2**
Quezaltenango *Guatemala* 14°50N 91°30W **88 D1**
Quezon City *Phil.* 14°37N 121°2E **37 B6**
Qufār *Si. Arabia* 27°26N 41°37E **44 E4**
Qui Nhon *Vietnam* 13°40N 109°13E **38 F7**
Quibala *Angola* 10°46S 14°59E **52 G2**
Quibaxe *Angola* 8°24S 14°27E **52 F2**
Quibdó *Colombia* 5°42N 76°40W **92 B3**
Quiberon *France* 47°29N 3°9W **20 C2**
Quiet L. *Canada* 61°5N 133°5W **70 A2**
Quiindy *Paraguay* 25°58S 57°14W **94 B4**
Quilá *Mexico* 24°23N 107°13W **86 C3**
Quilán, C. *Chile* 43°15S 74°30W **96 E2**
Quilcene *U.S.A.* 47°49N 122°53W **78 C4**
Quilimarí *Chile* 32°5S 71°30W **94 C1**
Quilino *Argentina* 30°14S 64°29W **94 C3**
Quillabamba *Peru* 12°50S 72°50W **92 F4**
Quillagua *Chile* 21°40S 69°40W **94 A2**
Quillota *Chile* 32°54S 71°16W **94 C1**
Quilmes *Argentina* 34°43S 58°15W **94 C4**
Quilon *India* 8°50N 76°38E **40 Q10**
Quilpie *Australia* 26°35S 144°11E **63 D3**
Quilpué *Chile* 33°5S 71°33W **94 C1**
Quilua *Mozam.* 16°17S 39°54E **55 F4**
Quimilí *Argentina* 27°40S 62°30W **94 B3**
Quimper *France* 48°0N 4°9W **20 B1**
Quimperlé *France* 47°53N 3°33W **20 C2**
Quinault → *U.S.A.* 47°21N 124°18W **78 C2**
Quincy *Calif., U.S.A.* 39°56N 120°57W **78 F6**
Quincy *Fla., U.S.A.* 30°35N 84°34W **85 F12**
Quincy *Ill., U.S.A.* 39°56N 91°23W **80 F8**
Quincy *Mass., U.S.A.* 42°14N 71°0W **83 D14**
Quincy *Wash., U.S.A.* 47°14N 119°51W **76 C4**
Quines *Argentina* 32°13S 65°48W **94 C2**
Quinga *Mozam.* 15°49S 40°15E **55 F5**
Quintana Roo □ *Mexico* 19°40N 88°30W **87 D7**
Quintanar de la Orden *Spain* 39°36N 3°5W **21 C4**
Quintero *Chile* 32°45S 71°30W **94 C1**
Quirihue *Chile* 36°15S 72°35W **94 D1**
Quirimbas △ *Mozam.* 12°30S 40°15E **55 E5**
Quirindi *Australia* 31°28S 150°40E **63 E5**
Quirinópolis *Brazil* 18°32S 50°30W **93 G8**
Quissanga *Mozam.* 12°24S 40°28E **55 E5**
Quissico *Mozam.* 24°42S 34°44E **57 C5**
Quitilipi *Argentina* 26°50S 60°13W **94 B3**
Quitman *U.S.A.* 30°47N 83°34W **85 F13**
Quito *Ecuador* 0°15S 78°35W **92 D3**
Quixadá *Brazil* 4°55S 39°0W **93 D11**
Quixaxe *Mozam.* 15°17S 40°4E **55 F5**
Qulan *Kazakhstan* 42°55N 72°43E **28 E8**
Qul'jā, Jazā'ir *Egypt* 24°22N 35°31E **44 E2**
Qulsary *Kazakhstan* 46°59N 54°1E **19 E9**
Qumbu *S. Africa* 31°10S 28°48E **57 E4**
Qŭqon *Uzbekistan* 40°31N 70°56E **28 E8**
Qurnat as Sawdā' *Lebanon* 34°18N 36°6E **46 A5**
Quşaybā' *Si. Arabia* 26°53N 43°35E **44 E4**
Quşaybah *Iraq* 34°24N 40°59E **44 C4**
Quseir *Egypt* 26°7N 34°16E **44 E2**
Qüshchī *Iran* 37°59N 45°3E **44 B5**
Quthing *Lesotho* 30°25S 27°36E **57 E4**
Qūţīābād *Iran* 35°47N 48°30E **45 C6**
Quwo *China* 35°38N 111°25E **34 G6**
Quyang *China* 38°35N 114°40E **34 E8**
Quynh Nhai *Vietnam* 21°49N 103°33E **38 B4**
Quyon *Canada* 45°31N 76°14W **83 A8**
Quzhou *China* 28°57N 118°54E **33 D6**
Quzi *China* 36°20N 107°20E **34 F4**
Qyzylorda *Kazakhstan* 44°48N 65°28E **28 E7**

R

Ra, Ko *Thailand* 9°13N 98°16E **39 H2**
Raahe *Finland* 64°40N 24°28E **8 D21**
Raalte *Neths.* 52°23N 6°16E **15 B6**
Raasay *U.K.* 57°25N 6°4W **11 D2**
Raasay, Sd. of *U.K.* 57°30N 6°8W **11 D2**
Raba *Indonesia* 8°36S 118°55E **37 F5**

Rába → *Hungary* 47°38N 17°38E **17 E9**
Rabai *Kenya* 3°50S 39°31E **54 C4**
Rabat = Victoria *Malta* 36°3N 14°14E **25 C1**
Rabat *Malta* 35°53N 14°24E **25 D1**
Rabat *Morocco* 34°2N 6°48W **50 B4**
Rabaul *Papua N. G.* 4°24S 152°18E **58 B8**
Rabbit Flat *Australia* 20°11S 130°1E **60 D5**
Rabbit Lake Mine *Canada* 58°4N 104°5W **71 B8**
Rabi *Fiji* 16°30S 179°59W **59 a**
Rābigh *Si. Arabia* 22°50N 39°5E **47 C2**
Rābor *Iran* 29°17N 56°55E **45 D8**
Rabwah = Chenab Nagar *Pakistan* 31°45N 72°55E **42 D5**
Race, C. *Canada* 46°40N 53°5W **73 C9**
Rach Gia *Vietnam* 10°5N 105°5E **39 G5**
Rachid *Mauritania* 18°45N 11°35W **50 E3**
Racibórz *Poland* 50°7N 18°18E **17 C10**
Racine *U.S.A.* 42°44N 87°47W **80 D2**
Rackerby *U.S.A.* 39°26N 121°22W **78 F5**
Radama, Nosy *Madag.* 14°0S 47°47E **57 A8**
Radama, Saikanosy *Madag.* 14°16S 47°53E **57 A8**
Rădăuţi *Romania* 47°50N 25°59E **17 E13**
Radcliff *U.S.A.* 37°51N 85°57W **81 G11**
Radekhiv *Ukraine* 50°25N 24°32E **17 C13**
Radekhov = Radekhiv *Ukraine* 50°25N 24°32E **17 C13**
Radford *U.S.A.* 37°8N 80°34W **81 G13**
Radhanpur *India* 23°50N 71°38E **42 H4**
Radhwa, Jabal *Si. Arabia* 24°34N 38°18E **44 E3**
Radisson *Qué., Canada* 53°47N 77°37W **72 B4**
Radisson *Sask., Canada* 52°30N 107°20W **71 C7**
Radium Hot Springs *Canada* 50°35N 116°2W **70 C5**
Radnor Forest *U.K.* 52°17N 3°10W **13 E4**
Radom *Poland* 51°23N 21°12E **17 C11**
Radomsko *Poland* 51°5N 19°28E **17 C10**
Radomyshl *Ukraine* 50°30N 29°12E **17 C15**
Radstock, C. *Australia* 33°12S 134°20E **63 E1**
Raduzhnyy *Russia* 62°5N 77°28E **28 C8**
Radville *Canada* 49°30N 104°15W **71 D8**
Radviliškis *Lithuania* 55°49N 23°33E **9 J20**
Rae *Canada* 62°50N 116°3W **70 A5**
Rae Bareli *India* 26°18N 81°20E **43 F9**
Rae Isthmus *Canada* 66°40N 87°30W **69 C11**
Raeren *Belgium* 50°41N 6°7E **15 D6**
Raeside, L. *Australia* 29°20S 122°0E **61 E3**
Raetihi *N.Z.* 39°25S 175°17E **59 C5**
Rafaela *Argentina* 31°10S 61°30W **94 C3**
Rafah *Gaza Strip* 31°18N 34°14E **46 D3**
Rafai *C.A.R.* 4°59N 23°58E **54 D4**
Rafḥā *Si. Arabia* 29°35N 43°35E **44 D4**
Rafsanjān *Iran* 30°30N 56°5E **45 D8**
Raft Pt. *Australia* 16°4S 124°26E **60 C3**
Râga *Sudan* 8°28N 25°41E **51 G11**
Ragachow *Belarus* 53°8N 30°5E **17 B16**
Ragama *Sri Lanka* 7°0N 79°50E **40 R11**
Ragged, Mt. *Australia* 33°27S 123°25E **61 F3**
Ragged Pt. *Barbados* 13°10N 59°26E **89 g**
Raghunathpalli *India* 22°14N 84°48E **43 H11**
Raghunathpur *India* 23°33N 86°40E **43 H12**
Raglan *N.Z.* 37°55S 174°55E **59 B5**
Ragusa *Italy* 36°55N 14°44E **22 F6**
Raha *Indonesia* 4°55S 123°0E **37 E6**
Rahaeng = Tak *Thailand* 16°52N 99°8E **38 D2**
Rahatgarh *India* 23°47N 78°22E **43 H8**
Rahimyar Khan *Pakistan* 28°30N 70°25E **42 E4**
Rāhjerd *Iran* 34°22N 50°22E **45 C6**
Rahole △ *Kenya* 0°5N 38°57E **54 B4**
Rahon *India* 31°3N 76°7E **42 D7**
Raiatéa, Î. *French Polynesia* 16°50S 151°25W **65 J12**
Raichur *India* 16°10N 77°20E **40 L10**
Raiganj *India* 25°37N 88°10E **43 G13**
Raigarh *India* 21°56N 83°25E **41 J13**
Raijua *Indonesia* 10°37S 121°36E **37 F6**
Raikot *India* 30°41N 75°42E **42 D6**
Railton *Australia* 41°25S 146°28E **63 G4**
Rainbow Bridge △ *U.S.A.* 37°5N 110°58W **77 H8**
Rainbow Lake *Canada* 58°30N 119°23W **70 B5**
Rainier *U.S.A.* 46°53N 122°41W **78 D4**
Rainier, Mt. *U.S.A.* 46°52N 121°46W **78 D5**
Rainy L. *Canada* 48°42N 93°10W **71 D10**
Rainy River *Canada* 48°43N 94°29W **71 D10**
Raippaluoto *Finland* 63°13N 21°14E **8 E19**
Raipur *India* 21°17N 81°45E **41 J12**
Raisen *India* 23°20N 77°48E **42 H8**
Raisio *Finland* 60°28N 22°11E **9 F20**
Raj Nandgaon *India* 21°5N 81°5E **41 J12**
Raj Nilgiri *India* 21°28N 86°46E **43 J12**
Raja, Ujung *Indonesia* 3°40N 96°25E **36 D1**
Raja Ampat, Kepulauan *Indonesia* 0°30S 130°0E **37 E8**
Rajahmundry *India* 17°1N 81°48E **41 L12**
Rajaji △ *India* 30°10N 78°20E **42 D8**
Rajang → *Malaysia* 2°30N 112°0E **36 D4**
Rajanpur *Pakistan* 29°6N 70°19E **42 E4**
Rajapalaiyam *India* 9°25N 77°35E **40 Q10**
Rajasthan □ *India* 26°45N 73°30E **42 F5**
Rajasthan Canal = Indira Gandhi Canal *India* 28°0N 72°0E **42 F5**
Rajauri *India* 33°25N 74°21E **43 C6**
Rajgarh *Mad. P., India* 24°2N 76°45E **42 G7**
Rajgarh *Raj., India* 27°14N 76°38E **42 F7**
Rajgarh *Raj., India* 28°40N 75°25E **42 E6**
Rajgir *India* 25°2N 85°25E **43 G11**
Rajkot *India* 22°15N 70°56E **42 H4**
Rajmahal Hills *India* 24°30N 87°30E **43 G12**
Rajpipla *India* 21°50N 73°30E **40 J8**
Rajpur *India* 22°18N 74°21E **42 H6**
Rajpura *India* 30°25N 76°32E **42 D7**
Rajshahi *Bangla.* 24°22N 88°39E **41 G16**
Rajshahi □ *Bangla.* 25°0N 89°0E **43 G13**
Rajula *India* 21°3N 71°26E **42 J4**
Rakaia *N.Z.* 43°45S 172°1E **59 E4**

Rakaia → *N.Z.* 43°36S 172°15E **59 E4**
Rakan, Ra's *Qatar* 26°10N 51°20E **45 E6**
Rakaposhi *Pakistan* 36°10N 74°25E **43 A6**
Rakata, Pulau *Indonesia* 6°10S 105°20E **36 F3**
Rakhiv *Ukraine* 48°3N 24°12E **17 D13**
Rakhni *Pakistan* 30°4N 69°56E **42 D3**
Rakhni → *Pakistan* 29°31N 69°36E **42 E3**
Rakiraki *Fiji* 17°22S 178°11E **59 a**
Rakitnoye *Russia* 45°36N 134°17E **30 B7**
Rakiura △ *N.Z.* 47°0S 167°50E **59 G1**
Rakops *Botswana* 21°1S 24°28E **56 C3**
Rakvere *Estonia* 59°20N 26°25E **9 G22**
Raleigh *U.S.A.* 35°47N 78°39W **85 D15**
Ralik Chain *Pac. Oc.* 8°0N 168°0E **64 G8**
Ralls *U.S.A.* 33°41N 101°24W **84 E4**
Ralston *U.S.A.* 41°30N 76°57W **82 E8**
Ram → *Canada* 62°1N 123°41W **70 A4**
Rām Allāh *West Bank* 31°55N 35°10E **46 D4**
Rama *Nic.* 12°9N 84°15W **88 D3**
Ramakona *India* 21°43N 78°50E **43 J8**
Rāmallāh = Rām Allāh *West Bank* 31°55N 35°10E **46 D4**
Raman *Thailand* 6°29N 101°18E **39 J3**
Ramanathapuram *India* 9°25N 78°55E **40 Q11**
Ramanetaka, B. de *Madag.* 14°13S 47°52E **57 A8**
Ramanujganj *India* 23°48N 83°42E **43 H10**
Ramat Gan *Israel* 32°4N 34°48E **46 C3**
Ramatlhabama *S. Africa* 25°37S 25°33E **56 D4**
Ramban *India* 33°14N 75°12E **43 C6**
Rambi = Rabi *Fiji* 16°30S 179°59W **59 a**
Rambipuji *Indonesia* 8°12S 113°37E **37 H15**
Rame Hd. *Australia* 37°47S 149°30E **63 F4**
Ramechhap *Nepal* 27°25N 86°10E **43 F12**
Ramganga → *India* 27°5N 79°58E **43 F8**
Ramgarh *Jharkhand, India* 23°40N 85°35E **43 H11**
Ramgarh *Raj., India* 27°16N 75°14E **42 F6**
Ramgarh *Raj., India* 27°30N 70°36E **42 F4**
Rāmhormoz *Iran* 31°15N 49°35E **45 D6**
Ramīān *Iran* 37°3N 55°16E **45 B7**
Ramingining *Australia* 12°19S 135°3E **62 A2**
Ramla *Israel* 31°55N 34°52E **46 D3**
Ramm = Rum *Jordan* 29°39N 35°26E **46 F4**
Ramm, Jabal *Jordan* 29°35N 35°24E **46 F4**
Ramnad = Ramanathapuram *India* 9°25N 78°55E **40 Q11**
Ramnagar *Jammu & Kashmir, India* 32°47N 75°18E **43 C6**
Ramnagar *Uttarakhand, India* 29°24N 79°7E **43 E8**
Râmnicu Sărat *Romania* 45°26N 27°3E **17 F14**
Râmnicu Vâlcea *Romania* 45°9N 24°21E **17 F13**
Ramona *U.S.A.* 33°2N 116°52W **79 M10**
Ramore *Canada* 48°30N 80°25W **72 C3**
Ramotswa *Botswana* 24°50S 25°52E **56 C4**
Rampur *H.P., India* 31°26N 77°43E **42 D7**
Rampur *Mad. P., India* 23°25N 73°53E **42 H5**
Rampur *Ut. P., India* 28°50N 79°5E **43 E8**
Rampur Hat *India* 24°10N 87°50E **43 G12**
Rampura *India* 24°30N 75°27E **42 G6**
Ramrama Tola *India* 21°52N 79°55E **43 J8**
Ramree I. *Burma* 19°0N 93°40E **41 K19**
Rāmsar *Iran* 36°53N 50°41E **45 B6**
Ramsey *I. of Man* 54°20N 4°22W **12 C3**
Ramsey *U.S.A.* 41°4N 74°9W **83 E10**
Ramsey L. *Canada* 47°13N 82°15W **72 C3**
Ramsgate *U.K.* 51°20N 1°25E **13 F9**
Ramtek *India* 21°20N 79°15E **40 J11**
Ramu *Kenya* 3°55N 41°10E **54 B5**
Rana Pratap Sagar Dam *India* 24°58N 75°38E **42 G6**
Ranaghat *India* 23°15N 88°35E **43 H13**
Ranahu *Pakistan* 25°55N 69°45E **42 G3**
Ranau *Malaysia* 6°2N 116°40E **36 C5**
Rancagua *Chile* 34°10S 70°50W **94 C1**
Rancheria → *Canada* 60°13N 129°7W **70 A3**
Ranchester *U.S.A.* 44°54N 107°10W **76 D10**
Ranchi *India* 23°19N 85°27E **43 H11**
Rancho Cordova *U.S.A.* 38°36N 121°18W **78 G5**
Rancho Cucamonga *U.S.A.* 34°10N 117°30W **79 L9**
Randalstown *U.K.* 54°45N 6°19W **10 B5**
Randers *Denmark* 56°29N 10°1E **9 H14**
Randfontein *S. Africa* 26°8S 27°45E **57 D4**
Randle *U.S.A.* 46°32N 121°57W **78 D5**
Randolph *Mass., U.S.A.* 42°10N 71°2W **83 D13**
Randolph *N.Y., U.S.A.* 42°10N 78°59W **82 D6**
Randolph *Utah, U.S.A.* 41°40N 111°11W **76 F8**
Randolph *Vt., U.S.A.* 43°55N 72°40W **83 C12**
Randsburg *U.S.A.* 35°22N 117°39W **79 K9**
Råneälven → *Sweden* 65°50N 22°20E **8 D20**
Rangae *Thailand* 6°19N 101°44E **39 J3**
Rangaunu B. *N.Z.* 34°51S 173°15E **59 A4**
Range, The *Zimbabwe* 19°2S 31°2E **55 F3**
Rangeley *U.S.A.* 44°58N 70°39W **83 B14**
Rangeley L. *U.S.A.* 44°55N 70°43W **83 B14**
Rangely *U.S.A.* 40°5N 108°48W **76 F9**
Ranger *U.S.A.* 32°28N 98°41W **84 E5**
Rangia *India* 26°28N 91°38E **41 F17**
Rangiora *N.Z.* 43°19S 172°36E **59 E4**
Rangitaiki → *N.Z.* 37°54S 176°49E **59 B6**
Rangitata → *N.Z.* 43°45S 171°15E **59 E3**
Rangitoto ke te tonga = D'Urville I., *N.Z.* 40°50S 173°55E **59 D4**
Rangkasbitung *Indonesia* 6°21S 106°15E **37 G12**
Rangon → *Burma* 16°28N 96°40E **41 L20**
Rangoon *Burma* 16°45N 96°20E **41 L20**
Rangpur *Bangla.* 25°42N 89°22E **41 G16**
Rangsang *Indonesia* 1°20N 103°30E **39 M4**
Rangsit *Thailand* 13°59N 100°37E **38 F3**
Ranibennur *India* 14°35N 75°30E **40 M9**
Raniganj *Ut. P., India* 27°3N 82°13E **43 F9**
Raniganj *W. Bengal, India* 23°40N 87°5E **41 H15**

Ranikhet *India* 29°39N 79°25E **43** E8
Raniwara *India* 24°50N 72°10E **42** G5
Rāniyah *Iraq* 36°15N 44°53E **44** B5
Ranka *India* 23°59N 83°47E **43** H10
Ranken → *Australia* 20°31S 137°36E **62** C2
Rankin *U.S.A.* 31°13N 101°56W **84** F4
Rankin Inlet *Canada* 62°30N 93°0W **68** C10
Rankins Springs
  Australia 33°49S 146°14E **63** E4
Rannoch, L. *U.K.* 56°41N 4°20W **11** E4
Rannoch Moor *U.K.* 56°38N 4°48W **11** E4
Ranobe, Helodranon' i
  Madag. 23°3S 43°33E **57** C7
Ranohira *Madag.* 22°29S 45°24E **57** C8
Ranomafana *Toamasina,*
  Madag. 18°57S 48°50E **57** B8
Ranomafana *Toliara,*
  Madag. 24°34S 47°0E **57** C8
Ranomafana △ *Madag.* 21°16S 47°25E **57** C8
Ranomena *Madag.* 23°25S 47°17E **57** C8
Ranong *Thailand* 9°56N 98°40E **39** H2
Ranotsara Nord *Madag.* 22°48S 46°36E **57** C8
Ränsa *Iran* 33°39N 48°18E **45** C6
Ransiki *Indonesia* 1°30S 134°10E **37** E8
Rantabe *Madag.* 15°42S 49°39E **57** B8
Rantauprapat *Indonesia* 2°15N 99°50E **36** D1
Rantemario *Indonesia* 3°15S 119°57E **37** E5
Ranthambore △ *India* 26°10N 76°30E **42** F7
Rantoul *U.S.A.* 40°19N 88°9W **80** E9
Raohe *China* 46°47N 134°0E **30** A7
Raoyang *China* 38°15N 115°45E **34** E8
Rap, Ko *Thailand* 9°19N 99°58E **39** b
Rapa *French Polynesia* 27°35S 144°20W **65** K13
Rapa Nui = Pascua, I. de
  Chile 27°7S 109°23W **65** K17
Rapallo *Italy* 44°21N 9°14E **20** D8
Rapar *India* 23°34N 70°38E **42** H4
Räpch *Iran* 25°40N 59°15E **45** E8
Rapel, Lago *Chile* 34°20S 71°14W **94** C1
Raper, C. *Canada* 69°44N 67°6W **69** C13
Rapid City *U.S.A.* 44°5N 103°14W **80** D2
Rapid River *U.S.A.* 45°55N 86°58W **80** C10
Rapla *Estonia* 59°1N 24°52E **9** G21
Rapti → *India* 26°18N 83°41E **43** F10
Raquette → *U.S.A.* 45°0N 74°42W **83** B10
Raquette Lake *U.S.A.* 43°49N 74°40W **83** C10
Rara △ *Nepal* 29°30N 82°10E **43** E10
Rarotonga *Cook Is.* 21°30S 160°0W **65** K12
Ra's al 'Ayn *Syria* 36°45N 40°12E **44** B4
Ra's al Khaymah *U.A.E.* 25°50N 55°59E **45** E7
Ra's at Tib *Tunisia* 37°1N 11°2E **22** F4
Rasa, Pta. *Argentina* 36°20S 56°41W **94** D4
Rasca, Pta. de la
  Canary Is. 27°59N 16°41W **24** G3
Raseiniai *Lithuania* 55°25N 23°5E **9** J20
Rashmi *India* 25°4N 74°22E **42** G6
Rasht *Iran* 37°20N 49°40E **45** B6
Rasi Salai *Thailand* 15°20N 104°9E **38** E5
Rason L. *Australia* 28°45S 124°25E **61** E3
Rasra *India* 25°50N 83°50E **43** G10
Rasul *Pakistan* 32°42N 73°34E **42** C5
Rat → *Canada* 49°35N 97°10W **71** D9
Rat Buri *Thailand* 13°30N 99°54E **38** F2
Rat Islands *U.S.A.* 52°0N 178°0E **74** a
Rat L. *Canada* 56°10N 99°40W **71** B9
Ratak Chain *Pac. Oc.* 1°0N 170°0E **64** G8
Ratangarh *India* 28°5N 74°35E **42** E6
Rataţawī *Iraq* 30°38N 47°13E **44** D5
Rath *India* 25°36N 79°37E **43** G8
Rath Luirc *Ireland* 52°21N 8°40W **10** D3
Rathangan *Ireland* 53°13N 7°1W **10** C4
Rathdrum *Ireland* 52°56N 6°14W **10** D5
Rathenow *Germany* 52°37N 12°19E **16** B7
Rathkeale *Ireland* 52°32N 8°56W **10** D3
Rathlin I. *U.K.* 55°18N 6°14W **10** A5
Rathmelton *Ireland* 55°2N 7°38W **10** A4
Ratibor = Racibórz
  Poland 50°7N 18°18E **17** C10
Ratlam *India* 23°20N 75°0E **42** H6
Ratnagiri *India* 16°57N 73°18E **40** L8
Ratodero *Pakistan* 27°48N 68°18E **42** F3
Raton *U.S.A.* 36°54N 104°24W **77** H11
Rattaphum *Thailand* 7°8N 100°16E **39** J3
Rattray Hd. *U.K.* 57°38N 1°50W **11** D7
Ratz, Mt. *Canada* 57°23N 132°12W **70** B2
Raub *Malaysia* 3°47N 101°52E **39** L3
Rauch *Argentina* 36°45S 59°5W **94** D4
Raudales *Mexico* 17°27N 93°39W **87** D6
Raufarhöfn *Iceland* 66°27N 15°57W **8** C6
Raufoss *Norway* 60°44N 10°37E **8** F14
Raukumara Ra. *N.Z.* 38°5N 177°55E **59** C6
Rauma *Finland* 61°10N 21°30E **8** F19
Raumo = Rauma
  Finland 61°10N 21°30E **8** F19
Raung, Gunung *Indonesia* 8°8S 114°3E **37** J17
Raurkela *India* 22°14N 84°50E **43** H11
Rausänsar *Iran* 34°43N 46°40E **44** C5
Rausu-Dake *Japan* 44°4N 145°7E **30** B12
Rava-Ruska *Ukraine* 50°15N 23°42E **17** C12
Rava Russkaya = Rava-Ruska
  Ukraine 50°15N 23°42E **17** C12
Ravalli *U.S.A.* 47°17N 114°11W **76** C6
Ravänsar *Iran* 34°43N 46°40E **44** C5
Rävar *Iran* 31°20N 56°51E **45** D8
Ravena *U.S.A.* 42°28N 73°49W **83** D11
Ravenna *Italy* 44°25N 12°12E **22** B5
Ravenna *Nebr., U.S.A.* 41°1N 98°55W **80** E4
Ravenna *Ohio, U.S.A.* 41°9N 81°15W **82** E3
Ravensburg *Germany* 47°46N 9°36E **16** E5
Ravenshoe *Australia* 17°37S 145°29E **62** B4
Ravensthorpe *Australia* 33°35S 120°2E **61** F3
Ravenswood *Australia* 20°6S 146°54E **62** C4
Ravenswood *U.S.A.* 38°57N 81°46W **81** F13
Ravi → *Pakistan* 30°35N 71°49E **42** D4
Rawalpindi *Pakistan* 33°38N 73°8E **42** C5
Rawang *Malaysia* 3°20N 101°35E **39** L3
Rawene *N.Z.* 35°25S 173°32E **59** A4
Rawlinna *Australia* 30°58S 125°28E **61** F4

Rawlins *U.S.A.* 41°47N 107°14W **76** F10
Rawlinson Ra. *Australia* 24°40S 128°30E **61** D4
Rawson *Argentina* 43°15S 65°5W **96** E3
Raxaul *India* 26°59N 84°51E **43** F11
Ray *U.S.A.* 48°21N 103°10W **80** A2
Ray, C. *Canada* 47°33N 59°15W **73** C8
Raya Ring, Ko *Thailand* 8°18N 98°29E **39** a
Rayadurg *India* 14°40N 76°50E **40** M10
Rayagada *India* 19°15N 83°20E **41** K13
Raychikhinsk *Russia* 49°46N 129°25E **29** E13
Rāyen *Iran* 29°34N 57°26E **45** D8
Rayleigh *U.K.* 51°36N 0°37E **13** F8
Raymond *Canada* 49°30N 112°35W **70** D6
Raymond *Calif., U.S.A.* 37°13N 119°54W **78** H7
Raymond *N.H., U.S.A.* 43°2N 71°11W **83** C13
Raymond *Wash.,*
  U.S.A. 46°41N 123°44W **78** D3
Raymondville *U.S.A.* 26°29N 97°47W **84** H6
Raymore *Canada* 51°25N 104°31W **71** C8
Rayón *Mexico* 29°43N 110°35W **86** B2
Rayong *Thailand* 12°40N 101°20E **38** F3
Raystown L. *U.S.A.* 40°25N 78°5W **82** F6
Rayville *U.S.A.* 32°29N 91°46W **84** E9
Raz, Pte. du *France* 48°2N 4°47W **20** C1
Razan *Iran* 35°23N 49°2E **45** C6
Razāzah, Buḥayrat ar
  Iraq 32°40N 43°35E **44** C4
Razāzah, L. = Razāzah, Buḥayrat
  ar *Iraq* 32°40N 43°35E **44** C4
Razdel'naya = Rozdilna
  Ukraine 46°50N 30°2E **17** E16
Razdolnoye *Russia* 43°30N 131°52E **30** C5
Razeh *Iran* 32°47N 48°9E **45** C6
Razgrad *Bulgaria* 43°33N 26°34E **23** C12
Razim, Lacul *Romania* 44°50N 29°0E **17** F15
Razmak *Pakistan* 32°45N 69°50E **42** C3
Re, Cu Lao *Vietnam* 15°22N 109°8E **38** E7
Ré, Î. de *France* 46°12N 1°30W **20** C3
Reading *U.K.* 51°27N 0°58W **13** F7
Reading *U.S.A.* 40°20N 75°56W **83** F9
Reading □ *U.K.* 51°27N 0°58W **13** F7
Realicó *Argentina* 35°0S 64°15W **94** D3
Ream *Cambodia* 10°34N 103°39E **39** G4
Ream △ *Cambodia* 10°30N 103°45E **39** G4
Reay Forest *U.K.* 58°22N 4°55W **11** C4
Rebecca, L. *Australia* 30°0S 122°15E **61** F3
Rebi *Indonesia* 6°23S 134°7E **37** F8
Rebiana *Libya* 24°12N 22°10E **51** D10
Rebiana, Sahrâ' *Libya* 24°30N 21°0E **51** D10
Reboly *Russia* 63°49N 30°47E **8** E24
Rebun-Tō *Japan* 45°23N 141°2E **30** B10
Recherche, Arch. of the
  Australia 34°15S 122°50E **61** F3
Rechna Doab *Pakistan* 31°35N 73°30E **42** D5
Rechytsa *Belarus* 52°21N 30°24E **17** B16
Recife *Brazil* 8°0S 35°0W **93** E12
Recife *Seychelles* 4°36S 55°42E **53** b
Recklinghausen *Germany* 51°37N 7°12E **15** C7
Reconquista *Argentina* 29°10S 59°45W **94** B4
Recreo *Argentina* 29°25S 65°10W **94** B2
Red → *U.S.A.* 31°1N 91°45W **84** F9
Red Bank *U.S.A.* 40°21N 74°5W **83** F10
Red Bay *Canada* 51°44N 56°25W **73** B8
Red Bluff *U.S.A.* 40°11N 122°15W **76** F2
Red Bluff Res. *U.S.A.* 31°54N 103°55W **84** F3
Red Cliffs *Australia* 34°19S 142°11E **63** E3
Red Cloud *U.S.A.* 40°5N 98°32W **80** E4
Red Creek *U.S.A.* 43°14N 76°45W **83** C8
Red Deer *Canada* 52°20N 113°50W **70** C6
Red Deer → *Alta.,*
  Canada 50°58N 110°0W **71** C7
Red Deer → *Man.,*
  Canada 52°53N 101°1W **71** C8
Red Deer L. *Canada* 52°55N 101°20W **71** C8
Red Hook *U.S.A.* 41°55N 73°53W **83** E11
Red Indian L. *Canada* 48°35N 57°0W **73** C8
Red L. *Canada* 51°3N 93°49W **71** C10
Red Lake *Canada* 51°3N 93°49W **71** C10
Red Lake Falls *U.S.A.* 47°53N 96°16W **80** B5
Red Lake Road *Canada* 49°59N 93°25W **71** C10
Red Lodge *U.S.A.* 45°11N 109°15W **76** D9
Red Mountain *U.S.A.* 35°37N 117°38W **79** K9
Red Oak *U.S.A.* 41°1N 95°14W **80** E6
Red River of the North →
  N. Amer. 49°0N 97°15W **80** A5
Red Rock *Canada* 48°55N 88°15W **72** C2
Red Rock, L. *U.S.A.* 41°22N 92°59W **80** E7
Red Rocks Pt. *Australia* 32°13S 127°32E **61** F4
Red Sea *Asia* 25°0N 36°0E **47** C2
Red Slate Mt. *U.S.A.* 37°31N 118°52W **78** H8
Red Sucker L. *Canada* 54°9N 93°40W **72** B1
Red Tower Pass = Turnu Roşu, P.
  Romania 45°33N 24°17E **17** F13
Red Wing *U.S.A.* 44°34N 92°31W **80** C7
Redang *Malaysia* 5°49N 103°2E **39** K4
Redange *Lux.* 49°46N 5°52E **15** E5
Redcar *U.K.* 54°37N 1°4W **12** C6
Redcar & Cleveland □
  U.K. 54°29N 1°0W **12** C7
Redcliff *Canada* 50°10N 110°50W **76** A8
Redcliffe *Australia* 27°12S 153°0E **63** D5
Redcliffe, Mt. *Australia* 28°30S 121°30E **61** E3
Reddersburg *S. Africa* 29°41S 26°10E **56** D4
Redditch *U.K.* 52°18N 1°55W **13** E6
Redfield *U.S.A.* 44°53N 98°31W **80** C4
Redford *U.S.A.* 44°38N 73°48W **83** B11
Redhead *Trin. & Tob.* 10°44N 60°58W **93** K16
Redlands *U.S.A.* 34°4N 117°11W **79** M9
Redmond *Oreg., U.S.A.* 44°17N 121°11W **76** D3
Redmond *Wash., U.S.A.* 47°40N 122°7W **78** C4
Redon *France* 47°40N 2°6W **20** C2
Redonda *Antigua & B.* 16°58N 62°19W **89** C7
Redondela *Spain* 42°15N 8°38W **21** A1
Redondo Beach *U.S.A.* 33°50N 118°23W **79** M8
Redruth *U.K.* 50°14N 5°14W **13** G2
Redvers *Canada* 49°35N 101°40W **71** D8

Redwater *Canada* 53°55N 113°6W **70** C6
Redwood *U.S.A.* 44°18N 75°48W **83** B9
Redwood △ *U.S.A.* 41°40N 124°5W **76** F1
Redwood City *U.S.A.* 37°30N 122°15W **78** H4
Redwood Falls *U.S.A.* 44°32N 95°7W **80** C6
Ree, L. *Ireland* 53°35N 8°0W **10** C3
Reed City *U.S.A.* 43°53N 85°31W **81** D11
Reed L. *Canada* 54°38N 100°30W **71** C8
Reedley *U.S.A.* 36°36N 119°27W **78** J7
Reedsburg *U.S.A.* 43°32N 90°0W **80** D8
Reedsport *U.S.A.* 43°42N 124°6W **76** E1
Reedsville *U.S.A.* 40°39N 77°35W **82** F7
Reefton *N.Z.* 42°6S 171°51E **59** E3
Reese → *U.S.A.* 40°48N 117°4W **76** F5
Refugio *U.S.A.* 28°18N 97°17W **84** G6
Regana, C. de *Spain* 39°25N 2°43E **24** B9
Regensburg *Germany* 49°1N 12°6E **16** D7
Reggâne = Zaouiet Reggâne
  Algeria 26°32N 0°3E **50** C6
Réggio di Calábria *Italy* 38°6N 15°39E **22** E6
Réggio nell'Emília *Italy* 44°43N 10°36E **22** B4
Reghin *Romania* 46°46N 24°42E **17** E13
Regina *Canada* 50°27N 104°35W **71** C8
Regina Beach *Canada* 50°47N 105°0W **71** C8
Registro *Brazil* 24°29S 47°49W **95** A6
Rehar → *India* 23°55N 82°40E **43** H10
Rehli *India* 23°38N 79°5E **43** H8
Rehoboth *Namibia* 23°15S 17°4E **56** B2
Rehovot *Israel* 31°54N 34°48E **46** D3
Reichenbach *Germany* 50°37N 12°17E **16** C7
Reid *Australia* 30°49S 128°26E **61** F4
Reidsville *U.S.A.* 36°21N 79°40W **85** C15
Reigate *U.K.* 51°14N 0°12W **13** F7
Reims *France* 49°15N 4°1E **20** B6
Reina Adelaida, Arch.
  Chile 52°20S 74°0W **96** G2
Reina Sofía, Tenerife ✈ (TFS)
  Canary Is. 28°3N 16°33W **24** F3
Reindeer → *Canada* 55°36N 103°11W **71** B8
Reindeer I. *Canada* 52°30N 98°0W **71** C9
Reindeer L. *Canada* 57°15N 102°15W **71** B8
Reinga, C. *N.Z.* 34°25S 172°43E **59** A4
Reinosa *Spain* 43°2N 4°15W **21** A3
Reitz *S. Africa* 27°48S 28°29E **57** D4
Reivilo *S. Africa* 27°36S 24°8E **56** D3
Reliance *Canada* 63°0N 109°20W **71** A7
Remanso *Brazil* 9°41S 42°4W **93** E10
Remarkable, Mt.
  Australia 32°48S 138°10E **63** E2
Rembang *Indonesia* 6°42S 111°21E **37** G14
Remedios *Panama* 8°15N 81°50W **88** E3
Remeshk *Iran* 26°55N 58°50E **45** E8
Remich *Lux.* 49°32N 6°22E **15** E6
Remscheid *Germany* 51°11N 7°12E **15** C7
Ren Xian *China* 37°8N 114°40E **34** F8
Rendang *Indonesia* 8°26S 115°25E **37** J18
Rendsburg *Germany* 54°17N 9°39E **16** A5
Renfrew *Canada* 45°30N 76°40W **83** A8
Renfrewshire □ *U.K.* 55°49N 4°38W **11** F4
Rengat *Indonesia* 0°30S 102°45E **36** E2
Rengo *Chile* 34°24S 70°50W **94** C1
Reni *Ukraine* 45°28N 28°15E **17** F15
Renmark *Australia* 34°11S 140°43E **63** E3
Rennell Sd. *Canada* 53°23N 132°35W **70** C2
Renner Springs
  Australia 18°20S 133°47E **62** B1
Rennes *France* 48°7N 1°41W **20** B3
Rennick Glacier
  Antarctica 70°30S 161°45E **5** D21
Rennie L. *Canada* 61°32N 105°35W **71** A7
Reno *U.S.A.* 39°31N 119°48W **78** F7
Reno → *Italy* 44°38N 12°16E **22** B5
Renovo *U.S.A.* 41°20N 77°45W **82** E7
Renqiu *China* 38°43N 116°5E **34** E9
Rensselaer *Ind., U.S.A.* 40°57N 87°9W **80** E10
Rensselaer *N.Y., U.S.A.* 42°38N 73°45W **83** D11
Renton *U.S.A.* 47°28N 122°12W **78** C4
Reotipur *India* 25°33N 83°45E **43** G10
Republic *Mo., U.S.A.* 37°7N 93°29W **80** G7
Republic *Wash., U.S.A.* 48°39N 118°44W **76** B4
Republican → *U.S.A.* 39°4N 96°48W **80** F5
Repulse B. *Australia* 20°35S 148°46E **62** J6
Repulse Bay *Canada* 66°30N 86°30W **69** C11
Requena *Peru* 5°5S 73°52W **92** E4
Requena *Spain* 39°30N 1°4W **21** C5
Resadiye = Datça *Turkey* 36°46N 27°40E **23** F12
Reserve *U.S.A.* 33°43N 108°45W **77** K9
Resht = Rasht *Iran* 37°20N 49°40E **45** B6
Resistencia *Argentina* 27°30S 59°0W **94** B4
Reşiţa *Romania* 45°18N 21°53E **17** F11
Reso = Raisio *Finland* 60°28N 22°11E **9** F20
Resolute *Canada* 74°42N 94°54W **69** B10
Resolution I. *Canada* 61°30N 65°0W **69** C13
Resolution I. *N.Z.* 45°40S 166°40E **59** F1
Ressano Garcia *Mozam.* 25°25S 32°0E **57** D5
Reston *Canada* 49°33N 101°6W **71** D8
Retalhuleu *Guatemala* 14°33N 91°46W **88** D1
Retenue, L. de
  Dem. Rep. of the Congo 11°0S 27°0E **55** E2
Retford *U.K.* 53°19N 0°56W **12** D7
Rethímno *Greece* 35°18N 24°30E **25** D6
Rethímno □ *Greece* 35°23N 24°28E **25** D6
Réunion ☑ *Ind. Oc.* 21°0S 56°0E **53** c
Reus *Spain* 41°10N 1°5E **21** B6
Reutlingen *Germany* 48°29N 9°12E **16** D5
Reval = Tallinn *Estonia* 59°22N 24°48E **9** G21
Revda *Russia* 56°48N 59°57E **18** C10
Revelganj *India* 25°50N 84°40E **43** G11
Revelstoke *Canada* 51°0N 118°10W **70** C5
Revillagigedo, Is. de
  Pac. Oc. 18°40N 112°0W **86** D2
Revuè → *Mozam.* 19°50S 34°0E **55** F3
Rewa *India* 24°33N 81°25E **43** G9
Rewari *India* 28°15N 76°40E **42** E7
Rexburg *U.S.A.* 43°49N 111°47W **76** E8
Rey *Iran* 35°35N 51°25E **45** C6

Rey, I. del *Panama* 8°20N 78°30W **88** E4
Rey, L. del *Mexico* 27°1N 103°26W **86** B4
Rey Malabo *Eq. Guin.* 3°45N 8°50E **52** D1
Reyðarfjörður *Iceland* 65°2N 14°13W **8** D6
Reyes, Pt. *U.S.A.* 38°0N 123°0W **78** H3
Reykjahlíð *Iceland* 65°40N 16°55W **8** D5
Reykjanes *Iceland* 63°48N 22°40E **8** E2
Reykjavík *Iceland* 64°10N 21°57W **8** D3
Reynolds Ra. *Australia* 22°30S 133°0E **60** D5
Reynoldsville *U.S.A.* 41°6N 78°53W **82** E6
Reynosa *Mexico* 26°7N 98°18W **87** B5
Rēzekne *Latvia* 56°30N 27°17E **9** H22
Rezvān *Iran* 27°34N 56°6E **45** E8
Rhayader *U.K.* 52°18N 3°29W **13** E4
Rhein → *Europe* 51°52N 6°2E **15** C6
Rhein-Main-Donau-Kanal
  Germany 49°1N 11°27E **16** D6
Rheine *Germany* 52°17N 7°26E **16** B4
Rheinland-Pfalz □ *Germany* 50°0N 7°0E **16** C4
Rhin = Rhein → *Europe* 51°52N 6°2E **15** C6
Rhine = Rhein → *Europe* 51°52N 6°2E **15** C6
Rhinebeck *U.S.A.* 41°56N 73°55W **83** E11
Rhineland-Palatinate =
  Rheinland-Pfalz □
  Germany 50°0N 7°0E **16** C4
Rhinelander *U.S.A.* 45°38N 89°25W **80** C9
Rhinns Pt. *U.K.* 55°40N 6°29W **11** F2
Rhino Camp *Uganda* 3°0N 31°22E **54** B3
Rhir, Cap *Morocco* 30°38N 9°54W **50** B4
Rhode Island □ *U.S.A.* 41°40N 71°30W **83** E13
Rhodes *Greece* 36°15N 28°10E **25** C10
Rhodope Mts. = Rhodopi Planina
  Bulgaria 41°40N 24°20E **23** D11
Rhodopi Planina
  Bulgaria 41°40N 24°20E **23** D11
Rhön *Germany* 50°24N 9°58E **16** C5
Rhondda *U.K.* 51°39N 3°31W **13** F4
Rhondda Cynon Taff □
  U.K. 51°42N 3°27W **13** F4
Rhône → *France* 43°28N 4°42E **20** E6
Rhum *U.K.* 57°0N 6°20W **11** E2
Rhyl *U.K.* 53°20N 3°29W **12** D4
Riachão *Brazil* 7°20S 46°37W **93** E9
Riasi *India* 33°10N 74°50E **43** C6
Riau □ *Indonesia* 0°0 102°35E **36** E2
Riau, Kepulauan
  Indonesia 0°30N 104°20E **36** D2
Riau Arch. = Riau, Kepulauan
  Indonesia 0°30N 104°20E **36** D2
Ribadeo *Spain* 43°35N 7°5W **21** A2
Ribas do Rio Pardo
  Brazil 20°27S 53°46W **93** H8
Ribauè *Mozam.* 14°57S 38°17E **55** E4
Ribble → *U.K.* 53°52N 2°25W **12** D5
Ribe *Denmark* 55°19N 8°44E **9** J13
Ribeira Brava *Madeira* 32°41N 17°4W **24** D2
Ribeira Grande *C. Verde Is.* 17°0N 25°4W **50** b
Ribeirão Prêto *Brazil* 21°10S 47°50W **95** A6
Riberalta *Bolivia* 11°0S 66°0W **92** F5
Riccarton *N.Z.* 43°32S 172°37E **59** E4
Rice *U.S.A.* 34°5N 114°51W **79** L12
Rice L. *Canada* 44°12N 78°10W **82** B6
Rice Lake *U.S.A.* 45°30N 91°44W **80** C8
Rich, C. *Canada* 44°43N 80°38W **82** B4
Richards Bay *S. Africa* 28°48S 32°6E **57** D5
Richardson → *Canada* 58°25N 111°14W **71** B6
Richardson Lakes
  U.S.A. 44°46N 70°58W **81** C18
Richardson Springs
  U.S.A. 39°51N 121°46W **78** F5
Riche, C. *Australia* 34°36S 118°47E **61** F2
Richey *U.S.A.* 47°39N 105°4W **76** C11
Richfield *U.S.A.* 38°46N 112°5W **76** G7
Richfield Springs
  U.S.A. 42°51N 74°59W **83** D10
Richford *U.S.A.* 45°0N 72°40W **83** B12
Richibucto *Canada* 46°42N 64°54W **73** C7
Richland *Ga., U.S.A.* 32°5N 84°40W **85** E12
Richland *Wash., U.S.A.* 46°17N 119°18W **76** C4
Richland Center *U.S.A.* 43°21N 90°23W **80** D8
Richlands *U.S.A.* 37°6N 81°48W **81** G13
Richmond *Australia* 20°43S 143°8E **62** C3
Richmond *N.Z.* 41°20S 173°12E **59** D4
Richmond *U.K.* 54°25N 1°43W **12** C6
Richmond *Calif., U.S.A.* 37°56N 122°21W **78** H4
Richmond *Ind., U.S.A.* 39°50N 84°53W **81** F11
Richmond *Ky., U.S.A.* 37°45N 84°18W **81** G11
Richmond *Mich., U.S.A.* 42°49N 82°45W **82** D2
Richmond *Mo., U.S.A.* 39°17N 93°58W **80** F7
Richmond *Tex., U.S.A.* 29°35N 95°46W **84** G7
Richmond *Utah, U.S.A.* 41°56N 111°48W **76** F8
Richmond *Va., U.S.A.* 37°33N 77°27W **81** G15
Richmond Hill *Canada* 43°52N 79°27W **82** C5
Richmond Ra. *Australia* 29°0S 152°45E **63** D5
Richmondville *U.S.A.* 42°38N 74°33W **83** D10
Richtersveld △ *S. Africa* 28°15S 17°10E **56** D2
Richville *U.S.A.* 44°25N 75°23W **83** B9
Richwood *U.S.A.* 38°14N 80°32W **81** F13
Ridder = Leninogorsk
  Kazakhstan 50°20N 83°30E **28** D9
Riddlesburg *U.S.A.* 40°9N 78°15W **82** F6
Ridgecrest *U.S.A.* 35°38N 117°40W **79** K9
Ridgefield *Conn., U.S.A.* 41°17N 73°30W **83** E11
Ridgefield *Wash.,*
  U.S.A. 45°49N 122°45W **78** E4
Ridgeland *Miss., U.S.A.* 32°26N 90°8W **85** E9
Ridgeland *S.C., U.S.A.* 32°29N 80°59W **85** E14
Ridgetown *Canada* 42°26N 81°52W **82** D3
Ridgewood *U.S.A.* 40°59N 74°7W **83** F10
Ridgway *U.S.A.* 41°25N 78°44W **82** E6
Riding Mountain △
  Canada 50°50N 100°0W **71** C9
Ridley, Mt. *Australia* 33°12S 122°7E **61** F3
Riebeek-Oos *S. Africa* 33°10S 26°10E **56** E4
Ried *Austria* 48°14N 13°30E **16** D7
Riesa *Germany* 51°17N 13°17E **16** C7

Riet → *S. Africa* 29°0S 23°54E **56** D3
Rietbron *S. Africa* 32°54S 23°10E **56** E3
Rietfontein *Namibia* 21°58S 20°58E **56** C3
Rieti *Italy* 42°24N 12°51E **22** C5
Rif = Er Rif *Morocco* 35°1N 4°1W **50** A5
Riffe L. *U.S.A.* 46°32N 122°26W **78** D4
Rifle *U.S.A.* 39°32N 107°47W **76** G10
Rift Valley *Africa* 7°0N 30°0E **48** G7
Rift Valley □ *Kenya* 0°20N 36°0E **54** B4
Rīga *Latvia* 56°53N 24°8E **9** H21
Riga, G. of *Latvia* 57°40N 23°45E **9** H20
Rīgān *Iran* 28°37N 58°58E **45** D8
Rīgas Jūras Līcis = Riga, G. of
  Latvia 57°40N 23°45E **9** H20
Rigaud *Canada* 45°29N 74°18W **83** A10
Rigby *U.S.A.* 43°40N 111°55W **76** E8
Rīgestān *Afghan.* 30°15N 65°0E **40** D4
Riggins *U.S.A.* 45°25N 116°19W **76** D5
Rigolet *Canada* 54°10N 58°23W **73** B8
Rihand Dam *India* 24°9N 83°2E **43** H10
Riihimäki *Finland* 60°45N 24°48E **8** F21
Riiser-Larsen-halvøya
  Antarctica 68°0S 35°0E **5** C4
Riiser-Larsen Ice Shelf
  S. Ocean 74°0S 19°0W **5** D2
Riiser-Larsen Sea *S. Ocean* 67°30S 22°0E **5** C4
Rijeka *Croatia* 45°20N 14°21E **16** F8
Rijssen *Neths.* 52°19N 6°31E **15** B6
Rikuchū-Kaigan △
  Japan 39°20N 142°0E **30** E11
Rikuzentakada *Japan* 39°0N 141°40E **30** E10
Riley *U.S.A.* 43°32N 119°28W **76** E4
Rima → *Nigeria* 13°4N 5°10E **50** F7
Rimah, Wadi ar →
  Si. Arabia 26°5N 41°30E **44** E4
Rimau, Pulau *Malaysia* 5°15N 100°16E **39** c
Rimbey *Canada* 52°35N 114°15W **70** C6
Rimersburg *U.S.A.* 41°3N 79°30W **82** E5
Rímini *Italy* 44°3N 12°33E **22** B5
Rimouski *Canada* 48°27N 68°30W **73** C6
Rimrock *U.S.A.* 46°40N 121°7W **78** D5
Rinca *Indonesia* 8°45S 119°35E **37** F5
Rincón de Romos
  Mexico 22°14N 102°18W **86** C4
Rinconada *Argentina* 22°26S 66°10W **94** A2
Rind → *India* 25°53N 80°33E **43** G9
Ringas *India* 27°21N 75°34E **42** F6
Ringgold Is. *Fiji* 16°15S 179°25W **59** a
Ringkøbing *Denmark* 56°5N 8°15E **9** H13
Ringvassøya *Norway* 69°56N 19°15E **8** B18
Ringwood *U.S.A.* 41°7N 74°15W **83** E10
Rinjani *Indonesia* 8°24S 116°28E **36** F5
Rio Branco *Brazil* 9°58S 67°49W **92** E5
Río Branco *Uruguay* 32°40S 53°40W **95** C5
Río Bravo *Mexico* 25°59N 98°6W **87** B5
Río Bravo → *N. Amer.* 29°2N 102°45W **86** B4
Río Bravo del Norte →
  Mexico 25°57N 97°9W **87** B5
Rio Brilhante *Brazil* 21°48S 54°33W **95** A5
Rio Claro *Brazil* 22°19S 47°35W **95** A6
Rio Claro *Trin. & Tob.* 10°20N 61°25W **89** D7
Río Colorado *Argentina* 39°0S 64°0W **96** D4
Río Cuarto *Argentina* 33°10S 64°25W **94** C3
Rio das Pedras *Mozam.* 23°8S 35°28E **57** C6
Rio de Janeiro *Brazil* 22°54S 43°12W **95** A7
Rio de Janeiro □ *Brazil* 22°50S 43°0W **95** A7
Rio do Sul *Brazil* 27°13S 49°37W **95** B6
Río Dulce △ *Guatemala* 15°43N 88°50W **88** C2
Río Gallegos *Argentina* 51°35S 69°15W **96** G3
Río Grande *Argentina* 53°50S 67°45W **96** G3
Rio Grande *Brazil* 32°0S 52°20W **95** C5
Río Grande *Mexico* 23°50N 103°2W **86** C4
Río Grande *Puerto Rico* 18°23N 65°50W **89** d
Río Grande → *N. Amer.* 25°58N 97°9W **84** J6
Rio Grande City *U.S.A.* 26°23N 98°49W **84** H5
Río Grande de Santiago →
  Mexico 21°36N 105°26W **86** C3
Rio Grande do Norte □
  Brazil 5°40S 36°0W **93** E11
Rio Grande do Sul □
  Brazil 30°0S 53°0W **95** C5
Río Hato *Panama* 8°22N 80°10W **88** E3
Río Lagartos *Mexico* 21°36N 88°10W **87** C7
Rio Largo *Brazil* 9°28S 35°50W **93** E11
Río Mulatos *Bolivia* 19°40S 66°50W **92** G5
Río Muni □ *Eq. Guin.* 1°30N 10°0E **52** D2
Río Negro *Brazil* 26°0S 49°55W **95** B6
Río Pardo *Brazil* 30°0S 52°30W **95** C5
Río Pilcomayo △
  Argentina 25°5S 58°5W **94** B4
Río Platano △ *Honduras* 15°45N 85°0W **88** C3
Río Rancho *U.S.A.* 35°14N 106°41W **77** J10
Río Segundo *Argentina* 31°40S 63°59W **94** C3
Río Tercero *Argentina* 32°15S 64°8W **94** C3
Rio Verde *Brazil* 17°50S 51°0W **93** G8
Río Verde *Mexico* 21°56N 99°59W **87** C5
Rio Vista *U.S.A.* 38°10N 121°42W **78** G5
Ríobamba *Ecuador* 1°50S 78°45W **92** D3
Ríohacha *Colombia* 11°33N 72°55W **92** A4
Ríosucio *Colombia* 7°27N 77°7W **92** B3
Riou L. *Canada* 59°7N 106°25W **71** B7
Ripley *Canada* 44°4N 81°35W **82** B3
Ripley *Calif., U.S.A.* 33°32N 114°39W **79** M12
Ripley *N.Y., U.S.A.* 42°16N 79°43W **82** D5
Ripley *Tenn., U.S.A.* 35°45N 89°32W **85** D10
Ripley *W. Va., U.S.A.* 38°49N 81°43W **81** F13
Ripon *U.K.* 54°9N 1°31W **12** C6
Ripon *Calif., U.S.A.* 37°44N 121°7W **78** H5
Ripon *Wis., U.S.A.* 43°51N 88°50W **80** D9
Rishâ', W. ar → *Si. Arabia* 25°33N 44°5E **44** E5
Rishiri-Rebun-Sarobetsu △
  Japan 45°26N 141°30E **30** B10
Rishiri-Tō *Japan* 45°11N 141°15E **30** B10
Rishon le Ziyyon *Israel* 31°58N 34°48E **46** D3
Rison *U.S.A.* 33°58N 92°11W **84** E8
Risør *Norway* 58°43N 9°13E **9** G13
Rita Blanca Cr. →
  U.S.A. 35°40N 102°29W **84** D3

Ritter, Mt. *U.S.A.* 37°41N 119°12W **78** H7
Rittman *U.S.A.* 40°58N 81°47W **82** F3
Ritzville *U.S.A.* 47°8N 118°23W **76** C4
Riva del Garda *Italy* 45°53N 10°50E **22** B4
Rivadavia *B. Aires,*
　Argentina 35°29S 62°59W **94** D3
Rivadavia *Mendoza,*
　Argentina 33°13S 68°30W **94** C2
Rivadavia *Salta, Argentina* 24°5S 62°54W **94** A3
Rivadavia *Chile* 29°57S 70°35W **94** B1
Rivas *Nic.* 11°30N 85°50W **88** D2
Rivash *Iran* 35°28N 58°26E **45** C8
River Cess *Liberia* 5°30N 9°32W **50** G4
River Jordan *Canada* 48°26N 124°3W **78** B2
Rivera *Argentina* 37°12S 63°14W **94** D3
Rivera *Uruguay* 31°0S 55°50W **95** C4
Riverbank *U.S.A.* 37°44N 120°56W **78** H6
Riverdale *U.S.A.* 36°26N 119°52W **78** J7
Riverhead *U.S.A.* 40°55N 72°40W **83** F12
Riverhurst *Canada* 50°55N 106°50W **71** C7
Rivers *Canada* 50°2N 100°14W **71** C8
Rivers Inlet *Canada* 51°42N 127°15W **70** C3
Riversdale *Canada* 44°5N 81°20W **82** B3
Riversdale *S. Africa* 34°7S 21°15E **56** E3
Riverside *U.S.A.* 33°59N 117°22W **79** M9
Riverton *Australia* 34°10S 138°46E **63** E2
Riverton *Canada* 51°1N 97°0W **71** C9
Riverton *N.Z.* 46°21S 168°0E **59** G2
Riverton *U.S.A.* 43°2N 108°23W **76** E9
Riviera *U.S.A.* 35°4N 114°35W **79** K12
Riviera di Levante *Italy* 44°15N 9°30E **20** D8
Riviera di Ponente *Italy* 44°10N 8°20E **20** D8
Rivière-au-Renard
　Canada 48°59N 64°23W **73** C7
Rivière-du-Loup *Canada* 47°50N 69°30W **73** C6
Rivière-Pentecôte *Canada* 49°57N 67°1W **73** C6
Rivière-Pilote *Martinique* 14°26N 60°53W **88** c
Rivière St-Paul *Canada* 51°28N 57°45W **73** B8
Rivière-Salée *Martinique* 14°31N 61°0W **88** c
Rivne *Ukraine* 50°40N 26°10E **17** C14
Rívoli *Italy* 45°3N 7°31E **20** D7
Rivoli B. *Australia* 37°32S 140°3E **63** F3
Riyadh = Ar Riyāḍ
　Si. Arabia 24°41N 46°42E **44** E5
Riyadh al Khabrā'
　Si. Arabia 26°2N 43°33E **44** E4
Rize *Turkey* 41°0N 40°30E **19** F7
Rizhao *China* 35°25N 119°30E **35** G10
Rizokarpaso *Cyprus* 35°36N 34°23E **25** D13
Rizzuto, C. *Italy* 38°53N 17°5E **22** E7
Rjukan *Norway* 59°54N 8°33E **9** G13
Road Town *Br. Virgin Is.* 18°27N 64°37W **89** e
Roan Plateau *U.S.A.* 39°20N 109°20W **76** G9
Roanne *France* 46°3N 4°4E **20** C6
Roanoke *Ala., U.S.A.* 33°9N 85°22W **85** E12
Roanoke *Va., U.S.A.* 37°16N 79°56W **81** G14
Roanoke → *U.S.A.* 35°57N 76°42W **85** D16
Roanoke I. *U.S.A.* 35°53N 75°39W **85** D17
Roanoke Rapids *U.S.A.* 36°28N 77°40W **85** C16
Roatán *Honduras* 16°18N 86°35W **88** C2
Robât Sang *Iran* 35°35N 59°10E **45** C8
Robāṭkarīm *Iran* 35°25N 50°59E **45** C6
Robbins I. *Australia* 40°42S 145°0E **63** G4
Robe → *Australia* 21°42S 116°15E **60** D2
Robert Bourassa, Rés.
　Canada 53°40N 76°55W **72** B4
Robert Lee *U.S.A.* 31°54N 100°29W **84** F4
Robertsdale *U.S.A.* 40°11N 78°6W **82** F6
Robertson *S. Africa* 33°46S 19°50E **56** E2
Robertson I. *Antarctica* 65°15S 59°30W **5** C18
Robertson Ra. *Australia* 23°15S 121°0E **60** D3
Robertstown *Australia* 33°58S 139°5E **63** E2
Roberval *Canada* 48°32N 72°15W **73** C5
Robeson Chan. *N. Amer.* 82°0N 61°30W **4** A4
Robesonia *U.S.A.* 40°21N 76°8W **83** F8
Robinson *U.S.A.* 39°0N 87°44W **80** F10
Robinson → *Australia* 16°3S 137°16E **62** B2
Robinson Crusoe I.
　Pac. Oc. 33°38S 78°52W **90** F2
Robinson Ra. *Australia* 25°40S 119°0E **61** E2
Robinvale *Australia* 34°40S 142°45E **63** E3
Roblin *Canada* 51°14N 101°21W **71** C8
Roboré *Bolivia* 18°10S 59°45W **92** G7
Robson, Mt. *Canada* 53°10N 119°10W **70** C5
Robstown *U.S.A.* 27°47N 97°40W **84** H6
Roca, C. da *Portugal* 38°40N 9°31W **21** C1
Roca Partida, I. *Mexico* 19°1N 112°2W **86** D2
Rocas, I. *Brazil* 4°0S 34°1W **93** D12
Rocha *Uruguay* 34°30S 54°25W **95** C5
Rochdale *U.K.* 53°38N 2°9W **12** D5
Rochefort *Belgium* 50°9N 5°12E **15** D5
Rochefort *France* 45°56N 0°57W **20** D3
Rochelle *U.S.A.* 41°56N 89°4W **80** E9
Rocher River *Canada* 61°23N 112°44W **70** A6
Rochester *U.K.* 51°23N 0°31E **13** F8
Rochester *Ind., U.S.A.* 41°4N 86°13W **80** E10
Rochester *Minn., U.S.A.* 44°1N 92°28W **80** C7
Rochester *N.H., U.S.A.* 43°18N 70°59W **83** C14
Rochester *N.Y., U.S.A.* 43°10N 77°37W **82** C7
Rock → *Canada* 60°7N 127°7W **70** A3
Rock, The *Australia* 35°15S 147°2E **63** F4
Rock Creek *U.S.A.* 41°40N 80°52W **82** E4
Rock Falls *U.S.A.* 41°47N 89°41W **80** E9
Rock Hill *U.S.A.* 34°56N 81°1W **85** D14
Rock Island *U.S.A.* 41°30N 90°34W **80** E8
Rock Port *U.S.A.* 40°25N 95°31W **80** E6
Rock Rapids *U.S.A.* 43°26N 96°10W **80** D6
Rock Sound *Bahamas* 24°54N 76°12W **88** B4
Rock Springs *Mont.,*
　U.S.A. 46°49N 106°15W **76** C10
Rock Springs *Wyo.,*
　U.S.A. 41°35N 109°14W **76** F9
Rock Valley *U.S.A.* 43°12N 96°18W **80** D5
Rockall *Atl. Oc.* 57°37N 13°42W **6** D3
Rockdale *Tex., U.S.A.* 30°39N 97°0W **84** F6
Rockdale *Wash., U.S.A.* 47°22N 121°28W **78** C5

Rockeby = Mungkan Kandju △
　Australia 13°35S 142°52E **62** A3
Rockefeller Plateau
　Antarctica 76°0S 130°0W **5** E14
Rockford *U.S.A.* 42°16N 89°6W **80** D9
Rockglen *Canada* 49°11N 105°57W **71** D7
Rockhampton *Australia* 23°22S 150°32E **62** C5
Rockingham *Australia* 32°15S 115°38E **61** F2
Rockingham *N.C.,*
　U.S.A. 34°57N 79°46W **85** D15
Rockingham *Vt.,*
　U.S.A. 43°11N 72°29W **83** C12
Rockingham B. *Australia* 18°5S 146°10E **62** B4
Rocklake *U.S.A.* 48°47N 99°15W **80** A4
Rockland *Canada* 45°33N 75°17W **83** A9
Rockland *Idaho, U.S.A.* 42°34N 112°53W **76** E7
Rockland *Maine, U.S.A.* 44°6N 69°7W **81** C19
Rockland *Mich., U.S.A.* 46°44N 89°11W **80** B9
Rocklin *U.S.A.* 38°48N 121°14W **78** G5
Rockly B. *Trin. & Tob.* 11°9N 60°46W **93** J16
Rockmart *U.S.A.* 34°0N 85°3W **85** D12
Rockport *Mass., U.S.A.* 42°39N 70°37W **83** D14
Rockport *Tex., U.S.A.* 28°2N 97°3W **84** G6
Rocksprings *U.S.A.* 30°1N 100°13W **84** F4
Rockville *Conn., U.S.A.* 41°52N 72°28W **83** E12
Rockville *Md., U.S.A.* 39°5N 77°9W **81** F15
Rockwall *U.S.A.* 32°56N 96°28W **84** E6
Rockwell City *U.S.A.* 42°24N 94°38W **80** D7
Rockwood *Canada* 43°37N 80°8W **82** C4
Rockwood *Maine,*
　U.S.A. 45°41N 69°45W **81** C19
Rockwood *Tenn.,*
　U.S.A. 35°52N 84°41W **85** D12
Rocky Ford *U.S.A.* 38°3N 103°43W **76** G12
Rocky Gully *Australia* 34°30S 116°57E **61** F2
Rocky Harbour *Canada* 49°36N 57°55W **73** C8
Rocky Island L. *Canada* 46°55N 83°0W **72** C3
Rocky Lane *Canada* 58°31N 116°22W **70** B5
Rocky Mount *U.S.A.* 35°57N 77°48W **85** D16
Rocky Mountain △
　U.S.A. 48°0N 105°45W **76** F11
Rocky Mountain House
　Canada 52°22N 114°55W **70** C6
Rocky Mts. *N. Amer.* 49°0N 115°0W **76** B6
Rocky Point *Namibia* 19°3S 12°30E **56** B2
Rod *Pakistan* 28°10N 63°5E **40** E3
Roda *Greece* 39°48N 19°46E **25** A3
Rødbyhavn *Denmark* 54°39N 11°22E **9** J14
Roddickton *Canada* 50°51N 56°8W **73** B8
Rodez *France* 44°21N 2°33E **20** D5
Ródhos = Rhodes
　Greece 36°15N 28°10E **25** C10
Rodia *Greece* 35°22N 25°1E **25** D7
Rodney *Canada* 42°34N 81°41W **82** D3
Rodney, C. *N.Z.* 36°17S 174°50E **59** B5
Rodopos *Greece* 35°34N 23°45E **25** D5
Rodriguez *Ind. Oc.* 19°45S 63°20E **3** E13
Roe → *U.K.* 55°6N 6°59W **10** A5
Roebling *U.S.A.* 40°7N 74°47W **83** F10
Roebourne *Australia* 20°44S 117°9E **60** D2
Roebuck B. *Australia* 18°5S 122°20E **60** C3
Roermond *Neths.* 51°12N 6°0E **15** C6
Roes Welcome Sd.
　Canada 65°0N 87°0W **69** C11
Roeselare *Belgium* 50°57N 3°7E **15** D3
Rogachev = Ragachow
　Belarus 53°8N 30°5E **17** B16
Rogagua, L. *Bolivia* 13°43S 66°50W **92** F5
Rogatyn *Ukraine* 49°24N 24°36E **17** D13
Rogers *U.S.A.* 36°20N 94°7W **84** C7
Rogers City *U.S.A.* 45°25N 83°49W **81** C12
Rogersville *Canada* 46°44N 65°26W **73** C6
Roggan → *Canada* 54°24N 79°25W **72** B4
Roggan L. *Canada* 54°8N 77°50W **72** B4
Roggeveen Basin
　Pac. Oc. 31°30S 95°30W **65** L18
Roggeveldberge *S. Africa* 32°10S 20°10E **56** E3
Rogoaguado, L. *Bolivia* 13°0S 65°30W **92** F5
Rogojampi *Indonesia* 8°19S 114°17E **37** J17
Rogue → *U.S.A.* 42°26N 124°26W **76** E1
Rohnert Park *U.S.A.* 38°16N 122°40W **78** G4
Rohri *Pakistan* 27°45N 68°51E **42** F3
Rohri Canal *Pakistan* 26°15N 68°27E **42** F3
Rohtak *India* 28°55N 76°43E **42** E7
Roi Et *Thailand* 16°4N 103°40E **38** D4
Roja *Latvia* 57°29N 22°43E **9** H20
Rojas *Argentina* 34°10S 60°45W **94** C3
Rojo, C. *Mexico* 21°33N 97°20W **87** C5
Rokan → *Indonesia* 2°0N 100°50E **36** D2
Rokiškis *Lithuania* 55°55N 25°35E **9** J21
Rolândia *Brazil* 23°18S 51°23W **95** A5
Rolla *Mo., U.S.A.* 37°57N 91°46W **80** G8
Rolla *N. Dak., U.S.A.* 48°52N 99°37W **80** A4
Rolleston *Australia* 24°28S 148°35E **62** C4
Rollingstone *Australia* 19°2S 146°24E **62** B4
Roma *Australia* 26°32S 148°49E **63** D4
Roma *Italy* 41°54N 12°28E **22** D5
Roma *Sweden* 57°32N 18°26E **9** H18
Roma-Los Saenz *U.S.A.* 26°24N 99°1W **84** H5
Romain, C. *U.S.A.* 33°0N 79°22W **85** E15
Romaine → *Canada* 50°18N 63°47W **73** B7
Roman *Romania* 46°57N 26°55E **17** E14
Romang *Indonesia* 7°30S 127°20E **37** F7
Români *Egypt* 30°59N 32°38E **46** E1
Romania ■ *Europe* 46°0N 25°0E **17** F12
Romano, Cayo *Cuba* 22°0N 77°30W **88** B4
Romans-sur-Isère *France* 45°3N 5°3E **20** D6
Romblon *Phil.* 12°33N 122°17E **37** B6
Rome = Roma *Italy* 41°54N 12°28E **22** D5
Rome *Ga., U.S.A.* 34°15N 85°10W **85** D12
Rome *N.Y., U.S.A.* 43°13N 75°27W **83** C9
Rome *Pa., U.S.A.* 41°51N 76°21W **83** E8
Romney *U.S.A.* 39°21N 78°45W **81** F14
Romney Marsh *U.K.* 51°2N 0°54E **13** F8
Rømø *Denmark* 55°10N 8°30E **9** J13
Romorantin-Lanthenay
　France 47°21N 1°45E **20** C4

Romsdalen *Norway* 62°25N 7°52E **8** E12
Romsey *U.K.* 51°0N 1°29W **13** G6
Ron *Vietnam* 17°53N 106°27E **38** D6
Rona *U.K.* 57°34N 5°59W **11** D3
Ronan *U.S.A.* 47°32N 114°6W **76** C6
Roncador, Cayos
　Colombia 13°32N 80°4W **88** D3
Roncador, Serra do
　Brazil 12°30S 52°30W **93** F8
Ronda *Spain* 36°46N 5°12W **21** D3
Rondane *Norway* 61°57N 9°50E **8** F13
Rondônia □ *Brazil* 11°0S 63°0W **92** F6
Rondonópolis *Brazil* 16°28S 54°38W **93** G8
Rondu *Pakistan* 35°32N 75°10E **43** B6
Rong, Koh *Cambodia* 10°45N 103°15E **39** G4
Ronge, L. la *Canada* 55°6N 105°17W **71** B7
Ronne *Denmark* 55°6N 14°43E **9** J16
Ronne Ice Shelf
　Antarctica 77°30S 60°0W **5** D18
Ronsard, C. *Australia* 24°46S 113°10E **61** E1
Ronse *Belgium* 50°45N 3°35E **15** D3
Roodepoort *S. Africa* 26°11S 27°54E **57** D4
Roof Butte *U.S.A.* 36°28N 109°5W **77** H9
Rooiboklaagte →
　Namibia 20°50S 21°0E **56** C3
Rooniu, Mt. *Tahiti* 17°49S 149°12W **59** d
Roorkee *India* 29°52N 77°59E **42** E7
Roosendaal *Neths.* 51°32N 4°29E **15** C4
Roosevelt *U.S.A.* 40°18N 109°59W **76** F9
Roosevelt → *Brazil* 7°35S 60°20W **92** E6
Roosevelt, Mt. *Canada* 58°26N 125°20W **70** B3
Roosevelt I. *Antarctica* 79°30S 162°0W **5** D12
Roper → *Australia* 14°43S 135°27E **62** A2
Roper Bar *Australia* 14°44S 134°44E **62** A1
Roque Pérez *Argentina* 35°25S 59°24W **94** D4
Roquetas de Mar *Spain* 36°46N 2°36W **21** D4
Roraima □ *Brazil* 2°0N 61°30W **92** C6
Roraima, Mt. *Venezuela* 5°10N 60°40W **92** B6
Røros *Norway* 62°35N 11°23E **8** E14
Rosa *Zambia* 9°33S 31°15E **55** D3
Rosa, Monte *Europe* 45°57N 7°53E **20** D7
Rosalia *U.S.A.* 47°14N 117°22W **76** C5
Rosamond *U.S.A.* 34°52N 118°10W **79** L8
Rosario *Argentina* 33°0S 60°40W **94** C3
Rosário *Brazil* 3°0S 44°15W **93** D10
Rosario *Baja Calif.,*
　Mexico 30°0N 115°50W **86** B1
Rosario *Sinaloa, Mexico* 22°58N 105°53W **86** C3
Rosario *Paraguay* 24°30S 57°35W **94** A4
Rosario de la Frontera
　Argentina 25°50S 65°0W **94** B3
Rosario de Lerma
　Argentina 24°59S 65°35W **94** A2
Rosario del Tala
　Argentina 32°20S 59°10W **94** C4
Rosário do Sul *Brazil* 30°15S 54°55W **95** C5
Rosarito *Mexico* 32°20N 117°2W **79** N9
Roscoe *U.S.A.* 41°56N 74°55W **83** E10
Roscommon *Ireland* 53°38N 8°11W **10** C3
Roscommon □ *Ireland* 53°49N 8°23W **10** C3
Roscrea *Ireland* 52°57N 7°49W **10** D4
Rose → *Australia* 14°16S 135°45E **62** A2
Rose, L. *Bahamas* 21°0N 73°30W **89** B5
Rose Belle *Mauritius* 20°24S 57°36E **53** d
Rose Blanche *Canada* 47°38N 58°45W **73** C8
Rose Hill *Mauritius* 20°14S 57°27E **53** d
Rose Pt. *Canada* 54°11N 131°39W **70** C2
Rose Valley *Canada* 52°19N 103°49W **71** C8
Roseau *Dominica* 15°17N 61°24W **89** C7
Roseau *U.S.A.* 48°51N 95°46W **80** A6
Rosebery *Australia* 41°46S 145°33E **63** G4
Rosebud *S. Dak., U.S.A.* 43°14N 100°51W **80** D3
Rosebud *Tex., U.S.A.* 31°4N 96°59W **84** F6
Roseburg *U.S.A.* 43°13N 123°20W **76** E2
Rosedale *U.S.A.* 33°51N 91°2W **85** E9
Rosehearty *U.K.* 57°42N 2°7W **11** D6
Roseires Res. *Sudan* 11°51N 34°23E **51** F12
Rosemary *Canada* 50°46N 112°5W **70** C6
Rosenberg *U.S.A.* 29°34N 95°49W **84** G7
Rosenheim *Germany* 47°51N 12°7E **16** E7
Roses, G. de *Spain* 42°10N 3°15E **21** A7
Rosetown *Canada* 51°35N 107°59W **71** C7
Roseville *Calif., U.S.A.* 38°45N 121°17W **78** G5
Roseville *Mich., U.S.A.* 42°30N 82°56W **82** D2
Roseville *Pa., U.S.A.* 41°51N 76°57W **83** E8
Rosewood *Australia* 27°38S 152°36E **63** D5
Roshkhvār *Iran* 34°58N 59°37E **45** C8
Rosignano Maríttimo
　Italy 43°24N 10°28E **22** C4
Rosignol *Guyana* 6°15N 57°30W **92** B7
Roșiori de Vede *Romania* 44°9N 25°0E **17** F13
Roskilde *Denmark* 55°38N 12°3E **9** J15
Roslavl *Russia* 53°57N 32°55E **18** D5
Rosmead *S. Africa* 31°29S 25°8E **56** E4
Ross *Australia* 42°2S 147°30E **63** G4
Ross *N.Z.* 42°53S 170°49E **59** E3
Ross Dependency
　Antarctica 76°0S 170°0W **5** D12
Ross I. *Antarctica* 77°30S 168°0E **5** D11
Ross Ice Shelf *Antarctica* 80°0S 180°0E **5** E12
Ross L. *U.S.A.* 48°44N 121°4W **78** B5
Ross-on-Wye *U.K.* 51°54N 2°34W **13** F5
Ross River *Australia* 23°44S 134°30E **62** C1
Ross River *Canada* 62°30N 131°30W **70** A2
Ross Sea *Antarctica* 74°0S 178°0E **5** D11
Rossall Pt. *U.K.* 53°55N 3°3W **12** D4
Rossan Pt. *Ireland* 54°42N 8°47W **10** B3
Rossano *Italy* 39°36N 16°39E **22** E7
Rossburn *Canada* 50°40N 100°49W **71** C8
Rosseau *Canada* 45°16N 79°39W **82** A5
Rosseau, L. *Canada* 45°10N 79°35W **82** A5
Rosses, The *Ireland* 55°2N 8°20W **10** A3
Rossignol, L. *Canada* 52°43N 73°40W **72** B5
Rossignol L. *Canada* 44°12N 65°10W **73** D6
Rossiya = Russia ■
　Eurasia 62°0N 105°0E **29** C11

Rossland *Canada* 49°6N 117°50W **70** D5
Rosslare *Ireland* 52°17N 6°24W **10** D5
Rosslare Harbour *Ireland* 52°15N 6°20W **10** D5
Rossmore *Canada* 44°8N 77°23W **82** B7
Rosso *Mauritania* 16°40N 15°45W **50** E2
Rossosh *Russia* 50°15N 39°28E **19** D6
Røssvatnet *Norway* 65°45N 14°5E **8** D16
Rosthern *Canada* 52°40N 106°20W **71** C7
Rostock *Germany* 54°5N 12°8E **16** A7
Rostov *Don, Russia* 47°15N 39°45E **19** E6
Rostov *Yaroslavl, Russia* 57°14N 39°25E **18** C6
Roswell *Ga., U.S.A.* 34°2N 84°22W **85** D12
Roswell *N. Mex.,*
　U.S.A. 33°24N 104°32W **77** K11
Rotan *U.S.A.* 32°51N 100°28W **84** E4
Rother → *U.K.* 50°59N 0°45E **13** G8
Rothera *Antarctica* 67°34S 68°8W **5** C17
Rotherham *U.K.* 53°26N 1°20W **12** D6
Rothes *U.K.* 57°32N 3°13W **11** D5
Rothesay *Canada* 45°23N 66°0W **73** C6
Rothesay *U.K.* 55°50N 5°3W **11** F3
Roti *Indonesia* 10°50S 123°0E **37** F6
Roto *Australia* 33°0S 145°30E **63** E4
Rotondo, Mte. *France* 42°14N 9°8E **20** E8
Rotoroa, L. *N.Z.* 41°55S 172°39E **59** D4
Rotorua *N.Z.* 38°9S 176°16E **59** C6
Rotorua, L. *N.Z.* 38°5S 176°18E **59** C6
Rotterdam *Neths.* 51°55N 4°30E **15** C4
Rotterdam *U.S.A.* 42°48N 74°1W **83** D10
Rottnest I. *Australia* 32°0S 115°27E **61** F2
Rottumeroog *Neths.* 53°33N 6°34E **15** A6
Rottweil *Germany* 48°9N 8°37E **16** D5
Rotuma *Fiji* 12°25S 177°5E **58** C10
Roubaix *France* 50°40N 3°10E **20** A5
Rouen *France* 49°27N 1°4E **20** B4
Rouleau *Canada* 50°10N 104°56W **71** C8
Round I. *Mauritius* 19°51S 57°45E **53** d
Round Mountain
　U.S.A. 38°43N 117°4W **76** G5
Round Mt. *Australia* 30°26S 152°16E **63** E5
Round Rock *U.S.A.* 30°31N 97°41W **84** F6
Roundup *U.S.A.* 46°27N 108°33W **76** C9
Rousay *U.K.* 59°10N 3°2W **11** B5
Rouses Point *U.S.A.* 44°59N 73°22W **83** B11
Rouseville *U.S.A.* 41°28N 79°42W **82** E5
Roussillon *France* 42°30N 2°35E **20** E5
Rouxville *S. Africa* 30°25S 26°50E **56** E4
Rouyn-Noranda *Canada* 48°20N 79°0W **72** C4
Rovaniemi *Finland* 66°29N 25°41E **8** C21
Rovereto *Italy* 45°53N 11°3E **22** B4
Rovigo *Italy* 45°4N 11°47E **22** B4
Rovinj *Croatia* 45°5N 13°40E **16** F7
Rovno = Rivne *Ukraine* 50°40N 26°10E **17** C14
Rovuma = Ruvuma →
　Tanzania 10°29S 40°28E **55** E5
Row'ān *Iran* 35°8N 48°51E **45** C6
Rowena *Australia* 29°48S 148°55E **63** D4
Rowley Shoals *Australia* 17°30S 119°0E **60** C2
Roxas *Phil.* 11°36N 122°49E **37** B6
Roxboro *U.S.A.* 36°24N 78°59W **85** C15
Roxborough
　Trin. & Tob. 11°15N 60°35W **93** J16
Roxburgh *N.Z.* 45°33S 169°19E **59** F2
Roxburgh *U.S.A.* 54°11N 131°39W **70** C2
Roxby Downs *Australia* 30°43S 136°46E **63** E2
Roy *Mont., U.S.A.* 47°20N 108°58W **76** C9
Roy *N. Mex., U.S.A.* 35°57N 104°12W **77** J11
Roy *Utah, U.S.A.* 41°10N 112°2W **76** F7
Royal Bardia △ *Nepal* 28°20N 81°20E **43** E9
Royal Canal *Ireland* 53°30N 7°13W **10** C4
Royal Chitawan △
　Nepal 26°30N 84°30E **43** F11
Royal Leamington Spa
　U.K. 52°18N 1°31W **13** E6
Royal Natal △ *S. Africa* 28°43S 28°51E **57** D4
Royal Tunbridge Wells
　U.K. 51°7N 0°16E **13** F8
Royale, Isle *U.S.A.* 48°0N 88°54W **80** B9
Royan *France* 45°37N 1°2W **20** D3
Royston *U.K.* 52°3N 0°0 **13** E7
Rozdilna *Ukraine* 46°50N 30°2E **17** E16
Rozhyshche *Ukraine* 50°54N 25°15E **17** C13
Rtishchevo *Russia* 52°18N 43°46E **18** D7
Ruacaná *Namibia* 17°20S 14°12E **56** B1
Ruaha △ *Tanzania* 7°41S 34°30E **54** D3
Ruahine Ra. *N.Z.* 39°55S 176°2E **59** C6
Ruapehu *N.Z.* 39°17S 175°35E **59** C5
Ruapuke I. *N.Z.* 46°46S 168°31E **59** G2
Ruâq, W. → *Egypt* 30°30N 33°49E **46** F2
Rub' al Khālī *Si. Arabia* 19°0N 48°0E **47** D4
Rubeho Mts. *Tanzania* 6°50S 36°25E **54** D4
Rubh a' Mhail *U.K.* 55°56N 6°8W **11** F2
Rubha Hunish *U.K.* 57°42N 6°20W **11** D2
Rubha Robhanais = Lewis, Butt of
　U.K. 58°31N 6°16W **11** C2
Rubicon → *U.S.A.* 38°53N 121°4W **78** G5
Rubio *Venezuela* 7°43N 72°22W **92** B4
Rubondo △ *Tanzania* 2°18S 31°58E **54** C3
Rubtsovsk *Russia* 51°30N 81°10E **28** D9
Ruby L. *U.S.A.* 40°10N 115°28W **76** F6
Ruby Mts. *U.S.A.* 40°30N 115°20W **76** F6
Rudall *Australia* 33°43S 136°17E **63** E2
Rudall → *Australia* 22°34S 122°13E **60** D3
Rudall River △
　Australia 22°38S 122°30E **60** D3
Rudbar *Iran* 36°48N 49°23E **45** B6
Rudewa *Tanzania* 10°7S 34°40E **55** E3
Rudnyy *Kazakhstan* 52°57N 63°7E **28** D7
Rudolfa, Ostrov *Russia* 81°45N 58°30E **28** A6
Rudyard *U.S.A.* 46°14N 84°36W **81** B11
Ruenya → *Africa* 16°24S 33°48E **55** F3
Ruffling Pt. *Br. Virgin Is.* 18°44N 64°27W **89** e

Rufiji → *Tanzania* 7°50S 39°15E **54** D4
Rufino *Argentina* 34°20S 62°50W **94** C3
Rufunsa *Zambia* 15°4S 29°34E **55** F2
Rugby *U.K.* 52°23N 1°16W **13** E6
Rugby *U.S.A.* 48°22N 100°0W **80** A4
Rügen *Germany* 54°22N 13°24E **16** A7
Ruhengeri *Rwanda* 1°30S 29°36E **54** C2
Ruhnu *Estonia* 57°48N 23°15E **9** H20
Ruhr → *Germany* 51°27N 6°43E **16** C4
Ruhuhu → *Tanzania* 10°31S 34°34E **55** E3
Ruidoso *U.S.A.* 33°20N 105°41W **77** K11
Ruivo, Pico *Madeira* 32°45N 16°56W **24** D3
Rujm Tal'at al Jamā'ah
　Jordan 30°24N 35°30E **46** E4
Ruk *Pakistan* 27°50N 68°42E **42** F3
Rukhla *Pakistan* 32°27N 71°57E **42** C4
Ruki →
　Dem. Rep. of the Congo 0°5N 18°17E **52** E3
Rukwa □ *Tanzania* 7°0S 31°30E **54** D3
Rukwa, L. *Tanzania* 8°0S 32°20E **54** D3
Rulhieres, C. *Australia* 13°56S 127°22E **60** B4
Rum = Rhum *U.K.* 57°0N 6°20W **11** E2
Rum *Jordan* 29°39N 35°26E **46** F4
Rum Cay *Bahamas* 23°40N 74°58W **89** B5
Rum Jungle *Australia* 13°0S 130°59E **60** B5
Ruma △ *Kenya* 0°39S 34°18E **54** C3
Rumāḥ *Si. Arabia* 25°29N 47°10E **44** E5
Rumania = Romania ■
　Europe 46°0N 25°0E **17** F12
Rumaylah *Iraq* 30°47N 47°37E **44** D5
Rumbêk *Sudan* 6°54N 29°37E **51** G11
Rumford *U.S.A.* 44°33N 70°33W **83** B14
Rumia *Poland* 54°37N 18°25E **17** A10
Rumoi *Japan* 43°56N 141°39E **30** C10
Rumonge *Burundi* 3°59S 29°26E **54** C2
Rumson *U.S.A.* 40°23N 74°0W **83** F11
Rumuruti *Kenya* 0°17N 36°32E **54** B4
Runan *China* 33°0N 114°30E **34** H8
Runanga *N.Z.* 42°25S 171°15E **59** E3
Runaway, C. *N.Z.* 37°32S 177°59E **59** B6
Runaway Bay *Jamaica* 18°27N 77°20W **88** a
Runcorn *U.K.* 53°21N 2°44W **12** D5
Rundu *Namibia* 17°52S 19°43E **56** B2
Rungwa *Tanzania* 6°55S 33°32E **54** D3
Rungwa → *Tanzania* 7°36S 31°50E **54** D3
Rungwa △ *Tanzania* 6°53S 34°2E **54** D3
Rungwe *Tanzania* 9°11S 33°32E **55** D3
Rungwe, Mt. *Tanzania* 9°8S 33°40E **52** F6
Runton Ra. *Australia* 23°31S 123°6E **60** D3
Ruo Shui → *China* 41°0N 100°16E **32** B5
Ruokolahti *Finland* 61°17N 28°50E **8** F23
Ruoqiang *China* 38°55N 88°10E **32** C6
Rupa *India* 27°15N 92°21E **41** F18
Rupar *India* 31°2N 76°38E **42** D7
Rupat *Indonesia* 1°45N 101°40E **36** D2
Rupen → *India* 23°28N 71°31E **42** H4
Rupert *U.S.A.* 42°37N 113°41W **76** E7
Rupert → *Canada* 51°29N 78°45W **72** B4
Rupert B. *Canada* 51°35N 79°0W **72** B4
Rupert House = Waskaganish
　Canada 51°30N 78°40W **72** B4
Rupsa *India* 21°37N 87°1E **43** J12
Rurrenabaque *Bolivia* 14°30S 67°32W **92** F5
Rusambo *Zimbabwe* 16°30S 32°4E **55** F3
Rusape *Zimbabwe* 18°35S 32°8E **55** F3
Ruschuk = Ruse
　Bulgaria 43°48N 25°59E **23** C12
Ruse *Bulgaria* 43°48N 25°59E **23** C12
Rush *Ireland* 53°31N 6°6W **10** C5
Rushan *China* 36°56N 121°30E **35** F11
Rushden *U.K.* 52°18N 0°35W **13** E7
Rushmore, Mt. *U.S.A.* 43°53N 103°28W **80** D2
Rushville *Ill., U.S.A.* 40°7N 90°34W **80** E8
Rushville *Ind., U.S.A.* 39°37N 85°27W **81** F11
Rushville *Nebr., U.S.A.* 42°43N 102°28W **80** D2
Russas *Brazil* 4°55S 37°50W **93** D11
Russell *Canada* 50°50N 101°20W **71** C8
Russell *Kans., U.S.A.* 38°54N 98°52W **80** F4
Russell *N.Y., U.S.A.* 44°27N 75°9W **83** B9
Russell *Pa., U.S.A.* 41°56N 79°8W **82** E5
Russell Cave △ *U.S.A.* 34°59N 85°49W **85** D12
Russell I. *Man., Canada* 56°15N 101°30W **71** B8
Russell L. *N.W.T.,*
　Canada 63°5N 115°44W **70** A5
Russellkonda *India* 19°57N 84°42E **41** K14
Russellville *Ala., U.S.A.* 34°30N 87°44W **85** D11
Russellville *Ark., U.S.A.* 35°17N 93°8W **84** D8
Russellville *Ky., U.S.A.* 36°51N 86°53W **80** G10
Russia ■ *Eurasia* 62°0N 105°0E **29** C11
Russian → *U.S.A.* 38°27N 123°8W **78** G3
Russkoye Ustye *Russia* 71°0N 149°0E **4** B15
Rustam *Pakistan* 34°25N 72°13E **42** B5
Rustam Shahr *Pakistan* 26°58N 66°6E **42** F2
Rustavi *Georgia* 41°30N 45°0E **19** F8
Rustenburg *S. Africa* 25°41S 27°14E **56** D4
Ruston *U.S.A.* 32°32N 92°38W **84** E8
Rutana *Burundi* 3°55S 30°0E **54** C3
Ruteng *Indonesia* 8°35S 120°30E **37** F6
Ruth *U.S.A.* 43°42N 82°45W **82** C2
Rutherford *U.S.A.* 38°26N 122°24W **78** G4
Rutland *U.S.A.* 43°37N 72°58W **83** C12
Rutland □ *U.K.* 52°38N 0°40W **13** E7
Rutland Water *U.K.* 52°39N 0°38W **13** E7
Rutledge → *Canada* 61°4N 112°0W **71** A6
Rutledge L. *Canada* 61°33N 110°47W **71** A6
Rutog *China* 33°27N 79°42E **32** C2
Rutshuru
　Dem. Rep. of the Congo 1°13S 29°25E **54** C2
Ruvu *Tanzania* 6°49S 38°43E **54** D4
Ruvu → *Tanzania* 6°23S 38°52E **54** D4
Ruvuba △ *Burundi* 3°3S 29°33E **54** C2
Ruvuma □ *Tanzania* 10°20S 36°0E **55** E4
Ruvuma → *Tanzania* 10°29S 40°28E **55** E5
Ruwais *U.A.E.* 24°5N 52°50E **45** E7
Ruwenzori *Africa* 0°30N 29°55E **54** B2
Ruwenzori △ *Uganda* 0°30N 30°0E **54** B2
Ruya → *Zimbabwe* 16°27S 32°5E **57** B5

Ruyigi *Burundi* 3°29S 30°15E **54** C3
Ružomberok *Slovak Rep.* 49°3N 19°17E **17** D10
Rwanda ■ *Africa* 2°0S 30°0E **54** C3
Ryan, L. *U.K.* 55°0N 5°2W **11** G3
Ryazan *Russia* 54°40N 39°40E **18** D6
Ryazhsk *Russia* 53°45N 40°3E **18** D7
Rybachiy Poluostrov *Russia* 69°43N 32°0E **8** B25
Rybachye = Balykchy *Kyrgyzstan* 42°26N 76°12E **32** B2
Rybinsk *Russia* 58°5N 38°50E **18** C6
Rybinskoye Vdkhr. *Russia* 58°30N 38°25E **18** C6
Rybnitsa = Râbniţa *Moldova* 47°45N 29°0E **17** E15
Rycroft *Canada* 55°45N 118°40W **70** B5
Ryde *U.K.* 50°43N 1°9W **13** G6
Ryderwood *U.S.A.* 46°23N 123°3W **78** D3
Rye *U.K.* 50°57N 0°45E **13** G8
Rye → *U.K.* 54°11N 0°44W **12** C7
Rye Bay *U.K.* 50°52N 0°49E **13** G8
Rye Patch Res. *U.S.A.* 40°28N 118°19W **76** F4
Ryegate *U.S.A.* 46°18N 109°15W **76** C9
Ryley *Canada* 53°17N 112°26W **70** C6
Rylstone *Australia* 32°46S 149°58E **63** E4
Ryn Peski = Naryn Qum *Kazakhstan* 47°30N 49°0E **28** E5
Ryōtsu *Japan* 38°5N 138°26E **30** E9
Rypin *Poland* 53°3N 19°25E **17** B10
Ryūgasaki *Japan* 35°54N 140°11E **31** G10
Ryukyu Is. = Ryūkyū-rettō *Japan* 26°0N 126°0E **31** M3
Ryūkyū-rettō *Japan* 26°0N 126°0E **31** M3
Rzeszów *Poland* 50°5N 21°58E **17** C11
Rzhev *Russia* 56°20N 34°20E **18** C5

S

Sa *Thailand* 18°34N 100°45E **38** C3
Sa Cabaneta *Spain* 39°37N 2°45E **24** B9
Sa Canal *Spain* 38°51N 1°23E **24** C7
Sa Conillera *Spain* 38°59N 1°13E **24** C7
Sa Dec *Vietnam* 10°20N 105°46E **39** G5
Sa Dragonera *Spain* 39°35N 2°19E **24** B9
Sa Kaeo *Thailand* 13°49N 102°4E **38** F4
Sa Mesquida *Spain* 39°55N 4°16E **24** B11
Sa Pa *Vietnam* 22°20N 103°47E **38** A4
Sa Savina *Spain* 38°44N 1°25E **24** C7
Sa'ādatābād *Fārs, Iran* 30°10N 53°5E **45** D7
Sa'ādatābād *Hormozgān, Iran* 28°3N 55°53E **45** D7
Sa'ādatābād *Kermān, Iran* 29°40N 55°51E **45** D7
Saale → *Germany* 51°56N 11°54E **16** C6
Saalfeld *Germany* 50°38N 11°21E **16** C6
Saanich *Canada* 48°29N 123°26W **78** B3
Saar → *Europe* 49°41N 6°32E **15** E6
Saarbrücken *Germany* 49°14N 6°59E **16** D4
Saaremaa *Estonia* 58°30N 22°30E **9** G20
Saarijärvi *Finland* 62°43N 25°16E **8** E21
Saariselkä *Finland* 68°16N 28°15E **8** B23
Sab 'Ābar *Syria* 33°46N 37°41E **44** C3
Saba *W. Indies* 17°38N 63°14W **89** C7
Šabac *Serbia* 44°48N 19°42E **23** B8
Sabadell *Spain* 41°28N 2°7E **21** B7
Sabah □ *Malaysia* 6°0N 117°0E **36** C5
Sabak *Malaysia* 3°46N 100°58E **39** L3
Sabalān, Kūhhā-ye *Iran* 38°15N 47°45E **44** B5
Sabalana, Kepulauan *Indonesia* 6°45S 118°50E **37** F5
Sábana de la Mar *Dom. Rep.* 19°7N 69°24W **89** C6
Sábanalarga *Colombia* 10°38N 74°55W **92** A4
Sabang *Indonesia* 5°50N 95°15E **36** C1
Sabará *Brazil* 19°55S 43°46W **93** G10
Sabarmati → *India* 22°18N 72°22E **42** H5
Sabattis *U.S.A.* 44°6N 74°40W **83** B10
Saberania *Indonesia* 2°5S 138°18E **37** E9
Sabhā *Libya* 27°9N 14°29E **51** C8
Sabi → *India* 28°29N 76°44E **42** E7
Sabie *S. Africa* 25°10S 30°48E **57** D5
Sabinal *Mexico* 30°57N 107°30W **86** A3
Sabinal *U.S.A.* 29°19N 99°28W **84** G5
Sabinas *Mexico* 27°51N 101°7W **86** B4
Sabinas → *Mexico* 27°37N 100°42W **86** B4
Sabinas Hidalgo *Mexico* 26°30N 100°10W **86** B4
Sabine → *U.S.A.* 29°59N 93°47W **84** G8
Sabine L. *U.S.A.* 29°53N 93°51W **84** G8
Sabine Pass *U.S.A.* 29°44N 93°54W **84** G8
Sablayan *Phil.* 12°50N 120°50E **37** B6
Sable *Canada* 55°30N 68°21W **73** A6
Sable, C. *Canada* 43°29N 65°38W **73** D6
Sable, C. *U.S.A.* 25°9N 81°8W **88** A3
Sable I. *Canada* 44°0N 60°0W **73** D8
Sabrina Coast *Antarctica* 68°0S 120°0E **5** C9
Sabulubbek *Indonesia* 1°36S 98°40E **36** E1
Sabzevār *Iran* 36°15N 57°40E **45** B8
Sabzvārān *Iran* 28°45N 57°50E **45** D8
Sac City *U.S.A.* 42°25N 95°0W **80** D6
Săcele *Romania* 45°37N 25°41E **17** F13
Sacheon *S. Korea* 35°0N 128°6E **35** G15
Sachigo → *Canada* 55°6N 88°58W **72** A2
Sachigo, L. *Canada* 53°50N 92°12W **72** B1
Sachimbo *Angola* 9°14S 20°16E **52** F4
Sachsen □ *Germany* 50°55N 13°10E **16** C7
Sachsen-Anhalt □ *Germany* 52°0N 12°0E **16** C7
Sackets Harbor *U.S.A.* 43°57N 76°7W **83** C8
Sackville *Canada* 45°54N 64°22W **73** C7
Saco *Maine, U.S.A.* 43°30N 70°27W **83** C14
Saco *Mont., U.S.A.* 48°28N 107°21W **76** B10
Sacramento *U.S.A.* 38°35N 121°29W **78** G5
Sacramento → *U.S.A.* 38°3N 121°56W **78** G5
Sacramento Mts. *U.S.A.* 32°30N 105°30W **77** K11
Sacramento Valley *U.S.A.* 39°30N 122°0W **78** G5
Sada-Misaki *Japan* 33°20N 132°5E **31** H6
Sadabad *India* 27°27N 78°3E **42** F8
Sadani *Tanzania* 5°58S 38°35E **54** D4
Sadao *Thailand* 6°38N 100°26E **39** J3
Sadd el Aali *Egypt* 23°54N 32°54E **51** D12
Saddle Mt. *U.S.A.* 45°58N 123°41W **78** E3
Sadimi *Dem. Rep. of the Congo* 9°25S 23°32E **55** D1
Sado *Japan* 38°0N 138°25E **30** F9
Sadra *India* 23°21N 72°43E **42** H5
Sadri *India* 25°11N 73°26E **42** G5
Sæby *Denmark* 57°21N 10°30E **9** H14
Saegertown *U.S.A.* 41°43N 80°9W **82** E4
Şafājah *Si. Arabia* 26°25N 39°0E **44** E3
Safata B. *Samoa* 14°0S 171°50W **59** b
Säffle *Sweden* 59°8N 12°55E **9** G15
Safford *U.S.A.* 32°50N 109°43W **77** K9
Saffron Walden *U.K.* 52°1N 0°16E **13** E8
Safi *Morocco* 32°18N 9°20W **50** B4
Şafīābād *Iran* 36°45N 57°58E **45** B8
Safid Dasht *Iran* 33°27N 48°11E **45** C6
Safid Kūh *Afghan.* 34°45N 63°0E **40** B3
Safid Rūd → *Iran* 37°23N 50°11E **45** B6
Safipur *India* 26°44N 80°21E **43** F9
Şāfītā *Syria* 34°48N 36°7E **44** C3
Safune *Samoa* 13°25S 172°21W **59** b
Şafwān *Iraq* 30°7N 47°43E **44** D5
Sag Harbor *U.S.A.* 41°0N 72°18W **83** F12
Saga *Japan* 33°15N 130°16E **31** H5
Saga □ *Japan* 33°15N 130°20E **31** H5
Sagae *Japan* 38°22N 140°17E **30** E10
Sagaing *Burma* 21°52N 95°59E **41** J19
Sagamore *U.S.A.* 40°46N 79°14W **82** F5
Saganaga L. *Canada* 48°14N 90°52W **80** A8
Sagar *Karnataka, India* 14°14N 75°6E **40** M9
Sagar *Mad. P., India* 23°50N 78°44E **43** H8
Sagara, L. *Tanzania* 5°20S 31°0E **54** D3
Sagarmatha = Everest, Mt. *Nepal* 28°5N 86°58E **43** E12
Sagarmatha △ *Nepal* 27°55N 86°45E **43** F12
Saginaw *U.S.A.* 43°26N 83°56W **81** D12
Saginaw B. *U.S.A.* 43°50N 83°40W **81** D12
Saglouc = Salluit *Canada* 62°14N 75°38W **69** C12
Sagone *France* 42°7N 8°42E **20** E8
Sagua la Grande *Cuba* 22°50N 80°10W **88** B3
Saguache *U.S.A.* 38°5N 106°8W **76** G10
Saguaro △ *U.S.A.* 32°12N 110°38W **77** K8
Saguenay → *Canada* 48°22N 71°0W **73** C5
Sagunt *Spain* 39°42N 0°18W **21** C5
Sagunto = Sagunt *Spain* 39°42N 0°18W **21** C5
Sagwara *India* 23°41N 74°1E **42** H6
Sahagún *Spain* 42°18N 5°2W **21** A3
Saḩam al Jawlān *Syria* 32°45N 35°55E **46** C4
Sahamandrevo *Madag.* 23°15S 45°35E **57** C8
Sahand, Kūh-e *Iran* 37°44N 46°27E **44** B5
Sahara *Africa* 23°0N 5°0E **50** D6
Saharan Atlas = Saharien, Atlas *Algeria* 33°30N 1°0E **50** B6
Saharanpur *India* 29°58N 77°33E **42** E7
Saharien, Atlas *Algeria* 33°30N 1°0E **50** B6
Saharsa *India* 25°53N 86°36E **43** G12
Sahasinaka *Madag.* 21°49S 47°49E **57** C8
Sahaswan *India* 28°5N 78°45E **43** E8
Saheira, W. el → *Egypt* 30°5N 33°25E **46** E2
Sahel *Africa* 16°0N 5°0E **50** E5
Sahibganj *India* 25°12N 87°40E **43** G12
Sāḩilīyah *Iraq* 33°43N 42°42E **44** C4
Sahiwal *Pakistan* 30°45N 73°8E **42** D5
Şaḩneh *Iran* 34°29N 47°41E **44** C5
Sahrawi = Western Sahara ■ *Africa* 25°0N 13°0W **50** D3
Sahuaripa *Mexico* 29°3N 109°14W **86** B3
Sahuarita *U.S.A.* 31°57N 110°58W **77** L8
Sahuayo de Díaz *Mexico* 20°4N 102°43W **86** C4
Sai → *India* 25°39N 82°47E **43** G10
Sai Buri *Thailand* 6°43N 101°45E **39** J3
Sai Kung *China* 22°23N 114°16E **33** G11
Sai Twong △ *Thailand* 15°56N 101°10E **38** E3
Sai Yok △ *Thailand* 14°25N 98°40E **38** E2
Sa'id Bundâs *Sudan* 8°24N 24°48E **51** G10
Sa'īdābād = Sīrjān *Iran* 29°30N 55°45E **45** D7
Sa'īdābād *Iran* 36°8N 54°11E **45** B7
Sa'īdīyeh *Iran* 36°20N 48°55E **45** B6
Saidpur *Bangla.* 25°48N 89°0E **41** G16
Saidpur *India* 25°33N 83°11E **43** G10
Saidu Sharif *Pakistan* 34°43N 72°24E **43** B5
Saigō *Japan* 36°12N 133°20E **31** F6
Saigon = Thanh Pho Ho Chi Minh *Vietnam* 10°58N 106°40E **39** G6
Saijō *Japan* 33°55N 133°11E **31** H6
Saikai △ *Japan* 33°12N 129°36E **31** H4
Saikanosy Masoala *Madag.* 15°45S 50°10E **57** B9
Saikhoa Ghat *India* 27°50N 95°40E **41** F19
Saiki *Japan* 32°58N 131°51E **31** H5
Şā'īl *Si. Arabia* 27°28N 41°45E **44** E4
Sailana *India* 23°28N 74°55E **42** H6
Sailolof *Indonesia* 1°15S 130°46E **37** E8
Saimaa *Finland* 61°15N 28°15E **8** F23
Saimen = Saimaa *Finland* 61°15N 28°15E **8** F23
Şa'in Dezh *Iran* 36°40N 46°25E **44** B5
St. Abb's Head *U.K.* 55°55N 2°8W **11** F6
St. Albans *Canada* 47°51N 55°50W **73** C8
St. Albans *U.K.* 51°45N 0°19W **13** F7
St. Albans *Vt., U.S.A.* 44°49N 73°5W **83** B11
St. Albans *W. Va., U.S.A.* 38°23N 81°50W **81** F13
St. Alban's Head *U.K.* 50°34N 2°4W **13** G5
St. Albert *Canada* 53°37N 113°32W **70** C6
St-André *Réunion* 20°57S 55°39E **53** c
St. Andrew's *Canada* 47°45N 59°15W **73** C8
St. Andrews *U.K.* 56°20N 2°47W **11** E6
St-Anicet *Canada* 45°8N 74°22W **83** A10
St. Annes *Canada* 49°40N 96°39W **71** D9
St. Anns B. *Canada* 46°22N 60°25W **73** C7
St. Ann's Bay *Jamaica* 18°26N 77°12W **88** a
St. Anthony *Canada* 51°22N 55°35W **73** B8
St. Anthony *U.S.A.* 43°58N 111°41W **76** E8
St-Antoine *Canada* 46°22N 64°45W **73** C7
St. Arnaud *Australia* 36°40S 143°16E **63** F3
St-Augustin *Canada* 51°13N 58°38W **73** B8
St-Augustin → *Canada* 51°16N 58°40W **73** B8
St. Augustine *U.S.A.* 29°54N 81°19W **85** G14
St. Austell *U.K.* 50°20N 4°47W **13** G3
St. Barbe *Canada* 51°12N 56°46W **73** B8
St-Barthélemy *W. Indies* 17°50N 62°50W **89** C7
St. Bees Hd. *U.K.* 54°31N 3°38W **12** C4
St. Bees I. *Australia* 20°56S 149°26E **62** J7
St-Benoît *Réunion* 21°2S 55°43E **53** c
St. Bride's *Canada* 46°56N 54°10W **73** C9
St. Brides B. *U.K.* 51°49N 5°9W **13** F2
St-Brieuc *France* 48°30N 2°46W **20** B2
St. Catharines *Canada* 43°10N 79°15W **82** C5
St. Catherines I. *U.S.A.* 31°40N 81°10W **85** F14
St. Catherine's Pt. *U.K.* 50°34N 1°18W **13** G6
St-Chamond *France* 45°28N 4°31E **20** D6
St. Charles *Ill., U.S.A.* 41°54N 88°19W **80** E9
St. Charles *Md., U.S.A.* 38°36N 76°56W **81** F15
St. Charles *Mo., U.S.A.* 38°47N 90°29W **80** F8
St. Charles *Va., U.S.A.* 36°48N 83°4W **81** G12
St. Christopher-Nevis = St. Kitts & Nevis ■ *W. Indies* 17°20N 62°40W **89** C7
St. Clair *Mich., U.S.A.* 42°50N 82°30W **82** D2
St. Clair *Pa., U.S.A.* 40°43N 76°12W **83** F8
St. Clair → *U.S.A.* 42°38N 82°31W **82** D2
St. Clair, L. *N. Amer.* 42°27N 82°39W **82** D2
St. Clairsville *U.S.A.* 40°5N 80°54W **82** F4
St. Claude *Canada* 49°40N 98°20W **71** D9
St. Clears *U.K.* 51°49N 4°31W **13** F3
St-Clet *Canada* 45°21N 74°13W **83** A10
St. Cloud *Fla., U.S.A.* 28°15N 81°17W **85** G14
St. Cloud *Minn., U.S.A.* 45°34N 94°10W **80** C6
St. Cricq, C. *Australia* 25°17S 113°6E **61** E1
St. Croix *U.S. Virgin Is.* 17°45N 64°45W **89** C7
St. Croix → *U.S.A.* 44°45N 92°48W **80** C7
St. Croix Falls *U.S.A.* 45°24N 92°38W **80** C7
St. David's *Canada* 48°12N 58°52W **73** C8
St. David's *U.K.* 51°53N 5°16W **13** F2
St. David's Head *U.K.* 51°54N 5°19W **13** F2
St-Denis *France* 48°56N 2°20E **20** B5
St-Denis *Réunion* 20°52S 55°27E **53** c
St-Denis ✈ (RUN) *Réunion* 20°53S 55°32E **53** c
St-Dizier *France* 48°38N 4°56E **20** B6
St. Elias, Mt. *U.S.A.* 60°18N 140°56W **68** C5
St. Elias Mts. *N. Amer.* 60°33N 139°28W **70** A1
St-Étienne *France* 45°27N 4°22E **20** D6
St. Eugène *Canada* 45°30N 74°28W **83** A10
St. Eustatius *W. Indies* 17°20N 63°0W **89** C7
St-Félicien *Canada* 48°40N 72°25W **72** C5
St-Flour *France* 45°2N 3°6E **20** D5
St. Francis *U.S.A.* 39°47N 101°48W **80** F3
St. Francis → *U.S.A.* 34°38N 90°36W **85** D9
St. Francis, C. *S. Africa* 34°14S 24°49E **56** E3
St. Francisville *U.S.A.* 30°47N 91°23W **84** F9
St-François, L. *Canada* 45°10N 74°22W **83** A10
St-Gabriel *Canada* 46°17N 73°24W **72** C5
St. Gallen = Sankt Gallen *Switz.* 47°26N 9°22E **20** C8
St-Gaudens *France* 43°6N 0°44E **20** E4
St. George *Australia* 28°1S 148°30E **63** D4
St. George *N.B., Canada* 45°11N 66°50W **73** C6
St. George *Ont., Canada* 43°15N 80°15W **82** C4
St. George *S.C., U.S.A.* 33°11N 80°35W **85** E14
St. George *Utah, U.S.A.* 37°6N 113°35W **77** H7
St. George, C. *Canada* 48°30N 59°16W **73** C8
St. George, C. *U.S.A.* 29°40N 85°5W **85** G12
St. George Ra. *Australia* 18°40S 125°0E **60** C4
St. George's *Canada* 48°26N 58°31W **73** C8
St-Georges *Canada* 46°8N 70°40W **73** C5
St. George's *Grenada* 12°5N 61°43W **89** D7
St. George's B. *Canada* 48°24N 58°53W **73** C8
St. Georges Basin *N.S.W., Australia* 35°7S 150°36E **63** F5
St. Georges Basin *W. Austral., Australia* 15°23S 125°2E **60** C4
St. George's Channel *Europe* 52°0N 6°0W **10** E6
St. Georges Hd. *Australia* 35°12S 150°42E **63** F5
St. Gotthard P. = San Gottardo, P. del *Switz.* 46°33N 8°33E **20** C8
St. Helena *Atl. Oc.* 15°58S 5°42W **48** H3
St. Helena *U.S.A.* 38°30N 122°28W **76** G2
St. Helena, Mt. *U.S.A.* 38°40N 122°36W **78** G4
St. Helena B. *S. Africa* 32°40S 18°10E **56** E2
St. Helens *Australia* 41°20S 148°15E **63** G4
St. Helens *U.K.* 53°27N 2°44W **12** D5
St. Helens *U.S.A.* 45°52N 122°48W **78** E4
St. Helens, Mt. *U.S.A.* 46°12N 122°12W **78** D4
St. Helier *U.K.* 49°10N 2°7W **13** H5
St-Hubert *Belgium* 50°2N 5°23E **15** D5
St-Hubert *Canada* 45°29N 73°25W **83** A11
St-Hyacinthe *Canada* 45°40N 72°58W **72** C5
St. Ignace *U.S.A.* 45°52N 84°44W **81** C11
St. Ignace I. *Canada* 48°45N 88°0W **72** C2
St. Ignatius *U.S.A.* 47°19N 114°6W **76** C6
St. Ives *Cambs., U.K.* 52°20N 0°4W **13** E7
St. Ives *Corn., U.K.* 50°12N 5°30W **13** G2
St. James *U.S.A.* 43°59N 94°38W **80** D6
St-Jean → *Canada* 50°17N 64°20W **73** B7
St-Jean, L. *Canada* 48°40N 72°0W **73** C5
St-Jean-Port-Joli *Canada* 47°15N 70°13W **73** C5
St-Jean-sur-Richelieu *Canada* 45°20N 73°20W **83** A11
St-Jérôme *Canada* 45°47N 74°0W **72** C5
St. John *Canada* 45°20N 66°8W **73** C6
St. John *U.S.A.* 38°0N 98°46W **80** F4
St. John → *N. Amer.* 45°12N 66°5W **81** C20
St. John, C. *Canada* 50°0N 55°32W **73** C8
St. John I. *U.S. Virgin Is.* 18°20N 64°42W **89** e
St. John's *Antigua & B.* 17°6N 61°51W **89** C7
St. John's *Canada* 47°35N 52°40W **73** C9
St. Johns *Ariz., U.S.A.* 34°30N 109°22W **77** J9
St. Johns *Mich., U.S.A.* 43°0N 84°33W **81** D11
St. Johns → *U.S.A.* 30°24N 81°24W **85** F14
St. John's Pt. *Ireland* 54°34N 8°27W **10** B3
St. Johnsbury *U.S.A.* 44°25N 72°1W **83** B12
St. Johnsville *U.S.A.* 43°0N 74°43W **83** C10
St. Joseph *Canada* 43°24N 81°42W **82** C3
St-Joseph *Martinique* 14°39N 61°4W **88** c
St-Joseph *Réunion* 21°22S 55°37E **53** c
St. Joseph *La., U.S.A.* 31°55N 91°14W **84** F9
St. Joseph *Mo., U.S.A.* 39°46N 94°50W **80** F6
St. Joseph → *U.S.A.* 42°7N 86°29W **80** D10
St. Joseph, I. *Canada* 46°12N 83°58W **72** C3
St. Joseph, L. *Canada* 51°10N 90°35W **72** B1
St-Jovite *Canada* 46°8N 74°38W **72** C5
St. Kilda *U.K.* 57°49N 8°34W **14** C2
St. Kitts & Nevis ■ *W. Indies* 17°20N 62°40W **89** C7
St. Laurent *Canada* 50°25N 97°58W **71** C9
St. Lawrence *Australia* 22°16S 149°31E **62** C4
St. Lawrence *Canada* 46°54N 55°23W **73** C8
St. Lawrence → *Canada* 49°30N 66°0W **73** C6
St. Lawrence, Gulf of *Canada* 48°25N 62°0W **73** C7
St. Lawrence I. *U.S.A.* 63°30N 170°30W **74** a
St. Lawrence Islands △ *Canada* 44°27N 75°52W **83** B9
St. Léonard *Canada* 47°12N 67°58W **73** C6
St-Leu *Réunion* 21°9S 55°18E **53** c
St. Lewis → *Canada* 52°26N 56°11W **73** B8
St-Lô *France* 49°7N 1°5W **20** B3
St-Louis *Guadeloupe* 15°56N 61°19W **88** b
St-Louis *Réunion* 21°16S 55°25E **53** c
St. Louis *Senegal* 16°8N 16°27W **50** E2
St. Louis *U.S.A.* 38°37N 90°11W **80** F8
St. Louis → *U.S.A.* 46°44N 92°9W **80** B7
St-Luc *Canada* 45°22N 73°18W **83** A11
St. Lucia ■ *W. Indies* 14°0N 60°57W **89** f
St. Lucia, L. *S. Africa* 28°5S 32°30E **57** D5
St. Lucia Channel *W. Indies* 14°15N 61°0W **89** D7
St. Maarten ⊠ *W. Indies* 18°0N 63°5W **89** C7
St. Magnus B. *U.K.* 60°25N 1°35W **11** A7
St-Malo *France* 48°39N 2°1W **20** B2
St-Marc *Haiti* 19°10N 72°41W **89** C5
St. Maries *U.S.A.* 47°19N 116°35W **76** C5
St-Martin ⊠ *W. Indies* 18°0N 63°0W **89** C7
St-Martin, C. *Martinique* 14°52N 61°14W **88** c
St. Martin, L. *Canada* 51°40N 98°30W **71** C9
St. Martins *Barbados* 13°5N 59°28W **89** g
St. Mary Pk. *Australia* 31°32S 138°34E **63** E2
St. Marys *Australia* 41°35S 148°11E **63** G4
St. Marys *Canada* 43°20N 81°10W **82** C3
St. Mary's *Corn., U.K.* 49°55N 6°18W **13** H1
St. Mary's *Orkney, U.K.* 58°54N 2°54W **11** C6
St. Marys *Ga., U.S.A.* 30°44N 81°33W **85** F14
St. Marys *Pa., U.S.A.* 41°26N 78°34W **82** E6
St. Mary's, C. *Canada* 46°50N 54°12W **73** C9
St. Mary's B. *Canada* 46°50N 53°50W **73** C9
St. Marys Bay *Canada* 44°25N 66°10W **73** D6
St-Mathieu, Pte. *France* 48°20N 4°45W **20** B1
St. Matthew I. *U.S.A.* 60°24N 172°42W **74** a
St-Maurice → *Canada* 46°21N 72°31W **72** C5
St. Mawes *U.K.* 50°10N 5°2W **13** G2
St-Nazaire *France* 47°17N 2°12W **20** C2
St. Neots *U.K.* 52°14N 0°15W **13** E7
St-Niklaas *Belgium* 51°10N 4°8E **15** C4
St-Omer *France* 50°45N 2°15E **20** A5
St-Pamphile *Canada* 46°58N 69°48W **73** C6
St-Pascal *Canada* 47°32N 69°48W **73** C6
St. Paul *Canada* 54°0N 111°17W **70** C6
St-Paul *Réunion* 20°59S 55°17E **53** c
St. Paul *Minn., U.S.A.* 44°56N 93°5W **80** C7
St. Paul *Nebr., U.S.A.* 41°13N 98°27W **80** E4
St-Paul → *Canada* 51°27N 57°42W **73** B8
St. Paul, I. *Ind. Oc.* 38°55S 77°34E **3** F13
St. Paul I. *Canada* 47°12N 60°9W **73** C7
St. Peter *U.S.A.* 44°20N 93°57W **80** C7
St. Peter Port *U.K.* 49°26N 2°33W **13** H5
St. Peters *N.S., Canada* 45°40N 60°53W **73** C7
St. Peters *P.E.I., Canada* 46°25N 62°35W **73** C7
St. Petersburg = Sankt-Peterburg *Russia* 59°55N 30°20E **9** G24
St. Petersburg *U.S.A.* 27°46N 82°40W **85** H13
St-Philippe *Réunion* 21°21S 55°44E **53** c
St-Pie *Canada* 45°30N 72°54W **83** A12
St-Pierre *Martinique* 14°45N 61°10W **88** c
St-Pierre *Réunion* 21°19S 55°28E **53** c
St-Pierre *St-P. & M.* 46°46N 56°12W **73** C8
St-Pierre, L. *Canada* 46°12N 72°52W **72** C5
St-Pierre-et-Miquelon ⊠ *N. Amer.* 46°55N 56°10W **73** C8
St-Quentin *Canada* 47°30N 67°23W **73** C6
St-Quentin *France* 49°50N 3°16E **20** B5
St. Regis *U.S.A.* 47°18N 115°6W **76** C6
St. Regis Falls *U.S.A.* 44°40N 74°32W **83** B10
St. Sebastien, Tanjon' i *Madag.* 12°26S 48°44E **57** A8
St-Siméon *Canada* 47°51N 69°54W **73** C6
St. Simons I. *U.S.A.* 31°12N 81°15W **85** F14
St. Simons Island *U.S.A.* 31°9N 81°22W **85** F14
St. Stephen *Canada* 45°16N 67°17W **73** C6
St. Thomas *Canada* 42°45N 81°10W **82** D3
St. Thomas I. *U.S. Virgin Is.* 18°20N 64°55W **89** e
St-Tite *Canada* 46°45N 72°34W **72** C5
St-Tropez *France* 43°17N 6°38E **20** E7
St-Troud = St. Truiden *Belgium* 50°48N 5°10E **15** D5
St. Truiden *Belgium* 50°48N 5°10E **15** D5
St. Vincent = São Vicente *C. Verde Is.* 17°0N 25°0W **50** b
St. Vincent, G. *Australia* 35°0S 138°0E **63** F2
St. Vincent & the Grenadines ■ *W. Indies* 13°0N 61°10W **89** D7
St. Vincent Passage *W. Indies* 13°30N 61°0W **89** D7
St-Vith *Belgium* 50°17N 6°9E **15** D6
St. Walburg *Canada* 53°39N 109°12W **71** C7
Ste-Agathe-des-Monts *Canada* 46°3N 74°17W **72** C5
Ste-Anne *Guadeloupe* 16°13N 61°24W **88** b
Ste-Anne *Seychelles* 4°36S 55°31E **53** b
Ste-Anne, L. *Canada* 50°0N 67°42W **73** B6
Ste-Anne-des-Monts *Canada* 49°8N 66°30W **73** C6
Ste. Genevieve *U.S.A.* 37°59N 90°2W **80** G8
Ste-Marguerite → *Canada* 50°9N 66°36W **73** B6
Ste-Marie *Canada* 46°26N 71°0W **73** C5
Ste-Marie *Martinique* 14°48N 61°1W **88** c
Ste-Marie *Réunion* 20°53S 55°33E **53** c
Ste-Marie, Ile = Nosy Boraha *Madag.* 16°50S 49°55E **57** B8
Ste-Rose *Guadeloupe* 16°20N 61°45W **88** b
Ste-Rose *Réunion* 21°8S 55°45E **53** c
Ste. Rose du Lac *Canada* 51°4N 99°30W **71** C9
Saintes *France* 45°45N 0°37W **20** D3
Saintes, Îs. des *Guadeloupe* 15°50N 61°35W **88** b
Saintfield *U.K.* 54°28N 5°49W **10** B6
Saintonge *France* 45°40N 0°50W **20** D3
Saipan *N. Marianas* 15°12N 145°45E **64** F6
Sairang *India* 23°50N 92°45E **41** H18
Sairecábur, Cerro *Bolivia* 22°43S 67°54W **94** A2
Saitama *Japan* 35°54N 139°38E **31** G9
Saitama □ *Japan* 36°25N 139°30E **31** F9
Saiyid *Pakistan* 33°7N 73°2E **42** C5
Sajama *Bolivia* 18°7S 69°0W **92** G5
Sajószentpéter *Hungary* 48°12N 20°44E **17** D11
Sajum *India* 33°20N 79°0E **43** C8
Sak → *S. Africa* 30°52S 20°25E **56** E3
Saka *Kenya* 0°9S 39°20E **54** B4
Sakai *Japan* 34°34N 135°27E **31** G7
Sakaide *Japan* 34°19N 133°50E **31** G6
Sakaiminato *Japan* 35°38N 133°11E **31** G6
Sakākah *Si. Arabia* 30°0N 40°8E **44** D4
Sakakawea, L. *U.S.A.* 47°30N 101°25W **80** B3
Sakami → *Canada* 53°40N 76°40W **72** B4
Sakami, L. *Canada* 53°15N 77°0W **72** B4
Sakania *Dem. Rep. of the Congo* 12°43S 28°30E **55** E2
Sakaraha *Madag.* 22°55S 44°32E **57** C7
Sakartvelo = Georgia ■ *Asia* 42°0N 43°0E **19** F7
Sakarya *Turkey* 40°48N 30°25E **19** F5
Sakashima-Guntō *Japan* 24°46N 124°0E **31** M2
Sakata *Japan* 38°55N 139°50E **30** E9
Sakchu *N. Korea* 40°23N 125°2E **35** D13
Sakeny → *Madag.* 20°0S 45°25E **57** C8
Sakha □ *Russia* 66°0N 130°0E **29** C14
Sakhalin *Russia* 51°0N 143°0E **29** D15
Sakhalinskiy Zaliv *Russia* 54°0N 141°0E **29** D15
Šakiai *Lithuania* 54°59N 23°2E **9** J20
Sakon Nakhon *Thailand* 17°10N 104°9E **38** D5
Sakrand *Pakistan* 26°10N 68°15E **42** F3
Sakri *India* 26°13N 86°5E **43** F12
Sakrivier *S. Africa* 30°54S 20°28E **56** E3
Sakti *India* 22°2N 82°58E **43** H10
Sakuma *Japan* 35°3N 137°49E **31** G8
Sakurai *Japan* 34°30N 135°51E **31** G7
Sal *C. Verde Is.* 16°45N 22°55W **50** b
Sal Rei *C. Verde Is.* 16°11N 22°53W **50** b
Sala *Sweden* 59°58N 16°35E **9** G17
Sala Consilina *Italy* 40°23N 15°36E **22** D6
Sala-y-Gómez *Pac. Oc.* 26°28S 105°28W **65** K17
Sala y Gómez Ridge *Pac. Oc.* 25°0S 98°0W **65** K18
Salaberry-de-Valleyfield *Canada* 45°15N 74°8W **83** A10
Salada, L. *Mexico* 32°20N 115°40W **77** K6
Saladas *Argentina* 28°15S 58°40W **94** B4
Saladillo *Argentina* 35°40S 59°55W **94** D4
Salado → *B. Aires, Argentina* 35°44S 57°22W **94** D4
Salado → *La Pampa, Argentina* 37°30S 67°0W **96** D3
Salado → *Santa Fe, Argentina* 31°40S 60°41W **94** C3
Salado → *Mexico* 26°52N 99°19W **84** H5
Salaga *Ghana* 8°31N 0°31W **50** G5
Sālah *Syria* 32°40N 36°45E **46** C5
Şalāḩ ad Dīn □ *Iraq* 34°35N 43°35E **44** C4
Salakos *Greece* 36°17N 27°57E **25** C9
Salālah *Oman* 16°56N 53°59E **47** D5
Salamanca *Chile* 31°46S 70°59W **94** C1
Salamanca *Spain* 40°58N 5°39W **21** B3
Salamanca *U.S.A.* 42°10N 78°43W **82** D6
Salāmatābād *Iran* 35°39N 47°50E **44** C5
Salamina *Greece* 37°56N 23°30E **23** F10
Salamis *Cyprus* 35°11N 33°54E **25** D12
Salar de Atacama *Chile* 23°30S 68°25W **94** A2
Salar de Uyuni *Bolivia* 20°30S 67°45W **92** H5
Salatiga *Indonesia* 7°19S 110°30E **37** G14
Salavat *Russia* 53°21N 55°55E **18** D10
Salaverry *Peru* 8°15S 79°0W **92** E3
Salawati *Indonesia* 1°7S 130°52E **37** E8
Salaya *India* 22°19N 69°35E **42** H3
Salayar *Indonesia* 6°7S 120°30E **37** F6
S'Albufera *Spain* 39°47N 3°7E **24** B10
Salcombe *U.K.* 50°14N 3°47W **13** G4
Saldanha *S. Africa* 33°0S 17°58E **56** E2
Saldanha B. *S. Africa* 33°6S 18°0E **56** E2
Saldus *Latvia* 56°38N 22°30E **9** H20
Sale *Australia* 38°6S 147°6E **63** F4
Salé *Morocco* 34°3N 6°48W **50** B4
Sale *U.K.* 53°26N 2°19W **12** D5
Salekhard *Russia* 66°30N 66°35E **28** C7
Salelologa *Samoa* 13°41S 172°11W **59** b
Salem *India* 11°40N 78°11E **40** P11
Salem *Ill., U.S.A.* 38°38N 88°57W **80** F9

Salem *Ind., U.S.A.* 38°36N 86°6W **80 F10**	Sam *India* 26°50N 70°31E **42 F4**	San Benito *U.S.A.* 26°8N 97°38W **84 H6**	San Ignacio *Belize* 17°10N 89°5W **87 D7**
Salem *Mass., U.S.A.* 42°31N 70°53W **83 D14**	Sam Neua *Laos* 20°29N 104°5E **38 B5**	San Benito → *U.S.A.* 36°53N 121°34W **78 J5**	San Ignacio *Bolivia* 16°20S 60°55W **92 G6**
Salem *Mo., U.S.A.* 37°39N 91°32W **80 G8**	Sam Ngao *Thailand* 17°18N 99°0E **38 D2**	San Benito Mt. *U.S.A.* 36°22N 120°37W **78 J6**	San Ignacio *Mexico* 27°27N 112°51W **86 B2**
Salem *N.H., U.S.A.* 42°45N 71°12W **83 D13**	Sam Rayburn Res. *U.S.A.* 31°4N 94°5W **84 F7**	San Bernardino *U.S.A.* 34°7N 117°19W **79 L9**	San Ignacio *Paraguay* 26°52S 57°3W **94 B4**
Salem *N.J., U.S.A.* 39°34N 75°28W **81 F16**	Sam Son *Vietnam* 19°44N 105°54E **38 C5**	San Bernardino Mts.	San Ignacio, L. *Mexico* 26°54N 113°13W **86 B2**
Salem *N.Y., U.S.A.* 43°10N 73°20W **83 C11**	Sam Teu *Laos* 19°59N 104°38E **38 C5**	*U.S.A.* 34°10N 116°45W **79 L10**	San Ildefonso, C. *Phil.* 16°0N 122°1E **37 A6**
Salem *Ohio, U.S.A.* 40°54N 80°52W **82 F4**	Sama de Langreo = Langreo	San Bernardino Str. *Phil.* 13°0N 125°0E **37 B6**	San Isidro *Argentina* 34°29S 58°31W **94 C4**
Salem *Oreg., U.S.A.* 44°56N 123°2W **76 D2**	*Spain* 43°18N 5°40W **21 A3**	San Bernardo *Chile* 33°40S 70°50W **94 C1**	San Jacinto *U.S.A.* 33°47N 116°57W **79 M10**
Salem *S. Dak., U.S.A.* 43°44N 97°23W **80 D6**	Samagaltay *Russia* 50°36N 95°3E **29 D10**	San Bernardo, I. de	San Jaime = Sant Jaume
Salem *Va., U.S.A.* 37°18N 80°3W **81 G13**	Samales Group *Phil.* 6°0N 122°0E **37 C6**	*Colombia* 9°45N 75°50W **92 B3**	*Spain* 39°54N 4°4E **24 B11**
Salerno *Italy* 40°41N 14°47E **22 D6**	Samana *India* 30°10N 76°13E **42 D7**	San Blas *Mexico* 26°5N 108°46W **86 B3**	San Javier *Misiones,*
Salford *U.K.* 53°30N 2°18W **12 D5**	Samana Cay *Bahamas* 23°3N 73°45W **89 B5**	San Blas, Arch. de	*Argentina* 27°55S 55°5W **95 B4**
Salgueiro *Brazil* 8°4S 39°6W **93 E11**	Samanga *Tanzania* 8°20S 39°13E **55 D4**	*Panama* 9°50N 78°31W **88 E4**	San Javier *Santa Fe,*
Salibabu *Indonesia* 3°51N 126°40E **37 D7**	Samangán □ *Afghan.* 36°15N 68°3E **40 B5**	San Blas, C. *U.S.A.* 29°40N 85°21W **85 G12**	*Argentina* 30°40S 59°55W **94 C4**
Salibea = Salybia	Samangwa	San Borja *Bolivia* 14°50S 66°52W **92 F5**	San Javier *Bolivia* 16°18S 62°30W **92 G6**
Trin. & Tob. 10°43N 61°2W **93 K15**	*Dem. Rep. of the Congo* 4°23S 24°10E **54 C1**	San Buenaventura = Ventura	San Javier *Chile* 35°40S 71°45W **94 D1**
Salida *U.S.A.* 38°32N 106°0W **74 C5**	Samani *Japan* 42°7N 142°56E **30 C11**	*U.S.A.* 34°17N 119°18W **79 L7**	San Jerónimo Taviche
Salihli *Turkey* 38°28N 28°8E **23 E13**	Samar *Phil.* 12°0N 125°0E **37 B7**	San Buenaventura	*Mexico* 16°44N 96°35W **87 D5**
Salihorsk *Belarus* 52°51N 27°27E **17 B14**	Samara *Russia* 53°8N 50°6E **18 D9**	*Mexico* 27°5N 101°32W **86 B4**	San Joaquin *U.S.A.* 36°36N 120°11W **78 J6**
Salima *Malawi* 13°47S 34°28E **53 G6**	Samaria = Shōmron	San Carlos = Sant Carles	San Joaquin *U.S.A.* 38°4N 121°51W **78 G5**
Salina *Italy* 38°34N 14°50E **22 E6**	*West Bank* 32°15N 35°13E **46 C4**	*Spain* 39°3N 1°34E **24 B8**	San Joaquin Valley
Salina *Kans., U.S.A.* 38°50N 97°37W **80 F6**	Samaria △ *Greece* 35°17N 23°58E **25 D5**	San Carlos *Argentina* 33°50S 69°0W **94 C2**	*U.S.A.* 37°20N 121°0W **78 J6**
Salina *Utah, U.S.A.* 38°58N 111°51W **76 G8**	Samarinda *Indonesia* 0°30S 117°9E **36 E5**	San Carlos *Chile* 36°10S 72°0W **94 D1**	San Jon *U.S.A.* 35°6N 103°20W **77 J12**
Salina Cruz *Mexico* 16°10N 95°12W **87 D5**	Samarkand = Samarqand	San Carlos *Baja Calif. S.,*	San Jordi = Sant Jordi
Salinas *Brazil* 16°10S 42°10W **93 G10**	*Uzbekistan* 39°40N 66°55E **28 F7**	*Mexico* 24°47N 112°7W **86 C2**	*Spain* 39°33N 2°46E **24 B9**
Salinas *Ecuador* 2°10S 80°58W **92 D2**	Samarqand *Uzbekistan* 39°40N 66°55E **28 F7**	San Carlos *Coahuila,*	San Jorge *Argentina* 31°54S 61°50W **94 C3**
Salinas *U.S.A.* 36°40N 121°39W **78 J5**	Sāmarrā' *Iraq* 34°12N 43°52E **44 C4**	*Mexico* 29°1N 100°51W **86 B4**	San Jorge, B. *Mexico* 31°20N 113°20W **86 A2**
Salinas → *Guatemala* 16°28N 90°31W **87 D6**	Samastipur *India* 25°50N 85°50E **43 G11**	San Carlos *Nic.* 11°12N 84°50W **88 D3**	San Jorge, G. *Argentina* 46°0S 66°0W **96 F3**
Salinas → *U.S.A.* 36°45N 121°48W **78 J5**	Samba	San Carlos *Phil.* 10°29N 123°25E **37 B6**	San José = San Josep
Salinas, B. de *Nic.* 11°4N 85°45W **88 D2**	*Dem. Rep. of the Congo* 4°38S 26°22E **54 C2**	San Carlos *Uruguay* 34°46S 54°58W **95 C5**	*Spain* 38°55N 1°18E **24 C7**
Salinas, Pampa de las	Samba *India* 32°32N 75°10E **43 C6**	San Carlos *Venezuela* 9°40N 68°36W **92 B5**	San José *Argentina* 32°12S 58°15W **94 C4**
Argentina 31°58S 66°42W **94 C2**	Sambalpur *India* 21°28N 84°4E **41 J14**	San Carlos de Bariloche	San José *Costa Rica* 9°55N 84°2W **88 E3**
Salinas Ambargasta	Sambar, Tanjung	*Argentina* 41°10S 71°25W **96 E2**	San Jose *Guatemala* 14°0N 90°50W **88 D1**
Argentina 29°0S 65°0W **94 B3**	*Indonesia* 2°59S 110°19E **36 E4**	San Carlos de Bolívar	San Jose *Mind. Occ., Phil.* 12°27N 121°4E **37 B6**
Salinas de Hidalgo	Sambas *Indonesia* 1°20N 109°20E **36 D3**	*Argentina* 36°15S 61°6W **94 D3**	San Jose *Nueva Ecija,*
Mexico 22°38N 101°43W **86 C4**	Sambava *Madag.* 14°16S 50°10E **57 A9**	San Carlos del Zulia	*Phil.* 15°45N 120°55E **37 A6**
Salinas Grandes *Argentina* 30°0S 65°0W **94 C3**	Sambawizi *Zimbabwe* 18°24S 26°13E **55 F2**	*Venezuela* 9°1N 71°55W **92 B4**	San Jose *U.S.A.* 37°20N 121°53W **78 H5**
Salinas Pueblo Missions ○	Sambhal *India* 28°35N 78°37E **43 E8**	San Carlos L. *U.S.A.* 33°11N 110°32W **77 K8**	San José, I. *Mexico* 25°0N 110°38W **86 C2**
U.S.A. 34°6N 106°4W **77 J10**	Sambhar *India* 26°52N 75°6E **42 F6**	San Clemente *Chile* 35°30S 71°29W **94 D1**	San José de Buenavista
Salinas Valley *U.S.A.* 36°15N 121°15W **78 J5**	Sambhar L. *India* 26°55N 75°12E **42 F6**	San Clemente *U.S.A.* 33°26N 117°37W **79 M9**	*Phil.* 10°45N 121°56E **37 B6**
Saline → *Ark., U.S.A.* 33°10N 92°8W **84 E8**	Sambiase *Italy* 38°58N 16°17E **22 E7**	San Clemente I. *U.S.A.* 32°53N 118°29W **79 N8**	San José de Chiquitos
Saline → *Kans., U.S.A.* 38°52N 97°30W **80 F5**	Sambir *Ukraine* 49°30N 23°10E **17 D12**	San Cristóbal = Es Migjorn Gran	*Bolivia* 17°53S 60°50W **92 G6**
Salines, C. de ses *Spain* 39°16N 3°4E **24 B10**	Sambor *Cambodia* 12°46N 106°0E **38 F6**	*Spain* 39°57N 4°3E **24 B11**	San José de Feliciano
Salinópolis *Brazil* 0°40S 47°20W **93 D9**	Samborombón, B.	San Cristóbal *Argentina* 30°20S 61°10W **94 C3**	*Argentina* 30°26S 58°46W **94 C4**
Salisbury *Australia* 34°46S 138°38E **63 E2**	*Argentina* 36°5S 57°20W **94 D4**	San Cristóbal *Dom. Rep.* 18°25N 70°6W **89 C5**	San José de Jáchal
Salisbury *U.K.* 51°4N 1°47W **13 F6**	Samburu □ *Kenya* 0°37N 37°31E **54 B4**	San Cristóbal *Solomon Is.* 10°30S 161°0E **58 C9**	*Argentina* 30°15S 68°46W **94 C2**
Salisbury *Md., U.S.A.* 38°22N 75°36W **81 F16**	Samcheok *S. Korea* 37°30N 129°10E **35 F15**	San Cristóbal *Venezuela* 7°46N 72°14W **92 B4**	San José de Mayo
Salisbury *N.C., U.S.A.* 35°40N 80°29W **85 D14**	Same *Tanzania* 4°2S 37°38E **54 C4**	San Cristóbal de las Casas	*Uruguay* 34°27S 56°40W **94 C4**
Salisbury I. *Canada* 63°30N 77°0W **69 C12**	Samfya *Zambia* 11°22S 29°31E **55 E2**	*Mexico* 16°45N 92°38W **87 D6**	San José del Cabo
Salisbury Plain *U.K.* 51°14N 1°55W **13 F6**	Samnah *Si. Arabia* 25°10N 37°15E **44 E3**	San Diego *Calif., U.S.A.* 32°42N 117°9W **79 N9**	*Mexico* 23°3N 109°41W **86 C3**
Şalkhad *Syria* 32°29N 36°43E **46 C5**	Samo Alto *Chile* 30°22S 71°0W **94 C1**	San Diego *Tex., U.S.A.* 27°46N 98°14W **84 H5**	San José del Guaviare
Salla *Finland* 66°50N 28°49E **8 C23**	Samoa ■ *Pac. Oc.* 14°0S 172°0W **59 b**	San Diego, C. *Argentina* 54°40S 65°10W **96 G3**	*Colombia* 2°35N 72°38W **92 C4**
Salliq = Coral Harbour	Samokov *Bulgaria* 42°18N 23°35E **23 C10**	San Diego de la Unión	San Josep *Spain* 38°55N 1°18E **24 C7**
Canada 64°8N 83°10W **69 C11**	Samos *Greece* 37°45N 26°50E **23 F12**	*Mexico* 21°28N 100°52W **86 C4**	San Juan *Argentina* 31°30S 68°30W **94 C2**
Sallisaw *U.S.A.* 35°28N 94°47W **84 D7**	Samothráki = Mathraki	San Diego Int. ✈ (SAN)	San Juan *Puerto Rico* 18°28N 66°7W **89 d**
Salluit *Canada* 62°14N 75°38W **69 C12**	*Greece* 39°48N 19°31E **25 A3**	*U.S.A.* 32°44N 117°11W **79 N9**	San Juan *Trin. & Tob.* 10°39N 61°29W **93 K15**
Salmās *Iran* 38°11N 44°47E **44 B5**	Samothraki *Greece* 40°28N 25°28E **23 D11**	San Dimitri, Ras *Malta* 36°4N 14°11E **25 C1**	San Juan □ *Argentina* 31°9S 69°0W **94 C2**
Salmo *Canada* 49°10N 117°20W **70 D5**	Sampacho *Argentina* 33°20S 64°50W **94 C3**	San Dimitri Point = San Dimitri,	San Juan → *Argentina* 32°20S 67°25W **94 C2**
Salmon *U.S.A.* 45°11N 113°54W **76 D7**	Sampalan *Indonesia* 8°41S 115°34E **37 K18**	Ras *Malta* 36°4N 14°11E **25 C1**	San Juan → *Nic.* 10°56N 83°42W **88 D3**
Salmon → *Canada* 54°3N 122°40W **70 C4**	Sampang *Indonesia* 7°11S 113°13E **37 G15**	San Estanislao *Paraguay* 24°39S 56°26W **94 A4**	San Juan → *U.S.A.* 37°16N 110°26W **77 H8**
Salmon → *U.S.A.* 45°51N 116°47W **76 D5**	Sampit *Indonesia* 2°34S 113°0E **36 E4**	San Felipe *Chile* 32°43S 70°42W **94 C1**	San Juan Bautista = Sant Joan de
Salmon Arm *Canada* 50°40N 119°15W **70 C5**	Sampit, Teluk *Indonesia* 3°5S 113°3E **36 E4**	San Felipe *Mexico* 31°1N 114°52W **86 A2**	Labritja *Spain* 39°5N 1°31E **24 B8**
Salmon Gums *Australia* 32°59S 121°38E **61 F3**	Samrong *Cambodia* 14°15N 103°30E **38 E4**	San Felipe *Venezuela* 10°20N 68°44W **92 A5**	San Juan Bautista
Salmon Pt. *Canada* 43°52N 77°15W **82 C7**	Samrong *Thailand* 15°10N 100°40E **38 E3**	San Felipe → *U.S.A.* 33°10N 115°49W **79 M11**	*Paraguay* 26°37S 57°6W **94 B4**
Salmon River Mts.	Samso *Denmark* 55°50N 10°35E **9 J14**	San Félix *Chile* 28°56S 70°28W **94 B1**	San Juan Bautista
U.S.A. 44°50N 115°30W **76 D6**	Samsun *Turkey* 41°15N 36°22E **19 F6**	San Félix *Pac. Oc.* 26°23S 80°0W **90 F2**	*U.S.A.* 36°51N 121°32W **78 J5**
Salmon River Res.	Samui, Ko *Thailand* 9°30N 100°0E **39 b**	San Fernando = Sant Ferran	San Juan Capistrano
U.S.A. 43°32N 75°55W **83 C9**	Samusole	*Spain* 38°42N 1°28E **24 C7**	*U.S.A.* 33°30N 117°40W **79 M9**
Salo *Finland* 60°22N 23°10E **9 F20**	*Dem. Rep. of the Congo* 10°2S 24°0E **55 E1**	San Fernando *Chile* 34°30S 71°0W **94 C1**	San Juan Cr. → *U.S.A.* 35°40N 120°22W **78 J5**
Salome *U.S.A.* 33°47N 113°37W **79 M13**	Samut Prakan *Thailand* 13°32N 100°40E **38 F3**	San Fernando *Mexico* 24°51N 98°10W **87 C5**	San Juan de Guadalupe
Salon *India* 26°2N 81°27E **43 F9**	Samut Songkhram	San Fernando *La Union,*	*Mexico* 24°38N 102°44W **86 C4**
Salon-de-Provence *France* 43°39N 5°6E **20 E6**	*Thailand* 13°24N 100°1E **38 F3**	*Phil.* 16°40N 120°23E **37 A6**	San Juan de la Costa
Salonica = Thessaloniki	Samwari *Pakistan* 28°30N 66°46E **42 E2**	San Fernando *Pampanga,*	*Mexico* 24°20N 110°41W **86 C2**
Greece 40°38N 22°58E **23 D10**	San *Mali* 13°15N 4°57W **50 F5**	*Phil.* 15°5N 120°37E **37 A6**	San Juan de los Lagos
Salonta *Romania* 46°49N 21°42E **17 E11**	San → *Cambodia* 13°32N 105°57E **38 F5**	San Fernando *Spain* 36°28N 6°17W **21 D2**	*Mexico* 21°15N 102°18W **86 C4**
Salpausselkä *Finland* 61°3N 26°15E **8 F22**	San → *Poland* 50°45N 21°51E **17 C11**	San Fernando	San Juan de los Morros
Salsacate *Argentina* 31°20S 65°5W **94 C2**	San Agustín, C. *Phil.* 6°20N 126°13E **37 C7**	*Trin. & Tob.* 10°16N 61°28W **89 D7**	*Venezuela* 9°55N 67°21W **92 B5**
Salsk *Russia* 46°28N 41°30E **19 E7**	San Agustín de Valle Fértil	San Fernando *U.S.A.* 34°17N 118°26W **79 L8**	San Juan del Norte *Nic.* 10°58N 83°40W **88 D3**
Salso → *Italy* 37°6N 13°57E **22 F5**	*Argentina* 30°35S 67°30W **94 C2**	San Fernando de Apure	San Juan del Norte, B. de
Salt → *Canada* 60°0N 112°25W **70 B6**	San Ambrosio *Pac. Oc.* 26°28S 79°53W **90 F3**	*Venezuela* 7°54N 67°15W **92 B5**	*Nic.* 11°0N 83°40W **88 D3**
Salt → *U.S.A.* 33°23N 112°19W **77 K7**	San Andreas *U.S.A.* 38°12N 120°41W **78 G6**	San Fernando de Atabapo	San Juan del Río *Mexico* 20°23N 100°0W **87 C5**
Salt Fork Red → *U.S.A.* 34°27N 99°21W **84 D5**	San Andrés, I. de	*Venezuela* 4°3N 67°42W **92 C5**	San Juan del Sur *Nic.* 11°20N 85°51W **88 D2**
Salt L. *Australia* 30°6S 142°8E **63 E3**	*Caribbean* 12°42N 81°46W **88 D3**	San Francisco *Argentina* 31°30S 62°5W **94 C3**	San Juan I. *U.S.A.* 48°32N 123°5W **78 B3**
Salt Lake City *U.S.A.* 40°45N 111°53W **76 F8**	San Andres Mts.	San Francisco *U.S.A.* 37°46N 122°23W **78 H4**	San Juan Island ○
Salt Range *Pakistan* 32°30N 72°25E **42 C5**	*U.S.A.* 33°0N 106°30W **77 K10**	San Francisco →	*U.S.A.* 48°35N 123°8W **78 B3**
Salta *Argentina* 24°57S 65°25W **94 A2**	San Andrés Tuxtla	*U.S.A.* 32°59N 109°22W **77 K9**	San Juan Mts. *U.S.A.* 37°30N 107°0W **77 H10**
Salta □ *Argentina* 24°48S 65°30W **94 A2**	*Mexico* 18°27N 95°13W **87 D5**	San Francisco, C. de	San Justo *Argentina* 30°47S 60°30W **94 C3**
Saltash *U.K.* 50°24N 4°14W **13 G3**	San Angelo *U.S.A.* 31°28N 100°26W **84 F4**	*Colombia* 6°18N 77°29W **90 C3**	San Kamphaeng *Thailand* 18°45N 99°8E **38 C2**
Saltburn by the Sea *U.K.* 54°35N 0°58W **12 C7**	San Anselmo *U.S.A.* 37°59N 122°34W **78 H4**	San Francisco, Paso de	San Lázaro, C. *Mexico* 24°50N 112°18W **86 C2**
Saltcoats *U.K.* 55°38N 4°47W **11 F4**	San Antonio *Belize* 16°15N 89°2W **87 D7**	*S. Amer.* 27°0S 68°0W **94 B2**	San Leandro *U.S.A.* 37°42N 122°9W **78 H4**
Saltee Is. *Ireland* 52°7N 6°37W **10 D5**	San Antonio *Chile* 33°40S 71°40W **94 C1**	San Francisco de Macorís	San Lorenzo = Sant Llorenç des
Saltfjellet *Norway* 66°40N 15°15E **8 C16**	San Antonio *N. Mex.,*	*Dom. Rep.* 19°19N 70°15W **89 C5**	Cardassar *Spain* 39°37N 3°17E **24 B10**
Saltfjorden *Norway* 67°15N 14°10E **8 C16**	*U.S.A.* 33°55N 106°52W **77 K10**	San Francisco del Monte de Oro	San Lorenzo *Argentina* 32°45S 60°45W **94 C3**
Saltillo *Mexico* 25°25N 101°0W **86 B4**	San Antonio *Tex.,*	*Argentina* 32°36S 66°8W **94 C2**	San Lorenzo *Ecuador* 1°15N 78°50W **92 C3**
Salto *Argentina* 34°20S 60°15W **94 C3**	*U.S.A.* 29°25N 98°29W **84 G5**	San Francisco del Oro	San Lorenzo *Paraguay* 25°20S 57°32W **94 B4**
Salto *Uruguay* 31°27S 57°50W **94 C4**	San Antonio → *U.S.A.* 28°30N 96°54W **84 G6**	*Mexico* 26°52N 105°51W **86 B3**	San Lorenzo → *Mexico* 24°15N 107°24W **86 C3**
Salto → *Italy* 42°26N 12°25E **22 C5**	San Antonio, C.	San Francisco Int. ✈ (SFO)	San Lorenzo, I. *Mexico* 28°38N 112°51W **86 B2**
Salto del Guaíra *Paraguay* 24°3S 54°17W **95 A5**	*Argentina* 36°15S 56°40W **94 D4**	*U.S.A.* 37°37N 122°22W **78 H4**	San Lorenzo, Mte.
Salton City *U.S.A.* 33°18N 115°57W **79 M11**	San Antonio, C. de *Cuba* 21°50N 84°57W **88 B3**	San Francisco Javier = Sant	*Argentina* 47°40S 72°20W **96 F2**
Salton Sea *U.S.A.* 33°15N 115°45W **79 M11**	San Antonio, Mt.	Francesc de Formentera	San Lucas = Cabo San Lucas
Saltsburg *U.S.A.* 40°29N 79°27W **82 F5**	*U.S.A.* 34°17N 117°38W **79 L9**	*Spain* 38°42N 1°26E **24 C7**	*Mexico* 22°53N 109°54W **86 C3**
Saluda → *U.S.A.* 34°1N 81°4W **85 D14**	San Antonio de los Baños	San Gabriel *Chile* 33°47S 70°15W **94 C1**	San Lucas *Bolivia* 20°5S 65°7W **92 H5**
Salūm *Egypt* 31°31N 25°7E **51 B11**	*Cuba* 22°54N 82°31W **88 B3**	San Gabriel Chilac	San Lucas *Mexico* 27°10N 112°14W **86 B2**
Salur *India* 18°27N 83°18E **41 K13**	San Antonio de los Cobres	*Mexico* 18°19N 97°21W **87 D5**	San Lucas, C. *Mexico* 22°52N 109°53W **86 C3**
Salvador *Brazil* 13°0S 38°30W **93 F11**	*Argentina* 24°10S 66°17W **94 A2**	San Gabriel Mts.	San Luis *Argentina* 33°20S 66°20W **94 C2**
Salvador *Canada* 52°10N 109°32W **71 C7**	San Antonio Oeste	*U.S.A.* 34°17N 118°0W **79 L9**	San Luis *Cuba* 20°13N 75°51W **88 B4**
Salvador, El ■	*Argentina* 40°40S 65°0W **96 E4**	San Gavino Monreale	San Luis *Guatemala* 16°14N 89°27W **88 C2**
Cent. Amer. 13°50N 89°0W **88 D2**	San Ardo *U.S.A.* 36°1N 120°54W **78 J6**	*Italy* 39°33N 8°47E **22 E3**	San Luis *Ariz., U.S.A.* 32°29N 114°47W **77 K6**
Salvador, L. *U.S.A.* 29°43N 90°15W **85 G9**	San Agustín *Canary Is.* 27°47N 15°32W **24 G4**	San German *Puerto Rico* 18°4N 67°4W **89 d**	San Luis Colo., U.S.A. 37°12N 105°25W **77 H11**
Salween → *Burma* 16°31N 97°37E **41 L20**	San Augustine *U.S.A.* 31°32N 94°7W **84 F7**	San Gorgonio Mt.	San Luis □ *Argentina* 34°0S 66°0W **94 C2**
Salyan *Azerbaijan* 39°33N 48°59E **45 B6**	San Bartolomé	*U.S.A.* 34°6N 116°50W **79 L10**	San Luis, I. *Mexico* 29°58N 114°26W **86 B2**
Salybia *Trin. & Tob.* 10°43N 61°2W **93 K15**	*Canary Is.* 28°59N 13°37W **24 F6**	San Gottardo, P. del	San Luis, Sierra de
Salzach → *Austria* 48°12N 12°56E **16 D7**	San Bartolomé de Tirajana	*Switz.* 46°33N 8°33E **20 C8**	*Argentina* 32°30S 66°10W **94 C2**
Salzburg *Austria* 47°48N 13°2E **16 E7**	*Canary Is.* 27°54N 15°34W **24 G4**	San Gregorio *Uruguay* 32°37S 55°40W **95 C4**	San Luis de la Paz
Salzgitter *Germany* 52°9N 10°19E **16 B6**	San Benedetto del Tronto	San Gregorio *U.S.A.* 37°20N 122°23W **78 H4**	*Mexico* 21°18N 100°31W **86 C4**
Salzwedel *Germany* 52°52N 11°10E **16 B6**	*Italy* 42°57N 13°53E **22 C5**	San Guillermo △	San Luis Obispo *U.S.A.* 35°17N 120°40W **79 K6**
	San Benedicto, I.	*Argentina* 27°50S 69°45W **94 B2**	San Luis Potosí *Mexico* 22°9N 100°59W **86 C4**
	Mexico 19°18N 110°49W **86 D2**		San Luis Potosí □ *Mexico* 23°0N 101°0W **86 C4**
			San Luis Res. *U.S.A.* 37°4N 121°5W **78 H5**
			San Luis Río Colorado
			Mexico 32°29N 114°58W **86 A2**
			San Manuel *U.S.A.* 32°36N 110°38W **77 K8**
			San Marcos *Guatemala* 14°59N 91°52W **88 D1**
			San Marcos *Calif.,*
			U.S.A. 33°9N 117°10W **79 M9**
			San Marcos *Tex., U.S.A.* 29°53N 97°56W **84 G6**
			San Marcos, I. *Mexico* 27°13N 112°6W **86 B2**
			San Marino *San Marino* 43°55N 12°30E **16 G7**
			San Marino ■ *Europe* 43°56N 12°25E **22 C5**
			San Martín *Antarctica* 68°11S 67°0W **5 C17**
			San Martín *Argentina* 33°5S 68°28W **94 C2**
			San Martín → *Bolivia* 13°8S 63°43W **92 F6**
			San Martín, L. *Argentina* 48°50S 72°50W **96 F2**
			San Martín de los Andes
			Argentina 40°10S 71°20W **96 E2**
			San Mateo = Sant Mateu
			Spain 39°3N 1°23E **24 B7**
			San Mateo *U.S.A.* 37°34N 122°19W **78 H4**
			San Matías *Bolivia* 16°25S 58°20W **92 G7**
			San Matías, G. *Argentina* 41°30S 64°0W **96 E4**
			San Miguel = Sant Miquel
			Spain 39°3N 1°26E **24 B7**
			San Miguel *El Salv.* 13°30N 88°12W **88 D2**
			San Miguel *Panama* 8°27N 78°55W **88 E4**
			San Miguel *U.S.A.* 35°45N 120°42W **78 K6**
			San Miguel → *Bolivia* 13°52S 63°56W **92 F6**
			San Miguel de Tucumán
			Argentina 26°50S 65°20W **94 B2**
			San Miguel del Monte
			Argentina 35°23S 58°50W **94 D4**
			San Miguel I. *U.S.A.* 34°2N 120°23W **79 L6**
			San Nicolás *Canary Is.* 27°58N 15°47W **24 G4**
			San Nicolás de los Arroyos
			Argentina 33°25S 60°10W **94 C3**
			San Nicolas I. *U.S.A.* 33°15N 119°30W **79 M7**
			San Onofre *U.S.A.* 33°22N 117°34W **79 M9**
			San Pablo *Bolivia* 21°43S 66°38W **94 A2**
			San Pablo *U.S.A.* 37°58N 122°21W **78 H4**
			San Pedro *B. Aires,*
			Argentina 33°40S 59°40W **94 C4**
			San Pedro *Misiones,*
			Argentina 26°30S 54°10W **95 B5**
			San Pedro *Chile* 33°54S 71°28W **94 C1**
			San Pedro *Ivory C.* 4°50N 6°33W **50 H4**
			San Pedro *Mexico* 23°55N 110°17W **86 C2**
			San Pedro □ *Paraguay* 24°0S 57°0W **94 A4**
			San Pedro → *Chihuahua,*
			Mexico 28°20N 106°10W **86 B3**
			San Pedro → *Nayarit,*
			Mexico 21°45N 105°30W **86 C3**
			San Pedro → *U.S.A.* 32°59N 110°47W **77 K8**
			San Pedro, Pta. *Chile* 25°30S 70°38W **94 B1**
			San Pedro Channel
			U.S.A. 33°30N 118°25W **79 M8**
			San Pedro de Atacama
			Chile 22°55S 68°15W **94 A2**
			San Pedro de Jujuy
			Argentina 24°12S 64°55W **94 A3**
			San Pedro de las Colonias
			Mexico 25°45N 102°59W **86 B4**
			San Pedro de Macorís
			Dom. Rep. 18°30N 69°18W **89 C6**
			San Pedro del Norte *Nic.* 13°4N 84°33W **88 D3**
			San Pedro del Paraná
			Paraguay 26°43S 56°13W **94 B4**
			San Pedro Mártir, Sierra
			Mexico 31°0N 115°30W **86 A1**
			San Pedro Mártir △
			Mexico 31°0N 115°21W **86 A1**
			San Pedro Ocampo = Melchor
			Ocampo *Mexico* 24°51N 101°39W **86 C4**
			San Pedro Pochutla
			Mexico 15°44N 96°28W **87 D5**
			San Pedro Sula *Honduras* 15°30N 88°0W **88 C2**
			San Pedro Tututepec
			Mexico 16°9N 97°38W **87 D5**
			San Pietro *Italy* 39°8N 8°17E **22 E3**
			San Rafael *Argentina* 34°40S 68°21W **94 C2**
			San Rafael *Calif., U.S.A.* 37°58N 122°32W **78 H4**
			San Rafael *N. Mex.,*
			U.S.A. 35°7N 107°53W **77 J10**
			San Rafael Mt. *U.S.A.* 34°41N 119°52W **79 L7**
			San Rafael Mts. *U.S.A.* 34°40N 119°50W **79 L7**
			San Ramón de la Nueva Orán
			Argentina 23°10S 64°20W **94 A3**
			San Remo *Italy* 43°49N 7°46E **20 E7**
			San Roque *Argentina* 28°25S 58°45W **94 B4**
			San Roque *Spain* 36°17N 5°21W **21 D3**
			San Rosendo *Chile* 37°16S 72°43W **94 D1**
			San Saba *U.S.A.* 31°12N 98°43W **84 F5**
			San Salvador *El Salv.* 13°40N 89°10W **88 D2**
			San Salvador de Jujuy
			Argentina 24°10S 64°48W **94 A3**
			San Salvador I. *Bahamas* 24°0N 74°40W **89 B5**
			San Sebastián = Donostia-San
			Sebastián *Spain* 43°17N 1°58W **21 A5**
			San Sebastián *Puerto Rico* 18°20N 66°59W **89 d**
			San Sebastián de la Gomera
			Canary Is. 28°5N 17°7W **24 F2**
			San Serra = Son Serra
			Spain 39°43N 3°13E **24 B10**
			San Severo *Italy* 41°41N 15°23E **22 D6**
			San Simeon *U.S.A.* 35°39N 121°11W **78 K5**
			San Simon *U.S.A.* 32°16N 109°14W **77 K9**
			San Telmo = Sant Elm
			Spain 39°35N 2°21E **24 B9**
			San Telmo *Mexico* 30°58N 116°6W **86 A1**
			San Tiburcio *Mexico* 24°8N 101°32W **86 C4**
			San Valentin, Mte. *Chile* 46°30S 73°30W **96 F2**
			San Vicente de Cañete
			Peru 13°8S 76°30W **92 F3**

160 San Vicente de la Barquera

INDEX TO WORLD MAPS

San Vicente de la Barquera *Spain* 43°23N 4°29W **21** A3
San Vito *Costa Rica* 8°50N 82°58W **88** E3
Sana' *Yemen* 15°27N 44°12E **47** D3
Sana → *Bos.-H.* 45°3N 16°23E **16** F9
Sanae IV *Antarctica* 70°20S 9°0W **5** D2
Sanaga → *Cameroon* 3°35N 9°38E **52** D1
Sanaloa, Presa *Mexico* 24°50N 107°20W **86** C3
Sanana *Indonesia* 2°4S 125°58E **37** E7
Sanand *India* 22°59N 72°25E **42** H5
Sanandaj *Iran* 35°18N 47°1E **44** C5
Sanandita *Bolivia* 21°40S 63°45W **94** A3
Sanawad *India* 22°11N 76°5E **42** H7
Sancellas = Sencelles *Spain* 39°39N 2°54E **24** B9
Sanchahe *China* 44°50N 126°2E **35** B14
Sánchez *Dom. Rep.* 19°15N 69°36W **89** C6
Sanchor *India* 24°45N 71°55E **42** G4
Sancti Spíritus *Cuba* 21°52N 79°33W **88** B4
Sancy, Puy de *France* 45°32N 2°50E **20** D5
Sand = Polokwane → *S. Africa* 22°25S 30°5E **57** C5
Sand Hills *U.S.A.* 42°10N 101°30W **80** D3
Sand Lakes ⌓ *Canada* 57°51N 98°32W **71** B9
Sand Springs *U.S.A.* 36°9N 96°7W **84** C6
Sanda *Japan* 34°53N 135°14E **31** G7
Sandakan *Malaysia* 5°53N 118°4E **36** C5
Sandan = Sambor *Cambodia* 12°46N 106°0E **38** F6
Sandanski *Bulgaria* 41°35N 23°16E **23** D10
Sanday *U.K.* 59°16N 2°31W **11** B6
Sandefjord *Norway* 59°10N 10°15E **9** G14
Sanders *U.S.A.* 35°13N 109°20W **77** J9
Sanderson *U.S.A.* 30°9N 102°24W **84** F3
Sandersville *U.S.A.* 32°59N 82°48W **85** E13
Sandfire Roadhouse *Australia* 19°45S 121°15E **60** C3
Sandfly L. *Canada* 55°43N 106°6W **71** B7
Sandfontein *Namibia* 23°48S 19°1E **56** C2
Sandheads, The *India* 21°10N 88°20E **43** J13
Sandía *Peru* 14°10S 69°30W **92** F5
Sandila *India* 27°5N 80°31E **43** F9
Sandnes *Norway* 58°50N 5°45E **9** G11
Sandnessjøen *Norway* 66°2N 12°38E **8** C15
Sandoa *Dem. Rep. of the Congo* 9°41S 23°0E **52** F4
Sandomierz *Poland* 50°40N 21°43E **17** C11
Sandover → *Australia* 21°43S 136°32E **62** C2
Sandoway = Thandwe *Burma* 18°20N 94°30E **41** K19
Sandoy *Færoe Is.* 61°52N 6°46W **8** F9
Sandpoint *U.S.A.* 48°17N 116°33W **76** B5
Sandray *U.K.* 56°53N 7°31W **11** E1
Sandringham *U.K.* 52°51N 0°31E **12** E8
Sandstone *Australia* 27°59S 119°16E **61** E2
Sandusky *Mich., U.S.A.* 43°25N 82°50W **82** C2
Sandusky *Ohio, U.S.A.* 41°27N 82°42W **82** E2
Sandveld *Namibia* 21°25S 20°0E **56** C3
Sandviken *Sweden* 60°38N 16°46E **8** F17
Sandwich, C. *Australia* 18°14S 146°18E **62** B4
Sandwich B. *Canada* 53°40N 57°15W **73** B8
Sandwich B. *Namibia* 23°25S 14°20E **56** C1
Sandy *Oreg., U.S.A.* 45°24N 122°16W **78** E4
Sandy *Pa., U.S.A.* 41°6N 78°46W **82** E6
Sandy *Utah, U.S.A.* 40°32N 111°50W **76** F8
Sandy Bay *Canada* 55°31N 102°19W **71** B8
Sandy Bight *Australia* 33°50S 123°20E **61** F3
Sandy C. *Queens., Australia* 24°42S 153°15E **62** C5
Sandy C. *Tas., Australia* 41°25S 144°45E **63** G3
Sandy Cay *Bahamas* 23°13N 75°18W **89** B4
Sandy Cr. → *U.S.A.* 41°51N 109°47W **76** F9
Sandy Creek *U.S.A.* 43°38N 76°5W **83** C8
Sandy L. *Canada* 53°2N 93°0W **72** B1
Sandy Lake *Canada* 53°0N 93°15W **72** B1
Sandy Valley *U.S.A.* 35°49N 115°38W **79** K11
Sanford *Fla., U.S.A.* 28°48N 81°16W **85** G14
Sanford *Maine, U.S.A.* 43°27N 70°47W **83** C14
Sanford *N.C., U.S.A.* 35°29N 79°10W **85** D15
Sanford → *Australia* 27°22S 115°53E **61** E2
Sanford, Mt. *U.S.A.* 62°13N 144°8W **68** C5
Sang-i-Masha *Afghan.* 33°8N 67°27E **42** C2
Sanga *Mozam.* 12°22S 35°21E **55** E4
Sanga → *Congo* 1°5S 17°0E **52** E3
Sangamner *India* 19°37N 74°15E **40** K9
Sangān *Iran* 34°23N 60°15E **45** C9
Sangar *Afghan.* 32°56N 65°30E **42** C1
Sangar *Russia* 64°2N 127°31E **29** C13
Sangar Sarai *Afghan.* 34°27N 70°35E **42** B4
Sangarh → *Pakistan* 30°43N 70°44E **42** D4
Sangay *Ecuador* 2°0S 78°20W **92** D3
Sange *Dem. Rep. of the Congo* 6°58S 28°21E **54** D2
Sangeang *Indonesia* 8°12S 119°6E **37** F5
Sanger *U.S.A.* 36°42N 119°33W **78** J7
Sangerhausen *Germany* 51°28N 11°18E **16** C6
Sanggan He → *China* 38°12N 117°15E **34** E9
Sanggau *Indonesia* 0°5N 110°30E **36** D4
Sanghar *Pakistan* 26°2N 68°57E **42** F3
Sangihe, Kepulauan *Indonesia* 3°0N 125°30E **37** D7
Sangihe, Pulau *Indonesia* 3°35N 125°30E **37** D7
Sangju *S. Korea* 36°25N 128°10E **35** F15
Sangkapura *Indonesia* 5°52S 112°40E **36** F4
Sangkhla Buri *Thailand* 14°57N 98°28E **38** E2
Sangkulirang *Indonesia* 0°59N 117°58E **36** D5
Sangla *Pakistan* 31°43N 73°23E **42** D5
Sangli *India* 16°55N 74°33E **40** L9
Sangmélima *Cameroon* 2°57N 12°1E **52** D2
Sangod *India* 24°55N 76°17E **42** G7
Sangre de Cristo Mts. *U.S.A.* 37°30N 105°20W **77** H11
Sangre Grande *Trin. & Tob.* 10°35N 61°8W **93** K15
Sangrur *India* 30°14N 75°50E **42** D6
Sangudo *Canada* 53°50N 114°54W **70** C6
Sangue → *Brazil* 11°1S 58°39W **92** F7
Sanibel *U.S.A.* 26°27N 82°1W **85** H13
Sanikluaq *Canada* 56°32N 79°14W **72** A4
Sanin-Kaigan △ *Japan* 35°39N 134°37E **31** G7
Sanirajak *Canada* 68°46N 81°12W **69** C11
Sanjawi *Pakistan* 30°17N 68°21E **42** D3
Sanje *Uganda* 0°49S 31°30E **54** C3
Sanjo *Japan* 37°37N 138°57E **30** F9
Sankh → *India* 22°15N 84°48E **43** H11
Sankt Gallen *Switz.* 47°26N 9°22E **20** C8
Sankt Michel = Mikkeli *Finland* 61°43N 27°15E **8** F22
Sankt Moritz *Switz.* 46°30N 9°51E **20** C8
Sankt-Peterburg *Russia* 59°55N 30°20E **9** G24
Sankt Pölten *Austria* 48°12N 15°38E **16** D8
Sankuru → *Dem. Rep. of the Congo* 4°17S 20°25E **52** E4
Sanliurfa *Turkey* 37°12N 38°50E **44** B3
Sanlúcar de Barrameda *Spain* 36°46N 6°21W **21** D2
Sanmenxia *China* 34°47N 111°12E **34** G6
Sanming *China* 26°15N 117°40E **33** D6
Sannicandro Gargánico *Italy* 41°50N 15°34E **22** D6
Sânnicolau Mare *Romania* 46°5N 20°39E **17** E11
Sannieshof *S. Africa* 26°30S 25°47E **56** D4
Sannīn, J. *Lebanon* 33°57N 35°52E **46** B4
Sanniquellie *Liberia* 7°19N 8°38W **50** G4
Sanok *Poland* 49°35N 22°10E **17** D12
Sanquhar *U.K.* 55°22N 3°54W **11** F5
Sans Souci *Trin. & Tob.* 10°50N 61°0W **93** K16
Sant Antoni de Portmany *Spain* 38°59N 1°19E **24** C7
Sant Carles *Spain* 39°3N 1°34E **24** B8
Sant Elm *Spain* 39°35N 2°21E **24** B9
Sant Feliu de Guíxols *Spain* 41°45N 3°1E **21** B7
Sant Ferran *Spain* 38°42N 1°28E **24** C7
Sant Francesc de Formentera *Spain* 38°42N 1°26E **24** C7
Sant Jaume *Spain* 39°54N 4°4E **24** B11
Sant Joan *Spain* 39°36N 3°4E **24** B10
Sant Joan de Labritja *Spain* 39°5N 1°31E **24** B8
Sant Jordi *Ibiza, Spain* 38°53N 1°24E **24** C7
Sant Jordi *Mallorca, Spain* 39°33N 2°46E **24** B9
Sant Jordi, G. de *Spain* 40°53N 1°2E **21** B6
Sant Llorenç des Cardassar *Spain* 39°37N 3°17E **24** B10
Sant Mateu *Spain* 39°3N 1°23E **24** B7
Sant Miquel *Spain* 39°3N 1°26E **24** B7
Sant Salvador *Spain* 39°27N 3°11E **24** B10
Santa Agnés *Spain* 39°3N 1°21E **24** B7
Santa Ana *Bolivia* 13°50S 65°40W **92** F5
Santa Ana *El Salv.* 14°0N 89°31W **88** D2
Santa Ana *Mexico* 30°33N 111°7W **86** A2
Santa Ana *U.S.A.* 33°46N 117°52W **79** M9
Sant' Antíoco *Italy* 39°4N 8°27E **22** E3
Santa Bárbara *Chile* 37°40S 72°1W **94** D1
Santa Bárbara *Honduras* 14°53N 88°14W **88** D2
Santa Bárbara *Mexico* 26°48N 105°49W **86** B3
Santa Barbara *U.S.A.* 34°25N 119°42W **79** L7
Santa Barbara Channel *U.S.A.* 34°15N 120°0W **79** L7
Santa Barbara I. *U.S.A.* 33°29N 119°2W **79** M7
Santa Catalina, Gulf of *U.S.A.* 33°10N 117°50W **79** N9
Santa Catalina, I. *Mexico* 25°40N 110°47W **86** B2
Santa Catalina I. *U.S.A.* 33°23N 118°25W **79** M8
Santa Catarina □ *Brazil* 27°25S 48°30W **95** B6
Santa Catarina, I. de *Brazil* 27°30S 48°40W **95** B6
Santa Cecília *Brazil* 26°56S 50°18W **95** B5
Santa Clara *Cuba* 22°20N 80°0W **88** B4
Santa Clara *Calif., U.S.A.* 37°21N 121°57W **78** H5
Santa Clara *N.Y., U.S.A.* 44°38N 74°27W **83** B10
Santa Clara *Utah, U.S.A.* 37°8N 113°39W **77** H7
Santa Clara de Olimar *Uruguay* 32°50S 54°54W **95** C5
Santa Clara Valley *U.S.A.* 36°50N 121°30W **78** J5
Santa Clarita *U.S.A.* 34°24N 118°33W **79** L8
Santa Clotilde *Peru* 2°33S 73°45W **92** D4
Santa Coloma de Gramenet *Spain* 41°27N 2°13E **21** B7
Santa Cruz *Bolivia* 17°43S 63°10W **92** G6
Santa Cruz *Chile* 34°38S 71°27W **94** C1
Santa Cruz *Costa Rica* 10°15N 85°35W **88** D2
Santa Cruz *Madeira* 32°42N 16°46W **24** D3
Santa Cruz *Phil.* 14°20N 121°24E **37** B6
Santa Cruz *U.S.A.* 36°58N 122°1W **78** J4
Santa Cruz → *Argentina* 50°10S 68°20W **96** G3
Santa Cruz de la Palma *Canary Is.* 28°41N 17°46W **24** F2
Santa Cruz de la Palma ✕ **(SPC)** *Canary Is.* 28°40N 17°45W **24** F2
Santa Cruz de Tenerife *Canary Is.* 28°28N 16°15W **24** F3
Santa Cruz del Norte *Cuba* 23°9N 81°55W **88** B3
Santa Cruz del Sur *Cuba* 20°44N 78°0W **88** B4
Santa Cruz do Rio Pardo *Brazil* 22°54S 49°37W **95** A6
Santa Cruz do Sul *Brazil* 29°42S 52°25W **95** B5
Santa Cruz I. *U.S.A.* 34°1N 119°43W **79** M7
Santa Cruz Is. *Solomon Is.* 10°30S 166°0E **58** C9
Santa Cruz Mts. *Jamaica* 17°58N 77°43W **88** a
Santa Domingo, Cay *Bahamas* 21°25N 75°15W **88** B4
Santa Elena *Argentina* 30°58S 59°47W **94** C4
Santa Elena, C. *Costa Rica* 10°54N 85°56W **88** D2
Santa Eulària des Riu *Spain* 38°59N 1°32E **24** C8
Santa Fé *Argentina* 31°35S 60°41W **94** C3
Santa Fe *U.S.A.* 35°41N 105°57W **77** J11
Santa Fé □ *Argentina* 31°50S 60°55W **94** C3
Santa Fé do Sul *Brazil* 20°13S 50°56W **93** H8
Santa Filomena *Brazil* 9°6S 45°50W **93** E9
Santa Gertrudis *Spain* 39°0N 1°26E **24** C7
Santa Inês *Brazil* 13°17S 39°48W **93** F11
Santa Inés, I. *Chile* 54°0S 73°0W **96** G2
Santa Isabel *Argentina* 36°10S 66°54W **94** D2
Santa Isabel do Morro *Brazil* 11°34S 50°40W **93** F8
Santa Lucía *Corrientes, Argentina* 28°58S 59°5W **94** B4
Santa Lucía *San Juan, Argentina* 31°30S 68°30W **94** C2
Santa Lucía *Uruguay* 34°27S 56°24W **94** C4
Santa Lucia Range *U.S.A.* 36°0N 121°20W **78** K5
Santa Luzia *C. Verde Is.* 16°50N 24°35W **50** b
Santa Margalida *Spain* 39°42N 3°6E **24** B10
Santa Margarita *Argentina* 38°28S 61°35W **94** D3
Santa Margarita *U.S.A.* 35°23N 120°37W **78** K6
Santa Margarita → *U.S.A.* 33°13N 117°23W **79** M9
Santa Margarita, I. *Mexico* 24°27N 111°50W **86** C2
Santa María *Argentina* 26°40S 66°0W **94** B2
Santa Maria *Azores* 36°58N 25°6W **50** a
Santa Maria *Brazil* 29°40S 53°48W **95** B5
Santa Maria *C. Verde Is.* 16°31N 22°53W **50** b
Santa Maria *U.S.A.* 34°57N 120°26W **79** L6
Santa María → *Mexico* 31°0N 107°14W **86** A3
Santa María, B. de *Mexico* 25°4N 108°6W **86** B3
Santa Maria da Vitória *Brazil* 13°24S 44°12W **93** F10
Santa María del Camí *Spain* 39°38N 2°47E **24** B9
Santa Maria di Léuca, C. *Italy* 39°47N 18°22E **23** E8
Santa Marta *Colombia* 11°15N 74°13W **92** A4
Santa Marta, Sierra Nevada de *Colombia* 10°55N 73°50W **92** A4
Santa Marta Grande, C. *Brazil* 28°43S 48°50W **95** B6
Santa Maura = Lefkada *Greece* 38°40N 20°43E **23** E9
Santa Monica *U.S.A.* 34°1N 118°29W **79** M8
Santa Monica Mts. ⌓ *U.S.A.* 34°4N 118°44W **79** L8
Santa Paula *U.S.A.* 34°21N 119°4W **79** L7
Santa Ponça *Spain* 39°30N 2°28E **24** B9
Santa Rosa *La Pampa, Argentina* 36°40S 64°17W **94** D3
Santa Rosa *San Luis, Argentina* 32°21S 65°10W **94** C2
Santa Rosa *Brazil* 27°52S 54°29W **95** B5
Santa Rosa *Calif., U.S.A.* 38°26N 122°43W **78** G4
Santa Rosa *N. Mex., U.S.A.* 34°57N 104°41W **77** J11
Santa Rosa and San Jacinto Mts. ⌓ *U.S.A.* 33°28N 116°20W **79** M10
Santa Rosa de Copán *Honduras* 14°47N 88°46W **88** D2
Santa Rosa de Río Primero *Argentina* 31°8S 63°20W **94** C3
Santa Rosa del Sara *Bolivia* 17°7S 63°35W **92** G6
Santa Rosa I. *Calif., U.S.A.* 33°58N 120°6W **79** M6
Santa Rosa I. *Fla., U.S.A.* 30°20N 86°50W **85** F11
Santa Rosa Range *U.S.A.* 41°45N 117°40W **76** F5
Santa Rosalía *Mexico* 27°19N 112°17W **86** B2
Santa Sylvina *Argentina* 27°50S 61°10W **94** B3
Santa Tecla = Nueva San Salvador *El Salv.* 13°40N 89°18W **88** D2
Santa Teresa *Argentina* 33°25S 60°47W **94** C3
Santa Teresa *Australia* 24°8S 134°22E **62** C1
Santa Teresa *Mexico* 25°17N 97°51W **87** B5
Santa Teresa △ *Uruguay* 33°57S 53°31W **95** C5
Santa Teresita *Argentina* 36°32S 56°41W **94** D4
Santa Vitória do Palmar *Brazil* 33°32S 53°25W **95** C5
Santa Ynez → *U.S.A.* 34°41N 120°36W **79** L6
Santa Ynez Mts. *U.S.A.* 34°30N 120°0W **79** L6
Santa Ysabel *U.S.A.* 33°7N 116°40W **79** M10
Santai *China* 31°5N 104°58E **32** C5
Santana *Madeira* 32°48N 16°52W **24** D3
Santana, Coxilha de *Brazil* 30°50S 55°35W **95** C4
Santana do Livramento *Brazil* 30°55S 55°30W **95** C4
Santander *Spain* 43°27N 3°51W **21** A4
Santander Jiménez *Mexico* 24°13N 98°28W **87** C5
Santanilla, Is. *Honduras* 17°22N 83°57W **88** C3
Santanyí *Spain* 39°20N 3°5E **24** B10
Santaquin *U.S.A.* 39°59N 111°47W **76** G8
Santarém *Brazil* 2°25S 54°42W **93** D8
Santarém *Portugal* 39°12N 8°42W **21** C1
Santaren Channel *W. Indies* 24°0N 79°30W **88** B4
Santee *U.S.A.* 32°50N 116°58W **79** N10
Santee → *U.S.A.* 33°7N 79°17W **85** E15
Santiago = Río Grande de Santiago → *Mexico* 21°36N 105°26W **86** C3
Santiago = São Tiago *C. Verde Is.* 15°0N 23°40W **50** b
Santiago *Brazil* 29°11S 54°52W **95** B5
Santiago *Canary Is.* 28°2N 17°12W **24** F2
Santiago *Chile* 33°26S 70°40W **94** C1
Santiago *Panama* 8°0N 81°0W **88** E3
Santiago → *Peru* 4°27S 77°38W **92** D3
Santiago de Compostela *Spain* 42°52N 8°37W **21** A1
Santiago de Cuba *Cuba* 20°0N 75°49W **88** C4
Santiago de los Caballeros *Dom. Rep.* 19°30N 70°40W **89** C5
Santiago del Estero *Argentina* 27°50S 64°15W **94** B3
Santiago del Estero □ *Argentina* 27°40S 63°15W **94** B3
Santiago del Teide *Canary Is.* 28°17N 16°48W **24** F3
Santiago Ixcuintla *Mexico* 21°49N 105°13W **86** C3
Santiago Jamiltepec *Mexico* 16°17N 97°49W **87** D5
Santiago Papasquiaro *Mexico* 25°3N 105°25W **86** C3
Santiago Pinotepa Nacional *Mexico* 16°19N 98°1W **87** D5
Santiaguillo, L. de *Mexico* 24°48N 104°48W **86** C4
Santo Amaro *Brazil* 12°30S 38°43W **93** F11
Santo Anastácio *Brazil* 21°58S 51°39W **95** A5
Santo André *Brazil* 23°39S 46°29W **95** A6
Santo Ângelo *Brazil* 28°15S 54°15W **95** B5
Santo Antão *C. Verde Is.* 16°52N 25°10W **50** b
Santo Antônio do Içá *Brazil* 3°5S 67°57W **92** D5
Santo Antônio do Leverger *Brazil* 15°52S 56°5W **93** G7
Santo Domingo *Dom. Rep.* 18°30N 69°59W **89** C6
Santo Domingo *Baja Calif., Mexico* 30°43N 116°2W **86** A1
Santo Domingo *Baja Calif. S., Mexico* 25°29N 111°55W **86** B2
Santo Domingo *Nic.* 12°14N 84°59W **88** D3
Santo Domingo de los Colorados *Ecuador* 0°15S 79°9W **92** D3
Santo Domingo Pueblo *U.S.A.* 35°31N 106°22W **77** J10
Santo Tomás *Mexico* 31°33N 116°24W **86** A1
Santo Tomás *Peru* 14°26S 72°8W **92** F4
Santo Tomé *Argentina* 28°40S 56°5W **95** B4
Santo Tomé de Guayana = Ciudad Guayana *Venezuela* 8°0N 62°30W **92** B6
Santoña *Spain* 43°29N 3°27W **21** A4
Santorini *Greece* 36°23N 25°27E **23** F11
Santos *Brazil* 24°0S 46°20W **95** A6
Santos Dumont *Brazil* 22°55S 43°10W **95** A7
Santuario de Aves Laguna Colorada △ *Bolivia* 22°10S 67°45W **94** A2
Sanur *Indonesia* 8°41S 115°15E **37** K18
Sanwer *India* 22°59N 75°50E **42** H6
Sanxiang *China* 22°21N 113°25E **33** G9
Sanya *China* 18°14N 109°29E **38** C7
Sanyuan *China* 34°35N 108°58E **34** G5
São Bernardo do Campo *Brazil* 23°45S 46°34W **95** A6
São Borja *Brazil* 28°39S 56°0W **95** B4
São Carlos *Brazil* 22°0S 47°50W **95** A6
São Cristóvão *Brazil* 11°1S 37°15W **93** F11
São Domingos *Brazil* 13°25S 46°19W **93** F9
São Filipe *C. Verde Is.* 15°2N 24°30W **50** b
São Francisco *Brazil* 16°0S 44°50W **93** G10
São Francisco → *Brazil* 10°30S 36°24W **93** F11
São Francisco do Sul *Brazil* 26°15S 48°36W **95** B6
São Gabriel *Brazil* 30°20S 54°20W **95** C5
São Gonçalo *Brazil* 22°48S 43°5W **95** A7
Sao Hill *Tanzania* 8°20S 35°12E **55** D4
São João da Boa Vista *Brazil* 22°0S 46°52W **95** A6
São João da Madeira *Portugal* 40°54N 8°30W **21** B1
São João del Rei *Brazil* 21°8S 44°15W **95** A7
São João do Araguaia *Brazil* 5°23S 48°46W **93** E9
São João do Piauí *Brazil* 8°21S 42°15W **93** E10
São Joaquim *Brazil* 28°18S 49°56W **95** B6
São Joaquim △ *Brazil* 28°12S 49°37W **95** B6
São Jorge *Azores* 38°38N 28°3W **50** a
São Jorge, Pta. de *Madeira* 32°50N 16°53W **24** D3
São José *Brazil* 27°38S 48°39W **95** B5
São José do Norte *Brazil* 32°1S 52°3W **95** C5
São José do Rio Preto *Brazil* 20°50S 49°20W **95** A6
São José dos Campos *Brazil* 23°7S 45°52W **95** A6
São Leopoldo *Brazil* 29°50S 51°10W **95** B5
São Lourenço *Brazil* 22°7S 45°3W **95** A6
São Lourenço → *Brazil* 17°53S 57°27W **93** G7
São Lourenço, Pta. de *Madeira* 32°44N 16°39W **24** D3
São Lourenço do Sul *Brazil* 31°22S 51°58W **95** C5
São Luís *Brazil* 2°39S 44°15W **93** D10
São Luís Gonzaga *Brazil* 28°25S 55°0W **95** B5
São Marcos → *Brazil* 18°15S 47°37W **93** G9
São Marcos, B. de *Brazil* 2°0S 44°0W **93** D10
São Mateus *Brazil* 18°44S 39°50W **93** G11
São Mateus do Sul *Brazil* 25°52S 50°23W **95** B5
São Miguel *Azores* 37°47N 25°30W **50** a
São Miguel do Oeste *Brazil* 26°45S 53°34W **95** B5
São Nicolau *C. Verde Is.* 16°20N 24°20W **50** b
São Paulo *Brazil* 23°32S 46°38W **95** A6
São Paulo □ *Brazil* 22°0S 49°0W **95** A6
São Paulo de Olivença *Brazil* 3°27S 68°48W **92** D5
São Roque *Madeira* 32°46N 16°48W **24** D3
São Roque, C. de *Brazil* 5°30S 35°16W **93** E11
São Sebastião, I. de *Brazil* 23°50S 45°18W **95** A6
São Sebastião do Paraíso *Brazil* 20°54S 46°59W **95** A6
São Tiago *C. Verde Is.* 15°0N 23°40W **50** b
São Tomé *São Tomé & Príncipe* 0°10N 6°39E **48** F4
São Tomé, C. de *Brazil* 22°0S 40°59W **95** A7
São Tomé & Príncipe ■ *Africa* 0°12N 6°39E **49** F4
São Vicente *Brazil* 23°57S 46°23W **95** A6
São Vicente *C. Verde Is.* 17°0N 25°0W **50** b
São Vicente *Madeira* 32°48N 17°3W **24** D2
São Vicente, C. de *Portugal* 37°0N 9°0W **21** D1
Saona, I. *Dom. Rep.* 18°10N 68°40W **89** C6
Saône → *France* 45°44N 4°50E **20** D6
Saonek *Indonesia* 0°22S 130°55E **37** E8
Sapam, Ao *Thailand* 8°0N 98°26E **39** a
Saparua *Indonesia* 3°33S 128°40E **37** E7
Sapele *Nigeria* 5°50N 5°40E **50** G7
Sapelo I. *U.S.A.* 31°25N 81°12W **85** F14
Sapi ⌓ *Zimbabwe* 15°48S 29°42E **55** F2
Saposoa *Peru* 6°55S 76°45W **92** E3
Sapphire *Australia* 23°28S 147°43E **62** C4
Sappho *U.S.A.* 48°4N 124°16W **78** B2
Sapporo *Japan* 43°0N 141°21E **30** C10
Sapulpa *U.S.A.* 35°59N 96°5W **84** D6
Saqqez *Iran* 36°15N 46°20E **44** B5
Sar Dasht *Āzarbāyjān-e Gharbī, Iran* 36°9N 45°28E **44** B5
Sar Dasht *Khuzestān, Iran* 32°32N 48°52E **45** C6
Sar-e Pol □ *Afghan.* 36°20N 65°50E **40** B4
Sar Gachīneh = Yāsūj *Iran* 30°31N 51°31E **45** D6
Sar Planina *Macedonia* 42°0N 21°0E **23** C9
Sara Buri = Saraburi *Thailand* 14°30N 100°55E **38** E3
Sarāb *Iran* 37°55N 47°40E **44** B5
Sarābādī *Iraq* 33°1N 44°48E **44** C5
Saraburi *Thailand* 14°30N 100°55E **38** E3
Saradiya *India* 21°34N 70°2E **42** J4
Saragossa = Zaragoza *Spain* 41°39N 0°53W **21** B5
Saraguro *Ecuador* 3°35S 79°16W **92** D3
Sarahs *Turkmenistan* 36°32N 61°13E **45** B9
Sarai Naurang *Pakistan* 32°50N 70°47E **42** C4
Saraikela *India* 22°42N 85°56E **43** H11
Sarajevo *Bos.-H.* 43°52N 18°26E **23** C8
Sarakhs = Sarahs *Turkmenistan* 36°32N 61°13E **45** B9
Saran, Gunung *Indonesia* 0°30S 111°25E **36** E4
Saranac Lake *U.S.A.* 44°20N 74°10W **83** B10
Saranac Lakes *U.S.A.* 44°20N 74°28W **83** B10
Saranda *Tanzania* 5°45S 34°59E **54** D3
Sarandí del Yí *Uruguay* 33°18S 55°38W **95** C4
Sarandí Grande *Uruguay* 33°44S 56°20W **94** C4
Sarangani B. *Phil.* 6°0N 125°13E **37** C7
Sarangani Is. *Phil.* 5°25N 125°25E **37** C7
Sarangarh *India* 21°30N 83°5E **41** J13
Saransk *Russia* 54°10N 45°10E **18** D8
Sarapul *Russia* 56°28N 53°48E **18** C9
Sarasota *U.S.A.* 27°20N 82°32W **85** H13
Saratoga *Calif., U.S.A.* 37°16N 122°2W **78** H4
Saratoga *Wyo., U.S.A.* 41°27N 106°49W **76** F10
Saratoga ⌓ *U.S.A.* 43°0N 73°38W **83** D11
Saratoga L. *U.S.A.* 43°1N 73°44W **83** C11
Saratoga Springs *U.S.A.* 43°5N 73°47W **83** C11
Saratok *Malaysia* 1°55N 111°17E **36** D4
Saratov *Russia* 51°30N 46°2E **19** D8
Sarāvān *Iran* 27°25N 62°15E **45** E9
Saravane *Laos* 15°43N 106°25E **38** E6
Sarawak □ *Malaysia* 2°0N 113°0E **36** D4
Saray *Turkey* 41°26N 27°55E **23** D12
Sarayköy *Turkey* 37°55N 28°54E **23** F13
Sarbāz *Iran* 26°38N 61°19E **45** E9
Sarbīsheh *Iran* 32°30N 59°40E **45** C8
Sarda → *India* 27°21N 81°23E **43** F9
Sardarshahr *India* 28°30N 74°29E **42** E6
Sardegna □ *Italy* 40°0N 9°0E **22** D3
Sardhana *India* 29°9N 77°39E **42** E7
Sardina, Pta. *Canary Is.* 28°9N 15°44W **24** F4
Sardinia = Sardegna □ *Italy* 40°0N 9°0E **22** D3
Sardis *Turkey* 38°28N 27°58E **23** E12
Sārdūīyeh = Dar Mazār *Iran* 29°14N 57°20E **45** D8
Saren *Indonesia* 8°26S 115°34E **37** J18
S'Arenal *Spain* 39°30N 2°45E **24** B9
Sarera, G. of *Indonesia* 2°0S 135°0E **58** B6
Sargasso Sea *Atl. Oc.* 27°0N 72°0W **66** G13
Sargodha *Pakistan* 32°10N 72°40E **42** C5
Sarh *Chad* 9°5N 18°23E **51** G9
Sārī *Iran* 36°30N 53°4E **45** B7
Saria *India* 21°38N 83°22E **43** J10
Sariab *Pakistan* 30°6N 66°59E **42** D2
Sarıgöl *Turkey* 38°14N 28°41E **23** E13
Sarikei *Malaysia* 2°8N 111°30E **36** D4
Sarila *India* 25°46N 79°41E **43** G8
Sarina *Australia* 21°22S 149°13E **62** C4
Sarita *U.S.A.* 27°13N 97°47W **84** H6
Sariwŏn *N. Korea* 38°31N 125°46E **35** E13
Sarju → *India* 27°21N 81°23E **43** F9
Sark *U.K.* 49°25N 2°22W **13** H5
Sarkari Tala *India* 27°39N 70°52E **42** F4
Şarköy *Turkey* 40°36N 27°6E **23** D12
Sarlat-la-Canéda *France* 44°54N 1°13E **20** D4
Sarmi *Indonesia* 1°49S 138°44E **37** E9
Sarmiento *Argentina* 45°35S 69°5W **96** F3
Särna *Sweden* 61°41N 13°8E **8** F15
Sarnia *Canada* 42°58N 82°23W **82** D2
Sarolangun *Indonesia* 2°19S 102°42E **36** E2
Saronikos Kolpos *Greece* 37°45N 23°45E **23** F10
Saros Körfezi *Turkey* 40°30N 26°15E **23** D12
Sarpsborg *Norway* 59°16N 11°7E **9** G14
Sarqan *Kazakhstan* 45°24N 79°55E **32** B2
Sarre = Saar → *Europe* 49°41N 6°32E **15** E6
Sarreguemines *France* 49°5N 7°4E **20** B7

Sarthe → *France* 47°33N 0°31W **20** C3
Saruna → *Pakistan* 26°31N 67°7E **42** F2
Sarvar *India* 26°4N 75°0E **42** F6
Sarvestān *Iran* 29°20N 53°10E **45** D7
Sary-Tash *Kyrgyzstan* 39°44N 73°15E **28** F8
Saryshaghan *Kazakhstan* 46°12N 73°38E **28** E8
Sasan Gir *India* 21°10N 70°36E **42** J4
Sasaram *India* 24°57N 84°5E **43** G11
Sasebo *Japan* 33°10N 129°43E **31** H4
Saser Kangri *India* 34°50N 77°50E **43** B7
Saskatchewan □
  Canada 54°40N 106°0W **71** C7
Saskatchewan →
  Canada 53°37N 100°40W **71** C8
Saskatoon *Canada* 52°10N 106°38W **71** C7
Saskylakh *Russia* 71°55N 114°1E **29** B12
Saslaya △ *Nic.* 13°45N 85°4W **88** D2
Sasolburg *S. Africa* 26°46S 27°49E **57** D4
Sasovo *Russia* 54°25N 41°55E **18** D7
Sassandra *Ivory C.* 4°55N 6°8W **50** H4
Sassandra → *Ivory C.* 4°58N 6°5W **50** H4
Sássari *Italy* 40°43N 8°34E **22** D3
Sassnitz *Germany* 54°29N 13°39E **16** A7
Sassuolo *Italy* 44°33N 10°47E **22** B4
Sasyk, Ozero *Ukraine* 45°45N 29°20E **17** F15
Sata-Misaki *Japan* 31°0N 130°40E **31** J5
Satadougou *Mali* 12°25N 11°25W **50** F3
Satakunda = Satakunta
  Finland 61°45N 23°0E **8** F20
Satakunta *Finland* 61°45N 23°0E **8** F20
Satara *India* 17°44N 73°58E **40** L8
Satara *S. Africa* 24°29S 31°47E **57** C5
Satbarwa *India* 23°55N 84°16E **43** H11
Satevó *Mexico* 27°57N 106°7W **86** B3
Satilla → *U.S.A.* 30°59N 81°29W **85** F14
Satka *Russia* 55°3N 59°1E **18** C10
Satmala Hills *Andhra Pradesh,*
  India 19°45N 78°45E **40** K11
Satmala Hills *Maharashtra,*
  India 20°15N 74°40E **40** J9
Satna *India* 24°35N 80°50E **43** G9
Sátoraljaújhely
  Hungary 48°25N 21°41E **17** D11
Satpura △ *India* 22°40N 78°15E **42** J7
Satpura Ra. *India* 21°25N 76°10E **40** J10
Satsuna-Shotō *Japan* 30°0N 130°0E **31** K5
Sattahip *Thailand* 12°41N 100°54E **38** F3
Satu Mare *Romania* 47°46N 22°55E **17** E12
Satui *Indonesia* 3°50S 115°27E **36** E5
Satun *Thailand* 6°43N 100°2E **39** J3
Satupa'itea *Samoa* 13°45S 172°18W **59** b
Saturnina → *Brazil* 12°15S 58°10W **92** F7
Sauce *Argentina* 30°5S 58°46W **94** C4
Sauceda *Mexico* 25°46N 101°19W **86** B4
Saucillo *Mexico* 28°1N 105°17W **86** B3
Sauda *Norway* 59°40N 6°20E **9** G12
Sauðárkrókur *Iceland* 65°45N 19°40W **8** D4
Saudi Arabia ■ *Asia* 26°0N 44°0E **44** B3
Sauerland *Germany* 51°12N 7°59E **16** C4
Saugeen → *Canada* 44°30N 81°22W **82** B3
Saugerties *U.S.A.* 42°5N 73°57W **83** D11
Saugus *U.S.A.* 34°25N 118°32W **79** L8
Sauk Centre *U.S.A.* 45°44N 94°57W **80** C6
Sauk Rapids *U.S.A.* 45°35N 94°10W **80** C6
Sault Ste. Marie *Canada* 46°30N 84°20W **72** C3
Sault Ste. Marie *U.S.A.* 46°30N 84°21W **81** B11
Saumlaki *Indonesia* 7°55S 131°20E **37** F8
Saumur *France* 47°15N 0°5W **20** C3
Saunders, C. *N.Z.* 45°53S 170°45E **59** F3
Saunders I. *Antarctica* 57°48S 26°28W **5** B1
Saunders Pt. *Australia* 27°52S 125°38E **61** E4
Saurimo *Angola* 9°40S 20°12E **52** F4
Sausalito *U.S.A.* 37°51N 122°29W **78** H4
Savá *Honduras* 15°32N 86°15W **88** C2
Sava → *Serbia* 44°50N 20°26E **23** B9
Savage *U.S.A.* 47°27N 104°21W **76** C11
Savage I. = Niue
  Pac. Oc. 19°2S 169°54W **65** J11
Savage River *Australia* 41°31S 145°14E **63** G4
Savai'i *Samoa* 13°28S 172°24W **59** b
Savalou *Benin* 7°57N 1°58E **50** G6
Savane *Mozam.* 19°37S 35°8E **55** F4
Savanna *U.S.A.* 42°5N 90°8W **80** D8
Savanna-la-Mar *Jamaica* 18°10N 78°10W **88** a
Savannah *Ga., U.S.A.* 32°5N 81°6W **85** E14
Savannah *Mo., U.S.A.* 39°56N 94°50W **80** F6
Savannah *Tenn., U.S.A.* 35°14N 88°15W **85** D10
Savannah → *U.S.A.* 32°2N 80°53W **85** E14
Savannakhet *Laos* 16°30N 104°49E **38** D5
Savant L. *Canada* 50°16N 90°44W **72** B1
Savant Lake *Canada* 50°14N 90°40W **72** B1
Save → *Mozam.* 21°16S 34°0E **57** C5
Sāveh *Iran* 35°2N 50°20E **45** C6
Savelugu *Ghana* 9°38N 0°54W **50** G5
Savo *Finland* 62°45N 27°30E **8** E22
Savoie □ *France* 45°26N 6°25E **20** D7
Savolax = Savo *Finland* 62°45N 27°30E **8** E22
Savona *Italy* 44°17N 8°30E **20** D8
Savona *U.S.A.* 42°17N 77°13W **82** D7
Savonlinna *Finland* 61°52N 28°53E **8** F23
Savoy = Savoie □ *France* 45°26N 6°25E **20** D7
Savur *Turkey* 37°34N 40°53E **44** B4
Savusavu *Fiji* 16°34S 179°15E **59** a
Savusavu B. *Fiji* 16°45S 179°15E **59** a
Sawahlunto *Indonesia* 0°40S 100°52E **36** E2
Sawai *Indonesia* 3°0S 129°5E **37** E7
Sawai Madhopur *India* 26°0N 76°25E **42** G7
Sawaleke *Fiji* 17°59S 179°18E **59** a
Sawang Daen Din
  Thailand 17°28N 103°28E **38** D4
Sawankhalok *Thailand* 17°19N 99°50E **38** D2
Sawara *Japan* 35°55N 140°30E **31** G10
Sawatch Range *U.S.A.* 39°0N 106°30W **76** G10
Sawel Mt. *U.K.* 54°50N 7°2W **10** B4
Sawi *Thailand* 10°14N 99°5E **39** G2
Sawmills *Zimbabwe* 19°30S 28°2E **55** F2
Sawtooth → *U.S.A.* 44°0N 114°50W **76** D6

Sawtooth Range *U.S.A.* 44°3N 114°58W **76** D6
Sawu *Indonesia* 10°35S 121°50E **37** F6
Sawu Sea *Indonesia* 9°30S 121°50E **37** F6
Saxby → *Australia* 18°25S 140°53E **62** B3
Saxmundham *U.K.* 52°13N 1°30E **13** E9
Saxony = Sachsen □
  Germany 50°55N 13°10E **16** C7
Saxony, Lower =
  Niedersachsen □
  Germany 52°50N 9°0E **16** B5
Saxton *U.S.A.* 40°13N 78°15W **82** F6
Sayabec *Canada* 48°35N 67°41W **73** C6
Sayaboury *Laos* 19°15N 101°45E **38** C3
Sayán *Peru* 11°8S 77°12W **92** F3
Sayan, Vostochnyy
  Russia 54°0N 96°0E **29** D10
Sayan, Zapadnyy *Russia* 52°30N 94°0E **32** A4
Sayanogorsk *Russia* 53°5N 91°23E **29** D10
Saydā *Lebanon* 33°35N 35°25E **46** B4
Sayhandulaan = Oldziyt
  Mongolia 44°40N 109°1E **34** B5
Sayḥūt *Yemen* 15°12N 51°10E **47** D5
Saylac *Somali Rep.* 11°21N 43°30E **47** E3
Saynshand = Buyant-Uhaa
  Mongolia 44°55N 110°11E **33** B6
Sayre *Okla., U.S.A.* 35°18N 99°38W **84** D5
Sayre *Pa., U.S.A.* 41°59N 76°32W **83** E8
Sayreville *U.S.A.* 40°28N 74°22W **83** F10
Sayula *Mexico* 19°52N 103°36W **86** D4
Sayward *Canada* 50°21N 125°55W **70** C3
Sazanit *Albania* 40°30N 19°20E **23** D8
Sázava → *Czech Rep.* 49°53N 14°24E **16** D8
Sazin *Pakistan* 35°35N 73°30E **43** B5
Scafell Pike *U.K.* 54°27N 3°14W **12** C4
Scalloway *U.K.* 60°9N 1°17W **11** A7
Scalpay *U.K.* 57°18N 6°0W **11** D3
Scandia *Canada* 50°20N 112°2W **70** C6
Scandicci *Italy* 43°45N 11°11E **22** C4
Scandinavia *Europe* 64°0N 12°0E **8** E15
Scapa Flow *U.K.* 58°53N 3°3W **11** C5
Scappoose *U.S.A.* 45°45N 122°53W **78** E4
Scarba *U.K.* 56°11N 5°43W **11** E3
Scarborough
  Trin. & Tob. 11°11N 60°42W **89** D7
Scarborough *U.K.* 54°17N 0°24W **12** C7
Scariff I. *Ireland* 51°44N 10°15W **10** E1
Scarp *U.K.* 58°1N 7°8W **11** C1
Scebeli = Shabeelle →
  Somali Rep. 2°0N 44°0E **47** G3
Schaffhausen *Switz.* 47°42N 8°39E **20** C8
Schagen *Neths.* 52°49N 4°48E **15** B4
Schaghticoke *U.S.A.* 42°54N 73°35W **83** D11
Schefferville *Canada* 54°48N 66°50W **73** B6
Schelde → *Belgium* 51°15N 4°16E **15** C4
Schell Creek Ra. *U.S.A.* 39°25N 114°40W **76** G6
Schellsburg *U.S.A.* 40°3N 78°39W **82** F6
Schenectady *U.S.A.* 42°49N 73°57W **83** D11
Schenevus *U.S.A.* 42°33N 74°50W **83** D10
Schiedam *Neths.* 51°55N 4°25E **15** C4
Schiermonnikoog *Neths.* 53°30N 6°15E **15** A6
Schio *Italy* 45°43N 11°21E **22** B4
Schiphol, Amsterdam ✈ (AMS)
  Neths. 52°18N 4°45E **15** B4
Schleswig *Germany* 54°31N 9°34E **16** A5
Schleswig-Holstein □
  Germany 54°30N 9°30E **16** A5
Schœlcher *Martinique* 14°36N 61°7W **88** c
Schoharie *U.S.A.* 42°40N 74°19W **83** D10
Schoharie Cr. →
  U.S.A. 42°57N 74°18W **83** D10
Scholls *U.S.A.* 45°24N 122°56W **78** E4
Schouten I. *Australia* 42°20S 148°20E **63** G4
Schouten Is. = Supiori
  Indonesia 1°0S 136°0E **37** E9
Schouwen *Neths.* 51°43N 3°45E **15** C3
Schreiber *Canada* 48°45N 87°20W **72** C2
Schroffenstein *Namibia* 27°11S 18°42E **56** D2
Schroon Lake *U.S.A.* 43°50N 73°46W **83** C11
Schuler *Canada* 50°20N 110°6W **71** C6
Schumacher *Canada* 48°30N 81°16W **72** C3
Schurz *U.S.A.* 38°57N 118°49W **76** G4
Schuyler *U.S.A.* 41°27N 97°4W **80** E5
Schuylerville *U.S.A.* 43°6N 73°35W **83** C11
Schuylkill → *U.S.A.* 39°53N 75°12W **83** G9
Schuylkill Haven *U.S.A.* 40°37N 76°11W **83** F8
Schwäbische Alb
  Germany 48°20N 9°30E **16** D5
Schwaner, Pegunungan
  Indonesia 1°0S 112°30E **36** E4
Schwarzrand *Namibia* 25°37S 16°50E **56** D2
Schwarzwald *Germany* 48°30N 8°20E **16** D5
Schwedt *Germany* 53°3N 14°16E **16** B8
Schweinfurt *Germany* 50°3N 10°14E **16** C6
Schweiz = Switzerland ■
  Europe 46°30N 8°0E **20** C8
Schweizer-Reneke
  S. Africa 27°11S 25°18E **56** D4
Schwenningen = Villingen-
  Schwenningen *Germany* 48°3N 8°26E **16** D5
Schwerin *Germany* 53°36N 11°22E **16** B6
Schwyz *Switz.* 47°2N 8°39E **20** C8
Sciacca *Italy* 37°31N 13°3E **22** F5
Scilla *Italy* 38°15N 15°43E **22** E6
Scilly, Isles of *U.K.* 49°56N 6°22W **13** H1
Scioto → *U.S.A.* 38°44N 83°1W **81** F12
Scituate *U.S.A.* 42°12N 70°44W **83** D14
Scobey *U.S.A.* 48°47N 105°25W **76** B11
Scone *Australia* 32°5S 150°52E **63** E5
Scone *U.K.* 56°25N 3°24W **11** E5
Scoresbysund = Ittoqqortoormiit
  Greenland 70°20N 23°0W **4** B6
Scotia *Calif., U.S.A.* 40°29N 124°6W **76** F1
Scotia *N.Y., U.S.A.* 42°50N 73°58W **83** D11
Scotia Sea *Antarctica* 56°5S 56°0W **5** B18
Scotland *Canada* 43°1N 80°22W **82** C4
Scotland □ *U.K.* 57°0N 4°0W **11** E5
Scott *Antarctica* 77°0S 165°0E **5** D11

Scott, C. *Australia* 13°30S 129°49E **60** B4
Scott City *U.S.A.* 38°29N 100°54W **80** F3
Scott Glacier *Antarctica* 66°15S 100°5E **5** C8
Scott I. *Antarctica* 67°0S 179°0E **5** C11
Scott Is. *Canada* 50°48N 128°40W **70** C3
Scott L. *Canada* 59°55N 106°18W **71** B7
Scott Reef *Australia* 14°0S 121°50E **60** B3
Scottburgh *S. Africa* 30°15S 30°47E **57** E5
Scottdale *U.S.A.* 40°6N 79°35W **82** F5
Scottish Borders □ *U.K.* 55°35N 2°50W **11** F6
Scotts Valley *U.S.A.* 37°3N 122°1W **78** H4
Scottsbluff *U.S.A.* 41°52N 103°40W **80** E2
Scottsboro *U.S.A.* 34°40N 86°2W **85** D11
Scottsburg *U.S.A.* 38°41N 85°47W **81** F11
Scottsdale *Australia* 41°9S 147°31E **63** G4
Scottsdale *U.S.A.* 33°40N 111°53W **77** K8
Scottsville *Ky., U.S.A.* 36°45N 86°11W **85** C11
Scottsville *N.Y., U.S.A.* 43°2N 77°47W **82** C7
Scottville *U.S.A.* 43°58N 86°17W **80** D10
Scranton *U.S.A.* 41°25N 75°40W **83** E9
Scugog, L. *Canada* 44°10N 78°55W **82** B6
Scunthorpe *U.K.* 53°36N 0°39W **12** D7
Scutari = Shkodër
  Albania 42°4N 19°32E **23** C8
Sea Is. *U.S.A.* 31°30N 81°7W **85** F14
Seabrook, L. *Australia* 30°55S 119°40E **61** F2
Seaford *U.K.* 50°47N 0°7E **13** G8
Seaford *U.S.A.* 38°39N 75°37W **81** F16
Seaforth *Australia* 20°55S 148°57E **62** J6
Seaforth *Canada* 43°35N 81°25W **82** C3
Seaforth, L. *U.K.* 57°52N 6°36W **11** D2
Seaham *U.K.* 54°50N 1°20W **12** C6
Seal → *Canada* 59°4N 94°48W **71** B10
Seal L. *Canada* 54°20N 61°30W **73** B7
Sealy *U.S.A.* 29°47N 96°9W **84** G6
Searchlight *U.S.A.* 35°28N 114°55W **79** K12
Searcy *U.S.A.* 35°15N 91°44W **84** D9
Searles L. *U.S.A.* 35°44N 117°21W **79** K9
Seascale *U.K.* 54°24N 3°29W **12** C4
Seaside *Calif., U.S.A.* 36°37N 121°50W **78** J5
Seaside *Oreg., U.S.A.* 46°0N 123°56W **78** E3
Seaspray *Australia* 38°25S 147°15E **63** F4
Seattle *U.S.A.* 47°36N 122°19W **78** C4
Seattle-Tacoma Int. ✈ (SEA)
  U.S.A. 47°27N 122°18W **78** C4
Seaview Ra. *Australia* 18°40S 145°45E **62** B4
Sebago L. *U.S.A.* 43°52N 70°34W **83** C14
Sebago Lake *U.S.A.* 43°51N 70°34W **83** C14
Sebastián Vizcaíno, B.
  Mexico 28°0N 114°30W **86** B2
Sebastopol = Sevastopol
  Ukraine 44°35N 33°30E **19** F5
Sebastopol *U.S.A.* 38°24N 122°49W **78** G4
Sebewaing *U.S.A.* 43°44N 83°27W **81** D12
Sebha = Sabhā *Libya* 27°9N 14°29E **51** C8
Şebinkarahisar *Turkey* 40°22N 38°28E **19** F6
Sebring *Fla., U.S.A.* 27°30N 81°27W **85** H14
Sebring *Ohio, U.S.A.* 40°55N 81°2W **82** F3
Sebringville *Canada* 43°24N 81°4W **82** C3
Sebta = Ceuta *N. Afr.* 35°52N 5°18W **21** E3
Sebuku *Indonesia* 3°30S 116°25E **36** E5
Sebuku, Teluk *Malaysia* 4°0N 118°10E **36** D5
Sechelt *Canada* 49°25N 123°42W **70** D4
Sechura, Desierto de *Peru* 6°0S 80°30W **92** E2
Secretary I. *N.Z.* 45°15S 166°56E **59** F1
Secunderabad *India* 17°28N 78°30E **40** L11
Security *U.S.A.* 38°45N 104°45W **76** G11
Sedalia *U.S.A.* 38°42N 93°14W **80** F7
Sedan *France* 49°43N 4°57E **20** B6
Sedan *U.S.A.* 37°8N 96°11W **80** G6
Sedbergh *U.K.* 54°20N 2°31W **12** C5
Seddon *N.Z.* 41°40S 174°7E **59** D5
Seddonville *N.Z.* 41°33S 172°1E **59** D4
Sedé Boqér *Israel* 30°52N 34°47E **46** E3
Sedeh *Fārs, Iran* 30°45N 52°11E **45** D7
Sedeh *Khorāsān, Iran* 33°20N 59°14E **45** C8
Sederot *Israel* 31°32N 34°37E **46** D3
Sédhiou *Senegal* 12°44N 15°30W **50** F2
Sedley *Canada* 50°10N 104°0W **71** C8
Sedona *U.S.A.* 34°52N 111°46W **77** J8
Sedro-Woolley *U.S.A.* 48°30N 122°14W **78** B4
Seeheim *Namibia* 26°50S 17°45E **56** D2
Seeis *Namibia* 22°29S 17°39E **56** C2
Seekoei → *S. Africa* 30°18S 25°1E **56** E4
Seeley's Bay *Canada* 44°29N 76°14W **83** B8
Seferihisar *Turkey* 38°10N 26°50E **23** E12
Seg-ozero *Russia* 63°20N 33°46E **18** B5
Segamat *Malaysia* 2°30N 102°50E **39** L4
Segesta *Italy* 37°56N 12°50E **22** F5
Seget *Indonesia* 1°24S 130°58E **37** E8
Segezha *Russia* 63°44N 34°19E **18** B5
Ségou *Mali* 13°30N 6°16W **50** F4
Segovia = Coco →
  Cent. Amer. 15°0N 83°8W **88** D3
Segovia *Spain* 40°57N 4°10W **21** B3
Segre → *Spain* 41°40N 0°43E **21** B6
Séguéla *Ivory C.* 7°55N 6°40W **50** G4
Seguin *U.S.A.* 29°34N 97°58W **84** G6
Segundo → *Argentina* 30°53S 62°44W **94** C3
Segura → *Spain* 38°3N 0°44W **21** C5
Seh Konj, Kūh-e *Iran* 30°6N 57°30E **45** D8
Seh Qal'eh *Iran* 33°40N 58°24E **45** C8
Sehitwa *Botswana* 20°30S 22°30E **56** C3
Sehlabathebe △ *Lesotho* 29°53S 29°7E **57** D4
Sehore *India* 23°10N 77°5E **42** H7
Sehwan *Pakistan* 26°28N 67°53E **42** F2
Seikan Tunnel *Japan* 41°28N 140°10E **30** D10
Seil *U.K.* 56°18N 5°38W **11** E3
Seiland *Norway* 70°25N 23°15E **8** A20
Seiling *U.S.A.* 36°9N 98°56W **84** C5
Seinäjoki *Finland* 62°40N 22°51E **8** E20
Seine → *France* 49°26N 0°26E **20** B4
Seistan = Sīstān *Asia* 30°50N 61°0E **45** D9
Seistan, Daryācheh-ye = Sīstān,
  Daryācheh-ye *Iran* 31°0N 61°0E **45** D9

Sekayu *Indonesia* 2°51S 103°51E **36** E2
Seke *Tanzania* 3°20S 33°31E **54** C3
Sekenke *Tanzania* 4°18S 34°11E **54** C3
Sekondi-Takoradi *Ghana* 4°58N 1°45W **50** H5
Sekudai *Malaysia* 1°32N 103°39E **39** d
Sekuma *Botswana* 24°36S 23°50E **56** C3
Selah *U.S.A.* 46°39N 120°32W **76** C3
Selama *Malaysia* 5°12N 100°42E **39** K3
Selaru *Indonesia* 8°9S 131°0E **37** F8
Selatan, Selat *Malaysia* 5°15N 100°20E **39** c
Selby *U.K.* 53°47N 1°5W **12** D6
Selby *U.S.A.* 45°31N 100°2W **80** C3
Selçuk *Turkey* 37°56N 27°22E **23** F12
Selden *U.S.A.* 39°33N 100°34W **80** F3
Sele → *Italy* 40°29N 14°56E **22** D6
Selebi-Phikwe *Botswana* 21°58S 27°48E **57** C4
Selemdzha → *Russia* 51°42N 128°53E **29** D13
Selenga = Selenge Mörön →
  Asia 52°16N 106°16E **32** A5
Selenge Mörön → *Asia* 52°16N 106°16E **32** A5
Seletan, Tanjung
  Indonesia 4°10S 114°40E **36** E4
Sélibabi *Mauritania* 15°10N 12°15W **50** E3
Seligman *U.S.A.* 35°20N 112°53W **77** J7
Selima, El Wâhât el
  Sudan 21°22N 29°19E **51** D11
Selinda Spillway →
  Botswana 18°35S 23°10E **56** B3
Selinsgrove *U.S.A.* 40°48N 76°52W **82** F8
Selkirk *Canada* 50°10N 96°55W **71** C9
Selkirk *U.K.* 55°33N 2°50W **11** F6
Selkirk I. = Horse I.
  Canada 53°20N 99°6W **71** C9
Selkirk Mts. *Canada* 51°15N 117°40W **68** D8
Sellafield *U.K.* 54°25N 3°29W **12** C4
Sellia *Greece* 35°12N 24°23E **25** D6
Sells *U.S.A.* 31°55N 111°53W **77** L8
Selma *Ala., U.S.A.* 32°25N 87°1W **85** E11
Selma *Calif., U.S.A.* 36°34N 119°37W **78** J7
Selma *N.C., U.S.A.* 35°32N 78°17W **85** D15
Selmer *U.S.A.* 35°10N 88°36W **85** D10
Selous △ *Tanzania* 8°37S 37°42E **55** D4
Selowandoma Falls
  Zimbabwe 21°15S 31°50E **55** G3
Selpele *Indonesia* 0°1S 130°5E **37** E8
Selsey Bill *U.K.* 50°43N 0°47W **13** G7
Seltso *Russia* 53°22N 34°4E **18** D5
Selu *Indonesia* 7°32S 130°55E **37** F8
Selva *Argentina* 29°50S 62°0W **94** B3
Selva *Spain* 39°46N 2°54E **24** B9
Selva Lancandona = Montes
  Azules △ *Mexico* 16°21N 91°3W **87** D6
Selvagens, Ilhas *Madeira* 30°5N 15°55W **50** B2
Selvas *Brazil* 6°30S 67°0W **92** E5
Selwyn L. *Canada* 60°0N 104°30W **71** B8
Selwyn Mts. *Canada* 63°0N 130°0W **68** C6
Selwyn Ra. *Australia* 21°10S 140°0E **62** C3
Seman → *Albania* 40°47N 19°30E **23** D8
Semarang *Indonesia* 7°0S 110°26E **37** G14
Sembabule *Uganda* 0°4S 31°25E **54** C3
Sembawang *Singapore* 1°27N 103°50E **39** d
Sembung *Indonesia* 8°28S 115°11E **37** J18
Semenanjung Blambangan
  Indonesia 8°42S 114°29E **37** K17
Semeru *Indonesia* 8°4S 112°55E **37** H15
Semey *Kazakhstan* 50°30N 80°10E **28** D9
Seminoe Res. *U.S.A.* 42°9N 106°55W **76** E10
Seminole *Okla., U.S.A.* 35°14N 96°41W **84** D6
Seminole *Tex., U.S.A.* 32°43N 102°39W **84** E3
Seminole Draw →
  U.S.A. 32°27N 102°20W **84** E3
Semipalatinsk = Semey
  Kazakhstan 50°30N 80°10E **28** D9
Semirara Is. *Phil.* 12°0N 121°20E **37** B6
Semitau *Indonesia* 0°29N 111°57E **36** D4
Semmering P. *Austria* 47°41N 15°45E **16** E8
Semnān *Iran* 35°40N 53°23E **45** C7
Semnān □ *Iran* 36°0N 54°0E **45** C7
Semporna *Malaysia* 4°30N 118°33E **37** D5
Semuda *Indonesia* 2°51S 112°58E **36** E4
Sen → *Cambodia* 12°32N 104°28E **38** F5
Sena *Iran* 28°27N 51°36E **45** D6
Sena *Mozam.* 17°25S 35°0E **55** F4
Sena Madureira *Brazil* 9°5S 68°45W **92** E5
Senador Pompeu *Brazil* 5°40S 39°20W **93** E11
Senang, Pulau *Singapore* 1°11N 103°52E **39** d
Senanga *Zambia* 16°7S 23°16E **53** H4
Senatobia *U.S.A.* 34°37N 89°58W **85** D10
Sencelles *Spain* 39°39N 2°54E **24** B9
Sendai *Kagoshima, Japan* 31°50N 130°20E **31** J5
Sendai *Miyagi, Japan* 38°15N 140°53E **30** E10
Sendai-Wan *Japan* 38°15N 141°0E **30** E10
Sendhwa *India* 21°41N 75°6E **42** J6
Seneca *U.S.A.* 34°41N 82°57W **85** D13
Seneca Falls *U.S.A.* 42°55N 76°48W **83** D8
Seneca L. *U.S.A.* 42°40N 76°54W **82** D8
Senecaville L. *U.S.A.* 39°55N 81°25W **82** G3
Senegal ■ *W. Afr.* 14°30N 14°30W **50** F3
Senegal → *W. Afr.* 15°48N 16°32W **50** E2
Senegambia *Africa* 12°45N 12°0W **48** E2
Senekal *S. Africa* 28°20S 27°36E **57** D4
Senga Hill *Zambia* 9°19S 31°11E **55** D3
Senge Khambab = Indus →
  Pakistan 24°20N 67°47E **42** G2
Sengua → *Zimbabwe* 17°7S 28°5E **55** F2
Senhor-do-Bonfim
  Brazil 10°30S 40°10W **93** F10
Senigállia *Italy* 43°43N 13°13E **22** C5
Senj *Croatia* 45°0N 14°58E **16** F8
Senja *Norway* 69°25N 17°30E **8** B17
Senkaku-Shotō
  E. China Sea 25°45N 123°30E **31** M1
Senkuang *Indonesia* 1°11N 104°2E **39** d
Senlis *France* 49°13N 2°35E **20** B5
Senmonorom *Cambodia* 12°27N 107°12E **38** F6
Senneterre *Canada* 48°25N 77°15W **72** C4

Seno *Laos* 16°35N 104°50E **38** D5
Sens *France* 48°11N 3°15E **20** B5
Senta *Serbia* 45°55N 20°3E **23** B9
Sentani *Indonesia* 2°36S 140°37E **37** E10
Sentery = Lubao
  Dem. Rep. of the Congo 5°17S 25°42E **54** D2
Sentinel *U.S.A.* 32°52N 113°13W **77** K7
Sentosa *Singapore* 1°16N 103°50E **39** d
Seo de Urgel = La Seu d'Urgell
  Spain 42°22N 1°23E **21** A6
Seogwipo *S. Korea* 33°13N 126°34E **35** H14
Seohara *India* 29°15N 78°33E **43** E8
Seonath → *India* 21°44N 82°28E **43** J10
Seohara *India* 26°9N 78°48E **43** F8
Seongnam *S. Korea* 37°26N 127°8E **35** F14
Seoni *India* 22°5N 79°30E **43** H8
Seoni Malwa *India* 22°27N 77°28E **42** H8
Seonsan *S. Korea* 36°14N 128°17E **35** F15
Seosan *S. Korea* 36°47N 126°27E **35** F14
Seoul *S. Korea* 37°31N 126°58E **35** F14
Sepīdān *Iran* 30°20N 52°5E **45** D7
Sep'o *N. Korea* 38°57N 127°25E **35** E14
Sepone *Laos* 16°45N 106°13E **38** D6
Sept-Îles *Canada* 50°13N 66°22W **73** B6
Sequoia △ *U.S.A.* 36°30N 118°30W **78** J8
Seraing *Belgium* 50°35N 5°32E **15** D5
Serakhis → *Cyprus* 35°13N 32°55E **25** D11
Seram *Indonesia* 3°10S 129°0E **37** E7
Seram Sea *Indonesia* 2°30S 128°30E **37** E7
Serang *Indonesia* 6°8S 106°10E **37** G12
Serangoon *Singapore* 1°23N 103°54E **39** d
Serasan *Indonesia* 2°29N 109°4E **36** D3
Serbia □ *Serbia* 43°30N 21°0E **23** C9
Serbia ■ *Europe* 43°20N 20°0E **23** B9
Serdar *Turkmenistan* 39°4N 56°23E **45** B8
Serdobsk *Russia* 52°28N 44°10E **18** D7
Seremban *Malaysia* 2°43N 101°53E **39** L3
Serengeti △ *Tanzania* 2°11S 35°0E **54** C3
Serengeti Plain *Tanzania* 2°40S 35°0E **54** C4
Serenje *Zambia* 13°14S 30°15E **55** E3
Sereth = Siret →
  Romania 45°24N 28°1E **17** F14
Sergeya Kirova, Ostrova
  Russia 77°30N 90°0E **29** B10
Sergino *Russia* 62°25N 65°12E **28** C7
Sergipe □ *Brazil* 10°30S 37°30W **93** F11
Sergiyev Posad *Russia* 56°20N 38°10E **18** C6
Serhetabat *Turkmenistan* 35°20N 62°18E **45** C9
Seria *Brunei* 4°37N 114°23E **36** D4
Serian *Malaysia* 1°10N 110°31E **36** D4
Seribu, Kepulauan
  Indonesia 5°36S 106°33E **36** F3
Sericho *Kenya* 1°5N 39°5E **54** B4
Serifos *Greece* 37°9N 24°30E **23** F11
Sérigny → *Canada* 56°47N 66°0W **73** A6
Seringapatam Reef
  Australia 13°38S 122°5E **60** B3
Seririt *Indonesia* 8°12S 114°56E **37** J17
Sermata *Indonesia* 8°15S 128°50E **37** F7
Sermersuaq *Greenland* 79°30N 62°0W **4** B4
Serov *Russia* 59°29N 60°35E **18** C11
Serowe *Botswana* 22°25S 26°43E **56** C4
Serpentine Lakes
  Australia 28°30S 129°10E **61** E4
Serpent's Mouth = Sierpe, Bocas
  de la *Venezuela* 10°0N 61°30W **93** L15
Serpukhov *Russia* 54°55N 37°28E **18** D6
Serra do Navio *Brazil* 0°59N 52°3W **93** C8
Serrania San Luís △
  Paraguay 22°35S 57°22W **94** A4
Serranía San Rafael △
  Paraguay 26°30S 56°0W **95** B4
Serres *Greece* 41°5N 23°31E **23** D10
Serrezuela *Argentina* 30°40S 65°20W **94** C2
Serrinha *Brazil* 11°39S 39°0W **93** F11
Sertanópolis *Brazil* 23°4S 51°2W **95** A5
Serua *Indonesia* 6°18S 130°1E **37** F8
Serui *Indonesia* 1°53S 136°10E **37** E9
Serule *Botswana* 21°57S 27°20E **56** C4
Ses Salines *Spain* 39°21N 3°3E **24** B10
Sese Is. *Uganda* 0°20S 32°20E **54** C3
Sesepe *Indonesia* 1°30S 127°59E **37** E7
Sesfontein *Namibia* 19°7S 13°39E **56** B1
Sesheke *Zambia* 17°29S 24°13E **56** B3
S'Espalmador *Spain* 38°47N 1°26E **24** C7
S'Espardell *Spain* 38°48N 1°29E **24** C7
S'Estanyol *Spain* 39°22N 2°54E **24** B9
Setana *Japan* 42°26N 139°51E **30** C9
Sète *France* 43°25N 3°42E **20** E5
Sete Lagoas *Brazil* 19°27S 44°16W **93** G10
Sétif *Algeria* 36°9N 5°26E **50** A7
Seto *Japan* 35°14N 137°6E **31** G8
Setonaikai *Japan* 34°20N 133°30E **31** G6
Setonaikai △ *Japan* 34°15N 133°15E **31** G6
Settat *Morocco* 33°0N 7°40W **50** B4
Setting L. *Canada* 55°0N 98°38W **71** C9
Settle *U.K.* 54°5N 2°16W **12** C5
Settlement, The
  Br. Virgin Is. 18°43N 64°22W **89** e
Settlers *S. Africa* 25°2S 28°30E **57** C4
Setúbal *Portugal* 38°30N 8°58W **21** C1
Setúbal, B. de *Portugal* 38°40N 8°56W **21** C1
Seul, Lac *Canada* 50°20N 92°30W **72** B1
Sevan, Ozero = Sevana Lich
  Armenia 40°30N 45°20E **44** A5
Sevana Lich *Armenia* 40°30N 45°20E **44** A5
Sevastopol *Ukraine* 44°35N 33°30E **19** F5
Seven Sisters *Canada* 54°56N 128°10W **70** C3
Severn → *Canada* 56°2N 87°36W **72** A2
Severn → *U.K.* 51°35N 2°40W **13** F5
Severnaya Zemlya
  Russia 79°0N 100°0E **29** B11
Severnyye Uvaly *Russia* 60°0N 50°0E **18** C8
Severo-Kurilsk *Russia* 50°40N 156°8E **29** D16
Severo-Yeniseyskiy
  Russia 60°22N 93°1E **29** C10

162 Severo-Zapadnyy INDEX TO WORLD MAPS

Severo-Zapadnyy □ Russia 65°0N 40°0E 28 C4
Severobaykalsk Russia 55°39N 109°19E 29 D11
Severodvinsk Russia 64°27N 39°58E 18 B6
Severomorsk Russia 69°5N 33°27E 8 B25
Severouralsk Russia 60°9N 59°57E 18 B10
Seversk Russia 56°36N 84°49E 28 D9
Sevier → U.S.A. 39°4N 113°6W 76 G7
Sevier Desert U.S.A. 39°40N 112°45W 76 G7
Sevier L. U.S.A. 38°54N 113°9W 76 G7
Sevilla Spain 37°23N 5°58W 21 D2
Seville = Sevilla Spain 37°23N 5°58W 21 D2
Sevlievo Bulgaria 43°2N 25°6E 23 C11
Sewani India 28°58N 75°39E 42 E6
Seward Alaska, U.S.A. 60°7N 149°27W 68 C5
Seward Nebr., U.S.A. 40°55N 97°6W 80 E5
Seward Pa., U.S.A. 40°25N 79°1W 82 F5
Seward Peninsula U.S.A. 65°30N 166°0W 74 a
Sewell Chile 34°10S 70°23W 94 C1
Sewer Indonesia 5°53S 134°40E 37 F8
Sewickley U.S.A. 40°32N 80°12W 82 F4
Sexsmith Canada 55°21N 118°47W 70 B5
Seychelles ■ Ind. Oc. 5°0S 56°0E 53 b
Seyðisfjörður Iceland 65°16N 13°57W 8 D7
Seydişehir Turkey 37°25N 31°51E 19 G5
Seydvān Iran 38°34N 45°2E 44 B5
Seyhan → Turkey 36°43N 34°53E 44 B2
Seym → Ukraine 51°27N 32°34E 19 D5
Seymour Australia 37°2S 145°10E 63 F4
Seymour S. Africa 32°33S 26°46E 57 E4
Seymour Conn., U.S.A. 41°24N 73°4W 83 E11
Seymour Ind., U.S.A. 38°58N 85°53W 81 F11
Seymour Tex., U.S.A. 33°35N 99°16W 84 E5
Sfântu Gheorghe Romania 45°52N 25°48E 17 F13
Sfax Tunisia 34°49N 10°48E 51 B8
Sha Tau Kok China 22°33N 114°13E 33 F11
Sha Tin China 22°23N 114°12E 33 G11
Shaanxi □ China 35°0N 109°0E 34 G5
Shaba = Katanga □ Dem. Rep. of the Congo 8°0S 25°0E 54 D2
Shaba ⌓ Kenya 0°38N 37°48E 54 B4
Shabeelle → Somali Rep. 2°0N 44°0E 47 G3
Shabogamo L. Canada 53°15N 66°30W 73 B6
Shabunda Dem. Rep. of the Congo 2°40S 27°16E 54 C2
Shache China 38°20N 77°10E 32 C2
Shackleton Fracture Zone S. Ocean 60°0S 60°0W 5 B18
Shackleton Ice Shelf Antarctica 66°0S 100°0E 5 C8
Shackleton Inlet Antarctica 83°0S 160°0E 5 E11
Shādegān Iran 30°40N 48°38E 45 D6
Shadi India 33°24N 77°14E 43 C7
Shadrinsk Russia 56°5N 63°32E 28 D7
Shadyside U.S.A. 39°58N 80°45W 82 G4
Shafter U.S.A. 35°30N 119°16W 79 K7
Shaftesbury U.K. 51°0N 2°11W 13 F5
Shaftsbury U.S.A. 43°0N 73°11W 83 D11
Shagram Pakistan 36°24N 72°20E 43 A5
Shah Alam Malaysia 3°5N 101°32E 39 L3
Shah Alizai Pakistan 29°25N 66°33E 42 E2
Shah Bunder Pakistan 24°13N 67°56E 42 G2
Shahabad Punjab, India 30°10N 76°55E 42 D7
Shahabad Raj., India 25°15N 77°11E 42 G7
Shahabad Ut. P., India 27°36N 79°56E 43 F8
Shahadpur Pakistan 25°55N 68°35E 42 G3
Shahbā' Syria 32°52N 36°38E 46 C5
Shahdād Iran 30°30N 57°40E 45 D8
Shahdād, Namakzār-e Iran 30°20N 58°20E 45 D8
Shahdadkot Pakistan 27°50N 67°55E 42 F2
Shahdol India 23°19N 81°26E 43 H9
Shahe China 37°0N 114°32E 34 F8
Shahganj India 26°3N 82°44E 43 F10
Shahgarh India 27°15N 69°50E 42 F3
Shahjahanpur India 27°54N 79°57E 43 F8
Shahpur = Salmās Iran 38°11N 44°47E 44 B5
Shahpur India 22°12N 77°58E 42 H7
Shahpur Baluchistan, Pakistan 28°46N 68°27E 42 E3
Shahpur Punjab, Pakistan 32°17N 72°26E 42 C5
Shahpur Chakar Pakistan 26°9N 68°39E 42 F3
Shahpura Mad. P., India 23°10N 80°45E 43 H9
Shahpura Raj., India 25°38N 74°56E 42 G6
Shahr-e Bābak Iran 30°7N 55°9E 45 D7
Shahr-e Kord Iran 32°15N 50°55E 45 C6
Shāhrakht Iran 33°38N 60°16E 45 C9
Shahrezā = Qomsheh Iran 32°0N 51°55E 45 D6
Shahrig Pakistan 30°15N 67°40E 42 D2
Shāhrud = Emāmrūd Iran 36°30N 55°0E 45 B7
Shahukou China 40°20N 112°18E 34 D7
Shaikhabad Afghan. 34°2N 68°45E 42 B3
Shajapur India 23°27N 76°21E 42 H7
Shajing China 22°44N 113°48E 33 F10
Shakargarh Pakistan 32°17N 75°10E 42 C6
Shakawe Botswana 18°28S 21°49E 56 B3
Shaker Heights U.S.A. 41°28N 81°32W 82 E3
Shakhtersk Russia 49°10N 142°8E 29 E15
Shakhty Russia 47°40N 40°16E 19 E7
Shakhunya Russia 57°40N 46°46E 18 C8
Shaki Nigeria 8°41N 3°21E 50 G6
Shaksam Valley Asia 36°0N 76°20E 43 A7
Shallow Lake Canada 44°36N 81°5W 82 B3
Shalqar Kazakhstan 47°48N 59°39E 28 E6
Shaluli Shan China 30°40N 99°55E 32 C4
Shām Iran 26°39N 57°21E 45 E8
Shām, Bādiyat ash Asia 32°0N 40°0E 44 C3
Shamâl Sînî □ Egypt 30°30N 33°30E 46 E2
Shamattawa Canada 55°51N 92°5W 72 A1
Shamattawa → Canada 55°1N 85°23W 72 A2
Shamīl Iran 27°30N 56°55E 45 E8
Shāmkūh Iran 35°47N 57°50E 45 C8
Shamli India 29°32N 77°18E 42 E7
Shammar, Jabal Si. Arabia 27°40N 41°0E 44 E4
Shamo = Gobi Asia 44°0N 110°0E 34 C6
Shamo, L. Ethiopia 5°45N 37°30E 47 F2
Shamokin U.S.A. 40°47N 76°34W 83 F8
Shamrock Canada 45°23N 76°50W 83 A8
Shamrock U.S.A. 35°13N 100°15W 84 D4
Shamva Zimbabwe 17°20S 31°32E 55 F3
Shan □ Burma 21°30N 98°30E 41 J21
Shan Xian China 34°50N 116°5E 34 G9
Shanchengzhen China 42°20N 125°20E 35 C13
Shāndak Iran 28°28N 60°27E 45 D9
Shandon U.S.A. 35°39N 120°23W 78 K6
Shandong □ China 36°0N 118°0E 35 G10
Shandong Bandao China 37°0N 121°0E 35 F11
Shandur Pass Pakistan 36°4N 72°31E 43 A5
Shang Xian = Shangzhou China 33°50N 109°58E 34 H5
Shangalowe Dem. Rep. of the Congo 10°50S 26°30E 55 E2
Shangani Zimbabwe 19°41S 29°20E 57 B4
Shangani → Zimbabwe 18°41S 27°10E 55 F2
Shangbancheng China 40°50N 118°1E 35 D10
Shangdu China 41°30N 113°30E 34 D7
Shanghai China 31°15N 121°26E 33 C7
Shanghe China 37°20N 117°10E 35 F9
Shangnan China 33°32N 110°50E 34 H6
Shangqiu China 34°26N 115°36E 34 G8
Shangrao China 28°25N 117°59E 33 D6
Shangshui China 33°42N 114°35E 34 H8
Shangzhi China 45°22N 127°56E 35 B14
Shangzhou China 33°50N 109°58E 34 H5
Shanhetun China 44°33N 127°15E 35 B14
Shanklin U.K. 50°38N 1°11W 13 G6
Shannon N.Z. 40°33S 175°25E 59 D5
Shannon → Ireland 52°35N 9°30W 10 D2
Shannon ✈ (SNN) Ireland 52°42N 8°57W 10 D3
Shannon, Mouth of the Ireland 52°30N 9°55W 10 D2
Shannon △ Australia 34°35S 116°25E 61 F2
Shannonbridge Ireland 53°17N 8°3W 10 C3
Shansi = Shanxi □ China 37°0N 112°0E 34 F7
Shantar, Ostrov Bolshoy Russia 55°9N 137°40E 29 D14
Shantipur India 23°17N 88°25E 43 H13
Shantou China 23°18N 116°40E 33 D6
Shantung = Shandong □ China 36°0N 118°0E 35 G10
Shanxi □ China 37°0N 112°0E 34 F7
Shanyang China 33°31N 109°55E 34 H5
Shanyin China 39°25N 112°56E 34 E7
Shaoguan China 24°48N 113°35E 33 D6
Shaoxing China 30°0N 120°35E 33 D7
Shaoyang China 27°14N 111°25E 33 D6
Shap U.K. 54°32N 2°40W 12 C5
Shapinsay U.K. 59°3N 2°51W 11 B6
Shaqra' Si. Arabia 25°15N 45°16E 44 E5
Shaqrā' Yemen 13°22N 45°44E 47 E4
Sharafkhāneh Iran 38°11N 45°29E 44 B5
Sharbot Lake Canada 44°46N 76°41W 83 B8
Shari Japan 43°55N 144°40E 30 C12
Sharjah = Ash Shāriqah U.A.E. 25°23N 55°26E 45 E7
Shark B. Australia 25°30S 113°32E 61 E1
Shark Bay ⌓ Australia 25°30S 113°30E 61 E1
Sharm el Sheikh Egypt 27°53N 34°18E 51 C12
Sharon Canada 44°6N 79°26W 82 B5
Sharon Mass., U.S.A. 42°7N 71°11W 83 D13
Sharon Pa., U.S.A. 41°14N 80°31W 82 E4
Sharon Springs Kans., U.S.A. 38°54N 101°45W 80 F3
Sharon Springs N.Y., U.S.A. 42°48N 74°37W 83 D10
Sharp Pt. Australia 10°58S 142°43E 62 A3
Sharpe L. Canada 54°24N 93°40W 72 B1
Sharpsville U.S.A. 41°15N 80°29W 82 E4
Sharqi, Al Jabal ash Lebanon 33°40N 36°10E 46 B5
Sharya Russia 58°22N 45°20E 18 C8
Shashemene Ethiopia 7°13N 38°33E 47 F2
Shashi Botswana 21°15S 27°27E 57 C4
Shashi China 30°25N 112°14E 33 C6
Shashi → Africa 21°14S 29°20E 55 G2
Shasta, Mt. U.S.A. 41°25N 122°12W 76 F2
Shasta L. U.S.A. 40°43N 122°25W 76 F2
Shatsky Rise Pac. Oc. 34°0N 157°0E 64 D7
Shatt al Arab Asia 29°57N 48°34E 45 D6
Shaunavon Canada 49°35N 108°25W 71 D7
Shaver L. U.S.A. 37°9N 119°18W 78 H7
Shaw → Australia 20°21S 119°17E 60 D2
Shaw I. Australia 20°30S 149°2E 62 J7
Shawanaga Canada 45°31N 80°17W 82 A4
Shawangunk Mts. U.S.A. 41°35N 74°30W 83 E10
Shawano U.S.A. 44°47N 88°36W 80 C9
Shawinigan Canada 46°35N 72°50W 72 C5
Shawmari, J. ash Jordan 30°35N 36°35E 46 E5
Shawnee U.S.A. 35°20N 96°55W 84 D6
Shay Gap Australia 20°30S 120°10E 60 D3
Shaybārā Si. Arabia 25°26N 36°47E 44 E3
Shaykh, J. ash Lebanon 33°25N 35°50E 46 B4
Shaykh Miskīn Syria 32°49N 36°9E 46 C5
Shaykh Sa'd Iraq 32°34N 46°17E 44 C5
Shāzand Iran 33°56N 49°24E 45 C6
Shchūchinsk Kazakhstan 52°56N 70°12E 28 D8
She Xian China 36°30N 113°40E 34 F7
Shebele = Shabeelle → Somali Rep. 2°0N 44°0E 47 G3
Sheboygan U.S.A. 43°46N 87°45W 80 D10
Shediac Canada 46°14N 64°32W 73 C7
Sheelin, L. Ireland 53°48N 7°20W 10 C4
Sheep Haven Ireland 55°11N 7°52W 10 A4
Sheep Range U.S.A. 36°35N 115°15W 79 J11
Sheerness U.K. 51°26N 0°47E 13 F8
Sheet Harbour Canada 44°56N 62°31W 73 D7
Sheffield U.K. 53°23N 1°28W 12 D6
Sheffield Ala., U.S.A. 34°46N 87°41W 85 D11
Sheffield Mass., U.S.A. 42°5N 73°21W 83 D11
Sheffield Pa., U.S.A. 41°42N 79°3W 82 E5
Sheikhpura India 25°9N 85°53E 43 G11
Shekhupura Pakistan 31°42N 73°58E 42 D5
Shekou China 22°30N 113°55E 33 G10
Shelburne N.S., Canada 43°47N 65°20W 73 D6
Shelburne Ont., Canada 44°4N 80°15W 82 B4
Shelburne U.S.A. 44°23N 73°14W 83 B11
Shelburne B. Australia 11°50S 142°50E 62 A3
Shelburne Falls U.S.A. 42°36N 72°45W 83 D12
Shelby Mich., U.S.A. 43°37N 86°22W 80 D10
Shelby Miss., U.S.A. 33°57N 90°46W 85 E9
Shelby Mont., U.S.A. 48°30N 111°51W 76 B8
Shelby N.C., U.S.A. 35°17N 81°32W 85 D14
Shelby Ohio, U.S.A. 40°53N 82°40W 82 F2
Shelbyville Ill., U.S.A. 39°24N 88°48W 80 F9
Shelbyville Ind., U.S.A. 39°31N 85°47W 81 F11
Shelbyville Ky., U.S.A. 38°13N 85°14W 81 F11
Shelbyville Tenn., U.S.A. 35°29N 86°28W 85 D11
Sheldon U.S.A. 43°11N 95°51W 80 D6
Sheldrake Canada 50°20N 64°51W 73 B7
Shelikhova, Zaliv Russia 59°30N 157°0E 29 D16
Shell Lakes Australia 29°20S 127°30E 61 E4
Shellbrook Canada 53°13N 106°24W 71 C7
Shellharbour Australia 34°31S 150°51E 63 E5
Shelter I. U.S.A. 41°4N 72°20W 83 E12
Shelton Conn., U.S.A. 41°19N 73°5W 83 E11
Shelton Wash., U.S.A. 47°13N 123°6W 78 C3
Shen Xian China 36°15N 115°40E 34 F8
Shenandoah Iowa, U.S.A. 40°46N 95°22W 80 E6
Shenandoah Pa., U.S.A. 40°49N 76°12W 83 F8
Shenandoah Va., U.S.A. 38°29N 78°37W 81 F14
Shenandoah → U.S.A. 39°19N 77°44W 81 F15
Shenandoah △ U.S.A. 38°35N 78°22W 81 F14
Shenchi China 39°8N 112°10E 34 E7
Shendam Nigeria 8°49N 9°30E 50 G7
Shendī Sudan 16°46N 33°22E 51 E12
Shengfang China 39°3N 116°42E 34 E9
Shenjingzi China 44°40N 124°30E 35 B13
Shenmu China 38°50N 110°29E 34 E6
Shenqiu China 33°25N 115°5E 34 H8
Shensi = Shaanxi □ China 35°0N 109°0E 34 G5
Shenyang China 41°48N 123°27E 35 D12
Shenzhen China 22°32N 114°5E 33 F10
Shenzhen ✈ (SZX) China 22°41N 113°49E 33 F10
Shenzhen Shuiku China 22°34N 114°8E 33 F11
Shenzhen Wan China 22°27N 113°55E 33 G10
Sheo India 26°11N 71°15E 42 F4
Sheopur Kalan India 25°40N 76°40E 42 G7
Shepetivka Ukraine 50°10N 27°10E 17 C14
Shepparton Australia 36°23S 145°26E 63 F4
Sheppey, I. of U.K. 51°25N 0°48E 13 F8
Shepton Mallet U.K. 51°11N 2°33W 13 F5
Sheqi China 33°12N 112°57E 34 H7
Sher Qila Pakistan 36°7N 74°2E 43 A6
Sherborne U.K. 50°57N 2°31W 13 G5
Sherbro I. S. Leone 7°30N 12°40W 50 G3
Sherbrooke N.S., Canada 45°8N 61°59W 73 C7
Sherbrooke Qué., Canada 45°28N 71°57W 83 A13
Sherburne U.S.A. 42°41N 75°30W 83 D9
Shergarh India 26°20N 72°18E 42 F5
Sherghati India 24°34N 84°47E 43 G11
Sheridan Ark., U.S.A. 34°19N 92°24W 84 D8
Sheridan Wyo., U.S.A. 44°48N 106°58W 76 D10
Sheringham U.K. 52°56N 1°13E 12 E9
Sherkin I. Ireland 51°28N 9°26W 10 E2
Sherkot India 29°22N 78°35E 43 E8
Sherlovaya Gora Russia 50°34N 116°15E 29 D12
Sherman N.Y., U.S.A. 42°9N 79°35W 82 D5
Sherman Tex., U.S.A. 33°38N 96°36W 84 E6
Sherpur India 25°34N 83°47E 43 G10
Sherridon Canada 55°8N 101°5W 71 B8
Sherwood Forest U.K. 53°6N 1°7W 12 D6
Sherwood Park Canada 53°31N 113°19W 70 C6
Sheslay → Canada 58°48N 132°5W 70 B2
Shethanei L. Canada 58°48N 97°50W 71 B9
Shetland □ U.K. 60°30N 1°30W 11 A7
Shetland Is. U.K. 60°30N 1°30W 11 A7
Shetrunji → India 21°19N 72°7E 42 J5
Sheung Shui China 22°31N 114°7E 33 F11
Shey-Phoksundo △ Nepal 29°30N 82°45E 43 E10
Sheyenne → U.S.A. 47°2N 96°50W 80 B5
Shiashkotan, Ostrov Russia 48°49N 154°6E 29 E16
Shibām Yemen 15°59N 48°36E 47 D4
Shibata Japan 37°57N 139°20E 30 F9
Shibecha Japan 43°17N 144°36E 30 C12
Shibetsu Japan 44°10N 142°23E 30 B11
Shibogama L. Canada 53°35N 88°15W 72 B2
Shibushi Japan 31°25N 131°8E 31 J5
Shickshinny U.S.A. 41°9N 76°9W 83 E8
Shickshock Mts. = Chic-Chocs, Mts. Canada 48°55N 66°0W 73 C6
Shidao China 36°50N 122°25E 35 F12
Shido Japan 34°19N 134°10E 31 G7
Shiel, L. U.K. 56°48N 5°34W 11 E3
Shield, C. Australia 13°20S 136°20E 62 A2
Shīeli Kazakhstan 44°20N 66°15E 28 E7
Shiga □ Japan 35°20N 136°0E 31 G8
Shiguaigou China 40°52N 110°15E 34 D6
Shihchiachuangi = Shijiazhuang China 38°2N 114°28E 34 E8
Shihezi China 44°15N 86°2E 32 B3
Shijiazhuang China 38°2N 114°28E 34 E8
Shikarpur India 28°17N 78°7E 42 E8
Shikarpur Pakistan 27°57N 68°39E 42 F3
Shikohabad India 27°6N 78°36E 43 F8
Shikoku □ Japan 33°30N 133°30E 31 H6
Shikoku-Sanchi Japan 33°30N 133°30E 31 H6
Shikotan, Ostrov Asia 43°47N 146°44E 29 E15
Shikotsu-Ko Japan 42°45N 141°25E 30 C10
Shikotsu-Tōya △ Japan 42°44N 145°8E 30 C10
Shiliguri India 26°45N 88°25E 41 F16
Shiliu = Changjiang China 19°20N 108°55E 38 C7
Shilka Russia 52°0N 115°55E 29 D12
Shilka → Russia 53°20N 121°26E 29 D13
Shillelagh Ireland 52°45N 6°32W 10 D5
Shillington U.S.A. 40°18N 75°58W 83 F9
Shillong India 25°35N 91°53E 41 G17
Shilo West Bank 32°4N 35°18E 46 C4
Shilou China 37°0N 110°48E 34 F6
Shimabara Japan 32°48N 130°20E 31 H5
Shimada Japan 34°49N 138°10E 31 G9
Shimane □ Japan 35°0N 132°30E 31 G6
Shimanovsk Russia 52°15N 127°30E 29 D13
Shimba Hills ⌓ Kenya 4°14S 39°25E 54 C4
Shimizu Japan 35°0N 138°30E 31 G9
Shimla India 31°2N 77°9E 42 D7
Shimodate Japan 36°20N 139°55E 31 F9
Shimoga India 13°57N 75°32E 40 N9
Shimoni Kenya 4°38S 39°20E 54 C4
Shimonoseki Japan 33°58N 130°55E 31 H5
Shimpuru Rapids Namibia 17°45S 19°55E 56 B2
Shin, L. U.K. 58°5N 4°30W 11 C4
Shinano-Gawa → Japan 36°50N 138°30E 31 F9
Shināş Oman 24°46N 56°28E 45 E8
Shīndand Afghan. 33°12N 62°8E 40 C3
Shinglehouse U.S.A. 41°58N 78°12W 82 E6
Shingū Japan 33°40N 135°55E 31 H7
Shingwidzi S. Africa 23°5S 31°25E 57 C5
Shinjō Japan 38°46N 140°18E 30 E10
Shinkolobwe Dem. Rep. of the Congo 11°10S 26°40E 52 G5
Shinshār Syria 34°36N 36°43E 46 A5
Shinyanga Tanzania 3°45S 33°27E 54 C3
Shinyanga □ Tanzania 3°50S 34°0E 54 C3
Shio-no-Misaki Japan 33°25N 135°45E 31 H7
Shiogama Japan 38°19N 141°1E 30 E10
Shiojiri Japan 36°6N 137°58E 31 F8
Shipchenski Prokhod Bulgaria 42°45N 25°15E 23 C11
Shiping China 23°45N 102°23E 32 D5
Shippagan Canada 47°45N 64°45W 73 C7
Shippensburg U.S.A. 40°3N 77°31W 82 F7
Shippenville U.S.A. 41°15N 79°28W 82 E5
Shiprock U.S.A. 36°47N 108°41W 77 H9
Shiqma, N. → Israel 31°37N 34°30E 46 D3
Shiquan China 33°5N 108°15E 34 H5
Shiquan He = Indus → Pakistan 24°20N 67°47E 42 G2
Shīr Kūh Iran 31°39N 54°3E 45 D7
Shiragami-Misaki Japan 41°24N 140°12E 30 D10
Shirakawa Fukushima, Japan 37°7N 140°13E 31 F10
Shirakawa Gifu, Japan 36°17N 136°56E 31 F8
Shirane-San Gumma, Japan 36°48N 139°22E 31 F9
Shirane-San Yamanashi, Japan 35°42N 138°9E 31 G9
Shiraoi Japan 42°33N 141°21E 30 C10
Shīrāz Iran 29°42N 52°30E 45 D7
Shire → Africa 17°42S 35°19E 55 F4
Shiretoko-Misaki Japan 44°21N 145°20E 30 B12
Shirinab → Pakistan 30°15N 66°28E 42 D2
Shiriya-Zaki Japan 41°25N 141°30E 30 D10
Shiroishi Japan 38°0N 140°37E 30 F10
Shirshov Ridge Pac. Oc. 58°0N 170°0E 64 B8
Shīrvān Iran 37°30N 57°50E 45 B8
Shirwa, L. = Chilwa, L. Malawi 15°15S 35°40E 55 F4
Shivpuri India 25°26N 77°42E 42 G7
Shixian China 43°5N 129°50E 35 C15
Shiyan China 22°42N 113°56E 33 F10
Shiyan Shuiku China 22°42N 113°54E 33 F10
Shizuishan China 39°15N 106°50E 34 E4
Shizuoka Japan 34°57N 138°24E 31 G9
Shizuoka □ Japan 35°15N 138°40E 31 G9
Shklov = Shklow Belarus 54°16N 30°15E 17 A16
Shklow Belarus 54°16N 30°15E 17 A16
Shkodër Albania 42°4N 19°32E 23 C8
Shkumbini → Albania 41°2N 19°31E 23 D8
Shmidta, Ostrov Russia 81°0N 91°0E 29 A10
Shō-Gawa → Japan 36°47N 137°4E 31 F8
Shoal L. Canada 49°33N 95°1W 71 D9
Shoal Lake Canada 50°30N 100°35W 71 C8
Shōdo-Shima Japan 34°30N 134°15E 31 G7
Sholapur = Solapur India 17°43N 75°56E 40 L9
Shōmrōn West Bank 32°15N 35°13E 46 C4
Shoreham U.S.A. 43°53N 73°18W 83 C11
Shoreham by Sea U.K. 50°50N 0°16W 13 G7
Shori → Pakistan 28°29N 69°44E 42 E3
Shorkot Pakistan 30°50N 72°0E 42 D5
Shorkot Road Pakistan 30°47N 72°15E 42 D5
Shoshone Calif., U.S.A. 35°58N 116°16W 79 K10
Shoshone Idaho, U.S.A. 42°56N 114°25W 76 E6
Shoshone L. U.S.A. 44°22N 110°43W 76 D8
Shoshone Mts. U.S.A. 39°20N 117°25W 76 G5
Shoshong Botswana 22°56S 26°31E 56 C4
Shoshoni U.S.A. 43°14N 108°7W 76 E9
Shouguang China 37°52N 118°45E 35 F10
Shouyang China 37°54N 113°8E 34 F7
Show Low U.S.A. 34°15N 110°2W 77 J8
Shqipëria = Albania ■ Europe 41°0N 20°0E 23 D9
Shreveport U.S.A. 32°31N 93°45W 84 E8
Shrewsbury U.K. 52°43N 2°45W 13 E5
Shri Mohangarh India 27°17N 71°18E 42 F4
Shrirampur India 22°44N 88°21E 43 H13
Shropshire □ U.K. 52°36N 2°45W 13 E5
Shū Kazakhstan 43°36N 73°42E 28 E8
Shuangcheng China 45°20N 126°15E 35 B14
Shuanggou China 34°2N 117°30E 35 G9
Shuangliao China 43°29N 123°30E 35 C12
Shuangshanzi China 40°20N 119°8E 35 D10
Shuangyang China 43°28N 125°40E 35 C13
Shuangyashan China 46°28N 131°5E 33 B8
Shuguri Falls Tanzania 8°33S 37°22E 55 D4
Shuiye China 36°7N 114°8E 34 F8
Shujalpur India 23°18N 76°46E 42 H7
Shukpa Kunzang India 34°22N 78°22E 43 B8
Shulan China 44°28N 127°0E 35 B14
Shule China 39°25N 76°3E 32 C2
Shule He → China 40°20N 92°50E 32 B4
Shumagin Is. U.S.A. 55°7N 160°30W 74 a
Shumen Bulgaria 43°18N 26°55E 23 C12
Shumikha Russia 55°10N 63°15E 28 D7
Shuo Xian = Shuozhou China 39°20N 112°33E 34 E7
Shuozhou China 39°20N 112°33E 34 E7
Shūr → Fārs, Iran 28°30N 55°0E 45 D7
Shūr → Kermān, Iran 30°52N 57°37E 45 D8
Shūr → Yazd, Iran 31°45N 55°15E 45 D7
Shūr Āb Iran 34°23N 51°11E 45 C6
Shūr Gaz Iran 29°10N 59°20E 45 D8
Shūrāb Iran 33°43N 56°29E 45 C8
Shūrjestān Iran 31°24N 52°25E 45 D7
Shurugwi Zimbabwe 19°40S 30°0E 55 F3
Shūsf Iran 31°50N 60°5E 45 D9
Shūshtar Iran 32°0N 48°50E 45 D6
Shuswap L. Canada 50°55N 119°3W 70 C5
Shuyang China 34°10N 118°42E 35 G10
Shūzū Iran 29°52N 54°30E 45 D7
Shwebo Burma 22°30N 95°45E 41 H19
Shwegu Burma 24°15N 96°26E 41 G20
Shweli → Burma 23°45N 96°45E 41 H20
Shymkent Kazakhstan 42°18N 69°36E 28 E7
Shyok India 34°13N 78°12E 43 B8
Shyok → Pakistan 35°13N 75°53E 43 B6
Si Kiang = Xi Jiang → China 22°5N 113°20E 33 D6
Si Lanna △ Thailand 19°17N 99°12E 38 C2
Si Nakarin Res. Thailand 14°35N 99°0E 38 E2
Si-ngan = Xi'an China 34°15N 109°0E 34 G5
Si Prachan Thailand 14°37N 100°9E 38 E3
Si Racha Thailand 13°10N 100°48E 38 F3
Si Xian China 33°30N 117°50E 35 H9
Siachen Glacier Asia 35°20N 77°30E 43 B7
Siahaf → Pakistan 29°3N 68°57E 42 E3
Siahan Range Pakistan 27°30N 64°40E 40 F4
Siaksriindrapura Indonesia 0°51N 102°0E 36 D2
Sialkot Pakistan 32°32N 74°30E 42 C6
Siam = Thailand ■ Asia 16°0N 102°0E 38 E4
Sian = Xi'an China 34°15N 109°0E 34 G5
Sian Ka'an ⌓ Mexico 19°35N 87°40W 87 D7
Siantan Indonesia 3°10N 106°15E 36 D3
Sīāreh Iran 28°5N 60°14E 45 D9
Siargao I. Phil. 9°52N 126°3E 37 C7
Siari Pakistan 34°55N 76°40E 43 B7
Siasi Phil. 5°34N 120°50E 37 C6
Siau Indonesia 2°50N 125°25E 37 D7
Šiauliai Lithuania 55°56N 23°15E 9 J20
Sibâi, Gebel el Egypt 25°45N 34°10E 44 E2
Sibang Indonesia 8°34S 115°13E 37 K18
Sibay Russia 52°42N 58°39E 18 D10
Sibayi, L. S. Africa 27°20S 32°45E 57 D5
Šibenik Croatia 43°48N 15°54E 22 C6
Siberia = Sibirskiy □ Russia 58°0N 90°0E 29 D10
Siberia Russia 60°0N 100°0E 4 D13
Siberut Indonesia 1°30S 99°0E 36 E1
Sibi Pakistan 29°30N 67°54E 42 E2
Sibil = Oksibil Indonesia 4°59S 140°35E 37 E10
Sibiloi ⌓ Kenya 4°0N 36°20E 54 B4
Sibirskiy □ Russia 58°0N 90°0E 29 D10
Sibirtsevo Russia 44°12N 132°26E 30 B5
Sibiti Congo 3°38S 13°19E 52 E2
Sibiu Romania 45°45N 24°9E 17 F13
Sibley U.S.A. 43°24N 95°45W 80 D6
Sibolga Indonesia 1°42N 98°45E 36 D1
Siborongborong Indonesia 2°13N 98°59E 39 L2
Sibsagar India 27°0N 94°36E 41 F19
Sibu Malaysia 2°18N 111°49E 36 D4
Sibuco Phil. 7°20N 122°10E 37 C6
Sibuguey B. Phil. 7°50N 122°45E 37 C6
Sibut C.A.R. 5°46N 19°10E 52 C3
Sibutu Phil. 4°45N 119°30E 37 D5
Sibutu Passage E. Indies 4°50N 120°0E 37 D6
Sibuyan I. Phil. 12°25N 122°40E 37 B6
Sibuyan Sea Phil. 12°30N 122°20E 37 B6
Sicamous Canada 50°49N 119°0W 70 C5
Siccus → Australia 31°55S 139°17E 63 E2
Sichon Thailand 9°0N 99°54E 39 H2
Sichuan □ China 30°30N 103°0E 32 C5
Sicilia Italy 37°30N 14°30E 22 F6
Sicily = Sicilia Italy 37°30N 14°30E 22 F6
Sicily, Str. of Medit. S. 37°35N 11°56E 22 F4
Sico → Honduras 15°58N 84°58W 88 C3
Sicuani Peru 14°21S 71°10W 92 F4
Sidari Greece 39°47N 19°41E 25 A3
Siddhapur India 23°56N 72°25E 42 H5
Siddipet India 18°5N 78°51E 40 K11
Sideros, Akra Greece 35°19N 26°19E 25 D8
Sidhauli India 27°17N 80°50E 43 F9
Sidhi India 24°25N 81°53E 43 G9
Sidi-bel-Abbès Algeria 35°13N 0°39W 50 A5
Sidi Ifni Morocco 29°29N 10°12W 50 C3
Sidikalang Indonesia 2°45N 98°19E 39 L2
Sidlaw Hills U.K. 56°32N 3°2W 11 E5
Sidley, Mt. Antarctica 77°2S 126°2W 5 D14
Sidmouth U.K. 50°40N 3°15W 13 G4
Sidmouth, C. Australia 13°25S 143°36E 62 A3
Sidney Canada 48°39N 123°24W 70 D4
Sidney Mont., U.S.A. 47°43N 104°9W 76 C11

Sidney *N.Y., U.S.A.* 42°19N 75°24W **83** D9
Sidney *Nebr., U.S.A.* 41°8N 102°59W **80** E2
Sidney *Ohio, U.S.A.* 40°17N 84°9W **81** E11
Sidney Lanier, L. *U.S.A.* 34°10N 84°4W **85** D12
Sidoarjo *Indonesia* 7°27S 112°43E **37** G15
Sidon = Saydā *Lebanon* 33°35N 35°25E **46** B4
Sidra, G. of = Surt, Khalīj
    Libya 31°40N 18°30E **51** B9
Siedlce *Poland* 52°10N 22°20E **17** B12
Sieg → *Germany* 50°46N 7°6E **16** C4
Siegen *Germany* 50°51N 8°0E **16** C5
Siem Pang *Cambodia* 14°7N 106°23E **38** E6
Siem Reap = Siemreab
    Cambodia 13°20N 103°52E **38** F4
Siemreab *Cambodia* 13°20N 103°52E **38** F4
Siena *Italy* 43°19N 11°21E **22** C4
Sieradz *Poland* 51°37N 18°41E **17** C10
Sierpe, Bocas de la
    Venezuela 10°0N 61°30W **93** L15
Sierra Blanca *U.S.A.* 31°11N 105°22W **84** F2
Sierra Blanca Peak
    U.S.A. 33°23N 105°49W **77** K11
Sierra City *U.S.A.* 39°34N 120°38W **78** F6
Sierra Colorada
    Argentina 40°35S 67°50W **96** E3
Sierra de Agalta △
    Honduras 15°1N 85°48W **88** C2
Sierra de Bahoruco △
    Dom. Rep. 18°10N 71°25W **89** C5
Sierra de La Culata △
    Venezuela 8°45N 71°10W **89** E5
Sierra de Lancandón △
    Guatemala 16°59N 90°23W **88** C1
Sierra de las Quijadas △
    Argentina 32°29S 67°5W **94** C2
Sierra de San Luis △
    Venezuela 11°20N 69°43W **89** D6
Sierra de San Pedro Mártir,
  Parque Nacional △
    Mexico 31°10N 115°30W **86** A1
Sierra Gorda *Chile* 22°50S 69°15W **94** A2
Sierra Leone ■ *W. Afr.* 9°0N 12°0W **50** G3
Sierra Madre *Mexico* 16°0N 93°0W **87** D6
Sierra Madre Occidental
    Mexico 27°0N 107°0W **86** B3
Sierra Madre Oriental
    Mexico 25°0N 100°0W **86** C5
Sierra Mojada *Mexico* 27°18N 103°41W **86** B4
Sierra Nevada *Spain* 37°3N 3°15W **21** D4
Sierra Nevada *U.S.A.* 39°0N 120°30W **78** H8
Sierra Nevada △
    Venezuela 8°35N 70°45W **89** E5
Sierra Nevada de Santa Marta △
    Colombia 10°56N 73°36W **89** D5
Sierra Vista *U.S.A.* 31°33N 110°18W **77** L8
Sierraville *U.S.A.* 39°36N 120°22W **78** F6
Sifnos *Greece* 37°0N 24°45E **23** F11
Sifton *Canada* 51°21N 100°8W **71** C8
Sifton Pass *Canada* 57°52N 126°15W **70** B3
Sig *Algeria* 35°32N 0°12W **50** A5
Sigatoka *Fiji* 18°8S 177°32E **59** a
Sighetu-Marmaţiei
    Romania 47°57N 23°52E **17** E12
Sighişoara *Romania* 46°12N 24°50E **17** E13
Sigli *Indonesia* 5°25N 96°0E **36** C1
Siglufjörður *Iceland* 66°12N 18°55W **8** C4
Signal de Botrang *Belgium* 50°29N 6°4E **15** D6
Signal Pk. *U.S.A.* 33°20N 114°2W **79** M12
Signy I. *Antarctica* 60°43S 45°36W **5** C18
Sigsig *Ecuador* 3°0S 78°50W **92** D3
Sigüenza *Spain* 41°3N 2°40W **21** B4
Siguiri *Guinea* 11°31N 9°10W **50** F4
Sigulda *Latvia* 57°10N 24°55E **9** H21
Sihora *India* 23°29N 80°6E **43** H9
Siikajoki → *Finland* 64°50N 24°43E **8** D21
Siilinjärvi *Finland* 63°4N 27°39E **8** E22
Sijarira Ra. = Chizarira
    Zimbabwe 17°36S 27°45E **55** F2
Sika *India* 22°26N 69°47E **42** H3
Sikanni Chief →
    Canada 57°47N 122°15W **70** B4
Sikao *Thailand* 7°34N 99°21E **39** J2
Sikar *India* 27°33N 75°10E **42** F6
Sikasso *Mali* 11°18N 5°35W **50** F4
Sikeston *U.S.A.* 36°53N 89°35W **80** G9
Sikhote Alin, Khrebet
    Russia 45°0N 136°0E **30** B8
Sikhote Alin Ra. = Sikhote Alin,
    Khrebet *Russia* 45°0N 136°0E **30** B8
Sikinos *Greece* 36°40N 25°8E **23** F11
Sikkim □ *India* 27°50N 88°30E **41** F16
Sil → *Spain* 42°27N 7°43W **21** A2
Silacayoapan *Mexico* 17°30N 98°9W **87** D5
Silawad *India* 21°54N 74°54E **42** J6
Silchar *India* 24°49N 92°48E **41** G18
Siler City *U.S.A.* 35°44N 79°28W **85** D15
Silesia = Śląsk *Poland* 51°0N 16°30E **16** C9
Silgarhi Doti *Nepal* 29°15N 81°0E **43** E9
Silghat *India* 26°35N 93°0E **41** F18
Silhouette *Seychelles* 4°29S 55°12E **53** b
Silifke *Turkey* 36°22N 33°58E **44** B2
Siliguri = Shiliguri *India* 26°45N 88°25E **41** F16
Siling Co *China* 31°50N 89°20E **32** C3
Silistra *Bulgaria* 44°6N 27°19E **23** B12
Silivri *Turkey* 41°4N 28°14E **23** D13
Siljan *Sweden* 60°55N 14°45E **8** F16
Silkeborg *Denmark* 56°10N 9°32E **9** H13
Silkwood *Australia* 17°45S 146°2E **62** B4
Sillajhuay, Cordillera
    Chile 19°46S 68°40W **92** G5
Sillamäe *Estonia* 59°24N 27°45E **9** G22
Silloth *U.K.* 54°52N 3°23W **12** C4
Siloam Springs *U.S.A.* 36°11N 94°32W **84** C7
Silopi *Turkey* 37°15N 42°27E **44** B4
Silsbee *U.S.A.* 30°21N 94°11W **84** F7
Šilutė *Lithuania* 55°21N 21°33E **9** J19
Silvan *Turkey* 38°7N 41°2E **44** B4

Silvani *India* 23°18N 78°25E **43** H8
Silver City *U.S.A.* 32°46N 108°17W **77** K9
Silver Cr. → *U.S.A.* 43°16N 119°13W **76** E4
Silver Creek *U.S.A.* 42°33N 79°10W **82** D5
Silver L. *U.S.A.* 38°39N 120°6W **78** G6
Silver Lake *Calif.,*
    U.S.A. 35°21N 116°7W **79** K10
Silver Lake *Oreg., U.S.A.* 43°8N 121°3W **76** E3
Silvermine Mts. *Ireland* 52°47N 8°15W **10** D3
Silverton *Colo., U.S.A.* 37°49N 107°40W **77** H10
Silverton *Tex., U.S.A.* 34°28N 101°19W **84** D4
Silvies *U.S.A.* 43°34N 119°2W **76** E4
Simaltala *India* 24°43N 86°33E **43** G12
Simanggang = Sri Aman
    Malaysia 1°15N 111°32E **36** D4
Simard, L. *Canada* 47°40N 78°40W **72** C4
Simav *Turkey* 39°4N 28°58E **23** E13
Simba *Tanzania* 2°10S 37°36E **54** C4
Simbirsk = Ulyanovsk
    Russia 54°20N 48°25E **18** D8
Simbo *Tanzania* 4°51S 29°41E **54** C2
Simcoe *Canada* 42°50N 80°23W **82** D4
Simcoe, L. *Canada* 44°25N 79°20W **82** B5
Simdega *India* 22°37N 84°31E **43** H11
Simeria *Romania* 45°51N 23°1E **17** F12
Simeulue *Indonesia* 2°45N 95°45E **36** D1
Simferopol *Ukraine* 44°55N 34°3E **19** F5
Simi *Greece* 36°35N 27°50E **23** F12
Simi Valley *U.S.A.* 34°16N 118°47W **79** L8
Simikot *Nepal* 30°0N 81°50E **43** E9
Simla = Shimla *India* 31°2N 77°9E **42** D7
Simlipal △ *India* 21°45N 86°30E **43** J12
Simmie *Canada* 49°56N 108°6W **71** D7
Simmler *U.S.A.* 35°21N 119°59W **79** K7
Simo älv = Simojoki →
    Finland 65°35N 25°1E **8** D21
Simojoki → *Finland* 65°35N 25°1E **8** D21
Simojovel *Mexico* 17°12N 92°38W **87** D6
Simonette → *Canada* 55°9N 118°15W **70** B5
Simonstown *S. Africa* 34°14S 18°26E **56** E2
Simpang Empat *Malaysia* 5°27N 100°29E **39** c
Simplonpass *Switz.* 46°15N 8°3E **20** C8
Simpson Desert *Australia* 25°0S 137°0E **62** D2
Simpson Desert △
    Australia 24°59S 138°21E **62** C2
Simpson Pen. *Canada* 68°34N 88°45W **69** C11
Simrishamn *Sweden* 55°33N 14°22E **9** J16
Simsbury *U.S.A.* 41°53N 72°48W **83** E12
Simushir, Ostrov
    Russia 46°50N 152°30E **29** E16
Sin Cowe I. *S. China Sea* 9°53N 114°19E **36** C4
Sina Dhago *Somali Rep.* 5°50N 47°0E **47** F4
Sinabang *Indonesia* 2°30N 96°24E **36** D1
Sinai = Es Sînâ' *Egypt* 29°0N 34°0E **46** F3
Sinai, Mt. = Mûsa, Gebel
    Egypt 28°33N 33°59E **44** D2
Sinaloa □ *Mexico* 25°0N 107°30W **86** C3
Sinaloa de Leyva
    Mexico 25°50N 108°14W **86** B3
Sinarades *Greece* 39°34N 19°51E **25** A3
Sincelejo *Colombia* 9°18N 75°24W **92** B3
Sinch'ang *N. Korea* 40°7N 128°28E **35** D15
Sinch'ŏn *N. Korea* 38°25N 125°21E **35** E13
Sinclair *U.S.A.* 41°47N 107°7W **76** F10
Sinclair Mills *Canada* 54°5N 121°40W **70** C4
Sinclair's B. *U.K.* 58°31N 3°5W **11** C5
Sinclairville *U.S.A.* 42°16N 79°16W **82** D5
Sincorá, Serra do *Brazil* 13°30S 41°0W **93** F10
Sind = Sindh □ *Pakistan* 26°0N 69°0E **42** G3
Sind → *Jammu & Kashmir,*
    India 34°18N 74°45E **43** B6
Sind → *Mad. P., India* 26°26N 79°13E **43** F8
Sind Sagar Doab *Pakistan* 32°0N 71°30E **42** D4
Sindangan *Phil.* 8°10N 123°5E **37** C6
Sindangbarang *Indonesia* 7°27S 107°1E **37** G12
Sinde *Zambia* 17°28S 25°51E **55** F2
Sindh □ *Pakistan* 26°0N 69°0E **42** G3
Sindhnur *India* 15°45N 76°45E **40** M10
Sindri *India* 23°45N 86°42E **43** H12
Sines *Portugal* 37°56N 8°51W **21** D1
Sines, C. de *Portugal* 37°58N 8°53W **21** D1
Sineu *Spain* 39°38N 3°1E **24** B10
Sing Buri *Thailand* 14°53N 100°25E **38** E3
Singa *Sudan* 13°10N 33°57E **51** F12
Singalila △ *India* 27°10N 88°5E **43** F13
Singapore ■ *Asia* 1°17N 103°51E **39** d
Singapore, Straits of *Asia* 1°15N 104°0E **39** d
Singapore Changi ✈ (SIN)
    Singapore 1°23N 103°59E **39** M4
Singaraja *Indonesia* 8°7S 115°6E **37** J18
Singatoka = Sigatoka *Fiji* 18°8S 177°32E **59** a
Singida *Tanzania* 4°49S 34°48E **54** C3
Singida □ *Tanzania* 6°0S 34°30E **54** D3
Singkaling Hkamti
    Burma 26°0N 95°39E **41** G19
Singkang *Indonesia* 4°8S 120°1E **37** E6
Singkawang *Indonesia* 1°0N 108°57E **36** D3
Singkep *Indonesia* 0°30S 104°25E **36** E2
Singkil *Indonesia* 2°17N 97°49E **39** L1
Singleton *Australia* 32°33S 151°0E **63** E5
Singleton, Mt. *N. Terr.,*
    Australia 22°0S 130°46E **60** D5
Singleton, Mt. *W. Austral.,*
    Australia 29°27S 117°15E **61** E2
Singoli *India* 25°0N 75°22E **42** G6
Singora = Songkhla
    Thailand 7°13N 100°37E **39** J3
Sinhŭng *N. Korea* 40°11N 127°34E **35** D14
Siniscóla *Italy* 40°34N 9°41E **22** D3
Sinjai *Indonesia* 5°7S 120°20E **37** F6
Sinjär *Iraq* 36°19N 41°52E **44** B4
Sinkat *Sudan* 18°55N 36°49E **51** E13
Sinkiang = Xinjiang Uygur
    Zizhiqu □ *China* 42°0N 86°0E **32** C3
Sinmak *N. Korea* 38°25N 126°14E **35** E14
Sinmi-do *N. Korea* 39°33N 124°53E **35** E13

Sinnamary *Fr. Guiana* 5°25N 53°0W **93** B8
Sinni → *Italy* 40°8N 16°41E **22** D7
Sinop *Turkey* 42°1N 35°11E **19** F6
Sinor *India* 21°55N 73°20E **42** J5
Sinp'o *N. Korea* 40°0N 128°13E **35** E15
Sinsk *Russia* 61°8N 126°48E **29** C13
Sintang *Indonesia* 0°5N 111°35E **36** D4
Sinton *U.S.A.* 28°2N 97°31W **84** G6
Sintra *Portugal* 38°47N 9°25W **21** C1
Sinŭiju *N. Korea* 40°5N 124°24E **35** D13
Siocon *Phil.* 7°40N 122°10E **37** C6
Siófok *Hungary* 46°54N 18°3E **17** E10
Sion *Switz.* 46°14N 7°20E **20** C7
Sion Mills *U.K.* 54°48N 7°29W **10** B4
Sioux Center *U.S.A.* 43°5N 96°11W **80** D5
Sioux City *U.S.A.* 42°30N 96°24W **80** D5
Sioux Falls *U.S.A.* 43°33N 96°44W **80** D5
Sioux Lookout *Canada* 50°10N 91°50W **72** B1
Sioux Narrows *Canada* 49°25N 94°10W **71** D10
Sipadan *Malaysia* 7°6N 118°38E **37** D5
Siparia *Trin. & Tob.* 10°8N 61°31W **93** K15
Siping *China* 43°8N 124°21E **35** C13
Sipiwesk L. *Canada* 55°5N 97°35W **71** B9
Siple *Antarctica* 75°0S 74°0W **5** D7
Sipra → *India* 23°55N 75°28E **42** H6
Sipura *Indonesia* 2°18S 99°40E **36** E1
Siquia → *Nic.* 12°10N 84°20W **88** D3
Siquijor *Phil.* 9°12N 123°35E **37** C6
Siquirres *Costa Rica* 10°6N 83°30W **88** D3
Şīr Abū Nu'ayr *U.A.E.* 25°20N 54°20E **45** E7
Şīr Banī Yās *U.A.E.* 24°19N 52°37E **45** E7
Sir Edward Pellew Group
    Australia 15°40S 137°10E **62** B2
Sir Graham Moore Is.
    Australia 13°53S 126°34E **60** B4
Sir James MacBrien, Mt.
    Canada 62°7N 127°41W **68** C7
Sira → *Norway* 58°23N 6°34E **9** G12
Siracusa *Italy* 37°4N 15°17E **22** F6
Sirajganj *Bangla.* 24°25N 89°47E **43** G13
Sirathu *India* 25°39N 81°19E **43** G9
Sīrdān *Iran* 36°39N 49°12E **45** B6
Siren *U.S.A.* 45°47N 92°24W **80** C7
Sirer *Spain* 38°56N 1°22E **24** C7
Siret → *Romania* 45°24N 28°1E **17** F14
Sirghāyā *Syria* 33°51N 36°8E **46** B5
Sirinat △ *Thailand* 8°6N 98°17E **39** a
Sirmaur *India* 24°51N 81°23E **43** G9
Sirohi *India* 24°52N 72°53E **42** G5
Sironj *India* 24°5N 77°39E **42** G7
Síros = Syros *Greece* 37°28N 24°57E **23** F11
Sirr, Nafud as *Si. Arabia* 25°33N 44°35E **44** E5
Sirsa *India* 29°33N 75°4E **42** E6
Sirsa → *India* 26°51N 79°4E **43** F8
Sisak *Croatia* 45°30N 16°21E **16** F9
Sisaket *Thailand* 15°8N 104°23E **38** E5
Sishen *S. Africa* 27°47S 22°59E **56** D3
Sishui *Henan, China* 34°48N 113°15E **34** G7
Sishui *Shandong, China* 35°42N 117°18E **35** G9
Sisipuk L. *Canada* 55°45N 101°50W **71** B8
Sisophon *Cambodia* 13°38N 102°59E **38** F4
Sisseton *U.S.A.* 45°40N 97°3W **80** C5
Sīstān *Asia* 30°50N 61°0E **45** D9
Sīstān, Daryācheh-ye *Iran* 31°0N 61°0E **45** D9
Sīstān va Balūchestān □
    Iran 27°0N 62°0E **45** E9
Sisters *U.S.A.* 44°18N 121°33W **76** D3
Sisters, The *Seychelles* 4°16S 55°52E **53** b
Siswa Bazar *India* 27°9N 83°46E **43** F10
Sitamarhi *India* 26°37N 85°30E **43** F11
Sitampiky *Madag.* 16°41S 46°6E **57** B8
Sitapur *India* 27°38N 80°45E **43** F9
Siteki *Swaziland* 26°32S 31°58E **57** D5
Sitges *Spain* 41°17N 1°47E **21** B6
Sitia *Greece* 35°13N 26°6E **25** D8
Sitito-Ozima Ridge
    Pac. Oc. 23°0N 143°0E **64** E6
Sitka *U.S.A.* 57°3N 135°20W **70** B1
Sitoti *Botswana* 23°15S 23°40E **56** C3
Sittang Myit → *Burma* 17°20N 96°45E **41** L20
Sittard *Neths.* 51°0N 5°52E **15** C5
Sittingbourne *U.K.* 51°21N 0°45E **13** F8
Sittoung = Sittang Myit →
    Burma 17°20N 96°45E **41** L20
Sittwe *Burma* 20°18N 92°45E **41** J18
Situbondo *Indonesia* 7°42S 114°0E **37** G16
Si'umu *Samoa* 14°1S 171°48W **59** b
Siuna *Nic.* 13°37N 84°45W **88** D3
Siuri *India* 23°50N 87°34E **43** H12
Sīvand *Iran* 30°5N 52°55E **45** D7
Sivas *Turkey* 39°43N 36°58E **44** B3
Siverek *Turkey* 37°50N 39°19E **44** B3
Sivomaskinskiy *Russia* 66°40N 62°35E **18** A11
Sivrihisar *Turkey* 39°30N 31°35E **19** G5
Sīwa *Egypt* 29°11N 25°31E **51** C11
Sīwa, El Wâhât es *Egypt* 29°10N 25°30E **48** D6
Siwa Oasis = Sīwa, El Wâhât es
    Egypt 29°10N 25°30E **48** D6
Siwalik Range *Nepal* 28°0N 83°0E **43** F10
Siwan *India* 26°13N 84°21E **43** F11
Six Cross Roads *Barbados* 13°7N 59°28W **89** g
Sixmilebridge *Ireland* 52°44N 8°46W **10** D3
Sixth Cataract *Sudan* 16°20N 32°42E **51** E12
Siyah Kuh, Kavīr-e *Iran* 32°55N 53°55E **45** C7
Siziwang Qi *China* 41°25N 111°40E **34** D6
Sjælland *Denmark* 55°30N 11°30E **9** J14
Sjumen = Shumen
    Bulgaria 43°18N 26°55E **23** C12
Skadarsko Jezero *Europe* 42°10N 19°20E **23** C8
Skaftafell *Iceland* 64°1N 16°41W **8** D5
Skaftafell △ *Iceland* 64°0N 16°50W **8** D5
Skagafjörður *Iceland* 65°54N 19°35W **8** D4
Skagastølstindane
    Norway 61°28N 7°52E **8** F12

Skagaströnd *Iceland* 65°50N 20°19W **8** D3
Skagen *Denmark* 57°43N 10°35E **9** H14
Skagerrak *Denmark* 57°30N 9°0E **9** H13
Skagit → *U.S.A.* 48°23N 122°22W **78** B4
Skagway *U.S.A.* 59°28N 135°19W **68** D6
Skala-Podilska *Ukraine* 48°50N 26°15E **17** D14
Skalat *Ukraine* 49°23N 25°55E **17** D13
Skåne *Sweden* 55°59N 13°30E **9** J15
Skaneateles *U.S.A.* 42°57N 76°26W **83** D8
Skaneateles L. *U.S.A.* 42°51N 76°22W **83** D8
Skardu *Pakistan* 35°20N 75°44E **43** B6
Skarżysko-Kamienna
    Poland 51°7N 20°52E **17** C11
Skeena → *Canada* 54°9N 130°5W **70** C2
Skeena Mts. *Canada* 56°40N 128°30W **70** B3
Skegness *U.K.* 53°9N 0°20E **12** D8
Skeldon = Corriverton
    Guyana 5°55N 57°20W **92** B7
Skeleton Coast *Namibia* 20°0S 13°0E **53** J2
Skeleton Coast △ *Namibia* 20°0S 13°0E **56** C1
Skellefteå *Sweden* 64°45N 20°50E **8** D19
Skellefteälven →
    Sweden 64°45N 21°10E **8** D19
Skelleftehamn *Sweden* 64°40N 21°9E **8** D19
Skerries, The *U.K.* 53°25N 4°36W **12** D3
Skibbereen *Ireland* 51°33N 9°16W **10** E2
Skiddaw *U.K.* 54°39N 3°9W **12** C4
Skidegate *Canada* 53°15N 132°1W **70** C2
Skien *Norway* 59°12N 9°35E **9** G13
Skierniewice *Poland* 51°58N 20°10E **17** C11
Skíkhist, Mt. *Canada* 50°12N 121°54W **70** C4
Skikda *Algeria* 36°50N 6°58E **50** A7
Skilloura *Cyprus* 35°14N 33°10E **25** D12
Skipton *U.K.* 53°58N 2°3W **12** D5
Skirmish Pt. *Australia* 11°59S 134°17E **62** A1
Skiros *Greece* 38°55N 24°34E **23** E11
Skive *Denmark* 56°33N 9°2E **9** H13
Skjálfandafljót → *Iceland* 65°59N 17°25W **8** D5
Skjálfandi *Iceland* 66°5N 17°30W **8** C5
Skole *Ukraine* 49°3N 23°30E **17** D12
Skopelos *Greece* 39°9N 23°47E **23** E10
Skopi *Greece* 35°11N 26°2E **25** D8
Skopje *Macedonia* 42°1N 21°26E **23** C9
Skövde *Sweden* 58°24N 13°50E **9** G15
Skovorodino *Russia* 54°0N 124°0E **29** D13
Skowhegan *U.S.A.* 44°46N 69°43W **81** C19
Skull *Ireland* 51°32N 9°34E **10** E2
Skunk → *U.S.A.* 40°42N 91°7W **80** E8
Skuodas *Lithuania* 56°16N 21°33E **9** H19
Skvyra *Ukraine* 49°44N 29°40E **17** D15
Skye *U.K.* 57°15N 6°10W **11** D2
Skykomish *U.S.A.* 47°42N 121°22W **76** C3
Skyros = Skiros *Greece* 38°55N 24°34E **23** E11
Slade Pt. *Australia* 21°5S 149°13E **62** K7
Slættaratindur *Faroe Is.* 62°18N 7°1E **8** E9
Slagelse *Denmark* 55°23N 11°19E **9** J14
Slamet *Indonesia* 7°16S 109°8E **37** G13
Slane *Ireland* 53°42N 6°33W **10** C5
Slaney → *Ireland* 52°26N 6°33W **10** D5
Slangberge *S. Africa* 31°32S 20°48E **56** E3
Slate Is. *Canada* 48°40N 87°0W **72** C2
Slatina *Romania* 44°28N 24°22E **17** F13
Slatington *U.S.A.* 40°45N 75°37W **83** F9
Slave → *Canada* 61°18N 113°39W **70** A6
Slave Coast *W. Afr.* 6°0N 2°30E **50** G6
Slave Lake *Canada* 55°17N 114°43W **70** B6
Slave Pt. *Canada* 61°11N 115°56W **70** A5
Slavgorod *Russia* 53°1N 78°37E **28** D8
Slavonski Brod *Croatia* 45°11N 18°1E **23** B8
Slavuta *Ukraine* 50°15N 27°2E **17** C14
Slavyanka *Russia* 42°53N 131°21E **30** C5
Slavyansk = Slovyansk
    Ukraine 48°55N 37°36E **19** E6
Slawharad *Belarus* 53°27N 31°0E **17** B16
Sleaford *U.K.* 53°0N 0°24W **12** D7
Sleaford B. *Australia* 34°55S 135°45E **63** E2
Sleat, Sd. of *U.K.* 57°5N 5°47W **11** D3
Sleeper Is. *Canada* 58°30N 81°0W **69** D11
Sleeping Bear Dunes △
    U.S.A. 44°50N 86°5W **80** C10
Sleepy Eye *U.S.A.* 44°18N 94°43W **80** C6
Slemon L. *Canada* 63°13N 116°4W **70** A5
Slide Mt. *U.S.A.* 42°0N 74°25W **83** E10
Slidell *U.S.A.* 30°17N 89°47W **85** F10
Sliema *Malta* 35°55N 14°30E **25** D2
Slieve Aughty *Ireland* 53°4N 8°30W **10** C3
Slieve Bloom *Ireland* 53°4N 7°40W **10** C4
Slieve Donard *U.K.* 54°11N 5°55W **10** B6
Slieve Gamph *Ireland* 54°6N 9°0W **10** B3
Slieve Gullion *U.K.* 54°7N 6°26W **10** B5
Slieve League *Ireland* 54°40N 8°42W **10** B3
Slieve Mish *Ireland* 52°12N 9°50W **10** D2
Slievenamon *Ireland* 52°25N 7°34W **10** D4
Sligeach = Sligo *Ireland* 54°16N 8°28W **10** B3
Sligo *Ireland* 54°16N 8°28W **10** B3
Sligo *U.S.A.* 41°6N 79°29W **82** E5
Sligo □ *Ireland* 54°8N 8°42W **10** B3
Sligo B. *Ireland* 54°18N 8°40W **10** B3
Slippery Rock *U.S.A.* 41°4N 80°3W **82** E4
Slite *Sweden* 57°42N 18°48E **9** H18
Sliven *Bulgaria* 42°42N 26°19E **23** C12
Sloan *U.S.A.* 35°57N 115°13W **79** K11
Sloansville *U.S.A.* 42°45N 74°22W **83** D10
Slobodskoy *Russia* 58°40N 50°6E **18** C9
Slobozia *Romania* 44°34N 27°23E **17** F14
Slocan *Canada* 49°48N 117°28W **70** D5
Slonim *Belarus* 53°4N 25°19E **17** B13
Slough *U.K.* 51°30N 0°36W **13** F7
Slough □ *U.K.* 51°30N 0°36W **13** F7
Sloughhouse *U.S.A.* 38°26N 121°12W **78** G5
Slovak Rep. ■ *Europe* 48°30N 20°0E **17** D10
Slovakia = Slovak Rep. ■
    Europe 48°30N 20°0E **17** D10

Slovakian Ore Mts. = Slovenské
    Rudohorie *Slovak Rep.* 48°45N 20°0E **17** D10
Slovenia ■ *Europe* 45°58N 14°30E **16** F8
Slovenija = Slovenia ■
    Europe 45°58N 14°30E **16** F8
Slovenská = Slovak Rep. ■
    Europe 48°30N 20°0E **17** D10
Slovenské Rudohorie
    Slovak Rep. 48°45N 20°0E **17** D10
Slovyansk *Ukraine* 48°55N 37°36E **19** E6
Sluch → *Ukraine* 51°37N 26°38E **17** C14
Sluis *Neths.* 51°18N 3°23E **15** C3
Słupsk *Poland* 54°30N 17°3E **17** A9
Slurry *S. Africa* 25°49S 25°42E **56** D4
Slutsk *Belarus* 53°2N 27°31E **17** B14
Slyne Hd. *Ireland* 53°25N 10°10W **10** C1
Slyudyanka *Russia* 51°40N 103°40E **29** D11
Småland *Sweden* 57°15N 15°25E **9** H16
Smalltree L. *Canada* 61°0N 105°0W **71** A8
Smallwood Res. *Canada* 54°5N 64°30W **73** B7
Smarhon *Belarus* 54°20N 26°24E **17** A14
Smartt Syndicate Dam
    S. Africa 30°45S 23°10E **56** E3
Smartville *U.S.A.* 39°13N 121°18W **78** F5
Smeaton *Canada* 53°30N 104°49W **71** C8
Smederevo *Serbia* 44°40N 20°57E **23** B9
Smerwick Harbour
    Ireland 52°12N 10°23W **10** D1
Smethport *U.S.A.* 41°49N 78°27W **82** E6
Smidovich *Russia* 48°36N 133°49E **29** E14
Smith *Canada* 55°10N 114°0W **70** B6
Smith Center *U.S.A.* 39°47N 98°47W **80** F4
Smith River △ *U.S.A.* 41°54N 124°8W **76** F1
Smithburne → *Australia* 17°3S 140°57E **62** B3
Smithers *Canada* 54°45N 127°10W **70** C3
Smithfield *S. Africa* 30°9S 26°30E **57** E4
Smithfield *N.C., U.S.A.* 35°31N 78°21W **85** D15
Smithfield *Utah, U.S.A.* 41°50N 111°50W **76** F8
Smiths Falls *Canada* 44°55N 76°0W **83** B9
Smithton *Australia* 40°53S 145°6E **63** G4
Smithville *Canada* 43°6N 79°33W **82** C5
Smithville *U.S.A.* 30°1N 97°10W **84** F6
Smoke Creek Desert
    U.S.A. 40°30N 119°40W **76** F4
Smoky → *Canada* 56°10N 117°21W **70** B5
Smoky Bay *Australia* 32°22S 134°13E **63** E1
Smoky Hill → *U.S.A.* 39°4N 96°48W **80** F5
Smoky Hills *U.S.A.* 39°15N 99°30W **80** F4
Smoky Lake *Canada* 54°10N 112°30W **70** C6
Smøla *Norway* 63°23N 8°3E **8** E13
Smolensk *Russia* 54°45N 32°5E **18** D5
Smolikas, Oros *Greece* 40°9N 20°58E **23** D9
Smolyan *Bulgaria* 41°36N 24°38E **23** D11
Smooth Rock Falls
    Canada 49°17N 81°37W **72** C3
Smoothstone L. *Canada* 54°40N 106°50W **71** C7
Smorgon = Smarhon
    Belarus 54°20N 26°24E **17** A14
Smyrna = İzmir *Turkey* 38°25N 27°8E **23** E12
Smyrna *U.S.A.* 39°18N 75°36W **81** F16
Snæfell *Iceland* 64°48N 15°34W **8** D6
Snaefell *I. of Man* 54°16N 4°27W **12** C3
Snæfellsjökull *Iceland* 64°49N 23°46W **8** D2
Snake → *U.S.A.* 46°12N 119°2W **76** C4
Snake I. *Australia* 38°47S 146°33E **63** F4
Snake Range *U.S.A.* 39°0N 114°20W **76** G6
Snake River Plain
    U.S.A. 42°50N 114°0W **76** E7
Snåsavatnet *Norway* 64°12N 12°0E **8** D15
Sneek *Neths.* 53°2N 5°40E **15** A5
Sneem *Ireland* 51°50N 9°54W **10** E2
Sneeuberge *S. Africa* 31°46S 24°20E **56** E3
Snelling *U.S.A.* 37°31N 120°26W **78** H6
Snežka *Europe* 50°41N 15°50E **16** C8
Snizort, L. *U.K.* 57°33N 6°28W **11** D2
Snøhetta *Norway* 62°19N 9°16E **8** E13
Snohomish *U.S.A.* 47°55N 122°6W **78** C4
Snoqualmie Pass
    U.S.A. 47°25N 121°25W **78** C5
Snoul *Cambodia* 12°4N 106°26E **39** F6
Snover *U.S.A.* 43°27N 82°58W **82** C2
Snow Hill *U.S.A.* 38°11N 75°24W **81** F16
Snow Lake *Canada* 54°52N 100°3W **71** C8
Snow Mt. *Calif., U.S.A.* 39°23N 122°45W **78** F4
Snow Mt. *Maine, U.S.A.* 45°18N 70°48W **83** A14
Snow Shoe *U.S.A.* 41°2N 77°57W **82** E7
Snowbird L. *Canada* 60°45N 103°0W **71** A8
Snowdon *U.K.* 53°4N 4°5W **12** D3
Snowdonia △ *U.K.* 53°7N 3°59W **12** D4
Snowdrift = Łutsel K'e
    Canada 62°24N 110°44W **71** A6
Snowdrift → *Canada* 62°24N 110°44W **71** A6
Snowflake *U.S.A.* 34°30N 110°5W **77** J8
Snowshoe Pk. *U.S.A.* 48°13N 115°41W **76** B6
Snowtown *Australia* 33°46S 138°14E **63** E2
Snowville *U.S.A.* 41°58N 112°43W **76** F7
Snowy → *Australia* 37°46S 148°30E **63** F4
Snowy Mt. *U.S.A.* 43°42N 74°23W **83** C10
Snowy Mts. *Australia* 36°30S 148°20E **63** F4
Snug Corner *Bahamas* 22°33N 73°52W **89** B5
Snug Harbour *Canada* 45°22N 80°17W **82** A4
Snyatyn *Ukraine* 48°27N 25°38E **17** D13
Snyder *Okla., U.S.A.* 34°40N 98°57W **84** H5
Snyder *Tex., U.S.A.* 32°44N 100°55W **84** E4
Soahanina *Madag.* 18°42S 44°13E **57** B7
Soalala *Madag.* 16°6S 45°20E **57** B8
Soaloka *Madag.* 18°32S 45°15E **57** B8
Soan → *Pakistan* 33°1N 71°44E **42** C4
Soanierana-Ivongo
    Madag. 16°55S 49°35E **57** B8
Soanindraniny *Madag.* 19°54S 47°14E **57** B8
Soavina *Madag.* 20°23S 46°56E **57** C8
Soavinandriana *Madag.* 19°9S 46°45E **57** B8
Sobat, Nahr → *Sudan* 9°22N 31°33E **51** G12
Sobhapur *India* 22°47N 78°17E **42** H8
Sobradinho, Represa de
    Brazil 9°30S 42°0W **93** E10

Sobral *Brazil* 3°50S 40°20W **93** D10
Soc Giang *Vietnam* 22°54N 106°1E **38** A6
Soc Trang *Vietnam* 9°37N 105°50E **39** H5
Socastee *U.S.A.* 33°41N 78°59W **85** E15
Soch'e = Shache *China* 38°20N 77°10E **32** C2
Sochi *Russia* 43°35N 39°40E **19** F6
Société, Îs. de la
  French Polynesia 17°0S 151°0W **65** J12
Society Is. = Société, Îs. de la
  French Polynesia 17°0S 151°0W **65** J12
Socompa, Portezuelo de
  Chile 24°27S 68°18W **94** A2
Socorro *N. Mex., U.S.A.* 34°4N 106°54W **77** J10
Socorro *Tex., U.S.A.* 31°39N 106°18W **84** F1
Socorro, I. *Mexico* 18°45N 110°58W **86** D2
Socotra *Yemen* 12°30N 54°0E **47** E5
Soda L. *U.S.A.* 35°10N 116°4W **77** J5
Soda Plains *India* 35°30N 79°0E **43** B8
Soda Springs *U.S.A.* 42°39N 111°36W **76** E8
Sodankylä *Finland* 67°29N 26°40E **8** C22
Soddy-Daisy *U.S.A.* 35°17N 85°10W **85** D12
Söderhamn *Sweden* 61°18N 17°10E **8** F17
Söderköping *Sweden* 58°31N 16°20E **9** G17
Södermanland *Sweden* 58°56N 16°55E **9** G17
Södertälje *Sweden* 59°12N 17°39E **9** G17
Sodiri *Sudan* 14°27N 29°0E **51** F11
Sodus *U.S.A.* 43°14N 77°4W **82** C7
Sodwana Bay △ *S. Africa* 27°35S 32°43E **57** D5
Soekmekaar = Morebeng
  S. Africa 23°30S 29°55E **57** C4
Soest *Neths.* 52°9N 5°19E **15** B5
Sofala □ *Mozam.* 19°30S 34°30E **57** B5
Sofia = Sofiya *Bulgaria* 42°45N 23°20E **23** C10
Sofia → *Madag.* 15°27S 47°23E **57** B8
Sofiya *Bulgaria* 42°45N 23°20E **23** C10
Sōfu-Gan *Japan* 29°49N 140°21E **31** K10
Sogamoso *Colombia* 5°43N 72°56W **92** B4
Sogār *Iran* 25°53N 58°6E **45** E8
Sogndalsfjøra *Norway* 61°14N 7°5E **8** F12
Søgne *Norway* 58°5N 7°48E **9** G12
Sognefjorden *Norway* 61°10N 5°50E **8** F11
Soh *Iran* 33°26N 51°27E **45** C6
Sohâg *Egypt* 26°33N 31°43E **51** C12
Sohagpur *India* 22°42N 78°12E **42** H8
Sohar = Ṣuḥār *Oman* 24°20N 56°40E **45** E8
Soignies *Belgium* 50°35N 4°5E **15** D4
Soissons *France* 49°25N 3°19E **20** B5
Sōja *Japan* 34°40N 133°45E **31** G6
Sojat *India* 25°55N 73°45E **42** G5
Sokal *Ukraine* 50°31N 24°15E **17** C13
Sokcho *S. Korea* 38°12N 128°36E **35** E15
Söke *Turkey* 37°48N 27°28E **23** F12
Sokelo
  Dem. Rep. of the Congo 9°55S 24°36E **55** D1
Sokhumi *Georgia* 43°0N 41°0E **19** F7
Soko Is. *China* 22°10N 113°54E **33** G10
Sokodé *Togo* 9°0N 1°11E **50** G6
Sokol *Russia* 59°30N 40°5E **18** C7
Sokółka *Poland* 53°25N 23°30E **17** B12
Sokołów Podlaski
  Poland 52°25N 22°15E **17** B12
Sokoto *Nigeria* 13°2N 5°16E **50** F7
Sol Iletsk *Russia* 51°10N 55°0E **18** D10
Solai *Kenya* 0°2N 36°12E **54** B4
Solan *India* 30°55N 77°7E **42** D7
Solana Beach *U.S.A.* 32°58N 117°16W **79** N9
Solander I. *N.Z.* 46°34S 166°54E **59** G1
Solapur *India* 17°43N 75°56E **40** L9
Soldotna *U.S.A.* 60°29N 151°3W **68** C4
Soléa *Cyprus* 35°5N 33°4E **25** D12
Soledad *Colombia* 10°55N 74°46W **92** A4
Soledad *U.S.A.* 36°26N 121°20W **78** J5
Soledad *Venezuela* 8°10N 63°34W **92** B6
Solent, The *U.K.* 50°45N 1°25W **13** G6
Solfonntaggen *Norway* 60°2N 6°57E **9** F12
Solhan *Turkey* 38°57N 41°3E **44** B4
Soligalich *Russia* 59°5N 42°10E **18** C7
Soligorsk = Salihorsk
  Belarus 52°51N 27°27E **17** B14
Solihull *U.K.* 52°26N 1°47W **13** E6
Solikamsk *Russia* 59°38N 56°50E **18** C10
Solila *Madag.* 21°25S 46°37E **57** C8
Solimões = Amazonas →
  S. Amer. 0°5S 50°0W **93** D8
Solingen *Germany* 51°10N 7°5E **16** C4
Sollefteå *Sweden* 63°12N 17°20E **8** E17
Sóller *Spain* 39°46N 2°43E **24** B9
Solo → *Indonesia* 6°47S 112°22E **37** G15
Sologne *France* 47°40N 1°45E **20** C4
Solok *Indonesia* 0°45S 100°40E **36** E2
Sololá *Guatemala* 14°49N 91°10W **88** D1
Sololo *Kenya* 3°33N 38°39E **54** B4
Solomon, N. Fork →
  U.S.A. 39°29N 98°26W **80** F4
Solomon, S. Fork →
  U.S.A. 39°25N 99°12W **80** F4
Solomon Is. ■ *Pac. Oc.* 6°0S 155°0E **58** B8
Solomon Rise *Pac. Oc.* 1°0N 157°0E **64** G7
Solon *China* 46°32N 121°10E **33** B7
Solon Springs *U.S.A.* 46°22N 91°49W **80** B8
Solor *Indonesia* 8°27S 123°0E **37** F6
Solothurn *Switz.* 47°13N 7°32E **20** C7
Šolta *Croatia* 43°24N 16°15E **22** C7
Solṭānābād *Khorāsān,*
  Iran 34°13N 59°58E **45** C8
Solṭānābād *Khorāsān, Iran* 36°29N 58°5E **45** B8
Solunska Glava
  Macedonia 41°44N 21°31E **23** D9
Solvang *U.S.A.* 34°36N 120°8W **79** L6
Solvay *U.S.A.* 43°3N 76°13W **83** C8
Sölvesborg *Sweden* 56°5N 14°35E **9** H16
Solway Firth *U.K.* 54°49N 3°35W **12** C4
Solwezi *Zambia* 12°11S 26°21E **55** E2
Sōma *Japan* 37°45N 140°50E **30** F10
Soma *Turkey* 39°10N 27°35E **23** E12
Somabhula *Zimbabwe* 19°42S 29°40E **57** B4

Somali Pen. *Africa* 7°0N 46°0E **48** F8
Somali Rep. ■ *Africa* 7°0N 47°0E **47** F4
Somalia = Somali Rep. ■
  Africa 7°0N 47°0E **47** F4
Somaliland □ *Somali Rep.* 9°0N 46°0E **47** F4
Sombor *Serbia* 45°46N 19°9E **23** B8
Sombra *Canada* 42°43N 82°29W **82** D2
Sombrerete *Mexico* 23°38N 103°39W **86** C4
Sombrero *Anguilla* 18°37N 63°30W **89** C7
Somdari *India* 25°47N 72°38E **42** G5
Somers *U.S.A.* 48°5N 114°13W **76** B6
Somerset *Ky., U.S.A.* 37°5N 84°36W **81** G11
Somerset *Mass., U.S.A.* 41°47N 71°8W **83** E13
Somerset *Pa., U.S.A.* 40°1N 79°5W **82** F5
Somerset □ *U.K.* 51°9N 3°0W **13** F5
Somerset East *S. Africa* 32°42S 25°35E **56** E4
Somerset I. *Canada* 73°30N 93°0W **68** B10
Somerset West *S. Africa* 34°8S 18°50E **56** E2
Somersworth *U.S.A.* 43°16N 70°52W **83** C14
Somerton *U.S.A.* 32°36N 114°43W **77** K6
Somerville *U.S.A.* 40°35N 74°38W **83** F10
Someş → *Romania* 47°49N 22°43E **17** D12
Somme → *France* 50°11N 1°38E **20** A4
Somnath *India* 20°53N 70°22E **42** J4
Somosierra, Puerto de
  Spain 41°4N 3°35W **21** B4
Somosomo *Fiji* 16°47S 179°58W **59** a
Somosomo Str. *Fiji* 16°0S 180°0E **59** a
Somoto *Nic.* 13°28N 86°37W **88** D2
Somport, Tunnel de
  Spain 42°48N 0°31W **20** E3
Son → *India* 25°42N 84°52E **43** G11
Son Ha *Vietnam* 15°3N 108°34E **38** E7
Son Hoa *Vietnam* 13°2N 108°58E **38** F7
Son La *Vietnam* 21°20N 103°50E **38** B4
Son Morrell *Spain* 39°44N 3°20E **24** B10
Son Rapinya *Spain* 39°35N 2°37E **24** B9
Son Sardina *Spain* 39°37N 2°40E **24** B9
Son Serra *Spain* 39°43N 3°13E **24** B10
Son Tay *Vietnam* 21°8N 105°30E **38** B5
Soná *Panama* 8°0N 81°20W **88** E3
Sonamarg *India* 34°18N 75°21E **43** B6
Sonamukhi *India* 23°18N 87°27E **43** H12
Sonar → *India* 24°24N 79°56E **43** G8
Sönch'ŏn *N. Korea* 39°48N 124°55E **35** E13
Sondags → *S. Africa* 33°44S 25°51E **56** E4
Sondar *India* 33°28N 75°56E **43** C6
Sønderborg *Denmark* 54°55N 9°49E **9** J13
Sóndrio *Italy* 46°10N 9°52E **20** C8
Sone *Mozam.* 17°23S 34°55E **55** F3
Sonepur *India* 20°55N 83°50E **41** J13
Song *Thailand* 18°28N 100°11E **38** C3
Song Cau *Vietnam* 13°27N 109°18E **38** F7
Song Hong → *Vietnam* 22°0N 104°0E **32** D5
Song Xian *China* 34°12N 112°8E **34** G7
Songan *Indonesia* 8°13S 115°24E **37** J18
Songea *Tanzania* 10°40S 35°40E **55** E4
Songgang *China* 22°46N 113°50E **33** F10
Songhua Hu *China* 43°35N 126°50E **35** C14
Songhua Jiang →
  China 47°45N 132°30E **33** B8
Songimvelo △ *S. Africa* 25°50S 31°2E **57** D5
Söngjin = Kimch'aek
  N. Korea 40°40N 129°10E **35** D15
Songkhla *Thailand* 7°13N 100°37E **39** J3
Songnim *N. Korea* 38°45N 125°39E **35** E13
Songo *Mozam.* 15°34S 32°38E **55** F3
Songo *Sudan* 9°47N 24°21E **51** G10
Songpan *China* 32°40N 103°30E **32** C5
Songwe
  Dem. Rep. of the Congo 3°20S 26°16E **54** C2
Songwe → *Africa* 9°44S 33°58E **55** D3
Sonhat *India* 23°29N 82°31E **43** H10
Sonid Youqi *China* 42°45N 112°48E **34** C7
Sonipat *India* 29°0N 77°5E **42** E7
Sonkach *India* 22°59N 76°21E **42** H7
Sonmiani *Pakistan* 25°25N 66°40E **42** G2
Sonmiani B. *Pakistan* 25°15N 66°30E **42** G2
Sono → *Brazil* 9°58S 48°11W **93** E9
Sonoma *U.S.A.* 38°18N 122°28W **78** G4
Sonora *Calif., U.S.A.* 37°59N 120°23W **78** H6
Sonora *Tex., U.S.A.* 30°34N 100°39W **84** F4
Sonora □ *Mexico* 29°20N 110°40W **86** B2
Sonora → *Mexico* 29°5N 110°55W **86** B2
Sonoran Desert
  U.S.A. 33°40N 113°30W **79** L12
Sonoyta *Mexico* 31°51N 112°50W **86** A2
Sonsonate *El Salv.* 13°43N 89°44W **88** D2
Soochow = Suzhou
  China 31°19N 120°38E **33** C7
Sooke *Canada* 48°13N 123°43W **78** B3
Soomaaliya = Somali Rep. ■
  Africa 7°0N 47°0E **47** F4
Sop Hao *Laos* 20°33N 104°27E **38** B5
Sop Prap *Thailand* 17°53N 99°20E **38** D2
Sopi *Indonesia* 2°34N 128°28E **37** D7
Sopot *Poland* 54°27N 18°31E **17** A10
Sopron *Hungary* 47°45N 16°32E **17** E9
Sopur *India* 34°18N 74°27E **43** B6
Sør-Rondane *Antarctica* 72°0S 25°0E **5** D4
Sorah *Pakistan* 27°13N 68°56E **42** F3
Soraon *India* 25°37N 81°51E **43** G9
Sorel *Canada* 46°0N 73°10W **72** C5
Sórgono *Italy* 40°1N 9°6E **22** D3
Soria *Spain* 41°43N 2°32W **21** B4
Soriano *Uruguay* 33°24S 58°19W **94** C4
Sorkh, Kuh-e *Iran* 35°40N 58°30E **45** C8
Soroca *Moldova* 48°8N 28°12E **17** D15
Sorocaba *Brazil* 23°31S 47°27W **95** A6
Sorochinsk *Russia* 52°26N 53°10E **18** D9
Soroki = Soroca *Moldova* 48°8N 28°12E **17** D15
Sorong *Indonesia* 0°55S 131°15E **37** E8
Soroni *Greece* 36°21N 28°1E **25** C10
Soroti *Uganda* 1°43N 33°35E **54** B3
Sørøya *Norway* 70°40N 22°30E **8** A20
Sørøysundet *Norway* 70°25N 23°0E **8** A20
Sorrell *Australia* 42°47S 147°34E **63** G4

Sorrento *Italy* 40°37N 14°22E **22** D6
Sorsele *Sweden* 65°31N 17°30E **8** D17
Sorsogon *Phil.* 13°0N 124°0E **37** B6
Sortavala *Russia* 61°42N 30°41E **8** F24
Sortland *Norway* 68°42N 15°25E **8** B16
Soscumica, L. *Canada* 50°15N 77°27W **72** B4
Sosnogorsk *Russia* 63°37N 53°51E **18** B9
Sosnowiec *Poland* 50°20N 19°10E **17** C10
Sossus Vlei *Namibia* 24°40S 15°23E **56** C2
Sôsura *N. Korea* 42°16N 130°36E **35** C16
Sot → *India* 27°27N 79°37E **43** F8
Sotavento *C. Verde Is.* 15°0N 25°0W **50** b
Sotik *Kenya* 0°41S 35°7E **54** C4
Sotkamo *Finland* 64°8N 28°23E **8** D23
Soto la Marina *Mexico* 23°46N 98°13W **87** C5
Soto la Marina →
  Mexico 23°45N 97°45W **87** C5
Sotuta *Mexico* 20°36N 89°1W **87** C7
Souanké *Congo* 2°10N 14°3E **52** D2
Souda *Greece* 35°29N 24°4E **25** D6
Soudas, Ormos *Greece* 35°25N 24°10E **25** D6
Souderton *U.S.A.* 40°19N 75°19W **83** F9
Soufrière *Guadeloupe* 16°5N 61°40W **88** b
Soufrière *St. Lucia* 13°51N 61°3W **89** f
Soufrière Bay *Dominica* 15°13N 61°22W **89** f
Soukhouma *Laos* 14°38N 105°48E **38** E5
Sŏul = Seoul *S. Korea* 37°31N 126°58E **35** F14
Sound, The *U.K.* 50°20N 4°10W **13** G3
Sources, Mt. aux *Lesotho* 28°45S 28°50E **57** D4
Soure *Brazil* 0°35S 48°30W **93** D9
Souris *Man., Canada* 49°40N 100°20W **71** D8
Souris *P.E.I., Canada* 46°21N 62°15W **73** C7
Souris → *N. Amer.* 49°40N 99°34W **80** A4
Sousa *Brazil* 6°45S 38°10W **93** E11
Sousse *Tunisia* 35°50N 10°38E **51** A8
South → *S. Africa* 31°35S 18°24E **56** E2
South Africa ■ *Africa* 32°0S 23°0E **56** E3
South America 10°0S 60°0W **90** E5
South Aulatsivik I.
  Canada 56°45N 61°30W **73** A7
South Australia □
  Australia 32°0S 139°0E **63** E2
South Australian Basin
  Ind. Oc. 38°0S 126°0E **64** L4
South Ayrshire □ *U.K.* 55°18N 4°41W **11** F4
South Baldy Pk. *U.S.A.* 34°6N 107°11W **77** J10
South Bass I. *U.S.A.* 41°39N 82°49W **82** E2
South Bend *Ind., U.S.A.* 41°41N 86°15W **80** E10
South Bend *Wash.,*
  U.S.A. 46°40N 123°48W **78** D3
South Boston *U.S.A.* 36°42N 78°54W **81** G14
South Branch *Canada* 47°55N 59°2W **73** C8
South Brook *Canada* 49°26N 56°5W **73** C8
South Bruny I. *Australia* 43°20S 147°15E **63** G4
South Carolina □ *U.S.A.* 34°0N 81°0W **85** E14
South Charleston
  U.S.A. 38°22N 81°44W **81** F13
South China Sea *Asia* 10°0N 113°0E **36** C4
South Cumberland Is. △
  Australia 20°42S 149°11E **62** J7
South Dakota □ *U.S.A.* 44°15N 100°0W **80** C4
South Dayton *U.S.A.* 42°21N 79°3W **82** D5
South Deerfield *U.S.A.* 42°29N 72°37W **83** D12
South Downs *U.K.* 50°52N 0°25W **13** G7
South East C. *Australia* 43°40S 146°50E **63** G4
South East Is. *Australia* 34°17S 123°30E **61** F3
South Esk → *U.K.* 56°43N 2°31W **11** E6
South Fiji Basin *Pac. Oc.* 26°0S 175°0E **64** K9
South Foreland *U.K.* 51°8N 1°24E **13** F9
South Fork American →
  U.S.A. 38°57N 120°59W **78** G5
South Fork Feather →
  U.S.A. 39°17N 121°36W **78** F5
South Fork Grand →
  U.S.A. 45°43N 102°17W **80** C2
South Fork Milk →
  U.S.A. 48°4N 106°19W **76** B10
South Fork Republican →
  U.S.A. 40°3N 101°31W **80** E3
South Georgia *Antarctica* 54°30S 37°0W **96** G4
South Gloucestershire □
  U.K. 51°32N 2°28W **13** F5
South Hadley *U.S.A.* 42°16N 72°35W **83** D12
South Haven *U.S.A.* 42°24N 86°16W **80** D10
South Henik L. *Canada* 61°30N 97°20W **71** A9
South Horr *Kenya* 2°12N 36°56E **54** B4
South I. *Kenya* 2°35N 36°35E **54** B4
South I. *N.Z.* 44°0S 170°0E **59** F3
South Indian Lake
  Canada 56°47N 98°56W **71** B9
South Invercargill *N.Z.* 46°26S 168°23E **59** G2
South Island △ *Kenya* 2°39N 36°35E **54** B4
South Kitui △ *Kenya* 1°48S 38°46E **54** C4
South Knife → *Canada* 58°55N 94°37W **71** B10
South Koel → *India* 22°32N 85°14E **43** H11
South Korea ■ *Asia* 36°0N 128°0E **35** G15
South Lake Tahoe
  U.S.A. 38°57N 119°59W **78** G6
South Lanarkshire □
  U.K. 55°37N 3°53W **11** F5
South Loup → *U.S.A.* 41°4N 98°39W **80** E4
South Luangwa △ *Zambia* 13°0S 31°20E **55** E3
South Magnetic Pole
  Antarctica 64°8S 138°8E **5** C9
South Milwaukee
  U.S.A. 42°55N 87°52W **80** D10
South Molton *U.K.* 51°1N 3°51W **13** F4
South Moose L. *Canada* 53°49N 100°1W **71** C8
South Nahanni →
  Canada 61°3N 123°21W **70** A4
South Nation → *Canada* 45°34N 75°6W **83** A9
South Natuna Is. = Natuna
  Selatan, Kepulauan
  Indonesia 2°45N 109°0E **36** D3
South Negril Pt. *Jamaica* 18°16N 78°22W **88** a
South Orkney Is.
  Antarctica 63°0S 45°0W **5** C18

South Ossetia □ *Georgia* 42°21N 44°2E **19** F7
South Otselic *U.S.A.* 42°38N 75°46W **83** D9
South Pagai, I. = Pagai Selatan,
  Pulau *Indonesia* 3°0S 100°15E **36** E2
South Paris *U.S.A.* 44°14N 70°31W **83** B14
South Pittsburg *U.S.A.* 35°1N 85°42W **85** D12
South Platte → *U.S.A.* 41°7N 100°42W **80** E3
South Pole *Antarctica* 90°0S 0°0 **5** E
South Porcupine *Canada* 48°30N 81°12W **72** C3
South Portland *U.S.A.* 43°38N 70°15W **81** D18
South Pt. *Barbados* 13°2N 59°32W **89** g
South Pt. *U.S.A.* 13°2N 59°32W **89** g
South River *Canada* 45°52N 79°23W **72** C4
South River *U.S.A.* 40°27N 74°23W **83** F10
South Ronaldsay *U.K.* 58°48N 2°58W **11** C6
South Sandwich Is.
  Antarctica 57°0S 27°0W **5** B1
South Sandwich Trench
  Atl. Oc. 56°0S 24°0W **5** B1
South Saskatchewan →
  Canada 53°15N 105°5W **71** C7
South Seal → *Canada* 58°48N 98°8W **71** B9
South Shetland Is.
  Antarctica 62°0S 59°0W **5** C18
South Shields *U.K.* 55°0N 1°25W **12** C6
South Sioux City *U.S.A.* 42°28N 96°24W **80** D5
South Sister *U.S.A.* 44°4N 121°51W **76** D3
South Talpatti = New Moore I.
  Ind. Oc. 21°37N 89°10E **43** J13
South Taranaki Bight
  N.Z. 39°40S 174°5E **59** C5
South Tasman Rise
  S. Ocean 48°0S 146°0E **5** A10
South Thompson →
  Canada 50°40N 120°20W **70** C4
South Twin I. *Canada* 53°7N 79°52E **72** B4
South Tyne → *U.K.* 54°59N 2°8W **12** C5
South Uist *U.K.* 57°20N 7°15W **11** D1
South Valley *U.S.A.* 35°1N 106°41W **77** J10
South Wellesley Is.
  Australia 16°58S 139°17E **62** B2
South West C. *Australia* 43°34S 146°3E **63** G4
South West C. *N.Z.* 47°17S 167°28E **59** G1
South Williamsport
  U.S.A. 41°13N 77°0W **82** E8
South Yorkshire □ *U.K.* 53°27N 1°36W **12** D6
Southampton *Canada* 44°30N 81°25W **82** B3
Southampton *U.K.* 50°54N 1°23W **13** G6
Southampton *U.S.A.* 40°53N 72°23W **83** F12
Southampton □ *U.K.* 50°54N 1°23W **13** G6
Southampton I. *Canada* 64°30N 84°0W **69** C11
Southaven *U.S.A.* 34°59N 90°0W **85** D9
Southbank *Canada* 54°2N 125°46W **70** C3
Southbridge *N.Z.* 43°48S 172°16E **59** E4
Southbridge *U.S.A.* 42°5N 72°2W **83** D12
Southend *Canada* 56°19N 103°22W **71** B8
Southend-on-Sea *U.K.* 51°32N 0°44E **13** F8
Southend-on-Sea □ *U.K.* 51°32N 0°44E **13** F8
Southern = Yuzhnyy □
  Russia 44°0N 40°0E **28** E5
Southern □ *Malawi* 15°0S 35°0E **55** F4
Southern □ *Zambia* 16°20S 26°20E **55** F2
Southern Alps *N.Z.* 43°41S 170°11E **59** E3
Southern Cross
  Australia 31°12S 119°15E **61** F2
Southern Indian L.
  Canada 57°10N 98°30W **71** B9
Southern Lau Group
  Fiji 18°40S 178°40W **59** a
Southern Ocean *Antarctica* 62°0S 60°0E **5** C6
Southern Pines *U.S.A.* 35°11N 79°24W **85** D15
Southern Uplands *U.K.* 55°28N 3°52W **11** F5
Southington *U.S.A.* 41°36N 72°53W **83** E12
Southland □ *N.Z.* 45°30S 168°0E **59** F1
Southold *U.S.A.* 41°4N 72°26W **83** E12
Southport *Australia* 27°58S 153°25E **63** D5
Southport *U.K.* 53°39N 3°0W **12** D4
Southport *U.S.A.* 42°3N 76°49W **82** D8
Southwest △ *Australia* 43°8S 146°5E **63** G4
Southwest Pacific Basin
  Pac. Oc. 40°0S 140°0W **5** A12
Southwold *U.K.* 52°20N 1°41E **13** E9
Southwood △ *Australia* 27°48S 150°8E **63** D5
Soutpansberg *S. Africa* 23°0S 29°30E **57** C4
Sovetsk *Kaliningrad, Russia* 55°6N 21°50E **9** J19
Sovetsk *Kirov, Russia* 57°38N 48°53E **18** C8
Sovetskaya Gavan
  Russia 48°58N 140°18E **29** E15
Soweto *S. Africa* 26°14S 27°52E **57** D4
Sowma'eh Sarā *Iran* 37°17N 49°18E **45** B6
Sōya-Kaikyō = La Perouse Str.
  Asia 45°40N 142°0E **30** B11
Sōya-Misaki *Japan* 45°30N 141°55E **30** B10
Soyo *Angola* 6°13S 12°20E **52** F2
Sozh → *Belarus* 51°57N 30°48E **17** B16

Spassk Dalniy *Russia* 44°40N 132°48E **30** B6
Spatha, Akra *Greece* 35°42N 23°43E **25** D5
Spatsizi → *Canada* 57°42N 128°7W **70** B3
Spatsizi Plateau Wilderness △
  Canada 57°40N 128°0W **70** B3
Spean → *U.K.* 56°55N 4°59W **11** E4
Spearfish *U.S.A.* 44°30N 103°52W **80** C2
Spearman *U.S.A.* 36°12N 101°12W **84** C4
Speculator *U.S.A.* 43°30N 74°22W **83** C10
Speightstown *Barbados* 13°15N 59°39W **89** g
Speke Gulf *Tanzania* 2°20S 32°50E **54** C3
Spence Bay = Taloyoak
  Canada 69°32N 93°32W **68** C10
Spencer *Idaho, U.S.A.* 44°22N 112°11W **76** D7
Spencer *Iowa, U.S.A.* 43°9N 95°9W **80** D6
Spencer *N.Y., U.S.A.* 42°13N 76°30W **83** D8
Spencer *Nebr., U.S.A.* 42°53N 98°42W **80** D4
Spencer, C. *Australia* 35°20S 136°53E **63** F2
Spencer B. *Namibia* 25°30S 14°47E **56** D1
Spencer G. *Australia* 34°0S 137°20E **63** E2
Spencerville *Canada* 44°51N 75°33W **83** B9
Spences Bridge *Canada* 50°25N 121°20W **70** C4
Spennymoor *U.K.* 54°42N 1°36W **12** C6
Spenser Mts. *N.Z.* 42°15S 172°45E **59** E4
Sperrin Mts. *U.K.* 54°50N 7°0W **10** B5
Spey → *U.K.* 57°40N 3°6W **11** D5
Speyer *Germany* 49°29N 8°25E **16** D5
Spezand *Pakistan* 29°59N 67°0E **42** E2
Spiddle *Ireland* 53°15N 9°18W **10** C2
Spili *Greece* 35°13N 24°31E **25** D6
Spin Būldak *Afghan.* 31°1N 66°25E **42** D2
Spinalonga *Greece* 35°18N 25°44E **25** D7
Spirit Lake *U.S.A.* 46°15N 122°9W **78** D4
Spirit River *Canada* 55°45N 118°50W **70** B5
Spiritwood *Canada* 53°24N 107°33W **71** C7
Spithead *U.K.* 50°45N 1°10W **13** G6
Spitzbergen = Svalbard
  Arctic 78°0N 17°0E **4** B8
Spjelkavik *Norway* 62°28N 6°22E **8** E12
Split *Croatia* 43°31N 16°26E **22** C7
Split L. *Canada* 56°8N 96°15N **71** B9
Split Lake *Canada* 56°8N 96°15N **71** B9
Spofford *U.S.A.* 29°10N 100°25W **84** G4
Spokane *U.S.A.* 47°40N 117°24W **76** C5
Spoleto *Italy* 42°44N 12°44E **22** C5
Spooner *U.S.A.* 45°50N 91°53W **80** C8
Sporyy Navolok, Mys
  Russia 75°50N 68°40E **28** B7
Sprague *U.S.A.* 47°18N 117°59W **76** C5
Spratly I. *S. China Sea* 8°38N 111°55E **36** C4
Spratly Is. *S. China Sea* 8°20N 112°0E **36** C4
Spray *U.S.A.* 44°50N 119°48W **76** D4
Spree → *Germany* 52°32N 13°12E **16** B7
Sprengisandur *Iceland* 64°52N 18°7W **8** D4
Spring City *U.S.A.* 40°11N 75°33W **83** F9
Spring Creek *U.S.A.* 40°44N 115°35W **76** F6
Spring Garden *U.S.A.* 39°52N 120°47W **78** F6
Spring Hall *Barbados* 13°18N 59°36W **89** g
Spring Hill *U.S.A.* 28°27N 82°41W **85** G13
Spring Mts. *U.S.A.* 36°0N 115°45W **79** J11
Spring Valley *Calif.,*
  U.S.A. 32°44N 116°59W **79** N10
Spring Valley *Nev.,*
  U.S.A. 36°6N 115°14W **79** J11
Springbok *S. Africa* 29°42S 17°54E **56** D2
Springboro *U.S.A.* 41°48N 80°22W **82** E4
Springdale *Canada* 49°30N 56°6W **73** C8
Springdale *U.S.A.* 36°11N 94°8W **84** C7
Springer *U.S.A.* 36°22N 104°36W **77** H11
Springerville *U.S.A.* 34°8N 109°17W **77** J9
Springfield *Canada* 42°50N 80°56W **82** D4
Springfield *N.Z.* 43°19S 171°56E **59** E3
Springfield *Colo.,*
  U.S.A. 37°24N 102°37W **77** H12
Springfield *Ill., U.S.A.* 39°48N 89°39W **80** F10
Springfield *Mass., U.S.A.* 42°6N 72°35W **83** D12
Springfield *Mo., U.S.A.* 37°13N 93°17W **80** G7
Springfield *Ohio, U.S.A.* 39°55N 83°49W **81** F12
Springfield *Oreg., U.S.A.* 44°3N 123°1W **76** D2
Springfield *Tenn.,*
  U.S.A. 36°31N 86°53W **85** C11
Springfield *Vt., U.S.A.* 43°18N 72°29W **83** C12
Springfontein *S. Africa* 30°15S 25°40E **56** E4
Springhill *Canada* 45°40N 64°4W **73** C7
Springhill *U.S.A.* 33°0N 93°28W **84** E8
Springhouse *Canada* 51°56N 122°7W **70** C4
Springs *S. Africa* 26°13S 28°25E **57** D4
Springsure *Australia* 24°8S 148°6E **62** C4
Springvale *U.S.A.* 43°28N 70°48W **83** C14
Springville *Calif., U.S.A.* 36°8N 118°49W **78** J8
Springville *N.Y., U.S.A.* 42°31N 78°40W **82** D6
Springville *Utah, U.S.A.* 40°10N 111°37W **76** F8
Springwater *U.S.A.* 42°38N 77°35W **82** D7
Spruce-Creek *U.S.A.* 40°36N 78°9W **82** F6
Spruce Knob-Seneca Rocks △
  U.S.A. 38°50N 79°30W **81** F14
Spruce Mt. *U.S.A.* 44°12N 72°19W **83** B12
Sprucedale *Canada* 45°29N 79°28W **82** A5
Spur *U.S.A.* 33°28N 100°52W **84** E4
Spurn Hd. *U.K.* 53°35N 0°8E **12** D8
Spuzzum *Canada* 49°37N 121°23W **70** D4
Squam L. *U.S.A.* 43°45N 71°32W **83** C13
Squamish *Canada* 49°45N 123°10W **70** D4
Square Islands *Canada* 52°47N 55°47W **73** B8
Squires, Mt. *Australia* 26°14S 127°28E **61** E4
Srbija = Serbia ■ *Europe* 43°20N 20°0E **23** B9
Sre Ambel *Cambodia* 11°8N 103°46E **39** G4
Sre Khtum *Cambodia* 12°10N 106°52E **39** F6
Sre Umbell = Sre Ambel
  Cambodia 11°8N 103°46E **39** G4
Srebrenica *Bos.-H.* 44°6N 19°18E **23** B8
Sredinny Ra. = Sredinnyy Khrebet
  Russia 57°0N 160°0E **29** D17
Sredinnyy Khrebet
  Russia 57°0N 160°0E **29** D17
Srednekolymsk *Russia* 67°27N 153°40E **29** C16
Śrem *Poland* 52°6N 17°2E **17** B9

Sremska Mitrovica
Serbia 44°59N 19°38E **23** B8
Srepok → Cambodia 13°33N 106°16E **38** F6
Sretensk Russia 52°10N 117°40E **29** D12
Sri Aman Malaysia 1°15N 111°32E **36** D4
Sri Lanka ■ Asia 7°30N 80°50E **40** R12
Srikakulam India 18°14N 83°58E **41** K13
Srinagar India 34°5N 74°50E **43** B6
Srono Indonesia 8°24S 114°16E **37** J17
Staaten → Australia 16°24S 141°17E **62** B3
Staaten River △
Australia 16°15S 142°40E **62** B3
Stade Germany 53°35N 9°29E **16** B5
Stadskanaal Neths. 53°4N 6°55E **15** A6
Staffa U.K. 56°27N 6°21W **11** E2
Stafford U.K. 52°49N 2°7W **12** E5
Stafford U.S.A. 37°58N 98°36W **80** G4
Stafford Springs U.S.A. 41°57N 72°18W **83** E12
Staffordshire □ U.K. 52°53N 2°10W **12** E5
Staines U.K. 51°26N 0°29W **13** F7
Stakhanov Ukraine 48°35N 38°40E **19** E6
Stalida Greece 35°17N 25°25E **25** D7
Stalowa Wola Poland 50°34N 22°3E **17** C12
Stalybridge U.K. 53°28N 2°3W **12** D5
Stamford Australia 21°15S 143°46E **62** C3
Stamford U.K. 52°39N 0°29W **13** E7
Stamford Conn., U.S.A. 41°3N 73°32W **83** E11
Stamford N.Y., U.S.A. 42°25N 74°38W **83** D10
Stamford Tex., U.S.A. 32°57N 99°48W **84** E5
Stampriet Namibia 24°20S 18°28E **56** C2
Stamps U.S.A. 33°22N 93°30W **84** E8
Standerton S. Africa 26°55S 29°7E **57** D4
Standish U.S.A. 43°59N 83°57W **81** D12
Stanford S. Africa 34°26S 19°29E **56** E2
Stanford U.S.A. 47°9N 110°13W **76** C8
Stanger S. Africa 29°27S 31°14E **57** D5
Stängsläsen = Salpausselkä
Finland 61°3N 26°15E **8** F22
Stanislaus → U.S.A. 37°40N 121°14W **78** H5
Stanke Dimitrov
Bulgaria 42°17N 23°9E **23** C10
Stanley Australia 40°46S 145°19E **63** G4
Stanley China 22°13N 114°12E **33** G11
Stanley Falk. Is. 51°40S 59°51W **96** G5
Stanley U.K. 54°53N 1°41W **12** C6
Stanley Idaho, U.S.A. 44°13N 114°56W **76** D6
Stanley N. Dak., U.S.A. 48°19N 102°23W **80** A2
Stanley N.Y., U.S.A. 42°48N 77°6W **82** D7
Stanley Mission
Canada 55°25N 104°33W **71** B8
Stannards U.S.A. 42°5N 77°55W **82** D7
Stanovoy Khrebet
Russia 55°0N 130°0E **29** D14
Stanovoy Ra. = Stanovoy Khrebet
Russia 55°0N 130°0E **29** D14
Stansmore Ra. Australia 21°23S 128°33E **60** D4
Stansted, London ✈ (STN)
U.K. 51°54N 0°14E **13** F8
Stanthorpe Australia 28°36S 151°59E **63** D5
Stanton U.S.A. 32°8N 101°48W **84** E4
Stanwood U.S.A. 48°15N 122°23W **78** B4
Staples Canada 42°10N 82°35W **82** D2
Staples U.S.A. 46°21N 94°48W **80** B7
Stapleton U.S.A. 41°29N 100°31W **80** E3
Star City Canada 52°50N 104°20W **71** C8
Star Lake U.S.A. 44°10N 75°2W **83** B9
Stara Planina Bulgaria 43°15N 23°0E **23** C10
Stara Zagora Bulgaria 42°26N 25°39E **23** C11
Starachowice Poland 51°3N 21°2E **17** C11
Staraya Russa Russia 57°58N 31°23E **18** C5
Starbuck I. Kiribati 5°37S 155°55W **65** H12
Starcke △ Australia 14°56S 145°2E **62** A4
Stargard Szczeciński
Poland 53°20N 15°0E **16** B8
Staritsa Russia 56°33N 34°55E **18** C5
Starke U.S.A. 29°57N 82°7W **85** G4
Starkville U.S.A. 33°28N 88°49W **85** E10
Starogard Gdański
Poland 53°59N 18°30E **17** B10
Starokonstantinov =
Starokonstantyniv
Ukraine 49°48N 27°10E **17** D14
Starokonstantyniv
Ukraine 49°48N 27°10E **17** D14
Start Pt. U.K. 50°13N 3°39W **13** G4
Staryy Chartoriysk
Ukraine 51°15N 25°54E **17** C13
Staryy Oskol Russia 51°19N 37°55E **19** D6
State College U.S.A. 40°48N 77°52W **82** F7
Stateline U.S.A. 38°57N 119°56W **78** G7
Staten, I. = Estados, I. de Los
Argentina 54°40S 64°30W **96** G4
Staten I. U.S.A. 40°35N 74°9W **83** F10
Statesboro U.S.A. 32°27N 81°47W **85** E14
Statesville U.S.A. 35°47N 80°53W **85** D14
Statia = St. Eustatius
W. Indies 17°20N 63°0W **89** C7
Stauffer U.S.A. 34°45N 119°3W **79** L7
Staunton Ill., U.S.A. 39°1N 89°47W **80** F9
Staunton Va., U.S.A. 38°9N 79°4W **81** F14
Stavanger Norway 58°57N 5°40E **9** G11
Staveley N.Z. 43°40S 171°32E **59** E3
Stavelot Belgium 50°23N 5°55E **15** D5
Stavern Norway 59°0N 10°1E **9** G14
Stavoren Neths. 52°53N 5°22E **15** B5
Stavropol Russia 45°5N 42°0E **19** E7
Stavros Cyprus 35°1N 32°38E **25** D11
Stavros Greece 35°12N 24°45E **25** D6
Stavros, Akra Greece 35°26N 24°58E **25** D6
Stawell Australia 37°5S 142°47E **63** F3
Stawell → Australia 20°20S 142°55E **62** C3
Stayner Canada 44°25N 80°5W **82** B4
Stayton U.S.A. 44°48N 122°48W **76** D2
Steamboat Springs
U.S.A. 40°29N 106°50W **76** F10
Steele U.S.A. 46°51N 99°55W **80** B4
Steelton U.S.A. 40°14N 76°50W **82** F8

Steen River Canada 59°40N 117°12W **70** B5
Steens Mt. U.S.A. 42°35N 118°40W **76** E4
Steenwijk Neths. 52°47N 6°7E **15** B6
Steep Pt. Australia 26°8S 113°8E **61** E1
Steep Rock Canada 51°30N 98°48W **71** C9
Stefanie L. = Chew Bahir
Ethiopia 4°40N 36°50E **47** G2
Stefansson Bay Antarctica 67°20S 59°8E **5** C5
Steiermark □ Austria 47°26N 15°0E **16** E8
Steilacoom U.S.A. 47°10N 122°36W **78** C4
Steilrandberge Namibia 17°45S 13°20E **56** B1
Steinbach Canada 49°32N 96°40W **71** D9
Steinhausen Namibia 21°49S 18°20E **56** C2
Steinkjer Norway 64°1N 11°31E **8** D14
Steinkopf S. Africa 29°18S 17°43E **56** D2
Stellarton Canada 45°32N 62°30W **73** C7
Stellenbosch S. Africa 33°58S 18°50E **56** E2
Stendal Germany 52°36N 11°53E **16** B6
Steornabhaigh = Stornoway
U.K. 58°13N 6°23W **11** C2
Stepanakert = Xankändi
Azerbaijan 39°52N 46°49E **44** B5
Stephens Creek
Australia 31°50S 141°30E **63** E3
Stephens I. Canada 54°10N 130°45W **70** C2
Stephens L. Canada 56°32N 95°0W **71** B9
Stephenville Canada 48°31N 58°35W **73** C8
Stephenville U.S.A. 32°13N 98°12W **84** E5
Steppe Asia 50°0N 50°0E **26** C7
Sterkstroom S. Africa 31°32S 26°32E **56** E4
Sterling Colo., U.S.A. 40°37N 103°13W **76** F12
Sterling Ill., U.S.A. 41°48N 89°42W **80** E9
Sterling Kans., U.S.A. 38°13N 98°12W **80** F4
Sterling City U.S.A. 31°51N 101°0W **84** F4
Sterling Heights U.S.A. 42°35N 83°2W **81** D12
Sterling Run U.S.A. 41°25N 78°12W **82** E6
Sterlitamak Russia 53°40N 56°0E **18** D10
Sternes Greece 35°30N 24°9E **25** D6
Stettin = Szczecin Poland 53°27N 14°27E **16** B8
Stettiner Haff Germany 53°47N 14°15E **16** B8
Stettler Canada 52°19N 112°40W **70** C6
Steubenville U.S.A. 40°22N 80°37W **82** F4
Stevenage U.K. 51°55N 0°13W **13** F7
Stevens Point U.S.A. 44°31N 89°34W **80** C9
Stevenson U.S.A. 45°42N 121°53W **78** E5
Stevenson → Australia 27°6S 135°33E **63** D2
Stevenson L. Canada 53°55N 96°0W **71** C9
Stevensville U.S.A. 46°30N 114°5W **76** C6
Stewart Canada 55°56N 129°57W **70** B3
Stewart U.S.A. 39°5N 119°46W **78** F7
Stewart → Canada 63°19N 139°26W **68** C6
Stewart, C. Australia 11°57S 134°56E **62** A1
Stewart, I. Chile 54°50S 71°15W **96** G2
Stewart I. N.Z. 46°58S 167°54E **59** G1
Stewarts Point U.S.A. 38°39N 123°24W **78** G3
Stewartville U.S.A. 43°51N 92°29W **80** D7
Stewiacke Canada 45°9N 63°22W **73** C7
Steynsburg S. Africa 31°15S 25°49E **56** E4
Steyr Austria 48°3N 14°25E **16** D8
Steytlerville S. Africa 33°17S 24°19E **56** E3
Stigler U.S.A. 35°15N 95°8W **84** D7
Stikine → Canada 56°40N 132°30W **70** B2
Stilfontein S. Africa 26°51S 26°50E **56** D4
Stillwater N.Z. 42°27S 171°20E **59** E3
Stillwater N.Y., U.S.A. 42°55N 73°41W **83** D11
Stillwater Okla., U.S.A. 36°7N 97°4W **84** C6
Stillwater Range U.S.A. 39°50N 118°5W **76** G4
Stillwater Res. U.S.A. 43°54N 75°3W **83** C9
Stilwell U.S.A. 35°49N 94°38W **84** D7
Stînga Nistrului □
Moldova 47°20N 29°15E **17** E15
Ştip Macedonia 41°42N 22°10E **23** D10
Stirling Canada 44°18N 77°33W **82** B7
Stirling U.K. 56°8N 3°57W **11** E5
Stirling □ U.K. 56°12N 4°18W **11** E4
Stirling Ra. Australia 34°23S 118°0E **61** F2
Stirling Range △
Australia 34°26S 118°20E **61** F2
Stittsville Canada 45°15N 75°55W **83** A9
Stjernøya Norway 70°20N 22°40E **8** A20
Stjørdalshalsen Norway 63°29N 10°51E **8** E14
Stockerau Austria 48°24N 16°12E **16** D9
Stockholm Sweden 59°19N 18°4E **9** G18
Stockport U.K. 53°25N 2°9W **12** D5
Stocksbridge U.K. 53°29N 1°35W **12** D6
Stockton Calif., U.S.A. 37°58N 121°17W **78** H5
Stockton Kans., U.S.A. 39°26N 99°16W **80** F4
Stockton Mo., U.S.A. 37°42N 93°48W **80** G7
Stockton-on-Tees U.K. 54°35N 1°19W **12** C6
Stockton-on-Tees □
U.K. 54°35N 1°19W **12** C6
Stockton Plateau
U.S.A. 30°30N 102°30W **84** F3
Stoeng Treng Cambodia 13°31N 105°58E **38** F5
Stoer, Pt. of U.K. 58°16N 5°23W **11** C3
Stoke-on-Trent U.K. 53°1N 2°11W **12** D5
Stoke-on-Trent □ U.K. 53°1N 2°11W **12** D5
Stokes △ Australia 33°45S 121°11E **61** F3
Stokes Bay Canada 45°0N 81°28W **82** B3
Stokes Pt. Australia 40°10S 143°56E **63** G3
Stokes Ra. Australia 15°50S 130°50E **60** C5
Stokksnes Iceland 64°14N 14°58W **8** D6
Stokmarknes Norway 68°34N 14°54E **8** B16
Stolac Bos.-H. 43°5N 17°59E **23** C7
Stolbovoy, Ostrov
Russia 74°44N 135°14E **29** B14
Stolbtsy = Stowbtsy
Belarus 53°30N 26°43E **17** B14
Stolin Belarus 51°53N 26°50E **17** C14
Stomio Greece 39°52N 22°45E **25** E10
Stone U.K. 52°55N 2°9W **12** E5
Stoneboro U.S.A. 41°20N 80°7W **82** E4
Stonehaven U.K. 56°59N 2°12W **11** E6
Stonehenge Australia 24°22S 143°17E **62** C3
Stonehenge U.K. 51°9N 1°45W **13** F6
Stonewall Canada 50°10N 97°19W **71** C9
Stony I. U.S.A. 43°53N 76°19W **83** C8

Stony L. Man., Canada 58°51N 98°40W **71** B9
Stony L. Ont., Canada 44°30N 78°5W **82** B6
Stony Point U.S.A. 41°14N 73°59W **83** E11
Stony Pt. U.S.A. 43°50N 76°18W **83** C8
Stony Rapids Canada 59°16N 105°50W **71** B7
Stony Tunguska = Tunguska,
Podkamennaya →
Russia 61°50N 90°13E **29** C10
Stonyford U.S.A. 39°23N 122°33W **78** F4
Stora Lulevatten Sweden 67°10N 19°30E **8** C18
Storavan Sweden 65°45N 18°10E **8** D18
Stord Norway 59°52N 5°23E **9** G11
Store Bælt Denmark 55°20N 11°0E **9** J14
Storm B. Australia 43°10S 147°30E **63** G4
Storm Lake U.S.A. 42°39N 95°13W **80** D6
Stormberge S. Africa 31°16S 26°17E **56** E4
Stormsrivier S. Africa 33°59S 23°52E **56** E3
Stornoway U.K. 58°13N 6°23W **11** C2
Storozhinets = Storozhynets
Ukraine 48°14N 25°45E **17** D13
Storozhynets Ukraine 48°14N 25°45E **17** D13
Storrs U.S.A. 41°49N 72°15W **83** E12
Storsjön Sweden 63°9N 14°30E **8** E16
Storuman Sweden 65°5N 17°10E **8** D17
Storuman, L. Sweden 65°13N 16°50E **8** D17
Stouffville Canada 43°58N 79°15W **82** C5
Stoughton Canada 49°40N 103°0W **71** D8
Stour → Dorset, U.K. 50°43N 1°47W **13** G6
Stour → Kent, U.K. 51°18N 1°22E **13** F9
Stour → Suffolk, U.K. 51°57N 1°4E **13** F9
Stourbridge U.K. 52°28N 2°8W **13** E5
Stout L. Canada 52°0N 94°40W **71** C10
Stove Pipe Wells Village
U.S.A. 36°35N 117°11W **79** J9
Stow U.S.A. 41°10N 81°27W **82** E3
Stowbtsy Belarus 53°30N 26°43E **17** B14
Stowmarket U.K. 52°12N 1°0E **13** E9
Strabane U.K. 54°50N 7°27W **10** B4
Strahan Australia 42°9S 145°20E **63** G4
Stralsund Germany 54°18N 13°4E **16** A7
Strand S. Africa 34°9S 18°48E **56** E2
Stranda Møre og Romsdal,
Norway 62°19N 6°58E **8** E12
Stranda Nord-Trøndelag,
Norway 63°33N 10°14E **8** E14
Strangford L. U.K. 54°30N 5°37W **10** B6
Stranorlar Ireland 54°48N 7°46W **10** B4
Stranraer U.K. 54°54N 5°1W **11** G3
Strasbourg Canada 51°4N 104°55W **71** C8
Strasbourg France 48°35N 7°42E **20** B7
Stratford N.Z. 39°20S 174°19E **59** C5
Stratford Calif., U.S.A. 36°11N 119°49W **78** J7
Stratford Conn., U.S.A. 41°12N 73°8W **83** E11
Stratford Tex., U.S.A. 36°20N 102°4W **84** C3
Stratford-upon-Avon
U.K. 52°12N 1°42W **13** E6
Strath Spey U.K. 57°9N 3°49W **11** D5
Strathalbyn Australia 35°13S 138°53E **63** F2
Strathaven U.K. 55°40N 4°5W **11** F4
Strathcona △ Canada 49°38N 125°40W **70** D3
Strathmore Canada 51°5N 113°18W **70** C6
Strathmore U.K. 56°37N 3°7W **11** E5
Strathmore U.S.A. 36°9N 119°4W **78** J7
Strathnaver Canada 53°20N 122°33W **70** C4
Strathpeffer U.K. 57°35N 4°32W **11** D4
Strathroy Canada 42°58N 81°38W **82** D3
Strathy Pt. U.K. 58°36N 4°1W **11** C4
Strattanville U.S.A. 41°12N 79°19W **82** E5
Stratton U.S.A. 45°8N 70°26W **83** A14
Stratton Mt. U.S.A. 43°4N 72°55W **83** C12
Straubing Germany 48°52N 12°34E **16** D7
Straumnes Iceland 66°26N 23°8E **8** C2
Strawberry → U.S.A. 40°10N 110°24W **76** F8
Streaky B. Australia 32°48S 134°13E **63** E1
Streaky Bay Australia 32°51S 134°18E **63** E1
Streator U.S.A. 41°8N 88°50W **80** E9
Streetsboro U.S.A. 41°14N 81°21W **82** E3
Streetsville Canada 43°35N 79°42W **82** C5
Streng → Cambodia 13°12N 103°37E **38** F4
Streymoy Færoe Is. 62°8N 7°5W **8** E9
Strezhevoy Russia 60°42N 77°34E **28** C8
Strimonas → Greece 40°46N 23°51E **23** D10
Strokestown Ireland 53°46N 8°7W **10** C3
Strómboli Italy 38°47N 15°13E **22** E6
Stromeferry U.K. 57°21N 5°33W **11** D3
Stromness U.K. 58°58N 3°17W **11** C5
Stromsburg U.S.A. 41°7N 97°36W **80** E5
Strömstad Sweden 58°56N 11°10E **9** G14
Strömsund Sweden 63°51N 15°33E **8** E16
Strongsville U.S.A. 41°19N 81°50W **82** E3
Stronsay U.K. 59°7N 2°35W **11** B6
Stroud U.K. 51°45N 2°13W **13** F5
Stroud Road Australia 32°18S 151°57E **63** E5
Stroudsburg U.S.A. 40°59N 75°12W **83** F9
Stroumbi Cyprus 34°53N 32°29E **25** E11
Struer Denmark 56°30N 8°35E **9** H13
Strugi Krasnyye Russia 58°21N 29°1E **9** G23
Strumica Macedonia 41°28N 22°41E **23** D10
Struthers Canada 48°41N 85°51W **72** C2
Struthers U.S.A. 41°4N 80°39W **82** E4
Stryker U.S.A. 48°41N 114°46W **76** B6
Stryy Ukraine 49°16N 23°48E **17** D12
Strzelecki Cr. →
Australia 29°37S 139°59E **63** D2
Strzelecki Desert
Australia 29°30S 140°0E **63** D3
Stuart Fla., U.S.A. 27°12N 80°15W **85** H14
Stuart Nebr., U.S.A. 42°36N 99°8W **80** D4
Stuart → Canada 54°0N 123°35W **70** C4
Stuart Bluff Ra.
Australia 22°50S 131°52E **60** D5
Stuart L. Canada 54°30N 124°30W **70** C4
Stuart Ra. Australia 29°10S 134°56E **63** D1
Stull L. Canada 54°24N 92°34W **72** B1
Stung Treng = Stoeng Treng
Cambodia 13°31N 105°58E **38** F5

Stupart → Canada 56°0N 93°25W **72** A1
Sturgeon B. Canada 52°0N 97°50W **71** C9
Sturgeon Bay U.S.A. 44°50N 87°23W **80** C10
Sturgeon Falls Canada 46°25N 79°57W **72** C4
Sturgeon L. Alta., Canada 55°6N 117°32W **70** B5
Sturgeon L. Ont., Canada 50°0N 90°45W **72** C1
Sturgeon L. Ont., Canada 44°28N 78°43W **82** B6
Sturgis Canada 51°56N 102°36W **71** C8
Sturgis Mich., U.S.A. 41°48N 85°25W **81** E11
Sturgis S. Dak., U.S.A. 44°25N 103°31W **80** C2
Sturt △ Australia 27°17S 141°37E **63** D3
Sturt Cr. → Australia 19°8S 127°50E **60** C4
Sturt Stony Desert
Australia 28°30S 141°0E **63** D3
Stutterheim S. Africa 32°33S 27°28E **56** E4
Stuttgart Germany 48°48N 9°11E **16** D5
Stuttgart U.S.A. 34°30N 91°33W **84** D9
Stuyvesant U.S.A. 42°23N 73°45W **83** D11
Stykkishólmur Iceland 65°2N 22°40W **8** D2
Styria = Steiermark □
Austria 47°26N 15°0E **16** E8
Su Xian = Suzhou
China 33°41N 116°59E **34** H9
Suakin Sudan 19°8N 37°20E **51** E13
Suan N. Korea 38°42N 126°22E **35** E14
Suar India 29°2N 79°3E **43** E8
Şubā Si. Arabia 27°10N 35°40E **44** E2
Subang Indonesia 6°34S 107°45E **37** G12
Subansiri → India 26°48N 93°50E **41** F18
Subarnarekha → India 22°34N 87°24E **43** H12
Subayhah Si. Arabia 30°2N 38°50E **44** D3
Subi Indonesia 2°58N 108°50E **36** D3
Subotica Serbia 46°6N 19°39E **23** A8
Suceava Romania 47°38N 26°16E **17** E14
Suchan = Partizansk
Russia 43°8N 133°9E **30** C6
Suchil Mexico 23°38N 103°55W **86** C4
Suchou = Suzhou
China 31°19N 120°38E **33** C7
Süchow = Xuzhou
China 34°18N 117°10E **35** G9
Suck → Ireland 53°17N 8°3W **10** C3
Sucre Bolivia 19°0S 65°15W **92** G5
Sucuriú → Brazil 20°47S 51°38W **93** H8
Sud, Pte. du Canada 49°3N 62°14W **73** C7
Sud-Kivu
Dem. Rep. of the Congo 3°0S 28°30E **54** C2
Sud-Ouest, Pte. Canada 49°23N 63°36W **73** C7
Sud Ouest, Pte. Mauritius 20°28S 57°18E **53** d
Sudan ■ Africa 15°0N 30°0E **51** E11
Sudbury Canada 46°30N 81°0W **72** C3
Sudbury U.K. 52°2N 0°45E **13** E8
Sûdd Sudan 8°20N 30°0E **51** G12
Sudeten Mts. = Sudety
Europe 50°20N 16°45E **17** C9
Sudety Europe 50°20N 16°45E **17** C9
Suðuroy Færoe Is. 61°32N 6°50W **8** F9
Sudi Tanzania 10°11S 39°57E **55** E4
Sudirman, Pegunungan
Indonesia 4°30S 137°0E **37** E9
Sudong, Pulau Singapore 1°13N 103°44E **39** d
Sueca Spain 39°12N 0°21W **21** C5
Suemez I. U.S.A. 55°15N 133°20W **70** B2
Suez = El Suweis Egypt 29°58N 32°31E **51** C12
Suez, G. of = Suweis, Khalig el
Egypt 28°40N 33°0E **51** C12
Suez Canal = Suweis, Qanâ es
Egypt 31°0N 32°20E **51** B12
Suffield Canada 50°12N 111°10W **70** C6
Suffolk U.S.A. 36°44N 76°35W **81** G15
Suffolk □ U.K. 52°16N 1°0E **13** E9
Sugar Grove U.S.A. 41°59N 79°20W **82** E5
Sugarcreek U.S.A. 41°25N 79°52W **82** E5
Sugarive → India 26°16N 86°24E **43** F12
Sugluk = Salluit
Canada 62°14N 75°38W **69** C12
Şuḩār Oman 24°20N 56°40E **45** E8
Sühbaatar Mongolia 50°17N 106°10E **32** A5
Sühbaatar □ Mongolia 45°30N 114°0E **34** B8
Suhl Germany 50°36N 10°42E **16** C6
Sui Pakistan 28°37N 69°19E **42** E3
Sui Xian China 34°25N 115°2E **34** G8
Suide China 37°30N 110°12E **34** F6
Suifenhe China 44°25N 131°10E **35** B16
Suihua China 46°32N 126°55E **33** B7
Suining Jiangsu, China 33°56N 117°58E **35** H9
Suining Sichuan, China 30°26N 105°35E **32** C5
Suiping China 33°10N 113°59E **34** H7
Suir → Ireland 52°16N 7°9W **10** D4
Suisse = Switzerland ■
Europe 46°30N 8°0E **20** C8
Suisun City U.S.A. 38°15N 122°2W **78** G4
Suiyang China 44°30N 97°50W **71** C9
Suizhong China 40°21N 120°20E **35** D11
Sujangarh India 27°42N 74°31E **42** F6
Sukabumi Indonesia 6°56S 106°50E **37** G12
Sukadana Indonesia 1°10S 110°0E **36** E4
Sukagawa Japan 37°17N 140°23E **31** F10
Sukaraja Indonesia 2°28S 110°25E **36** E4
Sukawati Indonesia 8°35S 115°17E **37** K18
Sukch'ŏn N. Korea 39°22N 125°35E **35** E13
Sukhona → Russia 61°15N 46°39E **18** C6
Sukhothai Thailand 17°1N 99°49E **38** D2
Sukhumi = Sokhumi
Georgia 43°0N 41°0E **19** F7
Sukkur Pakistan 27°42N 68°54E **42** F3
Sukkur Barrage Pakistan 27°40N 68°54E **42** F3
Sukri → India 25°4N 71°43E **42** G4
Sukumo Japan 32°56N 132°44E **31** H6
Sukunka → Canada 55°45N 121°15W **70** B4
Sula, Kepulauan Indonesia 1°45S 125°0E **37** E7
Sulaco → Honduras 15°2N 87°44W **88** C2
Sulaiman Range
Pakistan 30°30N 69°50E **42** D3
Şūlār Iran 31°53N 51°54E **45** D6
Sulawesi Indonesia 2°0S 120°0E **37** E6

Sulawesi Barat □ Indonesia 3°0S 119°0E **37** E5
Sulawesi Sea = Celebes Sea
Indonesia 3°0N 123°0E **37** D6
Sulawesi Selatan □
Indonesia 2°30S 120°0E **37** E6
Sulawesi Tengah □
Indonesia 1°30S 121°0E **37** E6
Sulawesi Tenggara □
Indonesia 3°50S 122°0E **37** E6
Sulawesi Utara □ Indonesia 1°0N 124°0E **37** D6
Sulima S. Leone 6°58N 11°32W **50** G3
Sulina Romania 45°10N 29°40E **17** F15
Sulitjelma Norway 67°9N 16°3E **8** C17
Sullana Peru 4°52S 80°39W **92** D2
Sullivan Ill., U.S.A. 39°36N 88°37W **80** F9
Sullivan Ind., U.S.A. 39°6N 87°24W **80** F10
Sullivan Mo., U.S.A. 38°13N 91°10W **80** F8
Sullivan Bay Canada 50°55N 126°50W **70** C3
Sullivan I. = Lanbi Kyun
Burma 10°50N 98°20E **39** G2
Sullom Voe U.K. 60°27N 1°20W **11** A7
Sulphur La., U.S.A. 30°14N 93°23W **84** F8
Sulphur Okla., U.S.A. 34°31N 96°58W **84** D6
Sulphur Pt. Canada 60°56N 114°48W **70** A6
Sulphur Springs U.S.A. 33°8N 95°36W **84** E7
Sultan Canada 47°36N 82°47W **72** C3
Sultan U.S.A. 47°52N 121°49W **78** C5
Sultan Hamud Kenya 2°1S 37°22E **54** C4
Sultanābād = Arāk Iran 34°0N 49°40E **45** C6
Sultanpur Mad. P., India 23°9N 77°56E **42** H8
Sultanpur Punjab, India 31°13N 75°11E **42** D6
Sultanpur Ut. P., India 26°18N 82°4E **43** F10
Sulu Arch. Phil. 6°0N 121°0E **37** C6
Sulu Sea E. Indies 8°0N 120°0E **37** C6
Suluq Libya 31°44N 20°14E **51** B10
Sulzberger Ice Shelf
Antarctica 78°0S 150°0W **5** E13
Sumalata Indonesia 1°0N 122°31E **37** D6
Sumampa Argentina 29°25S 63°29W **94** B3
Sumatera Indonesia 0°40N 100°20E **36** D2
Sumatera Barat □
Indonesia 1°0S 101°0E **36** E2
Sumatera Utara □
Indonesia 2°30N 98°0E **36** D1
Sumatra = Sumatera
Indonesia 0°40N 100°20E **36** D2
Sumba Indonesia 9°45S 119°35E **37** F5
Sumba, Selat Indonesia 9°0S 118°40E **37** F5
Sumbawa Indonesia 8°26S 117°30E **36** F5
Sumbawa Besar
Indonesia 8°30S 117°26E **36** F5
Sumbawanga □ Tanzania 8°0S 31°30E **52** F6
Sumbe Angola 11°10S 13°48E **52** G2
Sumbu △ Zambia 8°43S 30°22E **55** D3
Sumburgh Hd. U.K. 59°52N 1°17W **11** B7
Sumdeo India 31°26N 78°44E **43** D8
Sumdo China 35°6N 78°41E **43** B8
Sumedang Indonesia 6°52S 107°55E **37** G12
Sumen = Shumen
Bulgaria 43°18N 26°55E **23** C12
Sumenep Indonesia 7°1S 113°52E **37** G15
Sumgait = Sumqayit
Azerbaijan 40°34N 49°38E **19** F8
Summer L. U.S.A. 42°50N 120°45W **76** E3
Summerland Canada 49°32N 119°41W **70** D5
Summerside Canada 46°24N 63°47W **73** C7
Summersville U.S.A. 38°17N 80°51W **81** F13
Summerville Ga.,
U.S.A. 34°29N 85°21W **85** D12
Summerville S.C., U.S.A. 33°1N 80°11W **85** E14
Summit Lake Canada 54°20N 122°40W **70** C4
Summit Peak U.S.A. 37°21N 106°42W **77** H10
Sumner Iowa, U.S.A. 42°51N 92°6W **80** D7
Sumner Wash., U.S.A. 47°12N 122°14W **78** C4
Sumoto Japan 34°21N 134°54E **31** G7
Šumperk Czech Rep. 49°59N 16°59E **17** D9
Sumqayit Azerbaijan 40°34N 49°38E **19** F8
Sumter U.S.A. 33°55N 80°21W **85** E14
Sumy Ukraine 50°57N 34°50E **19** D5
Sun City S. Africa 25°17S 27°3E **56** D4
Sun City Ariz., U.S.A. 33°35N 112°16W **79** M7
Sun City Calif., U.S.A. 33°43N 117°11W **79** M9
Sun City Center U.S.A. 27°43N 82°21W **85** H13
Sun Lakes U.S.A. 33°10N 111°52W **77** K8
Sun Valley U.S.A. 43°42N 114°21W **76** E6
Sunagawa Japan 43°29N 141°55E **30** C10
Sunan N. Korea 39°15N 125°40E **35** E13
Sunart, L. U.K. 56°42N 5°43W **11** E3
Sunburst U.S.A. 48°53N 111°55W **76** B8
Sunbury Australia 37°35S 144°44E **63** F3
Sunbury U.S.A. 40°52N 76°48W **83** F8
Sunchales Argentina 30°58S 61°35W **94** C3
Suncheon S. Korea 34°52N 127°31E **35** G14
Suncho Corral Argentina 27°55S 63°27W **94** B3
Sunch'ŏn N. Korea 39°24N 125°47E **35** E13
Suncook U.S.A. 43°8N 71°27W **83** C13
Sunda, Selat Indonesia 6°20S 105°30E **36** F3
Sunda Is. Indonesia 5°0S 105°0E **64** H2
Sunda Str. = Sunda, Selat
Ind. Oc. 6°20S 105°30E **36** F3
Sunda Trench = Java Trench
Ind. Oc. 9°0S 105°0E **36** F3
Sundance Canada 56°32N 94°4W **71** B10
Sundance U.S.A. 44°24N 104°23W **76** D11
Sundar Nagar India 31°32N 76°53E **42** D7
Sundarbans Asia 22°0N 89°0E **41** J16
Sundargarh △ India 22°0N 88°45E **43** J13
Sundargarh India 22°4N 84°5E **41** H14
Sundays = Sondags →
S. Africa 33°44S 25°51E **56** E4
Sunderland Canada 44°16N 79°4W **82** B5
Sunderland U.K. 54°55N 1°23W **12** C6
Sundown △ Australia 28°55S 151°34E **63** D5
Sundre Canada 51°49N 114°38W **70** C6
Sundsvall Sweden 62°23N 17°17E **8** E17
Sung Hei Vietnam 10°20N 106°2E **39** G6
Sungai Acheh Malaysia 5°8N 100°30E **39** c

Sungai Kolok *Thailand* 6°2N 101°58E **39** J3
Sungai Lembing *Malaysia* 3°55N 103°3E **39** L4
Sungai Petani *Malaysia* 5°37N 100°30E **39** K3
Sungaigerong *Indonesia* 3°0S 104°52E **36** E2
Sungailiat *Indonesia* 1°51S 106°8E **36** E3
Sungaipenuh *Indonesia* 2°1S 101°20E **36** E2
Sungari = Songhua Jiang → *China* 47°45N 132°30E **33** B8
Sunghua Chiang = Songhua Jiang → *China* 47°45N 132°30E **33** B8
Sunland Park *U.S.A.* 31°50N 106°40W **77** L10
Sunndalsora *Norway* 62°40N 8°33E **8** E13
Sunnyside *U.S.A.* 46°20N 120°0W **76** C4
Sunnyvale *U.S.A.* 37°23N 122°2W **78** H4
Sunrise Manor *U.S.A.* 36°12N 115°4W **79** J11
Suntar *Russia* 62°15N 117°30E **29** C12
Suomenselkä *Finland* 62°52N 24°0E **8** E21
Suomi = Finland ■ *Europe* 63°0N 27°0E **8** E22
Suomussalmi *Finland* 64°54N 29°10E **8** D23
Suoyarvi *Russia* 62°3N 32°20E **18** A5
Supai *U.S.A.* 36°15N 112°41W **77** H7
Supaul *India* 26°10N 86°40E **43** F12
Superior *Ariz., U.S.A.* 33°18N 111°6W **77** K8
Superior *Mont., U.S.A.* 47°12N 114°53W **76** C6
Superior *Nebr., U.S.A.* 40°1N 98°4W **80** E4
Superior *Wis., U.S.A.* 46°44N 92°6W **80** B7
Superior, L. *N. Amer.* 47°0N 87°0W **72** C2
Suphan Buri *Thailand* 14°14N 100°10E **38** E3
Suphan Dağı *Turkey* 38°54N 42°48E **44** B4
Supiori *Indonesia* 1°0S 136°0E **37** E9
Supung Shuiku *China* 40°35N 124°50E **35** D13
Sūq ash Shuyūkh *Iraq* 30°53N 46°28E **44** D5
Sūq Suwayq *Si. Arabia* 24°23N 38°27E **44** E3
Suqian *China* 33°54N 118°8E **35** H10
Suquţra = Socotra *Yemen* 12°30N 54°0E **47** E5
Sūr *Lebanon* 33°19N 35°16E **46** B4
Şūr *Oman* 22°34N 59°32E **47** C6
Sur, Pt. *U.S.A.* 36°18N 121°54W **78** J5
Sura → *Russia* 56°6N 46°0E **18** C8
Surab *Pakistan* 28°25N 66°15E **42** E2
Surabaja = Surabaya *Indonesia* 7°17S 112°45E **37** G15
Surabaya *Indonesia* 7°17S 112°45E **37** G15
Surakarta *Indonesia* 7°35S 110°48E **37** G14
Surat *Australia* 27°10S 149°6E **63** D4
Surat *India* 21°12N 72°55E **40** J8
Surat Thani *Thailand* 9°6N 99°20E **39** H2
Suratgarh *India* 29°18N 73°55E **42** E5
Şuraymilā *Si. Arabia* 25°7N 46°7E **44** E5
Surendranagar *India* 22°45N 71°40E **42** H4
Surf *U.S.A.* 34°41N 120°36W **79** L6
Surfers Paradise *Australia* 28°0S 153°25E **63** D5
Surgut *Russia* 61°14N 73°20E **28** C8
Suriapet *India* 17°10N 79°40E **40** L11
Surigao *Phil.* 9°47N 125°29E **37** C7
Surin *Thailand* 14°50N 103°34E **38** E4
Surin Nua, Ko *Thailand* 9°30N 97°55E **39** H1
Surinam = Suriname ■ *S. Amer.* 4°0N 56°0W **93** C7
Suriname ■ *S. Amer.* 4°0N 56°0W **93** C7
Suriname → *Suriname* 5°50N 55°15W **93** B7
Sürmaq *Iran* 31°3N 52°48E **45** D7
Surrey *Canada* 49°7N 122°45W **78** A4
Surrey □ *U.K.* 51°15N 0°31W **13** F7
Sursand *India* 26°39N 85°43E **43** F11
Sursar → *India* 26°14N 87°3E **43** F12
Surt *Libya* 31°11N 16°39E **51** B9
Surt, Khalīj *Libya* 31°40N 18°30E **51** B9
Surtanahu *Pakistan* 26°22N 70°0E **42** F4
Surtsey *Iceland* 63°20N 20°30W **8** E3
Suruga-Wan *Japan* 34°45N 138°30E **31** G9
Susaki *Japan* 33°22N 133°17E **31** H6
Süsangerd *Iran* 31°35N 48°6E **45** D6
Susanville *U.S.A.* 40°25N 120°39W **76** F3
Susner *India* 23°57N 76°5E **42** H7
Susquehanna *U.S.A.* 41°57N 75°36W **83** E9
Susquehanna → *U.S.A.* 39°33N 76°5W **81** F15
Susques *Argentina* 23°35S 66°25W **94** A2
Sussex *Canada* 45°45N 65°37W **73** C6
Sussex *U.S.A.* 41°13N 74°37W **83** E10
Sussex, E. □ *U.K.* 51°0N 0°20E **13** G8
Sussex, W. □ *U.K.* 51°0N 0°30W **13** G7
Sustut → *Canada* 56°20N 127°30W **70** B3
Susuman *Russia* 62°47N 148°10E **29** C15
Susunu *Indonesia* 3°7S 133°39E **37** E8
Susurluk *Turkey* 39°54N 28°8E **23** E13
Sutay Uul *Asia* 46°35N 93°38E **32** B4
Sutherland *S. Africa* 32°24S 20°40E **56** E3
Sutherland *U.K.* 58°12N 4°50W **11** C4
Sutherland *U.S.A.* 41°10N 101°8W **80** E4
Sutherland Falls *N.Z.* 44°48S 167°46E **59** F1
Sutherlin *U.S.A.* 43°23N 123°19W **76** E2
Suthri *India* 23°3N 68°55E **42** H3
Sutlej → *Pakistan* 29°23N 71°3E **42** E4
Sutter *U.S.A.* 39°10N 121°45W **78** F5
Sutter Buttes *U.S.A.* 39°12N 121°49W **78** F5
Sutter Creek *U.S.A.* 38°24N 120°48W **78** G6
Sutton *Canada* 45°6N 72°37W **83** A12
Sutton *Nebr., U.S.A.* 40°36N 97°52W **80** E6
Sutton *W. Va., U.S.A.* 38°40N 80°43W **81** F13
Sutton → *Canada* 55°15N 83°45W **72** A3
Sutton Coldfield *U.K.* 52°35N 1°49W **13** E6
Sutton in Ashfield *U.K.* 53°8N 1°16W **12** D6
Sutton L. *Canada* 54°15N 84°42W **72** B3
Suttor → *Australia* 21°36S 147°2E **62** C4
Suttsu *Japan* 42°48N 140°14E **30** C10
Suva *Fiji* 18°6S 178°30E **59** a
Suva Planina *Serbia* 43°10N 22°5E **23** C10
Suvorov Is. = Suwarrow Is. *Cook Is.* 13°15S 163°5W **65** J11
Suwałki *Poland* 54°8N 22°59E **17** A12
Suwana *Indonesia* 8°44S 115°36E **37** K18
Suwannaphum *Thailand* 15°33N 103°47E **38** E4
Suwannee → *U.S.A.* 29°17N 83°10W **85** G13
Suwanose-Jima *Japan* 29°38N 129°43E **31** K4

Suwarrow Is. *Cook Is.* 13°15S 163°5W **65** J11
Suweis, Khalîg el *Egypt* 28°40N 33°0E **51** C12
Suweis, Qanâ es *Egypt* 31°0N 32°20E **51** B12
Suwon *S. Korea* 37°17N 127°1E **35** F14
Suzdal *Russia* 56°29N 40°26E **18** C7
Suzhou *Anhui, China* 33°41N 116°59E **34** H9
Suzhou *Jiangsu, China* 31°19N 120°38E **33** C7
Suzu *Japan* 37°25N 137°17E **31** F8
Suzu-Misaki *Japan* 37°31N 137°21E **31** F8
Suzuka *Japan* 34°55N 136°36E **31** G8
Svalbard *Arctic* 78°0N 17°0E **4** B8
Svalbard Radio = Longyearbyen *Svalbard* 78°13N 15°40E **4** B8
Svappavaara *Sweden* 67°40N 21°3E **8** C19
Svartisen *Norway* 66°40N 13°59E **8** C15
Svay Chek *Cambodia* 13°48N 102°58E **38** F4
Svay Rieng *Cambodia* 11°9N 105°45E **39** G5
Svealand □ *Sweden* 60°20N 15°0E **9** F16
Svendborg *Denmark* 55°4N 10°35E **9** J14
Sverdlovsk = Yekaterinburg *Russia* 56°50N 60°30E **28** D7
Sverdrup Chan. *Canada* 79°56N 96°25W **69** B10
Sverdrup Is. *Canada* 79°0N 97°0W **69** B10
Sverige = Sweden ■ *Europe* 57°0N 15°0E **9** H16
Svetlaya *Russia* 46°33N 138°18E **30** A9
Svetlogorsk = Svyetlahorsk *Belarus* 52°38N 29°46E **17** B15
Svir → *Russia* 60°30N 32°48E **18** B5
Svishtov *Bulgaria* 43°36N 25°23E **23** C11
Svislach *Belarus* 53°3N 24°2E **17** B13
Svizzera = Switzerland ■ *Europe* 46°30N 8°0E **20** C8
Svobodnyy *Russia* 51°20N 128°0E **29** D13
Svolvær *Norway* 68°15N 14°34E **8** B16
Svyetlahorsk *Belarus* 52°38N 29°46E **17** B15
Swabian Alps = Schwäbische Alb *Germany* 48°20N 9°30E **16** D5
Swaffham *U.K.* 52°39N 0°42E **13** E8
Swains I. *Amer. Samoa* 11°11S 171°4W **65** J11
Swainsboro *U.S.A.* 32°36N 82°20W **85** E13
Swakop → *Namibia* 22°38S 14°36E **56** C2
Swakopmund *Namibia* 22°37S 14°30E **56** C1
Swale → *U.K.* 54°5N 1°20W **12** C6
Swan → *Australia* 32°3S 115°45E **61** F2
Swan → *Canada* 52°30N 100°45W **71** C8
Swan Hill *Australia* 35°20S 143°33E **63** F3
Swan Hills *Canada* 54°43N 115°24W **70** C5
Swan Is. = Santanilla, Is. *Honduras* 17°22N 83°57W **88** C3
Swan L. *Man., Canada* 52°30N 100°40W **71** C8
Swan L. *Ont., Canada* 54°16N 91°11W **72** B1
Swan Ra. *U.S.A.* 48°0N 113°45W **76** C7
Swan River *Canada* 52°10N 101°16W **71** C8
Swanage *U.K.* 50°36N 1°58E **13** G6
Swansea *Australia* 42°8S 148°4E **63** G4
Swansea *Canada* 43°38N 79°28W **82** C5
Swansea *U.K.* 51°37N 3°57W **13** F4
Swansea □ *U.K.* 51°38N 4°3W **13** F3
Swartberge *S. Africa* 33°20S 22°0E **56** E3
Swartmodder *S. Africa* 28°1S 20°32E **56** D3
Swartnossob → *Namibia* 23°8S 18°42E **56** C2
Swartruggens *S. Africa* 25°39S 26°42E **56** D4
Swastika *Canada* 48°7N 80°6W **72** C3
Swat → *Pakistan* 34°40N 72°5E **43** B5
Swatow = Shantou *China* 23°18N 116°40E **33** D6
Swaziland ■ *Africa* 26°30S 31°30E **57** D5
Sweden ■ *Europe* 57°0N 15°0E **9** H16
Sweet Grass *U.S.A.* 48°59N 111°58W **76** B8
Sweet Home *U.S.A.* 44°24N 122°44W **76** D2
Sweetwater *Nev., U.S.A.* 38°27N 119°9W **78** G7
Sweetwater *Tenn., U.S.A.* 35°36N 84°28W **85** D12
Sweetwater *Tex., U.S.A.* 32°28N 100°25W **84** E4
Sweetwater → *U.S.A.* 42°31N 107°2W **76** E10
Swellendam *S. Africa* 34°1S 20°26E **56** E3
Świdnica *Poland* 50°50N 16°30E **17** C9
Świdnik *Poland* 51°13N 22°39E **17** C12
Świebodzin *Poland* 52°15N 15°31E **16** B8
Świecie *Poland* 53°25N 18°30E **17** B10
Swift Current *Canada* 50°20N 107°45W **71** C7
Swift Current → *Canada* 50°38N 107°44W **71** C7
Swilly, L. *Ireland* 55°12N 7°33W **10** A4
Swindon *U.K.* 51°34N 1°46W **13** F6
Swindon □ *U.K.* 51°34N 1°46W **13** F6
Swinemünde = Świnoujście *Poland* 53°54N 14°16E **16** B8
Swinford *Ireland* 53°57N 8°58W **10** C3
Świnoujście *Poland* 53°54N 14°16E **16** B8
Switzerland ■ *Europe* 46°30N 8°0E **20** C8
Swords *Ireland* 53°28N 6°13W **10** C5
Swoyerville *U.S.A.* 41°18N 75°53W **83** E9
Sydenham → *Canada* 42°33N 82°25W **82** D2
Sydney *Australia* 33°52S 151°12E **63** E5
Sydney *Canada* 46°7N 60°7W **73** C7
Sydney L. *Canada* 50°41N 94°25W **71** C10
Sydney Mines *Canada* 46°18N 60°15W **73** C7
Sydprøven = Alluitsup Paa *Greenland* 60°30N 45°35W **4** C5
Sydra, G. of = Surt, Khalîj *Libya* 31°40N 18°30E **51** B9
Sykesville *U.S.A.* 41°3N 78°50W **82** E6
Syktyvkar *Russia* 61°45N 50°40E **18** B9
Sylacauga *U.S.A.* 33°10N 86°15W **85** E11
Sylarna *Sweden* 63°2N 12°13E **8** E15
Sylhet *Bangla.* 24°54N 91°52E **41** G17
Sylhet □ *Bangla.* 24°50N 91°50E **41** G17
Sylt *Germany* 54°54N 8°22E **16** A5
Sylvan Beach *U.S.A.* 43°12N 75°44W **83** C9
Sylvan Lake *Canada* 52°20N 114°3W **70** C6
Sylvania *Ga., U.S.A.* 32°45N 81°38W **85** E14
Sylvania *Ohio, U.S.A.* 41°43N 83°42W **81** E12
Sylvester *U.S.A.* 31°32N 83°50W **85** F13
Sym *Russia* 60°20N 88°18E **28** C9
Synnot Ra. *Australia* 16°30S 125°20E **60** C4

Syowa *Antarctica* 68°50S 12°0E **5** C5
Syracuse *Kans., U.S.A.* 37°59N 101°45W **80** G3
Syracuse *N.Y., U.S.A.* 43°3N 76°9W **83** C8
Syracuse *Nebr., U.S.A.* 40°39N 96°11W **80** E5
Syrdarya → *Kazakhstan* 46°3N 61°0E **28** E7
Syria ■ *Asia* 35°0N 38°0E **44** C3
Syrian Desert = Shām, Bādiyat ash *Asia* 32°0N 40°0E **44** C3
Syros *Greece* 37°28N 24°57E **23** F11
Syzran *Russia* 53°12N 48°30E **18** D8
Szczecin *Poland* 53°27N 14°27E **16** B8
Szczecinek *Poland* 53°43N 16°41E **17** B9
Szczeciński, Zalew = Stettiner Haff *Germany* 53°47N 14°15E **16** B8
Szczytno *Poland* 53°33N 21°0E **17** B11
Szechwan = Sichuan □ *China* 30°30N 103°0E **34** B5
Szeged *Hungary* 46°16N 20°10E **17** E11
Székesfehérvár *Hungary* 47°15N 18°25E **17** E10
Szekszárd *Hungary* 46°22N 18°42E **17** E10
Szentes *Hungary* 46°39N 20°21E **17** E11
Szolnok *Hungary* 47°10N 20°15E **17** E11
Szombathely *Hungary* 47°14N 16°38E **17** E9

T

Ta Khli *Thailand* 15°15N 100°21E **38** E3
Ta Khli Khok *Thailand* 15°18N 100°20E **38** E3
Ta Lai *Vietnam* 11°24N 107°23E **39** G6
Tabacal *Argentina* 23°15S 64°15W **94** A3
Tabaco *Phil.* 13°22N 123°44E **37** B6
Ţābah *Si. Arabia* 26°55N 42°38E **44** E4
Tabanan *Indonesia* 8°32S 115°8E **37** K18
Tabas *Khorāsān, Iran* 32°48N 60°12E **45** C9
Tabas *Yazd, Iran* 33°35N 56°55E **45** C8
Tabasará, Serranía de *Panama* 8°35N 81°40W **88** E3
Tabasco □ *Mexico* 18°0N 92°40W **87** D6
Tābāsīn *Iran* 31°12N 57°54E **45** D8
Tabatinga, Serra da *Brazil* 10°30S 44°0W **93** F10
Taber *Canada* 49°47N 112°8W **70** D6
Tablas *Phil.* 12°25N 122°2E **37** B6
Table, Pte. de la *Réunion* 21°14S 55°48E **53** c
Table B. *Canada* 53°40N 56°25W **73** B8
Table B. *S. Africa* 33°35S 18°25E **56** E2
Table Mt. *S. Africa* 33°58S 18°26E **56** E2
Table Rock L. *U.S.A.* 36°36N 93°19W **80** G7
Tabletop, Mt. *Australia* 23°24S 147°11E **62** C4
Tábor *Czech Rep.* 49°25N 14°39E **16** D8
Tabora *Tanzania* 5°2S 32°50E **54** D3
Tabora □ *Tanzania* 5°0S 33°0E **54** D3
Tabou *Ivory C.* 4°30N 7°20W **50** H4
Tabrīz *Iran* 38°7N 46°20E **44** B5
Tabuaeran *Kiribati* 3°51N 159°22W **65** G12
Tabūk *Si. Arabia* 28°23N 36°36E **44** D3
Tabūk □ *Si. Arabia* 27°40N 36°50E **44** E3
Tacámbaro de Codallos *Mexico* 19°14N 101°28W **86** D4
Tacheng *China* 46°40N 82°58E **32** B3
Tach'ing Shan = Daqing Shan *China* 40°40N 111°0E **34** D6
Tacloban *Phil.* 11°15N 124°58E **37** B6
Tacna *Peru* 18°0S 70°20W **92** G4
Tacoma *U.S.A.* 47°14N 122°26W **78** C4
Tacuarembó *Uruguay* 31°45S 56°0W **95** C4
Tademaït, Plateau du *Algeria* 28°30N 2°30E **50** C6
Tadjoura *Djibouti* 11°50N 42°55E **47** E3
Tadmor *N.Z.* 41°27S 172°45E **59** D4
Tadoule L. *Canada* 58°36N 98°20W **71** B9
Tadoussac *Canada* 48°11N 69°42W **73** C6
Tadzhikistan = Tajikistan ■ *Asia* 38°30N 70°0E **28** F8
Taegu = Daegu *S. Korea* 35°50N 128°37E **35** G15
Taegwan *N. Korea* 40°13N 125°12E **35** D13
Taejŏn = Daejeon *S. Korea* 36°20N 127°28E **35** F14
Taen, Ko *Thailand* 9°22N 99°57E **39** b
Tafalla *Spain* 42°30N 1°41W **21** A5
Tafelbaai = Table B. *S. Africa* 33°35S 18°25E **56** E2
Tafermaar *Indonesia* 6°47S 134°10E **37** F8
Tafí Viejo *Argentina* 26°43S 65°17W **94** B2
Tafihān *Iran* 29°25N 52°39E **45** D7
Tafresh *Iran* 34°45N 49°57E **45** C6
Taft *Iran* 31°45N 54°14E **45** D7
Taft *Phil.* 11°57N 125°30E **37** B7
Taft *U.S.A.* 35°8N 119°28W **79** K7
Taftan *Pakistan* 29°0N 61°30E **40** E2
Taftān, Kūh-e *Iran* 28°40N 61°0E **45** D9
Taga *Uruguay* 34°21S 55°46W **95** C4
Taga Dzong *Bhutan* 27°5N 89°55E **41** F16
Taganrog *Russia* 47°12N 38°50E **19** E6
Tagbilaran *Phil.* 9°39N 123°51E **37** C6
Tagish *Canada* 60°19N 134°16W **70** A2
Tagish L. *Canada* 60°10N 134°20W **70** A2
Tagliamento → *Italy* 45°38N 13°6E **22** B5
Tagomago *Spain* 39°2N 1°39E **24** B8
Taguatinga *Brazil* 12°27S 46°22W **93** F10
Tagum *Phil.* 7°33N 125°53E **37** C7
Tagus = Tejo → *Europe* 38°40N 9°24W **21** C1
Tahakopa *N.Z.* 46°30S 169°23E **59** G2
Tahan, Gunung *Malaysia* 4°34N 102°17E **39** K4
Tahat *Algeria* 23°18N 5°33E **50** D7
Tāherī *Iran* 27°43N 52°20E **45** E7
Tahiti *French Polynesia* 17°37S 149°27W **59** d
Tahiti, I. *Tahiti* 17°37S 149°27W **59** d
Tahlequah *U.S.A.* 35°55N 94°58W **84** D7
Tahoe, L. *U.S.A.* 39°6N 120°2W **78** G6
Tahoe City *U.S.A.* 39°10N 120°9W **78** F6
Tahoka *U.S.A.* 33°10N 101°48W **84** E4
Taholah *U.S.A.* 47°21N 124°17W **78** C2
Tahoua *Niger* 14°57N 5°16E **50** F7

Tahrūd *Iran* 29°26N 57°49E **45** D8
Tahsis *Canada* 49°55N 126°40W **70** D3
Tahta *Egypt* 26°44N 31°32E **51** C12
Tahulandang *Indonesia* 2°27N 125°23E **37** D7
Tahuna *Indonesia* 3°38N 125°30E **37** D7
Tai Au Mun *China* 22°18N 114°17E **33** G11
Tai Mo Shan *China* 22°25N 114°7E **33** G11
Tai O *China* 22°15N 113°52E **33** G10
Tai Pang Wan *China* 22°33N 114°24E **33** F11
Tai Po *China* 22°27N 114°10E **33** G11
Tai Rom Yen △ *Thailand* 8°45N 99°30E **39** H2
Tai Shan *China* 36°12N 117°0E **35** F9
Tai Yue Shan = Lantau I. *China* 22°15N 113°56E **33** G10
Tai'an *China* 36°12N 117°8E **35** F9
Taiarapu, Presqu'île de *Tahiti* 17°47S 149°14W **59** d
Taibei = T'aipei *Taiwan* 25°4N 121°29E **33** D7
Taibique *Canary Is.* 27°42N 17°58W **24** G2
Taibus Qi *China* 41°54N 115°22E **34** D8
T'aichung *Taiwan* 24°9N 120°37E **33** D7
Taieri → *N.Z.* 46°3S 170°12E **59** G3
Taigu *China* 37°28N 112°30E **34** F7
Taihang Shan *China* 36°0N 113°30E **34** G7
Taihape *N.Z.* 39°41S 175°48E **59** C5
Taihe *China* 33°20N 115°42E **34** H8
Taikang *China* 34°5N 114°50E **34** G8
Tailem Bend *Australia* 35°12S 139°29E **63** F2
Taimyr Peninsula = Taymyr, Poluostrov *Russia* 75°0N 100°0E **29** B11
Tain *U.K.* 57°49N 4°4W **11** D4
T'ainan *Taiwan* 23°0N 120°10E **33** D7
Taipa *China* 22°10N 113°33E **33** G10
T'aipei *Taiwan* 25°4N 121°29E **33** D7
Taiping *Malaysia* 4°51N 100°44E **39** K3
Taipingzhen *China* 33°35N 111°42E **34** H6
Tairbeart = Tarbert *U.K.* 57°54N 6°49W **11** D2
Taita Hills *Kenya* 3°25S 38°15E **54** C4
Taitao, Pen. de *Chile* 46°30S 75°0W **96** F2
T'aitung *Taiwan* 22°43N 121°4E **33** D7
Taivalkoski *Finland* 65°33N 28°12E **8** D23
Taiwan ■ *Asia* 23°30N 121°0E **33** D7
Taiyiba *Israel* 32°36N 35°27E **46** C4
Taiyuan *China* 37°52N 112°33E **34** F7
Taizhong = T'aichung *Taiwan* 24°9N 120°37E **33** D7
Ta'izz *Yemen* 13°35N 44°2E **47** E3
Tājābād *Iran* 30°2N 54°24E **45** D7
Tajikistan ■ *Asia* 38°30N 70°0E **28** F8
Tajima *Japan* 37°12N 139°46E **31** F9
Tajo = Tejo → *Europe* 38°40N 9°24W **21** C1
Tajrīsh *Iran* 35°48N 51°25E **45** C6
Tak *Thailand* 16°52N 99°8E **38** D2
Takāb *Iran* 36°24N 47°7E **44** B5
Takachiho *Japan* 32°42N 131°18E **31** H5
Takachu *Botswana* 22°37S 21°58E **56** C3
Takada *Japan* 37°7N 138°15E **31** F9
Takahagi *Japan* 36°43N 140°45E **31** F10
Takaka *N.Z.* 40°51S 172°50E **59** D4
Takamaka *Seychelles* 4°50S 55°30E **53** b
Takamatsu *Japan* 34°20N 134°5E **31** G7
Takaoka *Japan* 36°47N 137°0E **31** F8
Takapuna *N.Z.* 36°47S 174°47E **59** B5
Takasaki *Japan* 36°20N 139°0E **31** F9
Takatsuki *Japan* 34°51N 135°37E **31** G7
Takaungu *Kenya* 3°38S 39°52E **54** C4
Takayama *Japan* 36°18N 137°11E **31** F8
Take-Shima *Japan* 30°49N 130°26E **31** J5
Takefu *Japan* 35°50N 136°10E **31** G8
Takengon *Indonesia* 4°45N 96°50E **36** D1
Takeo *Japan* 33°12N 130°1E **31** H5
Takeshima = Tokdo *Asia* 37°15N 131°52E **31** F5
Tākestān *Iran* 36°0N 49°40E **45** C6
Taketa *Japan* 32°58N 131°24E **31** H5
Takev *Cambodia* 10°59N 104°47E **39** G5
Takh *India* 33°6N 77°32E **43** C7
Takhmau *Cambodia* 11°29N 104°57E **39** G5
Takht-Sulaiman *Pakistan* 31°40N 69°58E **42** D3
Takikawa *Japan* 43°33N 141°54E **30** C10
Takla L. *Canada* 55°15N 125°45W **70** B3
Takla Landing *Canada* 55°30N 125°50W **70** B3
Takla Makan *China* 38°0N 83°0E **32** C3
Taklamakan Shamo = Takla Makan *China* 38°0N 83°0E **32** C3
Taksimo *Russia* 56°20N 114°52E **29** D12
Taku → *Canada* 58°30N 133°50W **70** B2
Takua Pa *Thailand* 8°52N 98°21E **39** H2
Takua Thung *Thailand* 8°24N 98°27E **39** a
Tal Halāl *Iran* 28°54N 55°1E **45** D7
Tala *Uruguay* 34°21S 55°46W **95** C4
Talagang *Pakistan* 32°55N 72°25E **42** C5
Talagante *Chile* 33°40S 70°50W **94** C1
Talamanca, Cordillera de *Cent. Amer.* 9°20N 83°20W **88** E3
Talampaya △ *Argentina* 29°43S 67°42W **94** B2
Talara *Peru* 4°38S 81°18W **92** D2
Talas *Kyrgyzstan* 42°30N 72°13E **28** E8
Talāta *Egypt* 30°36N 32°20E **46** E1
Talaud, Kepulauan *Indonesia* 4°30N 126°50E **37** D7
Talaud Is. = Talaud, Kepulauan *Indonesia* 4°30N 126°50E **37** D7
Talavera de la Reina *Spain* 39°55N 4°46W **21** C3
Talayan *Phil.* 6°52N 124°24E **37** C6
Talbandh *India* 22°3N 86°20E **43** H12
Talbot, C. *Australia* 13°48S 126°43E **60** B4
Talbragar → *Australia* 32°12S 148°37E **63** E4
Talca *Chile* 35°28S 71°40W **94** D1
Talcahuano *Chile* 36°40S 73°10W **94** D1
Talcher *India* 20°55N 85°18E **41** J14

Tālesh *Iran* 37°58N 48°58E **45** B6
Tālesh, Kūhhā-ye *Iran* 37°42N 48°55E **45** B6
Tali Post *Sudan* 5°55N 30°44E **51** G12
Taliabu *Indonesia* 1°50S 125°0E **37** E6
Talibon *Phil.* 10°9N 124°20E **37** B6
Talihina *U.S.A.* 34°45N 95°3W **84** D7
Taliwang *Indonesia* 8°50S 116°55E **36** F5
Tall 'Afar *Iraq* 36°22N 42°27E **44** B4
Tall Kalakh *Syria* 34°41N 36°15E **46** A5
Talladega *U.S.A.* 33°26N 86°6W **85** E11
Tallahassee *U.S.A.* 30°27N 84°17W **85** F12
Tallangatta *Australia* 36°15S 147°19E **63** F4
Tallering Pk. *Australia* 28°6S 115°37E **61** E2
Talli *Pakistan* 29°32N 68°8E **42** E3
Tallinn *Estonia* 59°22N 24°48E **9** G21
Tallmadge *U.S.A.* 41°6N 81°27W **82** E3
Tallulah *U.S.A.* 32°25N 91°11W **84** E9
Talnakh *Russia* 69°29N 88°22E **29** C9
Taloyoak *Canada* 69°32N 93°32W **68** C10
Talpa de Allende *Mexico* 20°23N 104°51W **86** C4
Talparo *Trin. & Tob.* 10°30N 61°17W **93** K15
Talsi *Latvia* 57°10N 22°30E **9** H20
Taltal *Chile* 25°23S 70°33W **94** B1
Taltson → *Canada* 61°24N 112°46W **70** A6
Talwood *Australia* 28°29S 149°29E **63** D4
Talyawalka Cr. → *Australia* 32°28S 142°22E **63** E3
Tam Ky *Vietnam* 15°34N 108°29E **38** E7
Tam Quan *Vietnam* 14°35N 109°3E **38** E7
Tama *U.S.A.* 41°58N 92°35W **80** E7
Taman Negara △ *Malaysia* 4°38N 102°26E **39** K4
Tamano *Japan* 34°29N 133°59E **31** G6
Tamanrasset *Algeria* 22°50N 5°30E **50** D7
Tamaqua *U.S.A.* 40°48N 75°58W **83** F9
Tamar → *U.K.* 50°27N 4°15W **13** G3
Tamarin *Mauritius* 20°19S 57°20E **53** d
Tamarinda *Spain* 39°55N 3°49E **24** B10
Tamashima *Japan* 34°32N 133°40E **31** G6
Tamatave = Toamasina *Madag.* 18°10S 49°25E **57** B8
Tamaulipas □ *Mexico* 24°0N 98°45W **87** C5
Tamaulipas, Sierra de *Mexico* 23°30N 98°20W **87** C5
Tamazula *Mexico* 24°57N 106°57W **86** C3
Tamazunchale *Mexico* 21°16N 98°47W **87** C5
Tambach *Kenya* 0°36N 35°31E **54** B4
Tambacounda *Senegal* 13°45N 13°40W **50** F3
Tambelan, Kepulauan *Indonesia* 1°0N 107°30E **36** D3
Tambellup *Australia* 34°4S 117°37E **61** F2
Tambo *Australia* 24°54S 146°14E **62** C4
Tambo de Mora *Peru* 13°30S 76°8W **92** F3
Tambohorano *Madag.* 17°30S 43°58E **57** B7
Tambora *Indonesia* 8°12S 118°5E **36** F5
Tambov *Russia* 52°45N 41°28E **18** D7
Tambuku *Indonesia* 7°8S 113°40E **37** G15
Tâmega → *Portugal* 41°5N 8°21W **21** B1
Tamenglong *India* 25°0N 93°35E **41** G18
Tamiahua, L. de *Mexico* 21°35N 97°35W **87** C5
Tamil Nadu □ *India* 11°0N 77°0E **40** P10
Tamluk *India* 22°18N 87°58E **43** H12
Tammerfors = Tampere *Finland* 61°30N 23°50E **8** F20
Tammisaari *Finland* 60°0N 23°26E **9** G20
Tamo Abu, Banjaran *Malaysia* 3°10N 115°5E **36** D5
Tampa *U.S.A.* 27°56N 82°27W **85** H13
Tampa, Tanjung *Indonesia* 8°55S 116°12E **37** K19
Tampa B. *U.S.A.* 27°50N 82°30W **85** H13
Tampere *Finland* 61°30N 23°50E **8** F20
Tampico *Mexico* 22°13N 97°51W **87** C5
Tampin *Malaysia* 2°28N 102°13E **39** L4
Tampoi *Malaysia* 1°30N 103°39E **39** d
Tamu *Burma* 24°13N 94°12E **41** G19
Tamworth *Australia* 31°7S 150°58E **63** E5
Tamworth *Canada* 44°29N 77°0W **82** B8
Tamworth *U.K.* 52°39N 1°41W **13** E6
Tan An *Vietnam* 10°32N 106°25E **39** G6
Tan-Tan *Morocco* 28°29N 11°1W **50** C3
Tana → *Kenya* 2°32S 40°31E **54** C5
Tana → *Norway* 70°30N 28°14E **8** A23
Tana, L. *Ethiopia* 13°5N 37°30E **47** E2
Tana River Primate △ *Kenya* 1°55S 40°7E **54** C5
Tanabe *Japan* 33°44N 135°22E **31** H7
Tanafjorden *Norway* 70°45N 28°25E **8** A23
Tanahbala *Indonesia* 0°30S 98°30E **36** E1
Tanahgrogot *Indonesia* 1°55S 116°15E **36** E5
Tanahjampea *Indonesia* 7°10S 120°35E **37** F6
Tanahmasa *Indonesia* 0°12S 98°39E **36** E1
Tanahmerah *Indonesia* 6°5S 140°16E **37** F10
Tanakpur *India* 29°5N 80°7E **43** E9
Tanakura *Japan* 37°10N 140°20E **31** F10
Tanami Desert *Australia* 18°50S 132°0E **60** C5
Tanami Mine *Australia* 19°59S 129°43E **60** C4
Tananarive = Antananarivo *Madag.* 18°55S 47°31E **57** B8
Tánaro → *Italy* 44°55N 8°40E **20** D8
Tancheng *China* 34°25N 118°20E **35** G10
Tanch'ŏn *N. Korea* 40°27N 128°54E **35** D15
Tanda *Ut. P., India* 26°33N 82°35E **43** F10
Tanda *Ut. P., India* 28°57N 78°56E **43** E8
Tanda *Phil.* 9°4N 126°9E **37** C7
Tandaia *Tanzania* 9°25S 34°15E **55** D3
Tandaué *Angola* 16°58S 18°5E **56** B2
Tandil *Argentina* 37°15S 59°6W **94** D4
Tandil, Sa. del *Argentina* 37°30S 59°0W **94** D4
Tandlianwala *Pakistan* 31°3N 73°9E **42** D5
Tando Adam *Pakistan* 25°45N 68°40E **42** G3
Tando Allahyar *Pakistan* 25°28N 68°43E **42** G3
Tando Mohommed Khan *Pakistan* 25°8N 68°32E **42** G3

Tandou L. *Australia* 32°40S 142°45E **63 E3**
Tandoureh △ *Iran* 37°50N 59°0E **44 B8**
Tandragee *U.K.* 54°21N 6°24W **10 B5**
Tane-ga-Shima *Japan* 30°30N 131°0E **31 J5**
Taneatua *N.Z.* 38°4S 177°1E **59 C6**
Tanen Tong Dan = Dawna Ra.
Burma 16°30N 98°30E **38 D2**
Tanezrouft *Algeria* 23°9N 0°11E **50 D6**
Tang, Koh *Cambodia* 10°16N 103°7E **39 G4**
Tang, Ra's-e *Iran* 25°21N 59°52E **45 E8**
Tang Krasang *Cambodia* 12°34N 105°3E **38 F5**
Tanga *Tanzania* 5°5S 39°2E **54 D4**
Tanga □ *Tanzania* 5°20S 38°0E **54 D4**
Tanganyika, L. *Africa* 6°40S 30°0E **54 D3**
Tanger *Morocco* 35°50N 5°49W **50 A4**
Tangerang *Indonesia* 6°11S 106°37E **37 G12**
Tanggu *China* 39°2N 117°40E **35 E9**
Tanggula Shan *China* 32°40N 92°10E **32 C4**
Tanggula Shankou
China 32°42N 92°27E **32 C4**
Tanghe *China* 32°47N 112°50E **34 H7**
Tanghla Range = Tanggula Shan
China 32°40N 92°10E **32 C4**
Tangier = Tanger
Morocco 35°50N 5°49W **50 A4**
Tangjia *China* 22°22N 113°35E **33 G10**
Tangjia Wan *China* 22°21N 113°36E **33 G10**
Tangorin *Australia* 21°47S 144°12E **62 C3**
Tangorombohitr'i Makay
Madag. 21°0S 45°15E **57 C8**
Tangra Yumco *China* 31°0N 86°38E **32 C3**
Tangshan *China* 39°38N 118°10E **35 E10**
Tangtou *China* 35°28N 118°30E **35 G10**
Tanimbar, Kepulauan
Indonesia 7°30S 131°30E **37 F8**
Tanimbar Is. = Tanimbar,
Kepulauan *Indonesia* 7°30S 131°30E **37 F8**
Taninthari = Tenasserim
Burma 12°6N 99°3E **39 F2**
Tanjay *Phil.* 9°30N 123°5E **37 C6**
Tanjong Malim *Malaysia* 3°42N 101°31E **39 L3**
Tanjong Pelepas *Malaysia* 1°21N 103°33E **39 d**
Tanjore = Thanjavur
India 10°48N 79°12E **40 P11**
Tanjung *Indonesia* 8°21S 116°9E **37 J19**
Tanjung *Phil.* 2°10S 115°25E **36 E5**
Tanjung Tokong *Malaysia* 5°28N 100°18E **39 c**
Tanjungbalai *Indonesia* 2°55N 99°44E **36 D1**
Tanjungbatu *Indonesia* 2°23N 118°3E **36 D5**
Tanjungkarang Telukbetung =
Bandar Lampung
Indonesia 5°20S 105°10E **36 F3**
Tanjungpandan
Indonesia 2°43S 107°38E **36 E3**
Tanjungpinang *Indonesia* 1°5N 104°30E **36 D2**
Tanjungredeb *Indonesia* 2°9N 117°29E **36 D5**
Tanjungselor *Indonesia* 2°55N 117°38E **36 D5**
Tank *Pakistan* 32°14N 70°25E **42 C4**
Tankhala *India* 21°58N 73°47E **42 J5**
Tankwa-Karoo △
S. Africa 32°14S 19°50E **56 E2**
Tannersville *U.S.A.* 41°3N 75°18W **83 E9**
Tannu Ola *Asia* 51°0N 94°0E **29 D10**
Tannum Sands
Australia 23°57S 151°22E **62 C5**
Tanout *Niger* 14°50N 8°55E **50 F7**
Tanta *Egypt* 30°45N 30°57E **51 B12**
Tantoyuca *Mexico* 21°21N 98°14W **87 C5**
Tantung = Dandong
China 40°10N 124°20E **35 D13**
Tanunda *Australia* 34°30S 139°0E **63 E2**
Tanzania ■ *Africa* 6°0S 34°0E **54 D3**
Tanzhou *China* 22°16N 113°28E **33 G9**
Tanzilla → *Canada* 58°8N 130°43W **70 B2**
Tao, Ko *Thailand* 10°5N 99°52E **39 G2**
Tao'an = Taonan
China 45°22N 122°40E **35 B12**
Tao'er He → *China* 45°45N 124°5E **35 B13**
Taole *China* 38°48N 106°40E **34 E4**
Taonan *China* 45°22N 122°40E **35 B12**
Taos *U.S.A.* 36°24N 105°35W **77 H11**
Taoudenni *Mali* 22°40N 3°55W **50 D5**
Tapa *Estonia* 59°15N 25°50E **9 G21**
Tapa Shan = Daba Shan
China 32°0N 109°0E **33 C5**
Tapachula *Mexico* 14°54N 92°17W **87 E6**
Tapah *Malaysia* 4°12N 101°15E **39 K3**
Tapajós → *Brazil* 2°24S 54°41W **93 D8**
Tapaktuan *Indonesia* 3°15N 97°10E **36 D1**
Tapanahoni → *Suriname* 4°20N 54°25W **93 C8**
Tapanui *N.Z.* 45°56S 169°18E **59 F2**
Tapauá → *Brazil* 5°40S 64°21W **92 E6**
Tapes *Brazil* 30°40S 51°23W **95 C5**
Tapeta *Liberia* 6°29N 8°52W **50 G4**
Taphan Hin *Thailand* 16°13N 100°26E **38 D3**
Tapirapecó, Serra
Venezuela 1°10N 65°0W **92 C6**
Tapo-Capara △ *Venezuela* 7°55N 71°15W **89 E5**
Tapti → *India* 21°8N 72°41E **40 J8**
Tapuae-o-Uenuku *N.Z.* 42°0S 173°39E **59 E4**
Tapul Group *Phil.* 5°35N 120°50E **37 C6**
Tapurucuará *Brazil* 0°24S 65°2W **92 D5**
Taqtaq *Iraq* 35°53N 44°35E **44 C5**
Taquara *Brazil* 29°36S 50°46W **95 B5**
Taquari → *Brazil* 19°15S 57°17W **92 G7**
Tara *Australia* 27°17S 150°31E **63 D5**
Tara *Canada* 44°28N 81°9W **82 B3**
Tara *Russia* 56°55N 74°24E **28 D8**
Tara *Zambia* 16°58S 26°45E **55 F2**
Tara → *Montenegro* 43°21N 18°51E **23 C8**
Tarābulus *Lebanon* 34°31N 35°50E **46 A4**
Tarābulus *Libya* 32°49N 13°7E **51 B8**
Taradehi *India* 23°18N 79°27E **43 H8**
Tarajalejo *Canary Is.* 28°12N 14°7W **24 F5**
Tarakan *Indonesia* 3°2N 117°35E **36 D5**

Tarakit, Mt. *Kenya* 2°2N 35°10E **54 B4**
Tarama-Jima *Japan* 24°39N 124°42E **31 M2**
Taran, Mys *Russia* 54°56N 19°59E **9 J18**
Taranagar *India* 28°43N 74°50E **42 E6**
Taranaki □ *N.Z.* 39°25S 174°30E **59 C5**
Taranaki, Mt. *N.Z.* 39°17S 174°5E **59 C5**
Tarancón *Spain* 40°1N 3°1W **21 B4**
Tarangire △ *Tanzania* 4°21S 36°7E **54 C4**
Taransay *U.K.* 57°54N 7°0W **11 D1**
Táranto *Italy* 40°28N 17°14E **22 D7**
Táranto, G. di *Italy* 40°8N 17°20E **22 D7**
Tarapacá *Colombia* 2°56S 69°46W **92 D5**
Tarapacá □ *Chile* 20°45S 69°30W **94 A2**
Tarapoto *Peru* 6°30S 76°20W **92 E3**
Tararua Ra. *N.Z.* 40°45S 175°25E **59 D5**
Tarashcha *Ukraine* 49°30N 30°31E **17 D16**
Tarauacá *Brazil* 8°6S 70°48W **92 E4**
Tarauacá → *Brazil* 6°42S 69°48W **92 E5**
Taravao *Tahiti* 17°43S 149°19W **59 d**
Taravao, Isthme de
Tahiti 17°43S 149°19W **59 d**
Tarawa *Kiribati* 1°30N 173°0E **64 G9**
Tarawera *N.Z.* 39°2S 176°36E **59 C6**
Tarawera, L. *N.Z.* 38°13S 176°27E **59 C6**
Taraz *Kazakhstan* 42°54N 71°22E **28 E8**
Tarazona *Spain* 41°55N 1°43W **21 B5**
Tarbagatay, Khrebet
Kazakhstan 48°0N 83°0E **28 E9**
Tarbat Ness *U.K.* 57°52N 3°47W **11 D5**
Tarbela Dam *Pakistan* 34°8N 72°52E **42 B5**
Tarbert *Ireland* 52°34N 9°22W **10 D2**
Tarbert *Argyll & Bute,*
U.K. 55°52N 5°25W **11 F3**
Tarbert *W. Isles, U.K.* 57°54N 6°49W **11 D2**
Tarbes *France* 43°15N 0°3E **20 E4**
Tarboro *U.S.A.* 35°54N 77°32W **85 D16**
Tarcoola *Australia* 30°44S 134°36E **63 E1**
Tarcoon *Australia* 30°15S 146°43E **63 E4**
Taree *Australia* 31°50S 152°30E **63 E5**
Tarfaya *Morocco* 27°55N 12°55W **50 C3**
Târgoviște *Romania* 44°55N 25°27E **17 F13**
Târgu Jiu *Romania* 45°5N 23°19E **17 F12**
Târgu Mureș *Romania* 46°31N 24°38E **17 E13**
Tarif *U.A.E.* 24°3N 53°46E **45 E7**
Tarifa *Spain* 36°1N 5°36W **21 D3**
Tarija *Bolivia* 21°30S 64°40W **94 A3**
Tarija □ *Bolivia* 21°30S 63°30W **94 A3**
Tariku → *Indonesia* 2°55S 138°26E **37 E9**
Tarim Basin = Tarim Pendi
China 40°0N 84°0E **32 B3**
Tarim He → *China* 39°30N 88°30E **32 C3**
Tarim Pendi *China* 40°0N 84°0E **32 B3**
Taritatu → *Indonesia* 2°54S 138°27E **37 E9**
Tarka → *S. Africa* 32°10S 26°0E **56 E4**
Tarka La *Bhutan* 27°12N 89°44E **43 F13**
Tarkhankut, Mys
Ukraine 45°25N 32°30E **19 E5**
Tarko Sale *Russia* 64°55N 77°50E **28 C8**
Tarkwa *Ghana* 5°20N 2°0W **50 G5**
Tarlac *Phil.* 15°29N 120°35E **37 A6**
Tarma *Peru* 11°25S 75°45W **92 F3**
Tarn → *France* 44°5N 1°6E **20 E4**
Târnăveni *Romania* 46°19N 24°13E **17 E13**
Tarnobrzeg *Poland* 50°35N 21°41E **17 C11**
Tarnów *Poland* 50°3N 21°0E **17 C11**
Tarnowskie Góry
Poland 50°27N 18°54E **17 C10**
Țărom *Iran* 28°11N 55°46E **45 D7**
Taroom *Australia* 25°36S 149°48E **63 D4**
Taroudannt *Morocco* 30°30N 8°52W **50 B4**
Tarpon Springs *U.S.A.* 28°9N 82°45W **85 G13**
Tarrafal *C. Verde Is.* 15°18N 23°39W **50 b**
Tarragona *Spain* 41°5N 1°17E **21 B6**
Tarraleah *Australia* 42°17S 146°26E **63 G4**
Tarrasa = Terrassa *Spain* 41°34N 2°1E **21 B7**
Tarrytown *U.S.A.* 41°4N 73°52W **83 E11**
Tarshiha = Me'ona *Israel* 33°1N 35°15E **46 B4**
Tarsus *Turkey* 36°58N 34°55E **44 B2**
Tartagal *Argentina* 22°30S 63°50W **94 A3**
Tartu *Estonia* 58°20N 26°44E **9 G22**
Tartús *Syria* 34°55N 35°55E **44 C2**
Tarumizu *Japan* 31°29N 130°42E **31 J5**
Tarutao = Ko Tarutao △
Thailand 6°31N 99°26E **39 J2**
Tarutao, Ko *Thailand* 6°33N 99°40E **39 J2**
Tarutung *Indonesia* 2°0N 98°54E **36 D1**
Taseko → *Canada* 52°8N 123°45W **70 C4**
Tash-Kömür *Kyrgyzstan* 41°40N 72°10E **28 E8**
Tash-Kumyr = Tash-Kömür
Kyrgyzstan 41°40N 72°10E **28 E8**
Tashauz = Dashoguz
Turkmenistan 41°49N 59°58E **28 E6**
Tashi Chho Dzong = Thimphu
Bhutan 27°31N 89°45E **41 F16**
Țashk, Daryācheh-ye
Iran 29°45N 53°35E **45 D7**
Tashkent = Toshkent
Uzbekistan 41°20N 69°10E **28 E7**
Tashtagol *Russia* 52°47N 87°53E **28 D9**
Tasiilaq *Greenland* 65°40N 37°20W **4 C6**
Tasik Kenyir *Malaysia* 5°5N 102°50E **39 K4**
Tasikmalaya *Indonesia* 7°18S 108°12E **37 G13**
Tåsjön *Sweden* 64°15N 15°40E **8 D16**
Taskan *Russia* 62°59N 150°20E **29 C16**
Tasman B. *N.Z.* 40°59S 173°25E **59 D4**
Tasman Basin *Pac. Oc.* 46°0S 158°0E **64 M7**
Tasman Mts. *N.Z.* 41°3S 172°25E **59 D4**
Tasman Pen. *Australia* 43°10S 148°0E **63 G4**
Tasman Sea *Pac. Oc.* 36°0S 160°0E **58 E9**
Tasmania □ *Australia* 42°0S 146°30E **63 G4**
Tasmanian Wilderness World
Heritage Area △
Australia 43°0S 146°0E **63 G4**
Tassili n'Ajjer △ *Algeria* 25°47N 8°1E **50 C7**
Tassili-Oua-n-Ahaggar
Algeria 20°41N 5°30E **50 D7**

Tat Ton △ *Thailand* 15°57N 102°2E **38 E4**
Tata *Morocco* 29°46N 7°56W **50 C4**
Tatabánya *Hungary* 47°32N 18°25E **17 E10**
Tatahouine *Tunisia* 32°56N 10°27E **51 B8**
Tataouine *Tunisia* 32°57N 10°29E **51 B8**
Tatar Republic = Tatarstan □
Russia 55°30N 51°30E **18 C9**
Tatarbunary *Ukraine* 45°50N 29°39E **17 F15**
Tatarsky Proliv *Russia* 50°0N 141°0E **29 E15**
Tatarstan □ *Russia* 55°30N 51°30E **18 C9**
Tatatua, Pte. *Tahiti* 17°44S 149°8W **59 d**
Tateyama *Japan* 35°0N 139°50E **31 G9**
Tathlina L. *Canada* 60°33N 117°39W **70 A5**
Tathra *Australia* 36°44S 149°59E **63 F4**
Tatinnai L. *Canada* 60°55N 97°40W **71 A9**
Tatla Lake *Canada* 52°0N 124°20W **70 C4**
Tatnam, C. *Canada* 57°16N 91°0W **71 B10**
Tatra = Tatry *Slovak Rep.* 49°20N 20°0E **17 D11**
Tatry *Slovak Rep.* 49°20N 20°0E **17 D11**
Tatshenshini →
Canada 59°28N 137°45W **70 B1**
Tatsuno *Japan* 34°52N 134°33E **31 G7**
Tatta *Pakistan* 24°42N 67°55E **42 G2**
Tatuĩ *Brazil* 23°25S 47°53W **95 A6**
Tatum *U.S.A.* 33°16N 103°19W **77 K12**
Tat'ung = Datong *China* 40°6N 113°18E **34 D7**
Tatvan *Turkey* 38°31N 42°15E **44 B4**
Ta'ū *Amer. Samoa* 14°15S 169°30W **59 b**
Taubaté *Brazil* 23°0S 45°36W **95 A6**
Tauern *Austria* 47°15N 12°40E **16 E7**
Taumarunui *N.Z.* 38°53S 175°15E **59 C5**
Taumaturgo *Brazil* 8°54S 72°51W **92 E4**
Taung *S. Africa* 27°33S 24°47E **56 D3**
Taungdwingyi *Burma* 20°1N 95°40E **41 J19**
Taunggyi *Burma* 20°50N 97°0E **41 J20**
Taungup *Burma* 18°51N 94°14E **41 K19**
Taunsa *Pakistan* 30°42N 70°39E **42 D4**
Taunsa Barrage *Pakistan* 30°42N 70°50E **42 D4**
Taunton *U.K.* 51°1N 3°5W **13 F4**
Taunton *U.S.A.* 41°54N 71°6W **83 E13**
Taunus *Germany* 50°13N 8°34E **16 C5**
Taupo *N.Z.* 38°41S 176°7E **59 C6**
Taupo, L. *N.Z.* 38°46S 175°55E **59 C5**
Tauragė *Lithuania* 55°14N 22°16E **9 J20**
Tauranga *N.Z.* 37°42S 176°11E **59 B6**
Tauranga Harb. *N.Z.* 37°30S 176°5E **59 B6**
Taureau, Rés. *Canada* 46°46N 73°50W **72 C5**
Taurianova *Italy* 38°21N 16°1E **22 E7**
Taurus Mts. = Toros Dağları
Turkey 37°0N 32°30E **44 B2**
Tautira *Tahiti* 17°44S 149°9W **59 d**
Tauyskaya Guba
Russia 59°20N 150°20E **29 D16**
Tavan Bogd Uul
Mongolia 49°10N 87°49E **32 B3**
Tavastehus = Hämeenlinna
Finland 61°0N 24°28E **8 F21**
Tavda *Russia* 58°7N 65°8E **28 D7**
Tavda → *Russia* 57°47N 67°18E **28 D7**
Taveta *Kenya* 3°23S 37°37E **54 C4**
Taveuni *Fiji* 16°51S 179°58W **59 a**
Tavira *Portugal* 37°8N 7°40W **21 D2**
Tavistock *Canada* 43°19N 80°50W **82 C4**
Tavistock *U.K.* 50°33N 4°9W **13 G3**
Tavoy *Burma* 14°2N 98°12E **38 E2**
Tavrichanka *Russia* 43°18N 131°59E **30 C5**
Tavua *Fiji* 17°37S 177°5E **59 a**
Tavuki *Fiji* 19°7S 178°8E **59 a**
Taw → *U.K.* 51°4N 4°4W **13 F3**
Tawa → *India* 22°48N 77°48E **42 H8**
Tawas City *U.S.A.* 44°16N 83°31W **81 C12**
Tawau *Malaysia* 4°20N 117°55E **36 D5**
Tawi-Tawi *Phil.* 5°10N 120°15E **37 C6**
Taxco *Mexico* 18°33N 99°36W **87 D5**
Taxila *Pakistan* 33°42N 72°52E **42 C5**
Taxkorgan Tajik Zizhixian
China 37°49N 75°14E **32 C2**
Tay → *U.K.* 56°37N 3°38W **11 E5**
Tay, Firth of *U.K.* 56°25N 3°8W **11 E5**
Tay, L. *Australia* 32°55S 120°48E **61 F3**
Tay, L. *U.K.* 56°32N 4°8W **11 E4**
Tay Ninh *Vietnam* 11°20N 106°5E **39 G6**
Tayabamba *Peru* 8°15S 77°16W **92 E3**
Taygetos Oros *Greece* 37°0N 22°23E **23 F10**
Taylakova *Russia* 59°13N 74°0E **28 D8**
Taylor *Canada* 56°13N 120°40W **70 B4**
Taylor *Nebr., U.S.A.* 41°46N 99°23W **80 E4**
Taylor *Pa., U.S.A.* 41°23N 75°43W **83 E9**
Taylor *Tex., U.S.A.* 30°34N 97°25W **84 F6**
Taylor, Mt. *U.S.A.* 35°14N 107°37W **77 J10**
Taylorville *U.S.A.* 39°33N 89°18W **80 F9**
Taymā *Si. Arabia* 27°35N 38°45E **44 E3**
Taymyr, Oz. *Russia* 74°20N 102°0E **29 B11**
Taymyr, Poluostrov
Russia 75°0N 100°0E **29 B11**
Tayport *U.K.* 56°27N 2°52W **11 E6**
Tayrona △ *Colombia* 11°20N 74°2W **89 D5**
Tayshet *Russia* 55°58N 98°1E **29 D10**
Taytay *Phil.* 10°45N 119°30E **37 B5**
Taza *Morocco* 34°16N 4°6W **50 B5**
Tāza Khurmātū *Iraq* 35°18N 44°20E **44 C5**
Tazawa-Ko *Japan* 39°43N 140°40E **30 E10**
Tazerbo *Libya* 25°45N 21°0E **51 C10**
Tazin → *Canada* 59°48N 109°55W **71 B7**
Tazin L. *Canada* 59°44N 108°42W **71 B7**
Tazovskiy *Russia* 67°30N 78°44E **28 C8**
Tbilisi *Georgia* 41°43N 44°50E **19 F7**
Tchad = Chad ■ *Africa* 15°0N 17°15E **51 F8**
Tchad, L. *Chad* 13°30N 14°30E **51 F8**
Tch'eng-tou = Chengdu
China 30°38N 104°2E **32 C5**
Tchentlo L. *Canada* 55°15N 125°0W **70 B4**

Tchibanga *Gabon* 2°45S 11°0E **52 E2**
Tch'ong-k'ing = Chongqing
China 29°35N 106°25E **32 D5**
Tczew *Poland* 54°8N 18°50E **17 A10**
Te Anau, L. *N.Z.* 45°15S 167°45E **59 F1**
Te Aroha *N.Z.* 37°32S 175°44E **59 B5**
Te Awamutu *N.Z.* 38°1S 175°20E **59 C5**
Te Ika a Maui = North I.
N.Z. 38°0S 175°0E **59 C5**
Te Kuiti *N.Z.* 38°20S 175°11E **59 C5**
Te Puke *N.Z.* 37°46S 176°22E **59 B6**
Te Waewae B. *N.Z.* 46°13S 167°33E **59 G1**
Te Wai Pounamu = South I.
N.Z. 44°0S 170°0E **59 E3**
Teague *U.S.A.* 31°38N 96°17W **84 F6**
Teahupoo *Tahiti* 17°50S 149°16W **59 d**
Teapa *Mexico* 17°33N 92°57W **87 D6**
Tebakang *Malaysia* 1°6N 110°30E **36 D4**
Teberu *Malaysia* 1°30N 103°42E **39 d**
Tébessa *Algeria* 35°22N 8°8E **50 A7**
Tebicuary → *Paraguay* 26°36S 58°16W **94 B4**
Tebingtinggi *Riau,*
Indonesia 1°0N 102°45E **36 E2**
Tebingtinggi *Sumatera Utara,*
Indonesia 3°20N 99°9E **36 D1**
Tecate *Mexico* 32°34N 116°38W **79 N10**
Tecka *Argentina* 43°29S 70°48W **96 E2**
Tecomán *Mexico* 18°55N 103°53W **86 D4**
Tecopa *U.S.A.* 35°51N 116°13W **79 K10**
Tecoripa *Mexico* 28°37N 109°57W **86 B3**
Tecuala *Mexico* 22°23N 105°27W **86 C3**
Tecuci *Romania* 45°51N 27°27E **17 F14**
Tecumseh *Canada* 42°19N 82°54W **82 D2**
Tecumseh *Mich., U.S.A.* 42°0N 83°57W **81 D12**
Tecumseh *Okla., U.S.A.* 35°15N 96°56W **84 D6**
Tedzhen = Tejen
Turkmenistan 37°23N 60°31E **28 F7**
Tees → *U.K.* 54°37N 1°10W **12 C6**
Tees B. *U.K.* 54°40N 1°9W **12 C6**
Teeswater *Canada* 43°59N 81°17W **82 C3**
Tefé *Brazil* 3°25S 64°50W **92 D6**
Tegal *Indonesia* 6°52S 109°8E **37 G13**
Tegallalang *Indonesia* 8°27S 115°17E **37 J18**
Tegalsari *Indonesia* 8°25S 114°8E **37 J17**
Tegid = Bala, L. *U.K.* 52°53N 3°37W **12 E4**
Tegucigalpa *Honduras* 14°5N 87°14W **88 D2**
Tehachapi *U.S.A.* 35°8N 118°27W **79 K8**
Tehachapi Mts. *U.S.A.* 35°0N 118°30W **79 L8**
Teheran = Tehrān *Iran* 35°41N 51°25E **45 C6**
Tehoru *Indonesia* 3°23S 129°30E **37 E7**
Tehrān *Iran* 35°41N 51°25E **45 C6**
Tehrān □ *Iran* 35°30N 51°30E **45 C6**
Tehri *India* 30°23N 78°29E **43 D8**
Tehuacán *Mexico* 18°27N 97°23W **87 D5**
Tehuantepec *Mexico* 16°21N 95°13W **87 D5**
Tehuantepec, G. de
Mexico 15°50N 95°12W **87 D5**
Tehuantepec, Istmo de
Mexico 17°15N 94°30W **87 D6**
Teide, Pico de *Canary Is.* 28°15N 16°38W **24 F3**
Teifi → *U.K.* 52°5N 4°41W **13 E3**
Teign → *U.K.* 50°32N 3°32W **13 G4**
Teignmouth *U.K.* 50°33N 3°31W **13 G4**
Tejakula *Indonesia* 8°8S 115°20E **37 J18**
Tejam *India* 29°57N 80°11E **43 E9**
Tejen *Turkmenistan* 37°23N 60°31E **28 F7**
Tejen → *Turkmenistan* 37°24N 60°38E **45 B9**
Tejo → *Europe* 38°40N 9°24W **21 C1**
Tejon Pass *U.S.A.* 34°49N 118°53W **79 L8**
Tekamah *U.S.A.* 41°47N 96°13W **80 E5**
Tekapo, L. *N.Z.* 43°53S 170°33E **59 E3**
Tekax *Mexico* 20°12N 89°17W **87 C7**
Tekeli *Kazakhstan* 44°50N 79°0E **28 E8**
Tekirdağ *Turkey* 40°58N 27°30E **23 D12**
Tekkali *India* 18°37N 84°15E **41 K14**
Tekoa *U.S.A.* 47°14N 117°4W **76 C5**
Tekong Besar, Pulau
Singapore 1°25N 104°3E **39 d**
Tel Aviv ✈ (TLV) *Israel* 32°5N 34°49E **46 C3**
Tel Aviv-Yafo *Israel* 32°4N 34°48E **46 C3**
Tel Lakhish *Israel* 31°34N 34°51E **46 D3**
Tel Megiddo *Israel* 32°35N 35°11E **46 C4**
Tela *Honduras* 15°40N 87°28W **88 C2**
Telanaipura = Jambi
Indonesia 1°38S 103°30E **36 E2**
Telavi *Georgia* 42°0N 45°30E **19 F8**
Telde *Canary Is.* 27°59N 15°25W **24 G4**
Telegraph Creek *Canada* 58°0N 131°10W **70 B2**
Telekhany = Tsyelyakhany
Belarus 52°30N 25°46E **17 B13**
Telemark *Norway* 59°15N 7°40E **9 G12**
Telén *Argentina* 36°15S 65°31W **94 D2**
Teleng *Iran* 25°47N 61°3E **45 E9**
Teles Pires → *Brazil* 7°21S 58°3W **92 E7**
Telescope Pk. *U.S.A.* 36°10N 117°5W **79 J9**
Telfer Mine *Australia* 21°40S 122°12E **60 C3**
Telford *U.K.* 52°40N 2°27W **13 E5**
Telford and Wrekin □
U.K. 52°45N 2°27W **12 E5**
Telkwa *Canada* 54°41N 127°5W **70 C3**
Tell City *U.S.A.* 37°57N 86°46W **80 G10**
Tellicherry *India* 11°45N 75°30E **40 P9**
Telluride *U.S.A.* 37°56N 107°49W **77 H10**
Teloloapán *Mexico* 18°21N 99°51W **87 D5**
Telpos Iz *Russia* 63°16N 59°13E **18 B10**
Telsen *Argentina* 42°30S 66°50W **96 E3**
Telšiai *Lithuania* 55°59N 22°14E **9 J20**
Teluk Anson = Teluk Intan
Malaysia 4°3N 101°0E **39 K3**
Teluk Bahang *Malaysia* 5°28N 100°12E **39 c**
Teluk Betung = Bandar Lampung
Indonesia 5°20S 105°10E **36 F3**
Teluk Intan *Malaysia* 4°3N 101°0E **39 K3**
Telukbutun *Indonesia* 4°13N 108°12E **36 D3**
Telukdalam *Indonesia* 0°33N 97°50E **36 D1**
Tema *Ghana* 5°41N 0°0 **50 G5**

Temagami, L. *Canada* 47°0N 80°10W **72 C3**
Temax *Mexico* 21°9N 88°56W **87 C7**
Temba *S. Africa* 25°20S 28°17E **57 D4**
Tembagapura *Indonesia* 4°20S 137°0E **37 E9**
Tembe
Dem. Rep. of the Congo 0°16S 28°14E **54 C2**
Tembe *S. Africa* 26°51S 32°24E **57 D5**
Temblor Range *U.S.A.* 35°20N 119°50W **79 K7**
Teme → *U.K.* 52°11N 2°13W **13 E5**
Temecula *U.S.A.* 33°30N 117°9W **79 M9**
Temengor, Tasik
Malaysia 5°24N 101°18E **39 K3**
Temerloh *Malaysia* 3°27N 102°25E **39 L4**
Teminabuan *Indonesia* 1°26S 132°1E **37 E8**
Temir *Kazakhstan* 49°1N 57°14E **19 E10**
Temirtau *Kazakhstan* 50°5N 72°56E **32 A2**
Temirtau *Russia* 53°10N 87°30E **28 D9**
Témiscamie → *Canada* 50°59N 73°5W **73 B5**
Témiscaming *Canada* 46°44N 79°5W **72 C4**
Témiscamingue, L.
Canada 47°10N 79°25W **72 C4**
Temosachic *Mexico* 28°57N 107°51W **86 B3**
Tempe *U.S.A.* 33°24N 111°54W **77 K8**
Tempiute *U.S.A.* 37°39N 115°38W **78 H11**
Temple *U.S.A.* 31°6N 97°21W **84 F6**
Temple B. *Australia* 12°15S 143°3E **62 A3**
Templemore *Ireland* 52°47N 7°51W **10 D4**
Templeton *U.S.A.* 35°33N 120°42W **78 K6**
Templeton → *Australia* 21°0S 138°40E **62 C2**
Tempoal de Sánchez
Mexico 21°31N 98°23W **87 C5**
Temuco *Chile* 38°45S 72°40W **96 D2**
Temuka *N.Z.* 44°14S 171°17E **59 F3**
Tenabo *Mexico* 20°3N 90°14W **87 C6**
Tenaha *U.S.A.* 31°57N 94°15W **84 F7**
Tenakee Springs
U.S.A. 57°47N 135°13W **70 B1**
Tenali *India* 16°15N 80°35E **41 L12**
Tenancingo de Degollado
Mexico 18°58N 99°36W **87 D5**
Tenango del Valle
Mexico 19°7N 99°33W **87 D5**
Tenaro, Akra *Greece* 36°22N 22°27E **23 F10**
Tenasserim *Burma* 12°6N 99°3E **39 F2**
Tenasserim □ *Burma* 14°0N 98°30E **38 F2**
Tenby *U.K.* 51°40N 4°42W **13 F3**
Tenda, Colle di *France* 44°7N 7°36E **20 D7**
Tendaho *Ethiopia* 11°48N 40°54E **47 E3**
Tendukhera *India* 23°24N 79°33E **43 H8**
Teneguía, Volcanes de
Canary Is. 28°28N 17°51W **24 F2**
Ténéré, Erg du *Niger* 17°35N 10°55E **51 E8**
Tenerife *Canary Is.* 28°15N 16°35W **24 F3**
Tenerife, Pico *Canary Is.* 27°43N 18°1W **24 G1**
Tenerife Norte ✈ (TFN)
Canary Is. 28°28N 16°17W **24 F3**
Tenerife Sur ✈ (TFS)
Canary Is. 28°3N 16°33W **24 F3**
Teng Xian *China* 35°5N 117°10E **35 G9**
Tengah, Kepulauan
Indonesia 7°5S 118°15E **36 F5**
Tengchong *China* 25°0N 98°28E **32 D4**
Tengchowfu = Penglai
China 37°48N 120°42E **35 F11**
Tenggarong *Indonesia* 0°24S 116°58E **36 E5**
Tengger Shamo *China* 38°0N 104°0E **34 E3**
Tenggol, Pulau *Malaysia* 4°48N 103°41E **39 K4**
Tengiz Köli *Kazakhstan* 50°30N 69°0E **32 A1**
Teniente Enciso △
Paraguay 21°5S 61°8W **94 A3**
Teniente Rodolfo Marsh
Antarctica 62°30S 58°0W **5 C18**
Tenino *U.S.A.* 46°51N 122°51W **78 D4**
Tenkasi *India* 8°55N 77°20E **40 Q10**
Tenke *Katanga,*
Dem. Rep. of the Congo 11°22S 26°40E **55 E2**
Tenke *Katanga,*
Dem. Rep. of the Congo 10°32S 26°7E **55 E2**
Tennant Creek
Australia 19°30S 134°15E **62 B1**
Tennessee □ *U.S.A.* 36°0N 86°30W **85 D11**
Tennessee → *U.S.A.* 37°4N 88°34W **80 G9**
Teno, Pta. de *Canary Is.* 28°21N 16°55W **24 F3**
Tenom *Malaysia* 5°4N 115°57E **36 C5**
Tenosique *Mexico* 17°29N 91°26W **87 D6**
Tenryū-Gawa → *Japan* 35°39N 137°48E **31 G8**
Tenterden *U.K.* 51°4N 0°42E **13 F8**
Tenterfield *Australia* 29°0S 152°0E **63 D5**
Teófilo Otoni *Brazil* 17°50S 41°30W **93 G10**
Tepa *Indonesia* 7°52S 129°31E **37 F7**
Tepalcatepec →
Mexico 18°35N 101°59W **86 D4**
Tepehuanes *Mexico* 25°21N 105°44W **86 B3**
Tepetongo *Mexico* 22°28N 103°9W **86 C4**
Tepic *Mexico* 21°30N 104°54W **86 C4**
Teplice *Czech Rep.* 50°40N 13°48E **16 C7**
Tepoca, C. *Mexico* 30°20N 112°25W **86 A2**
Tequila *Mexico* 20°54N 103°47W **86 C4**
Ter → *Spain* 42°2N 3°12E **21 A7**
Ter Apel *Neths.* 52°53N 7°5E **15 B7**
Téra *Niger* 14°0N 0°45E **50 F6**
Teraina *Kiribati* 4°43N 160°25W **65 G12**
Téramo *Italy* 42°39N 13°42E **22 C5**
Terang *Australia* 38°15S 142°55E **63 F3**
Terang, Teluk *Indonesia* 8°44S 116°0E **37 K19**
Terceira *Azores* 38°43N 27°13W **50 a**
Tercero → *Argentina* 32°58S 61°47W **94 C3**
Terebovlya *Ukraine* 49°18N 25°44E **17 D13**
Terek → *Russia* 44°0N 47°30E **19 F8**
Terepaima △ *Venezuela* 9°58N 69°17W **89 E6**
Teresina *Brazil* 5°9S 42°45W **93 E10**
Terewah, L. *Australia* 29°52S 147°35E **63 D4**
Teridgerie Cr. →
Australia 30°25S 148°50E **63 E4**
Termas de Río Hondo
Argentina 27°29S 64°52W **94 B3**
Termez = Termiz
Uzbekistan 37°15N 67°15E **28 F7**

Términi Imerese *Italy* 37°59N 13°42E **22 F5**
Términos, L. de *Mexico* 18°37N 91°33W **87 D6**
Termiz *Uzbekistan* 37°15N 67°15E **28 F7**
Térmoli *Italy* 42°0N 15°0E **22 C6**
Ternate *Indonesia* 0°45N 127°25E **37 D7**
Terneuzen *Neths.* 51°20N 3°50E **15 C3**
Terney *Russia* 45°3N 136°37E **30 B8**
Terni *Italy* 42°34N 12°37E **22 C5**
Ternopil *Ukraine* 49°30N 25°40E **17 D13**
Ternopil = Ternopil
  Ukraine 49°30N 25°40E **17 D13**
Terowie *Australia* 33°8S 138°55E **63 E2**
Terra Bella *U.S.A.* 35°58N 119°3W **79 K7**
Terra Nova △ *Canada* 48°33N 53°55W **73 C9**
Terrace *Canada* 54°30N 128°35W **70 C3**
Terrace Bay *Canada* 48°47N 87°5W **72 C2**
Terracina *Italy* 41°17N 13°15E **22 D5**
Terralba *Italy* 39°43N 8°39E **22 E3**
Terrassa *Spain* 41°34N 2°1E **21 B7**
Terre Haute *U.S.A.* 39°28N 87°25W **81 F10**
Terrebonne B. *U.S.A.* 29°5N 90°35W **85 G9**
Terrell *U.S.A.* 32°44N 96°17W **84 E6**
Terrenceville *Canada* 47°40N 54°44W **73 C9**
Terry *U.S.A.* 46°47N 105°19W **76 C11**
Terryville *U.S.A.* 41°41N 73°3W **83 E11**
Terschelling *Neths.* 53°25N 5°20E **15 A5**
Teruel *Spain* 40°22N 1°8W **21 B5**
Tervola *Finland* 66°6N 24°49E **8 C21**
Teryaweynya L.
  Australia 32°18S 143°22E **63 E3**
Teshio *Japan* 44°53N 141°44E **30 B10**
Teshio-Gawa → *Japan* 44°53N 141°45E **30 B10**
Tesiyn Gol → *Mongolia* 50°40N 93°20E **32 A4**
Teslin *Canada* 60°10N 132°43W **70 A2**
Teslin → *Canada* 61°34N 134°35W **70 A2**
Teslin L. *Canada* 60°15N 132°57W **70 A2**
Tessalit *Mali* 20°12N 1°0E **50 D6**
Tessaoua *Niger* 13°47N 7°56E **50 F7**
Test → *U.K.* 50°56N 1°29W **13 G6**
Testigos, Is. Los *Venezuela* 11°23N 63°7W **89 D7**
Tetachuck L. *Canada* 53°18N 125°55W **70 C3**
Tetas, Pta. *Chile* 23°31S 70°38W **94 A1**
Tete *Mozam.* 16°13S 33°33E **55 F3**
Tete □ *Mozam.* 15°15S 32°40E **55 F3**
Teterev → *Ukraine* 51°1N 30°5E **17 C16**
Teteven *Bulgaria* 42°58N 24°17E **23 C11**
Tethul → *Canada* 60°35N 112°12W **70 A6**
Tetiyev *Ukraine* 49°22N 29°38E **17 D15**
Teton → *U.S.A.* 47°56N 110°31W **76 C8**
Tétouan *Morocco* 35°35N 5°21W **50 A4**
Tetovo *Macedonia* 42°1N 20°59E **23 C9**
Tetufera, Mt. *Tahiti* 17°40S 149°26W **59 d**
Teuco → *Argentina* 25°35S 60°11W **94 B3**
Teulon *Canada* 50°23N 97°16W **71 C9**
Teun *Indonesia* 6°59S 129°8E **37 F7**
Teuri-Tō *Japan* 44°26N 141°19E **30 B10**
Teutoburger Wald
  Germany 52°5N 8°22E **16 B5**
Tevere → *Italy* 41°44N 12°14E **22 D5**
Teverya *Israel* 32°47N 35°32E **46 C4**
Teviot → *U.K.* 55°29N 2°38W **11 F6**
Tewantin *Australia* 26°27S 153°3E **63 D5**
Tewkesbury *U.K.* 51°59N 2°9W **13 F5**
Texada I. *Canada* 49°40N 124°25W **70 D4**
Texarkana *Ark., U.S.A.* 33°26N 94°2W **84 E7**
Texarkana *Tex., U.S.A.* 33°26N 94°3W **84 E7**
Texas *Australia* 28°49S 151°9E **63 D5**
Texas □ *U.S.A.* 31°40N 98°30W **84 F5**
Texas City *U.S.A.* 29°24N 94°54W **84 G7**
Texel *Neths.* 53°5N 4°50E **15 A4**
Texline *U.S.A.* 36°23N 103°2W **84 G3**
Texoma, L. *U.S.A.* 33°50N 96°34W **84 E6**
Teyateyaneng *Lesotho* 29°7S 27°34E **53 K5**
Tezin *Afghan.* 34°24N 69°30E **42 B3**
Teziutlán *Mexico* 19°49N 97°21W **87 D5**
Tezpur *India* 26°40N 92°45E **41 F18**
Tezzeron L. *Canada* 54°43N 124°30W **70 C4**
Tha-anne → *Canada* 60°31N 94°37W **71 A10**
Tha Deua *Laos* 17°57N 102°53E **38 D4**
Tha Deua *Laos* 19°26N 101°50E **38 C3**
Tha Li *Thailand* 17°37N 101°25E **38 D3**
Tha Pla *Thailand* 17°48N 100°32E **38 D3**
Tha Rua *Thailand* 14°34N 100°44E **38 E3**
Tha Sala *Thailand* 8°40N 99°56E **39 H2**
Tha Song Yang *Thailand* 17°34N 97°55E **38 D1**
Thaba Putsoa *Lesotho* 29°45S 28°0E **57 D4**
Thabana Ntlenyana
  Lesotho 29°30S 29°16E **57 D4**
Thabazimbi *S. Africa* 24°40S 27°21E **57 C4**
Thādiq *Si. Arabia* 25°18N 45°52E **44 E5**
Thai Binh *Vietnam* 20°35N 106°1E **38 B6**
Thai Muang *Thailand* 8°24N 98°16E **39 H2**
Thai Nguyen *Vietnam* 21°35N 105°55E **38 B5**
Thailand ■ *Asia* 16°0N 102°0E **38 E4**
Thailand, G. of *Asia* 11°30N 101°0E **39 G3**
Thakhek *Laos* 17°25N 104°45E **38 D5**
Thal *Pakistan* 33°28N 70°33E **42 C4**
Thal Desert *Pakistan* 31°10N 71°30E **42 D4**
Thala La = Hkakabo Razi
  Burma 28°25N 97°23E **41 E20**
Thalabarivat *Cambodia* 13°33N 105°57E **38 F5**
Thallon *Australia* 28°39S 148°49E **63 D4**
Thalu, Ko *Thailand* 9°26N 99°54E **39 b**
Thames *N.Z.* 37°7S 175°34E **59 B5**
Thames → *Canada* 42°20N 82°25W **82 D2**
Thames → *U.K.* 51°29N 0°34E **13 F8**
Thames → *U.S.A.* 41°18N 72°5W **83 E12**
Thames Estuary *U.K.* 51°29N 0°52E **13 F8**
Thamesford *Canada* 43°4N 81°0W **82 C4**
Thamesville *Canada* 42°33N 81°59W **82 D3**
Than *India* 22°34N 71°11E **42 H4**
Than Uyen *Vietnam* 22°0N 103°54E **38 B4**
Thana Gazi *India* 27°25N 76°19E **42 F7**
Thandla *India* 23°0N 74°34E **42 H6**
Thandwe *Burma* 18°20N 94°30E **41 K19**
Thane *India* 19°12N 72°59E **40 K8**
Thanesar *India* 30°1N 76°52E **42 D7**

Thanet, I. of *U.K.* 51°21N 1°20E **13 F9**
Thangool *Australia* 24°38S 150°42E **62 C5**
Thanh Hoa *Vietnam* 19°48N 105°46E **38 C5**
Thanh Hung *Vietnam* 9°55N 105°43E **39 H5**
Thanh Pho Ho Chi Minh
  Vietnam 10°58N 106°40E **39 G6**
Thanh Thuy *Vietnam* 22°55N 104°51E **38 A5**
Thanjavur *India* 10°48N 79°12E **40 P11**
Thano Bula Khan
  Pakistan 25°22N 67°50E **42 G2**
Thaolintoa L. *Canada* 61°30N 96°25W **71 A9**
Thap Lan △ *Thailand* 14°15N 102°16E **38 E4**
Thap Sakae *Thailand* 11°30N 99°37E **39 G2**
Thap Than *Thailand* 15°27N 99°54E **38 E2**
Thar Desert *India* 28°0N 72°0E **42 F5**
Tharad *India* 24°30N 71°44E **42 G4**
Thargomindah
  Australia 27°58S 143°46E **63 D3**
Tharp Fracture Zone
  S. Ocean 54°0S 135°0W **5 B14**
Tharrawaddy *Burma* 17°38N 95°48E **41 L19**
Tharthār, Buḩayrat ath
  Iraq 34°0N 43°15E **44 C4**
Tharthar, L. = Tharthār,
  Buḩayrat ath *Iraq* 34°0N 43°15E **44 C4**
Tharthār, W. ath → *Iraq* 34°32N 43°4E **44 C4**
Thasos *Greece* 40°40N 24°40E **23 D11**
That Khe *Vietnam* 22°16N 106°28E **38 b**
Thatcher *Ariz., U.S.A.* 32°51N 109°46W **77 K9**
Thatcher *Colo., U.S.A.* 37°33N 104°7W **77 H11**
Thaton *Burma* 16°55N 97°22E **41 L20**
Thaungdut *Burma* 24°30N 94°40E **41 G19**
Thayer *U.S.A.* 36°31N 91°33W **80 G8**
Thayetmyo *Burma* 19°20N 95°10E **41 K19**
Thazi *Burma* 21°0N 96°5E **41 J20**
Thbeng Meanchey
  Cambodia 13°49N 104°58E **38 F5**
The Broads *U.K.* 52°45N 1°30E **12 E9**
The Everglades *U.S.A.* 25°50N 81°0W **85 J14**
The Gulf = Persian Gulf
  Asia 27°0N 50°0E **45 E6**
The Hague = 's-Gravenhage
  Neths. 52°7N 4°17E **15 B4**
The Pas *Canada* 53°45N 101°15W **71 C8**
The Wash *U.K.* 52°58N 0°20E **12 E8**
The Weald *U.K.* 51°4N 0°20E **13 F8**
Thebes = Thiva *Greece* 38°19N 23°19E **23 E10**
Thebes *Egypt* 25°40N 32°35E **51 C12**
Thedford *Canada* 43°9N 81°51W **82 C3**
Theebine *Australia* 25°57S 152°34E **63 D5**
Thekulthili L. *Canada* 61°3N 110°0W **71 A7**
Thelon → *Canada* 64°16N 96°4W **71 A8**
Theodore *Australia* 24°55S 150°3E **62 C5**
Theodore *Canada* 51°26N 102°59W **71 C8**
Theodore *U.S.A.* 30°33N 88°10W **85 F10**
Theodore Roosevelt △
  U.S.A. 47°0N 103°25W **80 B2**
Theodore Roosevelt L.
  U.S.A. 33°40N 111°10W **77 K8**
Thepha *Thailand* 6°52N 100°58E **39 J3**
Theresa *U.S.A.* 44°13N 75°48W **83 B9**
Thermopolis *U.S.A.* 43°39N 108°13W **76 E9**
Thermopylae *Greece* 38°48N 22°35E **23 E10**
Thessalon *Canada* 46°20N 83°30W **72 C3**
Thessalonica, Gulf of =
  Thessaloniki Kolpos
  Greece 40°15N 22°45E **23 D10**
Thessaloniki *Greece* 40°38N 22°58E **23 D10**
Thessaloniki Kolpos
  Greece 40°15N 22°45E **23 D10**
Thetford *U.K.* 52°25N 0°45E **13 E8**
Thetford Mines *Canada* 46°8N 71°18W **73 C5**
Theun → *Laos* 18°19N 104°0E **38 C5**
Theunissen *S. Africa* 28°26S 26°43E **56 D4**
Thevenard *Australia* 32°9S 133°38E **63 E1**
Thibodaux *U.S.A.* 29°48N 90°49W **85 G9**
Thicket Portage *Canada* 55°19N 97°42W **71 B9**
Thief River Falls *U.S.A.* 48°7N 96°10W **80 A5**
Thiel Mts. *Antarctica* 85°15S 91°0W **5 E16**
Thiers *France* 45°52N 3°33E **20 D5**
Thiès *Senegal* 14°50N 16°51W **50 F2**
Thika *Kenya* 1°1S 37°5E **54 C4**
Thimphu *Bhutan* 27°31N 89°45E **41 F16**
Thina → *S. Africa* 31°18S 29°13E **57 E4**
Þingvallavatn *Iceland* 64°11N 21°9W **8 D3**
Thionville *France* 49°20N 6°10E **20 B7**
Thira = Santorini
  Greece 36°23N 25°27E **23 F11**
Third Cataract *Sudan* 19°42N 30°20E **51 E12**
Thirsk *U.K.* 54°14N 1°19W **12 C6**
Thiruvananthapuram =
  Trivandrum *India* 8°41N 77°0E **40 Q10**
Thisted *Denmark* 56°58N 8°40E **9 H13**
Thistle I. *Australia* 35°0S 136°8E **63 F2**
Thithia = Cicia *Fiji* 17°45S 179°18W **59 a**
Thiva *Greece* 38°19N 23°19E **23 E10**
Þjórsá → *Iceland* 63°47N 20°48W **8 E3**
Thlewiaza → *Canada* 60°29N 94°40W **71 A10**
Thmar Puok *Cambodia* 13°57N 103°4E **38 F4**
Tho Vinh *Vietnam* 19°16N 105°42E **38 C5**
Thoa → *Canada* 60°31N 109°47W **71 A7**
Thoen *Thailand* 17°43N 99°12E **38 D2**
Thoeng *Thailand* 19°41N 100°12E **38 C3**
Thohoyandou *S. Africa* 22°58S 30°29E **57 C5**
Tholdi *Pakistan* 35°5N 76°6E **43 B7**
Thomas *U.S.A.* 35°45N 98°45W **84 D5**
Thomas, L. *U.S.A.* 26°4S 137°58E **63 D2**
Thomaston *U.S.A.* 32°53N 84°20W **85 E12**
Thomasville *Ala.,
  U.S.A.* 31°55N 87°44W **85 F11**
Thomasville *Ga., U.S.A.* 30°50N 83°59W **85 F13**
Thomasville *N.C., U.S.A.* 35°53N 80°5W **85 D14**
Thompson *Canada* 55°45N 97°52W **71 B9**
Thompson *U.S.A.* 41°52N 75°31W **83 E9**
Thompson → *Canada* 50°15N 121°24W **70 C4**
Thompson → *U.S.A.* 39°46N 93°37W **80 F7**
Thompson Falls *U.S.A.* 47°36N 115°21W **76 C6**

Thompson Pk. *U.S.A.* 41°0N 123°2W **76 F2**
Thompson Springs
  U.S.A. 38°58N 109°43W **76 G9**
Thompsontown *U.S.A.* 40°33N 77°14W **82 F7**
Thomson *U.S.A.* 33°28N 82°30W **85 E13**
Thomson → *Australia* 25°11S 142°53E **62 C3**
Thong Yang *Thailand* 9°28N 99°56E **39 b**
Þórisvatn *Iceland* 64°20N 18°55W **8 D4**
Thornaby on Tees *U.K.* 54°33N 1°18W **12 C6**
Thornbury *Canada* 44°34N 80°26W **82 B4**
Thorne *U.K.* 53°37N 0°57W **12 D7**
Thornton *Canada* 44°16N 79°43W **82 B5**
Thornton *U.S.A.* 39°52N 104°58W **76 G11**
Thorold *Canada* 43°7N 79°12W **82 C5**
Thouin, C. *Australia* 20°20S 118°10E **60 D2**
Thousand Islands *U.S.A.* 44°20N 76°0W **83 B9**
Thousand Oaks *U.S.A.* 34°10N 118°50W **79 L8**
Thrace *Turkey* 41°0N 27°0E **23 D12**
Three Forks *U.S.A.* 45°54N 111°33W **76 D8**
Three Hills *Canada* 51°43N 113°15W **70 C6**
Three Hummock I.
  Australia 40°25S 144°55E **63 G3**
Three Pagodas Pass *Asia* 15°20N 98°30E **38 E2**
Three Points, C. *Ghana* 4°42N 2°6W **50 H5**
Three Rivers *Calif.,
  U.S.A.* 36°26N 118°54W **78 J8**
Three Rivers *Tex.,
  U.S.A.* 28°28N 98°11W **84 G5**
Three Springs *Australia* 29°32S 115°45E **61 E2**
Throssell, L. *Australia* 27°33S 124°10E **61 E3**
Throssell Ra. *Australia* 22°3S 121°43E **60 D3**
Thrushton △ *Australia* 27°47S 147°40E **63 D4**
Thua → *Kenya* 1°31S 39°30E **54 C4**
Thuan Hoa *Vietnam* 8°58N 105°30E **39 H5**
Thubun Lakes *Canada* 61°30N 112°0W **71 A6**
Thuin *Belgium* 50°20N 4°17E **15 D4**
Thule = Qaanaaq
  Greenland 77°40N 69°0W **4 B4**
Thule Air Base = Uummannaq
  Greenland 77°28N 69°13W **4 B4**
Thun *Switz.* 46°45N 7°38E **20 C7**
Thunder B. *U.S.A.* 45°0N 83°20W **82 B1**
Thunder Bay *Canada* 48°20N 89°15W **72 C2**
Thung Salaeng Luang △
  Thailand 16°43N 100°30E **38 D3**
Thung Song *Thailand* 8°10N 99°40E **39 H2**
Thunkar *Bhutan* 27°55N 91°0E **41 F17**
Thuong Tra *Vietnam* 16°2N 107°42E **38 D6**
Thüringer Wald *Germany* 50°35N 11°0E **16 C6**
Thurles *Ireland* 52°41N 7°49W **10 D4**
Thurrock □ *U.K.* 51°31N 0°23E **13 F8**
Thursday I. *Australia* 10°30S 142°3E **62 A3**
Thurso *Canada* 45°36N 75°15W **72 C4**
Thurso *U.K.* 58°36N 3°32W **11 C5**
Thurso → *U.K.* 58°36N 3°32W **11 C5**
Thurston I. *Antarctica* 72°0S 100°0W **5 D16**
Thutade L. *Canada* 57°0N 126°55W **70 B3**
Thyolo *Malawi* 16°7S 35°5E **55 F4**
Ti-Tree *Australia* 22°5S 133°22E **62 C1**
Tian Shan *Asia* 40°30N 76°0E **32 B3**
Tianjin *China* 39°7N 117°12E **35 E9**
Tianshifu *China* 41°17N 124°22E **35 D13**
Tianshui *China* 34°32N 105°40E **34 G3**
Tianyar *Indonesia* 8°12S 115°30E **37 J18**
Tianzhen *China* 40°24N 114°5E **34 D8**
Tianzhuangtai *China* 40°43N 122°5E **35 D12**
Tiarei *Tahiti* 17°32S 149°20W **59 d**
Tiaret *Algeria* 35°20N 1°21E **50 A6**
Tibagi *Brazil* 24°30S 50°24W **95 A5**
Tibagi → *Brazil* 22°47S 51°1W **95 A5**
Tibastī, Sarīr *Libya* 22°50N 18°30E **51 D9**
Tibati *Cameroon* 6°22N 12°30E **52 C2**
Tiber = Tevere → *Italy* 41°44N 12°14E **22 D5**
Tiber Res. *U.S.A.* 48°19N 111°6W **76 B8**
Tiberias = Teverya *Israel* 32°47N 35°32E **46 C4**
Tiberias, L. = Yam Kinneret
  Israel 32°45N 35°35E **46 C4**
Tibesti *Chad* 21°0N 17°30E **51 D9**
Tibet = Xizang Zizhiqu □
  China 32°0N 88°0E **32 C3**
Tibet, Plateau of *Asia* 32°0N 86°0E **26 E10**
Tibni *Syria* 35°36N 39°50E **44 C3**
Tibooburra *Australia* 29°26S 142°1E **63 D3**
Tiburón, I. *Mexico* 29°0N 112°25W **86 B2**
Ticino → *Italy* 45°9N 9°14E **20 D8**
Ticonderoga *U.S.A.* 43°51N 73°26W **83 C11**
Ticul *Mexico* 20°24N 89°32W **87 C7**
Tidaholm *Sweden* 58°12N 13°58E **9 G15**
Tiddim *Burma* 23°28N 93°45E **41 H18**
Tidioute *U.S.A.* 41°41N 79°24W **82 E5**
Tidjikja *Mauritania* 18°29N 11°35W **50 E3**
Tidore *Indonesia* 0°40N 127°25E **37 D7**
Tiefa *China* 42°28N 123°26E **35 C12**
Tiegang Shuiku *China* 22°37N 113°53E **33 F10**
Tiel *Neths.* 51°53N 5°26E **15 C5**
Tieling *China* 42°20N 123°55E **35 C12**
Tielt *Belgium* 51°0N 3°20E **15 C3**
Tien Shan = Tian Shan
  Asia 40°30N 76°0E **32 B3**
Tien-tsin = Tianjin
  China 39°7N 117°12E **35 E9**
Tien Yen *Vietnam* 21°20N 107°24E **38 B6**
T'ienching = Tianjin
  China 39°7N 117°12E **35 E9**
Tienen *Belgium* 50°48N 4°57E **15 D4**
Tientsin = Tianjin *China* 39°7N 117°12E **35 E9**
Tieri *Australia* 23°2S 148°21E **62 C4**
Tierra Amarilla *Chile* 27°28S 70°18W **94 B1**
Tierra Amarilla
  U.S.A. 36°42N 106°33W **77 H10**
Tierra Colorada *Mexico* 17°11N 99°32E **87 D5**
Tierra de Campos *Spain* 42°10N 4°50W **21 A3**
Tierra del Fuego, I. Grande de
  Argentina 54°0S 69°0W **96 G3**
Tiétar → *Spain* 39°50N 6°1W **21 C3**
Tieté → *Brazil* 20°40S 51°35W **95 A5**

Tiffin *U.S.A.* 41°7N 83°11W **81 E12**
Tifton *U.S.A.* 31°27N 83°31W **85 F13**
Tifu *Indonesia* 3°39S 126°24E **37 E7**
Tighina *Moldova* 46°50N 29°30E **17 E15**
Tigil *Russia* 57°49N 158°40E **29 D16**
Tignish *Canada* 46°58N 64°2W **73 C7**
Tigre → *Peru* 4°30S 74°10W **92 D4**
Tigre → *Venezuela* 9°20N 62°30W **92 B6**
Tigris = Dijlah, Nahr →
  Asia 31°0N 47°25E **44 D5**
Tigyaing *Burma* 23°45N 96°10E **41 H20**
Tīhāmah *Asia* 15°3N 41°55E **47 D3**
Tijara *India* 27°56N 76°31E **42 F7**
Tijuana *Mexico* 32°32N 117°1W **79 N10**
Tikal *Guatemala* 17°13N 89°24W **88 C2**
Tikal △ *Guatemala* 17°23N 89°34W **88 C2**
Tikamgarh *India* 24°44N 78°50E **43 G8**
Tikhoretsk *Russia* 45°56N 40°5E **19 E7**
Tikhvin *Russia* 59°35N 33°30E **18 C5**
Tikirarjuaq = Whale Cove
  Canada 62°10N 92°34W **71 A10**
Tikrīt *Iraq* 34°35N 43°37E **44 C4**
Tiksi *Russia* 71°40N 128°45E **29 B13**
Tilamuta *Indonesia* 0°32N 122°23E **37 D6**
Tilburg *Neths.* 51°31N 5°6E **15 C5**
Tilbury *Canada* 42°17N 82°23W **82 D2**
Tilbury *U.K.* 51°27N 0°22E **13 F8**
Tilcara *Argentina* 23°36S 65°23W **94 A2**
Tilden *U.S.A.* 42°3N 97°50W **80 D5**
Tilhar *India* 28°0N 79°45E **43 F8**
Tilichiki *Russia* 60°27N 166°5E **29 C17**
Tilissos *Greece* 35°20N 25°1E **25 D7**
Till → *U.K.* 55°41N 2°13W **12 B5**
Tillamook *U.S.A.* 45°27N 123°51W **76 D2**
Tillsonburg *Canada* 42°53N 80°44W **82 D4**
Tillyeria *Cyprus* 35°6N 32°40E **25 D11**
Tilos *Greece* 36°27N 27°27E **23 F12**
Tilpa *Australia* 30°57S 144°24E **63 E3**
Tilt → *U.K.* 56°46N 3°51W **11 E5**
Tilton *U.S.A.* 43°27N 71°36W **83 C13**
Tiltonsville *U.S.A.* 40°10N 80°41W **82 F4**
Timanfaya △ *Canary Is.* 29°0N 13°46W **24 F6**
Timanskiy Kryazh *Russia* 65°58N 50°5E **18 A9**
Timaru *N.Z.* 44°23S 171°14E **59 F3**
Timau *Kenya* 0°4N 37°15E **54 B4**
Timbaki *Greece* 35°4N 24°45E **25 D6**
Timber Creek *Australia* 15°35S 130°29E **60 C5**
Timber Lake *U.S.A.* 45°26N 101°5W **80 C3**
Timber Mt. *U.S.A.* 37°6N 116°28W **78 H10**
Timbuktu = Tombouctou
  Mali 16°50N 3°0W **50 E5**
Timi *Cyprus* 34°44N 32°31E **25 E11**
Timimoun *Algeria* 29°14N 0°16E **50 C6**
Timiris, Râs *Mauritania* 19°21N 16°30W **50 E2**
Timiskaming, L. =
  Témiscamingue, L.
  Canada 47°10N 79°25W **72 C4**
Timişoara *Romania* 45°43N 21°15E **17 F11**
Timmins *Canada* 48°28N 81°25W **72 C3**
Timok → *Serbia* 44°10N 22°40E **23 B10**
Timor *Asia* 9°0S 125°0E **37 F7**
Timor Leste = East Timor ■
  Asia 8°50S 126°0E **37 F7**
Timor Sea *Ind. Oc.* 12°0S 127°0E **60 B4**
Tin Can Bay *Australia* 25°56S 153°0E **63 D5**
Tin Mt. *U.S.A.* 36°50N 117°10W **78 J9**
Tina → *S. Africa* 31°18S 29°13E **57 E4**
Tina, Khalig el *Egypt* 31°10N 32°40E **46 D1**
Tinaca Pt. *Phil.* 5°30N 125°25E **37 C7**
Tinajo *Canary Is.* 29°4N 13°42W **24 E6**
Tindal *Australia* 14°31S 132°22E **60 B5**
Tindouf *Algeria* 27°42N 8°10W **50 C3**
Tinfunque △ *Paraguay* 23°55S 60°17W **94 A3**
Tinggi, Pulau *Malaysia* 2°18N 104°7E **39 L5**
Tingo María *Peru* 9°10S 75°54W **92 E3**
Tingrela *Ivory C.* 10°27N 6°25W **50 F4**
Tinh Bien *Vietnam* 10°36N 104°57E **39 G5**
Tinian *N. Marianas* 15°0N 145°38E **64 F6**
Tinnevelly = Tirunelveli
  India 8°45N 77°45E **40 Q10**
Tinogasta *Argentina* 28°5S 67°32W **94 B2**
Tinos *Greece* 37°33N 25°8E **23 F11**
Tinpahar *India* 24°59N 87°44E **43 G12**
Tintina *Argentina* 27°2S 62°45W **94 B3**
Tintinara *Australia* 35°48S 140°2E **63 F3**
Tioga *N. Dak., U.S.A.* 48°24N 102°56W **80 A2**
Tioga *Pa., U.S.A.* 41°55N 77°8W **82 E7**
Tioman, Pulau *Malaysia* 2°50N 104°10E **39 L5**
Tionesta *U.S.A.* 41°30N 79°28W **82 E5**
Tipperary *Ireland* 52°28N 8°10W **10 D3**
Tipperary □ *Ireland* 52°37N 7°55W **10 D4**
Tipton *Calif., U.S.A.* 36°4N 119°19W **78 J7**
Tipton *Iowa, U.S.A.* 41°46N 91°8W **80 E8**
Tipton Mt. *U.S.A.* 35°32N 114°12W **79 K12**
Tiptonville *U.S.A.* 36°23N 89°29W **85 C10**
Tīrān *Iran* 32°45N 51°8E **45 C6**
Tiranë *Albania* 41°18N 19°49E **23 D8**
Tirari Desert *Australia* 28°22S 138°7E **63 D2**
Tiraspol *Moldova* 46°55N 29°35E **17 E15**
Tire *Turkey* 38°5N 27°45E **23 E12**
Tirebolu *Turkey* 40°58N 38°45E **19 F6**
Tiree *U.K.* 56°31N 6°55W **11 E2**
Tiree, Passage of *U.K.* 56°30N 6°30W **11 E2**
Tîrgovişte = Târgovişte
  Romania 44°55N 25°27E **17 F13**
Tîrgu Jiu = Târgu Jiu
  Romania 45°5N 23°19E **17 F12**
Tîrgu Mureş = Târgu Mureş
  Romania 46°31N 24°38E **17 E13**
Tirich Mir *Pakistan* 36°15N 71°55E **40 A7**
Tiritiri o te Moana = Southern
  Alps *N.Z.* 43°41S 170°11E **59 E3**
Tirnavos *Greece* 39°45N 22°18E **23 E10**
Tirodi *India* 21°40N 79°44E **43 J8**
Tirol □ *Austria* 47°3N 10°43E **16 E6**
Tirso → *Italy* 39°53N 8°32E **22 E3**

Tiruchchirappalli *India* 10°45N 78°45E **40 P11**
Tirunelveli *India* 8°45N 77°45E **40 Q10**
Tirupati *India* 13°39N 79°25E **40 N11**
Tiruppur *India* 11°5N 77°22E **40 P10**
Tiruvannamalai *India* 12°15N 79°5E **40 N11**
Tisa → *Serbia* 45°15N 20°17E **23 B9**
Tisa = Tisza → *Serbia* 45°15N 20°17E **23 B9**
Tisdale *Canada* 52°50N 104°0W **71 C8**
Tishomingo *U.S.A.* 34°14N 96°41W **84 D6**
Tisza = Tisa → *Serbia* 45°15N 20°17E **23 B9**
Tit-Ary *Russia* 71°55N 127°2E **29 B13**
Tithwal *Pakistan* 34°21N 73°50E **43 B5**
Titicaca, L. *S. Amer.* 15°30S 69°30W **92 G5**
Titiwa *Nigeria* 12°14N 12°53E **51 F8**
Titule
  Dem. Rep. of the Congo 3°15N 25°31E **54 B2**
Titusville *Fla., U.S.A.* 28°37N 80°49W **85 G14**
Titusville *Pa., U.S.A.* 41°38N 79°41W **82 E5**
Tivaouane *Senegal* 14°56N 16°45W **50 F2**
Tiverton *Canada* 44°16N 81°32W **82 B3**
Tiverton *U.K.* 50°54N 3°29W **13 G4**
Tívoli *Italy* 41°58N 12°45E **22 D5**
Tizi-Ouzou *Algeria* 36°42N 4°3E **50 A6**
Tizimín *Mexico* 21°9N 88°9W **87 C7**
Tiznit *Morocco* 29°48N 9°45W **50 C4**
Tjeggelvas *Sweden* 66°37N 17°45E **8 C17**
Tjieggelvas = Tjeggelvas
  Sweden 66°37N 17°45E **8 C17**
Tjirebon = Cirebon
  Indonesia 6°45S 108°32E **37 G13**
Tjluring *Indonesia* 8°25S 114°13E **37 J17**
Tjörn *Sweden* 58°0N 11°35E **9 H14**
Tlacotalpan *Mexico* 18°37N 95°40W **87 D5**
Tlahualilo de Zaragoza
  Mexico 26°7N 103°27W **86 B4**
Tlaquepaque *Mexico* 20°39N 103°19W **86 C4**
Tlaxcala *Mexico* 19°19N 98°14W **87 D5**
Tlaxcala □ *Mexico* 19°30N 98°20W **87 D5**
Tlaxiaco *Mexico* 17°25N 97°35W **87 D5**
Tlemcen *Algeria* 34°52N 1°21W **50 B5**
To Bong *Vietnam* 12°45N 109°16E **38 F7**
Toa Payoh *Singapore* 1°20N 103°51E **39 d**
Toad → *Canada* 59°25N 124°57W **70 B4**
Toad River *Canada* 58°51N 125°14W **70 B3**
Toamasina *Madag.* 18°10S 49°25E **57 B8**
Toamasina □ *Madag.* 18°0S 49°0E **57 B8**
Toay *Argentina* 36°43S 64°38W **94 D3**
Toba *Japan* 34°30N 136°51E **31 G8**
Toba, Danau *Indonesia* 2°30N 97°30E **36 D1**
Toba Kakar *Pakistan* 31°30N 69°0E **42 D3**
Toba Tek Singh *Pakistan* 30°55N 72°25E **42 D5**
Tobago *Trin. & Tob.* 11°10N 60°30W **89 D7**
Tobelo *Indonesia* 1°45N 127°56E **37 D7**
Tobermory *Canada* 45°12N 81°40W **82 A3**
Tobermory *U.K.* 56°38N 6°5W **11 E2**
Tobi *Pac. Oc.* 2°40N 131°10E **37 D8**
Tobin, L. *Australia* 21°45S 125°49E **60 D4**
Tobin, L. *Canada* 53°35N 103°30W **71 C8**
Toboali *Indonesia* 3°0S 106°25E **36 E3**
Tobol → *Russia* 58°10N 68°12E **28 D7**
Toboli *Indonesia* 0°38S 120°5E **37 E6**
Tobolsk *Russia* 58°15N 68°10E **28 D7**
Tobruk = Tubruq *Libya* 32°7N 23°55E **51 B10**
Tobyhanna *U.S.A.* 41°11N 75°25W **83 E9**
Tobyl = Tobol → *Russia* 58°10N 68°12E **28 D7**
Tocantinópolis *Brazil* 6°20S 47°25W **93 E9**
Tocantins □ *Brazil* 10°0S 48°0W **93 F9**
Tocantins → *Brazil* 1°45S 49°10W **93 D9**
Toccoa *U.S.A.* 34°35N 83°19W **85 D13**
Tochi → *Pakistan* 32°49N 70°41E **42 C4**
Tochigi *Japan* 36°25N 139°45E **31 F9**
Tochigi □ *Japan* 36°45N 139°45E **31 F9**
Toco *Trin. & Tob.* 10°49N 60°57W **93 K16**
Toconao *Chile* 23°11S 68°1W **94 A2**
Tocopilla *Chile* 22°5S 70°10W **94 A1**
Tocumwal *Australia* 35°51S 145°31E **63 F4**
Tocuyo → *Venezuela* 11°3N 68°23W **89 D6**
Todd → *Australia* 24°52S 135°48E **62 C2**
Todeli *Indonesia* 1°40S 124°29E **37 E6**
Todenyang *Kenya* 4°35N 35°56E **54 B4**
Todgarh *India* 25°42N 73°58E **42 G5**
Todos os Santos, B. de
  Brazil 12°48S 38°38W **93 F11**
Todos Santos *Mexico* 23°26N 110°13W **86 C2**
Toe Hd. *U.K.* 57°50N 7°8W **11 D1**
Tofield *Canada* 53°25N 112°40W **70 C6**
Tofino *Canada* 49°11N 125°55W **70 D3**
Tofua *Tonga* 19°45S 175°5W **59 c**
Tōgane *Japan* 35°33N 140°22E **31 G10**
Togian, Kepulauan
  Indonesia 0°20S 121°50E **37 E6**
Togliatti *Russia* 53°32N 49°24E **18 D8**
Togo ■ *W. Afr.* 8°30N 1°35E **50 G6**
Togtoh *China* 40°15N 111°10E **34 D6**
Tohiea, Mt. *Moorea* 17°33S 149°49W **59 d**
Tōhoku □ *Japan* 39°50N 141°45E **30 E10**
Tōhōm *Mongolia* 44°27N 108°2E **34 B5**
Toinya *Sudan* 6°17N 29°46E **51 G11**
Toiyabe Range *U.S.A.* 39°30N 117°0W **76 G5**
Tojikiston = Tajikistan ■
  Asia 38°30N 70°0E **28 F8**
Tojo *Indonesia* 1°20S 121°15E **37 E6**
Tōjō *Japan* 34°53N 133°16E **31 G6**
Tok *U.S.A.* 63°20N 142°59W **68 C5**
Tokachi-Dake *Japan* 43°17N 142°5E **30 C11**
Tokachi-Gawa →
  Japan 42°44N 143°42E **30 C11**
Tokala *Indonesia* 1°30S 121°40E **37 E6**
Tōkamachi *Japan* 37°8N 138°43E **31 F9**
Tokanui *N.Z.* 46°34S 168°56E **59 G2**
Tokara-Rettō *Japan* 29°37N 129°43E **31 K4**
Tokarahi *N.Z.* 44°56S 170°39E **59 F3**
Tokashiki-Shima *Japan* 26°11N 127°21E **31 L3**
Tokat *Turkey* 40°22N 36°35E **19 F6**
Tokch'ŏn *N. Korea* 39°45N 126°18E **35 E14**
Tokdo *Asia* 37°15N 131°52E **31 F5**

Tokeland U.S.A. 46°42N 123°59W 78 D3
Tokelau Is. Pac. Oc. 9°0S 171°45W 64 H10
Tokmak Kyrgyzstan 42°49N 75°15E 28 E8
Toko Ra. Australia 23°5S 138°20E 62 C2
Tokoro-Gawa → Japan 44°7N 144°5E 30 B12
Toku Tonga 18°10S 174°11W 59 c
Tokuno-Shima Japan 27°56N 128°55E 31 L4
Tokushima Japan 34°4N 134°34E 31 G7
Tokushima □ Japan 33°55N 134°0E 31 H7
Tokuyama Japan 34°3N 131°50E 31 G5
Tōkyō Japan 35°43N 139°45E 31 G9
Tolaga Bay N.Z. 38°21S 178°20E 59 C7
Tolbukhin = Dobrich Bulgaria 43°37N 27°49E 23 C12
Toledo Brazil 24°44S 53°45W 95 A5
Toledo Spain 39°50N 4°2W 21 C3
Toledo Ohio, U.S.A. 41°39N 83°33W 81 E12
Toledo Oreg., U.S.A. 44°37N 123°56W 76 D2
Toledo Wash., U.S.A. 46°26N 122°51W 76 C2
Toledo, Montes de Spain 39°33N 4°20W 21 C3
Toledo Bend Res. U.S.A. 31°11N 93°34W 84 F8
Tolga Australia 17°15S 145°29E 62 B4
Toliara Madag. 23°21S 43°40E 57 C7
Toliara □ Madag. 21°0S 45°0E 57 C8
Tolima Colombia 4°40N 75°19W 92 C3
Tolitoli Indonesia 1°5N 120°50E 37 D6
Tollhouse U.S.A. 37°1N 119°24W 78 H7
Tolmachevo Russia 58°56N 29°51E 9 G23
Tolo, Teluk Indonesia 2°20S 122°10E 37 E6
Tolo Harbour China 22°27N 114°12E 33 G11
Toluca Mexico 19°17N 99°40W 87 D5
Tom Burke S. Africa 23°5S 28°0E 57 C4
Tom Price Australia 22°40S 117°48E 60 D2
Tomah U.S.A. 43°59N 90°30W 80 D8
Tomahawk U.S.A. 45°28N 89°44W 80 C9
Tomakomai Japan 42°38N 141°36E 30 C10
Tomales U.S.A. 38°15N 122°53W 78 G4
Tomales B. U.S.A. 38°15N 123°58W 78 G3
Tomanivi Fiji 17°37S 178°1E 59 a
Tomar Portugal 39°36N 8°25W 21 C1
Tomaszów Mazowiecki Poland 51°30N 20°2E 17 C10
Tomatlán Mexico 19°56N 105°15W 86 D3
Tombador, Serra do Brazil 12°0S 58°0W 92 F7
Tombigbee → U.S.A. 31°8N 87°57W 85 F11
Tombouctou Mali 16°50N 3°0W 50 E5
Tombstone U.S.A. 31°43N 110°4W 77 L8
Tombua Angola 15°55S 11°55E 56 B1
Tomé Chile 36°36S 72°57W 94 D1
Tomelloso Spain 39°10N 3°2W 21 C4
Tomini Indonesia 0°30N 120°30E 37 D6
Tomini, Teluk Indonesia 0°10S 121°0E 37 E6
Tomintoul U.K. 57°15N 3°23W 11 D5
Tomkinson Ranges Australia 26°11S 129°5E 61 E4
Tommot Russia 59°4N 126°20E 29 D13
Tomnop Ta Suos Cambodia 11°20N 104°15E 39 G5
Tomo → Colombia 5°20N 67°48W 92 B5
Toms Place U.S.A. 37°34N 118°41W 78 H8
Toms River U.S.A. 39°58N 74°12W 83 G10
Tomsk Russia 56°30N 85°5E 28 D9
Tonalá Chiapas, Mexico 16°4N 93°45W 87 D6
Tonalá Jalisco, Mexico 20°37N 103°14W 86 C4
Tonantins Brazil 2°45S 67°45W 92 D5
Tonasket U.S.A. 48°42N 119°26W 76 B4
Tonawanda U.S.A. 43°1N 78°53W 82 D6
Tonb Iran 26°15N 55°15E 45 E7
Tonbridge U.K. 51°11N 0°17E 13 F8
Tondano Indonesia 1°35N 124°54E 37 D6
Tondoro Namibia 17°45S 18°50E 56 B2
Tone → Australia 34°25S 116°25E 61 F2
Tone-Gawa → Japan 35°44N 140°51E 31 F9
Tonekābon Iran 36°45N 51°12E 45 B6
Tong Xian China 39°55N 116°35E 34 E9
Tong-Yeong S. Korea 34°50N 128°20E 35 G15
Tonga ■ Pac. Oc. 19°50S 174°30W 59 c
Tonga Trench Pac. Oc. 18°0S 173°0W 64 J10
Tongaat S. Africa 29°33S 31°9E 57 D5
Tongareva = Penrhyn Cook Is. 9°0S 158°0W 65 H12
Tongariro △ N.Z. 39°8S 175°33E 59 C5
Tongatapu Tonga 21°10S 175°10W 59 c
Tongatapu Group Tonga 21°0S 175°0W 59 c
Tongchuan China 35°6N 109°3E 34 G5
Tongeren Belgium 50°47N 5°28E 15 D5
Tonggu Jiao China 22°22N 113°37E 33 G10
Tongguan China 34°40N 110°25E 34 G6
Tonghua China 41°42N 125°58E 35 D13
Tongjosŏn Man N. Korea 39°30N 128°0E 35 E15
Tongking, G. of = Tonkin, G. of Asia 20°0N 108°0E 38 C7
Tongliao China 43°38N 122°18E 35 C12
Tongling China 30°55N 117°48E 33 C6
Tongobory Madag. 23°32S 44°20E 57 C7
Tongoy Chile 30°16S 71°31W 94 C1
Tongres = Tongeren Belgium 50°47N 5°28E 15 D5
Tongsa Dzong Bhutan 27°31N 90°31E 41 F17
Tongshi China 18°30N 109°20E 38 C7
Tongue U.K. 58°29N 4°25W 11 C4
Tongue → U.S.A. 46°25N 105°52W 76 C11
Tongwei China 35°0N 105°5E 34 G3
Tongxin China 36°59N 105°58E 34 F3
Tongyang N. Korea 39°9N 126°53E 35 E14
Tongyu China 44°45N 123°4E 35 B12
Tonj Sudan 7°20N 28°44E 51 G11
Tonk India 26°6N 75°54E 42 F6
Tonkawa U.S.A. 36°41N 97°18W 84 C6
Tonkin = Bac Phan Vietnam 22°0N 105°0E 38 B5
Tonkin, G. of Asia 20°0N 108°0E 38 C7
Tonle Sap Cambodia 13°0N 104°0E 38 F5
Tono Japan 39°19N 141°32E 30 E10
Tonopah U.S.A. 38°4N 117°14W 77 G5
Tonosí Panama 7°20N 80°20W 88 E3
Tons → Haryana, India 30°30N 77°39E 42 D7
Tons → Ut. P., India 26°1N 83°33E 43 F10
Tønsberg Norway 59°19N 10°25E 9 G14
Tonto △ U.S.A. 33°39N 111°7W 77 K8
Tonumea Tonga 20°30S 174°30W 59 c
Toobanna Australia 18°42S 146°9E 62 B4
Toodyay Australia 31°34S 116°28E 61 F2
Tooele U.S.A. 40°32N 112°18W 76 F7
Toompine Australia 27°15S 144°19E 63 D3
Toora Australia 38°39S 146°23E 63 F4
Toora-Khem Russia 52°28N 96°17E 29 D10
Toowoomba Australia 27°32S 151°56E 63 D5
Top Springs Australia 16°37S 131°51E 60 C5
Topaz U.S.A. 38°41N 119°30W 78 G7
Topeka U.S.A. 39°3N 95°40W 80 F6
Topley Canada 54°49N 126°18W 70 C3
Topocalma, Pta. Chile 34°10S 72°2W 94 C1
Topock U.S.A. 34°46N 114°29W 79 L12
Topol'čany Slovak Rep. 48°35N 18°12E 17 D10
Topolobampo Mexico 25°36N 109°3W 86 B3
Topozero, Ozero Russia 65°35N 32°0E 8 D25
Toppenish U.S.A. 46°23N 120°19W 76 C3
Toraka Vestale Madag. 16°20S 43°58E 57 B7
Torata Peru 17°23S 70°1W 92 G4
Torbalı Turkey 38°10N 27°21E 23 E12
Torbat-e Heydārīyeh Iran 35°15N 59°12E 45 C8
Torbat-e Jām Iran 35°16N 60°35E 45 C9
Torbay Canada 47°40N 52°42W 73 C9
Torbay □ U.K. 50°26N 3°31W 13 G4
Tordesillas Spain 41°30N 5°0W 21 B3
Torfaen □ U.K. 51°43N 3°3W 13 F4
Torgau Germany 51°34N 13°0E 16 C7
Torhout Belgium 51°5N 3°7E 15 C3
Tori-Shima Japan 30°29N 140°19E 31 J10
Torino Italy 45°3N 7°40E 20 D7
Torit Sudan 4°27N 32°31E 51 H12
Torkamān Iran 37°35N 47°23E 44 B5
Tormes → Spain 41°18N 6°29W 21 B2
Tornado Mt. Canada 49°55N 114°40W 70 D6
Torneå = Tornio Finland 65°50N 24°12E 8 D21
Torneälven → Europe 65°50N 24°12E 8 D21
Torneträsk Sweden 68°24N 19°15E 8 B18
Tornio Finland 65°50N 24°12E 8 D21
Tornionjoki = Torneälven → Europe 65°50N 24°12E 8 D21
Tornquist Argentina 38°8S 62°15W 94 D3
Toro Spain 39°59N 4°8E 24 B11
Toro, Cerro del Chile 29°10S 69°50W 94 B2
Toro ⌓ Uganda 1°5N 30°22E 54 C3
Toro Pk. U.S.A. 33°34N 116°24W 79 M10
Toronto Canada 43°39N 79°20W 82 C5
Toronto U.S.A. 40°28N 80°36W 82 F4
Toronto Lester B. Pearson Int. ✈ (YYZ) Canada 43°46N 79°35W 82 C5
Toropets Russia 56°30N 31°40E 18 C5
Tororo Uganda 0°45N 34°12E 54 B3
Toros Dağları Turkey 37°0N 32°30E 44 B2
Torpa India 22°57N 85°6E 43 H11
Torquay U.K. 50°27N 3°32W 13 G4
Torrance U.S.A. 33°50N 118°20W 79 M8
Torre de Moncorvo Portugal 41°12N 7°8W 21 B2
Torre del Greco Italy 40°47N 14°22E 22 D6
Torrejón de Ardoz Spain 40°27N 3°29W 21 B4
Torrelavega Spain 43°20N 4°5W 21 A3
Torremolinos Spain 36°38N 4°30W 21 D3
Torrens, L. Australia 31°0S 137°50E 63 E2
Torrens Cr. → Australia 22°23S 145°9E 62 C4
Torrens Creek Australia 20°48S 145°3E 62 C4
Torrent Spain 39°27N 0°28W 21 C5
Torreón Mexico 25°33N 103°26W 86 B4
Torres Brazil 29°21S 49°44W 95 B5
Torres Mexico 28°46N 110°47W 86 B2
Torres Strait Australia 9°50S 142°20E 58 B7
Torres Vedras Portugal 39°5N 9°15W 21 C1
Torrevieja Spain 37°59N 0°42W 21 D5
Torrey U.S.A. 38°18N 111°25W 76 G8
Torridge → U.K. 51°0N 4°13W 13 G3
Torridon, L. U.K. 57°35N 5°50W 11 D3
Torrington Conn., U.S.A. 41°48N 73°7W 83 E11
Torrington Wyo., U.S.A. 42°4N 104°11W 76 E11
Tórshavn Færoe Is. 62°5N 6°56W 8 E9
Tortola Br. Virgin Is. 18°19N 64°45W 89 e
Tortosa Spain 40°49N 0°31E 21 B6
Tortosa, C. Spain 40°41N 0°52E 21 B6
Tortue, Î. de la Haiti 20°5N 72°57W 89 B5
Tortuguero △ Costa Rica 10°31N 83°29W 88 D3
Torūd Iran 35°25N 55°5E 45 C7
Toruń Poland 53°2N 18°39E 17 B10
Tory Hill Canada 44°58N 78°16W 82 B6
Tory I. Ireland 55°16N 8°14W 10 A3
Tosa Japan 33°24N 133°23E 31 H6
Tosa-Shimizu Japan 32°52N 132°58E 31 H6
Tosa-Wan Japan 33°15N 133°30E 31 H6
Toscana □ Italy 43°25N 11°0E 22 C4
Toshka Lakes Egypt 22°50N 31°0E 51 D12
Toshkent Uzbekistan 41°20N 69°10E 28 E7
Tostado Argentina 29°15S 61°50W 94 B3
Tostón, Pta. de Canary Is. 28°42N 14°2W 24 F5
Tosu Japan 33°22N 130°31E 31 H5
Toteng Botswana 20°22S 22°58E 56 C3
Totma Russia 60°0N 42°40E 18 C7
Totnes U.K. 50°26N 3°42W 13 G4
Totness Suriname 5°53N 56°19W 93 B7
Totonicapán Guatemala 14°58N 91°12W 88 D1
Totoya, I. Fiji 18°57S 179°50W 59 a
Totten Glacier Antarctica 66°45S 116°10E 5 C8
Tottenham Australia 32°14S 147°21E 63 E4
Tottenham Canada 44°1N 79°49W 82 B5
Tottori Japan 35°30N 134°15E 31 G7
Tottori □ Japan 35°30N 134°12E 31 G7
Toubkal, Djebel Morocco 31°0N 8°0W 50 B4
Tougan Burkina Faso 13°11N 2°58W 50 F5
Touggourt Algeria 33°6N 6°4E 50 B7
Toul France 48°40N 5°53E 20 B6
Toulon France 43°10N 5°55E 20 E6
Toulouse France 43°37N 1°27E 20 E4
Toummo Niger 22°45N 14°8E 51 D8
Toungoo Burma 19°0N 96°30E 41 K20
Touraine France 47°20N 0°30E 20 C4
Tourcoing France 50°42N 3°10E 20 A5
Touriñán, C. Spain 43°3N 9°18W 21 A1
Tournai Belgium 50°35N 3°25E 15 D3
Tournon-sur-Rhône France 45°4N 4°50E 20 D6
Tours France 47°22N 0°40E 20 C4
Toussoro, Mt. C.A.R. 9°7N 23°14E 52 C4
Touws → S. Africa 33°45S 21°11E 56 E3
Touwsrivier S. Africa 33°20S 20°2E 56 E3
Towada Japan 40°37N 141°13E 30 D10
Towada-Hachimantai △ Japan 40°20N 140°55E 30 D10
Towada-Ko Japan 40°28N 140°55E 30 D10
Towanda U.S.A. 41°46N 76°27W 83 E8
Tower U.S.A. 47°48N 92°17W 80 B7
Towerhill Cr. → Australia 22°28S 144°35E 62 C3
Towner U.S.A. 48°21N 100°25W 80 A3
Townsend U.S.A. 46°19N 111°31W 76 C8
Townshend I. Australia 22°10S 150°31E 62 C5
Townsville Australia 19°15S 146°45E 62 B4
Towraghondī Afghan. 35°13N 62°16E 40 B3
Towson U.S.A. 39°24N 76°36W 81 F15
Towuti, Danau Indonesia 2°45S 121°32E 37 E6
Toya-Ko Japan 42°35N 140°51E 30 C10
Toyama Japan 36°40N 137°15E 31 F8
Toyama □ Japan 36°45N 137°30E 31 F8
Toyama-Wan Japan 37°0N 137°30E 31 F8
Toyapakeh Indonesia 8°41S 115°29E 37 K18
Toyohashi Japan 34°45N 137°25E 31 G8
Toyokawa Japan 34°48N 137°27E 31 G8
Toyonaka Japan 34°46N 135°28E 31 G7
Toyooka Japan 35°35N 134°48E 31 G7
Toyota Japan 35°3N 137°7E 31 G8
Tozeur Tunisia 33°56N 8°8E 50 B7
Trá Li = Tralee Ireland 52°16N 9°42W 10 D2
Tra On Vietnam 9°58N 105°55E 39 H5
Trabzon Turkey 41°0N 39°45E 19 F6
Tracadie Canada 47°30N 64°55W 73 C7
Tracy Canada 46°1N 73°9W 72 C5
Tracy Calif., U.S.A. 37°44N 121°26W 78 H5
Tracy Minn., U.S.A. 44°14N 95°37W 80 C6
Trafalgar, C. Spain 36°10N 6°2W 21 D2
Trail Canada 49°5N 117°40W 70 D5
Trainor L. Canada 60°24N 120°17W 70 A4
Trakai △ Lithuania 54°30N 25°10E 9 J21
Trákhonas Cyprus 35°12N 33°21E 25 D12
Tralee Ireland 52°16N 9°42W 10 D2
Tralee B. Ireland 52°17N 9°55W 10 D2
Tramore Ireland 52°10N 7°10W 10 D4
Tramore B. Ireland 52°9N 7°10W 10 D4
Tramuntana, Serra de Spain 39°48N 2°54E 24 B9
Tran Ninh, Cao Nguyen Laos 19°30N 103°10E 38 C4
Tranås Sweden 58°3N 14°59E 9 G16
Trancas Argentina 26°11S 65°20W 94 B2
Trang Thailand 7°33N 99°38E 39 J2
Trangahy Madag. 19°7S 44°31E 57 B7
Trangan Indonesia 6°40S 134°20E 37 F8
Trangie Australia 32°4S 148°0E 63 E4
Trani Italy 41°17N 16°25E 22 D7
Tranoroa Madag. 24°42S 45°4E 57 C8
Tranqueras Uruguay 31°13S 55°45W 95 C4
Transantarctic Mts. Antarctica 85°0S 170°0W 5 E12
Transilvania Romania 46°30N 24°0E 17 E12
Transilvanian Alps = Carpaţii Meridionali Romania 45°30N 25°0E 17 F13
Transnistria = Stînga Nistrului □ Moldova 47°20N 29°15E 17 E15
Transylvania = Transilvania Romania 46°30N 24°0E 17 E12
Trápani Italy 38°1N 12°29E 22 E5
Trapper Pk. U.S.A. 45°54N 114°18W 76 D6
Traralgon Australia 38°12S 146°34E 63 F4
Trasimeno, L. Italy 43°8N 12°6E 22 C5
Trat Thailand 12°14N 102°33E 39 F4
Tratani → Pakistan 29°19N 68°20E 42 E3
Traun Austria 48°14N 14°15E 16 D8
Travellers L. Australia 33°20S 142°0E 63 E3
Travemünde Germany 53°57N 10°52E 16 B6
Travers, Mt. N.Z. 42°1S 172°45E 59 E4
Traverse City U.S.A. 44°46N 85°38W 81 C11
Travis, L. U.S.A. 30°24N 97°55W 84 F6
Travnik Bos.-H. 44°17N 17°39E 23 B7
Trawbreaga B. Ireland 55°20N 7°25W 10 A4
Trébbia → Italy 45°4N 9°41E 20 D8
Třebíč Czech Rep. 49°14N 15°55E 16 D8
Trebinje Bos.-H. 42°44N 18°22E 23 C8
Trebonne Australia 18°37S 146°5E 62 B4
Tregaron U.K. 52°14N 3°56W 13 E4
Tregrosse Is. Australia 17°41S 150°43E 62 B5
Treherne Canada 49°38N 98°42W 71 D9
Treinta y Tres Uruguay 33°16S 54°17W 95 C5
Trelawney Zimbabwe 17°30S 30°30E 57 B5
Trelew Argentina 43°10S 65°20W 96 E3
Trelleborg Sweden 55°20N 13°10E 9 J15
Tremadog Bay U.K. 52°51N 4°18W 12 E3
Tremonton U.S.A. 41°43N 112°10W 76 F7
Tremp Spain 42°10N 0°52E 21 A6
Trenche → Canada 47°46N 72°53W 72 C5
Trenčín Slovak Rep. 48°52N 18°4E 17 D10
Trenggalek Indonesia 8°3S 111°43E 37 H14
Trenque Lauquen Argentina 36°5S 62°45W 94 D3
Trent → Canada 44°6N 77°34W 82 B7
Trent → U.K. 53°41N 0°42W 12 D7
Trento Italy 46°4N 11°8E 22 A4
Trenton Canada 44°10N 77°34W 82 B7
Trenton Mo., U.S.A. 40°5N 93°37W 80 E7
Trenton N.J., U.S.A. 40°14N 74°46W 83 F10
Trenton Nebr., U.S.A. 40°11N 101°1W 80 E3
Trepassey Canada 46°43N 53°25W 73 C9
Tres Arroyos Argentina 38°26S 60°20W 94 D3
Três Corações Brazil 21°44S 45°15W 95 A6
Três Lagoas Brazil 20°50S 51°43W 93 H8
Tres Lomas Argentina 36°27S 62°51W 94 D3
Tres Montes, C. Chile 46°50S 75°30W 96 F1
Tres Pinos U.S.A. 36°48N 121°19W 78 J5
Três Pontas Brazil 21°23S 45°29W 95 A6
Tres Puentes Chile 27°50S 70°15W 94 B1
Tres Puntas, C. Argentina 47°0S 66°0W 96 F3
Três Rios Brazil 22°6S 43°15W 95 A7
Tres Valles Mexico 18°15N 96°8W 87 D5
Tresco U.K. 49°57N 6°20W 13 H1
Treviso Italy 45°40N 12°15E 22 B5
Triabunna Australia 42°30S 147°55E 63 G4
Trianda Greece 36°25N 28°10E 25 C10
Triangle Zimbabwe 21°2S 31°28E 57 C5
Tribal Areas □ Pakistan 33°0N 70°0E 42 C4
Tribulation, C. Australia 16°5S 145°29E 62 B4
Tribune U.S.A. 38°28N 101°45W 80 F3
Trichinopoly = Tiruchchirappalli India 10°45N 78°45E 40 P11
Trichur India 10°30N 76°18E 40 P10
Trida Australia 33°1S 145°1E 63 E4
Trier Germany 49°45N 6°38E 16 D4
Trieste Italy 45°40N 13°46E 22 B5
Triglav Slovenia 46°21N 13°50E 16 E7
Trikala Greece 39°34N 21°47E 23 E9
Trikomo Cyprus 35°17N 33°52E 25 D12
Trikora, Puncak Indonesia 4°15S 138°45E 37 E9
Trim Ireland 53°33N 6°48W 10 C5
Trimmu Dam Pakistan 31°10N 72°8E 42 D5
Trincomalee Sri Lanka 8°38N 81°15E 40 Q12
Trindade Brazil 16°40S 49°30W 93 G9
Trindade, I. Atl. Oc. 20°20S 29°50W 2 F8
Trinidad Bolivia 14°46S 64°50W 92 F6
Trinidad Cuba 21°48N 80°0W 88 B4
Trinidad Trin. & Tob. 10°30N 61°15W 89 D7
Trinidad Uruguay 33°30S 56°50W 94 C4
Trinidad U.S.A. 37°10N 104°31W 77 H11
Trinidad → Mexico 17°49N 95°9W 87 D5
Trinidad & Tobago ■ W. Indies 10°30N 61°20W 89 D7
Trinity Canada 48°59N 53°55W 73 C9
Trinity U.S.A. 30°57N 95°22W 84 F7
Trinity → Calif., U.S.A. 41°11N 123°42W 76 F2
Trinity → Tex., U.S.A. 29°45N 94°43W 84 G7
Trinity B. Canada 48°20N 53°10W 73 C9
Trinity Hills Trin. & Tob. 10°7N 61°7W 93 K15
Trinity Is. U.S.A. 56°33N 154°25W 74 a
Trinity Range U.S.A. 40°10N 118°40W 76 F4
Trinkitat Sudan 18°45N 37°51E 51 E13
Trinway U.S.A. 40°9N 82°1W 82 F2
Triolet Mauritius 20°4S 57°32E 53 d
Tripoli = Tarābulus Lebanon 34°31N 35°50E 46 A4
Tripoli = Tarābulus Libya 32°49N 13°7E 51 B8
Tripoli Greece 37°31N 22°25E 23 F10
Tripolitania = Tarābulus N. Afr. 31°0N 13°0E 51 B8
Tripura □ India 24°0N 92°0E 41 H18
Tripylos Cyprus 34°59N 32°41E 25 E11
Tristan da Cunha Atl. Oc. 37°6S 12°20W 49 K2
Trisul India 30°19N 79°47E 43 D8
Trivandrum India 8°41N 77°0E 40 Q10
Trnava Slovak Rep. 48°23N 17°35E 17 D9
Trochu Canada 51°50N 113°13W 70 C6
Trodely I. Canada 52°15N 79°26W 72 B4
Troglav Croatia 43°56N 16°36E 22 C7
Troilus, L. Canada 50°50N 74°35W 72 B5
Trois-Pistoles Canada 48°5N 69°10W 73 C6
Trois-Rivières Canada 46°25N 72°34W 72 C5
Trois-Rivières Guadeloupe 15°57N 61°40W 88 b
Troitsk Russia 54°10N 61°35E 28 D7
Troitsko Pechorsk Russia 62°40N 56°10E 18 B10
Trölladyngja Iceland 64°54N 17°16W 8 D5
Trollhättan Sweden 58°17N 12°20E 9 G15
Trollheimen Norway 62°46N 9°1E 8 E13
Trombetas → Brazil 1°55S 55°35W 93 D7
Tromsø Norway 69°40N 18°56E 8 B18
Tron Thailand 17°28N 100°7E 38 D3
Trona U.S.A. 35°46N 117°23W 79 K9
Tronador, Mte. Argentina 41°10S 71°50W 96 E2
Trøndelag Norway 64°17N 11°50E 8 D14
Trondheim Norway 63°36N 10°25E 8 E14
Trondheimsfjorden Norway 63°35N 10°30E 8 E14
Troodos Cyprus 34°55N 32°52E 25 E11
Troon U.K. 55°33N 4°39W 11 F4
Tropic U.S.A. 37°37N 112°5W 77 H7
Trostan U.K. 55°3N 6°10W 10 A5
Trou Gras Pt. St. Lucia 13°51N 60°53W 89 f
Trout → Canada 61°19N 119°51W 70 A5
Trout L. N.W.T., Canada 60°40N 121°14W 70 A4
Trout L. Ont., Canada 51°20N 93°15W 71 C10
Trout Lake Canada 56°30N 114°32W 70 B6
Trout Lake U.S.A. 46°0N 121°32W 78 E5
Trout River Canada 49°29N 58°8W 73 C8
Trout Run U.S.A. 41°23N 77°3W 82 E7
Trouville-sur-Mer France 49°21N 0°5E 20 B4
Trowbridge U.K. 51°18N 2°12W 13 F5
Troy Turkey 39°57N 26°12E 23 E12
Troy Ala., U.S.A. 31°48N 85°58W 85 F12
Troy Kans., U.S.A. 39°47N 95°5W 80 F6
Troy Mo., U.S.A. 38°59N 90°59W 80 F8
Troy Mont., U.S.A. 48°28N 115°53W 76 B6
Troy N.Y., U.S.A. 42°44N 73°41W 83 D11
Troy Ohio, U.S.A. 40°2N 84°12W 81 E11
Troy Pa., U.S.A. 41°47N 76°47W 83 E8
Troyes France 48°19N 4°3E 20 B6
Truchas Pk. U.S.A. 35°58N 105°39W 77 J11
Trucial States = United Arab Emirates ■ Asia 23°50N 54°0E 45 F7
Truckee U.S.A. 39°20N 120°11W 78 F6
Trudovoye Russia 43°17N 132°5E 30 C6
Trujillo Honduras 16°0N 86°0W 88 C2
Trujillo Peru 8°6S 79°0W 92 E3
Trujillo Spain 39°28N 5°55W 21 C3
Trujillo U.S.A. 35°32N 104°42W 77 J11
Trujillo Venezuela 9°22N 70°38W 92 B4
Truk Micronesia 7°25N 151°46E 64 G7
Trumann U.S.A. 35°41N 90°31W 85 D9
Trumansburg U.S.A. 42°33N 76°40W 83 D8
Trumbull, Mt. U.S.A. 36°25N 113°19W 77 H7
Trundle Australia 32°53S 147°35E 63 E4
Trung-Phan = Annam Vietnam 16°0N 108°0E 38 E7
Truro Canada 45°21N 63°14W 73 C7
Truro U.K. 50°16N 5°4W 13 G2
Truskavets Ukraine 49°17N 23°30E 17 D12
Trutch Canada 57°44N 122°57W 70 B4
Truth or Consequences U.S.A. 33°8N 107°15W 77 K10
Trutnov Czech Rep. 50°37N 15°54E 16 C8
Tryonville U.S.A. 41°42N 79°48W 82 E5
Tsandi Namibia 17°42S 14°50E 56 B1
Tsaratanana Madag. 16°47S 47°39E 57 B8
Tsaratanana, Mt. de = Maromokotro Madag. 14°0S 49°0E 57 A8
Tsaratanana ⌓ Madag. 13°57S 48°52E 57 A8
Tsau Botswana 20°8S 22°22E 56 C3
Tsavo Kenya 2°59S 38°28E 54 C4
Tsavo East △ Kenya 2°44S 38°47E 54 C4
Tsavo West △ Kenya 3°19S 37°57E 54 C4
Tsentralnyy □ Russia 52°0N 40°0E 28 D4
Tses Namibia 25°58S 18°8E 56 D2
Tsetserleg Mongolia 47°36N 101°32E 32 B5
Tsévié Togo 6°25N 1°20E 50 G6
Tshabong Botswana 26°2S 22°29E 56 D3
Tshane Botswana 24°5S 21°54E 56 C3
Tshela Dem. Rep. of the Congo 4°57S 13°4E 52 E2
Tshesebe Botswana 21°51S 27°32E 57 C4
Tshibeke Dem. Rep. of the Congo 2°40S 28°35E 54 C2
Tshibinda Dem. Rep. of the Congo 2°23S 28°43E 54 C2
Tshikapa Dem. Rep. of the Congo 6°28S 20°48E 52 F4
Tshilenge Dem. Rep. of the Congo 6°17S 23°48E 54 D1
Tshinsenda Dem. Rep. of the Congo 12°20S 28°0E 55 E2
Tshofa Dem. Rep. of the Congo 5°13S 25°16E 54 D2
Tshwane = Pretoria S. Africa 25°44S 28°12E 57 D4
Tshwane Botswana 22°24S 22°1E 56 C3
Tsigara Botswana 20°22S 25°54E 56 C4
Tsihombe Madag. 25°10S 45°41E 57 D8
Tsiigehtchic Canada 67°15N 134°0W 68 C6
Ts'il-os ⌓ Canada 51°9N 123°59W 70 C4
Tsimlyansk Res. = Tsimlyanskoye Vdkhr. Russia 48°0N 43°0E 19 E7
Tsimlyanskoye Vdkhr. Russia 48°0N 43°0E 19 E7
Tsinan = Jinan China 36°38N 117°1E 34 F9
Tsineng S. Africa 27°5S 23°5E 56 D3
Tsing Yi China 22°21N 114°6E 33 G11
Tsinghai = Qinghai □ China 36°0N 98°0E 32 C4
Tsingtao = Qingdao China 36°5N 120°20E 35 F11
Tsingy de Bemaraha ⌓ Madag. 18°35S 45°25E 57 B8
Tsingy de Namoroka ⌓ Madag. 16°29S 45°25E 57 B8
Tsinjoarivo Madag. 19°37S 47°40E 57 B8
Tsinjomitondraka Madag. 15°40S 47°8E 57 B8
Tsirigo = Kythira Greece 36°8N 23°0E 23 F10
Tsiroanomandidy Madag. 18°46S 46°2E 57 B8
Tsitondroina Madag. 21°19S 46°0E 57 C8
Tsitsikamma △ S. Africa 34°3S 23°40E 56 E3
Tsivory Madag. 24°4S 46°5E 57 C8
Tskhinvali Georgia 42°14N 44°1E 19 F7
Tsna → Russia 54°55N 41°58E 18 D7
Tso Moriri, L. India 32°50N 78°20E 43 C8
Tsobis Namibia 19°27S 17°30E 56 B2
Tsodilo Hill Botswana 18°49S 21°43E 56 B3
Tsogttsetsiy = Baruunsuu Mongolia 43°43N 105°35E 34 C3
Tsolo S. Africa 31°18S 28°37E 57 E4
Tsomo S. Africa 32°0S 27°42E 57 E4
Tsu Japan 34°45N 136°25E 31 G8
Tsu L. Canada 60°40N 111°52W 70 A6
Tsuchiura Japan 36°5N 140°15E 31 F10
Tsuen Wan China 22°22N 114°6E 33 G11
Tsugaru-Kaikyō Japan 41°35N 141°0E 30 D10
Tsumeb Namibia 19°9S 17°44E 56 B2
Tsumis Namibia 23°39S 17°29E 56 C2
Tsuruga Japan 35°45N 136°2E 31 G8
Tsurugi-San Japan 33°51N 134°6E 31 H7
Tsuruoka Japan 38°44N 139°50E 30 E9
Tsushima Gifu, Japan 35°10N 136°43E 31 G8
Tsushima Nagasaki, Japan 34°20N 129°20E 31 G4
Tsuyama Japan 35°3N 134°0E 31 G7
Tsyelyakhany Belarus 52°30N 25°46E 17 B13
Tual Indonesia 5°38S 132°44E 37 F8
Tualatin U.S.A. 45°23N 122°45W 78 E4
Tuam Ireland 53°31N 8°51W 10 C3
Tuamotu, Îs. French Polynesia 17°0S 144°0W 65 J13
Tuamotu Arch. = Tuamotu, Îs. French Polynesia 17°0S 144°0W 65 J13
Tuamotu Ridge Pac. Oc. 20°0S 138°0W 65 K14
Tuan Giao Vietnam 21°35N 103°25E 38 B4
Tuao Phil. 17°55N 121°22E 37 A4
Tuapse Russia 44°5N 39°10E 19 F6
Tuas Singapore 1°19N 103°39E 39 d

Tuatapere *N.Z.* 46°8S 167°41E **59** G1
Tuba City *U.S.A.* 36°8N 111°14W **77** H8
Tuban *Indonesia* 6°54S 112°3E **37** G15
Tubani *Botswana* 24°46S 24°18E **56** D3
Tubarão *Brazil* 28°30S 49°0W **95** B6
Tübās *West Bank* 32°20N 35°22E **46** C4
Tübingen *Germany* 48°31N 9°4E **16** D5
Tubou *Fiji* 18°13S 178°48W **59** a
Tubruq *Libya* 32°7N 23°55E **51** B10
Tubuaï, Îs.
French Polynesia 25°0S 150°0W **65** K13
Tuc Trung *Vietnam* 11°1N 107°12E **39** G6
Tucacas *Venezuela* 10°48N 68°19W **92** A5
Tuchitua *Canada* 60°55N 129°13W **70** A3
Tuchodi → *Canada* 58°17N 123°42W **70** B4
Tuckanarra *Australia* 27°7S 118°5E **61** E2
Tucson *U.S.A.* 32°13N 110°58W **77** K8
Tucumán □ *Argentina* 26°48S 66°2W **94** B2
Tucumcari *U.S.A.* 35°10N 103°44W **77** J12
Tucupita *Venezuela* 9°2N 62°3W **92** B6
Tucuruí *Brazil* 3°42S 49°44W **93** D9
Tucuruí, Represa de
Brazil 4°0S 49°30W **93** D9
Tudela *Spain* 42°4N 1°39W **21** A5
Tudmur *Syria* 34°36N 38°15E **44** C3
Tudor, L. *Canada* 55°50N 65°25W **73** A6
Tuen Mun *China* 22°24N 113°59E **33** G10
Tugela → *S. Africa* 29°14S 31°30E **57** D5
Tuguegarao *Phil.* 17°35N 121°42E **37** A6
Tugur *Russia* 53°44N 136°45E **29** D14
Tui *Spain* 42°3N 8°39W **21** A1
Tuineje *Canary Is.* 28°19N 14°3W **24** F5
Tukangbesi, Kepulauan
Indonesia 6°0S 124°0E **37** F6
Tukarak I. *Canada* 56°15N 78°45W **72** A4
Tukayyid *Iraq* 29°47N 45°36E **44** D5
Tuktoyaktuk *Canada* 69°27N 133°2W **68** C6
Tukums *Latvia* 56°58N 23°10E **9** H20
Tukuyu *Tanzania* 9°17S 33°35E **55** D3
Tula *Hidalgo, Mexico* 20°3N 99°21W **87** C5
Tula *Tamaulipas, Mexico* 23°0N 99°40W **87** C5
Tula *Russia* 54°13N 37°38E **18** D6
Tulancingo *Mexico* 20°5N 98°22W **87** C5
Tulare *U.S.A.* 36°13N 119°21W **78** J7
Tulare Lake Bed *U.S.A.* 36°0N 119°48W **78** K7
Tularosa *U.S.A.* 33°5N 106°1W **77** K10
Tulbagh *S. Africa* 33°16S 19°6E **56** E2
Tulcán *Ecuador* 0°48N 77°43W **92** C3
Tulcea *Romania* 45°13N 28°46E **17** F15
Tulchyn *Ukraine* 48°41N 28°49E **17** D15
Tüleh *Iran* 34°35N 52°33E **45** C7
Tulemalu L. *Canada* 62°58N 99°25W **71** A9
Tuli *Zimbabwe* 21°58S 29°13E **55** G2
Tulia *U.S.A.* 34°32N 101°46W **84** D4
Tulita *Canada* 64°57N 125°30W **68** C7
Ţülkarm *West Bank* 32°19N 35°2E **46** C4
Tulla *Ireland* 52°53N 8°46W **10** D3
Tullahoma *U.S.A.* 35°22N 86°13W **85** D11
Tullamore *Australia* 32°39S 147°36E **63** E4
Tullamore *Ireland* 53°16N 7°31W **10** C4
Tulle *France* 45°16N 1°46E **20** D4
Tullow *Ireland* 52°49N 6°45W **10** D5
Tully *Australia* 17°56S 145°55E **62** B4
Tully → *U.S.A.* 42°48N 76°7W **83** D8
Tulsa *U.S.A.* 36°10N 95°55W **84** C7
Tulsequah *Canada* 58°39N 133°35W **70** B2
Tuluá *Colombia* 4°6N 76°11W **92** C3
Tulun *Russia* 54°32N 100°35E **29** D11
Tulungagung *Indonesia* 8°5S 111°54E **37** H14
Tuma → *Nic.* 13°6N 84°35W **88** D3
Tumacacori ∴ *U.S.A.* 31°35N 111°6W **77** L8
Tumaco *Colombia* 1°50N 78°45W **92** C3
Tumatumari *Guyana* 5°20N 58°55W **92** B7
Tumba *Sweden* 59°12N 17°48E **9** G17
Tumba, L.
Dem. Rep. of the Congo 0°50S 18°0E **52** E3
Tumbarumba *Australia* 35°44S 148°0E **63** F4
Tumbaya *Argentina* 23°50S 65°26W **94** A2
Tumbes *Peru* 3°37S 80°27W **92** D2
Tumbler Ridge *Canada* 55°8N 121°0W **70** B4
Tumbwe
Dem. Rep. of the Congo 11°25S 27°15E **55** E2
Tumby Bay *Australia* 34°21S 136°8E **63** E2
Tumd Youqi *China* 40°30N 110°30E **34** D6
Tumen *China* 43°0N 129°50E **30** C4
Tumen Jiang → *China* 42°20N 130°35E **35** C16
Tumeremo *Venezuela* 7°18N 61°30W **92** B6
Tumkur *India* 13°18N 77°6E **40** N10
Tump *Pakistan* 26°7N 62°16E **40** F3
Tumpat *Malaysia* 6°11N 102°10E **39** J4
Tumu *Ghana* 10°56N 1°56W **50** F5
Tumucumaque, Serra
Brazil 2°0N 55°0W **93** C8
Tumut *Australia* 35°16S 148°13E **63** F4
Tumwater *U.S.A.* 47°1N 122°54W **78** C4
Tuna *India* 22°59N 70°5E **42** H4
Tunapuna *Trin. & Tob.* 10°38N 61°24W **93** K15
Tunas de Zaza *Cuba* 21°39N 79°34W **88** B4
Tunbridge Wells = Royal
Tunbridge Wells *U.K.* 51°7N 0°16E **13** F8
Tuncurry *Australia* 32°17S 152°29E **63** E5
Tundla *India* 27°12N 78°17E **42** F8
Tunduru *Tanzania* 11°8S 37°25E **55** E4
Tundzha → *Bulgaria* 41°40N 26°35E **23** C11
Tung Chung *China* 22°17N 113°57E **33** G10
Tung Lung Chau
China 22°15N 114°17E **33** G11
Tungabhadra → *India* 15°57N 78°15E **40** M11
Tungla *Nic.* 13°24N 84°21W **88** D3
Tungsten *Canada* 61°57N 128°16W **70** A3
Tunguska, Nizhnyaya →
Russia 65°48N 88°4E **29** C9
Tunguska, Podkamennaya →
Russia 61°50N 90°13E **29** C10
Tunica *U.S.A.* 34°41N 90°23W **85** D9
Tunis *Tunisia* 36°50N 10°11E **50** A7

Tunisia ■ *Africa* 33°30N 9°10E **51** A7
Tunja *Colombia* 5°33N 73°25W **92** B4
Tunkhannock *U.S.A.* 41°32N 75°57W **83** E9
Tunliu *China* 36°13N 112°52E **34** F7
Tunnel Creek △
Australia 17°41S 125°18E **60** C4
Tunnsjøen *Norway* 64°45N 13°25E **8** D15
Tunungayualok I. *Canada* 56°0N 61°0W **73** A7
Tunuyán *Argentina* 33°35S 69°0W **94** C2
Tunuyán → *Argentina* 33°33S 67°30W **94** C2
Tuolumne *U.S.A.* 37°58N 120°15W **78** H6
Tuolumne → *U.S.A.* 37°36N 121°13W **78** H5
Tūp Āghāj *Iran* 36°3N 47°50E **44** B5
Tupã *Brazil* 21°57S 50°28W **95** A5
Tupelo *U.S.A.* 34°16N 88°43W **85** D10
Tupinambarana, Ilha
Brazil 3°0S 58°0W **92** D7
Tupiza *Bolivia* 21°30S 65°40W **94** A2
Tupman *U.S.A.* 35°18N 119°21W **79** K7
Tupper *Canada* 55°32N 120°1W **70** B4
Tupper L. *U.S.A.* 44°10N 74°32W **83** B10
Tupper Lake *U.S.A.* 44°14N 74°28W **83** B10
Tupungato, Cerro
S. Amer. 33°15S 69°50W **94** C2
Tuquan *China* 45°18N 121°38E **35** B11
Túquerres *Colombia* 1°5N 77°37W **92** C3
Tura *Russia* 64°20N 100°17E **29** C11
Turabah *Si. Arabia* 28°20N 43°15E **44** D4
Türän *Iran* 35°39N 56°42E **45** C8
Tura *Russia* 51°55N 94°0E **29** D10
Turayf *Si. Arabia* 31°41N 38°39E **44** D3
Turda *Romania* 46°34N 23°47E **17** E12
Turek *Poland* 52°3N 18°30E **17** B10
Turén *Venezuela* 9°17N 69°6W **92** B5
Turfan = Turpan *China* 43°58N 89°10E **32** B3
Turfan Basin = Turpan Pendi
China 42°40N 89°25E **32** B3
Turfan Depression = Turpan
Pendi *China* 42°40N 89°25E **32** B3
Turgeon → *Canada* 50°0N 78°56W **72** C4
Türgovishte *Bulgaria* 43°17N 26°38E **23** C12
Turgutlu *Turkey* 38°30N 27°43E **23** E12
Turgwe → *Zimbabwe* 21°33S 32°15E **57** C5
Turia → *Spain* 39°27N 0°19W **21** C5
Turiaçu *Brazil* 1°40S 45°19W **93** D9
Turiaçu → *Brazil* 1°36S 45°19W **93** D9
Turin = Torino *Italy* 45°3N 7°40E **20** D7
Turkana, L. *Africa* 3°30N 36°5E **54** B4
Turkestan = Türkistan
Kazakhstan 43°17N 68°16E **28** E7
Turkey ■ *Eurasia* 39°0N 36°0E **19** G6
Turkey Creek = Warmun
Australia 17°2S 128°12E **60** C4
Türkistan *Kazakhstan* 43°17N 68°16E **28** E7
Türkmenabat
Turkmenistan 39°6N 63°34E **45** B9
Türkmenbashi
Turkmenistan 40°5N 53°5E **45** A7
Turkmenistan ■ *Asia* 39°0N 59°0E **28** F6
Turks Island Passage
W. Indies 21°30N 71°30W **89** B5
Turku *Finland* 60°30N 22°19E **9** F20
Turkwel → *Kenya* 3°6N 36°6E **54** B4
Turlock *U.S.A.* 37°30N 120°51W **78** H6
Turnagain → *Canada* 59°12N 127°35W **70** B3
Turnagain, C. *N.Z.* 40°28S 176°38E **59** D6
Turneffe Is. *Belize* 17°20N 87°50W **87** D7
Turner *U.S.A.* 48°51N 108°24W **76** B9
Turner Pt. *Australia* 11°47S 133°32E **62** A1
Turner Valley *Canada* 50°40N 114°17W **70** C6
Turners Falls *U.S.A.* 42°36N 72°33W **83** D12
Turnhout *Belgium* 51°19N 4°57E **15** C4
Turnor L. *Canada* 56°35N 108°35W **71** B7
Tŭrnovo = Veliko Tŭrnovo
Bulgaria 43°5N 25°41E **23** C11
Turnu Măgurele
Romania 43°46N 24°56E **17** G13
Turnu Roşu, P.
Romania 45°33N 24°17E **17** F13
Turpan *China* 43°58N 89°10E **32** B3
Turpan Pendi *China* 42°40N 89°25E **32** B3
Turriff *U.K.* 57°32N 2°27W **11** D6
Tursäq *Iraq* 33°27N 45°47E **44** C5
Turtle Head I. *Australia* 10°56S 142°37E **62** A3
Turtle L. *Canada* 53°36N 108°38W **71** C7
Turtle Lake *U.S.A.* 47°31N 100°53W **80** B3
Turtleford *Canada* 53°23N 108°57W **71** C7
Turuépano △ *Venezuela* 10°34N 62°43W **89** D7
Turukhansk *Russia* 65°21N 88°5E **29** C9
Tuscaloosa *U.S.A.* 33°12N 87°34W **85** E11
Tuscany = Toscana □
Italy 43°25N 11°0E **22** C4
Tuscarawas → *U.S.A.* 40°24N 81°25W **82** F3
Tuscarora Mt. *U.S.A.* 40°55N 77°55W **82** F7
Tuscola *Ill., U.S.A.* 39°48N 88°17W **80** F9
Tuscola *Tex., U.S.A.* 32°12N 99°48W **84** E5
Tuscumbia *U.S.A.* 34°44N 87°42W **85** D11
Tuskegee *U.S.A.* 32°25N 85°42W **85** E12
Tuticorin *India* 8°50N 78°12E **40** Q11
Tutóia *Brazil* 2°45S 42°20W **93** D10
Tutong *Brunei* 4°47N 114°40E **36** D4
Tutrakan *Bulgaria* 44°2N 26°40E **23** B12
Tuttle Creek L. *U.S.A.* 39°15N 96°36W **80** F5
Tuttlingen *Germany* 47°58N 8°48E **16** E5
Tutuala *E. Timor* 8°25S 127°15E **37** F7
Tutuila *Amer. Samoa* 14°19S 170°50W **59** b
Tutume *Botswana* 20°30S 27°5E **53** J5
Tuul Gol → *Mongolia* 48°30N 104°25E **32** B5
Tuva □ *Russia* 51°30N 95°0E **29** D10
Tuvalu ■ *Pac. Oc.* 8°0S 178°0E **58** H9
Tuxpan *Mexico* 20°57N 97°24W **87** C5
Tuxtla Gutiérrez *Mexico* 16°45N 93°7W **87** D6
Tuy = Tui *Spain* 42°3N 8°39W **21** A1
Tuy An *Vietnam* 13°17N 109°16E **38** F7
Tuy Duc *Vietnam* 12°15N 107°27E **39** F6
Tuy Hoa *Vietnam* 13°5N 109°10E **38** F7

Tuy Phong *Vietnam* 11°14N 108°43E **39** G7
Tuya L. *Canada* 59°7N 130°35W **70** B2
Tuyen Hoa *Vietnam* 17°50N 106°10E **38** D6
Tuyen Quang *Vietnam* 21°50N 105°10E **38** B5
Tüysärkän *Iran* 34°33N 48°27E **45** C6
Tuz Gölü *Turkey* 38°42N 33°18E **19** G5
Tūz Khurmātū *Iraq* 34°56N 44°38E **44** C5
Tuzigoot △ *U.S.A.* 34°46N 112°2W **77** J7
Tuzla *Bos.-H.* 44°34N 18°41E **23** B8
Tver *Russia* 56°55N 35°55E **18** C6
Twain *U.S.A.* 40°1N 121°3W **78** E5
Twain Harte *U.S.A.* 38°2N 120°14W **78** G6
Tweed *Canada* 44°29N 77°19W **82** B7
Tweed → *U.K.* 55°45N 2°0W **11** F6
Tweed Heads *Australia* 28°10S 153°31E **63** D5
Tweedsmuir △ *Canada* 53°0N 126°20W **70** C3
Twentynine Palms
U.S.A. 34°8N 116°3W **79** L10
Twillingate *Canada* 49°42N 54°45W **73** C9
Twin Bridges *U.S.A.* 45°33N 112°20W **76** D7
Twin Falls *Canada* 53°30N 64°32W **73** B7
Twin Falls *U.S.A.* 42°34N 114°28W **76** E6
Twin Valley *U.S.A.* 47°16N 96°16W **80** B5
Twinsburg *U.S.A.* 41°19N 81°26W **82** E3
Twitchell Res. *U.S.A.* 34°59N 120°19W **79** L6
Two Harbors *U.S.A.* 47°2N 91°40W **80** B8
Two Hills *Canada* 53°43N 111°52W **70** C6
Two Rivers *U.S.A.* 44°9N 87°34W **80** C10
Two Rocks *Australia* 31°30S 115°35E **61** F2
Twofold B. *Australia* 37°8S 149°59E **63** F4
Tyachiv *Ukraine* 48°1N 23°35E **17** D12
Tychy *Poland* 50°9N 18°59E **17** C10
Tyler *Minn., U.S.A.* 44°17N 96°8W **80** C5
Tyler *Tex., U.S.A.* 32°21N 95°18W **84** E7
Tynda *Russia* 55°10N 124°43E **29** D13
Tyndall *U.S.A.* 43°0N 97°50W **80** D5
Tyne → *U.K.* 54°59N 1°32W **12** C6
Tyne & Wear □ *U.K.* 55°6N 1°17W **12** B6
Tynemouth *U.K.* 55°1N 1°26W **12** B6
Tyre = Sūr *Lebanon* 33°19N 35°16E **46** B4
Tyrifjorden *Norway* 60°2N 10°8E **9** F14
Tyrol = Tirol □ *Austria* 47°3N 10°43E **16** E6
Tyrone *U.S.A.* 40°40N 78°14W **82** F6
Tyrone □ *U.K.* 54°38N 7°11W **10** B4
Tyrrell → *Australia* 35°26S 142°51E **63** F3
Tyrrell, L. *Australia* 35°20S 142°50E **63** F3
Tyrrell L. *Canada* 63°7N 105°27W **71** A7
Tyrrhenian Sea *Medit. S.* 40°0N 12°30E **22** E5
Tysfjorden *Norway* 68°7N 16°25E **8** B17
Tyulgan *Russia* 52°22N 56°12E **18** D10
Tyumen *Russia* 57°11N 65°29E **28** D7
Tywi → *U.K.* 51°48N 4°21W **13** F3
Tywyn *U.K.* 52°35N 4°5W **13** E3
Tzaneen *S. Africa* 23°47S 30°9E **57** C5
Tzermiado *Greece* 35°12N 25°29E **25** D7
Tzukong = Zigong
China 29°15N 104°48E **32** D5

U

U.S.A. = United States of
America ■ *N. Amer.* 37°0N 96°0W **74** C7
U.S. Virgin Is. □ *W. Indies* 18°20N 65°0W **89** e
Uanle Uen = Wanleweyne
Somali Rep. 2°37N 44°54E **47** G3
Uatumā → *Brazil* 2°26S 57°37W **92** D7
Uaupés *Brazil* 0°8S 67°5W **92** D5
Uaupés → *Brazil* 0°2N 67°16W **92** C5
Uaxactún *Guatemala* 17°25N 89°29W **88** C2
Ubá *Brazil* 21°8S 43°0W **95** A7
Ubaitaba *Brazil* 14°18S 39°20W **93** F11
Ubangi = Oubangi →
Dem. Rep. of the Congo 0°30S 17°50E **52** E3
Ubauro *Pakistan* 28°15N 69°45E **42** E3
Ubayyiḍ, W. al → *Iraq* 32°34N 43°48E **44** C4
Ube *Japan* 33°56N 131°15E **31** H5
Úbeda *Spain* 38°3N 3°23W **21** C4
Uberaba *Brazil* 19°50S 47°55W **93** G9
Uberlândia *Brazil* 19°0S 48°20W **93** G9
Ubin, Pulau *Singapore* 1°24N 103°57E **39** d
Ubly *U.S.A.* 43°42N 82°55W **82** C2
Ubolratna Res. *Thailand* 16°45N 102°30E **38** D4
Ubombo *S. Africa* 27°31S 32°4E **57** D5
Ubon Ratchathani
Thailand 15°15N 104°50E **38** E5
Ubondo
Dem. Rep. of the Congo 0°55S 25°42E **54** C2
Ubort → *Belarus* 52°6N 28°30E **17** B15
Ubud *Indonesia* 8°30S 115°16E **37** J18
Ubundu
Dem. Rep. of the Congo 0°22S 25°30E **54** C2
Ucayali → *Peru* 4°30S 73°30W **92** D4
Uchab *Namibia* 19°47S 17°42E **56** B2
Uchiura-Wan *Japan* 42°25N 140°40E **30** C10
Uchquduq *Uzbekistan* 41°50N 62°50E **28** E7
Uchur → *Russia* 58°48N 130°35E **29** D14
Ucluelet *Canada* 48°57N 125°32W **70** D3
Uda → *Russia* 54°42N 135°14E **29** D14
Udachnyy *Russia* 66°25N 112°24E **29** C12
Udagamandalam *India* 11°30N 76°44E **40** P10
Udainagar *India* 22°33N 76°13E **42** H7
Udaipur *India* 24°36N 73°44E **42** G5
Udaipur Garhi *Nepal* 27°0N 86°35E **43** F12
Udala *India* 21°35N 86°34E **43** J12
Uddevalla *Sweden* 58°21N 11°55E **9** G14
Uddjaure *Sweden* 65°56N 17°49E **8** D17
Uden *Neths.* 51°40N 5°37E **15** C5
Udgir *India* 18°25N 77°5E **40** K10
Udhampur *India* 33°0N 75°5E **43** C6
Údine *Italy* 46°3N 13°14E **22** A5
Udintsev Fracture Zone
S. Ocean 71°0S 145°0W **5** B13
Udmurtia □ *Russia* 57°30N 52°30E **18** C9
Udon Thani *Thailand* 17°29N 102°46E **38** D4
Udong *Cambodia* 11°48N 104°45E **38** G5
Udskaya Guba *Russia* 54°50N 135°45E **29** D14

Udu Pt. *Fiji* 16°9S 179°57W **59** a
Udupi *India* 13°25N 74°42E **40** N9
Udzungwa △ *Tanzania* 7°52S 36°35E **54** D4
Udzungwa Range
Tanzania 9°30S 35°10E **55** D4
Ueda *Japan* 36°24N 138°16E **31** F9
Uedineniya, Os. *Russia* 78°0N 85°0E **4** B12
Uele →
Dem. Rep. of the Congo 3°45N 24°45E **52** D4
Uelen *Russia* 66°10N 170°0W **29** C19
Uelzen *Germany* 52°57N 10°32E **16** B6
Ufa *Russia* 54°45N 55°55E **18** D10
Ufa → *Russia* 54°40N 56°0E **18** D10
Ugab → *Namibia* 20°55S 13°30E **56** C1
Ugalla → *Tanzania* 5°8S 30°42E **54** D3
Ugalla River △ *Tanzania* 5°50S 31°54E **54** D3
Uganda ■ *Africa* 2°0N 32°0E **54** B3
Ugie *S. Africa* 31°10S 28°13E **57** E4
Uglegorsk *Russia* 49°5N 142°2E **29** E15
Ugljan *Croatia* 44°12N 15°10E **16** F8
Ugolnye Kopi *Russia* 64°44N 177°42E **29** C18
Uhlenhorst *Namibia* 23°45S 17°55E **56** C2
Uhrichsville *U.S.A.* 40°24N 81°21W **82** F3
Uibhist a Deas = South Uist
U.K. 57°20N 7°15W **11** D1
Uibhist a Tuath = North Uist
U.K. 57°40N 7°15W **11** D1
Uig *U.K.* 57°35N 6°21W **11** D2
Uíge *Angola* 7°30S 14°40E **52** F2
Uiha *Tonga* 19°54S 174°25W **59** c
Uijeongbu *S. Korea* 37°44N 127°2E **35** F14
Ŭiju *N. Korea* 40°15N 124°35E **35** D13
Uinta Mts. *U.S.A.* 40°45N 110°30W **76** F8
Uis *Namibia* 21°8S 14°49E **56** C1
Uiseong *S. Korea* 36°21N 128°45E **35** F15
Uitenhage *S. Africa* 33°40S 25°28E **56** E4
Uithuizen *Neths.* 53°24N 6°41E **15** A6
Uji → *India* 32°10N 75°18E **42** C6
Ujhani *India* 28°0N 79°6E **43** F8
Uji-guntō *Japan* 31°15N 129°25E **31** J4
Ujjain *India* 23°9N 75°43E **42** H6
Ujung Pandang *Indonesia* 5°10S 119°20E **37** F5
Uka *Russia* 57°50N 162°0E **29** D17
Ukara I. *Tanzania* 1°50S 33°0E **54** C3
Uke-Shima *Japan* 28°2N 129°14E **31** K4
Ukerewe I. *Tanzania* 2°0S 33°0E **54** C3
Ukhrul *India* 25°10N 94°25E **41** G19
Ukhta *Russia* 63°34N 53°41E **18** B9
Ukiah *U.S.A.* 39°9N 123°13W **78** F3
Ukmergė *Lithuania* 55°15N 24°45E **9** J21
Ukraine ■ *Europe* 49°0N 32°0E **19** E5
Ukwi *Botswana* 23°29S 20°30E **56** C3
Ulaan-Uul *Mongolia* 44°13N 111°10E **34** B6
Ulaanbaatar *Mongolia* 47°55N 106°53E **32** B5
Ulaangom *Mongolia* 50°5N 92°10E **32** A4
Ulaanjirem *Mongolia* 45°5N 105°30E **34** B3
Ulamba
Dem. Rep. of the Congo 9°3S 23°38E **55** D1
Ulan Bator = Ulaanbaatar
Mongolia 47°55N 106°53E **32** B5
Ulan Ude *Russia* 51°45N 107°40E **29** D11
Ulaya *Morogoro, Tanzania* 7°3S 36°55E **54** D4
Ulaya *Tabora, Tanzania* 4°25S 33°30E **54** C3
Ulcinj *Montenegro* 41°58N 19°10E **23** D8
Ule älv = Oulujoki →
Finland 65°1N 25°30E **8** D21
Ule träsk = Oulujärvi
Finland 64°25N 27°15E **8** D22
Uleåborg = Oulu *Finland* 65°1N 25°29E **8** D21
Ulefoss *Norway* 59°17N 9°16E **9** G13
Ulhasnagar *India* 19°15N 73°10E **40** K8
Uliastay *Mongolia* 47°56N 97°28E **32** B4
Uljin *S. Korea* 36°59N 129°24E **35** F15
Ulladulla *Australia* 35°21S 150°29E **63** F5
Ullapool *U.K.* 57°54N 5°9W **11** D3
Ulleungdo *S. Korea* 37°30N 130°30E **31** F5
Ullswater *Canada* 45°12N 79°29W **82** A5
Ullswater *U.K.* 54°34N 2°52W **12** C5
Ulm *Germany* 48°23N 9°58E **16** D5
Ulmarra *Australia* 29°37S 153°4E **63** D5
Ulonguè *Mozam.* 14°37S 34°19E **55** E3
Ulricehamn *Sweden* 57°46N 13°26E **9** H15
Ulsan *S. Korea* 35°20N 129°15E **35** G15
Ulsta *U.K.* 60°30N 1°9W **11** A7
Ulster □ *U.K.* 54°35N 6°30W **10** B5
Ulubat Gölü *Turkey* 40°9N 28°35E **23** D13
Uludağ *Turkey* 40°4N 29°13E **23** D13
Uluguru Mts. *Tanzania* 7°15S 37°40E **54** D4
Ulungur He → *China* 47°1N 87°24E **32** B3
Ulungur Hu *China* 47°20N 87°10E **32** B3
Uluru *Australia* 25°23S 131°5E **61** E5
Uluru-Kata Tjuta △
Australia 25°19S 131°1E **61** E5
Ulutau *Kazakhstan* 48°39N 67°1E **28** E7
Uluwatu *Indonesia* 8°50S 115°5E **37** K18
Ulva *U.K.* 56°29N 6°13W **11** E2
Ulverston *U.K.* 54°13N 3°5W **12** C4
Ulverstone *Australia* 41°11S 146°11E **63** G4
Ulya *Russia* 59°10N 142°0E **29** D15
Ulyanovsk *Russia* 54°20N 48°25E **18** D8
Ulyasutay = Uliastay
Mongolia 47°56N 97°28E **32** B4
Ulysses *Kans., U.S.A.* 37°35N 101°22W **80** G3
Ulysses *Pa., U.S.A.* 41°54N 77°46W **82** E7
Ulysses, Mt. *Canada* 57°20N 124°5W **70** B4
Umala *Bolivia* 17°25S 68°5W **92** G5
'Umān = Oman ■ *Asia* 23°0N 58°0E **47** C6
Uman *Ukraine* 48°40N 30°12E **17** D16
Umaria *India* 23°35N 80°50E **43** H9
Umarkot *Pakistan* 25°15N 69°40E **42** G3
Umarpada *India* 21°27N 73°30E **42** J5
Umatilla *U.S.A.* 45°55N 119°21W **76** D4
Umba *Russia* 66°42N 34°11E **18** A5
Umbagog L., U.S.A. 44°46N 71°3W **83** B13
Umbakumba *Australia* 13°47S 136°50E **62** A2
Umbrella Mts. *N.Z.* 45°35S 169°5E **59** F2

Umeå *Sweden* 63°45N 20°20E **8** E19
Umeälven → *Sweden* 63°45N 20°20E **8** E19
Umera *Indonesia* 0°12S 129°37E **37** E7
Umfuli → *Zimbabwe* 17°30S 29°23E **55** F2
Umgusa *Zimbabwe* 19°29S 27°52E **55** F2
Umgwenya → *Mozam.* 25°14S 32°18E **57** D5
Umiujaq *Canada* 56°33N 76°33W **72** A4
Umkomaas *S. Africa* 30°13S 30°48E **57** E5
Umlazi *S. Africa* 29°59S 30°54E **53** L6
Umm ad Daraj, J. *Jordan* 32°18N 35°48E **46** C4
Umm al Qaywayn
U.A.E. 25°30N 55°35E **45** E7
Umm al Qittayn *Jordan* 32°18N 36°40E **46** C5
Umm Bāb *Qatar* 25°12N 50°48E **45** E6
Umm Durman = Omdurmân
Sudan 15°40N 32°28E **51** E12
Umm el Fahm *Israel* 32°31N 35°9E **46** C4
Umm el Qadr → *Sudan* 13°33N 26°35E **51** F11
Umm Lajj *Si. Arabia* 25°0N 37°23E **44** E3
Umm Qasr *Iraq* 30°1N 47°58E **44** D5
Umm Ruwaba *Sudan* 12°50N 31°20E **51** F12
Umnak I. *U.S.A.* 53°15N 168°20W **74** a
Umniati → *Zimbabwe* 16°49S 28°45E **55** F2
Umpqua → *U.S.A.* 43°40N 124°12W **76** E1
Umreth *India* 22°41N 73°4E **42** H5
Umtata = Mthatha
S. Africa 31°36S 28°49E **57** E4
Umuarama *Brazil* 23°45S 53°20W **95** A5
Umvukwe Ra. *Zimbabwe* 16°45S 30°45E **55** F3
Umzimvubu *S. Africa* 31°38S 29°33E **57** E4
Umzingwane →
Zimbabwe 22°12S 29°56E **55** G2
Umzinto = eMuziwezinto
S. Africa 30°15S 30°45E **57** E5
Una *India* 20°46N 71°8E **42** J4
Una → *Bos.-H.* 45°0N 16°20E **16** F9
Unadilla *U.S.A.* 42°20N 75°19W **83** D9
Unalakleet *U.S.A.* 63°52N 160°47W **74** a
Unalaska *U.S.A.* 53°53N 166°32W **74** a
Unalaska I. *U.S.A.* 53°35N 166°50W **74** a
'Unayzah *Si. Arabia* 26°6N 43°58E **44** E4
'Unayzah, J. *Asia* 32°12N 39°18E **44** C3
Uncía *Bolivia* 18°25S 66°40W **92** G5
Uncompahgre Peak
U.S.A. 38°4N 107°28W **76** G10
Uncompahgre Plateau
U.S.A. 38°20N 108°15W **76** G9
Undara Volcanic △
Australia 18°14S 144°41E **62** B3
Underbool *Australia* 35°10S 141°51E **63** F3
Underwood *Canada* 44°18N 81°29W **82** B3
Ungarie *Australia* 33°38S 146°56E **63** E4
Ungarra *Australia* 34°12S 136°2E **63** E2
Ungava, Pén. d' *Canada* 60°0N 74°0W **69** C12
Ungava B. *Canada* 59°30N 67°30W **69** D13
Ungeny = Ungheni
Moldova 47°11N 27°51E **17** E14
Unggi *N. Korea* 42°16N 130°28E **35** C16
Ungheni *Moldova* 47°11N 27°51E **17** E14
Ungwana B. *Kenya* 2°45S 40°20E **54** C5
União da Vitória *Brazil* 26°13S 51°5W **95** B5
Unimak I. *U.S.A.* 54°45N 164°0W **74** a
Union *Miss., U.S.A.* 32°34N 89°7W **85** E10
Union *Mo., U.S.A.* 38°27N 91°0W **80** F8
Union *S.C., U.S.A.* 34°43N 81°37W **85** D14
Union City *Calif., U.S.A.* 37°36N 122°1W **78** H4
Union City *N.J., U.S.A.* 40°45N 74°2W **83** F10
Union City *Pa., U.S.A.* 41°54N 79°51W **82** E5
Union City *Tenn., U.S.A.* 36°26N 89°3W **85** C10
Union Dale *U.S.A.* 41°43N 75°29W **83** E9
Union Gap *U.S.A.* 46°33N 120°28W **76** C3
Union Springs *Ala.,
U.S.A.* 32°9N 85°43W **85** E12
Union Springs *N.Y.,
U.S.A.* 42°50N 76°41W **83** D8
Uniondale *S. Africa* 33°39S 23°7E **56** E3
Uniontown *U.S.A.* 39°54N 79°44W **81** F14
Unionville *U.S.A.* 40°29N 93°1W **80** E7
United Arab Emirates ■
Asia 23°50N 54°0E **45** F7
United Kingdom ■ *Europe* 53°0N 2°0W **14** E6
United States of America ■
N. Amer. 37°0N 96°0W **74** C7
Unity *Canada* 52°30N 109°5W **71** C7
University Park
U.S.A. 32°17N 106°45W **77** K10
University Place *U.S.A.* 47°14N 122°33W **78** C4
Unjha *India* 23°46N 72°24E **42** H5
Unnao *India* 26°35N 80°30E **43** F9
Unsengedsi → *Zimbabwe* 15°43S 31°14E **55** F3
Unst *U.K.* 60°44N 0°53W **11** A8
Unuk → *Canada* 56°5N 131°3W **70** B2
Unzen-Amakusa △
Japan 32°15N 130°10E **31** H5
Uozu *Japan* 36°48N 137°24E **31** F8
Upata *Venezuela* 8°1N 62°24W **92** B6
Upemba, L.
Dem. Rep. of the Congo 8°30S 26°20E **55** D2
Upemba △
Dem. Rep. of the Congo 9°0S 26°35E **55** D2
Upernavik *Greenland* 72°49N 56°20W **4** B5
Upington *S. Africa* 28°25S 21°15E **56** D3
Upleta *India* 21°46N 70°16E **42** J4
'Upolu *Samoa* 13°58S 172°0W **59** b
Upper Alkali L. *U.S.A.* 41°47N 120°8W **76** F3
Upper Arrow L. *Canada* 50°30N 117°50W **70** C5
Upper Darby *U.S.A.* 39°55N 75°16W **81** F16
Upper Foster L. *Canada* 56°47N 105°20W **71** B7
Upper Hutt *N.Z.* 41°8S 175°5E **59** D5
Upper Klamath L.
U.S.A. 42°25N 121°55W **76** E3
Upper Lake *U.S.A.* 39°10N 122°54W **78** F4
Upper Liard *Canada* 60°3N 128°54W **70** A3
Upper Manzanilla
Trin. & Tob. 10°31N 61°4W **93** K15
Upper Missouri Breaks △
U.S.A. 47°50N 109°55W **76** C9

Upper Musquodoboit
　Canada　45°10N 62°58W **73** C7
Upper Red L. *U.S.A.*　48°8N 94°45W **80** A6
Upper Sandusky
　U.S.A.　40°50N 83°17W **81** E12
Upper Volta = Burkina Faso ■
　Africa　12°0N 1°0W **50** F5
Uppland *Sweden*　59°59N 17°48E **9** G17
Uppsala *Sweden*　59°53N 17°38E **9** G17
Upshi *India*　33°48N 77°52E **43** C7
Upstart, C. *Australia*　19°41S 147°45E **62** B4
Upton *U.S.A.*　46°N 104°38W **76** D11
Uqsuqtuuq = Gjoa Haven
　Canada　68°38N 95°53W **68** C10
Ur *Iraq*　30°55N 46°25E **44** D5
Urad Qianqi *China*　40°40N 108°30E **34** D5
Urakawa *Japan*　42°9N 142°47E **30** C11
Ural = Uralskiy □ *Russia*　64°0N 70°0E **28** C7
Ural = Zhayyq ➜
　Kazakhstan　47°0N 51°48E **19** E9
Ural *Australia*　33°21S 146°12E **63** E4
Ural Mts. = Uralskie Gory
　Eurasia　60°0N 59°0E **18** C10
Uralla *Australia*　30°37S 151°29E **63** E5
Uralsk = Oral *Kazakhstan* 51°20N 51°20E **19** D9
Uralskie Gory *Eurasia*　60°0N 59°0E **18** C10
Uralskiy □ *Russia*　64°0N 70°0E **28** C7
Urambo *Tanzania*　5°4S 32°0E **54** D3
Urandangi *Australia*　21°32S 138°14E **62** C2
Uranium City *Canada*　59°34N 108°37W **71** B7
Urapuntja = Utopia
　Australia　22°14S 134°33E **62** C1
Uraricoera ➜ *Brazil*　3°2N 60°30W **92** C6
Urasoe *Japan*　26°15N 127°43E **31** L3
Urawa = Saitama *Japan* 35°54N 139°38E **31** G9
Uray *Russia*　60°5N 65°15E **28** C7
'Uray'irah *Si. Arabia*　25°57N 48°53E **45** E6
Urbana *Ill., U.S.A.*　40°7N 88°12W **80** E9
Urbana *Ohio, U.S.A.*　40°7N 83°45W **81** E12
Urbandale *U.S.A.*　41°38N 93°43W **80** E7
Urbino *Italy*　43°43N 12°38E **22** C5
Urbión, Picos de *Spain*　42°1N 2°52W **21** A4
Urcos *Peru*　13°40S 71°38W **92** F4
Urdinarrain *Argentina* 32°37S 58°52W **94** C4
Ure ➜ *U.K.*　54°5N 1°20W **12** C6
Urengoy *Russia*　65°58N 78°22E **28** C8
Ures *Mexico*　29°26N 110°24W **86** B2
Urewera △ *N.Z.*　38°29S 177°7E **59** C6
Urfa = Şanlıurfa *Turkey*　37°12N 38°50E **44** B3
Urganch *Uzbekistan*　41°40N 60°41E **28** E7
Urgench = Urganch
　Uzbekistan　41°40N 60°41E **28** E7
Ürgüp *Turkey*　38°38N 34°56E **44** B2
Uri *India*　34°8N 74°2E **43** B6
Uribia *Colombia*　11°43N 72°16W **92** A4
Uriondo *Bolivia*　21°41S 64°41W **94** A3
Urique *Mexico*　27°13N 107°55W **86** B3
Urique ➜ *Mexico*　26°29N 107°58W **86** B3
Urk *Neths.*　52°39N 5°36E **15** B5
Urla *Turkey*　38°20N 26°47E **23** E12
Urmia = Orūmīyeh *Iran*　37°40N 45°0E **44** B5
Uroševac *Serbia*　42°23N 21°10E **23** C9
Uroyan, Montanas de
　Puerto Rico　18°12N 67°0W **89** d
Uruaçu *Brazil*　14°30S 49°10W **93** F9
Uruapan *Mexico*　19°24N 102°3W **86** D4
Urubamba ➜ *Peru*　10°43S 73°48W **92** F4
Urucará *Brazil*　2°32S 57°45W **92** D7
Uruçuí *Brazil*　7°20S 44°28W **93** E10
Uruguai ➜ *Brazil*　26°0S 53°30W **95** B5
Uruguaiana *Brazil*　29°50S 57°0W **94** B4
Uruguay ■ *S. Amer.*　32°30S 56°30W **94** C4
Uruguay ➜ *S. Amer.*　34°12S 58°18W **94** C4
Urumchi = Ürümqi
　China　43°45N 87°45E **32** B3
Ürümqi *China*　43°45N 87°45E **32** B3
Urup, Ostrov *Russia*　46°0N 151°0E **29** E16
Ürzhar *Kazakhstan*　47°5N 81°38E **28** E9
Usa ➜ *Russia*　66°16N 59°49E **18** A10
Uşak *Turkey*　38°43N 29°28E **19** G4
Usakos *Namibia*　21°54S 15°31E **56** C2
Usedom *Germany*　53°55N 14°2E **16** B8
Useless Loop *Australia*　26°8S 113°23E **61** E1
Ushakova, Ostrov *Russia*　82°0N 80°0E **29** A8
Ushant = Ouessant, Î. d'
　France　48°28N 5°6W **20** B1
Ushashi *Tanzania*　1°59S 33°57E **54** C3
'Ushayrah *Si. Arabia*　25°35N 45°47E **44** E5
Ushibuka *Japan*　32°11N 130°1E **31** H5
Üshtöbe *Kazakhstan*　45°16N 78°0E **28** E8
Ushuaia *Argentina*　54°50S 68°23W **96** G3
Ushumun *Russia*　52°47N 126°32E **29** D13
Usinsk *Russia*　65°57N 57°27E **28** C6
Usk *Canada*　54°38N 128°26W **70** C3
Usk ➜ *U.K.*　51°33N 2°58W **13** F5
Uska *India*　27°12N 83°7E **43** F10
Usman *Russia*　52°5N 39°48E **18** D6
Usoke *Tanzania*　5°8S 32°24E **54** D3
Usolye-Sibirskoye
　Russia　52°48N 103°40E **29** D11
Uspallata, P. de
　Argentina　32°37S 69°22W **94** C2
Ussuriysk *Russia*　43°48N 131°59E **30** C5
Ussurka *Russia*　45°12N 133°31E **30** B6
Ust-Chaun *Russia*　68°47N 170°30E **29** C18
Ust-Ilimsk *Russia*　58°3N 102°39E **29** D11
Ust-Ishim *Russia*　57°45N 71°10E **28** D8
Ust-Kamchatsk *Russia* 56°10N 162°28E **29** D17
Ust-Kamenogorsk = Öskemen
　Kazakhstan　50°0N 82°36E **28** E9
Ust-Khayryuzovo
　Russia　57°15N 156°45E **29** D16
Ust-Kut *Russia*　56°50N 105°42E **29** D11
Ust-Kuyga *Russia*　70°1N 135°43E **29** B14
Ust-Maya *Russia*　60°30N 134°28E **29** C14
Ust-Mil *Russia*　59°40N 133°11E **29** D14
Ust-Nera *Russia*　64°35N 143°15E **29** C15

Ust-Nyukzha *Russia*　56°34N 121°37E **29** D13
Ust-Olenek *Russia*　73°0N 120°5E **29** B12
Ust-Omchug *Russia*　61°9N 149°38E **29** C15
Ust-Port *Russia*　69°40N 84°26E **28** C9
Ust-Tsilma *Russia*　65°28N 52°11E **18** A9
Ust-Urt = Ustyurt Plateau
　Asia　44°0N 55°0E **28** E6
Ust-Usa *Russia*　66°2N 56°57E **18** A10
Ust-Vorkuta *Russia*　67°24N 64°0E **18** A11
Ústí nad Labem *Czech Rep.* 50°41N 14°3E **16** C8
Ústica *Italy*　38°42N 13°11E **22** E5
Ustinov = Izhevsk
　Russia　56°51N 53°14E **18** C9
Ustyurt Plateau *Asia*　44°0N 55°0E **28** E6
Usu *China*　44°27N 84°40E **32** B3
Usuki *Japan*　33°8N 131°49E **31** H5
Usulután *El Salv.*　13°25N 88°28W **88** D2
Usumacinta ➜ *Mexico* 18°24N 92°38W **87** D6
Usumbura = Bujumbura
　Burundi　3°16S 29°18E **54** C2
Usure *Tanzania*　4°40S 34°22E **54** C3
Usutuo ➜ *Mozam.*　26°48S 32°7E **57** D5
Uta *Indonesia*　4°33S 136°0E **37** E9
Utah □ *U.S.A.*　39°20N 111°30W **76** G8
Utah L. *U.S.A.*　40°12N 111°48W **76** F8
Utara, Selat *Malaysia*　5°28N 100°20E **39** c
Utarni *India*　26°5N 71°58E **42** F4
Utatlan *Guatemala*　15°2N 91°11W **88** C1
Ute Creek ➜ *U.S.A.* 35°21N 103°50W **77** J12
Utena *Lithuania*　55°27N 25°40E **9** J21
Utete *Tanzania*　8°0S 38°45E **54** D4
Uthai Thani *Thailand* 15°22N 100°3E **38** E3
Uthal *Pakistan*　25°44N 66°40E **42** G2
Utiariti *Brazil*　13°0S 58°10W **92** F7
Utica *N.Y., U.S.A.*　43°6N 75°14W **83** C9
Utica *Ohio, U.S.A.*　40°14N 82°27W **82** F2
Utikuma L. *Canada*　55°50N 115°30W **70** B5
Utila *Honduras*　16°6N 86°56W **88** C2
Utopia *Australia*　22°14S 134°33E **62** C1
Utrecht *Neths.*　52°5N 5°8E **15** B5
Utrecht □ *S. Africa*　27°38S 30°20E **57** D5
Utrecht □ *Neths.*　52°6N 5°7E **15** B5
Utrera *Spain*　37°12N 5°48W **21** D3
Utsjoki ➜ *Finland*　69°51N 26°59E **8** B22
Utsunomiya *Japan*　36°30N 139°50E **31** F9
Uttar Pradesh □ *India*　27°0N 80°0E **43** F9
Uttaradit *Thailand*　17°36N 100°5E **38** D3
Uttarakhand □ *India*　30°0N 79°30E **43** D8
Utterson *Canada*　45°12N 79°19W **82** A5
Uttoxeter *U.K.*　52°54N 1°52W **12** E6
Utuado *Puerto Rico*　18°16N 66°42W **89** d
Uummannaq *Avannaarsua,*
　Greenland　77°28N 69°13W **4** B4
Uummannaq *Kitaa,*
　Greenland　70°58N 52°17W **4** B5
Uummannarsuaq = Nunap Isua
　Greenland　59°48N 43°55W **66** D15
Uusikaarlepyy *Finland* 63°32N 22°31E **8** E20
Uusikaupunki *Finland*　60°47N 21°25E **8** F19
Uva *Russia*　56°59N 52°13E **18** C9
Uvalde *U.S.A.*　29°13N 99°47W **84** G5
Uvat *Russia*　59°5N 68°50E **28** D7
Uvinza *Tanzania*　5°5S 30°24E **54** D3
Uvira *Dem. Rep. of the Congo* 3°22S 29°3E **54** C2
Uvs Nuur *Mongolia*　50°20N 92°30E **32** A4
'Uwairidh, Ḥarrat al
　Si. Arabia　26°50N 38°0E **44** E3
Uwajima *Japan*　33°10N 132°35E **31** H6
Uwanda △ *Tanzania*　7°46S 32°0E **54** D3
Uweinat, Jebel *Sudan*　21°54N 24°58E **51** D10
Uxbridge *Canada*　44°6N 79°7W **82** B5
Uxin Qi *China*　38°50N 109°5E **34** E5
Uxmal *Mexico*　20°22N 89°46W **87** C7
Üydzin *Mongolia*　44°9N 107°0E **34** B5
Uyo *Nigeria*　5°1N 7°53E **50** G7
Uyûn Mûsa *Egypt*　29°53N 32°40E **46** F1
Uyuni *Bolivia*　20°28S 66°47W **92** H5
Uzbekistan ■ *Asia*　41°30N 65°0E **28** E7
Uzboy ➜ *Turkmenistan* 39°30N 55°0E **45** B7
Uzen *Kazakhstan*　43°29N 52°54E **19** F9
Uzen, Bolshoi = Uzen, Mal ➜
　Kazakhstan　49°4N 49°44E **19** E8
Uzen, Mal ➜ *Kazakhstan* 49°4N 49°44E **19** E8
Uzerche *France*　45°25N 1°34E **20** D4
Uzh ➜ *Ukraine*　51°15N 30°12E **17** C16
Uzhgorod = Uzhhorod
　Ukraine　48°36N 22°18E **17** D12
Uzhhorod *Ukraine*　48°36N 22°18E **17** D12
Užice *Serbia*　43°55N 19°50E **23** C8
Uzunköprü *Turkey*　41°16N 26°43E **23** D12

V

Vaal ➜ *S. Africa*　29°4S 23°38E **56** D3
Vaal Dam *S. Africa*　27°0S 28°14E **57** D4
Vaalbos △ *S. Africa*　28°22S 24°20E **56** D3
Vaalwater *S. Africa*　24°15S 28°8E **57** C4
Vaasa *Finland*　63°6N 21°38E **8** E19
Vác *Hungary*　47°49N 19°10E **17** E10
Vacaria *Brazil*　28°31S 50°52W **95** B5
Vacata *Fiji*　17°15S 179°31W **59** a
Vacaville *U.S.A.*　38°21N 121°59W **78** G5
Vach = Vakh ➜ *Russia*　60°45N 76°45E **28** C8
Vache, Î. à *Haiti*　18°2N 73°35W **89** C5
Vacoas *Mauritius*　20°18S 57°29E **53** d
Vadnagar *India*　23°47N 72°40E **42** H5
Vadodara *India*　22°20N 73°10E **42** H5
Vadsø *Norway*　70°3N 29°50E **8** A23
Vaduz *Liech.*　47°8N 9°31E **20** C8
Værøy *Norway*　67°40N 12°40E **8** C15
Vágar *Færoe Is.*　62°5N 7°15W **8** E9
Vagia, Akra *Greece*　36°15N 28°11E **25** C10
Vågsfjorden *Norway*　68°50N 16°50E **8** B17
Váh ➜ *Slovak Rep.*　47°43N 18°7E **17** D9
Vahsel B. *Antarctica*　75°0S 35°0W **5** D1

Váhtjer = Gällivare
　Sweden　67°9N 20°40E **8** C19
Vaï *Greece*　35°15N 26°18E **25** D8
Vaihiria, L. *Tahiti*　17°40S 149°25W **59** d
Vail *U.S.A.*　39°40N 106°20W **74** C5
Vairao *Tahiti*　17°47S 149°17W **59** d
Vaisali *India*　26°28N 78°53E **43** f
Vaitogi *Amer. Samoa*　14°24S 170°44W **59** b
Vakh ➜ *Russia*　60°45N 76°45E **28** C8
Val-d'Or *Canada*　48°7N 77°47W **72** C4
Val Marie *Canada*　49°15N 107°45W **71** D7
Valaam *Russia*　61°22N 30°57E **8** F24
Valahia *Romania*　44°35N 25°0E **17** F13
Valandovo *Macedonia*　41°19N 22°34E **23** D10
Valatie *U.S.A.*　42°24N 73°40W **83** D11
Valchета *Argentina*　40°40S 66°8W **96** E3
Valdai Hills = Valdayskaya
　Vozvyshennost *Russia* 57°0N 33°30E **18** C5
Valdayskaya Vozvyshennost
　Russia　57°0N 33°30E **18** C5
Valdepeñas *Spain*　38°43N 3°25W **21** C4
Valdés, Pen. *Argentina*　42°30S 63°45W **96** E4
Valdez *U.S.A.*　61°7N 146°16W **68** C5
Valdivia *Chile*　39°50S 73°14W **96** D2
Valdivia Abyssal Plain
　S. Ocean　62°30S 70°0E **5** C6
Valdosta *U.S.A.*　30°50N 83°17W **85** F13
Valdres *Norway*　61°5N 9°5E **8** F13
Vale *U.S.A.*　43°59N 117°15W **76** E5
Vale of Glamorgan □
　U.K.　51°28N 3°25W **13** F4
Valemount *Canada*　52°50N 119°15W **70** C5
Valença *Brazil*　13°20S 39°5W **93** F11
Valença do Piauí *Brazil* 6°20S 41°45W **93** E10
Valence *France*　44°57N 4°54E **20** D6
Valencia *Spain*　39°27N 0°23W **21** C5
Valencia *Trin. & Tob.*　10°39N 61°11W **93** K15
Valencia *U.S.A.*　34°48N 106°43W **77** J10
Valencia *Venezuela*　10°11N 68°0W **92** A5
Valencia □ *Spain*　39°20N 0°40W **21** C5
Valencia, G. de *Spain*　39°30N 0°20E **21** C6
Valencia de Alcántara
　Spain　39°25N 7°14W **21** C2
Valencia I. *Ireland*　51°54N 10°22W **10** E1
Valenciennes *France*　50°20N 3°34E **20** A5
Valentim, Sa. do *Brazil* 6°0S 43°30W **93** E10
Valentin *Russia*　43°8N 134°17E **30** C7
Valentine *Nebr., U.S.A.* 42°52N 100°33W **80** D3
Valentine *Tex., U.S.A.* 30°35N 104°30W **84** F2
Valera *Venezuela*　9°19N 70°37W **92** B4
Valga *Estonia*　57°47N 26°2E **9** H22
Valier *U.S.A.*　48°18N 112°16W **76** B7
Valjevo *Serbia*　44°18N 19°53E **23** B8
Valka *Latvia*　57°46N 26°3E **9** H22
Valkeakoski *Finland*　61°16N 24°2E **8** F21
Valkenswaard *Neths.*　51°21N 5°29E **15** C5
Vall de Uxó = La Vall d'Uixó
　Spain　39°49N 0°15W **21** C5
Valladolid *Mexico*　20°41N 88°12W **87** C7
Valladolid *Spain*　41°38N 4°43W **21** B3
Valldemossa *Spain*　39°43N 2°37E **24** B9
Valle de la Pascua
　Venezuela　9°13N 66°0W **92** B5
Valle de las Palmas
　Mexico　32°20N 116°43W **79** N10
Valle de Santiago
　Mexico　20°23N 101°12W **86** C4
Valle de Zaragoza
　Mexico　27°25N 105°50W **86** B3
Valle Fértil, Sierra del
　Argentina　30°20S 68°0W **94** C2
Valle Gran Rey *Canary Is.* 28°5N 17°20W **24** F2
Valle Hermoso *Mexico* 25°35N 97°40W **87** B5
Valle Nacional *Mexico* 17°47N 96°18W **87** D5
Valledupar *Colombia*　10°29N 73°15W **92** A4
Vallehermoso *Canary Is.* 28°10N 17°15W **24** F2
Vallejo *U.S.A.*　38°7N 122°14W **78** G4
Vallenar *Chile*　28°30S 70°50W **94** B1
Valletta *Malta*　35°54N 14°31E **25** D2
Valley Center *U.S.A.*　33°13N 117°2W **79** M9
Valley City *U.S.A.*　46°55N 98°0W **80** B4
Valley Falls *Oreg.,*
　U.S.A.　42°29N 120°17W **76** E3
Valley Falls *R.I., U.S.A.* 41°54N 71°24W **83** E13
Valley of Flowers △
　India　30°50N 79°40E **43** D8
Valley Springs *U.S.A.* 38°12N 120°50W **78** G6
Valley View *U.S.A.*　40°39N 76°33W **83** F8
Valley Wells *U.S.A.*　35°27N 115°46W **79** K11
Valleyview *Canada*　55°5N 117°17W **70** B5
Vallimanca, Arroyo
　Argentina　35°40S 59°10W **94** D4
Valls *Spain*　41°18N 1°15E **21** B6
Valmiera *Latvia*　57°37N 25°29E **9** H21
Valognes *France*　49°30N 1°28W **20** B3
Valona = Vlorë *Albania* 40°32N 19°28E **23** D8
Valozhyn *Belarus*　54°3N 26°30E **17** A14
Valparaíso *Chile*　33°2S 71°40W **94** C1
Valparaíso *Mexico*　22°46N 103°34W **86** C4
Valparaíso *U.S.A.*　41°28N 87°4W **80** E10
Valparaíso □ *Chile*　33°2S 71°40W **94** C1
Vals ➜ *S. Africa*　27°23S 26°30E **56** D4
Vals, Tanjung *Indonesia* 8°26S 137°25E **37** F9
Valsad *India*　20°40N 72°58E **40** J8
Valverde *Canary Is.*　27°48N 17°55W **24** G2
Valverde del Camino
　Spain　37°35N 6°47W **21** D2
Vammala *Finland*　61°20N 22°54E **8** F20
Vamos *Greece*　35°24N 24°13E **25** D6
Van *Turkey*　38°30N 43°20E **44** B4
Van, L. = Van Gölü
　Turkey　38°30N 43°0E **44** B4
Van Alstyne *U.S.A.*　33°25N 96°35W **84** E6
Van Blommestein Meer
　Suriname　4°45N 55°5W **93** C7
Van Buren *Canada*　47°10N 67°55W **73** C6
Van Buren *Ark., U.S.A.* 35°26N 94°21W **84** D7

Van Buren *Maine,*
　U.S.A.　47°10N 67°58W **81** B20
Van Buren *Mo., U.S.A.* 37°0N 91°1W **80** G8
Van Canh *Vietnam*　13°37N 109°0E **38** F7
Van Diemen, C. *N. Terr.,*
　Australia　11°9S 130°24E **60** B5
Van Diemen, C. *Queens.,*
　Australia　16°30S 139°46E **62** B2
Van Diemen G. *Australia* 11°45S 132°0E **60** B5
Van Gölü *Turkey*　38°30N 43°0E **44** B4
Van Horn *U.S.A.*　31°3N 104°50W **84** F2
Van Ninh *Vietnam*　12°42N 109°14E **38** F7
Van Rees, Pegunungan
　Indonesia　2°35S 138°15E **37** E9
Van Wert *U.S.A.*　40°52N 84°35W **81** E11
Van Yen *Vietnam*　21°4N 104°42E **38** B5
Vanadzor *Armenia*　40°48N 44°30E **19** F7
Vanavara *Russia*　60°22N 102°16E **29** C11
Vancouver *Canada*　49°15N 123°7W **78** A3
Vancouver *U.S.A.*　45°38N 122°40W **78** E4
Vancouver, C. *Australia* 35°2S 118°11E **61** G2
Vancouver I. *Canada*　49°50N 126°0W **78** B2
Vancouver Int. ✈ (YVR)
　Canada　49°10N 123°10W **78** A3
Vanda = Vantaa *Finland* 60°18N 24°56E **9** F21
Vandalia *Ill., U.S.A.*　38°58N 89°6W **80** F9
Vandalia *Mo., U.S.A.*　39°19N 91°29W **80** F8
Vandenberg Village
　U.S.A.　34°43N 120°28W **79** L6
Vanderbijlpark *S. Africa* 26°42S 27°54E **57** D4
Vandergrift *U.S.A.*　40°36N 79°34W **82** F5
Vanderhoof *Canada*　54°0N 124°0W **70** C4
Vanderkloof Dam
　S. Africa　30°4S 24°40E **56** E3
Vanderlin I. *Australia*　15°44S 137°2E **62** B2
Vänern *Sweden*　58°47N 13°30E **9** G15
Vänersborg *Sweden*　58°26N 12°19E **9** G15
Vang Vieng *Laos*　18°58N 102°32E **38** C4
Vanga *Kenya*　4°35S 39°12E **54** C4
Vangaindrano *Madag.*　23°21S 47°36E **57** C8
Vanguard *Canada*　49°55N 107°20W **71** D7
Vanino *Russia*　48°50N 140°5E **29** E15
Vankleek Hill *Canada*　45°32N 74°40W **83** A10
Vännäs *Sweden*　63°58N 19°48E **8** E18
Vannes *France*　47°40N 2°47W **20** C2
Vannøya *Norway*　70°6N 19°50E **8** A18
Vanrhynsdorp *S. Africa* 31°36S 18°44E **56** E2
Vansbro *Sweden*　60°32N 14°15E **9** F16
Vansittart B. *Australia* 14°3S 126°17E **60** B4
Vantaa *Finland*　60°18N 24°56E **9** F21
Vanua Balavu *Fiji*　17°12S 178°55W **59** a
Vanua Levu *Fiji*　16°33S 179°15E **59** a
Vanua Vatu *Fiji*　18°22S 179°15W **59** a
Vanuatu ■ *Pac. Oc.*　15°0S 168°0E **58** C9
Vanwyksvlei *S. Africa*　30°18S 21°49E **56** E3
Vanzylsrus *S. Africa*　26°52S 22°4E **56** D3
Vapnyarka *Ukraine*　48°32N 28°45E **17** D15
Var ➜ *France*　43°39N 7°12E **20** E7
Varāmīn *Iran*　35°20N 51°45E **45** C6
Varāmīn *Iran*　35°18N 51°35E **45** B6
Varanasi *India*　25°22N 83°0E **43** G10
Varangerfjorden *Norway* 70°3N 29°25E **8** A23
Varangerhalvøya
　Norway　70°25N 29°30E **8** A23
Varaždin *Croatia*　46°20N 16°20E **16** E9
Varberg *Sweden*　57°6N 12°20E **9** H15
Vardak □ *Afghan.*　34°0N 68°0E **40** B6
Vardar = Axios ➜
　Greece　40°57N 22°35E **23** D10
Varde *Denmark*　55°38N 8°29E **9** J13
Vardø *Norway*　70°23N 31°5E **8** A24
Varella, Mui *Vietnam*　12°54N 109°26E **38** F7
Varèna *Lithuania*　54°12N 24°30E **9** J21
Varese *Italy*　45°48N 8°50E **20** D8
Varginha *Brazil*　21°33S 45°25W **95** A6
Varillas *Chile*　24°0S 70°10W **94** A1
Varkaus *Finland*　62°19N 27°50E **8** E22
Varna *Bulgaria*　43°13N 27°56E **23** C12
Värnamo *Sweden*　57°10N 14°3E **9** H16
Vars *Canada*　45°21N 75°21W **83** A9
Varysburg *U.S.A.*　42°46N 78°19W **82** D6
Varzaneh *Iran*　32°25N 52°40E **45** C7
Vasa = Vaasa *Finland* 63°6N 21°38E **8** E19
Vasa Barris ➜ *Brazil* 11°10S 37°10W **93** F11
Vascongadas = País Vasco □
　Spain　42°50N 2°45W **21** A4
Vasht = Khāsh *Iran* 28°15N 61°15E **45** D9
Vasilevichi *Belarus*　52°15N 29°50E **17** B15
Vasilkov = Vasylkiv
　Ukraine　50°7N 30°15E **17** C16
Vaslui *Romania*　46°38N 27°42E **17** E14
Vassar *Canada*　49°10N 95°55W **71** D9
Vassar *U.S.A.*　43°22N 83°35W **81** D12
Västerås *Sweden*　59°37N 16°38E **9** G17
Västerbotten *Sweden*　64°36N 20°4E **8** D19
Västerdalälven ➜ *Sweden* 60°30N 14°7E **8** F16
Västervik *Sweden*　57°43N 16°33E **9** H17
Västmanland *Sweden*　59°45N 16°20E **9** G17
Vasto *Italy*　42°8N 14°40E **22** C6
Vasylkiv *Ukraine*　50°7N 30°15E **17** C16
Vatersay *U.K.*　56°55N 7°32W **11** E1
Vati *Greece*　35°57N 27°53E **25** D9
Vatican City ■ *Europe* 41°54N 12°27E **22** D5
Vatili *Cyprus*　35°6N 33°40E **25** D12
Vatiu = Atiu *Cook Is.*　20°0S 158°10W **65** J12
Vatnajökull *Iceland*　64°30N 16°48W **8** D5
Vatolakkos *Greece*　35°27N 23°53E **25** D5
Vatoloha *Madag.*　17°52S 47°48E **57** B8
Vatomandry *Madag.*　19°20S 48°59E **57** B8
Vatra-Dornei *Romania* 47°22N 25°22E **17** E13
Vatrak ➜ *India*　23°9N 73°2E **42** H5
Vättern *Sweden*　58°25N 14°30E **9** G16
Vatu Vara *Fiji*　17°26S 179°31W **59** a
Vatulele *Fiji*　18°33S 177°37E **59** a
Vaudreuil-Dorion
　Canada　45°23N 74°3W **83** A10
Vaughn *Mont., U.S.A.* 47°33N 111°33W **76** C8

Vaughn *N. Mex.,*
　U.S.A.　34°36N 105°13W **77** J11
Vaujours L. *Canada*　55°27N 74°15W **72** A5
Vaupés = Uaupés ➜
　Brazil　0°2N 67°16W **92** C5
Vaupés □ *Colombia*　1°0N 71°0W **92** C4
Vauxhall *Canada*　50°5N 112°9W **70** C6
Vav *India*　24°22N 71°31E **42** G4
Vavatenina *Madag.*　17°28S 49°12E **57** B8
Vava'u *Tonga*　18°36S 174°0W **59** c
Vava'u Group *Tonga* 18°40S 174°0W **59** c
Vawkavysk *Belarus*　53°9N 24°30E **17** B13
Växjö *Sweden*　56°52N 14°50E **9** H16
Vaygach, Ostrov *Russia* 70°0N 60°0E **28** C7
Veaikevárri = Svappavaara
　Sweden　67°40N 21°3E **8** C19
Vechte ➜ *Neths.*　52°34N 6°6E **15** B6
Vedea ➜ *Romania*　43°42N 25°41E **17** G13
Vedia *Argentina*　34°30S 61°31W **94** C3
Veendam *Neths.*　53°5N 6°52E **15** A6
Veenendaal *Neths.*　52°2N 5°34E **15** B5
Vefsna ➜ *Norway*　65°48N 13°10E **8** D15
Vega *Norway*　65°40N 11°55E **8** D14
Vega *U.S.A.*　35°15N 102°26W **84** D3
Vega Baja *Puerto Rico* 18°27N 66°23W **89** d
Vegreville *Canada*　53°30N 112°5W **70** C6
Vejer de la Frontera
　Spain　36°15N 5°59W **21** D3
Vejle *Denmark*　55°43N 9°30E **9** J13
Velas, C. *Costa Rica*　10°21N 85°52W **88** D2
Velasco, Sierra de
　Argentina　29°20S 67°10W **94** B2
Velddrif *S. Africa*　32°42S 18°11E **56** E2
Velebit Planina *Croatia* 44°50N 15°20E **16** F8
Veles *Macedonia*　41°46N 21°47E **23** D9
Vélez-Málaga *Spain*　36°48N 4°5W **21** D3
Vélez Rubio *Spain*　37°41N 2°5W **21** D4
Velhas ➜ *Brazil*　17°13S 44°49W **93** G10
Velika Kapela *Croatia* 45°10N 15°5E **16** F8
Velikaya ➜ *Russia*　57°48N 28°10E **9** H23
Velikaya Kema *Russia* 45°30N 137°12E **30** B8
Veliki Ustyug *Russia*　60°47N 46°20E **18** B8
Velikiye Luki *Russia*　56°25N 30°32E **18** C5
Veliko Tŭrnovo *Bulgaria* 43°5N 25°41E **23** C11
Velikonda Range *India* 14°45N 79°10E **40** M11
Velletri *Italy*　41°41N 12°47E **22** D5
Vellore *India*　12°57N 79°10E **40** N11
Velsk *Russia*　61°10N 42°5E **18** B7
Veluwezoom △ *Neths.*　52°5N 6°0E **15** B6
Velva *U.S.A.*　48°4N 100°56W **80** A4
Venado *Mexico*　22°56N 101°6W **86** C4
Venado Tuerto *Argentina* 33°50S 62°0W **94** C3
Vendée □ *France*　46°50N 1°35W **20** C3
Vendôme *France*　47°47N 1°3E **20** C4
Venézia *Italy*　45°27N 12°21E **22** B5
Venézia, G. di *Italy*　45°15N 13°0E **22** B5
Venezuela ■ *S. Amer.*　8°0N 66°0W **92** B5
Venezuela, G. de
　Venezuela　11°30N 71°0W **92** A4
Vengurla *India*　15°53N 73°45E **40** M8
Venice = Venézia *Italy* 45°27N 12°21E **22** B5
Venice *U.S.A.*　27°6N 82°27W **85** H13
Venkatapuram *India* 18°20N 80°30E **41** K12
Venlo *Neths.*　51°22N 6°11E **15** C6
Vennachar Junction
　Canada　45°5N 77°14W **82** A7
Vennesla *Norway*　58°15N 7°59E **9** G12
Venray *Neths.*　51°31N 6°0E **15** C6
Ventana, Punta de la
　Mexico　24°4N 109°48W **86** C3
Ventana, Sa. de la
　Argentina　38°0S 62°30W **94** D3
Ventersburg *S. Africa*　28°7S 27°9E **56** D4
Venterstad *S. Africa*　30°47S 25°48E **56** E4
Ventnor *U.K.*　50°36N 1°12W **13** G6
Ventotene *Italy*　40°47N 13°25E **22** D5
Ventoux, Mt. *France*　44°10N 5°17E **20** D6
Ventspils *Latvia*　57°25N 21°32E **9** H19
Ventuari ➜ *Venezuela*　3°58N 67°2W **92** C5
Ventucopa *U.S.A.*　34°50N 119°29W **79** L7
Ventura *U.S.A.*　34°17N 119°18W **79** L7
Vénus, Pte. *Tahiti*　17°29S 149°29W **59** d
Venus B. *Australia*　38°40S 145°42E **63** F4
Venustiano Carranza
　Mexico　30°25N 115°53W **86** A1
Vera *Argentina*　29°30S 60°20W **94** B3
Vera *Spain*　37°15N 1°51W **21** D5
Veracruz *Mexico*　19°11N 96°8W **87** D5
Veracruz □ *Mexico*　19°0N 96°15W **87** D5
Veraval *India*　20°53N 70°27E **42** J4
Verbánia *Italy*　45°56N 8°33E **20** D8
Vercelli *Italy*　45°19N 8°25E **20** D8
Verdalsøra *Norway*　63°48N 11°30E **8** E14
Verde ➜ *Argentina*　41°56S 65°5W **96** E3
Verde ➜ *Goiás, Brazil* 18°1S 50°14W **93** G8
Verde ➜ *Mato Grosso do Sul,*
　Brazil　21°25S 52°20W **93** H8
Verde ➜ *Chihuahua,*
　Mexico　26°29N 107°58W **86** B3
Verde ➜ *Oaxaca, Mexico* 15°59N 97°50W **87** D5
Verde ➜ *Veracruz,*
　Mexico　21°10N 102°50W **86** C4
Verde ➜ *Paraguay*　23°9S 57°37W **94** A4
Verde ➜ *U.S.A.*　33°33N 111°40W **74** D4
Verde, C. *Senegal*　14°45N 17°30W **48** F2
Verden *Germany*　52°55N 9°14E **16** B5
Verdi *U.S.A.*　39°31N 119°59W **78** F7
Verdon *France*　49°9N 5°24E **20** B6
Vereeniging *S. Africa*　26°38S 27°57E **57** D4
Verga, C. *Guinea*　10°30N 14°10W **50** F3
Vergara *Uruguay*　32°56S 53°57W **95** C5
Vergemont Cr. ➜
　Australia　24°16S 143°16E **62** C3
Vergennes *U.S.A.*　44°10N 73°15W **83** C11
Veria *Greece*　40°34N 22°12E **23** D10
Verín *Spain*　41°57N 7°27W **21** B2
Verkhnetulomskoye Vdkhr.
　Russia　68°36N 31°12E **8** B24

Verkhnevilyuysk
  Russia 63°27N 120°18E **29** C13
Verkhniy Baskunchak
  Russia 48°14N 46°44E **19** E8
Verkhoyansk *Russia* 67°35N 133°25E **29** C14
Verkhoyansk Ra. =
  Verkhoyanskiy Khrebet
  Russia 66°0N 129°0E **29** C13
Verkhoyanskiy Khrebet
  Russia 66°0N 129°0E **29** C13
Vermilion *Canada* 53°20N 110°50W **71** C6
Vermilion *U.S.A.* 41°25N 82°22W **82** E2
Vermilion ➤ *Canada* 53°22N 110°51W **71** C6
Vermilion B. *U.S.A.* 29°42N 92°0W **84** G9
Vermilion Bay *Canada* 49°51N 93°34W **71** D10
Vermilion Bay *U.S.A.* 29°45N 91°55E **25** A3
Vermilion L. *U.S.A.* 47°53N 92°26W **80** B7
Vermillion *U.S.A.* 42°47N 96°56W **80** D5
Vermillion ➤ *Canada* 47°38N 72°56W **72** C5
Vermont □ *U.S.A.* 44°0N 73°0W **83** C12
Vernadsky *Antarctica* 65°0S 64°0W **5** C17
Vernal *U.S.A.* 40°27N 109°32W **76** F9
Vernalis *U.S.A.* 37°36N 121°17W **78** H5
Verner *Canada* 46°25N 80°8W **72** C3
Verneukpan *S. Africa* 30°0S 21°0E **56** E3
Vernon *Canada* 50°20N 119°15W **70** C5
Vernon *U.S.A.* 34°9N 99°17W **84** D5
Vernonia *U.S.A.* 45°52N 123°11W **78** E3
Vero Beach *U.S.A.* 27°38N 80°24W **85** H14
Véroia = Veria *Greece* 40°34N 22°12E **23** D10
Verona *Canada* 44°29N 76°42W **83** B8
Verona *Italy* 45°27N 10°59E **22** B4
Versailles *France* 48°48N 2°7E **20** B5
Vert, C. *Senegal* 14°45N 17°30W **50** F2
Verulam *S. Africa* 29°38S 31°2E **57** D5
Verviers *Belgium* 50°37N 5°52E **15** D5
Veselovskoye Vdkhr.
  Russia 46°58N 41°25E **19** E7
Vesoul *France* 47°40N 6°11E **20** C7
Vesterålen *Norway* 68°45N 15°0E **8** B16
Vestfjorden *Norway* 67°55N 14°0E **8** C16
Vestmannaeyjar *Iceland* 63°27N 20°15W **8** E3
Vestspitsbergen *Svalbard* 78°40N 17°0E **4** B8
Vestvågøya *Norway* 68°18N 13°50E **8** B15
Vesuvio *Italy* 40°49N 14°26E **22** D6
Vesuvius, Mt. = Vesuvio
  Italy 40°49N 14°26E **22** D6
Veszprém *Hungary* 47°8N 17°57E **17** E9
Vetlanda *Sweden* 57°24N 15°3E **9** H16
Vetlugu ➤ *Russia* 56°36N 46°4E **18** C8
Vettore, Mte. *Italy* 42°49N 13°16E **22** C5
Veurne *Belgium* 51°5N 2°40E **15** C2
Veys *Iran* 31°30N 49°0E **45** D6
Vezhen *Bulgaria* 42°50N 24°20E **23** C11
Vi Thanh *Vietnam* 9°42N 105°26E **39** H5
Viacha *Bolivia* 16°39S 68°18W **92** G5
Viamão *Brazil* 30°5S 51°0W **95** C5
Viana *Brazil* 3°13S 44°55W **93** D10
Viana do Alentejo
  Portugal 38°17N 7°59W **21** C2
Viana do Castelo *Portugal* 41°42N 8°50W **21** B1
Vianden *Lux.* 49°56N 6°12E **15** E6
Viangchan = Vientiane
  Laos 17°58N 102°36E **38** D4
Vianópolis *Brazil* 16°40S 48°35W **93** G9
Vianos *Greece* 35°2N 25°21E **25** D7
Viaréggio *Italy* 43°52N 10°14E **22** C4
Vibo Valéntia *Italy* 38°40N 16°6E **22** E7
Viborg *Denmark* 56°27N 9°23E **9** H13
Vic *Spain* 41°58N 2°19E **21** B7
Vicenza *Italy* 45°33N 11°33E **22** B4
Vich = Vic *Spain* 41°58N 2°19E **21** B7
Vichada ➤ *Colombia* 4°55N 67°50W **92** C5
Vichy *France* 46°9N 3°26E **20** C5
Vicksburg *Ariz.,*
  U.S.A. 33°45N 113°45W **79** M13
Vicksburg *Miss., U.S.A.* 32°21N 90°53W **85** E9
Victor *India* 21°0N 71°30E **42** J4
Victor Harbor *Australia* 35°30S 138°37E **63** F2
Victoria *Argentina* 32°40S 60°10W **94** C3
Victoria *Canada* 48°30N 123°25W **78** B3
Victoria *Chile* 38°13S 72°20W **96** D2
Victoria *China* 22°17N 114°9E **33** G1
Victoria *Malta* 36°3N 14°14E **25** C1
Victoria *Seychelles* 4°38S 55°28E **53** b
Victoria *Kans., U.S.A.* 38°52N 99°9W **80** F4
Victoria *Tex., U.S.A.* 28°48N 97°0W **84** G6
Victoria □ *Australia* 37°0S 144°0E **63** F3
Victoria ➤ *Australia* 15°10S 129°40E **60** C4
Victoria, Grand L.
  Canada 47°31N 77°30W **72** C4
Victoria, L. *Africa* 1°0S 33°0E **54** C3
Victoria, L. *Australia* 33°57S 141°15E **63** E3
Victoria, Mt. *Burma* 21°14N 93°55E **41** J18
Victoria Beach *Canada* 50°40N 96°35W **71** C9
Victoria de Durango = Durango
  Mexico 24°3N 104°39W **86** C4
Victoria de las Tunas = Las Tunas
  Cuba 20°58N 76°59W **88** B4
Victoria Falls *Zimbabwe* 17°58S 25°52E **55** F2
Victoria Harbour
  Canada 44°45N 79°45W **82** B5
Victoria I. *Canada* 71°0N 111°0W **68** B8
Victoria L. *Canada* 48°20N 57°27W **73** C8
Victoria Ld. *Antarctica* 75°0S 160°0E **5** D11
Victoria Nile ➤ *Uganda* 2°14N 31°26E **54** B3
Victoria Pk. *Belize* 16°48N 88°37W **87** D7
Victoria River *Australia* 15°25S 131°0E **60** C5
Victoria Str. *Canada* 69°31N 100°30W **68** B9
Victoria West *S. Africa* 31°25S 23°4E **56** E3
Victoriaville *Canada* 46°4N 71°56W **73** C5
Victorica *Argentina* 36°20S 65°30W **94** D2
Victorville *U.S.A.* 34°32N 117°18W **79** L9
Vicuña *Chile* 30°0S 70°50W **94** C1
Vicuña Mackenna
  Argentina 33°53S 64°25W **94** C3
Vidal *U.S.A.* 34°7N 114°31W **79** L12
Vidal Junction *U.S.A.* 34°11N 114°34W **79** L12

Vidalia *U.S.A.* 32°13N 82°25W **85** E13
Vidin *Bulgaria* 43°59N 22°50E **23** C10
Vidisha *India* 23°28N 77°53E **42** H7
Vidos *Greece* 39°38N 19°55E **25** A3
Vidzy *Belarus* 55°23N 26°37E **9** J22
Viedma *Argentina* 40°50S 63°0W **96** E4
Viedma, L. *Argentina* 49°30S 72°30W **96** F2
Vielsalm *Belgium* 50°17N 5°54E **15** D5
Vieng Pou Kha *Laos* 20°41N 101°4E **38** B3
Vienna = Wien *Austria* 48°12N 16°22E **16** D9
Vienna *Canada* 42°41N 80°48W **82** D4
Vienna *Ill., U.S.A.* 37°25N 88°54W **80** G9
Vienna *Mo., U.S.A.* 38°11N 91°57W **80** F8
Vienne *France* 45°31N 4°53E **20** D6
Vienne ➤ *France* 47°13N 0°5E **20** C4
Vientiane *Laos* 17°58N 102°36E **38** D4
Vientos, Paso de los
  Caribbean 20°0N 74°0W **89** C5
Vieques *Puerto Rico* 18°8N 65°25W **89** d
Vierge Pt. *St. Lucia* 13°49N 60°53W **89** f
Vierzon *France* 47°13N 2°5E **20** C5
Viet Tri *Vietnam* 21°18N 105°25E **38** B5
Vietnam ■ *Asia* 19°0N 106°0E **38** C6
Vieux Fort *St. Lucia* 13°46N 60°58W **89** f
Vigan *Phil.* 17°35N 120°28E **37** A6
Vigévano *Italy* 45°19N 8°51E **20** D8
Viglas, Akra *Greece* 35°54N 27°51E **25** D9
Vigia *Brazil* 0°50S 48°5W **93** D9
Vigo *Spain* 42°12N 8°41W **21** A1
Vihowa *Pakistan* 31°8N 70°30E **42** D4
Vihowa ➤ *Pakistan* 31°8N 70°41E **42** D4
Vijayawada *India* 16°31N 80°39E **41** L12
Vijosë ➤ *Albania* 40°37N 19°24E **23** D8
Vík *Iceland* 63°25N 19°1W **8** E4
Vikeke = Viqueque
  E. Timor 8°52S 126°23E **37** F7
Viking *Canada* 53°7N 111°50W **70** C6
Vikna *Norway* 64°55N 10°58E **8** D14
Vila da Maganja *Mozam.* 17°18S 37°30E **55** F4
Vila da Ribeira Brava
  C. Verde Is. 16°32N 24°25W **50** b
Vila do Bispo *Portugal* 37°5N 8°53W **21** D1
Vila Franca de Xira
  Portugal 38°57N 8°59W **21** C1
Vila Gamito *Mozam.* 14°12S 33°0E **55** E3
Vila Gomes da Costa
  Mozam. 24°20S 33°37E **57** C5
Vila Machado *Mozam.* 19°15S 34°14E **55** F3
Vila Mouzinho *Mozam.* 14°48S 34°25E **55** E3
Vila Nova de Gaia *Portugal* 41°8N 8°37W **21** B1
Vila Real *Portugal* 41°17N 7°48W **21** B2
Vila-Real *Spain* 39°55N 0°3W **21** C5
Vila Real de Santo António
  Portugal 37°10N 7°28W **21** D2
Vila Vasco da Gama
  Mozam. 14°54S 32°14E **55** E3
Vila Velha *Brazil* 20°20S 40°17W **95** A7
Vilagarcía de Arousa
  Spain 42°34N 8°46W **21** A1
Vilaine ➤ *France* 47°30N 2°27W **20** C2
Vilanandro, Tanjona
  Madag. 16°11S 44°27E **57** B7
Vilanculos *Mozam.* 22°1S 35°17E **57** C6
Vilanova i la Geltrú *Spain* 41°13N 1°40E **21** B6
Vilcheka, Ostrov *Russia* 80°0N 58°31E **28** B6
Vilcheka, Zemlya *Russia* 80°30N 60°30E **4** A11
Vileyka *Belarus* 54°30N 26°53E **17** A14
Vilhelmina *Sweden* 64°35N 16°39E **8** D17
Vilhena *Brazil* 12°40S 60°5W **92** F6
Viliya = Neris ➤
  Lithuania 55°8N 24°16E **9** J21
Viljandi *Estonia* 58°28N 25°30E **9** G21
Vilkitskogo, Proliv
  Russia 78°0N 103°0E **29** B11
Vilkovo = Vylkove
  Ukraine 45°28N 29°32E **17** F15
Villa Abecia *Bolivia* 21°0S 68°18W **94** A2
Villa Ana *Argentina* 28°28S 59°40W **94** B4
Villa Angela *Argentina* 27°34S 60°45W **94** B3
Villa Bella *Bolivia* 10°25S 65°22W **92** F5
Villa Cañas *Argentina* 34°0S 61°35W **94** C3
Villa Constitución
  Argentina 33°15S 60°20W **94** C3
Villa de Arriaga *Mexico* 21°56N 101°20W **86** C4
Villa de María *Argentina* 29°55S 63°43W **94** B3
Villa de Méndez *Mexico* 25°7N 98°34W **87** B5
Villa Dolores *Argentina* 31°58S 65°15W **94** C2
Villa Frontera *Mexico* 26°56N 101°27W **86** B4
Villa Gesell *Argentina* 37°15S 56°55W **94** D4
Villa Guillermina
  Argentina 28°15S 59°29W **94** B4
Villa Hayes *Paraguay* 25°5S 57°20W **94** B4
Villa Hidalgo *Mexico* 24°15N 99°26W **87** C5
Villa Iris *Argentina* 38°12S 63°12W **94** D3
Villa María *Argentina* 32°20S 63°10W **94** C3
Villa Mazán *Argentina* 28°40S 66°30W **94** B2
Villa Montes *Bolivia* 21°10S 63°30W **94** A3
Villa Ocampo *Argentina* 28°30S 59°20W **94** B4
Villa Ocampo *Mexico* 26°27N 105°31W **86** B3
Villa Ojo de Agua
  Argentina 29°30S 63°44W **94** B3
Villa San Martín
  Argentina 28°15S 64°9W **94** B3
Villa Unión *Mexico* 23°12N 106°14W **86** C3
Villacarlos *Spain* 39°53N 4°17E **24** B11
Villacarrillo *Spain* 38°7N 3°3W **21** C4
Villach *Austria* 46°37N 13°51E **16** E7
Villafranca de Bonany
  Spain 39°34N 3°5E **24** B10
Villagrán *Mexico* 24°29N 99°29W **87** C5
Villaguay *Argentina* 32°0S 59°0W **94** C4
Villahermosa *Mexico* 17°59N 92°55W **87** D6
Villajoyosa *Spain* 38°30N 0°12E **21** C5
Villalba *Spain* 43°26N 7°40W **21** A2
Villanueva *U.S.A.* 35°16N 105°22W **77** J11
Villanueva de la Serena
  Spain 38°59N 5°50W **21** C3

Villanueva y Geltrú = Vilanova i
  la Geltrú *Spain* 41°13N 1°40E **21** B6
Villarreal = Vila-Real
  Spain 39°55N 0°3W **21** C5
Villarrica *Chile* 39°15S 72°15W **96** D2
Villarrica *Paraguay* 25°40S 56°30W **94** B4
Villarrobledo *Spain* 39°18N 2°36W **21** C4
Villavicencio *Argentina* 32°28S 69°0W **94** C2
Villavicencio *Colombia* 4°9N 73°37W **92** C4
Villaviciosa *Spain* 43°32N 5°27W **21** A3
Villazón *Bolivia* 22°0S 65°35W **94** A2
Ville-Marie *Canada* 47°20N 79°30W **72** C4
Ville Platte *U.S.A.* 30°41N 92°17W **84** F8
Villena *Spain* 38°39N 0°52W **21** C5
Villeneuve-d'Ascq *France* 50°38N 3°9E **20** A5
Villeneuve-sur-Lot *France* 44°24N 0°42E **20** D4
Villiers *S. Africa* 27°2S 28°36E **57** D4
Villingen-Schwenningen
  Germany 48°3N 8°26E **16** D5
Villmanstrand = Lappeenranta
  Finland 61°3N 28°12E **8** F23
Vilna *Canada* 54°7N 111°55W **70** C6
Vilnius *Lithuania* 54°38N 25°19E **9** J21
Vilvoorde *Belgium* 50°56N 4°26E **15** D4
Vilyuchinsk *Russia* 52°55N 158°24E **29** D16
Vilyuy ➤ *Russia* 64°24N 126°26E **29** C13
Vilyuysk *Russia* 63°40N 121°35E **29** C13
Viña del Mar *Chile* 33°0S 71°30W **94** C1
Vinarós *Spain* 40°30N 0°27E **21** B6
Vincennes *U.S.A.* 38°41N 87°32W **80** F10
Vincennes Bay *S. Ocean* 66°0S 109°0E **5** C8
Vincent *U.S.A.* 34°33N 118°11W **79** L8
Vinchina *Argentina* 28°45S 68°15W **94** B2
Vindelälven ➤ *Sweden* 63°55N 19°50E **8** E18
Vindeln *Sweden* 64°12N 19°43E **8** D18
Vindhya Ra. *India* 22°50N 77°0E **42** H7
Vineland *U.S.A.* 39°29N 75°2W **81** F16
Vinh *Vietnam* 18°45N 105°38E **38** C5
Vinh Linh *Vietnam* 17°4N 107°2E **38** D6
Vinh Long *Vietnam* 10°16N 105°57E **39** G5
Vinh Yen *Vietnam* 21°21N 105°35E **38** B5
Vinita *U.S.A.* 36°39N 95°9W **84** C7
Vinkovci *Croatia* 45°19N 18°48E **23** B8
Vinnitsa = Vinnytsya
  Ukraine 49°15N 28°30E **17** D15
Vinnytsya *Ukraine* 49°15N 28°30E **17** D15
Vinson Massif *Antarctica* 78°35S 85°25W **5** D16
Vinton *Calif., U.S.A.* 39°48N 120°10W **78** F6
Vinton *Iowa, U.S.A.* 42°10N 92°1W **80** D7
Vinton *La., U.S.A.* 30°11N 93°35W **84** F8
Viqueque *E. Timor* 8°52S 126°23E **37** F7
Virac *Phil.* 13°30N 124°20E **37** B6
Virachey *Cambodia* 13°59N 106°49E **38** E6
Virachey △ *Cambodia* 14°14N 106°55E **38** E6
Virago Sd. *Canada* 54°0N 132°30W **70** C2
Viramgam *India* 23°5N 72°0E **42** H5
Virananşehir *Turkey* 37°13N 39°45E **44** B3
Virawah *Pakistan* 24°31N 70°46E **42** G4
Virden *Canada* 49°50N 100°56W **71** D8
Vire *France* 48°50N 0°53W **20** B3
Vírgenes, C. *Argentina* 52°19S 68°21W **96** G3
Virgin ➤ *U.S.A.* 36°28N 114°21W **77** H6
Virgin Gorda *Br. Virgin Is.* 18°30N 64°26W **89** e
Virgin Is. (British) ☑
  W. Indies 18°30N 64°30W **89** e
Virgin Is. (U.S.) ☑
  W. Indies 18°20N 65°0W **89** e
Virgin Islands △
  U.S. Virgin Is. 18°21N 64°43W **89** C7
Virginia *S. Africa* 28°8S 26°55E **56** D4
Virginia *U.S.A.* 47°31N 92°32W **80** B7
Virginia □ *U.S.A.* 37°30N 78°45W **81** G14
Virginia Beach *U.S.A.* 36°49N 76°9W **81** F16
Virginia City *Mont.,*
  U.S.A. 45°18N 111°56W **76** D8
Virginia City *Nev.,*
  U.S.A. 39°19N 119°39W **78** F7
Virginia Falls *Canada* 61°38N 125°42W **70** A3
Virginiatown *Canada* 48°9N 79°36W **72** C4
Viroqua *U.S.A.* 43°34N 90°53W **80** D8
Virovitica *Croatia* 45°51N 17°21E **22** B7
Virpur *India* 21°51N 70°42E **42** J4
Virton *Belgium* 49°35N 5°32E **15** E5
Virudunagar *India* 9°30N 77°58E **40** Q10
Virunga △
  Dem. Rep. of the Congo 0°5N 29°38E **54** B2
Vis *Croatia* 43°4N 16°10E **22** C7
Visalia *U.S.A.* 36°20N 119°18W **78** J7
Visayan Sea *Phil.* 11°30N 123°30E **37** B6
Visby *Sweden* 57°37N 18°18E **9** H18
Viscount Melville Sd.
  Canada 74°10N 108°0W **69** B9
Visé *Belgium* 50°44N 5°41E **15** D5
Vise, Ostrov *Russia* 79°33N 76°50E **28** B8
Viségrad *Bos.-H.* 43°47N 19°17E **23** C8
Viseu *Brazil* 1°10S 46°5W **93** D9
Viseu *Portugal* 40°40N 7°55W **21** B2
Vishakhapatnam *India* 17°45N 83°20E **41** L13
Visnagar *India* 23°45N 72°32E **42** H5
Viso, Mte. *Italy* 44°38N 7°5E **20** D7
Visokoi I. *Antarctica* 56°43S 27°15W **5** B1
Vista *U.S.A.* 33°12N 117°14W **79** M9
Vistula = Wisła ➤
  Poland 54°22N 18°55E **17** A10
Vitebsk = Vitsyebsk
  Belarus 55°10N 30°15E **18** C5
Viterbo *Italy* 42°25N 12°6E **22** C5
Viti Levu *Fiji* 17°30S 177°30E **59** a
Vitigudino *Spain* 41°1N 6°26W **21** B2
Vitim *Russia* 59°28N 112°35E **29** D12
Vitim ➤ *Russia* 59°26N 112°34E **29** D12
Vitória *Brazil* 20°20S 40°22W **93** H10
Vitória da Conquista
  Brazil 14°51S 40°51W **93** F10
Vitória de São Antão
  Brazil 8°10S 35°20W **93** E11
Vitoria-Gasteiz *Spain* 42°50N 2°41W **21** A4

Vitsyebsk *Belarus* 55°10N 30°15E **18** C5
Vittória *Italy* 36°57N 14°32E **22** F6
Vittório Véneto *Italy* 45°59N 12°18E **22** B5
Viveiro *Spain* 43°39N 7°38W **21** A2
Vivian *U.S.A.* 32°53N 93°59W **84** E8
Viwa *Fiji* 17°10S 177°58E **59** a
Vizcaíno, Desierto de
  Mexico 27°30N 113°45W **86** B2
Vizcaíno, Sierra *Mexico* 27°30N 114°0W **86** B2
Vize *Turkey* 41°34N 27°45E **23** D12
Vizianagaram *India* 18°6N 83°30E **41** K13
Vladikavkaz *Russia* 43°0N 44°35E **19** F7
Vladimir *Russia* 56°15N 40°30E **18** C7
Vladimir Volynskiy = Volodymyr-
  Volynskyy *Ukraine* 50°50N 24°18E **17** C13
Vladivostok *Russia* 43°10N 131°53E **30** C5
Vlieland *Neths.* 53°16N 4°55E **15** A4
Vlissingen *Neths.* 51°26N 3°34E **15** C3
Vlorë *Albania* 40°32N 19°28E **23** D8
Vltava ➤ *Czech Rep.* 50°21N 14°30E **16** D8
Vo Dat *Vietnam* 11°9N 107°31E **39** G6
Voe *U.K.* 60°21N 1°16W **11** A7
Vogelkop = Doberai, Jazirah
  Indonesia 1°25S 133°0E **37** E8
Vogelsberg *Germany* 50°31N 9°12E **16** C5
Voghera *Italy* 44°59N 9°1E **20** D8
Vohibinany *Madag.* 18°49S 49°4E **57** B8
Vohilava *Madag.* 21°4S 48°0E **57** C8
Vohimarina = Iharana
  Madag. 13°25S 50°0E **57** A9
Vohimena, Tanjon' i
  Madag. 25°36S 45°8E **57** D8
Vohipeno *Madag.* 22°22S 47°51E **57** C8
Voi *Kenya* 3°25S 38°32E **54** C4
Voiron *France* 45°22N 5°35E **20** D6
Voisey B. *Canada* 56°15N 61°50W **73** A7
Vojmsjön *Sweden* 65°0N 16°24E **8** D17
Vojvodina □ *Serbia* 45°20N 20°0E **23** B9
Volborg *U.S.A.* 45°51N 105°41W **76** D11
Volcán de Colima △
  Mexico 19°30N 103°40W **86** D4
Volcano Is. = Kazan-Rettō
  Pac. Oc. 25°0N 141°0E **64** E6
Volcans △ *Rwanda* 1°30S 29°26E **54** C2
Volda *Norway* 62°9N 6°5E **8** E12
Volga ➤ *Russia* 46°0N 48°30E **19** E8
Volga Hts. = Privolzhskaya
  Vozvyshennost *Russia* 51°0N 46°0E **19** D8
Volgodonsk *Russia* 47°33N 42°5E **19** E7
Volgograd *Russia* 48°40N 44°25E **19** E7
Volgogradskoye Vdkhr.
  Russia 50°0N 45°20E **19** D8
Volkhov ➤ *Russia* 60°8N 32°20E **18** B5
Volkovysk = Vawkavysk
  Belarus 53°9N 24°30E **17** B13
Volksrust *S. Africa* 27°24S 29°53E **57** D4
Volochanka *Russia* 71°0N 94°28E **29** B10
Volodymyr-Volynskyy
  Ukraine 50°50N 24°18E **17** C13
Vologda *Russia* 59°10N 39°45E **18** C6
Volos *Greece* 39°24N 22°59E **23** E10
Volosovo *Russia* 59°27N 29°32E **9** G23
Volovets *Ukraine* 48°43N 23°11E **17** D12
Volozhin = Valozhyn
  Belarus 54°3N 26°30E **17** A14
Volsk *Russia* 52°5N 47°22E **18** D8
Volta □ *Ghana* 5°46N 0°41E **48** F4
Volta ➤ *Ghana* 5°46N 0°41E **48** F4
Volta, L. *Ghana* 7°30N 0°0E **50** G6
Volta Redonda *Brazil* 22°31S 44°5W **95** A7
Voltaire, C. *Australia* 14°16S 125°35E **60** B4
Volterra *Italy* 43°24N 10°51E **22** C4
Volturno ➤ *Italy* 41°1N 13°55E **22** D5
Volzhskiy *Russia* 48°56N 44°46E **19** E7
Vomo *Fiji* 17°30S 177°15E **59** a
Vondrozo *Madag.* 22°49S 47°20E **57** C8
Vopnafjörður *Iceland* 65°45N 14°50W **8** D6
Vorkuta *Russia* 67°48N 64°20E **18** A11
Vormsi *Estonia* 59°1N 23°13E **9** G20
Voronezh *Russia* 51°40N 39°10E **19** D6
Vorōts Järv *Estonia* 58°16N 26°3E **9** G22
Võru *Estonia* 57°48N 26°54E **9** H22
Vosges *France* 48°20N 7°10E **20** B7
Voss *Norway* 60°38N 6°26E **8** F12
Vostok *Antarctica* 78°30S 106°50E **5** D8
Vostok I. *Kiribati* 10°5S 152°23W **65** J12
Votkinsk *Russia* 57°0N 53°55E **18** C9
Votkinskoye Vdkhr.
  Russia 57°22N 55°12E **18** C10
Votsuri-Shima *Japan* 25°45N 123°39E **31** M1
Vouga ➤ *Portugal* 40°41N 8°40W **21** B1
Vouxa, Akra *Greece* 35°37N 23°32E **25** D5
Voyageurs △ *U.S.A.* 48°32N 93°0W **80** A7
Voynitsa *Russia* 65°10N 30°20E **8** D24
Voyvozh *Russia* 62°56N 54°56E **18** B10
Vozhe, Ozero *Russia* 60°45N 39°0E **18** B6
Voznesensk *Ukraine* 47°35N 31°21E **19** E5
Voznesenye *Russia* 61°0N 35°28E **18** B6
Vrangel *Russia* 42°43N 133°5E **30** C6
Vrangelya, Ostrov
  Russia 71°0N 180°0E **29** B18
Vranje *Serbia* 42°34N 21°54E **23** C9
Vratsa *Bulgaria* 43°15N 23°30E **23** C10
Vrbas ➤ *Bos.-H.* 45°8N 17°29E **22** B7
Vrede *S. Africa* 27°24S 29°6E **57** D4
Vredefort *S. Africa* 27°0S 26°22E **56** D4
Vredenburg *S. Africa* 32°56S 18°0E **56** E2
Vredendal *S. Africa* 31°41S 18°35E **56** E2
Vrindavan *India* 27°37N 77°40E **42** F7
Vrises *Greece* 35°23N 24°13E **25** D6
Vršac *Serbia* 45°8N 21°30E **23** B9
Vryburg *S. Africa* 26°55S 24°45E **56** D3
Vryheid *S. Africa* 27°45S 30°47E **57** D5
Vu Liet *Vietnam* 18°43N 105°23E **38** C5
Vukovar *Croatia* 45°21N 18°59E **23** B8

Vuktyl *Russia* 63°52N 57°20E **28** C6
Vulcan *Canada* 50°25N 113°15W **70** C6
Vulcan *Romania* 45°23N 23°17E **17** F12
Vulcaneşti *Moldova* 45°41N 28°18E **17** F15
Vulcano *Italy* 38°24N 14°58E **22** E6
Vulkaneshty = Vulcaneşti
  Moldova 45°41N 28°18E **17** F15
Vunduzi ➤ *Mozam.* 18°56S 34°1E **55** F3
Vung Tau *Vietnam* 10°21N 107°4E **39** G6
Vunidawa *Fiji* 17°50S 178°21E **59** a
Vunisea *Fiji* 19°3S 178°10E **59** a
Vwaza △ *Malawi* 10°58S 33°25E **55** E3
Vyartsilya *Russia* 62°8N 30°45E **8** E24
Vyatka = Kirov *Russia* 58°35N 49°40E **18** C8
Vyatka ➤ *Russia* 55°37N 51°28E **18** C9
Vyatskiye Polyany *Russia* 56°14N 51°5E **18** C9
Vyazemskiy *Russia* 47°32N 134°45E **29** E14
Vyazma *Russia* 55°10N 34°15E **18** C5
Vyborg *Russia* 60°43N 28°47E **8** F23
Vychegda ➤ *Russia* 61°18N 46°36E **18** B8
Vychodné Beskydy
  Europe 49°20N 22°0E **17** D11
Vyg-ozero *Russia* 63°47N 34°29E **18** B6
Vylkove *Ukraine* 45°28N 29°32E **17** F15
Vynohradiv *Ukraine* 48°9N 23°2E **17** D12
Vyrnwy, L. *U.K.* 52°48N 3°31W **12** E4
Vyshniy Volochek
  Russia 57°30N 34°30E **18** C5
Vyshzha = imeni 26 Bakinskikh
  Komissarov
  Turkmenistan 39°22N 54°10E **45** B7
Vyškov *Czech Rep.* 49°17N 17°0E **17** D9
Vytegra *Russia* 61°0N 36°27E **18** B6

W

W.A.C. Bennett Dam
  Canada 56°2N 122°6W **70** B4
Wa *Ghana* 10°7N 2°25W **50** F5
Waal ➤ *Neths.* 51°37N 5°0E **15** C5
Waalwijk *Neths.* 51°42N 5°4E **15** C5
Wabakimi △ *Canada* 50°43N 89°29W **72** B2
Wabana *Canada* 47°40N 53°0W **73** C9
Wabasca ➤ *Canada* 58°22N 115°20W **70** B5
Wabasca-Desmarais
  Canada 55°57N 113°56W **70** B6
Wabash *U.S.A.* 40°48N 85°49W **81** E11
Wabash ➤ *U.S.A.* 37°48N 88°2W **80** G9
Wabigoon L. *Canada* 49°44N 92°44W **71** D10
Wabowden *Canada* 54°55N 98°38W **71** C9
Wabuk Pt. *Canada* 55°20N 85°5W **72** A2
Wabush *Canada* 52°55N 66°52W **73** B6
Waco *U.S.A.* 31°33N 97°9W **84** F6
Waconichi, L. *Canada* 50°8N 74°0W **72** B5
Wad Hamid *Sudan* 16°30N 32°45E **51** E12
Wad Medanî *Sudan* 14°28N 33°30E **51** F12
Wad Thana *Pakistan* 27°22N 66°23E **42** F2
Wadai *Africa* 12°0N 19°0E **48** E5
Wadayama *Japan* 35°19N 134°52E **31** G7
Waddeneilanden *Neths.* 53°25N 5°10E **15** A5
Waddenzee *Neths.* 53°6N 5°10E **15** A5
Waddington *U.S.A.* 44°52N 75°12W **83** B9
Waddington, Mt.
  Canada 51°23N 125°15W **70** C3
Waddy Pt. *Australia* 24°58S 153°21E **63** C5
Wadebridge *U.K.* 50°31N 4°51W **13** G3
Wadena *Canada* 51°57N 103°47W **71** C8
Wadena *U.S.A.* 46°26N 95°8W **80** B6
Wadeye *Australia* 14°28S 129°52E **60** B4
Wadhams *Canada* 51°30N 127°30W **70** C3
Wadhwan *India* 22°42N 71°41E **42** H4
Wâdî as Sîr *Jordan* 31°56N 35°49E **46** D4
Wadi Halfa *Sudan* 21°53N 31°19E **51** D12
Wadi Rum △ *Jordan* 29°30N 35°20E **46** F4
Wadsworth *Nev.,*
  U.S.A. 39°38N 119°17W **76** G4
Wadsworth *Ohio, U.S.A.* 41°2N 81°44W **82** E3
Waegwan *S. Korea* 35°59N 128°23E **35** G15
Wafangdian *China* 39°38N 121°58E **35** E11
Wafrah *Kuwait* 28°33N 47°56E **44** D5
Wageningen *Neths.* 51°58N 5°40E **15** C5
Wager B. *Canada* 65°26N 88°40W **69** C11
Wagga Wagga *Australia* 35°7S 147°24E **63** F4
Waghete *Indonesia* 4°10S 135°50E **37** E9
Wagin *Australia* 33°17S 117°25E **61** F2
Wagner *U.S.A.* 43°5N 98°18W **80** D4
Wagon Mound *U.S.A.* 36°1N 104°42W **77** H11
Wagoner *U.S.A.* 35°58N 95°22W **84** D7
Wah *Pakistan* 33°45N 72°40E **42** C5
Wahai *Indonesia* 2°48S 129°35E **37** E7
Wahiawā *U.S.A.* 21°30N 158°2W **75** L8
Wâhid *Egypt* 30°48N 32°21E **46** E1
Wahnai *Afghan.* 32°40N 65°50E **42** C1
Wahoo *U.S.A.* 41°13N 96°37W **80** E6
Wahpeton *U.S.A.* 46°16N 96°36W **80** B6
Waiau ➤ *N.Z.* 42°47S 173°22E **59** E4
Waibeem *Indonesia* 0°30S 132°59E **37** E8
Waigeo *Indonesia* 0°20S 130°40E **37** E8
Waihi *N.Z.* 37°23S 175°52E **59** B5
Waihou ➤ *N.Z.* 37°15S 175°40E **59** B5
Waika
  Dem. Rep. of the Congo 2°22S 25°42E **54** C2
Waikabubak *Indonesia* 9°45S 119°25E **37** F5
Waikaremoana, L. *N.Z.* 38°49S 177°9E **59** C6
Waikari *N.Z.* 42°58S 172°41E **59** E4
Waikato ➤ *N.Z.* 37°23S 174°43E **59** B5
Waikerie *Australia* 34°9S 140°0E **63** E3
Waikokopu *N.Z.* 39°3S 177°52E **59** C6
Waikouaiti *N.Z.* 45°36S 170°41E **59** F3
Wailangilala *China* 22°6N 114°2E **33** G12
Wailuku *U.S.A.* 20°53N 156°30W **74** b
Waimakariri ➤ *N.Z.* 43°24S 172°42E **59** E4
Waimate *N.Z.* 44°45S 171°3E **59** F3
Wainganga ➤ *India* 18°50N 79°55E **40** K11
Waingapu *Indonesia* 9°35S 120°11E **37** F6
Waini ➤ *Guyana* 8°20N 59°50W **92** B7

Wainwright *Canada*	52°50N 110°50W	71 C6
Waiouru *N.Z.*	39°28S 175°41E	59 C5
Waipara *N.Z.*	43°3S 172°46E	59 E4
Waipawa *N.Z.*	39°56S 176°38E	59 B5
Waipiro *N.Z.*	38°2S 178°22E	59 C7
Waipoua Forest *N.Z.*	35°39S 173°33E	59 A4
Waipu *N.Z.*	35°59S 174°29E	59 A5
Waipukurau *N.Z.*	40°1S 176°33E	59 D6
Wairakei *N.Z.*	38°37S 176°6E	59 C6
Wairarapa, L. *N.Z.*	41°14S 175°15E	59 D5
Wairoa *N.Z.*	39°3S 177°25E	59 C6
Waitaki → *N.Z.*	44°56S 171°7E	59 F3
Waitangi *N.Z.*	35°16S 174°5E	59 A5
Waitara *N.Z.*	38°59S 174°14E	59 C5
Waitomo Caves *N.Z.*	38°16S 175°7E	59 C5
Waitsburg *U.S.A.*	46°16N 118°9W	76 C4
Waiuku *N.Z.*	37°15S 174°45E	59 B5
Wajima *Japan*	37°30N 137°0E	31 F8
Wajir *Kenya*	1°42N 40°5E	54 B5
Wakasa *Japan*	35°20N 134°24E	31 G7
Wakasa-Wan *Japan*	35°40N 135°30E	31 G7
Wakatipu, L. *N.Z.*	45°5S 168°33E	59 F2
Wakaw *Canada*	52°39N 105°44W	71 C7
Wakaya *Fiji*	17°37S 179°0E	59 a
Wakayama *Japan*	34°15N 135°15E	31 G7
Wakayama □ *Japan*	33°50N 135°30E	31 H7
Wake Forest *U.S.A.*	35°59N 78°30W	85 D15
Wake I. *Pac. Oc.*	19°18N 166°36E	64 F8
WaKeeney *U.S.A.*	39°1N 99°53W	80 F4
Wakefield *Jamaica*	18°26N 77°42W	88 a
Wakefield *U.S.A.*	41°24S 173°5E	59 D4
Wakefield *U.K.*	53°41N 1°29W	12 D6
Wakefield *Mass., U.S.A.*	42°30N 71°5W	83 D13
Wakefield *Mich., U.S.A.*	46°29N 89°56W	80 B9
Wakkanai *Japan*	45°28N 141°35E	30 B10
Wakkerstroom *S. Africa*	27°24S 30°10E	57 D5
Wakool *Australia*	35°28S 144°23E	63 F3
Wakool → *Australia*	35°5S 143°33E	63 F3
Wakre *Indonesia*	0°19S 131°5E	37 E8
Wakuach, L. *Canada*	55°34N 67°32W	73 A6
Walamba *Zambia*	13°30S 28°42E	55 E2
Wałbrzych *Poland*	50°45N 16°18E	16 C9
Walbury Hill *U.K.*	51°21N 1°28W	13 F6
Walcha *Australia*	30°55S 151°31E	63 E5
Walcheren *Neths.*	51°30N 3°35E	15 C3
Walcott *U.S.A.*	41°46N 106°51W	76 F10
Wałcz *Poland*	53°17N 16°27E	16 B9
Waldburg Ra. *Australia*	24°40S 117°35E	61 D2
Walden *Colo., U.S.A.*	40°44N 106°17W	76 F10
Walden *N.Y., U.S.A.*	41°34N 74°11W	83 E10
Waldport *U.S.A.*	44°26N 124°4W	76 D1
Waldron *U.S.A.*	34°54N 94°5W	84 D7
Walebing *Australia*	30°41S 116°13E	61 F2
Wales □ *U.K.*	52°19N 4°43W	13 E3
Walgett *Australia*	30°0S 148°5E	63 E4
Walgreen Coast *Antarctica*	75°15S 105°0W	5 D15
Walker *U.S.A.*	47°6N 94°35W	80 B6
Walker, L. *Canada*	50°20N 67°11W	73 B6
Walker L. *Canada*	54°42N 95°57W	71 C9
Walker L. *U.S.A.*	38°42N 118°43W	76 G4
Walkerston *Australia*	21°11S 149°8E	62 K7
Walkerton *Canada*	44°10N 81°10W	82 B3
Wall *U.S.A.*	44°0N 102°8W	80 C2
Walla Walla *U.S.A.*	46°4N 118°20W	76 C4
Wallace *Idaho, U.S.A.*	47°28N 115°56W	76 C6
Wallace *N.C., U.S.A.*	34°44N 77°59W	85 D16
Wallaceburg *Canada*	42°34N 82°23W	82 D2
Wallachia = Valahia *Romania*	44°35N 25°0E	17 F13
Wallal *Australia*	26°32S 146°7E	63 D4
Wallam Cr. → *Australia*	28°40S 147°20E	63 D4
Wallambin, L. *Australia*	30°57S 117°35E	61 F2
Wallangarra *Australia*	28°56S 151°58E	63 D5
Wallaroo *Australia*	33°56S 137°39E	63 E2
Wallenpaupack, L. *U.S.A.*	41°25N 75°15W	83 E9
Wallingford *Conn., U.S.A.*	41°27N 72°50W	83 E12
Wallingford *Vt., U.S.A.*	43°28N 72°58W	83 C12
Wallis & Futuna, Is. *Pac. Oc.*	13°18S 176°10W	58 C11
Wallowa *U.S.A.*	45°34N 117°32W	76 D5
Wallowa Mts. *U.S.A.*	45°20N 117°30W	76 D5
Walls *U.K.*	60°14N 1°33W	11 A7
Walls of Jerusalem △ *Australia*	41°56S 146°15E	63 G4
Wallula *U.S.A.*	46°5N 118°54W	76 C4
Wallumbilla *Australia*	30°57S 149°9E	63 D4
Walmsley L. *Canada*	63°25N 108°36W	71 A7
Walney, I. of *U.K.*	54°6N 3°15W	12 C4
Walnut Canyon △ *U.S.A.*	35°15N 111°20W	77 J8
Walnut Creek *U.S.A.*	37°54N 122°4W	78 H4
Walnut Ridge *U.S.A.*	36°4N 90°57W	85 C9
Walpole *Australia*	34°58S 116°44E	61 F2
Walpole *U.S.A.*	42°9N 71°15W	83 D13
Walpole-Nornalup △ *Australia*	35°0S 116°45E	61 G2
Walsall *U.K.*	52°35N 1°58W	13 E6
Walsenburg *U.S.A.*	37°38N 104°47W	77 H11
Walsh *U.S.A.*	37°23N 102°17W	77 H12
Walsh → *Australia*	16°31S 143°42E	62 B3
Walsingham *Canada*	42°40N 80°31W	82 D4
Walter F. George Res. *U.S.A.*	31°38N 85°4W	85 F12
Walterboro *U.S.A.*	32°55N 80°40W	85 E14
Walters *U.S.A.*	34°22N 98°19W	84 D5
Waltham *U.S.A.*	42°23N 71°14W	83 D13
Waltman *U.S.A.*	43°4N 107°12W	76 E10
Walton *U.S.A.*	42°10N 75°8W	83 D9
Walton-on-the-Naze *U.K.*	51°51N 1°17E	13 F9
Walvis Bay *Namibia*	23°0S 14°28E	56 C1
Walvisbaai = Walvis Bay *Namibia*	23°0S 14°28E	56 C1
Wamba *Dem. Rep. of the Congo*	2°10N 27°57E	54 B2
Wamba *Kenya*	0°58N 37°19E	54 B4
Wamego *U.S.A.*	39°12N 96°18W	80 F5
Wamena *Indonesia*	4°4S 138°57E	37 E9
Wampsville *U.S.A.*	43°4N 75°42W	83 C9
Wamsutter *U.S.A.*	41°40N 107°58W	76 F10
Wamulan *Indonesia*	3°27S 126°7E	37 E7
Wan Xian *China*	38°47N 115°7E	34 E8
Wana *Pakistan*	32°20N 69°32E	42 C3
Wanaaring *Australia*	29°38S 144°9E	63 D3
Wanaka *N.Z.*	44°42S 169°9E	59 F2
Wanaka, L. *N.Z.*	44°33S 169°7E	59 F2
Wanapitei L. *Canada*	46°45N 80°40W	72 C3
Wandel Sea = McKinley Sea *Arctic*	82°0N 0°0	4 A7
Wanderer *Zimbabwe*	19°36S 30°1E	55 F3
Wandhari *Pakistan*	27°42N 66°48E	42 F2
Wandoan *Australia*	26°5S 149°55E	63 D4
Wanfu *China*	40°8N 122°38E	35 D12
Wang → *Thailand*	17°8N 99°2E	38 D2
Wang Noi *Thailand*	14°13N 100°44E	38 E3
Wang Saphung *Thailand*	17°18N 101°46E	38 D3
Wang Thong *Thailand*	16°50N 100°26E	38 D3
Wanga *Dem. Rep. of the Congo*	2°58N 29°12E	54 B2
Wangal *Indonesia*	6°8S 134°9E	37 F8
Wanganella *Australia*	35°6S 144°49E	63 F3
Wanganui *N.Z.*	39°56S 175°3E	59 C5
Wangaratta *Australia*	36°21S 146°19E	63 F4
Wangary *Australia*	34°35S 135°29E	63 E2
Wangdu *China*	38°40N 115°7E	34 E8
Wangerooge *Germany*	53°47N 7°54E	16 B4
Wangiwangi *Indonesia*	5°22S 123°37E	37 F6
Wangqing *China*	43°12N 129°42E	35 C15
Wankaner *India*	22°35N 71°0E	42 H4
Wanless *Canada*	54°11N 101°21W	71 C8
Wanleweyne *Somali Rep.*	2°37N 44°54E	47 G3
Wanneroo *Australia*	31°42S 115°46E	61 F2
Wanning *China*	18°48N 110°22E	38 C8
Wanon Niwat *Thailand*	17°38N 103°46E	38 D4
Wanqinsha *China*	22°43N 113°33E	33 F10
Wanquan *China*	40°50N 114°40E	34 D8
Wanrong *China*	35°25N 110°50E	34 G6
Wanshan Qundao *China*	21°57N 113°45E	33 G10
Wantage *U.K.*	51°35N 1°25W	13 F6
Wanxian *China*	30°42N 108°20E	32 C5
Wanzai *China*	22°12N 113°31E	33 G10
Wapakoneta *U.S.A.*	40°34N 84°12W	81 E11
Wapato *U.S.A.*	46°27N 120°25W	76 C3
Wapawekka L. *Canada*	54°55N 104°40W	71 C8
Wapikopa L. *Canada*	52°56N 87°53W	72 B2
Wapiti → *Canada*	55°5N 118°18W	70 B5
Wappingers Falls *U.S.A.*	41°36N 73°55W	83 E11
Wapsipinicon → *U.S.A.*	41°44N 90°19W	80 E8
Wapusk △ *Canada*	57°46N 93°22W	71 B10
Warangal *India*	17°58N 79°35E	40 L11
Waraseoni *India*	21°45N 80°2E	43 J9
Waratah *Australia*	41°30S 145°30E	63 G4
Waratah B. *Australia*	38°54S 146°5E	63 F4
Warburton *Vic., Australia*	37°47S 145°42E	63 F4
Warburton *W. Austral., Australia*	26°8S 126°35E	61 E4
Warburton → *Australia*	28°4S 137°28E	63 D2
Warburton Ra. *Australia*	25°55S 126°28E	61 E4
Ward *N.Z.*	41°49S 174°11E	59 D5
Ward → *Australia*	26°28S 146°6E	63 D4
Ward Mt. *U.S.A.*	37°12N 118°54W	78 H8
Warden *S. Africa*	27°50S 29°0E	57 D4
Wardha *India*	20°45N 78°39E	40 J11
Wardha → *India*	19°57N 79°11E	40 K11
Wardsville *Canada*	42°39N 81°45W	82 D3
Ware *U.K.*	51°49N 0°0	13 F8
Ware *U.S.A.*	42°16N 72°14W	83 D12
Waregem *Belgium*	50°53N 3°27E	15 D3
Wareham *U.S.A.*	41°46N 70°43W	83 E14
Waremme *Belgium*	50°43N 5°15E	15 D5
Warialda *Australia*	29°29S 150°33E	63 D5
Wariap *Indonesia*	1°30S 134°5E	37 E8
Warin Chamrap *Thailand*	15°12N 104°53E	38 E5
Warkopi *Indonesia*	1°12S 134°9E	37 E8
Warm Springs *U.S.A.*	38°10N 116°20W	77 G5
Warman *Canada*	52°19N 106°30W	71 C7
Warmbad = Bela Bela *S. Africa*	24°51S 28°19E	57 C4
Warmbad *Namibia*	28°25S 18°42E	56 D2
Warminster *U.K.*	51°12N 2°10W	13 F5
Warminster *U.S.A.*	40°12N 75°6W	83 F9
Warmun *Australia*	17°2S 128°12E	60 C4
Warner Mts. *U.S.A.*	41°40N 120°15W	76 F3
Warner Robins *U.S.A.*	32°37N 83°36W	85 E13
Waroona *Australia*	32°50S 115°58E	61 F2
Warracknabeal *Australia*	36°9S 142°26E	63 F3
Warragul *Australia*	38°10S 145°58E	63 F4
Warrego → *Australia*	30°24S 145°21E	63 E4
Warrego Ra. *Australia*	24°58S 146°0E	62 C4
Warren *Australia*	31°42S 147°51E	63 E4
Warren *Ark., U.S.A.*	33°37N 92°4W	84 E8
Warren *Mich., U.S.A.*	42°28N 83°1W	81 D12
Warren *Minn., U.S.A.*	48°12N 96°46W	80 A5
Warren *Ohio, U.S.A.*	41°14N 80°49W	82 E4
Warren *Pa., U.S.A.*	41°51N 79°9W	82 E5
Warrenpoint *U.K.*	54°6N 6°15W	10 B5
Warrensburg *Mo., U.S.A.*	38°46N 93°44W	80 F7
Warrensburg *N.Y., U.S.A.*	43°29N 73°46W	83 C11
Warrenton *S. Africa*	28°9S 24°47E	56 D3
Warrenton *U.S.A.*	46°10N 123°56W	78 D3
Warri *Nigeria*	5°30N 5°41E	50 G7
Warrina *Australia*	28°12S 135°50E	63 D2
Warrington *U.K.*	53°24N 2°35W	12 D5
Warrington *U.K.*	30°23N 87°17W	85 F11
Warrington □ *U.K.*	53°24N 2°35W	12 D5
Warrnambool *Australia*	38°25S 142°30E	63 F3
Warroad *U.S.A.*	48°54N 95°19W	80 A6
Warruwi *Australia*	11°36S 133°20E	62 A1
Warsa *Indonesia*	0°47S 135°55E	37 E9
Warsak Dam *Pakistan*	34°11N 71°19E	42 B4
Warsaw = Warszawa *Poland*	52°14N 21°0E	17 B11
Warsaw *Ind., U.S.A.*	41°14N 85°51W	81 E11
Warsaw *N.Y., U.S.A.*	42°45N 78°8W	82 D6
Warsaw *Ohio, U.S.A.*	40°20N 82°0W	82 F3
Warszawa *Poland*	52°14N 21°0E	17 B11
Warta → *Poland*	52°35N 14°39E	16 B8
Warthe = Warta → *Poland*	52°35N 14°39E	16 B8
Waru *Indonesia*	3°30S 130°36E	37 E8
Warwick *Australia*	28°10S 152°1E	63 D5
Warwick *U.K.*	52°18N 1°35W	13 E6
Warwick *N.Y., U.S.A.*	41°16N 74°22W	83 E10
Warwick *R.I., U.S.A.*	41°42N 71°28W	83 E13
Warwickshire □ *U.K.*	52°14N 1°38W	13 E6
Wasaga Beach *Canada*	44°31N 80°1W	82 B4
Wasagaming *Canada*	50°39N 99°58W	71 C9
Wasatch Ra. *U.S.A.*	40°0N 111°30W	76 F8
Wasbank *S. Africa*	28°15S 30°9E	57 D5
Wasco *Calif., U.S.A.*	35°36N 119°20W	79 K7
Wasco *Oreg., U.S.A.*	45°36N 120°42W	76 D3
Waseca *U.S.A.*	44°5N 93°30W	80 C7
Wasekamio L. *Canada*	56°45N 108°45W	71 B7
Wash, The *U.K.*	52°58N 0°20E	12 E8
Washburn *Canada*	44°45N 79°20W	82 B5
Washburn *N. Dak., U.S.A.*	47°17N 101°2W	80 B3
Washburn *Wis., U.S.A.*	46°40N 90°54W	80 B8
Washim *India*	20°3N 77°0E	40 J10
Washington *U.K.*	54°55N 1°30W	12 C6
Washington *D.C., U.S.A.*	38°53N 77°2W	81 F15
Washington *Ga., U.S.A.*	33°44N 82°44W	85 E13
Washington *Ind., U.S.A.*	38°40N 87°10W	80 F10
Washington *Iowa, U.S.A.*	41°18N 91°42W	80 E8
Washington *Mo., U.S.A.*	38°33N 91°1W	80 F8
Washington *N.C., U.S.A.*	35°33N 77°3W	85 D16
Washington *Pa., U.S.A.*	40°10N 80°15W	82 F4
Washington *Utah, U.S.A.*	37°8N 113°31W	77 H7
Washington □ *U.S.A.*	47°30N 120°30W	76 C3
Washington, Mt. *U.S.A.*	44°16N 71°18W	83 B13
Washington Court House *U.S.A.*	39°32N 83°26W	81 F12
Washington I. *U.S.A.*	45°23N 86°54W	80 C10
Washougal *U.S.A.*	45°35N 122°21W	78 E4
Washpool △ *Australia*	29°22S 152°20E	63 D5
Wasian *Indonesia*	1°47S 133°19E	37 E8
Wasilla *U.S.A.*	61°35N 149°26W	68 C5
Wasior *Indonesia*	2°43S 134°30E	37 E8
Wāsiṭ □ *Iraq*	32°50N 45°50E	44 C5
Waskaganish *Canada*	51°30N 78°40W	72 B4
Waskaiowaka L. *Canada*	56°33N 96°23W	71 B9
Waskesiu Lake *Canada*	53°55N 106°5W	71 C7
Wasserkuppe *Germany*	50°29N 9°55E	16 C5
Waswanipi *Canada*	49°40N 76°29W	72 C4
Waswanipi, L. *Canada*	49°35N 76°40W	72 C4
Watampone *Indonesia*	4°29S 120°25E	37 E6
Watamu *Kenya*	3°23S 40°0E	54 C5
Watarrka △ *Australia*	24°20S 131°30E	60 D5
Water Park Pt. *Australia*	22°56S 150°47E	62 C5
Water Valley *U.S.A.*	34°10N 89°38W	85 D10
Waterberg Plateau △ *Namibia*	20°25S 17°18E	56 C2
Waterberge *S. Africa*	24°10S 28°0E	57 C4
Waterbury *Conn., U.S.A.*	41°33N 73°3W	83 E11
Waterbury *Vt., U.S.A.*	44°20N 72°46W	83 B12
Waterbury L. *Canada*	58°10N 104°22W	71 B8
Waterdown *Canada*	43°20N 79°53W	82 C5
Waterford *Canada*	42°56N 80°17W	82 D4
Waterford *Ireland*	52°15N 7°8W	10 D4
Waterford *Calif., U.S.A.*	37°38N 120°46W	78 H6
Waterford *Pa., U.S.A.*	41°57N 79°59W	82 E5
Waterford □ *Ireland*	52°10N 7°40W	10 D4
Waterford Harbour *Ireland*	52°8N 6°58W	10 D5
Waterhen L. *Canada*	52°10N 99°40W	71 C9
Waterloo *Belgium*	50°43N 4°25E	15 D4
Waterloo *Ont., Canada*	43°30N 80°32W	82 C4
Waterloo *Qué., Canada*	45°22N 72°32W	83 A12
Waterloo *Ill., U.S.A.*	38°20N 90°9W	80 F8
Waterloo *Iowa, U.S.A.*	42°30N 92°21W	80 D7
Waterloo *N.Y., U.S.A.*	42°54N 76°52W	82 D8
Watersmeet *U.S.A.*	46°16N 89°11W	80 B9
Waterton Lakes △ *Canada*	48°45N 115°0W	70 D6
Watertown *Conn., U.S.A.*	41°36N 73°7W	83 E11
Watertown *N.Y., U.S.A.*	43°59N 75°55W	83 C9
Watertown *S. Dak., U.S.A.*	44°54N 97°7W	80 C5
Watertown *Wis., U.S.A.*	43°12N 88°43W	80 D9
Waterval-Boven *S. Africa*	25°40S 30°18E	57 D5
Waterville *Canada*	45°16N 71°54W	83 A13
Waterville *Maine, U.S.A.*	44°33N 69°38W	81 C19
Waterville *N.Y., U.S.A.*	42°56N 75°23W	83 D9
Waterville *Pa., U.S.A.*	41°19N 77°21W	82 E7
Waterville *Wash., U.S.A.*	47°39N 120°4W	76 C3
Watervliet *U.S.A.*	42°44N 73°42W	83 D11
Wates *Indonesia*	7°51S 110°10E	37 G14
Watford *Canada*	42°57N 81°53W	82 D3
Watford *U.K.*	51°40N 0°24W	13 F7
Watford City *U.S.A.*	47°48N 103°17W	80 B2
Wathaman → *Canada*	57°16N 102°59W	71 B8
Wathaman L. *Canada*	56°58N 103°44W	71 B8
Watheroo *Australia*	30°15S 116°5E	61 F2
Watheroo △ *Australia*	30°19S 115°48E	61 F2
Wating *China*	35°40N 106°38E	34 G4
Watkins Glen *U.S.A.*	42°23N 76°52W	82 D8
Watling I. = San Salvador I. *Bahamas*	24°0N 74°40W	89 B5
Watonga *U.S.A.*	35°51N 98°25W	84 D5
Watrous *Canada*	51°40N 105°25W	71 C7
Watrous *U.S.A.*	35°48N 104°59W	77 J11
Watsa *Dem. Rep. of the Congo*	3°4N 29°30E	54 B2
Watseka *U.S.A.*	40°47N 87°44W	80 E10
Watson *Canada*	52°10N 104°30W	71 C8
Watson Lake *Canada*	60°6N 128°49W	70 A3
Watsontown *U.S.A.*	41°5N 76°52W	82 E8
Watsonville *U.S.A.*	36°55N 121°45W	78 J5
Wattiwarriganna Cr. → *Australia*	28°57S 136°10E	63 D2
Watuata = Batuata *Indonesia*	6°12S 122°42E	37 F6
Watubela, Kepulauan *Indonesia*	4°28S 131°35E	37 E8
Watubela Is. = Watubela, Kepulauan *Indonesia*	4°28S 131°35E	37 E8
Wau = Wâw *Sudan*	7°45N 28°1E	51 G11
Waubamik *Canada*	45°27N 80°1W	82 A4
Waubay *U.S.A.*	45°20N 97°18W	80 C5
Wauchope *N.S.W., Australia*	31°28S 152°45E	63 E5
Wauchope *N. Terr., Australia*	20°36S 134°15E	62 C1
Wauchula *U.S.A.*	27°33N 81°49W	85 H14
Waukarlycarly, L. *Australia*	21°18S 121°56E	60 D3
Waukegan *U.S.A.*	42°22N 87°50W	80 D10
Waukesha *U.S.A.*	43°1N 88°14W	80 D9
Waukon *U.S.A.*	43°16N 91°29W	80 D8
Waupaca *U.S.A.*	44°21N 89°5W	80 C9
Waupun *U.S.A.*	43°38N 88°44W	80 D9
Waurika *U.S.A.*	34°10N 98°0W	84 D6
Wausau *U.S.A.*	44°58N 89°38W	80 C9
Wautoma *U.S.A.*	44°4N 89°18W	80 C9
Wauwatosa *U.S.A.*	43°2N 88°0W	80 D9
Wave Hill = Kalkarindji *Australia*	17°30S 130°47E	60 C5
Wave Rock △ *Australia*	26°5S 118°53E	61 F2
Waveney → *U.K.*	52°35N 1°39E	13 E9
Waverley *N.Z.*	39°46S 174°37E	59 C5
Waverly *Iowa, U.S.A.*	42°44N 92°29W	80 D7
Waverly *N.Y., U.S.A.*	42°1N 76°32W	83 E8
Wavre *Belgium*	50°43N 4°38E	15 D4
Wâw *Sudan*	7°45N 28°1E	51 G11
Wāw al Kabīr *Libya*	25°20N 16°43E	51 C9
Wawa *Canada*	47°59N 84°47W	72 C3
Wawanesa *Canada*	49°36N 99°40W	71 D9
Wawona *U.S.A.*	37°32N 119°39W	78 H7
Waxahachie *U.S.A.*	32°24N 96°51W	84 E6
Way, L. *Australia*	26°45S 120°16E	61 E3
Waya *Fiji*	17°19S 177°10E	59 a
Waycross *U.S.A.*	31°13N 82°21W	85 F13
Wayland *U.S.A.*	42°34N 77°35W	82 D7
Wayne *Nebr., U.S.A.*	42°14N 97°1W	80 D5
Wayne *W. Va., U.S.A.*	38°13N 82°27W	81 F12
Waynesboro *Ga., U.S.A.*	33°6N 82°1W	85 E13
Waynesboro *Miss., U.S.A.*	31°40N 88°39W	85 F10
Waynesboro *Pa., U.S.A.*	39°45N 77°35W	81 F15
Waynesboro *Va., U.S.A.*	38°4N 78°53W	81 F14
Waynesburg *U.S.A.*	39°54N 80°11W	81 F13
Waynesville *U.S.A.*	35°28N 82°58W	85 D13
Waynoka *U.S.A.*	36°35N 98°53W	84 C5
Wazirabad *Pakistan*	32°30N 74°8E	42 C6
We *Indonesia*	5°51N 95°18E	36 C1
Weald, The *U.K.*	51°4N 0°20E	13 F8
Wear → *U.K.*	54°55N 1°23W	12 C6
Weatherford *Okla., U.S.A.*	35°32N 98°43W	84 D5
Weatherford *Tex., U.S.A.*	32°46N 97°48W	84 E6
Weaverville *U.S.A.*	40°44N 122°56W	76 F2
Webb City *U.S.A.*	37°9N 94°28W	80 G6
Webequie *Canada*	52°59N 87°21W	72 B2
Webster *Mass., U.S.A.*	42°3N 71°53W	83 D13
Webster *N.Y., U.S.A.*	43°13N 77°26W	82 C7
Webster *S. Dak., U.S.A.*	45°20N 97°31W	80 C5
Webster City *U.S.A.*	42°28N 93°49W	80 D7
Webster Springs *U.S.A.*	38°29N 80°25W	81 F13
Weda *Indonesia*	0°21N 127°50E	37 D7
Weda, Teluk *Indonesia*	0°20N 128°0E	37 D7
Weddell Abyssal Plain *S. Ocean*	65°0S 20°0W	5 C2
Weddell I. *Falk. Is.*	51°50S 61°0W	96 G4
Weddell Sea *Antarctica*	72°30S 40°0W	5 D1
Wedderburn *Australia*	36°26S 143°33E	63 F3
Wedgeport *Canada*	43°44N 65°59W	73 D6
Wedza *Zimbabwe*	18°40S 31°33E	55 F3
Wee Waa *Australia*	30°11S 149°26E	63 E4
Weed *U.S.A.*	41°25N 122°23W	76 F2
Weed Heights *U.S.A.*	38°59N 119°13W	78 G7
Weedsport *U.S.A.*	43°2N 76°33W	83 C8
Weedville *U.S.A.*	41°17N 78°30W	82 E6
Weenen *S. Africa*	28°48S 30°7E	57 D5
Weert *Neths.*	51°15N 5°43E	15 C5
Wei He → *Hebei, China*	36°10N 115°45E	34 F8
Wei He → *Shaanxi, China*	34°38N 110°15E	34 G6
Weichang *China*	41°58N 117°49E	35 D9
Weichuan *China*	34°20N 113°59E	34 G7
Weiden *Germany*	49°41N 12°10E	16 D7
Weifang *China*	36°44N 119°7E	35 F10
Weihai *China*	37°30N 122°6E	35 F12
Weimar *Germany*	50°58N 11°19E	16 C6
Weinan *China*	34°31N 109°29E	34 G5
Weipa *Australia*	12°40S 141°50E	62 A3
Weir → *Australia*	28°20S 149°50E	63 D4
Weir → *Canada*	56°54N 93°21W	71 B10
Weir River *Canada*	56°49N 94°6W	71 B10
Weirton *U.S.A.*	40°24N 80°35W	82 F4
Weiser *U.S.A.*	44°15N 116°58W	76 D5
Weishan *China*	34°47N 117°5E	35 G9
Weiyuan *China*	35°7N 104°10E	34 G3
Wejherowo *Poland*	54°35N 18°12E	17 A10
Wekusko L. *Canada*	54°40N 99°50W	71 C9
Welch *U.S.A.*	37°26N 81°35W	81 G13
Welford △ *Australia*	25°5S 143°16E	62 D3
Welkom *S. Africa*	28°0S 26°46E	56 D4
Welland *Canada*	43°0N 79°15W	82 D5
Welland → *U.K.*	52°51N 0°5W	13 E7
Wellesley Is. *Australia*	16°42S 139°30E	62 B2
Wellingborough *U.K.*	52°19N 0°41W	13 E7
Wellington *Australia*	32°35S 148°59E	63 E4
Wellington *Canada*	43°57N 77°20W	82 C7
Wellington *N.Z.*	41°19S 174°46E	59 D5
Wellington *S. Africa*	33°38S 19°1E	56 E2
Wellington *Somst., U.K.*	50°58N 3°13W	13 G4
Wellington *Telford & Wrekin, U.K.*	52°42N 2°30W	13 E5
Wellington *Colo., U.S.A.*	40°42N 105°0W	76 F11
Wellington *Kans., U.S.A.*	37°16N 97°24W	80 G5
Wellington *Nev., U.S.A.*	38°45N 119°23W	78 G7
Wellington *Ohio, U.S.A.*	41°10N 82°13W	82 E2
Wellington *Tex., U.S.A.*	34°51N 100°13W	84 D4
Wellington, I. *Chile*	49°30S 75°0W	96 F2
Wellington, L. *Australia*	38°6S 147°20E	63 F4
Wellington Chan. *Canada*	75°0N 93°0W	69 B10
Wells *U.K.*	51°13N 2°39W	13 F5
Wells *Maine, U.S.A.*	43°20N 70°35W	83 C14
Wells *N.Y., U.S.A.*	43°24N 74°17W	83 C10
Wells *Nev., U.S.A.*	41°7N 114°58W	76 F6
Wells, L. *Australia*	26°44S 123°15E	61 E3
Wells, Mt. *Australia*	17°25S 127°8E	60 C4
Wells Gray △ *Canada*	52°30N 120°15W	70 C4
Wells-next-the-Sea *U.K.*	52°57N 0°51E	12 E8
Wells River *U.S.A.*	44°9N 72°4W	83 B12
Wellsboro *U.S.A.*	41°45N 77°18W	82 E7
Wellsburg *U.S.A.*	40°16N 80°37W	82 F4
Wellsville *N.Y., U.S.A.*	42°7N 77°57W	82 D7
Wellsville *Ohio, U.S.A.*	40°36N 80°39W	82 F4
Wellsville *Utah, U.S.A.*	41°38N 111°56W	76 F8
Wellton *U.S.A.*	32°40N 114°8W	77 K6
Wels *Austria*	48°9N 14°1E	16 D8
Welshpool *U.K.*	52°39N 3°8W	13 E4
Welwyn Garden City *U.K.*	51°48N 0°12W	13 F7
Wem *U.K.*	52°52N 2°44W	12 E5
Wembere → *Tanzania*	4°10S 34°15E	54 C3
Wemindji *Canada*	53°0N 78°49W	72 B4
Wemyss *Canada*	44°52N 76°23W	83 B8
Wen Xian *China*	34°55N 113°5E	34 G7
Wenatchee *U.S.A.*	47°25N 120°19W	76 C3
Wenchang *China*	19°38N 110°42E	38 C8
Wenchi *Ghana*	7°46N 2°8W	50 G5
Wenchow = Wenzhou *China*	28°0N 120°38E	33 D7
Wenden *U.S.A.*	33°49N 113°33W	79 M13
Wendeng *China*	37°15N 122°5E	35 F12
Wendesi *Indonesia*	2°30S 134°17E	37 E8
Wendover *U.S.A.*	40°44N 114°2W	76 F6
Wenlock → *Australia*	12°2S 141°55E	62 A3
Wenshan *China*	23°20N 104°18E	32 D5
Wenshang *China*	35°45N 116°30E	34 G9
Wenshui *China*	37°26N 112°1E	34 F6
Wensleydale *U.K.*	54°17N 2°0W	12 C6
Wensu *China*	41°15N 80°10E	32 B3
Wensum → *U.K.*	52°40N 1°15E	12 E8
Wentworth *Australia*	34°2S 141°54E	63 E3
Wentzel L. *Canada*	59°2N 114°28W	70 B6
Wenut *Indonesia*	3°11S 133°19E	37 E8
Wenxi *China*	35°20N 111°10E	34 G6
Wenxian *China*	32°43N 104°36E	34 H3
Wenzhou *China*	28°0N 120°38E	33 D7
Weott *U.S.A.*	40°20N 123°55W	76 F2
Wepener *S. Africa*	29°42S 27°3E	56 D4
Werda *Botswana*	25°24S 23°15E	56 D3
Weri *Indonesia*	3°10S 132°38E	37 E8
Werra → *Germany*	51°24N 9°39E	16 C5
Werrimull *Australia*	34°25S 141°38E	63 E3
Werris Creek *Australia*	31°18S 150°38E	63 E5
Weser → *Germany*	53°36N 8°28E	16 B5
Wesiri *Indonesia*	7°30S 126°30E	37 F7
Weslaco *U.S.A.*	26°10N 97°58W	84 H6
Weslemkoon L. *Canada*	45°2N 77°25W	82 A7
Wesleyville *Canada*	49°9N 53°33W	73 C9
Wesleyville *U.S.A.*	42°9N 80°1W	82 D4
Wessel, C. *Australia*	10°59S 136°46E	62 A2
Wessel Is. *Australia*	11°10S 136°45E	62 A2
Wessington Springs *U.S.A.*	44°5N 98°34W	80 C4
West *U.S.A.*	31°48N 97°6W	84 F6
West → *U.S.A.*	42°52N 72°33W	83 D12
West Allis *U.S.A.*	43°1N 88°0W	80 D9
West Antarctica *Antarctica*	80°0S 90°0W	5 D15
West Baines → *Australia*	15°38S 129°59E	60 C4
West Bank ■ *Asia*	32°6N 35°13E	46 C4
West Bend *U.S.A.*	43°25N 88°11W	80 D9
West Bengal □ *India*	23°0N 88°0E	43 H13
West Berkshire □ *U.K.*	51°25N 1°17W	13 F6
West Beskids = Západné Beskydy *Europe*	49°30N 19°0E	17 D10
West Branch *U.S.A.*	44°17N 84°14W	81 C11
West Branch Susquehanna → *U.S.A.*	40°53N 76°48W	83 F8
West Bromwich *U.K.*	52°32N 1°59W	13 E6
West Burra *U.K.*	60°5N 1°21W	11 A7
West Canada Cr. → *U.S.A.*	43°1N 74°58W	83 C10
West Caroline Basin *Pac. Oc.*	4°0N 138°0E	64 G5

West Chazy *U.S.A.* 44°49N 73°28W **83** B11
West Chester *U.S.A.* 39°58N 75°36W **83** G9
West Coast ⌂ *Namibia* 21°53S 14°14E **56** C1
West Coast △ *S. Africa* 33°13S 18°0E **56** E2
West Columbia *U.S.A.* 29°9N 95°39W **84** G7
West Covina *U.S.A.* 34°4N 117°54W **79** L9
West Des Moines *U.S.A.* 41°35N 93°43W **80** E7
West Dunbartonshire □ *U.K.* 55°59N 4°30W **11** F4
West End *Bahamas* 26°41N 78°58W **88** A4
West Falkland *Falk. Is.* 51°40S 60°0W **96** G4
West Fargo *U.S.A.* 46°52N 96°54W **80** B5
West Fiji Basin *Pac. Oc.* 17°0S 173°0E **64** J9
West Fjord = Vestfjorden *Norway* 67°55N 14°0E **8** C16
West Fork Trinity → *U.S.A.* 32°48N 96°54W **84** E6
West Frankfort *U.S.A.* 37°54N 88°55W **80** G9
West Grand L. *U.S.A.* 45°14N 67°51W **81** C20
West Hartford *U.S.A.* 41°45N 72°44W **83** E12
West Haven *U.S.A.* 41°17N 72°57W **83** E12
West Hazleton *U.S.A.* 40°58N 76°0W **83** F9
West Helena *U.S.A.* 34°33N 90°38W **85** D9
West Hurley *U.S.A.* 41°59N 74°7W **83** E10
West Ice Shelf *Antarctica* 67°0S 85°0E **5** C7
West Indies *Cent. Amer.* 15°0N 65°0W **89** D7
West Jordan *U.S.A.* 40°36N 111°56W **76** F8
West Lamma Channel *China* 22°14N 114°4E **33** G11
West Linn *U.S.A.* 45°21N 122°36W **78** E4
West Lorne *Canada* 42°36N 81°36W **82** D3
West Lothian □ *U.K.* 55°54N 3°36W **11** F5
West Lunga → *Zambia* 13°6S 24°39E **55** E1
West MacDonnell △ *Australia* 23°38S 132°59E **60** D5
West Mariana Basin *Pac. Oc.* 15°0N 137°0E **64** F5
West Memphis *U.S.A.* 35°8N 90°10W **85** D9
West Midlands □ *U.K.* 52°26N 2°0W **13** E6
West Mifflin *U.S.A.* 40°21N 79°52W **82** F5
West Milford *U.S.A.* 41°8N 74°22W **83** E10
West Milton *U.S.A.* 41°1N 76°50W **82** E8
West Monroe *U.S.A.* 32°31N 92°9W **84** E8
West Newton *U.S.A.* 40°14N 79°46W **82** F5
West Nicholson *Zimbabwe* 21°2S 29°20E **55** G2
West Odessa *U.S.A.* 31°50N 102°30W **84** F3
West Palm Beach *U.S.A.* 26°43N 80°3W **85** H14
West Plains *U.S.A.* 36°44N 91°51W **80** G8
West Point *Miss., U.S.A.* 33°36N 88°39W **85** E10
West Point *N.Y., U.S.A.* 41°24N 73°58W **83** E11
West Point *Nebr., U.S.A.* 41°51N 96°43W **80** E5
West Point *Va., U.S.A.* 37°32N 76°48W **81** G15
West Point L. *U.S.A.* 33°8N 85°0W **85** E12
West Pt. = Ouest, Pte. de l' *Canada* 49°52N 64°40W **73** C7
West Pt. *Australia* 35°1S 135°56E **63** F2
West Road → *Canada* 53°18N 122°53W **70** C4
West Rutland *U.S.A.* 43°38N 73°3W **83** C11
West Schelde = Westerschelde → *Neths.* 51°25N 3°25E **15** C3
West Seneca *U.S.A.* 42°51N 78°48W **82** D6
West Siberian Plain *Russia* 62°0N 75°0E **26** B9
West Sussex □ *U.K.* 50°55N 0°30W **13** G7
West-Terschelling *Neths.* 53°22N 5°13E **15** A5
West Valley City *U.S.A.* 40°42N 111°58W **76** F8
West Virginia □ *U.S.A.* 38°45N 80°30W **81** F13
West-Vlaanderen □ *Belgium* 51°0N 3°0E **15** D2
West Walker → *U.S.A.* 38°54N 119°9W **78** G7
West Wyalong *Australia* 33°56S 147°10E **63** E4
West Yellowstone *U.S.A.* 44°40N 111°6W **76** D8
West Yorkshire □ *U.K.* 53°45N 1°40W **12** D6
Westall, Pt. *Australia* 32°55S 134°4E **63** E1
Westbrook *U.S.A.* 43°41N 70°22W **81** D18
Westbury *Australia* 41°30S 146°51E **63** G4
Westby *U.S.A.* 48°52N 104°3W **76** B11
Westend *U.S.A.* 35°42N 117°24W **79** K9
Westerland *Germany* 54°54N 8°17E **16** A5
Westerly *U.S.A.* 41°22N 71°50W **83** E13
Western □ *Kenya* 0°30N 34°30E **54** B3
Western □ *Zambia* 15°0S 24°4E **55** F1
Western Australia □ *Australia* 25°0S 118°0E **61** E2
Western Cape □ *S. Africa* 34°0S 20°0E **56** E3
Western Dvina = Daugava → *Latvia* 57°4N 24°3E **9** H21
Western Ghats *India* 14°0N 75°0E **40** N9
Western Isles □ *U.K.* 57°30N 7°10W **11** D1
Western Sahara ■ *Africa* 25°0N 13°0W **50** D3
Western Samoa = Samoa ■ *Pac. Oc.* 14°0S 172°0W **59** b
Western Sierra Madre = Madre Occidental, Sierra *Mexico* 27°0N 107°0W **86** B3
Westernport *U.S.A.* 39°29N 79°3W **81** F14
Westerschelde → *Neths.* 51°25N 3°25E **15** C3
Westerwald *Germany* 50°38N 7°56E **16** C4
Westfield *Mass., U.S.A.* 42°7N 72°45W **83** D12
Westfield *N.Y., U.S.A.* 42°20N 79°35W **82** D5
Westfield *Pa., U.S.A.* 41°55N 77°32W **82** E7
Westhill *U.K.* 57°9N 2°19W **11** D6
Westhope *U.S.A.* 48°55N 101°1W **80** A3
Westland △ *N.Z.* 43°16S 170°16E **59** E2
Westland Bight *N.Z.* 42°55S 170°5E **59** E3
Westlock *Canada* 54°9N 113°55W **70** C6
Westmar *Australia* 27°55S 149°44E **63** D4
Westmeath □ *Ireland* 53°33N 7°34W **10** C4
Westminster *Calif., U.S.A.* 33°45N 118°0W **79** M8
Westminster *Colo., U.S.A.* 39°50N 105°2W **76** G11
Westminster *Md., U.S.A.* 39°34N 76°59W **81** F15
Westmont *U.S.A.* 40°19N 78°58W **82** F6
Westmoreland *Barbados* 13°13N 59°37W **89** g
Westmorland *U.S.A.* 33°2N 115°37W **79** M11
Weston *Oreg., U.S.A.* 45°49N 118°26W **76** D4
Weston *W. Va., U.S.A.* 39°2N 80°28W **81** F13
Weston I. *Canada* 52°33N 79°36W **72** B4
Weston-super-Mare *U.K.* 51°21N 2°58W **13** F5
Westover *U.S.A.* 40°45N 78°40W **82** F6
Westport *Canada* 44°40N 76°25W **83** B8
Westport *Ireland* 53°48N 9°31W **10** C2
Westport *N.Z.* 41°46S 171°37E **59** D3
Westport *N.Y., U.S.A.* 44°11N 73°26W **83** B11
Westport *Oreg., U.S.A.* 46°8N 123°23W **78** D3
Westport *Wash., U.S.A.* 46°53N 124°6W **78** D2
Westray *Canada* 53°36N 101°24W **71** C8
Westray *U.K.* 59°18N 3°0W **11** B5
Westree *Canada* 47°26N 81°34W **72** C3
Westville *U.S.A.* 39°8N 120°42W **78** F6
Westwood *U.S.A.* 40°18N 121°0W **76** F3
Wetar *Indonesia* 7°48S 126°30E **37** F7
Wetaskiwin *Canada* 52°55N 113°24W **70** C6
Wete *Tanzania* 5°4S 39°43E **52** F7
Wetherby *U.K.* 53°56N 1°23W **12** D6
Wethersfield *U.S.A.* 41°42N 72°40W **83** E12
Wetteren *Belgium* 51°0N 3°53E **15** D3
Wetzlar *Germany* 50°32N 8°31E **16** C5
Wewoka *U.S.A.* 35°9N 96°30W **84** D6
Wexford *Ireland* 52°20N 6°28W **10** D5
Wexford □ *Ireland* 52°20N 6°25W **10** D5
Wexford Harbour *Ireland* 52°20N 6°25W **10** D5
Weyburn *Canada* 49°40N 103°50W **71** D8
Weymouth *Canada* 44°30N 66°1W **73** D6
Weymouth *U.K.* 50°37N 2°28W **13** G5
Weymouth *U.S.A.* 42°13N 70°58W **83** D14
Weymouth, C. *Australia* 12°37S 143°27E **62** A3
Wha Ti *Canada* 63°8N 117°16W **68** C8
Whakaari = White I. *N.Z.* 37°30S 177°13E **59** B6
Whakatane *N.Z.* 37°57S 177°1E **59** B6
Whale → *Canada* 58°15N 67°40W **73** A6
Whale Cove *Canada* 62°10N 92°34W **71** A10
Whales, B. of *Antarctica* 78°0S 160°0W **5** D12
Whalsay *U.K.* 60°22N 0°59W **11** A8
Whangamata *N.Z.* 37°12S 175°53E **59** B5
Whangamomona *N.Z.* 39°8S 174°44E **59** C5
Whanganui △ *N.Z.* 39°17S 174°53E **59** C5
Whangarei *N.Z.* 35°43S 174°21E **59** A5
Whangarei Harb. *N.Z.* 35°45S 174°28E **59** A5
Wharekauri = Chatham Is. *Pac. Oc.* 44°0S 176°40W **64** M10
Wharfe → *U.K.* 53°51N 1°9W **12** D6
Wharfedale *U.K.* 54°6N 2°1W **12** C5
Wharton *N.J., U.S.A.* 40°54N 74°35W **83** F10
Wharton *Pa., U.S.A.* 41°31N 78°1W **82** E6
Wharton *Tex., U.S.A.* 29°19N 96°6W **84** G6
Wharton Basin *Ind. Oc.* 22°0S 92°0E **64** K1
Wheatland *Calif., U.S.A.* 39°1N 121°25W **78** F5
Wheatland *Wyo., U.S.A.* 42°3N 104°58W **76** E11
Wheatley *Canada* 42°6N 82°27W **82** D2
Wheaton *Md., U.S.A.* 39°3N 77°3W **81** F15
Wheaton *Minn., U.S.A.* 45°48N 96°30W **80** C5
Wheelbarrow Pk. *U.S.A.* 37°26N 116°5W **78** H10
Wheeler *Oreg., U.S.A.* 45°41N 123°53W **76** D2
Wheeler *Tex., U.S.A.* 35°27N 100°16W **84** D4
Wheeler → *Canada* 57°2N 67°13W **73** A6
Wheeler L. *U.S.A.* 34°48N 87°23W **85** D11
Wheeler Pk. *N. Mex., U.S.A.* 36°34N 105°25W **77** H11
Wheeler Pk. *Nev., U.S.A.* 38°57N 114°15W **76** G6
Wheeler Ridge *U.S.A.* 35°0N 118°57W **79** L8
Wheelersburg *U.S.A.* 38°44N 82°51W **81** F12
Wheeling *U.S.A.* 40°4N 80°43W **82** F4
Whernside *U.K.* 54°14N 2°24W **12** C5
Whiddy I. *Ireland* 51°41N 9°31W **10** E2
Whim Creek *Australia* 20°50S 117°49E **60** D2
Whiskey Jack L. *Canada* 58°23N 101°55W **71** B8
Whiskeytown-Shasta-Trinity ⌂ *U.S.A.* 40°45N 122°15W **76** F2
Whistleduck Cr. → *Australia* 20°15S 135°18E **62** C2
Whistler *Canada* 50°7N 122°58W **70** C4
Whitby *Canada* 43°52N 78°56W **82** C6
Whitby *U.K.* 54°29N 0°37W **12** C7
White → *Ark., U.S.A.* 33°57N 91°5W **84** E9
White → *Ind., U.S.A.* 38°25N 87°45W **80** F10
White → *S. Dak., U.S.A.* 43°42N 99°27W **80** D4
White → *Tex., U.S.A.* 33°14N 100°56W **84** E4
White → *Utah, U.S.A.* 40°4N 109°41W **76** F9
White → *Vt., U.S.A.* 43°37N 72°20W **83** C12
White → *Wash., U.S.A.* 47°12N 122°15W **78** C4
White, L. *Australia* 21°9S 128°56E **60** D4
White B. *Canada* 50°0N 56°35W **73** C8
White Bird *U.S.A.* 45°46N 116°18W **76** D5
White Butte *U.S.A.* 46°23N 103°18W **80** B2
White City *U.S.A.* 42°26N 122°51W **76** E2
White Cliffs *Australia* 30°50S 143°10E **63** E3
White Hall *U.S.A.* 39°26N 90°24W **80** F8
White Haven *U.S.A.* 41°4N 75°47W **83** E9
White Horse, Vale of *U.K.* 51°37N 1°30W **13** F6
White I. *N.Z.* 37°30S 177°13E **59** B6
White L. *Canada* 45°18N 76°31W **83** A8
White L. *U.S.A.* 29°44N 92°30W **84** G8
White Lake *Canada* 45°21N 76°29W **83** A8
White Mountain Peak *U.S.A.* 37°38N 118°15W **77** H4
White Mts. *Calif., U.S.A.* 37°30N 118°15W **78** H8
White Mts. *N.H., U.S.A.* 44°15N 71°15W **83** B13
White Mts. △ *Australia* 20°43S 145°12E **62** C4
White Nile = Nîl el Abyad → *Sudan* 15°38N 32°31E **51** E12
White Otter L. *Canada* 49°5N 91°55W **72** C1
White Pass *U.S.A.* 46°38N 121°24W **78** D5
White Plains *U.S.A.* 41°2N 73°46W **83** E11
White River *Canada* 48°35N 85°20W **72** C2
White River *S. Africa* 25°20S 31°0E **57** D5
White River *U.S.A.* 43°34N 100°45W **80** D3
White Rock *Canada* 49°2N 122°48W **78** A4
White Rock *U.S.A.* 35°50N 106°12W **77** J10
White Russia = Belarus ■ *Europe* 53°30N 27°0E **17** B14
White Sands ⌂ *U.S.A.* 32°46N 106°20W **77** K10
White Sea = Beloye More *Russia* 66°30N 38°0E **8** C25
White Sulphur Springs *Mont., U.S.A.* 46°33N 110°54W **76** C8
White Sulphur Springs *W. Va., U.S.A.* 37°48N 80°18W **81** G13
White Swan *U.S.A.* 46°23N 120°44W **78** D6
Whitecliffs *N.Z.* 43°26S 171°55E **59** E3
Whitecourt *Canada* 54°10N 115°45W **70** C5
Whiteface Mt. *U.S.A.* 44°22N 73°54W **83** B11
Whitefield *U.S.A.* 44°23N 71°37W **83** B13
Whitefish *U.S.A.* 48°25N 114°20W **76** B6
Whitefish B. *U.S.A.* 46°40N 84°55W **72** C3
Whitefish L. *Canada* 62°41N 106°48W **71** A7
Whitefish Pt. *U.S.A.* 46°45N 84°59W **81** B11
Whitegull, L. = Goélands, L. aux *Canada* 55°27N 64°17W **73** A7
Whitehall *Mich., U.S.A.* 43°24N 86°21W **80** D10
Whitehall *Mont., U.S.A.* 45°52N 112°6W **76** D7
Whitehall *N.Y., U.S.A.* 43°33N 73°24W **83** C11
Whitehall *Wis., U.S.A.* 44°22N 91°19W **80** C8
Whitehaven *U.K.* 54°33N 3°35W **12** C4
Whitehorse *Canada* 60°43N 135°3W **70** A1
Whitemark *Australia* 40°7S 148°3E **63** G4
Whiteriver *U.S.A.* 33°50N 109°58W **77** K9
Whitesand → *Canada* 60°9N 115°45W **70** A5
Whitesands *S. Africa* 34°23S 20°50E **56** E3
Whitesboro *N.Y., U.S.A.* 43°7N 75°18W **83** C9
Whitesboro *Tex., U.S.A.* 33°39N 96°54W **84** E6
Whiteshell ⌂ *Canada* 50°0N 95°40W **71** D9
Whiteville *U.S.A.* 34°20N 78°42W **85** D15
Whitewater *U.S.A.* 42°50N 88°44W **80** D9
Whitewater Baldy *U.S.A.* 33°20N 108°39W **77** K9
Whitewater L. *Canada* 50°50N 89°10W **72** B2
Whitewood *Australia* 21°28S 143°30E **62** C3
Whitewood *Canada* 50°20N 102°20W **71** C8
Whithorn *U.K.* 54°44N 4°26W **11** G4
Whitianga *N.Z.* 36°47S 175°41E **59** B5
Whitman *U.S.A.* 42°5N 70°56W **83** D14
Whitney *Canada* 45°31N 78°14W **82** A6
Whitney, Mt. *U.S.A.* 36°35N 118°18W **78** J8
Whitney Point *U.S.A.* 42°20N 75°58W **83** D9
Whitstable *U.K.* 51°21N 1°3E **13** F9
Whitsunday I. *Australia* 20°15S 149°4E **62** J7
Whitsunday Islands △ *Australia* 20°15S 149°0E **62** J7
Whitsunday Passage *Australia* 20°16S 148°51E **62** J6
Whittier *U.S.A.* 33°58N 118°2W **79** M8
Whittlesea *Australia* 37°27S 145°9E **63** F4
Wholdaia L. *Canada* 60°43N 104°20W **71** A8
Whyalla *Australia* 33°2S 137°30E **63** E2
Wiang Kosai △ *Thailand* 17°54N 99°29E **38** D2
Wiang Sa *Thailand* 18°34N 100°45E **38** C3
Wiarton *Canada* 44°40N 81°10W **82** B3
Wiay *U.K.* 57°24N 7°13W **11** D1
Wibaux *U.S.A.* 46°59N 104°11W **76** C11
Wichian Buri *Thailand* 15°39N 101°7E **38** E3
Wichita *U.S.A.* 37°42N 97°20W **80** G5
Wichita Falls *U.S.A.* 33°54N 98°30W **84** E5
Wick *U.K.* 58°26N 3°5W **11** C5
Wickenburg *U.S.A.* 33°58N 112°44W **77** K7
Wickepin *Australia* 32°50S 117°30E **61** F2
Wickham *Australia* 20°42S 117°11E **60** D2
Wickham, C. *Australia* 39°35S 143°57E **63** F3
Wickliffe *U.S.A.* 41°36N 81°28W **82** E3
Wicklow *Ireland* 52°59N 6°3W **10** D5
Wicklow □ *Ireland* 52°57N 6°25W **10** D5
Wicklow Hd. *Ireland* 52°58N 6°0W **10** D6
Wicklow Mts. *Ireland* 52°58N 6°26W **10** C5
Wicklow Mts. △ *Ireland* 53°6N 6°21W **10** C5
Widgeegoara Cr. → *Australia* 28°51S 146°34E **63** D4
Widgiemooltha *Australia* 31°30S 121°34E **61** F3
Widnes *U.K.* 53°23N 2°45W **12** D5
Wieluń *Poland* 51°15N 18°34E **17** C10
Wien *Austria* 48°12N 16°22E **16** D9
Wiener Neustadt *Austria* 47°49N 16°16E **16** E9
Wiesbaden *Germany* 50°4N 8°14E **16** C5
Wigan *U.K.* 53°33N 2°38W **12** D5
Wiggins *Colo., U.S.A.* 40°14N 104°4W **76** F11
Wiggins *Miss., U.S.A.* 30°51N 89°8W **85** F10
Wight, I. of *U.K.* 50°41N 1°17W **13** G6
Wigston *U.K.* 52°35N 1°6W **13** E6
Wigton *U.K.* 54°50N 3°10W **12** C4
Wigtown *U.K.* 54°53N 4°27W **11** G4
Wigtown B. *U.K.* 54°46N 4°15W **11** G4
Wilber *U.S.A.* 40°29N 96°58W **80** E5
Wilberforce *Canada* 45°2N 78°13W **82** A6
Wilberforce, C. *Australia* 11°54S 136°35E **62** A2
Wilburton *U.S.A.* 34°55N 95°19W **84** D7
Wilcannia *Australia* 31°30S 143°26E **63** E3
Wilcox *U.S.A.* 41°35N 78°41W **82** E6
Wildrose *U.S.A.* 36°14N 117°11W **79** J9
Wildspitze *Austria* 46°53N 10°53E **16** E6
Wilge → *S. Africa* 27°3S 28°20E **57** D4
Wilhelm II Coast *Antarctica* 68°0S 90°0E **5** C7
Wilhelmshaven *Germany* 53°31N 8°7E **16** B5
Wilhelmstal *Namibia* 21°58S 16°21E **56** C2
Wilkes-Barre *U.S.A.* 41°15N 75°53W **83** E9
Wilkes Land *Antarctica* 69°0S 120°0E **5** D9
Wilkie *Canada* 52°27N 108°42W **71** C7
Wilkinsburg *U.S.A.* 40°26N 79°52W **82** F5
Wilkinson Lakes *Australia* 29°40S 132°39E **61** E5
Willandra Creek → *Australia* 33°22S 145°52E **63** E4
Willapa B. *U.S.A.* 46°40N 124°0W **76** C1
Willapa Hills *U.S.A.* 46°35N 123°25W **78** D3
Willard *U.S.A.* 41°3N 82°44W **82** E2
Willcox *U.S.A.* 32°15N 109°50W **77** K9
Willemstad *Neth. Ant.* 12°5N 68°55W **89** D6
William → *Canada* 59°8N 109°19W **71** B7
William 'Bill' Dannelly Res. *U.S.A.* 32°6N 87°24W **85** E11
William Creek *Australia* 28°58S 136°22E **63** D2
Williams *Australia* 33°2S 116°52E **61** F2
Williams *Ariz., U.S.A.* 35°15N 112°11W **77** J7
Williams *Calif., U.S.A.* 39°9N 122°9W **78** F4
Williams Harbour *Canada* 52°33N 55°47W **73** B8
Williams Lake *Canada* 52°10N 122°10W **70** C4
Williamsburg *Ky., U.S.A.* 36°44N 84°10W **81** G11
Williamsburg *Pa., U.S.A.* 40°28N 78°12W **82** F6
Williamsburg *Va., U.S.A.* 37°16N 76°43W **81** G15
Williamson *N.Y., U.S.A.* 43°14N 77°11W **82** C7
Williamson *W. Va., U.S.A.* 37°41N 82°17W **81** G12
Williamsport *U.S.A.* 41°15N 77°1W **82** E7
Williamston *U.S.A.* 35°51N 77°4W **85** D16
Williamstown *Australia* 37°51S 144°52E **63** F3
Williamstown *Ky., U.S.A.* 38°38N 84°34W **81** F11
Williamstown *Mass., U.S.A.* 42°43N 73°12W **83** D11
Williamstown *N.Y., U.S.A.* 43°26N 75°53W **83** C9
Willimantic *U.S.A.* 41°43N 72°13W **83** E12
Willingboro *U.S.A.* 40°3N 74°54W **81** E16
Williston *S. Africa* 31°20S 20°53E **56** E3
Williston *Fla., U.S.A.* 29°23N 82°27W **85** G13
Williston *N. Dak., U.S.A.* 48°9N 103°37W **80** A2
Williston L. *Canada* 56°0N 124°0W **70** B4
Willits *U.S.A.* 39°25N 123°21W **76** G2
Willmar *U.S.A.* 45°7N 95°3W **80** C6
Willmore Wilderness ⌂ *Canada* 53°45N 119°30W **70** C5
Willoughby *U.S.A.* 41°39N 81°24W **82** E3
Willow Bunch *Canada* 49°20N 105°35W **71** D7
Willow L. *Canada* 62°10N 119°8W **70** A5
Willow Wall, The *China* 42°10N 122°0E **35** C12
Willowick *U.S.A.* 41°38N 81°28W **82** E3
Willowlake → *Canada* 62°42N 123°8W **70** A4
Willowmore *S. Africa* 33°15S 23°30E **56** E3
Willows *U.S.A.* 39°31N 122°12W **78** F4
Willowvale = Gatyana *S. Africa* 32°16S 28°31E **57** E4
Wills, L. *Australia* 21°25S 128°51E **60** D4
Wills Cr. → *Australia* 22°43S 140°2E **62** C3
Willsboro *U.S.A.* 44°21N 73°24W **83** B11
Willunga *Australia* 35°15S 138°30E **63** F2
Wilmette *U.S.A.* 42°4N 87°42W **80** D10
Wilmington *Australia* 32°39S 138°7E **63** E2
Wilmington *Del., U.S.A.* 39°45N 75°33W **81** F16
Wilmington *N.C., U.S.A.* 34°14N 77°55W **85** D16
Wilmington *Ohio, U.S.A.* 39°27N 83°50W **81** F12
Wilmington *Vt., U.S.A.* 42°52N 72°52W **83** D12
Wilmslow *U.K.* 53°19N 2°13W **12** D5
Wilpena Cr. → *Australia* 31°25S 139°29E **63** E2
Wilsall *U.S.A.* 45°59N 110°38W **76** D8
Wilson *N.C., U.S.A.* 35°44N 77°55W **85** D16
Wilson *N.Y., U.S.A.* 43°19N 78°50W **82** C6
Wilson *Pa., U.S.A.* 40°41N 75°15W **83** F9
Wilson → *Australia* 16°48S 128°16E **60** C4
Wilson Bluff *Australia* 31°41S 129°0E **61** F4
Wilson Inlet *Australia* 35°0S 117°22E **61** G2
Wilsons Promontory *Australia* 38°59S 146°23E **63** F4
Wilton *U.S.A.* 47°10N 100°47W **80** B3
Wilton → *Australia* 14°45S 134°33E **62** A1
Wiltshire □ *U.K.* 51°18N 1°53W **13** F6
Wiltz *Lux.* 49°57N 5°55E **15** E5
Wiluna *Australia* 26°36S 120°14E **61** E3
Wimborne Minster *U.K.* 50°48N 1°59W **13** G6
Wimmera → *Australia* 36°8S 141°56E **63** F3
Winam G. *Kenya* 0°20S 34°15E **54** C3
Winburg *S. Africa* 28°30S 27°2E **56** D4
Winchendon *U.S.A.* 42°41N 72°3W **83** D12
Winchester *U.K.* 51°4N 1°18W **13** F6
Winchester *Conn., U.S.A.* 41°53N 73°9W **83** E11
Winchester *Idaho, U.S.A.* 46°14N 116°38W **76** C5
Winchester *Ind., U.S.A.* 40°10N 84°59W **81** E11
Winchester *Ky., U.S.A.* 37°59N 84°11W **81** G11
Winchester *N.H., U.S.A.* 42°46N 72°23W **83** D12
Winchester *Nev., U.S.A.* 36°7N 115°7W **79** J11
Winchester *Tenn., U.S.A.* 35°11N 86°7W **85** D11
Winchester *Va., U.S.A.* 39°11N 78°10W **81** F14
Wind → *U.S.A.* 43°12N 108°12W **76** E9
Wind Cave △ *U.S.A.* 43°32N 103°17W **80** D2
Wind River Range *U.S.A.* 43°0N 109°30W **76** E9
Windau = Ventspils *Latvia* 57°25N 21°32E **9** H19
Windber *U.S.A.* 40°14N 78°50W **82** F6
Winder *U.S.A.* 34°0N 83°45W **85** D13
Windermere *U.K.* 54°23N 2°55W **12** C5
Windhoek *Namibia* 22°35S 17°4E **56** C2
Windjana Gorge △ *Australia* 17°51S 125°0E **60** C3
Windom *U.S.A.* 43°52N 95°7W **80** D6
Windorah *Australia* 25°24S 142°36E **62** D3
Window Rock *U.S.A.* 35°41N 109°3W **77** J9
Windrush → *U.K.* 51°43N 1°24W **13** F6
Windsor *Australia* 33°37S 150°50E **63** E5
Windsor *N.S., Canada* 44°59N 64°5W **73** D7
Windsor *Ont., Canada* 42°18N 83°0W **82** D2
Windsor *U.K.* 51°29N 0°36W **13** F7
Windsor *Calif., U.S.A.* 38°33N 122°49W **76** G2
Windsor *Colo., U.S.A.* 40°29N 104°54W **76** F11
Windsor *Conn., U.S.A.* 41°50N 72°39W **83** E12
Windsor *Mo., U.S.A.* 38°32N 93°31W **80** F7
Windsor *N.Y., U.S.A.* 42°5N 75°37W **83** D9
Windsor *Vt., U.S.A.* 43°29N 72°24W **83** C12
Windsor & Maidenhead □ *U.K.* 51°29N 0°40W **13** F7
Windsorton *S. Africa* 28°16S 24°44E **56** D3
Windward Is. *W. Indies* 13°0N 61°0W **89** D7
Windward Passage = Vientos, Paso de los *Caribbean* 20°0N 74°0W **89** C5
Winefred L. *Canada* 55°30N 110°30W **71** B6
Winfield *U.S.A.* 37°15N 96°59W **80** G5
Wingate Mts. *Australia* 14°25S 130°40E **60** B5
Wingham *Australia* 31°48S 152°22E **63** E5
Wingham *Canada* 43°55N 81°20W **82** C3
Winisk → *Canada* 55°17N 85°5W **72** A2
Winisk L. *Canada* 52°55N 87°22W **72** B2
Wink *U.S.A.* 31°45N 103°9W **84** F3
Winkler *Canada* 49°10N 97°56W **71** D9
Winlock *U.S.A.* 46°30N 122°56W **78** D4
Winneba *Ghana* 5°25N 0°36W **50** G5
Winnebago, L. *U.S.A.* 44°0N 88°26W **80** D9
Winnecke Cr. → *Australia* 18°35S 131°34E **60** C5
Winnemucca *U.S.A.* 40°58N 117°44W **76** F5
Winnemucca L. *U.S.A.* 40°7N 119°21W **76** F4
Winner *U.S.A.* 43°22N 99°52W **80** D4
Winnett *U.S.A.* 47°0N 108°21W **76** C9
Winnfield *U.S.A.* 31°56N 92°38W **84** F8
Winnibigoshish, L. *U.S.A.* 47°27N 94°13W **80** B6
Winnipeg *Canada* 49°54N 97°9W **71** D9
Winnipeg → *Canada* 50°38N 96°19W **71** C9
Winnipeg, L. *Canada* 52°0N 97°0W **71** C9
Winnipeg Beach *Canada* 50°30N 96°58W **71** C9
Winnipegosis *Canada* 51°39N 99°55W **71** C9
Winnipegosis L. *Canada* 52°30N 100°0W **71** C9
Winnipesaukee, L. *U.S.A.* 43°38N 71°21W **83** C13
Winnisquam L. *U.S.A.* 43°33N 71°31W **83** C13
Winnsboro *La., U.S.A.* 32°10N 91°43W **84** E9
Winnsboro *S.C., U.S.A.* 34°23N 81°5W **85** D14
Winnsboro *Tex., U.S.A.* 32°58N 95°17W **84** E7
Winokapau, L. *Canada* 53°15N 62°50W **73** B7
Winona *Minn., U.S.A.* 44°3N 91°39W **80** C8
Winona *Miss., U.S.A.* 33°29N 89°44W **85** E10
Winooski *U.S.A.* 44°29N 73°11W **83** B11
Winooski → *U.S.A.* 44°32N 73°17W **83** B11
Winschoten *Neths.* 53°9N 7°3E **15** A7
Winsford *U.K.* 53°12N 2°31W **12** D5
Winslow = Bainbridge Island *U.S.A.* 47°38N 122°32W **78** C4
Winslow *U.S.A.* 35°2N 110°42W **77** J8
Winsted *U.S.A.* 41°55N 73°4W **83** E11
Winston-Salem *U.S.A.* 36°6N 80°15W **85** C14
Winter Garden *U.S.A.* 28°34N 81°35W **85** G14
Winter Haven *U.S.A.* 28°1N 81°44W **85** G14
Winter Park *U.S.A.* 28°36N 81°20W **85** G14
Winterhaven *U.S.A.* 32°44N 114°38W **79** N12
Winters *U.S.A.* 38°32N 121°58W **78** G5
Winterset *U.S.A.* 41°20N 94°1W **80** E6
Wintersville *U.S.A.* 40°23N 80°42W **82** F4
Winterswijk *Neths.* 51°58N 6°43E **15** C6
Winterthur *Switz.* 47°30N 8°44E **20** C8
Winthrop *U.S.A.* 48°28N 120°10W **76** B3
Winton *Australia* 22°24S 143°3E **62** C3
Winton *N.Z.* 46°8S 168°20E **59** G2
Wirrulla *Australia* 32°24S 134°31E **63** E1
Wisbech *U.K.* 52°41N 0°9E **13** E8
Wisconsin □ *U.S.A.* 44°45N 89°30W **80** C9
Wisconsin → *U.S.A.* 43°0N 91°15W **80** D8
Wisconsin Rapids *U.S.A.* 44°23N 89°49W **80** C9
Wisdom *U.S.A.* 45°37N 113°27W **76** D7
Wishaw *U.K.* 55°46N 3°54W **11** F5
Wishek *U.S.A.* 46°16N 99°33W **80** B4
Wisła → *Poland* 54°22N 18°55E **17** A10
Wismar *Germany* 53°54N 11°29E **16** B6
Wisner *U.S.A.* 41°59N 96°55W **80** E5
Witbank = eMalahleni *S. Africa* 25°51S 29°14E **57** D4
Witdraai *S. Africa* 26°58S 20°48E **56** D3
Witham *U.K.* 51°48N 0°40E **13** F8
Witham → *U.K.* 52°59N 0°2W **12** E7
Withernsea *U.K.* 53°44N 0°1E **12** D8
Witjira △ *Australia* 26°22S 135°37E **63** D2
Witless Bay *Canada* 47°17N 52°50W **73** C9
Witney *U.K.* 51°48N 1°28W **13** F6
Witnossob → *Namibia* 23°55S 18°45E **56** D3
Wittenberge *Germany* 53°0N 11°45E **16** B6
Wittenoom *Australia* 22°15S 118°20E **60** D2
Witu *Kenya* 2°23S 40°26E **54** C5
Witvlei *Namibia* 22°23S 18°32E **56** C2
Wiwon *N. Korea* 40°54N 126°3E **35** D14
Wkra → *Poland* 52°27N 20°44E **17** B11
Wlingi *Indonesia* 8°5S 112°25E **37** H15
Włocławek *Poland* 52°40N 19°3E **17** B10
Włodawa *Poland* 51°33N 23°31E **17** C12
Woburn *U.S.A.* 42°29N 71°9W **83** D13
Wodian *China* 32°50N 112°35E **34** H7
Wodonga *Australia* 36°5S 146°50E **63** F4
Wokam *Indonesia* 5°45S 134°28E **37** F8
Woking *U.K.* 51°19N 0°34W **13** F7
Wokingham *U.K.* 51°24N 0°49W **13** F7
Wokingham □ *U.K.* 51°25N 0°51W **13** F7
Wolf → *Canada* 60°17N 132°33W **70** A2
Wolf Creek *U.S.A.* 47°0N 112°4W **76** C7
Wolf L. *Canada* 60°24N 131°40W **70** A2
Wolf Point *U.S.A.* 48°5N 105°39W **76** B11

Wolfe I. *Canada* 44°7N 76°20W **83 B8**
Wolfeboro *U.S.A.* 43°35N 71°13W **83 C13**
Wolfsberg *Austria* 46°50N 14°52E **16 E8**
Wolfsburg *Germany* 52°25N 10°48E **16 B6**
Wolin *Poland* 53°50N 14°37E **16 B8**
Wollaston, Is. *Chile* 55°40S 67°30W **96 H3**
Wollaston L. *Canada* 58°7N 103°10W **71 B8**
Wollaston Lake *Canada* 58°3N 103°33W **71 B8**
Wollaston Pen. *Canada* 69°30N 115°0W **68 C8**
Wollongong *Australia* 34°25S 150°54E **63 E5**
Wolmaransstad *S. Africa* 27°12S 25°59E **56 D4**
Wolseley *S. Africa* 33°26S 19°7E **56 E2**
Wolsey *U.S.A.* 44°25N 98°28W **80 C4**
Wolstenholme, C.
  Canada 62°35N 77°30W **66 C12**
Wolvega *Neths.* 52°52N 6°0E **15 B6**
Wolverhampton *U.K.* 52°35N 2°7W **13 E5**
Wondai *Australia* 26°20S 151°49E **63 D5**
Wongalarroo L. *Australia* 31°32S 144°0E **63 E3**
Wongan Hills *Australia* 30°51S 116°37E **61 F2**
Wonju *S. Korea* 37°22N 127°58E **35 F14**
Wonosari *Indonesia* 7°58S 110°36E **37 G14**
Wonosobo *Indonesia* 7°22S 109°54E **37 G13**
Wonowon *Canada* 56°44N 121°48W **70 B4**
Wŏnsan *N. Korea* 39°11N 127°27E **35 E14**
Wonthaggi *Australia* 38°37S 145°37E **63 F4**
Wood Buffalo △ *Canada* 59°0N 113°41W **70 B6**
Wood Is. *Australia* 16°24S 123°19E **60 C3**
Wood L. *Canada* 55°17N 103°17W **71 B8**
Woodah, I. *Australia* 13°27S 136°10E **62 A2**
Woodbourne *U.S.A.* 41°46N 74°36W **83 E10**
Woodbridge *Canada* 43°47N 79°36W **82 C5**
Woodbridge *U.K.* 52°6N 1°20E **13 E9**
Woodburn *U.S.A.* 45°9N 122°51W **76 D2**
Woodenbong *Australia* 28°24S 152°39E **63 D5**
Woodend *Australia* 37°20S 144°33E **63 F3**
Woodford *Australia* 26°58S 152°47E **63 D5**
Woodfords *U.S.A.* 38°47N 119°50W **78 G7**
Woodlake *U.S.A.* 36°25N 119°6W **78 J7**
Woodland *Calif., U.S.A.* 38°41N 121°46W **78 G5**
Woodland *Maine, U.S.A.* 45°9N 67°25W **81 C20**
Woodland *Pa., U.S.A.* 41°0N 78°21W **82 F6**
Woodland *Wash.,*
  U.S.A. 45°54N 122°45W **78 E4**
Woodland Caribou △
  Canada 51°0N 94°45W **71 C10**
Woodlands *Singapore* 1°26N 103°46E **39 d**
Woodlands, The *U.S.A.* 30°9N 95°29W **84 F7**
Woodonga *Australia* 36°10S 146°50E **63 F4**
Woodridge *Canada* 49°20N 96°9W **71 D9**
Woodroffe, Mt.
  Australia 26°20S 131°45E **61 E5**
Woods, L. *Australia* 17°50S 133°30E **62 B1**
Woods, L. of the
  Canada 49°15N 94°45W **71 D10**
Woods Bay *Canada* 45°8N 79°59W **82 A5**
Woodstock *Australia* 19°35S 146°50E **62 B4**
Woodstock *N.B., Canada* 46°11N 67°37W **73 C6**
Woodstock *Ont., Canada* 43°10N 80°45W **82 C4**
Woodstock *U.K.* 51°51N 1°20W **13 F6**
Woodstock *Ill., U.S.A.* 42°19N 88°27W **80 D9**
Woodstock *N.Y., U.S.A.* 42°2N 74°7W **83 D10**
Woodstock *Vt., U.S.A.* 43°37N 72°31W **83 C12**
Woodsville *U.S.A.* 44°9N 72°2W **83 B13**
Woodview *Canada* 44°35N 78°8W **82 B6**
Woodville *N.Z.* 40°20S 175°53E **59 D5**
Woodville *Miss., U.S.A.* 31°6N 91°18W **84 F9**
Woodville *Tex., U.S.A.* 30°47N 94°25W **84 F7**
Woodward *U.S.A.* 36°26N 99°24W **84 C5**
Woody *U.S.A.* 35°42N 118°50W **79 K8**
Woody → *Canada* 52°31N 100°51W **71 C8**
Woolacombe *U.K.* 51°10N 4°13W **13 F3**
Woolamai, C. *Australia* 38°30S 145°23E **63 F4**
Wooler *U.K.* 55°33N 2°1W **12 B5**
Woolgoolga *Australia* 30°6S 153°11E **63 E5**
Woomera *Australia* 31°5S 136°50E **63 E2**
Woonsocket *R.I., U.S.A.* 42°0N 71°31W **83 E13**
Woonsocket *S. Dak.,*
  U.S.A. 44°3N 98°17W **80 C4**
Wooramel → *Australia* 25°47S 114°10E **61 E1**
Wooramel Roadhouse
  Australia 25°45S 114°17E **61 E1**
Wooroonooran △
  Australia 16°25S 146°1E **62 B4**
Wooster *U.S.A.* 40°48N 81°56W **82 F3**
Worcester *S. Africa* 33°39S 19°27E **56 E2**
Worcester *U.K.* 52°11N 2°12W **13 E5**
Worcester *Mass.,*
  U.S.A. 42°16N 71°48W **83 D13**
Worcester *N.Y., U.S.A.* 42°36N 74°45W **83 D10**
Worcestershire □ *U.K.* 52°13N 2°10W **13 E5**
Workington *U.K.* 54°39N 3°33W **12 C4**
Worksop *U.K.* 53°18N 1°7W **12 D6**
Workum *Neths.* 52°59N 5°26E **15 B5**
Worland *U.S.A.* 44°1N 107°57W **76 D10**
Worms *Germany* 49°37N 8°21E **16 D5**
Worsley *Canada* 56°31N 119°8W **70 B5**
Wortham *U.S.A.* 31°47N 96°28W **84 F6**
Worthing *Barbados* 13°5S 59°35W **89 g**
Worthing *U.K.* 50°49N 0°21W **13 G7**
Worthington *Minn.,*
  U.S.A. 43°37N 95°36W **80 D6**
Worthington *Pa., U.S.A.* 40°50N 79°38W **82 F5**
Wosi *Indonesia* 0°15S 128°0E **37 E7**
Wote *Kenya* 1°47S 37°38E **54 C4**
Wou-han = Wuhan
  China 30°31N 114°18E **33 C6**
Wousi = Wuxi *China* 31°33N 120°18E **33 C7**
Wowoni *Indonesia* 4°5S 123°5E **37 E6**
Wrangel I. = Vrangelya, Ostrov
  Russia 71°0N 180°0E **29 B18**
Wrangell *U.S.A.* 56°28N 132°23W **70 B2**
Wrangell Mts. *U.S.A.* 61°30N 142°0W **68 B5**
Wrath, C. *U.K.* 58°38N 5°1W **11 C3**
Wray *U.S.A.* 40°5N 102°13W **76 F12**
Wrekin, The *U.K.* 52°41N 2°32W **13 E5**
Wrens *U.S.A.* 33°12N 82°23W **85 E13**

Wrexham *U.K.* 53°3N 3°0W **12 D4**
Wrexham □ *U.K.* 53°1N 2°58W **12 D5**
Wright *Fla., U.S.A.* 30°27N 86°38W **85 F11**
Wright *Wyo., U.S.A.* 43°45N 105°28W **76 E11**
Wright Pt. *Canada* 43°48N 81°44W **82 C3**
Wrightson, Mt. *U.S.A.* 31°42N 110°51W **77 L8**
Wrightsville *U.S.A.* 32°44N 82°43W **85 E13**
Wrightwood *U.S.A.* 34°22N 117°38W **79 L9**
Wrigley *Canada* 63°16N 123°37W **68 C7**
Wrocław *Poland* 51°5N 17°5E **17 C9**
Września *Poland* 52°21N 17°36E **17 B9**
Wu Jiang → *China* 29°40N 107°20E **32 D5**
Wu Kau Tang *China* 22°30N 114°14E **33 F11**
Wu'an *China* 36°40N 114°15E **34 F8**
Wubin *Australia* 30°6S 116°37E **61 F2**
Wubu *China* 37°28N 110°42E **34 F6**
Wuchang *China* 44°55N 127°5E **35 B14**
Wucheng *China* 37°12N 116°20E **34 F9**
Wuchuan *China* 41°5N 111°28E **34 D6**
Wudi *China* 37°40N 117°35E **35 F9**
Wuding He → *China* 37°2N 110°23E **34 F6**
Wudinna *Australia* 33°0S 135°22E **63 E2**
Wudu *China* 33°22N 104°54E **34 H3**
Wuguishan *China* 22°25N 113°25E **33 G9**
Wuhai *China* 39°47N 106°52E **32 C5**
Wuhan *China* 30°31N 114°18E **33 C6**
Wuhe *China* 33°10N 117°50E **35 H9**
Wuhsi = Wuxi *China* 31°33N 120°18E **33 C7**
Wuhu *China* 31°22N 118°21E **33 C6**
Wukari *Nigeria* 7°51N 9°42E **50 G7**
Wulajie *China* 44°6N 126°33E **35 B14**
Wulanbulang *China* 41°5N 110°55E **34 D6**
Wular L. *India* 34°20N 74°30E **43 B6**
Wulian *China* 35°40N 119°12E **35 G10**
Wuliaru *Indonesia* 7°27S 131°0E **37 F8**
Wulumuchi = Ürümqi
  China 43°45N 87°45E **32 B3**
Wundanyi *Kenya* 3°24S 38°22E **54 C4**
Wunnummin L. *Canada* 52°55N 89°10W **72 B2**
Wuntho *Burma* 23°55N 95°45E **41 H19**
Wupatki △ *U.S.A.* 35°35N 111°20W **77 J8**
Wuppertal *Germany* 51°16N 7°12E **16 C4**
Wuppertal *S. Africa* 32°13S 19°12E **56 E2**
Wuqing *China* 39°23N 117°4E **35 E9**
Wurtsboro *U.S.A.* 41°35N 74°29W **83 E10**
Würzburg *Germany* 49°46N 9°55E **16 D5**
Wushan *China* 34°43N 104°53E **34 G3**
Wushi *China* 41°9N 79°13E **32 B2**
Wutai *China* 38°40N 113°12E **34 E7**
Wuting = Huimin
  China 37°27N 117°28E **35 F9**
Wutonghaolai *China* 42°50N 120°5E **35 C11**
Wutongqiao *China* 29°22N 103°50E **32 D5**
Wuwei *China* 37°57N 102°34E **32 C5**
Wuxi *China* 31°33N 120°18E **33 C7**
Wuxiang *China* 36°49N 112°50E **34 F7**
Wuyang *China* 33°25N 113°35E **34 H7**
Wuyi *China* 37°46N 115°56E **34 F8**
Wuyi Shan *China* 27°0N 117°0E **33 D6**
Wuyuan *China* 41°2N 108°20E **34 D5**
Wuzhai *China* 38°54N 111°48E **34 E6**
Wuzhi Shan *China* 18°45N 109°45E **38 C7**
Wuzhong *China* 38°2N 106°12E **34 E4**
Wuzhou *China* 23°30N 111°18E **33 D6**
Wyaaba Cr. →
  Australia 16°27S 141°35E **62 B3**
Wyalkatchem *Australia* 31°8S 117°22E **61 F2**
Wyalusing *U.S.A.* 41°40N 76°16W **83 E8**
Wyandotte *U.S.A.* 42°12N 83°9W **81 D12**
Wyandra *Australia* 27°12S 145°56E **63 D4**
Wyangala, L. *Australia* 33°54S 149°0E **63 E4**
Wyara, L. *Australia* 28°42S 144°14E **63 D3**
Wycheproof *Australia* 36°5S 143°17E **63 F3**
Wycliffe Well *Australia* 20°48S 134°14E **62 C1**
Wye → *U.K.* 51°38N 2°40W **13 F5**
Wyemandoo *Australia* 28°28S 118°29E **61 E2**
Wymondham *U.K.* 52°35N 1°7E **13 E9**
Wymore *U.S.A.* 40°7N 96°40W **80 E5**
Wyndham *Australia* 15°33S 128°3E **60 C4**
Wyndham *N.Z.* 46°20S 168°51E **59 G2**
Wynne *U.S.A.* 35°14N 90°47W **85 D9**
Wynyard *Australia* 41°5S 145°44E **63 G4**
Wynyard *Canada* 51°45N 104°10W **71 C8**
Wyola L. *Australia* 29°8S 130°17E **61 E5**
Wyoming *Canada* 42°57N 82°7W **82 D2**
Wyoming □ *U.S.A.* 43°0N 107°30W **76 E10**
Wyomissing *U.S.A.* 40°20N 75°59W **83 F9**
Wyong *Australia* 33°14S 151°24E **63 E5**
Wytheville *U.S.A.* 36°57N 81°5W **81 G13**

X

Xaafuun *Somali Rep.* 10°25N 51°16E **47 E5**
Xaafuun, Ras *Somali Rep.* 10°27N 51°24E **47 E5**
Xaçmaz *Azerbaijan* 41°31N 48°42E **19 F8**
Xai-Xai *Mozam.* 25°6S 33°31E **57 D5**
Xainza *China* 30°58N 88°35E **32 C3**
Xalapa *Mexico* 19°32N 96°55W **87 D5**
Xangongo *Angola* 16°45S 15°5E **56 B2**
Xankändi *Azerbaijan* 39°52N 46°49E **44 B5**
Xanthi *Greece* 41°10N 24°58E **23 D11**
Xanxerê *Brazil* 26°53S 52°23W **95 B5**
Xapuri *Brazil* 10°35S 68°35W **92 F5**
Xar Moron He →
  China 43°25N 120°35E **35 C11**
Xàtiva *Spain* 38°59N 0°32W **21 C5**
Xau, L. *Botswana* 21°15S 24°44E **56 C3**
Xavantina *Brazil* 21°15S 52°48W **95 A5**
Xenia *U.S.A.* 39°41N 83°56W **81 F12**
Xeropotamos →
  Cyprus 34°42N 32°33E **25 E11**
Xhora *S. Africa* 31°55S 28°38E **57 E4**
Xhumo *Botswana* 21°7S 24°35E **56 C3**
Xi Jiang → *China* 22°5N 113°20E **33 D6**
Xi Xian *China* 36°41N 110°58E **34 F6**

Xia Xian *China* 35°8N 111°12E **34 G6**
Xiachengzi *China* 44°40N 130°18E **35 B16**
Xiaguan *China* 25°32N 100°16E **32 D5**
Xiajin *China* 36°56N 116°0E **34 F9**
Xiamen *China* 24°25N 118°4E **33 D6**
Xi'an *China* 34°15N 109°0E **34 G5**
Xian Xian *China* 38°12N 116°6E **34 E9**
Xiang Jiang → *China* 28°55N 112°50E **33 D6**
Xiangcheng *Henan,*
  China 33°29N 114°52E **34 H8**
Xiangcheng *Henan,*
  China 33°50N 113°27E **34 H7**
Xiangfan *China* 32°2N 112°8E **33 C6**
Xianggang = Hong Kong □
  China 22°11N 114°14E **33 G11**
Xianghuang Qi *China* 42°2N 113°50E **34 C7**
Xiangning *China* 35°58N 110°50E **34 G6**
Xiangquan *China* 36°30N 113°1E **34 F7**
Xiangquan He = Sutlej →
  Pakistan 29°23N 71°3E **42 E4**
Xiangshui *China* 34°12N 119°33E **35 G10**
Xiangtan *China* 27°51N 112°54E **33 D6**
Xianyang *China* 34°20N 108°40E **34 G5**
Xiao Hinggan Ling *China* 49°0N 127°0E **33 B7**
Xiao Xian *China* 34°15N 116°55E **34 G9**
Xiaoyi *China* 37°8N 111°48E **34 F6**
Xiawa *China* 42°35N 120°38E **35 C11**
Xiayi *China* 34°15N 116°10E **34 G9**
Xichang *China* 27°51N 102°19E **32 D5**
Xichuan *China* 33°0N 111°30E **34 H6**
Xieng Khouang *Laos* 19°17N 103°25E **38 C4**
Xifei He → *China* 32°45N 116°40E **34 H9**
Xifeng *Gansu, China* 35°40N 107°40E **34 G4**
Xifeng *Liaoning, China* 42°42N 124°45E **35 C13**
Xifengzhen = Xifeng
  China 35°40N 107°40E **34 G4**
Xigazê *China* 29°5N 88°45E **32 D3**
Xihe *China* 34°2N 105°20E **34 G3**
Xihua *China* 33°45N 114°30E **34 H8**
Xili Shuiku *China* 22°36N 113°57E **33 F10**
Xiliao He → *China* 43°32N 123°35E **35 C12**
Xilinhot *China* 43°52N 116°2E **34 C9**
Xin Xian = Xinzhou
  China 38°22N 112°46E **34 E7**
Xinavane *Mozam.* 25°2S 32°47E **57 D5**
Xinbin *China* 41°40N 125°2E **35 D13**
Xincun *China* 38°15N 117°45E **35 E9**
Xing Xian *China* 38°27N 111°7E **34 E6**
Xing'an *China* 25°38N 110°40E **33 D6**
Xingcheng *China* 40°40N 120°45E **35 D11**
Xinghe *China* 40°55N 113°55E **34 D7**
Xinghua *China* 32°58N 119°48E **35 H10**
Xinglong *China* 40°25N 117°30E **35 D9**
Xingping *China* 34°20N 108°28E **34 G5**
Xingtai *China* 37°3N 114°32E **34 F8**
Xingu → *Brazil* 1°30S 51°53W **93 D8**
Xingyang *China* 34°45N 112°52E **34 G7**
Xinhe *China* 37°30N 115°15E **34 F8**
Xining *China* 36°34N 101°40E **32 C5**
Xinjiang *China* 35°34N 111°11E **34 G6**
Xinjiang Uygur Zizhiqu □
  China 42°0N 86°0E **32 C3**
Xinjin = Pulandian
  China 39°25N 121°58E **35 E11**
Xinkai He → *China* 43°32N 123°35E **35 C12**
Xinken *China* 22°39N 113°36E **33 F10**
Xinle *China* 38°25N 114°40E **34 E8**
Xinmin *China* 41°59N 122°50E **35 D12**
Xintai *China* 35°55N 117°45E **35 G9**
Xinwan *China* 22°47N 113°40E **33 F10**
Xinxiang *China* 35°18N 113°50E **34 G7**
Xinzhan *China* 43°50N 127°18E **35 C14**
Xinzheng *China* 34°20N 113°45E **34 G7**
Xinzhou *Hainan, China* 19°43N 109°17E **38 C7**
Xinzhou *Shanxi, China* 38°22N 112°46E **34 E7**
Xiongyuecheng *China* 40°12N 122°5E **35 D12**
Xiping *Henan, China* 33°22N 114°5E **34 H8**
Xiping *Henan, China* 33°25N 111°8E **34 H6**
Xique-Xique *Brazil* 10°50S 42°40W **93 F10**
Xisha Qundao = Paracel Is.
  S. China Sea 15°50N 112°0E **36 A4**
Xiuyan *China* 40°18N 123°11E **35 D12**
Xixabangma Feng
  China 28°20N 85°40E **43 E11**
Xixia *China* 33°25N 111°29E **34 H6**
Xixiang *China* 33°0N 107°44E **33 F10**
Xixón = Gijón *Spain* 43°32N 5°42W **21 A3**
Xiyang *China* 37°38N 113°38E **34 F7**
Xizang Zizhiqu □ *China* 32°0N 88°0E **32 C3**
Xlendi *Malta* 36°1N 14°12E **25 C1**
Xochob *Mexico* 19°21N 89°48W **87 D7**
Xuan Loc *Vietnam* 10°56N 107°14E **39 G6**
Xuanhua *China* 40°40N 115°2E **34 D8**
Xuchang *China* 34°2N 113°48E **34 G7**
Xun Xian *China* 35°42N 114°33E **34 G8**
Xunyang *China* 32°48N 109°22E **34 H5**
Xunyi *China* 35°8N 108°20E **34 G5**
Xúquer → *Spain* 39°5N 0°10W **21 C5**
Xushui *China* 39°2N 115°40E **34 E8**
Xuyen Moc *Vietnam* 10°34N 107°25E **39 G6**
Xuzhou *China* 34°18N 117°10E **35 G9**
Xylophagou *Cyprus* 34°54N 33°51E **25 E12**

Y

Ya Xian = Sanya *China* 18°14N 109°29E **38 C7**
Yaamba *Australia* 23°8S 150°22E **62 C5**
Yaapeet *Australia* 35°45S 142°3E **63 F3**
Yablonovyy Khrebet
  Russia 53°0N 114°0E **29 D12**
Yablonovyy Ra. = Yablonovyy
  Khrebet *Russia* 53°0N 114°0E **29 D12**
Yabrai Shan *China* 39°40N 103°0E **34 E2**
Yabrūd *Syria* 33°58N 36°39E **46 B5**

Yabucoa *Puerto Rico* 18°3N 65°53W **89 d**
Yacambú △ *Venezuela* 9°42N 69°27W **89 E6**
Yacheng *China* 18°22N 109°6E **38 C7**
Yacuiba *Bolivia* 22°0S 63°43W **94 A3**
Yacuma → *Bolivia* 13°38S 65°23W **92 F5**
Yadgir *India* 16°45N 77°5E **40 L10**
Yadkin → *U.S.A.* 35°23N 80°4W **85 D14**
Yadua *Fiji* 16°49S 178°18E **59 a**
Yaeyama-Rettō *Japan* 24°30N 123°40E **31 M1**
Yagasa Cluster *Fiji* 18°57S 178°28W **59 a**
Yagodnoye *Russia* 62°33N 149°40E **29 C15**
Yahila
  Dem. Rep. of the Congo 0°13N 24°28E **54 B1**
Yahk *Canada* 49°6N 116°10W **70 D5**
Yahuma
  Dem. Rep. of the Congo 1°0N 23°10E **52 D4**
Yaita *Japan* 36°48N 139°56E **31 F9**
Yaiza *Canary Is.* 28°57N 13°46W **24 F6**
Yakima *U.S.A.* 46°36N 120°31W **76 C3**
Yakima → *U.S.A.* 46°15N 119°14W **76 C4**
Yakishiri-Jima *Japan* 44°26N 141°25E **30 B10**
Yakobi I. *U.S.A.* 58°0N 136°30W **70 B1**
Yakovlevka *Russia* 44°26N 133°28E **30 B6**
Yaku-Shima *Japan* 30°20N 130°30E **31 J5**
Yakumo *Japan* 42°15N 140°16E **30 C10**
Yakutat *U.S.A.* 59°33N 139°44W **68 C6**
Yakutia = Sakha □
  Russia 66°0N 130°0E **29 C14**
Yakutsk *Russia* 62°5N 129°50E **29 C13**
Yala *Thailand* 6°33N 101°18E **39 J3**
Yalboroo *Australia* 20°50S 148°40E **62 J6**
Yale *U.S.A.* 43°8N 82°48W **82 C2**
Yalgoo *Australia* 28°16S 116°39E **61 E2**
Yalgorup △ *Australia* 32°39S 115°38E **61 F2**
Yalinga *C.A.R.* 6°33N 23°10E **52 C4**
Yalkabul, Pta. *Mexico* 21°32N 88°37W **87 C7**
Yalleroi *Australia* 24°3S 145°42E **62 C4**
Yalobusha → *U.S.A.* 33°33N 90°10W **85 E9**
Yalong Jiang → *China* 26°40N 101°55E **32 D5**
Yalova *Turkey* 40°41N 29°15E **23 D13**
Yalta *Ukraine* 44°30N 34°10E **19 F5**
Yalu Jiang → *China* 39°55N 124°19E **35 E13**
Yam Ha Melaḥ = Dead Sea
  Asia 31°30N 35°30E **46 D4**
Yam Kinneret *Israel* 32°45N 35°35E **46 C4**
Yamada *Japan* 33°33N 130°49E **31 H5**
Yamagata *Japan* 38°15N 140°15E **30 E10**
Yamagata □ *Japan* 38°30N 140°0E **30 E10**
Yamaguchi *Japan* 34°10N 131°32E **31 G5**
Yamaguchi □ *Japan* 34°20N 131°40E **31 G5**
Yamal, Poluostrov *Russia* 71°0N 70°0E **28 B8**
Yamal Pen. = Yamal, Poluostrov
  Russia 71°0N 70°0E **28 B8**
Yamanashi □ *Japan* 35°40N 138°40E **31 G9**
Yamanie Falls △
  Australia 18°29S 146°9E **62 B4**
Yamantau, Gora *Russia* 54°15N 58°6E **18 D10**
Yamato Ridge
  Sea of Japan 39°20N 135°0E **30 E7**
Yamba *Australia* 29°26S 153°23E **63 D5**
Yambarran Ra.
  Australia 15°10S 130°25E **60 C5**
Yâmbiô *Sudan* 4°35N 28°16E **51 H11**
Yambol *Bulgaria* 42°30N 26°30E **23 C12**
Yamburg *Russia* 68°21N 77°8E **28 C8**
Yamdena *Indonesia* 7°45S 131°20E **37 F8**
Yame *Japan* 33°13N 130°35E **31 H5**
Yamethin *Burma* 20°29N 96°18E **41 J20**
Yamma Yamma, L.
  Australia 26°16S 141°20E **63 D3**
Yamoussoukro *Ivory C.* 6°49N 5°17W **50 G4**
Yampa → *U.S.A.* 40°32N 108°59W **76 F9**
Yampi Sd. *Australia* 16°8S 123°38E **60 C3**
Yampil *Moldova* 48°15N 28°15E **17 D15**
Yampol = Yampil
  Moldova 48°15N 28°15E **17 D15**
Yamuna → *India* 25°30N 81°53E **43 G9**
Yamunanagar *India* 30°7N 77°17E **42 D7**
Yamzho Yumco *China* 28°48N 90°35E **32 D4**
Yana → *Russia* 71°30N 136°0E **29 B14**
Yanagawa *Japan* 33°10N 130°24E **31 H5**
Yanai *Japan* 33°58N 132°7E **31 H6**
Yan'an *China* 36°35N 109°26E **34 F5**
Yanaul *Russia* 56°25N 55°0E **18 C10**
Yanbu 'al Baḥr *Si. Arabia* 24°0N 38°5E **44 F3**
Yanchang *China* 36°43N 110°1E **34 F6**
Yancheng *Henan, China* 33°35N 114°0E **34 H8**
Yancheng *Jiangsu, China* 33°23N 120°8E **35 H11**
Yanchep *Australia* 31°33S 115°37E **61 F2**
Yanchi *China* 37°48N 107°20E **34 F4**
Yanchuan *China* 36°51N 110°10E **34 F6**
Yanco Cr. → *Australia* 35°14S 145°35E **63 F4**
Yandicoogina *Australia* 22°49S 119°12E **60 D2**
Yandoon *Burma* 17°0N 95°40E **41 L19**
Yang Xian *China* 33°15N 107°30E **34 H4**
Yang-yang *S. Korea* 38°4N 128°38E **35 E15**
Yangambi
  Dem. Rep. of the Congo 0°47N 24°24E **54 B1**
Yangcheng *China* 35°28N 112°22E **34 G7**
Yangch'ü = Taiyuan
  China 37°52N 112°33E **34 F7**
Yanggao *China* 40°21N 113°55E **34 D7**
Yanggu *China* 36°8N 115°43E **34 F8**
Yangliuqing *China* 39°2N 117°5E **35 E9**
Yangon = Rangoon
  Burma 16°45N 96°20E **41 L20**
Yangpingguan *China* 32°58N 106°5E **34 H4**
Yangquan *China* 37°58N 113°31E **34 F7**
Yangtse = Chang Jiang →
  China 31°48N 121°10E **33 C7**
Yangtze Kiang = Chang Jiang →
  China 31°48N 121°10E **33 C7**
Yangyuan *China* 40°1N 114°10E **34 D8**
Yangzhou *China* 32°21N 119°26E **33 C6**
Yanji *China* 42°59N 129°30E **35 C15**
Yankton *U.S.A.* 42°53N 97°23W **80 D5**
Yanonge
  Dem. Rep. of the Congo 0°35N 24°38E **54 B1**

Yanqi *China* 42°5N 86°35E **32 B3**
Yanqing *China* 40°30N 115°58E **34 D8**
Yanshan *China* 38°4N 117°22E **35 E9**
Yanshou *China* 45°28N 128°22E **35 B15**
Yantabulla *Australia* 29°21S 145°0E **63 D4**
Yantai *China* 37°34N 121°22E **35 F11**
Yantian *China* 22°35N 114°16E **33 F11**
Yanuca *Fiji* 18°24S 178°0E **59 a**
Yanzhou *China* 35°35N 116°49E **34 G9**
Yao Noi, Ko *Thailand* 8°7N 98°37E **39 a**
Yao Xian *China* 34°55N 108°59E **34 G5**
Yao Yai, Ko *Thailand* 8°0N 98°35E **39 a**
Yaoundé *Cameroon* 3°50N 11°35E **52 D2**
Yaowan *China* 34°15N 118°3E **35 G10**
Yap *Pac. Oc.* 9°30N 138°10E **64 G8**
Yapen *Indonesia* 1°50S 136°0E **37 E9**
Yapen, Selat *Indonesia* 1°20S 136°10E **37 E9**
Yapero *Indonesia* 4°59S 137°11E **37 E9**
Yappar → *Australia* 18°22S 141°16E **62 B3**
Yaqaga *Fiji* 16°35S 178°36E **59 a**
Yaqui → *Mexico* 27°37N 110°39W **86 B2**
Yar-Sale *Russia* 66°50N 70°50E **28 C8**
Yaraka *Australia* 24°53S 144°3E **62 C3**
Yaransk *Russia* 57°22N 47°49E **18 C8**
Yare → *U.K.* 52°35N 1°38E **13 E9**
Yarí → *Colombia* 0°20S 72°20W **92 D4**
Yarkand = Shache
  China 38°20N 77°10E **32 C2**
Yarkant He → *China* 40°26N 80°59E **32 B3**
Yarker *Canada* 44°23N 76°46W **83 B8**
Yarkhun → *Pakistan* 36°17N 72°30E **43 A5**
Yarlung Ziangbo Jiang =
  Brahmaputra →
  Asia 23°40N 90°35E **43 H13**
Yarmouth *Canada* 43°50N 66°7W **73 D6**
Yarmūk → *Syria* 32°42N 35°40E **46 C4**
Yaroslavl *Russia* 57°35N 39°55E **18 C6**
Yarqa, W. → *Egypt* 30°0N 33°49E **46 F2**
Yarra Yarra Lakes
  Australia 29°40S 115°45E **61 E2**
Yarram *Australia* 38°29S 146°39E **63 F4**
Yarraman *Australia* 26°50S 152°0E **63 D5**
Yarras *Australia* 31°25S 152°20E **63 E5**
Yarrie *Australia* 20°40S 120°12E **60 D3**
Yartsevo *Russia* 60°20N 90°0E **29 C10**
Yarumal *Colombia* 6°58N 75°24W **92 B3**
Yasawa *Fiji* 16°47S 177°31E **59 a**
Yasawa Group *Fiji* 17°0S 177°23E **59 a**
Yaselda *Belarus* 52°7N 26°28E **17 B14**
Yasin *Pakistan* 36°24N 73°23E **43 A5**
Yasinski, L. *Canada* 53°16N 77°35W **72 B4**
Yasinya *Ukraine* 48°16N 24°21E **17 D13**
Yasothon *Thailand* 15°50N 104°10E **38 E5**
Yass *Australia* 34°49S 148°54E **63 E4**
Yāsūj *Iran* 30°31N 51°31E **45 D6**
Yatağan *Turkey* 37°20N 28°10E **23 F13**
Yates Center *U.S.A.* 37°53N 95°44W **80 G6**
Yathkyed L. *Canada* 62°40N 98°0W **71 A9**
Yatsushiro *Japan* 32°30N 130°40E **31 H5**
Yatta Plateau *Kenya* 2°0S 38°0E **54 C4**
Yauco *Puerto Rico* 18°2N 66°51W **89 d**
Yavari → *Peru* 4°21S 70°2W **92 D4**
Yávaros *Mexico* 26°42N 109°31W **86 B3**
Yavatmal *India* 20°20N 78°15E **40 J11**
Yavne *Israel* 31°52N 34°45E **46 D3**
Yavoriv *Ukraine* 49°55N 23°20E **17 D12**
Yavorov = Yavoriv
  Ukraine 49°55N 23°20E **17 D12**
Yawatahama *Japan* 33°27N 132°24E **31 H6**
Yawri B. *S. Leone* 8°22N 13°0W **50 G3**
Yaxian = Sanya *China* 18°14N 109°29E **38 C7**
Yazd *Iran* 31°55N 54°27E **45 D7**
Yazd □ *Iran* 32°0N 55°0E **45 D7**
Yazd-e Khvāst *Iran* 31°31N 52°7E **45 D7**
Yazman *Pakistan* 29°8N 71°45E **42 E4**
Yazoo → *U.S.A.* 32°22N 90°54W **85 E9**
Yazoo City *U.S.A.* 32°51N 90°25W **85 E9**
Ybycuí △ *Paraguay* 26°5S 56°46W **94 B4**
Ybytyruzú △ *Paraguay* 25°51S 56°11W **95 B4**
Ye *Burma* 15°15N 97°15E **38 E1**
Ye Xian *China* 33°35N 113°25E **34 H7**
Yebyu *Burma* 14°15N 98°13E **38 E2**
Yecheng *China* 37°54N 77°26E **32 C2**
Yecheon *S. Korea* 36°39N 128°27E **35 F15**
Yecla *Spain* 38°35N 1°5W **21 C5**
Yécora *Mexico* 28°20N 108°58W **86 B3**
Yedintsy = Edineţ
  Moldova 48°9N 27°18E **17 D14**
Yegros *Paraguay* 26°20S 56°25W **94 B4**
Yehbuah *Indonesia* 8°23S 114°45E **37 J17**
Yehuda, Midbar *Israel* 31°35N 35°15E **46 D4**
Yei *Sudan* 4°9N 30°40E **51 H12**
Yekaterinburg *Russia* 56°50N 60°30E **28 D7**
Yelarbon *Australia* 28°33S 150°38E **63 D5**
Yelets *Russia* 52°40N 38°30E **18 D6**
Yelizavetgrad = Kirovohrad
  Ukraine 48°35N 32°20E **19 E5**
Yelizovo *Russia* 53°11N 158°23E **29 D16**
Yell *U.K.* 60°35N 1°5W **11 A7**
Yell Sd. *U.K.* 60°33N 1°15W **11 A7**
Yellow = Huang He →
  China 37°55N 118°50E **35 F10**
Yellow Sea *China* 35°0N 123°0E **35 G12**
Yellowhead Pass
  Canada 52°53N 118°25W **70 C5**
Yellowknife *Canada* 62°27N 114°29W **70 A6**
Yellowknife → *Canada* 62°31N 114°19W **70 A6**
Yellowstone □
  U.S.A. 47°59N 103°59W **76 C12**
Yellowstone △ *U.S.A.* 44°40N 110°30W **76 D8**
Yellowstone L. *U.S.A.* 44°27N 110°22W **76 D8**
Yelsk *Belarus* 51°50N 29°10E **17 C15**
Yemen ■ *Asia* 15°0N 44°0E **47 E3**
Yen Bai *Vietnam* 21°42N 104°52E **38 B5**
Yenangyaung *Burma* 20°30N 95°0E **41 J19**

Yenbo = Yanbu 'al Baḥr
  Si. Arabia 24°0N 38°5E 44 F3
Yenda Australia 34°13S 146°14E 63 E4
Yeni Erenköy = Yialousa
  Cyprus 35°32N 34°10E 25 D13
Yenice Turkey 39°55N 27°17E 23 E12
Yenisey → Russia 71°50N 82°40E 28 B9
Yeniseysk Russia 58°27N 92°13E 29 D10
Yeniseyskiy Zaliv Russia 72°20N 81°0E 28 B9
Yenyuka Russia 57°57N 121°15E 29 D13
Yeo → U.K. 51°2N 2°49W 13 G5
Yeo, L. Australia 28°0S 124°30E 61 E3
Yeo I. Canada 45°24N 81°48W 82 A3
Yeoju S. Korea 37°20N 127°35E 35 F14
Yeola India 20°2N 74°30E 40 J9
Yeong-wol S. Korea 37°11N 128°28E 35 F15
Yeongcheon S. Korea 35°58N 128°56E 35 G15
Yeongdeok S. Korea 36°24N 129°22E 35 F15
Yeongdeungpo
  S. Korea 37°31N 126°54E 35 F14
Yeongdong S. Korea 36°10N 127°46E 35 F14
Yeongju S. Korea 36°50N 128°40E 35 F15
Yeosu S. Korea 34°47N 127°45E 35 G14
Yeovil U.K. 50°57N 2°38W 13 G5
Yeppoon Australia 23°5S 150°47E 62 C5
Yerbent Turkmenistan 39°30N 58°50E 28 F6
Yerbogachen Russia 61°16N 108°0E 29 C11
Yerevan Armenia 40°10N 44°31E 44 A5
Yerington U.S.A. 38°59N 119°10W 76 G4
Yermak Kazakhstan 52°2N 76°55E 28 D8
Yermo U.S.A. 34°54N 116°50W 79 L10
Yeropol Russia 65°15N 168°40E 29 C17
Yeroskipos Cyprus 34°46N 32°28E 25 E11
Yershov Russia 51°23N 48°27E 19 D8
Yerushalayim = Jerusalem
  Israel/West Bank 31°47N 35°10E 46 D4
Yes Tor U.K. 50°41N 4°0W 13 G4
Yesan S. Korea 36°41N 126°51E 35 F14
Yeso U.S.A. 34°26N 104°37W 77 J11
Yessey Russia 68°29N 102°10E 29 C11
Yetman Australia 28°56S 150°48E 63 D5
Yeu, Î. d' France 46°42N 2°20W 20 C2
Yevpatoriya Ukraine 45°15N 33°20E 19 E5
Yeysk Russia 46°40N 38°12E 19 E6
Yezd = Yazd Iran 31°55N 54°27E 45 D7
Ygatimí Paraguay 24°5S 55°40W 95 A4
Yhati Paraguay 25°45S 56°35W 94 B4
Yhú Paraguay 25°0S 56°0W 95 B4
Yí → Uruguay 33°7S 57°8W 94 C4
Yi 'Allaq, G. Egypt 30°21N 33°31E 46 E2
Yi He → China 34°10N 118°8E 35 G10
Yi Xian Hebei, China 39°20N 115°30E 34 E8
Yi Xian Liaoning, China 41°30N 121°22E 35 D11
Yialiás → Cyprus 35°9N 33°44E 25 D12
Yialousa Cyprus 35°32N 34°10E 25 D13
Yibin China 28°45N 104°32E 32 D5
Yichang China 30°40N 111°20E 33 C6
Yicheng China 35°42N 111°40E 34 G6
Yichuan China 36°2N 110°10E 34 F6
Yichun China 47°44N 128°52E 33 B7
Yidu China 36°43N 118°28E 35 F10
Yijun China 35°28N 109°8E 34 G5
Yıldız Dağları Turkey 41°48N 27°36E 23 D12
Yilehuli Shan China 51°20N 124°20E 33 A7
Yimianpo China 45°7N 128°2E 35 B15
Yinchuan China 38°30N 106°15E 34 E4
Yindarlgooda, L.
  Australia 30°40S 121°52E 61 F3
Ying He → China 32°30N 116°30E 34 H9
Ying Xian China 39°32N 113°10E 34 E7
Yingkou China 40°37N 122°18E 35 D12
Yining China 43°58N 81°10E 32 B3
Yinmabin Burma 22°10N 94°55E 41 H19
Yirga Alem Ethiopia 6°48N 38°22E 47 F2
Yirrkala Australia 12°14S 136°56E 62 A2
Yishan China 24°28N 108°38E 32 D5
Yishui China 35°47N 118°30E 35 G10
Yishun Singapore 1°26N 103°51E 39 d
Yitong China 43°13N 125°20E 35 C13
Yixing China 31°21N 119°48E 33 C6
Yiyang Henan, China 34°27N 112°10E 34 G7
Yiyang Hunan, China 28°35N 112°18E 33 D6
Yli-Kitka Finland 66°8N 28°30E 8 C23
Ylitornio Finland 66°19N 23°39E 8 C20
Ylivieska Finland 64°4N 24°28E 8 D21
Yoakum U.S.A. 29°17N 97°9W 84 G6
Yog Pt. Phil. 14°6N 124°12E 37 B6
Yogyakarta Indonesia 7°49S 110°22E 37 G14
Yogyakarta □ Indonesia 7°48S 110°22E 37 G14
Yoho △ Canada 51°25N 116°30W 70 C5
Yojoa, L. de Honduras 14°53N 88°0W 88 D2
Yok Don △ Vietnam 12°50N 107°40E 38 F6
Yokadouma Cameroon 3°26N 14°55E 52 D2
Yokkaichi Japan 34°55N 136°38E 31 G8
Yoko Cameroon 5°32N 12°20E 52 C2
Yokohama Japan 35°27N 139°28E 31 G9
Yokosuka Japan 35°20N 139°40E 31 G9
Yokote Japan 39°20N 140°30E 30 E10
Yola Nigeria 9°10N 12°29E 51 G8
Yolaina, Cordillera de
  Nic. 11°30N 84°0W 88 D3
Yólöten Turkmenistan 37°18N 62°21E 45 B9
Yom → Thailand 15°35N 100°1E 38 E3
Yonago Japan 35°25N 133°19E 31 G6
Yonaguni-Jima Japan 24°27N 123°0E 31 M1
Yŏnan N. Korea 37°55N 126°11E 35 F14
Yonezawa Japan 37°57N 140°4E 30 F10
Yong Peng Malaysia 2°0N 103°3E 39 M4
Yong Sata Thailand 7°8N 99°41E 39 J2
Yongamp'o N. Korea 39°56N 124°23E 35 E13
Yongcheng China 33°55N 116°20E 34 H9
Yongdeng China 36°38N 103°25E 34 F2
Yonghe China 36°46N 110°38E 34 F6
Yongji China 34°52N 110°28E 34 G6
Yongnian China 36°47N 114°29E 34 F8
Yongning China 38°15N 106°14E 34 E4

Yongqing China 39°25N 116°28E 34 E9
Yonibana S. Leone 8°30N 12°19W 50 G3
Yonkers U.S.A. 40°56N 73°52W 83 F11
Yonne → France 48°23N 2°58E 20 B5
York Australia 31°52S 116°47E 61 F2
York U.K. 53°58N 1°6W 12 D6
York Ala., U.S.A. 32°29N 88°18W 85 E10
York Nebr., U.S.A. 40°52N 97°36W 80 E5
York Pa., U.S.A. 39°58N 76°44W 81 F15
York, C., Australia 10°42S 142°31E 62 A3
York, City of □ U.K. 53°58N 1°6W 12 D6
York, Kap Greenland 75°55N 66°25W 4 B4
York, Vale of U.K. 54°15N 1°25E 12 C6
York Sd. Australia 15°0S 125°5E 60 C4
Yorke Pen. Australia 34°50S 137°40E 63 E2
Yorkshire Dales △ U.K. 54°12N 2°10W 12 C5
Yorkshire Wolds U.K. 54°8N 0°31W 12 C7
Yorkton Canada 51°11N 102°28W 71 C8
Yorkville U.S.A. 38°52N 123°13W 78 G3
Yoro Honduras 15°9N 87°7W 88 C2
Yoron-Jima Japan 27°2N 128°26E 31 L4
Yos Sudarso, Pulau = Dolak,
  Pulau Indonesia 8°0S 138°30E 37 F9
Yosemite △ U.S.A. 37°45N 119°40W 78 H7
Yosemite Village
  U.S.A. 37°45N 119°35W 78 H7
Yoshino-Kumano △
  Japan 34°12N 135°55E 31 H8
Yoshkar Ola Russia 56°38N 47°55E 18 C8
Yotvata Israel 29°55N 35°2E 46 F4
Youbou Canada 48°53N 124°13W 78 B2
Youghal Ireland 51°56N 7°52W 10 E4
Youghal B. Ireland 51°55N 7°49W 10 E4
Young Australia 34°19S 148°18E 63 E4
Young Canada 51°47N 105°45W 71 C7
Young Uruguay 32°44S 57°36W 94 C4
Younghusband, L.
  Australia 30°50S 136°5E 63 E2
Younghusband Pen.
  Australia 36°0S 139°25E 63 F2
Youngstown Canada 51°35N 111°10W 71 C6
Youngstown N.Y., U.S.A. 43°15N 79°3W 82 C5
Youngstown Ohio, U.S.A. 41°6N 80°39W 82 E4
Youngsville U.S.A. 41°51N 79°19W 82 E5
Youngwood U.S.A. 40°14N 79°34W 82 F5
Youyu China 40°10N 112°20E 34 D7
Yozgat Turkey 39°51N 34°47E 19 G5
Ypacaraí △ Paraguay 25°18S 57°19W 94 B4
Ypané → Paraguay 23°29S 57°19W 94 A4
Ypres = Ieper Belgium 50°51N 2°53E 15 D2
Yreka U.S.A. 41°44N 122°38W 76 F2
Ystad Sweden 55°26N 13°50E 9 J15
Ysyk-Köl = Balykchy
  Kyrgyzstan 42°26N 76°12E 32 B2
Ysyk-Köl Kyrgyzstan 42°25N 77°15E 28 E8
Ythan → U.K. 57°19N 1°59W 11 D7
Ytyk-Kyuyel Russia 62°30N 133°45E 29 C14
Yu Jiang → China 23°22N 110°3E 33 D6
Yu Xian = Yuzhou
  China 34°10N 113°28E 34 G7
Yu Xian Hebei, China 39°50N 114°35E 34 E8
Yu Xian Shanxi, China 38°5N 113°20E 34 E7
Yuan Jiang → China 28°55N 111°50E 33 D6
Yuanqu China 35°18N 111°40E 34 G6
Yuanyang China 35°3N 113°58E 34 G7
Yuba → U.S.A. 39°8N 121°36W 78 F5
Yuba City U.S.A. 39°8N 121°37W 78 F5
Yūbari Japan 43°4N 141°59E 30 C10
Yūbetsu Japan 44°13N 143°50E 30 B11
Yucatán □ Mexico 20°50N 89°0W 87 C7
Yucatán, Canal de
  Caribbean 22°0N 86°30W 88 B2
Yucatán, Península de
  Mexico 19°30N 89°0W 66 H11
Yucatan Basin Cent. Amer. 19°0N 86°0W 87 D7
Yucatan Channel = Yucatán,
  Canal de Caribbean 22°0N 86°30W 88 B2
Yucca U.S.A. 34°52N 114°9W 79 L12
Yucca Valley U.S.A. 34°8N 116°27W 79 L10
Yucheng China 36°55N 116°32E 34 F9
Yuci China 37°42N 112°46E 34 F7
Yuen Long China 22°26N 114°2E 33 G11
Yuendumu Australia 22°16S 131°49E 60 D5
Yugorenok Russia 59°47N 137°40E 29 D14
Yugoslavia = Serbia ■
  Europe 43°20N 20°0E 23 B9
Yukon U.S.A. 35°31N 97°45W 84 D6
Yukon → U.S.A. 62°32N 163°54W 74 a
Yukon Territory □
  Canada 63°0N 135°0W 68 C6
Yukta Russia 63°26N 105°42E 29 C11
Yukuhashi Japan 33°44N 130°59E 31 H5
Yulara Australia 25°10S 130°55E 61 E5
Yule → Australia 20°41S 118°17E 60 D2
Yuleba Australia 26°37S 149°24E 63 D4
Yulin Hainan, China 18°10N 109°31E 38 C7
Yulin Shaanxi, China 38°20N 109°30E 34 E5
Yuma Ariz., U.S.A. 32°43N 114°37W 79 N12
Yuma Colo., U.S.A. 40°8N 102°43W 76 F12
Yuma, B. de Dom. Rep. 18°20N 68°35W 89 C6
Yumbe Uganda 3°28N 31°15E 54 B3
Yumbi
  Dem. Rep. of the Congo 1°12S 26°15E 54 C2
Yumen China 39°50N 97°30E 32 C4
Yuna → Australia 28°20S 115°0E 61 E2
Yuncheng Henan, China 35°36N 115°57E 34 G8
Yuncheng Shanxi, China 35°2N 111°0E 34 G6
Yungas Bolivia 17°0S 66°0W 92 G5
Yungay Chile 37°10S 72°5W 94 D1
Yunnan □ China 25°0N 102°0E 32 D5
Yunxi China 33°0N 110°22E 34 H6
Yupanqui Basin Pac. Oc. 11°0S 101°0W 65 J17
Yuraygir △ Australia 29°45S 153°15E 63 D5
Yurga Russia 55°42N 84°51E 28 D9
Yurimaguas Peru 5°55S 76°7W 92 E3
Yurubí △ Venezuela 10°26N 68°42W 89 D6
Yuscarán Honduras 13°58N 86°45W 88 D2

Yushe China 37°4N 112°58E 34 F7
Yushu Jilin, China 44°43N 126°38E 35 B14
Yushu Qinghai, China 33°5N 96°55E 32 C4
Yutai China 35°0N 116°45E 34 G9
Yutian Hebei, China 39°53N 117°45E 35 E9
Yutian Sinkiang-Uigur,
  China 36°52N 81°42E 32 C3
Yuxari Qarabağ =
  Nagorno-Karabakh □
  Azerbaijan 39°55N 46°45E 44 B5
Yuxi China 24°30N 102°35E 32 D5
Yuzawa Japan 39°10N 140°30E 30 E10
Yuzhno-Kurilsk Russia 44°1N 145°51E 29 E15
Yuzhno-Sakhalinsk
  Russia 46°58N 142°45E 29 E15
Yuzhnyy □ Russia 44°0N 40°0E 28 E5
Yuzhou China 34°10N 113°28E 34 G7
Yvetot France 49°37N 0°44E 20 B4

Z

Zaanstad Neths. 52°27N 4°50E 15 B4
Zāb al Kabīr → Iraq 36°1N 43°24E 44 B4
Zāb aş Şaghīr → Iraq 35°17N 43°29E 44 C4
Zabaykalsk Russia 49°40N 117°25E 29 E12
Zābol Iran 31°0N 61°32E 45 D9
Zābol □ Afghan. 32°0N 67°0E 40 D5
Zāboli Iran 27°10N 61°35E 45 E9
Zabrze Poland 50°18N 18°50E 17 C10
Zacapa Guatemala 14°59N 89°31W 88 D2
Zacapu Mexico 19°50N 101°43W 86 D4
Zacatecas Mexico 22°47N 102°35W 86 C4
Zacatecas □ Mexico 23°0N 103°0W 86 C4
Zacatecoluca El Salv. 13°29N 88°51W 88 D2
Zachary U.S.A. 30°39N 91°9W 84 F9
Zacoalco de Torres
  Mexico 20°14N 103°35W 86 C4
Zacualtipán Mexico 20°39N 98°36E 87 C5
Zadar Croatia 44°8N 15°14E 16 F8
Zadetkyi Kyun Burma 10°0N 98°25E 39 G2
Zafarqand Iran 33°11N 52°29E 45 C7
Zafra Spain 38°26N 6°30W 21 C2
Żagań Poland 51°39N 15°22E 16 C8
Zagaoua Chad 15°30N 22°24E 51 E10
Zagazig Egypt 30°40N 31°30E 51 B12
Zāgheh Iran 33°30N 48°42E 45 C6
Zagreb Croatia 45°50N 15°58E 16 F9
Zāgros, Kūhhā-ye Iran 33°45N 48°5E 45 C6
Zagros Mts. = Zāgros, Kūhhā-ye
  Iran 33°45N 48°5E 45 C6
Zahamena △ Madag. 17°37S 48°49E 57 B8
Zāhedān Fārs, Iran 28°46N 53°52E 45 D7
Zāhedān Sīstān va Balūchestān,
  Iran 29°30N 60°50E 45 D9
Zahlah Lebanon 33°52N 35°50E 46 B4
Zaïre = Congo → Africa 6°4S 12°24E 52 F2
Zaječar Serbia 43°53N 22°18E 23 C10
Zaka Zimbabwe 20°20S 31°29E 57 C5
Zakamensk Russia 50°23N 103°17E 29 D11
Zakhodnaya Dzvina =
  Daugava → Latvia 57°4N 24°3E 9 H21
Zākhū Iraq 37°10N 42°50E 44 B4
Zakinthos = Zakynthos
  Greece 37°47N 20°54E 23 F9
Zakopane Poland 49°18N 19°57E 17 D10
Zakros Greece 35°6N 26°10E 25 D8
Zakynthos Greece 37°47N 20°54E 23 F9
Zalaegerszeg Hungary 46°53N 16°47E 17 E9
Zalari Russia 53°33N 102°30E 29 D11
Zalău Romania 47°12N 23°3E 17 E12
Zaleshchiki = Zalishchyky
  Ukraine 48°45N 25°45E 17 D13
Zalew Wiślany Poland 54°20N 19°50E 17 A10
Zalingei Sudan 12°51N 23°29E 51 F10
Zalishchyky Ukraine 48°45N 25°45E 17 D13
Zama L. Canada 58°45N 119°5W 70 B5
Zambeke
  Dem. Rep. of the Congo 2°8N 25°17E 54 B2
Zambeze → Africa 18°35S 36°20E 55 F4
Zambezi = Zambeze →
  Africa 18°35S 36°20E 55 F4
Zambezi Zambia 13°30S 23°15E 55 G3
Zambezi △ Zimbabwe 17°54S 25°41E 55 F2
Zambezia □ Mozam. 16°15S 37°30E 55 F4
Zambia ■ Africa 15°0S 28°0E 55 F2
Zamboanga Phil. 6°59N 122°3E 37 C6
Zamora Mexico 19°59N 102°16W 86 D4
Zamora Spain 41°30N 5°45W 21 B3
Zamość Poland 50°43N 23°15E 17 C12
Zanda China 31°32N 79°50E 32 D2
Zandvoort Neths. 52°22N 4°32E 15 B4
Zanesville U.S.A. 39°56N 82°1W 82 G2
Zangābād Iran 38°26N 46°44E 44 B5
Zangue → Mozam. 17°50S 35°21E 55 F4
Zanjan Iran 36°40N 48°35E 45 B6
Zanjan □ Iran 37°20N 49°30E 45 B6
Zanjan → Iran 37°8N 47°47E 45 B6
Zante = Zakynthos
  Greece 37°47N 20°54E 23 F9
Zanthus Australia 31°2S 123°34E 61 F3
Zanzibar Tanzania 6°12S 39°12E 54 D4
Zaouiet El-Kala = Bordj Omar
  Driss Algeria 28°10N 6°40E 50 C7
Zaouiet Reggâne Algeria 26°32N 0°3E 50 C6
Zaozhuang China 34°50N 117°35E 35 G9
Zap Suyu = Zāb al Kabīr →
  Iraq 36°1N 43°24E 44 B4
Zapadnaya Dvina = Daugava →
  Latvia 57°4N 24°3E 9 H21
Západné Beskydy Europe 49°30N 19°0E 17 D10
Zapala Argentina 39°0S 70°5W 96 D2
Zapaleri, Cerro Bolivia 22°49S 67°11W 94 A2
Zapata U.S.A. 26°55N 99°16W 84 M5
Zapolyarnyy Russia 69°26N 30°51E 8 B24
Zapopán Mexico 20°43N 103°24W 86 C4
Zaporizhzhya Ukraine 47°50N 35°10E 19 E6
Zaporozhye = Zaporizhzhya
  Ukraine 47°50N 35°10E 19 E6

Zara Turkey 39°58N 37°43E 44 B3
Zaragoza Coahuila,
  Mexico 28°29N 100°55W 86 B4
Zaragoza Nuevo León,
  Mexico 23°58N 99°46W 87 C5
Zaragoza Spain 41°39N 0°53W 21 B5
Zarand Kermān, Iran 30°46N 56°34E 45 D8
Zarand Markazī, Iran 35°18N 50°25E 45 C6
Zaranj Afghan. 30°55N 61°55E 40 D2
Zarasai Lithuania 55°40N 26°20E 9 J22
Zárate Argentina 34°7S 59°0W 94 C4
Zard, Kūh-e Iran 32°22N 50°4E 45 C6
Zāreh Iran 35°7N 49°9E 45 C6
Zaria Nigeria 11°0N 7°40E 50 F7
Zarneh Iran 33°55N 46°10E 44 C5
Zaros Greece 35°8N 24°54E 25 D6
Zarqā', Nahr az →
  Jordan 32°10N 35°37E 46 C4
Zarrīn Iran 32°46N 54°37E 45 C7
Zaruma Ecuador 3°40S 79°38W 92 D3
Żary Poland 51°37N 15°10E 16 C8
Zarzis Tunisia 33°31N 11°2E 51 B8
Zaskar → India 34°13N 77°20E 43 B7
Zaskar Mts. India 33°15N 77°30E 43 C7
Zastron S. Africa 30°18S 27°7E 56 E4
Zavāreh Iran 33°29N 52°28E 45 C7
Zave Zimbabwe 17°6S 30°1E 55 F3
Zavitinsk Russia 50°10N 129°20E 29 D13
Zavodovski, I. Antarctica 56°0S 27°45W 5 B1
Zawiercie Poland 50°30N 19°24E 17 C10
Zāwiyat al Baydā = Al Bayḍā
  Libya 32°50N 21°44E 51 B10
Zāyā Iraq 33°33N 44°13E 44 C5
Zāyandeh → Iran 32°35N 52°0E 45 C7
Zaysan Kazakhstan 47°28N 84°52E 32 B3
Zaysan Köli Kazakhstan 48°0N 83°0E 28 E9
Zayü China 28°48N 97°27E 32 D4
Zazafotsy Madag. 21°11S 46°21E 57 C8
Zbarazh Ukraine 49°43N 25°44E 17 D13
Zdolbuniv Ukraine 50°30N 26°15E 17 C14
Zduńska Wola Poland 51°37N 18°59E 17 C10
Zeballos Canada 49°59N 126°50W 70 D3
Zebediela S. Africa 24°20S 29°17E 57 C4
Zeebrugge Belgium 51°19N 3°12E 15 C3
Zeehan Australia 41°52S 145°25E 63 G4
Zeeland □ Neths. 51°30N 3°50E 15 C3
Zeerust S. Africa 25°31S 26°4E 56 D4
Zefat Israel 32°58N 35°29E 46 C4
Zehak Iran 30°53N 61°42E 45 D9
Zeil, Mt. Australia 23°30S 132°23E 60 D5
Zeila = Saylac
  Somali Rep. 11°21N 43°30E 47 E3
Zeist Neths. 52°5N 5°15E 15 B5
Zeitz Germany 51°2N 12°7E 16 C7
Zelenogorsk Russia 60°12N 29°43E 8 F23
Zelenograd Russia 56°1N 37°12E 18 C6
Zelienople U.S.A. 40°48N 80°8W 82 F4
Zémio C.A.R. 5°2N 25°5E 54 A2
Zempoala Mexico 19°27N 96°23W 87 D5
Zemun Serbia 44°51N 20°25E 23 B9
Zenica Bos.-H. 44°10N 17°57E 23 B7
Zepče Bos.-H. 44°28N 18°2E 23 B8
Zevenaar Neths. 51°56N 6°5E 15 C6
Zeya Russia 53°48N 127°14E 29 D13
Zeya → Russia 51°42N 128°53E 29 D13
Zêzere → Portugal 39°28N 8°20E 21 C1
Zghartā Lebanon 34°21N 35°53E 46 A4
Zgorzelec Poland 51°10N 15°0E 16 C8
Zhabinka Belarus 52°13N 24°2E 17 B13
Zhambyl = Taraz
  Kazakhstan 42°54N 71°22E 28 E8
Zhangaqazaly Kazakhstan 45°48N 62°6E 28 E7
Zhangbei China 41°10N 114°45E 34 D8
Zhangguangcai Ling
  China 45°0N 129°0E 35 B15
Zhangjiabian China 22°33N 113°28E 33 F9
Zhangjiagang China 31°55N 120°30E 37 B13
Zhangjiakou China 40°48N 114°55E 34 D8
Zhangwu China 42°43N 123°52E 35 C12
Zhangye China 38°50N 100°23E 32 C5
Zhangzhou China 24°30N 117°35E 33 D6
Zhanhua China 37°40N 118°8E 35 F10
Zhanjiang China 21°15N 110°20E 33 D6
Zhannetty, Ostrov
  Russia 76°43N 158°0E 29 B16
Zhanyi China 25°38N 103°48E 32 D5
Zhanyu China 44°30N 122°30E 35 B12
Zhao Xian China 37°43N 114°45E 34 F8
Zhaocheng China 36°22N 111°38E 34 F6
Zhaotong China 27°20N 103°44E 32 D5
Zhaoyuan Heilongjiang,
  China 45°27N 125°0E 35 B13
Zhaoyuan Shandong,
  China 37°20N 120°23E 35 F11
Zhari Namco China 31°6N 85°36E 32 C3
Zharkent Kazakhstan 44°10N 80°0E 28 E9
Zhashkiv Ukraine 49°15N 30°5E 17 D16
Zhashui China 33°40N 109°8E 34 H5
Zhayylma Kazakhstan 51°37N 61°33E 28 D7
Zhayyq → Kazakhstan 47°0N 51°48E 19 E9
Zhdanov = Mariupol
  Ukraine 47°5N 37°31E 19 E6
Zhecheng China 34°7N 115°20E 34 G8
Zhejiang □ China 29°0N 120°0E 33 D7
Zheleznodorozhnyy
  Russia 62°35N 50°55E 18 B9
Zheleznogorsk-Ilimskiy
  Russia 56°34N 104°8E 29 D11
Zhen'an China 33°27N 109°9E 34 H5
Zhengding China 38°8N 114°32E 34 E8
Zhengzhou China 34°45N 113°34E 34 G7
Zhenlai China 45°50N 123°5E 35 B12
Zhenping China 33°10N 112°16E 34 H7
Zhenyuan China 35°35N 107°30E 34 G4
Zhetiqara Kazakhstan 52°11N 61°12E 28 D7
Zhezqazghan Kazakhstan 47°44N 67°40E 28 E7
Zhidan China 36°48N 108°48E 34 F5
Zhigansk Russia 66°48N 123°27E 29 C13

Zhilinda Russia 70°0N 114°20E 29 C12
Zhitomir = Zhytomyr
  Ukraine 50°20N 28°40E 17 C15
Zhlobin Belarus 52°55N 30°0E 17 B16
Zhmerynka Ukraine 49°2N 28°2E 17 D15
Zhob Pakistan 31°20N 69°31E 42 D3
Zhob → Pakistan 32°4N 69°50E 42 C3
Zhodzina Belarus 54°5N 28°17E 17 A15
Zhokhova, Ostrov
  Russia 76°4N 152°40E 29 B16
Zhongdian China 27°48N 99°42E 32 D4
Zhongning China 37°29N 105°40E 34 F3
Zhongshan Antarctica 69°0S 39°50E 5 C6
Zhongshan China 22°35N 113°29E 33 F9
Zhongshankong China 22°35N 113°29E 33 F9
Zhongtiao Shan China 35°0N 111°10E 34 G6
Zhongwei China 37°30N 105°12E 34 F3
Zhongyang China 37°20N 111°11E 34 F6
Zhosaly Kazakhstan 45°29N 64°8E 28 E7
Zhoucun China 36°47N 117°48E 35 F9
Zhouzhi China 34°10N 108°12E 34 G5
Zhuanghe China 39°40N 123°0E 35 E12
Zhucheng China 36°0N 119°27E 35 G10
Zhugqu China 33°40N 104°30E 34 H3
Zhuhai China 22°17N 113°34E 33 G10
Zhujiang Kou China 22°20N 113°45E 33 G10
Zhumadian China 32°59N 114°2E 34 H8
Zhuo Xian = Zhuozhou
  China 39°28N 115°58E 34 E8
Zhuolu China 40°20N 115°12E 34 D8
Zhuozhou China 39°28N 115°58E 34 E8
Zhuozi China 41°0N 112°25E 34 D7
Zhytomyr Ukraine 50°20N 28°40E 17 C15
Ziarat Pakistan 30°25N 67°49E 42 D2
Zibo China 36°47N 118°3E 35 F10
Zichang China 37°18N 109°40E 34 F5
Zidi = Wandhari
  Pakistan 27°42N 66°48E 42 F2
Zielona Góra Poland 51°57N 15°31E 16 C8
Zierikzee Neths. 51°40N 3°55E 15 C3
Zigong China 29°15N 104°48E 32 D5
Ziguéy Chad 14°43N 15°50E 51 F9
Ziguinchor Senegal 12°35N 16°20W 50 F2
Zihuatanejo Mexico 17°39N 101°33W 86 D4
Žilina Slovak Rep. 49°12N 18°42E 17 D10
Zillah Libya 28°30N 17°33E 51 C9
Zima Russia 54°0N 102°5E 29 D11
Zimapán Mexico 20°43N 99°21W 87 C5
Zimba Zambia 17°20S 26°11E 55 F2
Zimbabwe Zimbabwe 20°16S 30°54E 55 G3
Zimbabwe ■ Africa 19°0S 30°0E 55 F3
Zimnicea Romania 43°40N 25°22E 17 G13
Zinave △ Mozam. 21°35S 33°40E 57 C5
Zinder Niger 13°48N 9°0E 50 F7
Zinga Tanzania 9°16S 38°49E 54 D4
Zion □ U.S.A. 37°15N 113°5W 77 H7
Ziros Greece 35°5N 26°8E 25 D8
Zirreh, Gowd-e Afghan. 29°45N 62°0E 40 E3
Zitácuaro Mexico 19°24N 100°22W 86 D4
Zitundo Mozam. 26°48S 32°47E 57 D5
Ziwa Maghariba = Kagera □
  Tanzania 2°0S 31°30E 54 C3
Ziway, L. Ethiopia 8°0N 38°50E 47 F2
Ziyang China 32°32N 108°31E 34 H5
Zlatograd Bulgaria 41°22N 25°7E 23 D11
Zlatoust Russia 55°10N 59°40E 18 C10
Zlín Czech Rep. 49°14N 17°40E 17 D9
Zmeinogorsk Kazakhstan 51°10N 82°13E 28 D9
Znojmo Czech Rep. 48°50N 16°2E 16 D9
Zobeyrī Iran 34°10N 46°40E 44 C5
Zobia
  Dem. Rep. of the Congo 3°0N 25°59E 54 B2
Zoetermeer Neths. 52°3N 4°30E 15 B4
Zohreh → Iran 30°16N 51°15E 45 D6
Zolochiv Ukraine 49°45N 24°51E 17 D13
Zomba Malawi 15°22S 35°19E 55 F4
Zongo
  Dem. Rep. of the Congo 4°20N 18°35E 52 D3
Zonguldak Turkey 41°28N 31°50E 19 F5
Zonqor Pt. Malta 35°52N 14°34E 25 D2
Zorritos Peru 3°43S 80°40W 92 D2
Zou Xiang China 35°30N 116°58E 34 G9
Zouar Chad 20°30N 16°32E 51 D9
Zouérate = Zouîrât
  Mauritania 22°44N 12°21W 50 D3
Zouîrât Mauritania 22°44N 12°21W 50 D3
Zoutkamp Neths. 53°20N 6°18E 15 A6
Zrenjanin Serbia 45°22N 20°23E 23 B9
Żufār Oman 17°40N 54°0E 47 D5
Zug Switz. 47°10N 8°31E 20 C8
Zugspitze Germany 47°25N 10°59E 16 E6
Zuid-Holland □ Neths. 52°0N 4°35E 15 C4
Zuidbeveland Neths. 51°30N 3°50E 15 C3
Zuidhorn Neths. 53°15N 6°23E 15 A6
Zula Eritrea 15°17N 39°40E 47 D2
Zumbo Mozam. 15°35S 30°26E 55 F3
Zumpango Mexico 19°48N 99°6W 87 D5
Zunhua China 40°18N 117°58E 35 D9
Zuni Pueblo U.S.A. 35°4N 108°51W 77 J9
Zunyi China 27°42N 106°53E 32 D5
Zurbātīyah Iraq 33°9N 46°3E 44 C5
Zürich Switz. 47°22N 8°32E 20 C8
Zutphen Neths. 52°9N 6°12E 15 B6
Zuurberg △ S. Africa 33°12S 25°32E 56 E4
Zuwārah Libya 32°58N 12°1E 51 B8
Żūzan Iran 34°22N 59°53E 45 C8
Zvishavane Zimbabwe 20°17S 30°2E 55 G3
Zvolen Slovak Rep. 48°33N 19°10E 17 D10
Zwettl Austria 48°35N 15°9E 16 D8
Zwickau Germany 50°44N 12°30E 16 C7
Zwolle Neths. 52°31N 6°6E 15 B6
Zwolle U.S.A. 31°38N 93°39W 84 F8
Żyrardów Poland 52°3N 20°28E 17 B11
Zyryan Kazakhstan 49°43N 84°20E 28 E9
Zyryanka Russia 65°45N 150°51E 29 C16
Zyryanovsk = Zyryan
  Kazakhstan 49°43N 84°20E 28 E9
Żywiec Poland 49°42N 19°10E 17 D10

World: Regions in the News

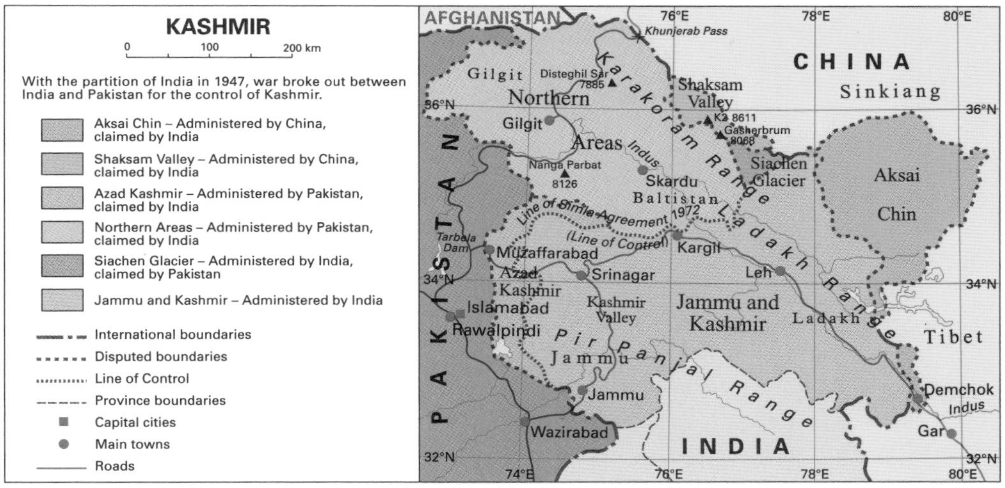

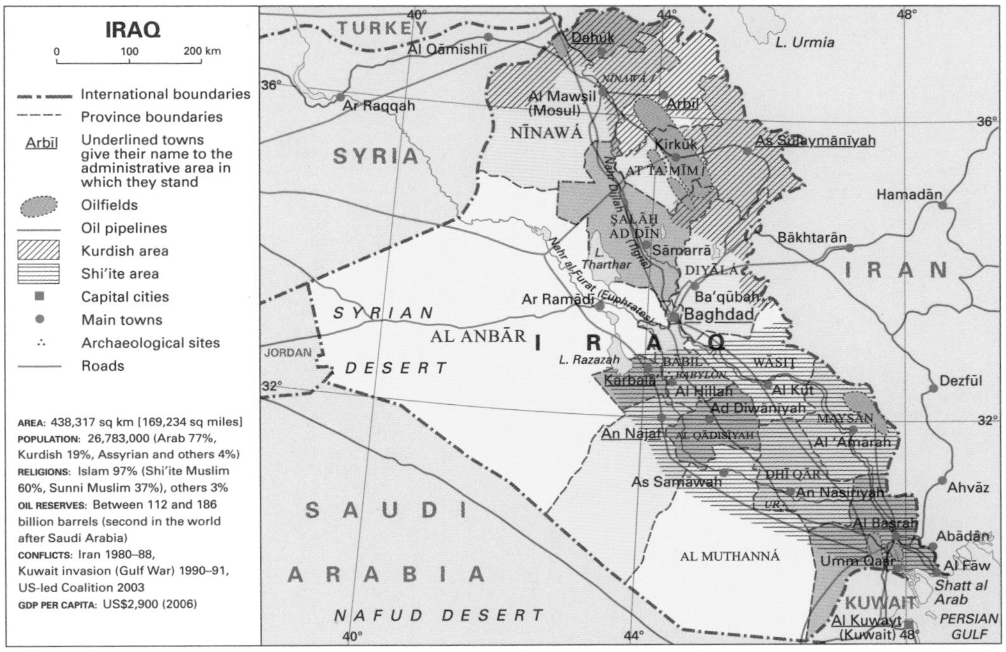

KASHMIR

0   100   200 km

With the partition of India in 1947, war broke out between India and Pakistan for the control of Kashmir.

- Aksai Chin – Administered by China, claimed by India
- Shaksam Valley – Administered by China, claimed by India
- Azad Kashmir – Administered by Pakistan, claimed by India
- Northern Areas – Administered by Pakistan, claimed by India
- Siachen Glacier – Administered by India, claimed by Pakistan
- Jammu and Kashmir – Administered by India

- — ·· — International boundaries
- ····· Disputed boundaries
- ········· Line of Control
- — — — Province boundaries
- ▪ Capital cities
- ● Main towns
- —— Roads

Map labels: AFGHANISTAN, Khunjerab Pass, 76°E, 78°E, 80°E, CHINA, Gilgit, Disteghil Sar 7885, Shaksam Valley, K2 8611, Gasherbrum 8068, Sinkiang, 36°N, Northern, Gilgit, Areas, Karakoram Range, Siachen Glacier, Aksai Chin, Nanga Parbat 8126, Indus, Ladakh Range, Skardu, Baltistan, Line of Birila Agreement 1972 (Line of Control), Tarbela Dam, Muzaffarabad, Kargil, Leh, 34°N, Azad Kashmir, Srinagar, Jammu and Kashmir, Ladakh, Tibet, Islamabad, Kashmir Valley, Rawalpindi, Pir Panjal Range, Jammu, Demchok, Indus, Jammu, Wazirabad, Gar, PAKISTAN, INDIA, 32°N, 74°E, 76°E, 78°E, 80°E

IRAQ

0   100   200 km

- — ·· — International boundaries
- — — — Province boundaries
- *Arbil* Underlined towns give their name to the administrative area in which they stand
- Oilfields
- Oil pipelines
- Kurdish area
- Shi'ite area
- ▪ Capital cities
- ● Main towns
- ∴ Archaeological sites
- —— Roads

AREA: 438,317 sq km [169,234 sq miles]
POPULATION: 26,783,000 (Arab 77%, Kurdish 19%, Assyrian and others 4%)
RELIGIONS: Islam 97% (Shi'ite Muslim 60%, Sunni Muslim 37%), others 3%
OIL RESERVES: Between 112 and 186 billion barrels (second in the world after Saudi Arabia)
CONFLICTS: Iran 1980–88, Kuwait invasion (Gulf War) 1990–91, US-led Coalition 2003
GDP PER CAPITA: US$2,900 (2006)

Map labels: TURKEY, 40°, 44°, 48°, Dehūk, L. Urmia, Al Qāmishli, NINAWĀ, 36°, Al Mawşil (Mosul), Arbīl, Ar Raqqah, SYRIA, Kirkūk, As Sulaymānīyah, AT TA'MĪM, 36°, Hamadān, SALĀH AD DĪN, L. Tharthar, Sāmarrā, Bākhtarān, DIYĀLĀ, IRAN, Al Furat (Euphrates), Ba'qūbah, Ar Ramādī, Baghdad, JORDAN, SYRIAN DESERT, AL ANBĀR, IRAQ, BĀBIL, WĀSIT, L. Razazah, BABYLON, Al Kūt, Karbalā', Al Hillah, Ad Dīwānīyah, MAYSĀN, 32°, 32°, An Najaf, AL QĀDISĪYAH, Al 'Amārah, Dezfūl, SAUDI, DHĪ QĀR, Ahvāz, As Samāwah, An Nāsirīyah, ARABIA, AL MUTHANNĀ, Al Başrah, Abādān, NAFUD DESERT, Umm Qasr, Al Faw, Shatt al Arab, PERSIAN GULF, KUWAIT, Al Kuwayt (Kuwait), 40°, 44°, 48°

AFGHANISTAN

0   100   200 km

- — ·· — International boundaries
- — — — Province boundaries
- ▪ Capital cities
- ● Main towns
- →—← Roads and road tunnel
- Land over 3,000 m
-)(Mountain passes

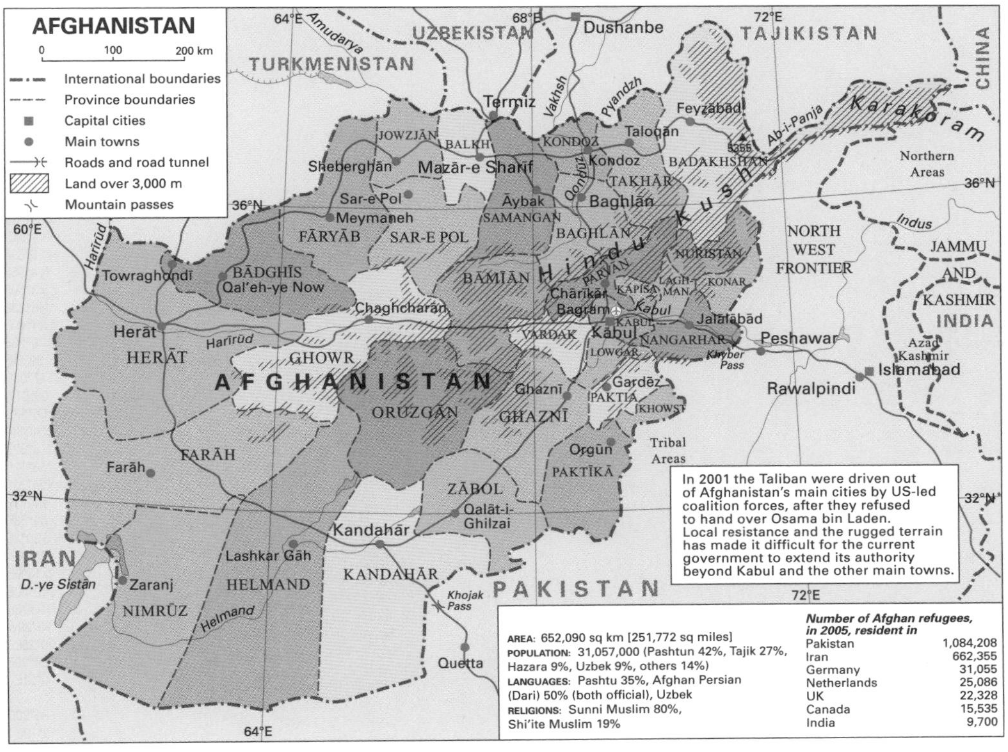

In 2001 the Taliban were driven out of Afghanistan's main cities by US-led coalition forces, after they refused to hand over Osama bin Laden. Local resistance and the rugged terrain has made it difficult for the current government to extend its authority beyond Kabul and the other main towns.

AREA: 652,090 sq km [251,772 sq miles]
POPULATION: 31,057,000 (Pashtun 42%, Tajik 27%, Hazara 9%, Uzbek 9%, others 14%)
LANGUAGES: Pashtu 35%, Afghan Persian (Dari) 50% (both official), Uzbek
RELIGIONS: Sunni Muslim 80%, Shi'ite Muslim 19%

Number of Afghan refugees, in 2005, resident in

Pakistan	1,084,208
Iran	662,355
Germany	31,055
Netherlands	25,086
UK	22,328
Canada	15,535
India	9,700

Map labels: 64°E, 68°E, 72°E, UZBEKISTAN, Dushanbe, TAJIKISTAN, Amudarya, TURKMENISTAN, Termiz, Vakhsh, Pyandzh, Feyzābād, CHINA, JOWZJĀN, BALKH, Kondūz, Talōqan, Āb-i-Panja, Karakoram, Sheberghān, Mazār-e Sharīf, KONDŪZ, BADAKHSHĀN, Sar-e Pol, Aybak, SAMANGAN, BAGHLĀN, TAKHĀR, Northern Areas, 36°N, Meymaneh, Baghlān, Indus, FĀRYĀB, SAR-E POL, NURISTĀN, Hindu Kush, 60°E, Towraghondī, BĀDGHĪS, Qal'eh-ye Now, BĀMIĀN, PARVĀN, KAPISA, LAGHMĀN, KONAR, NORTH WEST FRONTIER, JAMMU, Chaghcharān, Chārīkār, Bāgrām, Jalālābād, AND, Herāt, Harīrūd, GHOWR, BĀMIĀN, Kabul, NANGARHĀR, Peshawar, KASHMIR, HERĀT, VARDAK, LOWGAR, Khyber Pass, Azad Kashmir, INDIA, Ghaznī, Gardēz, Islamabad, Harīrūd, AFGHANISTAN, PAKTIA, KHOWST, Rawalpindi, ORŪZGĀN, GHAZNĪ, Orgūn, Tribal Areas, FARĀH, Farāh, ZĀBOL, PAKTĪKĀ, 32°N, IRAN, D.-ye Sīstān, Zaranj, Qalāt-i-Ghilzai, NIMRŪZ, Lashkar Gāh, Khojak Pass, HELMAND, KANDAHĀR, Kandahār, Helmand, PAKISTAN, 72°E, Quetta, 64°E

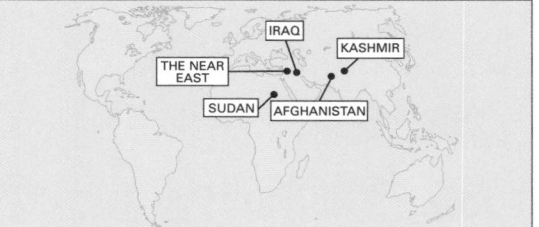

Locator map labels: IRAQ, KASHMIR, THE NEAR EAST, SUDAN, AFGHANISTAN

THE NEAR EAST

0   25   50 km

- — · — 1949 Armistice Line
- — ·· — 1950 Armistice Line
- — — — 1974 Cease-fire Line
- Palestinian control
- Joint Israeli/Palestinian control
- *Efrata* ● Main Jewish settlements
- *Halhul* □ Main Palestinian Arab towns
- Israeli security fence (April 2006)
- Israeli security fence subject to further ministerial examination

ISRAEL
POPULATION: 6,352,000 (inc. Israeli settlers in West Bank and Golan Heights)
INFANT MORTALITY: 6.7 deaths per 1,000 births
RELIGIONS: Jewish 76.4%, Muslim 16%, Christian 2.1%
GDP PER CAPITA: US$26,200 (2006)

WEST BANK
POPULATION: 2,460,000 (Muslim 75%, Jewish 17%)
INFANT MORTALITY: 18.7 deaths per 1,000 births
GDP PER CAPITA: US$1,100 (2003)

GAZA STRIP
POPULATION: 1,429,000 (Muslim 98.7% Christian 0.7%, Jewish 0.6%)
INFANT MORTALITY: 21.9 deaths per 1,000 births
GDP PER CAPITA: US$600 (2003)

JORDAN
POPULATION: 5,907,000 (Palestinian Arab 50%)

LEBANON
POPULATION: 3,874,000 (Palestinian Arab 11%)

Map labels: 35°E, Saydā, Bekaa Valley, LEBANON, Litani, SYRIA, Sūr (Tyre), Qiryat Shemona, Golan Heights (under Israeli occupation), Nahariyya, 33°N, Akko, Zefat, Yam Kinneret, Hefa, Terverya, Nazerat, Disengagement Zone, ISRAEL, Irbid, Baka al Sharqiya, Jenin, Hadera, WEST, Tūbās, Netanya, Shavel Shomron, Elon More, Kedumim, Nabulus, Qalqilya, Imanuel, Karne Shomron, Kfar Tapuah, MEDITERRANEAN SEA, Elkana, Ariēl, Shiloh, Tel Aviv-Yafo, Manuel, 32°N, 32°N, BANK, Rām Allah, Beit El, 'Ammān, Rehovot, Al Birah, El Arihā (Jericho), Ashdod, Maale Adumim, Jerusalem, Bayt Lahm, Ashqelon, Efrata, Bethlehem, Dead Sea, Gaza, Halhul, Tkoa, GAZA STRIP, Al Khalīl (Hebron), Qiryat Arba, Be'er Sheva, JORDAN, Khān Yūnis, EGYPT, 35°E

SUDAN

0   250   500 km

- ● Refugee sites
- ● IDP sites (Internally Displaced Persons)
- Area of damaged/destroyed villages
- — — — Regional boundaries
- ▪ Capital cities
- ● Main towns

AREA: 2,505,813 sq km [967,494 sq miles]
POPULATION: 41,236,000 (Black 52%, Arab 39%, Beja 6%, others 3%)
RELIGIONS: Sunni Muslim 70% (mostly in the north), indigenous beliefs 25%, Christian 5% (mostly in the south)

Sudan has more internally displaced people than any other country (5.3 million in 2006) and there are 229,000 Sudanese refugees in neighbouring Chad. Up to 400,000 people are estimated to have been killed since conflict began in the Darfur region in early 2003.

Map labels: Tropic of Cancer, 30°, Aswān, Red Sea, EGYPT, LIBYA, Nile, Jedda, 20°, Port Sudan, NORTHERN, CHAD, DARFUR, Khartoum, Omdurmān, Wād Medani, Abéché, El Fâsher, ERITREA, SUDAN, EASTERN, CENTRAL, El Obeid, KORDOFAN, Nyālā, Atbara, White Nile, Blue Nile, BAHR EL GHAZAL, UPPER NILE, ETHIOPIA, Wâw, CONGO (DEM. REP. OF THE), EQUATORIA, Juba, UGANDA, KENYA, 10°

KEY TO EUROPEAN MAP PAGES

 **Large scale maps**
(>1:2 500 000)

 **Medium scale maps**
(1:2 800 000 – 1:9 900 000)

 **Small scale maps**
(<1:10 000 000)

ICELAND

WORLD COUNTRY INDEX

Country	Page
Afghanistan	40
Albania	23
Algeria	50
Angola	52–53
Argentina	94, 96
Armenia	19
Australia	60–63
Austria	16–17
Azerbaijan	19
Bahamas	88–89
Bahrain	45
Bangladesh	41
Barbados	89
Belarus	17, 18–19
Belgium	15
Belize	88
Benin	50
Bhutan	41
Bolivia	92
Bosnia-Herzegovina	22–23
Botswana	56
Brazil	92–93, 95
Brunei	36
Bulgaria	23
Burkina Faso	50
Burma (Myanmar)	41
Burundi	54
Cambodia	38–39
Canary Is.	24
Cameroon	52
Canada	68–73
Central African Republic	52
Chad	51
Chile	94, 96–97
China	32–35
Colombia	92
Congo	52
Congo, Dem. Rep. of the	52–53, 54–55
Costa Rica	88
Croatia	22–23
Cuba	88–89
Cyprus	25
Czech Republic	16–17
Denmark	9
Djibouti	47
Dominican Republic	89
Ecuador	92
Egypt	51
El Salvador	88
England	12–13
Equatorial Guinea	52
Eritrea	47
Estonia	9
Ethiopia	47, 52
Fiji	59
Finland	8–9
France	20–21
French Guiana	93
Gabon	52
Gambia	50
Georgia	19
Germany	16
Ghana	50
Greece	23
Greenland	4
Guadeloupe	88
Guatemala	88
Guinea	50
Guinea-Bissau	50
Guyana	92
Haiti	89
Honduras	88
Hungary	17
Iceland	8
India	40–43
Indonesia	36–37
Iran	44–45
Iraq	44–45
Irish Republic	10
Israel	46
Italy	22–23
Ivory Coast	50
Jamaica	88
Japan	30–31
Jordan	46
Kazakhstan	28
Kenya	54
Korea, North	35
Korea, South	35
Kuwait	44–45
Kyrgyzstan	28
Laos	38
Latvia	9
Lebanon	46
Lesotho	57
Liberia	50
Libya	51
Lithuania	9
Luxembourg	15
Macedonia	23
Madagascar	57
Malawi	55
Malaysia	36–37, 39
Mali	50
Malta	25
Martinique	88
Mauritania	50
Mexico	86–87
Moldova	17
Mongolia	32
Montenegro	23
Morocco	50
Mozambique	55, 57
Namibia	56
Nepal	43
Netherlands	15
New Zealand	59
Nicaragua	88
Niger	50–51
Nigeria	50–51
Northern Ireland	10
Norway	8–9
Oman	47
Pakistan	40, 42
Panama	88
Papua New Guinea	64
Paraguay	94–95
Peru	92
Philippines	37
Poland	16–17
Portugal	21
Puerto Rico	89
Qatar	45
Romania	17
Russia	18–19, 28–29
Rwanda	54
St. Lucia	89
Samoa	59
Saudi Arabia	44–45, 47
Scotland	11
Senegal	50
Serbia	23
Sierra Leone	50
Singapore	39
Slovak Republic	17
Slovenia	22
Solomon Is.	64
Somali Republic	47
South Africa	56–57
Spain	21
Sri Lanka	40
Sudan	51
Suriname	92–93
Swaziland	57
Sweden	8–9
Switzerland	16
Syria	44, 46
Taiwan	33
Tajikistan	28
Tanzania	54–55
Thailand	38–39
Togo	50
Tonga	59
Trinidad and Tobago	93
Tunisia	50–51
Turkey	19
Turkmenistan	28
Uganda	54
Ukraine	18–19
United Arab Emirates	47
United Kingdom	10–13
USA	74–85
Uruguay	94–95
Uzbekistan	28
Vanuatu	64
Venezuela	92–93
Vietnam	38–39
Wales	12–13
Yemen	47
Zambia	55, 56–57
Zimbabwe	55

8

14

11

11

12

10

16

15

20

N

IRELAND

UNITED KINGDOM

B

21

FRANCE

ANDORRA

PORTUGAL

SPAIN

24

MOROCCO

ALG